THE HUTCHINSON  *Concise* ENCYCLOPEDIA

UPDATED
–1994–
EDITION

Helicon

© Helicon Publishing 1993

First published 1989
Second edition 1991
Updated edition 1993

Maps and diagrams copyright © Helicon Publishing 1993

Helicon Publishing Ltd
42 Hythe Bridge Street
Oxford OX1 2EP

Printed and bound in Great Britain by
Jarrold and Sons Ltd, Norwich

ISBN 0 09 177646 5

British Library Cataloguing in Publication Data

A catalogue record for this book is available from the
British Library.

PREFACE

The *Hutchinson Concise Encyclopedia* is an illustrated single-volume companion to world events, history, arts, and sciences, for home, school, or library use. The aim throughout has been to provide up-to-date, readable entries, using clear and non-technical language.

Arrangement of entries

Entries are ordered alphabetically, as if there were no spaces between words. Thus, entries for words beginning 'national' follow the order:

> national insurance
> nationalism
> National Party

However, we have avoided a purely mechanical alphabetization in cases where a different order corresponds more with human logic. For example, sovereigns with the same name are grouped according to country before number, so that King George II of England is placed before George III of England, and not next to King George II of Greece. Words beginning 'Mc' and 'Mac' are treated as if they begin 'Mac'; and 'St' and 'Saint' are both treated as if they were spelt 'Saint'.

Foreign names and titles

Names of foreign sovereigns and places are usually shown in their English form, except where the foreign name is more familiar; thus, there are entries for Charles V of Spain, but Juan Carlos (not John Charles), and for Florence, not Firenze. Entries for titled people are under the name by which they are best known to the general reader: thus, Anthony Eden, not Lord Avon. Cross-references have been provided in cases where confusion is possible.

Cross-references

These are shown by a ◊ symbol immediately preceding the reference. Cross-referencing is selective; a cross-reference is shown when another entry contains material directly relevant to the subject matter of an entry, and where the reader may not otherwise think of looking. To assist the reader, we have avoided as far as possible entries which consist only of a cross-reference; even the shortest cross-reference gives some indication of the subject involved. Common alternative spellings, where there is no agreed consistent form, are also shown; thus there is a cross-reference to Muhammad at Mohammed.

Units

SI (metric) units are used throughout for scientific entries. Measurements of distances, temperatures, sizes, and so on, usually include an approximate imperial equivalent.

Science and technology

Entries are generally placed under the better-known name (thus, acetylene is placed under A and not under its technically correct name ethyne), but the technical term is also given. To aid comprehension, particularly for the non-specialist, technical terms are frequently explained when used within the text of an entry, even though they may have their own entry elsewhere.

Chinese names

Pinyin, the preferred system for transcribing Chinese names of people and places, is generally used: thus, there is an entry at Mao Zedong, not Mao Tse-tung; an exception is made for a few names which are more familiar in their former (Wade–Giles) form, such as Sun Yat-sen and Chiang Kai-Shek. Where confusion is likely, Wade–Giles forms are given as cross-references.

Comments and suggestions

We welcome comments from readers on suggested improvements or alterations to the Encyclopedia.

CONTRIBUTORS

David Armstrong PhD
Christine Avery PhD
John Ayto MA
Paul Bahn
Mark Bindley
David Black
Malcolm Bradbury MA, PhD, Hon D Litt, FRSL
Brendan Bradley MA, MSc, PhD
Tia Cockerell LLB
Sue Cusworth
Nigel Davis MSc
Ian D Derbyshire PhD
J Denis Derbyshire PhD, FBIM
Col Michael Dewar
Dougal Dixon BSc, MSc
Nigel Dudley
Suzanne Duke
George du Boulay FRCR, FRCP, Hon FACR
Ingrid von Essen
Anna Farkas
Jane Farron BA
Peter Fleming PhD
Kent Fedorowich BA, MA, PhD
Derek Gjertsen BA
Lawrence Garner BA
Joseph Harrison BA, PhD
Michael Hitchcock PhD
Stuart Holroyd
H G Jerrard PhD
Robin Kerrod FRAS
Charles Kidd
Stephen Kite B Arch, RIBA
Peter Lafferty MSc
Chris Lawn BA, MA
Mike Lewis MBCS
Graham Ley MPhil
Carol Lister PhD, FSS
Graham Littler BSc, MSc, FSS
Robin Maconie MA
Morven MacKillop
Tom McArthur PhD
Isabel Miller, BA, PhD
Karin Mogg MSc, PhD
Bob Moore PhD
David Munro PhD
Joanne O'Brien
Roger Owen MA, DPhil
Robert Paisley PhD
Michael Pudlo MSc, PhD
Tim Pulleine
Ian Ridpath FRAS
Adrian Room MA
Simon Ross
Julian Rowe PhD
Paul Rowntree
Jack Schofield BA, MA
Mark Slade MA
Steve Smyth
Joe Staines
Glyn Stone
Callum Storrie
Michael Thum
Stephen Webster BSc, MPhil
Liz Whitelegg BSc

EDITORS

Editorial Director
Michael Upshall

Project Editor
Hilary McGlynn

Update Editor
Louise Jones

Picture Research
Michael Nicholson

Cartography
Jones Sewell Associates

Production
Tony Ballsdon

A1 abbreviation for *first class* (of ships).

AA abbreviation for the British *Automobile Association*.

Aalborg (Danish *Ålborg*) port in Denmark 32 km/20 mi inland from the Kattegat, on the south shore of the Limfjord; population (1983) 155,400. One of Denmark's oldest towns, it has a castle and the fine Budolfi church. It is the capital of Nordjylland county in Jylland (Jutland); the port is linked to Nørresundby on the N side of the fjord by a tunnel built 1969.

Aalto Alvar 1898–1976. Finnish architect and designer. One of Finland's first modernists, his architectural style was unique, characterized by asymmetry, curved walls, and contrast of natural materials. Buildings include the Hall of Residence, Massachusetts Institute of Technology, Cambridge, Massachusetts 1947–49; Technical High School, Otaniemi 1962–65; Finlandia Hall, Helsinki 1972. He also invented a new form of laminated bent plywood furniture in 1932.

aardvark nocturnal mammal *Orycteropus afer* found in central and southern Africa. A timid, defenceless animal about the size of a pig, it has a long head, pig-like snout, and large asinine ears. It feeds on termites which it licks up with its long sticky tongue.

aardwolf nocturnal mammal *Proteles cristatus* of the ◊hyena family. It is found in E and S Africa, usually in the burrows of the aardvark, and feeds on termites.

Aarhus (Danish *Århus*) second city of Denmark, on the East coast overlooking the Kattegat; population (1983) 248,500. It is the capital of Aarhus county in Jylland (Jutland), and a shipping and commercial centre.

Aaron in the Bible, the elder brother of Moses and leader with him of the Israelites in their march from Egypt to the Promised Land of Canaan. He made the Golden Calf for the Israelites to worship when they despaired of Moses' return from Mount Sinai.

abacus method of calculating with a handful of stones on 'a flat surface' (Latin *abacus*), familiar to the Greeks and Romans, and used by earlier peoples, possibly even in ancient Babylon; it still survives in the more sophisticated beadframe form of the Russian *schoty* and the Japanese *soroban*. The abacus has now been replaced by electronic calculators, based on the same principle.

abalone snail-like marine mollusc, genus *Haliotis* (also known from its shape as the ear shell), with a bluish mother-of-pearl used in ornamental work.

Abbas I *the Great* c. 1557–1629. Shah of Persia from 1588. He expanded Persian territory by conquest, defeating the Uzbeks near Herat in 1597 and also the Turks. The port of Bandar-Abbas is named after him. At his death his empire reached from the river Tigris to the Indus. He was a patron of the arts.

Abbas II Hilmi 1874–1944. Last ◊khedive of Egypt, 1892–1914. On the outbreak of war between Britain and Turkey in 1914, he sided with Turkey and was deposed following the establishment of a British protectorate over Egypt.

Abbasid dynasty dynasty of the Islamic empire who reigned as ◊caliphs in Baghdad 750–1258. They were descended from Abbas, the prophet Muhammad's uncle, and some of them, such as Harun al-Rashid and Mamun (reigned 813–33), were outstanding patrons of cultural development. Later their power dwindled, and in 1258 Baghdad was burned by the Tatars. From then until 1517 the Abbasids retained limited power as caliphs of Egypt.

Abbé (French 'priest') a cleric who wears the clothes of a priest but who has no ecclesiastical function.

Abbey Theatre playhouse in Dublin associated with the Irish literary revival of the early 1900s. The theatre, opened in 1904, staged the works of a number of brilliant dramatists, including Lady Gregory, Yeats, J M Synge, and Sean O'Casey. Burned out in 1951, it was rebuilt 1966.

Abd el-Kader c. 1807–1883. Algerian nationalist. Emir (Islamic chieftain) of Mascara from 1832, he led a struggle against the French until his surrender in 1847.

Abd el-Krim el-Khettabi 1881–1963. Moroccan chief known as the 'Wolf of the ◊Riff'. With his brother Muhammad, he led the *Riff revolt* against the French and Spanish invaders, inflicting disastrous defeat on the Spanish at Anual in 1921, but surrendered to a large French army under Pétain in 1926. Banished to the island of Réunion, he was released in 1947 and died in Cairo.

abdication renunciation of an office or dignity, usually the throne, by a ruler or sovereign.

abdomen the part of the vertebrate body containing the digestive organs; the hind part of the body in insects and other arthropods. In mammals, the abdomen is separated from the chest (◊thorax) by the diaphragm, a sheet of muscular tissue; in arthropods, commonly by a narrow constriction. In insects and spiders, the abdomen is characterized by the absence of limbs.

Abdul-Hamid II 1842–1918. Last sultan of Turkey 1876–1909. In 1908 the ◊Young Turks under Enver Pasha forced Abdul-Hamid to restore the constitution of 1876, and in 1909 insisted on his deposition. He died in confinement. For his part in the ◊Armenian massacres suppressing the revolt of 1894–96 he was known as the Great Assassin and still motivates Armenian violence against the Turks.

Abdullah ibn Hussein 1882–1951. King of Jordan from 1946. He worked with the British guerrilla leader T E ◊Lawrence in the Arab revolt of World War I. Abdullah became king of Transjordan 1946; on the incorporation of Arab Palestine (after the 1948–49 Arab-Israeli War) he renamed the country the Hashemite Kingdom of Jordan. He was assassinated.

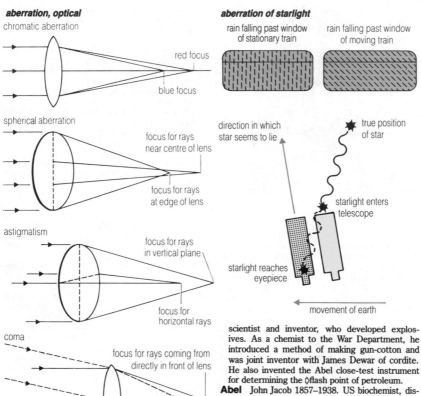

aberration, optical

chromatic aberration

red focus

blue focus

spherical aberration

focus for rays
near centre of lens

focus for rays
at edge of lens

astigmatism

focus for rays
in vertical plane

focus for
horizontal rays

coma

focus for rays coming from
directly in front of lens

focus for rays
coming at an angle

aberration of starlight

rain falling past window
of stationary train

rain falling past window
of moving train

direction in which
star seems to lie

true position
of star

starlight enters
telescope

starlight reaches
eyepiece

movement of earth

scientist and inventor, who developed explosives. As a chemist to the War Department, he introduced a method of making gun-cotton and was joint inventor with James Dewar of cordite. He also invented the Abel close-test instrument for determining the ◊flash point of petroleum.

Abel John Jacob 1857–1938. US biochemist, discoverer of ◊adrenaline. He studied the chemical composition of body tissues, and this led, in 1898, to the discovery of adrenaline, the first hormone to be identified, which Abel called epinephrine. He later became the first to isolate ◊amino acids from blood.

Abelard Peter 1079–1142. French scholastic philosopher noted for his work on logic and theology. Details of his controversial life are contained in the autobiographical *Historia Calamitatum Mearum/ The History of My Misfortunes*. He opposed realism in the debate over universals, and propounded 'conceptualism' whereby universal terms have only a mental existence.

Abercromby Ralph 1734–1801. Scots soldier who in 1801 commanded an expedition to the Mediterranean, charged with the liquidation of the French forces left behind by Napoleon in Egypt. He fought a brilliant action against the French at Aboukir Bay in 1801, but was mortally wounded at the battle of Alexandria a few days later.

Aberdeen city and seaport on the E coast of Scotland, administrative headquarters of Grampian region; population (1986) 214,082. Industries include manufacturing, and engineering for offshore oilfields in the North Sea.

Aberdeen George Hamilton Gordon, 4th Earl of Aberdeen 1784–1860. British Tory politician, prime minister 1852–55, resigned because of the Crimean War losses. Although a Tory, he supported Catholic emancipation and followed Peel in his conversion to free trade.

Aberdeenshire former county in E Scotland, merged in 1975 into Grampian region.

Abdullah Sheikh Muhammad 1905–1982. Indian politician, known as the 'Lion of Kashmir'. He headed the struggle for constitutional government against the Maharajah of Kashmir, and in 1948 became prime minister of Kashmir. He agreed to the accession of the state to India to halt ethnic infiltration, but was dismissed and imprisoned from 1953 (with brief intervals) until 1966, when he reaffirmed the right of the people 'to decide the future of the state' (see ◊Kashmir). He became chief minister of Jammu and Kashmir 1975, accepting the sovereignty of India.

Abdul Mejid I 1823–1861. Sultan of Turkey from 1839. During his reign the Ottoman Empire was increasingly weakened by internal nationalist movements and the incursions of the other great powers.

Abdul Rahman Tuanku 'King' 1903– . Malaysian politician who negotiated 1961–62 the formation of the federation of Malaysia; he was its first prime minister 1963–70.

Abel in the Old Testament, second son of Adam and Eve; as a shepherd, he made burnt offerings of meat to God which were more acceptable than the fruits offered by his brother Cain; he was killed by the jealous Cain.

Abel Frederick Augustus 1827–1902. British

Aberfan mining village in Mid Glamorgan, Wales. Coal waste overwhelmed a school and houses in 1966; of 144 dead, 116 were children.

aberration of starlight the apparent displacement of a star from its true position, due to the combined effects of the speed of light and the speed of the Earth in orbit around the Sun (about 30 km/18.5 mi per sec).

aberration, optical any of a number of defects that impair the image in an optical instrument. In *chromatic aberration* the image is surrounded by coloured fringes, because light of different colours is brought to different focal points by a lens. In *spherical aberration* the image is blurred because different parts of the lens or mirror have different focal lengths. In *astigmatism* the image appears elliptical or cross-shaped. In *coma*, the images appear progressively elongated towards the edge of the field of view. Optical aberration occurs because of minute variations in the glass and because different parts of the light ◊spectrum are reflected or refracted by varying amounts.

abeyance doctrine whereby a peerage falls into a state of suspension between a number of co-heirs or co-heiresses; in the UK the only peerages that can fall into abeyance are baronies that have been created by writ.

Abidja'n port and former capital (until 1983) of the Republic of Ivory Coast, W Africa; population (1982) 1,850,000. Products include coffee, palm oil, cocoa, and timber (mahogany).

ab init. abbreviation for *ab initio* (Latin 'from the beginning').

ablative in the grammar of certain inflected languages, such as Latin, the ablative case is the form of a noun, pronoun or adjective used to indicate the agent in passive sentences or the instrument, manner, or place of the action described by the verb.

ABM abbreviation for *anti-ballistic missile*; see under ◊nuclear warfare.

abolitionism in UK and US history, a movement in the late 18th and early 19th centuries, first to end the slave trade, and then to abolish the institution of ◊slavery and emancipate slaves.

In the UK, the leading abolitionist was William ◊Wilberforce, who secured passage of a bill abolishing the slave trade in 1807. In the USA, slavery was officially abolished by the Emancipation Proclamation 1863 of President Abraham ◊Lincoln, but it could not be enforced until 1865 after the Union victory in the ◊Civil War. See also ◊black history.

abominable snowman legendary creature, said to resemble a human, with long arms and a thick-set body covered with reddish-grey hair. Reports of its existence in the Himalayas, where it is known as the *yeti*, have been current since 1832, but gained substance from a published photograph of a huge footprint in the snow in 1951.

aborigine any indigenous inhabitant of a country. The word also refers to the original peoples of countries colonized by Europeans, and especially to ◊Australian Aborigines.

abortion the ending of a pregnancy before the fetus is developed sufficiently to survive outside the womb. Abortion may be accidental (miscarriage) or deliberate (termination of pregnancy).

Aboukir Bay, Battle of also known as the Battle of the Nile: naval battle between the UK and France, in which Admiral Nelson defeated Napoleon's fleet at the Egyptian seaport of Aboukir on 1 Aug 1798.

Abraham *c.* 2300 BC. According to the Bible, founder of the Jewish nation. Jehovah promised him heirs and land for his people in Canaan, renamed him Abraham ('father of many nations') and once tested him by a command (later retracted) to sacrifice his son Isaac or, in the Koran, Ishmael.

Abraham, Plains/Heights of plateau near Quebec, Canada, where the British commander ◊Wolfe defeated the French under ◊Montcalm, 13 Sept 1759.

abrasive substance used for cutting and polishing or for removing small amounts of the surface of hard materials. There are two types: natural and artificial abrasives, and their hardness is measured using the ◊Mohs scale.

Abruzzi mountainous region of S central Italy, comprising the provinces of L'Aquila, Chieti, Pescara, and Teramo. Gran Sasso d'Italia, 2,914 m/9,560 ft, is the highest point of the ◊Apennines.

Absalom in the Old Testament, favourite son of King David; when defeated in a revolt against his father he fled on a mule, but was caught up by his hair in a tree branch and killed by Joab, one of David's officers.

abscess a collection of pus in the tissues forming in response to infection. Its presence is signalled by pain and inflammation.

abscissa in ◊coordinate geometry, the horizontal or *x* coordinate, that is, the distance of a point from the vertical or *y*-axis. For example, a point with the coordinates (3,4) has an abscissa of 3.

abscission in botany, the controlled separation of part of a plant from the main plant body – most commonly, the falling of leaves or the dropping of fruit. In ◊deciduous plants the leaves are shed before the winter or dry season, whereas ◊evergreen plants drop their leaves continually throughout the year. Fruit-drop, the abscission of fruit while still immature, is a naturally ocurring process.

absolute zero zero degrees Kelvin, equivalent to $-273.16°C$, the lowest temperature that can possibly exist, at which molecules have no energy. Near this temperature, the physical properties of materials change substantially; for example, some metals lose their electrical resistance (become superconductive).

absolutism or *absolute monarchy* a system of government in which the ruler or rulers have unlimited power. The principle of an absolute monarch, given a right to rule by God (see ◊divine right of kings), was extensively used in Europe during the 17th and 18th centuries. Absolute monarchy is contrasted with limited or constitutional monarchy, in which the sovereign's powers are defined or limited.

absorption scientific term with several meanings. It most commonly describes the taking up of one substance by another, such as a liquid by a solid (ink by blotting-paper) or a gas by a liquid (ammonia by water). In optics, absorption is the phenomenon by which a substance retains radiation of particular wavelengths; for example, a piece of blue glass absorbs all visible light except the wavelengths in the blue part of the spectrum. In nuclear physics, absorption is the capture by elements such as boron of neutrons produced by fission in a reactor.

abstract art non-representational art. Ornamental art without figurative representation occurs in most cultures. The modern abstract movement in sculpture and painting emerged in Europe and North America between 1910 and 1920. Two approaches produce very different abstract styles: images that have been 'abstracted' from nature to the point

Academy Award winners (Oscars)

Year

1975 Best Picture: One Flew Over the Cuckoo's Nest
      Best Director: Milos Forman One Flew Over the
                Cuckoo's Nest
      Best Actor: Jack Nicholson One Flew Over the
                Cuckoo's Nest
      Best Actress: Louise Fletcher One Flew Over the
                Cuckoo's Nest

1976 Best Picture: Rocky
      Best Director: John G. Avildsen Rocky
      Best Actor: Peter Finch Network
      Best Actress: Faye Dunaway Network

1977 Best Picture: Annie Hall
      Best Director: Woody Allen Annie Hall
      Best Actor: Richard Dreyfuss The Goodbye Girl
      Best Actress: Diane Keaton Annie Hall

1978 Best Picture: The Deer Hunter
      Best Director: Michael Cimino The Deer Hunter
      Best Actor: Jon Voight Coming Home
      Best Actress: Jane Fonda Coming Home

1979 Best Picture: Kramer vs Kramer
      Best Director: Robert Beaton Kramer vs Kramer
      Best Actor: Dustin Hoffman Kramer vs Kramer
      Best Actress: Sally Field Norma Rae

1980 Best Picture: Ordinary People
      Best Director: Robert Redford Ordinary People
      Best Actor: Robert de Niro Raging Bull
      Best Actress: Sissy Spacek Coalminer's Daughter

1981 Best Picture: Chariots of Fire
      Best Director: Warren Beaty Reds
      Best Actor: Henry Fonda On Golden Pond
      Best Actress: Katharine Hepburn On Golden Pond

1982 Best Picture: Gandhi
      Best Director: Richard Attenborough Gandhi
      Best Actor: Ben Kingsley Gandhi
      Best Actress: Meryl Streep Sophie's Choice

1983 Best Picture: Terms of Endearment
      Best Director: James L. Brooks Terms of Endearment
      Best Actor: Robert Duvall Tender Mercies
      Best Actress: Shirley MacLaine Terms of Endearment

1984 Best Picture: Amadeus
      Best Director: Milos Forman Amadeus
      Best Actor: F Murray Abraham Amadeus
      Best Actress: Sally Field Places in the Heart

1985 Best Picture: Out of Africa
      Best Director: Sidney Pollack Out of Africa
      Best Actor: William Hurt Kiss of the Spider Woman
      Best Actress: Geraldine Page The Trip to Bountiful

1986 Best Picture: Platoon
      Best Director: Oliver Stone Platoon
      Best Actor: Paul Newman The Color of Money
      Best Actress: Marlee Matlin Children of a Lesser God

1987 Best Picture: The Last Emperor
      Best Director: Bernardo Bertolucci The Last Emperor
      Best Actor: Michael Douglas Wall Street
      Best Actress: Cher Moonstruck

1988 Best Picture: Rain Man
      Best Director: Barry Levinson Rain Man
      Best Actor: Dustin Hoffman Rain Man
      Best Actress: Jodie Foster The Accused

1989 Best Picture: Driving Miss Daisy
      Best Director: Oliver Stone Born on the 4th of July
      Best Actor: Daniel Day-Lewis My Left Foot
      Best Actress: Jessica Tandy Driving Miss Daisy

1990 Best Picture: Dances with Wolves
      Best Director: Kevin Costner Dances with Wolves
      Best Actor: Jeremy Irons Reversal of Fortune
      Best Actress: Kathy Bates Misery

1991 Best Picture: The Silence of the Lambs
      Best Director: Jonathan Demme The Silence of the Lambs
      Best Actor: Anthony Hopkins The Silence of the Lambs
      Best Actress: Jodie Foster The Silence of the Lambs

1992 Best Picture: Unforgiven
      Best Director: Clint Eastwood Unforgiven
      Best Actor: Al Pacino Scent of a Woman
      Best Actress: Emma Thompson Howards End

where they no longer reflect a conventional reality; and non-objective or 'pure' art forms, supposedly without reference to reality.

Abstract Expressionism US movement in abstract art that emphasized the act of painting, the expression inherent in paint itself, and the interaction of artist, paint, and canvas. Abstract Expressionism first emerged in New York in the early 1940s. Gorky, Kline, Pollock, and Rothko are associated with the movement.

Absurd, Theatre of the drama originating with a group of playwrights in the 1950s, including Beckett, Ionesco, Genet, and Pinter. Their work expressed the belief that in a godless universe human existence has no meaning or purpose and therefore all communication breaks down. Logical construction and argument gives way to irrational and illogical speech and to its ultimate conclusion, silence, as in Beckett's play **Breath** 1970.

Abu Bakr or **Abu-Bekr** 573–634. 'Father of the virgin', name used by Abd-el-Ka'aba from about 618 when the prophet Muhammad married his daughter Aisha. On Muhammad's death, he became the first ◊caliph and proved a vigorous ruler, adding Mesopotamia to the Muslim world.

Abu Dhabi sheikhdom in SW Asia, on the Arabian Gulf, capital of the ◊United Arab Emirates. Formerly under British protection, it has been ruled since 1971 by Sheikh Zayed Bin Al-Nahayan, who is also president of the Supreme Council of Rulers of the United Arab Emirates.

Abuja newly built city in Nigeria which is planned to replace Lagos as capital. Shaped like a crescent, it was designed by Kenzo ◊Tange.

Abú Nuwás Hasan ibn Háni 762–c. 815. Arab poet. His work was based on old forms, but the new freedom with which he used them, his eroticism, and his ironic humour, have contributed to his reputation as perhaps the greatest of Arab poets.

Abu Simbel former site of two ancient temples in S Egypt, built during the reign of Rameses II and commemorating him and his wife Nefertari; before the site was flooded by the Aswan High Dam, the temples were moved, in sections, 1966–67.

abyssal zone dark ocean area 2–6,000 m/6,500–19,500 ft deep; temperature 4°C/39°F. Some fish and crustaceans living there may be blind or have their own light sources.

Abyssinia former name of ◊Ethiopia.

a/c abbreviation for **account**.

accelerator

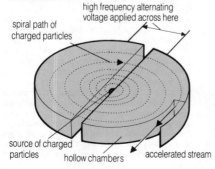

spiral path of
charged particles

high frequency alternating
voltage applied across here

source of charged
particles

hollow chambers

accelerated stream

accumulator

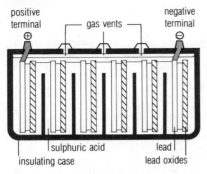

positive terminal ⊕ — gas vents — negative terminal ⊖

sulphuric acid   lead
insulating case   lead oxides

AC in physics, abbreviation for ◊*alternating current.*

acacia one of a large group of shrubs and trees of the genus *Acacia*, belonging to the pea family. Acacias include the thorn trees of the African savannah, and the **gum arabic tree** *Acacia senegal* of N Africa.

Academy Award annual cinema award given from 1927 onwards by the American Academy of Motion Pictures, nicknamed 'Oscar' (1931).

Academy, French or *Académie Française.* Literary society founded by ◊Richelieu in 1635; it is especially concerned with maintaining the purity of the French language; membership is limited to 40 'immortals' at a time.

Academy of Sciences, Soviet society founded in 1725 by Catherine the Great in Leningrad; it has been responsible for such achievements as ◊Sputnik, and has branches in the Ukraine (welding, cybernetics), Armenia (astrophysics), and Georgia (mechanical engineering).

acanthus herbaceous plant with handsome leaves. Some 20 species are found in the Mediterranean region and the Old World tropics, including *bear's breech Acanthus mollis*, whose leaves were used as a motif in classical architecture.

a cappella (Italian 'in the style of the chapel') choral music which is sung without instrumental accompaniment.

Acapulco or *Acapulco de Juarez* port and holiday resort in Mexico; population (1985) 638,000.

ACAS abbreviation for *Advisory, Conciliation and Arbitration Service*, an independent organization set up by the UK government 1975 to advise and arbitrate in industrial disputes between staff and employers.

Accad alternative form of ◊Akkad, ancient city of Mesopotamia.

accelerated freeze drying see ◊AFD.

acceleration the rate of increase in the velocity of a moving body.

accelerator device to bring charged particles (such as protons) up to high kinetic energies. To give particles the energies needed requires many successive applications of a high voltage to electrodes placed in the path of the particles. Accelerators have uses in industry, medicine, and in pure physics. In 1988 the USA announced the Ronald Reagan Center for High Energy Physics, in Waxahachie, Texas, which will house Superconducting Super Collider (SSC), an accelerator 85 km/53 mi in circumference, to be completed by 1996.

accelerometer apparatus for measuring ◊acceleration or deceleration – that is, the rate of increase or decrease in the ◊velocity of a moving object.

accent a way of speaking that identifies a person with a particular country, region, language, social class, linguistic style, or some mixture of these. People often describe only those who belong to groups other than their own as having accents and may give them special names; for example, an Irish brogue, a Northumbrian burr.

accessory in law, accessories are criminal accomplices who may be either 'before the fact' (inciting another to commit a crime) or 'after the fact' (giving assistance after the crime). An accomplice present when the crime is committed is an 'abettor'. In English law these distinctions no longer apply: all those involved in the commission of a crime are punishable in the same way.

access time in computing, the 'reaction time': the time taken after being given an instruction before the computer reads from, or writes to, ◊memory.

acclimation or *acclimatization* the physiological changes induced in an organism by exposure to new environmental conditions. When humans move to higher altitudes, for example, the number of red blood cells rises to increase the oxygen-carrying capacity of the blood, in order to compensate for the lower levels of oxygen in the air.

accomplice a person who is associated with another in the commission of a crime. In English law, the word is used both for persons who played a minor part in the crime and for the principal offenders. See also ◊accessory.

accordion a musical instrument, box-like in form, small enough to be portable, comprising a pair of bellows with many folds and a keyboard of up to 50 keys. When the keys are pressed and the bellows worked, wind is admitted to metal reeds, whose length and thickness determine the notes emitted. It was invented by Cyrill Damien (1772–1847) in Vienna 1829.

accountancy financial management of businesses and other organizations, from balance sheets to policy decisions. Forms of ◊inflation accounting, such as CCA (current cost accounting) and CPP (current purchasing power) are aimed at providing valid financial comparisons over a period in which money values change.

Accra capital and port of Ghana; population of Greater Accra region (1984) 1,420,000. The port trades in cacao, gold, and timber. Industries include engineering, brewing and food processing. Osu (Christiansborg) Castle is the presidential residence, and the University of Ghana is at nearby Legon.

accumulator in electricity, a storage battery – that is, a group of rechargeable secondary cells. An ordinary 12-volt car battery is an accumulator consisting of six lead-acid cells which are continually recharged by the car's alternator or dynamo. It has electrodes of lead and lead oxide in an electrolyte of sulphuric acid.

accusative in the grammar of some inflected languages, such as Latin, Greek, or Russian, the accusative case is the form of a noun, pronoun, or adjective used to indicate that it is the direct object of a verb. It is also used with certain prepositions.

Acer genus of trees and shrubs of N temperate regions with over 115 species. *Acer* includes the ◊sycamores and ◊maples.

acetaldehyde common name for ◊ethanal.

acetate common name for ◊ethanoate.

acetic acid common name for ◊ethanoic acid.

acetone common name for ◊propanone.

acetylene common name for ◊ethyne.

acetylsalicylic acid chemical name for the painkilling drug ◊aspirin.

Achaea in ancient Greece, and also today, an area of the N Peloponnese; the **Achaeans** were the predominant group in the Mycenaean period, and are said by Homer to have taken part in the siege of Troy.

Achaean League union in 275 BC of most of the cities of the N Peloponnese, which managed to defeat Sparta, but was itself defeated by the Romans 146 BC.

Achaemenid dynasty rulers of the Persian Empire 550–330 BC, named after Achaemenes, ancestor of Cyrus the Great, founder of the empire. His successors included Cambyses, Darius I, Xerxes, and Darius III, who, as the last Achaemenid ruler, was killed after defeat in battle against Alexander the Great in 330 BC.

Achebe Chinua 1930– . Nigerian novelist, whose themes include the social and political impact of European colonialism on African people, and the problems of newly independent African nations. His first novel, *Things Fall Apart* 1958, was widely acclaimed; *Anthills of the Savannah* 1987 is also set in a fictional African country.

achene a dry, one-seeded ◊fruit that develops from a single ◊ovary and does not split open to disperse the seed. Achenes commonly occur in groups, for example the fruiting heads of buttercup (*Ranunculus*) and clematis. The outer surface may be smooth, spiny, ribbed, or tuberculate, depending on the species.

Acheson Dean (Gooderham) 1893–1971. US politician; as undersecretary of state 1945–47 in Truman's Democratic administration, he was associated with George C ◊Marshall in preparing the Marshall Plan, and succeeded him as secretary of state 1949–53. He helped establish NATO, and criticized Britain for having 'lost an empire and not yet found a role'.

Achilles Greek hero of the *Iliad* attributed to Homer. He was the son of Peleus, king of the Myrmidons in Thessaly, and the sea nymph Thetis, who rendered him invulnerable, except for the heel by which she held him, by dipping him in the river Styx. Achilles killed Hector in the Trojan War, and was himself killed by Paris with a poisoned arrow in the heel.

Achilles tendon the tendon pinning the calf muscle to the heelbone. It is one of the largest in the human body.

achromatic lens combination of lenses made from glasses of different refractive index, constructed in such a way as to minimize chromatic aberration (which in a single lens causes coloured fringes round images because the lens diffracts the different wavelengths in white light to slightly different extents).

acid a substance which, in solution in an ionizing solvent (usually water), gives rise to hydrogen ions (H^+ or protons). Acids react with alkalis to form salts, and they act as solvents. Strong acids are corrosive; dilute acids have a sour or sharp taste.

acid house a type of ◊house music.

acid rain acidic rainfall thought to be caused principally by the release into the atmosphere of sulphur dioxide (SO_2) from coal-burning power stations. Acid gases, especially those of nitrogen oxides, are also contributed from other industrial activities and automobile exhaust fumes.

aclinic line the magnetic equator, an imaginary line near the equator, where the compass needle has no 'dip' or magnetic inclination.

acne skin eruption caused by inflammation of the sebaceous glands which secrete an oily substance (sebum), the natural lubricant of the skin. Sometimes their openings become stopped and they swell; the contents decompose and pimples form.

Aconcagua an extinct volcano in the Argentine Andes, the highest peak in the Americas. Height 6960 m/22,834 ft. It was first climbed by Vines and Zeebruggen in 1897.

aconite herbaceous plant *Aconitum napellus* of the buttercup family, with hooded blue-mauve flowers, commonly known as **monkshood**. It produces aconitine, a powerful alkaloid with narcotic and analgesic properties.

acorn fruit of the oak tree, a nut growing in a shallow cup.

acoustics in general, the experimental and theoretical science of sound; in particular, that branch of the science that has to do with the phenomena of sound in space.

acquired character a feature of the body that develops during the lifetime of an individual, usually as a result of repeated use or disuse, such as the enlarged muscles of a weightlifter. ◊Lamarck's theory of evolution assumed that acquired characters were passed from parent to offspring.

acquired immune deficiency syndrome full name for the disease ◊AIDS.

acquittal in law, the setting free of someone charged with a crime after a trial. In English courts it follows a verdict of 'not guilty', but in Scotland the verdict may be either 'not guilty' or 'not proven'. Acquittal by the jury must be confirmed by the judge.

acre traditional English land measure (4,047 sq m/4,840 sq yd/0.405 ha). Originally meaning a field, it was the size that a yoke of oxen could plough in a day.

Acre seaport in Israel; population (1983) 37,000. Taken by the ◊Crusaders in 1104, it was captured by ◊Saladin in 1187 and retaken by ◊Richard I (the Lionheart) in 1191. Napoleon failed in a siege in 1799; General ◊Allenby captured it in 1918; and it became part of Israel in 1948.

acre-foot unit sometimes used to measure large volumes of water, such as the capacity of a reservoir (equal to its area in acres multiplied by its average depth in feet). 1 acre-foot equals 1,233.5 m^3.

acridine an organic compound which occurs in crude anthracene oil, extracted by dilute acids. It is also obtained synthetically. It is used to make many dye-stuffs and some valuable drugs.

acronym a word formed from the initial letters and/or syllables of other words, intended as a pronounceable abbreviation, for example *NATO* (North Atlantic Treaty Organization).

acrophobia a ◊phobia involving fear of heights.

acropolis citadel of an ancient Greek town. Best known is the Acropolis at Athens, famous for the ruins of the Parthenon, built there during the great days of the Athenian empire. The term is also used for analogous structures, as in the massive granite-built ruins of Great ◊Zimbabwe.

acrostic a number of lines of writing, especially verse, whose initial letters (read downwards) form a word, phrase, or sentence. A *single acrostic* is formed by the initial letters of lines only, while a *double acrostic* is formed by both initial and final letters.

acrylic acid common name for ◊propenoic acid.

ACTH (*adreno-cortico-tropic hormone*) a ◊hormone, secreted by the ◊pituitary gland, which controls the production of corticosteroid

acid rain

As industry has expanded since the industrial revolution, the quantity of waste gases and smoke given off by factories has increased enormously. As a result more and more chemical pollutants are being added to the atmosphere. Fossil fuels, such as coal, oil, and gas, contain sulphur which is given off when they are burnt. The chemicals produced can alter the acidity of the rain and cause severe damage to plant life, lakes, and the water supply.

A tree is damaged in a number of ways. The bark and leaves are damaged by the direct effects. The change in pH of the ground water makes the roots less effective. Fewer nutrients pass up into the tree, making it more susceptible to damage. Leaves and needles fall off and the crowns thin and die.

Sulphur dioxide (SO_2) and nitrogen oxides (NO_2) are given off with the smoke when fossil fuels burn.

H_2SO_4

HNO_3

SO_2 NO_2

Some of the gases go directly into plants and into the ground, but most are oxidized to sulphuric acid (H_2SO_4) and nitric acid (HNO_3).

These acids, dissolved in rainwater, rain down often a great distance away.

Direct effects of chemicals in the atmosphere are felt within a few kilometres of the emission. These include the deterioration of buildings and harm to human health.

Indirect effects, due to chemical changes in the ground water, can be felt thousands of kilometres away.

Sometimes lime is dropped into an acid lake to neutralize it, but this is only a temporary measure.

Acidity is measured in pH. The lower the pH value the higher the acidity. In a lake (or river) affected by acid rain, different creatures die at different pH values.

death in lakes and rivers

1. Crustaceans and snails die
2. Salmon and trout die

3. Sensitive insects die
4. Whitefish and grayling die

5. Perch and pike die
6. Eel and brook trout die

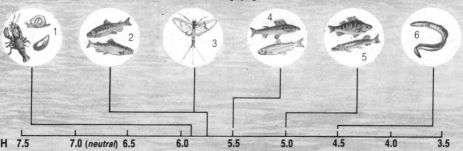

| pH | 7.5 | | 7.0 (neutral) 6.5 | | 6.0 | 5.5 | 5.0 | 4.5 | 4.0 | 3.5 |

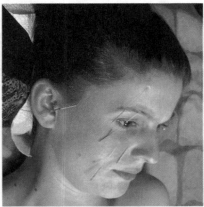

acupuncture a woman patient being treated for per-sistent headaches by acupuncture.

hormones by the ◊adrenal gland. It is commonly produced as a response to stress.

actinide chemical element with atomic numbers 89–105. All actinides are radioactive, and synthetic above uranium (atomic number 92). They are grouped because of their chemical similarities, and also by analogy with the rare-earth elements (lanthanides).

actinium rare radioactive element, atomic number 89, relative atomic mass of most stable isotope 227; the first of the ◊actinide series and a weak emitter of high-energy alpha-rays. It is made by bombarding radium with neutrons.

action in law, one of the proceedings whereby a person enforces his or her rights in a law court. Actions fall into three principal categories, namely civil (such as the enforcement of a debt), penal (where a punishment is sought for the person sued), and criminal (where in Britain the Crown prosecutes a person accused of an offence).

action and reaction in physical mechanics, equal and opposite effects produced by a force acting on an object. For example, the pressure of expanding gases from the burning of fuel in a rocket motor (a force) produces an equal and opposite reaction which causes the rocket to move.

action painting or *gesture painting* in US art, the most dynamic school of Abstract Expressionism. It emphasized the importance of the physical act of painting, sometimes expressed with both inventiveness and aggression, and on occasion performed for the camera. Jackson Pollock was the leading exponent.

action potential in biology, a change in the potential difference (voltage) across the membrane of a nerve cell when an impulse passes along it. The potential change (from about –60 to +45 millivolts) accompanies the passage of sodium and potassium ions across the membrane.

Actium, Battle of naval battle in which ◊Augustus defeated the combined fleets of ◊Mark Antony and ◊Cleopatra in 31 BC. The site is modern Akri, a promontory in western Greece.

act of Congress in the USA, a bill or resolution passed by both houses of Congress, the Senate and the House of Representatives, which then becomes law unless it is vetoed by the president. If vetoed, it may still become a law if it is returned to Congress again and passed by a majority of two-thirds in each house.

act of God legal term meaning some sudden and irresistible act of nature which could not reasonably have been foreseen, such as extraordinary storms, snow, frost, or sudden death.

act of Parliament in Britain, a change in the law originating in Parliament and called a statute. Such acts may be either public (of general effect), local, or private. Before an act receives the royal assent and becomes law it is a 'bill'. The body of English statute law comprises all the acts passed by Parliament: the existing list opens with the Statute of Merton, passed in 1235. An act (unless it is stated to be for a definite period and then to come to an end) remains on the statute book until it is repealed. See also ◊act of Congress.

Actors' Studio theatre workshop in New York City, established 1947 by Cheryl Crawford, Elia Kazan, and Lee Strasberg for the study of Stanislavsky's ◊Method of acting.

actuary a mathematician who makes statistical calculations concerning human life expectancy and other risks, on which insurance premiums are based. Professional bodies are the Institute of Actuaries (England, 1848), Faculty of Actuaries (Scotland, 1856), and Society of Actuaries (US, 1949, by a merger of two earlier bodies).

acupuncture system developed in ancient China of inserting needles into the body at predetermined points to relieve pain and assist healing. The method, increasingly popular in the West, is thought to work partly by stimulating the brain's own painkillers, or endorphins.

acute in medicine, a condition which develops and resolves quickly, for example the common cold, or meningitis. In contrast, a *chronic* condition develops over a long period.

AD abbreviation for *anno Domini* (Latin 'in the year of the Lord').

ADA computer-programming language developed in the early 1980s to meet the need of reacting to events in the world as they happen.

Adam family of Scottish architects and designers. *William Adam* (1689–1748) was the leading Scottish architect of his day, and his son *Robert Adam* (1728–92) is considered the greatest British architect of the late 18th century. He transformed the prevailing Palladian fashion in architecture to a Neo-Classical style. He designed interiors for many great country houses (Harewood House, Yorkshire; Luton Hoo, Luton;) and with his brother *James Adam* (1732–94) developed the area known as the Adelphi in London.

Adam in the Old Testament, founder of the human race. Formed by God from the dust and given the breath of life, Adam was placed in the Garden of Eden, where ◊Eve was given to him as a companion. With her, he tasted the forbidden fruit of the Tree of Knowledge of Good and Evil, and they were expelled from the Garden.

Adams Ansel 1902–1984. US photographer, who produced superbly printed images of dramatic landscapes and organic forms of the American West. He was associated with the ◊Zone System of exposure estimation.

Adams John 1735–1826. 2nd president of the USA 1797–1801, and vice president 1789–97. Born at Quincy, Massachusetts. He was a member of the Continental Congress, 1774–78, and signed the Declaration of Independence. In 1779 he went to France and negotiated the treaties that ended the War of American Independence. In 1785 he became the first US ambassador in London.

Adams American photographer Ansel Adams.

Adams John Coolidge 1947– . US composer and conductor, director of the New Music Ensemble 1972–81. His works include *Heavy Metal* 1971, *Bridge of Dreams* 1982, and the opera *Nixon in China* 1988.

Adams John Couch 1819–1892. English astronomer, who deduced the existence of the planet Neptune 1845.

Adams John Quincy 1767–1848. 6th president of the USA 1825–29. Eldest son of President John ◊Adams, he was born at Quincy, Massachusetts, and became US minister in The Hague, Berlin, St Petersburg, and London. In 1817 he became ◊Monroe's secretary of state, formulated the ◊Monroe doctrine 1823, and succeeded him in the presidency, despite receiving fewer votes than his main rival, Andrew ◊Jackson. As president, Adams was an advocate of strong federal government.

Adams Richard 1920– . British novelist. A civil servant 1948–72, he achieved fame with *Watership Down* 1972, a tale of a rabbit community, which was popular with adults and children. Later novels include *The Plague Dogs* 1977 and *Girl on a Swing* 1980.

Adams Roger 1889–1971. US organic chemist, best known for his painstaking analytical work to determine the composition of naturally occuring substances such as complex vegetable oils and plant ◊alkaloids.

Adams Samuel 1722–1803. US politician, second cousin of President John Adams; he was the chief prompter of the Boston Tea Party (see War of ◊American Independence). He was also a signatory of the Declaration of Independence, and anticipated the French emperor Napoleon in calling the British a 'nation of shopkeepers'.

Adamson Robert R 1821–1848. Scottish photographer who, with David Octavius Hill, turned out 2,500 ◊calotypes (mostly portraits) in five years from 1843.

Adana capital of Adana (Seyhan) province, S Turkey. A major cotton-growing centre, it is Turkey's fourth largest city. Population (1985) 776,000.

adaptation in biology, any change in the structure or function of an organism that allows it to survive and reproduce more effectively in its environment. In ◊evolution, adaptation occurs as a result of random variation in the genetic make-up of organisms (produced by ◊mutation and ◊recombination) coupled with natural selection.

adaptive radiation in evolution, the production of several new ◊species, with ◊adaptations to different ways of life, from a single parent stock. Adaptive radiation is likely to occur whenever a species enters a new habitat that contains few, if any, similar species.

ADB abbreviation for ◊*Asian Development Bank*.

ADC abbreviation for *aide-de-camp*.

Addams Charles 1912–1988. US cartoonist, creator of the Gothically ghoulish Addams family in the *New Yorker* magazine. There was a successful television series based on the cartoon in the 1960s.

addax light-coloured ◊antelope *Addax nasomaculatus* of the Sahara desert, where it exists on the scanty vegetation without drinking. It is about 1.1 m/3.5 ft at the shoulder and both sexes have spirally twisted horns.

added value in economics, the difference between the cost of producing something and the price at which it is sold. Added value is the basis of VAT (◊value-added tax), a tax on the value added at each stage of the production process of a commodity.

addendum (Latin) something to be added.

adder venomous European snake *Vipera berus*, belonging to the viper family. Growing to about 60 cm/2 ft long, it has a thick body, triangular head, a characteristic V-shaped mark on its head, and often, zig-zag markings along the back. A shy animal, it feeds on small mammals and lizards. The *puff adder Bitis arietans* is a large yellowish thick-bodied viper up to 1.6 m/5 ft long living in Africa and Arabia.

addiction state of dependence on drugs, alcohol, or other substances.

Addis Ababa or *Adis Abeba* capital of Ethiopia; population (1984) 1,412,000. It was founded in 1887 by Menelik, chief of Shoa, who ascended the throne of Ethiopia in 1889. His former residence, Menelik Palace, is now occupied by the chairperson of the Provisional Military Council; the city is the headquarters of the Organization of African Unity.

Addison Joseph 1672–1719. British writer. He contributed to the *Tatler*, begun by Richard ◊Steele, and co-founded with him in 1711 the *Spectator*.

Addison's disease rare deficiency of the ◊adrenal glands which is treated with hormones. It is named after Thomas Addison, the London physician who first described it in 1855.

additive in food, a chemical added to prolong shelf life (such as salt), alter colour, or improve food value (such as vitamins or minerals). Many chemical additives are used in the manufacture of food. They are subject to regulation since individuals may be affected by constant exposure to even

adder

puff adder

small concentrations of certain additives and suffer side effects such as hyperactivity. Within the European Community, approved additives are given an official number (◊E number).

address in a computer memory, a number indicating a specific location. At each address, a single piece of data can be stored. For microcomputers, this normally amounts to one byte (enough to represent a single character such as a letter or number).

Adelaide 1792–1849. Queen consort of ◊William IV of England. Daughter of the Duke of Saxe-Meiningen, she married William, then Duke of Clarence, in 1818. No children of the marriage survived infancy.

Adelaide capital and industrial city of South Australia; population (1986) 993,100. Industries include oil refining, shipbuilding, and the manufacture of electrical goods and cars. Grain, wool, fruit, and wine are exported. Founded in 1836, Adelaide was named after William IV's queen.

Aden (Arabic *'Adan*) capital of South Yemen, on a rocky peninsula at the SW corner of Arabia, commanding the entrance to the Red Sea; population (1984) 264,300. It comprises the new administrative centre Madinet al-Sha'ab; the commercial and business quarters of Crater and Tawahi, and the harbour area of Ma'alla. The city's economy is based on oil refining, fishing, and shipping. A British territory from 1839, Aden became part of independent South Yemen in 1967.

Adenauer Konrad 1876–1967. German Christian Democrat politician, chancellor of the Federal Republic 1949–63. With the French president de Gaulle he achieved the postwar reconciliation of France and Germany and strongly supported all measures designed to strengthen the Western bloc in Europe.

adenoids masses of lymphoid tissue, similar to ◊tonsils, located in the upper part of the throat. They are part of a child's natural defences against the entry of germs but usually shrink and disappear by the age of ten years.

Ader Clement 1841–1925. French aviation pioneer whose first steam-driven aeroplane, the *Éole*, made the first powered take-off in history (1890), but it could not fly. In 1897, with his *Avion III*, he failed completely, despite false claims made later.

adhesion in medicine, the abnormal binding of two tissues as a result of inflammation. The moving surfaces of joints or internal organs may merge together if they have been inflamed.

adhesive substance that sticks two surfaces together. Natural adhesives include gelatine in its crude industrial form (made from bones, hide fragments and fish offal), and vegetable gums. Synthetic adhesives include thermoplastic and thermosetting resins, which are often stronger than the substances they join; mixtures of epoxy resin and hardener that set by chemical reaction; and elastomeric (stretching) adhesives for flexible joints.

adiabatic the expansion or contraction of a gas in which a change takes place in the pressure or volume, although no heat is allowed to enter or leave.

Adi Granth or *Guru Granth Sahib* the holy book of Sikhism.

ad infinitum (Latin) to infinity, endlessly.

adipose tissue a type of ◊connective tissue of ◊vertebrates, the main energy store of the body. It is commonly called fat tissue, and consists of large spherical cells filled with ◊fat. In mammals, major layers are in the inner

Adenauer German politician Konrad Adenauer, 1949.

layer of skin, and around the ◊kidneys and ◊heart.

adj. abbreviation for *adjective*.

adjective the grammatical ◊part of speech for words that describe nouns (for example, *new* and *enormous*, as in 'a new hat' and 'an enormous dog'). Adjectives generally have three degrees (grades or levels for the description of relationships): the positive degree (*new*; *enormous*, the comparative degree (*newer*; *more enormous*), and the superlative degree (*newest*; *most enormous*).

Adler Alfred 1870–1937. Austrian psychologist. Adler saw the 'will to power' as more influential in accounting for human behaviour than the sexual drive theory. Over this theory he parted company with ◊Freud after a ten-year collaboration. His books include *Organic Inferiority and Psychic Compensation* 1907 and *Understanding Human Nature* 1927.

Adler Larry 1914– . US musician, a virtuoso performer on the harmonica.

ad lib(itum) (Latin) as much as desired.

administrative law the law concerning the powers, and control, of government agencies (for example, ministers, government departments, and local authorities). These agencies have powers which include making quasi-judicial decisions (such as determining planning applications) and delegated legislation (making statutory instruments and orders). The vast increase in these powers in the 20th century in many countries has been criticised by lawyers.

admiral highest-ranking naval officer; in the UK Royal Navy (in descending order) admiral of the fleet, admiral, vice admiral, rear admiral; in the US Navy, fleet admiral, admiral, vice admiral, rear admiral.

admiral name for several species of butterfly related to the tortoiseshells. The red admiral *Vanessa atalanta*, wingspan 6 cm/2 in, migrates each year to the Mediterranean from N Europe, where it cannot survive the winter.

Admiral's Cup sailing series first held in 1957 and held biennially. National teams consisting of three boats compete over three inshore courses (in the Solent) and two offshore courses (378 km/235 mi across the Channel from Cherbourg to the Isle of Wight and 1,045 km/650 mi from Plymouth to Fastnet lighthouse off Ireland, and back). The highlight is the Fastnet race.

Admiralty, Board of the in Britain, the controlling department of state for the Royal Navy from the reign of Henry VIII until 1964, when most of its functions – apart from that of management – passed to the Ministry of Defence. The 600-year-old office of Lord High Admiral reverted to the sovereign.

ad nauseam (Latin) to the point of disgust.

Adonis in Greek mythology, a beautiful youth beloved by ◊Aphrodite. He was killed while boar-hunting, but from his blood sprang the anemone. He was allowed to return from the lower world for six months every year to rejoin her.

adoption the permanent legal transfer of parental rights and duties in respect of a child from one person to another. It was first legalized in England in 1926; in 1958 an adopted child was enabled to inherit on parental intestacy. The Children's Act 1975 enables an adopted child at the age of 18 to know its original name. See also ◊custody of children.

adrenal gland a ◊gland situated on top of the kidney. The adrenals are soft and yellow, and consist of two parts. The *cortex* (outer part) secretes various steroid ◊hormones, controls salt and water metabolism, and regulates the use of carbohydrates, proteins, and fats. The *medulla* (inner part) secretes the hormones epinephrine and norepinephrine (adrenalin and noradrenalin) which constrict the blood vessels of the belly and skin so that more blood is available for the heart, lungs, and voluntary muscles, an emergency preparation for the stress reaction 'fight or flight'.

adrenaline hormone, also called *epinephrine*, secreted by the medulla of the ◊adrenal glands.

Adrian IV (Nicholas Breakspear) *c.* 1100–1159. Pope 1154–59, the only British pope. He secured the execution of ◊Arnold of Brescia; crowned Frederick I Barbarossa as German emperor; refused Henry II's request that Ireland should be granted to the English crown in absolute ownership; and was at the height of a quarrel with the emperor when he died.

Adriatic Sea large arm of the Mediterranean Sea, lying NW to SE between the Italian and the Balkan peninsulas. The western shore is Italian; the eastern is Croatian, Yugoslav, and Albanian. The sea is about 805 km/500 mi long, and its area is 135,250 sq km/52,220 sq mi.

adsorption the taking up of a gas or liquid by the surface of a solid (for example, activated charcoal adsorbs gases). It involves molecular attraction at the surface, and should be distinguished from ◊absorption (in which a uniform solution results from a gas or liquid being incorporated into the bulk structure of a liquid or solid).

adultery voluntary sexual intercourse by a married person with someone other than his or her legal partner. It is one factor which may prove 'irretrievable breakdown' of marriage in actions for ◊judicial separation or ◊divorce in Britain. It is almost universally recognized as grounds for divorce in the USA, and is theoretically a punishable offence in some states.

Aduwa, Battle of defeat of the Italians by the Ethiopians at Aduwa in 1896 under Emperor ◊Menelik II. It marked the end of Italian ambitions in this part of Africa until Mussolini's reconquest in 1935.

adv. abbreviation for ◊*adverb*.

advanced gas-cooled reactor (AGR) a type of ◊nuclear reactor, widely used in Britain. The AGR uses a fuel of enriched uranium dioxide in stainless steel cladding and a moderator of graphite. Carbon dioxide gas is pumped through the reactor core to extract the heat produced by the ◊fission of the uranium. The heat is transferred to water in a steam generator, and the steam drives a turbogenerator to produce electricity.

Advent in the Christian calendar, the preparatory season for Christmas, including the four Sundays preceding it, beginning with the Sunday that falls nearest (before or after) St Andrew's Day (30 Nov).

Adventist a person who believes that Christ will return to make a second appearance on the earth. Expectation of the Second Coming of Christ is found

advanced gas-cooled reactor

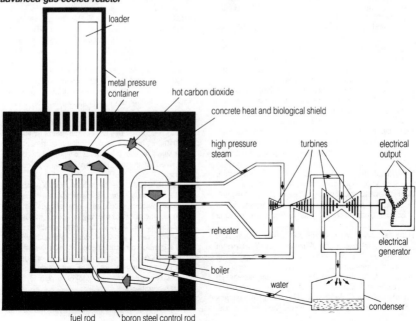

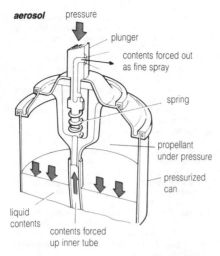

aerosol

pressure

plunger

contents forced out
as fine spray

spring

propellant
under pressure

pressurized
can

liquid
contents

contents forced
up inner tube

in New Testament writings generally. Adventist views are held by the Seventh-Day Adventists, Christadelphians, Jehovah's Witnesses, and the Four Square Gospel Alliance.

adverb the grammatical part of speech for words that modify or describe verbs ('She ran *quickly*'), adjectives ('a *beautifully* clear day'), and adverbs ('They did it *really* well'). Most adverbs are formed from adjectives or past participles by adding -ly (*quick: quickly; or -ally (automatic: automatically*).

advertising any of various methods used by a company to increase the sales of its products or to promote a brand name. Advertising can be seen by economists as both beneficial (since it conveys information about a product and so brings the market closer to a state of ◊perfect competition) and also as a hindrance to perfect competition, since it attempts to make illusory distinction (such as greater sex appeal) between essentially similar products.

Advertising Standards Authority (ASA) an organization founded by the UK advertising industry 1962 to promote higher standards of advertising in the media (excluding television and radio, which have their own authority). It is financed by the advertisers, who pay 0.1% supplement on the cost of advertisements. It recommends to the media that advertisements which might breach the British Code of Advertising Practice are not published, but has no statutory power.

advocate (Latin *advocatus*, one summoned to one's aid, especially in a court of justice) a professional pleader in a court of justice. The English term is ◊barrister or counsel, but advocate is retained in Scotland and in other countries, such as France, whose legal systems are based on Roman law.

Advocates, faculty of the professional organization for Scottish advocates, the equivalent of English ◊barristers. It was incorporated in 1532 under James V.

Aegean civilization the cultures of Bronze Age Greece, including the *Minoan civilization* of Crete and the *Mycenaean civilization* of the eastern Peloponnese.

Aegean Sea branch of the Mediterranean between Greece and Turkey; the Dardanelles connect it with the Sea of Marmara. The numerous islands in the Aegean Sea include Crete, the Cyclades, the Sporades, and the Dodecanese. There is political tension between Greece and Turkey over sea limits claimed by Greece around such islands as Lesvos, Chios, Samos, and Kos.

Aelfric c. 955–1020. English writer. He is celebrated for his writings in vernacular Old English prose, particularly for his two collections of homilies and the *Lives of the Saints*.

Aeneas in classical legend, a Trojan prince who became the ancestral hero of the Romans. According to Homer, he was the son of Anchises and the goddess Aphrodite. During the Trojan war he owed his life several times to the intervention of the gods. The legend on which Virgil's *Aeneid* is based describes his escape from Troy and eventual settlement in Latium.

Aeniad, The epic poem by Virgil, written in 12 books of hexameters and composed during the last 11 years of his life (30–19 bc). It celebrates the development of the Roman Empire through the legend of Aeneas. After the fall of Troy, Aeneas wanders for seven years and becomes shipwrecked off Africa. He is received by Dido, queen of Carthage, and they fall in love. Aeneas, however, renounces their love and sails on to Italy where he settles as founder of Latium and the Roman state.

Aeolian harp a wooden sound box, rectangular and fitted with loose gut strings which vibrate in the wind to produce a chordal impression. It became popular in parts of Europe in the 19th century.

aepyornis type of huge extinct flightless bird living in Madagascar until a few thousand years ago. Some stood 3 m/10 ft high and laid eggs with a volume of 9 litres/2 gallons.

Aequi an Italian people, originating around the river Velino, who were turned back from their advance on Rome in 431 bc, and conquered in 304 bc, during the Samnite Wars. They subsequently adopted Roman customs and culture.

aerenchyma a plant tissue with numerous air-filled spaces between the cells. It occurs in the stems and roots of many aquatic plants where it aids buoyancy and facilitates transport of oxygen around the plant.

aerial or *antenna* in radio broadcasting, a conducting device that radiates or receives radio waves. The design of an aerial depends principally on the wavelength of the radio signal. Long waves (hundreds of metres) may employ long wire aerials; short waves (several centimetres wavelength) may employ rods and dipoles; microwaves may also use dipoles – often with reflectors arranged like a toast rack – or highly directional parabolic dish aerials. Because microwaves travel in straight lines, giving line-of-sight communication, microwave aerials are usually located at the tops of tall masts or towers.

aerobic in biology, a description of those living organisms which use molecular oxygen (usually dissolved in water) for the efficient release of energy.

aerodynamics the branch of fluid physics that studies the flow of gases, particularly as it applies to solid objects (such as land vehicles, bullets, rockets, and aircraft) moving at speed through air. For maximum efficiency, the aim is usually to design the shape of an object to produce a streamlined flow, with a minimum of turbulence in the moving air.

aeronautics the science of travel through the Earth's atmosphere, including aerodynamics, aircraft structures, jet and rocket propulsion, and aerial navigation.

aeroplane a powered heavier-than-air craft supported in flight by fixed wings. Aeroplanes are

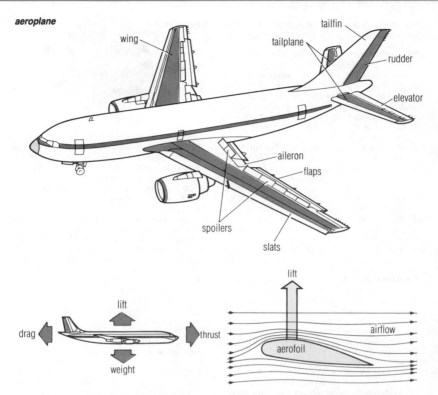

aeroplane

propelled by the thrust of a jet engine or airscrew (propeller). They must be designed aerodynamically, as streamlining ensures maximum flight efficiency. The shape of a plane depends on its operating speed – aircraft operating at well below the speed of sound need not be so streamlined as supersonic aircraft.

aerosol particles of liquid or solid suspended in a gas. Fog is a common natural example. Aerosol cans, which contain pressurized gas mixed with a propellant, are used to spray liquid in the form of tiny drops for products such as insecticides. Many commercial aerosols use chlorofluorocarbons (CFCs) as propellants, but British companies controlling most of the UK aerosol market agreed to phase out CFC's by the end of 1989 as it was believed they are responsible for the destruction of the ◊ozone layer in the Earth's ◊atmosphere. Unfortunately, many 'ozone friendly' aerosols have the disadvantage of using flammable butane or propane as propellants.

Aeschylus *c.* 525–*c.* 456 BC. Greek dramatist, widely regarded as the founder of Greek tragedy. By the introduction of a second actor he made true dialogue and dramatic action possible. Aeschylus wrote some 90 plays between 499 and 458 BC of which seven survive. These are: *The Suppliant Women* peformed about 490, *The Persians* 472, *Seven against Thebes* 467, *Prometheus Bound* (about 460) and the *Oresteia* trilogy 458 which won first prize at the festival of Dionysus. The three plays – *Agamemnon, Choephori,* and *Eumenides* – deal with the curse on the house of Agamemnon.

Aesir principal gods of Norse mythology whose dwelling place was Asgard.

Aesop traditional writer of Greek fables. According to Herodotus he lived in the reign of Amasis of Egypt (mid-6th century BC) and was a slave of Iadmon, a Thracian. The fables, for which no evidence of his authorship exists, are anecdotal stories using animal characters to illustrate moral or satirical points.

Aesthetic movement English artistic movement of the late 19th century, dedicated to the doctrine 'art for art's sake' - that is, art as self-sufficient, not needing to justify its existence by serving any particular use. Artists associated with the movement include Beardsley and Whistler.

aesthetics the branch of philosophy which deals with the nature of beauty, especially in art. It emerged as a distinct branch of enquiry in the mid-18th century.

aestivation in zoology, a state of inactivity and reduced metabolic activity, similar to ◊hibernation, that occurs during the dry season in species such as lungfish and snails. In botany, the term is used to describe the way in which flower petals and sepals are folded in the buds. It is an important feature in ◊plant classification.

aet. abbreviation for *aetatis* (Latin 'of the age').

Aetolia district of ancient Greece on the NW of the gulf of Corinth. The *Aetolian League* was a confederation of the cities of Aetolia which, following the death of Alexander the Great, was the chief rival of the Macedonian power and the Achaean League.

AFD abbreviation for *accelerated freeze drying*, a common method of food preservation. See also ◊food technology.

affidavit a legal document, used in court applications and proceedings, in which a person swears that certain facts are true. In England, the oath is usually sworn before a solicitor or Commissioner for Oaths.

affiliation order in English law, formerly a court order for maintenance against the alleged father of an illegitimate child. Under the Family Law Reform Act 1987, either parent can apply for a court order for maintenance of children, no distinction being made between legitimate and illegitimate children. Genetic fingerprinting was first used in 1988 in Britain to prove paternity and thereby allow immigration to the UK.

affinity in law, relationship by marriage not blood, for example between step-parent and stepchild, which may legally preclude their marriage. It is distinguished from consanguinity or blood relationship. In Britain the right to marry was extended to many relationships formerly prohibited, by the Marriage (Prohibited Degrees of Relationship) Act 1986.

affinity in chemistry, the force of attraction between chemical elements, which helps to keep them in combination in a molecule.

affirmation a solemn declaration made instead of taking the oath by a person who has no religious belief or objects to taking an oath.

affirmative action in the USA, a government-endorsed policy of positive ◊discrimination in favour of members of minority ethnic groups and women in such areas as employment and education, designed to counter the effects of long-term discrimination against them. The policy has been controversial, and in the 1980s it has been less rigorously enforced.

affluent society a society in which most people have money left over after satisfying their basic needs such as food and shelter. They are then able to decide how to spend their excess ('disposable') income, and become 'consumers'. The term was popularized by the US economist John Kenneth ◊Galbraith.

Afghan inhabitant of Afghanistan. The most dominant group, particularly in Kabul, are the Pathans. The Tajiks, a smaller ethnic group, are predominantly traders and farmers in the province of Herat and around Kabul, and the Hazaras, another farming group, are found in the southern mountain ranges of the Hindu Kush.

Afghan hound dog resembling the saluki, though less thickly coated, first introduced to Britain by army officers serving on the North-West Frontier in the late 19th century.

Afghanistan mountainous, landlocked country in S central Asia, bounded by Tajikistan, Turkmenistan, and Uzbekistan to the north, Iran to the west, and Pakistan to the south and east.

Afghan Wars wars waged between Britain and Afghanistan to counter the threat to British India from expanding Russian influence in Afghanistan.
First Afghan War 1838–42, when the British garrison at Kabul was wiped out.
Second Afghan War 1878–80, when Gen ◊Roberts captured Kabul and relieved Kandahar.
Third Afghan War 1919, when peace followed the dispatch by the UK of the first aeroplane ever seen in Kabul.

AFL-CIO abbreviation for *American Federation of Labor and Congress of Industrial Organizations*, a federation of North American trade unions, representing (1992) about 20% of the workforce in North America. The AFL was founded in 1886, superseding the Federation of Organized Trades and Labor Unions of the US and Canada, and the CIO in 1935, known then as the Committee on

African violet

Industrial Organization (it adopted its present title in 1927 after expulsion from the AFL for its opposition to the AFL policy of including only skilled workers). A merger reunited them in 1955, bringing most unions into the national federation.

Africa second largest of the continents, and three times the area of Europe.
area 30,097,000 sq km/11,617,000 sq mi
largest cities Cairo, Algiers, Lagos, Kinshasa, Abidjan, Tunis, Cape Town, Nairobi
physical dominated by a central plateau, which includes the world's largest desert (◊Sahara); Nile and Zaïre rivers, but generally there is a lack of rivers, and also of other inlets, so that Africa has proportionately the shortest coastline of all the continents; comparatively few offshore islands; 75% is within the tropics; Great Rift Valley; immensely rich fauna and flora
exports has 30% of the world's minerals; crops include coffee (Kenya), cocoa (Ghana, Nigeria), cotton (Egypt, Uganda)
population (1988) 610 million; annual growth rate 3%
language Hamito-Semitic in the north; Bantu below the Sahara; Xhosa languages with 'click' consonants in the far south.
religion Islam in the north; animism below the Sahara, which survives alongside Christianity (both Catholic and Protestant) in many central and southern areas.

African art the art of sub-Saharan Africa, from prehistory onwards, ranging from the art of ancient civilizations to the new styles of post-imperialist African nations. Among the best-known examples of African art are bronze figures from Benin and Ife (in modern Nigeria) dating from about 1500 and, also on the W coast, bronze or brass figures for measuring gold, made by the Ashanti.

African National Congress (ANC) multiracial nationalist organization formed in South Africa 1912 to extend the franchise to the whole population and end all racial discrimination there. Its president is Nelson ◊Mandela. Although nonviolent, it was banned by the government in 1960, and in exile in Mozambique developed a military wing, *Umkhonto we Sizwe*, which engaged in sabotage and guerrilla training. The armed struggle was suspended 1990 after the ANC's headquarters were moved from Zambia to Johannesburg. Talks between the ANC and the South African government have taken place intermittently since 1991, with the proposed aim of creating a nonracial constitution.

African violet herbaceous plant *Saintpaulia ionantha* from tropical central and E Africa, with velvety green leaves and scentless purple flowers. Different colours and double varieties have been bred.

Afrikaans language along with English, an official language of the Republic of South Africa. Spoken mainly by the Afrikaners, descendants of Dutch and other 17th-century colonists, it is a variety of the Dutch language, modified by circumstance and the influence of German, French, and other immigrant and local languages. It became a standardized written language *c*. 1875.

Afrika Korps the German army in the Western Desert of N Africa in World War II 1941–43. They first came into contact with British troops at El Agheila on 24 Mar 1941, and were driven out of N Africa by May 1943.

Afrikaner (formerly known as *Boer*) inhabitant of South Africa descended from the original Dutch and ◊Huguenot settlers of the 17th century. Comprising approximately 60% of the white population in the Republic, they were originally farmers but have now become mainly urbanized. Their language is Afrikaans.

Afro-Caribbean person of African descent from the West Indies. Afro-Caribbeans are the descendants of West African prisoners of war and others kidnapped purposely, who were shipped to the West Indies by European slave traders. Since World War II many Afro-Caribbeans have migrated to Europe, especially Britain and the Netherlands, and also to North America.

after-burning method of increasing the thrust of a gas turbine (jet) aero engine by spraying additional fuel between the turbojet and the tail pipe. Used for short-term increase of power during take-off, or combat in military aircraft.

after-image persistence of an image on the retina of the eye after the object producing it has been removed. This leads to persistence of vision, a necessary phenomenon for the illusion of continuous movement in films and television. The colours of an after-image are often complementary to those producing it.

after-ripening the process undergone by the seeds of some plants before germination can occur.

The length of the after-ripening period in different species may vary from a few weeks to many months. It helps seeds to germinate at a time when conditions are most favourable for growth. In some cases the embryo is not fully mature at the time of dispersal and must develop further before germination can take place. Other seeds do not germinate even when the embryo is mature, probably owing to growth-inhibitors within the seed which must be leached out or broken down before germination can begin.

AG abbreviation for *Aktiengesellschaft* (German 'limited company').

Agadir most southern seaport in Morocco; near the mouth of the river Sus. Population (1984) 110,500. It was rebuilt after being destroyed by an earthquake in 1960.

Agadir Incident international crisis provoked by Kaiser Wilhelm II of Germany. By sending the gunboat *Panther* to demand territorial concessions from the French, he hoped to drive a wedge into the Anglo-French entente. In fact, German aggression during the second Moroccan crisis merely served to reinforce Anglo-French fears of Germany's intentions. The crisis also gave rise to the term 'gunboat diplomacy'.

Aga Khan IV 1936– . Spiritual head (*imam*) of the *Ismaili* Muslim sect (see ◊Islam). He succeeded his grandfather in 1957.

agama type of lizard. There are about 280 varied species in the agama family, living in Africa, Asia, and Australia. The *Agama stellio* is 30 cm/1 ft long, can change colour, and feeds on insects.

Agamemnon in Greek mythology, a Greek hero, son of Atreus, King of Mycenae. He married Clytemnestra, and their children included Electra, Iphigenia, and Orestes. He led the capture of Troy,

Afghanistan
Republic of
Jamhuria Afghanistan

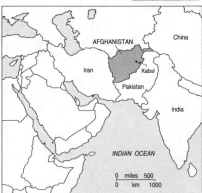

area 652,090 sq km/251,707 sq mi
capital Kabul
towns Kandahár, Herát
physical mountainous; rivers and desert areas
head of state Burhanuddin Rabbani from 1992
head of government to be announced
political system emergent democracy
exports dried fruit, rare minerals, natural gas, karakul lamb skins, Afghan coats
currency afgháni

population (1989) 15,590,000; annual growth rate 0.6%
life expectancy men 43, women 41
language Pushtu
religion Muslim: 80% Sunni, 20% Shi'ite
literacy 39% male/8% female (1985 est)
GNP $3.3 bn (1985); $275 per head
chronology
1747 Afghanistan became an independent emirate.
1838–1919 Afghan Wars waged between Afghanistan and Britain to counter the threat to British India from expanding Russian influence in Afghanistan.
1919 Afghanistan recovered full independence following Third Afghan War.
1953 Lt-Gen Daud Khan became prime minister and introduced reform programme.
1963 Daud Khan forced to resign and constitutional monarchy established.
1973 Monarchy overthrown in coup by Daud Khan.
1978 Daud Khan ousted by Taraki and the People's Democratic Party (PDP) of Afghanistan.
1979 Soviet invasion installed Babrak Karmal in power.
1986 Replacement of Karmal as leader by Dr Najibullah Ahmadzai. Partial Soviet troop withdrawal.
1988 New non-Marxist constitution adopted.
1989 Withdrawal of Soviet troops; civil war.
1991 UN peace efforts failed.
1992 Najibullah regime overthrown. Burhanuddin Rabbani named interim head of state. Islamic law introduced.
1993 Renewed bombardment of Kabul by rebel forces.

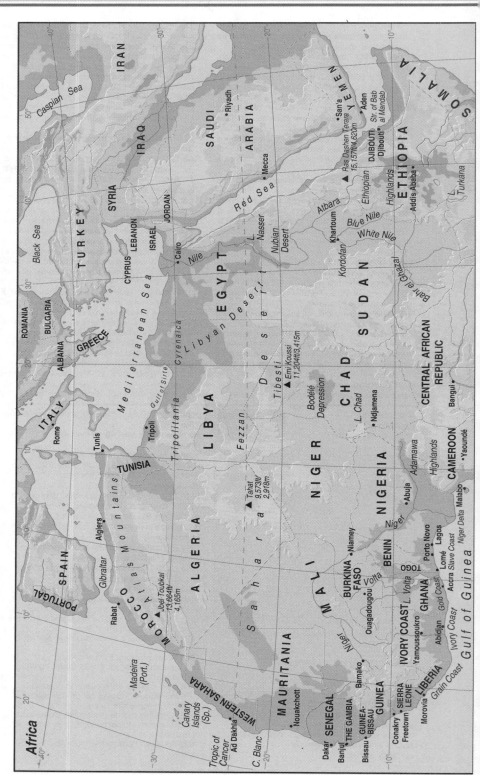

Africa

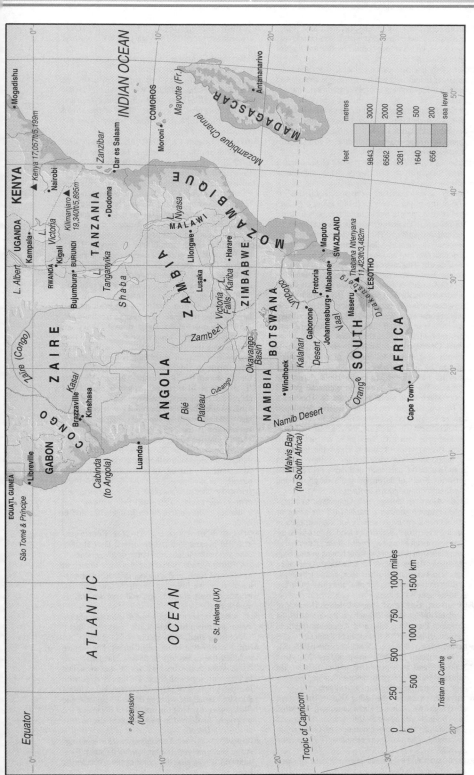

Equator

ATLANTIC

OCEAN

° Ascension
(UK)

° St. Helena (UK)

Tristan da Cunha

Tropic of Capricorn

São Tomé & Príncipe
EQUATL. GUINEA
•Libreville
GABON

CONGO

Zaire (Congo)

ZAIRE

Brazzaville•
Kasai
Kinshasa

Cabinda
(to Angola)

•Luanda

ANGOLA

Bié
Plateau

Cubango

Namib Desert

Walvis Bay
(to South Africa)

NAMIBIA

•Windhoek

Okavango
Basin

Kalahari
Desert

Zambezi

Cape Town•

Orange

SOUTH
AFRICA

BOTSWANA

Limpopo

•Gaborone
Johannesburg•
Vaal

Pretoria•
•Mbabane
Maseru•
LESOTHO

SWAZILAND
•Maputo

Thabana Ntlenyana
▲11,423ft/3,482m

Drakensberg

ZIMBABWE

•Harare

Victoria
Falls•
L.
Kariba

Lusaka•

ZAMBIA

Shaba

L.
Tanganyika

MOZAMBIQUE

L.
Nyasa

MALAWI

•Lilongwe

Bujumbura•
BURUNDI

Kigali•
RWANDA

L.
Victoria

Kampala•
UGANDA

L. Albert

TANZANIA

Kilimanjaro▲
19,340ft/5,895m

•Dodoma

•Nairobi

▲Kenya 17,057ft/5,199m

KENYA

•Mogadishu

Zanzibar

•Dar es Salaam

INDIAN OCEAN

Mozambique Channel

COMOROS
•Moroni

Mayotte (Fr.)

MADAGASCAR

•Antananarivo

metres		feet
3000		9843
2000		6562
1000		3281
500		1640
200		656
sea level		

0   250   500   750   1000 miles

0   500   1000   1500 km

0°   0°   10°   20°   30°   40°   50°

received Priam's daughter Cassandra as a prize, and was murdered by Clytemnestra and her lover, Aegisthus, on his return home. Orestes and Electra later killed the guilty couple.

agar jelly-like substance obtained from seaweed and used mainly as a culture medium in biology and medicine for growing bacteria and other microorganisms.

agaric type of ◊fungus, of typical mushroom shape, with a rounded cap, radially arranged gills, and a central stalk. Agarics include the **field mushroom** *Agaricus campestris* and the **horse mushroom** *Agaricus arvensis*.

agate a banded or cloudy type of chalcedony, a silica, SiO$_2$, used for ornamental stones and objects of art.

ageing in common usage, the period of deterioration of the physical condition of a living organism that leads to death; in biological terms, the entire life-process. Three current theories attempt to account for ageing. The first suggests that the process is genetically determined, to remove individuals that can no longer reproduce by causing their death. The second suggests that it is due to the accumulation of mistakes during the replication of ◊DNA at cell division. The third suggests that it is actively induced by pieces of DNA which move between cells, or cancer-causing viruses; these may become abundant in old cells and induce them to produce unwanted ◊proteins or interfere with the control functions of their DNA.

Agent Orange a selective ◊weedkiller, subsequently discovered to contain highly poisonous ◊dioxin as a by-product. It became notorious after its widespread use in the 1960s during the Vietnam War by US forces to eliminate ground cover which could protect communists. Thousands of US troops who had handled it later developed cancer or fathered deformed babies.

agglutination in medicine, the clumping together of ◊antigens, such as blood cells or bacteria, to form larger, visible masses, under the influence of ◊antibodies. As each antigen clumps only in response to its particular antibody, agglutination provides a way of determining ◊blood groups and the identity of unknown bacteria.

aggression in biology, behaviour used to intimidate or injure another organism (of the same or of a different species), usually for the purposes of gaining a territory, a mate, or food. Aggression often involves an escalating series of threats aimed at intimidating an opponent without having to engage in potentially dangerous physical contact. Aggressive signals include roaring in red deer, snarling by dogs, fluffing up the feathers in birds, and raising the fins in some species of fish.

Agincourt, Battle of battle in which Henry V of England defeated the French on 24 Oct 1415, St Crispin's Day. The village of Agincourt (modern *Azincourt*) is south of Calais, in N France.

Agnew Spiro 1918– . US vice president 1969–73. A Republican, he was governor of Maryland 1966–69, and vice president under ◊Nixon. He resigned in 1973, shortly before pleading 'no contest' to a charge of income-tax evasion.

agnostic a person believing that in the nature of things we cannot know anything of what lies behind or beyond the world of natural phenomena; thus, the existence of God cannot be proved. The word was coined by T H ◊Huxley in 1869.

agoraphobia a ◊phobia involving fear of open spaces and crowded places.

Agostini Giacomo 1943– . Italian motor cyclist. He won a record 122 grands prix and 15 world titles.

AGR abbreviation for ◊advanced gas-cooled reactor, a type of ◊nuclear reactor.

Agra city of Uttar Pradesh, republic of India, on the river Jumna, 160 km/100 mi SE of Delhi; population (1981) 747,318. A commercial and university centre, it was the capital of the Mogul empire 1527–1628, from which period dates the Taj Mahal.

Agricola Gnaeus Julius 37–93 AD. Roman general and politician. Born in Provence, he became Consul in 77 AD, and then governor of Britain 78–85 AD. He extended Roman rule to the Firth of Forth in Scotland, and won the battle of Mons Graupius (site uncertain, but in the Grampian mountains), before being recalled by ◊Domitian, who had grown jealous. His fleet sailed round the north of Scotland and proved Britain an island. His daughter married the historian ◊Tacitus in 78 AD.

agriculture cultivation of land by people. There are two main categories: raising crops and raising animals. Crops are for human nourishment, animal fodder, or commodity crops such as cotton and sisal. Animals are raised for wool, milk, leather, dung (as fuel), or meat. The units for managing agricultural production vary from crofting, small holdings, and farms to collective farms run by entire communities. Agriculture developed in Egypt at least 7,000 years ago. Re-organization along more scientific and productive lines was a feature of 18th-century Britain in response to dramatic population growth. Mechanization made considerable progress in the USA and Europe during the 19th century. After World War II, there was an explosive growth in agricultural chemicals: herbicides, insecticides, fungicides, and fertilizers. In the 1960s there was development of high-yielding species, especially in the ◊**green revolution** in the Third World, and the industrialized countries began intensive farming of cattle, poultry, and pigs. In the 1980s, hybridization by genetic engineering methods was developed, and pest control by the use of chemicals plus ◊pheromones.

agrimony herbaceous plant *Agrimonia eupatoria* of the rose family, with small yellow flowers on a slender spike. It grows on hedgebanks and in fields.

Agrippa Marcus Vipsanius 63–12 BC. Roman general. He commanded the victorious fleet at ◊Actium and married Julia, daughter of ◊Augustus.

agronomy study of crops and soils, a branch of agricultural science. Agronomy includes such topics as selective breeding (of plants and animals), irrigation, pest control, and soil analysis and its modification.

AH with reference to the Muslim calendar, abbreviation for **anno hegirae** (Latin 'year of the flight' - of ◊Muhammad, from Mecca to Medina).

Ahab c. 875–854 BC. King of Israel. His empire included the suzerainty of Moab, and Judah was his subordinate ally, but his kingdom was weakened by constant wars with Syria. By his marriage with Jezebel, princess of Sidon, Ahab was led to introduce into Israel the worship of the Phoenician god Baal, thus provoking the hostility of Elijah and the prophets. Ahab died in battle against the Syrians at Ramoth Gilead.

Ahasuerus (Greek *Xerxes*) several Persian kings in the Bible, notably the husband of ◊Esther. Traditionally it was also the name of the ◊Wandering Jew.

aircraft *NASA's ER-2 research aircraft in flight, which is used for collecting data from the ozone layer in the upper atmosphere.*

Ahmadabad or *Ahmedabad*   capital of Gujarat, India; population (1981) 2,515,195. A cotton-manufacturing centre, it has many edifices of the Hindu, Muslim, and Jain faiths.

Ahmadiyya   Islamic religious movement founded by Mirza Ghulam Ahmad (1839–1908). His followers reject the doctrine that Muhammad was the last of the prophets and accept Ahmad's claim to be the Mahdi and Promised Messiah. In 1974 the Ahmadis were denounced by their coreligionists as non-Muslims.

Ahmad Shah   1724–1773. First ruler of Afghanistan. Elected king in 1747, he had made himself master of the Punjab by 1751. He defeated the Mahrattas at Panipat in 1761, and then the Sikhs.

Ahriman   in Zoroastrianism, the supreme evil spirit, lord of the darkness and death, waging war with his counterpart Ahura Mazda (Ormuzd) until a time when human beings choose to lead good lives and Ahriman is finally destroyed.

Ahura Mazda or *Ormuzd*   in Zoroastrianism, the spirit of supreme good. As god of life and light, he will finally prevail over his enemy, Ahriman.

AI(D)   abbreviation for *artificial insemination (by donor)*. AIH is *artificial insemination by husband*.

Aidan, St   *c.* 600–651. Irish monk from Iona who converted Northumbria to Christianity and founded Lindisfarne monastery on Holy Island. His feast day is 31 Aug.

aid, foreign   financial and other assistance given by richer, usually industrialized, countries to developing states. Official development aid (ODA) may be given for idealistic, commercial, or political reasons, or a combination of the three, as through the ◊International Development Association and ◊International Finance Corporation.

AIDS   abbreviation for *acquired immune deficiency syndrome*, the newest and gravest of sexually transmitted diseases (◊STDs). It is caused by the human immunodeficiency virus (HIV), now known to be a ◊retrovirus, a complex organism first identified in 1983. A 1989 UK government survey estimated that 1.6% of all British males aged around 30 will die of AIDS-related diseases. In the USA it is estimated that one million Americans are infected with the HIV virus. Worldwide cases of AIDS reached 215,500 by Jan 1990.

Aiken   Howard 1900–   . US mathematician. He began work in 1937 on the first electromechanical computer, and initiated the concept of 'time-sharing'.

aikido   Japanese art of self defence; one of the ◊martial arts. Two main systems of aikido are tomiki and uyeshiba.

Ainu   aboriginal people of Japan. In the 4th century AD, they were driven N by ancestors of the modern Japanese. Some 16,000 inhabit the island of Hokkaido in N Japan; other groups live on Sakhalin and the Kuril islands of the USSR. The Ainu language is unrelated to any other.

air   see under ◊atmosphere.

air conditioning   a system that controls the state of the air inside a building or vehicle. A complete air-conditioning unit controls the temperature and ◊humidity of the air, removes dust and odours from it and circulates it by means of a fan. US inventor W H Carrier developed the first effective air-conditioning unit in 1902.

aircraft   aeronautical vehicle, which may be lighter than air (supported by buoyancy) or heavier than air (supported by the dynamic action of air on its surfaces). Balloons and airships are lighter-than-air craft. Heavier-than-air craft include the ◊aeroplane, glider, and helicopter.

aircraft carrier   sea-going base for aircraft. The first purpose-designed aircraft carrier was HMS *Hermes*, completed 1913. In World War II the most famous was HMS *Ark Royal*, completed 1938. After World War II the cost and vulnerability of such large vessels was considered to outweigh their advantages. However, by 1980 the need to have a means of destroying aircraft beyond the range of a ship's own weapons, especially on convoy duty, led to a widespread revival of aircraft carriers in the 20-30,000 tonne range.

air cushion vehicle   (ACV) a craft supported by a layer, or cushion, of high-pressure air. The ◊hovercraft is the best-known form of ACV.

Airedale terrier   large ◊terrier dog with a rough red-brown coat. It originated about 1850 in the Aire and Wharfedale districts of Yorkshire, England, as a cross of the otter hound and Irish and Welsh terriers.

air force   a nation's fighting aircraft, and the organization to maintain them.

airglow   a faint and variable light in the Earth's ◊atmosphere produced by chemical reactions in the ionosphere.

airlock   airtight chamber that allows people to pass between areas at different pressure; also an air-bubble in a pipe that impedes fluid flow.

air raid   aerial attack, usually on a civilian population. In World War II, raids were usually made by bomber aircraft, but many thousands were killed in London in 1944 by German V1 and V2 rockets. The air raids on Britain 1940–41 became known as *the Blitz*.

air sac   in birds, a thin-walled extension of the ◊lungs. There are nine of these and they extend into the abdomen and bones, effectively increasing lung capacity. In mammals, it is another name for the alveoli in the lungs, and, in some insects, widenings of the ◊tracheae.

airship   a power-driven ◊balloon. All airships have streamlined envelopes or hulls, which contain the inflation gas (originally hydrogen, now helium) and are non-rigid, semi-rigid, or rigid.

Ajaccio   capital and second largest port of Corsica; population (1982) 55,279. Founded by the Genoese in 1492, it was the birthplace of Napoleon; it has been French since 1768.

Ajax   Greek hero in ◊Homer. Son of Telamon, king of Salamis, he was second only to Achilles among the Greek heroes in the Trojan War. When Agamemnon awarded the armour of the dead Achilles to Odysseus, Ajax is said to have gone mad with jealousy, and then committed suicide in shame.

AIDS

Many questions remain to be answered on the effects of the human immuno-deficiency virus (HIV). It is not known if the virus can remain dormant indefinitely. Nor is it understood why some people develop intermediate illnesses such as persistent generalised lymphadenopathy – with swollen glands and malaise which may last for months – and AIDS-related complex (ARC), marked by increased susceptibility to disease, lethargy, diarrhoea, weight loss, and night sweats.

HIV (coloured orange) binds to a protein (CD4) on the inside surface of human T4 lymphocytes. *These blood cells have a key role in the immune system. Once inside the T4 cell, the virus uses the enzyme reverse transcriptase to insert its genetic material into the host's DNA. This provirus may remain latent for years. When it multiplies, it destroys the T4 cell and matures as it is released into the blood.*

glycoprotein, GP120

lipio membrane (fat)

glycoprotein, GP41

core protein, P24

core protein, P18

genetic template, RNA

reverse transcriptase

the AIDS virus in cross-section

AIDS is the name given to a constellation of opportunistic infections – bacterial, viral, fungal and parasitic diseases and tumours. HIV also acts directly to destroy blood and other cells of the body.

digestive tract
Severe thrush affecting the mouth and oesophagus makes eating difficult. Chronic diarrhoea and opportunistic intestinal infection can lead to dehydration and malnutrition.

lungs
Lung diseases, such as tuberculosis, are characteristic of AIDS, and *Pneumocystis carinii*, rarely affecting healthy individuals, is common.

skin
Kaposi's sarcoma, a skin cancer usually seen in elderly men, occurs in AIDS in a highly malignant form. Other skin conditions include rashes and eczema.

brain
Compromised immunity, the indirect cause of disease, increases the risk of encephalitis and tumour. Dementia complex is the direct result of HIV infection.

central nervous system
The virus causes widespread damage to the central nervous system, with progressive intellectual, neuromuscular and psychological dysfunction.

pregnancy
HIV can be transmitted across the placenta or during birth; and both mother and baby are at increased risk of developing full-blown AIDS.

a cure?
Drugs are being developed to treat HIV and opportunistic infection, but they cause severe side-effects and so far do not actually cure AIDS.

***Akihito** The emperor and his wife on their wedding day.*

Akbar Jellaladin Muhammad 1542–1605. Mughal emperor of N India from 1556, when he succeeded his father. He gradually established his rule throughout the whole of India N of the Deccan. He is considered the greatest of the Mughal emperors, and the firmness and wisdom of his rule won him the title 'Guardian of Mankind'; he was a patron of the arts.

A Kempis Thomas   see ◊Thomas à Kempis, religious writer.

Akhetaton capital of ancient Egypt established by the monotheistic pharaoh ◊Ikhnaton as the centre for his cult of the Aten, the sun's disc; it is the modern Tell el Amarna 300 km/190 mi S of Cairo. His palace had formal enclosed gardens. After his death it was abandoned, and the ◊*Amarna tablets,* found in the ruins, were probably discarded by his officials.

Akhmatova Anna, pen name of Anna Andreevna Gorenko 1889–1966. Russian poet. Among her most notable poems are the cycle *Requiem* 1963 (written in the 1930s), which deals with the Stalinist terror, and *Poem without a hero* 1962 (begun in 1940).

Akhenaton another name for ◊Ikhnaton, pharaoh of Egypt.

Akihito 1933–. Emperor of Japan from 1989, succeeding his father Hirohito (Showa). His reign is called the Heisei ('achievement of universal peace') era.

Akkad northern Semitic people who conquered the Sumerians in 2350 BC and ruled Mesopotamia. The ancient city of Akkad in central Mesopotamia, founded by ◊Sargon I, was an imperial centre in the 3rd millennium BC; the site is unidentified, but it was on the Euphrates.

Akkaia alternative form of ◊Achaea.

Aksum ancient Greek-influenced Semitic kingdom which flourished 1st–6th centuries AD and covered a large part of modern Ethiopia as well as the Sudan. The ruins of its capital, also called Aksum, lie NW of Aduwa, but the site has been developed as a modern city.

Alabama state of southern USA; nicknamed Heart of Dixie/Camellia State
area 131,994 sq km/50,983 sq mi
capital Montgomery
towns Birmingham, Mobile
physical the state comprises the Cumberland Plateau in the north; the Black Belt, or Canebrake, which is excellent cotton-growing country, in the centre; and south of this, the coastal plain of Piny Woods. The main river is the river Alabama.
products cotton no longer prime crop, though still important; soybeans, peanuts; wood products; coal, iron; chemicals; textiles; paper
population (1980) 3,893,888
famous people Nat King Cole, Helen Keller, Joe Louis, Jesse Owens, Booker T Washington
history first settled by the French in the early 18th century, it was ceded to Britain in 1763, passed to the USA in 1783, and became a state in 1819. It was one of the ◊Confederate States in the American Civil War.

air sac

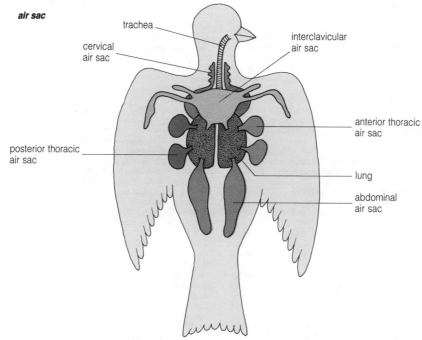

trachea

cervical air sac

interclavicular air sac

anterior thoracic air sac

posterior thoracic air sac

lung

abdominal air sac

Albania
Republic of
(Republika e Shqipërisë)

area 28,748 sq km/11,100 sq mi
capital Tirana
towns Shkodër, Vlorë, chief port Durrës
physical mainly mountainous, with rivers flowing
E–W, and a small coastal plain
head of state Sali Berisha from 1992

head of government Alexander Meksi from 1992
political system emergent democracy
exports crude oil, bitumen, chrome, iron ore,
nickel, coal, copper wire, tobacco, fruit
currency lek
population (1990 est) 3,270,000; annual growth
rate 1.9%
life expectancy men 69, women 73
languages Albanian, Greek
religion Muslim 70%, although all religion banned
1967–90
literacy 75% (1986)
GNP $2.8 bn (1986 est); $900 per head
chronology
1912 Albania achieved independence from Turkey.
1925 Republic proclaimed.
1928–39 Monarchy of King Zog.
1939–44 Under first Italian and then German rule.
1946 Communist republic proclaimed under the
leadership of Enver Hoxha.
1949 Admitted into Comecon.
1961 Break with Khrushchev's USSR.
1978 Break with 'revisionist' China.
1985 Death of Hoxha.
1987 Normal diplomatic relations restored with
Canada, Greece, and West Germany.
1990 One-party system abandoned. First
opposition party formed.
1991 Multiparty elections held.
1992 Totalitarian and communist parties banned.
Sali Berisha elected president.

alabaster a naturally occurring fine-grained translucent form of ◊gypsum. It is a soft material, used for carvings.

Alain-Fournier pen name of Henri-Alban Fournier 1886–1914. French novelist. His haunting semi-autobiographical fantasy *Le Grand Meaulnes/ The Lost Domain* 1913 was a cult novel of the 1920s and 1930s.

Alamein, El, battles of in World War II, two battles in the Western Desert, N Egypt. In the *First Battle of El Alamein* 1–27 Jul 1942 the British 8th Army under ◊Auchinleck held the German and Italian forces under Rommel. In the *Second Battle of El Alamein* 23 Oct–4 Nov 1942 ◊Montgomery defeated Rommel. These battles were a turning point of the war.

Alamo, the mission fortress in San Antonio, Texas, USA; besieged 23 Feb–6 Mar 1836 by ◊Santa Anna and 4,000 Mexicans; they killed the garrison of about 180, including Davy ◊Crockett and Jim ◊Bowie.

Alamogordo town in New Mexico, USA. The first atom bomb was exploded nearby at Trinity Site 16 Jul 1945. It is now a test site for guided missiles.

Alanbrooke Alan Francis Brooke, 1st Viscount Alanbrooke 1883–1963. British army officer, chief of staff in World War II and largely responsible for the strategy that led to the German defeat.

Alarcón Pedro Antonio de 1833–1891. Spanish journalist and writer. The acclaimed masterpiece *Diario/Diary* was based upon his experiences as a soldier in Morocco. His *El Sombrero de tres picos/ The Three-Cornered Hat* 1874 was the basis of Manuel de Falla's ballet.

Alaric *c.* 370–410. King of the Visigoths. In 396 he invaded Greece and retired with much booty to Illyria. In 400 and 408 he invaded Italy, and in 410 captured and sacked Rome, but died the same year on his way to invade Sicily. The river Busento was

diverted by his soldiers so that he could be buried in its course with his treasures; the labourers were killed to keep the secret.

Alaska largest state of the USA, in the Pacific NW
area 1,500,000 sq km/586,400 sq mi; largest state of USA
capital Juneau
towns Anchorage, Fairbanks, Fort Yukon, Holy Cross
physical much of Alaska is mountainous and includes Mount McKinley, 6,194 m/20,320 ft, the highest peak in North America, surrounded by a national park. Reindeer thrive in the Arctic tundra and elsewhere there are extensive forests.
products oil and natural gas; coal, copper, iron, gold, and tin; fur; salmon fisheries and canneries; lumbering.
population (1990) 550,000, including 9% American Indians, Aleuts, and Inuits.
history the first European to visit Alaska was Vitus ◊Bering in 1741. Alaska was a Russian colony from 1744 until purchased by the USA in 1867 for $7,200,000; it became a state in 1959.

albacore name loosely applied to several sorts of fish found in warm regions of the Atlantic and Pacific oceans, in particular to a large tunny and to several species of mackerel.

Albania country in SE Europe, bounded N and E by Yugoslavia, SE by Greece, and W and SW by the Adriatic Sea.

Alban, St died 303 AD. First Christian martyr in England. In 793 King Offa founded a monastery on the site of Alban's martyrdom, and round this the city of St Albans grew up.

albatross large seabird, genus *Diomedea*, with narrow wings up to 3 m/10 ft long adapted for gliding, mainly found in the S hemisphere. It belongs to the ◊petrel group.

albedo the fraction of the incoming light reflected by a body such as a planet. A body with a high albedo, near 1, is very bright, while a body with a low albedo, near 0, is dark.

Albee Edward 1928– . US playwright. His internationally performed plays are associated with the theatre of the absurd and include *The Zoo Story* 1960, *The American Dream* 1961, *Who's Afraid of Virginia Woolf?* 1962 (filmed with Elizabeth Taylor and Richard Burton as the quarrelling, alcoholic, academic couple 1966), *Tiny Alice* 1965, and *A Delicate Balance* 1966.

Albéniz Isaac 1860–1909. Spanish composer and pianist, born in Catalonia. He composed the suite *Iberia* and other piano pieces, making use of traditional Spanish tunes.

Alberoni Giulio 1664–1752. Spanish-Italian priest and politician. Born in Parma, Italy. Philip V made him prime minister of Spain in 1715. In 1717 he became a cardinal. He introduced many reforms, but was forced to flee to Italy in 1719, when his foreign policies failed.

Albert Prince Consort 1819–1861. Husband of Queen ◊Victoria of the UK from 1840; a patron of arts and science. Albert was the second son of the Duke of Saxe-Coburg-Gotha and first cousin to Queen Victoria. He planned the Great Exhibition of 1851, which made a handsome profit (£186,000); this was used to buy the sites in London of all the South Kensington museums and colleges and the Royal Albert Hall, built 1871. Albert popularized the Christmas tree in England. He was regarded by the British people with groundless suspicion because of his German connections. He died of typhoid.

Albert I 1875–1934. King of the Belgians from 1909, the younger son of Philip, Count of Flanders, and the nephew of Leopold II. In 1900 he married Duchess Elisabeth of Bavaria. In World War I he commanded the Allied army that conquered the Belgian coast in 1918, re-entering Brussels in triumph on 22 Nov. He was killed while mountaineering.

Alberta province of W Canada
area 661,188 sq km/255,219 sq mi
capital Edmonton
towns Calgary, Lethbridge, Medicine Hat, Red Deer
physical the Rocky Mountains; dry, treeless prairie in the centre and south; towards the north this merges into a zone of poplar, then mixed forest.
products coal; wheat, barley, oats, sugar-beet in the south; more than a million head of cattle; oil and natural gas.
population (1986) 2,366,000
history in the 17th century much of its area was part of a grant to the ◊Hudson's Bay Company for the fur trade. It became a province in 1905.

Alberti Leon Battista 1404–1472. Italian ◊Renaissance architect and theorist, noted for his recognition of the principles of classical architecture and their modification for Renaissance practice in *On Architecture* 1452.

Albigenses heretical sect of Christians (associated with the ◊Cathars) who flourished in S France near Albi and Toulouse during the 11th–13th centuries. They adopted the Manichean belief in the duality of good and evil and pictured Jesus as being a rebel against the cruelty of an omnipotent God.

albinism rare hereditary condition in which the body fails to synthesize the pigment known as melanin, normally found in the skin, hair and eyes. As a result, the hair is white, and the skin and eyes are pink. The skin and eyes are abnormally sensitive to light, and vision is often impaired.

Albinoni Tomaso 1671–1751. Italian Baroque composer and violinist, whose work was studied and adapted by Bach. He composed over 40 operas.

Albion ancient name for Britain used by the Greeks and Romans. It was mentioned by Pytheas of Massilia (4th century BC), and is probably of Celtic origin, but the Romans, having in mind the white cliffs of Dover, assumed it to be derived from *albus* (white). The kindred name of Albany was given to the Scottish Highlands in the 10th century.

albumin or *albumen* sulphur-containing ◊protein substance, best known in the form of egg white. It also occurs in milk, and as a major component of serum.

Albuquerque Alfonso de 1453–1515. Viceroy and founder of the Portuguese East Indies 1508–15, when the king of Portugal replaced him by his worst enemy and he died at sea on the way home; his ship *Flor del Mar* was lost between Malaysia and India with all his treasure.

alcázar Moorish palace (Arabic 'fortress') in Spain; one of five in Toledo was defended by the Nationalists against the Republicans for 71 days in 1936 during the Spanish ◊Civil War.

Alcazarquivir, Battle of battle on 4 Aug 1578 between the forces of Sebastian, king of Portugal (1554-1578), and those of the Berber kingdom of Fez. Sebastian's death on the field of battle paved the way for the incorporation of Portugal into the Spanish kingdom of Philip II.

alchemy the supposed art, transmuting base metals, such as lead and mercury, into silver and gold by the philosopher's stone, a hypothetical substance, to which was also attributed the power to give eternal life. It flourished in Europe during the Middle Ages before falling into disrepute.

Alcibiades 450–404 BC. Athenian general. Handsome and dissolute, he became the archetype of capricious treachery for his military intrigues against his native state with the Spartans and Persians; the Persians eventually had him assassinated. He had been brought up by ◊Pericles and was a friend of ◊Socrates, whose reputation as a teacher suffered from the association.

Alcmene in Greek mythology, the wife of Amphitryon, and mother of Heracles (the father was Zeus, who visited Alcmene in the form of her husband).

Alcock John William 1892–1919. British aviator. On 14 Jun 1919 in a Vickers-Vimy biplane, he and Lt Whitten-Brown made the first nonstop transatlantic flight. Alcock died after an aeroplane accident in the same year.

alcohol member of a group of organic chemical compounds characterized by the presence of one or more OH (hydroxyl) groups in the molecule. The main uses of alcohols are in alcoholic drinks (ethanol), as solvents for gums and resins, in lacquers and varnishes, in the making of dyes, for essential oils in perfumery and for medical substances in pharmacy.

alcoholic liquor an intoxicating drink. Ethyl alcohol, a colourless liquid, C_2H_5OH, is the basis of all common intoxicants:
wines, ciders, sherry contain alcohol produced by direct fermentation using yeasts of the sugar content in the relevant fruit.
malt liquors are beers and stouts, in which the starch of the grain is converted to sugar by malting, and the sugar then fermented into alcohol by yeasts. Fermented drinks contain less than 20% alcohol.
spirits are distilled from malted liquors or wines, and can contain up to 55% alcohol. A concentration

alcohol
The systematic naming of simple straight-chain organic molecules

Alkane	Alcohol	Aldehyde	Ketone	Carboxylic acid	Alkene
CH_4 methane	$CH_3 OH$ methanol	$HCHO$ methanal	–	$HCO_2 H$ methanoic acid	–
$CH_3 CH_3$ ethane	$CH_3 CH_2 OH$ ethanol	$CH_3 CHO$ ethanal	–	$CH_3 CO_2 H$ ethanoic acid	$CH_2 CH_2$ ethene
$CH_3 CH_2 CH_3$ propane	$CH_3 CH_2 CH_2 OH$ propanol	$CH_3 CH_2 CHO$ propanal	$CH_3 CO CH_3$ propanone	$CH_3 CH_2 CO_2H$ propanoic acid	$CH_2 CH CH_3$ propene
methane	methanol	methanal	propanone	methanoic acid	ethene

of 0.15% alcohol in the blood causes mild intoxication; 0.3% definite drunkenness and partial loss of consciousness; 0.6% endangers life.

Alcoholics Anonymous voluntary self-help organization established in 1934 in the USA to combat alcoholism; organizations now exist in many other countries.

alcoholism dependence on alcoholic liquor. It is characterized as an illness when consumption of alcohol interferes with normal physical or emotional health, and may produce physical and psychological addiction. The cost of alcoholism is very high in medical and social terms, and the condition is notoriously difficult to treat.

Alcott Louisa M(ay) 1832–1888. US author of the children's classic *Little Women* 1869, which drew on her own home circumstances, the heroine Jo being a partial self-portrait. *Good Wives* 1869 was among its sequels.

Alcuin 735–804. English scholar. Born in York, he went to Rome in 780, and in 782 took up his residence at Charlemagne's court in Aachen. From 796 he was abbot of Tours. He disseminated Anglo-Saxon scholarship, organized education and learning in the Frankish empire, gave a strong impulse to the Carolingian Renaissance, and was a prominent member of Charlemagne's academy.

Aldebaran brightest star in the constellation Taurus, and marking the eye of the 'bull'. It is a red giant 68 light years away, shining with a true luminosity of about 100 times that of the Sun.

aldehyde group of organic chemical compounds prepared by oxidation of primary alcohols, so that the OH (hydroxyl) group loses its hydrogen to give an oxygen joined by a double bond to a carbon atom (the aldehyde group having the formula CHO).

alder tree *Alnus glutinosa* allied to the birch and found in wet habitats in Europe and N Asia. About 30 other species of alder occur in the northern hemisphere and S America.

Aldermaston site of the Atomic Weapons Establishment (AWE) in Berkshire, England. In 1958–63 the Campaign for Nuclear Disarmament made it the focus of an annual Easter protest march.

Aldiss Brian 1925– . British science-fiction writer, anthologist, and critic. His novels include *Non-Stop* 1958, *Helliconia Summer* 1983, and *Trillion Year Spree* 1986.

aleatory music method of composition (pioneered by John ◊Cage) from about 1945 in which the elements are assembled by chance, for example by using dice (Latin *alea*) or by computer.

Aleppo former name of ◊Haleb, a town in Syria.

Aletsch most extensive glacier in Europe, 23.6 km/14.7 mi long, beginning on the southern slopes of the Jungfrau in the Bernese Alps, Switzerland.

Aleutian Islands volcanic island chain in the N Pacific, stretching 1,900 km/1,200 mi SW of Alaska, of which it forms part. Population 6,000 Inuit (Eskimo), most of whom belong to the Greek Orthodox Church, plus a large US defence establishment. There are 14 large and over 100 small islands, running along the ◊Aleutian Trench. The islands are mountainous, barren, and treeless; they are ice-free all the year round, but are often foggy.

A level (Advanced level) in the UK, examinations taken by some students in no more than four subjects, usually at the age of 18 after two years' study. Two A level passes are normally required for entry to a university degree course.

Alexander eight popes, including:

Alexander III died 1181. Pope 1159–81; his authority was opposed by ◊Frederick I Barbarossa, but Alexander eventually compelled him to render homage in 1178. He supported Henry II of England in his invasion of Ireland, but subjugated him after the murder of Thomas ◊Becket.

Alexander VI (Rodrigo Borgia) 1431–1503. Pope 1492–1503. He was of Spanish origin, and bribed his way to the papacy, where he furthered the advancement of his illegitimate children, who included Cesare and Lucrezia ◊Borgia. When ◊Savonarola preached against his corrupt practices Alexander had him executed, and he is said to have died of poison he had prepared for his cardinals. He was a great patron of the arts.

Alexander three tsars of Russia:

Alexander I 1777–1825. Tsar of Russia from 1801. Defeated by Napoleon at Austerlitz 1805, he made peace at Tilsit 1807, but economic crisis led to a break with Napoleon's ◊continental system, and the opening of Russian ports to British trade; this led to Napoleon's ill-fated invasion of Russia. He gave a constitution to Poland.

Alexander II 1818–1881. Tsar of Russia from 1855. He is remembered as 'the Liberator' for his emancipation of the serfs in 1861, but the revolutionary element remained unsatisfied, and Alexander became increasingly autocratic and reactionary. He was assassinated by ◊Nihilists.

Alexander III 1845–1894. Tsar of Russia from 1881, when he succeeded his father, Alexander II. He pursued a reactionary policy, persecuting the Jews and promoting Russification.

Alexander three kings of Scotland:

Alexander I c. 1078–1124. King of Scotland from 1107, known as the *Fierce*.

Alexander II 1198–1249. King of Scotland from 1214, when he succeeded his father William the Lion. Alexander supported the English barons in their struggle with King John after Magna Carta. By the treaty of Newcastle in 1244 he acknowledged Henry III of England as his liege lord.

Alexander III 1241–1285. King of Scotland from 1249, son of Alexander II. In 1263 he extended his authority over the Western Isles, which had been dependent on Norway, and strengthened the power of the central Scottish government.

Alexander I Karageorgevich 1888–1934. Regent of Serbia 1912–21 and king of Yugoslavia 1921–34, as dictator from 1929; assassinated, possibly by Italian Fascists.

Alexander Nevski, St 1220–1263. Russian military leader, son of the grand duke of Novgorod; in 1240 he defeated the Swedes on the banks of the Neva (hence Nevski), and in 1242 defeated the Teutonic Knights on frozen Lake Peipus.

Alexander Obrenovich 1876-1903. King of Serbia from 1889 while still a minor, on the abdication of his father, King Milan. He took power into his own hands in 1893, and in 1900 married a widow, Draga Mashin. In 1903 Alexander and his queen were murdered, and ◊Peter I Karageorgevich was placed on the throne.

Alexander the Great 356–323 BC. King of Macedonia and conqueror of the Persian empire. As commander of the vast Macedonian army he conquered Greece in 336 BC. He defeated Darius the Persian king in Asia Minor in 333, then moved on to Egypt where he founded Alexandria, future centre of the Hellenistic civilization. He defeated the Persians again in Assyria in 331, then advanced further east to reach the Indus. He conquered the Punjab before diminished troops forced his retreat.

Alexandra 1936– . Princess of the UK. Daughter of the Duke of Kent and Princess Marina, she married Angus Ogilvy (1928–), younger son of the earl of Airlie. They have two children, James (1964–) and Marina (1966–).

Alexandra 1844–1925. Queen consort of ◊Edward VII of the UK, whom she married in 1863. She was the daughter of Christian IX of Denmark. An annual Alexandra Rose Day in aid of hospitals commemorates her charitable work.

Alexandra 1872–1918. Last tsarina of Russia, 1894–1917; the former Princess Alix of Hesse, granddaughter of Queen Victoria, she married ◊Nicholas II. From 1907 she fell under the spell of ◊Rasputin, brought to the palace to try to cure her son of haemophilia. She was shot with the rest of her family by the Bolsheviks in the Russian Revolution.

Alexandria, School of the writers and scholars of Alexandria who from about 331 BC to 642 AD made the city the chief centre of culture in the Western world. They include the poets Callimachus, Apollonius Rhodius, and Theocritus; Euclid, pioneer of geometry; Eratosthenes, the geographer; Hipparchus, who developed a system of trigonometry; Ptolemy, who gave his name to the Ptolemaic system of astronomy that endured for over 1,000 years; and Philo, the Jewish philosopher. The Gnostics and Neo-Platonists also flourished in Alexandria.

Alexandria or *El Iskandariya* city, chief port, and second largest city of Egypt, situated between the Mediterranean and Lake Maryut; population (1986) 5,000,000. It is linked by canal with the Nile and is an industrial city (oil refining, and cotton and grain trading). Founded in 331 BC by Alexander the Great, Alexandria was for over 1,000 years the capital of Egypt.

Alexeev Vasiliy 1942– . Russian weightlifter who broke 80 world records 1970-77, a record for any sport. He has been Olympic superheavyweight champion twice, world champion seven times, and European champion on eight occasions.

Alexius I Comnenus 1048–1118. Byzantine emperor 1081–1118. The Latin (W European) Crusaders helped him repel Norman and Turkish invasions, and he devoted great skill to buttressing the threatened empire. His daughter ◊Anna Comnena chronicled his reign.

alfalfa or *lucerne* a perennial tall herbaceous plant *Medicago sativa* of the pea family, with spikes of small purple flowers in late summer. Native to Eurasia, it is now an important fodder crop, and is generally processed into hay, meal, or silage.

al-Fatah a Palestinian nationalist organization founded in 1956 to bring about an independent state of Palestine. Also called the Palestine National Liberation Movement, it is the main component of the ◊Palestine Liberation Organization. Its leader is Yassir ◊Arafat.

Alfonsín Foulkes Raúl 1926– . Argentine politician, member of the Radical Union Party (UCR), elected president 1983 when civilian government was returned; replaced 1989 by Carlos Menem. Alfonsín, a lawyer, was imprisoned for his political activities in 1953 under the rightwing military ruler Perón. He was a member of the Chamber of Deputies 1963–66 and 1973–76. While president, he set up investigations into allegations of human-rights violations by the army. In 1986 he was the joint winner of the Human Rights Prize of the Council of Europe.

Alfonso eleven kings of Castile, including:

Alfonso X called *el Sabio* 'the Wise' 1221–1284. King of Castile from 1252, whose reign was politically unsuccessful but who is remembered for his contribution to learning: he made Castilian the official language of the country, and commissioned a history of Spain and an encyclopedia, as well as several translations from Arabic.

Alfonso two kings of Spain, including:

Alfonso XIII 1886–1941. King of Spain 1886–1931. Assumed power 1906 and married Princess Ena, granddaughter of Queen Victoria of the UK, in the same year. He abdicated soon after the fall of the Primo de Rivera dictatorship and Spain became a republic.

Alfred the Great c. 848–c. 900. King of Wessex from 871, he defended England against Danish invasion, made legal reforms, and encouraged literacy.

algae a diverse group of plants (including those commonly called seaweeds) that shows great variety of form, ranging from the lowest type of only a single cell to the higher seaweeds of considerable size and complexity of structure.

Algeria
Democratic and Popular Republic of
(al-Jumhuriya al-Jazairiya ad-Dimuqratiya ash-Shabiya)

area 2,381,741 sq km/919,352 sq mi
capital al-Jazair/Algiers
towns Qacentina/Constantine; ports are Ouahran/Oran, Annaba
physical coastal plains, mountain plateau, desert
head of state Ali Kafi from 1992
head of government Belnid Absessalem from 1992

political system semi-military rule
exports oil, natural gas, iron, wine, olive oil
currency dinar
population (1990 est) 25,715,000 (83% Arab, 17% Berber); annual growth rate 3.0%
life expectancy men 59, women 62
language Arabic (official), Berber, French
religion Sunni Muslim
literacy 63% male/37% female (1985 est)
GNP $64.6 bn; $2,796 per head
chronology
1954 War for independence from France led by the National Liberation Front (FLN).
1962–3 Independence achieved. Ben Bella elected president.
1965 Ben Bella deposed by military, led by Col Houari Boumédienne.
1976 New constitution approved.
1978 Death of Boumédienne.
1979 Bendjedid Chadli elected president. Ben Bella released from house arrest.
1981 Algeria helped in securing release of US prisoners in Iran.
1983 Chadli re-elected.
1988 170 killed during riots in protest at government policies. Reform programme introduced.
1989 In a referendum, Algerians voted for an end to one-party rule.
1991 Fundamentalist Islamic Salvation Front (FIS) won first round of multiparty elections.
1992 Military took control of government and FIS ordered to disband.

Algarve ancient kingdom in S Portugal, the modern district of Faro, a popular holiday resort; population (1981) 323,500.

algebra system of arithmetic applying to any set of non-numerical symbols, and the axioms and rules by which they are combined or operated upon.

Algeciras Conference a conference held in Jan 1906 when the European Great Powers of France, Germany, Britain, Russia, and Austria-Hungary, together with the USA, Spain, the Low Countries, Portugal, and Sweden met to settle the question of Morocco. The conference was prompted by increased German demands in what had traditionally been seen as a French area of influence, but resulted in a reassertion of Anglo-French friendship, and the increased isolation of Germany.

Alger Horatio 1834–1899. US writer of children's books. He wrote over 100 didactic moral tales in which the heroes rise from poverty to riches through hard work and good deeds, including the series 'Ragged Dick' from 1867 and 'Tattered Tom' from 1871.

Algeria country in N Africa, bounded to the E by Tunisia and Libya, to the SE by Niger, to the SW by Mali, to the NW by Morocco, and to the N by the Mediterranean Sea.

Al-Ghazzali 1058–1111. Muslim philosopher and one of the most famous Sufis (Muslim mystics). He was responsible for easing the conflict between the Sufi and the Ulema, a body of Muslim religious and legal scholars.

Algiers (Arabic *Al-Jezair*, French *Alger*) capital of Algeria, N Africa, situated on the narrow coastal plain between the Atlas mountains and the Mediterranean; population (1984) 2,442,300.

Algiers, Battle of the bitter conflict in Algiers 1954–62 between the Algerian nationalist population and the French army and French settlers. The conflict ended with Algerian independence in 1962.

alginate salt of alginic acid, obtained from brown seaweeds, and used in textiles, paper, food products, and pharmaceuticals.

Algol in computing, an early high-level programming language, developed in the 1950s and 1960s, for scientific applications. Although a general-purpose language, Algol (short for algorithmic language) is best suited for mathematical work and has an algebraic style. It is no longer in common use.

Algol an ◊eclipsing binary, a pair of rotating stars in the constellation Perseus, one of which eclipses the other every 69 hours, causing its brightness to drop by two-thirds. It is also known as Beta Persei.

Algonquin N American Indians of the subarctic region. They lived formerly along the Ottawa River and the northern tributaries of the St Lawrence, but now inhabit reserves in E Ontario and W Quebec.

algorithm a procedure or series of steps by which a problem can be solved. In computer science, where the term is most often used, algorithm describes the logical sequence of operations to be performed by a computer program. A ◊flow chart is a visual algorithm.

Alhambra fortified palace at Granada, Spain, built by Moorish kings mainly between 1248 and 1354. The finest example of Moorish architecture, it stands on a rocky hill.

Ali c. 600–661. 4th caliph of Islam. He was born in Mecca, the son of Abu Talib, uncle to the prophet Muhammad, who gave him his daughter Fatima in marriage. On Muhammad's death in 632, Ali had a claim to succeed him, but this was not conceded until 656. After a stormy reign, he was assassinated. Around Ali's name has raged the controversy of the Sunnites and the Shi'ites (see ◊Islam), the former denying his right to the caliphate and the latter supporting it.

Ali (Ali Pasha) 1741–1822. Turkish politician, known as *Arslan* (the Lion). An Albanian, he was appointed pasha (governor) of the Janina region (now Ioánnina, Greece) in 1788. His court was visited by the British poet Byron. He was murdered by the sultan's order.

Ali Muhammad 1942– . US boxer. Olympic light-heavyweight champion in 1960, he went on to become world professional heavyweight champion in 1964, and was the only man to regain the title twice. He was known for his quickness and extrovert nature.

Alia Ramiz 1925– . Albanian communist politician, head of state 1982–92. Under his stewardship, policy relaxations and a gradual opening-out of the country began.

alibi the legal defence that the accused was at some other place when the crime was committed (from Latin 'elsewhere'). In Britain it can usually only be used as a defence in a ◊Crown Court trial if the prosecution is supplied with details before the trial.

Alicante seaport and tourist resort in Valencia, SE Spain; population (1986 est) 265,500. The wine and fruit trade passes through the port.

Alice's Adventures in Wonderland a children's story by Lewis Carroll, published 1865. Alice dreams she follows the White Rabbit down a rabbit-hole and meets fantastic characters such as the Cheshire Cat, the Mad Hatter, and the King and Queen of Hearts.

alien in law, a person who is not a citizen of a particular state. In the UK, under the British Nationality Act 1981, an alien is anyone who is neither a British Overseas citizen (for example Commonwealth) nor a member of certain other categories; citizens of the Republic of Ireland are not regarded as aliens. Aliens may not vote or hold public office in the UK.

Alien and Sedition Acts laws passed by the US Congress in 1798, when war with France seemed likely. The acts lengthened the period of residency required for US citizenship, gave the president the power to expel 'dangerous' aliens, and severely restricted criticism of the government. They were controversial because of the degree of power exercised by central government; they are now also seen as an early manifestation of US xenophobia (fear of foreigners).

alienation a sense of frustration, isolation, and powerlessness; a feeling of loss of control over one's life; a sense of estrangement either from society or from oneself. As a sociological concept it was developed by the German philosophers Hegel and Marx; the latter used it as a description and criticism of the condition of workers in capitalist society.

alimentary canal long tube extending from the mouth to the anus, about 9 m/33 ft long in a human adult. Its function is to convey and digest food, and it consists of the oesophagus (gullet), stomach, duodenum, and the small and large intestines.

alimony in the US and formerly in the UK, money allowance given by court order to a former wife or husband after separation or divorce; in the UK the legal term is ◊maintenance. In some legal systems the right has been extended outside marriage and is colloquially termed 'palimony'.

aliphatic compound any organic chemical compound that is made up of chains of carbon atoms, rather than rings (as in cyclic compounds). The chains may be linear, as in hexane C_6H_{14}, or branched, as in propan-2-ol (isopropanol) $(CH_3)_2CHOH$.

alkali chemical compound classed as a base which is soluble in water. Alkalis neutralize acids and are soapy to the touch.

alkali metals group of elements in the periodic table of the elements – group I or group Ia: lithium (Li), sodium (Na), potassium (K), rubidium (Rb), caesium (Cs), and francium (Fr). In general, the elements of this group are reactive, soft, low-melting-point metals.

alkaline earth elements a group of elements in the periodic table of the elements – group II or IIa: beryllium (Be), magnesium (Mg), calcium (Ca), strontium (Sr), barium (Ba), and radium (Ra). All the elements are metallic but none occurs free in nature. They and their compounds are used to make alloys, oxidizers, and drying agents.

alkaloid a physiologically active and frequently poisonous substance contained in certain plants. It is usually a base, forming salts with acids and, when soluble, giving an alkaline solution.

al-Khwarizmi Muhammad ibn-Musa 780–c. 850. Arab mathematician who lived and worked in Baghdad. He introduced the ◊algorithm (a word based on his name), the word ◊algebra (al-jabr, in an adaptation of an earlier Indian text), the Hindu decimal system, and the concept of zero into Arab mathematics. He compiled astronomical tables, and put forward Arabic numerals.

Allah Islamic name for God, Arabic al-Ilah 'the God'.

allegory in literature, the description or illustration of one thing in terms of another; a work of poetry or prose in the form of an extended metaphor or parable which makes use of symbolic fictional characters.

Allegri Gregorio 1582–1652. Italian Baroque composer, who became a priest and entered the Sistine chapel choir in 1629. His *Miserere* for nine voices was reserved for performance by the chapel choir until ◊Mozart (at 14) wrote out the music from memory.

allegro (Italian 'merry, lively') in music, a lively or quick passage, movement, or composition.

allele an alternative form of a given ◊gene. Thus, blue and brown eyes are determined by different alleles of the gene for eye colour.

Allen Woody, pseudonym of Allen Stewart Konigsberg 1935– . US film director and actor, known for his cynical, witty, often self-deprecating parody and off-beat humour. His films include *Play It Again Sam* 1972, *Annie Hall* 1977 (for which he won three Academy Awards), and *Hannah and her Sisters* 1986 – all of which he also directed.

Allende (Gossens) Salvador 1908–1973. Chilean left-wing politician. Elected president in 1970 as the candidate of the Popular Front alliance, Allende never succeeded in keeping the electoral alliance together in government. His failure to solve the country's economic problems or to deal with political subversion allowed the army to stage the 1973 coup which brought about the death of Allende and many of his supporters.

allergy special sensitivity of the body which makes it react, with an exaggerated response of the natural immune defence mechanism, to the introduction of an otherwise harmless foreign substance termed an allergen.

Alliance the loose union 1981–87 formed by the British ◊Liberal Party and ◊Social Democratic Party (SDP) for electoral purposes.

Allied Mobile Force (AMF) permanent multinational military force established 1960 to move immediately to any NATO country under threat of attack; headquarters in Heidelberg, West Germany.

Allies, the in World War I, the 23 countries allied against Germany, notably the UK, France, Italy, Russia, and the USA; and in World War II the 49 countries allied against the ◊Axis (Germany, Italy, and Japan), including the UK, USA, and USSR.

alligator type of reptile resembling a crocodile. There are two species: *Alligator mississipiensis* of the southern states of the USA, and *Alligator sinensis* from the swamps of the lower Chang Jiang river in China. The former grows to about 4 m/12 ft, but the latter only to 1.5 m/5 ft. Alligators swim well with lashing movements of the tail, and feed on fish and mammals but seldom attack people.

alliteration in poetry and prose, the use within a line or phrase of words beginning with the same sound. It was a common device in Old English poetry, and its use survives in many traditional English phrases such as 'kith and kin', 'hearth and home', and so on.

allium genus of plants belonging to the lily family. They are usually acrid in their properties, but form bulbs in which sugar is stored. Cultivated species include onion, garlic, chives, and leek.

allopathy the treatment of disease of one kind by exciting a disease process of another kind or in another part.

allopurinol a drug prescribed for the treatment of ◊gout, which acts by reducing levels of ◊uric acid in the blood.

allotment a small plot of rented land, used for growing vegetables and flowers. Allotments originated in Britain during the 18th and 19th centuries, when much of the common land was enclosed, and efforts were made to provide plots for poor people to use for cultivation. Later, Acts of Parliament made this provision obligatory for local councils. In 1978 in Britain, there were some 0.5 million allotment plots.

allotrope different forms of the same element, for example the two forms of oxygen: 'normal' oxygen (O_2) and ozone (O_3), which have different molecular configurations.

alloy metal blended with some other metallic or non-metallic substance in order to give it special qualities, such as resistance to corrosion, greater hardness and tensile strength. Useful alloys include bronze, brass, cupronickel, duralumin, German silver, gunmetal, pewter, solder, steel and stainless steel. The most recent alloys include the superplastics, which may stretch 100% at specific temperatures, permitting, for example, their injection into moulds as easily as plastic.

All Saints' Day festival on 1 Nov for all Christian saints and martyrs who have no special day of their own. Also known as All-Hallows or Hallowmas.

All Souls' Day festival in the Catholic church, held on 2 Nov (following All Saints' Day) in the conviction that the faithful by prayer and self-denial can hasten the deliverance of souls expiating their sins in purgatory.

allspice spice prepared from dried berries of the pimento tree *Pimenta dioica*, cultivated chiefly in Jamaica.

Allston Washington 1779–1843. US painter, a pioneer of the Romantic movement in America. Allston painted classical, religous, and historical subjects, but is probably best known for his Romantic sea- and landscapes. His mastery of light and colour earned him the title 'the American Titian'.

alluvial deposit a layer of broken rocky matter, formed from material that has been washed along by a river or stream and dropped as the current changed. River plains and deltas are made entirely of alluvial deposits, but smaller pockets can be found in the beds of upland torrents.

Alma-Ata (former name to 1921 *Vernyi*) capital of the Republic of Kazakh, USSR; population (1983) 1,023,000. Industries include engineering, printing, tobacco processing, textile manufacturing and leather products.

Alma, Battle of the battle in 1854 between Russian forces and those of Britain, France, and Turkey in the Crimean War of 1854–56.

alma mater Latin 'bounteous mother'. It can be applied to universities and schools as though they are the 'foster-mothers' of their students.

Almansa, Battle of in the War of the Spanish Succession, battle on 25 Apr 1707 in which British, Portuguese, and Spanish forces were defeated by the French under the Duke of Berwick at a Spanish town in Albacete, about 80 km/50 mi NW of Alicante.

Alma-Tadema Laurence 1836–1912. Dutch painter who settled in the UK in 1870. He painted romantic, idealized scenes from Greek, Roman, and Egyptian life in a distinctive, detailed style.

Almeida Francisco de *c.* 1450–1510. First viceroy of Portuguese India 1505–08. He was killed in a skirmish with the Hottentots at Table Bay, S Africa.

Almohad a Berber dynasty 1130–1269 founded by the Berber prophet Muhammad ibn Tumart (*c.* 1080–1130). They ruled much of Morocco and Spain, which they took by defeating the ◊Almoravids; they later took the area which today forms Algeria and Tunis. Their policy of religious 'purity' involved the forced conversion and massacre of the Jewish population of Spain. They were themselves defeated by the Christian kings of Spain in 1212, and in Morocco in 1269.

almond seed of the almond tree *Prunus dulcis*, which is closely related to the peach and the apricot. Originally a native of N Africa and the Middle East, the almond tree was long ago introduced into Europe.

Almoravid a Berber dynasty 1056–1147 founded by the prophet Abdullah ibn Tashfin, ruling much of Morocco and Spain in the 11th–12th centuries. They came from the Sahara and in the 11th century began laying the foundations of an empire covering

alpaca

the whole of Morocco and parts of Algeria; their capital was the newly founded Marrakesh. In 1086 they defeated Alfonso VI of Castile to gain much of Spain. They were later overthrown by the ◊Almohads.

aloe genus of African plants of the family Liliaceae, distinguished by their long fleshy leaves. The drug, aloes, a powerful cathartic, is prepared from the juice of the leaves of several of the species.

alpaca domesticated South American member of the camel family found in Chile, Peru, and Bolivia, and herded at high elevations in the Andes. About 1 m/3 ft tall, it is mainly bred for its long fine wool, and like the llama was probably bred from the wild ◊guanaco.

alpha and omega first (α) and last (Ω) letters of the Greek alphabet, hence the beginning and end, or sum total, of anything.

alphabet a set of conventional symbols for the purpose of writing, so called from *alpha* and *beta*, the names of the first two letters of the classical Greek alphabet.

Alpha Centauri the brightest star in the constellation of Centaurus. It is actually a triple star (see ◊binary star); the two brighter stars orbit each other every 80 years, and the third, Proxima Centauri, 4.3 light years away, is the closest star to the Sun.

alpha particle positively charged particle ejected with very great velocity from the nucleus of an ◊atom. It is one of the products of the spontaneous disintegration of radioactive substances such as radium and thorium, and is identical with the nucleus of a helium atom, that is, it consists of two protons and two neutrons.

Alps mountain chain, the barrier between N Italy and France, Germany and Austria.
famous peaks include *Mont Blanc* the highest at 4,807 m/15,772 ft, first climbed by Jacques Balmat and Michel Paccard 1786;
Matterhorn in the Pennine Alps 4,477 m/14,688 ft, first climbed by Edward Whymper 1865 (four of the party of seven were killed when the rope broke during their descent);
Eiger in the Bernese Alps/Oberland, 3,970 m/13,101 ft, with a near-vertical rock wall on the north face;
Jungfrau 4,166 m/13,668 ft, of exceptional beauty, and *Finsteraarhorn* 4,274 m/14,014 ft.
famous passes include *Brenner* the lowest, Austria/Italy;
Great St Bernard the highest, 2,472 m/8,110 ft, Italy/Switzerland (by which Napoleon marched into Italy 1800);

Alps The French Alps, showing left to right, Aiguille du Chardonnet, Aiguil le Verte and Aiguille du Dru.

alphabet

Egyptian Hieroglyphics

ДБВГД
ЕЖЅЗИ
ІКЛМН
Cyrillic

ABCDEF F
HIKΓMN
OΓQRST
Greek

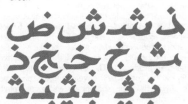
Arabic

Hebrew

Little St Bernard Italy/France (which Hannibal is thought to have used), and *St Gotthard* S Switzerland, which Suvorov used when ordered by the tsar to withdraw his troops from Italy. All have been superseded by all-weather road/rail tunnels. The Alps extend into Yugoslavia with the Julian and Dinaric Alps.

Alsace-Lorraine area of NE France, lying to the W of the river Rhine. It forms the modern French regions of *Alsace* capital Strasbourg; population

(1982) 1,566,000 and **Lorraine** capital Nancy; population (1982) 2,320,000. The former iron and steel industries are being replaced by electronics, chemicals, and precision engineering. The German dialect spoken does not have equal rights with French, and there is autonomist sentiment.

Alsatia the old name for Alsace, now part of Alsace-Lorraine, formerly part of Germany.

alsatian breed of dog known officially from 1977 as the German shepherd. It has a wolflike appearance, a thick coat with many varieties of colouring, and distinctive gait. Alsatians are used as police dogs because of their high intelligence.

Altamira cave near the Spanish village of Santillana del Mar in Santander province where in 1879 Palaeolithic wall paintings were discovered.

Altdorfer Albrecht c.1480–1538. German painter and printmaker, active in Regensburg, Bavaria. Altdorfer's work, influenced by the linear, classical style of the Italian Renaissance, often depicts dramatic landscapes that are out of scale with the figures in the paintings. His use of light creates tension and effects of movement. Many of his works are of religious subjects.

alternate angles in geometry one of a pair of angles that lie on opposite sides of a transversal (a line cutting two other lines). If the two other lines are parallel, the alternate angles are equal.

alternating current (AC) electric current that flows for an interval of time in one direction and then in the opposite direction, that is, a current that flows in alternately reversed directions through or round a circuit. Electric energy is usually generated as alternating current in a power station, and alternating currents may be used for both power and lighting.

alternation of generations the typical lifecycle of terrestrial plants and some seaweeds, in which there are two distinct forms occurring alternately: ◊diploid and ◊haploid. Diploid produces haploid spores by ◊meiosis, and is called the sporophyte (spore-producer), while haploid produces ◊gametes (sex cells), and is called the gametophyte (gamete-producer). The gametes fuse to form a diploid ◊zygote which develops into a new sporophyte, thus the sporophyte and gametophyte alternate.

alternative energy sources of energy that are renewable and ecologically safe, as opposed to sources that are expendable, and often have toxic by-products, such as coal, oil, or gas (fossil fuels) and uranium (for nuclear power). The most important alternative energy source is **hydroelectric power (HEP)**, which harnesses the energy in flowing water. Other sources include **tidal power**; **windmills**; **wind turbines**; **solar power** (already successfully exploited in many parts of the world); **wave power**, and **geothermal energy**.

alternator an electricity ◊generator, which produces an alternating current.

Altgeld John Peter 1847–1902. US political and social reformer. Born in Prussia, he was taken in infancy to the USA. During the Civil War he served in the Union army. He was a judge of the Supreme Court in Chicago 1886–91, and as governor of Illinois 1893–97 was a champion of the worker against the government-backed power of big business.

Althing the parliament of Iceland, established about 930 and the oldest in the world.

altimeter an instrument commonly used in aircraft that measures altitude, or height above sea level. The common type is a form of aneroid ◊barometer, which works by sensing the differences in air pressure at different altitudes. This type must continually be recalibrated because of the change in air pressure with changing weather conditions. The ◊radar altimeter measures the height of the aircraft above the ground, measuring the time it takes for radio pulses emitted by the aircraft to be reflected.

altitude in two-dimensional geometry, the perpendicular distance from a vertex (corner) of a triangle to the base (the side opposite the vertex).

Altmark incident naval skirmish in World War II. The *Altmark*, a German auxiliary cruiser, was intercepted on 15 Feb 1940 by HM destroyer *Intrepid* off the coast of Norway. It was carrying the captured crews of Allied merchant ships sunk by the German battleship *Admiral Graf Spee* in the S Atlantic, and took refuge in Jösing fjord. There it was cornered by HMS *Cossack*, under Captain Vian, and ran aground. Vian's men released 299 British sailors.

alto (Italian 'high') (1) low-register female voice also called **contralto**; (2) high adult male voice, also known as a counter tenor; (3) (French) viola.

altruism the giving of help or charity without expectation of return. In biology, altruism often means helping another individual to reproduce more effectively, as a direct result of which the altruist may leave fewer offspring itself. Female honey bees behave altruistically by rearing sisters in order to help their mother, the queen bee, reproduce, and forego any possibility of reproducing themselves.

ALU *arithmetic and logic unit* in a computer, the part of the ◊CPU (central processing unit) that performs simple arithmetic or logical operations on data.

alum a white crystalline powder readily soluble in water; a double sulphate of potassium and aluminium.

alumina oxide of aluminium, AC_2O_3, sometimes called corundum, which is widely distributed in clays, slates, and shales. It is formed by the decomposition of the feldspars in granite, and used as an abrasive.

aluminium the most abundant metal, symbol Al, atomic number 13, relative atomic mass 26.98. Pure aluminium is a soft white metal. It oxidizes rapidly, and is valuable for its light weight, its specific gravity being 2.70, and for this reason is widely used in shipbuilding and aircraft. In the pure state it is a weak metal, but if combined with other elements such as copper, silicon, or magnesium, it forms alloys of great strength.

Alva or **Alba** Ferdinand Alvarez de Toledo, Duke of Alva 1508–1582. Spanish politician and general. He commanded the Spanish armies of the Holy Roman emperor Charles V and Philip II of Spain, and in 1567 was appointed governor of the Netherlands, where he set up a reign of terror to suppress the revolt against demands for increased taxation, reductions in local autonomy, and the Inquisition. In 1573 he retired, and returned to Spain.

Alvarado Pedro de c. 1485–1541. Spanish conquistador. In 1519 he accompanied Hernando Cortez, and distinguished himself in the conquest of Mexico. In 1523–24 he conquered Guatemala.

Alvarez Luis Walter 1911–1988. US physicist who headed the research team which discovered the Xi-zero atomic particle in 1959. He worked on the US atomic bomb project for two years, at Chicago and Los Alamos, during World War II. Nobel Prize 1968.

alveolus one of the many thousands of tiny air sacs in the ◊lung in which exchange of oxygen and carbon dioxide takes place between air and blood.

Alzheimer's disease the commonest manifestation of ◊dementia, estimated to afflict 5–10% of the aged population. Attacking the brain's 'grey matter', Alzheimer's is a disease of mental processes rather than physical function, characterized by memory loss and progressive intellectual impairment. It was first described by Alois Alzheimer in 1906. The cause is unknown, although a link with high levels of aluminium in drinking water was discovered in 1989. There is as yet no treatment, but recent insights into the molecular basis of the disease may aid the search for a drug to counter its effects.

a.m. abbreviation for *ante meridiem* (Latin 'before noon').

AM in physics, abbreviation for amplitude ◊modulation, one way in which radio waves are altered for the transmission of broadcasting signals.

Amal a radical Lebanese ◊Shi'ite military force, established by Musa Sadr in the 1970s; their headquarters are at Borj al-Barajneh. The movement split into extremist and moderate groups in 1982, but both sides agreed on the aim of increasing Shi'ite political representation in Lebanon. Amal guerrillas were responsible for many of the attacks and kidnappings in Lebanon during the 1980s.

Amalekite in the Old Testament, member of an ancient Semitic people of SW Palestine and the Sinai peninsula. According to Exodus 17 they harried the rear of the Israelites after their crossing of the Red Sea, were defeated by Saul and David, and finally crushed in the reign of Hezekiah.

amalgam an alloy of mercury with other metals. Most metals will form amalgams, the notable exceptions being iron and platinum. The most familiar form of amalgam is used in dentistry for filling teeth, and usually contains copper, silver, and zinc as the main alloying ingredients. The amalgam is pliable when first mixed and then sets hard.

Amanita genus of fungi. It is distinguished by having a ring, or *volva*, round the stem, warty patches on the cap, and by the clear white colour of the gills. Many of the species are brightly coloured and highly poisonous.

Amanullah Khan 1892–1960. Emir (ruler) of Afghanistan 1919–29. Third son of Habibullah Khan, he seized the throne on his father's assassination and concluded a treaty with the British, but his policy of westernization led to rebellion in 1928. Amanullah had to flee, abdicated in 1929, and settled in Rome, Italy.

Amar Das 1495–1574. Third guru (teacher) of Sikhism 1552–74. He laid strong emphasis on equality and opposed the caste system. He initiated the custom of the *langar* (communal meal).

Amarna tablets collection of Egyptian clay tablets with cuneiform inscriptions, found in the ruins of the ancient ◊Akhetaton on the east bank of the Nile. The majority of the tablets, which comprise royal archives and letters of 1411–1375 BC, are in the British Museum. They may have been discarded as inessential documents when the city was abandoned.

Amaterasu in Japanese mythology, the sun-goddess, grandmother of Jimmu Tenno, first ruler of Japan, from whom the emperors claimed to be descended.

Amati Italian family of violin-makers, working in Cremona, *c.* 1550–1700.

amatol an explosive consisting of ammonium nitrate and TNT (trinitrotoluene) in almost any proportions.

Amazon South American river, the world's second longest, 6,570 km/4,080 mi, and the largest in volume of water. Its main headstreams, the Marañ́in and the Ucayali, rise in central Peru and unite to flow eastwards across Brazil for about 4,000 km/2,500 mi. It has 48,280 km/30,000 mi of navigable waterways, draining 7,000,000 sq km/2,750,000 sq mi, nearly half the South American land mass. It reaches the Atlantic on the Equator, its estuary 80 km/50 mi wide, discharging a volume of water so immense that 64 km/40 mi out to sea fresh water remains at the surface.

Amazon in Greek mythology, a member of a group of legendary female warriors living near the Black Sea, who cut off their right breasts to use the bow more easily; their queen, Penthesilea, was killed by ◊Achilles at the siege of Troy. The term has come to mean a strong, fierce woman.

Amazonian Indian the indigenous inhabitants of the Amazon Basin in South America. The majority of the peoples belong to small societies whose traditional livelihood includes hunting and gathering, fishing, and shifting cultivation. A wide range of indigenous languages are spoken.

ambassador officer of the highest rank in the diplomatic service, who represents the head of one sovereign state at the court or capital of another.

amber fossilized gum from coniferous trees of the Middle Tertiary period, often washed ashore on the Baltic coast with plant and animal specimens preserved in it. Ranging in colour from red to yellow, it is used in jewellery making.

ambergris fatty substance, resembling wax, found in the stomach and intestines of the sperm ◊whale, which was used in perfumery as a fixative.

amblyopia reduced vision without apparent disorder in the eye concerned.

Ambrose, St *c.* 340–397. One of the early Christian leaders and writers known as the Fathers of the Church. He was bishop of Milan, Italy, and wrote on theological subjects. Feast day 7 Dec.

ambrosia Greek 'immortal', the food of the gods, supposed to confer eternal life upon all who ate it.

amen Hebrew word signifying affirmation ('so be it'), commonly used at the close of a Jewish or Christian prayer or hymn. As used by Jesus Christ in the New Testament it was traditionally translated 'verily'.

Amenhotep four Egyptian pharaohs, including:

Amenhotep III *c.* 1400 BC– . King of Egypt who built great monuments at Thebes, including the temples at Luxor. Two portrait statues at his tomb were known to the Greeks as the colossi of Memnon; one was cracked, and when the temperature changed at dawn it gave out an eerie sound, then thought supernatural. His son *Amenhotep IV* changed his name to ◊Ikhnaton.

America the western hemisphere of the earth, containing the continents of ◊North America and ◊South America, with Central America in between. This great land mass extends from the Arctic to the Antarctic, from beyond 75° N to past 55° S. The area is about 42,000,000 sq km/16,000,000 sq mi, and the estimated population is over 500,000,000.

American Civil War 1861–65; see ◊Civil War, American.

American Federation of Labor and Congress of Industrial Organizations *AFL–CIO* federation of North American trade unions, created 1955 from the AFL (founded 1866), initially a union of skilled craftworkers, and the CIO, formed 1938 as a dissenting offshoot of the AFL.

American football see ◊football, American.

American Independence, War of the revolt 1775–83 of the British North American colonies that resulted in the establishment of the USA. It was caused by colonial resentment at the contemporary attitude that commercial or industrial interests of any colony should be subordinate to those of the mother country; and the unwillingness of the colonists to pay for a standing army.

American Indian an aboriginal of the Americas. They were called Indians by Columbus because he believed he had found, not the New World, but a new route to India. They are thought to have entered N America from Asia via the former land-bridge, Beringia, 60,000–35,000 BC.

American Legion community organization in USA, originally for ex-servicemen of World War I, founded in 1919.

American Samoa see ◊Samoa, American.

American System, the in US history, a federal legislative programme following the War of ◊1812 that was designed to promote an integrated national economy. It introduced tariffs to protect American industry from foreign competition, internal improvements to the transport network, and a national bank to facilitate economic growth.

America's Cup international yacht-racing trophy contested every three or four years. It is a seven-race series. The USA have dominated the race since its beginning in 1870, losing only once in its 130-year history, to Australia in 1983.

americium artificial element which is a member of the ◊actinide group, atomic number 95. It is produced by bombarding plutonium with neutrons.

Amerindian an abbreviated form of American Indian used to describe the indigenous peoples of the Americas.

amethyst a variety of quartz, SiO_2, coloured violet by the presence of small quantities of manganese, and used as a semiprecious stone.

Amhara person of Amhara culture from the central Ethiopian plateau. They comprise approximately 25% of Ethiopia's population. The Amhara language belongs to the Semitic branch of the Afro-Asiatic family.

amicus curiae (Latin 'friend of the court') in law, someone advising the court in a legal case as a neutral person, not representing either side.

Amida Buddha the 'Buddha of immeasurable light'. Japanese name for *Amitābha*, the transhistorical Buddha venerated in Pure Land Buddhism, who presides over the Western Paradise where, through his infinite compassion, believers hope to be reborn.

Amies Hardy 1909– . British couturier, one of Queen Elizabeth II's dressmakers. Noted from 1934 for his tailored clothes for women, he also designed successfully for men from 1959.

Amin Dada Idi 1925– . Ugandan politician, president 1971–79. He led the coup that deposed Milton Obote in 1971, expelled the Asian community in 1972, and exercised a reign of terror over his people. He fled when insurgent Ugandan and Tanzanian troops invaded the country in 1979.

amines class of organic chemical compounds derived from ammonia, one or more of the hydrogen atoms of ammonia being replaced by other groups of atoms.

amino acid a water-soluble ◊molecule mainly composed of carbon, oxygen, hydrogen, and nitrogen. When joined in chains, amino acids form ◊peptides and ◊proteins.

Amis Kingsley 1922– . British novelist and poet. His works include *Lucky Jim* 1954, a comic portrayal of life in a provincial university, and *Take a Girl Like You* 1960. He won the Booker Prize in 1986 for *The Old Devils*.

Amis Martin 1949– . British novelist, son of Kingsley Amis. His works include *The Rachel Papers* 1974 and *Money* 1984.

Amman capital and chief industrial centre of Jordan; population (1980) 1,232,600. An important communications centre, the city now houses many Palestinian refugees.

ammeter an instrument that measures electric current, usually in ◊amperes.

Ammon in Egyptian mythology, the king of the gods; the name is also spelt Amen/Amun, as in the name of the pharaoh Tutankh*amen*.

ammonia NH_3 a colourless pungent-smelling gas about two-thirds as dense as air. It is used mainly to produce nitrogenous fertilizers.

ammonite extinct ◊cephalopod mollusc akin to the modern nautilus. The shell was curled in a plane spiral and made up of numerous gas-filled chambers, the outermost containing the body of the animal. Many species flourished between 200 million and 65 million years ago, ranging in size from that of a small coin to 2 m/6 ft across.

ammonium chloride NH_4Cl (also known as *sal ammoniac*) a volatile salt, it forms white crystals around volcanic craters, and is prepared synthetically for use in 'dry-cell' batteries.

amnesia a loss or impairment of memory. As a clinical condition it may be caused by disease or injury to the brain; in some cases it may be a symptom of an emotional disorder.

Amnesty International human-rights organization established in the UK 1961 to campaign for the release of political prisoners worldwide. It is politically unaligned. Nobel prize 1977.

amniocentesis sampling the amniotic fluid of a fetus for diagnostic purposes (the amniotic fluid surrounds the fetus in the womb). It is used to detect Down's syndrome and other abnormalities.

amnion innermost of three membranes that enclose the embryo within the egg (reptiles and birds) or within the uterus (mammals). It contains amniotic fluid which cushions the embryo.

amoeba (plural *amoebae*) one of the simplest living animals, consisting of a single cell and belonging to the group ◊Protozoa. The body consists of colourless protoplasms. Its activities are controlled by its nucleus, and it feeds by flowing round and engulfing organic debris. It reproduces by ◊binary fission.

Amorites ancient people of Semitic or Indo-European origin, who were among the inhabitants of ◊Canaan at the time of the Israelite invasion. They provided a number of Babylonian kings.

amortization in finance, the ending of a debt by paying it off gradually. The term is used to describe either the paying off of a cash debt, or the accounting procedure by which the value of an asset is progressively reduced ('depreciated') over a number of years.

Amos book of the Old Testament written c. 750 BC. One of the ◊prophets, Amos was a shepherd who foretold the destruction of Israel because of the people's abandonment of their faith.

ampere (usually abbreviated to *amp*) unit (symbol A) of electrical current producing a force between long, straight parallel conductors, one metre apart in a vacuum, of 2×10^7 ◊newtons per metre length.

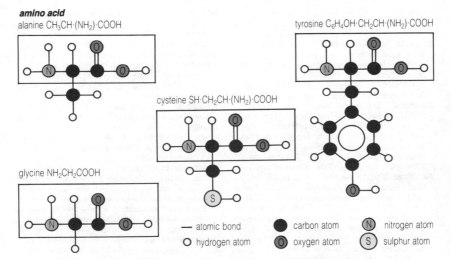

amino acid

alanine CH₃CH·(NH₂)·COOH

tyrosine C₆H₄OH·CH₂CH·(NH₂)·COOH

cysteine SH·CH₂CH·(NH₂)·COOH

glycine NH₂CH₂COOH

— atomic bond   ● carbon atom   Ⓝ nitrogen atom

○ hydrogen atom   ◉ oxygen atom   Ⓢ sulphur atom

amphetamine synthetic ◊stimulant. Used in World War II to help soldiers overcome combat fatigue, its effects made it a popular drug in the post-war years. Doctors prescribed it as an anorexic (appetite suppressant) for weight loss; as an antidepressant, to induce euphoria; as a stimulant, to increase alertness. Indications for its use today are very restricted because of severe side effects, including addiction and abuse.

amphibian member of the class of vertebrates which generally spend their larval ('tadpole') stage in fresh water, transferring to land at maturity, although they generally return to water to breed. Like fish and reptiles, they continue to grow throughout life, and cannot maintain a temperature greatly differing from that of their environment. The class includes caecilians, worm-like in appearance; salamanders, frogs, and toads.

amphibole any one of a large group of rock-forming silicate minerals, closely related to pyroxene.

amphioxus filter-feeding animal about 6 cm/2 in long with a fish-like shape and a notochord (a flexible rod which forms the supporting structure of its body). A primitive relative of vertebrates, it lacks organs such as heart or eye, and lives half-buried in the sea floor.

amphitheatre large oval or circular building used by the Romans for gladiatorial contests, fights of wild beasts, and other similar spectacles; the arena of an amphitheatre is completely surrounded by the seats of the spectators, hence the name (Greek *amphi*, around). The Romans built many amphitheatres. The ◊Colosseum in Rome, completed 80 AD, held 50,000 spectators.

amphora large pottery storage jar in the Graeco-Roman world used for wine, oil, and dry goods.

amplitude maximum displacement of an oscillation from the equilibrium position. For a wave motion, it is the height of a wave (or the depth of a trough). With a sound wave, for example, amplitude corresponds to the intensity (loudness) of the sound. In AM (amplitude modulation) radio

amoeba

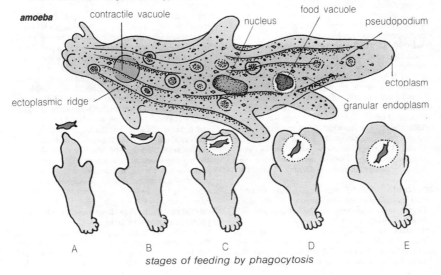

contractile vacuole   nucleus   food vacuole   pseudopodium

ectoplasm

ectoplasmic ridge   granular endoplasm

A   B   C   D   E

stages of feeding by phagocytosis

broadcasting, the required audiofrequency signal is made to modulate (vary slightly) the amplitude of a continuously transmitted radio carrier wave.

ampulla small vessel with a round body and narrow neck, used for holding oil, perfumes, and so on, used by the Greeks and Romans for toilet purposes.

amputation loss of part or all of a limb or other body appendage through surgery or mishap.

Amritsar city in the Punjab, India; population (1981) 594,844. It is the holy city of ◊Sikhism, with the Guru Nanak University, named after the first Sikh guru, and the Golden Temple from which armed demonstrators were evicted by the Indian army under Gen Dayal in 1984, 325 being killed. In 1919 it was the scene of the Amritsar Massacre.

Amritsar Massacre the killing of 379 Indians (and wounding of 1,200) in Amritsar in the Punjab 1919, when British troops under Gen Edward Dyer (1864–1927) opened fire without warning on an angry crowd of some 10,000, assembled to protest against the arrest of two Indian National Congress (see ◊Congress Party) leaders.

Amsterdam capital of the Netherlands; population (1990) 695,100. Canals cut through the city link it with the North Sea and the Rhine, and as a port it is second only to Rotterdam. There is shipbuilding, printing, food processing, banking, and insurance.

Amundsen Roald 1872–1928. Norwegian explorer, who in 1906, was the first person to navigate the ◊North-West Passage. Beaten to the North Pole by ◊Peary in 1910, he reached the South Pole ahead of ◊Scott in 1911.

Amur river in E Asia. Formed by the Argun and the Shilka, the Amur enters the Sea of Okhotsk. At its mouth at Nikolaevsk it is 16 km/10 mi wide. For much of its course of over 4,400 km/2,730 mi it forms, together with its tributary, the Ussuri, the boundary between Russia and China.

amyl alcohol common name for ◊pentanol.

amylase one of a group of ◊enzymes that break down ◊starches into their component molecules (sugars) for use in the body. It occurs widely in both plants and animals. In humans, it is found in pancreatic juices and saliva.

Anabaptist a member of any of various 16th-century Protestant sects who believed in adult rather than child baptism, and sought to establish utopian communities. Anabaptist groups were widespread in N Europe; in Münster, Germany, Anabaptists controlled the city 1534–35.

anabolic steroid ◊hormone which stimulates tissue growth. Its use in medicine is limited to the treatment of some ◊anaemias and breast cancers; it may help to break up blood clots. Side effects include aggressive behaviour, masculinization in women, and, in children, reduced height.

anabolism the process of building up body tissue, promoted by the influence of certain hormones.

anabranch stream which branches from a main river, then reunites with it. For example, the Great Anabranch in New South Wales, Australia, leaves the Darling near Menindee, and joins the Murray below the Darling-Murray confluence.

anaconda South American ◊snake *Eunectes murinus* allied to the boa constrictor. One of the largest snakes, growing to 9 m/30 ft or more, it is found in and near water.

anaemia a condition caused by a shortage of ◊haemoglobin, the oxygen-carrying component of the blood. It arises either from abnormal loss or defective production of haemoglobin.

anaerobic in biology, a description of those living organisms that do not require oxygen for the release of energy food. Anaerobic organisms include many bacteria, yeasts, and internal parasites.

anaesthetic a drug which produces loss of sensation or consciousness; the resulting state is *anaesthesia*, in which the patient is insensitive to stimuli. Anaesthesia may also happen as a result of nerve disorder.

Analects the most important of the four books that contain the teachings and ideas of ◊Confucianism.

analgesia relief of pain, the sensation which is felt when electrical stimuli travel along a nerve pathway, from peripheral nerve fibres to the brain via the spinal cord.

analogue computer early computing device which performs calculations through the interaction of continuously varying physical quantities such as voltages. Such a computer is said to operate in 'real time', and can therefore be used to monitor and control other things, or events, as they are happening.

analysis branch of mathematics concerned with limiting processes on axiomatic number systems; ◊calculus of variations and infinitesimal calculus is now called analysis. In chemistry, analysis is the determination of the composition or properties of substances (see ◊analytical chemistry).

analytic in philosophy, a term derived from ◊Kant: the converse of ◊synthetic. In an analytic judgement, the subject is contained in the predicate, and the judgement therefore provides no new knowledge, for example: 'All bachelors are unmarried'.

analytical chemistry branch of chemistry that deals with the determination of the chemical composition of substances.

analytical engine a mechanical computer, designed but never completed by Charles ◊Babbage. Using a program on punched cards to determine the exact type of calculation to be performed, it would have been the first true computer.

analytical geometry another name for ◊coordinate geometry.

Ananda 5th century BC. Favourite disciple of the Buddha. At his plea, a separate order was established for women. He played a major part in collecting the teachings of the Buddha after his death.

anaphylaxis a severe allergic response involving the whole body. Typically, the air passages become constricted, the blood pressure falls rapidly, and the victim collapses. Rare in humans, anaphylaxis is most often seen following wasp or bee stings, or treatment with some drugs.

anarchism the political belief that society should have no government, laws, police, or other authority, but should be a free association of all its members. It does not mean 'without order'; most theories of anarchism imply an order of a very strict and symmetrical kind, but they maintain that such order can be achieved by cooperation, and that other methods of achieving order, which rely on authority, are morally reprehensible and politically unstable. Anarchism must not be confused with nihilism, a purely negative and destructive activity directed against society as such: it is essentially a pacifist movement.

Anastasia 1901–1918. Russian Grand Duchess, youngest daughter of ◊Nicholas II. She was murdered with her parents, but it has been alleged that Anastasia escaped, and of those who claimed her identity the most famous was Anna Anderson (1902–1984). Alleged by some to be a Pole,

Franziska Schanzkowski, she was rescued from a Berlin canal in 1920: the German Federal Supreme Court found no proof of her claim in 1970.

anastomosis a normal or abnormal communication between two vessels (usually blood vessels) in the body. Surgical anastomosis is the deliberate joining of two vessels or hollow parts of an organ, for example, when part of the intestine has been removed, and the remaining free ends are brought together and stitched.

anatomy the study of the structure of the body, especially the ◊human body, as distinguished from physiology, which is the study of its functions.

Anaximander 610–*c.* 547 BC. Greek astronomer and philosopher. He is thought to have been the first to determine solstices and equinoxes, to have invented the sundial, and to have produced the first geographical map. He believed that the universe originated as a formless mass (*apeiron*, 'indefinite') containing within itself the contraries of hot and cold, and wet and dry, from which land, sea, and air were formed out of the union and separation of these opposites.

ANC abbreviation for ◊*African National Congress*.

ancestor worship religious attitude to deceased members of a group or family. Adherents believe that the souls of the dead remain involved in this world, and are capable of influencing events if appealed to.

Anchorage port and largest town of Alaska, USA, at the head of Cook Inlet. Population (1984) 244,030. Established 1918, Anchorage is an important centre of administration, communication, and commerce. Industries include salmon canning, and coal and gold are mined.

anchovy small fish *Engraulis encrasicholus* of the ◊herring family. It is fished extensively, being abundant in the Mediterranean, and is also found on the Atlantic coast of Europe and in the Black Sea. It grows to 20 cm/8 in.

ancien régime the old order, especially the feudal, absolute monarchy in France before the French Revolution 1789.

ancient art art of prehistoric cultures and the ancient civilizations in the western hemisphere that predate the classical world of Greece and Rome, for example Egyptian, W Asian, and Aegean art. Artefacts range from simple relics of the Palaeolithic period, such as pebbles carved with symbolic figures, to the sophisticated art forms of ancient Egypt and Assyria, for example mural paintings, sculpture, and jewellery.

Ancient Mariner, The Rime of the a poem by Samuel Taylor Coleridge, published 1798, describing the curse which falls upon a mariner and his ship when he shoots an albatross.

Andalusia (Spanish *Andalucía*) fertile autonomous region of S Spain, including the provinces of Almería, Cádiz, Córdoba, Granada, Huelva, Jaeva, Málaga, and Seville; population (1981) 6,442,000. Malaga, Cadiz, and Algeciras are the chief ports and industrial centres. The *Costa del Sol* on the S coast is famous for its tourist resorts, including Marbella and Torremolinos.

Andaman Islands group of islands in the Bay of Bengal, between India and Burma, forming (with the Nicobar Islands) a territory of the Republic of India. Area 6,500 sq km/2,500 sq mi; population (1981) 188,254. The economy is based on fishing and the production of rubber, fruit, rice, and timber.

andante in music, a passage or movement to be performed at a walking pace; that is, at a moderately slow tempo.

Andean Group (Spanish *Grupo Andino*) South American organization aimed at economic and social cooperation between member states. It was established under the Treaty of Cartagena 1969, by Bolivia, Chile, Colombia, Ecuador, and Peru; Venezuela joined 1973, but Chile withdrew in 1977. The organization is based in Peru.

Andean Indian indigenous inhabitant of the Andes Mountains in South America. The Incas extended their control over much of the Andean region 1200–1525. Pachacuti (1438–1463), the ninth Inca and first emperor, imposed the Quechua language in order to unify the different conquered groups. It is now spoken by over 10,000,000, and is a member of the Andean-Equatorial family.

Andersen Hans Christian 1805–1875. Danish writer. His novel *The Improvisatore* 1835 was followed by fairy tales such as 'The Ugly Duckling', 'The Emperor's New Clothes', and 'The Snow Queen', which gained him international fame and have been translated into many languages.

Anderson Carl David 1905– . US physicist, who discovered the positive electron or positron in 1932; he shared a Nobel prize 1936.

Anderson Elizabeth Garrett 1836–1917. The first English woman to qualify in medicine. Refused entry into medical school, Anderson studied privately and was licensed by the Society of Apothecaries in London in 1865. She was physician to the Marylebone Dispensary for Women and Children (later renamed the Elizabeth Garrett Anderson Hospital), now staffed by women and serving women patients.

Anderson Marian 1902– . US contralto singer, born in Philadelphia. She toured Europe in 1930, but in 1939 she was barred from singing at Constitution Hall, Washington, because she was black. In 1955 she sang at the Metropolitan Opera, the first black singer to appear there. Her voice was noted for its range and richness.

Anderson Sherwood 1876–1941. US writer, born in

Andersen *Danish writer Hans Christian Andersen author of* The Snow Queen.

Andorra
Principality of
(Principat d'Andorra)

area 465 sq km/190 sq mi
capital Andorra-la-Vella

physical mountainous, with narrow valleys
head of state Joan Marti i Alanis (bishop of Seo de Urgel, Spain) and François Mitterrand (president of France)
head of government Oscar Riba Reig from 1989
political system semi-feudal co-principality
exports main industries tourism and tobacco
currency French franc and Spanish peseta
population (1990) 51,000 (30% Andorrans, 61% Spanish, 6% French)
language Catalan (official); French, Spanish
religion Roman Catholic
literacy 100% (1987)
GDP $300 million (1985)
chronology
1970 Extension of franchise to third-generation women and second-generation men.
1976 First political party formed.
1977 Franchise extended to first-generation Andorrans.
1981 First prime minister appointed by General Council.
1982 Executive and legislative powers separated with the appointment of an Executive Council.
1991 Andorra's first constitution planned. Links with the EC formalized.

Ohio and best known for his sensitive, experimental and poetic stories of small-town Midwestern life, *Winesburg, Ohio* 1919.

Andes the great mountain system or *cordillera* that forms the western fringe of South America, extending through some 67° of latitude and the republics of Colombia, Venezuela, Ecuador, Peru, Bolivia, Chile, and Argentina. The mountains exceed 3,600 m/12,000 ft for half their length of 6,500 km/4,000 mi. Most of the individual mountains are volcanic, with some still active.

andesite a volcanic igneous rock intermediate in silicon content between rhyolite and basalt. It is characterized by a large quantity of the mineral ◊feldspar, giving it a light colour. Andesite erupts from volcanoes at destructive plate margins (where one plate of the earth's surface is being drawn down beneath another; see ◊plate tectonics), including the Andes, from which it gets its name.

Andhra Pradesh state in E central India
area 276,814 sq km/106,285 sq mi
capital Hyderabad
towns Secunderabad
products chief agricultural crops are rice, sugar cane, tobacco, groundnuts, and cotton
population (1991) 66,304,900
languages Telugu, Urdu, and Tamil
history formed in 1953 from the Telugu-speaking areas of ◊Madras, and enlarged in 1956 from the former Hyderabad state.

Andorra landlocked country in the E Pyrenees, bounded to the north by France and to the south by Spain.

André Carl 1935– . US sculptor, a Minimalist, who often uses industrial materials and basic geometrical forms. An example is the notorious *Equivalent VIII* 1976, a simple rectangle of bricks (Tate Gallery, London).

André John 1751–1880. British army major in the War of American Independence, who covertly negotiated the surrender of West Point with Benedict ◊Arnold, and was caught and hanged by the Americans.

Andrea del Sarto 1486–1531. Italian Renaissance painter active in Florence, one of the finest portraitists and religious painters of his time. His style is serene and noble, characteristic of High Renaissance art.

Andreas Capellanus Latin name for ◊André le Chapelain.

André le Chapelain 12th century. French priest and author. He wrote *De Arte Honest Amandi/The Art of Honest Love*, a seminal work in ◊courtly love literature, at the request of ◊Marie de France, while he was chaplain at her court in Troyes, E France.

Andrew (full name Andrew Albert Christian Edward) 1960– . Prince of the UK, Duke of York, second son of Queen Elizabeth II. He married Sarah Ferguson 1986; their first daughter, Princess Beatrice, was born 1988 and their second daughter, Princess Eugenie, was born 1990. The couple separated 1992.

Andrewes Lancelot 1555–1626. Church of England bishop successively of Chichester (1605), Ely (1609), and Winchester (1618). He took part in preparing the text of the Authorized Version of the Bible, and was known for his fine preaching.

Andrew, St New Testament apostle, martyred on an X-shaped cross (*St Andrew's cross*). He is the patron saint of Scotland. Feast day 30 Nov.

Andrić Ivo 1892–1974. Yugoslavian novelist and ardent nationalist. A diplomat, he was ambassador to Berlin in 1940. *Na Drini ćuprija/The Bridge on the Drina* 1945, an epic history of a small Bosnian town, is his best work. Nobel prize 1961.

Androcles 1st century AD. Roman slave. Traditionally, he fled from a cruel master to the African desert, where he drew a thorn from the paw of a crippled lion. Recaptured, and sentenced to combat a lion in the arena, he found his adversary was his old friend. ◊Tiberius was said to have freed them both.

androecium the male part of a flower, comprising a number of ◊stamens.

androgen a general name for any male sex hormone, of which ◊testosterone is the most important. They are all ◊steroids and are principally involved in the production of male ◊secondary sexual characters (such as facial hair).

Andromache heroine of Homer's *Iliad*; the wife of Hector, who was killed in combat with Achilles, and mother of the boy Astyanax, whom the Greeks ordered to be killed. After the fall of Troy she was awarded to Neoptolemus, Achilles' son.

Andromeda a major constellation of the northern hemisphere, best placed for viewing in autumn. Its main feature is the ◊Andromeda galaxy. The star Alpha Andromedae forms one corner of the Square of Pegasus. It represents the princess of Greek mythology.

Andromeda Galaxy a spiral galaxy 2.2 million light years away in the constellation of Andromeda, and the most distant object visible to the naked eye. It is similar in nature to our own ◊Milky Way but contains about twice as many stars. It is the largest member of the ◊Local Group of galaxies.

Andropov Yuri 1914–1984. Soviet communist politician, president 1983–84. As chief of the KGB 1967–82, he established a reputation for efficiently suppressing dissent.

anemone plant of the buttercup family Ranunculaceae. The white-petalled *wood anemone Anemone nemorosa*, or *wind-flower*, grows in shady woods, flowering in spring. The *garden anemone* is *Anemone coronaria*.

anemophily a type of ◊pollination in which the pollen is carried on the wind (also known as *wind-pollination*). Anemophilous flowers are usually unscented, either have very reduced petals and sepals or lack them altogether, and do not produce nectar. In some species they are borne in ◊catkins. Male and female reproductive structures are commonly found in separate flowers. The male flowers have numerous exposed stamens, often on long filaments; the female flowers have long, often branched, feathery stigmas.

aneroid a kind of ◊barometer.

aneurysm a weakening in the wall of an artery, causing it to balloon outwards, with the risk of rupture and serious blood loss. If detected in time, some aneurysms can be excised.

Angad 1504–1552. second guru (teacher) of Sikhism 1539–52, succeeding Nanak. He is best known for popularizing the alphabet known as *Gurmukhi*, in which the Sikh scriptures are written.

angel in Christian, Jewish, and Muslim belief, supernatural being intermediate between God and humans. The Christian hierarchy has nine orders: *Seraphim*, *Cherubim*, *Thrones* (who contemplate God and reflect his glory), *Dominations*, *Virtues*, *Powers* (who regulate the stars and the Universe), *Principalities*, *Archangels*, and *Angels* (who minister to humanity). In traditional Catholic belief, every human being has a guardian angel. The existence of angels was reasserted by the Pope in 1986.

angel dust popular name for *phencyclidine* (PCP), an animal tranquillizer often used illegally as a psychedelic drug.

angelfish name for a number of unrelated fishes. The freshwater *angelfish*, genus *Pterophyllum* of South America is a tall flattened fish with a striped body, up to 26 cm/10 in tall, but usually smaller in captivity. The *angelfish* or *monkfish Squatina* is a bottom-living shark up to 1.8 m/6 ft long with a body flattened from top to bottom. The *marine angelfish, Pomacanthus* and others, are

Angelou US writer Maya Angelou.

tall narrow-bodied fish, often brilliantly coloured, up to 65 cm/2 ft long, living around coral reefs in the tropics.

angelica plant of the umbelliferous family. *Angelica sylvestris*, the species found in Britain, is a tall perennial herb, with wedge-shaped leaves and clusters of white, pale violet, or pinkish flowers.

Angelico Fra *c.* 1400–1455. Italian painter active in Florence. Fra Angelico, a Dominican friar, was one of the best-known religious painters of the 14th century. His outstanding achievement was a series of frescoes at the monastery of S Marco, Florence, begun after 1436. He also produced several altarpieces in sweet colours and a delicately simple style.

Angell Norman 1872–1967. British writer on politics and economics. In *The Great Illusion* 1910 he maintained that any war must prove ruinous to the victors as well as to the vanquished. Nobel Peace prize 1933.

Angelou Maya (born Marguerite Johnson) 1928– US novelist, poet, playwright, and short-story writer. Her powerful autobiographical work, *I Know Why the Caged Bird Sings* 1970 and its sequels, tell of the struggles towards physical and spiritual liberation of a black woman growing up in the US South.

Angevin relating to the reigns of the English kings Henry II, and Richard I (also known, with the later English kings up to Richard III, as the *Plantagenets*); derived from ◊Anjou, the region in France controlled by English kings at this time. The *Angevin Empire* comprised the territories (including England) that belonged to the Anjou dynasty.

angina or *angina pectoris*. Severe pain in the chest due to impaired blood supply to the heart muscle because a coronary artery is narrowed (◊atheroma). The pain seems to shoot across the chest and arm, rather than appearing to come from the heart.

angiography a technique for X-raying major blood vessels. A radio-opaque dye is injected into the bloodstream so that the suspect vessel is clearly silhouetted on the X-ray film.

angiosperm flowering plant in which the seeds are enclosed within an ovary, which ripens to a fruit.

Angiosperms are divided into ◊monocotyledons (single seed-leaf in the embryo) and ◊dicotyledons (two seed-leaves in the embryo). They include the vast majority of flowers, herbs, grasses, and trees except conifers.

Angkor in Cambodia, the ruins of the ancient capital of the Khmer Empire. The remains date mainly from the 10–12th century AD, and comprise temples originally dedicated to the Hindu gods, shrines associated with Theravada Buddhism, and royal palaces. Many are grouped within the great enclosure called **Angkor Thom**, but the great temple of **Angkor Wat** (early 12th century) lies outside. Angkor was abandoned in the 15th century, and the ruins were overgrown by jungle and not adequately described until 1863.

angle in geometry, an amount of turn. Angles are measured in ◊degrees or ◊radians. An angle of 90° (90 degrees) is a right angle. Angles of less than 90° are called *acute angles*; angles of more than 90° but less than 180° are *obtuse angles*. A *reflex angle* is an angle of more than 180° but less than 360°. Angles can be measured using a protractor.

angler fish *Lophius piscatorius*, also known as the frogfish or monkfish. It lives in the N Atlantic and Mediterranean, grows to 2 m/6.5 ft, and has a flattened body and broad head and jaws. Camouflaged against the sea bottom, it waits, twitching the enlarged tip of the thread-like first ray of the dorsal fin to entice prey.

Anglesey Henry William Paget, 1st Marquess of Anglesey 1768–1854. British cavalry leader during the Napoleonic wars. He was twice Lord Lieutenant of Ireland, and succeeded his father as earl of Uxbridge in 1812. At the Battle of Waterloo he led a great charge, lost a leg, and was made a marquess for his conspicuous services.

Anglican Communion family of Christian churches including the Church of England, the US Episcopal Church, and those holding the same essential doctrines, that is the Lambeth Quadrilateral 1888 Holy Scripture as the basis of all doctrine, the Nicene and Apostles' Creeds, Holy Baptism and Holy Communion, and the historic episcopate.

angling fishing with rod and line in many popular forms. *Freshwater* and *sea-fishing* are the most popular forms. Fishing is the biggest participant sport in the United Kingdom.

Anglo a combining form with several related meanings. In 'Anglo-Saxon' it refers to the Angles, a Germanic people who invaded Britain in the 5th to 7th centuries. In 'Anglo-Welsh' it refers to England or the English. In 'Anglo-American' it may refer either to England and the English, or commonly but less accurately to Britain and the British; it may also refer to the English language and to the Anglo-Saxon element in American society (often in contrast to 'Hispano-American'). In many parts of the world 'an Anglo' is a person of Anglo-Saxon background or type and/or someone who speaks English.

Anglo-Irish Agreement or *Hillsborough Agreement* a concord reached in 1985 between the UK and Irish premiers, Margaret Thatcher and Garret FitzGerald. One sign of the improved relations between the two countries was increased cross-border co-operation between police and security forces across the border with Northern Ireland. However, the agreement was rejected by Northern Ireland Unionists as a step towards a renunciation of British sovereignty. In Mar 1988 talks led to further strengthening of the agreement.

Anglo-Saxon the Germanic invaders (Angles, Saxons and Jutes) who conquered much of Britain between the 5th and 7th centuries. The Angles settled in East Anglia, Mercia, and Northumbria; the Saxons in Essex, Sussex, and Wessex; and the Jutes in Kent and S Hampshire. After the conquest a number of kingdoms were set up, commonly referred to as the **Heptarchy**; these were united in the early 9th century under the overlordship of Wessex.

Anglo-Saxon art the painting, sculpture, and architecture of England from the 7th century to 1066. Sculpted crosses and ivories, manuscript painting, and gold and enamel jewellery survive; the relics of the Sutton Hoo ship burial, 7th century, and the Lindisfarne Gospels, *c.* 690 (both British Museum, London), have typical Celtic ornamental patterns, but in manuscripts of S England a different style emerged in the 9th century, with delicate, lively pen-and-ink figures and heavily decorative foliage borders.

Anglo-Saxon Chronicle a history of England from the Roman invasion to the 11th century, in the form of a series of chronicles written in Old English by monks, begun in the 9th century (during the reign of King Alfred), and continuing to the 12th century.

Anglo-Saxon language the group of dialects spoken by the Anglo-Saxon peoples who in the 5th to 7th centuries invaded and settled in Britain (in what became England and Lowland Scotland). Anglo-Saxon is traditionally known as Old English. See ◊English language.

Angola country in SW Africa, bounded to the west by the Atlantic ocean, to the north and northeast by Zaïre, to the east by Zambia, and to the south by Namibia.

Angry Young Men a group of British writers who emerged about 1950 after the creative hiatus which followed World War II. They included Kingsley Amis, John Wain, John Osborne, and Colin Wilson. Also linked to the group were Iris Murdoch and Kenneth Tynan.

angst (German 'anxiety') an emotional state of anxiety without a specific cause. In ◊Existentialism, the term refers to general human anxiety at having free will, that is, of being responsible for one's actions.

Angström Anders Jonas 1814–1874. Swedish physicist, who worked in spectroscopy and solar physics. The *angstrom unit*, used to express the wavelength of electromagnetic radiation (light, radiant heat, X-rays), is one ten-millionth of a millimetre (10^{-7} mm).

Anguilla island in the E Caribbean
area 90 sq km/35 sq mi
capital The Valley
exports lobster, salt
currency Eastern Caribbean dollar
population (1984) 7,000
language English and Creole
government from 1982, governor, executive council, and legislative house of assembly (chief minister Emile Gumbs from 1984)
recent history a British colony from 1650, Anguilla was long associated with St ◊Christoper-Nevis, but revolted against alleged domination by the larger island, and in 1969 declared itself a republic. A small British force restored order, and Anguilla retained a special position at its own request, since 1980 a separate dependency of the UK.

Angola
People's Republic of
(República Popular de Angola)

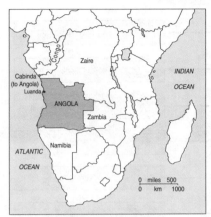

area 1,246,700 sq km/481,350 sq mi
capital and chief port Luanda
towns Lobito and Benguela, also ports
physical elevated plateau, desert in the S
head of state and government José Eduardo dos Santos from 1979
political system socialist republic
exports oil, coffee, diamonds, palm oil, sisal, iron ore, fish
currency kwanza
population (1989 est) 9,733,000 (largest ethnic group Ovimbundu); annual growth rate 2.5%
life expectancy men 40, women 44
language Portuguese (official), Umbundu, Kimbundu
religion Roman Catholic 68%, Protestant 20%, animist 12%
literacy 20%
GDP $7.9 bn (1982); $620 GNP per head

chronology
1951 Angola became an overseas territory of Portugal.
1956 The People's Movement for the Liberation of Angola (MPLA) formed.
1961 Unsuccessful independence rebellion.
1962 The National Front for the Liberation of Angola (FNLA) formed.
1966 The National Union for the Total Independence of Angola (UNITA) formed.
1975 Transitional government of independence formed from representatives of MPLA, FNLA, UNITA, and Portuguese government. MPLA supported by USSR and Cuba, FNLA by non-left power groups of southern Africa, and UNITA by Western powers. Angola declared independent. MPLA proclaimed People's Republic under the presidency of Dr Agostinho Neto. FNLA and UNITA proclaimed People's Democratic Republic of Angola.
1976 MPLA gained control of most of the country. South African troops withdrawn but Cuban units remained.
1977 MPLA restructured to become the People's Movement for the Liberation of Angola-Workers' Party (MPLA-PT).
1979 Death of Neto, succeeded by José Eduardo dos Santos.
1980 Constitution amended to provide for an elected people's assembly. UNITA guerrillas, aided by South Africa, continued to operate South African raids on the South West Africa People's Organization's bases in Angola.
1984 Lusaka agreement.
1985 South African forces withdrawn.
1986 Further South African raids into Angola.
1988 Peace treaty signed with South Africa and Cuba.
1990 Peace offer by rebels. Return to multiparty politics promised.
1991 Peace agreement officially ended civil war between MPLA-PT and UNITA.
1992 MPLA's general-election victory fiercely disputed by UNITA. Continued fighting renewed the civil war.

Angus former county and modern district on the E coast of Scotland, merged in 1975 in Tayside region.

Anhui (former name *Anhwei*) province of E China, watered by the Chiang Jiang (Yangtze River) and producing cereals in the north and cotton, rice, and tea in the south. There are coal mines, and iron and steel works. The capital is Hofei. Area 139,900 sq km/54,000 sq mi; population (1982) 49,665,700.

aniline $C_6H_5NH_2$ (modern name **phenylamine**) the simplest aromatic chemical known. When pure, it is a colourless oily liquid; it has a characteristic odour, and turns brown in contact with air. It occurs in coal tar, and is used in the rubber industry and to make drugs and dyes. It is highly poisonous.

animal behaviour the scientific study of the behaviour of animals, either by comparative psychologists (with an interest mainly in the mental processes involved in the control of behaviour) or by ethologists (with an interest in the biological context and relevance of behaviour).

animal kingdom one of the major kingdoms of living things, the science of which is zoology. Animals are all ◊heterotrophs (that is they obtain their energy from organic substances produced by other organisms); they have ◊eukaryotic cells (the genetic material is contained within a distinct nucleus) bounded by a thin cell membrane rather than a thick cell wall. In the past, it was common to include the single-celled ◊protozoa with the animals, but these are now classified as protists. Thus all animals are multicellular. Most are capable of moving around but some, such as sponges and corals, are stationary.

animism in psychology and physiology, the view of human personality which rejects materialistic mechanism as a valid explanation of human behaviour. In religious theory, the conception of spiritual reality behind the material one: for example, beliefs in the soul as a shadowy duplicate of the body capable of independent activity, both in life and death.

anion ion carrying a negative charge. An electrolyte, such as the salt zinc chloride, is dissociated in aqueous solution or in the molten state into doubly-charged Zn^2h+ zinc ◊cations and singly-charged $Clh-$ anions. During electrolysis, the zinc cations flow to the cathode (to become discharged and liberate zinc metal) and the chloride anions flow to the anode (to liberate chlorine gas).

anise umbelliferous plant *Pimpinella anisum* whose fruits, aniseeds, are used to flavour foods. Aniseed oil is used in cough medicines.

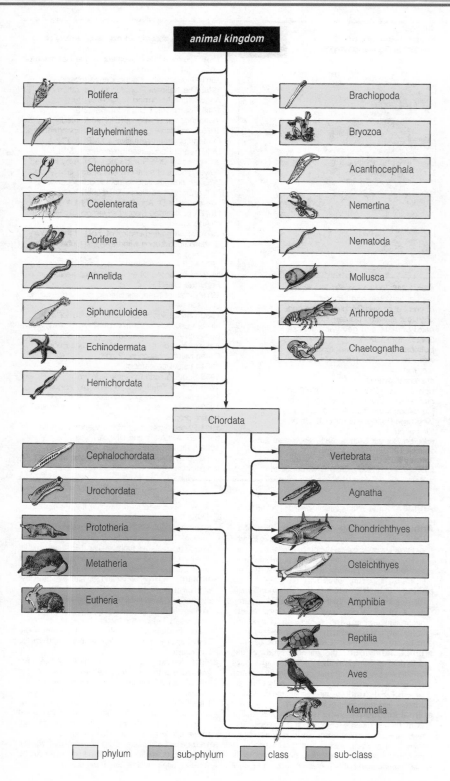

Ankara (former name *Angora*) capital of Turkey; population (1990) 2,559,500. Industries include cement, textiles, and leather products. It replaced Istanbul (then in Allied occupation) as capital in 1923.

Anna Comnena 1083–after 1148. Byzantine historian, daughter of the emperor ◊Alexius I, and chiefly remembered as the historian of her father's reign. After a number of abortive attempts to alter the imperial succession in favour of her husband, Nicephorus Bryennius (*c.* 1062–1137), she retired to a convent to write her major work, the *Alexiad*. This dealt with the period 1069–1118 and followed on from the writings of her husband. It describes the Byzantine view of public office, as well as religious and intellectual life of the period.

Annapurna mountain 8,075 m/26,502 ft in the Himalayas, Nepál. The north face was climbed by a French expedition (Maurice Herzog) in 1950 and the south by a British one in 1970.

Anne Queen of Great Britain and Ireland 1665–1714. Second daughter of James, Duke of York, who became James II, and Anne Hyde, she received a Protestant upbringing, and in 1683 married Prince George of Denmark. Of their many children only one survived infancy, William, Duke of Gloucester, who died at the age of 11. She succeeded William on the throne in 1702. The outstanding events of her reign were the War of the Spanish Succession (1702–13), Marlborough's victories at Blenheim, Ramillies, Oudenarde, and Malplaquet, and the union of the English and Scottish parliaments in 1707.

Anne (full name Anne Elizabeth Alice Louise) 1950– . Princess of the UK. Second child of Queen ◊Elizabeth II, she was declared Princess Royal in 1987. She is an excellent horsewoman, winning a gold medal at the 1976 Olympics, and is actively involved in global charity work, especially for children. In 1973 she married Captain Mark Phillips (1949–); they separated 1989 and were divorced 1992. She married commander Tim Lawrence the same year.

annealing process of heating a material (usually glass or metal) for a given time at a given temperature, followed by slow cooling, to increase ductility and strength. It is a common form of ◊heat treatment.

annelid general name for a segmented worm of the phylum Annelida. Annelids include earthworms, leeches, and marine worms such as lugworms. There is a distinct head and the soft body is divided into a number of similar segments shut off from one another internally by membranous partitions, but there are no jointed appendages.

Anne of Austria 1601–1666. Queen of France from 1615 and regent 1643–61. Daughter of Philip III of Spain, she married Louis XIII of France and on his death became regent for their son, Louis XIV, until his majority.

Anne of Cleves 1515–1557. Fourth wife of ◊Henry VIII of England. She was the daughter of the Duke of Cleves, and was recommended to Henry as a wife by Thomas ◊Cromwell, who wanted an alliance with German Protestantism against the Holy Roman Emperor. Henry did not like her looks, had the marriage declared void after six months and pensioned her.

Anne of Denmark 1574–1619. Queen consort of Great Britain. Daughter of Frederick II of Denmark and Norway, she married in 1589 James VI of Scotland, who became James I of Great Britain in 1603. Anne was suspected of Catholic leanings, and was notably extravagant.

anno domini (Latin 'in the year of our Lord') in the Christian chronological system, dates since the birth of Christ, denoted by the letters AD. There is no year 0, so AD 1 follows immediately after the year 1 BC (before Christ). The system became the standard reckoning in the Western world when adopted by the English historian Bede in the 8th century. The abbreviations CE (Common Era) and BCE (before Common Era) are increasingly used instead.

annual plant a plant that completes its life-cycle within one year, during which time it germinates, grows to maturity, bears flowers, produces seed and then dies. Examples include the common poppy (*Papaver rhoeas*) and groundsel (*Senecio vulgaris*). Among garden plants, some that are described as 'annuals' are actually perennials, although usually cultivated as annuals because they cannot survive winter frosts. See also ◊ephemeral, ◊biennial, ◊perennial.

annual rings or *growth rings* the concentric rings visible on a cut tree trunk or other woody stem. In spring and early summer, spring wood is formed which has larger and more numerous vessels than the autumn wood produced when growth is slowing down. The result is a clear boundary between the paler spring wood and the dark, dense autumn wood. The annual rings may be used to estimate the age of the plant (see ◊dendrochronology), but occasionally more than one growth ring is produced in a given year.

Annunciation in the New Testament, the announcement to Mary by the angel Gabriel that she was to be the mother of Christ; the feast of the Annunciation is 25 Mar, also known as Lady Day.

anode the electrode towards which negative particles (anions, electrons) move within a device such as the cells of a battery, electrolytic cells, and diodes.

anodizing a process that increases the resistance to ◊corrosion of a metal such as aluminium by building up a protective oxide layer on the surface. The natural corrosion resistance of aluminium is provided by a thin film of aluminium oxide; anodizing increases the thickness of this film and thus the corrosion protection.

anorexia lack of desire to eat, especially the pathological condition of *anorexia nervosa*, found particularly in adolescent females, who may be obsessed with the desire to lose weight. It is the opposite of ◊bulimia.

Anouilh Jean 1910–1987. French playwright. His plays, influenced by neoclassical tradition, include *Antigone* 1942, *L'Invitation au château/Ring Round the Moon* 1947, *Colombe* 1950, and *Becket* 1959, about Thomas à Becket and Henry II.

anoxia shortage of oxygen in the tissues.

Anschluss the union of Austria with Germany, accomplished by the German Chancellor Hitler on 12 Mar 1938.

Anselm, St *c.* 1033–1109. Medieval priest. Educated at the abbey of Bec in Normandy, which as an abbot (from 1078) he made the greatest centre of scholarship in Europe, he was appointed archbishop of Canterbury by William II in 1093, but was later forced into exile. He holds an important place in the development of ◊Scholasticism.

ANSI abbreviation for *American National Standards Institution*, the US national standards body. It sets official procedures in (amongst other areas) computing and electronics.

Anson George, 1st Baron Anson 1697–1762. British admiral, who sailed around the world 1740–44.

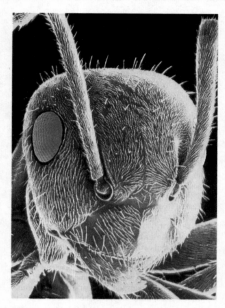

ant Electron microscope picture of the head of a black garden ant. (×46)

In 1740 he commanded the squadron attacking the Spanish colonies and shipping in South America; he returned home, by circumnavigating the world, with £500,000 of Spanish treasure; He carried out important reforms at the Admiralty.

ant insect belonging to the family Formicidae, and to the same order (Hymenoptera) as bees and wasps. They are characterized by a conspicuous 'waist' and elbowed antennae. About 10,000 different species are known, all social in habit, and all construct nests of various kinds.

antacid a substance that neutralizes stomach acid. It may be taken between meals to relieve symptoms of hyperacidity, such as pain, bloating, nausea, and 'heartburn'. Excessive or prolonged need for antacids should be investigated medically.

Antananarivo former name *Tananarive* capital of Madagascar, on the interior plateau, with a rail link to Tamatave; population (1985) 662,585.

Antarctica the Antarctic continent
area 13,727,000 sq km/5,300,000 sq mi
physical the continent, once part of ◊Gondwanaland, is a vast plateau, of which the highest point is the Vinson Massif in the Ellsworth mountains, 5,139 m/16,860 ft high. The Ross Ice Shelf is formed by several glaciers coalescing in the Ross Sea, and Mount Erebus on Ross Island is the world's southernmost active volcano. There is less than 50 mm/2 in of rainfall a year (less than the Sahara). Little more than 1% is ice-free, the temperature falling to -70°C/-100°F and below, and in places the ice is 5,000 m/16,000 ft deep, comprising over two-thirds of the world's fresh water. It covers extensive mineral resources, including iron, coal, and with indications of uranium and other strategic metals, as well as oil.
population settlement is limited to scientific research stations with changing personnel.
history in 1988, nine countries signed the Minerals Convention, laying Antarctica open to commercial exploitation.

anteater

Antarctic Circle an imaginary line that runs round the South Pole at latitude 66°33'S. The line encompasses the continent of Antarctica and the Antarctic Ocean.

Antarctic Treaty agreement signed 1959 between 12 nations with an interest in Antarctica (including Britain), and today with 35 countries party to it. Its provisions (covering the area south of latitude 60°S) neither accepted nor rejected any nation's territorial claims, but barred any new ones; imposed a ban on military operations and large-scale mineral extraction, and allowed for free exchange of scientific data from bases. Since 1980 the Treaty has been extended to conserve marine resources within the larger area bordered by the Antarctic Convergence.

Antares brightest star in the constellation of Scorpius. It is a red supergiant several hundred times larger than the Sun, lies about 400 light years away, and fluctuates slightly in brightness.

anteater South American animal *Myrmecophaga tridactyla* that lives almost entirely on ants and termites. It has toothless jaws, an extensile tongue, and claws for breaking into nests of their prey. It is about 50 cm/2 ft high and common in Brazil.

antebellum in US usage, the period just before the Civil War (1861–65); for example, an antebellum Southern mansion. The term 'pre-war' would be used when describing the period before any other war.

antelope any of a number of distinct kinds of even-toed hoofed wild mammals belonging to the cow family. Most are lightly built and good runners. They are grazers or browsers, and chew the cud. They range in size from the dik-diks and duikers, only 30 cm/1 ft high, to the eland, which can be 1.8 m/6 ft at the shoulder.

antenna in zoology, an appendage ('feeler') on the head. Insects, centipedes, and millipedes each have one pair of antennae, but there are two pairs in crustaceans, such as shrimps. In insects, the antennae are usually involved with the senses of smell and touch. They are frequently complex structures with large surface areas which increase the ability to detect scents.

antenna in radio, another name for ◊aerial.

anthelmintic a class of drugs effective against a range of ◊parasites.

anthem in music, a short, usually elaborate, religious choral composition, sometimes accompanied by the organ.

anther in a flower, the terminal part of a stamen in which the ◊pollen grains are produced. It is usually borne on a slender stalk, or filament, and has two lobes, each containing two chambers or pollen sacs within which the pollen is formed.

antheridium an organ producing the male gametes (◊antherozoids) in algae, bryophytes (mosses and lichens), and pteridophytes (ferns and horsetails). It may be either single-celled, as in most algae, or multicellular, as in bryophytes and pteridophytes.

antherozoid a motile (or independently moving) male gamete produced by algae, bryophytes (mosses and liverworts), pteridophytes (ferns and horsetails), and some gymnosperms (notably the cycads). Antherozoids are formed in an ◊antheridium and, after being released, swim by means of one or more ◊flagella, to the female gametes. Higher plants have non-motile male gametes contained within ◊pollen grains.

Anthony Susan B(rownell) 1820–1906. American pioneering feminist, who also worked for the antislavery and temperance movements. Her campaigns included demands for equality of pay for female teachers, the married women's property act and women's suffrage. In 1869 with Elizabeth Cady Stanton she founded the National Woman Suffrage Association.

Anthony, St c. 251–356. Founder of Christian monasticism. Born in Egypt, he renounced at the age of 20 all his possessions and lived in a tomb, and at 35 sought further solitude on a mountain in the desert. Anthony's temptations in the desert were a popular subject in art; he is also often depicted with a pig.

anthracite a hard, dense, glossy variety of coal, containing over 90 per cent of fixed carbon and a low percentage of ash and volatile matter, which causes it to burn without flame, smoke, or smell.

anthrax cattle and sheep disease occasionally transmitted to humans, usually via infected hides and fleeces. It may develop as a skin lesion or as a severe pneumonia. Treatment is with antibiotics.

anthropology scientific study of humankind. The study was developed following 19th-century evolutionary theory to deal with the human species biologically, physically, socially, and culturally. Anthropology overlaps with sociology, linguistics, and psychology, archaeology, zoology, and medicine.

anthropomorphism the attribution of human characteristics to animals, inanimate objects, or deities. It appears as a feature in the mythologies of many cultures, and as a literary device in ◊fable and ◊allegory.

antibiotic a drug which kills or inhibits the growth of bacteria and fungi. It is derived from living organisms such as fungi or other bacteria, which distinguishes it from other antibacterials.

antibody a protein molecule produced by ◊lymphocytes in response to the presence of invading substances, or ◊antigens, including the proteins carried on the surface of bacteria and viruses. Antibody production is just one aspect of ◊immunity in vertebrates.

anticholinergic drug which blocks the passage of certain nerve impulses in the ◊central nervous system.

Antichrist in Christian theology, the great opponent of Christ, by whom he is finally to be conquered. The idea of conflict between Light and Darkness is present in Persian, Babylonian, and Jewish literature, and influenced early Christian thought.

anticline geological term for a fold in the rocks of the Earth's crust in which the layers or beds bulge upwards forming a sort of arch, which, however, is seldom preserved intact. The opposite of an anticline is a syncline.

anticoagulant a substance which suppresses the formation of ◊blood clots. Common anticoagulants are heparin, produced by the liver and lungs, and derivatives of coumarin. Anticoagulants are used medically, in treating heart attacks, for example. They are also produced by blood-feeding animals such as mosquitoes, leeches, and vampire bats, to keep the victim's blood flowing.

Anti-Comintern Pact or *Anti-Communist Pact* agreement signed between Germany and Japan on 25 Nov 1936, opposing communism as a menace to peace and order. The pact was later signed by Italy in 1937 and by Hungary, Spain, and the Japanese puppet state of Manchukuo in 1939.

anticonvulsant a drug used to prevent epileptic seizures (convulsions or fits).

anticyclone an area of high atmospheric pressure caused by descending air, which becomes warm and dry. Winds radiate from a calm centre, taking a clockwise direction in the northern hemisphere, and an anticlockwise direction in the southern hemisphere.

antidepressant a drug used to relieve symptoms in depressive illness. The two most important groups are the tricyclic antidepressants (TCADs) and the monoamine oxidase inhibitors (MAOIs), which act by altering chemicals available to the central nervous system. Both may produce serious side effects.

Antietam, Battle of indecisive engagement of the American Civil War on 17 Sept 1862 at Antietam Creek, off the Potomac River. The Union general McClellan blocked the advance of the Confederates under Robert E Lee on Washington DC.

antifreeze a substance added to a car's water-cooling system, for example, to prevent it freezing in cold weather. The most common types of antifreeze contain the chemical ethylene ◊glycol, or $(CH_2OH.CH_2OH)$, an organic alcohol with a freezing point of about −15°C.

antifungal a drug that acts against fungal infection, such as ringworm and athlete's foot.

antigen any substance which causes production of ◊antibodies. Common antigens include the proteins carried on the surface of bacteria, viruses, and pollen grains. The proteins of incompatible blood groups or tissues also act as antigens, which has to be taken into account in medical procedures such as blood transfusion and organ transplants.

Antigone in Greek legend, a daughter of Jocasta, by her son ◊Oedipus.

Antigua and Barbuda three islands (Antigua, Barbuda, and uninhabited Redonda) in the eastern Caribbean.

antihistamine a drug which counteracts the effects of ◊histamine.

antihypertensive therapy to control ◊hypertension. The first step is usually a change in diet to reduce salt and, if necessary, caloric intake. If further measures are required, a drug regimen may be prescribed.

anti-inflammatory a substance that reduces swelling in soft tissues.

Antilles the whole group of West Indian islands, divided north-south into the *Greater Antilles* (Cuba, Jamaica, Haiti-Dominican Republic, Puerto Rico) and *Lesser Antilles*, sub-divided into the Leeward Islands (Virgin Islands, St Kitts-Nevis, Antigua and Barbuda, Anguilla, Montserrat and Guadeloupe) and the Windward Islands (Dominica, Martinique, St Lucia, St Vincent and the Grenadines, Barbados, and Grenada).

antimatter in physics, a form of matter in which all the attributes of an ordinary atomic particle, such as electrical charge and spin, are reversed.

antimony in chemistry, a metallic element, symbol Sb, atomic number 51, relative atomic mass 121.76. In the ordinary form it is a silver-white metal, brittle, and readily powdered. It occurs chiefly as stibnite, and is used in a number of alloys, and in photosensitive substances in colour photography and optical electronics.

Antioch ancient capital of the Greek kingdom of Syria, founded 300 BC by Seleucus Nicator in

Antigua and Barbuda
State of

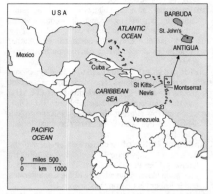

area Antigua 280 sq km/108 sq mi, Barbuda 160 sq km/62 sq mi, plus Redonda 1 sq km/0.4 sq mi
capital and chief port St John's
physical tropical island country

head of state Elizabeth II from 1981 represented by governor general
head of government Vere C Bird from 1981
political system liberal democracy
exports sea-island cotton, rum
currency East Caribbean dollar
population (1989) 83,500; annual growth rate 1.3%
life expectancy 70
language English
religion Christian
literacy 90% (1985)
GDP $173 million (1985); $2,200 per head
chronology
1967 Antigua and Barbuda became an associated state within the Commonwealth, with full internal independence.
1971 Progressive Labour Movement (PLM) won the general election by defeating the Antigua Labour Party (ALP).
1976 PLM called for early independence but ALP urged caution. ALP won the general election.
1981 Full independence.
1983 Assisted US invasion of Grenada.
1984 ALP won the general election.
1985 ALP re-elected.
1989 ALP re-elected.
1991 Vere Bird remained in power despite calls for his resignation.

memory of his father Antiochus, and for long famed for its splendour and luxury. Under the Romans it was an early centre of Christianity. The site is now occupied by the Turkish town of Antakiyah; population (1970) 57,600.

Antiochus 13 kings of Syria of the Seleucid dynasty, including:

Antiochus I 324–?261 BC. King of Syria from 281 BC, son of Seleucus, one of the generals of Alexander the Great. He earned the title of Antiochus Soter or Saviour by his defeat of the Gauls in Galatia 278 BC.

Antiochus II 286–?246 BC. King of Syria 261–246 BC, son of Antiochus I. He was known as Antiochus Theos, the Divine. During his reign the eastern provinces broke away from the Graeco-Macedonian rule and set up native princes.

Antiochus III the Great c. 241–187 BC. King of Syria from 223 BC, grandson of Antiochus II. He secured a loose suzerainty over Armenia and Parthia 209, overcame Bactria, received the homage of the Indian king of the Kabul valley, and returned by way of the Persian Gulf 204 BC. He took possession of Palestine, entering Jerusalem in 198 BC. He crossed into NW Greece, but was decisively defeated by the Romans at Thermopylae in 191 and at Magnesia in 190 BC. He had to abandon his domains in Anatolia, and perished at the hands of the people of Elymais.

Antiochus IV ?215–164 BC. King of Syria from 175 BC, known as Antiochus Epiphanes, the Illustrious; second son of Antiochus III. He occupied Jerusalem about 170 BC, seizing much of the Temple treasure, and instituted worship of the Greek type in the Temple. This produced the revolt of the Jewish people under the Maccabees, and Antiochus died before he could suppress it.

Antiochus VII Sidetes 2nd century BC. King of Syria 138–129 BC. The last strong ruler of the Seleucid dynasty, he took Jerusalem in 134 BC, reducing the Maccabees to subjection, and fought successfully against the Parthians.

antiparticle in nuclear physics, a particle that differs from another fundamental particle in having the opposite charge or magnetic moment. For example, an electron carries a negative charge whereas its antiparticle, the positron, carries a positive one. In all other respects, such as mass, the particles are identical.

antipodes places exactly opposite on the globe (Greek 'opposite feet'). In Britain, Australia and New Zealand are called the Antipodes.

antipope a rival claimant to the elected pope for the leadership of the Roman Catholic church, for instance in the Great Schism 1378–1417 when there were rival popes in Rome and Avignon.

antipruritic skin preparation or drug administered to relieve itching.

antipsychotic a drug used to treat the symptoms of severe mental disorder, also known as a *neuroleptic*.

antipyretic a drug, such as aspirin, used to reduce fever.

anti-racism and anti-sexism active opposition to ◊racism and ◊sexism; positive action or a set of policies designed to counteract racism and sexism, often on the part of an official body or an institution, such as a school, a business, or a government agency.

antirrhinum or **snapdragon** plant belonging to the same family, Scrophulariaceae, as the foxglove and toadflax. *Antirrhinum majus*, a native of the Mediterranean region, is a familiar garden flower.

anti-Semitism literally, prejudice against Semitic people (see ◊Semite), but in practice it has meant prejudice or discrimination against, and persecution of, the Jews as an ethnic group. It has been practised for almost 2,000 years by some European Christians. Anti-Semitism was a tenet of Hitler's Germany and in the Holocaust of 1933–45 about 6 million Jews died in concentration camps. Anti-Semitism occurs in eastern Europe and Islamic nations, and is fostered by extreme right-wing groups elsewhere. It is a form of ◊racism.

antiseptic substance killing or hindering the growth of microorganisms. The use of antiseptics was pioneered by Joseph ◊Lister.

antispasmodic drug which reduces motility, the activity of the muscular intestine walls. Anticholinergics act indirectly by way of the autonomic nervous system, which controls involuntary movement. Other drugs act directly on the smooth muscle to relieve spasm (contraction).

anti-trust laws in economics, regulations preventing or restraining trusts, monopolies, or any business practice considered to be unfair or uncompetitive. In the US, anti-trust laws prevent mergers and acquisitions which might create a monopoly situation, or one in which restrictive practices might be stimulated.

antitussive substance administered to suppress a cough. Coughing, however, is an important reflex in clearing secretions from the airways, and its suppression is usually unnecessary and possibly harmful.

antiviral a drug that acts against viruses, usually preventing them from multiplying. Most virus infections are not susceptible to antibiotics. Antivirals have been difficult drugs to develop, and do not necessarily cure the diseases.

anti-vivisection opposition to vivisection, that is, experiments on living animals, which is practised in the pharmaceutical and cosmetics industries on the grounds that it may result in discoveries of importance to medical science. Anti-vivisectionists argue that it is immoral to inflict pain on helpless creatures, and that it is unscientific, in that results achieved with animals may not be paralleled with human beings.

antler the 'horn' of a deer, often branched, and made of bone rather than horn. Antlers are shed and regrown each year. ◊Caribou of both sexes grow them, but in all other types of deer, only the males have antlers.

ant lion larva of one of the insects of the family Myrmeleontidae which traps insects by waiting at the bottom of a pit it digs in sandy soil. Ant lions are mainly tropical, but also occur in some parts of Europe.

Antonello da Messina c. 1430–1479. Italian painter, born in Messina, Sicily, known as a pioneer of the technique of oil painting, which he is said to have introduced to Italy from N Europe. Flemish influence is reflected in his technique, his use of light, and sometimes in imagery. Surviving works include bust-length portraits and sombre religious paintings.

Antonine Wall Roman line of fortification 142–200 ad, the Roman Empire's NW frontier, between the Clyde and Forth, Scotland.

Antoninus Pius 86–161 AD. Roman emperor, who had been adopted in 138 as Hadrian's heir, and succeeded him later that year; he enjoyed a prosperous reign. His daughter married ◊Marcus Aurelius.

Antonioni Michelangelo 1912– . Italian film director, famous for his subtle analysis of neuroses and personal relationships of the leisured classes. His work includes *L'Avventura* 1960, *Blow Up* 1967, and *The Passenger* 1975.

Antony and Cleopatra a tragedy by William Shakespeare, written and first performed 1607–08. Mark Antony falls in love with the Egyptian queen Cleopatra in Alexandria, but returns to Rome when his wife, Fulvia, dies. He then marries Octavia to heal the rift between her brother Octavius Caesar and himself. Antony returns to Egypt and Cleopatra, but is finally defeated by Caesar. Believing Cleopatra dead, Antony kills himself and Cleopatra takes her life rather than surrender to Caesar.

antonymy near or precise oppositeness between or among words. 'Good' and 'evil' are antonyms, 'good' and 'bad' are also antonyms, and therefore 'evil' and 'bad' are synonyms in this context. Antonymy may vary with context and situation; in discussing the weather, 'dull' and 'bright' are antonymous, but when talking about knives and blades the opposite of 'dull' is 'sharp'.

Antrim county of Northern Ireland
area 2,831 sq km/1093 sq mi
towns Belfast (county town), port of Larne
products potatoes, oats; linen, and synthetic textiles
population (1981) 642,267.

Antwerp (Flemish *Antwerpen*, French *Anvers*) port in Belgium on the river Scheldt; population (1985) 486,500. One of the world's busiest ports, it has shipbuilding, oil-refining, petrochemical, textile, and diamond-cutting industries. The home of Rubens is preserved, and many of his works are in the Gothic cathedral.

Anubis in Egyptian mythology, the jackal-headed god of the dead.

anxiety an emotional state of fear or apprehension. Normal anxiety is a response to dangerous situations. Abnormal anxiety can either be free-floating, when the person may feel anxious much of the time in a wide range of situations, or it may be phobic, when the person is excessively afraid of an object or situation.

anxiolytic drug which reduces an anxiety state.

ANZAC acronym from the initials of the *Australian and New Zealand Army Corps*, applied in general to all troops of both countries serving in World War I and to some extent those in World War II. The date of their landing in Gallipoli, Turkey, 25 Apr 1915, is marked by a public holiday, *Anzac Day*, in both Australia and New Zealand.

Anzio, Battle of in World War II, the beachhead invasion of Italy 22 Jan–23 May 1944 by Allied troops; failure to use information gained by deciphering German signals (see ◊Ultra) led to Allied troops being stranded for a period after German attacks.

ANZUS acronym for *Australia, New Zealand, and the United States* (Pacific Security Treaty), a military alliance established in 1951. It was replaced in 1954 by the ◊South East Asia Treaty Organization.

aorta the chief ◊artery – the dorsal blood vessel carrying oxygenated blood from the left ventricle of the heart in birds and mammals. It branches to form smaller arteries which in turn supply all body organs except ◊lungs. In fish, the ventral aorta carries deoxygenated blood from the heart to the ◊gills, and the dorsal aorta carries oxygenated blood from the gills to other parts of the body.

Aouita Said 1960– . Moroccan runner. Outstanding at middle and long distances, he won the 1984 Olympic and 1987 World Championship 5000 metres title, and has set many world records.

Apache one of the North ◊American Indian peoples, related to the Navajo, who now number about 10,000. The surviving Apaches live in reservations in Arizona (the Apache state), SW Oklahoma, and New Mexico.

apartheid the racial-segregation policy of the government of South Africa. Apartheid was legally first formulated in 1948, when the Afrikaner National Party gained power. Non-whites do not share full rights of citizenship with the 4.5 million

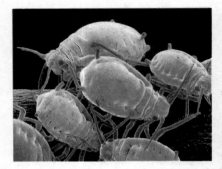

aphid *Electron microscope picture of a group of wingless aphids (green fly) feeding on a plant stem. (x32)*

whites and many public facilities and institutions are restricted to the use of one race only; the establishment of ◊Black National States is another manifestation of apartheid. In 1991 President de Klerk repealed the key elements of apartheid legislation.

apatite a calcium phosphate mineral, $Ca_5(PO_4CO_3)_3$ (F, OH, Cl), green or purple, used in manufacturing fertilizer. It rates 5 on the Mohs scale of hardness.

ape any of those ◊primates most closely related to humans, including gibbon, orang-utan, chimpanzee, and gorilla.

Apelles 4th century BC. Greek painter, said to have been the greatest in antiquity. He was court painter to Philip of Macedonia and his son Alexander the Great. None of his work survives.

Apennines chain of mountains stretching the length of the Italian peninsula. A continuation of the Maritime Alps, from Genoa it swings across the peninsula to Ancona on the E coast, and then back to the W coast and into the 'toe' of Italy. The system is continued across the Strait of Messina along the N Sicilian coast, then across the Mediterranean sea in a series of islands to the Atlas mountains of North Africa.

aperture in photography, an opening in the camera that allows light to pass through the lens to strike the film. Controlled by shutter speed and the iris diaphragm, it can be set mechanically or electronically at various diameters.

aphasia difficulty in speaking, writing, and reading, caused by damage to the brain.

aphelion the point at which an object, travelling in an elliptical orbit around the Sun, is at its furthest from the Sun.

aphid small insect that lives by sucking sap from plants. There are many species, often adapted to particular plants.

Aphrodite in Greek mythology, the goddess of love (Roman Venus, Phoenician Astarte, Babylonian Ishtar); said to be either a daughter of ◊Zeus (in Homer) or sprung from the foam of the sea (in Hesiod). She was the unfaithful wife of ◊Hephaestus and the mother of ◊Eros.

Apia capital and port of Western Samoa, on the north coast of Upolu island, in the West Pacific; population (1981) 33,170.

Apis ancient Egyptian god with a bull's head, linked with Osiris (and later merged with him into the Ptolemaic god Serapis); his cult centres were Memphis and Heliopolis, where sacred bulls were mummified.

Apocrypha an appendix to the Old Testament of

Aphrodite *An 18th century cast of the Medici Venus, Greek 2nd century BC.*

the Bible, not included in the final Hebrew canon but recognized by Roman Catholics. There are also disputed New Testament texts known as Apocrypha.

apogee the point at which an object, travelling in an elliptical orbit around the Earth, is at its furthest from the Earth.

Apollinaire Guillaume. Pen name of Guillaume Apollinaire de Kostrowitsky 1880–1918. French poet of aristocratic Polish descent. He was a leader of the *avant garde* in Parisian literary and artistic circles. His novel *Le Poète assassiné/The Poet Assassinated* 1916, followed by the experimental poems *Alcools/Alcohols* 1913 and *Calligrammes/Word Pictures* 1918, show him as a representative of the Cubist and Futurist movements.

Apollo in Greek mythology, the god of sun, music, poetry, prophecy, agriculture, and pastoral life, and leader of the Muses. He was the twin child (with ◊Artemis) of ◊Zeus and Leto. Ancient statues show Apollo as the embodiment of the Greek ideal of male beauty.

Apollo asteroid a member of a group of ◊asteroids whose orbits cross that of the Earth. They are named after the first of their kind, Apollo, discovered 1932, and then lost until 1973. Apollo asteroids are so small and faint that they are difficult to see except when close to Earth.

Apollonius of Rhodes *c.* 220–180 BC. Greek poet, author of the epic *Argonautica*, which tells the story of Jason and the Argonauts.

Apollo of Rhodes the Greek statue of Apollo generally known as the ◊Colossus of Rhodes.

Apollo project US space project to land a person on the Moon, achieved by Apollo 11 in Jul 1969, when Neil Armstrong was the first to set foot there. The program was announced 1961 by President Kennedy. The world's most powerful rocket, Saturn V, was built to launch the Apollo spacecraft, which carried three astronauts. When the Apollo spacecraft was in orbit around the Moon, two astronauts entered the Lunar Module in which they descended to the lunar surface. The first Apollo mission carrying a crew, Apollo 7 in October 1968, was a test flight in orbit around the Earth. After three other preparatory flights, Apollo 11 made

Apollo project Ed Aldrin, one of the first astronauts to walk on the moon, 1969 .

the first lunar landing. Five more manned landings followed, the last in 1972.

aposematic coloration in biology, the technical name for ◊warning coloration markings that make a dangerous, poisonous, or foul-tasting animal particularly conspicuous and recognizable to a predator. Examples include the yellow and black stripes of bees and wasps, and the bright red or yellow colours of many poisonous frogs; see also ◊mimicry.

a posteriori (Latin 'from the latter') in logic, an argument which deduces causes from their effects; inductive reasoning; the converse of ◊a priori.

apostle in the New Testament, the 12 chief ◊disciples namely, Andrew Bartholomew, James (the Great), James (the Less), John, Jude (or Thaddeus), Matthew, Peter, Philip, Simon, Thomas, and Judas Iscariot: after the latter's death his place was taken by Matthias. In the earliest days of Christianity the term was extended to include some who had never known Jesus in the flesh, notably St Paul.

Apostles discussion group founded 1820 at Cambridge University, UK; members have included the poet Tennyson, the philosophers G E Moore and Bertrand Russell, the writers Lytton Strachey and Leonard Woolf, the economist J M Keynes, and the spies Guy Burgess and Anthony Blunt.

Apostles' Creed one of the three ancient ◊creeds of the Christian church.

apostolic succession the doctrine in the Christian church that certain spiritual powers were received by the first apostles direct from Christ, and have been handed down in the ceremony of 'laying on of hands' from generation to generation of bishops.

apostrophe a punctuation mark ('). In English it either denotes a missing letter (mustn't for must not), or indicates possession (John's camera, the girl's dress). Correct use of the apostrophe has caused controversy for centuries and its possessive use is in decline.

apothecary a person who prepares and dispenses medicines, a pharmacist. The word retains its original meaning in the USA and other countries, but in England apothecary came to mean a licensed medical practitioner. In 1815, the Society of Apothecaries was given the right to grant licences to practise medicine in England and Wales.

Appalachians mountain system of eastern North America, stretching about 2,400 km/1,500 mi from Alabama in the SW to Quebec province in the NE composed of very ancient eroded rocks. The chain includes the Allegheny, Catskill and Blue Ridge mountains, the later having the highest peak, Mount Mitchell, 2,045 m/6,684 ft. The eastern edge has a fall line to the coastal plain

where Philadelphia, Baltimore and Washington stand.

appeasement the conciliatory policy adopted by the British government, particularly under Neville Chamberlain, towards the Nazi and Fascist dictators in Europe in the 1930s. It was opposed by Winston Churchill, but the ◊Munich Agreement 1938 was almost universally hailed as its justification. Appeasement ended when Germany occupied Bohemia-Moravia in March 1939.

appendicitis inflammation of the small, blind extension of the bowel in the lower right abdomen, the *appendix*. In an acute attack, the appendix may burst, causing a potentially lethal spread of infection (see ◊peritonitis). Treatment is by removal (appendectomy).

apple fruit of *Malus pumila*, a tree of the family Rosaceae. It has been an important food-plant in Europe from the earliest times, the cultivated varieties being derived from the wild crab apple.

Appleseed, Johnny character in US folk legend who wandered through the country for 40 years sowing apple seeds from which apple trees grew. The legend seems to be based on a historical figure, the US pioneer John Chapman (1774–1845).

Appleton layer a band containing ionized gases in the Earth's upper atmosphere, above the Heaviside layer. It can act as a reflector of radio signals, although its ionic composition varies with the sunspot cycle. It was named after the British physicist Edward Appleton.

application in computing, a job that can be performed by a specialist program designed for the non-expert user. The term is also used to describe such a program. Typical applications include stock control, payroll, and word processing. Application programs differ from systems programs, which perform functions within the machine that are normally invisible to the user (the computer's internal 'housekeeping').

appliqué a type of embroidery used to create pictures or patterns by 'applying' pieces of material to a background fabric. The pieces are cut into the appropriate shapes and sewn on, providing decoration for wall hangings, furnishing textiles, and sometimes clothes.

Appomattox village in Virginia, USA, scene of the surrender on 9 Apr 1865 of the Confederate army under Robert E Lee to the Union army under Ulysses S Grant, which ended the American Civil War.

apricot fruit of *Prunus armeniaca*, a tree closely related to the almond, peach, plum, and cherry. It has yellow-fleshed fruit. A native of the Far East, it has long been cultivated in Armenia, from where it was introduced into Europe and the USA.

April Fools' Day the first day of April, when it is customary in Western Europe and the USA to expose people to ridicule by causing them to believe some falsehood or to go on a fruitless errand.

a priori a Latin term meaning 'from what comes before'. In philosophy an a priori proposition is one that is known to be true, or false, without reference to experience; the converse of ◊a posteriori.

Apuleius Lucius *c.* 160 AD. Roman lawyer, philosopher and author, whose picaresque adventure tale *Metamorphoses, or The Golden Ass*, is sometimes called the world's first novel. The work preserved several ancient legends, notably the story of Cupid and ◊Psyche.

Apulia or *Puglia* region of Italy, the south eastern 'heel'; area 19,346 sq km/7472 sq mi; capital Bari. Products include wheat, grapes, almonds, olives and vegetables; the chief industrial centre is Taranto. Population (1981) 3,871,617.

Aqaba, Gulf of gulf extending for 160 km/100 mi between the Negev and the Red Sea; its coastline is uninhabited except at its head, where the frontiers of Israel, Egypt, Jordan, and Saudi Arabia converge. Here are the two ports Eilat (Israeli Elath) and Aqaba, Jordan's only port.

Aquae Sulis Roman name of the city of ◊Bath in W England.

aqualung self-contained underwater breathing apparatus (scuba) worn by divers, developed in the early 1940s by the French diver Jacques Cousteau. The aqualung provides air to the diver at the same pressure as that of the surrounding water (which increases with increasing depth). Air comes from compressed-air cylinders on the diver's back, regulated by a valve system.

aquamarine blue variety of the mineral ◊beryl. It is used in jewellery.

aquaplaning phenomenon in which the tyres of a road vehicle cease to make direct contact with the road surface, caused by the presence of a thin film of water. As a result, the vehicle can go out of control (particularly if the steered wheels are involved).

Aquarius a zodiac constellation in the southern hemisphere near Pegasus. The Sun passes through Aquarius from late Feb to early Mar. It is represented as a man pouring water from a jar.

aquatint print-making technique, a method combined with etching to produce prints with subtle, grainy effects, as well as more precisely etched lines. Aquatint became popular in the late 18th century.

aqueduct artificial channel or conduit for water, commonly an elevated structure of stone, wood, or iron built for conducting water across a valley.

aqueous humour watery fluid found in the space between the cornea and lens of the vertebrate eye. Similar to blood serum in composition, it is renewed every four hours.

aquifer any ◊bed of rock containing water that can be extracted by a well. The rock of an aquifer must be porous and permeable (full of interconnected holes) so that it can absorb water.

Aquila a constellation of the equatorial region of the sky. Its brightest star is the first-magnitude ◊Altair, flanked by the stars Beta and Gamma Aquilae. It is represented by an eagle.

Aquinas St Thomas *c.* 1226–1274. Neapolitan philosopher and theologian. His *Summa Contra Gentiles/Against the Errors of the Infidels* 1259–64, argues that reason and faith are compatible. His most significant contribution to philosophy was to synthesize the thought of Aristotle and Christian doctrine.

Aquino (Maria) Corazón (born Cojuangco) 1933– Populist president of the Philippines 1986–92. She was instrumental in the nonviolent overthrow of President Marcos 1986. She sought to rule in a conciliatory manner, but encountered opposition from left (communist guerrillas) and right (army coup attempts), and her land reforms were seen as inadequate.

Aquitaine region of SW France, capital Bordeaux; area 41,308 sq km/15,955 sq mi; population (1986) 2,718,000. It comprises the *départements* of Dordogne, Gironde, Landes, Lot-et-Garonne, and Pyrénées-Atlantiques. Red wines (Margaux, St Julien) are produced in the Medoc district, bordering the Gironde. Aquitaine was an English possession 1152–1452.

Arab speakers of Arabic, the major Semitic

Aquino *President Corazón Aquino campaigning in Angeles City, Philippines, Jan 1987.*

language of the Afro-Asiatic family. The homeland of the Arabs comprises Saudi Arabia, Qatar, Kuwait, Bahrain, United Arab Emirates, Oman, South Yemen, and North Yemen.

Arab Emirates see ◊United Arab Emirates.

arabesque a pose in which the dancer stands on one leg, straight or bent, with the other leg raised behind, fully extended. The arms are held in a harmonious position to give the longest possible line from fingertips to toes.

Arabian Nights oriental tales in oral circulation among Arab storytellers from the 10th century, and probably having roots in India. They are also known as *The Thousand and One Nights* and include *Ali Baba, Aladdin,* and *Sindbad.*

Arabian sea the NW branch of the ◊Indian Ocean.

Arabic language a Hamito-Semitic language of W Asia and North Africa, originating among the Arabs of the Arabian peninsula. Arabic script is written from right to left.

arabic numerals the signs 0,1,2,3,4,5,6,7,8,9, which were in use among the Arabs before being adopted by the peoples of Europe during the Middle Ages in place of Roman numerals. They appear to have originated in India, and reached Europe by way of Spain.

Arab-Israeli Wars a series of wars between Israel and various Arab states in the Middle East since the founding of the state of Israel in 1948. *First Arab-Israeli War* 15 May 1948–13 Jan/24 Mar 1949. As soon as the independent state of Israel had been proclaimed it was invaded by combined Arab forces. The Israelis defeated them and went on to annex more territory, so that they controlled 75 per cent of Palestine. *Second Arab-Israeli War* 29 Oct–4 Nov 1956. After Egypt had taken control of the Suez Canal, Israel invaded and captured Sinai and the Gaza Strip, from which it withdrew after the entry of a UN force. *Third Arab-Israeli War* 5–10 Jun 1967, the *Six-Day War*. It resulted in the Israeli capture of the Golan Heights from Syria; Old Jerusalem and the West Bank from Jordan; and, in the south, occupation of the Gaza Strip and Sinai Peninsula as far as the Suez Canal. *Fourth Arab-Israeli War* 6–24 Oct 1973, the 'October War' or *Yom Kippur War,* so called because the Israeli forces were taken by surprise on the Day of ◊Atonement. It resulted in the recrossing of the Suez Canal

Arafat *Leader of the Palestine Liberation Organization from 1969, Yassir Arafat.*

by Egyptian forces and initial gains, though there was some later loss of ground by the Syrians in the north. *Fifth Arab-Israeli War* From 1978 the presence of Palestinian guerrillas in Lebanon led to alternate Arab raids on Israel and Israeli retaliatory incursions, but on 6 Jun 1982 Israel launched a full-scale invasion. By 14 Jun Beirut was encircled, and PLO and Syrian forces were evacuated (mainly to Syria) 21–31 Aug, but in Feb 1985 there was a unilateral Israeli withdrawal from the country without any gain or losses incurred. Despite this, Israeli incursions into Lebanon have continued.

Arabistan former name of the Iranian province of Khuzestan, revived in the 1980s by the 2 million Sunni Arab inhabitants who demand autonomy. Unrest and sabotage 1979–80 led to a pledge of a degree of autonomy by Ayatollah ◊Khomeni.

Arab League an organization of Arab states established in Cairo in 1945 to promote Arab unity, especially in opposition to Israel. The original members were Egypt, Syria, Iraq, Lebanon, Transjordan (Jordan 1949), Saudi Arabia, and Yemen. In 1979 Egypt was suspended and the league's headquarters transferred to Tunis in protest against the Egypt-Israeli peace, but Egypt was readmitted as a full member 1989, and in 1990 its headquarters returned to Cairo.

Arachne (Greek 'spider') in Greek mythology, a Lydian girl who was so skilful a weaver that she challenged the goddess Athena to a contest. Athena tore Arachne's beautiful tapestries to pieces and Arachne hanged herself. She was transformed into a spider, and her weaving became a cobweb.

Arafat Yassir 1929– Palestinian nationalist politician, cofounder of ◊al-Fatah 1956 and president of the ◊Palestine Liberation Organization (PLO) from 1969. His support for Saddam Hussein after Iraq's invasion of Kuwait 1990 weakened his international standing, but he has since been influential in Middle East peace talks.

Aragón autonomous region of NE Spain including the provinces of Huesca, Teruel, and Zaragoya. Capital Saragossa; population (1986) 1,215,000. Products include almonds, figs, grapes, and olives. Aragón was an independent kingdom 1035–1479.

Aragon Louis 1897–1982. French poet and novelist. Beginning as a Dadaist, he became one of the leaders of Surrealism, published volumes of verse and in 1930 joined the Communist Party. Taken prisoner in World War II he escaped to join the Resistance, experiences reflected in the poetry of *Le Crève-coeur* 1942 and *Les Yeux d'Elsa* 1944.

Aral Sea inland sea divided between Kazakhstan and Uzbekistan; the world's fourth largest lake; former area 62,000 sq km/24,000 sq mi, but decreasing. Water from its tributaries, the Amu Darya and Syr Darya, has been diverted for irrigation and city use, and the sea is disappearing, with long-term consequences for the climate.

Aramaic language a Hamito-Semitic language of W Asia, the everyday language of Palestine in the time of Christ.

Ararat double-peaked mountain on the Turkish-Iranian border; the higher, Great Ararat, 5,156 m/17,000 ft, was the reputed resting place of Noah's Ark after the Flood.

araucaria coniferous tree allied to the firs. It is native to the southern hemisphere, and often attains a gigantic size: Araucarias include the *monkey-puzzle tree Araucaria araucana*, the *Australian bunya bunya pine Araucaria bidwillii*, and the *Norfolk Island pine Araucaria heterophylla*.

Arawak indigenous American people of the Caribbean and Amazon basin, dating from approximately AD 1000–1550. They lived mainly by shifting cultivation in tropical forests. They were driven out of the Lesser Antilles by another American Indian people, the Caribs, shortly before the arrival of the Spanish in the 16th century.

arbitrageur in international finance, a person who buys securities (such as currency or commodities) in one country or market for immediate resale in another market, to take advantage of different prices. Arbitrage became widespread during the 1970s and 1980s with the increasing ◊deregulation of financial markets.

arbitration submission of a dispute to a third, unbiased party for settlement. It may be personal litigation, trade-union issues, or international disputes (as the case of the warship ◊*Alabama*).

arboretum a collection of trees. An arboretum may have many species or just different varieties of one species, for example different types of pine tree.

Arbuthnot John 1667–1735. Scottish physician, attendant on Queen Anne 1705–14. He was a friend of Pope, Gray, and Swift, and was the chief author of the satiric *Memoirs of Martinus Scriblerus*. He created the national character of John Bull, a prosperous farmer, in his *The History of John Bull* 1712, pamphlets advocating peace with France.

arbutus genus of evergreen shrubs, family Ericaceae. The strawberry tree *Arbutus unedo* is grown for its ornamental strawberry-like fruit.

arc in geometry, a section of a curve. A ◊circle has two kinds of arcs. An arc that is less than a semicircle is called a *minor arc*; an arc that is greater than a semicircle is a *major arc*.

Arc de Triomphe triumphal arch in the Place de l'Etoile, Paris, France, begun by Napoleon in 1806 and completed in 1836. It was intended to commemorate the French victories of 1805–06. Beneath it rests France's 'Unknown Soldier'.

arch a curved structure consisting of several wedge-shaped stones or other hard blocks which are supported by their mutual pressure. The term is also applied to any curved structure which is an arch in form only.

Arch Joseph 1826–1919. British Radical Member of Parliament and trade unionist, founder of the National Agricultural Union (the first of its kind) in 1872.

Archaean or *Archaeozoic* earliest period of geological time; the first part of the Precambrian era, from the formation of Earth up to 2.5 billion years

arch (Top left) the Arch of Titus on Via Sacra in the Forum, Rome. (Top right) the Arch of Septimus Severus in the Forum, Rome.

ago. Traces of life have recently been found in Archaean rocks.

archaebacteria three groups of bacteria whose DNA differs significantly from that of other bacteria (called the 'eubacteria'). All are strict anaerobes, that is, they are killed by oxygen. This is a primitive condition, and shows that the archaebacteria are related to the earliest life forms, which appeared about 4,000 million years ago, when there was little oxygen in the Earth's atmosphere.

archaeology the study of prehistory and ancient periods of history, based on the examination of physical remains.

archaeopteryx fossil from the limestone of Bavaria about 160 million years old, and popularly known as 'the first bird'. *Archaeopteryx* was about the size of a crow and had feathers and wings, but in many respects its skeleton is reptilian (long bony tail, teeth) and very like some small dinosaurs of the time.

archbishop in the Christian church, a bishop of superior rank, who has authority over other bishops in his jurisdiction and often over an ecclesiastical province. In the Church of England there are two archbishops – the archbishop of Canterbury ('Primate of All England') and the archbishop of York ('Primate of England').

archdeacon originally an ordained dignitary of the Christian church charged with the supervision of the deacons attached to a cathedral. Today in the Roman Catholic church the office is purely titular; in the Church of England an archdeacon still has many business duties, such as the periodic inspection of the churches.

archegonium the female sex organ found in bryophytes (mosses and liverworts), pteridophytes (ferns and horsetails), and some gymnosperms. It is a multicellular, flask-shaped structure consisting of two parts, the swollen base or venter containing the egg cell, and the long, narrow neck. When the egg cell is mature the cells of the neck dissolve, allowing the passage of the male gametes, or ◊antherozoids.

Archer Frederick 1857–1886. British jockey. He rode 2,748 winners in 8,084 races between 1870 and 1886, including 21 classic winners.

Archer Jeffrey 1940– . British author and politician. A Conservative Member of Parliament 1969–74, he lost a fortune in a disastrous investment, but recouped it as a best-selling novelist. Works include *Not a Penny More, Not a Penny Less* 1975 and *First Among Equals* 1984. In 1985 he became deputy chairman of the Conservative party but in Nov 1986 resigned after a scandal involving a payment to a prostitute.

archaeopteryx

Wing structure of a flying reptile

Wing structure of a bird

archaeology

14–16th cent.	Renaissance interest in clasical art, for example, Cellini.
1748	Pompeii rediscovered, and aroused the interest of connoisseurs.
1790	John Frere identified Old Stone Age tools and large extinct animals.
1822	Champollion deciphered Egyptian hieroglyphics.
1832	Charles and John Deane pioneered the recording of underwater finds, such as *Mary Rose.*
1836	C J Thomsen devised the Stone, Bronze, and Iron Age classification.
1840s	Layard excavated the Assyrian capital, Nineveh.
1868	Great Zimbabwe ruins first seen by Europeans.
1871	Schliemann began work at Troy.
1879	Stone Age paintings were first discovered at Altamira.
1880s	Pitt-Rivers developed the technique of stratification (identificaton of successive layers of soil with different archaelogical periods).
1891	Petrie began excavating Tell el Amarna (Akhetaton).
1899–1935	A J Evans excavated Minoan Knossos in Crete.
1911	Hiram Bingham discovered the Inca city of Machu Picchu.
1911–12	Piltdown skull 'discovered'; proved a fake in 1949.
1914–18	Osbert Crawford developed the technique of aerial survey of sites.
1922	Tutankhamen's tomb opened by Howard Carter.
1935	A E Douglas developed dendrochronology (dating events in the distant past by counting tree rings).
1939	Anglo-Saxon ship-burial treasure found at Sutton Hoo.
1947	First of the Dead Sea Scrolls discovered.
1948	Proconsul apeman discovered by Mary Leakey in Kenya.
1953	Ventris deciphered Minoan 'Linear B'.
1960s	Radiocarbon dating and thermoluminescence developed.
1961	Swedish warship *Wasa* raised at Stockholm.
1963	W B Emery pioneered 'rescue archaeology' at Abu Simbel.
1974	Tomb of Shi Huangdi discovered in China.
1978	Tomb of Philip of Macedon (Alexander's father) discovered.
1979	Aztec capital Tenochtitlán excavated beneath Mexico city.
1982	Henry VIII's warship *Mary Rose* raised.
1985	Major work on wreck of the Dutch East Indiaman *Amsterdam* near Hastings begun, and tomb of Maya, Tutankhamen's treasurer, discovered at Saqqara.

archerfish surface-living fish, genus *Toxotes*, living in brackish mangrove swamps of SE Asia and Australia. It grows to about 25 cm/10 in and is able to shoot down insects up to 1.5 m/5 ft above the water by spitting a water-jet from its mouth.

Archimedes *c.* 287–212 BC. Greek mathematician, who made important discoveries in geometry, hydrostatics, and mechanics. He formulated a law of fluid-displacement ($\Diamond$Archimedes' principle), and is credited with the invention of the Archimedes screw, a cylindrical device for raising water.

Archimedes' principle law stating that an object totally or partly submerged in a fluid displaces a volume of fluid which weighs the same as the apparent loss in weight of the object (which equals the upthrust on it).

Archimedes screw one of the earliest kinds of pump, thought to have been invented by Archimedes. It consists of a spiral screw revolving inside a close-fitting cylinder. It is used, for example, to raise water for irrigation.

archipelago a group of islands, or an area of sea containing a group of islands. The islands of an archipelago are often volcanic in origin, caused by a rise in sea level flooding a hilly landscape.

Archipenko Alexander 1887–1964. Russian-born abstract sculptor, who lived in France from 1908 and in the USA from 1923. He pioneered Cubist works composed of angular forms and spaces, and later experimented with clear plastic and sculptures incorporating lights.

architecture the art of building structures. The term covers the design of any structure for living or working in: houses, churches, temples, palaces, castles; and also, the style of building of any particular country at any period of history. Some theorists include under the term architecture only structures designed by a particular architect; others include so-called vernacular architecture: traditional buildings such as the cottages and farms of particular areas that have evolved slowly through the centuries but can claim no particular designer.

archives a collection of historically valuable records, ranging from papers and documents to films, videotapes, and sound recordings.

archon (Greek 'ruler') in ancient Greece, the title of the chief magistrate in many cities. In Athens, there were originally three: the king Archon, the eponymous Archon (who gave his name to the year, hence the modern use of the word), and the polemarch. Their numbers were later increased

architecture

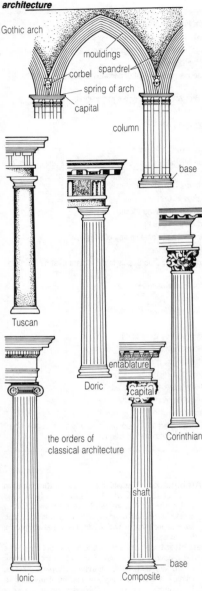

Gothic arch

mouldings
spandrel
corbel
spring of arch
capital

column

base

Tuscan

entablature

Doric

capital

Corinthian

the orders of
classical architecture

shaft

Ionic

base

Composite

classical temple

cornice

tympanum

cornice

frieze

architrave triglyph metope

capital

abacus

shaft

entablature pediment

column

to nine, with the extra six keeping a record of judgements.

arc lamp an electric light that uses the illumination of an electric arc. Humphry ◊Davy developed an arc lamp in 1808, and its major use in recent years has been in cinema projectors. The lamp consists essentially of two carbon electrodes, between which a very high voltage is maintained. Electric current arcs (jumps) between the two, creating a brilliant light.

arc minute and **arc second** units for measuring small angles, used in geometry, surveying and map-making, and astronomy. An arc minute is one-sixtieth of a degree, and an arc second one-sixtieth of an arc minute. Small distances in the sky, as between two close stars or the apparent width of a planet's disc, are expressed in minutes and seconds of arc.

Arctic, the region north of the Arctic Circle. There is no Arctic continent, merely pack ice (which breaks into ice floes in summer) surrounding the Pole and floating on the Arctic Ocean. Pack ice is carried by the south-flowing current into the Atlantic Ocean as ◊icebergs. In winter the Sun disappears below the horizon for a time (and in summer, which only lasts up to two months, remains above it), but the cold is less severe than in parts of E Siberia or the Antarctic. Land areas in the Arctic have mainly stunted tundra vegetation, with an outburst of summer flowers. Animals include reindeer, caribou, musk ox, fox, hare, lemming, and wolf, polar bear, seal, and walrus. There are few birds, except in summer, when insects, especially mosquitoes, are plentiful. The aboriginal people are the ◊Inuit of the American/Canadian Arctic and Greenland. The most valuable resource is oil.

Arctic Circle an arbitrary line drawn round the North Pole at 66° 32′ N.

Arctic Ocean ocean surrounding the North Pole; area 14,000,000 sq km/5,400,000 sq mi. Because of the Siberian and North American rivers flowing into it, it has comparatively low salinity and freezes readily.

Arcturus brightest star in the constellation Bootes, and the fourth-brightest star in the sky. It is a red giant, 36 light years away.

Arden John 1930– . British playwright. His early plays *Serjeant Musgrave's Dance* 1959 and *The Workhouse Donkey* 1963 show the influence of ◊Brecht. Subsequent works, often written in collaboration with his wife, Margaretta D'Arcy, show increasing concern with the political situation in Northern Ireland and a dissatisfaction with the professional and subsidized theatre world.

Ardennes wooded plateau in NE France, SE Belgium and N Luxembourg, cut through by the river Meuse; there was heavy fighting here in both world wars. See ◊Champagne-Ardenne.

area a measure of surface. A unit of area is the metre squared. The area of geometrical plane shapes with straight edges are determined from the area of a rectangle. Integration may be used to determine the area of shapes enclosed by curves.

areca genus of palms. The ◊betel nut comes from the species *Areca catechu*.

Arecibo site in Puerto Rico of the world's largest single-dish ◊radio telescope, 305 m/1,000 ft in diameter. It is built in a natural hollow, and uses the rotation of the Earth to scan the sky. It has been used both for radar work on the planets and for conventional radio-astronomy, and is operated by Cornell University, USA.

Arctic habitat

Arctic wildlife is rich and varied, especially in the warmer months. As the Arctic seas warm up in spring, tiny floating plants, the phytoplankton, grow and multiply in huge quantities. They are an almost never-ending supply of food for fish and krill, which in turn support large numbers of seals, walruses, whales, and seabirds. Large meat-eaters, such as polar bears, prey on aquatic animals as these venture out on to land to breed. Smaller carnivores, such as the Arctic fox, prey on small mammals and birds.

seagulls

Arctic foxes

walruses

polar bear

razorbills

fish

killer whale

ringed seals

With the onset of winter, a pregnant female polar bear digs out a den in a snowdrift mound. There, in December, she gives birth to her young. She suckles them until they are three months old. Then mother and young emerge from the den – just when baby seals, the bears' favourite diet, are plentiful.

cross-section through polar bear den

ventilation shaft

surface

entrance hole

upper area

lower area

Argentina
Republic of
(República Argentina)

area 2,780,092 sq km/1,073,080 sq mi
capital Buenos Aires (to move to Viedma)
towns Rosario, Córdoba, Tucumán, Mendoza,
Santa Fé; ports are La Plata and Bahía Blanca
physical mountains in the W, forest in the N and E,
pampas (treeless plains) in the central area; rivers
Colorado, Paraná, Uruguay, Rio de la Plata estuary
territories part of Tierra del Fuego; disputed claims
to S Atlantic islands and part of Antarctica
head of state and government Carlos Menem
from 1989
political system emergent democracy
exports beef, livestock, cereals, wool, tannin,
groundnuts, linseed oil, minerals (coal, copper,
molybdenum, gold, silver, lead, zinc, barium,
uranium), and the country has huge resources of
oil, natural gas, and hydroelectric power
currency peso = 10,000 australs
population (1990 est) 32,686,000 (mainly of
Spanish or Italian origin, only about 30,000 American
Indians surviving); annual growth rate 1.5%

life expectancy men 66, women 73
language Spanish
religion Roman Catholic (state-supported)
literacy 96% male/95% female (1985 est)
GNP $70.1 bn (1990); $2,162 per head
chronology
1816 Achieved independence from Spain.
1946 Juan Perón elected president, supported by
his wife 'Evita'.
1955 Perón overthrown and civilian administration
restored.
1966 Coup brought back military rule.
1973 Perónist party won the presidential and
congressional elections. Perón returned from exile
in Spain as president, with his third wife, 'Isabelita',
as vice-president.
1974 Perón died. Succeeded by 'Isabelita'.
1976 Coup resulted in rule by a military junta led by
Lt-Gen Jorge Videla. Congress dissolved.
1976–78 Ferocious campaign against left-wing
elements. The start of the 'dirty war'.
1978 Videla retired. Succeeded by Gen Roberto
Viola, who promised a return to democracy.
1981 Viola died suddenly. Replaced by Gen
Leopoldo Galtieri.
1982 With a deteriorating economy, Galtieri sought
popular support by ordering an invasion of the
British-held Falkland Islands. After losing the short
war, Galtieri was removed and replaced by Gen
Reynaldo Bignone.
1983 Amnesty law passed and 1853 democratic
constitution revived. General elections won by Dr
Raúl Alfonsín and his party.
1984 Commission on the Disappearance of
Persons (CONADEP) reported on over 8,000
people who had disappeared during the 'dirty war'
of 1976–83.
1985 A deteriorating economy forced Alfonsín to
seek help from the IMF and introduce a harsh
austerity programme.
1988 Unsuccessful army coup attempt.
1989 Carlos Menem, a Perónist, elected president.
1990 Full diplomatic relations with the UK restored.
Revolt by army officers thwarted.
1992 New currency introduced.

Arequipa city in Peru at the base of the volcano
El Misti. Founded by Pizarro in 1540, it is the
cultural focus of S Peru, and a busy commercial
(soap, textiles) centre; population (1990 est)
965,000.
Ares in Greek mythology, the god of war (Roman
◊Mars). The son of Zeus and Hera, he was worshipped chiefly in Thrace.
arête a sharp narrow ridge separating two ◊glacier
valleys (a French term; in the USA often called
a *combe-ridge*; in German a *grat*). The typical U-
shaped cross-sections of glacier valleys give arêtes
very steep sides.
Aretino Pietro 1492–1556. Italian writer, born in
Arezzo. His *Letters* 1537–57 are a unique record of
the cultural and political events of his time, and
illustrate his vivacious, exuberant character. He
also wrote poems and comedies.
Argand diagram a method for representing
complex numbers by cartesian co-ordinates (*x*, *y*).
The *x* axis represents the real numbers, and the *y*
axis the non-real, or 'imaginary', numbers.
Argentina country in South America, bounded by

Chile to the south and west, Bolivia to the northwest, and Paraguay, Brazil, Uruguay, and the Atlantic Ocean to the east.
argon a chemically inert gaseous element, symbol Ar, atomic number 18, relative atomic mass
39.944. It is used in electric discharge lamps (see
◊discharge tube) and in argon lasers.
argonaut type of pelagic octopus, genus
Argonauta.
Argonauts in Greek legend, the band of heroes
who accompanied ◊Jason when he set out in the
ship *Argo* to fetch the Golden Fleece.
Argos city in ancient Greece, at the head of the
Gulf of Nauplia. In the Homeric age the name
Argives was sometimes used instead of Greeks.
It was once a cult centre of the goddess ◊Hera.
argument in mathematics, a specific value of
the independent variable of a ◊function of *x*. Argument is also the name given to the angle θ between
the position vector of a ◊complex number and
the limb of the real axis, usually written arg *z*
for the complex number $z = r(\cos \theta + i \sin \theta)$.

Argus in Greek mythology, a giant with a hundred eyes, which ◊Hera eventually transplanted to the tail of her favourite bird, the peacock.

Argyll Archibald Campbell, 5th Earl of, 1530–1573. Adherent of the Scottish presbyterian, John ◊Knox. A supporter of Mary Queen of Scots from 1561 on her return from France, he commanded her forces during the days following her escape from Lochleven Castle in 1568. He revised his position and became Lord High Chancellor of Scotland in 1572.

aria (Italian 'air') solo vocal piece in opera or oratorio, often in three sections, the third repeating the first after a contrasting central section.

Ariadne in Greek mythology, the daughter of Minos, king of Crete. When Theseus came from Athens as one of the victims offered to the Minotaur, she fell in love with him and gave him the ball of thread which enabled him to find his way out of the labyrinth.

Ariane a series of launch vehicles built by the European Space Agency to place satellites into Earth orbit (first flight 1979). The launch site is at Kouru in French Guiana.

Arianism a system of Christian theology which denied the complete divinity of Christ. It was founded *c.* 310 by ◊Arius, and condemned as heretical at the Council of Nicaea in 325.

arid zone infertile area with a small, infrequent rainfall that rapidly evaporates because of high temperatures. There are arid zones in Morocco, Pakistan, Australia, USA, and elsewhere.

Aries a zodiac constellation, in the northern hemisphere near Auriga, seen as representing the legendary ram whose golden fleece was sought by Jason and the Argonauts. Its most distinctive feature is a curve of three stars of decreasing brightness. The Sun passes through Aries from late Apr to mid-May.

aril an accessory seed-cover other than a ◊fruit; it may be fleshy and sometimes brightly coloured, woody or hairy. In flowering plants (◊angiosperms) it is often derived from the stalk which originally attached the ovule to the ovary wall. Examples of arils include the bright red, fleshy layer surrounding the yew seed (yews are ◊gymnosperms, so they lack true fruits), and the network of hard filaments which partially covers the nutmeg seed; it is the latter which yields the spice known as mace.

Ariosto Ludovico 1474–1533. Italian poet. He wrote Latin poems and comedies on Classical lines, and published the *Orlando Furioso* in Ferrara in 1516. This is a romantic epic, dealing with the wars of Charlemagne against the Saracens, and the love of Orlando (Roland) for Angelica, a princess of Cathay. The perfection of its style and its unflagging narrative interest place Ariosto among the great Italian poets.

Aristarchus of Samos *c.* 310–264 BC. Greek astronomer. The first to argue that the Earth moves round the Sun, he was ridiculed for his beliefs.

Aristides *c.* 530–468 BC. Athenian politician. He was one of the ten Athenian generals at the battle of ◊Marathon in 490 BC and was elected chief archon, or magistrate. Later he came into conflict with the democratic leader Themistocles, and was exiled around 483 BC. He returned to fight against the Persians at Salamis in 480 BC, and next year commanded the Athenians at Plataea.

Aristophanes *c.* 448–380 BC. Greek dramatist, one of the founders of comedy. Of his 11 extant plays (of a total of over 40), the early comedies are remarkable for the violence of the satire with which he ridiculed the democratic war leaders. He also satirized contemporary issues such as the new learning of Socrates in *The Clouds* 423 and the power of women in *Lysistrata* 411. The chorus plays a prominent role, frequently giving the play its title, as in *The Birds* 414, *The Wasps* 422, and *The Frogs* 405.

Aristotle 384–322 BC. Greek philosopher, who studied under ◊Plato. Aristotle maintained that sense-experience is our only source of knowledge, and that by reasoning we can discover the essences of things, that is, their distinguishing qualities. In his works on ethics and politics, Aristotle suggested that human happiness consists in living in conformity with nature, according to reason and moderation. He derived his political theory from the recognition that mutual aid is natural to humankind, and refused to set up any one constitution as universally ideal. Of Aristotle's works some 22 treatises survive, dealing with logic, metaphysics, physics, astronomy, meteorology, biology, psychology, ethics, politics, and literary criticism.

arithmetic branch of mathematics involving the study of numbers. The fundamental operations of arithmetic are addition, subtraction, multiplication, division, and, dependent on these four, raising to ◊powers and extraction of roots. Percentages, fractions, and ratio are developed from these operations. Fractions arise in the process of measurement.

arithmetic sequence or *arithmetic progression* or *arithmetic series* sequence of numbers or terms that have a common difference between any one term and the next in the sequence. For example, 2, 7, 12, 17, 22, 27, ... is an arithmetic sequence with a common difference of 5. The general formula for the nth term is $a + (n - 1)d$, where a is the first term and d is the common difference. The sum s of n terms is: $s = n/2\,[2a + (n - 1)d]$.

Arius *c.* 256–336. Egyptian priest whose ideas gave rise to ◊Arianism, a Christian belief which denied the complete divinity of Christ. He was condemned at the Council of Nicaea in 325.

Arizona state in SW USA; nickname Grand Canyon State
area 295,023 sq km/113,909 sq mi
capital Phoenix
towns Tucson, Flagstaff
physical Colorado Plateau in the N and E, desert basins and mountains in the S and W; Colorado River; Grand Canyon
products cotton under irrigation, livestock, copper, molybdenum, silver, electronics, aircraft
population (1980) 2,718,000 including over 150,000 American Indians (Navajo, Hopi, Apache), who still own a quarter of the state
famous people Geronimo, Barry Goldwater, Zane Grey, Frank Lloyd Wright
history part of New Spain 1715; part of Mexico 1824; passed to USA after Mexican War 1848; territory 1863; state 1912.

Arjan died 1606. Fifth guru (teacher) of Sikhism from 1581. He built the Golden Temple in ◊Amritsar and compiled the *Adi Granth*, the first volume of Sikh scriptures. He died in Muslim custody.

Arjuna Indian prince, one of the two main characters in the Hindu epic *Mahābhārata*.

Arkansas state in S central USA; nickname Wonder State/Land of Opportunity
area 135,403 sq km/52,299 sq mi
capital Little Rock
towns Fort Smith

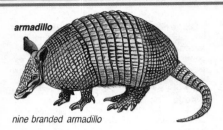

armadillo

nine branded armadillo

physical Ozark mountains in the west; lowlands in the east; Arkansas River; many lakes

products cotton, soya beans, rice, oil, natural gas, bauxite, timber, processed foods

population (1990) 2,350,700

history explored by ◊de Soto 1541; European settlers 1648, who traded with local Indians; part of Louisiana Purchase 1803; state 1836.

Ark of the Covenant in the Old Testament or Hebrew Bible, the chest which contained the Tablets of the Law as given to Moses. It is also the cupboard in a synagogue in which the ◊Torah scrolls are kept.

Arkwright Richard 1732–1792. British inventor and manufacturing pioneer. After experimenting in machine-designing he set up his 'spinning frame' at Preston, Lancashire in 1768. He installed steam power in his Nottingham works in 1790.

Armada fleet sent by Philip II of Spain against England in 1588. See ◊Spanish Armada.

armadillo mammal with an armour of bony plates on its back. Some 20 species live from Texas to Patagonia and range in size from the fairy armadillo at 13 cm/5 in to the giant armadillo, 1.5 m/4.5 ft long. They feed on insects, fruit, and carrion. Some can roll into an armoured ball if attacked; others rely on burrowing for protection.

Armageddon in the New Testament (Revelation 16), the site of the final battle between the nations which will end the world; it has been identified with ◊Megiddo in Israel.

Armagh county of Northern Ireland

area 1,254 sq km/484 sq mi

population (1981) 118,820

towns county town Armagh; Lurgan, Portadown

physical flat in the north, with many bogs; low hills in the south; Lough Neagh

products chiefly agricultural: apples, potatoes, flax

armature in a motor or dynamo, the wire-wound coil which carries the current and rotates in a magnetic field. It is also the name given to the pole-piece of a permanent magnet or electromagnet. The moving, iron part of a solenoid, especially if it acts as a switch, may also be referred to as an armature.

Armenia country in W Asia, bounded E by Azerbaijan, N by Georgia, W by Turkey, and S by Iran.

Armenian member of the largest ethnic group inhabiting Armenia. There are Armenian minorities in Azerbaijan, as well as in Turkey and Iran. Christianity was introduced to the ancient Armenian kingdom in the 3rd century. There are 4–5 million speakers of Armenian, which belongs to the Indo-European family of languages.

Armenian church form of Christianity adopted in Armenia in the 3rd century. The Catholicos, or exarch, is the supreme head, and Echmiadzin (near Yerevan) is his traditional seat.

Armenian language one of the main divisions of the Indo-European language family. Old Armenian, the classic literary language, is still used in the liturgy of the Armenian church. Contemporary Armenian, with modified grammar and enriched

---

Armenia
Republic of

area 29,800 sq km/11,500 sq mi

capital Yerevan

towns Kumayri (formerly Leninakan)

physical mainly mountainous (including Mount Ararat), wooded

head of state Levon Ter-Petrossian from 1990

head of government Gagik Arutyunyan from 1991

political system emergent democracy

products copper, molybdenum, cereals, cotton, silk

currency rouble

population (1991) 3,580,000 (90% Armenian, 5% Azeri, 2% Russian, 2% Kurd)

language Armenian

religion traditionally Armenian Christian

chronology

1918 Became an independent republic.

1920 Occupied by the Red Army.

1936 Became a constituent republic of the USSR.

1988 Demonstrations called for the transfer of Nagorno-Karabakh from Azerbaijan to Armenian control. Earthquake claimed around 25,000 lives and caused extensive damage.

1989 Pro-autonomy Armenian National Movement founded. Civil war erupted with Azerbaijan over Nagorno-Karabakh.

1990 Nationalists secured control of Armenian supreme soviet; independence declared.

1991 Independence received overwhelming support in a referendum. Armenia joined new Commonwealth of Independent States (CIS) and was granted diplomatic recognition by USA.

1992 Armenia was admitted into Conference on Security and Cooperation in Europe (CSCE) and joined United Nations (UN). Conflict over Nagorno-Karabakh worsened.

with words from other languages, is used by a group of 20th century writers.

Armenian massacres series of murders of Armenians by Turkish soldiers between 1895 and 1915. Reforms promised to Armenian Christians by Turkish rulers never materialized; unrest broke out and there were massacres by Turkish troops in 1895. Again in 1909 and 1915, the Turks massacred altogether more than a million Armenians, and deported others into the N Syrian desert, where they died of starvation; those who could fled to Russia or Persia, and only some 100,000 were left.

Arminius 17 BC–21 AD. German chieftain. An ex-soldier of the Roman army, he annihilated a Roman force led by Varus in the Teutoburger Wald area in 9 AD, and saved Germany from becoming a Roman province. He thus ensured that the empire's frontier did not extend beyond the Rhine.

Arminius Jacobus. Latinized name of Jakob Harmensen 1560–1609. Dutch Protestant priest who founded Arminianism, a school of Christian theology opposed to Calvin's doctrine of predestination. His views were developed by Simon Episcopius (1583–1643). Arminianism is the basis of Wesleyan ◊Methodism in the UK.

Armistice Day in the UK, the anniversary of the armistice signed 11 Nov 1918, ending World War I; it is today commemorated on the same day as ◊Remembrance Sunday.

armour body protection worn in battle. Body armour is depicted in Greek and Roman art; chain mail was developed in the Middle Ages but the craft of the armourer in Europe reached its height in design in the 15th century, when knights were completely encased in plate armour which still allowed freedom of movement. Medieval Japanese armour was articulated, made of iron, gilded metal, leather, and silk.

Armstrong Edwin Howard 1890–1954. American radio engineer, who developed superheterodyne tuning for reception over a very wide spectrum of radio frequencies and frequency ◊modulation for static-free reception.

Armstrong Louis ('Satchmo') 1900–1971. US jazz trumpet player and singer, born in New Orleans. His Chicago recordings in the 1920s with the Hot Five and Hot Seven made him known for his warm

armour A late 15th-century suit of plate armour.

and pure trumpet tone, his improvisation and gravelly voice.

Armstrong Neil Alden 1930– . US astronaut. In 1969, he was the first person to set foot on the Moon, and said, 'That's one small step for a man, one giant leap for mankind.'

Armstrong William George 1810–1900. British engineer, who developed a revolutionary method of making gun barrels in 1855, by building a breechloading artillery piece with a steel and wrought iron barrel (previous guns were muzzle loaded and had cast bronze barrels). By 1880 the 150 mm/16 in Armstrong gun was the standard for all British ordnance.

Arne Thomas Augustus 1710–1778. British composer, whose musical drama *Alfred* includes the song 'Rule Britannia!'.

Arnhem, Battle of in World War II, airborne operation by the Allies, 17–26 Sept 1944, to secure a bridgehead over the Rhine, thereby opening the

aromatic compounds

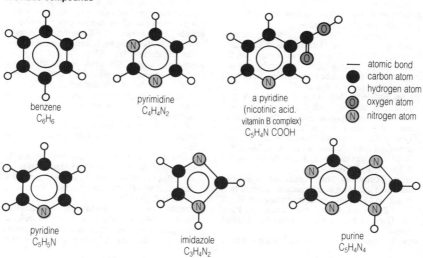

benzene
C_6H_6

pyrimidine
$C_4H_4N_2$

a pyridine
(nicotinic acid,
vitamin B complex)
$C_5H_4N\ COOH$

— atomic bond
● carbon atom
○ hydrogen atom
◉ oxygen atom
Ⓝ nitrogen atom

pyridine
C_5H_5N

imidazole
$C_3H_4N_2$

purine
$C_5H_4N_4$

artesian well

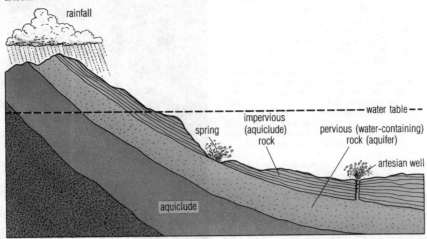

rainfall

water table

spring

impervious (aquiclude) rock

pervious (water-containing) rock (aquifer)

artesian well

aquiclude

way for a thrust towards the Ruhr and a possible early end to the war. It was only partly successful.

Arnim Ludwig Achim von 1781–1831. German Romantic poet and novelist. His finest work, the historical novel *Die Kronenwächter* 1817, was unfinished.

Arnold Benedict 1741–1801. American soldier, who betrayed the American side in the War of American Independence. A merchant in Newhaven, Connecticut, he joined the colonial forces, but in 1780 plotted to betray the strategic post at West Point to the British. Maj André was sent by the British to discuss terms with him, but was caught and hanged as a spy. Arnold escaped to the British, who gave him an army command.

Arnold Matthew 1822–1888. British poet and critic, son of Thomas ◊Arnold. His poems, characterized by their elegiac mood and pastoral themes, include 'The Forsaken Merman' 1849, 'Thyrsis' 1867 (commemorating his friend Arthur Hugh ◊Clough), 'Dover Beach' 1867, and 'The Scholar Gypsy' 1853. Arnold's critical works include '*Essays in Criticism*' 1865 and 1888, and '*Culture and Anarchy*' 1869, which attacks 19th-century philistinism.

aromatic compounds organic chemical compounds derived from benzene.

Arp Hans/Jean 1887–1966. French abstract painter and sculptor. He was one of the founders of Dada in 1915, and later associated with the Surrealists. His innovative wood sculptures use organic shapes in bright colours. Also remarkable are his torn-paper collages.

Arras, Battle of battle of World War I, April–May 1917. Effective but costly British attack on German forces in support of French offensive, which was only partially successful, on the ◊Siegfried Line. British casualties totalled 84,000 as compared to 75,000 German casualties. In World War II the town was captured 1940 by the Germans in the advance on Dunkirk.

Arras, Congress and Treaty of a meeting convened under papal and conciliar auspices in N France in 1435 between representatives of Henry VI of England, Charles VII of France, and Philip the Good of Burgundy, to settle the Hundred Years' War.

arrest deprivation of personal liberty with a view to detention. In Britain an arrest in civil proceedings now takes place only on a court order, usually for ◊contempt of court. In criminal proceedings an arrest may be made on a magistrate's warrant, but a police constable is empowered to arrest without warrant in all cases where he or she has reasonable ground for thinking a serious offence has been committed. Private persons may, and are indeed bound to, arrest anyone committing a serious offence or breach of the peace in their presence. In the USA police and private persons have similar rights and duties.

arrhythmia a disturbance of the natural rhythm of the heart. There are various kinds of arrhythmia, some indicative of heart disease.

arrowroot starchy substance derived from the roots and tubers of various plants. The true arrowroot *Maranta arundinacea* was used by the Indians of South America as an antidote against the effects of poisoned arrows.

arsenic a greyish-white semi-metallic crystalline element, symbol As, atomic number 33, relative atomic mass 74.91. It occurs in many ores, and is widely distributed, being present in minute quantities in the soil, the sea, and the human body. It is poisonous. The chief source of arsenic compounds is as a by-product from metallurgical processes.

arson the malicious and wilful setting fire to property, crops, possessions, in Britain covered by the Criminal Damage Act (1971).

Artaud Antonin 1896–1948. French theatre director. Although his play, *Les Cenci/The Cenci* 1935, was a failure, his concept of the 'Theatre of Cruelty', intended to release feelings usually repressed in the unconscious, has been an important influence on modern dramatists such as Camus, Genet, and in the productions of Peter Brook. Declared insane in 1936, he was confined in an asylum.

Art Deco style in art and architecture, originating in France in 1925, and continuing through the 1930s, using rather heavy, geometric simplification of form, for example Radio City Music Hall, New York.

Artemis in Greek mythology, the goddess (Roman ◊Diana) of chastity, childbirth, and the young; she was envisaged as a virgin huntress; her cult centre was at ◊Ephesus. She was later

arthritis X-ray of the hands of a person with extreme rheumatoid arthritis.

also identified with ◊Selene, goddess of the Moon.

arteriosclerosis hardening of the arteries, with thickening and loss of elasticity. It is associated with smoking, ageing and a diet high in saturated fats.

artery a vessel which conveys blood from the hearts of vertebrates to the body tissues. The largest of the arteries is the aorta, which in mammals leads from the left ventricle of the heart, up over the heart and down through the diaphragm into the belly. Arteries are flexible, elastic tubes consisting of three layers, the middle of which is muscular; by its rhythmic contraction this aids the pumping of blood around the body.

artesian well a well in which water rises from its ◊aquifer under natural pressure. Such a well may be drilled into an aquifer that is confined by impermeable beds both above and below. If the water table (the top of the region of water saturation) in that aquifer is above the level of the well head, hydrostatic pressure will force the water to the surface.

arthritis inflammation of the joints. More common in women, *rheumatoid arthritis* usually begins in middle age in the small joints of the hands and feet, causing a greater or lesser degree of deformity and painfully restricted movement. It is alleviated by drugs, and surgery may be performed to correct deformity.

arthropod invertebrate animal with jointed legs and a segmented body with a horny or chitinous casing, the latter being shed periodically and replaced as the animal grows. This definition includes arachnids such as spiders and mites, as well as crustaceans, millipedes, centipedes, and insects.

Arthur 6th century AD. Legendary English 'king' and hero in stories of ◊Camelot and the quest for the Holy Grail. Arthur is said to have been born at Tintagel and be buried at Glastonbury. He may have been a Romano-British leader against pagan Saxon invaders.

Arthur Chester Alan 1830–1886. 21st president of the USA. He was born in Vermont, son of a Baptist minister, and became a lawyer and Republican political appointee in New York. In 1880, Arthur was chosen as ◊Garfield's vice president, and was his successor when Garfield was assassinated the following year. Arthur held office until 1885.

Arthur Duke of Brittany 1187–1203. Grandson of Henry II of England and nephew of King ◊John, who is supposed to have had him murdered, 13 Apr 1203, as a rival for the crown.

Arthur Prince of Wales 1486–1502. Eldest son of Henry VII of England. He married ◊Catherine of Aragon in 1501, when he was 16 and she was 15, but died the next year.

artichoke two plants of the family Compositae. The *common* or *globe artichoke Cynara scolymus* is tall, with purplish blue flowers; the bracts of the unopened flower are eaten. The *Jerusalem artichoke Helianthus tuberosus* has edible tubers.

article a grammatical ◊part of speech, of which there are two in English: the *definite article* 'the', which serves to specify or identify a noun (as in 'This is the book I need'), and the *indefinite article* 'a' or 'an') (before vowels), which indicates a single unidentified noun ('They gave me a piece of paper and an envelope').

artificial insemination mating achieved by mechanically injecting semen into the womb without genital contact. It is commonly used with cattle because it allows the farmer to select the type and quality of bull required for the herd, and to exert greater control over the timing and organization of the breeding programme. The practice of artificially inseminating pigs has also become much more widespread in recent years.

artificial intelligence (AI) a branch of cognitive science concerned with creating computer programs that can perform actions comparable with those of an intelligent human. Current AI research covers areas such as planning (for robot behaviour), language understanding, pattern recognition, and knowledge representation.

artificial limb a device to replace a limb that has been removed by surgery or one that is malformed because of genetic defects. It is one form of ◊prosthesis.

artificial respiration the maintenance of breathing when the natural process is suspended.

artificial selection in biology, selective breeding of individuals that exhibit particular characters which a plant or animal breeder wishes to develop. The development of particular breeds of cattle for improved meat production (such as the Aberdeen-Angus) or milk production (such as Jerseys) are examples.

artillery collective term for large military ◊firearms.

14th century cannons came into general use, and were most effective in siege warfare.

16th century the howitzer, halfway between a gun and a mortar (muzzle-loading cannon), was first used in sieges.

early 19th century in the Napoleonic period, field artillery became smaller and more mobile.

1914—18 in World War I, howitzers were used to demolish trench systems. Giant cannons were particularly useful in the entrenched conditions of the Western Front, and at sea against the lumbering, heavily armoured battleships, but the fire accuracy on small or moving targets was poor.

1970s introduction of electronically operated target devices and remote-control firing; on battleships gun turrets no longer needed an operator.

1980s howitzers became self-mobile and computer-controlled. Shells may be made to home in automatically on an unseen target, such as a tank, but so far cannot distinguish tanks already disabled.

Art Nouveau art style developed in France in the 1890s, marked by sinuous lines and stylized flowers and foliage. Also known as Jugendstil (Germany); Stile Liberty (Italy). Exponents included ◊Beardsley, ◊Gaudí, ◊Gilbert, C R ◊Mackintosh, René ◊Lalique.

Arts and Crafts movement a social movement based in design and architecture, founded by William ◊Morris in the latter half of the 19th century and supported by A W ◊Pugin and John ◊Ruskin,

artificial respiration

This technique – mouth-to-mouth resuscitation – delivers a continuous supply of oxygen to the lungs of an unconscious person who is not breathing.

Any person who fails to breathe spontaneously requires artificial respiration immediately. If the vital air supply is interrupted for more than four minutes, brain, heart and other tissues begin to suffer irreversible damage. Warning signs include absence of chest movements and blue-grey pallor.

Often the mouth and throat are blocked by blood, stomach contents, or dentures. The victim should be turned onto one side, which may clear the airway. Any obstruction can be removed with the fingers wrapped in a clean cloth. If the person is still not breathing artificial resuscitation should be started at once.

When an unconscious person is placed in the supine position the tongue may drop into the back of the throat, filling the airway and preventing air from reaching the lungs. An open airway must be established before artificial respiration is given. The head is tilted backwards until neck and chest are in a line. Then the jaw is extended to lift the tongue. The position is maintained by keeping one hand on the forehead and the other under the chin.

An airtight seal is created by pinching the nostrils between the fingers of the hand on the forehead and placing the lips around the victim's mouth. The lungs are expanded with a steady, gentle breath, and the chest rises visibly. Exhalation occurs naturally, as the victim's mouth is uncovered. For adults, the procedure is repeated 12 times per minute.

As soon as spontaneous breathing begins the victim should be placed in the recovery position. This keeps the airway clear.

The lips are placed around the nose and mouth of an infant to obtain an airtight seal. No more than little puffs are required to fill the lungs, at a rate of 20 per minute.

stressing the importance of manual processes and largely anti-machine in spirit.

Arts Council of Great Britain UK arts organization, incorporated in 1945, which aids music, drama, and visual arts from government funds.

Aruba island in the Caribbean, the westernmost of the Lesser Antilles; an overseas part of the Netherlands
area 193 sq km/74.5 sq mi
population (1983) 67,000
history Aruba obtained separate status from the other Netherlands Antilles in 1986 and has full internal autonomy.

arum plant of the family Araceae. The species *Arum maculatum*, known as **cuckoopint** or **lords-and-ladies**, is a common British hedgerow plant. The arum or trumpet lily *Zantedeschia aethiopica*, a well-known ornamental plant, is a native of South Africa.

Arunachal Pradesh union territory of the republic of India, in the Himalayas on the borders of Tibet and Burma; area 83,578 sq km/32,282 sq mi; population (1981) 628,000. It produces rubber, coffee, spices, fruit, and timber.

Aryan member of an ancient people who were believed to have lived between Central Asia and E Europe, and to have reached India about 1500 BC. In the ◊Nazi period Hitler and other German theorists erroneously propagated the idea of the Aryans as a white-skinned, blue-eyed, fair-haired master-race.

Aryan language any of the languages of the Aryan peoples of India; a 19th-century name for the ◊Indo-European languages.

Arya Samaj Hindu religious sect founded by Dayanand Saraswati (1825–88) about 1875. He renounced idol-worship and urged a return to the purer principles of the Rig Veda (Hindu scriptures). The movement believes that ◊caste should be determined by merit rather than birth.

ASA abbreviation for *Association of Southeast Asia* (1961–67), replaced by ASEAN (◊*Association of Southeast Asian Nations*).

ASA in photography, a numbering system for rating the speed of films, devised by the American Standards Association. It has now been superseded by *ISO*, the International Standards Organization.

Asante or *Ashanti* person of Asante culture from central Ghana, west of Lake Volta. The Asante language belongs to the Kwa branch of the Niger-Congo family.

a.s.a.p. abbreviation for *as soon as possible*.

ASAT acronym for *anti-satellite weapon*.

asbestos any of several related minerals of fibrous structure which offer great heat resistance because of their non-flammability and poor conductivity. Commercial asbestos is generally made from chrysolite, a kind of ◊serpentine mineral found in Quebec, the USSR, and Zimbabwe. Asbestos usage is now strictly controlled as exposure to asbestos dust can cause cancer.

Ascension British island of volcanic origin in the S Atlantic, a dependency of ◊St Helena since 1922; population (1982) 1,625. The chief settlement is Georgetown.

Ascension Day or *Holy Thursday* in the Christian calendar, the feast day commemorating Christ's ascension into heaven. It is the 40th day after Easter.

Ascham Roger *c.* 1515–1568. English scholar and royal tutor, author of *The Scholemaster* 1570 on the art of education.

ash

ASCII American Standard Code for Information Interchange in computing, a seven- or eight-digit binary code for communicating alphabetic, numeric and other characters (a ◊binary number system). For example, the ASCII code for A is 01000001, for B 01000010, and for C 01000011. The eighth bit (binary digit) is not needed for the code, but is sometimes used to check for errors or allow special characters to be included.

ascorbic acid (or *vitamin C*) a relatively simple organic acid found in fresh fruits and vegetables. It is soluble in water and destroyed by prolonged boiling, so soaking or overcooking of vegetables reduces their vitamin C content. Lack of ascorbic acid results in scurvy.

ASEAN abbreviation for ◊*Association of Southeast Asian Nations*.

asepsis The practice of ensuring that bacteria are excluded from open sites during surgery, wound dressing, blood sampling, and other procedures. So-called aseptic technique is a first line of defence against infection.

asexual reproduction a biological term applied to reproductive processes which are not ◊sexual and thus do not involve fusion of ◊gametes. They include ◊binary fission, in which the parent organism splits into two or more 'daughter' organisms, or ◊budding, in which a new organism is formed initially as an outgrowth of the parent organism.

ash tree of the genus *Fraxinus*, belonging to the family Oleaceae. *F. excelsior* is the European species; its timber is of importance. The **mountain ash** or **rowan** *Sorbus aucuparia* belongs to the family Rosaceae.

Ashbee C(harles) R(obert) 1863–1942. British designer, architect, and writer, one of the major figures of the ◊Arts and Crafts movement. He founded a 'Guild and School of Handicraft' in the East End of London in 1888, but later modified his views, accepting the importance of machinery and design for industry.

Ashcan school group of US painters active *c.* 1908–14, whose members included Robert Henri (1865–1929), George Luks (1867–1933), William Glackens (1870–1938), Everett Shinn (1876–1953), and John Sloan (1871–1951). Their style is realist; their subjects centred on modern city life, the poor and the outcast.

Ashcroft Peggy 1907– . British actress. Her many leading roles include Desdemona, in Shakespeare's *Othello* (with Paul Robeson), and appearances in the TV series *The Jewel in the Crown* 1984 and the film *A Passage to India* 1985.

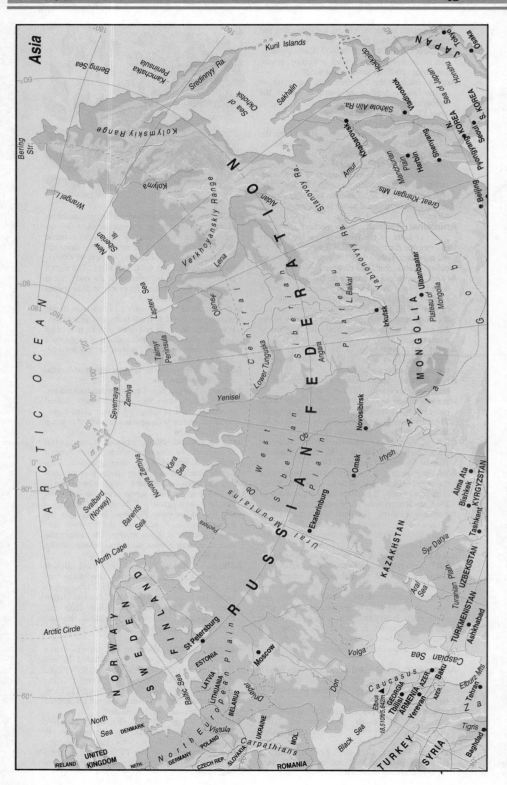

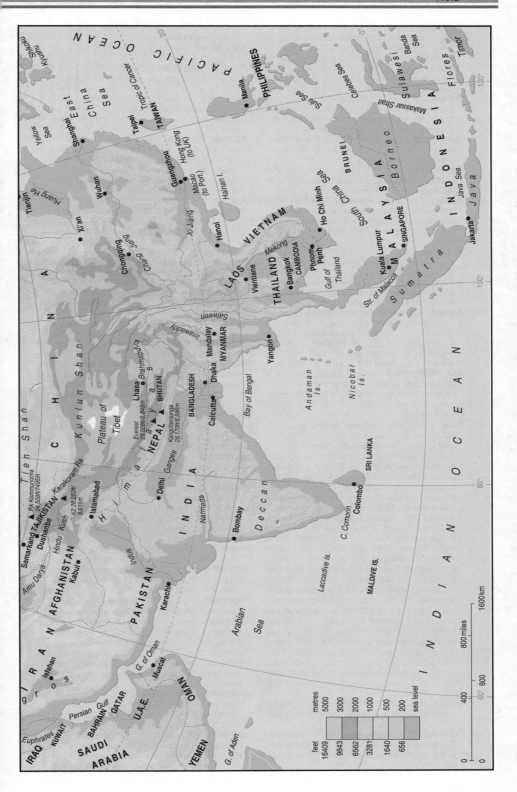

Ashdown 'Paddy' (Jeremy John Durham) 1941–
English politician, leader of the merged Social and
Liberal Democrats from 1988. He served in the
Royal Marines as a commando, leading a Special
Boat Section in Borneo, and was a member of the
Diplomatic Service 1971–76. He became a Liberal
MP 1983. His constituency is Yeovil, Somerset.

Ashes, the cricket trophy theoretically held by the
winning team in the England-Australia test series.
The trophy is permanently held at ◊Lord's cricket
ground no matter who wins the series.

Ashkenazi a Jew of German or East European
descent, as opposed to Sephardi, of Spanish,
Portuguese, or N African descent.

Ashkhabad capital of Turkmenistan; population
(1989) 402,000. Industries include glass and cotton;
'Bukhara' carpets are made here.

Ashley Laura (born Mountney) 1925–1985. Welsh
designer, who established and gave her name to a
neo-Victorian country style in clothes and furnishings from 1953. She had an international chain of
shops.

Ashmole Elias 1617–1692. British antiquary,
whose collection forms the basis of the Ashmolean
Museum, Oxford.

ashram an Indian community whose members
lead a simple life of discipline and self-denial, and
devote themselves to social service.

Ashton Frederick 1904–1988. British dancer and
choreographer. Born in Ecuador, he studied with
◊Massine and ◊Rambert before joining the Vic-
Wells in 1935 as chief choreographer, creating
several roles for Margot ◊Fonteyn. He was
director of the Royal Ballet, London, 1963–70.

Ash Wednesday first day of Lent, the period in
the Christian calendar leading up to Easter; in the
Catholic church the foreheads of the congregation
are marked with a cross in ash, as a sign of
penitence.

Asia largest of the continents, forming the eastern
part of Eurasia to the east of the Ural mountains, one
third of the total land surface of the world.
area 44,000,000 sq km/17,000,000 sq mi
largest cities (over 5 million) Tokyo, Shanghai,
Osaka, Beijing, Seoul, Calcutta, Bombay, Jakarta,
Bangkok, Tehran, Hong Kong
physical five main divisions: (1) central triangular
mountain mass, including the Himalayas; to the N
the great Tibetan plateau, bounded by the Kunluu
mountains, to the N of which lie further ranges, as
well as the Gobi Desert. (2) The SW plateaux and
ranges, forming Afghanistan, Baluchistan, Iran. (3)
The northern lowlands, from the central mountains
to the Arctic Ocean, much of which is frozen for
several months each year. (4) The eastern margin
and islands, where much of the population is concentrated. (5) The southern plateau and river
plains, including Arabia, the Deccan, and the alluvial
plains of the Euphrates, Tigris, Indus, Ganges, and
Irrawaddy. The climate shows great extremes and
contrasts, the heart of the continent becoming
bitterly cold in winter and very hot in summer. This,
with the resulting pressure and wind systems,
accounts for the Asiatic monsoons, bringing heavy
rain to all SE Asia, China, and Japan, between May
and October.
population (1988) 2,996 million the most densely
populated of the continents; annual growth rate
1.7%
language predominantly tonal languages
(Chinese, Japanese) in the east, Indo-Iranian languages in central India and Pakistan (Hindi/Urdu),
and Semitic (Arabic) in the SW

religion Hinduism, Islam, Buddhism, Christianity,
Confucianism, Shintoism.

Asia Minor historical name for **Anatolia**, the
Asian part of Turkey.

Asian Development Bank (ADB) a bank
founded 1966 to stimulate growth in Asia and the Far
East by administering direct loans and technical
assistance. Members include 30 countries within
the region, and 14 countries of W Europe and
N America. The headquarters are in Manila, Philippines.

Asiento, Treaty of agreement between the UK
and Spain 1713, whereby British traders were
permitted to introduce 144,000 black slaves into the
Spanish-American colonies in the course of the next
30 years. In 1750 the right was bought out by the
Spanish government for $100,000.

Asimov Isaac 1920–1992. US science-fiction
writer and writer on science, born in the USSR. He
has published about 200 books, and is possibly best
known for his *I, Robot* 1950 and the Foundation
trilogy 1951–53, continued in *Foundation's Edge*
1983.

AS Level General Certificate of Education
Advanced Supplementary examinations introduced
in the UK 1988, equivalent to 'half an ◊A Level',
intended as a means of broadening the sixth form
(age 16–18) curriculum, and including more
students in the examination system.

Asmara or *Asmera* capital of Eritrea, Ethiopia;
64 km/40 mi SW of Massawa on the Red Sea;
population (1984) 275,385. Products include beer,
clothes, and textiles.

Asoka reigned 264–228 BC. Indian emperor, who
was a Buddhist convert. He had edicts enjoining the
adoption of his new faith carved on pillars and rock
faces, throughout his dominions, and many survive.
In Patna there are the remains of a hall built by him.

asp any of several venomous snakes, including
Vipera aspis of S Europe allied to the ◊adder, and the
Egyptian cobra *Naja haje*, reputed to have been
used by Cleopatra for her suicide.

asparagus plant of the family Liliaceae. *Asparagus officinalis* is cultivated, and the young shoots
are eaten as a vegetable.

Aspasia *c.* 440 BC. Greek courtesan, the mistress
of the Athenian politician ◊Pericles. The philosopher ◊Socrates visited her salon, a meeting place
for the celebrities of Athens. Her free thinking led to
a charge of impiety from which Pericles had to
defend her.

aspen a variety of ◊poplar tree. *Populus tremula* is
small-leaved with thin flexible branches.

asphalt a mixture of different hydrocarbons forming a semi-solid brown or black bitumen, used in the
construction industry.

asphodel genus of plants belonging to the family
Liliaceae. *Asphodelus albus*, the **white asphodel**
or *king's spear*, is found in Italy and Greece,
sometimes covering large areas, and providing
grazing for sheep. *Asphodeline lutea* is the yellow
asphodel.

asphyxia suffocation; a lack of oxygen which
produces a build-up of carbon dioxide waste in the
tissues.

aspidistra Asiatic plant of the Liliaceae family.
The Chinese *Aspidistra elatior* has broad, lanceolate
leaves and, like all members of the genus, grows
well in warm indoor conditions.

aspirin acetylsalicylic acid, a popular ◊analgesic
developed in the early 20th century, for headaches
and arthritis. In the long term, even moderate use
may involve side effects including kidney damage

and hearing defects, and it is no longer considered suitable for children under 12, because of a suspected link with a rare disease, Reye's syndrome. Recent medical research suggests that aspirin may be of value in preventing heart attack (myocardial infarction) and thrombosis.

Asquith Herbert Henry, 1st Earl of Oxford and Asquith 1852–1928. British Liberal politician, prime minister 1908–16. As chancellor of the Exchequer he introduced old-age pensions 1908. He limited the powers of the House of Lords and attempted to give Ireland Home Rule.

ass domesticated donkey, or the wild form from which it was derived, the African wild ass *Equus asinus*; also the Asian wild ass *Equus hemionus*. They differ from horses in their smaller size, larger ears, tufted tail, dorsal stripes, and characteristic bray.

Assad Hafez al 1930– . Syrian Ba'athist politician; he became prime minister after the bloodless military coup in 1970, and in 1971 was the first president to be elected by popular vote; re-elected 1978. He is a Shia (Alawite) Muslim.

Assam state of NE India
area 78,523 sq km/30,310 sq mi
capital Dispur
towns Shilling
products half India's tea is grown here, and half its oil produced; rice, jute, sugar, cotton, coal
population (1981) 19,900,000, including 12,000,000 Assamese (Hindus), 5,000,000 Bengalis (chiefly Muslim immigrants from Bangladesh), and Nepális; and 2,000,000 native people (Christian and traditional religions)
language Assamese
history a thriving region from 1000 BC; later emigrants came from China and Burma; after Burmese invasion 1826, Britain took control; made a separate province 1874; included in the Dominion of India, except for most of the Muslim district of Silhet, which went to Pakistan 1947; the Gara, Khasi, and Jaintia tribal hill districts became the state of ◊Meghalaya 1970; the Mizo hill district became the union territory of Mizoram 1972; massacres of Muslim Bengalis by Hindus 1983.

assassination murder, especially of a political, royal, or public person. The term derives from a sect of Muslim fanatics in the 11th and 12th centuries, who were reputed to take cannabis (Arabic *hashshashin* 'takers of hashish') before their expeditions.

assault an act or threat of physical violence against a person without their consent. In English law it is both a crime and a ◊tort (a civil wrong). The kinds of criminal assault are: common (ordinary); aggravated (more serious, such as causing actual bodily harm); or indecent (of a sexual nature).

assault ship naval vessel with a platform for helicopters, a dock for large landing craft, tank decks, troop accommodation, and defended by missiles, machine guns, and anti-aircraft guns.

assaying the determination of the quantity of a given chemical substance present in a sample. Usually it refers to determining the purity of precious metals.

assembly code computer-programming language closely related to the internal codes of the machine itself. It consists chiefly of a set of short mnemonics which are translated, by a program called an assembler, into ◊machine code for the computer's CPU (central processing unit) to follow directly. In assembly language, for example, JMP means 'jump' and LDA is 'load accumulator'. Used by programmers who need to write very fast or efficient programs.

assembly line a method of mass production in which a product is built up step by step by successive workers adding one part at a time.

asset a business accounting term which covers the land or property of a company or individual, payments due from bills, investments, and anything else owned that can be turned into cash. On a company's balance sheet, total assets must be equal to liabilities (money and services owed).

Assisted Places Scheme in UK education, a scheme established in 1980 by which the government assists parents with the cost of fees at ◊independent schools, on a means-tested basis.

assize in medieval Europe, the passing of laws, either by the king with the consent of nobles, as in the Constitutions of ◊Clarendon by Henry II, 1164, or as a complete system, such as the *Assizes of Jerusalem*, a compilation of the law of the feudal kingdom of Jerusalem in the 13th century. The term remained in use in the UK for the courts held by judges of the High Court in each county; they were abolished under the Courts Act 1971.

association football see ◊football, association.

Association of Southeast Asian Nations (ASEAN) regional alliance formed in Bangkok in 1967; it took over the nonmilitary role of the Southeast Asia Treaty Organization in 1975. Its members are Indonesia, Malaysia, the Philippines, Singapore, Thailand, and (from 1984) Brunei; headquarters Jakarta, Indonesia.

associative law in mathematics, the law that states that the result of performing certain consecutive operations is independent of the order in which they are performed. Thus addition is associative because, for example $3 + (4 + 5)$ gives the same sum as $(3 + 4) + 5$. Multiplication is also associative, for example $2 \times (3 \times 4)$ gives the same product as $(2 \times 3) \times 4$. Subtraction and division are not associative.

assortative mating in ◊population genetics, selective mating between individuals that are genetically related or have similar characteristics. If sufficiently consistent, assortative mating can eventually result in the evolution of two or more new species.

Assyria empire in the Middle East *c.* 2500–612 BC, in N Mesopotamia (now Iraq); capital Niniveh. It was initially subject to ◊Sumeria and intermittently to ◊Babylon. The Assyrians adopted in the main the Sumerian religion and structure of society. At its greatest extent the empire included Egypt and stretched from the E Mediterranean coast to the Persian Gulf.

Astaire Fred 1899–1987. US dancer, who starred in the films *Top Hat* 1935, *Easter Parade* 1948, and *Funny Face* 1957, all of which contained many sequences he designed himself. Most famous of his dancing partners was Ginger Rogers.

Astarte alternative name for the Babylonian and Assyrian goddess ◊Ishtar.

aster plant of the family Compositae, belonging to the same subfamily as the daisy. The sea aster *Aster tripolium* grows wild on sea cliffs in the S of England. Other species are familiar as cultivated garden flowers, including the Michaelmas daisy *Aster nova-belgii*.

asterisk a star-like punctuation mark (*) used to link the asterisked word with a note at the bottom of a page; to mark that certain letters are missing from a word (especially a taboo word such as f**k); or to indicate that a word or usage is nonexistent,

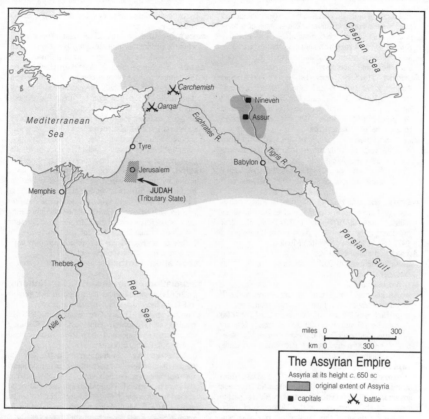

The Assyrian Empire

Assyria at its height c. 650 BC

original extent of Assyria

■ capitals ✕ battle

Mediterranean Sea

Carchemish

Qarqar

Nineveh

Assur

Euphrates R.

Tigris R.

Tyre

Babylon

Jerusalem

JUDAH
(Tributary State)

Memphis

Thebes

Red Sea

Nile R.

Caspian Sea

Persian Gulf

miles 0   300
km 0   300

astronaut *Bruce McCandless floats free above the Earth in his manned manoeuvring unit (MMU), Feb 7 1984.*

for example, 'In English we say three boys and not three *boy'.

asteroid or *minor planet* any of many thousands of small bodies, composed of rock and iron, that orbit the Sun. Most asteroids lie in a belt between the orbits of Mars and Jupiter. Asteroids are thought to be fragments left over from the formation of the ◊solar system. About 100,000 may exist, but their total mass is only a few hundredths the mass of the Moon. They include Ceres (the largest asteroid, 1,000 km/620 mi in diameter), and Vesta (which has a light-coloured surface, and is the brightest as seen from Earth).

asthenosphere a division of the Earth's structure lying beneath the ◊lithosphere, at a depth of approximately 70 km/45 mi to 250 km/160 mi. It is thought to be the soft, relatively mobile layer of the ◊mantle on which the rigid plates of the Earth's surface move to produce the motions of ◊plate tectonics.

asthma difficulty in breathing due to spasm of the bronchi (air passages) in the lungs. Attacks may be provoked by allergy, infection, stress, or emotional upset. Treatment is with ◊bronchodilators to relax the bronchial muscles and thereby ease the breathing.

astigmatism an optical distortion, usually caused by an irregular curvature of the cornea, the transparent front 'window' of the eye.

Aston Francis William 1877–1945. British physicist, who developed the mass spectrometer, which separates ◊isotopes by projecting their ions (charged atoms) through a magnetic field.

athletics *Florence Joyner Griffiths (US) running at Cologne, in the Mobil Grand Prix, 1987.*

Astor prominent American and British family. *John Jacob Astor* (1763–1848) was an American millionaire. *Waldorf Astor*, 2nd Viscount Astor (1879–1952), was Conservative Member of Parliament for Plymouth 1910–19, when he succeeded to the peerage. He was chief proprietor of the British *Observer* newspaper. His wife was Nancy Witcher Langhorne (1879–1964) *Lady Astor*, the first woman Member of Parliament to take her seat in the House of Commons in 1919, when she succeeded her husband for the constituency of Plymouth. She was also a temperance fanatic and great political hostess. Government policy was said to be decided at Cliveden, their country home.

astrolabe ancient navigational instrument, forerunner of the sextant. Astrolabes usually consisted of a flat disc with a sighting rod which could be pivoted to point at the Sun or bright stars. From the altitude of the Sun or star above the horizon, the local time could be estimated.

astrology study of the relative position of the planets and stars in the belief that they influence events on earth. The astrologer casts a ◊horoscope based on the time and place of the subject's birth. Astrology has no proven scientific basis, but has been widespread since ancient times. Western astrology is based on the signs of the zodiac; Chinese astrology is based on a 60-year cycle and lunar calendar.

astrometry the measurement of the precise positions of stars, planets, and other bodies in space. Such information is needed for practical purposes including accurate timekeeping, surveying and navigation, and calculating orbits and measuring distances in space. Astrometry is not concerned with the surface

astronaut Western term for a person making flights into space; the Soviet term is cosmonaut.

astronomical unit the average distance of the Earth from the Sun: 149,597,870 km/ 92,955,800 mi.

astronomy the science of the celestial bodies: the Sun, the Moon and planets; the stars and galaxies; and all other objects in the Universe. It is concerned with their positions, motions, distances, and physical conditions; and with their origins and evolution. Astronomy thus divides into fields such as astrophysics, celestial mechanics, and cosmology.

astrophysics the study of the physical nature of stars, galaxies, and the Universe. It began with the development of spectroscopy in the 19th century, which allowed astronomers to analyse the composition of stars from their light.

Asturias autonomous region of N Spain; area 10,565 sq km/4,081 sq mi; population (1981) 1,130,000. Half of Spain's coal is produced from the mines of Asturias. Agricultural produce includes maize, fruit, and livestock. Oviedo and Gijon are the main industrial towns.

Asturias Miguel Angel 1899–1974. Guatemalan author and diplomat. He published poetry, Guatemalan legends, and novels, such as *El Presidente/The President* 1946, attacking Latin-American dictatorships and 'Yankee imperialism'. Nobel prize 1967.

Asunción capital and port of Paraguay, on the Paraguay river; population (1983) 708,000. It produces textiles, footwear, and food products.

Aswan winter resort town in Upper Egypt; population (1976) 144,000. It is near the High Dam 1960–70, which keeps the level of the Nile constant throughout the year without flooding. It produces steel and textiles.

asymptote in ◊coordinate geometry, a straight line towards which a curve approaches more and more closely but never reaches. A ◊hyperbola has two asymptotes, which in the case of a rectangular hyperbola are at right angles to each other.

Atacama desert in N Chile; area about 80,000 sq km/31,000 sq mi. Inland are mountains, and the coastal area is rainless and barren. There are silver and copper mines, and extensive nitrate deposits.

Atahualpa *c.* 1502–1533. Last emperor of the Incas of Peru. He was taken prisoner in 1532 when the Spaniards arrived, and agreed to pay a huge ransom, but was accused of plotting against the conquistador Pizarro and sentenced to be burned. On his consenting to Christian baptism, the sentence was commuted to strangulation.

Atatürk Kemal. Name assumed in 1934 by Mustafa Kemal Pasha 1881–1938. Turkish politician and general, first president of Turkey from 1923. After World War I he established a provisional rebel government and in 1921–22 the Turkish armies under his leadership expelled the Greeks who were occupying Turkey. He is the founder of the modern republic, which he ruled as virtual dictator, with a policy of consistent and radical westernization.

atavism (Latin *atavus* 'ancestor') in ◊genetics, the reappearance of a characteristic not apparent in the immediately preceding generations; in psychology, the manifestation of primitive forms of behaviour.

ataxia loss of muscular coordination due to neurological damage or disease.

Atget Eugène 1857–1927. French photographer. He took up photography at the age of 40, and for 30 years documented urban Paris, leaving a huge body of work.

astronomy: chronology

2300 BC	Chinese astronomers made their earliest observations.
2000 BC	Babylonian priests made their first observational records.
1900 BC	Stonehenge was constructed: first phase.
365 BC	The Chinese observed the satellites of Jupiter with the naked eye.
3rd cent. BC	Aristarchus argued that the Sun is the centre of the solar system.
2nd cent. AD	Ptolemy's Earth-centred system was promulgated
1543 AD	Copernicus revived the ideas of Aristarchus in *De Revolutionibus*.
1608	Lippershey invented the telescope, which was first used by Galileo in 1609.
1609	Kepler's first two laws of planetary motion were published (the third in 1619).
1632	Leiden established the world's first official observatory.
1633	Galileo's theories were condemned by the inquisition.
1675	The Royal Greenwich Observatory was founded in England.
1687	Newton's *Principia* was published, including his law of universal gravitation.
1704	Halley predicted the return of the comet now named after him, which duly reappeared in 1758: it was last seen in 1986.
1781	Herschel discovered Uranus and recognized stellar systems beyond our galaxy.
1796	Laplace elaborated his theory of the origin of the solar system.
1801	Piazzi discovered the first asteroid, Ceres.
1814	Fraunhofer first studied absorption lines in the solar spectrum.
1846	Neptune was discovered by Galle and D'Arrest.
1859	Kirchhoff explained dark lines in the Sun's spectrum.
1887	The earliest photographic star charts were produced.
1889	E E Barnard took the first photographs of the Milky Way.
1890	The first photograph of the spectrum was taken.
1908	The Tunguska comet fell in Siberia.
1920	Eddington began the study of interstellar matter.
1923	Hubble proved that the galaxies are systems independent of the Milky Way, and by 1930 had confirmed that the universe is expanding.
1930	Pluto was discovered by Clyde Tombaugh at the Lowell Observatory, Arizona.
1931	Jansky founded radioastronomy.
1945	Radar contact with the Moon was established.
1948	The 200-inch Hale reflector telescope was installed at Mount Palomar, California.
1955	The Jodrell Bank radioastronomy dish in England was completed.
1957	The first Sputnik satellite (USSR) opened the age of space observation.
1962	The first X-ray source was discovered in Scorpio.
1963	The first quasar was discovered by Mount Palomar Observatory.
1967	The first pulsar was identified by Jocelyn Bell and Antony Hewish, in England.
1969	The first manned Moon landing was made by US astronauts.
1970	The black hole theory was confirmed for the first time.
1976	A 236-inch reflector telescope was installed at Mount Semirodniki (USSR); Viking probes (USA) soft-landed on Mars; experiments indicated no signs of life.
1977	Uranus was discovered to have rings; the spacecraft *Voyager 1* and *2* were launched, the latter passing Jupiter and Saturn 1979–81, and Uranus 1986; due Neptune 1989.
1978	The spacecraft *Pioneer Venus 1* and *2* reached Venus; a satellite of Pluto, Charon, was discovered by James Christie of the US Naval Observatory; Herculina was discovered to be the first asteroid with a satellite.
1979	The UK infra-red telescope (UKIRT) was established on Hawaii.
1986	Halley's comet returned. Voyager 2 discovered six new moons around Uranus.
1987	Bright supernovae were visible to the naked eye for the first time since 1604.
1989	*Voyager 2* flew by Neptune and discovered eight moons and three rings.
1990	Hubble Space Telescope was launched into orbit by the US space shuttle.
1991	The space probe *Galileo* flew past the asteroid Gaspra.
1992	COBE satellite detected ripples from the Big Bang that mark the first stage in the formation of galaxies.

Athanasian creed one of the three ancient ◊creeds of the Christian church. Mainly a definition of the Trinity and incarnation, it was written many years after the death of Athanasius, but was attributed to him as the chief upholder of Trinitarian doctrine.

Athanasius, St 298–373. Christian bishop of Alexandria, supporter of the doctrines of the Trinity and incarnation. He was a disciple of St Anthony the hermit, and an opponent of ◊Arianism in the great Arian controversy. Arianism was officially condemned at the Council of Nicaea in 325, and in 328 Athanasius was appointed bishop of Alexandria. The ◊Athanasian creed was not actually written by him, although it reflects his views.

atheism non-belief in, or the positive denial of, the existence of a god or gods.

Athelstan c. 895–939. King of the Mercians and West Saxons. Son of Edward the Elder and grandson of Alfred the Great, he was crowned king in 925 at Kingston-upon-Thames. He subdued parts of Cornwall and Wales, and in 937 defeated the Welsh, Scots, and Danes at Brunanburh.

Athena in Greek mythology, the goddess (Roman ◊Minerva) of war, wisdom, and the arts and crafts, who was supposed to have sprung fully armed from the head of ◊Zeus. Her chief cult centre was Athens, where the Parthenon was dedicated to her.

Athens (Greek *Athinae*) capital city of modern Greece and of ancient Attica; population (1981) 885,000, metropolitan area 3,027,000. Situated 8 km/5 mi NE of its port of Piraeus on the Gulf of Aegina, it is built around the rocky hills of the Acropolis 169 m/412 ft and the Areopagus 112 m/370 ft, and is overlooked from the NE by the hill of Lycabettus 277 m/909 ft. It lies in the south of the central plain of Attica, watered by the mountain streams of Cephissus and Ilissus.

atheroma furring up of the interior of an artery by deposits, mainly of cholesterol, within its walls.

atherosclerosis thickening and hardening of the walls of the arteries, associated with ◊atheroma.

athletics competitive track and field events consisting of running, throwing, and jumping disciplines. *Running events* range from sprint races (100 metres) to the marathon (26 miles 385 yards). *Jumping events* are the high jump, long jump, triple jump and pole vault (men only). *Throwing events* are javelin, discus, shot putt, and hammer throw (men only).

Atlanta capital and largest city of Georgia, USA; population (1980) 422,000, metropolitan area 2,010,000. There are Ford and Lockheed assembly plants, and it is the headquarters of Coca-Cola.

Atlantic, Battle of the German campaign during World War I to prevent merchant shipping from carrying food supplies across the Atlantic. By 1917, some 875,000 tons of shipping had been lost. The odds were only turned by the belated use of naval *convoys* and the use of *depth charges* to deter submarine attack.

Atlantic, Battle of the continuous battle fought in the Atlantic Ocean throughout World War II (1939–45) by the sea and air forces of Britain and Germany. The total number of U-boats destroyed by the Allies during the whole war was nearly 800. At least 2,200 convoys of 75,000 merchant ships crossed the Atlantic.

Atlantic Charter declaration issued during World War II by the British prime minister Churchill and the US president Roosevelt after meetings in Aug 1941. It stressed their countries' good intentions

and was largely a propaganda exercise to demonstrate public solidarity between the Allies.

Atlantic Ocean sea lying between Europe and Africa to the east and the Americas to the west, probably named after ◊Atlantis; area of basin 81,500,000 sq km/31,500,000 sq mi; including Arctic Ocean, and Antarctic seas, 106,200,000 sq km/41,000,000 sq mi. The average depth is 3 km/2 mi; greatest depth the Puerto Rico Trench 9,219 m/27,498 ft. The Mid-Atlantic Ridge, of which the Azores, Ascension, St Helena, and Tristan da Cunha form part, divides it from north to south. Lava welling up from this central area annually increases the distance between South America and Africa. The North Atlantic is the saltiest of the main oceans, and it has the largest tidal range. In the 1960s–1980s average wave heights have increased by 25%, the largest from 12 m to 18 m.

Atlas in Greek mythology, one of the ◊Titans who revolted against the gods; as a punishment Atlas was compelled to support the heavens upon his head and shoulders. Growing weary, he asked Perseus to turn him into stone, and he was transformed into Mount Atlas.

atlas a book of maps. The first modern atlas was the *Theatrum orbis terrarum* 1570; the first English atlas has a collection of the counties of England and Wales by Christopher Saxten 1579.

Atlas Mountains mountain system of NW Africa, stretching 2,400 km/1,500 mi from the Atlantic coast of Morocco to the Gulf of Gabes, Tunisia, and lying between the Mediterranean on the north and the Sahara on the south. The highest peak is Mount Toubkal 4,165 m/13,664 ft.

atman in Hinduism, the individual soul or the eternal essential self.

atmosphere the mixture of gases that surrounds the Earth, prevented from escaping by the pull of the Earth's gravity. Atmospheric pressure decreases with height in the atmosphere. In its lowest layer, the atmosphere consists of nitrogen (78%) and oxygen (21%), both in molecular form (two atoms bounded together). The other 1% is largely argon, with very small quantities of other gases, as well as water vapour.

atmosphere a unit of pressure (atm) equal to 14.7 lb/in^2, 101,325 pascals or 760 torr. The actual pressure exerted by the atmosphere fluctuates around this value, which is the standard at sea level and 0°C used with reference to very high pressures.

atom the very small, discrete particles of which all matter is composed. There are 92 kinds of atom occurring naturally, which correspond to the 92 elements. They differ in chemical behaviour and cannot be broken up by chemical means to anything simpler.

atom bomb bomb deriving its explosive force from nuclear fission (see ◊nuclear energy) as a result of a neutron chain reaction, developed in the 1940s in the UK and USA for use in World War II, and superseded in the 1950s by the hydrogen bomb. See ◊nuclear warfare.

atomic energy another name for ◊nuclear energy.

atomic number the number of electrons or the positive charge on the nucleus of an atom. The 105 elements are numbered 1 (hydrogen) to 105 (hahnium) in the periodic table of elements.

The Earth's atmosphere

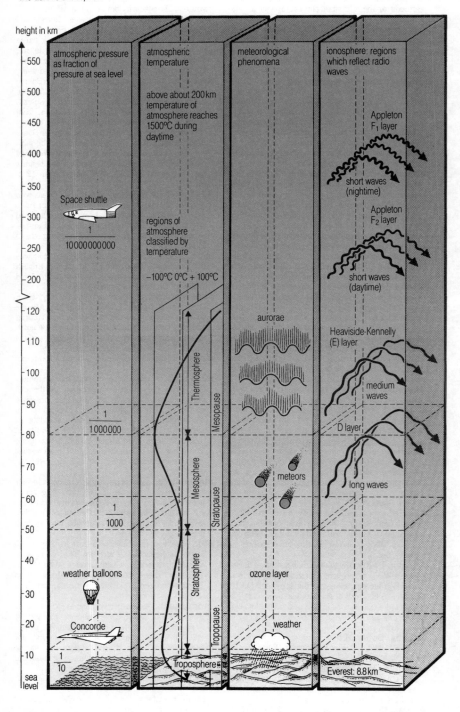

atomic time   the time as given by atomic clocks, which are regulated by natural resonance frequencies of particular atoms, and display a continuous count of seconds.

atomic weight   another name for ◊relative atomic mass.

Aton   in ancient Egypt, the sun's disc as an emblem of the single deity whose worship was enforced by ◊Ikhnaton.

atonality   in music, a modern system of composition, in which there is an absence of ◊key. Exponents of atonality include Schoenberg, Berg, Webern, Stockhausen, Boulez, and many other modern composers.

atonement   in Christian theology, the doctrine that Christ suffered on the cross to bring about reconciliation and forgiveness between God and humans.

Atonement, Day of   Jewish holy day (*Yom Kippur*) held on the tenth day of Tishri (Sept–Oct), the seventh month of the Jewish year. It is a day of fasting, penitence, and cleansing from sin.

ATP   (*adenosine triphosphate*) nucleotide molecule found in all cells. It can yield large amounts of energy, used to drive many biological processes, including muscle contraction and the synthesis of complex molecules needed by the cell. ATP is formed during photosynthesis in plants, or by the breakdown of food molecules during ◊metabolism in animals.

atrium   in architecture, an inner, open courtyard.

atrophy   in medicine, a diminution in size and function, or output, of a body tissue or organ. It is usually due to nutritional impairment or disease.

attainder, bill of   a legislative device that allowed the English Parliament to declare guilt and impose a punishment on an individual without bringing the matter before the courts. Such bills were used intermittently from the Wars of the Roses until 1798. Some acts of attainder were also passed by American colonial legislators during the War of Independence to deal with 'loyalists' who continued to support the English crown.

attar of roses   perfume derived from the essential oil of roses, obtained by crushing and distilling the petals of the flowers.

attempt   criminal offence in the UK under the Criminal Attempts Act 1981, which repealed the 'suspected person offence', commonly known as the 'sus' law. The offence must involve 'more than a mere preparatory act'; that is, it must include at least a partial or unsuccessful performance of the crime.

Attenborough   Richard 1923– . British film director. Originally an actor, he starred in *Brighton Rock* 1947 and *10 Rillington Place* 1970. He has directed *Oh! What a Lovely War* 1968, *Gandhi* 1982, and *Cry Freedom* 1987.

Attica (Greek *Attiki*)   region of Greece comprising Athens and the district around it; area 3,381 sq km/1,305 sq mi; population (1981) 342,000. It is noted for its language, art, and philosophical thought in Classical times. It is a prefecture of modern Greece with Athens as its capital.

Attila   *c.* 406–453. King of the Huns from 434, called the 'Scourge of God'. He em   barked on a career of vast conquests ranging from the Rhine to Persia. In 451 he invaded Gaul, but was defeated on the ◊Catalaunian Fields by the Roman and Visigothic armies under Aëtius (died 454) and Theodoric I. In 452 he led his Huns into Italy and only the personal intervention of Pope Leo I prevented the sacking of Rome.

Attlee Clement Attlee, British prime minister 1945–51.

Attila Line   line dividing Greek and Turkish Cyprus, so called because of a fanciful identification of the Turks with the Huns.

Attis   in Classical mythology, a Phrygian god, whose death and resurrection symbolized the end of winter and the arrival of spring.

Attlee   Clement (Richard), 1st Earl 1883–1967. British Labour politician. In the coalition government during World War II he was Lord Privy Seal 1940–42, dominions secretary 1942–43 and Lord President of the Council 1943–45, as well as deputy prime minister from 1942. As prime minister 1945–51 he introduced a sweeping programme of nationalization and a whole new system of social services.

attorney   a person who represents another in legal matters. In the USA, attorney is the formal title for a lawyer, who combines the functions performed in the UK by a barrister and a solicitor. This use of the term is largely obsolete in Britain except in Attorney General. See also ◊power of attorney.

Attorney General   in England, principal law officer of the Crown and head of the English Bar; the post is one of great political importance. In the USA, the chief law officer of the government and head of the Department of Justice.

Atwood   Margaret (Eleanor) 1939–   . Canadian novelist, short-story writer, and poet. Her novels, which often treat feminist themes with wit and irony, include *The Edible Woman* 1969, *Life Before Man* 1979, *Bodily Harm* 1981, *The Handmaid's Tale* 1986, and *Cat's Eye* 1989.

aubergine   a plant, member of the family Solanaceae. The *eggplant*, *Solanum melongena*, is native to tropical Asia. Its purple-skinned,

Atwood Canadian novelist and poet Margaret Atwood.

sometimes white, fruits are eaten as a vegetable.

aubrieta spring-flowering dwarf perennial plant of the family Cruciferae. It has a trailing habit and bears purple flowers.

Auckland largest city in New Zealand, situated in N North Island; population (1986) 888,000. It fills the isthmus that separates its two harbours (Waitemata and Manukau), and its suburbs spread north across the Harbour Bridge. It is the country's chief port and leading industrial centre, having iron and steel plants, engineering, car assembly, textiles, food-processing, sugar-refining, and brewing.

Auckland George Eden, 1st Earl of Auckland 1784–1849. British Tory politician for whom Auckland, New Zealand, is named. He became a Member of Parliament in 1810, and 1835–41 was governor general of India.

auction bridge card game played by two pairs of players using all 52 cards. The chief characteristic is the selection of trumps by a preliminary bid or auction.

Auden W(ystan) H(ugh) 1907–1973. US poet of British origin. He wrote some of his most original poetry, such as *Look, Stranger!* 1936, in the 1930s when he led the influential left-wing literary group that included MacNeice, Spender, and Day Lewis. Later, after moving to the US in 1939, he adopted a more conventional Christian viewpoint in *The Age of Anxiety* 1947.

audiometer an electrical instrument used to test hearing.

audit the official inspection of a company's accounts by a qualified accountant as required each year by law, to ensure the company balance sheet reflects the true state of its affairs.

Audit Commission independent body in the UK established by the Local Government Finance Act 1982. It administers the District Audit Service (established 1844) and appoints auditors for the accounts of all UK local authorities. The Audit Commission consists of 15 members: its aims include finding ways of saving costs, and controlling illegal local-authority spending.

Audubon John James 1785–1851. US naturalist. In 1827, he published the first part of his *Birds of North America*, with a remarkable series of colour plates. Later, he produced a similar work on American quadrupeds.

Augsburg, Confession of statement of the Protestant faith as held by the German Reformers composed by Philip ◊Melanchthon. Presented to Charles V, Holy Roman Emperor, at the conference known as the Diet of Augsburg in 1530, it is the creed of the modern Lutheran church.

Augsburg, Peace of religious settlement following the Diet of Augsburg 1555, which established the right of princes in the Holy Roman Empire (rather than the emperor himself, Ferdinand I) to impose a religion on their subjects – later summarized by the maxim *cuius regio, eius religio*. It initially applied only to Lutherans and Catholics.

augur member of a college of Roman priests who interpreted the will of the gods from signs or 'auspices' such as the flight of birds, the condition of entrails of sacrificed animals, and the direction of thunder and lightning. Their advice was sought before battle and on other important occasions.

Augustan age the golden age of the Roman emperor ◊Augustus 63 BC–14 AD, noted for its art, particularly literature. The name was also given to later periods which used Classical ideals, such as that of Queen Anne in England.

Augustine of Hippo, St 354–430. One of the early Christian leaders and writers known as the Fathers of the Church. He was converted to Christianity by Ambrose in Milan and became bishop of Hippo (modern Annaba, Algeria) 396. Among Augustine's many writings are his *Confessions*, a spiritual autobiography, and the influential *De Civitate Dei/The City of God* vindicating the Christian church and divine providence in 22 books.

Augustine, St died 604. First archbishop of Canterbury, England. He was sent from Rome to convert England to Christianity by Pope Gregory I. Landing at Ebbsfleet, Thanet, in 597, he soon baptized Ethelbert, King of Kent. He was consecrated bishop of the English at Arles 597 and appointed archbishop in 601. Feast day 26 May.

Augustinian of a religious community that follows the Rule of St ◊Augustine of Hippo. It includes the Canons of St Augustine, Augustinian Friars and Hermits, Premonstratensians, Gilbertines, and Trinitarians.

Augustus 63 BC–14 AD. Title of Octavian (Gaius Julius Caesar Octavianus), first of the Roman emperors. He joined forces with Mark Antony and Lepidus in the Second Triumvirate. Following Mark Antony's liaison with Cleopatra, Augustus defeated the Egyptian queen at Actium in 31 BC. As emperor (from 27 BC) he reformed the government of the empire, the army and Rome's public services, and was a noted patron of the arts.

auk any member of the family of marine diving birds that includes ◊razorbills, ◊puffins, and ◊guillemots. Confined to the N hemisphere they feed on fish, and use their wings to 'fly' underwater in pursuit.

Aung San 1914–1947. Burmese politician. As leader of the Anti-Fascist People's Freedom League he became vice president of the executive council in Sept 1946. During World War II he had collaborated first with Japan and then with the UK.

Aurangzeb or *Aurungzebe* 1618–1707. Mughal emperor of N India from 1658. Third son of Shah Jahan, he made himself master of the court by a palace revolution. His reign was the most brilliant period of the Mughal dynasty, but by despotic tendencies and Muslim fanaticism he aroused much opposition. His latter years were spent in war with the princes of Rajputana and Mahrattas.

Aurelian (Lucius Domitius Aurelianus) *c.* 214–275. Roman emperor from 270. A successful soldier, he was chosen emperor by his troops on the death of Claudius II. He defeated the Goths and Vandals, defeated and captured ◊Zenobia of Palmyra, and was planning a campaign against Parthia when he was murdered. The *Aurelian Wall*, a fortification surrounding Rome, was built by Aurelian in 271. It was made of concrete, and substantial ruins exist. The *Aurelian Way* ran from Rome through Pisa and Genoa to Antipolis (Antibes) in Gaul.

Aurelius (Antoninus) Marcus Roman emperor; see ◊Marcus Aurelius.

Auric Georges 1899–1983. French composer. He was one of the musical group known as ◊Les Six, who were influenced by Erik ◊Satie. Auric composed a comic opera, several ballets, and incidental music.

auricula a plant, the *primrose Primula auricula*. It is a native of the Alps, but has been grown in English gardens for three centuries.

Auriga constellation of the northern hemisphere, represented as a man driving a chariot. Its brightest star is first-magnitude Capella; Epsilon Aurigae is an ◊eclipsing binary star, with a period of

aurora The aurora borealis showing multiple bands near Fairbanks, Alaska.

27 years, the longest of its kind (last eclipse 1983).

Aurignacian in archaeology, an Old Stone Age culture which came between the Mousterian and the Solutrian in the Upper Palaeolithic. It is derived from a cave at Aurignac in the Pyrenees, France.

Auriol Vincent 1884–1966. French socialist politician. He was president of the two Constituent Assemblies of 1946 and first president of the Fourth Republic 1947–54.

aurora coloured light in the night sky, *aurora borealis*, 'northern lights', in the northern hemisphere, and *aurora australis* in the southern. Auroras are usually in the form of a luminous arch with its apex towards the magnetic pole followed by arcs, bands, rays, curtains, and coronas, usually green, but often showing shades of blue and red, and sometimes yellow or white. Aurorae are caused at a height of 100 km/60 mi by a fast stream of charged particles, originating in the sun. These enter the upper atmosphere and, by bombarding the gases in the atmosphere, cause them to emit visible light.

Aurora Roman goddess of the dawn. The Greek equivalent is *Eos*.

Auschwitz Polish *Oswiecim* town near Krakow in Poland, the site of a camp used by the Nazis in World War II to exterminate Jews as part of the ◊'final solution'. Each of the four gas chambers could hold 6,000 people.

auscultation evaluation of internal organs by listening, usually with the aid of a stethoscope.

Australia, Commonwealth of

State (Capital)	Area sq km
New South Wales (Sydney)	801,600
Queensland (Brisbane)	1,727,200
South Australia (Adelaide)	984,000
Tasmania (Hobart)	67,800
Victoria (Melbourne)	227,600
Western Australia (Perth)	2,525,500
Territories	
Northern Territory (Darwin)	1,346,200
Capital Territory (Canberra)	2,400
	7,682,300
External territories	
Ashmore and Cartier Islands	5
Australian Antarctic Territory	6,044,000
Christmas Island	140
Cocos (Keeling) Islands	14
Coral Sea Islands	1,000,000
Heard Island and McDonald Islands	410
Norfolk Island	40

Ausgleich the compromise between Austria and Hungary of 8 Feb 1867 that established the Austro Hungarian Dual Monarchy under Hapsburg rule. It endured until the collapse of ◊Austria-Hungary in 1918.

Austen Jane 1775–1817. British novelist, noted for her domestic novels of manners. All her novels are set within the confines of middle-class provincial society, and show her skill at drawing characters and situations with delicate irony. These include *Sense and Sensibility* 1811, *Pride and Prejudice* 1813, and *Mansfield Park* 1814.

Austerlitz, Battle of battle on 2 Dec 1805 in which the French forces of Emperor Napoleon defeated those of Alexander I of Russia and Francis II of Austria at a small town in Czechoslovakia, formerly in Austria, 19 km/12 mi E of Brno.

Austin Herbert, 1st Baron Austin 1866–1941. British pioneer car manufacturer. He began manufacturing cars in 1905 at Northfield, Birmingham, notably the 'Austin Seven' in 1921.

Australasia loosely applied geographical term, usually meaning Australia, New Zealand, and neighbouring islands.

Australia the smallest continent and largest island in the world, situated south of Indonesia, between the Pacific and Indian oceans.

Australia Day national holiday in Australia, the anniversary of Captain Phillip's arrival in Sydney 26 Jan 1788 and the founding of the first colony.

Australian Aborigine indigenous inhabitant of the continent of Australia. They speak several hundred different languages, the most important being Aranda (Arunta), spoken in central Australia, and Murngin, spoken in Arnhem Land. In recent years there has been a movement for the recognition of Aborigine rights, campaigning against racial discrimination in housing, education, wages, and inadequate medical facilities.

Australian Prime Ministers

Took office	Name	Party
1901	Sir Edmund Barton	Protectionist
1903	Alfred Deakin	Protectionist
1904	John Watson	Labor
1904	Sir G Reid	Free Trade
1905	Alfred Deakin	Protectionist
1908	Andrew Fisher	Labor
1909	Alfred Deakin	Protectionist-Free Trade alliance
1910	Andrew Fisher	Labor
1913	Sir J Cook	Liberal
1914	Andrew Fisher	Labor
1915	W M Hughes	Labor
1917	W M Hughes	Nationalist Labor
1923	S M Bruce	Nationalist
1929	J H Scullin	Labor
1932	J A Lyons	United Australia Party
1939	Sir Earle Page	Country Party
1939	R G Menzies	United Australia Party
1941	A W Fadden	Country Party
1941	John Curtin	Labor
1945	F M Forde	Labor
1945	J B Chifley	Labor
1949	R G Menzies	Liberal-Country Party
1966	Harold Holt	Liberal-Country Party
1967	John McEwen	Liberal-Country Party
1968	J G Gorton	Liberal-Country Party
1971	William McMahon	Liberal-Country Party
1972	Gough Whitlam	Labor
1975	Malcolm Fraser	Liberal-Country Party
1983	Robert Hawke	Labor
1991	Paul Keating	Labor

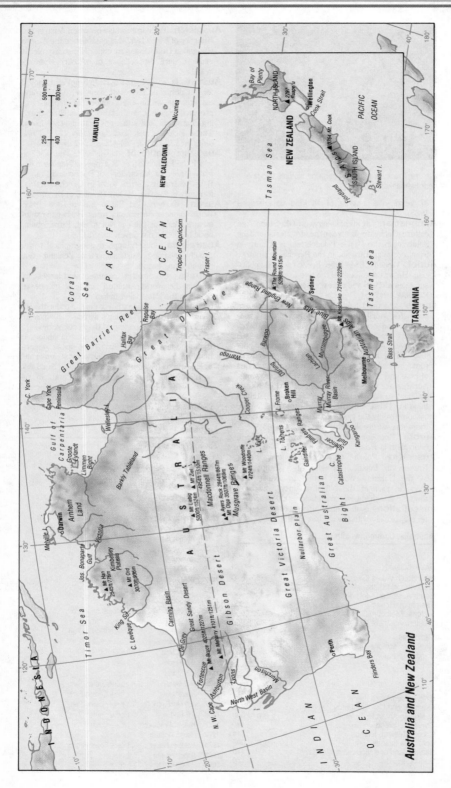

Australia and New Zealand

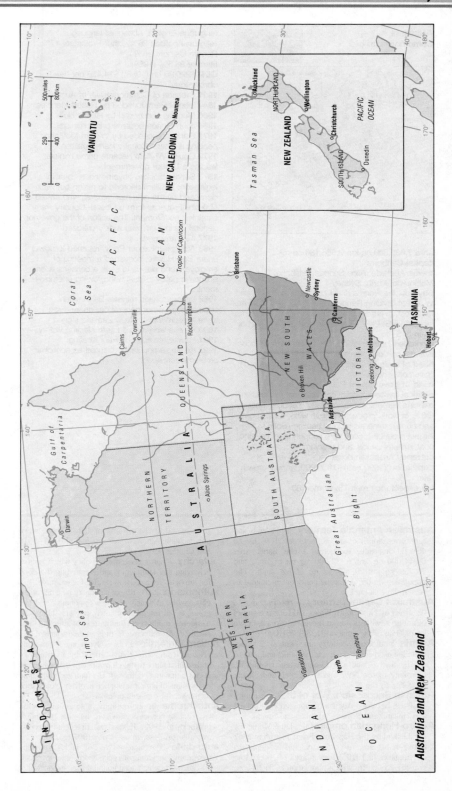

Australia and New Zealand

Australia
Commonwealth of

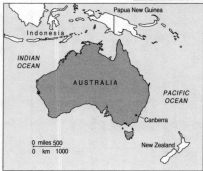

Papua New Guinea

Indonesia

INDIAN
OCEAN

AUSTRALIA

PACIFIC
OCEAN

Canberra

0 miles 500
0 km 1000

New Zealand

area 7,682,300 sq km/2,966,136 sq mi
capital Canberra
towns Adelaide, Alice Springs, Brisbane, Darwin, Melbourne, Perth, Sydney
physical the world's driest continent, arid in N and W, Great Dividing Range in the E; NE peninsula has rainforest; rivers N–S and Darling River and Murray system E–S; Lake Eyre basin and fertile Nullarbor Plain in S
territories Norfolk Island, Christmas Island, Cocos Islands; part of Antarctica
head of state Elizabeth II from 1952 represented by governor general
head of government Paul Keating from 1991
political system federal constitutional monarchy
exports cereals, meat and dairy products; wool (30% of world production); fruit, wine, nuts, sugar, and honey; minerals include bauxite (world's largest producer), coal, iron, copper, lead, tin, zinc, opal, mineral sands, and uranium
currency Australian dollar
population (1990 est)16,650,000; annual growth rate 1.5%
life expectancy men 75, women 80

language English; Aboriginal languages
religion Anglican 26%, other Protestant 17%, Roman Catholic 26%
literacy 98.5% (1988)
GDP $220.96 bn (1988); $14,458 per head
chronology
1901 Creation of Commonwealth of Australia.
1944 Liberal Party founded by Robert Menzies.
1966 Menzies succeeded by Harold Holt.
1968 John Gorton became prime minister.
1971 Gorton succeeded by William McMahon, heading a Liberal-Country Party coalition.
1972 Gough Whitlam became prime minister, leading a Labour government.
1975 Senate blocked government's financial legislation; Whitlam declined to resign but was dismissed by the governor general, who invited Malcolm Fraser to form a Liberal–Country Party caretaker government. The action of the governor general, John Kerr, was widely criticized.
1977 Kerr resigned.
1983 Australian Labour Party, returned to power under Bob Hawke, convened a meeting of employers and unions to seek a consensus on economic policy to deal with growing unemployment.
1988 Labour foreign minister Bill Hayden appointed governor general designate. Free trade agreement with New Zealand signed.
1990 Hawke won record fourth election victory.
1991 Hawke replaced by Paul Keating.
1992 Keating's popularity declined as economic problems continued.

Australian Antarctic Territory the islands and territories south of 60° S, between 160° E and 45° E longitude, excluding Adélie Land; area 6,044,000 sq km/2,332,900 sq mi of land, and 75,759 sq km/29,243 sq mi of ice shelf. The population on the Antarctic continent is limited to research personnel.

Australian Capital Territory territory ceded to Australia by New South Wales 1911 for the site of ◊Canberra, with its port at Jervis Bay area 2,432 sq km/939 sq mi; population (1987) 261,000.

Austria landlocked country in central Europe, bounded by Hungary to the E, Slovenia and Italy to the S, Switzerland and Lechtenstein to the W, Germany to the NW, and the Czech and Slovak republics to the N.

Austrian Succession, War of the war fought 1740–48 between Austria (supported by England and Holland and Prussia, France, and Spain).

Austro-Hungarian empire the Dual Monarchy established by the Hapsburg Franz Joseph in 1867 between his empire of Austria and his kingdom of Hungary. In 1910 it had an area of 100,864 sq km/261,239 sq mi with a population of 51 million.

It collapsed in the autumn of 1918. There were only two king-emperors: Franz Joseph 1867–1916 and Charles 1916–18.

autarchy a national economic policy which aims at achieving self-sufficiency and eliminating the need for imports (by imposing tariffs, for example).

authoritarianism rule of a country by a dominant elite, who ruthlessly repress opponents and the press to maintain their own power. They are frequently indifferent to activities not affecting their security. An extreme form is ◊totalitarianism.

autism, infantile a rare syndrome, generally present from birth, characterized by a withdrawn state and a failure to develop normally in language or social behaviour, although the autistic child may show signs of high intelligence in other areas, such as music. Its cause is unknown.

autochrome in photography, a single-plate additive colour process devised by the ◊Lumière brothers in 1903. It was the first commercially available process, in use from 1907 to 1935.

auto-da-fé (Portuguese 'act of faith') religious ceremony, including a procession, solemn mass, and sermon, which accompanied the sentencing of

Austria
Republic of
(Republik Österreich)

area 83,500 sq km/32,375 sq mi
capital Vienna
towns Graz, Linz, Salzburg, Innsbruck
physical mountainous, with the Danube river basin in the E
head of state Thomas Klestil from 1992
head of government Franz Vranitzky from 1986

political system democratic federal republic
exports minerals, manufactured goods
currency schilling
population (1990 est) 7,595,000; annual growth rate 0.1%
life expectancy men 70, women 77
language German
religion Roman Catholic 85%
literacy 98% (1983)
GDP $183.3 bn (1987); $11,337 per head
chronology
1918 Hapsburg rule ended, republic proclaimed.
1938 Incorporated into German Third Reich.
1945 1920 constitution reinstated and coalition government formed by the Socialist Party of Austria (SPÖ) and the Austrian People's Party (ÖVP).
1955 Allied occupation ended and the independence of Austria formally necognized.
1966 ÖVP in power with Josef Klaus as chancellor.
1970 SPÖ formed a minority government, with Dr Bruno Kreisky as chancellor.
1983 Kreisky resigned and was replaced by Dr Fred Sinowatz, leading a coalition.
1986 Dr Kurt Waldheim elected president. Sinowatz resigned and was succeeded by Franz Vranitzky. No party won an overall majority in the general election.
1989 Austria sought EC membership.
1990 Vranitzky re-elected.
1991 Bid for EC membership endorsed by the Community.
1992 Klestil replaced Waldheim as president.

---

heretics by the Spanish ◊Inquisition before they were handed over to the secular authorities for punishment, usually burning.

autogiro or **autogyro** a heavier-than-air craft that supports itself in the air with a rotary wing, or rotor. The Spanish aviator Juan de la ◊Cierva designed the first successful autogiro in 1923. The autogiro's rotor provides only lift and not propulsion, unlike in a ◊helicopter where the rotor provides both. The autogiro is propelled by an orthodox ◊propeller.

autoimmunity a situation where the body's immune responses are mobilized not against 'foreign' matter, such as invading germs, but against the body itself. So-called autoimmune diseases include ◊myasthenia gravis, pernicious ◊anaemia, rheumatoid ◊arthritis, and ◊lupus erythematosus.

autolysis in biology, the destruction of a ◊cell after its death by the action of its own ◊enzymes, which break down its structural molecules.

automatic pilot a control device that keeps an aeroplane flying automatically on a given course at a given height and speed. Devised by American businessman Lawrence Sperry in 1912, the automatic pilot contains a set of ◊gyroscopes that provide reference for the plane's course. Sensors detect when the plane deviates from this course and send signals to the control surfaces – the ailerons, elevators, and rudder – to take the appropriate action.

automation the widespread use of self-regulating machines in industry. Automation involves the addition of control devices, using electronic sensing and computing techniques, which often follow the pattern of human nervous and brain functions, to already mechanized physical processes of production and distribution, for example, steel processing, mining, chemical production, and road, rail, and air control.

automatism the performance of actions without awareness or conscious intent. It is seen in sleep-walking and in some (relatively rare) psychotic states.

automaton a mechanical figure imitating human or animal performance. Automatons are usually designed for decorative appeal as opposed to purely functional robots.

autonomic nervous system in mammals, the part of the nervous system which controls the involuntary activities of the smooth muscles (of the digestive tract, blood vessels), the heart, and the glands. The **sympathetic** system is involved in response to stress, when it speeds the heart rate, increases blood pressure and generally prepares the body for action. The **parasympathetic** system is more important when the body is at rest, since it slows the heart rate, decreases blood pressure, and stimulates the digestive system.

Autonomisti semi-clandestine amalgam of Marxist student organizations, linked with guerrilla groups and such acts as the kidnapping and murder of Italian premier Aldo Moro by the Red Brigade in 1978.

autopsy (or **post-mortem**) examination of a cadaver to determine the cause of death.

autosome any ◊chromosome in the cell other than a sex chromosome.

auto-suggestion conscious or unconscious acceptance of an idea as true, without demanding rational proof, but with potential subsequent effect for good or ill. Pioneered by ◊Coué in healing, it is used in modern psychotherapy to conquer nervous habits, dependence on tobacco, alcohol, and so on.

autotroph any living organism which synthesizes ◊organic substances from inorganic molecules using light or chemical energy. All green plants and many ◊planktonic organisms are autotrophs, using sunlight to convert carbon dioxide and water into sugars by ◊photosynthesis.

autumnal equinox see ◊equinox.

autumn crocus member of the family Liliaceae. One species, the mauve *meadow saffron* *Colchicum autumnale* yields *colchicine*, which is used in treating gout and in plant breeding (it causes plants to double the numbers of their chromosomes).

Auvergne ancient province of central France and a modern region (*départements* Allier, Cantal, Haute-Loire, and Puy-de-Dôme); area 26,013 sq km/10,044 sq mi; population (1982) 1,333,000. Its capital is Clermont-Ferrand. Mountainous, it lies in the heart of the Central Plateau, composed chiefly of volcanic rocks in several masses.

auxin a ◊plant hormone that promotes stem and root growth in plants. Auxins influence many aspects of plant growth and development, including cell enlargement, inhibition of development of axillary buds, ◊tropisms, and the initiation of roots. *Synthetic auxins* are used in rooting powders for cuttings, and in some weedkillers.

Ava ancient capital of Burma, on the river Irrawaddy, founded by Thadomin Payä in 1364 AD. Thirty kings reigned there until 1782, when a new capital, Amarapura, was founded by Bodaw Payä. In 1823 the site of the capital was transferred back to Ava by King Baggidaw.

avalanche (French *avaler*, to swallow) a fall of a mass of snow and ice down a steep slope. Avalanches occur because of the unstable nature of snow masses in mountain areas.

Avalokiteśvara in Mahāyāna Buddhism, one of the most important bodhisattvas, seen as embodying compassion. Known as *Guanyin* in China, *Kwannon* in Japan. One of the attendants of Amida Buddha.

Avalon in Celtic legend, the island of the blessed or paradise, and in the Arthurian legend the land of heroes, to which the dead king was conveyed. It has been associated with Glastonbury, in S W England.

avant-garde (French 'vanguard') in the arts, those artists or works which are in the forefront of new developments in their medium (and often in consequence considered 'difficult'). The term was introduced (as was 'reactionary') after the French Revolution, when it was used to describe any socialist political movement.

Avatar in Hindu mythology, the descent of a deity to earth in a visible form. Most famous are the ten Avatars of ◊Vishnu.

Avebury Europe's largest stone circle (diameter 412 m/450 yd), Wiltshire, England; probably constructed in the Neolithic period 3,500 years ago; it is linked with nearby ◊Silbury Hill. The village of Avebury was built within the circle, and many of the stones were used for building material.

Avebury John Lubbock, 1st Baron Avebury 1834–1913. British banker. Liberal (from 1886 Liberal Unionist) Member of Parliament 1870–1900, he was largely responsible for the Bank Holidays Act 1871 introducing statutory public holidays.

Ave Maria (Latin 'Hail, Mary') Christian prayer to the Virgin Mary, which takes its name from the archangel Gabriel's salutation of the Virgin Mary (Luke 11:28) when announcing that she would be the mother of the Messiah.

avens several low-growing plants of the rose family. *Wood avens* or *herb bennet Geum urbanum* grows in woods and shady places on damp soils, through most of Europe, N Asia and

North Africa. It has yellow five-petalled flowers and pinnate leaves.

average number that represents the typical member of a group of numbers. The simplest include the arithmetic and geometric ◊mean; the ◊median and the ◊root-mean-square are more complex averages.

Averroes (Arabic *Ibn Rushd*) 1126–1198. Arabian philosopher, who argued for the eternity of matter, and denied the immortality of the individual soul. His philosophical writings, including commentaries on Aristotle and Plato's *Republic*, became known to the West through Latin translations. He influenced Christian and Jewish writers, and reconciled Islamic and Greek thought.

Avignon city in Provence, France, capital of Vaucluse *département*, on the river Rhône NW of Marseilles. An important Gallic and Roman city, it has its 14th-century walls, the famous 12th-century bridge (only half still standing), a 13th-century cathedral, and the palace built 1334–42 during the residence here of the popes. Avignon was papal property 1348–1791. Population (1983) 88,650.

avocado tree of the laurel family. *Persia americana* is a native to Central America. Its dark green pear-shaped fruit have buttery-textured flesh and are used in salads.

avocet wading bird, genus *Recurvirostra*, with characteristic long narrow upturned bill used in sifting water as it feeds in the shallows. It is about 45 cm/1.5 ft long, has long legs, partly-webbed feet, and black and white plumage. There are four species.

Avogadro's hypothesis in chemistry, the law which states that equal volumes of all gases, when at the same temperature and pressure, have the same numbers of molecules. This law was first propounded by Count Amadeo Avogadro.

avoirdupois system of weights based on the pound (0.45 kg), which consists of 16 ounces (each of 16 drams) or 7,000 grains (each equal to 65 mg).

Avon any of several rivers in England and Scotland. The Avon in Warwickshire is associated with Shakespeare.

Avon county of SW England, area 1,347 sq km/520 sq mi; population (1981) 915,176. Created in 1974, it includes Bristol, the southern part of Gloucestershire, and a large part of Somerset, including Bath, Weston-super-Mare, Radstock, and Clevedon.

AWAC acronym for *Airborne Warning And Control System*.

Awe longest (37 km/23 mi) of the Scottish freshwater lochs, in Strathclyde, SE of Oban. It is drained by the river Awe into Loch Etive.

Axis the alliance of Nazi Germany and Fascist Italy before and during World War II. The *Rome-Berlin Axis* was formed in 1936, when Italy was being threatened with sanctions because of its invasion of Abyssinia, and became a full military and political alliance in May 1939. A 10-year alliance between Germany, Italy, and Japan (*Rome-Berlin-Tokyo Axis*) was signed in Sept 1940, and was subsequently joined by Hungary, Bulgaria, Romania, and the puppet states of Slovakia and Croatia. The Axis collapsed with the fall of Mussolini and the surrender of Italy in 1943.

axolotl aquatic larval form ('tadpole') of the Mexican salamander *Ambystoma mexicanum* which may reach 30 cm/1 ft long and breed without changing to the adult form.

axon the long thread-like extension of a ◊nerve cell.

Axum alternative transliteration of ◊Aksum, an ancient kingdom in Ethiopia.

ayatollah honorific title awarded to Shi'ite Muslims in Iran by popular consent, as, for example, to Ayatollah Ruhollah ◊Khomeini.

Ayckbourn Alan 1939– . British playwright and theatre director. His prolific output, characterized by his acute ear for comic dialogue, includes the trilogy *The Norman Conquests* 1974, *A Woman in Mind* 1986, and *A Small Family Business* 1987. Later works include *Man of the Moment* 1988.

aye-aye nocturnal tree-climbing ◊lemur *Daubentonia madagascariensis* of Madagascar. It has gnawing, rodent-like teeth and a long middle finger with which it probes for insects. Just over 1 m/3 ft long, it is now very rare through loss of its forest habitat.

Ayer A(lfred) J(ules) 1910–1989. British philosopher. He wrote *Language, Truth, and Logic* 1936, an exposition of the theory of 'logical positivism', presenting a criterion by which meaningful statements (essentially truths of logic, as well as statements derived from experience) could be distinguished from meaningless metaphysical utterances (for example, claims that there is a God, or that the world external to our own minds is illusory).

Ayers Rock vast ovate mass of pinkish rock in Northern Territory, Australia; 335 m/1,100 ft high and 9 km/6 mi round.

Ayesha 611–678. Third and favourite wife of the prophet Muhammad, whom he married when she was nine. Her father, Abu Bakr, became ◊caliph on Muhammad's death in 632, and she bitterly opposed the later succession to the caliphate of Ali, who had once accused her of infidelity.

Ayrshire former county of SW Scotland, with a 113 km/70 mi coastline on the Firth of Clyde. In 1975 the major part was merged in the region of Strathclyde, the remaining sector, approximately south of the Water of Girvan and including Girvan itself, became part of Dumfries and Galloway.

Ayurveda ancient Hindu system of medicine, the main principles of which are derived from the Vedas, and still practised in India in Ayurvedic hospitals and dispensaries.

azalea plant of the family Ericaceae, closely related to *Rhododendron*, in which genus they are now generally included. There are several species native to Asia and North America, and from these many cultivated varieties have been derived

Azaña Manuel 1880–1940. Spanish politician and first prime minister 1931–33 of the second Spanish republic. He was last president of the republic during the Civil War 1936–39, before the establishment of a dictatorship under Francisco Franco.

Azerbaijan country in W Asia, bounded S by Iran, E by the Caspian Sea, W by Armenia and Georgia, and N by Russia.

Azerbaijan, Iranian two provinces of NW Iran, Eastern Azerbaijan (capital Tabriz), population (1986) 4,114,000, and Western Azerbaijan (capital Orúmiyeh), population 1,972,000. Azerbaijanis in Iran, as in the Republic of Azerbaijan, are mainly Shi'ite Muslim ethnic Turks, descendants of followers of the Khans from the ◊Mongol Empire.

Azhar, El Muslim university and mosque in Cairo, Egypt. Founded in 970 by Jawhar, commander in chief of the army of the Fatimid caliph, it is claimed to be the oldest university in the world. It became the centre of Islamic learning, with several subsidiary foundations, and is now primarily a school of Koranic teaching.

azimuth in the sky, the angular distance eastwards along the horizon, measured from due north, of an object through which a meridian (vertical circle) passes through that object.

Azores group of nine islands in the N Atlantic; area 2,335 sq km/922 sq mi; population (1987) 254,000. They are outlying peaks of the Mid-Atlantic Ridge, and are volcanic in origin. The capital is Ponta Delgada on the main island, San Miguel.

Azerbaijan
Republic of

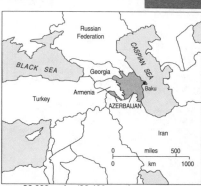

area 86,600 sq km/33,400 sq mi
capital Baku
towns Gyandzha (formerly Kirovabad), Sumgait
physical Caspian Sea; the country ranges from semidesert to the Caucasus Mountains
head of state Albulfaz Elchibey from 1992
head of government to be appointed
political system emergent democracy
products oil, iron, copper, fruit, vines, cotton, silk, carpets
currency rouble

population (1990) 7,145,600 (83% Azeri, 6% Russian, 6% Armenian)
language Turkic
religion traditionally Shi'ite Muslim
chronology
1917–18 A member of the anti-Bolshevik Transcaucasian Federation.
1918 Became an independent republic.
1920 Occupied by the Red Army.
1922–36 Formed part of the Transcaucasian Federal Republic with Georgia and Armenia.
1936 Became a constituent republic of the USSR.
1988–89 Dispute with neighbouring Armenia over Nagorno-Karabakh resulted in violent clashes.
1990 Soviet troops dispatched to Baku to restore order and state of emergency declared. Secession from the USSR was announced.
1991 Independence declared and Azerbaijan joined the new Commonwealth of Independent States (CIS). Nagorno-Karabakh declared its independence.
1992 Azerbaijan was admitted into Conference on Security and Cooperation in Europe (CSCE); became a member of the United Nations (UN); and was accorded diplomatic recognition by the USA. Albulfaz Elchibey, leader of the Popular Front, was elected president. The fight for Nagorno-Karabakh intensified.
1993 Prime Minister Rakham Guseinov resigned over differences with President Elchibey.

Azorín pen name of José Martínez Ruiz 1873–1967. Spanish novelist and poet. His works include the autobiographical *La voluntad/The Choice* 1902 and *Antonio Azorín* 1903 – the author adopted the latter name as his pen name.

Azov (Russian *Azovskoye More*) inland sea of Europe, forming a gulf in the NE of the Black Sea, between Ukraine and Russia. It is an important source of freshwater fish.

AZT drug, now known as zidovudine, used in the treatment of ◊AIDS.

Aztec member of a Mexican ◊American Indian people who migrated from further north in the 12th century, and in 1325 began reclaiming lake marshland to build their capital, Tenochtitlán, on the site of modern Mexico City. Under Montezuma I (reigned from 1440), they created an empire in central and southern Mexico.

BA in education, abbreviation for *Bachelor of Arts*.

Baader-Meinhof gang popular name for the West German guerrilla group the *Rote Armee Fraktion*/Red Army Faction, active from 1968 against what it perceived as US imperialism. Its two leaders were Andreas Baader (1943–77) and Ulrike Meinhof (1934–76).

Baal Semitic word meaning 'lord' or 'owner', used as a divine title of their chief male gods by the Phoenicians, or Canaanites. Their worship as deities of fertility, often orgiastic and of a phallic character, was strongly denounced by the Hebrew prophets.

Baalbek city of ancient Syria, in modern Lebanon, 60 km/36 mi NE of Beirut, 1,150 m/3,000 ft above sea level. Originally a centre of Baal worship. The Greeks identified Baal with Helios, the sun, and renamed Baalbek *Heliopolis*. Its ruins, including Roman temples, survive; the Temple of Bacchus, built in the 2nd century AD, is still almost intact.

Ba'ath Party socialist party aiming at the extended union of all Arab countries, active in Iraq and Syria.

Bab, the Mirza Ali Mohammad 1819–1850. Persian religious leader, born in Shiraz, founder of ◊Babism. In 1844 he proclaimed that he was a gateway to the Hidden Imam, a new messenger of Allah who was to come. He gained a large following whose activities caused the Persian authorities to fear a rebellion, and who were therefore persecuted. The Bab was executed for heresy.

Babbage Charles 1792–1871. British mathematician credited with being the inventor of the computer. He designed an ◊analytical engine, a general-purpose computing device for performing different calculations according to a program input on punched cards (an idea borrowed from the Jacquard loom). This device was never built, but it embodied many of the principles on which modern digital computers are based.

Babbit metal an ◊alloy of tin, copper and antimony used to make bearings, developed by the American inventor Isaac Babbit in 1839.

babbler bird of the thrush family Muscicapidae with a loud babbling cry. Babblers, subfamily Timaliinae, are found in the Old World, and there are some 250 species in the group.

Babel Hebrew name for the city of ◊Babylon, chiefly associated with the *Tower of Babel*

which, in the Genesis story in the Old Testament, was erected in the plain of Shinar by the descendants of Noah. It was a ziggurat or staged temple seven storeys high (100 m/300 ft) with a shrine of Marduk on the summit. It was built by Nabopolassar, father of Nebuchadnezzar, and was destroyed when Sennacherib sacked the city 689 BC.

Babel Isaak Emmanuilovich 1894–1939/40. Russian writer. Born in Odessa, he was an ardent supporter of the Revolution and fought with Budyenny's cavalry in the Polish campaign of 1921–22, an experience which inspired *Konarmiya/Red Cavalry* 1926. Best known of his other works is *Odesskie rasskazy/Stories from Odessa* 1924, which portrays the life of the Odessa Jews.

Baber (Arabic 'lion') title given to ◊Zahir ud-din Muhammad, founder of the Mughal Empire in N India.

Babeuf François Noël 1760–1797. French revolutionary journalist, a pioneer of practical socialism. In 1794 he founded a newspaper in Paris, later known as the *Tribune of the People*, in which he demanded the equality of all people. He was guillotined for conspiring against the Directory (see ◊French Revolution).

Babi faith alternative name for ◊Baha'i faith.

Babington Anthony 1561–1586. English traitor who hatched a plot to assassinate Elizabeth I and replace her by ◊Mary, Queen of Scots; its discovery led to Mary's execution and his own.

Babism religious movement founded by Mirza Ali Mohammad ('the Bab'). An offshoot of Islam, its main difference is the belief that Muhammad was not the last of the prophets. The movement split into two groups after the death of the Bab: Baha'ullah, the leader of one of these groups, founded the ◊Baha'i faith.

Babi Yar site of a massacre of Jews by the Germans in 1941, near Kiev, USSR.

baboon type of large monkey, genus *Papio*, with a long dog-like muzzle and large canine teeth,

Babbage This prototype of a complex calculating machine was created by English mathematician Charles Babbage.

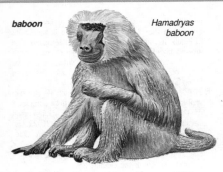

baboon — *Hamadryas baboon*

spending much of its time on the ground in open country. Males, with head and body up to 1.1 m/3.5 ft long, are larger than females and dominant males rule the 'troops' in which baboons live. They inhabit Africa and SW Arabia.

Babylon capital of ancient Babylonia, on the left bank of the Euphrates. The site is in modern Iraq, 88 km/55 mi S of Baghdad and 8 km/5 mi N of Hilla, which is built chiefly of bricks from the ruins of Babylon. The *hanging gardens of Babylon,* one of the seven wonders of the world, were probably erected on a vaulted stone base, the only stone construction in the mud-built city.

Babylonian captivity the exile of Jewish deportees to Babylon after Nebuchadnezzar II's capture of Jerusalem in 586 BC.

Baccalauréat the French examination providing the school-leaving certificate and qualification for university entrance, also available on an international basis as an alternative to English ◊A Levels.

Bacchus in Greek and Roman mythology, the god of fertility (see ◊Dionysus) and of wine; his rites (*Bacchanalia*) were orgiastic.

Bach Johann Sebastian 1685–1750. German composer. Appointments included positions at the courts of Weimar and Anhalt-Köther, and from 1723 until his death musical director at St Thomas's choir school in Leipzig. Bach was a master of contrapuntal technique, and his music marks the culmination of the Baroque polyphonic style. His orchestral music includes the six *Brandenburg concertos*, other concertos for clavier and for violin, and four orchestral suits. Bach's keyboard music, for clavier and for organ, is of equal importance. He also wrote chamber music and songs.

bacillus a group of rod-like ◊bacteria that occur everywhere in the soil and air, and are responsible for diseases such as anthrax as well as causing food spoilage.

backgammon a popular boardgame revived in the 1970s. The children's version is Ludo. The Old English form was 'back game'.

background radiation the electromagnetic radiation, also known as the 3° radiation, left over from the original formation of the Universe in the Big Bang around 15,000 million years ago. It corresponds to an overall background temperature of 3K, or 3° above absolute zero.

back to the land a movement in late Victorian England which emphasized traditional values and rural living as a reaction against industrialism and urban society.

Bacon Francis 1561–1626. English statesman, philosopher, and essayist. He became Lord Chancellor 1618, and the same year confessed to bribe-taking, was fined £40,000 (which was paid by the king), and spent four days in the Tower of London. His works include *Essays* 1597, *The Advancement of Learning* 1605, and *The New Atlantis* 1626.

Bacon Francis 1909–1992. British painter, born in Dublin. He came to London in 1925 and taught himself to paint. He practised abstract art, then developed a distorted Expressionist style, with tortured figures presented in loosely defined space. Since 1945 he has focused on studies of figures, as in his series of screaming popes based on the portrait of Innocent X by Velázquez.

bacteria microscopic unicellular organisms with prokaryotic cells (see ◊prokaryote). They reproduce by ◊binary fission, and since this may occur approximately every 20 minutes, a single bacterium is potentially capable of producing 16 million copies of itself in a day. Bacteria mutate readily, a characteristic which accounts for the rapid emergence of strains which are resistant to antibiotics. Although generally considered harmful, certain types of bacteria are essential in many food and industrial processes.

bacteriophage a ◊virus that attacks bacteria.

Bactria former region of central Asia (now divided between Afghanistan, Pakistan, and Tajikistan) which was partly conquered by ◊Alexander the Great; in the 3rd–6th centuries BC it was a great centre of E–W trade and cultural exchange.

Bactrian one of the two species of ◊camel, found in Asia.

Babylon The Ishtar Gate surrounded by ruins in Babylon, now Iraq.

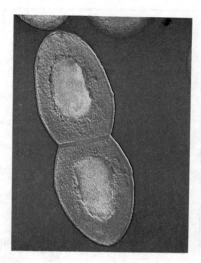

bacteria transmission electron micrograph showing a bacterium (*Streptococcus*) in the final stages of division by binary fission.

Baden former state of SW Germany, which had Karlsruhe as its capital. Baden was captured from the Romans in 282 by the Alemanni; later it became a margravate, and in 1806 a grand duchy. A state of the German empire 1871–1918, then a republic, and under Hitler a *Gau* (province), it was divided between the *Länder* of Württemberg-Baden and Baden in 1945, and in 1952 made part of ◊Baden-Württemberg.

Baden-Powell Robert Stephenson Smyth, 1st Baron Baden-Powell 1857–1941. British general, founder of the Scout Association. He distinguished himself in the defence of Mafeking, Bophuthatswana, South Africa, during the Second South African War. After 1907 he devoted his time to developing the Scout movement, which rapidly spread throughout the world.

Baden-Württemberg administrative region (German *Land*) of Germany
area 35,750 sq km/13,805 sq mi
capital Stuttgart
towns Karlsruhe, Mannheim, Freiburg, Heidelberg
physical Black Forest; Rhine boundary south and west; source of the Danube; see also ◊Swabia
products wine, jewellery, watches, clocks, musical instruments, textiles, chemicals, iron, steel, electrical equipment, surgical instruments
population (1988) 9,390,000
history formed in 1952 (following a plebiscite) by

badger

American badger

the merger of the *Länder* Baden, Württemberg-Baden, and Württemberg-Hohenzollern.

Bader Douglas 1910–1982. British fighter pilot. He lost both legs in a flying accident in 1931, but had a distinguished flying career in World War II. He was knighted in 1976 for his work for disabled people.

badger large mammal of the weasel family with molar teeth of a crushing type adapted to a partly vegetable diet, and short strong legs with long claws suitable for digging. The Eurasian *common badger Meles meles* is about 1 m/3 ft long, with long coarse greyish hair on the back, and a white face with a broad black stripe along each side. Mainly a woodland animal, it is harmless and nocturnal, and spends the day in a system of burrows called a 'sett'. It feeds on roots, a variety of fruits and nuts, insects, worms, mice, and young rabbits.

badlands a barren landscape cut by erosion into a maze of ravines, pinnacles, gullies, and sharp-edged ridges. The best-known badland region is in South Dakota and Nebraska, USA.

badminton indoor racket game played on a court with a feathered shuttlecock instead of a ball. Similar to lawn ◊tennis but played on a smaller court, the object is the same: to force the opponent(s) to be unable to return the shuttlecock.

Badoglio Pietro 1871–1956. Italian soldier and Fascist politician. A veteran of campaigns against the peoples of Tripoli and Cyrenaica, in 1935 he became commander in chief in Ethiopia, adopting ruthless measures to break patriot resistance, and being created viceroy of Ethiopia and duke of Addis Ababa in 1936. He succeeded Mussolini as prime minister of Italy from July 1943 to June 1944.

Baedeker Karl 1801–1859. German publisher of foreign-travel guides; these are now based in Hamburg (before World War II in Leipzig).

Baekeland Leo Hendrik 1863–1944. US chemist, the inventor of ◊bakelite, the first commercial plastic. He later made a photographic paper, Velox, which could be developed in artificial light.

Baffin William 1584–1622. English navigator and explorer. In 1616, he and Robert Bylot discovered Baffin Bay and reached latitude 77° 45′ which for 236 years remained the 'furthest north'.

BAFTA abbreviation for *British Academy of Film and Television Arts.*

Baggara a Bedouin people of the Nile Basin, principally in Kordofan, Sudan, W of the White Nile. They are Muslims, traditionally occupied in cattle-breeding and big-game hunting.

Baghdad historic city and capital of Iraq, on the Tigris; population (1985) 4,649,000. Industries include oil refining, distilling, tanning, tobacco processing, and the manufacture of textiles and cement. Founded in 762, it became Iraq's capital in 1921. During the Gulf War 1991, it was badly damaged by air raids by the UN coalition forces.

Baghdad Pact military treaty of 1955 concluded by the UK, Iran, Iraq, Pakistan, and Turkey, with the USA cooperating; it was replaced by the ◊Central Treaty Organization (CENTO) when Iraq withdrew in 1959.

bagpipe ancient musical instrument of many countries, known to the Romans and ancient Egyptians and found in different forms in various parts of Europe. It consists of a chanter (melody) pipe and drones (which emit invariable notes to supply a ground bass) and sound is emitted when a windbag in inflated by the performer.

Baha'i religion founded in the 19th century from a Muslim splinter group, ◊Babism, by the Persian

badminton

A volleying game played on an indoor court with rackets and a shuttlecock. It is played as singles or pairs and the object is to play the shuttle over the raised net and to score points by grounding the shuttle in the opponent's half of the court or by forcing an error. Only the server can score points. A game is won when one side reaches 15 points (11 in women's singles).

Shuttles
Shuttles come in two forms. They can be either synthetic or made with 16 goose feathers. The feathered cock is the one used in major tournament play while the plastic cock is used at junior level and for practice.

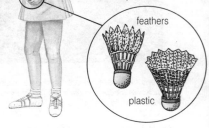

feathers

plastic

grips

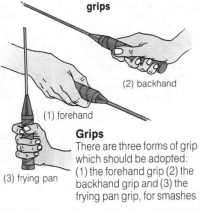

(2) backhand

(1) forehand

(3) frying pan

Grips
There are three forms of grip which should be adopted: (1) the forehand grip (2) the backhand grip and (3) the frying pan grip, for smashes

Service
The shuttle is dropped from the hand onto the racket and the service must be underhand and hit over the net. Overhand serving, like that in lawn tennis, is not permitted in badminton.

dimensions of the badminton court

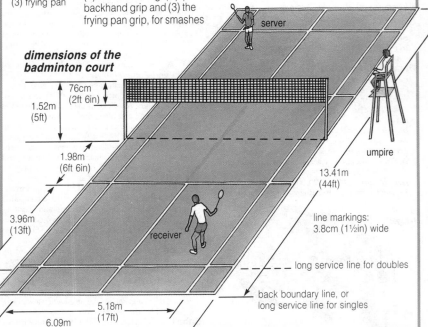

server

umpire

76cm (2ft 6in)

1.52m (5ft)

1.98m (6ft 6in)

3.96m (13ft)

76.2cm (2ft 6in)

receiver

13.41m (44ft)

line markings: 3.8cm (1½in) wide

– – – – long service line for doubles

back boundary line, or long service line for singles

5.18m (17ft)

6.09m (20ft)

Bahamas
Commonwealth of the

area 13,864 sq km/5,352 sq mi
capital Nassau on New Providence
physical comprises 700 tropical coral islands and about 1,000 cays

head of state Elizabeth II from 1973 represented by governor general
head of government Hubert Ingraham from 1992
political system constitutional monarchy
exports cement, pharmaceuticals, petroleum products, crawfish, rum, pulpwood; over half the islands' employment comes from tourism
currency Bahamian dollar
population (1990 est) 251,000; annual growth rate 1.8%
language English and some Creole
religion Christian
literacy 95% (1986)
GDP $2.7 bn (1987); $11,261 per head
chronology
1964 Internal self-government attained.
1967 First national assembly elections.
1972 Constitutional conference to discuss full independence.
1973 Full independence achieved.
1983 Allegations of drug trafficking by government ministers.
1984 Deputy prime minister and two cabinet ministers resigned. Pindling denied any personal involvement and was endorsed as party leader.
1987 Pindling re-elected despite claims of fraud.
1992 Hubert Ingraham won absolute majority in assembly elections.

◊Baha'ullah. The most important principle of his message was that all great religious leaders are manifestations of the unknowable God and all scriptures are sacred. There is no priesthood: all Baha'is are expected to teach, and to work towards world unification. There are about 4.5 million Baha'is worldwide.

Bahamas group of islands in the Caribbean, off the SE coast of Florida.

Baha'ullah Title of Mirza Hosein Ali 1817–1892. Persian founder of the ◊Baha'i religion.

Bahrain group of islands in the Arabian Gulf, between Saudi Arabia and Iran.

Baikal Russian *Baykal Ozero* largest freshwater lake in Asia 31,500 sq km/12,150 sq mi and deepest in the world (up to 1,740 m/5,710 ft), in S Siberia, Russia. Fed by more than 300 rivers, it is drained only by the Lower Angara. It has sturgeon fisheries and rich fauna.

Baikonur launch site for spacecraft, at Tyuratam, Kazakhstan, near the Aral Sea. All Soviet space probes and crewed Soyuz missions were launched from here.

bail the setting at liberty of a person in legal custody on an undertaking, (usually backed by some security, given either by that person or by someone else), to attend at a court at a stated time and place. If the person does not attend, the bail may be forfeited. The Bail Act of 1976 presumes that a suspect will be granted bail, unless the police can give good reasons why not, for example, by showing that a further offence may take place.

Bailey Donald Coleman 1901–1985. British engineer, inventor in World War II of the portable *Bailey bridge*, made of interlocking, interchangeable, adjustable and easily transportable units.

bailiff term originating in Normandy as the name for a steward of an estate. It retained this meaning in England throughout the Middle Ages, and could also denote a sheriff's assistant.

Bainbridge Beryl 1933– . British novelist, originally an actress, whose works have the drama and economy of a stage-play. They include *The*

Dressmaker 1973, *The Bottle Factory Outing* 1974, the collected short stories in *Mum and Mr Armitage* 1985 and *The Birthday Boys* 1991.

Baird John Logie 1888–1946. British electrical engineer, who pioneered television. In 1925 he gave the first public demonstration of television, and in 1926, pioneered fibre optics, radar (in advance of Robert ◊Watson-Watt) and infra-red television for the long-distance detection of objects.

Bakelite the first synthetic ◊plastic, discovered by Leo ◊Baekeland in 1909. Bakelite is hard, tough and heatproof, and is used as an electrical insulator. It is made by the reaction together of phenol and formaldehyde, first producing a powdery resin which sets solid when heated. Objects are made by subjecting the resin to compression moulding (simultaneous heat and pressure in a mould).

Baker Benjamin 1840–1907. British engineer, who designed (with British engineer John Fowler 1817–1898) London's first underground railway (the Metropolitan and District) in 1869, the Forth Bridge, Scotland, 1890, and the original Aswan Dam on the River Nile, Egypt.

Baker Kenneth (Wilfrid) 1934– . British Conservative politician, home sectretary 1990–92, and

Baird John Baird engaged in his pioneering work with television, 1943

Bahrain
State of
(Dawlat al Bahrayn)

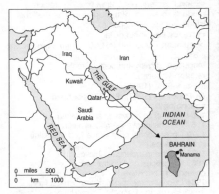

area 688 sq km/266 sq mi
capital Manama on the largest island (also called Bahrain)
towns oil port Mina Sulman
physical 33 islands, flat and hot

head of state and government Sheikh Isa bin Sulman Al-Khalifa (1933–) from 1961
political system absolute emirate
exports oil and natural gas
currency Bahrain dinar
population (1990 est) 512,000 (two-thirds are nationals); annual growth rate 4.4%
life expectancy men 67, women 71
language Arabic, Farsi
religion Muslin (Shi'ite 60%, Sunni 40%)
literacy 79% male/64% female (1985 est)
GDP $3.5 bn (1987); $7,772 per head
chronology
1816 Under British protection.
1968 Britain announced its intention to withdraw its forces. Bahrain formed, with Qatar and the Trucial States, the Federation of Arab Emirates.
1971 Qatar and the Trucial States left the federation and Bahrain became an independent state.
1973 New constitution adopted, with an elected national assembly.
1975 Prime minister resigned and national assembly dissolved. Emir and his family assumed virtually absolute power.
1986 Gulf University established in Bahrain. A causeway (24 km/15 mi long) linking the island with Saudi Arabia was opened.
1991 Bahrain joined the UN coalition opposing Iraq in the Gulf War.

chair of the Conservative Party 1989–90. Under prime minister John Major he was made home secretary.

Baker III James Addison 1930– . US politician. He was White House Chief of Staff under Reagan 1980–84, Treasury Secretary 1984–88, managed Bush's presidential campaign in 1988, and was Secretary of State 1989–92.

Bakewell Robert 1725–1795. Pioneer improver of farm livestock. From his home in Leicestershire, England, he developed the Dishley or 'New Leicester' breed of sheep and also worked on raising the beef-producing qualities of Longhorn cattle.

Bakke Allan 1940– . US student who, in 1978, gave his name to a test case claiming 'reverse discrimination' when appealing against his exclusion from medical school, since less well-qualified blacks were to be admitted as part of a special programme for ethnic minorities. He won his case against quotas before the Supreme Court.

Bakst Leon. Stage name of Russian artist Leon Rosenberg 1866–1924. He was a talented theatrical designer. From 1900–09 he was scenic artist to the Imperial theatres; then scenery painter and costume designer for ◊Diaghilev's ballets.

Baku capital city of the Republic of Azerbaijan, and industrial port (oil refining) on the Caspian Sea; population (1987) 1,741,000. Baku is a major oil centre, and is linked by pipelines with Batumi on the Black Sea.

Bakunin Mikhail 1814–1876. Russian anarchist, active in Europe. In 1848 he was expelled from France as a revolutionary agitator. In Switzerland in the 1860s he became recognized as the leader of the anarchist movement. In 1869 he joined the First International (a coordinating socialist body) but, after stormy conflicts with Karl Marx, was expelled 1872.

Balaclava, Battle of in the Crimean War, an engagement on 25 Oct 1854 near a town in Ukraine, 10 km/6 mi SE of Sevastopol. It was the scene of the ill-timed but gallant *Charge of the*

Light Brigade of British cavalry againt the Russian entrenched artillery. Of the 673 soldiers who took part, there were 272 casualties.

Balakirev Mily Alexeyevich 1837–1910. Russian composer. He wrote orchestral and piano music, songs, and a symphonic poem 'Tamara'. He was leader of the group known as The Five or The Mighty Handful and taught its members, Mussorgsky, Rimsky-Korsakov and Borodin.

balalaika Russian musical instrument, resembling a guitar. It has a triangular sound box and two, three, or four strings.

balance an apparatus for weighing or measuring mass. The various types include a beam balance, consisting of a centrally-pivoted lever with pans hanging from each end, and a spring balance in which the object to be weighed stretches (or compresses) a vertical coil spring fitted with a pointer that indicates the weight on a scale. Kitchen and bathroom scales are balances.

balance of nature in ecology, the idea that there is an inherent stability in most ◊ecosystems, and that human interference can disrupt this stability. Organisms in the ecosystem are adapted to each other, waste products produced by one species are used by another, resources used by some are replenished by others, and so on.

balance of payments in economics, a tabular account of a country's debit and credit transactions with other countries. Items are divided into the *current account,* which includes both visible trade (imports and exports) and invisible trade (such as transport, tourism, interest, and dividends), and the *capital account* which includes investment in and out of the country, international grants and loans. Deficits or surpluses on these accounts are brought into balance by buying and selling reserves of foreign currencies.

balance of power in politics, the theory that the best way of ensuring international order is to have power so distributed among states that no single state is able to achieve a preponderant position.

The term, which may also refer more simply to the actual distribution of power, is one of the most enduring concepts in international relations. Since the development of nuclear weapons, it has been asserted that the balance of power has been replaced by a *balance of terror*.

balance of trade the balance of trade transactions of a country recorded in its current account; it forms one component of the country's ◊balance of payments.

balance sheet a statement of the financial position of a company or individual on a specific date, showing both ◊assets and ◊liabilities.

Balanchine George 1904–1983. US choreographer, born in Russia. His many works include *Apollon Musagète* 1928 and *The Prodigal Son* 1929 for Diaghilev, several works for music by Stravinsky such as *Agon* 1957 and *Duo Concertante* 1972 and musicals such as *On Your Toes* 1936 and *The Boys from Syracuse* 1938.

Balboa Vasco Núñez de 1475–1517. Spanish ◊conquistador, the first European to see the Pacific Ocean, on 29 Sept 1513, from the isthmus of Darien (now Panama). He was made admiral of the Pacific and governor of Panama, but was removed by Spanish court intrigue, imprisoned and executed.

Balder in Norse mythology, the son of Odin and Frigga and husband of Nanna, the best, wisest, and most loved of all the gods. He was killed, at Loki's instigation, by a twig of mistletoe shot by the blind god Hodur.

Baldung Grien Hans 1484/85–1545. German Renaissance painter, engraver, and designer, based in Strasbourg. His best-known theme is *Death and the Maiden*, of which he painted several versions.

Baldwin James 1924–1987. US writer, born in Harlem, New York, who portrayed the condition of black Americans in contemporary society. His works include the novels *Go Tell It on the Mountain* 1953, *Another Country* 1962, and *Just Above My Head* 1979; the play *The Amen Corner* 1955; and the autobiographical essays *Notes of a Native Son* 1955 and *The Fire Next Time* 1963.

Baldwin Stanley, 1st Earl Baldwin of Bewdley 1867–1947. British Conservative politician, prime minister 1923–24, 1924–29, and 1935–37; he weathered the general strike 1926, secured complete adult suffrage 1928, and handled the abdication crisis of Edward VIII 1936.

Balearic Islands (Spanish *Baleares*) Mediterranean group of islands forming an autonomous region of Spain; including Majorca, Minorca, and Ibiza
area 5,014 sq km/1,935 sq mi
capital Palma; on Majorca
products figs, olives, oranges, wine, brandy, coal, iron, slate, tourism is important
population (1981) 685,088
history a Roman colony from 123 BC, the Balearic Islands were an independent Moorish kingdom 1009–1232; the islands were conquered by Aragon in 1343.

Balewa alternative title of Nigerian politician ◊Tafawa Balewa.

Balfour Arthur James, 1st Earl of Balfour 1848–1930. British Conservative politician, prime minister 1902–05 and foreign secretary 1916–19, when he issued the ◊Balfour Declaration and was involved in peace negotiations after World War I.

Balfour Declaration a letter, dated 2 Nov 1917, from the British foreign secretary, A J Balfour, to Lord Rothschild (chair, British Zionist Federation) stating: 'HM government view with favour the establishment in Palestine of a national home for the Jewish people' but without prejudicing non-Jewish peoples; it led to the foundation of Israel in 1948.

Bali island of Indonesia, E of Java, one of the Sunda Islands
area 5,800 sq km/2,240 sq mi
capital Denpasar
physical volcanic mountains
products gold and silver work, woodcarving, weaving, copra, salt, coffee
population (1980) 2,470,000
history Bali's Hindu culture goes back to the 7th century; the Dutch gained control of the island by 1908.

Balkans peninsula of SE Europe, stretching into the Mediterranean between the Adriatic and Aegean Seas, comprising Albania, Bulgaria, Greece, Romania, Turkey-in-Europe, and Yugoslavia. It is joined to the rest of Europe by an isthmus 1,200 km/750 mi wide between Rijeka on the W and the mouth of the Danube on the Black Sea to the E.

Balkan Wars two wars 1912–13 and 1913 which resulted in the expulsion by the Balkan states of Ottoman Turkey from Europe except for a small area around Istanbul.

ballad type of popular poem which tells a story, primarily intended for singing at the communal ring-dance, the refrains representing the chorus. Poets of the Romantic movement both in England and in Germany were greatly influenced by the ballad revival, for example, the *Lyrical Ballads* 1798 of Wordsworth and Coleridge.

ballade in music, an instrumental piece based on a story; a form used in piano works by Chopin and Liszt. In literature, a poetic form developed in France in the later Middle Ages from popular ◊ballad, generally consisting of one or more groups

Ballesteros Seve Ballesteros playing to win at the British Open, 1988.

Bandaranaike *Sirimavo Bandaranaike, who became prime minister of Sri Lanka in 1960, was the world's first woman prime minister.*

Banda *Hastings Banda, first president of Malawi.*

of three stanzas of seven or eight lines each, followed by a shorter stanza or envoy, the last line being repeated as a chorus.

Ballard J(ames) G(raham) 1930– . British novelist, whose works include science fiction on the theme of disaster, such as *The Drowned World* 1962, and *High-Rise* 1975, and the partly autóbiographical *Empire of the Sun* 1984, dealing with his internment in China during World War II.

Ballesteros Severiano 'Seve' 1957– . Spanish golfer who came to prominence 1976 and has been dominant in Europe, as well as winning leading tournaments in the US. He has won the British Open three times 1979, 1984, 1988.

ballet a theatrical representation in dance form where music also plays a major part in telling a story or conveying a mood. In the 20th century Russian ballet has had a vital influence on the classical tradition in the West, and modern ballet has developed in the USA through the work of George Balanchine and Martha Graham, and in England through the influence of Marie Rambert.

ballet blanc (French 'white ballet') a ballet in which the female dancers wear calf-length white dresses, such as *Giselle*. The costume was introduced by Marie ◊Taglioni in *La Sylphide* 1832.

ballistics study of the motion of projectiles.

balloon impermeable fabric bag which rises when filled with gas lighter than the surrounding air. In 1783, the first successful human ascent was in Paris, in a hot-air balloon designed by the ◊Montgolfier brothers. During the French Revolution balloons were used for observation; in World War II they were used to defend London against low-flying aircraft. They are now used for sport, and as a means of meteorological, infra-red, gamma ray, and ultra-violet observation. The first transatlantic crossing by balloon was made 11–17 Aug 1978 by a US team.

ballroom dancing collective term for social dances such as the foxtrot, quickstep, tango, and waltz.

ball valve a valve used in lavatory cisterns to cut off the water supply when it reaches the correct level. It consists of a flat rubber washer at one end of a pivoting arm and a hollow ball at the other. The ball floats on the water surface, rising as the cistern fills, and at the correct level the rubber washer is pushed against the water-inlet pipe, cutting off the flow.

Balmoral Castle residence of the British royal family in Scotland on the river Dee, 10.5 km/6¹/2 mi NE of Braemar, Grampian region.

balsam garden plants of the genus *Impatiens*, which are usually annuals with red or white flowers.

Baltic, Battle of the naval battle fought off Copenhagen on 2 Apr 1801, in which a British fleet under Sir Hyde Parker, with ◊Nelson as second-in-command, annihilated the Danish navy.

Baltic Sea large shallow arm of the North Sea, extending NE from the narrow Skagerrak and Kattegat, between Sweden and Denmark, to the Gulf of Bothnia between Sweden and Finland. Its coastline is 8,000 km/5,000 mi long, and its area, including the gulfs of Riga, Finland and Bothnia, is 422,300 sq km/163,000 sq mi. Its shoreline is shared by Denmark, Germany, Poland, USSR, Finland, and Sweden.

Baltimore industrial port and largest city in Maryland, USA, on the W shore of Chesapeake Bay, NE of Washington DC; population (1980) 787,000. Industries include shipbuilding, oil refining, food processing, and the manufacture of steel, chemicals and aerospace equipment.

Baluch inhabitant of Baluchistan, SW Asia. The common religion is Islam, and they speak Baluchi (a member of the Iranian branch of the Indo-European language family).

Baluchistan mountainous desert area, comprising a province of Iran (capital Zahedan),a province of Pakistan of the same name, and a small area of Afghanistan, total population (1981) 4,332,000. Total area 347 200 sq km/134 100 sq mi. The port of Gwadar in Pakistan is strategically important, on the Indian Ocean and the Strait of Hormuz.

Balzac Honoré de 1799–1850. French novelist. His first success was *Les Chouans/The Chouans* 1829, inspired by Scott. This was the beginning of the long series of novels, *La Comédie humaine/The Human Comedy*, which he intended to consist of 143 volumes depicting 19th-century French life in every conceivable aspect, but of which about 80 were completed.

Bamako capital and port of Mali on the River Niger; population (1976) 404,022. It produces pharmaceuticals, chemicals, textiles, tobacco and metal products.

bamboo plant of the group Bambuseae, belonging to the grass family, Gramineae, mainly found in tropical and sub-tropical countries, and remarkable for the gigantic size which some species can attain.

Bangkok the Royal Palace in Bangkok contains within its 1900 m perimeter walls fine temples, including the Chapel Royal of the Emerald Buddha.

banana tree-like tropical plants 8 m/25 ft high, of the family Musaceae, which include the commercial *banana,* sterile hybrid forms of the genus *Musa.*

band music group, usually falling into a specialist category, for example, *military* comprising woodwind, brass, percussion; *brass,* solely brass and percussion, which are especially typical of the north of England; *marching,* a variant of the brass, which developed as an adjunct of American football and has been introduced to Britain: *dance, jazz, rock and pop* generally electric guitar, bass, and drums (or drum machine), variously augmented; and *steel* popular in the West Indies, especially Trinidad, using percussion instruments made from oildrums.

Banda Hastings Kamuzu *c.* 1902– . Malawi politician, president from 1966. He led his country's independence movement and was prime minister of Nyasaland (the former name of Malawi) from 1963. He became Malawi's first president 1966 and 1971 and was named president for life; his rule has been authoritarian. Despite civil unrest during 1992, he has resisted calls for free, multiparty elections.

Bandaranaike Sirimavo (born Ratwatte) 1916– . Sri Lankan politician, who succeeded her husband Solomon Bandaranaike to become the world's first woman prime minister 1960–65 and 1970–177, but was expelled from parliament in 1980 for abuse of her powers while in office. She was largely responsible for the new constitution in 1972.

Bandaranaike Solomon West Ridgeway Dias 1899–1959. Sri Lankan nationalist politician. In 1951 he founded the Sri Lanka Freedom Party and in 1956 became prime minister, pledged to a socialist programme and a neutral foreign policy. He failed to satisfy extremists and was assassinated by a Buddhist monk.

bandicoot type of small marsupial mammal inhabiting Australia and New Guinea. There are about 11 species, family Peramelidae, rat or rabbit-sized and living in burrows. They have long snouts, eat insects, and are nocturnal.

banding term used in UK education for the division of school pupils into broad streams by ability. Banding is used by some local authorities to ensure that comprehensive schools receive an intake of children spread right across the ability range. Banding is used internally by some schools as a means of avoiding groups of very wide mixed ability.

Bandung commercial city and capital of Jawa Barat province on the island of Java, Indonesia; population (1980) 1,201,000. Bandung is the third-largest city in Indonesia and was the administrative centre when the country was the Netherlands East Indies.

Bandung Conference the first conference 1955 of the Afro-Asian nations, proclaiming anti-colonialism and neutrality between East and West.

Bangalore capital of Karnataka state, S India; population (1981) 2,914,000. Industries include electronics, aircraft and machine tools construction, and coffee.

Bangkok capital and port of Thailand, on the river Chao Phraya; population (1990) 6,019,000. Products include paper, ceramics, cement, textiles, and aircraft. It is the headquarters of the SE Asia Treaty Organization.

Bangladesh country in S Asia, surrounded on three sides by India, and bounded to the S by the bay of Bengal.

Bangui capital and port of the Central African Republic on the River Ubangi; population (1988) 597,000. Industries include beer, cigarettes, office machinery, and timber and metal products.

banjo resonant stringed musical instrument, with a long neck and circular drum-type sound box; it is played with a plectrum. It originated in the USA with black slaves, and, introduced to Britain in 1846, became a popular amateur instrument.

Banjul capital and chief port of Gambia, on an island at the mouth of the river Gambia; population (1983) 44,536. It was known as Bathurst until 1973. It was established as a settlement for freed slaves in 1816.

bank a financial institution which uses funds deposited with it to lend money to companies or individuals, and which also provides financial services to its customers. A *central bank* (in the UK, the Bank of England) issues currency for the government, in order to provide cash for circulation and exchange. In terms of assets, seven of the world's top 10 banks were Japanese in 1988.

Bank for International Settlements (BIS) a bank established 1930 to handle German reparations settlements from World War I. The BIS (based in Basel, Switzerland) is today an important centre for economic and monetary research and assists cooperation of central banks. Its financial activities are essentially short term.

Bankhead Tallulah 1903–1968. US actress, noted for her wit and flamboyant lifestyle; she starred in *The Little Foxes* 1939.

Bank of England UK central bank founded by Act of Parliament in 1694. It was entrusted with note issue in 1844, and nationalized in 1946. It is banker to the UK government and assists in implementing financial and monetary policies through intervention in financial and foreign exchange markets.

bank rate interest rate fixed by the Bank of England as a guide to mortgage, hire purchase rates, and so on, which was replaced in 1972 by the *minimum lending rate* (lowest rate at which the Bank acts as lender of last resort to the money market), which from 1978 was again a 'bank rate' set by the Bank.

Bangladesh
People's Republic of
(Gana Prajatantri Bangladesh)

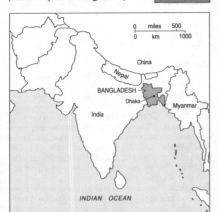

0 miles 500
0 km 1000

China
Nepal
BANGLADESH
Dhaka
Myanmar
India
INDIAN OCEAN

area 143,000 sq km/55,000 sq mi
capital Dhaka (formerly Dacca)
towns ports Chittagong, Khulna
physical flat delta of rivers Ganges and Brahmaputra; annual rainfall of 2,540 mm/100 in; vulnerable to flooding and cyclones
head of state Abdur Rahman Biswas from 1991
head of government Begum Khaleda Zia from 1991
political system emergent democratic republic

exports jute (50% of world production), tea
currency taka
population (1991 est) 107,992,100; annual growth rate 2.17%
life expectancy men 48, women 47
language Bangla (Bengali)
religion Sunni Muslim 85%, Hindu 14%
literacy 43% male/22% female (1985 est)
GDP $17.6 bn (1987); $172 per head
chronology
1947 Formed into E province of Pakistan.
1970 Half a million killed in flood.
1971 Independent Bangladesh emerged under Sheikh Mujib ur-Rahman after civil war.
1975 Assassination of Sheikh Mujib. Martial law imposed.
1976–77 Maj-Gen Zia ur-Rahman assumed power.
1981 Assassination of Maj-Gen Zia.
1982 Lt-Gen Ershad assumed power in army coup. Martial law imposed.
1986 Elections disputed. Martial law ended.
1987 State of emergency declared in response to opposition demonstrations.
1988 Assembly elections boycotted by main opposition parties. State of emergency lifted. Islam made state religion. Monsoon floods and a cyclone left 35 million homeless.
1990 Mass antigovernment protests.
1991 Cyclone killed over 100,000 and left up to 10 million homeless. Parliamentary government restored.

bankruptcy the process by which the property of a person unable to pay debts is taken away under a court order and divided fairly among his or her creditors, after preferential payments such as taxes and wages. Proceedings may be instituted either by the debtor (voluntary bankruptcy), or by any creditor for a substantial sum (involuntary bankruptcy). Until 'discharged', a bankrupt is severely restricted in financial activities. When 'discharged' he or she becomes free of most debts dating from the time of bankruptcy.

banksia genus of shrubs and trees, family Proteaceae, which are native to Australia and include the honeysuckle tree; they are named after Joseph ◊Banks.

Bannister Roger Gilbert 1929– . British athlete who became the first man to run the mile in under four minutes. He achieved this feat at Oxford, England on 6 May 1954 in a time of 3 min 59.4 sec. He was knighted 1975.

Bannockburn, Battle of battle in central Scotland, near Stirling, on 24 Jun 1314, when ◊Robert I (also known as Robert the Bruce) defeated the English under ◊Edward II.

bantam small variety of domestic chicken. This can either be a small version of one of the large breeds, or a separate type. Some are prolific layers, and bantam cocks have a reputation as spirited fighters.

Banting Frederick Grant 1891–1941. Canadian physician who discovered insulin in 1921 when, experimentally, he tied off the ducts of the ◊pancreas in order to determine the function of the islets of Langerhans. He was helped by Charles ◊Best and John J R Macleod, with whom he shared the 1923 Nobel Prize for Medicine.

Bantu languages a group of related languages spoken widely over the greater part of Africa S of the Sahara, including Swahili, Xhosa and Zulu. Meaning 'people' in Zulu, the word Bantu itself illustrates a characteristic use of prefixes: *mu-ntu*, 'man', *ba-ntu*, 'people'.

Bantustan (or Bantu homelands) name until 1978 for the ◊Black National States in the Republic of South Africa.

banyan tropical tree *Ficus benghalensis* of the family Moraceae. It produced aerial roots which grow down from its spreading branches, forming supporting pillars which have the appearance of separate trunks.

baobab tree *Adansonia digitata*, family Bombacaceae. It has root-like branches, hence its nickname 'upside-down tree', and edible fruit known as monkey bread.

baptism immersion in or sprinking with water as a religious rite of initiation. It was practised long

Bannister British athlete Roger Bannister.

Barbados

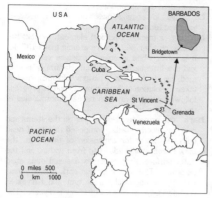

area 430 sq km/166 sq mi
capital Bridgetown
physical most easterly island of the West Indies; surrounded by coral reefs
head of state Elizabeth II from 1966 represented by governor general
head of government Erskine Lloyd Sandiford from 1987

political system constitutional monarchy
exports sugar, rum, oil
currency Barbados dollar
population (1990 est) 260,000; annual growth rate 0.5%
life expectancy men 70, women 75
language English and Bajan
religion Christian
literacy 99% (1984)
GDP $1.4 bn (1987); $5,449 per head
chronology
1951 Universal adult suffrage introduced. The Barbados Labour Party (BLP) won the general election.
1954 Ministerial government established.
1961 Full internal self-government. Democratic Labour Party (DLP), led by Errol Barrow, in power.
1966 Barbados achieved full independence within the Commonwealth. Barrow became the new nation's first prime minister.
1972 Diplomatic relations with Cuba established.
1976 BLP, led by Tom Adams, returned to power.
1983 Barbados supported US invasion of Grenada.
1985 Adams died suddenly. Bernard St John became prime minister.
1986 DLP, led by Barrow, returned to power.
1987 Barrow died, succeeded by Erskine Lloyd Sandiford.
1989 National Democratic Party (NDP) formed.
1991 DLP, under Erskine Sandiford, won general election.

---

before the beginning of Christianity. In the Christian baptism ceremony, sponsors or godparents make vows on behalf of the child which are renewed by the child at confirmation. The *amrit* ceremony in Sikhism is sometimes referred to as baptism.

Baptist member of any of several Christian sects practising baptism by immersion of believers only on profession of faith. Baptists stand in the Protestant and evangelical tradition and seek their authority in the Bible. Baptism originated among English Dissenters who took refuge in the Netherlands in the early 17th century, and spread by emigration and, later, missionary activity. Of the world total of approximately 31 million, some 26.5 million are in the USA and 265,000 in the UK.

bar ◊cgs unit of pressure (symbol bar) equal to 10^5 pascals or 10^6 dynes/cm², approximately 750 mmHg or 0.986 atm. Its diminutive, the *millibar* is commonly used by meteorologists.

Barabbas in the New Testament, a robber released from prison at Passover instead of Jesus Christ.

barb general name for fish of the genus *Barbus* and some related genera of the family Cyprinidae. As well as the ◊barbel, barbs include many small tropical Old World species, some of which are familiar aquarium species. They are active egglaying species, usually of 'typical' fish shape and with barbels at the corner of the mouth.

Barbados island in the Caribbean, one of the Lesser Antilles.

Barbarossa nickname 'red beard' given to the German emperor ◊Frederick I, and also to two brothers who were Barbary pirates: *Horuk* was killed by the Spaniards in 1518; *Khair-ed-Din* took Tunis in 1534 and died in Constantinople in 1546.

Barbarossa, Operation German codename for the plan to invade Russia during World War II in 1941.

Barbary ape tailless yellowish-brown macaque monkey *Macaca sylvanus*, found in the mountains and wilds of Algeria and Morocco. It was introduced to Gibraltar, where legend has it that the British will leave if the colony dies out.

barbastelle insect-eating bat *Barbastella barbastellus* with 'frosted' black fur and a wingspan of about 25 cm/10 in, occasionally found in the UK but more common in Europe.

barbed wire a cheap fencing material made of strands of galvanized wire (see ◊galvanizing), with sharp barbs wound upon them at intervals. In 1873 Joseph Glidden in the USA devised a machine to mass produce barbed wire.

Barbie *Klaus Barbie, the Nazi SS commander in Lyon, France, during World War II.*

barbel freshwater fish *Barbus barbus* found in fast-flowing rivers with sand or gravel bottoms in Britain and Europe. Long-bodied, and up to 1 m/3 ft long, the barbel has four *barbels* ('little beards' – sensory fleshy filaments) near the mouth.

barber's shop unaccompanied close-harmony singing, which originated among waiting customers in barber's shops in 19th-century USA.

barbet type of small, often brightly coloured bird found in forests throughout the tropics. There are some 78 species of barbet in the family Capitonidae, about half living in Africa. It eats insects and fruits. Distant relations of woodpeckers, barbets drill nest holes with their beaks. The name comes from the 'little beard' of bristles at the base of the beak.

Barbican, the arts and residential complex in the City of London. The Barbican Arts Centre 1982 contains theatres, cinemas, exhibitions and concert halls.

Barbie Klaus 1913– . German Nazi, a member of the ◊SS from 1936. During World War II he was involved in the deportation of Jews from the occupied Netherlands 1940–42 and in tracking down Jews and Resistance workers in France 1942–45. He was arrested 1983 and convicted of crimes against humanity in France 1987.

barbiturate a hypnosedative drug, commonly called 'sleeping pills'. Tolerance develops quickly in the user so that increasingly large doses are required to induce sleep. Its action persists for hours or days, causing confused, aggressive behaviour or disorientation.

Barbizon school French school of landscape painters of the mid-19th century, based at Barbizon in the forest of Fontainebleau. Members included J F Millet, Diaz de la Peña (1807–76), and Théodore Rousseau (1812–67). They aimed to paint fresh, realistic scenes, sketching and painting their subjects in the open air.

Barcelona capital, industrial city (textiles, engineering, chemicals), and port of Catalonia, NE Spain; population (1981) 1,755,000. As the chief centre of anarchism and Catalonian nationalism it was prominent in the overthrow of the monarchy 1931, and was the last city of the republic to surrender to Franco 1939.

Bardeen John 1908– . US physicist, who won a Nobel prize 1956, with Walter Brattain and William Shockley, for the development of the transistor in 1948. In 1972, he was the first double winner of a Nobel prize in the same subject (with Leon Cooper and John Schrieffer) for his work on superconductivity.

Bardot Brigitte 1934– . French film actress, whose sensual appeal did much to popularize French cinema internationally. Her films include *And God Created Woman* 1950.

Bardo Thodol also known as the *Book of the Dead* a Tibetan Buddhist text giving instructions to the newly dead about the Bardo, or state between death and rebirth.

Barebones Parliament the English assembly called by Oliver ◊Cromwell to replace the 'Rump Parliament' Jul 1653.

Barenboim Daniel 1942– . Israeli pianist and conductor, born in Argentina. Appointed July 1987, he was sacked from his post as artistic director of the Opéra Bastille, Paris, a few months before its opening in July 1989.

Barents Willem 1550–1597. Dutch explorer, who made three expeditions to seek the ◊North-East Passage; he died on the last. The Barents Sea is named after him.

Bari capital of Apulia region, S Italy, and industrial port on the Adriatic; population (1981) 371,022. It is the site of Italy's first nuclear power station; the part of the town known as Tecnopolis is the Italian equivalent of ◊Silicon Valley.

baritone lower-range male voice midway between bass and tenor.

barium a metallic chemical element, symbol Ba, atomic number 56, relative atomic mass 137.36. It is silver-white in colour, oxidizes very easily, and is a little harder than lead. Barium is used in medicine, in the form of barium sulphate, which is taken in solution (a 'barium meal') and its progress followed using X-rays, to reveal abnormalities of the digestive tract.

bark the protective outer layer on the stems and roots of woody plants, composed mainly of dead cells. To allow for expansion of the stem, the bark is continually added to from within, and the outer surface often becomes fissured or is shed as scales. The bark from the cork oak (*Quercus ruber*) is economically important and harvested commercially, usually about every ten years. The spice ◊cinnamon, and the drugs cascara (used as a laxative and stiumlant) and ◊quinine all come from bark.

Barker Clive 1952– . British horror writer, whose *Books of Blood* 1984–85 are in the sensationalist tradition of horror fiction.

barley

barley cereal belonging to the family Gramineae. The cultivated barley *Hordeum vulgare* comprises three varieties – six-rowed barley, four-rowed barley or Scotch Bigg, and two-rowed barley. Barley was one of the earliest cereals to be cultivated, and no other cereal can thrive in so wide a range of climate. Polar barley is sown and reaped well within the Arctic circle in Europe. Barley is no longer much used in bread-making, but its high protein form finds a wide use for animal feeding. Its main importance, however, is in brewing and distilling, for which low protein varieties are used.

bar mitzvah in Judaism, initiation of a boy, which takes place at the age of 13, into the adult Jewish community; less common is the *bat* or *bas mitzvah* for girls at age 12. The boy reads a passage from the Torah in the synagogue on the Sabbath, and is subsequently regarded as a full member of the congregation.

Barnabas, St in the New Testament, a 'fellow-labourer' with St Paul; he went with St Mark on a

barometer
measure to top of meniscus

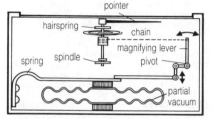

Torricellian vacuum

atmospheric
pressure in
mm of mercury

barometer tube

mercury

atmospheric pressure

pointer

hairspring

chain

magnifying lever

spring   spindle   pivot

partial
vacuum

missionary journey to Cyprus, his birthplace. Feast day 11 Jun.

barnacle marine crustacean of the subclass Cirripedia. The larval form is free-swimming, but when mature, it fixes itself by the head to rock or floating wood. The animal then remains attached, enclosed in a shell through which the cirri (modified legs) protrude to sweep food into the mouth.

Barnard Christiaan Neethling 1922– . South African surgeon who performed the first human heart transplant in 1967 in Cape Town. The patient, 54-year-old Louis Washkansky, lived for 18 days.

Barnardo Thomas John 1845–1905. British philanthropist, who was known as Dr Barnardo, although not medically qualified. He opened the first of a series of homes for destitute children in 1867 in Stepney, London.

Barnard's star second-closest star to the Sun, 6 light years away in the constellation Ophiuchus. It is a faint red dwarf of 9th magnitude, visible only through a telescope.

Barnet, Battle of in the English Wars of the ◊Roses, the defeat of Lancaster by York on 14 Apr 1471 in Barnet, Hertfordshire (now NW London).

Barnum P(hineas) T(aylor) 1810–1891. US showman. In 1871 he established the 'Greatest Show on Earth' (which included the midget 'Tom Thumb') comprising circus, menagerie, and exhibition of 'freaks', conveyed in 100 rail cars. He coined the phrase'there's a sucker born every minute'.

barograph device for recording variations in atmospheric pressure.

barometer instrument which measures atmospheric pressure as an indication of weather. Most often used are the **mercury barometer** and the **aneroid barometer**.

baron rank in the ◊peerage of the UK, above a baronet and below a viscount. The first English barony by patent was created in 1387, but barons by 'writ' existed earlier. Life peers, created under the Act of 1958, are always of this rank.

baronet hereditary title in the UK below the rank of baron, but above that of knight; the first creations were in 1611 by James I, who needed funds from their sale to finance an army in Ulster. A baronet does not have a seat in the House of Lords, but is entitled to the style *Sir* before his Christian name.

Barons' Wars civil wars in England:
1215–17 between King ◊John and his barons, over his failure to honour ◊Magna Carta;
1264–67 between ◊Henry III (and the future ◊Edward I) and his barons (led by Simon de ◊Montfort);
1264 14 May **Battle of Lewes** at which Henry III was defeated and captured;
1265 4 Aug Simon de Montfort was defeated by Edward I at Evesham and killed.

Baroque style of art and architecture characterized by extravagance in ornament and great expressiveness. It dominated European **art** for most of the 17th century, with artists like the painter Rubens and the sculptor Bernini. In **architecture** it often involved large-scale designs, such as Bernini's piazza in Rome and the palace of Versailles in France. In **music** the Baroque era lasted from about 1600 to 1750, and its major composers included Monteverdi, Vivaldi, J S Bach, and Handel.

barracuda large predatory fish *Sphyraena barracuda* found in the warmer seas of the world. It can grow over 2 m/6 ft long, and has a superficial resemblance to a pike. Young fish shoal but the older ones are solitary. The barracuda has very sharp shearing teeth, and may attack people.

Barranquilla seaport in N Colombia, on the river Magdalena; population (1985) 1,120,900. Products include chemicals, tobacco, textiles, furniture and footwear.

Barras Paul François Jean Nicolas, Count Barras 1755–1829. French revolutionary. He was elected to the National Convention in 1792, and helped to overthrow Robespierre 1794. In 1795 he became a member of the Directory (see ◊French Revolution). In 1796 he brought about the marriage of his former mistress, Joséphine de Beauharnais, with Napoleon, and assumed dictatorial powers. After Napoleon's coup d'état of 19 Nov 1799, Barras fell into disgrace.

Barrault Jean Louis 1910– . French actor and director. His films include *La Symphonie fantastique* 1942, *Les Enfants du Paradis* 1944, and *La Ronde* 1950.

Barre the wooden bar running along the walls of a ballet studio at waist height, designed to help dancers find their balance while going through the initial daily exercises.

Barre Raymond 1924– . French politician, member of the centre-right Union pour la Démocratie Française; prime minister 1976–81, when he also held the Finance Ministry portfolio and gained a reputation as a tough and determined budget-cutter (nicknamed Monsieur Economy).

barrel a unit of liquid capacity, used particularly for measuring petroleum. A barrel of petroleum contains 159 litres/35 gallons.

Barrie J(ames) M(atthew) 1860–1937. Scottish playwright and novelist, author of *The Admirable Crichton* 1902 and *Peter Pan* 1904.

barrier reef a ◊coral reef that lies offshore, separated from the mainland by a shallow lagoon. The Great Barrier Reef, off the coast of N E Australia, is a spectacular example.

barrister in the UK, a lawyer qualified by study at the ◊Inns of Court to plead for a client in court. In Scotland they are called ◊advocates. Barristers act for clients through the intermediary of ◊solicitors. In the highest courts, only barristers can represent litigants but this distinction between barristers and solicitors seems likely to change in the 1990s. In the USA an attorney (lawyer) may serve both functions. See also ◊Queen's Counsel.

barrow a burial mound, usually composed of earth but sometimes of stones, examples of which are found in many parts of the world. There are two main types, *long,* dating from the New Stone Age, and *round,* from the early Bronze Age.

Barry Charles 1795–1860. British architect of the neo-Gothic Houses of Parliament at Westminster, London, 1840–60, in collaboration with ◊Pugin.

Barstow Stan 1928– . English novelist. Born in W Yorkshire, his novels describe northern working-class life including *A Kind of Loving* 1960.

Barth Karl 1886–1968. Swiss Protestant theologian. Socialist in his political views, he attacked the Nazis. His *Church Dogmatics* 1932–62 makes the resurrection of Jesus the focal point of Christianity.

Barthes Roland 1915–1980. French critic. He was an influential theorist of ◊semiology, the science of signs and symbols. One of the French 'new critics', he attacked traditional literary criticism in works such as *Sur Racine/On Racine* 1963, and set out his own theories in *Eléments de sémiologie* 1964.

Bartholomew, Massacre of St start of French religious persecution 24 Aug 1572; see ◊St Bartholomew, Massacre of.

Bartholomew, St in the New Testament, one of the apostles. Legends relate that after the Crucifixion he took Christianity to India, or that he was a missionary in Anatolia and Armenia, where he suffered martyrdom by being flayed alive. Feast day 24 Aug.

Bartók Béla 1881–1945. Hungarian composer. Regarded as a child prodigy, he studied music at Budapest, and collaborated with ◊Kodály in research into Hungarian folk music, which influenced his later compositions and led him to develop a new musical language making tonal use of the 12 notes of the chromatic scale. His large output includes string quartets, violin and piano concertos, orchestral suites, and operas. When Hungary joined Germany in World War II, Bartók went to the USA.

Bartolommeo Fra, also called Baccio della Porta *c.* 1472–*c.* 1517. Italian religious painter of the High Renaissance, active in Florence. His painting of the *Last Judgment* 1499 (Museo di S Marco, Florence) greatly influenced Raphael.

Barton Edmund 1849–1920. Australian politician. He was leader of the Federation movement from 1896, and first prime minister of Australia 1901–03. On his retirement he became a high-court judge.

Baruch Bernard (Mannes) 1870–1965. US financier. He was a friend of the British premier Churchill and a self-appointed, unpaid adviser to US presidents Wilson, F D Roosevelt, and Truman. He strongly advocated international control of nuclear energy.

Baryshnikov Mikhail 1948– . Latvian-born dancer, now based in the USA. He joined the Kirov Ballet in 1967 and soon became acclaimed worldwide as a soloist. After defecting from the former USSR 'on artistic, not political grounds' while on

Bartók Hungarian composer Béla Bartók.

tour in Canada 1974, he danced with various companies, and later joined the American Ballet Theater (ABT) as principal dancer. He left to join the New York City Ballet 1978–80, but rejoined ABT as director 1980–90. From 1990 he has danced for various companies.

basalt the commonest volcanic ◊igneous rock, and the principal rock type on the ocean floor; it is basic, that is, it contains relatively little silica: 45–50%. It is usually dark grey.

bascule bridge type of movable bridge in which one or two counterweighted deck members pivot upwards to allow shipping to pass underneath. One example is Tower Bridge, in London.

base in mathematics, the number of different single-digit symbols used in a particular number system. Thus our usual (decimal) counting system of numbers has the base 10 (using the symbols 0,1,2,3,4,5,6,7,8,9). In the ◊binary number system, which has only the numbers 1 and 0, the base is 2. A base is also a number which, when raised to a particular power (that is, when multiplied by itself a particular number of times as in $10^2 = 10 \times 10 = 100$), has a ◊logarithm equal to the power. For example, the logarithm of 100 to the base 10 is 2.

base

binary (base 2)	octal (base 8)	decimal (base 10)	hexadecimal (base 16)
0	0	0	0
1	1	1	1
10	2	2	2
11	3	3	3
100	4	4	4
101	5	5	5
110	6	6	6
111	7	7	7
1000	10	8	8
1001	11	9	9
1010	12	10	A
1011	13	11	B
1100	14	12	C
1101	15	13	D
1110	16	14	E
1111	17	15	F
10000	20	16	10
11111111	377	255	FF
11111010001	3721	2001	7D1

baseball national summer game of USA, possibly derived from the English game of ◊rounders. According to tradition it was invented in Cooperstown, New York, by Abner Doubleday in 1839.

Basel or *Basle* (French *Bâle*) financial, commercial, and industrial centre in Switzerland; population (1990) 171,000.

base lending rate the rate of interest to which most bank lending is linked, the actual rate depending on the status of the borrower. A prestigious company might command a rate only 1% above base rate while an individual would be charged several points above. An alternative method of interest rates is ◊LIBOR.

base pair the linkage of two base (purine or pyrimidine) molecules in ◊DNA. One base of each pair lies on one of the two strands of the DNA double helix, and one on the other strand, so the base pairs link the two strands, rather like the rungs of a ladder. In DNA, there are four bases: adenine and guanine (purines) and cytosine and thymine (pyrimidines). Adenine always pairs with thymine and cytosine with guanine.

Bashkir autonomous republic of Russia, with the Ural Mountains on the E
area 143,600 sq km/55,430 sq mi
capital Ufa
products minerals, oil, natural gas
population (1982) 3,876,000
history annexed by Russia 1557; became the first Soviet Autonomous Republic 1919. Since 1989 Bashkirs have demanded greater independence.

Bashō pen name of Japanese poet Matsuo Munefusa 1644–1694. He was master of the *haiku*, a 17-syllable poetic form with lines of 5, 7 and 5 syllables, which he infused with subtle allusiveness and made the accepted form of poetic expression in Japan. His most famous work is *Oku-no-hosomichi/The Narrow Road to the Deep North* 1694, an account of a visit to northern Japan, which consists of haikus interspersed with prose passages.

BASIC Beginner's All-purpose Symbolic Instruction Code a computer-programming language, developed in 1971 for ◊Fortran and designed for ease of use. BASIC uses an interpreter (enabling programs to be entered and run line by line with no preparation) rather than a compiler (which involves having to write complete programs before they can be tested). Most home computers (micros) operate using BASIC.

basic-oxygen process the most widely used method of steel-making, involving the blasting of oxygen into molten pig iron. Pig iron from a blast furnace, together with steel scrap, is poured into a converter, and a jet of oxygen is then projected into the mixture at supersonic speed. The excess carbon in the mix and other impurities quickly burn out or form a slag, and the converter is emptied by tilting. It takes only about 45 minutes to refine 350 tonnes of steel.

basidiocarp the spore-bearing body or 'fruiting body' of all basidiomycete ◊fungi, except the rusts and smuts. A well-known example is the edible mushroom. Other types include globular basidiocarps (puffballs) or flat ones that project from tree trunks (brackets). They are made up of a mass of tightly packed, intermeshed ◊hyphae.

Basie 'Count' (William) 1904–1984. US band leader, pianist, and organist, who was popular for his simplified, swinging style of music. He developed the big-band sound and led impressive groups of musicians in a career spanning more than 50 years.

basic-oxygen process

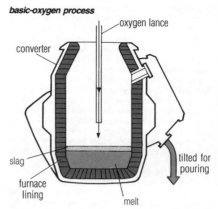

basil plant *Ocimum basilicum* of the family Labiatae. A native of the tropics, it is cultivated in Europe as a culinary herb.

Basil II *c.* 958–1025. Byzantine emperor from 976. His achievement as emperor was to contain, and later decisively defeat, the Bulgarians, earning for himself the title *Bulgar-Slayer* after a victory 1014. After the battle he blinded almost all 15,000 of the defeated, leaving only a few men with one eye to lead their fellows home. The Byzantine empire reached its greatest extent at the time of his death.

basilica type of Roman public building; a large roofed hall flanked by columns, generally with an aisle on each side, used for judicial or other public business. The earliest known basilica, at Pompeii, dates from the 2nd century BC. The type was adopted by the early Christians for their churches.

basilisk a S American lizard genus *Basiliscus*. It is able to run bipedally when travelling fast (about 11 kph/7 mph) and may dash a short distance across the surface of water. The male has a well-developed crest on the head, body, and tail.

basidiocarp

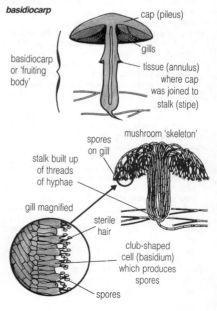

Basil, St *c.* 330–379. Cappadocian monk, known as 'the Great', founder of the Basilian monks. Elected bishop of Caesarea 370, Basil opposed the heresy of ◊Arianism. He wrote many theological works and composed the 'Liturgy of St Basil', in use in the Eastern Orthodox Church. Feast day 2 Jan.

basketball ball game between two teams of five players on an indoor enclosed court.

basketry an ancient craft used to make a wide range of objects from containers and baskets to furniture by interweaving or plaiting rushes, cane or other equally strong, natural fibres. *Wickerwork* is a more rigid type of basketry worked onto a sturdy frame, usually made from willow twigs.

Basle alternative form of ◊Basel, city in Switzerland.

Basov Nikolai Gennadievich 1912– . Soviet physicist who in 1953, with his compatriot Alexander Prokhorov, developed the microwave amplifier called a ◊maser. They were awarded the Nobel Prize in Physics 1964, which they shared with the American Charles Townes.

Basque a member of a people who occupy the autonomous Basque region (created 1980) of N Spain and the French *département* of Pyrénées-Atlantiques. During the Spanish Civil War 1936–39, they were on the Republican side, and were defeated by Franco. The Basque separatist movement ETA (*Euskadi ta Azkatasuna*/Basque Nation and Liberty) and the French organization *Enbata*/Ocean Wind, engaged in guerrilla activity from 1968 in an unsuccessful attempt to secure a united Basque state.

Basque Country (Spanish *Vascongadas*, Basque *Euskadi*) autonomous region of NW Spain; area 7,250 sq km/2,800 sq mi; population (1981) 2,142,000.

Basque language a language of W Europe known to its speakers, the Basques, as *Euskara*, and apparently unrelated to any other language on earth. It is spoken by some half a million people in N Spain and SW France, around the Bay of Biscay ('the Basque bay'), as well as by emigrants.

Basra (Arabic *al-Basrah*) only port in Iraq, in the Shatt-al-Arab delta, 97 km/60 mi from the Persian Gulf; population (1970) 450,000. Exports include wool, oil, cereal and dates.

bass long-bodied scaly sea fish *Morone labrax* found in the N Atlantic and Mediterranean, growing to 1 m/3 ft, often seen in shoals, and penetrating to brackish water. Other fish of the same family (Serranidae) are also called bass, as are N American freshwater fishes of the family Centrarchidae.

bass 1) lowest range of male voice; 2) lower regions of musical pitch.

basset type of dog with a long low body, wrinkled forehead, and long pendulous ears, originally bred in France for hunting hares.

basset horn a musical ◊wind instrument resembling a clarinet.

bassoon woodwind instrument, the bass of the oboe family. It is descended from the bass pommer, which was approximately 2 m/6 ft in length and perfectly straight, whereas the bassoon is doubled back on itself in a tube about 2.5 m/7.5 ft long. Its tone is rich and deep.

Bass Strait shallow but turbulent channel between Australia and Tasmania, named after British explorer George Bass (1760-1812); oil was discovered in the 1960s.

Bastille the castle of St Antoine, part of the fortifications of Paris, which was used for centuries as a state prison; it was singled out for the initial attack by the mob that set the French Revolution in motion 14 Jul 1789. Only seven prisoners were found in the castle; the governor and most of the garrison were killed, and the Bastille was razed.

Basutoland former name for ◊Lesotho.

bat flying mammal in which the forelimbs are developed as wings capable of rapid and sustained flight. These wings consist of a thin hairless skin stretched between the four fingers of the hand, and from the last finger down to the hindlimb. The thumb is free and has a sharp claw to help in climbing. The hind feet have five toes with sharp hooked claws which suspend the animal head downwards when resting. Bats are nocturnal, and those native to temperate countries hibernate in winter. There are about 1,000 species of bats forming the order Chiroptera, making this the second-largest mammal order.

Batak a number of distinct but related peoples of N Sumatra in Indonesia. Numbering approximately 2,500,000, the Batak speak languages belonging to the Austronesian family.

Batavian Republic republic set up by France in the ◊Netherlands 1795; it lasted until the establishment of the kingdom of the Netherlands 1814 at the end of the Napoleonic Wars.

batch system in computing, a system for processing large volumes of data. Quantities of data are collected into a 'batch' and processed during regular 'runs' (for example, each night, or at weekends). This enables efficient use of the computer and is well suited to applications of a repetitive nature, such as a company payroll.

Bateman H(enry) M(ayo) 1887–1970. British cartoonist, born in Australia. During the 1920s and 1930s he had enormous success with cartoons based on themes of social embarrassment in such series as *The Man who...* (as in *The Guardsman who dropped his rifle*).

Bates H(enry) W(alter) 1825–1892. British naturalist and explorer, who identified 8,000 new species of insects. He made a special study of ◊camouflage in animals, and his observation of insect imitation of species unpleasant to predators is known as 'Batesian mimicry'.

Bath, Order of the British order of knighthood, believed to have been founded in the reign of Henry IV (1399–1413). Formally instituted 1815, it included civilians from 1847 and women from 1970. There are three grades: Knights of the Grand Cross (GCB), Knights Commanders (KCB), and Knights Companions (CB).

bathyscaph or *bathyscaphe* or *bathyscape* submersible vessel with an observation capsule underneath, used to investigate animal life and conditions at great depths in the ocean. One of the most famous descents was made by the bathyscaph *Trieste*, which descended nearly 11,000 m/6.8 mi into Challenger Deep in the Pacific Ocean 1960.

bathysphere a steel sphere used for observation in deep-sea diving. It is lowered into the ocean by cable.

batik Javanese technique of hand-applied colour design for fabric; areas undyed in any colour are successively sealed with wax. Practised throughout Indonesia, the craft was introduced into Europe by the Dutch.

Batista Fulgencio 1901–1973. Cuban dictator 1933–44 and 1952–59, whose authoritarian methods enabled him to jail his opponents and amass a large personal fortune. He was overthrown by rebel forces led by Fidel ◊Castro 1957.

Batten Jean 1909–1982. New Zealand aviator, who made the first return solo flight by a

basketball

An indoor sport played on a court by five members per side. The object is, via a series of dribbling and passing moves with the hands, to get the ball into the opposing half and score goals by throwing the ball into the opposing basket.

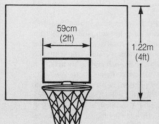

59cm (2ft)

1.22m (4ft)

The basket

The basket is a piece of netting which hangs from a metal rim and is open at both ends to allow the ball to pass through. The rim is attached to a backboard and points can be scored by rebounding the ball off the backboard.

Play

Play is started with a jumpball. Two players, one from each team, face each other and the referee tosses the ball into the air between the two players who attempt to knock the ball to a teammate. The ball can only be played after it has reached its greatest height. A player in the jumpball can only play the ball twice after which it must be played to a player not involved.

dimensions of the court

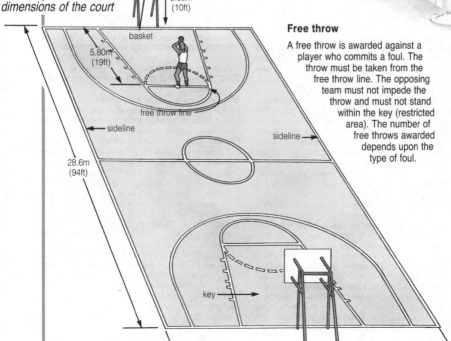

3.05m (10ft)

basket

5.80m (19ft)

free throw line

← sideline

28.6m (94ft)

sideline →

Free throw

A free throw is awarded against a player who commits a foul. The throw must be taken from the free throw line. The opposing team must not impede the throw and must not stand within the key (restricted area). The number of free throws awarded depends upon the type of foul.

key →

50.24m (50ft)

battery
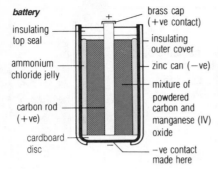
- brass cap (+ve contact)
- insulating top seal
- insulating outer cover
- ammonium chloride jelly
- zinc can (−ve)
- mixture of powdered carbon and manganese (IV) oxide
- carbon rod (+ve)
- cardboard disc
- −ve contact made here

woman Australia–Britain 1935, and established speed records.

battery energy storage device allowing release of electricity on demand. A battery is made up of one or more cells, each containing two conducting ◊electrodes (one positive, one negative) immersed in a liquid ◊electrolyte, in a container. When an outside connection (such as through a light bulb) is made between the electrodes, a current flows through the circuit, and chemical reactions releasing energy take place within the cells.

battleship warship, formerly predominating over all others in armour and firepower, but obsolete from World War II.

baud unit measuring the rate at which electrical signals are sent between electronic devices such as telegraphs and computers.

Baudelaire Charles Pierre 1821–1867. French poet, whose work combined rhythmical and musical perfection with a morbid romanticism and eroticism, often using oriental imagery and finding beauty in decadence and evil. His first book of verse, *Les Fleurs du mal/Flowers of Evil* 1857, caused a scandal, and was condemned by the censor as endangering public morals.

Baudouin 1930– . King of the Belgians. In 1950 his father, ◊Leopold III, relinquished his own constitutional powers, and Baudouin was known until his succession in Jul 1951 as *Le Prince Royal*. In 1960 he married Fabiola de Mora y Aragón (1928–), member of a Spanish noble family.

Bauhaus a German school founded 1919 by the architect Walter ◊Gropius at Weimar, in an attempt to fuse all the arts and crafts in a unified whole. Moved to Dessau under political pressure 1925, it was closed by the Nazis 1933. Associated with the Bauhaus were Klee, Kandinsky, and Ludwig Mies van der Rohe. The tradition never died, and in 1972 the *Bauhaus Archive* was installed in new premises in Berlin.

Bāul member of Bengali mystical sect that emphasizes freedom from compulsion, from doctrine, and from social caste; they avoided all outward forms of religious worship. Not ascetic, they aim for harmony between physical and spiritual needs.

Baum L(yman) Frank 1856–1919. US writer, best known for the children's fantasy *The Wonderful Wizard of Oz* 1900.

bauxite the principal ore of aluminium, consisting of a mixture of hydrated aluminium oxides and hydroxides, generally contaminated with compounds of iron, which give it a red colour.

Bavaria (German *Bayern*) administrative region (German *Land*) of Germany.
area 70,550 sq km/27,230 sq mi
capital Munich
towns Augsburg, Nuremberg, Regensburg

products beer, electronics, electrical engineering, optics, cars, aerospace, chemicals, plastics, oil-refining, textiles, glass, toys
population (1988) 11,000,000
famous people Lucas Cranach, Hitler, Franz Josef Strauss, Richard Strauss
religion 70% Roman Catholic, 26% Protestant
history the last king, Ludwig III, abdicated in 1918, and Bavaria declared itself a republic.

bay name given to various species of laurel *Laurus* and some other plants. Its aromatic evergreen leaves are used for flavouring in cookery, and there is also a golden-leaved variety.

Bayern German name for ◊Bavaria, region of Germany.

Bayesian statistics a form of statistics which uses the knowledge of prior probability together with the probability of actual data to determine posterior probabilities, using Bayes' theorem.

Bayeux Tapestry a linen hanging 70 m/231 ft long, and 50 cm/20 in wide, made about 1067–70, which gives a vivid pictorial record of the invasion of England by ◊William I (the Conqueror) 1066. It is an embroidery rather than a true tapestry, sewn with woollen threads in blue, green, red, and yellow, and contains 72 separate scenes with descriptive wording in Latin.

Bayliss William Maddock 1860–1924. English physiologist, who discovered the hormone secretin with E H ◊Starling in 1902. Secretin plays an important part in digestion. During World War I, he introduced the use of saline (salt water) injections to help the injured recover from ◊shock.

Bay of Pigs inlet on the S coast of Cuba, about 145 km/90 mi SW of Havana, the site of an unsuccessful invasion attempt by 1,500 US-sponsored Cuban exiles 17–20 Apr 1961; 1,173 were taken prisoner.

bayonet a short sword attached to the muzzle of a firearm. Initially the bayonet was placed inside the barrel of the muzzle-loading muskets of the late 17th century. The sock or ring bayonet, invented 1700, allowed a weapon to be fired without interruption, leading to the abolition of the pike.

BBC abbreviation for *◊British Broadcasting Corporation*.

BC abbreviation for *before Christ*.

BCG abbreviation for *bacillus of ◊Calmette and Guérin*, used as a vaccine to confer active immunity to ◊tuberculosis.

beach strip of land bordering the sea, normally consisting of boulders and pebbles on exposed coasts or sand on sheltered coasts. It is usually defined by the high and low water marks. In Britain, beaches free of industrial pollution, litter and sewage, and with water of the highest quality, have the right (since 1988) to fly a blue flag.

Beach Boys, the US pop group formed 1961. They began as exponents of vocal-harmony surf music with Chuck Berry guitar riffs (hits include 'Surfin' USA' 1963, 'Help Me, Rhonda' 1965) but the compositions, arrangements, and production by Brian Wilson (1942–) became highly complex under the influence of psychedelic rock, peaking with 'Good Vibrations' 1966.

beagle short-haired hound with pendant ears, sickle tail, and bell-like voice for hunting hares on foot ('beagling').

beak the horn-covered projecting jaws of a bird, or other horny jaws such as those of the tortoise or octopus. The beaks of birds are adapted by shape and size to specific diets.

bear

polar bear

beaker people   people of Iberian origin who spread out over Europe in the 2nd millenium BC, and who began Stonehenge in England. Their remains include earthenware beakers.

beam weapon   a weapon capable of destroying a target by means of a high-energy beam. Beam weapons similar to the 'death ray' of science fiction have been explored, particularly during Ronald Reagan's presidential term in the USA.

bean   the seed of numerous leguminous plants. Beans, which are rich in nitrogenous or protein matter, are grown both for human consumption and as food for cattle and horses. Varieties of bean are grown throughout Europe, the USA, South America, China, Japan and SE Asia.

bear   large mammal with a heavily built body, short powerful limbs, and very short tail. Bears breed once a year, producing one to four cubs. In northern regions they hibernate, and the young are born in the winter den. They are found mainly in N America and N Asia. The skin of the polar bear is black to conserve 80–90% of the solar energy trapped and channelled down the hollow hairs of its fur.

bear   a speculator who sells stocks or shares on the stock exchange expecting a fall in the price in order to buy them back at a profit, the opposite of a ◊bull. In a bear market, prices fall and bears prosper.

Beardsley   Aubrey (Vincent) 1872–1898. British illustrator, whose meticulously executed black-and-white work displays the sinuous line and decorative mannerisms of Art Nouveau and was often charged with being grotesque and decadent. He became known through the *Yellow Book* magazine and his drawings for Oscar Wilde's *Salome* 1893.

Beatles, the (Left to right) John Lennon, Ringo Starr, George Harrison and Paul McCartney in 1963, at the start of their highly successful career.

bearing   a device used in a machine to allow free movement between two parts, typically the rotation of a shaft in a housing. The *sleeve* or *journal bearing* is used for the big-end and main bearings on a car ◊crankshaft. *Ball-bearings* are widely used to support shafts, as in the spindle in the hub of a bicycle wheel.

Beat Generation   the beatniks of the 1950s and 1960s, characterized by dropping out of conventional life styles and opting for life on the road, drugs, and anti-materialist values; and the associated literary movement whose members included William S Burroughs, Allen Ginsberg, and Jack Kerouac (who is credited with coining the term).

beatification   in the Catholic church, the first step towards ◊canonization. Persons who have been beatified can be prayed to, and the title 'Blessed' can be put before their names.

Beatitudes   in the New Testament, the sayings of Jesus reported in Matthew 6: 1–12; Luke 6: 20–38, depicting the spiritual qualities which characterize members of the Kingdom of God.

Beatles, the   English pop group 1960–70. The members, all born in Liverpool, were John Lennon (1940–80, rhythm guitar, vocals), Paul McCartney (1942– , bass, vocals), George Harrison (1943– , lead guitar, vocals), and Ringo

Beaufort scale

Number and description	Features	Air speed mi per hr	m per sec
0 calm	smoke rises vertically; water smooth	less than 1	less than 0.3
1 light air	smoke shows wind direction; water ruffled	1–3	0.3–1.5
2 slight breeze	leaves rustle; wind felt on face	4–7	1.6–3.3
3 gentle breeze	loose paper blows around	8–12	3.4–5.4
4 moderate	branches sway	13–18	5.5–7.9
5 fresh breeze	small trees sway, leaves blown off	19–24	8.0–10.7
6 strong breeze	whistling in telephone wires; sea spray	25–31	10.8–13.8
7 moderate gale	large trees sway	32–38	13.9–17.1
8 fresh gale	twigs break from trees	39–46	17.2–20.7
9 strong gale	branches break from trees	47–54	20.8–24.4
10 whole gale	trees uprooted, weak buildings collapse	55–63	24.5–28.4
11 storm	widespread damage	64–72	28.5–32.6
12 hurricane	widespread structural damage	above 73	above 32.7

Beauvoir *Simone de Beauvoir, the distinguished French literary figure and philosopher of the feminist movement.*

Starr (formerly Richard Starkey, 1940– , drums). Using songs written by Lennon and McCartney, they brought the ◊Mersey beat to prominence with worldwide hits including 'She Loves You' 1963, 'I Want To Hold Your Hand' 1963, and 'Can't Buy Me Love' 1964.

Beaton Cecil 1904–1980. British portrait and fashion photographer, designer, illustrator, diarist, and conversationalist. He produced notable portrait studies and also designed scenery and costumes for ballets, and sets for plays and films.

Beatrix 1936– . Queen of the Netherlands. The eldest daughter of Queen ◊Juliana, she succeeded to the throne on her mother's abdication 1980. In 1966 she married W German diplomat Claus von Amsberg (1926–), who was created a prince of the Netherlands. Her heir is Prince Willem Alexander (1967–).

Beaufort scale system of recording wind velocity, devised 1806 by Francis Beaufort. It is a numerical scale ranging from 0 to 17, calm being indicated by 0 and a hurricane by 12; 13–17 indicate degrees of hurricane force.

Beaumarchais Pierre Augustin Caron de 1732–1799. French dramatist. His great comedies *Le Barbier de Seville* 1775 and *Le Mariage de Figaro* (1778, but prohibited until 1784) form the basis of operas by ◊Rossini and ◊Mozart.

Beaumont Francis 1584–1616. English dramatist and poet. From about 1608 he collaborated with John ◊Fletcher. Their joint plays include *Philaster* 1610, *The Maid's Tragedy* c. 1611, and *A King and No King* c. 1611. *The Woman Hater* c. 1606 and *The Knight of the Burning Pestle* c. 1607 are ascribed to Beaumont alone.

Beauvoir Simone de 1908–1986. French socialist, feminist, and writer, who taught philosophy at the Sorbonne 1931–43. Her book *Le Deuxième sexe/The Second Sex* 1949 is a classic text which became a seminal work for many feminists.

beaver aquatic rodent *Castor fiber* with webbed hind feet, broad flat scaly tail and thick waterproof fur. It has very large incisor teeth and fells trees to feed on the bark and to use the logs to construct the 'lodge', in which the young are reared, food is stored, and where much of the winter is spent.

Beaverbrook William Maxwell Aitken, 1st Baron Beaverbrook 1879–1964. British newspaper proprietor and politician, born in Canada. Between World War I and II he used his newspapers, especially the *Daily Express*, to campaign for Empire free trade and against Prime Minister Baldwin.

Bebel August 1840–1913. German socialist and founding member of the *Verband deutsche Arbeitervereine* (League of Workers' Clubs), together with Wilhelm Liebknecht. Also known as the Eisenach Party, it was based in Saxony and SW Germany before being incorporated into the SPD (*Sozialdemokratische Partei Deutschlands*) 1875.

bebop or *bop* a rhythmically complex, highly improvisational, 'hot' jazz style which was developed in the USA in the 1940s by Charlie Parker, Dizzy Gillespie, Thelonius Monk, and other musicians.

Bechuanaland former name until 1966 of ◊Botswana.

Becket St Thomas 1118–1170. English priest and politician. He was chancellor to ◊Henry II 1155–62, when he was appointed archbishop of Canterbury. The interests of the church soon conflicted with those of the crown, and Becket was assassinated; he was canonized 1172.

Beckett Samuel 1906–1989. Irish novelist and dramatist, who writes in French and English. *En attendant Godot/Waiting for Godot* 1952, is possibly the best-known example of Theatre of the ◊Absurd. This predicament is explored to further extremes in *Fin de Partie/Endgame* 1957, and *Happy Days* 1961. Nobel prize 1969.

Beckford William 1760–1844. British author and eccentric. Forced out of England by scandals about his private life, he published *Vathek* 1787 in Paris, a fantastic Arabian Nights tale, and on returning to England in 1796, rebuilt his home, Fonthill Abbey in Wiltshire, as a Gothic fantasy.

Beckmann Max 1884–1950. German Expressionist painter, who fled the Nazi regime in 1933 for the USA. After World War I his art was devoted to themes of cruelty in human society, portraying sadists and their victims with a harsh, cartoon-like style of realism.

becquerel the ◊SI unit of radioactivity, equivalent to the number of atoms of a radioactive substance that disintegrate per second.

Becquerel Antoine Henri 1852–1908. French physicist, who discovered penetrating, invisible radiation coming from uranium salts, the first indication of ◊radioactivity, and shared a Nobel prize with the ◊Curies in 1903.

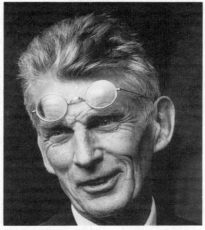

Beckett *Irish novelist and dramatist Samuel Beckett, winner of the Nobel Prize for Literature 1969.*

bee The head of a honey worker bee. (×5).

bed in geology, the unitary 'building block' of ◊sedimentary rock. A bed consists of a simple layer of rock, often separated above and below from other beds by well-defined partings called bedding planes.

bedbug flattened wingless red-brown insect *Cimex lectularius* with piercing mouthparts. It hides by day in crevices or bedclothes and emerges at night to suck human blood.

Bede *c.* 673–735. English theologian and historian, known as **the Venerable Bede**, active in Durham and Northumbria. He wrote many scientific, theological, and historical works. His *Historia Ecclesiastica Gentis Anglorum/Ecclesiastical History of the English People* 731 is an important source for early English history.

Bedfordshire county in central S England
area 1,235 sq km/477 sq mi
towns administrative headquarters Bedford; Luton, Dunstable
products cereals, vegetables, agricultural machinery, electrical goods
population (1986) 521,000
famous people John Bunyan.

Bedlam popular abbreviation of the name, Bethlehem, of the earliest mental hospital in Europe; it was opened in the 14th century in a former priory in Bishopsgate, London, and the hospital is now in Surrey.

Bedouin member of a nomadic people of Arabia and N Africa, now becoming increasingly settled. Their traditional trade was the rearing of horses and camels.

bee four-winged insect of the super-family Apoidea in the order Hymenoptera, usually with a sting. There are over 12,000 species, of which less than 1 in 20 are social in habit.

beech genus of trees *Fagus*, of the family Fagaceae. The *Common beech Fagus sylvaticus*, found in European forests, has a smooth grey trunk and edible nuts or 'mast' which are used as animal feed or processed for oil. The timber is used in furniture.

Beecher Harriet unmarried name of Harriet Beecher ◊Stowe, author of *Uncle Tom's Cabin*.

Beecher Lyman 1775–1863. US Presbyterian minister, one of the most influential pulpit orators of his time. He was the father of Harriet Beecher ◊Stowe and Henry Ward Beecher. As pastor from 1847 of Plymouth church, Brooklyn, New York, he was a leader in the movement for the abolition of slavery.

Beeching Richard, Baron Beeching 1913–1985. British scientist and administrator. He was chair of British Railways Board 1963–65, producing the controversial *Beeching Report* 1963 planning concentration on inter-city passenger traffic and a freight system.

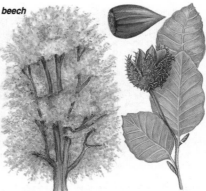

beech

bee-eater one of 23 species of bird *Merops apiaster* found in Africa, S Europe, and Asia. It feeds on a variety of insects, including bees, which it catches in its long narrow bill. Chestnut, yellow and blue-green, it is gregarious, and generally nests in river banks and sandpits.

beer alcoholic drink made from malt (fermented barley or other grain), flavoured with hops. Beer contains 1–6% alcohol. One of the oldest alcoholic drinks, it was brewed in ancient Egypt and Babylon.

beet plants of the genus *Beta*, family Chenapodiaceae, which includes the **common beet** *Beta vulgaris*. One variety of *Beta vulgaris* is used to produce sugar, and another, the mangelwurzel, grown as cattle fodder; the **beetroot** or **red beet** *Beta rubra* is a salad plant.

Beethoven Ludwig van 1770–1827. German composer. In a career which spanned the transition from Classicism to Romanticism, his mastery of musical expression in every genre made him the dominant influence in 19th-century music, especially the symphony. His works include piano and violin concertos, piano sonatas, string quartets, sacred music and nine symphonies. From 1801 he was hampered by deafness but continued his composition.

beetle common name of insects in the order Coleoptera (Greek 'sheath-winged') with leathery forewings folding down in a protective sheath over the membranous hindwings which are those used for flight. They pass through a complete metamorphosis. They include some of the largest and smallest

Beeton, Mrs Isabella Beeton, who became a byword for household management as 'Mrs Beeton'.

of all insects; the largest is the **Hercules beetle** *Dynastes hercules* of the S American rainforests, 15 cm/6 in long, the smallest only 0.05 cm/0.02 in. The largest order in the animal kingdom, beetles number some 370,000 named species, with many not yet described.

Beeton, Mrs (Isabella Mary Mayson) 1836–1865. British writer on cookery and domestic management. *Beeton's Household Management* 1859 was the first comprehensive work on domestic science.

Begin Menachem 1913– . Israeli politician, leader of the extremist Irgun Zvai Leumi organization in Palestine from 1942; prime minister of Israel 1977–83, as head of the right-wing Likud party. In 1978 he shared a Nobel Peace Prize with President Sadat of Egypt for work on the ◊Camp David Agreements for a Middle East peace settlement.

begonia genus of the tropical and subtropical plant family Begoniaceae. Begonias have fleshy and succulent leaves, and some have large brilliant flowers. There are numerous species native to the tropics, in particular South America and India.

Behan Brendan 1923–1964. Irish dramatist. His early experience of prison and knowledge of the workings of the ◊IRA (recounted in his autobiography *Borstal Boy* 1958) provided him with two recurrent themes in his plays. *The Quare Fellow* 1954 was followed by the tragicomedy *The Hostage* 1958, first written in Gaelic.

behaviourism school of psychology originating in USA. Behaviourists maintain that all human activity can ultimately be explained in terms of conditioned reactions or reflexes and habits formed in consequence. Leading behaviourists include ◊Pavlov, B F Skinner and John B Watson.

behaviour therapy in psychology, the application of behavioural principles, derived from learning theories, to the treatment of clinical conditions such as ◊phobias, ◊obsessions, sexual and inter-

personal problems. For example, in treating a phobia the person is taken into the situation that he or she is afraid of, in gradual steps.

Behn Aphra 1640–1689. English novelist and playwright, the first professional female English writer. Her writings were criticized for their sexual explicitness. Her novel *Oronooko*, an attack on slavery, was published 1688.

Behrens Peter 1868–1940. German architect. He pioneered the adaptation of architecture to modern industry, and designed the AEG turbine factory in Berlin 1909, a landmark in industrial design. He influenced ◊Le Corbusier and ◊Gropius.

Beiderbecke Bix (Leon Bismarck) 1903–1931. US jazz cornetist, composer, and pianist. He was greatly inspired by the classical composers Debussy, Ravel, and Stravinsky. A romantic soloist with Paul Whiteman's orchestra. His reputation grew after his early death.

Beijing (formerly Peking) capital of China; part of its NE border is formed by the Great Wall of China; population (1989) 6,800,000. Industries include textiles, petrochemicals, steel, and engineering. The Forbidden City, built 1406–20 as Gu Gong (Imperial Palace) of the Ming emperors, and the Summer Palace are here.

Beirut or **Beyrouth** capital and port of Lebanon, devastated by civil war in the 1970s and 1980s and occupied by armies of neighbouring countries; population (1988 est) 1,500,000.

Belarus or **Byelorussia** or **Belorussia** country in E central Europe, bounded S by Ukraine, E by Russia, W by Poland, and N by Latvia and Lithuania.

bel canto term which usually refers to the 18th-century Italian style of singing with great emphasis on perfect technique and beautiful tone.

Belfast industrial port (shipbuilding, engineering, electronics, textiles, tobacco) and capital of North-

Belarus
Republic of

area 207,600 sq km/80,100 sq mi
capital Minsk (Mensk)
towns Gomel, Vitebsk, Mogilev, Bobruisk, Grodno, Brest
physical more than 25% forested; rivers W Dvina, Dnieper and its tributaries, including the Pripet and Beresina; the Pripet Marshes in the E; mild and damp climate
head of state Stanislav Shushkevich from 1991

head of government Vyacheslav Kebich from 1990
political system emergent democracy
products peat, agricultural machinery, fertilizers, glass, textiles, leather, salt, electrical goods, meat, dairy produce
currency rouble and dukat
population (1990) 10,200,000 (77% Byelorussian 'Eastern Slavs', 13% Russian, 4% Polish, 1% Jewish)
language Byelorussian, Russian
religion Roman Catholic, Russian Orthodox, with Baptist and Muslim minorities
chronology
1919 Proclaimed a Soviet republic.
1937–41 More than 100,000 people were shot in mass executions ordered by Stalin.
1941–44 Occupied by Nazi Germany.
1945 Became a founding member of the United Nations.
1986 Fallout from the Chernobyl nuclear reactor in Ukraine contaminated a large area.
1989 Byelorussian Popular Front established as well as a more extreme nationalist organization, the Tolaka group.
1990 Byelorussian established as state language and republican sovereignty declared.
1991 Independence from the Soviet Union was declared in the wake of failed anti-Gorbachev coup. Shushkevich elected president. Commonwealth of Independent States (CIS) formed in Minsk. Belarus was accorded diplomatic recognition by USA.
1992 Belarus was admitted into Conference on Security and Cooperation in Europe (CSCE).

ern Ireland since 1920; population (1985) 300,000. Since 1968 the city has been badly damaged by civil disturbances.

Belgian Congo   former name 1908–60 of ◊Zaïre.

Belgium   country in northern Europe, bounded to the northwest by the North Sea, to the southwest by France, to the east by Luxembourg and Germany, and to the northeast by the Netherlands.

Belgrade   (Serbo-Croat *Beograd*) capital of Yugoslavia and Serbia, and Danube river port linked with the port of Bar on the Adriatic; population (1981) 1,470,000. Industries include light engineering, food processing, textiles, pharmaceuticals and electrical goods.

Belisarius   c. 505–565. Roman general under Emperor ◊Justinian I.

Belize   country in Central America, bounded to the north by Mexico, to the west and south by Guatemala, and to the east by the Caribbean Sea.

Belize City   chief port of Belize, and capital until 1970; population (1980) 40,000. It was destroyed by a hurricane 1961 and it was decided to move the capital inland, to Belmopan.

Bell   Alexander Graham 1847–1922. British scientist, and inventor of the telephone. He patented his invention in 1876, and later experimented with a type of phonograph and in aeronautics invented the tricycle undercarriage.

belladonna   plant of the genus *Atropa*. The dried powdered leaves of *Atropa bella-donna* or **deadly nightshade** contain the alkaloids hyoscyamine, atropine, hyoscine, and belladonnine. Belladonna acts as an ◊anticholinergic, and is highly toxic in large doses.

Bellini   family of Italian painters, founders of the Venetian school. The greatest is *Giovanni Bellini* (c. 1430–1516), who produced varied devotional pictures of the Madonna. He introduced softness in tone, harmony in composition, and a use of luminous colour that greatly influenced the next generation of painters (especially Giorgione and Titian). He worked in oil rather than tempera.

Bellini   Vincenzo 1801–1835. Italian composer, born in Catania, Sicily. His best-known operas include *La sonnambula* 1831, *Norma* 1831, and *I puritani* 1835.

Bellow   Saul 1915–   . US novelist. Canadian-born of Russian descent, he settled in Chicago with his family at the age of nine. His works include *Humboldt's Gift* 1975, *The Dean's December* 1982, and *More Die of Heartbreak* 1987. Nobel Prize 1976.

bell ringing   the art of ringing church bells. *Change ringing* by hand (by means of a rope fastened to the wheel of the bell mechanism) is an English art perfected in the 17th century. Mathematical permutations are rung on 5–12 bells, and ringers are organized in guilds. The *carillon* method, popular in Europe and in the USA, involves a series of up to 70 bells being played by the

Belgium
Kingdom of (French *Royaume de Belgique*, Flemish *Koninkrijk België*)

area 30,513 sq km/11,779 sq mi
capital Brussels
towns Ghent, Liège, Charleroi, Bruges, Mons, Blankenburghe, Knokke; ports are Antwerp, Ostend, Zeebrugge
physical mostly flat, with hills and forest in SE
head of state King Baudouin from 1951
head of government Jean-Luc Dehaene from 1992
political system liberal democracy
exports iron and steel, textiles, manufactured goods, petrochemicals
currency Belgian franc
population (1990 est) 9,895,000 (Flemings and Walloons); annual growth rate 0.1%
life expectancy men 72, women 78
language in the N (Flanders) Flemish (a Dutch dialect, known as *Vlaams*) 55%, in the S (Wallonia) Walloon (a French dialect) 32%, with 11% bilingual, and German (E border 0.6%); all are official
religion Roman Catholic 75%
literacy 98% (1984)
GDP $111 bn (1986); $9,230 per head
chronology
1830 Belgium became an independent kingdom.
1914 Invaded by Germany.
1940 Again invaded by Germany.
1948 Belgium became founder member of Benelux Customs Union.
1949 Founder member of Council of Europe.
1951 Leopold III abdicated in favour of his son Baudouin.
1952 Belgium became founder member of European Coal and Steel Community (ECSC).
1957 Belgium became founder member of the European Community (EC).
1971 Steps towards regional autonomy taken.
1972 German-speaking members of the cabinet included for the first time.
1973 Linguistic parity achieved in government appointments.
1974 Separate regional councils and ministerial committees established.
1978 Wilfried Martens succeeds Leo Tindemans as prime minister.
1980 Open violence over language divisions. Regional assemblies for Flanders and Wallonia and a three-member executive for Brussels created.
1981 Short lived coalition led by Mark Eyskens was followed by the return of Martens.
1987 Martens head of caretaker government after breakup of coalition.
1988 Following a general election, Martens formed a new coalition.
1992 Dehaene formed a new coalition. It was announced that a federal system would be introduced.

Bellini The Doge Leonardo Loredan painted by Venetian artist Giovanni Bellini (c. 1501) National Gallery, London.

use of a 'keyboard' linked only to the clapper of the bells. *Handbell* ringing is played solo or by a team of ringers selecting from a range of lightweight bells of pure tone resting on a table.

bells nautical term applied to half-hours of watch. A day is divided into seven watches, five of four hours each and two of two hours.

Belmopan capital of Belize from 1970; population

Bellow US novelist Saul Bellow.

(1991) 4,000. It replaced Belize City as administrative centre of the country.

Belo Horizonte industrial city (steel, engineering, textiles) in SE Brazil, capital of the fast-developing state of Minas Gerais; population (1991) 2,103,300. Built in the 1890s, it was Brazil's first planned modern city.

Belorussia or *Byelorussia* former name 1919–91 of the Republic of ◊Belarus.

Belsen site of a Nazi ◊concentration camp in Lower Saxony, West Germany.

Belshazzar in the Old Testament, the last king of Babylon, son of Nebuchadnezzar. During a feast (known as *Belshazzar's Feast*) the king saw a message, interpreted by ◊Daniel as prophesying the fall of Babylon and death of Belshazzar, all of which is said to have happened that same night

---

Belize
(formerly *British Honduras*)

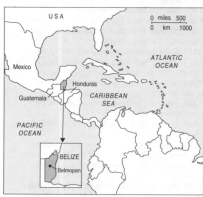

area 22,963 sq km/8,864 sq mi
capital Belmopan
towns port Belize City
physical half the country is forested, much of it high rain forest
head of state Elizabeth II from 1981 represented by governor general

head of government George Price from 1989
political system constitutional monarchy
exports sugar, citrus fruits, rice, lobster
currency Belize dollar
population (1990 est) 180,400 (including Maya minority in the interior); annual growth rate 2.5%
language English (official) and Spanish
religion Roman Catholic 60%, Protestant 35%
literacy 93% (1988)
GDP $176 million (1983); $1,000 per head
chronology
1862 Belize became a British colony.
1954 Constitution adopted, providing for limited internal self-government. General election won by George Price.
1964 Full internal self-government granted.
1965 Two-chamber national assembly introduced, with Price as prime minister.
1970 Capital moved from Belize City to Belmopan.
1975 British troops sent to defend the frontier with Guatemala.
1977 Negotiations undertaken with Guatemala but no agreement reached.
1980 United Nations called for full independence.
1981 Full independence achieved. Price became prime minister.
1984 Price defeated in general election. Manuel Esquivel formed the government. Britain reaffirmed its undertaking to defend the frontier.
1989 Price (PUP) won the general election.
1991 Diplomatic relations with Guatemala established.

Benedict, St Italian St Benedict, the founder of Western monasticism.

when the city was invaded by the Medes and Persians (539 BC).

Bemba people of Bemba origin. Their homeland is the northern province of Zambia, though many reside in urban areas such as Lusaka and Copperbelt. The Bemba language belongs to the Bantu branch of the Niger-Congo family.

Benares a transliteration of ◊Varanasi, holy city in India.

Ben Bella Ahmed 1916– . Algerian leader of the National Liberation Front (FLN) from 1952; he was prime minister of independent Algeria 1962–65, when he was overthrown by ◊Boumédienne and detained till 1979. He founded a new party, Mouvement pour la Démocratie en Algérie, 1985.

bends popular name for paralytic affliction of divers, arising from too rapid release of nitrogen after solution in the blood under pressure. Immediate treatment is compression and slow decompression in a special chamber.

Benedictine order religious order of monks and nuns in the Roman Catholic church, founded by St ◊Benedict at Subiaco, Italy, in the 6th century. St Augustine brought the order to England. At the beginning of the 14th century it was at the height of its prosperity, and had a strong influence on medieval learning.

benediction blessing recited at the end of a Christian service, particularly the Mass.

Benedict, St c. 480–c. 547. Founder of Christian monasticism in the West, and of the ◊Benedictine order. He founded the monastery of Monte Cassino, Italy. Here he wrote out his rule for monastic life, and was visited shortly before his death by the Ostrogothic king Totila, whom he converted to the Christian faith. Feast day 11 Jul.

Benelux customs union of *Be*lgium, *Ne*therlands and *Lux*embourg (agreed 1944, fully effective 1960); precursor of the European Economic Community.

Beneš Eduard 1884–1948. Czech politician. President of the republic from 1935 until forced to resign by the Germans, he headed a government in exile in London during World War II. Returning home as president in 1945, he resigned again in 1948.

Bengal former province of British India, divided 1947 into ◊West Bengal, a state of India, and East Bengal, from 1972 ◊Bangladesh. The famine in 1943, caused by a slump in demand for jute and a bad harvest, resulted in over 3 million deaths.

Bengali language a member of the Indo-Iranian branch of the Indo-European language family, the official language of Bangladesh and of the state of Bengal in India.

Benghazi or *Banghazi* historic city and industrial port in N Libya on the Gulf of Sirte; population (1982) 650,000. It was controlled by Turkey between the 16th century and 1911, and by Italy 1911–1942.

Benin
People's Republic of
(République Populaire du Benin)

area 112,600 sq km/43,480 sq mi
capital Porto Novo
towns Abomey, Natitingou; chief port Cotonou
physical flat, humid, with dense vegetation
head of state and government Nicéphore Soglo from 1991

political system socialist pluralist republic
exports cocoa, peanuts, cotton, palm oil
currency CFA franc
population (1990 est) 4,840,000; annual growth rate 3%
life expectancy men 42, women 46
language French (official); Fon 47% and Yoruta 9% in the S; six major tribal languages in the N
religion animist 65%, Christian 17%, Muslim 13%
literacy 37% male/16% female (1985 est)
GDP $1.6 bn (1987); $365 per head
chronology
1958 Became self-governing French dominion.
1960–72 Acute political instability.
1972 Military regime established by Gen Mathieu Kerekou.
1974 Kerekou announced that the country would follow a path of 'scientific socialism'.
1975 Name of country changed from Dahomey to Benin.
1977 Return to civilian rule.
1980 Kerekou formally elected president.
1989 Marxist-Leninism dropped as official ideology. Opposition to Kerekou grew.
1990 Referendum support for multiparty elections.
1991 Multiparty elections held. Kerekou defeated in presidential elections by Soglo.

Bentham English philosopher Jeremy Bentham, founder of utilitarianism.

Ben-Gurion David. Adopted name of David Gruen 1886–1973. Israeli socialist politician, the country's first prime minister 1948–53, and again in 1955–63. He was born in Poland.

Benin country in W Africa, sandwiched between Nigeria on the east and Togo on the west, with Burkina Faso to the northwest, Niger to the northeast, and the Atlantic Ocean to the south.

Benin former African kingdom 1200–1897, now part of Nigeria.

Benn Tony (Anthony Wedgwood) 1925– . English Labour politician, formerly the leading figure on the party's left wing. He was minister of technology 1966–70 and of industry 1974–75, but his campaign against entry to the European Community led to his transfer to the Department of Energy 1975–79. He unsuccessfully contested the Labour Party leadership 1988.

Bennett (Enoch) Arnold 1867–1931. English novelist. Coming from one of the 'five towns' of the Potteries which formed the setting of his major books, he became a London journalist in 1893, and editor of *Woman*, in 1896. His books include *Anna of the Five Towns* 1904, *Sacred and Profane Love* 1905, *The Old Wives' Tale* 1908, and the trilogy *Clayhanger, Hilda Lessways* and *These Twain* 1910–15.

Bennett Alan 1934– . English playwright. His works (set in his native north of England), treat subjects such as senility, illness and death, with macabre comedy. His work includes TV films, for example, *An Englishman Abroad* 1982, the cinema film, *A Private Function* 1984, and plays *Kafka's Dick* 1986 and *The Madness of George III* 1991.

Bennett Richard Rodney 1936– . British composer of jazz, film music including *Far from the Madding Crowd* 1967, *Nicholas and Alexandra* 1971, *Murder on the Orient Express* 1974 (all three scores receiving Oscar nominations), symphonies, and operas.

Ben Nevis highest mountain in the British Isles (1,342 m/4,406 ft), in the Grampians, Scotland.

Bentham Jeremy 1748–1832. English philosopher, legal and social reformer, founder of ◊utilitarianism. The essence of his moral philosophy is found in the pronouncement of his *Principles of Morals and Legislation* (written 1780, published 1789), that the object of all legislation should be 'the greatest happiness for the greatest number'.

bentwood originally a country style of wooden furniture, mainly chairs, made by steam-heating and then bending rods of wood to form the backs, legs and seat frame. It has been popular since the 19th century, although more recently designers such as Marcel ◊Breuer and Alvar ◊Aalto have

benzene

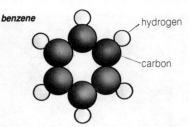

developed a different form by bending sheets of plywood.

Benz Karl 1844–1929. German automobile engineer, who produced the world's first petrol driven motor car. He built his first model engine in 1878 and the petrol driven car in 1885.

benzaldehyde C_6H_5CHO in chemistry, a clear colourless liquid with the characteristic odour of almonds. It is used as a solvent, and to make perfumes and dyes.

Benzedrine trade name for ◊amphetamine, a stimulant drug.

benzene C_6H_6 a clear liquid hydrocarbon of characteristic odour, occurring in coal tar. It is used as a solvent in the synthesis of many important chemicals.

benzodiazepine a ◊tranquillizer, which may also be used as a ◊hypnotic. Developed as a muscle relaxant, it came to be widely prescribed for its ◊anxiolytic effect. However, addiction has emerged as a serious side effect of long-term or indiscriminate use.

benzoic acid $C_6H_5CO_2H$ a white crystalline solid, sparingly soluble in water, and used as a preservative for certain foods. It is obtained chemically by the direct oxidation of benzaldehyde, and occurs in certain natural resins, some essential oils, and as hippuric acid.

benzoin a resin obtained by making incisions in the bark of *Styrax benzoin*, a tree native to the E Indies. Benzoin is used in the preparation of cosmetics, perfumes, and incense.

Ben Zvi Izhak 1884–1963. Israeli politician, president 1952–63. He was born in Poltava, Russia, and became active in the Zionist movement in the Ukraine. In 1907 he went to Palestine but was deported together with ◊Ben Gurion in 1915 and, with him, served in the Jewish Legion under Gen Allenby, who commanded the British forces in the Middle East.

Beograd the Serbo-Croatian form of ◊Belgrade, capital of Yugoslavia.

Berg Austrian composer Alban Berg.

Bergius German chemist and Nobel prizewinner for chemistry in 1931.

Beowulf Anglo-Saxon poem (composed *c.* 700), the only complete surviving example of Germanic folk-epic. It is extant in a single manuscript copied *c.* 1000 in the Cottonian collection of the British Museum.

Berber a people of N Africa, who since prehistoric times have inhabited Barbary, the Mediterranean coastlands from Egypt to the Atlantic. Their language is Berber, spoken by about one-third of Algerians and nearly two-thirds of Moroccans.

Bérégovoy Pierre 1925– . French socialist politician, prime minister from 1992. A close ally of François Mitterrand, he was named chief of staff 1981 after managing the successful presidential campaign. He was social affairs minister 1982–84 and finance minister 1984–86 and 1988–92.

Berg Alban 1885–1935. Austrian composer who studied under ◊Schoenberg, and was associated with him as one of the leaders of the serial, or 12-tone, school of composition. His output includes orchestral, chamber, vocal music, and two operas, *Wozzeck* 1925, a grim story of working-class life, and an unfinished opera, *Lulu.*

bergamot tree *Citrus bergamia*; from the rind of its fruit a fragrant orange-scented essence used as a perfume is obtained. The sole source of supply is S Calabria, but the name comes from the town of Bergamo, in Lombardy.

Bergen industrial port (shipbuilding, engineering, fishing) in SW Norway; population (1991) 213,300. Founded in 1070, Bergen was a member of the Hanseatic League.

Bergius Friedrich Karl Rudolph 1884–1949. German research chemist who invented processes for converting coal into oil, and wood into sugar.

Bergman Ingmar 1918– . Swedish film producer and director. His work deals with complex moral, psychological, and metaphysical problems and is often heavily tinged with pessimism. His films include *Wild Strawberries* 1957, *Persona* 1966, and *Fanny and Alexander* 1982.

Bergan Ingrid 1917–1982. Swedish actress, whose early films include *Casablanca* and *For Whom the Bell Tolls* both 1943. By leaving her husband for film producer Roberto Rossellini, she broke an unofficial moral code of Hollywood 'star' behaviour and was ostracized for many years. She was re-admitted to make the award-winning *Anastasia* 1956.

Bergman Swedish actress Ingrid Bergman, 1971.

Bergson Henri 1859–1941. French philosopher, who believed that time, change, and development were the essence of reality. He thought that time was not a succession of distinct and separate instants, but a continuous process in which one period merged imperceptibly into the next.

Beria Lavrenti 1899–1953. Soviet politician, who became head of the Soviet police force and minister of the interior in 1938. On Stalin's death in 1953, he was shot after a secret trial.

Bering Vitus 1681–1741. Danish explorer, the first European to sight Alaska. He died on Bering Island in the Bering Sea, both named after him, as are Bering Strait and Beringia.

Bering Sea section of the N Pacific between Alaska and Siberia, from the Aleutian Islands N to Bering Strait.

Bering Strait strait between Alaska and Siberia, linking the N Pacific and Arctic oceans.

Berio Luciano 1925– . Italian composer. His style has been described as graceful ◊serialism, and he has frequently experimented with electronic music and taped sound.

Berkeley Busby 1895–1976. US film director, famous for his ingeniously extravagant sets and his use of female dancers to create large-scale pattern effects through movement and costume, as in *Gold Diggers of 1933.*

berkelium an artificially-made radioactive element, symbol Bk, atomic number 97. It was discovered at Berkeley, USA, in 1949 by Seaborg and others.

Berkshire or *Royal Berkshire* county in S central England

area 1,259 sq km/486 sq mi

towns administrative headquarters Reading; Eton, Slough, Maidenhead, Ascot, Bracknell, Newbury, Windsor

products general agricultural and horticultural electronics, plastics, pharmaceuticals

population (1991) 716,500

famous people King Alfred, Stanley Spencer.

Berlin industrial city (machine tools, electrical goods, paper and printing) and capital of the Federal Republic of Germany; population (1990) 3,102,500. The ◊Berlin Wall divided the city from 1961 to 1989, but in Oct 1990 Berlin became the capital of a unified Germany once more, with East and West Berlin reunited as the 16th *Land* (state) of the Federal Republic.

Berlin Irving. Adopted name of Israel Baline 1888–1989. Russian-born American composer, whose hits include 'Alexander's Ragtime Band', 'Always', 'God Bless America', and 'White Christmas', and the musicals *Top Hat* 1935, *Annie Get Your Gun* 1950, and *Call Me Madam* 1953. He also wrote the scores of films, such as *Blue Skies.*

Berlin blockade in June 1948, the closing of entry to Berlin from the west by Soviet forces. It was an attempt to prevent the other Allies (USA, France, and Britain) unifying the western part of Germany. The British and US forces responded by sending supplies to the city by air for over a year (the *Berlin airlift*). In May 1949 the blockade was lifted; the airlift continued until Sept. The blockade marked the formal division of the city into Eastern and Western sectors.

Berlin, Congress of congress of the European powers (Russia, Turkey, Austria-Hungary, Britain, France, Italy, and Germany) held at Berlin in 1878 to determine the boundaries of the Balkan states after the Russo-Turkish war. Prime Minister Disraeli attended as Britain's chief envoy, and declared on his return to England that he had brought back 'peace with honour'.

Berlinguer Enrico 1922–1984. Italian Communist who freed the party from Soviet influence. By 1976 he was near to the premiership, but the ◊Red Brigade murder of Aldo Moro, the prime minister, revived the socialist vote.

Berlin Wall the dividing line between East and West Berlin which, from 13 Aug 1961, was reinforced by the Russians with armed guards and barbed wire to prevent the escape of unwilling inhabitants of East Berlin to the rival political system of West Berlin. The interconnecting link between East and West Berlin was *Checkpoint Charlie*, where both sides used to exchange captured spies. Escapers from East to West were shot on sight. The Wall was dismantled in Nov 1989.

Berlioz (Louis) Hector 1803–1869. French Romantic composer and the founder of modern orchestration. Much of his music was inspired by drama and literature and has a theatrical quality. He wrote symphonic works such as *Symphonie fantastique* and *Roméo et Juliette*, dramatic cantatas including *La Damnation de Faust* and *L'Enfance du Christ*, sacred music and three operas, *Béatrice et Bénédict*, *Benvenuto Cellini*, and *Les Troyens*.

Bermuda British colony in the NW Atlantic
area 54 sq km/21 sq mi
capital and chief port Hamilton
products Easter lilies, pharmaceutical; tourism and banking are important
currency Bermuda dollar
population (1980) 54,893
language English
religion Christian
government under the constitution of 1968, Bermuda is a fully self-governing British colony, with a Governor, Senate and elected House of Assembly (premier from 1982 John Swan, United Bermuda Party).
recent history the islands were named after Juan de Bermudez, who visited them in 1515, and were settled by British colonists in 1609. Racial violence in 1977 led to intervention, at the request of the government, by British troops.

Bern (French *Berne*) capital of Switzerland and of Bern canton, in W Switzerland on the Aar; industries include textiles, chocolate, pharmaceuticals, light metal and electrical goods; population (1984) 140,600. It joined the Swiss confederation in 1353 and became the capital 1848.

Bernadette, St 1844–1879. French saint, born in Lourdes in the French Pyrenees. In Feb 1858 she had a vision of the Virgin Mary in a grotto, and it became a centre of pilgrimage. Many sick people who were dipped in the waters were said to have been cured. Feast day 16 Apr.

Bernard Claude 1813–1878. French physiologist and founder of experimental medicine. Bernard first demonstrated that digestion is not restricted to the stomach, but takes place throughout the small intestine. He discovered the digestive input of the pancreas, several functions of the liver, and the vasomotor nerves which dilate and contract the blood vessels and thus regulate body temperature.

Bernard of Clairvaux, St 1090–1153. Christian founder in 1115 of Clairvaux monastery in Champagne, France, he reinvigorated the ◊Cistercian order; he preached the Second Crusade in 1146, and had the scholastic philosopher Abelard condemned for heresy. He is often depicted with a beehive. Feast day 20 Aug.

Bernard of Menthon, St or *Bernard of Montjoux* 923–1008. Christian priest, founder of the hospices for travellers on the Alpine passes that bear his name. The large, heavily built *St Bernard dogs* formerly used to find travellers lost in the snow were also called after him. He is the patron saint of mountaineers. Feast day 28 May.

Bernese Oberland or *Bernese Alps* the mountainous area in the S of Berne canton which includes some of the most famous peaks, such as the Jungfrau, Eiger, and Finsteraarhorn. Interlaken is the chief town.

Bernhard Prince of the Netherlands 1911– . Formerly Prince Bernhard of Lippe-Biesterfeld, he married Princess ◊Juliana in 1937. When Germany invaded the Netherlands in 1940, he escaped to England. In 1976 he was widely censured for his involvement in the purchase of Lockheed aircraft by the Netherlands.

Bernhardt Sarah. Stage name of French tragic actress Rosine Bernard 1845–1923. Dominating the stage of her day, she frequently performed at the Comédie-Française. Her most famous roles were as Cordelia in *King Lear*, ◊Racine's *Phèdre*, Dona Sol in ◊Hugo's *Hernani*, and in the male roles of Hamlet, and of Napoleon's son in ◊Rostand's *L'Aiglon*.

Bernini Giovanni Lorenzo 1598–1680. Italian sculptor, architect, and painter, a leading figure in the development of the Baroque style. His work in Rome includes the colonnaded piazza in front of St Peter's Basilica (1656), fountains (as in the Piazza Navona), and papal monuments. His sculpture includes *The Ecstacy of St Theresa* 1645–52 (S Maria della Vittoria, Rome), and numerous portrait busts.

Bernouilli effect

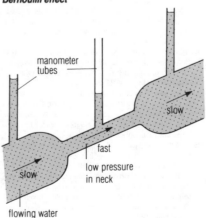

manometer tubes

slow

fast

low pressure in neck

slow

flowing water

Bernoulli Swiss family of mathematicians. *Jacques* (1654–1705) discovered Bernoullian numbers, a series of complex fractions used in higher mathematics. *Jean* (1667–1748) found the equation of the ◊catenary (1690) and developed exponential ◊calculus (1691). Jean's son *Daniel* (1700–82) made important contributions in hydrodynamics (the study of fluids).

Bernoulli effect a drop in hydraulic pressure, such as that in a fluid flowing through a constriction in a pipe. It is also responsible for the pressure differences on each surface of an aerofoil, which gives lift to the wing of an aircraft. The effect was named after the Swiss physicist Daniel ◊Bernoulli.

Bernstein Leonard 1918–1990. US composer, conductor and pianist. He conducted major orchestras throughout the world. His works, which established a vogue for realistic, contemporary themes, included symphonies such as *The Age of Anxiety* 1949; ballets such as *Fancy Free* 1944; scores for musicals including *Wonderful Town* 1953, *West Side Story* 1957; and a *Mass* 1971 in memory of J F Kennedy.

berry a fleshy, many-seeded ◊fruit that does not split open to release the seeds. The outer layer of tissue, the exocarp, forms an outer skin which is often brightly coloured to attract birds to eat the fruit and thus disperse the seeds. Examples of berries are the tomato and the grape.

Berry Chuck (Charles Edward) 1931– . US rock-and-roll singer, prolific songwriter, and guitarist. His characteristic guitar riffs became staples of rock music, and his humorous storytelling lyrics were also influential. He had a string of hits in the 1950s beginning with 'Maybellene' 1955.

Berryman John 1914–1972. US poet, whose complex and personal works include *Homage to Mistress Bradstreet* 1956, *77 Dream Songs* 1964 (Pulitzer Prize), and *His Toy, His Dream, His Rest* 1968.

berserker legendary Scandinavian warrior whose frenzy in battle transformed him into a wolf or bear howling and foaming at the mouth (hence 'to go berserk'), and rendered him immune to sword and flame.

Bertholet Claude Louis 1748–1822. French chemist, who carried out research on dyes and bleaches (introducing the use of ◊chlorine as a bleach) and determined the composition of ◊ammonia.

Bertolucci Bernardo 1940– . Italian director, whose work combines political and historical satire with an elegant visual appeal. His films include *The Spider's Stratagem* 1970, *Last Tango in Paris* 1972, and *The Last Emperor* 1987, for which he received an Academy Award.

beryl a mineral, beryllium aluminium silicate, $Be_3Al_2Si_6O_{18}$, which forms crystals chiefly in granite. It is the chief ore of ◊beryllium. Two of its gem forms are *aquamarine* (light-blue crystals) and *emerald* (dark-green crystals).

beryllium a light silvery hard metallic element, symbol Be, atomic number 4, relative atomic mass 9.013. It is used as a source of neutrons when bombarded, to make windows for X-ray tubes, to toughen copper for high-grade gearwheels and spark-free tools, and as a neutron reflector, ◊moderator, and uranium sheathing in nuclear reactors.

Berzelius Jöns Jakob 1779–1848. Swedish chemist who specialized in the determination of atomic and molecular weights. He invented (1813–14) the system of chemical symbols now in use and did valuable work on ◊catalysts.

Bessel Friedrich Wilhelm 1784–1846. German astronomer and mathematician, the first person to find the approximate distance to a star by direct methods when he measured the ◊parallax of 61 Cygni in 1838.

Bessemer process the first cheap method of making ◊steel, invented by Henry Bessemer in England in 1856. It has since been superseded by more efficient steelmaking processes, particularly the ◊basic-oxygen process. In the Bessemer process compressed air is blown into the bottom of a converter, a furnace shaped rather like a cement mixer, containing molten pig iron. The excess carbon in the iron burns out, other impurities form a slag, and the furnace is emptied by tilting.

Best Charles Herbert 1899–1978. Canadian physiologist, one of the team of Canadian scientists including Frederick ◊Banting, whose researches resulted in 1922 in the discovery of insulin as a treatment for diabetes.

bestiary in medieval times, a book with stories and illustrations which depicted real and mythical animals or plants to illustrate a (usually Christian) moral. The stories were initially derived from the Greek *Physiologus* (c. 2nd century AD), a collection of 48 such stories, written in Alexandria.

bestseller a book written and merchandised for the maximum market, frequently, thanks to the system of newspaper charting of sales, in a very short time. The Bible is the great bestseller, but more popular and commercial examples include, in the USA, Charles Monroe Seldon's *In His Steps* 1897, Margaret Mitchell's *Gone With the Wind* 1936, and Dale Carnegie's *How to Win Friends and Influence People* 1937.

beta-blocker a drug that blocks impulses which stimulate certain nerve endings (beta receptors) serving the heart muscles. This reduces the heart rate and the force of contraction. This, in turn, reduces the amount of oxygen (and therefore the blood supply) required by the heart. They are banned from use in competitive sport.

beta particle an electron or positron emitted from a radioactive substance whilst undergoing spontaneous disintegration. Beta particles do not exist in the nucleus, but are created on disintegration when a neutron converts to a proton to emit an electron, or a proton converts to a neutron to emit a positron.

Betelgeuse a red supergiant star in the constellation of Orion, over 300 times the diameter of the Sun, about the same size as the orbit of Mars. It lies 650 light years away.

betel nut fruit of the areca palm (*Areca catechu*), used as a masticatory by peoples of the East: chewing it results in blackened teeth and a deep red stained mouth.

Bethlehem (Hebrew *Beit-Lahm*) town on the W bank of the river Jordan, S of Jerusalem. Occupied by Israel in 1967; population (1980) 14,000. In the New Testament it was the birthplace of Jesus Christ and associated with King David.

Bethmann Hollweg Theobald von 1856–1921. German politician, imperial chancellor 1909–17, largely responsible for engineering popular support for World War I in Germany, but his power was gradually superseded by a military dictatorship under ◊Ludendorff.

Betjeman John 1906–1984. English poet and essayist, originator of a peculiarly English light verse, nostalgic and delighting in Victorian and Edwardian architecture. His *Collected Poems* appeared in 1968 and a verse autobiography *Summoned by Bells* in

Bevan *Aneurin Bevan when minister of health, 1945.*

1960. He was knighted in 1969 and became Poet Laureate in 1972.

betony plant of the family Labiatae, *Betonica officinalis* is a hedgerow weed in Britain. It has a hairy stem and leaves and reddish-purple flowers.

Beuys Joseph 1921–1986. German sculptor and performance artist. By the 1970s he had gained an international reputation. His sculpture makes use of unusual materials such as felt and fat. He was strongly influenced by his wartime experiences.

Bevan Aneurin 1897–1960. British Labour politician. Son of a Welsh miner, and himself a miner at 13, he became Member of Parliament for Ebbw Vale 1929–60. As minister of health 1945–51, he inaugurated the National Health Service (NHS); he was minister of labour Jan–Apr 1951, when he resigned (with Harold Wilson) on the introduction of NHS charges and led a Bevanite faction against the government. He was noted as an orator.

beverage plant product used to impart pleasant flavours and stimulants to people's fluid intake. Examples include tea, coffee, cocoa, cola nuts, and hops.

Beveridge William Henry, 1st Baron Beveridge 1879–1963. British economist. A civil servant, he acted as Lloyd George's lieutenant in the social legislation of the Liberal government before World War I. The Beveridge Report 1942 formed the basis of the welfare state in Britain.

Bevin Ernest 1881–1951. British Labour politician. Chief creator of the Transport and General Workers' Union, he was its general secretary 1921–40, when he entered the war cabinet as minister of labour and National Service. He organized the 'Bevin boys', chosen by ballot to work in the coal mines as war service, and was foreign secretary in the Labour government 1945–51.

Bewick Thomas 1753–1828. British wood engraver, excelling in animal subjects. His illustrated *General History of Quadrupeds* 1790 and *History of British Birds* 1797, 1804 display his skill.

Beza Théodore (properly De Bèsze) 1519-1605. French church reformer. He settled in Geneva, Switzerland, where he worked with the Protestant leader J Calvin and succeeded him 1564–1600 as head of the reformed church there. He wrote in defence of the burning of ◊Servetus (1554) and translated the New Testament into Latin.

BFI abbreviation for *British Film Institute*.

BFPO abbreviation for *British Forces Post Office*.

Bhagavad-Gītā (Hindu 'the Song of the Blessed'). Religious and philosophical Sanskrit poem, dating from around 300 BC, forming an episode in the sixth book of the *Mahābhārata*, one of the two great Hindu epics. It is the supreme religious work of ◊Hinduism.

bhakti (Sanskrit 'devotion') in Hinduism, a tradition of worship that emphasizes love and devotion rather than ritual, sacrifice, or study.

bhangra pop music evolved in the UK in the late 1970s from traditional Punjabi music, combining electronic instruments and ethnic drums.

bhikku a Buddhist monk who is totally dependent on alms and the monastic community (*sangha*).

Bhindranwale Sant Jarnail Singh 1947–1984. Indian Sikh fundamentalist leader, who campaigned for the creation of a separate state of Khalistan during the early 1980s, precipitating a bloody Hindu-Sikh conflict in the Punjab. He was killed in the siege of the Golden Temple in ◊Amritsar.

Bhopal industrial city (textiles, chemicals, electrical goods, jewellery); capital of Madhya Pradesh, central India; population (1981) 672,000. In 1984 some 2,000 people died after an escape of poisonous gas from a factory owned by the US company Union Carbide.

Bhumibol Adulyadej 1927– . King of Thailand from 1946. Educated in Bangkok and Switzerland, he succeeded on the assassination of his brother, formally taking the throne in 1950. In 1973 he was active, with popular support, in overthrowing the military government of Field Marshal Kittachorn, and ending a sequence of army-dominated regimes in power from 1932.

Bhutan mountainous, landlocked country in SE Asia, bordered to the N by China and to the S by India.

Bhutto Benazir 1953– . Pakistani politician, leader of the Pakistan People's Party (PPP) from 1984 (in exile until 1986), and prime minister of Pakistan 1988–90. The first female leader of a Muslim state, she was accused of corruption and incompetence and overthrown by President Ghulam Ishaq Khan 1990.

Bhutto Zulfiqar Ali 1928–1979. Pakistani politician, president 1971–73 and then prime minister until the 1977 military coup led by Gen ◊Zia ul Haq. In 1978 he was sentenced to death for conspiracy to murder a political opponent, and was hanged.

Biafra, Republic of state proclaimed in 1967 when fears that Nigerian central government was

Bhutto *Benazir Bhutto in Islamabad, Dec 1988.*

Bhutan
Kingdom of
(*Druk-yul*)

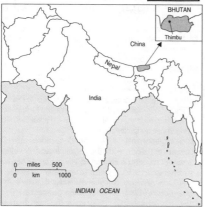

China

Thimbu

Nepal

India

BHUTAN

Thimbu

| 0 | miles | 500 |
| 0 | km | 1000 |

INDIAN OCEAN

area 46,600 sq km/18,000 sq mi
capital Thimphu
physical occupies S slopes of the Himalayas, and is cut by valleys of tributaries of the Brahmaputra
head of state and government Jigme Singye Wangchuk from 1972

political system absolute monarchy
exports timber, minerals
currency ngultrum; also Indian currency
population 1,566,000 (1990 est); annual growth rate 2%
life expectancy men 44, women 43
language Dzongkha (official; a Tibetan dialect), Nepáli, and English
religion Mahayana Buddhist
literary 5%
GDP $250 million (1987); $170 per head
chronology
1865 Trade treaty with Britain signed.
1907 First hereditary monarch installed.
1910 Anglo-Bhutanese Treaty signed.
1945 Indo-Bhutan Treaty of Friendship signed.
1952 King Jigme Dorji Wangchuk installed.
1953 National assembly established.
1959 4,000 Tibetan refugees given asylum.
1968 King established first cabinet.
1972 King died and was succeeded by his son Jigme Singye Wangchuk.
1979 Tibetan refugees told to take up Bhutanese citizenship or leave. Most stayed.
1983 Bhutan became a founder member of the South Asian Regional Cooperation organization (SARC).
1988 King imposed 'code of conduct' suppressing Nepalese customs.
1990 Hundreds of people allegedly killed during prodemocracy demonstrations.

Billy the Kid *Historic photograph of American outlaw William Bonney, Billy the Kid.*

increasingly in the hands of the rival Hausa tribe led the predominantly Ibo Eastern Region of Nigeria to secede under Lt-Col Odumegwu Ojukwu,

an Oxford-educated Ibo. On the proclamation of Biafra, civil war ensued with the rest of the federation, and in a bitterly fought campaign federal forces had confined the Biafrans to a shrinking area of the interior by 1968, and by 1970 Biafra ceased to exist.

Bible the sacred book of the Jewish and Christian religions. The Hebrew Bible, recognized by both Jews and Christians, is called the ◊*Old Testament* by Christians. The ◊*New Testament* comprises books recognized by the Christian church from the 4th century as canonical. The Roman Catholic Bible also includes the ◊*Apocrypha.* The first English translation of the entire Bible was by a priest, Miles Coverdale, 1535; the Authorized Version or *King James Bible* 1611 was long influential in the clarity and beauty of its language. A revision of the Authorized Version carried out in 1959 by the British and Foreign Bible Society produced the widely-used Revised Standard Version. A new translation into English from the original Hebrew and Greek texts was the New English Bible (New Testament 1961, Old Testament and Apocrypha 1970). Missionary activity led to the translation of the Bible into the language of native populations, and by 1975 parts of the Bible had been translated into over 1500 different languages, with 261 complete translations.

bicarbonate of soda a white crystalline solid ($NaHCO_3$) more properly called sodium hydrogen carbonate (sodium barcarbonate). It neutralizes acids and is used in medicine to treat acid indigestion. It is also used in baking powders and effervescent drinks.

Bichat Marie François Xavier 1771–1802. French physician and founder of ◊histology. He studied the organs of the body, their structure, and the ways in which they are affected by disease. This led to his discovery and naming of 'tissues', a basic medical concept. He argued that disease does not affect the whole organ but only certain of its constituent tissues.

bicycle a pedal-driven two-wheeled vehicle used in ◊cycling.

biennial plant a plant that completes its life cycle in two years. During the first year it grows vegetatively and the surplus food produced is stored in its ◊perennating organ, usually the root. In the following year these food reserves are used for the production of leaves, flowers and seeds, after which the plant dies. Many root vegetables are biennials, including the carrot *Daucus carota* and parsnip *Pastinaca sativa*. Some garden plants which are grown as biennials are actually perennials, for example the wallflower *Cheiranthus cheiri*.

bigamy in law, the offence of marrying a person whilst already lawfully married. In some countries marriage to more than one wife or husband is lawful; see also ◊polygamy.

big band description of jazz sound created in the late 1930s and 1940s by bands of 15 or more players, such as those of Duke ◊Ellington and Benny ◊Goodman, where there is more than one instrument to some of the parts.

Big Bang in astronomy, the hypothetical 'explosive' event which marked the origin of the Universe as we know it. At the time of the Big Bang, the entire Universe was squeezed into a hot, superdense state. The Big Bang explosion threw this material outwards, producing the expanding Universe (see ◊red shift). The cause of the Big Bang is unknown; observations of the current rate of expansion of the Universe suggest that it took place between 10 billion and 20 billion years ago. See also ◊cosmology.

Big Bang in economics, popular term for the major changes instituted in late 1986 to the organization and practices of the City of London as Britain's financial centre, with the aim of ensuring that London retained its place as one of the leading world financial centres. Facilitated in part by computerization and on-line communications, the changes included the liberalization of the London ◊Stock Exchange. This involved merging the functions of jobber (dealer in stocks and shares) and broker (who mediates between the jobber and the public), introducing negotiated commission rates, and allowing foreign banks and financial companies to own British brokers/jobbers, or themselves to join the London Stock Exchange.

Big Ben a bell in the clock tower of the Houses of Parliament in London, cast at the Whitechapel Bell Foundry in 1858, and known as 'Big Ben' after Benjamin Hall, First Commissioner of Works at the time.

Bihar or *Behar* state of NE India
area 173,876 sq km/67,132 sq mi
capital Patna
products copper, iron, coal, rice, jute, sugarcane, grain, oilseed
population (1981) 70,000,000
language Hindi, Bihari
famous people Chandragupta, Asoka
history the ancient kingdom of Magadha roughly corresponded to central and S Bihar.

Bikini atoll in the ◊Marshall Islands, N Pacific, where in 1946–63 atom-bomb tests were carried out by the USA.

Biko Steve 1946–1977. South African civil-rights leader. An active opponent of ◊apartheid, he was arrested in Sept 1977 and died in detention six days later.

bilateralism in economics, a trade agreement between two countries or groups of countries in which they give each other preferential treatment. Usually the terms agreed result in balanced trade and are favoured by countries with limited foreign exchange reserves. Bilateralism is incompatible with free trade.

Bilbao industrial port (iron and steel, chemicals, cement, food) in N Spain, capital of Biscay province; population (1981) 433,000.

bilberry plant *Vaccinium myrtillus* of the family Ericaceae closely resembling the cranberry, but distinguished by its bluish berries.

bilby a rabbit-eared bandicoot *Macrotis lagotis*, a lightly-built marsupial with big ears and long nose. This burrowing animal is mainly carnivorous. Its pouch opens backwards.

Bildungsroman (German 'education novel') novel that deals with the psychological development of its central character, tracing his or her life from inexperienced youth to maturity. ◊Goethe's *Wilhelm Meisters Lehrjahr/Wilhelm Meister's Apprenticeship* 1795–96 established the genre.

bile a brownish fluid produced by the liver. In most vertebrates, it is stored in the gall bladder and emptied into the small intestine as food passes through. *Bile salts* assist the digestion of fats; *bile pigments* are the breakdown products of old red blood cells which are passed into the gut to be eliminated with the faeces.

bilharziasis or *schistosomiasis* disease causing anaemia, inflammation, diarrhoea, dysentery, enlargement of the spleen and liver, and cirrhosis of the liver. It is contracted by bathing in water contaminated with human sewage.

billabong (Aboriginal Australian *billa bung* 'dead river') a waterhole, originally part of a river, formed by the drying up of the channel connecting it to the river.

billet doux (French 'sweet note') a letter to or from one's lover.

billiards indoor game played with tapered poles called cues and composition balls (one red, two white) on a rectangular table covered with a green baize cloth with six pockets, one at each corner and in each of the long sides at the middle. Played normally by two players, scoring strokes are made by potting the red ball, potting your opponent's ball, or potting another ball off one of these two.

billion a thousand million (1,000,000,000). In Britain, this number was formerly known as a milliard, and a million million (1,000,000,000,000) as a billion, but the first definition is more prevalent.

Bill of Exchange a form of commercial credit instrument, or IOU, used in international trade. In Britain, a Bill of Exchange is defined by the Bills of Exchange Act, 1882, as an unconditional order in writing addressed by one person to another, signed by the person giving it, requiring the person to whom it is addressed to pay on demand or at a fixed or determinable future time a certain sum in money to or to the order of a specified person, or to the bearer. US practice is governed by the Uniform Negotiable Instruments Law, drafted on the same lines as the British, and accepted by all states by 1927.

Bill of Rights in Britain, Act of 1689 embodying the Declaration of Rights presented by the House of Commons to William and Mary before they replaced James II on the throne. It made illegal the suspension of laws by royal authority without Parliament's consent; the power to dispense with laws; the establishment of special courts of law; levying money by royal prerogative without Parliament's consent; a standing army in peacetime without Parliament's consent. It also asserted a right to petition the sovereign, freedom of parliamentary elections, freedom of speech in parliamentary debates, and the necessity of frequent parliaments. See also ◊Constitution. In the USA, the first ten amendments (1791) to the American constitution:

1 giving freedom of worship, of speech, of the press, of assembly, and to petition the government;

2 asserting the right to keep and bear arms (which has hindered modern attempts to control illicit use of arms);

3 prohibiting billeting of soldiers in private homes in peacetime;

4 forbidding unreasonable search and seizure;

5 asserting that none are to be 'deprived of life, liberty or property without due process of law' or be compelled in any criminal case to be a witness against himself (frequently quoted in the McCarthy era);

6 giving the right to speedy trial, to call witnesses, and have defence counsel;

7 giving the right to trial by jury;

8 outlawing excessive bail or fines, or 'cruel and unusual punishment', not to be inflicted (used in recent times to oppose the death penalty);

9 and 10 safeguarding to the states and people all rights not specifically delegated to the central government.

Billy the Kid nickname of William H Bonney 1859–1881. US outlaw, a leader in the Lincoln County cattle war in New Mexico, who allegedly killed his first man at 12. He was sentenced to death for murdering a sheriff, but escaped (killing two guards), and was finally shot by Sheriff Pat Garrett while trying to avoid recapture.

bimetallic strip strip made from two metals each having a different coefficient of thermal expansion which therefore bends when subjected to a change in temperature.

bimetallism monetary system in which two metals, traditionally gold and silver, both circulate at a ratio fixed by the state, are coined by the ◊mint on equal terms, and are legal tender to any amount. The system was in use in the 19th century.

binary fission in biology, a form of asexual reproduction, whereby a single-celled organism divides into two smaller 'daughter' cells. It can also occur in a few simple multicellular organisms, such as sea anemones, producing two smaller sea anemones of equal size.

binary number system or *binary number code* a system of numbers to base 2 using combinations of the two digits 1 and 0. Binary numbers play a key role in modern digital computers, where they form the basis of the internal coding of information, the values of bits (short for 'binary digits') being represented as on/off (1 and 0) states of switches and high/low voltages in circuits.

binary star a pair of stars moving in orbit around their common centre of mass. Observations show that most stars are binary, or even multiple, for example the nearest star system to the Sun, ◊Alpha Centauri.

binary weapon in chemical warfare, weapon consisting of two substances that in isolation are harmless but when mixed together form a poisonous nerve gas.

binding energy in physics, the amount of energy needed to break the nucleus of an atom into the neutrons and protons that make it up.

binoculars

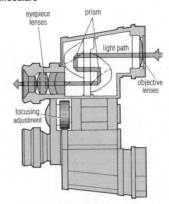

eyepiece lenses   prism

light path

objective lenses

focusing adjustment

binoculars an optical instrument for viewing an object in magnification with both eyes, for example, field-glasses and opera-glasses. Binoculars consist of two telescopes containing lenses and prisms, which produce a stereoscopic effect as well as magnifying the image. Use of prisms has the effect of 'folding' the light path, allowing for a compact design.

binomial in algebra, an expression consisting of two terms, such as $a + b$, $a - b$. The **binomial theorem**, discovered by Isaac ◊Newton and first published in 1676, is a formula whereby any power of a binomial quantity may be found without performing the progressive multiplications.

binomial system of nomenclature in biology, the system in which all organisms are identified by a two-part Latinized name. Devised by the biologist ◊Linnaeus, it is also known as the Linnean System. The first name identifies the ◊genus, the second the ◊species within that genus.

binturong shaggy-coated mammal *Arctitis binturong*, the largest member of the mongoose family, nearly 1 m/3 ft long excluding a long muscular tail with a prehensile tip. Mainly nocturnal and tree-dwelling, the binturong is found in the forests of SE Asia, feeding on fruit, eggs, and small animals.

biochemistry science concerned with the chemistry of living organisms: the structure and reactions of proteins (especially enzymes), nucleic acids, carbohydrates, and lipids.

biodegradable material capable of being broken down by living organisms, principally bacteria and fungi. Biodegradable substances, for example fruit, vegetables, and sewage, can be rendered harmless by natural processes. Non-biodegradable substances, such as most plastics and heavy metals, eventually accumulate in the environment and may cause serious problems of ◊pollution.

bioengineering the application of engineering to biology and medicine. Common applications include the design and use of artificial limbs, joints and organs, including hip joints and heart valves.

biofeedback modification or control of a biological system by its results or effects, for example, a change in the position or ◊trophic level of one species affects all levels above it.

biogenesis biological term coined 1870 by T H Huxley to express the hypothesis that living matter always arises out of other similar forms of living matter. It superseded the opposite idea of ◊spontaneous generation or abiogenesis (that is, that living things may arise out of non-living matter).

biography an account of a person's life. When it is written by that person, it is an ◊autobiography. Biography can be simply a factual narrative, but it was also established as a literary form in the 18th and 19th centuries.

Bioko island in the Bight of Bonny, West Africa, part of Equatorial Guinea; area 2,017 sq km/786 sq mi; produces coffee, cacao and copra; population (1983) 57,190. Formerly a Spanish possession, as Fernando Po, it was known 1973–79 as Macías Nguema Bijogo.

biological clock a regular internal rhythm of activity, produced by unknown mechanisms, and not dependent on external time-signals. Such clocks are known to exist in almost all animals, and also in many plants, fungi and unicellular organisms. In higher organisms, there appears to be a series of clocks of graded importance. For example, although body temperature and activity cycles in human beings are normally 'set' to 24 hours, the two cycles may vary independently, showing that two clock mechanisms are involved.

biological control the control of pests such as insects and fungi through biological means, rather than the use of chemicals. This can include breeding resistant crop strains, inducing infertility in the pest, breeding viruses that attack the pest species, or introducing the pest's natural predator. Biological control tends to be naturally self-regulating, but as living systems are so complex it is difficult to predict all the consequences of introducing a biological controlling agent.

biological oxygen demand (BOD) the amount of dissolved oxygen taken up by micro-organisms in a sample of water. Since these micro-organisms live by decomposing organic matter, and the amount of oxygen used is proportional to their number and metabolic rate, BOD can be used as a measure of the extent to which the water is polluted with organic compounds.

biological shield a shield around a nuclear reactor that protects personnel from the effects of ◊radiation. It usually consists of a thick wall of steel and concrete.

biological warfare use of living organisms, or of infectious material derived from them, to bring about death or disease in humans, animals, or plants. It was condemned by the Geneva Convention 1925, to which the United Nations has urged all states to adhere. See also ◊chemical warfare.

biology the science of life. Strictly speaking, biology includes all the life sciences, for example, anatomy and physiology, cytology, zoology and botany, ecology, genetics, biochemistry and biophysics, animal behaviour, embryology, and plant breeding.

bioluminescence the production of light by living organisms. It is a feature of many fish, crustaceans, and other marine animals, especially deep-sea organisms. On land, bioluminescence is seen in some nocturnal insects such as glowworms and fireflies, and in certain bacteria and fungi. Light is usually produced by the oxidation of luciferin, a reaction catalysed by the ◊enzyme luciferase. This reaction is unique, being the only known biological oxidation which does not produce heat. Animal luminescence is involved in communication, camouflage, or luring prey, but its function in other organisms is unclear.

biomass the gross weight of organisms present in a given area. It may be specified for one particular species (such as earthworm biomass), for a category of species (for example, herbivore biomass) or for all species (total biomass).

biome a large-scale natural assemblage of plants and animals living in a particular type of environment. Examples include the tundra biome and the desert biome.

bionics the design and development of artificial systems that imitate those of living things. The artificial bionic arm, for example, uses electronics to amplify minute electrical signals generated in body muscles to work electric motors, which operate the joints of artificial fingers and wrist.

biophysics the application of physical laws to the properties of living organisms. Examples include using the principles of ◊mechanics to calculate the strength of bones and muscles, and ◊thermodynamics to study plant and animal energetics.

biopsy removal of a tissue sample from the body for diagnostic examination.

biorhythms rhythmic changes, mediated by ◊hormones, in the physical state and activity patterns of certain plants and animals which have seasonal activities. Examples include winter hibernation, spring flowering or breeding, and periodic migration. The hormonal changes themselves are often a response to changes in day length (◊photoperiodism); they signal the time of year to the animal or plant. Other biorhythms are innate, and continue even if external stimuli such as day-length are removed. These include a 24-hour or ◊circadian rhythm, a 28-day or circalunar rhythm (corresponding to the phases of the moon), and even a year-long rhythm in some organisms.

biosphere or *ecosphere* that region of the earth's surface (land and water), and the atmosphere above it, which can be occupied by living organisms.

biosynthesis the synthesis of ◊organic chemistry from simple inorganic ones by living cells. One important biosynthetic reaction is the conversion of carbon dioxide and water to glucose by plants, during ◊photosynthesis. Other biosynthetic reactions produce cell constituents including ◊proteins and ◊fats.

biotechnology the industrial use of living organisms, to produce food, drugs or other products. Historically biotechnology has largely been restricted to the brewing and baking industries, using ◊fermentation by yeast, but the most recent advances involve ◊genetic engineering, in which single-celled organisms with modified ◊DNA are used to produce substances such as insulin.

biotin a vitamin of the B-complex; it is found in many different kinds of food, with egg-yolk, liver and yeast containing large amounts.

birch tree of the genus *Betula*, including about 40 species found in cool temperate parts of the northern hemisphere. The white or silver birch *Betula pendula* is of industrial importance, as its timber is quick-growing and durable. The bark is used for tanning and dyeing leather.

bird backboned animal of the class Aves, the biggest group of land vertebrates, characterized by warm blood, feathers, wings, breathing through lungs, and egg-laying by the female. Most birds fly, but some groups (such as ostriches) are flightless. Many communicate by sounds or visual displays. Birds have highly developed patterns of instinctive behaviour. Hearing and eyesight are well developed, but the sense of smell is usually poor. Typically the eggs are brooded in a nest, and, on hatching,,the young receive a period of parental care. There are nearly 8,500 species of birds.

bird of paradise one of 40 species of crow-like birds, family *Paradiseidae*, native to New Guinea

Bismarck *Prusso-German politician Prince Otto von Bismarck in army uniform.*

and neighbouring islands. Females are drably coloured, but the males have bright and elaborate plumage used in courtship display. Hunted almost to extinction for their plumage, they are now being conserved.

Birkenhead Frederick Edwin Smith, 1st Earl of Birkenhead 1872–1930. British Conservative politician. A flamboyant character, known as FE, he joined with Baron Carson in organizing armed resistance in Ulster to Irish Home Rule; he was Lord Chancellor 1919–22, and a much criticized secretary for India 1924–28.

Birmingham industrial city in the West Midlands, second largest city of the UK; population (1986) 1,006,527, metropolitan area 2,632,000. Industries include motor vehicles, machine tools, aerospace control systems, plastics, chemicals, food.

Birmingham industrial city (iron, steel, chemicals, building materials, computers, cotton textiles) and commercial centre in Alabama, USA; population (1984) 280,000.

Biro Lazlo 1900–1985. Hungarian-born Argentinian who invented a ballpoint pen in 1944. His name became generic for ballpoint pens in the UK.

Birtwistle Harrison 1934– . British composer. He has specialized in chamber music, for example, his chamber opera *Punch and Judy* 1967.

Biscay, Bay of bay of the Atlantic Ocean between N Spain and W France, known for rough seas and exceptionally high tides.

bishop priest next in rank to an archbishop in the Roman Catholic, Eastern Orthodox, and Anglican churches. A bishop has charge of a district called a *diocese*.

Bismarck Otto Eduard Leopold, Prince von Bismarck 1815–1898. German politician, prime minister of Prussia 1862–90 and chancellor of the German Empire 1871–90. He pursued an aggressively expansionist policy, with wars against Denmark 1863–64, Austria 1866, and France 1870–71, which brought about the unification of Germany.

Bismarck Archipelago group of over 200 islands in SW Pacific Ocean, part of ◊Papua New Guinea; area 49,660 sq km/19,200 sq mi. Largest island New Britain.

bismuth a pinkish-white metallic element, symbol Bi, atomic number 83, relative atomic mass 208.98. It is a poor conductor of heat and electricity, and is used in alloys of low melting point, and in medical compounds to soothe gastric ulcers.

bison large hoofed mammal of the bovine family. There are two species, the *European bison* or *wisent*, *Bison bonasus*, of which only a few protected herds survive. It is about 2 m/7 ft high and weighs a tonne. The *North American bison* (often known as 'buffalo') *Bison bison* is slightly smaller, with a heavier mane and more sloping hindquarters. Both species are brown. Formerly roaming the prairies in vast numbers, it was almost exterminated in the 19th century, but survives in protected areas.

Bissau capital and chief port of Guinea-Bissau, on an island at the mouth of the Geba river; population (1979) 109,500. Originally a fortified slave-trading centre, Bissau became a free port 1869.

bit in computing, a unit of information; a binary digit or place in a binary number. A ◊byte is eight bits.

bit in building and construction, a tool used for drilling or boring, as in a carpenter's brace and bit. It also refers to the cutting part of any tool, for example the blade of a plane.

bittersweet alternative name for the woody ◊nightshade plant.

bitumen an impure mixture of hydrocarbons, including such deposits as petroleum, ◊asphalt and natural gas, although sometimes the term is restricted to a soft kind of pitch resembling asphalt.

bivalent in biology, a pair of homologous chromosomes during reduction division (◊meiosis). In chemistry the term is sometimes used to describe an element or group with a ◊valency of two, although the term 'divalent' is more common.

bivalve marine or freshwater mollusc. The body is enclosed between two shells hinged together by a ligament on the dorsal side of the body.

Bizet Georges (Alexandre César Léopold) 1838–1875. French composer of operas, among them *Les Pêcheurs de perles/The Pearl Fishers* 1863, and *La Jolie Fille de Perth/The Fair Maid of Perth* 1866. He also wrote the concert overture *Patrie*, and incidental music to Daudet's *L'Arlésienne*. His operatic masterpiece *Carmen* was produced a few months before his death in 1875.

Bjelke-Peterson Joh(annes) 1911– . Australian politician, leader of Queensland National Party (QNP) and Premier of Queensland 1968–87.

black term used to describe Africans south of the Sahara, today distributed around the world. In the UK and some other countries (but not the US) the term is sometimes used for people originally from the Indian sub-continent. In Australia it is also often used to refer to Australian Aborigines.

Black Joseph 1728–1799. Scottish physicist and chemist, who in 1754 discovered carbon dioxide (which he called fixed air). By his investigations (1761) of latent and specific heat, he laid the foundation for the work of his pupil James Watt.

Black and Tans nickname of a specially raised force of military police employed by the British in 1920–21 to combat the Sinn Feiners (Irish nationalists) in Ireland; the name was derived from the colours of the uniforms.

blackberry fruit of the bramble *Rubus fruticosus*, a prickly shrub, closely allied to the raspberry, that is native to northern parts of Europe. It produces pink or white blossoms and edible, black, compound fruits. There are 400 or so types of bramble found in Britain. In the past some have been regarded as distinct species.

blackbird bird *Turdus merula* of the thrush family. The male is black with yellow bill and eyelids, the female dark brown with a dark beak. About 25 cm/10 in long, it lays three to five blue-green eggs with brown spots. Its song is rich and flute-like.

black body a hypothetical object in physics that completely absorbs any falling radiation. It is also a perfect emitter of temperature-dependent radiation.

black box popular name for the robust box, usually orange-painted for easy recovery, containing an aeroplane's flight and voice recorders. It monitors the plane's behaviour and the crew's conversation, thus providing valuable clues as to the cause of a disaster.

blackbuck antelope *Antilope cervicapra* found in central and north-west India. It is related to the gazelle, from which it differs in having the horns spirally twisted. The male is black above and white beneath, whereas the female and young are fawn-coloured above. It is about 76 cm/2.5 ft in height.

blackcap ◊warbler *Sylvia atricapilla*. The male has a black cap, the female a reddish-brown one. About 14 cm/5.5 in long, the blackcap likes wooded areas, and is a summer visitor to N Europe.

blackcock large grouse *Lyrurus tetrix* found on moors and in open woods in N Europe and Asia. The male is mainly black with a lyre-shaped tail, and up to 54 cm/1.7 ft in height. The female is speckled brown and only 40 cm/1.3 ft high.

Black Country central area of England, around and to the north of Birmingham. Heavily industrialized, it gained its name in the 19th century from its belching chimneys, but pollution laws have given it a changed aspect.

Black Death modern name (first used in England in the early 19th century) for the great epidemic of bubonic ◊plague, which ravaged Europe in the 14th century, killing between one-third and one-half of the population. The cause of the Black Death was the bacterium *Pasteurella postis*, transmitted by rat fleas.

black economy the unofficial economy of a country, which includes undeclared earnings from a second job ('moonlighting'), and enjoyment of undervalued goods and services (such as company 'perks'), designed for tax evasion purposes. In industrialized countries, it has been estimated to equal about 10% of ◊gross domestic product.

blackfly plant-sucking insect, a type of ◊aphid.

Blackfoot member of a ◊Plains Indian people who now live predominantly in Saskatchewan, Canada. Their name is derived from their black moccasins, and their language belongs to the Algonquian family.

Black Forest (German *Schwarzwald*) mountainous region of coniferous forest in Baden-Württemberg, West Germany. Bounded west and south by the Rhine, which separates it from the Vosges, it has an area of 4,660 sq km/1,800 sq mi and rises to 1,493 m/4,905 ft in the Feldberg. Parts of the forest have recently been affected by ◊acid rain.

black hole an object whose gravity is so great that nothing can escape from it, not even light. They are thought to form when massive stars shrink at the ends of their lives. A black hole can grow by sucking in more matter, including other stars, from the space around it. Matter that falls into a black hole is squeezed to infinite density at the centre of the hole. Black holes can be detected because gas falling towards them becomes so hot that it emits X-rays.

Black Hole of Calcutta incident in Anglo-Indian history: according to tradition Suraj- ud-Dowlah, the nawab of Bengal, confined 146 British prisoners on the night of 20 Jun 1756 in one small room, of whom only 23 allegedly survived; later research reduced the deaths to 43, a result of negligence rather than intention.

Black James 1924– . British physiologist, director of therapeutic research at Wellcome Laboratories (near London) from 1978. He was active in the development of ◊beta-blockers and anti-ulcer drugs. He was knighted 1981, and awarded a Nobel Prize 1988.

blackmail the criminal offence of the unwarranted demanding of money with menaces of violence, or threats of detrimental action such as exposure of some misconduct on the part of the victim.

Black Monday worldwide stock market crash on 19 October 1987, prompted by the announcement of worse than expected US trade figures and the response by US Secretary of the Treasury Baker who indicated that the sliding dollar needed to decline further. This caused a world panic as fears of the likely impact of a US recession were voiced by the major industrialized countries. The expected world recession did not occur and by the end of 1988 it was clear that the main effect had been a steadying in stock market activity and only a slight slowdown in world economic growth.

Black Muslim member of a religious group founded 1929 in the USA and led from 1934 by Elijah Muhammad (1897–1975) (then Elijah Poole) after a vision of Allah. Its growth from 1946 as a black separatist organization was due to Malcolm X (1926–65), son of a Baptist minister, who in 1964 broke away and founded his own Organization for Afro-American Unity, preaching 'active self-defence'.

Black National State an area in the Republic of South Africa set aside for development to self-government by black Africans in accordance with ◊apartheid. Before 1980 these areas were known as black homelands or *bantustans*. They comprise less than 14 per cent of the country; tend to be in arid areas, though some have mineral wealth; and may be in scattered blocks. Those that have so far reached nominal independence are Transkei 1976, Bophuthatswana 1977, Venda 1979, Ciskei 1981. They are not recognized outside South Africa because of their racial basis, and 11 million blacks live permanently in the country's white-designated areas.

Blackpool seaside resort in Lancashire, England, 45 km/28 mi north of Liverpool; population (1981) 148,000. Amusement facilities include 11 km/7 mi of promenades, known for their 'illuminations' of coloured lights, fun fairs, and a tower 152 m/500 ft high.

Black Power a movement towards black separatism in the USA during the 1960s, embodied in the *Black Panther Party* founded 1966 by Huey Newton and Bobby Seale. Its ultimate aim was the establishment of a separate black state in the USA established by a black plebiscite under the aegis of the UN. Following a National Black Political Convention in 1972, a National Black Assembly was established to exercise pressure on the Democratic and Republican parties.

Black Prince name given to ◊Edward, Prince of Wales, eldest son of Edward III of England.

Black Sea (Russian *Chernoye More*) inland sea in SE Europe, linked with the seas of Azov and Marmara, and via the Dardanelles with the

Mediterranean. Uranium deposits beneath it are among the world's largest.

Black September a guerrilla splinter group of the ◊Palestine Liberation Organization formed in 1970. Operating from bases in Syria and the Lebanon, it was responsible for the kidnap attempts at the Munich Olympics 1972 which led to the deaths of 11 Israelis, and more recent hijack and bomb attempts carried out by individuals such as Leila Khaled.

blacksnake name given to several species of snake. The Australian **blacksnake** *Pseudechis porphyriacus* is a venomous snake of the cobra family found in damp forests and swamps in E Australia. The American **blacksnake** *Coluber constrictor* from the E USA is a relative of the grass snake about 1.2 m/4 ft long, and without venom.

Black Stone in Islam, sacred stone built into the east corner of the ◊Kaaba which is a focal point of the *hajj*, or pilgrimage, to Mecca. There are a number of stories concerning its origin, one of which states that it was sent to Earth at the time of the first man, Adam; Muhammad declared that it was given to Abraham by Gabriel. It has been suggested that it is of meteoric origin.

Black Stump, the in Australia, an imaginary boundary between civilization and the outback, as in the phrase *this side of the black stump*.

blackthorn densely branched spiny bush, *Prunus spinosa*, family Rosaceae. It produces white blossom on black, leafless branches in early spring; its sour blue-black fruit, sloes, may be used to flavour gin.

Black Thursday name given to the day of the Wall Street stock market crash on 29 Oct 1929, which was followed by the worst economic depression in American history.

Blackwell Elizabeth 1821–1910. First British woman to qualify in medicine, in 1849.

black widow N American spider *Latrodectus mactans*. The male is small and harmless, but the female is 1.3 cm/0.5 in long with a red patch below the abdomen and a powerful venomous bite. The bite causes pain and fever in human victims, but they usually recover.

bladder hollow elastic-walled organ in the ◊urinary systems of amphibians, mammals, and some reptiles. Urine enters the bladder through two ureters, one leading from each kidney, and leaves it through the urethra.

bladderwort carnivorous aquatic plant, genus *Utricularia*, of the family Lentibulariaceae, which feeds on small crustacea.

Blake Robert 1599–1657. British admiral of the Parliamentary forces. Appointed 'general-at-sea' 1649, he destroyed Prince Rupert's privateering fleet off Cartagena, Spain, in the following year. In 1652 he won several engagements against the Dutch. In 1654 he bombarded Tunis, the stronghold of the Barbary corsairs, and in 1657 captured the Spanish treasure fleet in Santa Cruz.

Blake William 1757–1827. British painter, engraver, poet, and mystic, a leading figure in the Romantic period. His visionary, symbolic poems include *Songs of Innocence* 1789 and *Songs of Experience* 1794. He engraved the text and illustrations for his works and hand-coloured them, mostly in watercolour. He also illustrated works by others, including the poet Milton, and created a highly personal style.

Blamey Thomas Albert 1884–1951. The first Australian field marshal. Born in New South Wales, he served at Gallipoli and on the Western Front in World War I, and in World War II was commander in chief of the Allied Land Forces in the SW Pacific 1942–45.

Blanc Louis 1811–1882. French socialist. In 1839 he founded the *Revue du progrès*, in which he published his *Organisation du travail*, advocating the establishment of cooperative workshops and other socialist schemes. He was a member of the provisional government of 1848 (see ◊revolutions of 1848) and from its fall lived in the UK until 1871.

blank verse in literature, the unrhymed iambic pentameter or ten-syllable line of five stresses. Originated by the Italian Gian Giorgio Trissino in his tragedy *Sofonisba* 1514–15, it was introduced to England about 1540 by the Earl of Surrey, and developed by Marlowe. More recent exponents of blank verse in English include Thomas Hardy, T S Eliot, and Robert Frost.

Blanqui Louis Auguste 1805–1881. French revolutionary politician. He formulated the theory of the 'dictatorship of the proletariat', used by Karl Marx, and spent a total of 33 years in prison for insurrection. He became a martyr figure for the French workers' movement.

Blantyre-Limbe the chief industrial and commercial centre of Malawi, in the Shire highlands; population (1985) 355,000. It produces tea, coffee, rubber, tobacco, and textiles.

Blarney small town in County Cork, Republic of Ireland, possessing, inset in the wall of the 15th-century castle, the **Blarney Stone**, reputed to give persuasive speech to those kissing it.

blasphemy written or spoken insult directed against religious belief or sacred things with deliberate intent to outrage believers. Blasphemy against the Christian church is still an offence in English common law, despite several recommendations (for example by the Law Commission in 1985) that it should be abolished or widened to apply to all religious faiths. In 1989 Salman Rushdie was accused by orthodox Muslims of blasphemy against the Islamic faith in his book *The Satanic Verses*.

blast furnace furnace in which temperature is raised by the injection of an air blast. It is employed in the extraction of metals from their ores, particularly pig-iron from iron ore.

blastocyst in mammals, a stage in the development of the ◊embryo that is roughly equivalent to the ◊blastula of other animal groups.

blastomere in biology, a cell formed in the early stages as a fertilised ovum splits; see also blastocyst.

blastula an early stage in the development of a fertilized egg, when the egg changes from a solid mass of cells to a hollow ball of cells (the blastula), containing a fluid-filled cavity (the **blastocoel**). See also ◊embryology.

Blaue Reiter, der (German 'The Blue Rider') a group of German Expressionist painters based in Munich, some of whom had left die ◊Brücke. They were interested in the value of colours, in folk art, and in the necessity of painting 'the inner, spiritual side of nature', but styles were highly varied. Wassily Kandinsky and Franz Marc published a book of their views in 1912 and there were two exhibitions (1911, 1912).

bleaching decolorization of coloured materials. The two main types of bleaching agent are the *oxidizing bleaches*, which add oxygen and remove hydrogen, and include the ultraviolet rays in sunshine, hydrogen peroxide, and chlorine in household bleaches, and the *reducing bleaches* which add hydrogen or remove oxygen, for example sulphur dioxide.

bleeding loss of blood from the circulation; see ◊haemorrhage.

Blenheim, Battle of battle on 13 Aug 1704 in which English troops under ◊Marlborough defeated the French and Bavarians near the Bavarian village of Blenheim (now in West Germany) on the left bank of the Danube.

Blériot Louis 1872–1936. French aviator who, in a monoplane of his own construction, made the first flight across the English Channel on 25 Jul 1909.

Bligh William 1754–1817. British admiral. Bligh accompanied Captain ◊Cook on his second voyage 1772–74, and in 1787 commanded HMS *Bounty* on an expedition to the Pacific. On the return voyage the crew mutinied 1789, and Bligh was cast adrift in a boat with 18 men. He was appointed governor of New South Wales in 1805, where his discipline again provoked a mutiny 1808. He returned to Britain, and was made an admiral in 1811.

blindness complete absence or impairment of sight. It may be caused by heredity, accident, disease, or deterioration with age.

blind spot the area where the optic nerve and blood vessels pass through the retina of the ◊eye. No visual image can be formed as there are no light-sensitive cells in this part of the retina.

Blitzkrieg (German 'lightning war') a swift military campaign, as used by Germany at the beginning of World War II. The abbreviation *Blitz* was applied to the German air raids on London 1940–41.

Blixen Karen, born Karen Dinesen 1885–1962. Danish writer. Her autobiography *Out of Africa* 1937 is based on her experience of running a coffee plantation in Kenya. She wrote fiction, mainly in English, under the pen name Isak Dinesen.

bloc (French) a group, especially used of politically allied countries, as in 'the Soviet bloc'.

block and tackle a type of ◊pulley.

Bloemfontein capital of the Orange Free State and judicial capital of the Republic of South Africa; population (1985) 204,000. Founded 1846, the city produces canned fruit, glassware, furniture, and plastics.

Blok Alexander Alexandrovich 1880–1921. Russian poet who, as a follower of the French Symbolist movement, used words for their symbolic rather than actual meaning. He backed the 1917 Revolution, as in his most famous poems *The Twelve* 1918, and *The Scythians* 1918, the latter appealing to the West to join in the revolution.

Blomberg Werner von 1878–1946. German soldier and Nazi politician, minister of defence 1933–35 and minister of war and head of the *Wehrmacht* (army) 1935–38 under Hitler's chancellorship. He was discredited by his marriage to a prostitute and dismissed in Jan 1938, enabling Hitler to exercise more direct control over the armed forces. In spite of his removal from office, Blomberg was put on trial for war crimes in 1946 at Nuremberg.

blood liquid circulating in the arteries, veins, and capillaries of vertebrate animals. In humans it makes up 5% of the body weight, occupying a volume of 5.5 l/10 pt. It consists of a colourless, transparent liquid called *plasma*, containing microscopic cells of three main varieties. *Red cells* form nearly half the volume of the blood, with 5,000 billion cells per litre. Their red colour is caused by ◊haemoglobin. Some *white cells* (◊leucocytes) ingest invading bacteria and so protect the body from disease; these also help to repair injured tissues. Others (◊lymphocytes) produce antibodies, which help provide immunity. Blood *platelets* assist in the clotting of blood.

Blood Thomas 1618–1680. Irish adventurer, known as Colonel Blood, who attempted to steal the crown jewels from the Tower of London, England, 1671.

blood-brain barrier a theoretical term for the mechanism which prevents many substances circulating in the bloodstream (including some germs) from invading the brain.

blood group the classification of blood types according to antigenic activity. Red blood cells of one individual may carry molecules on their surface which act as ◊antigens in another individual whose red blood cells lack these molecules. The two main antigens are designated A and B. These give rise to four blood groups: having A only (A), having B only (B), having both (AB), and having neither (O). Each of these groups may or may not contain the ◊rhesus factor. Correct typing of blood groups is vital in transfusion since incompatible types of donor and recipient blood will result in blood clotting, with possible death of the recipient.

bloodhound ancient breed of dog. Black and tan in colour, it has long, pendulous ears, and distinctive wrinkles on the head. Its excellent powers of scent have been employed in tracking and criminal work from very early times.

blood pressure the pressure, or tension, of the blood in the arteries and veins of the ◊circulatory system, due to the muscular activity of the heart.

blood test a laboratory evaluation of a blood sample. There are numerous blood tests, from simple typing to establish its group (in case a ◊transfusion is needed) to sophisticated biochemical assays of substances, such as hormones, present in the blood only in minute quantities.

bloom whitish powdery or wax-like coating over the surface of certain fruits that easily rubs off when handled. It often contains ◊yeasts which live on the sugars in the fruit. The term bloom is also used to describe a rapid increase in number of certain species of algae found in lakes and ponds.

Bloomer Amelia Jenks 1818–1894. US campaigner for women's rights. She introduced in 1849, when unwieldy crinolines were the fashion, a knee-length skirt combined with loose trousers gathered at the ankles, which became known as *bloomers* (also called 'rational dress'). She published the magazine *The Lily* 1849–54, which campaigned for women's rights and dress reform, and lectured with Susan B ◊Anthony in New York, USA.

Bloomsbury Group a group of writers and artists based in ◊Bloomsbury, London, between the world wars. The group included the artists ◊Duncan Grant and Vanessa Bell, and the writers Lytton ◊Strachey and Leonard and Virginia ◊Woolf.

Blow John 1648–1708. British composer. He taught ◊Purcell, and wrote church music, for example the anthem 'I Was Glad when They Said unto Me' 1697. His masque *Venus and Adonis* 1685 is sometimes called the first English opera.

blowfly fly, genus *Calliphora*, also known as *bluebottle*, or one of the related genus *Lucilia*, *greenbottle*. It lays its eggs in dead flesh, on which the maggots feed.

blubber the thick layer of ◊fat under the skin of marine mammals, which provides an energy store and an effective insulating layer, preventing the loss of body heat to the sea. Blubber has been used (when boiled down) in engineering, food processing, cosmetics and printing, but all of these products can now be produced synthetically, thus saving the lives of animals.

Blücher Gebhard Leberecht von 1742–1819. Prussian general and field marshal, popular as 'Marshal

bluebell

Forward'. He took an active part in the patriotic movement, and in the War of German Liberation defeated the French as commander in chief at Leipzig 1813, crossed the Rhine to Paris 1814, and was made prince of Wahlstadt (Silesia). In 1815 he was defeated by Napoleon at Ligny, but played a crucial role in the British commander Wellington's triumph at Waterloo, near Brussels.

Bluebeard folktale character, popularized by the writer Charles Perrault in France about 1697, and historically identified with Gilles de ◊Rais. He murdered six wives for disobeying his command not to enter a locked room, but was himself killed before he could murder the seventh.

bluebell name given in Scotland to the harebell *Campanula rotundifolia*, and in England to the wild hyacinth *Endymion nonscriptus*, belonging to the family Liliaceae.

bluebird North American bird, genus *Sialia*, belonging to the thrush family. The **eastern bluebird** *Sialia sialis* is regarded as the herald of spring. Slightly larger than a robin, it has a similar reddish breast, the upper plumage being sky-blue, and a distinctive song.

blue chip in business and finance, a stock which is considered strong and reliable in terms of the dividend yield and capital value. Blue chip companies are favoured by stock market investors more interested in security than risk taking.

Blue Division the Spanish volunteers who fought with the German army against the USSR during World War II.

bluegrass dense, spreading grass, *Poa compressa*, which is blue-tinted and grows in clumps. It provides pasture for horses and is abundant in Kentucky, USA, which is known as the bluegrass state.

blue-green algae single-celled, primitive organisms that resemble bacteria in their internal cell organization, sometimes joined together in colonies or filaments. Blue-green algae are among the oldest known living organisms; remains have been found in rocks up to 3,500 million years old. They are widely distributed in aquatic habitats, on the damp surfaces of rocks and trees, and in the soil.

blue gum Australian tree *Eucalyptus globulus* with bluish bark, a chief source of eucalyptus oil.

Blue Mountains part of the ◊Great Divide, New South Wales, Australia, ranging 600–1,100 m/2000–03,600 ft and blocking Sydney from the interior until the crossing 1813 by surveyor William Lawson, Gregory Blaxland, and William Wentworth.

blueprint process widely used for copying engineering drawings and architectural plans, so called because it produces a white copy of the original against a blue background.

Blue Ridge Mountains range extending from West Virginia to Georgia, USA, and including Mount Mitchell 2,045 m/6,712 ft; part of the ◊Appalachians.

blues 12-bar folk song in which, typically, the second line of the three-line verse is a repetition of the first, with variations, so giving the singer time to improvise the third line. It originated among American blacks in the rural South in the late 19th century, and the words are often melancholy.

blue shift in astronomy, a manifestation of the ◊Doppler effect in which an object appears bluer when it is moving towards the observer or the observer is moving towards it (blue light is of a higher frequency than other colours in the spectrum). The blue shift is the opposite of the ◊red shift.

Blum Léon 1872–1950. French politician. He was converted to socialism by the ◊Dreyfus affair (1899), and in 1936 became the first socialist prime minister of France. He was again premier for a few weeks in 1938. Imprisoned under the Vichy government as a danger to French security in 1942, he was released by the Allies in 1945. He again became premier for a few weeks in 1946.

Blunt Anthony 1907–1983. British art historian and double agent. As a Cambridge don, he recruited for the Soviet secret service, and, as a member of the British Secret Service 1940–45, passed information to the Russians. In 1951 he assisted the defection to the USSR of the British agents Guy ◊Burgess and Donald Maclean (1913–83). He was author of many respected works on French and Italian art.

Blyton Enid 1897–1968. British writer of children's books. Originally a teacher, she created the character Noddy, and the adventures of the 'Famous Five' and 'Secret Seven', but has been criticized by educationalists for social, racial, and sexual stereotyping.

BMA abbreviation for *British Medical Association*.

BNF abbreviation for *British Nuclear Fuels*.

boa type of non-venomous snake that kills its prey by constriction. The **boa constrictor** *Constrictor constrictor*, can be up to 5.5 m/18.5 ft long, but is rarely more than 4 m/12 ft. It feeds mainly on small mammals and birds. Other boas include the ◊anaconda and the **emerald tree boa** *Boa canina*, about 2 m/6 ft long and bright green.

Boadicea alternative spelling of British queen ◊Boudicca.

boar name used for some wild members of the pig family, such as the Eurasian **wild boar** *Sus scrofa*, from which domestic breeds derive. The wild boar is sturdily built, being 1.5 m/4.5 ft long and 1 m/3 ft high, and possesses formidable tusks. Of gregarious nature and mainly woodland-dwelling, it feeds on roots, nuts, and some carrion and insects.

boardsailing a watersport combining elements of surfing and sailing; also called sailboarding and *Windsurfing* which is a tradename. The boardsailer stands on a board, (2.5–4m/8–13 ft) long, that is propelled and steered by means of a sail attached to a mast which is articulated at the foot. Developed by Hoyle Schweitzer and Jim Drake in the USA in 1968, the sailboard was first devised in 1958 by Peter Chilvers (1946–) of England.

boat people those Vietnamese who left their country by sea following the takeover of South Vietnam 1975 by North Vietnam. Many have been attacked by Thai pirates.

Boat Race annual UK rowing race between the crews of Oxford and Cambridge universities. It is held during the Easter vacation over a 6.8 km/4.25 mi course on the River Thames between Putney and Mortlake.

bobcat cat *Felis rufa* living in a variety of habitats from S Canada through to S Mexico. It is similar to the lynx, but only 75 cm/2.5 ft long, with reddish fur and less well-developed ear-tufts.

Boccaccio Des Cas des Nobles Hommes et Femmes *illustrating part of Boccaccio's* Decameron.

Bogart American film actor, Humphrey Bogart.

bobsleighing or *bobsledding* the sport of racing steel-bodied, steerable toboggans, manned by two or four people, down mountain ice-chutes at speeds of up to 130 kmph/80 mph. It was introduced as an Olympic event in 1924 and world championships have been held every year since 1931.

Boccaccio Giovanni 1313–1375. Italian poet. His great work is the *Decameron* 1348–53, a hundred tales told by ten young people seeking refuge in the country from the plague. Its bawdiness and exuberance as well as narrative skill and characterization made the work enormously popular and influential, inspiring the English writers Chaucer and Shakespeare among many others.

Boccherini (Ridolfo) Luigi 1743–1805. Italian composer and cellist. He studied in Rome, made his mark in Paris 1768, and was court composer in Prussia and Spain. Boccherini composed some 350 instrumental works, an opera, and oratorios.

Bode Johann Elert 1747–1826. German astronomer. He published the first atlas of all stars visible to the naked eye, *Uranographia* 1801.

Bodhidharma 6th century AD. Indian Buddhist. He entered China from S India *c.* 520, and was the founder of **Zen**, the school of Mahāyāna ◊Buddhism in which intuitive meditation, prompted by contemplation, leads to enlightenment.

bodhisattva in Mahāyāna Buddhism, someone who seeks ◊enlightenment in order to help other living beings. A bodhisattva is free to enter ◊nirvana but voluntarily chooses to be reborn until all other beings have attained it.

Bodichon Barbara (born Leigh-Smith) 1827–1891. English feminist, and campaigner for women's education and suffrage. In 1852 she opened a primary school in London. She wrote *Women and Work* 1857, and was a founder of the magazine *The Englishwoman's Journal* in 1858.

Bodley Thomas 1545–1613. English scholar and diplomat after whom the Bodleian Library in Oxford is named. After retiring from Queen Elizabeth I's service in 1597, he began to restore the library at Oxford which had originally been founded in the 15th century. It was opened as the Bodleian Library 1602.

Boeing William Edward 1881–1956. US industrialist, and founder of the Boeing Airplane Company 1917. Its military aircraft include the flying fortress bombers used in World War II, and the Chinook helicopter; its commercial craft include the ◊jetfoil, and the Boeing 747 and 707 jets.

Boeotia ancient district of central Greece, of which ◊Thebes was the chief city; the *Boeotian League* (formed by ten city states in the 6th century BC) superseded ◊Sparta in the leadership of Greece in the 4th century.

Boer a Dutch settler or descendant of Dutch and Huguenot settlers in South Africa; see also ◊Afrikaner.

Boer War war between the Dutch settlers in South Africa and the British; see ◊South African Wars.

bog an area of soft, wet, spongy ground consisting of decaying vegetable matter (◊peat). Bogs occur on cold uplands where drainage is poor.

Bogarde Dirk. Stage-name of Derek van den Bogaerde 1921– . Dutch-born British actor, who acquired an international reputation for complex roles in films such as *Death in Venice* 1971, and *A Bridge Too Far* 1977.

Bogart Humphrey 1899–1957. US film actor, who achieved fame with his portrayal of a gangster in *The Petrified Forest* 1936. He became a cult figure as the romantic, tough 'loner' in such films as *The Maltese Falcon* 1941, and *Casablanca* 1943.

Bogomils heretics who originated in 10th-century Bulgaria and spread throughout the Byzantine empire. They take their name from Bogomilus, or Theophilus, who taught in Bulgaria 927–950. Despite persecution, they were only expunged by the Ottomans after the fall of Constantinople 1453.

Bogotá capital of Colombia, South America; 2,640 m/8,660 ft above sea level on the edge of the plateau of the E Cordillera; population (1985) 4,185,000. It was founded 1538.

Bohemia kingdom of central Europe from the 9th century, under Hapsburg rule 1526–1918, when it was included in ◊Czechoslovakia. The name Bohemia derives from the Celtic Boii, its earliest known inhabitants.

Bohr Niels Henrik David 1885–1962. Danish physicist. He founded the Institute of Theoretical Physics in Copenhagen, of which he became director in 1920. Nobel prize 1922. In 1952, he helped to set up ◊CERN in Geneva.

boil small abscess originating around a hair root or in a sweat gland.

Boileau Nicolas 1636–1711. French poet and critic. After a series of contemporary satires, his *Epîtres/Epistles* 1669–77 led to his joint appointment with Racine as royal historiographer in 1677. Later works include *L'Art poétique/The Art of Poetry* 1674, and the mock-heroic *Le Lutrin/The Lectern* 1674–83.

Bokassa *Marshal Jean Bokassa changed his country's name to the Central African Empire, and crowned himself emperor in 1977.*

boiler a vessel which converts water into steam. Boilers are used in conventional power stations to generate steam to feed steam ◊turbines, which drive the electricity generators. They are also used in steam ships which are propelled by steam turbines and steam locomotives. Every boiler has a furnace in which fuel (coal, oil or gas) is burned to produce hot gases, and a system of tubes in which heat is transferred from the gases to the water.

boiling point for any given liquid, the temperature at which the application of heat raises the temperature of the liquid no further, but converts it to vapour.

Bokassa Jean-Bédel 1921– . President and later self-proclaimed emperor of the Central African Republic 1966–79. Commander in chief from 1963, in Dec 1965 he led a military coup which gave him the presidency, and on 4 Dec 1977 he proclaimed the Central African Empire with himself as emperor for life. His regime was characterized by arbitrary state violence and cruelty. In exile 1979–86, he was sentenced to death but later commuted to life imprisonment 1988.

bolero a Spanish dance in triple time for a solo dancer or a couple, usually with castanet accompaniment. Also the title of a one-act ballet score by Ravel, choreographed by Nijinsky for Ida Rubinstein in 1928.

boletus European fungus, resembling the mushroom, and belonging to the class Basidiomycetes. *Boletus edulis* is edible, but some species are poisonous.

Boleyn Anne 1507–1536. Queen of England. Second wife of King Henry VIII, she was married to him in 1533 and gave birth to the future Queen Elizabeth I in the same year. Accused of adultery and incest with her half-brother (a charge invented by Thomas Cromwell), she was beheaded.

Bolingbroke Henry John, Viscount Bolingbroke 1678–1751. British Tory politician and philosopher. He was foreign secretary 1710–14 and a Jacobite conspirator.

Bolingbroke Henry of Bolingbroke   title of ◊Henry IV of England.

Bolívar Simón 1783–1830. South American nationalist, leader of revolutionary armies, known as *the Liberator*. He fought the Spanish colonial forces in several uprisings and eventually liberated his native Venezuela 1821, Colombia and Ecuador 1822, Peru 1824, and Bolivia (a

Boleyn *Portrait of Henry VIII's second wife, Anne Boleyn, by an unknown artist (1530s) National Portrait Gallery, London.*

new state named after him, formerly Upper Peru) 1825.

Bolivia landlocked country in South America, bordered to the north and east by Brazil, to the southeast by Paraguay, to the south by Argentina, and to the west by Chile and Peru.

Böll Heinrich 1917–1985. West German novelist. A radical Catholic and anti-Nazi, he attacked Germany's political past and the materialism of its contemporary society. His books include *Billard um Halbzehn/Billiards at Half-Past Nine* 1959 and *Gruppenbild mit Dame/Group Portrait with Lady* 1971. Nobel Prize for Literature 1972.

boll-weevil small American beetle *Anthonomus grandis* of the weevil family. The female lays eggs in the unripe pods or 'bolls' of the cotton plant, and on these the larva feeds, causing great destruction.

Bologna industrial city and capital of Emilia-Romagna, Italy, 80 km/50 mi north of Florence; population (1984) 442,307. It was the site of an Etruscan town, later of a Roman colony, and became a republic in the 12th century. It came under papal rule 1506, and was united with Italy 1860.

bolometer sensitive ◊thermometer which measures the energy of radiation by registering the change in electrical resistance of a fine wire when it is exposed to heat or light.

Bolshevik member of the majority (Russian *bolshinstvo* 'majority') of the Russian Social Democratic Party, who split from the ◊Mensheviks 1903. The Bolsheviks advocated the destruction of capitalist political and economic institutions, and the setting-up of a socialist state with power in the hands of the workers. The Bolsheviks effected the ◊Russian Revolution 1917.

bomb an explosive projectile used in warfare. Initially dropped from aeroplanes (from World War I), bombs were in World War II also launched by rocket (◊V1, V2). New developments since the 1960s concern missiles launched from aircraft, land sites, or submarines. In the 1970s laser guidance systems were developed to hit small targets with accuracy. There are also ◊incendiary bombs and nuclear bombs and missiles (see ◊warfare). Any object designed to cause damage by explosion can be called a bomb (car bombs, letter bombs).

Bombay former province of British India. Together with a number of interspersed princely states, it was included in the domain of India in 1947, and the major part became in 1960 the two new states of ◊Gujarat and ◊Maharashtra. The capital was the city of ◊Bombay.

Bolivia
Republic of
(República de Bolivia)

Brazil
La Paz
Peru
BOLIVIA
Paraguay
PACIFIC OCEAN
Sucre
ATLANTIC OCEAN
Chile
Argentina

0 miles 500
0 km 1000

area 1,098,581 sq km/424,052 sq mi
capital La Paz (seat of government), Sucre (legal capital and seat of judiciary)
towns Santa Cruz, Cochabamba
physical high plateau between mountain ridges; forest and lowlands in the E
head of state and government Jaime Paz Zamora from 1989
political system emergent democratic republic
exports tin (second largest world producer), other non-ferrous metals, oil, gas (piped to Argentina), agricultural products, coffee, sugar, cotton
currency boliviano
population (1990 est) 6,730,000; (Quechua 25%, Aymara 17%, Mestizo 30%, European 14%); annual growth rate 2.7%
language Spanish; Aymara, Quechua, all official
religion Roman Catholic (state-recognized)
literacy 84% male/65% female (1985 est)

GDP $4.2 bn (1987); $617 per head
chronology
1825 As Upper Peru, achieved independence from Spain.
1952 Dr Víctor Paz Estenssoro elected president.
1956 Dr Hernan Siles Zuazo became president.
1960 Estenssoro returned to power.
1964 Army coup led by vice-president.
1966 Gen René Barrientos became president.
1967 Uprising, led by 'Che' Guevara, put down with US help.
1969 Barrientos killed in air crash; vice-president Siles Salinas succeeded, but deposed by army coup.
1970 Army coup put Gen Juan Torres Gonzalez in power.
1971 Torres replaced by Col Hugo Banzer.
1973 Banzer promised democratic government.
1974 After attempted coup, Banzer postponed elections and banned political and trade-union activity.
1978 Elections declared invalid after allegations of fraud.
1980 More inconclusive elections followed by a coup led by Gen Garcia; allegations of corruption and drug trafficking led to cancellation of US and EC aid.
1981 Garcia forced to resign; replaced by Gen Celso Torrelio Villa
1982 Torrelio resigned; replaced by military junta led by Gen Vildoso; worsening economy prompted Vildoso to ask congress to install civilian administration; Dr Siles Zuazo chosen as president.
1983 Economic aid from USA and EC resumed.
1984 New coalition government formed by Siles; abduction of president by right-wing officers; the president undertook a five-day hunger strike.
1985 President Siles resigned; elections inconclusive; Dr Paz Estenssoro, now 77, chosen by congress.
1989 Jaime Paz Zamora (MIR) elected president in power-sharing arrangement with Hugo Banzer Suarez; pledges to maintain fiscal and monetary discipline and preserve free-market policies.

Bombay industrial port (textiles, engineering, pharmaceuticals, diamonds), commercial centre, and capital of Maharashtra, W India; population (1981) 8,227,000. It is the centre of the Hindi film industry.

Bonaparte Corsican family of Italian origin, which gave rise to the Napoleonic dynasty: see ◊Napoleon

I, ◊Napoleon II, and ◊Napoleon III. Other well-known members were the brothers and sister of Napoleon I:

Joseph 1769–1844, whom Napoleon made king of Naples 1806 and Spain 1808.

Lucien 1775–1840, whose handling of the Council of Five Hundred on 10 Nov 1799 ensured Napoleon's future.

Louis 1778–1846, made king of Holland 1806–10, who was the father of Napoleon III.

Bonar Law See ◊Law, Andrew Bonar, British Conservative politician.

Bonaventura, St (John of Fidanza) 1221–1274. Italian Roman Catholic theologian. He entered the Franciscan order in 1243, became professor of theology at Paris, France, and in 1256 general of his order. In 1273 he was created cardinal and bishop of Albano. His eloquent writings earned him the title of the 'Seraphic Doctor'. Feast day 15 Jul.

bond chemical result of the forces of attraction that hold together atoms of an element or elements to form a molecule.

bond in commerce, a security issued by a government, local authority, company, bank, or other

bomb fireball resulting from the test detonation of a hydrogen bomb at Bikini Atoll on May 21 1956.

institution on fixed interest. Usually a long-term security, a bond may be irredeemable, secured or unsecured. Property bonds are non-fixed securities with the yield fixed to property investment.

Bond Alan 1938– . Australian businessman. Born in London, he emigrated to Western Australia in 1951. By the age of 19, he had started his own business and, later, heading the Bond Corporation, expanded into newspapers, breweries, television, oil, gas and gold mining. His leisure interests included sailing and in 1983 his syndicate's yacht 'Australia II' won the America's Cup from the US. By the late 1980s it was evident that the Bond empire had overstretched itself and in Sept 1990 he surrendered the chairmanship of the group.

Bond Edward 1935– . British dramatist, whose work has aroused controversy because of the savagery of some of his themes, for example the brutal killing of a baby, symbol of a society producing unwanted children, in *Saved* 1965. His later works include *Black Mass* 1970 about apartheid, *Bingo* 1973, and *The Sea* 1973.

Bondfield Margaret Grace 1873–1953. British socialist. Originally a shop assistant, she became a trade-union organizer to improve working conditions for women. She was the first woman to enter the cabinet – as minister of labour, 1929–31.

Bondi Beach Australian beach on the E coast of the southern side of Sydney Harbour, celebrated for its surf.

bone hard connective tissue of most vertebrate animals consisting of a network of collagen fibres impregnated with calcium phospate. In strength, the

bone

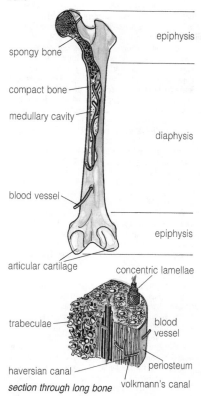

spongy bone

compact bone

medullary cavity

epiphysis

diaphysis

blood vessel

epiphysis

articular cartilage

concentric lamellae

trabeculae

blood vessel

haversian canal

periosteum

volkmann's canal

section through long bone

toughest bone is comparable with reinforced concrete. Bones develop initially from ◊cartilage. Humans have about 206 distinct bones in the ◊skeleton.

bone china or *softpaste* semi-porcelain made of bone ash and china clay (kaolin); first made in the West in imitation of Chinese porcelain.

bongo Central African antelope *Boocercus eurycerus*, living in dense humid forests. Up to 1.4 m/4.5 ft at the shoulder, its spiral-shaped horns may grow to 80 cm/2.6 ft or more. The chestnut body has narrow white stripes running down the sides, and a black belly.

Bonhoeffer Dietrich 1906–1945. German Lutheran theologian and opponent of Nazism. Involved in an anti-Hitler plot, he was executed by the Nazis in Flossenburg concentration camp. His *Letters and Papers from Prison*, published 1953, became the textbook of modern radical theology, anticipating the prospect of a 'religionless' Christianity.

Boniface name of nine popes, including:

Boniface VIII Benedict Caetani *c.* 1228–1303. Pope from 1294. He clashed unsuccessfully with Philip IV of France over his taxation of the clergy, and also with Henry III of England.

Boniface, St 680–754. English monk, known as the 'Apostle of Germany'. Originally named Wynfrith, he was born in Devon and became a Benedictine monk. After a missionary journey to Frisia in 716, he was given the task of bringing Christianity to Germany by Pope Gregory II in 718, and was appointed archbishop of Mainz in 746. He returned to Frisia in 754 and was martyred near Dockum. Feast day 5 Jun.

Bonn industrial city (chemicals, textiles, plastics, aluminium), capital of West Germany, 18 km/15 mi SSE of Cologne, on the left bank of the Rhine; population (1985) 289,900.

Bonnard Pierre 1867–1947. French Post-Impressionist painter. With other members of *les ◊Nabis*, he explored the decorative arts (posters, stained glass, furniture). He painted domestic interiors and nudes.

Bonneville Salt Flats bed of a prehistoric lake in Utah, USA, of which the Great Salt Lake is the surviving remnant. It has been used for motor speed records.

bonsai (Japanese 'bowl cultivation') the art of producing miniature trees by selective pruning. It originated in China many centuries ago, and later spread to Japan. Some specimens in the Imperial Japanese collection are over 300 years old.

Bonus Expeditionary Force in US history, a march on Washington DC by unemployed ex-servicemen during the great depression to lobby Congress for immediate cash payment of a promised war veterans' bonus. During the spring of 1932, some 15,000 veterans camped by the river Potomac or squatted in disused government buildings. They were eventually dispersed by troops.

booby tropical seabird, genus *Sula*, closely related to the northern ◊gannet. There are six species, including the circumtropical brown booby *Sula leucogaster*. They dive into the sea for food.

boogie-woogie a form of jazz played on the piano, using a repeated motif in the left hand. It was common in the USA from around 1900 to the 1940s. Notable boogie-woogie players included Pinetop Smith, Mead 'Lux' Lewis, and Jimmy Yancey.

bookbinding the art or craft of securing the pages of a book between protective covers by sewing and/or gluing. Modern cloth binding, common to England and the USA, was first introduced in 1822, but since World War II synthetic bindings have been increasingly employed.

Booker Prize British literary prize of £15,000 awarded annually (from 1969) by the Booker company (formerly Booker McConnell) to a novel published in the UK during the previous year.

booklouse tiny wingless insect *Atropus pulsatoria* which lives in books and papers, feeding on starches and moulds.

Book of the Dead ancient Egyptian book, known as the *Book of Coming Forth by Day*, and buried with the dead as a guide to reaching the kingdom of Osiris, the god of the underworld.

Boole George 1814–1864. English mathematician, whose work *The Mathematical Analysis of Logic* 1847 established the basis of modern mathematical logic, and whose *Boolean algebra* can be used in designing computers.

boomerang hand-thrown wooden missile shaped in a curved angle, developed by the Australian Aborigines to kill game. It can return to the thrower if the target is missed.

Boone Daniel 1734–1820. American pioneer, who explored the Wilderness Road (East Virginia/Kentucky) in 1775 and paved the way for the first westward migration of settlers.

booster the first-stage rockets of a space-launching vehicle, or additional rockets strapped on to the main rocket to assist take-off.

Boötes constellation of the northern hemisphere representing a herdsman driving a bear (Ursa Major) around the pole. Its brightest star is ◊Arcturus.

Booth Charles 1840–1916. British sociologist, author of the study *Life and Labour of the People in London* 1891–1903, and pioneer of an old-age pension scheme.

Booth John Wilkes 1839–1865. US actor and fanatical Confederate who assassinated President ◊Lincoln 14 Apr 1865; he escaped with a broken leg and was later shot in a barn in Virginia.

Booth William 1829–1912. British founder of the ◊Salvation Army in 1878, and its first 'general'.

Boothby Robert John Graham, Baron Boothby 1900–1986. Scottish politician. He became a Unionist Member of Parliament in 1924 and was parliamentary private secretary to Churchill 1926–29. He advocated Britain's entry into the European Community, and was a noted speaker.

bootlegging the illegal manufacture, distribution, or sale of a product. The term is said to have originated in the USA, when the sale of alcohol to American Indians was illegal and bottles were hidden for sale in the legs of the jackboots of unscrupulous traders. It was later used for all illegal liquor sales in the period of ◊Prohibition in the USA 1920–33, and is often applied to unauthorized commercial tape recordings and copying of computer software.

bop short for ◊*bebop*, a style of jazz.

Bophuthatswana Republic of
area 40,330 sq km/15,571 sq mi
capital Mmbatho or Sun City, a casino resort frequented by many white South Africans
exports platinum, chrome, vanadium, asbestos, manganese
currency South African rand
population (1980) 1,328,637
language Setswana, English
religion Christian
government executive president elected by the Assembly: Chief Lucas Mangope
recent history first 'independent' Black National State from 1977, but not recognized by any country other than South Africa.

borage salad plant *Borago officinalis* cultivated in

Britain and occasionally naturalized. It has small blue flowers and hairy leaves.

Borah William Edgar 1865–1940. US Republican politician. Born in Illinois, he was a senator for Idaho from 1906. An arch-isolationist, he was one of those chiefly responsible for the USA's repudiation of the League of Nations.

borax hydrated sodium borate, $Na_2B_4O_7.10H_2O$, found as soft, whitish crystals or incrustations on the shores of hot springs and lakes associated with recent volcanoes. It provides a starting material for *perborates* (used in bleaches and washing powders).

Bordeaux port on the Garonne, capital of Aquitaine, SW France, a centre for the wine trade, oil refining, aeronautics and space industries; population (1982) 640,000. Bordeaux was under the English crown for three centuries until 1453. In 1870, 1914, and 1940 the French government was moved here because of German invasion.

Border Allan 1955– . Australian cricketer, captain of the Australian team from 1985. He has played for New South Wales and Queensland and in England for Gloucestershire and Essex. He made his Test debut for Australia 1978-79.

Borders region of Scotland
area 4,672 sq km/1,803 sq mi
towns administrative headquarters Newtown St Boswells; Hawick, Jedburgh
products knitted goods, tweed, electronics, timber
population (1983) 101,202
famous people Duns Scotus, Mungo Park.

bore a surge of tidal water up an estuary or a river, caused by the funnelling of the rising tide by a narrowing river mouth. A particularly high tide, possibly fanned by wind, may build up when it is held back by a river current in the river mouth. The result is a broken wave, a metre or so high.

Borelli Giovanni Alfonso 1608–1679. Italian scientist who explored the links between physics and medicine, and showed how mathematical, geometrical, and mechanical principles could be applied to animal ◊physiology. This approach, known as *iatrophysics*, has proved to be basic to understanding how the mammalian body works.

Borg Bjorn 1956– . Swedish lawn tennis player who won the men's singles title at Wimbledon five times 1976-80, a record since the abolition of the challenge system in 1922.

Borges Jorge Luis 1899–1986. Argentinian poet and short-story writer. In 1961 he became director of the National Library, Buenos Aires, and was professor of English literature at the university there. He is known for his fantastic and paradoxical work *Ficciones/Fictions* 1944.

Borgia Cesare 1476–1507. Italian general, illegitimate son of Pope Alexander VI. Made a cardinal at 17 by his father, he resigned to become captain-general of the papacy, campaigning successfully against the city republics of Italy. Ruthless and treacherous in war, he was an able ruler of conquered territory (the model of Machiavelli's *The Prince*), but his power crumbled on the death of his father. He was a patron of artists.

Borgia Lucrezia 1480–1519. Duchess of Ferrara from 1501. She was the illegitimate daughter of Pope ◊Alexander VI and sister of Cesare Borgia. She was married at 12 and again at 13 to further her father's ambitions, both marriages being annulled by him. Her final marriage was to the son and heir of the Duke of Ferrara. She made the court a centre of culture and was a patron of authors and artists such as Ariosto and Titian.

Bosnia-Herzegovina
Republic of

area 51,129 sq km/19,745 sq mi
capital Sarajevo
towns Banja Luka, Mostar, Prijedor, Tuzla, Zenica
physical barren, mountainous country
population (1990) 4,300,000 including 44%
Muslims, 33% Serbs, 17% Croats; a complex
patchwork of ethnically mixed communities

head of state Alija Izetbegović from 1990
head of government Mile Akmadzic from 1992
political system emergent democracy
products citrus fruits, vegetables, iron, steel,
leather goods, textiles
language Serbian variant of Serbo-Croatian
religion Sunni Muslim, Serbian Orthodox, Roman
Catholic
chronology
1918 Incorporated in the future Yugoslavia.
1941 Occupied by Nazi Germany.
1945 Became republic within Yugoslav Socialist
Federation.
1980 Upsurge in Islamic nationalism.
1990 Ethnic violence erupted between Muslims
and Serbs. Communists defeated in multiparty
elections.
1991 May: Serbia–Croatia conflict spread disorder
into Bosnia-Herzegovina. Serbian enclaves
established by force.
1992 Muslims and Croats voted overwhelmingly in
favour of independence; referendum boycotted by
Serbs. Ethnic hostilities escalated, with Serb
forces occupying E and Croatian forces much of
W. A state of emergency was declared; all-out civil
war ensued. UN and EC mediators vainly sought
truce. Fighting continued, with accusations of
'ethnic cleansing' being practised, particularly by
Serbs.
1993 UN–EC peace plan accepted in principle by
Serbs and Croats but fighting continued. USA
began airdrops of food and medical supplies.

boric acid also called boracic acid. H_3BO_3 an acid formed by the combination of hydrogen and oxygen with non-metallic boron. It is a weak antiseptic.

Boris Godunov 1552–1605. See Boris ◊Godunov, tsar of Russia from 1598.

Bormann Martin 1900–1945. German Nazi leader. He took part in the abortive Munich ◊putsch of 1923, and rose to high positions in the National Socialist Party, becoming party chancellor in May 1941. He was believed to have escaped the fall of Berlin in May 1945, and was tried in his absence and sentenced to death at Nuremberg 1945–46. A skeleton discovered in Berlin in 1972 was officially recognized as his by forensic experts in 1973.

Born Max 1882–1970. German physicist, who received a Nobel Prize in 1954 for fundamental work on the ◊quantum theory.

Borneo third largest island in the world, one of the Sunda Islands in the W Pacific; area 754,000 sq km/290,000 sq mi. It comprises the Malaysian territories of ◊*Sabah* and ◊*Sarawak*: ◊*Brunei;* and, occupying by far the largest part, the Indonesian territory of ◊*Kalimantan*. It is mountainous and densely forested. In coastal areas the people of Borneo are mainly of Malaysian origin, with a few Chinese, and the interior is inhabited by the indigenous Dayaks. It was formerly under both Dutch and British colonial influence until Sarawak was formed in 1841.

Borodin Alexander Porfir'yevich 1833–1887. Russian composer. Born in St Petersburg, the illegitimate son of a Russian prince. His principal work is the opera *Prince Igor*; left unfinished, was completed by Rimsky-Korsakov and Glazunov.

boron a chemical element, symbol B, atomic number 5, relative atomic mass 10.81. It is used to harden steel and, because it absorbs slow neutrons, to make control rods for nuclear reactors.

Bosch Hieronymus (Jerome) 1460–1516. Netherlandish painter. His fantastic visions of weird and

hellish creatures, as shown in *The Garden of Earthly Delights, c.* 1505–10 (Prado, Madrid), show astonishing imagination and a complex imagery. His religious subjects focused not on the holy figures but on the mass of ordinary witnesses.

Bosnia-Herzegovina (Serbo Croatian *Bosna-Hercegovina*) country in central Europe, bounded to the north and west by Croatia, to the east by Serbia, and to the east and south by the Yugoslavian republic of Montenegro.

Bosnian Crisis period of international tension 1908 when Austria attempted to capitalize on Turkish weakness after the ◊Young Turk revolt by annexing the provinces of Bosnia and Herzegovina. Austria obtained Russian approval in exchange for conceding Russian access to the Bosporus straits.

Bosporus (Turkish *Karadeniz Boğazı*) strait 27 km/17 mi long joining the Black Sea with the Sea of Marmara and forming part of the water division between Europe and Asia. Istanbul stands on its W side.

Boston industrial and commercial centre, capital of Massachusetts, USA; population (1990) 574,300; metropolitan area 4,171,600. It is a publishing centre, and Harvard University and Massachusetts Institute of Technology are nearby.

Boston Tea Party American colonists' protest 1773 against the British tea tax before the War of ◊American Independence.

Boswell James 1740–1795. Scottish biographer and man-of-letters. He was a member of Samuel Johnson's London Literary Club, and in 1773 the two men travelled to Scotland together, as recorded in Boswell's *Journal of a Tour to the Hebrides* 1785. His *Life of Samuel Johnson* was published 1791.

Bosworth, Battle of last battle of the Wars of the Roses, fought on 22 Aug 1485 near the village of Market Bosworth, 19 km/12 mi W of Leicester, England. Richard III, the Yorkist king, was defeated and slain by Henry of Richmond, who became Henry VII, the first Tudor monarch.

Botswana
Republic of

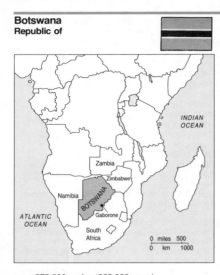

area 575,000 sq km/222,000 sq mi
capital Gaborone
physical desert in SW, plains in E, fertile lands and swamp in N.

head of state and government Quett Ketamile Joni Masire from 1980
political system democratic republic
exports diamonds, copper, nickel, meat
currency pula
population 1,218,000 (1990 est) (80% Bamangwato, 20% Bangwaketse); annual growth rate 3.5%
life expectancy 59 (1988)
language English (official); Setswana (national)
religion Christian 50%, animist 50%
literacy 84% (1988)
GDP $2.0 bn (1988); $1,611 per head
chronology
1885 Became a British protectorate.
1960 New constitution created a legislative council.
1963 End of high-commission rule.
1965 Capital transferred from Mafeking to Gaborone. Internal self-government granted. Seretse Khama elected head of government.
1966 Full independence achieved. New constitution came into effect. Name changed from Bechuanaland to Botswana. Seretse Khama elected president.
1980 Seretse Khama died and was succeeded by Vice-President Quett Masire.
1985 South African raid on Gaborone.
1987 Joint permanent commission with Mozambique established, to improve relations.
1989 Masire re-elected.

botany the study of plants. It is subdivided into a number of specialized studies, such as the identification and classification of plants (taxonomy), their external formation (plant morphology), their internal arrangement (plant anatomy), their microscopic examination (histology), their life history (plant physiology), and their distribution over the earth's surface in relation to their surroundings (plant ecology). Palaeobotany concerns the study of fossil plants, while economic botany deals with the utility of plants. Horticulture, agriculture, and forestry are specialized branches of botany.

Botany Bay inlet on the E coast of Australia, 8 km/5 mi S of Sydney, New South Wales. Chosen in 1787 as the site for a penal colony, it proved unsuitable. Sydney now stands on the site of the former settlement.

botfly type of fly, family Oestridae. The larvae are parasites which feed on the skin (warblefly of cattle) or in the nasal cavity (nostril-flies of sheep, deer). The horse botfly, family Gasterophilidae, has a parasitic larva which feeds in the horse's stomach.

Botha Louis 1862–1919. South African soldier and politician. In 1907 Botha became premier of the Transvaal and in 1910 of the first Union government. On the outbreak of World War I in 1914 he rallied South Africa to the Commonwealth, suppressed a Boer revolt under Gen de Wet, and conquered German South West Africa.

Botha P(ieter) W(illem) 1916– . South African politician. Prime minister 1978–84 and president 1984–89, he initiated a modification of apartheid which later slowed in the face of Afrikaner (Boer) opposition. In 1984 he became the first executive state president. In 1989 he resigned his leadership after suffering a stroke, to be succeeded by F W de Clerk.

Botham Ian Terence 1955– . England cricketer, and former test captain. Prolific all-rounder, but often controversial. He has played county cricket for Somerset, Worcestershire and Durham, as well as playing in Australia. He played for England 1977–89 and 1991.

Bothwell James Hepburn, 4th Earl of Bothwell *c.* 1536–1578. Scottish nobleman, husband of ◊Mary, Queen of Scots, 1567–70, alleged to have arranged the explosion that killed Darnley, her previous husband, in 1567.

Botswana landlocked country in central southern Africa, bounded to the south and east by South Africa, to the west and north by Namibia, and to the northeast by Zimbabwe.

Botticelli Sandro 1445–1510. Florentine painter

Botticelli The Mystic Nativity *(1500) National Gallery, London.*

of religious and mythological subjects. He was patronized by the ruling Medici family, for whom he painted *Primavera* 1478 and *The Birth of Venus* c. 1482–84 (both in the Uffizi, Florence). From the 1490s he was influenced by the religious fanatic Savonarola and developed a harshly expressive and emotional style.

bottlebrush trees and shrubs common in Australia, belonging to the genera *Melaleuca* and *Callistemon*, with characteristic cylindrical, composite flowerheads, often brightly coloured.

Bottomley Virginia 1948– . British conservative politician, health secretary from April 1992, member of Parliament for Surrey Southwest from 1984.

botulism a rare but often fatal type of food poisoning. It is caused by the bacterium *Clostridium botulinum*, sometimes found in canned food.

Boudicca died 60 AD. Queen of the Iceni (native Britons), often referred to by the Latin form *Boadicea*. Her husband, King Prasutagus, had been a tributary of the Romans, but on his death 61 AD, the territory of the Iceni was violently annexed, Boudicca was scourged and her daughters raped. Boudicca raised the whole of SE England in revolt, and before the main Roman armies could return from campaigning in Wales she burned London and Colchester. Later the British were virtually annihilated somewhere between London and Chester, and Boudicca poisoned herself.

Boudin Eugène 1824–1898. French painter, a forerunner of Impressionism, noted for his fresh seaside scenes painted in the open air.

Bougainville Louis Antoine de 1729–1811. French navigator who made the first systematic observations of longitude.

bougainvillea genus of South American climbing plants, family Nyctaginaceae, now cultivated in warm countries throughout the world for the red and purple bracts which cover the flowers. They are named after Louis Bougainville.

Boulanger Nadia (Juliette) 1887–1979. French music teacher. A pupil of Fauré, and admirer of Stravinsky, she included among her pupils at the Conservatoire Américain de Fontainebleau in Paris (from 1921) Aaron Copland, Walter Piston and Lennox Berkeley.

boules (French 'balls') a French game (also *boccie* and *pétanque* played between two players or teams; it is similar to bowls.

Boulez Pierre 1925– . French composer and conductor. He studied with ◊Messiaen, and is a pioneer of electronic music. His works include *Le Visage nuptial* 1946–52, for two solo voices, female choir and orchestra; *Le Marteau sans maître* 1955, a cantata; *Pli selon pli* 1962 for soprano and orchestra; and *Répons* 1981 for chamber orchestra and electronics.

Boulton Matthew 1728–1809. British factory-owner, who helped to finance James ◊Watt's development of the steam engine.

Boumédienne Houari. Adopted name of Mohammed Boukharouba 1925–1978. Algerian politician who brought the nationalist leader Ben Bella to power by a revolt in 1962, and superseded him as president 1965–78 by a further coup.

Bounty, Mutiny on the Pacific mutiny in 1789 against British captain William ◊Bligh.

Bourbon French royal house (succeeding that of ◊Valois) beginning with Henry IV, and ending with Louis XVI, with a brief revival under Louis XVIII, Charles X, and Louis Philippe. The Bourbons also ruled Spain almost uninterruptedly from Philip V to Alfonso XIII, and were restored in

1975 (◊Juan Carlos); as well as Naples and several Italian duchies.

Bourbon Charles, Duke of Bourbon 1490–1527. He was made Constable of France for his courage at the Battle of Marignano 1515. Later he served the Holy Roman emperor Charles V, and helped to drive the French from Italy. In 1526 he was made duke of Milan, and in 1527 allowed his troops to sack Rome. He was killed by a shot the artist Cellini claimed to have fired.

Bourbon, duchy of originally a seigniory created in the 10th century in the county of Bourges, central France. It became a duchy in 1327, and was held by the dukes of Bourbon until they died out at the end of the 12th century.

Bourgeois Léon Victor Auguste 1851–1925. French politician. Entering politics as a Radical, he was prime minister in 1895, and later served in many cabinets. He was one of the pioneer advocates of the League of Nations. Nobel Peace prize 1920.

bourgeoisie (French) the middle classes. The French word originally meant the freemen of a borough. Hence it came to mean the whole class above the workers and peasants, and below the nobility. Bourgeoisie (and *bourgeois*) has also acquired a contemptuous sense, as implying commonplace, philistine respectability. By socialists it is applied to the whole propertied class, as distinct from the proletariat.

Bourgogne region of France; area 31,582 sq km/12,194 sq mi; capital Dijon. It includes the *départements* of Côte-d'Or, Nièvre, Sâone-et-Loire, and Yonne. Population (1986) 1,607,000. It is famous for its wines, such as Chablis and Nuits-Saint-Georges, and for its cattle (the Charolais herdbook is maintained at Nevers). A former independent kingdom and duchy (see ◊Burgundy), it was incorporated into France in 1477.

Bourguiba Habib ben Ali 1903– . Tunisian politician, first president of Tunisia 1957–87. He was frequently imprisoned by the French for his nationalist aims as leader of the Néo-Destour party. He became prime minister in 1956, president (for life from 1974) and prime minister of the Tunisian republic in 1957; overthrown in a coup 1987.

Bournonville August 1805–1879. Danish dancer and choreographer. He worked with the Royal Danish Ballet for most of his life, giving Danish ballet a worldwide importance. His ballets, many of which have been revived in the last 50 years, include *La Sylphide* 1836 (music by Lövenskjold) and *Napoli* 1842.

Boutros-Ghali Boutros 1922– . Egyptian diplomat and politician, deputy prime minister 1991–92. He worked towards peace in the Middle East in the foreign ministry posts he held 1977–91. He became secretary general of the United Nations 1992, and during his first year of office had to deal with the war in Bosnia-Herzegovina and famine in Somalia.

Bouvines, Battle of a victory for Philip II (Philip Augustus) of France in 1214, near the village of Bouvines in Flanders, over the Holy Roman emperor Otto IV and his allies. The battle ensured the succession of Frederick II as emperor, and confirmed Philip as ruler of the whole of N France and Flanders; it led to the renunciation of all English claims to the region.

Bovine Somato Tropin (*BST*) a hormone which increases an injected cow's milk yield by 10–40%. It is a protein naturally occurring in milk, and breaks down within the human digestive tract into harmless amino acids. However, following trials in the UK in 1988, doubts have arisen as to whether such a degree of protein addition could in the long term be guaranteed 'harmless' to either cattle or humans.

bovine spongiform encephalopathy (BSE) disease of cattle, allied to ◊scrapie, which renders the brain spongy and may drive an animal mad. It has been identified only in the UK, but with more than 13,000 cases confirmed since the first diagnosis in November 1986, it poses a threat to the valuable export trade in livestock. The disease has also killed wildlife park animals.

Bow Clara 1905–1965. US silent film actress, known as the 'It' girl after her vivacious performance in *It* 1927.

bower-bird Australian bird related to the ◊birds of paradise. The males are dully-coloured, and build elaborate bowers of sticks and grass, decorated with shells, feathers, or flowers to attract the females. There are 17 species in the family Ptilonorhynchidae.

bowfin N American fish *Amia calva* with a swimbladder highly developed as an air sac, enabling it to breathe air.

bowhead Arctic whale *Balaena mysticetus* with huge curving upper jaw bones supporting the plates of baleen which it uses to sift the water for planktonic crustaceans. Averaging 15 m/50 ft long and 90 tonnes in weight, these slow-moving, placid whales were once extremely common, but by the 17th century were already becoming scarce through hunting. Only an estimated 3,000 remain and continued hunting by the Inuit may result in extinction.

Bowie David. Stage name of David Jones 1947– . British pop singer and songwriter, born in Brixton, London. He became a glitter-rock star with the album *The Rise and Fall of Ziggy Stardust and the Spiders from Mars* 1972, and collaborated in the mid-1970s with the electronic virtuoso Brian Eno (1948–) and Iggy ◊Pop. He has also acted in plays and films, including Nicolas Roeg's *The Man Who Fell to Earth* 1976.

Bowie James 'Jim' 1796–1836. US frontiersman and folk hero. A colonel in the Texan forces during the Mexican War, he is said to have invented the single-edge, guarded hunting and throwing knife known as a *Bowie knife*. He was killed in the battle of the ◊Alamo.

bowls outdoor and indoor game popular in England and Commonwealth countries. It has been played in Britian since the 13th century at least and was popularized by Sir Francis Drake who is reputed to have played bowls on Plymouth Hoe as the Spanish Aramada arrived in 1588.

box small evergreen trees and shrubs, genus *Buxus*, of the family Buxaceae. The **common box**, *B. sempervirens*, is slow growing, and ideal for hedging.

boxer breed of dog, about 60 cm/2 ft tall, with a smooth coat and a set-back nose, which is generally given a docked tail. It is usually brown but may be brindled or white.

Boxer member of the *I Ho Ch'üan*/*Society of Harmonious Fists*, Chinese nationalists who in 1900 at the instigation of the empress dowager besieged the foreign legations in Beijing and murdered European missionaries and thousands of Chinese Christian converts (the **Boxer Rebellion**). An international punitive force was dispatched, Beijing was captured on 14 Aug 1900, and China agreed to pay a large indemnity.

boxfish type of fish which has scales that are hexagonal bony plates fused to form a box covering the body, only the mouth and fins being free of the armour.

boxing fighting with fists. The modern sport dates from the 18th century when fights were with bare knuckles and with untimed rounds. Each round ended with a knockdown. Fighting with gloves became the accepted form in the latter part of the 19th century after the formulation of the Queensberry Rules in 1867. The last bare-knuckle fight was in 1889 between John L Sullivan and Jake Kilrain.

Boycott Charles Cunningham 1832–1897. Land agent in County Mayo, Ireland, who strongly opposed the demands for agrarian reform by the Irish Land League 1879–81, with the result that the peasants refused to work for him; hence the word 'boycott'.

Boyer Charles 1899–1977. French film actor, who made his name in Hollywood in the 1930s as a screen 'lover' in films such as *Mayerling* 1937.

Boyle's law in physics, law stating that the volume (V) of a given mass of gas at a constant temperature is inversely proportional to its pressure (p). It was discovered in 1662 by Robert Boyle.

Boyne, Battle of the battle fought 1 Jul 1690 in E Ireland, in which James II was defeated by William III. It was the decisive battle of the War of English Succession, confirming a Protestant ascendancy. It took its name from the river Boyne in the Republic of Ireland 113 km/70 mi long, flowing past Drogheda into the Irish Sea.

Boy Scout a member of the ◊Scout movement.

BP abbreviation for *British Petroleum*.

Brabant (Flemish *Braband*) former duchy of W Europe, comprising the Belgian provinces of Brabant and Antwerp and the Dutch province of North Brabant, divided when Belgium became independent (1830).

brachiopod phylum of marine clamlike creatures with about 300 species. They are suspension feeders, ingesting minute food particles from water. A single internal organ, the iophophore, handles feeding, aspiration, and excretion.

bracken species of fern *Pteridium aquilinum*, abundant in most parts of Europe. It has a perennial root-stock which throws up large fronds.

bracket fungus ◊fungus of the class Basidiomycetes, with bracket-shaped fruiting body, often seen on tree trunks.

bract a leaf-life structure, in whose ◊axil a flower or inflorescence develops. They are generally green and smaller thàn the true leaves. However, in some plants the bracts may be brightly coloured and conspicuous, taking over the role of attracting pollinating insects to the flowers, whose own petals are small; examples include poinsettia (*Euphorbia pulcherrima*) and Bougainvillea.

Bradbury Malcolm 1932– . British novelist and critic, noted for his comic and satiric portrayals of academic life. His best-known work is *The History Man* 1975, set in a provincial English university.

Bradbury Ray 1920– . US writer, born in Illinois. He was one of the first science-fiction writers to make the genre 'respectable' to a wider readership. His work shows nostalgia for small-town Midwestern life, and includes *The Martian Chronicles* 1950, *Fahrenheit 451* 1953, and *Something Wicked This Way Comes* 1962.

Bradford industrial city (engineering, machine tools, electronics, printing) in West Yorkshire, England, 14 km/9 mi W of Leeds; population (1981) 280,500. From the 13th century, Bradford developèd as a great wool- and, later, cloth-manufacturing

brain

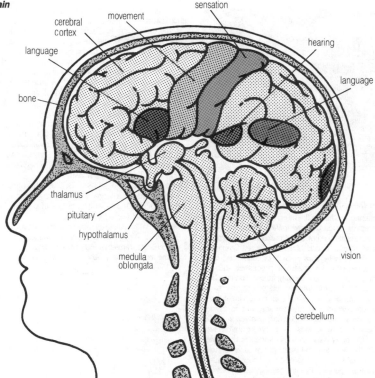

centre, but the industry declined from the 1970s with Third World and Common Market competition. The city has received a succession of immigrants, Irish in the 1840s, German merchants in the mid-19th century, then Poles and Ukrainians, and more recently West Indians and Asians.

Bradley Omar Nelson 1893–1981. US general in World War II. In 1943 he commanded the 2nd US Corps in Tunisia and Sicily, and in 1944 led the US troops in the invasion of France. He was chief of staff of the US Army 1948–49 and chair of the joint chiefs of staff 1949–53. He was appointed general of the army in 1950.

Bradman Donald George 1908– . Australian test cricketer with the highest average in test history. From 52 test matches he averaged 99.94 runs per innings. To counter him, the 1932-33 English team devised the 'bodyline' bowling attack, which limited him to more modest scores.

Bragança name of the royal house of Portugal whose members reigned 1640–1853; another branch were emperors of Brazil 1822–89.

Brahe Tycho 1546–1601. Danish astronomer, who made accurate observations of the planets from which ◊Kepler proved that planets orbit the Sun in ellipses. His discovery and report of the 1572 supernova made him famous, and his observations of the comet of 1577 proved that it moved on an orbit among the planets, thus disproving the Greek view that comets were in the Earth's atmosphere.

Brahma in Hinduism, the creator of the cosmos, who forms with Vishnu and Siva the Trimurti, or three aspects of the absolute spirit. Also an alternative form of ◊Brahman.

Brahman in Hinduism, the supreme being, an impersonal spirit into whom the *atman*, or soul, will eventually be absorbed when its cycle of rebirth is ended.

Brahmanism the earliest stage in the development of ◊Hinduism. Its sacred scriptures are the ◊*Vedas*, with their accompanying literature of comment and explanation known as Brahmanas, Aranyakas, and Upanishads.

Brahmaputra river in Asia 2,900 km/1,800 mi long, a tributary of the Ganges.

Brahma Samaj Indian monotheistic religious movement, founded in 1830 in Calcutta by Ram Mohun Roy, who attempted to recover the simple worship of the Vedas and purify Hinduism. The movement had split into a number of sects by the end of the 19th century and is now almost defunct.

Brahms Johannes 1833–1897. German composer, pianist, and conductor. Ranked as one of the greatest composers of symphonic music and of songs, his works include four symphonies; *Lieder*; concertos for piano and for violin; chamber music; works for piano; and the choral *A German Requiem* 1868. He was renowned as a performer and conductor of his own works.

Braille a system of writing for the blind. Letters are represented by a combination of raised dots on paper or other materials, which are then read by touch. It was invented in 1829 by *Louis Braille* (1809–52), who was blind from the age of three.

brain in higher animals, a mass of interconnected ◊nerve cells, forming the anterior part of the ◊central nervous system, whose activities it coordinates and controls. In ◊vertebrates, the brain

Brahms The composer in his study.

is contained by the skull. An enlarged portion of the upper spinal cord, the *medulla oblongata*, contains centres for the control of respiration, heartbeat rate and strength, and blood pressure. Overlying this is the *cerebellum*, which is concerned with coordinating complex muscular processes such as maintaining posture and moving limbs. The cerebral hemispheres (*cerebrum*) are paired outgrowths of the front end of the forebrain, in early vertebrates mainly concerned with the senses, but in higher vertebrates greatly developed and involved in intelligent behaviour. In humans, the nerves from the two sides of the body cross over as they enter the brain, so that the left cerebral hemisphere is associated with the right side of the body and vice versa. In right-handed people, the left hemisphere seems to be more important in controlling verbal and mathematical skills while the right hemisphere is more important in spatial perception, musical appreciation, and other artistic skills. In the brain, nerve impulses are passed across ◊synapses by neurotransmitters, in the same way as in other parts of the nervous system.

brain damage impairment which can be caused by trauma (for example, accidents) or disease (such as encephalitis), or which may be present at birth. Depending on the area of the brain which is affected, language, movement, sensation, judgement, or other abilities may be impaired.

brainstem the central core of the brain, where the top of the spinal cord merges with the undersurface of the brain.

brainstem the central core of the brain, where the top of the spinal cord merges with the undersurface of the brain.

brake a device used to slow down or stop the movement of a moving body or vehicle. The mechanically applied caliper brake used on bicycles uses a scissor action to press hard rubber blocks against the wheel rim. The main braking system of a car works hydraulically, or by means of liquid pressure. When the driver depresses the brake pedal, liquid pressure forces pistons to apply brakes on each wheel.

Bramah Joseph 1748–1814. British inventor of a flushing water closet (1778), an 'unpickable' lock (1784), and the hydraulic press (1795). The press made use of ◊Pascal's principle (that pressure in fluid contained in a vessel is evenly distributed) and employed water as the hydraulic fluid; it enabled the 19th-century bridge-builders to lift massive girders.

Bramante Donato *c.* 1444–1514. Italian Renaissance architect and artist. Inspired by Classical designs, he was employed by Pope Julius II in re-building part of the Vatican and St Peter's.

Brancusi Constantin 1876–1957. Romanian sculptor, active in Paris from 1904, a pioneer of abstract forms and conceptual art. He was one of the first sculptors in the 20th century to carve directly from his material, working with marble, granite, wood and other materials. He developed increasingly simplified natural or organic forms,

Brandenburg former Prussian and German province, capital Potsdam. It was divided 1945 between Poland and East Germany.

Brando Marlon 1924– . US actor, whose casual mumbling speech and use of ◊method acting earned him a place as one of the most distinctive screen actors. His films include *A Streetcar Named Desire* 1951, *Julius Caesar* 1953, *The Godfather* and *Last Tango in Paris* both 1972.

Brandt Bill 1905–1983. British photographer, who produced a large body of richly-printed and romantic black and white studies of people, London life, and social behaviour.

Brandt Willy. Adopted name of Karl Herbert Frahm 1913– . West German socialist politician, federal chancellor (premier) 1969–74. He played a key role in the remoulding of the Social Democratic Party

brake

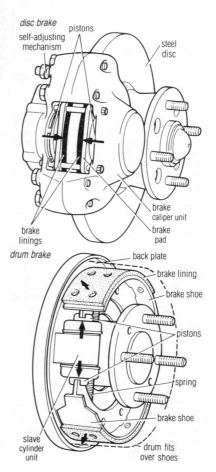

disc brake
- self-adjusting mechanism
- pistons
- steel disc
- brake caliper unit
- brake linings
- brake pad

drum brake
- back plate
- brake lining
- brake shoe
- pistons
- spring
- brake shoe
- slave cylinder unit
- drum fits over shoes

Brando Marlon Brando as the rebellious biker Johnny in The Wild One 1954.

(SPD) as a moderate socialist force (chair 1964–87). As mayor of West Berlin 1957–66, Brandt became internationally known during the Berlin Wall crisis of 1961. Nobel Peace Prize 1971.

Brandt Commission officially the Independent Commission on International Development Issues, established in 1977 and chaired by the former West German chancellor Willy ◊Brandt. Consisting of 18 eminent persons acting independently of governments, the Commission examined the problems of developing countries and sought to identify corrective measures that would command international support. It was disbanded in 1983.

Branson Richard 1950– . British businessman and entrepreneur, whose Virgin company developed quickly, diversifying from retailing records to the airline business.

Braque Georges 1882–1963. French painter, who, with Picasso, founded the Cubist movement around 1908–10. They worked together at L'Estaque in the south of France and in Paris. Braque soon began to experiment in collages, and invented a technique of gluing paper, wood, and other materials to canvas. His later work became more decorative.

Brasília capital of Brazil from 1960, some 1,000 m/3,000 ft above sea level; population (1980)

Branson British businessman and entrepreneur Richard Branson, 1986.

411,500. It was designed by Lucio Costa (1902–63), with Oscar Niemeyer as chief architect, as a completely new city to bring life to the interior.

Braşov (Hungarian *Brassó*, German *Krondstadt*) industrial city (machine tools, industrial equipment, chemicals, cement, woollens) in central Romania at the foot of the Transylvanian Alps; population (1983) 331,240. It belonged to Hungary until 1920.

brass an ◊alloy of copper and zinc, with not more than 5% or 6% of other metals. The zinc content ranges from 20% to 45%, and the colour of brass varies accordingly from coppery to whitish yellow. Brasses are characterized by the ease with which they may be shaped and machined; they are strong and ductile, resist many forms of corrosion, and are used for electrical fittings, ammunition cases, screws, household fittings, and ornaments.

brass in music, instruments made of brass, which are directly blown through a 'cup' or 'funnel' mouthpiece. They comprise:
symphony orchestra:
French horn a descendant of the natural hunting horn, valved and curved into a circular loop, with a wide bell;
trumpet a cylindrical tube curved into an oblong, with a narrow bell and three valves (the state *fanfare trumpet* has no valves);
trombone instrument with a 'slide' to vary the effective length of the tube (the *sackbut*, common from the 14th century, was its forerunner);
tuba normally the lowest toned instrument of the orchestra; valved and with a very wide bore to give sonority, its bell points upward.
brass band (in descending order of pitch):
cornet three-valved instrument, looking like a shorter, broader trumpet, and with a wider bore;
flugelhorn valved instrument, rather similar in range to the cornet;

brass instruments

trumpet

cornet

trombone

tuba

French horn

tenor horn;
B-flat baritone;
euphonium;
trombone;
bombardon (bass tuba).

A brass band normally also includes bass and side drums, triangle, and cymbals.

brassica genus of plants of the family Cruciferae. The best-known species is the common cabbage *Brassica oleracea* with its varieties broccoli, cauliflower, kale, brussels sprouts.

Bratislava (German *Pressburg*) capital of the Slovak Republic and industrial port (engineering, chemicals, oil refining) on the river Danube; population (1991) 441,500. It was the capital of Hungary 1526–1784.

Brattain Walter Houser 1902–1987. US physicist. In 1956, he was awarded a Nobel prize jointly with William Shockley and John Bardeen for their work on the development of the transistor, which replaced the comparatively costly and clumsy vacuum tube in electronics.

Brauchitsch Walther von 1881–1948. German field marshal. A staff officer in World War I, he became in 1938 commander in chief of the army and a member of Hitler's secret cabinet council. He was dismissed after his failure to invade Moscow 1941. Captured in 1945, he died before being tried.

Braun Eva 1910–1945. German Nazi. Born in Munich. Secretary to Hitler's photographer and personal friend, Heinrich Hoffmann, she was Hitler's mistress for years, and married him in the air-raid shelter of the Chancellery in Berlin on 29 Apr 1945. They then committed suicide together.

Brazil country in South America, bounded to the southwest by Uruguay, Argentina, Paraguay and Bolivia, to the west by Peru and Colombia, to the north by Venezuela, Guyana, Suriname and French Guiana, and to the west by the Atlantic Ocean.

Brazil nut seed, rich in oil and highly nutritious, of the South American tree *Bertholletia excelsa*. The seeds are enclosed in a hard outer casing, each fruit containing 10–20 arranged like the segments of an orange. The timber of the tree is also valuable.

brazing a method of joining two metals by melting an ◊alloy into the joint. It is similar to soldering but takes place at a much higher temperature. Copper and silver alloys are widely used for brazing, at temperatures up to about 900°C.

Brazzaville capital of the Congo, industrial port (foundries, railway repairs, shipbuilding, shoes, soap, furniture, bricks) on the river Zaïre, opposite Kinshasa; population (1984) 595,000. It was the African headquarters of the Free (later Fighting) French during World War II.

bread food made with ground cereals, usually wheat, and water, though with many other variants of the contents. The dough may be unleavened or raised (usually with yeast) and then baked.

breadfruit fruit of a tree *Artocarpus communis* of the mulberry family Moraceae. When toasted, it is said to taste like bread. It is native to the South Sea Islands and is an important local article of food.

Breakspear Nicholas original name of ◊Adrian IV, the only English pope.

bream deep-bodied, flattened fish *Abramis brama* of the carp family, growing to about 50 cm/1.6 ft, typically found in lowland rivers across Europe.

breast organ on upper front of the human female, also known as a ◊mammary gland. Each of the two breasts contains milk-producing cells, and a network of tubes or ducts which lead to an opening in the nipple.

breast

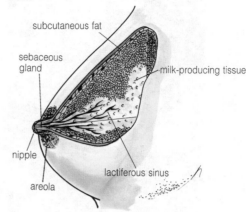

subcutaneous fat

sebaceous gland

milk-producing tissue

nipple

lactiferous sinus

areola

Breathalyzer instrument for on-the-spot checking by the police of the amount of alcohol in the blood of a suspect driver, who breathes into a plastic bag connected to a tube containing a chemical (such as a diluted solution of potassium dichromate in 50% sulphuric acid) which changes colour. Another method is to use a gas chromatograph, again from a breath sample.

breathing in terrestrial animals, the process of taking air into the lungs for ◊gas exchange. It is sometimes referred to as external respiration, for true respiration is a cellular (internal) process.

breccia a coarse sedimentary rock, made up of broken fragments of pre-existing rocks (a clastic sedimentary rock).

Brecht Bertolt 1898–1955. German dramatist and poet, who aimed to destroy the 'suspension of disbelief' usual in the theatre, and to express Marxist ideas. His first notable work was an adaptation of John Gay's *Beggar's Opera* as *Die Dreigroschenoper/The Threepenny Opera* 1928, set to music by Kurt Weill. Later plays include *Mutter Courage/Mother Courage* 1941 and *Der kaukasische Kreidekreis/The Caucasian Chalk Circle* 1949.

Breda, Treaty of 1667 treaty that ended the Second Anglo-Dutch War (1664–67). By the terms of the treaty, England gained New Amsterdam, which was renamed New York.

Brecht German dramatist and poet Bertolt Brecht.

Brazil
Federative Republic of
(*República Federativa do Brasil*)

area 8,512,000 sq km/3,286,000 sq mi
capital Brasília
towns São Paulo, Belo Horizonte, Curitiba, Fortaleza; ports are Rio de Janeiro, Recife, Pôrto Alegre, Salvador
physical the densely forested Amazon basin covers the N half of the country with a network of rivers; the S is fertile; enormous energy resources, both hydroelectric (Itaipú dam on the Paraná, and Tucuruí on the Tocantins) and nuclear (uranium ores)
head of state and government Hamar Franco from 1992
political system emergent democratic federal republic
exports coffee, sugar, cotton, textiles, motor vehicles, iron, chrome, manganese, tungsten and other ores, as well as quartz crystals, industrial diamonds
currency cruzado
population 153,770,000 (1990 est) (including

200,000 Indians mostly living on reserves); annual growth rate 2.2%
life expectancy men 61, women 66
language Portuguese; 120 Indian languages.
religion Roman Catholic 89%, Indian faiths
literacy 79% male/76% female (1985 est)
GDP $352 bn (1988); $2,434 per head
chronology
1822 Brazil became an independent empire, ruled by Dom Pedro, son of the refugee King João VI of Portugal.
1889 Monarchy abolished and republic established.
1891 Constitution for a federal state adopted.
1930 Dr Getulio Vargas became president.
1945 Vargas deposed by the military.
1950 Vargas returned to office.
1954 Vargas committed suicide.
1956 Juscelino Kubitschek became president.
1960 Capital moved to Brasília.
1961 João Goulart became president.
1964 Bloodless coup made Gen Castelo Branco president. He assumed dictatorial powers, abolishing free political parties.
1967 New constitution adopted. Branco succeeded by Marshal da Costa e Silva.
1969 Da Costa e Silva resigned and a military junta took over.
1974 Gen Ernesto Geisel became president.
1978 Gen Baptista de Figueiredo became president.
1979 Political parties legalized again.
1984 Mass calls for a return to fully democratic government.
1985 Tancredo Neves became first civilian president for 21 years. Neves died and was succeeded by the vice-president, José Sarney.
1988 New constitution approved, transferring power from the president to the congress. Measures announced to half large-scale burning of Amazonian rainforest.
1989 Forest Protection Service and Ministry for Land Reform abolished. Fernando Collar elected president.
1992 Earth Summit, global conference on the environment, held in Rio de Janeiro. Collar impeached for corruption and replaced by vice president Hamar Franco.

breed a recognizable group of domestic animals, within a species, with distinctive characteristics that have been produced by ◊artificial selection.

breeder reactor a ◊nuclear reactor which produces more fuel than it consumes. Breeder reactor is an alternative name for the fast reactor.

breeding in biology, the rearing of animals or the cultivation of plants, using planned crossing and selection to change the characteristics of an existing ◊breed or ◊cultivar (variety), or to produce a new one.

breeding in nuclear physics, process in a reactor in which more fissionable material is produced than is consumed in running the reactor.

Bremen industrial port (iron and steel, oil refining, chemicals, aircraft, shipbuilding, cars) in Germany, on the River Weser 69 km/43 mi from open sea; population (1988) 522,000.

Bremen administrative region (German *Land*) of Germany, consisting of the cities of Bremen and Bremerhaven; area 404 sq km/156 sq mi; population 652,000.

Brenner Sidney 1927– . British scientist, born in South Africa, one of the pioneers of genetic engineering. Brenner discovered messenger

◊RNA (a link between ◊DNA and ◊ribosomes, where proteins are synthesized) in 1960.

Brenner Pass lowest of the Alpine passes, 1,370 m/4,495 ft; it leads from Trentino-Alto Adige, Italy, to the Austrian Tirol, and is 19 km/12 mi long.

Brenton Howard 1942– . British dramatist, noted for *The Romans in Britain* 1980, and a translation of Brecht's *The Life of Galileo*.

Brescia historic and industrial city (textiles, engineering, firearms, metal products) in N Italy, 84 km/52 mi E of Milan; population (1988) 199,000. It has medieval walls and two cathedrals (12th and 17th century). Ancient name *Brixia*.

Breslau German name of ◊Wroclaw, town in Poland.

Brest naval base and industrial port (electronics, engineering, chemicals) on *Rade de Brest* (Brest Roads), a great bay at the W extremity of Brittany, France; population (1983) 166,500. Occupied as a U-boat base by the Germans 1940–44, the town was destroyed by Allied bombing and rebuilt.

Brest-Litovsk, Treaty of treaty signed 3 Mar 1918 between Russia and Germany, Austria-Hungary, and their allies. Under it, Russia agreed to recognize the independence of the Baltic states, Georgia, the Ukraine, and Poland, and pay heavy compensation. Under the Nov 1918 Armistice that ended World War I, it was annulled.

Bretagne French name for ◊Brittany, region of W France.

Brétigny, Treaty of treaty made between Edward III of England and John II of France in 1360 at the end of the first phase of the Hundred Years' War, under which Edward received Aquitaine and its dependencies in exchange for renunciation of his claim to the French throne.

Breton André 1896–1966. French author, among the leaders of ◊Dada. *Les Champs magnétiques/ Magnetic Fields* 1921, an experiment in automatic writing, was one of the most notable products of the movement. He was also a founder of ◊Surrealism, publishing *Le Manifeste de surréalisme/Surrealist Manifesto* 1924.

Breton language a member of the Celtic branch of the Indo-European language family; the language of Brittany in France, related to Welsh and Cornish, and descended from the speech of Celts who left Britain as a consequence of the Anglo-Saxon invasions of the 5th and 6th centuries. Officially neglected for centuries, Breton is now a recognized language of France.

Bretton Woods township in New Hampshire, USA, where the United Nations Monetary and Financial Conference was held in 1944 to discuss post-war international payments problems. The agreements reached on financial assistance and measures to stabilize exchange rates led to the creation of the International Bank for Reconstruction and Development in 1945 and the International Monetary Fund.

Breuer Josef 1842–1925. Viennese physician, one of the pioneers of psychoanalysis. He applied it successfully to cases of hysteria, and collaborated with Freud in *Studien über Hysterie/Studies in Hysteria* 1895.

Breuer Marcel l902– . Hungarian-born architect and designer, who studied and taught at the ◊Bauhaus. His tubular steel chair, 1925, was the first of its kind. He moved to England, then to the USA, where he was in partnership with Gropius 1937–40. His buildings show an affinity with natural materials; the best known is the Bijenkorf, Rotterdam (with Elzas) 1953.

Breuil Henri 1877–1961. French prehistorian, professor of historic ethnography and director of research at the Institute of Human Palaeontology, Paris, from 1910. He established the genuine antiquity of Palaeolithic cave art and stressed the anthropological approach to the early human history.

breviary in the Roman Catholic church, the book of instructions for reciting the daily services. It is usually in four volumes, one for each season.

Brezhnev Leonid Ilyich 1906–1982. Soviet leader. A protégé of Stalin and Khrushchev, he came into power as general secretary of the Soviet Communist Party (CPSU) 1964–82 and was president 1977–82. Domestically he was conservative, abroad he established the USSR as a military and political superpower, extending its influence in Africa and Asia.

Brezhnev Doctrine Soviet doctrine 1968 designed to justify the invasion of Czechoslovakia. It laid down for the USSR as a duty the direct maintenance of 'correct' socialism in countries within the Soviet sphere of influence. In 1979 it was extended, by the invasion of Afghanistan, to the direct establishment of 'correct' socialism in countries not already within its sphere.

Brian known as *Brian Boru* ('Brian of the Tribute') 926–1014. King of Ireland from 976, who took Munster, Leinster, and Connacht, to become ruler of all Ireland. He defeated the Norse at Clontarf, thus ending Norse control of Dublin, although he was himself killed.

Briand Aristide 1862–1932. French radical socialist politician. He was prime minister 1909–11, 1913, 1915–17, 1921–22, 1925–26, and 1929, and foreign minister 1925–32. In 1925 he concluded the ◊Locarno Pact and in 1928 the ◊Kellogg Pact; in 1930 he outlined a scheme for a United States of Europe.

brick a common building material, rectangular in shape, made of clay that has been fired in a kiln. Bricks are made by kneading a mixture of crushed clay and other materials into a stiff mud and extruding it into a ribbon. The ribbon is cut into individual bricks which are fired at a temperature up to about 1,000°C. Bricks may alternatively be pressed into shape in moulds.

bridge a construction which provides a continuous path or road over water, valleys, ravines, or above other roads. Bridges may be classified into four main groups: *arch* for example, Sydney Harbour bridge (steel arch) with a span of 503 m/1,650 ft; *beam or girder* for example, Rio-Niteroi (1974) Guanabara Bay, Brazil, centre span 300 m/984 ft;

bridge

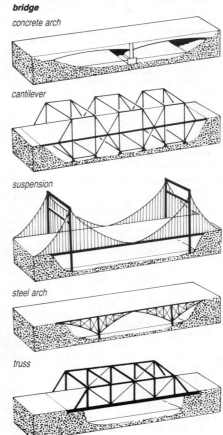

concrete arch

cantilever

suspension

steel arch

truss

length 13,900 m/8 mi 3,363 ft; *cantilever* for example, Forth rail bridge, Scotland, which is 1,658 m/5,440 ft long with two main spans, two cantilevers each, one from each tower; *suspension* for example, Humber bridge, England, with a centre span of 1,410 m/4,626 ft.

bridge card game derived from whist and introduced into Britain about 1880. It is played in two forms ◊auction bridge and ◊contract bridge.

Bridgetown port and capital of Barbados, founded 1628, population (1985) 253,055. Sugar is exported through the nearby deep-water port.

Bridget, St 453–523. A patron saint of Ireland, also known as St Brigit or *St Bride*. She founded a church and monastery at Kildare, and is said to have been the daughter of a prince of Ulster. Feast day 1 Feb.

Bridgewater Francis Egerton, 3rd Duke of Bridgewater 1736–1803. Pioneer of British inland navigation. With James ◊Brindley as his engineer, he constructed 1762–72 the Bridgewater canal from Worsley to Manchester, to the Mersey, a distance of 67.5 km/42 mi.

Bright John 1811–1889. British Liberal politician, a campaigner for free trade, peace, and social reform. A Quaker millowner, he was among the founders of the Anti-Corn Law League in 1839, and was largely instrumental in securing the passage of the Reform Bill of 1867.

brill flatfish *Scophthalmus laevis* which lives in shallow water over sandy bottoms in the NE Atlantic and Mediterranean. It is a freckled sandy brown, and grows to 60 cm/2 ft.

Brindley James 1716–1772. British canal builder, the first to employ tunnels and aqueducts extensively, in order to reduce the number of locks on a direct-route canal. His 580 km/360 mi of canals included the Bridgewater (Manchester-Liverpool) and Grand Union (Manchester-Potteries) canals.

Brinell hardness test test for the hardness of a substance according to the area of indentation made by a 10 mm/0.4 in hardened steel or sintered tungsten carbide ball under standard loading conditions in a test machine. It is equal to the load (kg) divided by the surface area (mm^2).

Brisbane industrial port (brewing, engineering, tanning, tobacco, shoes; oil pipeline from Moonie), capital of Queensland, E Australia, near the mouth of Brisbane river, dredged to carry ocean-going ships; population (1986) 1,171,300

Brisbane Thomas Makdougall 1773–1860. Scottish soldier, colonial administrator, and astronomer. After serving in the Napoleonic Wars under Wellington, he was governor of New South Wales 1821–25, and Brisbane in Queensland is named after him.

Brissot Jacques Pierre 1754–1793. French revolutionary leader. He became a member of the legislative assembly and the National Convention, but his party of moderate republicans – the ◊Girondins, or Brissotins – fell foul of Robespierre and Brissot was guillotined.

bristletail primitive wingless insect, order Thysanura. Up to 2 cm/0.8 in long, bristletails have a body tapering from front to back, two long antennae and three 'tails' at the rear end.

Bristol industrial port (aircraft engines, engineering, microelectronics, tobacco, chemicals, paper, printing), administrative headquarters of Avon, SW England; population (1981) 388,000.

Britain, Ancient the name Britain, indicating present-day England, Scotland, and Wales, is derived from the Roman name Britannia, which is in its turn derived from the ancient Celtic. Britain was inhabited for thousands of years by people who kept livestock and grew corn; they built stone circles and buried their chiefs in ◊barrow mounds. After 1000 BC Britain was conquered by the ◊Celts.

Britain, Battle of World War II air battle between German and UK air forces over Britain which lasted from 10 Jul to 12 Oct 1940. It has been divided into five phases: 10 July–7 Aug, the preliminary phase; 8–23 Aug, attack on coastal targets; 24 Aug–6 Sept, attack on Fighter Command airfields; 7–30 Sept, daylight attack on London, chiefly by heavy bombers; and 1–31 Oct, daylight attack on London, chiefly by fighter-bombers.

Britannicus Tiberius Claudius *c.* 41–55 AD. Roman prince, son of the Emperor Claudius and Messalina, so-called from his father's expedition to Britain. He was poisoned by Nero.

British Antarctic Territory colony created in 1962 and comprising all British territories S of latitude 60°S: the British sector of the Antarctic continent (Graham Land and areas round the Weddell Sea) approximately 388,500 sq km/150,000 sq mi; the South Orkneys, 722 sq km/240 sq mi, and South Shetlands, 337 sq km/130 sq mi. Scientific personnel are the only population: about 300.

British Broadcasting Corporation (BBC) in the UK, the state-owned broadcasting network. It operates television, national and local radio stations, and is financed solely by the sale of television viewing licences. It is not allowed to carry advertisements, but overseas radio broadcasts (World Service) have a government subsidy.

British Columbia province of W Canada on the Pacific
area 948,599 sq km/366,255 sq mi
capital Victoria
towns Vancouver, Prince George, Kamloops, Kelowna
physical Rocky Mountains and Coast Range; the coast is deeply indented; rivers include the Fraser and Columbia; there are more than 80 lakes; more than half the land is forested
products fruit and vegetables; timber and wood products; fish; coal, copper, iron, lead; oil and natural gas, and hydroelectricity
population (1986) 2,889,000
history Captain Cook explored the coast in 1778; a British colony was founded on Vancouver Island in 1849, and the gold rush of 1858 extended settlement to the mainland; it became a province in 1871.

(British) Commonwealth (of Nations) former official name of the ◊Commonwealth.

British Council government organization set up 1935 (royal charter 1940) to promote a wider knowledge of the UK, excluding politics and commerce, and to develop cultural relations with other countries.

British Empire, Order of the British order of chivalry, instituted by George V in 1917. There are military and civil divisions, and the ranks are GBE, Knight Grand Cross or Dame Grand Cross; KBE, Knight Commander; DBE, Dame Commander; CBE, Commander; OBE, Officer; MBE, Member.

British Empire the various territories all over the world conquered or colonized by Britain from about 1600, most now independent or lost to other powers; the British Empire was at its largest at the end of World War I, with over 25% of the world's population and area. The ◊Commonwealth is composed of former and remaining territories of the British Empire.

British Empire

Current name	Colonial names and history	Colonized	Independent
India	British E India Co. 18th cent.–1858	18th cent.	1947
Pakistan	British E India Co. 18th cent.–1858	18th cent.	1947
Sri Lanka	Portuguese, Dutch 1602–1796; Ceylon 1802–1972	16th cent.	1948
Ghana	Gold Coast	1618	1957
Nigeria		1861	1960
Cyprus	Turkish to 1878, then British rule	1878	1960
Sierra Leone	British protectorate	1788	1961
Tanzania	German E Africa to 1921; British mandate from League of Nations/UN as Tanganyika	19th cent.	1961
Jamaica	Spanish to 1655	16th cent.	1962
Trinidad & Tobago	Spanish 1532–1797; British 1797–1962	1532	1962
Uganda	British protectorate	1894	1962
Kenya	British colony from 1920	1895	1963
Malaysia	British interests from 1786; Federation of Malaya 1957–63	1874	1963
Malawi	British protectorate of Nyasaland 1907–53; Federation of Rhodesia & Nyasaland 1953–64	1891	1964
Malta	French 1798–1814	1798	1964
Zambia	N Rhodesia – British protectorate; Federation of Rhodesia & Nyasaland 1953–64	1924	1964
The Gambia		1888	1965
Singapore	Federation of Malaya 1963–65	1858	1965
Guyana	Dutch to 1796; British Guiana 1796–1966	1620	1966
Botswana	Bechuanaland – British protectorate	1885	1966
Lesotho	Basutoland	1868	1966
Bangladesh	British E India Co. 18th cent.–1858; British India 1858–1947; E Pakistan 1947–71	18th cent.	1971
Zimbabwe	S Rhodesia from 1923; UDI 1965–79 under Ian Smith	1895	1980

British Expeditionary Force (BEF) a British army which served in France in World War I 1914–18, under first J French and then D Haig. Also the army of World War II 1939–40, which was evacuated from Dunkirk, France; commander Gen Gort.

British Honduras former name of ◊Belize, a country in Central America.

British Indian Ocean Territory British colony in the Indian Ocean directly administered by the Foreign and Commonwealth Office. It consists of the Chagos Archipelago some 1,900 km/1,200 mi NE of Mauritius
area 60 sq km/23 sq mi
products copra, salt fish, tortoiseshell
population (1982) 3,000
history purchased in 1965 for $3 million by Britain from Mauritius to provide a joint US/UK base

British Isles group of islands off the NW coast of Europe, consisting of Great Britain (England, Wales, and Scotland), Ireland, the Channel Islands, Orkney and Shetlands, Isle of Man, and many others which are included in various counties, such as the Isle of Wight, Scilly Isles, Lundy Island, and the Inner and Outer Hebrides. The islands are divided from Europe by the North Sea, Strait of Dover, and English Channel, and face the Atlantic to the W.

British Library the national library of the UK. Created 1973, it comprises the *reference division* (the former library departments of the British Museum, being rehoused at the Euston Road, London, site); *lending division* at Boston Spa, Yorkshire, from which full text documents and graphics can be sent, using a satellite link, to other countries; and *bibliographic services division* (incorporating the British National Bibliography).

British Museum largest museum of the UK. Founded in 1753 with the purchase of Hans Sloane's library and art collection, and the subsequent acquisition of the Cottonian, Harleian, and other libraries, the British Museum was opened at Montagu House, Bloomsbury, in 1759.

British Standards Institute (BSI) the UK national standards body. Although government funded, the Institute is independent. The BSI interprets international technical standards for the UK, and also sets its own. For consumer goods, it sets standards which products should reach (the BS standard), as well as testing products to see that they conform to that standard (as a result of which the product may be given the BSI 'kite' mark).

British Telecom a British company that formed part of the Post Office until 1980, and was privatized in 1984. It is responsible for ◊telecommunications, including the telephone network, and radio and television broadcasting. Previously a monopoly, it now faces commercial competition for some of its services. It operates Britain's ◊viewdata network called ◊Prestel.

British thermal unit (BTU) imperial unit of heat, defined as the amount of heat required to raise the temperature of 0.45 kg/1 lb of water by 1°F. It is now replaced in the ◊SI system by the joule (1 BTU = 1,055.06 joules) but still used by some public utilities.

Brittain Vera 1894–1970. British socialist writer, a nurse to the troops overseas 1915–19, as told in her *Testament of Youth* 1933; *Testament of Friendship* 1950 commemorated Winifred ◊Holtby.

Brittan Leon 1939– . British Conservative politician and lawyer. Chief secretary to the Treasury 1981–83, Home Secretary 1983–85, Secretary for trade and industry 1985–86, (resigned over his part in the ◊Westland affair) and senior European Commissioner from 1988.

Brittany (French *Bretagne*) region of NW France in the Breton peninsula between the Bay of Biscay and the English Channel
area 27,208 sq km/10,505 sq mi
capital Rennes

Britten British composer and pianist Benjamin Britten.

Brontë Emily, Anne, and Charlotte, painted by their brother, Patrick Branwell, c. 1835.

population (1982) 2,707,886

history originally the Gallo-Roman province of Armorica, after being conquered by Julius Caesar in 56 BC, it was devastated by Norsemen after the Roman withdrawal. During the Anglo-Saxon invasion of Britain so many Celts migrated across the Channel that it gained the name of Brittany. There is now some separatist feeling.

Britten (Edward) Benjamin, Baron Britten 1913–1976. British composer. He wrote for the individual voice, for example Peter Pears (1910–1986) and Janet ◊Baker, and is also known for his operas. *Peter Grimes* 1945 based on a tale by Crabbe, the chamber opera *The Rape of Lucretia* 1946, *Billy Budd* 1951, *A Midsummer Night's Dream* 1960, and *Death in Venice* 1973.

brittle star type of ◊starfish, with a small central rounded body and long flexible spiny arms used for walking. The *small brittle-star Amphipholis squamata* is greyish, about 4.5 cm/2 in across, and found on the seabed almost worldwide. It broods its young, and its arms can be luminous.

Brno industrial city in the Czech republic (chemicals, arms, textiles, machinery), population (1984) 380,800. Founded in the 10th century, Brno was formerly capital of the Austrian crownland of Moravia.

broadcasting the transmission of sound and vision programmes by radio and television. Broadcasting may be organized under complete state control, as in the former USSR, or private enterprise, as in the USA, or may operate under a compromise system, as in Britain, where there is a television and radio service controlled by the state-regulated ◊British Broadcasting Corporation, and also the commercial Independent Television Commission (the Independent Broadcasting Authority before 1991).

broad-leaved tree another name for a tree belonging to the ◊angiosperms, such as ash, beech, oak, maple or birch. Their leaves are generally broad and flat, in contrast to the needle-like leaves of most ◊conifers. See also ◊deciduous tree.

Broadmoor special hospital (established 1863) in Crowthorne, Berkshire, England, for those formerly described as 'criminally insane'.

Broads, Norfolk area of some twelve interlinked freshwater lakes in E England, created about 600 years ago by the digging out of peat deposits; they are noted for wildlife and boating facilities.

Broadway major street of Manhattan, New York, famous for its theatres.

broccoli a variety of ◊cabbage.

broderie anglaise literally 'English embroidery', although popular in many other countries also. A type of embroidered fabric, usually white cotton, in which holes are cut in patterns and oversewn, often to decorate shirts and skirts.

Brodsky Joseph 1940– . Russian poet, who emigrated to the USA in 1972. His work, often dealing with themes of exile, is admired for its wit and economy of language. Many of his poems, written in Russian, have been translated into English (*A Part of Speech* 1980). More recently he has also written in English. Nobel prize 1987.

brome general name for annual grasses of the genus *Bromus* and some related grasses.

bromeliad plant of the family Bromeliaceae, to which the pineapple belongs. Bromeliads originate in tropical America, where there are some 1,400 species. Many are terrestrial, growing in habitats ranging from scrub desert to tropical forest floor. Many, however, are epiphytes and grow on trees.

bromine an element that exists as a red, volatile liquid at room temperature; symbol Br, atomic number 35, relative atomic mass 79.909. Bromine is poisonous and a member of the halogen series of elements.

bronchitis inflammation of the bronchi (air passages) of the lungs, usually caused initially by a viral infection, such as a cold or flu. It is aggravated by environmental pollutants.

bronchodilator a drug that relieves obstruction of the airways by causing the bronchi and bronchioles to relax and widen. It is most useful in the treatment of asthma.

Brontë family of English writers, including the three sisters *Charlotte* (1816–55), *Emily Jane* (1818–48) and *Anne* (1820–49), and their brother *Patrick Branwell* (1817–48). Their best-known works are Charlotte Brontë's *Jane Eyre* 1847 and Emily Brontë's *Wuthering Heights* 1847. Later works include Anne's *The Tenant of Wildfell Hall* 1848, and Charlotte's *Shirley* 1849, and *Villette* 1853.

Brontosaurus large plant-eating dinosaur, now called *Apatosaurus*, which flourished about 145 million years ago. Up to 21 m/69 ft long and 30 tonnes in weight, it stood on four elephant-like legs and had a long tail, long neck, and small head. It probably snipped off low-growing vegetation with peg-like front teeth, and swallowed it whole to be ground by pebbles in the stomach.

bronze ◊alloy of copper and tin, yellow or brown in colour. It is harder than pure copper, more suitable for ◊casting, and also resists ◊corrosion. Bronze may contain as much as 25 per cent tin, together with small amounts of other metals, particularly lead.

Bronze Age period of early history and prehistory when bronze was the chief material used for tools and weapons. It lies between the Stone Age and the Iron Age and may be dated 5000–1200 BC in the Middle East, and about 2000–500 BC in Europe. Recent discoveries in Thailand suggest that the Far East, rather than the Middle East, was the cradle of the Bronze Age.

Bronzino Agnolo 1503–1572. Italian painter active in Florence, court painter to Cosimo I, Duke of Tuscany. He painted in an elegant, frigid Mannerist style, and is best known for portraits and the allegory *Venus, Cupid, Folly and Time c.* 1545 (National Gallery, London).

Brook Peter 1925– . British theatrical producer and director. Known for his experimental productions with the Royal Shakespeare Company in England, he has worked with the Paris-based Le Centre International de Créations Théâtrales since 1970. Films he has directed include *Lord of the Flies* 1962 and *Meetings with Remarkable Men* 1979.

Brooke Rupert Chawner 1887–1915. English poet, symbol of the World War I 'lost generation'. His poems, the best-known being the five war sonnets (including 'Grantchester' and 'The Great Lover'), were published posthumously.

Brookeborough Basil Brooke, Viscount Brookeborough 1888–1973. Unionist politician of Northern Ireland. He entered Parliament in 1929, held ministerial posts 1933–45, and was prime minister of Northern Ireland 1943–63. He was a staunch advocate of strong links with Britain.

Brooklands former motor racing track near Weybridge, Surrey. One of the world's first purpose-built circuits, it was opened in 1907 as a testing ground for early motor-cars. It was the venue for the first British Grand Prix (then known as the RAC Grand Prix) in 1926.

Brookner Anita 1928– . British novelist and art historian, whose novels include *Hotel du Lac* 1984, winner of the Booker prize, *A Misalliance* 1986, and *Latecomers* 1988.

Brooks Louise 1906–1985. US actress, known for her roles in silent films such as *Die Büchse der Pandora/Pandora's Box* and *Das Tagebuch einer Verlorenen/Diary of a Lost Girl* both 1929, and directed by G W ◊Pabst.

Brooks *Louise Brooks as Lulu in Pandora's Box 1928.*

Brooks Mel, born Melvin Kaminsky 1926– . US film director, whose comic films include *Blazing Saddles* 1974, and *History of the World Part I* 1981.

broom shrub of the family Leguminosae, especially species of *Cytisus*, such as the yellow-flowered *common broom Cytisus scoparius* of Britain.

Brouwer Adriaen 1605–1638. Flemish painter who studied with Frans Hals. He excelled in scenes of peasant revelry.

Brown Capability 1715–1783. English landscape gardener, real name Lancelot Brown. One of the most famous garden designers, he acquired his nickname because of his continual enthusiam for the 'capabilities' of natural landscapes. He advised on gardens of stately homes including Blenheim, Stowe, and Petworth, sometimes also contributing to the architectural designs.

Brown Charles Brockden 1771–1810. US novelist, magazine editor. He is called the 'father of the American novel' for his *Wieland* 1798, *Ormond* 1799, *Edgar Huntly* 1799, and *Arthur Mervyn* 1800. His works also pioneered the Gothic and fantastic tradition of American fiction.

Brown Ford Madox 1821–1893. British painter, associated with the ◊Pre-Raphaelite Brotherhood. His pictures include *The Last of England* 1855 (Birmingham Art Gallery) and *Work* 1852–65 (City Art Gallery, Manchester), packed with realistic detail and symbolic incident.

Brown George, Baron George-Brown 1914–1985. British Labour politician. He entered Parliament in 1945, was briefly minister of works in 1951 and contested the leadership of the party on the death of Gaitskell, but was defeated by Harold Wilson. He was secretary for economic affairs 1964–66 and foreign secretary 1966–68. He was created a life peer in 1970.

Brown John 1800–1859. US slavery abolitionist. With 18 men, he seized, on the night of 16 Oct 1859, the government arsenal at Harper's Ferry in W Virginia, apparently intending to distribute weapons to runaway slaves who would then defend the mountain stronghold, which Brown hoped would become a slave republic. On 18 Oct the arsenal was stormed by US marines under Colonel Robert E ◊Lee. Brown was tried and hanged on 2 Dec, becoming a martyr, and the hero of the popular song 'John Brown's Body' *c.* 1860.

Browne Robert 1550–1633. English Puritan religious leader, founder of the Brownists. He was imprisoned several times in 1581–82 for attacking Episcopalianism. He founded a community in Norwich and the Netherlands which continued on ◊Nonconformist lines, developing into modern ◊Congregationalism.

Browne Thomas 1605–1682. English author and physician. His dense, allusive writings include *Religio Medici/The Religion of a Doctor* 1643, *Urn Burial* and *The Garden of Cyrus* both 1658, and *Christian Morals* 1717.

Brownian movement continuous random motion of particles in a fluid medium (gas or liquid) as they are subject to impact from the molecules of the medium. This was observed in 1827 by the Scottish botanist Robert Brown (1773–1858), but not convincingly explained until ◊Einstein in 1905.

Browning Elizabeth Barrett 1806–1861. English poet. In 1844 she published *Poems* (including 'The Cry of the Children'), which led to her friendship and secret marriage with Robert Browning 1846. The *Sonnets from the Portuguese* 1847 were written during their courtship.

Brunei
Islamic Sultanate of
(Negara Brunei Darussalam)

area 5,800 sq km/2,226 sq mi
capital and chief port Bandar Seri Begawan
physical 75% of the area is forested; the Limbang valley splits Brunei in two, and its cession to Sarawak in 1890 is disputed by Brunei
head of state and of government Muda Hassanal Bolkiah Mu'izzaddin Waddaulah, Sultan of

Brunei, from 1968
political system absolute monarchy
exports liquefield natural gas (world's largest producer) and oil, both expected to be exhausted by 2000 AD
currency Brunei dollar
population 372,000 (1990 est) (65% Malay, 20% Chinese – few Chinese granted citizenship); annual growth rate 12%
language Malay (official) English, Chinese
religion Muslim (60%; official)
literacy 95%
GDP $3.4 bn (1985); $20,000 per head
chronology
1888 Brunei became a British protectorate.
1941–45 Occupied by Japan.
1959 Written constitution made Britain responsible for defence and external affairs.
1962 Sultan began rule by decree.
1963 Proposal to join Malaysia abandoned.
1967 Sultan abdicated in favour of his son Hassanal Bolkiah.
1971 Brunei given internal self-government.
1975 UN resolution called for independence for Brunei.
1984 Full independence achieved, with Britain maintaining a small force to protect the oil and gas fields.
1985 A 'loyal and reliable' political party, the Brunei National Democratic Party (BNDP), legalized.
1986 Death of former sultan, Sir Omar.
1988 BNDP banned.

Browning Robert 1812–1889. English poet. His work is characterized by the use of dramatic monologue and an interest in obscure literary and historical figures. His work includes the play *Pippa Passes* 1841, and the poems 'The Pied Piper of Hamelin', 'My Last Duchess' both 1842, 'Home Thoughts from Abroad' 1845, and 'Rabbi Ben Ezra' 1864.

Brownshirts the SA (*Sturm-Abteilung*), or Storm Troops, the private army of the German Nazi party; so called from the colour of their uniform.

Bruce name, of Norman origin, of one of the most important Scottish noble houses. In 1290, Robert

Bruce Robert Bruce, crowned king of Scotland in 1306.

VI tried unsuccessfully to seize the throne, but his grandson ◊Robert and great-grandson David were both kings of Scotland.

Bruce James 1730–1794. Scottish explorer, the first European to reach the source of the Blue Nile 1770, and to follow the river downstream to Cairo by 1773.

Bruce Robert 1274–1329. Scottish hero. He was the grandson of Robert de Bruce 1210–95, who unsuccessfully claimed the Scottish throne in 1290. Bruce shared in the national rising led by ◊Wallace, and soon after the latter's execution in 1305 he rose again against Edward I of England, and was crowned king of Scotland in 1306. He defeated Edward II at Bannockburn in 1314, and in 1329 the treaty of Northampton recognized Scottish independence, and Bruce as king. See also ◊Robert, kings of Scotland.

Bruce Stanley Melbourne, 1st Viscount Bruce of Melbourne 1883–1967. Australian National Party politician and lawyer, prime minister 1923–29. He was elected to parliament in 1918. As prime minister and minister for external affairs in a National–Country Party coalition, he introduced unemployment insurance and other social and welfare measures.

Brücke, die German Expressionist art movement 1905–13, formed in Dresden. Ernst Ludwig Kirchner was one of its founders and Emil Nolde a member 1906–07. Strongly influenced by African art, they strove for spiritual significance, using raw colours to express different emotions. In 1911 the ◊Blaue Reiter took over as the leading group in German art.

Bruckner (Joseph) Anton 1824–1896. Austrian Romantic composer. He was cathedral organist at Linz 1856–68, and his compositions were much influenced by ◊Wagner. From 1868 he was at Vienna, where he became professor at the Conservatoire. His works include many choral pieces, and ten symphonies, the last unfinished.

Brueghel family of Flemish painters, the eldest of whom, *Pieter Brueghel* (*c.* 1525–69), was one of the greatest artists of his time. He is noted for satirical and humorous pictures of peasant life, many of which include symbolic details illustrating folly and inhumanity, and for a series of Months (5 of 12 survive), including *Hunters in the Snow* (Kunsthistorisches Museum, Vienna).

Bruges (Flemish *Brugge*) historic city in NW Belgium; capital of W Flanders province, 16 km/10 mi from the North Sea, with which it is connected by canal; population (1991) 117,100. Bruges was the capital of medieval ◊Flanders, and was the chief European wool manufacturing town as well as its chief market.

Brummell George Bryan 1778–1840. British dandy and leader of fashion, known as Beau Brummell. A friend of the Prince of Wales, the future George IV, he later quarrelled with him, and was driven by gambling losses to exile in France in 1816.

Brundtland Gro Harlem 1939– . Norwegian Labour politician, prime minister 1981, 1986, and 1990. Educated at Oslo and Harvard universities, she entered politics with the Norwegian Labour Party and became its leader in 1981. She was defeated in the 1989 elections by Conservative prime minister Jan Syse. The *Brundtland Report* 1987 was produced by the World Commission on Environment and Development, chaired by her.

Brunei country on the N coast of Borneo, surrounded to the landward side by Sarawak, and bounded to the N by the South China Sea.

Brunel Isambard Kingdom 1806–1859. British engineer and inventor. In 1833 he became engineer to the Great Western Railway, which adopted the 2.1 m/7ft gauge on his advice. He built the Clifton Suspension Bridge over the river Avon at Bristol and the Saltash Bridge over the river Tamar near Plymouth. His ship-building designs include the *Great Western* 1838, the first steamship to cross the Atlantic regularly; the *Great Britain* 1845, the first large iron ship to have a screw propeller; and the *Great Eastern* 1858, which laid the first transatlantic telegraph cable.

Brunel Marc Isambard 1769–1849. British engineer and inventor, who constructed the Rotherhithe tunnel under the river Thames from Wapping to Rotherhithe 1825–1843.

Brunelleschi Filippo 1377–1446. Italian Renaissance architect. One of the earliest and greatest Renaissance architects, he pioneered the scientific use of perspective. He was responsible for the construction of the dome of Florence Cathedral (completed 1438), a feat deemed impossible by many of his contemporaries.

Brunel Isambard Kingdom Brunel.

Bruning Heinrich 1885–1970. German politician. Elected to the Reichstag (parliament) in 1924, he led the Catholic Centre Party from 1929 and was federal chancellor (premier) 1930–32, when political and economic crisis forced his resignation.

Bruno Giordano 1548–1600. Italian philosopher. He became a ◊Dominican in 1563, but his sceptical attitude to Catholic doctrines forced him to flee Italy in 1577. After visiting Geneva and Paris, he lived in England 1583–85, where he wrote some of his finest works. After returning to Europe, he was arrested by the ◊Inquisition in 1593 in Venice, and burned at the stake for his adoption of Copernican astronomy and his heretical religious views.

Bruno, St 1030–1101. German founder of the monastic Catholic ◊Carthusian order. He was born in Cologne, became a priest, and controlled the cathedral school of Rheims 1057–76. Withdrawing to the mountains near Grenoble after an ecclesiastical controversy, he founded the monastery at Chartreuse in 1084. Feast day 6 Oct.

Brunswick (German *Braunschweig*) industrial city in Lower Saxony, Germany (chemical engineering, precision engineering, food processing); population (1988) 248,000. It was one of the chief cities of N Germany in the Middle Ages, and a member of the ◊Hanseatic League. It was capital of the duchy of Brunswick from 1671.

Brussels (Flemish *Brussel*/French *Bruxelles*) capital of Belgium, industrial city (lace, textiles, machinery, chemicals); population (1987) 974,000 (80% French-speaking, the suburbs Flemish-speaking). It is the headquarters of the European Economic Community and since 1967 of the international secretariat of NATO. First settled in the 6th century AD, and a city from 1321, Brussels became the capital of the Spanish Netherlands 1530 and of Belgium 1830.

Brussels sprout one of the small edible buds along the stem of a variety of ◊cabbage.

Brussels, Treaty of pact of economic, political, cultural, and military alliance established 17 Mar 1948 for 50 years by Britain, France, and the Benelux countries, joined by W Germany and Italy in 1955. It was the forerunner of the North Atlantic Treaty Organization and the European Community.

Brussilov Aleksei Alekseevich 1853–1926. Russian general, military leader in World War I, who achieved major successes against the Austro-Hungarian forces in 1916. Later he was commander of the Red Army 1920 which drove the Poles to within a few miles of Warsaw before being repulsed.

Brutus Marcus Junius *c.* 78–42 BC. Roman soldier, a supporter of ◊Pompey (against Caesar) in the Civil War. Pardoned by ◊Caesar, and raised to high office by him, he nevertheless plotted Caesar's assassination to restore the purity of the Republic. When Brutus was defeated (with ◊Cassius) by ◊Mark Antony, Caesar's lieutenant, at Philippi in 42 BC, he committed suicide.

Bruxelles French form of ◊Brussels, capital of Belgium.

Bryan William Jennings 1860–1925. US politician, who campaigned unsuccessfully for the presidency three times: as the Populist and Democratic nominee 1896, as an anti-imperialist Democrat 1900, and as a Democratic tariff reformer 1908. He served as President Wilson's secretary of state 1913–1915.

bryony two hedgerow climbing plants found in Britain: *white bryony Bryonia cretica* belonging to the gourd family Cucurbitaceae, and *black bryony Tamus communis* of the yam family Dioscoreaceae.

bryophyte a member of the Bryophyta, a division of the plant kingdom containing three classes, the Hepaticae (◊liverwort), Musci (◊moss), and Anthocerotae (◊hornwort). Bryophytes are generally small, low-growing, terrestrial plants with no ◊vascular (water-conducting) system as in higher plants. Their lifecycle shows a marked ◊alternation of generations. Bryophytes chiefly occur in damp habitats and require water for the dispersal of the male gametes (◊antherozoids).

BSc abbreviation for *Bachelor of Science*.

BSI abbreviation for ◊*British Standards Institute*.

BST abbreviation for *British Summer Time*.

BT abbreviation for *British Telecom*.

Btu abbreviation for ◊*British thermal unit*.

bubble chamber a vessel filled with a transparent highly superheated liquid, through which an ionizing particle moves. A violent boiling along its path shown by a string of tiny bubbles may start. Photographic study of these tracks gives much information about the nature and movement of atomic particles and the interaction of particles and radiations. By using a pressurized liquid medium instead of a gas, it overcomes drawbacks inherent in the earlier ◊cloud chamber.

bubble memory in computing, a memory device based on the creation of small magnetic 'bubbles' on a ◊chip. Bubble-memory chips typically store up to four megabits (4 million ◊bits) of information. They are not sensitive to shock and vibration, unlike other memory devices such as disk drives, yet, like magnetic disks, they do not lose their information when the computer is switched off.

Bucaramanga industrial (coffee, tobacco, cacao, cotton) and commercial city in N central Colombia; population (1985) 493,929. Founded by the Spanish in 1622.

buccaneer a member of various groups of seafarers off the Spanish American coast in the 17th century, who plundered Spanish ships and colonies. Because they were acting on (sometimes spurious) commission, they distinguished themselves from true ◊pirates.

Bucer Martin 1491–1551. German Protestant reformer, regius professor of divinity at Cambridge University from 1549, who tried to reconcile the views of his fellow Protestants Luther and Zwingli and the significance of the eucharist.

Buchan John, Baron Tweedsmuir 1875–1940. Scottish politician and author. Called to the Bar in 1901, he was Conservative member of parliament for the Scottish universities 1927–35, and governor general of Canada 1934–40. He published adventure stories which won wide popularity and included *Prester John* 1910, *The Thirty-Nine Steps* 1915, *Greenmantle* 1916, *Huntingtower* 1922, *The Three Hostages* 1924, and *The House of the Four Winds* 1935.

Buchanan Jack 1891–1957. British musical comedy actor. His songs such as 'Good-Night Vienna' epitomized the period between World Wars I and II.

Bucharest (Romanian *Bucureşti*) capital and largest city of Romania; population (1983) 1,995,000. Originally a citadel built by Vlad the Impaler (see ◊Dracula) to stop the advance of the Ottoman invasion in the 14th century. It became the capital of the princes of Wallachia 1698 and of Romania 1861.

Buchenwald site of a Nazi concentration camp 1937–45 at a village NE of Weimar, East Germany.

Buck Pearl S 1892–1973. US novelist. Daughter of missionaries to China, she wrote novels about Chinese life, such as *East Wind–West Wind* 1930 and *The Good Earth* 1931. Nobel Prize for Literature 1938.

Buckingham George Villiers, 1st Duke of Buckingham 1592–1628. English courtier, adviser to James I and later Charles I. After Charles's accession, Buckingham attempted to form a Protestant coalition in Europe which led to war with France, but he failed to relieve the Protestants besieged in La Rochelle 1627. This added to his unpopularity with Parliament, and he was assassinated.

Buckingham George Villiers, 2nd Duke of Buckingham 1628–1687. English politician, a member of the ◊Cabal under Charles II. A dissolute son of the 1st duke, he was brought up with the royal

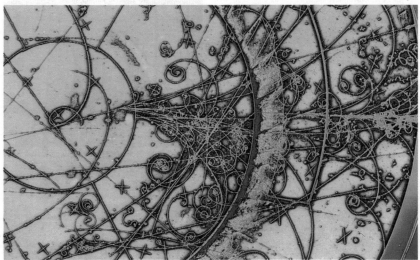

bubble chamber *Artificially coloured bubble chamber photograph taken at CERN, the European particle physics laboratory outside Geneva.*

children. His play *The Rehearsal* satirized the style
of the poet Dryden, who portrayed him as Zimri in
Absalom and Achitophel.

Buckingham Palace London home of the British
sovereign, built 1703 for the duke of Buckingham,
but bought by George III in 1762 and reconstructed
by ◊Nash 1821–36; a new front was added in
1913.

Buckinghamshire county in SE central England
area 1,883 sq km/727 sq mi
towns administrative headquarters Aylesbury;
Buckingham, High Wycombe, Beaconsfield, Olney
products furniture, especially beech; agricultural
population (1986) 617,900.

Buckley William 1780–1856. Australian convict,
who escaped from Port Phillip and lived 1803–35
among the Aborigines before giving himself up,
hence *Buckley's chance* meaning an 'outside
chance'.

Bucks abbreviation for ◊*Buckinghamshire*.

buckthorn thorny shrubs of the family Rhamnaceae,
of which two species, the buckthorn *Rhamnus
catharticus* and the alder buckthorn *Frangula alnus*,
are native to Britain.

buckwheat high nutritive value grain plant
Fagopyrum esculentum, of the family Polygonaceae.
The plant grows to about 1 m/3 ft, and the seeds are
either eaten whole or ground into flour. It is eaten
both by humans and animals. Buckwheat can grow
on poor soil in a short summer.

bud an undeveloped shoot usually enclosed by
protective scales; inside is a very short stem and
numerous undeveloped leaves, or flower parts,
or both. Terminal buds are found at the tips of
shoots, while axillary buds develop in the ◊axils
of the leaves, often remaining dormant unless the
terminal bud is removed or damaged. Adventitious
buds may be produced anywhere on the plant, their
formation sometimes stimulated by an injury, such
as that caused by pruning.

Budapest capital of Hungary, industrial city (chemicals, textiles) on the Danube; population (1983)
2,064,000. Buda, on the right bank of the Danube,
became the Hungarian capital in 1867 and was joined
with Pest, on the left bank, in 1872.

Buddha 'enlightened one', title of Prince *Gautama
Siddhārtha c.* 563–483 BC. religious leader,
founder of Buddhism, born at Lumbini in Nepál.
At the age of 29, he left a life of luxury, and his wife
and son, to seek a way of escape from the burdens
of existence. After six years of austerity he realized
that asceticism, like overindulgence, was futile, and
chose the middle way of meditation. He became
enlightened under a bo tree near Buddh Gaya in
Bihar, India. He began teaching at Varanasi, and
founded the Sangha, or order of monks. He spent
the rest of his life moving around N India and died
at Kusinagara in Uttar Pradesh.

Buddh Gaya village in Bihar, India, where
Gautama became ◊Buddha while sitting beneath
a bo (*bodhi*, wisdom) tree; a descendant of the

original bo tree (*Ficus religiosa*, peepul tree) is
preserved.

Buddhism one of the great world religions, which
originated in India about 500 BC. It derives from
the teaching of Buddha, who is regarded as one
of a series of such enlightened beings; there are
no gods. The most important doctrine is that of
karma, good or evil deeds meeting an appropriate
reward or punishment either in this life or (through
reincarnation) a long succession of lives. The main
divisions are *Theravāda* (or Hīnayāna) in SE Asia
and *Mahāyāna* in N Asia; *Lamaism* in Tibet and
Zen in Japan are among the many Mahāyāna sects.
Its symbol is the lotus. There are over 247.5 million
Buddhists worldwide.

budding a type of ◊asexual reproduction in which
a bubble-like outgrowth develops from a cell, enlarges, and eventually becomes detached to form
a new individual. The majority of yeasts reproduce
in this way. In horticulture, the term is used for
a technique of plant propagation whereby a bud
(or scion) and a sliver of bark from one plant are
transferred to an incision made in the bark of another plant (the stock). This method of ◊grafting
is often used for roses.

buddleia genus of shrubs and trees, family
Buddleiaceae, of which the best-known is the
butterfly bush Buddleia davidii. Its purple or
white flowerheads are attractive to insects.

Budge Donald 1915– . US tennis player. The
first person to perform the Grand Slam when
he won Wimbledon, French, US and Australian
championships in 1938.

budgerigar small Australian parakeet *Melopsittacus
undulatus* which feeds mainly on grass seeds. Normally it is bright green, but varieties with yellow,
white, blue, and mauve have been produced.

budget an estimate of income and expenditure for
some future period, used in the financial planning
of a business or country. National budgets set out
estimates of government income and expenditure
and generally include changes in taxation. Interim

Buddha 13th century Thai bronze Buddha.

Budapest The Parliament building on the eastern side
of the Danube.

Buenos Aires *The Congress National, Plaza Congress in Buenos Aires, Argentina .*

budgets are not uncommon, particularly when dramatic changes in economic conditions occur.

Buenos Aires   capital and industrial city of Argentina, on the south bank of the River Plate; population (1980) 9,927,000. It was founded 1536, and became the capital 1853.

buffalo   name given to two species of wild cattle. The Asiatic *water buffalo Bubalis bubalis* is found domesticated all across S Asia and wild in parts of Bengal, Assam, and Nepál. It likes moist conditions. Usually grey or black, up to 1.8 m/6 ft high, both sexes carry large horns. The *African buffalo Syncerus caffer* is found in Africa S of the Sahara where there is grass, water, and cover in which to retreat. There are various types, the biggest up to 1.6 m/5 ft high, black, and with massive horns set close together over the head.

bug   in computing, an error in a program. It can be an error in the logical structure of a program or a syntactic error such as a spelling mistake. Either can cause serious problems in major applications such as controlling a power station. *Debugging is the process of finding bugs and eliminating them from a program.

bug   in entomology, name sometimes applied indiscriminately to insects, but strictly only those belonging to the order Hemiptera. All these have piercing mouthparts adapted for sucking the juices of plants or animals, the 'beak' being tucked under the body when not in use.

bugle   in music, a wind instrument of the brass family, with a shorter tube and less expanded bell than the trumpet. Constructed of copper plate with brass, it has long been used as a military instrument.

bugle   low-growing perennial plant *Ajuga reptans*, family Labiatae, with two-lipped blue flowers in a purplish spike. The leaves may be smooth edged or faintly toothed, the lower ones with a long stalk. Bugle is found across Europe and N Africa, usually in damp woods or pastures.

bugloss   name of several plants of the family Boraginaceae, distinguished by their rough bristly leaves and small blue flowers.

building society   financial institution which attracts investment, in order to lend money, repayable at interest, for the purchase or building of a house on security of a mortgage. Since the 1970s building societies in the UK have considerably expanded their services and in many ways now compete with clearing banks.

Bukharest   alternative form of ◊Bucharest, capital of Romania.

Bukharin   Nikolai Ivanovich 1888–1938. Russian politician and theorist. A moderate, he was the

most influential Bolshevik thinker after ◊Lenin. Executed on Stalin's orders for treason in 1936, he was posthumously rehabilitated in 1988.

Bulawayo   industrial city and railway junction in Zimbabwe at an altitude of 1,355 m/4,450 ft on the river Matsheumlope, a tributary of the Zambezi; population (1982) 414,000. It produces agricultural and electrical equipment. The former capital of Matabeleland, Bulawayo developed with the exploitation of goldmines in the neighbourhood.

bulb   instrument of vegetative reproduction consisting of a modified leaf bud with fleshy leaves containing a reserve food supply; roots form from its base. It is a characteristic of many monocotyledenous plants such as the daffodil, snowdrop, and onion. Bulbs are grown on a commercial scale in temperate countries, especially England and Holland.

bulbul   small fruit-eating bird of the family Pycnonotidae. There are about 120 species, mainly in the forests of the Old World tropics.

Bulganin   Nikolai 1895–1975. Russian military leader and politician. He helped to organize Moscow's defence in World War II, became a marshal of the USSR 1947, and was minister of defence 1947–49 and 1953–55. On the fall of Malenkov he became prime minister (chair of Council of Ministers) 1955–58 until ousted by Khrushchev.

Bulgaria   country in SE Europe, bounded to the N by Romania, to the W by Yugoslavia, to the S by Greece, to the SW by Turkey, and to the E by the Black Sea.

bulimia   (Greek 'ox hunger') counteraction of stress or depression by uncontrollable overeating, compensated for by forced vomiting or an overdose of laxatives.

bull   a speculator who buys stocks or shares on the stock exchange expecting a rise in the price in order to sell them later at a profit, the opposite of a ◊bear. In a bull market, prices rise and bulls profit.

Bull John   typical Englishman, especially as represented in cartoons. The name came into popular use after the publication of Dr John Arbuthnot's *History of John Bull* 1712 advocating the Tory policy of peace with France.

Bull   John *c.* 1562–1628. British composer, organist, and virginalist, one of the finest keyboard players of his time. Most of his output is for keyboard, and includes ◊'God Save the King'. He also wrote sacred vocal music.

bull papal   document or edict issued by the pope; so called from the circular seals (medieval Latin *bulla*) attached to them. Famous papal bulls include Leo X's condemnation of Luther in 1520 and Pius IX's proclamation of papal infallibility in 1870.

bulldog   British dog of ancient but uncertain origin. The head is broad and square, with a deeply wrinkled skull, small folded ears, and nose laid back between the eyes.

bulldozer   an earth-moving machine widely used in construction work for clearing rocks and tree stumps and levelling a site. The bulldozer is a kind of ◊tractor with a powerful engine and a curved blade at the front, which can be lifted and forced down by hydraulic rams. It usually has crawler, or ◊caterpillar tracks so that it can move easily over rough ground.

Buller   Redvers Henry 1839–1908. British commander against the Boers in the South African War 1899–1902. He was defeated at Colenso and Spion Kop, but relieved Ladysmith; he was superseded by Lord Roberts.

Bulgaria
Republic of
(*Republika Bulgaria*)

area 110,912 sq km/42,812 sq mi
capital Sofia
towns Plovdiv, Ruse; Burgas and Varna are Black Sea Ports
physical Balkan and Rhodope mountains; Danube River in the N
head of state Zhelyu Zhelev from 1990
head of government Lyuben Berov from 1992
political system emergent democratic republic

exports textiles, chemicals, non-ferrous metals, timber, minerals, machinery
currency lev
population (1990 est) 8,978,000 (including 900,000–1,500,000 ethnic Turks); annual growth rate 0.1%
language Bulgarian, Turkish
religion Eastern Orthodox Christian 90%, Sunni Muslim 10%
literacy 98%
GDP $25.4 bn (1987); $2,836 per head
chronology
1908 Bulgaria became a kingdom independent of Turkish rule.
1944 Soviet invasion of German-occupied Bulgaria.
1946 Monarchy abolished; Communist-dominated people's republic proclaimed.
1954 Election of Todor Zhivkov as Communist Party general secretary.
1971 Constitution modified; Zhivkov elected president.
1985–88 Large-scale administrative and personnel changes made haphazardly under Soviet stimulus.
1987 Introduction of multi-candidate elections.
1989 310,000 ethnic Turks fled in opposition to the 'Bulgarianization' campaign. Opposition parties allowed to form.
1991 New constitution adopted. Formation of first noncommunist government.
1992 Zhelev became Bulgaria's first directly-elected president.

bullfighting the national 'sport' of Spain, it involvs the taunting of a bull in a circular ring, until its eventual death at the hands of the matador. Originally popular in Greece and Rome, it was introduced into Spain by the Moors in the 11th century.

bullfinch bird *Pyrrhula pyrrhula* of the finch family, with a thick head and neck, and short heavy bill. It is small, blue-grey or black, the males being reddish and the females brown on the breast. They are 14.5 cm/6 in long, and usually seen in pairs.

bullroarer musical instrument consisting of a piece of wood fastened by one of its pointed ends to a cord. It is twirled round the head to make a whirring noise, and is used by Australian Aborigines during religious rites.

Bull Run, Battles of in the American Civil War, two victories for the Confederate army under Gen Robert E Lee at *Manassas* Junction, NE Virginia:
1st Battle of Bull Run 21 Jul 1861.
2nd Battle of Bull Run 29–30 Aug 1862.

bull-terrier heavily built, smooth-coated breed of dog, usually white, originating as a cross between terrier and bulldog.

Bülow Prince Bernhard von 1849–1929. German diplomat and politician. He was chancellor of the German Empire 1900–09 under Kaiser Wilhelm II and, holding that self-interest was the only rule for any state, adopted attitudes to France and Russia which unintentionally reinforced the trend towards opposing European power groups: the ◊Triple Entente (Britain, France, Russia) and ◊Triple Alliance (Germany, Austria-Hungary, Italy).

bulrush two plants: the *great reed-mace* or *cat's tail Typha latifolia* with chocolate-brown tight-packed flower spikes reaching up to 15cm/6in long, and a type of sedge *Scirpus lacustris* with tufts of reddish-brown flowers at the top of a rounded, rush-like stem.

bumble-bee large ◊bee, usually dark coloured but banded with yellow, orange or white, belonging to the genus *Bombus*.

Bunche Ralph 1904–1971. US diplomat, specializing in African and colonial affairs. Bunche, grandson of a slave, was principal director of the UN Department of Trusteeship 1947–54, and then UN under-secretary acting as mediator in Palestine 1948–49 and as special representative in the Congo 1960. In 1950 he was awarded the Nobel Peace Prize.

Bundelas Rajput clan which became prominent in the 14th century and gave its name to the Bundelkhand in N Central India. The clan had replaced the ◊Chandelā in the 11th century and continued to resist the attacks of other Indian rulers until coming under British control after 1812.

Bunker Hill, Battle of the first considerable engagement in the War of ◊American Independence, 17 Jun 1775, near a small hill in Charlestown (now part of Boston), Massachusetts, USA; although the colonists were defeated they were able to retreat to Boston and suffered far fewer casualties than the British.

Bunsen Robert Wilhelm von 1811–1899. German chemist, credited with the invention of the *Bunsen burner*. His name is also given to the carbon–zinc electric cell, which he invented in 1841 for use in arc-lamps. In 1859 he discovered two new elements, caesium and rubidium.

bunting name given to a number of sturdy, finch-like birds with short thick bills, of the family Emberizidae. Most live in the Americas.

Buñuel Luis 1900–1983. Spanish ◊surrealist film director. He collaborated with Salvador ◊Dali in

Bunyan Portrait of John Bunyan by Thomas Sadler (1684-85) National Portrait Gallery, London.

Un Chien Andalou 1928, and established his solo career with *Los Olvidados/The Young and the Damned* 1950. His works are often controversial and anti-clerical, with black humour and erotic imagery. Later films include *Le Charme discret de la Bourgeoisie/The Discreet Charm of the Bourgeoisie* 1972 and *Cet Obscur Objet du Désir/That Obscure Object of Desire* 1977.

Bunyan John 1628–1688. English author. A Baptist, he was imprisoned in Bedford Gaol 1660-72 for preaching. During a second gaol sentence in 1675 he started to write *Pilgrim's Progress*, the first part of which was published in 1678. Other works include *Grace Abounding* 1666, *The Life and Death of Mr Badman* 1680, and *The Holy War* 1682.

bunyip mythical animal of the Australian Aborigines; it is a river creature, rather like a slender, long-necked hippopotamus. The word has been adopted in Australian English to mean 'fake' or 'impostor'.

buoy a floating object used to mark channels for shipping or warn of hazards to navigation. Buoys come in different shapes, such as a pole (spar buoy), cylinder (car buoy), and cone (nun buoy). Light buoys carry a small tower surmounted by a flashing lantern, and bell buoys house a bell, which rings as the buoy moves up and down with the waves.

buoyancy the lifting effect of a fluid on a body wholly or partly immersed in it. This was studied by ◊Archimedes in the 3rd century BC.

bur or **burr** in botany, a type of 'false fruit' or ◊pseudocarp, surrounded by numerous hooks; for instance, that of burdock (*Arctium*) where the hooks are formed from bracts surrounding the flower-head. The term is also used to include any type of fruit or seed bearing hooks, such as that of goosegrass (*Galium aparine*) and wood avens (*Geum urbanum*). Burs catch in the feathers or fur of passing animals, and thus may be dispersed over considerable distances.

Burbage Richard *c.* 1567–1619. English actor, thought to have been Shakespeare's original Hamlet, Othello, and Lear. He also appeared in first productions of works by Ben ◊Jonson, ◊Kyd, and ◊Webster. His father **James Burbage** (c. 1530–97) built the first English playhouse, known as 'The Theatre'; his brother **Cuthbert Burbage** (c. 1566–1636) built the original ◊Globe Theatre 1599 on Bankside, Southwark, London.

burbot long, rounded fish *Lota lota* of the cod family, the only one living entirely in fresh water. Up to 1 m/3 ft, it lives on the bottom of clear lakes and rivers, often in holes or under rocks.

Burckhardt Jacob 1818–1897. Swiss art historian, professor of history at Basel University 1858–93. His *The Civilization of the Renaissance in Italy* 1860, intended as part of a study of world cultural history, has been highly influential.

burden of proof in court proceedings, the duty of a party to produce sufficient evidence to prove that his case is true. In English law a higher standard of proof is required in criminal cases (beyond all reasonable doubt), than in civil cases (on the balance of probabilities).

burdock plant *Arctium lappa* of the family Compositae. A bushy herb, it is a common roadside weed in Britain. It has hairy leaves, and its ripe fruit are enclosed in hooked burs.

bureaucracy an organization whose structure and operations are governed to a high degree by written rules and a hierarchy of offices: in its broadest sense, all forms of administration; in its narrowest, rule by officials.

Burgenland federal state of SE Austria, extending from the Danube S along the W border of the Hungarian plain
area 3,966 sq km/1,531 sq mi
capital Eisenstadt
products timber; lignite, antimony, limestone, wine, sugar, fruit
population (1981) 272,300.

Bürger Gottfried 1747–1794. German Romantic poet, remembered for his ballad 'Lenore' 1773.

Burges William 1827–1881. British Gothic revivalist architect. Main works are Cork Cathedral 1862–76, additions to and remodelling of Cardiff Castle 1865 and Castle Coch near Cardiff c. 1875. His work is characterized by sumptuous interiors with carving, painting, and gilding.

Burgess Anthony, pen name of Anthony John Burgess Wilson 1917– . British novelist, critic, and composer. His prolific work includes *A Clockwork Orange* 1962, set in a future London terrorized by teenage gangs, and the panoramic *Earthly Powers* 1980. His vision has been described as bleak and pessimistic, but his work is also comic and satiric, as in his novels featuring the poet Enderby.

Burgess Guy (Francis de Moncy) 1910–1963. British spy, a diplomat recruited by the USSR as agent; linked with Kim ◊Philby, Donald Maclean (1913–83), and Anthony ◊Blunt.

Burgess Shale Site the site of unique fossil-bearing rock formations in Yoho National Park, British Colombia, Canada. The shales in this corner of the Rocky Mountains contain more than 120 species of marine invertebrate fossils. Although discovered in 1909 by Charles Walcott, the Burgess Shales have only recently been used as evidence in the debate concerning the evolution of life.

burgh former unit of Scottish local government, abolished in 1975; the terms **burgh** and **royal burgh** once gave mercantile privilege but are now only an honorary distinction.

burgh (**burh** or **borough**) a term originating in Germanic lands 9th–10th centuries referring to a fortified settlement, usually surrounding a monastery or castle. Later, it was used to mean new towns, or towns which enjoyed particular privileges relating to government and taxation, and whose citizens were called ◊burghers.

Burgh Hubert de died 1243. English ◊justiciar and regent of England. He began his career in the administration of Richard I, and was promoted to the justiciarship by King John and remained in that position under Henry III from 1216 until his dismissal. He was a supporter of King John against the barons, and ended French intervention in England by his defeat of the French fleet in the Strait of Dover in 1217. He re-organized royal administration and the Common Law.

burgher a term used from the 11th century to describe citizens of ◊burghs who were freemen of the burgh, and had the right to participate in its government. They usually had to possess a house within the burgh.

Burghley William Cecil, Baron Burghley 1520–1598. English politician, chief adviser to Elizabeth I as secretary of state from 1558 and Lord High Treasurer from 1572. He was largely responsible for the religious settlement of 1559, and took a leading role in the èvents preceding the execution of Mary, Queen of Scots, in 1587.

burglary in UK law, the offence of entering a building as a trespasser with the intent to commit theft or other serious crime; the maximum sentence is 14 years, though aggravated burglary (involving the use of firearms or other weapons) can mean life imprisonment.

Burgos city in Castilla-León, Spain, 217 km/135 mi north of Madrid; population (1991) 169,300. It produces textiles, motor parts, and chemicals. It was capital of the old kingdom of Castile and the national hero El Cid is buried in the Gothic cathedral, built 1221–1567.

Burgoyne John 1722–1792. British general and dramatist. He served in the American War of Independence and surrendered to the Americans at Saratoga in 1777. He wrote comedies, among them *The Maid of the Oaks* 1775 and *The Heiress* 1786. He figures in George Bernard Shaw's play *The Devil's Disciple*.

Burgundy ancient kingdom and duchy in the valley of the rivers Saône and Rhône, France. The Burgundi were a Teutonic tribe and overran the country about 400. From the 9th century to the death of Duke ◊Charles the Bold in 1477, it was the nucleus of a powerful principality. On Charles's death the duchy was incorporated into France. The capital of Burgundy was Dijon. The modern region to which it corresponds is ◊Bourgogne.

Buridan's ass a problem in medieval *scholastic* philosophy, in which a donkey is midway between two bundles of hay; since it cannot choose which of the two to eat first, it dies of hunger. The problem was invented by Jean Buridan (1300–c. 1366), who taught at the University of Paris, to demonstrate the absence of free choice.

Burke Edmund 1729–1797. British Whig politician and political theorist. In Parliament from 1765, he opposed the government's attempts to coerce the American colonists, for example in *Thoughts on the Present Discontents* 1770, and supported the emancipation of Ireland, but denounced the French Revolution, for example in *Reflections on the Revolution in France* 1790.

Burke John 1787–1848. First publisher, in 1826, of ◊*Burke's Peerage*.

Burke Martha Jane *c.* 1852–1903. Real name of American heroine ◊Calamity Jane.

Burke Robert O'Hara 1820–1861. Australian explorer who made the south–north crossing of Australia (Victoria–Gulf of Carpentaria), with William Wills (1834–61). Both died on the return journey, only one man of their party surviving. Burke was born in Galway, Ireland, and became a police inspector in the goldfields of Victoria.

Burke William 1792–1829. Irish murderer. He and his partner *William Hare,* living in Edinburgh, dug up the dead to sell for dissection. They increased their supplies by murdering at least 15 people. Burke was hanged on the evidence of Hare. Hare is said to have died a beggar in London in the 1860s.

Burke's Peerage Popular name of the *Genealogical and Heraldic History of the Peerage, Baronetage, and Knightage of the United Kingdom*, first issued by John Burke in 1826. The most recent edition was in 1970.

Burkina Faso landlocked country in W Africa, bounded to the E by Niger, to the NW and W by Mali, to the S by Ivory Coast, Ghana, Togo and Benin.

burlesque in the 17th and 18th centuries, a form of satirical comedy parodying a particular play or dramatic genre. For example, ◊Gay's *The Beggar's Opera* 1728 is a burlesque of 18th-century opera, and ◊Sheridan's *The Critic* 1777 satirizes the sentimentality in contemporary drama. In the US in the mid 19th century, burlesque referred to a sex and comedy show invented by Michael Bennett Leavitt [in 1866] with acts including acrobats, chorus and comedy numbers; during the 1920s striptease was introduced to counteract the growing popularity of the cinema, with Gypsy Rose Lee its most famous artiste. Burlesque was banned in New York in 1942.

Burlington Richard Boyle, 3rd Earl of 1694–1753. British architectural patron and architect; one of the premier exponents of Palladianism in Britain. His buildings, such as Chiswick House in London (1725–29), are characterized by absolute adherence to the Classical rules. His major protégé was William Kent.

Burma former name (to 1989) of ◊Myanmar

Burman member of the largest ethnic group in Myanmar. The Burmans migrated from the hills of Tibet and had settled in the area around Mandalay by the 11th century AD. They speak a Sino-Tibetan language.

burn in medicine, destruction of body tissue by extremes of temperature, corrosive substances, electricity or radiation. *First-degree burns* may cause reddening; *second-degree burns* cause blistering and irritation but usually heal spontaneously; *third-degree burns* are disfiguring and may be life-threatening.

Burnaby Frederick 1842–1885. English soldier, traveller, and founder of the weeky critical journal *Vanity Fair*. His writings include *On Horseback*

Burlington Based on Pallacio's Villa Rotunda, Italy, Chiswick House, London was designed by Lord Burlington 1725–29, and set in a garden designed by William Kent.

Burkina Faso
The People's Democratic Republic of

area 274,000 sq km/106,000 sq mi
capital Ouagadougou
towns Bobo-Doiulasso
physical landlocked plateau, savannah country; headwaters of the river Volta
head of state and government Blaise Compaoré from 1987
political system transitional
exports cotton, groundnuts, livestock, hides, skins
currency CFA franc
population (1990 est) 8,541,000; annual growth rate 2.4%

life expectancy men 44, women 47
language French (official); about 50 native languages.
religion animist 53%, Sunni Muslim 36%, Roman Catholic 11%
literacy 21% male/6% female (1985 est)
GDP $1.6 bn (1987); $188 per head
chronology
1958 Became a self-governing republic within the French Community.
1960 Full independence achieved
1966 Military coup led by Col Lamizana.
1970 Referendum approved a new constitution leading to a return to civilian rule.
1974 After experimenting with a mixture of military and civilian rule, Lamizana reassumed full power.
1977 Ban on political activities removed. Referendum approved a new constitution based on civilian rule.
1978 Lamizana elected president.
1980 Lamizana overthrown in a bloodless coup led by Col Zerbo.
1982 Zerbo ousted in a coup by junior officers. Maj Ouédraogo became president and Thomas Sankara prime minister.
1983 Sankara seized complete power.
1984 Upper Volta renamed Burkina Faso.
1987 Sankara killed in coup led by Blaise Compaoré.
1991 New constitution approved. Compaoré re-elected president.
1992 Multiparty elections held amid opposition claims of electoral fraud.

---

through Asia Minor 1877. He joined the British Nile expedition to relieve Gen ◊Gordon, in Khartoum, Sudan, and was killed in action at the battle of Abu Klea.

Burne-Jones Edward Coley 1833–1898. British painter. Influenced by William Morris and the Pre-Raphaelite Rossetti, he was inspired by legend and myth, as in *King Cophetua and the Beggar Maid* 1880–84 (Tate Gallery, London), but moved towards Symbolism. He also designed tapestries and stained glass.

burnet herb *Sanguisorba minor* of the rose family, also known as *salad burnet.* It smells of cucumber and can be used in salads.

Burnet Gilbert 1643–1715. British historian and bishop, author of *History of His Own Time* 1723–24. His Whig views having brought him into disfavour, he retired to The Hague on the accession of James II, and became the confidential adviser of William of Orange, with whom he sailed to England in 1688. He was appointed bishop of Salisbury in 1689.

Burnet Macfarlane 1899–1985. Australian physician, authority on immunology and viral diseases. He was awarded the Order of Merit in 1958 in recognition of his work on such diseases as influenza, polio and cholera.

Burnett Frances Eliza Hodgson 1849–1924. British writer, living in the USA from 1865, who wrote children's stories including the rags-to-riches tale *Little Lord Fauntleroy* 1886, and the sentimental *The Secret Garden* 1909.

Burney Frances (Fanny) 1752–1840. British novelist and diarist, daughter of the musician Dr Charles Burney (1726–1814). She achieved success with *Evelina,* published anonymously 1778, became a member of Dr ◊Johnson's circle, received a post at court from Queen Charlotte, and

in 1793 married the émigré General D'Arblay. She published two further novels, *Cecilia* 1782, and *Camilla* 1796, and her diaries and letters appeared in 1842.

Burnham Forbes 1923–1985. Guyanese Marxist Leninist politician. He was prime minister 1964–80, leading the country to independence 1966, and declaring it the world's first cooperative republic 1970. He was executive president 1980–85. Resistance to the US landing in Grenada in 1983 was said to be due to his forewarning the revolutionaries of the attack.

Burns John 1858–1943. British labour leader, sentenced to six weeks' imprisonment for his part in the Trafalgar Square demonstration on 'Bloody Sunday' 13 Nov 1887, and leader of the strike in 1889 securing the dockers' tanner (wage of 6d per hour). An Independent Labour member of parliament 1892–1918, he was the first person from the labouring classes to be a member of the Cabinet, as president of the Local Government Board 1906–14.

Burns Robert 1759–1796. Scottish poet, notable for his use of the Scots dialect at a time when it was not considered suitably 'elevated' for literature. Burns' first volume, *Poems, Chiefly in the Scottish Dialect,* appeared in 1786. In addition to his poetry Burns wrote or adapted many songs, including 'Auld Lang Syne'.

burr alternative name for ◊bur.

Burr Aaron 1756–1836. US politician. He was on George Washington's staff during the War of Independence. He tied with Thomas Jefferson in the presidential election of 1800, but Alexander ◊Hamilton influenced the House of Representatives to vote Jefferson in, Burr becoming vice president. He killed Hamilton in a duel in 1804, became a social outcast, and had to leave the USA for some years following the 'Burr conspiracy', which implicated him variously in a scheme to conquer Mexico, or part of Florida, or to rule over a seceded Louisiana.

Burroughs Edgar Rice 1875–1950. US novelist, born in Chicago. He wrote *Tarzan of the Apes* 1914, the story of an aristocratic child lost in the jungle and reared by chimpanzees, and many other thrillers.

Burroughs William S 1914– . US novelist, born in St Louis, Missouri. He dropped out and, as part of the ◊beat generation, wrote *Junkie* 1953, *The Naked Lunch* 1959, *The Soft Machine* 1961, and *Dead Fingers Talk* 1963. Later novels include *Queer* 1986.

Burroughs William Steward 1857–1898. American industrialist, who invented the first hand-operated adding machine to give printed results.

Bursa city in NW Turkey, with a port at Mudania; population (1990) 834,600. It was the capital of the Ottoman Empire 1326–1423.

Burt Cyril Lodowic 1883–1971. British psychologist. A specialist in child and mental development, he argued in *The Young Delinquent* 1925 the importance of social and environmental factors in delinquency. After his death it was discovered that he falsified some of his experimental results in an attempt to prove his theory that intelligence is largely inherited.

Burton Richard Francis 1821–1890. British traveller, master of 35 oriental languages, and translator of the *Arabian Nights* 1885–88. In 1853 he made the pilgrimage to Mecca in disguise; in 1856 he was commissioned by the Foreign Office to explore the sources of the Nile, and (with ◊Speke) reached Lake Tanganyika 1858.

Burton Richard. Stage name of Welsh actor Richard Jenkins 1925–1984. He was remarkable for his voice and for his marital and acting partnership with Elizabeth Taylor, with whom he appeared in the films *Cleopatra* 1962, and *Who's Afraid of Virginia Woolf?* 1966. His later works include *Equus* 1977 and *1984* 1984.

Burton Robert 1577–1640. English philosopher, who wrote an analysis of depression, *Anatomy of Melancholy* 1621, a compendium of information on the medical and religious opinions of the time, much used by later authors. Born in Leicester, he was educated at Oxford, and remained there for the rest of his life as a fellow of Christ Church.

Burundi country in E central Africa, bounded to the north by Rwanda, to the west by Zaïre, to the south by Lake Tanganyika, and to the southeast and east by Tanzania.

Bush George 1924– . 41st president of the USA 1989–93, a Republican. He was director of the Central Intelligence Agency (CIA) 1976–81, and US vice president 1981–89. As president, his sending of US troops to depose General Noriega of Panama, and success in the 1991 Gulf War, were popular moves at home. However, domestic economic problems 1991–92 were followed by his defeat in the 1992 presidential elections by Democrat Bill Clinton.

bushbuck antelope *Tragelaphus scriptus* found over most of Africa S of the Sahara. Up to 1 m/3 ft high, the males have keeled horns twisted into spirals, and are brown to blackish. The females are generally hornless, lighter and redder. All have white markings, including stripes or vertical rows of dots down the sides. Rarely far from water, bushbuck live in woods and thick brush.

bushel dry or liquid measure equal to 8 gallons (2219.36 cu in) in Britain; some US states have

---

Burundi
Republic of
(Republika y'Uburundi)

area 27,834 sq km/10,747 sq mi
capital Bujumbura
towns Kitega
physical grassy highland
head of state and government Pierre Buyoya from 1987
political system one-party military republic
exports coffee, cotton, tea, nickel, hides, livestock; there are also 500 million tonnes of peat reserves in the basin of the Akanyaru river
currency Burundi franc
population (1990 est) 5,647,000 (of whom 15% are Nilotic Tutsi, still holding most of the land and political power, and the remainder Bantu Hutu); annual growth rate 2.8%
life expectancy men 45, women 48
language Kirundi (a Bantu language) and French (both official); Kiswahili
religion Roman Catholic 62%, Protestant 5%, Muslim 1%, animist 32%
literacy 43% male/26% female (1985)
GDP $1.1 bn (1987); $230 per head
chronology
1962 Separated from Rwanda-Urundi, as Burundi, and given independence as a monarchy under King Mwambutsa IV.
1966 King deposed by his son Charles, who became Ntare V and was in turn deposed by his prime minister, Capt Michel Micombero, who declared Burundi a republic.
1972 Ntare V killed, allegedly by the Hutu ethnic group. Massacres of 150,000 Hutus by the rival Tusi ethnic group, of which Micombero was a member.
1973 Micombero made president and prime minister.
1974 Union for National Progress (UPRONA) declared the only legal political party, with the president as its secretary general.
1976 Army coup deposed Micombero. Col Jean-Baptiste Bagaza appointed president.
1981 New constitution adopted, providing for a national assembly.
1984 Bagaza elected president as sole candidate.
1987 Bagaza deposed in coup in Sept. Maj Pierre Buyoya headed new Military Council for National Redemption.
1988 Some 24,000 majority Hutus killed by Tutsis. First Hutu prime minister appointed.
1992 New constitution approved.

different standards according to the goods measured.

bushido chivalric code of honour of the Japanese military caste, the ◊samurai; the term dates only from the 17th century, and became a nationalist, militarist slogan in the years before World War II.

bushman former term for the Kung, an aboriginal people of southern Africa, still living to some extent nomadically, especially in the Kalahari Desert. Formerly numerous, only some 26,000 remain. They are traditionally hunters and gatherers, and speak a Khoisan language. Their early art survives in cave paintings.

bushmaster large snake *Lachesis muta* related to the rattlesnakes. Up to 4 m/12 ft long, found in wooded areas of South and Central America, it has a powerful venomous bite. When alarmed, it produces a noise by vibrating its tail amongst dry leaves.

bushranger Australian armed robber of the 19th century. The first bushrangers were escaped convicts. The last gang was led by *Ned ◊Kelly* and his brother Dan in 1878–80. They form the subject of many Australian ballads.

business plan a key management tool which focuses on business objectives, the products or services involved, estimated market potential, expertise in the firm, projected financial results, the money required from investors, and the likely investment return.

business school institution for training in management and marketing, such as London Business School (LBS), Harvard in the USA, Insead in France.

Busoni Ferruccio (Dante Michelangiolo Benvenuto) 1866–1924. Italian pianist, composer, and music critic. In 1891–93 he was at the Conservatoire of Boston, USA, and later lived in Berlin, Bologna, and Zürich. Much of his music was for the piano, but he also composed several operas including *Doktor Faust*, completed by a pupil after his death.

bust in finance, a failure or bankruptcy.

Bustamante (William) Alexander (born Clarke) 1884–1977. Jamaican Labour politician. As leader of the Labour Party, he was first prime minister of independent Jamaica 1962–67.

bustard type of bird, family Otididae, related to cranes but with rounder bodies, thicker necks and relatively short beaks, found on the ground on open plains and fields.

butadiene CH_2:CHCH:CH_2 (modern name *buta-1,3-diene*) an inflammable gas derived from petroleum, and used in making synthetic rubber.

butane C_4H_1dO an alkane (paraffin hydrocarbon) gas, a by-product of petroleum manufacture or from natural gas. Liquefied under pressure, it is used as a fuel for industrial and domestic purposes, for example in portable cookers.

Bute John Stuart, 3rd Earl of Bute 1713–1792. British Tory politician, prime minister 1762–63. On the accession of George III in 1760, he became the chief instrument in the king's policy for breaking the power of the Whigs and establishing the personal rule of the monarch through Parliament.

Buthelezi Chief Gatsha 1928– . Zulu leader and politician, chief minister of KwaZulu, a black 'homeland' in the Republic of South Africa from 1970. He is founder and president of ◊*Inkatha* 1975, a paramilitary organization for attaining a nonracial democratic political system.

Butler Joseph 1692–1752. British priest, who became dean of St Paul's in 1740 and bishop of Durham in 1750; his *Analogy of Religion* 1736 argued that it

is no more rational to accept ◊deism, arguing for God as the first cause, than revealed religion (not arrived at by reasoning).

Butler Josephine (born Gray) 1828–1906. British social reformer. She promoted women's education and the Married Women's Property Act, and campaigned against the Contagious Diseases Acts of 1862–70, which made women in garrison towns liable to compulsory examination for venereal disease. As a result of her campaigns the acts were repealed in 1883.

Butler Richard Austen, Baron Butler 1902–1982. British Conservative politician, known from his initials as Rab. As minister of education 1941–45, he was responsible for the Education Act 1944; he was chancellor of the Exchequer 1951–55, Lord Privy Seal 1955–59, and foreign minister 1963–64. As a candidate for the premiership, he was defeated by Harold Macmillan in 1957 (under whom he was home secretary 1957–62), and by Douglas-Home in 1963. He was master of Trinity College, Cambridge, 1965–78.

Butler Samuel 1612–1680. English satirist. His poem *Hudibras*, published in three parts in 1663, 1664 and 1678, became immediately popular for its biting satire against the Puritans.

Butler Samuel 1835–1902. British author, who made his name in 1872 with his satiric attack on contemporary utopianism, *Erewhon* ('nowhere' reversed), but is now best remembered for his autobiographical *The Way of All Flesh* written 1872–85 and published 1903.

Butlin (William) Billy 1899–1980. British holiday-camp entrepreneur. Born in South Africa, he went in early life to Canada, but later entered the fair business in the UK. He originated a chain of camps that provide accommodation, meals, and amusements at an inclusive price. He was knighted in 1964.

butter foodstuff made from the fatty portion of milk. Making butter by hand, which is done by skimming off the cream and churning it, was traditionally a convenient means of preserving milk.

buttercup species of the genus *Ranunculus* with divided leaves and yellow flowers, which include the *common buttercup Ranunculus acris* and the *creeping buttercup Ranunculus repens*.

butterfly insect belonging, like moths, to the order Lepidoptera, in which the wings are covered with tiny scales, often brightly coloured. There are some 15,000 species of butterfly.

butterfly fish name for several fishes, not all related. The freshwater *butterfly fish Pantodon buchholzi* of W Africa can leap from the water and glide for a short distance on its large wing-like pectoral fins. Up to 10 cm/4 in long, it lives in stagnant water. The tropical marine *butterfly fishes*, family Chaetodontidae, are brightly coloured with laterally flattened bodies, often with long snouts

butterfly

Byrd English composer William Byrd.

which they poke into crevices in rocks and coral when feeding.

butterwort insectivorous plant, genus *Pinguicula*, with purplish flowers and a rosette of leaves covered with a sticky secretion that traps insects.

Buxtehude Diderik 1637–1707. Danish composer and organist at Lübeck, Germany, who influenced Bach and Handel. He is remembered for his organ works and cantatas written for his evening concerts or *Abendmusiken*.

buyer's market a market having an excess of goods and services on offer and where prices are likely to be declining. The buyer benefits from the wide choice and competition available.

buzzard name given to a number of species of medium-sized hawks with broad wings, often seen soaring.

Byblos ancient Phoenician city (modern Jebeil), 32 km/20 mi N of Beirut, Lebanon. Known to the Assyrians and Babyonians as Gubla. It had a thriving export of cedar and pinewood to Egypt as early as 1500 BC. In Roman times called Byblos, it boasted an amphitheatre, baths, and a temple dedicated to an unknown male god, and was noted for its celebration of the resurrection of Adonis, worshipped as a god of vegetation.

Byng George, Viscount Torrington 1663–1733. British admiral. He captured Gibraltar in 1704, commanded the fleet that prevented an invasion of England by the 'Old Pretender' James Edward Stuart in 1708, and destroyed the Spanish fleet at Messina in 1718. John ◊Byng was his fourth son.

Byng John 1704–1757. British admiral. Byng failed in the attempt to relieve Fort St Philip when in 1756 the island of Minorca was invaded by France. He was court-martialled and shot. As the French writer Voltaire commented, it was done 'to encourage the others'.

Byrd Richard Evelyn 1888–1957. US explorer. He flew to the North (1926) and South Pole (1929), and led five overland expeditions in Antarctica.

Byrd William 1543–1623. British composer, who composed secular vocal and instrumental music, but his church choral music (set to Latin words, as he was a firm Catholic) represents his most important work.

Byrds, the US pioneering folk-rock group 1964–73. Best remembered for their 12-string guitar sound and the hits 'Mr Tambourine Man' 1965 (a version of Bob Dylan's song) and 'Eight Miles High' 1966, they moved towards country rock in the late 1960s.

Byron Ada Augusta 1815–1851. British mathematician, daughter of Lord Byron. She was the world's first computer programmer, working with ◊Babbage's mechanical invention, and in 1983

a new high-level computer language, ADA, was named after her.

Byron George Gordon, 6th Baron Byron 1788–1824. British poet, who became the symbol of Romanticism and political liberalism throughout Europe in the 19th century. His reputation was established with the first two cantos of *Childe Harold* 1812. Later works include *The Prisoner of Chillon* 1816, *Beppo* 1818, *Mazeppa* 1819, and, most notably, *Don Juan* 1819–24. He left England in 1816, spending most of his later life in Italy.

byte in computing, a sequence or string of usually eight bits (binary digits) constituting a unit of memory or a character (a letter, number or symbol). A byte is the number of bits needed to represent a single character (eight bits in extended ASCII).

Byzantine Empire the *Eastern Roman Empire* 395–1453, with its capital at Constantinople (Byzantium).
330 Emperor Constantine removed his capital to Constantinople.
395 The Roman Empire was divided into eastern and western halves.
476 The Western Empire was overrun by barbarian invaders.
527–565 Justinian I temporarily recovered Italy, N Africa, and parts of Spain.
7th–8th century Syria, Egypt, and N Africa were lost to the Arabs, who twice besieged Constantinople (673–77, 718), but the Byzantines maintained their hold on Anatolia.
8th–11th centuries The ◊Iconoclastic controversy brought the emperors into conflict with the papacy, and in 1054 the Greek Orthodox church broke with the Roman.
867–1056 Under the Macedonian dynasty the Byzantine Empire reached the height of its prosperity; the Bulgars proved a formidable danger, but after a long struggle were finally crushed in 1018 by ◊Basil II ('the Bulgar-Slayer'). After Basil's death the Byzantine Empire declined due to internal factions.
1071–73 The Seljuk Turks conquered most of Anatolia.
1204 The Fourth Crusade sacked Constantinople and set Baldwin of Flanders (1171–1205) on the throne.
1261 The Latin (W European) Empire was overthrown; the Byzantine Empire maintained a precarious existence.
1453 The Turks captured Constantinople.

Byzantine style a style in the visual arts and architecture, which originated in Byzantium (4th–5th

Byron A portrait of Lord Byron by Thomas Phillips (signed 1835) National Portrait Gallery, London.

centuries) and spread to Italy, throughout the Balkans, and to Russia, where it survived for many centuries. It is characterized by heavy stylization, strong linear emphasis, the use of rigid artistic stereotypes and sometimes rich colours, particularly gold. Byzantine artists excelled in mosaic work, and manuscript painting. In architecture the dome supported on pendentives was in widespread use.

Byzantium ancient Greek city on the Bosphorus (modern Istanbul), founded as a colony of the Greek city of Megara, near Corinth about 660 BC. In 330 AD the capital of the Roman Empire was transferred there by Constantine the Great, who renamed it ◊Constantinople.

cactus

C abbreviation for *centum* (Latin 'hundred'); *century*; *centigrade*; ◊*Celsius*.

C a general-purpose computer-programming language popular on minicomputers. Developed in the early 1970s from an earlier language called BCPL, C is closely associated with the development of the operating system ◊Unix. It is especially good for writing fast and efficient systems programs, such as operating systems (which control the operations of the computer).

c. abbreviation for *circa* (Latin 'about').

cabbage plant *Brassica oleracea* of the family Cruciferae, allied to the turnip and wild charlock. It is an important table vegetable, and the numerous cultivated varieties – all probably descended from the wild cabbage – include kale, Brussels sprouts, common cabbage, savoy, cauliflower, sprouting broccoli, and kohlrabi.

cabbala alternative spelling of ◊kabbala.

caber, tossing the Scottish athletic sport requiring great strength. The contestant has to toss a caber (a tapering tree-trunk) 6.1 m/20 ft long, until it rotates through 180 degrees.

cabinet the group of ministers holding a country's most important executive offices who decide the government's policy. In Britain the cabinet system originated under the Stuarts; under William III it became customary for the king to select his ministers from the party with a parliamentary majority. The US cabinet, unlike the British, does not initiate legislation, and its members, appointed by the president, may not be members of Congress.

cable car a method of transporting passengers up steep slopes by cable. In the *cable railway*, passenger cars are hauled along rails by a cable wound by a powerful winch. A pair of cars usually operates together on the funicular principle, one going up as the other goes down. The other main type is the *aerial cable car*, properly called a téléphérique, where the passenger car is suspended from a trolley that runs along an aerial cableway.

cable television distribution of broadcast signals through cable relay systems. Narrowband systems were originally used to deliver services to areas with poor 'off-air' reception; modern systems with wider bandwith coaxial and fibre optic cable are increasingly used for distribution of satellite channels and the development of home-based interactive services.

Caboto Giovanni, or *John Cabot* 1450–1498. Italian navigator. Commissioned with his three sons by Henry VII to discover unknown lands, he arrived at Cape Breton Island on 24 Jun 1497, thus, according to tradition, becoming the first European to reach the North American mainland (he thought he was in NE Asia). In 1498, he sailed again, touched Greenland, and probably died on the voyage.

cactus in botany, plant of the family Cactaceae, but in common speech applied to many different succulent and prickly plants. True cacti have a woody axis overlaid with an enlarged fleshy stem, which assumes various forms and is usually covered with spines.

CAD *computer-aided design* the use of computer facilities for creating and editing design drawings. CAD also allows such things as automatic testing of designs and multiple or animated three-dimensional views of designs. CAD systems are widely used in architecture, electronics, and engineering, especially in the motor-vehicle industry where cars designed by computer are now commonplace. A related development is ◊CAM (computer-assisted manufacture).

Cadarache French nuclear research site, NE of Aix-en-Provence.

caddis fly insect of the order Trichoptera. Adults are generally dull brown, moth-like, with wings covered in tiny hairs. Mouthparts are poorly developed, and many do not feed as adults. They are usually found near water.

Cádiz Spanish city and naval base, capital and seaport of the province of Cádiz, standing on Cádiz Bay, an inlet of the Atlantic, 103 km/64 mi S of Seville. Population (1981) 157,766. After the discovery of America 1492, Cádiz became one of the most important ports in Europe. Francis Drake burnt a Spanish fleet here in 1587 to prevent the sailing of the ◊Armada.

cadmium a metallic element, symbol Cd, atomic number 48, relative atomic mass 112.41. Cadmium is a soft, silver-white, highly toxic metal. It is used in electroplating, as a constituent of one of the lowest-melting alloys, and in bearing alloys with low coefficients of friction. Cadmium is also used in control rods in nuclear reactors owing to its high absorption of neutrons.

Cadwalader 7th century. Welsh hero. The son of Cadwallon, king of Gwynedd, N Wales, he defeated and killed Eadwine of Northumbria in

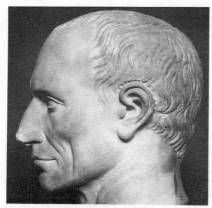

Caesar *Roman statesman and military commander, Julius Caesar.*

633. About a year later he was killed in battle.

Caedmon 7th century. Earliest known English poet. According to the Northumbrian historian Bede, when Caedmon was a cowherd at the Christian monastery of Whitby, he was commanded to sing by a stranger in a dream, and on waking produced a hymn on the Creation. The original poem is preserved in some manuscripts. Caedmon became a monk and may have composed other religious poems.

Caesar powerful family of ancient Rome which included Gaius Julius ◊Caesar, whose grand-nephew and adopted son ◊Augustus assumed the name of Caesar, and in turn passed it on to his adopted son ◊Tiberius. Henceforth, it was borne by the successive emperors, becoming a title of the Roman rulers. The titles Tsar in Russia and Kaiser in Germany are both derived from the name Caesar.

Caesar Gaius Julius *c.* 102–44 BC. Roman statesman and general. He formed with Pompey and Crassus the First Triumvirate. He conquered Gaul 58–50 BC, and invaded Britain in 55 and 54. He fought against Pompey 49–48 BC, defeating him at Pharsalus. After a period in Egypt Caesar returned to Rome as dictator from 46 BC. He was assassinated on the Ides of March 44 BC.

Caesarea alternative form of ◊Qisaraya, port in Israel.

Caesarean section a surgical operation to deliver a baby by way of an incision in the mother's abdominal wall. It may be recommended for almost any obstetric complication implying a threat to mother or baby.

caesium a chemical element, symbol Cs, atomic number 55, relative atomic mass 132.91. It is used in the manufacture of photoelectric cells.

Caetano Marcello 1906–1980. Portuguese right-wing politician. He succeeded the dictator Salazar as prime minister from 1968 until his exile after the revolution of 1974.

caffeine one of a group of organic substances called ◊alkaloids. Caffeine is found in tea and coffee, and is partly responsible for their stimulant effect.

Cage John 1912–1992. US composer. A pupil of Schoenberg, he reassessed musical aesthetics and defined the role of music as 'purposeless play'. All sounds that can be heard are to be available for musical purposes, for example electrical buzzers and tin cans as used in *Imaginary Landscape No 3*.

Cagliari capital and port of Sardinia, Italy, on the Gulf of Cagliari; population (1988) 222,000.

Cain in the Old Testament, the first-born son of Adam and Eve. He murdered his brother Abel from motives of jealousy, as Abel's sacrifice was more acceptable to God than his own.

Cain James M(allahan) 1892–1977. US novelist. He was the author of thrillers, including *The Postman Always Rings Twice* 1934, *Mildred Pierce* 1941, and *Double Indemnity* 1943.

Caine Michael. Stage-name of Maurice Micklewhite 1933– . British actor, noted for his dry, laconic Cockney style. His long cinematic career includes the films *Alfie* 1966, *California Suite* 1978, *Educating Rita* 1983, and *Hannah and her Sisters* 1986.

Cairo Arabic *El Qahira* capital of Egypt, on the east bank of the Nile 13 km/8 mi above the apex of the Delta and 160 km/100 mi from the Mediterranean; the largest city in Africa and in the Middle East; population (1985) 6,205,000, Greater Cairo (1987) 13,300,000. El Fustat (Old Cairo) was founded by Arabs about 64 AD, Cairo itself about 1000 by the ◊Fatimid ruler Gowhar. The Great Pyramids and Sphinx are at nearby Giza.

caisson a cylindrical or boxlike structure, usually of reinforced ◊concrete, that is sunk into a river bed to form the foundations of a bridge.

Cajun member of a French-speaking community of Louisiana, USA, descended from French-Canadians who in the 18th century were driven there from Nova Scotia (then known as Acadia, from which the name Cajun comes). *Cajun music* has a lively rhythm and features steel guitar, fiddle, and accordion.

calabash evergreen tree, *Crescentia cujete*, family Bignoniaceae, found in South America, India and Africa. They produce gourds which are used as water containers.

Calabria mountainous earthquake region occupying the 'toe' of Italy, comprising the provinces of Catanzaro, Cosenza and Reggio; the capital is Catanzaro, Reggio is the industrial centre. Area 15,080 sq km/5,820 sq mi. Population (1990) 2,153,700.

calamine a zinc mineral. When referring to skin-soothing lotions and ointments, calamine means a pink powder of zinc oxide and 0.5% iron (II) oxide, used, for example, in treating eczema, measles rash, and insect bites or stings.

Calamity Jane nickname of Martha Jane Burke c. 1852–1903. US heroine of Deadwood, South Dakota, mining camps. She worked as a teamster, transporting supplies to the camps, adopted male dress and, as an excellent shot, promised 'calamity' to any aggressor. Her renown was spread by many fictional accounts of the 'wild west' which featured her exploits.

calcite a common, colourless or white rock-forming mineral, calcium carbonate, $CaCO_3$. It is the main constituent of limestone and marble.

calcium a silvery-white metallic element, one of the alkaline earth metals; symbol Ca, atomic number 20, relative atomic mass 40.07. It is very widely distributed, mainly in the form of its carbonate $CaCO_3$ which occurs in a fairly pure condition as ◊calcite in chalk and limestone. Calcium is an essential component of bones, teeth, shells, milk and leaves, and it forms 1.5% of the human body. Calcium compounds are important to the chemical industry.

calculator an electronic computing device for performing numerical calculations. It can add, subtract, multiply, and divide; many also have squares, roots, and advanced trigonometric and statistical functions.

Input is by a small keyboard and results are shown on a one-line screen (VDU) which is typically a ◊liquid crystal display (LCD).

calculus branch of mathematics that permits the manipulation of continuously varying quantities, applicable to practical problems involving such matters as changing speeds, problems of flight, varying stresses in the framework of a bridge, and electrical circuits with varying currents and voltages. *Integral calculus* deals with the method of summation or adding together the effects of continuously varying quantities. *Differential calculus* deals in a similar way with rates of change.

Calcutta largest city of India, on the Hooghly, the most westerly mouth of the Ganges, some 130 km/80 mi N of the Bay of Bengal. It is the capital of West Bengal; population (1981) 9,166,000. Chiefly a commercial and industrial centre (engineering, shipbuilding, jute, and other textiles). Calcutta was the seat of government of British India 1773–1912.

Calder Alexander 1898–1976. US abstract sculptor, the inventor of *mobiles*, suspended shapes that move in the lightest current of air. In the 1920s he began making wire sculptures and *stabiles* (static mobiles), coloured abstract shapes attached by lines of wire.

caldera in geology, a very large basin-shaped ◊crater. Calderas are found at the tops of volcanoes, where the original peak has collapsed into an empty chamber beneath. The basin, many times larger than the original volcanic vent, may be flooded, producing a crater lake, or the flat floor may contain a number of small volcanic cones, showing where the volcanic activity continued after the collapse.

Calderón de la Barca Pedro 1600–1681. Spanish dramatist and poet. After the death of Lope de Vega, he was considered to be the leading Spanish dramatist. Most famous of some 118 plays is the philosophical *La Vida es sueño/Life is a Dream* 1635.

Caldwell Erskine (Preston) 1903–1987. US novelist, whose *Tobacco Road* 1932 and *God's Little Acre* 1933, are earthy and vivid presentations of the poverty-stricken Southern sharecroppers.

calendar the divisions of the ◊year and the method of ordering the years. From year one, an assumed date of the birth of Jesus, dates are reckoned backwards (BC or BCE, 'before common era') and forwards (AD, Latin *anno domini*, in the year of the Lord or CE, 'common era'). The *lunar month* (period between one new moon and the next) averages naturally 29.5 days, but the Western calendar uses for convenience a *calendar month* with a complete number of days, 30 or 31 (Feb has 28). Since there are slightly fewer than six extra hours a year left over, they are added to Feb as a 29th day every 4th year (*leap year*).

Calgary city in Alberta, Canada, on the Bow, in the foothills of the Rockies; at 1,048 m/3,440 ft it is one of the highest Canadian towns; population (1984) 619,814. The centre of a large agricultural region, it is the oil and financial centre of Alberta and W Canada.

Calhoun John Caldwell 1782–1850. US politician, born in South Carolina. He was vice president 1825–29 under John Quincy Adams and 1829–33 under Andrew Jackson. Throughout his life he was a defender of the *states' rights* against the federal government, and of the institution of black slavery.

Cali city in SW Colombia, in the Cauca Valley 975 m/3,200 ft above sea level, founded in 1536. Cali has textile, sugar and engineering industries. Population (1985) 1,398,276.

California Pacific state of the USA; nicknamed the Golden State, originally because of its gold mines, but more recently because of its sunshine
area 406,377 sq km/156,962 sq mi
capital Sacramento
towns Los Angeles, San Diego, San Francisco
physical Sierra Nevada (including Yosemite and Sequoia National Parks, Lake Tahoe and Mount Whitney, 4,418 m/14,494 ft, the highest mountain in the continental USA excluding Alaska); and the Coast Range; Death Valley 86 m/282 ft below sea level; Colorado and Mojave deserts (Edwards Air Force base is in the latter)
products leading agricultural state with fruit, nuts, wheat, vegetables, cotton, rice; beef cattle; timber; fish; oil and natural gas; aerospace, electronics (see ◊Silicon Valley), food-processing; films and television programmes. There are also great reserves of energy (geothermal) in the hot water which lies beneath much of the state
population (1980) 23,667,902, largest of the USA, 66% non-Hispanic white; 20% Hispanic; 7.5% Black; 7% Asian (including many Vietnamese)
famous people Bret Harte, W R Hearst, Jack London, Marilyn Monroe, Richard Nixon, William Saroyan, John Steinbeck
history colonized by Spain in 1769, it was ceded to the USA after the Mexican War of 1848, and became a state in 1850. Gold had been discovered in the Sierra Nevada in Jan 1848, and was followed by the gold rush 1849–56.

California current the cold ocean ◊current in the East Pacific Ocean flowing southwards down the west coast of North America. It is part of the North Pacific ◊gyre (a vast, circular movement of ocean water).

californium a transuranic element, symbol Cf, atomic number 98. It is a radioactive metal produced in very small quantities and used in nuclear reactors as a neutron source.

Caligula Gaius Caesar 12–41 AD. Roman emperor, son of Germanicus, and successor to Tiberius in 37 AD; a tyrant and alleged to be mad, he was assassinated by an officer of his guard.

calima dust cloud (Spanish 'haze') in Europe, coming from the Sahara Desert, which sometimes causes heatwaves and eye irritation.

caliph title of civic and religious head of the world of Islam. The first caliph was ◊Abu Bakr. Nominally elective, the office became hereditary, held by the Ummayyad dynasty 661–750 and then by the ◊Abbasids. During the 10th century the political and military power passed to the leader of the caliph's Turkish bodyguard; about the same time an independent ◊Fatimid caliphate . sprang up in Egypt. After the death of the last Abbasid (1258) the title was claimed by a number of Muslim chieftains in Egypt, Turkey, and India. The most powerful of these were the Turkish sultans of the Ottoman Empire.

calla another name for ◊arum lily.

Callaghan (Leonard) James 1912– . British Labour politician. As chancellor of the Exchequer 1964-67, he introduced corporation and capital-gains tax, and resigned following devaluation. He was home secretary 1967-70 and prime minister 1976–79 in a period of increasing economic stress.

Callaghan Morley 1903– . Canadian novelist and short story writer, whose realistic novels include *Such Is My Beloved* 1934, *More Joy*

In Heaven 1937, and *Close To The Sun Again* 1977.

Callao chief commercial and fishing port of Peru, 12 km/7 mi SW of Lima ; population (1984) 411,200. Founded in 1537, it was destroyed by an earthquake in 1746. It is Peru's main naval base, and produces fertilizers.

Callas Maria. Stage name of Maria Kalogeropoulou 1923–1977. US lyric soprano, born in New York of Greek parents. With a voice of fine range and a gift for dramatic expression, she excelled in operas including *Norma, Madame Butterfly, Aïda, Lucia di Lammermoor* and *Medea*.

calligraphy the art of handwriting, regarded in China and Japan as the greatest of the visual arts, and playing a large part in Islamic art because the depiction of the human and animal form is forbidden.

callipers a measuring instrument used, for example, to measure the internal and external diameter of pipes. Some callipers are made like a pair of compasses, having two legs, often curved, pivoting about a screw at one end. The ends of the legs are placed in contact with the object to be measured, and the gap between the ends is then measured against a rule. The slide calliper looks like an adjustable spanner, and carries a scale for direct measuring, usually with a ◊vernier scale for accuracy.

Callisto second-largest moon of Jupiter, 4,800 km/ 3,000 miles in diameter, orbiting every 16.7 days at a distance of 1.9 million km/1.2 million mi from the planet. Its surface is covered with large craters.

callus in botany, a tissue that forms at a damaged plant surface. Composed of large, thin-walled ◊parenchyma cells, it grows over and around the wound, eventually covering the exposed area.

Calmette Albert 1863–1933. French bacteriologist. A student of Pasteur, who developed (with Camille Guérin 1872–1961) the ◊BCG vaccine against tuberculosis in 1921.

calomel mercury (I) (mercurous) chloride, Hg_2Cl_2, a white, heavy powder formerly used as a laxative, now used as a pesticide and fungicide.

calorie unit of heat (that is, the quantity of heat required to raise the temperature of 1 gram of water by 1°C), which has now been replaced by the ◊joule, equivalent to 0.24 calories. In dietetics, the Calorie or kilocalorie is equal to 1,000 calories.

calorific value the amount of heat generated by a given mass of fuel when it is completely burned. It is measured in joules per kilogram. Calorific values are measured experimetally using a bomb ◊calorimeter.

calorimeter an instrument used in physics to measure heat. A simple calorimeter consists of a heavy copper vessel which is polished (to reduce heat losses by radiation) and lagged with insulating material (to reduce losses by convection and conduction).

calotype a paper-based photograph using a wax paper negative, the first example of the ◊negative/positive process invented by Fox ◊Talbot around 1834.

Calvary in the New Testament, the site of Christ's crucifixion at Jerusalem. Two chief sites are suggested: one is where the Church of the Sepulchre now stands; the other is the hill beyond the Damascus gate. The name Calvary is also applied to any monument commemorating the Crucifixion.

Calvin John 1509–1564. French-born Swiss Protestant church reformer and theologian. He was a

Calvin The founder of Presbyterianism, John Calvin.

leader of the Reformation in Geneva and set up a strict religious community there. His theological system is known as Calvinism, and his church government as ◊Presbyterianism. Calvin wrote (in Latin) *Institutes of the Christian Religion* 1536 and commentaries on the New Testament and much of the Old Testament.

Calvin Melvin 1911– . US chemist who, using radioactive carbon-14 as a tracer, determined the biochemical processes of ◊photosynthesis, in which green plants use ◊chlorophyll to convert carbon dioxide and water into sugar and oxygen. Nobel Prize for chemistry 1961.

Calvinism Christian doctrine as interpreted by John Calvin and adopted in Scotland, parts of Switzerland, and the Netherlands. Its central doctrine is predestination, under which certain souls (the elect) are predestined by God through the sacrifice of Christ to salvation, and the rest to damnation. Although Calvinism is rarely accepted today in its strictest interpretation, the 20th century has seen a Neo-Calvinist revival through the work of Karl ◊Barth.

Calypso in Greek mythology, a sea ◊nymph who waylaid the homeward-bound Odysseus for seven years.

calypso in music, a type of West Indian satirical ballad with a syncopated beat.

calyptra in mosses and liverworts, a layer of cells that encloses and protects the young sporophyte (spore capsule), forming a sheathlike hood around the capsule. Also used to describe the root cap, a layer of ◊parenchyma cells covering the end of a root that gives protection to the root tip as it grows through the soil. This is constantly being worn away and replaced by new cells from a special ◊meristem, the calyptrogen.

calyx the collective term for the ◊sepals of a flower, forming the outermost whorl of the ◊perianth. It surrounds the other flower parts, and protects them while in bud. In some flowers, for example, the campions (*Silene*), the sepals are fused along their sides, forming a calyx-tube.

cam a part of a machine that transmits a regular movement to another part when it rotates. The most common type of cam, often called an *edge cam*, is in a car engine, in the form of a rounded projection on a shaft, the camshaft. When the camshaft turns, the cams press against linkages (followers) that open the valves in the cylinders. A *face cam* is a disc with a groove in its face, in which the follower travels. A *cylindrical cam* carries

Cameroon
Republic of
(*République du Cameroun*)

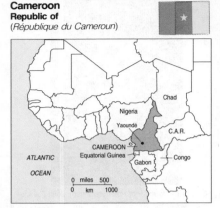

area 474,000 sq km/183,580 sq mi
capital Yaoundé
towns chief port Douala
physical desert in the far N in the Lake Chad basin, dry savannah plateau in the intermediate area, and in the S dense tropical rainforest
head of state and of government Paul Biya from 1982
political system emergent democratic republic
exports cocoa, coffee, bananas, cotton, timber, rubber, groundnuts, gold, aluminium, crude oil
currency CFA franc
population 10,190,000 (1985); annual growth rate 2.7%
life expectancy men 49, women 53
language French and English in pidgin variations

(official); there are 163 indigenous peoples with many African languages
religion Roman Catholic 35%, animist 25%, Muslim 22%, Protestant 18%
literacy 68% male/45% female (1985 est)
GDP 12.7 bn (1987); $1,170 per head
chronology
1884 Under German rule.
1916 Captured by Allied forces in World War I.
1922 Divided between Britain and France.
1946 French and British Cameroons made UN trust territories.
1960 French Cameroon became the independent Republic of Cameroon. Ahmadou Ahidjo elected president.
1961 N part of British Cameroon merged with Nigeria and S part joined the Republic of Cameroon to become the Federal Republic of Cameroon.
1966 A one-party regime was introduced.
1972 New constitution made Cameroon a unitary state, the United Republic of Cameroon.
1973 New national assembly elected.
1982 Ahidjo succeeded by Paul Biya.
1983 Biya began to remove his predecessor's supporters and was accused by Ahidjo of trying to create a police state.
1984 Biya re-elected and defeated a plot to overthrow him. Country's name changed to Republic of Cameroon.
1988 Biya re-elected.
1990 Widespread public disorder. Biya granted amnesty to political prisoners.
1991 Constitutional changes made.
1992 Ruling RDPC party won in first multiparty elections in 28 years. Biya's presidential victory challenged by opposition.

---

angled parallel grooves which impart a to-and-fro motion to the follower when it rotates.

CAM *computer-aided manufacture* the use of computers to control production processes; in particular, the control of machine tools and ◊robots in factories.

Camargue the marshy area of the ◊Rhône delta, S of Arles, France: area about 780 sq km/300 sq mi. Bulls and horses are bred there, and the nature reserve, which is known for its bird life, forms the southern part.

cambium a layer of actively dividing cells (lateral ◊meristem), found within stems and roots, which gives rise to ◊secondary growth in perennial plants, causing an increase in girth. There are two main types of cambium: vascular cambium which gives rise to secondary xylem and phloem tissues, and cork cambium or phellogen which gives rise to secondary cortex and cork tissues (see ◊bark).

Cambodia (formerly *Khmer Republic* 1970–76, *Democratic Kampuchea* 1976–79, and *People's Republic of Kampuchea* 1979–89) country in SE Asia, bounded N and NW by Thailand, N by Laos, E and SE by Vietnam, and SW by the Gulf of Thailand.

Cambrai, Battles of two battles in World War I at Cambrai in NE France; in the *First Battle*, Nov–Dec 1917, the town was almost captured by the British when large numbers of tanks were used for the first time; in the *Second Battle*, 25 Aug–5 Oct 1918, the town was taken during the final British offensive.

Cambrian the period of geological time between 590 and 505 million years ago; the first period of the ◊Palaeozoic era. All invertebrate phyla appeared, and marine algae were widespread. The earliest fossils with hard shells, such as trilobites, date from this period.

Cambridge English city, the administrative headquarters of Cambridgeshire, on the river Cam (a river sometimes called by its earlier name, Granta), 82 km/51 mi N of London; population (1989) 101,000. The city is centred on Cambridge University (founded 12th century).

Cambridgeshire county in E England,
area 3,409 sq km/1,316 sq mi
towns administrative headquarters Cambridge; Ely, Huntingdon, Peterborough
products mainly agricultural
population (1991) 640,700

Camden Town group school of British painters 1911–13, based in Camden Town, London, in part inspired by ◊Sickert. The work of Spencer Gore (1878–1914) and Harold Gilman (1876–1919) is typical of the group.

camel large cud-chewing mammal of the even-toed hoofed order Artiodactyla. Unlike typical ruminants, it has a three-chambered stomach. It has two toes which have broad soft soles for walking on sand, and hoofs resembling nails. There are two species, the single-humped *Arabian camel* (*Camelus dromedarius*), and the twin-humped *Bactrian camel* (*Camelus bactrianus*) from Asia. They carry a food reserve of fatty tissue in the hump, can go without drinking for long periods, can feed on

Cambodia
State of

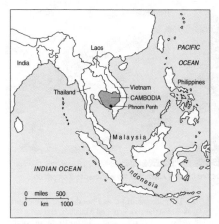

area 181,000 sq km/71,000 sq mi
capital Phnom Penh
towns Battambang, and the seaport Kompong Som
physical mostly forested; flat, with mountains in S
head of state Prince Norodom Sihanouk from 1991
head of government Hun Sen from 1985
political system transitional
exports rubber, rice, pepper, wood, cattle
currency Cambodian riel
population (1990 est) 6,993,000; annual growth rate 2.2%
life expectancy men 42, women 45
language Khmer (official), French
religion Theravada Buddhist 95%
literacy 78% male/39% female (1980 est)
GDP $100 per head (1984)
chronology
1863–1941 French protectorate.
1953 Granted full independence.
1970 Prince Sihanouk overthrown by Lon Nol.
1975 Lon Nol overthrown by Khmer Rouge.
1978–79 Vietnamese invasion and installation of Heng Samrin government.
1987 Vietnamese troop withdrawal began.
1991 Peace agreement signed in Paris. Communism abandoned.
1992 Khmer Rouge refused to disarm; UN imposed limited trade embargo on areas controlled by Khmer Rouge.

---

salty vegetation, and can withstand extremes of heat and cold, thus being well adapted to desert conditions.

camellia oriental evergreen shrub of the family Theaceae, closely allied to the tea plant. Numerous species, including *Camellia japonica* and *Camellia reticulata*, have been introduced into Europe.

Camelot legendary capital of King ◊Arthur. A possible site is the hill fort of South Cadbury Castle, near Yeovil in Somerset, England.

camera apparatus used in ◊photography.

camera obscura a darkened box with a tiny hole for projecting the inverted image of the scene outside on a screen inside.

Cameroon country in W Africa, bounded NW by Nigeria, NE by Chad, E by the Central African Republic, S by Congo, Gabon, and Equatorial Guinea, and W by the Atlantic.

Camoens or *Camões*, Luís Vaz de 1524–1580. Portuguese poet and soldier. His poem, *Os Lusiades/The Lusiads*, published in 1572, tells the story of the explorer Vasco da Gama, incorporating much Portuguese history.

Camorra Italian secret society formed about 1820 by criminals in the dungeons of Naples, and continued once they were outside. It dominated politics from 1848, was suppressed in 1911, but many members eventually surfaced in the US ◊Mafia. The Camorra still operates in the Naples area.

camouflage colours or structures that allow an animal to blend with its surroundings, to avoid detection by other animals. Camouflage can take the form of matching the background colour, of countershading (darker on top, lighter below, to counteract natural shadows) or of irregular patterns that break up the outline of the animal's body. More elaborate camouflage involves closely resembling a feature of the natural environment.

Campaign for Nuclear Disarmament (CND) non-political British organization advocating worldwide abolition of nuclear weapons. It seeks unilateral British initiatives to help start the multilateral process and end the arms race. It was founded 1958.

Campania agricultural region (wheat, citrus, wine, vegetables, tobacco) of S Italy, including the volcano, ◊Vesuvius, capital Naples, industrial centres Benevento, Caserta and Salerno; population (1990) 5,853,900. Ancient sites at Pompeii, Herculaneum, Paestum.

Campbell Colin, 1st Baron Clyde 1792–1863. British field marshal. He commanded the Highland Brigade at ◊Balaclava in the Crimean War, and as commander in chief during the Indian Mutiny raised the siege of Lucknow and captured Cawnpore.

Campbell Donald Malcolm 1921–1967. British car and speedboat enthusiast. In 1964 he set the world water-speed record of 444.7 kph/276.3 mph on Lake Dumbleyung, Australia, with the turbo-jet hydroplane *Bluebird*, and achieved the land-speed record of 648.7 kph/403.1 mph at Lake Eyre salt flats, Australia. He was killed in an attempt to raise his water-speed record on Coniston Water, England.

Campbell Malcolm 1885–1948. British racing driver who at one time held both land and water speed records. His car and boat were both called *Bluebird*.

Campbell-Bannerman Henry 1836–1908. British Liberal politician, prime minister 1905–08. He granted self-government to the South African colonies, and passed the Trades Disputes Act 1906.

Camp David official country home of US presidents in the Appalachian mountains, Maryland; it was originally named Shangri-la by F D Roosevelt, but was renamed Camp David by Eisenhower.

Camp David Agreements two framework agreements signed 1978 by the Israeli prime minister Begin and president Sadat of Egypt, at the instance of US president Carter, covering a phased withdrawal of Egypt from Sinai, which was completed in 1982, and an overall Middle East settlement including the election by the Palestinians of the West Bank and Gaza Strip of a 'self-governing authority'.

camphor a volatile, aromatic ◊ketone substance ($C_{10}H_{16}O$) obtained from the camphor tree. It is distilled from chips of the wood of the root, trunk, and branches. It is used in insect repellents and in the manufacture of celluloid.

Campbell Donald Campbell in his jet boat Bluebird just before his fatal attempt at the water-speed record on 5 Jan 1967.

campion several plants of the genera *Lychnis* and *Silene*, belonging to the family Caryophyllaceae, which include the garden campion *Lychnis coronaria*, the wild white and red campions *Silene alba* and *Silene dioica*, and the bladder campion *Silene vulgaris*.

Campion Edmund 1540–1581. English Jesuit and Roman Catholic martyr. In 1573 he became a Jesuit in Rome, and in 1580 was sent to England as a missionary. He was betrayed as a spy in 1581, imprisoned in the Tower of London, and hanged, drawn, and quartered as a traitor.

Campion Thomas 1567–1620. English poet and musician. He was the author of the critical *Art of English Poesie* 1602, and four *Bookes of Ayres*, for which he composed both words and music.

Campo-Formio, Treaty of peace settlement during the Revolutionary Wars in 1797 between Napoleon and Austria, by which France gained the region of modern Belgium and Austria was compensated with Venice and part of modern Yugoslavia.

Camus Albert 1913–1960. Algerian-born French writer. A journalist in France, he was active in the Resistance during World War II. His novels include *L'Étranger/The Outsider* 1942, *La Peste/The Plague* 1948, and *L'Homme Révolté/The Rebel* 1952, a study of revolutionary ideals corrupted by murder and oppression. Sartre. Nobel prize 1957.

Canaan an ancient region between the Mediterranean and the Dead Sea, in the Bible the 'Promised Land' of the Israelites. Occupied as early as the 3rd millennium BC by the Canaanites, a Semitic-speaking people who were known to the Greeks of the 1st millennium BC as Phoenicians. The capital was Ebla (the modern Tell Mardikh, Syria).

Canada country occupying the northern part of the North American continent, bounded to the south by the USA, to the north by the Arctic, to the east by the Atlantic Ocean, to the northwest by Alaska, and to the west by the Pacific Ocean.

canal artificial waterway constructed for drainage, irrigation, or navigation. *Irrigation canals* carry water for irrigation from rivers, reservoirs, or wells, and are carefully designed to maintain an even flow of water over the whole length. *Navigation and ship canals* are constructed at one level between locks, and frequently link with other forms of waterway – rivers and sea links – to form a waterway system. The world's two major international ship canals are the Suez canal and the Panama canal which provide invaluable short cuts for shipping between Europe and the East and between the east and west coasts of the Americas.

Canaletto Antonio (Giovanni Antoni Canal) 1697–1768. Italian painter celebrated for his paintings of views (*vedute*) of Venice and for views of the Thames and London 1746–56.

Canaries current the cold ocean current in the North Atlantic Ocean flowing SW from Spain along the NW coast of Africa. It meets the northern equatorial current at a latitude of 20°N.

canary bird *Serinus canaria* of the finch family, found wild in the Canary Islands and Madeira. It is greenish with a yellow underside. Canaries have

Canada: Provinces

Province (Capital)	Area sq km
Alberta (*Edmonton*)	661,187
British Columbia (*Victoria*)	948,599
Manitoba (*Winnipeg*)	650,088
New Brunswick (*Fredericton*)	73,437
Newfoundland (*St John's*)	404,517
Nova Scotia (*Halifax*)	54,558
Ontario (*Toronto*)	1,068,587
Prince Edward Island (*Charlottetown*)	5,657
Québec (*Québec*)	1,540,676
Saskatchewan (*Regina*)	651,901
Territories	
Northwest Territories (*Yellowknife*)	3,379,689
Yukon Territory (*Whitehorse*)	536,327
	9,975,223

Camus French novelist and dramatist Albert Camus.

Canaletto The Bacino di S. Marco on Ascension Day *(c. 1740) Royal Collection, London.*

been bred as cage-birds in Europe since the 15th century, and many domestic varieties are yellow or orange.

Canary Islands (Spanish *Canarias*) group of volcanic islands 100 km/60 mi off the NW coast of Africa, forming the Spanish provinces of Las Palmas and Santa Cruz de Tenerife; area 7273 sq km/2808 sq mi; population (1986) 1,615,000.

Canberra capital of Australia (since 1908), situated in the Australian Capital Territory enclosed within New South Wales, on a tributary of the Murrumbidgee; area (Australian Capital Territory

Canada
Dominion of

area 9,975,223 sq mi/3,851,809 sq mi
capital Ottawa
towns Toronto, Montréal, Vancouver, Winnipeg, Edmonton, Quebec, Hamilton, Calgary
physical St Lawrence Seaway, Mackenzie river; Great Lakes; Arctic Archipelago; Rocky Mountains; Great Plains or Prairies; Canadian Shield
territories Arctic sector N of mainland
head of state Elizabeth II from 1952 represented by governor general
head of government Brian Mulroney from 1984
political system federal constitutional monarchy
exports wheat; timber; pulp and newsprint, fish, furs, oil and natural gas, aluminium, asbestos,

coal, copper, iron, nickel
currency Canadian dollar
population (1990 est) 26,527,000 (including 300,000 American Indians, some 300,000 Métis (people of mixed race) and 19,000 Inuit (or Eskimo). Annual growth rate 1.1%
life expectancy men 72, women 79
language English, French (both official); N American Indian languages and the Inuit Inuktitut
religion Roman Catholic 46%, Protestant 35%
literacy 99%
GDP 412 bn (1987); $15,910 per head
chronology
1957 Progressive Conservatives returned to power after 36 years in opposition.
1963 Liberals elected under Lester Pearson.
1968 Pearson suceeded by Pierre Trudeau.
1979 Joe Clark, leader of the Progressive Conservatives, formed a minority government.
1980 Clark defeated on budget proposals. Liberals under Trudeau returned with a large majority.
1982 Canada Act removed Britain's last legal control over Canadian affairs.
1983 Clark replaced as leader of the Progressive Conservatives by Brian Mulroney.
1984 Trudeau retired and was succeeded as Liberal leader and prime minister by John Turner. Progressive Conservatives won the general election and Brian Mulroney became prime minister.
1988 Conservatives re-elected. Free trade agreement with USA signed.
1990 Canada joined the coalition opposing Iraq's invasion of Kuwait.
1991 Constitutional reform package (the Charlottetown agreement) proposed.
1992 Self-governing homeland for Inuit approved. The Charlottetown agreement rejected in national referendum.
1993 Mulroney resigned leadership of Conservative Party but remained prime minister until a successor was appointed.

Canadian Prime Ministers

1867	John A Macdonald (*Conservative*)
1873	Alexander Mackenzie (*Liberal*)
1878	John A Macdonald (*Conservative*)
1891	John J Abbott (*Conservative*)
1892	John S D Thompson (*Conservative*)
1894	Mackenzie Bowell (*Conservative*)
1896	Charles Tupper (*Conservative*)
1896	Wilfred Laurier (*Liberal*)
1911	Robert L Bordern (*Conservative*)
1920	Arthur Meighen (*Conservative*)
1921	William Lyon Mackenzie King (*Liberal*)
1926	Arthur Meighen (*Conservative*)
1926	William Lyon Mackenzie King (*Liberal*)
1930	Richard Bedford Bennett (*Conservative*)
1935	William Lyon Mackenzie King (*Liberal*)
1948	Louis Stephen St Laurent (*Liberal*)
1957	John G Diefenbaker (*Conservative*)
1963	Lester Bowles Pearson (*Liberal*)
1968	Pierre Elliot Trudeau (*Liberal*)
1979	Joseph Clark (*Progressive Conservative*)
1980	Pierre Elliot Trudeau (*Liberal*)
1984	John Turner (*Liberal*)
1984	Brian Mulroney (*Progressive Conservative*)

Canetti Elias Canetti, the first Bulgarian to win the Nobel Prize for literature (1981).

including the port at Jervis Bay) 2,432 sq km/939 sq mi; population (1986) 285,800.

cancan high-kicking stage dance for women (solo or line of dancers) originating in Paris about 1830. The music usually associated with the cancan is the *galop* from Offenbach's *Orpheus in the Underworld*.

cancer a group of diseases characterized by abnormal proliferation of cells. Regardless of where the cancer arises, its cells are usually degenerate, capable only of reproducing themselves (tumour formation) so as to outnumber the surrounding healthy cells. Also, malignant cells tend to spread from their site of origin by the process known as metastasis.

Cancer the faintest zodiac constellation (its brightest stars are fourth magnitude), through which the Sun passes during late Jul and early Aug. It is represented as a crab, and its main feature is the star cluster Praesepe, popularly known as the Beehive. It is in the northern hemisphere, near Ursa Major.

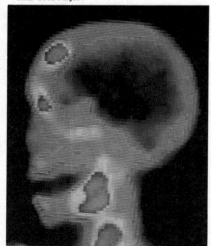

cancer Skull of a person suffering from bone cancer, showing the areas of cancerous bone in red.

candela SI unit of luminous intensity (cd). It replaces units such as the candle or standard candle.

candle means of producing light consisting typically of a vertical cylinder of wax (such as tallow or paraffin wax) with a central wick of string. A flame applied to the end of the wick melts the wax, and the burning wax produces a luminous flame. The wick is treated with a substance such as alum so that it carbonizes but does not rapidly burn out.

cane the reedlike stem of various plants such as the sugar cane and bamboo, and particularly of the group of palms called rattans, consisting of the genus *Calamus* and its allies. Their slender stems are dried and used for making walking sticks, baskets, and furniture.

Canetti Elias 1905– . Bulgarian-born writer. He was exiled from Austria as a Jew in 1938, and settled in England in 1939. His books, written in German, include the novel *Die Blendung/Auto da Fé*; and an autobiography. He was concerned with crowd behaviour and the psychology of power. Nobel prize 1981.

Canis Major· brilliant constellation of the southern hemisphere, representing one of the two dogs following at the heel of Orion. Its main star is Sirius, the 'dog star', and the brightest star in the sky.

Canis Minor small constellation of the equatorial region, representing the second of the two dogs of Orion (the other dog is represented by ◊Canis Major). Its brightest star is Procyon.

cannabis the dried leaf and female flowers (marijuana) and resin (hashish) of certain varieties of ◊*hemp Cannabis sativa* which are smoked or eaten and have an intoxicating and stimulating effect.

cannibalism the practice of eating human flesh, also called anthropophagy. The name is derived from the Caribs, a South American and West Indian people, alleged by the conquering Spaniards to eat their captives.

canning food preservation in hermetically sealed containers by the application of heat. Originated by Nicolas Appert in France in 1809 with glass containers, it was developed by Peter Durand in England in 1810 with tin cans, which are actually made of sheet steel with a thin coating of tin to postpone corrosion.

Canning George 1770–1827. British Tory politician, foreign secretary 1807–10 and 1822–27, and prime minister 1827 in coalition with the Whigs. He was largely responsible during the Napoleonic Wars for the seizure of the Danish fleet and British intervention in the Spanish peninsula.

Cannizzaro Stanislao 1826–1910. Italian chemist who revived interest in the work of Avogadro (1811) which had revealed the difference between ◊atoms and ◊molecules, and so established atomic and molecular weights as the basis of chemical calculations.

Cano Juan Sebastian del c. 1476–1526. Spanish voyager. It is claimed that he was the first person to sail around the world. He sailed with Magellan in 1519, and after the latter's death in the Philippines, brought the *Victoria* safely home to Spain.

canoeing sport of propelling a lightweight, shallow boat, pointed at both ends, by paddles or sails. Modern-day canoes are made from fibre-glass, but original boats were of wooden construction covered in bark or skin. Canoeing was popularized as a sport in the 19th century and the Royal Canoe Club in Britain was founded in 1866.

canon a type of priest in the Roman Catholic and Anglican churches. Canons, headed by the dean, are attached to a cathedral and constitute the *chapter*.

canon in theology, the collection of writings that is accepted as authoritative in a given religion, such as the *Tripitaka* in Theravāda Buddhism. In the Christian church, it comprises the books of the ◊Bible.

canon in music, a form for a number of 'voices' or parts in which each enters successively, at fixed time intervals, in exact imitation of each other. The parts may then end together or continue their repetition as in a round.

canonical hours in the Catholic church, seven set periods of devotion: *matins* and *lauds*, *prime*, *terce*, *sext*, *nones*, *evensong* or *vespers*, *compline*. In the Anglican church, the period 8 am–6 pm within which marriage can be legally performed in a parish church without a special licence.

canonization in the Catholic church, the admission of one of its members to the Calendar of ◊Saints. The evidence before the candidate's exceptional piety is contested before the Congregation for the Causes of Saints by the Promotor Fidei, popularly known as the *devil's advocate*. Papal ratification of a favourable verdict results in ◊beatification, and full sainthood (conferred in St Peter's basilica, the Vatican) follows after further proof.

canon law the rules and regulations of the Christian church, especially the Greek Orthodox, Roman Catholic, and Anglican churches. Its origin is sought in the declarations of Christ and the apostles. In 1983 Pope John Paul II issued a new canon-law code reducing offences carrying automatic excommunication, extending the grounds for annulment of marriage, removing the ban on marriage with non-Catholics, and banning trade-union and political activity by priests.

Canopus second-brightest star in the sky, magnitude –0.7, lying in the constellation Carina. It is a yellow-white supergiant about 200 light years away.

Canossa ruined castle 19 km/12 mi SW of Reggio, Italy. The Holy Roman emperor Henry IV did penance here before Pope ◊Gregory VII in 1077

for having opposed him in the question of investitures.

Canova Antonio 1757–1822. Italian Neoclassical sculptor, based in Rome from 1781. His highly finished marble portrait busts and groups soon proved popular, and he received commissions from popes, kings, and emperors. He made several portraits of Napoleon.

Cánovas del Castillo Antonio 1828–1897. Spanish politician and chief architect of the political system known as the *turno politico* through which his own conservative party, and that of the liberals under Práxedes Sagasta, alternated in power. Elections were rigged to ensure the appropriate majorities. Cánovas was assassinated in 1897 in a reprisal attack carried out by anarchists.

Cantab abbreviation for *Cantabrigiensis* (Latin 'of Cambridge').

Cantabria autonomous region of N Spain (coextensive with the province of ◊Santander; area 5,289 sq km/2,043 sq mi; population (1981) 511,000; capital Santander.

cantaloupe several small varieties of melon, *Cucumis melo*, distinguished by their small, round, ribbed fruits.

cantata in music, an extended work for voices, from Italian, meaning 'sung', as opposed to ◊sonata ('sounded') for instruments. A cantata can be sacred or secular, sometimes with solo voices, and usually with orchestral accompaniment.

Canterbury city in Kent, England, on the Stour, 100 km/62m south east of London; population (1984) 39,000.

history the Saxon capital of Kent, Canterbury has been the metropolis of the Anglican Communion since Augustine's mission to England was welcomed by KIng Ethelbert in 597. The present cathedral was begun by Lanfranc in the 11th century. St Thomas à Becket was murdered in the cathedral in 1170.

Canterbury, archbishop of primate of all England, archbishop of the Church of England, and first peer of the realm, ranking next to royalty. He crowns the sovereign, has a seat in the House of Lords, and is a member of the Privy Council. He is appointed by the prime minister. His seat is Lambeth Palace, London, with a second residence at the Old Palace, Canterbury. Robert ◊Runcie was appointed 1980.

Canterbury Tales an unfinished collection of stories in prose and verse (c. 1387) by Geoffrey Chaucer, told by a group of pilgrims on their way to Thomas Becket's tomb at Canterbury. The tales and preludes are notable for their vivid character portrayal and colloquial language.

cantilever a beam or structure that is fixed at one end only, though it may be supported partway along its length, for example a diving board. The cantilever principle, widely used in construction engineering, eliminates the need for a second main support at the free end of the beam, allowing for more elegant structures and reducing the amount of materials required. Many large-span ◊bridges have been built on the cantilever principle.

Canton former name of Kwangchow or ◊Guangzhou in China.

cantor in Judaism, the prayer leader in a synagogue; the cantor is not a rabbi, and the position can be taken by any lay person.

Canute c. 995–1035. King of England from 1016, Denmark from 1018, and Norway from 1028. Having invaded England with his father, Sweyn, king of Denmark, 1013, Canute defeated ◊Edmund

Ironside 1016, invaded Scotland, and conquered Norway. According to legend, Canute deflated his flattering courtiers by showing that the sea would not retreat at his command.

Canute (Cnut VI) 1163–1202. King of Denmark from 1182, son and successor of Waldemar Knudsson. With the aid of his brother and successor, Waldemar II and Absalon, archbishop of Lund, he resisted Frederick Barbarossa's northward expansion, established Denmark as the dominant power in the Baltic, and presided over the transformation of his country from a Viking to a feudal society.

canyon a deep narrow hollow running through mountains. Canyons are cut by river action, usually in areas of low rainfall, where the river receives water from outside the area.

Cao Chan 1719–1763. Chinese novelist (formerly Ts'ao Chan) whose tragic love story *The Dream of the Red Chamber*, which involves the downfall of a Manchu family, is semi-autobiographical.

cap. abbreviation for *capital*.

CAP abbreviation for *Common Agricultural Policy*.

capacitance, electrical ratio of the electric charge on a body to the resultant change of potential. See ◊capacitor.

capacitor device for storing electric charge, used in electronic circuits; it consists of two metal plates separated by an insulating 'dielectric'.

Cape Canaveral promontory on the Atlantic coast of Florida, USA, 367 km/228 mi N of Miami, used as a rocket launch site by ◊NASA.

Cape Cod peninsula in SE Massachusetts, USA, where in 1620 the English ◊Pilgrims landed at Provincetown.

Cape Horn most southerly point of South America, in the Chilean part of the archipelago of ◊Tierra del Fuego; notorious for gales and heavy seas. It was named in 1616 by its Dutch discoverer Willem Schouten 1580–1625 after his birthplace (Hoorn).

Čapek Karel (Matelj) 1890–1938. Czech playwright, who wrote *R.U.R.* (Rossum's Universal Robots) 1921, in which robots (a term he coined) rebel against their masters, and *The Insect Play*.

Capella brightest star in the constellation Auriga, and the sixth-brightest star in the sky. It consists of a pair of yellow giant stars 45 light years away orbiting each other every 104 days.

Cape of Good Hope South African headland forming a peninsula between Table Bay and False Bay, Cape Town. The first European to sail round it was Bartholomew ◊Diaz in 1488.

Cape Province (Afrikaans *Kaapprovinsie*) largest province of the Republic of South Africa, named after the Cape of Good Hope.

area 641,379 sq km/247,638 sq mi, excluding Walvis Bay

capital Cape Town

towns Port Elizabeth, East London, Kimberley, Grahamstown, Stellenbosch

physical Orange river, Drakensberg, Table Mountain (highest point Maclear's Beacon 1087 m/3567 ft); Great Karoo Plateau, Walvis Bay

products fruit, vegetables, wine; meat, ostrich feathers; diamonds, copper, asbestos, manganese

population (1985) 5,041,000, officially including 2,226,200 coloured; 1,569,000 black; 1,264,000 white; 32,120 Asian

history the Dutch occupied the Cape in 1652, but it was taken by the British in 1795 after the French Revolutionary armies had occupied the Netherlands, and was sold to Britain for £6 million in 1814. The Cape was given self-government in 1872. It was an original province of the Union in 1910.

caper shrub *Capparis spinosa*, native to the Mediterranean and belonging to the family Capparidaceae. Its flower buds are preserved in vinegar as a condiment.

capercaillie large bird *Tetrao urogallus* of the grouse type found in coniferous woodland in Europe and N Asia. At nearly 1 m/3 ft long, the male is the biggest gamebird in Europe, with a largely black plumage and rounded tail which is fanned out in courtship. The female is speckled brown and about 60 cm/2 ft.

Capet Hugh 938–996. King of France from 987, when he claimed the throne on the death of Louis V. He founded the *Capetian dynasty*,

---

Cape Verde
Republic of
(*República de Cabo Verde*)

area 4,033 sq km/1,557 sq mi
capital Praia
physical archipelago of ten islands 565 km/350 mi

W of Senegal
head of state Mascarenhas Monteiro from 1991
head of government Carlos Viega from 1991
political system socialist pluralist state
exports bananas, salt, fish
currency Cape Verde escudo
population (1990 est) 375,000 (including 100,000 Angolan refugees); annual growth rate 1.9%
life expectancy men 57, women 61
language Creole dialect of Portuguese
religion Roman Catholic 80%
literacy 61% male/39% female (1985)
GDP $158 million (1987); $454 per head
chronology
1974 Moved towards independence through a transitional Portuguese-Cape Verde government.
1975 Full independence achieved. National people's assembly elected. Aristides Pereira became the first president.
1980 Constitution adopted providing for eventual union with Guinea-Bissau.
1981 Union with Guinea-Bissau abandoned and the constitution amended; became one-party state.
1991 First multiparty elections held.

of which various branches continued to reign until the French Revolution, for example, ◊Valois and ◊Bourbon.

Cape Town (Afrikaans *Kaapstad*) port and oldest town in South Africa, situated in the SW on Table Bay; population (1985) 776,617. Industries include horticulture and trade in wool, wine, fruit, grain, and oil. It is the legislative capital of the Republic of South Africa, and capital of Cape Province, and was founded in 1652.

Cape Verde group of islands in the Atlantic, off the coast of Senegal.

capillary in anatomy, a fine blood vessel, between 8 and 20 thousandths of a millimetre in diameter, that connects the ◊arteries and ◊veins of vertebrates. Water, proteins, soluble food substances, gases, and white blood cells pass through the capillary wall (consisting of a single layer of cells) between the fluid (◊lymph) bathing the body tissue outside the capillary and the ◊blood within the capillary.

capillary in physics, a very narrow, thick-walled tube, usually made of glass, such as in a thermometer. Properties of fluids such as surface tension and viscosity can be studied using capillary tubes. The movement of liquids through tubes and pores, such as the upward flow of liquid in filter paper (used in a form of chromatography) is known as capillarity.

capital in architecture, a stone placed on the top of a column, pier, or pilaster, and usually wider on the upper surface than the diameter of the supporting shaft. It consists of three parts: the top member called the *abacus*, a block which acts as the supporting surface to the superstructure; the middle portion known as the bell or *echinus*; and the lower part called the necking or *astragal*. See also ◊order.

capital in economics, accumulated or inherited wealth held in the form of assets (such as stocks and shares, property, and bank deposits). In stricter terms, capital is defined as the stock of goods used in the production of other goods, and may be *fixed capital* (such as buildings, plant and machinery) which is durable, or *circulating capital* (raw materials and components) which is used up quickly.

capital bond an investment bond, which is purchased by a single payment, set up for a fixed period, and offered for sale by a life insurance company. The emphasis is on capital growth of the lump sum invested rather than on income.

capital expenditure spending on fixed assets such as plant and equipment, trade investments or the purchase of other businesses.

capital gains tax an income tax levied on the change of value of a person's assets, often property.

capitalism economic system in which the principal means of production, distribution, and exchange are in private (individual or corporate) hands, and competitively operated for profit. A *mixed economy* combines the private enterprise of capitalism and a degree of state monopoly, as in nationalized industries.

capital punishment punishment by death. It was abolished in Britain in 1965 for all crimes except treason. It is retained in many other countries, including the USA (certain states), France, and the USSR.

capitulum in botany, an inflorescence consisting of a flattened or rounded head of numerous, small, stalkless flowers. The capitulum is surrounded by a whorl of bracts, and has the appearance of a large, single flower. It is characteristic of plants belonging

Capote US novelist and journalist Truman Capote.

to the daisy family Compositae such as the daisy *Bellis perennis* and the garden marigold *Calendula officinalis*; but is also seen in parts of other families, such as scabious *Knautia* and teasels *Dipsacus*. The individual flowers are known as ◊florets.

Capodimonte village, N of Naples, Italy, where porcelain known by the same name was first produced under King Charles III of Naples about 1740. The porcelain is usually white, decorated with folk figures, landscapes, or flowers.

Capone Al(phonse) 1898–1947. US gangster, born in Brooklyn, New York, the son of an Italian barber. During the ◊Prohibition period Capone built up a criminal organization in the city of Chicago. He was imprisoned 1931–39, for income-tax evasion, the only charge that could be sustained against him. His nickname was *Scarface*.

Capote Truman. Pen name of Truman Streckfuss Persons 1924–1984. US novelist. He wrote *Breakfast at Tiffany's* 1958; set a trend with *In Cold Blood* 1966, reconstructing a Kansas killing; and mingled recollection and fiction in *Music for Chameleons* 1980.

Cappadocia ancient region of Asia Minor, in modern E central Turkey. The area includes over 600 Byzantine cave churches cut into volcanic rock, dating mainly from the 10th and 11th centuries. It was conquered by the Persians in 584 BC but in the 3rd century BC became an independent kingdom. The region was annexed as a province of the Roman Empire in 17 AD.

Capricorn in astrology, the tenth sign of the zodiac, ruled by the planet Saturn. The Sun is in this sign from Dec 22 to Jan 19.

Capricornus zodiac constellation in the southern hemisphere near Sagittarius. It is represented as a fish-tailed goat, and its brightest stars are third magnitude.

Caprivi Strip NE access strip for ◊Namibia to the Zambezi river.

capsicum plant of the nightshade family Solanaceae, native to Central and South America. The differing species produce green-to-red fruits which vary in size. The small ones are used whole to give the hot flavour of chilli, or ground to produce cayenne pepper; the large pointed or squarish pods, known as sweet peppers, are mild flavoured and used as a vegetable.

capsule in botany, a dry, usually many-seeded ◊fruit formed from an ovary composed of two or more fused ◊carpels, that splits open to release the seeds. The same term is also used for the spore-containing structure of mosses and liverworts; this is borne at the top of a long stalk or seta.

Caracalla Roman emperor 211-17.

Capuchin a member of the ◊Franciscan order of monks in the Roman Catholic church, instituted by Matteo di Bassi (died 1552), an Italian monk who wished to return to the literal observance of the rule of St Francis; their rule was drawn up in 1529. The brown habit with the pointed hood (French *capuche*) which he adopted gave his followers the name.

capuchin type of monkey, genus *Cebus* found in Central and South America, so called because the hairs on the head resemble the cowl of a capuchin monk. Capuchins live in small groups, feed on fruit and insects, and have a tail which is semi-prehensile and can give support when climbing through the trees.

capybara largest rodent *Hydrochoerus hydrochaeris*, up to 1.3 m/4 ft long and 50 kg/110 lb in weight. It is found in South America, and belongs to the guinea-pig family. It inhabits marshes and dense vegetation around water. It has thin yellowish hair, swims well, and can rest underwater with just eyes, ears, and nose above the surface.

Caracalla Marcus Aurelius Antoninus 186–217. Roman emperor. His nickname derived from the celtic cloak (caracella) that he wore. He succeeded his father Septimus Severus in 211, ruled with cruelty and extravagance, and was assassinated.

Caracas chief city and capital of Venezuela; situated on the Andean slopes, 13 km/8 mi S of its port La Guaira on the Caribbean coast; population of metropolitan area (1981) 1,162,952. Founded in 1567 it is now a major industrial and commercial centre, notably for oil companies.

Caractacus died *c.* 54 AD. British chieftain, who headed resistance to the Romans in SE England

43–51 AD, but was defeated on the Welsh border. Shown in Claudius's triumphal procession, he was released in tribute to his courage and died in Rome.

carat (US karat) unit of purity in gold. Pure gold is 24-carat; 22-carat (the purest used in jewellery) is 22 parts gold and two parts alloy (to give greater strength). The metric carat of 0.200 grams is the unit of weight for diamonds and other precious stones.

Caravaggio Michelangelo Merisi da 1573–1610. Italian painter of the early Baroque period, active in Rome 1592–1606 (which he left after killing a man), then in Naples and finally Malta. He created a forceful style, using great contrasts of light and shade and focusing closely on the subject figures, sometimes using dramatic foreshortening.

caraway plant *Carum carvi* of the umbelliferous family. It is grown for its aromatic fruit, which is used in cookery, medicine, and perfumery.

carbides compounds of carbon and one other chemical element, usually a metal, silicon, or boron.

carbohydrates a group of chemical compounds composed of carbon, hydrogen, and oxygen, all with the basic formula $C_m(H_2O)_n$.

carbolic acid common name for the aromatic compound ◊phenol.

carbon one of the most widely distributed non-metallic elements; symbol C, atomic number 6, relative atomic mass 12.011. It occurs on its own as diamonds and graphite (crystalline forms), in carbonaceous rocks such as chalk and limestone, as carbon dioxide in the atmosphere, as hydrocarbons in petroleum, coal, and natural gas, and as a constituent of all organic substances.

Carbonari a political secret revolutionary society in S Italy in the first half of the 19th century. They later played a part in ◊Mazzini's nationalist 'Young Italy' movement.

carbonates an important group of chemical compounds formed by the combination of a carbonate group (CO_3) with another element, usually a metal.

carbon cycle the sequence by which ◊carbon circulates and is recycled through the natural world. The carbon element from carbon dioxide in the atmosphere is taken up during the process of ◊photosynthesis, and the oxygen component is released back into the atmosphere. Today, the carbon cycle is being altered by the increased consumption of fossil fuels, and burning of large tracts of tropical forests, as a result of which levels of carbon dioxide are building up in the atmosphere and probably contributing to the ◊greenhouse effect.

carbohydrate
  polysaccharide

glucose molecules linked to form
polysaccharide glycogen
(animal starch)

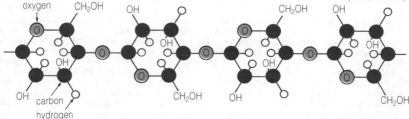

carbon

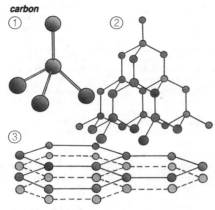

1. the basic unit of the diamond structure
2. *diamond* a giant three dimensional structure
3. *graphite* a two dimensional structure

carbon dating another name for ◊radiocarbon dating.

carbon dioxide a colourless gas (CO_2) formed by the oxidation of carbon. It is produced during the process of respiration by living things.

carbon fibre a fine, black silky filament of pure carbon produced by heat treatment from a special grade of Courtelle acrylic fibre, used for reinforcing plastics. The resulting ◊composite is very stiff and weight-for-weight has four times the strength of high-tensile steel. It is used in aerospace, cars, electrical and sports equipment.

Carboniferous the period of geological time between 360 and 286 million years ago, the fifth period of the Palaeozoic era. In the USA it is regarded as two periods – the Mississippian (lower) and the Pennsylvanian (upper). Typical of the lower Carboniferous rocks are shallow-water ◊limestones, while upper Carboniferous have ◊delta deposits with ◊coal (hence the name). Amphibians were abundant, and reptiles evolved.

carbon monoxide a colourless, odourless gas (CO) formed when carbon is oxidized in a limited supply of air. It is a poisonous constituent of car exhaust fumes, forming a stable compound with haemoglobin in the blood, thus preventing the haemoglobin from transporting oxygen to the body tissues.

carborundum silicon carbide (SiC), an artificial compound of carbon and silicon. It is a hard, black substance, used as an abrasive.

carbuncle a bacterial infection of the skin, similar to a ◊boil, but deeper and more widespread. It may only be cleared with antibiotics.

carburation regular combustion, usually in a closed space, of carbon compounds such as petrol, kerosene, or fuel oil.

Carchemish (modern Karkamis, Turkey) centre of the ◊Hittite New Empire (c. 1400–1200 BC) on the Euphrates, 80 km/50 mi NE of Aleppo, and taken by Sargon II of Assyria 717 BC. Nebuchadnezzar II of Babylon defeated the Egyptians here 605 BC.

carcinogenic liable to precipitate cancerous change in the body tissues. Many carcinogens have now been identified, including chemical substances, such as tar products, and some forms of radiation.

Cárdenas Lazaro 1895–1970. Mexican general and politician. In early life a civil servant, he took part in the revolutionary campaigns 1915–29 that followed the fall of President Diaz (1830–1915), was president of the republic 1934–40, and introduced many socialist measures.

cardiac pertaining to the heart.

Cardiff capital of Wales (from 1955), and administrative headquarters of S and Mid Glamorgan, at

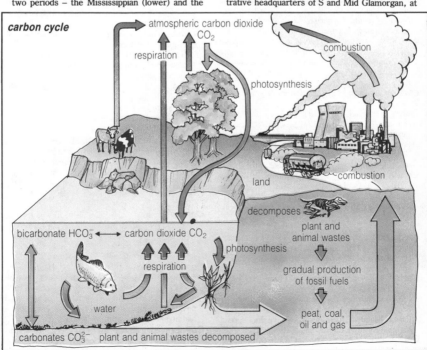

carbon cycle

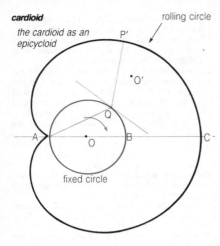

cardioid

the cardioid as an epicycloid

rolling circle

P'

O'

Q

A B C

O

fixed circle

the mouth of the Taff, Rhymney, and Ely rivers; population (1983) 279,800. Besides steelworks, there are automotive component, flour milling, paper, cigar, and other industries. The city dates from Roman times, the later town being built round a Norman castle.

Cardiganshire former county of Wales, since 1974 part of Dyfed.

Cardin Pierre 1922– . French women's and men's fashion designer, the first to show a collection for men, in 1960.

cardinal in the Roman Catholic church, the highest rank next to the pope. They act as an advisory body to the pope and elect him. Their red hat is the badge of office. The number of cardinals has varied (there were 151 in 1989).

cardinal number in mathematics, one of the series of numbers 0,1,2,3,4 . . . Cardinal numbers relate to quantity, whereas ordinal numbers (first, second, third, fourth . . .) relate to order.

cardioid heart-shaped curve traced out by a point on the circumference of a circle which rolls around the edge of another circle of the same diameter. The polar equation of the cardioid is of the form $r = a(1 + cos$ gT).

care order a court order which places a child in the care of a local authority.

Carey George Leonard 1935– . 103rd archbishop of Canterbury from 1991. A product of a Liberal evangelical background, he was appointed bishop of Bath and Wells 1987. His support of the ordination of women caused disagreement during his first meeting with Pope John Paul II 1992.

Carey Peter 1943– . Australian novelist. He has combined work in advertising with a writing career since 1962, and his novels include *Bliss* 1981, *Illywhacker* (Australian slang for 'con man') 1985, and *Oscar and Lucinda* 1988, which won the Booker prize.

cargo cult Melanesian religious movement, dating from the 19th century. Adherents believe the arrival of cargo is through the agency of a messianic spirit figure, and heralds a new paradise.

Carib a member of a group of ◊American Indian aboriginal people of South America and the islands of the West Indies in the Caribbean Sea. In 1796 the English in the West Indies deported most of them to Roatan Island off Honduras. They have since spread extensively in Honduras and Nicaragua.

Caribbean Community *(CARICOM)* organ-

ization for economic and foreign policy coordination in the Caribbean region, established by the Treaty of Chaguaramas in 1973. Its members are Antigua, Bahamas, Barbados, Belize, Dominica, Grenada, Guyana, Jamaica, Montserrat, St Christopher-Nevis, St Lucia, St Vincent and the Grenadines, and Trinidad and Tobago. Its headquarters are in Kingston, Jamaica.

Caribbean Sea part of the Atlantic Ocean between the N coasts of South and Central America and the West Indies, about 2,740 km/1,700 mi long and between 650 km/400 mi–1,500 km/900 mi wide. It is here that the ◊Gulf Stream turns towards Europe.

caribou the ◊reindeer of North America.

caricature exaggerated portrayal of individuals or types, aiming to ridicule or otherwise expose the subject. Exponents include Rowlandson, Daumier, and Grosz.

CARICOM abbreviation for ◊*Caribbean Community*.

caries decay and disintegration of the substance of teeth or bone.

Carina constellation of the southern hemisphere, representing a ship's keel. Its brightest star is Canopus; it also contains Eta Carinae, a massive and highly luminous star embedded in a gas cloud. It has varied unpredictably in the past; some astronomers think it is likely to explode as a supernova within 10,000 years.

Carinthia (German *Kärnten*) an alpine federal state of SE Austria, bordering Italy and Yugoslavia in the S; capital Klagenfurt; area 9,533 sq km/3,681 sq mi; population (1987) 542,000.

Carl Gustaf XVI 1946– . King of Sweden from 1973. He succeeded his grandfather Gustaf VI, his father having been killed in an air crash in 1947. Under the new Swedish constitution which became effective on his grandfather's death, the monarchy was effectively stripped of all power at his accession.

Carlist a supporter of the claims of the Spanish pretender Don Carlos de Bourbon (1788–1855), and his descendants, to the Spanish crown. The Carlist revolt continued, especially in the Basque provinces, until 1839.

Carlos I 1863–1908. King of Portugal, of the Braganza-Coburg line, from 1889 until he was assassinated in Lisbon with his elder son Luis. He was succeeded by his younger son Manoel.

Carlos kings of Spain; see ◊Charles.

Carlos Don 1545–1568. Spanish prince. Son of Philip II, he was recognized as heir to the thrones of Castile and Aragon, but became mentally unstable and had to be placed under restraint following a plot to assassinate his father. His story was the subject of plays by Schiller, Alfieri, Otway, and others.

Carlow county in the Republic of Ireland (county town Carlow), in the province of Leinster; area 896 sq km/346 sq mi; population (1991) 40,900. Mostly flat except for mountains in the south, the land is fertile, and dairy farming is important.

Carlson Chester 1906–1968. US scientist, who invented ◊xerography. A research worker with Bell Telephone, he was sacked from his post in 1930 during the Depression, and set to work on his own to develop an efficient copying machine. By 1938 he had invented the Xerox photocopier.

Carlsson Ingvar (Gösta) 1934– . Swedish socialist politician, leader of the Social Democratic Party, deputy prime minister 1982–86 and prime minister from 1986.

Carlucci Frank (Charles) 1930– . US politician, a pragmatic moderate. A former diplomat and deputy director of the CIA, he was national security adviser 1986–87 and defence secretary from Nov 1987 under Reagan, supporting Soviet-US arms reduction.

Carlyle Thomas 1795–1881. Scottish essayist and social critic. His works include *Sartor Resartus* 1836, describing his loss of Christian belief, *French Revolution* 1837, *Chartism* 1839, and *Past and Present* 1843.

Carmarthenshire former county of S Wales, and formerly also the largest Welsh county. It was merged in 1974, together with Cardigan and Pembroke, into Dyfed.

Carmelite order mendicant order of friars in the Roman Catholic church. The first congregation was founded on Mount Carmel in Palestine by Berthold, a crusader from Calabria, about 1155, and spread to Europe in the 13th century. The Carmelites have devoted themselves largely to missionary work and mystical theology. They are known from their white overmantle (over a brown habit) as *White Friars*.

Carmichael 'Hoagy' (Hoagland Howard) 1899–1981. US composer, pianist, singer, and actor. His best-known songs include 'Stardust' 1927, 'Rockin' Chair' 1930, 'Lazy River' 1931, and 'In the Cool, Cool, Cool of the Evening' 1951 (Academy Award).

Carmina Burana medieval lyric miscellany compiled from the work of wandering 13th-century scholars, and including secular (love songs and drinking songs) as well as religious verse. A cantata (1937) by Carl Orff was based on the material.

carnation numerous double-flowered cultivated varieties of the clove-pink *Dianthus caryophyllus*. They are divided into flake, bizarre, and picotees, according to whether the petals exhibit one or more colours on their white ground, have the colour dispersed in strips, or have a coloured border to the petals.

Carnegie Andrew 1835–1919. American industrialist and philanthropist, born in Scotland, who developed the Pittsburgh iron and steel industries. He endowed public libraries, education, and various research trusts.

Carnegie Dale 1888–1955. US author and teacher, best known for the book *How to Win Friends and Influence People* 1938.

carnelian semi-precious gemstone consisting of quartz (silica) with iron impurities which give it a translucent red colour. It is also called cornelian, and comes mainly from Brazil, India and Japan.

carnivore an animal which eats other animals. Sometimes confined to animals that eat the flesh of ◊vertebrate prey, it is often used more broadly, to include animals that eat any other animals, even microscopic ones. Carrion-eaters may or may not be included. Additionally, the name carnivore is sometimes used to refer to members of the mammalian group *Carnivora*, which includes cats, dogs, bears, badgers, and weasels.

Carnot Marie François Sadi 1837–1894. French president from 1887. He successfully countered the Boulangist anti-German movement (see ◊Boulanger) and in 1892 the scandals arising out of French financial activities in Panama. He was assassinated by an Italian anarchist at Lyons.

Carnot Nicolas Leonard Sadi 1796–1832. French soldier-scientist, who founded ◊thermodynamics;

his pioneering work was *Réflexions sur la puissance motrice du feu/On the Motive Power of Fire*.

Carnot cycle changes in the physical condition of a gas in a reversible heat engine, necessarily in the following order: (1) isothermal expansion (without change of temperature), (2) adiabatic expansion (without change of heat content), (3) isothermal compression, and (4) adiabatic compression.

carnotite important radioactive ore of vanadium and uranium with traces of radium. A yellow powdery mineral, it is mined chiefly in the W United States and the USSR.

carob small tree of the Mediterranean region, *Ceratonia siliqua*, also known as the *locust* tree. Its 20 cm/8 in pods are used as animal fodder; they are also the source of a chocolate substitute.

carol song, in medieval times associated with a round dance. The term came later to be applied to popular songs (as distinct from hymns) associated with the great annual festivals, such as May Day, the New Year, Easter, and Christmas.

Carol two kings of Romania:

Carol I 1839–1914. First king of Romania, 1881–1914. A prince of the house of Hohenzollern-Sigmaringen, he was invited to become prince of Romania, then under Turkish suzerainty, in 1866. In 1877, in alliance with Russia, he declared war on Turkey, and the Congress of Berlin 1878 recognized Romanian independence.

Carol II 1893–1953. King of Romania 1930–40. Son of King Ferdinand, he married Princess Helen of Greece and they had a son, Michael. In 1925 he renounced the succession and settled in Paris with his mistress, Mme Lupescu. Michael succeeded to the throne in 1927, but in 1930 Carol returned to Romania and was proclaimed king. In 1938 he introduced a new constitution under which he became practically absolute. He was forced to abdicate by the pro-Nazi ◊Iron Guard in Sept 1940.

Carolina two separate states of the USA; see ◊North Carolina and ◊South Carolina.

Caroline of Anspach 1683–1737. Queen of George II of Great Britain. The daughter of the Margrave of Brandenburg-Anspach, she married George, Electoral Prince of Hanover, in 1705, and followed him to England in 1714 when his father became King George I. She was the patron of many leading writers and politicians.

Caroline of Brunswick 1768–1821. Queen of George IV of Great Britain, who unsuccessfully attempted to divorce her on his accession to the throne 1820.

Carolines scattered archipelago in Micronesia, Pacific Ocean, consisting of over 500 coral islets; area 1,200 sq km/463 sq mi. The chief islands are Ponape, Kusai, and Truk in the eastern group, and Yap and Belau in the western.

Carolingian dynasty Frankish dynasty descending from ◊Pepin the Short (died 768) and named after his son Charlemagne; its last ruler was Louis V of France (reigned 966–87), who was followed by Hugh Capet.

carotene a naturally occurring pigment of the ◊carotenoid group. Carotenes produce the orange, yellow and red colours of carrots, tomatoes, oranges, and shellfish. They are also involved in photosynthesis as adjuncts to ◊chlorophyll. In animals, carotenes can be converted to vitamin A if that vitamin is lacking in the diet.

carotenoids a group of yellow, orange, red or brown pigments found in many living organisms, particularly in the ◊chloroplasts and other plastids of plants. There are two main types, the carotenes and the xanthophylls. Some carotenoids act as accessory pigments in photosynthesis, and in certain algae they are the principal light-absorbing pigments functioning more efficiently than ◊chlorophyll in low-intensity light. Carotenes can also occur in organs such as petals, roots and fruits, giving them their characteristic colour, as in the yellow and orange petals of wallflowers. They are also responsible for the autumn colours of leaves, persisting longer than the green chlorophyll, which masks them during the summer.

Carothers Wallace 1896–1937. US chemist, whose research into polymerization led to the discovery in 1930 that some polymers were fibre-forming, and in 1937 produced nylon.

carp fish *Cyprinus carpio* found all over the world. It commonly grows to 50 cm/1.8 ft and 3 kg/7 lb, but may be very much larger. It lives in lakes, ponds and slow rivers. The wild form is drab, but cultivated forms may be golden, or may have few large scales (mirror carp) or be scaleless (leather carp).

Carpaccio Vittorio 1450/60–1525/26. Italian painter of detailed scenes of his native Venice, as in the series *The Legend of St Ursula* 1490–98 (Accademia, Venice).

Carpathian Mountains Central European mountain system, forming a semi-circle through the Czech Republic-Poland-Ukraine-Romania, 1450 km/900 mi long. The central *Tatra mountains* on the Czech-Polish frontier include the highest peak, Gerlachovka, 2663 m/8737 ft.

carpe diem (Latin 'seize the day') live for the present.

carpel a female reproductive unit in flowering plants (◊angiosperms). It usually comprises an ◊ovary containing one or more ovules, the stalk or style, and a ◊stigma at its top which receives the pollen. A flower may have one or more carpels, and they may be separate or fused together. Collectively the carpels of a flower are known as the ◊gynoecium.

carpetbagger in US history, derogatory name for the entrepreneurs and politicians from the North who moved to the Southern states during ◊Reconstruction after the Civil War of 1861–65.

Carracci Italian family of painters in Bologna, noted for murals and ceilings. The foremost of them, *Annibale Carracci* (1560–1609), decorated the Farnese Palace, Rome, with a series of mythological paintings united by simulated architectural ornamental surrounds (completed 1604).

carragheen species of deep reddish branched seaweed, *Chondrus crispus*. Named after Carragheen in Ireland, it is found elsewhere in N Europe. It is exploited commercially in food and medicinal preparations, and as cattle feed.

Carrel Alexis 1873–1944. French-US surgeon, whose experiments paved the way for organ transplantation. Working at the Rockefeller Institute, Carrel devised a way of joining blood vessels end to end (anastomosing). This was important in the development of transplant surgery, as was his work on keeping organs viable outside the body.

Carrhae, Battle of battle in which the invading Roman general Crassus was defeated and killed by the Parthians in 53 BC. The ancient town of Carrhae was near modern Haran, Turkey.

carrier anyone who harbours an infectious organism without ill effects, but who can, however, pass the infection to others.

Carrington Peter Alexander Rupert, 6th Baron Carrington 1919– . British Conservative politician. While foreign secretary 1979–82, he negotiated independence for Zimbabwe, but resigned after failing to anticipate the Falklands crisis. He was secretary-general of NATO 1984–88.

Carroll Lewis. Pen name of Charles Lutwidge Dodgson 1832–1898. English mathematician and writer of children's books. Although he published mathematics books (under his own name) he is best known for the children's classics *Alice's Adventures in Wonderland* 1865, and its sequel *Through the Looking Glass* 1872, published under the pen name Lewis Carroll.

carrot hardy European biennial *Daucus carota* of the family Umbelliferae. Grown since the 16th century for its edible root, it has a high sugar content and also contains carotene, which can be converted by the human liver to vitamin A.

carrying capacity in ecology, the maximum number of animals of a given species that a particular area can support. When the carrying capacity is exceeded, there is insufficient food (or other resources) for all members of the population. The population may then be reduced by emigration, reproductive failure, or death through starvation.

Carson Christopher 'Kit' 1809–68. US frontiersman, guide, and Indian agent, who later fought for the Federal side in the Civil War; Carson City was named after him.

Carson Edward Henry, Baron Carson 1854–1935. Irish politician and lawyer, who played a decisive part in the trial of the writer Oscar Wilde. In the years before World War I he led the movement in Ulster to resist Irish ◊Home Rule by force of arms if need be.

Cartagena or *Cartagena de los Indes* port and industrial city in NW Colombia: population (1985) 531,000. Plastics and chemicals are produced here.

carte blanche (French 'white paper') no instructions, complete freedom to do as one wishes.

cartel firms which remain independent but which enter into agreement to set mutually acceptable prices for their products. A cartel may restrict output or raise prices in order to prevent entrants to the market and increase member profits. They therefore represent a form of ◊oligopoly.

Carter Elliott (Cook) 1908– . US composer. His early works show the influence of Stravinsky, but his musical language has moved on to become tough and dissonant. His works include four string quartets, the *Symphony for Three Orchestras* 1967, and *A Mirror on Which to Dwell* 1975.

Carter Jimmy (James Earl) 1924– . 39th president of the USA 1977–81, a Democrat. Born in Plains, Georgia, he served in the navy, studied nuclear physics, and after a spell as a peanut farmer entered politics in 1953. In 1976 he narrowly wrested the presidency from Ford. Features of his presidency were the return of the Panama Canal Zone to Panama, the Camp David Agreements for peace in the Middle East, and the Iranian seizure of US embassy hostages. He was defeated by Reagan in 1980.

Carter Doctrine assertion in 1980 by President Carter of a vital US interest in the Persian Gulf region (prompted by Soviet invasion of Afghanistan): any outside attempt at control would be met by force if necessary.

Cartesian coordinates in ◊coordinate geometry, a system used to represent vectors or to denote the position of a point on a plane (two dimensions) or in space (three dimensions) with reference to a set of two or more axes. The Cartesian coordinate system can be extended to any finite number of dimensions (axes), and is used thus in theoretical mathematics. It is named after Descartes.

Carthage ancient Phoenician port in N Africa, 16 km/10 mi N of modern Tunis, Tunisia. An important trading centre, from the 6th century BC it was in conflict with Greece, and then with Rome, and was destroyed 146 BC at the end of the ◊*Punic Wars*. About 45 BC Roman colonists settled in Carthage, and it rose to be the wealthy and important capital of the province of Africa. After its capture by the Vandals in 439 AD it was little more than a pirate stronghold.

Carthusian order Roman Catholic order of monks and, later, nuns, founded by St Bruno in 1084 at Chartreuse, near Grenoble, France. Living chiefly in unbroken silence, they ate one vegetarian meal a day and supported themselves by their own labours; the rule is still one of severe austerity.

Cartier Georges Etienne 1814–1873. French-Canadian politician. He fought against the British in the rebellion of 1837, and was joint prime minister with John Macdonald 1858–62. He brought Quebec into the Canadian federation in 1867.

Cartier Jacques 1491–1557. French navigator, who sailed up the St Lawrence river in 1534, and named the site of Montreal, later exploring Canada further.

Cartier-Bresson Henri 1908– . French photographer, considered the greatest of photographic artists. His documentary work was achieved using a small format camera.

cartilage flexible bluish-white connective ◊tissue made up of the protein collagen. In cartilaginous fish, it forms the skeleton; in other vertebrates, it forms the embryonic skeleton which is replaced by ◊bone in the adult, except in areas of wear such as bone endings, and the discs between the backbones. It also supports the larynx, nose, and external ear of mammals.

Cartland Barbara 1904– . English romantic novelist. She published her first book *Jigsaw* in 1921, and since then has produced a prolific stream of stories of chastely romantic love, usually in idealized or exotic settings, for a mainly female audience (such as *Love Climbs In* 1978 and *Moments of Love* 1981).

cartography the art and practice of drawing ◊maps, sometimes involving ◊projection.

cartomancy the practice of telling fortunes by cards, often ◊tarot cards.

cartoon a humorous or satirical drawing or caricature; a strip cartoon or ◊comic strip; traditionally, the base design for a large fresco, mosaic, or tapestry. Surviving examples include Leonardo da Vinci's *Virgin and St Anne* (National Gallery, London).

Cartwright Edmund 1743–1823. British inventor. He patented the power loom 1785, built a weaving mill 1787, and patented a wool-combing machine 1789.

Caruso Enrico 1873–1921. Italian operatic tenor. In 1902 he achieved a great success in Monte Carlo, in Puccini's *La Bohème*. He subsequently won worldwide fame and is today chiefly remembered for performances as Canio in *Pagliacci*, and the Duke in *Rigoletto*.

Carver George Washington 1864–1943. US agricultural chemist. Born a slave in Missouri, he devoted his life to improving the economy of the American South and the condition of blacks. He

caryatid The Erectheon, Porch of the Caryatids at the Parthenon, Athens.

advocated the diversification of crops, promoted peanut production, and was a pioneer in the field of plastics.

caryatid building support or pillar in the shape of a woman; a male figure is a *telamon* or *atlas*.

caryopsis a dry, one-seeded ◊fruit in which the wall of the seed becomes fused to the carpel wall during its development. It is a type of ◊achene, and therefore develops from one ovary and does not split open to release the seed.

Casablanca (Arabic *Dar el-Beida*) port, commercial and industrial centre on the Atlantic coast of Morocco; population (1980) 2,175,000. It trades in fish, phosphates, and manganese.

Casablanca Conference World War II meeting of the UK and US leaders Churchill and Roosevelt, 14–24 Jan 1943, at which the Allied demand for the unconditional surrender of Germany, Italy, and Japan was issued.

Casals Pablo 1876–1973. Spanish Catalan cellist, composer and conductor. He left Spain in 1939 to lived in Prades, in the French Pyrenees, where he founded an annual music festival.

Casanova de Seingalt Giovanni Jacopo 1725–1798. Italian adventurer, spy, violinist, librarian, and, according to his *Memoirs*, one of the world's great lovers. From 1774 he was a spy in the Venetian police service. In 1782 a libel got him into trouble, and after more wanderings he was in 1785 appointed Count Waldstein's librarian at his castle of Dûx in Bohemia, where he wrote his *Memoirs* (published 1826–38).

casein main protein of milk, from which it can be separated by the action of acid, rennin, or bacterial action (souring); also the main component of cheese. Commercially used in cosmetics, glues, and as a sizing for coating paper.

Casement Roger David 1864–1916. Irish nationalist. While in the British consular service he exposed the exploitation of the people of the Belgian Congo and in Peru. He was hanged for treason by the British for his part in the Irish republican Easter Rising.

Cash Johnny 1932– . US country singer, songwriter, and guitarist. His early hits, recorded for Sun Records in Memphis, Tennessee, include the million-selling 'I Walk the Line' 1956.

Cash Pat 1965– . Australian tennis player. With his powerful serve and attacking play, he won the 1986 Davis Cup for Australia and won Wimbledon in 1987.

cash crop crop grown solely for sale rather than for the farmer's own use, for example coffee, cotton, or sugar beet. Many Third World countries must grow

cassowary

cash crops to meet their debt repayments rather than grow food for their people. The price for these crops depends on Western financial interests such as multinational companies and the International Monetary Fund. In Britain, the most widespread cash crop is the potato.

cashew tree of tropical America *Anacardium occidentale*, family Anacardiaceae. Extensively cultivated in India and Africa, it produces edible kidney-shaped nuts.

cashmere a natural fibre originating from the goats of Kashmir. Used for shawls and woollens, it can also be imitated artificially.

Caslavska Vera 1943– . Czechoslovakian gymnast. She was the first of the great modern-day stylists. She won a record 21 world, Olympic and European gold medals 1959-68 (she also won 8 silver medals and 3 bronze medals).

Caspian Sea world's largest inland sea, divided between Iran, Azerbaijan, Russia, Kazakhstan, and Turkmenistan; area about 400,000 sq km/ 155,000 sq mi, with a maximum depth of 1,000 m/ 3,250 ft. The chief ports are Astrakhan and Baku. It is now approximately 28 m/90 ft below sea level due to drainage in the north, and the damming of the Volga and Ural rivers for hydroelectric power.

Cassandra in Greek mythology, the daughter of ◊Priam, king of Troy. Her prophecies (for example of the fall of Troy) were never believed, because she had rejected the love of Apollo. She was murdered with Agamemnon by Clytemnestra.

cassava plant *Manihot utilissima*, also known as **manioc**, belonging to the family Euphorbiaceae. Native to South America, it is now widely grown in the tropics for its starch-containing roots. The bitter cassava yields a flower called Brazilian arrowroot, from which tapioca and bread are made.

cassia bark of a plant, *Cinnamomum cassia*, of the family Lauraceae. It is aromatic, and closely resembles the true cinnamon, for which it is a widely used substitute. *Cassia* is also a genus of plants of the family Leguminosae, many of which have strong purgative properties; *Cassia senna* is the source of the laxative senna.

Cassiopeia prominent constellation of the northern hemisphere, representing the mother of Andromeda. It has a distinctive W-shape, and contains one of the most powerful radio sources in the sky, Cassiopeia A, the remains of a ◊supernova (star explosion), as well as open and globular clusters.

cassiterite chief ore of tin, consisting of black stannic oxide (SnO_2), usually found in granite rocks. It was formerly extensively mined in Cornwall; today Malaysia is the world's major supplier.

Cassius Gaius died 42 BC. Roman soldier, one of the conspirators who killed Julius ◊Caesar. He fought at Carrhae 53 BC, and with the republicans against Caesar at Pharsalus 48 BC, was pardoned and appointed praetor, but became a leader in the conspiracy of 44 BC, and after Caesar's death joined Brutus. He committed suicide after his defeat at ◊Philippi 42 BC.

Cassivelaunus chieftain of the British tribe, the Catuvellauni, who led the British resistance to Caesar in 54 BC.

cassowary large flightless bird, genus *Casuarius*, found in New Guinea and N Australia, usually in forests. Cassowaries are related to emus, but have a bare head with a horny casque, or helmet, on top, and brightly coloured skin on the neck. The loose plumage is black and the wings are tiny, but cassowaries can run and leap well, and defend themselves by kicking. They stand up to 1.5 m/5 ft tall.

castanets Spanish percussion instrument made of two hollowed wooden shells, held in the hand to produce a rhythmic accompaniment to dance.

caste grouping of Hindu society from ancient times into four main classes from which some 3,000 subsequent divisions derive: *Brahmans* (priests), *Kshatriyas* (nobles and warriors), *Vaisyas* (traders and farmers), and *Sudras* (servants); plus a fifth class, *Harijan* (untouchables).

Castelo Branco Camilo 1825–1890. Portuguese novelist. His work fluctuates between mysticism and Bohemianism, and includes *Amor de perdição/Love of Perdition* 1862, written during his imprisonment for adultery, and *Novelas do Minho* 1875, stories of the rural north.

Castiglione Baldassare, Count Castiglione 1478–1529. Italian author and diplomat, who described the perfect Renaissance gentleman in *Il Cortegiano/The Courtier* 1528.

Castile kingdom founded in the 10th century, occupying the central plateau of Spain. Its union with Aragon in 1479 was the foundation of the Spanish state. It comprised the two great basins separated by the Sierra de Gredos and the Sierra de Guadarrama, known traditionally as Old and New Castile. The area now forms the modern regions of ◊Castilla-León and ◊Castilla-La Mancha.

Castilian language a member of the Romance branch of the Indo-European language family originating in NW Spain, in the provinces of Old and New Castile. It is the basis of present-day

Castro (Ruz) *Cuban revolutionary and premier Fidel Castro, 1972*

castle (Top left) Stokesay Castle in Shropshire, England, was built between the 12th and 13th century. (Top right) Bodiam Castle, built by Edward Dalyngrigge in the 14th century.

standard Spanish (see ◊Spanish language) and is often seen as the same language, the terms *castellano* and *español* being used interchangeably in both Spain and the Spanish-speaking countries of the Americas.

Castilla Ramón 1797–1867. President of Peru 1841–51 and 1855–62. He dominated Peruvian politics for over two decades, bringing political stability. Income from guano exports was used to reduce the national debt and improve transport and educational facilities. He abolished the head tax on Indians and black slavery.

Castilla-La Mancha autonomous region of central Spain; population (1986) 1,665,000; area 79,230 sq km/30,591 sq mi. It includes the provinces of Albacete, Ciudad Real, Cuenca, Guadalajara, and Toledo. Irrigated land produces grain and chickpeas, and merino sheep graze here.

Castilla-León autonomous region of central Spain; population (1986) 2,600,000; area 94,147 sq km/36,350 sq mi. It includes the provinces of Avila, Burgos, León, Palencia, Salamanca, Segovia, Soria, Valladolid, and Zamora. Irrigated land produces wheat and rye. Cattle, sheep, and fighting bulls are bred in the uplands.

casting the process of producing solid objects by pouring molten material into a shaped mould and allowing it to cool. Casting is used to shape such materials as glass, plastics, and especially metals and alloys.

cast iron a cheap but invaluable constructional material, most commonly used for car engine blocks. Cast iron is partly refined pig (crude) iron, which is very fluid when molten and highly suitable for shaping by casting, as it contains too many impurities, especially carbon, to be readily shaped in any other way. Solid cast iron is heavy and can absorb great shock, but is very brittle.

castle the private fortress of a king or noble. The earliest castles in Britain were built following the Norman Conquest, and the art of castle building reached a peak in the 13th century. By the 15th century, the need for castles for domestic defence had largely disappeared, and the advent of gunpowder made them largely useless against attack. See also ◊château.

Castle Barbara, Baroness Castle (born Betts) 1911– . British Labour politician, a cabinet minister in the Labour governments of the 1960s and 1970s. She led the Labour group in the European Parliament 1979–89.

Castle Hill rising Irish convict revolt in New South Wales, Australia, 4 Mar 1804; a number were killed while parleying with the military under a flag of truce.

Castlereagh Robert Stewart, Viscount Castle-

reagh 1769–1822. British Tory politician. As chief secretary for Ireland 1797–1801, he suppressed the rebellion of 1798, and helped the younger Pitt secure the union of England Scotland, and Ireland in 1801. As foreign secretary 1812–22, he repressed the Reform movement, coordinated European opposition to Napoleon, and represented Britain at the Congress of Vienna 1814–15.

Castor and Pollux/Polydeuces in Greek mythology, twin sons of Leda (by ◊Zeus), brothers of ◊Helen and ◊Clytemnestra. Protectors of mariners, they were transformed at death to the constellation Gemini.

castor oil plant tall tropical and subtropical shrub *Ricinus communis*, also known as **Palma Christi**, family Euphorbiaceae. The seeds yield the purgative castor oil, and also ricin, one of the most powerful poisons known, which can be targeted to destroy cancer cells, while leaving normal cells untouched.

castration the removal of the testicles. It prevents reproduction, and also much modifies the secondary sexual characteristics: for instance, the voice may remain high as in childhood, and growth of hair on the face and body may become weak or cease, owing to the removal of the hormones normally secreted by the testes.

Castries port and capital of St Lucia, on the NW coast of the island; population (1988) 53,000. It produces textiles, chemicals, wood products, tobacco, and rubber products.

Castro Cipriano 1858–1924. Venezuelan dictator, known as 'the Lion of the Andes'. He seized power in 1899 and ruled for nine years of political chaos. When he refused to pay off foreign debts in 1902, British, German, and Italian ships blockaded the country. He presided over a remarkably corrupt government, there were frequent rebellions during his rule, and opponents of his regime were exiled or murdered.

Castro (Ruz) Fidel 1927– . Cuban Communist politician, prime minister 1959–76 and president from 1976. He led two successful coups against the right-wing Batista regime and led the revolution that overthrew the dictator 1959. He raised the standard of living for most Cubans but dealt harshly with dissenters.

casuarina genus of trees and shrubs with many species native to Australia and New Guinea, but also found in Africa and Asia. The river she-oak, *Casuarina cunninghamiana*, has fronded branches resembling cassowary feathers, hence the Latin name.

cat small domesticated carnivorous mammal *Felis catus* often kept as a pet and for catching small pests

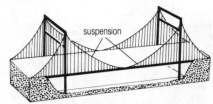

A suspension bridge takes up a catenary curve

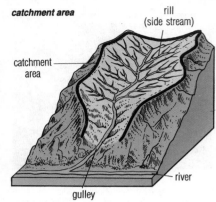

catchment area rill (side stream)

catchment area

river

gulley

such as rodents. Found in many colour variants, it may have short, long, or no hair, but the general shape and size is constant. All cats walk on the pads of their toes, and have retractile claws. They have strong limbs, large eyes, and acute hearing. The canine teeth are long and well-developed, as are the shearing teeth in the side of the mouth.

catacomb underground cemetery. Those of the early Christians beneath the basilica of St Sebastian in Rome, where bodies were buried in niches in the walls of the tunnels, are particularly well-known.

Catalan language a member of the Romance branch of the Indo-European language family, an Iberian language closely related to Provençal in France. It is spoken in Catalonia in NE Spain, the Balearic Isles, Andorra, and a corner of SW France.

Catalaunian Fields plain near Troyes, France, scene of the defeat of Attila the Hun by the Romans and Goths under the Roman general Aëtius (died 454) in 451.

Catalonia (Spanish *Cataluña*) autonomous region of NE Spain; population (1981) 5,938,208; area 31,960 sq km/12,340 sq mi. It includes Barcelona (the capital), Gerona, Lérida, and Tarragona. Industries include wool and cotton textiles, and hydroelectric power is produced.

catalpa tree found in N America, China, and West Indies, belonging to the Bignoniaceae family. The Indian bean tree, *Catalpa bignoniodes*, has been introduced into Europe. It has large, heart-shaped leaves, and white, yellow and purple streaked bell-shaped flowers.

catalyst a substance which alters the speed of a chemical or biochemical reaction but which remains unchanged at the end of the reaction. ◊Enzymes are biochemical catalysts. In practice most catalysts are used to speed up reactions.

catamaran a twin-hulled sailing vessel, based on the aboriginal craft of South America and the Indies, made of logs lashed together, with an outrigger. A similar vessel with three hulls is known as a trimaran.

cataract opacity of the lens of the eye. Fluid accumulates between the fibres of the lens and gives place to deposits of albumen; these coalesce into rounded bodies; the lens fibres break down, and areas of the lens become filled with opaque products of degeneration.

catarrh inflammation of the mucous membrane of the nose, with excessive production of mucus.

catastrophe theory mathematical theory developed by René Thom in 1972, in which he showed that the growth of an organism proceeds by a series of gradual changes, which are triggered by, and in turn trigger, large-scale changes or 'catastrophic' jumps. It also has applications in engineering; for example, the gradual strain on the structure of a bridge which eventually results in a sudden collapse, and has been extended to economic and psychological events.

Catch-22 black-humour novel by Joseph Heller, published 1961, about a US squadron flying absurd bombing missions in Italy in World War II; the crazed military justifications involved made the phrase 'catch-22' represent all false authoritarian logic.

catch crop crop that is inserted between two principal crops in a rotation in order to provide some quick livestock grazing at a time when the land would otherwise be lying idle.

Catcher in the Rye, The 1951 novel of a young man's growing up and his fight to maintain his integrity in a 'phoney' adult world; written by J D Salinger, it became an international student classic.

catchment area area from which water is collected by a river; hence area from which a school draws pupils, for instance.

Cateau-Cambresis, Treaty of treaty that ended the dynastic wars between the Valois of France and the Hapsburg Empire, 2–3 Apr 1559.

catechism teaching by question and answer on the Socratic method, but especially as a means of instructing children in the basics of the Christian creed.

categorical imperative a technical term in Kant's moral philosophy designating the supreme principle of morality for rational beings. The Imperative orders us to act only in such a way that we can will a maxim, or subjective principle, of our action to be a universal law.

category in philosophy, a fundamental concept applied to being, which cannot be reduced to anything more elementary. Aristotle listed ten categories: substance, quantity, quality, relation, place, time, position, state, action, passion.

catenary a curve taken up by a flexible cable suspended between two points, under gravity. The term is used to describe the curve of overhead suspension cables that hold the conductor wire of an electric railway or tramway.

caterpillar larval stage of a butterfly or moth.

caterpillar track a track on which track-laying vehicles such as tanks and bulldozers run, which takes the place of ordinary tyred wheels. It consists of an endless flexible belt of metal plates. A track-laying vehicle has a track each side, and its engine drives small cog wheels that run along the top of the track in contact with the ground. The advantage of such tracks over wheels is that they distribute the vehicle's weight over a wider area, and are thus ideal for use in soft and waterlogged ground conditions.

catfish fish belonging to the order Siluriformes, in which barbels (feelers) on the head are

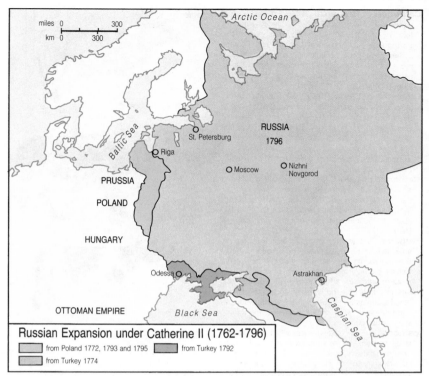

Russian Expansion under Catherine II (1762-1796)

from Poland 1772, 1793 and 1795   from Turkey 1792

from Turkey 1774

well-developed, so giving a resemblance to the whiskers of a cat. Catfishes are found worldwide, mainly but not exclusively in fresh water, and are especially plentiful in South America.

Cathar member of a sect in medieval Europe usually numbered among the Christian heretics. They started about the 10th century in the Balkans where they were called Bogomils, spread to SW Europe where they were often identified with the ◊Albigenses, and by the middle of the 14th century had been destroyed or driven underground by the Inquisition. They believed in reincarnation for everyone except their members.

cathedral Christian church containing the throne of a bishop or archbishop, which is usually situated on the south side of the choir. A cathedral is governed by a dean and chapter.

Catherine I 1683–1727. Empress of Russia from 1724. A Lithuanian peasant girl, born Martha Skavronsky, she married a Swedish dragoon and eventually became the mistress of Peter the Great. In 1703 she was rechristened as Katarina Alexeievna, and in 1711 the tsar divorced his wife and married Catherine. She accompanied him in his campaigns, and showed tact and shrewdness. In 1724 she was proclaimed empress, and after Peter's death 1725 she ruled capably with the help of her ministers. She allied Russia with Austria and Spain in an anti-English bloc.

Catherine II *the Great* 1729–1796. Empress of Russia from 1762, and daughter of the German prince of Anhalt-Zerbst. In 1745, she married the Russian grand duke Peter. Catherine was able to dominate him, and six months after he became tsar 1762 he was put out of the way and Catherine ruled alone. During her reign Russia extended its

boundaries to include territory from Turkey 1774, and profited also by the partitions of Poland.

Catherine de' Medici 1519–1589. French queen consort of Henry II, whom she married 1533, and mother of Francis II, Charles IX, and Henry III. At first outshone by Henry's mistress Diane de Poitiers (1490–1566), she became regent 1560–63 for Charles IX, and was politically powerful until his death 1574.

Catherine of Alexandria, St Christian martyr. According to legend she disputed with 50 scholars, refusing to give up her faith and marry Emperor Maxentius. Her emblem is a wheel, on which her persecutors tried to kill her (the wheel broke and she was beheaded). Feast day 25 Nov.

Catherine of Aragon 1485–1536. First queen of Henry VIII of England, 1509–33, and mother of Mary I; Henry divorced her without papal approval.

Catherine de' Medici During her regency Catherine de' Medici virtually ruled France.

Catherine of Braganza 1638–1705. Queen of Charles II of England 1662–85. The daughter of John IV of Portugal (1604–56), she brought the Portuguese possessions of Bombay and Tangier as her dowry. Her childlessness and practice of her Catholic faith were unpopular, but Charles resisted pressure for divorce. She returned to Lisbon 1692.

Catherine of Siena 1347–1380. Catholic mystic, born in Siena, Italy. She attempted to reconcile the Florentines with the Pope, and persuaded Gregory XI to return to Rome from Avignon 1376. In 1375 she is said to have received on her body the stigmata, the impression of Christ's wounds. Her *Dialogue* is a classic mystical work. Feast day 29 Apr.

Catherine of Valois 1401–1437. queen of Henry V of England, whom she married 1420, and the mother of Henry VI. After the death of Henry V, she secretly married Owen Tudor (*c.* 1400–61) about 1425, and their son became the father of Henry VII.

catheter a fine tube inserted into the body to introduce or remove fluids. The original catheter was the urinary one, passed by way of the urethra (which ducts urine away from the bladder). In modern practice, catheters are inserted into blood vessels, either in the limbs or trunk, to provide blood samples and local pressure measurements, and to deliver drugs and/or nutrients directly into the bloodstream.

cathode the electrode towards which positive particles (cations) move within a device such as the cells of a battery, electrolytic cells, and diodes.

cathode-ray tube a form of vacuum tube in which a beam of electrons is produced and focused on to a fluorescent screen. It is an essential component of television receivers, computer visual display units, and oscilloscopes.

Catholic church the whole body of the Christian church, though usually applied to the ◊Roman Catholicism.

Catholic Emancipation acts passed in Britain 1780–1829 to relieve Catholics of restrictions imposed from the time of Henry VIII.

Catiline (Lucius Sergius Catilina) *c.* 108–62 BC. Roman politician. Twice failing to be elected to the consulship in 64/63 BC, he planned a military coup, but ◊Cicero exposed his conspiracy. He died at the head of the insurgents.

cation an ion carrying a positive charge. During electrolysis, cations in the electrolyte move to the cathode (negative electrode).

Cato Marcus Porcius 234–149 BC. Roman politician. Appointed censor (senior magistrate) in 184, he excluded from the senate those who did not meet his high standards, and was so impressed by the power of ◊Carthage, on a visit in 157, that he ended every speech by saying 'Carthage must be destroyed.' His farming manual is the earliest surviving work in Latin prose.

Cato Street Conspiracy unsuccessful plot hatched in Cato Street, Edgware Road, London, to murder the Tory foreign secretary Castlereagh and his ministers on 20 Feb 1820. The leader, the Radical Arthur Thistlewood (1770–1820), who intended to set up a provisional government, was hanged with four others.

CAT scan or *CT scan* (computerized *a*xial *t*omography) a sophisticated method of diagnostic imaging. Quick and non-invasive, CAT scanning is an important aid to diagnosis, pinpointing disease without the need for exploratory surgery.

cattle

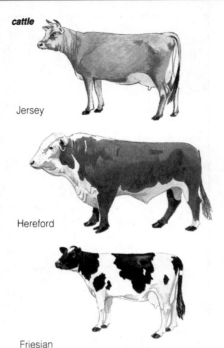

Jersey

Hereford

Friesian

cat's-eyes reflective studs used to mark the limits of traffic lanes, invented by the Englishman Percy Shaw as a road safety device in 1934.

cattle large, ruminant, even-toed, hoofed mammals of the family Bovidae, including wild species such as buffalo, bison, yak, gaur, gayal, and banteng, as well as domestic breeds.

Catullus Gaius Valerius *c.* 84–54 BC. Roman lyric poet, born in Verona of a well-to-do family. He moved in the literary and political society of Rome and wrote lyrics describing his unhappy love affair with Clodia, probably the wife of the consul Metellus, calling her Lesbia. His longer poems include two wedding-songs. Many of his poems are short verses to his friends.

Caucasoid or *Caucasian* former racial classification used for any of the light-skinned peoples; so named because the German anthropologist J F Blumenbach (1752–1840) theorized that they originated in the Caucasus.

Caucasus series of mountain ranges between the Caspian and Black Seas, in the republics of Russia, Georgia, Armenia, and Azerbaijan; 1200 km/750 mi long. The highest is Elbruz, 5642 m/18,480 ft.

caucus in the USA a closed meeting of regular party members, for example to choose a candidate for office. The term was originally used in Boston, Massachusetts, in the 18th century. In the UK it was first applied to the organization introduced by the Liberal politician Joseph Chamberlain in 1878 and is generally used to mean a local party committee.

cauliflower variety of cabbage *Brassica oleracea*, distinguished by its large flattened head of fleshy, aborted flowers. It is similar to broccoli but less hardy.

caustic soda former name for *sodium hydroxide*, NaOH.

cauterization the use of special instruments to burn or fuse small areas of body tissue with a minimum bleeding. Tiny blood vessels are cauterized to minimize blood loss in surgery.

Cauthen Steve 1960– . US jockey. He rode *Affirmed* to the US Triple Crown in 1978 at the age of 18 and won 487 races in 1977. He has ridden in England since 1979 and has twice won the Derby, on *Slip Anchor* in 1985 and on *Reference Point* in 1987. He was champion jockey in 1984, 1985 and 1987.

Cauvery or *Kaveri* river of S India, rising in the W Ghats and flowing 765 km/475 mi SE to meet the Bay of Bengal in a wide delta. It has been a major source of hydroelectric power since 1902 when India's first hydropower plant was built on the river.

Cavaco Silva Anibal 1939– . Portuguese politician. He became prime minister with a minority victory in the 1985 elections, soon after being elected leader of the Social Democratic Party (PSD). His government fell in 1987, but an election later that year gave him Portugal's first absolute majority since democracy was restored.

cavalier horseman of noble birth, but in particular a supporter of Charles I in the English Civil War, typically with courtly dress and long hair (as distinct from a Roundhead); also a supporter of Charles II after the Restoration.

Cavalier poet a poet of Charles II's court, including Thomas Carew, Robert Herrick, Richard Lovelace, and Sir John Suckling.

Cavalli (Pietro), Francesco 1602–1676. Italian composer, organist at St Mark's, Venice, and the first to make opera a popular entertainment with, for example, *Xerxes* 1654, later performed in honour of Louis XIV's wedding in Paris. Twenty-seven of his operas survive.

Cavan agricultural inland county of the Republic of Ireland, in the province of Ulster; population (1991) 52,800; area 1,890 sq km/730 sq mi.

cave a hollow in the Earth's crust produced by the action of underground water or by waves on a sea coast. Caves of the former type commonly occur in limestone, but not in chalk country where the rocks are soluble in water. A *pothole* is a vertical hole in rock caused by water descending a crack.

caveat emptor (Latin 'let the buyer beware') the buyer is responsible for checking the quality of goods purchased.

Cavell Edith Louisa 1865–1915. British matron of a Red Cross hospital in Brussels, Belgium, in World War I, who helped Allied soldiers escape to the Dutch frontier. She was court-martialled by the Germans and condemned to death. Her last words were: 'Patriotism is not enough. I must have no hatred or bitterness towards anyone.'

Cavendish Henry 1731–1810. British physicist. He discovered hydrogen, which he called 'inflammable air' (1766), the composition of water, and the composition of nitric acid.

Cavendish experiment measurement of the gravitational attraction between lead and gold spheres, which enabled Henry Cavendish to calculate a mean value for the mass and density of Earth, using Newton's Law of Universal Gravitation.

cave temple example of rock architecture, such as Ajanta in western India; Alamira, near Santander, Spain.

caviar the salted roes of the sturgeon. Caviar is prepared by beating and straining the fish ovaries until the eggs are free from fats and adding salt. The USSR and Iran are its main exporters.

cavitation the formation of cavities in fluids with loss of pressure at high velocities, in accordance with the ◊Bernoulli effect. This can result in vibra-

Cavour As prime minister of Piedmont, Cavour was largely responsible for achieving the unification of Italy in 1861.

tion, noise, and damage to, for instance, propellers or other machine parts of hydraulic engines.

Cavour Camillo Benso, Count 1810–1861. Italian nationalist politician. Prime minister of Piedmont 1852–59 and 1860–61. With British and French support, he achieved his idea of a united Italy in 1861 having expelled the Austrians 1859 and helped Garibaldi in liberating S Italy 1860.

cavy a type of short-tailed South American rodent, family Caviidae, of which the *guinea-pig* *Cavia porcellus* is an example. Wild cavies are greyish or brownish with rather coarse hair. They live in small groups in burrows.

Cawnpore old spelling of ◊Kanpur, Indian city.

Caxton William *c.* 1422–1491. First English printer. He learned the art of printing in Cologne 1471 and set up a press in Bruges, producing the first book printed in English, his version of French romance, *Recuyell of the Historyes of Troye* 1474. Returning to England in 1476 he established himself in Westminster, London, where he produced the first book printed in England, *Dictes or Sayengis of the Philosophres* 1477.

Cayenne capital and chief port of French Guiana, on Cayenne island at the mouth of the river Cayenne; population (1990) 41,700.

cayenne pepper condiment derived from the dried fruits of ◊*Capsicum*, a genus of plants of the family Solanaceae. It is wholly distinct in its origin from black or white pepper, which is derived from a different plant (*Piper nigrum*).

Cayley Arthur 1821–1895. British mathematician, who developed matrix algebra, used by ◊Heisenberg to elucidate quantum mechanics.

Cayley George 1773–1857. British aviation pioneer, inventor of the first piloted glider in 1853, and the caterpillar tractor.

Cayman Islands British island group in the West Indies.
area 260 sq km/100 sq mi
exports farmed green turtle; seawhip coral, a source of ◊prostaglandins
currency CI dollar
population (1988) 22,000
language English
government governor, executive council, and legislative assembly

cedar

history settled by military deserters in the 17th century, the islands became a pirate lair in the 18th century. Administered with Jamaica until 1962, when they became a separate colony, they are now a tourist resort, international financial centre, and tax haven.

CB abbreviation for *Citizens' Band* (radio).

CBI abbreviation for ◊*Confederation of British Industry*.

cc abbreviation for *cubic centimetres*; also abbreviation for *carbon copy/copies*.

CD abbreviation for *Corps Diplomatique* (French, 'Diplomatic Corps'); *compact disc.*

CE abbreviation for ◊*Church of England* (often *C of E*); Common Era (see under ◊calendar).

Ceauşescu Nicolae 1918–1989. Romanian politician, leader of Romanian Communist Party (RCP), in power from 1967. He pursued a policy line independent of and critical of the USSR. He promoted family members, including his wife, Elena, to senior state and party posts. Both were tried and executed following a popular uprising in Dec 1989.

Cebu chief city and port of the island of Cebu in the Philippines; population (1980) 490,000; area 5,086 sq km/1,964 sq mi.

Cecil Robert, 1st Earl of Salisbury 1563–1612. secretary of state to Elizabeth I of England, succeeding his father, Lord Burghley; he was afterwards chief minister to James I, who created him earl of Salisbury in 1605.

Cecilia Christian patron saint of music, martyred in Rome in the 2nd or 3rd century, who is said to have sung hymns under torture. Feast day 22 Nov.

cedar type of coniferous tree. The best-known is the cedar of Lebanon *Cedrus libani*, which grows to a great height and age in the mountains of Syria and Asia Minor. Of the famous forests on Mount Lebanon itself, only a few groups of trees remain. Together with the Himalayan cedar *Cedrus deodara* and the Atlas cedar *Cedrus atlantica*, it has been introduced into England.

Ceefax one of Britain's two ◊teletext systems (the other is Oracle), or 'magazines of the air', developed by the BBC and first broadcast in 1973. 'Ceefax' is a corruption of 'see facts'.

CEGB abbreviation for *Central Electricity Generating Board.*

celandine two plants belonging to different families, and resembling each other only in their bright yellow flowers. The greater celandine *Chelidonium majus* belongs to the Papaveraceae family, and is common in hedgerows. The lesser celandine *Ranunculus ficaria* is a wayside and meadow plant belonging to the buttercup family.

Celebes English name for ◊Sulawesi, an island of Indonesia.

celery plant *Apium graveolens* of the family Umbelliferae. It grows in ditches and salt-marshes, and has a coarse texture and acrid taste. Cultivated celery has its acrid qualities removed by blanching.

celestial mechanics the branch of astronomy that deals with the calculation of the orbits of celestial bodies, their gravitational attractions (such as those that produce Earth's tides), and also the orbits of artificial satellites and space probes.

celibacy a way of life involving voluntary abstinence from sexual intercourse. In some religions, such as Christianity and Buddhism, celibacy is a requirement for certain religious roles, such as the priesthood or a monastic life. Other religions, including Judaism, strongly discourage celibacy.

cell in biology, a discrete, membrane-bound portion of living matter, the smallest unit capable of an independent existence. All living organisms consist of one or more cells, with the exception of ◊viruses. Bacteria, protozoa and many other microorganisms consist of single cells, whereas a human is made up of billions of cells. Essential features of a cell are the membrane which encloses it and restricts the flow of substances in and out, the jelly-like material within, known as ◊protoplasm, the ◊ribosomes that carry out protein synthesis, and the ◊DNA that forms the hereditary material.

cell, electric in physics, apparatus in which chemical energy is converted into electrical energy; the popular name is 'battery', but this is actually a collection of cells in one unit. Electric cells can be divided into *primary*, which cannot be replenished; and *secondary*, or accumulators, which are so constituted that the action is reversible, and the original condition can be restored by an electric current.

Cellini Benvenuto 1500–1571. Italian sculptor and goldsmith working in the Mannerist style; author of an arrogant autobiography. His works include a magnificent gold saltcellar made for Francis I of France 1540–43 (Kunsthistorisches Museum, Vienna).

cello short for *violoncello*, a member of the ◊violin family of bowed string musical instruments.

cellophane a transparent wrapping film made from wood ◊cellulose, widely used for packaging, first produced by the Swiss chemist Jacques Edwin Brandenberger in 1908.

cellular radio a system of radiotelephony for vehicles that uses an interconnected network of low-powered transmitters, with each transmitter serving a limited area, or cell, about 5 km/3 mi across. The transmitters are linked to the telephone system via a central computer, which switches a telephone call to the receiver vehicle's cell.

cellulite fatty compound alleged by some dietitians to be produced in the body by liver disorder and to cause lumpy obesity. Medical opinion generally denies its existence.

cellulitis inflammation of body tissue, accompanied by swelling, redness, and pain.

celluloid transparent or translucent highly inflammable plastic material once used in photographic film, now replaced by the non-inflammable cellulose acetate.

cellulose a complex ◊carbohydrate composed of long chains of glucose units. It is the principal constituent of the cell wall of higher plants. Molecules of cellulose are organized into long, unbranched microfibrils which give support to the cell wall.

cell

Cells are the building units of living things. Most of them are tiny, measuring less than .03mm in diameter. Animal and plant cells have similar internal structures and composition, but plant cells, because of their rigid cellulose walls, are more regular in shape. Animal cells lack chloroplasts, the photosynthesizing structures of plant cells.

In animal and plant embryos, all cells tend to be identical, but gradually they change into various distinct types.

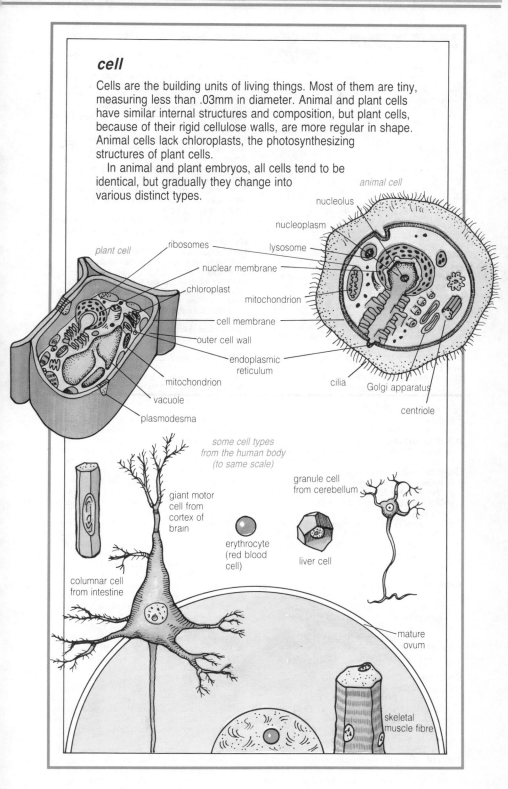

animal cell

nucleolus
nucleoplasm
lysosome
mitochondrion
cell membrane
endoplasmic reticulum
cilia
Golgi apparatus
centriole

plant cell
ribosomes
nuclear membrane
chloroplast
outer cell wall
mitochondrion
vacuole
plasmodesma

some cell types from the human body (to same scale)

giant motor cell from cortex of brain

granule cell from cerebellum

erythrocyte (red blood cell)

liver cell

columnar cell from intestine

mature ovum

skeletal muscle fibre

Central African Republic
(*République Centrafricaine*)

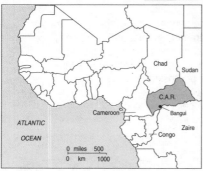

area 625,000 sq km/240,000 sq mi
capital Bangui
physical most of the country is on a plateau, with rivers flowing N and S. The N is dry and there is rainforest in the SW
head of state and government André Kolingba from 1981
political system one-party military republic
exports diamonds, uranium, coffee, cotton, timber
currency CFA franc
population (1990 est) 2,879,000; annual growth rate 2.3%
life expectancy men 41, women 45

language Sangho, French (official) Arabic, Hunsa, Swahili
religion 25% Protestant, 25% Roman Catholic, 10% Muslim, 10% animist
literacy 53% male/29% female (1985 est)
GDP $1 bn (1987) $374 per head
chronology
1960 Central African Republic achieved independence from France with David Dacko elected president.
1962 The republic made a one-party state.
1965 Dacko ousted in a military coup led by Col Bokassa.
1966 Constitution rescinded and national assembly dissolved.
1972 Bokassa declared himself president for life.
1976 Bokassa made himself emperor of the Central African Empire.
1979 Bokassa deposed by Dacko following violent repressive measures by the self-styled emperor, who went into exile.
1981 Dacko deposed in a bloodless coup, led by Gen André Kolingba, and an all-military government established.
1983 Clandestine opposition movement formed.
1984 Amnesty for all political party leaders announced. President Mitterrand of France paid a state visit.
1985 New constitution, with some civilians in the government, promised.
1986 Trial of Bokassa started for his part in the killing of schoolchildren 1979. Gen Kolingba re-elected.
1988 Bokassa found guilty and received death sentence, later commuted to life imprisonment.
1992 Abortive debate on political reform; multiparty elections promised but then postponed.

Cellulose is the most abundant substance found in the plant kingdom.

cellulose nitrate an ◊ester made by the action of nitric acid and sulphuric acid on cellulose, and used to make lacquers and explosives ('gun cotton').

Celsius a temperature scale in which one division or degree is taken as one hundredth part of the interval between the freezing point (0°C) and the boiling point (100°C) of water at standard atmospheric pressure.

Celt a people whose first known territory was in central Europe about 1200 BC, in the basin of the upper Danube and S Germany. They developed a transitional culture between the Bronze and Iron Ages, 9th–5th centuries BC (the Hallstatt culture, from its site SW of Salzburg).

Celtic art a style of art which originated in about 500 BC, probably on the Rhine, and spread with the Celts. Masterpieces of metalwork using curving incised lines and coloured enamel and coral survived at La Tène, a site at Lake Neuchâtel, Switzerland. Celtic manuscript illumination and sculpture from Ireland and Anglo-Saxon Britain of the 6th–8th centuries has intricate spiral and geometric ornament.

Celtic languages a branch of the Indo-European family, further divided into two groups: the *Brythonic* or *P-Celtic* (Welsh, Cornish, Breton, and Gaulish) and the *Goidelic* or *Q-Celtic* (Irish, Scottish, and Manx Gaelic). Celtic languages once stretched from the Black Sea to Britain, but have been in decline for centuries limited to the so called 'Celtic Fringe' of W Europe.

cement a bonding agent used to unite particles in one mass or to cause one surface to adhere to another; especially Portland cement, a powder obtained from burning together a mixture of lime (or chalk) and clay, which is the universal medium for building in brick or stone or for the production of concrete. In geology, a chemically precipitated material such as carbonate which occupies the interstices of clastic rocks.

cenotaph monument to commemorate a person or persons not actually buried at the site, as in the Whitehall Cenotaph, London, commemorating the dead of both World Wars.

Cenozoic or *Caenozoic* era of geological time that began about 65 million years ago and is still in process. It is divided into the Tertiary and Quaternary periods. The Cenozoic has seen the emergence of land animals, of mammals as a dominant group, and the formation of the mountain chains of the Himalayas and the Alps.

censor in ancient Rome, either of two senior magistrates, high officials elected every five years to hold office for 18 months. Their responsibilities included public morality, a census of the citizens, and a revision of the Senatorial list.

censor in Freudian psychology, the psychic function which prevents unconscious impulses that are unacceptable from reaching the conscious mind, that is, so-called ◊repression.

censorship the suppression by authority of material considered immoral, heretical, subversive, libellous, damaging to state security, or otherwise offensive. It is generally more stringent under totalitarian or strongly religious regimes and in wartime.

census official count of the population of a country, originally for military call-up, later for assessment of social trends as other information regarding age, sex, and occupation of each individual was included.

central nervous system

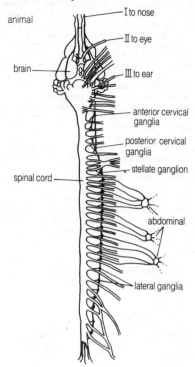

animal
— I to nose
— II to eye
brain
— III to ear
— anterior cervical ganglia
— posterior cervical ganglia
— stellate ganglion
spinal cord
— abdominal
— lateral ganglia

The first American census was taken in 1790 and the first in Britain in 1801.

centaur in Greek mythology, a creature half man and half horse. Centaurs were supposed to live in Thessaly, and be wild and lawless; the mentor of Hercules, Chiron, was an exception.

Centaurus large bright constellation of the southern hemisphere, represented as a centaur. It contains the closest star to the Sun, Proxima Centauri. Omega Centauri, the largest and brightest globular cluster of stars in the sky, is 16,000 light years away. Centaurus A, a peculiar galaxy 15 million light years away, is a strong source of radio waves and X-rays.

centigrade alternative name for the ◊Celsius temperature scale.

centipede jointed-legged animal of the group Chilopoda, members of which have a distinct head and a single pair of long antennae. Their bodies are composed of segments (which may number nearly 200), each of similar form and bearing a single pair of legs. Most are small, but the tropical *Scolopendra gigantea* may reach 30 cm/1 ft in length. *Millipedes*, class Diplopoda, have fewer segments (up to 100), but have two pairs of legs on each.

CENTO abbreviation for ◊*Central Treaty Organization*.

Central African Republic landlocked country in Central Africa, bordered NE and E by the Sudan, S by Zaïre and the Congo, W by Cameroon, and NW by Chad.

Central America the part of the Americas which links Mexico with the Isthmus of Panama, comprising Belize, Costa Rica, El Salvador, Guatemala, Honduras, Nicaragua, and Panama.

Central Asian Republic group of five republics (Kazakhstan, Kyrgyzstan, Tajikistan, Turkmenis-

tan, and Uzbekistan. Formerly part of the Soviet Union, their independence was recognized 1991. They have a large Muslim population.

Central Criminal Court in the UK, Crown Court in the City of London, able to try all treasons and serious offences committed in the City or Greater London. First established 1834, it is popularly known as the Old Bailey after part of the medieval defences of London; the present building is on the site of Newgate Prison.

central dogma in genetics and evolution, the fundamental belief that ◊genes can affect the nature of the physical body, but that changes in the body (for example, through use or accident) cannot be translated into changes in the genes.

central heating a system of heating from a central source, typically of a house, as opposed to heating each room individually with a separate fire. The most common type of central heating used in British houses is the hot-water system. Water is heated in a furnace burning oil, gas or solid fuel, and is then pumped through radiators in each room. The level of temperature can be selected by adjusting a ◊thermostat.

Central Intelligence Agency (CIA) US intelligence organization established in 1947 by President Truman. It has actively intervened overseas, generally to undermine left-wing regimes or to protect US financial interests, for example in the Congo (now Zaïre) and Nicaragua. Robert James Woolsey became CIA director 1993.

central nervous system the part of the nervous system with a concentration of ◊nerve cells which coordinates various body functions. In ◊vertebrates, the central nervous system consists of a brain and a dorsal nerve cord (the spinal cord) within the spinal column. In worms, insects, and crustaceans, it consists of two central nerve cords with concentrations of nerve cells, known as ◊*ganglia* in each segment, and a small brain in the head.

Central Scotland region of Scotland, formed 1975 from the counties of Stirling, S Perthshire, and W Lothian.
area 2,631 sq km/1,016 sq mi
towns administrative headquarters Stirling; Falkirk, Alloa, Grangemouth
products agriculture; industries including brewing and distilling, engineering, electronics
population (1991) 268,000
famous people Rob Roy Macgregor (1671–1734).

Central Treaty Organization (CENTO) military alliance which replaced the ◊Baghdad Pact in 1959; it collapsed when the withdrawal of Iran, Pakistan, and Turkey in 1979 left the UK as the only member.

Centre region of N central France; area 39,151 sq km/15,112 sq mi; population (1986) 2,324,000. It includes the departments of Cher, Eure-et-Loire, Indre, Indre-et-Loire, Loire-et-Cher, and Loiret. Its capital is Orléans.

centre of mass also called *centre of gravity*, the point in or near an object from which its total weight appears to originate and can be assumed to act. A symmetrical homogeneous object such as a sphere or cube has its centre of mass at its physical centre; a hollow shape (such as a cup) may have its centre of mass in space inside the hollow.

centrifugal force a useful (but unreal) concept in physics. It may be regarded as a force that acts radially outwards from a spinning or orbiting object, thus balancing the (real) inwardly-directed ◊centripetal force. For an object of mass m moving with a velocity v in a circle of radius

Cézanne Mountains in Provence *(c. 1886) National Gallery, London.*

r, the centrifugal force F equals mv^2/r (outwards).

centrifuge apparatus for rotating containers at high speeds. One use is for separating mixtures of substances of different densities.

centriole a structure found in the ◊cells of animals that plays an important role in the processes of ◊meiosis and ◊mitosis (cell division).

centripetal force force that acts radially inwards on an object moving in a curved path. For example, with a weight whirled in a circle at the end of a length of string, the centripetal force is the tension in the string. For an object of mass m moving with a velocity v in a circle of radius r, the centripetal force F equals mv^2/r (inwards). The reaction to this force is the ◊centrifugal force.

cephalopod type of predatory marine mollusc with the mouth and head surrounded by tentacles. They are the most intelligent, the fastest-moving, and the largest of all animals without backbones, and there are remarkable luminescent forms which swim or drift at great depths. Cephalopods have the most highly developed nervous and sensory systems of all invertebrates, the eye in some paralleling closely that found in vertebrates. Examples include octopus, squid, and cuttlefish. Shells are rudimentary or absent in most cephalopods.

cephalosporin class of broad-spectrum antibiotics. The first one was extracted from sewage-contaminated water, and other naturally-occurring ones have been isolated from moulds taken from soil samples. Synthetic cephalosporins can be designed to be effective against a particular ◊pathogen.

Cepheus constellation of the north polar region, representing King Cepheus of Greek mythology, husband of Cassiopeia and father of Andromeda. It contains the Garnet Star, Mu Cephei, a red supergiant of variable brightness that is one of the reddest-coloured stars known, and Delta Cephei, prototype of the ◊Cepheid variables.

ceramic non-metallic mineral used in articles created from powder and sintered at high temperatures. Ceramics are divided into heavy clay products (bricks, roof tiles, drainpipes, sanitary ware), refractories or high-temperature materials (linings for furnaces used in steel-making, fuel elements in nuclear reactors), and ◊pottery, which uses china clay, ball clay, china stone, and flint. Super-ceramics, such as silicon carbide, are lighter, stronger, and more heat-resistant than steel for use in motor and aircraft engines, and have to be cast to shape since they are too hard to machine.

Cerberus in Greek mythology, the three-headed dog guarding the entrance to ◊Hades, the underworld.

cereal grass grown for its edible starch seeds. The term refers primarily to barley and wheat, but may also refer to oats, maize, rye, millet, and rice. They store easily, and contain about 75% carbohydrate and 10% protein. In 1984, world production exceeded 1.8 billion tonnes. Between 1975–85, cereal yields in Britain doubled, and now commonly exceed six tonnes per hectare. If all the world's cereal crop was consumed directly by humans, everyone could obtain adequate protein and carbohydrate; however, a large proportion of cereal production, especially in affluent nations, is used as animal feed to boost the production of meat, milk, butter, and eggs.

cerebral pertaining to that part of the brain known as the cerebral hemispheres, concerned with higher brain functions.

cerebral haemorrhage the bursting of a blood vessel in the brain, caused by factors such as high blood pressure combined with hardening of the arteries, or chronic poisoning with lead or alcohol. It may cause death, or damage parts of the brain and lead to paralysis or mental impairment. The effects are usually long-term.

cerebral palsy abnormality of the brain caused by oxygen deprivation before birth, injury during birth, haemorrhage, meningitis, viral infection, or faulty development. It is characterized by muscle spasm, weakness, and lack of coordination and impaired movement.

cerebrum part of the vertebrate ◊brain, formed from two paired cerebral hemispheres. In birds and mammals, it is the largest part of the brain. It is covered with an infolded layer of grey matter, the cerebral cortex, which integrates brain function. The cerebrum coordinates the senses, and is responsible for learning and other higher mental faculties.

Ceres the largest asteroid, 1,020 km/634 mi in diameter, and the first to be discovered (by Giuseppe Piazzi 1801). Ceres is a rock that orbits the Sun every 4.6 years at an average distance of 420,000,000 km/260,000,000 mi. Its mass is about one-sixtieth that of the Moon.

Ceres in Roman mythology, the goddess of agriculture (Greek ◊Demeter).

cerium chemical element, symbol Ce, atomic number 58. It is a metal in the ◊lanthanide series, and used as a sparking component in lighter flints.

cermet a heat-resistant material containing ceramics and metal, widely used in jet engines. Cermets behave much like metals but have the great heat resistance of ceramics. Tungsten carbide, molybdenum boride, and aluminium oxide are among the ceramics used; iron, cobalt, nickel, and chromium are among the metals.

CERN nuclear research organization founded 1954 as a cooperative enterprise among European governments. It has laboratories at Meyrin, near Geneva, in Switzerland. It was originally known as the *Conseil Européen pour la Recherche Nucléaire*, but subsequently renamed *Organisation Européene pour la Recherche Nucléaire*

Cervantes Saavedra, Miguel de 1547–1616. Spanish novelist, playwright, and poet, whose masterpiece, *Don Quijote* (in full *El ingenioso hidalgo Don Quijote de la Mancha*) was published 1605. A spurious second part of *Don Quijote* prompted Cervantes to bring out his own authentic second part in 1615.

cervical cancer ◊cancer of the cervix (the neck of the womb).

Chad
Republic of
(*République du Tchad*)

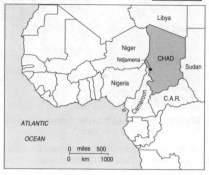

area 1,284,000 sq km/495,600 sq mi
capital N'djamena
physical savanna and part of Sahara Desert in the
N; rivers in the S flow N to Lake Chad in the marshy E
head of state and government Idriss Deby from
1990
political system emergent democratic republic
exports cotton, meat, livestock, hides, skins
currency CFA franc
population 5,064,000 (1990 est); annual growth
rate 2.3%
life expectancy men 42, women 45
language French and Arabic (both official); over
100 African languages
religion 44% Muslim (N), 33% Christian, 23%
animist (S)
literacy 40% male/11% female (1985 est)
GDP $980 million (1986); $186 per head

chronology
1960 Independence from France achieved with
François Tombalbaye as president.
1963 Violent opposition in the Muslim N, led by the
Chadian National Liberation Front (Frolinat),
backed by Libya.
1975 Tambalbaye killed in military coup led by Felix
Malloum. Frolinat continued its resistance.
1978 Malloum brought the former Frolinat leader
Hissenè Habré into his government but they were
unable to work together.
1979 Malloum forced to leave the country. An
interim government was set up under Gen
Goukouni. Habré continued his opposition with
his Army of the North (FAN).
1981 Habré was now in control of half the country,
forcing Goukouni to flee to Cameroon and then
Algeria, where, with Libyan support, he set up a
'government in exile'.
1983 Habré's regime recognized by the
Organization for African Unity (OAU) but in the
north Goukouni's supporters, with Libyan help,
fought on. Eventually a ceasefire was agreed,
dividing the country into two halves either side of
latitude 16° N.
1984 Libya and France agreed a withdrawal of
forces.
1985 Fighting between Libyan-backed and
French-backed forces intensified.
1987 Chad, France, and Libya agree on ceasefire
proposed by OAU.
1988 Full diplomatic relations with Libya restored.
1990 Habré ousted in a coup led by Idriss Déby.
New constitution adopted.
1992 Anti-government coup foiled. Two new
opposition parties approved.

---

cervical smear removal of a small sample of
tissue from the cervix to screen for changes implying a likelihood of cancer. The procedure is also
known as the 'Pap' test after its originator, George
Papanicolau.

CET abbreviation for *Central European Time*.

Cetewayo (Cetshwayo) *c.* 1829–1884. King of
Zululand, S Africa 1873–83, whose rule was
threatened by British annexation of the Transvaal
1877. Although he defeated the British at Isan-
dhlwana 1879, he was later that year defeated by
them at Ulundi. Restored to his throne 1883, he was
then expelled by his subjects.

Ceylon former name of ◊Sri Lanka.

Cézanne Paul 1839–1906. French Post-
Impressionist painter. He broke away from the
Impressionists' spontaneous vision to develop a
style that captured not only light and life, but the
structure of natural forms, in landscapes, still lifes,
portraits, and his series of bathers.

cf. abbreviation for *confer* (Latin 'compare').

CFC abbreviation for ◊*chlorofluorocarbon*.

c.g.s. system system of units based on the centimetre, gram, and second, as units of length, mass,
and time. It has been replaced for scientific work by
the ◊SI system to avoid inconsistencies in definition
of the thermal calorie and electrical quantities.

Chad, Lake lake on the NE boundary of Nigeria. It
varies in extent between rainy and dry seasons from
50,000 sq km/20,000 sq mi to 20,000 sq km/7,000
sq mi. The Lake Chad basin is being jointly developed by Cameroon, Chad, Niger and Nigeria.

Chad landlocked country in central N Africa,
bounded to the north by Libya, to the east by Sudan,
to the south by the Central African Republic, and to
the west by Cameroon, Nigeria, and Niger.

Chadli Benjedid 1929– . Algerian socialist politician, president 1979–92. An army colonel, he supported Boumédienne in the overthrow of Ben Bella
1965, and succeeded Boumédienne 1979, pursuing
more moderate policies.

chador all-enveloping black garment for women worn
by some Muslims and Hindus. It dates from the 6th
century BC and was revived by Khomeini in Iran in
response to the Koran request for 'modesty' in dress.

Chadwick James 1891–1974. British physicist. In
1932, he discovered the particle in an atomic nucleus which became known as the neutron because
it has no electric charge.

chafer type of beetle, family Scarabaeidae. The
adults eat foliage or flowers, and the underground
larvae feed on roots, especially of grasses and
cereals, and can be very destructive.

chaffinch bird *Fringilla coelebs* of the finch family,
common throughout much of Europe and W Asia.
About 15 cm/6 in long, the male is olive-brown
above, with a bright chestnut breast, a bluish-grey
cap, and two white bands on the upper part of the
wing; the female is duller.

Chagall Marc 1887–1985. French painter and
designer, born in Russia; much of his highly-
coloured, fantastic imagery was inspired by
the village life of his boyhood. He designed
stained glass (notably a chapel at Vence, in the

Chagall The Blue Circus *(1950) Tate Gallery, London.*

south of France, 1950s), tapestries, and stage sets.

Chain Ernst Boris 1906–1979. German biochemist who worked on the development of penicillin. After the discovery of ◊penicillin by Alexander Fleming, Chain worked to isolate and purify it. For this work, he shared the 1945 Nobel Prize for Medicine with Fleming and Howard Florey. He also discovered penicillinase, an enzyme which destroys penicillin.

chain reaction in nuclear physics, a fission reaction which is maintained because neutrons released by the splitting of some atomic nuclei themselves go on to split others, releasing even more neutrons. Such a reaction can be controlled (as in a nuclear reactor) by using moderators to absorb excess neutrons. Uncontrolled, a chain reaction produces a nuclear explosion (as in an atomic bomb).

Chaka alternative spelling of ◊Shaka, Zulu chief.

chalcedony a form of quartz, SiO_2, in which the crystals are so fine-grained that they are impossible to distinguish with a microscope (cryptocrystalline). It often contains large numbers of semiprecious stones such as agate.

Chaldaea an ancient region of ◊Babylonia.

chalice cup, usually of precious metal, used in celebrating the ◊Eucharist in the Christian church.

chalk *Cliffs near Lulworth, Dorset provide some of the finest coastal scenery in England.*

Chamberlain Neville Chamberlain waving the Munich Agreement that he negotiated with Hitler 1938.

chalk a soft, fine-grained, whitish rock composed of carbonate of lime, $CaCO_3$, extensively quarried for use in cement, lime, and mortar, and in the manufacture of cosmetics and toothpaste. It is not used for blackboard chalk, which is in fact ◊gypsum.

Chamberlain (Arthur) Neville 1869–1940. British Conservative politician, son of Joseph Chamberlain. He was prime minister 1937–40; his policy of appeasement towards the fascist dictators Mussolini and Hitler (with whom he concluded the ◊Munich Agreement 1938) failed to prevent the outbreak of World War II.

Chamberlain (Joseph) Austen 1863–1937. British Conservative politician, elder son of Joseph Chamberlain; as foreign secretary 1924–29 he negotiated the Pact of ◊Locarno, for which he won the Nobel Peace Prize 1925, and signed the ◊Kellogg-Briand pact 1928.

Chamberlain Joseph 1836–1914. British politician, reformist mayor of and Member of Parliament for Birmingham; in 1886 he disagreed with Gladstone's policy of Home Rule for Ireland, resigned from the cabinet, and led the revolt of the Liberal-Unionists.

chamber music music suitable for performance in a small room or chamber, rather than in the concert hall. The term is applied to music written for a small combination of instruments, played with one instrument to a part. Many such combinations are possible, but of these the string quartet is one of the most common.

Chambers William 1726–1796. British architect, popularizer of Chinese influence (as in the pagoda, Kew Gardens, London) and designer of Somerset House, London.

chameleon type of lizard, comprising some 80 or so species, which form the family Chameleontidae. Some species have highly developed colour-changing abilities, which are caused by changes in the intensity of light, of temperature, and of emotion, which affect the dispersal of pigment granules in the layers of cells beneath the outer skin.

chameleon

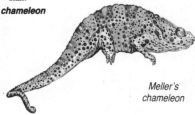

Meller's chameleon

chamois goat-like mammal *Rupicapra rupicapra* found in the mountain ranges of S Europe and Asia Minor. It is brown, with dark patches running through the eyes, and can be up to 80 cm/2.6 ft high. Chamois are very sure footed, and live in herds of up to 30 members.

champagne French sparkling wine, produced from fine grapes and blended wines, the former grown in a strictly defined area of the Marne region around Reims and Epernay in Champagne. Fermentation takes place after the bottle has been sealed, which causes the effervescence.

Champaigne Philippe de 1602–1674. French artist, the leading portrait painter of the court of Louis XIII. Of Flemish origin, he went to Paris 1621, and gained the patronage of Richelieu. His style is elegant, cool, and restrained.

champignon fungus *Marasmius oreades*, family Agaricaceae, which is edible, and a popular food in France. It is known as the fairy-ring champignon because mushrooms occur in rings around the outer edge of the underground mass of fungus.

Champlain Samuel de 1567–1635. French pioneer, soldier, and explorer in Canada. Having served in the army of Henry IV and on an expedition to the West Indies, he began his exploration of Canada 1603. In a third expedition 1608 he founded and named Quebec, and was appointed lieutenant-governor of French Canada 1612.

Champollion Jean François, le Jeune 1790–1832. French Egyptologist who in 1822 deciphered Egyptian hieroglyphics with the aid of the ◊Rosetta Stone.

Chancellor, Lord High UK state official, originally the royal secretary, today a member of the cabinet, whose office ends with a change of government. The Lord High Chancellor acts as speaker of the House of Lords, may preside over the court of appeal, and is head of the judiciary.

chancellor of the Duchy of Lancaster in the UK, honorary post held by a cabinet minister who has other nondepartmental responsibilities. The chancellor of the Duchy of Lancaster was originally the monarch's representative controlling the royal lands and courts within the duchy.

chancellor of the Exchequer in the UK, senior cabinet minister responsible for the national economy. The office, established under Henry III, originally entailed keeping the Exchequer seal.

Chancery in the UK, a division of the high court which deals with such matters as the administration of the estates of deceased persons, the execution of trusts, the enforcement of sales of land, and ◊foreclosure of mortgages. Before reorganization of the court system in 1875, it administered the rules of ◊equity as distinct from ◊common law.

Chandelā or **Candella** a Rajput dynasty which ruled the Bundelkhand region of central India from the 9th to the 11th century. They fought against Muslim invaders, until they were replaced by the Bundelās.

Chandigarh city of N India, in the foothills of the Himalayas; population (1981) 371,992.

Chandler Raymond 1888–1959. US crime writer, who created the 'private eye' hero Philip Marlowe, a hard-boiled detective, in such novels as *The Big Sleep* 1939, *Farewell, My Lovely* 1940, and *The Long Goodbye* 1954.

Chandragupta Maurya ruler of N India *c.* 321–*c.* 297 BC, founder of the Maurya dynasty (in modern Bihar, India). He overthrew the Nanda dynasty 325, and then conquered the Punjab 322 after the death of ◊Alexander, expanding his

Chanel *The French couturier 'Coco' Chanel in 1929.*

empire to the borders of Persia. He is credited as having united most of India under one administration.

Chanel Coco (Gabrielle) 1883–1971. French fashion designer, creator of the 'little black dress', informal cardigan suit, and perfumes.

Changchun industrial city and capital of Jilin province, China; population (1984) 1,809,200. Machinery and motor vehicles are manufactured. It is also the centre of an agricultural district.

change of state in physics, when a gas condenses to a liquid or a liquid freezes to a solid. Similar changes take place when a solid melts to form a liquid or a liquid vaporizes (evaporates) to produce gas. The first set of changes are brought about by cooling, the second set by heating. In the unusual change of state called sublimation, a solid changes directly to a gas without passing through the liquid state. For example, solid carbon dioxide (dry ice) sublimes to carbon dioxide gas.

Chang Jiang longest river (formerly Yangtze Kiang) of China, flowing about 6,300 km/3,900 mi from Tibet to the Yellow Sea. It is a major commercial waterway.

Changsha river port, on the Chang Jiang, capital of Hunan province, China; population (1984) 1,123,900. It trades in rice, tea, timber, and nonferrous metals; works antimony, lead, and silver; and produces chemicals, electronics, porcelain, and embroideries.

Channel, English stretch of water between England and France, leading in the west to the Atlantic Ocean, and in the east via the Strait of Dover to the North Sea; also known as La Manche (French 'the sleeve') from its shape.

Channel Islands *area* 194 sq km/75 sq mi
islands Jersey, Guernsey, Alderney, Great and Little Sark, with the lesser Herm, Brechou, Jethou, and Lihou
exports flowers, early potatoes, tomatoes, butterflies
population (1981) 128,878
language official language French (◊Norman French) but English more widely used
religion chiefly Anglican
famous people Lily Langtry
history originally under the duchy of Normandy, they are the only part still held by Britain. The islands came under the same rule as England 1066, and are dependent territories of the English Crown.

Channel swimming popular test of endurance since Capt Matthew Webb (1848–1883) first swam from Dover to Calais in 1875. His time was 21 hr 45 min for the 34 km/21 mi journey.

Channel tunnel

The rail link between the UK and France has the potential to reduce the travel time between London and Paris to about three hours, matching the total time of a journey by air. An Anglo-French consortium raised money for work to begin at both ends of the projected route in 1987, with a deadline for completion of 1993.

The machines used to bore the Channel tunnel each weigh 500 tonnes/492 tons. They have rotating heads with tungsten-carbide "picks", and special trains travel behind them to deliver equipment and remove spoil. 700,000 concrete segments will form the tunnel lining, and trackwork, mechanical and electrical equipment and signals will be installed.▶

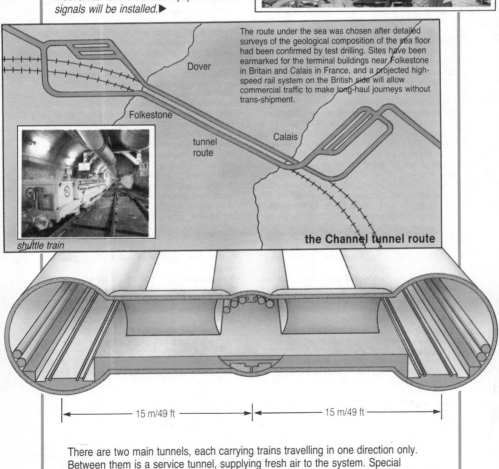

Dover

Folkestone

tunnel route

Calais

The route under the sea was chosen after detailed surveys of the geological composition of the sea floor had been confirmed by test drilling. Sites have been earmarked for the terminal buildings near Folkestone in Britain and Calais in France, and a projected high-speed rail system on the British side will allow commercial traffic to make long-haul journeys without trans-shipment.

shuttle train

the Channel tunnel route

←——— 15 m/49 ft ———→ ←——— 15 m/49 ft ———→

There are two main tunnels, each carrying trains travelling in one direction only. Between them is a service tunnel, supplying fresh air to the system. Special precautions are being taken to prevent rabid animals from using the tunnel to reach Britain, which is rabies-free.

Chaplin *Charlie Chaplin in* The Gold Rush *1925.*

Channel tunnel   a tunnel being built beneath the English Channel, linking Britain with mainland Europe. It will comprise twin rail tunnels 50 km/31 mi long and 7.3 m/24 ft in diameter located 40 m/130 ft beneath the seabed. Specially designed shuttle trains carrying cars and lorries will run every few minutes between terminals at Folkestone, Kent, and near Calais, France. The French and English sections were linked Dec 1990 and the tunnel is scheduled to be operational 1993.

chant   word used in common speech to denote any vocal melody or song, especially of a slow and solemn character; in music applied specifically to a type of simple melody used in services of the Christian Church, for singing the psalms and canticles and in some forms of Buddhism. The Ambrosian and ◊Gregorian chants are forms of ◊plainsong melody.

chanterelle   edible fungus *Cantharellus cibarius* which is bright yellow and funnel shaped. It grows in deciduous woodland.

chantry   in medieval Europe, a religious ceremony in which, in return for an endowment of land, the souls of the donor, his family, and his friends would be prayed for. A chantry could be held at an existing altar, or in a specially-constructed chantry chapel, in which the donor's body was usually buried.

chaos theory   branch of mathematics used to deal with chaotic systems, for example, an engineered structure, such as an oil platform, which is subjected to irregular, unpredictable wave stress.

Chaplin   Charles Spencer ('Charlie') 1889–1977. English actor-director. He made his reputation as a tramp with smudge moustache, bowler hat, and cane in silent films from the mid-1910s, including *The Rink* 1916, *The Kid* 1921, and *The Gold Rush* 1925. His works often contrast buffoonery with pathos, and later films combine dialogue with mime and music, such as *The Great Dictator* 1940, and *Limelight* 1952.

Chapman   George 1559–1634. English poet-dramatist. His translations of Homer (completed 1616) were celebrated; his plays include the comedy *Eastward Ho!* (with Jonson and Marston) 1605, and the tragedy *Bussy d'Amboise* 1607.

char   fish *Salvelinus alpinus* related to the trout, living in the Arctic coastal waters, and also in Europe and North America in some freshwaters, especially upland lakes.

charcoal   black, porous form of ◊carbon, produced by heating wood or other organic materials in the absence of air (a process called destructive distillation). It is used as a fuel, for smelting metals such as copper and zinc; in the form of *activated charcoal* for purifying and filtration of drinking water and other liquids and gases; and by artists for making black line drawings.

Charlemagne's Kingdom

☐ Frankish tributaries   ✗ battle
☐ Frankish Kingdoms at 768
☐ areas conquered by Charlemagne

Charlemagne

charge-coupled device *CCD* ◊semiconductor logic circuit component, employed in computers, which usually consists of alternate layers of metal, silicon dioxide, and silicon.

charged particle beam high-energy beam of electrons or protons, which does not burn through the surface of its target like a ◊laser, but cuts through it. Such beams are being developed as weapons.

Charge of the Light Brigade disastrous charge of British Light Brigade of cavalry against the Russian entrenched artillery on 25 October 1854 during the Crimean War at ◊Balaclava.

charismatic a recent movement within the Christian church that emphasizes the role of the Holy Spirit in the life of the individual believer, and in the life of the Church. See ◊Pentecostal movement.

Charlemagne Charles I, the Great 742–814. King of the Franks from 768 and Holy Roman emperor from 800. By inheritance (his father was ◊Pepin the Short) and extensive campaigns of conquest, he united most of W Europe by 804, when after 30 years of war the Saxons came under his control. He reformed the legal, judicial, and military systems, established schools, promoted Christianity, commerce, agriculture, arts, and literature.

Charles Jacques Alexandre César 1746–1823. French physicist, who studied gases and made the first ascent in a hydrogen-filled balloon 1783. His work on the expansion of gases led to the formation of Charles' law.

Charles Ray 1930– . US singer, songwriter, and pianist, whose first hits were 'I've Got A Woman' 1955, 'What'd I Say' 1959, and 'Georgia on My Mind' 1960. He has recorded gospel, blues, rock, soul, country, and rhythm and blues.

Charles two kings of Great Britain:

Charles I 1600–1649. King of Great Britain and Ireland from 1625, the son of James I of England (James VI of Scotland). He accepted the ◊Petition of Right 1628, but then dissolved Parliament and ruled without one 1629–40. His advisers were Strafford and Laud, who persecuted the Puritans and provoked the Scots to revolt. The ◊Short Parliament, summoned 1640, refused funds, and the ◊Long Parliament later that year rebelled. Charles declared war on Parliament 1642 but surrendered 1646 and was beheaded 1649.

Charles II 1630–1685. King of Great Britain and Ireland from 1660, when Parliament accepted the restoration of the monarchy; he was the son of Charles I. His chief minister Clarendon arranged his marriage 1662 with Catherine of Braganza, but was replaced 1667 with the cabal of advisers. His plans to restore Catholicism in Britain led to war with the Netherlands 1672–74 and a break with Parliament, which he dissolved 1681.

Charles (full name Charles Philip Arthur George) 1948– . Prince of the UK, heir to the British throne, and Prince of Wales since 1958 (invested 1969). He is the first-born child of Queen Elizabeth II and the Duke of Edinburgh. He studied at Trinity College, Cambridge, 1967–70, before serving in the Royal Air Force and Royal Navy. He is the first royal heir since 1659 to have an English wife, Lady Diana Spencer, daughter of the 8th Earl Spencer. They have two sons and heirs, William (1982–) and Henry (1984–). Charles and Diana separated 1992.

Charles ten kings of France, including:

Charles I see the emperor ◊Charlemagne.

Charles II *the Bald*; see ◊Charles, rulers of the Holy Roman Empire.

Charles III *the Fat*; see ◊Charles, rulers of the Holy Roman Empire.

Charles V *the Wise* 1337–1380. King of France from 1364. He was regent during the captivity of his father, John II, in England 1356–60, and became king on John's death. He reconquered nearly all France from England 1369–80.

Charles VI *the Mad* or *the Well-Beloved* 1368–1422. King of France from 1380, succeeding his father Charles V, he was under the regency of his uncles until 1388. He became mentally unstable in 1392, and civil war broke out between the dukes of Orleans and Burgundy. Henry V of England invaded France in 1415, conquering Normandy, and in 1420 forcing Charles to sign the Treaty of Troyes, recognizing Henry as his successor.

Charles VII 1403–1461. King of France from 1429. Son of Charles VI, he was excluded from the succession by the Treaty of Troyes, but recognized by the South of France. In 1429 Joan of Arc raised the siege of Orléans and had him crowned at Reims. He organized France's first standing army and by 1453 he had expelled the English from all of France except Calais.

Charles VIII 1470–1498. King of France from 1483, when he succeeded his father, Louis XI. In 1494 he unsuccessfully tried to claim the Neapolitan crown, and when he entered Naples 1495 was forced to withdraw by a coalition of Milan, Venice, Spain, and the Holy Roman Empire. He defeated them at Fornovo, but lost Naples. He died while preparing a second expedition.

Charles IX 1550–1574. King of France from 1560. Second son of Henry II and Catherine de'Medici, he succeeded his brother Francis II at the age of ten, but remained under the domination of his mother for ten years while France was torn by religious

Charles I A portrait by Daniel Mytens (1631), National Portrait Gallery, London.

wars. In 1570 he fell under the influence of the ◊Huguenot leader Admiral Coligny (1517–72); alarmed by this, Catherine instigated his order for the Massacre of St ◊Bartholomew, which led to a new religious war.

Charles X 1757–1836. King of France from 1824. Grandson of Louis XV and brother of Louis XVI and Louis XVIII, he was known as the Count of Artois before his accession. He fled to England at the beginning of the French Revolution, and when he came to the throne on the death of Louis XVIII, he attempted to reverse the achievements of the Revolution. A revolt ensued 1830, and he again fled to England. He died at Gorizia.

Charles seven rulers of the Holy Roman Empire:

Charles I better known as ◊Charlemagne.

Charles II *the Bald* 823–877. Holy Roman emperor from 875 and (as Charles II) king of France from 843.

Charles III *the Fat* 832–888. Holy Roman emperor 881–87; he became king of the West Franks 885, thus uniting for the last time the whole of Charlemagne's dominions, but was deposed.

Charles IV 1316–1378. Holy Roman emperor from 1355 and king of Bohemia from 1346. Son of John of Luxembourg, king of Bohemia, he was elected king of Germany 1346 and ruled all Germany from 1347.

Charles V 1500–1558. Holy Roman emperor 1519–56. Son of Philip of Burgundy and Joanna of Castile, he inherited vast possessions which led to rivalry from Francis I of France, whose alliance with the Ottoman Empire brought Vienna under siege in 1529 and 1532. Charles was also in conflict with the Protestants in Germany until the Treaty of ◊Passau 1552.

Charles VI 1685–1740. Holy Roman emperor from 1711, father of ◊Maria Theresa, whose succession to his Austrian dominions he tried to ensure, and himself claimant to the Spanish throne 1700; see War of the ◊Spanish Succession.

Charles VII 1697–1745. Holy Roman emperor from 1742, opponent of ◊Maria Theresa's claim to the Austrian dominions of Charles VI.

Charles (Karl Franz Josef) 1887–1922. Emperor of Austria and king of Hungary from 1916, the last of the Hapsburg emperors. He succeeded his great-uncle, Franz Josef, in 1916, but was forced to withdraw to Switzerland 1918, although he refused to abdicate.

Charles (Spanish *Carlos*) four kings of Spain:

Charles I 1500–1558. See ◊Charles V, Holy Roman emperor.

Charles II 1661–1700. King of Spain from 1665; second son of Philip IV, he was the last of the Spanish Hapsburg kings. Mentally handicapped from birth, he bequeathed his dominions to Philip of Anjou, grandson of Louis XIV, which led to the War of the ◊Spanish Succession.

Charles III 1716–1788. King of Spain from 1759, son of Philip V. On the death of his half-brother Ferdinand VI (1713–1759), he became king of Spain, handing over Naples and Sicily to his son Ferdinand (1751–1825). During his reign Spain was twice at war with Britain: during the Seven Years' War, when he sided with France and lost Florida; and when he backed the Americans in the War of Independence and regained it. At home he carried out a programme of reforms and expelled the Jesuits.

Charles IV 1748–1819. King of Spain from 1788, when he succeeded his father, Charles III, but left the government in the hands of his wife and her lover, the minister Manuel de Godoy (1767–1851). In 1808 Charles was induced to abdicate by Napoleon's machinations in favour of his son Ferdinand VII (1784–1833), who was subsequently deposed by Napoleon's brother Joseph.

Charles (Swedish *Carl*) 15 kings of Sweden. The first six were local chieftains.

Charles IX 1550–1611. King of Sweden from 1604. Regent for his nephew Sigismund, king of Poland from 1592, Charles was elected king of Sweden to depose the Polish king 1604. This involved him in war with Poland and Denmark.

Charles X 1622–1660. King of Sweden from 1654, when he succeeded his cousin Christina. He waged war with Poland and Denmark, and in 1657 invaded Denmark by leading his army over the frozen sea.

Charles XII 1682–1718. King of Sweden from 1697, when he succeeded his father, Charles XI. From 1700 he was involved in wars with Denmark, Poland, and Russia. He won a succession of victories, until in 1709 while invading Russia, he was defeated at Poltava in Ukraine, and forced to take refuge in Turkey until 1714. He was killed while besieging Fredrikshall.

Charles XIII 1748–1818. King of Sweden from 1809, when he was elected; he became the first king of Sweden and Norway 1814.

Charles XIV (Jean Baptiste Jules ◊Bernadotte) 1763–1844. King of Sweden and Norway from 1818. A former marshal in the French army, in 1810 he was elected crown prince of Sweden, under the name of Charles John (*Carl Johan*). Loyal to his adopted country, he brought Sweden into the alliance against Napoleon 1813, as a reward for which Sweden received Norway. He succeeded to the throne on the death of Charles XIII, and was the founder of the present dynasty.

Charles Albert 1798–1849. King of Sardinia from 1831. He showed liberal sympathies in early life, and after his accession introduced some reforms. On the outbreak of the 1848 revolution he granted a constitution and declared war on Austria. His troops were defeated at Custozza and Novara. In 1849 he abdicated in favour of his son Victor Emmanuel and retired to a monastery, where he died.

Charles Edward Stuart 1720–1788. British prince, known as the Young Pretender or Bonnie Prince Charlie, grandson of James II. In the Jacobite rebellion 1745 Charles won the support of the Scottish Highlanders and his army invaded England, but was beaten back by the Duke of ◊Cumberland and routed at ◊Culloden 1746.

Charles Martel *c.* 688–741. Frankish ruler (◊Mayor of the Palace) of the east of the Frankish kingdom from 717 and the whole kingdom from 731. His victory against the Moors 732 between Poitiers and Tours earned him his nickname of Martel, 'the Hammer', and halted the Islamic advance into Europe. An illegitimate son of Pepin of Heristal (Pepin II, Mayor of the Palace *c.* 640–714), he was grandfather of Charlemagne.

Charles' law law stated by Jacques Charles in 1787, and independently by Joseph Gay-Lussac (1778–1850) in 1802, which states that the volume of a given mass of gas at constant pressure increases by $1/273$ of its volume at $0°C$ for each degree C rise of temperature, that is, the coefficient of expansion of all gases is the same. The law is only approximately true and the coefficient of expansion is generally taken as 0.003663 per degree C.

Charleston a popular back-kicking dance of the 1920s which originated in Charleston, South

château *The château of Azay le Rideau, France.*

Carolina, and became a national craze in the USA.

charlock plant *Sinapis arvensis* of the family Cruciferae, also known as **wild mustard**. It is a common annual weed in Britain, reaching a height of 60 cm/2 ft, with yellow flowers.

Charlotte Sophia 1744–1818. British queen consort. The daughter of the German duke of Mecklenburg-Strelitz, she married George III of Great Britain and Ireland 1761, and bore him nine sons and six daughters.

Charlton Robert 'Bobby' 1937– . English footballer who scored a record 49 goals in 106 appearances for his country. He spent most of his playing career with Manchester United.

Charon in Greek mythology, the boatman who ferried the dead over the river Styx to the underworld.

Charpentier Marc-Antoine 1645–1704. French composer. His music is mostly sacred, and includes a number of masses; other works include the opera *Médée* 1693.

Charter 88 British political campaign which began 1988, calling for a written constitution to prevent what it termed the development of 'an elective dictatorship'. Those who signed the Charter, including many figures from the arts, objected to what they saw as the autocratic premiership of Prime Minister Margaret Thatcher.

Chartism radical British democratic movement, mainly of the working classes, which flourished around 1838–50. It derived its name from the People's Charter, a programme comprising six points: universal male suffrage, equal electoral districts, vote by ballot, annual parliaments, abolition of the property qualification for, and payment of, Members of Parliament.

Chartreuse, La Grande the original home of the Carthusian order of Roman Catholic monks, established by St Bruno around 1084, in a remote valley 23 km/14 mi NNE of Grenoble (in the modern *département* of Isère), France. The present buildings date from the 17th century.

Charybdis in Greek mythology, a whirlpool formed by a monster of the same name on one side of the narrow straits of Messina, Sicily, opposite the monster Scylla.

chasing indentation of a design on metal by small chisels and hammers. This method of decoration was familiar in ancient Egypt, Assyria, and Greece.

château term originally applied to a French medieval castle, but now used to describe a country house or important residence in France. The château was first used as a domestic building in the late 15th century; by the reign of Louis XIII (1610–43) fortifications such as moats and keeps were no longer used.

Chateaubriand François René, vicomte de 1768–1848. French author. In exile from the French Revolution 1794–99, he wrote *Atala* 1801 (written after his encounters with N American Indians); and the autobiographical *René*, which formed part of *Le Génie de Christianisme/The Genius of Christianity* 1802.

Chatterton Thomas 1752–1770. English poet, whose medieval-style poems were to inspire English Romanticism. Born in Bristol, he studied ancient documents he found in the Church of St Mary Redcliffe, and composed poems he ascribed to a 15th-century monk, 'Thomas Rowley', which were accepted as genuine. He committed suicide in London, after becoming destitute.

Chatwin Bruce 1940–1989. British writer. His works include *The Songlines* 1987, written after living with nomadic Aborigines, and *Utz* 1988, a novel based in Prague.

Chaucer Geoffrey c. 1340–1400. English poet. Author of *The Canterbury Tales* about 1387, a collection of tales told by pilgrims on their way to the Thomas Becket shrine, he was the most influential English poet of the Middle Ages. The popularity of his work assured the dominance of southern English in literature. Chaucer's other work includes the French-influenced *Romance of the Rose* and an adaptation of Boccaccio's *Troilus and Criseyde*.

chauvinism a warlike patriotism, as exhibited by Nicholas Chauvin, one of Napoleon I's veterans and his fanatical admirer. In the mid-20th century the expression **male chauvinism** was coined to mean the belief in superiority of the male sex over the female.

Chávez (y Ramírez) Carlos (Antonio de Padua) 1899–1978. Mexican composer. A student of the piano and of the complex rhythms of his country's folk music, he founded the Mexico Symphony Orchestra. His works include a number of ballets, seven symphonies, and concertos for both violin and piano.

cheese the curd of milk (from cows, goats, or sheep), separated from the whey and variously treated to produce three main types:

Chaucer *Posthumous portrait by an unknown artist, National Portrait Gallery, London.*

cheese

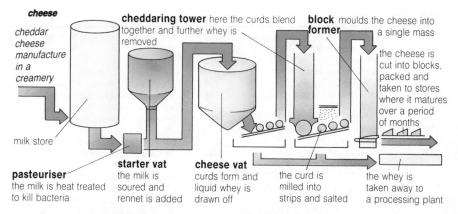

cheddar cheese manufacture in a creamery

cheddaring tower here the curds blend together and further whey is removed

block former moulds the cheese into a single mass

the cheese is cut into blocks, packed and taken to stores where it matures over a period of months

milk store

pasteuriser the milk is heat treated to kill bacteria

starter vat the milk is soured and rennet is added

cheese vat curds form and liquid whey is drawn off

the curd is milled into strips and salted

the whey is taken away to a processing plant

hard-pressed: Cheddar, Cheshire, Parmesan, Gruyère, which are the most important nutritionally and economically.
semi-hard: Stilton, Gorgonzola, Wensleydale, Roquefort, Pont l'Evêque, Gouda.
soft: Camembert, Brie, Quark/Fromou.

cheetah large wild cat *Acinonyx jubatus* native to Africa, Arabia, and SW Asia, but now rare in some areas. It is yellowish with black spots, and has a slim lithe build. It is up to 1 m/3 ft tall at the shoulder, and up to 1.5 m/5 ft long. It can reach 110 kph/70 mph, but tires after about 400 metres. Cheetahs live in open country where they hunt small antelopes, hares, and birds.

Cheka secret police operating in the USSR 1918–23. It originated from the tsarist Okhrana and became successively the OGPU (GPU) 1923–34, NKVD 1934–46, MVD 1946–53, and the ◊KGB from 1954.

Chekhov Anton (Pavlovich) 1860–1904. Russian dramatist and writer. He began to write short stories and comic sketches as a medical student. His plays concentrate on the creation of atmosphere and delineation of internal development, rather than external action. His first play *Ivanov* 1887 was a failure, as was *The Seagull* 1896 until revived by Stanislavsky 1898 at the Moscow Arts Theatre, for which Chekhov went on to write his major plays *Uncle Vanya* 1899, *The Three Sisters* 1901 and *The Cherry Orchard* 1904.

chela in Hinduism, a follower or pupil of a guru (teacher).

Chelsea porcelain factory English porcelain factory, thought to be the first. Based in southwest London, it dates from the 1740s and produced softpaste porcelain. Later items are distinguishable from the anchor mark on the base. The factory was taken over by William Duesbury of Derby 1769 (after which the so-called 'Chelsea-Derby' was produced), and pulled down 1784.

Chekhov *Russian writer Anton Chekhov.*

Chelyabinsk industrial town and capital of Chelyabinsk region, W Siberia, Russia; population (1987) 1,119,000. It has iron and engineering works, and makes chemicals, motor vehicles, and aircraft.

chemical element another name for ◊element.

chemical equation method of indicating the reactants and products of a chemical reaction using chemical symbols and formulae. These may indicate atoms, ions, radicals, or molecules.

chemical warfare use of gaseous, liquid, or solid substances with toxic effect on humans, animals, or plants; together with biological warfare, it was banned 1925 although this has not always been observed. In 1989, the 149-nation Conference on Chemical Weapons unanimously voted to outlaw chemical weapons.

irritant gases may cause permanent injury or death. Examples include chlorine, phosgene (Cl_2CO), and mustard gas ($C_4H_8Cl_2S$), used in World War I and allegedly in Afghanistan, Laos, and by Iraq against Iran.

tear gases for example, CS gas used in riot control, are intended to have less permanent effect.

nerve gases are organophosphorus compounds allied to insecticides which are taken into the body through the skin and lungs, and break down the action of the nervous system. Developed by the Germans for World War II, they were not used.

incapacitants are drugs designed to put an enemy temporarily out of action by, for example, impairing vision or inducing hallucinations. They have not so far been used.

toxins are poisons to be eaten, drunk, or injected, for example, ricin (derived from the castor oil plant) and the botulism toxin. Ricin has been used in individual cases, and other toxins were allegedly used by the former USSR in Afghanistan and by the Vietnamese in Kampuchea.

herbicides are defoliants used to destroy vegetation sheltering guerrillas and the crops of hostile populations. They were used in Malaya by the UK, and in Vietnam by the USA. Agent Orange (see ◊dioxin) became notorious because of later allegations that it caused cancer and birth abnormalities among Vietnam War veterans and US factory staff. Some stocks are held by a number of countries for retaliation or the development of preventative measures.

binary weapons are two chemical components that become toxic in combination, when the shell containing them is fired. See also ◊biological warfare.

chemistry: chronology

1AD	Gold, silver, copper, lead, iron, tin, and mercury were known.	**1850**	Ammonia was first made from coal-gas.
1100	Alcohol was first distilled.	**1858**	Cannizzaro's method of atomic weights was expounded.
1242	Gunpowder was introduced to Europe from the Far East.	**1866**	Nobel invented dynamite.
1604	Italian mathematician, astronomer and physicist Galileo invented the thermometer.	**1868**	The first plastic substance – celluloid – was made.
1649	Carbon, sulphur, antimony, and arsenic were known.	**1869**	Mendeleyev expounded his Periodic Table.
1660	Law concerning effect of pressure on gas (*Boyle's Law*) was established by English chemist Robert Boyle.	**1879**	Saccharin was discovered.
		1886	French chemist Ferdinand Moissan isolated fluorine.
1742	Invention of the Centigrade scale.	**1894**	Ramsay and Rayleigh discovered inert gases.
1746	Lead chamber process developed for manufacturing sulphuric acid; German chemist Andreas Marggraf discovered zinc.	**1897**	The electron was discovered by English physicist Sir Joseph Thomson.
		1898	The Curies discovered radium.
1750	Swedish chemist Axel Cronstedt discovered cobalt and nickel.	**1912**	Vitamins were discovered by British biochemist Gowland Hopkins; British physicist Lawrence Bragg demonstrated that crystals have a regular arrangement of atoms.
1756	Scottish chemist and physicist Joseph Black discovered carbon dioxide.		
1772	German chemist Karl Scheele discovered oxygen, two years before Priestley.	**1919**	Artificial disintegration of atoms by Rutherford.
1774	Scheel discovered chlorine; Swedish chemist Johan Gahn discovered manganese	**1920**	Rutherford discovered the proton.
		1927	British chemist Neil Sidgwick's *theory of valency* was announced.
1777	Lavoisier explained burning; sulphur was known to be an element.	**1932**	Deuterium (heavy water) was discovered; Chadwick discovered the neutron.
1779	Dutch scientist Jan Ingenhousz demonstrated photosynthesis.		
1781	English scientist Henry Cavendish showed water to be a compound.	**1933**	British chemist Norman Haworth synthesized Vitamin C.
1792	Italian physicist Alessandro Volta demonstrated the electrochemical series.	**1942**	Plutonium was first synthesized.
		1945	The atomic bomb was exploded.
1800	Volta designed his electric battery.	**1953**	Hydrogen was converted to helium.
1803	Dalton expounded his atomic theory.	**1954**	Einsteinium and fermium were synthesized.
1807	Sodium and potassium were first prepared by Davy.	**1955**	Ilya Prigogine described the thermodynamics of irreversible processes.
1811	Publication of Italian physicist Amedeo Avogadro's hypothesis on the relationship of volumes of gases and numbers of molecules to temperature and pressure.	**1962**	Neil Bartlett prepared the first compound of an inert gas, xenon hexafluoroplatinate.
		1965	Robert B Woodward synthesized complex organic compounds.
1813	French chemist Bernard Courtois discovered iodine.	**1982**	Element 109, unnilennium, synthesized.
1818	Berzelius's atomic symbols were elaborated.	**1985**	Fullerenes were discovered by Harold Kroto and David Walton at the University of Sussex, England.
1819	French scientists Henri Dulong and Alexis-Thérèse Petit's *law of atomic heats* was demonstrated.	**1987**	US chemists Donald Cram and Charles Pederson, and Jean-Marie Lehn of France created artificial molecules that mimic the vital chemical reactions of life processes.
1828	The first organic compounds, alcohol and urea, were synthesized.		
1834	Faraday expounded the *laws of electrolysis*.		
1836	Acetylene was discovered.	**1990**	Jean-Marie Lehn, Ulrich Koert, and Margaret Harding reported the synthesis of a new class of compounds, called nucleohelicates, that mimic the double helical structure of DNA, turned inside out.
1840	Liebig expounded the carbon and nitrogen cycles.		
1846	Scottish chemist Thomas Graham's *law of diffusion* (*Graham's Law*) was expounded.		

Chernobyl The damage caused to the Chernobyl nuclear reactor following the 1986 disaster.

chemiluminescence alternative term for ◊bioluminescence.

chemisorption in chemistry, the attachment, by chemical means, of a single layer of molecules, atoms, or ions of gas to the surface of a solid or, less frequently, a liquid. It is the basis of catalysis and of great industrial importance.

chemistry the science concerned with the composition of matter, and of the changes which take place in it under certain conditions.

Chemnitz (formerly *Karl-Marx-Stadt*) industrial city (engineering, textiles, chemicals) in Germany, on the river Chemnitz, 65 km/40 mi SSE of Leipzig; population (1990) 310,000.

chemosynthesis method of making ◊protoplasm (contents of a cell) using the energy from chemical reactions, in contrast to the use of light energy employed for the same purpose in ◊photosynthesis. The process is used by certain bacteria, which can synthesize organic compounds from carbon dioxide and water using the energy from special methods of ◊respiration.

Chengdu formerly *Chengtu* ancient city capital of Sichuan province, China; population (1989) 2,780,000. It is an important rail junction and has railway workshops, textile, electronics, and engineering industries.

cheque (US *check*) an order written by the drawer to a bank to pay a specific sum on demand.

cheque card card issued from 1968 by savings and clearings banks in Europe, which guarantees payment by the issuing bank when it is presented with a cheque for payment of goods or service.

Chequers country home of the prime minister of the UK. It is an Elizabethan mansion in the Chiltern hills near Princes Risborough, Buckinghamshire, and was given to the nation by Lord Lee of Fareham under the Chequers Estate Act 1917, which came into effect Jan 1921.

Cherenkov Pavel 1904– . Soviet physicist. In 1934, he discovered *Cherenkov radiation*; this occurs as a bluish light when charged atomic particles pass through water or other media at a speed in excess of that of light in that medium.

Chernenko Konstantin 1911–1985. Soviet politician, leader of the Soviet Communist Party (CPSU) and president 1984–85. He was a protégé of Brezhnev and from 1978 a Politburo member.

Chernobyl town in central Ukraine. In Apr 1986, a leak, caused by overheating, occurred in a nonpressurized boiling-water nuclear reactor. The resulting clouds of radioactive isotopes were traced as far away as Sweden; many people were killed or disabled, and thousands of square kilometres contaminated.

Cherokee North ◊American Indian people, formerly living in the mountain country of Alabama, the Carolinas, Georgia, and Tennessee. They now live mainly in North Carolina and Oklahoma, where they established their capital at Tahlequah. Their language belongs to the Iroquoian family.

cherry tree of the genus *Prunus*, distinguished from plums and apricots by its fruit, which is spherical and smooth and not covered with a bloom.

chervil plants, genus *Chaerophyllum*, of the Umbelliferous family. The garden chervil *Chaerophyllum cerefolium* has leaves with a sweetish odour, somewhat resembling parsley. It is used as a garnish, and as a pot-herb.

Chesapeake Bay largest of the inlets on the Atlantic coast of the USA, bordered by Maryland and Virginia. Its wildlife is threatened by urban and industrial development.

chess

the way each piece can move

arrangement of the chessmen

chestnut

Chiang Kai-shek General and president of the Chinese republic under the Nationalist government.

Cheshire county in NW England
area 2,328 sq km/899 sq mi
towns administrative headquarters Chester, Warrington, Crewe, Widnes, Macclesfield, Congleton
physical chiefly a fertile plain; Mersey, Dee, and Weaver rivers
products textiles, chemicals, dairy products
population (1986) 942,400

chess board game originating at least as early as the 2nd century AD. Two players use 16 pieces each, on a board of 64 squares of alternating colour, to try and force the opponent into a position where the main piece (the king) is threatened and cannot move to another position without remaining threatened.

Chesterfield Philip Dormer Stanhope, 4th Earl of Chesterfield 1694–1773. English politician and writer, author of *Letters to his Son* 1774 – his illegitimate son, Philip Stanhope (1732–68).

Chesterton G(ilbert) K(eith) 1874–1936. British novelist and satirical poet. His novels include the series featuring the naive priest-detective 'Father Brown' (1911–   ), *The Napoleon of Notting Hill* 1904, and *The Man Who Knew Too Much* 1922; poems include *Wine, Water and Song* 1915.

chestnut tree, genus *Castanea*, belonging to the same family, Fagaceae, as the oak and beech. The Spanish or sweet chestnut, *Castanea sativa*, produces a fruit that is a common article of diet in Europe and the USA; its timber is also valuable. The horse chestnut or conker tree, *Aesculus hippocastanum*, is quite distinct, belonging to a different family.

chewing gum confectionery mainly composed of chicle (juice of the sapodilla tree *Achras Zapota* of Central America, flavoured, especially with mint, and usually sweetened. The first patent was taken out in the USA 1871.

Chiang Ching former name of the Chinese actress ◊Jiang Qing, third wife of Mao.

Chiang Ching-kuo 1910–1988. Taiwanese politician, son of Chiang Kai-shek. Prime minister from 1971, he became president from 1978.

Chiang Kai-shek (Pinyin *Jiang Jie Shi*) 1887–1975. Chinese ◊Guomindang (Kuomintang) general and politician, president of China 1928–31 and 1943–49, and of Taiwan from 1949, where he set up a breakaway right-wing government on his expulsion from the mainland by the communist forces. He was a commander in the civil war that lasted from the end of imperial rule 1911 to the Second ◊Sino-Japanese War and beyond, having split with the communist leader Mao Zedong 1927.

Chicago financial and industrial (iron, steel, chemicals, textiles) city in Illinois, USA, on Lake Michigan; population (1980) 3,005,000, metropolitan area 7,581,000. The famous stockyards are now closed.

Chicano a Spanish-speaking American of Mexican descent in the SW USA. The term was originally used for those who became US citizens because of the ◊Mexican War. The word probably derives from the Spanish word *Mexicanos*.

Chichen Itzá Mayan city in Yucatán, Mexico, which flourished 11th–13th centuries. Excavated 1924–40 by Sylvanus Griswold Morley, the remains include temples with sculptures and colour reliefs, an observatory, and a sacred well into which sacrifices, including human beings, were cast.

Chichester Francis 1901–1972. English sailor and navigator. In 1931, he made the first E-W crossing of the Tasman Sea in *Gipsy Moth*, but earned greater fame for his circumnavigation of the world in his yacht *Gipsy Moth IV* 1966-67.

chicken pox a common but mild disease, also known as varicella, caused by a virus of the ◊herpes group, and transmitted by airborne droplets. Chicken pox chiefly attacks children under 10. The incubation period is 2–3 weeks.

chickpea seeds of the annual *Cicer arietinum*, family Leguminosae, which is grown for food in India and the Middle East.

chicory plant *Cichorium intybus*, family Compositae. It grows wild in Britain, mainly on chalky soils, and has large, usually blue, flowers. Its long taproot is used dried and roasted as a coffee substitute. The blanched leaves are used in salads.

chiffchaff bird *Phylloscopus collybita* of the warbler family, found in woodlands and thickets in Europe and N Asia during the summer, migrating south for winter. About 11 cm/4.3 in long, olive above,

Chichen Itzá The main pyramid of Chichen Itzá, Mexico.

Chile
Republic of
(*República de Chile*)

area 756,950 sq km/292,257 sq mi
capital Santiago
towns Concepción, Vina del Mar, Temuco; ports are Valparaiso, Antofagasta, Arica, Iquique
physical Andes mountains along E border, Atacama Desert in N, arable land and forest in the S
territories Easter Island, Juan Fernandez Island, half of Tierra del Fuego, and part of Antarctica
head of state and government Patricio Aylwin from 1990
political system emergent democratic republic
exports copper, iron, nitrate, paper and pulp
currency peso
population (1990 est) 13,000,000 (the majority mesitzo, of mixed American Indian and Spanish descent); annual growth rate 1.6%
life expectancy men 64, women 73
language Spanish
religion Roman Catholic 89%
literacy 95.4% (1988)
GDP $18.9 bn (1987); $6,512 per head
chronology
1818 Achieved independence from Spain.
1864 Christian Democrats formed government under Eduardo Frei.
1970 Dr Salvador Allende became the first democratically elected Marxist president.
1973 Government overthrown by the CIA-backed military, led by Gen Augusto Pinochet. Allende killed. Policy of repression began during which all opposition was put down.
1983 Growing opposition to the regime from all sides, with outbreaks of violence.
1988 Plebiscite asking whether Pinochet should serve a further term resulted in a clear 'No' vote.
1989 Pinochet agreed to constitutional reform. Aylwin elected president.
1990 Aylwin reached accord on end to military government. Pinochet censured by president.

greyish below, with an eyestripe and usually dark legs, it looks similar to a willow-warbler but has a distinctive song.

Chifley Joseph Benedict 'Ben' 1885–1951. Australian Labor prime minister 1945–49. He was minister of postwar reconstruction 1942–45 under Curtin, when he succeeded him as prime minister. He united the party in fulfilling a welfare and nationalization programme 1945–49 (although he failed in an attempt to nationalize the banks 1947), and initiated an immigration programme and the Snowy Mountains hydroelectric scheme.

Chihuahua capital of Chihuahua state, Mexico, 1,285 km/800 mi NW of Mexico City; population (1984) 375,000. Founded in 1707, it is the centre of a mining district.

chihuahua smallest breed of dog, developed in the USA from Mexican origins. It may weigh only 1 kg/2.2 lb. The domed head and wide set ears are characteristic, and the skull is large compared to the body. It can be almost any colour, and occurs in both smooth (or even hairless) and long-coated varieties.

chilblain painful inflammation of the skin of the feet or hands, due to cold. The parts turn red, swell, itch violently, and are very tender. In bad cases, the skin cracks, blisters, or ulcerates.

child abuse the molesting of children by parents and other adults. In the UK, it can give rise to various criminal charges, such as gross indecency with children. A local authority can take abused children away from their parents under care orders. Controversial methods of diagnosis of sexual abuse led to a public inquiry in Cleveland, England, 1988, which severely criticized the handling of such cases.

Childers (Robert) Erskine 1870–1922. Irish Sinn Féin politician, author of the novel *The Riddle of the Sands* 1903, who was executed as a Republican guerrilla.

Children's Crusade a ◊Crusade by some 10,000 children from France, the Low Countries and Germany, in 1212, to recapture Jerusalem. Motivated by religious piety, many of them were sold into slavery or died of disease.

Chile South American country, bounded to the north by Peru and Bolivia, to the east by Argentina, and to the south and west by the Pacific Ocean.

chilli (North American *chili*) the pod, or powder made from the pod, of a variety of ◊Capsicum, *Capsicum frutescens*.

Chiltern Hundreds stewardship of in the UK, a nominal office of profit under the crown. British Members of Parliament may not resign; therefore, if they wish to leave office during a parliament they may apply for this office, a formality which disqualifies them from being an MP.

chimaera fish of the group Holocephali. They have thick bodies which taper to a long thin tail, large fins, smooth skin, and a cartilaginous skeleton. They can grow to 1.5 m/4.5 ft. Most chimaeras are deep-water fish, and even *Chimaera monstrosa*, a relatively shallow-living form caught commonly round European coasts, lives at a depth of 300–500 m/1000–1600 ft.

chimera in biology, an organism composed of tissues that are genetically different. Chimeras can develop naturally if a ◊mutation occurs in a cell of a developing embryo but are more commonly produced artificially by implanting cells from one organism into the embryo of another.

chimpanzee highly intelligent African ape *Pan troglodytes* that lives mainly in rain forests but sometimes in wooded savannah. They are covered in thin but long black body hair, except for the face, hands, and feet, which may be pink or black skin. Chimpanzees normally walk on all fours, supporting the front of the body on the knuckles of the fingers, but can stand or walk upright for a short distance.

China
People's Republic of
(*Zhonghua Renmin Gonghe Guo*)

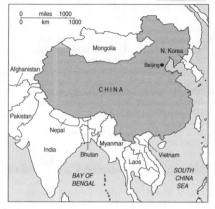

area 9,596,960 sq km/3,599,975 sq mi
capital Beijing (Peking)
towns Chongqing (Chungking), Shenyang
(Mukden), Wuhan, Nanjing (Nanking), Harbin;
ports Tianjin (Tientsin), Shanghai, Qingdao
(Tsingtao), Lüda (Lü-ta), Guangzhou (Canton)
physical two-thirds of China is mountains (in the N
and SW) or desert; the E is irrigated by rivers Huang
He (Yellow River), Chang Jiang (Yangtze-Kiang), Xi
Jiang (Si Kiang)
head of state Yang Shangkun from 1988
head of government Li Peng from 1987
political system communist republic
exports tea; livestock and animal products;
textiles (silk and cotton); oil, minerals, chemicals;
light industrial goods
currency yuan
population (1990 est) 1,130,065,000 (of whom the
majority are Han or ethnic Chinese; the 67 million
of other ethnic groups, including Tibetan, Uigur,
and Zhuang, live in border areas). The number of
people of Chinese origin outside China, Taiwan,
and Hong Kong is estimated at 15–24 million.
Annual growth rate 1.2%
life expectancy men 67, women 69
language Chinese
religion officially atheist, but traditionally Taoist,
Confucianist, and Buddhist; Muslim 13 million;

Catholic 3–6 million; Protestant 3 million
literacy 82% male/66% female (1985 est)
GDP $293.4 bn (1987); $274 per head
chronology
1949 People's Republic of China proclaimed by
Mao Zedong.
1954 Soviet-style constitution adopted.
1956–57 Hundred Flowers Movement
encouraged criticism of the government.
1958–60 Great Leap Forward commune
experiment to achieve 'true communism'.
1962 Sino-Indian border war.
1962–65 Economic recovery programme under
Liu Shaoqi; Maoist 'socialist education movement'
rectification campaign.
1966–68 Great Proletarian Cultural Revolution
and overthrow of Liu Shaoqi.
1970–76 Reconstruction under Mao and Zhou
Enlai; purge of extreme left.
1971 Entry into United Nations.
1972 US president Nixon visited Beijing.
1975 New state constitution. Unveiling of Zhou's
Four Modernizations programme.
1976 Death of Zhou Enlai and Mao Zedong;
appointment of Hua Guofeng as prime minister
and Communist Party chair. Deng in hiding. Gang
of Four arrested.
1977 Rehabilitation of Deng Xiaoping.
1979 Economic reforms introduced. Diplomatic
relations opened with USA. Punitive invasion of
Vietnam.
1980 Zhao Ziyang appointed prime minister.
1981 Hu Yaobang succeeded Hua as party chair.
Imprisonment of Gang of Four.
1986 Student demonstrations for democracy.
1987 Hu was replaced as party leader by Zhao, with
Li Peng as prime minister. Deng left the Politburo
but remained influential.
1988 Yang Shankun became state president.
Economic reforms encountered increasing
problems; inflation rocketing.
1989 Over 2,000 killed in prodemocracy
demonstrations in Tiananman Square;
international sanctions imposed.
1991 EC and Japanese sanctions lifted.
1992 China promised to sign 1968 Nuclear Non-
Proliferation Treaty. Relations with former USSR
and Vietnam normalized.
1993 Jiang Zemin set to replace Yang Shangkun as
president.

They can grow to 1.4 m/4.5 ft tall, and weigh 50 kg/
110 lb. They are very strong, and climb well, but
spend time on the ground. They live in loose social
groups. The bulk of the diet is fruit, with some
leaves, insects, and occasional meat. Chimpanzees
can use 'tools', fashioning twigs to extract termites
from their nests.

Chimu South American civilization that flourished
in Peru about 1250–1470, when they were conquered by the Incas. They produced fine work in
gold, realistic portrait pottery, savage fanged images in clay, and possibly a system of writing or
recording by painting beans in particular patterns.
They built aqueducts carrying water many miles,
and the maze-like city of Chan Chan, 36 sq km/14 sq
mi, on the coast near Trujillo.

China country in SE Asia, bounded N by Mongolia,
NW by Kazakhstan, NE by the Russian Federation,
SW by India and Nepál, S by Bhutan, Myanmor,

Laos, and Vietnam, SE by the South China Sea, and
E by the East China Sea, North Korea, and the
Russian Federation.

china clay a clay mineral formed by the decomposition of feldspars. The alteration of aluminium
silicates results in the formation of kaolinite, from
which **kaolin**, or white china clay, is derived.

China, history *500,000 BC* The earliest human
remains found in China are those of 'Peking man'
(*Sinanthropus pekingensis*).
18,000 Humans of the modern type are first known
to have inhabited the region.
5000 A simple agricultural society was established.
c. 2800–c. 2200 The **Sage kings**, a period of
agricultural development, known only from legend.
c. 2000–c. 1500 The **Xia dynasty**, a bronze age
with further agricultural developments, including
irrigation, and the first known use of writing.

Chinese dynasties

Dynasty	Date	Major events
Xia (Hsia)	c.2000–c.1500 BC	Agriculture, bronze, first writing.
Shang (Yin)	c.1500–c.1066 BC	First major dynasty; first Chinese calendar.
Zhou (Chou)	c.1066–c.221 BC	Developed society using money, iron, written laws; age of Confucius.
Qin (Ch'in)	221–206 BC	Unification after period of Warring States, building of Great Wall began, roads built.
Han	206 BC–220 AD	First centralized and effectively administered empire; introduction of Buddhism.
San Kuo (Three Kingdoms)	220–280	Division into three parts, prolonged fighting and eventual victory of Wei over Chu and Wu; Confucianism superseded by Buddhism and Taoism.
Western Jin (Chin)	265–316	Internal warfare; beginning of Hun invasions in the north. Developments in arts and science; Buddhism and Taoism continued to spread.
Eastern Jin (Chin)	317–439	
Southern and Northern	386–581	
Sui	581–618	Reunification; barbarian invasions stopped; Great Wall refortified.
Tang (T'ang)	618–907	Centralized government; empire greatly extended; period of excellence in sculpture, painting, and poetry.
Wu Tai (Five Dynasties)	907–960	Economic depression and loss of territory in northern China, central Asia, and Korea; first use of paper money.
Song (Sung)	960–1279	Period of calm and creativity; printing developed (movable type); central government restored; northern and western frontiers neglected and Mongol incursions began.
Yuan	1279–1368	Beginning of Mongol rule in China, under Kublai Khan; Marco Polo visited China; dynasty brought to an end by widespread revolts, centred in Mongolia.
Ming	1368–1644	Mongols driven out by native Chinese, Mongolia captured by 2nd Ming emperor; period of architectural development; Beijing flourished as new capital.
Manchu or Qing (Ch'ing)	1644–1911	China once again under non-Chinese rule, conquered by nomads from Manchuria; initially trade and culture flourished, but conservatism led to a decline, culminating in the dynasty's overthrow by revolutionaries led by Sun Yat-sen.

Pinyin spellings are given here, following official adoption of the *Pinyin* system in 1979, with the older romanized forms in brackets.

c. 1500–c. 1066 The **Shang dynasty** is the first of which we have documentary evidence; bronze vases survive of its art.

1066–221 During the **Zhou dynasty**, the feudal structure of society broke down in a period of political upheaval, though iron, money, and written laws were all in use, and philosophy flourished (see ◊Confucius). The dynasty ended in the 'Warring States' period (403–221 BC), with the country divided into small kingdoms.

221–206 The shortest and most remarkable of the dynasties, the **Qin**, corresponds to the reign of Shih Huang Ti, who curbed the feudal nobility and introduced orderly government; he built roads and canals, and began the ◊Great Wall of China to keep out invaders from the north.

206 BC–220 AD The **Han dynasty** was a long period of peace, during which territory was expanded, the keeping of historical records was systematized, and an organized civil service set up. Art and literature flourished, and ◊Buddhism was introduced.

220–439 The country was divided under **Three Kingdoms**: the Wei, Chu, and Wu, of which the Wei became the most powerful, eventually founding the **Jin dynasty** (265–439), which expanded to take over from the barbarian invaders who ruled much of China at that time, but lost the territory they had gained to the Tatar invaders from the north.

581–618 Reunification came with the **Sui dynasty** when the government was reinstated and the Great Wall refortified.

618–907 During the **Tang dynasty** the system of government became more highly developed than ever before, and the empire covered most of SE and much of central Asia. Art and literature (especially poetry) flourished again.

907–960 The period known as the **Five Dynasties and Ten Kingdoms** held war, economic depression, and loss of territory. Printing was developed.

960–1279 During the **Song dynasty** central government was restored. Mongol invasions began in the north.

1279–1368 The Mongols reigned (the **Yuan dynasty**); there were widespread revolts.

1368–1644 The Mongols were expelled by the first of the **Ming dynasty**, who expanded the empire. Portuguese explorers reached Canton 1517, and other Europeans followed.

1644–1912 The last of the dynasties was the **Manchu**, which gave several great rulers to China, up to the empress dowager Tz'e Hsi (died 1908). During the 19th century it seemed likely that China would be partitioned among the European powers, all trade being conducted through treaty ports in their control. The ◊**Boxer Rebellion** 1900 against Western influence was suppressed by European troops.

1911–12 Revolution broke out, and the infant emperor Henry ◊Pu Yi was deposed. For history 1911–present, see ◊Chinese Revolution and ◊China.

China Sea area of the Pacific Ocean bordered by China, Vietnam, Borneo, the Philippines, and

China Part of the Sacred Way to the Ming Tombs is lined with statues of courtiers, soldiers, politicians, and animals.

Japan. Various groups of small islands and shoals, including the Paracels, 500 km/300m E of Vietnam, have been disputed by China and other powers because they lie in oil-rich areas.

chinchilla South American rodent *Chinchilla laniger* found in high, rather barren areas of the Andes in Bolivia and Chile. About the size of a small rabbit, it has long ears and a long bushy tail, and shelters in rock crevices. These gregarious animals have very thick soft siver-grey fur, and were hunted almost to extinction for it.

Chinese inhabitant of China or a person of Chinese descent. They comprise approximately 25% of the world's population, and the Chinese language is the largest member of the Sino-Tibetan family.

Chinese language depending upon definition, a language or group of languages of the Sino-Tibetan family, spoken in China, Taiwan, Hongkong, Singapore, and Chinese communities throughout the world. Varieties of spoken Chinese differ greatly, but share a written form using thousands of ideographic symbols which have changed little in 2,000 years. Nowadays, *putonghua* ('common speech'), based on the educated Beijing dialect known as 'Mandarin' Chinese, is promoted throughout China as the national spoken and written language.

Chinese Revolution a series of major political upheavals in China 1911–49. A nationalist revolt overthrew the imperial dynasty 1912. Led by Sun Yat-sen 1923–25, and by Chiang Kai-shek 1925–49, the nationalists, or Guomindang, came under increasing pressure from the growing communist movement. The 10,000 km/6,000 mi *Long March* of the communists 1934–35 to escape from the nationalist forces saw Mao Zedong emerge as leader. After World War II, the conflict expanded into open civil war 1946–49, until the Guomindang were defeated at Nanking. This effectively established communist rule in China under the leadership of Mao.

chinook a warm dry wind that blows downhill on the eastern side of the Rocky Mountains. It often occurs in winter and spring when it produces a rapid

China, People's Republic of

Province	Former name	Capital	Area sq km
Anhui	Anhwei	Hefei	139
Fujian	Fukien	Fuzhou	121
Gansu	Kansu	Lanzhou	454
Guangdong	Kwangtung	Guangzhou	212
Guizhou	Kweichow	Guiyang	176
Hebei	Hopei	Shijiazhuang	188
Heilongjiang	Heilungkiang	Harbin	469
Henan	Honan	Zhengzhou	167
Hubei	Hupeh	Wuhan	186
Hunan	Hunan	Changsha	210
Jiangsu	Kiangsu	Nanjing	103
Jiangxi	Kiangsi	Nanchang	169
Jilin	Kirin	Changchun	187
Liaoning	Liaoning	Shenyang	146
Quinghai	Tsinghai	Xining	721
Shaanxi	Shensi	Xian	206
Shanxi	Shansi	Taiyuan	156
Shandong	Shantung	Jinan	153
Sichuan	Szechwan	Chengdu	567
Yunnan	Yunnan	Kunming	394
Zhejiang	Chekiang	Hangzhou	102
Autonomous Regions			
Guangxi Zhuang	Kwangsi Chuang	Nanning	236
Nei Monggol	Inner Mongolia	Hohhot	1,183
Ningxia Hui	Ningshia Hui	Yinchuan	66
Xinjiang Uygur	Sinkiang Uighur	Urumqi	1,600
Xizang	Tibet	Lhasa	1,228
Municipalities			
Beijing	Peking		17
Shanghai	Shanghai		6
Tianjin	Tientsin		11
		Total	9,571

thaw, and so is important to the agriculture of the area. The name is a native Indian word meaning 'snow-eater'.

chip a complete electronic circuit on a slice of silicon (or other ◊semiconductor) crystal only a few millimetres square. It is also called ◊silicon chip and ◊integrated circuit.

chipmunk name for a number of species of small ground squirrel with characteristic stripes along its side. They live in North America and E Asia, in a variety of habitats, usually wooded, and take shelter in burrows. They have pouches in their cheeks for carrying food. They climb well but spend most of their time on or near the ground.

Chippendale Thomas *c.* 1718–1779. English furniture designer. His book *The Gentleman and Cabinet Maker's Director* 1754 was a significant contribution to furniture design. He favoured Louis XVI, Chinese, Gothic, and neo-Classical styles, and worked mainly in mahogany.

Chirac Jacques 1932– . French conservative politician, prime minister 1974–76 and 1986–88. He established the neo-Gaullist Rassemblement pour la République (RPR) 1976, and became mayor of Paris 1977.

Chirico Giorgio de 1888–1978. Italian painter born in Greece, the founder of Metaphysical painting, a style that presaged Surrealism in its use of enigmatic imagery and dream-like settings. Early examples date from 1910.

Chiron an outer asteroid discovered by Charles Kowal 1977, orbiting between Saturn and Uranus. It appears to have a dark surface resembling that of asteroids in the inner solar system, probably consists of a mixture of ice and dark stony material, and may have a diameter of about 200 km/120 mi.

chiropractic manipulation of the spine and other parts to relieve apparently non-related conditions, claimed to be caused by pressure on the nerves. It is not fully recognized by orthodox medicine.

Chissano Joaquim 1939– . Mozambique nationalist politician, president from 1986. In Oct 1992 Chissano signed a peace accord with the leader of the rebel Mozambique National Resistance (MNR) party, bringing to an end 16 years of civil war.

chitin a complex long-chain compound, or ◊polymer; a nitrogenous derivative of glucose. Chitin is found principally in the ◊exoskeleton of insects and other arthropods. It combines with protein to form a covering that can be hard and tough, as in scorpions, or soft and flexible, as in caterpillars. In crustaceans such as crabs, it is impregnated with calcium carbonate for extra strength.

Chittagong city and port in Bangladesh, 16 km/10 mi from the mouth of the Karnaphuli river, on the Bay of Bengal; population (1981) 1,388,476. Industries include steel, engineering, chemicals, and textiles.

chivalry the code of gallantry and honour that medieval knights were supposed to observe. The word originally meant the knightly class of the feudal Middle Ages.

chive plant *Allium schoenoprasum* that grows wild in a few places in Britain, and is cultivated as a salad vegetable or garnish.

chlamydia single-celled organism that can only live parasitically in animal cells. They are considered to be descendants of bacteria which have lost certain metabolic processes. In humans, chlamydias cause ◊trachoma, a disease found mainly in the tropics (a leading cause of blindness), and psittacosis, which is contracted from birds by inhaling particles of dried droppings.

chloral (modern name *trichloroethanal*) an oily colourless liquid with a characteristic pungent smell.

chip

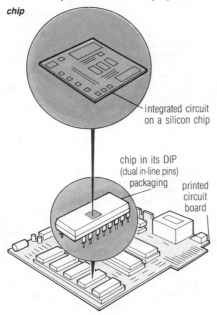

integrated circuit
on a silicon chip

chip in its DIP
(dual in-line pins)
packaging   printed
circuit
board

It is very soluble in water, and its compound, chloral hydrate, is a powerful sleep-inducing agent.

chloramphenicol first of the broad-spectrum antibiotics to be used commercially. It was discovered in a Peruvian soil sample. Because of its toxicity, its use is limited to treatment of life-threatening infection, such as meningitis and typhoid fever.

chlorates in chemistry, salts whose acid contains both chlorine and oxygen (ClO, ClO_2, ClO_3, and ClO_4). Common chlorates are those of sodium, potassium, and barium. Certain chlorates are used in weedkillers.

chlorides salts of hydrochloric acid (HCl), commonly formed by its action on various metals or by the direct combination of the metal and chlorine. Sodium chloride (NaCl) is common table salt.

chlorine a chemical element, a greenish-yellow gas with an irritating, suffocating smell; symbol Cl, atomic number 17, relative atomic mass 35.457. It is an important bleaching agent and is used as a germicide for drinking and swimming-pool water. It is also an oxidizing agent and finds many applications in organic chemistry.

chlorofluorocarbon or *CFC* man-made chemical, which is odourless, non-toxic, non-flammable, and chemically inert. CFCs are used as propellants in aerosol cans, refrigerants in refrigerators and air conditioners, in the manufacture of foam boxes for take-away food cartons, and as cleaning substances in the electronics industry. They are partly responsible for the destruction of the ozone layer.

chloroform $CHCl_3$ (modern name *trichloromethane*) a clear, colourless, toxic liquid with a characteristic, pungent, sickly-sweet smell and taste, formerly used as an anaesthetic. It is used as a solvent and in the synthesis of organic chemical compounds.

chlorophyll the green pigment present in the majority of plants which is responsible for the absorption of light energy during the light reaction of ◊photosynthesis. It absorbs the red and blue-violet parts of sunlight but reflects the green, thus giving the characteristic colour to most plants.

chloroplast a structure (organelle) within a plant cell containing the green pigment chlorophyll. Chloroplasts occur in most cells of the green plant which are exposed to light, often in large numbers. Typically, they are flattened and disc-like, with a double membrane enclosing the stroma, a gel-like matrix. Within the stroma are stacks of flat vesicles, or grana, where ◊photosynthesis occurs.

chlorosis an abnormal condition of green plants in which the stems and leaves turn pale green or yellow. The yellowing is due to a reduction in the levels of the green chlorophyll pigments. It may be caused by a deficiency in essential elements (such as magnesium, iron, or manganese), a lack of light, genetic factors, or virus infection.

chocolate a drink or confectionery derived from ◊cocoa.

choke in physics, a coil employed as an electrical ◊inductance, particularly the type used as a 'starter' in the circuit of fluorescent lighting.

cholera intestinal infection caused by a bacterium (*Vibrio cholerae*), and characterized by violent diarrhoea.

cholesterol a ◊steroid substance that forms part of all cell membranes, and plays a vital role in stabilizing them. When made by the body, it is transported in the blood. Cholesterol in foodstuffs boosts the blood concentration, which leads to it being deposited on the artery walls; this can

Chopin A daguerrotype of the composer.

contribute to heart trouble. Cholesterol is broken down in the liver into bile salts.

Chomsky Noam 1928– . US professor of linguistics. He proposed a theory of transformational generative grammar, which attracted widespread interest outside linguistics because of the claims it made about the relationship between language and the mind, and the universality of an underlying language structure. He is also a leading spokesman against imperialist tendencies of the US government.

Chongqing or *Chungking*, also known as *Pahsien* city in Sichuan province, China, which stands at the confluence of the ◊Chang Jiang and the Jialing Jiang; population (1984) 2,733,700. Industries include iron, steel, chemicals, synthetic rubber, and textiles.

Chopin Frédéric (François) 1810–1849. Polish composer and pianist, who made his debut as a pianist at the age of eight. As a performer Chopin revolutionized the technique of pianoforte-playing, and concentrated on solo piano pieces. His pieces for piano solo, including two piano concertos, are characterized by their lyrical and poetic quality.

Chopin Kate 1851–1904. US novelist and story writer. Her novel *The Awakening* 1899 is now regarded as a classic of feminist sensibility.

chorale a traditional hymn tune of the German Protestant Church.

chord in geometry, a straight line joining any two points on a curve. The chord that passes through the centre of a circle (the longest chord) is the diameter. The longest and shortest chords of an ellipse (a regular oval) are called the major and minor axes.

chordate animal belonging to the phylum Chordata, which includes vertebrates, sea squirts, amphioxus, and others. All these animals, at some stage of their lives, have a supporting rod of tissue (notochord or backbone) running down their bodies.

chorea a disease of the nervous system marked by involuntary movements of the face muscles and limbs, formerly called St Vitus' dance.

choreography the art of creating and arranging ballet and dance for performance; originally, in the 18th century, the art of dance notation.

chorion outermost of the three membranes enclosing the embryo of reptiles, birds, and mammals; see also ◊amnion.

Chou En-lai former name for Chinese politician ◊Zhou Enlai.

chough bird *Pyrrhocorax pyrrhocorax* of the crow family, about 38 cm/15 in long, black-feathered, and with red bill and legs. It lives on sea-cliffs and mountains from Europe to E Asia, but is now rare.

Christ see ◊Jesus Christ.

christening Christian ceremony of ◊baptism of infants, including giving a name.

Christian follower of ◊Christianity, the religion derived from the teachings of ◊Jesus. In the New Testament, Acts 11:26, it is stated that the first to be called Christians were the disciples in Antioch (modern Antakiyah, Turkey).

Christian ten kings of Denmark and Norway, including:

Christian I 1426–1481. King of Denmark from 1448, and founder of the Oldenburg dynasty. In 1450 he established the union of Denmark and Norway which lasted until 1814.

Christian VIII 1786–1848. King of Denmark 1839–48. He proved to be unpopular because of his opposition to reform. His attempt to encourage the Danish language and culture in Schleswig and Holstein led to an insurrection there shortly after his death. He was succeeded by Frederick VII.

Christian IX 1818–1906. King of Denmark from 1863. In 1864 he lost the duchies of Schleswig and Holstein after a war with Austria and Prussia.

Christian X 1870–1947. King of Denmark and Iceland from 1912, when he succeeded his father Frederick VIII. He married Alexandrine, Duchess of Mecklenburg-Schwerin, and was popular for his democratic attitude. During World War II he was held prisoner by the Germans in Copenhagen.

Christianity world religion derived from the teaching of Jesus Christ in the first third of the 1st century, with a present-day membership of about 1 billion. Its main divisions are the ◊Roman Catholic, Eastern ◊Orthodox, and ◊Protestant churches.

beliefs An omnipotent God the Father is the fundamental concept, together with the doctrine of the Trinity, that is, the union of the three persons of the Father, Son, and Holy Spirit in one Godhead. Christians believe that Jesus died for the sins of the people, and his divinity is based on the belief of his resurrection after death, and his ascension into Heaven. The main commandments are to love God and to love one's neighbour as oneself.

history

1st century The Christian church is traditionally said to have originated on the first Whitsun Day, but was separated from the parent Jewish church by the declaration of Saints Barnabas and Paul that the distinctive rites of Judaism were not necessary for entry into the Christian church.

3rd century Christians were persecuted under the Roman emperors Severus, Decius, and Diocletian.

312 Emperor Constantine established Christianity as the religion of the Roman Empire.

4th century A settled doctrine of Christian belief evolved, with deviating beliefs condemned as heresies. Questions of discipline threatened disruption within the church; to settle these, Constantine called the Council of Arles 314, followed by the councils of Nicaea 325, and Constantinople 381.

5th century Councils of Ephesus 431 and Chalcedon 451. Christianity was carried northwards by figures such as Saints Colomba and Augustine in England.

800 Holy Roman Emperor Charlemagne crowned by the Pope. The church assisted the growth of the feudal system of which it formed the apex.

1054 The *Eastern Orthodox Church* split from the Roman Catholic Church.

11th–12th centuries Secular and ecclesiastical jurisdiction were often in conflict, for example, Emperor Henry IV and Pope Gregory VII,

Henry II of England and his archbishop Becket.

1096–1291 The church supported a series of wars in the Middle East, the **Crusades**.

1229 The **Inquisition** was established to suppress heresy.

14th century Increasing worldliness (against which the foundation of the Dominican and Franciscan monastic orders was a protest) and ecclesiastical abuses led to dissatisfaction in the 14th century and the appearance of the reformers Wycliffe and Huss.

15th–17th centuries Thousands of women were accused of witchcraft and executed.

early 16th century The Renaissance brought a re-examination of Christianity in N Europe by the humanists Erasmus, More, and Colet.

1517 The German priest Martin Luther started the **Reformation**, an attempt to return to primitive Christianity, and became leader of the **Protestant** movement.

1519–64 In Switzerland the Reformation was carried out by Calvin and Zwingli.

1529 Henry VIII renounced papal supremacy and proclaimed himself head of the **Church of England**.

1545–63 The **Counter-Reformation** was initiated by the Catholic church at the Council of Trent.

1560 The **Church of Scotland** was established according to Calvin's Presbyterian system.

16th–18th centuries Missionaries in the Third World suppressed indigenous religions.

18th century During the Age of Reason, Christianity was questioned, and the Bible examined on the same basis as secular literature. In England the Church of England suffered the loss of large numbers of Nonconformists.

19th century The evolutionary theories of Darwin and others challenged orthodox belief.

1948 The World Council of Churches was founded as part of the **ecumenical movement**. Protestant evangelicism grew rapidly in the USA, spread by television.

1969 A **liberation theology** of freeing the poor from oppression emerged in South America, and attracted papal disapproval.

1972 The United Reformed Church was formed.

1989 Barbara Harris, first female bishop, ordained in the USA.

1992 The Church of England general synod voted in favour of the ordination of women priests.

Christian Science   a sect, the Church of Christ, Scientist, established in the USA by Mary Baker Eddy 1879. Christian Scientists believe that since God is good and is spirit, matter and evil are not truly real. Consequently they refuse all medical treatment.

Christie   Agatha 1890–1976. English detective novelist who created the characters Hercule Poirot and Miss Jane Marple. Her prolific output included the novels *The Murder of Roger Ackroyd* 1926 and *Ten Little Indians* 1939, and the play *The Mousetrap* 1952.

Christina   1626–1689. Queen of Sweden 1632–54. Succeeding her father Gustavus Adolphus at the age of six, she assumed power 1644, but disagreed with the former regent ◊Oxenstjerna. Refusing to marry, she eventually nominated her cousin Charles Gustavus (Charles X) as her successor. As a secret convert to Roman Catholicism, which was then illegal in Sweden, she had to abdicate

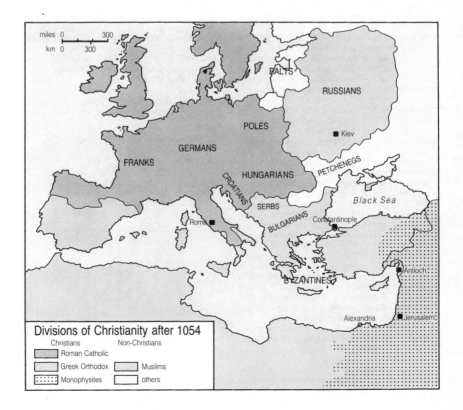

Divisions of Christianity after 1054

Christians — Roman Catholic; Greek Orthodox; Monophysites. Non-Christians — Muslims; others.

chromatography

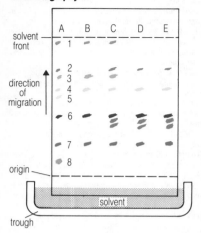

chromatography

solvent front

direction of migration

origin

trough

	A	B	C	D	E
1					
2					
3					
4					
5					
6					
7					
8					

solvent

1654, and went to live in Rome, twice returning to Sweden unsuccessfully to claim the throne. She ended her life on a pension from the Pope.

Christmas 25 Dec, a holiday throughout the Western world, traditionally marked by feasting and gift-giving. In the Christian church, it is the day on which the birth of Christ is celebrated, although the actual birth date is unknown. Many of its customs have a non-Christian origin.

Christmas rose see ◊hellebore.

Christmas tree type of tree brought indoors and decorated for Christmas, usually the Norway spruce *Picea abies*. The custom was a medieval German tradition and is now practised in many Western countries.

Christophe Henri 1767–1820. Black slave in the West Indies who was one of the leaders of the revolt against the French 1790, and was crowned king of Haiti 1812. His reign saw the distribution of plantations to military leaders. He shot himself when his troops deserted him because of his alleged cruelty.

Christopher, St the patron saint of travellers. His feast day on 25 Jul was dropped from the Roman Catholic liturgical calendar 1969.

chromatic scale a musical scale proceeding by semitones. All 12 notes in the octave are used rather than the 7 notes of the diatonic scale.

chromatography an important technique used especially in biochemistry, for separating mixtures into their components for analysis and quantification. For example, if a protein has been broken down into its constituent amino acids, chromatography can be used to separate and identify those amino acids.

chromium a chemical element, symbol Cr, atomic number 24, relative atomic mass 52.01. It is a bluish-white metal capable of taking a high polish, and with a high melting-point. It is used decoratively and, alloyed with nickel, for electrical heating wires. Resistant to abrasion and corrosion, it is used to harden steel, and is a constituent of stainless steel and many other useful alloys. It is used extensively in chromium plating and as a ◊catalyst.

chromosome a structure in a cell nucleus responsible for the transmission of hereditary characteristics, by means of a ◊genetic code.

chromosphere a layer of mostly hydrogen gas about 10,000 km/6,000 mi deep above the visible surface of the Sun (the photosphere). Its name

means 'colour sphere'; it appears pinkish-red during ◊eclipses of the Sun.

chronic in medicine, describing a condition which is of slow onset, and which then runs a prolonged course, such as rheumatoid arthritis or chronic bronchitis. In contrast, an **acute** condition develops and is resolved quickly.

Chronicles two books of the Old Testament or Hebrew Bible containing genealogy and history.

chronicles, medieval books modelled on the Old Testament Books of Chronicles. Until the later Middle Ages, they were usually written in Latin by churchmen, who borrowed extensively from each other.

chronometer instrument for measuring time, especially used at sea. It is designed to remain accurate through all conditions of temperature and pressure. The first accurate marine chronometer, capable of an accuracy of half a minute a year, was made 1761 by John Harrison in England.

chrysanthemum plant of the family Compositae, with about 200 species. There are many cultivated varieties but some uncertainty as to the wild species from which they have been evolved. In the Far East the common chrysanthemum has been cultivated for more than 2,000 years, and is the national emblem of Japan.

chrysolite an alternative name for the mineral ◊olivine.

chub freshwater fish *Leuciscus cephalus* of the carp family. Rather thickset and cylindrical, it grows up to 60 cm/2 ft, is dark greenish or grey on the back, silvery yellow below, with metallic flashs on the flanks. It lives generally in clean rivers, from Britain to the USSR.

Chun Doo-Hwan 1931– . South Korean military ruler who seized power 1979; president 1981–87 as head of the newly formed Democratic Justice Party.

church a building designed as a Christian place of worship.

Churchill Caryl 1938– . British playwright, whose predominantly radical and feminist works include *Cloud Nine* 1979, *Top Girls* 1982, and *Serious Money* 1987.

Churchill Randolph (Henry Spencer) 1849–1895. British Conservative politician, chancellor of the

church

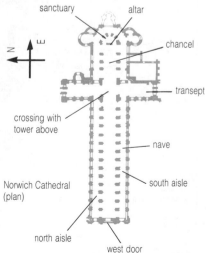

sanctuary altar chancel

N E

transept

crossing with tower above

nave

Norwich Cathedral (plan)

south aisle

north aisle west door

Churchill *Winston Churchill photographed at his desk, March 1944.*

Exchequer and leader of the House of Commons 1886, father of Winston Churchill.

Churchill Winston (Leonard Spencer) 1874–1965. British Conservative politician. In Parliament from 1900, as a Liberal until 1923, he held a number of ministerial offices, including 1st Lord of the Admiralty 1911–15 and chancellor of the Exchequer 1924–29. Absent from the cabinet in the 1930s, he returned Sep 1939 to lead a coalition government 1940–45, negotiating with Allied leaders in World War II; he was again prime minister 1951–55. He won the Nobel Prize for Literature 1953.

Church in Wales the Welsh Anglican church; see ◊Wales, Church in.

Church of England the established form of Christianity in England, a member of the Anglican Communion. It was dissociated from the Roman Catholic Church 1534. There were approximately 1,100,000 regular worshippers 1988.

history
2nd century Christianity arrived in England during the Roman occupation.
597 St Augustine became first archbishop of Canterbury.
1529–34 At the ***Reformation*** the chief change was political: the sovereign (Henry VIII) replaced the pope as head of the church and assumed the right to appoint archbishops and bishops.
1536–40 Dissolution of the monasteries.
1549 First publication of the ***Book of Common Prayer***, the basis of worship throughout the Anglican Church.
1563–1604 The ***Thirty-Nine Articles***, the Church's doctrinal basis, were drawn up, enforced by Parliament, and revised.
17th–18th centuries Colonizers took the Church of England to North America (where three US bishops were consecrated after the War of Independence, whose successors still lead the Episcopal Church in the USA), Australia, New Zealand, and India.
19th century Missionaries were active in Africa. The ***Oxford Movement***, led by the academic priests Newman, Keble, and Pusey, eventually developed into Anglo-Catholicism.
20th century There were moves towards reunion with the Methodist and Roman Catholic churches. Modernism, a liberal movement, attracted attention 1963 through a book by a bishop, J A T Robinson. The ***ordination of women*** was accepted by some overseas Anglican churches, for example the US

Episcopal Church 1976; in 1992 the Anglican churches of England and Australia voted in favour of the ordination of women.

Church of Scotland the established form of Christianity in Scotland, first recognized by the state 1560. It is based on the Protestant doctrines of the reformer Calvin and governed on Presbyterian lines. The Church went through several periods of episcopacy in the 17th century, and those who adhered to episcopacy after 1690 formed the Episcopal Church of Scotland, an autonomous church in communion with the Church of England. In 1843, there was a split in the Church of Scotland (the Disruption), in which almost a third of its ministers and members left and formed the Free Church of Scotland. Its membership 1988 was about 850,000.

CIA abbreviation for ◊*Central Intelligence Agency*.

Cibachrome in photography, a process of printing directly from transparencies. Distinguished by rich, saturated colours, it can be home-processed and is one of the most permanent processes. It was introduced 1963.

cicada insect of the family Cicadidae. Most species are tropical, but a few occur in Europe and North America. Young cicadas live underground, for up to 17 years in some species. The adults live on trees, whose juices they suck. The males produce a loud, almost continuous, chirping by vibrating membranes in resonating cavities in the abdomen.

Cicero 106–43 BC. Roman orator, writer, and statesman. His speeches, and philosophical and rhetorical works are models of Latin prose, and his letters provide a picture of contemporary Roman life. As consul 63 BC he exposed Catiline's conspiracy in four major orations.

cichlid freshwater fish of the family Cichlidae. Cichlids are somewhat perch-like, but have a single nostril on each side instead of two. They are mostly predatory fishes, and have deep, colourful bodies, flattened from side to side so that some are almost disc shaped. Many are territorial in the breeding season and may show care of the young. There are more than 1000 species found in South and Central America, Africa, and India.

CID abbreviation for ◊*Criminal Investigation Department*.

Cid Rodrigo Diaz de Bivar 1040–1099. Spanish soldier, nicknamed *El Cid* ('the lord') by the Moors. Born in Castile of a noble family, he fought against the king of Navarre, and won his nickname *el Campeador* (the Champion) by killing the Navarrese champion in single combat. Essentially a mercenary, fighting both with and against the Moors, he died while defending Valencia against them, and in subsequent romances became Spain's national hero.

cider in the UK, a fermented drink made from the juice of the apple; in the USA the term cider usually refers to unfermented (non-alcoholic) apple juice. Cider has been known for more than 2,000 years, and for many centuries has been a popular drink in France and England, which are now its main centres of production.

cif in economics, abbreviation for *cost, insurance, and freight* or *charged in full*. Many countries value their imports on this basis while exports are usually valued ◊*fob*.

cigar a compact roll of tobacco leaves for smoking. It was originally a sheath of palm leaves filled with tobacco, smoked by the Indians of Central and North America. Cigar smoking was introduced into

Spain soon after 1492, and spread all over Europe in the next few centuries. From about 1890 cigar smoking was gradually supplanted in popularity in Britain by cigarette smoking.

cigarette a thin paper tube stuffed with shredded tobacco for smoking, usually plugged with a filter. The first cigarettes were the *papelitos* smoked in

South America about 1750. The habit spread to Spain, and then throughout the world, and is today the most general form of tobacco smoking.

cilia (singular *cilium*) small thread-like organs on the surface of some cells, composed of contractile fibres which produce rhythmic waving movements. Some single-celled organisms move by means of

cinema: chronology

1826–34	Various machines were invented to show moving images: the stroboscope, zoetrope, and thaumatrope.
1872	Eadweard Muybridge demonstrated movement of horses' legs using 24 cameras.
1877	Invention of Praxinoscope; developed as a projector of successive images on screen in 1879 in France.
1878–95	Marey, a French physiologist, developed various forms of camera for recording human and animal movements.
1887	Augustin le Prince produced the first series of images on a perforated film; Thomas Edison took the first steps in developing a motion-picture recording and reproducing device to accompany recorded sound.
1888	William Friese-Green showed the first celluloid film and patented a movie camera.
1889	Edison invented 35mm film.
1890–94	Edison, using perforated film, perfected his Kinetograph camera and Kinetoscope individual viewer.
1895	The Lumière brothers, Auguste (1862–1954) and Louis (1864–1948), projected a film of a train arriving at a station. Some of the audience fled in terror.
1896	Pathé introduced the Berliner gramophone, using discs in synchronization with film. Lack of amplification, however, made the performances ineffective.
1899	Edison tried to improve amplification by using banks of phonographs.
1900	Attempts to synchronize film and disc were made by Gaumont in France and Goldschmidt in Germany.
1902	Georges Méliès (1861–1938) made *Le Voyage dans la lune/A Trip to the Moon*.
1903	The first 'western' was made in the USA: *The Great Train Robbery* by Edwin S Porter.

1906	The earliest colour film (Kinemacolor) was patented in Britain by George Albert Smith.
1908–1911	In France, Emile Cohl experimented with film animation.
1910	With the dominating influence of the Hollywood Studios, film actors and actresses began to be recognized as international stars.
1912	In Britain, Eugene Lauste designed experimental 'sound on film' systems.
1914–18	Full newsreel coverage of World War I.
1915	*The Birth of a Nation*, D W Griffith's epic on the American civil war, was released in the USA.
1918–19	A sound system called Tri-Ergon was developed in Germany which led to sound being recorded on film photographically. The photography of sound was also developed by Lee De Forrest in his Phonofilm system.
1923	The first sound film (as Phonofilm) was demonstrated.
1927	Release of the first major sound film, *The Jazz Singer*, Warners in New York. The first Academy Awards (Oscars) were given.
1928	Walt Disney released his first Mickey Mouse cartoon, *Steamboat Willie*.
1932	Technicolor (three-colour) process was used for a Walt Disney cartoon film.
1952	Cinerama (wide-screen presentation) was introduced in New York.
1953	Commercial 3-D (three-dimensional cinema) and wide screen Cinemascope were launched in the USA.
1959	The first film in Smell-O-Vision, *The Scent of Mystery*, was released. The process did not catch on.
1980	Most major films were released in Dolby stereo.
1982	Walt Disney's *Tron* was one of the first and most effective feature-length, computer-generated animation films.
1988	Robert Zemickis's *Who Framed Roger Rabbit* set new technical standards in combining live action with cartoon animation.

cilia. In multicellular animals, they keep lubricated surfaces clear of debris.

Cimabue Giovanni (Cenni de Peppi) c. 1240–1302. Italian painter, active in Florence, traditionally styled the 'father of Italian painting'. Among the works attributed to him are *Madonna and Child* (Uffizi, Florence), a huge Gothic image.

cinchona shrub or tree of the family Rubiaceae, found growing wild in the Andes. ◊Quinine is produced from the bark of some species and its culture has been introduced into India, Sri Lanka, the Philippines, and Indonesia.

Cincinnatus Lucius Quintus, lived 5th century BC. Early Roman general, known for his frugal lifestyle. Appointed dictator in 458 BC he defeated the Aequi in a brief campaign, then resumed life as a yeoman farmer.

ciné camera a camera which takes a rapid sequence of still photographs – 24 frames (pictures) each second. When the pictures are projected one after the other at the same speed on to a screen, they appear to show movement, because our eyes hold on to the image of one picture before the next one appears.

cinema a modern form of art and entertainment, consisting of 'moving pictures' projected on to a screen. Cinema borrows from the other arts, such as music, drama, and literature, but is entirely dependent for its origins on technological developments, including the technology of film.

CinemaScope trade name for a wide-screen process using anamorphic lenses, in which images are compressed during filming and then extended during projection over an area wider than the normal screen. The first film to be made in CinemaScope was *The Robe* 1953.

cinema vérité a style of film-making that aims to capture truth on film by observing, recording, and presenting real events and situations as they occur without exercising any directorial, editorial, or technical control.

Cinerama a wide-screen process devised in 1937 by Fred Waller of Paramount's special-effects department. Originally three 35mm cameras and three projectors were used to record and project a single image. Three aspects of the image were recorded and then projected on a large curved screen with the result that the images blended together to produce an illusion of vastness. The first Cinerama film was *How the West Was Won* 1962. It was eventually abandoned in favour of a single-lens 70mm process.

cinnabar mercuric sulphide, HgS, the only important ore of mercury. It is deposited in veins and impregnations near recent volcanic rocks and hot springs. The mineral itself is used as a red pigment, commonly known as **vermilion**. Cinnabar is found in Spain (Almadén), the USA (California), Peru, Italy, and Yugoslavia.

cinnamon bark of a tree *Cinnamomum zeylanicum*, grown in India and Sri Lanka. The bark is ground to make the spice used in curries and confectionery. Oil of cinnamon is obtained from waste bark, and is used as flavouring in food and medicine.

Cinque Ports group of ports in S England, originally five, Sandwich, Dover, Hythe, Romney, and Hastings, later including Rye, Winchelsea, and others. Probably founded in Roman times, they rose to importance after the Norman conquest, and until the end of the 15th century were bound to supply the ships and men necessary against invasion.

circadian rhythm the metabolic rhythm found in most organisms, which generally coincides with the 24 hour day. Its most obvious manifestation is the regular cycle of sleeping and waking, but body temperature and the concentration of ◊hormones which influence mood and behaviour also vary over the day.

Circe in Greek mythology, an enchantress. In the *Odyssey* of Homer she turned the followers of Odysseus into pigs when she held their leader captive.

circle path followed by a point which moves so as to keep a constant distance, the **radius**, from a fixed point, the **centre**. The longest distance in a straight line from one side of a circle to the other, passing through the centre, is called the **diameter**. It is twice the radius. The ratio of the distance all the way round the circle (the **circumference**) to the diameter is an ◊irrational number called π (*pi*), roughly equal to 3.14159. A circle of diameter d has a circumference C equal to πd, or $C = 2\pi r$, and an area $A = \pi r^2$.

circuit breaker a switching device designed to protect an electric circuit from excessive current. It has the same action as a ◊fuse, and many houses now have a circuit-breaker between the incoming mains supply and the domestic circuits.

circulatory system the system of vessels in an animal's body which transports essential substances (blood or other circulatory fluid) to and from the different parts of the body. Except for simple animals such as sponges and coelenterates (jellyfish, sea anemones, corals), all animals have a circulatory system.

circumcision surgical removal of part of the foreskin (prepuce) of the penis, usually performed in the newborn.

circumference in geometry, the curved line that encloses a plane figure, for example, a circle or an

circle

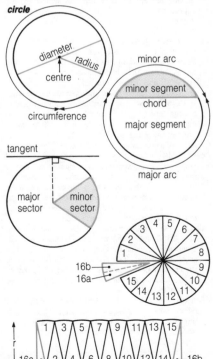

circulatory system

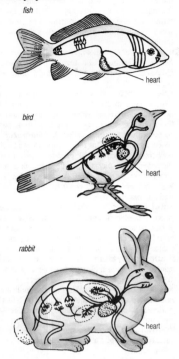

fish

heart

bird

heart

rabbit

heart

ellipse. Its length varies according to the nature of the curve, and may be ascertained by the appropriate formula. Thus, the circumference of a circle is $2\pi r$, where r is the radius and $\pi = 3.1415927...$

circumnavigation sailing round the world. The first ship to do so was the *Victoria*, one of the Spanish squadron of five vessels that sailed from Seville in Aug 1519 under Magellan.

circus (Latin 'circle') originally, in Roman times, an arena for chariot races and gladiatorial combats. In modern times, an entertainment, often held in a large tent ('big top'), involving performing animals, acrobats and clowns. In 1871, P T ◊Barnum created the 'Greatest Show on Earth'. The popularity of animal acts has decreased in the 1980s.

cirrhosis a liver disorder characterized by partial degeneration and scarring in response to damage. It may be caused by an infection such as viral hepatitis, by chronic alcoholism, congestive heart failure, or malnutrition. If cirrhosis is diagnosed early enough, it can be arrested by treating the cause; otherwise it will progress and may prove fatal.

Cisalpine southern region of the Roman province of Gallia, (N Italy); the northern, Transalpine Gaul, comprised modern Belgium, France, Netherlands and Switzerland. The *Cisalpine Republic* was the creation of Napoleon in N Italy in 1797, known as the Italian Republic 1802–04 and the Kingdom of Italy 1804–15.

Ciskei, Republic of a Bantu homeland in South Africa, which became independent 1981, although this is not recognized by any other country.
area 7,700 sq km/2,974 sq mi
capital Bisho
products pineapples, timber, metal products, leather, textiles

population (1984) 903,681
language Xhosa
government president (Lennox Sebe from 1981), with legislative and executive councils.

Cistercian order Roman Catholic monastic order established at Cîteaux 1098 by St Robert de Champagne, abbot of Molesme, as a stricter form of the Benedictine order. Living mainly by agricultural labour, the Cistercians made many advances in farming methods in the Middle Ages. The *Trappists*, so called from the original house at La Trappe in Normandy (founded by Dominique de Rancé 1664), follow a particularly strict version of the rule (including the maintenance of silence, manual labour, and a vegetarian diet).

cistron in genetics, the segment of ◊DNA that is required to synthesize a complete polypeptide chain. It is the molecular equivalent of a ◊gene.

CITES abbreviation for (*Convention on International Trade in Endangered Species*) an international agreement signed by 81 countries under the auspices of the ◊IUCN to regulate the trade in ◊endangered species of animals and plants.

cithara ancient musical instrument, resembling a lyre but with a flat back. It was strung with wire and plucked with a plectrum or (after the 16th century) with the fingers. The bandurria and laud, still popular in Spain, are instruments of the same type.

Citizens Advice Bureaux (CAB) UK organization established 1939 to provide information and advice to the public on any subject, such as personal problems, financial, house purchase, or consumer rights. If required, the bureaux will act on behalf of citizens, drawing on its own sources of legal and other experts. There are more than 600 bureaux located all over the UK.

citizens' band (CB) short-range radio communication (around 27 MHz) facility used by members of the public in USA and many European countries to chat or call for assistance in emergency.

citric acid an organic acid widely distributed in the plant kingdom, especially in citrus fruits. It is a white powder with a sharp acid taste. At one time it was prepared from concentrated lemon juice, but now the main source is the fermentation of sugar with certain moulds.

citronella lemon-scented oil used in cosmetics and insect-repellants, obtained from the S Asian grass *Cymbopogon nardus*.

citrus genus of trees and shrubs, family Rutaceae, found in the warmer parts of the world, particularly Asia. They are evergreen and aromatic, and several species – the orange, lemon, lime, citron and grapefruit – are cultivated for fruit.

city generally, a large and and important town; in the UK one awarded the title by the crown, and traditionally a cathedral town. In ancient Europe cities were states in themselves. In the early Middle Ages, cities were usually those towns which were episcopal sees (seats of bishops).

City, The the financial centre of London.

city technology college in the UK, a planned network of some 20 schools, financed jointly by government and industry, designed to teach technological subjects in inner-city areas to students aged 11–18.

Ciudad Juárez city on the Rio Grande, in Chihuahua state, N Mexico, on the border with the USA. Population (1980) 567,300. It is a centre for cotton.

civet type of small to medium-sized carnivorous mammal found in Africa and Asia, belonging to the family Viverridae, which also includes ◊**mongooses** and ◊**genets**. Distant relations of cats, they generally have longer jaws and more teeth. All have a scent gland in the inguinal (groin) region.

civil aviation the operation of passenger and freight transport by air. With increasing traffic, control of air space is a major problem, and in 1963 Eurocontrol was established by Belgium, Britain, France, West Germany, Luxembourg, and the Netherlands to supervise both military and civil movement in the air space over member countries. There is also a tendency to co-ordinate services and other facilities between national airlines, for example, the establishment of Air Union by France (Air France), W Germany (Lufthansa), Italy (Alitalia) and Belgium (Sabena) 1963.

civil defence organization of the civilian population of a state to mitigate the effects of enemy attack.

civil disobedience the deliberate breaking of laws considered unjust, a form of nonviolent direct action; the term was coined by the US writer Thoreau in an essay of that name 1849. It was advocated by Mahatma Gandhi to prompt peaceful withdrawal of British power from India. Civil disobedience has since been employed by, for instance, the US civil-rights movement in the 1960s and the peace movement in the 1980s.

civil engineering the branch of engineering that is concerned with the construction of roads, bridges, aqueducts, water-works, tunnels, canals, irrigation works, and harbours.

civil law the legal system based on ◊Roman law. It is one of the two main European legal systems, English (common) law being the other.

civil list in the UK, the annual sum provided from public funds to meet the official expenses of the sovereign and immediate dependants; private expenses are met by the ◊privy purse.

civil-list pension in the UK, a pension originally paid out of the sovereign's civil list, but granted separately since the accession of Queen Victoria. These are paid to persons in need, who have just claims on the royal beneficence, who have rendered personal service to the crown, or who have rendered service to the public by their discoveries in science and attainments in literature, art, or the like. The recipients are nominated by the prime minister, and the list is approved by Parliament.

civil rights the rights of the individual citizen. In many countries they are specified (as in the Bill of Rights of the US constitution) and guaranteed by law to ensure equal treatment for all citizens. In the USA, the struggle to obtain civil rights for former slaves and their descendants, both through legislation and in practice, has been a major theme since the Civil War.

civil service the body of administrative staff appointed to carry out the policy of a government. Members of the UK civil service may not take an active part in politics, and do not change with the government.

civil war war between rival groups within the same country.

Civil War, American (also called *the War Between the States*) war 1861–65 between the Southern or Confederate States of America and the Northern or Union states. The former wished to maintain their 'states' rights', in particular the institution of slavery, and claimed the right to secede from the Union; the latter fought initially to maintain the Union, and later (1863) to emancipate the slaves.

1861 Seven Southern states set up the Confederate States of America (president Jefferson Davis) 8 Feb; ◊Fort Sumter, Charleston, captured 12–14 Apr; Robert E Lee (Confederate) was victorious at the *1st Battle of Bull Run* 21 Jul.

1862 Battle of *Shiloh* 6–7 Apr was indecisive. Gen Grant (Unionist) captured New Orleans in May, but the Confederates were again victorious at the *2nd Battle of Bull Run* 29–30 Aug. Lee's advance was then checked by Gen McClellan at ◊Antietam 17 Sep.

1863 The Emancipation Proclamation was issued by President Lincoln on 1 Jan, freeing the slaves; *Battle of Gettysburg* (Union victory) 1–4 Jul marked the turning point of the war; Grant overran the Mississippi states, capturing *Vicksburg* 4 Jul.

1864 In the *Battle of Cold Harbor* near Richmond, Virginia, 1–12 Jun, Lee delayed Grant in his advance on Richmond. The Union Gen Sherman marched through Georgia to the sea, taking *Atlanta* 1 Sep and Savannah 22 Dec.

1865 Lee surrendered to Grant at *Appomattox* courthouse 9 Apr; Lincoln was assassinated 14 Apr; last Confederate troops surrendered 26 May. There were 359,528 Union dead and 258,000 Confederate dead.

Civil War, English in British history, the struggle in the middle years of the 17th century between the king and the Royalists (Cavaliers) on one side, and the Parliamentarians (also called Roundheads) on the other.

1642 On 22 Aug Charles I raised his standard at Nottingham. The Battle of ◊Edgehill on 23 Oct was indecisive.

1644 The Battle of ◊Marston Moor on 2 July was a victory for the Parliamentarians under ◊Cromwell.

1645 The Battle of ◊Naseby on 14 June was a decisive victory for Cromwell.

1646 On 5 May 1646 Charles surrendered to the Scottish army.

1648 A Royalist and Presbyterian rising in Mar to Aug was soon crushed by Cromwell and his New Model Army.

1649–50 Cromwell's invasion of Ireland.

1650 Cromwell defeated the Royalists under the future Charles II at Dunbar, Scotland.

1651 The Battle of Worcester was another victory for Cromwell.

Civil War, Spanish war 1936–39 precipitated by a military revolt led by Gen Franco against the Republican government. Franco's insurgents (Nationalists, who were supported by Fascist Italy and Nazi Germany) seized power in the S and NW, but were suppressed in areas such as Madrid and Barcelona by the workers' militia. The loyalists (Republicans) were aided by the USSR and the volunteers of the International Brigade, which included several writers, among them George Orwell. Inferior military capability led to the gradual defeat of the Republicans by 1939.

1937 Bilbao and the Basque country were bombed into submission by the Nationalists.

1938 Catalonia was cut off from the main Republican territory.

1939 Barcelona fell in Jan and Madrid in Apr, and Franco established a dictatorship.

cladistics a method of biological ◊classification (taxonomy) which uses a formal step-by-step procedure for objectively assessing the extent to which organisms share particular characters, and for assigning them to taxonomic groups. These

clam

giant clam

taxonomic groups (◊species, ◊genus, family, and so on) are termed *clades*.

cladode a flattened stem that is leaf-like in appearance and function. It is an adaptation to dry conditions because a stem contains fewer ◊stomata than a leaf, and water loss is thus minimized. The true leaves are usually reduced to spines or small scales. Examples of plants with cladodes are butcher's broom *Ruscus aculeatus*, *Asparagus*, and certain cacti. Cladodes may bear flowers or fruit on their surface and this distinguishes them from leaves.

Clair René, pseudonym of René-Lucien Chomette 1898–1981. French film-maker, originally a poet, novelist, and journalist. His *Sous les Toits de Paris/Under the Roofs of Paris* 1930 was one of the first sound films.

clam name used to include any ◊bivalve mollusc. The *giant clam Tridacna gigas* of the Indopacific can weigh, with the shell, 225 kg/500 lb.

clan social grouping based on ◊kinship, most familiar in the Highland clans of Scotland, theoretically each descended from a single ancestor from whom the name is derived, for example, clan MacGregor ('son of Gregor'). Rivalry between clans were often bitter, and they played a large role in the Jacobite revolts of 1715 and 1745, after which their individual tartan Highland dress was banned 1746–82.

Clapton Eric 1945– . English blues and rock guitarist, singer, and composer, member of the Yardbirds 1963–65 and Cream 1966–68. Originally a blues purist, then one of the pioneers of heavy rock with Cream and on the album *Layla* 1970 (released under the name Derek and the Dominos) he later adopted a more laid-back style in his solo career, as on *Journeyman* 1989.

Clare county on the west coast of the Republic of Ireland, in the province of Munster; area 3,188 sq km/1,231 sq mi; population (1991) 90,800. Shannon airport is here.

Clare John 1793–1864. English poet. His work includes *Poems Descriptive of Rural Life* 1820, *The Village Minstrel* 1821, and *Shepherd's Calendar* 1827. Clare's work was largely rediscovered in the 20th century.

Clarendon, Constitutions of in English history, a series of resolutions agreed by a council

Clapton *Eric Clapton (right) with George Harrison (left) at the Live Aid concert, 1985.*

summoned by Henry II at Clarendon in Wiltshire 1164. The Constitutions aimed at limiting the secular power of the clergy, and were abandoned after the murder of Thomas Becket. They form an important early English legal document.

Clare, St *c.* 1194–1253. Christian saint. Born in Assisi, Italy, she became at 18 a follower of St Francis, who founded for her the convent of San Damiano. Here she gathered the first members of the **Order of Poor Clares**. In 1958 she was proclaimed by Pius XII the patron saint of television. Feast day 12 Aug.

claret English term for the red wines of Bordeaux, since the 17th century.

clarinet a musical ◊woodwind instrument with a single reed, and a cylindrical tube, broadening at the end, developed in Germany in the 18th century. At the lower end of its range it has a rich 'woody' tone, which becomes increasingly brilliant toward the upper register.

Clark Joe (Joseph) Charles 1939– . Canadian Progressive Conservative politician, born in Alberta. He became party leader 1976, and defeated Trudeau 1979 to become the youngest prime minister in Canada's history. Following the rejection of his government's budget, he was defeated in a second election in Feb 1980. He became Secretary of State for External Affairs (foreign minister) in the Mulroney government (1984–).

Clark Mark (Wayne) 1896–1984. US general in World War II. In 1942 he became chief of staff for ground forces, led a successful secret mission by submarine to get information in N Africa preparatory to the Allied invasion, and commanded the 5th Army in the invasion of Italy.

Clarke Arthur C(harles) 1917– . English science fiction and non-fiction writer, who originated the plan for the modern system of communications satellites 1945. His works include *Childhood's End* 1953 and the screen play of *2001: A Space Odyssey* 1968.

Clarke Kenneth (Harry) 1940– . British Conservative politician, member of Parliament from 1970, a cabinet minister from 1985, education secretary 1990–92, home secretary 1992–93, Chancellor of the Exchequer from 1993.

Clarke orbit an alternative name for ◊geostationary orbit, an orbit 35,900 km/22,300 mi high, in which satellites circle at the same speed as the Earth turns. This orbit was first suggested by space writer Arthur C ◊Clarke in 1945.

Clarkson Thomas 1760–1846. British philanthropist. From 1785 he devoted himself to a campaign against slavery. He was one of the founders of the Anti-Slavery Society 1823 and was largely responsible for the abolition of slavery in British colonies 1833.

class in sociology, the main form of social stratification in industrial societies, based primarily on economic and occupational factors, but also referring to people's style of living or sense of group identity.

class in biological classification, a group of related ◊orders. For example, all mammals belong to the class Mammalia and all birds to the class Aves. Among plants, all class names end in 'idae' (such as Asteridae) and among fungi in 'mycetes'; there are no equivalent conventions among animals. Related classes are grouped together in a ◊phylum.

classical economics school of economic thought which dominated 19th century thinking. It originated with Adam Smith's *The Wealth of Nations* 1776 which embodied many of the basic concepts and principles of the classical school. Smith's theories were further developed in the writings of John Stuart Mill and David Ricardo. Central to the theory was economic freedom, competition and laissez faire government. The idea that economic growth could best be promoted by free trade, unassisted by government, was in conflict with ◊mercantilism.

Classicism in literature, music, and art, a style that emphasizes the qualities traditionally considered characteristic of ancient Greek and Roman art, that is, reason, balance, objectivity, restraint, and strict adherence to form. The term Classicism is often used to characterize the culture of 18th-century Europe, and contrasted with the 19th century Romanticism.

classification in biology, the arrangement of organisms into a hierarchy of groups, on the basis of their similarities in biochemical, anatomical or physiological characters. The basic grouping is a ◊species, several of which may constitute a ◊genus, which in turn are grouped into families, and so on up through orders, classes, phyla (or, in plants, divisions) to kingdoms.

clathrates compounds formed by small molecules filling in the holes in the structural lattice of another compound, for example, sulphur dioxide molecules in ice crystals. Clathrates are, therefore, intermediate between mixtures and compounds.

Claude Lorrain (Claude Gellée) 1600–1682. French landscape painter, active in Rome from 1627. His subjects are mostly mythological and historical, with insignificant figures lost in great expanses of poetic scenery, as in *The Enchanted Castle* 1664 (National Gallery, London).

Claudian or Claudius Claudianus *c.* 370–404. Last of the great Latin poets of the Roman empire. He was probably born at Alexandria, and wrote official panegyrics, epigrams, and the epic *The Rape of Proserpine*.

Claudius 10 BC–54 AD. Nephew of ◊Tiberius, made Roman emperor by his troops in 41, after the murder of Caligula, though more inclined to scholarly pursuits. During his reign the Roman Empire was considerably extended, and in 43 he took part in the invasion of Britain. He was long dominated by his third wife, Messalina, whom ultimately he had executed, and is thought to have been poisoned by his fourth wife, Agrippina the Younger.

Clause 28 in British law, a controversial clause in the Local Government Bill 1988 (now section 28 of the Local Governenment Act 1988) which prohibits local authorities promoting homosexuality by publishing material, or by promoting the teaching in state schools of the acceptability of homosexuality as a 'pretended family relationship'. It became law despite widespread opposition.

Clausewitz Karl von 1780–1831. Prussian officer and writer on war, born near Magdeburg. He is known mainly for his book *Vom Kriege/On War* 1833.

Clausius Rudolf Julius Emaneul 1822–1888. German physicist, one of the founders of the science of thermodynamics. In 1850, he enunciated its second law: heat cannot of itself pass from a colder to a hotter body.

claustrophobia a ◊phobia involving fear of enclosed spaces.

Claverhouse John Graham, Viscount Dundee 1649–1689. Scottish soldier. Appointed by Charles II to suppress the ◊Covenanters from 1677, he was routed at Drumclog 1679, but three weeks later won the battle of Bothwell Bridge, by which

the rebellion was crushed. Until 1688 he was engaged in continued persecution and became known as 'Bloody Clavers', regarded by the Scottish people as a figure of evil. Then his army joined the first Jacobite rebellion and defeated the loyalist forces in the pass of Killiecrankie, where he was mortally wounded.

clavichord stringed keyboard instrument, popular in Renaissance Europe and in 18th-century Germany until the early 19th century. Notes are sounded by a metal blade striking the string. It was a forerunner of the pianoforte.

claw a hard, hooked pointed outgrowth of the digits of mammals, birds, and some reptiles. Claws are composed of the protein keratin, and grow continuously from a bundle of cells in the lower skin layer. Hooves and nails are modified structures with the same origin as claws.

clay a mud that has undergone a greater or lesser degree of consolidation. It may be white, grey, red, yellow, blue-ish, or black, and consists essentially of hydrated silicates of alumina, together with sand, lime, iron, oxides, magnesium, potassium, soda, and organic substances. When moistened it is rendered plastic. It hardens on heating, which renders it impermeable.

Clay Cassius Marcellus original name of boxer Muhammad ◊Ali.

Cleese John 1939– . English actor and comedian. For television he has written for the satirical *That Was The Week That Was* and *The Frost Report*, and the comic *Monty Python's Flying Circus* and *Fawlty Towers*. His films include *A Fish Called Wanda* 1988.

clef in music, the symbol used to indicate the pitch of the lines of the staff in musical notation.

cleft palate fissure of the roof of the mouth, often accompanied by a hare lip, the result of a genetic defect.

Cleisthenes ruler of Athens. Inspired by Solon, he is credited with the establishment of democracy in Athens 507 BC.

cleistogamy the production of flowers which never fully open and are automatically self-fertilized. Cleistogamous flowers are often formed late in the year, after the production of normal flowers, or during a period of cold weather, as seen in several species of *Viola*.

clematis genus of temperate woody climbers with showy flowers, family Ranunculaceae. The wild *traveller's joy* or *old man's beard*, *Clematis vitalba*, is the only British species, although

Cleese English actor John Cleese in A Fish Called Wanda 1988.

Bill Clinton

many have been introduced, and garden hybrids bred.

Clemenceau Georges 1841–1929. French politician and journalist (prominent in defence of ◊Dreyfus). After World War I he presided over the Peace Conference in Paris that drew up the Treaty of ◊Versailles, but failed to secure for France the Rhine as a frontier.

Clement VII 1478–1534. Pope 1523–34. He refused to allow the divorce of Henry VIII of England and Catherine of Aragon. He was the illegitimate son of a brother of Lorenzo di Medici, the ruler of Florence.

Cleopatra *c.* 68–30 BC. Queen of Egypt from 51 BC. In 49 BC the Roman general Julius Caesar arrived in Egypt and she became his mistress, bore him a son, Caesarion, and accompanied him to Rome. After Caesar's murder 44 BC she returned to Alexandria and resumed her position as queen of Egypt. From 40 BC one of Caesar's successors, Mark Antony, lived with her. Rome declared war on Egypt 32 BC and scored a decisive victory in the naval Battle of Actium the following year; Mark Antony and Cleopatra killed themselves.

Cleopatra's Needle either of two ancient Egyptian granite obelisks erected at Heliopolis in the 15th century BC by Thothmes III, and removed to Alexandria by the Roman emperor Augustus about 14 BC. They have no connection with Cleopatra's reign. One of the pair was taken to London 1878 and erected on the Victoria Embankment; it is 21 m/68.5 ft high. The other was given by the khedive of Egypt to USA, and erected in Central Park, New York, 1881.

Clermont-Ferrand city, capital of Puy-de-Dôme *département,* in the Auvergne region of France; population (1990) 140,200. It is a centre for agriculture, and its rubber industry is the largest in France.

Cleveland county in NE England
area 583 sq km/225 sq mi
towns administrative headquarters Middlesbrough; Stockton on Tees, Billingham, Hartlepool
products steel, chemicals
population (1987) 555,000

Cleveland largest city of Ohio, USA, on Lake Erie at the mouth of the river Cuyahoga; population (1981) 574,000, metropolitan area 1,899,000. Its chief industries are the iron and steel works, and petroleum refining.

Cleveland (Stephen) Grover 1837–1908. 22nd and 24th president of the USA, 1885–89 and 1893–97; notable as the first Democratic president elected after the Civil War, and as the only president to hold office for two nonconsecutive terms. He attempted to check corruption in public life, and in 1895 initiated arbitration proceedings which eventually settled a territorial dispute with Britain concerning the Venezuelan boundary.

climate weather conditions at a particular place over a period of time. Climate encompasses all the meteorological elements and the factors that influence them. The primary factors that determine the variations of climate over the surface of the Earth are: (a) the effect of latitude and the tilt of the Earth's axis to the plane of the orbit about the Sun ($66\ 1/2°$); (b) the difference between land and sea; (c) contours of the ground; and (d) location of the area in relation to ocean currents. Catastrophic variations to climate may be caused by the impact of another planetary body, or clouds resulting from volcanic activity.

climax community an assemblage of plants and animals that is relatively stable in its environment (for example, oak woods in Britain). It is brought about by ecological ◊succession, and represents the point at which succession ceases to occur.

climax vegetation the state of equilibrium that is reached after a series of changes have occurred in the vegetation of a particular habitat. It is the final stage in a ◊succession, where the structure and species of a habitat do not develop further, providing conditions remain unaltered.

clinical psychology discipline dealing with the understanding and treatment of health problems, particularly mental disorders. The main problems dealt with include anxiety, phobias, depression, obsessions, sexual and marital problems, drug and alcohol dependence, childhood behavioural problems, psychoses (such as schizophrenia), mental handicap and brain damage (such as dementia).

Clinton Bill (William Jefferson) 1946– . 42nd president of the USA from 1993. A Democrat, he served as governor of Arkansas 1979–81 and 1983–93, establishing a liberal and progressive reputation. He won a successful 1992 presidential campaign against the incumbent George ◊Bush by centring on domestic issues and economic recovery. He became the first Democrat in the White House for 13 years.

Clive Robert, Baron Clive of Plassey 1725–1774. British general and administrator, who established British rule in India by victories over the French at Arcot in the Carnatic (a region in SE India) 1751 and over the nawab of Bengal, Suraj-ud-Dowlah, at Calcutta and Plassey 1757. On his return to Britain his wealth led to allegations that he had abused his power.

cloaca the common opening of the digestive, urinary and reproductive tracts; a cloaca is found in most vertebrates; placental mammals, however, have a separate anus and urinogenital opening instead of one posterior opening to the body, the cloacal aperture. The cloaca forms a chamber in which products can be stored before being voided from the body via a muscular opening.

clone group of cells or organisms arising by asexual reproduction from a single 'parent' individual. Clones therefore have exactly the same genetic make-up. The term has been adopted by computer technology, in which it describes a (non-existent) device that mimics an actual one to enable certain software programs to run correctly.

closed-circuit TV (CCTV) a localized television system in which programmes are sent over relatively short distances, the camera, receiver and controls being linked by cable. Closed-circuit TV systems are used in department stores and large offices as a means of internal security, monitoring peoples' movement.

closed shop a company or firm, public corporation, or other body that requires its employees to be members of the appropriate trade union. The practice became legally enforceable in the UK 1976, but was rendered largely inoperable by the Employment Acts 1980 and 1982. Usually demanded by unions, the closed shop may be preferred by employers as simplifying negotiation, but it was condemned by the European Court of Human Rights 1981. In the USA the closed shop was made illegal by the Taft-Hartley Act 1947, passed by Congress over Truman's veto.

cloud water vapour condensed into minute water particles that float in masses in the atmosphere. Like fogs or mists, from which clouds are distinguished by the height at which they occur above the ground, they are formed by the cooling of air charged with water vapour which condenses generally on tiny dust particles.

cloud chamber apparatus for tracking ionized particles. It consists of a vessel filled with air or other gas, saturated with water vapour. When suddenly expanded, this cools and a cloud of tiny droplets forms on any nuclei, dust, or ions present. If single fast-moving ionizing particles collide with the air or gas molecules, they show as visible tracks.

Clouet François c. 1515–1572. French portrait painter, who succeeded his father Jean Clouet (1486-1541 as court painter. He worked in the fashionable Italian style of Mannerism. His half-nude portrait of Diane de Poitiers, *The Lady in her Bath c.* 1540 (National Gallery, Washington), is a piece of refined eroticism.

clove the unopened flower bud of the clover tree *Eugenia caryophyllus*. A member of the family Myrtaceae, the clover tree is a native of the Moluccas. Cloves are used for flavouring in cookery and confectionery. Oil of cloves, which has tonic and carminative qualities, is employed in medicine.

clover leguminous plant, of which there are a great number of species which mostly belong to the genus *Trifolium*. Found mainly in temperate regions, clover plants have trifoliate leaves and roundish flowerheads or a spike of small flowers. Many species are cultivated as fodder plants.

Clovis 465–511. Merovingian King of the Franks from 481. He succeeded his father Childeric as king of the Salian (northern) Franks, defeated the Gallo-Romans (Romanized Gauls) near Soissons 486, ending their rule in France, and defeated the Alemanni, a confederation of Germanic tribes, near Cologne in 496. He embraced Christianity and subsequently proved a powerful defender of orthodoxy against the Arian ◊Visigoths, whom he defeated at Poitiers 507. He made Paris his capital.

club an association of persons for social purposes, indulgence in sport or hobbies, or discussion of matters of common interest. The London men's clubs of today developed from the taverns and coffee-houses of the 17th and 18th centuries. The oldest is White's, evolved from a chocolate-house of the same name in 1693.

Club of Rome informal international organization, set up after a meeting at the Accademia dei Lincei, Rome, in 1968, which aims to promote greater understanding of the interdependence of global economic, political, natural, and social systems.

cloud

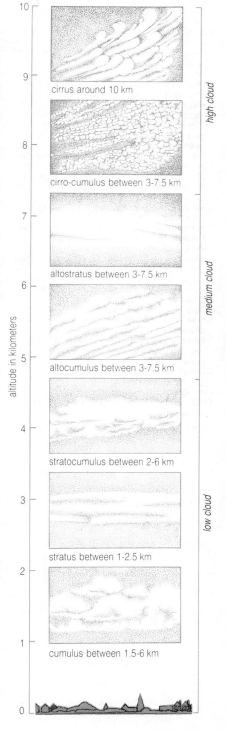

cirrus around 10 km

cirro-cumulus between 3-7.5 km

altostratus between 3-7.5 km

altocumulus between 3-7.5 km

stratocumulus between 2-6 km

stratus between 1-2.5 km

cumulus between 1.5-6 km

altitude in kilometers

high cloud

medium cloud

low cloud

clubroot a disease affecting cabbages, turnips, and allied plants of the Cruciferae family. It is caused by a ◊slime mould *Plasmodiophora brassicae*. This attacks the roots of the plant, which send out knotty outgrowths, hence the popular name of finger-and-toe disease; eventually the whole plant decays.

Clunies-Ross family that established a benevolently paternal rule in the Cocos Islands. John Clunies-Ross settled on Home Island in 1827: the family's rule ended in 1978 with the purchase of the Cocos by the Australian government.

clutch a device for disconnecting rotating shafts, particularly in a car's transmission system. In a car with a manual gearbox, the driver depresses the clutch when changing gear, thus disconnecting the engine from the gearbox. The clutch consists of two main plates, a pressure plate and a driven plate, which is mounted on a shaft leading to the gearbox. When the clutch is engaged, the pressure plate presses the driven plate against the engine ◊flywheel and drive goes to the gearbox. Depressing the clutch springs the pressure plate away, freeing the driven plate.

Clwyd county in N Wales
area 2,426 sq km/937 sq mi
towns administrative headquarters Mold; Flint, Denbigh, Wrexham; seaside resorts Colwyn Bay, Rhyl, Prestatyn
physical rivers Dee and Clwyd; Clwydian Range with Offa's Dyke along the main ridge
products dairy and meat products, optical glass, chemicals, limestone, microprocessors, plastics
population (1981) 391,000
language 19% Welsh-speaking; English

Clyde river in Strathclyde, Scotland; 170 km/103 mi long. The Firth of Clyde and Firth of Forth are linked by the Forth and Clyde canal, 56 km/35 mi long. The shipbuilding yards have declined in recent years.

Clytemnestra in Greek mythology, the wife of ◊Agamemnon.

cm abbreviation for *centimetre*.

CND abbreviation for *Campaign for Nuclear Disarmament*.

Cnossus alternative form of ◊Knossos.

c/o abbreviation for *care of*.

CO abbreviation for *Commanding Officer*.

co. abbreviation for *company*.

coal mineral substance of fossil origin, the result of the transformation of ancient plant matter under progressive compression. It is classified according to the proportion of carbon and volatiles it contains. The main types are ◊anthracite (bright, with more than 90% carbon), *bituminous coal* (bright and dull patches), ◊*lignite* (woody, grading into peat), and ◊*peat* (no woody structure but only 70% cent carbon).

coal gas gas produced when ◊coal is destructively distilled or heated out of contact with the air. Its main constituents are methane, hydrogen and carbon monoxide. Coal gas has been superseded by ◊natural gas for domestic purposes.

coalition an association of political groups, usually for some limited or short-term purpose, such as fighting an election or forming a government when one party has failed to secure a majority in a legislature.

coaltar black oily material resulting from the destructive distillation of coal.

coastal erosion the sea erodes the land by the constant battering of the waves. This produces two effects. The first is a hydraulic effect, in which the force of the wave compresses air pockets in the rocks and cliffs, and the air can then expand explosively. The second is the effect of abrasion, in which rocks and pebbles are flung against the cliffs, wearing them away. In areas where there are beaches, the waves cause longshore drift, in which the sand and stone fragments are carried in a particular direction parallel to the shore.

coati climbing mammal related to the ◊raccoon, with a long flexible pig-like snout used for digging, a good sense of smell, and long claws and long tail. They live in packs in the forests of S and Central America.

co-axial cable an electric cable that consists of a central conductor surrounded by a conducting tube or sheath. It can transmit the high-frequency

clutch

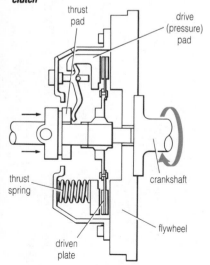

thrust pad
drive (pressure) pad
thrust spring
crankshaft
driven plate
flywheel

disengaged (pedal pressed down)

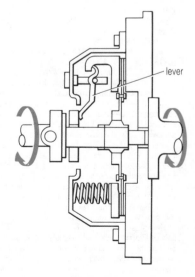

lever

engaged (pedal up)

coastal erosion

The sea erodes the land by the constant battering of waves. The force of the waves creates a hydraulic effect, compressing air to form explosive pockets in the rocks and cliffs. The waves also have an abrasive effect, flinging rocks and pebbles against the cliff faces and wearing them away.

In areas where there are beaches, the waves cause longshore drift, in which sand and stone fragments are carried in a particular direction parallel to the shore.

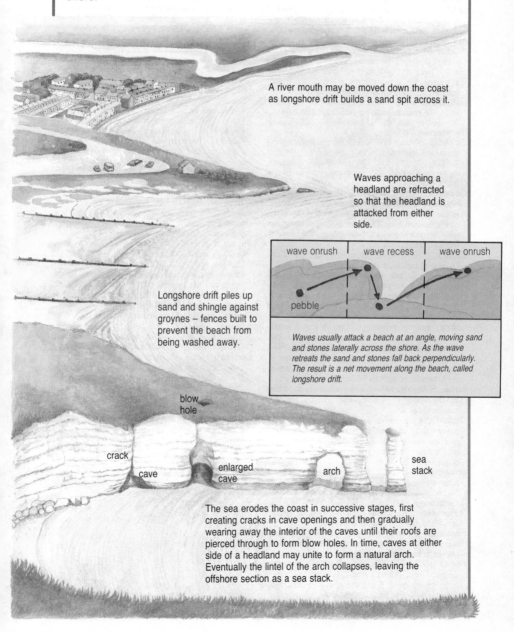

A river mouth may be moved down the coast as longshore drift builds a sand spit across it.

Waves approaching a headland are refracted so that the headland is attacked from either side.

Longshore drift piles up sand and shingle against groynes – fences built to prevent the beach from being washed away.

wave onrush | wave recess | wave onrush

pebble

Waves usually attack a beach at an angle, moving sand and stones laterally across the shore. As the wave retreats the sand and stones fall back perpendicularly. The result is a net movement along the beach, called longshore drift.

blow hole

crack

cave

enlarged cave

arch

sea stack

The sea erodes the coast in successive stages, first creating cracks in cave openings and then gradually wearing away the interior of the caves until their roofs are pierced through to form blow holes. In time, caves at either side of a headland may unite to form a natural arch. Eventually the lintel of the arch collapses, leaving the offshore section as a sea stack.

cobra

Indian cobra

signals used in television, telephone and other telecommunications transmissions.

cobalt metallic element, closely resembling nickel in appearance, symbol Co, atomic number 27, relative atomic mass 58.94. It occurs in a number of ores, and is used as a pigment and in alloys. Cobalt-60 is a radioactive (half-life 5.3 years) substance produced by neutron radiation in heavy-water reactors, and used in large quantities as a source for gamma rays in cancer therapy, substituting for the much more costly radium.

cobalt ore cobalt extracted from a number of minerals, the main ones being **smaltite**, $(Co,Ni)As_2$; **linnaeite**, $(Co,Ni)_3S_4$; **cobaltite**, CoAsS; and **erythrite**, $Co_3(AsO_4)_2 \cdot 8H_2O$.

Cobbett William 1763–1835. British Radical politician and journalist, who published the weekly *Political Register* 1802–35. His crusading essays on farmers' conditions were collected as *Rural Rides* 1830.

Cobden Richard 1804–1865. British Liberal politician and economist, co-founder with John Bright of the Anti-Corn Law League 1839. A Member of Parliament from 1841, he opposed class and religious privileges and believed in disarmament and free trade.

COBOL (*CO*mmon *B*usiness-*O*riented *L*anguage) a computer-programming language, designed in the late 1950s especially for business use. COBOL facilitates the writing of programs that deal with large computer files and handle business arithmetic, and has become the major language for commercial data processing.

cobra type of venomous, smooth-scaled snake found in Africa and S Asia, species of which can grow from 1 m/3 ft to over 4.3 m/14 ft. The neck stretches into a 'hood' when the snake is alarmed. Their venom contains nerve toxins which are powerful enough to kill humans.

coca S American shrub *Erythroxylon coca*, family Erythroxylaceae, whose dried leaves are the source of cocaine.

Coca-Cola a sweetened, fizzy drink, originally flavoured by coca and cola nuts, containing caramel and caffeine. Invented 1886, Coca-Cola was sold in every state of the USA by 1895 and in 155 countries by 1987.

cocaine a stimulant, it is an alkaloid extracted from the leaves of the coca tree. It has very limited medical application, mainly as a local anaesthetic agent which is readily absorbed by mucous membranes (lining tissues) of the nose and throat. It is toxic, addictive, and illegal.

cockatiel Australian parrot *Nymphicus hollandicus*, about 20 cm/8 in long, with greyish plumage, yellow cheeks, a long tail, and a crest like a cockatoo.

cockatoo type of ◊parrot, usually white with tinges of red, yellow, or orange, with an erectile crest on the head. They are native to Australia, New Guinea, and nearby islands.

cockchafer beetle *Melolontha melolontha*, also known as **maybug**, up to 3 cm/1.2 in long, with heavy, clumsy, buzzing flight, seen on early summer evenings. They damage trees by feeding on the foliage and flowers, and the larvae, sometimes called **rookworms**, live underground, feeding on grass and cereal roots.

Cockcroft John Douglas 1897–1967. British physicist. In 1932, he and E T S Walton succeeded in splitting the nucleus of the atom for the first time, and in 1951 they were jointly awarded a Nobel prize.

Cockerell Christopher 1910– . British engineer, who invented the ◊hovercraft 1959.

cockle bivalve mollusc with ribbed, heart-shaped shell. The **common cockle** *Cerastoderma edule* is up to 5 cm/2 in across, and is found low on shores and in estuaries around N European and Mediterranean coasts in sand or mud.

cockroach insect of the family Blattidae, distantly related to the mantises. There are 3,500 species, mainly in the tropics. They have long antennae and biting mouthparts, and can fly, but rarely do so.

cocoa and chocolate food products made from the cacao (or cocoa) bean, fruit of a tropical tree *Theobroma cacao*, which grows chiefly in W Africa (Ghana, Nigeria), parts of S America, the West Indies, Java, and Sri Lanka, but is indigenous to S America. Chocolate was introduced to Europe as a drink in the 16th century; eating chocolate was first produced in the late 18th century.

cultivation The cacao tree grows to some 6 m/20 ft high. It begins bearing fruit about the fifth year; this matures rapidly as a pod, 12.5–22.5 cm/5–9 in) long, containing 20 to 40 seeds (beans) embedded in juicy white pulp. The trees bear all the year round and there are two, sometimes three, harvests.

coconut fruit of the coconut palm *Cocos nucifera*, which grows throughout the lowland tropics. The fruit has a large outer husk of fibres which is split off and used for coconut matting and ropes. Inside this is the nut exported to temperate countries. Its hard shell contains white flesh and coconut milk which makes a nourishing drink.

Cocos group of 27 small coral islands in the Indian Ocean, about 1,770 km/1,080 mi NW of Perth, Australia; area 14 sq km/5.5 sq mi; population (1984) 584. They are owned by Australia.

Cocteau Jean 1889–1963. French poet, dramatist, film director, and critic. A leading figure in European modernism, he worked with Picasso, Diaghilev and Stravinsky. He produced many volumes of poetry, ballets such as *Le Boeuf sur le toit/The Nothing Doing Bar* 1920, plays, for example, *Orphée/Orpheus* 1926, and a mature novel of bourgeois French life, *Les*

coconut

Cocteau *French playwright, novelist, poet, film director and artist, Jean Cocteau in 1929.*

Enfants terribles 1929, which he made into a film 1950.

cod sea fish *Gadus morhua* found in the N Atlantic and Baltic. Brown to grey with spots, white below, it can grow to 1.5 m/5 ft.

COD abbreviation for *cash on delivery*.

coda (Italian 'tail') in music, a concluding section of a movement added to indicate finality.

codeine an opium derivative which provides ◊analgesia in mild to moderate pain. It is also effective in suppressing coughs.

codex an ancient book, with pages stitched together and bound. During the 2nd century AD codices began to replace the earlier rolls.

cod liver oil oil obtained by subjecting fresh cod livers to pressure at a temperature of about 85°C. It is highly nutritious, being a valuable source of the vitamins A and D. Overdose can be harmful.

codon in ◊genetics, triplet of bases (see ◊base pair) in a molecule of ◊DNA or ◊RNA that codes for a particular ◊amino acid during the process of protein synthesis; see also ◊genetic code.

Cody Samuel Franklin 1862–1913. US aviation pioneer. He made his first powered flight on 16 Oct 1908 at Farnborough, England, in a machine of his own design. He was killed in a flying accident.

Cody William Frederick 1846–1917. US scout and performer, known as *Buffalo Bill* from his contract to supply buffalo carcasses to railway labourers (over 4,000 in 18 months). From 1883 he toured USA and Europe with a Wild West show.

Coe Sebastian 1956– . English middle distance runner. He was Olympic 1500 metre champion 1980 and 1984. Between 1979–81 he broke eight individual world records at 800, 1000, 1500 metres, and one mile.

coefficient the number part in front of an algebraic term, signifying multiplication. For example, in the expression $4x^2 + 2xy - x$, the coefficient of x^2 is 4 (because $4x^2$ means $4 \times x^2$), that of xy is 2, and that of x is –1 (because $-1 \times x = -x$).

coefficient of relationship the probability that any two individuals share a given ◊gene by virtue of being descended from a common ancestor. In ◊sexual reproduction of ◊diploid species, an individual shares half its genes with each parent, with its offspring, and (on average) with each sibling, but only a quarter (on average) with its grandchildren or its siblings' offspring, an eighth with its great-grandchildren, and so on.

coelacanth lobe-finned fish *Latimeria chalumnae* up to 2 m/6 ft long. They have bone and muscle at the base of the fins, and are distantly related to the lobefins which were the ancestors of all land animals with backbones. They live in deep water surrounding the Comoro Islands, off the coast of Madagascar. They were believed to be extinct, but were rediscovered 1938.

coeliac disease a disorder of the absorptive surface of the small intestine. It is mainly associated with an intolerance to gluten, a constituent of wheat.

coelom in all but the simplest animals, the fluid-filled cavity which separates the body wall from the gut and associated organs, and allows the gut muscles to contract independently of the rest of the body.

coffee a drink made from the roasted and ground seeds or berries of any of several species of the Coffea shrub, cultivated in the tropics. It contains a stimulant, ◊caffeine. Coffee drinking began in Arab countries in the 14th century but did not become common in Europe until 300 years later. In the 17th century the first coffee houses were opened in London.

cultivation Naturally about 5 m/17 ft, the shrub is pruned to about 2 m/7 ft, is fully fruit-bearing in five or six years and lasts for 30 years. Coffee grows best on frost-free hillsides with moderate rainfall. The world's largest producers are Brazil, Colombia, and Ivory Coast.

cogito, ergo sum (Latin) 'I think, therefore I am' quotation from French philosopher René Descartes.

cognition in psychology, a general term covering the functions involved in dealing with information, for example, perception (seeing, hearing, and so on) attention, memory, and reasoning.

cognitive therapy a treatment for emotional disorders, particularly ◊depression and ◊anxiety, developed by Professor Aaron T Beck in the USA. This approach encourages the client to challenge the distorted and unhelpful thinking that is characteristic of these problems. The treatment includes ◊behaviour therapy and has been particularly helpful for people suffering from depression.

coherence in physics, two or more waves of a beam of light or other ◊electromagnetic radiation having the same frequency, and the same ◊phase or a constant phase difference.

cohesion in physics, a phenomenon in which interaction between two surfaces of the same material in contact makes them cling together (with two different materials the similar phenomenon is called adhesion). According to kinetic theory, cohesion is caused by attraction between particles at the atomic or molecular level. Surface tension, which causes liquids to form spherical droplets, is caused by cohesion.

COI abbreviation for *Central Office of Information*.

coin a form of ◊money. In modern times the right to make and issue coins is a state monopoly and the great majority are tokens, in that their face value is greater than that of the metal of which they consist. A milled edge, originally used on gold and silver coins to avoid fraudulent 'clipping' of the edges of precious metal coins, is retained in some modern token coinage.

coke a clean, light fuel produced by the carbonization of certain types of coal. When this coal is strongly heated in airtight ovens, in order to release all volatile constituents, the brittle, silver-grey coke is left. It comprises 90 per cent carbon together with very small quantities of water, hydrogen, and oxygen, and makes a useful industrial and domestic fuel.

Coke Edward 1552–1634. Lord Chief Justice of England 1613–17. Against Charles I he drew up

Coleridge English poet and critic Samuel Taylor
Coleridge.

the ◊Petition of Right 1628. His *Institutes* are a legal
classic, and he ranks as the supreme common
lawyer.

Coke Thomas William 1754–1842. British pioneer
and promoter of the new improvements associated
with the Agricultural Revolution. His innovations
included regular manuring of the soil, the cultivation
of fodder crops in association with corn, and the
drilling of wheat and turnips.

cola or *kola* genus of tropical trees, family
Sterculiaceae. Their nuts are chewed in W Africa for
their high caffeine content, and in the West are used
with coca leaves to flavour soft drinks.

Colbert Jean-Baptiste 1619–1683. French
politician. Chief minister to Louis XIV, and
controller-general (finance minister) from 1665. He
reformed the Treasury, by protectionist measures
he promoted French industry and commerce, and
tried to make France a naval power equal to England
or the Netherlands, but favoured a peaceful foreign
policy.

cold, common minor disease caused by a variety
of viruses. Symptoms are headache, chill, nasal
discharge, sore throat and occasionally cough. Research indicates that the virulence of a cold depends
on psychological factors and either reduction or
increase of social or work activity as a result of
stress in the previous six months.

cold-blooded common name for ◊*poikilothermy*.

Colditz town in E Germany, near Leipzig, site of a
castle used as a high-security prisoner-of-war camp
(Oflag IVC) in World War II. Among daring escapes
was that of British Capt Patrick Reid and others in
Oct 1942. In 1990 the castle was converted into a
hotel.

cold war hostilities short of armed conflict, consisting of tensions, threats, and subversive political
activities; particularly the Cold War 1945–90 between the USSR and the West.

cold-working method of shaping metal at or near
atmospheric temperature.

Cole Thomas 1801–1848. US painter, founder of
the *Hudson River school* of landscape artists.

Coleman Ornette 1930– . US alto saxophonist
and composer. In the late 1950s he rejected the
established structural principles of jazz for free
avant-garde improvisation.

coleoptile the protective sheath which surrounds
the young shoot tip of a grass during its passage
through the soil to the surface. Although of relatively simple structure, most coleoptiles are very

sensitive to light, ensuring that seedlings grow
upwards.

Coleridge Samuel Taylor 1772–1834. English
poet, one of the founders of the Romantic movement. His poems include 'The Ancient Mariner',
'Christabel', and 'Kubla Khan'; critical works, some
of the finest in English, include *Biographia Literaria*
1817 and notes on Shakespeare's plays.

Colette Sidonie-Gabrielle 1873–1954. French
writer. At 20 she married Henri Gauthier-Villars, a
journalist known as 'Willy', and under this name her
four 'Claudine' novels, based on her own early life,
were published. Divorced in 1906, she was a striptease and mime artist for a while, but continued to
write, for example, *Chéri* 1920, *La Fin de Chéri/
The End of Chéri* 1926, and *Gigi* 1944.

colic a spasmodic attack of pain in the abdomen.
Colicky pains are usually caused by the blockage,
and subsequent distension, of a hollow organ, for
example the bowel, gall bladder (biliary colic) or
ureter (renal colic). Characteristically the pain is
very severe during contraction of the muscular wall
of the organ, then recedes temporarily as the
muscle tires.

Coligny Gaspard de 1517–1572. French admiral
and soldier, and prominent ◊Huguenot. About 1557
he joined the Protestant party, helping to lead the
Huguenot forces during the Wars of Religion. After
the Treaty of St. Germain 1570, he became a
favourite of the young king Charles IX, but on the
eve of the massacre of St Bartholomew's Day was
killed by a servant of the Duke of Guise.

colitis inflammation of the colon (large intestine).
Sulphonamides are among the drugs used in its
treatment. It may be due to food poisoning or some
types of dysentery.

collage a technique of pasting paper to create a picture. Several artists in the early 20th century used
collage: Arp, Braque, Ernst, and Schwitters, among
others. Many also experimented with *photomontage*, creating compositions from pieces of photographs rearranged with often disturbing effects.

collateral security available in return for a loan.
Usually stocks, shares, property, or life assurance
policies will be accepted as collateral.

collective farm a farm in which a group of farmers
pool their land, domestic animals, and agricultural
implements, retaining as private property enough
only for its own requirements. The profits of the
farm are divided among its members in proportion
to work done.

collective security a system for achieving international stability by an agreement among all states
to unite against any aggressor. Such a commitment
was embodied in the post-World War I League of
Nations and also in the United Nations Organization,
although neither body was able to live up to the
ideals of its founders.

collective unconscious in psychology, the
term used for the shared pool of memories inherited
from ancestors which Carl Jung suggested co-
existed with individual ◊unconscious recollections,
and which might be active both for evil in precipitating mental disturbance or for good in prompting
achievements (for example, in the arts).

collenchyma a plant tissue composed of somewhat elongated cells with thickened cell walls,
especially at the corners where adjacent cells meet.
It is a supporting and strengthening tissue found in
non-woody plants, particularly in the stems and
leaves.

collie type of sheepdog originally bred in Britain. The *rough* and *smooth collies* are about

60 cm/2 ft tall, and have long narrow heads and muzzles. The **border collie** is a working dog, often black and white, about 45 cm/1.5 ft tall, with a dense coat. The **bearded collie** is a little smaller, and rather like an Old English sheepdog in appearance.

Collier Jeremy 1650–1726. British Anglican cleric, a ◊Nonjuror, who was outlawed in 1696 for granting absolution on the scaffold to two men who had tried to assassinate William III. His *Short View of the Immorality and Profaneness of the English Stage* 1698 was aimed at the dramatists Congreve and Vanbrugh.

collimator 1. a small telescope attached to a larger optical instrument to fix its line of sight. 2. an optical device for producing a nondivergent beam of light. 3. any device for limiting the size and angle of spread of a beam of radiation or particles.

Collingwood Cuthbert, Baron Collingwood 1750–1810. British admiral, who served with Horatio Nelson in the West Indies against France and blockading French ports 1803–05; after Nelson's death he took command at the Battle of Trafalgar.

Collins (William) Wilkie 1824–1889. English novelist, author of mystery and suspense novels, including *The Woman in White* 1860 (with its fat villain Count Fosco), often called the first English detective novel, and *The Moonstone* 1868 (with Sergeant Cuff, one of the first detectives in English literature).

Collins Michael 1890–1992. Irish Sinn Féin leader, a founder and director of intelligence of the Irish Republican Army 1919, minister for finance in the Provisional government of the Irish Free State 1922, commander of the Free State forces and for ten days head of state; killed in the civil war.

Collins Phil 1951– . English pop singer, drummer, and actor. A member of the group Genesis from 1970, he has also pursued a successful solo career from 1981, with hits (often new versions of old songs) including 'In the Air Tonight' 1981 and 'Groovy Kind of Love' 1988.

Collodi Carlo, pen name of Carlo Lorenzini 1826–1890. Italian writer, born in Florence. In 1881–83 wrote *The Adventure of Pinocchio*, the children's story of a wooden puppet who became a human body.

colloid a substance composed of extremely small particles whose size is between those in suspension and those in true solution (between 1 and 1,000 microns across). The two components are known as the continuous phase, which has the second (dispersed) phase distributed in it. There are various types of colloids: those involving gases include an aerosol (a dispersion of a liquid or solid in a gas, as in fog or smoke) and a foam (a dispersion of a gas in a liquid). Liquids form both the dispersed and continuous phases in an emulsion.

Cologne (German **Köln**) industrial and commercial port in North Rhine-Westphalia, Germany, on the left bank of the Rhine, 35 km/22 mi from Düsseldorf; population (1988) 914,000. To the north is the Ruhr coalfield, on which many of Cologne's industries are based. They include motor vehicles, railway wagons, chemicals, and machine tools.

Colombia country in South America, bounded N and W by the Caribbean and the Pacific, and having borders with Panama to the NW, Venezuela to the E and NE, Brazil to the SE, and Peru and Ecuador to the SW.

Collins *English rock star Phil Collins.*

Colombo capital and principal seaport of Sri Lanka, on the west coast near the mouth of the Kelani river; population (1990) 615,000. It trades in tea, rubber, and cacao. It has iron and steel works, and an oil refinery.

Colombo Matteo Realdo *c.* 1516–1559. Italian anatomist who discovered pulmonary circulation, that is, the process of blood circulating from the heart to the lungs and back.

Colombo Plan plan for cooperative economic development in S and SE Asia, established 1951. The member countries meet annually to discuss economic and development plans such as irrigation, hydro-electric schemes, and technical training.

colon in punctuation, a mark (:) intended to direct the reader's attention forward, usually because what follows explains or develops what has just been written (for example, the farmer owned a variety of dogs: a spaniel, a pointer, a terrier, a border collie, and three mongrels).

colon in anatomy, the part of the large ◊intestine between the caecum and rectum, where water and mineral salts are absorbed from digested food, and the residue formed into ◊faeces or faecal pellets.

Colón second largest city in Panama, at the Caribbean end of the Panama Canal; population (1990) 140,900

colonialism another name for ◊imperialism.

Colorado state of the central W USA; nickname Centennial State
area 270,240 sq km/104,247 sq mi
capital Denver
towns Colorado Springs, Pueblo
physical Great Plains in the E; the main ranges of the Rocky Mountains; high plateaux of the Colorado Basin in the west
products cereals, meat and dairy products; oil, coal, molybdenum, uranium; iron, steel, machinery
population (1990) 3,294,400
famous people Jack Dempsey, Douglas Fairbanks
history it first attracted fur traders, and Denver was founded following the discovery of gold 1858. Colorado became a state 1876.

coloratura in music, a rapid ornamental vocal passage with runs, and trills. A *coloratura soprano* has a light, high voice suited to such music.

Colosseum ruined amphitheatre in ancient Rome, begun by the emperor Vespasian to replace the

Colombia
Republic of
(*República de Colombia*)

area 1,141,748 sq km/440,715 sq mi
capital Bogotá
towns Medellín, Cali, Bucaramanga; ports Barranquilla, Cartagena
physical the Andes mountains run N–S; plains in the E; Magdalena River runs N to the Caribbean
head of state and government Cesar Gaviria Trujillo from 1990
political system emergent democratic republic
exports emeralds (world's largest producer), coffee (second largest world producer), cocaine, bananas, cotton, meat, sugar, oil, skins, hides
currency peso
population (1990 est) 32,598,800 (mestizo 68%, white 20%, Amerindian 1%); annual growth rate 2.2%
life expectancy men 61, women 66, Indians 34
language Spanish

religion Roman Catholic 95%
literacy 89% male/87% female/40% Indian (1987)
GDP $31.9 bn (1987); $1,074 per head
chronology
1886 Full independence achieved.
1948 Left-wing mayor of Bogotá assassinated. Widespread outcry.
1949 Start of near civil war, La Violencia, during which 280,000 people died.
1957 Hoping to halt the violence, Conservatives and Liberals agreed to form a National Front, sharing the presidency.
1970 National Popular Alliance (ANAPO) formed as a left-wing opposition to the National Front.
1974 National Front accord temporarily ended.
1975 Civil unrest because of disillusionment with the government.
1978 Liberals, under Julio Turbay, revived the accord and began an intensive fight against drug dealers.
1982 Liberals maintained their control of Congress but lost the presidency. The Conservative president, Belisario Betancur, attempted to end the violence by granting left-wing guerrillas an amnesty, freeing political prisoners, and embarking on a large public works programme.
1984 Minister of justice assassinated by, it was suspected, drug dealers. Campaign against them was stepped up.
1986 Virgilio Barco Vargas, Liberal, elected president by a record margin
1989 Drug cartel assassinated leading presidential candidate. Vargas declared antidrug war.
1990 Trujillo elected president.
1991 New constitution prohibited extradition of Colombians wanted for trial in other countries; several drug barons arrested. Liberal party won the general election.
1992 One of the leading drug barons, Pablo Escobar, escaped from prison.

---

amphitheatre destroyed by fire in the reign of Nero, and completed by Titus 80 AD, it was 187 m/615 ft long and 49 m/160 ft high, and seated 50,000 people. Early Christians were martyred here by lions and gladiators. It could be flooded for mimic sea battles.

Colossus of Rhodes bronze statue of Apollo erected at the entrance to the harbour at Rhodes 292–280 BC. Said to have been about 30 m/100 ft high, it was counted as one of the Seven Wonders of the World, but in 224 BC fell as a result of an earthquake.

colour blindness an incurable defect of vision which reduces the ability to discriminate one colour from another. 2–6% of men, and less than 1% of women have colour blindness.

colours, military flags or standards carried by British military regiments, so called because of the various combinations of colours employed to distinguish one regiment from another. Each battalion carries the sovereign's colour and the regimental colour which bears the title, crest, and motto of the regiment with the names of battle honours.

Colt Samuel 1814–1862. US gunsmith who invented the revolver 1835 that bears his name.

Coltrane John (William) 1926–1967. US jazz saxophonist, in 1955 a member of the Miles Davis quintet. His performances were noted for experimentation, and his quartet was highly regarded for its innovations in melody and harmony.

colugo SE Asian climbing mammal of the order Dermoptera, about 60 cm/2 ft long including tail. It glides between forest trees using a flap of skin which extends from head to forelimb to hindlimb to tail. It may glide 130 m or more, losing little height. It feeds largely on buds and leaves, and rests hanging upside down under branches.

Columba, St 521–597. Irish Christian abbot, missionary to Scotland. Born in County Donegal

Colosseum The Colosseum in Rome, Italy.

Columbus An engraving of the portrait by Sebastiano del Piombo; the original is in the Uffizi, Florence.

of royal descent, he founded monasteries and churches in Ireland. In 563 he sailed with 12 companions to Iona, and built there a monastery which was to play an important part in the conversion of Britain. Feast day 9 Jun.

Columban, St 543–615. Irish Christian abbot. Born in Leinster, he studied at Bangor, and about 585 went to the Vosges, France, with 12 other monks and founded the monastery of Luxeuil. He went to Italy, where he built the abbey of Bobbio in the Apennines. Feast day 23 Nov.

Columbia, District of seat of the federal government of the USA, bordering the capital, Washington; area 178 sq km/69 sq mi. Situated on the Potomac river, it was ceded by Maryland as the national capital site 1790.

columbine plant *Aquilegia vulgaris*, family Ranunculaceae. It is a perennial herb, with deeply divided leaves, and purple flowers with spurred petals. It grows wild in woods and is a familiar garden plant.

columbium former name for the chemical element ◊niobium.

Columbus Christopher 1451–1506. Italian navigator and explorer (Spanish name Cristobal Colon) who made four voyages to the New World. In 1492, he reached San Salvador Island, Cuba, and Haiti. From 1493–96, he reached Guadaloupe, Montserrat, Antigua, Puerto Rico, and Jamaica. In 1498, he visited Trinidad, and the mainland of South America. From 1502–04, he visited Honduras and Nicaragua.

column in architecture, a structure, round or polygonal in plan, erected vertically as a support for some part of a building. Cretan paintings reveal the existence of wooden columns in Aegean architecture, about 1500 BC. The Hittites, Assyrians, and Egyptians also used wooden columns, and in modern times they are a feature of the monumental architecture of China and Japan. In classical architecture there are five principal types of column; see ◊order.

coma in medicine, a state of deep unconsciousness from which the subject cannot be roused. There are many possible causes, including head injury, cerebral haemorrhage, and drug overdose.

coma In optics, one of the geometrical aberrations of a lens, whereby skew rays from a point object make a comet-shaped spot on the image plane instead of meeting at a point, hence the name. In astronomy,

the hazy cloud of gas and dust that surrounds the nucleus of a ◊comet.

combination in mathematics, a selection of a number of objects from some larger number of objects. Combinatorial analysis is important in the study of ◊probability.

Combination Laws laws passed in Britain in 1799 and 1800 making trade unionism illegal, introduced after the French Revolution for fear that the unions would become centres of political agitation. The unions continued to exist, but claimed to be friendly societies or went underground, until the acts were repealed 1824, largely due to the radical Francis Place.

combine a machine used for harvesting cereals and other crops, so called because it combines the actions of reaping – cutting the crop, and threshing – beating the ears so that the grain separates.

combustion burning, defined in chemical terms as rapid combination of a substance with oxygen accompanied by the evolution of heat and usually light. A slow-burning candle flame and the explosion of a mixture of petrol vapour and air are extreme examples of combustion.

Comecon (Council for Mutual Economic Cooperation, or CMEA) economic organization 1949–91, linking the USSR with Bulgaria, Czechoslovakia, Hungary, Poland, Romania, East Germany (1950–90), Mongolia (from 1962), Cuba (from 1972), and Vietnam (from 1978). Yugoslavia was an associate member; Albania also belonged 1949–61. Its establishment was prompted by the ◊Marshall Plan.

Comédie Française The French national theatre (for both comedy and tragedy) in Paris, founded 1680 by Louis XIV. Its base is the Salle Richelieu on the right bank of the Seine, and the Théâtre de l'Odéon, on the left bank, is a testing-ground for avant-garde ideas.

comedy in the simplest terms, a drama with a happy or amusing ending, as opposed to tragedy. The comic tradition has enjoyed many changes since its Greek and Roman roots; although some comedies are timeless, such as those of Shakespeare and Molière, others are very representative of a particular era, relying upon topical allusion and current fashion.

comet a small, icy body orbiting the Sun on a usually highly elliptical path. A comet consists of a central nucleus a few kilometres across, often likened to a dirty snowball because it consists mostly of ice mixed with dust. As the comet approaches the Sun the nucleus heats up, releasing gas and dust which form a tenuous ◊*coma* up to 100,000 km/60,000 mi wide, around the nucleus. Gas and dust stream away from the coma to form one or more tails, which may extend for millions of kilometres.

comfrey tall perennial *Symphytum officinale*, family Boraginaceae. Up to 1.2 m/4 ft tall, it has hairy, winged stems and lanceolate (tapering) leaves; the flowers grow in drooping clusters and are bell shaped. They may be white, yellowish, purple or pink.

comic strip or *strip cartoon* a sequence of several frames of drawings in ◊cartoon style. Strips may work independently or form instalments of a serial and are usually humorous or satirical in intent. Longer stories in comic-strip form are published separately as comic books (see under ◊magazine).

Comines Philippe de c. 1445–1509. French diplomat in the service of Charles the Bold, Louis XI, and Charles VIII, author of *Mémoires* 1489–98.

Cominform *Com*munist *Inform*ation Bureau 1947–56, established by the Soviet politician Andrei Zhdanov (1896–1948) to exchange information between European communist parties. Yugoslavia was expelled in 1948.

Comintern abbreviation of *Com*munist ◊*Intern*ational.

comma a punctuation mark (,), intended to provide breaks or pauses inside a sentence; commas may come at the end of a clause, after a phrase, or in lists (for example, apples, pears, plums, and pineapples.

command language in computing, a set of commands and the rules governing their use by which ◊end users (nonspecialists) control a program. For example, an ◊operating system may have commands such as SAVE and DELETE, or a payroll program may have commands for adding and amending staff records.

Commando member of British troop of Combined Operations Command who raided enemy-occupied territory in World War II after the evacuation of Dunkirk 1940. At the end of the war the army Commandos were disbanded, but the organization was carried on by the Royal Marines.

commando member of a specially trained amphibious military unit. The term originated in S Africa, where it was used for Boer military reprisal raids against Africans, and later, in the South African War, against the British. Commando units carry out guerrilla raids.

commedia dell'arte popular form of Italian improvised drama in the 16th and 17th centuries; performed by trained troupes of actors with stock characters and situations. It exerted considerable influence on writers such as Molière and on the English genres ◊pantomime, harlequinade, and the ◊Punch and Judy show. It laid the foundation for a tradition of mime, particularly in France, which has continued with the contemporary mime of Jean-Louis Barrault and Marcel Marceau.

comme il faut (French 'as it should be') socially correct and acceptable.

committal proceedings in the UK, a preliminary hearing in a magistrate's court to decide whether there is a case to answer before a higher court. From 1967 the proceedings were unreported unless a defendant, or one of them, wished the restriction lifted.

commodity things produced for sale. They may be *consumer goods* like radios, or *producer goods* such as copper bars. *Commodity markets* deal in raw or semi-raw materials which are amenable to grading and which can be stored for considerable periods without deterioration.

Commodus Lucius Aelius Aurelius 161–192. Roman emperor from 180. Son of Marcus Aurelius, he was a tyrant and was strangled by members of his household.

common in the UK, unenclosed wasteland and pasture used in common by the inhabitants of a parish or district or the community at large. It originated in the Middle Ages, when every manor had a large area of unenclosed, uncultivated land over which freeholders and copyholders had certain rights to take or use what the soil naturally produced.

Common Agricultural Policy (CAP) system that allows the twelve member countries of the European Economic Community to jointly organize and control agricultural production within their boundaries.

common law that part of the English law not embodied in legislation. It consists of rules of law based on common custom and usage and on judicial decisions. English common law became the basis of law in the USA and many other English-speaking countries.

Common Market popular name for the EEC or European Economic Community; see ◊European Community.

Common Prayer, Book of the service book of the Church of England, based largely on the Roman breviary. The first Book of Common Prayer in English was known as the First Prayer Book of Edward VI, published in 1549, and is the basis of the Book of Common Prayer still, although not exclusively, in use.

Commons, House of the lower but more powerful of the two parts of the British and Canadian ◊parliaments.

Commonwealth, the (British) association of states that have been or still are ruled by Britain (see ◊British Empire). Independent states are full 'members of the Commonwealth', while dependent territories, such as colonies and protectorates, rank as 'Commonwealth countries'. Very small self-governing countries may have special status, for example, Nauru.

Commonwealth a body politic founded on law for the common 'weal' or good. 17th-century political philosophers such as Thomas Hobbes and John Locke used the term to mean an organized political community. Specifically, it was applied to the Cromwellian regime 1649-60.

Commonwealth conference any consultation between the prime ministers (or defence, finance, foreign, or other ministers) of the sovereign independent members of the Commonwealth. These are informal discussion meetings and the implementation of policies is decided by individual governments. Notable recent Commonwealth conferences have been Singapore 1971, the first outside the UK; Sydney 1978, the first regional meeting; Lusaka 1979, the first regular session in Africa; and Vancouver 1987.

Commonwealth Development Corporation organization founded in 1948 as the Colonial Development Corporation to aid the development of dependent Commonwealth territories; the change of name and extension of its activities to include those now independent were announced in 1962.

Commonwealth Games multi-sport gathering of competitors from Commonwealth countries. Held every four years, the first meeting (known as the British Empire Games) was at Hamilton, Canada in Aug 1930.

Commune, Paris two periods of government in France. See ◊Paris Commune.

communication in biology, the signalling of information by one organism to another, usually with the intention of altering the recipient's behaviour. Signals used in communication may be visual (such as a smile), auditory (for example, the whines or barks of a dog), olfactory (such as the odours released by the scent glands of a deer), electrical (as in the pulses emitted by electric fish) or tactile (for example, the nuzzling of male and female elephants).

communications satellite a relay station in space for sending telephone, television, telex, and other messages around the world. Messages are sent to and from the satellites via ground stations. Most modern communications satellites are in ◊geostationary orbit, appearing to hang fixed over one point on the Earth's surface.

Communion, Holy in the Christian church, another name for the ◊Eucharist.

Commonwealth, British

Country   *Capital*   (Area in 1,000 sq km)

IN AFRICA
Botswana   *Gaborone*   (575)
British Indian Ocean Terr.   *Victoria*   (0.2)
Gambia   *Banjul*   (11)
Ghana   *Accra*   (239)
Kenya   *Nairobi*   (583)
Losotho   *Maseru*   (30)
Malawi   *Zomba*   (117)   ·
Mauritius   *Port Louis*   (2)
Nigeria   *Lagos*   (924)
St Helena   *Jamestown*   (0.1)
Seychelles   *Victoria*   (65)
Sierra Leone   *Freetown*   (73)
Swaziland   *Mbabane*   (17)
Tanzania   *Dodoma*   (943)
Uganda   *Kampala*   (236)
Zambia   *Lusaka*   (752)
Zimbabwe   *Salisbury*   (391)

IN THE AMERICAS
Anguilla   *The Valley*   (0.09)
Antigua   *St John's*   (0.4)
Bahamas   *Nassau*   (14)
Barbados   *Bridgetown*   (0.4)
Belize   *Belmopan*   (23)
Bermuda   *Hamilton*   (0.05)
Brit. Virgin Is.   *Road Town*   (0.2)
Canada   *Ottawa*   (9,976)
Cayman Islands   *Georgetown*   (0.3)
Dominica   *Roseau*   (0.7)
Falkland Is.   *Stanley*   (12)
Grenada   *St George's*   (0.3)
Guyana   *Georgetown*   (210)
Jamaica   *Kingston*   (12)
Montserrat   *Plymouth*   (0.1)
St Christopher-Nevis   *Basseterre Charlestown*   (0.4)
St Lucia   *Castries*   (0.6)
St Vincent and the Grenadines   *Kingstown*   (0.2)
Trinidad and Tobago   *Port of Spain*   (0.5)
Turks and Caicos Is.   *Grand Turk*   (0.4)

IN THE ANTARCTIC
Australian Antarctic Terr.   (5,403)
Brit. Antarctic Terr.   (390)
Falklands Is. Dependencies   (1.6)
(N.Z.) Ross Dependency   (453)

Country   *Capital*   (Area in 1,000 sq km)

IN ASIA
Bangladesh   *Dacca*   (143)
Brunei   *Bandar Seri Begawan*   (6)
Cyprus   *Nicosia*   (9)
Hong Kong   *Victoria*   (1.2)
India   *Delhi*   (3,215)
Malaysia, Rep. of   *Kuala Lumpur*   (332)
Maldives   *Malé*   (0.3)
Singapore   *Singapore*   (0.6)
Sri Lanka   *Colombo*   (66)

IN AUSTRALASIA AND THE PACIFIC
Australia   *Canberra*   (7,704)
Norfolk Island   (0.03)
Fiji   *Suva*   (18)
Kiribati   *Tarawa*   (0.7)
*Nauru   (0.02)
New Zealand   *Wellington*   (269)
Cook Islands   (0.2)
Niue Island   (0.3)
Tokelau Islands   (0.01)
Papua New Guinea   *Port Moresby*   (475)
Pitcairn   (0.005)
Solomon Islands   *Honiara*   (30)
Tonga   *Nuku'alofa*   (0.7)
*Tuvalu   *Funafuti*   (0.02)
Vanuatu   *Vila*   (15)
Western Samoa   *Apia*   (3)

IN EUROPE
*United Kingdom
England   *London*   (131)
Wales   *Cardiff*   (21)
Scotland   *Edinburgh*   (79)
N. Ireland   *Belfast*   (14)
Isle of Man   *Douglas*   (0.5)
Channel Islands   (0.2)
Gibraltar   *Gibraltar*   (0.006)
Malta   *Valletta*   (0.3)

TOTAL (33,932)
*Special members

---

communism revolutionary socialism based on the theories of the political philosophers Karl Marx and Friedrich Engels, emphasizing common ownership of the means of production and a planned economy. The principle held is that each should work according to their capacity and receive according to their needs. Politically, it seeks the overthrow of capitalism through a proletarian revolution. The first communist state was the USSR after the revolution of 1917. Revolutionary socialist parties and groups united to form communist parties in other countries (in the UK 1920). After World War II, communism was enforced in those countries that came under Soviet occupation. China emerged after 1961 as a rival to the USSR in world communist leadership, and other countries attempted to adapt communism to their own needs. The late 1980s saw a movement for more individual freedoms in many communist countries, culminating in the abolition or overthrow of communist rule in Eastern European countries and Mongolia, and further state repression in China. The failed hard-line coup in the USSR against President Gorbachev 1991 resulted in the effective abandonment of communism there.

Communism Peak alternative form of Pik Kommunizma, the highest mountain in the ◊Pamirs.

community in ecology, an assemblage of plants, animals and other organisms living within a circum-scribed area. Communities are usually named by reference to a dominant feature such as a characteristic plant species (for example, beech wood community), or prominent physical feature (for example, a freshwater pond community).

community council in Wales, name for a ◊parish council.

community service scheme introduced in Britain by the Criminal Justice Act 1972, under which minor offenders are sentenced to spare time work in the service of the community (aiding children, the elderly or the handicapped), instead of prison. The offender must consent, be 16 or over, and have committed no violence.

commutator a device in a DC (direct current) electric motor that reverses the current flowing in the armature coils as the armature rotates. A DC generator, or ◊dynamo, uses a commutator to convert the AC (alternating current) generated in the armature coils into DC. A commutator consists of opposite pairs of conductors insulated from one another, and contact to an external circuit is provided by carbon or metal brushes.

Comoros group of islands comprising Njazidja, Nzwani, and Mwali, situated in the Indian Ocean between Madagascar and the E coast of Africa. The fourth island in the group, Mayotte, is a French dependency.

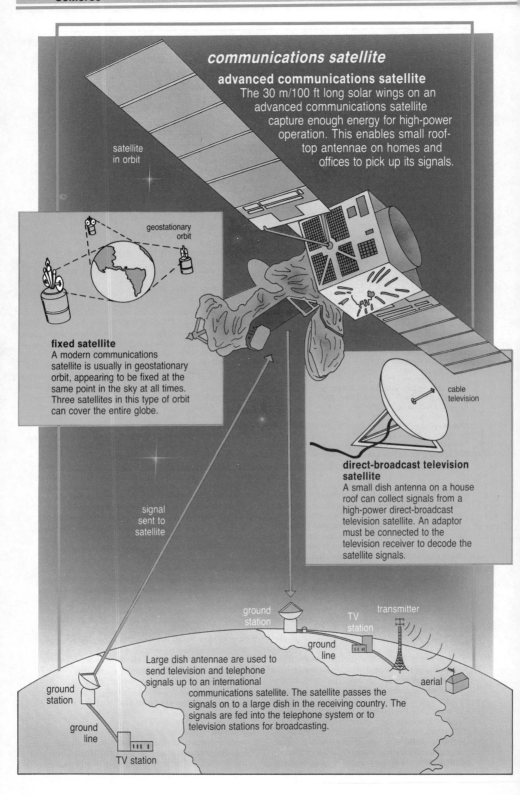

communications satellite

advanced communications satellite
The 30 m/100 ft long solar wings on an advanced communications satellite capture enough energy for high-power operation. This enables small roof-top antennae on homes and offices to pick up its signals.

satellite in orbit

geostationary orbit

fixed satellite
A modern communications satellite is usually in geostationary orbit, appearing to be fixed at the same point in the sky at all times. Three satellites in this type of orbit can cover the entire globe.

cable television

direct-broadcast television satellite
A small dish antenna on a house roof can collect signals from a high-power direct-broadcast television satellite. An adaptor must be connected to the television receiver to decode the satellite signals.

signal sent to satellite

ground station

TV station

transmitter

ground line

aerial

ground station

ground line

TV station

Large dish antennae are used to send television and telephone signals up to an international communications satellite. The satellite passes the signals on to a large dish in the receiving country. The signals are fed into the telephone system or to television stations for broadcasting.

Comoros
Federal Islamic Republic of
(*Jumhuríyat al-Qumur al-Itthadíya al Islãmíyah*)

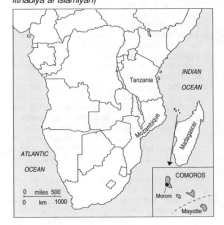

area 1,862 sq km/719 sq mi
capital Moroni
physical comprises the islands of Njazídja, Nzwani, and Mwali (formerly Grand Comoro,

Anjouan, Maheli); poor soil
head of state Said Mohammad Djohar from 1989
head of government Halidi Abderamane Ibrahim from 1993
political system authoritarian nationalism
exports copra, vanilla, cocoa, sisal, coffee, cloves
currency CFA franc
population 459,000 (1990 est); annual growth rate 3.1%
life expectancy men 48, women 52
language Arabic (official), Comorian, Makua, French
religion Muslim (official) 86%, Roman Catholic 14%
literacy 15%
GDP $198 million (1987); $468 per head
chronology
1975 Independence achieved, but Mayotte remained part of France. Ahmed Abdallah elected president. The Comoros joined United Nations.
1976 Abdallah overthrown by Ali Soilih.
1978 Soilih killed by mercenaries. Islamic republic proclaimed; Abdallah elected president.
1979 The Comoros became a one-party state.
1989 Abdallah killed by French mercenaries who took control of government before turning authority over to French administration and interim president Djohar.
1990 Antigovernment coup failed.
1992 Third transitional government appointed.

compact disc disc for storing digital information, about 12 cm/4.5 in across, mainly used for music. Entirely different from a conventional LP (gramophone) record, the compact disc is silvery in colour with a transparent plastic coating; the metal disc underneath the plastic coating is etched by a ◊laser beam with microscopic pits, which carry a digital code that represents the music. During playback, a laser beam reads the code and produces
compact disc

signals that are changed into near-exact replicas of the original sounds.

Companion of Honour British order of chivalry, founded by George V 1917. It is of one class only, and carries no title, but Companions append 'CH' to their names. The number is limited to 65 and the award is made to both men and women.

company a number of people grouped together as a business enterprise. Various types of companies

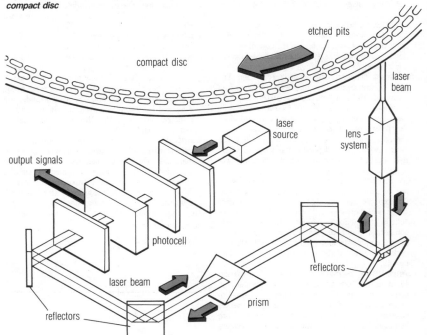

compact disc

compass

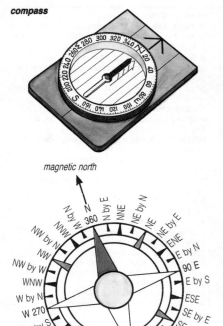

magnetic north

include public limited companies, partnerships, joint ventures, sole proprietors, and branches of foreign companies. Most companies are private and unlike public companies, cannot offer their shares to the general public.

comparative advantage law of international trade first elaborated by David ◊Ricardo showing that trade becomes advantageous if the cost of production of particular items differs between one country and another.

compass an instrument for finding direction. The most commonly used is a magnetic compass, consisting of a thin piece of magnetic material with the north-seeking pole indicated, free to rotate on a pivot and mounted on a compass card on which the points of the compass are marked. When the compass is properly adjusted and used, the north-seeking pole will point to the magnetic north, from which true north can be found from tables of magnetic corrections.

competition in ecology, the interaction between two or more organisms, or groups of organisms (for example, species), that use a common resource which is in short supply. Competition invariably results in a reduction in the numbers of one or both competitors, and has played an important role in ◊evolution, contributing both to the decline of certain species, and to the evolution of ◊adaptations.

competition, perfect in economics, a market situation in which there are many potential and actual buyers and sellers, each being too small to be an individual influence on the price; the market is open to all and the products being traded are homogeneous. At the same time, the producers

are seeking the maximum profit and consumers the best value for money.

compiler a computer program, invented by Grace Murray Hopper at the Remington Rand Corporation 1951, that translates other programs, written in high-level (easy-to-use) programming languages, into a code executable by the computer.

complementation in genetics, the interaction that can occur between two different mutant forms of a gene in a ◊diploid organism, to make up for each other's deficiencies and allow the organism to function normally.

complex in psychology, a group of ideas and feelings which have become repressed because they are distasteful to the person in whose mind they arose; but which are still active in the depths of the person's unconscious mind, continuing to affect his or her life and actions, even though he or she is no longer fully aware of their existence. Typical examples include the ◊Oedipus complex and the inferiority complex.

complex number in mathematics, a number written in the form $a + ib$, where a and b are ◊real numbers and i is the square root of -1 (that is, $i^2 = -1$); i used to be known as the imaginary part of the complex number. Some equations in algebra, such as those of the form $x^2 + 5 = 0$, cannot be solved without recourse to complex numbers, because the real numbers do not include square roots of negative numbers.

compliance in the UK, abiding by the terms of the Financial Services Act 1986. Companies undertaking any form of investment business are regulated by the Act and must fulfil their obligations to investors under it, under four main headings: efficiency, competitiveness, confidence, and flexibility.

componential analysis in linguistics, the analysis of the elements of a word's meaning. The word *boy*, for example, might be said to have three basic meaning elements (or semantic properties): 'human', 'young,' and 'male'; and so might the word *murder*: 'kill', 'intentional', and 'illegal'.

Compositae the daisy family; dicotyledonous flowering plants characterized by flowers borne in composite heads. It is the largest family of flowering plants, the majority being herbaceous. Birds seem to favour the family for use in nest 'decoration', possibly because many species either repel or kill insects (see ◊pyrethrum). Species include the daisy and dandelion; food plants artichoke, lettuce, safflower; and the garden chrysanthemum, dahlia, daisybush, and zinnia.

composite in industry, a purpose-designed engineering material created by combining single materials with complementary properties into a composite form. Most composites have a structure in which one component consists of discrete elements such as fibres (for example, asbestos, glass or carbon steel in continuous or short lengths, or 'whiskers', specially grown

complex number

Argand diagram

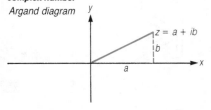

computer

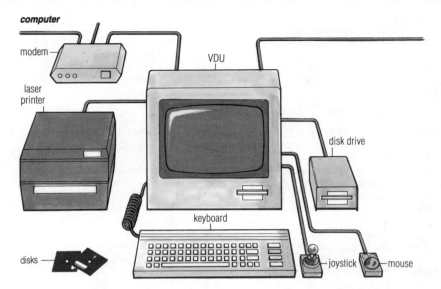

crystals a few mm long, such as silicon carbide)
dispersed in a continuous matrix, such as plastics,
concrete, steel.

compos mentis (Latin) of sound mind.

compost ◊biodegradable vegetation, such as
leaves, fruit, and vegetables, that breaks down
as a result of the action of bacteria, fungi, and
other ◊decomposers.

compound chemical substance made up of two or
more ◊elements bonded together, so that they
cannot be separated by physical means. They
may be made up of electrovalent or covalent
bonds.

compound interest interest calculated by increasing the original capital by the amount of interest each time the interest becomes due. When
simple interest is calculated, only the interest on
the original capital is added.

comprehensive school in the UK, a secondary school which admits pupils of all abilities, and
therefore without any academic selection procedure.

compressor a machine designed to compress a
gas, usually air, commonly used to power pneumatic tools, such as road drills, paint sprayers and
dentists' drills.

Compromise of 1850 in US history, legislative
proposals designed to resolve sectional conflict
between north and south over the admission
of California to the union in 1850. Slavery was
prohibited in California, but a new fugitive slave
law was passed to pacify the slave states. The
Senate debate on the compromise lasted nine
months: acceptance temporarily revitalized the
union.

computer a programmable, electronic device for
performing calculations and other symbol manipulation tasks. There are three types: the *digital
computer* which manipulates information coded
as ◊binary numbers, the *analogue computer* (a
task-oriented computer) and the *hybrid computer*
which has components of both analogue and digital
computers.

computer game computer-controlled game in
which the computer (usually) opposes the human player. Also known as video games, they

typically employ fast, animated graphics on a
◊VDU (screen) and ◊synthesized sound. Computer games became possible with the advent of
the ◊microprocessor in the mid-1970s and rapidly
became popular as arcade games.

computer simulation representation of a problem
or situation mathematically on a computer, possibly
involving complex graphics, so that the effects of
varying one or more of the definitive parameters
can be observed and the problem solved or a design
modified.

computer terminal a screen and a keyboard,
sometimes combined in one unit, connected to a
computer. It is a ◊peripheral device.

computing device any device built to perform
or help perform computations, such as the abacus,
slide rule, or computer.

computer memory

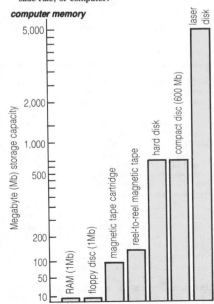

computing

1614	Scottish mathematician John Napier invented logarithms.		**1951**	Ferranti Mark I: the first commercially produced computer; 'Whirlwind', the first real-time computer.
1615	William Oughtred (1575–1660) invented the slide rule.		**1952**	EDVAC (Electronic Discrete Variable Computer) completed at the Institute for Advanced Study, Princeton, USA
1623	Wilhelm Schickard (1592–1635) invented the first mechanical calculating machine.		**1953**	Magnetic core memory developed.
1645	Blaise Pascal produced a calculator.		**1957**	FORTRAN, the first high-level computer language, developed by IBM.
1672–74	Leibniz built his first calculator, the Stepped Reckoner.			
1801	Joseph-Marie Jacquard developed an automatic loom controlled by punched cards.		**1958**	The first integrated circuit.
			1963	The first minicomputer built by Digital Equipment (DEC); the PDP-8; the first electronic calculator (Bell Punch Company).
1820	First mass-produced calculator (the Arithmometer, by Charles Thomas de Colmar 1785–1870).			
1822	Charles Babbage's first model for the Difference Engine.		**1964**	IBM System/360; the first compatible family of computers.
1830s	Babbage created the first design for the Analytical Engine.		**1965**	The first supercomputer: the Control Data CD6600.
1890	Herman Hollerith developed the punched card ruler for the US census.		**1970**	The first microprocessor: the Intel 4004.
			1974	CLIP-4, the first computer with a parallel architecture.
1936	Alan Turing published the mathematical theory of computing.		**1975**	The first personal computer: Altair 8800.
1938	Konrad Zuse constructed the first binary calculator, using Boolean algebra.		**1981**	The Xerox Start system, the first WIMP system (Windows, Icons, Menus and Pointing devices).
1943	'Colossus' electronic code-breaker developed at Bletchley Park, England.		**1985**	The Inmos T414 Transputer, the first 'off the shelf' RISC microprocessor for building parallel computers.
1945	ENIAC (Electronic Numerator, Integrator, Analyser, and Computer) completed at the University of Pennsylvania.		**1988**	The first optical microprocessor, which uses light instead of electricity.
			1989	Wafer-scale silicon memory chips, able to store 200 million characters.
1948	Manchester University (England) Mark I completed: first stored-program computer.		**1990**	Microsoft released Windows 3.
			1992	Philips launched the CD-I (compact disc-interactive) player.

Comte Auguste 1798–1857. French philosopher, generally regarded as the founder of sociology, a term he coined 1830. He sought to establish sociology as an intellectual and 'scientific' discipline, using ◊positivism as the basis of a new science of social order and social development.

Conakry capital and chief port of the Republic of Guinea; population (1983) 705,300. It is on the island of Tumbo, linked with the mainland by a causeway and by rail with Kankan, 480 km/300 mi NE. Bauxite and iron ore are mined nearby.

concave lens a converging ◊lens – that is, a parallel beam of light gets wider as it passes through such a lens. A concave lens is thinner at its centre than at the edges. Common forms include biconcave (with both surfaces curved inwards) and plano-concave (with one flat surface and one concave). The whole lens may be further curved overall (making a convexo-concave or diverging meniscus lens, as in some spectacle lenses).

concentration camp a prison camp devised by the British during the Boer War in South Africa 1899 for the detention of Afrikaner women and children. The system of concentration camps was developed by the Nazis in Germany to imprison political and ideological opponents. Several hundred camps were established in Germany and occupied Europe, the most infamous being the extermination camps of Auschwitz, Belsen, Maidanek, Sobibor, and Treblinka. The total number of people murdered at the camps may have exceeded 6 million, and some inmates were subjected to medical experimentation before being killed.

concertina a wind musical instrument with free reeds consisting of two keyboards connected by expandable and folding bellows. It is played by compressing and expanding the bellows while at the same time pressing the knobs on the keyboard so that air is admitted to the reeds, which are set in vibration.

concerto composition, usually in three movements, for solo instrument (or instruments) and orchestra. It developed from the concerto grosso form for string orchestra, in which a group of solo instruments is contrasted with a full orchestra.

concentration camp Auschwitz: the most infamous Nazi concentration camp, liberated by the American 7th Army, 3 May 1945.

Conchobar in Celtic mythology, king of Ulster whose intended bride, Deirdre, eloped with Noísi. She died of sorrow when Conchobar killed her husband and his brothers.

concilliar movement the 15th century attempt to urge the supremacy of church councils over the popes, particularly with regard to the ◊Great Schism, and the reformation of the church.

conclave any secret meeting, in particular the gathering of cardinals in Rome to elect a new pope. They are locked away in the Vatican Palace until they have reached a decision. The result of each ballot is announced by a smoke signal – black for an indecisive vote and white when the choice is made.

concordance book containing an alphabetical list of the words in some important work with references to the places in which they occur. The first concordance was one prepared to the Vulgate by a Dominican in the 13th century.

concordat agreement regulating relations between the papacy and a secular government, for example, that for France between Pius VII and the emperor Napoleon, which lasted 1801–1905; Mussolini's concordat, which lasted 1929–78 and safeguarded the position of the church in Italy; and one of 1984 in Italy in which Roman Catholicism ceased to be the Italian state religion.

Concorde the only successful ◊supersonic airliner, which cruises at Mach 2, or twice the speed of sound, about 2,170 kph/1,350 mph. *Concorde*, the result of Anglo-French cooperation, made its first flight in 1969, and entered commercial service seven years later. It is 62 m/202 ft long and has a wing span of nearly 26 m/84 ft.

concrete a building material composed of cement, stone, sand, and water. It has been used since Roman and Egyptian times.

Concorde The British built Concorde 002 takes off for the first time, from Filton, near Bristol, Apr 1969.

Condé Louis de Bourbon, Prince of Condé 1530–1569. Prominent French ◊Huguenot leader. Founder of the house of Condé and uncle of Henry IV of France. He distinguished himself in the wars between Henry II and the Holy Roman emperor Charles V, particularly in the defence of Metz.

Condé Louis II 1621–1686. Prince of Condé called the *Great Condé*. French commander, who won brilliant victories during the Thirty Years' War at Rocroi 1643 and Lens, France, in 1648, but rebelled 1651 and entered the Spanish service. Pardoned 1660, he commanded Louis XIV's armies against the Spanish and the Dutch.

condenser in optics, a short focal-length convex ◊lens or combination of lenses used for concentrating a light source onto a small area, as used in a slide projector or microscope sub-stage lighting unit. A condenser can also be made using a concave mirror.

conditioning in psychology, two major principles of behaviour modification. In *classical conditioning*, described by Pavlov, a new stimulus can evoke an automatic response by being repeatedly associated with a stimulus that naturally provokes a response. For example, a bell repeatedly associated with food will eventually trigger salivation, even if presented without food. In *operant conditioning*, described by Thorndike and Skinner, the frequency of a voluntary response can be increased by following it with a reinforcer or reward.

condominium the joint rule of a territory by two or more states, for example, Canton and Enderbury islands, in the South Pacific Phoenix group (under the joint control of Britain and USA for 50 years from 1939). The term has also come into use in N America to describe a type of joint property ownership of, for example, a block of flats.

condor a large flying bird *Vultur gryphus*, a South American ◊vulture, with wingspan up to 3 m/10 ft, weight up to 13 kg/28 lb, and length up to 1.2 m/3.8 ft. It is black, with some white on the wings and a white frill at the base of the neck. It lives in the Andes and along the South American coast, and feeds on carrion. The *Californian condor Gymnogyps californianus* is a similar bird, and on the verge of extinction. It only lays one egg at a time and may not breed every year. It is the subject of a special conservation effort.

Condorcet Marie Jean Antoine Nicolas Caritat, Marquis de Condorcet 1743–1794. French philosopher and politician, associated with the ◊Encyclopédistes. One of the ◊Girondins, he opposed the execution of Louis XVI, and was imprisoned and poisoned himself. His *Esquisse d'un tableau des progrès de l'esprit humain/Historical Survey of the Progress of Human Understanding* 1795 envisaged inevitable future progress, though not the perfectibility of human nature.

conductance the ability of a material to carry an electrical current, usually given the symbol G. For a direct current, it is the reciprocal of resistance: a conductor of resistance R has a conductance of $1/R$. For an alternating current, conductance is the resistance (R) divided by the impedence Z: $G = R/Z$. Conductance was formerly expressed in reciprocal ohms (or mhos); the modern SI unit is the Siemens.

conductor in physics, a material that conducts heat or electricity (as opposed to a non-conductor or insulator). A good conductor has a high electrical or thermal conductivity, generally a substance rich in free electrons such as a metal. A poor conductor

Congo
Republic of
(*République du Congo*)

area 342,000 sq km/132,000 sq mi
capital Brazzaville
towns chief port Pointe Noire
physical Zaïre (Congo) river on the border; half the country is rainforest
head of state and government Pascal Lissouba from 1992
political system emergent democratic republic
exports timber, petroleum, cocoa
currency CFA franc

population (1990 est) 2,305,000 (chiefly Bantu); annual growth rate 2.6%
life expectancy men 45, women 48
language French (official), African languages
religion animist 50%, Christian 48%, Muslim 2%
literacy 79% male/55% female (1985 est)
GDP $2.1 bn (1983); $500 per head
chronology
1960 Achieved full independence from France, with Abbe Youlou as the first president.
1963 Youlou forced to resign. New constitution approved, with Alphonse Massamba-Débat as president.
1964 The Congo became a one-party state.
1968 Military coup, led by Capt Marien Ngouabi, ousted Massamba-Débat.
1970 A Marxist state, the People's Republic of the Congo, was announced, with the Congolese Labour Party (PCT) as the only legal party.
1977 Ngouabi assassinated. Col Yhombi-Opango became president.
1979 Yhombi-Opango handed over the presidency to PCT, who chose Col Denis Sassou-Ngessou as his successor.
1984 Sassou-Ngessou elected for another five-year term.
1990 The PCT abandoned Marxist-Leninism.
1991 1979 constitution suspended. Country renamed The Republic of Congo.
1992 New constitution approved and multiparty elections held.

has few free electrons (such as the non-metals glass and porcelain). Carbon is exceptional in being non-metallic and yet (in some of its forms) a relatively good conductor of heat and electricity.

cone in geometry, a solid or surface generated by rotating an isosceles triangle or framework about its line of symmetry. It can also be formed by the set of all straight lines passing through a fixed point and the points of a circle or ellipse whose plane does not contain the point.

cone in botany, the reproductive structure of the conifers, and cycads, also known as a ◊strobilus. It consists of a central axis surrounded by numerous, overlapping, scale-like sporophylls, modified leaves which bear the reproductive organs. Usually there are separate male and female cones, the former bearing pollen sacs containing pollen grains, and the larger female cones bearing the ovules which contain the ova or egg cells. The pollen is carried from male to female cones by wind (◊anemophily). The seeds develop within the female cone, and are released as the scales open in dry atmospheric conditions, which favour seed dispersal.

cone

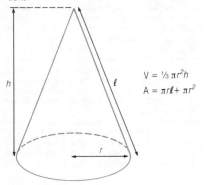

$$V = \tfrac{1}{3}\pi r^2 h$$
$$A = \pi r \ell + \pi r^2$$

Confederacy in US history, popular name for the *Confederate States of America*, the government established by the Southern US states Feb 1861 when they seceded from the Union, precipitating the ◊Civil War. Richmond, Virginia, was the capital, and Jefferson Davies the president. The Confederacy fell after its army was defeated 1865 and Gen Robert E Lee surrendered.

Confederation, Articles of in US history, the means by which the 13 former British colonies created a form of national government. Ratified 1781, the Articles established a unicameral legislature, Congress, with limited powers of raising revenue, regulating currency, and conducting foreign affairs, but the individual states retained significant autonomy. It was superseded by the US Constitution 1788.

Confederation of British Industry (CBI) UK organization of employers, established 1965, combining the former Federation of British Industries (founded 1916), British Employers' Confederation, and National Association of British Manufacturers.

conference system a system of international conferences in the 19th century promoted principally by the German chancellor Bismarck to ease the integration of a new powerful German state into the 'concept of Europe'. The conferences were intended to settle great power disputes, mainly related to the Balkans, the Middle East, and the designation of colonies in Africa and Asia. Most important of these was the Congress of ◊Berlin 1878. The system fell into disuse with the retirement of Bismarck and the pressures of new European alliance blocks.

confession a religious practice, the confession of sins, practised in Roman Catholic, Orthodox, and most Oriental Christian churches and since the early 19th century revived in Anglican and Lutheran churches. The Lateran Council of 1215 made auricular confession (self-accusation by the penitent to a priest, who in Catholic doctrine is divinely invested with authority to give absolution) obligatory once a year.

confirmation rite practised by a number of Christian denominations, including Roman Catholic, Anglican, and Orthodox, in which a previously baptized person is admitted to full membership of the church. In Reform Judaism there is often a confirmation service several years after the bar or bat mitzvah (initiation into the congregation).

Confucianism the body of beliefs and practices that are based on the Chinese classics and supported by the authority of the philosopher Confucius (Kong Zi). For some 2,500 years most of the Chinese people have derived from Confucianism their ideas of cosmology, political government, social organization, and individual conduct. Human relationships follow the patriarchal pattern. The origin of things is seen in the union of *yin* and *yang*, the passive and active principles.

Confucius 551–479 BC. (Latinized form of Kong Zi, meaning Kong the master) Chinese philosopher whose name is given to ◊Confucianism. He devoted his life to relieving suffering of the poor through governmental and administrative reform. His emphasis on tradition and ethics attracted a growing number of pupils during his lifetime; *The Analects of Confucius*, a compilation of his teachings, was published after his death.

conga a popular Latin American dance, originally from Cuba, in which the participants, usually in a line, take three steps forwards or backwards and then kick.

conger a large eel *Conger conger* found in the N Atlantic and Mediterranean. It is often 1.8 m/6 ft long, and sometimes as much as 2.7 m/9 ft. It lives in shallow water, hiding in crevices during the day and active by night, feeding on fish and other animals.

conglomerate a coarse sedimentary rock, made up of broken fragments of pre-existing rocks (a clastic sedimentary rock).

Congo country in W central Africa, bounded to the north by Cameroon and the Central African Republic, to the east and south by Zaïre, to the west by the Atlantic Ocean, and to the northwest by Gabon.

Congregationalism form of church government adopted by those Protestant Christians known as Congregationalists, who let each congregation manage its own affairs. The first Congregationalists were the Brownists, named after Robert Browne, who in 1580 defined the congregational principle.

Congress national legislature of the USA, consisting of the House of Representatives (435 members, apportioned to the states of the Union on the basis of population, and elected for two-year terms) and the Senate (100 senators, two for each state, elected for six years, one-third elected every two years). Both representatives and senators are elected by direct popular vote. Congress meets in Washington DC, in the Capitol. An ◊act of Congress is a bill passed by both houses.

Congress of Racial Equality (CORE) US non-violent civil-rights organization, founded in Chicago 1942.

Congress Party Indian political party, founded 1885 as a nationalist movement. It played an important part in throwing off British rule and was the governing party from independence 1947 until 1977, when Indira Gandhi lost the leadership she had held since 1966. Heading a splinter group, known as *Congress (I)*, she achieved an overwhelming victory in the elections of 1980, and

reduced the main Congress Party in turn to a minority.

congress system developed from the Congress of Vienna, a series of international meetings in Aachen, Germany (1818), Troppali, Austria (1820), and Verona, Italy (1822). British opposition to the repressive intentions of the congresses effectively ended them as a system of international arbitration, although congresses continued to meet into the 1830s.

Congreve William 1670–1729. English dramatist and poet. His first success was the comedy *The Old Bachelor* 1693, followed by *The Double Dealer* 1694, *Love for Love* 1695 and the tragedy *The Mourning Bride* 1697. *The Way of the World* 1700 was at the time a failure. His plays, which satirize the social affectations of the time, are noted for the elegance of their construction and prose style.

congruence in geometry, having the same shape and size, as applied to two-dimensional or solid figures. With plane congruent figures, one figure will fit on top of the other exactly though this may first require rotation and/or reflection (making a mirror image) of one of the figures.

conic section curve obtained when a conical surface is intersected by a plane. If the intersecting plane cuts both extensions of the cone it yields a ◊hyperbola; if it is parallel to the side of the cone it produces a parabola. Other intersecting planes produce a ◊circle or an ◊ellipse.

conidium (plural *conidia*) an asexual spore formed by some fungi at the tip of a specialized ◊hypha or conidiophore. The conidiophores grow erect, and cells from their ends round off and separate into conidia, often forming long chains. Conidia easily become detached and are dispersed by air movements.

conifer trees and shrubs of the class Coniferales, in the gymnosperm group, which are often pyramidal in form, with leaves that are either scaled or made up of needles. Conifers include pines, firs, yews, monkey-puzzles and larches. Most are evergreen.

conjugation in biology, the bacterial equivalent of sexual reproduction. A fragment of the ◊DNA from one bacterium is passed along a thin tube, the pilus, into the cell of another bacterium.

conjunction a grammatical ◊part of speech that serves to connect words, phrases and clauses; for example *and* in 'apples and pears' and *but* in 'we're going but they aren't'.

conjunction in astronomy, there are several different forms of conjunction. *Inferior conjunction* occurs when an ◊inferior planet (or other object) passes between the Earth and Sun, and has an identical right ascension to the Sun. *Superior conjunction* occurs when a ◊superior planet (or other object) passes behind, or on the far side of, the Sun, and has the same right ascension as the Sun. *Planetary conjunction* takes place when a planet is closely aligned with another celestial object, such as the Moon, a star, or another planet, as seen from Earth.

conjunctivitis inflammation of the conjunctiva, the delicate membrane which lines the inside of the eyelids and covers the front of the eye. It may be caused by infection, allergy, or other irritant.

Connacht province of the Republic of Ireland, comprising the counties of Mayo, Galway, Roscommon, Sligo, and Leitrim; area 17,122 sq km/6,611 sq mi; population (1981) 424,410. The chief towns are Galway, Roscommon, Castlebar, Sligo, and

Carrick-on-Shannon. Mainly lowland, it is agricultural and stock-raising country, with poor land in the west.

Connecticut state in New England, USA; nickname Constitution State/Nutmeg State
area 12,667 sq km/4,889 sq mi
capital Hartford
towns Bridgeport, New Haven
physical highlands in the NW; Connecticut river
products market garden, dairy, and poultry products; tobacco; watches, clocks, silverware; helicopters, jet engines, nuclear submarines
population (1980) 3,107,576
famous people Phineas T Barnum, Katharine Hepburn, Harriet Beecher Stowe, Mark Twain
history settled by Puritan colonists from Massachusetts 1635, it was one of the Thirteen Colonies, and became a state in 1788.

connective tissue in animals, tissue made up of a noncellular substance, the ◊extracellular matrix, in which some cells are embedded. The skin, bones, tendons, cartilage and adipose tissue (fat) are the main connective tissues. There are also small amounts of connective tissue in organs such as the brain and liver, where they maintain shape and structure.

conquistador Spanish word for 'conqueror', applied to such explorers and adventurers in the Americas as Cortes and Pizarro.

Conrad Joseph 1857–1924. British novelist, of Polish parentage, born Teodor Jozef Konrad Korzeniowski in the Ukraine. His novels include *Almayer's Folly* 1895, *Lord Jim* 1900, *Heart of Darkness* 1902, *Nostromo* 1904, *The Secret Agent* 1907, and *Under Western Eyes* 1911. His works vividly evoked for English readers the mysteries of sea life and exotic foreign settings, and explored the psychological isolation of the 'outsider'.

Conrad several kings of the Germans, and Holy Roman Emperors, including:

Conrad II died 1039. King of the Germans from 1024, Holy Roman emperor from 1027. He ceded the march Sleswick, south of the Jutland peninsula, to King Canute, but extended his rule into Lombardy and Burgundy.

Conrad III 1093–1152. Holy Roman emperor from 1138 the first king of the Hohenstaufen dynasty. Throughout his reign there was a fierce struggle between his followers, the *Ghibellines*, and the *Guelphs*, the followers of Henry the Proud, duke of Saxony and Bavaria (1108–1139). Henry's son Henry the Lion (1129–1195) continued the struggle.

Conrad V (Conradin) 1252–1268. son of Conrad IV, recognized as king of the Germans, Sicily, and Jerusalem by German supporters of the ◊Hohenstaufens in 1254. He led Ghibelline forces against Charles of Anjou at the battle of Tagliacozzo, N Italy 1266, and was captured and executed.

Conran Terence 1931– . British retailer of furnishings, fashion, and household goods. Chairman of the Habitat and Conran companies, he was knighted 1983.

conscientious objector person refusing compulsory service, usually military, on moral, religious, or political grounds.

conscription system under which all able-bodied male citizens (and female in some countries, such as Israel) are legally liable to serve with the armed forces. It originated in France 1792, and in the 19th century it became the established practice in almost all European states.

consent, age of the age at which consent may legally be given to sexual intercourse by a girl or boy. In the UK it is 16.

conservation in the life sciences, care for, and protection of, the ◊biosphere. Since the 1950s it has been increasingly realized that the earth, together with its atmosphere, animal and plant life, mineral and agricultural resources, form an interdependent whole which is in danger of irreversible depletion and eventual destruction unless positive measures are taken to conserve a balance.

conservatism an approach to government and economic management identified with a number of Western political parties, such as the British Conservative, West German Christian Democratic, and Australian Liberal parties. It tends to be explicitly nondoctrinaire and pragmatic but generally emphasizes free-enterprise capitalism, minimal government intervention in the economy, rigid law and order, and the importance of national traditions.

Conservative Party UK political party, one of the two historic British parties; the name replaced *Tory* in general use from 1830 onwards. Traditionally the party of landed interests, it broadened its political base under Disraeli's leadership in the 19th century. The modern Conservative Party's free-market capitalism is supported by the world of finance and the management of industry; its economic policies have increased the spending power of the majority, but also the gap between rich and poor; nationalized industries are sold off (see ◊privatization); military spending and close alliance with the USA are favoured.

conspicuous consumption selection and purchase of goods for the effect they create rather than their inherent value. These might include items with an obviously expensive brand name tag.

Constable John 1776–1837. English landscape painter. The scenes of his native Suffolk include *The Haywain* 1821 (National Gallery, London), but he travelled widely in Britain, depicting castles, cathedrals, landscapes, and coastal scenes.

Constance, Council of council held by the Roman Catholic church 1414–17 in Constance, Germany. It elected Pope Martin V, which ended the Great Schism 1378–1417 when there were rival popes in Rome and Avignon.

constant in mathematics, a fixed quantity or one that does not change its value in relation to ◊variables. For example, in the algebraic expression $y^2 = 5x - 3$, the number 3 is a constant. In physics, certain quantities are regarded as universal constants, for example, the speed of light in a vacuum.

constantan a high-resistance alloy of approximately 40% nickel and 60% copper with a very low temperature coefficient. It is used in electrical resistors.

Constantine II 1940– . King of the Hellenes (Greece). In 1964 he succeeded his father Paul I, went into exile 1967, and was formally deposed 1973.

Constantine the Great 274–337. First Christian emperor of Rome and founder of Constantinople. He defeated Maxentius, joint-emperor at Rome 321,and 313 formally recognized Christianity. Now sole emperor of the West of the Empire, he defeated Licinius, emperor of the East, to become ruler of the Roman world 324. He presided over the Church's first council at Nicaea in 325. In 330 Constantine moved his capital to Byzantium, renaming it Constantinople.

Constable Salisbury Cathedral and Archdeacon Fisher's House from the River *(1820) National Gallery, London.*

Constantinople former name of Istanbul, Turkey, 330–1453. It was founded by the Roman emperor Constantine the Great by the enlargement of the Greek city of Byzantium 328, and became the capital of the Byzantine Empire 330. Its elaborate fortifications enabled it to resist a succession of sieges, but it was captured by crusaders 1204, and was the seat of a Latin (W European) kingdom until recaptured by the Greeks 1261. An attack by the Turks 1422 proved unsuccessful, but it was taken by another Turkish army 29 May 1453 after nearly a year's siege, and became the capital of the Ottoman Empire.

constant prices a series of prices adjusted to reflect real purchasing power. If wages were to rise by 15% from £100 per week (to £115) and the rate of inflation was 10% (requiring £110 to maintain spending power), the real wage would have risen by 5%. An index used to create a constant price series, unlike ◊current prices.

constellation in astronomy, one of the 88 areas into which the sky is divided for the purposes of identifying and naming objects. The first constellations were simple patterns of stars in which early civilizations visualized gods, sacred beasts, and mythical heroes.

constitution the fundamental laws of a state, laying down the system of government and defining the relations of the legislature, executive, and judiciary to each other and to the citizens. Since the French Revolution almost all countries (the UK is one exception), have adopted written constitutions; that of the USA (1787) is the oldest.

Constructivism revolutionary art movement founded in Moscow 1917 by the Russians Naum Gabo, Antoine Pevsner (1886–1962), and Vladimir Tatlin (1885–1953). Tatlin's abstract sculptures, using wood, metal, and clear plastic, were hung on walls or suspended from ceilings.

consul the chief magistrate of ancient Rome following the expulsion of the last king in 510 BC. The Consuls were two annually elected magistrates, both of equal power; they jointly held full civil power at Rome, and the chief military command in the field.

After the establishment of the Roman Empire the office became purely honorary. The term consul is also used for a state official, with political and commercial responsibilities, who looks after their country's citizens in major foreign cities)

consumer durable a good which is required to satisfy personal requirements and which has a long life, such as furniture and electrical goods, as opposed to food and drink which are perishables and have to be replaced frequently.

consumer protection laws and measures designed to ensure fair trading for buyers. The movement in the 20th century has been to shift the burden to check goods and services for quality, safety and suitability, away from the consumer to the producer.

consumers' association a group formed to protect consumer interests usually where the quality and price of goods or services is concerned.

consumption the purchasing and using of goods and services. In economics, it means a country's total expenditure over a given period (usually a year) on goods and services (including expenditure on raw materials and defence).

consumption former name for the disease ◊tuberculosis.

contact lens a lens placed in contact with the eye, separated in most cases only by a film of tears. Contact lenses may be used as a substitute for spectacles for the correction of defective vision or, in special circumstances, as protective shells or for cosmetic purposes, for example, changing eye colour.

contact process the main method of manufacturing sulphuric acid, one of the most important industrial chemicals. In the contact process a mixture of sulphur dioxide and air is passed over a hot (450°C) catalyst of vanadium/vanadium oxide. The sulphur trioxide produced is then absorbed by a spray of dilute acid.

Contadora Group an alliance formed between Colombia, Mexico, Panama, and Venezuela in Jan 1983 to establish a general peace treaty for Central America. The process was designed to include the

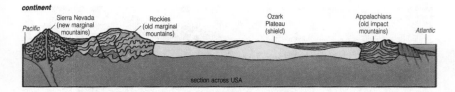

continent

Pacific — Sierra Nevada (new marginal mountains) — Rockies (old marginal mountains) — Ozark Plateau (shield) — Appalachians (old impact mountains) — Atlantic

section across USA

formation of a Central American parliament (similar to the European parliament).

contempt of court behaviour which shows contempt for the authority of a court, such as: disobeying a court order; behaviour which disrupts, prejudices or interferes with court proceedings; and abuse of judges, inside or outside a court. The court may punish contempt with a fine or imprisonment.

continent any one of the large land masses of the Earth, as distinct from ocean. They are Asia, Africa, North and South America, Europe, Australia, and Antarctica. Continents are constantly moving and evolving (see ◊plate tectonics). A continent does not end at the coastline. Its boundary is the edge of the shallow continental shelf (part of the continental ◊crust, made of ◊sial) which may extend several hundred kilometres out to sea.

Continental Congress in US history, the federal legislature of the original 13 states, acting as a provisional revolutionary government during the War of ◊American Independence. It was convened in Philadelphia 1774–1789, when the constitution was adopted. The second Continental Congress, convened May 1775, was responsible for drawing up the Declaration of Independence.

continental drift theory in geology first proposed 1915 by the German meteorologist Alfred Wegener that about 200 million years ago the Earth consisted of a single large continent (he called it ◊Pangaea) which subsequently broke apart to form the continents known today. The theory of ◊plate tectonics has provided a convincing explanation of how such vast movement may have occurred.

Continental System the vast system of economic preference and protection within Europe created by the French emperor Napoleon in order to exclude British trade. Apart from its function as economic warfare, the system also reinforced the French economy at the expense of other European states.

continuum a ◊set which is infinite and and everywhere continuous, for example, the set of points on a line.

contraceptive drug, device, or technique that interferes with reproduction. Some types of pill prevent the ripening and release of an egg cell (ovum) or prevent the sperm fertilizing the egg; barrier methods, such as the condom or diaphragm, stop the sperm reaching the egg; intrauterine devices (IUDs) halt the implantation of the embryo in the wall of the womb.

contract bridge popular card game first played 1925. Following a much publicised match 1930 it quickly outgrew auction bridge in popularity.

contractile root a thickened root at the base of a corm, bulb or other organ that helps position it at an appropriate level in the ground. Contractile roots are found, for example, on the corms of *Crocus*. After they have become anchored in the soil the upper portion contracts, pulling the plant deeper into the ground.

contralto another name for the female alto voice.

contrapuntal in music, term used to describe a work employing ◊counterpoint.

Contras right-wing guerrilla force operating in Nicaragua to overthrow the democratically-elected Sandinista government 1979–90; they were estimated to number some 15,000 in 1985. Covert US funding of Contra forces since 1984 was revealed by the ◊Irangate hearings 1986–87.

convection a type of heat energy transfer that involves the movement of a fluid (gas or liquid). According to the kinetic theory, molecules of fluid in contact with the source of heat expand and tend to rise within the bulk of the fluid. Less energetic, cooler molecules sink to take their place, setting up convection currents. This is the principle of natural convection in many domestic hot-water systems and room space-heating.

convent religious house for ◊nuns.

convergence in mathematics, property of a series of numbers in which the difference between consecutive terms gradually decreases. The sum of a converging series approaches a limit as the number of terms tends to ◊infinity.

convergent evolution the independent evolution of similar structures in species (or other taxonomic groups) that are not closely related, as a result of living in a similar way. Thus, birds and bats have

continental drift

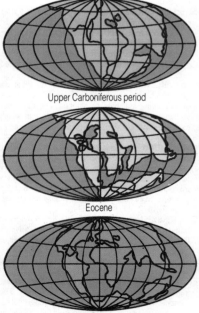

Upper Carboniferous period

Eocene

Lower Quaternary

convergent evolution

bird wing

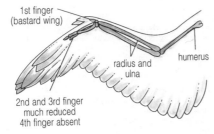

1st finger
(bastard wing)

radius and
ulna

humerus

2nd and 3rd finger
much reduced
4th finger absent

bat wing

1st finger
(claw)

radius and
ulna

humerus

other four fingers hold wing out

wings, not because they are descended from a common winged ancestor, but because their respective ancestors independently evolved flight.

convex lens a converging ◊lens – that is, a parallel beam of light passing through it converges and is eventually brought to a focus; it can therefore produce a real image on a screen. Such a lens is wider at its centre than at the edges. Common forms include *biconvex* (with both surfaces curved towards) and *plano-convex* (with one flat surface and one convex). The whole lens may be further curved overall, making a *concavo-convex* or converging meniscus lens, used in spectacles.

conveyancing the administrative process involved in transferring title to land, usually on its sale or purchase. In England and Wales, conveyancing is usually by solicitors, but, since 1985, can also be done by licensed conveyancers.

conveyor a device used for transporting materials. Very widely used throughout industry is the *conveyor belt*, usually a rubber or fabric belt running on rollers. Trough-shaped belts are used, for example in mines, for transporting ores and coal. *Chain conveyors* are also used in coal mines to remove coal from the cutting machines. Overhead endless chain conveyors are used to carry components and bodies in car assembly works. Other types include *bucket conveyors* and *screw conveyors*, powered versions of ◊Archimedes screw.

convict system British penal system of transporting convicted people to the British colonies, usually Australia. The first fleet arrived at Sydney Cove in Jan 1788. About 137,000 male and 25,000 female convicts were transported to Australia 1788-1868.

convocation in the Church of England, the synods (councils) of the clergy of the provinces of Canterbury and York. The General Synod established 1970 took over the functions and authority of the Convocation of Canterbury and York which continued only in a restricted form.

convolvulus or *bindweed* genus of plants of the

family Convolvulaceae. They are characterized by their twining stems, and by their petals which are united into a tube.

convoy system grouping of ships to sail together under naval escort in wartime. In World War I UK navy escort vessels were at first used only to accompany troopships, but the convoy system was adopted for merchant shipping when the unrestricted German submarine campaign opened in 1917. In World War II it was widely used by the Allies, and was generally successful.

convulsion a series of violent contractions of the muscles over which the patient has no control. It may be associated with loss of consciousness.

Cook, Mount highest point, 3,764 m/12,349 ft of Southern ◊Alps, range of mountains running through New Zealand.

Cook James 1728–1779. British naval explorer. He made three voyages: 1769–71 to Tahiti, New Zealand, and Australia; 1772–75 to the South Pacific; and 1776–79 to the South and North Pacific, attempting to find the NW Passage, and charting the Siberian coast. He was killed on Hawaii. Cook made enormous additions to geographical knowledge, and was responsible for Britain's acquisition of the Australasian territories.

Cook Thomas 1808–1892. Pioneer British travel agent, founder of Thomas Cook & Son. He organized his first tour, to Switzerland, in 1863, and introduced traveller's cheques (then called 'circular notes'), in the early 1870s.

Cook Islands group of six large and a number of smaller Polynesian islands 2,600 km/1,560 mi NE of Auckland, New Zealand; area 238 sq km/92 sq mi; population (1981) 17,754. Their main products are fruit, copra and crafts. They became a self-governing overseas territory of New Zealand 1964.

Cook Strait strait dividing North and South Island, New Zealand. A submarine cable carries electricity from South to North Island.

Coolidge (John) Calvin 1872–1933. 30th president of the USA 1923–29, a Republican. As governor of Massachusetts 1919, he was responsible for crushing a Boston police strike. He became vice president 1921 and president on the death of Harding. He was re-elected 1924, and his period of office was marked by great economic prosperity.

Cooper Gary 1901–1962. American actor, who epitomized the lean, true-hearted Yankee, slow of speech but capable of outdoing the 'badmen' in *Sergeant York* 1940 (Academy Award 1941), and *High Noon* 1952.

Cook British navigator and explorer Captain James Cook.

Cooper James Fenimore 1789–1851. US writer, the first great US novelist. He wrote some 50 novels, first becoming popular with *The Spy* 1821. The volumes of ◊*Leatherstocking Tales* describe the frontier hero Leatherstocking and American Indians before and after the American Revolution, including *The Last of the Mohicans* 1826.

co-operative movement the banding together of groups of people for mutual assistance in trade, manufacture, the supply of credit, or other services. The original principles of co-operative movement were laid down in 1844 by the Rochdale Pioneers, under the influence of Robert Owen, and by Charles Fourier in France. In the UK the 1970s and 1980s have seen a growth in the number of workers' co-operatives, set up in factories otherwise threatened by closure due to economic depression.

Co-operative Party political party founded in Britain in 1918 by the co-operative movement, to maintain its principles in parliamentary and local government. A written constitution was adopted in 1938. The party had strong links with the Labour Party; from 1946 Co-operative Party candidates stood in elections as Co-operative and Labour Candidates, and after the 1959 general election agreement was reached to limit the party's candidates to 30.

Co-operative Wholesale Society (CWS) a British concern, the largest co-operative organization in the world, owned and controlled by the numerous co-operative retail societies, which are also its customers. Founded in 1863, it acts as wholesaler, manufacturer, and banker, and owns factories, farms and estates, in addition to offices and warehouses.

coordinate geometry a system of geometry, also called analytical geometry, in which points, lines, shapes, and surfaces are represented by algebraic expressions. In plane (two-dimensional) coordinate geometry, the plane is usually defined by two axes at right angles to each other, the horizontal x-axis and the vertical y-axis, meeting at O, the origin. A point on the plane can be represented by a pair of ◊Cartesian coordinates, which define its position in terms of its distance along the x-axis and along the y-axis from O. These distances are respectively the x and y coordinates of the point.

coot water bird *Fulica atra* belonging to the rail family. About 38 cm/1.2 ft long, and mainly black, it has a stark white forehead and big feet with lobed toes. They are found in Europe, Asia, N Africa. and Australia on inland waters, feeding on plants, insects, and small fish.

Coote Eyre 1726–1783. Irish general in British India. His victory in 1760 at Wandiwash, followed by the capture of Pondicherry, ended French hopes of supremacy in India. He returned to India as commander in chief 1779, and several times defeated ◊Hyder Ali, sultan of Mysore.

Copenhagen (Danish **København**) capital of Denmark, on the islands of Zealand and Amager; population (1985) 1,350,000 (including suburbs).

Copenhagen, Battle of naval victory on 2 Apr 1801 by a British fleet under Sir Hyde Parker (1739–1807) and ◊Nelson over the Danish fleet. Nelson put his telescope to his blind eye and refused to see Parker's signal for withdrawal.

Copepoda subclass of ◊crustaceans, mainly microscopic, and found in plankton.

Copernicus Nicolaus 1473–1543. Polish astronomer, who believed that the Sun, not the Earth, is at the centre of the Solar System, thus defying established doctrine. For 30 years he worked on the hypothesis that the rotation and the orbital motion of the Earth was responsible for the apparent movements of the heavenly bodies. His great work *De Revolutionibus Orbium Coelestium* was not published until the year of his death.

Copland Aaron 1900–1990. US composer. Copland's early works, such as the piano concerto of 1926, were in the jazz idiom then popular in the USA, but he gradually developed a gentler style with a regional flavour drawn from American folk music.

copper a chemical element, and one of the earliest metals used by humans. Chemical symbol Cu, atomic number 29, relative atomic mass 63.54. It is orange-pink in colour, very malleable and ductile, and used principally on account of its toughness, softness, pliability, high thermal and electrical conductivity, and resistance to corrosion.

copper ore any mineral from which copper is extracted, including **native copper**, Cu; **chalcocite**, Cu_2O; **chalcopyrite**, $CuFeS_2$; **bornite**, $FeS.2Cu_2S.CuS$; **azurite**, $2CuCO_3.Cu(OH)_2$; **malachite**, $CuCO_3.Cu(OH)_2$; and **chrysocolla**, $CuSiO_3.2H_2O$.

coppicing a severe type of pruning where trees are cut down to near ground level at regular intervals, typically every 3–20 years, to promote the growth of numerous shoots from the base. This form of woodland management used to be commonly practised, especially on hazel, to produce large quantities of thin branches for firewood, fencing, and so on. The resulting thicket was known as a coppice or copse. See also ◊pollarding.

Coppola Francis Ford 1939– . US film director and screenwriter. He directed *The Godfather* in 1972, which became one of the biggest money-makers of all time. Other films include *Apocalypse Now* 1979, and *The Cotton Club* 1984.

copra dried kernel of the ◊coconut.

Copt a descendant of the ancient Egyptians who accepted Christianity in the 1st century and refused to adopt Islam after the Arab conquest. They now form a small minority (about 5 per cent) of Egypt's population. The head of the Coptic Church is the Patriarch of Alexandria, currently Shenonda III (1923–), 117th pope of Alexandria. He was imprisoned by President Sadat 1981 and is opposed by Muslim fundamentalists.

Coptic language a member of the Hamito-Semitic language family and a minority language of Egypt. It is descended from the language of the ancient Egyptians and is the ritual language of the Coptic Christian Church. It is written in the Greek alphabet with some additional characters derived from Demotic script.

Coppola *American film director and screenwriter Francis Coppola, 1979.*

coral

static island

sea level

fringing reef

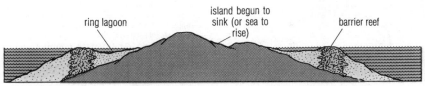

ring lagoon

island begun to
sink (or sea to
rise)

barrier reef

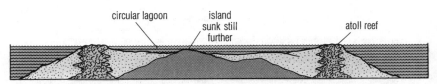

circular lagoon

island
sunk still
further

atoll reef

copyright law applying to literary, musical and artistic works (including plays, recordings, films, radio and television broadcasts, and, in the USA and Britain, computer programs), which prevents the reproduction of the work, in whole or in part, without the author's consent.

coral marine organism related to sea anemones, and belonging to the class Anthozoa of the phylum Cnidaria. It has a skeleton of lime (calcium carbonate) extracted from the surrounding water. Corals exist in warm, salt seas, at moderate depths with sufficient light.

Coral Sea or *Solomon Sea* part of the Pacific Ocean lying between NE Australia, New Guinea, the Solomon Islands, New Hebrides, and New Caledonia. It contains numerous coral islands and reefs.

cor anglais or *English horn* musical instrument; not a horn but a woodwind, a member of the ◊oboe family, whose English origin is doubtful. A metal tube, bent backwards to the mouth of the player, contains the double reed. Introduced into the orchestra in the time of Wagner, it has an expressive tone, and is normally used in slow melodic passages.

Corday Charlotte 1768–1793. French Girondin (right-wing republican during the French Revolution). After overthrow of the Girondins by the more extreme Jacobins in May 1793, she stabbed to death the Jacobin leader, Marat, with a bread knife as he sat in his bath in July of the same year. She was guillotined.

cordillera a group of mountain ranges and their valleys, all running in a specific direction, formed by the convergence of two ◊tectonic plates along a line.

Cordilleras, the the mountainous western section of North America, with the Rocky Mountains and the coast ranges parallel to the contact between the North American and the Pacific plates.

core the innermost part of the structure of the Earth. It is divided into an inner core, the upper boundary of which is 1,600 km/940 mi from the centre, and an outer core, 1,820 km/1,060 mi thick. Both parts are thought to be made of nickel and iron,

with the inner core being solid and the outer core being liquid. The temperature may be 3,000°C.

Corfu (Greek *Kérkira*) most northerly, second largest of the Ionian islands, off the coast of Epirus in the Ionian Sea; area 1,072 sq km/414 sq mi; population (1981) 96,500. Its businesses include tourism, fruit, olive oil, and textiles. Its largest town is the port of Corfu (Kérkira), population (1981) 33,560. Corfu was colonized by Corinthians about 700 BC, Venice held it 1386–1797, Britain from 1815–64.

Corinth ancient Greek city-state, which played an important part in the Peloponnesian War, later conquered by the Romans (146 BC). The modern port of Corinth (Greek *Kórinthos*) stands on an isthmus dissected by the Corinth canal, opened 1893.

Cork largest county of the Republic of Ireland, in the province of Munster; area 7,459 sq km/2,880 sq mi; population (1981) 402,000. It is agricultural but there is also some copper and manganese mining, marble quarrying, and river and sea fishing. Natural gas and oil fields are found off the S coast at Kinsale. The county town is Cork, population (1981) 150,000.

cork the light, waterproof, outer layers of the bark of the stems and roots of almost all trees and shrubs. The cork oak *Quercus suber*, a native of S Europe and N Africa, is cultivated in Spain and Portugal; the corky outer layers of its bark provide the cork for commercial use.

corm a short, swollen, underground plant stem, surrounded by protective scale-leaves, as seen in *Crocus*. It stores food, provides a means of ◊vegetative reproduction, and acts as a ◊perennating organ. During the year the corm gradually withers as the food reserves are used for the production of leafy, flowering shoots formed from axillary buds. Several new corms are formed at the base of these shoots, above the old corm.

cormorant seabird *Phalacrocorax carbo* about 90 cm/3 ft long, with webbed feet, long neck and beak, and glossy black plumage. There are some 30 species of cormorant worldwide including a flightless form *Nannopterum harrisi* in the Galapagos Islands.

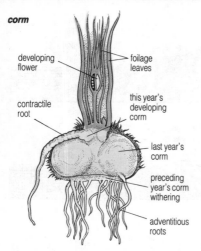

corm

developing flower

foilage leaves

contractile root

this year's developing corm

last year's corm

preceding year's corm withering

adventitious roots

It generally feeds on bottom-living fish in shallow water.

corncrake bird *Crex crex* of the rail family. About 25 cm/10 in long, it is drably coloured, shy, and has a persistent rasping call. It lives in meadows and crops, but has become rare where mechanical methods of cutting corn are used. It lives in the milder regions of all continents.

Corneille Pierre 1606–1684. French dramatist. His many tragedies such as *Oedipe* 1659 glorify the strength of will governed by reason, and established the French classical dramatic tradition for the next two centuries. His most famous play, *Le Cid* 1636, a tragi-comedy, was attacked by the Academicians although achieving huge public success. Later plays were based on Aristotle's unities, and again favoured by Richelieu.

cornet musical instrument. Originally the name of a family of woodwind instruments; it now refers to the *cornet à pistons*. Like a shorter, broader trumpet, with a wider bore, it is without fixed notes. Notes of different pitch are obtained by over-blowing and by means of three pistons. It is chiefly used in military and brass bands.

cornflour in the UK, the purified starch content of maize (Indian corn), used as a thickener in cooking; in the USA it is called cornstarch.

cornflower plant *Centaurea cyanus* of the family Compositae. It is distinguished from the knapweeds by its deep azure blue flowers, and was formerly a common weed in cornfields in Britain.

Cornforth John 1917– . Australian chemist. In 1975 he shared a Nobel prize with Vladimir Prelog for work utilizing ◊radioisotopes as 'markers' to find out how enzymes synthesize chemicals which are mirror images of one another (stereo isomers).

Corn Laws in Britain, laws to regulate the export or import of cereals, in order to maintain an adequate supply for the consumers and a secure price for the producers. For centuries the Corn Laws formed an integral part of the mercantile system in England, and it was not until after the Napoleonic wars, with mounting pressure from a growing urban population, that they aroused any strong opposition because of their tendency to drive up the price. They were modified 1828 and 1842 and, partly as a result of the Irish famine, practically repealed by Robert Peel 1846, as being an unwarranted tax on food and a hindrance to British exports.

Cornwall county in SW England including Scilly Islands (Scillies)
area (excluding Scillies) 3,548 sq km/1,370 sq mi
towns administrative headquarters Truro; Camborne, Launceston; resorts of Bude, Falmouth, Newquay, Penzance, St Ives
physical Bodmin Moor (including Brown Willy 419 m/1,375 ft), Land's End peninsula, St Michael's Mount, rivers Tamar, Fowey, Fal, and Camel
products growing electronics industry; spring flowers; tin (mined since Bronze Age, some workings renewed in 1960s, though the industry has all but disappeared), kaolin (St Austell); fish
population (1986) 441,900
famous people John Betjeman, Humphry Davy, Daphne du Maurier, William Golding.

Cornwallis Charles, 1st Marquess Cornwallis 1738–1805. British soldier, eldest son of the 1st Earl Cornwallis. He led the British forces in the War of ◊American Independence until 1781, when his surrender at Yorktown ended the war.

corolla collective name for the ◊petals of a flower. In some plants the petal margins are partially or completely fused to form a *corolla-tube*, for example in bindweed *Convolvulus arevensis*.

corona a faint halo of hot (about 2,000,000K) and tenuous gas around the Sun, which boils from the surface. It is visible at solar ◊eclipses or through a *coronagraph*, an instrument that blocks light from the Sun's brilliant disc. The gas flows away from the corona to form the ◊solar wind.

coronary artery disease condition in which the fatty deposits of ◊atherosclerosis form in, and therefore narrow, the coronary arteries which supply the heart muscle.

coronation the ceremony of investing a sovereign with the emblems of royalty, as a symbol of inauguration in office. Since the coronation of Harold in 1066, English sovereigns have been crowned in Westminster Abbey, London. The kings of Scotland were traditionally crowned at Scone; French kings in Reims.

coroner in England, an official who investigates the deaths of persons who have died suddenly by acts of violence, or under suspicious circumstances, by holding an inquest or ordering a post-mortem examination. They may also inquire into instances of ◊treasure trove.

Corot Jean-Baptiste-Camille 1796–1875. French painter, creator of a distinctive landscape style with cool colours and soft focus. His early work, particularly Italian scenes in the 1820s, influenced the Barbizon school of painters, and like them Corot

corona *The corona, the Sun's outer atmosphere, can only be seen during a total solar eclipse.*

worked out of doors, but he also continued a conventional academic tradition with more romanticized paintings.

corporal punishment physical punishment of wrongdoers, for example by whipping. It was abolished as a punishment for criminals in Britain in 1967 but only became illegal for punishing schoolchildren in state schools in 1986. It is still used as a punishment for criminals in many countries, especially under Islamic law.

corporation an organisation which has its own legal identity, distinct from that of its members, for example a ◊company. The term is more commonly used in the USA than in Britain. In English law corporations can be either: a corporation aggregate, consisting of a number of members who may vary from time to time, as in a company; or a corporation sole, consisting of one person and his successors, for example a monarch or a bishop.

corporation tax a tax levied on a company's profits by public authorities. It is a form of income tax, and rates vary according to country, but there is usually a flat rate. It is an important source of revenue for governments.

corporative state state in which the members are organized and represented not on a local basis as citizens, but as producers working in a particular trade, industry, or profession. Originating with the syndicalist workers' movement, the idea was superficially adopted by the fascists in the 1920s and 1930s. Catholic social theory, as expounded in some papal encyclicals, also favours the corporative state as a means of eliminating class conflict.

Corpus Christi feast celebrated in the Roman Catholic and Greek Orthodox churches, and to some extent in the Anglican Church, on the Thursday after Trinity Sunday. It was instituted in the 13th century.

corpuscular theory hypothesis about the nature of light championed by Isaac ◊Newton, who postulated that it consists of a stream of particles or corpuscles. The theory was superseded at the beginning of the 19th century by Thomas ◊Young's wave theory. Modern ◊quantum theory and wave mechanics embody both concepts.

Correggio Antonio Allegri da *c.* 1494–1534. Italian painter of the High Renaissance, whose style followed the classical grandeur of Leonardo and Titian but anticipated the Baroque in its emphasis on movement, softer forms, and contrasts of light and shade.

Corregidor an island at the mouth of Manila Bay, Luzon, the Philippines, where survivors of the ◊Bataan campaign were defeated by the Japanese, 9 Apr–6 May 1942; the USA recaptured it on 15 Feb 1945.

correlation a relationship or form of interdependence between two sets of data. In ◊statistics, such relationships are measured by the calculation of ◊coefficients. These generally measure correlation on a scale with 1 indicating perfect positive correlation, 0 no correlation at all, and -1 perfect inverse correlation.

corrie (Scottish; Welsh *cwm*; French *cirque*) a hollow in the mountainside in a glaciated area representing the source of a melted glacier. The weight of the ice has ground out the bottom and worn back the sides. It is open at the front, and its sides and back are formed of ◊arêtes. There may be a lake in the bottom.

corroboree Australian Aboriginal dance. Some corroborees record events in history; others have a religious significance, connected with

corrie *A perfect corrie overlooking Loch Broom, in the Scottish Highlands.*

fertility and rejuvenation, or are theatrical entertainment.

corrosion the eating away and eventual destruction of metals and alloys by chemical attack. The rusting of ordinary iron and steel is the commonest form of corrosion. Rusting takes place in moist air, the iron combines with oxygen and water to form a brown-orange deposit of ◊rust, hydrated iron oxide. The rate of corrosion is increased where the atmosphere is polluted with sulphur dioxide. Salty roads or atmospheres accelerate the rusting of car bodies.

corsair a pirate based on the N African Barbary Coast. From the 16th century onward the corsairs plundered shipping in the Mediterranean and Atlantic, holding the hostages for ransom or selling them as slaves. Although many punitive expeditions were sent against them, they were not suppressed until France occupied Algiers in 1830.

Corsica (French *Corse*) island region of France, in the Mediterranean off the W coast of Italy, immediately N of Sardinia

area 8,680 sq km/3350 sq mi

capital and port Ajaccio

exports wine, olive oil

population (1984) 244,600, of whom just under 50% are native Corsicans; there are about 400,000 *émigrés*, mostly in Mexico and Central America, who return to retire

language French (official); the majority speak Corsican, an Italian dialect

famous people Napoleon

government its special status involves a regional assembly from 1982 with uncertain powers.

Cort Henry 1740–1800. British iron manufacturer. For the manufacutre of ◊wrought iron, he invented the puddling process and developed the rolling mill, both of which were of vast importance in the Industrial Revolution.

Cortés Hernándo (Ferdinand) 1485–1547. Spanish conquistador. He overthrew the Aztec empire 1519–21, and secured Mexico for Spain.

corticosteroid any of several hormones secreted by the adrenal cortex; also synthetic forms with similar properties. Corticosteroids have anti-inflammatory and ◊immunosuppressive effects and may be used to treat a number of conditions including rheumatoid arthritis, severe allergies, asthma, some skin diseases, and some cancers. Side-effects can be serious. Therapy must be withdrawn very gradually.

cortisone a corticosteroid with anti-inflammatory qualities. It is commonly used in the treatment of rheumatism.

Cortona Pietro da see ◊Pietro da Cortona, Italian Baroque painter.

corundum Al_2O_3 a native aluminium oxide, occurring in cleavable masses or in pyramidal crystals.

Costa Rica
Republic of
(República de Costa Rica)

area 50,997 sq km/19,690 sq mi
capital San José
towns ports Limón, Puntarenas
physical high central plateau and tropical coast
head of state and government Rafael Calderón from 1990
political system liberal democracy
exports coffee, bananas, cocoa, sugar
currency colón
population (1990 est) 3,032,000 (including 1,200 Guaymi Indians); annual growth rate 2.6%

life expectancy men 71, women 76
language Spanish (official)
religion Roman Catholic 95%
literacy 94% male/93% female (1985 est)
GDP $4.3 bn (1986); $1,550 per head
chronology
1821 Independence achieved from Spain.
1949 New constitution adopted. National army abolished. José Figueres, co-founder of the National Liberation Party (PLN), was elected president. He embarked on an ambitious socialist programme.
1958–73 Mainly Conservative administrations returned.
1974 PLN regained the presidency and returned to socialist policies.
1978 Rodrigo Carazo, Conservative, elected president. Sharp deterioration in the state of the economy.
1982 Luis Alberto Monge of the PLN elected president. Harsh austerity programme introduced to rebuild the economy. Pressure from the USA to abandon neutral stance and condemn the Sandinista regime in Nicaragua.
1983 Policy of neutrality reaffirmed.
1985 Following border clashes with Sandinista forces, a US-trained anti-guerrilla guard was formed.
1986 Oscar Arias Sanchez won the presidency on a neutralist platform.
1987 Oscar Arias Sanchez won Nobel Peace Prize.
1990 Rafael Calderón, the pro-US candidate, elected president.

cosecant in trigonometry, a ◊function of an angle in a right-angled triangle found by dividing the length of the hypotenuse (the longest side) by the length of the side opposite the angle. Thus, a cosecant of an angle *A*, usually shortened to *cosec A*, is always greater than 1. It is the reciprocal of the sine of the angle, that is, *cosec A* = 1/*sin A*.

Cosgrave Liam 1920– . Irish Fine Gael politician, prime minister of the Republic of Ireland 1973–77. As party leader 1965–77, he headed a Fine Gael–Labour coalition government from 1973. Relations between the Irish and UK governments improved under his premiership.

Cosgrave William Thomas 1880–1965. Irish politician. He took part in the Easter Rising 1916, and sat in the Sinn Féin cabinet of 1919–21. Head of the Free State government 1922–33, he founded and led the Fine Gael opposition 1933–44. His eldest son is Liam Cosgrave.

cosine in trigonometry, a ◊function of an angle in a right-angled triangle found by dividing the length

of the side adjacent to the angle by the length of the hypotenuse (the longest side). It is usually shortened to *cos*.

cosmic radiation radiation caused by space-originating high-energy particles, consisting of protons and light nuclei, which collide with atomic nuclei in the earth's atmosphere.

cosmology the study of the structure of the Universe. Modern cosmology began in the 1920s with the discovery that the Universe is expanding, which suggested that it began in an explosion, the ◊Big Bang. The **steady state theory** was an alternative view in which the Universe has no origin, but is expanding because new matter is being continually created.

Cosmos name used since the early 1960s for nearly all Soviet artificial satellites. Nearly 2000 Cosmos satellites have been launched.

Cossack member of any of several, formerly horse-raising groups, of S and SW Russia, Ukraine and Poland, predominantly of Russian or Ukrainian origin, who took in escaped serfs and lived in independent communal settlements (military brotherhoods) from the 15th to the 19th century. Later they held land in return for military service in the cavalry under Russian and Polish rulers. After 1917, Cossack communities were incorporated into the Soviet administrative and collective system.

Costa Rica country in central America, bounded to the N by Nicaragua, to the S by Panama, to the E by the Caribbean, and to the W by the Pacific Ocean.

cost benefit analysis the process whereby a project is assessed for its social and welfare benefits rather than a straightforward financial return on investment. For example, this might take into account the environmental impact of an

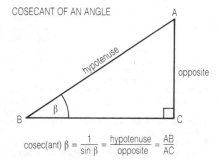

COSECANT OF AN ANGLE

$$\text{cosec(ant)} \ \beta = \frac{1}{\sin \beta} = \frac{\text{hypotenuse}}{\text{opposite}} = \frac{AB}{AC}$$

Cosmonaut Soviet pioneers of space flight photographed in 1965 including Yuri Gagarin (bottom left).

industrial plant, or convenience for users of a new railway.

Costello Elvis. Stage name of Declan McManus 1954– . English rock singer, songwriter, and guitarist, noted for his stylistic range and intricate lyrics. His albums with his group the Attractions include *Armed Forces* 1979, *Trust* 1981, and *Blood and Chocolate* 1986.

cost of living the cost of goods and services needed for an average standard of living.

cotangent in trigonometry, a ◊function of an angle in a right-angled triangle found by dividing the length of the side adjacent to the angle by the length of the side opposite it. It is usually written as *cotan*, or *cot* and it is the reciprocal of the tangent of the angle, so that *cotan A* = 1/*tan A*, where *A* is the angle in question.

cot death death of an apparently healthy baby during sleep, formally known as Sudden Infant Death Syndrome (SIDS).

Côte d'Ivoire (English *Ivory Coast*) country in W Africa, bounded to the N by Mali and Burkina Faso, E by Ghana, S by the Gulf of Guinea, and W by Liberia and Guinea.

Cotman John Sell 1782–1842. British landscape painter, with Crome a founder of the *Norwich school*, a group of realistic landscape painters influenced by Dutch examples. He painted bold

designs in simple flat washes of colour, such as *Greta Bridge, Yorkshire* 1805 (British Museum, London).

cotoneaster genus of trees and shrubs, family Rosaceae, closely allied to the hawthorn and medlar. Its fruits, small and unpalatable, are usually bright red and conspicuous, often persisting through the winter.

Cotonou chief port and largest city of Benin, on the Bight of Benin; population (1982) 487,000. Palm products and timber are exported.

cottage industry an industry undertaken by employees in their homes and often using their own equipment. Cottage industries frequently utilize a traditional craft such as weaving or pottery, but may also use high technology.

cotton tropical and sub-tropical herbaceous plant of the genus *Gossypium*, family Malvaceae. Fibres surround the seeds inside its ripened fruit, or boll, and these are spun into yarn for cloth.

cotton gin a machine that separates cotton fibres from the seed boll. The invention of the gin by the American Eli ◊Whitney in 1793 was a milestone in ◊textile history.

cottonwood name given to several species of N American poplar with fluffy seeds. Also, Australian tree *Bedfordia salaoina* with downy leaves.

cotyledon a structure in the embryo of a seed plant which may form a 'leaf' after germination and is commonly known as a seed leaf. The number of cotyledons present in an embryo is an important character in the classification of flowering plants (◊angiosperms).

couch grass plant *Agropyron repens*, one of the commonest of the Gramineae grasses. It is closely allied to wheat, but is generally regarded as a weed.

cougar alternative name for the ◊puma, a large American cat.

coulomb the practical unit of electrical charge; the quantity of electricity conveyed by a current of one ampere in one second.

Coulomb Charles Auguste de 1736–1806. French scientist, inventor of the torsion balance for measuring the force of electric and magnetic attraction. The coulomb was named after him.

council in local government in England and Wales, a popularly elected local assembly charged with the government of the area within its boundaries. Under the Local Government Act of 1972, they comprise three types: ◊county councils, ◊district councils, and ◊parish councils.

Council for Mutual Economic Assistance (CMEA) full name for ◊Comecon, organization established in 1949 by Eastern bloc countries.

Council of Europe body constituted in 1949 to secure 'a greater measure of unity between the European countries'. The first session of the *Consultative Assembly* opened at Strasbourg, France (still its headquarters), in Aug 1949, the members then being the UK, France, Italy, Belgium, the Netherlands, Sweden, Denmark, Norway, the Republic of Ireland, Luxembourg, Greece, and Turkey; Iceland, West Germany, Austria, Cyprus, Switzerland, Malta, Portugal, Spain, and Liechtenstein joined subsequently. The widest association of European states, it has a *Committee* of foreign ministers, a *Parliamentary Assembly* (with members from national parliaments), and a *European Commission* investigating violations of human rights.

counterfeiting fraudulent imitation, especially of banknotes. It is countered by special papers,

cotangent

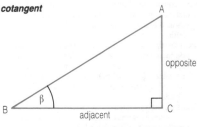

$$\text{cot(angent) } \beta = \frac{1}{\tan \beta} = \frac{\cos \beta}{\sin \beta} = \frac{\text{adjacent}}{\text{opposite}} = \frac{BC}{AC}$$

elaborate watermarks, and skilled printing, sometimes also insertion of a metallic strip. See also ◊forgery.

counterpoint in music, the simultaneous combination of two or more separate melodies to form a harmonious whole. It originated in ◊plainsong, with two independent vocal lines sung simultaneously.

Counter-Reformation a movement initiated by the Catholic church at the Council of Trent 1545–63 to counter the spread of the ◊Reformation. Extending into the 17th century, its dominant forces included the rise of the Jesuits as an educating and missionary group and the deployment of the Spanish ◊Inquisition in other countries.

countertenor highest natural male voice. It was revived in the UK by Alfred Deller (1912–79).

countervailing power in economics, the belief that too much power held by one group or company can be balanced or neutralized by another, creating a compatible relationship, such as trade unions in the case of strong management in a large company, or an opposition party facing an authoritarian government.

country and western the popular music of the white US South and Southwest, evolved from the folk music of the English, Irish, and Scottish settlers with a strong blues influence. Characteristic instruments are slide guitar, mandolin, and fiddle. Lyrics typically extol family values and traditional sex roles. Country music encompasses a variety of regional styles, and ranges from mournful ballads to fast and intricate dance music.

Country Party (official name *National Country Party* from 1975) Australian political party representing the interests of the farmers and people of the smaller towns; it holds the power balance between Liberals and Labor. It developed from about 1860, gained strength after the introduction of preferential voting (see ◊vote) in 1918, and has been in coalition with the Liberals from 1949.

Countryside Commission an official conservation body, created for England and Wales under the Countryside Act 1968. It replaced the National Parks Commission, and had by 1980 created over 160 Country Parks.

county administrative unit of a country or state. In the UK it is nowadays synonymous with 'shire', although historically the two had different origins. Many of the English counties can be traced back to Saxon times. In the USA a county is a subdivision of a state; the power of counties differs widely between states. The Republic of Ireland has 26 geographical and 27 administrative counties.

county council in the UK, a unit of local government, whose responsibilities include broad planning policy, highways, education, personal social services, and libraries; police, fire and traffic control; and refuse disposal.

county court English court of law created by the County Courts Act 1846 and now governed by the Act of 1984. It exists to try civil cases, such as actions on ◊contract and ◊tort where the claim does not exceed £5,000, and disputes about land, such as between landlord and tenant. County courts are presided over by one or more Circuit Judges. An appeal on a point of law lies to the Court of Appeal.

coup d'état or *coup* forcible takeover of the government of a country by elements from within that country. It differs from a revolution in typically being carried out by a small group (for example of army officers or opposition politicians) to install their leader as head of government, rather than being a mass uprising by the population at large.

Couperin François 1668–1733. French composer, called *le Grand*, as the most famous of a distinguished musical family. Born in Paris, he held various court appointments and wrote vocal, chamber, and harpsichord music.

couplet in literature, a pair of lines of verse, usually of the same length and rhymed.

Courbet Gustave 1819–1877. French artist, a portrait, genre, and landscape painter. His *Burial at Ornans* 1850 (Louvre, Paris), showing ordinary working people gathered round a village grave, shocked the public and the critics with its 'vulgarity'.

coursing chasing of hares by greyhounds, not by scent but by sight, as a 'sport', and as a test of the greyhound's speed. It is one of the most ancient of field sports. Since the 1880s it has been practised on enclosed or park courses.

court a body which hears legal actions and the building where this occurs. See ◊law court and particular kinds of court, for example ◊County Court, and ◊Small Claims Court.

Court Margaret (born Smith) 1942– . Australian tennis player. The most prolific winner in the women's game, she won a record 66 Grand Slam titles, including a record 24 at singles.

Courtauld Samuel 1793–1881. British industrialist who developed the production of viscose rayon and other synthetic fibres from 1904.

courtesy title in the UK, title given to the progeny of members of the peerage. For example, the eldest son of a duke, marquess or earl may bear one of his father's lesser titles; thus the Duke of Marlborough's son is the Marquess of Blandford. They are not peers and do not sit in the House of Lords.

courtly love a medieval code of amorous conduct between noble men and women.

court-martial court convened for the trial of persons subject to military discipline. British court martials are governed by the code of the service concerned – Naval Discipline, Army, or Air Force Acts – and in 1951 an appeal court was established for all three services by the Courts Martial (Appeals) Act. The procedure prescribed for the US services is similar, being based on British practice.

Court of Session the supreme Civil Court in Scotland, established 1532. Cases come in the first place before one of the judges of the Outer House, and from that decision an appeal lies to the Inner House which sits in two divisions called the First and Second Division. From the decisions of the Inner House an appeal lies to the House of Lords. The court sits in Edinburgh.

Court of the Lord Lyon Scottish heraldic authority composed of one King of Arms, three Heralds, and three Pursuivants who specialize in genealogical work. It embodies the High Sennachie of Scotland's Celtic kings.

courtship behaviour exhibited by animals as a prelude to mating. The behaviour patterns vary considerably from one species to another, but are often ◊ritualized forms of behaviour quite unrelated to courtship or mating (for example, courtship feeding in birds).

Cousteau Jacques-Yves 1910– . French oceanographer, celebrated for his researches in command of the *Calypso* from 1951; he pioneered the invention of the aqualung 1943 and techniques in underwater filming.

covalency in chemistry, a form of ◊valency in which two atoms unite by sharing a pair of electrons.

Covenanter in English history, one of the Presbyterian Christians who swore to uphold their forms of worship in a National Covenant, signed on 28 Feb 1638, when Charles I attempted to introduce a liturgy on the English model into Scotland.

Coventry industrial city in West Midlands, England; population (1981) 313,800. Manufacturing includes cars, electronic equipment, machine tools, and agricultural machinery.

Coverdale Miles 1488–1569. English Protestant priest whose translation of the Bible was the first to be printed in English (1535). His translation of the psalms is that retained in the Book of Common Prayer.

Coward Noel 1899–1973. English playwright, actor, producer, director and composer, who epitomized the witty and sophisticated man of the theatre. From his first success with *The Young Idea* 1923, he wrote and appeared in plays and comedies such as *Hay Fever* 1925; *Private Lives* 1930, with Gertrude Lawrence; *Design for Living* 1933; *Blithe Spirit* 1941.

cowfish type of ◊boxfish.

Cowley Abraham 1618–1667. British poet. He introduced the Pindaric ode (based on the Greek poet Pindar) to English poetry, and published metaphysical verse with elaborate imagery, as well as essays.

cow parsley tall perennial plant *Anthriscus sylvestris* of the carrot family. Up to 1 m/3 ft tall, its pinnate leaves, hollow furrowed stems and heads of white flowers in early summer are familiar in hedgerows and shady places. Also known as keck, it can be found in Europe, N Asia and N Africa.

Cowper William 1731–1800. English poet, who trained as a lawyer, but suffered a mental breakdown in 1763 and entered an asylum, where he underwent an evangelical conversion. He later wrote hymns (for example 'God moves in a mysterious way'). His verse includes the six books of *The Task* 1785, and the comic poem 'John Gilpin'.

cowrie marine snail-like mollusc, in which the interior spiral form is concealed by a double outer lip. The shells are hard, shiny, and often coloured. Most cowries are shallow-water forms, and are found in many parts of the world, particularly the tropical Indopacific.

coyote wild dog *Canis latrans*, in appearance like a small wolf, living from Alaska to Central America. Its head and body are about 90 cm/3 ft long, and brown flecked with grey or black. Coyotes live in open country and can run at 65 kph/40 mph. Its main foods are rabbits and rodents.

coypu South American water rodent *Myocastor coypus*, about 60 cm/2 ft long and weighing up to 9 kg/20 lb. It has a scaly, rat-like tail, webbed hind feet, a blunt-muzzled head, and large orange incisors. The fur is reddish brown. It feeds on vegetation, and lives in burrows in river and lake banks.

Cozens John Robert 1752–1797. British landscape painter, a watercolourist whose Romantic views of Europe painted on tours in the 1770s and 1780s influenced Girtin and Turner.

CPU or *processor* central processing unit of a computer: the part that reads the program, fetches data, performs operations on the data in accordance with the program, and outputs its results.

Cousteau French underwater explorer Jacques Cousteau.

CPVE (Certificate of Pre-Vocational Education) in the UK, educational qualification introduced in 1986 for students over 16 in schools and colleges who want a one-year course of preparation for work or further vocational study.

crab name given to many decapod (ten-legged) crustaceans of the suborder Reptantia ('walking'), related to ◊lobsters and ◊crayfish. Mainly marine, some crabs live in fresh water or on land. They are alert carnivores and scavengers. They have a typical sideways walk, and strong pincers on the first pair of legs, the other four pairs being used for walking. Periodically, the outer shell is cast to allow for growth. The true crabs (division Brachyura) have a broad, rather round, upper body shell (carapace), and a small ◊abdomen tucked beneath the body.

crab apple wild form *Malus sylvestris* from which the cultivated apple has been derived; it differs chiefly in the smaller size and bitter flavour of the fruit, used in crab apple jelly.

Crabbe George 1754–1832. British poet. Originally a doctor, he became a clergyman in 1781, and wrote grimly realistic verse of the poor of his own time: *The Village* 1783, *The Parish Register* 1807, and *The Borough* 1810 (which includes the story used in the Britten opera *Peter Grimes*).

Crab Nebula cloud of gas 6,000 light years away, in the constellation of Taurus, the remains of a star that exploded as a ◊supernova (observed as a brilliant point of light on Earth in 1054). At its centre is a ◊pulsar that flashes 30 times a second. The name comes from its crab-like appearance.

crack ◊cocaine in crystal solids; it is heated and inhaled, and said to be more addictive than cocaine snorted in powdered form.

cracking method of distilling ◊petroleum products; see also ◊fractionation.

Cracow alternative form of ◊Kraków, Polish city.

Craig Edward Gordon 1872–1966. British director and stage designer. His innovations and theories on

CPU

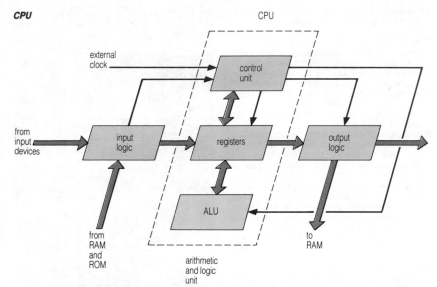

CPU

external clock

control unit

from input devices

input logic

registers

output logic

from RAM and ROM

ALU

to RAM

arithmetic and logic unit

stage design and lighting effects, expounded in *On the Art of the Theatre* 1911, had a huge influence on stage production in Europe and the USA.

Craig James 1871–1940. Ulster Unionist politician, the first prime minister of Northern Ireland 1921–40. Craig became a Member of Parliament in 1906, and was a highly effective organizer of Unionist resistance to Home Rule. As prime minister he carried out systematic discrimination against the Catholic minority, abolishing proportional representation in 1929 and redrawing constituency boundaries to ensure Protestant majorities.

crake any of several small birds related to the ◊corncrake.

Cranach Lucas 1472–1553. German painter, etcher, and woodcut artist, a leading light in the German Renaissance. He is best known for full-length nudes and precise and polished portraits, such as *Martin Luther* 1521 (Uffizi, Florence).

cranberry plant *Vaccinium oxycoccos* allied to the bilberry, and belonging to the heath family Ericaceae. It is a small evergreen, growing in marshy places, and bearing small, acid, edible, crimson berries.

crane in engineering, a machine for raising, lowering or placing in position heavy loads. The three main types are the jib crane, the overhead travelling crane and the tower crane. Most cranes have the machinery mounted on a revolving turntable. They may be mounted on trucks or be self-propelled, often being fitted with ◊caterpillar tracks.

crane in zoology, bird of the family Gruidae, with long legs and neck, and powerful wings. They are marsh and plain-dwelling birds, feeding on plants as well as insects and small animals. They fly well and are usually migratory. They are found in all parts of the world except S America.

Crane (Harold) Hart 1899–1932. US poet. His long mystical poem *The Bridge* (1930) uses the Brooklyn Bridge as a symbol. He drowned after jumping overboard from a steamer bringing him back to the USA after a visit to Mexico.

Crane Stephen 1871–1900. US writer, who introduced grim realism into the US novel. Born in New Jersey, he became a journalist, and wrote *Red Badge of Courage* 1895, dealing vividly with the US Civil War.

crane fly type of fly, often known as *daddy-longlegs*, with long, slender, and very fragile legs. The larvae live in the soil, or in water.

cranesbill plant of the genus *Geranium*, which contains about 400 species. The plant is named after the long, beak-like process which is attached to its seed vessels. When ripe, this splits into coiling spirals, which jerk the seeds out, assisting in their distribution.

craniotomy an operation to remove or turn back a small flap of skull bone to give access to the living brain.

crank a device which converts rotary movement to reciprocating (back-and-forwards or up-and-down) movement, or vice versa.

crankshaft an essential component of piston engines, which converts the up-and-down (reciprocating) motion of the pistons into useful rotary motion. The familiar car crankshaft carries a number of cranks. The pistons are connected to the cranks by connecting rods and ◊bearings; when the pistons move up and down, the connecting rods force the offset crank pins to describe a circle, thereby rotating the crankshaft.

Cranmer Thomas 1489–1556. English priest, archbishop of Canterbury from 1533. A Protestant convert, under Edward VI he helped to shape the doctrines of the Church of England. He was responsible for the issue of the Prayer Books of 1549 and 1552, and supported the succession of Lady Jane Grey.

Crassus Marcus Licinius *c*. 108–53 BC. Roman general who crushed the ◊Spartacus rising in 71 BC. In 60 BC he joined with Caesar and Pompey in the first Triumvirate and in 55 BC obtained command in the East. Invading Mesopotamia, he was defeated by the Parthians at the battle of Carrhae, captured, and put to death.

crater a bowl-shaped topographic feature, usually round and with steep sides. Craters are formed by explosive events such as the eruption of a volcano or by the impact of a meteorite. A ◊caldera is a much larger feature.

craton or *shield* the core of a continent, a vast tract of very ancient ◊metamorphic rock around which the continent has been built. In Precambrian times there may have been mountains here, but now these mountains have been worn down and the land is flat.

Crawford Joan 1908–1977. US actress, who made her name from 1925 in dramatic films such as *Mildred Pierce* 1945, and *Whatever Happened to Baby Jane?* 1962.

crawling peg in economics, also known as sliding- or moving-parity, a method of achieving a desired adjustment in a currency exchange rate (up or down) by small percentages over a given period, rather than by a major one-off revaluation or devaluation.

Craxi Bettino 1934– . Italian socialist politician, leader of the Italian Socialist Party (PSI) from 1976, prime minister 1983–87.

crayfish freshwater crustacean structurally similar to, but smaller than, the lobster. They are brownish-green scavengers which are found in all parts of the world except Africa.

Crazy Horse 1849–1877. Sioux Indian chief, one of the Indian leaders at the massacre of ◊Little Bighorn. He was killed when captured.

creationism a theory concerned with the origins of matter and life, claiming, as does the Bible in Genesis, that the world and humanity were created by a supernatural Creator, not more than 6,000 years ago. It was developed in response to Darwin's theory of ◊evolution; it is not recognized by scientists as having a factual basis.

Crécy, Battle of first important battle of the Hundred Years' War, 1346. Philip VI of France was defeated by Edward III of England at the village of Crécy-en-Ponthieu, now in Somme *département*, France, 18 km/11 mi NE of Abbeville.

credit in economics, means by which goods or services are obtained without immediate payment, usually by agreeing to pay interest. The three main forms are consumer credit (usually extended to individuals by retailers), bank credit (such as overdrafts or personal loans) and trade credit (common in the commercial world both within countries and internationally).

credit in education, the system of evaluating courses so that a partial qualification from one institution is accepted by another on transfer to complete a course. In North America, the term also refers to the successful completion of a course.

credit card card issued by an organization, such as a retail outlet or a bank, which enables the holder to obtain goods or services on credit (usually to a specified limit).

credit rating measure of the willingness or ability to pay for goods, loans, or services rendered by an individual, company, or country. A country with a good credit rating will attract loans on favourable terms.

Cree an indigenous North American people whose language belongs to the Algonquian family. The Cree are distributed over a vast area: in Canada, from Quebec to Alberta. In the USA the majority of Cree live in the Rocky Boys reservation in Montana.

creed a system of belief; in the Christian church the verbal confessions of faith expressing the accepted doctrines of the church. The different forms are the *Apostles' Creed*, the *Nicene Creed*, and the *Athanasian Creed*. The only creed recognized by the Eastern Orthodox Church is the Nicene.

Creed Frederick George 1871–1957. Canadian inventor, who developed the teleprinter. He perfected the Creed telegraphy system (teleprinter), first used in Fleet Street in 1912 and now,

usually known as Telex, in offices throughout the world.

creep in civil and mechanical engineering, the property of a solid – typically a metal – under continuous stress that causes it to deform below its yield point (the point at which any elastic solid normally stretches without any increase in load or stress). Lead, tin, and zinc, for example, exhibit creep at ordinary temperatures, seen in the movement of the lead sheeting on the roofs of old buildings.

cremation disposal of the dead by burning. The custom was universal among ancient Indo-European peoples, for example, the Greeks, Romans, and Teutons, but was discontinued among Christians until the late 19th century on account of their belief in the bodily resurrection of the dead. The first crematorium in the UK was opened in 1885 in Woking, Surrey.

crème de la crème (French 'the cream of the cream') the elite, the very best.

Creole in the West Indies and Spanish America, originally someone of European descent born in the New World; but also someone of mixed European and African descent. In Louisiana and other states on the Gulf of Mexico, it applies either to someone of French or Spanish descent or (popularly) to someone of mixed European and African descent.

Creole languages term for ◊pidgin languages which have ceased to be simply trade jargons in ports and markets and have become the mother tongues of particular communities. Having begun with the characteristics of pidgin languages, many creoles have developed into distinct languages with incipient literatures of their own, for example, Jamaican Creole, Haitian Creole, Krio in Sierra Leone, and Tok Pisin in Papua-New Guinea.

creosote general name for several of the fractions of coal tar; they are used as wood preservatives. Medicinal creosote is derived from wood tar.

crescent the curved shape of the Moon when it appears less than half illuminated. It also refers to any object or symbol resembling the crescent moon. Often associated with Islam, it was first used by the Turks on their standards after the capture of Constantinople 1453, and appears on the flags of many Muslim countries. The *Red Crescent* is the Muslim equivalent of the Red Cross.

cress several plants, mostly belonging to the Cruciferae family, and characterized by a pungent taste. The common garden cress *Lepidium sativum* is cultivated in Europe, N Africa, and parts of Asia; the young plants are grown along with white mustard to be eaten while in the seed leaf stage as 'mustard and cress'.

Cresson Edith 1934– . French politician and founder member of the Socialist Party, prime minister 1991–92. Her government was troubled by a struggling economy, a series of strikes, and unrest in many of the country's poor suburban areas, which eventually forced her resignation.

Cretaceous period of geological time 144–65 million years ago. It is the last period of the Mesozoic era, during which angiosperm (seed-bearing) plants evolved and dinosaurs and other reptiles reached a peak before almost complete extinction at the end of the period.

Crete (Greek *Kríti*) the largest Greek island, in the E Mediterranean Sea, 100 km/62 mi SE of Greece.
area 8,378 sq km/3,234 sq mi
capital Khaniá (Canea)
towns largest town Iráklion
products citrus fruit, olives, wine

Croatia
Republic of

area 56,538 sq km/21,824 sq mi
capital Zagreb
towns chief port: Rijeka (Fiume); other ports: Zadar, Sibenik, Split, Dubrovnik
physical Adriatic coastline with large islands; very mountainous, with part of the Karst region and the Julian and Styrian Alps; some marshland
head of state Franjo Tudjman from 1990
head of government Hrvoje Sarinic from 1992
political system emergent democracy

products cereals, potatoes, tobacco, fruit, livestock, metal goods, textiles
currency Croatian dinar
population (1990) 4,760,000 including 75% Croats, 12% Serbs, and 1% Slovenes
language Croatian variant of Serbo-Croatian
religion Roman Catholic (Croats); Orthodox Christian (Serbs)
GNP $7.9 bn (1990); $1,660 per head
chronology
1918 Became part of the kingdom which united the Serbs, Croats, and Slovenes.
1929 The kingdom of Croatia, Serbia, and Slovenia became Yugoslavia. Croatia continued its campaign for autonomy.
1941 Became a Nazi puppet state following German invasion.
1945 Became constituent republic of Yugoslavia.
1970s Separatist demands resurfaced. Crackdown against anti-Serb separatist agitators.
1989 Formation of opposition parties permitted.
1990 Communists defeated by Tudjman-led Croatian Democratic Union (HDZ) in first free election since 1938. New constitution adopted.
1991 Croatia declared independence and later formally seceded from Yugoslavia. Military conflict with Serbia resulted in civil war.
1992 United Nations peace accord reached in Sarajevo. UN peacekeeping forces drafted into Croatia. Tudjman directly elected president; HDZ won assembly elections.
1993 Croatian forces launched offensive to retake parts of Serb-held Krajina, violating the 1992 UN peace accord.

population (1991) 536,900
language Cretan dialect of Greek
history it has the remains of the ◊Minoan civilization 3000–1400 BC, (see ◊Knossos), and then came successively under Roman, Byzantine, Venetian, and Turkish rule. The island was annexed by Greece in 1913.
crib death North American term for ◊cot death.
Crick Francis 1916– . British molecular biologist. From 1949 he researched into DNA's molecular structure, and the means whereby characteristics are transmitted from one generation to another. For this work he was awarded a Nobel prize (with Maurice Wilkins 1916– and James D Watson).
cricket the national summer sport in England. The game is played between two sides of 11 players each on a pitch 20 m/22 yds long with a wicket at each end. The object of the game is to score more runs than the opponents. A run is normally scored by the batsman after striking the ball and exchanging ends with his partner, or by hitting the ball to the boundary line for an automatic four or six runs.
cricket in zoology, a type of insect belonging to the order Orthoptera and related to grasshoppers. Crickets are somewhat flattened and have long antennae. The males make a chirping noise by rubbing together special areas on the wings. The females have a long needle-like egglaying organ (ovipositor). There are 900 species known worldwide.
Crimea northern peninsula on the Black Sea, an autonomous republic of ◊Ukraine
area 27,000 sq km/10,400 sq mi
capital Simferopol
towns Sevastopol, Yalta
products iron, oil
population 2.5 million (70% Russian, despite return of 150,000 Tatars since 1989)

recent history Under Turkish rule 1475–1774, a subsequent brief independence was ended by Russian annexation in 1783. It was the republic of Taurida 1917–20, and the Crimean Autonomous Soviet Republic from 1920 until occupied by Germany Jul 1942–May 1944. It was then reduced to a region, its Tatar people being deported to Uzbekistan for collaboration.
Crimean War war 1853–56 between Russia and the allied powers of England, France, Turkey, and Sardinia. The war arose from British and French mistrust of Russia's ambitions in the Balkans. It began with an allied Anglo-French expedition to the Crimea to attack the Russian Black Sea city of Sevastopol. The battles of the River Alma, Balaclava (including the charge of the Light Brigade), and Inkerman in 1854 led to a siege which, due to military mismanagement, lasted for a year until Sept 1855. The war was ended by the Treaty of Paris in 1856, but the scandal surrounding French and British losses through disease led to the organization of proper military nursing services by Florence Nightingale.
Criminal Injuries Compensation Board UK board established 1964 to administer financial compensation by the state for victims of crimes of violence. Victims can claim compensation for their injuries, but not for damage to property.
Criminal Investigation Department (New Scotland Yard) detective branch of the London Metropolitan Police, established 1878, and comprising a force of about 4,000 men and women, recruited entirely from the uniformed police and controlled by an Assistant Commissioner. Such branches are now also found in the regional police forces.
criminal law the body of law which defines the

cricket Imran Khan playing in the second one-day international for Pakistan against England, at Nottingham, 1988.

public wrongs (crimes) which are punishable by the state and establishes methods of prosecution and punishment. It is distinct from civil law which deals with legal relationships between individuals (including organizations) such as contract law.

Cripps (Richard) Stafford 1889–1952. British Labour politician. A founder of the Socialist League, he was expelled from the Labour party 1939–45 for supporting a 'Popular Front' against Chamberlain's appeasement policy. He was ambassador to Moscow 1940–42, minister of aircraft production 1942–45, and chancellor of the Exchequer 1947–50.

critical angle in optics, for a ray of light passing from a denser to a less dense medium (such as from glass to air), the smallest angle of incidence at which the emergent ray grazes the surface of the denser medium – at an angle of refraction of 90°. The ray does not pass out into the less dense medium (when

critical angle

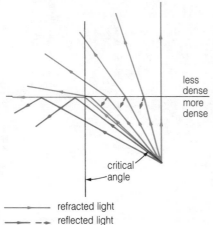

less dense
more dense

critical angle

— refracted light
— – – reflected light

the angle of incidence has to be less than the critical angle), nor is it internally reflected back into the denser medium (when the angle of incidence has to be greater than the critical angle).

critical mass in nuclear physics, the minimum mass of fissile material that can undergo a continuous ◊chain reaction. Below this mass, too many ◊neutrons escape from the surface for a chain reaction to carry on; above the critical mass, the reaction may accelerate into a nuclear explosion.

critical path analysis procedure used in the management of complex projects to minimize the amount of time taken. The analysis shows which projects can run in parallel with each other, and which have to be completed before other subprojects can follow on. Computer applications packages for critical path analysis are widely used to help reduce the time and effort involved in critical path analysis.

critical temperature temperature above which a particular gas cannot be converted into a liquid by pressure alone. It is also the temperature at which a magnetic material loses its magnetism (the Curie point).

Crivelli Carlo 1435/40–1495/1500. Italian painter in the early Renaissance style, active in Venice. He painted extremely detailed, decorated religious works, sometimes festooned with garlands of fruit.

Croatia (Serbo-Croat *Hrvatska*) country in central Europe, bounded N by Slovenia and Hungary, W by the Adriatic Sea, and E by Bosnia-Herzegovina and the Yugoslavian republic of Serbia.

Croce Benedetto 1866–1952. Italian philosopher and literary critic, an opponent of fascism.

crochet a technique similar to both knitting and lacemaking, in which one hooked needle is used to produce a loosely looped network of wool or cotton. Dating from the 19th century, crochet can be almost as fine and complex as lace.

Crockett Davy 1786–1836. US folk hero, a Democrat Congressman 1827–31 and 1833–35. A series of books, of which he may have been part-author, made him into a mythical hero of the frontier, but their Whig associations cost him his office. He died in the battle of the ◊Alamo during the war for Texan independence.

crocodile large aquatic carnivorous reptile, related to alligators and caimans, but distinguished from them by a more pointed snout, and a notch in the upper jaw into which the fourth tooth in the lower jaw fits. They can grow up to 6 m/20 ft, and have long powerful tails which propel them when swimming. They can live up to 100 years.

crocus genus of plants, family Iridaceae, native to N parts of the Old World, especially S Europe and Asia Minor. During the dry season of the year they remain underground in the form of a corm, and produce fresh shoots and flowers in spring or autumn. At the end of the season of growth fresh corms are produced.

Croesus died *c.* 546 BC. Last king of Lydia, famed for his wealth. His court included ◊Solon, who warned him that no man could be called happy until his life had ended happily. When Croesus was overthrown by Cyrus the Great in 546 BC and condemned to be burnt to death, he called out Solon's name. Cyrus, having learnt the reason, spared his life.

croft a small farm in the Highlands of Scotland, traditionally farming common land co-operatively;

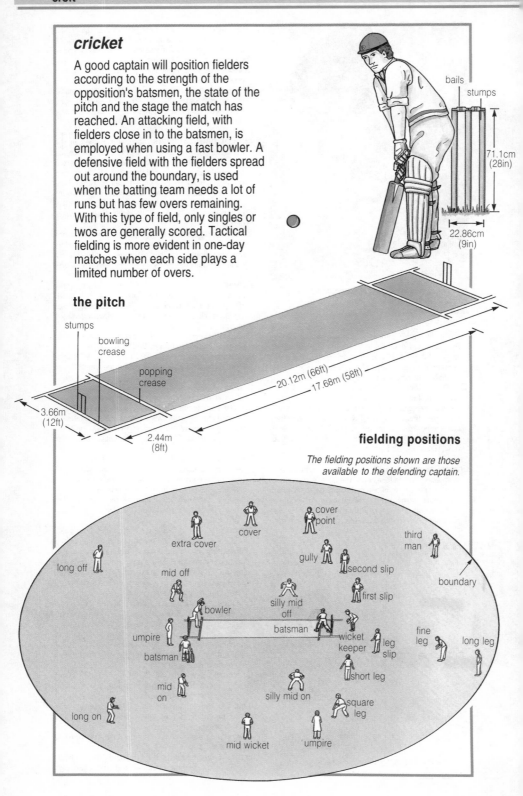

cricket

A good captain will position fielders according to the strength of the opposition's batsmen, the state of the pitch and the stage the match has reached. An attacking field, with fielders close in to the batsmen, is employed when using a fast bowler. A defensive field with the fielders spread out around the boundary, is used when the batting team needs a lot of runs but has few overs remaining. With this type of field, only singles or twos are generally scored. Tactical fielding is more evident in one-day matches when each side plays a limited number of overs.

bails
stumps

71.1cm
(28in)

22.86cm
(9in)

the pitch

stumps

bowling
crease

popping
crease

20.12m (66ft)
17.68m (58ft)

3.66m
(12ft)

2.44m
(8ft)

fielding positions

The fielding positions shown are those available to the defending captain.

cover
point

cover

extra cover

third
man

long off

gully

second slip

boundary

mid off

first slip

silly mid
off

bowler

umpire

batsman

wicket
keeper

fine
leg

long leg

batsman

leg
slip

mid
on

short leg

silly mid on

square
leg

long on

mid wicket

umpire

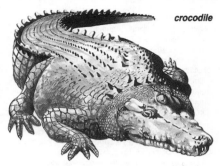
crocodile

the 1886 Crofters Act gave security of tenure to crofters. Today, although grazing land is still shared, arable land is typically enclosed.

Cro-magnon a type of prehistoric human, the first skeletons of whic were found in 1868 in the Cro-magnon cave near Les Eyzies, in the Dordogne region of France. They are thought to have superseded the Neanderthals, and lived between 40,000 and 35,000 years ago. Although biologically modern, they were larger in build than modern humans. Their culture produced flint and bone tools, jewellery, and cave paintings.

Crompton Richmal, pen name of British writer R C Lamburn 1890–1969. She is remembered for her stories about the mischievous schoolboy 'William'.

Crompton Samuel 1753–1827. British inventor at the time of the Industrial Revolution. He invented the 'spinning mule' 1779, combining the ideas of ◊Arkwright and ◊Hargreaves. Though widely adopted, his invention brought him little financial return.

Cromwell Oliver 1599–1658. English general and politician, Puritan leader of the Parliamentary side in the ◊Civil War. He raised cavalry forces (later called *Ironsides*) which aided the victories at Edgehill 1642 and ◊Marston Moor 1644, and organized the New Model Army, which he led (with Gen Fairfax) to victory at Naseby 1645. As **Lord Protector** (ruler) from 1653, he established religious toleration, and Britain's prestige in Europe on the basis of an alliance with France against Spain.

Cromwell Richard 1626–1712. son of Oliver Cromwell, he succeeded his father as Protector, but resigned in May 1659, living in exile after the Restoration until 1680, when he returned to England.

Cromwell Thomas, Earl of Essex *c.* 1485–1540. English politician. Originally in Lord Chancellor Wolsey's service, he became secretary to Henry VIII in 1534 and the real director of government policy. He had Henry proclaimed head of the church, suppressed the monasteries, ruthlessly crushed all opposition, and favoured Protestantism, which upheld the divine right of the pope. His mistake in arranging Henry's marriage to Anne of Cleves

crocus

(to cement an alliance with the German Protestant princes against France and the Holy Roman Empire) led to his being accused of treason and beheaded.

Crookes William 1832–1919. British scientist, whose many chemical and physical discoveries included the metal thallium 1861, the radiometer 1875, and Crooke's high vacuum tube used in X-ray techniques.

crop in birds, the thin-walled enlargement of the digestive tract between the oesophagus and stomach. It is an effective storage organ especially in seed-eating birds; a pigeon's crop can hold about 500 cereal grains. Digestion begins in the crop, by the moisturizing of food. A crop also occurs in insects and annelid worms.

crop a plant grown for human use. Over 80 crops are grown worldwide, providing people with the majority of their food, and supplying fibres, rubber, pharmaceuticals, dyes, and other materials. There are four main groups of crops:

food crops are grown specifically to feed people, and provide the bulk of people's food worldwide. The major types are cereals, roots, pulses, vegetables, fruits, oil crops, tree nuts, sugar, beverages, and spices. Cereals make the most important contribution to human nutrition.

forage crops are crops like grass, clover, and kale, which are grown to feed livestock. Forage crops cover a greater area of the world than food crops. Grass, which dominates this group, is the world's most abundant crop, though much of it is still in an unimproved state.

fibre crops produce vegetable fibres. Temperate areas produce flax and hemp, but the most important fibre crops are cotton, jute, and sisal, which are grown mostly in the tropics. Cotton dominates fibre crop production.

Cromwell *A portrait after Samuel Cooper (1656), National Portrait Gallery, London.*

miscellaneous crops include tobacco, rubber, ornamental flowers, and plants used in perfumery, pharmaceuticals, and dye. See also ◊catch crop.

crop circle circular area of flattened grain found in fields – especially in SE England – with increasing frequency ever since 1980. The cause is unknown. Most of the research into crop circles has been conducted by dedicated amateur investigators. Physicists who have studied the phenomenon have suggested that an electromagnetic whirlwind, or 'plasma vortex', can explain both the crop circles and some UFO sightings, but this does not account for the increasing geometric complexity of crop circles, nor for the fact that until 1990 they were unknown outside the UK.

crop rotation in agriculture, the system of regularly changing the crop grown on a piece of ground, and growing the different crops in a particular order to fully utilize the nutrients in the soil and to prevent the build-up of insect and fungal pests. In the 18th century, a four-year rotation was widely adopted with autumn-sown cereal, followed by a root crop, then spring cereal, and ending with a leguminous crop. Since then, more elaborate rotations have been devised with two, three, or four successive cereal crops, and with the root break replaced by a cash crop such as sugar beet or potatoes, or by a legume such as peas or beans.

croquet outdoor game played with mallets and balls on a level hooped lawn measuring 27 m/90 ft by 18 m/60 ft. It first became popular in France in the 16th–17th centuries.

Crosby 'Bing' (Harry Lillis) 1904–1977. US singer and actor, who began as a danceband singer in 1925 and gained success with his distinctive style of crooning in such songs as 'Pennies from Heaven', and 'White Christmas' – both featured in films with the same titles. He specialised in light comedy roles.

crossbill type of ◊finch *Loxia curvirostra* in which the hooked tips of the upper and lower beak cross one another, an adaptation for extracting the seeds from conifer cones. It is found in northern parts of Europe, Asia, and N America.

crossing over in biology, a process that occurs during ◊meiosis. While the ◊chromosomes are lying alongside each other in pairs, each partner may break, and then link up with the segment from the other partner, so exchanging corresponding sections. It is a form of genetic ◊recombination, which increases variation and thus provides the raw material of evolution.

croup inflammation (usually viral) of a child's larynx and trachea, with croaking breathing and a cough.

crow any of 35 species of the genus *Corvus* found worldwide. They are usually 45 cm/1.5 ft long, black, with a strong bill, feathered at the base, and omnivorous with a bias towards animal food. They are considered to be very intelligent.

crowding out in economics, a situation in which an increase in government expenditure, by generating price rises and thus a reduction in the real money supply, results in a fall in private consumption and/ or investment. Crowding out has been used in recent years as a justification of privatization of state-owned services and industries.

Crowley John 1942– . US writer of science fiction and fantasy, notably *Little, Big* 1980 and *Aegypt* 1987, which contains esoteric knowledge and theoretical puzzles.

crown an official head-dress worn by a king or queen. The modern crown originated with the diadem, an embroidered fillet worn by eastern rulers, for which a golden band was later substi-

tuted. A laurel crown was granted by the Greeks to a victor in the games, and by the Romans to a triumphant general. Crowns came into use among the Byzantine emperors and the European kings after the fall of the Western Empire.

crown colony any British colony that is under the direct legislative control of the crown and does not possess its own system of representative government. Crown colonies are administered either by a crown-appointed governor or by elected or nominated legislative and executive councils with an official majority. Usually the crown retains rights of veto and of direct legislation by orders in council.

Crown Courts in England and Wales, a court where more serious criminal cases are heard after referral from ◊magistrates' courts after ◊committal proceedings. Appeals against conviction or sentence at magistrates' courts may be heard in Crown Courts. Appeal from a Crown Court is to the Court of Appeal.

Crown Estate title (from 1956) of land in UK formerly owned by the monarch but handed to Parliament (by George III in 1760) in exchange for an annual payment (called the civil list). It owns valuable sites in central London, and 268,400 acres in England and Scotland.

crown jewels popular name for ◊regalia.

Crown Proceedings Act an Act of Parliament which provided that the Crown (as represented by, for example, government departments) could from 1948 be sued like a private individual.

crucifixion death by fastening to a cross, a form of capital punishment used by the ancient Romans, Persians, and Carthaginians, and abolished by the Roman emperor Constantine. The Crucifixion refers to the death of Jesus in this manner.

Cruelty, Theatre of a theory advanced by Antonin ◊Artaud in his book *Le Théâtre et son double* 1938 and adopted by a number of writers and directors including Peter Brook. It aims to shock the audience into an awareness of primitive human nature, through the release of feelings that are conventionally repressed.

Crufts Charles 1852–1938. British dog expert. He organized his first dog show in 1886; annual shows bearing his name have since been held in the UK.

cruise missile a pilotless aircraft derived from the German V-1 of World War II. Initial trials in the 1950s demonstrated the limitations of cruise missiles which included high fuel consumption and relatively slow speeds (when compared to Intercontinental Ballistic Missiles ICBMs) as well as inaccuracy and a small warhead. Improvements to guidance systems by the use of Terrain Contour Matching (TERCOM) ensured pin-point accuracy on low-level flights after launch from a mobile ground launcher (Ground Launched Cruise Missile – GLCM), from an aircraft (Air Launched Cruise Missile – ALCM) or from a submarine or ship (Sea Launched Cruise Missile – SLCM).

Crusade a war against non-Christians and heretics, sanctioned by the pope; in particular, a series of wars 1096–1291 undertaken by European rulers to recover Palestine from the Muslims, motivated by religious zeal and the desire for more land, and by the trading ambitions of the major Italian cities.

crust the outermost part of the structure of the ◊Earth, consisting of two distinct parts, the oceanic crust and the continental crust. The *oceanic* crust averages about 10 km/6.2 mi thick and is fairly even in composition. The *continental* crust is complex. Because of the movements of ◊plate tectonics, the ocean crust is not older than about 200 million years. Parts of the continental crust are more than ten times that age.

crystal

sodium chloride

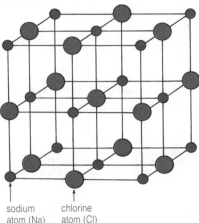

sodium   chlorine
atom (Na)   atom (Cl)

crustacean one of the class of arthropods that includes crabs, lobsters, shrimps, woodlice, and barnacles. The external skeleton is made of protein and chitin hardened with lime. Each segment bears a pair of appendages which may be modified as antennae, for feeding, swimming, walking or grasping.

Crux constellation of the southern hemisphere, popularly known as the Southern Cross, the smallest of the 88 constellations. Its brightest star, Alpha Crucis, is a ◊double star. Near Beta Crucis lies a glittering star cluster known as the Jewel Box. The constellation also contains the Coalsack, a dark cloud of dust silhouetted against the bright starry background of the Milky Way.

cryolite a rare crystalline mineral, Na_3AlF_6, found in Greenland, used in refining aluminium.

cryptogam an obsolete name applied to the lower plants. It included the algae, liverworts, mosses and ferns (plus the fungi and bacteria in very early schemes of classification).

cryptography science of codes, for example, that produced by the Enigma coding machine used by the Germans in World War II (as in ◊Ultra), and those used in commerce by banks encoding electronic fund transfer messages, business firms sending computer-conveyed memos between headquarters, and in the growing field of electronic mail. No method of encrypting is completely unbreakable, but decoding can be made extremely complex.

crystal a substance with an orderly three-dimensional arrangement of its atoms or molecules, thereby creating an external surface of clearly defined smooth faces having characteristic angles between them. Examples are common salt and quartz.

crystallography the scientific study of ◊crystals. In 1912, it was found that the shape and size of the unit cell of a crystal can be discovered by X-rays, thus opening up an entirely new way of 'seeing' atoms. This means of determining the atomic patterns in a crystal is known as X-ray diffraction. By this method it has been found that many substances have unit cells or boxes which are exact cubes, for example ordinary table salt (sodium chloride). It has been shown that even purified biomolecules, such as proteins and DNA, can form crystals, and

such compounds may now be studied by the same method.

Crystal Palace glass and iron building designed by Joseph Paxton, housing the Great Exhibition of 1851 in Hyde Park, London; later rebuilt in modified form at Sydenham Hill in 1854 (burnt down 1936).

CSE *Certificate of Secondary Education* the examinations taken by the majority of secondary school pupils in the UK, who were not regarded as academically capable of GCE ◊O Level, until the introduction of the common secondary examination system, ◊GCSE, in 1988.

Ctesiphon ruined royal city of the Parthians, and later capital of the Sassanian Empire, 19 km/12 mi SE of Baghdad, Iraq.

cu abbreviation for *cubic* (measure).

Cuba island in the Caribbean, the largest of the West Indies, off the south coast of Florida.

Cuban missile crisis a crisis in international relations in 1962 when Soviet rockets were installed in Cuba and US President Kennedy compelled Khrushchev, by an ultimatum, to remove them. The drive by the USSR to match the USA in nuclear weaponry dates from this event.

cube in geometry, a solid figure whose faces are all squares. It has six equal-area faces and 12 equal-length edges. If the length of one edge is l, the volume of the cube $V = l^3$ and its surface area $A = 6l^2$.

cubic measure a measure of volume, indicated either by the prefix cubic followed by a linear measure, as in cubic foot, or the suffix cubed, as in metre-cubed.

Cubism revolutionary movement in modern painting, pioneering abstract art. Its founders Braque and Picasso were admirers of Cézanne and were inspired by his attempt to create a structure on the surface of the canvas. The Cubists began to 'abstract' images from nature, gradually releasing themselves from the imitation of reality. Cubist painters include Juan Gris, Fernand Léger, and Robert Delaunay.

Cuchulain in Celtic mythology, a legendary hero, the chief figure in an important cycle of Irish legends. He is associated with his uncle Conchobar, king of Ulster; his exploits are described in the epic saga *Cow-reiving of Cuailgne*.

cuckoo any of about 200 species of bird of the family Cuculidae, whose name derives from its characteristic call. Somewhat hawk-like, it is about 33 cm/1.1 ft long, bluish-grey and barred beneath (females sometimes reddish), and has a long rounded tail. It is a 'brood parasite', laying its eggs singly, at intervals of about 48 hours, in the nests of small insectivorous birds. As soon as the young cuckoo hatches, it ejects all other young birds or eggs from the nest, and is tended by 'foster-parents' until fledging. Cuckoos feed on insects, particularly hairy caterpillars which are distasteful to most birds.

cuckoo flower or *Lady's Smock* perennial plant *Cardamine pratensis*, family Cruciferae. Native to Britain, it is common in moist meadows and marshy woods. It bears pale lilac flowers, which later turn white from April to June.

cuckoo-pint *wake-robin* or *lords-and-ladies* perennial plant *Arum maculatum* of the Araceae family. The large arrow-shaped leaves appear in early spring, and the flower-bearing stalks are enveloped by a bract, or spathe. In late summer the bright red, berry-like fruits, which are poisonous, make their appearance.

Cuba
Republic of
(*República de Cuba*)

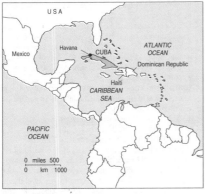

area 110,860 sq km/42,820 sq mi
capital Havana
physical comprises Cuba, the largest and westernmost of the West Indian islands, and smaller islands including Isle of Youth; low hills; Sierra Maestra mountains in E
head of state and government Fidel Castro Ruz from 1959
political system communist republic
exports sugar, tobacco, coffee, nickel, fish
currency Cuban peso
population (1990 est) 10,582,000; 37% are white of Spanish descent; 51% mulatto; 11% of African origin; annual growth rate 0.6%
life expectancy men 72, women 75
language Spanish
religion Roman Catholic 85%
literacy 96% male/95% female (1979)
disposable national income $15.8 bn (1983); $1,590 per head
chronology
1901 Cuba achieved independence.
1933 Fulgencia Batista seized power.
1944 Batista retired.

1952 Batista seized power again to begin an oppressive regime.
1953 Fidel Castro led an unsuccessful coup against Batista.
1956 Castro led a second unsuccessful coup.
1959 Batista overthrown by Castro. Constitution of 1940 replaced by a 'Fundamental Law', making Castro prime minister, his brother Raul Castro his deputy, and Che Guevara his number three.
1960 All US businesses in Cuba appropriated without compensation. USA broke off diplomatic relations.
1961 USA sponsored an unsuccessful invasion, the Bay of Pigs episode. Castro announced that Cuba had become a communist state, with a Marxist-Leninist programme of economic development.
1962 Cuba expelled from the Organization of American States (OAS). Soviet nuclear missiles removed from Cuba at US insistence.
1965 Cuba's sole political party renamed Cuban Communist Party (PCC). With Soviet help, Cuba began to make considerable economic and social progress.
1972 Cuba became a full member of the Moscow-based Council for Mutual Economic Assistance (CMEA).
1976 New socialist constitution approved and Castro elected president.
1976–81 Castro became involved in extensive international commitments, assisting Third World countries, particularly in Africa.
1982 Cuba joined other Latin American countries in giving moral support to Argentina in its dispute with Britain.
1984 Castro tried to improve US-Cuban relations by discussing the exchange of US prisoners in Cuba with Cuban 'undesirables' in the USA.
1988 Peace accord with South Africa signed, agreeing to withdrawal of Cuban troops from Angola.
1991 Soviet troops withdrawn.
1992 Castro affirmed continuing support of communism.

cucumber plant *Cucumis sativus*, family Cucurbitaceae, producing long, green-skinned fruit with crisp, translucent, edible flesh. Small cucumbers, especially the fruit of *Cucumis anguria*, are pickled as gherkins.

Culdees an ancient order of Christian monks which existed in Ireland and Scotland from before the 9th century to about the 12th century AD, when the Celtic Church, to which they belonged, was forced to conform to Roman usages. Some survived until the 14th century, while at Armagh in Northern Ireland they remained until the dissolution of the monasteries in 1541.

Culloden, Battle of defeat in 1746 of the Jacobite rebel army of the British Prince ◊Charles Edward Stuart by the Duke of ◊Cumberland on a stretch of moorland in Inverness-shire, Scotland.

cultivar a variety of a plant developed by horticultural or agricultural techniques. The term is derived from 'cultivated variety'.

Cultural Revolution a movement begun by Chinese communist party chairman Mao Zedong in 1966 and directed against bureaucracy and university intellectuals. Intended to 'purify' Chinese

communism, it was also an attempt by Mao to restore his political and ideological pre-eminence inside China.

culture in sociology, the way of life of a particular society or group of people, including patterns of thought, beliefs, behaviour, customs, traditions, rituals, dress, and language, as well as art, music, and literature.

culture in biology, the growing of living cells and tissues in laboratory conditions.

Cumae ancient city in Italy, on the coast 16 km/10mi W of Naples. It was famous in the ancient world as the seat of the oracle of the Cumaean Sibyl.

Cuman member of the powerful Turki federation of the Middle Ages, which dominated the steppes in the 11th and 12th centuries and built an empire reaching from the Volga to the Danube.

Cumberland former county of NW England, merged in 1974 with ◊Cumbria.

Cumberland Ernest Augustus, Duke of Cumberland 1771–1851. King of Hanover from 1837, the fifth son of George III of Britain. He was intensely unpopular, being a high Tory and an opponent of all reforms. On the death of William IV he became king of Hanover, where his attempts to suppress the constitution met with open resistance which had to be put down by force.

Cumberland William Augustus, Duke of Cumberland 1721–1765. British general, who ended the Jacobite rising in Scotland with the Battle of Culloden 1746; his brutal repression of the Highlanders earned him the nickname of 'Butcher'. Third son of George II, he was created Duke of Cumberland in 1726. He fought in the War of the Austrian Succession at ◊Dettingen in 1743 and ◊Fontenoy in 1745. In the Seven Years' War he surrendered with his army at Kloster-Zeven 1757.

Cumbria county in NW England
area 6,810 sq km/2,629 sq mi
towns administrative headquarters Carlisle, Barrow, Kendal, Whitehaven, Workington, Penrith
physical Lake District National Park, including Scafell Pike 978 m/3,210 ft, highest mountain in England; Helvellyn 950 m/3,118 ft; Lake Windermere, the largest lake in England, 17 km/10.5 mi long, 1.6 km/1 mi wide
products the traditional coal, iron, and steel of the coast towns has been replaced by newer industries including chemicals, plastics, and electronics; in the N and E there is dairying, and West Cumberland Farmers is the country's largest agricultural co-operative
population (1991) 486,900

cumin seed-like fruit of the plant *Cuminum cyminum*, with a bitter flavour. It is used as a spice in cooking.

Cummings E(dward) E(stlin) 1894–1962. US poet. His poems initially gained notoriety for their idiosyncratic punctuation and typography (he always wrote his name 'e. e. cummings', for example), but their lyric power has gradually been recognized.

cuneiform an ancient system of writing formed of combinations of wedge-shaped strokes, usually impressed on clay. It was probably invented by the Sumerians, and was in use in Mesopotamia as early as the middle of the 4th millennium BC. The decipherment of the cuneiform scripts was pioneered by the German G F Grotefend (1802) and the British orientalist H C Rawlinson (1846)

Cunha Euclydes da 1866–1909. Brazilian writer. His novel *Os Sertoes/Rebellion in the Backlands* 1902 describes the Brazilian *sertao* (backlands), and how a small group of rebels resisted government troops.

Cupid in Roman mythology, the god of love, identified with the Greek god ◊Eros.

cuprite Cu₂O a red oxide of copper in crystalline form.

cupro-nickel a copper alloy (75% copper and 25% nickel).

Curaçao island in the West Indies, one of the ◊Netherlands Antilles; area 444 sq km/171 sq mi; population (1988) 148,500. The principal industry, dating from 1918, is the refining of Venezuelan petroleum. Curaçao was colonized by Spain 1527, annexed by the Dutch West India Company 1634, and gave its name from 1924 to the group of islands renamed Netherlands Antilles in 1948. Its capital is the port of Willemstad.

curare poison, extracted from the bark of the South American tree *Strychnus toxifera*. Used on arrowheads, it was used to paralyse prey by blocking nerve stimulation of the muscles. Derivatives are used medically as muscle relaxants during surgery and when a patient is receiving mechanically assisted ventilation.

curate in the Christian church, literally, a priest who has the cure of souls in a parish, and so used in Europe. In England it is generally applied to an unbeneficed cleric who acts as assistant to a parish priest, more exactly as 'assistant curate'.

Curia Romana the judicial and administrative bodies through which the pope carries on the government of the Roman Catholic Church.

Curie Marie (born Sklodovska) 1867–1934. Polish scientist, famous for her investigations into radioactivity, and for discovering radium with her husband Pierre (1859–1906).

curium a metallic element, atomic number 96, relative atomic mass 247. It is radioactive and does not occur naturally, but is produced from americium.

curlew wading bird of the genus Numenius 55 cm/1.8 ft tall, with mottled brown plumage, long legs and a long thin downcurved bill. Several species live in N Europe, Asia, and N America. The name derives from its haunting flute-like call.

curling game played on ice with stones; sometimes described as 'bowls on ice'. One of the national games of Scotland, where it probably originated, it has spread to many countries. It can also be played on artificial (cement or tarmacadam) ponds.

currant berry of a small seedless variety of grape, grown on a large scale in Greece and California and used dried in cake-making. Because of the similarity of the fruit, the same name is given to several species of shrubs in the genus *Ribes*, family Grossulariaceae.

current the flow of a body of water or air moving in a definite direction. Oceanic currents may be:
drift currents, broad and slow-moving;
stream currents, narrow and swift-moving;
upwelling currents, which bring cold, nutrient-rich water from the ocean bottom.

current account in economics, that part of the balance of payments concerned with current transactions, as opposed to capital movements. It includes trade (visibles) and service transactions such as investment, insurance, shipping, and tourism (invisibles). The state of the current account is regarded as a barometer of overall economic health.

current prices a series of prices which express values pertaining to a given time but which do not take account of the changes in purchasing power, unlike ◊constant prices.

curriculum vitae (CV) (Latin 'the course of life') an account of one's education and previous employment, attached to a job application.

Curtin John 1885–1945. Australian Labor politician, prime minister from 1941. Born in Victoria. He rose to prominence as a trade-union leader and journalist, and was elected leader of the Labor Party in 1935. As prime minister, he organized the mobilization

Curie Marie Curie in her Paris laboratory.

of Australia's resources to meet the danger of Japanese invasion during World War II.

curve in geometry, the ◊locus of a point moving according to specified conditions. The circle is the locus of all points equidistant from a given point (the centre). Other common geometrical curves are the ◊ellipse, ◊parabola, and ◊hyperbola, which are also produced when a cone is cut by a plane at different angles. Many curves have been invented for the solution of special problems in geometry and mechanics, for example, the cissoid (the inverse of a parabola) and the ◊cycloid.

Curzon George Nathaniel, 1st Marquess Curzon of Kedleston 1859–1925. British Conservative politician. Viceroy of India from 1899, he resigned in 1905 following a controversy with Kitchener, and was foreign secretary 1919–22.

Curzon Line Polish-Russian frontier proposed after World War I by the territorial commission of the Versailles conference in 1919, based on the eastward limit of areas with a predominantly Polish population. It acquired its name after Lord ◊Curzon suggested in 1920 that the Poles, who had invaded Russia, should retire to this line pending a Russo-Polish peace conference. The frontier established in 1945 in general follows the Curzon Line.

Cushing Harvey Williams 1869–1939. US neurologist who pioneered modern neurosurgery. He developed a range of techniques for the surgical treatment of brain tumours, and also studied the link between the ◊pituitary gland and conditions such as dwarfism.

custard apple several tropical fruits produced by trees and shrubs of the genus *Annona*, family Annonaceae. *Annona reticulata*, **the bullock's heart**, bears a large dark-brown fruit, containing a sweet reddish-yellow pulp; it is a native of the West Indies.

Custer George A(rmstrong) 1839–1876. US Civil War general. He subsequently campaigned against the Sioux from 1874, and was killed with a detachment of his troops by the forces of Sioux chief Sitting Bull in the Battle of Little Big Horn, Montana: *Custer's last stand*, 25 Jun 1876.

custodianship in the UK, legal status granted to an adult for the care of children not one's own by birth, separate from adoption. In 1984 in the UK effect was given to the provision under the Children's Act of 1975 for 'custodianship' by step-parents, or foster-parents. It transfers many parental rights needed by a permanent guardian without affecting the legal status of the real parents.

custody of children in the UK, the legal control of a minor by an adult. Parents usually have joint custody of their children, but this may be altered by a court order, which may be made in various different circumstances. In all cases, the court gives the welfare of the child paramount consideration.

Customs and Excise custom duties are taxes levied on certain imports, for example, tobacco, wine and spirits, perfumery and jewellery; excise duties are levied on certain goods produced (such as beer) and include VAT; or on licences to carry on certain trades (such as sale of wines and spirits) or other activities (theatrical entertainments, betting, and so on) within a country.

Cuthbert, St died 687. Christian saint. He travelled widely as a missionary and because of his alleged miracles was known as the 'wonderworker of Britain'. He became prior of Lindisfarne (◊Holy Island), but retired in 676 to Farne Island. In 684 he became bishop of Hexham and later of Lindisfarne. Feast day 20 Mar.

cuticle in zoology, the horny noncellular surface layer of many invertebrates such as insects; in botany, the waxy surface layer on those parts of plants that are exposed to the air, continuous except for the ◊stomata and ◊lenticels. All these different types are secreted by the cells of the ◊epidermis. A cuticle reduces water loss and, in arthropods, acts as an ◊exoskeleton.

cuttle-fish small squid with an internal calcareous shell (cuttlebone). The **common cuttle** *Sepia officinalis* of the Atlantic and Mediterranean, is up to 30 cm/1 ft long, swims actively by means of the fins into which the sides of its oval, flattened body are expanded, and also jerks itself backwards by shooting a jet of water from its 'siphon'. It is capable of rapid changes of colour and pattern. The large head has conspicuous eyes, and the ten arms are provided with suckers. Two arms are very much elongated, and with them the cuttle seizes its prey. It has an 'ink-sac' from which a dark fluid can be discharged into the water, distracting predators from the cuttle itself.

Cutty Sark British sailing ship, one of the tea clippers that used to compete in the 19th century to bring their cargoes fastest from China to Britain.

Cuvier Georges, Baron Cuvier 1769–1832. French comparative anatomist. In 1799 he proved extinction (the phenomenon that some species have ceased to exist) by reconstructing extinct giant animals which he believed were destroyed in a series of giant deluges.

Cuyp Aelbert 1620–1691. Dutch painter of countryside scenes, seascapes, and portraits. His idyllically peaceful landscapesba thed in golden light include *A Horseman with Cowherds in a Landscape* (National Gallery, London).

Cuzco city in S Peru, capital of Cuzco department, in the Andes, over 3,350 m/11,000 ft above sea level some 560 km/350 mi SE of Lima; population (1981) 181,500. Ancient capital of the ◊Inca empire.

CV abbreviation for *curriculum vitae*.

cwt abbreviation for *hundredweight*, a unit of weight equal to 50.802 kg/112 lb.

cyanide in chemistry, a salt of hydrocyanic acid (or hydrogen cyanide, HCN) produced when this

Cuzco The Inca capital has many Spanish buildings alongside the older Inca structures.

cycling The 1988 Tour de France.

is neutralized by alkalis, for example potassium cyanide, KCN. The principal cyanides are potassium, sodium, calcium, mercuric, gold, and cupric. Certain cyanides are infamous as poisons.

cyanosis bluish discoloration of the skin, especially around the mouth, due to diminished uptake of oxygen. It is most often seen in disease of the heart or lungs.

Cybele in Phrygian mythology, an earth goddess, identified by the Greeks with ◊Rhea and honoured in Rome.

cybernetics science concerned with how systems organize, regulate, and reproduce themselves, and also how they evolve and learn. In the laboratory, inanimate objects are created that behave like living systems. Uses range from the creation of electronic artificial limbs to the running of the fully-automated factory where decision-making machines operate at up to managerial level.

cycad plant of the order Cycadales belonging to the Gymnosperms. Some have a superficial resemblance to palms, others to ferns. There are ten genera and about 80–100 species, native to tropical and sub-tropical countries. The stems of many species yield an edible starchy substance resembling sago.

cyclamate derivative of cyclohexysulphamic acid, formerly used as an artificial sweetener. Its use in foods was banned in UK and USA from 1970, when studies showed that massive doses caused cancer in rats.

cyclamen genus of perennial plants, family Primulaceae, with heart-shaped leaves and petals which are twisted at the base and bent back. The flowers are usually white or pink, and several species are cultivated.

cyclic compounds organic chemicals that have rings of atoms in their molecules.

cycling riding a bicycle for sport, pleasure, or transport. The first bicycle was seen in Paris in 1791 and was a form of hobby-horse. The first treadle-propelled cycle was designed by Kirkaptrick Macmillan (Scotland) in 1839. By the end of the 19th century wire wheels, metal frames (replacing wood) and pneumatic tyres had been added. One of the most popular bicycles of that time was the

front-wheel driven 'Penny Farthing' with a large front wheel.

cycloid in geometry, a curve resembling a series of arches traced out by a point on the circumference of a circle that rolls along a straight line. Its applications include the study of the motion of wheeled vehicles along roads and tracks.

cyclone an area of low atmospheric ◊pressure. Cyclones are formed by the mixture of cold, dry polar air with warm, moist equatorial air. These masses of air meet in temperate latitudes; the warm air rises over the cold, resulting in rain.

Cyclops in Greek mythology, one of a legendary nation of giants who lived in Sicily, had a single eye, and lived as shepherds; Odysseus encountered them in Homer's *Odyssey*.

cyclosporin ◊immunosuppressive, derived from fungi. In use by 1978, it revolutionized transplant surgery by reducing the incidence and severity of rejection of donor organs.

cyclotron type of particle ◊accelerator.

Cygnus large prominent constellation of the northern hemisphere, representing a swan. Its brightest star is first-magnitude Deneb.

cylinder in geometry, commonly interpreted as a surface generated by a set of lines which are parallel to a fixed line and passing through a plane curve not in the plane of the fixed line; a tubular solid figure with a circular base, ordinarily understood to be a right cyclinder, that is, having its curved surface at right angles to the base. The volume of a cylinder is given by: $V = \pi r^2 h$ where V is the volume, r is the radius, and h is the height. Its total surface area A has the formula: $A = 2\pi r\,(h + r)$ where $2\pi rh$ is the curved surface area, and $2\pi r^2$ is the area of both circular ends.

cymbal musical instrument of percussion, consisting of a round metal plate with a drumstick, struck or clashed against another cymbal.

Cymbeline another name for *Cunobelin*, king of the Catuvellauni (5–40 AD), who fought unsuccessfully against the Roman invasion of Britain. His capital was at Colchester.

Cymru Celtic name for ◊Wales.

Cynewulf lived early 8th century. Anglo-Saxon poet. He is thought to have been a Northumbrian monk, and is the undoubted author of 'Juliana'

cylinder

$$V = \pi r^2 h$$
$$A = 2\pi rh + 2\pi r^2$$

cycloid

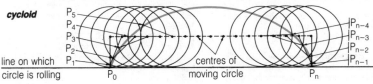

line on which P_1 centres of
circle is rolling P_0 moving circle P_n

P_5, P_4, P_3, P_2, P_{n-4}, P_{n-3}, P_{n-2}, P_{n-1}

Cyprus
Greek **Republic of Cyprus**
(*Kypriakí Dimokratía*) in the S and
Turkish **Republic of Northern
Cyprus** (*Kibris Cumhuriyeti*) in the N

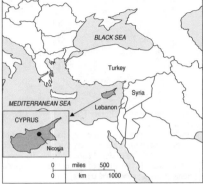

area 9,251 sq km/3,572 sq mi, 37% in Turkish
hands
capital Nicosia (divided between Greeks and
Turks)
towns ports Paphos, Limassol, and Larnaca
(Greek); Morphou, and ports Kyrenia and
Famagusta (Turkish)
physical central plain between two E–W mountain
ranges
head of state and government Glafkoş Clerides
(Greek) from 1993, Rauf Denktas (Turkish) from 1976
political system divided democratic republic
exports citrus fruits, grapes, Cyprus sherry,
potatoes, clothing, footwear
currency Cyprus pound and Turkish lira
population (1990 est) 708,000 (Greek Cypriot 78%,
Turkish Cypriot 18%; annual growth rate 1.2%
life expectancy men 72, women 76
language Greek and Turkish (official); English

religion Greek Orthodox 78%, Sunni Muslim 18%
literacy 99% (1984)
GDP $3.7 bn (1987); $5,497 per head
chronology
1955 Guerrilla campaign for enosis, or union with
Greece, started by Archbishop Makarios and Gen
Grivas.
1956 Makarios and enosis leaders deported.
1959 Compromise agreed and Makarios returned
to be elected president of an independent Greek-
Turkish Cyprus.
1960 Full independence achieved, with Britain
retaining its military bases.
1963 Turks set up their own government in N
Cyprus. Fighting broke out between the two
communities.
1964 UN peacekeeping force installed.
1971 Grivas returned to start a guerrilla war
against the Makarios government.
1975 A military coup deposed Makarios, who fled
to Britain. Nicos Sampson appointed president.
Turkish army sent to N Cyprus to confirm the
Turkish Cypriots' control. The military regime in S
Cyprus collapsed and Makarios returned. N
Cyrpus declared itself the Turkish Federated State
of Cyprus (TFSC), with Rauf Denktaş as president.
1977 Makarios died and was succeeded by Spyros
Kyprianou.
1983 An independent Turkish Republic of
Northern Cyprus (TRNC) was proclaimed but was
recognized only by Turkey.
1984 UN peace proposals rejected.
1985 Summit meeting between Kyprianou and
Denktaş failed to reach agreement.
1988 Georgios Vassilou elected president. Talks
with Denktaş, under UN auspices, began.
1989 Vassilou and Denktas met to draft an
agreement on the reunification of the island,
but talks were abandoned.
1991 Turkish offer of peace talks rejected by
Cyprus and Greece.
1992 UN-sponsored peace talks collapsed.
1993 Clerides replaced Vassilou as Greek
president.

and part of the 'Christ' in the Exeter Book (a
collection of poems now in Exeter Cathedral), and of
the 'Fates of the Apostles' and 'Elene' in the Vercelli
Book (a collection of Old English manuscripts
housed at Vercelli, Italy), in all of which he inserted
his name in the form of runic acrostics.

Cynic a school of Greek philosophy, founded in
Athens about 400 BC by Antisthenes, a disciple of
Socrates, who advocated a stern and simple morality, and a complete disregard of pleasure and comfort.

cypress coniferous tree or shrub of the genera
Cupressus and Chamaecyparis, family Cupressaceae. There are about 20 species found mainly in the
temperate regions of the N hemisphere and many
more ornamental varieties. They have minute
scale-like leaves and small globular cones made up of
woody scales and containing an aromatic resin.

Cyprian, St *c.* 210–258. Christian martyr, one of
the earliest Christian writers and bishop of Carthage
about 249. He wrote a treatise on the unity of the
church. Feast day 16 Sept.

Cyprus island in the Mediterranean, off the S coast
of Turkey.

Cyrano de Bergerac Savinien de 1619–1655.
French writer. He joined a corps of guards at 19, and
performed heroic feats which made him famous. He

is the hero of a classic play by Rostand, in which his
notoriously long nose is used as a counterpoint to his
chivalrous character.

Cyrenaic a school of Greek ◊hedonistic philosophy founded about 400 BC by Aristippus of Cyrene.
He regarded pleasure as the only absolutely worth-
while thing in life, but taught that self-control and intelligence were necessary to choose the best pleasures.

Cyrenaica area of E Libya, colonized by the Greeks
in 7th century BC, and later held by the Egyptians,
Romans, Arabs, Turks, and Italians. Modern cities
in the region are Benghazi, Derna, and Tobruk.

Cyril and Methodius two brothers, both Christian saints: Cyril 826–869 and Methodius 815–885.
They invented a Slavonic alphabet, and translated
the Bible and the liturgy from Greek to Slavonic.
The language (known as ***Old Church Slavonic***)
remained in use in churches and for literature among
Bulgars, Serbs, and Russians up to the 17th century. The ***cyrillic alphabet*** is named after Cyril
and may also have been invented by him. Feast day
14 Feb.

Cyril of Alexandria, St 376–444. Bishop of
Alexandria from 412, persecutor of Jews and other
non-Christians. He was suspected of ordering the
murder of Hypatia (*c.*370–*c.*415) the woman
philosopher.

Czech Republic
(*Česká Republika*)

area 78,864 sq km/30,461 sq mi
capital Prague
towns Brno, Ostrava, Olomouc, Liberec, Plzeň, Ustí nad Labem, Hradec Králové
physical mountainous; rivers: Morava, Labe (Elbe), Vltava (Moldau)
head of state Václav Havel from 1993
head of government Václav Klaus from 1993
political system emergent democracy
exports machinery, vehicles, coal, iron and steel, chemicals, glass, ceramics, clothing
currency new currency based on koruna

population (1991) 10,298,700 (with German and other minorities); annual growth rate 0.4%
life expectancy men 68, women 75
language Czech (official)
religion Roman Catholic (75%), Protestant, Hussite, Orthodox
literacy 100%
GDP $26,600 m (1990); $2,562 per head
chronology
1526–1918 Under Habsburg domination.
1918 Independence achieved from Austro-Hungarian Empire; Czechs joined Slovaks in forming Czechoslovakia as independent nation.
1948 Communists assumed power in Czechoslovakia.
1968 Czech Socialist Republic created under new federal constitution.
1989 Pro-democracy demonstrations in Prague. New political parties formed, including Czech-based Civic Forum under Václav Havel. Communist Party stripped of powers and political parties legalized. Havel appointed state president.
1990 Havel re-elected president in multiparty elections.
1991 Civic Forum split into CDP and CM; evidence of increasing Czech and Slovak separatism.
1992 Václav Klaus, leader of the Czech-based CDP, became prime minister; Havel resigned following Slovak gains in assembly elections. Creation of separate Czech and Slovak states agreed.
1993 Czech Republic became sovereign state, with Klaus as prime minister. Havel elected president of the new republic.

Cyrus the Great Founder of the Persian Empire. King of Persia, originally as vassal to the ◊Medes, whose empire he overthrew in 550 BC, he captured ◊Croesus in 546 BC, and conquered all Asia Minor, adding Babylonia (including Syria and Palestine) to his empire in 539 BC. The exiled Jews were allowed to return to Jerusalem. He died fighting in Afghanistan.

cystic fibrosis hereditary disease involving defects of various tissues, including the sweat glands, the mucous glands of the bronchi (air passages) and the digestive glands. The sufferer experiences repeated chest infections and digestive disorders, and generally fails to thrive.

cystitis inflammation of the bladder, usually caused by bacterial infection, and resulting in frequent and painful urination.

cytochrome a type of protein, responsible for part of the process of ◊respiration by which food molecules are broken down in ◊aerobic organisms. Cytochromes are part of the electron transport chain, which uses energized electrons to reduce molecular oxygen (O_2) to oxygen ions (O^{2h-}). These then combine with hydrogen ions (H^{h+}) to form water (H_2O), the end product of aerobic respiration. As electrons are passed from one cytochrome to another energy is released and used to make ◊ATP.

cytology the study of ◊cells, especially in relation to their functions. Major advances have been made possible in this field by the development of ◊electron microscopes.

cytoplasm the part of the cell outside the ◊nuc-leus. Strictly speaking, this includes all the ◊organelles (mitochondria, chloroplasts, and so on) but often cytoplasm refers to the jelly-like matter in which the organelles are embedded (correctly termed the cytosol). In many cells, the cytoplasm is made up of two parts, the ectoplasm or plasma-gel, a dense gelatinous outer layer concerned with cell movement, and the endoplasm or plasmasol, a more fluid inner part where most of the organelles are found.

cytoskeleton in a living cell, a matrix of protein filaments and tubules that occurs within the cytosol (the liquid part of the ◊cytoplasm). It gives the cell a definite shape, transports vital substances around the cell, and may also be involved in cell movement.

Czechoslovakia *The Soviet occupation of Czechoslovakia, 1968.*

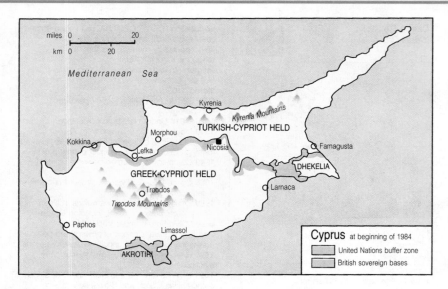

miles 0   20

km 0   20

Mediterranean Sea

Kyrenia

Kyrenia Mountains

TURKISH-CYPRIOT HELD

Morphou

Kokkina

Lefka   Nicosia

Famagusta

DHEKELIA

GREEK-CYPRIOT HELD

Larnaca

Troodos

Troodos Mountains

Paphos

Limassol

AKROTIRI

Cyprus at beginning of 1984

United Nations buffer zone

British sovereign bases

cytotoxic drug   drug that kills or damages cells. Although used specifically to kill the cells of a malignant tumour, or as an ◊immunosuppressive following organ transplantation, it may damage healthy cells as well. Side effects include nausea, vomiting, hair loss, and bone marrow damage.

czar   alternative form of tsar, an emperor of pre-Revolutionary Russia.

Czechoslovakia   former country in E central Europe, a federation of the ◊Czech Republic and the ◊Slovak Republic 1968–93.

Czech Republic   country in E central Europe, bounded NE by Poland, E by the Slovak Republic, SW by Austria, and W by Germany.

d. abbreviation for *day; diameter; died.*

D abbreviation for *five hundred* (Roman).

DA abbreviation for *District Attorney.*

dab marine flatfish *Limanda limanda* of the plaice family found in the NE Atlantic. Light brown or grey, with dark brown spots and rough-scaled on the coloured side, it grows to about 25 cm/10 in.

Dacca former spelling (until 1984) of ◊Dhaka, capital of Bangladesh.

dace freshwater fish *Leuciscus leuciscus* of the carp family. Common in England, and also in Europe, it is silvery and reaches a length of 30 cm/1 ft.

Dachau site of a ◊concentration camp during World War II at a town in Bavaria, Germany.

dachshund small hound of German origin (German 'badger-dog') bred originally for badger digging. It is long in body and short-legged. Several varieties are bred, standard size (up to 10 kg/22 lb) and miniature (5 kg/11 lb or less), and long-haired, smooth-haired, and wire-haired.

Dada artistic and literary movement founded 1915 in Zürich, Switzerland, by the Romanian poet Tristan Tzara (1896–1963) and others in a spirit of rebellion and disillusion during World War I. Other Dadaist groups were soon formed by the artists ◊Duchamp and Man ◊Ray in New York and ◊Picabia in Barcelona. Dada had a considerable impact on early 20th-century art, questioning established artistic rules and values.

Dadd Richard 1817–1887. British painter. In 1843 he murdered his father and was confined as insane, but continued to paint minutely detailed pictures of fantasies and fairy tales, such as *The Fairy Feller's Master-Stroke* 1855–64 (Tate Gallery, London).

daddy-longlegs popular name for a ◊crane fly.

Dadra and Nagar Haveli since 1961 a Union Territory of West India; capital Silvassa; population (1989) 138,500. Formerly part of Portuguese Daman, it produces rice, wheat, millet, and timber.

Daedalus in Greek mythology, an Athenian craftsman supposed to have constructed for King Minos the labyrinth in which the ◊Minotaur was imprisoned. He fled from Crete with his son ◊Icarus using wings made from feathers fastened with wax.

daffodil several species of the genus *Narcissus*, distinguished by their trumpet-shaped corollas. The common daffodil of N Europe *Narcissus pseudonarcissus* has large yellow flowers, and

grows from a large bulb. There are numerous cultivated forms.

Dafydd ap Gwilym *c.* 1340–*c.* 1400. Welsh poet. His work is notable for its complex but graceful style, its concern with nature and love rather than with heroic martial deeds, and for its references to classical and Italian poetry. He was born into an influential Cardiganshire gentry family, and is traditionally believed to have led a life packed with amorous adventures.

Dagestan autonomous republic of S Russia, situated E of the ◊Caucasus, bordering the Caspian Sea. Capital Makhachkala; area 50,300 sq km/14,700 sq mi; population (1982) 1,700,000. It is mountainous, with deep valleys, and its numerous ethnic groups speak a variety of distinct languages. Annexed from Iran in 1723, which strongly resisted Russian conquest, it became an autonomous republic in 1921.

Daguerre Louis Jacques Mande 1787–1851. French pioneer of photography. Together with Niepce, he is credited with the invention of photography (though others were reaching the same point simultaneously). He invented the daguerreotype in 1838, a one-off image process, superseded ten years later by Fox Talbot's negative/positive process.

Dahl Roald 1916–1990. British writer, celebrated for short stories with a twist, for example, *Tales of the Unexpected* 1979, and for children's books including *Charlie and the Chocolate Factory* 1964.

dahlia genus of perennial plants, family Compositae, comprised of 20 species and many cultivated forms. Native to Mexico, the dahlia is a stocky plant with showy flowers that come in a wide range of colours.

Dahomey the former name (until 1975) of the People's Republic of ◊Benin.

Dáil Eireann the lower house of the legislature of the Republic of Ireland. It consists of 148 members elected by adult suffrage on a basis of proportional representation.

Daimler Gottlieb 1834–1900. German engineer who pioneered the modern motor car. In 1886 he produced his first motor vehicle and a motorbicycle. He later joined forces with Karl ◊Benz and was one of the pioneers of the high-speed 4-stroke petrol engine.

daisy genus of hardy perennials, family Compositae. The *common daisy Bellis perennis* has a single white or pink flower rising from a rosette of leaves. It is a common lawn weed.

daisy bush genus *Olearia* of Australian and New Zealand shrubs, family Compositae, with flowers like daisies and felted or holly-like leaves.

Dakar capital and chief port (with artificial harbour) of Senegal; population (1984) 1,000,000.

Dalai Lama 14th incarnation 1935– . Spiritual and temporal head of the Tibetan state until 1959,

daffodil

Dali Autumnal Cannibalism *(1936) Tate Gallery,*
London

when he went into exile in protest against Chinese
annexation and oppression. Tibetan Buddhists believe that each Dalai Lama is a reincarnation of
his predecessor and also of ◊Avalokitesvara (see
◊Lamaism).

Dalgarno George 1626–1687. Scottish schoolmaster and inventor of the first sign language
alphabet 1680.

Dalhousie James Andrew Broun Ramsay, 1st Marquess and 10th Earl of Dalhousie 1812–1860. British
administrator, governor general of India 1848–56. In
the second Sikh War he annexed the Punjab 1849,
and, after the second Burmese War, Lower Burma
1853. He reformed the Indian army and civil service
and furthered social and economic progress.

Dali Salvador 1904–1989. Spanish painter. In 1928
he collaborated with Buñuel on the film *Un Chien
Andalou.* In 1929 he joined the Surrealists and soon
became notorious for his flamboyant eccentricity.
Influenced by the psychiatric theories of Freud, he
developed a repertoire of dramatic images, such as
the distorted human body, limp watches, and burning giraffes. These are painted with a meticulous,
polished clarity. He also painted religious themes
and many portraits of his wife Gala.

Dallapiccola Luigi 1904–1975. Italian composer.
In his early years he was a ◊neoclassicist in the
manner of Stravinsky, but he soon turned to
◊serialism, which he adapted to his own style.
His works include the operas *Il Prigioniero/The
Prisoner* 1949 and *Ulisse/Ulysses* 1968, as well as
many vocal and instrumental compositions.

Dallas commercial city in Texas, USA; population (1980) 904,000. Industries include banking,
insurance, oil, aviation, aerospace and electronics.
Dallas–Fort Worth Regional Airport (opened 1973)
is one of the world's largest. John F ◊Kennedy was
assassinated on a visit here in 1963.

dalmatian breed of dog, about 60 cm/2 ft tall, white
with spots that are black or brown. It was formerly
used as a coach dog.

Dalton Hugh, Baron Dalton 1887–1962. British
economist and Labour politician. Chancellor of the
Exchequer 1945, he resigned 1947 following a disclosure to a lobby correspondent before a budget
speech. He was created a life peer 1960.

Dalton John 1776–1844. British chemist, the first
to propose the existence of atoms, which he considered to be the smallest parts of matter. Extending
the range of compounds, he produced the first list of
relative atomic masses, *Absorption of Gases* 1805.

He was also the first scientist to note and record
colour-blindness.

dam a structure built to hold back water, in order
to prevent flooding, provide water for irrigation and
storage, and to provide ◊hydroelectric power. The
world's biggest dams are of the earth- and rock-fill
type, also called ***embankment dams.*** Such dams
are generally built on broad valley sites. Deep,
narrow gorges dictate a ***concrete dam,*** where
the enormous strength of reinforced concrete can
withstand the water pressures involved. A valuable development in arid regions, as in parts of
Brazil, is the ***underground dam,*** where water
is stored among sand and stones on a solid rock
base, with a wall to ground level, so avoiding rapid
evaporation.

damages in English law, compensation for a ◊tort
(such as personal injuries caused by negligence) or
for a breach of contract. In the case of breach of
contract the complainant can claim all the financial loss he or she has suffered. Damages for
personal injuries include compensation for loss
of earnings, as well as for the injury itself.
The court might reduce the damages if the
claimant was partly to blame. In the majority
of cases, the parties involved reach an 'out of

dam

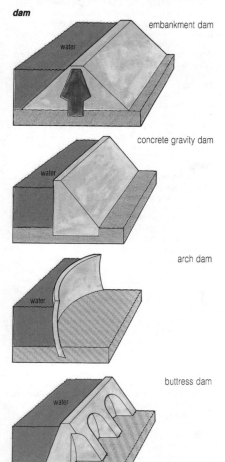

embankment dam

concrete gravity dam

arch dam

buttress dam

court settlement' (a compromise without going to court.)

Damascus (Arabic *Dimashq*) capital of Syria, on the river Barada, SE of Beirut; population (1981) 1,251,028. Produces silk, wood products and brass and copper ware. Said to be the oldest still inhabited city of the world, Damascus an ancient city even in Old Testament times; most notable of the old buildings is the Great Mosque, completed as a Christian church in the 5th century.

Dame title of a woman who has been awarded the Order of the Bath, Order of St Michael and St George, Royal Victorian Order, or Order of the British Empire. Legal title of the wife or widow of a knight or baronet, placed before her name.

damnation in Christian and Muslim belief, a state of eternal punishment which will be undergone by those who are not worthy of salvation, sometimes equated with ◊hell.

Damocles lived 4th century BC. A courtier of the elder Dionysius, ruler of Syracuse. Having extolled the happiness of his sovereign, Damocles was invited by him to a great feast, during which he saw above his head a sword suspended by a single hair. He recognized this as a symbol of the insecurity of the great.

damper incorrectly called shock absorber, a device for reducing the vibration of, for example, a spring. Dampers are used in conjunction with coil springs in most car suspension systems, and are usually of the telescopic type, consisting of a piston in an oil-filled cylinder. The resistance to movement of the piston through the oil creates the damping effect.

Dampier William 1652–1715. English explorer who circumnavigated the world three times.

damselfly a predatory, winged, often colourful insect with two pairs of similar wings which are generally folded back over the body when at rest, large, prominent eyes, and long, slender bodies.

damson type of plum tree *Prunus damascena*, distinguished by its small, oval fruit, which is dark purple or blue to black in colour.

Danby Thomas Osborne, Earl of Danby 1631–1712. British Tory politician. He acted 1673–78 as Charles II's chief minister and in 1674 was created earl of Danby, but was imprisoned in the Tower of London 1678–84. In 1688 he signed the invitation to William of Orange to take the throne; he was again chief minister 1690–95.

dance rhythmic movement of the body, usually performed in time to music. Its primary purpose may be religious, magical, martial, social or artistic – the last two being characteristic of contemporary societies. The pre-Christian era had a strong tradition of ritual dance and Greek dance still exerts an influence on dance movement today. Although Western folk and social dances have a long history the Eastern dance tradition long predates the Western. The European classical tradition dates from the 15th Century in Italy, the first printed text from France in the 16th century and the first dance school in Paris in the 17th century. The 18th century saw the development of European classical ◊ballet as we know it today and the 19th century the rise of Romantic ballet. The 20th century has seen the development of many divergent styles and ideas growing from a willingness to explore different techniques and amalgamate different traditions.

dandelion wild flower *Taraxacum officinale* belonging to the Compositae family. The stout stalk rises from a rosette of leaves that are deeply indented like a lion's teeth, hence the name (from French *dent de lion*). The flowerheads are bright yellow.

Danelaw extent of Danish rule in England by 886

area subject to Norsemen

The fruit is surmounted by the hairs of the calyx which constitute the familiar dandelion 'puff'.

Dandolo Venetian family which produced four doges (rulers), of whom the most outstanding, *Enrico Dandolo* (c. 1120–1205), became doge in 1193. He greatly increased the dominions of the Venetian republic and accompanied the crusading army that took Constantinople in 1203.

danegeld Norman name for the tax imposed from 991 by Anglo-Saxon kings to pay for tribute to the Vikings, and which continued to be levied until 1162. The Normans used it to finance military operations.

Danelaw name given 11th century to the area of N and E England settled by the Vikings 9th century. It stretched from the river Tees to the river Thames, and occupied about half of England. Within its bounds, Danish law, customs, and language prevailed. Its linguistic influence is still apparent.

dangling participle see ◊participle.

Daniel 6th century BC. Jewish folk hero and prophet at the court of Nebuchadnezzar; also the name of a book of the Old Testament or Jewish Bible, probably compiled in the 2nd century BC. It includes stories about Daniel and his companions Shadrach, Meshach, and Abednego, set during the Babylonian captivity of the Jews.

Daniell John Frederic 1790–1845. British chemist and meteorologist, who invented a primary electrical cell in 1836. In its original form, the Daniell cell consists of a central zinc cathode dipping into a porous pot containing zinc sulphate solution. The porous pot is, in turn, immersed in a solution of copper sulphate contained in a copper can, which acts as the cell's anode. The use of a porous barrier prevents polarization (the covering of the anode with small bubbles of hydrogen gas) and allows the cell to generate a continuous current of electricity.

Danish language a member of the North Germanic group of the Indo-European language family, spoken in Denmark and Greenland and related to Icelandic, Faroese, Norwegian, and Swedish. As one of the languages of the Vikings, who invaded and settled in parts of Britain during the 9th to 11th centuries, Old Danish had a strong influence on English.

dance: chronology

1909	The first Paris season given by Diaghilev's troupe of Russian dancers, later to become known as the Ballets Russes, marked the beginning of one of the most exciting periods in Western ballet.
1913	The première of Stravinsky's *The Rite of Spring* provoked a scandal in Paris.
1914	The foxtrot was introduced in England.
1926	Martha Graham, one of the most innovative figures in modern ballet, gave her first recital in New York. In England, students from the Rambert School of Ballet, opened by Marie Rambert in 1920, gave their first public performance in *A Tragedy of Fashion*, the first ballet to be choreographed by Frederick Ashton.
1928	The first performance of George Balanchine's *Apollon Musagète* in Paris, by the Ballets Russes, marked the birth of neoclassicism in ballet.
1931	Ninette de Valois' Vic-Wells ballet gave its first performance in London. In 1956 the company became the Royal Ballet.
1933	The Hollywood musical achieved artistic independence through Busby Berkeley's kaleidoscopic choreography in *Forty-Second Street* and Dave Gould's airborne finale in *Flying down to Rio*, in which Fred Astaire and Ginger Rogers appeared together for the first time.
1940	The Dance Notation Bureau was established in New York for recording ballets and dances.
1948	The New City Ballet was founded with George Balanchine as principal choreographer. The immensely popular film *The Red Shoes* appeared, choreographed by Massine and Robert Helpmann and starring Moira Shearer.
1950	The Festival Ballet, later to become the London Festival Ballet, was created by Alicia Markova and Anton Dolin who had first danced together with the Ballets Russes in 1929.
1952	Gene Kelly starred and danced in the film *Singin' in the Rain*.
1953	The American experimental choreographer Merce Cunningham, who often worked with the composer John Cage, formed his own troupe.
1954	Bill Haley's *Rock Around the Clock* heralded the age of rock and roll.
1956	The Bolshoi Ballet opened its first season in the West at Covent Garden in London, with Galina Ulanova dancing in *Romeo and Juliet*, startling audiences with its dramatic style.
1957	Jerome Robbins choreographed Leonard Bernstein's *West Side Story*, demonstrating his ability to work in both popular and classical forms.
1960	The progressive French choreographer Maurice Béjart became director of the Brussels-based *Ballet du XXième Siècle* company.
1961	Rudolf Nureyev defected while dancing with the Kirov Ballet in Paris. He was to have a profound influence on male dancing in the West. The South-African-born British choreographer John Cranko became director of the Stuttgart Ballet for which he was to produce several major ballets.
1962	Glen Tetley's ballet *Pierrot Lunaire*, in which he was one of the three dancers, was premièred in New York. In the same year he joined the Nederlands Dans Theater.
1965	American choreographer Twyla Tharp produced her first works.
1966	The School of Contemporary Dance was founded in London, from which Robin Howard and the choreographer Robert Cohan created the London Contemporary Dance Theatre. The choreographer Norman Morrice joined the Ballet Rambert and the company began to concentrate on contemporary works.
1968	Arthur Mitchell, the first black dancer to join the New York City Ballet, founded the Dance Theatre of Harlem.
1974	Mikhail Baryshnikov defected while dancing with a Bolshoi Ballet group in Toronto.
1978	The release of Robert Stigwood's film *Saturday Night Fever* popularized disco dancing worldwide.
1980	Natalia Makarova, who had defected in 1979, staged the first full-length revival of Petipa's *La Bayadère* in the West with the American Ballet Theatre in New York.
1982	Wayne Sleep, previously principal dancer with the Royal Ballet, starred as lead dancer in Andrew Lloyd-Webber's musical *Cats*, choreographed by Gillian Lynne.
1983	Break dancing was established as a cult with the release of the film *Flashdance*.
1984	The avant-garde group Michael Clark and Company made its debut in London.
1990	*Maple Leaf Rag*, Martha Graham's final work, was premièred in New York City.

Dante Alighieri 1265–1321. Italian poet. His works include the prose philosophical treatise *Convivio* 1306–08; *Monarchia* 1310–13, expounding his political theories; *De vulgari eloquentia/Concerning the Vulgar Tongue* 1304–06, an original Latin work on Italian, its dialects, and kindred languages; *Canzoniere/Lyrics*, containing his scattered lyrics; and his masterpiece *Divina Commedia/The Divine Comedy c.* 1300–21 an imaginary journey through Hell, Purgatory, and Paradise, under the guidance of Reason and Faith. It is generally considered the greatest poem of the Middle Ages.

Danton Georges Jacques 1759–1794. French revolutionary. A lawyer, during the early years of the Revolution he was one of the most influential men in Paris. He organized the rising of 10 Aug 1792 that overthrew the monarchy, roused the country to expel the Prussian invaders, and formed in Apr 1793 the revolutionary tribunal and the **Committee of Public Safety**, of which until Jul he was the real leader. Thereafter he lost power, and when he attempted to recover it, he was arrested and guillotined.

Danube (German *Donau*) second longest of European rivers, rising on the east slopes of the Black Forest, and flowing 2,820 km/1,750 mi across Europe to enter the Black Sea in Romania by a swampy delta.

Danzig German name for the Polish port of ◊Gdańsk.

Daphne in Greek mythology, a nymph, changed into a laurel tree to escape from Apollo's amorous pursuit.

Daqing oilfield near ◊Harbin, China.

D'Arblay, Madame married name of Fanny ◊Burney.

Darby Abraham 1677–1717. English ironmaster who developed a process for smelting iron ore using coke instead of the more expensive charcoal. He employed the cheaper iron to cast strong thin pots for domestic use as well as the huge cylinders required by the new steam pumping-engines.

Dardanelles Turkish strait connecting the Sea of Marmara with the Aegean Sea (ancient name Hellespont, Turkish name *Canakkale Boğazi*); its shores are formed by the ◊Gallipoli peninsula on the NW and the mainland of Turkey-in-Asia on the SE. It is 75 km/47 mi long and 5–6 km/3–4 mi wide.

Dar es Salaam (Arabic 'haven of peace'); chief seaport in Tanzania, on the Indian Ocean, and capital of Tanzania until its replacement by ◊Dodoma in 1974; population (1985) 1,394,000.

Darius I *the Great c.* 558–486 BC. King of Persia 521–485 BC. A member of a younger branch of the Achaemenid dynasty, he won the throne from the usurper Gaumata (d. 522 BC), reorganized the government, and in 512 BC marched against the Scythians, a people N of the Black Sea, and subjugated Thrace and Macedonia.

Darlan Jean François 1881–1942. French admiral and politician. He commanded the French navy 1939–40, took part in the evacuation of Dunkirk, and entered the Pétain cabinet as naval minister. In 1941 he was appointed vice-premier, and became strongly anti-British and pro-German, but in 1942 he was dropped from the cabinet by Laval and was sent to N Africa, where he was assassinated.

Darling Grace 1815–1842. British heroine. She was the daughter of a lighthouse keeper on the Farne Islands, off Northumberland. On 7 Sept 1838 the *Forfarshire* was wrecked, and Grace Darling and her father rowed through a storm to the wreck,

CHARLES ROBERT DARWIN, LL.D., F.R.S.

IN HIS *DESCENT OF MAN* HE BROUGHT HIS OWN SPECIES DOWN AS LOW AS POSSIBLE—*I.E.*, TO "A HAIRY QUADRUPED FURNISHED WITH A TAIL AND POINTED EARS, AND PROBABLY *ARBOREAL* IN ITS HABITS"—WHICH IS A REASON FOR THE VERY GENERAL INTEREST IN A "FAMILY TREE." HE HAS LATELY BEEN TURNING HIS ATTENTION TO THE "POLITIC WORM."

Darwin Cartoon of Charles Robert Darwin by Linley Sambourne.

saving nine lives. She was awarded a medal for her bravery.

Darnley Henry Stewart or Stuart, Lord Darnley 1545–1567. second husband of Mary, Queen of Scots, from 1565, and father of James I of England (James VI of Scotland). By the advice of her secretary, David ◊Rizzio, Mary refused Darnley the crown matrimonial; in revenge Darnley led a band of nobles who murdered Rizzio in Mary's presence. Darnley was assassinated 1567.

Darrow Clarence (Seward) 1857–1938. US lawyer, counsel for the defence in the Dayton, Tennessee, **monkey trial** 1925, in which a teacher, John T Scopes, was tried for teaching Darwin's theory of evolution, and fined $100.

Dart Raymond 1893–1988. Australian anthropologist. He discovered the fossil remains of the 'southern African ape' *Australopithecus africanus* 1924, near Taungs in Botswana.

darts indoor game played on a circular board. Darts (like small arrow shafts) approx 13cm/5in in length are thrown at segmented targets and score points values according to their landing place.

Darwin capital and port in Northern Territory, Australia, in NW Arnhem Land; population (1981) 56,500. It serves the uranium mining site at Rum Jungle to the south. Destroyed in 1974 by a cyclone, the city was rebuilt on the same site.

Darwin Charles Robert 1809–1882. British scientist, who developed the modern theory of ◊evolution, and proposed the principle of ◊natural selection. Following much research in South America and the Galapagos Islands as naturalist on HMS *Beagle* 1831–36, Darwin published *On the Origin of Species by Means of Natural Selection or the Preservation of Favoured Races in the Struggle for Life* 1859. This explained the evolutionary process through the principles of natural and sexual selection, refuting earlier theories. It aroused bitter controversy because it disagreed with the literal interpretation of the Book of Genesis.

Darwinism, Social in US history, an influential social theory, drawing upon the work of Charles Darwin and Herbert Spencer, which claimed to offer a scientific justification for late 19th-century laissez faire capitalism (the principle of unrestricted freedom in commerce). Popularized by academics and by businessmen like Andrew ◊Carnegie, social Darwinism naturalized competitive individualism and a market economy unregulated by government.

Dasam Granth a collection of the writings of the tenth Sikh guru (teacher), Gobind Singh, and of poems by a number of other writers. The script is Gurmukhi, the written form of Punjabi popularized by Guru Angad. It contains a retelling of the Krishna legends, devotional verse and diverting anecdotes.

dasyure type of marsupial, also known as a 'native cat', found in Australia and New Guinea. Various species have body lengths from 25 cm/10 in to 75 cm/2.5 ft. They have long bushy tails, and have dark coats with white spots. They are agile, nocturnal carnivores, able to move fast and climb.

data information, often in tabular or graphic form, especially that stored on computers.

database in computing, a structured, centralized collection of data, organized to allow access by several or many different user programs. The data is held in ◊files and arranged into hierarchies, networks, or relations - the three main types of database structure.

data-flow diagram in computing, another name for ◊flow chart.

data processing (DP) the commercial use of computers, typically to handle access to a database and the manipulation of large volumes of data, or for batch processing of homogeneous (of similar nature) data on a large scale. DP (sometimes called EDP, electronic data processing) is normally carried out on a mainframe computer.

data protection the safeguarding of information about individuals stored on computers, ensuring privacy. The Council of Europe adopted in 1981 a Data Protection Convention which led in the UK to the Data Protection Act 1984. This requires computer databases containing personal information to be registered, and users to process only accurate information and to retain the information only for a necessary period and for specified purposes. Individuals have a right of access, and sometimes of correction or erasure.

date palm of the genus *Phoenix*. The female tree produces the fruit, dates, in bunches weighing 9–11 kg/20–25 lb.

dating the science of determining the age of geological structures, rocks, and fossils, and placing them in the context of geological time.

dative in the grammar of certain inflected languages such as Latin, the dative case is the form of a noun, pronoun, or adjective used when it is the indirect object of a verb. It is also used with some prepositions.

datura genus of plants, family Solanaceae, such as the thorn apple, with handsome trumpet-shaped blooms. They have narcotic properties.

Daumier Honoré 1808–1879. French artist. He became famous for his sharply dramatic and satirical cartoons, dissecting Parisian society. His output was enormous and included 4,000 lithographs and, mainly after 1860, powerful satirical oil paintings that were little appreciated in his lifetime.

dauphin title of the eldest sons of the kings of France, derived from the personal name of a count, whose lands, the *Dauphiné* (capital Grenoble), traditionally passed to the heir to the throne from 1349 to 1830.

David c. 1060–970 BC. Second king of Israel. According to the Bible he played the harp before King Saul to banish his melancholy, and later slew the Philistine giant Goliath with a sling and stone. After Saul's death David was anointed king at Hebron, took Jerusalem and made it his capital. David sent Uriah (a soldier in his army) to his death in the front line of battle in order that he might marry his widow, Bathsheba. Their son Solomon later became king.

David Elizabeth 1914–1992. British cookery writer. Her *Mediterranean Food* 1950 and *French Country Cooking* 1951 helped to spark an interest in foreign cuisine in Britain, and also inspired a growing school of informed, highly literate writing on food and wine.

David Gerard c. 1450–1523. Netherlandish painter active chiefly in Bruges from about 1484. His style follows that of van der Weyden, but he was also influenced by the new taste in Antwerp for Italianate ornament. *The Marriage at Cana* c. 1503 (Louvre, Paris) is a good example of his work.

David Jacques Louis 1748–1825. French painter in the Neoclassical style. He was an active supporter of and unofficial painter to the republic during the French Revolution, for which he was imprisoned 1794–95. He was later appointed court painter to the emperor Napoleon, of whom he created well-known images such as the horseback figure of *Napoleon Crossing the Alps* 1800 (Louvre, Paris).

David two kings of Scotland:

David I 1082–1153. King of Scotland from 1124. The youngest son of Malcolm III Canmore and St ◊Margaret, he was brought up in the English court of Henry I, and married in 1113 Matilda, widow of the 1st earl of Northampton. He invaded England 1138 in support of Queen ◊Matilda, but was defeated at Northallerton in the Battle of the Standard, and again 1141.

David II 1324–1371. King of Scotland from 1329, son of Robert the Bruce. David was married at the age of four to Joanna, daughter of Edward II of England. After the defeat of the Scots by Edward III at Halidon Hill, David and Joanna were sent to France for safety. They returned 1341.

Davis *Hollywood legend Bette Davis.*

Davis *Steve Davis playing in the World Snooker Championships, 1981.*

In 1346 David invaded England, was captured at the battle of Neville's Cross and imprisoned for 11 years. On Joanna's death 1362 David married Margaret Logie, but divorced her 1370.

David Copperfield a novel by Charles Dickens, published 1849–50. The story follows the orphan David Copperfield from his schooldays and early poverty to eventual fame as an author.

David, St or *Dewi* 5th–6th century. Patron saint of Wales, Christian abbot and bishop. According to legend he was the son of a prince of Cardiganshire and uncle of King Arthur, and responsible for the adoption of the leek as the national emblem of Wales, but his own emblem is a dove. Feast day 1 Mar.

Davies Peter Maxwell 1934– . British composer and conductor, a pioneer of British music-theatre. He has composed much music for chamber ensembles, and combines medieval musical techniques with his own idiom. His opera *Taverner* is based on the life of the 16th-century composer and heretic John Taverner.

Davies Robertson 1913– . Canadian novelist. He gained an international reputation with *Fifth Business* 1970, the first novel of his Deptford trilogy, a panoramic work blending philosophy, humour, the occult, and ordinary life.

Da Vinci see ◊Leonardo da Vinci, Italian Renaissance artist.

Davis Angela 1944– . US left-wing activist for black rights, prominent in the student movement of the 1960s. In 1970 she went into hiding after being accused of supplying guns used in the murder of a judge who had been seized as a hostage in an attempt to secure the release of three black convicts (known as the *Soledad brothers* from the name of their prison). She was captured, tried, and acquitted.

Davis Bette 1908–1989. US actress. She entered films in 1930, and established a reputation with *Of Human Bondage* 1934 as a forceful dramatic actress. Later films included *Dangerous* 1935 and *Jezebel* 1938, both winning her Academy Awards, and *Whatever Happened to Baby Jane?* 1962.

Davis Jefferson 1808–1889. US politician, president of the short-lived Confederate States of America 1861–65. He was a leader of the Southern Democrats in the US Senate from 1857, and a defender of 'humane' slavery; in 1860 he issued a declaration in favour of secession from the USA. During the Civil War he assumed strong political leadership, but often disagreed with military policy. He was imprisoned for two years after the war, one of the very few cases of judicial retribution against Confederate leaders.

Davis Miles (Dewey Jr) 1926–1991. US jazz trumpeter, composer, and band leader. He recorded bebop with Charlie Parker 1945, pioneered cool jazz in the 1950s and jazz-rock fusion from the late 1960s. His influential albums include *Birth of the Cool* 1949, *Sketches of Spain* 1959, *Bitches' Brew* 1970 and *Tutu* 1985.

Davis Steve 1957– . English snooker player who has won every major honour in the game since turning professional in 1978. He has been world champion six times, including 1989.

Davis Cup annual lawn tennis tournament for men's international teams, first held 1900 after Dwight Filley Davis (1879–1945) donated the trophy.

Davison Emily 1872–1913. English militant suffragette, who died while trying to stop the King's horse at the Derby at Epsom (she was trampled by the horse). She joined the Women's Social and Political Union in 1906 and served several prison sentences for militant action such as stone throwing, setting fire to pillar boxes, and bombing Lloyd George's country house.

Davitt Michael 1846–1906. Irish Fenian revolutionary. He joined the Fenians 1865, and was sentenced 1870 to 15 years' prison for treason. After his release 1877, he and Charles Parnell founded the Land League 1879. Davitt was imprisoned several times for his share in the land-reform agitation. He was a member of Parliament 1895–99.

Davy Humphry 1778–1829. English chemist. While a laboratory assistant at Bristol in 1799, he discovered the respiratory effects of 'laughing gas' (nitrous oxide). He discovered, by electrolysis, the metals sodium, potassium, calcium, magnesium, strontium, and barium. He invented the 'safety lamp' for use in mines where methane was present, in effect enabling the miners to work in previously unsafe conditions.

Dawes Charles Gates 1865–1951. US Republican politician. In 1923 he was appointed by the Allied Reparations Commission president of the committee that produced the *Dawes Plan*, a $200 million loan that enabled Germany to pay enormous war debts after World War I. It was superseded by the Young Plan (which reduced the total reparations bill) 1929. Dawes was elected vice president of the USA 1924, received the Nobel peace prize 1925, and was ambassador to Britain 1929–32.

dawn raid in business, sudden and unexpected buying of a significant proportion of a company's shares, usually as a prelude to a takeover bid.

Davison *Militant suffragette Emily Davison, who was trampled on and killed by the King's horse at the Epsom Derby in 1913.*

DDT

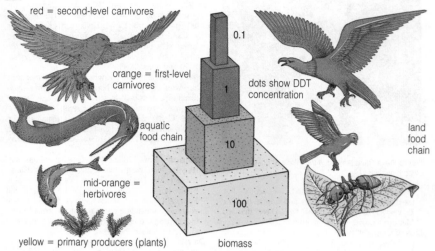

red = second-level carnivores

orange = first-level carnivores

0.1

dots show DDT concentration

1

aquatic food chain

10

land food chain

mid-orange = herbivores

100

yellow = primary producers (plants)

biomass

The aim is to prevent the target company having time to organize opposition to the takeover. The number of shares bought is often just below 5%, the figure above which the ownership of a block of shares must be disclosed under the Companies Act 1985.

day the time taken for the Earth to rotate once on its axis. The *solar day* is the time that the Earth takes to rotate once relative to the Sun. It is divided into 24 hours, and is the basis of our civil day. The *sidereal day* is the time that the Earth takes to rotate once relative to the stars. It is 3 minutes 56 seconds shorter than the solar day, because the Sun's position against the background of stars as seen from Earth changes as the Earth orbits it.

Dayak several indigenous peoples of Indonesian Borneo and Sarawak, including the Bahau of central and E Borneo, the Land Dayak of SW Borneo and the Iban of Sarawak. Their language belongs to the Austronesian family.

Dayan Moshe 1915–1981. Israeli general and politician. As minister of defence 1967 and 1969–74, he was largely responsible for the victory in the 1967 Six-Day War, but was criticized for Israel's alleged unpreparedness in the 1973 October War, and resigned with Golda Meir. Foreign minister from 1977, he resigned in 1979 in protest over the refusal of the Begin government to negotiate with the Palestinians.

Day Lewis Cecil 1904–1972. British poet, poet laureate 1968–1972. With ◊Auden and ◊Spender he was one of the influential left-wing poets of the 1930s.

DBE abbreviation for *Dame Commander of the Order of the British Empire*.

DC in music, the abbreviation for *da capo* (Italian 'from the beginning'; in physics, the abbreviation for *direct current* (electricity).

DD abbreviation for *Doctor of Divinity*.

D-day 6 June 1944, the day the Allied invasion of Europe took place during World War II. It was originally fixed for 5 June, but because of unfavourable weather the invasion was postponed for 24 hours. D-day was also military jargon for any day on which a crucial operation was planned.

DDT abbreviation for *dichloro-diphenyl-trichloroethane*, an insecticide discovered in 1939 by Swiss chemist Paul Müller. It is useful in the control of insects that spread malaria, but resistant strains develop. DDT is highly toxic, and persists in

the environment and in living tissue. Its use is now banned in most countries.

deacon in the Roman Catholic and Anglican churches, an ordained minister who ranks immediately below a priest. In the Protestant churches, a deacon is in training to become a minister or is a lay assistant. In England deaconesses may not administer the sacrament, but may conduct public worship and preach. Male deacons become priests after a year but women do not.

Dead Sea large lake, partly in Israel and partly in Jordan; area 1,020 sq km/394 sq mi; lying 394 m/1,293 ft below sea-level. The chief river entering it is the Jordan; it has no outlet to the sea, and the water is very salty.

Dead Sea Scrolls collection of ancient scrolls (some intact in their jars) and fragments of scrolls found 1947–56 in caves on the W side of the Jordan 12 km/7 mi S of Jericho and 2 km/1 mi from the N end of the Dead Sea, at ◊Qumran. They date mainly from *c.* 150 BC–68 AD, when the monastic community that owned them was destroyed by the Romans because of its support for a revolt against their rule. They include copies of Old Testament books a thousand years earlier than those previously known to be extant.

deafness lack or deficiency in the sense of hearing, either because of an inborn deficiency, or caused by injury or disease of the inner ear.

Deakin Alfred 1856–1919. Australian politician. He was attorney general in the first federal cabinet of 1901, and prime minister 1903–04, 1905–08, and 1909–10. In his second administration, he enacted wide-ranging legislation on defence and the provision of pensions.

dean *education* in universities and medical schools, the head of administration; in the colleges of Oxford and Cambridge, member of the teaching staff charged with the maintenance of discipline; *Anglican Communion* head of the chapter of a cathedral or collegiate church; a rural dean presides over a division of an archdeaconry; *Roman Catholic* senior cardinal bishop, head of the college of cardinals.

Dean James. Stage-name of James Byron 1931–1955. US actor. Killed in a road accident after only his first film, *East of Eden* 1955, had

Dean US cult hero of the fifties, James Dean.

been shown, he posthumously became a cult hero with *Rebel Without a Cause* and *Giant*, both 1956. He became a symbol of teenage rebellion against American middle-class values.

death a permanent ending of all the functions needed to keep an organism alive. Death used to be pronounced when a person's breathing and heartbeat stopped. The advent of mechanical aids has made this point difficult to determine, and a person is now pronounced dead when the brain ceases to control the vital functions.

death cap fungus ◊*Amanita phalloides*, the most poisonous mushroom known.

Death of a Salesman 1949 Broadway play by Arthur Miller, the story of the defeated salesman Willy Loman which captured the limitations and deceptions of the American dream of success.

Death Valley depression 225 km/140 mi long and 6–26 km/4–16 mi wide, in SE California, USA. At 85 mi/280 ft below sea level, it is the lowest point in North America. Bordering mountains rise to 3,000 mi/10,000 ft. It is one of the world's hottest places, with an average annual rainfall of 35 mm/ 1.4 in.

death-watch beetle *Xestobium rufovillosum* of the 'woodworm' family. The larvae live in oaks and willows, and can also cause damage by boring in old furniture or structural timbers. To attract the female, the male produces a ticking sound by striking his head upon a wooden surface, and this is taken by the superstitious as a warning of approaching death.

de Bono Edward 1933– . British doctor. Lecturer at the Department of Investigative Medicine, Cambridge University, from 1976, he is best known for his concept in *The Use of Lateral Thinking* 1967, which involves thinking round a problem rather than tackling it head-on.

Deborah in the Old Testament or Jewish Bible, a prophet and judge (leader). She helped lead an Israelite army against the Canaanite general Sisera, who was killed trying to flee; her song of triumph at his death is regarded as an excellent example of early Hebrew poetry.

Debray Régis 1941– . French Marxist theorist. He was associated with Che Guevara in the revolutionary movement in Latin America in the 1960s, and in 1967 was sentenced to 30 years' imprisonment in Bolivia, but was released after three years. His writings on Latin American politics include *Strategy for Revolution* 1970. He became a specialist

adviser to President Mitterrand of France on Latin American affairs.

Debrecen third largest city in Hungary, 193 km/ 120 mi E of Budapest, in the Great Plain (*Alföld*) region; population (1980) 193,000. Produces tobacco, agricultural machinery and pharmaceuticals. ◊Kossuth declared Hungary independent of the ◊Hapsburgs here in 1849.

Debrett John 1753–1822. London publisher of a directory of the Peerage from 1802, Baronetage in 1808, and Knightage 1866–73/4; the books are still called by his name.

debridement the removal of dead or contaminated tissue from a wound.

de Broglie Louis, 7th Duc de Broglie 1892–1987. French theoretical physicist. In 1929, he was awarded a Nobel Prize, having established that all particles can be described either by particle equations or by wave equations, thus laying the foundations of wave mechanics.

de Broglie Maurice, 6th Duc de Broglie 1875–1960. French physicist, brother of Louis ◊de Broglie. He worked on X-rays and gamma rays, and helped to establish the Einsteinian description of light in terms of photons.

Debs Eugene V(ictor) 1855–1926. US labour leader and Socialist, who organized the Social Democratic party 1897. He was Socialist candidate for the presidency in every election from 1900 to 1920, except that of 1916. He polled nearly one million votes in 1920, the highest Socialist vote ever in US presidential elections, despite having to conduct the campaign from a federal penitentiary in Atlanta, Georgia.

debt something which is owed by a person or organization, usually money, goods, or services. Debt usually occurs as a result of borrowing *credit*. *Debt servicing* is the payment of interest on a debt. The *national debt* of a country is the total money owed by the government to private individuals, banks, and so on; *international debt*, the money owed by one country to another, began on a large scale with the investment in foreign countries by newly industrialized countries in the late 19th–early 20th centuries. International debt became a global problem as a result of the oil crisis of the 1970s.

debt crisis any situation in which an individual, company or country owes more to others than they can repay or service when required; more specifically, the term refers to the massive indebtedness of many developing countries which became acute in the 1980s, threatening the stability of the international banking system as many debtor countries became unable to service their debts.

debugging finding and removing errors (called ◊bugs) from a computer program or system. The behaviour of a particular program can be investigated using a software device called a debugging tool, which allows examination and if necessary modification of the program at predetermined breakpoints.

death-watch

Debussy (Achille-) Claude 1862–1918. French composer, who won fame with *Prélude à l'après-midi d'un faune* 1894. His opera *Pelléas et Mélisande* was first performed 1902. He wrote orchestral music and numerous piano pieces, chamber music, ballets, and songs. His style reflects impressionist paintings and poetry in orchestral colour (for example the three seascapes of *La Mer*). Debussy is often considered the first of the modern composers because of his rejection of classical diatonic harmony.

de Castella Robert 1957- . Australian marathon runner. He set a world record of 2 hrs 8 mins 18 secs in the 1981 Japanese marathon and is the only person to have won the Commonwealth Games marathon title twice, in 1982 and 1986. He was voted Australian of the Year in 1983.

decathlon a two-day athletic competition for men consisting of ten events. The ten events are: 100 metres, long jump, shot put, high jump, 400 metres (day one); 110 metres hurdles, discus, pole vault, javelin, 1500 metres (day two). Points are awarded for performances and the winner is the athlete with the greatest aggregate score. The decathlon is an Olympic event.

decay, radioactive the process of continuous disintegration undergone by the nuclei of radioactive elements, such as radium and various isotopes of uranium and the transuranic elements. The associated radiation consists of alpha-rays, beta-rays, or gamma-rays (or a combination of these), and it takes place with a characteristic half-life, which is the time taken for half of any mass of a radioactive isotope to decay completely.

decibel a unit (dB), used originally to compare sound densities, and subsequently electrical or electronic power outputs; now also used to compare voltages. An increase of 10 decibels is equivalent to a 10-fold increase in intensity or power, and a 20-fold increase in voltage.

deciduous describing trees and shrubs that shed their leaves before the onset of winter or a dry season (see ◊abscission). In temperate regions there is little water available during winter, and leaf-fall is an adaptation to reduce ◊transpiration. Examples of deciduous trees are oak and beech. Most deciduous trees belong to the ◊angiosperms, and the term 'deciduous tree' is sometimes used to mean 'angiosperm tree', despite the fact that many angiosperms are evergreen, especially in the tropics, and a few ◊gymnosperms (such as larches) are deciduous. The term ◊broad-leaved is now preferred to 'deciduous tree' for this reason.

decision table in computing, a method of describing a procedure for a program to follow, based on comparing possible decisions and their consequences. It is often used in systems design.

Decius Gaius Messius Quintus Traianus 201–251. Roman emperor from 249. He fought a number of campaigns against the ◊Goths, but was finally beaten and killed by them near Abritum. He ruthlessly persecuted the Christians.

Declaration of Independence historic US document stating the theory of government on which the USA was founded, based on the right 'to life, liberty, and the pursuit of happiness'. The statement was issued by the American Continental Congress on 4 Jul 1776, renouncing all allegiance to the British crown and ending the political connection with Britain.

Declaration of Rights in Britain, the statement issued by the Convention Parliament Feb 1689, laying down the conditions under which the crown was to be offered to ◊William III and Mary. Its

clauses were incorporated in the ◊Bill of Rights.

decomposer in biology, an organism that feeds on excreta, or dead plant and animal matter. Decomposers include dung-beetle larvae, earthworms, certain bacteria, and fungi. They play a vital role in ecological systems by freeing important chemical substances, such as nitrogen compounds, locked up in dead organisms or excreta.

decomposition the process whereby a chemical compound is reduced to its component substances. In biology, it is the destruction of dead organisms by chemical reduction or by ◊decomposers.

decompression sickness an illness brought about by a sudden and substantial change in atmospheric pressure. It is caused by a too rapid release of nitrogen which has been absorbed into the bloodstream under pressure. It causes breathing difficulties, joint and muscle pain, and cramp, and is experienced mostly by deep-sea divers who surface too quickly. It is known as 'the bends'.

Decorated in architecture, the second period of English Gothic, covering the latter part of the 13th century and the 14th century. Characteristics include ornate window tracery, the window being divided into lights by vertical bars called mullions; sharp spires ornamented with crockets and pinnacles; complex church vaulting and slender arcade piers. Exeter Cathedral is a notable example.

dedicated computer a computer built into another device for the purpose of controlling or supplying information to it. Their use has increased dramatically since the advent of the ◊microprocessor: washing machines, digital watches, cars, and video recorders all have their own processors.

Dee John 1527–1608. English alchemist and mathematician, who claimed to have transmuted metals into gold, although he died in poverty. He long enjoyed the favour of Elizabeth I, and was employed as a secret diplomatic agent.

deed a legal document which passes an interest in property or binds a person to perform or abstain from some action. Deeds are of two kinds: indentures and deeds poll. Indentures bind two or more parties in mutual obligations. A deed poll is made by one party only, such as where a person changes his or her name.

Deep-Sea Drilling Project a research project initiated by the USA 1968 to sample the rocks of the ocean ◊crust. The operation became international 1975, with Britain, France, Germany, Japan, and the USSR involved.

deep sea trench steep-sided valley of the seabed indicating the junction of two of the giant curved plates that make up the Earth's surface. See ◊ocean trench, ◊plate tectonics.

deer ruminant, even-toed, hoofed mammal belonging to the family Cervidae. The male typically has a pair of antlers, shed and regrown each year. Most species of deer are forest-dwellers, found throughout Europe, Asia, and N America, but absent from Australia and Africa south of the Sahara.

deerhound large rough-coated dog, formerly used for hunting and killing deer. Slim and long-legged, it is 75 cm/2.5 ft or more tall, usually with a bluish-grey coat.

de facto (Latin) in fact.

de Falla Manuel Spanish composer. See ◊Falla, Manuel de.

defamation in law, an attack on a person's reputation by ◊libel or ◊slander.

default in commerce, failure to meet an obligation, usually financial.

Defence, Ministry of British government department created 1964 from a temporary Ministry

Degas Woman at her Toilet *(c.* 1894) Tate Gallery, London.

de Gaulle French general and wartime leader Charles de Gaulle.

of Defence established after World War II together with the Admiralty, Air Ministry, and War Office. It is headed by the secretary of state for defence with undersecretaries for the Royal Navy, Army, and Royal Air Force. This centralization was influenced by the example of the US Department of ◊Defense.

Defender of the Faith one of the titles of the English sovereign, conferred on Henry VIII 1521 by Pope Leo X in recognition of the king's treatise against the Protestant Luther. It appears on British coins in the abbreviated form *F.D.* (Latin *Fidei Defensor*).

Defense, Department of US government department presided over by a secretary of defence with a seat in the president's cabinet; each of the three services has a civilian secretary, not of cabinet rank, at its head. It was established when the army, navy, and air force were unified by the National Security Act 1947.

defibrillation the use of electrical stimulation to restore a chaotic heart beat to a rhythmical pattern. In fibrillation, which may occur in most kinds of heart disease, the heart muscle quivers instead of beating; the heart is no longer working as a pump. Paddles are applied to the chest wall, and one or more electric shocks are delivered to normalize the beat.

deficit financing in economics, a planned excess of expenditure over income, dictated by government policy, creating a shortfall of public revenue which is met by borrowing. The decision to create a deficit is taken to stimulate an economy by increasing consumer purchasing, and at the same time create more jobs.

deflation in economics, a reduction in the level of economic activity, usually caused by an increase in interest rates and reduction in the money supply, increased taxation, or a decline in government expenditure.

Defoe Daniel 1660–1731. English novelist and journalist, who wrote *Robinson Crusoe* 1719, which was greatly influential in the development of the novel. An active pamphleteer and political critic, he was imprisoned 1702–1704 following publication of the ironic *The Shortest Way With Dissenters*. Other works include the novel *Moll Flanders* 1722, and narratives including *A Journal of the Plague Year* 1724.

deforestation the destruction of forest for timber and clearing for agriculture, without planting new trees to replace those lost (reafforestation). Deforestation causes fertile soil to be blown away

or washed into rivers, leading to soil ◊erosion, drought, and flooding.

Degas (Hilaire Germain) Edgar 1834–1917. French Impressionist painter and sculptor. He devoted himself to lively, informal studies of ballet, horse racing, and young women working, often using pastels. From the 1890s he turned increasingly to sculpture, modelling figures in wax in a fluent, naturalistic style.

de Gaulle Charles 1890–1970. French conservative politician and general. He organized the ◊Free French troops fighting the Nazis 1940–44, was head of the provisional French government 1944–46, and leader of his own Gaullist party. In 1958 the national assembly asked him to form a government during France's economic recovery, and to solve the crisis in Algeria. He was president 1959–69, having changed the constitution.

degaussing neutralization of the magnetic field of a body by encircling it with a conductor through which a current is maintained. Ships were degaussed in the World War II to avoid them detonating magnetic mines.

degree in mathematics, a unit of measurement of an angle, written as °. A circle is divided into 360°; a degree is subdivided into 60 minutes. *Temperature* is also measured in degrees, which are divided decimally. See also ◊Celsius and ◊circle.

de Havilland Geoffrey 1882–1965. British aircraft designer who designed the *Moth*, the *Mosquito* fighter-bomber of World War II, and the post-war *Comet* – the world's first jet-driven airliner to enter commercial service.

dehydration a process to preserve food. Moisture content is reduced to 10–20% in fresh produce, and this provides good protection against moulds. Bacteria are not inhibited by drying so the quality of raw materials is vital. A major benefit to food manufacturers is reduction of weight and volume of the food products, lowering distribution cost.

Deighton Len 1929– . British author of spy fiction, including *The Ipcress File* 1963, and the trilogy *Berlin Game, Mexico Set, London Match* 1983–85, featuring the spy Bernard Samson.

Dei gratia (Latin) by the grace of God.

Deimos one of the two moons of Mars. It is irregularly shaped, 15 × 12 × 11 km/9 × 7.5 × 7 mi, orbits at a height of 24,000 km/15,000 mi every 1.26 days, and is not as roughly-featured as ◊Phobos. It was discovered by US astronomer Asaph Hall 1877, and is thought to be an asteroid captured by Mars' gravity.

deindustrialization a decline in the share of manufacturing industries in a country's economy. It is typified by the closing down and non-replacement of industrial plants, and an increase in service industries.

deism belief in a supreme being; but the term usually refers to a movement of religious thought in Britain in the 17th–18th centuries, characterized by belief in the 'religion of nature' as opposed to the revealed religion of Christianity.

déjà vu (French 'already seen') the feeling that something being seen for the first time has in fact been seen before.

de jure (Latin) according to law.

Dekker Thomas *c.* 1572–*c.* 1632. English dramatist and pamphleteer, who wrote mainly in collaboration with others. His plays include *The Shoemaker's Holiday* 1600, and *The Witch of Edmonton* (with Ford and Rowley).

Delacroix Eugène 1798–1863. French Romantic painter. His prolific output includes religious and historical subjects and portraits of friends, among them the musicians Paganini and Chopin. Against French academic tradition, he evolved a highly coloured, fluid style, as in *The Death of Sardanapalus* 1827 (Louvre, Paris).

de la Mare Walter 1873–1956. English poet, best known for his verse for children, such as *Songs of Childhood* 1902, which appeared under the pseudonym Walter Ramal.

de la Roche Mazo 1885–1961. Canadian novelist, author of the 'Whiteoaks' family saga.

Delaunay Robert 1885–1941. French painter, a pioneer in abstract art. With his wife Sonia Delaunay-Terk (1885–1979) he invented *Orphism*, an early variation on Cubism, focusing on the effects of pure colour.

Delaware state of NE USA; nickname The First State or Diamond State
area 5,023 sq km/1,939 sq mi
capital Dover
physical divided into two physical areas, one hilly and wooded, and the other gently undulating.
towns Wilmington
population (1980) 594,300
products dairy, poultry and market garden produce; chemicals, motor vehicles, textiles
famous people J P Marquand.

de la Warr Thomas West, Baron de la Warr 1577–1618. US colonial administrator, known as Delaware. Appointed governor of Virginia 1609, he arrived 1610 just in time to prevent the desertion of the Jamestown colonists, and by 1611 had reorganized the settlement. Both the river and state are named after him.

Delcassé Théophile 1852–1923. French politician. He became foreign minister 1898, but had to resign 1905 because of German hostility; he held that post again 1914–15. To a large extent he was responsible for the ◊*Entente Cordiale* with Britain.

De Lesseps Ferdinand, Vicomte 1805–1894. French engineer, who constructed the ◊Suez Canal 1859–1869. He reluctantly began the ◊Panama Canal 1881, but failed when he tried to construct it without locks.

Delhi union territory of the Republic of India from 1956; capital Delhi; area 1,484 sq km/573 sq mi; population (1981) 6,196,400. It produces grains, sugar cane, fruits, and vegetables.

Delilah in the Old Testament or Jewish Bible, the Philistine mistress of ◊Samson.

delirium a state of confusion in which the subject is incoherent, frenzied, and out of touch with

Delphi Tholos in the Sanctuary of Athena ('Marmaria') in Delphi, Greece.

reality. It is often accompanied by delusions or hallucinations.

Delius Frederick (Theodore Albert) 1862–1934. British composer, whose works include choral works (*Appalachia, Sea Drift, A Mass of Life, A Song of the High Hills*); the opera *A Village Romeo and Juliet* 1906 and music for the play *Hassan* 1923; orchestral works such as *Brigg Fair* and *In a Summer Garden*; chamber music and songs.

Delors Jacques 1925– . French socialist politician, finance minister 1981–84. As president of the European Commission from 1984 he has overseen significant budgetary reform and the move towards a free European Community market in 1992, with increased powers residing in Brussels.

Delphi city of ancient Greece, situated in a rocky valley to the north of the gulf of Corinth, on the southern slopes of Mount Parnassus, site of a famous oracle. Here in the temple of Apollo was the *Omphalos* or conical stone supposed to stand at the centre of the earth; the oracle was interpreted by priests from the inspired utterances of the Pythian priestess until it was closed down by Emperor ◊Theodosius in 390 AD.

delphinium plant belonging to the Ranunculaceae family. There are some 250 species including the **great flowered larkspur** *Delphinium grandiflorum*, an Asian form and one of the ancestors of the garden delphinium. Most species have blue, purple, or white flowers in a long spike.

del Sarto Andrea 1486–1531. See ◊Andrea del Sarto, Italian Renaissance painter.

delta a triangular tract of land at a river's mouth, formed by deposited silt or sediment. Familiar

delta

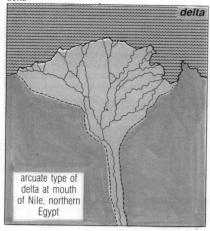

arcuate type of delta at mouth of Nile, northern Egypt

Demosthenes Athenian orator and politician.

examples of large deltas are those of the Mississippi, Ganges and Brahmaputra, Rhône, Po, Danube, and Nile; the shape of the Nile delta is like the Greek letter GD, and thus gave rise to the name.

Delta Force US anti-guerrilla force, based at Fort Bragg, N Carolina, and modelled on the British ◊Special Air Service.

delta wing an aircraft wing shaped like the Greek letter GD. It is a design that enables an aircraft to pass through the ◊sound barrier with little effect. The supersonic airliner Concorde and the Space Shuttle have delta wings.

demand in economics, the quantity of a product or service which customers want to buy at any given price.

dementia mental deterioration as a result of physical changes in the brain. It may be due to degenerative change, circulatory disease, infection, injury, or chronic poisoning.

demesne in the Middle Ages, land kept in the lord's possession, not leased out, but worked by ◊villeins to supply the lord's household.

Demeter in Greek mythology, goddess of agriculture (identified with Roman ◊Ceres), daughter of Kronos and Rhea, and by Zeus mother of Persephone. She is identified with the Egyptian goddess Isis and had a temple dedicated to her at Eleusis where ◊mystery religions were celebrated.

Demetrius Donskoi ('of the Don') 1350–1389. Grand Prince of Moscow from 1363. He achieved the first Russian victory over the Tatars on the plain of Kulikovo, next to the Don (hence his nickname) 1380.

de Mille Cecil B(lount) 1881–1959. US film director. He entered films with Jesse L Lasky 1913 (with whom he later established Paramount), and was one of the founders of Hollywood. He specialized in biblical epics, such as *The Sign of the Cross* 1932 and *The Ten Commandments* 1956.

democracy government by the people, usually through elected representatives. In the modern world democracy has developed from the American and French revolutions. The Western concept of democracy differs from that in communist countries: the former emphasizes the control of the government by the electorate, and freedom of speech and the press; in the latter both political and economic power rest in the Communist Party.

Democratic Party one of the two main political parties of the USA. It tends to be the party of the

working person, as opposed to the Republicans, the party of big business, but the divisions between the two are not clear-cut. Its stronghold has traditionally been the Southern states. In the 1960s the Northern Democrats ('Presidential wing') pressed for civil-rights reform, while Southern Democrats ('Congressional wing') voted against the president on social issues.

Democrats common name for the ◊Social and Liberal Democrats.

demodulation in radio, the technique of separating a transmitted audio frequency signal from its modulated radio carrier wave. At the transmitter the audio frequency signal (representing speech or music, for example) may be made to modulate the amplitude (AM broadcasting) or frequency (FM broadcasting) of a continuously transmitted radiofrequency carrier wave. At the receiver, the signal from the aerial is demodulated to extract the required speech or sound component. In early radio systems, this process was called detection.

demography the study of the size, structure, and development of human populations to establish reliable statistics on such factors as birth and death rates, marriages and divorces, life expectancy, and migration.

demonstration public show of support for, or opposition to, a particular political or social issue, typically by a group of people holding a rally, displaying placards, and making speeches. They usually seek some change in official policy by drawing attention to their cause. Demonstrations can be static or take the form of elementary street theatre or processions. A specialized type of demonstration is the *picket*, in which striking or dismissed workers try to dissuade others from using or working in the premises of the employer.

Demosthenes *c.* 384–322 BC. Athenian orator and politician. From 351 BC he led the party which advocated resistance to the growing power of ◊Philip of Macedon, and in his 'Philippics' incited the Athenians to war. This policy resulted in the defeat of Chaeronea 338, and the establishment of Macedonian supremacy. After the death of Alexander he organized a revolt, and when it failed took poison to avoid capture by the Macedonians.

Demotic Greek the common or vernacular variety of the modern ◊Greek language.

demotic script a form of cursive (joined) writing derived from Egyptian hieratic script, itself a cursive form of ◊hieroglyphic. Demotic documents are known from the 6th century BC to about 470 AD. It was written horizontally, from right to left.

Denbighshire former county of Wales, largely merged in 1974, together with Flint and part of Merioneth, in Clwyd; a small area along the W border was included in Gwynedd. Denbigh, in the Clwyd valley (population (1981) 9,000) was the county town.

Dench Judi 1934– . British actress, who made her debut as Ophelia in *Hamlet* 1957 with the Old Vic Company. Her many roles include Portia in *Twelfth Night, The Duchess of Malfi*, Lady Macbeth, and Cleopatra. She is also a versatile comedy actress, and has appeared in films, for example *A Room with a View*, and on television.

dendrochronology the analysis of the annual rings of trees to date past events. Samples of wood can be obtained by means of a narrow metal tube that is driven into a tree to remove a core extending from the bark to the centre. Samples taken from timbers at an archaeological site can be compared with cores from old, living trees, and the year when they were

Denmark
Kingdom of
(*Kongeriget Danmark*)

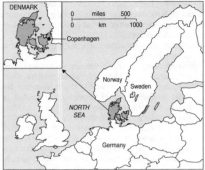

area 43,075 sq km/16,627 sq mi
capital Copenhagen
towns Aarhus, Odense, Aalborg, Esbjerg (ports)
physical flat land, comprises the Jutland peninsula
and about 500 islands (100 inhabited).
territories Faeroe Islands and Greenland
head of state Queen Margrethe II from 1972
head of government Poul Nyrup Rasmussen from 1993

political system liberal democracy
exports bacon, dairy produce, eggs, fish, mink
pelts, car and aircraft parts, electrical equipment,
textiles, chemicals
currency kroner
population (1990 est) 5,134,000; growth rate 0% pa
life expectancy men 72, women 78
language Danish (official)
religion Lutheran 97%
literacy 99% (1983)
GDP $85.5 bn (1987); $16,673 per head
chronology
1940–45 Occupied by Germany.
1945 Iceland's independence recognized.
1947 Frederik IX succeeded Christian X.
1948 Home rule granted for Faeroe Islands.
1960 Joined European Free Trade Association (EFTA).
1972 Margrethe II became Denmark's first queen in
nearly 600 years.
1973 Left EFTA and joined European Community.
1979 Home rule granted for Greenland.
1985 Strong non-nuclear movement in evidence.
1990 General election; another coalition
government formed.
1992 Rejection of Maastricht Treaty in national
referendum.
1993 Poul Nyrup Rasmussen led new coalition
government. Second referendum accepted
Maastricht Treaty.

felled can be determined by locating the point where
the rings of the two samples correspond.

Dene North American Indian people of the Northwest Territories, Canada.

Deng Xiaoping (formerly *Teng Hsiao-ping*)
1904– . Chinese political leader. A member of the
Chinese Communist Party (CCP) from the 1920s,
he took part in the Long March 1934–36. He was in
the Politburo from 1955 until ousted in the Cultural
Revolution 1966–69 Reinstated in the 1970s, he
gradually took power and introduced a radical economic modernization programme. He resigned
1990, but remained influential behind the scenes.

Den Haag Dutch form of The ◊Hague.

denier system of measuring fine yarns, both natural and synthetic, derived from the old French silk
industry. The denier was an old French silver coin.
Thus 9,000 metres of 15 denier nylon, commonly
used in nylon stockings, weighs 15 g/0.5 oz, and in
this case the thickness of thread would be 0.00425
mm/0.0017 in.

De Niro Robert 1943– . US actor. He won Oscars
for *The Godfather Part II* 1974 and *Raging Bull*
1979. Other films include *Taxi Driver* 1976, *The
Deer Hunter* 1978, and *The Untouchables* 1987.

Denmark peninsula and islands in N Europe,
bounded to the north by the Skagerrak, to the east
by the Kattegat, to the south by Germany, and to
the west by the North Sea.

Denning Alfred Thompson, Baron Denning of
Whitchurch 1899– . British judge, Master of the
Rolls 1962–82. In 1963 he conducted the inquiry
into the ◊Profumo scandal. A vigorous and highly
innovative civil lawyer, he was controversial in his
defence of the rights of the individual against the
state, the unions, and big business.

density measure of the compactness of a substance; the mass per unit volume, measured in kg per
cubic metre/lb per cubic foot. *Relative density* is
the ratio of the density of a substance to that of water
at 4°C.

dentistry the care and treatment of the teeth and
their supporting tissues.

denudation general term for the natural loss of
soil and rock debris, blown away by wind or washed
away by running water, that lays bare the rock
below. Over millions of years, denudation causes a
general levelling of the landscape.

Denver city of Colorado, USA, on the South Platte
river, near the foothills of the Rocky Mountains;
population (1990) 467,600, Denver-Boulder metropolitan area 1,848,300. It is a processing and distribution centre for a large agricultural area, and for
natural resources (minerals, oil, gas). It was the
centre of a gold and silver boom in the 1870s and
1880s, and for oil in the 1970s.

Deo gratias (Latin) 'thanks to God'.

deontology an ethical theory which argues that
the rightness of an action consists in its conformity
to duty, regardless of the consequences which may
result from it. Deontological ethics is thus opposed
to any form of utilitarianism.

deoxyribonucleic acid the full name of ◊DNA.

deposit account in banking, an account where
money is left to attract interest, sometimes for a fixed
term. Unlike a current account, the depositor does not
have constant access through a chequebook.

depreciation in economics, decline of a currency's value in relation to other currencies. Depreciation also describes the fall in value of an asset
(such as factory machinery) resulting from age, wear,
or other factors. It is an important factor in
assessing company profit.

depression an emotional state characterized by
sadness, unhappy thoughts, apathy, and dejection.
Sadness is a normal response to major losses such
as bereavement, and unemployment. However,
clinical depression, which is prolonged or unduly
severe, often requires treatment, such as antidepressant medication, cognitive therapy or, in very
rare cases, electro-convulsive therapy (ECT), in which
an electrical current is passed through the brain.

Depression in economics, a period of low output and investment, with high unemployment. Specifically, the term describes two periods of crisis in the world economies 1873–96 and 1929–mid 1930s.

de profundis (Latin 'from the depths') a cry from the depths of misery. From Psalm 130 *De profundis clamavi ad te* 'Out of the depths have I cried to thee'.

de Quincey Thomas 1785–1859. English author, a friend of ◊Wordsworth and ◊Coleridge, whose works include *Confessions of an English Opium-Eater* 1821, and the essays *On The Knocking at the Gate in Macbeth* 1823, and *Murder Considered as One of the Fine Arts* 1827.

Derain André 1880–1954. French painter, who experimented with strong, almost primary colours and exhibited with the Fauves, but later developed a more sombre landscape style. His work includes costumes and scenery for Diaghilev's *Ballets Russes*.

Derby industrial city in Derbyshire, England; population (1981) 216,000. Rail locomotives, Rolls-Royce cars and aero-engines, chemicals, paper, electrical, mining and engineering equipment are manufactured here.

Derby the ◊Blue Riband of the English horse racing season. It is run over 2.4 km/1.5 mi at Epsom every June. Established 1780 and named after 12th Earl of Derby. Most countries that stage racing have a Derby; in the US it is the *Kentucky Derby*.

Derby Edward Geoffrey Smith Stanley, 14th Earl of Derby 1799–1869. British politician. Originally a Whig, he became secretary for the colonies 1830, and introduced the bill for the abolition of slavery. He joined the Tories 1834, and the split in the Tory Party over Robert Peel's free-trade policy gave Derby the leadership for 20 years. He was prime minister 1852, 1858–59, and 1866–68, with the future prime minister Disraeli as his lieutenant in the Commons.

Derbyshire county in N central England
area 2,631 sq km/1,016 sq mi
towns administrative headquarters Matlock; Derby, Chesterfield, Ilkeston
products cereals; dairy and sheep farming. There have been pit and factory closures, but the area is being redeveloped, and there are large reserves of fluorspar.
population (1986) 911,700.

deregulation action to abolish or reduce state controls and supervision over private economic activities, as with the deregulation of the US airline industry 1978. Its purpose is to improve competitiveness. In Britain the major changes in the City of London 1986 (the ◊Big Bang) were in part deregulation.

de rigueur (French 'of strictness') demanded by the rules of etiquette.

dermatitis inflammation of the skin, usually related to allergy.

derrick a simple lifting machine, consisting of a pole carrying a block and tackle. Derricks are commonly to be seen on ships such as freighters. In the oil industry the tower used for hoisting the drill pipes is known as a derrick.

derris climbing plant of SE Asia *Derris elliptica*, family Leguminosae. Its roots contain rotenone, a strong insecticide.

Derry another name for ◊Londonderry.

dervish in Iran and Turkey, a religious mendicant, and throughout the rest of Islam a member of an

Islamic religious brotherhood, not necessarily mendicant in character. The Arabic equivalent is *fakir*. There are various orders of dervishes, each with its rule and special ritual. The 'whirling dervishes' claim close communion with the deity through ecstatic dancing; the 'howling dervishes' gash themselves with knives to demonstrate the miraculous feats possible to those who trust in Allah.

Desai Morarji 1896– . Indian politician. An early follower of Mahatma Gandhi, he was prime minister, as leader of the ◊Janata Party 1977–79, after toppling Indira Gandhi. Party infighting led to his resignation of both the premiership and party leadership.

desalination the removal of salt, especially from sea water, to produce fresh water for irrigation. Distillation has usually been the method adopted, but in the 1970s, a cheaper process, using certain polymer materials which filter the molecules of salt from the water by reverse osmosis, was developed.

Descartes René 1596–1650. French mathematician and philosopher. He believed that commonly accepted knowledge was doubtful because of the subjective nature of the senses, and attempted to rebuild human knowledge using as foundation *'cogito ergo sum'* ('I think, therefore I am'). He also believed that the entire material universe could be explained in terms of mathematical physics. He is regarded as the discoverer of analytical geometry and the founder of the science of optics. He was also influential in shaping contemporary theories of astronomy and animal behaviour.

deselection in Britain, removal or withholding of a sitting Member of Parliament's official status as a candidate for a forthcoming election. The term came into use in the 1980s with the efforts of many local Labour parties to revoke the candidature of MPs viewed as too right-wing.

desert area without sufficient vegetation to support human life. Scientifically this term includes

Descartes *An engraving of French philosopher and mathematician René Descartes from a portrait by Frans Hals.*

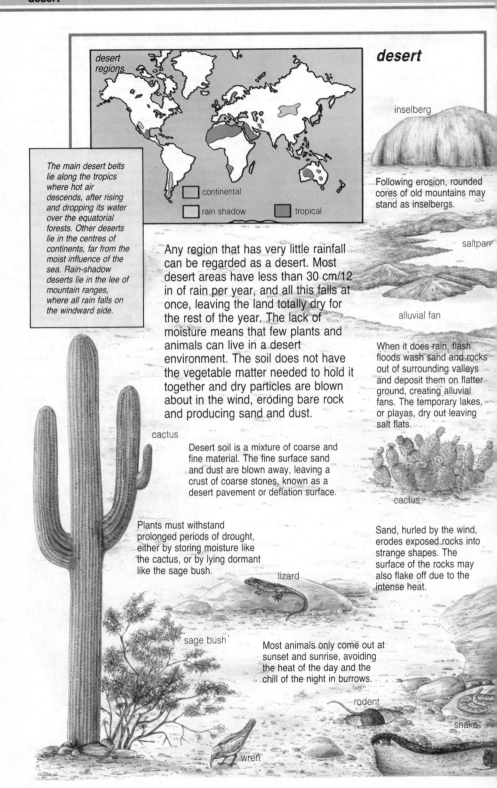

desert

desert regions

continental

rain shadow

tropical

The main desert belts lie along the tropics where hot air descends, after rising and dropping its water over the equatorial forests. Other deserts lie in the centres of continents, far from the moist influence of the sea. Rain-shadow deserts lie in the lee of mountain ranges, where all rain falls on the windward side.

Any region that has very little rainfall can be regarded as a desert. Most desert areas have less than 30 cm/12 in of rain per year, and all this falls at once, leaving the land totally dry for the rest of the year. The lack of moisture means that few plants and animals can live in a desert environment. The soil does not have the vegetable matter needed to hold it together and dry particles are blown about in the wind, eroding bare rock and producing sand and dust.

cactus

Desert soil is a mixture of coarse and fine material. The fine surface sand and dust are blown away, leaving a crust of coarse stones, known as a desert pavement or deflation surface.

Plants must withstand prolonged periods of drought, either by storing moisture like the cactus, or by lying dormant like the sage bush.

lizard

sage bush

Most animals only come out at sunset and sunrise, avoiding the heat of the day and the chill of the night in burrows.

rodent

wren

snake

inselberg

Following erosion, rounded cores of old mountains may stand as inselbergs.

saltpan

alluvial fan

When it does rain, flash floods wash sand and rocks out of surrounding valleys and deposit them on flatter ground, creating alluvial fans. The temporary lakes, or playas, dry out leaving salt flats.

cactus

Sand, hurled by the wind, erodes exposed rocks into strange shapes. The surface of the rocks may also flake off due to the intense heat.

the ice areas of the polar regions. Almost 33% of Earth's land surface is desert, and this proportion is increasing.

desertification the creation of deserts by changes in climate, or by human-aided processes, such as overgrazing, destruction of timber shelter belts, and the overpopulation which leads to exhaustion of the soil by too intensive cultivation without restoration of fertility. The process can be reversed by special planting (marram grass, trees) and by the use of water-absorbent plastic grains with the sand, a polymer absorbent of 40 times its own weight of water, which enables crops to be grown. About 135,000,000 people are affected, mainly in Africa, the Indian subcontinent, and South America.

Desert Rats nickname of the British 8th Army, in N Africa in World War II, originating in a military shoulder flash of a jerboa (N African rodent, capable of great leaps). In 1990 the Desert Rats were sent out to Saudi Arabia to oppose Iraq's occupation of Kuwait.

de Sica Vittorio 1902–1974. Italian director and actor. He achieved international fame with *Bicycle Thieves* 1948, a film of subtle realism. Later films included *Umberto D* 1952, *Two Women* 1960, and *The Garden of the Finzi-Continis* 1971.

Desmoulins Camille 1760–1794. French revolutionary, who summoned the mob to arms on 12 Jul 1789, so precipitating the revolt that culminated in the storming of the Bastille. A prominent ◊Jacobin, he was elected to the National Convention 1792. His *Histoire des Brissotins* was largely responsible for the overthrow of the ◊Girondins, but shortly after he was sent to the guillotine as too moderate.

de Soto Hernando *c.* 1496–1542. Spanish explorer. In his expedition of 1539, he explored Florida, Georgia, and the Mississippi River.

Desprez Josquin *c.* 1440–1521. Franco-Flemish composer. See ◊Josquin Desprez.

Dessalines Jean Jacques 1758–1806. Emperor of Haiti 1804–1806. Born in Guinea, he was taken to Haiti as a slave, where he succeeded ◊Toussaint L'Ouverture as leader of a revolt against the French, and made himself emperor. He was killed while suppressing a revolt provoked by his cruelty.

destroyer small, fast warship, originally introduced as a 'torpedo-boat destroyer'. In World War I they were developed for anti-submarine work, serving in this capacity with convoys in World War II. Modern guided-missile destroyers weigh 3,700–5,650 tonnes.

detective fiction novels or short stories in which a mystery is solved mainly by the action of a professional or amateur detective. Where the mystery to be solved concerns the commission of a crime, the work is called **crime fiction**. The earliest work of detective fiction as understood today was *Murders in the Rue Morgue* 1841 by Edgar Allen Poe, and his detective Dupin became the model for those who detected by deduction from a series of clues. The most popular deductive sleuth was Sherlock Holmes in the stories by Sir Arthur Conan Doyle.

détente (French) an easing of political tension between nations.

detergent a surface-active cleansing agent. The common detergents are made from fats (hydrocarbons) and sulphuric acid, and their long-chain molecules have a type of structure similar to that of soap molecules: a salt group at one end attached to a long hydrocarbon 'tail'. They have the advantage over soap in that they do not produce scum by forming insoluble salts with the calcium and magnesium ions present in hard water.

determinant in mathematics, an array of element written as a square, and denoted by two vertical lines enclosing the array. For a 2 × 2 matrix,

$$\begin{vmatrix} p & q \\ r & s \end{vmatrix}$$

the determinant is equal to $ps - qr$ (the difference between the products of the diagonal terms). Determinants are used to solve sets of ◊simultaneous equations by matrix methods.

determinism in philosophy, the view that denies human freedom of action. Because everything is strictly governed by the principle of cause and effect, human action is no exception. It is the opposite of free will, and rules out moral choice and responsibility.

deterrence the underlying conception of the nuclear arms race: the belief that a potential aggressor will be deterred from launching a 'first strike' nuclear attack by the knowledge that the adversary is capable of striking back. This doctrine is widely known as that of mutual assured destruction (MAD). Three essential characteristics of deterrence are: the 'capability to act', 'credibility', and the 'will to act'.

de Tocqueville Alexis 1805–1859. French politician, see ◊Tocqueville, Alexis de.

detonator also called blasting cap, a small explosive charge used to trigger off a main charge of high explosive. The relatively unstable compounds mercury fulminate and lead acid are often used in detonators, being set off by a lighted fuse, or more commonly by an electric current.

detritus in biology, the organic debris produced during the ◊decomposition of animals and plants.

Detroit city of Michigan, USA, situated on Detroit river; population (1980) 1,203,339, metropolitan area 4,353,000. It is an industrial centre with the headquarters of Ford, Chrysler, and General Motors, hence its nickname, Motown from 'motor town'.

de trop (French 'of too much') not wanted, in the way.

Dettingen, Battle of battle in the Bavarian village of that name where on 27 Jun 1743, in the War of the Austrian Succession, an army of British, Hanoverians, and Austrians under George II defeated the French under Adrien-Maurice, duc de Noailles (1678–1766).

deus ex machina (Latin 'a god from a machine') a far-fetched or unlikely event which resolves an intractable difficulty. The phrase was originally used in drama to mean a 'god' descending from heaven to resolve the plot.

deuterium a heavy isotope of hydrogen, mass number 2 (one proton and one neutron), discovered by ◊Urey 1932. Combined with oxygen, it produces 'heavy water', used in the nuclear industry.

deuteron the ion of deuterium ('heavy hydrogen'). It consists of one proton and one neutron, and thus has a positive charge.

Deuteronomy book of the Old Testament; 5th book of the ◊Torah. It contains various laws, including the ten commandments, and gives an account of the death of Moses.

de Valera Éamon 1882–1975. Irish politician, repeatedly imprisoned; he participated in the Easter Rising 1916 and was leader of ◊Sinn Féin 1917–26, when he formed the ◊Fianna Fáil party; he directed negotiations with Britain 1921 but refused to accept the partition of Ireland until 1937. He was prime minister of the Irish Free State/Eire/ Republic of Ireland 1932–48, 1951–54, and 1957–59, and president 1959–73.

de Valera *Eamon de Valera, Irish politician.*

de Valois Ninette 1898– . Irish dancer, choreographer and teacher, founder of the Vic-Wells Ballet 1931, which later became the Royal Ballet and Royal Ballet School. Among her works are *Job* 1931 and *Checkmate* 1937.

devaluation lowering of the official value of a currency against other currencies, so that exports become cheaper and imports dearer. Used when a country is badly in deficit in its balance of trade, it results in the goods the country produces being cheaper abroad, so that the economy is stimulated by increased foreign demand.

developing in photography, the process which produces a visible image on exposed photographic film. When film is exposed, invisible changes take place in the silver salts of the emulsion, which holds a latent or invisible image. Developing involves treating the emulsion with chemical developer, a reducing agent (such as hydroquinone) that changes the light-altered salts into dark metallic silver. The developed image is a negative – darkest where the strongest light hit the emulsion, lightest where the least light hit it.

development in the social sciences, the acquisition by a society of industrial techniques and technology; hence the common classification of the 'developed' nations of the First World and the poorer, 'developing' or 'underdeveloped' nations of the Third World. The assumption that development in the sense of industrialization was inherently good has been increasingly questioned since the 1960s.

developmental psychology the study of development of cognition and behaviour from birth to adulthood.

deviance abnormal behaviour; that is, behaviour that deviates from the norms or laws of a particular society or group, and so invokes social sanctions, controls, or stigma. The term may refer to minor abnormalities (such as nail-biting) as well as to criminal acts.

devil in Christian, Jewish, and Muslim theology, the supreme spirit of evil (*Beelzebub, Lucifer, Iblis*), or an evil spirit generally. The devil or Satan is mentioned only in the later books of the Old Testament, but the later Jewish doctrine is that found in the New Testament. In the Middle Ages the devil in popular superstition assumed the attributes of the horned fertility gods of paganism, and was regarded as the god of witches. In Muslim theology, Iblis is one of the *jinn*, beings created by Allah from fire, who refused to prostrate himself before Adam, and who tempted Adam and his wife Hawwa (Eve) to disobey Allah, an act which led to their expulsion from Paradise. He continues to try to lead people astray, but at the Last Judgment he and his hosts will be consigned to hell.

devil ray a large ray of the genera *Manta* and *Mobula*, in which two 'horns' project forward from the sides of the huge mouth. These flaps of skin guide the plankton on which the fish feeds into the mouth. The largest of these rays can be 7 m/23 ft across, and weigh 1000 kg/2,200 lb. They live in warm seas.

devil's coach horse large, black, long-bodied, omnivorous beetle *Ocypus olens*, about 3 cm/1.2 in long. It has powerful jaws and is capable of giving a painful bite. It emits an unpleasant smell when threatened.

Devil's Island smallest (Ile du Diable) of the Iles du Salut, off French Guiana, 43 km/27 mi NW of Cayenne. The group of islands was collectively and popularly known by the name Devil's Island, and formed a penal colony notorious for its terrible conditions.

devolution the delegation of authority and duties, especially in the later 20th century the movement to decentralize governmental power, as in the UK where a bill for the setting-up of Scottish and Welsh assemblies was introduced 1976 (rejected by a referendum in Scotland 1979).

Devolution, War of war waged 1667–68 by Louis XIV of France to gain Spanish territory in the Netherlands, of which ownership had allegedly 'devolved' on his wife Maria Theresa.

Devon or *Devonshire* county in SW England
area 6,711 sq km/2,590 sq mi
towns administrative headquarters Exeter; Plymouth, and the resorts Paignton, Torquay, Teignmouth, and Ilfracombe
products mainly agricultural, with sheep and dairy farming; cider and clotted cream; kaolin in the south; Honiton lace; Dartington glass
population (1986) 988,400
famous people Sir Francis Drake, Sir John Hawkins, Charles Kingsley, Robert F Scott.

Devonian the period of geological time 400–360 million years ago, the fourth period of the ◊Palaeozoic era. Many desert sandstones from N America and Europe date from this time. The first land plants flourished in the Devonian period, corals were abundant in the seas, and land invertebrates were present.

Devonshire Spencer Compton Cavendish, 8th Duke of Devonshire 1833–1908. British Liberal politician, known as Lord Hartington 1858–91, and leader of the Liberal Party 1874–80. He broke with Gladstone over Irish Home Rule 1885, and was president of the council 1895–1903 under Salisbury and Balfour. As a free-trader, he resigned from Balfour's cabinet.

dew precipitation in the form of moisture that collects on the ground, formed after the temperature of the ground has fallen below the ◊dew point of the air in contact with the ground. As the temperature falls during the night, the air and its water vapour become chilled, and condensation takes place on the cooled surfaces.

Dewey Melvil 1851–1931. US librarian. In 1876, he devised the *Dewey decimal system* of classification for books, now widely used in libraries.

dew point the temperature at which the water vapour in the air is saturated. At temperatures below the dew point, water vapour condenses out of the air as droplets, which if small form a suspension as mist or fog, or if larger become deposited on objects on or near the ground as ◊dew.

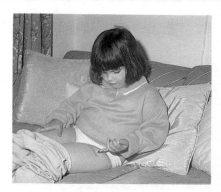

diabetes Diabetic child injecting herself with insulin.

Dhaka (formerly Dacca) capital of Bangladesh from 1971, in Dhaka region, W of the river Meghna; population (1984) 3,600,000. It trades in jute, oilseed, sugar, and tea, and produces textiles, chemicals, glass, and metal products.

dharma in Hinduism, consciousness of forming part of an ordered universe, and hence the moral duty of accepting one's station in life. In Buddhism, dharma is anything that increases generosity and wisdom, and so leads towards enlightenment.

dhole species of wild dog *Cuon alpinus* found in Asia from Siberia to Java. With head and body up to 1 m/3 ft long, variable in colour but often reddish above and lighter below, the dhole lives in groups from 3 up to 30 individuals.

DHSS abbreviation for *Department of Health and Social Security*, UK government department until divided 1988; see ◊social security.

diabetes a disease (*diabetes mellitus*) in which a deficiency in the islets of the pancreas prevents the body producing the hormone ◊insulin, so that it cannot use sugars properly.

Diaghilev Sergei Pavlovich 1872–1929. Russian ballet impresario, who in 1909 founded the *Ballets Russes* (headquarters Monte Carlo), which he directed for 20 years. Through the company he brought Russian ballet to the West, introducing and encouraging a dazzling array of dancers, choreographers and composers, such as Pavlova, Nijinsky, Fokine, Massine, Balanchine, Stravinsky, and Prokofiev.

dialect a variety of a language, either as spoken in a particular area ('Yorkshire dialect'), by a particular social group ('the dialect of educated Standard English'), or both ('the black American dialects of English').

dialectic a Greek term, originally associated with Socrates' method of argument through dialogue and conversation. *Hegelian dialectic* refers to an interpretive method in which the contradiction between a thesis and its antithesis is resolved through synthesis.

dialectical materialism the political, philosophical, and economic theory of Marx and Engels, also known as ◊Marxism.

dialysis a way of separating ◊colloidal particles from other non-colloidal ones in solution using a semi-permeable membrane (which allows the passage of the smaller non-colloidal particles but not the larger colloidal ones). Dialysis can thus separate, for example, salts from proteins in blood, which is the natural process in the filtration system of the kidneys, and the engineered equivalent in a dialysis (artificial kidney) machine.

diamond a colourless, transparent mineral, the crystalline form of carbon. It is regarded as a precious gemstone, the hardest natural substance known (10 on the ◊Mohs scale). Industrial diamonds are used for cutting (for example, the tungsten-carbide tools used in steel mills are cut with diamond tools), grinding, and polishing.

Diana in Roman mythology, goddess of hunting and the moon (Greek ◊Artemis), daughter of Jupiter and twin of Apollo.

Diana Princess of Wales 1961– . The daughter of the 8th Earl Spencer, she married Prince Charles at St Paul's Cathedral 1981, the first English bride of a royal heir since 1659. She is descended from the only sovereigns from whom Prince Charles is not descended, Charles II and James II. The couple have two sons, William (1982–) and Henry (1984–). Diana and Charles separated 1992.

DIANE the collection of information suppliers or 'hosts' for the European computer network, *D*irect *I*nformation *A*ccess *N*etwork for *E*urope.

dianetics a form of psychotherapy developed by L Ron Hubbard (1911–1986) in the USA, which formed the basis for ◊scientology. Hubbard believed that all mental illness and certain forms of physical illness are caused by 'engrams', or incompletely assimilated traumatic experiences, both pre- and post-natal.

diapause a period of suspended development that occurs in some species of insects, characterized by greatly reduced metabolism. Periods of diapause are often timed to coincide with the winter months, and improve the insect's chances of surviving adverse conditions.

diarrhoea excessive action of the bowels so that the motions are fluid or semi-fluid. It is caused by intestinal irritants (including some drugs and poisons), infection with harmful organisms (as in ◊dysentery or ◊cholera), or allergy.

diary an informal record of day-to-day events, observations, or reflections, usually not intended for a general readership. One of the earliest diaries extant is that of a Japanese noblewoman, the *Kagerō Nikki* 954–974, and the earliest diary extant in English is that of Edward VI (ruled 1547–53). Notable diaries include those of Samuel Pepys, the Quaker George Fox, Anne Frank, the novelist André Gide, and Katherine Mansfield.

Diaspora the dispersal of the Jews, initially from Palestine at the time of the Babylonian captivity 586 BC, but later meaning all the Jews living outside Israel.

diathermy the generation of heat in body tissues by the passage of high-frequency electric currents

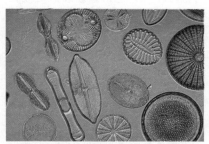

diatom Diatoms from a fundamental part of the food chain of both marine and freshwater environments. (×100)

Dickens *English novelist and writer Charles Dickens.*

Dietrich *Marlene Dietrich in* The Blue Angel *1930.*

between two electrodes placed on the body, used to relieve arthritic pain.

diatom microscopic alga of the division Bacillariophyta found in all parts of the world. They consist of single cells, sometimes grouped in colonies.

diatonic in music, a scale consisting of the seven notes of any major or minor key.

Díaz Bartolomeu *c.* 1450–1500. Portuguese explorer, the first European to reach the Cape of Good Hope 1488, and to establish a route around Africa.

Díaz Porfirio 1830–1915. Dictator of Mexico 1877–80 and 1884–1911. He lost the 1876 election, revolted, and seized power. He was supported by conservative landowners and foreign capitalists, who invested especially in railways and mines. He centralized the state at the expense of the peasants and Indians, and dismantled all local and regional leadership. He faced mounting opposition in his final years and was forced into exile 1911.

Dick Philip K(endred) 1928–1982. US science-fiction writer, whose works often deal with religion and the subjectivity of reality; his novels include *The Man in the High Castle* 1962 and *Do Androids Dream of Electric Sheep?* 1968.

Dickens Charles 1812–1870. English novelist, popular for his memorable characters and his portrayals of the social evils of Victorian England. In 1836 he published the first number of the *Pickwick Papers*, which established his position as a writer. This was followed by *Oliver Twist* 1838, the first of his 'reforming' novels; *Nicholas Nickleby* 1839; *Barnaby Rudge* 1840, *The Old Curiosity Shop* 1841, and *David Copperfield* 1849. Among his later books are *A Tale of Two Cities* 1859 and *Great Expectations* 1861.

Dickinson Emily 1830–1886. US poet. Born in Amherst, Massachusetts, she lived in near seclusion there from 1862. Almost none of her many short, mystical poems were published during her lifetime. Her concentrated work has only become well known in the 20th century.

dicotyledon a sub-class of the ◊angiosperms, containing the great majority of flowering plants. Dicotyledons are characterized by the presence of two seed-leaves or ◊cotyledons in the embryo, which is usually surrounded by an ◊endosperm.

They generally have broad leaves with net-like veins. Dicotyledons may be small plants such as daisies and buttercups, shrubs, or trees such as oak and beech. The other sub-class of the angiosperms is the ◊monocotyledons.

dictator an absolute ruler, overriding the constitution. (In ancient Rome a dictator was a magistrate invested with emergency powers for six months.) Although dictatorships were common in Latin America during the 19th century, the only European example during this period was the rule of Napoleon III. The crises following World War I produced many dictatorships, including the régimes of Atatürk and Pilł-sudski (nationalist), Mussolini, Hitler, Primo de Rivera, Franco, and Salazar (all right-wing) and Stalin (communist).

dictatorship of the proletariat Marxist term for a revolutionary dictatorship established during the transition from capitalism to ◊communism after a socialist revolution.

Diderot Denis 1713–1784. French philosopher of the Enlightenment and editor of the ◊*Encyclopédie* 1751–1780. He exerted an enormous influence on contemporary social thinking with his ◊materialism and anti-clericalism.

didjeridu musical wind instrument, made from a hollow bamboo section 1.5 m/4 ft long, and blown to produce rhythmic, booming notes. First developed and played by Australian Aborigines.

Dido Phoenician princess, legendary founder of Carthage, who committed suicide in order to avoid marrying a local prince. However Virgil records that it was because ◊Aeneas deserted her.

differential

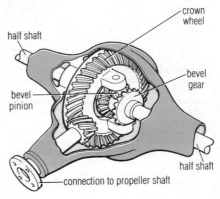

diecasting a major form of ◊casting, in which molten metal is injected into permanent metal moulds or dies.

Diefenbaker John George 1895–1979. Canadian Progressive Conservative politician, prime minister 1957–63, when he was defeated after criticism of the proposed manufacture of nuclear weapons in Canada.

dielectric a substance (an insulator such as ceramic or glass) capable of supporting electric stress. The dielectric constant, or relative permittivity, of a substance is the ratio of the capacity of a capacitor with the medium as dielectric to that of a similar capacitor in which the dielectric is replaced by a vacuum.

Dien Bien Phu, Battle of decisive battle in the ◊Indo-China War at a French fortress in North Vietnam, near the Laotian border, 320 km/200 mi from Hanoi. Some 10,000 French troops under Général de Castries were besieged 13 Mar–7 May 1954 by the communist Viet Minh. The fall of Dien Bien Phu resulted in the end of French control of Indo-China.

diesel engine a kind of ◊internal combustion engine that burns a lightweight oil. Diesel engines are piston-in-cylinder engines like the car ◊petrol engine, but just air (rather than an air/fuel mixture) is taken into the cylinder on the first piston stroke (down). The piston moves up and compresses the air until it is at a very high temperature. The fuel oil is then injected into the hot air, whereupon it burns, driving the piston down on its power stroke. For this reason the engine is called a compression-ignition engine (as opposed to the spark in a petrol engine).

diesel oil gas oil used in engines (when used in vehicle engines also known as *derv* – *d*iesel-*e*ngine *r*oad *v*ehicle). Like petrol, it is a petroleum product.

diet a meeting or convention of the princes and other dignitaries of the Holy Roman (German) Empire, for example, the Diet of Worms 1521 which met to consider the question of Luther's doctrines and the governance of the Empire under ◊Charles V.

diet a particular selection of ◊food, or a person's or people's regular food intake. A special diet may be recommended for medical reasons, undertaken to lose weight, or observed on religious grounds. An adequate diet is one that fills the body's nutritional requirements and gives an energy intake of around 2,400 calories a day. Some 450 million people in the world subsist on less than 1,500 calories, while in the developed countries the average daily intake is 3,300.

dietetics a specialized branch of human nutrition, dealing with the promotion of health through good nutrition.

Dietrich Marlene. Stage-name of Magdalene von Losch 1904–1992. German-American actress, born in Berlin. She first won fame by her appearance with Emil Jannings in *The Blue Angel* 1930, and went to Hollywood, becoming a US citizen in 1937. Later films include *Blonde Venus* 1932, and *Destry Rides Again* 1939. Her husky, sultry singing voice added to her appeal.

Dieu et mon droit (French 'God and my right') motto of the Royal Arms of Great Britain.

difference engine a mechanical calculating machine designed, but never completed, by the British mathematician Babbage about 1830. It was to calculate mathematical functions by solving the differences between values given to ◊variables within equations. Babbage designed the calculator so that once the initial values for the variables were set it would produce the next few thousand values without error.

differential an arrangement of gears in the final drive of a vehicle's transmission system that allows the driving wheels to turn at different speeds when cornering. The differential consists of sets of bevel gears and pinions within a cage attached to the crown wheel. When cornering, the bevel pinions rotate to allow the outer wheel to turn faster than the inner.

differential calculus a branch of ◊analysis involving the ◊differentiation of functions and their applications such as determination of maximum and minimum points and rates of change. See also ◊calculus, ◊integral calculus.

differentiation in mathematics, a procedure for determining the gradient of the tangent to a curve $f(x)$ at any point x. The first derivative is usually expressed as dy/dx. Applications of this procedure are rates of change, maximum and minimum points. When a ◊function $f(x)$ is differentiated, the result is a derived function (or derivative) written $f'(x)$. It may be regarded as the limit of the expression $[f(x + \delta x) - f(x)]/\delta x$ as δx tends to zero. Graphically, this is equivalent to the gradient (slope) of the curve represented by $y = f(x)$ at any point x.

differentiation in ◊embryology, the process whereby cells become increasingly different and specialized, giving rise to more complex structures which have particular functions in the adult organism. For instance, embryonic cells may develop into nerve, muscle or bone cells.

diffusion term used in physical chemistry to describe at least three processes: the spontaneous mixing of gases or liquids (classed together as *fluids* in scientific usage) when brought into contact without mechanical mixing or stirring; the spontaneous passage of fluids through membranes; and the spontaneous passage of dissolved materials both through the material in which they are dissolved and also through membranes.

diffraction the interference phenomena observed at the edges of opaque objects, or discontinuities between different media in the path of a wave train. The phenomena give rise to slight spreading of light into light and dark bands at the shadow of a straight edge. The diffraction grating is a device for separating a wave train such as a beam of incident light into its componenet frequencies (white light results in a spectrum). Sound waves can also be diffracted by a suitable array of solid objects.

differentiation

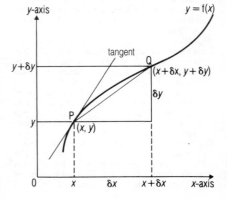

diffraction the diffraction effect created by the use of a cross-screen filter and two polarisers.

digestion the process whereby food eaten by an animal is broken down physically and chemically by ◊enzymes, usually in the ◊stomach and ◊intestines, to make the nutrients available for absorption and cell metabolism. In some single-celled organisms, such as amoebae, a food particle is engulfed by the cell and digested in a ◊vacuole within it.

digestive system the mouth, stomach, gut and associated glands of animals, which are responsible for digesting food. The food is broken down by physical and chemical means in the ◊stomach, and the soluble products absorbed in the ◊intestines. In birds, additional digestive organs are the ◊crop and ◊gizzard. In smaller, simpler animals such as jellyfish, the digestive system is simply a cavity (coelenteron or enteric cavity) with a 'mouth' into which food is taken; the digestive portion is dissolved and absorbed in this cavity and the remains are ejected back through the mouth.

digger an Australian term first coined to describe goldminers. It was adopted by Australian and New Zealand soldiers in France in 1916-17 and now generally means an Australian soldier, especially one who fought in World War I. In Australia it is also a term of friendly address, in the sense of 'mate'.

Diggers or *true ◊Levellers* an English 17th-century radical sect which became prominent in Apr 1649 when, headed by Gerrard Winstanley (*c.* 1609–60), it set up communal colonies near Cobham, Surrey, and elsewhere. They were broken up by mobs and, being pacifists, made no resistance. Their ideas considerably influenced the early ◊Quakers.

digital in electronics and computing, a term meaning 'coded as numbers'. A digital system uses two-state, either on/off or high/low voltage pulses, to encode, receive, and transmit information. A *digital computer* is a computing device that operates on a two-state system, using symbols that are internally coded as binary numbers (numbers made up of combinations of the digits 0 and 1), allowing very low-power circuits and very small electronic components.

digitalis plant of the genus *Digitalis*, family Scrophulariaceae, which includes the foxgloves. The leaves of the common foxglove *Digitalis purpurea* are the source of the drug *digitalis* used in the treatment of heart trouble. Digitalis therapy was pioneered in the late 1700s by William Withering, an English physician and botanist. Digitalis is extremely toxic.

digital sampling an electronic process used in ◊telecommunications for transforming a constantly varying (analogue) signal into one composed of discrete units, a digital signal. For example, a telephone microphone changes sound waves into an analogue signal that fluctuates up and down like a wave. In the digitizing process the waveform is sampled thousands of times a second and each part of the sampled wave is given a ◊binary code number related to the height of the wave at that point, which is transmitted along the telephone line. Using digital signals, messages can be transmitted quickly, accurately and economically.

dik-dik one of several species of tiny antelope, genus *Madoqua* found in Africa south of the Sahara in dry areas with scattered brush. About 60 cm/2 ft long and 35 cm/1.1 ft tall, dik-diks are often seen in pairs. Males possess short pointed horns. The name is derived from the alarm call of the animal.

dilatation and curettage (D and C) a common gynaecological procedure in which the cervix (neck of the womb) is widened or dilated, giving access so that the lining of the womb can be scraped away (curettage). It may be carried out to terminate a pregnancy, treat an incomplete miscarriage, or discover the cause of heavy menstrual bleeding.

dill umbelliferous herb *Anethum graveolens*.

dime novel yellow-backed cheap novel of a series started in the USA in the 1850s by Erastus F Beadle and frequently dealing with frontier adventure.

dik-dik

digestive system

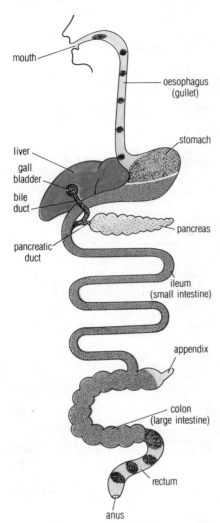

mouth
oesophagus (gullet)
liver
stomach
gall bladder
bile duct
pancreas
pancreatic duct
ileum (small intestine)
appendix
colon (large intestine)
rectum
anus

Like British 'penny dreadfuls', dime novels attained massive sales, especially with troops during the American Civil War. The 'Nick Carter' Library added detective stories to the genre.

dimension basic physical quantity such as mass, length, and time, which can be combined by multiplication or division to give the dimensions of derived quantities.

dimethyl sulphoxide by-product of the processing of wood to paper, used as an anti-freeze and industrial solvent.

diminishing returns, law of in economics, the principle that additional application of one factor of production, such as an extra machine or employee, at first results in rapidly increasing output, but then eventually yields declining returns, unless other factors are modified to sustain the increase.

Dimitrov Georgi 1882–1949. Bulgarian communist, prime minister from 1946. He was elected a deputy in 1913, and from 1919 was a member of the executive of the Comintern (see ◊International). In 1933 he was arrested in Berlin and tried with others in Leipzig for allegedly setting fire to the parliament building (see ◊Reichstag Fire). So forceful was his defence that he was acquitted, and he went to the USSR, where he became general secretary of the Comintern until its dissolution in 1943.

Dine Jim 1935– . US Pop artist. He experimented with combinations of paintings and objects, such as a washbasin attached to a canvas.

Dinesen Isak 1885–1962. Pen name of Danish writer Karen ◊Blixen.

Dingaan Zulu chief from 1828. He obtained the throne by murdering his predecessor, Shaka, and was known for his cruelty. In warfare with the Boer immigrants into Natal he was defeated on 16 Dec 1838 – 'Dingaan's Day'. He escaped to Swaziland, where he was deposed by his brother Mpande and subsequently murdered.

dingo wild dog of Australia. Descended from domestic animals brought from Asia by aborigines thousands of years ago, it belongs to the same species *Canis familiaris* as other domestic dogs. Reddish-brown, and with a bushy tail, it often hunts at night. It cannot bark.

Dinka person of Dinka culture from southern Sudan. Numbering approximately 1,000,000, the Dinka are primarily cattle herders, and inhabit the lands around the river system that flows into the White Nile. Their language belongs to the Chari-Nile family.

Dinorwig Europe's largest pumped-storage ◊hydroelectric scheme, completed in 1984, in Gwynedd, North Wales. Six turbogenerators together produce a maximum output of some 1,880 megawatts. The working head of water for the station is 530 m/1,740 ft.

dinosaur name given to the group of extinct reptiles living between 215 million and 65 million years ago. The name dinosaur, meaning 'terrible lizard', was given to the first specimens discovered, but the dinosaurs were not lizards. Their closest living relations are crocodiles and birds, the latter perhaps descended from the dinosaurs. There were many species of dinosaur that evolved during the millions of years they were the dominant large land animals. They disappeared 65 millon years ago, perhaps due to a significant change in climate.

Diocletian (Gaius Valerius Diocletianus) 245–313. Roman emperor 284–305, when he abdicated in favour of Galerius. He reorganized and sub-divided the Empire, with two joint and two subordinate emperors, and in 303 initiated severe persecution of the Christians.

diode a thermionic valve (vacuum tube) with two electrodes (negative cathode and positive anode) or its semi-conductor equivalent, which incorporates a p–n junction. Either device allows the passage of direct current in one direction only, and so is commonly used to rectify alternating current (AC), converting it to direct current (DC).

Diogenes *c.* 412–323 BC. Ascetic Greek philosopher of the Cynic school. He believed in freedom and self-sufficiency for the individual, and did not believe in social mores.

Dion Cassius 150–235. Roman historian. He wrote in Greek a Roman History in 80 books (of which 26 survive), covering the period from the foundation of the city to AD 229 including the only surviving account of Claudius' invasion of Britain.

Dionysia festivals of ◊Dionysus (Bacchus) celebrated in ancient Greece, especially in Athens.

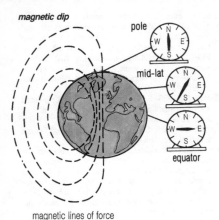

magnetic dip

pole

mid-lat

equator

magnetic lines of force

The most important were the lesser Dionysia in Dec, chiefly a rural festival and the greater Dionysia, at the end of Mar, when new plays were performed.

Dionysius name of two tyrants of the ancient Greek city of Syracuse in Sicily. *Dionysius the Elder* (432–367 BC) seized power in 405. His first two wars with Carthage further extended the power of Syracuse, but in a third (383–378 BC) he was defeated. He was succeeded by his son *Dionysius the Younger*. Driven out of Syracuse by Dion in 356, he was tyrant again in 353, but in 343 returned to Corinth.

Dionysus in Greek mythology, god of wine (son of Semele and Zeus), and also of orgiastic excess. He was identified with ◊Bacchus, whose rites were less savage. His festivals, the *Dionysia*, were particularly associated with Athens. Attendant on him were ◊maenads.

dioptre an optical unit in which the power of a lens is expressed as the reciprocal of its focal length in metres. The usual convention is that convergent lenses are positive and divergent lenses negative.

Dior Christian 1905–1957. French couturier. He established his own Paris salon in 1947, and made an impact with the 'New Look' – long and full-skirted – after war-time austerity.

dioxin common name for tetrachlorodibenzodioxin, one of a family of organic chemicals called dioxins. A highly toxic chemical, it was produced as a by-product of a defoliant used in the Vietnam War, and of the weedkiller 2,4,5-T. It causes a disfiguring skin complaint, chloracne, and has been linked with birth defects, miscarriages and cancer.

diphtheria infectious disease in which an occlusive membrane forms in the throat, threatening death by ◊asphyxia. Its incidence has been reduced greatly by immunization.

Diplock court in Northern Ireland, a type of court established in 1972 by the British government under Lord Diplock (1907–) to try offences linked with guerrilla violence. The right to jury trial was suspended and the court consisted of a single judge, since it was alleged that potential jurors were being intimidated and were refusing to serve. Despite widespread criticism, the Diplock courts have remained in operation.

diplodocus plant-eating dinosaur that lived about 145 million years ago, the fossils of which have been found in the western USA. Up to 27 m/88 ft long, most of this neck and tail, it weighed about 11 tonnes. It walked on four elephant-like legs, had nostrils on top of the skull, and peg-like teeth only at the front of the mouth.

diploid having two sets of ◊chromosomes in each cell. In sexually reproducing species, one set is derived from each parent, the ◊gametes, or sex cells, of each parent being ◊haploid (having only one set of chromosomes) due to ◊meiosis (cell division).

diplomacy the process by which states attempt to settle their differences through peaceful means such as negotiation or ◊arbitration. See ◊foreign relations.

dip, magnetic the angle between the horizontal and that taken up by a freely pivoted magnetic needle mounted vertically in the Earth's magnetic field. It is also called the angle of inclination. The dip needle parallels the lines of force of the magnetic field at any point. Thus at the north and south magnetic poles, the needle dips vertically and the angle of dip is 90°.

dipole in chemistry, a pair of equal and opposite charges located apart, as in some ionic molecules.

dipper bird *Cinclus cinclus* found in hilly and mountainous regions across Europe and Asia, where there are clear fast-flowing streams. It can swim, dive, or walk along the bottom using the pressure of water on its wings and tail to keep it down, while it searches for insect larvae and other small animals. About 18 cm/7 in long, it has chestnut plumage with white chin and breast, and a shape and cocked tail like a wren.

Dire Straits UK rock group formed 1977 by the guitarist, singer, and songwriter Mark Knopfler (1949–). In the 1980s they sold a record number of compact discs, including *Brothers in Arms* 1985 and *On Every Street* 1991.

direct current (DC) electric current that flows in one direction, and does not reverse its flow as ◊alternating current does. The electricity produced by a battery is direct current.

Director of Public Prosecutions (DPP) the head of the Crown Prosecution Service (established in 1985), responsible for the conduct of all criminal prosecutions in England and Wales. The DPP was formerly responsible only for the prosecution of certain serious crimes, such as murder.

Dis in Roman mythology, god of the underworld (Greek *Pluto*); ruler of Hades.

disarmament reduction of a country's weapons of war. Most disarmament talks since World War II have been concerned with nuclear-arms verification and reduction, but biological, chemical, and conventional weapons have also come under discussion at the United Nations and in other forums. Attempts to limit the arms race between the USA and (until its demise) the USSR included the ◊Strategic Arms Limitation Talks (SALT) of the 1970s and the ◊Strategic Arms Reduction Talks (START) of the 1980s–90s. Russia's president, Boris Yeltsin, continued the process of strategic arms reductions into 1992.

Disch Thomas M(ichael) 1940– . US writer and poet, noted for science-fiction novels such as *Camp Concentration* 1968 and *334* 1972.

discharge tube usually takes the form of a glass tube from which virtually all the air has been removed (so that it 'contains' a near vacuum), with

Disney Mickey Mouse, Walt Disney's first and most famous cartoon character, who made his debut in 1926.

electrodes at each end. When a high-voltage current is passed between the electrodes, the few remaining gas atoms in the tube (or some deliberately introduced ones) ionize and emit coloured light as they conduct the current along the tube. The light originates as electrons change energy levels in the ionized atoms. By coating the inside of the tube with a phosphor, invisible emitted radiation (such as ultraviolet light) can produce visible light; this is the principle of the fluorescent lamp.

disciple a follower, especially of a religious leader. The word is used in the Bible for the early followers of Jesus Christ. The twelve chief disciples of Jesus are known as the apostles.

discotheque club for dancing to pop music on records, which originated in the 1960s. The most famous, Studio 54 (1977–80) in Manhattan, New York, gained notoriety when its owner, Steve Rubell, operated a policy of selective admission. Its shortened form, *disco*, was used for an international style of recorded dance music of the 1970s with heavily emphasized beat, derived from ◊funk.

discrimination unequal distinction (social, economic, political, legal) between individuals or groups such that one has the power to treat the other unfavourably. Types of discrimination, often based on ◊stereotype, include anti-Semitism, apartheid, caste, racism, sexism, and slavery. *Positive discrimination*, or 'affirmative action', is sometimes practised in an attempt to counteract the effects of previous long-term discrimination against a minority group.

disinfectant agent which kills, or prevents the growth of, bacteria and other microorganisms. Chemical disinfectants include carbolic acid (phenol), used by Lister in surgery in the 1870s, ethanal, methanal, chlorine, and iodine.

disinvestment the withdrawal of investments in a country for political reasons. The term is also used in economics to describe non-replacement of stock as it wears out.

disk in computing, a common medium for storing large volumes of data. (The alternative is ◊magnetic tape.) A magnetic disk is rotated at high speed in a disk drive unit as a read/write (playback or record) head passes over its surfaces to record or to 'read' the magnetic variations that encode the data. There are several types, classified into fixed and removable disks.

dislocation in chemistry, a fault in the structure of a crystal.

Disney 'Walt' (Walter Elias) 1901–1966. US filmmaker, who became a pioneer of family entertainment. He established his own studio in Hollywood in 1923, and his first Mickey Mouse cartoon *Plane Crazy* appeared in 1928. He developed the 'Silly Symphony', a type of cartoon based on the close association of music with the visual image, such as *Fantasia* 1940. His many feature-length cartoons include *Snow White and the Seven Dwarfs* 1938, *Pinocchio* 1940, and *Dumbo* 1941.

dispersion in optics, dispersion describes the splitting of white light into a spectrum, for example when it passes through a prism or a diffraction grating. It occurs because the prism (or grating) bends each component wavelength to a slightly different extent. The natural dispersion of light through raindrops creates a rainbow. Dispersion also refers to the distribution of microscopic particles in a ◊colloid.

displacement activity in animal behaviour, an action that is performed out of its normal context, while the animal is in a state of stress, frustration or uncertainty. Birds, for example, often peck at grass when uncertain whether to attack or flee from an opponent; similarly, humans scratch their heads when nervous. See also ◊ethology.

Disraeli Benjamin, Earl of Beaconsfield 1804–1881. British Conservative politician and novelist. He was chancellor of the Exchequer under Lord Derby 1852, 1858–59, and 1866–68, and prime minister 1868 and 1874–80. His imperialist policies brought India directly under the crown and he personally purchased control of the Suez Canal. The central Conservative Party organization is his creation. His popular, political novels reflect an interest in social reform and include *Coningsby* 1844 and *Sybil* 1845.

Dissenter historically, one of those Protestants dissenting from the established Christian church, for example, Baptists, Presbyterians, and Independents (now known as Congregationalists).

Disraeli Benjamin Disraeli by John Everett Millais (1881) National Portrait Gallery, London.

Djibouti
Republic of
(*Jumhouriyya Djibouti*)

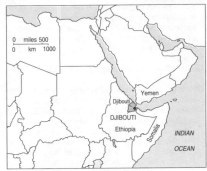

```
0   miles 500
0   km   1000
```

Yemen

Djibouti

DJIBOUTI

Ethiopia

Somalia

INDIAN

OCEAN

area 23,000 sq km/8,880 sq mi
capital and chief port Djibouti
physical mountains divide an inland plateau from

a coastal plain; hot and arid
head of state and government Hassan Gouled
Aptidon from 1977
political system authoritarian nationalism
exports acts mainly as a transit port for Ethiopia
currency Djibouti franc
population (1990 est) 337,000 (Issa 47%, Afar 37%,
European 8%, Arab 6%); annual growth rate 3.4%
language French (official), Somali, Afar, Arabic
religion Sunni Muslim
literacy 20% (1988)
GDP $378 million (1987); $1,016 per head
chronology
1977 Full independence achieved. Hassan Gouled
elected president.
1979 All political parties combined to form the
People's Progress Assembly (RPP).
1981 New constitution made RPP the only legal
party. Gouled re-elected. Treaties of friendship
signed with Ethiopia, Somalia, Kenya, and Sudan.
1984 Policy of neutrality reaffirmed.
1987 Gouled re-elected for a final term.
1991 Amnesty International accused secret police
of brutality.
1992 Djibouti elected member of UN Security
Council 1993–95.

---

dissident in one-party states, a person intellectually dissenting from the official line. Dissidents have been sent into exile, prison, labour camps, and mental institutions, or deprived of their jobs. In the former USSR the number of imprisoned dissidents declined from more than 600 in 1986 to fewer than 100 in 1990, of whom the majority were ethnic nationalists. In China the number of prisoners of conscience increased after the 1989 Tiananmen Square massacre, and in South Africa, despite the release of Nelson Mandela in 1990, numerous political dissidents remained in jail.

distributive law in mathematics, the law that states that if there are two binary operations '×' and '+' on a set S, then '×' distributes over '+' if for all a, b, $c \in S$, $a \times (b + c) = (a \times b) + (a \times c)$, and $(b + c) \times a = (b \times a) + (c \times a)$. Multiplication distributes over addition or subtraction; for example, $3 \times (4 + 5)$ is the same as $(3 \times 4) + (3 \times 5)$. See also ◊associative law.

distributor a device in a car engine's ignition system that distributes pulses of high-voltage electricity to the ◊spark plugs in the cylinders. The electricity is passed to the plug leads by the tip of a rotor arm, driven by the engine camshaft, and current is fed to the rotor arm from the ignition coil. The distributor also houses the contact-breaker, which opens and closes to interrupt the battery current to the coil, thus triggering off the high-voltage pulses. In modern cars with electronic ignition, it is absent.

district council unit of local government in England and Wales.

District of Columbia federal district of the USA, see ◊Washington.

diuretic drug that rids the body of excess fluid by increasing the output of urine by the kidneys. It may be used in the treatment of heart disease, high blood pressure, kidney and liver disease, and some endocrine disorders.

diver species of bird specialized for swimming and diving found in northern regions of the N hemisphere. The legs are set so far back that walking is almost impossible, and they come to land only to nest, but divers are powerful swimmers and good flyers. They have straight bills and long bodies, and feed on fish, crustaceans, and some water plants.

There are just four species, the largest, the *white-billed diver Gavia adamsii*, being an Arctic species 75 cm/2.5 ft long. Divers are also called *loons*.

divertissement (French 'entertainment') a dance, or group of dances, within a ballet or opera that have no connection with the plot, such as the character dances in the last act of *Coppélia* by Delibes.

dividend in business, the money which company directors decide should be taken out of profits for distribution to shareholders. It is usually declared as a percentage or fixed amount per share. Most companies pay dividends once or twice a year.

divination art of ascertaining future events or eliciting other hidden knowledge by supernatural or nonrational means. It generally involves the intuitive interpretation of the mechanical operations of chance or natural law, which can be as simple as observing the swing of a pendulum or based on a complex body of tradition, such as charting the planets in ◊astrology; *clairvoyance* is less dependent on external aids. Divination played a large part in the ancient civilizations of the Egyptians, Greeks (see ◊oracle), Romans, and Chinese (see ◊I Ching), and is still practised throughout the world.

Divine Comedy, The a poem by the Italian Dante Alighieri 1300–1321, describing a journey through Hell, Purgatory, and Paradise under the guidance of Reason and Faith. The poem makes great use of symbolism and illusion and influenced many English writers, including Milton and Byron.

Divine Light Mission religious movement founded in 1960. It proclaims *Guru Maharaj Ji* as the present age's successor to the gods or religious leaders Krishna, Buddha, Jesus, and Muhammad, who can provide his followers with the knowledge required to attain salvation.

divine right of kings Christian political doctrine that monarchy is divinely ordained as in the Bible, hereditary right cannot be forfeited, monarchs are accountable to God alone for their actions, and rebellion against the lawful sovereign is thus a sin against God. The court of Louis XIV of France pushed this to the limit.

diving the sport of entering the water either from a springboard (3 m/10 ft) above the water, or from a platform 10 m/33 ft above the water. Various differing starts are adopted, and twists and somersaults performed in mid-air. Points are awarded by judges and the level of difficulty of each dive is used as a multiplying factor.

diving apparatus an apparatus used to enable a person to spend time underwater. Diving bells were in use in the 18th century, the diver breathing air trapped in a bell-shaped chamber, followed by cumbersome diving suits in the early 19th century. Complete freedom of movement came with the ◊aqualung, invented by Jacques Cousteau in the early 1940s. For work at depths of several hundred metres the technique of saturation diving was developed in the 1970s, where divers live for a week or more breathing a mixture of helium and oxygen at the pressure existing on the seabed where they work. When they are not diving, they live in a compression chamber on board a support ship.

divorce the legal dissolution of a lawful marriage. It is distinct from a decree of nullity, which is a legal declaration that the marriage was invalid. The ease with which a divorce can be obtained in different countries varies considerably, and is also affected by different religious practices.

Diwali Hindu festival in Oct/Nov celebrating Lakshmi, goddess of light and wealth. It is marked by the lighting of lamps and candles, feasting, and exchange of gifts.

Dixie the Southern states of the USA. The word probably derives from the ◊Mason-Dixon line.

Dixieland jazz a jazz style which originated in New Orleans in the early 20th century.

Djakarta variant spelling of ◊Jakarta, capital of Indonesia.

Djibouti country on the E coast of Africa, at the S end of the Red Sea, bounded to the E by the Gulf of Aden, to the SE by the Somali Republic, and to the S, W, and N by Ethiopia.

Djibouti chief port and capital of the Republic of Djibouti, on a peninsula 240 km/149 mi SW of Aden and 565 km NE of Addis Ababa; population (1988) 290,000.

DM abbreviation for *Deutschmark*, the unit of currency in Germany.

DNA abbreviation for *deoxyribonucleic acid* a complex two-stranded molecule that contains, in chemically coded form, all the information needed to build, control and maintain a living organism. DNA is a double-stranded ◊nucleic acid that forms the basis of genetic inheritance in all organisms, except for a few viruses that depend on ◊RNA. In ◊eukaryotic organisms, it is organized into ◊chromosomes and contained in the cell nucleus.

Dnepropetrovsk city in Ukraine, on the right bank of the Dnieper; population (1987) 1,182,000. Centre of an important industrial region, with iron, steel, chemical, and engineering industries. It is linked with the Dnieper Dam, 60 km/37 mi downstream.

Dnieper or *Dnepr* Russian river rising in the Smolensk region and flowing S past Kiev, Dnepropetrovsk, and Zaporozhe, to enter the Black Sea E of Odessa. Total length 2,250 km/1,400 mi.

D-notice in the UK, a censorship notice issued by the Department of Defence to the media to prohibit the publication of information on matters of national security. The system dates from 1922.

do. abbreviation for *ditto*.

Dobermann or *Dobermann Pinscher* streamlined, smooth-coated dog with a docked tail, much used as a guard dog. It stands up to 70 cm/2.2 ft

DNA

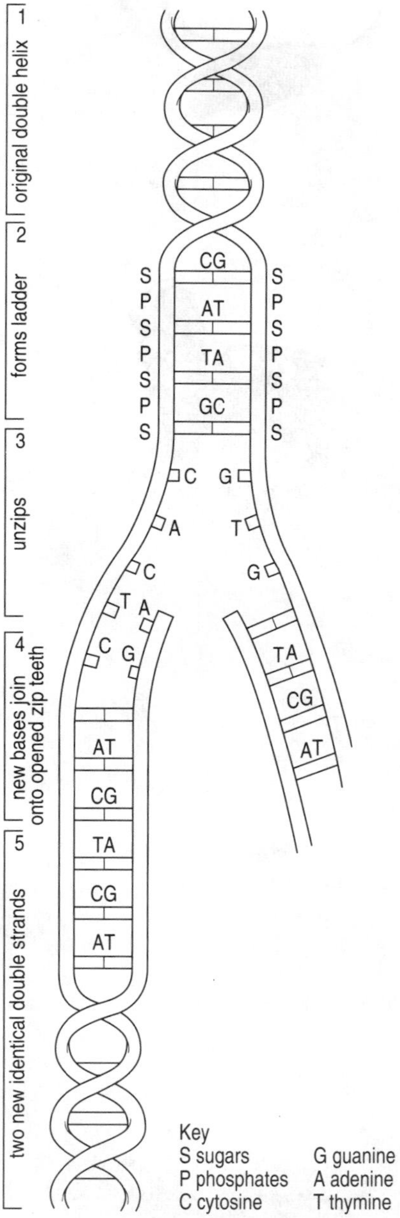

1 | original double helix
2 | forms ladder
3 | unzips
4 | new bases join onto opened zip teeth
5 | two new identical double strands

Key
S sugars   G guanine
P phosphates   A adenine
C cytosine   T thymine

tall, has a long head, flat, smooth skull, and is often black with brown markings. It takes its name from the man who bred it in 19th-century Germany.

Döblin Alfred 1878–1957. German novelist. *Berlin-Alexanderplatz* 1929 owes much to Joyce in its minutely detailed depiction of the inner lives of a city's inhabitants.

dock port accommodation for commercial and naval vessels, usually simple linear quayage adaptable to ships of any size, but with specialized equipment for

dog

Foxhound

Pekinese

Pug

Cocker spaniel

working collie

Labrador retriever

Egyptian greyhound

Jack Russell terrier

Chihuahua

Dobermann pinscher

bloodhound

Old English sheepdog

handling bulk cargoes, refrigerated goods, container traffic, and oil tankers. Flexible 'floating' docks are used for repairs.

dock in botany, name applied to a number of plants of the genus *Rumex*, family Polygonaceae. Commonly known as **sorrel**, they are annual to perennial herbs, often with lance-shaped leaves and small, greenish-coloured flowers.

Doctor Faustus a tragedy by Christopher Marlowe, published (in two versions) 1604 and 1616, first performed 1594. The play, based upon the medieval Faust legend, tells how Faustus surrenders his soul to the Devil in return for 24 years of life and the services of Mephistopheles, who will grant his every wish.

dodder genus of parasitic plants, *Cuscuta*, family Convolvulaceae, without leaves or roots. The thin stem twines round the host, and penetrating suckers withdraw nourishment.

Dodds Charles 1899–1973. British biochemist. He was largely responsible for the discovery of stilboestrol, the powerful synthetic hormone used in treating prostate conditions and also for fattening cattle.

dodecaphonic in music, a term applied to the 12-note system of composition.

Dodgson Charles Lutwidge. Real name of writer Lewis ◊Carroll.

dodo extinct bird *Raphus cucullatus* formerly found on Mauritius, but exterminated before the end of the 17th century. Related to the pigeons, it was larger than a turkey, with a bulky body and very short wings and tail. Flightless and trusting, it was easy prey to humans and the animals they introduced.

Dodoma capital (replacing Dar-es-Salaam in 1974) of Tanzania; 1,132 m/3,713 ft above sea level; population (1984) 180,000. Centre of communications, linked by rail with Dar-es-Salaam and Kigoma on Lake Tanganyika, and by road with Kenya to the N, and Zambia and Malawi to the S.

dog mammal *Canis familiaris* descended from the wolf or jackal, domesticated by humans, and bred into many different varieties for use as working animals and pets. As well as domestic dogs there are many species of wild dog in the dog family Canidae. Found in all continents except Antarctica, wild dogs are mostly hunters, running on the toes of the feet, and with long faces and keen noses.

doge the chief magistrate in the ancient constitutions of Venice and Genoa. The first doge of Venice was appointed in 697 with absolute power (modified in 1297), and from his accession dates Venice's prominence in history. The last Venetian doge, Lodovico Manin, retired in 1797.

dogfish small shark *Scyliorhinus caniculus* found in the NE Atlantic and Mediterranean. Bottom-living, it is sandy brown and covered with spots, and grows to about 75 cm/2.5 ft.

dog's mercury plant *Mercurialis perennis* of the family Euphorbiaceae. Dog's mercury carpets woodland floors in patches of a single sex. Male flowers are small, greenish yellow, and held on upright spike above the leaves. Female flowers droop below the upper leaves. Leaves are oval and light green. It is found across Europe.

dogwood deciduous shrub *Cornus sanguinea* growing up to 4 m/12 ft high. Several of the species are notable for their coloured bark: the **Westonbirt dogwood** *Cornus alba* has brilliant red stems in winter.

Doha capital and chief port of Qatar; population (1985) 150,000. Industries include oil refining,

dolphin

refrigeration plants, engineering and food processing. Centre of vocational training for all the Gulf states.

doldrums area of low atmospheric pressure along the equator, largely applied to oceans at the convergence of the NE and SE ◊trade winds. To some extent the area affected moves N and S with the sun.

Doll William Richard 1912– . British physician who proved the link between smoking and lung cancer.

Dollfuss Engelbert 1892–1934. Austrian Christian Socialist politician. He was appointed chancellor in 1932, and in 1933 suppressed parliament and ruled by decree. Negotiations for an alliance with the Austrian Nazis broke down. On 12 Feb 1934 he crushed the Social Democrats by force, and in May Austria was declared a ◊corporative state. The Nazis attempted a coup d'état on 25 Jul; the Chancellery was seized and Dollfuss murdered. He was known as the 'pocket chancellor' because of his small stature.

dolmen prehistoric monument in the form of a chamber built of large stone slabs, roofed over by a flat stone which they support. Dolmens are grave chambers of the Neolithic period, found in Europe and Africa, and occasionally in Asia as far as Japan. In Wales they are known as cromlechs.

dolphin highly intelligent marine mammal, a small toothed whale, of which many species exist. The **common dolphin** *Delphinus delphis* is found in all temperate and tropical seas. It is up to 2.5 m/8 ft long, and is dark above, white below, with bands of grey, white, and yellow on the sides, and has up to 100 teeth in its jaws which make the 15 cm/6 in 'beak' protrude forward from the rounded head. It feeds on fish and squid. They use sound in echolocation to navigate and find prey, as well as for communication. Some species can swim at up to 56 kph/35 mph, helped by special streamlining modifications of the skin. All power themselves by beating the tail up and down, and use the flippers to steer and stabilize. The US Navy began using dolphins 1960. In 1987 six dolphins were sent to detect mines in the Persian Gulf.

Domagk Gerhard 1895–1964. German pathologist, discoverer of antibacterial drugs. He found that a dye substance called prontosil red contains chemicals with powerful antibacterial properties. This became the first of the sulphonamide drugs, used to treat a wide range of conditions, including pneumonia and septic wounds.

Domenico Veneziano c. 1400–1461. Italian painter, active in Florence. His few surviving frescoes and altarpieces show a remarkably delicate use of colour and light (which recurs in the work of Piero della Francesca, who trained under him).

Dome of the Rock building in Jerusalem dating from the 7th century AD that enshrines the rock from which, in Muslim tradition, Muhammad ascended to heaven on his ◊Night Journey. It stands

Dominica
Commonwealth of

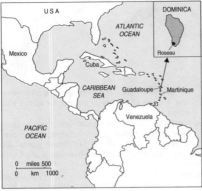

area 750 sq km/290 sq mi
capital Roseau, with a deepwater port
physical second largest of the Windward Islands, mountainous, tropical
head of state Clarence Seignoret from 1983

head of government Eugenia Charles from 1980
political system liberal democracy
exports bananas, coconuts, citrus, lime, bay oil
currency E Caribbean dollar, pound sterling, French franc
population (1990 est) 94,200 (mainly black African in origin, but with a small Carib reserve of some 500); annual growth rate 1.3%
language English (official), but the Dominican *patois* reflects earlier periods of French rule
religion Roman Catholic 80%
literacy 80%
GDP $91 million (1985); $1,090 per head
chronology
1978 Dominica achieved full independence within the Commonwealth. Patrick John, leader of the Dominica Labour Party (DLP), elected prime minister.
1980 Dominica Freedom Party (FDP), led by Eugenia Charles, won the general election.
1981 Patrick John was implicated in a plot to overthrow the government.
1982 John tried and acquitted.
1985 John retried and found guilty. Regrouping of left-of-centre parties resulted in the new Labour Party of Dominica (LPD). DFP, led by Eugenia Charles, re-elected.
1990 Charles elected to a third term.
1991 Integration into Windward Islands confederation proposed.

on the site of the Jewish national Temple and is visited by pilgrims.

Domesday Book record of the survey of England carried out in 1086 by officials of William the Conqueror, in order to assess land tax and other dues, ascertain the value of the crown lands, and enable the king to estimate the power of his vassal barons.

dominance in genetics, the concept that certain characteristics are dominant, that is, they mask the expression of other characteristics, known as recessives (see ◊recessivity). For example

if a person has one ◊allele (◊gene variant) for blue eyes and one for brown eyes, the brown colour will predominate. See also ◊heterozygous.

dominant in music, the fifth degree of the scale, for example G in C major.

Domingo Placido 1941– . Spanish tenor. One of a celebrated musical family, he emigrated with them to Mexico as a boy. He excels in romantic operatic roles.

Dominica island in the West Indies, between Guadeloupe and Martinique, the largest of the

Dominican Republic
(*República Dominicana*)

area 48,430 sq km/18,700 sq mi
capital Santo Domingo
physical comprises E part of island of Hispaniola; central mountain range; fertile valley in N
head of state and government Joaquin Ricardo Balaguer from 1986

political system democratic republic
exports sugar, gold, silver, tobacco, coffee
currency peso
population (1989 est) 7,307,000; annual growth rate 2.3%
life expectancy men 61, women 65
language Spanish (official)
religion Roman Catholic 95%
literacy 78% male/77% female (1985 est)
GDP $4.9 bn (1987); $731 per head
chronology
1930 Military coup established the dictatorship of Rafael Trujillo.
1961 Trujillo assassinated.
1962 First democratic elections resulted in Juan Bosch, founder of the Dominican Revolutionary Party (PRD) becoming president.
1963 Bosch overthrown in military coup.
1966 New constitution adopted. Joaquín Balaguer, leader of the Christian Social Reform Party (PRSC), became president.
1978 PRD returned to power, with Silvestre Antonio Guzmán as president.
1982 PRD re-elected, with Jorge Blanco as president.
1985 Blanco forced by IMF to adopt austerity measures to save the economy.
1986 PRSC returned to power, with Balaguer re-elected president.
1990 Balaguer re-elected by a small majority.

Windward Islands, with the Atlantic to the E and the Caribbean to the W.

Dominican order Roman Catholic order of friars founded 1215 by St Dominic; they are also known as Friars Preachers, Black Friars, or Jacobins. The order is worldwide and there is also an order of contemplative nuns; the habit is black and white.

Dominican Republic country in the West Indies, occupying the E of the island of Hispaniola, with Haiti to the W. The island is surrounded by the Caribbean Sea.

Dominic, St 1170–1221. Founder of the Roman Catholic Dominican order of preaching friars. It grew out of his mission to the Provençal Albigenses 1205–15. Feast day 7 Aug.

Dominions name formerly applied to self-governing divisions of the British Empire, for example Canada, now members of the ◊Commonwealth.

domino theory idea popularized by US president Eisenhower in 1954 that if one country came under communist rule, it was likely to be followed by adjacent countries becoming communist as well. Initially used to justify US intervention in Southeast Asia, it has also been invoked in reference to Central America.

Domitian (Titus Flavius Domitianus) 51–96 AD. Roman emperor. Born in Rome, he became emperor in 81 AD. He finalized the conquest of Britain (see ◊Agricola), strengthened the Rhine–Danube frontier, and suppressed immorality as well as freedom of thought in philosophy (see ◊Epictetus), and religion (Christians were persecuted). His reign of terror led to his assassination.

Don river in Russia, rising to the south of Moscow and entering the NE extremity of the Sea of Azov; length 1,900 km/1,180 mi. In its lower reaches the Don is 1.5 km/1 mi wide, and for about four months of the year it is closed by ice. Its upper course is linked with the Volga by a canal.

Donald Ian 1910–1987. English obstetrician who introduced ◊ultrasound scanning. He pioneered its use in obstetrics as a means of scanning the growing fetus without exposure to X-rays.

Donatello (Donato di Niccolo) 1386–1466. Italian sculptor of the early Renaissance, born in Florence. He was instrumental in reviving the Classical style, as in his graceful bronze statue of the youthful *David* (Bargello, Florence) and his equestrian statue of the general *Gattamelata* 1443 (Padua). The course of Florentine art in the 15th century was strongly influenced by his style.

Donation of Constantine the name given to the forged 8th-century document purporting to record Emperor Constantine's surrender of temporal sovereignty in W Europe to Pope Sylvester I (314–25).

Donatist a member of a puritanical Christian movement in 4th and 5th-century N Africa, named after Donatus of Casae Nigrae, a 3rd-century bishop, later known as Donatus of Carthage.

Donegal mountainous county in Ulster province in the NW of the Republic of Ireland, surrounded on three sides by the Atlantic; area 4,830 sq km/1,865 sq mi; population (1991) 127,900. The county town is Lifford; the market town and port of Donegal is at the head of Donegal Bay in the SW. Commercial activities include sheep and cattle raising, tweed and linen manufacture, and some deep-sea fishing.

Donetsk city in Ukraine, capital of Donetsk region, situated in the Donets Basin, a major coal mining area, 600 km/380 mi SE of Kiev; population (1987) 1,090,000. It has blast furnaces, rolling mills, and other heavy industries.

Dönitz Karl 1891–1980. German admiral, originator of the wolf-pack submarine technique which sank 15 million tonnes of Allied shipping in World War II. He succeeded Hitler in 1945, capitulated, and was imprisoned 1946–56.

Donizetti Gaetano 1797–1848. Italian composer, who composed more than 60 operas, including *Lucrezia Borgia* 1833, *Lucia di Lammermoor* 1835, *La Fille du régiment* 1840, *La Favorite* 1840, and *Don Pasquale* 1843. They show the influence of Rossini and Bellini, and their chief feature is their flow of expressive melodies.

Don Juan character of Spanish legend, Don Juan Tenorio, supposed to have lived in the 14th century, and notorious for his debauchery. Tirso de Molina, Molière, Mozart, Byron and G B Shaw have featured the legend.

donkey alternative name for ◊ass.

Donne John 1571–1631. British metaphyscial poet, whose work is characterized by subtle imagery and figurative language. In 1615 Donne took orders in the Church of England and as Dean of St Paul's was noted for his sermons. His poetry includes the sonnets 'No man is an island' and 'Death be not proud', elegies, satires and verse-letters.

Doolittle Hilda 1886–1961. US poet. She went to Europe in 1911, and was associated with Ezra Pound and the British writer Richard ◊Aldington (to whom she was married 1913–37), in founding the ◊Imagist school of poets. Her work includes the *Sea Garden* 1916 and *Helen in Egypt* 1916. She signed her work 'HD'.

Doomsday Book a variant spelling of ◊Domesday Book, English survey of 1086.

Doors, the US psychedelic rock group formed 1965 in Los Angeles by Jim Morrison (1943–71, vocals), Ray Manzarek (1935– , keyboards), Robby Krieger (1946– , guitar), and John Densmore (1944– , drums). Their first hit was 'Light My Fire' from their debut album *The Doors* 1967. They were noted for Morrison's poetic lyrics and flaunting performance.

doppelgänger (German 'double-goer') a ghostly apparition identical to a living person.

Doppler effect change in observed frequency (or wavelength) of waves due to relative motion between wave source and observer. It is responsible for the perceived change in pitch of a siren as it approaches and then recedes, and for the ◊red shift of light from distant stars. It is named after the Austrian physicist Christian Doppler (1803–53).

DORA in the UK, short for the Defence of the Realm Act, passed in Nov 1914, which conferred extraordinary powers on the government for the duration of World War I.

Dordogne river in SW France, rising in Puy-de-Dôme *département* and flowing 490 km/300 mi to join the Garonne, 23 km/14 mi N of Bordeaux. It gives its name to a *département* and is an important source of hydroelectric power.

Doré Gustave 1832–1883. French artist, a prolific illustrator, and also active as a painter, etcher, and sculptor. He produced closely worked engravings of scenes from, for example, Rabelais, Dante, Cervantes, the Bible, Milton, and Poe.

Dorian member of a people of ancient Greece. They entered Greece from the N and conquered most of the Peloponnese from the Achaeans and destroyed the ◊Mycenaean civilization; this invasion appears to have been completed before 1000 BC. Their chief cities were Sparta, Argos, and Corinth.

Dostoievsky Russian novelist Fyodor Dostoievsky.

dormancy in botany, a phase of reduced physiological activity exhibited by certain buds, seeds and spores. Dormancy can help a plant to survive unfavourable conditions, as in annual plants that pass the cold winter season as dormant seeds, and plants which form dormant buds. However, for various reasons many seeds exhibit a period of dormancy even when conditions are favourable for growth..

dormouse small rodent, akin to a mouse, with a hairy tail. There are about ten species, living in Europe, Asia, and Africa. They are arboreal (live in trees), nocturnal, and hibernate during winter in cold regions.

Dorset county in SW England
area 2,654 sq km/1,024 sq mi
towns administrative headquarters Dorchester; Poole, Shaftesbury, Sherborne; resorts Bournemouth, Lyme Regis, Weymouth
products Wytch Farm is the largest onshore oilfield in the UK.
population (1980 est) 655,700
famous people Thomas Hardy.

Dortmund industrial centre in the ◊Ruhr, Germany, 58 km/36 mi NE of Düsseldorf; population (1988) 568,000. Largest mining town of the Westphalian coalfield and the S terminus of the Dortmund-Ems canal. Industries include iron, steel, construction machinery, engineering, and brewing.

dory marine fish *Zeus faber* found in the Mediterranean and Atlantic. It grows up to 60 cm/2 ft, and has nine or ten long spines at the front of the dorsal fin, and four at the front of the anal fin. It is olive brown or grey, with a conspicuous black spot ringed with yellow on each side. It is a stalking predator, shooting out its mobile jaws to catch fish.

Dos Passos John 1896–1970. US author, born in Chicago. He made a reputation with the war novels *One Man's Initiation* 1919 and *Three Soldiers* 1921. His greatest work is the *USA* trilogy 1930–36, which gives a panoramic view of US life through the device of placing fictitious characters against the real setting of newspaper headlines and contemporary events.

Dostoievsky Fyodor Mihailovich 1821–1881. Russian novelist. Remarkable for their profound psychological insight, Dostoievsky's novels greatly influenced Russian writers, and since the beginning of the 20th century have been increasingly influential abroad. In 1849 he was sentenced to four years hard labour in Siberia,

followed by army service, for printing socialist propaganda. *The House of the Dead* 1861 recalls his prison experiences, followed by his major works *Crime and Punishment* 1866, *The Idiot* 1868–69 and *The Brothers Karamazov* 1880.

dotterel bird *Eudromias morinellus* of the plover family, nesting on high moors and tundra in Europe and Asia, migrating south for the winter. About 23 cm/9 in, it is clad in a pattern of black, brown, and white in summer, duller in winter, but always with white eyebrows and breastband. Females are larger than males, and the male incubates and rears the brood.

Dou Gerard 1613–1675. Dutch genre painter, a pupil of Rembrandt. He is known for small domestic interiors, minutely observed.

double bass a bowed string musical instrument, the bass of the ◊violin family.

double entendre (French 'double meaning') an ambiguous word or phrase.

double star two stars that appear close together. Most double stars attract each other due to gravity, and orbit each other, forming a genuine ◊binary star, but other double stars are at different distances from Earth, and lie in the same line of sight only by chance.

Douglas capital of the Isle of Man in the Irish Sea; population (1986) 20,400. A holiday resort and terminus of shipping routes to and from Fleetwood and Liverpool.

Douglas Gavin (or Gawain) 1475–1522. Scottish poet. A son of the Earl of Angus, he became bishop of Dunkeld in 1515, and was active in Scottish politics. He wrote two allegories, *The Palace of Honour* and *King Hart*, but is best known for his translation of Virgil's *Aeneid*, the first English versions.

Douglass Frederick c. 1817–1895. US anti-slavery campaigner. Born a slave in Maryland, he escaped 1838. His autobiographical *Narrative of the Life of Frederick Douglass* 1845 aroused support in northern states for the abolition of slavery. After the Civil War, he held several US government posts, including minister to Haiti.

Doukhobor member of a Christian sect of Russian origin, now mainly found in Canada, also known as 'Christians of the Universal Brotherhood'. Some of the Doukhobor teachings resemble those of the Quakers.

Doulton Henry 1820–1897. British ceramicist. He developed special wares for the chemical, electrical and building industries and in 1846 established the world's first stoneware drainpipe factory. From 1870 he created at Lambeth, in London, and Burslem, near Stoke-on-Trent, a reputation for art pottery and domestic tablewares.

Doumergue Gaston 1863–1937. French prime minister during the time leading up to World War I and again after the fall of Léon Blum's Popular Front government in 1937.

Douro (Spanish *Duero*) river rising in N central Spain and flowing through N Portugal to the Atlantic at Oporto; length 800 km/500 mi.

dove type of ◊pigeon.

Dover, Strait of (French *Pas-de-Calais*) stretch of water separating England from France, and connecting the English Channel with the North Sea. It is about 35 km/22 mi long and 34 km/21 mi wide at its narrowest part. It is one of the world's busiest sea lanes, and by 1972 increasing traffic, collisions, and shipwrecks had become so frequent that traffic-routeing schemes were enforced.

dowager the style given to the widow of a peer or baronet.

Doyle *Creator of the popular fictional duo of Sherlock Holmes and Dr Watson, Arthur Conan Doyle.*

Dowell Anthony 1943– . British ballet dancer, who was principal dancer with the Royal Ballet 1966–86, and director from 1986.

Dow Jones average a daily index of prices on New York's Wall Street stock exchange, based on 30 industrial stocks.

Dowland John 1563–1626. English composer. He failed to establish himself at the court of Queen Elizabeth – he was a Roman Catholic convert – but later reverted to Protestantism and from 1612 was patronized by the Stuart royal family. He is remembered for his songs to lute accompaniment.

Down county in the SE of Northern Ireland, facing the Irish Sea on the E; area 2,465 sq km/952 sq mi; population (1981) 53,193. In the S are the Mourne mountains, in the E Strangford sea lough. The county town is Downpatrick; the main industry is dairying.

Downing Street street in Westminster, London, leading from Whitehall to St James's Park, named after Sir George Downing (died 1684), a diplomat under Cromwell and Charles II. *Number 10* is the official residence of the prime minister, *number 11* is the residence of the chancellor of the Exchequer, and *number 12* the office of the government whips.

Down's syndrome chromosomal abnormality (the presence of an additional chromosome) which produces a rather flattened face, coarse, straight hair, and a fold of skin at the inner edge of the eye (hence the former name 'mongolism'). There is often mental retardation.

Doxiadis Constantinos 1913–1975. Greek architect and town planner; designer of ◊Islamabad.

Doyle Arthur Conan 1859–1930. British writer, creator of the detective Sherlock Holmes and his assistant Dr Watson, who featured in a number of stories, including *The Hound of the Baskervilles* 1902. Conan Doyle is also known for adventure novels, for example *The Lost World* 1912.

D'Oyly Carte Richard 1844–1901. British producer of the Gilbert and Sullivan operas at the Savoy Theatre, London, which he built. The old D'Oyly Carte Opera Company founded 1876 was disbanded 1982, but a new one opened its first season 1988.

DPhil abbreviation for *Doctor of Philosophy*.

DPP abbreviation for *Director of Public Prosecutions*.

Drabble Margaret 1939– . British writer. Her novels include *The Millstone* 1966, filmed as *The Touch of Love*, *The Middle Ground* 1980, and *The Radiant Way* 1987..

Draco 7th century BC–. Athenian statesman, the first to codify the laws of the Athenian city-state.

These were notorious for their severity; hence draconian, meaning particularly harsh.

Draco a large but faint constellation, representing a dragon coiled around the north celestial pole. The star Alpha Draconis (Thuban) was the pole star 4,800 years ago.

Dracula in the novel *Dracula* 1897, by Bram ◊Stoker, the caped count who, as a ◊vampire, drinks the blood of beautiful women.

draft in the USA, compulsory military service; also known as ◊conscription.

drag the resistance to motion a body experiences when passing through a fluid – gas or liquid. The aerodynamic drag aircraft experience when travelling through the air represents a great waste of power, so they must be carefully shaped, or streamlined to reduce drag to a minimum. Cars benefit from streamlining, and aerodynamic drag is used to slow down spacecraft returning from space. Boats travelling through water experience hydrodynamic drag on their hull, and the fastest vessels are ◊hydrofoils, whose hulls lift out of the water while cruising, thus minimizing hydrodynamic drag.

dragonfly type of insect with a long narrow body, two pairs of almost equally-sized, glassy wings with a network of veins, short, bristle-like antennae, powerful, 'toothed' mouthparts, and very large compound eyes (which may have up to 30,000 facets). They hunt other insects by sight, both as adults and as aquatic nymphs. The largest modern species have a wingspan of 18 cm/7 in, but fossils with wings up to 70 cm/2.3 ft across have been found.

dragoon a mounted soldier who carried an infantry weapon such as a 'dragon' or short musket used by the French in the 16th century. The name was retained by some later regiments after the original meaning became obsolete.

drag racing popular sport in the US. High-powered single-seater cars with large rear, and small front wheels are timed over a 402.3m/440-yard strip. Speeds of up to 450kph/280mph have been attained.

Drake Francis *c.* 1545–1596. English sea captain. Having enriched himself as a pirate against Spanish interests in the Caribbean 1567–72, he was sponsored by Elizabeth I for an expedition to the Pacific, sailing around the world 1577–80 in the *Golden Hind*. He was mayor of Plymouth 1582 and Member of Parliament 1584–85. In 1587 he raided the Spanish port of Cadiz. Against the ◊Spanish Armada 1588 he was vice-admiral.

Drake *Portrait of Sir Francis Drake by an unknown artist (1580-85), National Portrait Gallery, London.*

Dresden *Following the devastating bombing of Dresden in 1945, some ruins remain among the rebuilt quarters.*

drama a play performed by actors for an audience, an element of ◊theatre. The term is also used collectively to group plays into historical or stylistic periods, for example Greek drama, Restoration drama, as well as referring to the whole body of work written by a dramatist for performance. Drama is distinct from literature; it is a performing art open to infinite interpretation, the product not merely of the playwright but also of the collaboration of directors, designer, actors and many others.

dramatis personae (Latin) the characters in a play.

draughts board game (known in the USA and Canada as *checkers*) which has elements of a simplified form of chess. Each of the two players has 12 men (disc-shaped pieces), and attempts either to capture all the opponent's men or to block their movements.

Dravidian a group of non-Aryan peoples of the Deccan region of India and in N Sri Lanka. The Dravidian languages include Tamil, Telugu, Malayalam, and Kannada.

dream a series of events, or images, which occurs during sleep. For the purposes of (allegedly) foretelling the future, dreams fell into disrepute in the scientific atmosphere of the 18th century, but were given importance by ◊Freud who saw them as wish fulfilment (nightmares being failed dreams prompted by fears of 'repressed' impulses). Dreams occur in periods of rapid eye movement (REM) by the sleeper, when the cortex of the brain is approximately as active as in waking hours, and they occupy a fifth of sleeping time.

Dreamtime or *dreaming* the complex religious belief systems and stories of the creation of the Australian Aborigines. In Dreamtime, spiritual beings shaped the land; the first people were created and placed in their proper territories; and laws and rituals were established.

Dred Scott Case, The In US history, a Supreme Court case brought by a Missouri black slave, Dred Scott (*c.* 1800–1858), seeking to obtain his freedom on the grounds that his owner had taken him to reside temporarily in the free state of Illinois. The decision of the Supreme Court against Scott in 1857 intensified sectional discord before the Civil War.

Dreikaiserbund an informal alliance from 1872 between the emperors of Russia, Germany, and Austria-Hungary. It was at an end by 1879.

Dreiser Theodore 1871–1945. US novelist, formerly a Chicago journalist. He wrote the Naturalist novel *Sister Carrie* 1900 and *An American Tragedy* 1925, based on the real-life crime of a

Dreyfus *French army officer Alfred Dreyfus.*

young man who in 'making good' kills a shop assistant he has made pregnant.

Dresden city of E Germany, capital of Dresden district, formerly capital of Saxony; population (1982) 521,000. Manufactures include chemicals, machinery, glassware, and musical instruments. One of the most beautiful German cities prior to its devastation by Allied bombing in 1945; subsequently rebuilt.

Dreyfus Alfred 1859–1935. French army officer, victim of miscarriage of justice, and anti-Semitism. Employed in the War Ministry, in 1894 he was accused of betraying military secrets to Germany, court-martialled, and sent to ◊Devil's Island. When his innocence was discovered 1896 the military establishment tried to conceal it, and the implications of the Dreyfus affair were passionately discussed in the press until in 1906 he was exonerated.

drill large monkey *Mandrillus leucophaeus* living in forests of W Africa. Sombre-coated, black-faced, and stoutly built, with a very short tail, the male can have a head and body up to 75 cm/2.5 ft long, although females are smaller.

drilling a common woodworking and metal machinery process, which involves boring holes with a drill ◊bit. The commonest kind of drill bit is the fluted drill, which has spiral grooves around it to allow the cut material to escape. In the oil industry rotary drilling is used to bore oil wells. The drill bit usually consists of a number of toothed cutting wheels, which grind their way through the rock as the drill pipe is turned, and mud is pumped through the pipe to lubricate the bit and flush the ground-up rock to the surface.

dromedary type of Arabian ◊camel.

drought period of prolonged dry weather: in the UK, drought is defined as the passing of 15 days

dromedary

Dryden English poet, satirist, and dramatist John Dryden; a portrait by Kneller, 1693.

with less than 0.2 mm of rain. The area of the world subject to serious droughts, as in the Sahara, is increasing because of destruction of forests and so on, forming greater areas of desert.

drowning suffocation by fluid. Drowning may be due to inhaling external fluid, such as water, or to the presence of body fluids in the lungs.

drug and alcohol dependence individuals can become dependent on addictive drugs such as alcohol, nicotine (in cigarettes), tranquillizers, heroin, or stimulants (for example, amphetamines). Such substances can alter mood or behaviour. When dependence is established, sudden withdrawal from the drug can cause an unpleasant reaction, which can be dangerous.

Druidism religion of the Celtic peoples of pre-Christian Britain and Gaul. The word is usually derived from Greek *drus* oak, and they regarded this tree as sacred, one of their chief rites being the cutting from it of mistletoe with a golden sickle. They taught the immortality of the soul and a reincarnation doctrine, and were expert in astronomy. The Druids are thought to have offered human sacrifices.

drum percussion instrument, essentially a piece of skin (parchment, plastic or nylon) stretched over a resonator and struck with a stick, or the hands.

drupe a fleshy ◊fruit containing one or more seeds that are surrounded by a hard, protective layer, for example cherry, almond and plum. The wall of the fruit (◊pericarp) is differentiated into the outer skin (exocarp), the fleshy layer of tissues (mesocarp), and the hard layer surrounding the seed (endocarp). The coconut is a drupe, but here the pericarp becomes dry and fibrous at maturity. Blackberries are an aggregate fruit composed of a cluster of small drupes.

Druse or *Druze* a religious sect in the Middle East of some 500,000 people. They are monotheists, preaching that the Fatimid caliph al-Hakim (996–1021) is God; their scriptures are drawn from the Christian gospels, the Torah (the first five books of the Old Testament), the Koran, and Sufi allegories. Druse militia groups form one of the three main factions involved in the Lebanese civil war (the others are Amal Shi'ite Muslims and Christian Maronites). The Druse military leader (from his father's assassination in 1977) is Walid Jumblatt.

dryad in Greek mythology, a forest nymph or tree spirit.

dry cleaning a method of cleaning textiles based on the use of volatile solvents which dissolve grease, for example, trichloroethylene. First developed in France in 1849, the method is termed 'dry' because no water is used.

Dryden John 1631–1700. English poet and dramatist, noted for his satirical verse and for his use of the heroic couplet. His poetry includes the verse-satire *Absalom and Achitophel* 1681, 'Annus Mirabilis', and St Cecilia's Day' 1687; plays include the comedy *Marriage à la Mode* 1671 and *All for Love* 1678, a reworking of Shakespeare's *Antony and Cleopatra*. Critical works include *Essays on Dramatic Poesy* 1668.

dry point technique of engraving on copper, using a hard, sharp tool. The resulting lines tend to be fine and angular, with a strong furry edge created by the metal shavings. The technique is used in print making.

dry rot infection of timber in damp conditions by fungi, such as *Merulius lacrymans*, which forms a thread-like surface. Whitish at first, the fungi later reddens as reproductive spores are formed. Fungoid tentacles also enter the fabric of the timber, rendering it dry-looking and brittle. Dry rot spreads rapidly through a building.

Drysdale George Russell 1912–1969. Australian artist, who depicted the Australian outback, its drought, desolation, and poverty, and Aboriginal life.

DSO abbreviation for *Distinguished Service Order*.

DTI abbreviation for *Department of Trade and Industry*, UK government department.

Dual Entente an alliance between France and Russia which lasted from 1893 until the Bolshevik Revolution of 1917.

dualism in philosophy, the belief that reality is essentially dual in nature. ◊Descartes, for example, refers to thinking and material substance. These entities interact, but are fundamentally separate and distinct. Dualism is contrasted with ◊monism.

Dubai one of the ◊United Arab Emirates.

Dubček Alexander 1921–1992. Czechoslovak liberal socialist politician. As first secretary of the Communist Party 1967–69, he launched a liberalization campaign (called the Prague Spring). To stamp it out, the USSR invaded Czechoslovakia 1968; Dubček was arrested and, in 1970, expelled from the party. In 1989 he gave speeches at prodemocracy rallies and, after the fall of the hardline regime, was elected speaker of the national assembly, to which he was re-elected 1990. He died in a car crash.

Dublin county in Leinster province, Republic of Ireland, facing the Irish Sea; area 922 sq km/356 sq mi; population (1986) 1,021,000. Mostly level and low-lying, but rising in the south to 753 m/2,473 ft in Kippure, part of the Wicklow mountains.

Dublin (Gaelic *Baile Atha Cliath*) Capital and port on the E coast of the Republic of Ireland, at the mouth of the Liffey, facing the Irish Sea; population (1986) 502,700; Greater Dublin (including Dún Laoghaire) 921,000. It is the site of one of the world's largest breweries (Guinness); other industries include textiles, pharmaceuticals, electrical goods, and machine tools. It was the centre

Dubček Czech politician Alexander Dubček in 1968.

Dufy Deauville: Drying the Sails *(1933) Tate Gallery, London.*

of English rule from 1171 (exercised from Dublin Castle 1220) until 1922.

Dubuffet Jean 1901–1985. French artist. He originated *l'art brut*, raw or brutal art, in the 1940s. He used a variety of materials in his paintings and sculptures – plaster, steel wool, straw, and so on – and was inspired by graffiti and children's drawings. L'art brut emerged in 1945 with an exhibition of his own work and of paintings by psychiatric patients and naive or untrained artists.

Duccio di Buoninsegna *c.* 1255–1319. Italian painter, a major figure in the Sienese school. His greatest work is his altarpiece for Siena Cathedral, the *Maestà* 1308–11; the figure of the Virgin is Byzantine in style, with much gold detail, but Duccio also created a graceful linear harmony in drapery hems, for example, and this proved a lasting characteristic of Sienese style.

Duce (Italian 'leader') title bestowed on the Fascist dictator Mussolini by his followers, and later adopted as his official title.

Duchamp Marcel 1887–1968. US artist, born in France. He achieved notoriety with his *Nude Descending a Staircase* 1912 (Philadelphia Museum of Art), influenced by Cubism and Futurism. An active member of ◊Dada, he invented **readymades**, everyday items like a bicycle wheel on a kitchen stool, which he displayed as works of art.

duck short-legged waterbird with webbed feet and flattened bill of the family Anatidae, which also includes geese and swans. Ducks have the three front toes in a web, the hind toe free, and a skin-covered bill with a horny tip provided with little plates (lamellae) through which the birds are able to strain their food from water and mud. Most species of duck live in fresh water, feeding on worms and insects as well as vegetable matter.

duckweed tiny plant *Lemna minor* found floating on the surface of still water throughout most of the world, except the polar regions and tropics. Each plant consists of a flat circular leaf-like structure 0.4 cm/0.15 in or less across, with a single thin root below up to 15 cm/6 in long.

due process of law a legal principle, dating back to ◊Magna Carta (1215), and now enshrined in the fifth and fourteenth amendments of the American Constitution, that no person shall be deprived of his life, liberty or property without due process of law (a fair legal procedure). In the US, the provisions have been given a wide interpretation, to include for example, the right to representation by an attorney.

Dufay Guillaume 1400–1474. French composer. He is recognized as the foremost composer of his time,

both of secular songs and sacred music, including 84 songs, eight masses, motets, and antiphons. His work marks a transition between the music of the Middle Ages and that of the Renaissance, and is characterized by expressive melodies and rich harmonies.

Du Fu another name for the Chinese poet ◊Tu Fu.

Dufy Raoul 1877–1953. French painter and designer. He originated a fluent, brightly coloured style in watercolour and oils, painting scenes of gaiety and leisure, such as horse racing, yachting and life on the beach.

dugong marine mammal *Dugong dugong* found in the Red Sea, the Indian Ocean and W Pacific. It can grow to 3.6 m/11 ft long, and has a tapering body with a notched tail and two fore-flippers. It is herbivorous, feeding on sea grasses and seaweeds.

duiker (Afrikaans *diver*) a type of antelope common in Africa. Shy and nocturnal, they range from 30–70 cm/12–28 in tall. There are many species.

Dukakis Michael 1933–0000. US Democrat politician, governor of Massachusetts 1974–78 and from 1982, presiding over a high-tech economic boom, the 'Massachusetts miracle'. He was a presidential candidate in 1988.

Dukas Paul (Abraham) 1865–1935. French composer. He was professor of composition at the Paris Conservatoire, and composed the opera *Ariane et Barbe-Bleue* 1907, and the ballet *La Péri* 1912. His orchestral scherzo *L'Apprenti Sorcier/The Sorcer-er's Apprentice* 1897 is full of the colour and energy which characterizes much of his work.

duke highest title in the English peerage. It originated in England in 1337, when Edward III created his son Edward duke of Cornwall. The premier Scottish duke is the Duke of Hamilton (created 1643).

Dulce et decorum est pro patria mori (Latin 'it is sweet and noble to die for one's country') quotation from Horace's *Odes*, also used by Wilfred Owen as the title for his poem denouncing the First World War.

dulcimer musical instrument, consisting of a shallow box strung with wire strings which are struck with small wooden hammers. Of Eastern origin, it is still current in Hungary under the name cimbalom.

Dulles Alan 1893–1969. US lawyer, brother of John Foster ◊Dulles, and director of the Central Intelligence Agency (CIA) 1953–61.

Dulles John Foster 1888–1959. US politician. Senior US adviser at the founding of the United Nations, he

Dumas French dramatist and novelist Alexandre Dumas père.

largely drafted the Japanese peace treaty of 1951, and as secretary of state 1952–59, was critical of Britain in the Suez Crisis. He was the architect of US ◊Cold War foreign policy, securing US intervention in support of South Vietnam following the expulsion of the French in 1954.

Duma in Russia, before 1917, an elected assembly which met four times following the abortive 1905 revolution. With progressive demands the government could not accept, the Duma was largely powerless. After the abdication of Nicholas II the Duma directed the formation of a provisional government.

Dumas Alexandre 1802–1870. French author, known as Dumas *père* (the father). His play *Henri III et sa cour/Henry III and his Court* 1829 established French romantic historical drama, but today he is remembered for his romances, the reworked output of a 'fiction-factory' of collaborators. They include *Les Trois Mousquetaires/The Three Musketeers* 1844 and its sequels. Dumas *fils* was his illegitimate son.

Dumas Alexandre 1824–1895. French author, known as Dumas *fils* (the son), son of Dumas *père* and remembered for the play *La Dame aux camélias/The Lady of the Camellias* 1852, based on his own novel, and source of Verdi's opera *La traviata*.

Du Maurier Daphne 1907–1989. British novelist, whose romantic fiction includes *Jamaica Inn* 1936, *Rebecca* 1938, and *My Cousin Rachel* 1951.

Dumbarton Oaks an 18th-century mansion near Washington DC, USA, used as a centre for conferences and seminars. It was the scene of a conference held in 1944 which led to the foundation of the United Nations.

Dumfries and Galloway region of Scotland
area 6,500 sq km/2,510 sq mi
towns administrative headquarters Dumfries
products horses and cattle, for which the Galloway area was especially famous; sheep; timber
population (1990 est) 147,000
famous people home of Robert Burns at Dumfries; birthplace of Thomas ◊Carlyle at Ecclefechan.

Dumfriesshire former county of S Scotland, merged in 1975 in the region of Dumfries and Galloway.

Dumouriez Charles François du Périer 1739–1823. French general during the Revolution. In 1792 he was appointed foreign minister, supported the declaration of war against Austria, and after the

fall of the monarchy was given command of the army defending Paris; later he won the battle of Jemappes, but was defeated at Neerwinden (Austrian Netherlands) in 1793. After intriguing with the royalists he had to flee for his life, and from 1804 he lived in England.

dumping in international trade, when one country sells goods to another at below marginal cost or at a price below that in its own country. Countries dump in order to get rid of surplus produce or to improve their competitive position in the recipient country. The practice is widely condemned by protectionists (opponents of free trade) because of the unfair competition it represents.

Dumyat Arabic name for ◊Damietta, a town in Egypt.

Dunbar William c. 1460–c. 1520. Scottish poet at the court of James IV. His poems include a political allegory 'The Thrissel and the Rose' and the elegy 'Timor mortis conturbat me'.

Dunbartonshire former county of Scotland, bordering the N bank of the Clyde estuary, on which stand Dumbarton (the former county town), Clydebank and Helensburgh. It was merged in 1975 in the region of Strathclyde.

Duncan Isadora 1878–1927. American dancer and teacher. An influential pioneer of American modern dance, she adopted an expressive, free form, dancing barefoot and wearing a loose tunic, inspired by the ideal of Hellenic beauty. She toured extensively, often returning to Russia after her initial success

dune

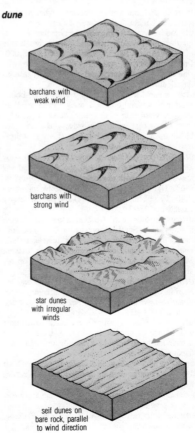

barchans with weak wind

barchans with strong wind

star dunes with irregular winds

seif dunes on bare rock, parallel to wind direction

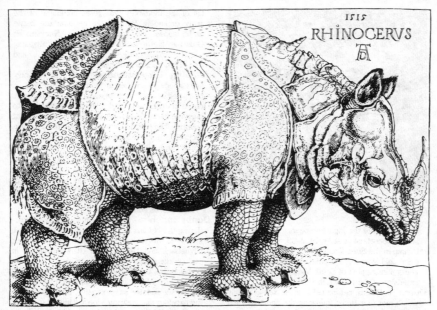

Dürer *Woodcut of a rhinoceros by Albrecht Dürer. The rhinoceros was described to him by a Portuguese artist in 1515.*

there in 1905, but died in an accident when her long scarf was caught in the wheel of a car.

Dundee city and fishing port, administrative headquarters of Tayside, Scotland, on the north side of the Firth of Tay; population (1981) 175,000. Important shipping and rail centre with jute, marine engineering, watch and clock, and textile industries.

dune a bank or a hill of wind-drifted sand. Loose sand is blown and bounced along by the wind, up the windward side of a dune. The sand particles then fall to rest on the lee side, while more are blown up from the windward. In this way a dune moves gradually downwind.

Dunedin port on Otago harbour, South Island, New Zealand; population (1986) 106,864. Also a road, rail and air centre, with engineering and textile industries. The city was founded in 1848 by members of the Free Church of Scotland and the university established 1869.

Dunfermline industrial town near the Firth of Forth in Fife region, Scotland; population (1981) 52,000. Site of the naval base of Rosyth; industries include engineering, shipbuilding, electronics, and textiles. Many Scottish kings, including Robert the Bruce, are buried in Dunfermline Abbey.

Dunham Katherine 1912– . American dancer, born in Chicago, noted for a free, strongly emotional method. She founded her own school and company in 1945.

Dun Laoghaire (former name Kingstown) port and suburb of Dublin, Republic of Ireland. It is a terminal for ferries to England, and there are fishing industries.

dunlin small wading bird *Calidris alpina* about 18 cm/7 in long, nesting along the far northern regions on moors and marshes. Chestnut above and black below in summer, it is greyish in winter. It is the commonest small sandpiper.

Dunlop John Boyd 1840–1921. Scottish inventor, who founded the rubber company that bears his name. In 1887, to help his child win a tricycle race, he bound on inflated rubber hose to the wheels. The same year he developed commercially practical pneumatic tyres (first patented by R W Thomson in 1846) for bicycles and cars.

dunnock European bird *Prunella modularis* similar in size and colouring to the sparrow, but with slate-grey head and breast, and more slender bill. It nests in bushes and hedges, and is often called 'hedge sparrow'.

Dunstable John *c.* 1385–1453. English composer. Little is known of his life, though he may have had some connection with St Albans Cathedral, and seems to have travelled widely in Europe, achieving a reputation also as a mathematician and astrologer. He wrote songs and anthems, and is generally considered one of the founders of Renaissance music.

duodecimal system system of arithmetic notation using 12 as a base, sometimes considered superior to the decimal system in that 12 has more factors than 10 (2, 3, 4, 6).

Du Pré Jacqueline 1945–1987. British cellist. Noted for her extraordinary technique and powerful interpretations of the classic cello repertory, particularly of Elgar. She had an international concert career while still in her teens, and made many recordings.

duralumin a lightweight aluminium ◊alloy widely used in aircraft construction, containing copper, magnesium and manganese.

Duras Marguerite 1914– . French writer. Her works include short stories (*Des Journées entières dans les arbres*), plays (*La Musica*), film scripts (*Hiroshima Mon Amour* 1960), and novels such as *Le Vice-Consul* 1966, evoking an existentialist world from the actual setting of Calcutta. Her autobiographical novel, *La Douleur*, is set in Paris in 1945.

Durban principal port of Natal, South Africa, and second port of the republic; population (1985)

634,300. Exports coal, maize, and wool; imports heavy machinery and mining equipment; also an important holiday resort.

Dürer Albrecht 1471–1528. German artist, the leading figure of the northern Renaissance. He was born in Nuremburg and travelled widely in Europe. Highly skilled in drawing and a keen student of nature, he perfected the technique of woodcut and engraving, producing woodcut series such as the *Apocalypse* 1498 and copperplate engravings such as *The Knight, Death and the Devil* 1513 and *Melancholia* 1514; he may also have invented etching. His paintings are relatively few; the altarpieces are inferior to the meticulously observed portraits (including many self-portraits).

Durga Hindu goddess; one of the many names for ◊*Mahadevi*.

Durham county in NE England
area 2,436 sq km/6,309 sq mi
towns administrative headquarters Durham; Darlington, and the new towns of Peterlee and Newton Aycliffe
products sheep and dairy produce; the county lies on one of Britain's richest coalfields.
population (1988 est) 596,800

Durham John George Lambton, 1st Earl of Durham 1792–1840. British politician. Appointed Lord Privy Seal in 1830. He drew up the first Reform Bill of 1832, and as governor general of Canada briefly in 1837 drafted the Durham Report which led to the union of Upper and Lower Canada.

Durkheim Emile 1858–1917. French sociologist, one of the founders of modern sociology, who also influenced social anthropology.

durra or *dourra* grass of the genus *Sorghum*, also known as Indian millet, grown as cereal in parts of Asia and Africa. *Sorghum vulgare* is the chief cereal in many parts of Africa.

Durrell Gerald Malcolm 1925– . British naturalist, brother of Lawrence Durrell. Director of Jersey Zoological Park, he is the author of travel and natural history books, and the humorous memoir *My Family and Other Animals* 1956.

Durrell Lawrence George 1912–1990. British novelist and poet. Born in India, he lived mainly in the East Mediterranean, the setting of his novels, including the Alexandria Quartet: *Justine, Balthazar, Mountolive* and *Clea* 1957–60. He was the brother of Gerald Durrell.

Dürrenmatt Friedrich 1921–1991. Swiss dramatist, author of grotesquely farcical tragi-comedies, for example *The Visit* 1956 and *The Physicists* 1962.

Durrës chief port of Albania, population (1983) 72,000. Main commercial and communications centre, with flour mills, soap and cigarette factories, distilleries, and an electronics plant. It was the capital of Albania 1912–21.

Dushanbe (1929–69) formerly *Stalinabad* capital of Tajikistan; population (1987) 582,000. Situated 160 km/100 mi N of the Afghan frontier, it is an important road, rail and air centre. Industries include cotton mills, tanneries, meat-packing factories, and printing works.

Düsseldorf industrial city of Germany, on the right bank of the Rhine, 26 km/16 mi NW of Cologne, capital of North Rhine-Westphalia; population (1988) 561,000. A river port and the commercial and financial centre of the Ruhr area, with food processing, brewing, agricultural machinery, textile, and chemical industries.

dust bowl area in the Great Plains region of North America (Texas to Kansas) that suffered extensive wind erosion as the result of bad farming practice in the once fertile soil. Much of the topsoil was blown away in the 1930s.

Dutch East India Company a trading company established in the Northern Netherlands in 1602 and given a trading monopoly in the Indonesian archipelago, with certain sovereign rights such as the creation of an army and a fleet. During the 17th and 18th centuries the company used its monopoly of East Indian trade to pay out high dividends, but wars with England and widespread corruption led to a suspension of payments in 1781 and an eventual takeover of the company by the Dutch government in 1798.

Dutch East Indies former Dutch colony which in 1945 became independent as ◊Indonesia.

Dutch elm disease a disease of elm trees (*Ulmus*), principally English elm and Dutch elm, caused by the fungus *Certocystis ulmi*. The fungus is usually spread from tree to tree by the elm bark beetle which lays its eggs beneath the bark. The disease has no cure and control methods involve injecting insecticide into the trees annually to prevent infection, or the destruction of all elms in a broad band around an infected area, to keep the beetles out.

Dutch Guiana former Dutch colony which in 1948 became independent as ◊Suriname.

Dutch language a member of the Germanic branch of the Indo-European language family, often referred to by scholars as Netherlandic and taken to include the standard language and dialects of the Netherlands (excluding Frisian) and also Flemish (in Belgium and northern France) and, more remotely, its off-shoot Afrikaans in South Africa.

Duvalier François 1907–1971. President of Haiti from 1959 until his death. Known as *Papa Doc*, he organized the Tontons Macoutes ('bogeymen') as a private army to cajole and assassinate opponents of his regime. He rigged the 1961 elections in order to have his term of office extended until 1967, and in 1964 declared himself president for life. He was excommunicated by the Vatican for harassing the Church, and was succeeded on his death by his son Jean-Claude.

Duvalier Jean Claude 1951– . President of Haiti 1971–86. Known as *Baby Doc*, he succeeded his father François Duvalier becoming, at the age of 19, the youngest president in the world. He was forced by the United States to moderate his father's tyrannical regime, yet no opposition was tolerated. He left Haiti in 1986 after mounting popular disturbances.

Duwez Pol 1907– . US scientist, born in Belgium, who in 1959 developed metallic glass with his team at the California Institute of Technology.

Dvořák Antonin (Leopold) 1841–1904. Czech composer. International success came with his series of Slavonic dances 1877–86 and he was Director of the National Conservatory, New York, 1892–95. Works such as his *New World Symphony* 1893 show his interest in black music. He wrote operas, including *Rusalka* 1901; large-scale choral works, the *Carnival* and other overtures, violin and cello concertos, chamber music, piano pieces, and songs. His music is in the classical tradition of Beethoven and Brahms, and strongly influenced by Czech folk music.

dwarf star a star on the ◊Hertzsprung-Russell diagram more commonly called a ◊main sequence star. See also ◊red dwarf and ◊white dwarf.

Dyck Anthony van 1599–1641. Flemish painter. An assistant to Rubens 1618–20, he then briefly worked in England at the court of James I, and

Dvořák *Czech composer Antonin Dvořák.*

moved to Italy in 1622. In 1626 he returned to Antwerp, where he continued to paint religious works and brilliant portraits. He painted his best-known portraits during his second period in England from 1632, for example, *Charles I on Horseback* c. 1638 (National Gallery, London).

dye substance which, applied in solution to fabrics, imparts a colour resistant to washing. *Direct dyes* combine with the material of the fabric, yielding a coloured compound; *indirect dyes* require the presence of another substance (a mordant), with which the fabric must first be treated; *vat dyes* are colourless soluble substances which on oxidation by exposure to air yield an insoluble coloured compound. Naturally occurring dyes include indigo, madder (alizarin), logwood, and cochineal, but industrial dyes (introduced in the 19th century) are usually synthetic; acid green was developed 1835, and bright purple 1856. Industrial dyes include azo-dye-stuffs, acridine, anthracene and aniline.

Dyfed county of SW Wales
area 5,768 sq km/2,226 sq mi
towns administrative headquarters Carmarthen; Aberystwyth, Cardigan, Lampeter
population (1991) 343,500

language English, Welsh (44%)
famous people Dafydd ap Gwilym

Dylan Bob. Adopted name of Robert Allen Zimmerman 1941– . US singer and songwriter, whose work in the 1960s, first in the folk-music tradition and from 1965 in an individualistic rock style, was highly influential on later pop music.

dynamics branch of mechanics that deals with the mathematical and physical study of the behaviour of bodies under the action of forces which produce changes of motion in them.

dynamite an explosive consisting of a mixture of nitroglycerine and kieselguhr; it was devised by Alfred Nobel.

dynamo a machine for transforming mechanical energy into electrical energy. It is also called a generator. A simple form of dynamo consists of a powerful field magnet, between the poles of which a suitable conductor, usually in the form of a coil (armature), is rotated. The mechanical energy of rotation is thus converted into an electric current in the armature.

dyscalculus a disability demonstrated by a poor aptitude with figures. A similar disability in reading and writing is called ◊dyslexia.

dysentery infection of the large intestine causing abdominal cramps and ◊diarrhoea.

dyslexia (Greek 'bad', 'pertaining to words'), a malfunction in the brain's synthesis and interpretation of sensory information, popularly 'word blindness'. It results in poor ability to read and write, though the person may otherwise excel, for example, in mathematics. A similar disability with figures is called ◊dyscalculus.

dyspnoea difficulty in breathing, or shortness of breath disproportionate to effort. It occurs if the supply of oxygen is inadequate or if carbon dioxide accumulates.

dysprosium an element, one of the yttrium group of rare earths (symbol Dy, atomic number 66, relative atomic mass 162.51).

Dzungarian Gates ancient route in central Asia on the border of Kazakhstan and Xinjiang Uygur region of China, 470 km/290 mi NW of Urümqi. The route was used by the Mongol hordes on their way to Europe.

eagle

bald eagle

E abbreviation for *east*.

eagle name given to a number of genera of large birds of prey of the family Accipitridae. The typical genus *Aquila* includes the golden eagle *Aquila chrysaetos*. It has a 2 m/6 ft wingspan and is dark brown.

Eanes António dos Santos Ramalho 1935– Portuguese politician. He helped plan the 1974 coup which ended the Caetano regime, and as army chief of staff put down a left-wing revolt in Nov 1975. He was president 1976–86.

ear the organ of hearing in animals. It responds to the vibrations that constitute sound, and these are translated into nerve signals and passed to the brain. A mammal's ear consists of three parts. The *outer ear* is a funnel which collects sound, directing it down a tube to the *ear drum* (tympanic membrane) which separates the outer and *middle ear*. Sounds vibrate this membrane, the mechanical movement of which is transferred to the membrane of the *inner ear* by three small bones, the auditory ossicles. Vibrations of the inner ear membrane move

fluid contained in the snail-shaped cochlea, which vibrates hair cells that stimulate the auditory nerve, connected to the brain. The fluid-filled labyrinth of the inner ear detects changes of position; this, with other sensory inputs, is responsible for the sense of balance.

Early English in architecture, name given by Thomas Rickman (1776–1841) to the first of the three periods of the English Gothic style. It covers the period from about 1189 to about 1280, and is characterized by tall, elongated windows (lancets) without mullions (horizontal bars), often grouped in threes, fives, or sevens; the pointed arch; pillars of stone centres surrounded by shafts of black Purbeck marble; and dog-tooth (zig-zag) ornament. Salisbury Cathedral is almost entirely Early English.

Earth the third planet from the Sun. It is almost spherical, flattened slightly at the poles, and has

ear

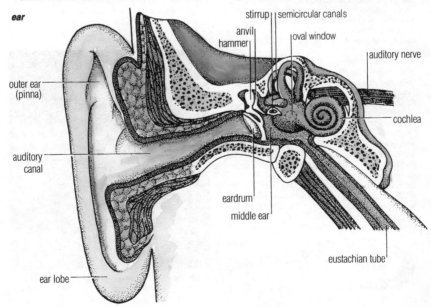

earthquake

Intensity value	Description
I	Only detected by instrument.
II	Felt by people resting.
III	Felt indoors; hanging objects swing; feels like passing traffic.
IV	Feels like passing heavy traffic; standing cars rock; windows, dishes, and doors rattle; wooden frames creak.
V	Felt outdoors; sleepers are woken; liquids spill; doors swing.
VI	Felt by everybody; people stagger; windows break; trees and bushes rustle; weak plaster cracks.
VII	Difficult to stand upright; noticed by vehicle drivers; plaster, loose bricks, tiles and chimneys fall; bells ring.
VIII	Car steering affected; some collapse of masonry; chimney stacks and towers fall; branches break from trees; cracks in wet ground.
IX	General panic; serious damage to buildings; underground pipes break; cracks and subsidence in ground.
X	Most buildings destroyed; landslides; water thrown out of canals.
XI	Rails bent; underground pipes totally destroyed.
XII	Damage nearly total; rocks displaced; objects thrown into air.

three geological zones: the ◊core, the ◊mantle, and the ◊crust. The surface is 70% covered with water, and surrounded by an atmosphere which supports life (Earth is the only planet on which life is known to exist).

mean distance from the Sun 149,500,000 km/ 93,000,000 mi

equatorial diameter 12,756 km/7,927 mi

circumference 40,070 km/24,900 mi

rotation period 23 hr 56 min 4.1 sec

year (complete orbit, or sidereal period) 365 days 5 hr 48 min 46 sec. Earth's average speed round the Sun is 30 km/18.5 mi per second; the plane of its orbit is inclined to its equatorial plane at an angle of 23.5°, the reason for the changing seasons

atmosphere nitrogen 78.09%, oxygen 20.95%, argon 0.93%, carbon dioxide 0.03%, and less than 0.0001% neon, helium, krypton, hydrogen, xenon, ozone, radon

surface land surface 150,000,000 sq km/ 57,500,000 sq mi (greatest height Mount Everest); water surface 361,000,000 sq km/139,400,000 sq mi (greatest depth Mariana Trench in Pacific). The interior is thought to be an inner core about 2,600

km/1,600 mi in diameter, of solid iron and nickel; an outer core about 2,250 km/1,400 mi thick, of molten iron and nickel; and a mantle of solid rock about 2,900 km/1,800 mi thick, separated by the ◊Mohorovičić discontinuity from the Earth's crust. The crust and the topmost layer of the mantle form about 12 major plates (on top of which the continents slowly drift)

age 4,600,000,000 years. The Earth was formed with the rest of the ◊Solar System by consolidation of interstellar dust. Life began about 4,000,000,000 years ago

satellite the ◊Moon.

earth in electricity, a connection between an appliance and the ground. In the event of a fault in an electrical appliance, for example, involving connection between the live part of the circuit and the outer casing, the current flows to earth, causing no harm to the user.

earthquake a shaking or convulsion of the Earth's surface, the scientific study of which is called ◊seismology. Earthquakes result from a build-up of stresses within rocks until strained to fracturing point. Most occur along ◊faults (fractures or breaks) in the Earth's strata. The force of an earthquake can be measured on the ◊Richter scale, and its effect on the Mercalli scale.

Earth Summit (official name *United Nations Conference on Environment and Development*) international meeting in Rio de Janeiro, Brazil, June 1992 which drew up measures towards world environmental protection. Treaties were made to combat global warming and protect wildlife ('biodiversity') (the latter was not signed by the USA).

earthworm annelid worm of the class Oligochaeta. Earthworms are hermaphrodite, and deposit their eggs in cocoons. They live by burrowing in the soil, feeding on the organic matter it contains. They play a most important role in the formation of humus by irrigating the soil.

earwig nocturnal insect of the order Dermaptera. The fore-wings are short and leathery, and serve to protect the hind-wings, which are large and are folded like a fan when at rest; the insects seldom fly. They are regarded as pests because they feed on flowers and fruit, but they also eat other insects, dead or alive. Eggs are laid beneath the soil, and

earthworm

Earth *View of the Earth rising over the surface of the Moon.*

earthquake

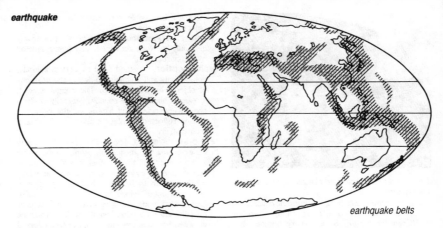

earthquake belts

the females cares for the young even after they have hatched.

easement in law, rights which a person may have over the land of another. The commonest example is a right of way; others are the right to bring water over another's land, and 'ancient lights', that is, the right to an uninterrupted flow of light to windows.

east one of the four cardinal points of the compass, indicating that part of the horizon where the Sun rises; when facing north, east is to the right.

East Anglia region of E England, formerly a Saxon kingdom, including Norfolk, Suffolk, and parts of Essex and Cambridgeshire. The University of East Anglia was founded at Norwich in 1962, and the Sainsbury Centre for the Visual Arts, opened in 1978, has a collection of ethnographic art and sculpture.

Easter feast of the Christian church, commemorating the Resurrection of Christ. The English name derives from Eostre, Anglo-Saxon goddess of spring, who was honoured in Apr. Easter eggs, symbolizing new life, are given as presents.

Easter Island or *Rapa Nui* Chilean island in the S Pacific Ocean, part of the Polynesian group, about 5,960 km/2,300 mi W of Chile; area about 166 sq km/64 sq mi; population (1985) 2,000. First reached by Europeans on Easter Sunday 1722. It is famous

earthquake: Mexico City, 19th Sept 1985.

for its huge carved statues and stone houses, the work of neolithic peoples of unknown origin. The chief centre is Hanga-Roa.

Easter Rising traditionally known as the *Easter Rebellion*. Republican insurrection in Dublin, Ireland, Apr 1916, against British rule in Ireland. It began on Easter Monday and was concluded a week later in the face of British artillery.

East India Company an English commercial company 1600–1858 that was chartered by Queen Elizabeth I and given a monopoly of trade between England and the Far East.

East India Company, Dutch see ◊Dutch East India Company.

Eastman George 1854–1932. US businessman and inventor who founded the Kodak photographic company. From 1888 he marketed daylight-loading flexible roll films (to replace the glass plates used previously) and portable cameras. By 1900 his company was selling a pocket camera for as little as $1.

East Sussex county in SE England
area 1,795 sq km/693 sq mi
towns administrative headquarters Lewes; cross-channel port of Newhaven; Brighton, Eastbourne, Hastings, Bexhill, Winchelsea, Rye
products electronics, gypsum, timber
population (1988 est) 698,000
famous people Henry James, Rudyard Kipling.

East Timor disputed territory on the island of ◊Timor in the Malay Archipelago; prior to 1975, a Portuguese colony for almost 460 years
area 14,760 sq km/5,700 sq mi
capital Dili
products coffee
population (1980) 555,000
history following Portugal's withdrawal in 1975, the left-wing Revolutionary Front of Independent East Timor (Fretilin) occupied the capital, Dili, calling for independence. In opposition, troops from neighbouring Indonesia invaded the territory, declaring East Timor (*Loro Sae*) the 17th province of Indonesia in Jul 1976. This claim is not recognized by the United Nations.

Eastwood Clint 1930– . US film actor and director. As the 'man with no name' caught up in Wild West lawlessness in *A Fistful of Dollars* 1964, he started the vogue for 'spaghetti westerns'. Later westerns include *High Plains Drifter* 1973, *Outlaw Josey Wales* 1976, and the Oscar-winning *Unforgiven* 1992.

EBCDIC extended binary coded decimal interchange code; in computing, a code used for storing and

Eastwood US film actor and director Clint Eastwood, photographed in 1970.

communicating alphabetic and numeric characters. It is an eight-digit code, representing up to 256 different characters by a ◊binary number system. It is still used in many mainframe computers, but almost all mini- and microcomputers now use ◊ASCII code.

ebony tropical hardwood tree, genus *Diospyros*, of the family Ebenaceae. Its very heavy, hard black timber polishes well and is used in cabinet-making, inlaying, and also for piano-keys and knife-handles.

EC abbreviation for ◊*European Community*.

eccentricity in geometry, a property of a ◊conic section (◊circle, ◊ellipse, ◊parabola, or ◊hyperbola). It is the distance of any point on the ◊curve from a fixed point (the focus) divided by the distance of that point from a fixed line (the directrix). A circle has an eccentricity of zero; for an ellipse it is less than one, for a parabola equal to one, and for a hyperbola greater than one.

Ecclesiastes aslo known as 'The Preacher', a book of the Old Testament or Hebrew Bible, traditionally attributed to ◊Solomon, on the theme of the vanity of human life.

ecdysis the periodic shedding of the ◊exoskeleton by insects and other arthropods to allow growth. Prior to shedding, a new soft and expandable layer is first laid down underneath the existing one. The old layer then splits, the animal moves free of it, and the new layer expands and hardens.

Echegaray José 1832–1916. Spanish dramatist. His dramas include *O locura o santidad/Madman or Saint* 1877, and *El gran Galeoto/The World and his Wife* 1881. Nobel Prize for Literature 1904.

echidna or *spiny ant-eater*. Several species of toothless, egg-laying, spiny mammals, in the order Monotremata, found in Australia and New Guinea. They feed entirely upon ants and termites which they dig out with their powerful claws and lick up with their prehensile tongue. When attacked, echidnas roll themselves into a ball, or try to hide by burrowing in the earth.

echinoderm marine invertebrate which has a basic body structure divided into five sectors. The phylum Echinodermata ('spiny-skinned') includes the starfish, brittlestars, sea-lilies, sea-urchins, and sea-cucumbers. The skeleton is external, made of a series of limy plates, and Echinodermata generally move using tube-feet – small water-filled sacs which can be protruded or pulled back to the body.

echo a reflection of a ◊sound wave, or of a ◊radar or ◊sonar signal. By accurately measuring the time taken for an echo to return to the transmitter, and by knowing the speed of a radar signal (the speed of light) or a sonar signal (the speed of sound in water), it is possible to calculate the range of the object causing the echo.

Echo in Greek mythology, a nymph who pined away until only her voice remained, after being rejected by Narcissus.

echolocation method used by certain animals, notably bats and dolphins, to detect the positions of objects by using sound. The animal emits a stream of high-pitched sounds, generally at ultrasonic frequencies, and listens for the returning echoes reflected off objects ahead to determine their distance.

echo-sounder a device that detects objects under water by means of ◊sonar – bouncing sound waves off them. Most boats are equipped with echo-sounders to measure the water depth beneath them. An echo-sounder consists of a transmitter, which emits an ultrasonic pulse (see ◊ultrasound), and a receiver, which detects the pulse after reflection from the seabed. The time between transmission and receipt of the reflected signal is a measure of the depth of water.

eclampsia convulsions occurring due to ◊toxaemia of pregnancy.

eclipse the passage of an astronomical body through the shadow of another. The term is usually used for solar and lunar eclipses, which may be either partial or total, but also, for example, for eclipses by Jupiter of its satellites. An eclipse of a star by a body in the Solar System is called an ◊occultation.

eclipsing binary a ◊binary (double) star in which the two stars periodically pass in front of each other as seen from Earth.

ecliptic the path, against the background of stars, that the Sun appears to follow each year as the Earth orbits the Sun. It can be thought of as marking the intersection of the plane of the Earth's orbit with the celestial sphere (imaginary sphere around the Earth).

Eco Umberto 1932– . Italian semiologist and literary critic (*The Role of the Reader* 1979), and author of the 'philosophical thriller' *The Name of the Rose* 1983.

ecology (from Greek *oikos*, house) the study of the relationship between an organism and the ◊environment in which it lives, including other living organisms and the non-living surroundings. The term was introduced by the biologist Ernst Haeckel in 1866.

econometrics the use of mathematical and statistical analysis to the study of economic relationships, including testing economic theories and making quantitative predictions.

economic community or *common market* an organization of autonomous countries formed to promote trade. Examples include the Caribbean Community (Caricom) 1973, Central African Economic Community 1985, European Economic Community (EEC) 1957, and Latin American Economic System 1975.

economics social science devoted to studying the production, distribution, and consumption of wealth. It consists of the disciplines of ◊*microeconomics*, the study of individual producers, consumers or markets, and ◊*macroeconomics*, the study of whole economies or systems (in particular, areas such as taxation and public spending).

economies of scale in economics, when production capacity is increased at a financial cost which is more than compensated for by the greater volume of output.

ecosystem in ◊ecology, an integrated unit consisting of the ◊community of living organisms and

eclipse

The Sun is much larger than the Moon, but is at such a distance from the Earth that their diameters appear the same. One of nature's most awesome events occurs when the Moon passes in front of the Sun, hiding our parent star from view.

solar eclipses

Total solar eclipses occur if the Sun, Moon and Earth are exactly aligned and the Sun is completely hidden; a partial eclipse takes place if only part of the Sun is obscured. Annular eclipses occur during an exact alignment if the Moon is at its furthest point from us. Its apparent diameter will be less, the Sun being seen as a ring around the Moon.

During a total solar eclipse the Sun's corona can be seen surrounding the lunar disc.

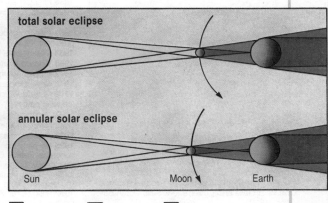

total solar eclipse

annular solar eclipse

Sun   Moon   Earth

sunlight   umbra   penumbra

lunar eclipses

Lunar eclipses take place when the Moon passes into the Earth's shadow. When this happens the lunar surface is plunged into darkness, although it is only very rarely that the Moon disappears completely from view. A small amount of sunlight is usually bent towards the lunar surface by the Earth's atmosphere.

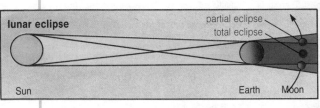

lunar eclipse

partial eclipse
total eclipse

Sun   Earth   Moon

sunlight

umbra

penumbra

Total solar eclipses (top) occur if the Moon passes through the umbra of the Earth's shadow. A partial eclipse (bottom) takes place when only part of the Moon enters this region. During a lunar eclipse, the curved shadow of the Earth can be seen crossing the lunar disc.

Ecuador
Republic of
(*República del Ecuador*)

area 301,150 sq km/116,270 sq mi
capital Quito
towns Cuenca; chief port Guayaquil
physical Andes mountains, divided by a central plateau, or Valley of the Volcanoes, including Chimborazo and Cotopaxi, which has a large share of the cultivable land and is the site of the capital
head of state and government Sixto Duran Ballen from 1992

political system emergent democracy
exports bananas, cocoa, coffee, sugar, rice, balsa wood, fish, petroleum
currency sucre
population (1989 est) 10,490,000; annual growth rate 2.9%
life expectancy men 62, women 66
language Spanish (official); Quechuan, Jivaroan
religion Roman Catholic 95%
literacy 85% male/80% female (1985 est)
GDP $ 10.6 bn (1987); $1,069 per head
chronology
1830 Ecuador became an independent republic.
1930–48 Great political instability.
1948–55 Liberals in power.
1956 First Conservative president for 60 years.
1960 Liberals returned, with José Velasco as president.
1961 Velasco deposed and replaced by the vice-president.
1963 Military junta installed.
1968 Velasco returned as president.
1972 A coup put the military back in power.
1978 New democratic constitution adopted.
1979 Liberals in power but opposed by right- and left-wing parties.
1982 Deteriorating economy provoked strikes, demonstrations and a state of emergency.
1983 Austerity measures introduced.
1985 No party with a clear majority in the national congress. Febres Cordero narrowly won the presidency for the Conservatives.
1988 Rodrigo Borja elected president for moderate left-wing coalition.
1992 Sixto Duran Ballen replaced Rodrigo Borja as president.

the physical environment in a particular area. The relationships between species in an ecosystem can be complex and finely balanced, and removal of a major predator, for example, can result in the destruction of the ecosystem through overgrazing by herbivores.

ecstasy or MDMA, 3.4 methylenedioxy-methamphetamine, an illegal drug increasingly in use in the USA and UK. It is a modified amphetamine with mild psychedelic effects. It can be synthesized from nutmeg oil, and works by depleting serotonin in the brain.

ECT abbreviation for ◊*electroconvulsive therapy*.

ectopic term applied to an anatomical feature which is displaced or found in an abnormal position. An ectopic pregnancy is one occurring outside the womb.

ectoplasm part of a cell's ◊cytoplasm.

ectotherm a 'cold-blooded' animal (see ◊poikilo-thermy) such as a lizard that relies on external warmth (ultimately from the sun) to raise its body temperature so that it can become active.

ECU abbreviation for European Currency Unit, official monetary unit of the EEC. It is based on the value of the different currencies used in the European Monetary System.

Ecuador country in South America, bounded to the north by Colombia, to the east and south by Peru, and to the west by the Pacific Ocean.

ecumenical council a meeting of church leaders to determine Christian doctrine; their results are binding on all church members. Seven such councils are accepted as ecumenical by both Eastern

and Western churches, while the Roman Catholic Church accepts a further 14 as ecumenical.

ecumenical movement movement for reunification of the various branches of the Christian church. It began in the 19th century with the extension of missionary work to the Third World, where the divisions created in Europe were incomprehensible, and gathered momentum from the need for unity in the face of growing secularism in Christian countries and of the challenge of such faiths as Islam. The *World Council of Churches* was founded 1948.

ecumenical patriarch the head of the Eastern Orthodox Church, the patriarch of Istanbul (Constantinople). The Bishop of Constantinople was recognized as having equal rights with the Bishop of Rome in 451, and first termed 'patriarch' in the 6th century. The office survives today but with only limited authority, mainly confined to the Greek and Turkish Orthodox churches.

eczema an inflammatory skin condition marked by dryness, rashes, and itching, the formation of blisters, and the exudation of fluid. It may be allergic in origin, and is sometimes complicated by infection.

Edda name given to two collections of early Icelandic literature, which together constitute our chief source for the Old Norse mythology. The term strictly applies to the *Younger* or *Prose Edda*, compiled by Snorri Sturluson, a priest, about 1230.

eddy current an electric current induced, in accordance with ◊Faraday's laws, in a conductor sited in a changing magnetic field. Eddy currents can cause much wasted energy in the cores of transformers and other electrical machines.

Eden British politician and prime minister, Anthony Eden.

Eden in the Old Testament book of Genesis and in the Koran, the 'garden' in which Adam and Eve were placed after their creation, and from which they were expelled for disobedience. Its location has often been identified with Mesopotamia, part of modern Iraq, and two of its rivers with the Euphrates and the Tigris.

Eden Anthony, 1st Earl of Avon 1897–1977. British Conservative politician, foreign secretary 1935–38, 1940–45, and 1951–55; prime minister 1955–57, when he resigned after the failure of the Anglo-French military intervention in the ◊Suez Crisis.

Edgehill, Battle of the first battle of the English Civil War. It took place in 1642, on a ridge in S Warwickshire, between Royalists under Charles I and Parliamentarians under the Earl of Essex. The result was indecisive.

Edinburgh capital of Scotland and administrative centre of the region of ◊Lothian, near the S shores of the Firth of Forth; population (1982) 447,741. A cultural centre, it is known for its annual festival of music and the arts; the university was established in 1583. Industries include printing, publishing, banking, insurance, chemical manufacture, distilling, brewing, and some shipbuilding.

Edison Thomas Alva 1847–1931. US scientist and inventor. His first invention was an automatic repeater for telegraphic messages. Later came the carbon transmitter (used as a microphone in the production of the Bell ◊telephone); the ◊phonograph; the electric filament lamp; a new type of storage battery; and the kinetoscopic camera, an early form of cinematography. He also anticipated the Fleming thermionic valve.

Edmonton capital of Alberta, Canada, on the N Saskatchewan river; population (1986) 789,000. Centre of an oil and mining area to the N; also an agricultural and dairying region. Petroleum pipelines link Edmonton with Superior, Wisconsin, USA, and Vancouver, British Columbia.

Edmund Ironside c. 989–1016. King of England, the son of Ethelred the Unready. He led the resistance to ◊Canute's invasion in 1015, and on Ethelred's death in 1016 was chosen as king by the citizens of London, while the Witan (the king's council) elected Canute. Edmund was defeated by Canute at Assandun (Ashington), Essex, and they divided the kingdom between them.

Edmund, St c. 840–870. King of East Anglia from 855. In 870 he was defeated and captured by the Danes at Hoxne, Suffolk, and martyred on refusing to renounce Christianity. He was canonized and his shrine at Bury St Edmunds became a place of pilgrimage.

education the process, beginning at birth, of developing intellectual capacity, manual skill, and social awareness, especially by giving instruction. In its more restricted sense, the term refers to the process of imparting literacy, numeracy, and a generally accepted body of knowledge.

Edward the Black Prince 1330–1376. Prince of Wales, eldest son of Edward III of England. The epithet supposedly derived from his black armour. During the Hundred Years' War he fought at the Battle of Crécy 1346 and captured the French king at Poitiers 1356. In 1367 he invaded Castile and restored to the throne the deposed king, Pedro the Cruel (1334–69).

Edward (full name Edward Antony Richard Louis) 1964– . Prince of the UK, third son of Queen Elizabeth II.

Edward ten kings of England or the UK:

Edward the Elder c. 870–924. King of the West Saxons. He succeeded his father ◊Alfred the Great in 899. He reconquered SE England and the Midlands from the Danes, uniting Wessex and ◊Mercia with the help of his sister, Athelflad. By the time Edward died, his kingdom was the most powerful in the British Isles. He was succeeded by his son ◊Athelstan.

Edward, St (the Martyr) c. 963–978. King of England from 975. Son of King Edgar, he was murdered at Corfe Castle, Dorset, probably at his stepmother Aelfthryth's instigation (she wished to secure the crown for her son, Ethelred). He was canonized 1001.

Edward, St (the Confessor) c. 1003–1066. King of England from 1042, the son of Ethelred II. He lived in Normandy until shortly before his accession. During his reign power was held by Earl ◊Godwin and his son ◊Harold, while the king devoted himself to religion. He was buried in Westminster Abbey, which he had rebuilt. He was canonized 1161.

Edward I 1239–1307. King of England from 1272, son of Henry III. Edward led the royal forces in the ◊Barons' War 1264–67, and was on a crusade when he succeeded to the throne. He established English rule over all Wales 1282–84, and secured recognition of his overlordship from the Scottish king, though the Scots (under Wallace and Bruce) fiercely resisted actual conquest. In his reign Parliament took its approximate modern form with the ◊Model Parliament of 1295.

Edward II 1284–1327. King of England from 1307. Son of Edward I and born at Caernarvon Castle, he was created the first prince of Wales in 1301.

Edison In his physics laboratory at West Orange, New Jersey, the inventor Thomas Edison holds an 'Edison Effect' lamp.

Edward VIII The Duke and Duchess of Windsor in a Sussex village, Sept 1939.

His invasion of Scotland in 1314 to suppress revolt resulted in defeat at ◊Bannockburn. He was deposed in 1327 by his wife Isabella (1292–1358), daughter of Philip IV of France, and her lover Roger de ◊Mortimer, and murdered in Berkeley Castle, Gloucestershire.

Edward III 1312–1377. King of England from 1327, son of ◊Edward II. He assumed the government 1330 from his mother, through whom in 1337 he laid claim to the French throne and thus began the ◊Hundred Years' War.

Edward IV 1442–1483. King of England 1461–70 and from 1471. Son of Richard, Duke of York. He succeeded Henry VI in the Wars of the ◊Roses, temporarily losing the throne to Henry when Edward fell out with his adviser ◊Warwick but regaining it at the Battle of Barnet.

Edward V 1470–1483. King of England 1483. Son of Edward IV, he was deposed three months after his accession in favour of his uncle (◊Richard III), and is traditionally believed to have been murdered (with his brother) in the Tower of London on Richard's orders.

Edward VI 1537–1553. King of England from 1547, son of Henry VIII and Jane Seymour. The government was entrusted to his uncle the Duke of Somerset, and after Somerset's fall in 1549 to the Earl of Warwick, later created Duke of Northumberland.

Edward VII 1841–1910. King of Great Britain and Ireland from 1901. As Prince of Wales he was a prominent social figure, but his mother Queen Victoria considered him too frivolous to take part in political life. In 1860 he made the first tour of Canada and the USA ever undertaken by a British prince.

Edward VIII 1894–1972. King of Great Britain and Northern Ireland Jan–Dec 1936, when he abdicated to marry Mrs Wallis Warfield Simpson (1896–1986), a US divorcee. He was created duke of Windsor and was governor of the Bahamas 1940–45, subsequently settling in France.

EEC abbreviation for *European Economic Community*; part of the ◊European Community.

eel any species of fish of the order Anguilliformes. They are snake-like, with elongated dorsal and anal fins. The males can reach 61 cm/2 ft, and the females 122 cm/4 ft.

efficiency in physics, the output of a machine (work done by the machine) divided by the input (work put into the machine), usually expressed as a percentage. Because of losses caused by friction, efficiency is always less than 100 per cent, although it can approach this for electrical machines with no moving parts (such as a transformer).

EFTA abbreviation for ◊European Free Trade Association.

e.g. abbreviation for *exempli gratia* (Latin 'for the sake of example').

egg in animals, the ovum, or female ◊gamete (reproductive cell). After fertilization by a sperm cell, it begins to divide to form an embryo. Eggs may be deposited by the female (◊oviparity) or they may develop within her body (◊vivipary and ◊ovovivipary). In the oviparous reptiles and birds, the egg is protected by a shell, and well supplied with nutrients in the form of yolk. In plants, the ovum is called an egg-cell.

ego (Latin 'I') in psychology, a general term for the processes concerned with the self and a person's conception of himself or herself, encompassing values and attitudes. In Freudian psychology, the term refers specifically to the element of the human mind that represents the conscious processes, concerned with reality, in conflict with the ◊id and the ◊superego.

egret type of heron with long feathers on the head or neck.

Egypt country in NE Africa, bounded to the north by the Mediterranean, to the east by the Suez Canal and Red Sea, to the south by Sudan, and to the west by Libya.

Egypt, ancient
5000 BC Egyptian culture already well established in the Nile Valley.

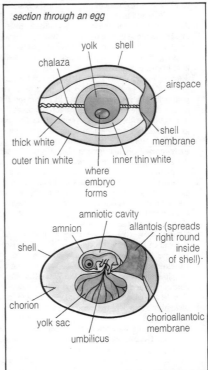

section through an egg

Egypt
Arab Republic of
(*Jumhuriyat Misr al-Arabiya*)

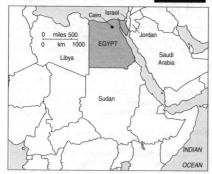

area 1,000,000 sq km/386,198 sq mi
capital Cairo
towns Gîza; ports Alexandria, Port Said
physical mostly desert; hills in E; fertile land along river Nile
head of state and government Hosni Mubarak from 1981
political system democratic republic
exports cotton and textiles, petroleum
currency Egyptian pound
population (1989 est) 54,779,000; annual growth rate 2.4%
life expectancy men 57, women 60
language Arabic (ancient Egyptian survives to some extent in Coptic)
religion Sunni Muslim 95%, Coptic Christian 5%
literacy 59% male/30% female (1985 est)
GDP $34.5 bn (1987); $679 per head
chronology
1914 Egypt became a British protectorate.
1936 Independence recognized. King Fuad succeeded by his son Farouk.

1946 Withdrawal of British troops except from Suez Canal Zone.
1952 Farouk overthrown by the army in a bloodless coup.
1953 Egypt declared a republic, with Gen Neguib as president.
1956 Neguib replaced by Col Gamal Nasser. Nasser announced nationalization of Suez Canal; Egypt attacked by Britain, France and Israel. Ceasefire agreed because of US intervention.
1958 Short-lived merger of Egypt and Syria as United Arab Republic (UAR).
1967 Six-Day War with Israel ended in Egypt's defeat and Israeli occupation of Sinai and the Gaza strip.
1970 Nasser was succeeded by Anwar Sadat.
1973 Attempt to regain territory lost to Israel led to fighting. Ceasefire arranged by US secretary of state Henry Kissinger.
1977 Visit by Sadat to Israel to address the Israeli parliament was criticized by Egypt's Arab neighbours.
1978–79 Camp David talks in the USA resulted in a treaty between Egypt and Israel. Egypt expelled from the Arab League.
1981 Sadat assassinated and succeeded by Hosni Mubarak.
1983 Improved relations between Egypt and the Arab world; only Libya and Syria maintained a trade boycott.
1984 Mubarak's party victorious in the people's assembly elections.
1987 Mubarak re-elected. Egypt readmitted to Arab League.
1988 Full diplomatic relations with Algeria restored.
1989 Improved relations with Libya; diplomatic relations with Syria restored.
1991 Participation in Gulf War on US-led side. Major force in convening Middle East peace conference in Spain.
1992 Outbreaks of violence between Muslims and Christians. Earthquake devastated Cairo.

3200 Menes united Lower Egypt (the delta) with his own kingdom of Upper Egypt
2800 ◊Imhotep built the step pyramid at Sakkara.
c. 2600 Old Kingdom reached the height of its power and the kings of the 4th dynasty built the pyramids at Gîza.
c. 2200–1800 Middle Kingdom, under which the unity lost towards the end of the Old Kingdom was restored.
1730 Invading Asiatic Hyksos people established their kingdom in the Nile Delta.
c. 1580 New Kingdom established by the 18th dynasty, following the eviction of the Hyksos, with its capital at ◊Thebes. High point of ancient Egyptian civilization under pharaohs ◊Thothmes, ◊Amenhotep, ◊Ikhnaton (who moved the capital to Akhetaton), and Tutankhamen.
c. 1321 19th dynasty: Rameses I built a temple at Karnak, Rameses II one at Abu Simbel.
1191 Rameses III defeated the Indo-European Sea Peoples, but after him there was decline, and power within the country passed from the pharaohs to the priests of Ammon.
1090–663 Late New Kingdom: Egypt was often divided between two or more dynasties; the nobles became virtually independent.
8–7th centuries Brief interlude of rule by kings from ◊Nubia.

666 The Assyrians under Ashurbanipal occupied Thebes.
663–609 Psammetichus I restored Egypt's independence and unity.
525 Egypt was conquered by ◊Cambyses, and became a Persian province.
c. 405–340 A period of independence.

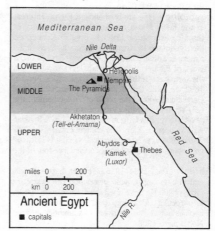

Ancient Egypt
■ capitals

egyptology Egyptian mask from the Ptolemaic period, 3rd-2nd century BC.

332 Conquest by ◊Alexander the Great. On the division of his empire, Egypt went to one of his generals, Ptolemy I, and his descendants.
30 Death of ◊Cleopatra and conquest by the Roman emperor Augustus: Egypt became a province of the Roman and Byzantine empires.
641 AD Conquest by the Arabs, so that the Christianity of later Roman rule was replaced by Islam. For modern history, see ◊Egypt.

Egyptian religion prehistoric Egyptian religion was based on the worship of totemic animals believed to be the ancestors of the clan. Totems later developed into gods, represented with animal heads. The cult of ◊Osiris was important. Immortality, conferred by the magical rite of mummification, was originally the sole prerogative of the king, but was extended under the New Kingdom to all who could afford it; they were buried with the ◊Book of the Dead.

egyptology the study of ancient Egypt. Interest in the subject was aroused by the discovery of the ◊Rosetta Stone 1799. Excavations continued throughout the 19th century, and gradually assumed a more scientific character, largely as a result of the work of Flinders ◊Petrie from 1880 onwards and the formation of the Egyptian Exploration Fund in 1892. In 1922 the British archaeologist Howard Carter discovered the tomb of Tutankhamen, the only royal tomb with all its treasures intact.

Ehrenburg Ilya Grigorievich 1891–1967. Russian writer, born in Kiev. His controversial work *The Thaw* 1954 depicts artistic circles in the USSR, and contributed to the growing literary freedom of the 1950s.

Ehrlich Paul 1854–1915. German bacteriologist and immunologist, who developed the first cure for syphilis. He developed the arsenic compounds, in particular salvarsan, used in the treatment of syphilis before the discovery of antibiotics. Shared Nobel prize 1908.

Eichendorff Joseph Freiherr von 1788–1857. German poet and novelist, born in Upper Silesia. He held various judicial posts, and wrote romantic stories, but is chiefly remembered as a lyric poet. His work was set to music by Schumann, Mendelssohn and Wolf.

Eichmann Karl Adolf 1906–1962. Austrian Nazi war criminal. As an ◊SS official during Hitler's regime he was responsible for atrocities against Jews and others, including the implementation of the 'final solution' – genocide. He managed to escape at the fall of Germany in 1945. He was discovered in Argentina in 1960, abducted from Argentina by Israeli agents, tried in Israel during 1961 for the extermination of 6 million Jews, and executed.

eider large marine duck, *Somateria mollissima*, highly valued for its soft down which is used in quilts and cushions for warmth. It is found on the coasts of the Atlantic and Pacific Oceans.

Eiffel Tower iron tower 320 m/1,050 ft high, designed by Gustave Alexandre Eiffel 1832–1923 for the Paris Exhibition of 1889. It stands in the Champ de Mars, Paris.

Einstein Albert 1879–1955. German-Swiss physicist, who formulated the theories of ◊relativity, and did important work in radiation physics and thermodynamics. In 1905 he published the special theory of relativity, and in 1915 issued his general theory of relativity. His latest conception of the basic laws governing the universe was outlined in his unified field theory, made public in 1953; and of the 'relativistic theory of the non-symmetric field', completed 1955. Einstein wrote that this simplified the derivations as well as the form of the field equations and made the whole theory thereby more transparent, without changing its content.

Einthoven Willem 1860–1927. Dutch physiologist and inventor of the electrocardiograph. He was able to show that particular disorders of the heart alter its electrical activity in characteristic ways.

Eire Gaelic name for the Republic of ◊Ireland.

Eisenhower Dwight D(avid) ('Ike') 1890–1969. 34th president of the USA 1953–60, a Republican. A general in World War II, he commanded the Allied forces in Italy 1943, then the Allied invasion of Europe, and from Oct 1944 all the Allied armies in the West. As president he promoted business

Einstein Albert Einstein in his Princeton residence, 1944.

interests at home and conducted the Cold War abroad. His vice president was Richard Nixon.

Eisenstein Sergei Mikhailovich 1898–1948. Latvian film director. He pioneered the use of montage (a technique of deliberately juxtaposing shots to create a particular meaning) as a means of propaganda, as in *The Battleship Potemkin* 1925. His *Alexander Nevsky* 1938 was the first part of an uncompleted trilogy, the second part, *Ivan the Terrible* 1944, being banned in Russia.

eisteddfod (Welsh 'sitting') traditional Welsh gathering for the encouragement of the bardic arts of music, poetry, and literature.

ejector seat device for propelling an aircraft pilot to safety in an emergency, invented by the British engineer James Martin (1893–1981). The first seats of 1945 were powered by a compressed spring; later seats used an explosive charge. By the early 1980s 35,000 seats had been fitted worldwide, and the lives of 5,000 pilots saved by their use.

Ekman spiral effect an application of the ◊Coriolis effect to ocean currents, whereby the currents flow at an angle to the winds that drive them. It derives its name from the Swedish oceanographer Vagn Ekman (1874-1954).

eland largest species of antelope, *Taurotragus oryx*. Pale fawn in colour, it is about 2 m/6 ft high, and both sexes have spiral horns about 45 cm/18 in long. It is found in central and southern Africa.

elasticity in economics, the measure of response of one variable to changes in another. If the price of butter is reduced by 10% and the demand increases by 20%, the elasticity measure is 2. Such measures are used to test the effects of changes in prices, incomes, and supply and demand. Inelasticity may exist in the demand for necessities, for example water, the demand for which will remain the same even if the price changes considerably.

elasticity in physics, the ability of a solid to recover its shape once deforming forces (stresses modifying its dimensions or shape) are removed. Metals are elastic up to a certain stress (the elastic limit), beyond which greater stress gives them a permanent deformation, as demonstrated by ◊Hooke's law.

Elbe one of the principal rivers of Germany, 1,166 km/725 mi long, rising on the S slopes of the Riesengebirge, Czech Republic, and flowing NW across the German plain to the North Sea.

Elbruz or *Elbrus* highest mountain, 5,642 m/18,510 ft, on the continent of Europe, in the ◊Caucasus, Georgia.

elder in botany, small tree or shrub of the genus *Sambucus*, family Caprifoliaceae. The common *Sambucus nigra*, found in Europe, N Africa, and W Asia, has pinnate leaves, and heavy heads of small, sweet-scented, white flowers in early summer. These are succeeded by clusters of small, black berries. The scarlet-berried *Sambucus racemosa* is found in parts of Europe, Asia and N America.

elder in the Presbyterian church, the elders or ruling elders are lay members who assist the minister (or teaching elder) in running the church.

El Dorado fabled city of gold believed by 16th-century Spaniards to exist somewhere in the Americas. The legend may be connected with the Chibchas people.

Eleanor of Castile Queen of Edward I of England, the daughter of Ferdinand III of Castile. She married Prince Edward in 1254, and accompanied him on his crusade in 1270. She died at Harby, Nottinghamshire, and Edward erected stone crosses in towns where her body rested on the funeral journey to London. Several *Eleanor Crosses* are still standing, for example at Northampton.

elector (German *Kurfürst*) any of originally seven (later ten) princes of the Holy Roman Empire who had the prerogative of electing the emperor (in effect, the king of Germany). Their constitutional status was formalized in 1356 in the document known as the *Golden Bull*, which granted them extensive powers within their own domains: acting as judges, issuing coins, and imposing tolls.

electoral college the indirect system of voting for the president and vice president of the USA. The people of each state officially vote not for the presidential candidate, but for a list of electors nominated by each party. The whole electoral-college vote of the state then goes to the winning party (and candidate).

electoral system see ◊vote and ◊proportional representation.

Electra in ancient Greek legend, the daughter of Clytemnestra and ◊Agamemnon, king of Mycenae, and sister of Iphigenia and Orestes. Her story is the subject of two plays of the 5th century BC by Sophocles and Euripides, which explore her role in the complex family tragedy which involved the deaths of her sister, both parents, and finally her brother.

electric arc a continuous electric discharge of high current between two electrodes, giving out a brilliant light and heat. The phenomenon is exploited in the carbon-arc lamp, once widely used in film projectors. In the electric-arc furnace an arc struck between huge carbon electrodes and the metal charge provides the heating. In arc ◊welding an electric arc provides the heat to fuse the metal.

electric charge property of some bodies that causes them to exert forces on each other. Two bodies both with positive or both with negative charges repel each other, while oppositely or 'unlike' charged bodies attract each other, since each is in the ◊*electric field* of the other. ◊Electrons possess a negative charge, and ◊protons an equal positive charge. The unit of electric charge is the *coulomb* (C).

electric current rate of flow of ◊electric charge. It is measured in amperes (coulombs per second).

electric field in physics, a region in which an ◊electric charge experiences a force due to the presence of another electric charge. It is a type of ◊electromagnetic field.

electricity a general term used for all phenomena caused by ◊electric charge, whether static or in motion. Electric charge is caused by an excess or deficit of electrons in the charged substance, and an electric current by the movement of electrons round a circuit. Substances may be electrical conductors, such as metals, which allow the passage of electricity through them, or insulators, such as rubber, which are extremely poor conductors. Substances with intermediate conductivities are known as ◊semiconductors.

electricity generation and supply electricity is the most useful and most convenient form of energy, readily convertible into heat and light and used to power machines. Electricity can be generated in one place and distributed anywhere because it readily flows through wires. It is generated at power stations where a suitable energy source is harnessed to drive ◊turbines that spin electricity generators. Current energy sources are coal, oil, water power (hydroelectricity), natural gas, and ◊nuclear power. Research is under way to increase the contribution of wind power, ◊tidal power and

electricity generation and supply

coal-fired power station (highly simplified)

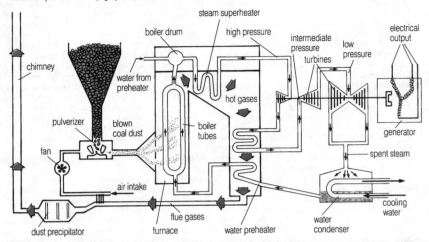

◊geothermal power. Nuclear fuel is a cheap source of electricity but environmental considerations may limit its future development.

electric light bulb the ◊incandescent filament lamp was first demonstrated by Joseph Swan in the UK in 1878 and Thomas Edison in the USA in 1879. The modern light bulb is a thin glass bulb filled with an inert mixture of nitrogen and argon gas. It contains a filament made of fine tungsten wire, and when electricity is passed through the wire, it glows white hot.

electric motor a machine that converts electrical energy into mechanical energy. Most direct-current and induction motors produce rotary motion. A linear induction motor produces linear (sideways) motion.

electrocardiogram (ECG) a recording of the electrical changes in the heart muscle, detected by electrodes attached to the chest. It is used to diagnose heart disease.

electroconvulsive therapy or *ECT* a treatment for ◊schizophrenia, and ◊depression, given under anaesthesia and with a muscle relaxant. An electric current is passed through the brain to induce alterations in the brain's electrical activity. The treatment can cause distress, and there is some controversy about its use and effectiveness.

electrocution death caused by electric current. It is used as a method of execution in some of the states of the USA. The criminal is strapped in a special electric chair and an electric shock at 1,800–2,000 volt is administered.

electrode conductor by which an electric current passes in or out of a substance, for example, in an electric-arc furnace or neon tube.

electrodynamics study of the interaction between charged particles and their emission and absorption of electromagnetic ◊radiation.
Quantum electrodynamics (QED) combines quantum ◊mechanics and ◊relativity theory, making exceedingly accurate predictions about subatomic processes involving charged particles.

electroencephalogram (EEG) a record of the electrical discharges of the brain, detected by electrodes attached to the scalp. The pattern of electrical activity revealed is diagnostic in some brain disorders, especially epilepsy.

electrolysis the production of chemical changes by passing an electric current through a solution (the electrolyte), resulting in the migration of the ions to the electrodes: positive cations to the negative electrode, or cathode, and negative anions to the positive electrode, or anode.

electrolyte a molten substance or solution in which an electric current is made to flow by the movement and discharge of ions in accordance with ◊Faraday's laws of electrolysis.

electromagnetic field in physics, the agency by which a particle with an ◊electric charge experiences a force in a particular region of space. If it does so only when moving, it is in a pure *magnetic field*, if it does so when stationary, it is in an *electric field*. Both can be present simultaneously.

electromagnetic induction in physics, the production of an ◊electromotive force (emf) in a circuit by a change of ◊magnetic flux through the circuit. The emf so produced is known as an induced emf, and any resulting current an induced current.

electromagnetic spectrum the complete range, over all wave lengths, of electromagnetic waves.

electromagnetic waves oscillating electric and magnetic fields travelling together through

electrolysis

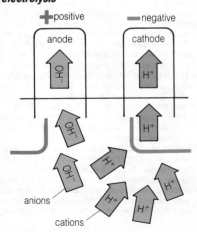

electromagnetic waves

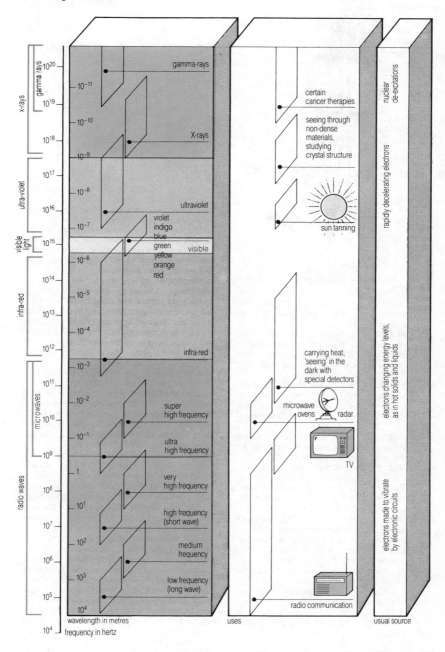

space at a speed of nearly 300 million metres per second. The (limitless) range of possible wavelengths or ◊frequencies of electromagnetic waves, which can be thought of as making up the *electromagnetic spectrum*, include radio waves, infrared radiation, visible light, ultraviolet radiation, X-rays, and gamma rays.

electromotive force (*emf*) in physics, the greatest potential difference which could be generated by a source of current. This is always greater than the measured potential difference generated, due to the resistance of the wires and components in the circuit.

electron stable, negatively charged ◊elementary particle, a constituent of all ◊atoms and the basic particle of electricity. A beam of electrons will

electron microscope

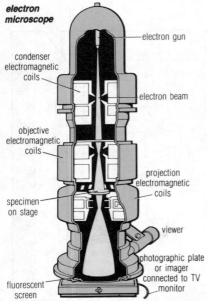

- electron gun
- condenser electromagnetic coils
- electron beam
- objective electromagnetic coils
- projection electromagnetic coils
- specimen on stage
- viewer
- photographic plate or imager connected to TV monitor
- fluorescent screen

electroscope

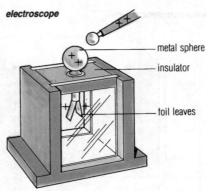

- metal sphere
- insulator
- foil leaves

undergo ◊diffraction (scattering), and produce interference patterns, in the same way as ◊electromagnetic waves such as light; hence they may also be regarded as waves.

electron gun a structure consisting of a series of ◊electrodes, including a cathode for producing an electron beam. It is an essential part of many electronic devices such as cathode-ray tubes (television tubes) and ◊electron microscopes.

electronic flash a discharge tube that produces a high-intensity flash of light for a few thousandths of a second. It is used in dim-light photography. The tube contains an inert gas such as krypton.

electronic mail a ◊telecommunications system that sends messages to people or computers via computer and telephone networks.

electronic music music produced since the 1950s in which composers work with electronically assembled or arranged sounds. Varèse, Boulez, and Stockhausen have pioneered the technique. See also ◊synthesizer.

electronics a branch of science that deals with the emission of ◊electrons from conductors and ◊semiconductors, with the subsequent manipulation of these electrons, and with the construction of electronic devices. The first electronic device was the ◊thermionic valve, or vacuum tube, in which electrons moved in a vacuum, and led to such inventions as ◊radio, ◊television, ◊radar, and the digital ◊computer. Replacement of valves with the comparatively tiny and reliable transistor in 1948 revolutionized electronic development. Modern electronic devices are based on minute integrated circuits and ◊silicon chips.

electron microscope an instrument that produces a magnified image by using a beam of ◊electrons instead of light rays as in an optical ◊microscope. The wavelength of the electron beam is much shorter than that of light, so much greater magnification and resolution (ability to distinguish detail) can be achieved.

electrophoresis the ◊diffusion of charged particles through a fluid under the influence of an electric field. It can be used in the biological sciences to separate ◊molecules of different sizes, which diffuse at different rates. In industry electrophoresis is used in paint-dipping operations to ensure that paint reaches awkward corners.

electroplating the deposition of metals upon metallic surfaces by electrolysis for decorative and/or protective purposes. It is used in the preparation of printers' blocks, 'master' audio discs, and in many other processes.

electroscope an apparatus for detecting ◊electric charge. The simple gold-leaf electroscope consists of a vertical conducting (metal) rod ending in a pair of rectangular pieces of gold foil, mounted inside and insulated from an earthed metal case. An electric charge applied to the end of the metal rod makes the gold leaves diverge, because they each receive a similar charge (positive or negative) and so repel each other.

electrostatics study of electric charges from stationary sources (not currents).

electrovalent bond type of chemical ◊bond in which the the combining atoms lose or gain electrons to form ions. It is also called an ionic bond.

electrum a naturally occurring alloy of gold and silver used by early civilizations to make the first coins, about the 6th century BC.

element a substance which cannot be split chemically into simpler substances. The atoms of a particular element all have the same number of protons in their nuclei. Elements are classified in the periodic table. Symbols are used to denote the elements, usually being the first letter or letters of the English or Latinized name of the element, for example C, carbon; Ca, calcium; Fe, iron (ferrum). These symbols represent one atom of the element.

elementary particle or *subatomic particle* a particle which combines with others to form an ◊atom. Elementary particles are the fundamental components of all matter. About 200 different ones have been identified, including protons and neutrons (in an atom's nucleus), and electrons (which may be regarded as orbiting the nucleus).

elephant the two surviving species of the Proboscidea, the Asiatic *Elephas maximus* and African *Loxodonta africana* elephant. The elephant can grow to 4 m/13 ft and 8 tons, has a thick, grey, wrinkled skin, a large head, a long trunk used to obtain food and water, and upper incisors or tusks, which grow very long. Elephants are herbivorous, highly intelligent, extremely social, and live in matriarchal herds.

elephantiasis in the human body, a gross local enlargement and deformity, especially of a leg, the scrotum, or a breast.

Elgar *The composer Edward Elgar.*

Eleusinian Mysteries   ceremonies in honor of ◊Demeter, ◊Persephone, and ◊Dionysus, celebrated in the remains of the temple of Demeter at Eleusis, Greece. Worshippers saw visions in the darkened temple, possibly connected with the underworld.

elevation of boiling point   a raising of the boiling point of a liquid above that of the pure solvent, caused by a substance being dissolved in it. The phenomenon is observed when salt is added to boiling water; the water ceases to boil because its boiling point has been elevated.

Elgar   Edward 1857–1934. English composer. He gained fame as a composer with his *Enigma Variations* in 1899, and although his most celebrated choral work, the oratorio setting of Newman's *The Dream of Gerontius*, was initially a failure, it was a great success at Düsseldorf in 1902. Many of his earlier works were then performed, including the popular *Pomp and Circumstance* marches.

Elgin marbles   collection of ancient Greek sculptures mainly from the Parthenon at Athens, assembled by the seventh Earl of Elgin, sent to England in 1812, and bought for the nation in 1816 for £35,000. They are now in the British Museum; Greece has asked for them to be returned to Athens.

Elijah   c. mid-9th century BC. in the Old Testament or Bible, a Hebrew prophet during the reigns of the Israelite kings Ahab and Ahaziah. He came from Gilead. He defeated the prophets of ◊Baal, and was said to have been carried up to heaven in a fiery chariot in a whirlwind. In Jewish belief, Elijah will return to Earth to herald the coming of the messiah.

Eliot   George, pen name of Mary Ann Evans 1819–1880. English novelist, who portrayed Victorian society, particularly its intellectual hypocrisy, with realism and irony. Her novels include *Adam Bede* 1859, *Mill on the Floss* 1860, and *Silas Marner* 1861. *Middlemarch* 1872 is now considered one of the greatest novels of the 19th century.

Eliot   John 1592–1632. English politician. He became a member of Parliament in 1614, and with the Earl of Buckingham's patronage was made a vice-admiral in 1619. In 1626 he was imprisoned in the Tower of London for demanding Buckingham's impeachment. In 1628 he was a formidable supporter of the ◊Petition of Right opposing Charles II, and with other parliamentary leaders was again imprisoned in the Tower of London in 1629, where he died.

Eliot   T(homas) S(tearns) 1888–1965. US-born poet and critic. His first volume of poetry *Prufrock and Other Observations* 1917 introduced new verse forms and rhythms; further collections include *The Waste Land* 1922, *The Hollow Men* 1925,

Eliot *Mary Ann Evans, otherwise known as the English novelist George Eliot.*

and *Old Possum's Book of Practical Cats* 1939. *Four Quartets* 1943 revealed his religious vision. He also wrote plays, including *Murder in the Cathedral* 1935 and *The Cocktail Party* 1949, and critical works, for example *The Sacred Wood* 1920. Nobel prize 1948.

Elizabeth   in the New Testament, mother of John the Baptist. She was a cousin of Jesus Christ's mother Mary, who came to see her shortly after the Annunciation; on this visit (called the Visitation), Mary sang the hymn of praise later to be known as the Magnificat.

Elizabeth   the Queen Mother 1900– . Wife of King George VI of England. She adopted the title Queen Elizabeth the Queen Mother after his death. She is the mother of ◊Elizabeth II and Princess ◊Margaret.

Elizabeth   two queens of England or the UK:

Elizabeth I   1533–1603. Queen of England 1558–1603, the daughter of Henry VIII and Anne Boleyn. Through her Religious Settlement of 1559 she enforced the Protestant religion by law and she had ◊Mary, Queen of Scots, executed 1587. Her conflict with Catholic Spain led to the defeat of the ◊Spanish Armada 1588. The Elizabethan age was expansionist in commerce and geographical exploration, and arts and literature flourished. The rulers of many European states made unsuccessful bids for Elizabeth's hand in marriage, and she used these bids to strengthen her power.

Elizabeth II   1926– . Queen of Great Britain and Northern Ireland from 1952, the elder daughter of George VI. She married her third cousin, Philip,

Elizabeth I *Portrait by an unknown artist (c. 1585–92) National Portrait Gallery, London.*

elk

ellipse

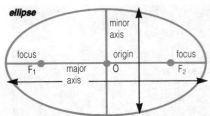

society cannot acknowledge; it encouraged the development of black literature after World War II.

Ellora archaeological site in the NW Deccan, Maharashtra State, India, with 35 cave temples – Buddhist, Hindu, and Jain – varying in date from the late 6th century to the 9th century. They include Visvakarma (a hall about 26 m/86 ft long containing a huge image of the Buddha), Tin Thal (a three-storeyed Buddhist monastery cave), the Rameswara cave (with beautiful sculptures), and Siva's Paradise, the great temple of Kailasa.

elm tree of the family Ulmaceae, found in temperate regions of the N hemisphere, and in mountainous parts of the tropics. The common English elm *Ulmus procera* is widely distributed throughout Europe, but numbers have been decimated by Dutch elm disease since the 1960s. It reaches 35 m/115 ft, with tufts of small, purplish-brown flowers which appear before the leaves.

El Nino (Spanish 'the child') warm ocean surge of the ◊Peru (Humboldt) Current, so called because it tends to occur at Christmas, recurring every ten years or so in the East Pacific off South America.

elongation the angular distance between either a planet or the Moon and the Sun. This angle is 0° at either inferior ◊conjunction or superior conjunction. ◊Quadrature occurs when the elongation angle is 90° and ◊opposition (opposite the Sun in the sky) when the angle is 180°.

El Paso city in Texas, USA, situated at the base of the Franklin Mountains, on the Rio Grande, opposite the Mexican city of Ciudad Juárez; population (1980) 425,200. Centre of an agricultural and cattle-raising area; industries based on local iron and copper mines, as well as oil refineries; also electronic, food processing and packing, and leather manufactures.

El Salvador country in central America, bounded N and E by Honduras, S and SW by the Pacific Ocean, and NW by Guatemala.

Elton Charles 1900– . British ecologist, a pioneer of the study of animal and plant life in their natural environment, and of animal behaviour as part of the complex pattern of life.

the Duke of Edinburgh, in 1947. They have four children: Prince Charles, Princess Anne, Prince Andrew, and Prince Edward.

Elizabeth 1709–1762. Empress of Russia from 1741, daughter of Peter the Great. She carried through a palace revolution and supplanted her cousin, the infant Ivan VI (1730–1764), on the throne. She continued the policy of westernization begun by Peter, and allied herself with Austria against Prussia.

Elizabethan term given to the period and style of Elizabeth I of England's reign, although also loosely applied to the preceding monarchs, Henry VIII, Edward VI and Mary.

elk large deer *Alces alces* inhabiting N Europe, Asia, Scandinavia, and North America, where it is known as the moose. It is brown in colour, stands about 2 m/6 ft at the shoulders, has very large palmate antlers, a fleshy muzzle, short neck, and long legs. It feeds on leaves and shoots. In North America, the ◊wapiti is called an elk.

Ellice Islands former name of ◊Tuvalu, a group of islands in the W Pacific Ocean.

Ellington 'Duke' (Edward Kennedy) 1899–1974. US pianist, and an outstanding composer and arranger of jazz. He wrote numerous pieces for his own jazz orchestra, and became one of the most important figures in jazz over a 55-year span. Compositions include 'Mood Indigo', 'Sophisticated Lady', and 'Black and Tan Fantasy'.

ellipse a curve joining all points (loci) around two fixed points (foci) such that the sum of the distances from those points is always constant. The diameter passing through the foci is the major axis, and the diameter bisecting this at right angles is the minor axis. An ellipse is one of a series of curves known as ◊conic sections. A slice across a cone that is not made parallel to, or does not pass through, the base will produce an ellipse.

Ellis (Henry) Havelock 1859–1939. British writer. Chiefly known as the author of many works on the psychology of sex, including *Studies in the Psychology of Sex* (seven volumes) 1898–1928. He was also a literary critic and essayist.

Ellis Island island off the shore of New Jersey, USA, former reception centre for steerage-class immigrants on arrival in New York between 1892 and 1943. No longer used, it was declared a National Historic Site in 1965 by President Johnson.

Ellison Ralph 1914– . US novelist. His *Invisible Man* 1952 portrays the plight of a black youth whom

elm

El Salvador
Republic of
(*República de El Salvador*)

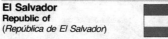

area 21,393 sq km/8,236 sq mi
capital San Salvador
physical flat in S, rising to mountains in N
head of state and government Alfredo Cristiani
from 1989
political system emergent democracy
exports coffee, cotton, sugar
currency colón

population (1989 est) 5,900,000 (mainly of mixed
Spanish-Indian ancestry; annual growth rate 2.9%
life expectancy men 63, women 66
language Spanish, Nahuatl
religion Roman Catholic 97%
literacy 75% male/69% female (1985 est)
GDP $4.7 bn (1987); $790 per head
chronology
1829 Achieved independence from Spain.
1961 Right-wing coup.
1972 Allegations of human-rights violations and
growth of left-wing guerrilla activities. Gen Carlos
Romero elected president.
1979 A coup replaced Romero with a military-
civilian junta.
1980 Archbishop Oscar Romero assassinated.
Country on verge of civil war. José Duarte became
president.
1981 The USA actively assisted the government
against the guerilla forces.
1982 Assembly elections boycotted by left-wing
parties and held amid considerable violence.
1986 Duarte sought a negotiated settlement with
the guerrillas.
1988 Duarte resigned.
1989 Alfredo Cristiani elected president.
1991 UN-sponsored peace accord signed by the
government and the socialist guerrilla group, the
FMLN.
1992 Peace accord validated. The FMLN became a
political party.

Elton published *Animal Ecology and Evolution*
1930 and *The Pattern of Animal Communities*
1966.

Eluard Paul, pen name of Eugène Grindel
1895–1952. French poet. He expressed the suffering of poverty in his verse, and was a leader
of the Surrealists. He fought in World War I, the
inspiration for *Poèmes pour la paix/Poems for Peace*
1918, and was a member of the Resistance in World
War II. His books include *Poésie et vérité/Poetry and
Truth* 1942 and *Au Rendezvous allemand/To the
German Rendezvous* 1944.

Elysée Palace (French *Palais de l'Elysée*) building in Paris erected in 1718 for Louis d'Auvergne,
Count of Evreux. It was later the home of Mme de
Pompadour, Napoleon I and Napoleon III, and in
1870 became the official residence of the presidents
of France.

Elysium or the *Elsyian Fields*. In classical
mythology, an afterworld or paradise (sometimes
called the Islands of the Blessed) for the souls of
those who found favour with the gods; it was
situated near the river Oceanus.

Elytis Odysseus, pen name of Odysseus Alepoudelis
1911– . Greek poet, born in Crete. He celebrates
the importance of the people's attempts to shape an
individual existence in freedom. His major work *To
Axion Esti/Worthy It Is* 1959, is a lyric cycle, parts
of which have been set to music by ◊Theodorakis.
Nobel Prize for Literature 1979.

Emancipation Proclamation, The in US
history, President Lincoln's Civil War announcement, 22 September 1862, stating that from the
beginning of 1863 all black slaves in states still
engaged in rebellion against the federal government
would be emancipated. Slaves in border states still
remaining loyal to the union were excluded.

embargo the legal prohibition by a government
of trade with another country, forbidding foreign
ships to leave or enter its ports. Trade embargoes

may be imposed on a country seen to be violating
international laws.

embolism blockage of an artery by an obstruction
called an embolus (usually a blood clot, fat particle,
or bubble of air).

embryo early development stage of animals and
plants following fertilization of an ovum (egg cell), or
activation of an ovum by ◊parthenogenesis.

embryology the study of the changes undergone
by living matter from its conception as a fertilized
ovum (egg) to its emergence into the world by
hatching or birth. It is mainly concerned with the
changes in cell organization in the ◊embryo and the
way in which these lead to the structures and organs
of the adult (◊differentiation).

embryo research the study of human embryos at an early stage, in order to detect
hereditary disease and genetic defects, and to
investigate the problems of subfertility and infertility.

embryo sac a large cell within the ovule of
flowering plants which represents the female
◊gametophyte when fully developed. It typically
contains eight nuclei. Fertilization occurs when one
of these nuclei, the egg nucleus, fuses with a male
◊gamete.

emerald green variety of the mineral ◊beryl.

emergence or *emergent evolution* a philosophical theory of the early 20th century postulating
that life 'emerges' or 'grows naturally' out of matter,
mind emerges out of life, and God emerges from
mind.

Emerson Ralph Waldo 1803–1882. US philosopher, essayist, and poet. He settled in Concord,
Massachusetts, which he made a centre of trans-
cendentalism, and wrote *Nature* 1836, which states
the movement's main principles. His two volumes of
Essays (1841, 1844) made his reputation. He was
greatly influenced by the Scottish philosopher and
historian Carlyle.

emery a variety of ◊corundum, greyish-black and opaque, containing a quantity of haematite and magnetite. It is much used as an ◊abrasive.

Emery Walter Bryan 1903–1971. British archaeologist, who in 1929–34 in Nubia, N Africa, excavated the barrows at Ballana and Qustol, rich royal tombs of the mysterious X-group people (3rd to 6th centuries AD). He also surveyed the whole region 1963–64 before it was flooded as a result of the building of the Aswan High Dam.

emf in physics, abbreviation for ◊*electromotive force*.

Emilia-Romagna region of N central Italy including much of the Po valley; area 22,126 sq km/8,546 sq mi, population (1981) 3,957,400. The capital is Bologna; other towns include Reggio, Rimini, Parma, Ferrara, and Ravenna. Agricultural produce includes fruit, wine, sugar beet, beef, and dairy products; oil and natural gas resources have been developed in the Po valley.

emotivism a philosophical position in the theory of ethics. Emotivists deny that moral judgments can be true or false; maintaining that they merely express an attitude or an emotional response.

Empedocles *c.* 490–430 BC. Greek philosopher universe into the four elements – fire, air, earth, and water – which through the action of love and discord are eternally constructed, destroyed, and constructed anew. According to tradition, he committed suicide by throwing himself into the crater of Mount Etna.

emphysema an incurable condition of extreme and disabling breathlessness. It is due to the progressive loss of the thin walls dividing the air spaces in the lungs, which reduces the area available for the exchange of oxygen.

empiricism in philosophy, the belief that all knowledge is ultimately derived from sense experience. It is suspicious of metaphysical schemes based on ◊*a priori* propositions, which are claimed to be true irrespective of experience. It is frequently contrasted with ◊rationalism.

employers' association an organization of employers formed for purposes of collective action. In the UK there were formerly three main organizations, which in 1965 combined as the ◊Confederation of British Industry.

employment exchange agency for bringing together employers requiring labour and workers seeking employment. Employment exchanges may be organized by central government or a local authority (known in the UK as Job Centres); or as private business ventures (employment agencies).

employment law law covering the rights and duties of employers and employees. In the UK, in the past, relations between employer and employee were covered mainly by the ◊common law, but statute law has become increasingly important in the 20th century, particularly in giving new rights to employees.

Empson William 1906–1984. English poet and critic. His critical work examined the potential variety of meaning in poetry, as in *Seven Types of Ambiguity* 1930 and *The Structure of Complex Words* 1951. His verse was published in *Collected Poems* 1955.

EMS abbreviation for ◊*European Monetary System.*

emu flightless bird *Dromaius novaehollandiae* native to Australia. It stands about 1.8 m/6 ft high, has coarse brown plumage, small rudimentary wings, short feathers on the head and neck, and powerful

enamel enamel plate showing Virgin and child.

legs, well adapted for running and kicking. The female has a curious bag or pouch in the windpipe that enables it to emit the characteristic loud booming note.

emulsion a type of ◊colloid, consisting of a stable dispersion of a liquid in another liquid, for example, oil and water in some cosmetic lotions.

enamel vitrified (glass-like) coating of various colours used for decorative purposes on a metallic or porcelain surface. In ◊*cloisonné* the various sections of the design are separated by thin metal wires or strips. In *champlevé* the enamel is poured into engraved cavities in the metal surface.

encaustic painting an ancient technique of painting, commonly used by the Egyptians, Greeks, and Romans, in which the coloured pigments were mixed with molten wax and painted on panels.

encephalitis inflammation of the brain, nearly always due to virus infection. It varies widely in severity, from short-lived, relatively slight effects to paralysis, coma, and death.

enclosure appropriation of common land as private property, or the changing of open-field systems to enclosed fields (often used for sheep). This process began in Britain in the 14th century, and became widespread in the 15th and 16th centuries. It caused poverty, homelessness, and rural depopulation, and resulted in revolts in 1536, 1569, and 1607.

encyclical a letter addressed by the pope to Roman Catholic bishops for the benefit of the people. The first was issued by Benedict XIV in 1740, but encyclicals became common only in the 19th century. They may be doctrinal (condemning errors), exhortative (recommending devotional activities), or commemorative.

encyclopedia a work of reference, either of all fields of knowledge or one specific subject. Although most encyclopedias are alphabetical with cross-references, some are organized thematically with indexes, in order to keep related subjects together.

Encyclopédie an encyclopedia written 1751–72 by a group of French scholars (Encyclopédistes) including D'Alembert and Diderot, inspired by the English encyclopedia produced by Ephraim Chambers in 1728. Religious scepticism and ◊Enlightenment social and political views were a feature of the work.

endemic term applied to a disease which is more or less prevalent in a given region or country all the time. It refers most often to tropical diseases, such as ◊malaria, which are particularly hard to eradicate.

endive hardy annual plant *Cichorium endivia*, family Compositae, the leaves of which are used in salads and cooking.

endocrine gland

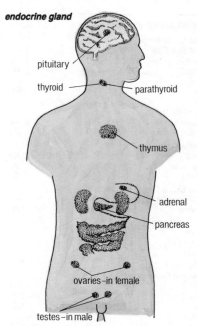

pituitary

thyroid

parathyroid

thymus

adrenal

pancreas

ovaries–in female

testes–in male

endocrine gland a type of gland which secretes hormones into the bloodstream to regulate body processes. Endocrine glands are most highly developed in vertebrates, but are also found in other animals, notably insects. In humans, the main endocrine glands are the pituitary, thyroid, parathyroid, adrenal, pancreas, ovary, and testis.

endometriosis a common gynaecological complaint in which patches of endometrium (the lining of the womb) are found outside the uterus.

endoplasm part of a cell's ◊cytoplasm.

endoplasmic reticulum a membranous structure in ◊eukaryotic cells, abbreviated as ER. It stores and transports proteins needed elsewhere in the cells and also carries various enzymes needed for the synthesis of ◊fats. It often bears ◊ribosomes which carry out protein synthesis.

endorphin a natural substance (a polypeptide) that modifies the action of nerve cells. Endorphins are produced by the pituitary gland and hypothalamus of vertebrates. They lower the perception of pain by reducing the transmission of signals between nerve cells.

endoscopy the examination of internal organs or tissues by direct vision. The instrument used (an endoscope) is equipped with an eyepiece, lenses, and its own light source to illuminate the field of vision.

endoskeleton the internal supporting structure of vertebrates, made up of cartilage or bone. It provides support, and acts as a system of levers to which muscles are attached to provide movement. Certain parts of the skeleton (the skull and ribs) give protection to vital body organs.

endosperm a nutritive tissue in the seeds of most flowering plants. It surrounds the embryo and is produced by an unusual process that parallels the ◊fertilization of the ovum by a male gamete. A second male gamete from the pollen grain fuses with two female nuclei within the ◊embryo sac. Thus the endosperm cells are triploid (having three sets of chromosomes). They contain food reserves

such as starch, fat and protein which are utilized by the developing seedling.

endotherm a 'warm-blooded', or homeothermic, animal.

endowment insurance a type of life insurance which may produce profits. An endowment policy will run for a fixed number of years during which it accumulates a cash value; it provides a savings plan for a retirement fund, and may be used to help with a house purchase, linked to a building society mortgage.

end user a user of a computer program, in particular someone who uses a program to perform a task (such as accounting or playing a computer game) rather than someone who writes programs (a programmer).

energy the capacity for doing work. *Potential energy* (PE) is energy deriving from position; thus a stretched spring has elastic PE; an object raised to a height above the earth's surface, or the water in an elevated reservoir, has gravitational PE; a lump of coal and a tank of petrol, together with the oxygen needed for their combustion, have chemical PE (due to relative positions of atoms). Other sorts of PE include electrical and nuclear. Moving bodies possess *kinetic energy* (KE). Energy can be converted from one form to another, but the total quantity stays the same (in accordance with the conservation laws that govern many natural phenomena). For example, as an apple falls, it loses gravitational PE but gains KE.

Engels Friedrich 1820–1895. German social and political philosopher, a friend of and collaborator with Karl ◊Marx on *The Communist Manifesto* 1848 and other key works. His later interpretations of Marxism, and his own philosophical and historical studies such as *Origins of the Family, Private Property, and the State* 1884 (which linked patriarchy with the development of private property), developed such concepts as historical materialism. His use of positivism and Darwinian ideas gave Marxism a scientific and deterministic flavour which was to influence Soviet thinking.

engineering the application of science to the design, construction and maintenance of works, machinery, roads, railways, bridges, harbour installations, engines, ships, aircraft and airports, spacecraft and space stations, and the generation, transmission and use of electrical power. The main divisions of engineering are aerospace, chemical, civil, electrical, electronic, gas, marine, materials, mechanical, mining, production, radio and structural engineering.

England largest division of the ◊United Kingdom.

Engels The German socialist philosopher Friedrich Engels.

area 130,763 sq km/50,487 sq mi
capital London
towns Birmingham, Cambridge, Coventry, Leeds, Leicester, Manchester, Newcastle-upon-Tyne, Nottingham, Oxford, Sheffield, York; ports Bristol, Dover, Felixstowe, Harwich, Liverpool, Portsmouth and Southampton
exports agricultural (cereals, rape, sugar beet, potatoes); meat and meat products; electronic (especially software), and telecommunications equipment (main centres Berkshire and Cambridge); scientific instruments; textiles and fashion goods; ◊North Sea oil and gas, petrochemicals, pharmaceuticals, fertilizers; beer; china clay, pottery, porcelain, and glass; film and television programmes, and sound recordings. Tourism is important. There are worldwide banking and insurance interests
currency pound sterling
population (1981) 46,229,955
language English, with more than 100 minority languages
religion Christian, with the Anglican Communion as the established church, 31,500,000; and various Protestant sects, of which the largest is the Methodist 1,400,000; Roman Catholic about 5,000,000; Jewish 410,000; Muslim 900,000; Sikh 175,000; Hindu 140,000.
For *government* and *history*, see ◊United Kingdom.

England: history
Old Stone Age Traces of human occupation at Cheddar Caves, Somerset.
New Stone Age Long barrows; remains of flint mining can be seen at Grimes Graves, Norfolk.
Bronze Age Round barrows.
c. 1800 Invasion of the Beaker people, who left traces of their occupation at Avebury and Stonehenge.
c. 450 Iron Age begins.
c. 400 Invasion by the Celts, who built hillforts, and left burial sites containing chariots.
55–54 Julius Caesar first visited England.
AD
43 Beginning of Roman conquest; surviving remains can be seen at Bath, Fishbourne (near Chichester), Hadrian's Wall, Watling Street, London (Temple of Mithras), Dover, St Alban's, and Dorchester.
407 Romans withdrew, but partially reoccupied the country *c.* 417–27 and *c.* 450.
5th–7th centuries Anglo-Saxons overran all England except Cornwall and Cumberland, forming independent kingdoms including Northumbria, Mercia, Kent, and Wessex.
c. 597 England converted to Christianity by St Augustine.
829 Egbert of Wessex accepted as overlord of all England.
878 Alfred ceded N and E England to the Danish invaders but kept them out of Wessex.
1066 Norman Conquest; England passed into French hands under William the Conqueror.
1172 Henry II became King of Ireland.
1215 King John forced to sign Magna Carta.
1284 Conquest of Wales, begun by the Normans, completed by Edward I.
1295 Model Parliament set up.
1338–1453 Hundred Years' War with France enabled parliament to secure control of taxation, and, by impeachment, of the king's choice of ministers.
1348–49 Black Death killed about 30% of the population.

English sovereigns from 900

West Saxon Kings

Edward the Elder	901
Athelstan	925
Edmund	940
Edred	946
Edwy	955
Edgar	959
Edward the Martyr	975
Ethelred II	978
Edmund Ironside	1016

Danish Kings

Canute	1016
Hardicanute	1040
Harold I	1035

West Saxon Kings (restored)

Edward the Confessor	1042
Harold II	1066

Norman Kings

William I	1066
William II	1087
Henry I	1100
Stephen	1135

House of Plantagenet

Henry II	1154
Richard I	1189
John	1199
Henry III	1216
Edward I	1272
Edward II	1307
Edward III	1327
Richard II	1377

House of Lancaster

Henry IV	1399
Henry V	1413
Henry VI	1422

House of York

Edward IV	1461
Richard III	1483
Edward V	1483

House of Tudor

Henry VII	1485
Henry VIII	1509
Edward VI	1547
Mary I	1553
Elizabeth I	1558

House of Stuart

James I	1603
Charles I	1625

The Commonwealth

House of Stuart (restored)

Charles II	1660
James II	1685
William III and Mary	1689
Anne	1702

House of Hanover

George I	1714
George II	1727
George III	1760
George IV	1820
William IV	1830
Victoria	1837

House of Saxe-Coburg

Edward VII	1901

House of Windsor

George V	1910
Edward VIII	1936
George VI	1936
Elizabeth II	1952

1381 Social upheaval led to the Peasants' Revolt, which was brutally repressed.

1399 Richard II deposed by parliament for absolutism.

1414 Lollard revolt repressed.

1455–85 Wars of the Roses.

1497 Henry VII ended the power of the feudal nobility with the suppression of the Yorkist revolts.

1529 Henry VIII became head of the English Church after breaking with Rome.

1536–43 Acts of Union united England and Wales after conquest.

1547 Edward VI adopted Protestant doctrines.

1553 Reversion to Roman Catholicism under Mary I.

1558 Elizabeth I adopted a religious compromise.

1588 Attempted invasion of England by the Spanish Armada.

1603 James I united the English and Scottish crowns; parliamentary dissidence increased.

1642–52 Civil War between royalists and parliamentarians.

1649 Charles I executed and the Commonwealth set up.

1653 Oliver Cromwell appointed Lord Protector.

1660 Restoration of Charles II.

1685 Monmouth rebellion.

1688 William of Orange invited to take the throne; flight of James II.

1707 Act of Union between England and Scotland under Queen Anne, after which the countries became known as Great Britain.

English language a member of the Germanic branch of the Indo-European language family. Developed through four major stages over about 1,500 years: *Old English* or *Anglo-Saxon* (*c.* 500–1050), rooted in the dialects of settling invaders (Jutes, Saxons, Angles then Danes); *Middle English* (*c.* 1050–1550), influenced by Norman French after the Conquest of 1066 and by ecclesiastical Latin; *Early Modern English* (*c.* 1550–1700), standardization of the diverse influences of Middle English, and *Late Modern English* (*c.*1700 onwards), the development and spread of current Standard English.

English law one of the major European legal systems, ◊Roman law being the other. English law has spread to many other countries, particularly former English colonies such as the USA, Canada, Australia, and New Zealand.

engraving the art of printmaking by means of blocks of metal, wood, or some other material, generally hard. The three main categories are: *relief prints*, made by cutting into the block so that the raised parts of the surface make the impression; *intaglio prints*, where the incised lines hold the ink for printing (intaglio prints are made mainly on metal, by line engraving, aquatint, dry point, etching, and mezzotint); and *whole-surface prints*, such as ◊lithography, where the design is made by painting or drawing on a stone surface.

Enlightenment a European intellectual movement, reaching its high point in the 18th century. Enlightenment thinkers were believers in social progress and in the liberating possibilities of rational and scientific knowledge. They were often critical of existing society and were hostile to religion, which they saw as keeping the human mind chained down by superstition.

enlightenment in Buddhism, the term used to translate the Sanskrit *bodhi*, awakening: perceiving the reality of the world, or the unreality of the self, and becoming liberated from suffering (Sanskrit *duhkha*). It is the gateway to ◊Nirvana.

Ennius Quintus 239–169 BC. Early Roman poet, who wrote tragedies based on the Greek pattern. His epic poem, the *Annales*, deals with Roman history.

enosis (Greek 'union') the movement, developed from 1930, for the union of ◊Cyprus with Greece.

entail in law, the settlement of land or other property on a successive line of people, usually succeeding generations of the original owner's family. An entail can be either *general*, in which case it simply descends to the heirs, or *special*, when it descends according to a specific arrangement, for example, to children by a named wife.

Entebbe town in Uganda, on the NW shore of Lake Victoria, 20 km/16 mi SW of Kampala, the capital; 1,779 m/3,863 ft above sea level; population (1983) 20,500. Founded in 1893, it was the administrative centre of Uganda 1894–1962.

Entente Cordiale (French 'friendly understanding') the agreement reached by Britain and France in 1904 recognizing British interests in Egypt and French interests in Morocco. It formed the basis for Anglo-French cooperation before the outbreak of World War I in 1914.

enterprise zone special zones designated by government to encourage industrial and commercial activity, usually in economically depressed areas. Investment is attracted by means of tax and other financial incentives.

entomology the study of ◊insects.

entrechat (French 'cross-caper') in ballet, a spring into the air during which the dancer criss-crosses his legs and feet a number of times. Wayne ◊Sleep broke ◊Nijinsky's record of an *entrechat dix* (ten times) with an *entrechat douze*(12 times) in 1973.

entrepreneur in business, a person who successfully manages and develops an enterprise through personal skill and initiative, and usually by taking financial risks. Notable examples include J D ◊Rockefeller and Henry ◊Ford.

entropy in ◊thermodynamics, a parameter representing the state of disorder of a system at the atomic, ionic, or molecular level; the greater disorder, the higher the entropy. Thus the fast-moving disordered molecules of water vapour have higher entropy than those of more ordered liquid water, which in turn have more entropy than the molecules in solid crystalline ice.

enucleation surgical removal of a complete organ, or tumour; for example, the eye from its socket.

E number any of various numbers preceded by the letter E (standing for European) which represent food ◊additives and which under EEC regulations must be displayed on the packaging of food that contains such additives. They cover preservatives, flavourings, and colourings (for example E150 is caramel colouring).

envelope in ◊geometry,* a curve that touches all the members of a family of lines or curves. For example, a family of three equal circles all touching each other and forming a triangular pattern (like a clover leaf) has two envelopes: a small circle that fits in the space in the middle, and a large circle that encompasses all three circles.

Enver Pasha 1881–1922. Turkish politician and soldier. He led the military revolt in 1908 which resulted in the Young Turk revolution (see ◊Turkey). He was killed fighting the Bolsheviks in Turkestan.

E–numbers

a selection of food additives authorized by the European Commission

number	name	typical use
	COLOURS	
E102	tartrazine	soft drinks
E104	quinoline yellow	
E110	sunset yellow FCF	biscuits
E120	cochineal	alcoholic drinks
E122	carmoisine	jams and preserves
E123	amaranth	
E124	ponceau 4R	dessert mixes
E127	erythrosine	glacé cherries
E131	patent blue V	
E132	indigo carmine	
E142	green S	pastilles
E150	caramel	beer, soft drinks, sauces, gravy browning
E151	black PN	
E160(b)	annatto; bixin; norbixin	crisps
E180	pigment rubine (lithol rubine BK)	
	ANTIOXIDANTS	
E310	propyl gallate	vegetable oils; chewing gum
E311	octyl gallate	
E312	dodecyl gallate	
E320	butylated hydroxynisole (BHA)	beef stock cubes; cheese spread
E321	butylated hydroxytoluene (BHT)	chewing gum
	EMULSIFIERS AND STABILIZERS	
E407	carageenan	quick setting jelly mixes; milk shakes
E413	tragacanth	salad dressings; processed cheese
	PRESERVATIVES	
E210	benzoic acid	
E211	sodium benzoate	beer, jam, salad cream, soft drinks, fruit pulp
E212	potassium benzoate	fruit-based pie fillings, marinated herring and mackerel
E213	calcium benzoate	
E214	ethyl para-hydroxy-benzoate	
E215	sodium ethyl para-hydroxy-benzoate	
E216	propyl para-hydroxy-benzoate	
E217	sodium propyl para-hydroxy-benzoate	
E218	methyl para-hydroxy-benzoate	
E220	sulphur dioxide	
E221	sodium sulphite	dried fruit, dehydrated vegetables, fruit juices
E222	sodium bisulphite	and syrups, sausages, fruit-based dairy
E223	sodium metabisulphate	desserts, cider, beer and wine; also used to prevent browning of raw
E224	potassium metabisulphite	peeled potatoes and to condition biscuit doughs
E226	calcium sulphite	
E227	calcium bisulphite	
E249	potassium nitrite	
E250	sodium nitrite	bacon, ham, cured meats, corned beef and
E251	sodium nitrate	some cheeses
E252	potassium nitrate	
	OTHERS	
E450(a)	disodium dihydrogen diphosphate; trisodium diphosphate; tetrasodium diphosphate; tetrapotassium diphosphate	buffers, sequestrants, emulsifying salts, stabilizers, texturizers, raising agents, used in whipping cream, fish
E450(b)	pentasodium triphosphate; pentapotassium triphosphate	and meat products, bread, processed cheese, canned vegetables
E450(c)	sodium polyphosphates; potassium polyphosphates	

environment in ecology, the sum of conditions affecting a particular organism, including physical surroundings, climate and influences of other living organisms; see also ◊biosphere and ◊habitat.

Environmentally Sensitive Area scheme introduced by the UK Ministry of Agriculture 1984 to protect ten of the most beautiful areas of the British countryside from the loss and damage caused by agricultural change. The ten areas are in the Pennine Dales, the North Peak District, the Norfolk Broads, the Breckland, the Suffolk River Valleys, the Test Valley, the South Downs, the Somerset Levels and Moors, West Penwith, Cornwall, the Shropshire Borders, the Cambrian Mountains, and the Lleyn Peninsular.

Environmental Protection Agency US agency set up 1970 to control water and air quality, industrial and commercial wastes, pesticides, noise, and radiation.

environment-heredity controversy a long-standing dispute among philosophers, psychologists, and scientists over the relative importance of environment (upbringing, experience, and learning) and heredity (genetic inheritance) in determining the make-up of an organism, especially as related to human personality and intelligence.

enzyme a biological ◊catalyst which converts one chemical to another, usually very swiftly, without itself being destroyed in the process. Enzymes are large, complex ◊proteins. They digest food, convert food energy into ◊ATP, help to manufacture all the molecular components of the body, produce copies of ◊DNA when the cell divides, and control the movement of substances into and out of cells.

Eocene second epoch of the Tertiary period of geological time, between 55 and 38 million years ago. The name means 'early recent', referring to the early forms of mammals evolving at the time, after the extinction of the dinosaurs.

EOKA an underground organization formed by Gen George Grivas in 1955 to fight for the independence of Cyprus from Britain and ultimately its union (*enosis*) with Greece. In 1971, 11 years after Cyprus's independence, Grivas returned to the island to form EOKA B, to resume the fight for *enosis* which had not been achieved by the Cypriot government.

eolith a chipped stone, once thought to have been manufactured as a primitive tool during the early Stone Age, but now generally believed to be the result of natural agencies.

Eos in Greek mythology, the goddess of the dawn, equivalent to the Roman name Aurora.

Epaminondas *c.* 420–362 BC. Theban general and politician, who won a decisive victory over the Spartans at Leuctra in 371, and was killed at the moment of victory at Mantinea.

ephedrine a drug which acts, adrenaline-like, on the sympathetic ◊nervous system (sympathomimetic). Once used to relieve bronchospasm in ◊asthma, it has been superseded by safer, more specific drugs. It is contained in some cold remedies as a decongestant. Side effects include tachycardia (rapid heartbeat), tremor, dry mouth, and anxiety.

ephemeral plant a plant with a very short life cycle, sometimes as little as six or eight weeks. It may complete several generations in one growing season. A number of common weeds are ephemerals, for example groundsel *Senecio vulgaris*, as are

epicycloid *a seven cusped epicycloid*

many desert plants. The latter take advantage of short periods of rain to germinate and reproduce, passing the dry season as dormant seeds.

Ephesus ancient Greek seaport in Asia Minor, a centre of the Ionian Greeks, with a temple of ◊Artemis destroyed by the Goths in 262 AD. St Paul visited the city, and addressed a letter (◊epistle) to the Christians there. In the 2nd century AD Ephesus had a population of 300,000, and it is now one of the world's largest archaeological sites.

epic a narrative poem or cycle of poems dealing with some great action, often the founding of a nation or the forging of national unity, and often using religious or cosmological themes. In the Western tradition, the crucial works are the *Iliad* and *Odyssey* attributed to Homer, works probably intended to be chanted in sections at feasts.

epicentre the point on the Earth's surface immediately above the seismic focus of an ◊earthquake. Most damage usually takes place at an earthquake's epicentre.The term is also used to refer to a point directly above or below a nuclear explosion ('ground zero').

Epictetus *c.* 55–135 AD. Greek Stoic philosopher, who encouraged people to refrain from self-interest, and to promote the common good of humanity. He believed that people were in the hands of an all-wise providence, and that they should endeavour to do their duty in the position to which they were called.

Epicureanism system of philosophy which says that soundly based human happiness is the highest good, so that its rational pursuit should be adopted.

Epicurus 341–270 BC. Greek philosopher, founder of Epicureanism, who taught at Athens from 306 BC.

epicyclic gear a gear system which consists of one or more gear wheels moving around another. This arrangement is also called a sun-and-planet gear. Epicyclic gears are found in bicycle hub gears and in automatic gearboxes.

epicycloid in geometry, a curve resembling a series of arches traced out by a point on the circumference of a circle that rolls around another circle of a different diameter. If the two circles have the same diameter, the curve is a ◊cardioid.

Epidaurus ancient Greek city and port on the E coast of Argolis, in the NE Peloponnèse. Originally famous for the temple of the god of healing, Aesculapius, Epidaurus is now noted for its

beautiful and well-preserved amphitheatre of the 4th century BC.

epidemic an outbreak of infectious disease affecting large numbers of people at the same time. A widespread epidemic which sweeps across many countries (such as the ◊Black Death in the late Middle Ages) is known as a pandemic.

epidermis the outermost layer of ◊cells on an organism's body. In plants and many invertebrates such as insects, it consists of a single layer of cells. In vertebrates, it consists of several layers of cells.

epigeal seed germination in which the ◊cotyledons are borne above the soil.

epigraphy (Greek *epigráphein* 'to write on') the art of writing with a sharp instrument on hard, durable materials such as stone, and also the scientific study of epigraphical writings or inscriptions.

epilepsy a group of disorders characterized by the occurrence of seizures. *Symptomatic epilepsy* is that arising from a known cause, such as a tumour or blood clot on the brain, head injury, or high fever. *Idiopathic epilepsy*, which is much more common, is a condition which develops without known cause.

Epiphany festival (6 Jan) of the Christian church, celebrating the coming of the ◊Magi, or Wise Men, to Bethlehem with gifts for the infant Jesus, and symbolizing the manifestation of Christ to the world. It is the 12th day after Christmas, and marks the end of the Christmas festivities.

epiphyte plant which grows on another plant or object above the surface of the ground, and which has no roots in the soil.

Epirus (Greek 'mainland') country of ancient Greece; the N part is in modern Albania; the remainder, in NW Greece, is divided into four provinces - Arta, Thesprotia, Yanina,and Preveza.

episcopacy in the Christian church, a system of government in which administrative and spiritual power over a district (diocese) is held by a bishop. The Roman Catholic, Eastern Orthodox, Anglican, and Episcopal (USA) churches are episcopalian; episcopacy also exists in some branches of the Lutheran Church, for example, in Scandinavia.

episiotomy an incision made in the perineum (the tissue bridging the vagina and rectum) to facilitate childbirth.

epistemology a branch of philosophy that examines the nature of knowledge and attempts to determine the limits of human understanding. Central issues include how knowledge is derived, and how it is to be validated and tested.

epistle in the New Testament, any of the 21 letters to individuals or to the members of various churches

Epidaurus *the Theatre in Epidaurus, Greece, was built by the architect Polycleitos and seats 14,000.*

Equatorial Guinea
Republic of
(*República de Guinea Ecuatorial*)

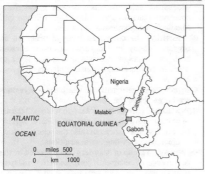

area 28,100 sq km/10, 852 sq mi
capital Malabo
physical comprises mainland Rio Muni, plus the small islands of Corisco, Elobey Grande and Elobey Chico, and Bioko Island (formerly Fernando Po) together with Annobón (formerly Pagalu)
head of state and government Teodoro Obiang Nguema Mbasogo from 1979

political system one-party military republic
exports coca, coffee, bananas, timber
currency ekuele; CFA franc
population (1988 est) 336,000; annual growth rate 2.2%
life expectancy men 44, women 48
language Spanish (official); pidgin English is widely spoken, and on Annobón (whose people were formerly slaves of the Portuguese) a Portuguese dialect
religion nominally Christian, mainly Catholic, but in 1978 Roman Catholicism was banned
literacy 55% (1984)
GDP $90 million (1987); $220 per head
chronology
1968 Achieved full independence from Spain. Francisco Macias Nguema became first president, soon assuming dictatorial powers.
1979 Macias overthrown and replaced by his nephew, Teodoro Obiang Nguema Mbasogo, who established a military regime. Macias tried and executed.
1982 Obiang elected president for another seven years. New constitution, promising a return to civilian government, adopted.
1989 Obiang re-elected president.
1992 New constitution adopted. Elections held, but president continued to nominate top government posts.

Epstein sculptor who worked in stone and marble. He is photographed next to his statue Lazarus.

written by Christian leaders. The best known are the 13 written by St ◊Paul. In modern usage the word is applied to letters with a suggestion of pomposity and literary affectation.

EPLF abbreviation for *Eritrean People's Liberation Front*.

epoxy resin a synthetic ◊resin used as an ◊adhesive and as an ingredient in paints. Household epoxy resin adhesives come in component form as two separate tubes of chemical, one tube containing resin, the other a curing agent (hardener). The two chemicals are mixed just before application, and the mix soon sets hard.

EPROM erasable programmable read-only memory; a computer memory device in the form of a chip that can record data and retain it indefinitely. The data can be erased by exposure to ultraviolet light and new data added. Other kinds of memory are ROM, PROM, and RAM.

Epsilon Aurigae an eclipsing binary star in the constellation Auriga. One of the pair is an 'ordinary' star, but the other seems to be a huge, distended object whose exact nature remains unknown. The period is 27 years, the longest of its kind. The last eclipse was 1982–84.

Epsom salts hydrated magnesium sulphate, $MgSO_4.7H_2O$, known as a saline purgative. The name is derived from a bitter saline spring at Epsom, Surrey, England, which contains the salt in solution.

Epstein Jacob 1880–1959. US sculptor. He experimented with abstract forms with some success, as in *Rock Drill* 1913–14 (Tate Gallery, London), but is better known, if not notorious, for stylized and muscular nude figures mainly sculpted in stone and coloured marble.

Equal Opportunities Commission commission established by the UK government in 1975 to implement the Sex Discrimination Act 1975. Its aim is to prevent discrimination, particularly on sexual or marital grounds.

***Erasmus** An engraving by the German painter Dürer of Desiderius Erasmus, the Renaissance Dutch scholar and theologian.*

equation mathematical expression that represents the equality of two expressions involving constants and/or variables, and thus usually includes an equals sign (=).

equator the *terrestrial equator* is the ◊great circle whose plane is perpendicular to the Earth's axis (the line joining the poles). Its length is 40,076 km/24,901.8 mi, divided into 360 degrees of longitude. The *celestial equator* is the circle in which the plane of the Earth's equator intersects the ◊celestial sphere.

Equatorial Guinea country in W central Africa, bounded N by Cameroon, E and S by Gabon, and W by the Atlantic Ocean; also several small islands off the coast and the larger island of Bioko off the coast of Cameroon.

equestrianism skill in horse riding, especially as practised under International Equestrian Federation rules. An Olympic sport, there are three main branches of equestrianism: *Show Jumping, Three Day Eventing, and Dressage*.

Equiano Olaudah 1745–1797. African anti-slavery campaigner and writer. A former slave, he travelled widely once free. His autobiography, *The Interesting Narrative of the Life of Olaudah Equiano or Gustavus Vassa the African* 1789, is the earliest significant work by an African written in English.

equilateral in geometry, refers to a figure having all sides of equal length. For example, a square and a rhombus are both equilateral four-sided figures. An equilateral triangle, to which the term is most often applied, has all three sides equal and all three angles equal (at 60°).

equilibrium in physics and chemistry, the state of a system in which the energy is balanced among the components in the most probable way, and there is no overall interaction between the components. An object is in thermal equilibrium when no heat enters or leaves it. Substances are in chemical equilibrium when the products of a reversible chemical reaction are formed at the same rate at which they decompose to form the reactants.

equinox the points in spring and autumn at which the Sun's path, the ◊ecliptic, crosses the celestial equator, so that the day and night are of approximately equal length on about 21 Mar, the *vernal equinox* and 23 Sept, the *autumnal equinox*.

equity a company's assets, less its liabilities, which are the property of the owner or shareholders. Popularly, equities are stocks and shares which, unlike debentures and preference shares, do not pay interest at fixed rates but pay dividends based on the company's performance. The value of equities tend to rise over the long term, but in the short term they are a risk investment because of fluctuating values.

equity a system of law supplementing the ordinary rules of law where the application of these would operate harshly in a particular case; sometimes it is regarded as an attempt to achieve 'natural justice'. So understood, equity appears as an element in most legal systems, and in a number of modern legal codes judges are instructed to apply both the rules of strict law and the principles of equity in reaching their decisions.

Equity in the UK theatre, a shortened term for the British Actors' Equity Association, the trade union for professional actors in theatre, film and television, founded in 1929. In the USA, its counterpart is the American Actors' Equity Association which, however, deals only with performers in the theatre.

Erasmus Desiderius *c.* 1466–1536. Dutch scholar and humanist. His pioneer edition of the Greek New Testament was published 1516, and his own *Colloquia* (dialogues on contemporary subjects) 1519.

Erastianism the belief that the church should be subordinated to the state. The name is derived from Thomas Erastus (1534–83), a German-Swiss theologian and opponent of Calvinism, who maintained in his writings that the church should not have the power of excluding people as a punishment for sin.

Eratosthenes *c.* 276–194 BC. Greek geographer and mathematician, whose map of the ancient world was the first to contain lines of latitude and longitude, and who calculated the earth's circumference with an error of less than 200 mi. His main mathematical achievements were his methods for duplicating the cube, and for finding prime numbers (Eratosthenes' 'sieve').

erbium a metallic element, symbol Er, atomic number 68, relative atomic mass 167.27. It is one of the rare earths, and was discovered in 1843 by Mosander.

Erebus, Mount the world's southernmost active volcano, 3,794 m/12,520 ft high, on Ross Island, Antarctica.

Erebus in Greek mythology, the god of darkness and the intermediate region between upper earth and ◊Hades.

Erfurt city in East Germany on the river Gera, capital of Erfurt district; population (1983) 214,000. A rich horticultural area, its manufactures include textiles, typewriters and electrical goods. The 12th–15th century cathedral has fine stained glass, and the Augustinian monastery where Martin ◊Luther spent some years is now an orphanage.

ergonomics the study of the relationship between people and the furniture, tools, and machinery they use at work. The object is to improve work performance by removing sources of muscular stress and general fatigue, for example by presenting data and control panels in easy-to-view form, making office furniture comfortable, and creating a pleasant environment.

ergot parasitic fungus *Claviceps purpurea* which attacks the rye plant. Ergot poisoning is caused by eating infected bread, resulting in burning pains, gangrene, and convulsions.

ergotamine ◊alkaloid administered to treat migraine. Isolated from ergot, a fungus that colonizes rye, it relieves symptoms by causing the cranial arteries to constrict. Its use is limited by severe side effects, including nausea and abdominal pain; there is a slight risk of addiction.

Erhard Ludwig 1897–1977. West German Christian Democrat politician, chancellor of the Federal Republic 1963–66. The 'economic miracle' of West Germany's recovery after World War II is largely attributed to Erhard's policy of social free enterprise (German *Marktwirtschaft*).

erica in botany, more commonly known as the heathers, the typical genus of the family Ericaceae. There are about 500 species, distributed mainly in South Africa and also Europe.

Ericsson Leif lived about 1000 AD. Norse explorer, son of Eric 'the Red', who sailed west from Greenland in about 1000 to find a country first sighted by Norsemen in 986. Landing with 35 companions in N America, he called it 'Vinland', because he discovered grape vines growing, and spent a winter there.

Eric 'the Red' 940–1010. allegedly the first European to find Greenland. According to a 13th-century saga, he was the son of a Norwegian chieftain, who was banished from Iceland about 982 for murder, sailed westward, and discovered a land which he called Greenland.

Eridanus the sixth-largest constellation, which meanders from the celestial equator deep into the southern hemisphere of the sky. Its most brilliant star, Achernar, is the ninth-brightest star in the entire sky. It represents a river.

Eridu ancient city of Mesopotamia about 5000 BC, according to tradition the cradle of Sumerian civilization. On its site is now the village of Tell Abu Shahrain, Iraq.

Erie, Lake fourth largest of the Great Lakes of North America, connected to Lake Ontario by the Niagara river, and by-passed by the Welland Canal; area 25,720 sq km/9,930 sq mi.

Erin poetic name for Ireland derived from the dative case Érinn of the Gaelic name Ériu, possibly derived from Sanskrit 'western'.

Eritrea province of N Ethiopia
area 118,500 sq km/45,745 sq mi
capital Asmara
towns ports Assab and Massawa are Ethiopia's outlets to the sea
physical coastline on the Red Sea 1,000 km/620 mi; narrow coastal plain which rises to an inland plateau
products coffee, salt, citrus fruits, grains, cotton
currency birr
population (1980) 2,426,200
language Amharic (official)
religion Islam
history part of an ancient Ethiopian kingdom until the 7th century; under Ethiopian influence until it fell to the Turks mid-16th century; Italian colony 1889–1941, where it was the base for Italian invasion of Ethiopia; under British administration 1941–52, when it became an autonomous part of Ethiopia; since 1962, when it became a region, various secessionist movements have risen; civil war 1970s, during which guerillas held most of Eritrea; Ethiopian government, backed by Soviet and Cuban forces, recaptured most towns 1978;

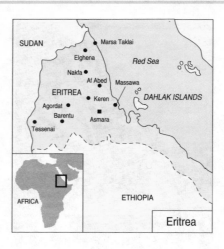

Eritrea

resistance continued in the 1980s, aided by conservative Gulf states, and some cooperation with guerillas in Tigré province.

ermine name given to the ◊stoat during the winter when its coat becomes white. In northern latitudes the coat becomes completely white, except for a black tip to the tail, but in warmer regions the back may remain brownish.

ERNIE (Electronic Random Number Indicator Equipment). In the UK, machine designed and produced by the Post Office Research Station to select a series of random 9-figure numbers to indicate prizewinners in the government's national lottery.

Ernst Max 1891–1976. German artist, who worked in France 1922–38 and in the USA from 1941. He was an active Dadaist, experimenting with collage, photomontage, and surreal images, and helped found the Surrealist movement 1924. His paintings are highly diverse.

Eros in astronomy, an asteroid, discovered 1898, 22 million km/14 million mi from the Earth at its nearest point. Eros was the first asteroid to be discovered whose orbit comes within that of Mars. It is elongated, measures about 36×12 km/22×7 mi, rotates around its shortest axis every 5.3 hours, and orbits the Sun every 1.8 years.

Eros in Greek mythology, boy-god of love (Roman *Cupid*), son of ◊Aphrodite, and armed with bow and arrows; he fell in love with ◊Psyche.

erosion the processes whereby the rocks and soil of the earth's surface are loosened, worn away, and transported (◊weathering does not involve transportation). There are two forms – chemical and physical. *Chemical erosion* involves the alteration of the mineral component of the rock, by means of rainwater or the substances dissolved in it, and its subsequent movement. *Physical erosion* involves the breakdown and transportation of exposed rocks by physical forces. In practice the two work together.

Ershad Hussain Mohammad 1930– . Military leader of Bangladesh from 1982–90. He became chief of staff in the Bangladesh army in 1979 and assumed power in a military coup in 1982. As president from 1983, Ershad introduced a successful rural-orientated economic programme. He was re-elected in 1986 and lifted martial law, but faced continuing political opposition.

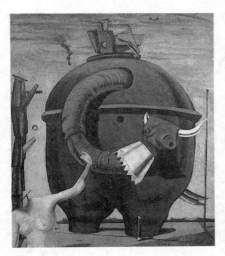

Ernst The Elephant Celebes *(1921) Tate Gallery, London.*

erysipelas an acute disease of the skin due to infection by a streptococcus. Starting at some point where the skin is broken or injured, the infection spreads, producing a swollen red patch with small blisters and generalized fever. The condition is now rare.

Esarhaddon died 669 BC. King of Assyria from 680, when he succeeded his father ◊Sennacherib. He conquered Egypt 671–74.

Esau in the Old Testament or Jewish Bible, the son of Isaac and Rebekah, and the elder twin brother of Jacob, who tricked Isaac into giving him the blessing intended for Esau by putting on goatskins. Earlier Esau had sold his birthright to Jacob for a 'mess of red pottage'. He was the ancestor of the Edomites.

escape velocity minimum velocity which an object such as a rocket must reach for it to escape from the gravitational pull of a planet or moon. The escape velocity of Earth is 11.2 km per sec/7 mi per sec; of the Moon 2.4 kps/1.5 mps; of Mars 5 kps/3.1 kps; and of Jupiter 62 kps/38 mps.

escheat a term used in feudal society to describe the reversion of lands to the lord in the event of the tenant dying without heirs or being convicted for treason. By the later Middle Ages in W Europe, tenants had insured against their lands escheating by granting them to trustees, or feoffees, who would pass them on to the grantor nominated in the will.

Escher Maurits Cornelis 1902–1972. Dutch graphic artist. His prints, often based on mathematical concepts, usually contain paradoxes and illusions. The lithograph *Ascending and Descending* 1960, with interlocking staircases creating a perspective puzzle, is typical.

Eskimo member (or language) of a people of the Arctic. The Eskimos of Greenland and Canada are ◊Inuit and their language Inuktitut; the Eskimos of South Alaska and Siberia are Yupik and their language Yuk.

Eskişehir city in Turkey, 200 km/125 mi W of Ankara; population (1985) 367,300. Produces meerschaum, chromium, magnesite, cotton goods, tiles, and also assembles aircraft.

esparto grass *Stipa tenacissima*, native to S Spain, S Portugal and the Balearics, but now widely grown in dry, sandy locations throughout the world. The plant is just over 1 m/3 ft high, producing greyish-green leaves, which are used for paper-making, ropes, baskets, mats, and cables.

Esperanto language devised 1887 by Dr Ludwig L Zamenhof (1859–1917) as an international auxiliary language. For its structure and vocabulary it draws on various European languages. Esperantists refer to Esperanto as a 'planned language' and to the natural languages of the world as 'ethnic languages'. Its spelling is phonetic.

espionage the practice of spying; a way to gather ◊intelligence.

ESS (evolutionary stable strategy) in ◊sociobiology, an assemblage of behavioural or physical characters (collectively termed a 'strategy') that is resistant to replacement by any forms bearing new traits, because these new traits will not be capable of successful reproduction.

essay short, literary piece of prose, dealing often from a fairly personal point of view with some particular subject. The essay first became a recognized genre and name with the first edition of the French writer Montaigne's *Essais* 1580. Bacon's essays 1597 are among the most famous in English. The essay was largely used in 19th-century Europe as a vehicle for literary criticism, but the personal essay is usually regarded as being particularly English in spirit.

Essen city in North Rhine-Westphalia, Germany; population (1988) 615,000. Administrative centre of the Ruhr, with textile, chemical, and electrical industries.

Essene member of a Jewish religious order that existed in the area near the Dead Sea *c.* 200 BC–200 AD, whose members lived an extremely simple life bound by strict rules; they believed that the day of judgment was imminent.

Essex county in SE England
area 3,672 sq km/1,417 sq mi
towns administrative headquarters Chelmsford; Colchester; ports Harwich, Tilbury; resorts Southend, Clacton
products dairying, cereals, fruit
population (1988 est) 1,529,500
famous people William Harvey.

Essex Robert Devereux, 2nd Earl of Essex 1566–1601. English soldier and politician. He fought in the Netherlands in 1585–86 and distinguished himself at the Battle of Zutphen. In 1596 he jointly commanded a force that siezed and sacked Cadiz. He became a favourite with Elizabeth I from 1587, but was executed because of his policies in Ireland.

estate in law, the rights which a person has in relation to any property. *Real estate* is an interest in any land; *personal estate* is an interest in any other kind of property.

estate in medieval and *ancien régime* Europe, an order of society which enjoys a prescribed share in government. In medieval theory, there were usually three estates – the *nobility*, the *clergy*, and the *commons* – with the particular functions of, respectively, defending society from foreign aggression and internal disorder, attending to its spiritual needs, and working to produce the wealth with which to support the other two orders.

ester an organic compound formed by the reaction between an alcohol and an acid, with the elimination of water. Esters are the organic equivalent of salts in inorganic chemistry.

Esther in the Old Testament or Jewish Bible, the wife of the Persian king Ahasuerus, who

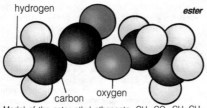

Model of the ester ethyl ethanoate, $CH_3 CO_2 CH_2 CH_3$

prevented the extermination of her people by the vizier Haman, a deliverance celebrated in the Jewish festival of Purim. Her story is told in the Old Testament book Esther.

Estonia country in N Europe, bounded E by Russia, S by Latvia, and N and W by the Baltic Sea.

etching a print from a metal (usually copper) plate, which is prepared with a waxy overlayer and then drawn on with an etching needle. The exposed areas are then 'etched', or bitten into, by a corrosive agent, so that they will hold ink for printing.

ethanal CH_2O (common name **acetaldehyde**) in chemistry, one of the chief members of the group of organic compounds known as ◊aldehydes. It is a colourless inflammable liquid boiling at 20.8°C (69.6°F). Ethanal is used to make many other organic chemical compounds.

ethane a colourless, odourless gas, C_2H_6. It is the second member of the series of paraffin hydrocarbons, the first being methane.

ethane-1,2-diol modern name for ◊glycol.

ethanoate CH_3CO_2 (common name **acetate**) in chemistry, salt of ethanoic (acetic) acid. In textiles, acetate rayon is a synthetic fabric made from modified cellulose (wood pulp) treated with acetic acid; in photography, acetate film is a non-flammable film made of cellulose acetate.

ethanoic acid CH_3CO_2H (common name **acetic acid**) in chemistry, one of the simplest members of

a series of organic acids called fatty acids. In the pure state it is a colourless liquid with an unpleasant pungent odour; it solidifies to an icelike mass of crystals at 16.7°C, and hence is often called glacial acetic acid. Vinegar is 3–6% ethanoic acid.

ethanol C_2H_5OH (common name **ethyl alcohol**) the chemical term for the alcohol found in beer, wine, cider, spirits, and other 'alcoholic drinks'. When pure, it is a colourless liquid with a pleasant odour, miscible with water or ether, and burning in air with a pale blue flame. The vapour forms an explosive mixture with air and may be used in high-compression internal combustion engines. It is produced naturally by the fermentation of carbohydrates by yeast cells. Industrially, it can be made by absorption of ethene and subsequent reaction with water, or by the reduction of ethanal in the presence of a catalyst, and is widely used as a solvent.

Ethelred II c. 968–1016. King of England from 978; nicknamed the **Unready**, that is, lacking in foresight. The son of King Edgar, he became king after the murder of his half-brother, Edward the Martyr. He tried to buy off the Danish raiders by paying ◊Danegeld, and in 1002 ordered the massacre of the Danish settlers – so provoking an invasion by Sweyn I of Denmark. War with Sweyn and Sweyn's son, Canute, occupied the rest of Ethelred's reign.

ethene C_2H_4 (common name **ethylene**) a colourless, flammable gas, the first member of the alkene series of hydrocarbons. It is the most widely used synthetic organic chemical and is used to produce polyethylene (polythene), dichloroethane, and polyvinyl chloride (PVC).

ether or **diethyl ether**. $C_2H_5OC_2H_5$ (modern name **ethoxyethane**) a colourless, volatile, inflammable liquid, slightly soluble in water, miscible with ethanol. It is prepared by treatment of ethanol with excess concentrated sulphuric acid at 140°C. It

Estonia
Republic of

area 45,000 sq km/17,000 sq mi
capital Tallinn
towns Tartu, Narva, Kohtla-Järve, Pärnu
physical lakes and marshes in a partly forested plain; 774 km/481 mi of coastline; mild climate
head of state Lennart Meri from 1992
head of government Tiit Vahl from 1992
political system emergent democracy
products oil and gas (from shale), wood products,
flax, dairy and pig products
currency kroon
population (1989) 1,573,000 (Estonian 62%, Russian 30%, Ukrainian 3%, Byelorussian 2%)
language Estonian, allied to Finnish
religion traditionally Lutheran
chronology
1918 Estonia declared its independence. Soviet troops took control after German withdrawal.
1919 Soviet rule overthrown with help of British navy; Estonia declared a democratic republic.
1934 Fascist coup replaced government.
1940 Estonia incorporated into USSR.
1941–44 German occupation during World War II.
1944 USSR regained control.
1980 Beginnings of nationalist dissent.
1988 Adopted own constitution, with power of veto on all centralized Soviet legislation.
1989 Estonian replaced Russian as main language.
1990 The Communist Party's monopoly of power was abolished. Pro-independence candidates secured a majority in multiparty elections.
1991 Full independence was declared after the abortive anti-Gorbachev coup in the USSR; the Communist Party was outlawed. Independence was recognized by the Soviet government and Western nations.
1992 New government formed by Tiit Vahl and new constitution approved. Meri chosen as new president by parliament.

Ethiopia
People's Democratic Republic of
(Amharic *Hebretesebawit Ityopia*, formerly also known as Abyssinia)

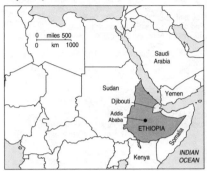

area 1,000,000 sq km/395,000 sq mi
capital Addis Ababa
towns Asmara (capital of Eritrea), Dire Dawa; ports are Massawa, Assab
physical a high plateau with mountains; plains in E; Blue Nile river
head of state and government Metes Zenawi from 1991
political system transitional to democratic socialist republic
exports coffee, pulses, oilseeds, hides, skins
currency birr
population (1989 est) 47,709,000 (Oromo 40%, Amhara 25%, Tigré 12%, Sidama 9%); annual growth rate 2.5%
life expectancy 38
language Amharic (official); Tigrinya, Orominga, Arabic
religion Christian (Ethiopian Orthodox church) 40%, Sunni Muslim 45%
literacy 35% (1988)
GDP $4.8 bn (1987); $104 per head
chronology
1974 Haile Selassie deposed and replaced by a military government led by Gen Teferi Benti. Ethiopia declared a socialist state.
1977 Teferi Benti killed and replaced by Col Mengistu Haile Mariam.
1985 Worst famine for more than a decade.
1987 New constitution adopted, Mengistu Mariam elected president. Provisional Military Administrative Council dissolved, and elected National Assembly introduced. New famine, with food aid supplies impeded by guerrillas.
1988 Mariam agreed to adjust his economic policies in order to secure IMF assistance. Influx of refugees from Sudan.
1989 Coup attempt against Mengistu foiled. Peace talks with Eritrean rebels reported some progress.
1990 Rebels captured port of Massawa. Mengistu announced reforms.
1991 Mengistu overthrown and replaced by Meles Zanawi. Eritrea's right to recede was recognized.
1993 An overwhelming majority voted in favour of Eritrean independence in a referendum.

---

is used as an anaesthetic by vapour inhalation and as an external cleansing agent before surgical operations. It is also used as a solvent, and in the extraction of oils, fats, waxes, resins, and alkaloids.

ether in science, formerly a hypothetical medium permeating all of space. The concept, originally Greek, was revived to explain the properties and propagation of light, which it was supposed must need a medium, the ether, in which to travel.

ethics the area of philosophy concerned with human values, and which studies the meanings of moral terms and theories of conduct and goodness.

Ethiopia country in E Africa, bounded NE by the Red Sea, E and SE by Somalia, S by Kenya, and W and NW by Sudan.

ethnology the study of contemporary peoples, concentrating on their geography and culture, as distinct from their social systems.

ethology the comparative study of ◊animal behaviour in its natural setting. Ethology is concerned with the causal mechanisms (both the stimuli that elicit behaviour and the physiological mechanisms controlling it), as well as the development of behaviour, its function, and its evolutionary history.

ethyne (CH)₂ (common name *acetylene*) in chemistry, a colourless inflammable gas. One important use is its conversion into the synthetic rubber neoprene. It is also used in oxyacetylene welding and cutting.

etiolation in botany, a form of growth seen in plants receiving insufficient light. It is characterized by long, weak stems, small leaves, and a pale yellowish colour (◊chlorosis) owing to a lack of chlorophyll. The rapid increase in height enables a plant to quickly reach a source of light, when a return to normal growth usually occurs.

Etna volcano on the E coast of Sicily, 3,323 m/10,902 ft – the highest in Europe.

etymology the study of the origin and history of words within and across languages. It has two major aspects: the study of the phonetic and written forms of words, and the semantics or meanings of those words.

Euboea (Greek *Evvoia*) mountainous island off the E coast of Greece, in the Aegean Sea; area 3,755 sq km/1,480 sq mi; about 177 km/110 mi long; population (1981) 188,410. Mount Delphi reaches 1,743 m/5,718 ft.

eucalyptus tree of the Myrtaceae family, native to Australia and Tasmania, where it is commonly known as a gum tree. About 90 per cent of Australian timber belongs to the eucalyptus group, which comprises about 500 species.

Eucharist chief Christian sacrament, in which bread is eaten and wine drunk as symbols of Christ's body and blood. Other names for it are the Lord's Supper, Holy Communion, and (among Roman Catholics) the Mass.

Euclid c. 330–c. 260 BC. Greek mathematician, who lived at Alexandria and wrote the *Stoicheia/Elements* in 13 books, of which nine deal with plane and solid geometry, and four with number theory.

eugenics the study of ways in which the physical and mental quality of a people can be controlled and improved by selective breeding. The idea was abused by the Nazi Party in Germany during the 1930s to justify the extermination of entire groups of people.

Eugénie 1826–1920. Empress of the French. Daughter of the Spanish count of Montijo, in 1853 she married Louis Napoleon (◊Napoleon III). She encouraged his intervention in Mexico and after his surrender to the Germans at Sedan, NE France, 1870, she fled to England.

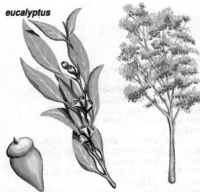
eucalyptus

eukaryote one of the two classes into which all living organisms (except bacteria and cyanobacteria) are divided. The other class is ◊prokaryote.

Eumenides ('kindly ones') in Greek mythology, appeasing name for the ◊Furies.

eunuch a castrated man. Originally eunuchs were simply bedchamber attendants in harems in the East (*eunoukhos* is Greek for 'one in charge of a bed') but as these were usually castrated so that they should not take too great an interest in their charges, the term became applied more generally. Eunuchs often filled high offices of state in China, India, and Persia.

euphemism a ◊figure of speech whose name in Greek means 'speaking well (of something)'. To speak or write euphemistically is to use a milder, more polite, less direct, or even less honest expression rather than one that is considered too blunt, vulgar, direct, or revealing.

euphonium type of ◊brass instrument, like a small tuba.

Euphrates (Arabic *Furat*) river, rising in E Turkey, flowing through Syria and Iraq and joining the Tigris above Basra to form the Shatt-el-Arab, at the head of the Persian/Arabian Gulf; 3,600 km/2,235 mi in length. The ancient cities of Babylon, Eridu, and Ur were situated along its course.

Eurasian in India and the East Indies, a term formerly used to denote a person born of mixed European and Asian parentage or ancestry.

Eureka 1) exclamation (Greek 'I've got it!') allegedly made by ◊Archimedes on his discovery of fluid

Euripides a bust of the ancient Greek dramatist Euripides.

Europe – history

3000 BC	Bronze Age civilizations: Minoan, Mycenaean.
6th–4th cent.	Greek civilization at its height; Alexander.
3rd cent.	Rome in control of the Italian peninsula.
146	Greece a Roman province, and Carthage destroyed.
1st cent.	Augustus made the Rhine and Danube the Roman Empire's northern frontiers; see Celts.
1st cent. AD	Britain brought within the Roman Empire.
2nd cent.	Roman Empire ceased to expand.
4th cent.	Christianity the established religion of the Roman Empire.
4th–6th cent.	W Europe overrun by Anglo-Saxons, Franks, Goths, Lombards.
7th–8th cent.	Christendom threatened by the Moors (Arabs).
800	Charlemagne given title of emperor by the Pope.
1073	Gregory VII begins 200 years of conflict between Empire and papacy.
1096–1272	Crusades.
12th cent.	Setting-up of German, Flemish, and Italian city states, which in the 14–15th centuries fostered the Renaissance.
1453	Constantinople captured by the Turks.
16th–17th cent.	Dominated by rivalry of France and the Hapsburgs, the Protestant Reformation, and the Catholic Counter-Reformation.
17th cent.	Absolute monarchy came to prevail (Louis XIV) in Europe, although in England supremacy of Parliament established by Civil War.
18th cent.	War of the Austrian Succession and Seven Years' War ended in the loss of the French colonial empire to Britain, and the establishment of Prussia as Europe's emergent power.
1789	French Revolution led to the united opposition of the rest of Europe in the Revolutionary and Napoleonic Wars.
1821–29	Greek War of Independence marked the end of Turkish control of the Balkans.
1848	Year of revolutions (see Louis Philippe, Metternich, Risorgimento).
1914–1918	World War I arose from the Balkan Question. Franco-German rivalry, and colonial differences; it destroyed the Austrian and Turkish empires and initiated that of the USSR.
1933	Hitler came to power.
1939–45	World War II resulted in decline of European colonial rule in Africa and Asia; full emergence of Soviet power, and Western forces organized under the aegis of the USA (NATO); the Cold War.
1957	Establishment of the European Economic Community, the 'Common Market'.
1973	Enlargement of the European Community to include Britain.
1979	First direct elections to the European Parliament.
1985	Accession to power in the USSR of Mikhail Gorbachev marked an apparent relaxation of political and economic bureaucracy.

displacement. 2) a plan for European technological cooperation, 1985. 3) alternative name for the copper-nickel alloy ◊constantan which is used in electrical equipment.

Euripides c.484–407 BC. Greek dramatist whose plays deal with ordinary people and social issues rather than the more grandiose themes used by his contemporaries. He wrote more than 80 plays, of which 18 survive, including *Alcestis* 438, *Medea* 431, *Andromache* 420, *Trojan Women* 415, *Electra* 413, *Iphigenia in Tauris* 413, *Iphigenia in Aulis* 405, and *Bacchae* 405.

Eurobond a bond underwritten by an international syndicate and sold in countries other than the country of the currency in which the issue is denominated. They provide longer-term financing than is possible with loans in ◊Eurodollars.

Eurodollar US currency deposited outside the US and held by individuals and institutions, not necessarily in Europe. They originated in the 1960s when E European countries deposited their US dollars in

W European banks. Banks holding Eurodollar deposits may lend in dollars, usually to finance trade, and often redeposit with other foreign banks. The practice is a means of avoiding credit controls and exploiting interest rate differentials.

Europa in astronomy, the fourth-largest moon of the planet Jupiter, diameter 3,100 km/1,900 mi, orbiting 671,000 km/417,000 mi from the planet every 3.55 days. It is covered by ice and crisscrossed by thousands of thin cracks, each some 50,000 km/30,000 mi long.

Europa in Greek mythology, the daughter of the king of Tyre, carried off by ◊Zeus (in the form of a bull); she personifies the continent of Europe.

Europe second smallest continent, comprising the land W of the Ural mountains; it has 8% of the Earth's surface, with 14.5% of world population.
area 10,400,000 sq km/4,000,000 sq mi
largest cities (over 2 million inhabitants) Moscow, London, Istanbul, St Petersburg, Madrid, Rome, Athens, Kiev, Budapest, Paris
population (1985) 496,000,000 (excluding Turkey and the ex-Soviet republics); annual growth rate 0.3%
languages mostly of Indo-European origin, with a few exceptions, including Finno-Ugrian (Finnish and Hungarian) and Basque
religion Christianity (Protestantism, Roman Catholicism, Greek Orthodox), Islam.

European inhabitant of the continent of Europe. The term is also sometimes applied to people of European descent living in other continents, especially in the Americas and Australia. Europe is culturally heterogeneous and although most of its languages belong to the Indo-European family, there are also speakers of Uralic (for example Hungarian), and Altaic (such as Turkish) languages, and Basque.

European Atomic Energy Commission (*EURATOM*) organization established by the second Treaty of Rome 1957, which seeks the cooperation of member states of the European Community in nuclear research and the rapid and large-scale development of non-military nuclear energy.

European Community (*EC*) political and economic alliance consisting of the European Coal and Steel Community (1952), European Economic Community (EEC, popularly called the Common Market, 1957), and the European Atomic Energy Commission (Euratom, 1957). The original six members – Belgium, France, West Germany, Italy, Luxembourg, and the Netherlands – were joined by the UK, Denmark, and the Republic of Ireland 1973, Greece 1981 and Spain and Portugal 1986). Association agreements – providing for free trade for ten years and the possibility of full EC membership – were signed with Czechoslovakia, Hungary and Poland 1991, subject to ratification, and with Romania 1992.

European Court of Justice the court of the European Community (EC) which is responsible for interpreting Community law and ruling on breaches by member states and others of such law. It sits in Luxembourg with judges from the member states.

European Economic Community (EEC) the ◊European Community.

European Free Trade Association (EFTA) an organization established 1960 consisting of Austria, Finland, Iceland, Norway, Sweden, Switzerland and (from 1991) Liechtenstein, previously a non-voting associate member. There are no import duties between members.

European Monetary System (EMS) an attempt by the European Community to bring financial cooperation and monetary stability to Europe. It was established 1979 in the wake of the 1974 oil crisis which brought growing economic disruption to European economies because of floating exchange rates. Central to the EMS is the ◊*Exchange Rate Mechanism* (ERM), a voluntary system of semi-fixed exchange rates based on the European Currency Unit (ECU).

European Parliament the parliament of the European Community, which meets in Strasbourg to comment on the legislative proposals of the Commission of the European Communities. Members are elected for a five-year term. The European Parliament has 518 seats, of which the UK, France, Germany, and Italy have 81 each, Spain 60, the Netherlands 25, Belgium, Greece, and Portugal 24 each, Denmark 16, the Republic of Ireland 15, and Luxembourg 6.

European Space Agency (ESA) an organization of European countries (Belgium, Denmark, France, Germany, Ireland, Italy, Netherlands, Spain, Sweden, Switzerland, and the UK) which engages in space research and technology. It was founded 1975, with headquarters in Paris.

europium a rare element, symbol Eu, atomic number 63, relative atomic mass 152. It is one of the lanthanide series of metals, used in lasers and in colour television.

eusociality form of social life found in insects such as honey bees and termites, in which the colony is made up of special castes (for example, workers, drones, and reproductives) whose membership is biologically determined. The worker castes do not usually reproduce. Only one mammal, the naked mole rat, has a social organization of this type.

Eutelsat abbreviation for *European Telecommunications Satellite Organization*.

eutrophication the over-enrichment of lake waters, primarily by nitrate fertilizers washed from soil by rain, and phosphates from detergents in municipal sewage. These encourage the growth of ◊algae which use up the oxygen, thereby making the water uninhabitable for fish and other animal life.

evangelicalism the beliefs of some Protestant Christian sects which stress fundamental biblical

European Community The signing of the Rome Treaties on 25 Mar 1957 in Palazzo dei Conservatori on the Capitoline Hill, which established the European Economic Community and Euratom.

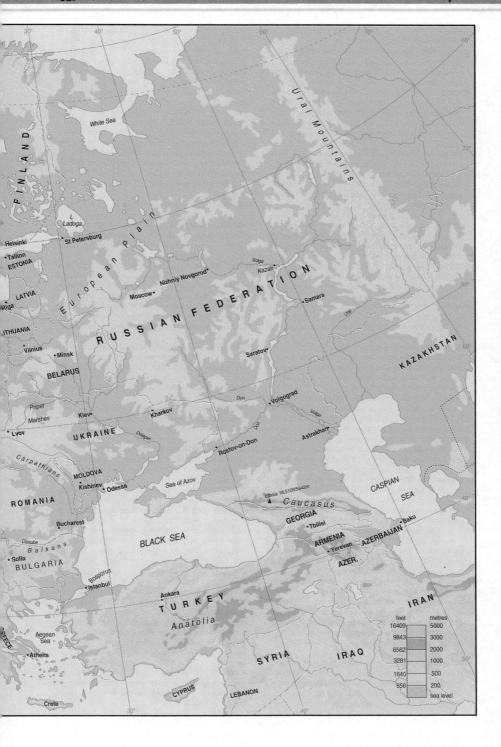

authority, faith, and the personal commitment of the 'born-again' experience.

evangelist person travelling to spread the Christian gospel, and especially the authors of the four Gospels in the New Testament: Matthew, Mark, Luke, and John.

Evans Arthur John 1851–1941. English archaeologist. His excavation of ◊Knossos on Crete resulted in the discovery of the pre-Phoenician Minoan script and proved the existence of the Minoan civilization of which all trace had disappeared except in legend.

Evans Walker 1903–1975. US photographer, best known for his documentary photographs of the people in the rural American south during the Great Depression of the 1930s. Many of his photographs appeared in James Agee's book *Let Us Now Praise Famous Men* 1941.

Eve in the Old Testament, the first woman, wife of ◊Adam, who was tempted by Satan in the form of a snake to eat the fruit of the Tree of Knowledge of Good and Evil, and thus brought about the expulsion from the Garden of Eden.

Evelyn John 1620–1706. English diarist and author. Of his 300-odd books the most important is his diary, first published in 1818, which covers the period 1640–1706.

evening primrose American plant of the family Onagraceae, naturalized in Europe. It is grown as a field crop for the oil it produces, which is used in treating eczema and premenstrual tension.

eventing sport (horse trials) giving an all-round test of a horse and rider in a three-day event: dressage, testing a horse's response to control; speed and endurance across country; and finally a modified showjumping contest.

Everest, Mount the world's highest mountain, in the Himalayas, on the China-Nepál frontier; height 8,872 m/29,108 ft. It was first climbed by Edmund ◊Hillary and Norghay ◊Tenzing in 1953.

evergreen plant, such as pine, spruce, or holly, that bears its leaves all year round. Most ◊conifers are evergreen. Plants that shed their leaves in winter are described as ◊deciduous.

everlasting flower flower head with coloured bracts which retains its colour when cut and dried, includes some species of *Ammobium, Helichrysum,* and *Xeranthemum.*

evidence the testimony of witnesses and production of documents and other material in court proceedings in order to prove or disprove facts at issue in the case. Witnesses must swear or affirm that their evidence is true. In English law, giving false evidence is the crime of ◊perjury.

evolution a slow process of change from one form to another, as in the evolution of the universe from its formation in the ◊Big Bang to its present state, or in the evolution of life on Earth. For human evolution, see ◊human species, origins of. Some Christians deny the theory of evolution as conflicting with the belief that God created all things (see ◊creationism).

exchange rate the price at which one currency is bought or sold in terms of other currencies, gold, or accounting units such as the special drawing right (SDR) of the ◊International Monetary Fund. Exchange rates may be fixed by international agreement or by government policy; or they may be wholly or partly allowed to 'float' (that is, find their own level) in world currency markets, as with most major currencies since the 1970s.

Exchange Rate Mechanism (ERM) voluntary system for controlling exchange rates within the European Community's ◊European Monetary System. The member currencies of the ERM are fixed against each other within a narrow band of fluctuation based on a central European Currency Unit (ECU) rate, but floating against nonmember countries. If a currency deviates significantly from the central ECU rate, the ◊European Monetary Cooperation Fund and the central banks concerned intervene to stabilize the currency.

exclamation mark or *exclamation point* a punctuation mark (!), used to indicate emphasis or strong emotion ('What a surprise!'). Usually the emphasis or emotion is built directly into the text, as part of a story, or dialogue, but the exclamation can also be placed in brackets to indicate that the writer is surprised by something, especially by something in a quotation.

exclusion principle in physics, a principle of atomic structure originated by Wolfgang ◊Pauli.

excommunication exclusion of an offender from the rights and privileges of the Roman Catholic Church; famous offenders include King John, Henry VIII, and Elizabeth I.

excretion the removal of waste products from the cells of living organisms. In plants and simple animals, waste products are removed by diffusion, but in higher animals by specialized organs. In mammals, for example, carbon dioxide and water are removed via the lungs, and nitrogenous compounds and water via the liver, kidneys, and urinary system.

executor in law, a person appointed in a will to carry out the instructions of the deceased. The executor has a duty to bury the deceased, prove the will, and obtain a grant of probate (that is, establish that the will is genuine and obtain official approval of his or her actions).

existentialism a branch of philosophy which emphasizes the existence of the individual. It is based on the concept that the universe is absurd, although humans have free will. Existentialists argue that philosophy must begin from the concrete situation of the individual in the world, and that this situation cannot be comprehended by any purely rational system.

exobiology the study of possible life-forms that may exist elsewhere in the Universe.

exocrine gland type of gland that discharges secretions, usually through a tube or a duct, on to a surface. Examples include sweat glands which release sweat on to the skin, and digestive glands which release digestive juices on to the walls of the intestine. Some animals also have ◊endocrine glands (ductless glands) that release hormones directly into the bloodstream.

Exodus in the Old Testament, the departure of the Israelites from slavery in Egypt, under the leadership of ◊Moses, for the Promised Land of Canaan. The journey included the miraculous parting of the Red Sea, Pharaoh's pursuing forces being drowned as the waters returned. Exodus is also the name of the book of the Bible that contains the story.

exorcism rite used in a number of religions for the expulsion of so-called 'evil spirits'. In Christianity it is employed, for example, in the Roman Catholic and Pentecostal churches.

exoskeleton the hardened external skeleton of insects, spiders, crabs, and other arthropods. It provides attachment for muscles and protection for the internal organs, as well as support. To permit growth it is a periodically shed in a process called ◊ecdysis.

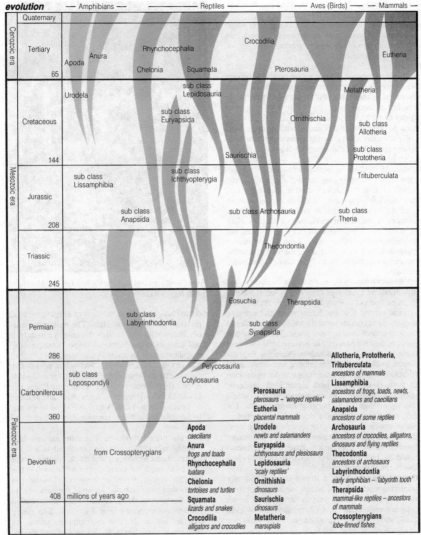

evolution — Amphibians — ————— Reptiles ————— — Aves (Birds) — — Mammals —

Allotheria, Prototheria, Trituberculata
ancestors of mammals

Lissamphibia
ancestors of frogs, toads, newts, salamanders and caecilians

Anapsida
ancestors of some reptiles

Pterosauria
pterosaurs – 'winged reptiles'

Eutheria
placental mammals

Archosauria
ancestors of crocodiles, alligators, dinosaurs and flying reptiles

Thecodontia
ancestors of archosaurs

Apoda
caecilians

Urodela
newts and salamanders

Labyrinthodontia
early amphibian – 'labyrinth tooth'

Anura
frogs and toads

Euryapsida
ichthyosaurs and plesiosaurs

Therapsida
mammal-like reptiles – ancestors of mammals

Rhynchocephalia
tuatara

Lepidosauria
'scaly reptiles'

Chelonia
tortoises and turtles

Ornithishia
dinosaurs

Crossopterygians
lobe-finned fishes

Squamata
lizards and snakes

Saurischia
dinosaurs

Crocodilia
alligators and crocodiles

Metatheria
marsupials

---

exosphere the uppermost layer of the ◊atmosphere. It is an ill-defined zone above the thermosphere, beginning at about 700 km and fading off into the vacuum of space.

expansion in physics, the increase in size of a constant mass of substance (a body) caused by, for example, increasing its temperature (thermal expansion) or its internal pressure. *Expansivity*, or coefficient of cubical (or thermal) expansion, is the expansion per unit volume per degree rise in temperature.

expectorant substance often added to cough mixture to help expel mucus from the airways. It is debatable whether it has an effect on lung secretions.

experiment in science, a practical test designed with the intention that its results will be relevant to a particular theory or set of theories. Although some experiments may be used merely for gathering more information about a topic which is already well understood, others may be of crucial importance in confirming a new theory or in undermining long-held beliefs.

experimental psychology the application of rigorous and objective scientific methods to the study of mental processes and behaviour.

expert system a computer program for giving advice which incorporates knowledge derived from human expertise. It is a kind of ◊knowledge-based system containing rules that can be applied to find the solution to a problem. It is a form of ◊artificial intelligence.

explanation in science, an attempt to make clear the cause of any natural event, by reference to physical laws and to observations.

Explorer one of a series of US scientific satellites. Explorer 1, launched Jan 1958, was the first US satellite in orbit and discovered the ◊Van Allen belts around the Earth.

explosive any material capable of a sudden release of energy and the rapid formation of a large volume of gas, leading when compressed to the development of a high-pressure wave (blast).

exponential in mathematics, a ◊function in which the variable quantity is an exponent, that is, an ◊index or power to which another number or expression is raised.

export goods or service produced in one country and sold to another. Exports may be visible (goods which are physically exported) or invisible (services provided in the exporting country but paid for in another country).

export credit loan, finance, or guarantee provided by a government or a financial institution enabling companies to export goods and services in situations where payment for them may be delayed or subject to risk.

exposure meter an instrument used in photography for indicating the correct exposure – the length of time the camera shutter should be open in given light conditions. Meters use substances such as cadmium sulphide and selenium as light sensors. These materials change electrically when light strikes them, the change being proportional to the intensity of the incident light. Many modern cameras have a built-in exposure meter that sets the camera controls automatically as the light conditions change.

Expressionism a style of painting, sculpture, and literature that expresses inner emotions; in particular, a movement in early 20th-century art in northern and central Europe. Expressionists tended to distort or exaggerate natural appearance in order to create a reflection of an inner world. The Norwegian painter Munch's *Skriket/The Scream* 1893 (National Gallery, Oslo) is a well-known example; Expressionist writers include Strindberg and Wedekind.

extinction in biology, the complete disappearance of a species. In the past extinctions generally occurred because species were unable to adapt quickly enough to a changing environment. Today, most extinctions are due to human activity. Some species, such as the ◊dodo of Mauritius, the ◊moas of New Zealand, and the passenger ◊pigeon of North America, have been exterminated by hunting. Others become extinct when their habitat is destroyed.

extracellular matrix a strong material naturally occurring in animals and plants, made up of protein and long-chain sugars (polysaccharides) in which cells are embedded. It is often called a 'biological glue', and forms an important part of ◊connective tissues such as bone and skin.

extradition the surrender, by one state to another, of a person accused of a criminal offence in the country to which they are extradited. It is usually governed by a treaty between the two states concerned. A state will not usually allow extradition for political offences or for an offence which it does not treat as a crime, even though it is a crime in the requesting state.

extraversion or *extroversion* a personality dimension described by ◊Jung and later by Eysenck. The typical extravert is sociable, impulsive, and carefree. The opposite of extraversion is introversion; the typical introvert is quiet, inward-looking, and reliable.

Extremadura autonomous region of W Spain including the provinces of Badajoz and Cáceres; area 41,602 sq km/16,063 sq mi; population (1981) 1,065,000. Irrigated land is used for growing wheat - the remainder is either oak forest or used for pig or sheep grazing.

Eyck Detail from Jan van Eyck's The Arnolfini Marriage (1434) National Gallery, London.

extrusion a common method of shaping metals, plastics, and other materials. The materials, usually hot, are forced through the hole in a metal die and take its cross-sectional shape. Rods, tubes, and sheets may be made in this way.

Eyck Jan van *c.* 1390-1441. Flemish painter of the early northern Renaissance, one of the first to work in oil. He served as court painter to Philip the Good, Duke of Burgundy, from 1425, and worked in Bruges from 1430. Van Eyck's paintings are technically brilliant and sumptuously rich in detail and colour.

eye the organ of vision. The *human eye* is a roughly spherical structure contained in a bony socket. Light enters it through the *cornea*, and passes through the circular opening (*pupil*) in the iris (the coloured part of the eye). The light is focused by the combined action of the curved cornea, the internal fluids, and the *lens* (the rounded transparent structure behind the iris). The ciliary muscles act on the lens to change its shape, so that images of objects at different distances can be focused on the *retina*. This is at the back of the eye, and is packed with light-sensitive cells (rods and cones), connected to the brain by the optic nerve.

In contrast, the *insect eye* is compound, that is, made up of many separate facets, each of which collects light and directs it separately to a receptor to build up an image. Lower invertebrates, such as worms and snails, have much simpler eyes, with no lens.

eyebright common wild flower of the genus *Euphrasia*, family Scrophulariaceae. It is 2–30 cm/1–12 in high, bearing whitish flowers streaked with purple.

Eyre, Lake Australia's largest lake, in central South Australia, which frequently runs dry, becoming a salt marsh in dry seasons; area up to 9,000 sq km/3,500 sq mi. It is the continent's lowest point, 12 m/39 ft below sea level.

Eyre Richard (Charles Hastings) 1943– . British stage and film director. He succeeded Peter Hall as artistic director of the National Theatre, London, in 1988. His films include *The Ploughman's Lunch* 1983 and *Laughterhouse* (US *Singleton's Pluck*) 1984.

Ezekiel born *c.* 622 BC. In the Old Testament, a Hebrew prophet. Carried into captivity in Babylon by ◊Nebuchadnezzar in 597, he preached that Jerusalem's fall was due to the sins of Israel. The book of Ezekiel is perhaps best known for the description of a vision of supernatural beings with which it begins.

Ezra in the Old Testament, a Jewish scribe who was allowed by Artaxerxes, king of Persia (probably Artaxerxes I, 464–423 BC), to lead his people back to Jerusalem from Babylon in 458 BC. He re-established the Mosaic law (laid down by Moses) and eradicated intermarriage.

eye

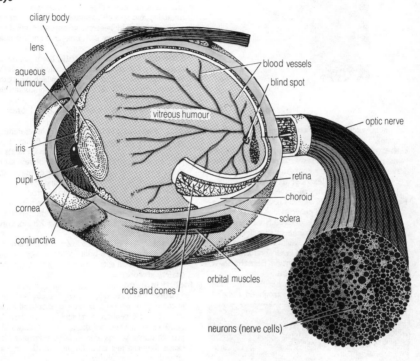

ciliary body
lens
aqueous humour
iris
pupil
cornea
conjunctiva
blood vessels
blind spot
vitreous humour
optic nerve
retina
choroid
sclera
rods and cones
orbital muscles
neurons (nerve cells)

°F abbreviation for ◊*Fahrenheit* (temperature scale).

Fabergé Peter Carl 1846–1920. Russian goldsmith and jeweller. Among his masterpieces was the series of jewelled Easter eggs, the first of which was commissioned by Alexander III for the Tsarina in 1884. Fabergé died in exile in Switzerland.

Fabian Society UK socialist organization for research, discussion and publication, founded in London in 1884. Its name is derived from the Roman commander Fabius Maximus, and refers to the evolutionary methods by which it hopes to attain socialism by a succession of gradual reforms. Early members included the playwright Bernard Shaw, and Beatrice and Sidney ◊Webb.

Fabius Laurent 1946– . French socialist politician, prime minister 1984–86. He introduced a liberal,

Fabergé A Fabergé egg.

freer-market economic programme, but his career was damaged by the 1985 ◊Greenpeace sabotage scandal.

Fabius Maximus name of an ancient Roman family of whom the best known is Quintus Fabius Maximus (died 203 BC), Roman general, known as Cunctator or 'Delayer' because of his tactics against ◊Hannibal 217–214 BC, when he continually harassed Hannibal's armies but never risked a set battle.

fable a story, either in verse or prose, in which animals or inanimate objects are endowed with the mentality and speech of human beings in order to point a moral. The best-known fables include those of Aesop (5th century BC), Phaedrus and Avianus, La Fontaine, Gay, and Lessing.

Fabricius Geronimo 1537–1619. Italian anatomist and embryologist. He made a detailed study of the veins, and discovered the valves which direct the bloodflow towards the heart. He also studied the development of chick ◊embryos.

facsimile transmission also called ◊*fax* or *telefax*.

factor a number which divides into another number exactly. For example, the factors of 64 are 1, 2, 4, 8, 16, 32, and 64. In algebra, certain kinds of polynomials (expressions consisting of several or many terms) can be factorized. For example, the factors of $x^2 + 3x + 2$ are $x + 1$ and $x + 2$.

factorial of a positive number, the product of all the whole numbers (integers) inclusive between 1 and the number itself. A factorial is indicated by the symbol !, $6! = 1 \times 2 \times 3 \times 4 \times 5 \times 6 = 720$. Factorial zero, 0!, is defined as 1.

factory act in Britain, an act of parliament governing conditions of work, hours of labour, safety, and sanitary provision in factories and workshops. See ◊safety at work.

factory farming the intensive rearing of poultry or animals for food, usually on high-protein foodstuffs in confined quarters. Chickens for eggs and meat, and calves for veal are commonly factory farmed. Some countries restrict the use of antibiotics and growth hormones as aids to factory farming, because they can persist in the flesh of the animals after they are slaughtered.

factory system the basis of manufacturing in the modern world. In the factory system workers are employed at a place where they carry out specific tasks, which together result in a product. This is called the division of labour. Usually these workers will perform their tasks with the aid of machinery. Such ◊mechanization is another feature of the modern factory system, which leads to ◊mass production. Richard ◊Arkwright pioneered the system in England in 1771, when he set up a cotton-spinning factory.

Fadden Arthur 'Artie' 1895–1973. Australian politician. He was leader of the Country Party 1941–58 and prime minister Aug–Oct 1941.

faeces remains of food and other debris passed out of the digestive tract of animals. Faeces consist of quantities of fibrous material, bacteria, and other microorganisms, rubbed-off lining of the digestive tract, bile fluids, undigested food, minerals, and water.

Faerie Queene, The a poem by Edmund Spenser, published 1590–96, dedicated to Elizabeth I. The poem, in six books, describes the adventures of six knights. Spenser used a new stanza form, later adopted by Keats, Shelley, and Byron.

Fahd 1921– . King of Saudi Arabia from 1982, when he succeeded his half-brother Khalid. As head of government he has been active in trying to bring about a solution to the Middle East conflicts.

Fahrenheit Gabriel Daniel 1686–1736. German physicist who devised the Fahrenheit temperature scale.

Fahrenheit scale a temperature scale invented by Gabriel Fahrenheit in 1714, no longer in scientific use. Intervals are measured in degrees (°F); °F = (°C × 9/5) + 32.

fainting a sudden, temporary loss of consciousness caused by reduced blood supply to the brain.

Fairbanks Douglas 1883–1939. US actor. He played swashbuckling heroes in silent films such as *The Three Musketeers* 1921, *The Thief of Baghdad* and *Don Quixote* 1925. He and Mary Pickford, whom he married in 1920, were idolized as 'the world's sweethearts'.

Fairbanks Douglas, Jnr 1909– . US actor, son of Douglas ◊Fairbanks. He achieved screen fame in *Catherine the Great* 1934 and *The Prisoner of Zenda* 1937.

Fairfax family Australian publishing dynasty founded by John Fairfax (1804-1877), a British-born printer and bookbinder, who went to Australia 1838 and became part-owner of the newspaper that became the *Sydney Morning Herald*. The family business, John Fairfax and Sons, one of the last remaining business dynasties founded in the 19th century, had interests in journalism, yachting and art and was noted for its philanthropy. In 1990, the John Fairfax Group went into receivership.

Fairfax Thomas, 3rd Baron Fairfax of Cameron 1612–1671. English general, commander in chief of the Parliamentary army in the English Civil War. With Cromwell he formed the ◊New Model Army, defeated Charles I at Naseby, and suppressed the Royalist and Presbyterian risings of 1648.

Faisal Ibn Abdul Aziz 1905–1975. King of Saudi Arabia from 1964. The younger brother of King Saud, on whose accession in 1953 he was declared crown prince. He was prime minister 1953–60 and from 1962 until his assassination.

fakir originally a Muslim mendicant of some religious order, but in India a general term for an ascetic.

Falange Española former Spanish Fascist Party, founded in 1933 by José Antonio de Rivera, son of the military ruler Miguel ◊Primo de Rivera. It was closely modelled in programme and organization on the Italian fascists and on the Nazis. In 1937, when ◊Franco assumed leadership, it was declared the only legal party, and altered its name to Traditionalist Spanish Phalanx.

Falasha a member of a small community of black Jews in Ethiopia. They suffered discrimination, but, after being accorded Jewish status by Israel in 1975, a gradual process of resettlement in Israel began, now only about 30,000 Falashas remain in Ethiopia.

falcon genus of birds of prey *Falco*, family Falconidae, order Falconiformes. Falcons are the smallest of the hawks (15-60 cm/6-24 in). They nest in high places, and kill their prey by swooping down at high speed. They include the peregrine and kestrel.

falconry the use of specially trained falcons and hawks to capture birds or small mammals.

Falkender Marcia, Baroness Falkender (Marcia Williams) 1932– . British political secretary to Labour prime minister Harold Wilson from 1956, she was influential in the 'kitchen cabinet' of the 1964-70 government, as described in her book *Inside No 10* 1972.

Fallopian tubes *The auricle (trumpet-shaped ending) of the Fallopian tube, which catches the eggs released from the ovary*

Falkland Islands British Crown Colony in the S Atlantic
area 12,173 sq km/4,700 sq mi, made up of two main islands: E Falkland 6,760 sq km/2,610 sq mi, and W Falkland 5,413 sq km/2,090 sq mi
capital Stanley; new port facilities were opened in 1984, and Mount Pleasant airport in 1985
exports wool, alginates (used as dyes and as a food additive) from seaweed beds.
population (1980) 1,813
history Argentina asserts its succession to the Spanish claim to the 'Islas Malvinas', but the inhabitants oppose cession. Occupied by Argentina Apr 1982, the islands were recaptured by British military forces in May–June of the same year. The cost of the British military presence was officially £257 million for 1987.

Falkland Islands, Battle of the British naval victory (under Admiral Sturdee) 8 Dec 1914 over the German Admiral von Spee.

Falla Manuel de 1876–1946. Spanish composer. His opera *La vida breve/Brief Life* 1905 (performed 1913) was followed by the ballets *El amor brujo/Love the Magician* 1915 and *El sombrero de tres picos/The Three-Cornered Hat* 1919, and his most ambitious concert work, *Noches en los jardines de España/Nights in the Gardens of Spain* 1916. He uses the folk-idiom of southern Spain.

Fallopian tubes in mammals, two tubes which carry eggs from the ovary to the uterus. An egg is fertilized by sperm in the Fallopian tubes, which are lined with cells whose ◊cilia move the egg towards the ovary.

fallout radioactive material released into the atmosphere in the debris of a nuclear explosion and descending to the surface. Such material can enter the food chain.

false-colour imagery a modern graphic technique that displays images electronically in false colours (not true to life) so as to enhance certain features. It is widely used in displaying electronic satellites like *Landsat*.

falsificationism in philosophy of science, the belief that a scientific theory must be under constant scrutiny, and that its merit lies only in how well it stands up to rigorous testing. First expounded by the philosopher Karl ◊Popper in his *Logic of Scientific Discovery* (1934), falsificationism in its crudest form suggests that a theory must be rejected or modified as soon as contradictory evidence emerges.

family in biological classification, a group of related genera (see ◊genus). Family names are not printed in italic (unlike genus and species names), and by convention they all have the ending -idae (animals) or -aceae (plants and fungi). For example, the genera of hummingbirds are grouped together in the hummingbird family, Trochilidae. Related families are grouped together in an ◊order.

family planning spacing or preventing the birth of children; see ◊contraceptive.

fan jet also known as *turbofan* or *turbojet*. The jet engine used by most airliners, so called because of its huge front fan. The fan sends air not only into the engine itself, but also around the engine. This results in a faster and more efficient propulsive jet. See ◊jet propulsion.

Fanon Frantz 1925–1961. French political writer. His experiences in Algeria during the war for liberation in the 1950s led to the writing of *Les Damnés de la terre/The Wretched of the Earth* 1964, which calls for violent revolution by the peasants of the Third World.

fantail type of domestic dove, often white, with a large widely fanning tail.

fantasy non-realistic fiction. Much of the world's fictional literature could be subsumed under this term, but as a commercial and literary genre fantasy started to thrive in the aftermath of the success of Tolkien's *Lord of the Rings* 1954–55 in the late 1960s. Earlier works by such writers as Lord Dunsany, Hope Mirrlees and E R Eddison, not classifiable in fantasy subgenres such as ◊science fiction, ◊horror or the ghost story, could be classified as fantasy.

Fantin-Latour (Ignace) Henri (Joseph Théodore) 1836–1904. French painter, excelling in delicate still lifes, flower paintings and portraits.

FAO abbreviation for ◊*Food and Agriculture Organization*.

farad ◊SI unit of electrical capacitance (symbol F). It is defined as the capacitance of a capacitor that, if charged with 1 coulomb, has a potential difference of 1 volt between its plates. It is named after Michael Faraday.

Faraday Michael 1791–1867. English chemist and physicist. In 1821 he began experimenting with electromagnetism, and ten years later discovered the induction of electric currents and made the first dynamo. He subsequently found that a magnetic field will rotate the plane of polarization of light. Faraday also investigated electrolysis.

Faraday's laws three laws of electromagnetic induction, and two laws of electrolysis, all proposed originally by Michael Faraday.

induction (1) a changing magnetic field induces an electromagnetic force in a conductor; (2) the electromagnetic force is proportional to the rate of change of the field; (3) the direction of the induced electromagnetic force depends on the orientation of the field.

electrolysis (1) the amount of chemical change during electrolysis is proportional to the charge passing through the liquid; (2) the amount of chemical change produced in a substance by a given amount of electricity is proportional to the electrochemical equivalent of that substance.

farandole an old French dance in six-eight time originating in Provence. The dancers join hands in a chain and follow the leader to the accompaniment of tambourine and pipe. There is a farandole in Act II of Tchaikovsky's *The Sleeping Beauty*.

farce a broad form of comedy involving stereotyped characters in complex, often improbable situations frequently revolving around extra-marital relationships, hence the term 'bedroom farce'.

Far East geographical term for all Asia east of the Indian subcontinent.

Farman Henry 1874–1958. Anglo-French air pioneer. After experiments in 1907, he designed and flew his classic biplane in 1909.

Farnaby Giles 1563–1640. English composer. He composed pieces for the virginal (an early keyboard instrument), psalms for Ravenscroft's Psalter 1621, and madrigals for voices.

Farnese an Italian family who held the duchy of Parma 1545–1731.

Faroe Islands, Faroes or *Faeroe Islands, Faeroes* island group (18 out of 22 inhabited) in the N Atlantic, forming an outlying part of ◊Denmark.

area 1,399 sq km/540 sq mi; largest islands are Stromo, Ostera, Vaego, Sudero and Sando.

capital Thorshavn on Stromo, population (1984) 15,000

exports fish, crafted goods

population (1986) 45,728

government since 1948 the islands have had full self-government

history first settled by Norsemen in the 9th century, they were a Norwegian province 1380–1709.

Farouk 1920–1965. King of Egypt 1936–52. He succeeded his father Fuad I. In 1952 he was compelled to abdicate, his son Fuad II being temporarily proclaimed in his stead.

Farquhar George 1677–1707. Irish dramatist. His most famous plays, *The Recruiting Officer* 1706, and *The Beaux' Stratagem* 1707, are in the tradition of the Restoration comedy of manners, although less robust.

Farrell James T(homas) 1904–1979. US novelist. His naturalistic *Studs Lonigan* trilogy 1932–35, comprising *Young Lonigan*, *The Young Manhood of Studs Lonigan*, and *Judgement Day*, describes the growing up of a young Catholic man in Chicago after World War I.

Faraday *English chemist and physicist Michael Faraday.*

fat

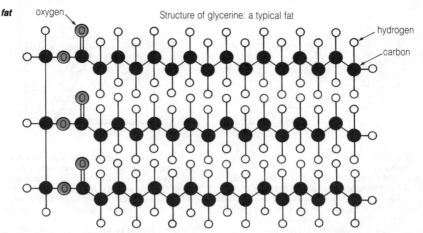

Structure of glycerine: a typical fat

oxygen

hydrogen

carbon

farthing formerly the smallest English coin, a quarter of a penny. It was introduced as a silver coin in Edward I's reign. The copper farthing became general in Charles II's time, and the bronze in 1860. It was dropped from use in 1961.

fasces in ancient Rome, bundles of rods carried in procession by the lictors in front of the chief magistrates, as a symbol of the latter's power over the lives and liberties of the people. An axe was included in the bundle. The fasces were revived as the symbol of ◊fascism.

fascism an ideology which denied all rights to individuals in their relations with the state, specifically, the totalitarian nationalist movement founded in Italy 1919 by ◊Mussolini. Fascism protected the existing social order by forcible suppression of the working-class movement and by providing scapegoats for popular anger in the Jew, the foreigner, or the black person; it also provided the machinery

Fassbinder *German film director Rainer Werner Fassbinder.*

for the economic and psychological mobilization for war. The atrocities committed by Nazi Germany and other fascist countries discredited fascism but neofascist groups still exist in many Western European countries.

Fashoda Incident dispute in 1898 in a town in the Sudan, now known as Kodok, then called Fashoda, in which French forces under Colonel Marchand clashed with British, under Lord Kitchener. Although originally a disagreement over local territorial claims, it almost led the two countries into war.

Fassbinder Rainer Werner 1946–1982. West German film director, who began his career as a fringe actor and founded his own 'anti-theatre' before moving into films. His works are mainly stylized indictments of contemporary German society. He made over 30 films, including *Die bitteren Tränen der Petra von Kant/The Bitter Tears of Petra von Kant* 1972 and *Die Ehe von Maria Braun/The Marriage of Maria Braun* 1979.

fast reactor a ◊nuclear reactor that makes use of fast neutrons to bring about fission. Unlike other reactors it has no little or no ◊moderator, to slow down neutrons. The reactor core is surrounded by a 'blanket' of uranium carbide. During operation, some of this uranium is converted into plutonium that can be extracted and later used as fuel; hence the alternative name *fast breeder reactor*.

fat in the broadest sense, an organic compound that is soluble in alcohol, but not in water; when used in this way, 'fat' is synonymous with lipid. The term is also used more specifically to denote triglycerides, and other esters of glycerol with fatty acids.

Fates in Greek and Roman mythology, the three famale figures, Antropos, Clotho, and Lachesis, envisaged as elderly spinners, who decided the length of human life, and analogous to the Roman Parcae and Norse ◊Norns.

Father of the Church any of certain teachers and writers of the early Christian church, particularly eminent for their learning and orthodoxy, experience, and sanctity of life, who lived during the period from the end of the 1st to the end of the 7th century, a period divided by the Council of Nicaea (325) into the Ante-Nicene and Post-Nicene Fathers.

fathom (Anglo-Saxon *faethm* 'to embrace') in mining, seafaring, and handling timber, unit of depth measurement (6 ft/1.829 m) used before metrication; it approximates to the distance between the

fault

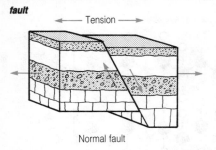

Normal fault

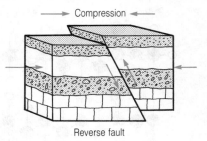

Reverse fault

hands when the arms are outstretched, hence its derivation.

Fatimid dynasty of Muslim Shi'ite caliphs founded in 909 by Obaidallah, who claimed to be a descendant of Fatima, the prophet Muhammad's daughter, and her husband Ali, in N Africa. In 969 the Fatimids conquered Egypt, and the dynasty continued until overthrown by Saladin in 1171.

fatty acid an organic compound consisting of a hydrocarbon chain, up to 24 carbon atoms long, with a carboxyl group (-CO_2H) at one end.

Faulkner Brian 1921–1977. Northern Ireland Unionist politician. He was the last prime minister of Northern Ireland 1971–72 before the Stormont Parliament was suspended.

Faulkner William 1897–1962. US novelist. His works include *The Sound and the Fury* 1929, dealing with a Southern US family in decline, As I Lay Dying 1930, *Light in August* 1932, a study of segregation, *The Unvanquished* 1938, stories of the Civil War, and *The Hamlet* 1940, *The Town* 1957, and *The Mansion* 1959, a trilogy covering the rise of the materialist Snopes family. He wrote in an experimental stream-of-consciousness style. Nobel Prize for literature 1949.

fault in geology, a crack in a rock along which the two sides have moved as a result of differing strains in the adjacent rock bodies. Displacement of rock masses horizontally or vertically along a fault may be microscopic, or it may be massive, causing major ◊earthquakes.

Faunus in Roman mythology, god of fertility and prophecy, with goat's ears, horns, tail and hind legs, identified with the Greek Pan.

Faust legendary magician. The historical Georg Faust appears to have been a wandering scholar and conjuror in Germany during the opening decade of the 16th century, but earlier figures such as Simon Magus (1st century AD, Middle Eastern practitioner of magic arts) contributed to the Faust legend.

Fauvism style of painting with a bold use of vivid colours, a short-lived but influential art movement originating in Paris 1903 with the founding of the Salon d'Automne by ◊Matisse and others.

Fawcett Millicent Garrett 1847–1929. English suffragette, younger sister of Elizabeth Garrett ◊Anderson. A non-militant, she rejected the violent acts of some of her contemporaries in the suffrage movement. She joined the first Women's Suffrage Committee 1867 and became president of the Women's Unionist Association 1889.

Fawkes Guy 1570–1606. English conspirator, born in York. He converted to Roman Catholicism as a youth, and joined in the Gunpowder Plot to blow up King James I and the members of both Houses of Parliament. He was arrested in the cellar underneath the House on 4 Nov 1605, tortured, and executed. The event is still commemorated in Britain with bonfires and fireworks on 5 Nov.

fax an alternative name for facsimile transmission or telefax; the transmission of images over a ◊telecommunications link, usually the telephone network. When placed on a fax machine, the original image is scanned by a transmitting device and converted into coded signals, which travel via the telephone lines to the receiving fax machine, where an image is created that is a copy of the original.

CONCILIVM SEPTEM NOBILIVM ANGLORVM CONIVRANTIVM IN NECEM IACOBI ·I·
MAGNÆ BRITANNIÆ REGIS TOTIVSQ· ANGLICI CONVOCATI PARLEMENTI·

Fawkes Britain's most famous subversive, Guy Fawkes, joined the Gunpowder Plot to blow up James I and both Houses of Parliament in 1605.

fax

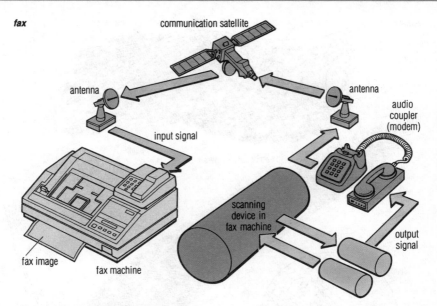

communication satellite

antenna

antenna

audio coupler (modem)

input signal

scanning device in fax machine

output signal

fax image

fax machine

Photographs as well as printed text and drawings can be sent.

FBI abbreviation of ◊*Federal Bureau of Investigation*, agency of the Department of Justice in the USA.

feather a rigid outgrowth of the outer layer of the skin of birds, made of the protein keratin. Feathers provide insulation, facilitate flight and are often important in camouflage, courtship and other displays. Feathers are replaced at least once a year.

feather star type of ◊echinoderm belonging to the class Crinoidea. The arms are branched into numerous projections (hence 'feather' star), and grow from a small cup-shaped body.

February Revolution the first stage of the ◊Russian Revolution 1917.

fecundity the rate at which an organism reproduces, as distinct from its ability to reproduce (◊fertility). In vertebrates, it is usually measured as the number of offspring produced by a female each year.

Federal Bureau of Investigation (FBI) agency of the Department of Justice in the USA which investigates violations of federal law not specifically assigned to other agencies, being particularly concerned with internal security.

Federal Deposit Insurance Corporation (FDIC) US government authority established in 1933 to regulate US banks and insure them against loss.

federalism a system of government where two or more separate states unite under a common central government while retaining a considerable degree of local autonomy. Switzerland, the USSR, the USA, Canada, Australia, and Malaysia are all examples of federal government, and many supporters of the European Community see it as the forerunner of a federal Europe.

Federalists, The in American history, those who advocated the ratification of the US constitution 1787–1788 in place of the Articles of ◊Confederation. The Federalists became in effect the ruling political party during the presidencies of George Washington and John Adams, 1789–1801,

legislating to strengthen the authority of the newly created federal government.

Federal Reserve System ('Fed') US central banking system and note issue authority, established in 1913 to regulate the country's credit and monetary affairs. The Fed consists of the 12 federal reserve banks and their 25 branches and other facilities throughout the countr.

feedback a principle used in self-regulating control systems. Information about what *is* happening in a system (such as level of temperature, engine speed or size of workpiece) is fed back to a controlling device, which compares it with what *should* be happening. If the two are different, the device takes suitable action (such as switching on a heater, allowing more steam to the engine, or resetting the tools).

feedback in biology, another term for ◊biofeedback.

Feininger Lyonel 1871–1956. US abstract artist, an early Cubist. He worked at the Bauhaus, Germany (a key centre of modern design), 1919–33, and later helped to found the Bauhaus in Chicago.

feldspar or *felspar* a type of rock-forming mineral, the chief constituent of ◊igneous rock. Feldspars contain aluminium silicate with varying proportions of silicates of sodium, potassium, calcium, and barium. It rates 6 on the ◊Mohs scale of hardness and is used in ceramics.

Fellini Federico 1920– . Italian film director, noted for his strongly subjective poetic imagery. His films include *I vitelloni/The Young and the Passionate* 1953, *La dolce vita/The Sweet Life* 1960, and *La città delle donne/City of Women* 1981.

felony in UK law, former term for an offence which is more serious than a ◊misdemeanour; in the USA, a felony is a crime punishable by imprisonment for a year or more. See also ◊criminal law.

felt matted fabric of wool, made by working fibres together under pressure, heat or by chemical action.

feminism a belief in equal rights and opportunities for women; see ◊women's movement.

fencing sport using the *foil*, derived from the light weapon used in practice duels; *épée*, a heavier

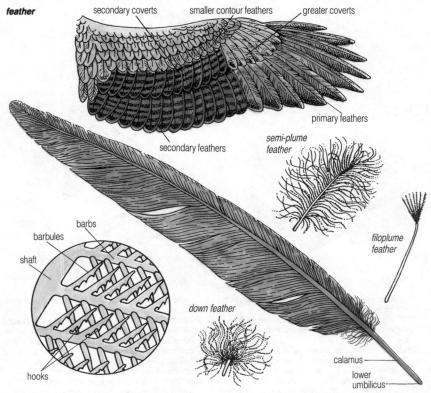

feather

secondary coverts · smaller contour feathers · greater coverts

primary feathers

secondary feathers

semi-plume feather

barbs

barbules

shaft

filoplume feather

hooks

down feather

calamus

lower umbilicus

weapon derived from the duelling sword proper; and *sabre*, in which cuts (it has two cutting edges) count as well as thrusts. Masks and protective jackets are worn, and hits are registered electronically in competitions.

Fender pioneering series of electric guitars and bass guitars. The first solid-body electric guitar on the market was the 1948 Fender Broadcaster (renamed the Telecaster 1950), and the first electric bass guitar was the Fender Precision 1951. The Fender Stratocaster guitar dates from 1954. Their designer, Leo Fender, began manufacturing amplifiers in the USA in the 1940s.

Fenian a member of an Irish-American republican secret society, founded in 1858 and named after the ancient Irish legendary warrior band of the Fianna. The collapse of the movement began when an attempt to establish an independent Irish republic by an uprising in Ireland 1867 failed, as did raids into Canada 1866 and 1870, and England 1867.

fennec small nocturnal desert ◊fox *Fennecus zerda* found in N Africa and Arabia. It has a head and body only 40 cm/1.3 ft long, and enormous ears which act as radiators to lose excess heat. It eats insects and small animals.

fennel perennial plant with feathery green leaves, family Umbelliferae. Fennels have an aniseed flavour. The thickened leafstalks of *sweet fennel Foeniculum dulce* are eaten, and the leaves and seeds of *Foeniculum vulgare* are used in seasoning.

Fens level, low-lying tracts of land in E England, west and south of the Wash, about 115 km/70 mi N–S and about 55 mi/34 mi E–W. They fall within the counties of Lincolnshire, Cambridgeshire, and

Norfolk, consisting of a huge area, formerly a bay of the North Sea, but now crossed by numerous drainage canals and forming some of the most productive agricultural land in Britain.

Fenton Roger 1819–1869. British photographer. The world's first war photographer, he went to the Crimea in 1855; he also founded the Royal Photographic Society in London.

Ferdinand 1861–1948. King of Bulgaria 1908–18. Son of Prince Augustus of Saxe-Coburg- Gotha, he was elected prince of Bulgaria 1887, and in 1908 proclaimed Bulgaria's independence of Turkey and assumed the title of tsar. In 1915 he entered World War I as Germany's ally, and in 1918 abdicated and retired to Coburg.

Ferdinand five kings of Castile, including:

Ferdinand I *the Great c.* 1016–1065. King of Castile from 1035. He began the reconquest of Spain from the Moors and united all NW Spain under his and his brothers' rule.

Ferdinand V 1452–1516. King of Castile from 1474, *Ferdinand II* of Aragon from 1479, and *Ferdinand III* of Naples from 1504; first king of all Spain. In 1469 he married his cousin ◊Isabella I, who succeeded to the throne of Castile 1474. They introduced the ◊Inquisition 1480, expelled the Jews, forced the surrender of the Moors at Granada 1492, and financed Columbus' expedition to the Americas.

Ferdinand three Holy Roman emperors, including:

Ferdinand II 1578–1637. King of Bohemia from 1617 and Hungary from 1618, Holy Roman emperor from 1619, when he succeeded his uncle Matthias. He was a zealous Catholic who provoked the Bohemian revolt that led to the Thirty Years' War.

fern

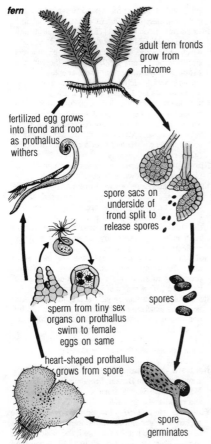

adult fern fronds grow from rhizome

fertilized egg grows into frond and root as prothallus withers

spore sacs on underside of frond split to release spores

spores

sperm from tiny sex organs on prothallus swim to female eggs on same

heart-shaped prothallus grows from spore

spore germinates

Ferdinand III 1608–1657. Holy Roman emperor from 1637 when he succeeded his father Ferdinand II; king of Hungary from 1625. Although anxious to conclude the Thirty Years' War, he did not give religious liberty to Protestants.

Ferdinand 1865–1927. King of Romania from 1914, when he succeeded his uncle Charles I. In 1916 he declared war on Austria. After the Allied victory in World War I, Ferdinand acquired Transylvania and Bukovina from Austria-Hungary, and Bessarabia from Russia. In 1922 he became king of Greater Romania.

Ferguson Harry 1884–1960. Irish engineer, who pioneered the development of the tractor, joining forces with Henry Ford in 1938 to manufacture it in the USA.

Fermanagh county in the southern part of Northern Ireland
area 1,676 sq km/647 sq mi
towns Enniskillen (county town), Lisnaskea, Irvinestown
physical in the centre is a broad trough of low-lying land, in which lie Upper and Lower Lough Erne
products mainly agricultural; livestock, tweeds, clothing
population (1981) 51,600.

Fermat Pierre de 1601–1665. French mathematician, who with Pascal founded the theory of ◊probability and the modern theory of numbers, and made contributions to analytical geometry.

fermentation the breakdown of sugars by bacteria and yeasts using a method of respiration without oxygen (◊anaerobic). These processes have long been utilized in baking bread, making beer and wine, and producing cheese, yoghurt, soy sauce, and many other foodstuffs.

Fermi Enrico 1901–1954. Italian physicist, who proved the existence of new radioactive elements produced by bombardment with neutrons, and discovered nuclear reactions produced by slow neutrons. He received the Nobel Prize for Physics in 1938.

fermium a metallic element, symbol Fm, atomic number 100. One of the actinide series, named after Fermi it has been produced only in minute quantities.

fern plant of the class Filicales, related to horsetails and clubmosses. Ferns are spore-bearing, not flowering, plants, and most are perennial herbs spreading by low-growing roots. The leaves, known as fronds, vary widely in size and shape. There are over 7,000 species.

Fernández Juan *c.* 1536–*c.* 1604. Spanish explorer and navigator. As a pilot on the Pacific coast of South America in 1563, he discovered the islands off the coast of Chile that now bear his name.

Fernel Jean François 1497–1558. French physician who introduced the words ◊physiology and ◊pathology into medicine.

Ferraro Geraldine 1935– . US Democrat politician, vice-presidential candidate in the 1984 election.

ferret domesticated variety of ◊polecat. About 35 cm/1.2 ft long, it usually has yellowish-white fur and pink eyes, and is used to hunt rabbits and rats.

ferro-alloy an alloy of iron with a high proportion of elements such as manganese, silicon, chromium and molybdenum. Ferro-alloys are used in the manufacture of alloy steels.

fertility an organism's ability to reproduce, as distinct from the rate at which it reproduces (see ◊fecundity). Individuals become infertile (unable to reproduce) when they cannot generate gametes (eggs or sperm) or when their gametes cannot yield a viable ◊embryo after ◊fertilization.

fertility drug any of a range of drugs taken to increase a female's fertility, developed in Sweden in the mid-1950s. Multiple births can result.

fertilization in ◊sexual reproduction, the union of two ◊gametes (sex cells, often called egg and sperm) to produce a ◊zygote, which combines the genetic material contributed by each parent. In self-fertilization the male and female gametes come from the same plant; in cross-fertilization they come from different plants. Self-fertilization occurs rarely in ◊hermaphrodite animals.

fertilizer a substance containing a range of the 20 or so chemical elements necessary for healthy plant growth, used to compensate the deficiencies of poor soil or of soil depleted by repeated cropping. Fertilizers may be *organic*, for example farmyard manure, composts, bonemeal, blood, and fishmeal; or *inorganic*, in the form of compounds, mainly of nitrogen, phosphate, and potash, which have come into use on a tremendously increased scale since 1945.

Fès former capital of Morocco 808–1062, 1296–1548, and 1662–1912, in a valley north of the Great Atlas mountains, 160 km/100 mi E of Rabat; population (1982) 448,823. Textiles, carpets, and leather are manufactured, and the fez, a brimless hat worn in S and E Mediterranean countries, is traditionally said to have originated here.

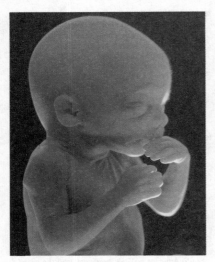

fetus *Human fetus about five months old.*

fescue widely distributed grass genus *Festuca*. Two common species in W Europe are meadow fescue up to 80 cm/2.6 ft high, and sheep's fescue up to 50 cm/1.6 ft high.

Fessenden Reginald Aubrey 1866–1932. American physicist, born in Canada, who patented the ◊modulation of radio waves (transmission of a signal using a carrier wave), an essential technique for voice transmission. In 1900, he devised a method of making audio-frequency speech (or music) signals modulate the amplitude of a transmitted radio-frequency carrier wave – the basis of AM radio broadcasting.

fetal surgery operation on the fetus to correct congenital conditions such as ◊hydrocephalus. Fetal surgery was pioneered in the USA in 1981. It leaves no scar tissue.

fetishism in anthropology, belief in the supernormal power of some inanimate object, which is known as a fetish. Fetishism in some form is common to most civilizations, and often has religio-magical significance. In psychology, the practice of associating an object with the sexual act, and transferring desire to the object (such as clothing) rather than the person.

fetus or *foetus* a stage in mammalian ◊embryo development. The human embryo is usually termed a fetus after the eighth week of development, when the limbs and external features of the head are recognizable.

feudalism the main form of social stratification in medieval Europe. A system based primarily on land, it involved a hierarchy of authority, rights, and power that extended from the monarch downwards. An intricate network of duties and obligations linked royalty, nobility, lesser gentry, free tenants, villeins, and serfs.

fever raised body temperature, usually due to infection.

Feyerabend Paul K 1924– . US philosopher of science, who rejected the attempt by certain philosophers (for instance ◊Popper) to find a methodology applicable to all scientific research.

Fianna Fáil Irish Republican Party, founded by the Irish nationalist de Valera in 1926. It has been the governing party in the Republic of Ireland 1932–48, 1951–54, 1957–73, 1977–81, 1982, and from 1987. It aims at the establishment of a united and completely independent all-Ireland republic.

Fibonacci Leonardo *c.* 1175–*c.* 1250. Italian mathematician. He published *Liber abaci* in Pisa 1202, which led to the introduction of Arabic notation into Europe. From 1960, interest increased in **Fibonacci numbers**, in their simplest form a series in which each number is the sum of its two predecessors (1, 1, 2, 3, 5, 8, 13,...).

fibreglass glass that has been formed into fine fibres. It can be produced as long continuous filaments or as a fluffy, short-fibred glass wool. Fibreglass has applications in the field of ◊fibre optics, and as a strengthener for plastics in ◊GRP (glass-reinforced plastics).

fibre optics transmission of light through glass or plastic fibres, known as ◊optical fibres.

fiction in literature, any work or type of work whose content is completely or largely invented. In the 20th century the term is applied to imaginative works of narrative prose (such as the novel or the short story), and contrasted with *non-fiction* such as history, biography, or works on practical subjects, and with *poetry*.

fief an estate held by a ◊vassal from his lord, given after the former had sworn homage, or fealty, promising to serve the lord. As a noble tenure, it carried with it rights of jurisdiction.

field in physics, an agency acting in a region of space, by which an object exerts a force on another non-touching object because of certain properties they both possess. For example, there is a force of attraction between any two objects that have mass, one of which is in the gravitational field of the other.

fieldfare bird *Turdus pilaris* of the thrush family, a winter migrant in Britain, breeding in Scandinavia, N Russia, and Siberia. It has a pale-grey lower back and neck, and a dark tail.

Fielding Henry 1707–1754. English novelist, whose narrative power influenced the form and technique of the novel and helped to make it the most popular form of literature in England. In 1742 he parodied Richardson's novel *Pamela* in his *Joseph Andrews*, which was followed by *Jonathan Wild the Great* 1743; his masterpiece *Tom Jones* 1749, which he described as a 'comic epic in prose'; and *Amelia* 1751.

field marshal the highest rank in certain armies. It was introduced to Britain from Germany by George II in 1736.

Field of the Cloth of Gold site between Guînes and Ardres near Calais, France, where a meeting took place between Henry VIII of England and Francis I of France in Jun 1520, remarkable for the lavish clothes worn and tent pavilions erected. Francis hoped to gain England's support in opposing the Holy Roman emperor, Charles V, but failed.

Fields Gracie. Stage-name of Grace Stansfield 1898–1979. British comedian and singer. Her humourously sentimental films include *Sally in our Alley* 1931 and *Sing as We Go* 1934. She was made a Dame of the British Empire 1979.

field studies study of ecology, geography, geology, history, archaeology, and allied subjects, in the natural environment, with emphasis on promoting a wider knowledge and understanding of the natural environment among the public.

fife a kind of small flute. Originally from Switzerland, it was known as the Swiss pipe and has long been used by British Army bands.

Fife region of E Scotland (formerly the county of Fife), facing the North Sea and Firth of Forth

Field of the Cloth of Gold *The Meeting of Henry VIII and the Emperor Maximilian I by an unknown artist. Royal Collection, Hampton Court.*

area 1,305 sq km/504 sq mi
towns administrative headquarters Glenrothes; Dunfermline, St Andrews, Kirkcaldy, Cupar
physical the only high land is the Lomond Hills, in the NW chief rivers Eden and Leven
products potatoes, cereals, electronics, petrochemicals (Mossmorran), light engineering
population (1981) 326,500.

Fifteen the ◊Jacobite rebellion of 1715, led by the 'Old Pretender' ◊James Edward Stuart and the Earl of Mar, in order to place the former on the English throne. Mar was checked at Sheriffmuir, Scotland, and the revolt collapsed.

fifth column a group within a country secretly aiding an enemy attacking from without. The term originated in 1936, during the Spanish Civil War, when Gen Mola boasted that Franco supporters were attacking Madrid with four columns, and that they had a 'fifth column' inside the city.

fifth-generation computer an anticipated new type of computer based on emerging microelectronic technologies. The basis will be very fast computing machinery, with many processors working in parallel made possible by very large-scale integration (◊VLSI) which can put many more circuits onto a ◊silicon chip. Such computers will run advanced 'intelligent' programs.

fig fruit of the W Asian tree *Ficus carica*, family Moraceae. Produced in two or three crops a year, and eaten fresh or dried, it has a high sugar content and laxative properties. It grows extensively in S Europe.

fighting fish small (6 cm/2 in long) fish *Betta splendens* and related species found in SE Asia. It can breathe air using an accessory breathing

Fiji

Papua New Guinea
Indonesia
FIJI
Suva
INDIAN OCEAN
AUSTRALIA
PACIFIC OCEAN
Tonga
New Zealand
0   500 miles
0   1000 km

area 18,272 sq km/7,055 sq mi
capital Suva on Viti Levu
physical comprises 844 Melanesian and Polynesian islands (about 110 inhabited), the largest being Viti Levu (10,386 sq km/400 sq mi) and Vanua Levu (5,535 sq km/2,137 sq mi)
head of state Ratu Sir Penaia Ganilau from 1987
head of government Col Sitiveni Rabuka from 1992

political system democratic republic
exports sugar, coconut oil, ginger, timber, canned fish; tourism is important
currency Fiji dollar
population (1989 est) 758,000 (46% Fijian, holding 80% of the land communally, and 49% Indians introduced in the 19th century to work the sugar crop); annual growth rate 2.1%
life expectancy men 67, women 71
language English (official); Fijian, Hindi
religion Hindu 50%, Methodist 44%
literacy 88% male/77% female (1980 est)
GDP $1.2 bn (1987); $1,604 per head
chronology
1970 Full independence achieved.
1987 General election in Apr brought to power an Indian-dominated coalition led by Dr Timoci Bavadra. Military coup in May by Col Sitiveni Rabuka removed new government at gunpoint. Governor General Ratu Sir Penaia Ganilau regained control within weeks. A second military coup by Rabuka in Sept proclaimed Fiji a republic and suspended the constitution. It was feared that ethnic rivalry would escalate and people of Indian extraction would be forced to emigrate. In Oct Fiji ceased to be a member of the Commonwealth. In Dec civilian government was restored.
1990 New constitution, favouring indigenous Fijians, introduced.
1992 General election produced coalition government; Col Rabuka named as president.

Finland
Republic of
(Suomen Tasavalta)

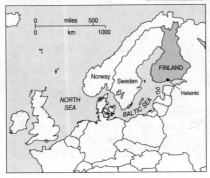

area 337,050 sq km/130,125 sq mi
capital Helsinki
towns Tampere, and the port of Turku
physical archipelago in S; most of the country is forest, with some 60,000 lakes; one third is within the Arctic Circle; mountains in the N

head of state Mauno Koivisto from 1982
head of government Esko Aho from 1991
political system democratic republic
exports metal, chemical and engineering products (icebreakers and oil rigs); paper, timber, and textiles; fine ceramics, glass, and furniture
currency Markka
population (1989 est) 4,990,000; annual growth rate 0.5%
life expectancy men 70, women 78
language Finnish, Swedish (official); Lapp
religion Lutheran 97%, Eastern Orthodox 1.2%
literacy 99%
GDP $77.9 bn (1987); $15,795 per head
chronology
1917 Independence declared.
1939 Defeated by USSR in Winter War.
1941 Joined Hitler in invasion of USSR.
1944 Concluded separate armistice with Allies.
1948 Finno-Soviet Pact of Friendship, Co-operation, and Mutual Assistance signed.
1973 Trade treaty with EEC signed.
1977 Trade agreement with USSR signed.
1982 Koivisto elected president; re-elected 1988.
1989 Finland joined Council of Europe.
1991 Swing to the centre in general election. New coalition government formed.
1992 Formal application for EC membership.

organ above the gill and can live in poorly oxygenated water. The male has large fins, and various colours, including shining greens, reds, and blues. The female is yellowish brown with short fins.

figurative language usage that departs from everyday factual, plain or literal language, and is commonly considered poetic, imaginative or ornamental. The transitional forms of figurative language, especially in literature, are the various figures of speech.

figure of speech a poetic, imaginative, or ornamental expression used for purposes of comparison, emphasis, or stylistic effect; usually one of a list of such forms dating from discussions of literary and rhetorical style in Greece in the 5th century BC. These figures include euphemism, hyperbole, metaphor, metonymy, onomatopoeia, oxymoron, personification, the pun, simile and synecdoche.

figwort plant of the genus *Scrophularia*. A perennial herb, it has square stems, opposite leaves, and open two-lipped flowers in a cluster at the top of the stem.

Fiji group of 332 islands in the SW Pacific, about 100 of which are inhabited.

file in computing, a collection of data or a program stored in a computer's external memory, for example on disk. *Serial files* hold information as a sequence of characters, so that, to read any particular item of data, the sequence before it must be read. *Random access files* allow the required record to be reached directly.

file transfer in computing, the transmission of a file (data stored for example on disk) from one machine to another. Both machines must be part of a computer ◊network, and both must be running appropriate communications software, so that the sending and receiving of the data can be coordinated.

Fillmore Millard 1800–1874. 13th president of the USA 1850–53, born into a poor farming family in New York state. A Whig, he supported a compromise on slavery 1850 to reconcile North and South, and failed to be renominated.

film, art of see ◊cinema.

film noir (French 'black film') a term originally used by French critics to describe any film characterized by pessimism, cynicism, and a dark, sombre tone. It has been used to describe Hollywood films of the 1940s and early 1950s portraying the seedy side of the criminal underworld.

film, photographic a strip of transparent material (usually cellulose acetate) coated with a light-sensitive emulsion, used in cameras to take pictures. The emulsion contains a mixture of light-sensitive silver halide salts (for example bromide or iodide) in gelatin. Films differ in their sensitivity to light, this being indicated by their speed. When the emulsion is exposed to light, the silver salts are invisibly altered, giving a latent image, which is then made visible by the process of ◊developing. Colour film consists of several layers of emulsion, each of which records a different colour in the light falling on it.

final solution (*Endlosung der Judenfrage*) euphemism used by the Nazis to describe the extermination of Jews and other opponents of the regime during World War II. See ◊holocaust.

Financial Times (FT) Index an indicator measuring the daily movement of 30 major industrial share prices on the London Stock Exchange (1935 = 100), issued by the London *Financial Times* newspaper.

finch bird of the family Fringillidae, in the order Passeriformes. They are seed-eaters with stout conical beaks, and include chaffinches, sparrows, and canaries.

Fine Gael Irish political party founded 1933 by W J ◊Cosgrave and led by Alan Dukes from 1987.

fingerprint the ridge pattern of the skin on a person's fingertips; this is constant through life and no two are exactly alike. Fingerprinting was first used as a means of identifying suspects in India, and was adopted by the English police in 1901; it is now widely employed in police and security work.

Finland country in Scandinavia, bounded N by Norway, E by Russia, S and W by the Baltic Sea, and NW by Sweden.

Finland, Gulf of eastern arm of the ◊Baltic Sea, separating Finland from Estonia.

finlandization political term coined by the Austrian politician Karl Gruber in 1953 to signify the limits set on the autonomy of a small state by a much more powerful neighbour, as on Finland by the former USSR.

Finney Albert 1936– . English stage and film actor. He created the title roles in Keith Waterhouse's *Billy Liar* 1960, and ◊Osborne's *Luther* 1961. His films include *Saturday Night and Sunday Morning* 1960, *Murder on the Orient Express* 1974, and *The Dresser* 1984.

Finney Thomas 'Tom' 1922– . British footballer, known as the 'Preston Plumber'. He played for England 76 times, and in every forward position. He was noted for his ball control and goal-scoring skill.

Finnish language a member of the Finno-Ugric language family, the national language of Finland and closely related to neighbouring Estonian, Livonian, Karelian, and Ingrian languages. At the beginning of the 19th century Finnish had no official status, Swedish being the language of education, government, and literature in Finland.

Finno-Ugric a group or family of more than 20 languages spoken by some 22 million people in scattered communities from Norway in the W to Siberia in the E and to the Carpathian mountains in the S. Speakers of these languages tend to live in enclaves surrounded by Germanic, Slavonic, or Turkish speakers, all of whom exercise influence upon the local Finno-Ugric varieties. The best-known members of the family are Finnish, Lapp, and Hungarian.

fiord alternative spelling of ◊fjord.

fir general term applied to ◊conifers, but the correct name for only a few species, such as the *silver fir Abies alba*, other *Abies* species, and the *Douglas fir Pseudotsuga menziesii*.

Firdausi Abdul Qasim Mansur *c.* 935–*c.* 1020. Persian poet, whose epic *Shahnama/The Book of Kings* relates the history of Persia in 60,000 verses. Among other episodes, it tells how Rustum unwittingly killed his son Sohrab in battle; this was used by Matthew ◊Arnold in his poem 'Sohrab and Rustum'.

firearm a weapon from which missiles are discharged by the combustion of an explosive. Firearms are generally divided into two main sections: ◊*artillery* (ordnance or cannon), with a bore greater than 2.54 cm/1 in, and ◊*small arms*, with a bore of less than 2.54 cm/1 in. Although gunpowder was known in Europe 60 years previously, the invention of guns dates from 1300–25, and is attributed to Berthold Schwartz, a German monk.

fireclay a clay with refractory characteristics (resistant to high temperatures), and hence suitable for lining furnaces. Its suitability is due its chemical composition, which contains a high percentage of silica and alumina, and a low percentage of oxides of sodium, potassium, iron, and calcium.

firedamp a gas which occurs in coal-mines and is explosive when mixed with air in certain proportions. It consists chiefly of methane CH_4 (natural gas or marsh gas), but always contains small quantities of other gases, such as nitrogen, carbon dioxide, and hydrogen, and sometimes ethane and carbon monoxide.

firefly winged nocturnal ◊beetle which emits light.

Firenze Italian form of ◊Florence.

fire protection methods available for fighting fires. In the UK, a public fire-fighting service is maintained by local authorities, and similar services operate in other countries. Industrial and commercial buildings are often protected by an automatic sprinkler system: heat or smoke opens the sprinkler heads on a network of water pipes and immediately sprays the seat of the fire. In certain circumstances water is ineffective and may be dangerous, for example, for oil and petrol storage tank fires, foam systems are used; for plants containing inflammable vapours, carbon dioxide is used; where electricity is involved, vaporizing liquids create a non-inflammable barrier; and for some chemicals only various dry powders can be used.

firework a device, originating in China, for producing a display of coloured lights (and sometimes noises) by burning chemicals. A firework consists of a container, usually cylindrical in shape, and of rolled paper, enclosing a mixture capable of burning independently of the oxygen in the air. One of the ingredients holds a separate supply of oxygen.

firmware a computer program held permanently in the machine in ◊ROM (read-only memory) chips. So called because a piece of software resident permanently in a piece of hardware needed a special name.

first aid action taken immediately after some traumatic event in order to save a victim's life, to prevent further damage, or facilitate later treatment. See also ◊resuscitation.

First Fleet eleven ships that brought the first white settlers from Britain to Australia. They set sail from Portsmouth May 1787 and arrived in Jan 1788.

First World War another name for ◊World War I, 1914–18.

fiscal policy that part of government policy devoted to achieving the desired level of revenue, notably through taxation, and deciding the priorities governing its expenditure.

fiscal year the financial year, which does not necessarily coincide with the calendar year.

Fischer Emil Hermann 1852–1919. German chemist. Working with Julius Tufel, he produced synthetic sugars and from these the various enzymes. His descriptions of the chemistry of the carbohydrates and peptides laid the foundations for the science of biochemistry. Nobel Prize for Chemistry 1902.

Fisher John Fisher, bishop of Rochester, was beheaded in 1535 for denying the royal supremacy.

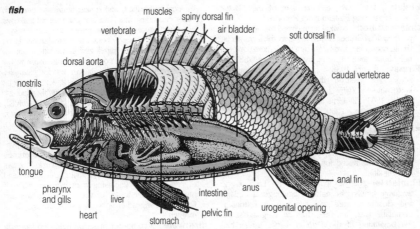

fish

muscles
spiny dorsal fin
vertebrate
air bladder
soft dorsal fin
dorsal aorta
caudal vertebrae
nostrils
tongue
anal fin
pharynx
and gills
liver
intestine
anus
heart
stomach
pelvic fin
urogenital opening

Fischer Hans 1881–1945. German chemist awarded the Nobel Prize for Chemistry in 1930 for his discovery of haemoglobin in blood.

fish aquatic vertebrate which breathes using gills. There are three main groups, not very closely related: the bony fishes (goldfish, cod, tuna); the cartilaginous fishes (sharks, rays); and the jawless fishes (hagfishes, lampreys).

Fisher John, St *c.* 1469–1535. English bishop. Created Bishop of Rochester in 1504. He was an enthusiastic supporter of the revival in the study of Greek, and a friend of the humanists More and Erasmus. In 1535 he was tried on a charge of denying the royal supremacy and beheaded.

fish farming also called *aquaculture* raising fish under controlled conditions in tanks and ponds, sometimes in offshore pens. It has been practised for centuries in the Far East, where Japan alone produces some 100,000 tonnes of fish a year. In the 1980s one-tenth of the world's consumption of fish was farmed, notably trout

drag net

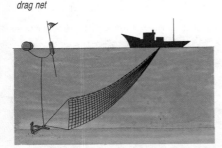

trawl net

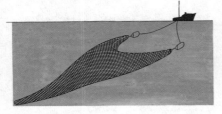

fish farming

and Atlantic salmon, turbot, eel, mussels, and oysters.

fission in physics, the splitting of the atomic nucleus (◊nuclear fission).

fistula an abnormal pathway developing between adjoining organs or tissues, or leading to the exterior of the body. A fistula developing between the bowel and the bladder, for instance, may give rise to urinary tract infection by organisms from the gut.

fitness in genetic theory, a measure of the success with which a genetically determined character can spread in future generations. By convention, the normal character is assigned a fitness of one, and variants (determined by other ◊alleles) are then assigned fitness values relative to this. Those with fitness greater than one will spread more rapidly and ultimately replace the normal allele; those with fitness less than one will gradually die out. See also ◊inclusive fitness.

Fitzgerald Ella 1918– . US jazz singer, recognized as one of the greatest voices of jazz, both in solo work and with big bands. She is particularly noted for her interpretations of Gershwin and Cole Porter songs.

Fitzgerald F(rancis) Scott (Key) 1896–1940. US novelist. His autobiographical novel *This Side of Paradise* 1920 made him known in the bright postwar society of the East Coast, and his most famous book, *The Great Gatsby* 1925, epitomizes the hedonistic Jazz Age. His wife Zelda's descent into madness forms the subject of *Tender is the Night* 1934.

FitzGerald Garret 1926– . Irish politician. As *Taoiseach* (prime minister) 1981–82 and again

Fitzgerald US novelist F Scott Fitzgerald and his wife Zelda on their honey moon.

flamingo

1982–86, he was noted for his attempts to solve
the Northern Ireland dispute, ultimately by participating in the Anglo-Irish agreement 1985. He tried
to remove some of the overtly Catholic features of
the constitution to make the Republic more attractive to Northern Protestants. He retired as leader
of the Fine Gael Party in 1987.

Fitzherbert   Maria Anne 1756–1837. wife of the
Prince of Wales, later George IV. She became Mrs
Fitzherbert by her second marriage in 1778 and,
after her husband's death in 1781, entered London
society. She secretly married the Prince of Wales
in 1785, and finally parted from him in 1803.

Fitzroy   family name of Dukes of Grafton; descended from King Charles II by his mistress
Barbara Villiers; seated at Euston Hall, Norfolk.

five pillars of Islam   the five duties required of
every Muslim:
repeating the creed which affirms that Allah is the
one God and Muhammad is his prophet; daily prayer
or ◊salat; fasting during the month of Ramadan; and,
if not prevented by ill health or poverty, the hajj, or
pilgrimage to Mecca, once in a lifetime.

fives   a game resembling squash played by two or
four players in a court enclosed on three or four
sides: the ball is struck with the hand.

Five-Year Plan   a long-term strategic plan for the
development of a country's economy. Five-year
plans were from 1928 the basis of economic planning in the USSR, aimed particularly at developing
heavy and light industry in a primarily agricultural
country. They have since been adopted by many
other countries.

Flaubert French novelist Gustave Flaubert.

fjord or **fiord**   name given to narrow sea inlets in
Norway, enclosed by high cliffs, and now to similar
formations elsewhere. *Fiordland* is the deeply indented SW coast of South Island, New Zealand; one
of the most magnificent inlets is Milford Sound.

flag   in botany, plant of the *Iris* genus. *Yellow
flag Iris pseudacorus* grows in damp places and
in marshes throughout Europe. It has a thick rhizome, stiff, blade-like monocotyledonous leaves,
and stems up to 150 cm/5 ft high. The flowers are
large and yellow.

flagellant   a religious fanatic who uses a whip on
him- or herself as a means of penance. Flagellation
is known in many religions from ancient times,
and there were notable outbreaks of this type
of extremist devotion in Christian Europe in the
11th–16th centuries.

flagellum   a small hair-like organ on the surface
of certain cells. Flagella are the motile organs of
certain protozoa and single-celled algae, and of the
sperm cells of higher animals. Unlike ◊cilia, flagella
usually occur singly or in pairs; they are also longer
and have a more complex whip-like action.

Flaherty   Robert 1884–1951. US film director. He
exerted great influence through his film of Inuit
(Eskimo) life *Nanook of the North* 1920. Later
films include *Man of Aran* 1934, and *Elephant
Boy* 1937.

flamboyant   in ◊architecture, term applied to the
late Gothic style of French architecture, contemporary with the ◊Perpendicular style in England.
It is characterized by flame-like decorative work
in windows, balustrades, and other projecting features.

flamen   a sacrificial priest in ancient Rome. The
office was held for life, but was terminated by
the death of the flamen's wife (who assisted him
at ceremonies) or by some misdemeanor. At first
there were three flamens for each deity, but another
12 were later added.

flame tree   smooth-stemmed semi-deciduous tree
Sterculia acerifolia with red/orange flowers, native
to Australia, but spread throughout the tropics.

flamingo   long-legged and long-necked wading
bird, family Phoenicopteridae, of the stork order Ciconiiformes. Largest of the family is the
greater or **roseate flamingo** *Phoenicopterus
ruber*, of both Africa and South America, with
delicate pink plumage, and 1.25 m/4 ft high.
They sift the mud for food with their downbent
bills, and build colonies of high, conelike mud
nests, with a little hollow for the eggs at the
top.

flea Electron microscope picture of a hedgehog flea
infested by parasitic mites.

flea

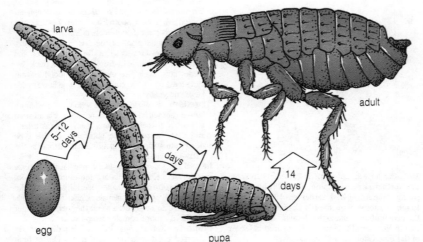

Flanagan Bud. Stage name of British comedian Robert Winthrop 1896–1968. Leader of the 'Crazy Gang' (1931–62), he also played in variety theatre all over the world and, with his partner Chesney Allen, popularized such songs as 'Underneath the Arches'.

Flanders a region of the Low Countries which in the 8th and 9th centuries extended from Calais to the Scheldt, and is now covered by the Belgian provinces of Oost Vlaanderen and West Vlaanderen (E and W Flanders), the French *département* of Nord, and part of the Dutch province of Zeeland. The language is Flemish.

flare, solar a brilliant eruption on the Sun above a ⟡sunspot, thought to be caused by release of magnetic energy. Flares reach maximum brightness within a few minutes, then fade away over about an hour. They eject a burst of atomic particles into space at up to 1,000 km/600 mi per second. When these particles reach Earth they can cause radio blackouts, disruptions of the Earth's magnetic field, and ⟡Aurora.

flash point in physics, the temperature at which a liquid heated under standard conditions gives off sufficient vapour to ignite on the application of a small flame.

flatworm invertebrate of the phylum Platyhelminthes. Some are free-living, but many are parasitic (for example tapeworms and flukes). The body is simple and bilaterally symmetrical, with one opening to the intestine. Many are hermaphrodite (with male and female sex organs).

Flaubert Gustave 1821–1880. French novelist, born in Rouen. His masterpiece *Madame Bovary* appeared in 1857 and aroused much controversy by its psychological portrayal of the wife of a country doctor, driven to suicide by a series of unhappy love affairs. *Salammbô* 1862 earned him the Legion of Honour in 1866, and was followed by *L'Education sentimentale/Sentimental Education* 1869, and *La Tentation de Saint Antoine/The Temptation of St Anthony* 1874.

flax plant of the family Linaceae which yields valuable commercial products. The common flax or linseed plant *Linum usitatissimum*, of almost worldwide distribution, has a stem up to 60 cm/2 ft high, small leaves and bright blue flowers.

flea black wingless insect, order Siphonaptera, with blood-sucking mouthparts. Fleas are parasitic on warm-blooded animals. Some fleas can jump 130 times their own height.

Fleming's rules

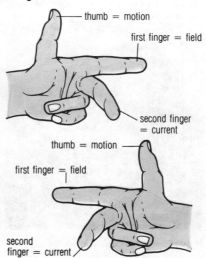

Fleming *Scottish bacteriologist Alexander Fleming.*

flight Pioneer aviator Sam Cody built this aeroplane in 1908 and he and his passengers, who totalled 334.8 kg/738 lbs, flew at Aldershot at a height of 21.3 m/70 ft for about seven miles.

fleabane plant of the genera *Erigeron* or *Pulicaria*, family Compositae. Common fleabane *Pulicaria dysenterica* has golden yellow flowerheads and grows in wet and marshy places.

Fleming Alexander 1881–1955. Scottish bacteriologist and discoverer in 1922 of lysozyme, and in 1928 of the antibiotic drug ◊penicillin. Nobel Prize for Physiology or Medicine, 1945.

Fleming Ian 1908–1964. English author of suspense novels featuring the ruthless, laconic James Bond, UK Secret Service agent No. 007.

floral diagram

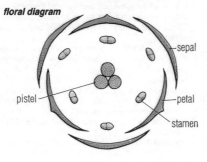

sepal

pistel

petal

stamen

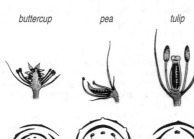

buttercup   pea   tulip

Fleming John Ambrose 1849–1945. English electrical physicist and engineer, who invented the thermionic valve in 1904.

Fleming's rules memory aids for the directions of the magnetic field, current, and motion in an electric generator or motor, using one's fingers. The three directions are represented by the thu*m*b (for *m*otion), *f*orefinger (for *f*ield) and second finger (*c*urrent), all held at right angles to each other. The right hand is used for generators, such as a dynamo, and the left for motors. They were named after the English physicist John Fleming.

Flemish A member of the W Germanic branch of the Indo-European language family, spoken in N Belgium and the Nord department of France. It is closely related to Dutch.

Fletcher John 1579–1625. English dramatist. He collaborated with ◊Beaumont, most notably producing *Philaster* 1609 and *The Maid's Tragedy* 1610–11. He is alleged to have collaborated with Shakespeare on *The Two Noble Kinsmen* and *Henry VIII* in 1612.

flight people first took to the air in ◊balloons and began powered flight in ◊airships, but the history of flying, both for civilian and military use, is dominated by the ◊aeroplane. Developed from glider design, the advent of the petrol engine saw the first powered flight by the American ◊Wright brothers 1903. This inspired the development of aircraft throughout Europe. Biplanes were succeeded by monoplanes in the 1930s and the first ◊jet plane, the German *Heinkel 178* in 1939. The 1950s saw the development of economical passenger airtravel with jetliners, and in the 1970s came the supersonic aircraft ◊Concorde.

flint a compact, hard, brittle mineral, brown, black, or grey in colour, found in nodules in chalk deposits. It consists of fine-grained silica, SiO_2, compressed into a homogeneous mass. Flint implements made by chipping one flint against another were widely used by Palaeolithic and Neolithic people.

Flodden, Battle of the defeat of the Scots under James IV by the English under the Earl of Surrey 9 Sept 1513 on a site 5 km/3 mi SE of Coldstream,

flower

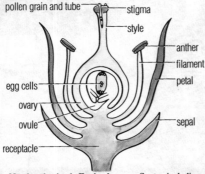

pollen grain and tube — stigma
style
anther
filament
petal
egg cells
ovary
ovule
sepal
receptacle

Northumberland, England; many Scots, including King James, were killed.

Flood, the in the Old Testament or Hebrew Bible and the Koran, disaster alleged to have obliterated all humanity except a chosen few (the family of ◊Noah).

floral diagram a diagram showing the arrangement and number of parts in a flower, drawn in cross-section. An ovary is drawn in the centre, surrounded by representations of the other floral parts, indicating the position of each at its base. If any parts such as the petals or sepals are fused, this is also indicated. Floral diagrams allow the structure of different flowers to be compared, and are usually presented with the floral formula.

floral formula a symbolic representation of the structure of a flower. Each kind of floral part is represented by a letter (K for calyx, C for corolla, P for perianth, A for androecium, G for gynoecium), and a number to indicate the quantity of the part present, for example, C5 for a flower with five petals. The number is in brackets if the parts are fused. If the parts are arranged in distinct whorls within the flower this is shown by two separate figures, such as A5 + 5, indicating two whorls of five stamens each.

Florence (Italian *Firenze*) capital of ◊Tuscany, N Italy, 88 km/55 mi from the mouth of the river Arno; population (1981) 448,330. It has printing, engineering, and optical industries, many crafts, including leather, gold and silver work, and embroidery, and is renowned for its art and architecture.

floret a small flower, usually making up part of a larger, composite inflorescence (or ◊capitulum) where numerous florets are grouped together into one flower-head. Florets are characteristic of the daisy family (Compositae). There are often two different types present on one flower-head: disc florets in the central area, and ray florets around the edge which usually have a single petal known as the ligule.

Florida most southeasterly state of the USA; mainly a peninsula jutting into the Atlantic, which it separates from the Gulf of Mexico; nickname Sunshine State.
area 151,939 sq km/58,560 sq mi
capital Tallahassee
towns Miami, Tampa, Jacksonville
physical 50% forested; lakes (including Okeechobee 1,800 sq km/700 sq mi); Everglades National Park (5,000 sq km/2,000 sq mi), birdlife, cypresses, alligators
products citrus fruit, melons, vegetables, fish and shellfish, phosphates (one third of world supply),

chemicals, largest US producer of uranium, space research
population (1980) 9,750,000.

flotation process a common method of mineral dressing (preparing ores for subsequent processing), making use of the different wetting properties of various ores. In the process the ore is finely ground and then mixed with water and a specially selected wetting agent. Air is bubbled through the mixture, forming a froth, the desired ore particles attach themselves to the bubbles and are skimmed off, while unwanted dirt or other ores remain behind.

flotsam, jetsam, and lagan *flotsam* goods found floating at sea after a shipwreck; *jetsam* those thrown overboard to lighten a sinking vessel; *lagan* those on the sea bottom, or secured to a buoy.

flounder small flatfish *Platichthys flesus* of the NE Atlantic and Mediterranean, although it sometimes lives in estuaries. It is dully coloured, and grows to 50 cm/1.6 ft.

flow chart a diagram, often used in computing, to show the possible paths through the logical structure of a sequence of events (or a computer program). Different symbols are used to indicate processing, decision-making, input, and output. These are connected by arrows showing the flow of control through the program, that is, the paths the computer can take when executing the program. It is a way of writing an ◊algorithm.

flower the reproductive unit of an ◊angiosperm or flowering plant, typically consisting of four whorls of modified leaves: the sepals, petals, stamens, and carpels. These are borne on a central axis or ◊receptacle. The many variations in size, colour, number and arrangement of parts are usually closely related to the method of pollination. Flowers adapted for wind-pollination typically have reduced or absent petals and sepals, and long, feathery stigmas which hang outside the flower to trap airborne pollen. In contrast, the petals of insect-pollinated flowers are usually conspicuous and brightly coloured.

flowering plant a term generally used for the ◊angiosperms, which bear flowers with various parts, including sepals, petals, stamens and carpels. Sometimes the term is used more broadly, to include both angiosperms and ◊gymnosperms, in which case the ◊cones of conifers and cycads may be referred to as 'flowers'.

flower power a youth movement of the 1960s; see ◊hippie.

flugelhorn type of ◊brass musical instrument.

fluid a liquid or gas, in which the molecules are relatively mobile and can 'flow'.

fluid, supercritical fluid brought by a combination of heat and pressure to the point at which, as a near vapour, it combines the properties of a gas and a liquid. Supercritical fluids are used as solvents in chemical processes, such as the extraction of lubricating oil from refinery residues or the decaffeination of coffee, because they avoid the energy-expensive need for phase changes (from liquid to gas and back again) required in conventional distillation processes.

fluke parasitic flatworm such as *Fasciola hepatica* that causes rot and dropsy of the liver in sheep, cattle, horses, dogs, and humans. Only the adult encysted stage of its life history is passed within the body, after ingestion by the host. The cyst dissolves in the stomach and the young fluke passes to the liver.

Flynn Erroll Flynn with Olivia de Havilland in The Charge of the Light Brigade.

fluorescence the process of emission of ◊electromagnetic radiation resulting from the absorption of certain types of energy; it ceases a minute fraction of a second after the exciting energy is removed. Fluorescence is also used to mean the radiation emitted as well as the emission process.

fluoride salt of hydrofluoric acid. Fluorides occur naturally in all water to a differing extent. Experiments in Britain, the USA and elsewhere have indicated that a concentration of fluoride of 1 part per million in water retards the decay of teeth in children by more than 50%.

fluorine chemical element, symbol F, atomic number 9, relative atomic mass 19. It occurs naturally as the minerals fluorspar (CaF_2) and cryolite (Na_3ALFe_6), and is the first member of the halogen group of elements. At ordinary temperatures it is a pale yellow, highly poisonous and reactive gas, and it unites directly with nearly all the elements.

fluorocarbon compound formed by replacing the hydrogen atoms of a hydrocarbon with fluorine. Fluorocarbons are used as inert coatings, refrigerants, synthetic resins, and as propellants in aerosols.

fluorspar or *fluorite*. A cubic mineral, CaF_2, usually violet-tinted.

flute member of a group of ◊woodwind musical instruments, including the piccolo, the concert flute, the bass or alto flute.

fly any insect of the order Diptera. A fly has one pair of wings, antennae, and compound eyes; the hindwings have become modified into knob-like projections (halteres) used to maintain equilibrium in flight. There are over 90,000 species.

flying dragon lizard *Draco volans* of SE Asia, which can glide on flaps of skin spread and supported by its ribs. This small (7.5 cm/3 in head and body) arboreal lizard can glide between trees for 6 m/20 ft or more.

flying fish Atlantic fish *Exocoetus volitans*, family Exocoetidae, of order Beloniformes, which can glide for 100 m/325 ft, over the surface of the sea on its expanded pectoral fins.

flying fox ◊bat of the order Megachiroptera.

flying lemur commonly used, but incorrect, name for ◊colugo.

flying lizard another name for ◊flying dragon.

flying squirrel name of many species of squirrel, not necessarily closely related. It is characterized by a membrane along the side of the body from forelimb to hindlimb, in some species running to neck and tail too, which allows it to glide through the air. Most species are E Asian. The giant flying squirrel *Petaurista* grows up to 1.1 m/3.5 ft including tail, and can glide 65 m/210 ft.

Flynn Errol 1909–1959. Australian actor. He is renowned for his portrayal of swashbuckling heroes in such films as *Captain Blood* 1935, *The Sea Hawk* 1940, and *The Master of Ballantrae* 1953.

flywheel a heavy wheel in an engine, which helps keep it running and smooths its motion. The ◊crankshaft in a petrol engine has a flywheel at one end, which keeps the crankshaft turning in between the intermittent power strokes of the pistons. It also comes into contact with the ◊clutch, serving as the connection between the engine and the car's transmission system.

FM in physics, the abbreviation for *frequency modulation*. Used in radio, FM is constant in

focal length

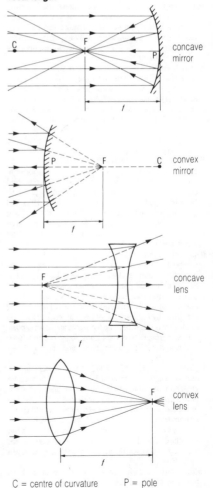

concave mirror

convex mirror

concave lens

convex lens

C = centre of curvature   P = pole
F = focus   *f* = focal length

fold

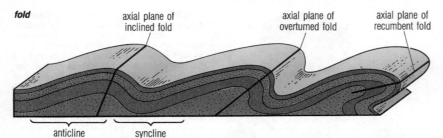

axial plane of inclined fold · axial plane of overturned fold · axial plane of recumbent fold

anticline · syncline

amplitude, and varies the frequency of the carrier wave. Its advantage over AM is its better signal-to-noise ratio.

FNLA abbreviation for *Front National de Libéra-tion de l'Angola* (French 'National Front for the Liberation of Angola').

Fo Dario 1926– . Italian playwright. His plays are predominantly political satires combining black humour with slapstick. They include *Morte accidentale di un anarchio/Accidental Death of an Anarchist* 1970, and *Non si paga non si paga/Can't Pay? Won't Pay!* 1975/1981.

fob abbreviation for *free-on-board*, used in commerce to describe a valuation of goods at point of embarkation, excluding transport and insurance costs. Export values are usually expressed fob for customs and excise purposes, while imports are usually valued ◊cif.

focal length the distance from the centre of a spherical mirror or lens to the focal point. For a concave mirror or convex lens, it is the distance at which parallel rays of light are brought to a focus to form a real image (for a mirror, this is half the radius of curvature). For a convex mirror or concave lens, it is the distance from the centre to the point at which a virtual image (an image produced by diverging rays of light) is formed.

Foch Ferdinand 1851–1929. Marshal of France during World War I. He was largely responsible for the first Allied victory of the ◊Marne, and commanded on the NW front Oct 1914–Sept 1916. He was appointed chief of general staff in 1917 and commander in chief of the Allied armies in the spring of 1918. He launched the Allied counter-offensive in July which brought about the negotiation of an armistice to end the war.

fog ◊cloud that collects at the surface of the Earth, composed of water vapour which has condensed on particles of dust in the atmosphere. Cloud and fog are both caused by the air temperature falling below ◊dew point. The thickness of fog depends on the number of water particles it contains. Usually, fog is formed by the meeting of two currents of air, one cooler than the other, or by warm air flowing over a cold surface. Sea fogs commonly occur where warm and cold currents meet, and the air above them mixes.

Fokine Mikhail 1880–1942. Russian dancer and choreographer, born in St Petersburg. He became chief choreographer to the Ballets Russes 1909–14, and with ◊Diaghilev revitalized and reformed the art of ballet, promoting the idea of artistic unity between dramatic, musical, and stylistic elements.

fold in geology, a bend in rock ◊beds. If the bend is arched up in the middle it is called an *anticline*; if it sags downwards in the middle it is called a *syncline*.

folic acid a ◊vitamin of the B-complex. It is found in liver and green leafy vegetables, and is also synthesized by the intestinal bacteria. It is essential for growth, and plays many other roles in the body. Lack of folic acid causes anaemia.

folklore the oral traditions and culture of a people, expressed in riddles, songs, tales, legends, and proverbs. The term was coined in 1846 by W J Thoms (1803–85), but the founder of the systematic study of the subject was Jacob ◊Grimm; see also ◊oral literature.

follicle in botany, a dry, usually many-seeded fruit which splits along one side only to release the seeds within. It is derived from a single ◊carpel and examples include the fruits of the *Delphinium* and columbine *Aquilegia*. It differs from a pod, which always splits open (dehisces) along both sides.

follicle in zoology, a small group of cells that surrounds and nourishes a structure such as a hair (hair follicle) or a cell such as an egg (Graafian follicle; see ◊menstrual cycle).

Fonda Henry 1905–1982. US actor, whose engaging style made him ideal in the role of the American pioneer and honourable man. His many films include *Grapes of Wrath* 1940, *My Darling Clementine* 1946, and *On Golden Pond* 1981.

Fonda Jane 1937– . American actress, daughter of Henry Fonda. Her early films include *Cat Ballou* 1965 and *Barbarella* 1968, and she won Academy Awards for *Klute* 1971 and *Coming Home* 1979.

Fontana Domenico 1543–1607. Italian architect. He was employed by Pope Sixtus V, and his principal works include the Vatican library, the completion of the dome of St Peter's, and the royal palace at Naples.

Fonteyn Margot stage name of Margaret Hookham 1919– . English ballet dancer. She made her debut with the Vic-Wells Ballet in *Nutcracker* in 1934 and first appeared as Giselle in 1937, eventually becoming prima ballerina of the Royal Ballet, London. Renowned for her perfect physique, musicality, and interpretive powers, she created several roles in ◊Ashton's ballets and formed one of the most famous ballet partnerships of all time with ◊Nureyev.

food general term for anything eaten by human beings and other animals to sustain life. Essential for humans are:

protein for body building and repair found in meat, milk, fish, eggs, and some vegetables;

fats (in moderation) to provide energy found in butter, oil, and lard;

carbohydrates also provide energy and are found in bread, potatoes, cereals, and sugar, which form the bulk of the diet;

vitamins required only in small quantities to assist the body to make full use of its food;

minerals which are also required in small quantities: salt; calcium (bone building) from milk; and iron (blood formation) from meats and green vegetables.

Essential foods also include water and fibre (for example, bran, green leaves for digestion) although

food chain

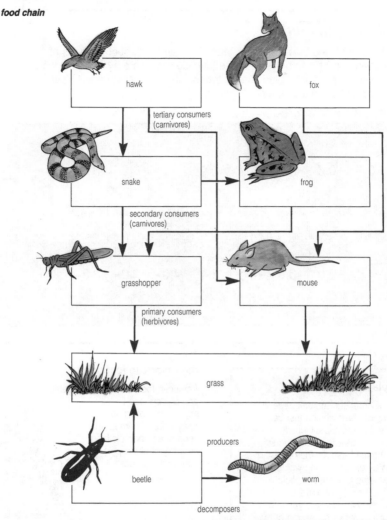

hawk

fox

tertiary consumers
(carnivores)

snake

frog

secondary consumers
(carnivores)

grasshopper

mouse

primary consumers
(herbivores)

grass

producers

beetle

worm

decomposers

these give little nourishment. The energy value of food is expressed in joules or calories.

Food and Agriculture Organization (FAO) agency of the United Nations concerned with investment in agriculture, also emergency food supplies; established in 1945, headquarters in Rome, Italy.

food chain or *food web* in ecology, the sequence of organisms through which energy and other nutrients are successively transferred. Since many organisms feed at several different levels (for example, omnivores feed on both fruit and meat), the relationships often form a complex web rather than a simple chain. See also ◊ecosystem and ◊heterotroph.

food poisoning acute illness caused by harmful bacteria (for example, ◊listeriosis), poisonous food (for example, certain mushrooms, puffer fish), or poisoned food (for example, lead or arsenic introduced accidentally during manufacture). The most frequent cause of food poisoning is the *salmonella* bacterium. This comes in many forms, and strains are found in a high percentage of cattle, pigs, and poultry.

food technology the application of scientific and engineering knowledge to the commercial processing and manufacture of foodstuffs, especially in preservation techniques such as ◊refrigeration, ◊deep freezing, ◊dehydration, ◊irradiation, ◊canning, and various forms of packaging, since foods are often consumed a great distance from where they were grown and harvested.

foot Imperial unit of length (ft), equivalent to 0.3048 m. Twelve inches comprise a foot, three feet make a yard.

Foot Michael 1913– . British Labour politician. A leader of the left-wing Tribune Group; he was secretary of state for employment 1974–76, Lord President of the Council and leader of the House 1976–79, and succeeded Callaghan as Labour Party leader 1980–83.

foot and mouth disease contagious eruptive viral fever which causes deterioration of milk yield and abortions in cattle.

football, American a contact sport similar to the English game of rugby. First match under Harvard

American football

A game played by 11 men per team. The aim is, through a series of passing or running plays, to score touchdowns (like a try in rugby) which are worth six points, plus one for the 'point-after' (conversion). Field goals (3 points) are another way of scoring.

the pitch with its 'grid-iron' effect

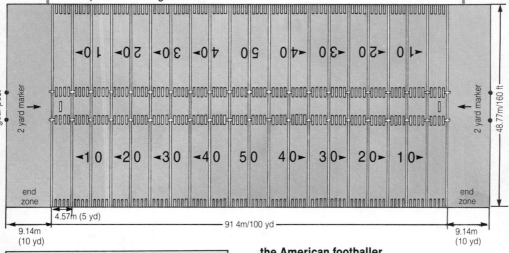

2 yard marker

48.77m/160 ft

goal post

2 yard marker

end zone

end zone

4.57m (5 yd)

91 4m/100 yd

9.14m (10 yd)

9.14m (10 yd)

series of plays

The tactics of American football depend upon a series of plays which must be choreographed in advance. Once in possession of the ball, the attacking side (the offense) must head for the opposing scoring area by either running with the ball, or by passing the ball to upfield players. In each series of plays the offense must gain at least ten yards in four plays or they lose possession of the ball.

the snap

After the scrimmage for the ball the snap is the first move made by the center to his quarterback, who then sets up an attacking move.

the American footballer

American football is a rough game, and players need maximum protection. They wear a helmet, and underneath their clothing an array of chest-, arm- and leg-pads.

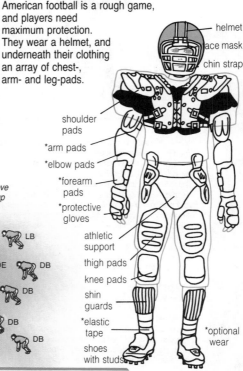

helmet

face mask

chin strap

shoulder pads

*arm pads

*elbow pads

*forearm pads

*protective gloves

athletic support

thigh pads

knee pads

shin guards

*elastic tape

shoes with studs

*optional wear

key:
B   running back
QB quarterback
E   end
T   tackle
G   guard
C   center
E   end
LB line backer
DE defensive end
DT defensive tackle
DB defensive back

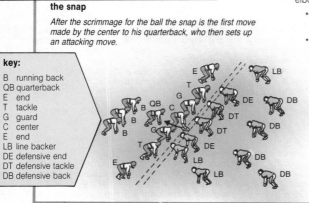

Ford *Henry Ford, founder of the Ford Motor Company.*

rules was between Harvard University and McGill University, Montreal in 1874.

football, association a form of football popularly known as soccer. Popular in England in the 14th century, it developed in the 19th century and the first set of rules were drawn up at Cambridge University in 1848.

football, Australian an 18-a-side game which is a cross between Gaelic football, rugby, and soccer, and is unique to Australia, although association and rugby football are also played there.

foot-poundal imperial unit of energy (ft-lb), defined as the work done when a force of 1 lb moves through a distance of 1 ft. It has been superseded for scientific work by the joule, and is equivalent to 0.04214 joule.

foraminifera single-celled marine animals, often classified as an order of Protozoa, which are enclosed by a thin shell. Some form part of ◊plankton, others live on the sea bottom.

force in physics, that influence which tends to change the state of rest or the uniform motion of a body in a straight line. It is measured by the rate of change of momentum of the body on which it acts, that is, the mass of the body multiplied by its acceleration: $F = ma$.

forces, fundamental in physics, the four fundamental interactions believed to be at work in the physical universe. There are two long-range forces: *gravity*, which keeps the planets in orbit around the Sun, and acts between all ◊particles that have mass; and the *electromagnetic force*, which stops solids from falling apart, and acts between all particles with ◊electric charge. There are two very short-range forces: the *weak force*, responsible for the reactions which fuel the

Sun, and for the emission of ◊beta particles from certain nuclei; and the *strong force*, which binds together the protons and neutrons in the nuclei of ◊atoms.

Ford Ford Madox. Adopted name of Ford Madox Hueffer 1873–1939. English writer. He is best remembered as editor of the *English Review* 1908 to which Thomas Hardy, D H Lawrence, and Joseph Conrad contributed, and for his novel *The Good Soldier* 1915.

Ford Gerald R(udolph) 1913– . 38th president of the USA 1974–77, a Republican. He was elected to the House of Representatives 1949, was nominated to the vice-presidency by ◊Nixon in 1973, and in 1974, when Nixon resigned, succeeded him as president. His decisions to give his predecessor a free pardon, and to give amnesty to those who resisted the draft for the Vietnam War, were controversial.

Ford Henry 1863–1947. US motor car manufacturer, who built his first car in 1893 and founded the Ford Motor Company in 1903. His model T (1908–27) was the first car to be constructed by purely mass-production methods, and 15 million of these historic cars were made.

Ford John 1586–1640. English poet and dramatist. He was noted for an imaginative and dramatic study of incest between brother and sister in *'Tis Pity She's a Whore* 1633.

Ford John. Assumed name of Sean O'Fearn 1895–1973. US film director. His films include *The Informer* 1935, *Stagecoach* 1939, and *The Grapes of Wrath* 1940.

foreclosure in British law, the transfer of a mortgaged property from the mortgagor to the mortgagee (for example a bank) where the mortgagor is in breach of the mortgage agreement, for example, by failing to keep up the repayments.

Foreign Legion a volunteer corps of foreigners within a country's army. The French *Légion Etrangère*, formed 1831, is the most famous of a number of such forces. Enlisted volunteers are of any nationality (about half are now French), but the officers are usually French. Headquarters until 1962 were Sidi Bel Abbés, Algeria; the main base is now Corsica, with reception headquarters at Aubagne, near Marseilles.

Forester C(ecil) S(cott) 1899–1966. British novelist. His reputation rests on his series of historical novels set in the Napoleonic era which, beginning with *The Happy Return* 1937, cover the career – from midshipman to admiral – of Horatio Hornblower.

forgery the making of a fake document, painting, or object with deliberate intention to deceive or defraud.

forget-me-not several plants of genus *Myosotis*, family Boraginaceae. The annual *common forget-me-not* has bright blue flowers; there are many other species.

forging one of the main methods of shaping metals, which involves hammering or the more gradual application of pressure. A blacksmith hammers red-hot metal into shape on an anvil, and the traditional place of work is called a forge. The blacksmith's mechanical equivalent is the drop forge. The metal is shaped by the blows from a falling hammer or ram, which is usually accelerated by steam or air pressure. Hydraulic presses forge by applying pressure gradually in a squeezing action.

formaldehyde common name for ◊methanol.

four-stroke cycle

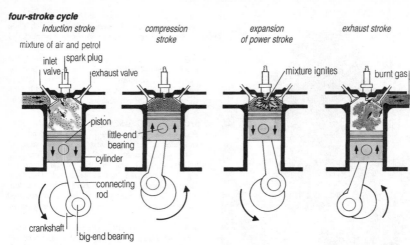

induction stroke

compression stroke

expansion of power stroke

exhaust stroke

mixture of air and petrol

inlet valve | spark plug

exhaust valve

mixture ignites

burnt gas

piston

little-end bearing

cylinder

connecting rod

crankshaft | big-end bearing

Formby George 1904–1961. English comedian. He established a stage and screen reputation as an apparently simple working lad, and sang such songs as 'Mr Wu' and 'Cleaning Windows', accompanying himself on the ukelele. His father was a music-hall star of the same name.

Formica trade name for a heat-proof plastic laminate, widely used for wipe-down kitchen surfaces. It is made from formaldehyde resins akin to ◊Bakelite.

formic acid common name for ◊methanoic acid.

formula in chemistry, a representation of a molecule, radical, or ion, in which chemical elements are represented by their symbols. A *molecular formula* gives the number of each type of element present in one molecule. A *structural formula* shows the relative positions of the atoms and the bonds between them. Formula is also another name for a ◊chemical equation.

Forrest John, 1st baron Forrest 1847–1918. Australian explorer who crossed Western Australia from west to east in 1870, when he went along the southern coast route, and in 1874, when he crossed much further north, exploring the Musgrave Ranges.

Forrestal James Vincent 1892–1949. US Democratic politician. As secretary of the navy from 1944, he organized its war effort, accompanying the US landings on the Japanese island Iwo Jima.

Forster E(dward) M(organ) 1879–1970. English novelist, concerned with the interplay of personality and the contrast betwen convention and instinct. His novels include *A Room with a View* 1908, *Howard's End* 1910, and *A Passage to India* 1924.

Forsyth Frederick 1938– . British thriller writer. His books include *The Day of the Jackal* 1970, *The Dogs of War* 1974, and *The Fourth Protocol* 1984.

forsythia genus of temperate E Asian shrubs, family Oleaceae, which bear yellow flowers in early spring before the leaves appear.

Fort-de-France capital, chief commercial centre, and port of ◊Martinique, West Indies; population (1982) 99,844.

Forth river in SE Scotland, with its headstreams rising on the NE slopes of Ben Lomond. It flows approximately 72 km/45 mi to Kincardine where the *Firth of Forth* begins. The Firth is approximately 80 km/50 mi long, and is 26 km/16 mi wide where it joins the North Sea.

Fortin Jean 1750–1831. French physicist and instrument-maker who invented a mercury barometer that bears his name. On this scale, normal atmospheric pressure is 760 mm of mercury.

Fort Knox US army post and gold depository in Kentucky, established 1917 as a training camp.

Fortran (from *formula translation*) computer-programming language particularly suited to mathematical and scientific computations. Developed in the mid-1950s, and one of the earliest languages, it is still widely used today.

Fort Sumter fort in Charleston harbour, South Carolina, USA, 6.5 km/4 mi SE of Charleston. The first shots of the American Civil War were fired here on 12 Apr 1861, after its commander had refused the call to surrender made by the Confederate Gen Beauregard.

Fort Ticonderoga fort in New York State, USA, on a route to Canada near Lake Champlain. It was the site 1758–59 of battles between the British and the French, and was captured from the British 10 May 1775 by Benedict Arnold and Ethan Allen (leading the ◊Green Mountain Boys).

Forty-Five the ◊Jacobite rebellion of 1745, led by Prince ◊Charles Edward Stuart. With his army of Highlanders 'Bonnie Prince Charlie' occupied Edinburgh and advanced into England as far as Derby, but then turned back. The rising was crushed by the Duke of Cumberland at Culloden in 1746.

fossil remains of an animal or plant from an earlier geological period preserved in rocks. Fossils may be formed by *refrigeration* (for example, Siberian ◊mammoths), preservation of the *skeleton* only, *carbonization* (leaves in coal), formation of a *cast* (dinosaur or human footprints in mud), or *mineralization* of bones or teeth.

fossil fuel fuel, such as coal or oil, formed from the fossilized remains of plants that lived hundreds of millions of years ago. Fossil fuels are a ◊non-renewable resource and will run out eventually. Extraction of coal causes considerable environmental pollution, and burning coal contributes to problems of ◊acid rain and the ◊greenhouse effect.

Foster Norman 1935– . British architect of the high-tech school. His works include the Willis Faber office, Ipswich 1978, the Sainsbury Centre for Visual Arts at the University of East Anglia 1979, and the headquarters of the Hongkong and Shanghai Bank, Hong Kong 1986.

Foucault Jean Bernard Léon 1819–1868. French physicist who used a pendulum to demonstrate the rotation of the Earth on its axis, and invented the gyroscope.

Foucault Michel 1926–1984. French philosopher, who rejected phenomenology and existentialism. His work was concerned with how forms of knowledge and forms of human subjectivity are constructed by specific institutions and practices.

Fouché Joseph, Duke of Otranto 1759–1820. French politician. He was elected to the National Convention (the post-Revolutionary legislature), and organized the conspiracy which overthrew the Jacobin leader Robespierre. Napoleon employed him as police minister.

fouetté (French 'whipped') in ballet, a type of *pirouette* in which the working leg whips out to the side and then into the knee while the dancer spins on the supporting leg. Odile performs 32 *fouettés* in Act III of *Swan Lake*.

Fountains Abbey Cistercian abbey in North Yorkshire, England. It was founded *c.* 1132, and suppressed in 1540. The ruins were incorporated into a Romantic landscape garden 1720–40 with lake, formal water garden, and temples, and a deer park.

four-colour process colour ◊printing using four printing plates, based on the principle that any colour is made up of differing proportions of the primary colours blue, red, and green. The first stage in preparing a colour picture for printing is to produce separate films, one each for the blue, red, and green respectively in the picture (colour separations). From these separations three printing plates are made, with a fourth plate for black. Ink colours complementary to those represented on the plates are used for printing – yellow for the blue plate, cyan for the red, and magenta for the green.

Fourdrinier machine a papermaking machine, patented by the Fourdrinier brothers Henry and Sealy in England in 1803. On the machine, liquid pulp flows onto a moving wire-mesh belt, and water drains and is sucked away, leaving a damp paper web. This is passed first through a series of steam-heated rollers, which dry it, and then between heavy calendar rollers, which give it a smooth finish. The machine can measure up to 90 m/300 ft in length, and is still in use.

Four Noble Truths in Buddhism, a summary of the basic concepts: life is suffering (Sanskrit *duhkha*, sour); suffering has its roots in desire (*trishna*, clinging or grasping); the cessation of desire is the end of suffering, *nirvana*; and this can be reached by the Noble Eightfold Path of *dharma* (truth).

four-stroke cycle the engine-operating cycle of most ◊petrol and ◊diesel piston engines. The 'stroke' is an upward or downward movement of a piston in a cylinder. In a petrol engine the cycle begins with the induction of a fuel mixture as the piston goes down on its first stroke. On the second stroke (up) the piston compresses the mixture in the top of the cylinder. An electric spark then ignites the mixture, and the gases produced force the piston down on its third, power stroke. On the fourth stroke (up) the piston expels the burnt gases from the cylinder into the exhaust.

Fourteen Points the terms proposed by President Wilson of the USA in his address to Congress on 8 Jan 1918, as a basis for the settlement of World War I that was about to reach its climax. They included: open diplomacy; freedom of the seas; removal of economic barriers; international disarmament; adjustment of colonial claims; German evacuation of Russian, Belgian, French, and Balkan territories; the restoration of Alsace-Lorraine to France; autonomy for the Austro-Hungarian peoples and those under Turkish rule; an independent Poland; and a general association of nations (which was to become the League of Nations).

fourth-generation language in computing, a programming language aimed at producing straightforward, commercial programs far more quickly than a more conventional language such as ◊COBOL. A fourth-generation language has facilities to support rapid screen design and easy use of databases. It follows three other generations of programming language: machine code (first generation), assembly language (second), and currently used languages such as ◊BASIC and ◊PASCAL (third).

Fourth of July in the USA, the anniversary of the day in 1776 when the ◊Declaration of Independence was adopted by the Continental Congress. It is a public holiday called *Independence Day*.

Fourth Republic the French constitutional regime which was established between 1944 and 1946, and lasted until 4 Oct 1958: from liberation after Nazi occupation during World War II to the introduction of a new constitution by Gen de Gaulle.

fowl name for a chicken or chickenlike bird. The *red jungle fowl Gallus gallus* is the ancestor of all domestic chickens.

Fowler (Peter) Norman 1938– . British Conservative politician. He was a junior minister in the Heath government, transport secretary in the first Thatcher administration 1979, social services secretary 1981, and employment secretary 1987–89. In May 1992 he succeeded Chris Patten as Conservative Party chairman.

Fowler Henry Watson 1858–1933 and his brother Francis George 1870–1918. British scholars and authors of a number of English dictionaries. *Modern English Usage* 1926, the work of Henry Fowler, has become a classic reference work for advice on matters of style and disputed usage.

fox name given to many of the smaller species of wild dog of the family Canidae, which live in Europe, North America, Asia, and Africa. It feeds on a wide range of animals from worms to rabbits, scavenges for food, and also eats berries. The fox is largely nocturnal, and makes an underground den or 'earth'. It is very adaptable, maintaining high populations in some urban areas.

Fox Charles James 1749–1806. English Whig politician. He entered Parliament 1769 as a supporter of the court, but went over to the opposition 1774. As secretary of state 1782, leader of the opposition to Pitt, and foreign secretary 1806, he welcomed the French Revolution and brought about the abolition of the slave trade.

Fox George 1624–1691. English founder of the Society of ◊Friends. He became a travelling preacher 1647, and in 1650 was imprisoned for blasphemy at Derby, where the name Quakers was first applied derogatorily to him and his followers, supposedly because he enjoined

fox

Fox *Portrait of Charles James Fox by K A Hickel (c. 1793) National Portrait Gallery, London.*

Judge Bennet to 'quake at the word of the Lord'.

Foxe John 1516–1587. English Protestant propagandist. He became a canon of Salisbury 1563. His *Book of Martyrs* 1563 luridly described persecutions under Queen Mary, reinforcing popular hatred of Roman Catholicism.

foxglove flowering plant of the genus *Digitalis*, family Scrophulariaceae, found in Europe and the Mediterranean region. It bears showy spikes of bell-like flowers, and can grow up to 1.5 m/5 ft high.

foxhound small keen-nosed hound. It is a combination of the old southern hound and other breeds, and has been bred in England for 300 years.

foxtrot ballroom dance originating in the USA about 1914. It has alternating long and short steps, supposedly like the movements of the fox.

f.p.s. system system of units based on the foot, pound, and second as units of length, mass, and time. It has now been replaced for scientific work by the ◊SI system.

fractal an irregular shape or surface produced by a procedure of repeated subdivision. Generated on a computer screen, fractals are used in creating models for geographical or biological processes (for example, the creation of a coastline by erosion or accretion, or the growth of plants).

fraction (from Latin *fractio* 'to break') in mathematics, a number that indicates one or more equal parts of a whole. Usually, the number of equal parts into which the unit is divided (denominator) is written below a horizontal line, and the number of parts comprising the fraction (numerator) is written above; thus ⅔ or ¾. Such fractions are called *vulgar* or *simple fractions*. The denominator can never be zero.

fractionation also known as *fractional distillation*, a process used to split complex mixtures (such as crude oil) into their components, usually by repeated heating, boiling, and condensation.

Fra Diavolo nickname of Michele Pezza 1771–1806. Italian brigand. A renegade monk, he led a gang in the mountains of Calabria for many years, and was eventually executed in Naples.

Fragonard Jean Honoré 1732–1806. French painter, the leading exponent of the Rococo style (along with his master Boucher). His light-hearted subjects include *The Swing* about 1766.

Frame Janet. Pen name of Janet Paterson Frame Clutha 1924– . New Zealand novelist. After being wrongly diagnosed as schizophrenic, she reflected her experiences 1945–54 in the novel *Faces in the Water* 1961, and the autobiographical *An Angel at My Table* 1984.

foxglove

France country in W Europe, bounded NE by Belgium and West Germany, E by Switzerland and Italy, S by the Mediterranean, SW by Spain and Andorra, and W by the Atlantic Ocean.

France Anatole. Pen name of Jacques Anatole Thibault 1844–1924. French writer, noted for the wit, urbanity, and style of his works. His earliest novel was *Le Crime de Sylvestre Bonnard* 1881; later books include the satiric *L'Ile des pingouins/Penguin Island* 1908, *Les Dieux ont soif/The Gods are Athirst* 1912, and the autobiographical series beginning with *Le Livre de mon ami/My Friend's Book* 1885.

Francesca Piero della   see ◊Piero della Francesca, Italian painter.

Franche-Comté region of E France; area 16,200 sq km/6,253 sq mi; population (1982) 1,081,000. Its capital is Besançon, and includes the *départements* of Doubs, Jura, Haute Saône, and Territoire de Belfort. In the mountainous Jura, there is farming and forestry, and elsewhere there are engineering and plastics industries.

franchise in business, the right given by a manufacturer to a distributor to market the manufacturer's product. Examples of franchise operations in the UK include Benetton and the Body Shop.

Francis or *François*   two kings of France:

Francis I 1494–1547. King of France from 1515. He succeeded his cousin Louis XII, and from 1519 European politics turned on the rivalry between him and the Holy Roman emperor Charles V, which led

Francis of Assisi, St *Founder of the Franciscan Order.*

France
French Republic
(*République Française*)

area (including Corsica) 551,553 sq km/212,960 sq mi
capital Paris
towns Lyon, Lille, Bordeaux, Toulouse, Nantes, Strasbourg; ports Marseille, Nice
physical rivers Seine, Loire, Garonne, Rhône, Rhine; mountain ranges Alps, Massif Central, Pyrenees, Jura, Vosges, Cévennes
territories Guadeloupe, French Guiana, Martinique, Réunion, St Pierre and Miquelon, Southern and Antarctic Territories, New Caledonia, French Polynesia, Wallis and Futuna
head of state François Mitterrand from 1981
head of government Edouard Balladur from 1993
political system liberal democracy
exports fruit (especially apples), wine, cheese, wheat, cars, aircraft, chemicals, jewellery, silk, lace
currency franc
population (1990 est) 56,184,000 (including 4,500,000 immigrants, chiefly from Portugal, Algeria, Morocco, and Tunisia); annual growth rate 0.3%
life expectancy men 71, women 79
language French (regional languages include Basque, Breton, and Catalan)
religion Roman Catholic 90%, Protestant 2%, Muslim 1%
literacy 99% (1984)
GNP $568 bn (1983); $7,179 per head
chronology
1944–46 De Gaulle provisional government. Commencement of Fourth Republic.
1954 Independence granted to Indochina.
1956 Moroccan and Tunisian independence.
1957 Entry into EEC.
1958 Recall of de Gaulle following Algerian crisis. Commencement of Fifth Republic.
1959 De Gaulle became president.
1962 Algerian independence granted.
1966 France withdrew from NATO.
1968 'May events' crisis.
1969 De Gaulle resigned following referendum defeat. Pompidou became president.
1974 Giscard d'Estaing elected president.
1981 Mitterrand elected Fifth Republic's first socialist president.
1988 Mitterrand re-elected.
1991 French forces joined the US-led coalition in the Gulf War. Edith Cresson became France's first female prime minister. Mitterrand's popularity fell.
1992 Socialist Party humiliated in regional and local elections. Cresson replaced by Bérégovoy. Referendum narrowly endorsed the Maastricht Treaty.
1993 Socialist Party suffered heavy defeat in National Assembly elections. Balladur appointed prime minister.

to war 1521–29, 1536–38, and 1542–44. In 1525 Francis was defeated and captured at Pavia, and released only after signing a humiliating treaty. At home, he developed absolute monarchy.

Francis II 1544–1560. King of France from 1559 when he succeeded his father, Henry II. He married Mary, Queen of Scots 1558. He was completely under the influence of his mother, ◊Catherine de' Medici.

Francis II 1768–1835. Holy Roman emperor 1792–1806. He became Francis I, Emperor of Austria 1804, and abandoned the title of Holy Roman emperor 1806. During his reign Austria was five times involved in war with France, 1792–97, 1798–1801, 1805, 1809, and 1813–14. He succeeded his father Leopold II.

Franciscan order Catholic order of friars, *Friars Minor* or *Grey Friars*, founded 1209 by ◊Francis of Assisi. Subdivisions were the strict Observants; the Conventuals, who were allowed to own property corporately; and the ◊Capuchins, founded 1529.

Francis of Assisi, St 1182–1226. Italian founder of the Roman Catholic Franciscan order of friars 1209 and, with St Clare, of the Poor Clares 1212. In 1224 he is said to have undergone a mystical experience during which he received the *stigmata* (five wounds of Christ). Many stories are told of his ability to charm wild animals, and he is the patron saint of ecologists. His feast day is 4 Oct.

Francis of Sales, St 1567–1622. French bishop and theologian. He became bishop of Geneva 1602, and in 1610 founded the order of the Visitation, an order of nuns. He is the patron saint of journalists and other writers. His feast day is 24 Jan.

francium a metallic element, symbol Fr, atomic number 87, relative atomic mass 223. It is a highly radioactive metal; the most stable isotope has a half-life of only 21 minutes. Francium was discovered by Mlle Perey 1939.

Franck César Auguste 1822–1890. Belgian composer. His music, mainly religious and Romantic in style, includes the Symphony in D minor 1866–68, *Symphonic Variations* 1885 for piano and orchestra, the violin sonata 1886, the oratorio *Les Béatitudes/The Beatitudes* 1879, and many organ pieces.

Franco (Bahamonde) Francisco 1892–1975. Spanish dictator from 1939. As a general, he led the insurgent Nationalists to victory in the Spanish ◊Civil War 1936–39, supported by Fascist Italy and Nazi Germany, and established a dictatorship. In 1942 Franco reinstated the Cortes (Spanish parliament), which in 1947 passed an act by which he became head of state for life.

Franco-German entente rapprochement between France and Germany, designed to erase the enmities of successive wars. It was initiated by the French president de Gaulle's visit to West Germany 1962, followed by the Franco-German Treaty of Friendship and Co-operation 1963.

France: former colonies

Current name	Colonial names and history	Colonized	Independent
Kampuchea	Cambodia to 1970	1863	1953
Laos	French Indo-China (protectorate)	1893	1954
Vietnam	Tonkin, Annam, Cochin-China to 1954; N&S Vietnam 1954–76	1858	1954
Burkina Faso	Upper Volta to 1984	1896	1960
Central African Republic	Ubangi-Shari	19th cent.	1960
Chad	French Equatorial Africa	19th cent.	1960
Côte d'Ivoire	Ivory Coast to 1986	1883	1960
Madagascar		1896	1960
Mali	French Sudan	19th cent.	1960
Niger		1912	1960
Algeria	Colonized in 19th cent. – incorporated into France 1881	c. 1840	1962

Franco-Prussian War war of 1870–71 between France and Prussia. The Prussian chancellor Bismarck put forward a German candidate for the vacant Spanish throne with the deliberate, and successful, intention of provoking the French emperor Napoleon III into declaring war. The Prussians defeated the French at ◊Sedan, then successfully besieged Paris. The Treaty of Frankfurt May 1871 gave to Prussia Alsace, Lorraine, and a large French indemnity. The war established Prussia, at the head of a unified Germany, as Europe's leading power.

Franglais the French language when mixed with (unwelcome) elements of modern, especially American, English (for example Evian mineral water described as *le fast drink des Alpes*).

France: rulers

Kings				Kings		
	Pepin III/Childerich III	751		Kings	Henri IV	1574
	Pepin III	752			Louis XIII	1610
	Charlemagne/Carloman	768			Louis XIV	1643
	Charlemagne (Charles I)	771			Louis XV	1715
	Louis I	814			Louis XVI	1774
	Lothair I	840			National Convention	1792
	Charles II (the Bald)	843			Directory (five members)	1795
	Louis II	877		First Consul	Napoléon Bonaparte	1799
	Louis III	879		Emperor	Napoléon I	1804
	Charles III (the Fat)	882		King	Louis XVIII	1814
	Odo	888		Emperor	Napoléon II	1815
	Charles III (the Simple)	893		Kings	Louis XVIII	1815
	Robert I	922			Charles X	1824
	Rudolf	923			Louis XIX	1830
	Louis IV	936			Henri V	1830
	Lothair II	954			Louis-Philippe	1830
	Louis V	986		Heads of	Philippe Buchez	1848
	Hugues Capet	987		State	Louis Cavaignac	1848
	Robert II	996		President	Louis Napoléon Bonaparte	1848
	Henri I	1031		Emperor	Napoléon III	1852
	Philippe I	1060		Presidents	Adolphe Thiers	1871
	Louis VI	1108			M. Patrice MacMahon	1873
	Louis VII	1137			Jules Grevy	1879
	Philippe II	1180			François Sadi-Carnot	1887
	Louis VIII	1223			Jean Casimir-Périer	1894
	Louis IX	1226			François Faure	1895
	Philippe III	1270			Emile Loubet	1899
	Philippe IV	1285			Armand Fallières	1913
	Louis X	1314			Raymond Poincaré	1913
	Jean I	1316			Paul Deschanel	1920
	Philippe V	1316			Alexandre Millerand	1920
	Charles IV	1322			Gaston Doumergue	1924
	Philippe VI	1328			Paul Doumer	1931
	Jean II	1350			Albert Le Brun	1932
	Charles V	1356			H. Philippe Pétain (Vichy government)	1940
	Charles VI	1380			provisional government	1944
	Charles VII	1422			Vincent Auriol	1947
	Louis XI	1461			René Coty	1954
	Charles VIII	1483			Charles de Gaulle	1959
	Louis XII	1498			Alain Poher	1969
	François I	1515			Georges Pompidou	1969
	Henri II	1547			Alain Poher	1974
	François II	1559			Valéry Giscard d'Estaing	1974
	Charles IX	1560			François Mitterrand	1981
	Henri III	1574				

Franklin Portrait of Benjamin Franklin after Joseph Siffred Duplessis (1783), National Portrait Gallery, London.

Francis I Unstable and vacillating, but remembered for the brilliance of his court.

Frank a member of the Germanic people prominent during the 3rd–8th centuries. They probably originated in Pomerania on the Black Sea, settled on the Rhine by the 3rd century, spread into the Roman Empire by the 4th century, and gradually conquered most of Gaul and Germany.

Frank Anne 1929–1945. German diarist who fled to the Netherlands with her family 1933 to escape Nazi anti-semitism. During the German occupation of Amsterdam, they remained in a sealed-off room 1942–44, when betrayal resulted in Anne's deportation and death in Belsen concentration camp. Her diary of her time in hiding was published 1947.

Frankfurt-am-Main city in Hessen, Germany, 72 km/45 mi NE of Mannheim; population (1988) 592,000. Frankfurt is an important commercial, banking and industrial centre, with electrical and machine industries, and an inland port on the River Main.

Frankfurt Parliament an assembly of liberal politicians and intellectuals which met for a few months in 1848 in the aftermath of the ◊revolutions of 1848 and the overthrow of monarchies in most of the German states.

frankincense resin of trees of the Old World genus *Boswellia*, burnt as incense and used in embalming.

Franklin Benjamin 1706–1790. US scientist and politician. He proved that lightning is a form of

Franz Joseph Emperor of Austria, Franz Joseph.

electricity, distinguished between positive and negative electricity, and invented the lightning conductor. He helped draft the Declaration of Independence and the US constitution, and was ambassador to France 1776–85.

Franklin John 1786–1847. British naval explorer who took part in expeditions to Australia, the Arctic, and N Canada, and in 1845 commanded an expedition to look for the ◊North-West Passage, on which he and his men perished.

Franklin Miles 1879–1954. Australian novelist who also used the pseudonym 'Brent of Bin Bin'. *My Brilliant Career* 1901, her first novel, was made into a successful film. An Australian literary award bearing her name is made annually.

Franklin Rosalind 1920–1958. English biophysicist, whose research on X-ray diffraction of DNA crystals helped Francis Crick and James D Watson to deduce the chemical structure of DNA.

Franz Ferdinand or Francis Ferdinand 1863–1914. Archduke of Austria. He became heir to his uncle, Emperor Franz Joseph, from 1884 but while visiting Sarajevo 28 Jun 1914, he and his wife were assassinated by Serbian nationalists. Austria used the episode to make unreasonable demands on Serbia which ultimately precipitated World War I.

Franz Joseph or Francis Joseph 1830–1916. Emperor of Austria-Hungary from 1848, when his uncle, Ferdinand I, abdicated. After the suppression of the 1848 revolution, Franz Joseph tried to establish an absolute monarchy, but had to grant Austria a parliamentary constitution 1861, and Hungary equality with Austria 1867. He was defeated in the Italian War 1859 and the Prussian War 1866. In 1914 he made the assassination of his nephew, Franz Ferdinand, the excuse for attacking Serbia.

Frasch process a process used to extract underground deposits of sulphur. Superheated steam is piped to the sulphur deposit and melts it. Compressed air is then pumped down to force the molten sulphur to the surface. It was developed in the USA by German-born Herman Frasch 1891.

Fraser Dawn 1937– . Australian sprint swimmer who won three successive gold medals at the Olympic Games (Melbourne 1956, Rome 1960, Tokyo 1964). She set 27 world records.

Fraser (John) Malcolm 1930– . Australian Liberal politician, prime minister 1975–83; nicknamed 'the Prefect' because of a supposed disregard for subordinates.

Fraser Peter 1884–1950. New Zealand Labour politician, born in Scotland. He joined the Independent Labour Party 1908. In 1910 he went to

New Zealand and soon became prominent in the Labour movement there. He held various cabinet posts 1935–40, and was prime minister 1940–49.

fraternity and sorority student societies (fraternity for men; sorority for women) in some US and Canadian universities and colleges. Although mainly social and residential, some are purely honorary, membership being on the basis of scholastic distinction, for example Phi Beta Kappa, earliest of the fraternities, founded at William and Mary College, Virginia 1776.

fraud in English law, an act of deception. To establish fraud it has to be demonstrated that: (1) a false representation (for example, a factually untrue statement) has been made, with the intention that it should be acted upon; (2) the person making the representation knows it is false or does not attempt to find out whether it is true or not; and (3) the person to whom the representation is made acts upon it to their detriment.

Fraunhofer Joseph von 1787–1826. German physicist, who did important work in optics. The dark lines in the solar spectrum (Fraunhofer lines), which revealed the chemical composition of the sun's atmosphere, were accurately mapped by him.

Frazer James George 1854–1941. Scottish anthropologist, and author of *The Golden Bough* 1890, a pioneer study of the origins of religion and sociology on a comparative basis. It exerted considerable influence on writers such as T S Eliot and D H Lawrence, but by the standards of modern anthropology many of its methods and findings are unsound.

Frederick IX 1899–1972. King of Denmark from 1947. He was succeeded by his daughter who became Queen ◊Margrethe II.

Frederick two Holy Roman emperors:

Frederick I *c.* 1123–1190. Holy Roman emperor from 1152, known as *Barbarossa* 'red- beard'. Originally duke of Swabia, he was elected emperor 1152, and was engaged in a struggle with Pope Alexander III 1159–77, which ended in his submission. Frederick joined the Third Crusade, and was drowned in Anatolia.

Frederick II 1194–1250. Holy Roman emperor from his election 1212, called 'the Wonder of the World'. He led a crusade 1228–29 which recovered Jerusalem by treaty without fighting. He quarrelled with the pope, who excommunicated him three times, and a feud began which lasted at intervals until the end of his reign.

Frederick three kings of Prussia, including:

Frederick II *the Great* 1712–1786. King of Prussia from 1740, when he succeeded his father Frederick William I. In that year he started the War of the ◊Austrian Succession by his attack on Austria. In the peace of 1745 he secured Silesia. The struggle was renewed in the ◊Seven Years' War 1756–63. He acquired West Prussia in the first partition of Poland 1772, and left Prussia as Germany's foremost state.

Frederick III 1831–1888. King of Prussia and emperor of Germany 1888. The son of Wilhelm I, he married the eldest daughter (Victoria) of Queen Victoria of the UK 1858, and, as a liberal, frequently opposed Chancellor Bismarck.

Frederick William 1620–1688. elector of Brandenburg from 1640, 'the Great Elector'. By successful wars with Sweden and Poland, he prepared the way for Prussian power in the 18th century.

Frederick William four kings of Prussia:

Frederick William I 1688–1740. King of Prussia from 1713, who developed Prussia's military might and commerce.

Frederick William II 1744–1797. King of Prussia from 1786. He was a nephew of Frederick II, but had little of his relative's military skill. He was unsuccessful in waging war on the French 1792–95, and lost all Prussia W of the Rhine.

Frederick William III 1770–1840. King of Prussia from 1797. He was defeated by Napoleon 1806, but contributed to his final overthrow 1813–15, and profited in territory allotted at the Congress of Vienna.

Frederick William IV 1795–1861. King of Prussia from 1840. He upheld the principle of the ◊divine right of kings, but was forced to grant a constitution 1850 after the Prussian revolution 1848. He suffered two strokes 1857, and became mentally debilitated.

Free Church the Protestant denominations in England and Wales that are not part of the Church of England, for example, the Methodist Church, Baptist Union, and United Reformed Church (Congregational and Presbyterian). These churches joined for common action in the Free Church Federal Council 1940.

Free Church of Scotland the body of Scottish Presbyterians who seceded from the Established Church of Scotland in the Disruption of 1843. In 1900 all but a small section that retains the old name, and is known as the Wee Frees, combined with the United Presbyterian Church to form the United Free Church, which reunited with the Church of Scotland 1929.

freedom of the city (or borough) honour bestowed on distinguished people by a city or borough in the UK and other countries. Historically, those granted freedom of a city (called 'freemen') had the right of participating in the privileges of the city or borough.

Freedom, Presidential Medal of the highest peacetime civilian honour in the USA. Instituted by J F Kennedy 1963, it is awarded to those 'who contribute significantly to the quality of American life'. A list of recipients is published each Independence Day.

free enterprise or *free market* an economic system where private capital is used in business with profits going to private companies and individuals. The term has much the same meaning as ◊capitalism.

free fall a state in which a body is falling freely under the influence of ◊gravity, as in free-fall parachuting. The term *weightless* is normally used to describe a body in free fall in space.

freefalling sport also known as ◊skydiving.

Free French in World War II, movement formed by Gen ◊de Gaulle in the UK Jun 1940, consisting of French soldiers who continued to fight against the Axis after the Franco-German armistice. They took part in campaigns in Africa, the Middle East, Italy, France, and Germany. Their emblem was the Cross of Lorraine, a cross with two bars.

freehold in England and Wales, ownership of land which is for an indefinite period. It is contrasted with a leasehold, which is always for a fixed period. In practical effect, a freehold is absolute ownership.

freeman one who enjoys the freedom of a borough. Since the early Middle Ages, a freeman has been allowed to carry out his craft or trade within the jurisdiction of the borough, and to participate in municipal government, but since the development of modern local government, such privileges have become largely honorary.

Freemasonry the beliefs and practices of a group of linked national organizations open to men over 21, united by the possession of a common code of morals and certain traditional 'secrets'. Modern Freemasonry began in 18th-century Europe. Freemasons do much charitable work, but have been criticized in recent years for their secrecy, their male exclusivity, and particularly their alleged use of influence within and between organizations (for example, the police or local government) to further each others' interests. There are approximately 6 million members.

free port a port where cargo may be accepted for handling, processing, and reshipment without the imposition of tariffs or taxes. Duties and tax become payable only if the products are for consumption in the country to which the free port belongs. Free ports are established to take advantage of a location with good trade links.

freesia genus of South African plants, family Iridaceae, commercially grown for their scented funnel-shaped flowers.

free thought post-Reformation movement opposed to Christian dogma, represented in Britain in the 17th and 18th century by ◊deists, in the 19th century by the radical thinker Richard Carlile (1790–1843), a pioneer of the free press, and the Liberal politicians Charles Bradlaugh and Lord Morley (1838-1923), and in the 20th century by Bertrand Russell.

Freetown capital of Sierra Leone, W Africa; population (1985) 469,000. It has an excellent commercial harbour. Industries include cement, plastics, footwear, and oil refining. Platinum, chromite, diamonds, and gold are traded.

free trade an economic system where governments do not interfere in the movement of goods between states; there are thus no taxes on imports. In the modern economy, free trade tends to hold within economic groups such as the European Community or the Warsaw Pact, but not generally, despite such treaties such as GATT (1948) and subsequent agreements to reduce tariffs. The opposite of free trade is ◊protectionism.

free verse poetry without metrical form. At the beginning of the 20th century, under the very different influences of Whitman and Mallarmé, many poets became convinced that the 19th century had done most of what could be done with regular metrical forms, and rejected regular metre in much the same spirit as Milton had rejected rhyme, preferring irregular metres which made it possible to express thought clearly and without distortion.

free will the doctrine that human beings are free to control their own actions, and that these actions are not fixed in advance by God or fate. Some Christian theologians assert that God gave humanity free will to choose between good and evil; others that God has decided in advance the outcome of all human choices (◊predestination, as in Calvinism).

freezing change from liquid to solid state, as when water becomes ice. For a given substance, freezing occurs at a definite temperature, known as the freezing point, that is invariable under similar conditions of pressure, and the temperature remains at this until all the liquid is frozen. The amount of heat per unit mass that has to be removed to freeze a substance is a constant for any given substance, and is known as the latent heat of fusion.

freezing point depression lowering of a solution's freezing point, below that of the pure solvent, which depends on the number of molecules of solute dissolved in it. Thus for a single solvent, such as pure water, all substances in the same molecular concentration produce the same lowering of freezing point. The depression d for a molar concentration C is given by the equation $d = KC$, where K is a constant for the particular solvent (called the cryoscopic constant). Measurement of freezing point depression is a useful method of determining molecular weights of solutes.

Frege Gottlob 1848–1925. German philosopher. The founder of modern mathematical logic, he published *Die Grundlagen der Arithmetik/The Foundations of Arithmetic* 1884, which was to influence ◊Russell and ◊Wittgenstein.

Frelimo (*F*ront for the *Li*beration of *Mo*zambique) nationalist group aimed at gaining independence for Mozambique from the occupying Portuguese. It began operating out of S Tanzania 1963, and continued until victory 1975.

French Community former association consisting of France and those overseas territories joined with it by the constitution of the Fifth Republic, following the 1958 referendum. Many of the constituent states withdrew during the 1960s, and it no longer formally exists, but in practice all former French colonies have close economic and cultural as well as linguistic links with France.

French Guiana (French *Guyane Française*) overseas department of France from 1976, on the N coast of South America, adjoining Suriname
area 91,000 sq km/35,120 sq mi
capital Cayenne
towns St Laurent
exports timber, shrimps, gold
population (1982) 73,000
language French, Creole, and Amerindian
history first settled by France 1604, the territory became a French possession 1817. A penal colony was established 1852. In 1935, the shipments of convicts from France ceased, and the status of it changed to an overseas department 1946.

French horn musical instrument. See ◊brass.

French India former French possessions in India – Pondicherry, Chandernagore, Karaikal, Mahé, and Yanaon (Yanam) – all transferred to India by 1954.

French language a member of the Romance branch of the Indo-European language family, spoken in France, Belgium, Luxembourg, and Switzerland in Europe, Canada (especially the province of Québec) in North America, and various Caribbean and Pacific Islands as well as certain N and W African countries (for example, Mali and Senegal).

French Polynesia French overseas territory (from 1961) in the S Pacific
total area 3,940 sq km/1,520 sq mi
capital Papeete on Tahiti
exports cultivated pearls, coconut oil, vanilla; tourism is important
population (1983) 166,000
languages Tahitian (official), French
government a High Commissioner and Council of Government; two deputies are returned to the National Assembly in France
recent history first visited by Europeans 1595; French Protectorate 1843; self-governing 1977; following demands for independence in ◊New Caledonia 1984–85, agitation increased also in Polynesia.

French Revolution the period between 1789 and 1795 which saw the end of the monarchy and its

Freud Francis Bacon (1952) Tate Gallery, London.

Freud Austrian psychiatrist and pioneer of psychoanalysis Sigmund Freud.

claim to absolute rule. On 5 May 1789, after the monarchy had attempted to increase taxation and control of affairs, the ◊States General (three 'estates' of nobles, clergy, and commons) met at Versailles to try to establish some constitutional controls. Divisions within the States General led to the formation of a National Assembly by the third (commons) estate 17 Jun. Repressive measures by ◊Louis XVI led to the storming of the Bastille by the Paris mob 14 Jul 1789. See also ◊Paris Commune.

On 20 Jun 1791 the royal family attempted to escape from the control of the Assembly, but Louis XVI was brought back a prisoner from Varennes and forced to accept a new constitution. War with Austria after 20 Apr 1792 threatened to undermine the revolution, but on 10 Aug the mob stormed the royal palace, and on 21 Sep the First French Republic was proclaimed.

On 21 Jan 1793, Louis XVI was executed. The moderate ◊Girondins were overthrown 2 Jun by the ◊Jacobins, and control of the country was passed to the infamous Committee of Public Safety, and ◊Robespierre. The mass executions of the ◊Reign of Terror began 5 Sep, and the excesses led to the overthrow of the Committee and Robespierre 27 Jul 1794 (9 Thermidor under the revolutionary calendar). The Directory was established to hold a middle course between royalism and Jacobinism. It ruled until Napoleon seized power 1799.

French Sudan former name (1898–1959) of ◊Mali, NW Africa.

French West Africa group of French colonies administered from Dakar 1895–1958. They have become the modern Senegal, Mauritania, Sudan, Burkina Faso, Guinea, Niger, Ivory Coast, and Benin.

frequency in physics, the number of cycles of a vibration occurring per unit of time. The unit of frequency is the hertz (Hz); 1 Hz = 1 cycle per second. Human beings can hear sounds from objects vibrating in the range 20 Hz to 15,000 Hz.

fresco mural painting technique using water-based paint on wet plaster. Some of the earliest frescoes (about 1750–1400 bc) were found in Knossos, Crete (now preserved in the Iráklion Museum). Fresco reached its finest expression in Italy from the 13th to the 17th century. Giotto, Masaccio, Michelangelo, and many other artists worked in the medium.

Freud Lucian 1922– . English painter, best known for realist portraits with the subject staring intently from an almost mask-like face, for example *Francis Bacon* 1952 (Tate Gallery, London). He is a grandson of Sigmund Freud.

Freud Sigmund 1865–1939. Austrian psychiatrist, born in Freiberg, Moravia. He developed the method of free association and interpretation of dreams which are still techniques of ◊psychoanalysis.

friar a monk of any order, but originally the title of members of the mendicant (begging) orders, the chief of which were the Franciscans or Minors (Grey Friars), the Dominicans or Preachers (Black Friars), the Carmelites (White Friars), and Augustinians (Austin Friars).

friction in physics, the force which opposes the relative motion of two bodies in contact. The *coefficient of friction* is the ratio of the force required to achieve this relative motion to the force pressing the two bodies together.

Friedan Betty 1921– . US liberal feminist. Her book *The Feminine Mystique* 1963 was one of the most influential books for the women's movement both in the USA and in Britain. She founded the National Organization for Women (NOW) 1966,

Fiedrich Winter landscape (c.1811) National Gallery, London.

the National Women's Political Caucus 1971, the First Women's Bank 1973, and called the First International Feminist Congress 1973.

Friedman Milton 1912– . American economist. The foremost exponent of ◊monetarism, he argues that a country's economy, and hence inflation, can be controlled through its money supply, although most governments lack the 'political will' to control inflation by cutting government spending and thereby increasing unemployment.

Friedrich Caspar David 1774–1840. German landscape painter in the Romantic style, active mainly in Dresden. He imbued his subjects – mountain scenes and moonlit seas – with great poetic melancholy, and was later much admired by Symbolist painters. *The Cross in the Mountains* 1807–08 (Dresden) made his reputation.

Friendly Islands another name for ◊Tonga.

friendly society (in the USA *benefit society*) an association designed to meet the needs of sickness and old age by money payments. There are some 6,500 registered societies in the UK. Among the largest are the National Deposit, Odd Fellows, Foresters, and Hearts of Oak. In the USA there are similar 'fraternal insurance' bodies, including the Modern Woodmen of America 1883 and the Fraternal Order of Eagles 1898.

Friends of the Earth (FoE or FOE) environmental pressure group, established in the UK in 1971, that aims to protect the environment and to promote the rational and sustainable use of the Earth's resources. It campaigns on issues such as acid rain; air, sea, river, and land pollution; recycling; disposal of toxic wastes; nuclear power and renewable energy; the destruction of rain forests; pesticides; and agriculture. FoE has branches in 30 countries.

Friends, Society of Christian Protestant sect popularly known as *Quakers*, founded by George ◊Fox in England in the 17th century. They were persecuted for their nonviolent activism, and many emigrated to form communities abroad, for example in Pennsylvania and New England, USA. They now form a worldwide movement of about 200,000. Their worship stresses meditation and the freedom of all to take an active part in the service (called a meeting, held in a meeting house). They have no priests or ministers.

Friesland N maritime province (capital Leeuwarden) of the Netherlands, which includes the Frisian Islands and land which is still being reclaimed from the former Zuyder Zee; area 3,352 sq km/1,294 sq mi; population (1990) 600,000. Friesian cattle originated here.

frigate warship, the most numerous type of larger surface vessel in the British Royal Navy. They are general-purpose anti-aircraft, anti-submarine escort vessels of up to 3,000 tonnes. Originally a frigate was a small, swift, undecked sailing vessel, used in the Mediterranean. The name was first applied to a type of warship in the 18th century.

Frigg also known as *Frigga* or *Freya*. In Scandinavian mythology, wife of Odin and mother of Thor, goddess of married love and the hearth. Friday is named after her.

fringe benefit in employment, payment in kind over and above wages and salaries. These may include a pension, subsidized lunches, company car, favourable loan facilities, and private health care.

fringe theatre in the UK, a term derived in the 1960s from the activities held on the 'fringe' of the Edinburgh Festival, and now denoting plays which are anti-establishment or experimental, in contrast to mainstream commercial theatre. Less formal and expensive than conventional theatre, fringe events are held in a variety of venues; university theatres, arts centres, converted warehouses or rooms in public houses. Notable 'fringe' writers include Howard ◊Brenton and David ◊Hare. The American equivalent is off-off-Broadway (off-Broadway is mainstream theatre which is not on Broadway).

fringing reef a ◊coral reef which is attached to the coast without an intervening lagoon.

Frink Elisabeth 1930–1993. English sculptor, best known for rugged, naturalistic bronzes, mainly based on animal forms, such as *Horseman* (opposite the Ritz Hotel, London). She was made a Dame of the British Empire 1982.

Frisch Karl von 1886–1982. German zoologist, founder with Konrad Lorenz of ◊ethology, the study of animal behaviour. He specialized in bees, discovering how they communicate the location of sources of nectar by 'dances' (see ◊communication).

Frisch Max 1911– . Swiss dramatist. Influenced by ◊Brecht, his early plays such as *Als der Krieg zu Ende war/When the War is Over* 1949, are more romantic in tone than his later symbolic dramas, such as *Andorra* 1962, which deal with questions of identity. His best-known play is *Biedermann und die brandstifter/The Fire Raisers* 1958, which deals with identity manipulation.

Frisch–Peierls memorandum a document revealing, for the first time, how small the ◊critical mass (the minimum quantity of substance required for a nuclear chain reaction to begin) of uranium needed to be if the isotope uranium-235 was separated from naturally occurring uranium; the memo thus implied the feasibility of using this isotope to make an atomic bomb. It was written by Otto ◊Frisch and Rudolf Peierls (1907–) at the University of Birmingham in 1940.

Frisian a member of a Germanic people of NW Europe. In Roman times they occupied the coast of Holland, and may have taken part in the Anglo-Saxon invasions of Britain. Their language was closely akin to the Anglo-Saxon, with which it formed the Anglo-Frisian branch of the West Germanic languages.

fritillary in entomology, type of butterfly of the family Nymphalidae. There are many species, most with a chequered (Latin *fritillaria*) pattern of black on orange.

fritillary in botany, plant of the genus *Fritillaria*, family Liliaceae. The snake's head fritillary *Fritillaria meleagris* has bell-shaped flowers with purple-chequered markings.

Friuli-Venezia Giulia autonomous agricultural and wine-growing region of NE Italy, bordered on the east by Slovenia; area 7,844 sq km/3,030 sq mi; population (1990) 1,201,000. It includes Gorizia, Pordenone, Trieste, and Udine.

Froebel Friedrich August Wilhelm 1782–1852. German educationist. He evolved a new system of education using instructive play, described in *Education of Man* 1826, and other works. In 1836 he founded the first kindergarten ('garden for children') in Blankenburg.

frog amphibian of the order Anura (Greek 'tail-less'). They usually have squat bodies, hind legs specialized for jumping, and webbed feet for swimming. Many frogs and ◊toads use their long, extensible tongues to capture insects. Frogs vary in size from the *Sminthillus limbatus*, 12 mm/0.5 in long, to the

frog

Wallace's
flying frog

giant frog *Telmatobius culeus* of Lake Titicaca,
50 cm/20 in.

frog-hopper type of leaping plant-bug, family
Cercopidae, which sucks the juice from plants.
The larvae are pale green, and protect themselves
(from drying out and from predators) by secreting
froth ('cuckoo-spit') from their anus.

frogmouth nocturnal bird, related to the nightjar, of
which the commonest species, *Podargus strigoides*,
is found throughout Australia, including Tasmania.
Well-camouflaged, it sits and awaits its prey.

Fromm Erich 1900–1980. German-American
psychoanalyst, driven from Germany in 1933.
His *The Fear of Freedom* 1941 and *The Sane
Society* 1955 were source books for modern alternative lifestyles.

frond a large leaf or leaf-like structure, especially
of ferns where it is often pinnately divided. The
term is also applied to the leaves of palms, and less
commonly to the plant bodies of certain seaweeds,
liverworts and lichens.

front in meteorology, the interface between two
air masses of different temperature or humidity.
Fronts are usually found when warm air from one
region of the Earth's surface meets cold air from
another.

frontier literature writing reflecting the US experience of frontier and pioneer life, long central
to American literature. James Fenimore Cooper's
Leatherstocking Tales, the frontier humour writing
of Artemus Ward, Bret Harte, and Mark Twain,

fruit

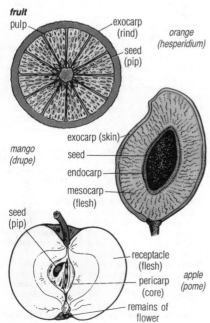

pulp

exocarp
(rind)

*orange
(hesperidium)*

seed
(pip)

exocarp (skin)

*mango
(drupe)*

seed

endocarp

mesocarp
(flesh)

seed
(pip)

receptacle
(flesh)

*apple
(pome)*

pericarp
(core)

remains of
flower

frustum

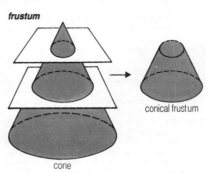

conical frustum

cone

dime novels, westerns, the travel records of Francis
Parkman, and the pioneer romances of Willa Cather
all come into this category, which has affected much
modern American writing.

front-line states the black nations of southern
Africa in the 'front line' of the struggle against the
racist policies of South Africa: namely Mozambique,
Tanzania, and Zambia.

frost condition of the weather when the air temperature is below freezing, 0°C/32°F. Water
in the atmosphere is deposited as ice crystals
on the ground or exposed objects. As cold air
is heavier than warm, *ground frosts* are more
common than *hoar frost*, which is formed by the
condensation of water particles in the same way as
◊dew collects.

Frost Robert (Lee) 1874–1963. US poet whose
verse, in traditional form, is written with an individual voice and penetrating vision; his best-known
poems include 'Mending Wall' ('Something there is
that does not love a wall'), 'The Road Not Taken',
and 'Stopping by Woods on a Snowy Evening'.

frostbite the freezing of skin or flesh, with formation
of ice crystals leading to tissue damage.

FRS abbreviation for *Fellow of the ◊Royal Society*.

fructose a fruit sugar, $C_6H_{12}O_6$, which occurs in
honey, the nectar of flowers, and many sweet fruits.
It is prepared from glucose on a large scale.

fruit in botany, the structure that develops from the
carpel of a flower, and encloses one or more seeds,
except in cases of ◊parthenocarpy. Its function is
to protect the seeds during their development and
to aid in their dispersal. They are often colourful,
sweet, juicy, and palatable. They provide vitamins
and minerals, but little protein, and are often regarded as a semi-luxury. Most fruits are borne by
perennial plants.

frustule the cell wall of a ◊diatom. Frustules are
intricately patterned on the surface with spots,
ridges, and furrows, each pattern being characteristic of a particular species.

fuchsia

frog

The life cycle of frogs, and of their close relatives, the toads, comprises several distinct stages. The young, or larvae, look unlike the adults and are said to undergo a complete metamorphosis "change of form". The adult common frog mates in water. From the fertilized eggs emerge the larvae, which at first breathe solely with gills and have no legs. As they grow, they become more adult-like and eventually are able to live and breathe on land.

Adult frogs breathe using their lungs, through the moist skin, and through the lining of their mouths. They feed on worms, beetles, and flies. The aquatic tadpoles at first feed on weeds and algae, but then change to a meat diet.

Parental care in some species of frogs and toads involves carrying the eggs or tadpoles (larvae) on the back. 1. Male stream frog with tadpoles. 2. Female Surinam toad with young. 3. Male midwife toad carrying eggs.

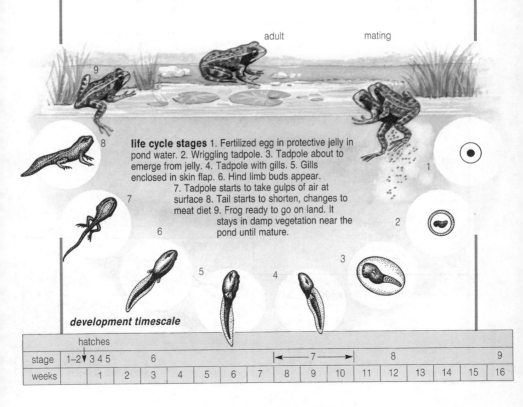

adult   mating

life cycle stages 1. Fertilized egg in protective jelly in pond water. 2. Wriggling tadpole. 3. Tadpole about to emerge from jelly. 4. Tadpole with gills. 5. Gills enclosed in skin flap. 6. Hind limb buds appear. 7. Tadpole starts to take gulps of air at surface 8. Tail starts to shorten, changes to meat diet 9. Frog ready to go on land. It stays in damp vegetation near the pond until mature.

development timescale

stage	1–2	3 4 5	6						←— 7 —→			8				9
weeks		1	2	3	4	5	6	7	8	9	10	11	12	13	14	15	16

hatches

front

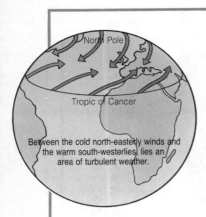

North Pole

Tropic of Cancer

Between the cold north-easterly winds and the warm south-westerlies, lies an area of turbulent weather.

The weather in North America and northern Europe is highly variable because both areas lie along the boundary between the cold air mass of the Arctic and the warm air mass at the Tropic of Cancer. Due to the rotation of the Earth, the polar winds blow from the north east and the tropical winds blow from the south west. Where they meet they spiral around one another, producing complex weather systems.

development of a frontal system

warm front

cold front

A

B

C

warm air rises to form occluded front

system starts again

A. As cold and hot air masses meet and begin to slide past one another, friction develops along the boundary line and their movement is slowed.

B. Eddies form, and the warm air rises upwards, sliding over the cold air mass. At the same time the cold air moves downwards, forcing its way under the warm air mass.

C. The moving boundary between the air masses is called a front. A warm front brings warm air into cool areas, while a cold front moves cold air into warm areas. Cold fronts eventually catch up with warm fronts to form occluded fronts, and the sequence starts all over again.

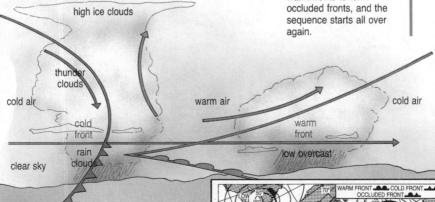

high ice clouds

thunder clouds

cold air

cold front

clear sky

rain clouds

warm air

warm front

cold air

low overcast

Different cloud and rain patterns occur along the moving fronts of hot and cold air masses.

On weather maps, cold and warm fronts are marked by different symbols.

The changeable weather patterns of northern Europe result from a succession of fronts.

WARM FRONT COLD FRONT
OCCLUDED FRONT

frustum in geometry, a 'slice' taken out of a solid figure by a pair of parallel planes. A conical frustum, for example, resembles a cone with the top cut off. The volume and area of a frustum are calculated by subtracting the volume or area of the 'missing' piece from those of the whole figure.

Fry Christopher 1907– . English dramatist. He was a leader of the revival of verse drama after World War II, notably *The Lady's Not for Burning* 1948, *Venus Observed* 1950, and *A Sleep of Prisoners* 1951. He has also written screen plays and made successful translations of Anouilh and Giraudoux.

Fry Elizabeth (born Gurney) 1780–1845. British Quaker philanthropist. She formed an association for the improvement of female prisoners in 1817, and worked with her brother, Joseph Gurney (1788–1847), on an influential report 1819 on prison reform.

Fry Roger Eliot 1866–1934. English artist and art critic, a champion of Post-Impressionism and a great admirer of Cézanne. He founded the Omega Workshops to improve design and to encourage young artists working in modern styles.

f-stop in photography, one of a series of numbers on the lens barrel designating the size of the variable aperture; it stands for focal length, and follows an internationally agreed scale.

FT Index abbreviation for ◊Financial Times Index, a list of leading share prices.

Fuad two kings of Egypt:

Fuad I 1868–1936. King of Eqypt. Son of the Khedive Ismail, he succeeded his elder brother, Hussein Kiamil, as sultan of Egypt in 1917, and when Egypt was declared independent in 1922 he assumed the title of king.

Fuad II 1952– . Grandson of Fuad I, he was king of Egypt 1952–53 between the abdication of his father ◊Farouk and the establishment of the republic.

Fuchs Klaus (Emil Julius) 1911–1988. German spy, who worked on atom-bomb research in the UK in World War II, and was imprisoned 1950–59 for passing information to the USSR. He resettled in East Germany.

fuchsia exotic plant of the Onagraceae family. Native to South and Central America and New Zealand, the genus contains a number of shrubs, small trees and herbaceous plants. The red, purple, or pink flowers hang downwards, and are bell-shaped.

fuel any source of heat or energy, embracing the entire range of all combustibles and including anything that burns. *Nuclear fuel* is any material which produces atomic energy in a nuclear reactor.

fuel cell cell converting chemical energy directly to electrical energy. It works on the same principle as a battery, but is continually fed with fuel, usually hydrogen. Fuel cells are silent and reliable (no moving parts), but expensive to produce.

fuel injection injecting fuel directly into the cylinders of an internal combustion engine. It is the standard method used in ◊diesel engines, and is now becoming popular for ◊petrol engines. In the diesel engine oil is injected into the hot compressed air at the top of the second piston stroke and explodes to drive the piston down on its power stroke. In the petrol engine petrol is injected into the cylinder at the start of the first induction stroke of the ◊four-stroke cycle. Such engines need no carburettor.

Fuentes Carlos 1928– . Mexican novelist, whose first novel *La región más transparente/Where the Air is Clear* 1958 encompasses the history of the country from the Aztecs to the present day.

fugue (Latin 'flight') in music, a complicated contrapuntal form (with two or more melodies) for a number of parts or 'voices' which enter successively in imitation of each other. It was used, for example, by J S Bach.

Führer, or Fuehrer German for 'leader'; the name adopted by Adolf ◊Hitler as leader of the National Socialist German Workers' (Nazi) Party.

Fujairah or *Fujayrah* one of the seven constituent member states of the ◊United Arab Emirates; area 1,150 sq km/450 sq mi; population (1980) 32,200.

Fujiyama or *Mount Fuji* Japanese volcano and highest peak, on Honshu Island; height 3,778 m/12,390 ft.

Fukuoka Japanese industrial town and port on the NW coast of Kyushu island; population (1980) 1,010,000. It produces chemicals, textiles, paper, and metal goods. It was formerly Najime.

Fulani person of Fulani culture from the southern Sahara and Sahel. Traditionally pastoralists and traders, Fulani groups are found in Senegal, Guinea, Mali, Burkina Faso, Niger, Nigeria, Chad, and Cameroon. The Fulani language is divided into four dialects, and belongs to the West Atlantic branch of the Niger-Congo family.

Fulbright William 1905– . US Democratic politician. He was responsible for the *Fulbright Act* 1946 which provided grants for thousands of Americans to study overseas and overseas students to enter the USA; he had studied at Oxford, UK, on a Rhodes scholarship.

full employment in economics, a state in which the only unemployment is frictional (that share of the labour force which is in the process of looking for, or changing to, a new job), and when everyone wishing to work is able to find employment.

Fuller (Richard) Buckminster 1895–1983. US architect and engineer. He invented the lightweight geodesic dome, a half-sphere of triangular components independent of buttress or vault.

fuller's earth a soft, greenish-grey rock resembling clay, but without clay's plasticity. It is formed largely of clay minerals, particularly montmorillonite, but a great deal of silica is also present.

full stop in punctuation another name for ◊period; it is also called full point.

fulmar several species of petrels of the family Procellariidae, which are similar in size and colour to the common gull. The northern fulmar (*Fulmarus glacialis*) is found in the N Atlantic and visits land only to nest, laying a single egg.

Fulton Robert 1765–1815. US engineer and inventor, who designed the first successful steamships. The first steam vessel of note, the *Clermont*, appeared on the Hudson in 1807, sailing between New York and Albany. The first steam warship was the *Fulton*, of 38 tonnes, built in 1814–15.

fumitory plant, genus *Fumeria*, family Fumariaceae, native to Europe and Asia. The common fumitory *F. officinalis* produces pink flowers tipped with blackish-red.

function in computing, those statements in a programming language that generate one value from another. *Function code* is a computer instruction in two parts: its function or operation code states what is to be done (add, subtract, and so on); the second part indicates on what (numbers, addresses). A *function key* on a keyboard performs a specific task when depressed: clear the screen, for example, or shift to lower-case letters.

function in mathematics, a function *f* is a set of ordered pairs ($x,f(x)$) of which no two can have

fungus

Fungi grow from spores as fine threads, or hyphae. These have no distinct cellular structure. Mushrooms and toadstools are the fruiting bodies formed by hyphae. Gills beneath the cap of these aerial structures produce masses of spores.

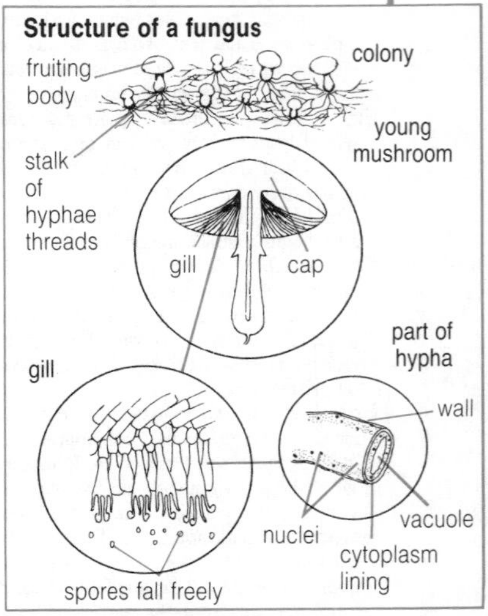

Structure of a fungus

Labels: fruiting body; colony; young mushroom; stalk of hyphae threads; gill; cap; gill; spores fall freely; part of hypha; wall; nuclei; vacuole; cytoplasm; lining

Common British fungi (and habitat)

1. Parasol mushroom (wood) 2. Oyster fungus (birch trees) 3. Deceiver (damp woods) 4. Beefsteak fungus (deciduous trees) 5. Jew's ear fungus (elder trees) 6. Honey fungus (beneath trees) 7. Wood blewitt (woods) 8. Field mushroom (meadows) 9. Cep fungus (woods) 10. Shaggy ink cap (rich soil) 11. Common puffball (woods) 12. Fairy rings (heaths) 13. Bracket fungus (oak, beech trunks) 14. Sickener (woods) 15. Stinkhorn (rich soil, woods) 16. Blusher (woods) 17. Tinder (birch trunks) 18. Razor strop (birch trunks) 19. Fly agaric (woods) 20. Death cap (deciduous woods) 21. Devil's boletus (chalkland) 22. Yellow-staining mushroom (meadows) 23. Panther cap (deciduous woods) 24. Destroying angel (woods) 25. Red-staining mushroom (woods)

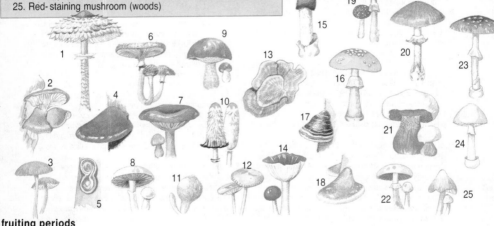

fruiting periods and edibility

	1	2	3	4	5	6	7	8	9	10	11	12	13	14	15	16	17	18	19	20	21	22	23	24	25
J		•	•		•								•				•	•							
F					•												•	•							
M					•												•	•							
A					•												•	•							
M					•											•	•	•							•
J					•					•				•	•	•	•	•							•
J	•		•	•	•	•				•	•	•	•	•	•	•	•	•		•					•
A	•		•	•	•	•	•		•		•	•	•	•	•	•	•	•	•	•	•	•	•	•	•
S	•	•	•	•	•	•	•		•		•	•	•	•	•	•	•	•	•	•	•	•	•	•	•
O	•	•	•	•	•	•	•		•		•	•	•	•	•	•	•	•	•	•	•	•	•	•	•
N		•	•	•	•						•	•	•	•	•	•	•	•	•						
D		•	•		•						•		•				•	•							

Column heading spans: edible (1–12) · inedible (13–18) · poisonous (19–25)

(left axis label: months)

the same first element. Hence, if $f(x) = x^2$, two ordered pairs are $(-2,4)$ and $(2,4)$. In the algebraic expression $y = 4x^3 + 2$, the dependent variable y is a function of the independent variable x, generally written as $f(x)$.

functionalism in the social sciences, the view of society as a system made up of a number of interrelated parts, all functioning on the basis of a common value system or consensus about basic values and common goals. Every social custom and institution is seen as having a function in ensuring that society works efficiently; deviance and crime are seen as a form of social sickness.

Functionalism in architecture and design, a 20th-century school, also called Modernism and International Style, characterized by a desire to exclude everything that serves no practical purpose. It was a reaction against the 19th century practice of imitating earlier styles, and its finest achievements are in the realm of industrial building.

fundamentalism in religion, an emphasis on basic principles or articles of faith. *Christian fundamentalism* emerged in the USA just after World War I and insists on belief in the literal truth of everything in the Bible; *Islamic fundamentalism* insists on strict observance of Muslim Shari'a law.

fungicide a chemical used to treat fungus diseases in plants and animals. Inorganic and organic compounds containing sulphur are widely used.

fungus (plural *fungi*) one of the group of organisms formerly included within the division Thallophyta, along with algae and bacteria, but now placed in the kingdom Fungi, separate from green plants. Fungi lack leaves and roots; they contain no chlorophyll, and reproduce by spores. Moulds, yeasts and mushrooms are all types of fungus.

funicular railway a railway with two cars connected by a wire cable wound around a drum at the top of a steep incline. In Britain, the system is used only in seaside cliff railways, but longer funicular railways of up to 1.5 km/1 mi exist in Switzerland.

funk a style of dance music of black American origin, relying on heavy percussion in polyrhythmic patterns. Leading exponents include James Brown (1928–) and George Clinton (1940–).

Furies in Greek mythology, the Erinyes, appeasingly called the Eumenides, ('kindly ones'). They were the daughters of Earth or of Night, represented as winged maidens, with serpents twisted in their hair. They punished such crimes as filial disobedience, murder, and inhospitality.

furlong unit of measurement, originating in Anglo-Saxon England, equivalent to 201 m/220 yd.

furnace a structure in which fuel such as coal, coke, gas, or oil is burned to produce heat for various purposes. Furnaces are used in conjunction with ◊boilers to produce hot water, for heating, and steam for driving turbines – in ships for propulsion and in power stations for generating electricity. The largest furnaces are those used for smelting and refining metals, such as the ◊blast furnace, electric furnace and ◊open-hearth furnace.

further education college college in the UK for students over school-leaving age which provides courses of a vocational or pre-vocational nature and general education at a level below that of a degree course.

Furtwängler (Gustav Heinrich Ernst Martin) Wilhelm 1886–1954. German conductor with the Berlin Philharmonic Orchestra 1922–54. His interpretations of the German romantic composers, especially Wagner, were regarded as classically definitive.

fuse in ◊explosives, a fuse is a cord impregnated with chemicals so that it burns slowly at a predetermined rate. It is used to set off a main explosive charge, sufficient length of fuse being left to allow the person lighting it to get away to safety. In electricity, *fuse wire* is wire designed to melt when excessive current passes through. It is a safety device to prevent surges of current that could damage equipment and cause fires.

fusel oil a liquid with a characteristic unpleasant smell, obtained as a by-product of the distillation of the product of any alcoholic fermentation, and used in paints, varnishes, essential oils, and plastics. Fusel oil is a mixture of fatty acids, alcohols, and esters.

fusion in physics, the fusing of the nuclei of light elements. Stars and hydrogen bombs work on the principle of nuclear fusion. So far no successful fusion reactor – one able to produce the required energy and contain the reaction – has been built.

future in business, a contract to buy or sell a specific quantity of a particular commodity or currency (or even a purely notional sum, such as the value of a particular stock index) at a particular date in the future. There is usually no physical exchange between buyer and seller. It is only the difference between the ground value and the market value which changes hands. The *futures market* trades in financial futures. The first organized futures exchange (rice futures only) was in Japan, 1730.

futures trading buying and selling commodities (usually cereals and metals) at an agreed price for delivery several months ahead.

Futurism a literary and artistic movement, 1909–14, originating in Paris. The Italian poet ◊Marinetti published the *Futurist Manifesto* in 1909 urging Italian artists to join him in Futurism. They eulogized the modern world and the 'beauty of speed and energy' in their works, trying to capture the dynamism of a speeding motor car or train by combining the shifting geometric planes of ◊Cubism with vibrant colours. As a movement it died out during World War I, but Futurists' exultation in war and violence was seen as an early manifestation of ◊fascism.

Fuzhou industrial port and capital of Fujian province, SE China; population (1984) 1,164,800. It is a centre for shipbuilding and steel production, and rice, sugar, tea, and fruit pass through the port. There are joint foreign and Chinese factories.

Fylingdales site in the North Yorkshire Moors National Park, England, of an early-warning radar station, linked with similar stations in Greenland and Alaska, to give a four-minute warning of nuclear attack.

g abbreviation for *gram*.

gabbro a basic (low-silica) ◊igneous rock formed deep in the Earth's crust. It contains pyroxene and calcium-rich feldspar, with smaller amounts of olivine and amphibole. Its coarse crystals of dull minerals give it a speckled appearance.

Gable Clark 1901–1960. US actor. He was a star for more than 30 years in 90 films, such as *It Happened One Night* 1934, *Gone with the Wind* 1939, and *The Misfits* 1961. He was nicknamed the 'King' of Hollywood.

Gabo Naum. Adopted name of Naum Neemia Pevsner 1890–1977. Russian abstract sculptor. One of the leading exponents of **Constructivism**, he taught at the Bauhaus in Berlin (a key centre of modern design). He often used transparent coloured plastics in his sculptures.

Gabon country in central Africa, bounded N by Cameroon, E and S by the Congo, W by the Atlantic Ocean, and NW by Equatorial Guinea.

Gaborone capital of Botswana from 1965, mainly an administrative centre; population (1990) 341,100. Light industry includes textiles.

Gabriel in the New Testament, the archangel who foretold the birth of John the Baptist to Zacharias and of Christ to the Virgin Mary. He is also mentioned in the Old Testament in the book of Daniel. In Muslim belief, Gabriel revealed the Koran to Muhammad and escorted him on his ◊Night Journey.

Gaddafi alternative form of ◊Khaddhafi, Libyan leader.

Gaddi family of Italian painters in Florence: *Gaddo Gaddi* (*c.* 1250–*c.*1330); his son *Taddeo Gaddi* (*c.* 1300–*c.* 1366), who painted the fresco cycle *Life of the Virgin* in Santa Croce, Florence; and grandson *Agnolo Gaddi* (active 1369–96), who also painted frescoes in Santa Croce, *The Story of the Cross* 1380s, and produced panel paintings in characteristic pale pastel colours.

gadolinium an element, symbol Gd, atomic number 64, relative atomic mass 157.25. It is a silvery-white metal, a member of the lanthanide series. It is found in the products of nuclear fission and used in electronic components, alloys, and products needing to withstand high temperatures.

Gadsden Purchase, The the purchase of approximately 77,720 sq km/30,000 sq mi in what is now New Mexico and Arizona by the USA in 1853. The land was bought from Mexico for $10,000,000 in a treaty negotiated by James Gadsden (1788–1858) of South Carolina in order to construct a transcontinental railroad route, the Southern Pacific, completed in the 1880s.

Gaelic language a member of the Celtic branch of the Indo-European language family, spoken in Ireland, Scotland, and (until 1974) the Isle of Man.

Gagarin Yuri (Alexeyevich) 1934–1968. Soviet cosmonaut, who in 1961 made the first manned space flight, in ◊Vostok 1.

Gaia or *Ge* in Greek mythology, the goddess of the Earth. She sprang from primordial Chaos and herself produced Uranus, by whom she was the mother of the Cyclopes and Titans.

Gaia hypothesis theory that the Earth's systems are regulated and kept adapted for life by living organisms themselves. Since life and environment are so closely linked, there is a need for humans

---

Gabon
Gabonese republic
(*République Gabonaise*)

Equatorial Guinea
São Tomé and Príncipe
Libreville
ATLANTIC OCEAN
GABON
Cameroon
Zaire
Congo
0 miles 500
0 km 1000

area 266,700 sq km/103,000 sq mi
capital Libreville
physical virtually the whole country is tropical rainforest; Ogooué River flows S–W

head of state and government Omar Bongo from 1967
political system emergent democracy
exports petroleum, manganese, iron, uranium
currency CFA franc
population (1988) 1,226,000; annual growth rate 1.6%
life expectancy men 47, women 51
language French (official), Bantu
religion Christian 96%, animist 3%, Muslim 1%
literacy 70% male/53% female (1985 est)
GDP $3.5 bn (1987); $3,308 per head
chronology
1960 Independence from France achieved. Léon M'ba became the first president.
1967 M'ba died and was succeeded by his protégé, Albert-Bernard Bongo.
1968 One-party state established.
1973 Bongo converted to Islam and changed his first name to Omar.
1989 Coup attempt against Bongo defeated.
1990 Bongo's Gabonese Democratic Party (PDG) won multiparty elections amid allegations of ballot-rigging.

Gainsborough Mrs Siddons *(1785) National Gallery, London.*

to maintain their environment and the living things around them; the theory was elaborated by James Lovelock in the 1970s.

Gainsborough Thomas 1727–1788. English landscape and portrait painter, one of the first British artists to follow the Dutch in painting realistic landscapes rather than imaginative Italianate scenery. *The Blue Boy* (San Marino) dates from his Bath period.

Gaitskell Hugh Todd Naylor 1906–1963. British Labour politician. In 1950 he became minister of economic affairs, and then chancellor of the Exchequer until Oct 1951. In 1955 he became party leader, and tried to reconcile internal differences on nationalization and disarmament.

Galatia ancient province of Asia Minor occupying part of the inland plateau; it was occupied in the 3rd century BC by the ◊Gauls, and was a Roman province from 25 BC.

galaxy a congregation of millions or billions of stars, held together by gravity. *Spiral galaxies*, such as the ◊Milky Way, are flattened in shape, with a central bulge of old stars surrounded by a disc of younger stars, arranged in spiral arms like a catherine wheel. *Barred spirals* are spiral galaxies that have a straight bar of stars across their centre, from the ends of which the spiral arms emerge. The arms of spiral galaxies contain gas and dust from which new stars are still forming. *Elliptical galaxies* contain old stars and very little gas. They include the most massive galaxies known, containing a trillion stars. There are also irregular galaxies. Most galaxies occur in clusters, containing anything from a few to thousands of members.

Galbraith John Kenneth 1908– . Canadian economist of the Keynesian school. His major works include *The Affluent Society* 1958 and *Economics and the Public Purpose* 1974. In the former he argued that advanced industrialized societies like the USA were suffering from private affluence accompanied by public squalor.

Galen *c.* 130–*c.* 200. Greek physician whose thinking dominated Western medicine for almost 1,500 years. He remained the highest medical authority until Andreas Vesalius and William Harvey exposed

the fundamental errors of his system. Central to his thinking were the theory of ◊humours and the threefold circulation of the blood.

galena chief ore of lead, consisting of lead sulphide, PbS. It may contain up to 1% silver, and so the ore is sometimes mined for both metals.

Galicia mountainous but fertile autonomous region of NW Spain, formerly an independent kingdom; area 29,434 sq km/11,362 sq mi. Industries include fishing and the mining of tungsten and tin. The language is similar to Portuguese.

Galilee region of N Israel (once a Roman province) which includes Nazareth and Tiberias, frequently mentioned in the Gospels of the New Testament.

Galilee, Sea of alternative name for Lake Tiberias in N Israel, into which the Jordan flows. It is 210 m/689 ft below sea level, and has an area of 165 sq km/64 sq mi.

Galileo (Galileo Galilei) 1564–1642. Italian mathematician, astronomer, and physicist. He developed the astronomical telescope and was the first to see sunspots, the four main satellites of Jupiter, mountains and craters on the Moon, and Venus' appearance going through 'phases', thus proving it was orbiting the Sun. In mechanics, Galileo discovered that freely falling bodies, heavy or light, had the same, constant acceleration (though the story of his dropping cannonballs from the Leaning Tower of Pisa is probably apocryphal), and that a body moving on a perfectly smooth horizontal surface would neither speed up nor slow down.

gall abnormal outgrowth on a plant which develops as a result of attack by insects or, less commonly, by bacteria, fungi, mites, or nematodes. The attack causes an increase in the number of cells, or an enlargement of existing cells in the plant.

gall bladder a small muscular sac attached to the underside of the liver and connected to the small intestine by the bile duct. It stores ◊bile from the liver.

galley ship powered by oars, and usually also with sails. Galleys typically had a crew of hundreds of oarsmen arranged in rows; they were used in warfare from antiquity until the 18th century. Louis XIV of France maintained a fleet of some 40 galleys, crewed by over 10,000 convicts, until 1748.

Gallipoli port in European Turkey, giving its name to the peninsula (ancient name *Chersonesus*) on which it stands. In World War I under British general Ian Hamilton there was an unsuccessful

Galileo The Italian mathematician, astronomer, and physicist, Galileo Galilei.

Gallipoli Men of the British Royal Naval Division and Australian troops sharing a trench. One man is using a periscope (left) and another a 'sniperscope'.

and costly attempt Feb 1915–Jan 1916 by Allied troops to force their way through the Dardanelles and link up with Russia. The campaign was fought mainly by Australian and New Zealand (◊ANZAC) forces, who suffered heavy losses.

gallium an element, symbol Ga, atomic number 31, relative atomic mass 69.75. It is a very scarce, grey metal which is liquid at room temperature. Gallium arsenide crystals are used in microelectronics, since electrons travel a thousand times faster through them than through silicon.

gallon imperial liquid or dry measure, equal to 4.546 litres, and subdivided into 4 quarts or 8 pints. The US gallon is equivalent to 3.785 litres.

gallstone a pebble-like, insoluble accretion formed in the human gall bladder from salts and other

Galtieri President Leopoldo Galtieri of Argentina in 1982.

substances present in the bile. Gallstones may be symptomless or they may cause pain, indigestion, or jaundice. If troublesome, they are removed, along with the gall bladder.

Gallup George Horace 1901–1984. US journalist and statistician, founder in 1935 of the American Institute of Public Opinion and deviser of the *Gallup Polls*, in which public opinion is gauged by questioning a number of representative individuals.

Galsworthy John 1867–1933. British novelist and dramatist, whose work examines the social issues of the Victorian period. He is best known for the series of novels in *The Forsyte Saga* 1922, and its sequel *A Modern Comedy* 1929.

Galtieri Leopoldo (Fortunato) 1926– . Argentinian general. Leading member of the right-wing military junta 1979–82 which ordered the seizure 1982 of the Falkland Islands (Malvinas). He and his fellow junta members were tried for abuse of human rights, and court-martialled for their conduct of the war; he was sentenced to 12 years in prison in 1986.

Galton Francis 1822–1911. English scientist, noted for his study of the inheritance of physical and mental attributes in humans which he called ◊eugenics.

galvanizing process for rendering iron rust-proof, by plunging it into molten zinc (the dipping method), or by electroplating it with zinc.

Gambia
Republic of The

Mauritania
Senegal
THE GAMBIA
Banjul
Guinea-Bissau
ATLANTIC
OCEAN
0 miles 500
0 km 1000

area 10,689 sq km/4,126 sq mi
capital Banjul
physical banks of the river Gambia

head of state and government Dawda Jawara from 1970
political system liberal democracy
exports groundnuts, palm oil, fish
currency dalasi
population (1990 est) 820,000; annual growth rate 1.9%
life expectancy 42 (1988 est)
language English (official) and African languages
religion Muslim 90%, with animist and Christian minorities
literacy 36% male/15% female (1985 est)
GDP $189 million (1987); $236 per head
chronology
1965 Achieved independence from Britain with Dawda K Jawara as prime minister.
1970 Gambia declared itself a republic.
1972 Jawara re-elected.
1981 Attempted coup foiled with the help of Senegal.
1982 Formed with Senegal the Confederation of Senegambia. Jawara re-elected.
1987 Jawara re-elected.
1989 Confederation of Senegambia dissolved.
1990 Gambian troops contributed to the stabilizing force in Liberia.

Gandhi Indira Gandhi, Nehru's daughter, twice prime minister of India.

Gandhi Mahatma ('Great Soul') Gandhi with his granddaughters.

galvanometer instrument for detecting small electric currents by their magnetic effect.

Galway county on the W coast of the Republic of Ireland, in the province of Connacht; area 5,939 sq km/2,293 sq mi; population (1991) 180,300.

Gama Vasco da 1460–1524. Portuguese navigator who commanded an expedition 1497 to discover the route to India round the Cape of Good Hope. He reached land on Christmas Day 1497, and named it Natal. He then crossed the Indian Ocean, and arrived at Calicut May 1498, returning to Portugal Sep 1499.

Gambetta Léon Michel 1838–1882. French politician, organizer of resistance during the Franco-Prussian War, and founder in 1871 of the Third Republic. In 1881–82 he was prime minister for a few weeks.

Gambia, The country in W Africa, surrounded to the N, E, and S by Senegal, and bordered to the W by the Atlantic Ocean.

gamelan orchestra a type of Indonesian orchestra, mainly using tuned metal percussion instruments, the music of which has influenced Western composers, such as Philip Glass.

gamete a cell which functions in sexual reproduction by merging with another gamete to form a ◊zygote. Examples of gametes include sperm and ova cells. In most organisms, the gametes are ◊haploid (they contain half the number of chromosomes of the parent), due to reduction division or ◊meiosis.

gametophyte the haploid generation in the life cycle of a plant that produces gametes; see ◊alternation of generations.

gamma radiation very high-frequency ◊electromagnetic radiation emitted by the nuclei of radioactive substances during decay. It is used to kill bacteria and other microorganisms, sterilize medical devices, and change the molecular structure of plastics to modify their properties (for example, to improve heat and abrasion resistance for insulation purposes).

Gandhi Indira 1917–1984. Indian politician. Prime minister of India 1966–77 and 1980–84, and leader of the ◊Congress Party 1966–77 and subsequently of the Congress (I) Party. She was assassinated by members of her Sikh bodyguard, resentful of her use of troops to clear malcontents from the Sikh temple at ◊Amritsar.

Gandhi Mohandas Karamchand, called *Mahatma* ('Great Soul') 1869–1948. Indian nationalist leader. A pacifist, he led the struggle for Indian independence from the UK by nonviolent noncooperation (*satyagraha*, defence of and by truth) from 1915. He

was several times imprisoned by the British authorities, and was influential in the nationalist ◊Congress Party and in the independence negotiations 1947. He was assassinated by a Hindu nationalist in the violence which followed Partition.

Gandhi Rajiv 1944–1991. Indian politician, prime minister from 1984 (following his mother Indira Gandhi's assassination) to 1989. As prime minister, he faced growing discontent with his party's elitism and lack of concern for social issues. He was assassinated by a bomb at an election rally.

Ganesa Hindu god, son of Siva and Parvati; he is represent as elephant-headed, and worshipped as a remover of obstacles.

Ganges (Hindi *Ganga*) major river of India and Bangladesh; length 2,506 km/1,557 mi. It is the most sacred river for ◊Hindus.

ganglion (*ganglia* plural) small, solid mass of nervous tissue containing many cell bodies and ◊synapses, usually enclosed in a tissue sheath; found in invertebrates and vertebrates.

Gang of Four the chief members of the radical faction that tried to seize power in China after the death of Mao Zedong 1976. It included his widow, ◊Jiang Quing; the other members were Zhang Chunjao, Wang Hungwen, and Yao Wenyuan. The coup failed, and they were soon arrested. In the UK the name was applied to the four members of the Labour Party who in 1981 resigned to form the Social Democratic Party (SDP): Roy Jenkins, David Owen, Shirley Williams, and William Rodgers.

Gandhi Indian prime minister Rajiv Gandhi in 1984.

Garbo The Swedish-born actress Greta Garbo in Anna Christie, *her first 'talkie' 1930.*

gangrene death and decay of body tissue due to bacterial action; the affected part gradually turns black.

gannet or *solan goose* a sea-bird *Sula bassana* in the family Sulidae, found in the N Atlantic. When fully grown, it is white with black-tipped wings having a span of 1.7 m/5.6 ft. The young are speckled. It breeds on cliffs in nests made of grass and seaweed. Only one (white) egg is laid.

Gansu province (formerly Kansu) of NW China
area 530,000 sq km/204,633 sq mi
capital Lanzhou
products coal, oil, hydroelectric power from the Huang He (Yellow) River
population (1990) 22,371,000, including many Muslims.

Ganymede in Greek mythology, a youth so beautiful he was chosen as cupbearer to Zeus.

Ganymede in astronomy, the largest moon of the planet Jupiter, and the largest moon in the Solar System, 5,300 km/3,300 mi in diameter (larger than the planet Mercury). It orbits Jupiter every 7.2 days at a distance of 1.1 million km/700,000 mi. Its surface is a mixture of cratered and grooved terrain.

Garbo Greta. Stage-name of Greta Lovisa Gustafsson 1905–1990. Swedish actress. She went to the USA in 1925, and her leading role in *The Torrent* 1926 made her one of Hollywood's first 'stars'. Her later films include *Queen Christina* 1933, *Anna Karenina* 1935, and *Ninotchka* 1939.

García Lorca Federico see ◊Lorca, Federico García.

García Márquez Gabriel 1928– . Colombian novelist, whose *Cien años de soledad/One Hundred Years of Solitude* 1967, the story of six generations of a family, is an example of magic realism, a technique for heightening the intensity of realistic portrayal of social and political issues by introducing grotesque or fanciful material. Nobel Prize for Literature 1982.

garden city in the UK, a town built in a rural area and designed to combine town and country advantages, with its own industries, controlled developments, private and public gardens, and cultural centre. The idea was proposed by Sir Ebenezer Howard (1850–1928), who in 1899 founded the Garden City Association, which established the first garden city, Letchworth (in Hertfordshire).

gardenia genus of subtropical and tropical trees and shrubs of Africa and Asia, family Rubiaceae, with

Garibaldi Italian hero of the Risorgimento, *Giuseppe Garibaldi.*

evergreen foliage and flattened rosettes of fragrant waxen-looking blooms, often white in colour.

Garfield James A(bram) 1831–1881. 20th president of the USA 1881, a Republican. He was elected president but held office for only four months before being assassinated in a Washington station by a disappointed office-seeker.

garfish type of fish with a long spear-like snout. The *common garfish Belone belone*, order Beloniformes, family Belonidae, has an elongated body 75 cm/2.5 ft long.

gargoyle spout projecting from the roof-gutter of a building with the purpose of directing water away from the wall. The term is usually applied to the ornamental forms found in Gothic architecture; these were carved in stone in the form of fantastic animals, angels, or human heads. They are often found on churches and cathedrals.

Garibaldi Giuseppe 1807–1882. Italian soldier who played an important role in the unification of Italy by conquering Sicily and Naples 1860. From 1834 a member of the nationalist Mazzini's ◊Young Italy society, he was forced into exile until 1848 and again 1849–54. He fought against Austria 1848–49, 1859, and 1866, and led two unsuccessful expeditions to liberate Rome from papal rule in 1862 and 1867.

Garland Judy (stage name of Frances Gumm) 1922–1969. US singer and actress. Her films include *The Wizard of Oz* 1939 (including the song 'Over the Rainbow'), *Meet Me in St Louis* 1944, and *A Star is Born* 1954.

garlic

Garvey *Jamaican-born Marcus Garvey, founder of the 'Back to Africa' movement, at a New York parade 1922.*

garlic perennial plant *Allium sativum*, family Liliaceae, with white flowers. The bulb, made of small segments, or cloves, is used in cookery, and its pungent essence contains allyl methyl trisulphide, which prevents blood clotting.

garnet a group of silicate minerals with the formula $X_3Y_2(SiO_4)_3$, when X is calcium, magnesium, iron, or manganese, and Y is iron, aluminium, chromium, or titanium, used as semiprecious gems (usually pink to deep red) and abrasives.

Garrick David 1717–1779. British actor and theatre manager. From 1747 he became joint patentee of the Drury Lane theatre with his own company, and instituted a number of significant theatrical conventions including concealed stage lighting and banishing spectators from the stage. He was noted for his Shakespearean performances as Richard III, Lear, Hamlet, and Benedick.

Garter, Order of the senior British order of knighthood, founded by Edward III in about 1347. Its distinctive badge is a garter of dark blue velvet, with the motto of the order, *Honi soit qui mal y pense* ('Shame be to him who thinks evil of it').

Garvey Marcus (Moziah) 1887–1940. Jamaican political thinker and activist, an early advocate of black nationalism. He founded the UNIA (Universal Negro Improvement Association) 1914, and moved to the USA 1916, where he established branches in New York and other Northern cities. He led a ***Back to Africa*** movement for black Americans to establish a black-governed country in Africa.

gas a form of matter in which the molecules move randomly in otherwise empty space, filling any size or shape of container into which the gas is put.

Gascoigne Paul, nicknamed 'Gazza' 1967– . English footballer who played for Tottenham Hotspur 1988–91 and for Lazio, Italy from 1992. At the 1989 World Cup semi-final against West Germany, he committed a foul for which he was booked (cautioned by the referee), meaning that he would be unable to play in the final, should England win. His tearful response drew public sympathy, and he was subsequently lionized by the British press.

Gascony ancient province of SW France. With Guienne it formed the duchy of Aquitaine in the 12th century; Henry II of England gained possession of it through his marriage to Eleanor of Aquitaine 1152, and it was often in English hands until 1451. It was ruled by the king of France until it was united with the French royal domain 1607 under Henry IV.

gas-cooled reactor see ◊advanced gas-cooled reactor.

gas engine type of internal combustion engine in which gas (coal gas, producer gas, natural gas, or gas from a blast furnace) is used as the fuel. The first practical gas engine was built 1860 by Jean Etienne Lenoir. It was developed by Nikolaus August Otto, who introduced the ◊four-stroke cycle.

gas exchange in biology, the exchange of gases between living organisms and the atmosphere; a process known in humans as ◊respiration.

gas laws physical laws concerning the behaviour of gases. They include Boyle's law and Charles' law, which are concerned with the relationships between the pressure, temperature, and volume of an ideal (i.e. hypothetical) gas.

gasohol a type of motor fuel that is 90% petrol and 10% ethanol (alcohol). The ethanol is usually obtained by fermentation, followed by distillation, using maize, wheat, potatoes, or sugar cane. It was used in early cars before petrol became cheap, and its use was revived during the energy shortage of the 1970s.

gasoline a mixture of hydrocarbons derived from petroleum, used mainly as a fuel for internal combustion engines. It is colourless and volatile.

Gasperi Alcide de 1881–1954. Italian politician. A founder of the Christian Democrat Party, he was prime minister 1945–53, and worked for European unification.

gastritis inflammation of the lining of the stomach. The term is applied to a range of conditions.

gastroenteritis inflammation of the stomach and intestines, giving rise to abdominal pain, vomiting, and diarrhoea. It may be caused by food or other poisoning, allergy, or infection.

gastro-enterology the medical speciality concerned with diseases of the alimentary tract.

gastropod very large class (Gastropoda) of ◊molluscs. They are single-shelled (in a spiral or modified spiral form), have eyes on stalks, and move on a flattened, muscular foot. Gastropods have well-developed heads and rough tongues. Some are marine, some freshwater, and others land creatures, but all tend to inhabit damp places. They include snails, slugs, limpets, and periwinkles.

gas turbine an engine in which burning fuel supplies hot gas to spin a ◊turbine. The most widespread application of gas turbines has been in aviation. All ◊jet engines are modified gas turbines, and some locomotives and ships also use gas turbines as a power source. They are used in industry for generating and pumping duties.

Gatling Richard Jordan 1818–1903. US inventor of a rapid-fire gun. Patented 1862, the Gatling gun had ten barrels arranged as a cylinder rotated by a hand crank. Cartridges from an overhead hopper or drum dropped into the breech mechanism, which loaded, fired, and extracted them at a rate of 320 rounds per minute.

GATT abbreviation for ◊***General Agreement on Tariffs and Trade***.

gaucho Indian-Spanish cattle herder, formerly working on Argentine and Uruguayan pampas.

Gaudí Antonio 1852–1926. Spanish architect. His spectacular Church of the Holy Family, Barcelona, begun 1883, is still under construction.

Gaudier-Brzeska Henri 1891–1915. French sculptor, active in London from 1911. He studied art in Bristol, Nuremberg, and Munich, and became a member of the English Vorticist movement.

gauge scientific measuring instrument, for example a wire-gauge or pressure-gauge. The term is also applied to the width of a railway or tramway track.

Gauguin Te Rerioa *'The Dream' (1897) Courtauld Collection, London.*

Gauguin Paul 1848–1903. French Post-Impressionist painter. His new style, **Synthetism**, was based on the use of powerful, expressive colours and boldly outlined areas of flat tone. He went to live in Tahiti 1891–93 and 1895–1901 and from 1901 in the Marquesas Islands. Influenced by Symbolism, he chose subjects reflecting his interest in the beliefs of other cultures.

Gaul member of the Celtic-speaking peoples who inhabited France and Belgium in Roman times. They were divided into several groupings, but united by a common religion controlled by the Druid priesthood. Certain Gauls invaded Italy around 400 BC, sacked Rome, and settled between the Alps and the Apennines; this district, Cisalpine Gaul, was conquered by Rome about 225 BC. The Romans conquered S Gaul between the Mediterranean and the Cevennes in about 125 BC and the remaining Gauls up to the Rhine were conquered by Julius ◊Caesar 58–51 BC.

Gaulle Charles de. See Charles ◊de Gaulle.

gaur Asiatic wild ox *Bos gaurus* which is dark greybrown with white 'socks', and 2 m/6 ft tall.

Gautier Théophile 1811–1872. French Romantic poet, whose later work emphasized the perfection of form and the 'polished' beauty of language and imagery (for example, *Emaux et Camées/Enamels and Cameos* 1852).

Gavaskar Sunil Manohar 1949– . Indian cricketer. Between 1971–87 he scored a record 10,122 test runs in a record 125 matches (including 106 consecutive).

Gay John 1685–1732. British poet and dramatist. *The Beggar's Opera* 1728, a 'Newgate pastoral' using traditional songs, was highly popular. Satiric political touches led to the banning of *Polly*, a sequel, until 1777.

Gaye Marvin 1939–1984. US pop singer and songwriter, whose hits, including 'Stubborn Kinda Fellow' 1962, 'I Heard It Through the Grapevine' 1968, and 'What's Going On' 1971 exemplified the Detroit ◊Motown sound.

Gaza Strip strip of Palestine under Israeli administration; capital Gaza; area 260 sq km/100 sq mi; population (1967) 365,000. It remains a volatile area for clashes between the Israeli authorities and the Palestinian people.

gazelle various species of lightly built fast-running antelopes found on the open plains of Africa and S Asia, especially those of the genus *Gazella*.

GCE (General Certificate of Education) in the UK, the public examination formerly taken at the age of 16 at Ordinary Level (O Level) and at 18 at Advanced Level (A Level). The GCE O Level examination, which was aimed at the top 20% of the ability range, was superseded in 1988 by the GCSE).

GCHQ (**Government Communications Headquarters**) the centre of the British government's electronic surveillance operations, in Cheltenham, Gloucestershire. It was established in World War I, and was successful in breaking the German Enigma code in 1940.

GCSE (General Certificate of Secondary Education) in the UK, from 1988, the new examination for 16-year old pupils, superseding both GCE O Level and CSE, and offering qualifications for up to 60% of school leavers in any particular subject.

Gdańsk (German *Danzig*) Polish port; population (1983) 464,600. Oil is refined, and textiles, televisions, and fertilizers are produced. It has become notable in the 1980s for strikes at the Lenin shipyards against the government.

GDP abbreviation for ◊*Gross Domestic Product*.

Geber Latinized form of Jabir ibn Hayyan *c.* 721–*c.* 776. Arabian alchemist. His influence lasted for more than 600 years, and in the late 1300s his name was adopted by a Spanish alchemist whose writings spread the knowledge and practice of alchemy throughout Europe.

gecko small soft-skinned lizard in the family Gekkonidae. It is common in warm climates, and has a large head, and short, stout body. Adhesive

gazelle

toe pads enable it to climb vertically and walk upside down on smooth surfaces in their search for flies, spiders, and other prey. The name is derived from the clicking sound which the animal makes.

Geddes Patrick 1854–1932. British town planner, who established the importance of surveys and research work, and properly planned 'diagnoses before treatment'. His major work is *City Development*, 1904.

Geiger counter device for detecting and/or counting nuclear radiation and particles. It detects the momentary current which passes between ◊electrodes in a suitable gas when a nuclear particle or a radiation pulse causes ionization in the gas. The electrodes are connected to electronic devices which enable the intensity of radiation or the number of particles passing to be measured. It is named after Hans Geiger (1882–1945).

geisha female entertainer (music, singing, dancing, and conversation) in Japanese teahouses and private parties. Geishas survive mainly as a tourist attraction. They are apprenticed from childhood and highly skilled in traditional Japanese arts and graces.

Geissler tube high-voltage ◊discharge tube in which traces of gas ionize and conduct electricity. It was developed in 1858 by the German physicist Heinrich Geissler (1814–1879).

gelatine water-soluble protein prepared from boiled hide and bone, used in cookery to set jellies, and in glues (see ◊adhesive) and photographic emulsions.

Geldof Bob 1954– . Irish fund-raiser and rock singer, leader of the group Boomtown Rats 1975–86. He instigated the charity Band Aid, which made a record in 1984 and organized Live Aid 1985: two simultaneous concerts, one in London and one in Philadelphia, broadcast live worldwide, which raised about £60 million for famine relief, primarily for Ethiopia.

gelignite a type of ◊dynamite.

Gell-Mann Murray 1929– . US physicist. In 1964, he formulated the theory of the ◊quark as the fundamental constituent of all matter, and smallest particle in the Universe.

gecko

Tokay gecko

gem a mineral precious by virtue of its composition, hardness, and rarity, cut and polished for ornamental use, or engraved. Of 120 minerals known to have been used as gemstones, only about 25 are in common use in jewellery; of these, the diamond, emerald, ruby, and sapphire are classified as precious, and the topaz, amethyst, opal, and aquamarine as semiprecious.

Gemayel Amin 1942– . Lebanese politician, a Maronite Christian; president 1982–88. He succeeded his brother, president-elect *Bechir Gemayel* (1947–1982), on his assassination 14 Sept 1982.

Gemeinschaft and Gesellschaft German terms (roughly, 'community' and 'association') coined by Ferdinand Tönnies 1887 to contrast social relationships in traditional rural societies with those in modern industrial societies. He saw *Gemeinschaft* as intimate and positive, and *Gesellschaft* as impersonal and negative.

Gemini prominent constellation of the zodiac, representing the twins Castor and Pollux. Its brightest star is Pollux, an orange giant 36 light years away. Castor is a system of six stars. The Sun passes through Gemini from late Jun to late Jul. Each Dec, the Geminid meteors radiate from Gemini.

Gemini project US space programme (1965–66) in which astronauts practised rendezvous and docking of spacecraft, and working outside their spacecraft, in preparation for the ◊Apollo Moon landings.

gemma (plural *gemmae*) a unit of ◊vegetative reproduction, consisting of a small group of undifferentiated green cells. Gemmae are found in certain mosses and liverworts, forming on the surface of the plant, often in cup-shaped structures, or gemmae cups. Gemmae are dispersed by splashes of rain, and can then develop into new plants. In many species gemmation is more common than reproduction by ◊spores.

gender in grammar, one of the categories into which nouns are divided in many languages, such as masculine, feminine, and neuter (as in Latin, German, and Russian), masculine and feminine (as in French, Italian, and Spanish), or animate and inanimate (as in North American Indian languages).

gene a unit of inherited material, situated on a strand of nucleic acid (◊DNA or ◊RNA). In higher organisms, genes are located on the ◊chromosomes. The term 'gene', coined by the Danish geneticist Wilhelm Johanssen in 1909, refers to the inherited factor that consistently affects a particular character in an individual, for example, the gene for eye colour. Also termed a Mendelian gene, after Gregor ◊Mendel, it may have several variants or ◊alleles, each specifying a particular form of that character,

Geldof Bob Geldof (right) and George Michael (left) at the finale of the Live Aid concert, London 1985.

for example, the alleles for blue or brown eyes. Some alleles show ◊dominance. These mask the effect of other alleles, known as ◊recessive.

gene pool the total sum of ◊alleles (variants of ◊genes) possessed by all the members of a given population or species alive at a particular time.

general senior military officer commanding a body of troops larger than a regiment, the ascending grades being in the UK and USA major general, lieutenant general, and general; in the USA the rank of general of the army is equivalent to the British ◊field marshal.

General Agreement on Tariffs and Trade (GATT) an organization within the United Nations founded 1948 with the aim of encouraging ◊free trade between nations through low tariffs, abolitions of quotas and export credits, and similar measures, outside customs unions and free trade areas. Thus it is opposed to food production subsidies such as the Common Agricultural Policy (CAP) of the European Community.

generator a machine that produces electrical energy from mechanical energy, as opposed to an ◊electric motor, which does the opposite.

Genesis first book of the Old Testament or Hebrew Bible, which includes the stories of the creation of the world, Adam and Eve, and the Flood, and the history of the Jewish patriarchs.

gene-splicing technique, invented 1973 by Stanley Cohen and Herbert Boyer (Stanford University/University of California), for inserting a foreign gene into bacteria in order to generate commercial biological products, for example, synthetic insulin, hepatitis-B vaccine, and interferon. It was patented in the USA 1984.

Genet Jean 1910–1986. French dramatist, novelist, and poet, an exponent of the Theatre of ◊Cruelty. His turbulent life and early years spent in prison are reflected in his drama, and are characterized by ritual, role-play, and illusion in which his characters come to act out their bizarre and violent fantasies. His plays include *Les Bonnes/The Maids* 1947, and *Les Paravents/The Screens* 1961.

gene therapy a proposed medical technique for curing or alleviating inherited diseases or defects. Although not yet a practical possibility, some of the basic techniques are available as a result of intensive research in genetic engineering. It may be useful for diseases such as haemoglobin irregularities, where only a relatively small group of cells – those in the bone marrow, which produce the red blood cells – need to be treated. The possibility of preventing genetic defects being passed on to the next generation, is more remote.

genetic code the way in which instructions for building proteins, the basic structural molecules of living matter, are 'written' in the genetic material DNA. This relationship between the sequence of bases (see ◊base pair), the sub-units in a DNA molecule, and the sequence of ◊amino acids, the sub-units of a protein molecule, is the basis of heredity. The code employs ◊codons of three bases each; it is the same in almost all organisms, except for a few minor differences recently discovered in some bacteria.

genetic diseases disorders caused at least partly by defective genes or chromosomes, of which there are some 3,000, including arthritis, autism, cleft palate, cystic fibrosis and Down's syndrome.

genetic engineering the deliberate manipulation of genetic material by biochemical techniques. It is often achieved by the introduction of new

DNA, usually by means of an infecting virus. This can be for pure research or to breed functionally specific plants or animals. It carries the major risk that new, more harmful bacteria could be produced which, if released from the laboratory, might start an uncontrollable epidemic.

genetic fingerprinting in genetic studies, a technique used to investigate how genes are mixed and matched during cell division. Like skin fingerprinting, it can accurately distinguish humans from one another, with the exception of identical twins.

genetics the study of inheritance and of the units of inheritance (genes). The founder of genetics was Gregor Mendel, whose experiments with plants, such as peas, showed that inheritance takes place by means of discrete 'particles', which later came to be called genes.

Geneva (French *Genève*) Swiss city, capital of Geneva canton, on the shore of Lake Geneva, largest of the central European lakes; population (1983) 370,000. It is a point of convergence of natural routes, and is a cultural and commercial centre. Industries include the manufacture of watches, scientific and optical instruments, foodstuffs, jewellery, and musical boxes.

Geneva Convention an international agreement 1864 regulating the treatment of those wounded in war, and later extended to cover the treatment of prisoners and the sick, and the protection of civilians in wartime. The rules were revised at conventions held 1906, 1929, and 1949, and by the 1977 Additional Protocols.

Geneva Protocol international agreement 1925, designed to prohibit the use of poisonous gases, chemical weapons, and bacteriological methods of warfare. It came into force 1928, but was not ratified by the USA until 1974.

Genghis Khan c.1160–1227. Mongol conqueror, ruler of all Mongol peoples from 1206. He began the conquest of N China 1213, overran the empire of the shah of Khiva 1219–25, and invaded N India, while his lieutenants advanced as far as the Crimea. When he died his empire ranged from the Yellow Sea to the Black Sea.

genitive in the grammar of certain inflected languages, the form of a word used for nouns, pronouns, or adjectives to indicate possession.

Genoa English form of ◊Genova, Italy.

genome the full complement of ◊genes carried by a single set of ◊chromosomes for a given species.

genome project an international programme of experimentation to identify, map and interpret the function of all the genes found in the human body. The total number of genes in the body is estimated at 50,000 to 100,000, and by 1986 more than 1,500 had been mapped. Fixing the position of genes for inherited conditions such as muscular dystrophy or cystic fibrosis raises the eventual possibility of therapy by gene replacement.

genotype the particular set of ◊alleles (variants of genes) possessed by a given organism. The term is usually used in conjunction with ◊phenotype, the product of the genotype and all environmental effects. See also ◊environment-heredity controversy.

Genova city in NW Italy, capital of Liguria; population (1981) 763,000. It is Italy's largest port; industries include oil-refining, chemicals, engineering, and textiles.

Genscher Hans-Dietrich 1927– . West German politician, chairman of the Free Democratic Party (FDP) 1974–85, foreign minister from 1974.

Gentili Alberico 1552–1608. Italian jurist. He practised law in Italy, but having adopted Protestantism was compelled to flee to England, where he lectured on Roman Law in Oxford. His publications, such as *De Jure Belli libri tres/On The Law Of War, Book Three* 1598, made him the first true international law writer and scholar.

Gentlemen-at-arms Honourable Corps of theoretically the main bodyguard of the sovereign; its functions are now ceremonial. Established 1509, the corps is, next to the Yeomen of the Guard, the oldest in the British army; it was reconstituted 1862.

gentry the lesser nobility, particularly in England and Wales. By the later Middle Ages, it included knights, esquires, and gentlemen, and after the 17th century, baronets.

genus group of ◊species with many characteristics in common. Thus, all dog-like species (including dogs, wolves, and jackals) belong to the genus *Canis* (Latin 'dog'). Species of the same genus are thought to be descended from a common ancestor species. Related genera are grouped into ◊families.

geochemistry the science of chemistry as it applies to geology. It deals with the relative and absolute abundances of the chemical ◊elements and their ◊isotopes in the Earth, and also with chemical changes that take place there.

geodesy methods of surveying the Earth for making maps and correlating geological, gravitational, and magnetic measurements. Geodesic surveys, formerly carried out by means of various measuring techniques on the surface, are now commonly made using radio signals and laser beams from orbiting satellites.

Geoffrey of Monmouth *c.* 1100–1154. Welsh writer and chronicler. He wrote *Historia Regum Britanniae/History of the Kings of Britain c.* 1139, which included accounts of the semi-legendary kings Lear, Cymbeline, and Arthur, and *Vita Merlini*, a life of the legendary wizard.

geography the science of Earth's surface; its topography, climate, and physical conditions, and how these factors affect civilization and society. It is usually divided into *physical geography*, dealing with landforms and climates; *biogeography*, dealing with the conditions that affect the distribution of animals and plants; and *human geography*, dealing with the distribution and activities of peoples on Earth.

geological time time scale embracing the history of Earth from its physical origin to the present day. Geological time is divided into eras (Precambrian, Palaeozoic, Mesozoic, Cenozoic), which in turn are divided in periods, epochs, ages, and finally chrons.

geology the science of the Earth, its origin, composition, structure, and history. It is divided into several branches: mineralogy (the minerals of Earth), petrology (rocks), stratigraphy (the deposition of successive beds of sedimentary rocks), palaeontology (fossils), and tectonics (the deformation and movement of the Earth's crust).

geometric progression/sequence/series in mathematics, a sequence of terms (progression) in which each term is a constant multiple (called the common ratio) of the one preceding it. For example, 3, 12, 48, 192, 768, . . . is a geometric sequence with a common ratio 4.

geometry branch of mathematics concerned with the properties of space, usually in terms of plane (two-dimensional) and solid (three-dimensional) figures. The subject is usually divided into *pure* geometry, which embraces roughly the plane and solid geometry dealt with in Euclid's *Elements*, and *analytical* or ◊*coordinate geometry*, in which problems are solved using algebraic methods. A third, quite distinct, type are the non-Euclidean geometries.

geophysics branch of geology using physics to study the Earth's surface, interior, and atmosphere.

George six kings of Great Britain:

George I 1660–1727. King of Great Britain from 1714. He was the son of the first elector of Hanover, Ernest Augustus (1629–1698), and his wife ◊Sophia. He succeeded to the electorate 1698, and became king on the death of Queen Anne. He attached himself to the Whigs, and spent most of his reign in Hanover, never having learned English.

George II 1683–1760. King of Great Britain from 1727, when he succeeded his father, George I. His victory at Dettingen 1743, in the War of the Austrian Succession, was the last battle commanded by a British king.

George III 1738–1820. King of Great Britain from 1760, when he succeeded his grandfather George II. He supported his ministers in a hard line towards the American colonies, and opposed Catholic emancipation and other reforms. Possibly suffering from porphyria, a rare hereditary metabolic disorder, he had repeated attacks of insanity, permanent from 1811.

George IV 1762–1830. King of Great Britain from 1820, when he succeeded his father George III, for whom he had been regent during the king's insanity 1811–20. Strictly educated, he reacted by entering into a life of debauchery, and in 1785 married a Catholic widow, Mrs ◊Fitzherbert, but in 1795 also married Princess ◊Caroline of Brunswick, in return for payment of his debts.

George V 1865–1936. King of Great Britain from 1910, when he succeeded his father Edward VII. He was the second son, and became heir 1892 on the death of his elder brother Albert, Duke of Clarence. In 1893, he married Princess Victoria Mary of Teck (Queen Mary), formerly engaged to his brother. In 1917 he abandoned all German titles for himself and his family.

George VI 1895–1952. King of Great Britain from 1936, when he succeeded after the abdication of his brother Edward VIII. Created duke of York 1920, he married in 1923 Lady Elizabeth Bowes-Lyon (1900–), and their children are Elizabeth II and Princess Margaret.

George II 1890–1947. King of Greece 1922–23 and 1935–47. He became king on the expulsion of his father Constantine I 1922, but was himself overthrown 1923. Restored by the military 1935, he set up a dictatorship under ◊Metaxas, and went into exile during the German occupation 1941–45.

George Cross/Medal UK awards to civilians for acts of courage.

George, St patron saint of England. The story of St George rescuing a woman by slaying a dragon, evidently derived from the ◊Perseus legend, first appears in the 6th century. The cult of St George was introduced into W Europe by the Crusaders. His feast day is 23 Apr.

Georgetown capital and port of Guyana; population (1983) 188,000. There is food processing and shrimp fishing.

Georgetown or *Penang* chief port of the Federation of Malaysia, and capital of Penang, on the Island of Penang; population (1980) 250,600. It produces textiles and toys.

George VI George VI succeeded to the throne after the unexpected abdication of his brother, Edward VIII in 1936.

Georgetown, Declaration of call in 1972, at a conference in Guyana of nonaligned countries, for a multipolar system to replace the two world power blocs, and for the Mediterranean Sea and Indian Ocean to be neutral.

Georgia state of the S USA; nickname Empire State of the South/Peach State
area 152,500 sq km/58,865 sq mi
capital Atlanta
towns Columbus, Savannah
products poultry, livestock, tobacco, maize, peanuts, cotton, china clay, crushed granite, textiles, carpets, aircraft
population (1990) 6,478,200
famous people Jim Bowie, Erskine Caldwell, Jimmy Carter, Martin Luther King, Margaret Mitchell
history named after George II of England, it was founded 1733 and was one of the original ◊Thirteen States of the USA.

Georgia county in the Caucasus of SE Europe, bounded N by Russia, E by Azerbaijan, S by Armenia, and W by the Black Sea.

Georgian a term which refers to a phase of English architecture and furniture making. The architecture is mainly classical in style, although external details and interiors were often rich in Rococo carving. Furniture was often made of mahogany and satinwood, and mass production became increasingly common. Designers included Thomas Chippendale, George Hepplewhite, and Thomas Sheraton.

geostationary orbit the circular path 35,900 km/ 22,300 mi above the Earth's equator on which a ◊satellite takes 24 hours to complete an orbit,

Georgia
Republic of

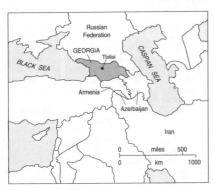

area 69,700 sq km/26,911 sq mi
capital Tbilisi
towns Kutaisi, Rustavi, Batumi, Sukhumi
physical largely mountainous with a variety of landscape from the subtropical Black Sea shores to the ice and snow of the crest line of the Caucasus; chief rivers are Kura and Rioni
features two autonomous republics, Abkhazia and Adzharia; one autonomous region, South Ossetia
interim head of state Eduard Shevardnadze from 1992
head of government Tengiz Sigua from 1992
political system transitional
products tea, citrus and orchard fruits, tung oil, tobacco, vines, silk, hydroelectricity
population (1990) 5,500,000 (70% Georgian, 8%

Armenian, 8% Russian, 6% Azeri, 3% Ossetian, 2% Abkhazian)
language Georgian
religion Georgian Church, independent of the Russian Orthodox Church since 1917
chronology
1918–21 Independent republic.
1921 Uprising quelled by Red Army and Soviet republic established.
1922–36 Linked with Armenia and Azerbaijan as the Transcaucasian Republic.
1936 Became separate republic within USSR.
1981–88 Increasing demands for autonomy, spearheaded from 1988 by the Georgian Popular Front.
1989 Abkhazians demanded secession from Georgia, provoking inter-ethnic clashes. Georgian Communist Party (GCP) leadership purged. State of emergency imposed in Abkhazia; inter-ethnic clashes in South Ossetia. Economic and political sovereignty declared.
1990 GCP monopoly ended and nationalist coalition triumphed in supreme soviet elections. Zviad Gamsakhurdia became president. GCP seceded from Communist Party of USSR; calls for Georgian independence.
1991 Independence declared and Gamsakhurdia popularly elected president. GCP outlawed and all relations with USSR severed. Anti-Gamsakhurdia demonstrations led to a state of emergency being declared. Georgia failed to join new Commonwealth of Independent States (CIS).
1992 Gamsakhurdia fled to Armenia and Sigua appointed prime minister. Eduard Shevardnadze appointed interim president. Georgia was admitted into United Nations (UN). Fighting started between Georgian troops and Abkhazian separatists in Abkhazia in NW. Shevardnadze elected chair of new parliament. Clashes in South Ossetia and Abkhazia continued.
1993 Inflation at 1,500%.

Germany
Federal Republic of
(*Bundesrepublik Deutschland*)

area 357,041 sq km/137,853 sq mi
capital Berlin
towns Cologne, Munich, Essen, Frankfurt-am-Main, Dortmund, Stuttgart, Düsseldorf, Leipzig, Dresden, Chemnitz, Magdeburg; ports Hamburg, Kiel, Cuxhaven, Bremerhaven, Rostock
physical flat in N, mountainous in S with Alps; rivers Rhine, Weser, Elbe flow N, Danube flows SE, Oder, Neisse flow N along Polish frontier; many lakes, including Müritz
head of state Richard von Weizsäcker from 1984
head of government Helmut Kohl from 1982
political system liberal democratic federal republic
exports machine tools (world's leading exporter), cars, commercial vehicles, electronics, industrial goods, textiles, chemicals, iron, steel, wine, lignite, uranium, coal, fertilizers, plastics
currency Deutschmark
population (1990) 78,420,000 (including nearly 5,000,000 guest workers (*Gastarbeiter*): 1,600,000 Turks, plus Yugoslavs, Italians, Greeks, Spanish, Portuguese); annual growth rate −0.7%
language German, Sorbian
religion Protestant 42%, Roman Catholic 35%
literacy 99% (1985)
GDP $1,250 bn (1989); $16,200 per head
chronology
1945 German surrender and division into four occupation zones (US, French, British, Soviet).
1948 Blockade of West Berlin.
1949 Federal Republic established under 'Basic Law' Constitution with Adenauer chancellor;

German Democratic Republic established as independent state.
1953 Riots in East Berlin suppressed by Soviet troops.
1954 West Germany granted full sovereignty.
1957 West Germany entered EC. Saarland recovery.
1961 Construction of Berlin Wall.
1963 Retirement of Chancellor Adenauer.
1964 East Germany signed Treaty of Friendship and Mutual Assistance with USSR.
1969 Willy Brandt became West German chancellor.
1971 Erich Honecker elected Socialist Unity Party (SED) leader in East Germany.
1972 West Germany and East Germany sign Basic Treaty.
1973 Basic Treaty ratified, normalizing relations between East and West Germany.
1974 Resignation of Brandt; Helmut Schmidt became chancellor of West Germany.
1975 East German friendship treaty with USSR renewed for 25 years.
1982 Helmut Kohl became West German chancellor.
1987 Official visit of Honecker to West Germany.
1988 Death of West German Bavarian CSU leader, Franz-Josef Strauss.
1989 West Germany: rising support for far right in local and European elections, declining support for Kohl. East Germany: mass exodus to West Germany began (344,000 left during 1989). Honecker replaced by Egon Krenz following mass demonstrations calling for reform soon after Gorbachev's visit to East Berlin. National borders, including Berlin Wall, opened in Nov. Reformist Hans Modrow appointed prime minister. Krenz replaced as party leader by Gysi and as president by Gerlach. Honecker placed under house arrest. Free multiparty elections promised for Mar 1990.
1990 Secret police (*Stasi*) headquarters in East Berlin stormed by demonstrators. East German multiparty elections won by the right-wing Christian Democratic Union (CDU). Official reunification of East and West Germany on 3 Oct. First all-German elections since 1932 held on 2 Dec, resulting in a victory for Kohl.
1991 Kohl's popularity declined after tax increase. The CDU lost its Bundesrat majority to the Social Democratic Party (SPD). Racist attacks on foreigners.
1992 Neo-Nazi riots against immigrants continued.
1993 Unemployment exceeded 7%. Honecker allowed to leave for exile in Chile.

---

thus appearing to hang stationary over one place on the Earth's surface. It is particularly used for communications satellites.

geothermal energy either subterranean hot water pumped to the surface and converted to steam or run through a heat exchanger, or dry steam, directed through turbines to produce electricity.

Gerald of Wales English name of ◊Giraldus Cambrensis, medieval Welsh bishop-historian.

geranium either a plant of the family Geraniaceae, having divided leaves, and pink or purple flowers, or of the family Pelargonium, having a hairy stem, and red, pink, or white flowers.

gerbil rodent of the family Cricetidae which has elongated back legs and good hopping or jumping ability. They range from mouse- to rat-size, and have hairy tails. Many of the 13 genera live in dry, sandy, or sparsely vegetated areas of Africa and Asia.

gerenuk antelope *Litocranius walleri* about 1 m/
3 ft at the shoulder, but with a greatly elongated
neck. It browses on leaves, often balancing on its
hind legs to do so. Sandy brown in colour, it is
well camouflaged in its E African habitat of dry
scrub.

geriatrics the branch of medicine concerned with
care of the elderly sick.

germ a colloquial term for a microorganism that
causes disease, such as certain ◊bacteria and
◊viruses. Formerly, it was also used to mean
something capable of developing into a complete
organism (such as a fertilized egg, or the ◊embryo
of a seed), and survives still in terms such as ◊germ
layer.

Germanic languages a branch of the Indo-
European language family, divided into *East Ger-
manic* (Gothic, now extinct), *North Germanic*
(Danish, Faroese, Icelandic, Norwegian, Swedish),
and *West Germanic* (Afrikaans, Dutch, English,
Flemish, Frisian, German, Yiddish).

Germanicus Caesar 15 BC–AD 19. Roman
general. Though he refused the suggestion of his
troops that he claim the throne on the death of
Augustus, his military successes in Germany made
Tiberius jealous. Sent to the east, he died near
Antioch, possibly murdered at the instigation of
Tiberius. He was the father of Caligula, and of
Agrippina, mother of Nero.

germanium a metallic element, symbol Ge,
atomic number 32, relative atomic mass 72.6. It is a
grey-white, brittle, crystalline metal in the silicon
group, with chemical and physical properties between those of silicon and tin. Germanium is a
semiconductor material and is widely used in the
manufacture of transistors and integrated circuits.
The oxide is transparent to infrared radiation, and is
used in military applications.

German language a member of the Germanic
group of the Indo-European language family, the
national language of Germany and Austria, and an
official language of Switzerland. There are many
spoken varieties of German, the best known distinction being between High German (*Hochdeutsch*) and
Low German (*Plattdeutsch*).

German measles or *rubella* a virus disease,
usually of children, having an incubation period of
two to three weeks. It is marked by a sore throat,
pinkish rash, and slight fever. If a woman contracts
it in the first three months of pregnancy, it may
cause serious damage to the unborn child. Immunization is recommended for girls who have not
contracted the disease, at about 12–14 months, or
at puberty.

German silver or *nickel silver* a silvery alloy of
nickel, copper, and zinc. It is widely used for cheap
jewellery and the base metal for silver plating. The
letters EPNS on silverware stand for electroplated
nickel silver.

Germany country in central Europe, bounded
N by the North and Baltic seas and Denmark, E
by Poland and the Czech Republic, S by Austria
and Switzerland, and W by France, Luxembourg,
Belgium, and the Netherlands. From 1949–
1990, Germany was divided into East and West
Germany.

Germany, East (German Democratic Republic)
country 1949–90, formed from the Soviet zone of
occupation in the partition of Germany following
World War II. East Germany became a sovereign
state 1954, and was reunified with West Germany
Oct 1990. For history after 1949, see ◊Germany,
Federal Republic of.

Germany, West (Federal Republic of Germany)
country 1949–90, formed from the British, US, and
French occupation zones in the partition of Ger-
many following World War II; reunified with East
Germany Oct 1990. For history after 1949 see
◊Germany, Federal Republic of.

germination the initial stages of growth in a
seed, spore, or pollen grain. Seeds germinate
when they are exposed to favourable external
conditions of moisture, light, and temperature, and
when any factors causing dormancy have been
removed.

germ layer in ◊embryology, a layer of cells that
can be distinguished during the development of a
fertilized egg. Most animals have three such layers,
the inner, middle, and outer.

Gerona town in Catalonia, NE Spain, capital
of Gerona province; population (1991) 66,900.
Industries include textiles and chemicals. There
are ferry links with Ibiza, Barcelona, and
Málaga.

Geronimo 1829–1909. Chief of the Chiricahua
Apache Indians and war leader. From 1875–1885,
he fought federal troops and settlers encroaching on
tribal reservations in the SW, especially SE Arizona
and New Mexico.

gerrymander in politics, the rearranging of constituency boundaries to give an unfair advantage
to the ruling party. The term derives from US
politician Elbridge Gerry (1744–1814), who, while
governor of Massachusetts 1812, reorganized an
electoral district (shaped like a salamander) in
favour of the Republicans.

Gershwin George 1898–1937. US composer,
who wrote the tone poem *An American in Paris*
1928, *Rhapsody in Blue* 1924, and the opera
Porgy and Bess 1935, in which he incorporated
the essentials of jazz. He also wrote popular
songs with his brother, the lyricist *Ira Gershwin*
(1896–1983).

Gertler Mark 1891–1939. English painter. He was a
pacifist and a noncombatant during World War I; his
Merry-Go-Round 1916 (Tate Gallery, London) is

Gertler Merry-Go-Round *(1916) Tate Gallery, London.*

Ghana
Republic of

area 238,537 sq km/92,100 sq mi
capital Accra
towns Kumasi, and ports Sekondi-Takoradi, Tema
physical mostly plains; bisected by river Volta
head of state and government Jerry Rawlings from 1981
political system military republic
exports cocoa, coffee, timber, gold, diamonds
currency cedi
population (1990 est) 15,310,000; annual growth rate 3.2%
life expectancy men 50, women 54
language English (official) and African languages
religion animist 38%, Muslim 30%, Christian 24%
literacy 64% male/43% female (1985 est)
GNP $3.9 bn (1983); $420 per head
chronology
1957 Independence achieved with Kwame Nkrumah as president.
1960 Ghana became a republic and a one-party state.
1966 Nkrumah replaced by Gen Joseph Ankrah.
1969 Ankrah replaced by Gen Akwasi Afrifa, who initiated a return to civilian government.
1970 Edward Akufo-Addo elected president.
1972 Another coup placed Col Acheampong at the head of a military government.
1978 Acheampong deposed. Another coup put Flight Lt Jerry Rawlings in power.
1979 Return to civilian rule under Hilla Limann.
1981 Rawlings seized power again. All political parties banned.
1989 Coup attempt foiled.
1992 New multiparty constitution approved. Rawlings elected president in national elections.
1993 Fourth republic of Ghana formally inaugurated.

often seen as an expressive symbol of militarism. He suffered from depression and committed suicide.

gerund in the grammar of certain languages, such as Latin, a noun formed from a verb, and functioning as a noun to express an action or state. In English, gerunds end in -ing.

gestalt the concept of a unified whole which is greater than, or different from, the sum of its parts; that is, a complete structure whose nature is not explained simply by analysing its constituent elements. The term was first used in psychology in Germany about 1910.

Gestapo abbreviated form of Geheime Staatspolizei, the German Nazi secret police, formed 1933, and under the direction of Heinrich Himmler from 1936. They used terrorism to stamp out anti-Nazi resistance.

gestation in all mammals except the monotremes (duck-billed platypus and spiny anteater), the period from the time of implantation of the embryo in the uterus to birth. This period varies between species; in humans, it is about 266 days, in elephants 18–22 months, and in some species of opossum as low as 12 days.

Gethsemane site of the garden where Judas Iscariot, according to the New Testament, betrayed Jesus. It is on the Mount of Olives, east of Jerusalem. When Jerusalem was divided between Israel and Jordan 1948, Gethsemane fell within Jordanian territory.

Getty J(ean) Paul 1892–1976. US oil billionaire, president of the Getty Oil Company from 1947, and founder of the **Getty Museum** (housing the world's best-funded art gallery) in Malibu, California. In 1985 his son **John Paul Getty Jr** (1932–) established an endowment fund of £50 million for the National Gallery, London.

Gettysburg site in Pennsylvania of a decisive battle of the American ◊Civil War in 1863, won by the North. The site is now a national cemetery, at the dedication of which President Lincoln delivered the **Gettysburg Address** 19 Nov 1863, a speech in which he reiterated the principles of freedom, equality, and democracy embodied in the US constitution.

Getz Stan(ley) 1927–1991. US tenor saxophonist of the 1950s 'cool jazz' school. He was the first US musician to be closely identified with the Latin American bossa nova sound.

geyser a natural spring which, at more or less regular intervals, explosively discharges a column of steam and hot water into the air.

G-forces the forces pilots and astronauts experience when their craft accelerate or decelerate rapidly. One G is the ordinary pull of gravity. Early astronauts were subjected to launch and re-entry forces up to six Gs or more. Pilots and astronauts wear G-suits that prevent their blood 'pooling' too much under severe G-forces, which can lead to unconsciousness.

Ghana country in W Africa, bounded to the N by Burkina Faso, E by Togo, S by the Gulf of Guinea, and W by the Ivory Coast.

Ghana, Ancient a great trading empire that flourished in NW Africa during the 5th–13th centuries. Founded by the Soninke people, the Ghana Empire was based, like the Mali Empire which superseded it, on the Saharan gold trade. At its peak in the 11th century, it occupied an area that includes parts of present-day Mali, Senegal, and Mauritania. Wars with the Berber tribes of the Sahara led to its fragmentation and collapse in the 13th century, when much of its territory was absorbed into Mali.

ghat in Hinduism, broad steps leading down to one of the sacred rivers. Some of these, known as 'burning ghats', are used for cremation.

Ghent (Flemish Gent, French Gand) city and port in East Flanders, NW Belgium; population (1991) 230,200. Industries include textiles, chemicals, electronics, and metallurgy.

gherkin a young or small green ◊cucumber.

ghetto area of a town where Jews were compelled to live, decreed by a law enforced by papal bull 1555. Ghettos were abolished, except in E Europe, in the

19th century, but the concept was revived by the Germans and Italians 1940–45. The term is now used generally for any deprived area occupied by a minority group.

Ghirlandaio Domenico *c.* 1449–1494. Italian fresco painter, head of a large and prosperous workshop in Florence. His fresco cycle 1486–90 in S Maria Novella, Florence includes portraits of Florentines and much contemporary detail.

GHQ abbreviation for *general headquarters*.

GI abbreviation for *government issue*, hence (in the USA) a common soldier.

Giacometti Alberto 1901–1966. Swiss sculptor and painter. In the 1930s, in his Surrealist period, he began to develop his characteristic spindly constructions. His mature style of emaciated single figures, based on wire frames, emerged in the 1940s.

Giant's Causeway stretch of columnar basalt forming a promontory on the N coast of Antrim, Northern Ireland. It was formed by an outflow of lava in Tertiary times which has solidified in polygonal columns.

Gibberd Frederick 1908–1984. British architect and town planner. His works include the new towns of Harlow, England, and Santa Teresa, Venezuela; the Catholic Cathedral, Liverpool; and the Central London mosque in Regent's Park.

gibberellin plant growth substance (see also ◊auxin) which mainly promotes stem growth but may also affect several other aspects of growth and development, including the breaking of dormancy in certain buds and seeds, and the induction of flowering. Application of gibberellin can stimulate the stems of dwarf plants to additional growth, delay the ageing process in leaves, and promote the production of seedless fruit (◊parthenocarpy).

gibbon type of small ape, genus *Hylobates*, of which there are several species. The *common* or *black-handed gibbon Hylobates lar* is about 60 cm/2 ft tall, with a body that is hairy except for the buttocks, which distinguishes it from other types of apes. Gibbons have long arms, no tail, and are arboreal in habit, but when on the ground walk upright. They are found from Assam through the Malay peninsula to Borneo.

Gibbon Edward 1737–1794. British historian, renowned author of *The History of the Decline and Fall of the Roman Empire* 1776–88.

Gibbon John Heysham 1903–1974. US surgeon who invented the heart-lung machine in 1953. It has since become indispensable in heart surgery, maintaining the circulation while the heart is temporarily inactivated.

Gibbs James 1682–1754. Scottish Neo-Classical architect whose works include St Martin's-in-the-Fields, London 1722–26, Radcliffe Camera, Oxford 1737–49, and Bank Hall, Cheshire 1750.

Gibraltar British dependency, situated on a narrow rocky promontory in S Spain.
area 5.9 sq km/2.2 sq mi
exports mainly a trading centre for the import and re-export of goods
population (1983) 29,000
recent history captured from Spain in 1704 by English admiral Sir George Rooke (1650–1709), it was ceded to Britain under the Treaty of Utrecht 1713. A referendum 1967 confirmed the wish of the people to remain in association with Britain, but Spain continues to claim sovereignty, and closed the border 1969–85. In 1989, Britain announced it would reduce the military garrison by half.

Gibraltar, Strait of strait between N Africa and Spain, with the Rock of Gibraltar on the north side and Jebel Musa on the south, the so-called Pillars of Hercules.

Gibson Mel 1956– . New York-born Australian actor who moved to Sydney when he was 12. His international stardom and sex symbol image are the result of roles in George Miller's *Mad Max* films (1979, 1982, 1985) and blockbusters such as *Lethal Weapon* 1987 and *Lethal Weapon 2* 1989. His other films include *The Year of Living Dangerously* 1983 and *Air America* 1991.

Gide André 1869–1951. French novelist, born in Paris. His work is largely autobiographical and concerned with the themes of self-fulfilment and renunciation. It includes *L'Immoraliste/The Immoralist* 1902, and *Les Faux-monnayeurs/The Counterfeiters* 1926; and an almost lifelong *Journal*. Nobel Prize for Literature 1947.

Gideon in the Old Testament, one of the Judges of Israel, who led a small band of Israelite warriors which routed an invading Midianite army of overwhelming number in a surprise night attack.

Gielgud John 1904– . British actor and director. He made his debut at the Old Vic in 1921, and created his most famous role as Hamlet in 1929. Film roles include Clarence in Shakespeare's *Richard III* 1955 and the butler in *Arthur* 1981 (for which he won an Oscar).

Gierek Edward 1913– . Polish communist politician. He entered the Politburo of the ruling Polish United Workers' Party (PUWP) 1956 and was party leader 1970–80. His industrialization programme plunged the country heavily into debt and sparked a series of ◊Solidarity-led strikes.

Giffard Henri 1825–1882. French inventor of the first passenger-carrying steerable airship, called a dirigible, built 1852. The hydrogen-filled airship was 45 m/150 ft long, its steam engine drove a propeller, and it was steered using a sail-like rudder. It flew at a speed of 8 kph/5 mph.

giga- prefix signifying multiplication by 10^9 (one thousand million, 1,000,000,000, or in current scientific terminology, one billion).

gila monster lizard *Heloderma suspectum* of SW USA and Mexico. Belonging to the only venomous genus of lizards, it has poison glands in its lower jaw, but the bite is not usually fatal to humans.

Gilbert Humphrey *c.* 1539–1583. English soldier and navigator who claimed Newfoundland (landing at St John's) for Elizabeth I in 1583. He died when his ship sank on the return voyage.

Gilbert W(illiam) S(chwenk) 1836–1911. British humorist and dramatist who collaborated with Arthur ◊Sullivan, providing the libretti for their series of light comic operas from 1871; they include *HMS Pinafore* 1878, *The Pirates of Penzance* 1879, and *The Mikado* 1885.

Gilbert William 1544–1603. Scientist and physician to Elizabeth I and (briefly) James I. He studied magnetism and static electricity, deducing that the Earth's magnetic field behaves as if a huge bar magnet joined the North and South poles. His book on magnets, published 1600, is the first printed scientific book based wholly on experimentation and observation.

Gilbert and Ellice Islands former British colony in the Pacific, known since independence in 1978 as ◊Tuvalu and ◊Kiribati.

Gilbert and George Gilbert Proesch 1943– and George Passmore 1942– . British painters and performance artists, who became famous in the 1960s for their presentation of themselves as works of art, *living sculpture*. Their work makes much use of photography.

Gill *The sculptor and engraver Eric Gill, self-portrait in wood, 1927.*

Gilded Age, the in US history, a derogatory term referring to the post-Civil War decades. It borrows the title of an 1873 political satire by Mark Twain and Charles Dudley Warner (1829–1900), which highlights the respectable veneer of a public life covering many scandals.

Gilgamesh hero of Sumerian, Hittite, Akkadian, and Assyrian legend. The 12 verse 'books' of the *Epic of Gilgamesh* were recorded in a standard version on 12 cuneiform tablets by the Assyrian king Ashurbanipal's scholars in the 7th century BC, and the epic itself is older than Homer's *Iliad* by at least 1,500 years. One-third mortal and two-thirds divine, Gilgamesh is Lord of the Sumerian city of Uruk, and his friend Enkidu (half beast, half man) dies for him. Its incident of the Flood is similar to the Old Testament account.

gill in biology, the main respiratory organ of most fish and immature amphibians, and of many aquatic invertebrates. In all types, water passes over the gills, and oxygen diffuses across the gill membrane into the circulatory system while carbon dioxide passes from the system out into the water.

gill imperial unit of volume for liquid measure, equal to one quarter of a pint, still used in selling alcoholic drinks.

Gill Eric 1882–1940. British sculptor and engraver. He designed the typefaces Perpetua 1925 and Gill Sans (without serifs) 1927, but is better known for monumental stone sculptures with clean, simplified outlines, such as *Prospero and Ariel* 1929–31 (on Broadcasting House, London).

Gillespie Dizzy. Stage name of John Birks Gillespie 1917–1993. US jazz trumpeter, together with Charlie Parker the chief creator and exponent of the ◊bebop style. Gillespie influenced many modern jazz trumpeters, including Miles Davis.

gilt-edged securities stocks and shares issued and guaranteed by the British government to raise funds and traded on the Stock Exchange. A relatively risk-free investment, gilts bear fixed interest and are usually redeemable on a specified date. According to the redemption date, they are described as short (up to five years), medium, or long (15 years or more).

gin (Dutch *jenever* 'juniper') alcoholic drink made by distilling a mash of maize, malt, or rye, with juniper flavouring. It was first produced in

Holland. In Britain, the low price of corn led to a mania for gin during the 18th century, resulting in the Gin Acts of 1736 and 1751 which reduced gin consumption to a quarter of its previous level.

ginger SE Asian reed-like perennial *Zingiber officinale*, family Zingiberaceae; the hot-tasting underground root is used in cooking.

ginger ale and beer sweetened, carbonated drinks containing ginger flavouring, sugar, and syrup; ginger beer also contains bitters.

ginkgo tree *Ginkgo biloba*, related to the conifers and also known, from the resemblance of its leaves to those of the maidenhair fern, as the maidenhair tree. In 200 years it may reach a height of 30 m/100 ft.

Ginsberg Allen 1926– . US poet. His *Howl* 1956 was the most influential poem produced by the ◊beat generation, criticizing the materialism of modern US society.

ginseng plant *Panax ginseng*, family Araliaceae, used in medicine in China.

Giolitti Giovanni 1842–1928. Italian liberal politician, born in Mondovi. He was prime minister 1892–93, 1903–05, 1906–09, 1911–14, and 1920–21. He opposed Italian intervention in World War I, and pursued a policy of broad coalitions, which proved ineffective in controlling Fascism after 1921.

Giorgione del Castelfranco *c.* 1475–1510. Italian Renaissance painter. His subjects are imbued with a sense of mystery and treated with a soft technique reminiscent of Leonardo's later works, as in *Tempest* (Accademia, Venice).

Giotto space probe built by the European Space Agency to study ◊Halley's comet. Launched by an Ariane rocket in Jul 1985, Giotto passed within 600 km/375 mi of the comet's nucleus on 13 Mar 1986.

Giotto di Bondone 1267–1337. Italian painter, active in Florence, Assisi, Padua, Rome, Naples, and elsewhere; he broke away from the conventional Gothic style of the time, and had an enormous influence on subsequent Italian painting. The interior of the Arena Chapel, Padua, is covered in a fresco cycle (completed by 1306) illustrating the life of Mary and the life of Christ.

giraffe tallest mammal, *Giraffa camelopardalis*. It stands over 5.5 m/18 ft tall, the neck accounting for nearly half this amount. The giraffe has two small skin-covered horns on the head and a long tufted tail. The skin has a mottled appearance and is reddish brown and cream. Giraffes are now found only in Africa, S of the Sahara Desert.

Girl Guides ◊Scout organization founded in the UK in 1910 by Baden-Powell and his sister Agnes. There are three branches: Brownie Guides (age

ginkgo

giraffe

7–11); Guides (10–16); Ranger Guides (14–20); and adult leaders – Guiders. The World Association of Girl Guides and Girl Scouts (as they are known in the USA) has over 6.5 million members.

giro system of making payments by direct transfer between one bank or post-office account and another.

Girondin member of the right-wing republican party in the French Revolution, so called because a number of their leaders came from the Gironde *département*. They were driven from power by the ◊Jacobins 1793.

Giscard d'Estaing Valéry 1926– . French conservative politician, president 1974–81. He was finance minister to de Gaulle 1962–66 and Pompidou 1969–74. As leader of the Union pour la Démocratie Française, which he formed in 1978, Giscard has sought to project himself as leader of a 'new centre'.

Gissing George (Robert) 1857–1903. British writer, who dealt with socialist ideas. Among his works are *New Grub Street* 1891 and the autobiographical *Private Papers of Henry Ryecroft* 1903.

Giza, El or *al-Jizah* site of the Great Pyramids and Sphinx, a suburb of ◊Cairo, Egypt; population (1983) 1,500,000. It has textile and film industries.

gizzard a muscular grinding organ of the digestive tract, below the ◊crop of birds, earthworms, and some insects, and forming part of the stomach. The gizzard of birds is lined with a hardened horny layer of the protein keratin, preventing damage to the muscle layer during the grinding process. Most birds swallow sharp grit which aids maceration of food in the gizzard.

glacier a mass of ice, originating in mountains in the snowfields above the snowline, that can move under pressure (glacier flow). It moves slowly down a valley or depression, and is constantly replenished from its source.

gladiator Roman professional fighter, recruited mainly from slaves, criminals, and prisoners of war, who fought to the death for the entertainment of the ancient Romans. The custom, which originated in the practice of slaughtering slaves on a chieftain's grave, was introduced into Rome from Etruria 264 BC and survived until the 5th century AD.

gladiolus genus of S European and African cultivated perennials, family Iridaceae, with brightly coloured, funnel-shaped flowers, borne in a spike; the sword-like leaves spring from a corm.

Gladstone William Ewart 1809–1898. British Liberal politician. He entered Parliament as a Tory 1833 and held ministerial office, but left the party 1846 and after 1859 identified himself with the Liberals. He was chancellor of the Exchequer 1852–55 and 1859–66, and prime minister 1868–74, 1880–85, 1886, and 1892–94. He introduced elementary education 1870 and vote by ballot 1872, and many reforms in Ireland, although he failed in his efforts to get a Home Rule Bill passed.

Glamorgan three counties of S Wales – ◊Mid, ◊South, and ◊West Glamorgan – created in 1974 from the former county of Glamorganshire.

gland a specialized organ of the body that manufactures and secretes enzymes, hormones, or other chemicals. In animals, glands vary in size from small (for example, tear glands) to large (for example, the pancreas), but in plants they are always small, and may consist of a single cell.

glandular fever viral disease (also known as *infectious mononucleosis*) characterized by fever and painfully swollen lymph nodes (in the neck); there may also be digestive upset, sore throat, and skin rashes. Lassitude persists and recovery is often slow.

Glasgow city and administrative headquarters of Strathclyde, Scotland; population (1991) 654,500. Industries include engineering, chemicals, printing, and distilling.

glasnost former Soviet leader ◊Gorbachev's policy of liberalizing various aspects of Soviet life and opening up Soviet relations with Western countries.

glass a brittle, usually transparent or translucent substance which is physically neither a solid nor a liquid. Glass is made by fusing certain types of sand (silica); this fusion occurs naturally in volcanic glass (see ◊obsidian).

Glass Philip 1937– . US composer. Strongly influenced by Indian music, his work is characterized by repeated rhythmic figures that are continually expanded and modified. His compositions include

Gladstone *The 19th-century British Liberal politician William Gladstone.*

glacier

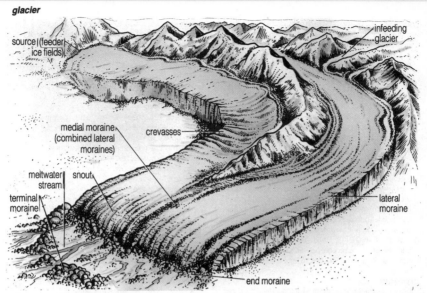

the operas *Einstein on the Beach* 1975, *Akhnaten* 1984, and *The Making of the Representative for Planet 8* 1988.

Glasse Hannah 1708–1770. British cookery writer whose *The Art of Cookery made Plain and Easy* 1747 is regarded as the first classic recipe book in Britain.

Glauber's salt in chemistry, crystalline sodium sulphate decahydrate $Na_2SO_4.10H_2O$, which melts at 31°C; the latent heat stored as it solidifies makes it a convenient thermal energy store. It is used in medicine.

glaucoma condition in which pressure inside the eye (intraocular pressure) is raised abnormally as excess fluid accumulates. It occurs when the normal flow of intraocular fluid out of the eye is interrupted. As pressure rises, the optic nerve suffers irreversible damage, leading to a reduction in the field of vision and, ultimately, loss of eyesight.

Glendower Owen *c.* 1359–1415. Welsh leader of a revolt against the English in N Wales, who defeated Henry IV in three campaigns 1400–02, though Wales was reconquered 1405–13.

Glenn John (Herschel) 1921– . US astronaut and politician. On 20 Feb 1962, he became the first American to orbit the Earth. After retiring from ◊NASA, he became a senator for Ohio 1974 and 1980, and unsuccessfully sought the Democratic presidential nomination 1984.

gliding the art of using air currents to fly unpowered aircraft. Technically speaking gliding involves the gradual loss of altitude; gliders designed for soaring flight (utilizing air rising up a cliff face or hill, warm air rising as a 'thermal' above sun-heated ground, and so on) are known as sail-planes. In **hang gliding**, perfected by a US engineer named Rogallo in the 1970s, the aeronaut is strapped into a carrier, attached to a sail wing of nylon stretched on an aluminium frame shaped like a paper dart, and jumps into the air from a high place.

Glinka Mikhail Ivanovich 1804–1857. Russian composer. He broke away from the contemporary prevailing Italian influence, and turned to Russian folk-music as the inspiration for his opera *A Life for the Tsar (Ivan Susanin)* 1836. His later works include

another opera *Ruslan and Lyudmila* 1842, and the orchestral *Kamarinskaya* 1848.

glissando in music, a rapid uninterrupted scale produced by sliding the finger across the keys or strings.

globefish another name for ◊puffer fish.

Globe Theatre octagonal theatre open to the sky, built by Cuthbert Burbage in 1599 on the Bankside, Southwark, London. It was the site for the first productions of most of Shakespeare's plays by Richard Burbage and his company. It was burned down 1613.

globular cluster a spherical ◊star cluster of between 10,000 and a million stars. More than a hundred globular clusters are distributed in a spherical halo around our Galaxy. They consist of old stars, formed early in our Galaxy's history. Globular clusters are also found around other galaxies.

Gloucestershire county in SW England
area 2,643 sq km/1,020 sq mi
towns administrative headquarters Gloucester; Stroud, Cheltenham, Tewkesbury, Cirencester
products cereals, fruit, dairy products; engineering, coal in the Forest of Dean
population (1986) 513,000.

glove box a form of protection used when handling certain dangerous materials, such as radioactive substances. Gloves fixed to ports in the walls of a box allow manipulation of objects within the box. The risk that the operator might inhale fine airborne particles of poisonous materials is removed by maintaining a vacuum inside the box, so that any airflow is inwards.

glow-worm the wingless female of various luminous beetles in the family Lampyridae. The luminous organs situated under the abdomen usually serve to attract winged males for mating. There are about 2,000 species, distributed throughout the tropics, Europe, and N Asia.

Gluck Christoph Willibald von 1714–1787. German composer. In 1762 his *Orfeo ed Euridice/Orpheus and Eurydice* revolutionized the 18th-century conception of opera by giving free scope to dramatic effect. *Orfeo* was followed by *Alceste/Alcestis* 1767 and *Paris ed Elena/Paris and Helen* 1770.

glucose $C_6H_{12}O_6$ a type of sugar or carbohydrate also known as grape-sugar or dextrose. It is present in the blood, and is found in honey and fruit juices. It is a source of energy for the body, being produced from other sugars and starches to form the 'energy currency' of many biochemical reactions also involving ◊ATP.

glue a kind of ◊adhesive.

glut an excess of goods in a market. A glut of agricultural produce often follows an exceptional harvest, causing prices to fall unless there is some form of intervention in the market.

glycerine $HOCH_2CH(OH)CH_2OH$ (common name for glycerol, or *trihydroxypropane*) a thick, colourless, odourless, sweetish liquid. It is obtained from vegetable and animal oils and fats (by treatment with acid, alkali, superheated steam, or an enzyme), or by fermentation of glucose, and is used in the manufacture of high explosives, in antifreeze solutions, to maintain moist conditions in fruits and tobacco, and in cosmetics.

glycine $CH_2(NH_2)COOH$ the simplest amino acid, and one of the main components of proteins. When purified, it is a sweet, colourless crystalline compound.

glycogen polymer (a polysaccaharide) of the sugar ◊glucose made and retained in the liver as a carbohydrate store, for which reason it is sometimes called animal starch. It is a source of energy when needed by muscles, in which it is converted back into glucose and metabolized under the action of the hormone ◊insulin.

glycol *dihydroxyethane* a thick, colourless, odourless, sweetish liquid also called ethylene glycol or ethanediol $(CH_2OH)_2$. Glycol is used in antifreeze solutions, in the preparation of ethers and esters, especially for explosives, as a solvent, and as a substitute for glycerine.

GMT abbreviation for ◊Greenwich Mean Time.

gnat small fly, especially of the family Culicidae, the mosquitoes. The eggs are laid in water, where they hatch into worm-like larvae, which pass through a pupal stage to emerge as perfect insects.

gneiss a ◊metamorphic rock, formed under conditions of extreme pressure, and often found in association with schists and granites.

Gnosticism esoteric cult of divine knowledge (a synthesis of Christianity, Greek philosophy, Hinduism, Buddhism, and the mystery cults of the Mediterranean), which was a rival to and influence on early Christianity. The medieval French ◊Cathar and the modern *Mandean* sects (in S Iraq) descend from Gnosticism.

GNP abbreviation for ◊*Gross National Product*.

gnu African antelope, also known as *wildebeest*, with a cow-like face, a beard, and mane, and heavy curved horns in both sexes. The body is up to 1.3 m/4.2 ft at the shoulder and slopes away to the hindquarters.

go game originating in China 3,000 years ago, and now the national game of Japan. It is played by placing small stones on a large grid. The object is to win territory and eventual superiority.

Goa, Daman, and Diu Union Territory of India comprising the former Portuguese coastal possessions of Goa and Daman, and the island of Diu, forcibly seized by India in 1961; area 3,813 sq km/1,472 sq mi; population (1981) 1,086,730. The capital is Panaji.

goat ruminant mammal, genus *Capra*, family Bovidae, closely related to the sheep. Both

males and females have horns and beards. They are sure-footed animals, and feed on shoots and leaves more than grass.

Gobbi Tito 1913–1984. Italian baritone singer, noted for his opera characterizations, especially of Figaro, Scarpia, and Iago.

Gobelins French tapestry factory, originally founded as a dyeworks in Paris by Gilles and Jean Gobelin about 1450. The firm began to produce tapestries in the 16th century, and in 1662 the establishment was bought by Colbert for Louis XIV. With the support of the French government it continues to make tapestries.

Gobi Asian desert divided between the Mongolian People's Republic and Inner Mongolia, China; 800 km/500 mi N–S, and 1,600 km/1,000 mi E–W. It is rich in fossil remains of extinct species.

Gobind Singh 1666–1708. the tenth and last guru (teacher) of Sikhism, 1675–1708, and founder of the Sikh brotherhood known as the ◊Khalsa. On his death the Sikh holy book, the *Guru Granth Sahib*, replaced the line of human gurus as the teacher and guide of the Sikh community.

God the concept of a supreme being, a unique personal creative entity, assumed to be completely good; basic to several religions (for example, ◊Christianity, ◊Islam, ◊Judaism).

Godard Jean-Luc 1930– . French film director, one of the leaders of ◊new wave cinema. His works are often characterized by experimental editing techniques, and an unconventional dramatic form. His films include *À bout de souffle*/Breathless 1960, *Weekend* 1968 and *Je vous salue, Marie*/Hail *Mary* 1985.

Goddard Robert Hutchings 1882–1945. US rocket pioneer. His first liquid-fuelled rocket was launched at Auburn, Massachusetts, USA, Mar 1926. By 1935 his rockets had gyroscopic control and carried cameras to record instrument readings.

Godfrey de Bouillon *c.* 1060–1100. Crusader, second son of Count Eustace II of Boulogne. He and his brothers (◊Baldwin and Eustace) led 40,000 Germans in the First Crusade 1096. When Jerusalem was taken 1099, he was elected its ruler, but refused the title of king.

God Save the King/Queen British national anthem. The melody resembles a composition by John Bull (1563–1628), and similar words are found from the 16th century. In its present form it dates from the 1745 Rebellion, when it was used as an anti-Jacobite Party song.

Godthaab (Greenlandic *Nuuk*) capital and largest town of Greenland; population (1982) 9,700. It is a storage centre for oil and gas, and the chief industry is fish processing.

Godunov Boris 1552–1605. Tsar of Russia from 1598. He was assassinated by a pretender to the throne. The legend that has grown up around this forms the basis of Pushkin's play *Boris Godunov* 1831 and Mussorgsky's opera of the same name 1874.

Goebbels Paul Josef 1897–1945. German Nazi leader. He joined the Nazi party in its early days, and was given control of its propaganda 1929. As minister of propaganda from 1933, he brought all cultural and educational activities under Nazi control. On the capture of Berlin by the Allies he poisoned himself.

Goering Hermann 1893–1946. German field marshal from 1938 and Nazi leader. Goering was part of Hitler's 'inner circle', and with Hitler's rise to power 1933, established the Gestapo and concentration camps. Appointed successor to Hitler 1939, he built

goldcrest

Gogh Self Portrait with Bandaged Ear *(1889)*
Courtauld Galleries, London.

a vast economic empire in occupied Europe, but later lost favour, and was expelled from the party 1945. Tried at Nuremberg, he poisoned himself before he could be executed.

Goes Hugo van der　died 1482. Flemish painter, active in Ghent. His *Portinari altarpiece c.* 1475 (Uffizi, Florence), is a huge oil painting of the Nativity, full of symbolism and naturalistic detail.

Goethe Johann Wolfgang von 1749–1832. German poet, novelist, and dramatist, generally considered the founder of modern German literature, and leader of the Romantic ◊*Sturm und Drang* movement. His works include the autobiographical *Die Leiden des Jungen Werthers*/*The Sorrows of the Young Werther* 1774 and *Faust* 1808, considered to be his masterpiece.

Gogh Vincent van 1853–1890. Dutch painter, a Post-Impressionist. He began painting in the 1880s. He met ◊Gauguin in Paris, and when he settled in Arles, Provence, 1888, Gauguin joined him there. After a quarrel van Gogh cut off part of his own earlobe, and in 1889 he entered an asylum; the following year he committed suicide. The Arles paintings vividly testify to his intense emotional involvement in his art; among the best known are *The Yellow Chair* and several *Sunflowers*.

Gogol Nicolai Vasilyevich 1809–1852. Russian writer. His first success was a collection of stories, *Evenings on a Farm near Dikanka* 1831–32, followed by *Mirgorod* 1835. Later works include *Arabesques* 1835, the comedy *The Inspector General* 1836, and the picaresque novel *Dead Souls* 1842.

goitre enlargement of the thyroid gland seen as a swelling on the neck. It is most pronounced in simple goitre, which is due to iodine deficiency. Much more common is toxic goitre (◊thyrotoxicosis), due to over-activity of the thyroid gland.

Gokhale Gopal Krishna 1866–1915. Political adviser and friend of Mohandas Gandhi, leader of the Moderate group in the Indian National Congress before World War I.

Golan Heights (Arabic *Jawlan*) plateau on the Syrian border with Israel, contested in the ◊Arab-Israeli Wars, and annexed by Israel 14 Dec 1981.

gold a heavy, precious, yellow metallic element; symbol Au, atomic number 79, atomic weight 197.0. It is unaffected by temperature changes and is highly resistant to acids. For manufacture, gold is alloyed with another strengthening metal, its purity being measured in ◊carats on a scale of 24.

Gold Coast former name for ◊Ghana, but historically the W coast of Africa from Cape Three Points to the Volta river, where alluvial gold is washed down.

Gold Coast resort region on the E coast of Australia, stretching 32 km/20 mi along the coast of Queensland and New South Wales, south of Brisbane; population (1986) 219,000.

goldcrest smallest British bird, *Regulus regulus*, about 9 cm/3.5 in long. It is olive green, with a bright yellow streak across the crown. This warbler builds its nest in conifers.

Golden Fleece in Greek mythology, fleece of the winged ram Chrysomallus, which hung on an oak tree at Colchis guarded by a dragon. It was stolen by Jason and the Argonauts.

Golden Horde the invading Mongol-Tatar army that first terrorized Europe from 1237 under the leadership of Batu Khan, a grandson of Genghis Khan. Tamerlane broke their power 1395.

goldenrod tall, leafy perennial, *Solidago virgaurea*, family Compositae, native to North America. It produces heads of many small yellow flowers.

golden section a proportion, approximately 8:13, used by artists, designers, and architects to form the basis for an aesthetically satisfying composition. It was known to the ancient Greeks.

goldfinch songbird *Carduelis carduelis* commonly found in Europe, W Asia, and N Africa. It is black, white, and red about the head, with gold and black wings.

goldfish fish of the carp family *Carassius auratus* found in E Asia. Greenish-brown in its natural state, it has for centuries been bred by the Chinese, taking on colourful and freakishly shaped forms.

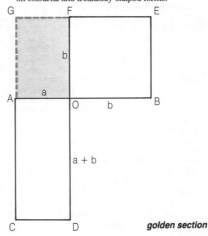

golden section

Golding William 1911–1993. British novelist, best known for his first book, *Lord of the Flies* 1954, in which savagery takes over among a group of English schoolboys marooned on a Pacific island. Later novels include *The Spire* 1964, *Rites of Passage* 1980, and *The Paper Men* 1984. Nobel Prize for Literature 1983.

Goldoni Carlo 1707–1793. Italian dramatist, born in Venice. He wrote popular comedies, including *La putta onorata/The Respectable Girl* 1749, *I pettegolezzi delle donne/Women's Gossip* 1750, and *L'Eventail/The Fan* 1763.

gold rush a large-scale influx of gold prospectors to an area where gold deposits have recently been discovered. The result is a dramatic increase in population. Cities such as Johannesburg, Melbourne, and San Francisco either originated or were considerably enlarged in a gold rush.

Goldsmith Oliver 1728–1774. English author, whose works include the novel *The Vicar of Wakefield* 1766 and the play *She Stoops to Conquer* 1773.

gold standard system under which a country's currency is exchangeable for a fixed weight of gold on demand at the central bank. It was almost universally applied 1870–1914, but by 1937 no single country was on the full gold standard. Britain abandoned the gold standard 1931; the USA abandoned it 1971. Holdings of gold are still retained because it is an internationally recognized commodity, which cannot be legislated upon or manipulated by interested countries.

Goldwater Barry 1909– . US Republican politician, presidential candidate in the 1964 election, when he was heavily defeated by Lyndon Johnson. Many of Goldwater's ideas were later adopted by the Republican right and the Reagan administration.

Goldwyn Samuel 1882–1974. US film producer. Born in Warsaw, he emigrated to the USA in 1896. He founded the Goldwyn Pictures Corporation 1917, precursor of the Metro-Goldwyn-Mayer Company 1925, later allied with United Artists. He was famed for his illogical aphorisms known as 'goldwynisms', for example 'Anyone who visits a psychiatrist should have his head examined'.

golf popular outdoor game in which a small rubber-cored ball is hit with a club (either wooden faced or iron faced). The club faces have varying angles and are styled for different types of shot. The ball is hit from a tee, a slightly elevated area, and the object of the game is to put the ball in a hole that can be anywhere between 91 m/100 yd and 457 m/500 yd away, in the least number of strokes.

Golgi apparatus or *Golgi body* a membranous structure found in the cells of ◊eukaryotes. It produces the membranes that surround the cell vesicles or ◊lysosomes. Named after the Italian physician Camillo Golgi (1844–1926).

Goliath in the Old Testament, champion of the ◊Philistines, who was said to have been slain with a stone from a sling by David in single combat in front of the opposing armies of Israelites and Philistines.

Gómez Juan Vicente 1864–1935. Venezuelan dictator 1908–35. He maintained good relations with foreign powers, including the Netherlands, UK, and USA, with their oil interests, and eliminated all foreign debts. He was reputed to be the richest man in South America. He used his well-equipped army to dominate the civilian population.

Gompers Samuel 1850–1924. US labour leader. His early career in the Cigarmakers' Union led him to found and lead the American Federation of ◊Labor 1882. Gompers advocated non-political activity within the existing capitalist system to secure improved wages and conditions for members.

Gomulka Wladyslaw 1905–1982. Polish communist politician, party leader 1943–48 and 1956–70. He introduced moderate reforms, including private farming and tolerance for Roman Catholicism.

gonadotrophin a ◊fertility drug.

Goncharov Ivan Alexandrovitch 1812–1891. Russian novelist. His first novel, *A Common Story* 1847, was followed in 1858 by his humorous masterpiece, *Oblomov*, which satirized the indolent Russian landed gentry.

Goncourt de, the brothers Edmond 1822–96 and Jules 1830–70. French writers. They collaborated in producing a compendium, *L'Art du XVIIIe siècle/18th-Century Art* 1859–75, historical studies, and a *Journal* 1887–96, which depicts French literary life of their day. Edmond de Goncourt founded the *Académie Goncourt*, opened in 1903, which awards an annual prize, the *Prix Goncourt*, to the author of the best French novel of the year.

Gonds a non-homogenous people of Central India, about half of whom speak unwritten languages belonging to the Dravidian family. There are over 4,000,000 Gonds, most of whom live in Madhya Pradesh, E Maharashtra, and N Andra Pradesh, though some are found in Orissa.

Gondwanaland land mass, including the continents of South America, Africa, Australia, and Antarctica, that formed the southern half of ◊Pangaea, the 'supercontinent' that may have existed between 250 and 200 million years ago. The northern half was ◊Laurasia.

gonorrhoea a common sexually transmitted disease arising from infection with the bean-shaped bacterium *Neisseria gonorrhoeae*. After an incubation period of two to ten days, infected men experience pain while urinating, and discharge from the penis; infected women often remain symptom-free.

González Márquez Felipe 1942– . Spanish socialist politician, leader of the Socialist Workers' Party (PSOE), prime minister from 1982. Although re-elected in the 1989 election, his popularity suffered from economic upheaval and allegations of corruption.

Good Friday in the Christian church, the Friday before Easter, which is kept in memory of the Crucifixion (the death of Jesus on the cross).

Good King Henry perennial plant *Chenopodium bonus-henricus* growing to 50 cm/1.6 ft, with triangular leaves which are mealy when young. Spikes of tiny greenish-yellow flowers appear above the leaves in midsummer.

Goodman 'Benny' (Benjamin David) 1909–1986. US clarinetist, nicknamed 'the King of Swing' for the new jazz idiom he introduced.

Goodman Paul 1911– . US writer and social critic, whose many writings (novels, plays, essays) express his anarchist, anti-authoritarian ideas. He studied youth offenders in *Growing up Absurd* 1960.

Goodyear Charles 1800–1860. US inventor, who developed vulcanized rubber 1839, particularly important for motor vehicle tyres.

Goonhilly British Telecom satellite tracking station in Cornwall, England. It is equipped with a communications satellite transmitter–receiver in permanent contact with most parts of the world.

goose name given to birds forming the genus *Anser*. Both genders are similar in appearance: they have short, webbed feet, placed nearer the front of the body than in other members of the order Anatidae,

Gorbachev *Soviet leader Mikhail Gorbachev on a visit to Britain, 1984.*

Gordon *British army general Charles Gordon.*

and the beak is slightly hooked. They feed entirely on grass and plants, 'grey' geese being very destructive to young crops.

gooseberry edible fruit of *Ribes uva-crispa*, a low-growing bush related to the currant. It is straggling in its growth, bearing straight sharp spines in groups of three, and rounded, lobed leaves. The flowers are green, and hang on short stalks. The fruits are generally globular, green, and hairy.

goosefoot plants of the family Chenopodiaceae, including fat-hen or white goosefoot, *Chenopodium album*, whose seeds were used as food in Europe from Neolithic times, and also from early times in the Americas. It grows to 1 m/3 ft tall and has lance- or diamond-shaped leaves and packed heads of small inconspicuous flowers.

gopher burrowing rodent of the family Geomyidae of North and Central America. It is grey or brown, grows to 30 cm/12 in, and has long teeth and claws.

Gorbachev Mikhail Sergeyevich 1931– . Soviet president, in power 1985–91. He was a member of the Politburo from 1980. As general secretary of the Communist Party (CPSU) 1985–91, and president of the Supreme Soviet 1988–91, he introduced liberal reforms at home (◊perestroika and ◊glasnost), proposed the introduction of multiparty democracy, and attempted to halt the arms race abroad. He became head of state 1989. He was awarded the Nobel Peace Prize 1990 but his international reputation suffered in the light of harsh state repression of nationalist demonstrations in the Baltic states. Following an abortive coup attempt by hardliners Aug 1991, international acceptance of independence for the Baltic states, and accelerated moves towards independence in other republics, Gorbachev's power base as Soviet president was greatly weakened and in Dec 1991 he resigned.

Gordian knot in Greek myth, the knot tied by King Gordius of Phrygia, only to be unravelled by the future conqueror of Asia. According to tradition, Alexander cut it with his sword 334 BC.

Gordimer Nadine 1923– . South African novelist, an opponent of apartheid. Her first novel, *The Lying Days*, appeared in 1953. She was awarded the Nobel Prize for literature in 1991.

Gordon Charles (George) 1833–1885. British general sent to Khartoum 1884 to rescue English garrisons that were under attack by the ◊Mahdi; he was himself besieged by the Mahdi's army. A relief expedition under Viscount Wolseley arrived 28 Jan 1885, to find that Khartoum, after a siege of ten months, had been captured, and Gordon killed, two days before.

Gore Albert 1948– . US Democratic politician, vice president from 1993. He served as congressman 1977–79, and as senator of Tennessee 1985–92. Like his running mate, Bill ◊Clinton, he is on the conservative wing of the party, but holds liberal views on such matters as women's rights and abortion.

Gorgon in Greek mythology, any of three sisters, Stheno, Euryale, and Medusa, who had wings, claws, enormous teeth, and snakes for hair. Medusa, the only one who was mortal, was killed by ◊Perseus, but even in death her head was still so frightful, it turned the onlooker to stone.

gorilla largest of the anthropoid apes, found in the dense forests of West Africa and mountains of Central Africa. The male stands about 2 m/6.5 ft, and weighs about 200 kg/450 lbs, females about half the size. The body is covered with blackish hair, silvered on the back in the male. Gorillas live in family groups of a senior male, several females, some younger males, and a number of infants. They are vegetarian, highly intelligent, and will attack only in self-defence.

Gorky (Russian *Gor'kiy*) name 1932–89 of ◊Nizhni Novgorod, city in central Russia.

Gorky Arshile 1904–1948. US painter, born in Armenia, who went to the USA in 1920. He painted Cubist abstracts before developing a more surreal Abstract Expressionist style.

Gorky Maxim. Pen name of Russian writer Alexei Peshkov 1868–1936. Born in Niznhi-Novgorod (renamed Gorky 1932–90 in his honour), he was exiled 1906–13 for his revolutionary principles. His works,

gorilla

Gorky *A committed, lifelong revolutionary, Maxim Gorky attracted official disapproval both before and after the 1917 Revolution.*

which include the play *The Lower Depths* 1902 and the recollections *My Childhood* 1913, combine realism with optimistic faith in the potential of the industrial proletariat.

gorse genus of plants *Ulex*, family Leguminosae, also known as **furze** or **whin**, consisting of thorny shrubs with spine-shaped leaves densely clustered along the stems, and bright yellow flowers.

Gorton John Grey 1911– . Australian Liberal politician. He was minister for education and science 1966–68, and then prime minister on the death of Holt until he resigned 1971.

goshawk bird *Accipiter gentilis* that is similar in appearance to the peregrine falcon, but with short wings and short legs.

Gospel in the New Testament generally, the message of Christian salvation; in particular the four written accounts of the life of Jesus Christ by Matthew, Mark, Luke, and John. The first three give approximately the same account or synopsis (giving rise to the name Synoptic Gospels), but differ from John.

gospel music a type of song developed in the 1920s in the black Baptist churches of the US South from spirituals, which were 18th- and 19th-century hymns joined to the old African pentatonic (five-note) scale.

Gossaert Jan Flemish painter, known as ◊Mabuse.

Gossamer Albatross the first human-powered aircraft to fly across the English Channel, in June 1979. It was designed by Paul MacCready and piloted and pedalled by Bryan Allen. The Channel crossing took 2 hours 49 minutes.

Göteborg port and industrial (ships, vehicles, chemicals) city on the W coast of Sweden, on the Göta Canal (built in 1832), which links it with Stockholm; population (1983) 424,186.

Goth E Germanic people who settled near the Black Sea around the 2nd century AD. They are divided into an eastern branch, the Ostrogoths, and a western branch, the Visigoths.

The *Ostrogoths* were conquered by the Huns in 372. They regained their independence in 454, and under ◊Theodoric the Great conquered Italy in 488–93; they disappeared as a nation after the Byzantine emperor ◊Justinian I reconquered Italy 535–55. The *Visigoths* migrated to Thrace. Under ◊Alaric they raided Greece and Italy 395–410, sacked Rome, and established a kingdom in S France. Expelled from there by the Franks, they established a Spanish kingdom which lasted until the Moorish conquest of 711.

Gothic architecture the various styles of architecture grouped under the heading of Gothic which have certain features in common: the vertical lines of tall pillars, spires, greater height in interior spaces, the pointed arch, rib vaulting, and the flying buttress.

Gothic art painting and sculpture in the style that dominated European art from the late 12th century until the early Renaissance. The great Gothic church façades held hundreds of sculpted figures and profuse ornament, and manuscripts were lavishly decorated. Stained glass replaced mural painting to some extent in N European churches. The *International Gothic* style in painting emerged in the 14th century, characterized by delicate and complex ornament and increasing realism.

Gothic novel genre established by Horace Walpole's *The Castle of Otranto* 1765, and marked by mystery, violence, and horror; an exponent of the genre was Edgar Allan Poe.

Gothic revival the modern resurgence of interest in Gothic architecture, especially as displayed in 19th-century Britain and the USA.

Götterdämmerung (German) in Scandinavian mythology, the end of the world.

Gottfried von Strassburg lived *c.* 1210. German poet, author of the unfinished epic *Tristan und Isolde* which inspired ◊Wagner.

Gould Shane Elizabeth 1957– . Australian sprint swimmer who, aged 15, won three gold medals at the 1972 Munich Olympics and became the only woman to have held all the world's freestyle records simultaneously. She was Australian of the Year 1972. She retired from competitive swimming 1973.

Gounod Charles François 1818–1893. French composer. His operas include *Sappho* 1851, *Faust* 1859, *Philémon et Baucis* 1860, and *Roméo et Juliette* 1867. He also wrote sacred songs, masses, and an oratorio, *The Redemption* 1882.

gourd name applied to various members of the family Cucurbitaceae, including the melon and pumpkin. In a narrower sense, the name applies only to the genus *Lagenaria*, of which the bottle gourd *Lagenaria siceraria* is best known.

gout disease marked by an excess of uric acid crystals in the tissues, causing pain and inflammation in one or more joints. The disease, more common in men, poses a long-term threat to the blood vessels and the kidneys, so ongoing treatment may be needed to minimize the levels of uric acid in the body fluids. Acute attacks are treated with ◊anti-inflammatories.

government system whereby political authority is exercised. Modern systems of government distinguish between liberal (Western) democracies, totalitarian (one-party) states, and autocracies (authoritarian, relying on force rather than ideology). Aristotle was the first to attempt a systematic classification of governments. His main distinctions were between government by one person, by few, and by many (monarchy, oligarchy, and democracy).

Government Communications Headquarters centre of the British government's electronic surveillance operations, popularly known as ◊GCHQ.

governor in engineering, a device that controls the speed of a machine or engine. James ◊Watt

Goya A Picnic *(late 1780s), National Gallery, London.*

invented the steam-engine governor in 1788. It works by means of heavy balls, which rotate on the end of linkages and move in or out because of ◊centrifugal force according to the speed of rotation. The movement of the balls closes or opens the steam valve to the engine. When the engine speed increases too much, the balls fly out, and cause the steam valve to close, so the engine slows down. The opposite happens when the engine speed drops too much.

Gowon Yakubu 1934– . Nigerian politician, head of state 1966–75. In the military coup of 1966 he seized power. After the Biafran civil war 1967–70, he reunited the country with his policy of 'no victor, no vanquished'. In 1975 he was overthrown by a military coup.

Goya Francisco José de Goya y Lucientes 1746–1828. Spanish painter and engraver. In 1789 he was court painter to Charles IV. His

grafting

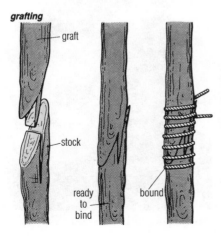

Grace The cricketer W G Grace, who helped establish cricket as England's national sport.

later works include portraits of four successive kings of Spain, and his etchings include *The Disasters of War*, depicting the French invasion of Spain 1810–14. Among his last works are the 'black paintings' (Prado, Madrid), with horrific images such as *Saturn Devouring One of his Sons* about 1822.

GP in medicine, the abbreviation for *general practitioner*.

GPU former name (1922–23) for ◊KGB, the Soviet secret police.

Graaf Regnier de 1641–1673. Dutch physician and anatomist who discovered the ovarian follicles, which were later named Graafian follicles. He gave exact descriptions of the testicles, and named the ovaries. He was also the first to isolate and collect the secretions of the pancreas and gall bladder.

Gracchus the brothers *Tiberius Sempronius* 163–133 BC and *Gaius Sempronius* 153–121 BC. Roman agrarian reformers. As ◊tribune in 133 BC, Tiberius tried to prevent the ruin of small farmers by making large slave-labour farms illegal, but was murdered. Gaius, tribune in 123 and 122 BC, revived his brother's legislation, and introduced other reforms, but was outlawed by the Senate and committed suicide.

Grace W(illiam) G(ilbert) 1848–1915. British cricketer and physician. Born at Downend, Bristol, he began playing first class cricket at the age of 15, and helped popularize the game in England.

Graces in Greek mythology, three goddesses (Aglaia, Euphrosyne, and Thalia), daughters of Zeus and Hera, the personification of grace and beauty and the inspirers of the arts and the sciences.

grafting the operation by which a piece of living tissue is removed from one organism and transplanted into the same or a different organism where it continues growing. In horticulture, it is a technique widely used for propagating plants, especially woody species. A bud or shoot on one plant, termed the scion, is inserted into another, the stock, so that they continue growing together, the tissues combining at the point of union.

Grafton Augustus Henry, 3rd Duke of Grafton 1735–1811. British politician. He became 1st Lord of the Treasury in 1766 and acting prime minister 1767–70.

Graham 'Billy' (William Franklin) 1918– . US Christian Protestant evangelist. His Evangelistic Association conducts worldwide 'crusades'.

Graham Martha 1893– . American choreographer. An innovative exponent of American modern dance, she had a major influence on choreographers in the contemporary dance movement.

Graham Thomas 1805–1869. Scottish chemist who laid the foundations of physical chemistry (the branch of chemistry concerned with changes in energy during a chemical transformation) by his work on the diffusion of gases and liquids. *Graham's Law* states that the diffusion rate of two gases varies inversely as the square root of their densities.

Grahame Kenneth 1859–1932. Scottish author. The early volumes of sketches of childhood, *The Golden Age* 1895 and *Dream Days* 1898, were followed by his masterpiece *The Wind in the Willows* 1908, an animal fantasy originally created for his young son, which was dramatized by A A Milne as *Toad of Toad Hall*.

gram metric unit of mass; one thousandth of a ◊kilogram.

grammar the principles of the correct use of language, dealing with the rules of structuring words into phrases, clauses, sentences, and paragraphs in an accepted way. Emphasis on the standardizing impact of print has meant that spoken or colloquial language is often perceived as less grammatical than written language, but all forms of a language, standard or otherwise, have their own grammatical systems of differing complexity.

grammar school in the UK, a secondary school catering for children of high academic ability, usually measured by the Eleven Plus examination. Most grammar schools have now been replaced by ◊comprehensive schools.

gramophone an old-fashioned English name for what is now called a record player, or stereo. Inventor Thomas Edison's original name for the machine, and the traditional US name, was *phonograph*.

Grampian region of Scotland
area 8,704 sq km/3,360 sq mi
towns administrative headquarters Aberdeen
products beef cattle (Aberdeen Angus and Beef Shorthorn); fishing, including salmon; North Sea oil service industries; tourism (winter skiing)
population (1984) 497,272.

Gramsci Antonio 1891–1937. Italian Marxist, who attempted to unify social theory and political practice. He helped to found the Italian Communist party in 1921, and was elected to parliament in 1924, but was imprisoned by Mussolini from 1926; his *Quaderni di carcere/Prison Notebooks* 1947 were published after his death.

Granada city in the Sierra Nevada in Andalucia, S Spain; population (1981) 262,100. It produces textiles, soap, and paper.

Granby John Manners, Marquess of Granby 1721–1770. British soldier. His head appears on many inn-signs in England as a result of his popularity as a commander of the British forces fighting in Europe in the Seven Years' War.

Gran Chaco large lowland plain in N Argentina, W Paraguay, and SE Bolivia; area 650,000 sq km/251,000 sq mi. It consists of swamps, forests (a source of quebracho timber), and grasslands, and there is cattle-raising.

grand opera a type of opera without any spoken dialogue (unlike the *opéra-comique*) as performed especially at the Paris *Opéra* from the 1820s to

granite Hay Tor (453 m/1,490 ft), one of Dartmoor's granite tors.

the 1880s. Using the enormous resources of the state-subsidized opera house, grand operas were extremely long (five acts), and included much incidental music, including a ballet.

Grand Banks continental shelf of the N Atlantic off SE Newfoundland, where the shallow waters are rich fisheries, especially for cod.

Grand Canal (Chinese *Da Yune*) the world's longest canal. It is 1,600 km/1,000 mi long, and runs north from Hangzhou to Tianjin, China. The earliest section was completed 486 BC, and the northern section was built 1282–92 AD, during the reign of Kublai Khan.

Grand Canyon vast gorge containing the Colorado river, Arizona, USA. It is 350 km/217 mi long, 6–29 km/4–18 mi wide, and reaches depths of over 1.5 km/1 mi.

Grand Design in history, a plan attributed by the French minister Sully to Henry IV of France (who was assassinated before he could carry it out) for a great Protestant union against the Holy Roman Empire; the term was also applied to President de Gaulle's vision of France's place in a united Europe.

Grande Dixence dam the world's highest dam, located in Switzerland, which measures 285 m/935 ft from base to crest. Completed in 1961, it contains 6 million cu m/8 million cu yd of concrete.

Grand Guignol genre of short horror play produced at the Grand Guignol theatre in Montmartre, Paris (called after the bloodthirsty character 'Guignol' in late 18th-century marionette plays).

Grant Hollywood film actor Cary Grant.

Grandi Dino 1895–1988. Italian politician, who challenged Mussolini for leadership of the Italian Fascist Party in 1921, but who was subsequently largely responsible for Mussolini's downfall in Jul 1943.

Grand National name given to several steeplechases, the most famous being run at Aintree, Merseyside during the Liverpool meeting in Mar or Apr over 7 km 242 m/4 mi 880 yd with 30 formidable jumps. It was first run in 1839.

Grand Remonstrance petition passed by the British Parliament in Nov 1641 which listed all the alleged misdeeds of Charles I and demanded parliamentary approval for the king's ministers and the reform of the church. Charles refused to accept the Grand Remonstrance and countered it by trying to arrest five leading members of the House of Commons (Pym, Hampden, Holles, Hesilrige, and Strode). The worsening of relations between king and Parliament led to the outbreak of the English Civil War in 1642.

Grange Movement, the in US history, a farmers' protest in the southern and midwestern states against economic hardship and exploitation. The National Grange of the Patrons of Husbandry, formed in 1867, was a network of local organizations, employing cooperative practices and advocating 'granger' laws. The movement petered out in the late 1870s, to be superseded by the ◊Greenbackers.

granite a plutonic ◊igneous rock, acidic in composition (containing a high proportion of silica), occurring in large-scale intrusions. The rock is coarsegrained, the characteristic minerals being quartz, feldspars, mica, and, particularly, orthoclase.

Grant Cary (stage-name of Archibald Leach) 1904–1986. US actor, born in Britain. His witty, debonair screen personality made him a favourite for more than three decades. His films include *Bringing Up Baby* 1937, *The Philadelphia Story* 1940, *Notorious* 1946, and *North by Northwest* 1959.

Grant Ulysses S(impson) 1822–1885. 18th president of the USA 1869–77. He was a Union general in the American Civil War and commander in chief from 1864. As a Republican president, he carried through a liberal ◊Reconstruction policy in the South, although he failed to suppress extensive political corruption within his own party and cabinet, which tarnished the reputation of his presidency.

granthi in Sikhism, the man or woman who reads from the holy book, the *Guru Granth Sahib*, during the service.

***Grant** General Ulysses S Grant, photographed in Jun 1864 at City Point, near Hopewell, Virginia, his headquarters during the American Civil War.*

graphics tablet or *bit pad* in computing an input device consisting of a pressure-sensitive tablet on which marks can be made with a stylus. The position of any mark is automatically identified and communicated to a computer for interpretation.

graphite a blackish-grey laminar crystalline form of ◊carbon, also known as *plumbago*, or black lead. It is widely used as a lubricant and as the active component of pencil lead.

grass plant of the large family, Gramineae, of monocotyledons, with about 9,000 species distributed worldwide except in the Arctic regions. The majority are perennial, with long, narrow leaves and hollow stems; hermaphroditic flowers are borne in spikelets.

Grass Günter 1927– . German writer. The grotesque humour and socialist feeling of his novels *Die Blechtrommel/The Tin Drum* 1959 and *Der Butt/The Flounder* 1977 characterize many of his poems.

grasshopper insect of the order Orthoptera, usually with strongly developed hind legs which enables it to leap. Members of the order include ◊locusts and ◊crickets.

grass of Parnassus plant *Parnassia palustris*, unrelated to grasses, found growing in marshes and on wet moors in Europe and Asia. It is low-growing, with a rosette of heart-shaped stalked leaves and has five-petalled, white flowers with conspicuous veins growing singly on stem tips in late summer.

grass-tree Australian plant of the genus *Xanthorrhoea*. The tall, thick stems have a grass-like tuft at the top and are surmounted by a flower-spike resembling a spear.

gravel mineral consisting of pebbles or small fragments of rock, originating in the beds of lakes and streams or on beaches. Gravel is quarried for use in roadbuilding, as ballast, and as an aggregate in concrete.

Graves Robert (Ranke) 1895–1985. English poet and author. He was severely wounded on the Somme in World War I, and his frank autobiography *Goodbye to All That* 1929 is one of the outstanding war books.

gravimetry the study of the Earth's gravitational field. Small variations in the gravitational field can be caused by varying densities of rocks and structure beneath the surface, a phenomenon called the *Bouguer anomaly*. These variations can

grass flower

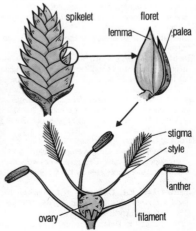

provide information about inaccessible subsurface conditions.

gravity the force of attraction between two objects because of their masses; for instance, the force we call gravity on Earth is the force of attraction between any object in the Earth's gravitational field and the Earth itself.

gravure one of the three main ◊printing methods, in which printing is done from a recessed surface. It is an ◊intaglio method, and is an economical process for high-volume printing which also reproduces illustrations well.

gray the derived SI unit of absorbed radiation dose (Gy). It is defined as the dose absorbed when the energy per unit mass imparted to matter by ionizing radiation is 1 joule/kg.

Gray Thomas 1716–1761. English poet, whose 'Elegy Written in a Country Churchyard' 1750 is one of the most quoted poems in English. Other poems include 'Ode on a Distant Prospect of Eton College', 'The Progress of Poesy', and 'The Bard'; these poems are now seen as the precursors of Romanticism.

grayling freshwater fish *Thymallus thymallus* of the family Salmonidae. It has a long multi-rayed dorsal fin, and exhibits a coloration shading from silver to purple. It is found in northern parts of North America, Europe, and Asia.

Graz capital of Styria province, and second largest city in Austria; population (1981) 243,400. Industries include engineering, chemicals, iron, and steel.

Great Australian Bight broad bay in S Australia, notorious for storms.

Great Barrier Reef chain of coral reefs and islands about 2,000 km/1,250 mi long, off the E coast of Queensland, Australia at a distance of 15–45 km/10–30 mi. It forms an immense natural breakwater, and the coral rock forms a structure larger than all human-made structures on Earth combined.

Great Bear Lake lake on the Arctic Circle, in the Northwest Territories, Canada; area 31,800 sq km/12,275 sq mi.

Great Britain official name for England, Scotland, and Wales, and the adjacent islands, from 1603 when the English and Scottish crowns were united under James I of England (James VI of Scotland). With Northern Ireland it forms the United Kingdom.

great circle a plane cutting through a sphere, and passing through the centre of the sphere, cuts the surface along a great circle. Thus, on the Earth, all meridians of longitude are half great circles; of the parallels of latitude, only the equator is a great circle.

Great Dane large short-haired dog, usually fawn in colour, standing up to 92 cm/36 in, and weighing up to 70 kg/154 lb. It has a long head, a large nose, and small ears.

Great Divide or *Great Dividing Range* E Australian mountain range, extending 3,700 km/2,300 mi N–S from Cape York Peninsula, Queensland, to Victoria.

Greater London official name for the City of London, which forms a self-governing enclave, and 32 surrounding boroughs. Certain powers were exercised over this whole area by the Greater London Council.

Greater London Council (GLC) in the UK, local authority that governed London 1965–86. The Labour Party had a majority of seats on the council after the 1964, 1973, and 1981 elections;

Great Leap Forward Silos on Shashiuyu commune near Tangshau, China.

the Conservative Party had a majority after the 1967, 1970, and 1977 elections. When the GLC was abolished in 1986 (see ◊local government) its powers either devolved back to the borough councils or were transferred to certain nonelected bodies.

Great Exhibition an exhibition held in Hyde Park, London, in 1851, proclaimed by its originator Prince Albert as 'the Great Exhibition of the Industries of All Nations'.

Great Expectations a novel by Charles Dickens, published 1860–61. Philip Pirrip ('Pip'), brought up by his sister and her husband, the blacksmith Joe Gargery, rejects his humble background and pursues wealth, which he believes comes from the elderly Miss Havisham. Ultimately he is forced by adversity to recognize the value of his origins.

Great Lakes series of five freshwater lakes along the USA–Canada border: Lakes Superior, Michigan, Huron, Erie, and Ontario; total area 245,000 sq km/94,600 sq mi. Interconnecting canals make them navigable by large ships, and they are drained by the ◊St Lawrence River.

Great Leap Forward the change in Chinese economic policy introduced under the second five-year plan of 1958–62. The basic idea, instigated by Mao Zedong, was to convert China into an industrially based economy by transferring resources away from agriculture. This coincided with the creation of people's communes. The inefficient and poorly planned allocation of state resources led to the collapse of the strategy by 1960 and a return to more adequate support for agricultural production.

Great Red Spot a prominent feature of ◊Jupiter.

Great Rift Valley longest 'split' in the Earth's surface, 8,000 km/5,000 mi long, running south from the Dead Sea (Israel/Jordan) to Mozambique.

Great Schism in European history, the period 1378–1417 in which there were rival popes in

Great Wall of China A derelict section of the Great Wall of China near Badaling, built from 214 BC, to repel Turkish and Mongol tribesmen.

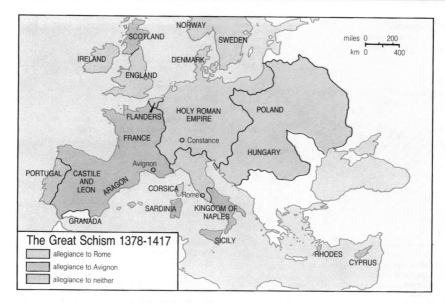

The Great Schism 1378-1417
- allegiance to Rome
- allegiance to Avignon
- allegiance to neither

Rome, Italy and Avignon, France; it was ended by the election of Martin V during the Council of Constance 1414–17.

Great Slave Lake lake in the Northwest Territories, Canada; area 28,450 sq km/10,980 sq mi.

Great Trek in South African history, the movement of 12,000–14,000 Boer (Dutch) settlers from Cape Colony in 1836 and 1837 to escape British rule. They established republics in Natal (1838–43) and the Transvaal. It is seen by many white South Africans as the main event in the founding of the present republic, and also as a justification for continuing whites-only rule.

Great Wall of China continuous defensive wall stretching from W Gansu to the Gulf of Liaodong (2,250 km/1,450 mi). It was once even longer. It was built under the Qin dynasty from 214 BC to prevent incursions by the Turkish and Mongol peoples. Some 8 m/25 ft high, it consists of a brick-faced wall of earth and stone, has a series of square watchtowers, and has been carefully restored.

Greco, El (Doménikos Theotokopoulos) 1541–1614. Spanish painter called 'the Greek' because he was born in Crete. He painted elegant portraits and intensely emotional religious scenes with increasingly distorted figures and flickering light, for example *The Burial of Count Orgaz* 1586 (Toledo).

Greece country in SE Europe, comprising the S Balkan peninsula; bounded N by Yugoslavia and Bulgaria, NE by Turkey, E by the Aegean Sea, S by the Mediterranean Sea, W by the Ionian Sea, and NW by Albania, and numerous islands to the S and E.

Greek art sculpture, mosaic, and crafts of ancient Greece (no large-scale painting survives). It is usually divided into three periods: *Archaic* (late 8th century–480 BC), showing Egyptian influence; *Classical* (480–323 BC), characterized by dignified realism; and *Hellenistic* (323–27 BC), more exuberant or dramatic. Sculptures of human figures dominate all periods, and vase painting was a focus for artistic development for many centuries.

Greek language a member of the Indo-European language family, *Modern Greek*, which is principally divided into the general vernacular (*Demotic Greek*) and the language of education and literature (*Katharevousa*), has a long and well-documented

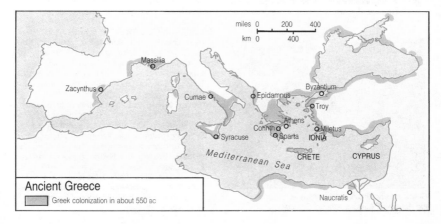

Ancient Greece
- Greek colonization in about 550 BC

Greece
Hellenic Republic
(*Elliniki Dimokratia*)

area 131,957 sq km/50,935 sq mi
capital Athens
towns Larisa; ports Piraeus, Thessaloniki, Patras, Iráklion
physical mountainous; a large number of islands, notably Crete, Corfu, and Rhodes
head of state Constantine Karamanlis from 1990
head of government Constantine Mitsotakis from 1990
political system democratic republic
exports tobacco, fruit, vegetables, olives, olive oil, textiles
currency drachma
population (1990 est) 10,066,000; growth rate 0.3% pa
life expectancy men 72, women 76
language Greek

religion Greek Orthodox 97%
literacy 96% male/89% female (1985)
GDP $40.9 bn (1987); $4,093 per head
chronology
1946 Civil war between royalists and communists; communists defeated.
1949 Monarchy re-established with Paul as king.
1964 King Paul succeeded by his son, Constantine.
1967 Army coup removed king; Col George Papadopoulos became prime minister; martial law imposed, all political activity banned.
1973 Republic proclaimed, with Papadopoulos as president.
1974 Former premier Constantine Karamanlis recalled from exile to lead government; martial law and ban on political parties lifted; restoration of the monarchy rejected by a referendum.
1975 New constitution made Greece a republic.
1980 Karamanlis resigned as prime minister and was elected president.
1981 Greece became a full member of the EC. Andreas Papandreou elected Greece's first socialist prime minister.
1983 Five-year defence and economic cooperation agreement signed with USA; ten-year economic cooperation agreement with USSR.
1985 Papandreou re-elected.
1988 Relations with Turkey improved; major cabinet reshuffle following criticism of Papandreou.
1989 Papandreou defeated in elections. Tzannis Tzannetakis became prime minister but his all-party government collapsed. Xenophon Zolotas formed new unity government. Papandreou charged with corruption.
1990 No outright majority in general election. Mitsotakis became premier and formed new all-party government. Karamanlis re-elected president.
1992 Papandreou acquitted. Greece opposed recognition of independence of the Yugoslav breakaway republic of Macedonia.

history: *Ancient Greek* from 14th to 12th century BC; *Archaic Greek* including Homeric epic language, until 800 BC; *Classical Greek* until 400 BC; Hellenistic Greek, the common language of Greece, Asia Minor, W Asia and Egypt to 4th century AD, and *Byzantine Greek* used until the 15th century and still the ecclesiastical language of the Greek orthodox Church.

Greenaway Kate 1846–1901. British illustrator, known for her drawings of children.

Greenbackers, the in US history, supporters of an alliance of agrarian and industrial organizations, known as the Greenback Labor Party, which campaigned for currency inflation by increasing the paper dollars (greenbacks) in circulation. The movement was superseded by ◊Populism.

Greene (Henry) Graham 1904–1991. British novelist. His works are often deeply concerned with religious issues, and include *Brighton Rock* 1938, *The Power and the Glory* 1940, *The Third Man* 1950, and *Monsignor Quixote* 1982.

greenfinch bird *Carduelis chloris*, common in Europe and N Africa. The male is green with a yellow breast, and the female a greenish-brown.

greenfly plant-sucking insect, a type of ◊aphid.

Greenham Common site of a continuous peace demonstration 1981–90 on common land near Newbury, Berkshire, UK, outside a US airbase. The women-only camp was established in Sept 1981 in protest against the siting of US cruise missiles in the UK. The demonstrations ended with the closure of the base.

greenhouse effect a phenomenon of the Earth's atmosphere by which solar radiation is absorbed by the Earth and, although re-emitted from the surface, is prevented from escaping from the atmosphere by ozone and carbon dioxide in the air. The result is to raise the Earth's temperature; in a garden greenhouse, the glass walls have the same effect. The United Nations Environment Programme estimates an increase in average world temperatures of 1.5 °C and a rise of 7.7 in/20 cm in sea level by 2025.

Greek art Phaidimus, *a 6th-century BC statue in the Acropolis Museum, Athens, Greece.*

Greene *British author Graham Greene.*

Greenland (Greenlandic *Kalaalit Nunaat*) world's largest island. It lies between the North Atlantic and Arctic Oceans.
area 2,175,600 sq km/840,000 sq mi
capital Godthaab (Greenlandic *Nuuk*) on W coast
exports fishing and fish processing industries
population (1983) 51,903; Inuit, Danish and other European
language Greenlandic
history Greenland was discovered *c.* 982 by ◊Eric the Red, who founded colonies on the W coast. It became a Danish colony in the 18th century, and following a referendum in 1979 was granted full internal self-government in 1981.

Green Mountain Boys in US history, irregular troops who fought to keep Vermont free from New York interference, and in the War of American Independence captured Fort Ticonderoga. Their leader was Ethan Allen (1738–89), who was later captured by the British.

Green Paper a publication issued by a British government department setting out various aspects of a matter on which legislation is contemplated, and inviting public discussion and suggestions. In due course it may be followed by a ◊White Paper, giving actual details of proposed legislation.

Green Party political party aiming to 'preserve the planet and its people', based on the premise that incessant economic growth is unsustainable. The leaderless party structure reflects a general commitment to decentralization. The British Green Party was founded 1973 as the Ecology Party (initially solely environmental). Green parties have sprung up in W Europe from the 1970s, linked to one another but unaffiliated to any pressure group. By 1989 the countries that had a number of parliamentary seats were: Austria 8, Belgium 11, Finland 4, Italy 20, Luxembourg 2, Republic of Ireland 1, Sweden 20, Switzerland 9, West Germany 42. Of the European Parliament, Belgian Green parties had 3 seats, French 9, Italian 3, Portuguese 1 and West German 8.

Greenpeace international environmental pressure group, founded 1971, with a policy of non-violent direct action backed by scientific research. During a protest against French atmospheric nuclear testing in the S Pacific 1985, its ship *Rainbow Warrior* was sunk by French intelligence agents.

green pound the exchange rate used by the European Community for the conversion of EEC agricultural prices to sterling. The prices for all EEC members are set in European Currency Units (ECUs) and are then converted into green currencies for each national currency.

green revolution in agriculture, a popular term for the change in methods of arable farming in developing countries, intended to provide more and better food for their populations and relying heavily on chemicals and machinery. It was instigated in the 1940s and 1950s, but abandoned by some countries in the 1980s.

greenshank greyish bird *Tringa nebularia* of the sandpiper group. It has long olive-green legs and a slightly upturned bill. It breeds in Scotland and N Europe.

Greenwich Mean Time (GMT) local time on the zero line of longitude (the *Greenwich meridian*), which passes through the Old Royal Observatory at Greenwich, London. It was replaced in 1986 by Coordinated Universal Time (UTC); see ◊time.

Greenwich Village section of New York's lower Manhattan which at the start of the 20th century became the bohemian and artistic quarter and, despite rising rentals, remains so.

Greer Germaine 1939– . Australian feminist, who became widely known on the publication of *The Female Eunuch* 1970. Later works include *The Obstacle Race* 1979, a study of contemporary women artists, and *Sex and Destiny: The Politics of Human Fertility* 1984.

Gregorian chant plainsong choral chants associated with Pope Gregory the Great (540–604), which became standard in the Roman Catholic Church.

Gregory Isabella Augusta (born Persse) 1852–1932. Irish playwright, associated with W B ◊Yeats in creating the ◊Abbey Theatre 1904. Her many plays include the comedy *Spreading the News* 1904 and the tragic *Gaol Gate* 1906.

Gregory name of 16 popes, including:

Gregory I St, the Great *c.* 540–604. Pope from 590, who asserted Rome's supremacy and exercised almost imperial powers. In 596 he sent St ◊Augustine to England. He introduced *Gregorian chant* (see ◊music) into the liturgy. Feast day 12 Mar.

Gregory XIII 1502–1585. Pope from 1572, who introduced the reformed *Gregorian ◊calendar*.

Gregory of Tours, St 538–594. French Christian bishop of Tours from 573, author of a *History of the Franks*. Feast day 17 Nov.

Grenada island in the Caribbean, the southernmost of the Windward Islands.

Grenadines chain of about 600 small islands in the Caribbean, part of the group known as the Windward Islands. They are divided between ◊St Vincent and ◊Grenada.

Grenville George 1712–1770. British Whig politician, prime minister and chancellor of the Exchequer 1763–65. His government prosecuted the Radical John ◊Wilkes in 1763, and passed the Stamp Act 1765 which precipitated the American War of Independence.

Grenville William Wyndham, Baron Grenville 1759–1834. British Whig politician, son of George Grenville. He was foreign secretary in 1791 and resigned along with Pitt in 1801 over King George III's refusal to assent to Catholic emancipation. He headed the 'All the Talents' coalition of 1806–07 which abolished the slave trade.

Grey Charles, 2nd Earl Grey 1764–1845. British Whig politician. He entered Parliament in 1786 and in 1806 became 1st Lord of the Admiralty, and foreign secretary soon afterwards. As prime minister 1830–34, he carried the Great Reform Bill in 1832, and the Act abolishing slavery throughout the British Empire in 1833.

Grenada

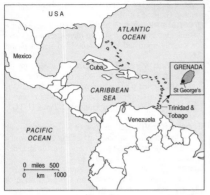

head of government Nicholas Braithwaite from 1990
political system emergent democracy
exports cocoa, nutmeg, bananas, mace
currency Eastern Caribbean dollar
population (1990 est) 84,000; annual growth rate −0.2%
language English (official) and French patois
religion Roman Catholic 60%
literacy 85% (1985)
GDP $139 million (1987); $1,391 per head
chronology
1974 Full independence achieved, with Eric Gairy elected prime minister.
1979 Gairy was removed in a bloodless coup led by Maurice Bishop. Constitution suspended and a people's revolutionary government established.
1983 Bishop was overthrown by left-wing opponents. A coup established the Revolutionary Military Council (RMC), which executed Bishop. The USA invaded Grenada, overthrowing the RMC.
1984 The newly formed New National Party (NNP) won 14 of the 15 seats in the house of representatives and its leader, Herbert Blaize, became prime minister.
1989 Blaize died and was replaced by Ben Jones.
1990 Nicholas Braithwaite of the NDC party became prime minister.
1991 Integration into the Windward Islands confederation proposed.

area (including the Grenadines, notably Carriacou) 344 sq km/133 sq mi
capital St George's
physical southernmost of the Windward Islands; mountainous
head of state Elizabeth II from 1974 represented by governor general

Grey Lady Jane 1537–1554. Queen of England 9–19 July 1553 and the great-granddaughter of Henry VII. She was married in 1553 to Lord Guildford Dudley (died 1554), son of the Duke of Northumberland. Since she was a Protestant, Edward VI was persuaded by Northumberland to set aside the claims to the throne of his sisters Mary and Elizabeth. When Edward died on 6 Jul, Jane reluctantly accepted the crown and was proclaimed queen four days later. Mary I, however, had the support of the populace and the Lord Mayor of London announced that she was queen on 19 Jul. Grey was executed on Tower Green.

greyhound ancient breed of dog, with a long narrow muzzle, slight build, and long legs, renowned for its swiftness, it is up to 75 cm/2.5 ft tall, and can exceed 60 kph/40 mph.

greyhound racing sport of greyhounds pursuing a mechanical dummy hare around a circular or oval track invented in the US, in 1919. It is popular in the UK and Australia, and attracts a lot of on- and off-course betting.

grid the network by which electricity is generated and distributed over a region or country. It contains many power stations and switching centres and allows, for example, high demand in one area to be met by surplus power generated in another. Britain has the world's largest grid system, with over 140 power stations able to supply up to 55,000 megawatts.

Grieg Edvard Hagerup 1843–1907. Norwegian composer. Much of his best music is small scale, particularly his songs, dances and piano works. Among his orchestral works are the *Piano Concerto* 1869, one of the most popular in the concert repertoire, and the incidental music for Ibsen's *Peer Gynt* 1876.

griffin mythical monster, the supposed guardian of hidden treasure, with the body, tail and hind legs of a lion, and the head, forelegs and wings of an eagle.

Griffith D(avid) W(ark) 1875–1948. US film director, generally regarded as one of the most influential figures in the development of cinema as an art.

Grey Portrait of Charles Grey attributed to Thomas Phillips (c. 1820) National Portrait Gallery, London.

Grey Portrait of Lady Jane Grey attributed to Master John (c. 1545) National Portrait Gallery, London.

Gris Violin and Fruit Dish *(1924) Tate Gallery, London.*

He made hundreds of 'one reelers' (12 minutes) 1908–13, in which he pioneered the techniques of the flash-back, cross-cut, close-up and longshot. After much experimentation with photography and new techniques came *Birth of a Nation* 1915.

griffon small breed of dog originating in Belgium, red, black, or black and tan in colour and weighing up to 5 kg/11 lb. They are square-bodied and round-headed, and there are rough and smooth-coated varieties.

griffon vulture *Gyps fulvus* a bird found in S Europe, W and Central Asia, and parts of Africa. It has a bald head with a neck ruff, and is 1.1 m/3.5 ft long with a wingspan of up to 2.7 m/9 ft.

Grignard François Auguste-Victor 1871–1935. French chemist. The so-called *Grignard reagents* (compounds containing a hydrocarbon radical, magnesium and a halogen such as chlorine) found important applications as some of the most versatile in organic synthesis.

Grimaldi Joseph 1779–1837. British clown, born in London, the son of an Italian actor. He appeared on the stage at two years old. He gave his name 'Joey' to all later clowns, and excelled as 'Mother Goose' performed at Covent Garden in 1806.

Grimm Jakob Ludwig Karl 1785–1863. Pioneer philologist (see ◊Grimm's Law) and collaborator with his brother Wilhelm Karl (1786–1859) in the *Fairy Tales* 1812–14, based on folk tales. Jakob's chief work was his *Deutsche Grammatick/German Grammar* 1819, which gave the first historical treatment of the ◊Germanic languages.

Grimm's Law in linguistics, the rule by which certain historical sound changes have occurred in some related European languages: for example Latin 'p' became English and German 'f', as in *pater/father, vater*.

Grimond Jo(seph), Baron Grimond 1913– . British Liberal politician. As leader of the party 1956–67, he aimed at making it 'a new radical party to take the place of the socialist party as an alternative to conservatism'.

Gris Juan 1887–1927. Spanish abstract painter, one of the earliest Cubists. He developed a distinctive geometrical style, often strongly coloured. He experimented with collage and made designs for Diaghilev's ballet 1922–23.

Grivas George 1898–1974. Greek Cypriot general who led ◊EOKA's attempts to secure the union (Greek ◊*enosis*) of Cyprus with Greece.

Gromyko Andrei 1909– . President of the USSR 1985–89. As ambassador to the USA from 1943, he took part in the Tehran, Yalta, and Potsdam conferences; as United Nations representative 1946–49, he exercised the Soviet veto 26 times, and was foreign minister 1957–85.

grooming in biology, the use by an animal of teeth, tongue, feet or beak to clean fur or feathers. Grooming also helps to spread essential oils for waterproofing. In many social species, notably monkeys and apes, grooming of other individuals is used to reinforce social relationships.

Gropius Walter Adolf 1883–1969. German architect. A founder-director of the ◊Bauhaus school in Weimar 1919–28, he was an advocate of team architecture and artistic standards in industrial production. His works include the Fagus-Werke (a shoe factory in Prussia), the Model Factory at the 1914 Werkbund exhibition in Cologne, and the Harvard Graduate Centre 1949–50.

grosbeak name of several thick-billed birds. The pine grosbeak *Pinicola enucleator*, also known as the pinefinch, breeds in Arctic forests. Its plumage is similar to that of the crossbill.

Gross Domestic Product (GDP) a measure (normally annual) of the total domestic output of a country, including exports, but not imports; see also ◊Gross National Product.

Grossmith George 1847–1912. British actor and singer. Turning from journalism to the stage, in 1877 he began a long association with the Gilbert and Sullivan operas, in which he created a number of parts. He collaborated with his brother Weedon Grossmith (1853–1919) in the comic *Diary of a Nobody* 1894.

Gross National Product (GNP) the most commonly used measurement of the wealth of a country. GNP is the ◊Gross Domestic Product plus income from abroad, minus income earned during the same period by foreign investors within the country. The national income of a country is the GNP minus

Grosz Suicide (1916), Tate Gallery, London.

whatever sum of money needs to be set aside to replace ageing capital stock.

Grosz Georg 1893–1959. German Expressionist painter and illustrator, a founder of the Berlin group of the Dada movement 1918. Grosz excelled in savage satirical drawings criticizing the government and the military establishment.

Grosz Károly 1930– . Hungarian communist politician, prime minister 1987–88, leader of the ruling Hungarian Socialist Workers' Party (HSWP) from 1988. He has sought to establish a flexible system of 'socialist pluralism'.

Grotius Hugo 1583–1645. Dutch jurist and politician. He became a lawyer, and later received political appointments. In 1618 he was arrested as a republican and sentenced to imprisonment for life: his wife contrived his escape 1620, and he settled in France, where he composed the *De Jure Belli et Pacis/On the Law of War and Peace* 1625, the foundation of international law.

groundnut South American annual plant, also known as the *peanut, earthnut* or *monkey nut Arachis hypogaea*, family Leguminosae. After flowering, the flowerstalks bend and force the pods into the earth so that they can ripen in near desert conditions without dessication. The nuts are a staple food in many tropical countries. They yield a valuable edible oil and are also used to make oilcake for cattle food.

grouper name given to a number of species of sea perch (Serranidae) found in warm waters. Some species grow to 2 m/6.5 ft long, and can weigh 300 kg/660 lbs.

grouse a fowl-like game bird of the family Tetraonidae, common in N America and N Europe. Grouse are mostly ground-living and are noted particularly for their courtship displays, known as ◊leks.

GRP glass-reinforced plastic. Although usually known as ◊fibreglass, this material is only strengthened by glass fibres, the rest being plastic. Products are usually moulded, mats of glass fibre being sandwiched between layers of a polyester plastic, which sets hard when mixed with a curing agent. GRP is now a favoured material for boat hulls and the bodies and some structural

components of performance cars; it is also used in saloon car-body manufacture.

Grünewald (Mathias Gothardt-Neithardt) c. 1475–1528. German painter, active in Mainz, Frankfurt, and Halle. He was court painter, architect, and engineer to the prince bishop elector of Mainz 1508–14. His few surviving paintings show an intense involvement with religious subjects.

Guadalajara industrial (textiles, glass, soap, pottery) capital of Jalisco state, W Mexico; population (1980) 2,244,715. It is a key communications centre.

Guadalcanal largest of the ◊Solomon Islands; area 6,475 sq km/2,500 sq mi; population (1984) 64,000. Gold, copra, and rubber are produced. During World War II it was the scene of a battle which was won by US forces after six months of fighting.

Guadeloupe an island group in the Leeward Islands, West Indies, an overseas department of France; area 1,779 sq km/687 sq mi; population (1982) 328,400. The main islands are Basse-Terre, on which is the chief town of the same name, and Grande-Terre. Sugar refining and rum distilling are the main industries.

Guam largest of the ◊Mariana islands in the W Pacific.

guan type of large, pheasant-like bird which lives in the forests of South and Central America. It is olive-green or brown.

guanaco wild member of the camel family *Lama guanacoe* found in South America on pampas and mountain plateaux. It grows to 1.2 m/4 ft at the shoulder, with head and body about 1.5 m/5 ft long. It is sandy-brown in colour, with a blackish face, and has fine wool. It lives in small herds and is the ancestor of the domestic llama.

Guangdong province of S China
area 231,400 sq km/89,320 sq mi
capital Guangzhou
products rice, sugar, tobacco, minerals, fish
population (1985) 61,600,000.

Guangxi autonomous region in S China
area 220,400 sq km/85,074 sq mi
capital Nanning
products rice, sugar, fruit
population (1985) 38,060,000 including the Zhuang people, allied to the Thai, who form China's largest ethnic minority.

Guangzhou (formerly Kwangchow/Canton) capital of Guangdong province, S China; population (1986) 3,290,000. Its industries include shipbuilding, engineering, chemicals, and textiles.

Guanyin in Chinese Buddhism, the goddess of mercy. In Japan she is *Kwannon* or Kannon, an attendant of the Amida Buddha (Amitābha). Her origins were in India as the male bodhisattva Avalokiteśvara.

guarana Brazilian woody climbing plant *Paullinia cupana*, family Sapindaceae. A drink made from its roasted seeds has a high caffeine content, and it is the source of the drug known as zoom in the USA. Starch, gum, and several oils are extracted from it for commercial use.

Guarneri celebrated family of violin-makers at Cremona, Italy, of whom (Bartolomeo) Giuseppe Guarneri 'del Gesù' (1698–1744) produced the finest models.

Guatemala country in central America, bounded N and NW by Mexico, E by Belize and the Caribbean Sea, SE by Honduras and El Salvador, and SW by the Pacific Ocean.

Guatemala
Republic of
(República de Guatemala)

area 108,889 sq km/42,042 sq mi
capital Guatemala City
towns Quezaltenango, Puerto Barrios (naval base)
physical mountainous, tropical
head of state and government Jorge Serrano Elías from 1991
political system democratic republic
exports coffee, bananas, cotton, sugar
currency quetzal
population (1990 est) 9,340,000 (Mayaquiche Indians 54%, mestizos 42%); annual growth rate 2.8%

life expectancy men 57, women 61
language Spanish (official) and Indian languages
religion Roman Catholic 80%, Protestant 20%
literacy 63% male/47% female (1985 est)
GDP $7 bn (1987); $834 per head
chronology
1839 Independent republic.
1954 Col Carlos Castillo became president in a US-backed coup, halting land reform.
1963 Military coup made Col Enrique Peralta president.
1966 Cesar Méndez elected president.
1970 Carlos Araña elected president.
1974 Gen Kjell Laugerud became president. Widespread political violence.
1978 Gen Fernando Romeo became president.
1981 Growth of anti-government guerrilla movement.
1982 Gen Angel Anibal became president. An army coup installed Gen Ríos Montt as head of a junta and then as president. Political violence continued.
1983 Montt removed in a coup led by Gen Mejía Victores, who declared amnesty for the guerrillas.
1985 New constitution adopted; Guatemalan Christian Democratic Party (PDCG) won congressional elections; Vincio Cerezo elected president.
1989 Coup attempt against Cerezo failed. Over 100,000 people killed, and 40,000 reported missing, since 1980.
1991 Elías of the Solidarity Action Movement elected president. Diplomatic relations with Belize established.

Guatemala City capital of Guatemala; population (1983) 1,300,000. It produces textiles, tyres, footwear, and cement.

guava tropical American tree *Psidium guajava*, family Myrtaceae; the astringent yellow pear-shaped fruit is used to make guava jelly, or it can be stewed or canned. It has a high vitamin C content.

Guayaquil city and chief port of ◊Ecuador; population (1986) 1,509,100.

Guderian Heinz 1888–1954. German general in World War II. He created the Panzer armoured divisions of the German army which formed the ground spearhead of Hitler's *Blitzkrieg* strategy, and achieved an important breakthrough at Sedan in Ardennes, France 1940 and the advance to Moscow 1941.

gudgeon freshwater cyprinid fish *Gobio gobio* found in Europe and N Asia on the gravel bottoms of streams. It is olive-brown, spotted with black, up to 20 cm/8 in long, and with a distinctive barbel at each side of the mouth.

guelder rose shrub or small tree *Viburnum opulus*, native to Europe and N Africa, with white flowers and shiny red berries.

Guelph and Ghibelline rival parties in medieval Germany and Italy, which supported the papal party and the Holy Roman emperors respectively.

Guérin Camille 1872–1961. French bacteriologist who, with Calmette, developed the Bacille Calmette-Guérin (BCG) vaccine for tuberculosis.

Guernsey second largest of the ◊Channel Islands; area 63 sq km/24.5 sq mi; population (1986) 55,500. The capital is St Peter Port. From 1975 it has been a major financial centre. Guernsey cattle originated here.

guerrilla irregular soldier fighting in a small unofficial unit, typically against an established or occupying power, and engaging in sabotage, ambush, and the like, rather than pitched battles against an opposing army. Guerrilla tactics have been used both by resistance armies in wartime (for example, the Vietnam War) and in peacetime by national liberation groups and militant political extremists.
Action Directe French group in alliance with Red Army Faction (see below); carries out bombings in Paris and elsewhere.
Amal Shi'ite Muslim militia in Lebanon.
Armed Revolutionary Nuclei NAR, neofascist; 1980 bomb in Bologna railway station, Italy, killed 76.
Black September Palestinian group named from the month when PLO guerrillas active in Jordan were suppressed by the Jordanian army; killed 11 Israelis at the Munich Olympic Games 1972.
Contras right-wing guerrillas in Nicaragua opposing the Sandinista government (see below); they receive funding from the USA.
ETA ◊Basque separatist movement in N Spain.
Hezbollah pro-Khomeini Shi'ite Muslim militia in Lebanon, the extremist wing of Amal (see above); backed by Syria and Iran.
Irish Republican Army IRA, organization committed to the formation of a unified Irish republic.
Palestine Liberation Organization PLO, organization committed to the creation of a separate Palestinian state.
Quebec Liberation Front FLQ separatist organization in Canada committed to the creation of an independent French-speaking Quebec; kidnapped and killed minister Pierre Laporte 1970.

Red Army Japan: killed 26 people at Lod airport in Israel 1972; attacked the US embassy in Indonesia 1986 and 1987.

Red Army Faction RAF, opposing 'US imperialism', formerly led by Andreas Baader and Ulrike Meinhof, active in West Germany from 1968.

Red Brigades Italy: kidnap and murder of Prime Minister Aldo Moro 1978; kidnap of US Brig-Gen James Lee Dozier 1981.

Sandinista National Liberation Front Marxist organization which overthrew the dictatorship in Nicaragua 1978–79 to form its own government.

Symbionese Liberation Army USA: kidnap of Patricia Hearst, granddaughter of the newspaper tycoon, 1974.

Tamil Tigers Tamil separatists in Sri Lanka.

Tupamaros left-wing urban guerrillas founded by Raoul Sendic in Montevideo, Uruguay, 1960; named after the Peruvian Indian leader Tupac Amaru.

Ulster Defence Association UDA Protestant anti-IRA organization in Northern Ireland, formed 1971; sometimes styled Ulster Freedom Fighters.

Guesdes Jules 1845–1922. French socialist leader from the 1880s who espoused Marxism and revolutionary change. His movement, the *Partie Ouvrier Français (French Workers' Party) was eventually incorporated in the foundation of the SF10 (Section Française de l'International Ouvrière/*French Section of International Labour) in 1905.

Guevara Ernesto 'Che' 1928–1967. Argentinian revolutionary. He was trained as a doctor, but in 1953 left Argentina because of his opposition to Perón. In effecting the Cuban revolution of 1959, he was second only to Castro and Castro's brother Raúl. In 1965 he moved on to fight against white mercenaries in the Congo, and then to Bolivia, where he was killed in an unsuccessful attempt to lead a peasant rising. He was an orthodox Marxist, and his guerrilla techniques were influential.

Guiana the NE part of South America, including ◊French Guiana, ◊Guyana, and ◊Suriname.

guild or *gild* medieval association, particularly of artisans or merchants, formed for mutual aid and protection and the pursuit of a common purpose, religious or economic. After the 16th century the position of the guilds was undermined by the growth of capitalism.

guillemot diving seabird of the auk family which breeds in large numbers on the rocky N Atlantic coasts. The *common guillemot Uria aalge* has a sharp bill and short tail, and sooty-brown and white plumage. Guillemots build no nest, but lay one large, almost conical egg on the rock.

guillotine beheading device consisting of a metal blade that descends between two posts. It was commonly in use in the Middle Ages, but was introduced in an improved design (by physician Joseph Ignace Guillotin 1738–1814) in France in 1792. It is still in use in some countries.

Guinea country in W Africa, bounded to the N by Senegal, NE by Mali, SE by the Ivory Coast, SW by Liberia and Sierra Leone, W by the Atlantic, and NW by Guinea-Bissau.

Guinea-Bissau country in W Africa, bounded to the N by Senegal, E and SE by Guinea, and SW by the Atlantic.

guinea fowl African game bird, family Numididae, especially the helmet guinea fowl *Numida meleagris*, which has a horny growth on the head, white-spotted feathers, and fleshy cheek wattles. It is the ancestor of the domestic fowl.

guinea pig a species of ◊cavy, a type of rodent.

Guinevere in Arthurian legend, the wife of King

Guinness *English actor Alec Guinness.*

Arthur. Her adulterous love affair with the knight ◊Lancelot led ultimately to Arthur's death.

Guinness Alec 1914– . English actor. His many stage appearances include Hamlet 1938 and Lawrence of Arabia in *Ross* 1960. In 1979 he gained a 'lifetime achievement' Oscar (films include *Kind Hearts and Coronets* 1949 and *The Bridge on the River Kwai* 1957).

Guinness affair in British law, a case of financial fraud during the takeover of Distillers by the brewing company Guinness in 1986. Those accused of acting illegally to sustain Guinness share prices include Ernest Saunders, former chief executive. The trial, lasting from Feb to Aug 1990, was widely seen as the first major test of the government's legislation increasing control of financial dealings on London's Stock Exchange. Ernest Saunders, Gerald Ronson, and Sir Jack Lyons were found guilty on a variety of theft and false-accounting charges.

Guise Henri 3rd Duke of Guise 1550–1588. French nobleman who persecuted the Protestant Huguenots and was largely responsible for the Massacre of St Bartholomew 1572. He was assassinated.

guitar six-stringed, flat-backed musical instrument plucked or strummed with the fingers, a development of the ◊lute, derived from a Moorish original.

Guiyang formerly *Kweiyang* capital and industrial city of ◊Guizhou province, S China; population (1989) 1,490,000. Industries include metals and machinery.

Guizhou formerly *Kweichow* province of S China
area 174,000 sq km/67,164 sq mi
capital Guiyang
products rice, maize; nonferrous minerals
population (1990) 32,392,000.

Guizot François Pierre Guillaume 1787–1874. French politician and historian. He wrote on the history of civilization, and became prime minister in 1847. His resistance to all reforms led to the revolution of 1848.

Gujarat state of W India
area 195,984 sq km/75,650 sq mi
capital Gandhinagar
products cotton, petrochemicals, oil, gas, rice, textiles
population (1991) 41,174,000
languages Gujarati, Hindi

Guinea
Republic of
(*République de Guinée*)

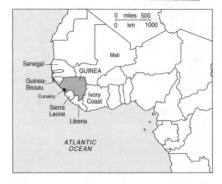

area 245,857 sq km/94,901 sq mi
capital Conakry
towns Labe, N'Zérékoré, Kankan
physical flat coastal plain with mountainous

interior; sources of rivers Niger, Gambia, and
Senegal; forest in SE
head of state and government Lansana Conté
from 1984
political system military republic
exports coffee, rice, palm kernels, alumina,
bauxite, diamonds
currency syli or franc
population (1990 est) 7,269,000 (chief peoples are
Fulani, Malinke, Susu); growth rate 2.3% pa
life expectancy men 39, women 42
language French (official), African languages
religion Muslim 85%, Christian 10%, local 5%
literacy men 40%/women 17% (1985 est)
GNP $1.9 bn (1987); $369 per head
chronology
1958 Full independence from France; Sékou
Touré elected president.
1977 Opposition to Touré's Marxist policies forced
him to accept return to mixed economy.
1980 Touré returned for fourth seven-year term.
1984 Touré died. Bloodless coup established a
military committee for national recovery, led by Col
Lansana Conté.
1985 Attempted coup against Conté failed
1990 Sent troops to join the multilateral force that
attempted to stabilize Liberia.
1991 Antigovernment general strike by National
Confederation of Guinea Workers.

Gujarati inhabitant of Gujarat on the NW seaboard
of India. The Gujaratis number approximately 27
million. Gujaratis are predominantly Hindu (90%),
with Muslim (8%) and Jain (2%) minorities.

Gujarati or Gujerati language a member of
the Indo-Iranian branch of the Indo-European
language family, spoken in and around the state
of Gujarat in India. Its script is a variant of the
Devanagari script used for Sanskrit and Hindi.

Gulf States oil-rich countries sharing the coastline of the Arabian/Persian Gulf (Iran, Iraq,
Bahrein, Kuwait, Oman, Qatar, Saudi Arabia, and
the United Arab Emirates).

Gulf Stream ocean ◊current arising from the
warm waters of the equatorial current, which

flows N from the Gulf of Mexico. It slows to a
broadening 'drift' off Newfoundland, splitting as it
flows E across the Atlantic, and tempering the
harshness of the climate of the British Isles and
Western Europe.

Gulf War *1* another name for the ◊Iran–Iraq War.
2 war 16 Jan–28 Feb 1991 between Iraq and a
coalition of 28 nations led by the USA. The invasion
and annexation of Kuwait by Iraq on 2 Aug 1990
provoked a build-up of US troops in Saudi Arabia,
eventually totalling over 500,000. The UK subsequently deployed 42,000 troops, France 15,000,
Egypt 20,000, and other nations smaller contin-
gents. An air offensive lasting six weeks, in which
'smart' weapons came of age, destroyed abut one-

Guinea-Bissau
Republic of (*Republica da
Guiné-Bissau*)

area 36,125 sq km/13,944 sq mi
capital and chief port Bissau
physical flat coastal plain rising to savanna in E
head of state and government João Bernardo
Vieira from 1980
political system socialist pluralist republic

exports rice, coconuts, peanuts, fish, salt, timber
currency peso
population (1989 est) 929,000; growth rate 2.4% pa
life expectancy 42 (1990)
language Portugese (official), Crioulo (Cape
Verdean dialect of Portuguese), African languages
religion animist 54%, Muslim 38%, Christian 8%
literacy men 46%/women 17% (1985 est)
GDP $135 million (1987); $146 per head
chronology
1956 PAIGC formed to secure independence from
Portugal.
1973 Two-thirds of the country declared
independent, with Luiz Cabral as president of a
state council.
1974 Independence achieved from Portugal.
1980 Cape Verde decided not to join a unified state.
Cabral deposed, and João Vieira became chair of a
council of revolution.
1981 PAIGC confirmed as the only legal party, with
Vieira as its secretary-general.
1982 Normal relations with Cape Verde restored.
1984 New constitution adopted, making Vieira
head of government as well as head of state.
1989 Vieira re-elected.
1991 Other parties legalized.
1992 Multiparty electoral commission established.

third of Iraqi equipment and inflicted massive casualties. A 100-hour ground war followed, which effectively destroyed the remnants of the 500,000-strong Iraqi army in or near Kuwait.

gull seabird of the family Laridae. Gulls are usually 25–75 cm/10–30 in long, white with grey or black on the back and wings, and with a large beak.

gum in botany, complex polysaccharides (carbohydrates) formed by plants and trees, particularly from dry regions. They form five main groups: plant exudates, for example, gum arabic; marine plant extracts, for example, agar; seed extracts; fruit and vegetable extracts; and synthetic gums. Gums are tasteless and odourless, insoluble in alcohol and ether but generally soluble in water. They have many uses. Gum is also a common name for the ◊eucalyptus tree.

gum arabic substance obtained from certain species of ◊acacia, with uses in medicine, confectionery, and adhesive manufacture.

gun name for all kinds of firearms; see also ◊artillery, ◊machine gun, ◊pistol, and ◊small arms.

gun metal a high-copper (88%) alloy, also containing tin and zinc, so called because it was once used to cast cannons. It is tough, hardwearing, and resists corrosion.

gunpowder the oldest known ◊explosive, a mixture of sulphur, sodium or potassium nitrate ($NaNO_3$ or KNO_3) and charcoal.

Gunpowder Plot the Catholic conspiracy to blow up James I of Britain and his parliament on 5 Nov 1605. It was discovered through an anonymous letter sent to Lord Monteagle (1575–1622), and Guy Fawkes was found in the cellar beneath the Palace of Westminster, ready to fire a store of explosives. Several of the conspirators were killed, and Fawkes and seven others were executed.

Guomindang Chinese National People's Party, founded 1894 by ◊Sun Yat-sen (Sun Zhong Shan), which overthrew the Manchu Empire 1912. From 1927 the right wing, led by ◊Chiang Kai-shek (Jiang Jie Shi), was in conflict with the left, led by Mao Zedong, until the Communist victory 1949 (except for the period of the Japanese invasion 1937–45). It survives as the sole political party of Taiwan, where it is still spelled *Kuomintang.*

gurdwara Sikh place of worship and meeting. As well as a room housing the *Guru Granth Sahib,* the holy book, the gurdwara contains a kitchen and eating area for the *langar,* or communal meal.

Gurkha soldiers of Nepálese origin, recruited since 1815 for the British Army. The Brigade of Gurkhas headquarters is in Hong Kong.

gurnard genus of tropic and temperate zone coastal fish (*Trigla*) in the family Trigilidae, which creep along the sea bottom by means of three finger-like appendages detached from the pectoral fins.

guru a Hindu or Sikh leader, or religious teacher.

Gush Emunim (Hebrew 'Bloc of the Faithful') Israeli fundamentalist group, founded in 1973, who claim divine right to the West Bank, Gaza Strip, and Golan Heights as part of Israel. The claim is sometimes extended to the Euphrates.

Gustaf V 1858–1950. King of Sweden from 1907, when he succeeded his father Oscar II. He married Princess Victoria, daughter of the Grand Duke of Baden, in 1881, thus uniting the reigning Bernadotte dynasty with the former royal house of Vasa.

Gustaf VI 1882–1973. King of Sweden from 1950, when he succeeded his father Gustaf V. He was an archaeologist and expert on Chinese art. He was succeeded by his grandson ◊Carl XVI Gustaf.

Gustavus Adolphus 1594–1632. King of Sweden from 1611, when he succeeded his father Charles IX. He waged successful wars with Denmark, Russia, and Poland, and in the ◊Thirty Years' War became a champion of the Protestant cause. Landing in Germany in 1630, he defeated the German general Wallenstein at Lützen, SW of Leipzig, on 6 Nov 1632, but was killed.

Gustavus Vasa 1496–1560. King of Sweden from 1523, when he was elected after leading the Swedish revolt against Danish rule. He united and

Gutenberg *The earliest illustration of a printing press, as invented by Johann Gutenberg. It is from the* Danse Macabre *printed by Mathias Lyons, 1499.*

Guyana
Cooperative Republic of

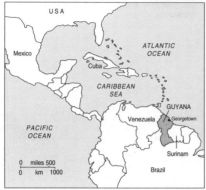

area 210,000 sq km/83,000 sq mi
capital and port Georgetown
physical mostly tropical rainforest

head of state Desmond Hoyte from 1985
head of government Cheddi Jagan from 1992
political system democratic republic
exports sugar, rice, rum, timber, diamonds
currency Guyanese dollar
population (1989 est) 846,000 (50% descendants of workers introduced from India, 30% black, 5% Amerindian); annual growth rate 2%
life expectancy men 66, women 71
language English (official), Hindi, Amerindian
religion Christian 57%, Hindu 33%, Sunni Muslim 9%
literacy 97% male/95% female (1985 est)
GNP $359 million (1987); $445 per head
chronology
1953 Assembly elections won by left-wing party (PPP). Britain installed interim administration, claiming fear of communist takeover.
1961 Internal self-government granted.
1966 Full independence achieved.
1970 Guyana became a republic within the Commonwealth.
1980 Forbes Burnham became the first executive president under new constitution.
1985 Burnham died and was succeeded by Desmond Hoyte.
1992 PPP won decisive victory in assembly elections; Jagan returned as prime minister.

pacified the country and established Lutheranism as the state religion.

Gutenberg Johann *c.* 1400–1468. German printer, considered the inventor of printing from moveable metal type. He is believed to have printed the Mazarin and the Bamberg Bibles.

Guthrie Woody. Stage name of Woodrow Wilson Guthrie 1912–1967. US folk singer and songwriter, whose left-wing protest songs, 'dustbowl ballads', and *talking blues* were an influence on, among others, Bob Dylan; they include 'Deportees', 'Hard Travelin', and 'This Land is Your Land'.

guttation the secretion of water onto the surface of leaves through specialized pores, or ◊hydathodes. The process occurs most frequently during conditions of high humidity when the rate of transpiration is low. Drops of water found on grass in early morning are often the result of guttation, rather than dew. Sometimes the water contains minerals in solution, such as calcium, which leaves a white crust on the leaf surface as it dries.

Guyana country in South America, bounded to the N by the Atlantic Ocean, E by Suriname, S and SW by Brazil, and NW by Venezuela.

Guzmán Blanco Antonio 1829–1899. Venezuelan dictator and military leader (*caudillo*). He seized power in 1870 and remained the absolute ruler until 1889. He modernized Caracas as the political capital and committed resources to education, communications, and agriculture, as well as encouraging foreign trade.

Gwent county of S Wales
area 1,376 sq km/531 sq mi
towns administrative headquarters Cwmbran; Abergavenny, Newport, Tredegar
products salmon and trout on the Wye and Usk; iron and steel at Llanwern
population (1991) 442,200
language 2.5% Welsh-speaking; English.

Gwyn Eleanor ('Nell') 1651–1687. English comedy actress from 1665, formerly an orange-seller at Drury Lane Theatre. From 1669 she was the mistress of Charles II (the elder of her two sons by him was created Duke of St Albans 1684), his last wish being 'Let not poor Nellie starve'.

Gwynedd county in NW Wales
area 3,867 sq km/1,493 sq mi
towns administrative headquarters Caernafon; Bangor; resorts Pwllheli, Barmouth
products cattle and sheep, gold (at Dolgellau), textiles, electronics, slate
population (1991) 235,450
language 61% Welsh-speaking; English.

gymnastics physical exercises, originally just for health and training (so-named from the way in which men of ancient Greece trained *gymnos* 'naked'). The *gymnasia* were schools for training competitors for public games.
Men's gymnastics includes high bar, parallel bars, horse vault, rings, pommel horse and floor exercises.
Women's gymnastics includes asymmetrical bars, side horse vault, balance beam and floor exercises.

gymnosperm in botany, any plant whose seeds are exposed, as opposed to the structurally more advanced ◊angiosperms, where they are inside an ovary. The group includes conifers and related plants such as cycads and ginkgos, whose seeds develop in ◊cones. Fossil gymnosperms have been found in rocks about 350 million years old.

gynaecology the medical speciality concerned with diseases of the female reproductive system.

gynoecium or *gynaecium* the collective term for the female reproductive organs of a flower, consisting of one or more ◊carpels, either free or fused together.

gypsum a common mineral, composed of hydrated calcium sulphate, $CaSO_4.2H_2O$. It rates 2 on Mohs scale of hardness. Gypsum has a number of commercial uses.

gyre a circular flow of ocean water; a type of current. Gyres are large and permanent, typically occupying half an ocean. Their movements are dictated by the prevailing winds and the ◊Coriolis effect. They move clockwise in the northern hemisphere and anticlockwise in the southern hemisphere.

gyroscope mechanical instrument, used as a stabilizing device, and consisting, in its simplest form, of a heavy wheel mounted on an axis fixed in a ring that can be rotated about another axis, which is also fixed in a ring capable of rotation about a third axis. Important applications of the gyroscope principle include the gyrocompass, the gyropilot for automatic steering, and gyro-directed torpedoes.

ha abbreviation for ◊*hectare*.

Haakon seven kings of Norway, including:

Haakon I (the Good) *c.* 915–961. King of Norway from about 935. The son of Harald Hárfagri ('Finehair') (*c.* 850–930), king of Norway, he was raised in England. He seized the Norwegian throne and tried unsuccessfully to introduce Christianity to Norway.

Haakon IV 1204–1263. King of Norway from 1217, the son of Haakon III. Under his rule, Norway flourished both militarily and culturally; he took control of the Faroe Islands, Greenland 1261, and Iceland 1262–64.

Haakon VII 1872–1957. King of Norway from 1905. Born Prince Charles, the second son of Frederick VIII of Denmark, he was elected king of Norway on separation from Sweden, and in 1906 he took the name Haakon. In World War II he refused to surrender to Germany and, when armed resistance in Norway was no longer possible, carried on the struggle from Britain until his return in 1945.

Haarlem industrial town in the W Netherlands, 20 km/12 mi W of Amsterdam; population (1984) 217,000. At Velsea to the N a road-rail tunnel runs under the North Sea Canal, linking N and S Holland. Industries include chemicals, pharmaceuticals, textiles, and printing.

habanera or *havanaise* a slow dance in two-four time originating in Havana, Cuba, which became popular when introduced into Spain during the 19th century. There is a famous example in Bizet's opera *Carmen*.

habeas corpus (Latin 'have the body'). In English law, a writ directed to someone who has custody of a prisoner, ordering them to bring the prisoner before the court issuing the writ, and to explain why the prisoner is detained in custody. Traditional rights to habeas corpus were embodied in law mainly due to Lord ◊Shaftesbury, in the Habeas Corpus Act (1679); the Scottish equivalent is the Wrongous Imprisonment Act (1701). The main principles were also adopted in the US constitution.

Haber Fritz 1868–1934. German chemist whose conversion of atmospheric nitrogen to ammonia opened the way for the synthetic fertilizer industry. His study of the combustion of hydrocarbons led to the commercial 'cracking' or fractionating of natural oil into its components, for example diesel, petrol, and paraffin. In electrochemistry he was the first to demonstrate that oxidation and reduction take place at the electrodes; from this he developed a general electrochemical theory.

habitat in ecology, the localized ◊environment in which an organism lives. Habitats are often described by the dominant plant type or physical feature, thus an oak-wood habitat or rocky seashore habitat.

Habsburg European royal family, former imperial house of Austria-Hungary. The name comes from the family castle in Switzerland. The Habsburgs held the title Holy Roman emperor 1273–91, 1298–1308, 1438–1740, and 1745–1806. They ruled Austria from 1278, under the title emperor 1806–1918.

hacker in computing, a person who uses a microcomputer linked to the telephone network to gain access without authorisation to confidential records held on large-scale computer installations. In the UK, hacking is legal, as long as no damage is done (a ruling given by the House of Lords in 1988).

haddock fish *Melanogrammus aeglefinus* of the cod family found off the N Atlantic coasts. It is brown with silvery underparts, and black markings above the pectoral fins. It can grow to a length of 1 m/3 ft.

Hades in Greek mythology, the underworld where spirits went after death, usually depicted as a cavern or pit underneath the earth. It was presided over by the god Hades or ◊Pluto (Roman ◊Dis).

Hadith a collection of the teachings of ◊Muhammad and stories about his life, regarded by Muslims as a guide to living second only to the ◊Koran.

Hadlee Richard John 1951– . New Zealand cricketer. In 1987 he equalled Ian Botham's world record of 373 wickets in test cricket.

Hadrian 76–138 AD. Roman emperor. Born in Spain, he was adopted by his kinsman, the emperor Trajan, whom he succeeded in 117. He abandoned Trajan's conquests in Mesopotamia, and adopted a defensive policy which included the building of Hadrian's Wall in Britain. Part of his Roman villa is now a museum.

Hadrian's Wall Roman fortification built 122–26 AD to mark England's northern boundary and abandoned about 383; it runs 185 km/115 mi from Wallsend on the river Tyne to Maryport, W Cumbria.

Haeckel Ernst Heinrich 1834–1919. German scientist and philosopher. His theory of 'recapitulation' (that embryonic stages represent past stages in the organism's evolution) has been superseded, but stimulated research in ◊embryology.

haematite a red or red-black mineral, the principal ore of iron, consisting mainly of iron (ferric)

Hadrian's Wall A section of Hadrian's Wall leading eastwards to Housesteads Fort.

oxide, Fe_2O_3 with a low proportion of phosphorous.

haematology branch of medicine concerned with disorders of the blood.

haemoglobin a protein which carries oxygen. In vertebrates it occurs in red blood cells, giving them their colour. Oxygen attaches to haemoglobin in the lungs or gills where the amount dissolved in the blood is high. This process effectively increases the amount of oxygen that can dissolve in the blood. The oxygen is later released in the body tissues where it is at low concentration.

haemolymph the circulatory fluid of those molluscs and insects that have an 'open' circulatory system. Haemolymph contains water, amino acids, sugars, salts, and white cells like those of blood. Circulated by a pulsating heart, its main functions are to transport digestive and excretory products around the body. In molluscs, it also transports oxygen and carbon dioxide.

haemolysis the destruction of red blood cells. Aged cells are constantly being lysed (broken down), but increased wastage of red cells is seen in some infections and blood disorders. It may result in ◊anaemia and ◊jaundice.

haemophilia an inherited disease in which normal blood clotting is impaired. The sufferer experiences prolonged bleeding from the slightest wound, as well as painful internal bleeding without apparent cause.

haemorrhage loss of blood from the circulation. It is 'manifest' when the blood can be seen, as when it flows from a wound, and 'occult' when the bleeding is internal, as from an ulcer or internal injury.

haemorrhoids distended (◊varicose) veins of the anus, popularly called piles.

haemostasis the natural mechanisms by which bleeding ceases of its own accord. The damaged vessel contracts, restricting the flow, and blood ◊platelets 'plug' the opening, releasing chemicals essential to clotting.

hafnium a metallic element, symbol Hf, atomic number 72, relative atomic mass 178.6. It occurs in zircon, and its properties and compounds closely resemble those of zirconium. It is highly absorbent of neutrons, and is used in control rods in nuclear reactors.

Haganah Zionist military organization in Palestine. It originated under Turkish rule before World War I to protect Jewish settlements, and many of its members served in the British forces in both world wars. After World War II it condemned guerrilla activity, opposing the British authorities only passively. It formed the basis of the Israeli army after Israel was established in 1948.

Haggadah in Judaism, the part of the Talmudic literature not concerned with to religious law (the *Halakah*) but devoted to folklore and stories of heroes.

Haggard H(enry) Rider 1856–1925. English novelist. Born in Norfolk, he held colonial service posts in Natal and the Transvaal 1875–79, then returned to England to train as a barrister. He used his South African experience in his romantic adventure tales, including *King Solomon's Mines* 1885 and *She* 1887.

Hague, The (Dutch *Gravenhage* or *Den Haag*) seat of the Netherlands government, linked by canal with Rotterdam and Amsterdam; population (1984) 672,100. It is also the seat of the United Nations International Court of Justice.

ha-ha in landscape gardening, a sunken boundary wall permitting an unobstructed view beyond a garden; a device much used by Capability ◊Brown.

Hahn Otto 1879–1968. West German physical chemist, who discovered ◊nuclear fission.

hahnium the former name for the element ◊unnilpentium.

Haifa port in NE Israel; population (1984) 227,000. Industries include oil refining and chemicals.

Haig Alexander (Meigs) 1924– . US general and Republican politician. He became President Nixon's White House chief of staff at the height of the ◊Watergate scandal, was NATO commander 1974–79, and was secretary of state to President Reagan 1981–82.

Haig Douglas, 1st Earl Haig 1861–1928. British army officer, commander in chief in World War I. His Somme (France) offensive in the summer of 1916 made considerable advances only at enormous cost, and his Passchendaele (Belgium) offensive (Jul–Nov 1917) achieved little at huge loss.

haiku 17-syllable Japanese verse form, usually divided into three lines of 5, 7, and 5 syllables. ◊Bashō popularized the form in the 17th century.

hail precipitation in the form of pellets of ice, (hailstones). It is caused by the circulation of moisture in strong convection currents, usually within cumulo-nimbus ◊cloud.

Haile Selassie Ras Tafari (the Lion of Judah) 1892–1975. Emperor of Ethiopia(1930-74). He pleaded unsuccessfully to the League of Nations against Italian conquest of his country 1935–36, and lived in the UK until his restoration in 1941. He was deposed by a military coup and died in captivity. Followers of ◊Rastafarianism believe that he was the Messiah, the incarnation of God (Jah).

Hainan island in the South China Sea; area 34,000 sq km/13,000 sq mi; population 2,700,000. The capital is Haikou. In 1987 Hainan was designated a Special Economic Zone, in 1988 it was separated from Guangdong and made a

Haile Selassie *Haile Selassie was emperor of Ethiopia until he was deposed in a military coup in 1974.*

Haiti
Republic of
(*République d'Haiti*)

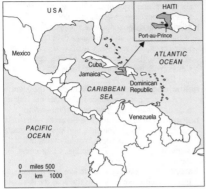

area 27,740 sq km/10,710 sq mi
capital Port-au-Prince
physical mainly mountainous and tropical
interim head of state Joseph Nerette from 1991
head of government Marc Bazin from 1992
political system transitional

exports coffee, sugar, sisal, cotton, cocoa, rice
currency gourde
population (1990 est) 6,409,000; annual growth
rate 1.7%
life expectancy men 51, women 54
language French (official) and creole
religion Christian 95%, voodoo 4%
literacy 40% male/35% female (1985 est)
GDP $2.2 bn (1987); $414 per head
chronology
1804 Independence from France achieved.
1957 Dr François Duvalier (Papa Doc) elected
president.
1964 Duvalier pronounced himself president for life.
1971 Duvalier died and was succeeded by his son,
Jean-Claude (Baby Doc).
1986 Duvalier deposed and replaced by Lt-Gen
Henri Namphy, as head of a governing council.
1988 Leslie Manigat became president in Feb.
Namphy staged a military coup in Jun, but another
coup in Sept led by Brig-Gen Prosper Avril
replaced him with a civilian government under
military control.
1989 Coup attempt against Avril foiled; US aid
resumed.
1990 Ertha Pascal-Trouillot became acting president.
1991 Jean-Bertrand Aristide elected president but
then overthrown in a military coup. Joseph Nerette
became interim head of state.
1992 Marc Bazin appointed president.

new province. It is China's second largest island.

Haiphong industrial port in N Vietnam; population
(1989) 456,000. It has shipyards, and industries include cement, plastics, phosphates, and
textiles.

hair a thread-like structure growing from mammalian skin. Each hair grows from a pit-shaped follicle
embedded in the second layer of the skin, the
dermis. It consists of dead cells impregnated with
the protein keratin. A coat of hair helps to insulate
land mammals by trapping air next to the body. It
also aids camouflage and protection, and its colouring or erection may be used for communication.

hairstreak one of a group of butterflies, belonging to the Blues (Lycaenidae), which live in both
temperate and tropical regions. Most of them are
brownish in their adult form, and they are nearly
all tailed.

Haiti country in the Caribbean, occupying the W
part of the island of Hispaniola, to the E is the
Dominican Republic.

hajj the pilgrimage to ◊Mecca which should be
undertaken by every Muslim at least once in a
lifetime, unless he or she is prevented by financial
or health difficulties.

hake fish *Merluccius merluccius* of the cod family,
found in N European, African, and American
waters. Its silvery, elongated body attains 1 m/3 ft.
It has two dorsal fins and one long anal fin.

Hakluyt Richard 1553–1616. English geographer
whose chief work is *The Principal Navigations,
Voyages and Discoveries of the English Nation*
1589–1600.

halal conforming to the rules laid down by Islam.
The term can be applied to all aspects of life, but
is usually used for food that is allowed under Muslim dietary laws; this includes meat from animals
that have been slaughtered in the correct ritual
fashion.

Haldane J(ohn) B(urdon) S(anderson) 1892–1964.
British scientist and writer. A geneticist, Haldane

was best known as a popular science writer of such
books as *The Causes of Evolution* 1933 and *New
Paths in Genetics* 1941.

Haldane Richard Burdon, Viscount Haldane
1856–1928. British Liberal politician. As secretary
for war 1905–12, he sponsored the army reforms
that established an expeditionary force, backed by a
territorial army and under the unified control of an
imperial general staff. He was Lord Chancellor
1912–15 and in the Labour government of 1924.
His writings on German philosophy led to popular
accusations of his being pro-German.

Hale George Ellery 1868–1938. US astronomer,
who made pioneer studies of the Sun and founded
three major observatories. In 1889, he invented the
spectroheliograph, a device for photographing the
Sun at particular wavelengths.

Hale Nathan 1755–1776. US nationalist, hanged by
the British as a spy in the War of American Independence. Reputedly his final words were 'I regret
that I have but one life to give for my country'.

Haleb Arabic name of ◊Aleppo, a city in Syria.

Halévy Ludovic 1834–1908. French novelist and
librettist. He collaborated with Hector Crémieux in
the libretto for Offenbach's *Orpheus in the Underworld*; and with Henri Meilhac on librettos for
Offenbach's *La Belle Hélène* and *La Vie parisienne*,
and for Bizet's *Carmen*.

Haley Bill 1927–1981. US pioneer of rock and roll,
originally a western-swing musician. His songs
'Rock Around the Clock' 1954 (recorded with his
group the Comets and featured in the 1955 film
Blackboard Jungle) and 'Shake, Rattle and Role'
1955 came to symbolize the beginnings of the rock-
and-roll era.

half-life during ◊radioactive decay, the time in
which the strength of a radioactive source decays to
half its original value. It may vary from millionths of a
second to billions of years.

halftone process a technique used in printing to
reproduce the full range of tones in a photograph
or other illustration. The intensity of the printed

colour is varied from full strength to the lightest shades, although only one colour of ink is used. The picture to be reproduced is photographed through a screen ruled with a rectangular mesh of fine lines, which breaks up the tones of the original into dots which vary in size according to the intensity of the tone. In the darker shades the dots are large and run together, in the lighter shades they are small and separate.

halibut fish *Hippoglossus hippoglossus* of the family Pleuronectidae found in the N Atlantic . Largest of the flatfish, it may reach over 2 m/6 ft and weigh 90–135 kg/200–300 lb. It is very dark mottled brown or green above and pure white beneath.

Halicarnassus ancient city in Asia Minor (now Bodrum in Turkey), where the tomb of Mausolus, built about 350 BC by widowed Queen Artemisia, was one of the Seven Wonders of the World. The Greek historian Herodotus was born here.

Halifax capital of Nova Scotia, E Canada's main port; population (1986) 296,000. Its industries include lumber, steel, and sugar refining.

Halifax Edward Frederick Lindley Wood, Earl of Halifax 1881–1959. British Conservative politician. He was viceroy of India 1926–31. As foreign secretary 1938–40 he was associated with Chamberlain's 'appeasement' policy. He received an earldom in 1944 for services to the Allied cause while ambassador to the USA 1941–46.

Hall Peter (Reginald Frederick) 1930– . British theatre, opera, and film director. He was director of the Royal Shakespeare Theatre at Stratford 1960–68 and developed the Royal Shakespeare Company as director 1968–73 until appointed director of the National Theatre 1973–88, succeeding Laurence Olivier.

Hall effect production of a voltage across a conductor or semiconductor carrying a current at right-angles to a surrounding magnetic field. It was discovered in 1897 by the US physicist Edwin Hall (1855–1938).

Haller Albrecht von 1708–1777. Swiss physician and scientist, one of the founders of modern ◊neurology. He studied the muscles and nerves, and concluded that nerves provide the stimulus which triggers muscle contraction. He also showed that it is the nerves, not muscle or skin, which permit sensation.

Halley Edmund 1656–1742. English scientist. In 1682 he observed Halley's comet, predicting its return in 1759.

Halley's comet a comet which orbits the Sun about every 76 years, named after Edmund Halley. It is the largest and brightest comet that reappears regularly, and orbits in the opposite direction to the planets in a range between the orbits of Venus and Neptune. Its appearance in 1986 was studied by space probes, which found it to have an elongated nucleus 15 km/10 mi by 8 km/5 mi covered with a dark crust of dust, through which jets of gas shoot at high speeds to produce its glowing head and tail. Records of Halley's comet go back to 240 BC, although the comet itself is much older. It is due to reappear 2061.

hallmark official mark on gold, silver, and (from 1913) platinum, instituted in the UK in 1327 (royal charter of London Goldsmiths) for the prevention of fraud. After 1363 personal marks of identification were added. Tests of metal content are carried out at authorized assay offices in London, Birmingham, Sheffield, and Edinburgh; each assay office has its distinguishing mark, to which is added a maker's mark, date letter, and mark guaranteeing standard.

Hallowe'en the evening of 31 Oct, immediately preceding the Christian Festival of Hallowmas or All Saints' Day. Customs associated with Hallowe'en in the USA and the UK include wearing masks or costumes, and 'trick or treating', going from house to house collecting sweets and money.

Hallstatt archaeological site in Upper Austria, SW of Salzburg. The salt workings date from prehistoric times, and in 1846 over 3,000 graves were discovered, belonging to a 9th–5th century BC Celtic civilization transitional between the Bronze and Iron ages.

hallucinogen substance which acts on the ◊central nervous system to produce hallucinations. Hallucinogens include LSD, peyote, and mescaline.

halogen one of a group of five elements with similar chemical bonding properties, and showing a gradation of physical properties. In order of reactivity, the elements are fluorine, F, chlorine, Cl, bromine, Br, iodine, I, and astatine, At.

halophyte a plant adapted to live where there is a high concentration of salt in the soil, for example, in saltmarshes and mudflats.

Hals Frans 1581/85–1666. Flemish-born painter of lively portraits, such as the *Laughing Cavalier* 1624 (Wallace Collection, London), and large groups of military companies, governors of charities, and others (many examples in the Frans Hals Museum, Haarlem).

Hamaguchi Hamaguchi Osachi, also known as Hamaguchi Yuko 1870–1931. Japanese politician and prime minister 1929–30, during the economic depression. His policies created social unrest and alienated military interests. His acceptance of the terms of the London Naval Agreement of 1930 was also unpopular. Shot by an assassin in November 1930, he died of his wounds 9 months later.

Hamburg largest port of Europe, in West Germany, on the Elbe; population (1986) 1,576,000. Industries include oil, chemicals, electronics, and cosmetics.

Hamilcar Barca *c.* 270–228 BC. Carthaginian general, father of ◊Hannibal. From 247 to 241 BC he harassed the Romans in Italy, and then led an expedition to Spain where he died in battle.

Hamilton capital (since 1815) of Bermuda, on Bermuda Island; population (1980) 1,617. It was founded in 1612.

Hamilton Alexander 1757–1804. US politician, who influenced the adoption of a constitution with a strong central government, and was the first secretary of the treasury 1789–95. He led the Federalist Party, and incurred the bitter hatred of Aaron ◊Burr when he voted against Burr and in favour of Jefferson for the presidency in 1801.

Hamilton Emma (born Amy Lyon) 1765–1815. British courtesan. After Admiral ◊Nelson's return from the Nile in 1798 she became his mistress and their daughter, Horatia, was born in 1801.

Hamilton James, 1st Duke of Hamilton 1606–1649. Scottish adviser to Charles I, he led an army against the ◊Covenanters 1639, and subsequently took part in the negotiations between Charles and the Scots. In the second Civil War he led the Scottish invasion of England, but was captured at Preston and executed.

Hamilton Richard 1922– . British artist, a pioneer of Pop art. His collage *Just what is it that makes today's homes so different, so appealing?* 1956 (Kunsthalle, Tübingen) is often cited as the first Pop art work.

Hamilton William Rowan 1805–1865. Irish mathematician, whose formulation of Isaac Newton's

hammerhead

mechanics proved adaptable to quantum theory, and whose 'quarternion' theory was a forerunner of the branch of mathematics known as vector analysis.

Hamite member of an African people, descended, according to tradition, from Ham, son of ◊Noah in the Bible: they include the ancient Egyptians, and the Berbers and Tuareg of N Africa. Hamitic languages are related to the Semitic.

Hamito-Semitic languages a family of languages spoken widely throughout the world but commonly associated with North Africa and Western Asia. It has two main branches, the *Hamitic* languages of North Africa and the *Semitic* languages originating in Syria and Mesopotamia, Palestine and Arabia but now found from Morocco in the west to the Arabian or Persian Gulf in the east.

Hamlet a tragedy by William Shakespeare, first performed in 1600 or 1601. Hamlet, after much hesitation, avenges the murder of his father, the king of Denmark, by the king's brother Claudius, but in the process his rejected lover Ophelia commits suicide and Hamlet and his mother die.

Hammarskjöld Dag 1905–1961. Swedish secretary-general of the United Nations 1953–61. Over the ◊Suez Crisis 1956 he opposed Britain. His attempts to solve the problem of Congo (now Zaïre), where he was killed in a plane crash, were criticized by the USSR. He won the Nobel Peace Prize in 1961.

hammerhead several species of shark in the genus *Sphyrna*, found in tropical seas, characterized by having eyes at the ends of a double-headed 'hammer'. It can grow to 4 m/13 ft.

Hammerstein Oscar II 1895–1960. Lyricist and librettist, who collaborated with Richard ◊Rodgers on some of the best known American musicals.

Hammett Dashiell 1894–1961. US crime novelist. His works *The Maltese Falcon* 1930, *The Glass Key* 1931, and the *The Thin Man* 1932 introduced the hard-bitten 'private eye' character.

Hammurabi King of Babylon from *c.* 1792 BC. He united his country and took it to the height of its power, although his consolidation of the legal code was bloodthirsty in its punishments.

Hampden John 1594–1643. English politician. He sat in the parliaments of 1621, 1625, and 1626, and became conspicuous when in 1627 he was imprisoned for refusing to pay a forced loan. His refusal in 1636 to pay ◊ship money made him a national figure. In the Short and Long parliaments he proved himself a skilful debater and parliamentary strategist. Charles's attempt to arrest him and four other leading MPs made the Civil War inevitable. He raised his own regiment on the outbreak of hostilities, and on 18 Jun 1643 was mortally wounded at the skirmish of Chalgrove Field in Oxfordshire.

Hampshire county of S England
area 3,777 sq km/1,458 sq mi

towns administrative headquarters Winchester; Southampton, Portsmouth, Gosport
products agricultural; oil from refineries at Fawley; chemicals, pharmaceuticals, electronics
population (1986) 1,509,500.

hamster type of rodent of the family Cricetidae with a thickset body, short tail and cheek pouches to carry food. A number of species are found across Asia and in SE Europe. Hamsters are often kept as pets.

Hancock John 1737–1793. American revolutionary politician. He advocated resistance to the British as president of the Continental Congress 1775–77, and was the first to sign the Declaration of Independence in 1776. He was governor of Massachusetts 1780–85 and 1787–93.

handball a team ball game now played indoors, popularized in Germany in the late 19th century. It is similar to association football, but played with the hands instead of the feet.

Handel Georg Friedrich 1685–1759. German composer. In 1712 he settled in England, where he established his popularity with works such as *Water Music* 1717 (written for George I). His great contribution is to choral music, such as *Messiah* 1742.

Hangchow former name for ◊Hangzhou, port in Zhejiang province, China.

hanging execution by suspension, usually with a drop of 0.6–2 m/2–6 ft, so that the powerful jerk of the tightened rope breaks the neck. This was once a common form of ◊capital punishment in Europe and was abolished in the UK 1965.

hanging participle see ◊participle.

Hangzhou port (formerly Hangchow), capital of Zhejiang province, China; population (1984) 1,223,000. It has jute, steel, chemical, tea, and silk industries.

Hannibal 247–182 BC. Carthaginian general from 221 BC, son of ◊Hamilcar Barca. His siege of Saguntum (modern Sagunto, near Valencia) precipitated the 2nd ◊Punic War. Following a brilliant campaign in Italy (after crossing the Alps in 218 BC with 57 elephants), Hannibal was the victor at Trasimene in 217 BC and Cannae in 216 BC, but failed to take Rome. In 203 BC he returned to Carthage to meet a Roman invasion, but was defeated at Zama in 202 BC, and was exiled in 196 BC at Rome's insistence.

Hanoi capital of Vietnam, on the Red River; population (1979) 2,571,000. Industries include textiles, paper, and engineering.

Hanover industrial city, capital of Lower ◊Saxony, West Germany; population (1984) 517,900. Industries include machinery, vehicles, electrical goods, rubber, textiles, and oil refining.

Handel Portrait by Thomas Hudson (1756) National Portrait Gallery, London.

Hanover German royal dynasty which ruled Great Britain and Ireland 1714–1901. Under the Act of ◊Settlement 1701, the succession passed to the ruling family of of Hanover, Germany, on the death of Queen Anne. On the death of Queen Victoria the crown passed to Edward VIII of Saxe-Coburg.

Hansard the official report of the proceedings of the British Parliament. Named after Luke Hansard (1752–1828), printer of the House of Commons *Journal* from 1774. The first official reports were published from 1803 by the political journalist Cobbett, who during his imprisonment of 1810–12 sold the business to his printer, Thomas Curson Hansard, son of Luke Hansard. The publication of the debates remained in the hands of the family until 1889, and is now the responsibility of the Stationery Office. The name *Hansard* was officially adopted 1943.

Hanseatic League a confederation of N European trading cities from the 12th century to 1669. At its height in the later 14th century the Hanseatic League included over 160 towns, among them Lübeck, Hamburg, Cologne, Breslau, and Cracow. The basis of its power was its monopoly of the Baltic trade and its relations with Flanders and England. The decline of the Hanseatic League from the 15th century was caused by the movement of trade routes and the development of national states.

Hansom Joseph Aloysius 1803–1882. British architect. His works include the Birmingham town hall 1831, but he is remembered as the introducer of the *hansom cab* in 1834, a two-wheel carriage with a seat for the driver on the outside.

Hanukkah eight-day festival in Judaism which takes place at the beginning of Dec. It celebrates the recapture of the Temple in Jerusalem by Judas Maccabees in 164 BC.

Hanuman in the Sanskrit epic ◊Rāmāyana, the Hindu monkey god and king of Hindustan (N India). He assisted Rama to recover his wife Sita, abducted by Ravana of Lanka (modern Sri Lanka).

haploid having one set of ◊chromosomes in each cell. Most higher organisms are ◊diploid, that is they have two sets, but most plants and many seaweeds are haploid, as are female honey bees (because they develop from eggs that have not been fertilized).

Hapsburg English form of ◊Habsburg, European royal family and former imperial house of Austria-Hungary.

Haq Fazlul 1873–1962. Leader of the Bengali Muslim peasantry. He was a member of the Viceroy's Defence Council, established in 1941, and later became Bengal's first Indian prime minister.

hara-kiri ritual suicide of the Japanese samurai (military caste) from the 12th century onwards. It was carried out to avoid dishonour or disgrace, either voluntarily or on the order of a feudal lord. The correct Japanese term is *seppuku*.

Harappa ruined city of a prehistoric Indian culture, the ◊Indus Valley Civilization.

Harare capital of Zimbabwe, on the Mashonaland plateau about 1,525 m/5,000 ft above sea level; population (1982) 656,000. It is the centre of a rich farming area (tobacco and maize), with metallurgical and food processing industries.

Harbin port on the Songhua river, NE China; the capital of ◊Heilongjiang province. It is a centre for metallurgical and machinery industries; population (1986) 2,630,000. Harbin was developed by Russian settlers after Russia was granted trading rights there in 1896, and more Russians

***Hardie** British socialist Keir Hardie.*

arrived as refugees after the October Revolution 1917.

Harcourt William Vernon 1827–1904. British Liberal politician. Under Gladstone he was home secretary 1880–85 and chancellor of the Exchequer 1886 and 1892–95. He is remembered for his remark in 1892: 'We are all Socialists now.'

hard copy output from a computer that is printed on paper rather than displayed on a screen.

Hardicanute c. 1019–1042. King of England from 1040. Son of Canute, he was king of Denmark 1028. In England he was known as a harsh ruler.

Hardie (James) Keir 1856–1915. Scottish socialist, Member of Parliament for West Ham, London, 1892–95 and for Merthyr Tydfil, Wales, from 1900. In 1888 he was the first Labour candidate to stand for Parliament; he entered Parliament independently as a Labour member in 1892 and was a chief founder of the ◊Independent Labour Party in 1893.

Harding Warren G(amaliel) 1865–1923. 29th president of the USA 1921–23, a Republican. Harding was born in Ohio, and entered the US Senate in 1914. As president he concluded the peace treaties of 1921 with Germany, Austria, and Hungary. He opposed US membership of the League of Nations, thus reinforcing the traditional US position of neutrality. There were charges of corruption among members of his cabinet (the ◊Teapot Dome Scandal).

hardness a physical property of materials that governs their use. Methods of heat treatment can increase the hardness of metals. A scale of hardness was devised by Friedrich ◊Mohs in the 1800s, based upon the hardness of certain minerals from soft talc (Mohs hardness 1) to diamond (10), the hardest of all materials. See also ◊Brinell hardness test.

hardware in computing, the mechanical, electrical and electronic components of a computer system, as opposed to the various programs which constitute ◊software and ◊firmware.

Hardy Oliver 1892–1957. US film comedian, member of the duo ◊Laurel and Hardy.

Hardy Thomas 1840–1928. English novelist and poet. His novels, set in rural 'Wessex' (based on his native Dorset) portray intense human relationships played out in a harshly indifferent natural world. They include *Far From the Madding Crowd* 1874, *The Mayor of Casterbridge* 1886, *Tess of the D'Urbervilles* 1891, and *Jude*

Harlow The American film star Jean Harlow, popularly known as the 'platinum blonde'.

the Obscure 1895. His poetry includes the *Wessex Poems* 1898 and the blank-verse epic *The Dynasts* 1904–1908.

hare any mammal of the genus *Lepus*, family Leporidae, larger than the ◊rabbit, with very long black-tipped ears, long hind legs, and short upturned tail.

harebell perennial plant *Campanula rotundifolia*, with bell-shaped blue flowers, found on dry grassland and heaths.

Hare Krishna popular name for a member of the ◊International Society for Krishna Consciousness, derived from their chant.

Hare's apparatus in physics, a specific kind of ◊hydrometer used to compare the relative densities of two liquids, or to find the density of one if the other is known. It was invented by the US chemist Robert Hare (1781–1858).

Hargobind 1595–1644. sixth guru (teacher) of Sikhism 1606–44. He encouraged Sikhs to develop military skills in response to growing persecution. At the festival of ◊Diwali Sikhs celebrate his release from prison.

Hargraves Edward Hammond 1816–1891. Australian prospector. In 1851 he found gold in the Blue Mountains of New South Wales, thus beginning the first Australian gold rush; he was made commissioner of crown lands and given a government award of £10,000.

Hargreaves James died 1778. British inventor. About 1764 he invented his 'spinning-jenny', which enabled a number of threads to be spun simultaneously by one person.

Harijan (Hindi 'children of god') member of the Indian ◊caste of untouchables. The name was coined by Mahatma Gandhi.

Harlem Globetrotters US touring basketball team who play exhibition matches worldwide. Comedy routines as well as their great skills are a feature of their games. They were founded by Abraham Saperstein (1903-1966) in 1927.

Harlem Renaissance a movement in US literature in the 1920s which used black life and traditional black culture as its subject matter; it was an early manifestation of black pride in the USA. The centre of the movement was the Harlem area of New York City.

Harlow Jean, born Harlean Carpentier 1911–1937. American film actress, the first 'platinum blonde'. Her films include *Hell's Angels* 1930 and *Saratoga* 1937.

harmattan in meteorology, a dry and dusty NE wind that blows over W Africa.

harmonica either *musical glasses* graded and filled with water, playable with small hammers, for which Mozart and Beethoven composed, or *mouth organ* invented by Wheatstone in 1829, in which small metal reeds of varied size, affixed to small slots in a narrow box, produce the notes when blown.

harmonics in music, the series of sounds of different pitches generated naturally by the vibration of a pipe or string when a note is played. This gives tone colour or timbre to an instrument.

harmonium portable, pipeless organ with a five-octave keyboard. Reeds are vibrated by air from foot-operated bellows.

harmony in music, any simultaneous combination of sounds, as opposed to melody, which is a succession of sounds. Although the term 'harmony' suggests a pleasant or agreeable sound, it is properly applied to any combination of notes, whether consonant or dissonant. Harmony deals with the formation of chords, their interrelation and logical progression.

Harold two kings of England:

Harold I died 1040. King of England from 1035. Known as *Harefoot* he was the illegitimate son of Canute, and claimed the throne 1035 when the legitimate heir Hardicanute was in Denmark. In 1037 he was elected king.

Harold II c. 1020–1066. King of England, elected in Jan 1066. In 1063 William of Normandy tricked him into swearing to support his claim to the English throne (see ◊William I), and when the Witan (council of Anglo-Saxon kings) elected Harold to succeed Edward the Confessor, William prepared to invade. Meanwhile, Harold's treacherous brother Tostig (died 1066) joined the king of Norway, Harald III Hardrada (1015–66), in invading Northumbria: Harold routed and killed them at Stamford Bridge on 25 Sept. Three days later William landed at Pevensey, Sussex; Harold was killed at the Battle of Hastings 14 Oct 1066.

harp plucked musical string instrument, with the strings stretched vertically within a wooden frame, normally triangular. It has up to 47 strings, and seven pedals set into the soundbox at the base to alter pitch.

Harpies in early Greek mythology, wind spirits; in later legend they have horrific women's faces and the bodies of vultures.

harpsichord keyboard musical instrument popular in the 16th–18th centuries, until superceded by the piano. The strings are plucked by quills, not struck by hammers. It was revived in the 20th century for authentic performance of early music.

harrier bird of prey of the genus *Circus* of the family Accipitridae. They have long wings and legs, short beaks and soft plumage. They are found throughout the world.

harrier breed of dog, a small hound originally used for hare-hunting.

Harrier the only truly successful vertical take-off and landing fixed-wing aircraft, often called the *jump jet*. Built in Britain, it made its first flight in 1966. It has a single ◊jet engine and a set of swivelling nozzles. These deflect the jet exhaust vertically downwards for take-off and landing, and to the rear for normal flight.

Harriman (William) Averell 1891–1986. US diplomat, administrator of ◊lend-lease in World War II, Democratic secretary of commerce in Truman's administration, 1946–1948, negotiator of the Nuclear Test Ban Treaty with the USSR in 1963.

Harris Arthur Travers 1892–1984. British marshal of the Royal Air Force in World War II. Known as 'Bomber Harris', he was commander in chief of Bomber Command 1942–45.

Harris Joel Chandler 1848–1908. US author of the tales of 'Uncle Remus', based on black folklore, about Br'er Rabbit and Tar-Baby.

Harrison Benjamin 1833–1901. 23rd president of the USA 1889–93, a Republican. He called the first Pan-American Conference, which led to the establishment of the Pan American Union, to improve inter-American cooperation, and develop commercial ties. In 1948 this became the ◊Organization of American States.

Harrison William Henry 1773–1841. 9th president of the USA 1841. Elected 1840 as a Whig, he died a month after taking office. Benjamin Harrison was his grandson.

harrow an agricultural implement used to break up the furrows left by the ◊plough and reduce the soil to a fine tilth. It is also used after sowing to cover the seeds. The traditional harrow consists of spikes set in a frame, and other harrows use sets of discs.

Hart Gary 1936– . US Democrat politician, senator for Colorado from 1974. In 1980 he contested the Democratic nomination for the presidency, and stepped down from his Senate seat in 1986 to stand, again unsuccessfully, in the 1988 presidential campaign.

hartebeest type of large African antelope *Alcelaphus buselaphus* with lyre-shaped horns set close on top of the head in both sexes. It may reach 1.5 m/5 ft at the rather humped shoulders, and up to 2 m/6 ft long. Clumsy-looking runners, hartebeest can still reach 65 kph/40 mph.

Hartley L(eslie) P(oles) 1895–1972. British novelist, noted for his exploration of the sinister. His books include *The Go-Between* 1953 and *The Hireling* 1957, both made into films.

hart's-tongue fern *Phyllitis scolopendrium*; its strap-like undivided fronds, up to 60 cm/2 ft long, have prominent brown spore-bearing organs in parallel lines on the underside of the leaf. It is found on walls, shady rocky places and in woods, especially in wet areas.

Harun al-Rashid 763–809. Caliph of Baghdad from 786 of the Abbasid dynasty, a lavish patron of music, poetry, and letters, known from the *Arabian Nights* stories.

harvestman arachnid of the order Opiliones. They are distinguished from true spiders by the absence of a waist or constriction in the oval body. They are carnivorous, and found from the Arctic to the tropics.

harvest-mite scarlet or rusty brown ◊mite common in summer and autumn. They are parasitic, and their bites are intensely irritating to humans.

Harvey William 1578–1657. English physician who discovered the circulation of blood. In 1628 he published his great book *De Motu Cordis* (*On the Motion of the Heart*). This contains a precise account of how the heart beats, and announces his discovery of the circulation of the blood.

Harwell the main research establishment of the United Kingdom Atomic Energy Authority, situated near the village of Harwell in Oxfordshire.

Haryana NW state of India
area 44,222 sq km/17,074 sq mi
capital Chandigarh
products sugar, cotton, oilseed, textiles, cement and iron ore
population (1991) 16,317,700
language Hindi.

Hasdrubal Barca died 207 BC, Carthaginian general, son of ◊Hamilcar Barca and brother of ◊Hannibal. He remained in command in Spain when Hannibal invaded Italy, and, after fighting there against the ◊Scipios until 208, marched to Hannibal's relief. He was defeated and killed in the Metaurus valley, NE Italy.

Hašek Jaroslav 1883–1923. Czech writer, who in 1915 deserted to the Russians, and eventually joined the Bolsheviks. His comic masterpiece is the unfinished *The Good Soldier Schweik* 1920–23.

hashish resinous form of the drug ◊cannabis.

Hassan II 1929– . King of Morocco from 1961; from 1976 he undertook the occupation of Western Sahara when it was ceded by Spain.

Hassidim or *Chasidim* a group of ultra-conservative Orthodox Jews, originating in an 18th-century movement that stressed intense emotion as a part of worship. Many of their ideas are based on the ◊kabbala.

Hastings, Battle of battle on 14 Oct 1066 at which William the Conqueror defeated Harold, king of England. The site is in fact 10 km/6 mi inland of Hastings, at Senlac, Sussex; it is marked by Battle Abbey.

Hathaway Anne 1556–1623. Wife of ◊Shakespeare from 1582.

Hathor in ancient Egyptian mythology, the sky-goddess, identified with ◊Isis.

Hatshepsut *c.* 1540–*c.* 1481 BC. Queen of Egypt during the 18th dynasty. She was the daughter of Thothmes I, with whom she ruled until the accession to the throne of her husband and half-brother Thothmes II. Throughout her reign real power lay with Hatshepsut, and she continued to rule after his death, as regent for her nephew Thothmes III.

Hattersley Roy 1932– . British Labour politician. On the right wing of the Labour Party, he was prices secretary 1976–79, and deputy leader of the party 1983–1992.

Haughey Charles 1925– . Irish Fianna Fáil politician of Ulster descent. Dismissed in 1970 from Jack Lynch's cabinet for alleged complicity in IRA gun-running, he was afterwards acquitted. Prime minister 1979–81, Mar–Nov 1982, and 1986–92, when he was replaced by Albert Reynolds.

Hausa Muslim people of N Nigeria, whose Afro-Asiatic language is a *lingua franca* of W Africa.

haustorium (plural *haustoria*) a specialized organ produced by a parasitic plant or fungus which penetrates the cells of its host to absorb nutrients. It may be either an outgrowth of ◊hyphae, as in the case of parasitic fungi, or of the stems of flowering parasitic plants, as seen in dodders (*Cuscuta*).

Havana capital and port of Cuba; population (1989) 2,096,100. Products include cigars and tobacco.

Havel Vaclav 1936– . Czech playwright and politician, president of Czechoslovakia 1989–92 and of the Czech Republic from 1993. His works include *The Garden Party* 1963, and *Largo Desolato* 1985, about a dissident intellectual. Havel became widely known as a human-rights activist. He was imprisoned 1979–83 and again 1989 for support of Charter 77, a human-rights manifesto. As president of Czechoslovakia he sought to preserve a united republic, but resigned in recognition of the breakup of the federation 1992.

Hawaii Pacific state of the USA; nickname Aloha State
area 16,764 sq km/6540 sq mi
capital Honolulu on Oahu
town Hilo
products sugar, coffee, pineapples, bananas and flowers; offshore cobalt, nickel and manganese

population (1990) 1,108,200 whom about 34% are European, 25% Japanese, 14% Filipino, 12% Hawaiian, and 6% Chinese
language English
religion Christianity; minority Buddhism
famous people Father Joseph Damien
history a kingdom until 1893, Hawaii became a republic 1894, ceded itself to the USA 1898, and became a state 1959.

hawfinch European finch *Coccothraustes coccothraustes* about 18 cm/7 in long. It is rather uncommon and spends most of its time in the treetops. It feeds on berries and seeds, and can crack cherry stones with its large and powerful bill.

hawk name of various small to medium-sized birds of prey, other than eagles and vultures, of the family Accipitridae. They have an untoothed hooked bill, short, broad wings, and keen eyesight.

Hawke Bob (Robert) 1929– . Australian Labor politician, prime minister 1983–91, on the right wing of the party. He was president of the Australian Council of Trade Unions 1970–80. He announced his retirement from politics 1992.

Hawking Stephen 1942– . English physicist, who has conducted important research into ◊black holes and gravitational field theory. His books include *A Brief History of Time* 1988.

Hawkins Coleman (Randolph) 1904–1969. US virtuoso tenor saxophonist. He was until 1934 a soloist in the swing band led by Fletcher Henderson (1898–1952), and was an influential figure in bringing the jazz saxophone to prominence as a solo instrument.

Hawkins John 1532–1595. English navigator, born in Plymouth. Treasurer to the navy 1573–89, he was knighted for his services as a commander against the Spanish Armada 1588.

Hawkins Richard *c.* 1562–1622. English navigator, son of John Hawkins. He held a command against the Spanish Armada in 1588; was captured in an expedition against Spanish possessions 1593–94 and not released till 1602; knighted in 1603.

hawk moth family of moths (Sphingidae) with some 1,000 species distributed throughout the world, but mainly tropical.

Hawks Howard 1896–1977. US director and producer of a wide range of films with popular appeal, including *The Big Sleep* 1946.

Hawksmoor Nicholas 1661–1736. English architect, assistant to ◊Wren in London churches and St

Hawking British physicist and mathematician Professor Stephen Hawking.

Paul's; joint architect with ◊Vanbrugh of Castle Howard and Blenheim Palace.

Haworth Norman 1883–1950. English organic chemist who was the first to synthesize a vitamin (vitamin C), in 1933.

hawthorn shrubs and trees of the *Crataegus* genus, family Rosaceae. The **common hawthorn, may** or **whitehorn** *Crataegus monogyna*, a thorny shrub or small tree, bears clusters of white or pink flowers followed by groups of red berries. Native to Europe, N Africa and W Asia, it has been naturalized in North America and Australia.

Hawthorne Nathaniel 1804–1864. US author of *The Scarlet Letter* 1850, a powerful novel of the Puritan Boston of 200 years earlier. He wrote three other novels, including *The House of the Seven Gables* 1851, and many short stories, including *Tanglewood Tales* 1853, classic legends retold for children.

hay a form of preserved grass used for winter livestock feed. The grass is cut and allowed to dry in the field before being removed for storage in a barn.

Hayden Williams 1933– . Australian Labor politician. Leader of the Australian Labor Party and of the opposition 1977–83, he became minister of foreign affairs 1983 and governor general 1989.

Haydn (Franz) Joseph 1732–1809. Austrian composer. A teacher of both Mozart and Beethoven, he was a major exponent of the classical sonata form in his numerous chamber and orchestral works (he wrote over 100 symphonies). He also wrote much choral music; the best-known including the oratorios *The Creation* 1798 and *The Seasons* 1801. He was the first great master of the string quartet.

Hayes Rutherford B(irchard) 1822–1893. 19th president of the USA 1877–81, a Republican. During his presidency federal troops (see ◊Reconstruction) were withdrawn from the Southern states and the Civil Service reformed.

hay fever an allergic reaction to pollen, causing sneezing and asthmatic symptoms. In those who are specially sensitive, powerful body chemicals, related to ◊histamine, are produced at the site of entry, causing irritation.

hazardous substances waste substances, usually generated by industry, that represent a hazard to the environment or to people living or working nearby. Examples include radioactive wastes, acidic resins, arsenic residues, residual hardening salts, lead, mercury, non-ferrous sludges, organic solvents, and pesticides.

hazel trees of the genus *Corylus*, family Corylaceae, including **common hazel** or **cobnut** *Corylus avellana* of which the **filbert** is the cultivated variety.

Hazlitt William 1778–1830. British essayist and critic, noted for his invective, scathing irony and gift for epigram. His critical essays include *Characters of Shakespeare's Plays* 1817–18, *Lectures on the English Poets* 1818–19, *English Comic Writers* 1819, and *Dramatic Literature of the Age of Elizabeth* 1820.

H-bomb abbreviated form of ◊hydrogen bomb.

headache pain in the head, which has causes ranging from minor eye strain, stress, infection and neck or jaw muscle strain to severe physical illness, for example brain tumour. It is marked by dilation of the cerebral blood vessels and irritation of the brain linings (meninges) and of the nerves.

Heal Ambrose 1872–1959. English cabinet-maker who took over the Heal's shop from his father and developed it into the famous London store in Tottenham Court Road. He initially designed

heart

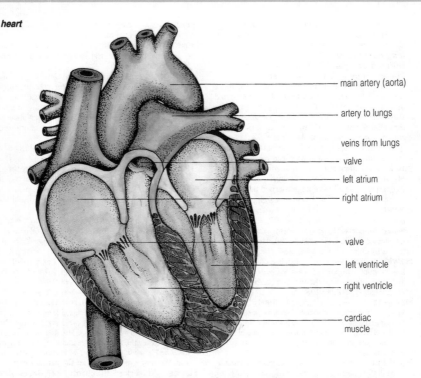

main artery (aorta)

artery to lungs

veins from lungs

valve

left atrium

right atrium

valve

left ventricle

right ventricle

cardiac muscle

furniture in the Arts and Crafts style, often in oak, and later, in the 1930s started using materials such as tubular steel.

Healey Denis (Winston) 1917– . British Labour politician. While minister of defence 1964–70 he was in charge of the reduction of British forces east of Suez. He was chancellor of the Exchequer 1974–79. In 1980 he contested the party leadership with James Callaghan, and was deputy to Michael Foot 1980–83. In 1987 he resigned from the shadow cabinet.

health service government provision of medical care on a national scale. From 1948 the UK has had a *National Health Service* (NHS) which includes hospital care, but charges are made for ordinary doctors' prescriptions, spectacles, and dental treatment, except for children and people on very low incomes. The USA has the federally subsidized schemes *Medicare* and *Medicaid*. See also ◊social security.

Heaney Seamus (Justin) 1939– . Irish poet, born in Londonderry, who has written powerful verse about the political situation in Northern Ireland. Collections include *North* 1975, *Field Work* 1979, and *Station Island* 1984.

hearing aid a device to improve the hearing of partially deaf people. The earliest aid was an ear trumpet. A typical modern aid consists of a battery-powered transistorized microphone/amplifier unit and earpiece.

hearsay evidence second-hand evidence, by a witness giving evidence of what another person has said. It is not acceptable as evidence in court.

Hearst William Randolph 1863–1951. US newspaper proprietor, celebrated for his introduction of banner headlines, lavish illustration, and the sensational approach known as 'yellow journalism'.

heart a muscular organ that rhythmically contracts to force blood around the body of an animal with a circulatory system. Annelid worms and some other invertebrates have simple hearts consisting of thickened sections of main blood vessels that pulse regularly. An earthworm has ten such hearts. Vertebrates have one heart. The fish's heart has two chambers – the thin-walled *atrium* (once called the auricle) that expands to receive blood, and the thick-walled *ventricle* which pumps it out. Amphibians and most reptiles have two atria and one ventricle; birds and mammals have two atria and two ventricles. The beating of the heart is controlled by the autonomic nervous systems, and by hormones.

heart-lung machine apparatus used during heart surgery to take over the functions of the heart and the lungs temporarily. It has a pump to circulate the blood around the body and facility for adding oxygen to the blood and removing carbon dioxide from it. A heart-lung machine was first used for open-heart surgery in the USA in 1953.

Heart of Darkness a story by Joseph Conrad, published 1902. Marlow, the narrator, tells of his journey by boat into the African interior to meet a company agent, Kurtz, who exercises great power over the indigenous people by barbaric means.

heat form of internal energy of a substance due to the kinetic energy in the motion of its molecules or atoms. It is measured by ◊temperature. Heat energy is transferred by conduction, convection, and radiation. Heat always flows from a region of higher temperature to one of lower temperature. Its effect on a substance may be simply to raise its temperature, to cause it to expand, to melt it if a solid, to vaporize it if a liquid, or to increase its pressure if a confined gas.

heat capacity in physics, the quantity of heat required to raise the temperature of a substance by one degree. The *specific heat capacity* of a substance is the heat capacity per unit of mass, measured in joules per kilogram per ◊kelvin (J kgh⁻¹ Kh⁻¹).

Heath Edward (Richard George) 1916– . British Conservative politician, party leader 1965–75. As prime minister 1970–74 he took the UK into the European Community, but was brought down by economic and industrial-relations crises at home.

heather low-growing evergreen shrub, common on sandy or acid soil. The *common heather* or *ling Calluna vulgaris* is a carpet-forming shrub, growing up to 60 cm/2 ft high, bearing pale pink-purple flowers in spikes in late summer, and small leaves on a shrubby stem. It is found over much of Europe, growing up to 750 m/2,400 ft above sea level. It may dominate large areas of heath or moorland, and other areas with well-drained acidic soil.

heat pump machine run by electricity or other power source which cools the interior of a building or, conversely, extracts energy from the atmosphere to provide space heating.

heat shield a material on the external surface of a spacecraft, which protects the astronauts and equipment inside from the heat of re-entry when returning to Earth. Air friction can generate temperatures of up to 1,500°C upon re-entry to the atmosphere.

heat storage means of storing heat for release later. It is usually achieved by using materials which undergo phase changes, for example, ◊Glauber's salt, and sodium pyrophosphate, which melts at 70°C. The latter is used to store off-peak heat in the home: the salt is liquefied by cheap heat during the night, and then freezes to give off heat during the day.

heat stroke or *sunstroke* illness caused by excessive exposure to heat. Mild heat stroke is experienced as lassitude and cramp, or simple fainting; recovery is prompt following rest and replenishment of salt lost in sweat. Severe heat stroke causes collapse akin to that seen in acute shock, and is potentially lethal without prompt treatment of cooling the body carefully and giving fluids to relieve dehydration.

heat treatment subjecting metals and alloys to controlled heating and cooling after fabrication to relieve internal stresses and improve their physical properties. Methods include ◊annealing, ◊quenching, and ◊tempering.

heaven in the theology of Christianity and some other religions, the destination after death of the virtuous. Many attempts have been made, particularly by Christian and Muslim writers, to describe its physical joys, but modern theologians usually describe it as a place or state in which the soul sees God as he really is.

heavy metal in music, a style of rock characterized by loudness, sex-and-violence imagery, and guitar solos. It developed out of the hard rock of the late 1960s and early 1970s (Led Zeppelin, Deep Purple). Bands include Motörhead, Def Leppard, and AC/DC. The term comes from *The Naked Lunch* by the US author William Burroughs.

heavy metal a metallic element of high relative atomic mass, for instance platinum, gold, and lead. Heavy metals are poisonous and tend to persist in living systems, causing, for example, gradual mercury poisoning in shellfish.

heavy water deuterium oxide (D_2O), water containing the isotope deuterium instead of hydrogen (relative molecular mass 20 as opposed to 18 for ordinary water).

Hebe in Greek mythology, the goddess of youth, daughter of Zeus and Hera, and handmaiden of the gods.

Hebei (formerly *Hopei* or *Hupei*) province of N China
area 202,700 sq km/78,240 sq mi
capital Shijiazhuang
products cereals, textiles, iron and steel
population (1985) 54,870,000.

Hebrew Bible the sacred writings of Judaism, known to Christians as the Old Testament. It includes the Torah (the first five books, ascribed to Moses), historical and prophetic books, and psalms, all in the Hebrew language.

Hebrew language a member of the ◊Hamito-Semitic language family spoken in W Asia by the ancient Hebrews, sustained for many centuries as the liturgical language of Judaism, and revived and developed in the 20th century as modern Israeli Hebrew, the national language of the State of Israel. It is the original language of the Old Testament of the Bible.

Hebrides group of over 500 islands (fewer than 100 inhabited) off W Scotland; total area 2,900 sq km/1,120 sq mi. The Hebrides were settled by Scandinavians in the 6th–9th centuries, and passed under Norwegian rule from about 890–1266.

The Inner Hebrides include Skye (area 1,665 sq km/643 sq mi), Mull, Jura, Islay, and Iona. The Outer Hebrides include Lewis-with-Harris, North Uist, South Uist, and Barra.

Hecate in Greek mythology, the goddess of witchcraft and magic, sometimes identified with ◊Artemis and the moon.

hectare unit of area in the metric system (Greek *hekaton* 100) equalling 100 ares (square decametres) or 10,000 square metres.

Hector in Greek mythology, a Trojan prince, son of King Priam, who, in the siege of Troy, was the foremost warrior on the Trojan side until he was killed by ◊Achilles.

Hecuba in Greek mythology, the wife of King Priam, and mother of ◊Hector and ◊Paris. She was captured by the Greeks after the fall of Troy.

hedgehog mammal of the genus *Erinaceus* common in Europe, W Asia, Africa, and India. The body, including the tail, is 30 cm/1 ft long. It is speckled-brown in colour, has a pig-like snout, and is covered with sharp spines. When alarmed it can roll the body into a ball. Hedgehogs feed on insects, slugs and carrion.

hedgerow a row of closely planted shrubs or low trees. It generally acts as a land division and windbreak; it also serves as a source of food, and refuge for wildlife. Hedgerows are an important part of the landscape in Britain, northern France, Ireland, and New England, but many have been destroyed in the last 40 years to accommodate altered farming practices and larger machinery.

hedge sparrow another name for ◊dunnock, a small bird.

hedonism the ethical theory that pleasure or happiness is, or should be, the main goal in life. Hedonist sects in ancient Greece were the Cyrenaics, who held that the pleasure of the moment is the only human good, and the Epicureans, who advocated the pursuit of pleasure under the direction of reason. Modern hedonistic philosophies, such as those of Bentham and Mill, regard the happiness of society, rather than that of the single individual, as the aim.

hedgerow

In Northern Europe, and especially in Britain, hedgerows are a traditional feature of the landscape. Hawthorn, blackthorn, elm and beech bushes were grown around the edges of farms and grazing land to define boundaries and to enclose cattle and sheep. With mechanized agriculture came the destruction of many hedgerows, along with the wildlife they support.

The dense growth and tough, thorny branches of hawthorn bushes are effective barriers to large mammals. But their foliage and flowers, and, those of the plants that grow around and beneath them, provide food for many caterpillars, butterflies, aphids and bees. The fruits are eaten by many birds and by voles and wood mice. Carnivorous birds feed on the insects and other small animals.

Life in the hedgerow
1. Peacock butterfly 2. Blackbird's nest
3. Seven-spot ladybird 4. Hollybush
5. Comma butterfly 6. Tiger moth
7. Field mouse 8. Warbler 9. Dog rose
10. Nettle 11. Orange-tip butterfly
12. Hawthorn 13. Wren
14. Hogweed 15. Bramble bush
16. Hawfinch 17. Wood mouse
18. Hedgehog 19. Primrose
20. Chickweed

helicopter

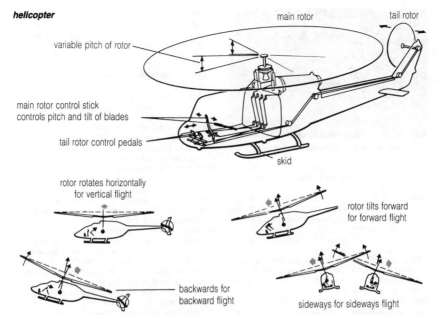

main rotor   tail rotor

variable pitch of rotor

main rotor control stick
controls pitch and tilt of blades

tail rotor control pedals

skid

rotor rotates horizontally
for vertical flight

rotor tilts forward
for forward flight

backwards for
backward flight

sideways for sideways flight

Hefei formerly *Hofei* capital of Anhui province, China; population (1984) 853,000. Products include textiles, chemicals, and steel.

Hegel Georg Wilhelm Friedrich 1770–1831. German philosopher, who conceived of consciousness and the external object as forming a unity, in which neither factor can exist independently, mind and nature being two abstractions of one indivisible whole. Hegel believed development took place through dialectic: contradiction and the resolution of contradiction. For Hegel, the task of philosophy was to comprehend the rationality of what already exists, but leftist followers, including Marx, used Hegel's dialectic to attempt to show the inevitability of radical change, and attacked both religion and the social order.

hegemony political dominance of one power over others in a group in which all are supposedly equal. The term was first used for the dominance of Athens over the other Greek city states, later applied to Prussia within Germany, and, in modern times, to the USA and USSR throughout the world.

Hegira see ◊Hijrah.

Heidegger Martin 1889–1976. German philosopher. In *Being and Time* 1927, he used the methods of ◊Husserl's phenomenology to explore the structures of human existence. His later writings meditated on the fate of a world dominated by science and technology.

Heilongjiang formerly *Heilungkiang* province of NE China, in ◊Manchuria
area 463,600 sq km/178,950 sq mi
capital Harbin
products cereals, gold, coal, copper, zinc, lead, cobalt
population (1985) 32,950,000.

Heine Heinrich 1797–1856. German romantic poet and journalist, who wrote *Reisebilder* 1826, and *Buch der Lieder/Book of Songs* 1827. From 1831 he lived mainly in Paris, as a correspondent for German newspapers.

Heinkel Ernst 1888–1958. German aircraft designer who pioneered jet aircraft. He founded his firm

1922, and built the first jet aircraft 1939 (developed independently of the Whittle jet of 1941). During World War II his company was Germany's biggest producer of warplanes.

Heisenberg Werner Carl 1901–1976. German physicist. He was an originator of ◊quantum mechanics and the formulator of the ◊uncertainty (indeterminacy) principle. Nobel prize 1932.

Hel or *Hela* in Norse mythology, the goddess of the underworld.

Helen in Greek mythology, the daughter of Zeus and Leda, and the most beautiful of women. She married Menelaus, king of Sparta, but during his absence eloped with Paris, prince of Troy. This precipitated the Trojan War. Afterwards she returned to Sparta with her husband.

Helena, St *c.* 248–328. Roman empress, mother of Constantine the Great, and a convert to Christianity. According to legend, she discovered the true cross of Christ in Jerusalem. Her feast day is 18 Aug.

helicopter an aircraft which achieves both lift and propulsion by means of a rotary wing, or rotor on top of the fuselage. It can take off and land vertically, move in any direction, or remain stationary in the air. The rotor of a helicopter has two or more blades, of aerofoil cross-section like an aeroplane's wings. Lift and propulsion are achieved by angling the blades as they rotate. Igor Sikorsky built the first practical single rotor craft in the USA 1939.

heliography old method of signalling, used by armies in the late 19th century, which employed sunlight reflected from a mirror to pass messages in ◊Morse code. On a clear day, a heliograph could send over distances in excess of 50 km/30 mi.

Heliopolis ancient Egyptian centre (biblical On) of the worship of the sun god Ra, NE of Cairo and near the modern village of Matariah.

Helios in Greek mythology, the sun-god and father of ◊Phaethon, thought to make his daily journey across the sky in a chariot.

heliotrope decorative plant, genus *Heliotropium*, family Boraginaceae, with distinctive spikes of

hell Stone carving of a medieval version of hell.

blue, lilac, or white flowers, especially the *Peruvian* or *cherry pie heliotrope Heliotropium peruvianum*.

helium a gaseous element, symbol He, atomic number 2, relative atomic mass 4.003. It is colourless, odourless, inert, non-inflammable, and very light. It is present in the Sun, in gases issuing from the Earth in radioactive minerals, and in small quantities in the atmosphere.

helix in mathematics, a three-dimensional curve resembling a spring, corkscrew, or screw thread. It is generated by a line that encircles a cylinder or cone at a constant angle.

hell in various religions, a place of posthumous punishment. In Hinduism, Buddhism, and Jainism, hell is a transitory stage in the progress of the soul, but in Christianity and Islam it is eternal (◊purgatory is transitory).

hellebore herbaceous plant of the genus *Helleborus*, family Ranunculaceae. The poisonous *stinking hellebore Helleborus foetidus* has greenish flowers early in the spring; the *Christmas rose Helleborus niger* has white flowers from Dec onwards.

helleborine temperate orchids of the genera *Epipactis* and *Cephalanthera*, including the *marsh helleborine Epipactis palustris*, with pink and white flowers.

Hellenic period (from *Hellas*, Greek name for Greece) the classical period of ancient Greek civilization, from the first Olympic Games 776 BC until the death of Alexander the Great 323 BC.

Hellenistic period the period in Greek civilization from the death of Alexander 323 BC until the accession of the Roman emperor Augustus 27 BC. Alexandria in Egypt was the centre of culture and commerce during this period, and Greek culture spread throughout the Mediterranean.

Heller Joseph 1923– . US novelist. He drew on his experiences in World War II to write ◊*Catch-22* 1961, satirizing war and bureaucratic methods.

Hellman Lillian 1907–1984. US playwright, whose plays are largely concerned with contemporary political and social issues. They include *The Children's Hour* 1934, *The Little Foxes* 1939, and *Toys in the Attic* 1960.

Helmholtz Hermann Ludwig Ferdinand von 1821–1894. German physiologist, physicist, and inventor of the ophthalmoscope. He was the first to explain how the cochlea of the inner ear works, and the first to measure the speed of nerve impulses. In physics, he formulated the law of conservation of energy, and did important work in thermodynamics.

Helmont Jean Baptiste van 1577–1644. Belgian doctor. He was the first to realize that gases exist apart from the atmosphere, and claimed to have coined the word 'gas' (from the Greek 'chaos').

Héloïse 1101–1164. Abbess of Paraclete in Champagne, correspondent and lover of ◊Abelard. She became deeply interested in intellectual study in her youth. After her affair with Abelard, and the birth of a son, Astrolabe, she became a nun 1229, and with Abelard's assistance, founded a nunnery at Paraclete. Her letters show her strong and pious character.

helot a class of slaves in ancient Sparta, who were probably the indigenous inhabitants. Their cruel treatment by the Spartans became proverbial.

Helsinki (Swedish *Helsingfors*) capital and port of Finland; population (1986) 488,000, metropolitan area 965,000. Industries include shipbuilding, engineering, and textiles.

Helsinki Conference international conference 1975 at which 35 countries, including the USSR and the USA, supposedly reached agreement on cooperation in security, economics, science, technology, and human rights. It is often regarded as marking the end of the ◊Cold War.

Helvetius Claude Adrien 1715–1771. French philosopher. In *De l'Esprit* 1758 he argued that self-interest, however disguised, is the mainspring of all human action, that since conceptions of good and evil vary according to period and locality there is no absolute good or evil. He also believed that intellectual differences are only a matter of education.

Hemingway Ernest 1898–1961. US writer. War, bullfighting, and fishing became prominent themes in his short stories and novels, which included *A Farewell to Arms* 1929, *For Whom the Bell Tolls* 1940, and *The Old Man and the Sea* 1952. His short, deceptively simple sentences attracted many imitators. Nobel prize 1954.

hemlock plant *Conium maculatum* of the family Umbelliferae, native to Europe, W Asia, and N Africa. Reaching up to 2 m/6 ft high, it bears umbels of small white flowers. The whole plant, and especially the root and fruit, is poisonous, causing paralysis of the nervous system. Hemlock is also the name of a type of conifer, genus *Tsuga*, whose crushed leaves have a similar smell.

Hemingway US novelist Ernest Hemingway.

hemp annual plant *Cannabis sativa*, family Cannabaceae. Originally from Asia, it is cultivated in most temperate countries for its fibres, produced in the outer layer of the stem, and used in ropes, twines and, occasionally, in a type of linen or lace. Cannabis is obtained from certain varieties of hemp.

Henan (formerly *Honan*) province of E central China
area 167,000 sq km/64,460 sq mi
capital Zhengzhou
products cereals and cotton
population (1985) 76,460,000.

henbane wild plant *Hyoscyamus niger*, found on waste ground through most of Europe and W Asia. A branching plant, up to 80 cm/2.6 ft high, it has hairy leaves and a nauseous smell. The yellow flowers are bell-shaped.

Hench Philip Showalter 1896–1965. US physician who introduced cortisone treatment for rheumatoid arthritis.

Henderson Arthur 1863–1935. British Labour politician, born in Glasgow. He was home secretary in the first Labour government, and was foreign secretary 1929–31, when he accorded the Soviet government full recognition. He was awarded a Nobel Peace Prize 1934.

Hendrix Jimi (James Marshall) 1942–1970. US rock guitarist, songwriter, and singer, legendary for his virtuoso experimental technique and flamboyance.

Hendry Stephen 1970– . Scottish snooker player of exceptional talent. He succeeded Steve Davis at the top of the world rankings during the 1989–90 season.

Hengist legendary leader, with his brother Horsa, of the Jutes, who originated in Jutland and settled in Kent about 450, the first Anglo-Saxon settlers in Britain.

Henlein Konrad 1898–1945. Sudeten-German leader of the Sudeten Nazi Party inside Czechoslovakia, and closely allied with Hitler's German Nazis. He was partly responsible for the destabilization of the Czech state 1938 which led to the ◊Munich Agreement and ceding of the Sudetenland.

Henley Royal Regatta rowing festival on the River ◊Thames inaugurated 1839. It is as much a social as a sporting occasion. Held in July, the principal events are the solo *Diamond Challenge Sculls*, and the *Grand Challenge Cup*.

henna small shrub *Lawsonia inermis* found in Iran, India, Egypt, and N Africa. The leaves and young twigs are ground up, mixed to a paste with hot water, and used to colour fingernails and hair.

Henrietta Maria 1609–1669. queen of England 1625–49. The daughter of Henry IV of France, she married Charles I of England 1625. As she used her influence to encourage him to aid Roman Catholics and make himself an absolute ruler, she became unpopular and had to go into exile 1644–60. She returned to England at the Restoration, but retired to France 1665.

henry ◊SI unit of inductance (H), named after Joseph ◊Henry. It is defined as the inductance of a closed circuit in which an electromotive force of 1 volt is produced when the electric current in the circuit varies uniformly at a rate of 1 ampere per second.

Henry Joseph 1797–1878. US physicist, inventor of the electromagnetic motor 1829, and a telegraphic apparatus. He also discovered the principle of electromagnetic induction, roughly at the same time as ◊Faraday, and the phenomenon

Hendrix Jimi Hendrix, Isle of Wight Pop Festival, 1970.

of self-induction. A unit of inductance (henry) is named after him.

Henry (Charles Albert David) known as *Harry* 1984– . Prince of the United Kingdom; second child of the Prince and Princess of Wales.

Henry Patrick 1736–1799. US politician, who in 1775 supported the arming of the Virginia militia against the British by a speech ending: 'Give me liberty or give me death!' He was governor of the state 1776–79 and 1784–86.

Henry William 1774–1836. English chemist. In 1803 he formulated *Henry's law*: when a gas is dissolved in a liquid at a given temperature, the mass which dissolves is in direct proportion to the gas pressure.

Henry eight kings of England:

Henry I 1068–1135. King of England from 1100. Youngest son of William I, he succeeded his brother William II. He won the support of the Saxons by granting them a charter and marrying a Saxon princess. An able administrator, he established a professional bureaucracy and a system of travelling judges.

Henry II 1133–1189. King of England from 1154, when he succeeded Stephen. He was the son of Matilda and Geoffrey of Anjou (1113–51). He curbed the power of the barons, but his attempt to bring the church courts under control had to be abandoned after the murder of ◊Becket. During his reign the English conquest of Ireland began.

Henry III 1207–1272. King of England from 1216, when he succeeded John, but he did not assume royal power until 1227. His subservience to the papacy and his foreign favourites led to de ◊Montfort's revolt 1264. Henry was defeated at Lewes, Sussex, and imprisoned. He was restored to the throne after royalist victory at Evesham 1265.

Henry IV (Bolingbroke) 1367–1413. King of England from 1399, the son of ◊John of Gaunt. In 1398 he was banished by Richard II for political activity, but returned 1399 to head a revolt and be accepted as king by Parliament.

Henry V 1387–1422. King of England from 1413, son of Henry IV. Invading Normandy 1415, he captured Harfleur, and defeated the French at ◊Agincourt. He invaded again 1417–19, capturing Rouen. He married ◊Catherine of Valois 1420, to gain recognition as heir to the French throne by his father-in-law Charles VI.

Henry VI 1421–1471. King of England from 1422, son of Henry V. He assumed royal power 1442, and identified himself with the party opposed to the continuation of the French war. After his marriage 1445, he was dominated by his wife, ◊Margaret

*Henry V Portrait by an unknown artist (c. 1518-23)
Royal Collection, Windsor.*

of Anjou. The unpopularity of the government, especially after the loss of the English conquests in France, encouraged Richard, Duke of ◊York to claim the throne, and though York was killed 1460, his son Edward proclaimed himself king 1461 (see Wars of the ◊Roses). Henry was captured 1465, temporarily restored 1470, but again imprisoned 1471 and then murdered.

Henry VII 1457–1509. King of England from 1485, son of Edmund Tudor, Earl of Richmond (c. 1430–56), and a descendant of ◊John of Gaunt. He spent his early life in Brittany until 1485, when he landed in Britain to lead the rebellion against Richard III which ended with Richard's defeat and death at ◊Bosworth. Yorkist revolts continued until 1497, but Henry restored order after the Wars of the ◊Roses by the ◊Star Chamber, and achieved independence from Parliament by amassing a private fortune through confiscations.

Henry VIII 1491–1547. King of England from 1509, when he succeeded his father Henry VII

*Henry VIII Portrait by an unknown artist (c. 1542)
National Portrait Gallery, London.*

and married Catherine of Aragon, the widow of his brother. His Lord Chancellor, Cardinal Wolsey, was replaced by Thomas More 1529, for failing to persuade the pope to grant Henry a divorce. After 1532 Henry broke with the Catholic church, proclaimed himself head of the church, and dissolved the monasteries. After divorcing Catherine, his wives were Anne Boleyn, Jane Seymour, Anne of Cleves, Catherine Howard, and Catherine Parr.

Henry four kings of France:

Henry I 1005–1060. King of France from 1031, who spent much of his reign in conflict with ◊William I the Conqueror, then duke of Normandy.

Henry II 1519–1559. King of France from 1547. He captured the fortresses of Metz and Verdun from the Holy Roman emperor Charles V, and Calais from the English. He was killed in a tournament.

Henry III 1551–1589. King of France from 1574. He fought both the ◊Huguenots (headed by his successor, Henry of Navarre) and the Catholic League (headed by the Duke of Guise). Guise expelled Henry from Paris 1588 but was assassinated. Henry allied with the Huguenots under Henry of Navarre to besiege the city, but was assassinated by a monk.

Henry IV 1553–1610. King of France from 1589. He was brought up as a Protestant, and from 1576 led the ◊Huguenots. On his accession he settled the religious question by adopting Catholicism while tolerating Protestantism. He restored peace and strong government to France, and brought back prosperity by measures for the promotion of industry and agriculture, and the improvement of communications. He was assassinated by a Catholic fanatic.

Henry seven Holy Roman emperors, including:

Henry I the Fowler c. 876–936. King of Germany from 919, and duke of Saxony from 912. He secured the frontiers of Saxony, ruled in harmony with its nobles, and extended German influence over the Hungarians, the Danes, and Slavonic tribes in the east.

Henry III the Black 1017–1056. King of Germany from 1028, Holy Roman emperor from 1039, who raised the empire to the height of its power, and extended its authority over Poland, Bohemia, and Hungary.

Henry V 1081–1125. Holy Roman emperor from 1106. He continued the struggle with the church until the settlement of the ◊investiture contest 1122.

Henry VI 1165–1197. Holy Roman emperor from 1190. As part of his plan for making the empire universal, he captured and imprisoned Richard I of England, and compelled him to do homage.

Henry O. Pen name of William Sydney Porter 1862–1910. US short story writer, whose collections include *Cabbages and Kings* 1904 and *The Four Million* 1906. His stories are in a colloquial style and noted for their skilled construction with twist endings.

Henry the Navigator 1394–1460. Portuguese prince. Under his patronage, Portuguese seamen explored and colonized Madeira and the Azores, and sailed down the African coast almost to Sierra Leone.

Henze Hans Werner 1926– . German composer whose large and varied output includes orchestral, vocal, and chamber music. He uses traditional symphony and concerto forms, and incorporates a wide range of styles including jazz.

Hepworth English sculptor Barbara Hepworth before her 1930 exhibition, with her stone Mother and Child.

heparin anticoagulant drug which acts to prevent clots from forming inside the blood vessels. It is often used after surgery, where there is risk of ◊thrombosis, or following pulmonary ◊embolism to ensure that no further clots form.

hepatitis inflammatory disease of the liver, usually caused by a virus. Other causes include systematic lupus erythematosus or amoebic dysentery.

Hepburn Audrey (Audrey Hepburn-Rushton) 1929–1993. British actress of Anglo-Dutch descent who often played innocent, childlike characters. She became a Hollywood star in such films as *Funny Face* 1957, *My Fair Lady* 1964, and *Robin and Marion* 1976.

Hepburn Katharine 1909– . US actress, who appeared in such films as *The African Queen* 1951, *Guess Who's Coming to Dinner* 1967, and *On Golden Pond* 1981. She won four Academy Awards.

Hepplewhite George died 1786. British furniture maker. He developed a simple, elegant style, especially in chairs which often had shield or heart-shaped backs. He worked mainly in mahogany or satinwood, adding inlaid or painted decorations of feathers, shells, or wheat-ears. His book of designs *The Cabinetmaker and Upholster's Guide* 1788, was published posthumously.

heptathlon a multi-event athletics discipline for women which consists of seven events over two days. The seven events, in order, are: 100 metres hurdles, high jump, shot put, 200 metres (day one); long jump, javelin, 800 metres (day two). Points are awarded for performances in each event like the ◊decathlon. It replaced the pentathlon in international competition 1981.

Hepworth Barbara 1903–1975. English sculptor. She developed a distinctive abstract style, creating hollowed forms of stone or wood with spaces bridged by wires or strings; many later works are in bronze.

Hera in Greek mythology, a goddess, sister-consort of Zeus, mother of Hephaestus, Hebe, and Ares; protector of women and marriage, and identified with Roman Juno.

Heracles in Greek mythology, a hero (Roman Hercules), son of Zeus and Alcmene, famed for strength. While serving Eurystheus, king of Argos, he performed 12 labours, including the cleansing of the Augean stables.

Heraclius *c.* 575–641. Byzantine emperor from 610. His reign marked a turning point in the empire's fortunes. Of Armenian descent, he recaptured Armenia 622, and other provinces 622–28 from the Persians, but lost them to the Arabs 629–41.

Heraklion alternative name for ◊Iráklion.

heraldry the decoration and insignia representing a person, family, or dynasty. Heraldry originated with simple symbols used on banners and shields for recognition in battle. By the 14th century, it had become a complex pictorial language with its own regulatory bodies (courts of chivalry), used by noble families, corporation, cities, and realms.

Herat capital of Herat province, Afghanistan, on the N banks of the Hari Rud; population (1980) 160,000. A principal road junction, it was a great city in ancient and medieval times.

herb any plant (usually a flowering plant) tasting sweet, bitter, aromatic, or pungent, used in cookery, medicine, or perfumery; technically, any plant whose aerial parts do not remain above ground at the end of the growing season.

herbarium a collection of dried, pressed plants used as an aid to identification of unknown plants and by taxonomists in the ◊classification of plants. The plant specimens are accompanied by information such as the date and place of collection.

Herbert Frank (Patrick) 1920–1986. US science-fiction writer, particularly noted for the *Dune* saga from 1965 onwards, broad-scale adventure stories containing serious ideas about ecology and philosophy.

Herbert George 1593–1633. English poet. His volume of religious poems, *The Temple*, appeared in 1633, shortly before his death from consumption. His poems depict his intense religious feelings in clear, simple language.

herbicide a type of ◊weedkiller.

herbivore an animal which feeds on green plants or their products, including seeds, fruit, and nectar, as well as ◊photosynthetic organisms in plankton. Herbivores are more numerous than other animals because their food is the most abundant. They form a vital link in the food chain between plants and carnivores.

herb Robert common wild flower *Geranium robertianum* found throughout Europe, central Asia, and naturalized in North America. About 30 cm/1 ft high, it bears hairy leaves and small pinkish to purplish flowers, and has a reddish hairy stem. When rubbed, the leaves have a strong smell.

Herculaneum ancient city of Italy between Naples and Pompeii. Herculaneum was overwhelmed during the eruption of Vesuvius AD 79, which also destroyed Pompeii. It was excavated from the 18th century onwards.

Hercules Roman form of ◊Heracles.

Hercules in astronomy, the fifth-largest constellation, lying in the northern hemisphere. Despite its size it contains no prominent stars. Its most important feature is a ◊globular cluster of stars 22,500 light years away, one of the best examples in the sky.

Herder Johann Gottfried von 1744–1803. German poet, critic, and philosopher. Herder's critical writings indicated his intuitive rather than reasoning trend of thought. He collected folk songs of all nations 1778 and in the *Ideen zur Philosophie der Geschichte der Menschheit/Outlines of a Philosophy of the History of Man* 1784–91 he outlined the stages of human cultural development.

heredity in biology, the transmission of traits from parent to offspring. See also ◊genetics.

Hereford and Worcester county in W central England
area 3,927 sq km/1,516 sq mi
towns administrative headquarters Worcester; Hereford, Kidderminster, Evesham, Ross-on-Wye, Ledbury
products mainly agricultural, apples, pears, and cider; hops and vegetables; Hereford cattle; carpets, porcelain, some chemicals and engineering
population (1991) 667,800
famous people Edward Elgar, A E Houseman, William Langland, John Masefield.

heresy (Greek *hairesis*, 'parties' of believers) doctrine opposed to orthodox belief, especially in religion. Those holding ideas considered heretical by the Christian church have included Gnostics, Arians, Pelagians, Montanists, Albigenses, Waldenses, Lollards, and Anabaptists.

Hereward the Wake 11th century. English leader of a revolt against the Normans 1070, whose stronghold in the Isle of Ely was captured by William the Conqueror 1071. Hereward escaped, but his fate is unknown.

Hergé Pen name of Georges Remi 1907–1983. Belgian artist, creator of the boy reporter Tintin who first appeared in strip-cartoon form as *Tintin in the Land of the Soviets* 1929–30.

hermaphrodite an organism which has both male and female sex organs. Hermaphroditism is the norm in species such as snails and oysters, and is standard in flowering plants. Pseudo-hermaphrodites have the internal sex organs of one sex, but the external appearance of the other. The true sex of the latter becomes apparent at adolescence when the normal hormone activity appropriate to the internal organs begin to function.

Hermaphroditus in Greek mythology, the son of Hermes and Aphrodite. He was loved by a nymph who prayed for eternal union with him, so that they became one body with dual sexual characteristics, hence the term ◊hermaphrodite

hermeneutics a philosophical tradition concerned with the nature of understanding and interpretation of human behaviour and social traditions.

Hermes in Greek mythology, a god, son of Zeus and Maia, and messenger of the gods; he has winged sandals, a wide-rimmed hat and a staff around which serpents coil. Identified with the Roman Mercury and ancient Egyptian Thoth, he protected thieves, travellers, and merchants.

hermit religious ascetic living in seclusion, often practising extremes of mortification (for example, the stylites, early Christians who lived on top of pillars).

hernia or *rupture* protrusion of part of an internal organ through a weakness in the surrounding muscular wall, usually in the groin or navel. The appearance is that of a rounded soft lump or swelling.

Hero and Leander in Greek mythology, a pair of lovers. Hero was a priestess of Aphrodite at Sestos on the Hellespont, in love with Leander on the opposite shore at Abydos. When he was drowned while swimming across during a storm, she threw herself into the sea out of grief.

Herod *the Great* 74–4 BC. King of the Roman province of Judaea, S Palestine, from 40 BC. With the aid of the triumvir Mark Antony he established his government in Jerusalem 37 BC. He rebuilt the Temple in Jerusalem, but his Hellenizing tendencies made him suspect to orthodox Jewry. His last years were a reign of terror, and St Matthew in the New Testament alleges that he ordered the slaughter of all the infants in Bethlehem to ensure the death of Jesus, whom he foresaw as a rival. He was the father of Herod Antipas.

Herod Agrippa I 10 BC–AD 44. Jewish ruler of Palestine from AD 41. His real name was Marcus Julius Agrippa, erroneously called 'Herod' in the *Bible*. Grandson of Herod the Great, he was made tetrarch (governor) of Palestine by the Roman emperor Caligula and king by Claudius in AD 41. He put St James to death and imprisoned St Peter, both apostles. His son was Herod Agrippa II.

Herod Agrippa II *c.* AD 40–93. King of Chalcis (now S Lebanon), son of Herod Agrippa I, he was appointed by Claudius about AD 50. In AD 60 he tried the apostle St Paul. He helped the Roman emperor Titus take Jerusalem AD 70, then went to Rome where he died.

Hertzsprung-Russell diagram

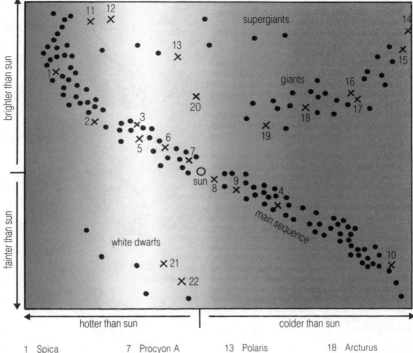

1	Spica	7	Procyon A	13	Polaris	18	Arcturus
2	Regulus	8	Tau Ceti	14	Betelgeuse	19	Pollux
3	Vega	9	61 Cygni A	15	Antares	20	Capella
4	61 Cygni B	10	Proxima Centauri	16	Mira	21	Sirius B
5	Sirius A	11	Rigel	17	Aldebaran	22	Procyon B
6	Altair	12	Deneb				

Herod Antipas 21 BC–39 AD. Tetrarch (governor) of the Roman province of Galilee, N Palestine, 4 BC–9 AD, son of Herod the Great. He divorced his wife to marry his niece Herodias, who got her daughter Salome to ask for John the Baptist's head when he reproved Herod's action. In 38 AD Herod Antipas went to Rome to try to get the emperor Caligula to give him the title of king, but was banished.

Herodotus *c.* 484–424 BC. Greek historian. His history deals with the Greek-Persian struggle which culminated in the defeat of the Persian invasion attempts 490 BC and 480 BC. Herodotus was the first historian to apply critical evaluation to his material.

heroin or *diamorphine* a powerful ◊opiate analgesic. It is more addictive than ◊morphine but causes less nausea. It has an important place in the control of severe pain in terminal illness, and is widely abused.

heron large wading bird of the family Ardeidae, which also includes bitterns, egrets, night-herons, and boatbills. They have sharp bills, broad wings, long legs and soft plumage. They are found mostly in tropical and subtropical regions, but also in temperate zones.

herpes infection by viruses of the herpes group. *Herpes simplex I* is the causative agent of a common inflammation, the cold sore. *Herpes simplex II* is responsible for genital herpes, a highly contagious, sexually transmitted disease characterized by painful blisters in the genital area. It can be transmitted in the birth canal from mother to newborn. *Herpes zoster* causes chickenpox and ◊shingles.

herring salt-water fish *Clupea harengus*, of the family Clupeidae. It swims close to the surface, and may be 25–40 cm/10–16 in long. A silvered greenish-blue, it has only one dorsal fin and one short ventral fin. The herring is found in large quantities off the shores of NE Europe, the E coast of North America, and the White Sea. Shoals have recently diminished, partly due to over-fishing, and pollution.

Herriot Édouard 1872–1957. French Radical politician. He was briefly prime minister 1924–25, 1926, and 1932. As president of the chamber of deputies in 1940 he opposed the policies of the right-wing Vichy government, was arrested and later taken to Germany until released 1945 by the Soviets.

Herschel John Fredrick William 1792–1871. English scientist and astronomer, who discovered thousands of close ◊double stars, clusters, and ◊nebulae, reported 1847. His inventions include astronomical instruments, sensitized photographic paper, and the use of sodium thiosulphite for fixing it.

Herschel William 1738–1822. German-born British astronomer. He was a skilled telescope-maker, and pioneered the study of binary stars and nebulae. In 1781, he discovered Uranus.

Hertfordshire county in SE England

area 1,634 sq km/631 sq mi
towns administrative headquarters Hertford; St Albans, Watford, Hatfield, Hemel Hempstead, Bishop's Stortford, Letchworth
products engineering, aircraft, electrical goods, paper and printing; general agricultural
population (1991) 951,500
famous people Graham Greene, Cecil Rhodes

hertz SI unit (Hz) of frequency (the number of repetitions of a regular occurrence in one second). Radio waves are often measured in megahertz (MHz), millions of hertz.

Hertz Heinrich 1857–1894. German physicist who produced and studied electromagnetic waves, showing that their behaviour resembled that of light and heat waves.

Hertzog James Barry Munnik 1866–1942. South African politician, prime minister 1924–39, founder of the Nationalist Party 1913 (the *United South African National Party* from 1933). He opposed South Africa's entry into both World Wars.

Hertzsprung-Russell diagram in astronomy, a graph on which the surface temperatures of stars are plotted against their luminosities. Most stars, including the Sun, fall into a narrow band called the ◊*main sequence*. When a star grows old it moves from the main sequence to the upper right part of the graph, into the area of the giants and supergiants. At the end of its life, as the star shrinks to become a white dwarf, it moves again, to the bottom left area. It is named after the Dane Ejnar Hertzpsrung and the American Henry Norris Russell, who independently devised it 1911–1913.

Herzegovina or *Hercegovina* part of ◊Bosnia-Herzegovina (a republic of Yugoslavia until 1991).

Herzl Theodor 1860–1904. Austrian founder of the *Zionist* movement. The ◊Dreyfus case convinced him that the only solution to the problem of anti-Semitism was the resettlement of the Jews in a state of their own. His book *Jewish State* 1896 launched political ◊Zionism, and he was the first president of the World Zionist Organization 1897.

Heseltine Michael (Ray Dibdin) 1933– . English Conservative politician, member of Parliament from 1966 (for Henley from 1974), secretary of state for trade and industry from 1992. As minister of defence from Jan 1983, he resigned Jan 1986 over the Westland affair (concerning the takeover of a British helicopter company) and was then seen as a major rival to Margaret Thatcher. However, in the 1990 leadership election he lost to John Major and became secretary of state for the environment 1990–92. In Oct 1992, adverse public reaction to his pit-closure programme forced the government to review their policy.

Hesiod lived 7th century BC. One of the earliest of the poets of ancient Greece. He is supposed to have lived a little later than Homer, and according to his own account he was born in Boeotia. He is the author of *Works and Days*, a poem that tells of the country life, and the *Theogony*, an account of the origin of the world and of the gods.

Hess (Walter Richard) Rudolf 1894–1987. German Nazi leader. In 1932 he was appointed deputy *Führer* to Hitler. On 10 May 1941 he landed by air in the UK with peace proposals, and was held a prisoner of war until 1945, when he was tried at Nuremberg. He was sentenced to life imprisonment and died in ◊Spandau prison, Berlin.

Hess Victor 1883–1964. Austrian physicist, who emigrated to the US shortly after sharing a Nobel prize in 1936 for the discovery of cosmic radiation.

Hesse (German *Hessen*) administrative region (German *Land*) of Germany
area 21,121 sq km/8,151 sq mi

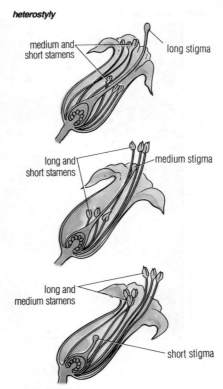

long stigma

medium and short stamens

long and short stamens

medium stigma

long and medium stamens

short stigma

capital Wiesbaden
towns Frankfurt-am-Main, Darmstadt, Kassel
products wine, timber; chemicals, cars, electrical engineering, optical instruments
population (1988) 5,550,000
religion Protestant 61%, Roman Catholic 33%.

Hesse Hermann 1877–1962. German-born writer who became a Swiss citizen 1923. He was a conscientious objector in World War I and a pacifist opponent of Hitler. His works include *Siddhartha* 1922 and *Steppenwolf* 1927. Later works, such as *Das Glasperlenspiel/The Glass Bead Game* 1943, tend towards the mystical. Nobel prize 1946.

Hestia in Greek mythology, the goddess (Roman Vesta) of the hearth, daughter of ◊Kronos (Roman Saturn) and Rhea.

heterosis or *hybrid vigour* an improvement in physical capacities that sometimes occurs in the ◊hybrid produced by mating two genetically different parents.

heterostyly in botany, having ◊styles of different lengths.

heterotroph any living organism that obtains its energy from organic substances which have been produced by other organisms. All animals and fungi are heterotrophs, and they include saprotorophs (which feed on dead animal and plant material).

heterozygous in a living organism, having two different ◊alleles (alternative forms) of the ◊gene for a given trait. In ◊homozygous organisms, by contrast, both chromosomes carry the same allele. An individual organism will generally be heterozygous for some genes but homozygous for others. For example in humans the allele for eye colour is heterozygous. A person who inherits an allele for brown eyes and an allele for blue eyes will be brown-eyed as a result of ◊dominance.

Hewish Antony 1924– . British radio-astronomer, who was awarded, with Martin ◊Ryle, the Nobel Prize for Physics 1974 for his work on ◊pulsars.

hexachlorophene a bactericide, used in minute quantities in soaps and surgical disinfectants.

hexadecimal number system a number system to the base 16, used in computing. In hex (as it is commonly known) the decimal numbers 0–15 are represented by the characters 0, 1, 2, 3, 4, 5, 6, 7, 8, 9, A, B, C, D, E, F. Hexadecimal numbers relate more closely than decimal numbers to a computer's internal ◊binary code.

Heydrich Reinhard 1904–1942. German Nazi. As head of party's security service and Heinrich ◊Himmler's deputy, he was instrumental in organizing the ◊final solution. While deputy 'protector' of Bohemia and Moravia from 1941, he was ambushed and killed by three members of the Czech forces in Britain, who had landed by parachute. Reprisals followed including several hundred executions and the massacre of ◊Lidice.

Heyerdahl Thor 1914– . Norwegian ethnologist, who sailed on the raft Kon Tiki 1947 from Peru to the Tuamotu Islands along the Humboldt Current, and in 1969–70 used ancient-Egyptian-style papyrus-reed boats to cross the Atlantic. He attempted to prove that ancient civilizations could have travelled the oceans.

Heywood Thomas c. 1570–c. 1650. English actor-dramatist. As well as acting he wrote or adapted over 220 plays, including the domestic tragedy *A Woman kilde with kindnesse* 1607.

Hezekiah died c. 699 BC. In the Old Testament, King of Judah from 719 BC until his death. Against the advice of the prophet Isaiah he rebelled against Assyrian suzerainty in alliance with Egypt, but was defeated by ◊Sennacherib. He carried out religious reforms.

HGV abbreviation for *heavy goods vehicle*.

Hiawatha legendary 16th-century North American Indian teacher and Onondaga chieftain, who is said to have welded the Six Nations of the ◊Iroquois into the league of the Long House, as the confederacy was known in what is now upper New York state.

hibernation a state of ◊dormancy in which certain animals spend the winter. It is associated with a dramatic reduction in body temperature, breathing, pulse rate and other metabolic processes.

hibiscus plant of the mallow family, ranging from large herbaceous plants to trees. Popular as ornamental plants because of their brilliantly coloured red through to white bell-shaped flowers, they include *Hibiscus syriacus* and *Hibiscus rosa-sinensis*.

Hick Graeme 1966– . Rhodesian-born cricketer who became Zimbabwe's youngest cricketer at the age of 17. A prolific batsman, he joined Worcestershire, England in 1984. He achieved the highest score in England in the 20th century in 1988 against Somerset, 405 not out.

Hickok (James Butler) 'Wild Bill' 1837–1876. US pioneer and law enforcer, a legendary figure in the Wild West. In the Civil War he was a sharpshooter and scout for the Union army, and then served as marshal in Kansas, killing many outlaws. He was shot from behind while playing poker in Deadwood, South Dakota.

hickory common tree of the genus *Carya*, native to N America and Asia. It provides a valuable timber, and all species produce nuts, although some are inedible. The pecan *Carya pecan* is widely cultivated in the southern states of the USA, and the shagbark *Carya ovata* in the northern states.

Hidalgo y Costilla Miguel 1743–1811. Catholic priest, known as the founder of Mexican independence.

hieroglyphic Egyptian writing system mid-4th millennium BC–3rd century AD, which combines picture signs with those indicating letters. The direction of writing is normally from right to left, the signs facing the beginning of the line. It was deciphered in 1822 by the French Egyptologist J F Champollion with the aid of the ◊*Rosetta Stone*, which has the same inscription carved in hieroglyphic, demotic, and Greek.

hi-fi the *high-fi*delity, or faithful reproduction of sound from a machine which plays recorded music or speech. A typical hi-fi system includes a turntable for playing vinyl records, a cassette tape deck to play magnetic tape recordings, a tuner to pick up radio broadcasts, an amplifier to serve all the equipment, possibly a compact disc player and two or more loudspeakers. Modern advances in mechanical equipment and electronics, such as digital recording techniques and compact discs, have made it possible to eliminate most distortions in the sound reproductive processes.

High Church Party a group in the Church of England which emphasizes aspects of Christianity usually associated with Catholics, such as ceremony and the church hierarchy. The term, first used in 1703 to describe those who opposed Dissenters, was most commonly used for groups such as the 19th-century ◊Oxford Movement.

high commissioner representative of one independent Commonwealth country in the capital of another, ranking with ambassador.

higher education in most countries, education beyond the age of 18 leading to a degree or similar qualification.

Highland Games traditional Scottish outdoor gathering which includes tossing the ◊caber, putting the shot, running, dancing and bagpipe playing. The most famous Highland Games is the Braemar Gathering.

Highland Region administrative region of Scotland

area 25,141 sq km/9,704 sq mi;

towns administrative headquarters Inverness; Thurso, Wick

products oil services and the provision of winter sports, timber, livestock, grouse and deer shooting and salmon fishing

population (1980) 200,000.

Highlands general name for the plateau of broken rock which covers almost all of Scotland, and extends S of the Highland region itself.

Highsmith Patricia 1921– . US crime novelist. Her first book *Strangers on a Train* 1950 was filmed by Hitchcock, and she excels in tension and psychological exploration of character, notably in her series dealing with the amoral Tom Ripley, including *The Talented Mr Ripley* 1956, *Ripley Under Ground* 1971, and *Ripley's Game* 1974.

highway in Britain, any road over which there is a right of way. In the USA, a term for a motorway.

highwayman in English history, a thief on horseback who robbed travellers on the highway; those who did so on foot were known as *footpads*. They continued to flourish well into the 19th century. Among the best-known highwaymen were Jonathan ◊Wild, Claude ◊Duval, John Nevison (1639–84), the original hero of the 'ride to York',

Hillary New Zealand mountaineer and explorer Edmund Hillary on Mount Everest, 1953.

Dick ◊Turpin, and his partner Tom King, and Jerry Abershaw (c. 1773–95).

hijacking the illegal seizure or taking control of a vehicle and/or its passengers or goods. The term is first recorded from 1923, and was originally used mainly to refer to the robbing of freight lorries. In recent times it (and its derivative, *skyjacking*), has been applied to the seizure of aircraft, usually in flight, by an individual or group, often with some political aim. International treaties (Tokyo 1963, the Hague 1970, and Montreal 1971) encourage international co-operation against hijackers and make severe penalties compulsory.

Hijrah (or *Hegira*) the trip from Mecca to Medina of the prophet Muhammad, which took place in 622 AD as a result of the persecution of the prophet and his followers. The Muslim calendar dates from this event, and the day of the Hijrah is celebrated as the Muslim New Year.

Hill David Octavius 1802–1870. Scottish photographer who, in collaboration with ◊Adamson, made extensive use of the ◊calotype process invented by Fox Talbot, in their large collection of portraits taken between 1843 and 1848 in Edinburgh.

Hill Rowland 1795–1879. British Post Office official who invented adhesive stamps, and in a pamphlet 'Post Office Reform' prompted the introduction of the penny prepaid post in 1840 (previously the addressee paid, according to distance, on receipt). He was secretary to the Post Office 1854–64.

Hillary Edmund 1919– . New Zealand mountaineer. In 1953, together with Norgay Tenzing, he conquered the summit of Mount Everest.

hillfort European Iron Age site with massive banks and ditches for defence, used not only as a military camp, but as a permanent settlement. An example is Maiden Castle in Dorset, England.

Hilliard Nicholas c. 1547–1619. English miniature portraitist and goldsmith, court artist to Elizabeth I from about 1579.

Hillsborough Agreement another name for the ◊Anglo-Irish Agreement 1985.

Himachal Pradesh NW state of India
area 55,673 sq km/21,490 sq mi
capital Simla
products timber, grain, rice, fruit
population (1981) 4,281,000, chiefly Hindu
language Pahari
history created as a union territory in 1948, it became a full state in 1971.

Himalayas vast mountain system of central Asia, extending from the Indian states of Kashmir in the W to Assam in the E, covering the S part of Tibet, Nepál, Sikkim, and Bhutan. It is the highest mountain range in the world. The two highest peaks are: *Mount Everest* and *Kangchenjunga*, third highest mountain in the world, on the Nepál-Sikkim border; height 8,597 m/28,208 ft; first climbed by a British expedition in 1955. Other major peaks include Makalu, Annapurna, and Nanga Parbat, all over 8,000 m/26,000 ft.

Himmler Heinrich 1900–1945. German Nazi leader, head of the ◊SS elite corps from 1929, the police and the Gestapo secret police from 1936. During World War II he replaced Göring as Hitler's second-in-command. He was captured in May 1945, and committed suicide.

Hīnayāna (Sanskrit 'lesser vehicle') name given by Mahāyāna Buddhists to ◊Theravāda Buddhism.

Hindemith Paul 1895–1963. German composer. His neo-classical, contrapuntal works include chamber ensemble and orchestral pieces, such as the *Symphonic Metamorphosis on Themes of Carl Maria von Weber* 1944, and the operas *Cardillac* 1926, revised 1952, and *Mathis der Maler/Mathis the Painter* 1938.

Hindenburg Paul Ludwig Hans von Beneckendorf und Hindenburg 1847–1934. German field marshal and right-wing politician. During World War I he was supreme commander and, together with Ludendorff, practically directed Germany's policy until the end of the war. He was president of Germany 1925–33, when Hitler took over.

Hindenburg Line German western line of World War I fortifications built 1916–17.

Hindi language a member of the Indo-Iranian branch of the Indo-European language family, the official language of the Republic of India, although resisted as such by the Dravidian-speaking states of the south. Hindi proper is used by some 30% of Indians, in such N states as Uttar Pradesh and Madhya Pradesh.

Hinduism Prambanan in central Java.

Hinduism religion originating in N India about 4,000 years ago, which is superficially and in some of its popular forms polytheistic, but has a concept of the supreme spirit, ◊Brahman, above the many divine manifestations. These include the triad of chief gods (the Trimurti): Brahma, Vishnu, and Siva (creator, preserver, and destroyer). Important ideas in Hinduism include reincarnation and ◊karma; the oldest scriptures are the *Vedas*. Temple worship is almost universally performed, and there are many festivals. There are over 805 million Hindus worldwide. Women are not regarded as the equals of men, but should be treated with kindness and respect. Muslim influence in N India led to veiling of women and the restriction of their movements from around the end of the 12th century.

Hindu Kush mountain range in central Asia; length 800 km/500 mi; greatest height Tirich Mir 7,690 m/25,230 ft, Pakistan. The *Khyber Pass*, a narrow defile (53 km/33 mi long), separates Pakistan from Afghanistan, and was used by ◊Zahir and other invaders of India.

Hindustani a member of the Indo-Iranian branch of the Indo-European language family, closely related to Hindi and Urdu and originating in the bazaars of Delhi. It serves as a lingua franca in many parts of the Republic of India.

Hine Lewis 1874–1940. US sociologist. He recorded in photographs child labour conditions in US factories at the beginning of this century, leading to a change in the law.

Hinkler Herbert John Louis 1892–1933. Australian pilot who in 1928 made the first solo flight from England to Australia. He was killed while making another attempt to fly to Australia.

hip-hop a style of popular music originating in New York in the early 1980s. It uses scratching (a percussive effect obtained by manually rotating a vinyl record) and heavily accented electronic drums behind a ◊rap vocal. The term 'hip-hop' also comprises break dancing and graffiti.

Hipparchus *c.* 555–514 BC. Greek tyrant. Son of ◊Pisistratus, he was associated with his elder brother Hippias as ruler of Athens 527–514 BC. His affection being spurned by Harmodius, he insulted her sister, and was assassinated.

Hipparchus *c.* 190–*c.* 120 BC. Greek astronomer, who invented trigonometry, calculated the lengths of the solar year and the lunar month, discovered the precession of the equinoxes, made a catalogue of 800 fixed stars, and advanced Eratosthenes' method of determining the situation of places on the Earth's surface by lines of latitude and longitude.

hippie a member of a youth movement of the mid- to late 1960s, which originated in San Francisco, California, and was characterized by nonviolent anarchy, concern for the environment, and rejection of Western materialism. The hippies formed an artistically prolific counterculture in the USA and UK. Their colourful psychedelic style, influenced by drugs such as ◊LSD, emerged especially in graphic art (see ◊poster) and music by bands such as Love (1965–71), the Grateful Dead (1965–), Jefferson Airplane (1965–74), and ◊Pink Floyd.

Hippocrates *c.* 460–*c.* 370 BC. Greek physician, often called the founder of medicine. Important Hippocratic ideas include cleanliness (for patients and physicians), moderation in eating and drinking, letting nature take its course, and living where the air is good.

Hippolytus in Greek mythology, the son of Theseus, who cursed him for his supposed dishonourable advances to his stepmother Phaedra.

hippopotamus

Killed by Poseidon as he rode near the sea in his chariot, he was restored to life when his innocence was proven.

hippopotamus (Greek 'river-horse') large herbivorous mammal of the family Hippopotamidae. The common hippopotamus *Hippopotamus amphibius* is found in Africa. It is over 4 m/13 ft long, 1.5 m/5 ft high, weighs about 4,500 kg/5 tons, and has a brown or slate-grey skin. It is a social and gregarious animal, and a good swimmer. It is an endangered species.

hire purchase (HP) a form of credit under which the buyer pays a deposit and makes instalment payments at fixed intervals over a certain period for a particular item. The buyer has immediate possession, but does not own the item until the final instalment has been paid. Credit cards are a modern alternative.

Hirohito 1901–1989. Emperor of Japan from 1926. He succeeded his father Yoshihito. After the defeat of Japan in 1945 he was made to reject belief in the divinity of the emperor and Japanese racial superiority, and accept the 1946 constitution greatly curtailing his powers. He was succeeded by his son ◊Akihito.

Hiroshige Andō 1797–1858. Japanese artist whose landscape prints, often using snow or rain to create atmosphere, were highly popular in his time, notably *Tōkaidō gojūsan-tsugi/53 Stations on the Tokaido Highway* 1833.

Hiroshima industrial city (cars) and port on the S coast of Honshu, Japan, largely rebuilt since

Hirohito Emperor Hirohito of Japan in ceremonial robes.

Hiroshima The total devastation caused by the atom bomb on Hiroshima towards the end of World War II.

6 Aug 1945 when it was the target of the first atom bomb to be used in wartime; population (1985)1,044,000.

Hiss Alger 1904– . US diplomat and liberal Democrat, a former State Department official, controversially imprisoned in 1950 for allegedly having spied for the USSR.

histamine an inflammatory substance, released in damaged tissues, which accounts for many of the symptoms of ◊allergy.

histogram a graph with the horizontal axis having discrete units or class boundaries with contiguous end points, and the vertical axis representing the frequency. Blocks are drawn such that their area is proportional to the frequencies within a class or across several class boundaries.

histology study of the microscopic structure of the tissues of organisms.

Hitchcock Suspense, melodrama and fleeting personal appearances are the hallmarks of Alfred Hitchcock's films.

histology the medical speciality concerned with the laboratory study of cells and tissues.

historical novel a fictional prose narrative set in the past. Literature set in the historic rather than immediate past has always abounded, but Sir Walter Scott began the modern tradition by setting imaginative romances of love, impersonation, and betrayal in a past based on known fact; his use of historical detail, and that of European imitators such as Manzoni, gave rise to the genre.

history the record of the development of human societies. The earliest surviving historical records are the inscriptions denoting the achievements of Egyptian and Babylonian kings. As a literary form in the Western world, historical writing or *historiography* began with the Greek Herodotus (c. 484–425 BC), who first passed beyond the limits of a purely national outlook.

Hitchcock Alfred 1899–1980. English film director, naturalized American in 1955. A master of suspense, he is noted for his camera work, and for making 'walk-ons' in his own works. His films include *The Thirty-Nine Steps* 1935, *The Lady Vanishes* 1939, *Rebecca* 1940, *Psycho* 1960, and *The Birds* 1963.

Hitler Adolf 1889–1945. German Nazi dictator, born in Austria. Führer (leader) of the ◊Nazi party from 1921, author of *Mein Kampf/My Struggle* 1925–27. Chancellor of Germany from 1933 and head of state from 1934, he created a dictatorship by playing party and state institutions against each other, and continually creating new offices and appointments. His position was not seriously challenged until the 'Bomb Plot' of 20 July 1944. In foreign affairs, he reoccupied the Rhineland and formed an alliance with Mussolini in 1936, annexed Austria 1938 and occupied Sudetenland under the ◊Munich Agreement. The rest of Czechoslovakia was annexed in Mar 1939. The Hitler-Stalin pact was followed in Sep by the invasion of Poland and the declaration of war by Britain and France. (see ◊World War II). He committed suicide as Berlin fell.

Hitler-Stalin pact non-aggression treaty between Germany and the USSR signed on 25 Aug 1939. It secretly allowed for the partition of Poland between the two countries and formed a sufficient security in the east for Hitler's declaration of war on Poland on 1 Sept 1939. This alliance of two apparently inimical ideologies was ended only by the German invasion of the USSR on 22 Jun 1941.

Hitler German Nazi leader Adolf Hitler at Berchtesgaden, Bavaria.

Hittite   member of a group of peoples who inhabited Anatolia and N Syria from the 3rd to the 1st millennium BC. The city of Hattusas (now Boğazköy in central Turkey) became the capital of a strong kingdom, which overthrew the Babylonian empire. After a period of eclipse the Hittite New Empire became a great power (about 1400–1200 BC) which successfully waged war with Egypt. The Hittite language is a Indo-European language.

HMSO   abbreviation for *His/Her Majesty's Stationery Office*.

hoatzin   tropical bird *Opisthocomus hoatzin* found only in the Amazon, resembling a small pheasant in size and appearance. Adults are olive with white markings above and red-brown below. The young are born with claws on their wings; these later fall off.

Hoban   James C 1762–1831. Irish-born architect who emigrated to the USA. His best known building is the White House, Washington DC, and he also worked on the Capitol and other public buildings.

Hobart   capital and port of Tasmania, Australia; population (1986) 180,000. Products include zinc, textiles, and paper.

Ho Chi Minh President Ho Chi Minh of Vietnam visiting Prague, Czechoslovakia , July 1957.

Hobbes   Thomas 1588–1679. English political philosopher. The first thinker since Aristotle to attempt to develop a comprehensive theory of nature, including human behaviour. In *The Leviathan* 1651 he advocates absolutist government as the only means of ensuring order and security; he saw this as deriving from the ◊social contract.

hobby   a small falcon *Falco subbuteo* found across Europe and N Asia. It is about 30 cm/1 ft long, with grey back, streaked front and chestnut thighs. It is found in open woods and heaths, and feeds on insects and small birds.

Ho Chi Minh   adopted name of Nguyen That Tan 1892–1969. North Vietnamese Communist politician, president from 1954. He was trained in Moscow, headed the communist Vietminh from 1941, and, having campaigned against the French colonizers 1946–54, became president and prime minister of the democratic republic at the armistice. Aided by the communist bloc, he did much to develop industrial potential. Although he relinquished the premiership in 1955, he was re-elected president in 1960.

Ho Chi Minh City   (formerly *Saigon*)   chief port and industrial city of southern Vietnam; population (1985) 3,500,000. Industries include shipbuilding, textiles, rubber, and food products. Saigon was the capital of the Republic of Vietnam (South Vietnam) 1954–76, when it was renamed.

Ho Chi Minh Trails   North Vietnamese troop and supply routes to South Vietnam via Laos, especially during the Vietnam War.

hockey   a game played with hooked sticks and a ball, the object being to hit the ball into the goal. It is played between two teams, each of not more than 11 players. Hockey has been an Olympic sport since 1908 for men and from 1980 for women.

Hockney   David 1937–   . British painter, printmaker, and designer. In the early 1960s he contributed to the Pop art movement. His portraits and views of swimming pools and modern houses reflects a preoccupation with surface pattern and effects of light. He has produced etchings, photo collages, and sets for opera.

Hodgkin's disease   rare form of cancer (also known as lymphadenoma), mainly affecting the lymph nodes and spleen. It undermines the immune system, leaving the sufferer more susceptible to infection. However, it responds well to radiotherapy and ◊cytotoxic drugs, and long-term survival is usual.

Hodza   Milan 1878–1944. Slovak politician and prime minister of Czechoslovakia from Feb 1936. He and President Beneš were forced to agree to the secession of the Sudeten areas of Czechoslovakia to the Germans before resigning on 22 Sep 1938 (see ◊Munich Agreement).

Hofei   former name of ◊Hefei, a city in China.

Hoffa   (James Riddle) 'Jimmy' 1913–?1975. US labour leader, president of the Teamsters Union (truckdrivers), jailed 1964–71 for attempted bribery of a federal court jury after he was charged with corruption. In 1975 he disappeared, and is generally believed to have been murdered.

Hoffman   Dustin 1937–   . US actor who popularized the role of the anti-hero in the 1960s and 1970s. He won Academy Awards for his performances in *Kramer vs Kramer* 1979 and *Rain Man* 1988. His other films include *The Graduate* 1967 and *Midnight Cowboy* 1969.

Hoffmann   E(rnst) T(heodor) A(madeus) 1776–1822. German composer and writer. A lawyer in Berlin, he enjoyed great success with his opera

hockey

An 11-a-side team game played either indoors or outdoors. The object is to score goals by passing a small ball (circumference about 228 mm/9 in) with the aid of a hooked stick. Goals are positioned at each end of the pitch.

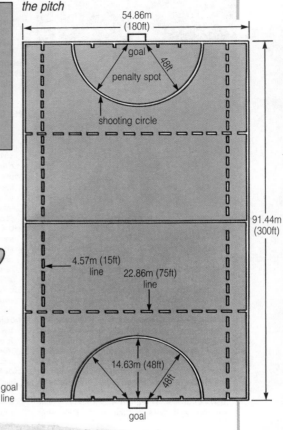

the pitch

54.86m (180ft)

goal

penalty spot

48ft

shooting circle

91.44m (300ft)

4.57m (15ft) line

22.86m (75ft) line

14.63m (48ft)

48ft

goal line

goal

the hockey stick
Hockey sticks are made of wood and must have a flat face. The rules do not restrict their length, but most are approximately 1.15 m/3 ft 9 in long.

the short corner

The short corner is a free stroke awarded to the attacking team. It is taken from a position not less than 9.14 m/30 ft from the goal. The attacking team should be outside the shooting circle and no more than six defenders should be behind their own goal line.

Hoffman Dustin Hoffman at the Oscar Award Ceremony, 1980.

Undine 1816, and his many fairy stories, including *Nüssknacker/Nutcracker* 1816. His stories inspired Offenbach's *Tales of Hoffmann.*

hog general name for a member of the ◊pig family.

Hogan Paul 1940– . Australian TV comic, film actor, and producer. The box-office hit *Crocodile Dundee* (considered the most profitable film in Australian history) 1986 and *Crocodile Dundee II* 1988 (of which he was co-writer, star, and producer) brought him international fame. His other films include *Almost an Angel* 1991.

Hogarth William 1697–1764. British painter and engraver, who produced portraits and moralizing genre scenes, such as *A Rake's Progress* 1735. His portraits are remarkably direct and full of character, for example *Heads of Six of Hogarth's Servants* c. 1750–55 (Tate Gallery, London).

Hogg James 1770–1835. Scottish novelist and poet, known as the 'Ettrick Shepherd'. Until the age of 30, he was illiterate. His novel *Confessions of a Justified Sinner* 1824 is a masterly portrayal of personified evil.

Hogmanay Scottish name for the last day of the year.

hogweed genus of plants *Heracleum*, family Umbelliferae; the **giant hogweed** *Heracleum mantegazzianum* grows over 3 m/9 ft high.

Hohenlinden, Battle of in the French ◊Revolutionary Wars, a defeat of the Austrians by the French on 3 Dec 1800 which, on top of the defeat at ◊Marengo, led the Austrians to make peace at the Treaty of Lunéville 1801.

Hohenstaufen Germany family of princes, several members of which were Holy Roman emperors 1138–1208 and 1214–54. They were the first German emperors to make use of associations with Roman law and tradition to aggrandize their office. Among the most notable were Conrad III, Frederick I (Barbarossa), the first to use the title Holy Roman emperor, Henry VI, and Frederick II. The last of the line, Conradin, was executed in 1268, with the approval of Pope Clement IV, while attempting to gain his Sicilian inheritance.

Hohenzollern Germany family, originating in Württemberg, the main branch of which held the titles of elector of Brandenburg from 1415, king of Prussia from 1701, and German emperor from 1871. The last emperor, Wilhelm II, was dethroned in 1918. Another branch of the family were kings of Romania 1881–1947.

Hohhot (formerly *Huhehot*) city and capital of Inner Mongolia (*Nei Mongol*) autonomous region, China; population (1989) 870,000. Industries include textiles, electronics, and dairy products.

Hokkaido most northerly of the four main islands of Japan, separated from Honshu to the S by Tsugaru Strait and from Sakhalin to the N by Soya Strait; area 83,513 sq km/32,246 sq mi, population (1986) 5,678,000. The capital is Sapporo. Natural resources include coal, mercury, manganese, oil and natural gas, timber, and fisheries. Coal mining and agriculture are the main industries.

Hokusai Katsushika 1760–1849. Japanese artist, the leading printmaker of his time. He is best known for *Fugaku Sanjūrokkei/36 Views of Mount Fuji* c. 1823–29, but he produced outstanding pictures of almost every kind of subject.

Holbein Hans, the Elder c. 1464–1524. German painter, active in Augsburg. His best-known works are altarpieces, such as that of *St Sebastian*, 1516 (Alte Pinakothek, Munich).

Holbein Hans, the Younger 1497/98–1543. German painter and woodcut artist. He was the son and pupil of Hans Holbein the Elder. He produced outstanding portraits of many famous names of the day, including Erasmus, Thomas More, and Thomas Cromwell.

holdfast an organ found at the base of many seaweeds, attaching them to the sea bed. It may be a flattened, sucker-like structure, or dissected and finger-like, growing into rock crevices.

holding company a company with a controlling shareholding in one or more subsidiaries.

holiday a period of allowed absence from work. Holidays (from medieval **holy days**, which were saint's days when no work was done) became a legal requirement in Britain under the Bank Holidays Acts 1871 and 1875. Under the Holidays with Pay Act 1938, paid holidays (initially one week) were made compulsory in many occupations.

Holiday Billie. Stage name of Eleanor Gough McKay 1915–1959. US jazz singer, also known as 'Lady Day'. She made her debut in Harlem clubs and became famous for her emotionally charged delivery and idiosyncratic phrasing. Songs she made her own include 'Strange Fruit' and 'I Cover the Waterfront'.

Holinshed Ralph c. 1520–c. 1580. English historian. He was probably born in Cheshire, went to London as assistant to a printer, and published in 1578 two volumes of the *Chronicles of England, Scotland and Ireland*, which were largely used by Shakespeare for his history plays.

holism philosophically, the concept that the whole is greater than the sum of its parts; also the idea that physical and mental wellbeing are inextricably linked.

Holland John Philip 1840–1914. Irish-born American engineer who developed some of the first submarines. He began work in Ireland in the late 1860s and emigrated to the USA in 1873. His first successful boat was launched in 1881 and, after several failures, he built the *Holland* in 1893 which was bought by the US Navy two years later.

Holland Sidney George 1893–1961. New Zealand politician, leader of the National Party 1940–57 and prime minister 1949–57. He suppressed union unrest and reduced government economic controls.

Hollar Wenceslaus 1607–1677. Bohemian engraver, active in England from 1637. He was the first landscape engraver to work in England, and recorded views of London before the Great Fire of 1666.

Hollerith Herman 1860–1929. US inventor of a mechanical tabulating machine, the first device for data processing. Hollerith's tabulator was widely publicized after being successfully used in the 1890 census. He established the Tabulating Machine Company, later one of the founding companies of International Business Machines (IBM).

holography

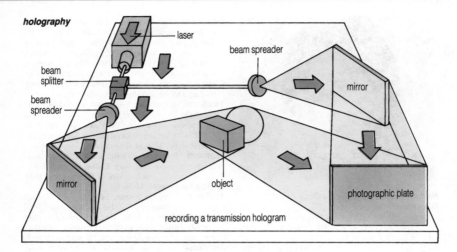

recording a transmission hologram

Hollis Roger 1905–1973. British civil servant, head of the secret intelligence service MI5 1956–65.

holly tree or shrub of genus *Ilex*, family Aquifoliaceae, including the **English Christmas holly** *Ilex aquifolium*, an evergreen with spiny, glossy leaves, small white flowers, and poisonous scarlet berries on the female tree, and the **Brazilian holly** *Ilex paraguayensis*, from the leaves of which the tea *yerba maté* is made.

Holly Buddy. Stage name of Charles Hardin Holley 1936–1959. US rock-and-roll singer, guitarist, and songwriter, born in Lubbock, Texas. He had a distinctive, hiccuping vocal style and was an early experimenter with recording techniques. Many of his hits with his band, the Crickets, such as 'That'll Be the Day' 1957, and 'Peggy Sue' 1957, have become classics. He was killed in a plane crash.

hollyhock plant of the genus *Althaea*, family Malvaceae. *Althaea rosea*, originally a native of Asia, produces spikes of large white, yellow or red flowers, 3 m/10 ft high when grown as a biennial.

Hollywood suburb of Los Angeles, California, USA, the centre of the US film industry from 1911.

Holmes à Court Michael Robert Hamilton 1937-1990. Australian entrepreneur born in South Africa, who had a reputation as a takeover specialist. He acquired interests in the media, the arts, mining and energy. He also founded some charitable institutions in Australia.

holmium a chemical element, symbol Ho, atomic number 67, relative atomic mass 164.94, discovered by Cleve in 1897. Holmium is one of the rare earth metals and occurs in various minerals such as gadolinite. It is used in electronic devices.

holocaust wholesale destruction; it is especially applied today to the annihilation of about 6 million Jews by the Hitler regime 1933–45 in the numerous concentration and extermination camps. Apart from the Jews, several million Russian civilians and gypsies, socialists and homosexuals, were also imprisoned and/or exterminated.

Holocene epoch of geological time that began 10,000 years ago, the second epoch of the Quaternary period. The glaciers retreated, and the climate became warmer.

holography a method of producing three-dimensional (3D) images by means of laser light. Although the possibility of holography was suggested as early as 1947, it could not be demonstrated until a pure coherent light source, the ◊laser, became available in 1963. Holography uses a photographic technique to produce a picture, or hologram, which contains 3D information about the object photographed. Some holograms show meaningless patterns in ordinary light and produce a 3D image only when laser light is shone through them, but reflection holograms produce images when ordinary light is reflected from them.

Holst Gustav(us Theodore von) 1874–1934. British composer. He composed operas including *Savitri* 1916, ballets, choral works including *Hymns from the Rig Veda* 1911, *The Hymn of Jesus* 1920, orchestral suites (such as *The Planets*, 1918), and songs.

Holt Harold Edward 1908–1967. Australian Liberal politician, prime minister 1966–67. He was minister of labour 1940–41 and 1949–58, and federal treasurer 1958–66, when he succeeded Menzies as prime minister. He was drowned in a swimming accident.

Holy Grail in Christian legend, the dish or cup used by Christ at the Last Supper, which, together with the spear with which he was wounded at the Crucifixion, appears as an object of quest by King Arthur's knights in certain stories incorporated in the Arthurian legend.

Holy Spirit the third part of the Christian ◊Trinity, also known as the Holy Ghost or the Paraclete. Usually depicted as a white dove.

Holy Alliance a 'Christian Union of Charity, Peace, and Love' initiated by Alexander I of Russia in 1815 and signed by every crowned head in Europe. Although designed to facilitate European cooperation through Christian principles, the alliance became associated with Russian attempts to preserve autocratic monarchies at any price, and an excuse to meddle in the internal affairs of other states. Ideas of an international army acting in the name of the alliance were rejected by Britain and Austria, in 1818 and in 1820.

Holy Communion another name for the ◊Eucharist, a Christian sacrament.

Holy Land another term for ◊Israel.

Holyoake Keith Jacka 1904–1983. New Zealand National Party politician, prime minister 1957 (for two months) and 1960–72, when he retired. He favoured a property-owning democracy.

holy orders Christian priesthood, as conferred by the laying on of hands by a bishop. The Anglican church has three orders (bishop, priest, and deacon); the Roman Catholic Church includes also subdeacon, acolyte, exorcist, reader, and door-keepers, and, outside the priesthood, ◊tertiary.

Holy Roman Empire name applied to the empire of ◊Charlemagne and his successors, and to the German empire 962–1806, both being regarded as a revival of the Roman Empire. At its height it comprised much of western and central Europe. See ◊Germany, history and ◊Habsburg.

Holyrood House royal residence in Edinburgh, Scotland. The palace was built 1498–1503 on the site of a 12th-century abbey by James IV. It has associations with Mary Queen of Scots and Charles Edward, the Young Pretender.

Holy See the diocese of the ◊pope.

Holy Week in the Christian church, the last week of ◊Lent, when Christians commemorate the events that led up to the crucifixion of Jesus. Holy Week begins on Palm Sunday and includes Maundy Thursday, which commemorates the Last Supper.

Home Alec Douglas- , Baron Home of the Hirsel 1903– . British Conservative politician. Foreign secretary 1960–63. When he succeeded Macmillan as prime minister in 1963, he renounced his peerage (as 14th Earl of Home) to fight (and lose) the general election of 1964; he resigned as party leader in 1965. He was again foreign secretary 1970–74, when he received a life peerage.

Home Counties the counties in close proximity to London, England: Hertfordshire, Essex, Kent, Surrey, and formerly Middlesex.

Home Guard unpaid force formed in Britain in May 1940 to repel the expected German invasion, and known until Jul 1940 as the Local Defence Volunteers. It consisted of men aged 17–65 who had not been called up, formed part of the armed forces of the crown, and was subject to military law.

Home Office British government department established in 1782 to deal with all the internal affairs of England except those specifically assigned to other departments. Responsibilities include the police, the prison service, immigration, race relations, and broadcasting. The home secretary, the head of the department, holds cabinet rank. There is a separate secretary of state for Scotland, and, since 1964, for Wales. The home secretary has certain duties in respect of the Channel Islands, and the Isle of Man.

homeopathy or *homoeopathy*. A system of medicine, introduced by the German physician Samuel Hahnemann (1755–1843), based on the treatment of a given disease by administering small quantities of a drug which produces the symptoms of that disease in a healthy person. It is contrasted with ◊allopathy.

homeostasis the maintenance of a constant state in an organism's internal environment. It includes regulation of the chemical composition of body fluids, as well as temperature and pressure.

homeothermy the maintenance of a constant body temperature in endothermic (warm-blooded) animals, by the use of chemical body processes to compensate for heat loss or gain when external temperatures change. Such processes include generation of heat by the breakdown of food and the contraction of muscles, and loss of heat by sweating, panting and other means.

Homer legendary Greek epic poet, according to tradition a blind minstrel and the author of the *Iliad* and the *Odyssey*. The *Iliad* tells of the siege of Troy, and the *Odyssey* of the adventures of Ulysses returning from it.

Homer Winslow 1836–1910. US painter and lithographer, best known for his seascapes, both oils and watercolours, which date from the 1880s and 1890s.

Home Rule the slogan of the Irish nationalist movement 1870–1914; it stood for the repeal of the Act of ◊Union 1801 and the establishment of an Irish parliament within the framework of the British Empire. The slogan was popularized after 1870 by Isaac Butt (1813–79) and ◊Parnell, his successor in the nationalist leadership. Gladstone's Home Rule bills of 1886 and 1893 were both defeated; Asquith's Home Rule bill became law in 1914, but was suspended during World War I. After 1918 the demand for an independent Irish republic replaced that for home rule.

home service force (HSF) force established in the UK in 1982, linked to the ◊Territorial Army and recruited from volunteers of ages 18–60 with previous military (TA or Regular) experience. It was introduced to guard key points and installations likely to be the target of enemy 'special forces' and saboteurs, so releasing other units for mobile defence roles.

Homestead Act, The in US history, an 1862 act of Congress to encourage the settlement of western lands by offering 65-hectare/160-acre plots cheaply or even free to those willing to cultivate and improve the land. By 1900 some 32,400,000 hectares/80,000,000 acres had been disposed of.

homicide in law, the killing of a human being. In British law this may be unlawful, lawful, or excusable, depending on the circumstance. Unlawful homicides are ◊murder, ◊manslaughter, ◊infanticide, and causing death by dangerous driving. Lawful homicide occurs where, for example, a police officer is justified in killing a criminal in the course of trying to arrest him. Excusable homicide occurs where the person was killed in self defence, or by accident.

homologous in biology, an organ or structure possessed by members of different taxonomic groups (for example, species, genera, families, orders) which, although now different in form or usage, originally derived from the same structure in a common ancestor. The wing of a bat, the arm of a monkey, and the flipper of a seal are homologous, because they all derive from the forelimb of an ancestral mammal.

homologous series various organic chemicals which form series whose consecutive members differ by a constant molecular weight.

homonymy an aspect of language in which two or more words may sound and look alike (*homonymy* proper; for example, a farmer's bull and a papal bull), may sound the same but look different (*homophony*; for example, air and heir; gilt and guilt), and may look the same but sound different (*homography*; for example the wind in the trees and roads that wind).

homosexuality sexual preference for, or attraction to, persons of one's own sex; in women it is referred to as ◊lesbianism. Men and women who are attracted to both sexes are referred to as bisexual.

homozygous in a living organism, having two identical ◊alleles of the ◊gene for a given trait. Homozygous individuals always breed true, that is they produce offspring that resemble them in appearance when bred with a genetically similar individual. ◊Recessive alleles are only expressed in the homozygous condition. See also ◊heterozygous.

Hon. abbreviation for *Honourable*.

Honduras
Republic of
(*República de honduras*)

```
0  miles  500
0  km     1000
```

area 112,088 sq km/43,227 sq mi
capital Tegucigalpa
towns San Pedro Sula; ports Henecan (on Pacific), La Ceiba
physical mountainous; 45% forest
head of state and government Rafael Leonardo

Callejas from 1990
political system democratic republic
exports coffee, bananas, timber (including mahogany, rosewood)
currency lempira
population (1989 est) 5,106,000 (90% mestizo, 10% Indians and Europeans); annual growth rate 3.1%
life expectancy men 58, women 62
language Spanish and Indian languages
religion Roman Catholic 97%
literacy 61% male/58% female (1985 est)
GDP $3.5 bn (1987); $758 per head
chronology
1838 Honduras achieved independence.
1980 After more than a century of mostly military rule, a civilian government was elected. The commander in chief of the army, Gen Gustavo Alvarez, retained considerable power.
1983 Close involvement with the USA allowing Nicaraguan counter-revolutionaries (Contras) to operate from Honduras.
1984 Alvares ousted in a coup led by junior officers, resulting in a review of policy towards the USA and Nicaragua.
1985 José Azeona elected president.
1989 Government and opposition declared their support for Central American peace plan to demobilize Nicaraguan Contras based in Honduas.
1990 Rafael Callejas inaugurated as president.
1992 Border dispute with El Salvador dating from 1861 finally resolved.

Honan former name of ◊Henan, a province of China.

Honduras country in central America, bounded to the N by the Caribbean, to the SE by Nicaragua, to the S by the Pacific, to the SW by El Salvador, and to the W and NW by Guatemala.

Honecker Erich 1912– . German communist politician, in power 1973–89, elected chair of the council of state (head of state) 1976. He governed in an austere manner and, while favouring East–West detente, was a loyal ally of the USSR. In Oct 1989, following a wave of pro-democracy demonstrations, he was replaced as leader of the Socialist Unity Party (SED) and head of state by Egon ◊Krenz, and in Dec expelled from the Communist Party. Following revelations of corruption during his regime, he was placed under house arrest, awaiting trial on charges of treason, corruption, and abuse of power. He was allowed to go into exile in Chile 1993.

Honegger Arthur 1892–1955. Swiss composer. In the 1920s he joined the group of French composers known as ◊Les Six. Later his work became deeply expressive, and varied in form, for example,

honeysuckle

opera (*Antigone* 1927), ballet (*Skating Rink* 1922), oratorio (*Le Roi David/King David*, and programme music *Pacific 231* 1923.

honey a sweep syrup made by honey ◊bees from the nectar of flowers. It is made in excess of their needs as food for the winter. Honey comprises various sugars, especially laevulose and dextrose, with enzymes, colouring matter, acids and pollen.

honey guides in botany, lines or spots on the petals of a flower which indicate to pollinating insects the position of the nectaries within the flower. The orange dot on the lower lip of the toadflax flower (*Linaria vulgaris*) is an example.

honeysuckle plants of the *Lonicera* genus, Caprifoliaceae family. The **common honeysuckle** or **woodbine** *Lonicera pericylmenum* is a climbing plant with sweet-scented flowers, reddish and yellow-tinted.

Hong Kong British crown colony in SE Asia, comprising Hong Kong Island, the Kowloon peninsula, and the mainland New Territories. It is due to revert to Chinese control 1997.
area 1,070 sq km/413 sq mi
capital Victoria (popularly Hong Kong City)
towns Kowloon, Tsuen Wan
exports textiles, clothing, electronic goods, clocks, watches, cameras, plastic products; tourism
currency Hong Kong dollar
population (1986) 5,431,000; 57% Hong Kong Chinese, most of the remainder refugees from the mainland
languages English and Chinese
religion Confucianist, Buddhist, Taoist, with Muslim and Christian minorities
government Hong Kong is a British dependency administered by a Crown-appointed governor Chris Patten from 1992 who presides over an unelected executive council, composed of four ex-officio and 11 nominated members, and a legislative council composed of three ex-officio

members, 29 appointees and 24 indirectly elected members.

history formerly part of ◊China, Hong Kong Island was occupied by Britain 1841, during the first of the ◊Opium Wars, and ceded by the Chinese government under the 1842 Treaty of Nanking. The Kowloon Peninsula was acquired under the 1860 Peking (Beijing) Convention and the New Territories secured on a 99-year lease from 1898.

The colony, which developed into a major *entrepôt* for Sino-British trade during the late 19th and early 20th centuries, was occupied by Japan 1941–45. The restored British administration promised, after 1946, to increase self-government. These plans were shelved, however, after the 1949 Communist revolution in ◊China. During the 1950s almost 1,000,000 Chinese (predominantly Cantonese) refugees fled to Hong Kong. Immigration continued during the 1960s and 1970s, raising the colony's population from 1,000,000 in 1946 to 5,000,000 in 1980, and forcing the imposition of strict border controls during the 1980s.

Hong Kong's economy expanded rapidly during the corresponding period, however, and the colony became one of Asia's major commercial, financial, and industrial centres. As the date (1997) for the termination of the New Territories' lease approached, negotiations on Hong Kong's future were opened between Britain and China during the early 1980s. These culminated in a unique agreement, signed in Beijing in 1984, in which Britain agreed to transfer full sovereignty of the Islands and New Territories to China in 1997 in return for a Chinese assurance that Hong Kong's social and economic freedom and capitalist lifestyle would be preserved for at least 50 years.

Honiara port and capital of the Solomon Islands, on the NW coast of Guadalcanal island; population (1984) 24,000.

honi soit qui mal y pense (French 'shame on him who thinks evil of it') the motto of the Order of the Garter.

Honolulu (Hawaiian 'sheltered bay') capital city and port of ◊Hawaii, USA, on the S coast of Oahu; population (1980) 365,000. It is a holiday resort, noted for its beauty and tropical vegetation, with some industry. 11 km/7 mi SW is Pearl Harbor with naval and military installations.

honours list military and civil awards approved by the Sovereign of the UK at New Year, and on her official birthday in June.

Honshu principal island of Japan. It lies between Hokkaido to the NE and Kyushu to the SW; area 230,448 sq km/88,839 sq mi, including 382 smaller islands; population (1980) 93,246,000. A chain of volcanic mountains runs along the island, which is subject to frequent earthquakes. The main cities are Tokyo, the capital of Japan, and Okohama, and the ports on the Inland Sea in the S Osaka, Kobe, Kure, and Hiroshima.

Honthorst Gerrit van 1590–1656. Dutch painter who used extremes of light and shade, influenced by Caravaggio; with Terbrugghen he formed the **Utrecht school**.

Hooch Pieter de 1629–1684. Dutch painter of harmonious domestic scenes and courtyards of his Delft period.

Hooke Robert 1635–1703. English scientist and inventor. He discovered that the tension in a lightly-stretched spring is proportional to its extension from its natural length (Hooke's law). His inventions included a telegraph system, a double-barrelled air-pump, the spirit-level, marine barometer, and sea gauge. He coined the term 'cell' in biology.

Hooker Joseph Dalton 1817–1911. British botanist who travelled to the Antarctic and made many botanical discoveries, documented in *Flora Antarctica* 1844–47. Among his other works are *Flora of British India* 1875–97 and *Genera Plantarum* 1862–63.

hookworm parasitic roundworm (see ◊worm) *Necator* which lives in tropic and subtropic regions, but also in humid sites in temperate climates where defecation occurs frequently. The eggs are hatched in damp soil, and the larvae bore into the human skin, usually through the feet. They make their way to the small intestine where they live by sucking blood. The eggs are expelled with faeces, and the cycle starts again.

Hooper John *c*. 1495–1555. English Protestant reformer and martyr. Born in Somerset, he adopted the views of ◊Zwingliand was appointed bishop of Gloucester 1550, and in 1555 was burned for heresy.

hoopoe bird *Upupa epops* in the order Coraciiformes. Slightly larger than a thrush, it has a long thin bill and a bright buff-coloured crest which expands into a fan shape. The wings are banded with black and white and the rest of the plumage is black, white, and buff. It is found in Europe, Asia, and Africa.

Hoover Herbert (Clark) 1874–1964. Thirty-first president of the USA 1929–33, a Republican. Secretary of commerce 1921–28, he was elected president but lost public confidence after the stock-market crash of 1929, when he opposed direct government aid for the unemployed in the depression that followed.

Hoover J(ohn) Edgar 1895–1972. US lawyer. As director of the Federal Bureau of Investigation (FBI) from 1924, he built up a powerful network for the detection of organized crime, including a national fingerprint collection. His drive against alleged communist activities after World War II, and his opposition to the Kennedy administration and others brought much criticism over abuse of power.

Hoover William Henry 1849–1932. US manufacturer who is best known for his association with the ◊vacuum cleaner. The Hoover vacuum cleaner soon became a generic name for the type.

Hoover dam the highest concrete dam in the USA, 221 m/726 ft, on the Colorado River at the Arizona-Nevada border, built 1931-1936. Known as Boulder Dam 1933–47, its name was restored by President Truman as Herbert ◊Hoover's reputation revived. It impounds Lake Meade, and has a hydro-electric power capacity of some 1,300 megawatts.

Hooverville colloquial term for any shantytown built by the unemployed and destitute in the USA during the Depression 1929–33, named after the US president Herbert Hoover, whose policies were blamed for the plight of millions.

Hope Anthony. Pen name of Anthony Hope Hawkins 1863–1933. British novelist, whose romance *The Prisoner of Zenda* 1894, and its sequel *Rupert of Hentzau* 1898, introduced the imaginary Balkan state of Ruritania.

Hope Bob. Stage-name of Leslie Townes Hope 1904– . US comedian, born in Britain, but taken to the USA in 1907. His film appearances include a series of 'Road' films made with Bing ◊Crosby.

Hopei former name of ◊Hebei, a province of China.

Hope's apparatus in physics, an apparatus used to demonstrate the temperature at which water has its maximum density. It is named after Thomas Charles Hope (1766–1844).

Hopewell North American Indian culture about 200 AD, noted for burial mounds up to 12 m/40 ft high, and also for Serpent Mound, Ohio; see also ◊moundbuilder.

Hopi indigenous American people, numbering approximately 6,000, who live mainly in the SW USA. Their language belongs to the Uto-Aztecan family. The Hopi reservation in Arizona, USA, is surrounded by the Dene reservation.

Hopkins Anthony 1937– . British actor. Notable stage appearances include *As You Like It* (with an all male cast), *Equus, Macbeth,* and *Pravda.* Films include *All Creatures Great and Small* and *A Bridge Too Far,* and television parts in *War and Peace* and *A Married Man.* His chilling portrayal of a serial killer in the film *Silence of the Lambs* 1991 won him an Academy Award and international stardom.

Hopkins Gerard Manley 1844–1889. British poet. His work, marked by its religious themes and use of natural imagery, includes 'The Wreck of the Deutschland' 1876, and 'The Windhover' 1877. His employment of 'sprung rhythm' has greatly influenced later 20th century poetry.

hoplite in ancient Greece, a heavily-armed infantry soldier.

Hopper Edward 1882–1967. US painter and etcher, whose views of New York in the 1930s and 1940s captured the loneliness and superficial glamour of city life, as in *Nighthawks* 1942 (Art Institute, Chicago).

hops female fruit-heads of the hop plant *Humulus lupulus,* family Cannabiaceae; these are dried and used as a tonic and in flavouring beer. In designated areas in Europe, no male hops may be grown, since seedless hops produced by the unpollinated female plant contain a greater proportion of alpha acid which gives beer its bitter taste.

Horace 65–8 BC. Roman lyric poet and satirist. He became a leading poet under the patronage of the emperor Augustus. His works include *Satires* 35–30 BC, the four books of *Odes c.* 24–25, *Epistles,* a series of verse letters, and a critical work *Ars Poetica.*

horehound genus of plants *Marrubium,* family Labiate. The *white horehound Marrubium vulgare,* found in Europe, N Africa, and W Asia and naturalized in North America, has a thick hairy stem and clusters of dull white flowers; it has medicinal uses.

horizon the limit to which one can see across the surface of the sea or a level plain, that is, about 5 km/3 mi at 1.5 m/5 ft above sea level, and about 65 km/40 mi at 300 m/1,000 ft.

hormone product of the endocrine glands, concerned with control of body functions. The main glands are the thyroid, parathyroid, pituitary, adrenal, pancreas, uterus, ovary, and testis. Hormones bring about changes in the functions of various organs according to the body's requirements. The pituitary gland, at the base of the brain, is the centre for overall coordination of hormone secretion; the thyroid hormones determine the rate of general body chemistry; the adrenal hormones prepare the organism for 'fight or flight' situations and the sexual hormones such as oestrogen govern reproductive functions.

horn family of musical instruments originating in

animal horns, of which the French horn is most widely used. See ◊brass.

Horn Philip de Montmorency, Count of Horn 1518–1568. Flemish politician. He held high offices under the Holy Roman emperor Charles V and his son Philip II, and from 1563 he was one of the leaders of the opposition to the rule of Cardinal Granvella (1517–1586) and to the introduction of the Inquisition. In 1567 he was arrested together with the Resistance leader Egmont, and both were beheaded in Brussels.

hornbeam a tree genus *Carpinus,* of the Betulaceae family. The *common hornbeam Carpinus betulus* is found in woods throughout the temperate regions of Europe and Asia. It has a twisted stem and smooth grey bark. The leaves are oval and hairy on the undersurface. It bears flowers in catkin form, followed by clusters of small nuts with distinctive winged bracts.

hornbill bird of the family of Bucerotidae, found in Africa, India, and Malaysia, and named for its powerful bill surmounted by a bony growth or casque. They are about 1 m/3 ft long, and omnivorous. During breeding season, the female walls herself into a hole in a tree, and does not emerge until the young are hatched.

hornblende any of various minerals consisting principally of calcium, iron, and magnesium silicate, found both in igneous and metamorphic rocks.

hornet a type of ◊wasp.

hornfels a ◊metamorphic rock formed by the heating of rocks in contact with a hot igneous body. It is fine-grained and brittle.

Horniman Annie Elizabeth Fredericka 1860–1937. British pioneer of repertory theatre, who subsidised the Abbey Theatre, Dublin, and founded the Manchester company.

hornwort underwater aquatic plants with pointed leaves, family Ceratophyllaceae, found in slow-moving water. They may be up to 2 m/7 ft long.

horoscope in astrology, a chart of the position of the Sun, Moon, and planets relative to the ◊zodiac at the moment of birth, used to assess a person's character and forecast future influences.

horror a modern genre of fiction and film, devoted primarily to scaring the reader, but often also aiming at a catharsis of common fears through their exaggeration into the bizarre and grotesque. Dominant figures in the horror tradition are Mary Shelley (*Frankenstein* 1818), Bram Stoker, and H P Lovecraft and, among contemporary writers, Stephen King and Clive Barker.

horse hoofed odd-toed grass-eating mammal, *Equus caballus* of the family Equidae (which also includes zebras and asses). The many breeds of *domestic horse* of Euro-Asian derivation range in colour through white, brown, and black. The yellow-brown *Mongolian wild horse Equus przewalskii* (named after its Polish 'discoverer' in about 1880) is the only surviving species of wild horse.

Horse, Master of the head of the department of the British royal household responsible for the royal stables. The Earl of Westmorland became Master of the Horse in 1978.

horse chestnut tree *Aesculus hippocastanatum,* originally from SE Europe but widely planted elsewhere. Its fruit contains the inedible conker. It is not related to the tree chestnut.

horse fly fly of the family Tabanidae. The females suck blood from horses, cattle, and humans. Males live on plants and suck nectar. The larvae are carnivorous. They are also

horse

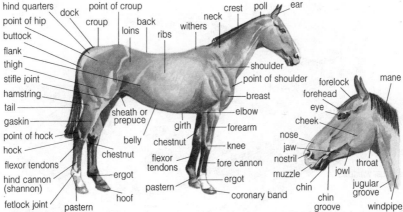

hind quarters · dock · point of croup · crest · poll · ear
point of hip · croup · back · neck · withers
buttock · loins · ribs
flank
thigh
stifle joint — shoulder
hamstring — point of shoulder · forelock · mane
tail — breast · forehead
gaskin · sheath or prepuce — elbow · eye
point of hock · girth · cheek
hock · belly · chestnut · forearm · nose
flexor tendons · chestnut · knee · jaw
hind cannon (shannon) · flexor tendons · fore cannon · nostril · throat
fetlock joint · ergot · pastern · ergot · muzzle · jowl
hoof · pastern · coronary band · chin · jugular groove
chin groove · windpipe

known as clegs or gadflies. There are over 2,500 species.

Horse Guards name given to a building in Whitehall, London, England, erected 1753 by Vardy from a design by Kent, on the site of the Tilt Yard of Whitehall palace. This spot has been occupied by the Household Cavalry or 'Horse Guards' since the Royal Horse Guards were formed in 1661.

horsepower an Imperial unit of power (hp) equivalent to 550 foot-pound force per second or 745.7 watts. It is a standard US unit equal to 746 watts.

horse racing the sport of racing mounted or driven horses. Two popular forms in Britain are *flat racing* for thoroughbred horses over a flat course, and *National Hunt* racing, in which the horses have to clear obstacles.

horseradish hardy perennial *Armoracia rusticana*, native to SE Europe but naturalized elsewhere, family Cruciferae. The thick, cream-coloured root is strong-tasting and made into a condiment to eat with meat.

horsetail plant of the class Equisetales, related to ferns and clubmosses. There are about 35 living species, bearing their spores on cones at the stem tip. The upright stems are ribbed, and often have spaced whorls of branches. Today they are of modest size, but hundreds of millions of years ago giant tree-like forms existed.

horsetail

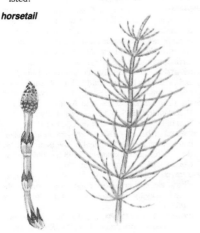

Horthy de Nagybánya Nicholas 1868–1957. Hungarian politician and admiral. Leader of the counter-revolutionary White government, he became regent in 1920, on the overthrow of the communist Bela Kun regime by Romanian intervention. He represented the conservative and military class, and retained power until World War II, trying (although allied to Hitler) to retain independence of action. In 1944 Hungary was taken over by the Nazis and he was deported to Germany.

horticulture the art and science of growing flowers, fruit, and vegetables. In Britain, over half a million acres are devoted to professional horticulture, and vegetables account for almost three quarters of the produce. Some areas, like the Vale of Evesham, have specialized in horticulture because they have the mild climate and light fertile soil most suited to these crops.

Horus in ancient Egyptian mythology, the hawkheaded sun god, son of Isis and Osiris, of whom the pharaohs were thought to be the incarnation.

Hospitaller a member of the Order of ◊St John.

host an organism that is parasitized by another. In ◊commensalism, the partner that does not benefit may also be called the host.

HOTOL (*Horizontal Take-Off and Landing*). British concept for a hypersonic transport and satellite launcher, which could be operational before the end of the century. It will be a single-stage vehicle with no boosters and will take off and land on a runway. It will feature a revolutionary air-breathing rocket engine which will enable it to carry much less oxygen than a conventional space plane.

hot spot in geology, a hypothetical region of high thermal activity in the Earth's ◊mantle. It is believed to be the origin of many chains of ocean islands, such as Polynesia (including Hawaii) and the Galapagos.

Hottentot South African people inhabiting the SW corner of the African continent when Europeans first settled there. The language bears a resemblance to Bushman, and has mainly monosyllabic roots with explosive consonants which produce clicking sounds.

Houdini Harry, stage name of Erich Weiss 1874–1926. US escapologist and conjuror. He attained fame by his escapes from ropes and handcuffs, and also reproduced some of the phenomena of spiritualist séances by purely mechanical means to expose fakes.

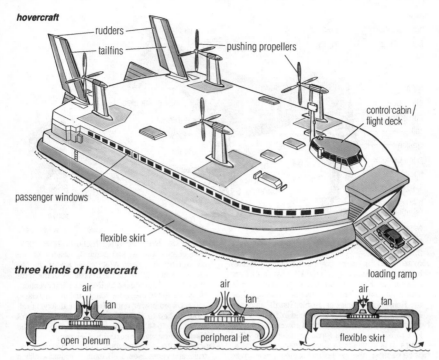

hovercraft

rudders

tailfins

pushing propellers

control cabin / flight deck

passenger windows

flexible skirt

three kinds of hovercraft

loading ramp

air

fan

open plenum

air

fan

peripheral jet

air

fan

flexible skirt

Houdon Jean-Antoine 1741–1828. French sculptor, a portraitist best known for his characterful studies of Voltaire and Neoclassical statue of George Washington, commissioned 1785.

Houphouët-Boigny Felix 1905– . Ivory Coast politician. He held posts in French ministries, and became president of the republic on independence in 1960. He was re-elected for a sixth term in 1985.

hour a period of time comprising 60 minutes; 24 hours make 1 calendar day.

Hours, Book of in medieval Europe, a collection of liturgical prayers for the use of the faithful, especially at home. Books of Hours appeared in England in the 13th century, and contained short prayers and illustrations, with each prayer suitable for a different hour of the day, in honour of the Virgin Mary. The enormous demand for Books of Hours was a stimulus for the development of Gothic illumination. A notable example is the *Très Riches Heures du Duc de Berry*, illustrated in the 14th–15th centuries by the Limbourg brothers.

house music a type of dance music of the 1980s originating in the inner-city clubs of Chicago, USA, combining funk with European high-tech pop, using dub, digital sampling, and cross-fading. *Acid house* has minimal vocal and melody, instead surrounding the mechanically emphasized 4/4 beat with found noises, strippeddown synthesizer riffs, and a wandering bass line.

housefly the most common type of fly of the family Muscidae. They are grey, and have mouthparts adapted for drinking liquids.

Housman A(lfred) E(dward) 1859–1936. British poet and classical scholar. His *A Shropshire Lad* 1896, a series of deceptively simple nostalgic ballad-like poems, was popular during World War I. This was followed by *Last Poems* 1922, and *More Poems* 1936.

Houston port in Texas, USA; population (1981) 1,595,000; linked by canal to the Gulf of Mexico. It is an agricultural centre, and industries include petrochemicals, chemicals, plastics, synthetic rubber, and electronics.

Houston Sam 1793–1863. American general who won Texan independence from Mexico 1836; Houston, Texas, is named after him. He was president of the Republic of Texas 1836–45.

hovercraft a vehicle that rides on a cushion of high-pressure air, free from all contact with the surface beneath, invented by British engineer Christopher Cockerell in 1959. Although hovercraft need a smooth terrain when operating overland at present hovercraft are best adapted to use on waterways, and are especially useful in places where harbours have not been established.

Howard Catherine c. 1520–1542. Queen consort of ◊Henry VIII of England from 1540. In 1541 the archbishop of Canterbury, Thomas Cranmer, accused her of being unchaste before marriage to Henry, and she was beheaded when Cranmer made further charges of adultery.

Howard Charles, 2nd Baron Howard of Effingham and 1st Earl of Nottingham 1536–1624. English admiral, a cousin of Queen Elizabeth I. He commanded the fleet against the Spanish Armada while Lord High Admiral 1585–1618, and cooperated with the Earl of Essex in the attack on Cádiz in 1596.

Howard Ebenezer 1850–1928. British town planner and founder of the ideal of the ◊garden city, through his book *Tomorrow* 1898 (republished as *Garden Cities of Tomorrow* in 1902).

Howard John 1726–1790. British philanthropist whose work to improve prison conditions is continued today by the *Howard League for Penal Reform*.

Howard Trevor (Wallace) 1916–1988. British film actor, whose work ranged from the quiet impact of

Brief Encounter 1945, to the bravura of *Conduct Unbecoming* 1975.

Howe Elias 1819–1867. US inventor in 1846 of a ◊sewing machine using double thread.

Howe Geoffrey 1926– . British Conservative politician. Under Heath he was solicitor-general 1970–72 and minister for trade 1972–74; under Thatcher chancellor of the Exchequer 1979–83; foreign secretary 1983-89; and deputy prime minister 1989-90. Increasing differences with Thatcher over monetary and political union with Europe caused him to resign Nov 1990. This exposed a deep division within the Conservative Party and opened the way for Michael Heseltine's leadership challenge.

Howe William, 5th Viscount Howe 1729–1814. British general. In the American War of Independence he won the Battle of Bunker Hill in 1775, and as commander in chief in America 1776–78 captured New York and defeated Washington at Brandywine and Germantown. He resigned in protest at lack of home government support.

howitzer a cannon, in use since the 16th century, with a steep angle of fire. It was used in World War I for demolishing the fortresses of the trench system. The multinational NATO FH70 field howitzer is mobile, with its own engine, and fires under computer control three 43 kg/95 lb shells at 32 km/20 mi range in 15 seconds.

Hoxha Enver 1908–1985. Albanian politician, the country's leader from 1954. Once a schoolmaster, he founded the Albanian Communist Party 1941, and headed the liberation movement 1939–44. He was prime minister 1944–54, combining with foreign affairs 1946–53, and from 1954 was first secretary of the Albanian Party of Labour. In policy he was a Stalinist, and independent of both Chinese and Soviet Communism.

Hoyle Fred(erick) 1915– . English astronomer and writer. In 1948 he joined with Hermann Bondi and Thomas Gold in developing the ◊steady state theory. In 1957, with Geoffrey and Margaret Burbidge and William Fowler, he showed that chemical elements heavier than hydrogen and helium are built up by nuclear reactions inside stars. He has created controversy by suggesting, with Chandra Wickramasinghe, that life originates in the gas clouds of space.

Hsuan Tung name adopted by Henry ◊P'u-i on becoming emperor of China in 1908.

Hua Guofeng formerly *Hua Kuofeng* 1920– . Chinese politician, leader of the Chinese Communist Party (CCP) 1976–81, premier 1976–80. He dominated Chinese politics1976–77, seeking economic modernization without major structural reform. From 1978 he was gradually eclipsed by Deng Xiaoping. Hua was ousted from the Politburo Sep 1982, but remained a member of the CCP Central Committee.

Huang He formerly *Hwang-ho* river in China; length 4,410 km/2,740 mi. It gains its name (meaning 'yellow river') from its muddy waters. Formerly known as 'China's sorrow' because of disastrous floods.

Hubbard L(afayette) Ron(ald) 1911–1986. US science-fiction writer of the 1930s–1940s, founder in 1954 of ◊Scientology.

Hubble Edwin Powell 1889–1953. US astronomer, who discovered the existence of other ◊galaxies outside our own, and classified them according to their shape. He first proposed that the Universe was expanding. *Hubble's constant* is a measure of the rate at which the Universe is expanding. (Modern observations suggest that galaxies are moving apart at a rate of 50–100 km/30–60 mi per second for every million ◊parsecs of distance.)

Hubble Space Telescope observatory in space, launched May 1990, developed jointly by ◊NASA and the European Space Agency. Orbiting at an altitude of 593 km/320 mi, it was designed to overcome the distortion and imperfections caused by the Earth's atmosphere, enabling objects not normally visible by telescope to be identified. However, soon after its launch a defective curvature was found in one or both of its 240 cm/94 in mirrors. Nevertheless, the telescope successfully photographed Supernova 1987A.

Hubei (formerly *Hupei*) province of central China, through which flow the Chang Jiang and its tributary the Han Shui; area 187,500 sq km/72,375 sq mi; population (1982) 47,804,000. The capital is Wuhan. Agricultural products include rice, cotton, cereals, beans, and vegetables. Copper, phosphorous, iron ore, salt, and gypsum are mined. Much of the province is low lying.

huckleberry berry-bearing bush of the genus *Vaccinium*, including the *bilberry Vaccinium myrtillus* in Britain, and blueberries in the USA.

Hudson Henry died 1611. English explorer. In Sept 1609, he reached New York Bay and sailed 240 km/150 mi up the river which now bears his name. In 1610, he sailed from London, England, in the *Discovery* and entered the Hudson Strait. After an icebound winter, Hudson and eight others were turned adrift by a mutinous crew.

Hudson Bay inland sea of NE Canada, linked with the Atlantic by *Hudson Strait*, and with the Arctic by Foxe Channel; area 1,233,000 sq km/476,000 sq mi. It is named after Henry Hudson.

Hudson's Bay Company a chartered company founded by Prince ◊Rupert in 1670 to trade in furs with the North American Indians. In 1783 the rival North-West Fur Company was formed, but in 1851 this became amalgamated with the Hudson's Bay Company, which lost its monopoly in 1859. It is still Canada's biggest fur company, but today has many other interests.

Hughes Howard 1905–1976. US tycoon. Inheriting wealth from his father, who had patented a successful oil-drilling bit, he created a legendary financial empire. A skilled pilot, he manufactured and designed aircraft, and made the classic film

Hoyle British astronomer Professor Fred Hoyle.

human body

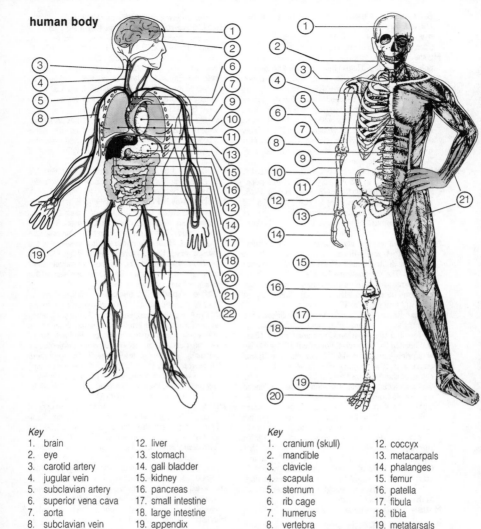

Key
1. brain
2. eye
3. carotid artery
4. jugular vein
5. subclavian artery
6. superior vena cava
7. aorta
8. subclavian vein
9. heart
10. lungs
11. diaphragm
12. liver
13. stomach
14. gall bladder
15. kidney
16. pancreas
17. small intestine
18. large intestine
19. appendix
20. bladder
21. femoral artery
22. femoral vein

Key
1. cranium (skull)
2. mandible
3. clavicle
4. scapula
5. sternum
6. rib cage
7. humerus
8. vertebra
9. ulna
10. radius
11. pelvis
12. coccyx
13. metacarpals
14. phalanges
15. femur
16. patella
17. fibula
18. tibia
19. metatarsals
20. phalanges
21. superficial (upper) layer of muscles

Hell's Angels 1930 about aviators of World War I.

Hughes Ted 1930– . British poet, Poet Laureate from 1984. His work includes *The Hawk in the Rain* 1957, *Lupercal* 1960, *Wodwo* 1967, and *River* 1983, and is characterized by its harsh portrayal of the crueller aspects of nature.

Hughes Thomas 1822–1896. British author, of the children's book *Tom Brown's School Days* 1857, a story of Rugby school under Thomas ◊Arnold.

Hughes William Morris 1862–1952. Australian politician, prime minister 1915–23; originally Labor, he headed a national cabinet. Born in London, he emigrated to Australia in 1884. He represented Australia in the peace conference after World War I at Versailles.

Hugo Victor (Marie) 1802–1885. French poet, novelist, and dramatist. The *Odes et poésies diverses* appeared in 1822, and his verse play *Hernani* 1830 established him as the leader of French Romanticism. More volumes of verse followed between his series of dramatic novels which included *The Hunchback of Notre Dame* 1831 and *Les Misérables* 1862.

Huguenot French Protestant (mainly Calvinist) in the 16th century. Severely persecuted under Francis I and Henry II, the Huguenots survived an attempt to exterminate them (24 Aug 1572) and the religious wars of the next 30 years. In 1598 Henry IV (himself formerly a Huguenot) granted them toleration under the *Edict of Nantes*. Louis XIV revoked the edict

human species, origins of

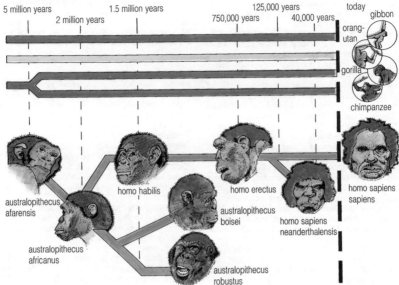

5 million years | 1.5 million years | 125,000 years | today | gibbon
2 million years | | 750,000 years | 40,000 years | orang-utan
| | | | gorilla
| | | | chimpanzee

australopithecus afarensis

homo habilis

homo erectus

homo sapiens sapiens

australopithecus africanus

australopithecus boisei

homo sapiens neanderthalensis

australopithecus robustus

1685, attempting their forcible conversion, and 400,000 emigrated.

Hull (officially *Kingston upon Hull*) city and port, through which the river Humber flows, administrative headquarters of Humberside, England; population (1986) 258,000. It is linked with the south bank of the estuary by the Humber Bridge. Industries include fish processing, vegetable oils, flour milling, electricals, textiles, paint, pharmaceuticals, chemicals, caravans, and aircraft.

Hull Cordell 1871–1955. US Democrat politician, born in Tennessee. He was a member of Congress 1907–33, and, as Roosevelt's secretary of state 1933–44, was identified with the Good Neighbour Policy of nonintervention in Latin America, and opposed German and Japanese aggression. In his last months of office he paved the way for a system of collective security, for which he was called 'father' of the United Nations. Nobel Peace Prize 1945.

hum, environmental a disturbing sound of frequency about 40 Hz, heard by individuals sensitive to this range, but inaudible to the rest of the population. It may be caused by industrial noise pollution, or have a more exotic origin, such as the jet stream, a fast-flowing high altitude (about 15,000 m/50,000 ft) mass of air.

human body the physical structure of the human being. It develops from the single cell of the fertilized ovum, is born at 40 weeks, and usually reaches sexual maturity between 11 and 18 years of age. The bony framework (skeleton) consists of more than 200 bones, over half of which are in the hands and feet. Bones are held together by joints, some of which allow movement, produced by muscles. The circulatory system supplies muscles and organs with blood, which provides oxygen and food, and removes waste products. Body functions are controlled by the nervous system and hormones. In the upper part of the trunk is the thorax, which contains the lungs and heart. Below this is the abdomen, inside which are the digestive system (stomach and intestines), the liver, spleen, and pancreas, the urinary system (kidneys, ureters, and bladder), and, in the woman, the reproductive organs (ovaries, uterus, and vagina). In the man, the prostate gland and seminal vesicles only of the reproductive system are situated in the abdomen, the testes being in the scrotum, which, with the penis, is suspended in front of and below the abdomen. The bladder empties through a small channel (urethra); this in the female opens in the upper end of the vulval cleft, which also contains the opening of the vagina, or birth canal. In the male, the urethra is continued into the penis. In both sexes, the lower bowel terminates in the anus, a ring of strong muscle situated between the buttocks.

human body: composition by weight

Class	Chemical/element or substance	% body weight
As pure elements or as minerals, salts, and so on	Oxygen	65
	Carbon	18
	Hydrogen	10
	Nitrogen	3
	Calcium	2
	Phosphorus	1.1
	Inorganic molecules	1
	Potassium	0.35
	Sulphur	0.25
	Sodium	0.15
	Chlorine	0.15
	Magnesium. Iron. Manganese. Copper. Iodine. Cobalt. Zinc	Traces
As water and solid matter	Water	60–80
	Total solid material	20–40
As organic molecules	Protein	15–20
	Lipid	3–20
	Carbohydrate	1–15
	Small organic molecules	0–1

human-computer interaction the exchange of information between a person and a computer, through the medium of a ◊user interface, studied as a branch of ergonomics.

Human Rights, Universal Declaration of charter of civil and political political rights drawn up by the United Nations in 1948. They include the right to life, liberty, education, and equality before the law; to freedom of movement, religion, association, and information; and to a nationality. Under the European Convention of Human Rights of 1950, the Council of Europe established the *European Commission of Human Rights* (headquarters in Strasbourg, France), which investigates complaints by states or individuals, and its findings are examined by the *European Court of Human Rights* (established 1959), whose compulsory jurisdiction has been recognized by a number of states.

human species, origins of evolution of humans from ancestral ◊primates. The African apes (gorilla and chimpanzee) are shown by anatomical and molecular comparisons to be our closest living relatives. Molecular studies put the date of the split between the human and African ape lines at 5 to 10 million years ago. There are no ape or *hominid* (of the human group) fossils from this period; the oldest known date from 3.5 million years ago, from Ethiopia and Tanzania. These creatures are known as *Australopithecus afarensis*, and they walked upright. They were either our direct ancestors, or an off-shoot of the line that led to modern humans. They might have been the ancestors of *Homo habilis*, who appeared about a million years later, had slightly larger bodies and brains, and were probably the first to use stone tools. Over 1.5 million years ago, *Homo erectus*, believed to be descended from *Homo habilis*, appeared in Africa. The erectus people had much larger brains, and were probably the first to use fire, and the first to move out of Africa. Their remains are found as far afield as China, Spain, and S Britain. Modern humans, *Homo sapiens sapiens*, and the Neanderthals *Homo sapiens neanderthalensis*, are probably descended from *Homo erectus*. Neanderthals were large-brained and heavily-built, probably adapted to the cold conditions of the ice ages. They lived in Europe and the Middle East, and died out about 40,000 years ago, leaving *Homo sapiens sapiens* as the only remaining species of the hominid group.

Creationists believe that the origin of the human species is as written in the book of Genesis in the Old Testament of the Bible.

Humber Bridge a suspension bridge with twin towers 163 m/533 ft high, which spans the estuary of the river Humber in NE England. When completed in 1980, it was the world's longest bridge with a span of 1,410 m/4,626 ft.

Humberside county of NE England
area 3,512 sq km/1,356 sq mi
towns administrative headquarters Beverley; Hull, Grimsby, Scunthorpe, Goole, Cleethorpes
products petrochemicals and refined oil; processed fish; cereals, root crops, cattle
population (1986) 849,000
famous people Amy Johnson, Andrew Marvell, John Wesley

Humboldt Friedrich Heinrich Alexander, Baron von Humboldt 1769–1859. German botanist and geologist who explored the regions of the Orinoco and the Amazon in S America 1800–04, and gathered 60,000 plant specimens. On his return, Humboldt devoted 21 years to writing an account of his travels.

Hume Basil 1923– . British Roman Catholic cardinal from 1976. A Benedictine monk, he was abbot of Ampleforth in Yorkshire 1963–76, and in 1976 became archbishop of Westminster.

Hume David 1711–1776. Scottish philosopher. *A Treatise of Human Nature* 1740 is a central text of British empiricism. Hume denies the possibility of going beyond the subjective experiences of 'ideas' and 'impressions'. The effect of this position is to invalidate metaphysics.

Hume Joseph 1777–1855. British Radical politician. Born at Montrose, Scotland, he went out to India as an army surgeon in 1797, made a fortune, and on his return bought a seat in Parliament. In 1818 he secured election as a Philosophic Radical and supported many progressive measures.

humidity the quantity of water vapour in a given volume of the atmosphere (absolute humidity), or the ratio of the amount of water vapour in the atmosphere to the saturation value at the same temperature (relative humidity); at ◊dew-point the latter is 100%.

hummingbird birds forming the family Trochilidae and found in the Americas. Their name is derived from the sound produced by the rapid vibration of their wings, and they are the only birds able to fly backwards. They are brilliantly coloured, and have long tongues to obtain nectar from flowers and capture insects. The Cuban *bee hummingbird Mellisuga helenae*, the world's smallest bird, is 5.5 cm/2 in long, and 2g/less than 1/10 oz.

humours, theory of theory prevalent in classical and medieval times that the human body was composed of four kinds of fluid: phlegm, blood, choler or yellow bile, and melancholy or black bile. A person's physical and mental characteristics could be accounted for by a different balance of humours in an individual.

Humperdinck Engelbert 1854–1921. German composer. He wrote the operas *Hänsel und Gretel* 1893, and *Königskinder/King's Children* 1910.

Humphries (John) Barry 1934– . Australian actor, author and comedian who created the caricature of Australian suburbia in housewife-superstar, Dame Edna Everage, from Moonee Ponds, Victoria. In the 1960s Humphries went to England where he published the Adventures of Barry McKenzie, a comic strip in the satirical magazine *Private Eye* 1963-74.

humus component of ◊soil consisting of decomposed or partly decomposed organic matter, dark in colour and usually richer towards the surface. It has a higher carbon content than the original material and a lower nitrogen content, and is a source of minerals in soil fertility.

Hun a member of any of a number of nomad Mongol peoples who first appeared in history in the 2nd century BC raiding across the Great Wall into China. They entered Europe about 372 AD, settled in Hungary, and imposed their supremacy on the Ostrogoths and other Germanic peoples. Under the leadership of Attila they attacked the Byzantine Empire, invaded Gaul, and threatened Rome, but after his death in 453 their power was broken by a revolt of their subject peoples. The *White Huns* or Ephthalites, a kindred people, raided Persia and N India in the 5th–6th centuries.

Hunan province of S central China
area 210,500 sq km/81,253 sq mi
capital Changsha
products rice, tea, tobacco, cotton; minerals
population (1985) 55,610,000.

hundred a subdivision within a shire in England, Ireland, and parts of the USA. The term was originally used by Germanic peoples to denote a

Hungary
Republic of
(Magyar *Köztársaság*)

```
0    miles    500
0    km       1000
```

NORTH
SEA

HUNGARY

Austria

Romania

Budapest

MEDITERRANEAN SEA

area 93,032 sq km/35,910 sq mi
capital Budapest
towns Miskolc, Debrecen, Szeged, Pécs
physical Great Hungarian Plain covers E half of country; Bakony Forest; Transdanubian Highlands in the W; rivers Danube, Tisza; Lake Balaton
head of state Arpád Göncz from 1990
head of government Jósef Antall from 1990
political system emergent democratic republic
exports machinery, vehicles, chemicals, textiles
currency forint
population (1990 est) 10,546,000 (Magyar 92%, Romany 3%, German 2.5%; annual growth rate 0.2%.

life expectancy men 67, women 74
language Hungarian (or Magyar)
religion Roman Catholic 67%, other Christian denominations 25%
literacy 99.3% male/98.5% female (1980)
GDP $26.1 bn (1987); $2.455 per head
chronology
1918 Independence from Austro-Hungarian Empire.
1919 Communist state formed for 133 days.
1920–44 Regency under Admiral Hartley, who joined Hitler's attack on USSR.
1945 Liberated by USSR.
1946 Republic proclaimed; Stalinist regime imposed.
1949 Soviet-style constitution adopted.
1956 Hungarian national uprising; workers' demonstrations in Budapest, democratization reforms by Imre Nagy overturned by Soviet tanks, Kádár installed as party leader.
1968 Economic decentralization reforms.
1983 Competition introduced into elections.
1987 VAT and income tax introduced.
1988 Kádár replaced by Károly Grosz; free trade union recognized; rival political parties legalized.
1989 Border with Austria opened. New 'transitional constitution' adopted, founded on multi-party democracy and new presidentialist executive. HSWP became Hungarian Socialist Party (HSP), led by Nyers. Kádár 'retired', later died; Nagy rehabilitated.
1990 HSP damaged by 'Danubegate' bugging scandal. Elections won by right-of-centre coalition.
1991 Legislation approved to compensate owners of land and property expropriated under communist government. Last Soviet troops deported. EC association pact signed.
1992 EC pact came into effect.

group of 100 warriors, also the area occupied by 100 families or equalling 100 hides (one hide being the amount of land necessary to support a peasant family).

hundred days in history, the period 20 Mar–28 Jun 1815, marking the French emperor Napoleon's escape from imprisonment on Elba to his departure from Paris after losing the battle of Waterloo on 18 Jun.

Hundred Years' War the series of conflicts between England and France 1337–1453.
1340 The English won the naval battle of Sluys.
1346 Battle of Crécy, another English victory.
1347 The English took Calais.
1356 Battle of Poitiers, where Edward the Black Prince defeated the French. King John of France was captured.
late 1350s–early 1360s France had civil wars, brigandage, and the popular uprising of the ◊Jacquerie.
1360 Treaty of Brétigny-Calais. France accepted English possession of Calais, and of an enlarged duchy of Gascony. John was ransomed for £500,000.
1369–1414 The tide turned in favour of the French, and when there was another truce in 1388, only Calais, Bordeaux, and Bayonne were in English hands. A state of half-war continued for many years.
1415 Henry V invaded France and won a victory at Agincourt, followed by conquest of Normandy.

1419 In the Treaty of Troyes, Charles VI of France was forced to disinherit his son, the Dauphin, in favour of Henry V, who was to marry Catherine, Charles' daughter. Most of N France was in English hands.
1422–28 After the death of Henry V his brother Bedford was generally successful.
1429 Joan of Arc raised the siege of Orléans, and the Dauphin was crowned Charles VII.
1430–53 After Joan's death the French continued their successful counter offensive, and in 1453 only Calais was left in English hands.

Hungarian language a member of the Finno-Ugric language group, spoken principally in Hungary but also in parts of the Slovak Republic, Romania, and Yugoslavia. Known as *Magyar* among its speakers, Hungarian is written in a form of the Roman alphabet in which *s* corresponds to English *sh*, and *sz* to *s*.

Hungary country in central Europe, bounded N by the Slovak Republic, NE by Ukraine, E by Romania, S by Yugoslavia and Croatia and W by Austria and Slovenia.

hunger march a procession of the unemployed, a feature of social protest in interwar Britain.

Hunt William Holman 1827–1910. British painter, one of the founders of the Pre-Raphaelite Brotherhood 1848. Obsessed with realistic detail, he travelled to Syria and Palestine to paint biblical subjects from 1854 onwards.

His best-known works include *The Awakening Conscience* 1853 (Tate Gallery, London) and *The Light of the World* 1854 (Keble College, Oxford).

Huntington's chorea a rare hereditary disease which begins in middle age. It is characterized by uncontrolled involuntary movements and rapid mental degeneration progressing to ◊dementia. There is no known cure.

Hunyadi János Corvinus 1387–1456. Hungarian politician and general. Born in Transylvania, reputedly the son of the emperor ◊Sigismund, he won battles against the Turks from the 1440s.

Hurd Douglas (Richard) 1930– . English Conservative politician, home secretary 1986–89, appointed foreign secretary 1989 in the reshuffle that followed Nigel Lawson's resignation as chancellor of the Exchequer. In Nov 1990 he was an unsuccessful candidate in the Tory leadership contest following Margaret Thatcher's unexpected resignation. He retained his post as foreign secretary in Prime Minister John Major's new cabinet formed after the 1992 general election.

hurling a team game played with 15 a side. It is a stick and ball game, popular in Ireland and first played over 3,000 years ago.

Huron second largest of the Great Lakes of North America, on the US-Canadian border; area 60,000 sq km/23,160 sq mi. It includes Georgian Bay, Saginaw Bay, and Manitoulin Island.

hurricane a revolving storm in tropical regions, called *typhoon* in the N Pacific. It originates between 5° and 20° N or S of the equator, when the surface temperature of the ocean is above 27°C/80°F. A central calm area, called the eye, is surrounded by inwardly spiralling winds (counterclockwise in the N hemisphere) of up to 320/ kph/ 200 mph. A hurricane is accompanied by lightning and torrential rain, and can cause extensive damage. In meteorology a hurricane is a wind of force 12 or more on the ◊Beaufort scale.

Husák Gustáv 1913–1991. Leader of the Communist Party of Czechoslovakia (CCP) 1969–87 and president 1975–89. After the 1968 Prague Spring of liberalization, his task was to restore control, purge the CCP, and oversee the implementation of a new, federalist constitution. He was deposed in the popular uprising of Nov–Dec 1989 and expelled from the Communist Party Feb 1990.

Huscarls Anglo-Danish warriors, in 10th-century Denmark and early 11th-century England. They formed the bulk of English royal armies until the Norman Conquest.

husky sledge dog used in Arctic regions, up to 70 cm/2 ft high, and 50 kg/110 lbs, with pricked ears, thick fur, and a bushy tail.

Huss John *c.* 1373–1415. Bohemian church reformer, who was excommunicated for attacks on ecclesiastical abuses. He was burned at the stake.

Hussein ibn Ali *c.* 1854–1931. Leader of the Arab revolt 1916–18 against the Turks. He proclaimed himself king of the Hejaz 1916, accepted the caliphate 1924, but after internal fighting he was deposed 1924 by Ibn Saud.

Hussein ibn Talal 1935– . King of Jordan from 1952. Great-grandson of Hussein ibn Ali, he became king after the mental incapacity of his father Talal. By 1967 he had lost all his kingdom west of the Jordan river in the ◊Arab-Israeli Wars, and in 1970 suppressed the ◊Palestine Liberation Organization acting as a guerrilla force against his rule on the remaining East Bank territories. He has become a moderating force in Middle Eastern politics.

Hussein Saddam 1937– . Iraqi politician, in power from 1968, president from 1979, progressively eliminating real or imagined opposition factions as he gained dictatorial control. He fought a bitter war against Iran 1980–88, with US economic aid, and dealt harshly with Kurdish rebels seeking independence, using chemical weapons against civilian populations. In 1990 he annexed Kuwait, to international condemnation, before being driven out by a US-dominated coalition army Feb 1991. After Iraq's defeat in the ◊Gulf War, the Kurds rebelled again, as did the Shi'ites in the south. Hussein used the remainder of his military force against them, causing hundreds of thousands of Kurds to flee their homes in N Iraq, and bombarding S Iraq until the UN imposed a 'No-fly zone' in the area.

Husserl Edmund (Gustav Albrecht) 1859–1938. German philosopher, regarded as the founder of ◊phenomenology, a philosophy concentrating on what is consciously experienced.

Hussite a follower of John ◊Huss. Opposed to both German and papal influence in Bohemia, the Hussites waged successful war against the Holy Roman Empire from 1419, but Roman Catholicism was finally re-established 1620.

Huston John 1906–1987. US film director, screenwriter, and actor. An impulsive and individualistic filmmaker, his work often deals with the themes of greed, treachery, human relationships, and the loner. His works as a director include *The Maltese Falcon* 1941, *The Treasure of the Sierra Madre* 1947 (Academy Award), and *The African Queen* 1951.

Hutton James 1726–1797. Scottish geologist, known as the 'founder of geology', who formulated the concept of ◊uniformitarianism.

Huxley Aldous (Leonard) 1894–1963. British writer. The satirical disillusion of his witty first novel, *Crome Yellow* 1921, continued throughout *Antic Hay* 1923, *Those Barren Leaves* 1925, and *Point Counter Point* 1928. His *Brave New World* 1932, concerns the reproduction of the human race by mass production in the laboratory.

Huxley Andrew 1917– . British physiologist, awarded the Nobel Prize for Medicine 1963, with Alan Hodgkin (1914–) and John Eccles (1903–), for work on nerve impulses.

Huxley Thomas Henry 1825–1895. British scientist and humanist. Following the publication of Charles Darwin's *On the Origin of Species* 1859, he won fame as 'Darwin's bulldog', and for many years was the most prominent and popular champion of

Huxley British novelist and writer, Aldous Huxley.

Huxley Biologist and humanist Thomas Henry Huxley was the foremost British exponent of Darwin's theory of evolution.

evolution. In 1869, he coined the word 'agnostic' to express his own religious attitude.

Hu Yaobang 1915–1989. Chinese politician, Communist Party (CCP) chairman 1981–87. A protégé of the communist leader Deng Xiaoping. Hu presided over a radical overhaul of the party structure and personnel 1982–86.

Huygens Christiaan 1629–1695. Dutch mathematical physicist and astronomer, who propounded the wave theory of light. He developed the pendulum clock, discovered polarization, and observed Saturn's rings.

Hwang-Ho former name of the ◊Huang He, a river in China.

hyacinth bulb-producing plant *Hyacinthus orientalis*, family Liliaceae, native to the E Mediterranean and Africa. The cultivated hyacinth has large, scented, cylindrical heads of pink, white, or blue flowers. The ◊water hyacinth, genus *Eichhornia*, is unrelated, a floating plant from South America.

Hyades V-shaped cluster of stars that forms the face of Taurus, the bull. It is 130 light years away and contains over 200 stars, although only about a dozen are visible to the naked eye.

hyaline membrane disease (HMD) disorder of premature babies, who are unable to produce enough pulmonary surfactant (lung surface conditioner) to enable them to breathe properly. The lungs become hard and glassy (Latin *hyalinus* 'glassy'). A synthetic replacement for surfactant has been developed.

hybrid the offspring from a cross between individuals of two different species, or two inbred lines within a species. In most cases, hybrids between species are infertile and unable to reproduce sexually. In plants, however, doubling of the chromosomes (see ◊polyploid) can restore the fertility of such hybrids.

hydathode a specialized pore, or less commonly, a hair, through which water is secreted by hydrostatic pressure from the interior of a plant leaf onto the surface. Hydathodes are found on many different plants and are usually situated around the leaf margin at vein endings. Each pore is surrounded by two crescent-shaped cells and resembles an open

◊stoma, but the size of the opening cannot be varied as in a stoma. The process of water secretion through hydathodes is known as ◊guttation.

Hyderabad capital city of the S central Indian state of Andhra Pradesh, on the Musi, population (1981) 2,528,000. Products include carpets, silks, and metal inlay work. It was formerly the capital of the state of Hyderabad. Buildings include the Jama Masjid mosque and Golconda fort.

Hyder Ali *c.* 1722–1782. Indian general, sultan of Mysore from 1759. In command of the army in Mysore from 1749, he became the ruler of the state 1759, and rivalled British power in the area until his triple defeat by Sir Eyre Coote 1781 during the Anglo-French wars.

hydra in zoology, genus of freshwater polyps, of the phylum *Cnidaria* (coelenterates). The body is a double-layered tube (with 6-10 hollow tentacles round the mouth), 1.25 cm/0.5 in extended, but capable of contracting to a small knob. They reproduce asexually in the summer, and sexually in the winter. It has no organs except those of reproduction. Usually fixed to waterweed, the hydra feeds on minute animals which are caught and paralysed by the stinging cells on the tentacles.

Hydra in astronomy, the largest constellation, winding across more than a quarter of the sky. Hydra represents the multi-headed monster slain by Heracles. Despite its huge size, it is not prominent; its brightest star is second-magnitude Alphard.

hydra in Greek mythology, a huge monster with nine heads. If one were cut off, two would grow in its place. One of the 12 labours of Heracles was to kill it.

hydrangea flowering shrub *Hydrangea macrophylla* of the Hydrangeaceae family, and native to Japan. It normally produces round heads of pink flowers, but these may be blue if certain chemicals, such as alum or iron, are in the soil. It is named from the Greek for water vessel, after its cup-like seed capsules.

hydraulics a field of study concerned with utilizing the properties of liquids, particularly the way they flow and transmit pressure. It applies the principles of ◊hydrostatics and hydrodynamics. The hydraulic principle of pressurised liquid increasing mechanical efficiency is commonly used on vehicle braking systems, the forging press, and the hydraulic systems of aircraft and excavators.

hydrocarbon one of a class of chemical compounds containing only hydrogen and carbon, for example

hydraulics

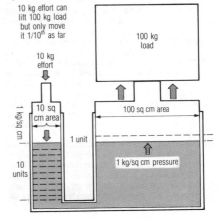

paraffin. Hydrocarbons are important in organic chemistry.

hydrocephalus a potentially serious increase in the volume of cerebrospinal fluid (CSF) within the ventricles of the brain. In infants, whose skull plates have not fused, it causes enlargement of the head, and there is a risk of brain damage from CSF pressure on the developing brain. Hydrocephalus may be due to mechanical obstruction of the outflow of CSF from the ventricles or to faulty reabsorption. Treatment usually involves surgical placement of a shunt system to drain the fluid into the abdominal cavity.

hydrochloric acid highly corrosive aqueous solution of hydrogen chloride (a colourless, corrosive gas HCl). It has many industrial uses, for example recovery of zinc from galvanized scrap iron, and the production of chlorides and chlorine. It is also produced in the stomachs of animals for the purposes of digestion.

hydrocyanic acid also called *prussic acid* a solution of hydrogen cyanide gas (HCN) in water. It is a colourless, highly poisonous, volatile liquid, smelling of bitter almonds.

hydrodynamics the science of non-viscous fluids (for example water, alcohol, ether) in motion.

hydroelectric power electricity generated by moving water. In a typical hydroelectric power (HEP) scheme, water stored in a reservoir, often created by damming a river, is piped into water ◊turbines, coupled to electricity generators. In ◊pumped storage plants, water flowing through the turbines is recycled. A ◊tidal power station is a HEP plant that exploits the rise and fall of the tides. About one-fifth of the world's electricity comes from hydroelectric power.

hydrofoil a wing that develops lift in the water in much the same way that an aeroplane wing develops lift in the air. A hydrofoil boat is one whose hull rises out of the water due to the lift.

hydrogen a gaseous element, symbol H, atomic number 1, relative atomic mass 1.00797. The lightest element known, it occurs on Earth chiefly in combination with oxygen as water. Hydrogen is the most common element in the Universe, and the fuel of fusion reactions which take place in the Sun and stars.

hydrogen bomb ◊bomb that works on the principle of nuclear ◊fusion. Large-scale explosion results from the thermonuclear release of energy when hydrogen nuclei are condensed to helium nuclei. The first hydrogen bomb was exploded at Eniwetok Atoll by the USA 1952.

hydrogen cyanide (HCN) a poisonous gas formed by the reaction of sodium cyanide with dilute sulphuric acid, used for fumigation.

hydrography study and charting of Earth's surface waters in seas, lakes, and rivers.

hydrology study of the location and movement of inland water, both frozen and liquid, above and below the surface of the ground. It is applied to major civil engineering projects such as irrigation schemes, dams and hydroelectric power, and in helping to plan measures for flood control and the supply of water for homes and industry.

hydrolysis a chemical reaction in which the action of water or its ions breaks down a substance into smaller molecules. Hydrolysis occurs in certain inorganic salts in solution, in nearly all non-metallic chlorides, in esters, and in other organic substances. It is important in the breakdown of food by the body.

hydrometer in physics, an instrument used to measure the density of liquids compared with that of water, usually expressed in grams per cubic centimetre. The hydrometer is based on ◊Archimedes' principle. It consists of a thin glass tube ending in a sphere which leads into a smaller sphere, the latter being loaded so that the hydrometer floats upright, sinking deeper into lighter liquids than heavier. It is used in brewing.

hydrophily a form of ◊pollination in which the pollen is carried by water. Hydrophily is very rare but occurs in a few aquatic species. In *Canadian pondweed Elodea* and *tape grass Vallisneria*, the male flowers break off whole and rise to the water surface where they encounter the female flowers which are borne on long stalks. In *eel grasses Zostera*, which are coastal plants growing totally submerged, the filamentous pollen grains are released into the water and carried by currents to the female flowers where they become wrapped around the stigmas.

hydrophobia another name for the disease ◊rabies.

hydrophyte a plant adapted to live in water, or in waterlogged soil. Hydrophytes may have leaves with a very reduced or absent ◊cuticle and no ◊stomata (since there is no need to conserve water), a reduced root and water-conducting system, and less supporting tissue since water buoys plants up. There are often numerous spaces between the cells in their stems and roots to make gas exchange with all parts of the plant body possible. Many have highly divided leaves, which lessens resistance to flowing water, for example *spiked water milfoil Myriophyllum spicatum*.

hydroplane on a submarine, a moveable fin angled downwards or upwards when the vessel is descending or ascending. It is also a specially designed, highly manoeuvrable motorboat or ◊hydrofoil boat that skims over the surface of the water when driven at high speed.

hydroponics the cultivation of plants without soil, using specially prepared solutions of mineral salts. The term was first coined by Professor W F Gericke, a US scientist. Beginning in the 1930s, large crops were grown by hydroponic methods, at first in California, but since then in many other parts of the world.

J von Sachs (1832–97) 1860 and W Knop 1865 developed a system of plant culture in water whereby the relation of mineral salts to plant growth could be determined, but it was not until about 1930 that large crops could be grown.

hydrosphere the water component of the Earth, usually encompassing the oceans, seas, rivers, streams, swamps, lakes, groundwater, and atmospheric water vapour.

hydrostatics in physics, the branch of ◊statics dealing with the mechanical problems of fluids in equilibrium, that is, in a static condition. Practical applications include shipbuilding and dam design.

hydroxides inorganic compounds containing one or more hydroxyl (OH) groups and generally combined with a metal. The most important hydroxides are caustic soda (sodium hydroxide NaOH), caustic potash (potassium hydroxide KOH), and slaked lime (calcium hydroxide $Ca(OH)_2$).

hydroxypropanoic acid modern name for ◊lactic acid.

hyena type of carnivorous mammal which lives in Africa and Asia. It has very strong limbs and jaws. It is a scavenger, although it will also attack and kill live prey.

hygrometer

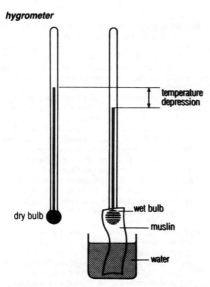

temperature depression

dry bulb

wet bulb

muslin

water

hyperbola

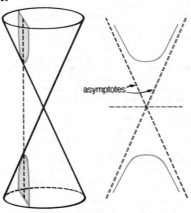

asymptotes

hygiene the science of the preservation of health and prevention of disease. It is chiefly concerned with such external conditions as the purity of air and water, bodily cleanliness, and cleanliness in the home and workplace.

hygrometer in physics, an instrument for measuring the humidity of a gas. A wet and dry bulb hygrometer consists of two vertical thermometers, with one of the thermometer bulbs covered in absorbent cloth dipped into water. As the water on the cloth evaporates, the bulb cools producing a temperature difference between the two thermometers. The amount of evaporation, and hence cooling of the wet bulb, depends on the relative humidity of the air.

Hymen in Greek mythology, either the son of Apollo and one of the Muses, or of Dionysus and Aphrodite. He was the god of marriage, and in art is represented as a youth carrying a bridal torch.

hymn song in praise of a deity. Examples include Ikhnaton's hymn to the Aton in ancient Egypt, the ancient Greek Orphic hymns, Old Testament psalms, extracts from the New Testament (such as Ave Maria), and hymns by the British writers John Bunyan ('Who would true valour see') and Charles Wesley ('Hark the herald angels sing'). ◊Gospel music is a form of Christian hymn-singing.

hyoscine a drug which acts on the autonomic nervous system, a derivative of ◊belladonna. It is frequently included in ◊premedication to dry up lung secretions and produce post-operative amnesia.

hyperactivity condition of excessive activity in children, combined with inability to concentrate and difficulty in learning. Modification of the diet may help, and in the majority of cases there is improvement at puberty. The cause is not known, although some food additives have come under suspicion.

hyperbola in geometry, a curve formed by cutting a right circular cone with a plane so that the angle between the plane and the base is greater than the angle between the base and the side of the cone. All hyperbolae are bounded by two ◊asymptotes.

hyperbole a ◊figure of speech whose Greek name suggests 'going over the top'. When people speak or write hyperbolically they exaggerate, usually to emphasize a point ('If I've told you once I've told you a thousand times not to do that').

hypercharge property of certain ◊elementary particles, analogous to electric charge, that accounts for the absence of some expected behaviour (such as decay) in terms of the short-range strong interaction force, which holds atomic nuclei together.

hyperinflation rapid and uncontrolled ◊inflation, or increases in prices, usually associated with political and/or social instability (as in Germany in the 1920s).

hypertension abnormally high ◊blood pressure, the smooth muscle cells of the walls of the arteries being constantly contracted. It increases the risk of severe illness including kidney disease, stroke, and heart attack.

hyperthyroidism or *thyrotoxicosis* overactivity of the thyroid gland due to enlargement or tumour. Symptoms include accelerated heart rate, sweating, anxiety, tremor, and weight loss. Treatment is by drugs or surgery.

hypha (plural *hyphae*) a delicate, usually branching filament, many of which collectively form the mycelium and fruiting bodies of a ◊fungus. Typically hyphae grow by increasing in length from the tips and by the formation of side-branches. Food molecules and other substances are transported along hyphae by the movement of the cytoplasm, known as 'cytoplasmic streaming.'

hyphen a punctuation mark (-) with two functions: (1) to join words, parts of words, syllables, and so on, for particular purposes, and (2) to mark the break in a word continued from the end of one line to the beginning of the next line.

hypnosis an artificially-induced state of relaxation in which suggestibility is heightened. The subject may carry out orders at once or long after being awakened, and may be made insensitive to pain. It is sometimes used to treat disorders such as addictions to tobacco or overeating, or to assist amnesia victims recall traumatic events.

hypnotic substance (such as ◊barbiturate, ◊benzodiazepine, alcohol) which depresses brain function, inducing sleep. Prolonged use may lead to tolerance and habituation; larger doses are required, and physical or psychological addiction occurs.

hypo in photography, a term for sodium thiosulphate, discovered 1819 by John ◊Herschel, and used as a fixative for photographic images from 1837.

hypocaust a floor raised on tile piers, heated by hot air circulating beneath it. It was first used by the Romans for baths in about 100 BC, and was later introduced to private houses.

hypocycloid in geometry, a cusped curve traced by a point on the circumference of a circle that rolls round the inside of another larger circle.

hypodermic an instrument used for injecting fluids beneath the skin. It consists of a small graduated tube of glass, metal, or plastic, with a close-fitting piston and a nozzle on to which a hollow needle can be fitted.

hypogeal a type of seed germination in which the ◊cotyledons remain below ground. The term can also refer to fruits which develop underground, for example peanuts (*Arachis hypogea*).

hypothalamus the region of the brain below the ◊cerebrum which regulates rhythmic activity and physiological stability within the body, including water balance and temperature. It controls the part of the nervous system which regulates the involuntary muscles, and also regulates the production of the pituitary gland's hormones by means of releasing or inhibiting hormones that affect the pituitary.

hypothermia a condition in which the deep temperature of the body drops abnormally low. If it continues untreated, coma and death ensue. Most at risk are babies (particularly if premature) and the aged.

hypothesis in science, an idea concerning an event and its possible explanation. The term is one favoured especially by the followers of the philosopher ◊Popper, who argue that the merit of a scientific hypothesis lies in its ability to make testable predictions, rather than in any apparent plausibility.

hyrax type of mammal, order *Hyracoidea*, that lives among rocks, in deserts, and in forests in Africa, Arabia, and Syria. It is about the size of a rabbit, with a plump body, short legs, short ears, long curved front teeth, and brownish fur. There are four toes on the front limbs, and three on the hind, each of which has a hoof. They are believed to be among the nearest living relatives of elephants.

hyssop aromatic herb *Hyssopus officinalis*, family Labiatae, found in Asia, S Europe, and around the Mediterranean. It has blue flowers, oblong leaves, and stems that are shrubby near the ground, but herbaceous above.

hysteria in psychology, a general term for an unreasonable reaction which is involuntary and largely unrealized. Symptoms are produced which are normally associated with physical illness, such as paralysis, blindness, recurrent cough, vomiting, and general malaise. The term is little used today in diagnosis.

ibis

iatrogenic caused by treatment; the term 'iatrogenic disease' may be applied to any pathological condition that is caused by what the doctor says or does.

IBA in the UK, abbreviation for *Independent Broadcasting Authority*.

Ibadan city in SW Nigeria and capital of Oyo state; population (1981) 2,100,000. Industries include chemicals, electronics, plastics, and vehicles.

Iban (formerly known as *Dayak*) a people of central Borneo. Approximately 250,000 Iban live in the interior uplands of Sarawak, while another 10,000 live in the border area of W Kalimantan. The Iban speak languages belonging to the Austronesian family.

Ibáñez Vincente Blasco 1867–1928. Spanish novelist and politician, born in Valencia. He was actively involved in revolutionary politics. His novels include *La barraca*/*The Cabin* 1898, the best of his regional works; *Sangre y arena*/*Blood and Sand* 1908, the story of a famous bullfighter; and *Los cuatro jinetes del Apocalipsis*/*The Four Horsemen of the Apocalypse* 1916, a product of the effects of World War I.

Ibarruri Dolores. Known as *La Pasionaria* ('the passion flower') 1895–   . Spanish Basque politician, journalist, and orator. In 1936 she helped to establish the Popular Front government, and was a Loyalist leader in the Civil War. When Franco came to power 1939 she left Spain for the USSR, where she was active in the Communist Party. She returned to Spain 1977 after Franco's death, and was re-elected to the Cortes.

ibex type of wild goat found in mountainous areas of Europe, NE Africa, and Central Asia. They grow to 100 cm/3.5 ft, and have brown or grey coats and heavy horns. They are herbivorous and live in small groups.

ibid. abbreviation for *ibidem* (Latin 'in the same place').

ibis type of wading bird, about 60 cm/2 ft tall, related to the storks and herons. It has long legs and neck, and a long curved beak. Various species occur in the warmer regions of the world.

Ibiza one of the ◊Balearic Islands, a popular tourist resort; area 596 sq km/230 sq mi; population (1986) 45,000.

Iblis the Muslim name for the ◊Devil.

Ibn Battuta 1304–1368. Arab traveller born in Tangiers. In 1325, he went on an extraordinary journey via Mecca to Egypt, E Africa, India, and China, returning some 30 years later. He subsequently travelled to Spain and Mali. The narrative of his travels, *The Adventures of Ibn Battuta*, was written with an assistant, Ibn Juzayy.

Ibn Saud 1880–1953. 1st king of Saudi Arabia from 1932. His father was the son of the sultan of Nejd, at whose capital, Riyadh, Ibn Saud was born. In 1891 a rival group seized Riyadh, and Ibn Saud went into exile with his father, who resigned his claim to the throne in his favour. In 1902 Ibn Saud recaptured Riyadh and recovered the kingdom, and by 1921 he had brought all central Arabia under his rule. In 1924 he invaded the Hejaz, of which he was proclaimed king 1926.

Ibo (or *Ebo*) person of Ibo culture from Nigeria's East-Central State. Primarily cultivators, they inhabit the richly forested tableland, bound by the River Niger to the W and the Cross River to the E. They are divided into five main divisions, and their languages belong to the Kwa branch of the Niger-Congo family.

Ibsen Henrik (Johan) 1828–1906. Norwegian playwright and poet, whose realistic and often controversial plays revolutionized European theatre. Driven into exile 1864–91 by opposition to the satirical *Love's Comedy* 1862, he wrote the verse dramas *Brand* 1866 and *Peer Gynt* 1867, followed by realistic social plays including *Pillars of Society* 1877, *A Doll's House* 1879, *Ghosts* 1881, *An Enemy of the People* 1882, and *Hedda Gabler* 1890.

Icarus in Greek mythology, the son of ◊Daedalus, who died when he flew too near the sun using wings made from feathers fastened with wax.

Ibsen *The Norwegian dramatist Henrik Ibsen.*

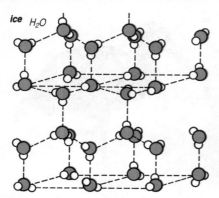

ice H_2O

the crystal structure of ice in which water molecules are held together by hydrogen bonds

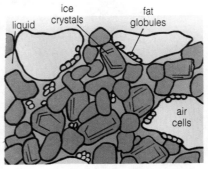

ice cream

ice crystals
liquid
fat globules
air cells

Icarus in astronomy, an ◊Apollo asteroid 1.5 km/1 mi in diameter, discovered 1949. It orbits the Sun every 409 days at a distance of between 2.0 and 0.19 astronomical units (about 150 million km). It is the only asteroid known to approach the Sun closer than the planet Mercury.

ICBM abbreviation for *intercontinental ballistic missile*; see ◊nuclear warfare.

ice the solid formed by water when it freezes. It is colourless and its crystals are hexagonal.

Ice Age any period of glaciation occurring in the Earth's history, but particularly that in the Pleistocene epoch, immediately preceding historic times. On the North American continent, ◊glaciers reached as far south as the Great Lakes, and an ice sheet spread over N Europe, leaving its remains as far south as Switzerland. There were several glacial advances separated by interglacial stages during which the ice melted and temperatures were higher than today.

Major Ice Ages
Name (European/US) date (years ago)
Pleistocene: Riss and Wurm/Wisconsin 80,000–10,000
Mindel/Illinoian 550,000–400,000
Gunz/Kansan 900,000–700,000
Danube/Nebraskan 1.7–1.3 million
Permo-Carboniferous 330–250 million
Ordovician 440–430 million
Verangian 615–570 million
Sturtian 820–770 million
Gnejso 940–880 million
Huronian 2,700–01,800 million

iceberg a floating mass of ice, about 5⁄6 of which is submerged, rising sometimes to 100 m/300 ft above sea level. Glaciers that reach the coast become extended into a broad foot; as this enters the sea, masses break off and drift towards temperate latitudes, becoming a danger to shipping.

ice cream a frozen liquid confectionery, commercially made from the early 20th century from various milk products and sugar, and in the UK also with 'non-milk' (animal or vegetable) fat, with usually artificial additives to give colour and flavour, and improve its keeping qualities and ease of serving. Water ices are frozen fruit juice.

history ideally made of cream, eggs, and sugar whipped together and frozen, ice cream was made in China before 1000 BC and probably introduced to Europe by Marco Polo; water ices were known in ancient Greece and Persia. Italy and Russia were noted for their ice cream even before it became a mechanized industry, first in the USA and in the 1920s in Britain. Technical developments from the 1950s made possible the mass distribution of a 'soft' ice cream resembling the original type in appearance.

ice hockey a game played on ice between two teams of six, developed in Canada from field hockey or bandy, with a puck (a rubber disc) in place of a ball. Players wear skates and protective clothing.

Iceland island in the N Atlantic, situated S of the Arctic Circle, between Greenland and Norway.

Icelandic language a member of the N Germanic branch of the Indo-European language family, spoken only in Iceland and the most conservative in form of the Scandinavian languages. Despite seven centuries of Danish rule, until 1918, Icelandic has remained virtually unchanged since the 12th century.

Iceni a people of E England, who revolted against occupying Romans under ◊Boudicca.

I Ching or *Book of Changes* an ancient Chinese book of divination based on 64 hexagrams, or patterns of six lines. The lines may be broken or whole (yin or yang) and are generated by throwing yarrow stalks or coins. The enquirer formulates a question before throwing, and the book gives interpretations of the meaning of the hexagrams.

ichneumon fly any parasitic wasp in the family Ichneumonidae. There are several thousand species in Europe, North America, and other regions. The eggs are laid in the eggs, larvae, or pupae of other insects, usually butterflies or moths.

icon in the Greek or Orthodox Eastern Church, a representation of Jesus, an angel, or a saint, in painting, low relief, or mosaic. A *riza*, or gold and silver covering which leaves only the face and hands visible and may be adorned with jewels presented by the faithful in thanksgiving, is often added as protection.

icon in computing, a small picture on a VDU (computer screen) representing an object or function that the user may manipulate or otherwise use. Icons make computers easier to use by allowing the user to point with the mouse arrow to pictures rather than type commands.

iconoclast literally, a person who attacks religious images; the Iconoclastic doctrine, rejecting the use of icons in churches, was given to the Christian party by the Byzantine emperor Leo III in 726. The same name was applied to those opposing the use of images at the Reformation, when there was much destruction in churches. Iconoclastic ideas had much in common with Islam and Judaism. Figuratively, the term is used for a person who attacks established ideals or principles.

iceberg icebergs in the Biscoe Islands, Antarctica.

iconography in art history, significance attached to conventional symbols which can help to identify subject matter (for example, a saint holding keys represents St Peter) and place a work of art in its historical context.

id in Freudian psychology, the instinctual element of the human mind, concerned with pleasure, which demands immediate satisfaction. It is regarded as the ◊unconscious element of the human psyche, and is said to be in conflict with the ◊ego and the ◊superego.

Idaho mountain state of NW USA; nickname Gem State
area 216,412 sq km/83,535 sq mi
capital Boise
towns Pocatello, Idaho Falls
products potatoes, wheat, livestock, timber, silver, lead, zinc, antimony
population (1990) 1,006,700

religion Christian, predominantly Mormon
history first permanently settled 1860 after the discovery of gold, Idaho became a state 1890.

Identikit a set of drawings of different parts of the face used to compose a likeness of a person for identification, first used by the police in Britain 1961. It has largely been replaced by ◊photofit, based on photographs, which produces a more realistic likeness.

ideology a set of ideas, beliefs, and opinions about the nature of people and society, providing a framework for a theory about how society is or should be organized.

Ides in the Roman calendar, the 15th day of Mar, May, Jul, and Oct, and 13th day of all other months (the word originally indicated the full moon); Julius Caesar was assassinated on the Ides of March 44 BC.

i.e. abbreviation for *id est* (Latin 'that is').

Iceland
Republic of
(*Lýdveldid Island*)

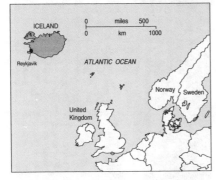

area 103,000 sq km/ 39,758 sq mi
capital Reykjavik
physical warmed by the Gulf Stream; glaciers and lava fields cover 75% of the country

head of state Vigdis Finnbogadóttir from 1980
head of government David Oddsson from 1991
political system democratic republic
exports cod and other fish products
currency krona
population (1990 est) 251,000; annual growth rate 0.8%
life expectancy men 74, women 80
language Icelandic
religion Evangelical Lutheran 95%
literacy 99.9% (1984)
GDP $3.9 bn (1986); $16,200 per head
chronology
1944 Independence from Denmark achieved.
1949 Joined NATO and the Council of Europe.
1953 Joined the Nordic Council.
1976 'Cod War' with the UK.
1979 Iceland announced a 200-mile exclusive fishing zone.
1987 New coalition government formed by Thorstein Palsson after general election.
1988 Vigdis Finnbogadóttir re-elected president for a third term.
1991 David Oddsson led new centre-right coalition and became prime minister after the general election.
1992 Iceland defied the world ban and resumed its whaling industry.

ignition coil

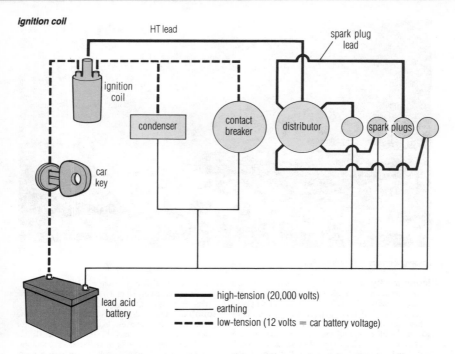

HT lead

spark plug
lead

ignition
coil

condenser

contact
breaker

distributor

spark plugs

car
key

lead acid
battery

━━━━ high-tension (20,000 volts)
──── earthing
━ ━ ━ low-tension (12 volts = car battery voltage)

Ifugao people of N Luzon in the Philippines, numbering approximately 70,000. Their language belongs to the Austronesian family.

Iglesias Pablo 1850–1925. Spanish politician, founder of the Spanish Socialist Party (*Partido Socialista Obrero Español*, PSOE) 1879 and in 1911 the first socialist deputy to be elected to the Cortes (parliament).

Ignatius Loyola, St 1491–1556. Spanish soldier converted 1521 to the Roman Catholic religious life after being wounded in battle, and founder of the ◊Jesuit order 1540. Feast day 31 Jul.

Ignatius of Antioch, St 1st–2nd century AD. Christian martyr. Traditionally a disciple of St John, he was bishop of Antioch, and was thrown to the wild beasts in Rome. He wrote seven epistles, important documents of the early Christian church. Feast day 1 Feb.

igneous rock a rock formed from cooling magma or lava, and solidifying from a molten state. Igneous rocks are classified according to their ◊feldspar content, grain size, texture, and chemical composition.

ignition coil a kind of ◊transformer that is an essential part of a petrol engine's ignition system. It consists of two wire coils wound around an iron core. The primary coil, which is connected to the car battery, has only a few turns. The secondary coil, connected via the ◊distributor to the ◊spark plugs, has many turns. The coil takes in a low voltage (usually 12 volts) from the battery and transforms it to a high voltage (about 20,000 volts) to ignite the engine.

Iguaçu falls or *Iguassú falls* waterfall on the border between Brazil and Argentina. The falls lie 19 km above the junction of the Iguaç with the Paraná. They are divided by forested rocky islands and form a spectacular tourist attraction. The water plunges in 275 falls. They have a

height of 82m/269 ft, and width about 4 km/2.5 mi.

iguana lizard of the family Iguanidae, which includes about 700 species and is chiefly confined to the Americas. The common iguana *Iguana iguana* of Central and South America may reach 2 m/6 ft.

IJsselmeer lake in the Netherlands, formed 1932 after the Zuider Zee was cut off by a dyke from the North Sea; freshwater since 1944; area 1,217 sq km/470 sq mi.

Iguaçu Falls The horseshoe-shaped Iguaçu Falls close to the Paraguyan border, comprising 275 separate waterfalls

iguana

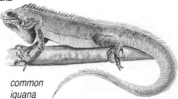

common
iguana

ikat the Indonesian term for a textile which is produced by resist-printing the warp or weft before ◊weaving. Ikat fabrics are produced in parts of Africa as well as Indonesia.

ikebana the Japanese art of flower arrangement. It dates from the 6th–7th century when arrangements of flowers were placed as offerings in Buddhist temples, a practice learned from China. In the 15th century, ikebana became a favourite pastime of the nobility. Oldest of modern Japanese ikebana schools is Ikenobo at Kyoto (7th century).

Ikhnaton or *Akhenaton* 14th century BC. King of Egypt of the 18th dynasty (*c.* 1379–62 BC), who may have ruled jointly for a time with his father Amenhotep III. He developed the cult of the sun, ◊Aton, rather than the rival cult of ◊Ammon. Some historians believe that his neglect of imperial defence for religious reforms led to the loss of most of Egypt's possessions in Asia. His favourite wife was Nefertiti, and two of his six daughters by her were married to his successors Smenkhare and Tutankaton (later known as Tutankhamen).

ILEA abbreviation for *Inner London Education Authority* body which administered education in London, England. It was abolished 1990 and replaced by smaller borough-based education authorities.

Île-de-France region of N France; area 12,012 sq km/4,637 sq mi; population (1986) 10,251,000. It includes Paris, Versailles, Sèvres, and St-Cloud. From here the early French kings extended their authority over the whole country.

Iliad Greek epic poem in 24 books, probably written before 700 BC, attributed to Homer. Its title is derived from Ilion, another name for Troy. Its subject is the wrath of Achilles, an incident during the tenth year of the Trojan War, when Achilles kills Hector to avenge the death of his friend Patroclus.

illegitimacy in law, the birth of a child to a mother who is not legally married; a child may be legitimated by subsequent marriage of the parents. Nationality of child is usually that of the mother. In the UK, recent acts have progressively removed many of the historic disadvantages of illegitimacy, for example, as regards inheritance, culminating in the Family Law Reform Act 1987 which removes, so far as possible, all remaining disadvantages. ◊Custody and ◊maintenance provisions are now the same as for legitimate children.

Illich Ivan 1926– . US radical philosopher and activist, born in Austria. His works, which include *Deschooling Society* 1971, *Towards a History of Need* 1978, and *Gender* 1983, are a critique against modern economic development, especially in the Third World.

Illinois midwest state of the USA; nickname Inland Empire/Prairie State
area 146,114 sq km/56,400 sq mi
capital Springfield
towns Chicago, Rockford, Peoria, Decatur
products mainly agricultural, soybeans, cereals, meat and dairy products; also machinery, electric and electronic equipment
population (1990) 11,430,600
famous people Walt Disney, James T Farrell, Ernest Hemingway, Edgar Lee Masters, Ronald Reagan, Frank Lloyd Wright
history ceded to Britain by the French in 1763, Illinois passed to American control in 1783, and became a state in 1818.

Illyria ancient name for the eastern coastal region on the Adriatic, N of the Gulf of Corinth, conquered by Philip of Macedon and a Roman province from AD 9. The Albanians are survivors of its ancient peoples.

imaginary number an unfortunate term sometimes used to describe the non-real element of a ◊complex number. For the complex number (*a* + *ib*), (*ib*) is the imaginary number where $i = \sqrt{-1}$, and *b* any real number.

Imagism a movement in Anglo-American poetry which flourished in London 1912–14 and affected much British and US poetry and critical thinking thereafter. A central figure was Ezra Pound, who asserted principles encouraging free verse, hard imagery, and poetic impersonality.

IMF abbreviation for ◊*International Monetary Fund.*

Imhotep *c.* 2800 BC. Egyptian physician and architect, adviser to King Zoser (3rd dynasty). He is thought to have designed the step pyramid at Sakkara, and his tomb (believed to be in the N Sakkara cemetery) became a centre of healing. He was deified as the son of ◊Ptah and was identified with Aesculapius, the Greek god of medicine.

Immaculate Conception in the Roman Catholic Church, the belief that the Virgin Mary was, by a special act of grace, preserved free from ◊original sin from the moment she was conceived. This article of the Catholic faith was for centuries the subject of heated controversy, opposed by St Thomas Aquinas and other theologians, but generally accepted from about the 16th century. It became a dogma in 1854.

immigration and emigration the movement of people from one country to another. Immigration is movement to a country; emigration is movement from a country. On a large scale it is often for economic reasons or because of persecution (which may create ◊refugees), and often prompts restrictive legislation by individual countries. The USA has received immigrants on a larger scale than any other country, more than 50 million during its history.

immunity the protection which animals have against the effects of foreign organisms and toxins on their body functions. Some white blood cells (◊phagocytes and ◊macrophages) engulf bacteria and other invading organisms, while others (natural killer cells) destroy body cells that have become infected. The T-lymphocytes are responsible for binding to specific invading organisms and killing them, or rendering them harmless. The B-lymphocytes produce ◊antibodies that are specific to particular micro-organisms. Against viruses, there is an additional form of defence, based on ◊interferons, which prevent them from replicating in the host's cells.

immunization conferring immunity to infectious disease by artificial methods. The most widely used technique is ◊vaccination.

immunoglobulin or *antibody* human ◊protein which can be separated from blood, and administered to confer immediate immunity on the recipient.

immunosuppressive drug that suppresses the body's normal immune responses to infection or foreign tissue. It is used in the treatment of auto-immune disease, as part of chemotherapy for leukaemias, lymphomas, and other cancers, and to help prevent rejection following organ transplantion.

impala African antelope *Aepyceros melampus* found from Kenya to South Africa in savannas and open woodlands. The body is sandy brown. The males have lyre-shaped horns up to 75 cm/2.5 ft long. Impala grow up to 1.5 m/5 ft long and 90 cm/3 ft tall. They live in herds and spring high in the air when alarmed.

impeachment in the UK, a judicial procedure by which the House of Commons from 1376 brought ministers and officers of state to trial before the House of Lords, for example Bacon 1621, Strafford 1640, and Warren Hastings 1788. In the USA the House of Representatives similarly may impeach offenders to be tried before the Senate, for example President Andrew Johnson 1868.

impedance the total opposition of a circuit to the passage of electric current.

imperialism the attempt by one country to dominate others, either by direct rule or by less obvious means such as control of markets for goods or raw materials. The latter is often called ◊neo-colonialism. In the 19th century imperialism was synonymous with the establishment of colonies (see ◊British Empire). Many socialist thinkers believe that the role of Western (especially US) finance capital in the Third World constitutes a form of imperialism.

Imperial system traditional system of units developed in the UK, based largely on the foot, pound, and second (◊f.p.s. system).

Imperial War Museum British military museum, founded in 1917, originally as a memorial to the men and women of the Empire in World War I. It now includes records of all operations fought by British forces since 1914. Its present building (formerly the Royal Bethlehem, or Bedlam, Hospital) in Lambeth Road, London, was opened 1936.

impetigo contagious bacterial infection (*Staphylococcus aureus*) of the skin which forms yellowish crusts; it is curable with antibiotics.

implantation in mammals, the process by which the developing ◊embryo attaches itself to the wall of the mother's uterus and stimulates the development of the ◊placenta.

import product or service which one country purchases from another for domestic consumption, or for processing and re-exporting (Hong Kong, for example, is heavily dependent on imports for its export business). If an importing country does not have a counterbalancing value of exports, it may experience balance-of-payments difficulties and accordingly consider restricting imports by some form of protectionism (such as an import tariff or imposing import quotas).

Importance of Being Earnest, The a romantic comedy by Oscar Wilde, first performed 1895. The courtship of two couples is comically complicated by confusions of identity and by the overpowering Lady Bracknell.

Impressionism movement in painting which originated in France in the 1860s and dominated European and North American painting in the late 19th century. The Impressionists wanted to depict real life, to paint straight from nature, and to capture the changing effects of light. The term was first used abusively to describe Monet's painting *Impression, Sunrise* 1872 (stolen from the Musée Marmottan, Paris); other Impressionists were Renoir and Sisley,

soon joined by Cézanne, Manet, Degas, and others.

imprinting in ◊ethology, the process whereby a young animal learns to recognize both specific individuals (for example, its mother) and its own species.

inbreeding in ◊genetics, the mating of closely related individuals. It is considered to be undesirable because it increases the risk that an offspring will inherit copies of rare deleterious recessive alleles from both parents (see ◊recessivity) and so suffer from disabilities.

Inca former ruling class of South American Indian people of Peru. The first emperor or 'Inca' (believed to be a descendant of the Sun) was Manco Capac about 1200 AD. Inca rule eventually extended from Quito in Ecuador to beyond Santiago in S Chile, but the civilization was destroyed by the Spanish conquest in the 1530s. The descendants of the Incas are the ◊Quechua.

incandescence emission of light from a substance in consequence of its high temperature. The colour of the emitted light from liquids or solids depends on their temperature, and for solids generally the higher the temperature the whiter the light. Gases may become incandescent through ◊ionizing radiation, as in the glowing vacuum ◊discharge tube.

incarnation assumption of living form (plant, animal, human) by a deity, for example the gods of Greece and Rome, Hinduism, Christianity (Jesus as the second person of the Trinity).

incendiary bomb a bomb containing inflammable matter. Usually dropped by aircraft, incendiary bombs were used in World War I, and in World War II were a major weapon in attacks on cities. To hinder firefighters, delayed-action high-explosive bombs were usually dropped with them. In the Vietnam War, the USA used napalm in incendiary bombs.

incest sexual intercourse between persons thought to be too closely related to marry; the exact relationships which fall under the incest taboo vary widely between societies. A biological explanation for the incest taboo is to avoid ◊inbreeding.

inch ◊Imperial measure of length, a twelfth of a ◊foot.

Inchon chief port of Seoul, South Korea; population (1984) 1,295,000. Produces steel and textiles.

inclination the angle between the ◊ecliptic and the plane of the orbit of a planet, asteroid, or comet. In the case of satellites orbiting a planet, it is the angle between the plane of orbit of the satellite and the equator of the planet.

inclusive fitness in ◊genetics, the success with which a given variant of a ◊gene (or allele) is passed on to future generations by a particular individual, after additional copies of the allele in the individual's relatives and their offspring have been taken into account, as well as those in its own offspring.

incomes policy a government-initiated exercise to curb ◊inflation by restraining rises in incomes, on either a voluntary or a compulsory basis; often linked with action to control prices, in which case it becomes a prices and incomes policy.

income tax a direct tax levied on personal income, mainly wages and salaries, but which may include the value of receipts other than in cash. In contrast, *indirect taxes* are duties payable whenever a specific product is purchased; examples include VAT and customs duties.

Inca Civilization

| | Inca Empire in 11th century |
| | Inca Empire in 1533 |

India: States

State	Capital	Area sq km
Andhra Pradesh	Hyderabad	276.814
Assam	Dispur	78.523
Bihar	Patna	173.876
Gujarat	Ahmedabad	195.984
Haryana	Chandigarh	44.222
Himachal Pradesh	Simla	55.673
Jammu and Kashmir	Srinagar	101.283
Karnataka	Bangalore	191.773
Kerala	Trivandrum	38.864
Madhya Pradesh	Bhopal	442.841
Maharashtra	Bombay	307.762
Manipur	Imphal	22.356
Meghalya	Shillong	22.489
Mizoram	Aizawl	21.087
Nagaland	Kohima	16.527
Orissa	Brubaneswar	155.782
Punjab	Chandigarh	50.362
Rajasthan	Jaipur	342.214
Sikkim	Gangtok	7.299
Tamil Nadu	Madras	130.069
Tripura	Agartala	10.477
Uttar Pradesh	Lucknow	294.413
West Bengal	Calcutta	87.853

incubus male spirit who in the popular belief of the Middle Ages had sexual intercourse with women in their sleep. Witches and demons were supposed to result. *Succubus* is the female equivalent.

indemnity in law, an undertaking to compensate another for damage, loss, trouble, or expenses, or the money paid by way of such compensation, for example under fire insurance agreements. An *act of indemnity* is passed by the UK Parliament to relieve offenders of penalties innocently incurred, as by ministers in the course of their duties.

Independence Day public holiday in the USA, commemorating the ◊Declaration of Independence 4 Jul 1776.

Independent Broadcasting Authority (IBA) in the UK, the corporate body established by legislation to provide commercially funded television (ITV from 1955) and local radio (ILR from 1973) services. During the 1980s this role was expanded to include the setting up of Channel 4 (launched 1982) and the provision of services broadcast directly by satellite into homes (DBS).

Independent Labour Party (ILP) British socialist party, founded in Bradford in 1893 by the Scottish Member of Parliament Keir Hardie. In 1900 it joined with trades unions and Fabians in founding the Labour Representation Committee, the nucleus of the ◊Labour Party. Many members left the ILP to join the Communist Party in 1921, and in 1932 all connections with the Labour Party were severed. After World War II the ILP consistently dwindled, eventually becoming extinct.

index (also known as *power* or *exponent*; plural *indices*) in mathematics, a number that indicates the number of times a term is multiplied by itself, for example $x^2 = x \times x$, $4^3 = 4 \times 4 \times 4$.

index in economics, an indicator of a general movement in wages, and prices over a specified period. For example, the retail price index (RPI) records changes in the ◊cost of living. The *Financial Times* share index indicates the general movement of the London Stock Exchange market in the UK; the USA equivalent is the Dow Jones Index.

Index Librorum Prohibitorum (Latin 'Index of Prohibited Books') the list of books formerly officially forbidden to members of the Roman Catholic church. The process of condemning books and bringing the Index up to date was executed by a congregation of cardinals, consultors, and examiners from the 16th century until it was finally abolished in 1966.

India country in S Asia, having borders to the N with Afghanistan, China, Nepál, and Bhutan, to the E with Burma, and to the NW with Pakistan.

Indiana state of the midwest USA; nickname Hoosier State
area 93,744 sq km/36,185 sq mi
capital Indianapolis
towns Fort Wayne, Gary, Evansville, South Bend
products cereals, building stone, machinery, electrical goods, coal, steel, iron, chemicals
population (1986) 5,503,000
famous people Theodore Dreiser, Cole Porter
history ceded to Britain by the French in 1763, Indiana passed under American control in 1783, and became a state in 1816.

Indian art the painting, sculpture, and architecture of India. Indian art dates back to the ancient Indus Valley civilization of about 3000 BC. Sophisticated artistic styles emerged from the 1st century AD. Buddhist art includes sculpture and murals. Hindu artists created sculptural schemes in caves and huge temple complexes; the Hindu style is lively, with voluptuous nude figures. The Islamic Mogul Empire of the 16th–17th centuries created an exquisite style of miniature painting, inspired by Persian examples.

Indian languages traditionally, the languages of the subcontinent of India; since 1947, the languages of the Republic of India. These number some 200, depending on whether a variety is classified as a language or a dialect, and divide into five main

India
Republic of
(Hindi *Bharat***)**

area 3,166,829 sq km/1,222,396 sq mi
capital New Delhi
towns Bangalore, Hyderabad, Ahmedabad; ports Calcutta, Bombay, Madras, Kanpur, Pune
physical Himalayas (mountains) on N border; plains around rivers Ganges, Indus, Brahmaputra; Deccan peninsula S of Narmada River forms a plateau between W and E Ghats mountains; desert in the W; Andaman and Nicobar Islands, Lakshadweep (Laccadive Islands)
head of state Shankar Dayal Sharma from 1992
head of government P V Narasimha Rao from 1991
political system democratic federal republic
exports tea, coffee, fish, iron, leather, textiles and steel
currency rupee

population (1991 est) 844,000,000 annual growth rate 2.0%
life expectancy men 56, women 55
language Hindi, English, Assamese, Bengali, Gujarati, Kannada, Kashmiri, Malayalam, Marathi, Oriya, Punjabi, Sanskrit, Sindhi, Tamil, Telugu, Urdu (all official);
religion Hindu 80%, Sunni Muslim 10%, Christian 2.5%, Sikh 2%
literacy (1985 est) 57% male/29% female
GDP $220.8 bn (1987); $283 per head
chronology
1947 Independence achieved from Britain.
1950 Federal republic proclaimed.
1962 Border skirmishes with China.
1964 Death of Prime Minister Nehru; border war with Pakistan over Kashmir.
1966 Indira Gandhi became prime minister.
1971 War with Pakistan; creation of Bangladesh.
1975–77 State of emergency proclaimed.
1980 Indira Gandhi returned in landslide victory.
1984 Assassination of Indira Gandhi; Rajiv Gandhi elected with record majority.
1987 Signing of 'Tamil' Colombo peace accord with Sri Lanka.
1988 Opposition party, Janata Dal, established by ex-finance minister V P Singh.
1989 Congress (I) lost majority in general election; Janata Dal minority government formed, with V P Singh prime minister.
1990 Central rule imposed in Jammu and Kashmir following separatist violence; V P Singh resigned; new minority Janata Dal government formed by Chandra Shekar.
1991 Central rule imposed in Tamil Nadu. Shekhar resigned. The assassination of Rajiv Gandhi in May delayed elections until June. P V Narasimha Rao led a minority government. Separatist violence continued.
1992 Communal violence killed over 1,200 people, mainly Muslims, following destruction of a mosque in N India by Hindu extremists.
1993 Sectarian violence in Bombay left 500 dead.

groups, the two most widespread of which are the Indo-European languages (mainly in the north) and the Dravidian languages (mainly in the south).

Indian Mutiny the revolt 1857–58 of the Bengal army against the British in India. The movement was confined to the north, from Bengal to the Punjab, and central India. Most support came from the army and recently dethroned princes, but in some areas it developed into a peasant rising or general revolt. The mutiny led to the end of rule by the East India Company.

Indian Ocean ocean between Africa and Australia, with India to the N, and the S boundary being an arbitrary line from Cape Agulhas to S Tasmania; area 73,500,000 sq km/28,371,000 sq mi; average depth 3,872 m/12,708 ft. The greatest depth is the Java Trench 7,725 m/25,353 ft.

India of the Princes the 562 Indian states ruled by princes during the period of British control. They occupied 45% of the total area of pre-partition India) and had a population of over 93 million. At the partition of British India in 1947 the princes were given independence by the British government, but were advised to adhere to either India or Pakistan. Between 1947 and 1950 all except ◊Kashmir were incorporated in either country.

indicator species a plant or animal whose presence or absence in an area indicates certain environmental conditions. For example, some lichens are sensitive to sulphur dioxide in the air, and absence of these species indicates atmospheric pollution.

indigo violet-blue vegetable dye obtained from plants of the genus *Indigofera*, family Leguminosae, but now replaced by a synthetic product.

indium a soft, silvery, rare metallic element, symbol In, atomic number 49, relative atomic mass 114.82. It occurs in minute traces in zinc ores, and is obtained by electrolysis from solutions of complex salts. Because it captures neutrons, indium is used to monitor the neutron emission from reactors. Other uses include the manufacture of junctions in semiconductor devices.

Indochina, French former collective name for Cambodia, Laos, and Vietnam, which became independent after World War II.

Indochina War war 1946–1954 between France, the occupying colonial power, and nationalist forces of what was to become Vietnam.
1945 Vietnamese nationalist communist leader Ho Chi Minh proclaimed an independent Vietnamese republic, which soon began an armed struggle against French forces.
1949 France in turn set up a noncommunist state.
1954 After the siege of ◊Dien Bien Phu, a ceasefire was agreed between France and China

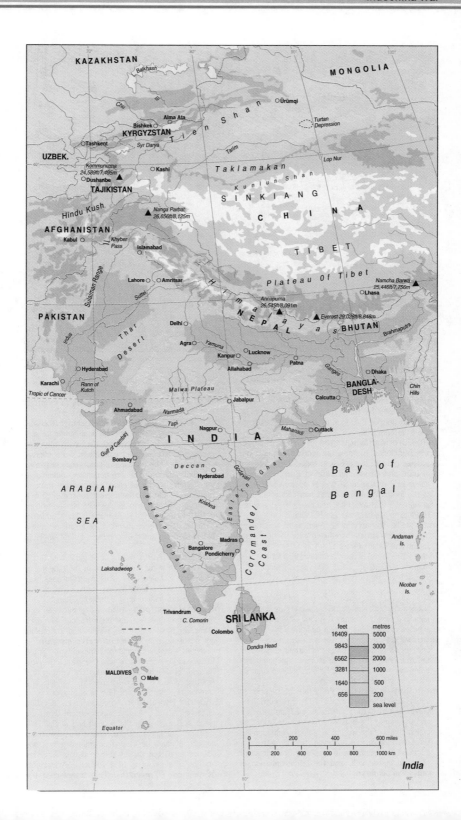

India

Indian Mutiny An early war photograph of the Indian Mutiny.

which resulted in the establishment of two separate Vietnamese states, North and South Vietnam, divided by the 17th parallel. Attempts at reunification of the country led subsequently to the ◊Vietnam War.

Indo-European languages A family of languages which includes some of the world's classical languages (Sanskrit and Pali in India, Zend Avestan in Iran, and Greek and Latin in Europe) as well as several of the most widely spoken languages of the modern world (English worldwide; Spanish in Iberia, Latin America, and elsewhere; and the Hindi group of languages in N India).

Indonesia country in SE Asia, made up of over 3,000 islands situated on the equator, between the Indian and Pacific Oceans.

Indra Hindu god of the sky, shown as a four-armed man on a white elephant, carrying a thunderbolt. The intoxicating drink ◊soma is associated with him.

indri largest living lemur *Indri indri* of Madagascar. Black and white, almost tailless, it has long arms and legs. It grows to 70 cm/2.3 ft long. It is diurnal and arboreal. Its howl is doglike or human in tone.

inductance in physics, the measure of the capability of an electronic circuit or circuit component to form a magnetic field or store magnetic energy when carrying a current. Its symbol is L, and its unit of measure is the ◊henry.

induction in obstetrics, deliberate intervention to initiate labour before it starts of its own accord. It involves rupture of the fetal membranes (amniotomy), and the use of the hormone oxytocin to stimulate contractions of the womb. In biology, induction is a term used for various processes, including the production of an ◊enzyme in response to a particular chemical in the cell, and the ◊differentiation of cells in an ◊embryo.

induction coil type of electrical transformer, similar to an ◊ignition coil, that produces an intermittent high voltage from a low-voltage supply.

indulgence in the Roman Catholic church, the total or partial remission of temporal punishment for sins which remain to be expiated after penitence and confession has secured exemption from eternal punishment. The doctrine of indulgence began as the commutation of church penances in exchange for suitable works of charity or money gifts to the church, and became a great source of church revenue. This trade in indulgences roused Luther in 1517 to initiate the Reformation. The Council of Trent in 1563 recommended moderate retention of indulgences, and they continue, notably in 'Holy Years'.

Indus river in Asia, rising in Tibet and flowing 3,059 km/1,901 mi to the Arabian Sea. In 1960 the use of its waters, including those of its five tributaries, was divided between India (rivers Ravi, Beas, Sutlej) and Pakistan (rivers Indus, Jhelum, Chenab).

industrial relations relationship between employers and employed, and their dealings with each other. In most industries wages and conditions are determined by *free collective bargaining* between employers and ◊trades unions. Some European countries have *worker participation* through profit-sharing and industrial democracy. Another solution is *co-ownership*, in which a company is entirely owned by its employees.

Industrial Revolution the sudden acceleration of technical and economic development that took place in Britain from the second half of the 18th century. The great initial invention was the steam engine, originally developed for draining mines (see ◊Newcomen) but rapidly put to use in factories and on the railways (see ◊Watt, ◊Arkwright, ◊Crompton, ◊Trevithick). This transferred the

Indonesia
Republic of
(*Republik Indonesia*)

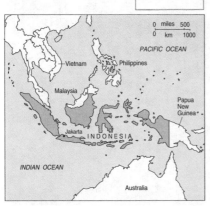

area 1,925,000 sq km/741,000 sq mi
capital Jakarta
towns ports Surabaya, Semarang
physical comprises 13,677 tropical islands of the
Greater Sunda group (including Java and Madura, part
of Borneo/Kalimantan, Sumatra, Sulawesi and
Belitung) and the Lesser Sundas/Nusa Tenggara
(including Bali, Lombok, Sumba, Timor), as well as
Malaku/Moluccas and part of New Guinea (Irian Jaya)
head of state and government T N J Suharto from
1967

political system authoritarian nationalist republic
exports coffee, rubber, timber, palm oil, coconuts,
tin, tea, tobacco, oil, liquid natural gas
currency rupiah
population (1989 est) 187,726,000 (including 300
ethnic groups); annual growth rate 2%
life expectancy men 52, women 55
language Indonesian (official)
religion Muslim 88%, Christian 10%, Buddhist and
Hindhu 2%
literacy 83% male/65% female (1985 est)
GDP $69.7 bn (1987); $409 per head
chronology
17th century Dutch rule established.
1942 Occupied by Japan. Nationalist government
established.
1945 Japanese surrender. Nationalists declare
independence under Sukarno.
1963 Western New Guinea (Irian Jaya) ceded by
Holland.
1965–66 Attempted communist coup: Gen
Suharto emergency administration.
1967 Sukarno replaced as president by Suharto.
1976 Annexation by force of East Timor.
1986 Institution of 'transmigration programme' to
resettle large numbers of Javanese.
1988 Suharto re-elected for fifth term.
1989 Foreign debt reached $50 billion. Western
creditors offered aid on condition that austerity
measures should be introduced.
1991 Democracy forums launched to promote
political dialogue. Massacre in East Timor.
1992 The ruling Gulkar party won the assembly
elections.
1993 President Suharto re-elected.

---

balance of political power from the landowner to the
industrial capitalist and created an urban working
class. From 1830 to the early 20th century, the
Industrial Revolution spread to Europe, its colonies, the USA, and Japan.

Indus Valley Civilization

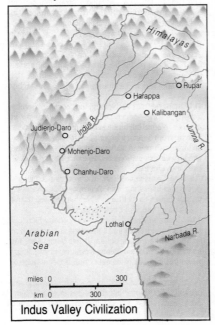

Indus Valley Civilization

industry the extraction and conversion of raw
materials, the manufacture of goods, and the
provision of services. Industry can be either low
technology, unspecialized and labour intensive as in
the less developed countries, or highly automated,
mechanized, and specialized, using advanced technology as in the 'industrialized' countries. The most
prominent trends in industrial activity over the last
20 years have been the growth of electronic and
microelectronic technologies, the expansion of the
off-shore oil industry, and particularly the prominence of Japan and the Pacific region countries
in manufacturing industry, electronics, and computers.

Indus Valley Civilization prehistoric culture
existing in the NW Indian subcontinent about
2500–1600 BC. Remains include soapstone seals
with engravings of elephants and snakes.

inert gases the group of six gaseous elements, so
named because of their unreactivity: argon, helium,
krypton, neon, radon, and xenon. They are also
called the noble gases. Some of them are used in
strip lighting and lasers.

inertia in physics, the tendency of an object to
remain in a state of rest or uniform motion until an
external force is applied, as postulated by ◊New-
ton's first law of motion.

INF abbreviation for *intermediate nuclear
forces*, as in the ◊Intermediate Nuclear Forces
Treaty.

infante and *infanta* in Spain and Portugal, the
sons (other than the heir apparent) and daughters
respectively of the sovereign. The heir apparent
in Spain bears the title of prince of Asturias.

infanticide killing of offspring in human
beings, often done to control population, and most

frequently of girls (India and China), though boys are killed in countries where bride-prices are high.

infant mortality rate a measure of the number of infants dying under one year of age. Improved sanitation, nutrition and medical care have considerably lowered figures throughout much of the world; for example in the 18th century in the UK 50% died, compared with under 2% in 1971. In much of the Third World, however, the infant mortality rate remains high.

infarct or *infarction* death and scarring of a portion of the tissue in an organ, as a result of congestion or blockage of a vessel serving it. A myocardial infarct (MI) is a technical term for a ◊heart attack.

infection invasion of the body by disease-causing organisms which become established, multiply, and produce symptoms.

inferiority complex in psychology, a ◊complex described by Adler based on physical inferiority; the term has been popularly used to refer to general feelings of inferiority.

inferior planet a planet (Mercury or Venus) whose orbit lies within that of the Earth, best observed when at its greatest elongation from the Sun, either at eastern elongation in the evening (setting after the Sun) or at western elongation in the morning (rising before the Sun).

infinite series in mathematics, a series of numbers consisting of a denumerably infinite sequence of terms. The sequence n, n^2, n^3, ... gives the series $n + n^2 + n^3 + ...$ For example, $1 + 2 + 3 + ...$ is a divergent infinite arithmetic series, and $8 + 4 + 2 + 1 + \frac{1}{2} + ...$ is a convergent infinite geometric series whose sum to infinity is 16.

infinity mathematical quantity that is larger than any fixed assignable quantity, given the symbol ∞. By convention, the result of dividing any number by zero is regarded as infinity.

inflammation a defensive reaction of the body tissues to disease or damage. Denoted by the suffix *-itis* (as in peritonitis), it may be acute or chronic, and may be accompanied by the formation of pus.

inflation in economics, a rise in the general level of prices. The many causes include *cost-push inflation* which occurred in 1974 as a result of the world price increase in oil, thus increasing production costs. *Demand-pull inflation* results when overall demand exceeds supply. Suppressed inflation occurs in controlled economies and is reflected in rationing, shortages and black market prices. Deflation, a fall in the general level of prices, is the reverse of inflation.

inflation tax tax imposed on companies that increase wages by more than an amount fixed by law (except to take account of increased profits or because of a profit-sharing scheme).

inflorescence a flower-bearing branch, or system of branches, in plants. Inflorescences can be divided into two main types. In a *cymose inflorescence*, the terminal growing point produces a single flower and subsequent flowers arise on lower lateral branches, as in forget-me-not (*Myosotis*) and chickweed (*Stellaria*); the oldest flowers are found at the apex. A *racemose inflorescence* consists of a main axis, bearing flowers along its length, with an active growing region at the apex; as in hyacinth and lupin, the oldest flowers are found near the base or, where the inflorescence has become flattened, towards the outside.

influenza a virus infection primarily affecting the air passages, but with ◊systemic effects such as fever, headache, joint pains, and lassitude.

infrared radiation Aerial infrared photograph of bends in the Mississippi River, USA. Healthy vegetation appears in shades of red.

infrared astronomy study of infrared radiation produced by relatively cool gas and dust in space, such as in the areas around forming stars. In 1983, the Infra-Red Astronomy Satellite (IRAS) surveyed the entire sky at infrared wavelengths. It found five new comets, thousands of galaxies undergoing bursts of star formation, and the possibility of planetary systems forming around several dozen stars.

infrared radiation invisible electromagnetic radiation of wavelength between about 0.75 ◊micrometres and 1 millimetre, that is, between the limit of the red end of the visible spectrum and the shortest microwaves. All bodies above the ◊absolute zero of temperature absorb and radiate infrared radiation. Infrared radiation is used in medical photography and treatment, in industry, astronomy, and criminology.

Ingres Jean Auguste Dominique 1780–1867. French painter, a leading exponent of the Neo-Classical style. He studied and worked in Rome about 1807–20, where he began the *Odalisque* series of sensuous female nudes. His portraits in the 1840s–50s are meticulously detailed and highly polished.

inhibition, neural in biology, the process whereby activity in one ◊nerve cell suppresses activity in another. Neural inhibition in networks of nerve cells leading from sensory organs, or to muscles, plays an important role in allowing an animal to make fine sensory discriminations and to exercise fine control over movements.

initiative device whereby the voters may play a direct part in making laws. A proposed law is drawn up and signed by petitioners, and submitted to the legislature. See also ◊referendum.

injunction in English law, a court order which forbids a person from doing something, or orders him or her to take certain action. It has been used, for example, to restrain unions from organising illegal picketing. Breach of an injunction is ◊contempt of court.

ink coloured liquid used for writing, drawing and printing. Traditional ink (blue, but later a permanent black), was produced from gallic acid and tannic acid, but modern inks are based on synthetic dyes.

Inkatha South African political organization formed 1975 by Chief Gatsha ◊Buthelezi, leader of six million Zulus, the country's biggest ethnic group. Inkatha aims to create a nonracial democratic political situation. Because Inkatha has tried to work with the white regime, Buthelezi has been regarded as a collaborator by blacks and the United Democratic Front. Fighting between Inkatha and African National Congress members cost more than 1,000 lives in the first five months of 1990.

Inkerman, Battle of a battle of the Crimean War, fought on 5 Nov 1854, during which an attack by the Russians on Inkerman Ridge, occupied by the British army besieging Sebastopol, was repulsed.

INLA abbreviation for ◊Irish National Liberation Army.

Innocent III 1161–1216. Pope from 1198. He asserted papal power over secular princes, especially over the succession of Holy Roman Emperors. He also made King ◊John of England his vassal, compelling him to accept ◊Langton as archbishop of Canterbury. He promoted the fourth Crusade and crusades against the non-Christian Livonians and Letts, and Albigensian heretics.

Innsbruck capital of Tirol State, W Austria, population (1981) 117,000. It is a tourist and winter sports centre, and a route junction for the Brenner Pass.

Inns of Court four private societies in London, England: Lincoln's Inn, Gray's Inn, Inner Temple, and Middle Temple. All English barristers must belong to one of these societies. They train law students and have power to call them to the English bar. Joint lectures are given, and there is a common examination board. Each is under the administration of a body of Benchers (judges and senior barristers).

Inoculation injection into the body of dead disease-carrying organisms, toxins, antitoxins, and so on, to produce immunity by inducing a mild form of a disease.

Inorganic chemistry the branch of chemistry dealing with the elements and their compounds, excluding the more complex carbon compounds

which are considered in ◊organic chemistry.

input device a device for entering information into a computer. Input devices include the electronic keyboard, joysticks, and vision systems.

inquest an inquiry held by a ◊coroner, especially into an unexplained death.

Inquisition tribunal of the Roman Catholic church established 1229 to suppress heresy (dissenting views), originally by excommunication. Sentence was pronounced during a religious ceremony, the ◊auto-da-fé. The Inquisition operated in France, Italy, Spain, and the Holy Roman Empire, and was especially active following the ◊Reformation; it was later extended to the Americas. Its trials were conducted in secret, under torture, and penalties ranged from fines, through flogging and imprisonment, to death by burning.

insanity popular and legal term for mental disorder. In medicine the term is ◊psychosis.

insect small invertebrate animal whose body is divided into head, thorax, and abdomen. The head bears a pair of feelers or antennae, and attached to the thorax are three pairs of legs and usually two pairs of wings.

insecticide a chemical used to kill insects. Among the most effective insecticides are synthetic organic chemicals such as ◊DDT and dieldrin, which are chlorinated hydrocarbons. These chemicals, however, have proved very persistent and can also poison higher animals, and are consequently banned in many countries. Other synthetic insecticides include organic phosphorus compounds such as malathion. Insecticides prepared from plants, such as derris and pyrethrum are safer to use, but need to be applied more frequently.

insectivore an animal whose diet is made up largely or exclusively of insects. In particular, the name is applied to mammals of the order Insectivora, which includes the shrews, hedgehogs, and moles.

insectivorous plant a plant that can capture and digest animals, to obtain nitrogen compounds which are lacking in its usual marshy habitat. Some are passive traps, for example, *pitcher plants Nepenthes*. One pitcher plant species has container-traps holding 2 1/3.5 pt of the liquid which 'digests' its insect food, and may even trap rats. Others,

insect

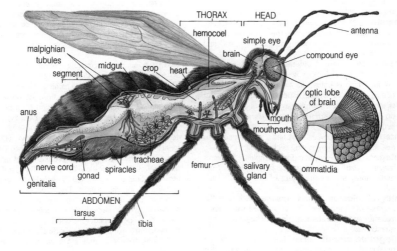

THORAX HEAD

hemocoel

malpighian tubules

midgut crop heart

segment

brain

simple eye

antenna

compound eye

optic lobe of brain

anus

mouth
mouthparts

tracheae

nerve cord gonad spiracles

genitalia

femur

salivary gland

ommatidia

ABDOMEN

tarsus

tibia

for example, **sundews** *Drosera*, **butterworts** *Pinguicula* and **Venus fly trap** *Dionaea muscipula*, have an active trapping mechanism; see ◊leaf.

inselberg a prominent steep-sided hill of resistant solid rock, such as granite, rising out of a plain, usually in a tropical area. Its rounded appearance is caused by so called onion-skin ◊weathering, in which the surface is eroded in successive layers.

insemination, artificial artificial introduction of semen into the female reproductive tract to bring about fertilization. Originally used by animal breeders to improve stock by the use of high-quality males, in the 20th century it has been developed for use in humans, to help the infertile. In 'in vitro' fertilization ('test-tube' babies), the egg is fertilized externally and then reimplanted in the womb; the first successful birth using this method was in the UK in 1978.

insider trading or **insider dealing** illegal use of privileged information in dealing on the stock exchanges, for example when a company takeover bid is imminent. Insider trading is in theory detected by the **Securities and Exchange Commission** (SEC) in the USA, and by the **Securities and Investment Board** (SIB) in the UK. Neither agency, however, has any legal powers other than public disclosure.

instalment credit a form of ◊hire purchase.

instinct in ◊ethology, behaviour found in all equivalent members of a given species (for example, all the males, or all the females with young) that is presumed to be genetically determined.

Institute for Advanced Study a department of Princeton University, USA, established 1933, to encourage gifted scientists to further their research uninterrupted by teaching duties or an imposed research scheme.

Instrument Landing System a landing aid for aircraft that uses ◊radio beacons on the ground and instruments on the flight deck. One beacon (localizer) sends out a vertical radio beam along the centre line of the runway. Another beacon (glide slope) transmits a beam in the plane at right-angles to the localiser beam at the ideal approach-path angle. The pilot can tell from the instruments how to manoeuvre to attain the correct approach path.

insulator poor ◊conductor of heat, sound, or electricity. Most substances lacking free (mobile) ◊electrons, such as non-metals, are electrical or thermal insulators.

insulin a ◊hormone, produced by specialized cells in the islets of Langerhans in the ◊pancreas, which regulates the ◊metabolism of glucose, fats, and proteins.

insurance contract indemnifying the payer of a premium against loss by fire, death, accident, and so on, which is known as **assurance** in the case of a fixed sum (in Britain especially when the event is inevitable, for example payment of a fixed sum on death), and **insurance** where the indemnity is proportionate to the loss.

intaglio a gem or seal that has a pattern cut into one surface; an ◊engraving technique.

integer a whole number, for example 3. Integers may be positive or negative; 0 is an integer. Formally, integers are members of the set Z = (... –2, –1, 0, 1, 2, ...)

integral calculus branch of mathematics using the process of ◊integration. It is concerned with finding volumes and areas and summing infinitesimally small quantities.

integrated circuit a complete electronic circuit produced on a single crystal of a ◊semiconductor (intermediate between an insulator and a conductor of electricity) such as silicon. The circuit might contain more than a million transistors, resistors, and capacitors and yet measure only 8 mm/0.3 in across. See also ◊silicon chip.

integration in mathematics, method in ◊calculus of evaluating definite or indefinite integrals. An example of a definite integral can be thought of as finding the area under a curve (as represented by an algebraic expression or function) between particular values of the function's variable.

intelligence in psychology, a general concept that summarizes the abilities of an individual in reasoning and problem solving, particularly in novel situations. These consist of a wide range of verbal and non-verbal skills and therefore some psychologists dispute a unitary concept of intelligence. See ◊intelligence test.

intelligence in military and political affairs, information, usually covertly or illegally obtained, about other countries. **Counter intelligence** is information on the activities of hostile agents. Much intelligence is gained by technical means, as at the UK electronic surveillance centre ◊GCHQ, Cheltenham.

intelligence test test which attempts to measure innate intellectual ability, rather than acquired ability.

intendant French term for official appointed by the French crown under Louis XIV to administer a territorial *département*. Their powers were extensive but counteracted to some extent by other local officials. The term was also used for certain administrators in Spain, Portugal, and Latin America.

interdict ecclesiastical punishment which excludes an individual, community, or realm from participation in spiritual activities except for communion. It was usually employed against heretics or realms whose ruler was an excommunicant.

i0.6l**interest** in finance, a sum of money paid by a borrower to a lender in return for the loan, usually expressed as a percentage per annum. **Simple interest** is interest calculated as a straight percentage of the amount loaned or invested. In **compound interest**, the interest earned over a period of time (for example, per annum) is added to the investment, so that at the end of the next period interest is paid on that total.

interference in physics, the phenomenon of two or more wave motions interacting and combining to produce a resultant wave of larger or smaller amplitude (depending on whether the combining waves are in or out of ◊phase with each other).

interferon naturally occurring protein which makes up part of the body's defences against disease. Three types (alpha, beta, and gamma) are produced to protect cells from viral infection. At present, only alpha interferon has any proven therapeutic value, and may be used to treat a rare type of ◊leukaemia.

Intermediate Nuclear Forces Treaty (INF) treaty signed 8 Dec 1987 between the USA and the USSR eliminating all ground-based intermediate nuclear missiles by 1989, thus reducing the countries' nuclear arsenals by some 2,000 (4% of the total). The treaty, seen as perhaps the most important ◊strategic arms-limitation treaty signed since nuclear weapons were first developed, included provisions for each country to inspect the other's nuclear installations to check that totals were not being exceeded.

intermediate technology the application of mechanics, electrical engineering, and other technologies, based on inventions and designs developed in scientifically sophisticated cultures, but utilizing materials, assembly, and maintenance methods found in technologically less advanced regions (known as the ◊Third World).

internal combustion engine a heat engine in which fuel is burned inside the engine, contrasting with an external combustion engine (like the steam engine) in which fuel is burned in a separate boiler. The petrol and diesel engine are both internal combustion engines. Gas turbines, jet and rocket engines are sometimes also considered to be internal combustion engines since they burn their fuel inside their combustion chambers.

International, the coordinating body established by labour and socialist organizations, including:

First International or *International Working Men's Association* 1864–72, formed in London under Karl ◊Marx.

Second International 1889-1914, founded in Paris.

Third (Socialist) International or *Comintern* 1919–43, formed in Moscow by the Soviet leader Lenin, advocating from 1933 a popular front (communist, socialist, liberal) against the German dictator Hitler.

Fourth International or *Trotskyist International* 1936, somewhat indeterminate, anti-Stalinist.

Revived *Socialist International* 1951, formed in Frankfurt, West Germany, a largely anticommunist association of social democrats.

International Atomic Energy Agency (IAEA) agency of the United Nations established in 1957, with headquarters in Vienna, Austria, and research centres in Austria, Monaco, and the International Centre for Theoretical Physics, Trieste, Italy.

International Brigade international volunteer force on the Republican side in the Spanish ◊Civil War 1936–39.

International Civil Aviation Organization agency of the ◊United Nations, established 1947 to regulate safety and efficiency and air law; headquarters Montreal.

International Court of Justice the main judicial organ of the ◊United Nations, at The Hague, the Netherlands.

International Date Line (IDL) a modification of the 180th meridian that marks the difference in time between E and W. The IDL was chosen at the International Meridian Conference in 1884.

Internationale international revolutionary socialist anthem; composed 1870 and first sung 1888. The words by Eugène Pottier (1816–1887) were written shortly after Napoleon III's surrender to Prussia, the music is by Pierre Degeyter. It was the Soviet national anthem 1917–44.

International Fund for Agricultural Development agency of the ◊United Nations, established 1977, to provide funds for benefiting the poor in developing countries.

International Geophysical Year (IGY) a research project sponsored by the International Council of Scientific Unions to find out as much as possible about the physical nature of the planet, Earth. It lasted between 1 Jul 1957 and 31 Dec 1958, to coincide with a period of intense sunspot activity, but was extended into 1959 as the International Geophysical Cooperation (IGC). Scientific knowledge of the Earth was expanded greatly during this time: in astronomy, the Van Allen radiation

belts were discovered; in oceanography, the deep ocean currents were found; in gravimetry, the presence of mountain roots in the Earth's crust was confirmed.

International Gothic a ◊Gothic style of painting prevalent in Europe in the 14th and 15th century.

international law body of rules generally accepted as governing the relations between countries, pioneered by Hugo ◊Grotius, especially in matters of human rights, territory, and war. Neither the League of Nations nor United Nations proved able to enforce it, successes being achieved only when the law coincided with the aims of a predominant major power, for example the ◊Korean War. The scope of the law is now extended to space, for example the 1967 treaty which (among other things) banned nuclear weapons from space.

International Maritime Organization a ◊United Nations agency concerned with world shipping. Established in 1958, it has its headquarters in London, England.

International Monetary Fund (IMF) specialized agency of the United Nations, headquarters Washington DC, established under the 1944 Bretton Woods agreement and operational since 1947. It seeks to promote international monetary cooperation, the growth of world trade, and to smooth multilateral payment arrangements among member states. IMF stand-by loans are available to members in balance of payments difficulties (the amount being governed by the member's quota), usually on the basis of acceptance of instruction on stipulated corrective measures.

International Society for Krishna Consciousness (ISKON) a Hindu sect based on the demonstration of intense love for Krishna (an incarnation of the god Vishnu), especially by chanting the mantra 'Hare Krishna'. Members wear distinctive yellow robes and men often have a large portion of their heads shaven. Their holy books are the Hindu scriptures and particularly the *Bhagavad-Gītā*, which they study daily.

internment the detention of suspected criminals without trial. Common with foreign citizens during wartime, internment was introduced for the detention of suspected terrorists in Northern Ireland by the UK Government 1971.

interplanetary matter gas and dust thinly spread through the solar system. The gas flows outwards from the Sun as the ◊solar wind. Fine dust lies in the plane of the solar system, scattering sunlight to cause the zodiacal light. Swarms of dust shed by comets enter the Earth's atmosphere to cause ◊meteor showers.

Interpol *Inter*national Criminal *Pol*ice Commission, founded following the Second International Judicial Police Conference 1923 with its headquarters in Vienna, but reconstituted after World War II with its headquarters in Paris. It has an international criminal register, fingerprint file, and methods index.

interpreter a computer program that translates statements from a ◊programming language into ◊machine code and causes them to be executed. Unlike a ◊compiler, which translates the whole program at once to produce an executable machine code program, an interpreter translates the programming language each time the program is run.

Interstate Commerce Commission US authority, established in 1887, which regulates all traffic between states. ICC regulations cover routes, services, bills of lading, mergers, and rates charged to users.

interstellar molecules over 50 different types of molecules existing in gas clouds in the Galaxy. Most have been detected by their radio emissions, but some have been found by the absorption lines they produce in the spectra of starlight. The most complex molecules, many of them based on ◊carbon, are found in the dense clouds where stars are forming. They may be significant for the origin of life elsewhere in space.

interval in music, the pitch difference between two notes, usually measured in terms of the diatonic scale.

intestacy the absence of a will at a person's death. In English law, special legal rules apply on intestacy for appointing administrators to deal with the deceased person's affairs, and for disposing of the deceased person's property in accordance with statutory provisions.

intestine in vertebrates, the digestive tract from the stomach outlet to the anus. The human *small intestine* is 6 m/20 ft long, 4 cm/1.5 in in diameter, and consists of the duodenum, jejunum, and ileum; the *large intestine* is 1.5 m/5 ft long, 6 cm/2.5 in in diameter, and includes the caecum, colon, and rectum. Both are muscular tubes comprising an inner lining which secretes alkaline digestive juice, a submucous coat containing fine blood vessels and nerves, a muscular coat, and a serous coat covering all, supported by a strong peritoneum, which carries the blood and lymph vessels, and the nerves. The contents are passed along slowly by ◊peristalsis.

Intifada popular name for *Popular Liberation Army of Palestine*, a loosely organized group of adult and teenage Palestinians active since 1987 in attacks on Israeli troops. Their campaign includes stone-throwing and petrol bombing.

intrusion a mass of ◊igneous rock that formed by 'injection' of molten rock into existing cracks beneath the surface of the Earth, as distinct from a volcanic rock mass which erupted from the surface.

intuition a rapid, unconscious thought process. In philosophy, intuition is that knowledge of a concept which does not derive directly from the senses. Thus, we may be said to have an intuitive idea of God, beauty, or justice. The concept of intuition is similar to Bertrand ◊Russell's theory of knowledge by acquaintance. In both cases, it is contrasted with ◊empirical knowledge.

Inuit people inhabiting the Arctic coasts of North America, the E islands of the Canadian Arctic, and the ice-free coasts of Greenland. They were first called Eskimos ('eaters of raw meat') by the Algonquin Indians. Their language, Inuktitut, belongs to the Eskimo-Aleut group.

Invalides, Hôtel des building in Paris, S of the Seine, founded in 1670 as a home for disabled soldiers. The church Dôme des Invalides contains the tomb of Napoleon I.

invar an alloy of iron containing 36% nickel, which scarcely expands or contracts when the temperature changes. It is used to make precision instruments (such as pendulums and tuning forks) whose dimensions must not alter.

Invergordon Mutiny incident in the British Atlantic Fleet, Cromarty Firth, Scotland, 15 Sep 1931. Ratings refused to prepare the ships for sea following the government's cuts in their pay; the cuts were consequently modified.

Inverness town in Highland region, Scotland, lying in a sheltered site at the mouth of the Ness; population (1985) 58,000. Industries include tourism, tweed, tanning, engineering, and distilling.

inverse square law in physics, the statement that the magnitude of an effect (usually a force) at a point is inversely proportional to the square of the distance between that point and the point location of its cause.

invertebrate an animal without a backbone. The invertebrates form a major division of the animal kingdom, and include the sponges, coelenterates, flatworms, nematodes, annelid worms, arthropods, molluscs, echinoderms, and primitive aquatic chordates such as sea-squirts and lancelets.

investiture contest the name given to the conflict between the papacy and the Holy Roman Empire 1075–1122, which centred on the right of lay rulers to appoint prelates.

investment in economics, the purchase of any asset with the potential to yield future financial benefit to the purchaser (such as a house, a work of art, stocks and shares, or even a private education). More strictly, it denotes expenditure on the stock of capital goods or resources of an enterprise or project, with a view to achieving profitable production for consumption at a later date.

investment trust a public company which makes investments in other companies on behalf of its shareholders. It may issue shares to raise capital and issue fixed interest securities.

in vitro fertilization literally, fertilization 'in glass', that is, allowing eggs and sperm to fuse in a laboratory to form embryos. The embryos produced may then either be reimplanted into the womb of the otherwise infertile mother, or used for research. The first baby to be produced in the UK by this method, Louise Brown, was born 1978.

involute of a circle, a ◊spiral that can be thought of as being traced by a point at the end of a taut non-elastic thread being wound onto or unwound from a spool.

INXS internationally-acclaimed Australian rock band, formed in Sydney in the late 1970s around lead singer Michael Hutchence. Their first worldwide hit album *Kick* was released in 1988.

Io in astronomy, the third-largest moon of the planet Jupiter, 3,600 km/2,240 mi in diameter, orbiting in 1.77 days at a distance of 413,000 km/257,000 mi. It is the most volcanically active body in the Solar System, covered by hundreds of vents that erupt sulphur.

iodine a non-metallic element, symbol I, atomic number 53, relative atomic mass 126.91. Not found in the free state, it occurs in saltpetre and as iodides in sea-water. Iodine is used in photography, in medicine as an antiseptic, and in chemicals and dyes. It collects in the thyroid gland, lack of it producing goitre. Iodine-131 (a radioactive isotope) is widely used in medicine.

iodoform CHI_3 (modern name *triiodomethane*) an antiseptic which crystallizes into yellow hexagonal plates. It is soluble in ether, alcohol, and chloroform.

ion atom, or group of atoms, which are either positively charged (*cation*) or negatively charged (*anion*), as a result of the loss or gain of electrons.

Iona an island in the Inner Hebrides; area 850 hectares. It is the site of a monastery founded 563 by St ◊Columba, and a centre of early Christianity. It later became a burial ground for Irish, Scottish, and Norwegian kings. It has a 13th-century abbey.

ion engine a rocket engine that uses ◊ions rather than hot gas for propulsion. Ion engines have been successfully tested in space, where they will eventually be used for gradual rather than sudden velocity

Iran
Islamic Republic of
(*Jomhori-e-Islami-e-Irân*;
until 1935 **Persia**)

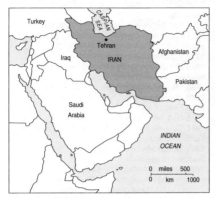

area 1,648,000 sq km/636,128 sq mi
capital Tehran
towns Isfahan, Mashhad, Tabriz, Shiraz, Ahwaz;
chief port Abadan
physical plateau surrounded by mountains,
including Elburz and Zagros; Lake Rezayeh;
Dasht-Ekavir Desert
Leader of the Islamic Revolution Seyed Ali
Khamenei from 1989
head of government Ali Akbar Rafsanjani from
1989
political system authoritarian Islamic republic
exports carpets, cotton textiles, metalwork,
leather goods, oil, petrochemicals, fruit

currency rial
population (1989 est) 51,005,000 (including
minorities in Azerbaijan, Baluchistan, Khuzestan/
Arabistan, and Kurdistan); annual growth rate
3.2%
life expectancy men 57, women 57
language Farsi (official), Kurdish, Turkish, Arabic,
English, French
religion Shi'ite Muslim (official) 92%
literacy 62% male/39% female (1985 est)
GDP $86.4 bn (1987); $1,756 per head
chronology
1946 British, US, and Soviet forces left Iran.
1953 Prime Minister Mossadeq deposed and the
shah took full control of the government
1975 The shah introduced a single-party system.
1978 Opposition to the shah organized from
France by Ayatollah Khomeini.
1979 Shah left the country and Khomeini returned
to create an Islamic state. Students seized US
hostages at embassy in Tehran.
1980 Start of Gulf War against Iraq.
1981 US hostages released.
1985 Gulf War fighting intensified.
1988 Ceasefire in Gulf War, talks with Iraq began.
1989 Khomeini called for the murder of British
writer Salman Rushdie. Khomeini died June. Ali
Khamenei elected interim Leader of the
Revolution. Speaker of the Iranian parliament Ali
Akbar Rafsanjani elected president.
1990 Peace treaty concluded with Iraq. Normal
relations with UK restored.
1991 Almost one million Kurds arrived in Iran from
Iraq, fleeing persecution by Saddam Hussein.
1992 Pro-Rafsanjani moderates won assembly
elections.

---

changes. In an ion engine atoms of mercury, for
example, are ionized – given an electric charge
by an electric field, and then accelerated at high
speed by a more powerful electric field.

Ionesco Eugène 1912– . Romanian-born French
dramatist, a leading exponent of the Theatre of the
◊Absurd. Most of his plays are in one act
and concern the futility of language as a means
of communication. These include *La Cantatrice
chauve/The Bald Prima Donna* 1950 and *La
Leçon/The Lesson* 1951.

Ionia in Classical times the W coast of Asia Minor,
settled about 1000 BC by the Ionians; it included the
cities of Ephesus, Miletus, and later Smyrna.

Ionian member of a Hellenic people from beyond
the Black Sea who crossed the Balkans around 1980
BC and invaded Asia Minor. Driven back by the
◊Hittites, they spread over mainland Greece, later
being supplanted by the ◊Achaeans.

ionic bond another name for ◊electrovalent bond.

ionizing radiation radiation which knocks electrons from atoms during its passage, thereby
leaving ions in its path. Electrons and alpha-
particles are much more ionizing than are neutrons
or ◊gamma radiation.

ionosphere ionized layer of Earth's outer
◊atmosphere (60–1,000 km/38–620 mi) that con-
taiuns sufficient free electrons to modify the way in
which radio waves are propagated.

ion plating method of applying corrosion-
resistant metal coatings. The article is placed in
argon gas, together with some coating metal, which
vaporizes on heating and becomes ionized (acquires

charged atoms) as it diffuses through the gas to form
the coating.

Iowa state of the midwest USA; nickname
Hawkeye State
area 145,790 sq km/56,275 sq mi
capital Des Moines
towns Cedar Rapids, Davenport, Sioux City
products cereals, soya beans, meat, wool, industrial products including chemicals, machinery and
electrical goods
population (1984) 2,837,000
famous people Buffalo Bill Cody
history part of the ◊Louisiana Purchase in 1803, it remains an area of small farms; it became a state in 1846.

ipecacuanha South American plant *Psychotria
ipecacuanha*, family Rubiaceae, used as an emetic
and in treating amoebic dysentery.

IQ intelligence quotient. It is the ratio between a
subject's 'mental age' and chronological age, multiplied by 100. 100 is considered average.

Iqbāl Muhammad 1875–1938. Islamic poet and
thinker. His literary works, in Urdu and Persian,
were mostly verse in the classical style, suitable for
public recitation.

IRA abbreviation for ◊Irish Republican Army.

Iráklion or *Heraklion* largest city and capital
(since 1971) of Crete, Greece; population (1981)
102,000.

Iran country in SW Asia, bounded N by Armenia,
Azerbaijan, the Caspian Sea, and Turkmenistan; E by
Afghanistan and Pakistan; S and SW by the Gulf of Oman
and the Persian Gulf; W by Iraq; and NW by Turkey.

Irangate or *Contragate* US political scandal in-

Iraq
Republic of
(*al Jumhouriya al 'Iraqia*)

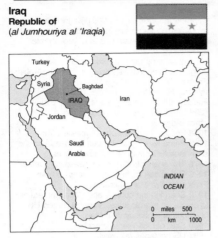

area 434,924 sq km/167,881 sq mi
apital Baghdad
towns Mosul and port of Basra
physical mountains in N, desert in W; wide valley of rivers Tigris and Euphrates NW-SE
head of state and government Saddam Hussein At-Takriti from 1979
political system one-party socialist republic
exports oil (prior to UN sanctions), wool, dates
currency Iraqi dinar
population (1989 est) 17,610,000 Arabs 77%, Kurds 19%, Turks 2%; annual growth rate 3.6%
life expectancy men 62, women 63

language Arabic (official)
religion Shi'ite Muslim 60%, Sunni Muslim 37%, Christian 3%
literacy 68% male/32% female (1980 est)
GDP $42.3 bn (1987); $3,000 per head
chronology
1920 Iraq became a British protectorate.
1921 Hashemite dynasty established, with Faisal I as king.
1932 Achieved full independence.
1958 Monarchy overthrown and Iraq became a republic.
1968 Military coup put Gen al-Bakr in power.
1979 Al-Bakr replaced by Saddam Hussein.
1980 Start of Iraq-Iran Gulf War.
1985 Gulf War fighting intensified.
1988 Ceasefire in Gulf War. Harsh repression of Kurdish rebels.
1989 Unsuccessful coup against President Saddam Hussein.
1990 Peace treaty favouring Iran agreed. Iraq invaded and annexed Kuwait, troops moved to Saudi Arabian Border. Multinational defence forces installed in Saudi Arabia. UN resolutions imposed total trade ban on Iraq and sanctioned the use of force.
1991 Jan: Iraq's infrastructure destroyed by bombing by US-led forces. Feb: land-sea-air offensive to free Kuwait successful. Uprisings of Kurds and Shi'ites brutally suppressed by Iraqi troops. Allied troops withdrew. Allies threatened to bomb strategic targets in Iraq if full information on nuclear facilities denied to UN.
1992 UN imposed a 'no-fly zone' over S Iraq to protect Shi'ites.
1993 Iraqi incursions into 'no-fly zone' prompted US-led alliance to bomb strategic Iraqi targets. Relations subsequently improved.

volving senior members of the Reagan administration. Congressional hearings 1986–87 revealed that the US government had secretly sold weapons to Iran in 1985 and traded them for hostages held in Lebanon by pro-Iranian militias, and used the profits to supply right-wing Contra guerrillas in Nicaragua with arms.

Iranian language   the main language of Iran, more commonly known as ◊Persian or Farsi.

Iran–Iraq War   or *Gulf War* war between Iran and Iraq 1980–88, claimed by the former to have begun with the Iraqi offensive of 21 Sep 1980, and by the latter with the Iranian shelling of border posts 4 Sep 1980. Occasioned by a boundary dispute over the ◊Shatt-al-Arab waterway, it fundamentally arose because of Iran's encouragement of the Shi'ite majority in Iraq to rise against the Sunni government of Saddam Hussein. An estimated 1 million people died in the war.

Iraq   country in SW Asia, bounded N by Turkey, E by Iran, SE by the Persian Gulf and Kuwait, S by Saudi Arabia, and W by Jordan and Syria.

Ireland   one of the British Isles, lying to the W of Great Britain, from which it is separated by the Irish Sea. It comprises the provinces of Ulster, Leinster, Munster, and Connacht, and is divided between the Republic of Ireland, which occupies the S, central, and NW of the island, and Northern Ireland, which occupies the NE corner and forms part of the United Kingdom.

Ireland, Northern
area 13,483 sq km/5,204 sq mi
capital Belfast
towns Londonderry, Enniskillen, Omagh, Newry, Armagh, Coleraine

exports engineering, especially shipbuilding including textile machinery, aircraft components; linen and synthetic textiles; processed foods, especially dairy and poultry products – all affected by the 1980s depression and political unrest
currency pound sterling
population (1988 est) 1,578,100
language English
religion Protestant 54%, Roman Catholic 31%

Northern Ireland
Protestant majority
R. Catholic majority

Ireland, Republic of
(Irish *Éire*)

area 70,282 sq km/27,146 sq mi
capital Dublin
towns ports Cork, Dún Laoghaire, Limerick, Waterford
physical central plateau surrounded by hills; rivers Shannon, Liffey, Boyne
head of state Mary Robinson from 1990
head of government Albert Reynolds from 1992
political system democratic republic
exports livestock, dairy products, Irish whiskey, microelectronic, mining, and engineering products, chemicals, clothing; tourism is important
currency punt

population (1989 est) 3,734,000; annual growth rate 0.1%
language Irish/Gaelic and English (both official)
religion Roman Catholic 94%
literacy 88% (1984)
GDP $21.9 (1987); $6,184 per head
chronology
1916 Easter Rising: nationalists proclaimed a republic. The revolt was suppressed by the British Army.
1918–21 Guerrilla warfare against British Army led to split in rebel forces.
1921 Anglo-Irish Treaty resulted in creation of the Irish Free State (Southern Ireland).
1937 Independence achieved from Britain.
1949 Eire left the Commonwealth and became the Republic of Ireland.
1973 Fianna Fáil Party defeated after 40 years in office.
1977 Fianna Fáil returned to power, with Jack Lynch as prime minister.
1979 Lynch resigned and was succeeded by Charles Haughey.
1981 Garret FitzGerald formed a coalition.
1983 New Ireland Forum formed, but rejected by the British government.
1985 Anglo-Irish Agreement signed.
1986 Protests by Ulster Unionists against the agreement.
1987 General election won by Charles Haughey.
1989 Haughey failed to win a majority in general election; progressive Democrats (a breakaway party of Fianna Fáil) given cabinet positions in a coalition government.
1990 Mary Robinson elected president.
1992 Haughey resigned and was replaced by Reynolds. National referendum approved ratification of the Maastricht Treaty. Reynolds lost confidence vote; election results inconclusive.
1993 Fianna Fáil–Labour coalition formed.

government there has been direct rule from the UK since 1972 because of the incidence of violence, though it can be argued that this has aggravated the situation. Northern Ireland is entitled to send 12 members to the Westminster Parliament.
recent history the creation of Northern Ireland dates from 1921 when the mainly Protestant counties of Ulster withdrew from the newly established Irish Free State. Spasmodic outbreaks of violence by the ◊IRA continued, but only in 1968–69 were there serious disturbances arising from Protestant political dominance and discrimination against the Roman Catholic minority in employment and housing. British troops were sent to restore peace and protect Catholics, but disturbances continued and in 1972 the parliament at Stormont was prorogued, and superseded by direct rule from Westminster.

Under the Anglo-Irish Agreement of 1985, the Republic of Ireland was given a consultative role (via an Anglo-Irish conference) in the government of Northern Ireland, but agreed that there should be no change in its status except by majority consent, and that there should be greater cooperation against terrorism. The agreement was approved by Parliament, but all 12 Ulster members gave up their seats, so that by-elections could be fought as a form of 'referendum' on the views of the province itself. A similar boycotting of the Northern Ireland Assembly led to its dissolution 1986 by the UK government. Between 1969 and 1991 violence had claimed almost 3,000 lives in Northern Ireland.

Ireland, Republic of country occupying the main part of the island of Ireland, off the NW coast of Europe. It is bounded to the E by the Irish Sea, to the S and W by the Atlantic, and to the NE by Northern Ireland.

Irene in Greek mythology, goddess of peace (Roman Pax). She was sometimes regarded as one of the Horae, who presided over the seasons and the order of nature, and were the daughters of Zeus and Themis.

Irene, St *c.* 752–*c.* 803. Byzantine emperor 797–802. The wife of Leo IV (750–780), she became regent for their son Constantine (771–805) on Leo's death. In 797 she deposed her son, had his eyes put out, and assumed full title of *basileus* (emperor), ruling in her own right until deposed and exiled to Lesvos by a revolt of 802. She was made a saint by the Greek Orthodox church for her attacks on the iconoclasts.

Ireton Henry 1611–1651. English Civil War general. He joined the parliamentary forces and fought at ◊Edgehill 1642, Gainsborough 1643, and ◊Naseby 1645. After the Battle of Naseby, Ireton, who was opposed to both the extreme republicans and ◊Levellers, strove for a compromise with Charles I, but then played a leading role in his trial and execution. He married his leader Cromwell's daughter in 1646. Lord Deputy in Ireland from 1650, he died after the capture of Limerick.

Irian Jaya the western portion of the island of New Guinea, part of Indonesia
area 420,000 sq km/162,000 sq mi
capital Jayapura

iris

population (1989) 1,555,700

history part of the Dutch East Indies 1828 as Western New Guinea; retained by Netherlands after Indonesian independence 1949, but ceded to Indonesia 1963 by the United Nations and remained part of Indonesia by an 'Act of Freer Choice' 1969; in the 1980s 700,000 acres were given over to Indonesia's controversial ***transmigration programme*** for the resettlement of farming families from overcrowded Java, causing destruction of rainforests and displacing indigenous people.

iridium an element, symbol Ir, atomic number 77, relative atomic mass 192.2. It is a metal of the platinum family, white, very hard and brittle, and usually alloyed with platinum or osmium. It is used for points of fountain-pen nibs, compass bearings, and in scientific, medical and electrical equipment.

iris in physiology, the coloured muscular diaphragm that controls size of the pupil in the vertebrate eye. It contains radial muscle which increases the pupil diameter and circular muscle which constricts pupil diameter. Both types of muscle respond involuntarily to light intensity.

iris in botany, perennial northern temperate flowering plants, family Iridaceae. The leaves are usually sword-shaped; the purple, white or yellow flowers have three upright inner petals and three outward-and downward-curving sepals.

Irish Gaelic first official language of the Irish Republic, but much less widely used than the second official language, English.

Irish National Liberation Army (INLA) guerrilla organization committed to the end of British rule in Northern Ireland and the incorporation of Ulster into the Irish Republic. The INLA was a 1974 offshoot of the Irish Republican Army.

Irish Republican Army (IRA) militant Irish nationalist organization, whose aim is to create a united Irish socialist republic including Ulster. The paramilitary wing of ◊Sinn Féin, it was founded in 1919, and fought a successful war against Britain 1919–21. It came to the fore again in 1939, with a bombing campaign in Britain, and was declared illegal in Eire. Its activities intensified from 1968 onwards, as the civil-rights disorders in Northern Ireland developed. In 1970 a group in the north broke away to become the ***Provisional IRA***; their commitment is to the expulsion of the British from Northern Ireland. In 1974 a further breakaway occurred, of the left-wing Irish Republican Socialist Party with its paramilitary wing, the Irish National Liberation Army. The IRA is committed to murderous and disruptive violence as a means of pursuing its objectives, and regularly carries out bombings and shootings in Britain and Eire.

Irkutsk city in the south of Russia; population (1985) 597,000. It produces coal, iron, steel, and machine tools. Founded in 1652, it began to grow after the Trans-Siberian railway reached it in 1898.

iron the most widely found metal, after aluminium; symbol Fe (Latin *ferrum*), atomic number 26, relative atomic mass 55.85. Iron is the basis of all steel, and as well as its constructional uses, when mixed with carbon and other elements, it has important chemical applications. In electrical equipment, it forms the basis of all permanent magnets and electromagnets, and the cores of transformers and magnetic amplifiers.

Iron Age the period when weapons and tools were made from iron. Iron was produced in Thailand by *c*. 1600 BC but was considered inferior in strength to bronze until *c*. 1000 BC when metallurgical techniques improved and steel was produced by adding carbon during the smelting process.

ironclad a wooden warship covered with armour plate. The first to begin construction was the French *Gloire* in 1858, but the first to be launched was the British HMS *Warrior* 1859. The design was replaced by battleships of all-metal construction in the 1890s.

Iron Cross medal awarded for valour in the German armed forces. Instituted in Prussia in 1813, it consists of a Maltese cross of iron, edged with silver.

Iron Curtain in Europe after World War II, the symbolic frontier between capitalist West and communist East. The term popularized by the UK prime minister Winston Churchill from 1945. In 1990, with the dissolution of the communist bloc, it ceased to exist.

Iron Guard pro-fascist group controlling Romania in the 1930s. To counter its influence, King Carol II established a dictatorship 1938 but the Iron Guard forced him to abdicate 1940.

iron ore mineral from which iron is extracted. The chief iron ores are: ◊***magnetite***, a black oxide; ◊***haematite***, or kidney ore, a red oxide; ◊***limonite***, a black oxide; and ***siderite***, a carbonaceous ore.

iron pyrites FeS_2 a common iron ore. Brassy yellow, and occurring in cubic crystals, it resembles gold nuggets and is often called 'fool's gold'.

Iroquois confederation of North American Indians, the Six Nations (Cayuga, Mohawk, Oneida, Onondaga, and Seneca, with the Tuscarora from 1715), traditionally formed by Hiawatha (actually a priestly title) in 1570.

irradiation in science, subjecting anything to radiation, including cancer tumours. Food can be sterilized by bombarding it with low-strength gamma rays. Although the process is now legal in several countries there remains fear about the possible long-term dangers to consumers of irradiated food.

irrational number a number that cannot be expressed as an exact ◊fraction. Irrational numbers include some square roots (for example, n12, n13 and n15 are irrational) and numbers such as π (the ratio of the circumference of a circle to its diameter, which is approximately equal to 3.14159) and *e*, the base of ◊natural logarithms (which is approximately 2.71828).

Irrawaddy chief river of Myanmar, flowing roughly N to S for 2,090 km/1,300 mi across the centre of the country into the Bay of Bengal. Its sources are the Mali and N'mai rivers; its chief tributaries are the Chindwin and Shweli.

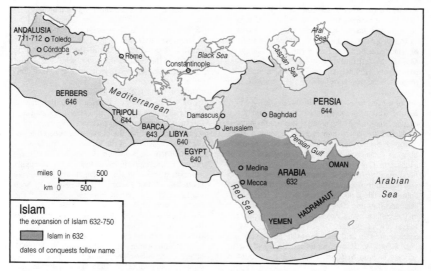

Islam
the expansion of Islam 632–750

■ Islam in 632

dates of conquests follow name

irredentist a person who wishes to reclaim the lost territories of a state. The term derives from an Italian political party founded about 1878 with a view to incorporating Italian-speaking areas into the Italian state.

Irving Henry. Stage name of English actor John Brodribb 1838–1905. He established his reputation from 1871, chiefly at the Lyceum Theatre in London, where he became manager from 1878. He staged a series of successful Shakespearean productions, including *Romeo and Juliet* 1882, with himself and Ellen ◊Terry playing the leading roles. In 1895 he was the first actor to be knighted.

Irving Washington 1783–1859. US essayist and short-story writer. He published a mock-heroic *History of New York* in 1809, supposedly written by the Dutchman 'Diedrich Knickerbocker'. In 1815 he went to England where his publications include the *Sketch Book of Geoffrey Crayon, Gent.* 1820, which contained such stories as 'Rip van Winkle' and 'Legend of Sleepy Hollow'.

Isaac in the Old Testament, Hebrew patriarch, son of ◊Abraham and Sarah, and father of Esau and Jacob.

Isaacs Alick 1921–1967. Scottish virologist who discovered ◊interferon 1957.

Isabella two Spanish queens:

Isabella I the Catholic 1451–1504. Queen of Castile from 1474, after the death of her brother Henry IV. By her marriage with Ferdinand of Aragon 1469, the crowns of two of the Christian states in the Spanish peninsula were united. In her reign the Moors were finally driven out of Spain; she introduced the ◊Inquisition into Castile, and the persecution of the Jews, and gave financial encouragement to ◊Columbus. Her youngest daughter was Catherine of Aragon, first wife of Henry VIII of England.

Isabella II 1830–1904. Queen of Spain from 1833, when she succeeded her father Ferdinand VII (1784–1833). The Salic Law banning a female sovereign had been repealed by the Cortes (Spanish parliament), but her succession was disputed by her uncle Don Carlos de Bourbon (1788–1855). After seven years of civil war the ◊Carlists were defeated. She abdicated in favour of her son Alfonso XII in 1868.

Isaiah 8th century BC. In the Old Testament, the first major Hebrew prophet. The son of Amos, he was probably of high rank, and lived largely in Jerusalem.

Isaurian an 8th-century Byzantine imperial dynasty, originating in Asia Minor.

ISBN abbreviation for *International Standard Book Number*.

Isherwood Christopher (William Bradshaw) 1904–1986. English novelist. He lived in Germany 1929–33 just before Hitler's rise to power, a period which inspired *Mr Norris Changes Trains* 1935 and *Goodbye to Berlin* 1939, creating the character of Sally Bowles (the basis of the musical *Cabaret* 1968).

Ishmael in the Old Testament, son of ◊Abraham and his wife Sarah's Egyptian maid Hagar; traditional ancestor of Muhammad and the Arab people. He and his mother were driven out by Sarah's jealousy. Muslims believe that it was Ishmael, not Isaac, whom God commanded Abraham to sacrifice, and that Ishmael helped Abraham build the ◊Kaaba in Mecca.

Ishtar goddess of love and war worshipped by the Babylonians and Assyrians, and personified as the legendary queen Semiramis.

Isidore of Seville *c.* 560–636. Writer and missionary. His *Etymologiae* was the model for later medieval encyclopedias and helped to preserve classical thought into the Middle Ages, and his *Chronica Maiora* remains an important source for the history of Visigothic Spain.

isinglass pure form of gelatin obtained from the cleaned and dried swim bladder of various fish, particularly the sturgeon. Isinglass is used in the clarification of wines and beer, and in cookery.

Isis the principal goddess of ancient Egypt. She was the daughter of Geb and Nut (earth and sky), and as the sister-wife of Osiris searched for his body after his death at the hands of his brother Set. Her son Horus then defeated and captured Set, but cut off his mother's head because she would not allow Set to be killed.

Islam religion founded in the Arabian peninsula in the early 7th century. The creed declares: there is no God but Allah, and ◊Muhammad is the Prophet or Messenger of Allah. Beliefs include Creation,

Fall of Adam, Angels and the ◊Jinn, Heaven and Hell, Day of Judgment, God's predestination of good and evil, and the succession of scriptures revealed to the prophets, including Moses and Jesus, but of which the perfect, final form is the *Koran* or *Quran* divided into 114 *suras* or chapters, said to have been divinely revealed to Muhammad, the original being preserved beside the throne of Allah in heaven.

sects there are two main Muslim sects:

Sunni whose members hold that the first three caliphs were all Muhammad's legitimate successors, and are in the majority. The name derives from the *Sunna*, Arabic 'rule', the body of traditional law evolved from the teaching and acts of Muhammad.

Shi'ite or *Shia* whose members believe that ◊Ali was Muhammad's first true successor; they number some 85 million, and are found in Iran, Iraq, Lebanon, and Bahrain. Holy men have greater authority in the Shi'ite sect. Breakaway sub-sects include the *Alawite* sect to which the ruling party in Syria belongs; and the *Ismaili* sect with the *Aga Khan* IV 1936– as its spiritual head. Later schools include *Sufism*, a mystical movement in 17th-century Iran.

organization there is no organized church or priesthood, though Muhammad's descendants (the Hashim family) and popularly recognized holy men, mullahs and ayatollahs, are accorded respect.

observances the 'Five Pillars of the Faith' are: recitation of the creed; worship five times a day facing the holy city of ◊Mecca (the call to prayer is given by a muezzin, usually from the minaret or tower of a ◊mosque); almsgiving; fasting sunrise to sunset through Ramadan (ninth month of the year, which varies with the calendar); and the pilgrimage to Mecca at least once in a lifetime.

Islamic law Islam embodies a secular Islamic Law (the Shari'a or 'Highway'), which is clarified for Shi'ites by reference to their own version of the *sunna*, 'practice' of the Prophet as transmitted by his companions; the Sunni sect also take into account *ijma'*, the endorsement by universal consent of practices and beliefs among the faithful. A *mufti* is a legal expert who guides the courts in their interpretation, and in Turkey (until the establishment of the republic in 1924) had supreme spiritual authority.

Islamabad capital of Pakistan from 1967, in the Potwar district, at the foot of the Margala Hills and immediately NW of Rawalpindi; population (1981) 201,000. The city was designed by Constantinos Doxiadis in the 1960s.

Islamic art art, architecture, and design of Muslim nations and territories. Because the Koran forbids representation in art, Islamic artistry was channelled into calligraphy and ornament. Despite this, there was naturalistic Persian painting, which inspired painters in the Mogul and Ottoman empires. Ceramic tiles decorated mosques and palaces from Spain (Alhambra, Granada) to S Russia and Mogul India (Taj Mahal, Agra). Wood, stone, and stucco sculpture ornamented buildings. Islamic artists produced excellent metalwork and, especially in Persia in the 16th–17th centuries, woven textiles and carpets.

Isle of Man see ◊Man, Isle of.

Isle of Wight see ◊Wight, Isle of.

Ismail 1830–1895. Khedive (governor) of Egypt 1866–79. A grandson of Mehemet Ali, he became viceroy of Egypt in 1863 and in 1866 received the title of khedive from the Ottoman sultan. In 1875 Britain, at Prime Minister Disraeli's suggestion, bought the khedive's Suez Canal shares for £3,976,582, and Anglo-French control of Egypt's finances was established.

Ismail I 1486–1524. Shah of Persia from 1501, founder of the *Safavi dynasty*, who established the first national government since the Arab conquest, and Shiite Islam as the national religion.

Ismaili a sect of ◊Shi'ite Muslims.

isobar a line drawn on maps and weather charts linking all places with the same atmospheric pressure (usually measured in millibars). When used in weather forecasting, the distance between the isobars is an indication of the barometric gradient.

isolationism in politics, concentration on internal rather than foreign affairs. In the USA, it is usually associated with the Republican Party, especially politicians of the Midwest. Intervention in both world wars was initially resisted, and after the fruitless wars in Korea and Vietnam, there was resistance to further involvement in Europe, the Pacific, or the Middle East.

isomer a chemical compound having the same molecular composition and mass as another, but with different properties, because of the different structural arrangement of the atoms in the molecules (for example, one being a 'mirror image' of another).

isoprene $CH_2:CH.C(CH_3):CH_2$ (modern name *methylbutadiene*) a volatile fluid obtained from petroleum and coal, used to make synthetic rubber.

isostasy the theoretical balance in buoyancy of all parts of the Earth's ◊crust, as though they were floating on a denser layer beneath. High mountains, for example, have very deep roots, just as an iceberg floats with most of its mass submerged.

isotherm a line on a map linking all places having the same temperature at a given time.

isotope one of two or more atoms which have the same atomic number (same number of protons), but which contain a different number of neutrons, so differ in their relative atomic mass. They may be stable or radioactive, natural or synthetic.

Israel country in SW Asia, bounded to the N by Lebanon, to the E by Syria and Jordan, to the S

isomer

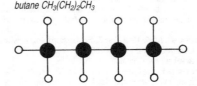

butane $CH_3(CH_2)_2CH_3$

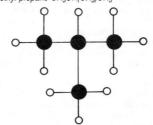

methyl propane $CH_3CH(CH_3)CH_3$

O hydrogen atom

● carbon atom

— atomic bond

Israel
State of
(*Medinat Israel*)

area 20,770 sq km/8,017 sq mi (as at 1949 armistice)
capital Jerusalem (not recognized by the UN)
towns ports Tel Aviv/Jaffa, Haifa, Eilat; Bat-Yam, Holon, Ramat Gan, Petach Tikva, Beersheba
physical coastal plain of Sharon between Haifa and Tel Aviv noted since ancient times for fertility; high arid region in S and centre; river Jordan Rift Valley along the E is below sea level
head of state Ezer Weizman from 1993
head of government Yitzhak Rabin from 1992
political system democratic republic
exports citrus and other fruit, avocados. chinese leaves, fertilizers, diamonds, plastics, petrochemicals, textiles, electronics, electro-optics, precision instruments, aircraft and missiles
currency shekel
population (1989 est) 4,477,000 (including some 750,000 Arabs as Israeli citizens and over 1 million Arabs in the occupied territories); under the Law of Return 1950, 'every Jew shall be entitled to come to Israel as an immigrant. About 500,000 Israeli-born Jews are resident in the USA. Annual growth rate 1.8%

life expectancy men 73, women 76
language Hebrew and Arabic (official); Yiddish, European and W Asian languages
religion Israel is a secular state, but the predominant faith is Judaism; also Sunni Muslim, Christian, and Druse
literacy Jewish 88%, Arab 70%
GDP $35 bn (1987); $8,011 per head
chronology
1948 Independent state of Israel proclaimed with Ben Gurion as prime minister.
1963 Ben Gurion succeeded by Levi Eshkol.
1964 Palestine Liberation Organization (PLO) founded.
1967 Israel victorious in the Six-Day War.
1968 Israel Labour Party formed, led by Golda Meir.
1969 Golda Meir became prime minister.
1974 Yom Kippur War. Golda Meir succeeded by Itzhak Rabin.
1977 Menachem Begin elected prime minister. Egyptian president addressed the Knesset.
1978 Camp David talks.
1979 Egyptian-Israeli agreement signed.
1982 Israel pursued PLO fighters into Lebanon.
1983 Agreement reached for withdrawal from Lebanon.
1985 Israeli prime minister Shimon Peres had secret talks with King Hussein of Jordan.
1986 Itzhak Shamir took over from Peres under power-sharing agreement.
1988 Criticism of Israel's handling of Palestinian uprising in occupied territories.
1989 New Likud-Labour coalition government formed under Shamir.
1990 Coalition collapsed. Widespread condemnation of Temple Mount killings. New Shamir right-wing coalition formed.
1991 Iraqi Scud missiles launched against Israel during the Gulf War. Middle East peace talks began in Barcelona.
1992 Shamir lost majority in Knesset; Rabin formed coalition after elections. 400 Palestinians expelled.
1993 100 of the expelled Palestinians allowed to return. Ban on contact with PLO formally lifted.

---

by the Gulf of Aqaba, and to the W by Egypt and the Mediterranean.

Issigonis Alec 1906–1988. Palestine-born British engineer who designed the Morris Minor 1948 and the Mini-Minor 1959 cars, thus creating modern economy motoring and adding the word 'mini' to the English language.

Istanbul city and chief seaport of Turkey; population (1990) 6,620,200. It produces textiles, tobacco, cement, glass, and leather. Founded as *Byzantium* about 660 BC, it was renamed *Constantinople* in 330, and was the capital of the ◊Byzantine Empire until captured by the Turks 1453. As *Istamboul* it was capital of the ◊Ottoman Empire until 1922.

Itagaki Taisuke 1837–1919. Japanese military and political leader, the founder of Japan's first political party, the Jiyuto (Liberal Party) in 1875. Involved in the overthrow of the Tokugawa shogunate and the Meiji restoration (see ◊Mutsuhito), Itagaki became a champion of democratic principles although continuing to serve in the government for short periods.

Italian language a member of the Romance branch of the Indo-European language family. With a strong

infusion of Latin for religious, academic and educational purposes, the written standard has tended to be highly formal and divorced from the many regional dialects (often mutually unintelligible) that are still largely the everyday usage of the general population.

italic style of printing in which the letters slope to the right, introduced by Aldus Manutius of Venice

Istanbul The Hagia Sophia in Istanbul, formerly a Christian church, converted to a mosque in 1453.

Italy
Republic of
(Repubblica Italiana)

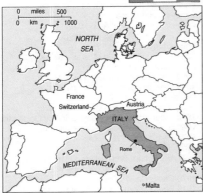

area 301,245 sq km/116,300 sq mi
capital Rome
towns Milan, Turin; ports Naples, Genoa, Palermo, Bari, Catania
physical mountainous (Maritime Alps, Dolomites, Apennines); rivers Po, Adige, Arno, Tiber, Rubicon; islands of Sicily, Sardinia, Elba, Capri, Ischia
exports wine, fruit, vegetables, textiles, clothing, leather goods, motor vehicles, electrical goods, chemicals, marble, sulphur, mercury, iron, steel

head of state Oscar Luigi Scalfaro from 1992
head of government Carlo Azeglio Ciampi from 1993
political system democratic republic
currency lira
population (1990 est) 57,657,000; annual growth rate 0.1%
life expectancy men 73, women 80 (1989)
language Italian
religion Roman Catholic (state religion)
literacy 97% (1989)
GDP $748 bn (1988); $13,052 per head
chronology
1946 Monarchy replaced by a republic.
1954 Trieste returned to Italy.
1976 Communists proposed the establishment of a broad-based, left-right government. Idea rejected by the Christian Democrats.
1978 Christian Democrat Aldo Moro kidnapped and murdered by Red Brigade guerrillas.
1983 Bettino Craxi became the socialist leader of a broad coalition government.
1987 Craxi resigned, and the succeeding coalition fell within months.
1988 Christian Democrats' leader, Ciriaco de Mita, established a five-party coalition
1989 De Mita succeeded by Ginlio Andreotti.
1991 Referendum approved electoral reform.
1992 President Cossiga resigned and was replaced by Scalfaro. Italy withdrew from the Exchange Rate Mechanism.
1993 Investigation of corruption exposed Mafia links with notable politicians, including Craxi and Andreotti. Referendum results showed that the Italian people were strongly in favour of a majority electoral system.

from 1501. It is usually used side by side with the erect Roman type, for purposes of emphasis and citation.

Italy country in S Europe, bounded N by Switzerland and Austria, E by Slovenia, Croatia, and the Adriatic Sea, S by the Ionian and Mediterranean Seas, and W by the Tyrrhenian and Ligurian Sea and France. It includes the Mediterranean islands of Sardinia and Sicily.

iteroparity in biology, the repeated production of offspring at intervals throughout the life cycle. It is usually contrasted with ◊semelparity, where each individual reproduces only once during its life. Most vertebrates are iteroparous.

Ito Hirobumi 1841–1909. Japanese politician, prime minister and a key figure in the modernization of Japan, he was also involved in the Meiji restoration under ◊Mutsuhito 1866–68 and in government missions to the USA and Europe in the 1870s. As minister for home affairs, he drafted the Meiji constitution in 1889 and oversaw its implementation as prime minister the following year.

Iturbide Augustin de 1783–1824. Mexican military leader (*caudillo*) who led the conservative faction in the nation's struggle for independence. In 1822 he crowned himself Augustin I. However his extravagance and failure to restore order led all other parties to turn against him. He reigned for less than a year.

IUCN (International Union for the Conservation of Nature) an organization established by the United Nations to promote the conservation of wildlife and habitats in the national policies of member states.

Ivan rulers of Russia, including:

Ivan III *the Great* 1440–1505. Grand duke of Muscovy from 1462, who revolted against Tatar overlordship by refusing tribute to Grand Khan

Ahmed in 1480. He claimed the title of tsar, and used the double-headed eagle as the Russian state emblem.

Ivan IV *the Terrible* 1530–1584. Grand duke of Muscovy from 1533, he assumed power 1544, and was crowned as first tsar of Russia 1547. He conquered Kazan 1552, Astrakhan 1556, and Siberia 1581. His last years alternated between debauchery and religious austerities.

Ives Charles (Edward) 1874–1954). US composer who experimented with ◊atonality, quarter tones, clashing time signatures, and quotations from popular music of the time. He wrote five symphonies, including *Holidays Symphony* 1904–13, chamber music, including the *Concord Sonata*, and the orchestral *Three Places in New England* 1903–14 and *The Unanswered Question* 1908.

Ives Frederic Eugene 1856–1937. American inventor who developed the ◊halftone process of printing photographs in 1878.

IVF abbreviation for *in vitro fertilization*.

ivory the hard white substance of which the teeth and tusks of certain animals are composed. Most valuable are elephants' tusks which are of unusual hardness and density. Ivory is used in carving and other decorative work, and is so valuable that poachers continue to destroy the remaining wild elephant herds in Africa to obtain it illegally.

Ivory Coast (French *Côte d'Ivoire*) country in W Africa, bounded to the N by Mali and Burkina Faso, E by Ghana, S by the Gulf of Guinea, and W by Liberia and Guinea.

ivy tree and shrub of the genus *Hedera*, family Araliaceae. The European ivy *Hedera helix* has shiny, evergreen, triangular or oval-shaped leaves and clusters of small, yellowish-green flowers, followed by black berries.

Ivory Coast
Republic of
(*République de la Côte d'Ivoire*)

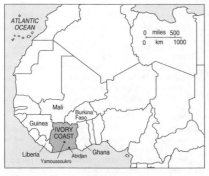

area 322, 463 sq km/127,000 sq mi
capital Abidjan; capital designate Yamoussouko

towns Bouaké, Daloa, Man
physical tropical rainforest (diminishing) in the S; savanna and low mountains in the N
head of state and government Félix Houphouët-Boigny from 1960
political system emergent democratic republic
exports coffee, cocoa, timber, petroleum
currency CFA franc
population (1990 est) 12,070,000; annual growth rate 3.3%
life expectancy men 52, women 55 (1989)
language French (official); native dialects
religion animist 65%, Muslim 24%, Christian 11%
literacy 35% (1988)
GDP $7.6 bn (1987); $687 per head
chronology
1958 Achieved internal self-government.
1960 Achieved full independence, with Félix Houphouët-Boigny as president of a one-party state.
1985 Houphouët-Boigny re-elected, unopposed.
1986 Name changed officially from Ivory Coast to Côte d'Ivoire.
1990 Houphouët-Boigny re-elected.

Ivy League a collective term for eight long-established East Coast private universities in the USA (Harvard, Yale, Princeton, Pennsylvania, Columbia, Brown, Dartmouth and Cornell).

IWW (Industrial Workers of the World) US labour movement founded 1905, popularly known as the **Wobblies**. The IWW was dedicated to the overthrow of capitalism but divided on tactics and gradually declined in popularity after 1917. At its peak 1912–15 the organization claimed to have 100,000 members, mainly in western mining and lumber areas, and in the textile mills of New England.

Demonstrations were violently suppressed by the authorities. See also ◊syndicalism.

Ixion in Greek mythology, a king whom Zeus punished for his crimes by binding him to a fiery wheel rolling endlessly through the underworld.

Izmir formerly *Smyrna* port and naval base in Turkey; population (1990) 1,747,400. Products include steel, electronics, and plastics. The largest annual trade fair in the Middle East is held here. Headquarters of ◊North Atlantic Treaty Organization SE Command.

J the symbol for joule, SI unit of energy.

jabiru species of stork *Jabiru mycteria* found in Central and South America. It is 1.5 m/5 ft high with white plumage. The head is black and red.

jacamar bird of the family Galbulidae of Central and South America. They have long sharp-pointed bills, long tails, and paired toes. The plumage is brilliantly coloured. The largest species grows to 30 cm/12 in.

jacana one of seven species of wading birds, family Jacanidae, with very long toes and claws enabling it to walk on the flat leaves of river plants, hence the name 'lily trotter'. It is found in South America, Africa, S Asia, and Australia.

jacaranda genus of American tropical ornamental trees, family Bignoniaceae, with fragrant wood and showy blue or violet flowers.

jack a tool or machine for lifting heavy weights such as vehicles. A *screw jack* uses the principle of the screw to magnify an applied effort; in a car jack, for example, turning the handle many times causes the lifting screw to rise slightly, and the effort is magnified to lift heavy weights. A *hydraulic jack* uses a succession of piston strokes to increase pressure in a liquid and force up a lifting ram.

jackal carnivorous member of the dog family found in S Asia, S Europe, and N Asia. It can grow to 80 cm/2.7 ft long, has greyish-brown fur, and a bushy tail.

Jackson English actress Glenda Jackson.

jackdaw bird *Corvus monedula* of the crow family, found in Europe and W Asia. It is black with a grey head, and about 33 cm/1.1 ft long. It nests in tree holes or on buildings.

Jackson Andrew 1767–1845. 7th president of the USA 1829–37, a Democrat. He defeated the British at New Orleans 1815, and was elected president 1828. In 1832 he vetoed the renewal of the US bank charter, and was re-elected, whereupon he continued his struggle against the power of finance.

Jackson Glenda 1936– . English actress. She has made many stage appearances and her films include the Oscar-winning *Women in Love* 1971. On television she played Queen Elizabeth I in *Elizabeth R* 1971. She was elected Labour member of parliament for Hampstead and Highgate (N London) 1992.

Jackson Jesse 1941– . US Democrat politician, campaigner for minority rights. He contested his party's 1984 and 1988 presidential nominations in an effort to increase voter registration and to put black issues on the national agenda. He is a notable public speaker.

Jackson John Hughlings 1835–1911. English neurologist and neurophysiologist. As a result of his studies of ◊epilepsy, Jackson was able to demonstrate that particular areas of the cerebral cortex (outer mantle of the brain) control the functioning of particular organs and limbs.

Jackson Michael 1958– . US singer and songwriter, noted for his meticulously choreographed performances. He had his first solo hit 1971 but his worldwide popularity reached a peak with the albums *Thriller* 1982 and *Bad* 1987.

Jackson Thomas Jonathan, known as 'Stonewall' Jackson 1824–1863. US Confederate general. In the American Civil War he acquired his nickname and his reputation at the Battle of Bull Run, from the firmness with which his brigade resisted the Northern attack. In 1862 he organized the Shenandoah valley campaign, and assisted Lee's invasion of Maryland. He helped to defeat Gen Joseph E Hooker's Union army at the battle of Chancellorsville, Virginia, but was fatally wounded by one of his own men in the confusion of battle.

Jacksonian Democracy in US history, a term describing the populist, egalitarian spirit pervading the presidencies of Andrew Jackson and Martin Van Buren, 1833–1841, which encouraged greater participation in the democratic process. Recent studies have questioned the professed commitment to popular control, emphasizing Jackson's alleged cult of personality.

Jack the Ripper popular name for the unidentified mutilator and murderer of five women prostitutes in the Whitechapel area of London 1888.

Jacob in the Old Testament, Hebrew patriarch, son of Isaac and Rebecca, who obtained the rights of seniority from his twin brother Esau by trickery. He married his cousins Leah and Rachel, serving their father Laban seven years for each, and at the time of famine in Canaan joined his son Joseph in Egypt. His 12 sons were the traditional ancestors of the 12 tribes of Israel.

Jacob François 1920– . French biochemist who, with Jacques ◊Monod, did pioneering research in molecular genetics and showed how the production of ◊proteins from ◊DNA is controlled.

Jacobean a style in the arts, particularly in architecture and furniture, during the reign of James I in England. Following the general lines of Elizabethan design, but using classical features more widely, it adopted many motifs from Italian Renaissance design.

jaguar

Jacobin member of an extremist republican club of the French Revolution founded at Versailles 1789, later using a former Jacobin friary as its Paris headquarters. Led by ◊Robespierre, it closed after his execution 1794.

Jacobite in Britain, a supporter of the royal house of Stuart after the deposition of James II 1688. They included the Scottish Highlanders, who rose un-successfully under ◊Claverhouse 1689; and those who rose in Scotland and N England under the leadership of James Francis Edward Stuart, the Old Pretender, in 1715, and followed his son ◊Charles Edward Stuart in an invasion of England which reached Derby 1745–46. After the defeat of ◊Cullo-den, Jacobitism disappeared as a political force.

Jacquard Joseph Marie 1752–1834. French textile manufacturer. In 1804 he constructed looms that used a series of punched cards which controlled the pattern of longitudinal warp threads depressed before each sideways passage of the shuttle. On later machines the punched cards were joined to form an endless loop which represented the 'pro-gram' for the repeating pattern of a carpet.

Jacquerie French peasant uprising 1358, caused by the ravages of the English army and French nobility, which reduced the rural population to destitution. The word derives from the nickname for French peasants, Jacques Bonhomme.

Jacuzzi Candido 1903–1986. US inventor and engineer, born in Italy. He invented the jacuzzi, a pump that enabled a whirlpool to be emulated in a domestic bath.

jade any of various glassy silicate minerals, especially jadeite, $NaAl(Si_2O_6)$, and nephrite, $Ca_2(Mg,Fe)_5Si_8O_{22}(OH)$, ranging from white to dark green according to the iron content. It is one of the hardest minerals known.

Jade Emperor in pantheistic Taoism, the supreme god, Yu Huang, who watches over human actions and is the rule of life and death.

Jaffa Biblical name *Joppa* port in W Israel, part of ◊Tel Aviv-Jaffa from 1950.

Jagan Cheddi 1918– . Guyanese left-wing poli-tician. Educated in British Guyana and the USA, he led the People's Progressive Party from 1950, and in 1961 he became the first prime minister of British Guyana. In 1992 he was victorious in the presiden-tial election, replacing Desmond Hoyte.

jaguar largest species of cat *Panthera onca* in the Americas. It can grow up to 2.5 m/8 ft long including the tail. The ground colour of the fur varies from creamy white to brown or black, and is covered with black spots. The jaguar is usually solitary.

jaguarundi wild cat *Felis yaguaroundi* found in forests in Central and South America. Up to 1.1 m/3.5 ft long, it is very slim, with rather short legs and short rounded ears. It is uniformly coloured dark brown or chestnut. A good climber, it feeds on birds and small mammals, and, unusually for a cat, has been reported to eat fruit.

Jahangir 'Conqueror of the World', name adopted by Salim 1569–1627. Third Mughal emperor of India from 1605, when he succeeded his father ◊Akbar the Great. He designed the Shalimar Gardens in Kashmir and buildings and gardens in Lahore.

Jahweh another spelling of ◊Jehovah, God in the Hebrew Bible or Old Testament.

jai alai another name for the ball-game ◊pelota.

Jainism Indian religion sometimes regarded as an offshoot from Hinduism. Jains believe in no god, that non-injury to living beings is the highest religion, and their ethical code is based on compassion. They also believe in ◊karma. Jainism, like Buddhism, is a monastic religion.

Jaipur capital of Rajasthan, India; population (1981) 1,005,000. Formerly the capital of the state of Jaipur, it was merged with Rajasthan 1949. Products include textiles and metal products.

Jakarta or *Djakarta* capital of Indonesia on the NW coast of Java; population (1980) 6,504,000. Industries include textiles, chemicals, and plastics; rubber, oil, tin, coffee, tea, and palm oil are among its exports.

Jakes Milos 1922– . Czech communist politician, a member of the Politburo from 1981 and party leader from 1987. A conservative, he supported the Soviet invasion of Czechoslovakia in 1968. He was forced to resign 1989 after a series of pro-democracy mass rallies.

Jamaica island in the Caribbean, to the S of Cuba, and to the W of Haiti.

James Henry 1843–1916. US novelist. The main theme of his novels was the impact of European culture on the US soul. They include *The Portrait of a Lady* 1881, *Washington Square* 1881, *The Bostonians* 1886, *The Ambassadors* 1903, and *The Golden Bowl* 1904. He also wrote more than a hundred shorter works of fiction, notably the supernatural tale *The Turn of the Screw* 1898.

Jainism The statue of Lord Bahubali (Gomateshvera) at Sravanabelagola, Tamil Nadu, one of the oldest and most important Jain pilgrimage centres in India.

Jamaica

area 11,525 sq km/4,411 sq mi
capital Kingston
towns Montego Bay, Spanish Town
physical mountainous tropical island
head of state Elizabeth II from 1962 represented by governor general

head of government P J Patterson from 1982
political system constitutional monarchy
exports sugar, bananas, bauxite, rum, coffee
currency Jamaican dollar
population (1990 est) 2,513,000; annual growth rate 2.2%
life expectancy men 75, women 78 (1989)
language English, Jamaican creole
religion Protestant 70%, Rastafarian
literacy 82% (1988)
GDP $2.9 bn (1989); $1,187 per head
chronology
1959 Granted internal self-government.
1962 Achieved full independence, with Alexander Bustamente of the Jamaica Labour Party (JLP) as prime minister.
1967 JLP re-elected under Hugh Shearer.
1972 Michael Manley of the People's National Party (PNP) became prime minister.
1980 JLP elected, with Edward Seaga as prime minister.
1983 JLP re-elected, winning all 60 seats.
1988 Island badly damaged by hurricane.
1989 PNP won a decisive victory with Michael Manley returning as prime minister.
1992 Manely resigned and was succeeded by P J Patterson.
1993 Landslide victory for PNP in general election.

James Jesse 1847–1882. US bank and train robber, born in Missouri and a leader (with his brother Frank) of the ◊Quantrill gang. Jesse was killed by an accomplice; Frank remained unconvicted and became a farmer.

James William 1842–1910. US psychologist and philosopher, brother of the novelist Henry James. He turned from medicine to psychology and taught at Harvard 1872–1907. His books include *Principles of Psychology* 1890, *Will to Believe* 1897, and *Varieties of Religious Experience* 1902, one of the most important works on the psychology of religion.

James I the Conqueror 1208–1276. King of Aragon from 1213, when he succeeded his father. He conquered the Balearic Islands and took Valencia from the Moors, dividing it with Alfonso X of Castile by a treaty 1244. Both these exploits are recorded in his autobiography *Llibre deis feyts*. He largely established Aragon as the dominant power in the Mediterranean.

James two kings of Britain:

James I 1566–1625. King of England from 1603 and Scotland (*James VI*) from 1567. The son of Mary, Queen of Scots, and Lord ◊Darnley, he succeeded on his mother's abdication from the Scottish throne, assumed power 1583, established a strong centralized authority, and in 1589 married Anne of Denmark (1574–1619). As successor to Elizabeth in England, he alienated the Puritans by his High Church views and Parliament by his assertion of divine right, and was generally unpopular because of his favourites, for example, ◊Buckingham, and because of his schemes for an alliance with Spain.

James II 1633–1701. King of England and Scotland (*James VII*) from 1685, second son of Charles I. He married Anne Hyde 1659 (1637–71, mother of Mary II and Anne) and ◊Mary of Modena 1673 (mother of James Francis Edward Stuart). He became a Catholic 1671, which led first to attempts to exclude him from the succession, then to the rebellions of ◊Monmouth and ◊Argyll, and finally to the Whig and Tory leaders' invitation to William of Orange to take the throne in 1688. James fled to France, led a rising in Ireland 1689, but after defeat at the Battle of the ◊Boyne 1690 remained in exile in France.

James seven kings of Scotland:

James I 1394–1437. King of Scotland 1406–37, who assumed power 1424. He was a cultured and strong monarch, whose improvements in the administration of justice brought him popularity among the common people. He was assassinated by a group of conspirators led by the Earl of Atholl.

James II 1430–1460. King of Scotland from 1437, assumed power 1449. He was accidentally killed while besieging Roxburgh Castle.

James III 1451–1488. King of Scotland from 1460, assumed power 1469. He was murdered during a rebellion.

James IV 1473–1513. King of Scotland from 1488, who married Margaret (1489–1541, daughter of Henry VII) 1503. He invaded England 1513, but was defeated and killed at ◊Flodden.

James V 1512–1542. King of Scotland from 1513, who assumed power 1528. Following an attack on Scottish territory by Henry VIII's forces, he was defeated near the border at Solway Moss 1542.

James VI of Scotland. See ◊James I of England.

James I The son of Mary, Queen of Scots, James I of England was already James VI of Scotland when he came to the throne in England in 1603.

Japan
(*Nippon*)

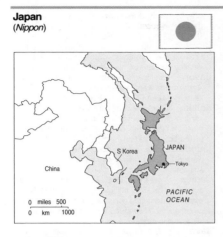

area 370,000 sq km/142,680 sq mi
capital Tokyo
towns Fukuoka, Kitakyushu, Kyoto, Sapporo;
ports Osaka, Nagoya, Yokohama, Kobe, Kawasaki
physical mountainous, volcanic; comprises over
1,000 islands, of which the chief are Hokkaido,
Honshu, Shikoku, Kyushu
head of state (figurehead) Emperor Akihito from
1989
head of government Kiichi Miyazawa from 1991
political system liberal democracy
exports electronic and electrical equipment, cars
and other vehicles, ships, iron and steel,
chemicals, textiles
currency yen
population (1990 est) 123,778,000; annual growth
rate 0.5%
life expectancy men 76, women 82 (1989)
language Japanese
religion Shinto and Buddhist (often combined),
Christian (minority).
literacy 99% (1989)
GDP $2.4 trillion (1989); $19,464 per head
chronology
1945 Japanese surrender. Allied control
commission in power.
1946 Framing of 'Peace Constitution'.
1952 Full sovereignty regained.
1958 Joined United Nations.
1972 Ryukyu Islands regained.
1974 Resignation of Prime Minister Tanaka over
Lockheed bribes scandal.
1982 Election of Yasuhiro Nakasone as prime
minister.
1987 Noboru Takeshita succeeded Nakasone.
1988 Recruit corporation insider-trading scandal
cast shadow over political parties.
1989 Emperor Hirohito died and was succeeded by
his son Akihito. Many cabinet ministers implicated
in Recruit scandal; Takeshita resigned.
1991 Japan contributed billions of dollars to the
Gulf War and its aftermath. Miyazawa became
prime minister.
1992 Over 100 politicians implicated in new
financial scandal.
1993 Worst recession of post-war era, though
trade surpluses remained high.

James VII of Scotland. See ◊James II of England.

James Francis Edward Stuart 1688–1766.
British prince, known as the Old Pretender (for
◊Jacobites James III). Son of James II, he was born
at St James's Palace and after the revolution of 1688
was taken to France. He landed in Scotland in 1715
to head a Jacobite rebellion, but withdrew for lack of
support.

Jameson Leander Starr 1853–1917. British
colonial administrator. In South Africa, early in
1896, he led the *Jameson Raid* from Mafeking into
Transvaal, in support of the non-Boer colonists
there, in an attempt to overthrow the government,
for which he served some months in prison. Returning to South Africa, he succeeded Cecil ◊Rhodes as
leader of the Progressive Party of Cape Colony,
where he was prime minister 1904–08.

James, St the Great died 44 AD. New Testament
apostle, originally a Galilean fisherman, the son of
Zebedee and brother of the apostle John. He was put
to death by ◊Herod Agrippa I. Patron saint of Spain.
Feast day 25 Jul.

James, St the Just 1st century AD. The New
Testament brother of Jesus, to whom Jesus
appeared after the Resurrection. Leader of the
Christian church in Jerusalem, he was the author of
the biblical Epistle of James.

Jammu and Kashmir state of N India
area 222,236 sq km/85,783 sq mi, of which 35%
is currently occupied by Pakistan, and 20% by
China.
capital Srinagar (winter); Jammu (summer)
towns Leh
products timber, grain, rice, fruit, silk, carpets
population (1991) 7,718,700 (Indian-occupied
territory)
history In 1947 Jammu was attacked by Pakistan
and chose to become part of the new state of India.
Dispute over the area caused further hostilities
1971 between India and Pakistan (ended by the
Simla agreement 1972).

Janáček Leoš 1854–1928. Czech composer. His
music, highly original and influenced by Moravian
folk music, includes arrangements of folk songs,
operas (*Jenufa* 1904, *The Cunning Little Vixen*
1924), and the choral *Glagolitic Mass* 1927.

Janam Sakhis a collection of stories about the life
of Nanak, the first guru (teacher) of Sikhism.

Janata alliance of political parties in India formed
1971 to oppose Indira Gandhi's Congress Party.
Victory in the election brought Morarji Desai to
power as prime minister but he was unable to
control the various groups within the alliance and
resigned 1979. His successors fared little better and
the elections of 1980 overwhelmingly returned
Indira Gandhi to office.

Jane Eyre a novel by Charlotte Brontë, published
1847. Jane, an orphan, is engaged as governess to
Mr Rochester's ward Adèle. Rochester and Jane fall
in love, but their wedding is prevented by the
revelation that Rochester already has a wife. Jane
flees, but later returns to find the house destroyed
by fire and Rochester blinded in a vain attempt to
save his wife. Jane and Rochester marry.

janissary bodyguard of the sultan, the Turkish
standing army 1330–1826. Until the 16th century
janissaries were Christian boys forcibly converted
to Islam; after this time they were allowed to marry,
and recruit their own children. The bodyguard
ceased to exist when it revolted against the

decision of the sultan in 1826 to raise a regular force.

Jansen Cornelius 1585–1638. Dutch Roman Catholic theologian, founder of Jansenism with his book *Augustinus* 1640.

Jansenism Christian teaching, which divided the Roman Catholic Church in France in the mid-17th century. Emphasizing the more predestinatory approach of Augustine's teaching, as opposed to that of the Jesuits, Jansenism was supported by the philosopher Pascal and Antoine Arnauld (a theologian linked with the abbey of Port Royal, SW of Paris). Jansenists were excommunicated 1719.

Jansky Karl Guthe 1905–1950. US radio engineer, who discovered that the Milky Way galaxy emanates radio waves.

Janus in Roman mythology, god of doorways and passageways, the patron of the beginning of the day, month, and year, after whom January is named; he is represented as two-faced, looking in opposite directions.

Japan country in E Asia, occupying a group of islands of which the four main ones are Hokkaido, Honshu, Kyushu, and Shikoku. Japan is situated in the N Pacific, to the E of North and South Korea.

Japan Current or *Kuroshio Current* warm ocean ◊current flowing from Japan to North America.

Japanese language a traditionally isolated language of E Asia, spoken almost exclusively in the islands of Japan. Possibly related to Korean, Japanese is culturally and linguistically influenced by Mandarin Chinese and written in Chinese-derived ideograms as well as syllabic alphabets.

Japji Sikh morning hymn which consists of verses from the beginning of the holy book *Guru Granth Sahib*.

Jarry Alfred 1873–1907. French satiric dramatist, whose *Ubu Roi* 1896 foreshadowed the Theatre of the ◊Absurd and the French surrealist movement.

Jaruzelski Wojciech 1923– . Polish general, communist leader from 1981, president 1985–90. He imposed martial law for the first year of his rule, suppressed the opposition and banned trade union activity, but later released many political prisoners. In 1989, elections in favour of the free trade union Solidarity forced Jaruzelski to speed up democratic reforms. He oversaw the transition to a new form of 'socialist pluralist' democracy and stepped down as president 1990.

Jarvik 7 the first successful artificial heart intended for permanent implantation in a human being. Made from polyurethane plastic and aluminium, it is powered by compressed air. Dr Barney Clark became the first person to receive a Jarvik 7 in Salt Lake City Dec 1982; it kept him alive for 112 days.

jasmine genus of plants *Jasminium*, family Oleaceae, with fragrant white/yellow flowers, and yielding jasmine oil, used in perfumes.

Jason in Greek mythology, leader of the *Argonauts* who sailed in the *Argo* to Colchis in search of the ◊Golden Fleece.

Jataka collections of Buddhist legends compiled at various dates in several countries; the oldest and most complete has 547 stories. They were collected before 400 AD.

jaundice the yellow discoloration of the skin caused by an excess of bile pigment in the bloodstream.

Jaurès Jean Léon 1859–1914. French socialist politician. In 1893 he joined the Socialist Party, established a united party, and in 1904 founded the newspaper *L'Humanité*, becoming its editor until his assassination.

Java or *Jawa* the most important island of Indonesia, situated between Sumatra and Bali.
area (with the island of Madura) 132,000 sq km/ 51,000 sq mi
capital Jakarta (also capital of Indonesia)
towns ports include Surabaja and Semarang
physical about half the island is under cultivation, the rest being thickly forested. Mountains and sea breezes keep temperatures down, but humidity is high, with heavy rainfall Dec–Mar.
exports rice, coffee, cocoa, tea, sugar, rubber, quinine, teak, and petroleum.
population (with Madura) (1989) 107,513,800; including people of Javanese, Sundanese, and Madurese origin, with differing languages
religion predominantly Muslim
history Occupied by Japan 1942–45 while under Dutch control, Java then became part of the republic of ◊Indonesia.

jaws the bony structures that form the framework of the mouth in all vertebrates except lampreys and hagfish (the agnathous or jawless vertebrates). They consist of the upper jaw bone or maxilla, and the lower jawbone, or mandible; the latter is hinged at each side to the bone of the temple by ◊ligaments.

jay genus of birds *Garrulus* of the crow family, common in Europe, Asia, and the Americas.

Jayawardene Janius Richard 1906– . Sri Lankan politician. Leader of the United Nationalist Party from 1973, he became prime minister 1977, and the country's first president.

jay

Japan A typical Japanese housing estate.

jazz polyphonic, syncopated music characterized by improvisation, which developed in the USA at the turn of this century out of black American and other indigenous popular music.
1880–1900 Originated chiefly in New Orleans from ragtime.
1920s Centre of jazz moved to Chicago (Louis Armstrong, Bix Beiderbecke) and St Louis.
1930s The *swing* bands used call-and-response arrangements with improvised solos (Paul Whiteman, Benny Goodman).
1940s Swing grew into the *big band* era (Glenn Miller, Duke Ellington); rise of *West Coast* jazz (Stan Kenton) and rhythmically complex, highly improvisational *bebop* (Charlie Parker, Dizzy Gillespie, Thelonius Monk).
1950s Jazz had ceased to be dance music; *cool jazz* (Stan Getz, Miles Davis, Modern Jazz Quartet) developed in reaction to the insistent, 'hot' bebop and *hard bop*.
1960s Free-form or free jazz (Ornette Coleman, John Coltrane).
1970s Jazz rock (US group Weather Report, formed 1970; British guitarist John McLaughlin, 1942–); jazz funk (US saxophonist Grover Washington Jr, 1943–); more eclectic free jazz (US pianist Keith Jarrett, 1945–).
1980s Resurgence of tradition (US trumpeter Wynton Marsalis, 1962– ; British saxophonist Courtney Pine, 1965–) and avant-garde (US chamber-music Kronos Quartet, formed 1978; anarchic British group Loose Tubes).

J-curve in economics, a graphic illustration of the likely effect of a currency devaluation on the balance of payments. Initially, there will be a deterioration as import prices increase and export prices decline, followed by a decline in import volume and upsurge of export volume. In statistics, it is called a frequency curve.

jeans denim trousers, traditionally blue, originating in jean cloth (from 'jene fustian', a heavy canvas material made in Genoa, Italy), which was first used in Liverpool, England, about 1850 to make working clothes. Levi Strauss (1830–1902), a Bavarian immigrant to the USA, made trousers for goldminers in San Francisco out of jean material intended for wagon covers. Hence they became known as 'Levis'. Later a French fabric *serge de Nîmes* (corrupted to 'denim') was used.

Jeans James Hopwood 1877–1946. English mathematician and scientist. In physics, he contributed work on the kinetic theory of gases, and forms of energy radiation; and in astronomy, on giant and dwarf stars, the nature of spiral nebulae, and the origin of the cosmos. He also did much to popularize astronomy.

Jedda alternative spelling for the Saudi Arabian port ◊Jiddah.

Jefferson Thomas 1743–1826. 3rd president of the USA 1801–09, founder of the Democratic Party. He published *A Summary View of the Rights of America* 1774 and as a member of the Continental Congresses 1775–76 was largely responsible for the drafting of the Declaration of Independence. He was governor of Virginia 1779–81, ambassador to Paris 1785–89, secretary of state 1789–93, and vice president 1797–1801.

Jeffrey Francis, Lord 1773–1850. Scottish lawyer and literary critic. Born at Edinburgh, he was a founder and editor of the *Edinburgh Review* 1802–29. In 1830 he was made Lord Advocate, and in 1834 a Scottish law lord. He was hostile to the Romantic poets, and

wrote of Wordsworth's *Excursion*: 'This will never do.'

Jeffreys George, 1st Baron 1648–1689. British judge. Born in Denbighshire, Scotland, he became Chief Justice of the King's Bench in 1683, and presided over many political trials, notably those of Sidney, Oates, and Baxter, becoming notorious for his brutality.

Jehosophat 4th king of Judah c. 873–849 BC; he allied himself with Ahab, king of Israel, in the war against Syria.

Jehovah also *Jahweh* in the Old Testament, another name for God; in the original Hebrew, it was YHVH, to which the vowels 'a o a' were later added.

Jehovah's Witness a member of a religious organization originating in the USA 1872 under Charles Taze Russell (1852–1916). Jehovah's Witnesses attach great importance to Christ's second coming, which Russell predicted would occur 1914, and which Witnesses still believe is imminent. All Witnesses are expected to take part in house-to-house preaching; there are no clergy. Membership (1986) about 1 million.

Jehu king of Israel c. 842–815 BC. He led a successful rebellion against the family of ◊Ahab and was responsible for the death of Jezebel. He was noted for his furious chariot-driving.

jellyfish marine animal of the phylum Cnidaria (coelenterates) with an umbrella-shaped body composed of a semi-transparent gelatinous substance, with a fringe of stinging tentacles. Most jellyfish move freely, but some are attached by a stalk to rocks or seaweed. They feed on small animals which are paralysed by their sting.

Jenkins Roy (Harris) 1920– . British politician. He became a Labour minister 1964, was home secretary 1965–67 and 1974–76, and chancellor of the Exchequer 1967–70. In 1981 he became one of the founders of the Social Democratic Party and was elected SDP Member of Parliament 1982, but lost his seat 1987.

Jenkins's Ear, War of war between Britain and Spain 1739 which later became part of the War of ◊Austrian Succession 1740–48. The name derives from the claim of Robert Jenkins, a merchant captain, that his ear had been cut off by Spanish coastguards near Jamaica. The incident was seized on by opponents of Robert ◊Walpole seeking to embarrass his government's anti-war policy and to force war with Spain.

Jenner Edward 1749–1823. English physician who pioneered vaccination. In Jenner's day, smallpox was a major killer. His discovery that inoculation with cowpox gives immunity to smallpox was a great medical breakthrough. He coined the word vaccination from the Latin word for cowpox *vaccina*.

Jerablus ancient Syrian city, adjacent to Carchemish on the Euphrates.

jerboa several genera of rodents, about 15–20 cm/6–8 in long, found in Africa, Asia, and E Europe. They are mainly herbivorous and nocturnal.

Jeremiah 7th century BC. Old Testament Hebrew prophet, whose ministry continued 626–586 BC. He was imprisoned during ◊Nebuchadnezzar's siege of Jerusalem on suspicion of intending to desert to the enemy. On the city's fall, he retired to Egypt.

Jericho Israeli-administered town in Jordan, N of the Dead Sea. It was settled by 8000 BC, and by 6000 BC had become a walled city with 2,000 inhabitants. In the Old Testament it was the first Canaanite stronghold captured by the Israelites, its walls, according to the Book of ◊Joshua, falling to the blast of Joshua's trumpets. Successive archaeological excavations since 1907 show that the walls of the city were destroyed many times.

Jeroboam first king of Israel c. 922–901 BC after the split with Judah.

Jerome Jerome K(lapka) 1859–1927. English journalist and writer. His works include the humorous essays *Idle Thoughts of an Idle Fellow* 1889, the novel *Three Men in a Boat* 1889, and the play *The Passing of the Third Floor Back* 1907.

Jerome, St c. 340–420. one of the early Christian leaders and scholars known as the Fathers of the Church. His Latin versions of the Old and New Testaments form the basis of the Roman Catholic Vulgate. He is usually depicted with a lion. Feast day 30 Sept.

Jersey largest of the ◊Channel Islands; capital St Helier; area 117 sq km/45 sq mi; population (1986) 80,000. Governed by a lieutenant-governor representing the English Crown and an assembly. Like Guernsey, it is famous for its cattle.

Jerusalem ancient city of Palestine, divided 1948 between Jordan and the new republic of Israel; area (pre-1967) 37.5 sq km/14.5 sq mi, (post-1967) 108 sq km/42 sq mi, including areas of the West Bank; population (1983) 479,000. In 1950 the western New City was proclaimed as the Israeli capital, and, having captured from Jordan the eastern Old City 1967, Israel affirmed 1980 that the united city was the country's capital; the United Nations does not recognize the claim.

Jervis John, Earl of St Vincent 1735–1823. English admiral. A rigid disciplinarian, he secured the blockage of Toulon in 1795, and the defeat of the Spanish fleet off Cape St Vincent

1797, in which Captain ◊Nelson played a key part.

Jesuit a member of the largest and most influential Roman Catholic religious order, also known as the *Society of Jesus*, founded by Ignatius Loyola 1534, dissolved 1773, re-established 1814. During the 16th and 17th centuries Jesuits achieved success as missionaries in Japan, China, Paraguay, and among the North American Indians. The order has about 29,000 members (15,000 priests plus students and lay members).

Jesus c. 4 BC–c. 30 AD. Jewish preacher on whose teachings ◊Christianity was founded. According to the accounts of his life in the four Gospels of the New Testament, he was born in Bethlehem, Palestine, son of God and the Virgin Mary, and brought up as a carpenter in Nazareth. After adult baptism, he gathered 12 disciples, but his preaching antagonized the authorities and he was executed. Three days after the Crucifixion there came reports of his resurrection and, later, ascension to heaven.

jet a mineral similar in composition to lignite and ◊anthracite. Ornaments made of jet have been found in Bronze Age tombs.

JET *J*oint *E*uropean *T*orus. A ◊tokamak machine built in England to conduct experiments on nuclear fusion. It is the focus of the European effort to produce a practical fusion power reactor.

jeté (French 'thrown') in dance, a jump from one foot on to the other. A *grand jeté* is a big jump in which the dancer pushes off on one foot, holds a brief pose in mid-air and lands lightly on the other foot.

jetfoil an advanced kind of ◊hydrofoil boat built by ◊Boeing, which is propelled by water jets. It features horizontal, fully submerged hydrofoils fore

jet propulsion

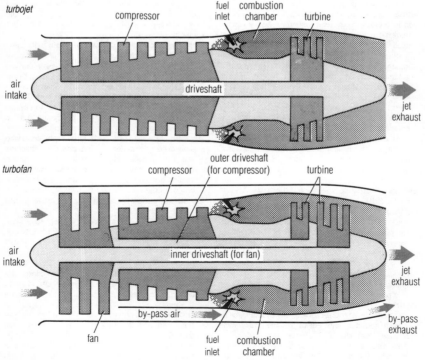

Jinnah *Muhammad Ali Jinnah, first governor general of Pakistan.*

and aft, and has a sophisticated computerized control system to maintain its stability in all waters.

jetlag effect of a sudden switch of time-zones in jet air travel, resulting in tiredness and feeling 'out of step' with day and night. See ◊circadian rhythm.

jet propulsion a method of propulsion in which an object is propelled in one direction by a jet, or stream of gases, moving in the other. This follows from ◊Newton's celebrated third law of motion 'to every action, there is an equal and opposite reaction'. The most widespread application of the jet principle is in the jet engine, the commonest kind of aero-engine.

jetsam goods deliberately sunk in the sea to lighten a vessel in a storm, or wreck. See under ◊flotsam.

jet stream a narrow band of very fast wind (velocities of over 150 kph/95 mph) found at altitudes of 10–16 km/6–10 mi in the upper troposphere or lower stratosphere. Jet streams usually occur about the latitudes of the Westerlies (35–60°).

Jew a follower of ◊Judaism, the Jewish religion. The term is also used to refer to members of the ethnic group, who may or may not practise the religion or identify with the cultural tradition. Prejudice against Jews is termed ◊anti-Semitism.

Jew's harp musical instrument, an iron frame held in the teeth, which has a steel strip twanged with the fingers. Different notes are obtained by changing the shape of the mouth.

Jezebel in the Old Testament, daughter of the king of Sidon. She married King Ahab of Israel, and was brought into conflict with the prophet Elijah by her introduction of the worship of Baal.

Jiang Jie Shi alternative transcription of Chinese leader ◊Chiang Kai-shek.

Jiang Qing formerly *Chiang Ching* 1913– Chinese communist politician, wife of the party leader Mao Zedong. In 1960 she became minister for culture, and played a key role in the 1966–69 Cultural Revolution as the leading member of the Shanghai-based Gang of Four, who attempted to seize power 1976. Jiang was imprisoned.

Jiangsu (formerly *Kiangsu*) province on the coast of E China.
area 102,200 sq km/39,450 sq mi
capital Nanjing
products cereals, rice, tea, cotton, soya, fish; silk; ceramics, textiles; coal, iron and copper; cement

population (1985) 61,710,000.

Jiangxi (formerly *Kiangsi*) province of SE China
area 164,800 sq km/63,613 sq mi
capital Nanchang
products rice, tea, cotton, tobacco; porcelain; coal, tungsten, uranium
population (1985) 34,210,000
history the province was ◊Mao Zedong's original base in the first phase of the Communist struggle against the Nationalists.

Jiddah or *Jedda* port in Hejaz, Saudi Arabia, on the E shore of the Red Sea; population (1982) 1,200,000. Industries include cement, steel, oil refining. Pilgrims pass through here on their way to Mecca.

jihad (Arabic 'conflict') a holy war undertaken by Muslims against non-believers.

Jilin (formerly Kirin) province of NE China in Central Manchuria.
area 187,000 sq km/72,180 sq mi
capital Changchun
population (1985) 22,840,000.

Jim Crow originally a derogatory US term for a black person. *Jim Crow laws* is a general term for the body of laws designed to deny civil rights to blacks or to enforce the policy of segregation, which existed in parts of the USA until Supreme Court decisions and civil-rights legislation of the 1950s and 1960s (Civil Rights Act 1964, Voting Rights Act 1965) denied their legality.

Jinan (formerly *Tsinan*) city and capital of Shandong province, China; population (1986) 1,430,000. It has food processing and textile industries.

jingoism truculent and blinkered patriotism. The term originated 1878, when British prime minister Disraeli's pro-Turkish policy nearly involved the UK in war with Russia. His supporters' war song included the line 'We don't want to fight, but by jingo if we do...'.

jinn in Muslim mythology, a spirit able to assume human or animal shape.

Jinnah Muhammad Ali 1876–1948. Indian politician, active in the creation of Pakistan as a separate, Muslim state; he was its first governor general from 1947. He advised the UK government on the need for a separate state of Pakistan in 1942, and at the 1946 conferences in London he insisted on the partition of British India into Hindu and Muslim states.

Jinsha Jiang river of China, which rises in SW China, and forms the Chang Jiang (Yangtze) at Yibin.

Jivaro American Indian peoples of E Ecuador and N Peru. They live by farming, hunting, fishing, and weaving; the Jivaro language belongs to the Andean-Equatorial family. They were formerly famous for preserving the hair and shrunken skin of the heads of their enemies as battle trophies.

jive an energetic dance popular in the USA from the 1940s.

Joan of Arc, St 1412–1431. French military leader. In 1429 at Chinon, NW France, she persuaded Charles VII that she had a divine mission to expel the English from France (see ◊Hundred Years' War) and secure his coronation. She raised the siege of Orléans, defeated the English at Patay, north of Orléans, and Charles was crowned in Reims. However, she failed to take Paris, and was captured May 1430 by the Burgundians, who sold her to the English. She was found guilty of witchcraft and heresy by a tribunal of French ecclesiastics who supported the English. She was burned in Rouen 30 May 1431. In 1920 she was canonized.

Job *c.* 5th century BC. in the Old Testament, Jewish leader who in the *Book of Job* questioned God's infliction of suffering on the righteous and endured great sufferings himself.

jobber former name (to Oct 1986) for a dealer on the London stock exchange who negotiated with a broker who, in turn, dealt with the general public.

Jodl Alfred 1892–1946. German general. In World War II he drew up the Nazi government's plan for the attack on Yugoslavia, Greece, and the USSR, and in Jan 1945 became chief of staff. He headed the delegation that signed Germany's surrender in Reims 7 May 1945. He was tried for war crimes in Nuremberg 1945–46, and hanged.

Jodrell Bank site in Cheshire, England, of the Nuffield Radio Astronomy Laboratories of the University of Manchester. Its largest instrument is the 76 m/250 ft radio dish, completed 1957 and modified 1970. A 38 m × 25 m/125 ft × 82 ft elliptical radio dish was introduced 1964, capable of working at shorter wavelengths.

Joffre Joseph Jacques Césaire 1852–1931. Marshal of France during World War I. The German invasion of Belgium 1914 took him by surprise, but his stand on the ◊Marne resulted in his appointment as supreme commander of all the French armies 1915. His failure to make adequate preparations at Verdun 1916 and the military disasters on the ◊Somme led to his replacement by Nivelle Dec 1916.

Johannesburg largest city of South Africa, situated on the Witwatersrand in Transvaal; population (1985) 1,609,400. It is the centre of a large gold mining industry; other industries include engineering works, meat-chilling plants, and clothing factories.

John Augustus (Edwin) 1878–1961. Welsh painter of landscapes and portraits, including *The Smiling Woman* 1910 (Tate Gallery, London) of his second wife, Dorelia. He was the brother of Gwen John.

John Elton. Stage name of Reginald Dwight 1947– . English pop singer, pianist, and composer, noted for his melodies and elaborate costumes and eyeglasses.

John Gwen 1876–1939. Welsh painter who lived in France for most of her life. Many of her paintings depict Dominican nuns (she converted to Catholicism 1913); she also painted calm, muted interiors.

John (John Lackland) 1167–1216. King of England from 1199. He lost Normandy and almost all of the other English possessions in France to the French, and succeeded in provoking Pope Innocent III to excommunicate England 1208–13. After the revolt of the barons he was forced to seal the Magna Carta 1215 at Runnymede on the Thames.

John two kings of France, including:

John II 1319–1364. King from 1350. He was defeated and captured by the Black Prince at Poitiers 1356. Released 1360, he failed to raise the money for his ransom and returned to England 1364, where he died.

John twenty-three popes, including:

John XXII 1249–1334. Pope 1316–34. He spent his papacy in Avignon, France, engaged in a long conflict with the Holy Roman emperor, Louis of Bavaria, and the Spiritual Franciscans, a monastic order who preached the absolute poverty of the clergy.

John XXIII (Baldassare Costa) died 1419. Antipope 1410–15. In an attempt to end the ◊Great Schism he was elected pope by a council of cardinals in Bologna, but was deposed by the Council of Constance 1415, together with the popes of Avignon and Rome. His papacy is not recognized by the church.

John XXIII Angelo Giuseppe Roncalli 1881–1963. Pope from 1958. He improved relations with the USSR in line with his encyclical *Pacem in Terris/Peace on Earth* 1963, established Roman Catholic hierarchies in newly emergent states, and summoned the Second Vatican Council, which reformed church liturgy and backed the ecumenical movement.

John three kings of Poland, including:

John III (Sobieski) 1624–1696. King of Poland from 1674. He became commander-in-chief of the army 1668 after victories over the Cossacks and Tatars. A victory over the Turks 1673 helped to get him elected to the Polish throne, and he saved Vienna from the besieging Turks 1683.

John six kings of Portugal, including:

John I 1357–1433. King of Portugal from 1385. An illegitimate son of Pedro I, he was elected by the Cortes. His claim was supported by an English army against the rival king of Castile, thus establishing the Anglo-Portuguese Alliance 1386. He married Philippa of Lancaster, daughter of ◊John of Gaunt.

John IV 1603–1656. King of Portugal from 1640. Originally Duke of Braganza, he was elected king when the Portuguese rebelled against Spanish rule. His reign was marked by a long war against Spain, which did not end until 1668.

John VI 1769–1826. King of Portugal, and regent for his insane mother *Maria I* from 1799 until her death 1816. He fled to Brazil when the French invaded Portugal 1807, and did not return until 1822. On his return Brazil declared its independence, with John's elder son Pedro as emperor.

John Bull an imaginary figure used as a personification of England. The name was popularized by Dr ◊Arbuthnot's *History of John Bull* 1712. He is represented as a prosperous farmer of the 18th century.

John of Damascus, St *c.* 676–*c.* 754. Eastern Orthodox theologian and hymn writer, a defender of image worship against the iconoclasts. Feast day 4 Dec. Contained in his *The Fountain of Knowledge* is *An Accurate Exposition of the Orthodox Faith*, an important chronicle of theology from the 4th–7th centuries.

John of Gaunt 1340–1399. English politician, born in Ghent, fourth son of Edward III, duke of Lancaster from 1362. During Edward's last years, and the years before Richard II attained the age

John Paul II The first Polish pope, John Paul II.

Johns Zero Through Nine *(1961) Tate Gallery, London.*

of majority, he acted as head of government, and Parliament protested against his corrupt rule. He supported the religious reformer Wycliffe against ecclesiastical influence at court.

John of Salisbury *c.* 1115–1180. English philosopher and historian. His *Policraticus* portrayed the church as the guarantee of liberty against the unjust claims of secular authority.

John Paul I Albino Luciani 1912–1978. Pope 26 Aug–28 Sept 1978. His name was chosen as the combination of his two immediate predecessors.

John Paul II Karol Wojtyla 1920– . Pope 1978– , the first non-Italian to be elected pope since 1522. He was born near Kraków, Poland. His reassertion of papal infallibility and condemnation of artificial contraception, female and married priests, and modern dress for monks and nuns have aroused criticism. He has warned against involvement of priests in political activity.

Johns Jasper 1930– . US painter, sculptor, and printmaker, a pioneer of Pop art and Minimal art. Works include the *Flags, Targets,* and *Numbers* series first exhibited 1958.

John, St 1st century AD. New Testament apostle. Traditionally, he wrote the fourth Gospel and the Johannine Epistles when bishop of Ephesus and the

Johnson *Ben Johnson at the Seoul Olympics, 1988.*

Book of Revelation while exiled to the Greek island of Patmos. His emblem is an eagle, his feast day 27 Dec.

Johnson Amy 1904–1941. English aviator. She made a solo flight from Croydon, S London, to Australia 1930, in 19½ days, and in 1932 made the fastest ever solo flight to Cape Town, South Africa. Her plane disappeared over the English Channel in World War II while she was serving with the Air Transport Auxiliary.

Johnson Andrew 1808–1875. 17th president of the USA 1865–69, a Democrat. He was a congressman from Tennessee 1843–53, governor of Tennessee 1853–57, senator 1857–62, and became vice-president 1864. He succeeded to the presidency on Lincoln's assassination. His conciliatory policy to the defeated South after the Civil War involved him in a feud with the radical Republicans, culminating in his impeachment before the Senate 1868, which failed to convict him by one vote.

Johnson Ben 1961– . Canadian sprinter. In 1987, he broke the world record for the 100 metres, running it in 9.83 seconds. At the Olympic Games 1988, he again broke the record, but was disqualified and suspended for using anabolic steroids to enhance his performance. He returned to competitive racing 1991, but in 1993 was banned for life after again testing positive for drug use.

Johnson Lyndon (Baines) 1908–1973. 36th president of the USA 1963–69, a Democrat. He was elected to Congress 1937–49 and to the Senate 1949–60. He stood as vice president 1960, bringing crucial Southern votes to J F Kennedy, after whose assassination he succeeded as president. The escalation of US involvement in the ◊Vietnam War eventually dissipated the support won by his *Great Society* legislation (civil rights, education, alleviation of poverty), and he declined to stand for re-election 1968.

Johnson *Amy Johnson, British pilot of the 1930s.*

Johnson *Lyndon B Johnson became president of the USA after Kennedy's assassination in 1963.*

Johnson *Portrait of Samuel Johnson by James Barry (c. 1777) National Portrait Gallery, London.*

Johnson Samuel, known as 'Dr Johnson' 1709–1784. English lexicographer, author, and critic, also noted as a brilliant conversationalist and the dominant figure in 18th-century London literary society. His *Dictionary*, published 1755, remained authoritative for over a century, and is still remarkable for the vigour of its definitions. In 1764 he founded the 'Literary Club' whose members included Reynolds, Burke, Goldsmith, Garrick, and ◊Boswell, Johnson's biographer.

Johnson Uwe 1934– . German novelist, who left East Germany for West Berlin 1959, and wrote of the division of Germany, in works such as *Anniversaries* 1977.

John the Baptist, St *c.* 12 BC–*c.* 27 AD. In the New Testament, an itinerant preacher. After preparation in the wilderness, he proclaimed the coming of Jesus Christ, baptized him in the river Jordan, and was executed by ◊Herod Antipas at the request of Salome. His emblem is a lamb. Feast day 24 Jun.

joie de vivre (French) joy of living.

joint in any animal with a skeleton, a point of movement or articulation. In invertebrates with an ◊exoskeleton, the joints are places where the exoskeleton is replaced by a more flexible outer covering, the arthrodial membrane, which allows the limb (or other body part) to bend at that point. In vertebrates, it is the point where two bones meet. Some joints allow no motion (the sutures of the skull), others allow a very small motion (the sacro-iliac joints in the lower back), but most allow a relatively free motion. Of these, some allow a gliding motion (one vertebra of the spine on another), some have a hinge action (elbow and knee), and others allow motion in all directions (hip and shoulder joints), by means of a ball-and-socket arrangement. The ends of the bones at a moving joint are covered with cartilage for greater elasticity and smoothness, and enclosed in an envelope (capsule) of tough white fibrous tissue lined with a membrane which secretes lubricating (◊synovial) fluid. The joint is further strengthened by ligaments.

Joint European Torus an experimental nuclear fusion machine, known as ◊JET.

joint venture in business, an undertaking in which an individual or legal entity of one country forms a company with those of another country, with risks being shared.

Joinville Jean, Sire de Joinville 1224–1317. French historian, born in Champagne. He accompanied Louis IX on the crusade of 1248–54, which he described in his *History of St Louis*.

joint

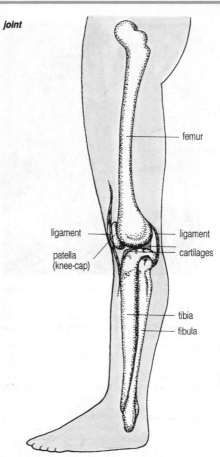

Jolson Al. Stage name of Asa Yoelson 1886–1950. US singer, born in Russia. He became famous as the star of the first sound-film, *The Jazz Singer* 1927.

Jonah 7th century BC. Hebrew prophet whose name is given to a book in the Old Testament. According to this, he fled by ship to evade his mission to prophesy the destruction of Nineveh. The crew threw him overboard in a storm, as a bringer of ill fortune, and he spent three days and nights in the belly of a whale before coming to land.

Jonathan Chief (Joseph) Leabua 1914–1987. Lesotho politician. As prime minister of Lesotho 1965–86, he played a pragmatic role, allying himself in turn with South Africa, then with the Organization of African Unity. His rule was ended by a coup in 1986.

Jones Inigo 1573–*c.* 1652. English architect. Born in London, he studied in Italy, and was influenced by the works of Palladio. He was employed by James I to design scenery for Ben Jonson's masques. In 1619 he designed his English Renaissance masterpiece, the banqueting-room at Whitehall, London.

Jones John Paul 1747–1792. American naval officer in the War of Independence in 1775. Heading a small French-sponsored squadron in the *Bonhomme Richard*, he captured the British warship *Serapis* 23 Sept 1779 in a bloody battle off Scarborough.

Jones Robert Tyre 'Bobby' 1902–1971. US golfer. He was the game's greatest amateur player who

Jones A drawing after Robert Van Voerst of English architect Inigo Jones, National Portrait Gallery, London.

never turned professional but won 13 major amateur and professional tournaments, including the Grand Slam of the amateur and professional opens of both the US and Britain in 1930.

Jonestown commune of the People's Temple Sect, NW of Georgetown, Guyana, established 1974 by Jim Jones (1933–78), who originally founded the sect among San Francisco's black community. Complaints of oppression of his black subjects led to a visit by a US congressman who was shot, with his companions. After this Jones enforced mass suicide on his followers by drinking cyanide; 914 died, including over 240 children.

jonquil a species of small daffodil *Narcissus*

jonquilla, family Amaryllidaceae, with yellow flowers. Native to Spain and Portugal, it is cultivated elsewhere.

Jönköping town at the S end of Lake Vättern, Sweden; population (1990) 111,500. It is an industrial centre in an agricultural and forestry region.

Jonson Ben(jamin) 1572–1637. English dramatist, poet, and critic. *Every Man in his Humour* 1598, established the English 'comedy of humours', in which each character embodies a 'humour' or vice such as green, lust, or avarice. This was followed by *Every Man out of his Humour* 1599, *Cynthia's Revels* 1600 and *Poetaster* 1601. His first extant tragedy is *Sejanus* 1603, with Burbage and Shakespeare as a member of the original cast.

The great plays of his middle years include *Volpone, or The Fox* 1606, *The Alchemist* 1610, and *Bartholomew Fair* 1614.

Joplin Janis 1943–1970. US blues and acid-rock singer, born in Texas, who became a symbol and victim of the 1960s drug culture. She was lead singer with the San Francisco group Big Brother and the Holding Company from 1966 and started a solo career in 1969 with the album *Kozmic Blues*. Her biggest hit, Kris Kristofferson's 'Me and Bobby McGee', was released on the posthumous *Pearl* LP 1971.

Joplin Scott 1868–1917. US pianist and composer in Chicago, the leading exponent of ⟨ragtime. His 'Maple Leaf Rag' 1899 was the first instrumental sheet music to sell a million copies, and 'The Entertainer', as the theme tune of the film *The Sting* 1973, revived his popularity. He was an

Jordan
Hashemite Kingdom of
(*Al Mamlaka al Urduniya al Hashemiyah*)

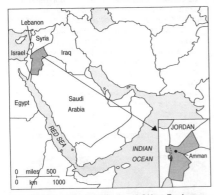

area 89,206 sq km/34,434 sq mi (West Bank, incorporated into Jordan 1950 but occupied by Israel since 1967, area 5,879 sq km/2,269 sq mi)
capital Amman
towns Zarqa, Irbid, Aqaba (the only port)
physical mostly desert
head of state King Hussein ibn Talai from 1952
head of government Mudar Badran from 1989
political system constitutional monarchy
exports potash, phosphates, citrus
currency Jordanian dinar
population (1990 est) 3,065,000 (including Palestinian refugees); West Bank (1988) 866,000; annual growth rate 3.6%
life expectancy men 67, women 71

language Arabic (official); English
religion Sunni Muslim 92%, Christian 8%
literacy 87% male/63% female (1985 est)
GDP $4.3 bn (1987); $1,127 per head
chronology
1946 Achieved full independence as Transjordan.
1949 New state of Jordan declared.
1953 Hussein ibn Talai became king of Jordan.
1958 Jordan and Iraq formed Arab Federation which ended when the Iraqi monarchy was deposed.
1976 Lower house dissolved, and elections postponed until further notice.
1982 Hussein tried to mediate in Arab-Israeli conflict.
1984 Women voted for the first time.
1985 Hussein put forward a framework for a Middle East peace settlement. Secret meeting between Hussein and Israeli prime minister.
1988 Hussein announced a decision to cease administering the West Bank as part of Jordan, passing responsibility to Palestine Liberation Organization, and the suspension of parliament.
1989 Prime minister Zaid al-Rifai resigned and Hussein promised new parliamentary elections following criticism of economic policies. Riots over price increases up to 50% following fall in oil revenues. 80-member parliament elected and Mudar Badran appointed prime minister.
1990 Hussein tried unsuccessfully to mediate after Iraq's invasion of Kuwait. Thousands of refugees fled to Jordan.
1991 Martial law ended and ban on political parties lifted.
1992 Political parties allowed to register.

influence on Jelly Roll Morton and other early jazz musicians.

Jordan country in SW Asia, bordered to the N by Syria, NE by Iraq, E and SE by Saudi Arabia, S by the Gulf of Aqaba, and W by Israel.

Joseph in the New Testament, the husband of the Virgin Mary, a descendant of King David, and a carpenter by trade. According to Roman Catholic tradition, he had a family by a previous wife, and was an elderly man when he married Mary.

Joseph in the Old Testament, the 11th and favourite son of ◊Jacob, sold into Egypt by his jealous half-brothers. After he had risen to power there, they and his father joined him to escape from famine.

Joseph Keith (Sinjohn) 1918– . British Conservative politician. A barrister; he entered Parliament in 1956. He held ministerial posts 1962–64, 1970–74, 1979–81, and (education and science) 1981–86.

Joseph two Holy Roman emperors:

Joseph I 1678–1711. Holy Roman emperor from 1705, and king of Austria, of the house of Hapsburg. He spent most of his reign involved in fighting the War of Spanish Succession.

Joseph II 1741–1790. Holy Roman emperor from 1765, son of Francis I (1708–1765). The reforms he carried out after the death of his mother, ◊Maria Theresa, in 1780, provoked revolts from those who lost privileges.

Josephine Marie Josèphe Rose Tascher de la Pagerie 1763–1814. Empress of France 1796–1809. Born on Martinique, she married in 1779 Alexandre de Beauharnais, and in 1796 Napoleon, who divorced her in 1809 because she had not produced children.

Joseph of Arimathaea, St 1st century AD. in the New Testament, a wealthy Jew, member of the Sanhedrin (supreme court), and secret supporter of Jesus Christ. On the evening of the Crucifixion he asked the Roman procurator Pilate for Jesus' body and buried it in his own tomb. Feast day 17 Mar.

Josephson Brian 1940– . British physicist, a leading authority on superconductivity. Working at Cambridge, in 1973 he shared a Nobel prize for his theoretical predictions of the properties of a supercurrent through a tunnel barrier.

Josephson junction a device used in 'superchips' to speed the passage of signals by a phenomenon called 'electron tunnelling'. Though these superchips respond a thousand times faster than the ◊silicon chip, they have the disadvantage that the components of the Josephson junctions operate only at temperatures close to ◊absolute zero. They are named after Brian Josephson.

Josephus Flavius 37–c. 100 AD. Jewish historian and general, born in Jerusalem. He became a Pharisee, and commanded the Jewish forces in Galilee in the revolt against Rome from 66 (which ended with the mass suicide at Masada). When captured, he gained the favour of Vespasian and settled in Rome as a citizen. He wrote *Antiquities of the Jews* to 66 AD; *The Jewish War*, and an autobiography.

Joshua 13th century BC. In the Old Testament, successor of Moses, who led the Jews in their conquest of the land of Canaan. The city of Jericho was the first to fall: according to the Book of Joshua, the walls crumbled to the blast of his trumpets.

Josquin Desprez or *des Prés* 1440–1521. Franco-Flemish composer. His music combines a technical mastery with the feeling for words which became a hallmark of Renaissance vocal music. His works, which include 18 masses, over 100 motets,

Joyce *Irish writer James Joyce.*

and secular vocal works, are characterized by their vitality and depth of feeling.

Joubert Petrus Jacobus 1831–1900. Boer general in South Africa. He opposed British annexation of the Transvaal in 1877, proclaimed its independence in 1880, led the Boer Commandos in the First ◊South African War against the British 1880–81, defeated ◊Jameson in 1896, and fought in the Second South African War.

joule unit (symbol J) of work and energy in MKS and SI units. It is the work done (the energy transferred) when the point of application of 1 Newton is displaced a distance of 1 metre in the direction of the force, also expressed as the work done in one second by the current of 1 amp across a potential difference of 1 volt.

Joule James Prescott 1818–1889. British physicist whose work on the relations between electrical, mechanical, and chemical effects led to the discovery of the first law of ◊thermodynamics.

Joule-Thomson effect in physics, the fall in temperature of a gas as it expands adiabatically (without loss or gain of heat to the system) through a narrow jet. It can be felt when, for example, compressed air escapes through the valve of an inflated bicycle tyre. Only hydrogen does not exhibit the effect.

Jovian 331–364. Roman emperor from 363. Captain of the imperial bodyguard, he was chosen as emperor by the troops after ◊Julian's death in battle with the Persians. He concluded an unpopular peace, and restored Christianity as the state religion.

Juan Carlos *King Juan Carlos of Spain.*

Joyce James (Augustine Aloysius) 1882–1941. Irish writer, who revolutionized the form of the English novel with his 'stream of consciousness' technique. His works include *Dubliners* 1914 (short stories), *Portrait of the Artist as a Young Man* 1916, *Ulysses* 1922 and *Finnegans Wake* 1938.

joystick in computing, an input device, similar to the joystick used to control the flight of an aircraft, which signals to a computer the direction and extent of displacement of a hand-held lever.

Juan Carlos 1938– . King of Spain. The son of Don Juan, pretender to the Spanish throne, he married in 1962 Princess Sofia, eldest daughter of King Paul of Greece. In 1969 he was nominated by Franco to succeed on the restoration of the monarchy intended to follow Franco's own death; his father was excluded because of his known liberal views. He became king 1975 and has sought to steer his country from dictatorship to democracy.

Juárez Benito 1806–1872. Mexican politician, president 1861–64 and 1867–72. In 1861 he suspended payouts on Mexico's foreign debts, which prompted a joint French, British, and Spanish expedition to exert pressure. French forces invaded and created an empire for ◊Maximilian, brother of the Austrian emperor. After their withdrawal in 1867, Maximilian was executed, and Juárez returned to the presidency.

Judah or Judaea. District of S Palestine. After the death of King Solomon 937 BC, Judah adhered to his son Rehoboam and the Davidic line, whereas the rest of Israel elected Jeroboam as ruler of the northern kingdom. In New Testament times, Judah was the Roman province of Judaea, and in modern Israeli usage it refers to the S area of the West Bank.

Judaism the religion of the Jews, according to tradition based on a covenant between God and Abraham (*c.* 2000 BC) and the renewal of the covenant with Moses (*c.* 1200 BC). It rests on the concept of one God, whose will is revealed in the *Torah* and who has a special relationship with the Jewish people. The Torah comprises the first five books of the Bible, also known as the Pentateuch. Outside Israel, there are large Jewish populations today in the USA, USSR, and the UK, and Jewish communities throughout the world: there are approximately 17 million Jews.

history

c. 2000 BC Led by Abraham, the Israelites emigrated from Mesopotamia to Canaan.

18th century–1580 Some settled on the borders of Egypt and were put to forced labour.

13th century They were rescued by Moses, who aimed at their establishment in Palestine. Moses gave the Ten Commandments to the people. The main invasion of Canaan was led by Joshua *c.* 1274.

12th–11th centuries During the period of Judges, ascendancy was established over the Canaanites.

c. 1000 Complete conquest of Palestine and the union of all Israel was achieved under David, and Jerusalem became the capital.

10th century Solomon, David's son, succeeded and enjoyed a reputation for great wealth and wisdom, but his lack of a constructive policy led after his death to the secession of the north (Israel) under Jeroboam, only Judah remaining under the house of David.

9th–8th centuries Assyria became the dominant power in the Middle East. Israel purchased safety by tribute, but the basis of the society was corrupt,

and prophets such as Amos, Isaiah, and Micah predicted destruction. At the hands of Tiglathpileser and his successor Shalmaneser IV, the northern kingdom was organized as Assyrian provinces after the fall of Samaria in 721, although Judah was spared as an ally.

586–458 Nebuchadnezzar took Jerusalem and carried off the major part of the population to Babylon. Judaism was retained during exile, and was reconstituted by their leader Ezra on the return to Jerusalem.

520 The Temple, originally built by Solomon, was restored.

c. 444 Ezra promulgated the legal code that was to govern the future of the Jewish people.

4th–3rd centuries After the conquest of the Persian Empire by Alexander the Great, the Syrian Seleucid rulers and Egyptian Ptolemaic dynasty struggled for Palestine, which came under the government of Egypt with a large measure of freedom.

2nd century With the advance of Syrian power Antiochus IV attempted intervention in Jewish internal quarrels, thus prompting a revolt in 165 led by the Maccabee family.

63 Judaea's near independence ended when internal dissension led to the Roman general Pompey's intervention and Roman suzerainty was established.

1st century AD A revolt led to the destruction of the Temple 66–70 by the Roman emperor Titus. Jewish national sentiment was encouraged by the work of Rabbi Johanan ben Zakkai (*c.* 20–90), and after his day the president of the Sanhedrin (supreme court) was recognized as the patriarch of Palestinian Jewry.

2nd–3rd centuries Greatest of the Sanhedrin presidents was Rabbi Judah (*c.* 135–220), who codified the traditional law in the Mishna. The Palestinian Talmud (*c.* 375) added the Gemara to the Mishna.

4th–5th centuries The intellectual leadership of Judaism passed to the descendants of the 6th-century exiles in Babylonia, who compiled the Babylonian Talmud.

8th–13th centuries Judaism enjoyed a golden era, producing the philosopher Saadiah, the poet Jehudah Ha-levi (*c.* 1075–1141), the codifier Moses Maimonides, and others.

14th–17th centuries Where Christianity was the dominant religion, the Jews were increasingly segregated from mainstream life and trade by anti-Semitism, which included restrictive legislation.

18th–19th centuries Outbreaks of persecution increased with the rise of European nationalism. The Reform movement, a rejection of religious orthodoxy and an attempt to interpret Judaism for modern times, began in Germany in 1810 and reached the UK in 1842.

20th century Zionism (founded 1896) was an attempt to create a homeland where the Jewish people would be free from persecution; this led to the establishment of the state of Israel 1948. Liberal Judaism (more radical than Reform) developed in the USA and founded its first UK synagogue in 1911. The Nazi regime 1933–45 killed 6 million European Jews.

Judas Iscariot 1st century. In the New Testament, the disciple who betrayed Jesus. At the last Passover he arranged, for 30 pieces of silver, to point out Jesus to the chief priests so that they could arrest him. Afterwards Judas was overcome with guilt and committed suicide.

Jude, St 1st century. supposed brother of Jesus Christ and writer of Epistle in the New Testament; patron saint of lost causes. Feast day 28 Oct.

judge a person invested with power to hear and determine legal disputes. In the UK, judges are chosen from barristers of long standing (for higher courts), and solicitors. Judges of the High Court, the crown courts, and the county courts are nominated by the Lord Chancellor, and those of the Court of Appeal and the House of Lords by the prime minister. In the USA, apart from the federal judiciary which are executive appointments, judges in most states are elected by popular vote.

judicial review in English law, action in the High Court to review the decisions of lower courts, tribunals, and administrative bodies. Various court orders can be made: *certiorari* (which quashes the decision); *mandamus* (which commands a duty to be performed); *prohibition* (which commands that an action should not be performed because it is unauthorized); a *declaration* (which sets out the legal rights or obligations); or an ◊*injunction*.

Judith 6th century BC. In the Old Testament Apocrypha, a Jewish heroine in the book of the same name, who saved her town by beheading Holofernes, the general of Nebuchadnezzar.

judo a type of wrestling of Japanese origin. The two combatants wear loose-fitting, belted jackets and trousers to facilitate holds, and the falls are broken by a square mat; when one has established a painful hold that the other cannot break, the latter signifies surrender by slapping the ground with a free hand. Degrees of proficiency are indicated by the colour of the belt: for novices white; after examination, brown (three degrees); and finally, black (nine degrees).

Juggernaut or *Jagannath* a name for Vishnu, the Hindu god, meaning 'Lord of the World'. His temple is at Puri, Orissa, India.

jugular vein one of two veins in the necks of vertebrates; they return blood from the head to the superior (or anterior) vena cava and thence to the heart.

jujitsu traditional Japanese form of self-defence; see ◊judo.

jujube tree of the *Zizyphus* genus, family Thamnaceae, with berry-like fruits.

Julian *c.* 331–363. Roman emperor, called the 'Apostate'. Born in Constantinople, the nephew of Constantine the Great, he was brought up as a Christian, but in early life became a convert to paganism. Sent by Constantius to govern Gaul in 355, he was proclaimed emperor by his troops in 360, and in 361 was marching on Constantinople when Constantius's death allowed him to succeed peacefully. He revived pagan worship, and refused to persecute heretics. He was killed in battle against the Persians.

Juliana 1909–. Queen of the Netherlands. The daughter of Queen Wilhelmina (1880–1962), she married Prince Bernhard of Lippe-Biesterfeld in 1937 and ruled 1948–80, when she abdicated and was succeeded by her daughter ◊Beatrix.

July Revolution the French revolution of 27–29 Jul 1830 in Paris which overthrew the restored Bourbon monarchy of Charles X and substituted the constitutional monarchy of Louis Philippe, whose rule (1830–48) is sometimes referred to as the July Monarchy.

jumbo jet popular name for a generation of huge wide-bodied airliners, particularly the *Boeing 747* which is 71 m/232 ft long, has a wing span of 60 m/196 ft, a maximum take-off weight

Jung Swiss psychiatrist and pioneer psychoanalyst Carl Jung.

of nearly 380 tonnes, and can carry over 400 passengers.

jumping hare long-eared S African rodent *Pedetes capensis*, similar in appearance and habits to the ◊jerboa, but with head and body about 40 cm/1.3 ft long, with a bushy tail about as long again. It is nocturnal and herbivorous.

Jung Carl Gustav 1875–1961. Swiss psychiatrist, who collaborated with ◊Freud until their disagreement in 1912 about the importance of sexuality in causing psychological problems. He studied religion and dream symbolism, and saw the unconscious as a source of spiritual insight. He also distinguished between introversion and extraversion. Works include *Modern Man in Search of a Soul* 1933.

jungle popular name for ◊rainforest.

juniper aromatic evergreen tree or shrub of the genus *Juniperus*, family Cupressaceae, found throughout temperate regions. Its berries are used to flavour gin.

junk bond derogatory term for a security, officially rated as 'below investment grade'. It is issued in order to raise a lot of capital in a short period, typically to finance a takeover. Junk bonds have a high yield, but are a high-risk investment.

Junkers Hugo 1859–1935. German aeroplane designer. In 1919 he founded in Dessau the aircraft works named after him. Junkers planes, including dive bombers, night fighters and troop carriers, were used by the Germans in World War II.

Juno principal goddess in Roman mythology (identified with the Greek Hera). The wife of Jupiter, the queen of heaven, she was concerned with all aspects of women's lives.

Jupiter The largest planet in the solar system.

Jurassic *Contorted Jurassic limestone strata in Jura, Switzerland.*

Jupiter in astronomy, the fifth planet from the Sun, and the largest in the Solar System (equatorial diameter 142,800 km/88,700 mi), with a mass over twice that of all the other planets combined, 318 times that of the Earth's. It takes 11.86 years to orbit the Sun, at an average distance of 778 million km/484 million mi, and has at least 16 moons. It is largely composed of hydrogen and helium, liquefied by pressure in its interior, and probably with a rocky core larger than the Earth. Its most notable feature is the Great Red Spot, a turbulent storm of rising gas 14,000 km/8,500 mi wide and some 30,000 km/20,000 mi long.

Jupiter or **Jōve** in mythology, chief god of the Romans, identified with the Greek ◊Zeus. He was god of the sky, associated with lightning and thunderbolt, protector in battle and bestower of victory. He was the son of Saturn, married his sister Juno, and reigned on Mount Olympus as lord of heaven.

Jura mountains series of parallel mountain ranges running SW–NE along the French-Swiss frontier between the Rhône and the Rhine, a distance of 250 km/156 mi. The highest peak is *Crête de la Neige*, 1,723 m/5,650 ft.

Jurassic period of geological time 213–144 million years ago; the middle period of the Mesozoic era. Climates worldwide were equable creating forests of conifers and ferns, dinosaurs were abundant, birds evolved, and limestones and iron ores were deposited.

jurisprudence the science of law in the abstract; that is, not the study of any particular laws or legal system, but of the principles upon which legal systems are founded.

justice of the peace in England, an unpaid magistrate appointed by the Lord Chancellor. Two or more sit to dispose of minor charges (formerly their jurisdiction was much wider), to commit more serious ones for trial by a higher court, and to grant licences for the sale of intoxicating liquor. In the USA, where they receive fees and are usually elected, their courts are the lowest in the States, and deal only with minor offences, such as traffic violations; they may also conduct marriages. See also ◊magistrates court.

justiciar the chief justice minister of Norman and early Angevin kings, second in power only to the king. By 1265, the government had been divided into various departments, such as the Exchequer and Chancery, which meant that it was no longer desirable to have one official in charge of all.

Justinian I 483–562. Byzantine emperor from 527. He recovered N Africa from the Vandals, SE Spain from the Visigoths, and Italy from the Ostrogoths, largely owing to his great general Belisarius. He ordered the codification of Roman law, which has exercised a great influence on European jurisprudence.

Justin Martyr *c.* 100–*c.* 163. One of the early Christian leaders and writers known as the Fathers of the Church. Born in Palestine of a Greek family, he was converted to Christianity and wrote two *Apologies* in its defence. He spent the rest of his life as an itinerant missionary, and was martyred in Rome. Feast day 1 Jun.

Jute member of a Germanic people who originated in Jutland but later settled in Frankish territory. They occupied Kent, England, about 450, according to tradition under Hengist and Horsa, and conquered the Isle of Wight and the opposite coast of Hampshire in the early 6th century.

jute fibre obtained from two plants of the genus *Corchorus*: *C. capsularis* and *C. olitorius*. Jute is used for sacks and sacking, upholstery, webbing, twine, and stage canvas.

Jutland Danish *Jylland*. A peninsula of N Europe; area 29,500 sq km/11,400 sq mi. It is separated from Norway by the Skagerrak, from Sweden by the Kattegat, with the North Sea to the W. The larger northern part belongs to Denmark, and the southern part to West Germany.

Jutland, Battle of naval battle of World War I, fought between England and Germany on 31 May 1916, off the W coast of Jutland. Its outcome was indecisive, but the German fleet remained in port for the rest of the war.

Juvenal *c.* 60–140 AD. Roman satirist and poet. His genius for satire brought him to the unfavourable notice of the emperor Domitian. Sixteen of his satires are extant, and they give an explicit and sometimes brutal picture of the decadent Roman society of his time.

juvenile delinquency offences against the law that are committed by young people. The Children and Young Persons Act 1969 introduced in Britain the gradual abolition of the prosecution of children up to the age of 14, and provided three options for Juvenile Courts in respect of all care and criminal proceedings involving children up to the age of 17: binding over of parents, supervision orders, and care orders.

K abbreviation for *kelvin* (temperature scale).

K abbreviation for thousand, as in a salary of £20K.

k symbol for *kilo–*, as in kg (kilogram) and km (kilometre).

K2 second highest mountain in the world, about 8,900 m/29,210 ft, in the Karakoram range, Kashmir, N India; it is also known as Dapsang (Hidden Peak) and formerly as Mount Godwin-Austen. It was first climbed 1954.

Kaaba (Arabic 'chamber') in Mecca, Saudi Arabia, the oblong building in the quadrangle of the Great Mosque, into the NE corner of which is built the Black Stone declared by the prophet Muhammad to have been given to Abraham by the archangel Gabriel, and revered by Muslims.

Kabardino-Balkar autonomous republic of Russia, in the N Caucasus Mountains; capital Nalchik; area 12,500 sq km/4,825 sq mi; population (1989) 760,000. Under Russian control from 1557, it was annexed 1827; it was an autonomous republic of the USSR 1936–91.

kabbala or *cabbala* (Hebrew 'tradition') ancient esoteric Jewish mystical tradition of philosophy containing strong elements of pantheism and akin to Neo-Platonism. Kabbalistic writing reached its peak period between the 13th and 16th centuries.

kabuki Japanese 'music-dance-play', popular drama on legendary themes, first developed about 1603 by the shrine maiden Okuni who gave performances with a chiefly female troupe: from 1629 only men were allowed to act, in the interests of 'propriety'.

Kabul capital of Afghanistan, 2,100 m/6,900 ft above sea level, on the river Kabul; population (1984) 1,179,300. Products include textiles, plastics, leather, and glass. It commands the strategic routes to Pakistan via the Khyber Pass.

Kabul has been in existence for over 3,000 years. It became the capital 1776, was captured by the British 1839 and 1879, and was under Soviet control 1979–89. In 1992 the city saw fierce fighting during the mujaheddin takeover and ousting of the Soviet-backed Najibullah regime. There is a university (1931), the tomb of Zahir (Babur), founder of the Mogul empire, and the Dar ol-Aman palace, which houses the parliament and government departments.

Kabwe town in central Zambia (formerly *Broken Hill*); population (1988) 200,300. It is a mining centre (copper, cadmium, lead, and zinc).

kabyle member of a group of Berber peoples of Algeria and Tunisia. As ◊Zouave they served in the French colonial forces, although many were notable in the fight for Algerian independence. Their language belongs to the Afro-Arabic family.

Kádár János 1912– . Hungarian Communist leader, in power from 1956, when he suppressed the national rising. As Hungarian Socialist Workers' Party (HSWP) leader and prime minister 1956–58 and 1961–65, Kádár introduced a series of market-socialist economic reforms, while retaining cordial political relations with the USSR. He was ousted as party general secretary 1988 and forced into retirement 1989.

Kafka Franz 1883–1924. Czech novelist, who wrote in German. His three unfinished allegorical novels *Der Prozess/The Trial* 1925, *Der Schloss/The Castle* 1926 and *Amerika/America* 1927, were posthumously published despite his instructions that they should be destroyed. The best known of his short stories is *Die Verwandlung/The Metamorphosis* 1915, in which a man turns into a beetle.

Kahn Louis 1901–1974. US architect, born in Estonia. A follower of Mies van der Rohe, he developed a classically romantic style, in which functional 'servant' areas, such as stairwells and air ducts, featured prominently, often as towerlike structures surrounding the main living and working, or 'served', areas. His projects are characterized by an imaginative use of concrete and brick and include the Salk Institute for Biological Studies, La Jolla, California, and the British Art Center at Yale University.

Kairouan Muslim holy city in Tunisia, N Africa, S of Tunis; population (1984) 72,200. It is a noted centre of carpet production. The city, said to have been founded AD 617, ranks after Mecca and Medina as a place of pilgrimage.

Kaiser a title formerly used by the Holy Roman emperors, Austrian emperors 1806–1918, and German emperors 1871–1918. The word, like the Russian tsar, is derived from the Latin *Caesar*.

Kaiser Georg 1878–1945. German playwright, the principal writer of German ◊Expressionism. His large output includes *Die Bürger von Calais/The Burghers of Calais* and *Gas* 1918–20.

kakapo a flightless parrot *Strigops habroptilus* which lives in burrows in New Zealand. It is green, yellow and brown, and is nocturnal. Because of the introduction of dogs and cats, it is in danger of extinction.

Kafka *Czech novelist Franz Kafka.*

Kalahari Desert semi-desert area forming most of Botswana and extending into Namibia, Zimbabwe, and South Africa; area about 900,000 sq km/347,400 sq mi. The only permanent river, the Okavango, flows into a delta in the NW forming marshes. The inhabitants of the Kalahari are the nomadic Bushmen.

Kalevala Finnish national epic poem compiled from legends and ballads by Elias Lönnrot in 1835; its hero is Väinamöinen, god of music and poetry.

Kalgan city in NE China, now known as ◊Zhangjiakou.

Kali in Hindu mythology, the goddess of destruction and death. She is the wife of ◊Siva.

Kālidāsa fl. 5th century AD. Indian epic poet and dramatist. His works, in Sanskrit, include the classic drama *Sakuntala*, the love story of King Dushyanta for the nymph Sakuntala.

Kalimantan provinces of the republic of Indonesia occupying part of the island of Borneo
area 543,900 sq km/210,000 sq mi
towns Banjermasin and Balikpapan
products petroleum, rubber, coffee, copra, pepper, timber
population (1989) 8,677,500

Kalinin Mikhail Ivanovich 1875–1946. Soviet politician, founder of the newspaper *Pravda*. He was prominent in the October Revolution, and in 1919 became head of state (president of the Central Executive Committee of the Soviet government until 1937, then president of the Presidium of the Supreme Soviet until 1946).

Kali-Yuga in Hinduism, the last of the four *yugas* (ages) that make up one cycle of creation. The Kali-Yuga, in which Hindus believe we are now living, is characterized by wickedness and disaster, and leads up to the destruction of this world in preparation for a new creation and a new cycle of *yugas*.

Kalki in Hinduism, the last avatar (manifestation) of Vishnu, who will appear at the end of the Kali-Yuga, or final age of the world, to destroy it in readiness for a new creation.

Kalmyk or *Kalmuck* autonomous republic in central Russia, on the Caspian Sea; area 75,900 sq km/29,300 sq mi; population (1989) 322,000; capital Elista. Industry is mainly agricultural. It was settled by migrants from China in the 17th century. The autonomous Soviet republic was abolished 1943–57 because of alleged collaboration of the people with the Germans during the siege of Stalingrad, but restored 1958.

Kaltenbrunner Ernst 1901–1946. Austrian Nazi leader. As head of the Security Police (SD) from 1943 he was responsible for the murder of millions of Jews (see ◊holocaust) and Allied soldiers in World War II. After the war, he was tried at Nuremberg, and hanged.

Kamchatka mountainous peninsula separating the Bering Sea and Sea of Okhotsk, forming (together with the Chukchi and Koryak national districts) a region of E Siberian Russia. Its capital Petropavlovsk is the only town; agriculture is possible only in the south.

Kamenev Lev Borisovich 1883–1936. Russian leader of the Bolshevik movement after 1917 who, with Stalin and Zinoviev, formed a ruling triumvirate in the USSR after Lenin's death in 1924. His alignment with the Trotskyists led to his dismissal from office and from the Communist Party by Stalin in 1926. Tried for plotting to murder Stalin, he was condemned and shot 1936.

Kamerlingh-Onnes Heike 1853–1926. Dutch physicist who worked mainly in the field of low-temperature physics. In 1911, he discovered the phenomenon of ◊superconductivity (enhanced electrical conductivity at very low temperatures), for which he was awarded the 1913 Nobel Prize for Physics.

kamikaze the pilots of the Japanese air force in World War II who deliberately crash-dived their planes, loaded with bombs, usually on ships of the US navy.

Kampala capital of Uganda; population (1983) 455,000. It is linked by rail with Mombasa. Products include tea, coffee, textiles, fruit, and vegetables.

Kampuchea former name (1975–89) of ◊Cambodia.

Kanchenjunga a variant spelling of ◊Kangchenjunga, a Himalayan mountain.

Kandinsky Wassily 1866–1944. Russian painter, a pioneer of abstract art. Born in Moscow, he travelled widely, settling in Munich 1896. Around 1910 he produced the first known examples of purely abstract work in 20th-century art. He was an originator of the ◊*Blaue Reiter* movement 1911–12. From 1921 he taught at the ◊Bauhaus school of design. He moved to Paris 1933, becoming a French citizen 1939.

Kandy city in central Sri Lanka, former capital of the kingdom of Kandy 1480–1815; population (1990) 104,000. Products include tea. One of the most sacred Buddhist shrines is situated at Kandy.

kangaroo any marsupial of the family Macropodidae found in Australia, Tasmania, and New Guinea. Kangaroos are plant-eaters and most live in groups. They are adapted to hopping, the vast majority of species having very large back legs and feet compared with the small forelimbs. The larger types can jump 9 m/30 ft at a single bound. Most are nocturnal. Species vary from small rat kangaroos, only 30 cm/1 ft long, through the medium-sized wallabies, to the large red and great grey kangaroos, which are the largest living marsupials. These may be 1.8 m/5.9 ft long with 1.1 m/3.5 ft tails.

kangaroo paw bulbous plant *Anigozanthos manglesii*, family Hameodoraceae, with a row of small white flowers emerging from velvety green tubes with red bases; floral emblem of W Australia.

Kangchenjunga Himalayan mountain on the Nepál–Sikkim border 8,598 m/20,208 ft high, 120 km/75 mi SE of Everest, first climbed by a British expedition 1955.

Ka Ngwane black homeland in Natal province, South Africa; achieved self-governing status 1971; population (1985) 392,800.

Kano capital of Kano state in N Nigeria, trade centre of an irrigated area; population (1983) 487,100.

kangaroo

Kano A gateway into the walled city of Kano, Nigeria.

Products include bicycles, glass, furniture, textiles, and chemicals. Founded about 1000 BC, Kano is a walled city, with New Kano extending beyond the walls.

Kanpur (formerly *Cawnpore*) capital of Kanpur district, Uttar Pradesh, India, SW of Lucknow, on the river Ganges; a commercial and industrial centre (cotton, wool, jute, chemicals, plastics, iron, steel); population (1981) 1,688,000.

Kansas state of central USA; nickname Sunflower State
area 213,063 sq km/82,264 sq mi
capital Topeka
towns Kansas City, Wichita, Hutchinson
products wheat, cattle; coal, petroleum, natural gas; aircraft
population (1989) 2,477,600.

Kansas City twin city in the USA at the confluence of the Missouri and Kansas rivers, partly in Kansas and partly in Missouri; important livestock centre. Kansas City, Missouri, has car assembly plants and Kansas City, Kansas, has the majority of offices; population (1989) of Kansas City (Kansas) 149,800, Kansas City (Missouri) 435,100.

Kansu alternative spelling for Chinese province ◊Gansu.

Kant Immanuel 1724–1804. German philosopher, who believed that knowledge is not merely an aggregate of sense impressions, but is dependent on the conceptual apparatus of the human understanding, which is not derived from experience. In ethics, Kant argued that right action cannot be based on feelings, but conforms to a law given by reason, *categorical imperative.*

KANU (Kenya African National Union) political party founded in 1944 and led by Jomo Kenyatta from 1947, when it was the Kenya African Union; it became KANU on independence. The party formed Kenyatta's political power base in 1963 when he became prime minister.

kaoliang variety of ◊sorghum.

kapok silky hairs produced round the seeds of certain trees, particularly the *kapok tree Bombax ceiba* of India and Malaysia, and the *silk-cotton tree Ceiba pentandra*, a native of tropical America. Kapok is used for stuffing cushions, mattresses, and for sound insulation; oil obtained from the seeds is used in food and soap preparation.

Karachi largest city and chief seaport of Pakistan, and capital of Sind province, NW of the Indus delta; industry (engineering, chemicals, plastics, textiles); population (1981) 5,208,000. It was the capital of Pakistan 1947–59.

Karajan Herbert von 1908–1989. Austrian conductor. He was conductor of the Berlin Philharmonic Orchestra 1955–89. He directed the

Salzburg Festival from 1964, and became director of the Vienna State Opera (artistic director 1956–64) in 1976.

Karakoram mountain range in central Asia, divided among China, Pakistan, and India. Peaks include K2, Masharbrum, Gasharbrum, and Mustagh Tower. *Ladakh* subsidiary range is in NE Kashmir on the Tibetan border.

Karamanlis Constantinos 1907– . Greek politician of the New Democracy Party. A lawyer and an anti-communist, he was prime minister Oct 1955–Mar 1958; May 1958–Sept 1961; and Nov 1961–Jun 1963, when he went into self-imposed exile. He was recalled as prime minister on the fall of the regime of the 'colonels' in Jul 1974, and was president 1980–85.

karate one of the ◊martial arts. Karate is a type of unarmed combat derived from kempo, a form of the Chinese Shaolin boxing. It became popular in the 1930s.

Karelia autonomous republic NW Russia
area 172,400 sq km/66,500 sq mi
capital Petrozavodsk
towns Vyborg
products fishing, timber, chemicals, coal
population (1989) 792,000
history constituted as an autonomous Soviet republic 1923, it was extended 1940 to include that part of Finnish Karelia ceded to the USSR. In 1946 the Karelo-Finnish Soviet Socialist Republic was set up but in 1956 the greater part of the republic returned to its former status as an autonomous Soviet socialist republic. A movement for the reunification of Russian and Finnish Karelia emerged in the late 1980s, as the Soviet regime crumbled.

Karen a people of the Far East, numbering approximately 2 million. They live in E Burma, Thailand, and the Irrawaddy delta. Their language belongs to the Sino-Thai family.

Karl-Marx-Stadt former name (1953–90) of ◊*Chemnitz* a city in Germany.

karma (Sanskrit 'fate') in Hinduism, the sum of a human being's actions, carried forward from one life to the next to result in an improved or worsened fate. Buddhism has a similar belief, except that no permanent personality is envisaged, the karma relating only to the physical and mental elements carried on from birth to birth, until the power holding them together disperses in the attainment of Nirvana.

Karmal Babrak 1929– . Afghani communist politician. In 1965 he formed what in 1977 became the banned People's Democratic Party of Afghanistan (PDPA). As president 1979–86, with Soviet backing, he sought to broaden the appeal of the PDPA but encountered wide resistance from the mujaheddin Muslim guerrillas. In 1991 he returned to Afghanistan from exile in Moscow.

Karnataka (known as *Mysore* until 1973) state in SW India
area 191,773 sq km/74,024 sq mi
capital Bangalore
products mainly agricultural, but its minerals include manganese, chromite, and India's only sources of gold and silver
population (1991) 44,817,400
language Kannada
famous people Hyder Ali, Tippu Sultan

karri giant eucalyptus tree *Eucalyptus diversifolia*, found in the extreme SW of Australia. It may reach over 120 m/400 ft. Its exceptionally strong timber is used for girders.

karyotype in biology, the set of ♢chromosomes characteristic of a given species. It is described as the number, shape, and size of the chromosomes in a single cell of an organism. In humans, for example, the karyotype consists of 46 chromosomes, in mice 40, crayfish 200, and in fruit flies 8.

Kashmir former part of Jammu state in the N of British India with a largely Muslim population, ruled by a Hindu maharajah, who joined it to the republic of India in 1947. There was fighting between pro-India and pro-Pakistan factions, the former being the Hindu ruling class and the latter the Muslim majority, and open war between the two countries 1965–66 and 1971. It remains divided: the NW is occupied by Pakistan, and the rest by India. Since 1990 it has been riven by Muslim separatist violence.

Kashmir Pakistan-occupied area in the NW of the former state of Kashmir, now ♢Jammu and Kashmir. Azad ('free') Kashmir, in the W, is self-governing; Pakistan governs the N and E regions, and the Northern Areas are claimed by India and Pakistan.

Katmandu or **Kathmandu** capital of Nepál; population (1981) 235,000. Founded in the 8th century on an ancient pilgrim and trade route from India to Tibet and China, it has a royal palace, Buddhist shrines, and monasteries.

Kato Kiyomasa 1562–1611. Japanese warrior and politician who was instrumental in the unification of Japan and the banning of Christianity in the country.

Katowice industrial city (anthracite, iron and coal mining, iron foundries, smelting works, machine shops) in Upper Silesia, S Poland; population (1990) 366,800.

Katsura Taro 1847–1913. Prince of Japan; an army officer, politician, and prime minister. During his first term as prime minister 1901–06, he was responsible for the Anglo-Japanese treaty of 1902, the successful prosecution of the war against Russia 1904–05, and in 1910 he was responsible for the annexation of Korea.

Katyn Forest forest near Smolensk, SW of Moscow, Russia, where 4,500 Polish officer prisoners of war (captured in the German–Soviet partition of Poland in 1940) were shot; 10,000 others were killed elsewhere. In 1989 the USSR accepted responsibility for the massacre.

Kaunda Kenneth (David) 1924– . Zambian politician. Imprisoned in 1958–60 as founder of the Zambia African National Congress, he became in 1964 first prime minister of Northern Rhodesia, then first president of Zambia. In 1973 he introduced one-party rule. He supported the nationalist movement in Southern Rhodesia, now Zimbabwe, and survived a coup attempt 1980. He was elected chair of the Organization of African Unity 1987. In 1990 he was faced with popular anti-government demonstrations, leading to the acceptance of a multiparty political system. He lost the first multiparty election, in Nov 1991, to Frederick Chiluba.

kauri pine New Zealand timber conifer *Agathis australis*, family Araucariaceae, whose fossilized gum deposits are especially valued in varnishes; the wood is used for carving and handicrafts.

Kautsky Karl 1854–1938. German socialist theoretician, who opposed the reformist ideas of Edouard ♢Bernstein from within the Social Democratic Party. In spite of his Marxist ideas he remained in the party when its left wing broke away to form the German Communist Party (KPD).

Kawabata Yasunari 1899–1972. Japanese novelist, translator of Lady ♢Murasaki, and author of *Snow Country* 1947 and *A Thousand Cranes* 1952. He was the first Japanese to win the Nobel Prize for Literature 1968.

Kawasaki industrial city (iron and steel, shipbuilding, chemicals, textiles) on Honshu island, Japan; population (1990) 1,173,600.

Kazakhstan
Republic of

area 2,717,300 sq km/1,049,150 sq mi
capital Alma-Ata
towns Karaganda, Semipalatinsk, Petropavlovsk
physical Caspian and Aral seas, Lake Balkhash; Steppe region
head of state Nursultan Nazarbayev from 1990
head of government Sergey Tereshchenko from 1991

political system emergent democracy
products grain, copper, lead, zinc, manganese, coal, oil
population (1990) 16,700,000 (40% Kazakh, 38% Russian, 6% Germans, 5% Ukrainians)
language Russian; Kazakh, related to Turkish
religion Sunni Muslim
chronology
1920 Autonomous republic in USSR.
1936 Joined the USSR and became a full union republic.
1950s Site of Nikita Khrushchev's ambitious 'Virgin Lands' agricultural extension programme.
1960s A large influx of Russian settlers turned the Kazakhs into a minority in their own republic.
1986 Riots in Alma-Alta after Gorbachev ousted local communist leader.
1989 Nazarbayev became leader of the Kazakh Communist Party (KCP) and instituted economic and cultural reform programmes.
1990 Nazarbayev became head of state.
1991 March: support pledged for continued union with USSR; Aug: Nazarbayev condemned attempted anti-Gorbachev coup; CP abolished and replaced by Independent Socialist Party of Kazakhstan (SPK). Dec: joined new Commonwealth of Independent States (CIS).
1992 Became a member of the United Nations (UN).
1993 New constitution adopted, increasing the authority of the president and making Kazakh the state language.

Keaton US comedy star Buster Keaton.

Kay John 1704–*c*. 1764. British inventor who developed the flying-shuttle, a machine to speed up the work of hand-loom weaving. In 1733 he patented his invention but was ruined by the litigation necessary for its defence.

Kaye Danny. Stage-name of Daniel Kaminski 1913–1987. US comedian and singer. He appeared in many films, including *Wonder Man* 1944, *The Secret Life of Walter Mitty* 1946, and *Hans Christian Andersen* 1952.

Kazakh a pastoral people of Kazakhstan. Kazakhs also live in China, Mongolia, and Afghanistan. The Kazakhs speak a Turkic language belonging to the Altaic family.

Kazakhstan country in central Asia, bounded N by Russia, W by the Caspian Sea, E by China, and S by Turkmenistan, Uzbekistan, and Kyrgyzstan.

Kazan capital of Tatarstan, central Russia, on the river Volga; a transport, commercial, and industrial centre (engineering, oil refining, petrochemical, textiles, large fur trade); population (1989) 1,094,000.

Kazan Elia 1909– . US stage and film director, reputed for his stage direction of *Skin of Our Teeth* 1942, *A Streetcar Named Desire* 1947, and *Cat on a Hot Tin Roof* 1955. He helped to found the ◊Actors' Studio. His films include *Gentlemen's Agreement* 1948, *East of Eden* 1954, and *The Visitors* 1972.

Kazantzakis Nikos 1885–1957. Greek writer of poems, for example, *I Odysseia/The Odyssey* 1938, which continues Homer's *Odyssey*, and novels, for example, *Zorba the Greek* 1946.

KBE abbreviation for *Knight (Commander of the Order) of the British Empire*.

KC abbreviation for *King's Counsel*.

kcal abbreviation for *kilocalorie*.

kea a hawk-like greenish parrot *Nestor notabilis* found in New Zealand, which eats insects, fruits, and sheep offal. The Maori name imitates its cry.

Kean Edmund 1787–1833. British tragic actor, noted for his portrayal of villainy in the Shakespearean roles of Shylock, Richard III, and Iago.

Keating Paul 1954– . Australian politician, Labour Party leader and prime minister from 1991. He was treasurer and deputy leader of the Labour Party 1983–91.

Keaton Buster. Stage name of Joseph Frank Keaton 1896–1966. US comedian and actor. One of the great comedians of the silent film era, with an inimitable deadpan expression. His films include *The General* 1927 and *The Cameraman* 1928.

Keats John 1795–1821. British poet, a leading figure of the Romantic movement. He published his first volume of poetry in 1817; this was followed in 1818 by *Endymion, Isabella*, and *Hyperion*, and in 1819 by 'The Eve of St Agnes' and his odes 'To

Autumn', and 'Lamia'. His final volume of poems appeared in 1820. He died of consumption.

Keillor Garrison 1942– . US novelist and humorist. His Lake Wobegon stories, including *Lake Wobegon Days* 1985 and *Leaving Home* 1987, often started as radio monologues about 'the town that time forgot, that the decades cannot improve'.

Keitel Wilhelm 1882–1946. German field marshal in World War II, chief of the supreme command from 1938. He signed Germany's surrender 8 May 1945. Tried at Nuremberg for war crimes, he was hanged.

Kekulé Friedrich August 1829–1896. German chemist whose theory (1858) of molecular structure revolutionized organic chemistry. He is best known for proposing two resonant forms of the ◊benzene ring.

Kellogg–Briand pact an agreement 1927 between the USA and France to renounce war and seek settlement of disputes by peaceful means. It took its name from the US secretary of state Frank B Kellogg (1856–1937) and the French foreign minister Aristide Briand (1862–1932). Other powers signed in Aug 1928, making a total of 67 signatories. The pact made no provision for measures against aggressors and became ineffective in the 1930s.

Kells, Book of an 8th-century illuminated manuscript of the Gospels produced at the monastery of Kells in County Meath, Ireland. It is now in Trinity College library, Dublin.

Kelly (Edward) Ned 1855–1880. Australian bushranger, who carried out bank robberies on the Victoria–New South Wales border. Kelly wore a distinctive home-made armour. In 1880 he was captured and hanged.

Kelly Grace (Patricia) 1928–1982. US film actress and later Princess of Monaco. She starred in *High Noon* 1952, *The Country Girl* 1954 for which she received an Academy Award, and *High Society* 1955. In 1956 she married Prince Rainier of Monaco.

kelp collective name for large seaweeds, particularly of the Fucaceae and Laminariaceae family. Kelp is also a term for the powdery ash of burned seaweeds, a source of iodine.

Kelvin William Thomson, 1st Baron Kelvin 1824–1907. Irish physicist, who pioneered the absolute scale of temperature. His work on the conservation of energy 1851 led to the second law of ◊thermodynamics.

kelvin scale of temperature (used by scientists) begins at ◊absolute zero (−273°C) but increases in the same way as the Celsius scale, that is, 0°C becomes 273 K and 100°C becomes 373 K.

Kemal Atatürk Mustafa Turkish politician; see ◊Atatürk.

Kelvin Irish physicist William Kelvin pioneered the Kelvin scale of temperature used by scientists.

Kennedy John F Kennedy 1962.

Kemble (John) Philip 1757–1823. British actor and theatre manager. He was famous for tragic roles, especially Shakespeare, including Hamlet and Coriolanus. As manager of Drury Lane 1788–1803 and Covent Garden 1803–17, in London, he introduced many innovations in theatrical management.

Kempe Margery c. 1373–c. 1439. English Christian mystic. She was converted to the religious life after a period of mental derangement, travelled widely as a pilgrim, and in the 1420s dictated her *Boke of Margery Kempe*, describing her experiences, both religious and worldly. It has been called the first autobiography in English.

Kempis Thomas à   medieval German monk and religious writer; see ◊Thomas à Kempis.

kendo Japanese armed ◊martial art in which combatants fence with bamboo replicas of samurai swords. Masks and padding are worn for protection. The earliest reference to kendo is 789 AD.

Keneally Thomas Michael 1935– . Australian novelist who won the Booker Prize 1982 with *Schindler's Ark*, based on the true account of Polish Jews saved during World War I by a German industrialist. He won the Miles Franklin Award on two occasions with *Bring Larks and Heroes* 1967 and *Three Cheers for the Paraclete* 1968.

Kennedy Edward (Moore) 1932– . US Democrat politician. He aided his brothers John and Robert Kennedy in the presidential campaign of 1960, and entered politics as a senator from Massachusetts in 1962. He failed to gain the presidential nomination in 1980, largely because of feeling about his delay in reporting a car crash at Chappaquiddick Island, near Cape Cod, Massachusetts, in 1969, in which his passenger, Mary Jo Kopechne, was drowned.

Kennedy John F(itzgerald) 1917–1963. 35th president of the USA 1961–63, a Democrat. Kennedy was the first Roman Catholic and the youngest person to be elected president. In foreign policy he carried through the unsuccessful ◊Bay of Pigs invasion of Cuba, and in 1963 secured the withdrawal of Soviet missiles from the island. Kennedy was assassinated on a visit to Dallas, Texas.

Kennedy Joseph (Patrick) 1888–1969. US industrialist and diplomat; ambassador to the UK 1937–40. A self-made millionaire, he groomed his four sons from an early age for careers in politics. His eldest son, Joseph Patrick Kennedy Jr (1915–44), was killed in action with the naval air force in World War II. His younger sons were John, Robert, and Edward.

Kennedy Robert F(rancis) 1925–1968. US Democrat politician and lawyer. He was campaign manager for his brother John F Kennedy in 1961, and as attorney general 1961–64 pursued a racket-busting policy and promoted the Civil Rights Act of 1964.

When Johnson preferred Hubert H Humphrey for the 1964 vice-president nomination, Kennedy resigned and was elected senator for New York. In 1968 he campaigned for the Democratic party's presidential nomination, but was assassinated.

Kennedy Space Center the ◊NASA launch site on Merritt Island, near Cape Canaveral, Florida, used for Apollo and Space Shuttle launches.

Kennelly-Heaviside layer former term for the E-layer, the lower regions of the ◊ionosphere which refract radio waves allowing their reception around the surface of the Earth. The Kennelly-Heaviside layer approaches the Earth by day, and recedes from it at night.

Kenneth I Kenneth McAlpin   King of Scotland. Traditionally, he is regarded as the founder of the Scottish kingdom by virtue of his final defeat of the Picts about 844, after which he reigned until his death in about 858.

Kent county in SE England, nicknamed the 'garden of England'
area 3,731 sq km/1,440 sq mi
towns administrative headquarters Maidstone; Canterbury, Chatham, Rochester, Tunbridge Wells; resorts Folkestone, Margate, Ramsgate
products hops, apples, soft fruit (on the weald); coal, cement, paper
population (1986) 1,501,000
famous people Charles Dickens, Christopher Marlowe.

Kent Bruce, 1929– . British peace campaigner who acted as general secretary for the Campaign for Nuclear Disarmament (CND) 1980–85. He was a Catholic priest until 1987.

Kent William 1685–1748. British architect, landscape gardener, and interior designer. In architecture he was foremost in introducing the Palladian style into Britain from Italy. As a gardener, he freed garden design from its earlier formalism.

Kentucky state of S central USA; nicknamed Blue Grass State
area 104,623 sq km/40,395 sq mi
capital Frankfort
towns Louisville, Lexington-Fayette
products tobacco, cereals, steel goods, textiles, transport vehicles
population (1980) 3,660,777
famous people Kit Carson, Jefferson Davis
history originally part of Virginia, it became a state in 1792.

Kenya country in E Africa, bordered to the N by the Sudan and Ethiopia, E by the Somali Republic, SE by the Indian Ocean, SW by Tanzania, and W by Uganda.

Kenyatta Jomo. Name assumed by Kamau Ngengi c. 1889–1978. Kenyan nationalist politician, prime

Kenyatta The first president of independent Kenya, Jomo Kenyatta.

Kenya
Republic of
(Jamhuri ya Kenya)

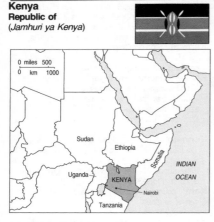

0 miles 500
0 km 1000

Sudan
Ethiopia
Somalia
INDIAN
OCEAN
Uganda
KENYA
Nairobi
Tanzania

area 583,000 sq km/224,960 sq mi
capital Nairobi
towns Kisumu, port Mombasa
physical mountains and highlands in the W and centre; coastal plain in S; the N is arid
head of state and government Daniel arap Moi

from 1978
political system authoritarian nationalism
exports coffee, tea, pineapples, petroleum products
currency Kenya shilling
population (1990 est) 25,393,000 (the dominant ethnic group is the Kikuyu); annual growth rate 4.2%
life expectancy men 59, women 63 (1989)
language Swahili, but English is in general use
religion Protestant 38%, Roman Catholic 28%, indigenous beliefs 26%, Muslim 6%
literacy 50% (1988)
GDP $6.9 bn (1987); $302 per head
chronology
1950 Mau Mau campaign began.
1953 Nationalist leader Jomo Kenyatta imprisoned.
1956 Mau Mau defeated, Kenyatta released.
1964 Full independence, Kenyatta president.
1978 Kenyatta succeeded by Daniel arap Moi.
1983 and **1988** Moi re-elected.
1989 Moi announced release of political prisoners.
1990 Despite riots, Moi refused multiparty politics.
1991 Increasing demand for political reform; Moi promised multiparty politics.
1992 Constitutional amendment passed. Moi re-elected in first direct elections amidst allegations of electoral fraud.

minister from 1963 as well as first president of Kenya from 1964 until his death. He led the Kenya African Union from 1947 (◊*KANU* from 1963) and was active in liberating Kenya from British rule.

Kepler Johann 1571–1630. German mathematician and astronomer. *Kepler's laws* of planetary motion are: (1) the orbit of each planet is an ellipse with the Sun at one of the foci; (2) the radius vector of each planet sweeps out equal areas in equal times; (3) the squares of the periods of the planets are proportional to the cubes of their mean distances from the Sun.

Kerala state of SW India, formed 1956 from the former princely states of Travancore and Cochin
area 38,864 sq km/15,002 sq mi
capital Trivandrum
products tea, coffee, rice, oilseed, rubber; textiles, chemicals, electrical goods
population (1991) 29,011,200
language Kannada, Malayalam, Tamil.

keratin fibrous protein found in the ◊skin of vertebrates and also in hair, nails, claws, hooves, feathers, and the outer coating of horns in animals such as cows and sheep.

Kerensky Alexander Feodorovich 1881–1970. Russian politician, premier of the second provisional government, before its collapse in Nov 1917, during the ◊Russian Revolution. He lived in the USA from 1918.

Kerkira Greek form of ◊Corfu, an island in the Ionian Sea.

Kern Jerome (David) 1885–1945. US composer. He wrote the popular operetta *Show Boat* 1927, which includes the song 'Ol' Man River'.

kernel the inner, softer part of a ◊nut, or of a seed within a hard shell.

kerosene a petroleum distillate, known in the UK as *paraffin*; a more highly refined form is used in jet aircraft fuel. It is a mixture of different hydrocarbons of the paraffin series.

Kerouac Jack 1923–1969. US novelist, who epitomized the ◊beat generation of the 1950s. His books include *On the Road* 1957, and *Big Sur* 1963.

Kerry county of Munster province, Republic of Ireland, E of Cork
area 4,701 sq km/1,815 sq mi
county town Tralee
physical W coastline deeply indented, N part low-lying, but in the S are the highest mountains in Ireland; many rivers and lakes
products engineering, woollens, shoes, cutlery; tourism is important
population (1991) 121,700

Kesselring Albert 1885–1960. German field marshal in World War II, commander of the Luftwaffe (air force) 1939–40. He later served under Field Marshal Rommel in N Africa, took command in Italy in 1943, and was commander in chief on the western front in Mar 1945. His death sentence for war crimes (1947) at the Nuremberg trials was commuted to imprisonment, and he was released in 1952.

kestrel hawk *Falco tinnunculus* of the family Falconidae, which breeds in Europe, Asia, and Africa. About 30 cm/1 ft long, the male has a head and tail of bluish-grey, and its back is a light chestnut-brown with black spots. The female is slightly larger and reddish-brown above, with bars. The kestrel hunts mainly by hovering in mid-air while searching for prey.

ketone member of the group of organic compounds containing the carbonyl group, CO, bonded to two atoms of carbon (instead of one carbon and one hydrogen as in aldehydes). They are liquids or low melting point solids, slightly soluble in water.

Kew Gardens popular name for the ◊Royal Botanic Gardens, Kew, Surrey, England.

key in music, the ◊diatonic scale around which a piece of music is written; for example, a passage in the key of C major will mainly use the notes of the C major scale. The term is also used for the lever activated by a keyboard player, such as a piano key.

keyboard in computing, an input device resembling a typewriter keyboard, which sends signals to a computer indicating which keys have been depressed.

Khaddhafi Libyan revolutionary Colonel Moamer al Khaddhafi.

Keynes John Maynard, 1st Baron Keynes 1883–1946. British economist, whose *The General Theory of Employment, Interest, and Money* 1936, proposed the prevention of financial crises and unemployment by adjusting demand through government control of credit and currency.

Keynesian economics the economic theory of J M Keynes which argues that a fall in national income, lack of demand for goods, and rising unemployment should be countered by increased government expenditure to stimulate the economy. It is opposed by monetarists (see ◊monetarism).

kg abbreviation for *kilogram*.

KG abbreviation for *Knight of the Order of the Garter*.

KGB the secret police of the USSR, the *Komitet Gosudarstvennoy Bezopasnosti*/Committee of State Security, which was in control of frontier and general security and the forced-labour system. KGB officers held ey appointments in all fields of daily life, reporting to administration offices in every major town. The KGB was superseded by the Russian Federal Security Agency on the demise of the Soviet Union 1991.

Khachaturian Aram Il'yich 1903–1978. Armenian composer, noted for folk-like themes, for example in the ballets *Gayaneh* 1942 and *Spartacus* 1956.

Khaddhafi or *Gaddafi* or *Qaddafi*, Maomer al 1942– . Libyan revolutionary leader. Overthrowing King Idris 1969, he became virtual president of a republic, although he nominally gave up all except an ideological role in 1974.

Khalifa the Sudanese dervish leader *Abdullah el Taaisha* 1846–1899. Successor to the Mahdi as Sudanese ruler from 1885, he was defeated at Omdurman 1898, and later killed in Kordofan.

Khalistan projected independent Sikh state. See ◊Sikhism.

Khalsa the brotherhood of the Sikhs, created by Guru Gobind Singh at the festival of Baisakhi in 1699. The Khalsa was originally founded as a militant group to defend the Sikh community from persecution.

Khama Seretse 1921–1980. Botswanan politician, prime minister of Bechuanaland 1965 and first president of Botswana from 1966 until his death.

Khan Jahangir 1963– . Pakistani squash player, who won the world open championship a record six times 1981–85 and 1988.

Khan Liaquat Ali 1895–1951. Indian politician,

deputy leader of the Muslim League Party 1941–47, first prime minister of Pakistan from 1947.

Kharkov capital of the Kharkov region, E Ukraine, 400 km/250 mi E of Kiev. It is a railway junction and industrial city (engineering, tractors), close to the Donets Basin coalfield and Krivoy Rog iron mines; population (1987) 1,587,000.

Khartoum capital and trading centre of Sudan, at the junction of the Blue and White Nile; population (1983) 476,218, and of Khartoum North, across the Blue Nile, 341,146. It was founded in 1830 by ◊Mehemet Ali.

khedive title granted by the Turkish sultan to his Egyptian viceroy 1867, retained by succeeding rulers until 1914.

Khe Sanh in the Vietnam War, US Marine outpost near the Loatian border and just S of the demilitarized zone in North Vietnam, Garrisoned by 4,000 Marines, it was attacked unsuccessfully by 20,000 North Vietnamese troops 21 Jan–7 Apr 1968.

Khirbet Qumran archaeological site in Jordan, see ◊Qumran.

Khmer or *Kmer* inhabitant of Kampuchea (Cambodia). Khmer minorities also live in E Thailand, and S Vietnam. The Khmer language belongs to the Mon Khmer family.

Khmer Republic former name of ◊Kampuchea, country in SE Asia.

Khmer Rouge communist movement in Kampuchea which opposed the US-backed regime led by Lon Nol 1970–75. By 1974 the Khmer Rouge controlled the countryside and in 1975 the capital Phnom Penh was captured and Sihanouk installed as head of state. Internal disagreements led to the creation of the Pol Pot government 1976 and mass deportations and executions. From 1978, when Vietnam invaded the country, the Khmer Rouge conducted a guerrilla campaign against the Vietnamese forces. Pol Pot retired as military leader 1985 and was succeeded by the more moderate Khieu Samphan. Pol Pot, however, continued in a leading role, despite officially resigning from all positions 1989. In 1991 the Khmer Rouge gained representation at government level.

Khomeini Iranian Shi'ite Muslim leader the Ayatollah Khomeini.

Khrushchev *The Soviet politician Nikita Khrushchev at the Quai d'Orsay, Paris.*

Khomeini Ayatollah Ruhollah 1900–1989. Iranian Shi'ite Muslim leader, born in Khomein, central Iran. Exiled for opposition to the Shah from 1964, he returned when the Shah left the country in 1979, and established a fundamentalist Islamic republic.

Khorana Har Gobind 1922– . Indian biochemist, who in 1976 led the team which first synthesized a biologically active gene.

Khrushchev Nikita Sergeyevich 1894–1971. Soviet politician, secretary general of the Communist Party 1953–64, premier 1958–64. He was the first official to denounce Stalin, 1956. A personal feud with Mao Zedong led to a breach in Soviet relations with China 1960. Khrushchev's foreign policy was one of peaceful coexistence with the West, marred by the crisis when he attempted to supply missiles to Cuba 1962.

Khufu *c.* 3000 BC. Egyptian king of Memphis, who built the largest of the pyramids, known to the Greeks as the pyramid of Cheops (the Greek form of Khufu).

Khyber Pass pass 53 km/33 mi long through the mountain range that separates Pakistan from Afghanistan. The Khyber Pass was used by many invaders of India.

Kiangsi former spelling of ◊Jiangxi, province of China.

Kiangsu former spelling of ◊Jiangsu, province of China.

kibbutz Israeli communal collective settlement, with collective ownership of all property and earnings, collective organization of work, and communal housing for children; a modified version, the *Moshav Shitufi*, is similar to the ◊collective farms of the USSR. Other Israeli co-operative rural settlements include the *Moshav Ovdim* which has equal opportunity, and the similar but less strict *Moshav* settlement.

Kidd William c.1645–1701. British pirate, popularly known as Captain Kidd. In 1696 he was commissioned to suppress pirates, but he became a pirate himself. Arrested in 1699, he was taken to England and hanged.

kidnapping the abduction of a person in order to gain money for their safe release. The practice arose in the 17th century with the abduction of young people to become indentured labourers in colonial plantations, from which they could be rescued by a ransom. In English common law it is an offence which carries a maximum sentence of life imprisonment.

kidney an organ of vertebrates responsible for water regulation, excretion of waste products, and maintaining the composition of the blood. In mammals, there is a pair of kidneys situated on the rear wall of the abdomen. Each one consists of a number of long tubules; the outer parts filter the aqueous components of blood, and the inner parts selectively reabsorb vital salts, leaving waste products in the remaining fluid (urine), which is passed through the ureter to the bladder.

Kierkegaard Søren Aabye 1813–1855. Danish philosopher, considered to be the founder of ◊existentialism. He disagreed with ◊Hegel, arguing that no system of thought could explain the unique experience of the individual. He defended Christianity, suggesting that God cannot be known through reason, but only through a 'leap of faith'. He believed that God and exceptional individuals were above moral laws.

Kiev capital of the Ukrainian republic, industrial centre (chemicals, clothing, leatherwork) and third largest city of the USSR, on the confluence of the Desna and Dnieper rivers; population (1985) 2,248,000. Founded in the 5th century, Kiev replaced ◊Novgorod as the capital of Slav-dominated Russia in 882.

Kigali capital of Rwanda, central Africa; population (1981) 156,650. Products include coffee and minerals.

Kikuyu person of Kikuyu culture from Kenya. They are Kenya's dominant ethnic group, and are primarily cultivators, though many are highly educated and have entered the professions. Their language belongs to the Bantu branch of the Niger-Congo family.

Kildare county of Leinster province, Republic of Ireland, S of Meath
area 1,694 sq km/654 sq mi
county town Naas
physical wet and boggy in the north
products oats, barley, potatoes; cattle rearing
population (1986) 116,000.

Kilimanjaro volcano in ◊Tanzania, the highest mountain in Africa, 5,900 m/19,365 ft.

Kilkenny county of Leinster province, Republic of Ireland, E of Tipperary
area 2,061 sq km/796 sq mi
county town Kilkenny
products agricultural; coal
population (1986) 73,000.

killerwhale a type of whale *Orcinus orca* found in all seas of the world. It is black on top, white below, and grows up to 9 m/30 ft long. It has been observed to prey on other whales, as well as seals and sea birds.

kiln high-temperature furnace used commercially for drying timber, roasting metal ores, or for making cement, bricks, and pottery. Oil- or gas-fired kilns are used to bake ceramics at up to 1,760°C/3,200°F; electric

kiln *Brick kilns near Lahore in Pakistan.*

kidney

Blood enters the kidney through the renal artery. The blood is filtered through the glomeruli to extract the urine. The urine flows through the ureter to the bladder; the cleaned blood flow leaves the kidney along the renal vein.

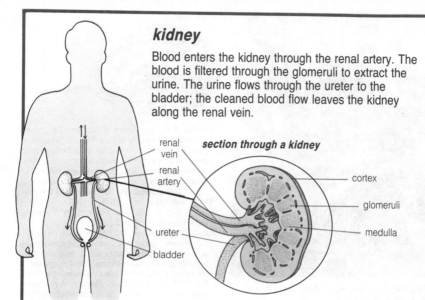

renal vein
renal artery
ureter
bladder

section through a kidney

cortex
glomeruli
medulla

The kidney machine is a copy of the glomerulus which acts as a coarse filtering mechanism in the kidney. Blood is pumped from the patient's body into an artificial kidney where it flows over a thin membrane placed between the blood and a cleaning fluid, called the dialysis fluid. There is a natural tendency, called dialysis, for impurities in the blood to flow across the membrane into the dialysis fluid.

artificial kidney (haemodializer)

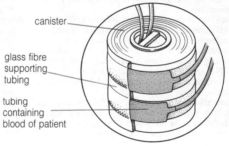

canister
glass fibre supporting tubing
tubing containing blood of patient

A man undergoing continuous ambulatory peritoneal dialysis, allowing a membrane inside the body to take over the kidney's function.▼

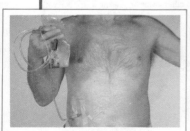

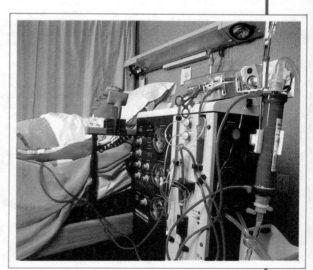

Elderly man undergoing renal dialysis on a kidney machine.

King *Civil Rights campaigner Martin Luther King,on the march in 1965.*

kilns do not generally reach such high temperatures.

kilo- prefix denoting multiplication by 1,000, hence *kilogram* unit of mass equal to 1,000 grams/2.2 lb; *kilometre* unit of length equal to 1,000 metres/3,280.89 ft (approx ⅝ of a mile); *kiloton* unit of explosive force equivalent to 1,000 tons of TNT, used in describing nuclear bombs; and *kilowatt* unit of power equal to about 1,000 watts/1.34 horsepower.

kilowatt-hour commercial unit of electrical energy (kWh), defined as the work done by a power of 1,000 watts in one hour; used to calculate the cost of electrical energy taken from the domestic supply.

Kim Il Sung 1912– . North Korean communist politician and marshal. He became prime minister in 1948 and president in 1972, but retained the presidency of the Communist Workers' Party. Known as the 'Great Leader' he has campaigned constantly for the reunification of Korea. His son Kim Chong Il (1942–) has been named as his successor.

kimberlite an igneous rock which is ultrabasic (containing very little silica). It is similar to peridotite and contains olivine and mica. Kimberlite represents the world's principal diamond source.

Kim Dae Jung 1924– . South Korean social-democratic politician. As a committed opponent of the regime of Gen Park Chung-Hee, he suffered imprisonment and exile. He was a presidential candidate in 1971 and 1987.

kimono traditional Japanese costume, still used by women for formal wear.

kinetic energy a form of ◊energy possessed by moving bodies. It is contrasted with ◊potential energy.

kinetics branch of ◊dynamics dealing with the action of forces producing or changing the motion of a body, as distinguished from kinematics, which deals with motion without reference to force or mass.

kinetics the branch of chemistry which investigates the rates of chemical reactions.

king crab

kinetic theory theory describing the physical properties of matter in terms of the behaviour – principally movement – of its component atoms or molecules. A gas consists of rapidly moving atoms or molecules and, according to kinetic theory, it is their continual impact on the walls of the containing vessel that accounts for the pressure of the gas.

King Billie Jean (born Moffitt) 1943– . US lawn tennis player. She won a record 20 Wimbledon titles between 1961 and 1979.

King Martin Luther, Jr 1929–1968. US civil-rights campaigner, black leader, and Baptist minister. He first came to national attention as leader of a bus boycott in 1955, and was one of the organizers of the massive (200,000 people) march on Washington DC 1963 to demand racial equality. A passionate advocate of nonviolence, he was awarded the Nobel Peace Prize 1964. He was assassinated. The third Monday in Jan is celebrated as *Martin Luther King Day*, a public holiday in the USA.

King William Lyon Mackenzie 1874–1950. Canadian Liberal politician, prime minister 1921-26, 1926-30, and 1935-48. He maintained the unity of the English- and French-speaking population, and was instrumental in establishing equal status for Canada with Britain.

king crab or *horseshoe crab* marine arthropod, subclass Xiphosura, class Arachnida, which lives on the Atlantic coast of North America, and the coasts of Asia. The upper side of the body is entirely covered with a rounded shell, and it has a long spine-like tail. It is up to 60 cm/2 ft long. It is unable to swim, and lays its eggs in the sand at the high-water mark.

kingdom the primary division in biological ◊classification. At one time only two kingdoms were recognized: animals and plants. Today most biologists prefer a five-kingdom system, even though it still involves grouping together organisms that are probably unrelated. One widely accepted scheme is: Kingdom Animalia (all multicellular animals); Kingdom Plantae (all plants, all seaweeds and other algae, including unicellular algae); Kingdom Fungi (all fungi, including the unicellular yeasts, but not slime moulds); Kingdom Protista or Protoctista (protozoa, diatoms, dinoflagellates, slime moulds, and various other lower organisms with eukaryotic

kingfisher

cells) and Kingdom Monera (all prokaryotes – the bacteria and cyanobacteria). The first four of these kingdoms comprise the eukaryotes.

kingfisher bird *Alcedo atthis* found in parts of Europe, Africa, and Asia. The plumage is brilliant blue-green on the back and chestnut beneath. Kingfishers feed upon fish and aquatic insects. The nest is made of fishbones in a hole in a river bank.

King Lear a tragedy by William Shakespeare, first performed 1605–06. Lear, king of Britain, favours his grasping daughters Goneril and Regan with shares of his kingdom but refuses his third, honest daughter, Cordelia, a share. Rejected by Goneril and Regan, the old and unbalanced Lear is reunited with Cordelia but dies of grief when she is murdered.

King's Council in medieval England, a court which carried out much of the king's daily administration. It was first established in the reign of Edward I, and became the Privy Council in 1534–36.

King's Counsel in England, a ◊barrister of senior rank; the term is used when a king is on the throne; and ◊Queen's Counsel when the monarch is a queen.

king's evil another name for the skin condition scrofula. In medieval England and France, it was thought that the touch of an anointed king could cure the condition.

Kingsley Charles 1819–1875. British author. Rector of Eversley, Hampshire 1842–75, he was known as the 'Chartist clergyman' because of such social novels as *Alton Locke* 1850. His historical novels include *Westward Ho!* 1855 and for children, *The Water-Babies* 1863.

Kingsley Mary Henrietta 1862–1900. British ethnologist. She made extensive expeditions in W Africa, and published lively accounts of her findings, for example, *Travels in West Africa* 1897. She died while nursing Boer prisoners during the South African war. She was the niece of the writer Charles Kingsley.

King's Proctor in England, the official representing the Crown in certain court cases; the term is used when a king is on the throne; and ◊Queen's Proctor when the monarch is a queen.

Kingston capital and principal port of Jamaica, West Indies; the cultural and commercial centre of the island; population (1983) 100,637. Founded in 1693, Kingston became the capital of Jamaica in 1872.

Kingston-upon-Hull official name of ◊Hull, city in Humberside in NE England.

Kingstown capital and principal port of St Vincent and the Grenadines, West Indies, in the SW of the island of St Vincent; population (1989) 29,400.

kinkajou Central and South American mammal *Potos flavus* of the raccoon family. Yellowish-brown, with a rounded face and slim body, the kinkajou grows to 55 cm/1.8 ft long with a 50 cm/1.6 ft tail, and has short legs with sharp claws. It spends its time in the trees and has a prehensile tail. It feeds largely on fruit.

Kinnock Neil 1942– . British Labour politician, party leader 1983–92. Born and educated in Wales, he was elected to represent a Welsh constituency in Parliament 1970 (Islwyn from 1983). He was further left than prime ministers Wilson and Callaghan, but as party leader (in succession to Michael Foot) adopted a moderate position, initiating a major policy review 1988–89. He resigned as party leader after Labour's defeat in the 1992 general election.

Kinsey Alfred 1894–1956. US researcher, whose studies of male and female sexual behaviour 1948–53, based on questionnaires, were the first serious published research on this topic.

Kinnock British Labour Party leader Neil Kinnock with his wife Glenys in Blackpool, Sept 1986.

Kinshasa formerly *Léopoldville* capital of Zaïre on the river Zaïre, 400 km/250 mi inland from Matadi; population (1984) 2,654,000. Industries include chemicals, textiles, engineering, food processing, and furniture. It was founded by the explorer Henry Stanley 1887.

kinship human relationship based on blood or marriage, and sanctified by law and custom. Kinship forms the basis for most human societies and for such social groupings as the family, clan, or tribe.

Kipling (Joseph) Rudyard 1865–1936. British writer, born in Bombay. His short stories include *Plain Tales from the Hills* 1888, the *Jungle Books* 1894–1895, *Stalky and Co* 1899, and the *Just So Stories* 1902. Other works include the novel *Kim* 1901, poetry, and an unfinished autobiography *Something of Myself* 1937.

Kirchner Ernst Ludwig 1880–1938. German Expressionist artist, a leading member of the group *die ◊Brücke* in Dresden from 1905 and in Berlin from 1911. He suffered a breakdown during World War I and settled in Switzerland, where he committed suicide.

Kirghiz member of a pastoral people numbering approximately 1.5 million. They inhabit the central Asian region bounded by the Hindu Kush, the Himalayas, and the Tian Shan mountains. The Kirghiz are Sunni Muslims and their Turkic language belongs to the Altaic family.

Kirghizia alternative form of ◊Kyrgyzstan, a country in central Asia.

Kipling British short story writer, novelist, and poet Rudyard Kipling.

Kiribati
Republic of

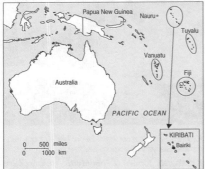

area 655 sq km/253 sq mi
capital and port Bairiki (on Tarawa Atoll)
physical comprises 33 Pacific islands: the Gilbert, Phoenix, and Line Islands, and Banaba (Ocean Island)

head of state and government Teatao Teannaki
political system liberal democracy
exports copra, fish
currency Australian dollar
population (1990 est); 65,600; annual growth rate 1.7%
language English (official) and Gilbertese
religion Roman Catholic 48%, Protestant 45%
literacy 90% (1985)
GDP $26 million (1987) $430 per head
chronology
1977 Gilbert Islands granted internal self-government.
1979 Achieved full independence, within the Commonwealth, as the Republic of Kiribati, with Ieremia Tabai as president.
1983 Tabai re-elected.
1985 Fishing agreement with Soviet state-owned company negotiated, prompting formation of Kiribati's first political party, the opposition Christian Democrats.
1987 Tabai re-elected.
1991 Tabai re-elected but not allowed under constitution to serve a further term; Trannaki elected president.

Kiribati   republic in the central Pacific, comprising three groups of coral atolls: the 16 Gilbert Islands, eight uninhabited Phoenix Islands, eight of the 11 Line Islands, and the volcanic island of Banaba.
Kirin   former name for ◊Jilin, Chinese province.
Kirk   Norman 1924–1974. New Zealand politician, known as 'Big Norm'. He led the Labour Party from 1965, and was prime minister 1972–74.
Kirkcaldy   seaport on the Firth of Forth, Fife region, Scotland; population (1987 est) 49,200. Products include floor coverings and paper. It is the birthplace of the economist Adam Smith and the architect Robert Adam.
Kirkcudbright   former county of S Scotland, merged 1975 in Dumfries and Galloway region. The county town was Kirkcudbright.
Kirov   Sergei Mironovich 1886–1934. Russian Bolshevik leader, who joined the party 1904 and took a prominent part in the 1917–20 civil war. His assassination 1934, possibly engineered by ◊Stalin, led to the political trials held during the next four years.
Kishi   Nobusuke 1896–1987. Japanese politician and prime minister 1957–60. A government minister during World War II and imprisoned 1945, he was never put on trial and returned to politics 1953. During his premiership, Japan began a substantial rearmament programme and signed a new treaty with the USA which gave greater equality between the two states.
Kishinev   Russian name for Chişinăn, the capital of Moldova. Population (1989) 565,000. It is a commercial and cultural centre; industries include cement, food processing, tobacco and textiles.
Kissinger   Henry 1923– . German-born US diplomat. In 1969 he was appointed assistant for National Security Affairs by President Nixon, and was secretary of state 1973–77. His missions to the USSR and China improved US relations with both countries, and he took part in negotiating US withdrawal from Vietnam 1973 and in Arab–Israeli peace negotiations 1973–75. He shared the Nobel Peace Prize 1973.
Kitakyushu   industrial (coal, steel, chemicals, cotton thread, plate glass, alcohol) city and port in Japan, on the Hibiki Sea, N Kyushu, formed 1963 by the amalgamation of Moji, Kokura, Tobata, Yawata, and Wakamatsu; population (1990) 1,026,500. A

tunnel opened 1942 links it with Honshu.
Kitasato   Shibasaburo 1852–1931. Japanese bacteriologist who discovered the plague bacillus. Kitasato was the first to grow the ◊tetanus bacillus in pure culture. He and Behring discovered that increasing non-lethal doses of tetanus toxin gives immunity to the disease.
Kitchener   Horatio Herbert. Earl Kitchener of Khartoum 1850–1916. British soldier and administrator. He defeated the Sudanese dervishes at Omdurman 1898 and re-occupied Khartoum. In South Africa, he was chief-of-staff 1900–02 during the Boer War, and commanded the forces in India 1902–09. He was appointed war minister on the outbreak of World War I, and drowned when his ship was sunk on the way to Russia.
kite   name of several birds of prey in the family Accipitridae, found in all parts of the world except the Americas. The red kite *Milvus milvus*, found in Europe, has a forked tail and narrow wings, and is about 60 cm/2 ft long. There are 50 known pairs in Wales, the only place in the UK where the kite is found. The darker and slightly smaller black kite *Milvus migrans* is found over most of the Old World. It scavenges in addition to hunting.

Kissinger *Henry Kissinger at a White House press conference, Oct 26 1972.*

Klee They're Biting (1920) Tate Gallery, London.

kiwi flightless bird *Apteryx* found only in New Zealand. It has long and hair-like brown plumage, a very long beak with nostrils at the tip, and is nocturnal and insectivorous. The egg is larger in relation to the bird's size (similar to a domestic chicken) than that of any other bird.

kiwi fruit plant *Actinidithia chinensis*, family Actinidiaceae, also known as *Chinese gooseberry*, with oval fruit of similar flavour to a gooseberry, and with a fuzzy brown skin. It is commercially grown on a large scale in New Zealand.

Klammer Franz 1953– . Austrian skier, who won a record 35 World Cup downhill races 1974-1985. Olympic gold medallist 1976.

Klaproth Martin Heinrich 1743–1817. German chemist who first identified the elements uranium, zirconium, cerium, and titanium.

Klee Paul 1879–1940. Swiss painter. He settled in Munich 1906, joined the ◊*Blaue Reiter* group 1912, and worked at the Bauhaus school of art and design 1920–31, returning to Switzerland 1933. His style in the 1920s-30s was dominated by humourous linear fantasies.

kleptomania (Greek *kleptēs* 'thief') a behavioural disorder characterized by an overpowering desire to steal. In kleptomania, as opposed to ordinary theft, there is no obvious need or use for what is stolen.

Klimt Gustav 1862–1918. Austrian painter, influenced by Art Nouveau; a founder member of the Vienna ◊*Sezession* group 1897. His works include mosaics, and his paintings achieve a similar jewelled effect.

Klondike former gold-mining area in ◊Yukon, Canada, and named after the river valley where gold was found 1896. About 30,000 people moved there during the following 15 years.

km abbreviation for *kilometre*.

knapweed plant *Centaurea nigra*, also known as *hardhead*, family Compositae. The hard, buds break into purple composite heads.

Kneller Godfrey 1646–1723. German-born painter, who lived in London from 1674. He was court portraitist to Charles II, James II, William III, and George I.

Knesset the Israeli parliament, consisting of a single chamber of 120 members elected for a period of four years.

Knighthood, Order of fraternity carrying with it the rank of knight, admission to which is granted as a mark of royal favour or as a reward for public services. During the Middle Ages such fraternities fell into two classes, religious and secular. The first class, including the ◊*Templars* and the *Knights of ◊St John*, consisted of knights who had taken religious vows and devoted themselves to military service against the Saracens or other non-Christians. The secular orders probably arose from bands of knights engaged in the service of a prince or great noble.

knitting method of making fabric by twining yarn with needles. Knitting may have developed from *crochet*, which uses a single hooked needle, or from *netting*, using a shuttle.

knocking phenomenon that occurs in a spark-ignition petrol engine when unburned fuel-air mixture explodes in the combustion chamber before being ignited by the spark. The resulting shock waves produce a metallic knocking sound. Loss of power occurs, which can be prevented by reducing the compression ratio, re-designing the geometry of the combustion chamber, or increasing the octane number of the petrol (usually by the use of lead tetraethyl anti-knock additives).

Knossos site near Iráklion of the chief city of ◊Minoan Crete, 6 km/4 mi SE of Candia. The remains, excavated by Arthur ◊Evans 1899–1935, date from the middle Minoan period, c. 2000 BC, and include the palace throne room and a labyrinth, legendary home of the Minotaur.

knot bird *Calidris canutus* of the sandpiper family. It is a wader, about 25 cm/10 in long. In the winter, it is grey above and white below, but in the breeding season, it is brick-red on the head and chest, and black on its wings and back. It feeds on insects and molluscs. Breeding in arctic regions, knots travel widely in winter, to be found as far south as South Africa, Australasia, and southern parts of South America.

knot unit by which a ship's speed is measured, equivalent to 1 ◊nautical mile per hour (1 knot = about 1½ miles per hour). It is also used in aviation, not yet having been replaced by the ◊SI unit, metres per second.

knowledge-based system (KBS) a computer program that uses an encoding of human knowledge to improve its problem-solving performance. It was first discovered in research into ◊artificial

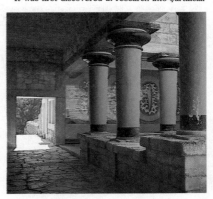

Knossos The Palace of Minos in Knossos, Crete.

***Knox** An engraving showing the 16th-century Scottish Protestant reformer John Knox.*

intelligence that adding heuristics (rules of thumb) enabled programs to tackle problems that were insoluble by the usual techniques of computer science.

Knox John *c.* 1505–1572. Scottish Protestant reformer, founder of the Church of Scotland. He spent several years in exile for his beliefs, including a period in Geneva where he met John ◊Calvin. He returned to Scotland 1559 to promote Presbyterianism.

koala marsupial *Phascolarctos cinereus* of the family Phalangeridae, found only in E Australia. It feeds almost entirely on eucalyptus shoots. It is about 60 cm/2 ft long, and resembles a bear. It has greyish fur which led to its almost complete extermination by hunters. Under protection from 1936, it has rapidly increased in numbers.

kōan in Zen Buddhism, a superficially nonsensical question or riddle used by a Zen master to help a pupil achieve satori (◊enlightenment). It is important in the Rinzai school.

Kobe deep water port in S Honshu, Japan; population (1985) 1,411,000. *Port Island*, created 1960–68 from the rock of nearby mountains, area 5 sq km/2 sq mi, is one of the world's largest construction projects.

Koch Robert 1843–1910. German bacteriologist. Koch and his assistants devised the means to culture bacteria outside the body, and formulated the rules for showing whether or not a bacterium is the cause of a disease.

Kodály Zoltán 1882–1967. Hungarian composer, born at Kecskemet. With ◊Bartók, he collected Magyar folk music, and wrote chamber and instrumental music, including the comic opera *Háry János* 1926, and 'Dances of Galanta'.

koala

Koestler Arthur 1905–1983. Hungarian author. Imprisoned by the Nazis in France 1940, he escaped to England. His novel *Darkness at Noon* 1941 is a fictional account of the Stalinist purges, and draws on his experiences as a prisoner under sentence of death during the Spanish Civil War. He also wrote extensively about creativity, parapsychology, politics, and culture. He committed suicide with his wife.

Koh-i-noor a famous diamond, originally part of the Aurangzeb treasure, seized by the shah of Iran from the Moguls in India 1739, taken back by Sikhs, and acquired by Britain 1849 when the Punjab was annexed.

kohl (Arabic) powdered antimony sulphide, used in Asia and the Middle East to darken the area around the eyes.

Kohl Helmut 1930– . West German conservative politician, leader of the Christian Democratic Union (CDU) from 1976, and chancellor from 1982. He skilfully managed the negotiations for the reunification of East and West Germany and was elected leader of a single German coalition government Dec 1990.

kohlrabi variety of kale *Brassica oleracea*. Leaves shoot from a swelling on the main stem; the globular portion is used for food, and resembles a turnip.

Kokoschka Oskar 1886–1980. Austrian Expressionist painter and writer, who lived in England from 1938. After World War I he worked in Dresden, then in Prague, and fled from the Nazis to England 1938. Initially influenced by the Vienna ◊*Sezession* painters, he developed a disturbing portrait style. He wrote several plays.

kola alternative spelling of ◊cola, genus of tropical tree.

Kolchak Alexander Vasilievich 1875–1920. Russian admiral, commander of the White forces in Siberia during the Russian civil war. He proclaimed himself Supreme Ruler of Russia 1918, but was later handed over to the Bolsheviks by his own men and shot.

Koller Carl 1857–1944. Austrian ophthalmologist who introduced local anaesthesia 1884.

Kollontai Alexandra 1872–1952. Russian revolutionary, politician, and writer. In 1905 she published *On the Question of the Class Struggle*, and was the only female member of the first Bolshevik government as Commissar for Public Welfare. She campaigned for domestic reforms such as simplification of divorce laws, and collective childcare.

Kollwitz Käthe 1867–1945. German artist, who made woodcuts, etchings, lithographs, and sculptures. Her early series of etchings of workers and

***Kohl** German chancellor Helmut Kohl, elected Dec 1990 in the first free all-German elections for 58 years.*

Kollwitz One of a series of large lithographs called Death *1934–35, by German artist Käthe Kollwitz.*

their environment are realistic and harshly expressive, for example *Weavers' Revolt* 1897–98. Later themes include war, death, and maternal love.

Kong Zi Pinyin form of ◊Confucius, Chinese philosopher.

Koniev Ivan Stepanovich 1898–1973. Soviet marshal, who in World War II liberated Ukraine from the German forces 1943, and advanced from the south on Berlin to link up with the British-US forces.

Konoe Fumimaro 1891–1946. Japanese politician and prime minister. Entering politics in the 1920s, Konoe was active in trying to curb the power of the army in government, and preventing an escalation of the war with China. He was prime minister for periods in the late 1930s, but finally resigned 1941 over differences with the army. He helped to engineer the fall of the ◊Tojo government 1944, but committed suicide after being suspected of war crimes.

Kon-Tiki legendary Sun King who ruled the country later occupied by the ◊Incas, and was supposed to have migrated out into the Pacific. The name was used by explorer Thor Heyerdahl for his raft which sailed from Peru to the Pacific Islands 1947.

kookaburra or *laughing jackass* the largest of the world's kingfishers *Dacelo novaeguineae*, with an extraordinary laughing call. It feeds on insects and other small creatures. The body and tail measure 45 cm/18 in, the head is greyish with a dark eye stripe, and the back and wings are flecked brown with grey underparts.

kora 21-string instrument of W African origin, with a harplike sound.

Koran (alternatively transliterated as *Quran*) the sacred book of Islam. Written in the purest Arabic, it contains 114 *suras* (chapters), and is stated to have been divinely revealed to the prophet Muhammad about 616.

Korea, history
1122–4th century The Chinese *Kija dynasty*.
10th century AD After centuries of internal war and invasion, Korea was united within its present boundaries.

16th century Japan invaded Korea for the first time, later withdrawing from a country it had devastated.

1905 Japan began to treat Korea as a protectorate.

1910 It was annexed by Japan. Many Japanese colonists settl ed in Korea, introducing both industrial and agricultural development.

1945 At the end of World War II, the Japanese in Korea surrendered, but the occupying forces at the ceasefire – the USSR north of the ◊38th parallel, and the USA south of it – resulted in a lasting division of the country as North and South Korea (see ◊Korea, North, and ◊Korea, South, for history since 1945).

Korean language the language of Korea, written from the 5th century AD in Chinese characters until the invention of an alphabet by King Sejong 1443. The linguistic affiliations of Korean are unclear, but it appears to be distantly related to Japanese.

Korea, North country in E Asia, bounded N by China, E by the Sea of Japan, S by South Korea, and W by the Yellow Sea.

Korean War US soldiers entrenched at the top of 'Old Baldy', Korea Sept 195 2.

Korea, North
Democratic People's Republic of
(*Chosun Minchu-chui Inmin
Konghwa-guk*)

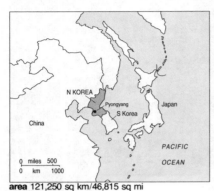

area 121,250 sq km/46,815 sq mi
capital Pyongyang
physical wide coastal plain rising to mountains
head of state Kim Il Sung from 1972
head of government Kang Song San from 1992

political system communism
exports coal, iron, copper, textiles, chemicals
currency won
population (1990 est) 23,059,000; annual growth
rate 2.5%
life expectancy men 67, women 73
language Korean
religion traditionally Buddhist and Confucian
literacy 99% (1989)
GDP $20 bn (1988); $3,450 per head
chronology
1948 Democratic People's Republic of Korea declared.
1950 North Korea invaded South to begin Korean War.
1953 Armistice agreed to end Korean War.
1961 Friendship and mutual assistance treaty
signed with China.
1972 New constitution, with executive president,
was adopted.
1989 Increasing evidence of nuclear weapons
development.
1991 Became a member of the UN. Signed non-
aggression agreement with South Korea; agreed
to ban nuclear weapons.
1992 Legislation passed which made foreign
investment in the country attractive.
1993 Government announced it was pulling out of
the Nuclear Non-Proliferation Treaty.

Korean War war 1950–53 between North Korea
(supported by China) and South Korea, aided by the
United Nations (including the UK, though the
troops were mainly US). North Korean forces
invaded the South 25 Jun 1950, and the Security
Council of the United Nations, owing to a walk-out
by the USSR, voted to oppose them. After a
campaign up and down the peninsula, which ended in
the restoration of the original boundary on the 38th
parallel, an armistice was signed with the North,
although South Korea did not participate.

Korea, South country in E Asia, bordered to the
N by North Korea, E by the Sea of Japan, S by the E
China Sea, and W by the Yellow Sea.

Korolev Sergei Pavlovich 1906–1966. Soviet designer of the first Soviet intercontinental missile,

used 1957 to launch the first ◊Sputnik satellite, and
1961 to launch the ◊Vostok spacecraft (also designed by Korolev).

Kosciusko highest mountain in Australia (2,229
m/7,316 ft), in New South Wales.

Kosciuszko Tadeusz 1746–1817. Polish revolutionary leader, defeated by combined Russian and
Prussian forces 1794, and imprisoned until 1796.

kosher of food, conforming to Mosaic law. Only
animals that chew the cud and have cloven hooves
(cows and sheep, but not pigs) are kosher. There
are rules governing their slaughter and preparation
(such as complete draining of blood), which also
apply to fowl. Only fish with scales and fins are
kosher; shellfish are not. Milk products may not be
cooked or eaten with meat or poultry.

Korea, South
Republic of
(*Daehan Minguk*)

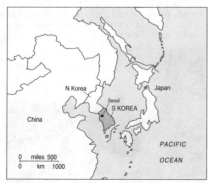

area 99,999 sq km/38,450 sq mi
capital Seoul
towns Taegu, ports Pusan, Inchon
physical mountainous
head of state Kim Young Sam from 1992

head of government Hwang In Sung from 1993
political system emergent democracy
exports steel, ships, chemicals, electronics
currency won
population (1990 est) 43,919,000; annual growth
rate 1.4%
life expectancy men 66, women 73
language Korean
religion traditionally Buddhist and Confucian
literacy 92% (1989)
GDP $171 bn (1988); $2,180 per head
chronology
1948 Republic proclaimed.
1950–53 War with North Korea.
1961 Military coup by Gen Park Chung-Hee.
1979 Assassination of President Park.
1980 Military coup by Gen Chun Doo-Hwan.
1987 Adoption of more democratic constitution.
1988 Former president Chun publicly apologized
for the misdeeds of his administration. Seoul
hosted summer Olympic Games.
1991 Violent mass demonstrations against the
government. Entered UN and signed non-
aggression pact with North Korea.
1992 Kim Young Sam won the presidential
election.

Kosygin *Soviet politician and prime minister, Alexei Kosygin at a press conference in Denmark, 1971.*

Kosovo autonomous region in Serbia, Yugoslavia; capital Priština; area 10,887 sq km/4,202 sq mi; population (1981) 1,584,000. Products include wine, nickel, lead, and zinc. Largely inhabited by Albanians and bordering on Albania, there are demands for unification with that country, while Serbians in 1988 were agitating for Kosovo to be merged with the rest of Serbia.

Kossuth Lajos 1802–1894. Hungarian nationalist. He proclaimed Hungarian independence of Hapsburg rule 1849, and when the Hungarians were later defeated, fled first to Turkey, and then to Britain.

Kosygin Alexei Nikolaievich 1904–1980. Soviet politician, prime minister 1964–80. He was elected to the Supreme Soviet 1938, became a member of the Politburo 1946, deputy prime minister 1960, and succeeded Khrushchev as premier.

koto rectangular 13-stringed musical instrument, plucked with the fingers, the main traditional instrument of Japan. It rests horizontally on the floor, the musician being seated behind it.

kouprey type of wild cattle *Bos sauveli* native to the forest of N Kampuchea. Only known to science since 1937, it is in great danger of extinction.

Kourou river and second-largest town of French Guiana, NW of Cayenne, site of the Guiana Space Centre of the European Space Agency. Situated near the equator, it is an ideal site for launches of satellites into ◊geostationary orbit.

Kowloon peninsula on the Chinese coast forming part of the British crown colony of Hong Kong; the town of Kowloon is a residential area.

kph or *km/h* abbreviation for *kilometres per hour*.

Kraków *Kraków's 14th-century Gothic cathedral.*

Kraków or *Cracow* city in Poland, on the Vistula; population (1985) 716,000. It is an industrial centre producing railway wagons, paper, chemicals, and tobacco. It was capital of Poland *c.* 1300–1595.

Krebs Hans 1900–1981. German-born British biochemist. In 1953 he shared a Nobel Prize in medicine for discovering the citric acid cycle, also known as Krebs' cycle, by which food is converted into energy in living tissues.

Krebs' cycle or *citric acid cycle* part of the chain of biochemical reactions through which organisms break down food using oxygen (aerobically) to release energy. It breaks down food molecules in a series of small steps, producing energy-rich molecules of ◊ATP.

kremlin citadel or fortress of Russian cities. The Moscow kremlin dates from the 12th century, and the name 'the Kremlin' is used as synonymous with the Soviet government.

krill Antarctic crustacean, the most common species being *Euphausia superba*. Shrimp-like, it is about 6 cm/2.5 in long, with two antennae, five pairs of legs, seven pairs of light organs along the body, and is coloured orange above and green beneath.

Krishna incarnation of the Hindu god ◊Vishnu, The devotion of the ◊bhakti movement is usually directed towards Krishna; an example of this is the ◊International Society for Krishna Consciousness. Many stories are told of Krishna's mischievous youth, and he is the charioteer of Arjuna in the *Bhagavad-Gītā*.

Kristallnacht the 'night of [broken] glass' 9–10 Nov 1938 when the Nazi Sturm Abteilung (SA) militia in Germany and Austria mounted a concerted attack on Jews, their synagogues, and their property. It followed the murder of a German embassy official in Paris by a Polish-Jewish youth. Subsequent measures included legislation against Jews owning businesses.

Kronos or *Cronus* in Greek mythology, ruler of the world and one of the ◊Titans. He was the father of Zeus, who overthrew him.

Kronstadt uprising revolt in Mar 1921 by sailors of the Russian Baltic Fleet at their headquarters in Kronstadt, outside Petrograd (now Leningrad). Red Army troops crossed the ice to the naval base and captured it.

Kropotkin Peter Alexeivich, Prince Kropotkin 1842–1921. Russian anarchist. Imprisoned for revolutionary activities 1874, he escaped to the UK in 1876, and later moved to Switzerland. Expelled from Switzerland, he went to France, where he was imprisoned 1883–86. He lived in Britain until 1917, when he returned to Moscow. Among his works are *Mutual Aid* 1902 and *Modern Science and Anarchism* 1903.

Kruger Stephanus Johannes Paulus 1825–1904. President of the Transvaal 1883–1900. He refused to remedy the grievances of the Uitlanders (English and other non-Boer white residents), and so precipitated the Second ◊South African War.

Kruger telegram message sent by Kaiser Wilhelm II of Germany to President Kruger of the Transvaal 3 Jan 1896 congratulating him on defeating the ◊Jameson raid of 1895. The text of the telegram provoked indignation, in Britain and elsewhere, and represented a worsening of Anglo-German relations, in spite of a German government retraction.

Krupp German steelmaking armaments firm, founded in the early 19th century, and developed by Alfred Krupp (1812–87) by pioneering the Bessemer steelmaking process. It developed

Kublai Khan

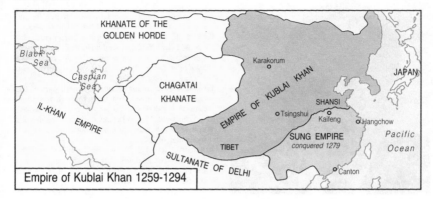

KHANATE OF THE GOLDEN HORDE

Black Sea

Caspian Sea

IL-KHAN EMPIRE

CHAGATAI KHANATE

Karakorum

EMPIRE OF KUBLAI KHAN

SHANSI

Tsingshui
Kaifeng
Hangchow

JAPAN

SUNG EMPIRE
conquered 1279

TIBET

SULTANATE OF DELHI

Canton

Pacific Ocean

Empire of Kublai Khan 1259-1294

the long-distance artillery used in World War I, and supported Hitler's regime in preparation for World War II, after which the head of the firm was imprisoned.

krypton a colourless, odourless, inert gas. It is an element, symbol Kr, atomic number 36, relative atomic mass 83.8. It was discovered in 1898 by Ramsay and Travers in the residue from liquid air. It occurs in the atmosphere at about 1½ parts per million, and is used to enhance brilliance in miners' electric lamps, and in some gas-filled electronic valves.

Kuala Lumpur capital of the Federation of Malaysia; population (1990) 1,237,900. The city developed after 1873 with the expansion of tin and rubber trading; these are now its major industries. Formerly within the state of Selangor, of which it was also the capital, it was created a federal territory in 1974.

Kuanyin transliteration of ◊Guanyin, goddess of mercy in Chinese Buddhism.

Kublai Khan 1216–1294. Mongol emperor of China from 1259. He completed his grandfather ◊Genghis Khan's conquest of N China from 1240, and on his brother Mungo's death in 1259, established himself as emperor of China. He moved the capital to Peking and founded the Yuan dynasty, successfully expanding his empire into Indochina, but was defeated in an attempt to conquer Japan 1281.

Kubrick Stanley 1928– . British film director, producer, and screenwriter, born in America. His films include *Dr Strangelove* 1964, *2001: A Space Odyssey* 1968, and *The Shining* 1979. More than any of his contemporaries, Kubrick achieved complete artistic control over his films, which have been ambitious in both scale and technique.

kudu African antelope *Tragelaphus strepsiceros*. It is fawn-coloured with thin white vertical stripes, and stands 1.3 m/4.2 ft at the shoulder, with head and body 2.4 m/8 ft long. Males have long spiral horns. The kudu is found in bush country from Angola to Ethiopia.

kudzu Japanese creeper *Pueraria lobata*, family Leguminosae, which helps fix nitrogen (see ◊nitrogen cycle) and can be used as fodder, but became a pest in the USA when introduced to check soil erosion.

Kuhn Thomas S 1922– . US historian and philosopher of science, who showed that social and cultural conditions affect the directions of science. *The Structure of Scientific Revolutions* 1962 argued that

even scientific knowledge is relative, dependent on the ◊*paradigm* (theoretical framework) that dominates a particular scientific field at that point in time. Such paradigms are so dominant that they are uncritically accepted as true, until a 'scientific revolution' creates a new orthodoxy. Kuhn's ideas have also influenced thinking in the social sciences.

Kuibyshev or *Kuybyshev* former name (1935–91) of ◊*Samara*, a city in W central Russia.

Ku Klux Klan US secret society dedicated to white supremacy, founded in 1866 in the southern states of the USA to oppose ◊Reconstruction after the Civil War and to deny political rights to the black population. Members wore hooded white robes to hide their identity, and burned crosses as a symbol. It was active in the 1960s in terrorizing civil rights activists and organizing racist demonstrations.

kulak Russian term for a peasant who could afford to hire labour, and often acted as village usurer. The kulaks resisted the Soviet government's policy of collectivization, and in 1930 they were 'liquidated as a class', with up to five million being either killed or deported to Siberia.

Kulturkampf German word for policy introduced by Chancellor Bismarck in Germany in 1873, which isolated the Catholic interest and attempted to reduce its power in order to create a political coalition of liberals and agrarian conservatives. The policy was abandoned after 1876 and replaced by an anti-Socialist policy.

Kun Béla 1885–1937. Hungarian politician who created a Soviet republic in Hungary Mar 1919, which was overthrown August of the same year by a Western blockade and Romanian military actions.

Kundera Milan 1929– . Czech writer, born in Brno. His first novel *The Joke* 1967 brought him into official disfavour in Prague, and, unable to publish further works, he moved to France. His novels include *The Book of Laughter and Forgetting* 1979 and *The Unbearable Lightness of Being* 1984.

Kung Hans 1928– . Swiss Roman Catholic theologian. Professor at Tübingen University, Germany, from 1963, he was barred by the Vatican from teaching in 1979 'in the name of the Church' because he had cast doubt on papal infallibility, and on whether Christ was the son of God.

kung fu The popular name for the Chinese art of unarmed combat (Mandarin *ch'üan fa*), one of the ◊martial arts. Practised in many forms, the most popular is *wing chun* 'beautiful springtime'. The basic principle is to use attack as a form of defence.

Kunming formerly *Yunnan* capital of Yunnan

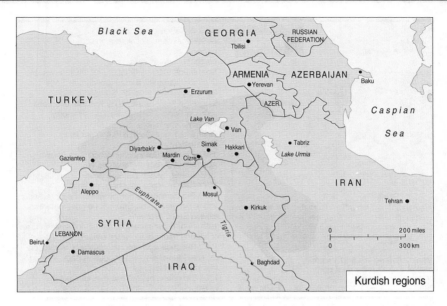

Kurdish regions

province, China, on Lake Dian Chi, about 2,000 m/6,300 ft above sea level; population (1989) 1,500,000. Industries include chemicals, textiles, and copper smelted with nearby hydroelectric power.

Kuomintang original name of Chinese nationalist party, now known (outside Taiwan) as ◊Guomindang.

kurchatovium another name for the element ◊rutherfordium.

Kurd member of the Kurdish culture, living mostly in the Taurus and Sagros mountains of W Iran and N Iraq in the region called Kurdistan. Although divided among more powerful states, the Kurds have nationalist aspirations; there are some 8 million in Turkey (where they suffer from discriminatory legislation), 5 million in Iran, 4 million in Iraq, 500,000 in Syria, and 500,000 in Azerbaijan, Armenia, and Georgia. Several million live elsewhere in Europe. Some 1 million Kurds were made homeless and 25,000 killed as a result of chemical-weapon attacks by Iraq 1984–89, and in 1991, in the wake of the Gulf War, more than 1 million were forced to flee their homes in N Iraq. The Kurdish languages (Kurmanji, Sorani Kurdish, Gurani, and Zaza) are members of the Indo-Iranian branch of the Indo-European family, and the Kurds are a non-Arab, non-Turkic ethnic group. The Kurds are predominantly Sunni Muslims, although there are some Shi'ites in Iran

Kurdistan or *Kordestan* hilly region in SW Asia in the neighbourhood of Mt Ararat, where the borders of Iran, Iraq, Syria, Turkey, Armenia, and Azerbaijan meet; area 192,000 sq km/74,600 sq mi.

Kuril Islands chain of about 50 small islands stretching from the NE of Hokkaido, Japan, to the S of Kamchatka, Russia; area 14,765 sq km/5,700 sq mi; population (1990) 25,000. Some of them are of volcanic origin.

Kuropatkin Alexei Nikolaievich 1848–1921. Russian general. He made his reputation during the Russo-Turkish War of 1877–78, was commander in chief in Manchuria in 1903, and resigned after his defeat at Mukden in the Russo-Japanese War. During World War I he commanded the armies on the N front until 1916.

Kutuzov Mikhail Larionovich, Prince of Smolensk 1745–1813. Commander of the Russian forces in the Napoleonic Wars. He commanded an army corps at ◊Austerlitz, and the retreating army in 1812. After the burning of Moscow he harried the French throughout their retreat, and later took command of the united Prussian armies.

Kuwait country in SW Asia, bordered N and NW by Iraq, E by the Gulf, and S and SW by Saudi Arabia.

Kuwait City (formerly *Qurein*) chief port and capital of the State of Kuwait, on the S shore of Kuwait Bay; population (1985) 44,300. It has been an important banking and investment centre since the development of oil in the 1940s.

Kuznetsov Anatoli 1930–1979. Russian writer. His novels *Babi Yar* 1966, describing the wartime execution of Jews at Babi Yar, near Kiev, and *The Fire* 1969, about workers in a large metallurgical factory, were seen as anti-Soviet.

kW abbreviation for *kilowatt*.

Kwakiutl (or Kwa-Gulth) indigenous American people who live on both sides of the northern entrance to the Queen Charlotte Strait. Their language belongs to the Wakashan family.

Kwangchow former name of ◊Guangzhou, city of China.

Kwangsi-Chuang former name of ◊Guanxi Zhuang, province of China.

Kwangtung former name of ◊Guangdong, province of China.

Kwannon or *Kannon* in Japanese Buddhism, a female form (known as the West as 'goddess of mercy') of the bodhisattva ◊Avalokiteśvara.

Kyd Thomas *c*.1557–1595. English dramatist, author in about 1588 of a bloody revenge tragedy *The Spanish Tragedy*, which anticipated elements present in *Hamlet*.

Kyoto former capital of Japan (794–1868) on Honshu island, linked by canal with Biwa Lake; population (1989) 1,407,300. University town; industries include silk weaving and manufacture, embroidery, porcelain, bronze and lacquer ware.

Kuwait
State of
(*Dowlat al Kuwait*)

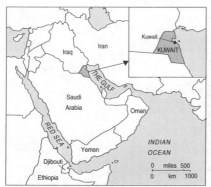

area 17,819 sq km/6,878 sq mi
capital Kuwait (also chief port)
physical hot desert
head of state and government Jabir al-Ahmad al-

Jabir al-Sabah from 1977
political system absolute monarchy
exports oil
currency Kuwaiti dinar
population (1990 est) 2,080,000 (40% Kuwaitis,
30% Palestinians); annual growth rate 5.5%
life expectancy men 72, women 76
language 78% Arabic, 10% Kurdish, 4% Farsi
religion Sunni Muslim, with Shi'ite minority
literacy 71% (1988)
GNP $19.1 bn (1988); $10,410 per head
chronology
1961 Achieved full independence, with Sheikh
Abdullah al-Salem al-Sabah as emir.
1965 Sheikh Sabah became emir.
1977 Crown Prince Jabi became emir.
1990 Pro-democracy demonstrations suppressed.
Iraq annexed Kuwait. Emir set up government in
exile in Saudi Arabia.
1991 Feb: Kuwait liberated by US-led forces. Trials
of alleged Iraqi collaborators criticized.
1992 Reconstituted national assembly elected on
restricted franchise, with opposition party winning
majority of seats.
1993 Incursions by Iraq into Kuwait created
tension; US-led air strikes restored calm.

Kyrgyzstan   country in central Asia, bounded N by
Kazakhstan, E by China, W by Uzbekistan, and S by
Tajikistan.

Kyrie eleison   (Greek 'Lord have mercy') the
words spoken or sung at the beginning of the mass in
the Catholic, Orthodox, and Anglican churches.

Kyushu   most southerly of the main islands of
Japan, separated from Shikoku and Honshu by
Bungo Channel and Suo Bay, but connected to
Honshu by bridge and rail tunnel.

area 42,084 sq km/16,249 sq mi including about
370 small islands
capital Nagasaki
towns Kagoshima, Kumamoto, Fukuoka
physical mountainous, volcanic, with sub-tropical
climate
products coal, gold, silver, iron, tin, rice, tea,
timber
population (1986) 13,295,000.

Kyrgyzstan
Republic of

area 198,500 sq km/76,641 sq mi
capital Bishkek (formerly Frunze)
towns Osh, Przhevalsk, Kyzyl-Kiya, Tormak
physical mountainous, an extension of the Tian
Shan range
head of state Askar Akayev from 1990

head of government Tursunbek Chyngyshev from
1991
political system emergent democracy
products cereals, sugar, cotton, coal, oil, sheep,
yaks, horses
population (1990) 4,400,000 (52% Kyrgyz, 22%
Russian, 13% Uzbek, 3% Ukrainian, 2% German)
language Kyrgyz, a Turkic language
religion Sunni Muslim
chronology
1917–1924 Part of independent Turkestan.
1924 Became autonomous republic within USSR.
1936 Became full union republic within USSR.
1990 Ethnic clashes resulted in state of emergency
being imposed in Bishkek. Askar Akayev chosen
as state president.
1991 March: Kyrgyz voters endorsed maintenance
of Union in USSR referendum. Aug: President
Akayev condemned anti-Gorbachev attempted
coup in Moscow; Kyrgyz Communist Party, which
supported the coup, suspended. Oct: Akayev
directly elected president. Dec: joined
Commonwealth of Independent States (CIS).
1992 Became a member of the United Nations
(UN).

L Roman numeral for 50; abbreviation for learner (driver).

l or **L** abbreviation for *litre*.

laager term used by Boers in South Africa to describe an enclosed encampment; now more widely applied to the siege mentality of sections of the Afrikaner population.

Lab. abbreviation for *Labour*.

Labanotation a comprehensive system of accurate and precise dance notation (*Kinetographie Laban* 1928) devised by Rudolf von Laban (1879–1958), dancer, choreographer and dance theorist.

labelled compound a chemical compound in which an ◊isotope (usually a radioactive one) is substituted for a normal atom. Thus labelled, the path taken by the compound through a system can be followed, for instance by measuring the radiation emitted.

labelling in sociology, defining or describing a person in terms of their behaviour; for example, describing someone who has broken a law as a criminal. Social labelling has been seen as a form of social control in that labels affect both a person's self-image and other people's reactions.

labellum the lower petal of an orchid flower, different in shape from the two lateral petals and giving the orchid its characteristic appearance. The labellum is more elaborate and usually larger than the other petals, and it often has a distinctive patterning to encourage insects to land on it when visiting the flower. Sometimes it is extended backwards to form a hollow spur containing nectar.

Labor, Knights of in US history, a national labor organization founded by Philadelphia tailor Uriah Stephens 1869 and committed to cooperative enterprise, equal pay for both sexes, and an eight-hour day. It grew rapidly in the mid-1880s under Terence V Powderly (1849–1924) but gave way to the American Federation of ◊Labor after 1886.

Labor Party in Australia, political party based on socialist principles. It was founded 1891 and first held office 1904. It formed governments 1929–31 and 1939–49, but in the intervening periods internal discord provoked splits, and reduced its effectiveness. It returned to power under Gough Whitlam 1972–75, again under Bob Hawke 1983–91, and yet again 1993 under Paul Keating, who had ousted Hawke as party leader 1991.

Labour Day annual festival of the Labour movement, often linked with 1 May, for example in England first Monday in May, and a bank holiday since 1976. In North America, **Labor Day** is celebrated on the first Monday in Sep, and is a public holiday.

labour market the market which determines the cost and conditions of the work force. This will depend on the demand of employers, the levels and availability of skills, and social conditions.

Labour Party in the UK, political party based on socialist principles, originally formed to represent the working class. It was founded 1900 and first held office 1924. The first majority Labour government 1945–51 introduced ◊nationalization and the National Health Service and expanded ◊social security. Labour was again in power 1964–70 and 1974–79. The party leader is elected by Labour Members of the Parliament.

labour theory of value in classical economics, the theory that the price (value) of a product directly reflects the amount of labour involved. According to theory, if the price of a product falls, either the share of labour in that product has declined, or that expended in other goods has risen.

Labrador mainland part of the province of Newfoundland, Canada, consisting primarily of a gently sloping plateau with irregular coastline, lying between Ungava Bay on the NW, the Atlantic on the E, and the Strait of Belle Isle on the SE; area 266,060 sq km/102,699 sq mi; population (1986) 28,741. It has important fisheries, large forests supporting a timber and pulp industry, and rich mineral resources. Hydroelectric resources include Churchill Falls on Churchill river, where one of the world's largest underground power houses is situated.

La Bruyère Jean de 1645–1696. French essayist. Born in Paris, he studied law, took a post in the revenue office, and in 1684 entered the service of the house of Condé. His *Caractères* 1688, satirical portraits of contemporaries, made him many enemies.

laburnum flowering tree *Laburnum anagyroides*, family Leguminosae, native to the mountainous parts of central Europe. The flowers, in long drooping clusters, are bright yellow and appear in early spring; some varieties have purple or reddish flowers. The seeds are poisonous.

Laccadive, Minicoy, and Amindivi islands former name of Indian island group ◊Lakshadweep.

lace a delicate, decorative textile fabric in openwork.

lacewing insect of the families Hemerobiidae (the brown lacewings) and Chrysopidae (the green lacewings) of the order Neuroptera. Found throughout the world, they are so named because of the veining of their two pairs of semi-transparent wings, and have narrow bodies and long thin antennae.

Laclos Pierre Choderlos de 1741–1803. French author and army officer. He wrote a single novel in letter form, *Les Liaisons dangereuses/Dangerous Acquaintances* 1782, an analysis of moral corruption.

lacquer a clear or coloured varnish used for decorating furniture and objets d'art. It was developed in China, probably as early as 4th century BC, and later adopted in Japan.

lacrosse Canadian ball game, adopted from the North American Indians, and named from a fancied resemblance of the lacrosse stick to a bishop's crozier. Thongs across its curved end form a pocket to carry the small rubber ball.

lactation the secretion of milk from the mammary glands of mammals. In late pregnancy, the cells lining the lobules inside the mammary glands undergo a change which makes them extract substances from the blood to produce milk. The supply of milk starts shortly after birth with the production of colostrum, a clear fluid consisting largely of water, protein, antibodies, and vitamins. The milk continues practically as long as the infant continues to suck.

lactic acid $CH_3CH(OH)CO_2H$ (modern name *hydroxypropanoic acid*) an organic acid, a colourless, almost odourless syrup, which is produced by certain bacteria during fermentation, and occurs in yoghurt, buttermilk, sour cream, wine, and certain plant extracts; it is also present in muscles when they are exercised hard, and in the stomach. It is used in food preservation, and the preparation of pharmaceuticals.

lactose a white sugar, found in solution in milk; it forms 5% of cow's milk. It is commercially prepared from the whey obtained in cheese-making.

Ladins ethnic community (about 16,000) in the Dolomites whose language (Ladin) derives directly from Latin; they descend from the Etruscans and other early Italian tribes, and have links with the speakers of ◊Romansch.

Ladoga (Russian *Ladozhskoye*) largest lake on the continent of Europe, in the USSR, just NE of Leningrad; area 18,400 sq km/7,100 sq mi. It receives the waters of the Svir, which drains Lake Onega, and other rivers, and runs to the Gulf of Finland by the river Neva.

Lady in the UK, the formal title of the daughter of an earl, marquis, or duke; and of any woman whose husband is above the rank of baronet or knight, as well as (by courtesy only) the wives of these latter ranks.

ladybird beetle of the family Coccinellidae, generally red or yellow in colour, with black spots. There are many species which, with their larvae, feed upon aphids and scale-insect pests.

Lady Day Christian festival (25 Mar) of the Annunciation of the Virgin Mary; until 1752 it was the beginning of the legal year in England, and is still a ◊quarter day.

lady's smock alternative name for the ◊cuckoo flower *Cardamine pratensis*.

Laënnec René Théophile Hyacinthe 1781–1826. French physician, inventor of the stethoscope 1814. He introduced it, along with the new diagnostic technique of ◊auscultation, in his book *De l'Auscultation Médiaté* 1819. It quickly became a medical classic.

Lafayette Marie Joseph Gilbert de Motier, Marquis de Lafayette 1757–1834. French soldier and politician. He fought against Britain in the American War of Independence. During the French Revolution he sat in the National Assembly as a constitutional royalist, and in 1789 was given command of the National Guard. In 1792 he fled the country after attempting to restore the monarchy, and was imprisoned by the Austrians until 1797. He supported Napoleon during the hundred days, sat in the chamber of deputies as a Liberal from 1818, and assisted the revolution of 1830.

Lafayette Marie-Madeleine, comtesse de Lafayette 1634–1693. French author. Her *La Princesse de Clèves* 1678 is the first French psychological novel and *roman à clef* (novel with a 'key') in that real-life characters are presented under fictitious names.

La Fontaine Jean de 1621–1695. French poet. His works include *Fables* 1668–94, and *Contes*

Lahore *the Lahore Fort was largely reconstructed . by the Mughal emperor Akbar, who reigned from 1556–1605.*

1665–74, a series of witty and bawdy tales in verse.

Laforgue Jules 1860–1887. French poet, who pioneered ◊free verse and who greatly influenced later French and English writers.

Lagash Sumerian city N of Shatra, Iraq, of great importance under independent and semi-independent rulers from about 3000 to 2700 BC. Besides objects of high artistic value, it has provided about 30,000 clay tablets giving detailed information on temple administration. It was discovered 1877 and excavated by Earnest de Sarzec, then French consul in Basra.

lager a type of ◊beer.

Lagerkvist Pär 1891–1974. Swedish author of lyric poetry, dramas including *The Hangman* 1935, and novels such as *Barabbas* 1950. Nobel prize 1951.

Lagerlöf Selma 1858–1940. Swedish novelist. Originally a schoolteacher, she won fame 1891 with a collection of stories of peasant life, *Gösta Berling's Saga*. She was the first woman to receive a Nobel prize, 1909.

lagoon a coastal body of shallow salt water, usually with limited access to the sea. The term is normally used to describe the shallow sea area cut off by a ◊coral reef or shingle ridge.

Lagos chief port and former capital (decision to create new capital at Abuja announced 1976) of Nigeria, W Africa; located at W end of an island in a lagoon and linked by bridges with the mainland via Iddo Island; population (1983) 1,097,000. Its products include chemicals, metal products, and fish.

Lagrange Joseph Louis 1736–1813. French mathematician, who predicted the existence of ◊Lagrangian points 1772. His *Mécanique analytique* 1788 applied mathematical analysis, using principles established by Newton, to such problems as the movements of planets when affected by each other's gravitational force.

Lagrangian points five points in space where a small body can remain in a stable orbit with two much more massive bodies. Three of the points, L1–L3, lie on a line joining the two bodies. The other two points, L4 and L5, which are the most stable, lie either side of the line. The *Trojan asteroids* lie at Lagrangian points L4 and L5 in Jupiter's orbit around the Sun. Clouds of dust and debris may lie at the Lagrangian points of the Moon's orbit around the Earth.

La Guardia Fiorello (Henrico) 1882–1947. US Republican politician, mayor of New York 1933–1945. Elected against the opposition of the powerful Tammany Hall Democratic Party organization, he cleaned up the administration, suppressed racketeering, and organized unemployment relief, slum-clearance schemes, and social services.

Lahore capital of the province of Punjab and second city of Pakistan; population (1981) 2,920,000. Industries include engineering, textiles, carpets, and chemicals. Associated with Mogul rulers Akbar, Jahangir, and Aurangzeb, whose capital it was in the 16th–17th centuries.

Lailat ul-Barah Muslim festival, the *Night of Forgiveness*, which takes place two weeks before the beginning of the fast of Ramadan (the ninth month of the Islamic year) and is a time for asking and granting forgiveness.

Lailat ul-Isra Wal Mi'raj Muslim festival which celebrates the prophet Muhammad's ◊Night Journey.

Lailat ul-Qadr Muslim festival, the *Night of Power*, which celebrates the giving of the Koran to Muhammad. It usually falls at the end of Ramadan.

Laing R(onald) D(avid) 1927–1990. Scottish psychoanalyst, originator of the 'social theory' of mental illness, for example that ◊schizophrenia is promoted by family pressure for its members to conform to standards alien to themselves. His books include *The Divided Self* 1960 and *The Politics of the Family* 1971.

laissez-faire theory that the state should refrain from all intervention in economic affairs, unless it was necessary to break up a monopoly. The phrase originated with the 18th-century French Economists, the Physiocrats, whose maxim was *laissez-faire et laissez-passer*, (literally 'let go and let pass', that is leave the individual alone, and let commodities circulate freely. The degree to which intervention should take place is one of the main problems of modern economics, both in capitalist and in communist regimes. See also Adam ◊Smith.

lake body of water without direct link to the sea. Lakes are common in formerly glaciated regions, along the courses of slow rivers, and in low land near the sea. The main classifications are by origin as follows: *glacial lakes* such as in the Alps; *barrier lakes* formed by landslides, valley glaciers, and the like; *crater lakes*; *tectonic lakes* occurring in natural fissures.

lake dwelling Stone Age village built on piles driven into the bottom of a lake. Such villages are found throughout Europe, in W Africa, South America, Borneo, and New Guinea. A lake village of the 1st centuries BC and AD has been excavated near Glastonbury, Somerset.

Lakshadweep group of coral islands, ten inhabited, in the Indian Ocean, 320 km/200 mi off the Malabar coast
area 28 sq km/11 sq mi
administrative headquarters Kavaratti Island
products coir, copra, fish
population (1981) 40,241
religion mainly Muslim
history British from 1877 until Indian independence; created a Union Territory of the Republic of India 1956. Formerly known as the Laccadive, Minicoy and Amindivi Islands, they were renamed Lakshadweep in 1973.

Lakshmi Hindu goddess of wealth and beauty, consort of Vishnu; her festival is ◊Diwali.

Lalique René 1860–1945. French designer of ◊Art Nouveau jewellery, glass, and house interiors.

Lallans a variant of 'lowlands' and a name for Lowland Scots, whether conceived as a language in its own right or as a northern dialect of English.

Lamaism the religion of Tibet and Mongolia, a form of Mahāyāna Buddhism. Buddhism was introduced into Tibet 640, but the real founder of Lamaism was the Indian missionary Padma Sambhava who began his activity about 750. The head of the church is the ◊Dalai Lama, who is considered an incarnation of the Bodhisattva Avalokitesvara.

Lamarck Jean Baptiste de 1744–1829. French naturalist. He proposed a theory of evolution, *Lamarckism*, and his works include *Philosophie Zoologique/Zoological Philosophy* 1809 and *Histoire naturelle des animaux sans vertèbres/Natural History of Invertebrate Animals* 1815–22.

Lamarckism a theory of evolution advocated during the early 19th century by Lamarck. It was based on the idea that ◊acquired characters were inherited: he argued that particular use of an organ or limb strengthens it, and that this development may be 'preserved by reproduction'.

Lamartine Alphonse de 1790–1869. French poet. His first volume of musically romantic poems, *Méditations* 1820 was followed by *Nouvelles Méditations/New Meditations* 1823 and *Harmonies* 1830. He entered the Chamber of Deputies 1833, and by his *Histoire des Girondins/History of the Girondins* 1847 influenced the revolution of 1848.

Lamb Charles 1775–1834. English essayist and critic. He collaborated with his sister Mary (1764–1847) on *Tales from Shakespeare* 1807, and his *Specimens of English Dramatic Poets* 1808 helped to revive interest in Elizabethan plays. As 'Elia' he contributed essays to the *London Magazine* from 1820 (collected 1823 and 1833).

Lambeth Conference meeting of bishops of the Anglican Communion every ten years, presided over by the archbishop of Canterbury; its decisions are not binding.

lamina in flowering plants (◊angiosperms), the blade of the ◊leaf on either side of the midrib. The lamina is generally thin and flattened, and is usually the primary organ of ◊photosynthesis. It has a network of veins through which water and nutrients are conducted. The term 'lamina' is also used more broadly to describe any thin, flat plant structure.

Lammas medieval festival ('loaf-mass') of harvest, celebrated on 1 Aug. It was an English ◊quarter day, and is still a quarter day in Scotland.

lammergeier bird of prey *Gypaetus barbatus*, also known as the bearded vulture, with a wingspan of 2.7 m/9 ft. It ranges over S Europe, N Africa, and Asia, in wild mountainous areas.

Lamming George 1927– . Barbadian novelist, author of the autobiographical *In the Castle of my Skin* 1953, describing his upbringing in a small village. He later moved to London and worked for the BBC.

Lamont Norman 1942– . British Conservative politician, member of Parliament for Kingston-upon-Thames from 1972. He was a junior minister in Margaret Thatcher's 1972 government, entering the cabinet in 1989 as Treasury chief secretary, succeeding John Major. His management of Major's campaign for the Conservative party leadership at the end of 1990 was rewarded with the post of chancellor of the Exchequer.

Lampedusa Giuseppe Tomasi di 1896–1957. Italian aristocrat, author of *The Leopard* 1958, a novel set in his native Sicily in the period after it was annexed by Garibaldi 1860, which chronicles the reactions of an aristocratic family to social and political upheavals.

lamprey eel-shaped jawless fish belonging to the family Petromyzontidae. Lampreys feed on other fish by fixing themselves by the round mouth to their host and boring into the flesh with their toothed tongue.

Lancashire county in NW England
area 3,063 sq km/1,182 sq mi

towns administrative headquarters Preston, which forms part of Central Lancashire New Town (together with Fulwood, Bamber Bridge, Leyland, and Chorley), Lancaster, Accrington, Blackburn, Burnley; ports Fleetwood and Heysham; seaside resorts Blackpool, Morecambe, and Southport
products formerly a world centre of cotton manufacture, this has been replaced with newer varied industries
population (1981) 1,376,500
famous people Kathleen Ferrier, Gracie Fields, George Formby, Rex Harrison.

Lancaster, Duchy and County Palatine of created in 1351, and attached to the crown since 1399. The office of Chancellor of the Duchy is actually a 'sinecure', usually held by a member of the Cabinet with a special role outside that of the regular ministries, for example, Harold Lever as financial adviser to the Wilson-Callaghan governments from 1974.

Lancaster House Agreement accord reached at a conference Sep 1979 at Lancaster House, London between Britain and representative groups of Rhodesia, including the Rhodesian government under Ian Smith, and black nationalist groups. The Agreement enabled a smooth transition to the independent state of ◊Zimbabwe 1980.

Lancaster, House of English royal house, branch of the Plantagenets.

lancelet marine animal, genus *Amphioxus* included in the ◊chordates, about 2.5 cm/1 in long. It has no skull, brain, eyes, heart, vertebral column, nor paired limbs, but has a notochord (supportive rod) which runs from end to end of the body, a tail, and a number of gillslits. Found in all seas, it burrows in the sand but when disturbed swims freely.

Lancelot of the Lake in British legend the most celebrated of King Arthur's knights, the lover of Queen Guinevere. Originally a folk-hero, he was introduced into the Arthurian cycle of tales in the 12th century.

Land federal unit (plural *Länder*) of West Germany.

Land Edwin 1909– . US inventor of the Polaroid camera 1947, which develops the film inside the camera and produces an instant photograph.

Land League Irish peasant organization, formed by Michael ◊Davitt 1879 to fight against evictions. It forced Gladstone's government, by its skilful use of the boycott against any man who took a farm from which another had been evicted, to introduce a law 1881 restricting rents and granting tenants security of tenure.

landlord and tenant in law, the relationship which exists between an owner of land or buildings (the landlord) gives to another (the tenant) the exclusive right of occupation for a definite limited period, whether it be a year, a term of years, a week or a month. When the terms of the contract are embodied in a deed they are said to be covenants, and the whole agreement is termed a lease. The relationship is also known as lessor and lessee.

Land Registry, HM an official body set up 1925 to register legal rights to land in England and Wales. There has been a gradual introduction, since 1925, of compulsory registration of land in different areas of the country. This requires the purchaser of land to register details of his title and all other rights (such as mortgages and ◊easements) relating to the land. Once registered, the title to the land is guaranteed by the Land Registry. This makes buying and selling of land easier and cheaper.

landslide

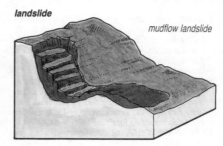

mudflow landslide

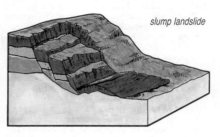

slump landslide

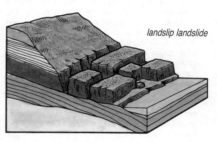

landslip landslide

Landsat a series of satellites used for monitoring earth resources. The first was launched 1972.

Landseer Edwin Henry 1802–1873. English painter and sculptor, who achieved popularity with sentimental studies of animals. His sculptures include the lions in Trafalgar Square, London, 1859.

landslide a sudden downward movement of a mass of soil or rocks from a cliff or steep slope. Landslides happen when a slope becomes unstable, usually because the base has been undercut or certain boundaries of materials within the mass have become wet and slippery.

Landsteiner Karl 1868–1943. Austrian immunologist, who discovered the ABO ◊blood group system 1900–02, and aided in the discovery of the Rhesus blood factors 1940. He discovered the polio virus.

Landtag legislature of each of the *Länder* (states) that form the federal republics of West Germany and Austria.

Lanfranc *c.* 1010–1089. Italian archbishop of Canterbury from 1070; he rebuilt the cathedral, replaced English clergy by Normans, enforced clerical celibacy, and separated the ecclesiastical from the secular courts.

Lang Andrew 1844–1912. Scottish historian and folklore scholar. His writings include historical works, anthropological essays, (such as *Myth, Ritual and Religion* 1887 and *The Making of Religion* 1898), novels, and a series of children's books, beginning with the *Blue Fairy Tale Book* 1889.

Lange New Zealand prime minister David Lange, 1988.

Lang Fritz 1890–1976. Austrian film director. His German films include *Metropolis* 1927, and the series of *Dr Mabuse* films, after which he fled from the Nazis to Hollywood 1936. His US films include *Fury* 1936, *You Only Live Once* 1937, and *The Big Heat* 1953.

Lange David (Russell) 1942– . New Zealand socialist politician, Labour Party leader from 1983, and prime minister 1983–89. Lange, a barrister, was elected to the House of Representatives 1977. Labour had a decisive win in the 1984 general election on a non-nuclear defence policy, which Lange immediately put into effect, despite criticism from the USA. He introduced a free-market economic policy and was re-elected 1987. He resigned 1989 over a disagreement with his finance minister.

Langland William *c.* 1332–*c.* 1400. English poet. His alliterative *Vision concerning Piers Plowman* appeared in three versions between about 1362 and 1398, but some critics believe he was only responsible for the first. It condemns the social and moral evils of 14th-century England.

Langobard alternative name for ◊Lombard, member of a Germanic people.

Langton Stephen *c.* 1150–1228. English priest. When in 1207 Innocent III secured his election as archbishop of Canterbury, King John refused to recognize him, and Langton was not allowed to enter England until 1213. He supported the barons in their struggle against John, and was mainly responsible for the ◊Magna Carta.

Langtry Lillie 1853–1929. English actress, and mistress of the future Edward VII. She was known as the 'Jersey lily' from her birthplace, and considered to be one of the most beautiful women of her time.

language the general name for human communication through speech or writing, or both. Different nationalities typically have different languages or their own variations on a particular language. The term is also used to indicate systems of communication with language-like qualities, such as *animal language* (the way animals communicate), *body language* (gestures and expressions used to communicate ideas), and *computer language* (such as BASIC and COBOL). One language may have various ◊dialects, which may be seen by users as languages in their own right.

Languedoc-Roussillon region of S France, comprising the *départements* of Aude, Lozère, Hérault, Pyrénées-Orientales, and Gard; area 27,400 sq km/10,576 sq mi; population (1986) 2,012,000. Its capital is Montpellier, and products include fruit, vegetables, wine, and cheese.

langur type of leaf-eating monkey that lives in trees in S Asia. It is related to the colobus monkey of Africa.

lanolin a sticky, purified wax obtained from sheep's wool, and used in cosmetics, soap, and leather preparation.

Lansbury George 1859–1940. British Labour politician, leader in the Commons 1931–35. In 1921, while Poplar borough mayor, he went to prison with most of the council rather than modify their policy of more generous unemployment relief. He was MP 1910–12, and 1922–40; he was leader of the parliamentary Labour party 1931–35, but resigned (as a pacifist) in opposition to the party's militant response to the Italian invasion of Abyssinia (present-day Ethiopia).

lanthanide one of the 15 chemically related elements of the lanthanide series. They are: lanthanum, cerium, praseodymium, neodymium, promethium, samarium, europium, gadolinium, terbium, dysprosium, holmium, erbium, thulium, ytterbium, and lutetium.

lanthanum in chemistry, a rare metallic element, symbol La, atomic number 57, relative atomic mass 138.9. It is the first element of the lanthanide series.

Lanzhou (formerly *Lanchow*) capital of Gansu province, China, on the Yellow River, 190 km/120 mi south of the Great Wall; population (1989) 1,480,000. Industries include oil refining, chemicals, fertilizers, and synthetic rubber.

Lao name given to people who live along the Mekong river system. There are approximately 9,000,000 Lao in Thailand and 2,000,000 in Laos. The Lao language is a member of the Sino-Tibetan family.

Laois or *Laoighis* county in Leinster province, Republic of Ireland.
area 1,720 sq km/664 sq mi
county town Port Laoise
physical flat except for the Slieve Bloom mountains in the NW
products sugar beet, dairy products, woollens, agricultural machinery
population (1991) 52,300

Laos landlocked country in SE Asia, bordered to the N by China, E by Vietnam, S by Kampuchea, and W by Thailand.

laparotomy an exploratory operation within the abdomen. The use of laparotomy, as of other exploratory surgery, has decreased sharply with medical advances such as the various modes of scanning, and the direct viewing technique known as ◊endoscopy.

La Paz the Bolivian seat of government.

Laos
People's Democratic Republic of
(*Saathiaranagroat Prachhathippatay Prachhachhon Lao*)

area 235,700 sq km/91,000 sq mi
capital Vientiane
towns Luang Prabang, the former royal capital
physical high mountains in the E; Mekong River in the W; jungle

head of state Nouhak Phoumsavan from 1992
head of government General Khamtay Siphandon from 1991
political system communism
exports teak, timber, coffee, electricity
currency new kip
population (1990 est) 4,024,000; annual growth rate 2.2%
life expectancy men 48, women 51 (1989)
language Lao (official), French
religion traditionally Theravada Buddhist
literacy 45% (1991)
GNP $500 million (1987); $180 per head
chronology
1893–1945 Laos became a French protectorate.
1954 Full independence achieved.
1960 Right-wing government seized power.
1962 Coalition government established; civil war continued.
1973 Vientiane ceasefire agreement.
1975 Communist-dominated republic proclaimed with Prince Souphanouvong as head of state.
1988 Plans announced to withdraw 40% of the Vietnamese forces stationed in the country.
1989 First general election in 13 years.
1991 Constitution approved. Kaysone Phomvihane elected president; Gen Khamtay Siphandon named premier.
1992 Phomvihane died and was replaced by Nouhak Phoumsavan. New national assembly created and general election held.

La Paz city in Bolivia, 3,800 m/12,400 ft above sea level; population (1988) 1,049,800. Products include textiles and copper. Founded by the Spanish 1548, it has been the seat of government since about 1900.

lapis lazuli deep-blue mineral consisting of a sodium aluminium silicate with sodium sulphide, 3(NaAlSiO₄)Na₂S. It is used in the manufacture of *ultramarine* pigment.

Laplace Pierre Simon, Marquis de Laplace 1749–1827. French astronomer and mathematician. In 1796, he theorized that the Solar System originated from a cloud of gas (the nebular hypothesis). He studied the motion of the Moon and planets, and published a five-volume survey of ◊celestial mechanics, *Traité de méchanique céleste* 1799–1825. Among his mathematical achievements was the development of probability theory.

Lapland region of Europe within the Arctic Circle in Norway, Sweden, Finland, and NW Russia, without political definition. Its chief resources are chromium, copper, iron, timber, hydroelectric power, and tourism. There are about 20,000 indigenous Saami (Lapps), who live by hunting, fishing, reindeer herding, and handicrafts.

La Plata capital of Buenos Aires province, Argentina; population (1980) 560,300. Industries include meat packing and petroleum refining. It was founded 1882.

La Plata, Rio de or *River Plate* estuary in South America into which the rivers Paraná and Uruguay flow; length 320 km/200 mi and width up to 240 km/150 mi. The basin drains much of Argentina, Bolivia, Brazil, Uruguay, and Paraguay, who all cooperate in its development.

lapwing bird *Vanellus vanellus* of the plover family, also known as the green plover, and from its call, as the peewit. Bottle-green above and white below, with a long thin crest and rounded wings, it is about

30 cm/1 ft long and inhabits moorland in Europe and Asia, making a nest scratched out of the ground.

larceny in the UK, formerly the name for ◊theft. Until 1827 larceny was divided into 'grand larceny', punishable by death or transportation for life, and 'petty larceny', when the stolen articles were valued at less than a shilling (5p). In the USA these terms are still used.

larch tree, genus *Larix*, of the family Pinaceae. The common large *Larix decidua* grows to 40 m/130 ft. It is one of the few ◊conifer trees to shed its leaves annually. The small needle-like leaves are replaced every year by new bright green foliage which later darkens.

lard edible fat high in saturated fatty acids. It is prepared from pigs and used in margarine, soap, and ointment.

Lares and Penates in Roman mythology, spirits of the farm and of the store cupboard, often identified with the family ancestors, whose shrine was the centre of family worship in Roman homes.

Largo Caballero Francisco 1869–1946. Spanish socialist and leader of the Spanish Socialist Party (PSOE). He became prime minister of the popular-front government elected Feb 1936 and remained in office for the first ten months of the Civil War before being replaced by Juan Negrin (1887–1956) May 1937.

La Rioja region of N Spain; see ◊Castile.

lark songbird of the family Alaudidae, found mainly in the Old World, but also in North America. It is usually about 17 cm/7 in long, and nests in the open.

Larkin Philip 1922–1985. English poet. His perfectionist, pessimistic verse includes *The North Ship* 1945, *The Whitsun Weddings* 1964, and *High Windows* 1974.

larkspur plant of genus ◊delphinium.

La Rochefoucauld François, duc de La Rochefoucauld 1613–1680. French writer. *Réflexions, ou sentences et maximes morales/Reflections, or Moral Maxims* 1665 is a collection of brief, epigrammatic, and cynical observations on life and society, with the epigraph 'Our virtues are mostly our vices in disguise'. He was a lover of Mme de ◊Lafayette.

Larousse Pierre 1817–1875. French grammarian and lexicographer. His encyclopedic dictionary, the *Grand Dictionnaire universel du XIXème siècle/Great Universal 19th-Century Dictionary* 1865–76, was an influential work and continues in subsequent revisions.

larva the stage between hatching and adulthood in those species in which the young have a different appearance and way of life from the adults. Examples include tadpoles (frogs) and caterpillars (butterflies). Larvae are typical of the invertebrates, and some (for example, shrimps) have two or more distinct larval stages. Among vertebrates, it is only the amphibians and some fish that have a larval stage.

laryngitis inflammation of the ◊larynx, causing soreness of the throat, dry cough, and hoarseness. The acute form is due to a cold, excessive use of the voice, or inhalation of irritating smoke, and may cause the voice to be completely lost. With rest the inflammation usually subsides in a few days.

larynx in mammals, a cavity at the upper end of the trachea (windpipe), containing the vocal cords. It is stiffened with cartilage and lined with mucous membrane. Amphibians and reptiles have much simpler larynxes, with no vocal cords. Birds have a similar cavity, called the *syrinx*, found lower down the trachea, where it branches to form the bronchi. It is very complex, with well-developed vocal cords.

la Salle René Robert Cavelier, Sieur de la Salle 1643–1687. French explorer. He made an epic voyage through North America exploring the Mississippi down to its mouth, and in 1682 founded Louisiana.

Las Casas Bartolomé de 1474–1566. Spanish missionary, historian, and colonial reformer. He was the first European to call for the abolition of Indian slavery in Latin America. He took part in the conquest of Cuba 1513, but subsequently worked for American Indian freedom in the Spanish colonies. *Historia de las Indias* (published 1875–76) is his account of the European oppression of the Indians.

Lascaux cave system near Montignac in the Dordogne, SW France, discovered 1940. It has rich paintings of buffalo, horses, and red deer of the Upper Palaeolithic period, about 18,000 BC.

laser acronym for *L*ight *A*mplification by *S*timulated *E*mission of *R*adiation. Device for producing a narrow beam of light, capable of travelling over vast distances without dispersion, of being focused to give enormous power densities (10^8 watts per cm² for high-energy lasers), and operating on a principle similar to that of the ◊maser. Uses of lasers include communications (a laser beam can carry much more information than radio waves), cutting, drilling, welding, satellite tracking, medical and biological research, and surgery.

Laski Harold 1893–1950. English political theorist. He taught a modified Marxism, and published *A Grammar of Politics* 1925 and *The American Presidency* 1940. He was chairman of the Labour Party 1945–46.

Las Palmas or *Las Palmas de Gran Canaria* tourist resort on the NE coast of Gran Canaria, Canary Islands; population (1981) 366,500. Products include sugar and bananas.

Lassa fever fever caused by a virus, first detected 1969, and spread by a species of rat found only in W Africa. There is no known cure, the survival rate being less than 50%.

Lassalle Ferdinand 1825–1864. German socialist. He was imprisoned for his part in the ◊revolution of 1848, during which he met ◊Marx, and in 1863 founded the General Association of German Workers (later the Social-Democratic Party). His publications include *The Working Man's Programme* 1862, and *The Open Letter* 1863. He was killed in a duel arising from a love affair.

Lassus (or *Lasso*) Roland de *c.* 1532–1594. Franco-Flemish composer of polyphonic sacred music, and of many songs and madrigals, including settings of poems by his friend ◊Ronsard.

latent heat in physics, heat which changes the state of a substance (for example, from solid to liquid) without changing its temperature.

lateral line system a system of sense organs in fishes and larval amphibians (tadpoles) which detects water movement. It usually consists of a row of interconnected pores on either side of the body and head.

Lateran Treaties a series of agreements that marked the reconciliation of the Italian state with the papacy 1929. The treaties involved recognition of the sovereignty of the ◊Vatican City State, the payment of an indemnity for papal possessions lost during unification 1870, and agreement on the role of the Catholic church within the Italian state in the form of a concordat between Pope Pius XI and the dictator Mussolini.

laterite a soft, friable, claylike rock, produced by the weathering of basalts, granites, and shales, and common in the tropics.

latex (Latin 'liquid') a lactiferous fluid of ◊angiosperm plants, an emulsion of various substances. Latex is exuded from the Para rubber tree and worked into rubber.

lateral line system

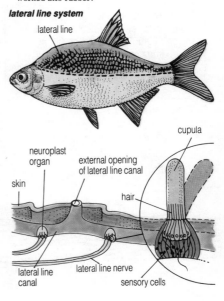

lateral line

cupula

neuroplast organ

external opening of lateral line canal

skin

hair

lateral line canal

lateral line nerve

sensory cells

laser

The laser was invented by US scientist, Theodore Maiman, who followed up a suggestion made by Charles Townes.

A laser beam is used to check quartz windows (centre) for cleanliness, used in electro-optical technology.

Technician working with a laser at an optical bench.

Mirrors reflecting the beam of an argon ion laser.

Gas laser

(1) In a gas laser, electrons moving between the electrodes pass energy to gas atoms. An energised atom emits a ray of light.

(2) The ray hits another energised atom causing it to emit a further ray of light.

(3) The rays bounce between the mirrors at each end causing a build-up of light. Eventually the beam becomes strong enough to pass through the half-silvered mirror at one end, producing a laser beam.

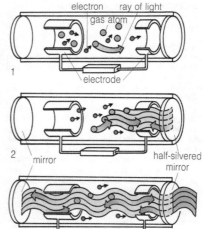

electron · ray of light · gas atom · electrode · mirror · half-silvered mirror

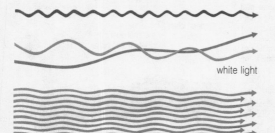

white light

laser beam

White light is a mixture of light waves of different wavelengths, corresponding to different colours. In a beam of white light, all the waves are out of step.

In a laser beam, all the waves are of the same wavelength, so the beam is a pure colour. All the waves in a laser beam are in step.

Latvia
Republic of

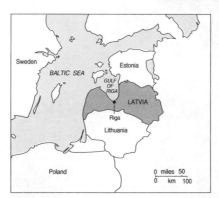

area 63,700 sq km/24,595 sq mi
capital Riga
towns Daugavpils, Liepāja, Jurmala, Jelgava, Ventspils
physical wooded lowland (highest point 312 m/1,024 ft), marshes, lakes; 472 km/293 mi of coastline; mild climate.
head of state Anatolijs Gorbunov from 1988
head of government Ivars Godmanis from 1990
political system emergent democratic republic
products electronic and communications equipment, motorcycles, consumer durables, timber, paper and woollen goods, meat and dairy products
currency Latvian rouble
population (1990) 2,700,000 (52% Latvian, 34% Russian, 5% Byelorussian, 3% Ukrainian)
language Latvian
religions mostly Lutheran Protestant, with a Roman Catholic minority
chronology
1918 Feb: Germany wrested Latvia from Soviet control. Nov: Latvia declared independence. Dec: Soviet rule restored after German withdrawal.
1919 Soviet rule overthrown by British naval and German forces May–Dec; democracy established.
1934 Coup replaced established government.
1939 German–Soviet secret agreement placed Latvia under Russian influence.
1940 Became constituent republic of USSR.
1941–44 Occupied by Germany.
1944 USSR regained control.
1988 Latvian Popular Front established to campaign for independence. Prewar flag readopted; official status given to Latvian language.
1989 Popular Front swept local elections.
1990 Jan: Communist Party's monopoly of power abolished. March–April: Popular Front secured majority in elections. May: unilateral declaration of independence from USSR.
1991 Aug: full independence declared at time of anti-Gorbachev coup; Communist Party outlawed. Sept: Became a member of the UN.
1992 US reopened its embassy in Latvia. Russia began pullout of ex-Soviet troops, to be completed 1994.

lathe a machine tool used for *turning*. The workpiece to be machined is held and rotated, while cutting tools are moved into it.

latifundium (plural latifundia) a large agricultural estate worked by low-paid labour in the interests of absentee landlords. The Latin term referred to estates in ancient Rome but has also been applied in Italy, Spain, and South America.

Latin an Indo-European language of ancient Italy. Latin has passed through four influential phases: as the language of (1) Republican Rome, (2) the Roman Empire, (3) the Roman Catholic Church, and (4) W European culture, science, philosophy and law during the Middle Ages and the Renaissance. During the third and fourth phases much Latin vocabulary entered the English language. It is the parent form of the ◊Romance languages, noted for its highly inflected grammar and conciseness of expression. The influence of Latin language and literature on many modern languages and literatures is still considerable.

Latin America countries of South and Central America (also including Mexico) in which Spanish, Portuguese, and French are spoken.

latitude and longitude points of measurement on the globe. *Latitude* is the angular distance of any point from the ◊equator, measured N or S along the Earth's curved surface. It is measured in degrees, minutes, and seconds, each minute equalling one sea-mile (1.85 km) in length. *Longitude* is the angle between the terrestrial meridian drawn from the pole, through a place, and a standard meridian at Greenwich, England. At the equator one degree of longitude measures approximately 112 km/70 mi.

La Tour Georges de 1593–1652. French painter of religious and genre scenes. Many of his pictures are illuminated by a single source of light.

Latter-day Saint member of a US-based Christian sect, the ◊Mormons.

Latvia country in N Europe, bounded E by Russia, N by Estonia, N and NW by the Baltic Sea, S by Lithuania and SE by Belarus.

Latvian language the language of Latvia; one of the two surviving members of the Baltic branch of the Indo-European language family.

Latynina Larissa Semyonovna 1935– . Soviet gymnast, who won 18 Olympic medals, including nine golds, 1956–64, more than any other person in any sport. She also won 3 world championships.

Laud A portrait of William Laud after Van Dyck.

Laurel and Hardy *The popular comic duo Laurel and Hardy, one of the most successful comedy teams in cinema history.*

Laud William 1573–1645. English priest. As archbishop of Canterbury from 1633, his High Church policy, support for Charles I's unparliamentary rule, censorship of the press, and persecution of the Puritans aroused bitter opposition, while his strict enforcement of the statutes against enclosures and of laws regulating wages and prices alienated the propertied classes. His attempt to impose the use of the Prayer Book on the Scots precipitated the English ♢Civil War. Impeached by Parliament 1640 he was imprisoned in the Tower, condemned to death, and beheaded.

laudanum alcoholic solution (tincture) of opium. Used formerly as a narcotic and for analgesia, freely available in the 19th century from Pharmacists on demand.

Lauder Harry 1870–1950. Stage name of Hugh MacLennan. A Scottish mill worker and miner, he became a successful music-hall comedian and singer.

Lauderdale John Maitland, Duke of Lauderdale 1616–1682. Scottish politician. Formerly a zealous ♢Covenanter, he joined the Royalists 1647, and as high commissioner for Scotland 1667–1679 persecuted the Covenanters. He was created duke of Lauderdale 1672.

Laughton Charles 1899–1962. English actor. Initially a classical stage actor, his film roles include the king in *The Private Life of Henry VIII* 1933, Captain Bligh in *Mutiny on the Bounty* 1935, and Quasimodo in *The Hunchback of Notre Dame* 1939.

Laurasia former land mass, formed by the fusion of North America, Greenland, Europe, and Asia, that made up the northern half of ♢Pangaea, the 'supercontinent' that is thought to have existed between 250 and 200 million years ago. The southern half was ♢Gondwanaland.

laurel evergreen tree *sweet bay Laurus nobilis*, family Lauraceae, of which the aromatic leaves are used in cookery. Ornamental shrub laurels, for example, *cherry laurel Prunus laurocerasus*, family Rosaceae, are poisonous.

Laurel and Hardy Stan Laurel (1890–1965) and Oliver Hardy (1892–1957) US film comedians (Laurel was English-born). Their films include many short, silent films, *Way Out West* 1937, and *A Chump at Oxford* 1940.

Laurence Margaret 1926–1987. Canadian novelist, whose books include *A Jest of God* 1966 and *The Diviners* 1974.

Laurier Wilfrid 1841–1919. Canadian Liberal prime minister 1896–1911, the first French-Canadian to hold the office. He supported imperial preference and the building of Canadian warships to cooperate with the British navy, and sent Canadian troops to serve in the Second South African War.

laurustinus evergreen shrub *Viburnum tinus* of the family Caprifoliaceae. Of Mediterranean origin, it has clusters of white flowers in the winter months.

Lausanne resort and capital of Vaud canton, W Switzerland, above the N shore of Lake Geneva; population (1983) 127,000. Industries include chocolate, scientific instruments, and publishing.

Lausanne, Treaty of peace settlement 1923 between Greece and Turkey after Turkey refused to accept the terms of the Treaty of Sèvres 1920, which would have made peace with the western allies. It involved the surrender by Greece of Smyrna (now Izmir) to Turkey and the enforced exchange of the Greek population of Smyrna for the Turkish population of Greece.

Lavoisier French chemist Antoine Lavoisier.

lava the molten material exuded from a ◊volcano which cools to form extrusive ◊igneous rock. A lava high in silica is very stiff and does not flow far, while low-silica lava can flow for long distances.

Laval Pierre 1883–1945. French right-wing politician. He was prime minister and foreign secretary 1931–32, and again 1935–36. In World War II he was vice-premier in Pétain's Vichy government Jun-Dec 1940, when he was dismissed. He was reinstated by Hitler's orders as head of the government and foreign minister 1942. After the war he was executed.

La Vallière Louise de la Baume le Blance, Duchesse de la Vallière 1644–1710. Mistress of the French king Louis XIV (by whom she had four children 1661–74).

lavender sweet-smelling herb, genus *Lavandula*, of the family Labiatae, a native of the W Mediterranean countries. The bushy low-growing *Lavandula angustifolia* has long, narrow, erect leaves of a silver-green colour. The flowers, borne on a terminal spike, vary in colour from lilac to deep purple and are covered with small fragrant oil glands.

Lavoisier Antoine Laurent 1743–1794. French chemist. He proved that combustion needed only a part of 'air' which he called oxygen, thereby destroying the theory of phlogiston (an imaginary 'fire element' released during combustion). With Laplace (1749-1827), he showed that water was a compound of oxygen and hydrogen. In this way he established the modern basic rules of chemical combination.

law the body of rules and principles under which justice is administered or order enforced in a state. In western Europe there are two main systems: ◊Roman law and ◊English law. The 1989 Green paper proposed 1) omitting the Bar's monopoly of higher courts, removing demarcation between barristers and solicitors; 2) cases to be taken on a no-win, no-fee' basis (as already happens in Scotland).

Law Andrew Bonar 1858–1923. British Conservative politician. Elected leader of the opposition 1911, he became colonial secretary in Asquith's coalition government 1915–16. He was chancellor of the Exchequer 1916–19, and Lord Privy Seal 1919–21 in Lloyd George's coalition, and formed a Conservative Cabinet 1922, but resigned on health grounds.

Lawrence Novelist and poet D H Lawrence.

Law Commissions in Britain, statutory bodies established in 1965 (one for England and Wales, and one for Scotland) which consider proposals for law reform and publish their findings. They also keep British law under constant review, looking for ways in which it can be simplified or finding obsolete law which should be repealed.

law courts the bodies which adjudicate in legal disputes. Civil and criminal cases are usually dealt with by separate courts. In most countries there is a hierarchy of courts which provide an appeal system.

law lords in England, the ten Lords of Appeal in Ordinary who, together with the Lord Chancellor and other peers, make up the House of Lords in its judicial capacity.

Lawrence D(avid) H(erbert) 1885–1930. English novelist and poet, who in his work expressed his belief in emotion and the sexual impulse as creative and true to human nature. His novels include *Sons and Lovers* 1913, *Women in Love* 1921, and *Lady Chatterley's Lover* 1928. He also wrote short stories, for example 'The Woman Who Rode Away', and poetry.

Lawrence Ernest O(rlando) 1901–1958. US physicist. His invention of the cyclotron pioneered the production of artificial radioisotopes.

Lawrence T(homas) E(dward) 1888–1935. British soldier, known as 'Lawrence of Arabia'. Appointed to the military intelligence department in Cairo during World War 1, he took part in negotiations for an Arab revolt against the Turks, and in 1916 attached himself a guerrilla leader of genius, combining raids on Turkish communications with the stirring up of revolt among the Arabs. In 1935 he was killed in a motorcycle accident.

Lawrence Thomas 1769–1830. British painter, the leading portraitist of his day. He became painter to George III in 1792 and president of the Royal Academy 1820.

lawrencium a synthetic radioactive element, symbol Lr, atomic number 103.

Lawrence Miss Caroline Fry *Tate Gallery, London.*

Lawson Nigel 1932– . British Conservative politician. A former financial journalist, he was financial secretary to the Treasury 1979–81, secretary of state for energy 1981–83, and chancellor of the Exchequer 1983-89. He resigned in 1989 after criticism of his policy of British membership of the European Monetary System by government adviser Alan Walters.

law, the rule of the principle that law (as administered by the ordinary courts) is supreme and that all citizens (including members of the government) are equally subject to it and equally entitled to its protection.

Laxness Halldor 1902– . Icelandic novelist, writing about Icelandic life in the style of the early sagas. Nobel prize 1955.

Layamon lived about 1200. English poet, author of the *Brut*, a chronicle of about 30,000 alliterative lines on the history of Britain from the legendary Brutus onwards, which gives the earliest version of the Arthurian story in English.

Lazarus Emma 1849–1887. US poet, author of the poem on the base of the Statue of Liberty which includes the words: 'Give me your tired, your poor, / Your huddled masses yearning to breathe free.'

Lazio (Roman *Latium*) region of W central Italy; area 17,203 sq km/6,642 sq mi; capital Rome; population (1981) 5,001,700. Products include olives, wine, chemicals, pharmaceuticals,

Lawson Nigel Lawson as Chancellor of the Exchequer in 1985.

and textiles. Home of the Latins from the 10th century BC, it was dominated by the Romans from the 4th century BC.

lb abbreviation for *pound* (weight).

lc in typography, the abbreviation for *lower case*, or 'small' letters, as opposed to capitals.

LCD abbreviation for ◊*liquid crystal display*.

L-dopa chemical, normally produced by the body, which is converted in the brain to dopamine, and is essential for local movement.

LEA in the UK, abbreviation for *Local Education Authority*.

Leach Bernard 1887–1979. British potter. His simple designs, influenced by a period of study in Japan, pioneered the modern revival of the art. He established the Leach Pottery at St Ives, Cornwall, in 1920.

leaching process by which substances are washed out of the ◊soil. Fertilizers leached out of the soil find their way into rivers and cause water ◊pollution. In tropical areas, leaching of the soil after ◊deforestation removes scarce nutrients and leads to a dramatic loss of soil fertility.

Leacock Stephen Butler 1869–1944. Canadian humorist, whose writings include *Literary Lapses* 1910, *Sunshine Sketches of a Little town* 1912, and *Frenzied Fiction* 1918.

lead one of the four most-used metallic elements. Symbol Pb (Latin *plumbum*), atomic number 82, relative atomic mass 207.21. It is bluish-grey, and the heaviest, softest, and weakest of the common metals; it lacks elasticity and is a poor conductor of electricity, but is resistant to corrosion by acids. Lead is used as a shield for radioactive sources, and in ammunition, batteries, glass, ceramics, and alloys such as pewter and solder. Lead is a cumulative poison within the body, and lead water pipes and lead-based paints are a health hazard, as is the use of lead in 'anti-knock' petrol additives. See ◊emission control.

lead-acid cell a type of ◊accumulator (storage battery).

lead ore a number of minerals are used to extract lead. The main primary ore is the sulphide galena, PbS. This is unstable and on prolonged exposure to the atmosphere it oxidizes into the minerals cerussite, $PbCO_3$, and anglesite, $PbSO_4$. Lead ores are usually associated with other metals, particularly silver – which can be mined at the same time – and zinc, which can cause problems during smelting.

leaf lateral outgrowth on the stem of a plant, and in most species the primary organ of ◊photosynthesis. The chief leaf types are ◊cotyledons (seed leaves), scale-leaves (on underground stems), foliage leaves, and ◊bracts (in the axil of which a flower is produced). A *simple leaf* is undivided, as in the beech or oak. A *compound leaf* is composed of several leaflets, as in the blackberry, horse-chestnut or ash tree (the latter being a ◊pinnate leaf). Leaves that fall in the autumn are termed *deciduous*, while evergreens are *persistent*.

leaf-hopper numerous species of ◊bug of the family Cicadellidae. They feed on the sap of leaves. Each species feeds on a limited range of plants.

leaf insect insect of the order Phasmida, about 10 cm/4 in long, with a green, flattened body, remarkable for closely resembling the foliage on which it lives. It is most common in SE Asia.

League of Nations international organization formed after World War I to solve international disputes by arbitration. Established in Geneva, Switzerland, 1920, the League included representatives from states throughout the world, but

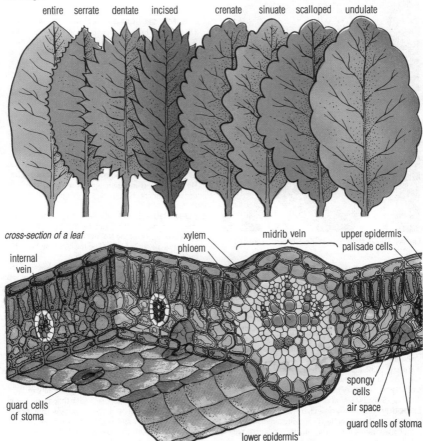

leaf

leaf margins

entire   serrate   dentate   incised   crenate   sinuate   scalloped   undulate

cross-section of a leaf   xylem   midrib vein   upper epidermis
                                             phloem   palisade cells
internal
vein

guard cells
of stoma   spongy
                                                                               cells
                                                                               air space
                                                                               guard cells of stoma

                              lower epidermis

was severely weakened by the US decision not to become a member, and has no power to enforce its decisions. It was dissolved in 1946. Its subsidiaries included the *International Labour Organization* and the *Permanent Court of International Justice* in The Hague, Netherlands, both now under the auspices of the ◊United Nations.

Leakey Louis (Seymour Bazett) 1903–1972. British archaeologist. Born in Kabete, Kenya, he was curator of Coryndon Museum, Nairobi, Kenya, 1945–61, and in 1958 discovered gigantic animal fossils in ◊Olduvai Gorge, as well as discovering many early remains of a human type with his wife Mary Leakey.

Leakey Mary 1913– . British archaeologist. She discovered in 1948, on Rusinga Island, Lake Victoria, E Africa, the prehistoric ape skull known as Proconsul, about 20 million years old; and human remains at Laetolil, to the south, about 3,750,000 years old.

Leakey Richard 1944– . British archaeologist, son of Louis and Mary Leakey. In 1972 he discovered at Lake Turkana, Kenya, an ape-form skull with some human characteristics and a brain capacity of 800 cm³, estimated to be about 2.9 million years old. In 1984 his team found an almost complete skeleton of *Homo erectus* some 1.6 million years old.

Lean David 1908–1991. British film director. His films, noted for their atmospheric quality, include *Brief Encounter* 1946, *The Bridge on the River Kwai* 1957 (Academy Award), *Lawrence of Arabia* 1962 (Academy Award), and *A Passage to India* 1984.

Lear Edward 1812–1888. British artist and humorist. He is best known for his *Book of Nonsense* 1846, which popularized the limerick. He travelled in Italy, Greece, Egypt and India, publishing books on his travels with his own illustrations, and spent most of his later life in Italy.

learning theory in psychology, a theory about how an organism acquires new behaviours. Two main theories are classical and operant ◊conditioning.

leasehold in law, land or property held by a tenant (lessee) for a specified period, usually at a rent from the landlord (lessor).

leather material prepared, mainly from the hides and skins of domesticated animals, by tanning with vegetables tannins and chromium salts. Leather is a durable and water-resistant material, and is used for bags, shoes, and clothing.

leaven element inducing fermentation; especially applied to the yeast added to dough in bread

Leakey *British archaeologist, Dr Richard Leakey in 1972.*

making. It is used figuratively to describe any pervasive influence, usually in a good sense, although in the Old Testament it symbolized corruption, and unleavened bread was used in sacrifice.

Leavis F(rank) R(aymond) 1895–1978. British literary critic and a lecturer at Cambridge university. He edited the controversial review *Scrutiny* 1932–53, championed the work of D H Lawrence and James Joyce, and in 1962 attacked C P Snow's theory of 'Two Cultures'. *New Bearings in English Poetry* 1932 and *The Great Tradition* 1948 are important critical works.

Lebanon country in W Asia, bordered N and E by Syria, S by Israel, and W by the Mediterranean.

Lebedev Peter Nikolaievich 1866–1912. Russian physicist. He succeeded in proving experimentally, and then measuring, the minute pressure which light exerts upon a physical body.

Lebensphilosophie (German) philosophy of life.

Lebenstraum (German, living space) theory developed by Hitler for the expansion of Germany into Eastern Europe, and used by the Nazis to justify their annexation of neighbouring states on the grounds that Germany was overpopulated.

Le Brun Charles 1619–1690. French artist, painter to Louis XIV from 1662. In 1663 he became director of the French Academy and of the Gobelin manufactory, which produced art, tapestries, and furnishings for the new palace of Versailles.

Le Carré John, pen name of British author David John Cornwell 1931– . His low-key realistic accounts of complex espionage include *The Spy Who Came in from the Cold* 1963, *Tinker Tailor Soldier Spy* 1974, *Smiley's People* 1980, *The Little Drummer Girl* 1983, and *The Russia House* 1989.

Le Chatelier's principle (or *Le Chatelier–Braun principle*) in science, the principle that if a change in conditions is imposed on a system in equilibrium, the system will react so as to counteract that change and restore the equilibrium.

lecithin a type of lipid (fat), containing nitrogen and phosphorus, which forms a vital part of the cell membranes of plant and animal cells. The name is from the Greek *lekithos*, (egg yolk – an important source).

Leclanché Georges 1839–1882. French engineer. In 1866, he invented a primary electrical ◊cell which is still the basis of most dry batteries.

Leconte de Lisle Charles Marie René 1818–1894. French poet. Born in Réunion, in the Indian Ocean, he settled 1846 in Paris. His work drew inspiration from the ancient world, as in *Poèmes antiques/Antique Poems* 1852, *Poèmes barbares/Barbaric Poems* 1862, and *Poèmes tragiques/Tragic Poems* 1884.

Le Corbusier assumed name of French architect Charles Edouard Jeanneret 1887–1965. He was noted for his functionalist approach to town planning in modern industrial society, based on the interrelation between modern machine forms and the techniques of modern architecture.

LED abbreviation for ◊*light-emitting diode*.

Leda in Greek mythology, wife of Tyndareus, by whom she was the mother of ◊Clytemnestra. By Zeus, who came to her as a swan, she was the mother of Helen of Troy, and Castor and Pollux.

Le Duc Tho 1911–1990. North Vietnamese diplomat, who was joint winner (with US secretary of state Kissinger) of the Nobel Peace Prize in 1973 for his part in negotiations to end the Vietnam War. He indefinitely postponed receiving it.

Lee Bruce. Stage name of Lee Yuen Kam 1941–1973. US 'Chinese Western' film actor, an expert in ◊kung fu who popularized the oriental martial arts in the West.

Lee Jennie, Baroness Lee 1904–1988. British socialist politician. On the left wing of the Labour Party, she was on its National Executive Committee 1958–70 and was minister of education 1967–70, founding the Open University 1969.

Lee Kuan Yew 1923– . Singaporean politician, prime minister from 1959. Lee, trained as a barrister in London, founded the moderate, anticommunist Socialist People's Action Party in 1954 and entered the Singapore legislative assembly in 1955. He was elected the country's first prime minister in 1959 and remained in power until he resigned in 1990. He was succeeded by Goh Chok Tong.

Lee Laurie 1914– . British writer. His works include the autobiographical novel *Cider with Rosie* 1959, a classic evocation of childhood; nature poetry such as *The Bloom of Candles* 1947; and travel writing including *A Rose for Winter* 1955.

Lee Robert E(dward) 1807–1870. US Confederate general in the ◊Civil War, a military strategist.

Lee *Singaporean politician and premier, Lee Kuan Yew in Feb 1972.*

Lebanon
Republic of
(al-Jumhouria al-Lubnaniya)

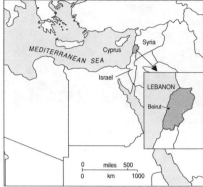

area 10,452 sq km/4,034 sq mi
capital and port Beirut
towns ports Tripoli, Tyre, Sidon
physical narrow coastal plain; Bekka valley N–S;
Labanon and Antilebanon mountain ranges
head of state Elias Hrawi from 1989
head of government Rafik at Hariri from 1992
political system emergent democratic republic
exports citrus and other fruit; industrial products
currency Lebanese pound
population (1990 est) 3,340,000 Lebanese 82%,
Palestinian 9%, Armenian 5%; growth rate −0.2% pa
life expectancy men 65, women 70 (1989)
language Arabic, French (both official), English,
Armenian
religion Muslim 57% (Shi'ite 33%, Sunni 24%),

Christian (Maronite/Orthodox) 40%, Druse 3%
literacy 86% male/69% female (1985 est)
GNP $1.8 bn (1986); $690 per head
chronology
1944 Independence achieved from France.
1964 Palestine Liberation Organization (PLO)
founded in Beirut.
1975 Civil war between Christians and Muslims.
1976 Ceasefire agreed.
1978 Israel invaded S Lebanon in search of PLO
fighters.
1979 Part of S Lebanon declared an 'independent
free Lebanon'.
1982 Bachir Gemayel became president, but
assassinated before he could assume office; his
brother, Amin Gemayel, became president.
1984 Most of international peacekeeping force
withdrawn.
1985 Lebanon nearing chaos; foreigners taken
hostage.
1987 Syrian troops sent into Beirut.
1988 Gemayel's last act in office was to establish a
military government; Selim El-Hoss set up a rival
government; partition threatened.
1989 Arab Peace Plan accepted by Muslims;
rejected by Maronite Christians led by Gen Michel
Aoun; National Assembly appointed Rene
Muawad president, replacing Aoun; car bomb
killed Muawad; succeeded by Elias Hrawi; Aoun
continued defiance.
1990 Irish hostage Brian Keenan released; Gen
Aoun surrendered; legitimate government
restored.
1991 Government extended control to the whole
county. Treaty of cooperation with Syria signed.
More Western hostages released.
1992 Remaining Western hostages released.
General election boycotted by many Christians.
Pro-Syrian administration re-elected with Rafik al-
Haririas prime minister.

In 1859 he suppressed John ◊Brown's raid on Harper's Ferry. On the outbreak of the Civil War he became military adviser to Jefferson ◊Davis, the president of the Confederacy, and in 1862 commander of the army of N Virginia. During 1862–63 he made several raids into Northern territory, but after his defeat at Gettysburg was compelled to take the defensive, and surrendered 1865 at Appomattox.

Lee Teng-Hui 1923– . Taiwanese right-wing politician, vice president 1984–88, president and Kuomintang party leader from 1988. Lee is viewed as a reforming technocrat.

leech worm in the class Hirudinea. Leeches inhabit fresh water, and in tropical countries infest damp forests. As blood-sucking animals they are injurious to people and animals, to whom they attach themselves by a strong suctorial mouth.

Leeds city in W Yorkshire, England, on the river Aire; population (1991 est) 674,400. Industries include engineering, printing, chemicals, glass, and woollens.

leek plant of the family Liliaceae. The cultivated leek is a variety of the wild *Allium ampeloprasum* of the Mediterranean area and Atlantic islands. The lower leaf-parts form the bulb which is eaten as a vegetable.

Leeward Islands (1) general term for the N half of the Lesser Antilles in the West Indies; (2) former British colony in the West Indies (1871–1956) comprising Antigua, Montserrat, St Christopher/St Kitts-Nevis, Anguilla, and the Virgin Islands; (3) group of islands in French Polynesia, S Pacific.

Le Fanu (Joseph) Sheridan 1814–1873. Irish writer, born in Dublin. He wrote mystery novels and short stories, such as *The House by the Churchyard* 1863, *Uncle Silas* 1864, and *In a Glass Darkly* 1872.

left wing in politics, the socialist parties. The term originated in the French National Assembly in 1789, where the nobles sat in the place of honour to the right of the president, and the commons sat to the left; this arrangement has become customary in European parliaments, where the progressives sit on the left and the conservatives on the right. It is also usual to speak of the right, left, and centre, when referring to the different elements composing a single party.

legacy in law, a gift of personal property made by a testator in a ◊will and passing on the testator's death to the legatee. *Specific* legacies are definite name objects; *general* legacies are sums of money or items not specially identified, a *residuary* legacy is all the remainder of the deceased's personal estate after their debts have been paid an the other legacies have been distributed.

legal aid public assistance with legal costs. In Britain it is given only to those below certain thresholds of income, only for certain cases, and may be for only part of the costs. It is administered by the Law Society and the Law Society of Scotland. Solicitors and barristers willing to do legal aid work belong to legal aid panels.

legal tender currency which must be accepted in payment of debt. Cheques and postal orders are not included. In most countries, limits are set on the amount of coinage, particularly of small denominations, which must legally be accepted.

legend (Latin *legere* 'to read') term originally applied to the books of readings designed for use in Divine Service, and afterwards extended to the stories of saints read at matins and at mealtimes in monasteries. The best-known collection of such stories was the 13th-century *Legenda Aurea* by Jacobus de Voragine. The term now also means traditional or undocumented stories about famous people.

Léger Fernand 1881–1955. French painter, strongly influenced by early Cubism. From around 1909 he evolved a characteristic style, painting abstract and semi-abstract works with cylindrical forms, reducing the human figure to robot-like components.

legionnaire's disease pneumonia-like disease, so called because it was first identified when it attacked a convention of American legionnaires (ex-servicemen) in 1976.

Legitimist the party in France that continued to support the claims of the house of ◊Bourbon after the revolution of 1830. When the direct line became extinct in 1883 the majority of the party transferred their allegiance to the house of Orléans.

Legnano, Battle of defeat of Holy Roman emperor Frederick I (Barbarosa) by members of the Lombard League in 1176 at Legnano, NW of Milan. It was the greatest setback to the emperor's plans for imperial domination in Italy, and showed for the first time the power of infantry against feudal cavalry.

Le Guin Ursula K(roeber) 1929– . US writer of science fiction and fantasy. Her novels include *The Left Hand of Darkness* 1969, which questions sex roles; the *Earthsea* trilogy 1968–72; and *The Dispossessed* 1974, which contrasts an anarchist and a capitalist society.

legumes plants of the family Leguminosae which have pods containing dry fruits. They are important in agriculture because of their nitrogen-rich roots, used to fix nitrogen in the soil.

Lehár Franz 1870–1948. Hungarian composer. He wrote many popular operettas, among them *The Merry Widow* 1905, *The Count of Luxembourg* 1909, *Gypsy Love* 1910, and *The Land of Smiles* 1929.

Le Havre industrial port (engineering, chemicals, oil refining) in Normandy, NW France, on the Seine; population (1990) 197,200

Lehmann Rosamond Nina 1903–1990. British novelist. Her books include *Invitation to the Waltz* 1932, *The Weather in the Streets* 1936, *The Echoing Grove* 1953, and *A Sea-Grape Tree* 1976.

Leibniz Gottfried Wilhelm 1646–1716. German mathematician and philosopher. Independently of, but concurrently with Newton, he developed ◊calculus. In his metaphysical works, such as *The Monadology* 1714, he argued that everything consisted of innumerable units, *monads*, whose individual properties determined its past, present, and future.

Leicester industrial city (food processing, hosiery, footwear, engineering, electronics, printing, plastics) and administrative headquarters of Leicestershire, England, on the river Soar; population (1991) 270,600.

Leicester Robert Dudley, Earl of Leicester *c.* 1532–1588. English courtier. Son of the duke of Northumberland, he was created Earl of Leicester in 1564. Queen Elizabeth I gave him command of the

Leicester *The controversial favourite of Elizabeth I, Robert Dudley, Earl of Leicester.*

army sent to the Netherlands in 1585–87, and of all the forces prepared to resist the threat of Spanish invasion in 1588.

Leicestershire county in central England
area 2,550 sq km/984 sq mi
towns administrative headquarters Leicester; Loughborough, Melton Mowbray, Market Harborough
products horses, cattle, sheep, dairy products, coal
population (1991) 860,500
famous people C P Snow.

Leichhardt Friedrich 1813–1848. Prussian-born Australian explorer. In 1843, he walked 965 km/600 mi from Sydney to Moreton Bay, Queensland, and in 1844 went from Brisbane to Arnhem Land, but disappeared during a further expedition from Queensland in 1848.

Leics abbreviation for ◊*Leicestershire*.

Leigh Mike 1943– . British playwright and director. He directs his own plays which evolve through improvisation before they are scripted; they include the comedies *Abigail's Party* 1977, and *Goose-Pimples* 1981. His work for television includes *Nuts in May* 1976, and *Home Sweet Home* 1982. His films include *High Hopes* 1989 and *Life is Sweet* 1991.

Leigh Vivien 1913–1967. British actress, born Vivien Mary Hartley. Noted for her fragile beauty and vivacity, she is remembered for her Oscar-winning roles as Scarlett O'Hara in *Gone With the Wind* 1939 and as Blanche du Bois in *A Streetcar Named Desire* 1951.

Leinster SE province of the Republic of Ireland, comprising the counties of Carlow, Dublin, Kildare, Kilkenny, Laois, Longford, Louth, Meath, Offaly, Westmeath, Wexford, Wicklow; area 19,630 sq km/7,577 sq mi; capital Dublin; population (1989) 1,860,000.

Leipzig city in W Saxony, Germany, 145 km/90 mi SW of Berlin; population (1986) 552,000. Products include furs, leather goods, cloth, glass, cars, and musical instruments.

leishmaniasis parasitic disease caused by microscopic protozoans (*Leishmania*), identified by William Leishman (1865–1926), and transmitted by sandflies. It may cause either localized infection or dangerous fever. It is prevalent in NE Africa and S Asia.

leitmotiv (German 'leading motive') in music, a recurring theme used to indicate a character or idea – a technique used frequently by Wagner in his operas.

Leitrim county in Connacht province, Republic of Ireland, bounded on the NW by Donegal Bay
area 1,530 sq km/591 sq mi

lemon

county town Carrick-on-Shannon
products potatoes, cattle, linen, woollens, pottery, coal, iron, lead
population (1991) 25,300

lek in biology, a closely spaced set of very small ◊territories each occupied by a single male during the mating season. Leks are found in the mating systems of several birds and a few antelopes.

Lely Peter. Adopted name of Pieter van der Faes 1618–1680. Dutch painter, born in Germany, active in the UK from 1641, who painted fashionable portraits in Baroque style. Subjects included Charles I, Cromwell, Charles II (who knighted him in 1679), and fashionable women of Charles II's court, for example *The Windsor Beauties* (Hampton Court).

Lemaître Georges Édouard 1894–1966. Belgian cosmologist who proposed the ◊Big Bang theory of the origin of the Universe 1927.

Le Mans industrial town in Sarthe *département*, France; population (1990) 148,500. It has a ◊motor racing circuit where the annual endurance 24-hour race (established 1923) for sports cars and their prototypes is held.

lemming small rodent found in northern regions. It is about 12 cm/5 in long, with thick brownish fur, small head, and short tail. Periodically, when their population exceeds the available food supply, lemmings undergo mass migrations.

lemon fruit of the lemon tree *Citrus limon*. It may have originated in NW India, and was introduced into Europe by the Spanish Moors in the 12th or 13th century. It is now grown largely in Italy, Spain, California, Florida, South Africa, and Australia.

Lenin *Soviet politician Vladimir Lenin in 1922 with his family.*

lemon balm perennial herb *Melissa officinalis* of the mint family Labiatae, with lemon-scented leaves. It is widely used in teas, liqueurs, and medicines.

lemur many species of ◊primate inhabiting Madagascar and the Comoro Islands. They are arboreal animals, and some species are nocturnal. They can grow to 1.2 m/4 ft long, have large eyes, and long, bushy tails. They feed upon fruit, insects, and small animals. Many are threatened with extinction as forests are cleared.

Lena longest river in Asiatic Russia, 4,400 km/2,730 mi. It rises near Lake Baikal and empties into the Arctic Ocean through a delta 400 km/240 mi wide. It is ice-covered for half the year.

Le Nain family of French painters, the brothers Antoine (1588–1648), Louis (1593–1648), and Mathieu (1607–1677). They were born in Laon, settled in Paris, and were among the original members of the French Academy in 1648. Attribution of works among them is uncertain. They chiefly painted sombre and dignified scenes of peasant life.

Lenclos Ninon de 1615–1705. French courtesan. As the recognized leader of Parisian society, she was the mistress in turn of many highly placed men, including Gen Condé and the writer La Rochefoucauld.

Lend-Lease an act of the US congress in March 1941 which gave the president power to order any defence article for the government of any country whose defence the president deemed vital to the defence of the US'. During World War II, the US negotiated many lend-lease agreements, most notably with Britain and the Soviet Union.

Lenglen Suzanne 1899–1938. French tennis player, Wimbledon singles and doubles champion 1919–23 and 1925, and Olympic champion 1921. She became professional in 1926. She also popularized sports clothes designed by Jean Patou (1880–1936).

Lenin Vladimir Ilyich. Adopted name of Vladimir Ilyich Ulyanov 1870–1924. Soviet communist politician and theoretician. Active in the 1905 Revolution, Lenin had to leave Russia when it failed, settling in Switzerland in 1914. He returned in Mar 1917 (see ◊Russian Revolution). With the Bolshevik revolution in Nov he became leader of a Soviet government, concluded peace with Germany, and organized a successful resistance to White (pro-tsarist) uprisings and foreign intervention. His modification of traditional Marxist doctrine to fit the objective conditions prevailing in Russia became known as Marxism-Leninism, the basis of communist ideology.

Leningrad former name of the Russian city ◊*St Petersburg*.

Lennon John 1940–1980. Rock singer and songwriter, former member of the ◊Beatles. Both before and after the band's break-up, he collaborated intermittently with his wife *Yoko Ono* (1933–). 'Give Peace a Chance' 1969, became an anthem of the peace movement. A 'fan' shot him dead.

Leno Dan 1861–1904. British comedian. A former acrobat, he became the idol of the music halls, and was considered the greatest of ◊pantomime 'dames'.

lens in optics, a piece of a transparent material such as glass with two polished surfaces – one concave or convex, and the other plane, concave or convex – to modify rays of light. A convex lens converges the light and a concave lens diverges it.

lens, gravitational in astronomy, object in space which, by its gravitational field, bends light in a similar way to a spectacle lens. As a result of this, one object, such as a quasar, can appear as two

lens

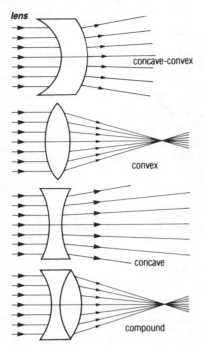

concave-convex

convex

concave

compound

images, where it is and where it appears to be. A gravitational lens also produces a magnifying effect; from a focal point 300 billion km out in space, objects behind the Sun would be magnified 20 million times.

Lent in the Christian church, the 40 days period of fasting which precedes Easter, beginning on Ash Wednesday, but omitting Sundays.

lenticel a small pore on the stems of woody plants or the trunks of trees. Lenticels are means of gas exchange between the stem interior and the atmosphere. They consist of loosely-packed cells with many air spaces between them, and are easily seen on smooth-barked trees such as cherries, where they form horizontal lines on the trunk.

lentil annual plant *Lens culinaris* of the Leguminosae family. The plant grows 15–45 cm/6–18 in high, and has white, blue, or purplish flowers. The seeds, contained in pods about 1.6 cm/0.6 in long, are widely used as food.

Lenz's law in physics, law stating that the direction of an ◊electromagnetically induced current (generated by moving a magnet near a wire or a wire in a magnetic field) will oppose the motion producing it.

Leo constellation of the zodiac, in the northern hemisphere near Ursa Major, through which the Sun passes from mid-Aug to mid-Sept. Its brightest star is first-magnitude Regulus, a blue-white star 85 light years away; Gamma Leonis is a double star. It represents a lion.

Leo III the Isaurian *c.* 680–740. Byzantine emperor, a soldier who seized the throne in 717. He successfully defended Constantinople against the Saracens in 717–18, and attempted to suppress the use of images in church worship.

Leo thirteen popes, including :

Leo I St (the Great) *c.* 390–461. Pope from 440. One of the most important of the early popes for establishing the Christian liturgy, Leo summoned

the Chalcedon Council where his ***Dogmatical Letter*** was accepted as the voice of St Peter. Acting as ambassador to the emperor Valentinian III (425–455), Leo saved Rome from devastation by the Huns by buying off their king, Attila.

Leo III *c.* 750–816. Pope from 795. After the withdrawal of the Byzantine emperors, the popes had become the real rulers in Rome. Leo III was forced to flee because of a conspiracy in Rome, and took refuge at the court of Charlemagne. He returned to Rome in 799, and crowned Charlemagne emperor in 800, establishing the secular sovereignty of the pope over Rome.

Leo X (Giovanni de' Medici) 1475–1521. Pope from 1513. The son of Lorenzo the Magnificent of Florence, he was created a cardinal at 13. He bestowed on Henry VIII of England the title of Defender of the Faith, but later excommunicated him. A patron of the arts, he sponsored the rebuilding of St Peter's Church, Rome. He raised funds for this by selling indulgences, a sale that led the religious reformer Martin Luther to rebel against papal authority.

León city in W Nicaragua, population (1981) 248,700. Industries include textiles and food processing. Founded 1524, it was capital of Nicaragua until 1855.

León industrial city (leather goods, footwear) in central Mexico; population (1980) 655,800.

Leonard Elmore 1925– . US author of westerns and thrillers, marked by vivid dialogue, for example *Stick* 1983 and *Freaky Deaky* 1988.

Leonard Sugar Ray 1956– . US boxer. In 1988 he became the first man to win world titles at five officially recognized weights.

Leonardo da Vinci 1452–1519. Italian painter, sculptor, architect, musician, engineer, and scientist, one of the greatest figures in the Italian Renaissance, active in Florence, Milan, and from 1516 in France. As state engineer and court painter to the duke of Milan, he produced the *Last Supper* mural about 1495 (S Maria delle Grazie, Milan). He was employed by Cesare Borgia in Florence when he painted the *Mona Lisa* about 1503–06

Leonardo da Vinci The Virgin and child with St Anne and St John the Baptist *(mid 1490s) National Gallery, London.*

Lesotho
Kingdom of

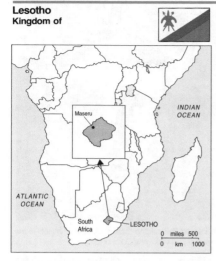

INDIAN
OCEAN

Maseru

ATLANTIC
OCEAN

South
Africa — LESOTHO

| 0 | miles | 500 |
| 0 | km | 1000 |

area 30,346 sq km/11,716 sq mi
capital Maseru

physical mountainous with plateau
head of state King Letsie III from 1990
head of government Ntsu Mokhele from 1993
political system emergent democracy
exports wool, mohair, diamonds
currency maluti
population (1990 est) 1,757,000; annual growth rate 2.7%
life expectancy men 59, women 62
language Sesotho and English (official)
religion Christian 70% (Roman Catholic 40%)
literacy 59% (1988)
GNP $408 million (1988); $410 per head
chronology
1966 Basutoland became independent, within the Commonwealth, as the Kingdom of Lesotho, with Chief Leabua Jonathan as prime minister.
1975 Members of the ruling party attacked by guerrillas backed by South Africa.
1986 South Africa imposed a border blockade, forcing the deportation of 60 African National Congress members. National assembly abolished.
1990 Mosheoshoe II deposed and replaced by his son Mohato as King Letsie III.
1991 Political parties permitted to operate.
1992 Moshoeshoe returned from exile.
1993 Free elections ended military rule.

Leonardo da Vinci Self-portrait of the artist.

(Louvre, Paris). His notebooks and drawings show an immensely inventive and enquiring mind, studying aspects of the natural world from anatomy to aerodynamics.

Leoncavallo Ruggiero 1857–1919. Italian operatic composer, born in Naples. He played in restaurants, composing in his spare time, until in 1892 *Pagliacci* was performed and immediately became popular. Of his other operas, only *La Bohème* 1897 (contemporary with Puccini's version) and *Zara* enjoyed some success.

Leonidas died 480 BC. King of Sparta. He was killed while defending the pass of ◊Thermopylae with 300 Spartans, 700 Thespians, and 400 Thebans against a huge Persian army.

Leonov Aleksei Arkhipovich 1934– . Soviet cosmonaut, the first person to walk in space in 1965, from his vehicle, *Voskhod 2*.

leopard member of the cat family *Panthera pardus* also known as the panther, found in Africa and Asia. The ground colour of the coat is golden and the black spots form rosettes which differ according to the variety; black panthers are simply mutants and retain the patterning as a 'watered-silk' effect. The leopard varies in size from 1.5–2.5 m/5–8 ft, including the tail, which may measure 1 m/3 ft.

Leopardi Giacomo, Court Leopardi 1798–1837. Italian romantic poet. He has been called the greatest Italian lyric poet since Dante. His first collection of his uniquely pessimistic poems, *Versi/ Verses*, appeared in 1824, and was followed by his philosophical *Operette Morali/Minor Moral Works* 1827, in prose, and *Canti/Lyrics* 1831.

Leopold three kings of Belgium:

Leopold I 1790–1865. King of Belgium from 1831, having been elected to the throne on the creation of an independent Belgium. Through his marriage, when prince of Saxe-Coburg, to Princess Charlotte Augusta, he was the uncle of Queen ◊Victoria, and exercised considerable influence over her.

Leopold II 1835–1909. King of Belgium from 1865, son of Leopold I. He financed the British journalist Stanley's explorations in Africa, which resulted in the foundation of the Congo Free State (now Zaïre), from which he extracted a huge fortune by ruthless exploitation.

Leopold III 1901–1983. King of Belgium from 1934, he surrendered to the Germans in 1940. Postwar charges against his conduct led to a regency by his brother Charles, and his eventual abdication in 1951 in favour of his son ◊Baudouin.

Leopold two Holy Roman emperors:

Leopold I 1640–1705. Holy Roman emperor from 1658, in succession to his father Ferdinand III. He warred against Louis XIV of France and the Ottoman Empire.

Leopold II 1747–1792. Holy Roman emperor in succession to his brother Joseph II, he was the son of Empress Maria Theresa. His hostility to the French Revolution led to the outbreak of war a few weeks after his death.

Léopoldville former name of ◊Kinshasa, city in Zaïre.

Lepanto, Battle of sea battle fought in the Mediterranean Gulf of Corinth off Lepanto, then in Turkish possession, on 7 Oct 1571, between the Ottoman Empire and forces from Spain, Venice, Genoa, and the Papal States, jointly commanded by Don John of Austria. The combined western fleets were known as the Christian League, instigated by Pope Pius V, and delivered a crushing blow to Muslim sea power.

Le Pen Jean-Marie 1928– . French extreme right-wing politician. In 1972 he formed the French National Front, supporting immigrant repatriation and capital punishment. The party gained 10% of the national vote in the 1986 election. Le Pen, a powerful orator, was elected to the European Parliament in 1984.

Lepenski Vir the site of Europe's oldest urban settlement (6th millenium BC), now submerged by an artificial lake on the Danube.

lepidoptera an order of insects, including ◊butterflies and ◊moths; the order consists of some 165,000 species.

leprosy a chronic disease caused by a bacterium which is closely related to that of ◊tuberculosis. The infection attacks skin and nerves.

Leptis Magna ruined city in Libya, 120 km/75 mi E of Tripoli. It was founded by the Phoenicians, then came under Carthage, and in 47 BC under Rome. Excavation in the 20th century revealed remains of fine Roman buildings.

lepton a type of sub-atomic or elementary ◊particle.

Lermontov Mikhail Yurevich 1814–1841. Russian romantic poet and novelist. In 1837 he was exiled to the Caucasus for a revolutionary poem on the death of ◊Pushkin, which criticized Court values. In 1838 he published his psychological novel *A Hero of Our Times* 1840 and a volume of poems *October* 1940.

Le Sage Alan René 1668–1747. French novelist and dramatist. Born in Brittany, he abandoned law for literature. His novels include *Le Diable boîteux/The Devil upon Two Sticks* 1707 and his picaresque masterpiece *Gil Blas* 1715–1735, much indebted to Spanish originals.

lesbianism homosexuality between women, so called from the Greek island of Lesbos (now Lesvos), the home of ◊Sappho the poet.

lesion a general term used to denote any change in a body tissue which is a manifestation of disease or injury.

Lesotho landlocked country in southern Africa, an enclave within South Africa.

less developed country (LDC) any country late in developing an industrial base, and dependent on cash crops and unprocessed minerals. The Group of 77 was established in 1964 to pressurize developed countries into giving greater aid to LDCs.

Lesseps Ferdinand, Vicomte de Lesseps 1805–1894. French engineer, constructor of the ◊Suez Canal 1859–69; he began the ◊Panama Canal in 1879, but failed when he tried to construct it without locks.

Lessing *Political and social themes predominate in the work of British novelist Doris Lessing.*

Lessing Doris (May) (born Taylor) 1919– . British novelist, born in Iran and brought up in Rhodesia. Much concerned with social and political themes, particularly the place of women in society, her work includes *The Grass is Singing* 1950, *The Golden Notebook* 1962, *The Good Terrorist* 1985, and the five-novel series *Children of Violence* 1952–69.

Lessing Gotthold Ephraim 1729–1781. German dramatist and critic. His dramatic masterpieces include *Miss Sara Sampson* 1755, *Minna von Barnhelm* 1767, *Emilia Galotti* 1772; and the verse play *Nathan der Weise* 1779. His works of criticism *Laokoon* 1766 and *Hamburgische Dramaturgie* 1767–68 had an important influence on German literature. He also produced many theological and philosophical writings.

Les Six French name ('the six') given in 1920 to a group of six French composers – Georges ◊Auric, Louis Durey (1888–1979), Arthur ◊Honegger, Darius ◊Milhaud, Francis ◊Poulenc, and Germaine Tailleferre (1892–1983) – dedicated to producing works free from foreign influences and reflecting the modern world.

Lethe in Greek mythology, a river of the underworld whose waters, when drunk, brought forgetfulness of the past.

letterpress the method of printing from raised type, pioneered by Johannes ◊Gutenberg in the 1450s.

lettres de cachet French term for an order signed by the king and closed with his seal (*cachet*); especially an order under which persons might be imprisoned or banished without trial. They were used as a means of disposing of politically dangerous persons or criminals of high birth without the embarrassment of a trial. The system was abolished during the French Revolution.

lettuce annual edible plant *Lactuca sativa*, family Compositae, believed to have been derived from the wild species, *Lactuca serriola*. There are many varieties, including the cabbage lettuce, with round or loose heads, and the Cos lettuce, with long, upright heads.

leucocyte a white blood cell. They are part of the body's defences and give immunity against disease. There are several different types of leucocyte. Some (◊*phagocytes* and ◊*macrophages*) engulf invading microorganisms, others kill infected

lever
first-order lever

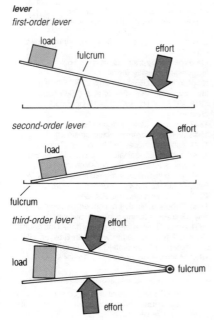

second-order lever

third-order lever

cells, while ◊*lymphocytes* produce more specific immune responses. Human blood contains about 11,000 leucocytes to the cubic millimetre – about one to every 500 red cells.

leucotomy or *frontal lobotomy* in medicine, an operation to severe the nerves in the frontal lobes of the brain in certain serious mental disorders. Always controversial, it is no longer practised. See also ◊psychosurgery.

leukaemia any one of a group of cancer-like diseases of the blood cells, with involvement of the bone marrow and other blood-forming tissue.

Le Vau Louis 1612–1670. French architect, who drafted the plan of Versailles, and built the Louvre and Les Tuileries in Paris.

levee a naturally-formed raised bank along the side of a river. When a river overflows its banks, the speed of the current in the flooded area is less than that in the channel, and silt is deposited. After the waters have withdrawn the silt is left as a bank that grows with successive floods. Eventually the river, contained by the levee, may be above the surface of the surrounding flood plain. Notable levees are found on the lower reaches of the Mississippi in America and the Po in Italy.

level a simple instrument for finding horizontal level, used in surveying and building construction. Often called a spirit, or bubble level, it consists of a coloured liquid in a glass tube, in which a bubble is trapped. When the tube is horizontal, the bubble moves to the centre.

Levellers the democratic party in the English Revolution. They found wide support among Cromwell's New Model Army and the yeoman farmers, artisans, and small traders, and proved a powerful political force 1647–49. Their programme included the establishment of a republic, government by a parliament of one house elected by male suffrage, religious toleration, and sweeping social reforms.

lever a simple machine consisting of a rigid rod pivoted at a fulcrum, used for shifting or raising a heavy load or applying force in a similar way. Levers

are classified into orders according to where the effort is applied, and the load-moving force developed, in relation to the position of the fulcrum.

leveraged buyout in business, the purchase of a controlling proportion of the shares of a company by its own management, financed almost exclusively by borrowing. It is so called because the ratio of a company's long-term debt to its equity (capital assets) is known as its 'leverage'.

Leverrier Urbain Jean Joseph 1811–1877. French astronomer, who predicted the existence and position of Neptune.

Lévesque René 1922–1987. French-Canadian politician. In 1968 he founded the Parti Québecois, with the aim of an independent Quebec, but a national referendum rejected the proposal in 1980. He was premier of Quebec 1976–85. In 1985 he resigned from the leadership of the party.

Levi Primo 1919–1987. Italian novelist, who joined the anti-Fascist resistance during World War II and was captured and sent to Auschwitz concentration camp. He wrote memorably of his experience as a Jewish survivor in *Se Questo e un uomo/If This is a Man* 1947.

leviathan in the Old Testament or Hebrew Bible, a mythical evil sea monster, identified by later commentators with the whale.

Levi-Montalcini Rita 1909– . Italian neurologist who discovered nerve growth factor, a molecule which controls how many cells make up the adult nervous system. Nobel prize for medicine 1986.

Lévi-Strauss Claude 1908–1990. French anthropologist, who sought to find a universal structure governing all societies, reflected in the way myths are created. His works include *Tristes Tropiques* 1955, and *Mythologiques/Mythologies* 1964–71.

levitation counteraction of gravitational forces on a body. As claimed by medieval mystics, spiritualist mediums, and practitioners of transcendental meditation, it is unproven. In the laboratory it can be produced scientifically, for example, electrostatic force and acoustical waves have been used to suspend water drops for microscopic study. It is also used in technology, for example, in magnetic levitation as in ◊maglev trains.

Lewes George Henry 1817–1878. English philosopher and literary critic, originally an actor. His works include a *Biographical History of Philosophy* 1845–46, and *Life and Works of Goethe* 1855.

Lewes, Battle of battle 1264 caused by the baronial opposition to Henry III, led by Simon de Montfort, earl of Leicester (1208–65). The king was defeated and captured at the battle.

Lewis (Harry) Sinclair 1885–1951. US novelist. He made a reputation with *Main Street* 1920, depicting American small-town life; *Babbitt* 1922, the story of a real-estate dealer caught in the conventions of his milieu; and *Arrowsmith* 1925, a study of a scientist. Nobel prize 1930.

Lewis Cecil Day see ◊Day Lewis.

Lewis Carl (Frederick Carleton) 1961– . US athlete. At the 1984 Olympic Games he equalled Jesse ◊Owens' performance, winning gold medals in the 100 and 200 metres, sprint relay, and long jump. In the 1988 Olympics, he repeated his golds in the 100 metres and long jump, and won a silver in the 200 metres. He failed to make the US 100- and 200-metre Olympic squads 1992, but won gold for the long jump and in the 400-metre relay team.

Lewis C(live) S(taples) 1898–1963. British academic, writer and author of children's books. He was a committed Christian and wrote essays in popular theology such as *The Screwtape Letters*

Liberia
Republic of

ATLANTIC
OCEAN

0   miles 500
0   km   1000

Guinea

Sierra   Ivory
Leone   Coast
Monrovia
LIBERIA

area 112,820 sq km/43,548 sq mi
capital and port Monrovia
physical forested highlands; swampy coast
head of state and government Amos Sawyer from 1990

political system democratic republic
exports iron ore, rubber, timber, diamonds, coffee
currency Liberian dollar
population (1990 est) 2,644,000; annual growth rate 3.2%
life expectancy men 53, women 56
language English (official)
religion animist 65%, Muslim 20%, Christian 15%
literacy 47% male/23% female (1985 est)
GNP $973 million (1987); $410 per head
chronology
1847 Founded as an independent republic.
1944 William Tubman elected president.
1971 Tubman succeeded by William Tolbert.
1980 Tolbert assassinated in a coup led by Samuel Doe, who suspended the constitution
1984 New constitution approved. National Democratic Party of Liberia (NDPL) founded by Doe.
1985 NDPL won general election.
1990 Rebels controlled almost entire country by July. Doe killed during a bloody civil war.
1991 Amos Sawyer elected president. Rebel leader Charles Taylor agreed to work with Sawyer. UN peacekeeping force drafted into the republic.
1992 Monrovia under siege by Taylor's rebel forces.

1942 and *Mere Christianity* 1952; and a series of books of Christian allegory for children.

Lewis Jerry Lee 1935– . US rock-and-roll and country singer and pianist. His trademark was the 'pumping piano' style in hits such as 'Whole Lotta Shakin' Going On' and 'Great Balls of Fire' 1957.

Lewis Hayley 1975– . Australian swimmer who, in 1990, became the first woman to win five gold metals in the Commonwealth Games.

Lewis Meriwether 1774–1809. US explorer. He was commissioned with William Clark (1770–1838) to find a land route to the Pacific. He followed the Missouri River to its source, crossed the Rocky Mountains, and followed the Columbia River to the Pacific, then returned overland to St Louis 1804–06.

Lewis (Percy) Wyndham 1886–1957. British writer and artist, who pioneered ◊Vorticism; and

Lewis US rock-and-roll, country singer, and pianist, Jerry Lew Lewis.

was noted for the hard and aggressive style of both his writing and painting. His literary works include the novels *Tarr* 1918, and *The Childermass* 1928, the essay *Time and Western Man* 1927 and autobiographies.

ley an area of temporary grassland which is sown to produce grazing and hay or silage for a period of one to ten years before being ploughed and cropped. Short term leys are often a component of modern systems of crop rotation.

Leyden Lucas van Dutch painter see ◊Lucas van Leyden.

Lhasa (the 'Forbidden City') capital of the autonomous region of Tibet, China, at 5,000 m/16,400 ft; population (1982) 105,000. Products include handicrafts and light industry.

Li Peng 1928– . Chinese communist politician, a member of the Politburo from 1985, and head of government from 1987.

Li Xiannian 1905– . Chinese politician, member of the Chinese Communist Party (CCP) Politburo from 1956. He fell out of favour during the 1966–69 Cultural Revolution, but was rehabilitated as finance minister 1973, supporting cautious economic reform. Li was appointed state president in Jun 1983.

liability in economics, a financial obligation. In accountancy liabilities are placed alongside assets on a balance sheet to show the wealth of the entity at a given date.

liana a woody, perennial climbing plant with very long stems, that grows around trees up to the canopy, where there is more sunlight. Lianas are especially common in tropical rain forests, where individual stems may grow up 70 m/255 ft long. They have an unusual stem structure which allows them to retain some flexibility.

Liaoning province of NE China
area 151,000 sq km/58,300 sq mi
capital Shenyang
towns Anshan, Fushun, Liaoyang
products cereals, coal, iron, salt, oil
population (1990) 39,460,000.

Liaquat Ali Khan 1895–1951. Indian Muslim nationalist politician, prime minister of Pakistan

Libya
Great Socialist People's Libyan Arab Jamahiriya
(al-Jamahiriya al-Arabiya al-Libya al-Shabiya al-Ishtirakiya al-Uzma)

area 1,780,000 sq km/680,000 sq mi
capital Tripoli
towns ports Benghazi, Misurata
physical desert; mountains in N and S

head of state and government Moamar al-Khaddhafi from 1969
political system one-party socialist state
exports oil, natural gas
currency Libyan dinar
population (1990 est) 4,280,000 (including 500,000 foreign workers); annual growth rate 3.1%
life expectancy men 64, women 69
language Arabic
religion Sunni Muslim
literacy 60% (1989)
GNP $20 bn (1988); $5,410 per head
chronology
1951 Achieved independence as the United Kingdom of Libya, under King Idris.
1969 King deposed in a coup led by Col Moamar Khaddhafi. Revolution Command Counsil set up and the Arab Socialist Union (ASU) proclaimed the one legal party.
1972 Proposed federation of Libya, Syria, and Egypt abandoned.
1980 Libyan troops began fighting in Chad.
1986 US bombing of Khaddhafi's headquarters.
1989 USA accused Libya of building a chemical-weapons factory and shot down two Libyan planes.
1992 Khaddafi under international pressure to extradite suspected Lockerbie bombers for trial outside Lebanon; sanctions imposed.

from independence 1947. The chief lieutenant of Muhammad ◊Jinnah, he was a leader of the Muslim League. He was assassinated.

Lib. abbreviation for *Liberal*.

Libby Willard Frank 1908–1980. US chemist, whose development of ◊radiocarbon dating 1947 won him a Nobel prize 1960.

libel in law, defamation in a permanent form, such as in a newspaper, book, or broadcast.

liberalism political and social theory that favours parliamentary government, freedom of the press, speech, and worship, the abolition of class privileges, a minimum of state interference in economic life, and international ◊free trade. It is historically associated with the Liberal Party in the UK and the Democratic Party in the USA.

Liberal Party in the UK, a political party, the successor to the ◊Whig Party, with an ideology of ◊liberalism. In the 19th century it was the party of the left, representing the interests of commerce and industry. Its outstanding leaders were Palmerston, Gladstone, and Lloyd George. From 1914 it declined, and the rise of the Labour Party pushed the Liberals into the middle ground. The Liberals joined forces with the Social Democratic Party (SDP) for the 1983 and 1987 elections. In the 1987 election the Alliance, as they were jointly known, achieved 22 seats and 22.6% of votes. In 1988, the SDP voted to merge with the Liberals to form the Social and Liberal Democrats.

Liberal Party, Australian political party established 1944 by Robert Menzies, after a Labor landslide, and derived from the former United Australia Party. After the voters rejected Labor's extensive nationalization plans, the Liberals were in power 1949–72 and 1975–83, and were led in succession by H E Holt, J G Gorton, Sir William McMahon (1908–), Sir Billy Sneddon (1926–), and Malcolm Fraser.

liberation theology Christian intellectual theory of Christ's primary importance as the 'Liberator', personifying the poor and devoted to freeing them from oppression (Matthew 19:21,

25:35, 40). Initiated by the Peruvian priest Gustavo Gutierrez in *The Theology of Liberation* 1969, and enthusiastically, and sometimes violently, adopted in Latin America, it embodies a Marxist interpretation of the class struggle.

Liberia country in W Africa, bounded to the N and NE by Guinea, E by the Ivory Coast, S and SW by the Atlantic, and NW by Sierra Leone.

liberty in its medieval sense, a franchise, or collection of privileges, granted to an individual or community by the king, and the area over which this franchise extended.

liberty, equality, fraternity (*liberté, egalité, fraternité*) motto of the French republic from 1793. It was changed 1940–44 under the Vichy regime to 'work, family, fatherland'.

LIBOR *London Interbank Offered Rates* loan rates for a specified period which are offered to first-class banks in the London interbank market. Banks link their lending to LIBOR as an alternative to the base lending rate when setting the rate for a fixed term, after which the rate may be adjusted.

Libra faint constellation of the zodiac, in the southern hemisphere near Scorpius. It represents the scales of justice. The Sun passes through Libra during Nov.

library a collection of information (usually in the form of books) held for common use. The earliest was at Ninevah in Babylonia times. The first public library was opened at Athens 330 BC. All ancient libraries were reference libraries; books could be consulted but not borrowed.

Libreville capital of Gabon, on the estuary of the river Gabon; population (1988) 352,000. Products include timber, oil, and minerals. It was founded 1849 as a refuge for slaves freed by the French.

Libya country in N Africa, bordered to the N by the Meditatean, E by Egypt, SE by the Sudan, S by Chad and Niger, and W by Algeria and Tunisia.

lichen organism of the group *Lichenes*, which consists of a fungus and an alga existing in a mutually beneficial relationship. Found on trees, rocks, and other substrates, lichen flourishes under very adverse conditions.

Lichfield Patrick Anson, 5th Earl of Lichfield 1939– . British photographer, known for portraits of the rich and famous.

Lichtenstein Roy 1923– . US Pop artist. He used advertising and comic-strip imagery, often focusing on popular ideals of romance and heroism, as in *Whaam!* 1963 (Tate Gallery, London).

Liddell Hart Basil 1895–1970. British military scientist. He was an exponent of mechanized warfare, and his ideas were adopted in Germany 1935 in creating the 1st Panzar Division, combining motorized infantry and tanks. From 1937 he advised the UK War Office on army reorganization.

Lidice Czechoslovakian mining village, replacing one destroyed by the Nazis 10 Jun 1942 as a reprisal for the assassination of ◊Heydrich. The men were shot, the women sent to concentration camps, and the children taken to Germany. The Sudeten German responsible was hanged 1946.

Lie Trygve (Halvdan) 1896–1968. Norwegian Labour politician and diplomat. He became the first secretary-general of the United Nations 1946–53, when he resigned over Soviet opposition to his handling of the Korean War.

Liebig Justus, Baron von Liebig 1803–1873. German chemist, a major contributor to agricultural chemistry. He introduced the theory of ◊radicals, and discovered chloroform and chloral.

Liebknecht Karl 1871–1919. German socialist, son of Wilhelm Liebknecht. A founder of the German Communist Party, originally known as the Spartacus League (see ◊Spartacist), he led an unsuccessful revolt in Berlin 1919, and was murdered by army officers.

Liebknecht Wilhelm 1826–1900. German socialist. A friend of the communist theoretician Marx, with whom he took part in the ◊revolution of 1848; he was imprisoned for opposition to the Franco-Prussian War.

Liechtenstein landlocked country in W central Europe, situated between Austria to the E, and Switzerland to the W.

lie detector popular name for a ◊polygraph.

Liège industrial city (weapons, textiles, paper, chemicals), capital of Liège province in Belgium,

SE of Brussels, on the Meuse; population (1991) 194,600.

liege in medieval times, a term used to describe the relationship between a lord and his vassal in the feudal system.

life the ability to grow, reproduce, and respond to such stimuli as light, heat, and sound. It is thought that life on Earth began about 4,000,000,000 years ago. It seems probable that the original atmosphere of Earth consisted of carbon dioxide, nitrogen, and water, and that complex organic molecules, such as ◊amino acids, were created when the atmosphere was bombarded by ultraviolet radiation or by lightning. Attempts to replicate these conditions in the laboratory have successfully shown that amino acids, purine and pyrimidine bases (◊base pairs in DNA), and other vital molecules can be created in this way.

lifeboat small land-based vessel specially built for saving life as sea, or a boat carried abroad a larger ship in case of shipwreck. In Britain the Royal National Lifeboat Institution (RNLI), founded 1824 at the instance of William Hillary, provides a voluntary manned and supported service. The US and Canadian Coast Guards are services of the governments.

life cycle in biology, the sequence of stages through which members of a given species pass. Most vertebrates have a simple life cycle consisting of ◊fertilization of sex cells or ◊gametes, a period of development as an ◊embryo, a period of juvenile growth after hatching or birth, an adulthood including ◊sexual reproduction, and finally death. Invertebrate life cycles are generally more complex and may involve major reconstitution of the individual's appearance (◊metamorphosis) and completely different styles of life. Thus, dragonflies live an aquatic life as larvae and an aerial life during the adult phase. In many other invertebrates and protozoa there are several different stages in the life cycle, and in parasites these often occur in different host organisms. Plants have a special type of life cycle with two distinct phases, known as an ◊alternation of generations.

life insurance an insurance policy that pays money on the death of the holder. It is correctly called assurance, as the policy covers an inevitable occurrence, not a risk.

Liechtenstein
Principality of
(*Fürstentum Liechtenstein*)

area 160 sq km/62 sq mi
capital Vaduz
physical Alpine; includes part of Rhine Valley
head of state Prince Hans Adam II from 1989
head of government Hans Brunhart from 1978
government constitutional monarchy
exports microchips, precision engineering, processed foods, postage stamps
currency Swiss franc
population (1990 est) 30,000 (33% foreign); annual growth rate 1.4%
life expectancy men 78, women 83
language German
religion Roman Catholic 87%
literacy 100% (1989)
GDP $1 bn (1987); $32,000 per head
chronology
1938 Prince Franz Josef II came to power.
1984 Vote extended to women in national elections.
1989 Prince Franz Josef II succeeded by Hans Adam II.
1990 Became a member of the UN.

life sciences scientific study of the living world as a whole, a new synthesis of several traditional scientific disciplines including ◊biology, ◊zoology, and ◊botany, and newer, more specialized areas of study such as ◊biophysics and ◊sociobiology.

life table in demography, a way of summarizing the probability that an individual will give birth or die during successive periods of life. From this the proportion of individuals who survive from birth to any given age (***survivorship***) and the mean number of offspring produced (***net reproductive rate***) can be determined. Insurance companies use life tables to estimate risk of death to set their premiums, while governments use them to determine future needs for education and health services.

LIFFE acronym for *L*ondon *I*nternational *F*inancial *F*utures *E*xchange, one of the exchanges in London when ◊futures contracts are traded. It opened Sep 1982 to provide a worldwide exchange for futures dealers and investors, and began options trading 1985. It was a forerunner of the ◊Big Bang in bringing US-style 'open-house' dealing (as opposed to telephone dealing) to the UK.

Liffey river in E Ireland, flowing from the Wicklow mountains to Dublin Bay; length 80 km/50 mi.

lift (North American ***elevator***) a device for lifting passengers and goods vertically, usually between the floors of a building. US inventor Elisha Graves ◊Otis developed the first passenger lift, installed 1857. The invention of the lift allowed the development of the ◊skyscraper from the 1880s.

Ligachev Egor (Kuzmich) 1920– . Soviet politician. He joined the Communist Party 1944, and became a member of the Politburo 1985. At one time chief conservative ideologist of the party he was replaced in this role by Vadim Medvedev 1988.

ligament a strong flexible connective tissue, made of the protein collagen, which joins bone to bone at moveable joints. Ligaments prevent bone dislocation (under normal circumstances), but permit joint flexion.

Ligeti György (Sándor) 1923– . Hungarian-born Austrian composer who developed a dense, highly chromatic, polyphonic style, in which melody and rhythm are sometimes lost in shifting blocks of sound. His works include *Aventures* 1962, *Requiem* 1965, an opera *Le Grand Macabre* 1978, and *Poème symphonique* 1962 for 100 metronomes.

light ◊electromagnetic radiation (waves) in the visible range, from about 400 nanometers in the extreme violet to about 770 nanometres in the extreme red. Light is considered to exhibit both particle and wave properties, and the fundamental particle of quantum of light is called the *photon*. The speed of light (and of all electromagnetic radiation) in a vacuum is approximately 300,000,000 metres per second/186,000 miles per second, and is a universal constant denoted by *c*.

light-emitting diode (LED) a means of displaying symbols in electronic instruments and devices. An LED is made of ◊semiconductor material, such as gallium arsenide phosphide, which glows when electricity is passed through it. The first digital watches and calculators had LED display, but now use ◊liquid crystal display (LCD).

lighthouse structure carrying a powerful light to warn ships or aeroplanes that they are approaching land. Dissolved acetylene or electricity is used, and the light of the burner or lamp is magnified and directed out to the horizon or up to the zenith by a series of mirrors or prisms.

lightning high-voltage electrical discharge between two charged rainclouds or between a cloud and the Earth, caused by the built-up of electrical charges. Air in the path of lightning ionizes (becoming conducting), and expands; the accompanying noise is heard as thunder. Currents of 20,000 amps and temperatures of 30,000°C/54,000°F are common.

light pen in computing, an ◊input device resembling an ordinary pen, used to indicate locations on a computer screen. With certain computer-aided design (CAD) programs, light pens are used to instruct computers to change shape, size, positions, and colours on a screen image.

light year in astronomy, the distance travelled by a beam of light in one calendar year, approximately 9,452,213,314,840 km/5,874,588,760,000 mi.

lignin a naturally occurring substance, produced by plants, to strength their tissues. It is the essential ingredient of all wood, and is therefore of great commercial importance. Chemically it is made up of thousands of rings of carbon atoms joined together in a long chain. The way in which they are linked up varies all along the chain, and this irregularity makes it difficult for ◊enzymes to attack lignin, so that most living organisms cannot digest wood.

lignite a type of ◊coal that is brown and fibrous, with a relatively low carbon content. In Scandinavia it is used to generate power.

lignocaine short-term local anaesthetic which is injected into tissues or applied to skin. It is particularly effective for brief, invasive procedures, such as dental care.

Likud alliance of right-wing Israeli political parties which defeated the Labour Party coalition in the May 1977 election, and brought Menachim Begin to power. In 1987, Likud were part of an uneasy national coalition with Labour, formed to solve Israel's economic crisis. In 1989, another coalition was formed under Shamir.

Lilburne John 1614–1657. English republican agitator. He was imprisoned 1638–40 for circulating Puritan pamphlets, fought in the Parliamentary army in the Civil War, and by his advocacy of a democratic republic won the leadership of the ◊Levellers. He was twice tried for sedition and acquitted, and after his acquittal he was imprisoned 1653–55.

Lilienthal Otto 1848–1896. German aviation pioneer, who inspired the ◊Wright brothers. He made and successfully flew many gliders before he was killed in a glider crash.

Lilith in the Old Testament, Assyrian female demon of the night. According to the ◊Talmud, she was the wife of Adam before Eve's creation.

Lille (Flemish ***Ryssel***) industrial city (textiles, chemicals, engineering, distilling), capital of Nord-Pas-de-Calais, France; population (1990) 178,300, metropolitan area 936,000. The world's first entirely automatic underground system was opened here 1982.

Lillee Dennis Keith 1949– . Australian cricketer. A fast bowler, he became Australia's highest Test wicket-taker, with a total of 355 wickets, an international record at the time of his retirement in 1984.

Lilongwe capital of Malawi since 1975; population (1987) 234,000. Products include tobacco and textiles.

lily plant of the genus *Lilium*, of which there are some 80 species, most with showy flowers growing from bulbs. The genus includes hyacinths tulips, asparagus, and plants of the onion genus.

lily of the valley common garden plant *Convallaria majalis*, family Liliaceae, growing in woods in

limestone Carboniferous limestone pavement near Ballynahowan, Ireland.

Europe, N Asia, and North America. The white flowers are scented.

Lima capital of Peru, and industrial city (textiles, chemicals, glass, cement), with its port at Callao; population (1983) 5,258,600. Founded by the conquistador Pizarro 1535, it was rebuilt after destruction by an earthquake 1746.

limbo in Christian theology, a region for the souls of those who were not admitted to the divine vision. *Limbus infantum* was a place where unbaptized infants enjoyed inferior blessedness; and *limbus patrum* was where the prophets and fathers of the Old Testament dwelt.

Limbourg brothers Franco-Flemish painters, *Pol*, *Herman*, and *Jan* (Hennequin, Janneken), active in the late 14th and early 15th century, first in Paris, then in the ducal court of Burgundy. They produced richly detailed manuscript illuminations, including the Book of ◊Hours.

lime calcium oxide CaO (also known as *quicklime*, or hydroxide, CaOH). A white powdery substance, it is used to reduce soil acidity. It is made commercially by heating calcium carbonate, $CaCO_3$, obtained from limestone or chalk.

lime small thorny bush *Citrus aurantifolia*, family Rutaceae, native to India. The white flowers are succeeded by light green or yellow fruits, limes, which resemble lemons but are more globular in shape.

lime or *linden* deciduous tree, genus *Tilia*, of the family Tiliaceae. The *common lime Tilia vulgaris* bears greenish-yellow fragrant flowers in clusters on a winged stalk, succeeded by small bobbly fruits.

Limerick county town of Limerick, Republic of Ireland, the main port of W Ireland, on the Shannon estuary; population (1981) 75,520. It was founded 12th century.

limerick five-line nonsense verse, which first appeared in England about 1820, and was popularized by Edward ◊Lear. An example is:
There was a young lady of Riga,
Who rode with a smile on a tiger;
They returned from the ride
With the lady inside,
And the smile on the face of the tiger.

Limerick county in SW Republic of Ireland, in Munster province
area 2,667 sq km/1,029 sq mi
county town Limerick
physical fertile, with hills in the south
products dairy products
population (1986) 108,000.

limestone a sedimentary rock chiefly composed of calcium carbonate, $CaCO_3$, usually in the form of the calcareous remains of freshwater or marine organisms, for example, crustacea, molluscs, foraminifera. Various types of limestone are used as building stone.

Limitation, Statutes of under English law, Acts of Parliament limiting the time within which legal action must be inaugurated. Actions for breach of contract and most other civil wrongs must be started within six years. Personal injury claims must usually be brought within three years.

limited company or *joint stock company* the usual type of company formation in the UK. It has its origins in the trading companies which began to proliferate 16th century. The capital of a limited company is divided into small units, and profits are distributed according to shareholding.

Limits, Territorial and Fishing see under ◊Maritime Law.

limnology study of lakes and other bodies of open fresh water, in terms of their plant and animal biology, and their physical properties.

limonite an iron ore, hydrated iron oxide, $2Fe_2O_33H_2O$. The mineral, also known as brown iron ore, is found in bog deposits.

limpet type of mollusc. It has a conical shell, and adheres firmly to rocks by the disc-like foot. Limpets are marine animals, and leave their fixed position only to graze on seaweeds, always returning to the same spot.

Lin Biao 1907–1971. Chinese politician and general. He joined the Communists 1927, became a commander of Mao Zedong's Red Army, and led the Northeast People's Liberation Army in the civil war after 1945. He became defence minister 1959, and as vice chairman of the party 1969, he was expected to be Mao's successor, but he lost favour.

Lincoln Abraham 1809–1865. Sixteenth president of the USA 1861–65. In the American ◊Civil War, his chief concern was the preservation of the Union from which the Confederate (Southern) slave states had seceded on his election. In 1863 he announced the freedom of the slaves with the *Emancipation Proclamation*. He was re-elected 1864 with victory for the North in sight, but assassinated by John Wilkes Booth at the end of the war.

Lincolnshire county in E England
area 5,885 sq km/2,272 sq mi
towns administrative headquarters Lincoln, resort Skegness
physical Lincoln Wolds, marshy coastline, the Fens in the SE, rivers Witham and Welland
products cattle, sheep, horses, cereals, flower bulbs, oil
population (1986) 567,000

Lincoln President of the USA Abraham Lincoln was assassinated by John Wilkes Booth.

Lindbergh US aviator Charles Lindbergh with his plane, Spirit of St Louis, in France 1927.

famous people Isaac Newton, Alfred Tennyson, Margaret Thatcher.

Lindbergh Charles (Augustus) 1902–1974. US aviator, who made the first solo non-stop flight across the Atlantic (New York–Paris) 1927 in the *Spirit of St Louis*.

linden another name for ◊lime.

linear accelerator in physics, a machine in which charged ◊particles are accelerated (as in an ◊accelerator) to high speed in passing down a straight evacuated tube or waveguide by electromagnetic waves in the tube or by electric fields.

linear equation in mathematics, an equation involving two variables, of the general form $y = mx + c$, where m and c are constants. In ◊coordinate geometry, such an equation plotted using ◊Cartesian coordinates gives a straight-line graph of slope m; c is the value of y where the line crosses the y-axis. Linear equations can be used to describe the behaviour of buildings, bridges, trusses, and other static structures.

linear motor type of ◊electric motor, an induction motor in which the stationary stator and moving armature are straight and parallel to each other (rather than being circular and one inside the other as in an ordinary induction motor). Linear motors are used, for example, to power sliding doors. There is a magnetic force between the stator and armature, and this has been used to support a vehicle, as in the experimental ◊maglev linear motor train.

linen the yarn spun and the textile woven from ◊flax.

ling deepwater long-bodied fish *Molva molva* of the cod family found in the seas off NW Europe. It reaches 2 m/6 ft long and 20 kg/45 lb in weight.

ling another name for common ◊heather.

lingam in Hinduism, phallic emblem of ◊Siva, the yoni being the female equivalent.

lingua franca any language that is used as a means of communication by groups who do not themselves normally speak that language; for example English is a lingua franca used by Japanese doing business in Finland, or Swedes in Saudi Arabia. Many of the world's lingua francas are ◊pidgin languages for example Bazaar Hindi (Hindustani).

linguistics the scientific study of language, from its origins, to the changing way it is pronounced (phonetics), derivation of words through various languages (etymology), development of meanings (semantics), and the arrangement and modifications of words to convey a message (grammar).

linkage in genetics, the association between two or more genes that tend to be inherited together because they are on the same chromosome. The closer together they are on the chromosome, the less likely they are to be separated by crossing over (one of the processes of ◊recombination) and they are then described as being 'tightly linked'.

Linlithgowshire former name of West Lothian, now included in Lothian region, Scotland.

Linnaeus Carolus (Carl von Linné) 1707–1778. Swedish naturalist and physician. His botanical work *Systema Naturae* 1758 contained his system for classifying plants and animals into groups depending on the number of stamens in their flowers, providing a much-needed framework for identification. He also devised the concise and precise system for naming plants and animals, using one Latin (or Latinized) word to represent the genus and a second to distinguish the species.

linnet bird of the finch family *Acanthis cannabina* common in Asia, NW Africa, and Europe. Mainly brown, the males have a crimson crown and breast in summer. It feeds on weed seeds and some insects. It is about 13 cm/5 in long.

Linotype typesetting machine once universally used for newspaper work, which sets complete lines (slugs) of metal type. It was invented in the USA in 1884 by German-born Ottmar ◊Mergenthaler.

Lin Piao alternative form of ◊Lin Biao.

linseed seeds of the flax plant *Linum usitatissimum*, from which linseed oil is expressed, the residue being used as feeding cake for cattle. The oil is used in paint, wood treatments and varnishes, and in the manufacture of linoleum.

Linz industrial port (iron, steel, metalworking) on the river Danube in N Austria; population (1981) 199,900.

lion member of the cat family *Panthera leo*, now only found in Africa and NW India. The coat is tawny, the young having darker spot markings which usually disappear in the adult. The male has a heavy mane and a tuft at the end of the tail. Head and body measure about 2 m/6 ft, plus 1 m/3 ft of tail, the lioness being slightly smaller.

lipid one of a group of organic compounds soluble in solvents such as ethanol (alcohol), but not in water. They include oils, fats, waxes, steroids, carotenoids, and other fatty substances.

Li Po 705–762. Chinese poet. He wrote in traditional forms, but his exuberance, the boldness of his imagination, and the intensity of his feeling have

liquid crystal display

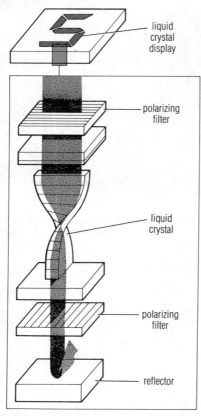

liquid crystal display

polarizing filter

liquid crystal

polarizing filter

reflector

won him recognition as perhaps the greatest of all Chinese poets. Although he was mostly concerned with higher themes, he is also noted for his celebration of the joys of drinking.

Lippi Filippino 1457–1504. Italian painter of the Florentine school, trained by Botticelli. He produced altarpieces and several fresco cycles, full of detail and drama, elegant and finely drawn. He was the son of Filippo Lippi.

Lippi Filippo 1406–1469. Italian Florentine painter, called *Fra* (Brother) Filippo, born in Florence and patronized by the Medici. He was a monk, but was tried in the 1450s for abducting a nun (the mother of his son Filippino). He is best known for his altarpieces, notably Madonnas and groups of saints.

Lippmann Gabriel 1845–1921. French doctor, who invented the direct colour process in photography. Nobel prize 1908.

liquid state of matter between a ◊solid and a ◊gas. A liquid forms a level surface and beneath the surface assumes the shape of its container. Its atoms do not occupy fixed postions as in a crystalline solid, nor do they have freedom of movement as in a gas. Unlike a gas, a liquid is difficult to compress since pressure applied at one point is equally transmitted throughout (Pascal's principle). ◊Hydraulics makes use of this property.

liquid air air that has been cooled so much that it has liquefied. This happens at temperatures below about –196°C. The various constituent gases

including nitrogen, oxygen, argon, and neon can be separated from liquid air by the technique of ◊fractionation.

liquidation in economics, the termination of a company by converting all its assets into money to pay off its liabilities.

liquid crystal display (LCD) a display of numbers (for example in a calculator) or picture (such as on a pocket television screen) produced by molecules of an organic substance in a semi-liquid state. The display is a blank until the application of an electric field which 'twists' the molecules so that they reflect or transmit light falling on them.

liquidity in economics, the state of possessing sufficient money and/or assets to be able to pay off all liabilities. *Liquid assets* are those which may be converted quickly into cash, such as shares, as opposed to property.

liquorice perennial European herb *Glycyrrhiza glabra*, family Leguminosae. The long sweet root yields an extract made into a hard black paste, used in confectionery and medicines.

Lisbon (Portuguese *Lisboa*) city and capital of Portugal, in the SW on the tidal lake and estuary formed by the Tagus; population (1981) 817,627. Industries include steel, textiles, chemicals, pottery, shipbuilding, and fishing. It has been capital since 1260, and reached its peak of prosperity in the 16th century.

Lisp a computer-programming language for list processing used primarily in artificial-intelligence (AI) research. Developed in the 1960s, and until recently common only in university laboratories, Lisp is more popular in the USA than in Europe, where the language ◊Prolog is often preferred for AI work.

Lister Joseph, 1st Baron Lister 1827–1912. British surgeon, and founder of antiseptic surgery. He introduced dressings soaked in carbolic acid and strict rules of hygiene to combat the increase in wound sepsis (the number of surgical operations had increased considerably, following the introduction of anaesthetics). He was influenced by Louis ◊Pasteur's work on bacteria.

listeriosis a disease of animals, which may occasionally infect humans with food poisoning, caused by the bacterium Listeria monocytogenes. As listeria bacteria breed at temperatures close to 0°C, they may flourish in ready-cooked frozen meals, if the cooking has not been thorough. It causes inflammation of the brain and its surrounding membranes, but can be treated with penicillin.

Lister British surgeon, Joseph Lister.

Lithuania
Republic of

area 65,200 sq km/25,174 sq mi
capital Vilnius
towns Kaunas, Klaipeda, Siauliai, Panevezys
physical central lowlands with gentle hills in W and higher terrain in SE; 25% forested; some 3,000 small lakes, marshes; complex sandy coastline
head of state Algirdas Brazauskas from 1993
head of government Bronislovas Lubys from 1992
political system emergent democracy
products heavy engineering, electrical goods, shipbuilding, cement, food processing, bacon, dairy products, cereals, potatoes
currency Lithuanian rouble
population (1990) 3,700,000 (Lithuanian 80%, Russian 9%, Polish 7%, Byelorussian 2%)
language Lithuanian
religion predominantly Roman Catholic

chronology
1918 Independence declared following withdrawal of German occupying troops at end of World War I; USSR attempted to regain power.
1919 Soviet forces overthrown by Germans, Poles, and nationalist Lithuanians; democratic republic established.
1920–39 Vilnius occupied by Poles.
1926 Coup; Antanas Smetona became president.
1939 Secret German–Soviet agreement brought most of Lithuania under Soviet influence.
1940 Incorporated into USSR as constituent republic.
1941 Revolt against USSR; rebel government established. German occupation.
1944 USSR resumed rule.
1944–52 Lithuanian guerrillas fought USSR.
1972 Demonstrations against Soviet government.
1980 Growth in nationalist dissent.
1988 Popular front formed, the Sajudis, to campaign for increased autonomy.
1989 Lithuanian declared the state language; flag of independent interwar republic readopted. Communist Party (CP) split into pro-Moscow and nationalist wings. Communist local monopoly of power abolished.
1990 Feb: nationalist Sajudis won elections. March: Vytautas Landsbergis became president; unilateral declaration of independence resulted in temporary Soviet blockade.
1991 Jan: Albertas Shiminas became prime minister. Sept: independence recognized by Soviet government and Western nations; Gediminas Vagnorius elected prime minister; CP outlawed; became a member of the UN.
1992 July: Aleksandras Abisala became prime minister. Nov: Democratic Labour Party, led by Algirdas Brazauskas, won majority vote.
1993 Brazauskas elected president.

Liszt Franz 1811–1886. Hungarian pianist and composer. An outstanding virtuoso he was an established concert artist by the age of 12. His expressive, romantic, and frequently chromatic work includes piano music, symphonies, and organ music.

litany in the Christian church, a form of prayer or supplication led by a priest with set responses by the congregation.

litchi or *lychee* tree *Litchi chinensis* of the family Sapindaceae. The delicately flavoured oval fruit is encased in a brownish rough outer skin and has a hard seed. The litchi is a native of S China, where it has been cultivated for 2,000 years.

literature words set apart in some way from ordinary everyday communication. In the ancient oral traditions, before stories and poems were written down, literature had a mainly public function – mythic and religious. As literary works came to be preserved in writing, and then printed, they became a vehicle for the exploration and expression of emotion and of the human situation.

lithium the lightest metallic element, symbol Li, atomic number 3, relative atomic mass 6,940. Lithium has a silvery lustre and tarnishes rapidly in air, so it is kept under naphtha. It is soft and ductile, and burns in air at 200°C. It is used as a reducing agent, in batteries, to harden alloys, and in producing tritium. Lithium compounds are used in medicine to treat depression.

lithography in printing, graphic reproduction by a process originated by Aloys ◊Senefelder, in which a drawing is made with greasy ink on an absorbent stone, which is then washed with water. The water then repels any ink applied to the surface, and the grease attracts it, so that the drawing can be printed. Modern lithographic printing is used in book production, and has developed this basic principle into complex processes.

lithosphere the topmost layer of the Earth's structure, forming the plates that take part in the movements of ◊plate tectonics. The lithosphere comprises the ◊crust and the upper ◊mantle. It is regarded as being rigid and moves about on the less rigid ◊asthenosphere. The lithosphere is probably about 75 km/47 mi thick.

Lithuania country in N Europe, bounded N by Latvia, E by Belarus, S by Poland and the Kaliningrad area of Russia, and W by the Baltic Sea.

Lithuanian language an Indo-European language spoken by the people of Lithuania that through its geographical isolation has retained many ancient features of the Indo-European language family. It acquired a written form in the 16th century, using the Latin alphabet.

litmus dye obtained from lichens, and used as an indicator to test the acidic or alkaline nature of aqueous solutions; it turns red in the presence of acid, and blue in the presence of alkali.

litre metric unit of volume (abbreviation l or L), formerly used to denote the volume occupied by 1 kg of pure water (equal to 1.76 pints) at 4°C at standard pressure. In ◊SI units it is the special name for the cubic decimetre.

Little Bighorn site in Montana, USA, of Gen

George ◊Custer's defeat by the ◊Sioux Indians 25 Jun 1876 under chiefs ◊Crazy Horse and Sitting Bull, known as ***Custer's last stand.***

liturgy in the Christian church, any service for public worship. The term was originally limited to the celebration of the ◊Eucharist.

Liu Shaoqi formerly ***Liu Shao-chi*** 1898–1969. Chinese communist politician, in effective control of government 1960–65. His advocacy of the Soviet line of development based around tight control, use of incentive gradings, and priority for industry over agriculture, was opposed by Mao Zedong, but Liu began to implement it while in power as state president 1960–65. In 1967, during the Cultural Revolution, Liu was brought down.

liver a large organ of vertebrates, which has many regulatory and storage functions. The human liver is situated in the upper abdomen, and weighs about 2 kg/4.5 lbs. It receives the products of digestion, converts glucose to glycogen (a long-chain carbohydrate used for storage), and breaks down fats. It removes excess amino acids from the blood, converting them to urea, which is excreted by the kidneys. The liver also synthesizes vitamins, produces bile and blood clotting factors, and removes damaged red cells and toxins from the blood.

Liverpool city, seaport, and administrative headquarters of Merseyside, NW England; population (1991) 448,300. In the 19th and early 20th century, it exported the textiles of Lancashire and Yorkshire, and is still Europe's chief Atlantic port with miles of specialized, mechanized quays on the river Mersey.

Liverpool Robert Banks Jenkinson, 2nd Earl Liverpool 1770–1825. British Tory politician. Foreign secretary 1801–03, home secretary 1804–06 and 1807–09, war minister 1809–12, and prime minister 1812–27. His government conducted the Napoleonic Wars to a successful conclusion, but its ruthless suppression of freedom of speech aroused such opposition that during 1815–20 revolution frequently seemed imminent.

liverwort plant of the class Hepaticae, related to mosses, found growing in damp places.

livery companies the ◊guilds of the City of London. Their role is now social rather than industrial, many administrating valuable charities.

Livia Drusilla 58 BC–AD 29. Roman empress, wife of ◊Augustus from 39 BC, she was the mother by her first husband of ◊Tiberius, and engaged in intrigue to secure his succession to the imperial crown. She remained politically influential to the end of her life.

Livingstone David 1813–1873. Scottish missionary explorer. In 1844, he went to Africa, reached Lake Ngami 1849, followed the Zambezi to its mouth and saw the Victoria Falls 1855, went to East and Central Africa 1858–64, reaching Lakes Shirwa and Malawi. From 1866, he tried to find the source of the Nile, and reached Ujiji in Oct 1871.

Livingstone Ken(neth) 1945– . British left-wing Labour politician, leader of the Greater London Council (GLC) 1981–86, Member of Parliament from 1987. He stood as a candidate for the Labour Party leadership 1992.

Livonia former region in Europe on the E coast of the Baltic Sea comprising most of present-day Latvia and Estonia. Conquered and converted to Christianity in the early 13th century by the crusading Livonian Knights. Livonia was independent till 1583, when it was divided between Poland and Sweden. In 1710, it was occupied by Russia, and in 1721 was ceded to Peter the Great.

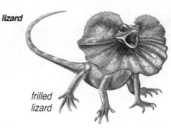

lizard

frilled lizard

Livy Titus Livius 59 BC–AD 17. Roman historian, famous for his narrative *History of Rome*, from the city's foundation to 9 BC, based partly on legend. It was composed of 142 books, of which 35 survive, covering the periods from the arrival of Aeneas in Italy to 293 BC and 218–167 BC.

lizard reptile of the suborder Lacertilia, belonging with the snakes in the order Squamata. Lizards are normally distinguishable from snakes by having four legs, moveable eyelids, eardrums and a fleshy tongue, but some lizards are legless and very snakelike in appearance. There are about 3,000 species of lizard worldwide.

Ljubljana (German *Laibach*) capital and industrial city (textiles, chemicals, paper, leather goods) of Slovenia; population (1981) 305,200. It has a nuclear research centre and is linked with S Austria by the Karawanken road tunnel under the Alps.

llama South American animal *Lama peruana*. Llamas can be white, brown, or dark, sometimes with spots or patches. They are very hardy, and require little food or water. They spit profusely when annoyed.

Llewellyn Richard, pen name of Richard Vivian Llewellyn, best known for *How Green Was My Valley* 1939, a novel about a S Wales mining family.

Llewelyn two kings of Wales:

Llewelyn I died 1240, king from 1194, who extended his rule to all Wales not in Norman hands

Llewelyn II *c.* 1225–82, king from 1246, grandson of Llewelyn I, who was compelled by Edward I in 1277 to acknowledge him as overlord and to surrender S Wales. His death while leading a national uprising ended Welsh independence.

Lloyd Selwyn See ◊Selwyn Lloyd, British Conservative politician.

Lloyd-George David, 1st Earl Lloyd George 1863–1945. Welsh Liberal politician, prime minister of a coalition government 1916–22. A pioneer of social reform, as chancellor of the Exchequer 1908–15 he introduced old-age pensions in 1908 and health and unemployment insurance in 1911. After

Lloyd-George *Portrait by William Orpen (1927) National Portrait Gallery, London.*

lock

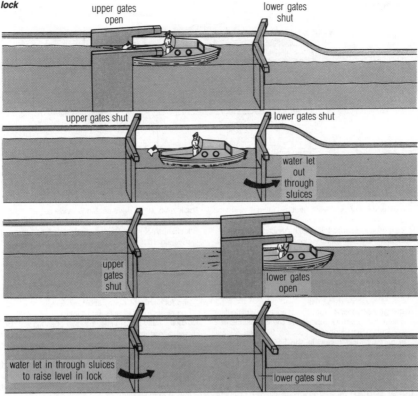

upper gates open | lower gates shut

upper gates shut | lower gates shut | water let out through sluices

upper gates shut | lower gates open

water let in through sluices to raise level in lock | lower gates shut

World War I he had a major role in the Versailles peace treaty.

Lloyd's Register of Shipping founded 1760, an international society for the survey and classification of merchant shipping which provides rules for the construction and maintenance of ships and their machinery.

Lloyd Webber Andrew 1948– . British composer. His early musicals, with lyrics by Tim Rice, include *Joseph and the Amazing Technicolor Dreamcoat* 1968, *Jesus Christ Superstar* 1970, and *Evita* 1978, based on the life of Eva Perón. He also wrote *Cats* 1981 and *The Phantom of the Opera* 1986.

loa a spirit in voodoo. They may be male or female, and include Maman Brigitte, the loa of death and cemeteries, and Aida-Wedo, the rainbow snake. Believers may be under the protection of one particular loa.

lobby individual or ◊pressure group that sets out to influence government action. The lobby is particularly prevalent in the USA, where the term originated in the 1830s from the practice of those wishing to influence state policy waiting for their electoral representative in the lobby of the Capitol. Under the UK lobby system, certain parliamentary journalists are given unofficial access to confidential news.

Lobengula 1833–1894. King of Matabeleland, (now part of Zimbabwe), 1870–93. After accepting British protection from internal and external threats to his leadership in 1888, he came under increasing pressure from British mining interests to allow

Yale lock

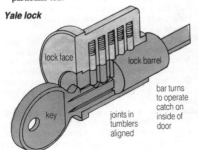

lock face | lock barrel

key | joints in tumblers aligned | bar turns to operate catch on inside of door

Locke English philosopher John Locke.

locomotive

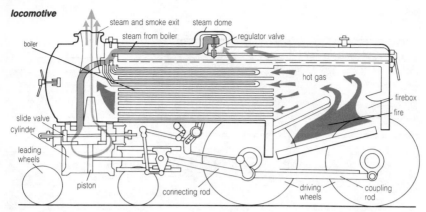

steam and smoke exit steam dome
steam from boiler regulator valve
boiler
hot gas
firebox
fire
slide valve
cylinder
leading
wheels
piston connecting rod driving wheels coupling rod

---

exploitation of goldfields near Bulawayo, and was overthrown in 1893 by a military expedition organized by Cecil ◊Rhodes' South African Company.

lobster marine member of the order Decapoda. Lobsters are grouped with the freshwater ◊crayfish in the suborder Reptantia ('walking'), though both lobsters and crayfish can also swim, using their fanlike tails. All have eyes on stalks and long antennae, and are mainly nocturnal. They scavenge and eat dead or dying fish.

local government that part of government dealing mainly with matters concerning the inhabitants of a particular district or place, usually financed at least in part by local taxes. In the USA and UK local government has had comparatively large powers and responsibilities. England and Wales are divided into counties (Scotland into regions) and these subdivided into districts.

Local Group in astronomy, a cluster of about three dozen galaxies that includes our own. Like other groups of galaxies, the Local Group is held together by the gravitational attraction between its members, and does not expand with the expanding Universe.

Locarno, Pact of a series of diplomatic documents initialled in Locarno on 16 Oct 1925 and formally signed in London on 1 Dec 1925. The pact settled the question of French security, and the signatories – Britain, France, Belgium, Italy, and Germany – guaranteed the existing frontiers between Germany and France, and Germany and Belgium. Following the pact, Germany was admitted to the League of Nations.

loc. cit. abbreviation for *loco citato* (Latin 'in the place cited').

Lochner Stephan died 1451. German painter, active in Cologne, a master of the International Gothic style. Most of his work is still in Cologne, for example the *Virgin in the Rose Garden*, about 1426 (Wallraf-Richartz Museum).

Loch Ness lake in Highland region, Scotland, forming part of the Caledonian Canal; 36 km/22.5 mi long, 229m/754 ft deep. There have been unconfirmed reports of a *Loch Ness monster* since the 15th century.

lock a gated chamber installed in canals, rivers and seaways that allows boats to sail from one level to another. A lock has gates at each end, and a boat sails in through one gate when the levels are the same outside and inside. Then water is allowed in (or out of) the lock until the water level rises (or falls) to the new level outside the other gate.

lock and key devices that provide security, usually fitted to a door of some kind. In 1778 English locksmith Robert Barron made the forerunner of the modern mortise lock, which contains levers that the key must raise to an exact height before the bolt can be moved. The Yale lock, a pin-tumbler design, was invented by Linus Yale Jr in 1865. More secure locks include combination locks, whose dial mechanism must be turned certain distances backwards and forwards to open, and time locks, which can be opened only at specific times.

Locke John 1632–1704. English philosopher. His *Essay concerning Human Understanding* 1690 maintained that experience was the only source of knowledge (empiricism), and that 'we can have knowledge no farther than we have ideas' prompted by such experience. *Two Treatises on Government* 1690 was influential in forming modern ideas of liberal democracy.

lockjaw popular name for ◊tetanus.

locomotive a machine for hauling trains on the railways. Richard ◊Trevithick built the first locomotive in 1804, a steam engine on wheels. Locomotive design did not radically improve until George ◊Stephenson built the *Rocket* 1829, which featured a multitube boiler and blastpipe, standard in all following *steam locomotives*. Most modern locomotives are diesel or electric: *diesel locomotives* have a powerful diesel engine, and *electric locomotives* collect their power either from an overhead cable or a 'third rail' alongside the ordinary track.

locus (Latin 'place') in mathematics, traditionally the path traced out by a moving point, but now defined as the set of all points on a curve satisfying given conditions. For example, the locus of a point that moves so that it is always at the same distance from another fixed point is a circle; the locus of a point that is always at the same distance from two fixed points is a straight line that perpendicularly bisects the line joining them.

locust swarming grasshopper, with short antennae and auditory organs on the abdomen, in the family Acrididae. As winged adults, flying in swarms, they may be carried by the wind hundreds of kilometres from their breeding grounds, and on landing devour all vegetation. Locusts occur in nearly every continent.

locust tree alternative name for the ◊carob, small tree of the Mediterranean region.

Lodge David (John) 1935– . British novelist, short story writer, and critic. Much of his fiction concerns the role of Catholicism in England, as in *The British*

Museum is Falling Down 1967, and *How Far Can You Go?* 1980.

Lodge Henry Cabot, Jr 1902–1985. US diplomat. He was Eisenhower's campaign manager, and US representative at the United Nations 1953–60. Ambassador to S Vietnam 1963–64 and 1965–67, he took over from Harriman as Nixon's negotiator in the Vietnam peace talks in 1969. He was a grandson of the elder Henry Cabot Lodge.

Lódź (Polish *Ll–ódź*) industrial town (textiles, machinery, dyes) in central Poland, 120 km/75 mi SW of Warsaw; population (1984) 849,000.

Loewe Frederick 1901–1988. US composer of musicals, born in Berlin. In 1942 he joined forces with the lyricist Alan Jay Lerner (1918–86), and their joint successes include *Brigadoon* 1947, *Paint Your Wagon* 1951, *My Fair Lady* 1956, *Gigi* 1958, and *Camelot* 1960.

Lofting Hugh 1886–1947. Anglo-US writer and illustrator of children's books, especially the 'Dr Doolittle' series, in which the hero can talk to animals.

log apparatus for measuring the speed of a ship; also the daily record of events on board a ship or aircraft.

loganberry hybrid between ◊blackberry and ◊raspberry with large, sweet, dull red fruit.

logarithm or *log* the exponent or ◊index of a number to a specified base. Logarithms are a mathematical process which make multiplication and division simpler by using the laws of indices. If $b^a = x$, then a is the logarithm of x to the base b.

logic a branch of philosophy which studies valid reasoning and argument. It is also the way in which one thing may be said to follow from or be a consequence of another (deductive logic). Logic is generally divided into the traditional formal logic of Aristotle, and the modern symbolic logic derived from Frege and Russell.

logical positivism the doctrine that the only meaningful propositions are those which can be empirically verifiable. Therefore, metaphysics, religion, and aesthetics are meaningless.

Logo a computer-programming language designed to teach mathematical concepts. Developed around 1970 at the Massachusetts Institute of Technology, it has become popular in schools and with home computer users because of its 'turtle graphics' feature. This allows the user to write programs that create line drawings on a computer screen, or drive a small mobile robot around the floor.

Lohengrin son of ◊Parsifal, hero of a late 13th-century legend, on which Wagner based his German opera *Lohengrin* 1847. He married Princess Elsa, who broke his condition that she never ask his origin, and he returned to the temple of the ◊Holy Grail.

Loire the longest river in France, rising in the Cévennes at 1,350 m/4,430 ft and flowing for 1,050 km/625 mi first N then W till it reaches the Bay of Biscay at St Nazaire, passing Nevers, Orléans, Tours, and Nantes. It gives its name to the *départements* of Loire, Haute-Loire, Loire-Atlantique, Indre-et-Loire, Maine-et-Loire, and Saône-et-Loire. There are many chateaux and vineyards along its banks.

Loki in Norse mythology, one of the Aesir (gods), but the cause of dissension among other gods, and the slayer of ◊Balder. His children are the Midgard serpent Jörmungander which girdles the earth, the wolf Fenris, and Hela, goddess of death.

Lollard a follower of the English religious reformer John ◊Wycliffe in the 14th century; The Lollards condemned transubstantiation, advocated the diversion of ecclesiastical property to charitable uses, and denounced war and capital punishment. They were active from about 1377; after the passing of the statute *De Heretico Comburendo* (of the necessity of burning of the heretic) 1401 many Lollards were burned, and in 1414 they raised an unsuccessful revolt in London.

Lombard or *Langobard* member of a Germanic people who invaded Italy in 568 and occupied Lombardy (named after them) and central Italy. Their capital was Monza. They were conquered by the Frankish ruler Charlemagne in 774.

Lombard league an association of N Italian communes established 1164 to maintain their independence against the Holy Roman emperors' claims of sovereignty.

Lombardy (Italian *Lombardia*) region of N Italy, including Lake Como; area 23,833 sq km/9,205 sq mi, and the country's chief industrial area (chemical, pharmaceuticals, engineering, textiles); capital Milan; population (1984) 8,885,000.

Lomé capital and port of Togo; population (1983) 366,476. A centre for gold, silver and marble crafts; major industries include steel production and oil refining.

Lomé Convention convention which in 1975 established economic cooperation between the EEC and African, Caribbean, and Pacific countries. It was renewed 1979, 1985.

lomentum a type of ◊fruit, similar to a pod but constricted between the seeds. When ripe, it splits into one-seeded units, as seen, for example, in the fruit of sainfoin (*Onobrychis viciifolia*) and radish (*Raphanus raphanistrum*). It is a type of ◊schizocarp.

Lomond, Loch largest freshwater Scottish lake, 37 km/23 mi long, area 70 sq km/25 sq mi, divided between Strathclyde and Central regions. It is overlooked by the mountain **Ben Lomond** 296.5 m/973 ft and linked to the Clyde estuary.

London the capital of England, and the United Kingdom, on the river Thames; area 1,580 sq km/610 sq mi; population (1984) 6,756,000, larger metropolitan area about 9,000,000. The *City of London*, known as the 'square mile', area 677 acres, is the financial and commercial centre of the UK. *Greater London* from 1965 comprises the City of London and 32 boroughs. Popular tourist attractions include the Tower of London, St Paul's Cathedral, Buckingham Palace, and Westminster Abbey. Roman Londinium was established soon after the Roman invasion 43 AD; in the 2nd century London became a walled city; by the 11th century, it was the main city of England and gradually extended beyond the walls to link with the originally separate Westminster.

London Jack (John Griffith) 1876–1916. US novelist, born in San Francisco. He is best known for adventure stories, for example, *The Call of the Wild* 1903, *The Sea Wolf* 1904, and *White Fang* 1906.

Londonderry or *Derry* county of N Ireland
area 2067 sq km/798 sq mi
towns Derry (county town, formerly Londonderry), Coleraine, Portstewart
products mainly agricultural, but farming is hindered by the very heavy rainfall; flax, dairy products; food processing, textiles, light engineering
population (1981) 186,751
famous people Joyce Cary.

Long Huey 1893–1935. US Democratic politician, nicknamed 'the Kingfish', governor of Louisiana

1928–31, US senator for Louisiana 1930–35. Legendary as a demagogue, he was also criticized for extravagance and corruption. He was assassinated.

Longfellow Henry Wadsworth 1807–1882. US poet, born in Portland, Maine. He is remembered for ballads ('Excelsior' 1839 and 'The Wreck of the Hesperus ' 1842), the narrative *Evangeline* 1847, and his metrically haunting *The Song of ◊Hiawatha* 1855.

Longford county of Leinster province, Republic of Ireland
area 1,044 sq km/403 sq mi
county town Longford
population (1981) 31,000.

Longinus Cassius 213–273. Greek philosopher. He taught in Athens for many years. Adviser to ◊Zenobia of Palmyra, he instigated her revolt against Rome, and was put to death when she was captured.

Longinus Dionysius lived 1st century AD. Greek critic, author of a treatise *On the Sublime* which influenced Dryden and Pope.

Long Island island off the coast of Connecticut and New York USA, separated from the mainland by Long Island Sound; area 3,627 sq km/1,400 sq mi. It includes two boroughs of New York City (Queens and Brooklyn), John F Kennedy airport, suburbs, and resorts.

longitude component of ◊latitude and longitude.

Long March, the in Chinese history, the 10,000 km/6,000 mi trek undertaken 1934– 35 by Mao Zedong and his communist forces from SE to NW China, under harassment from the Guomindang nationalist army.

Long Parliament the English Parliament 1640–60, which continued through the Civil War. After the Royalists withdrew in 1642, and the Presbyterian right were excluded in 1648, the remaining Rump ruled England until expelled by Cromwell in 1653. Reassembled 1659–60, the Long Parliament initiated the negotiations for the restoration of the monarchy.

loom a weaving machine, first used to weave sheep's wool at least 7,000 years ago. A loom is a frame on which a set of lengthwise threads (warp) is strung. Then a second set of threads (weft), carried in a shuttle, is inserted at right-angles over and under the warp. In practice the warp threads are separated as appropriate, to create a gap, or shed, through which the shuttle can be passed in a straight line. The warp threads are moved by means of a harness. A device called a reed presses each new line of weave tight against the previous ones.

loon N American name for the ◊diver.

Loos Adolf 1870–1933. Viennese architect. He rejected the ornamentation and curved lines of the Viennese Art Nouveau. His most important buildings are private houses on Lake Geneva 1904 and the Steiner House in Vienna 1910, but his main importance is as a polemicist; for example the article *Ornament and Crime* 1908.

Loos Anita 1888–1981. US writer, author of the humorous fictitious diary ◊*Gentlemen Prefer Blondes* 1925.

loosestrife plant of the family Primulaceae, including the *yellow loosestrife Lysimachia vulgaris*, with spikes of yellow flowers, and the low-growing *creeping jenny Lysimachia nummularia*. The striking *purple loosestrife Lythrum saclicaria* belongs to the family Lythraceae.

Lope de Vega (Carpio) Felix 1562–1635. Spanish poet and dramatist, one of the founders of modern Spanish drama. Born in Madrid, he served with the Armada in 1588, and in 1613 took holy orders. He wrote epics, pastorals, odes, sonnets, and novels, and over 1,500 plays, most of which are tragi-comedies. He set out his views on drama in *Arte nuevo de hacer comedias/The New Art of Writing Plays* c.1609, while reaffirming the classical form. His best known play is *Fuenteovejuna* 1614, acclaimed in this century as the first proletarian drama.

López Francisco Solano 1827–1870. Paraguayan dictator in succession to his father Carlos López. He involved the country in a war with Brazil, Uruguay, and Argentina during which five-sixths of the population died.

Lorca Federico García 1898–1936. Spanish poet. In 1929–30 he visited New York, and his experiences are reflected in *Poeta en Nuevo York*. Returning to Spain, he founded a touring theatrical company and wrote plays such as *Bodas de sangre/Blood Wedding* 1933, and *La casa de Bernarda Alba/The House of Bernarda Alba* 1936. His poems include *Lament* for the bullfighter Mejías.

Lord in the UK, prefix used informally as alternative to the full title of a marquess, earl, or viscount; normally also in speaking of a baron, and as a courtesy title before the forename and surname of younger sons of dukes and marquesses. A bishop is formally addressed as the Lord Bishop of –.

Lord Advocate chief law officer of the Crown in Scotland.

Lord Chancellor in Britain, a government minister who is also head of the judiciary, and Speaker of the House of Lords.

lord-lieutenant in the UK, the Sovereign's representative in a county, who recommends magistrates for appointment, and so on.

lord mayor in the UK, ◊mayor of a city.

Lord's one of England's test match grounds and the headquarters of cricket's governing body the Marylebone Cricket Club (MCC) since 1788.

Lords, House of the upper house of the UK ◊Parliament.

Lord's Prayer in the New Testament, prayer taught by Jesus Christ to his disciples. It is sometimes called Our Father or Paternoster from the opening words in English and Latin.

Lord's Supper in the Christian church, another name for the ◊Eucharist.

Lorenz Konrad 1903–1989. Austrian ethologist. Director of the Max Planck Institute for the Physiology of Behaviour in Bavaria 1961–73, he is known for his studies of animal behaviour, *King Solomon's Ring* 1952 and *On Aggression* 1966. In

Lorenz Austrian-born zoologist and biologist, Konrad Lorenz, Apr 1969.

1973 he shared a Nobel prize with N ◊Tinbergen and Karl von ◊Frisch, in recognition of their work in founding the science of ◊ethology.

Lorenz Ludwig Valentine 1829–1891. Danish mathematician and physicist. He developed mathematical formulae to describe phenomena such as the relationship between refraction of light and the density of a pure transparent substance, and the relationship between a metal's electrical and thermal conductivity and temperature.

lorikeet type of small brightly-coloured parrot, found in SE Asia and Australasia.

loris small Asian primate, of the Lorisidae family. Lorises are slow-moving, arboreal and nocturnal. They are 20-35 cm/8-14 in long, have very large eyes and are tailless.

Lorrain Claude 1600–1682. French painter; see ◊Claude Lorrain.

Lorraine region of France; see ◊Alsace-Lorraine.

Lorraine, Cross of heraldic cross with double crossbars, emblem of the medieval French nationalist Joan of Arc. It was adopted by the Free French forces in World War II.

Los Alamos town in New Mexico, USA, which has had a centre for atomic and space research since 1942. In World War II, the atom (nuclear fission) bomb was designed here (under ◊Oppenheimer), working on data from other research stations; the ◊hydrogen bomb was also developed here.

Los Angeles city and port in SW California, USA; population of urban area (1980) 2,967,000, the metropolitan area of Los Angeles-Long Beach 9,478,000. Industries include aerospace, electronics, chemical, clothing, printing, and food-processing. Features include the suburb of Hollywood, centre of the film industry since 1911; the Hollywood Bowl concert arena; observatories at Mt Wilson and Mt Palomar; Disneyland; the Huntingdon Art Gallery and Library; and the Getty Museum,

Losey Joseph 1909–1984. US film director. Blacklisted as a former Communist in the ◊McCarthy era, he settled in England, where his films included *The Servant* 1963 and *The Go-Between* 1971.

Lost Generation, the disoriented US literary generation of the 1920s, especially those who went to live in Paris. The phrase is attributed to the writer Gertrude Stein in Ernest Hemingway's novel of 1920s Paris, *The Sun Also Rises* 1926.

Lot in the Old Testament or Hebrew Bible, Abraham's nephew, who escaped the destruction of Sodom, although his wife was turned into a pillar of salt.

Lothair 825–869. King of Lotharingia (called after him, and later corrupted to Lorraine, now part of Alsace-Lorraine) from 855, when he inherited from his father, the Holy Roman emperor Lothair I, a district W of the Rhine, between the Jura mountains and the North Sea.

Lothair two Holy Roman emperors:

Lothair I 795–855. Holy Roman emperor from 817 in association with his father Louis I. On Louis' death, the empire was divided between Lothair and his brothers; Lothair took N Italy and the valleys of the rivers Rhône and Rhine.

Lothair II *c.* 1070–1137. Holy Roman emperor from 1133 and German king from 1125. His election as emperor, opposed by the Hohenstaufens, was the start of the feud between ◊Guelph and Ghibelline.

Lothian region of Scotland
area 1,755 sq km/677 sq mi
towns administrative headquarters Edinburgh; Livingston

loudspeaker

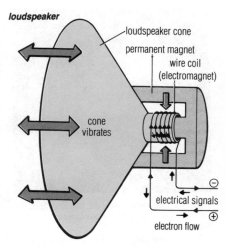

loudspeaker cone
permanent magnet
wire coil
(electromagnet)
cone vibrates
electrical signals
electron flow

products bacon, vegetables, coal, whisky, engineering, electronics
population (1984) 744,500
famous people birthplace of R L Stevenson in Howard Place, Edinburgh.

Lotto Lorenzo *c.* 1480–1556. Italian painter, born in Venice, active in Bergamo, Treviso, Venice, Ancona, and Rome. His early works were influenced by Giovanni Bellini; his mature style belongs to the High Renaissance. He painted dignified portraits, altarpieces, and frescoes.

lotus several different plants: those of the genus *Lotus*, family Leguminosae, including the bird's foot trefoil *Lotus corniculatus*; the shrub *Zizyphus lotus*, known to the ancient Greeks who used its fruit to make a type of bread and also a wine supposed to induce happy oblivion – hence *lotus-eaters*; the water-lily *Nymphaea lotus*, frequent in Egyptian art; and *Nelumbium nuciferum*, the sacred lotus of the Hindus.

Lotus Sūtra an important scripture of Mahāyāna Buddhism, particularly in China and Japan. It is Buddha Śākyamuni's final teaching, emphasizing that everyone can attain Buddhahood with the help of bodhisattvas. The original is in Sanskrit (*Saddharmapundarīka Sūtra*) and thought to date to some time after 100 BC.

loudspeaker an electromechanical device that converts electrical signals into sound waves. It is used in all sound-reproducing systems such as radios, record players, tape recorders, and televisions.

Louis, Prince of Battenberg 1854–1921. British admiral. A member of the Battenberg family, he took British nationality 1917. He was forced to resign as 1st Sea Lord 1912–14 because of anti-German sentiment. In 1917 he changed his name to Mountbatten, and was made marquess of Milford Haven in 1917. He was admiral of the fleet from 1921.

Louis Joe 1914–1981. US boxer born Joseph Louis Barrow. Nicknamed 'The Brown Bomber'. He was world heavyweight champion between 1937-49 and made a record 25 successful defences (a record for any weight).

Louis eighteen kings of France, including:

Louis I *the Pious* 788–840. Holy Roman emperor from 814, when he succeeded his father Charlemagne.

Louis II *the Stammerer* 846–879. King of France from 877, son of Charles the Bald,

Louis XIV This marble bust of the 'Sun King' Louis XIV of France, is by It alian sculptor Lorenzo Bernini.

he was dominated by the clergy and nobility.

Louis III 863–882. Son of Louis II, from 879 he ruled N France while his brother Carloman (866–84) ruled S France. His resistance to the Normans made him a hero of epic poems.

Louis IV (d'Outremer) 921–954. King of France from 936. His reign was marked by rebellion of nobles. As a result of his liberality they were able to build up powerful feudal lordships.

Louis V 966–987. King of France from 986, last of the ◊Carolingian dynasty.

Louis VII *c.* 1120–1180. King of France from 1137, who led the Second ◊Crusade.

Louis VIII 1187–1226. King of France from 1223, who unsuccessfully invaded England 1215–17.

Louis IX St 1214–1270. King of France from 1226, leader of the Seventh and Eighth ◊Crusades.

Louis X *the Stubborn* 1289–1316. King of France who succeeded his father Philip IV 1314. His reign saw widespread noble discontent.

Louis XI 1423–1483. King of France from 1461. He broke the power of the nobility (headed by ◊Charles the Bold) by intrigue and military power.

Louis XII 1462–1515. King of France from 1499, he was duke of Orléans until he succeeded his cousin Charles VIII to the throne. His reign was devoted to Italian wars.

Louis XIII 1601–1643. King of France from 1610 (in succession to his father Henry IV), assuming royal power in 1617; he was under the political control of ◊Richelieu from 1624–42.

Louis XIV *the Sun King* 1638–1715. King of France from 1643, when he succeeded his father Louis XIII. Until 1661 France was ruled by the chief minister, Mazarin, but later louis took absolute power. Throughout his reign he was engaged in unsuccessful expansionist wars – 1667–68, 1672–78, 1688–97, and 1701–13 (the War of the ◊Spanish Succession) – against various European alliances, always containing Britain and the Netherlands. He was a patron of the arts.

Louis XV 1710–1774. King of France from 1715, with the Duke of Orléans as regent until 1723. Great-grandson of Louis XIV. Indolent and frivolous, Louis left government in the hands of his ministers, the Duke of Bourbon and Cardinal Fleury (1653–1743). On the latter's death he attempted to rule alone, but became entirely dominated by his mistresses, Mme de ◊Pompadour and Mme

◊Du Barry. His foreign policy led to Canada and India being lost to France.

Louis XVI 1754–1793. King of France from 1774; grandson of Louis XV. He was dominated by his queen, ◊Marie Antoinette, and the finances fell into such confusion that in 1789 the ◊States General had to be summoned, and the ◊French Revolution began. Louis was sentenced for treason in Jan 1793, and guillotined.

Louis XVII 1785–1795. Nominal king of France, the son of Louis XVI. During the French Revolution he was imprisoned with his parents in 1792, and probably died in prison.

Louis XVIII 1755–1824. King of France 1814–24. Younger brother of Louis XVI; he assumed the title of king of France in 1795, having fled into exile in 1791 during the French Revolution, but became king only on the fall of Napoleon I in Apr 1814.

Louisiana southern state of the USA
area 125,675 sq km/48,523 sq mi
capital Baton Rouge
towns New Orleans, Shreveport
products rice, cotton, sugar, maize, oil, natural gas, sulphur, salt, processed foods, petroleum products, lumber, paper
population (1980) 4,206,000, which includes the Cajuns, descendants of 18th-century religious exiles from Canada, who speak a French dialect
famous people Louis Armstrong, Pierre Beauregard, Huey Long
history explored by La Salle, it was named after Louis XIV and claimed for France in 1682; was Spanish 1762–1800; passed to the USA under the ◊Louisiana Purchase in 1803, and was admitted to the Union as a state in 1812.

Louisiana Purchase the sale in 1803 by France to the USA of an area covering about 2,144,000 sq km/828,000 sq mi, including the present-day states of Louisiana, Missouri, Arkansas, Iowa, Nebraska, North and South Dakota, and Oklahoma. The purchase, which doubled the size of the USA, marked the end of Napoleon's plans for a colonial empire, and ensured free navigation on the Mississippi for the USA. The price was about $27 million.

Louis Philippe 1773–1850. King of France 1830–48. Son of Louis Philippe Joseph, Duke of Orléans 1747–93; both were known as *Philippe Egalité* from their support of the 1792 Revolution. He fled into exile 1793–1814, but became king after the 1830 revolution with the backing of the rich bourgeoisie. Corruption discredited his regime, and after his overthrow, he escaped to the UK and died there.

Lourdes town in SW France with a Christian shrine to St ◊Bernadette which has a reputation for miraculous cures; population (1982) 18,000.

Lourenço Marques former name of ◊Maputo, capital of Mozambique.

louse parasitic insect which lives on mammals, order Anoplura, with a flat, segmented body without wings, and a tube used for sucking blood from its host.

Louth smallest county (county town Dundalk) of the Republic of Ireland, province of ◊Leinster; area 821 sq km/317 sq mi; population (1981) 88,514.

love-in-a-mist perennial plant of S Europe *Nigella damascena*, family Ranunculaceae, with fern-like leaves, and blue or white flowers.

Lovelace Richard 1618–1658. English poet. Imprisoned in 1642 for petitioning for the restoration of royal rule, he wrote 'To Althea from Prison'.

Low Countries the region of Europe which consists of ◊Belgium and the ◊Netherlands, and usually includes ◊Luxembourg.

Lowell Amy (Lawrence) 1874–1925. US poet, who succeeded Ezra Pound as leader of the ◊Imagists. Her works, in free verse, include *Sword-Blades and Poppy Seed* 1916.

Lower Saxony (German *Niedersachsen* administrative region (*Land*) of N Germany
area 47,400 sq km/18,296 sq mi
capital Hanover
towns Brunswick, Göttingen, Oldenburg
products cereals, cars, machinery, electrical engineering
population (1988) 7,190,000
religion 75% Protestant, 20% Roman Catholic.

Lowry L(aurence) S(tephen) 1887–1976. British painter, born in Manchester. He painted northern industrial townscapes. His characteristic style of matchstick figures emerged in the 1920s.

Loyalist the one-third of the American population remaining loyal to Britain in the American War of Independence. Many went to Canada after 1783.

Loyalist a Northern Irish Protestant who opposes any kind of united Irish state.

Loyola see ◊Ignatius Loyola, founder of the Jesuits.

LSD *ly*sergic acid *d*iethylamide, a psychedelic drug and a hallucinogen. Colourless, odourless, and easily synthesized, it is non-addictive, but its effects are unpredictable. Its use is illegal in the UK.

LSI *large-scale integration* the technology by which whole electrical circuits can be etched into a piece of semiconducting material just a few millimetres square. By the late 1960s a complete computer processor could be integrated on a single ◊silicon chip, and in 1971 the US electronics company Intel produced the first commercially available ◊microprocessor (as such chips are called).

Ltd abbreviation for *Limited*; see ◊private limited company.

Luanda (formerly *Loanda*) capital and industrial port (cotton, sugar, tobacco, timber, paper, oil) of Angola; population (1988) 1,200,000. Founded in 1575 it became a Portuguese colonial administrative centre and a slaving outlet.

Lubbers Rudolph (Frans Marie) 1939– . Netherlands politician. He became minister for economic affairs in 1973 and prime minister in 1982.

Lubitsch Ernst 1892–1947. German-US film director, known for his stylish comedies, for example *Ninotchka* 1939, starring Greta ◊Garbo.

lubricant a substance used between moving surfaces to reduce friction. Those most used are carbon-based (organic) lubricants, often called grease and oil, recovered from petroleum distillation.

Lucan Marcus Annaeus Lucanus AD 39–65. Latin poet born in Cordova, a nephew of ◊Seneca and favourite of ◊Nero until the emperor became jealous of his verse. He then joined a republican conspiracy and committed suicide on its failure. His epic *Pharsalia* deals with the civil wars of ◊Caesar and ◊Pompey.

Lucas George 1944– . Us director and producer, who collaborated with Steven Spielberg on *Star Wars* 1977, *The Empire Strikes Back* 1980, and *Return of the Jedi* 1983. His other films, most of them box-office hits, include *Raiders of the Lost Ark* 1981 and *Indiana Jones and the Last Crusade* 1989.

Lucas van Leyden 1494–1533. Dutch artist, active in Leiden and Antwerp. He was an early pioneer of genre scenes. His woodcuts and engravings were greatly influenced by ◊Dürer, whom he met in Antwerp 1521.

lucerne another name for the plant ◊alfalfa.

Lucerne (German *Luzern*) capital and tourist centre of Lucerne canton, Switzerland, on the Reuss where it flows out of Lake Lucerne; population (1984) 62,000. It developed around the Benedictine monastery, established about 750, and owes its prosperity to its position on the St Gotthard road and railway.

Lucian *c.* 125–*c.* 190. Greek writer. Born at Samosata in Syria. He wrote satirical dialogues, in which he pours scorn on all religions.

Lucifer another name for the ◊devil.

Lucknow capital and industrial city (engineering, chemicals, textiles, many handicrafts) of the state of Uttar Pradesh, India; population (1981) 1,007,000. During the Indian Mutiny against British rule, it was besieged 2 Jul–16 Nov 1857.

Lowry Coming out of School 1927 Tate Gallery, London.

Lucretia (died *c.* 509 BC) in Roman history, the wife of Collatinus, said to have committed suicide after being raped by Sextus, son of ◊Tarquinius Superbus. Traditionally this led to the dethronement of Tarquinius and the establishment of the Roman republic in 509 BC.

Lucretius (Titus Lucretius Carus) *c.* 99–55 BC. Roman poet and ◊Epicurean philosopher, whose *De Rerum Natura/On the Nature of Things* envisaged the whole universe as a combination of atoms, and had some concept of evolutionary theory.

Lucullus Lucius Licinius 110–56 BC. Roman general. As commander against ◊Mithridates of Pontus 74–66 he showed himself one of Rome's ablest generals and administrators, until superseded by Pompey. He then retired from politics. Enormous wealth enabled him to live a life of luxury, and Lucullan feasts were famous.

Luddite a person taking part in the machine-wrecking riots in England of 1811–16. The main organizer of the Luddites, possibly an imaginary person, was referred to as General Ludd. The movement, which began in Nottinghamshire and spread to Lancashire, Cheshire, and Yorkshire, was primarily a revolt against the unemployment caused by the introduction of machines in the Industrial Revolution. Many Luddites were hanged or transported.

Ludendorff Erich von 1865–1937. German general, chief of staff to ◊Hindenburg in World War I, and responsible for the eastern-front victory at ◊Tannenberg in 1914. After Hindenburg's appointment as chief of general staff and Ludendorff's as quartermaster-general in 1916, he was also politically influential. He took part in the Nazi rising in Munich 1923, and sat in the Reichstag (parliament) as a right-wing Nationalist.

Ludwig Karl Friedrich Wilhelm 1816–1895. German physiologist who invented graphic methods of recording events within the body.

Ludwig three kings of Bavaria:

Ludwig I 1786–1868. King of Bavaria 1825–48. He succeeded his father Maximilian Joseph I. He made Munich an international cultural centre, but his association with the dancer Lola Montez led to his abdication in 1848.

Ludwig II 1845–1886. King of Bavaria from 1864, when he succeeded his father Maximilian II. He supported Austria during the Austro-Prussian War of 1866, but brought Bavaria into the Franco-Prussian War as Prussia's ally, and in 1871 offered the German crown to the king of Prussia. He was the composer Wagner's patron, and built the Bayreuth theatre for him. Declared insane in 1886, he drowned himself soon after.

Ludwig III 1845–1921. King of Bavaria from 1913; abdicated 1918.

Luftwaffe German air force in World War I and, as reorganized by the Nazi leader Goering in 1933, in World War II, when it also covered anti-aircraft defence and launching of the flying bombs ◊V1, V2.

lugworm genus *Arenicola* of marine worms (also known as lobworms) that grow up to 25 cm/10 in long, and are common between tide-marks.

Lu Hsün former name of Chinese writer ◊Lu Xun.

Lukács Georg 1885–1971. Hungarian philosopher, one of the founders of 'Western' or 'Hegelian' Marxism, a philosophical current opposed to the Marxism of the official communist movement.

Luke, St 1st century AD. Traditionally the compiler of the third Gospel and of the Acts of the Apostles in the New Testament. He is the patron saint of painters; his emblem is a winged ox, and his feast day 18 Oct.

Lully Jean-Baptiste 1632–1687. Adopted name of Giovanni Battista Lulli. French composer of Italian origin who was court composer to Louis XIV. He composed music for Molière's plays, established French opera, for example *Alceste* 1674, and *Armide et Renaud* 1686, and ballet.

lumbago pain in the lower region of the back, usually due to strain or faulty posture. If it occurs with ◊sciatica, it may be due to pressure on spinal nerves by a displaced vertebra. Treatment includes rest, application of heat, and skilled manipulation (see ◊osteopathy). Surgery may be needed in rare cases.

lumbar puncture the insertion of a hollow needle between two lumbar (lower back) vertebrae to withdraw a sample of cerebrospinal fluid (CSF) for testing. The procedure is also known as a spinal tap.

Normally clear and colourless, the CSF acts as a fluid buffer for the brain and spinal nerves. Changes in its quantity, colour, or composition may be diagnostic in neurological damage or disease.

Lumbini birthplace of ◊Buddha in the foothills of the Himalayas near the Nepalese-Indian frontier. A sacred garden and shrine were established 1970 by the Nepalese government.

lumen ◊SI unit of luminous flux (lm), equal to the amount of light emitted by a uniform point source of 1 candela in a solid angle of 1 steradian (the unit of solid angle). It is equivalent to 0.001471 watts.

Lumière Auguste Marie (1862–1954) and Louis Jean (1864–1948). French brothers who pioneered cinematography. In 1895 they patented their cinematograph, a combined camera and projector which operated at 16 frames per second. They opened the world's first cinema in Paris to show their films.

luminescence emission of light from a body when its atoms are excited by means other than raising its temperature.

luminous paint a preparation containing a mixture of pigment, oil, and a phosphorescent sulphide, usually calcium or barium. After exposure to light it appears luminous in the dark. The luminous paint used on watch faces is slightly radioactive and does not require exposure to light.

Lumumba Patrice 1926–1961. Congolese politician, prime minister of Zaïre 1960. Imprisoned by the Belgians, but released in time to attend the conference giving the Congo independence 1960, he led the National Congolese Movement to victory in the subsequent general election. He was deposed in a coup d'état, and murdered some months later.

lung a large cavity of the body, used for gas exchange. Most tetrapods have a pair of lungs, which occupy the thorax (the upper part of the trunk). Their function is to remove carbon dioxide dissolved in the blood and supply oxygen which is carried by ◊haemoglobin in red blood cells. The lung tissue, consisting of multitudes of air sacs and blood vessels, is very light and spongy. Air is drawn into the lungs through the trachea and bronchi by the expansion of the ribs and the contraction of the diaphragm.

lungfish freshwater fish; three genera of the order Dipnoi, found in Africa, South America, and Australia. They grow to about 2 m/6 ft, are eel shaped, long-lived, and in addition to gills have 'lungs' (modified swim bladders) with

lung

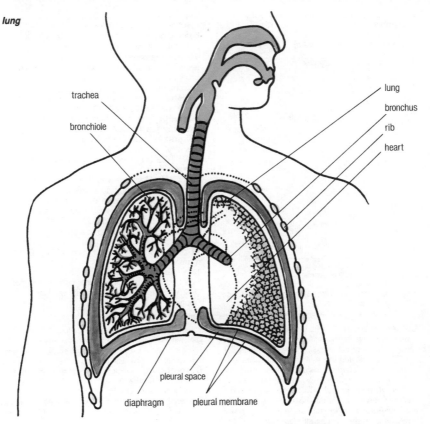

trachea

bronchiole

lung

bronchus

rib

heart

pleural space

diaphragm   pleural membrane

which they can breathe air in drought conditions.

Luo Guan-zhong formerly *Luo Kuan-chung* 14th-century Chinese novelist, who reworked popular tales into *The Romance of the Three Kingdoms* and *The Water Margin*.

Luo Kuan-chung earlier form of ◊Luo Guanzhong.

Lupercalia a Roman festival celebrated on 15 Feb. Goats and a dog were sacrificed, and the priests ran round the city carrying goatskin thongs, a blow from which was believed to cure sterility in women. The ritual probably combined fertility magic with charms conveying protection against wolves.

lupin plant of the genus *Lupinus*, which comprises about 300 species. They are native to Mediterranean regions and parts of N and S America, and some species are naturalized in Britain. The spikes of pea-like flowers may be white, yellow, blue or pink.

lupus erythematosus (LE) a connective tissue disease, one of several believed to be due to autoimmunity, an attack by the body on its own tissues.

Lurie Alison 1926– . US novelist and critic. Her subtly written and satirical novels include *Imaginary Friends* 1967, *The War Between the Tates* 1974, and *Foreign Affairs* 1985, a tale of transatlantic relations which won the Pulitzer Prize.

Lusaka capital of Zambia from 1964 (of N Rhodesia 1935–64), 370 km/230 mi NE of Livingstone; commercial and agricultural centre (flour mills, tobacco

factories, vehicle assembly, plastics and printing); population (1980) 538,469.

Lusitania Cunard liner sunk by German submarine on 7 May 1915 with the loss of some 1,200 lives, including some Americans; its destruction helped bring the USA into World War I.

lusophone the countries in which the ◊Portuguese language is spoken, or which were formerly ruled by Portugal.

lute family of stringed musical instruments of the 14th–18th centuries, which include the mandore, theorbo, and chitarrone. They are pear-shaped and plucked with the fingers.

lutetium silvery-white metallic element, symbol Lu, atomic number 71, relative atomic mass 174.97. Lutetium is the last of the ◊lanthanide series, and is used in the 'cracking' or breakdown of petroleum, and in other chemical processes.

lupin

Luxembourg
Grand Duchy of
(Grand-Duché de Luxembourg)

area 2,586 sq km/999 sq mi
capital Luxembourg
physical on the river Moselle; part of the Ardennes (Oesling) forest in the N

head of state Grand Duke Jean from 1964
head of government Jacques Santer from 1984
political system liberal democracy
exports iron and steel, chemicals, synthetic textiles; banking is very important; Luxembourg is economically linked with Belgium
currency Luxembourg franc
population (1990 est) 369,000; annual growth rate 0%
life expectancy men 71, women 78
language French (official); local Letzeburgesch; German
religion Roman Catholic 97%
literacy 100% (1983)
GNP $4.9 bn (1988); $13,380 per head
chronology
1948 With Belgium and the Netherlands, formed the Benelux customs union.
1958 Benelux became economic union.
1961 Prince Jean became acting head of state on behalf of his mother, Grand Duchess Charlotte.
1964 Grand Duchess Charlotte abdicated and Prince Jean became grand duke.
1974 Dominance of Christian Social Party (CSP) challenged by Socialists.
1979 CSP regained pre-eminence.
1991 Pact agreeing European free-trade area signed.
1992 Voted in favour of ratification of Maastricht Treaty.

Luther Martin 1483–1546. German Christian church reformer, regarded as the founder of the Protestantism. When a priest at the university of Wittenberg 1517, he attacked the sale of ◊indulgences in *95 theses* and defied papal condemnation; the Holy Roman emperor Charles V summoned him to the *Diet of Worms* in 1521, where he refused to retract anything. After the drawing up of the *◊Augsburg Confession* in 1530, he gradually retired from the Protestant leadership.

Lutheranism a form of Protestant Christianity derived from the life and teaching of Martin Luther; it is sometimes called Evangelical to distinguish it from the other main branch of European Protestantism, the Reformed. The most generally accepted statement of Lutheranism is that of the *Augsburg Confession* 1530 but Luther's Shorter Catechism also carries great weight. It is the largest Protestant body, including some 80 million persons.

Luthuli (or Lutuli) Albert 1899–1967. South African politician, president of the *African National Congress* from 1952. Luthuli, a Zulu tribal chief, preached nonviolence and multiracialism. Arrested in 1956, he was never actually tried for treason, although he suffered certain restrictions from 1959. Nobel Peace Prize 1960.

Lutosławski Witold 1913– . Polish composer. He has written chamber, vocal, and orchestral music, including three symphonies, *Livre pour orchestre* 1968 and *Mi-parti* 1976.

Lutyens Edwin Landseer 1869–1944. English architect, considered the greatest architect since Christopher ◊Wren. His designs ranged from picturesque to Renaissance style country houses and ultimately evolved into a classical style as in the Cenotaph, London, and the Viceroy's House, New Delhi.

lux ◊SI unit of illuminance (lx), equal to the illumination produced by a luminous flux of 1 lumen distributed uniformly over an area of 1 m^2.

Luxembourg capital of Luxembourg; population (1985) 76,000. The 16th-century Grand Ducal Palace, European Court of Justice, and European Parliament secretariat are situated here, but plenary sessions of the parliament are now held only in ◊Strasbourg. Products include steel, chemicals, textiles, and processed food.

Luxembourg landlocked country in W Europe, bordered to the N and W by Belgium, E by Germany, and S by France.

Luxembourg Accord French-initiated agreement in 1966 that a decision of the Council of Ministers

Luxor *The temple of Queen Hatshepsut in Luxor, Egypt, showing a bust of the queen on one of the columns.*

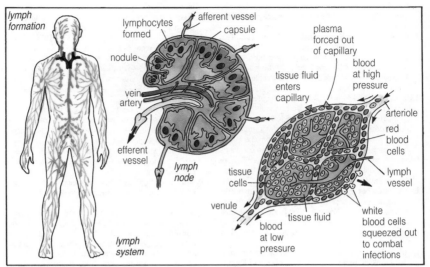

lymph formation

lymphocytes formed

afferent vessel

capsule

plasma forced out of capillary

nodule

blood at high pressure

tissue fluid enters capillary

vein

artery

arteriole

red blood cells

efferent vessel

lymph node

tissue cells

lymph vessel

venule

tissue fluid

white blood cells squeezed out to combat infections

lymph system

blood at low pressure

of the European Community may be vetoed by a member whose national interests are at stake.

Luxemburg Rosa 1870–1919. Polish-born German communist, collaborator with Karl Liebknecht in founding the *Spartacus League* in 1918 (see ◊Spartacist), and murdered with him during the Jan 1919 Berlin workers' revolt.

Luxor (Arabic *Al-Uqsur*) village in Egypt on the E bank of the Nile near the ruins of ◊Thebes.

Lu Xun pen name of Chon Shu-jêu 1881–1936. Chinese short story writer. His three volumes of satirically realistic stories, *Call to Arms*, *Wandering*, and *Old Tales Retold*, reveal the influence of Gogol. He is one of the most popular of modern Chinese writers.

Luzern German name of ◊Lucerne, town and lake in Switzerland.

Luzon largest island of the ◊Philippines; area 108,130 sq km/41,750 sq mi; capital Quezon City; population (1970) 18,001,270. The chief city is Manila, capital of the Philippines. Products include rice, timber, and minerals. It has US military bases.

LW abbreviation for *long wave*, a radio wave with a wavelength of over 1000 m; one of the main wavebands into which radio frequency transmissions are divided.

LWM abbreviation for *low water mark*.

lycanthropy folk belief in human transformation to a ◊werewolf; or, in psychology, a delusion involving this belief.

Lyceum an ancient Athenian gymnasium and garden, with covered walks, where ◊Aristotle taught. It was SE of the city, and named after the nearby temple of Apollo Lyceus.

lychee alternative spelling of ◊litchi.

Lycurgus Spartan lawgiver. He is said to have been a member of the royal house, who, while acting as regent, gave the Spartans their constitution and system of education. Many scholars believe him to be purely mythical.

Lydgate John *c.* 1370–*c.* 1450. English poet. He was a Benedictine monk, and later prior. His numerous works were often translations or adaptations, such as *Troy Book*, and *Falls of Princes*.

Lydia ancient kingdom in Anatolia (7th–6th centuries BC), with its capital at Sardis. The Lydians were the first Western people to use standard coinage. Their

last king, Croesus, was conquered by the Persians in 546 BC.

Lyell Charles 1797–1875. Scottish geologist. In his book *The Principles of Geology* 1830–33, he opposed ◊Cuvier's theory that the features of the Earth were formed by a series of catastrophes, and expounded ◊Hutton's view, known as ◊uniformitarianism, that past events were brought about by the same proscesses that occur today.

Lyly John *c.* 1553–1606. English playwright and author of the romance *Euphues, or the Anatomy of Wit* 1578. Its elaborate stylistic devices gave rise to the word 'euphuism' for an affected rhetorical style.

lymph the fluid found in the lymphatic system of vertebrates, which carries nutrients, oxygen, and white blood cells to the tissues, and waste matter away from them. It exudes from ◊capillaries into the tissue spaces between the cells and is made up of blood plasma, plus white cells.

lymph nodes small masses of lymphatic tissue in the body, which occur at various points along the major lymphatic vessels. Tonsils and adenoids are large lymph nodes. As the lymph fluid passes through them it is filtered, and bacteria and other micro-organisms are engulfed by cells known as macrophages. Lymph nodes are sometimes mistakenly called 'lymph glands', and the term 'swollen glands' refers to swelling of the lymph nodes caused by infection.

lymphocyte a type of white blood cell with a large nucleus, produced in the bone marrow of vertebrates. Most occur in the blood and lymph, and are also present in the body tissues. *B-lymphocytes* are responsible for the production of ◊antibodies which bind to specific ◊antigens, rendering them harmless. *T-lymphocytes*, formed from lymphocytes by the action of the ◊thymus, bind to specific antigens and destroy infected cells; they also help to activate the B-lymphocytes.

Lynch 'Jack' (John) 1917– . Irish politician, born in Cork. He became a noted Gaelic footballer and a barrister. In 1948 he entered the parliament of the republic as a Fianna Fáil member, and was prime minister 1966–73 and 1977–79.

lynx cat *Felis lynx* found in rocky and forested regions of North America and Europe. Larger than a wild cat, it has a short tail, tufted ears, and the long, silky fur is reddish brown or grey with dark spots.

Lyons (French *Lyon*) industrial city (textiles, chemicals, machinery, printing) and capital of Rhône *département*, Rhône-Alpes region and third largest city of France, at the confluence of the Rhône and Saône, 275 km/170 mi NNW of Marseilles; population (1982) 418,476.

Lyons Joseph 1848–1917. British entrepreneur, the founder of the catering firm of J Lyons in 1894. He popularized 'tea-shops', and the 'Corner Houses' incorporating several restaurants of varying types were long a feature of London life. From the 1970s the firm moved into other fields of mass catering.

lyophilization freeze-drying process used for foods and drugs, and in the preservation of organic archaeological remains.

Lyra small but prominent constellation of the northern hemisphere, representing the lyre of Orpheus. Its brightest star is Vega; Epsilon Lyrae, the 'double double', is a system of four linked stars; Beta Lyrae is an eclipsing binary. The Ring Nebula, M57, is a ◊planetary nebula.

lyre stringed instrument of great antiquity. It originated in Asia, and was used in Greece and Egypt. It consisted of a soundbox with two curved arms joined by a crosspiece. There were four to ten strings which were stretched from the crosspiece to a bridge near the bottom of the soundbox. It was played with a plectrum.

lyre-bird genus of Australian birds *Menura*. The male has a large lyre-shaped tail, brilliantly coloured. They nest on the ground, and feed on insects, worms, and snails.

Lysander Spartan general. He brought the Peloponnesian War to a successful conclusion by capturing the Athenian fleet at Aegospotami in 405 BC, and by starving Athens into surrender in the following year. He then aspired to make Sparta supreme in Greece, and himself in Sparta but was killed in battle with the Thebans.

Lysenko Trofim Denisovich 1898–1976. Soviet biologist, who believed in the inheritance of ◊acquired characters and used his position under Stalin to officially exclude ◊Mendel's theory of inheritance. He was removed from office after the fall of Premier Khrushchev in 1964.

Lysippus 4th century BC. Greek sculptor. He made a series of portraits of Alexander the Great (Roman copies survive) and is also known for the *Apoxyomenos*, an athlete (copy in the Vatican), and a colossal *Hercules* (lost). He was prolific, and proved a lasting influence on Greek sculpture.

lysis in biology, any process which destroys a cell by rupturing its lysis membrane (see under ◊lysosome).

lysosome a structure, or organelle, inside a ◊cell, principally found in animal cells. Lysosomes contain enzymes that can break down proteins and other biological substances. They are bounded by a *lysis membrane* that resists the attack of these enzymes and thus protects the cell from them. They play a part in digestion, and in the white blood cells known as phagocytes the lysosyme enzymes attack ingested bacteria.

Lytton Edward George Earle Lytton Bulwer, 1st Baron Lytton of Knebworth 1803–1873. British author. His novels successfully followed every turn of the public taste and include the Byronic *Pelham* 1828, *The Last Days of Pompeii* 1834, and *Rienzi* 1835. He sat in Parliament as a Liberal 1831–41, and as a Conservative 1852–66, and was Colonial Secretary 1858–59.

m   abbreviation for *metre*

M   Roman number for 1,000.

MA   in education, abbreviation for *Master of Arts*.

Maastricht Treaty   treaty on European union, signed 10 Dec 1991 by leaders of the European Community (EC) nations at Maastricht in the Netherlands, at a meeting convened to agree on terms for political union. The treaty was formally endorsed by the European parliament April 1992.

Mabuse   Jan. Adopted name of Jan Gosaert *c.* 1478–*c.* 1533. Flemish painter, active chiefly in Antwerp. His common name derives from his birthplace, Maubeuge. His visit to Italy in 1508 with Philip of Burgundy started a new vogue in Flanders for Italianate ornament and classical influence in painting, including sculptural nude figures.

McAdam   John Loudon 1756–1836. Scottish engineer. The word 'macadamizing' was coined for his system of constructing roads of broken granite.

Macao   Portuguese possession on the S coast of China, about 65 km/40 mi W of Hong Kong, from which it is separated by the estuary of the Canton river; it consists of a peninsula and the islands of Taipa and Colôane.
area 15.5 sq km/6 sq mi
capital Macao, on the peninsula
currency pataca
population (1986) 426,000
language Cantonese; Portuguese (official)
religion Buddhist, with 6% Catholic minority
government internal self-government with Consultative Council and Legislative Council under Portuguese governor
history a Portuguese trading post from 1537; recognised by China as a Portuguese colony from 1887; became an overseas province of Portugal 1951; by a treaty signed 1987 Macao will revert to Chinese control 1999.

macaque   type of monkey of the genus *Macaca*. Various species of these medium sized monkeys live in forests from the Far East to N Africa. They range from longtailed to tailless types, and have well-developed cheek pouches to carry food. The ◊rhesus and the ◊Barbary ape are part of this group.

MacArthur   Douglas 1880–1964. US general in World War II, commander of US forces in the Far East and, from Mar 1942, of the Allied forces in the SW Pacific. After the surrender of Japan he commanded the Allied occupation forces there. During 1950 he commanded the UN forces in Korea, but in April 1951, after expressing views contrary to US and UN policy, he was relieved of all his commands by President Truman.

Macaulay   Thomas Babington, Baron Macaulay 1800–1859. British historian, essayist, poet, and politician, secretary of war 1839–41. His *History of England* in five volumes 1849–55 celebrates the Glorious Revolution of 1668 as the crowning achievement of the Whig party.

macaw   large, brilliantly coloured, long-tailed tropical American ◊parrot.

Macbeth   King of Scotland from 1040. The son of Findlaech, hereditary ruler of Moray, he was commander of the forces of Duncan I, King of Scotia, whom he killed in battle in 1040. His reign was prosperous until Duncan's son Malcolm III led an invasion and killed him in Lumphanan. Shakespeare's tragedy *Macbeth*, first performed 1605–1606, was based on the 16th-century historian Holinshed's *Chronicles*.

Maccabees   Jewish family, sometimes known as the *Hasmonaeans*. It was founded by the priest Mattathias (died 166 BC) who with his sons led the struggle for Jewish independence against the Syrians in the 2nd century BC. Judas (died 161 BC) reconquered Jerusalem in 165 BC, and Simon (died 135 BC) established Jewish independence in 142 BC.

McCarthy   Joseph R(aymond), 'Joe' 1909–1957. US right-wing Republican politician, whose unsubstantiated claim 1950 that the State Department had been infiltrated by Communists started a wave of anticommunist hysteria, wild accusations, and blacklists, which continued until he was discredited in 1954.

McCartney   Paul 1942– . Rock singer and songwriter, former member of the ◊Beatles, and leader of Wings.

McClellan   George Brinton 1826–1885. US Civil War general, commander in chief of the Union forces 1861–62. He was dismissed by President Lincoln when he delayed five weeks in following up his victory over the Confederate general Lee at Antietam (see under ◊Civil War, American).

McClintock   Barbara 1902– . US geneticist, who concluded that ◊genes changed their position on the chromosome from generation to generation in a random way. This would explain how originally identical cells take on specialized functions as skin, muscle, bone, and nerve, and also how evolution could give rise to the multiplicity of species.

McClure   Robert John 1807–1873. British explorer. While on an expedition 1850–54 searching for

McCarthy US senator Joe McCarthy.

◊Franklin, he was the first to pass through the Northwest Passage.

MacCready Paul 1925– . US designer of the *Gossamer Condor* aircraft which made the first controlled flight by human power alone in 1977. His *Solar Challenger* flew from Paris to London under solar power.

McCullers Carson (Smith) 1917–1967. US novelist. Most of her writing (including her best known novels *The Heart is a Lonely Hunter* 1940 and *Reflections in a Golden Eye* 1941) is set in the southern states, where she was born, and deals with spiritual isolation, containing elements of violence.

McCullough Colleen (Margaretta) 1937– . Australian novelist, author of *The Thorn Birds* 1977, which set a record price for paperback and film rights. She was awarded the Burke Order in 1980 for services to people of the outback.

McDiarmid Hugh. Pen name of Christopher Murray Grieve 1892–1978. Scottish nationalist and Marxist poet. His works include *A Drunk Man looks at the Thistle* 1926 and two *Hymns to Lenin* 1930 and 1935.

Macdonald John Alexander 1815–1891. Glasgow-born Canadian Conservative politician. In 1857 he became prime minister of Upper Canada. He led the movement for federation, and in 1867 became Canada's first prime minister. Defeated in 1873, returned to office 1878–1891.

Macdonald Flora 1722–1790. Scottish heroine who rescued Prince Charles Edward Stuart, the Young Pretender, after his defeat at Culloden in 1746. She escorted him, disguised as her maid, to France. She was arrested, but released in 1747.

MacDonald (James) Ramsay 1866–1937. British Labour politician. He joined the ◊Independent Labour Party in 1894, and became first secretary of the new ◊Labour Party in 1900. In Parliament he led the party 1906–14 and 1922–31, and was prime minister of the first two Labour governments, Jan–Oct 1924 and 1929–31, and of a coalition 1931–35, for which he left the party.

Macedonia (Serbo)Croatian *Makedonija*) federal republic of Yugoslavia
area 25,700 sq km/9,920 sq mi
capital Skopje
physical mountainous; chief rivers Struma and Vardar
population (1981) 1,909,000, including 1,279,000 Macedonians, 377,000 Albanians, and 87,000 Turks
language Macedonian, closely allied to Bulgarian and written in Cyrillic
religion Macedonian Orthodox Christian
history Macedonia was an ancient country of SE Europe between Illyria, Thrace, and the Aegean Sea; settled by Slavs in the 6th century; conquered by Bulgars in the 7th century, by Byzantium 1014, by Serbia in the 14th century, and by the Ottoman Empire 1355; divided between Serbia, Bulgaria, and Greece after the Balkan Wars of 1912–13. Macedonia was united 1918 in what later became Yugoslavia, but nationalist demands for autonomy persisted. After increasing tensions, the republic declared independence from Yugoslavia 1992. EC leaders, at Greece's behest, have declined to recognize the republic unless it agrees to a name change, claiming that its name implies a territorial claim on the northern Greek province of Macedonia.

McEwan Ian 1948– . English novelist and short story writer. His tightly written works often have sinister undertones and contain elements of violence and bizarre sexuality, as in the short stories *First Love, Last Rites* 1975. His novels include *The*

Machiavelli *Italian diplomat and witer Niccolò Machiavelli, whose reputation rests largely on* The Prince.

Comfort of Strangers 1981 and *Black Dogs* 1992.

McGonagall William 1830–1902. Scottish poet, noted for the unintentionally humorous effect of his extremely bad serious verse, for example, his poem on the Tay Bridge disaster of 1879.

Machel Samora 1933–1986. Mozambique nationalist leader, president 1975–86. Machel was active in the liberation front Frelimo from its conception in 1962, fighting for independence from Portugal. He became Frelimo leader 1966, and Mozambique's first president, from independence until his death in a place crash near the South African border.

Machiavelli Niccolò 1469–1527. Italian politician and author, whose name is now synonymous with cunning nd cynical statecrafts. In his most important political works, *Il principe/The Prince* 1513 and *Discorsi/Discourses* 1531, he discusses ways in which rulers can advance selfish interests through amoral manipulation of other people.

machine code in computing, a ◊binary (two-state) code in which computer programs are expressed before being executed by the computer. All computer programs used to be written in machine code; later ◊assembly code and high-level programming languages were developed which are easier to use and can automatically be translated into machine code prior to execution.

machine gun a rapid-firing automatic gun.

machine politics the organization of a local political party to ensure its own election by controlling the electorate, and then to retain power through

Machu Picchu *The Inca city of Machu Picchu remained undiscovered until the 20th century.*

McKellen British actor Ian McKellen in the title role of the film Walter.

control of key committees and offices. The idea of machine politics was epitomized in the USA in the late 19th century, where it was used to control individual cities.

Mach number ratio of the speed of a body to the speed of sound in the undisturbed medium through which the body travels. Mach 1 is reached when a body (especially an aircraft) has a velocity greater than that of sound ('passes the sound barrier'). Named after Austrian physicist Ernst Mach (1838–1916).

Machtpolitik (German) power politics.

Machu Picchu a ruined Inca city in Peru, built *c.* 1500 AD, NW of Cuzco, discovered in 1911 by Hiram Bingham. It stands at the top of 300 m/1,000 ft high cliffs, and contains the well-preserved remains of houses and temples.

Macintosh Charles 1766–1843. Scottish manufacturing chemist who invented a waterproof fabric lined with a rubber that was used for raincoats – hence 'mackintosh'. Other waterproofing processes have now largely superseded this method.

McKellen Ian 1939– . British actor, whose stage roles include Richard II and Edward II, and Mozart in the stage version of *Amadeus*. His films include *Priest of Love* 1982 and *Plenty* 1985.

Mackensen August von 1849–1945. German field marshal. During ◊World War I he achieved the breakthrough at Gorlice and the conquest of Serbia 1915, and in 1916 played a major role in the overthrow of Romania. After the war Mackensen retained his popularity to become a folk hero of the German army.

Mackenzie, River river in the Northwest Territories, Canada, flowing from Great Slave Lake NW to the Arctic Ocean; about 1,800 km/1,120 mi long. It is the main channel of the Finlay-Peace-Mackenzie system, 4,200 km/2,600 mi long.

Mackenzie Compton 1883–1972. Scottish author. His first novel was *The Passionate Elopement* in 1911; later works were *Carnival* 1912, *Sinister Street* 1913–14 (an autobiographical novel), and the comic *Whisky Galore* 1947.

Mackenzie William Lyon 1795–1861. Canadian politician, born near Dundee. He emigrated to Canada in 1820, and in 1837 led a rising in Toronto against the oligarchic rule of establishment families, the Family Compact. After its failure he lived in the USA until 1849, and 1851–58 sat in the Canadian legislature as a Radical.

mackerel pelagic fish *scomber scombrus* found in the N Atlantic and Mediterranean. It is blue with irregular black bands down its sides, the latter and the under surface showing a metallic sheen.

McKinley, Mount peak in Alaska, USA, the highest in North America, 6,194 m/20,320 ft; named after William McKinley. See ◊Rocky Mountains.

McKinley William 1843–1901. 25th president of the USA 1897–1901, a Republican. Born in Ohio. He was elected to Congress in 1876. His period as president was marked by America's adoption of an imperialist policy, as exemplified by the Spanish-American War of 1898 and the annexation of the Philippines. He was assassinated in Buffalo, New York.

Mackintosh Charles Rennie 1868–1928. Scottish ◊Art Nouveau architect, designer, and painter, who exercised considerable influence on European design. His chief work includes the Glasgow School of Art 1896.

Maclean Alistair 1922–1987. Scottish adventure novelist. His first novel, *HMS Ulysses* 1955, was based on wartime experience. *The Guns of Navarone* 1957, and other novels were also successful as films.

Maclean Donald 1913–1983. English spy. He was educated at Cambridge, where he became a Communist. He worked for the UK Foreign Office in Washington (1944) and then Cairo (1948) before returning to London, from where he defected to the USSR in 1951.

MacLennan Robert (Adam Ross) 1936– Scottishcentrist politician. Member of parliament for Caithness and Sutherland from 1966. He left the Labour Party for the Social Democrats (SDP) 1981, and was SDP leader 1988 during merger negotiations with the Liberals. He then became a member of the new Social and Liberal Democrats.

McLuhan (Herbert) Marshall 1911–1980. Canadian theorist of communication, noted for his views on the effects of technology on modern society. He coined the phrase 'the medium is the message', meaning that the form rather than the content of information is crucial. His works include *The Gutenberg Galaxy* 1962 (in which he coined the phrase 'the global village' for the modern electronic society), *Understanding Media* 1964, and *The Medium is the Massage* (sic) 1967.

MacMahon Marie Edmé Patrice Maurice, Comte de MacMahon 1808–1893. Marshal of France. Captured at Sedan in 1870 during the Franco-Prussian War, he suppressed the Paris ◊Commune after his release, and as president of the republic 1873–79 worked for a royalist restoration until forced to resign.

Macmillan Conservative prime minister Harold Macmillan, 1957.

Madagascar
Democratic Republic of
(*Repoblika Demokratika n'i Madagaskar*)

area 594,000 sq km/228,500 sq mi
capital Antananarivo
towns chief port Toamasina
physical central highlands; humid valleys and coastal plains

head of state Albert Zafy from 1993
head of government Guy Razanamasy from 1991
political system emergent democratic republic
exports coffee, sugar, spice, textiles
currency Malagasy franc
population (1990 est) 11,802,000; annual growth rate 3.2%
life expectancy men 50, women 53
language Malagasy (official); French and English
religion animist 50%, Christian 40%, Muslim 10%
literacy 53% (1988)
GNP $2.1 bn (1987); $280 per head
chronology
1960 Achieved full independence
1972 Army took control of the government.
1975 Martial law imposed. New constitution proclaimed the Democratic Republic of Madagascar, with Didier Ratsiraka as president.
1976 Front-Line Revolutionary Organisation (AREMA) formed.
1977 National Front for the Defence of the Malagasy Socialist Revolution (FNDR) became the sole legal political organization.
1983 Ratsiraka re-elected, despite strong opposition.
1989 Ratsiraka re-elected.
1990 Political opposition legalized. 36 new parties created.
1991 Antigovernment demonstrations.
1992 Constitutional reform approved. First multiparty elections run by Democrat opposition.
1993 Albert Zafy elected president.

Macmillan (Maurice) Harold, 1st Earl of Stockton 1894–1986. British Conservative politician. As minister of housing 1951–54 he achieved the construction of 300,000 new houses per year. He was chancellor of the Exchequer 1955–57. He became prime minister 1957, on Eden's resignation after the Suez crisis. At home, he furthered domestic expansion. Internationally, he attempted unsuccessfully to negotiate British entry to the European Community, and encouraged the transition to independence of British colonies in Africa.

MacMillan Kenneth 1929–1992. Scottish choreographer. After studying at the Sadler's Wells Ballet School he was director of the Royal Ballet 1970–77 and then principal choreographer.

MacMillan Kirkpatrick died 1878. Scottish blacksmith, who invented the bicycle in 1839. His invention consisted of a 'hobby-horse' that was fitted with treadles and propelled by pedalling.

MacNeice Louis 1907–1963. British poet, born in Belfast. He made his debut with *Blind Fireworks* 1929 and developed a polished ease of expression, reflecting his classical training, as in *Autumn Journal* 1939. He was politically uncommitted.

Macpherson James 1736–1796. Scottish writer and forger, author of *Fragments of Ancient Poetry collected in the Highlands of Scotland* 1760, *Fingal* 1761 and *Temora* 1763, which he claimed as the work of the 3rd-century bard ◊Ossian.

Macquarie Lachlan 1762–1834. Scottish administrator in Australia. He succeeded ◊Bligh as governor of New South Wales in 1808, raised the demoralized settlements to prosperity, and did much to rehabilitate ex-convicts. He opened the first school for Aborigines. In 1821 he returned to Britain in poor health, exhausted by struggles with his opponents. Lachlan River, Macquarie River and Island and Macquarie University in Sydney are named after him.

McQueen Steve (Terence Steven) 1930–1980. US actor. He was one of the most popular film stars of the 1960s and 1970s, admired for his portrayals of the strong, silent loner, and noted for performing his own stunt work. After television success in the 1950s he became a film star with *The Magnificent Seven* 1960. His films include *The Great Escape* 1963, *Bullitt* 1968, *Papillon* 1973 and *The Hunter* 1980.

macramé the art of making decorative fringes and lacework with knotted threads. The name comes from the Arabic word for 'striped cloth', which is often decorated in this way.

Macready William Charles 1793–1873. British actor. He made his debut at Covent Garden, London

McQueen US actor, Steve McQueen.

in 1816. Noted for his roles as Shakespeare's tragic heroes (Macbeth, Lear, and Hamlet), he was partly responsible for persuading the theatre to return to the original texts of Shakespeare, and abandon the earlier bowdlerized versions.

macro in computing, an instruction in a programming language that is composed of a sequence of other instructions. Giving the computer a macro command causes it to obey the sequence of commands from which the macro was built. Macros allow a higher-level programming language to be created from the instructions of a lower-level language.

macrobiotics a dietary system of organically grown wholefoods. It originates in Zen Budhism, and attempts to balance the principles of ◊yin and yang, which are regarded as present in various foods in different proportions.

macroeconomics the division of economics concerned with the study of whole (aggregate) economies or systems, including such aspects as government income and expenditure, the balance of payments, fiscal policy, investment, inflation, and unemployment. It seeks to understand the influence of all relevant economic factors on each other and thus to quantify and predict aggregate national income.

macromolecule in chemistry, a very large molecule, generally of a polymer.

macrophage a type of white blood cell, or ◊leucocyte, found in all vertebrate animals. Macrophages specialize in the removal of bacteria and other microorganisms, or of cell debris after injury. Like phagocytes, they engulf foreign matter, but they are larger than phagocytes and have a longer life span. They are found throughout the body, but mainly in the lymph, connective tissues, and lungs; here they can also ingest inhaled particles.

MAD abbreviation for *mutual assured destruction*; the basis of the theory of ◊deterrence.

Madagascar island in the Indian Ocean, off the coast of E Africa, about 400 km/280 mi from Mozambique.

Madeira group of islands forming an autonomous region of Portugal off the NW coast of Africa, about 420 km/260 mi N of the Canary Islands. Madeira, the largest, and Porto Santo, are the only inhabited islands (capital Funchal). Their mild climate makes them an all-year-round resort.

Madeira river of W Brazil; length 3,250 km/2,020 mi. It is formed by the rivers Beni and Mamoré, and flows NE to join the Amazon.

Madhya Pradesh central state of India
area 442,841 sq km/170,936 sq mi
capital Bhopal
towns Indore, Jabalpur, Ujjain, Gwalior
products cotton, oilseed, and sugar; textiles, engineering, paper, and aluminium
population (1981) 52,131,720
language Hindi
history formed 1950 from the former British province of Central Provinces and Berar and the princely states of Makrai and Chattisgarh. In 1956 it lost some SW districts, including ◊Nagpur, and absorbed Bhopal, Madhya Bharat, and Vindhya Pradesh.

Madison James 1751–1836. 4th president of the USA 1809–17. In 1787 he became a member of the Philadelphia Constitutional Convention and took a leading part in drawing up the US constitution and the Bill of Rights. As secretary of state in Jefferson's government 1801–09, his main achievement was the ◊Louisiana Purchase. He was elected president in 1808 and re-elected 1812. During his period of office the War of 1812

with Britain took place.

Madoc, Prince legendary prince of Gwynned, Wales, supposed to have discovered America and been an ancestor of a group of light-skinned, Welsh-speaking Indians in the American West.

Madonna Italian name for the Virgin ◊Mary, meaning 'my lady'.

Madonna Stage name of Madonna Louise Veronica Ciccone 1959- . US pop singer and film actress of Italian extraction. Her style, a combination of overt sexuality and religious imagery, has been assiduously copied by a generation of teenagers. Her first major hit in the UK was 'Like a Virgin' 1984. By July 1990 she had accumulated 23 hit singles and eight albums, and had broken a record, previously held by the Beatles, of a run of 16 consecutive top five hits. She has also appeared in several films, such as *Desperately Seeking Susan* 1985 and *Shanghai Surprise* 1986.

Madras industrial port (cotton, cement, chemicals, iron and steel) and capital of Tamil Nadu, India, on the Bay of Bengal; population (1981) 4,277,000. Fort St George 1639 remains from the East India Company when Madras was the chief port on the E coast.

Madrid industrial city (leather, chemicals, furniture, tobacco, paper) and capital of Spain and Madrid province; population (1986) 4,855,000. Built on an elevated plateau in the centre of the country, at 655 m/2,183 ft it is the highest capital city in Europe and has excesses of heat and cold. Madrid began as a Moorish citadel captured by Castile 1083, and was designated capital 1561.

madrigal a form of secular song in four or five parts, usually sung without instrumental accompaniment. It originated in Italy around the beginning of the 14th century, and was popular in Elizabethan England. Madrigal composers include ◊Gabrieli, ◊Monteverdi, Thomas ◊Morley, and Orlando ◊Gibbons.

Madurai city in Tamil Nadu, India; site of the 16th–17th century Hindu temple of Sundareswara; cotton industry; population (1981) 904,000.

Maecenas Gaius Cilnius 69–8 BC. Roman patron of the arts. He was the friend and counsellor of

Madurai An elaborate gateway to the Dravidian Meenakshi temple at Madurai, Tamil Nadu, built between the 16th and 18th centuries.

Augustus, and encouraged the work of ◊Horace and ◊Virgil.

maenad in Greek mythology, a woman participant in the orgiastic rites of ◊Dionysus (also known as *Bacchae*).

Maeterlinck Maurice, Count Maeterlinck 1862–1949. Belgian poet and dramatist. His plays include *Pelléas et Mélisande* 1892, *L'Oiseau bleu/The Blue Bird* 1908, and *Le Bourgmestre de Stilmonde/The Burgomaster of Stilemonde* 1918 which celebrates Belgian resistance in World War I – a theme which caused his exile to America 1940. Nobel prize for Literature 1911.

Mafia secret society reputed to control organized crime such as gambling, loansharking, drug traffic, prostitution, and protection, chiefly in large US cities such as New York and Chicago; also known in the USA as *Cosa Nostra*. It originated in 15th-century Sicily as a secret society hostile to the law and avenging wrongs by means of terror and vendetta.

Magadha a kingdom of ancient India, roughly corresponding to the middle and southern parts of modern ◊Bihar. It was the scene of many incidents in the life of Buddha, and was the seat of the Maurya dynasty, founded by Chandragupta in the 3rd century BC.

magazine a publication brought out periodically, typically containing articles, essays, reviews, illustrations, and so on. The first magazine in the UK was the *Compleat Library* 1691; notable successors were Steele's *Tatler* 1709 and Addison's *Spectator* 1711.

Magdeburg industrial city and port (vehicles, paper, chemicals, iron, steel, textiles, and machinery) in East Germany on the river Elbe, capital of Magdeburg district; population (1981) 289,000. Magdeburg was a member of the Hanseatic League, and has a 13th-century Gothic cathedral.

Magellan Ferdinand 1480–1521. Portuguese navigator. In 1519 he sailed from Seville with the intention of reaching the East Indies by a westerly route. He sailed through the *Magellan Strait* at the tip of South America, crossed an ocean which he named the Pacific, and in 1521 reached the Philippines, where he was killed in a fight.

Magellanic Clouds in astronomy, the two nearest galaxies. They are irregularly shaped, and appear as detached parts of the ◊Milky Way, in the southern constellations Dorado and Tucana. The Large Magellanic Cloud is 160,000 light years away, and about a third the diameter of our Galaxy; the Small Magellanic Cloud 180,000 light years away, is about a fifth the diameter of our Galaxy.

maggot the footless larvae of an insect, a typical example being the larva of the blow-fly which is deposited as an egg on flesh.

Maghreb name for NW Africa (Arabic 'far west', 'sunset'). The Maghreb powers – Algeria, Libya, Morocco, Tunisia, and Western Sahara – agreed on economic coordination 1964–65, with Mauritania cooperating from 1970. Chad and Mali are sometimes included. See also ◊Mashraq.

magi priests of the Zoroastrian religion of ancient Persia. The term is used in the New Testament of the Latin Vulgate Bible where the Authorized Version gives 'wise men'. The magi who came to visit the infant Christ with gifts of gold, frankincense, and myrrh (the *Adoration of the Magi*) were in later tradition described as 'the three kings'; their names were Caspar, Melchior, and Balthazar.

magic the art of controlling the forces of nature by supernatural means such as charms and ritual. The central ideas are that like produces like (*sympathetic magic*) and that influence carries by *contagion* or association; for example, by the former principle an enemy could be destroyed through an effigy, by the latter principle through personal items such as hair or nail clippings. It is now generally accepted that most early religious practices and most early art are of magical origin, and there are similarities betwen magic and the use of symbolism in religious ritual. See also ◊witchcraft.

magic realism in literature, a fantastic situation realistically treated, as in the works of many Latin American writers, such as Isabel Allende, Borges, García Márquez; pioneered in Europe by E T A Hoffman and Hesse; and practised in the UK by, among others, Angela Carter. The term was coined in the 1920s to describe German paintings.

magic square in mathematics, a square array of different numbers in which the rows, columns, and diagonals add up to the same total. A simple example employing the numbers 1 to 9, with a total of 15, is:

$$\begin{matrix} 6 & 7 & 2 \\ 1 & 5 & 9 \\ 8 & 3 & 4 \end{matrix}$$

Maginot Line French fortification system along the German frontier from Switzerland to Luxembourg built 1929–36 under the direction of the war minister, André Maginot. It consisted of semi-underground forts armed with heavy guns, joined by underground passages, and protected by anti-tank defences; lighter fortifications continued the line to the sea. In 1940 the Germans pierced the Belgian frontier line and outflanked the Maginot Line.

magistrates' court in England and Wales, a local law court which mainly deals with minor criminal cases, but which also decides, in ◊committital proceedings, whether more serious criminal cases should be referred to the Crown Court. It also deals with some civil matters, such as certain matrimonial proceedings. A magistrates' court consists of between two and seven lay justices of the peace (who are advised on the law by a clerk to the justices), or a single paid lawyer called a stipendiary magistrate.

maglev short for magnetic levitation, a method of supporting, for example, a train above the track by magnetic forces.

magma molten material made up of solids and gases beneath the Earth's surface from which ◊igneous rocks are formed. Magma released by volcanoes is called ◊lava.

Magna Carta in English history, the charter granted by King John in 1215, traditionally seen as guaranteeing human rights against the excessive use of royal power. As a reply to the king's demands for excessive feudal dues and attacks on the privileges of the church, Archbishop Langton proposed to the barons the drawing up of a charter in 1213. John was forced to accept this at Runnymede (now in Surrey) on 15 Jun 1215.

magnesia common name for ◊magnesium oxide.

magnesium a light, white, fairly tough metallic element which burns with a bright flame. Symbol Mg, atomic number 12, relative atomic mass 24.32. It is widely distributed in its silicate, carbonate, and chloride forms. It is used in alloys, to strengthen aluminium for aircraft construction, and, with uranium, as a canning material in nuclear reactors. Its incendiary properties are used in flash photography, flares, and fireworks.

magnesium oxide (also called *magnesia*) MgO white powder or colourless crystals, formed when

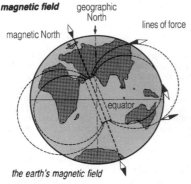

magnetic field   geographic North

magnetic North

lines of force

equator

the earth's magnetic field

magnesium is burned in air or oxygen. It is used to treat acidity of the stomach, and in some industrial processes.

magnetic field   a region around a permanent magnet, or around a conductor carrying an electric current, in which a force acts on a moving charge or on a magnet placed in the field. The field can be represented by lines of force, which by convention link north and south poles and are parallel to the directions of a small compass needle placed on them.

magnetic flux   a measurement of the strength of the magnetic field around electric currents and magnets. The amount of magnetic flux through an area equals the product of the area and the magnetic field strength at a point within that area. It is measured in ◊webers; one weber per square metre is equal to one ◊tesla.

magnetic resonance imaging   (MRI) a diagnostic scanning system based on the principles of magnetism. Claimed as the biggest breakthrough in diagnostic imaging since the discovery of X-rays, MRI yields finely detailed three-dimensional images of structures within the body.

magnetic storm   in meteorology, a sudden disturbance affecting the Earth's magnetic field, causing anomallies in radio transmissions and magnetic compasses. It is probably caused by ◊sunspot activity.

magnetic tape   a narrow plastic ribbon coated with an easily magnetizable material to record data. It is used in sound recording, audiovisual systems (videotape), and computing.

magnetism   branch of physics dealing with the properties of magnets and ◊magnetic fields. Magnetic fields are produced by moving charged particles; in electromagnets, electrons flow through a coil of wire connected to a battery; in magnets, atoms align to generate the field.

magnetite   a black iron ore, magnetic iron oxide, Fe_3O_4, found in igneous rocks. Under the name *lodestone*, it is familiar from its use as a compass since the 1st millennium BC.

magneto   a simple electric generator, often used to provide the electricity for the ignition system of motor cycles. It consists of a rotating magnet, which sets up an electric current in a coil.

magnetohydrodynamics   a field of science concerned with the behaviour of ionized gases in a magnetic field, also known as ◊MHD. Schemes have been developed that use MHD to generate electric power.

magnetosphere   the volume of space, surrounding a planet, controlled by the planet's magnetic field, and acting as a magnetic 'shell'. The Earth's extends

64,000 km/40,000 mi towards the Sun, but many times this distance on the side away from the Sun.

magnetron   a ◊thermionic valve (vacuum tube) for generating very high-frequency oscillations, used in radar and to produce microwaves in a microwave oven.

Magnificat   in the New Testament, the song of praise sung by Mary, the mother of Jesus Christ, on her visit to her cousin Elizabeth shortly after the Annunciation; it is used in the liturgy of some Christian churches.

magnification   a measure of the enlargement or reduction of an object in an imaging optical system. Linear magnification is the ratio of the size (height) of the image to that of the object. Angular magnification is the ratio of the angle subtended at the observer's eye by the image to the angle subtended by the object when viewed directly.

magnitude   in astronomy, measure of the brightness of a star or other celestial object. Faint objects have larger magnitudes, sixth magnitude being the faintest visible to the naked eye under good conditions. The brightest objects have negative magnitudes. *Apparent magnitude* is the brightness of an object as seen from Earth, *absolute magnitude* the brightness at a standard distance of 10 parsecs (32.6 light years).

magnolia   tree or shrub of the family Magnoliaceae, native to China, Japan, North America, and the Himalayas. They vary in height from 60 cm/2 ft to 30 m/150 ft. The large single flowers are white, rose, or purple.

Magnox   an early type of nuclear reactor used in the UK, for example in Calder Hall, the world's first commercial nuclear power station. This type of reactor uses uranium fuel encased in tubes of magnesium alloy called Magnox. Carbon dioxide gas is used as a coolant to extract heat from the reactor core. See also ◊nuclear energy.

magpie   genus of birds *Pica* in the crow family. It feeds on insects, snails, young birds, and carrion, and is found in Europe, Asia, N Africa, and W North America.

Magritte   René 1898–1967. Belgian Surrealist painter. His paintings focus on visual paradoxes and everyday objects taken out of context. Recurring motifs include bowler hats, apples, and windows.

Magyar   member of the largest ethnic group in Hungary, comprising 92% of the population. Magyars are of mixed Ugric and Turkish origin, and they arrived in Hungary towards the end of the 9th century. The Magyar language belongs to the Uralic group.

Mahābhārata   Sanskrit Hindu epic consisting of 18 books probably composed in its present form about

magnolia

300 BC. It forms with the *Rāmāyana* the two great epics of the Hindus. It deals with the fortunes o the rival families of the Kauravas and the Pandavas and contains the ◊*Bhagavad-Gītā*, or *Song of the Blessed*, an episode in the sixth book.

Mahādeva (Sanskrit 'great god') a title given to the Hindu god ◊Siva.

Mahādevī (Sanskrit 'great goddess') a title given to Sakti, the consort of the Hindu god Siva. She is worshipped in many forms, including her more active manifestations as Kali or Durga and her peaceful form as Parvati.

Maharashtra state in W central India
area 307,762 sq km/118,717 sq mi
capital Bombay
towns Pune, Nagpur, Sholapur
products cotton, rice, groundnuts, sugar, minerals
population (1981) 62,694,000
language Marathi 50%
religion Hindu 80%, Parsee, Jain, and Sikh minorities
history formed in 1960 from the S part of the former Bombay state.

maharishi Hindu guru, or spiritual leader.

mahatma (Sanskrit 'great soul') title conferred on Mohandas K ◊Gandhi by his followers as the first great national Indian leader.

Mahāyāna one of the two major forms of ◊Buddhism, common in N Asia (China, Korea, Japan, and Tibet). Veneration of Bodhisattvas is important in Mahāyāna, as is the idea that everyone has within them the seeds of Buddhahood.

Mahdi (Arabic 'he who is guided aright') in Islam, the title of a coming messiah who will establish the reign of justice on Earth. It has been assumed by many Muslim leaders, notably the Sudanese sheik Muhammad Ahmed (1848–85), who headed a revolt in 1881 against Egypt and in 1885 captured Khartoum. His great-grandson *Sadiq el Mahdi* (1936–   ), leader of the Umma party in the Sudan, was prime minister 1966–67. He was imprisoned 1969–74 for attempting to overthrow the military regime.

mah-jong (Chinese 'sparrows') originally an ancient Chinese card game, dating from the Song dynasty 960–1279. It is now usually played by four people with 144 small ivory tiles or 'dominoes', divided into six suits.

Mahler Gustav 1860–1911. Austrian Romantic composer. His nine symphonies, *Das Lied von der Erde/Song of the Earth* 1909, and his song cycles display a synthesis of Romanticism and new uses of chromatic harmonies and musical forms.

mahogany timber obtained from several genera of trees found in America and Africa. Mahogany wood is durable, has a warm red colour, and takes a high polish.

Mahratta or *Maratha* member of a people of Maharashtra, India. In the 17th and 18th centuries they formed a powerful military confederacy in rivalry with the Mogul emperors. The Afghan allies of the latter defeated them 1761, and, after a series of wars with the British 1779–1871, most of their territory was annexed. Their language is Marathi.

Maia in Greek mythology, daughter of Atlas and mother of Hermes.

Maiden Castle a prehistoric hill-fort and later earthworks on Fordington Hill, near Dorchester, Dorset, England. Ramparts, about 18 m/60 ft high, enclosed an area of 18 ha/45 acres. The site was inhabited from Neolithic times (about

2000 BC) and was stormed by the Romans in 43 AD.

maidenhair fern *Adiantum capillus-veneris* with hair-like fronds terminating in small kidney-shaped, spore-bearing pinnules.

maidenhair tree another name for ◊gingko, a genus of ornamental trees related to the conifers.

maid of honour in Britain, the closest attendant on a queen. They are chosen generally from the daughters and granddaughters of peers, but in the absence of another title bear that of Honourable.

Mailer Norman 1923–   . US writer and journalist. He gained wide attention with his novel of World War II *The Naked and the Dead* 1948.

Maillol Aristide Joseph Bonaventure 1861–1944. French artist who turned to sculpture in the 1890s. His work is devoted to the human figure, particularly the female nude. It shows the influence of classical Greek art, but tends towards simplified rounded forms.

mail order a type of business in which retail organizations sell their goods through catalogues, usually by post. Goods sold range from the cheapest household goods (in Europe) to motor cars (in Japan).

Maimonides Moses (Moses Ben Maimon) 1135–1204. Jewish rabbi and philosopher, born in Córdoba, Spain. Known as one of the greatest Hebrew scholars, he attempted to reconcile faith and reason; his philosophical classic is *More nevukhim/The Guide to the Perplexed* 1176–91, which helped to introduce the theories of Aristotle into medieval philosophy.

Maine north-easternmost state of the USA, largest of the New England states; nicknamed Pine Tree State
area 86,027 sq km/33,215 sq mi
capital Augusta
towns Portland
physical Appalachian Mountains; Acadia National Park; 80% of the state is forested
products dairy and market garden produce; paper, pulp and timber; textiles; tourism and fishing are also important
population (1983) 1,146,000
famous people Longfellow
history settled from 1623, it became a state in 1820.

mainframe a large computer used for commercial data processing and other large-scale operations. Because of the increase in computing power, the distinction between the mainframe, ◊minicomputer, and ◊microcomputer (home computer) is becoming less important. A ◊supercomputer is more powerful than a mainframe.

main sequence in astronomy, the part of the ◊Hertzsprung–Russell diagram that contains most of the stars, including the Sun. It runs diagonally from the top left of the diagram to the lower right. The most massive (and hence brightest) stars are at the top left, with the least massive (coolest) stars at the bottom right.

maintenance in law, payments to support children or a spouse, under the terms of an agreement, or by a court order. In Britain, financial provision orders are made on divorce, but a court action can also be brought for maintenance without divorce proceedings. Applications for maintenance of illegitimate children are now treated in the same way as for legitimate children.

Maintenon Françoise d'Aubigné, Marquise de Maintenon 1653–1719. Second wife of Louis XIV of France from 1684, and widow of the writer Paul Scarron (1610–60). Her political influence

Malawi
Republic of
(*Malaŵi*)

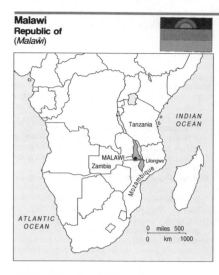

area 117,000 sq km/47,950 sq mi

capital Lilongwe
towns Blantyre-Limbe
physical mountainous W of Lake Malawi
head of state and government Hastings Kamusu Banda from 1966 for life
political system one-party republic
exports tea, tobacco, cotton, groundnuts, sugar
currency kwacha
population (1990 est) 9,080,000; annual growth rate 3.3%
life expectancy men 46, women 50
language English, Chichewa (both official)
religion Christian 75%; Muslim 20%
literacy 25% (1988)
GNP $1.2 bn (1987); $160 per head
chronology
1964 Achieved independence
1966 Became a one-party republic, with Hastings Banda as president.
1971 Banda was made president for life.
1977 Banda started a programme of moderate liberalization.
1986–89 Influx of over 650,000 refugees from Mozambique.
1992 Call for multiparty politics. Industrial riots caused many fatalities. Western aid suspended over human-rights violations.
1993 Commission appointed to supervise preparation for referendum.

was considerable, and, as a Catholic convert from Protestantism, her religious opinions were zealous.

Maitreya the Buddha to come, 'the kindly one', an important figure in all forms of Buddhism; he is known as *Mi-lo-fo* in China and *Miroku* in Japan. Buddhists believe that a Buddha appears from time to time to maintain knowledge of the true path; Maitreya is the next future Buddha.

maize plant *Zea mays* of the grass family. Grown extensively in all subtropical and warm temperate regions, its range has been extended to colder zones by hardy varieties developed in the 1960s.

majolica or *maiolica* a kind of enamelled ◊pottery, so named from Majorca, where such ware was made. The term is applied to the richly decorated enamel pottery produced in Italy in the 15th to 18th centuries.

Major John 1943– . British Conservative politician, prime minister from Nov 1990. He was foreign secretary 1989 and chancellor of the Exchequer 1989–90. His earlier positive approach to European Community matters was hindered during 1991 by divisions within the Conservative Party. Despite continuing public dissatisfaction with the poll tax, the National Health Service, and the recession, Major was returned to power in the April 1992 general election. His subsequent handling of a series of political crises called into question his effectiveness.

Majorca (Spanish *Mallorca*) largest to the ◊Balearic Islands, belonging to Spain, in the W Mediterranean
area 3,640 sq km/1,405 sq mi
capital Palma
products olives, figs, oranges, wine, brandy, timber, sheep; tourism in the mainstay of the economy
population (1981) 561,215
history captured 797 by the Moors, it became the kingdom of Majorca 1276, and was united with Aragon in 1343.

major-general after the English Civil War, one of the officers appointed by Oliver Cromwell in 1655 to oversee the 12 military districts into which England had been divided. Their powers were extensive.

Makarios III 1913–1977. Cypriot politician, Greek Orthodox archbishop 1950–77. A leader of the Resistance organization ◊EOKA, he was exiled

by the British to the Seychelles 1956–57 for supporting armed action to achieve union with Greece (*enosis*). He was president of the republic of Cyprus 1960–77 (briefly deposed by a Greek coup Jul–Dec 1974).

Makarova Natalia 1940– . Russian ballerina. She danced with the Kirov Ballet 1959–70, then sought political asylum in the West. Her roles include Giselle, and Aurora in *The Sleeping Beauty*.

Malabo port and capital of Equatorial Guinea, on the island of Bioko; population (1983) 15,253. It was founded in the 1820s by the British as Port Clarence. Under Spanish rule it was known as Santa Isabel (until 1973)

malachite a common ◊copper ore, and a source of green pigment.

Málaga industrial seaport (sugar refining, distilling, brewing, olive-oil pressing, shipbuilding) and holiday resort in Andalusia, Spain; capital of Málaga province on the Mediterranean; population (1991) 524,800.

Major John Major, unexpected victor in the 1990 Conservative Party leadership election.

history Founded by the Phoenicians and taken by the Moors 711, Málaga was capital of the Moorish kingdom of Malaga from the 13th century until captured 1487 by Ferdinand and Isabella.

Malagasy inhabitant of Madagascar. Primarily rice farmers, they make use of both irrigated fields and swidden (temporary plot) methods. The language belongs to the Austronesian family.

Malamud Bernard 1914–1986. US novelist. He first attracted attention with *The Natural* 1952. Later works, often dealing with Jewish immigrant tradition, include *The Assistant* 1957, *The Fixer* 1966, *Dubin's Lives* 1979, and *God's Grace* 1982.

malapropism an amusing slip of the tongue, arising from the confusion of similar-sounding words. Derived from the French *mal à propos* (inappropriate); it is associated with Mrs Malaprop, a character in Sheridan's play *The Rivals* 1775, who was the pineapple (pinnacle) of perfection in such matters.

malaria infectious parasitic disease transmitted by mosquitoes, marked by periodic fever and an enlarged spleen, which affects some 200 million people a year. When a female mosquito of the *Anopheles* genus bites a human with malaria, it takes in with the human blood the malaria parasite (*Plasmodium*). This matures within the insect, and is then transferred when the mosquito bites a new victim.

Malawi country in SE Africa, bordered N and NE by Tanzania, E, S and W by Mozambique, and W by Zambia.

Malawi, Lake (formerly *Lake Nyasa*) African lake, bordered by Malawi, Tanzania, and Mozambique, formed in a section of the Great ◊Rift Valley. It is about 500 m/1,500 ft above sea level and 560 km/350 mi long, with an area of 37,000 sq km/14,280 sq mi. It is intermittently drained to the south by the river Shiré into the Zambezi.

Malay person of Malay culture, comprising the majority population of the Malay peninsula and also found in S Thailand, and coastal Sumatra and Borneo.

Malay language a member of the Western or Indonesian branch of the ◊Malayo-Polynesian language family, used in the Malay peninsula and many of the islands of Malaysia and Indonesia. The Malay language can be written with either Arabic or Roman scripts. The dialect of the S Malay in Malaysia and Bahasa Indonesia, the official language of Indonesia. Bazaar Malay is a widespread pidgin variety used for trading and shopping.

Malayo-Polynesian also known as Austronesian, a family of languages spoken in Malaysia, the Indonesian archipelago, parts of Indochina, Taiwan, Madagascar, Melanesia, and Polynesia (excluding Australia and most of New Guinea). The group contains some 500 distinct languages.

Malaysia country in SE Asia, comprising the Malay Peninsula, bordered to the N by Thailand, and surrounded E, S, and W by the South China Sea; and the states of Sabah and Sarawak, which occupy the N part of the island of Borneo, the S being part of Indonesia.

Malcolm III called Canmore *c.* 1031–1093. King of Scotland from 1054, the son of Duncan I (died 1040); he was killed at Alnwick while invading Northumberland.

Maldives group of 1,196 islands in the N Indian Ocean, about 640 km/400 mi SW of Sri Lanka, only 203 of which are inhabited.

Malaysia

area 331,500 sq km/128,000 sq mi
capital Kuala Lumpur
towns Kuching in Sarawak and Kota Kinabalu in Sabah
physical comprises W Malaysia (the nine Malay states – Perlis, Kedah, Johore, Selangor, Perak, Negri Sembilan, Kelantan, Trengganu, Pahang – plus Penang and Malacca); and E Malaysia (Sarawak and Sabah); 75% of the area is covered in tropical jungle; there is a central mountain range; swamps in the E

head of state Rajah Azlan Shah (sultan of Perak) from 1989
head of government Mahathir bin Mohamad from 1981
political system liberal democracy
exports pineapples, palm oil, rubber, timber, petroleum (Sarawak), bauxite
currency ringgit
population (1990 est) 17,053,000 (Malaysian 47%, Chinese 32%, Indian 8%, others 13%); annual growth rate 2%
life expectancy men 65, women 70
language Malay (official)
religion Muslim (official)
literacy 80% (1989)
GNP $34.3 bn (1988); $1,870 per head
chronology
1963 Formation of federation of Malaysia.
1965 Secession of Singapore from federation.
1969 Anti-Chinese riots in Kuala Lumpur.
1971 Launch of Bumiputra 'new economic policy'.
1981 Election of Dr Mahathir bin Mohamad as prime minister.
1982 Mahathir bin Mohamed re-elected.
1986 Mahathir bin Mohamad re-elected.
1987 Arrest of over 100 opposition activists as Malay–Chinese relations deteriorated.
1988 Split in ruling UMNO party.
1989 Semangat '46 set up by former members of UMNO.
1990 Mahathir bin Mohamad re-elected.
1991 New economic growth programme launched.

Maldives
Republic of
(Divehi Jumhuriya)

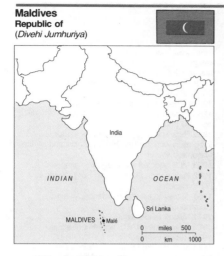

area 298 sq km/115 sq mi
capital Malé
physical comprises some 1,000 coral islands, largely flat, none bigger than 13 sq km/5 sq mi

head of state and government Maumoon Abdul Gayoom from 1978
political system authoritarian nationalism
exports coconuts, copra, bonito (fish related to tunny); tourism is important
currency Rufiya
population (1990 est) 219,000; annual growth rate 3.7%
language Divehi (Sinhalese dialect)
religion Sunni Muslim
literacy 36% (1989)
GNP $69 million (1987); $410 per head
chronology
1953 Originally a sultanate, the Maldive Islands became a republic within the Commonwealth.
1954 Sultanate restored.
1965 Achieved full independence outside the Commonwealth.
1968 Sultan deposed and a republic reinstated with Ibrahim Nasir as president.
1978 Nasir retired and was replaced by Maumoon Abdul Gayoom.
1982 Rejoined the Commonwealth.
1983 Gayoom re-elected.
1988 Gayoom re-elected. Unsuccessful coup attempt by mercenaries thought to have the backing of former president Nasir, was foiled by Indian troops.

Malé capital of the Maldives in the Indian Ocean; population (1990) 55,100. It trades in copra, breadfruit, and palm products.

Malenkov Georgi Maximilianovich 1901–1988. Soviet prime minister 1953–55, ousted by Khrushchev.

Malevich Kasimir 1878–1935. Russian abstract painter, born in Kiev. In 1912 he visited Paris and became a Cubist, and in 1913 he launched his own abstract movement, ◊*Suprematism*. Later he returned to figurative themes treated in a semi-abstract style.

Malherbe François de 1555–1628. French poet and grammarian, born in Caen. He became court poet about 1605 under Henry IV and Louis XIII. He advocated reform of language and versification,

and established the 12-syllable Alexandrine as the standard form of French verse.

Mali landlocked country in NW Africa, bordered to the NE by Algeria, E by Niger, SE by Burkina Faso, S by the Ivory Coast, SW by Senegal and Guinea, and W and N by Mauritania.

Mali, Ancient a Muslim empire in NW Africa during the 7th–15th centuries. Thriving on its trade in gold, it reached its peak in the 14th century under Mansa Musa (reigned 1312–37), when it occupied an area covering present-day Senegal, Gambia, Mali, and S Mauritania. Mali's territory was similar to (though larger than) that previously ruled by ancient Ghana; the Mali empire gave way in turn to the ◊Songhai Empire.

Mali
Republic of
(République du Mali)

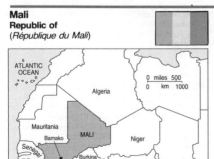

area 1,204,000 sq km/465,000 sq mi
capital Bamako
physical river Niger in S; savanna; part of the Sahara in N
head of state and government Alpha Oumar

Konare from 1992
political system emergent democratic republic
exports cotton, peanuts, livestock
currency CFA franc
population (1990 est) 9,182,000; annual growth rate 2.9%
life expectancy men 44, women 47
language French (official), Bambara
religion Sunni Muslim 90%, animist 9%
literacy 10% (1989)
GNP $1.6 bn (1987); $230 per head
chronology
1959 With Senegal, formed the Federation of Mali.
1960 Became the independent Republic of Mali, with Mobido Keita as president.
1968 Keita ousted in a coup by Moussa Traoré.
1974 New constitution made Mali a one-party state.
1976 New national party, the Malian People's Democratic Union, announced.
1983 Agreement between Mali and Guinea for eventual political and economic integration.
1991 Traoré ousted in a coup led by Lt-Col Amadon Toumani Touré. New constitution agreed subject to referendum.
1992 Referendum endorsed new democratic constitution. Konare elected president.

Malta
Republic of
(*Repubblika Ta'Malta*)

area 316 sq km/122 sq mi
capital Valletta
physical includes the island of Gozo 67 sq km/
26 sq mi and Comino 2.5 sq km/1 sq mi
head of state Vincent Tabone from 1989
head of government Eddie Fenech-Adami from 1987
political system liberal democracy
exports vegetables, knitwear, handmade lace,
plastics, electronic equipment

currency Maltese lira
population (1990 est) 373,000; annual growth rate
0.7%
life expectancy men 72, women 77
language Maltese, English
religion Roman Catholic 98%
literacy 90% (1988)
GNP $1.6 bn (1988); $4,750 per head
chronology
1947 Achieved self-government.
1955 Dom Mintoff of the Malta Labour Party (MLP)
became prime minister.
1956 Referendum approved proposal for
integration with the UK. Proposal opposed by the
Nationalist Party.
1958 MLP rejected the integration proposal.
1962 Nationalists elected, with Borg Olivier as
prime minister.
1964 Achieved full independence, within the
Commonwealth.
1971 Mintoff re-elected.
1972 Seven-year NATO agreement signed.
1974 Became a republic.
1984 Mintoff retired and was replaced by Mifsud
Bonnici as prime minister and MLP leader.
1987 Eddie Fenech-Adami (Nationalist) became
prime minister.
1989 Vincent Tabone elected president.
1990 Formal application made for EC
membership.
1992 Nationalist Party returned to power in general
election.

malic acid $C_4H_6O_5$ an organic compound that can
be extracted from apples, plums, cherries, grapes,
and other fruits. It occurs in all living cells, though
in smaller amounts, being one of the intermediates
of the ◊Krebs' cycle.

Malik Yakob Alexandrovich 1906–1980. Soviet
diplomat. He was permanent representative at the
United Nations 1948–53 and 1968–76, and it was
his walkout from the Security Council in Jan 1950
that allowed the authorization of UN intervention in
Korea (see ◊Korean War).

Malinowski Bronislaw 1884–1942. Polish
anthropologist, one of the founders of the theory of
◊functionalism in the social sciences. His study of
the peoples of Trobinand Islands led him to see
customs and practices in terms of their function in
creating and maintaining social order.

Malipiero Gian Francesco 1882–1973. Italian
composer, editor of Monteverdi and Vivaldi. His
own works include operas based on Shakespeare's
Julius Caesar 1934–35 and *Antony and Cleopatra*
1936–37 in a Neo-Classical style.

mallard common wild duck *Anas platyrhynchos*
found almost worldwide and from which domestic
ducks were bred. The male, which can grow to a
length of 60 cm/2 ft, usually has a green head and
brown breast, while the female is mottled brown.
They are omnivorous.

Mallarmé Stéphane 1842–1898. French poet,
who founded the Symbolist school with Verlaine.
His belief that poetry should be evocative and
suggestive was reflected in *L'Après-midi d'un
faune/Afternoon of a Faun* 1876, which inspired
Debussy. Later publications are *Poésies complètes/
Complete Poems* 1887, *Vers et prose/Verse and Prose*
1893, and the prose *Divagations/Digressions* 1897.

mallee small trees and shrubs of the genus *Eucalyptus* with many small stems and thick underground roots that retain water.

Mallorca Spanish form of ◊Majorca, an island in
the Mediterranean.

mallow flowering plant of the family Malvaceae,
including the European *common mallow Malva
sylvestris*; the *marsh mallow Althaea officinalis*.
See also ◊hollyhock. Most have pink or purple
flowers.

Malmö industrial port (shipbuilding, engineering, textiles) in SW Sweden; population (1990)
233,900.

Malory Thomas 15th century. English author of the
prose romance *Morte d'Arthur* (about 1470). It is a
translation from the French, modified by material
from other sources, and deals with the exploits of
Arthur's knights of the Round Table and the quest
for the Grail. Malory's identity is uncertain.

Malpighi Marcello 1628–1694. Italian physiologist, who made many discoveries (still known by his
name) in his microscope studies of animal and plant
tissues.

Malplaquet, Battle of victory of 1709 of the
British, Dutch, and Austrians, under Marlborough
and Prince Eugene of Savoy, over the French under
Villars, during the War of the ◊Spanish Succession.
The village of Malplaquet is in Nord *département*,
France.

malpractice term in US law for ◊negligence by a
professional person, usually a doctor, which may
lead to an action for damages by his client. Such legal
actions are more common in the USA than in Britain,
and result in doctors having high insurance costs
which are reflected in higher fees charged to their
patients.

Malraux André 1901–1976. French novelist. He
became involved in the nationalist/communist revolution in China in the 1920s, reflected in *La Condition humaine/Man's Estate* 1933; *L'Espoir/Days of
Hope* 1937 is set in Civil War Spain, where he was a
bomber-pilot in the International Brigade. In World

War II he supported the Gaullist Resistance, and was Minister of Cultural Affairs 1960–90.

malt in brewing, grain (barley, oats, or wheat) artificially germinated and then dried in a kiln. Fermented malts are used to make beers, or then distilled to produce spirits such as whisky.

Malta island in the Mediterranean, S of Sicily, E of Tunisia, and N of Libya.

Malta, Knights of another name for members of the military-religious order of the Hospital of ◊St John of Jerusalem.

Malthus Thomas Robert 1766–1834. British cleric and economist, whose *Essay on the Principle of Population* 1798 (revised 1803) argued for population control, since populations increase in geometric ratio, and food only in arithmetic ratio. He saw war, famine, and disease as necessary checks on population growth.

Maluku (or *Moluccas*) group of Indonesian islands
area 74,500 sq km/28,764 sq mi
capital Ambon, on Amboina
population (1989) 1,814,000
history as the Spice Islands, they were formerly part of the Netherlands E Indies, and the S Moluccas attempted secession from the newly created Indonesian Republic from 1949; exiles continue agitation in the Netherlands.

Malvinas Argentinian name for the ◊Falkland Islands.

mamba venomous snake of the cobra family found in Africa S of the Sahara. It can grow to a length of 3.4 m/11 ft.

Mameluke member of a powerful political class who dominated Egypt, originally descended from freed Turkish slaves. They formed the royal bodyguard in the 13th century, and in 1250 placed one of their own number on the throne. Mameluke sultans ruled Egypt until the Turkish conquest of 1517, and they remained the ruling class until 1811, when they were massacred by Mehemet Ali.

Mamet David 1947– . US playwright. His plays, with their vivid, freewheeling language and sense of ordinary American life, include *American Buffalo* 1977, *Sexual Perversity in Chicago* 1978, *Glengarry/ Glen Ross* 1984 (filmed 1992), and *Speed-the-Plow* 1988.

mammal a vertebrate animal which suckles its young and has hair, lungs, and a four-chambered heart. Mammals maintain a constant body temperature in varied surroundings. Most mammals give birth to live young, but the platypus and echidna lay eggs. There are over 4,000 species, adapted to almost every conceivable way of life. The smallest shrew weighs only 2 g/0.07 oz, the largest whale up to 150 tonnes.

mammary gland in female mammals, milk-producing gland derived from epithelial cells underlying the skin, active only after the production of young. In all but monotremes (egg-laying mammals), the mammary glands terminate in teats which aid infant suckling. The number of glands and their position vary between species.

mammography an X-ray procedure used to detect breast cancer at an early stage.

mammoth genus *Mammuthus* of extinct elephants whose remains are found worldwide, some being half as tall again as modern species.

management information system (MIS) in commercial organizations with computer support, a set of programs for abstracting and summarizing computer-held information for the purposes of management consumption. Such systems normally provide regular printed reports and, on request, particular reports and statistical analyses.

Managua capital and chief industrial city of Nicaragua, on the lake of the same name; population (1985) 682,000. It has twice been destroyed by earthquake and rebuilt, in 1931 and 1972; it was also badly damaged by civil war in the late 1970s.

manakin bird of the family Pipridae found in South and Central America, about 15 cm/6 in long and often brightly coloured. It feeds on berries and other small fruits.

Manama (Arabic *Al Manamah*) capital and free trade port of Bahrain, on Bahrain Island; handles oil and entrepôt trade; population (1988) 152,000.

manatee plant-eating aquatic mammal of the genus *Trichechus* belonging to the order Sirenia (sea-cows). Manatees are found on the eastern coasts of tropical North and South America, and around West Africa. They occur in fresh and sea water. The forelimbs are flippers; the hindlimbs are absent, but there is a short rounded dorso-ventrally flattened tail which is used for propulsion. They are in danger of becoming extinct.

Manaus capital of Amazonas, Brazil, on the Rio Negro, near its confluence with the Amazon; population (1991) 996,700. It can be reached by sea-going vessels, although 1,600 km/1,000 mi from the Atlantic. Formerly a centre of the rubber trade, it developed as a tourist centre in the 1970s.

Manchester port in NW England, on the river Irwell, 50 km/31 mi E of Liverpool. It is a manufacturing (textile machinery, chemicals, rubber, processed foods) and financial centre; population (1991) 397,400. It is linked by the Manchester Ship Canal, built 1894, to the river Mersey and the sea.

Manchu ruling dynasty in China 1644–1912. Originally a nomadic people from Manchuria, they established power through a series of successful invasions from the north.

Manchukuo former Japanese puppet state in ◊Manchuria 1932–45.

Manchuria European name for the NE region of China (provinces of Heilongjiang, Jilin, and Liaoning). It was united with China by the ◊Manchu dynasty 1644, but as the Chinese Empire declined Japan and Russia were rivals for its control. The Russians were expelled after the ◊Russo-Japanese War, and in 1932 Japan consolidated its position by creating a puppet state, *Manchukuo*, which disintegrated on the defeat of Japan in World War II.

mandala a symmetrical design in Hindu and Buddhist art which represents the Universe; used in some forms of meditation.

Mandalay chief town of the Mandalay division of Myanmar (formerly Burma), on the river Irrawaddy, about 495 km/370 mi N of Rangoon; population (1983) 533,000.

mandarin the Chinese language, historically deriving from the language spoken by mandarins, Chinese imperial officials, from the 7th century onwards. The form of it spoken in Beijing has become the standard language of China, used by 70% of the population.

mandarin variety of the tangerine orange *Citrus reticulata*.

mandate in history, a territory whose administration was entrusted to Allied states by the League of Nations under the Treaty of Versailles after World War I. Mandated territories were former German and Turkish possessions (including Iraq, Syria, Lebanon, and Palestine). When the United Nations replaced the League of Nations in 1945,

Mandela *Nelson Mandela, deputy leader of the African National Congress.*

mandates that had not achieved independence became known as ◊trust territories.

Mandela Nelson (Rolihlahla) 1918– . South African politician and lawyer, president of the ◊African National Congress (ANC) from 1991. As organizer of the then banned ANC, he was jailed for life in 1964. In prison he became a symbol of unity for the anti-apartheid movement. Following the lifting of the ban on the ANC by President F W de Klerk, he was released Feb 1990 and after negotiations, reached agreement 1992 with President de Klerk

on hastening the creation of an interim government under which reforms could take place to bring about a multiracial South Africa. In 1993 they agreed to the formation of a government of national unity after free elections in late 1993 or early 1994.

Mandela Winnie (Nomzamo) 1934– . Civil rights activist in South Africa and former wife of Nelson Mandela 1955–92. A leading spokesperson for the African National Congress since her husband's imprisonment 1964–90, she has been jailed for a year and put under house arrest several times. She was jailed for six years 1991 for kidnapping and assault, after the abduction and murder in 1989 of a teenage boy. In 1992 she and Nelson Mandela separated, and she resigned from her ANC leadership posts.

Mandelshtam Osip Emilevich 1891–1938. Russian poet. Son of a Jewish merchant, he was sent to a concentration camp by the Communist authorities in the 1930s, where he died. His posthumously published work with its classic brevity established his reputation.

mandolin musical instrument with four or five pairs of strings, descended from the ◊lute, and so called because it has an almond-shaped body (Italian *mandorla* 'almond').

mandrill large W African ground-living monkey *Mandrillus sphinx*. The nose is bright red and the cheeks striped with blue. There are red callosities on the buttocks; the fur is brown, apart from a yellow beard. It has large canine teeth.

Manet Edouard 1832–1883. French painter, active in Paris. Rebelling against the academic tradition, he developed a clear and unaffected Realist style, becoming a leading spirit in the Impressionist movement. His subjects were chiefly modern, such as *Un bar aux Folies-Bergère/Bar at the Folies-Bergère* 1882.

manganese a silvery-white metallic element, symbol Mn, atomic number 25, relative atomic mass 54.9. Manganese is among the most common metals in the Earth's crust and is used to make steels and bronzes, brass, and nickel alloys.

Manet *Bar at the Folies-Bergère (1882) Courtauld Collection, London.*

mango tree *Mangifera indica*, native to India but now widely cultivated for its oval fruits in other tropical and subtropical areas.

mangrove shrub or tree found growing in the muddy swamps of tropical coasts and estuaries where, by sending down aerial roots from its branches, it rapidly forms close-growing mangrove swamps. Its timber is impervious to water and resists marine worms.

Manhattan an island 20 km/12.5 mi long and 4 km/2.5 mi wide lying between the Hudson and East rivers and forming a borough of the city of ◊New York, USA; population (1980) 1,428,000. It includes the Wall Street business centre, and Broadway theatres.

Manhattan Project code name for the development of the atom bomb in the USA in World War II, to which the scientists Fermi and Oppenheimer contributed.

manic depression a mental disorder characterized by recurring periods of ◊depression which may or may not alternate with periods of inappropriate elation (mania) or overactivity. Sufferers may be genetically predisposed to the condition.

Manichaeism religion founded by the prophet Mani (Latinized as Manichaeus, *c.* 216–276). Despite persecution Manichaeism spread and flourished until about the 10th century. It held that the material world is an invasion of the realm of light by the powers of darkness: particles of goodness imprisoned in matter were to be rescued by messengers such as Jesus, and finally by Mani himself.

Manifest Destiny in US history, a phrase coined by journalist John L O'Sullivan in 1845 articulating the belief that Americans had a providential mission to extend both their territory and their democratic processes westwards across the continent. Reflecting this belief, Texas and California were shortly afterwards annexed by the USA.

Manila industrial port (textiles, tobacco, distilling, chemicals, shipbuilding) and capital of the Philippines, on the island of Luzon; population (1990) 1,598,000.

manioc another name for the plant ◊cassava.

Manipur NE state of India
area 22,400 sq km/8,646 sq mi
capital Imphal
products grain, fruit, vegetables, sugar, textiles, cement
population (1991) 1,826,700
language Hindi
religion Hindu 70%
history administered from the state of Assam until 1947 when it became a Union Territory. It became a state 1972.

Man, Isle of island in the Irish Sea, a dependency of the British crown, but not part of the UK
area 570 sq km/220 sq mi
capital Douglas
towns Ramsey, Peel, Castletown
exports light engineering products
currency the island produces its own coins and notes in UK currency denominations
population (1986) 64,300
language English (Manx, nearer to Scottish than Irish Gaelic, has been almost extinct since the 1970s)
government crown-appointed lieutenant-governor, a legislative council, and the representative House of Keys, which together make up the Court of Tynwald, passing laws subject to the royal assent. Laws passed at Westminster

only affect the island if specifically so provided
history Norwegian until 1266, when the island was ceded to Scotland; it came under UK administration in 1765.

Manitoba W prairie province in Canada
area 650,000 sq km/250,900 sq mi
capital Winnipeg
exports grain, manufactured foods, and beverages; machinery; furs, fish, minerals (nickel, zinc, copper, and the world's largest caesium deposits)
population (1991) 1,092,600
history known as Red River settlement until it joined Canada 1870, it was the site of the Riel Rebellion 1885.

Manley Michael 1924– . Jamaican politician, prime minister 1972–80 and 1989–91. He resigned and left parliament because of ill health 1992 and was succeeded by P J Patterson. His father, *Norman Manley* (1893–1969), was founder of the People's National Party and prime minister 1969–62.

Mann Heinrich 1871–1950. German novelist, who fled to the USA with his brother Thomas Mann. His books include *Im Schlaraffenland/In the Land of Cockaigne* 1901, *Professor Unrat/The Blue Angel of Cockaigne* 1904, depicting the sensual downfall of a schoolmaster, and a scathing trilogy dealing with the Kaiser's Germany *Das Kaiserreich/The Empire* 1918–25.

Mann Thomas 1875–1955. German novelist and critic, concerned with the theme of the artist's relation to society. His first novel *Buddenbrooks* 1901 dealt with an old Hanseatic family in his native Lübeck, and *Der Zauberberg/The Magic Mountain* 1924 led to a Nobel Prize 1929. Later works include *Dr Faustus* 1947 and *Die Bekenntnisse des Hochstaplers Felix Krull/Confessions of Felix Krull* 1954. Notable among his short stories is *Der Tod in Venedig/Death in Venice* 1913.

manna a sweetish exudation obtained from many trees such as the ash and larch, and used in medicine. The manna of the Bible is thought to have been from the tamarisk tree.

Mannerheim Carl Gustav Emil von 1867–1951. Finnish general and politician. After the establishment of a Finnish socialist republic in 1917 he formed a White (counter-revolutionary) army, crushed the socialists with German assistance, and during 1918–19 acted as regent. He commanded the Finnish army 1939–40 and 1941–44, and as president of Finland 1944–46 negotiated the peace settlement with the USSR.

Mannerism in painting and architecture, a term coined by ◊Vasari and used to describe the 16th-century reaction to the peak of ◊Renaissance classicism as achieved by Raphael, Leonardo, and early Michelangelo. It is characterized by a subtle but conscious breaking of the 'rules' of classical composition, for example, displaying the human body in a distorted pose, off-centre, and using harsh, non-blending colours.

Mannheim Karl 1893–1947. Hungarian sociologist, who settled in the UK 1933. In *Ideology and Utopia* 1929 he argued that all knowledge, except in mathematics and physics, is ideological, a reflection of class interests and values; that there is no such thing as objective knowledge or absolute truth.

Manoel two kings of Portugal:

Manoel I 1469–1521. King of Portugal from 1495, when he succeeded his uncle John II (1455–95). He was known as 'the Fortunate', because his reign was distinguished by the discoveries made

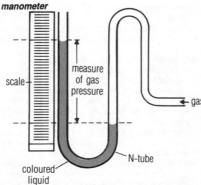

manometer

scale

measure of gas pressure

gas

N-tube

coloured liquid

by Portuguese navigators and the expansion of the Portuguese empire.

Manoel II 1889–1932. King of Portugal 1908–10. He ascended the throne on the assassination of his father, Carlos I, but was driven out by a revolution in 1910, and lived in England.

manometer instrument for measuring the pressure of liquids (including human blood pressure) or gases. In its basic form, it is a U-tube part-filled with coloured liquid; pressure of a gas entering at one side is measured by the level to which the liquid rises at the other.

Mansfield Katherine. Pen name of Kathleen Beauchamp 1888–1923. New Zealand writer, who lived most of her life in England. Her short stories include *In a German Pension* 1911, *Bliss* 1920 and *The Garden Party* 1923.

manslaughter in English law, the unlawful killing of a human being in circumstances not so culpable as ◊murder; for example, when the killer: suffers extreme provocation; is in some way mentally ill (diminished responsibility); did not intend to kill but did so accidentally in the course of another crime or by behaving with criminal recklessness; or is the survivor of a genuine suicide pact which involved killing the other person.

manta another name for the ◊devil ray.

Mantegna Andrea *c.* 1431–1506. Italian Renaissance painter and engraver, active chiefly in Padua and Mantua, where some of his frescoes remain. Paintings such as *The Agony in the Garden* 1455 reveal a dramatic linear style, mastery of perspective, and strongly Classical architectural detail.

mantis insect of the family Mantidae, related to cockroaches. There are about 2,000 species of mantis, some up to 20 cm/8 in long, mainly tropical.

mantle the layer of the Earth's structure between

Mantegna The Agony in the Garden *(c. 1455) National Gallery, London.*

the ◊crust and the ◊core. It is thought to consist of silicate rocks such as ◊olivine and ◊spinel. The mantle and the crust above it constitute the rigid plates of the ◊lithosphere.

mantra in Hindu or Buddhist belief, a word repeatedly intoned to assist concentration and develop spiritual power, for example *om*, which represents the names of Brahma, Vishnu, and Siva. Followers of a guru may receive their own individual mantra.

Manu in Hindu mythology, the founder of the human race, who was saved by ◊Brahma from a deluge.

Manx Gaelic see ◊Gaelic language.

Manzoni Alessandro, Count Manzoni 1785–1873. Italian poet and novelist, known for his historical romance, *I promessi sposi/The Betrothed* 1825–27. Verdi's *Requiem* commemorates him.

Maoism form of communism based on the ideas and teachings of the Chinese communist leader ◊Mao Zedong. It involves an adaptation of ◊Marxism to suit conditions in China and apportions a much greater role for agriculture and the peasantry in the building of socialism, thus effectively bypassing the capitalist (industrial) stage envisaged by Marx.

Maori member of a Polynesian people of New Zealand, who form about 10% of the population; (1981) 279,000. In recent years there has been increased Maori consciousness, and a demand for official status for the Maori language and review of the Waitangi Treaty of 1840 (under which the Maoris surrendered their lands to British sovereignty). The *Maori Unity Movement/Kotahitanga* was founded 1983 by Eva Rickard.

Maori language a member of the Polynesian branch of the Malayo-Polynesian language family, spoken by the Maori people of New Zealand. Only one-third use the language today, but efforts are being made to strengthen it after a long period of decline and official indifference.

Mao Zedong formerly *Mao Tse-tung* 1893–1976. Chinese political leader and marxist theoretician. A founder of the Chinese Communist Party (CCP) 1921, Mao soon emerged as its leader. He organized the ◊Long March 1934–36 and the war of liberation 1937–49, and headed the CCP and government until his death. His influence diminished with the failure of his 1958–60 ◊Great Leap Forward, but he emerged dominant again during the 1966–69 ◊Cultural Revolution.

map a diagrammatic representation of an area, for example part of the Earth's surface, or the distribution of the stars. Modern maps of the Earth are made using aerial photography; a series of overlapping stereoscopic photographs is taken which can then be used to prepare a three-dimensional image.

Mapai (Miphlegeth Poolei Israel) the Israeli Workers' Party or Labour Party, founded 1930. Its leading figure until 1965 was David Ben Gurion. In 1968, the party allied with two other democratic

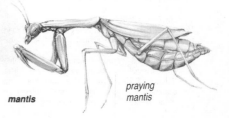

praying mantis

mantis

map

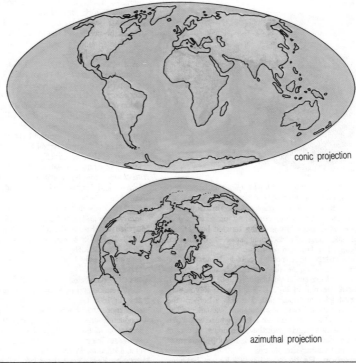

conic projection

azimuthal projection

cylindrical projection

Mao Zedong *Chairman Mao with vice chairman Lin Biao, who is holding the Little Red Book of Mao's thoughts.*

socialist parties to form the Israeli Labour Party, led initially by Levi Estikol and later Golda Meir.

maple deciduous tree of the genus *Acer* with lobed leaves and green flowers, followed by two-winged fruits, samaras. There are over 200 species, chiefly in north temperate regions.

Mappa Mundi a 13th-century map of the world, one of the best-known medieval world maps. It is circular, and shows Asia at the top, with Europe and Africa below, and Jerusalem at the centre. It was drawn by David de Bello, a canon at Hereford Cathedral, who left the map to the cathedral.

Maputo capital of Mozambique, and Africa's second largest port, on Delagoa Bay; population (1982) 786,000. Linked by rail with Zimbabwe and South

maple

Africa, it is a major outlet for minerals, steel, textiles, processed foods, and furniture.

maquis type of vegetation common in many Mediterranean countries, consisting of scrub woodland with many low-growing tangled bushes and shrubs, typically including species of broom, gorse, heather, and rockrose.

Maracaibo oil-exporting port in Venezuela, on the channel connecting Lake Maracaibo with the Gulf of Venezuela; population (1980) 929,000.

Marat Jean Paul 1743–1793. French Revolutionary leader and journalist. He was a hero of the Paris revolutionary crowds, and was elected in 1792 to the National Convention, where he carried on a long struggle with the ◊Girondins, ending in their overthrow in May 1793. In Jul he was murdered by Charlotte ◊Corday.

Marathon, Battle of 490 BC. Fought between the Greeks, who were ultimately victorious, and invading Persians on the plain of Marathon, 40 km/25 mi NE of Athens. Prior to the battle, news of the Persian destruction of the Greek city of Eretria was taken from Athens to Sparta by a courier, Pheidippides, who fell dead on arrival. His feat is commemorated by the *Marathon race*.

marathon athletics endurance race over 42.2 km/26 mi 385 yd. It was first included in the Olympic Games at Athens in 1896. The distance varied until it was standardized in 1924. More recently races have been opened to wider participation, including social runners as well as those competing at senior level, for example the London Marathon from 1981.

marble metamorphosed ◊limestone that takes and retains a good polish, and is used in building and sculpture. Mineral impurities give it various colours and patterns but in its pure form it is white, for example ◊Carrara marble.

Marble Arch triumphal arch in London designed by John ◊Nash to commemorate Nelson's victories. Intended as a ceremonial entry to Buckingham Palace, in 1851 it was moved to Hyde Park at the end of Oxford Street.

Marburg disease viral disease of central Africa, first occurring in Europe in 1967 among research workers in Germany working with African green monkeys, hence its common name **green monkey disease**. It is characterized by haemorrhage of the mucous membranes, fever, vomiting and diarrhoea; mortality is high.

Marc Franz 1880–1916. German Expressionist painter, associated with Kandinsky in founding the Blaue Reiter movement. Animals played an essential part in his view of the world and bold

semi-abstracts of red and blue horses feature in his major work, *Blue Horses* 1911.

Marceau Marcel 1923– . French mime artist. He is the creator of the clown-harlequin Bip, and of mime sequences such as 'Youth, Maturity, Old Age, and Death'.

Marchais Georges 1920– . Leader of the French Communist Party (PCF) from 1972. Under his leadership, the party committed itself to a 'transition to socialism' by democratic means and entered into a union of the left with the Socialist Party (PS). This was severed in 1977, and the PCF returned to a more orthodox pro-Moscow line.

Marche region of E central Italy consisting of the provinces of Ancona, Ascoli Piceno, Macerata, and Pesaro e Urbino; capital Ancona; area 9,692 sq km/3,742 sq mi; population (1981) 1,412,000.

marches the boundary areas of England with Wales, and England with Scotland. In the Middle Ages these troubled frontier regions were held by lords of the marches, sometimes called *marchiones* and later Earls of March.

Marciano Rocco Francis Marchegiano 'Rocky' 1923–1969. US boxer, world heavyweight champion 1952-56. He retired after 49 professional fights, the only heavyweight champion to retire undefeated.

Marconi Guglielmo 1874–1937. Italian pioneer in the invention and development of wireless telegraphy. In 1895 he achieved wireless communication over more than a mile, and in England in 1896 he conducted successful experiments that led to the formation of the company that became Marconi's Wireless Telegraph Company Ltd. He shared the Nobel Prize for Physics 1909.

Marcos Ferdinand 1919–1989. Filipino right-wing politician, president from 1965 until 1986, when he was forced into exile. He was backed by the USA when in power, but in 1988 US authorities indicted him for racketeering and embezzlement.

Marcus Aurelius Antoninus 121–180. Roman emperor and Stoic philosopher. Born in Rome, he was adopted, at the same time as Lucius Aurelius Verus, by his uncle, the emperor Antoninus Pius, whom he succeeded in 161. He conceded an equal share in the rule to Lucius Verus (died 169).

Mardi Gras (French 'fat Tuesday' from the custom of using up all the fat in the household before the beginning of ◊Lent) Shrove Tuesday. A festival

Marconi The Italian inventor Guglielmo Marconi.

was traditionally held on this day in Paris, and there are carnivals in many parts of the world, including Italy, New Orleans, and South America.

Marduk in Babylonian mythology, the sun-god, creator of Earth and man.

mare (plural *maria*) dark lowland plain on the Moon. The name comes from Latin, 'sea', because these areas were once wrongly thought to be areas of water.

Marengo, Battle of defeat of the Austrians by the French emperor Napoleon on 14 Jun 1800, as part of his Italian campaign, near the village of Marengo in Piedmont, Italy.

Margaret 1282–1290. Queen of Scotland from 1285, known as *the Maid of Norway*. Margaret was the daughter of Eric II, king of Norway, and Princess Margaret of Scotland. When only two years of age she became queen of Scotland on the death of her grandfather, Alexander III, but died in the Orkneys on a voyage to her kingdom.

Margaret of Anjou 1430–1482. Queen of England from 1445, wife of ◊Henry VI of England. After the outbreak of the Wars of the ◊Roses in 1455, she acted as the leader of the Lancastrians, but was defeated and captured at the battle of Tewkesbury 1471 by Edward IV.

Margaret (Rose) 1930–. Princess of the UK, younger daughter of George VI. In 1960 she married Anthony Armstrong-Jones, later created Lord Snowdon, but in 1976 they agreed to live apart, and were divorced in 1978. Their children are *David, Viscount Linley* (1961–) and *Lady Sarah Armstrong-Jones* (1964–).

Margaret, St 1045–1093. Queen of Scotland, the granddaughter of king Edmund Ironside of England. She went to Scotland after the Norman Conquest, and soon after married Malcolm III. The marriage of her daughter Matilda to Henry I united the Norman and English royal houses.

margarine a butter substitute, made from animal fats and vegetable oils. The French chemist Hippolyte Mège-Mouries invented margarine in 1889. Modern margarines are usually made with vegetable oils, such as sunflower oil, giving a product that is low in saturated fats.

margay small wild cat *Felis wiedi* found from S USA to South America in forested areas, where it hunts birds and small mammals. It is about 60 cm/2 ft long with a 40 cm/1.3 ft tail, has a rather rounded head, and black spots and blotches on a yellowish-brown coat.

marginal cost pricing in economics, the setting of a price based on the production cost plus the cost of producing another unit. In this way, the price of an item is kept to a minimum, reflecting only the extra cost of labour and materials.

marginal efficiency of capital in economics, effectively the rate of return on investment in a given business project compared with the rate of return if the capital were invested at prevailing interest rates.

marginal theory in economics, the study of the effect of increasing a factor by one more unit (known as the marginal unit). For example, if a firm's production is increased by one unit, its costs will increase also; the increase in costs is called the marginal cost of production. Marginal theory is a central tool of microeconomics.

marginal utility in economics, the measure of additional satisfaction (utility) gained by a consumer who receives one additional unit of a product or service. The concept is used to explain why consumers buy more of a product when the price falls.

margrave German title (equivalent of marquess) for the 'counts of the march', who guarded the frontier regions of the Holy Roman Empire from Charlemagne's time. Later the title was used by other territorial princes. The most important were the margraves of Austria and of Brandenburg.

Margrethe II 1940–. Queen of Denmark from 1972, when she succeeded her father Frederick IX. In 1967, she married the French diplomat Count Henri de Laborde de Monpezat, who took the title Prince Hendrik. Her heir is Crown Prince Frederick (1968–).

marguerite plant *Leucanthemum vulgare*, family Compositae. It is a shrubby perennial and bears white daisy-like flowers.

Marguerite of Navarre also known as *Margaret d'Angoulême* 1492–1549. Queen of Navarre from 1527, French poet, and author of the *Heptaméron* 1558, a collection of stories in imitation of Boccaccio's *Decameron*.

Mariana Islands or Marianas archipelago in the NW Pacific, divided politically into:
Guam unincorporated territory of the USA
area 535 sq km/206 sq mi
capital Agaña
towns port Apra
products sweet potatoes, fish; tourism is important
currency US dollar
population (1980) 106,000
language English, Chamorro (basically Malay-Polynesian)
religion Roman Catholic 96%
government popularly elected governor (Ricardo Bordallo from 1985) and single-chamber legislature
recent history Guam was ceded by Spain to the USA in 1898, and occupied by Japan 1941–44. Granted full US citizenship and self-government from 1950
Northern Marianas commonwealth in union with the USA of 16 mountainous islands, extending 560 km/350 mi N from Guam
area 479 sq km/185 sq mi
capital Garapan on Saipan
products sugar, coconuts, coffee
currency US dollar
population 16,780, mainly Micronesian
language Chamorro, English
religion mainly Roman Catholic
government own constitutional elected government
history sold to Germany by Spain in 1899. The islands were mandated to Japan in 1918, and taken by US Marines 1944–45 in World War II. They were under US trusteeship from 1947, and voted to become a commonwealth of the USA in 1978.

Mariana Trench the lowest region on the Earth's surface; the deepest part of the sea floor. The trench is 2,500 km/1,500 mi long and is situated 300 km/200 mi E of the Mariana Islands, in the NW Pacific Ocean. Its deepest part is the gorge known as the Challenger Deep, which extends 11,034 m/36,201 ft below sea level.

Maria Theresa 1717–1780. Empress of Austria from 1740, when she succeeded her father, the Holy Roman Emperor Charles VI; her claim to the throne was challenged and she became embroiled, first in the War of the ◊Austrian Succession 1740–48, then in the ◊Seven Years' War of 1756–63; she remained in possession of Austria but lost Silesia. The rest of her reign was peaceful and, with her son Joseph II, she introduced social reforms.

Marie 1875–1938. Queen of Romania. She was the daughter of the Duke of Edinburgh, second son of Queen ◊Victoria, and married Prince Ferdinand of Romania in 1893, who was king 1922–27. She wrote a number of literary works, notably *Story of My Life* 1934–35. Her son Carol became king of Romania, and her daughters, Elisabeth and Marie, queens of Greece and Yugoslavia respectively.

Marie Antoinette 1755–1793. Queen of France from 1774. She was the daughter of Empress Maria Theresa of Austria, and married ◊Louis XVI of France in 1770. With a reputation for frivolity and extravagance, she meddled in politics in the Austrian interest, and helped provoke the ◊French Revolution of 1789. She was tried for treason in Oct 1793 and guillotined.

Marie de France *c.* 1150–1215. French poet, thought to have been the half-sister of Henry II of England, and abbess of Shaftesbury 1181–1215. She wrote *Lais* (verse tales which dealt with Celtic and Arthurian themes) and *Ysopet*, a collection of fables.

Marie de' Medici 1573–1642. Queen of France, wife of Henry IV from 1600, and regent (after his murder) for their son Louis XIII. She left the government to her favourites, the Concinis, until in 1617 Louis XIII seized power and executed them. She was banished, but after she led a revolt in 1619, ◊Richelieu effected her reconciliation with her son, but when she attempted to oust him in 1630, she was exiled.

Marie Louise 1791–1847. Queen consort of Napoleon I from 1810 (after his divorce from Josephine), mother of Napoleon II. She was the daughter of Francis I of Austria (see Emperor ◊Francis II), and on Napoleon's fall returned to Austria.

Mariette Auguste Ferdinand François 1821–1881. French egyptologist, whose discoveries from 1850 included the 'temple' between the paws of the Sphinx. He founded the Egyptian Museum in Cairo.

marigold name for several members of the family Compositae, including *pot marigold Calendula officinalis*, and the tropical American *Tagetes patula*, commonly known as *French marigold*.

marijuana popular name for the dried leaves and flowers of the hemp plant ◊cannabis, used as a drug.

Mariner spacecraft series of US space probes that explored the planets Mercury, Venus, and Mars 1962–75.

marines a fighting force which operates both on land and at sea. The British *Corps of Royal Marines* (1664) is primarily a military force also trained for fighting at sea, and providing commando units, landing craft, crews, and frogmen. The *US Marine Corps* (1775) is primarily a naval force trained for fighting on land.

Marinetti Filippo Tommaso 1876–1944. Italian author, who in 1909 published the first manifesto of ◊Futurism, which called for a break with tradition in art, poetry, and the novel, and glorified the machine age.

Marini Marino 1901–1980. Italian sculptor. Influenced by ancient art, he developed a distinctive horse-and-rider theme and a dancers series, reducing the forms to an elemental simplicity. He also produced fine portraits in bronze.

marionette type of ◊puppet, a jointed figure controlled from above by wires or strings. Intricately crafted marionettes were used in Burma

and Ceylon, and later at the courts of Italian princes in the 16th–18th centuries. Haydn wrote an operetta *Dido* 1778 for the Esterhazy Marionette theatre. In the 20th century marionettes have enjoyed a revival, chiefly as television entertainment.

Maritime Law that part of the law dealing with the sea: in particular fishing areas, ships, and navigation. Seas are divided into: internal waters governed by a state's internal laws (such as harbours, inlets); ◊territorial waters (the area of sea adjoining the coast over which a state claims rights); the continental shelf (the sea bed and subsoil which the coastal state is entitled to exploit beyond the territorial waters); and the high seas, where international law applies.

Marius Gaius 155–86 BC. Roman military commander and politician. He was elected consul seven times, the first time in 107 BC. He defeated the Cimbri and the Teutons (Germanic tribes attacking Gaul and Italy) 102–101 BC. Marius tried to deprive Sulla of the command in the East against Mithridates, and as a result civil war broke out in 88 BC. Sulla marched on Rome, and Marius fled to Africa, but later Cinna held Rome for Marius, and together they created a reign of terror in Rome.

Marivaux Pierre Carlet de Chamblain de 1688–1763. French novelist and dramatist. His polished, sophisticated comedies include *Le Jeu de l'amour et du hasard/The Game of Love and Chance* 1730 and *Les Fausses confidences/False Confidences* 1737.

marjoram aromatic herb of the Labiatae family. Wild marjoram *Origanum vulgare* is found both in Europe and Asia and has become naturalized in the Americas; the culinary sweet marjoram is *Origanum majorana*.

Mark Antony 83–30 BC. Roman politician and soldier. He was tribune and later consul under Caesar. After Caesar's assassination he formed the Second Triumvirate with Octavius and Lepidus, and in 42 BC defeated Brutus and Cassius at Philippi. He took Egypt as his share of the empire, and formed a liaison with Cleopatra. He was defeated by Octavius at the battle of Actium in 31 BC.

marketing promoting goods and services to consumers. Marketing has in the 20th century become an increasingly important determinant of company policy, influencing product development, pricing, methods of distribution, advertising, and promotion techniques. Marketing skills are increasingly taught in schools and colleges.

market maker a stockbroker in the UK entitled to deal directly on the stock exchange. The role was created in Oct 1986, when the jobber (intermediary) disappeared from the stock exchange. Market makers trade in the dual capacity of broker and jobber.

markhor large wild goat *Capra falconeri*, with spirally twisted horns and long shaggy coat. It is found in the Himalayas.

Markievicz Constance Georgina, Countess Markievicz (born Gore Booth) 1868–1927. Irish nationalist, who married the Polish count Markievicz in 1900. Her death sentence for taking part in the Easter Rising of 1916 was commuted, and after her release from prison in 1917 she was elected to the Westminster Parliament as a Sinn Féin candidate in 1918 (technically the first British woman member of parliament), but did not take her seat.

Markova Alicia, stage name of Lilian Alicia Marks 1910– . British ballet dancer. Trained by ◊Pavlova, she was ballerina with ◊Diaghilev's company 1925–29, the Vic-Wells Ballet 1933–35,

Marley Reggae musician Bob Marley.

partnered Anton ◊Dolin in their own Markova-Dolin Company 1935–37, and danced with the Ballet Russe de Monte Carlo 1938–41 and Ballet Theatre, USA, 1941–46.

Marks Simon, 1st Baron of Broughton 1888–1964. British chain-store magnate. His father, Polish immigrant Michael Marks, had started a number of 'penny bazaars' with Yorkshireman Tom Spencer in 1887; Simon Marks entered the business in 1907 and built up an international chain of Marks and Spencer stores.

Mark, St 1st century AD. In the New Testament, Christian apostle and evangelist, whose name is given to the second Gospel. It was probably written 65–70 AD, and used by the authors of the first and third Gospels. He is the patron saint of Venice, and his emblem is a winged lion; feast day 25 Apr.

Marlborough John Churchill, 1st Duke of Marlborough 1650–1722. English soldier, created a duke 1702 by Queen Anne. In the War of the ◊Spanish Succession he defeated the French outside Vienna in the Battle of ◊Blenheim 1704, and achieved victories in Belgium at ◊Ramillies 1706 and ◊Oudenaarde 1708, and in France at ◊Malplaquet 1709. He was granted the Blenheim mansion in Oxfordshire in recognition of his services.

Marley Bob (Robert Nesta) 1945–1980. Jamaican reggae singer, a Rastafarian whose songs, many of which were topical and political, popularized reggae in the UK and the USA in the 1970s. One of his best-known songs is 'No Woman No Cry'; his albums include *Natty Dread* 1975 and *Exodus* 1977.

marlin or *spearfish* several genera of fish, family Istiophoridae, order Perciformes. Some 2.5 m/7 ft long, they are found in warmer waters, have elongated snouts, and high-standing dorsal fins.

Marlowe Christopher 1564–1593. English poet-dramatist. His work includes the blank-verse plays *Tamburlaine the Great* about 1587, *The Jew of Malta* about 1589, *Edward II* and *Dr Faustus*, both about 1592, the poem *Hero and Leander* 1598, and a translation of Ovid's *Amores*.

Marmara small inland sea separating Turkey in Europe from Turkey in Asia, connected through the Bosporus with the Black Sea, and through the Dardanelles with the Aegean; length 275 km/170 mi, breadth up to 80 km/50 mi.

Marmontel Jean François 1723–1799. French novelist and dramatist. He wrote tragedies and libretti,

and contributed to the *Encyclopédie* (see ◊encyclopedia); in 1758 he obtained control of the journal *Le Mercure/The Mercury*, in which his *Contes moraux/Moral Studies* 1761 appeared. Other works include *Bélisaire/Belisarius* 1767, and *Les Incas/The Incas* 1777.

marmoset small tree-dwelling monkey in the family Hapalidae found in South and Central America. Most species have characteristic tufted ears, and bear-like claws. The tail is not prehensile.

marmot large burrowing rodent of the genus *Marmota* which eats plants and insects. They are found from the Alps to the Himalayas, and also in North America. Marmots live in colonies, make burrows, one to each family, and hibernate. In North America they are called woodchucks or groundhogs.

Marne, Battles of the in World War I, two unsuccessful German offensives: *First Battle* 6–9 Sept 1914, von Moltke's advance was halted by the British Expeditionary Force and the French under Foch; *Second Battle* 15 Jul–4 Aug 1918, Ludendorff's advance was defeated by British, French, and US troops under Pétain, and German morale crumbled.

Maronite member of a Christian sect deriving from refugee Monothelites (Christian heretics) of the 7th century. They were subsequently united with the Roman Catholic Church, and number about 400,000 in Lebanon and Syria, with an equal number scattered overseas in S Europe and the Americas.

Maroon freed or escaped African slave, organized and armed by the Spanish. They were in Jamaica in the late 17th century and early 18th century. They harried the British with guerrilla tactics.

marquess or *marquis* title and rank of a nobleman who in the British peerage ranks below a duke and above an earl. The first English marquess was created in 1385, but the lords of the Scottish and Welsh 'marches' were known as *marchiones* before this date. The wife of a marquess is a marchioness.

marquetry the inlaying of different types of wood, usually on furniture, to create ornate patterns and pictures. Parquetry is the term used for geometrical inlaid patterns. The method is thought to have originated in Germany or Holland. Inlays can be of other materials, such as bone and ivory.

Marquette Jacques 1637–1675. French Jesuit missionary and explorer. He went to Canada in 1666, explored the upper lakes of the St Lawrence, and in 1673 made a voyage down the Mississippi.

Márquez Gabriel García see ◊García Márquez.

Marrakesh town in Morocco in the foothills of the Atlas mountains, about 210 km/130 mi S of Casablanca. It is a tourist centre, and has textile, leather, and food processing industries; population (1982) 482,500.

marram grass coarse perennial grass *Ammophila arenaria*, flourishing on sandy areas. Because of its tough, creeping rootstocks, it is widely used to hold coastal dunes in place, particularly in Holland.

Marrano one of the Spanish and Portuguese Jews converted by force to Christianity in the 14th and 15th centuries, many of whom secretly preserved their adherence to Judaism and carried out Jewish rites. Under the Spanish Inquisition thousands were burned at the stake.

marriage the legally or culturally sanctioned union of one man and one woman (monogamy); one man and two or more women (polygamy); one woman and two or more men (polyandry). The basis of marriage varies considerably in different societies (romantic love in the West; arranged marriages in some other societies), but most marriage ceremonies, contracts, or customs involve a set of rights and duties such as care and protection, and there is generally an expectation that children will be born of the union to continue the family line.

marrow trailing vine *Cucurbita pepo*, family Cucurbitaceae, producing large pulpy fruits, used as vegetables and in preserves; the young fruits of one variety are known as courgettes (USA zuchini).

Mars in Roman mythology, the god of war, after whom the month of March is named. He is equivalent to the Greek Ares.

Mars the fourth planet from the Sun, average distance 227,800,000 km/141,500,000 mi. It revolves around the Sun in 687 Earth days, and has a rotation period of 24 hr 37 min. It is much smaller than Venus or Earth, with diameter 6,780 km/4,210 mi, and mass 0.11 that of Earth. Mars is slightly pear-shaped, with a low, level northern hemisphere, comparatively uncratered and geologically 'young', and a heavily cratered 'ancient' southern hemisphere.

Marseillaise, La French national anthem; the words and music were composed in 1792 by the army officer Rouget de Lisle.

Marseille the chief seaport of France, industrial centre (chemicals, oil refining, metallurgy, shipbuilding, food processing), and capital of the *département* of Bouches-du-Rhône, on the Golfe du Lion, Mediterranea Sea; population (1990) 807,700.

Marsh Ngaio 1899–1982. New Zealand writer of detective fiction. Her first detective novel *A Man Lay Dead* 1934, in which she introduced her most famous character, Chief Inspector Roderick Alleyn, had many sequels.

marshal a title given in some countries to a high officer of state. The ◊Earl Marshal in England organizes state ceremonies; the office is hereditarily held by the Duke of Norfolk. The corresponding officer in Scotland was the Earl Marischal.

Marshal in the British Royal Air Force, a military rank corresponding to that of Admiral of the Fleet in the navy and Field Marshal in the army. In the French Army the highest officers bear the designation of Marshal of France.

Marshall George Catlett 1880–1959. US general and diplomat. He was army chief of staff in World War II, secretary of state 1947–49, and secretary of defence Sept 1950–Sept 1951. He initiated the ◊Marshall Plan 1947 and received the Nobel Peace prize 1953.

Marshall John 1755–1835. American jurist. As chief justice of the Supreme Court 1801–35, he established the power and independence of the Supreme Court. He laid down interpretations of the US constitution in a series of important decisions which have since become universally accepted.

Marshall John Ross 1912–1988. New Zealand National Party politician, noted for his negotiations of a free-trade agreement with Australia. He was deputy to K J Holyoake as prime minister and succeeded him Feb–Nov 1972.

Marshall William, 1st Earl of Pembroke *c.* 1146–1219. English knight, regent of England from 1216. After supporting the dying Henry II against Richard (later Richard I), he went on a crusade to Palestine, was pardoned by Richard, and was granted an earldom in 1189. On King John's death he was appointed guardian of the future Henry III, and

marsh marigold

defeated the French under Louis VIII to enable Henry to gain the throne.

Marshall Islands the Radak (13 islands) and Ralik (11 islands) chains in the W Pacific
area 180 sq km/70 sq mi
capital Majuro
products copra, phosphates, fish, tourism
population (1988) 41,000
government internally self-governing, with elected governments
recent history German 1906–19; administered by Japan until 1946 passed to the USA as part of the Pacific Islands Trust Territory in 1947. They were used for many atomic bomb tests 1946–63, and the islanders are demanding compensation.

Marshall Plan a programme of US financial aid to Europe, set up at the end of World War II, totalling $12,000 million 1948–52. Officially known as the European Recovery Programme, it was initiated by George ◊Marshall in a speech at Harvard in Jun 1947, but was in fact the work of a State Department group led by Dean ◊Acheson.

marsh gas a form of the gas ◊methane. It is produced in swamps and marshes by the action of bacteria.

marsh marigold plant *Caltha palustris* of the buttercup family Ranunculaceae, known as the king-cup in the UK and as the cowslip in the USA. It grows in moist sheltered spots, and has five-sepalled flowers of a brilliant yellow.

Marston Moor, Battle of battle fought in the English Civil War on 2 Jul 1644 on Marston Moor, 11 km/7 mi W of York. The royalists, under Prince Rupert and the Duke of Newcastle, were completely defeated by the Parliamentarians and Scots, under Cromwell and Lord Leven.

marsupial (Greek *marsupion*, little purse or bag) mammal in which the female has a pouch in which she carries her young for some considerable time after birth. Marsupials include the kangaroo, wombat, opossum, Tasmanian wolf, bandicoot, and wallaby.

marten small carnivorous mammal belonging to the weasel family Mustelidae, genus *Martes*. Martens live in North America, Europe, and Asia. The pinemarten *Martes martes* has long, brown fur, and is about 75 cm/2.5 ft long. It is found in Britain.

Martens Wilfried 1936– . Prime minister of Belgium 1979–92, member of Social Christian Party. He was president of the Dutch-speaking CVP 1972–79 and, as prime minister, headed six coalition governments in the period 1979–92, when he was replaced by Jean-Luc Dehaene.

Martial (Marcus Valerius Martialis) 41–104. Latin epigrammatist. His poetry, often bawdy, reflects contemporary Roman life, and is renowned for correctness of diction, versification, and form.

martial arts styles of armed and unarmed combat developed in the East from ancient techniques and arts. Common martial arts include aikido, judo, ju-jitsu, karate, kendo, and kung fu.

martial law the replacement of civilian by military authorities in the maintenance of order.

martin name of several genera of birds, related to the swallow, in the family Hirundinidae. The European house martin *Delichon urbica*, a summer migrant from Africa, is blue-black above and white below, distinguished from the swallow by its shorter, less forked tail.

Martin Richard 1754–1834. Irish landowner and lawyer known as 'Humanity Martin'. He founded the British Royal Society for the Prevention of Cruelty to Animals 1824.

Martin V 1368–1431. Pope from 1417. A member of the Roman family of Colonna, he was elected during the Council of Constance, and ended the Great Schism between the rival popes of Rome and Avignon.

Martineau Harriet 1802–1876. British moralist, journalist, economist, and novelist, who wrote popular works on economics, children's stories, and articles in favour of the abolition of slavery.

Martinet Jean died 1672. French inspector-general of infantry under Louis XIV, whose constant drilling brought the army to a high degree of efficiency – hence the use of his name to mean a strict disciplinarian.

Martínez Ruiz José. Real name of ◊Azorín, Spanish author.

Martini Simone *c.* 1284–1344. Italian painter, one of the great masters of the Sienese school. His patrons included the city of Siena, the king of Naples, and the pope. Two of his frescoes are in the Palazzo Pubblico in Siena.

Martinique French island in the West Indies (Lesser Antilles)
area 1,079 sq km/417 sq mi
capital Fort-de-France
products sugar, cocoa, rum, bananas, pineapples
population (1984) 327,000
history Martinique was reached by Spanish navigators in 1493, and became a French colony in 1635; since 1972 it has been a French overseas region.

Martinmas in the Christian calendar, the feast of St Martin, 11 Nov. Fairs were frequently held on this day, at which farmworkers were hired. In the Middle Ages it was also the day on which cattle were slaughtered and salted for winter consumption.

Martin, St 316–400. Bishop of Tours, France, from about 371, and founder of the first monastery in Gaul. He is usually represented as tearing his cloak to share it with a beggar.

MartinuBohuslav (Jan) 1890–1959. Czech composer, who studied in Paris. Works include the operas *Julietta* 1937 and *The Greek Passion* 1959, symphonies, and chamber music.

martyr one who voluntarily suffers death for refusing to renounce their faith. The first recorded Christian martyr was St Stephen, who was killed in Jerusalem shortly after Christ's alleged ascension.

Marvell Andrew 1621–1678. English metaphysical poet and satirist. His poems include 'To His Coy Mistress' and 'Horatian Ode upon Cromwell's Return from Ireland'. He was committed to the Parliamentary cause, and was member of parliament for Hull from 1659.

Marx Karl Heinrich 1818–1883. German philosopher, economist, and revolutionary social theorist. His three-volume *Das Kapital/Capital*

1867–94 is the fundamental text in Marxist economics.

Marx Brothers US film comedians *Leonard 'Chico'* (from the 'chicks' (girls) he chased) 1891–1961; *Arthur 'Harpo'* (from the harp he played) 1893–1964; *Julius 'Groucho'* 1890–1977; *Milton 'Gummo'* (from his gumshoes or galoshes) 1894–1977, who left the team early on, and *Herbert 'Zeppo'* (born at the time of the first zeppelins) 1901–79, part of the team until 1934. Their films include *Animal Crackers* 1932, *Duck Soup* 1933, *A Night at the Opera* 1935, and *Go West* 1937.

Marxism philosophical system, developed by the 19th-century German social theorists ◊Marx and ◊Engels, also known as *dialectical materialism*, under which matter gives rise to mind (materialism) and all is subject to change (from dialectic; see ◊Hegel). As applied to history, it supposes that the succession of feudalism, capitalism, socialism (called 'modes of production') is inevitable. The stubborn resistance of any existing system to change necessitates its complete overthrow in the *class struggle* – in the case of capitalism, by the proletariat – rather than gradual modification.

Mary in the New Testament, the mother of Jesus through divine intervention (see ◊Annunciation), wife of ◊Joseph. The Roman Catholic Church maintains belief in her ◊Immaculate Conception and bodily assumption into heaven, and venerates her as a mediator. Feast day 15 Aug.

Mary *Queen of Scots* 1542–1587. Queen of Scotland 1542–67. Also known as *Mary Stuart*, she was the daughter of James V. She was married three times: to Francis II of France 1558–60; to her cousin, the Earl of Darnley, 1565–67; and 1567–71 to the Earl of Bothwell, who was thought to have been Darnley's murderer. After her forced abdication she was imprisoned but escaped 1568 to England. Elizabeth I held her prisoner, while the Roman Catholics, who regarded Mary as rightful queen of England, formed many conspiracies to place her on the throne, and for complicity in one of these she was executed.

Mary Duchess of Burgundy 1457–1482. The daughter of Charles the Bold, she married Maximilian of Austria in 1477, thus bringing the Low Countries into the possession of the Hapsburgs and, ultimately, of Spain.

Mary Queen 1867–1953. Consort of George V of the UK. She was the daughter of the Duke and Duchess of Teck, the latter a granddaughter of George II.

Mary Portrait of Mary, Queen of Scots, after Nicholas Hilliard (c. 1610) National Portrait Gallery, London.

Mary two queens of England:

Mary I 1516–1558. Queen of England from 1553. She was born at Greenwich, the daughter of Henry VIII by Catherine of Aragon. When Edward VI died, she secured the crown without difficulty in spite of the conspiracy to substitute Lady Jane ◊Grey. In 1554 she married Philip II of Spain, and as a devout Catholic obtained the restoration of papal supremacy.

Mary II 1662–1694. Queen of England, Scotland, and Ireland from 1688. She was the elder daughter of ◊James II, and in 1677 was married to her cousin, ◊William III of Orange. After the 1688 revolution she accepted the crown jointly with William.

Maryland state of the E USA; nickname Old Line State or Free State
area 27,394 sq km/10,574 sq mi
capital Annapolis
towns Baltimore
products fruit, cereals, tobacco; fish and oysters
population (1984) 4,349,000
famous people Francis Scott Key, Stephen Decatur, H L Mencken, Upton Sinclair
history one of the original ◊Thirteen Colonies, first settled in 1634; it became a state in 1788.

Mary Magdalene, St woman who according to the New Testament was present at the Crucifixion and was the first to meet the risen Jesus. She is often identified with the woman of St Luke's gospel who anointed Christ's feet, and her symbol is a jar of ointment; feast day 22 Jul.

Mary of Modena 1658–1718. Queen consort of England and Scotland. She was the daughter of the Duke of Modena, Italy, and married James, Duke of York, later James II, in 1673. The birth of their son, James Francis Edward Stuart, popularly thought to have arrived in a warming pan, was the signal for the revolution of 1688 which overthrew James II. Mary of Modena fled to France.

Mary Rose greatest warship of Henry VIII of England, which sank off Southsea, Hampshire, on 19 Jul 1545. The wreck was located in 1971, and raised in 1982 for preservation in dry dock in Portsmouth harbour.

Masaccio (Tomaso di Giovanni di Simone Guidi) 1401–1428. Florentine painter, a leader of the early Italian Renaissance. His work on the frescoes in Santa Maria del Carmine, Florence, 1425–28, which he painted with Masolino da Panicale (c. 1384–1447), shows a decisive break with Gothic conventions. He was the first painter to apply the scientific laws of perspective, newly discovered by the architect Brunelleschi.

Masada rock fortress 396 m/1,300 ft above the west shore of the Dead Sea, Israel. When besieged by the Romans 72 AD, its population of 953 committed mass suicide. The site was excavated 1963–65, including the palace of Herod.

Masai member of an African people, whose territory is divided between Tanzania and Kenya. They were originally warriors and nomadic breeders of humped zebu cattle, but are now gradually adopting a more settled life. They speak a Nilotic language.

Masaryk Jan (Garrigue) 1886–1948. Czech politician, son of Tomáš Masaryk. He was foreign minister from 1940, when the Czech government was exiled in London in World War II. He returned in 1945, retaining the post, but as a result of communist political pressure committed suicide.

Masaryk Tomáš (Garrigue) 1850–1937. Czech nationalist politician. He directed the Czech revolutionary movement against the Austrian Empire, founding with Beneš and Stefanik the Czechoslovak National Council, and in 1918 was elected first president of the newly formed Czechoslovak Republic. Three times re-elected, he resigned in 1935 in favour of Beneš.

Mascagni Pietro 1863–1945. Italian composer of the one-act opera *Cavalleria rusticana/Rustic Chivalry*, first produced in Rome in 1890.

Masefield John 1878–1967. British poet and novelist. His works include novels (*Sard Harker* 1924),

Masaccio The Virgin and Child *(from the Pisa polyptych, 1426) National Gallery, London.*

Masaryk Tomáš Garrigue Masaryk, the first president *of Czechoslovakia.*

critical works (*Badon Parchments* 1947), and children's books (*The Box of Delights* 1935), and plays. He was Poet Laureate 1930–68.

maser acronym for **M**icrowave **A**mplification by **S**timulated **E**mission of **R**adiation. In physics, it is a high-frequency microwave amplifier or oscillator. The signal to be amplified is used to stimulate unstable atoms into emitting energy at the same frequency. The principle has been extended to other parts of the electromagnetic spectrum, as for example in the ◊laser.

Maseru capital of Lesotho, South Africa, on the Caledon river; population (1986) 289,000. It is a centre for trade and diamond processing.

Mashraq (Arabic 'east') the Arab countries of the E Mediterranean: Egypt, Sudan, Jordan, Syria, and Lebanon. The term is contrasted with ◊Maghreb, Arab countries of NW Africa.

Maskelyne Nevil 1732–1811. English astronomer, who accurately measured the distance from the Earth to the Sun by observing a transit of Venus across the Sun's face 1769. In 1774, he measured the density of the Earth from the deflection of a plumbline near a large mountain.

masochism a desire to subject oneself to physical or mental pain, humiliation, or punishment, for erotic pleasure, to alleviate guilt, or out of destructive impulses turned inwards. The term is derived from Leopold von ◊Sacher-Masoch.

Mason-Dixon Line in the USA, the boundary line between Maryland and Pennsylvania (latitude 39° 43′ 26.3′N), named after Charles Mason (1730–87) and Jeremiah Dixon (died 1777), English astronomers and surveyors who surveyed it 1763–67. It was popularly seen as dividing the North from the South.

masque a spectacular and essentially aristocratic 'entertainment' with a fantastic or mythological theme in which music, dance, and extravagant costumes and scenic design were more important than plot. Originating in Italy, it reached its height of popularity at the English court between 1600 and 1640, with the collaboration of Ben ◊Jonson as writer and Inigo ◊Jones as stage designer.

mass in physics, the quantity of matter in a body. Mass determines the acceleration produced in a body by a given force acting on it, the acceleration being inversely proportional to the mass of the body. The mass also determines the force exerted on a body by ◊gravity on Earth, although this attraction varies slightly from place to place. In the SI system, the base unit of mass is the kilogram.

Mass in Christianity, the celebration of the ◊Eucharist.

Mass in music, the setting of the invariable parts of the Christian Mass, that is *Kyrie, Gloria, Credo, Sanctus* with *Benedictus*, and *Agnus Dei*. A notable example is Bach's *Mass in B Minor*.

Massachusetts New England state of the USA; nickname Bay State or Old Colony
area 21,385 sq km/8,257 sq mi
capital Boston
towns Worcester, Springfield, Nantucket
products mainly industrial, especially electronic and communications equipment, shoes, textiles, machine tools; building stone; cod
population (1984) 5,741,000
famous people Samuel Adams, Louisa May Alcott, Emily Dickinson, Emerson, Hawthorne, Poe, Revere, Thoreau, Whistler
history one of the original ◊Thirteen Colonies, it was first settled in 1620 by the Pilgrims at Plymouth, and became a state 1788.

Masséna André 1756–1817. Marshal of France. He served in the French Revolutionary Wars, and under the emperor Napoleon was created a marshal of France in 1804, duke of Rivoli in 1808, and prince of Essling in 1809. He was in command in Spain 1810–11 in the Peninsular War, and was defeated by British troops under Wellington.

mass-energy equation ◊Einstein's equation $E = mc^2$, denoting the equivalence of mass and energy, where E is the energy in joules, m is the mass in kilograms, and c is the speed of light, in vacuum, in metres per second.

Massenet Jules Emile Frédéric 1842–1912. French composer. His many operas include *Hérodiade* 1881, *Manon* 1884, *Le Cid* 1885, and *Thaïs* 1894. He also composed ballets, oratorios, and orchestral suites, including *Scènes pittoresques* 1874.

Massey Vincent 1887–1967. A Liberal, he was the first Canadian to become governor general of Canada (1952–59). He helped to establish the Massey Foundation 1918 which funded the building of Massey College and the University of Toronto.

Massif Central mountainous plateau region of S central France; area 93,000 sq km/36,000 sq mi, highest peak Puy de Sancy 1,886 m/6,188 ft. It is a source of hydroelectricity and includes the ◊Auvergne and ◊Cevennes.

Massine Léonide 1895–1979. Russian choreographer and dancer. He was a creator of comedy in ballet, and also symphonic ballet using concert music. He succeeded ◊Fokine at the Ballets Russes and continued with the company after ◊Diaghilev's death, later working in both America and Europe. His works include the first Cubist-inspired ballet *Parade* 1917, *La Boutique Fantastique* 1919, and *The Three Cornered Hat* 1919.

Massorah a collection of philological notes on the Hebrew text of the Old Testament. It was at first an oral tradition, but was committed to writing in the Aramaic language at Tiberias, Palestine, between the 6th and 9th centuries.

mass production the manufacture of goods on a large scale, a technique that aims for low unit cost and high sales. In modern factories mass production is achieved by a variety of means, such as the division and specialization of labour, and ◊mechanization. This speeds up production and allows the manufacture of near-identical, or interchangeable parts. Such parts can then be assembled quickly into a finished product on an ◊assembly line.

mass spectrometer in physics, an apparatus for analysing chemical composition. Positive ions (charged particles) of a substance are separated by an electromagnetic system, which permits accurate measurement of the relative concentrations of the various ionic masses present, particularly isotopes.

Master of the King's/Queen's Musick appointment to the British royal household, the holder composing appropriate music for state occasions. The first was Nicholas Lanier, appointed by Charles I in 1626; the composer Malcolm ◊Williamson was appointed in 1975.

Master of the Rolls title of an English judge ranking immediately below the Lord Chief Justice. He presides over the Court of Appeal, besides being responsible for ◊Chancery records and for the admission of solicitors.

mastiff British dog, usually fawn in colour, originally bred for sporting purposes. It can grow up to 90 cm/3 ft at the shoulder, and weighs about 100 kg/220 lb.

mastodon primitive elephant, whose fossil remains have been discovered in all the continents

Matterhorn *The Matterhorn, first climbed by the British mountaineer Edward Whymper in 1865.*

except Australia, particularly in deposits from the Pleistocene Age in the USA and Canada. It resembled the modern elephant, but was lower and longer; its teeth suggest that it ate leaves in the primeval swamps and forests.

Mastroianni Marcello 1924– . Italian film actor, famous for his carefully understated roles as an unhappy romantic lover in such films as *La Dolce Vita* 1959 and *La Notte/The Night 1961.*

Mata Hari ('Eye of the Day'), stage name of Gertrud Margarete Zelle 1876–1917. Dutch courtesan, dancer, and probable spy. In World War I she appears to have been a double agent, in the pay of both France and Germany. She was shot by the French on espionage charges.

matamata South American freshwater turtle or terrapin *Chelys fimbriata* with a shell up to 40 cm/15 in long. The head is flattened, with a 'snorkel' nose, and the neck has many projections of skin.

match a small strip of wood or paper, tipped with combustible material for producing fire. Friction matches containing phosphorus were first made by John Walker of Stockton-on-Tees, about 1826.

maté dried leaves of the Brazilian holly *Ilex paraguensis*, an evergreen shrub akin to the common holly, that grows in Paraguay and Brazil. The roasted powdered leaves are made into a tea.

materialism the philosophical theory that there is nothing in existence over and above matter and matter in motion. Such a theory excludes the possibility of deities. It also sees mind as an attribute of the physical, denying idealist theories which see mind as something independent of body, for example Descartes' theory of 'thinking substance'.

mathematical induction a formal method of proof in which the proposition $P(n + 1)$ is proved true on the hypothesis that the proposition $P(n)$ is true. The proposition is then shown to be true for a particular value of n, say k, and therefore by induction the proposition must be true for $n = k + 1$, $k + 2$, $k + 3$, ... In many cases $k = 1$, so the proposition is true for all positive integers.

mathematics the science of spatial and numerical relationships. The main divisions of *pure mathematics* include geometry, arithmetic, algebra, calculus, and trigonometry. Mechanics, statistics, numerical analysis, computing, the mathematical theories of astronomy, electricity, optics, thermodynamics, and atomic studies come under the heading of *applied mathematics.*

Mather Cotton 1663–1728. American theologian and writer. He was a Puritan minister in Boston, and a man of great learning, writing over 400 works of theology, history, science, and annals. Mather appears to have supported the Salem witch-hunts.

Matilda 1102–1167. Queen of England 1141–53. Recognized during the reign of her father ◊Henry I as his heir, she married first the Holy Roman emperor Henry V, and after his death Geoffrey ◊Plantagenet, Count of Anjou. On her father's death in 1135, the barons elected her cousin Stephen to be king. In order to press her claim to the throne Matilda invaded England 1139, and was crowned 1141. Civil war ensued until in 1153 Stephen was finally recognized as king, with Henry II (Matilda's son) as his successor.

Matisse Henri 1869–1954. French painter, sculptor, illustrator, and designer. His work concentrates on designs that emphasize curvaceous surface patterns, linear arabesques, and brilliant colour.

Mato Grosso (Portuguese 'dense forest') area of SW Brazil, now forming two states, with their capitals at Cuiaba and Campo Grande. The forests, now depleted, supplied rubber and rare timbers; diamonds and silver are mined.

matriarchy a form of social organization in which women head the family, and descent and relationship are reckoned through the female line. In matrilineal societies, powerful positions are usually held by men but acceded to through female kin. Matriarchy, often associated with polyandry (one wife with several husbands), occurs in certain parts of India, in the South Pacific, Central Africa, and among some N American Indian peoples.

matrix in mathematics, the name given to a square ($n \times n$) or rectangular ($m \times n$) array of elements (numbers or algebraic variables). They are a means of condensing information about mathematical systems, and can be used for, among other things, solving simultaneous linear equations and transformations.

matrix in biology, usually refers to the ◊extracellular matrix.

Matsudaira Tsuneo 1877–1949. Japanese diplomat and politician who negotiated for Japan at the London Naval Conference of 1930 and acted as imperial household minister 1936–45, advising the emperor, but was unsuccessful in keeping Japan out of a war with the Western powers. He became first chairman of the Japanese Diet (parliament) after World War II.

Matsukata Masayoshi 1835–1924. Prince of Japan. As a politician, he successfully combated inflation and restored government finances in the 1880s, paving the way for the modernization of the Japanese economy.

Matsuoka Yosuke 1880–1946. Japanese politician. As foreign minister 1927–29, he was largely responsible for the increasingly belligerent attitude towards China. His attempts to deal with Japan's worsening economic situation led to inflation and civil unrest.

Matsys (also *Massys* or *Metsys*) Quentin *c.* 1464–1530. Flemish painter, active in Antwerp. He is known for religious subjects such as the *Lamentation* 1511 (Musées Royaux, Antwerp) and portraits set against landscapes or realistic interiors.

matter in physics, the material of which all objects outside the mind are considered to be composed. The history of science and philosophy is largely taken up with accounts of theories of matter, ranging from the hard 'atoms' of

mathematical symbols

$a \rightarrow b$	a implies b
∞	infinity
lim	limiting value
$a \sim b$	numerical difference between a and b
$a \approx b$	a approximately equal to b
$a = b$	a equal to b
$a \equiv b$	a identical with b (for formulae only)
$a > b$	a greater than b
$a < b$	a smaller than b
$a \neq b$	a not equal to b
$b < a < c$	a greater than b and smaller than c, that is a lies between the values b & c but cannot equal either.
$a \geq b$	a equal to or greater than b, that is, a at least as great as b
$a \leq b$	a equal to or less than b, that is, a at most as great as b
$b \leq a \leq c$	a lies between the values b & c and could take the values b and c.
$\|a\|$	absolute value of a; this is always positive, for example $\|-5\| = 5$
$+$	addition sign, positive
$-$	subtraction sign, negative
$\times$ or $\odot$	multiplication sign, times
$:$ or $\div$ or $/$	division sign, divided by
$a + b = c$	$a + b$, read as 'a plus b', denotes the addition of a and b. The result of the addition, c, is also known as the sum.
$\int$	indefinite integral
$\int_a^b f(x)dx$	definite integral, or integral between $x = a$ and $x = b$
$a - b = c$	$a - b$, read as 'a minus b', denotes subtraction of b from a.
	$a - b$, or c, is the difference. Subtraction is the opposite of addition.
$a \times b = c$ $ab = c$ $a.b = c$	$a \times b$, read as 'a multiplied by b', denotes multiplication of a by b. $a \times b$, or c, is the product, a and b are factors of c.
$a : b = c$ $a \div b = c$ $a/b = c$	$a : c$, read as 'a divided by b', denotes division. a is the dividend, b is the divisor; $a : b$, or c, is the quotient. One aspect of division – repeated subtraction, is the opposite of multiplication – repeated addition. In fractions, $\frac{a}{b}$ or a/b, a is the numerator ($=$ dividend), b the denominator ($=$ divisor).
$a^b = c$	a^b, read as 'a to the power b'; a is the base, b the exponent.
$\sqrt[b]{a} = c$	$\sqrt[b]{a}$, is the bth root of a, b being known as the root exponent. In the special case of $\sqrt[2]{a} = c$, $\sqrt[2]{a}$ or c is known as the square root of a, and the root exponent is usually omitted, that is, $\sqrt[2]{a} = \sqrt{a}$.
e	exponential constant and is the base of natural (napierian) logarithms $= 2.7182818284\ldots\ldots$
π	ratio of the circumference of a circle to its diameter $= 3.1415925535\ldots\ldots$

Democritus to the 'waves' of modern quantum theory.

Matterhorn (French *le Cervin* Italian *il Cervino*) mountain peak in the Alps on the Swiss-Italian border; 4,478 m/14,690 ft.

Matthews Stanley 1915– . English footballer who played for Stoke City, Blackpool, and England. He played nearly 700 Football League games, and won 54 international caps. He was the first European Footballer of the Year 1956, and the first footballer to be knighted.

Matthew, St Christian apostle and evangelist, the traditional author of the first Gospel. He is usually identified with Levi, who was a tax collector in the service of Herod Antipas, and was called by Jesus to be a disciple as he sat by the Lake of Galilee receiving customs dues. His emblem is a man with wings; feast day 21 Sept.

Matthias Corvinus 1440–1490. King of Hungary from 1458. His aim of uniting Hungary, Austria, and Bohemia involved him in long wars with the Holy Roman emperor and the kings of Bohemia and Poland, during which he captured Vienna 1485 and made it his capital. His father was János ◊Hunyadi.

Maugham (William) Somerset 1874–1965. British writer. His work includes the novels *Of Human Bondage* 1915, *The Moon and Sixpence* 1919, and *Cakes and Ale* 1930; short stories *The Trembling of a Leaf* 1921, *Ashenden* 1928; and plays *Lady Frederick* 1907, *Our Betters* 1923.

Mau Mau name given by white settlers to a Kenyan secret guerrilla society with nationalist aims 1952–60, an offshoot of the Kikuyu Central Association banned in World War II. Attacks on other Kikuyu (about 1,000 killed) were far more common than on whites (about 100 killed).

Maundy Thursday in the Christian church, the Thursday before Easter. The ceremony of washing the feet of pilgrims on that day was instituted in

Mauritania
Islamic Republic of
(*République Islamique de Mauritanie*)

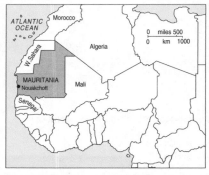

area 1,030,000sq km/419,000 sq mi
capital Nouakchott
physical valley of river Senegal in S; the rest is arid
head of state and government Moaouia Ould Sidi Ahmed Taya from 1984
political system emergent democratic republic
exports iron ore, fish, gypsum

currency ouguiya
population (1990 est) 2,038,000 (30% Arab Berber, 30% black Africans, 30% Haratine – descendants of black slaves, who remained slaves till 1980); annual growth rate 3%
life expectancy men 43, women 48
language French (official)
religion Sunni Muslim
literacy 17% (1987)
GNP $843 million (1988); $480 per head
chronology
1960 Achieved full independence, with Moktar Ould Daddah, as president.
1975 Western Saraha ceded by Spain. Mauritania occupied the southern part and Morocco the rest. Polisario Front formed in Sahara to resist the occupation by Mauritania and Morocco.
1978 Daddah deposed in bloodless coup and replaced by Mohamed Khouni Ould Haidalla. Peace agreed with Polisario Front.
1981 Diplomatic relations with Morocco broken.
1984 Haidalla overthrown by Moaouia Ould Sidi Ahmed Taya. Palisario regime formerly recognized.
1985 Relations with Morocco restored.
1989 Violent clashes between Mauritanians and Senegalese in Nouakchott and Dakar.
1991 Amnesty for political prisoners.
1992 First multiparty elections won by ruling PRDS.

commemoration of Jesus' washing of the apostles' feet and observed 4th century–1754. In the UK it was performed by the English sovereigns until the time of William III, and *Maundy money* is still presented by the sovereign to poor people each year.

Maupassant Guy de 1850–1893. French author, born in Normandy. A civil servant, he was encouraged as a writer by ◊Flaubert, and established a reputation with the short story 'Boule de Suif/Ball of Fat' 1880 (he wrote some 300 short stories). His novels include *Une Vie/A Woman's Life* 1883 and *Bel-Ami* 1885.

Mauriac François 1885–1970. French novelist. His novel *Le Baiser au lépreux/A Kiss for the Leper* 1922 describes the conflict of an unhappy marriage. The irreconcilability of Christian practice and human nature are examined in *Fleuve de feu/River of Fire* 1923, *Le Désert de l'amour/The Desert of Love* 1925, and *Thérèse Desqueyroux* 1927. Nobel Prize for Literature 1952.

Mauritania country in NW Africa, bordered to the NE by Algeria, E and S by Mali, SW by Senegal, W by the Atlantic Ocean, and NW by Western Sahara.

Mauritius island in the Indian Ocean, E of Madagascar.

Mauritius
Republic of

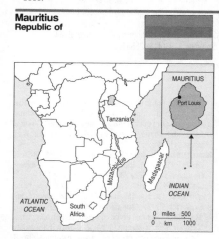

area 1,865 sq km/720 sq mi; the island of Rodrigues is part of Mauritius and there are several small island dependencies
capital Port Louis
physical a mountainous, volcanic island surrounded by coral reefs.

interim head of state Veerasamy Ringadoo from 1992
head of government Aneerood Jugnauth from 1982
political system liberal democratic republic
exports sugar, knitted goods, tea
currency Mauritius rupee
population (1990 est) 1,141,900; annual growth rate 1.5%
life expectancy men 64, women 71 (1989)
language English (official); creole French
religion Hindu 51%, Christian 30%, Muslim 17%
literacy 94% (1989)
GNP $1.4 bn (1987); $1,810 per head
chronology
1968 Achieved full independence within the Commonwealth.
1982 Aneerood Jugnauth prime minister.
1983 Jugnauth formed a new party, the Mauritius Socialist Movement, pledged to make Mauritius a republic within the Commonwealth, but Assembly refused. Ramgoolam appointed governor general. Judnauth formed a new coalition government.
1985 Ramgoolam died, succeeded by Ringadoo.
1987 Jugnath's coalition re-elected.
1990 Attempt to create a republic failed.
1992 Mauritius became a republic while remaining a member of the Commonwealth. Ringadoo became interim president.

Maurois André. Pen name of Emile Herzog 1885–1967. French novelist and writer, whose works include the semi-autobiographical *Bernard Quesnay* 1926, and fictionalized biographies, such as *Ariel* 1923, a life of Shelley.

Mauroy Pierre 1928– . French socialist politician, prime minister 1981–84. He oversaw the introduction of a radical reflationary programme.

Maury Matthew Fontaine 1806–1873. US naval officer, founder of the US Naval Oceanographic Office. His system of recording oceanographic information is still used today.

Maurya Dynasty Indian dynasty *c.* 321–*c.* 185 BC, founded by Chandragupta Maurya (321–*c.* 279 BC) who ruled much of India until the murder of the emperor Brhadratha in 185 BC and the creation of the Suringa dynasty. The Emperor Asoka (*c.* 270–232 BC) left a legacy of administrative reform and a series of edicts in stone which were erected throughout the kingdom. These are some of the oldest deciphered texts in India. Asoka was a convert to Buddhism.

Mawson Douglas 1882–1958. Australian explorer, born in Britain, who reached the South Magnetic Pole on Shackleton's expedition 1907–09.

max. abbreviation for *maximum*.

Maxim Hiram Stevens 1840–1916. US-born (naturalized British) inventor of the first automatic machine gun 1884.

Maximilian 1832–1867. Emperor of Mexico 1864–67. He accepted the title of emperor of Mexico when the French emperor Napoleon III's troops occupied the country, but encountered resistance from the deposed president ◊Juárez, and in 1866, after the French troops withdrew on the insistence the USA, Maximilian was captured by the republicans and shot.

Maximilian I 1459–1519. Holy Roman emperor from 1493, the son of Emperor Frederick III. He had acquired the Low Countries through his marriage with Mary of Burgundy in 1477; he married his son Philip I (the Handsome) to the heiress to the Spanish throne, and undertook long wars with Italy and Hungary in attempts to extend Hapsburg power. He was the patron of the artist Dürer.

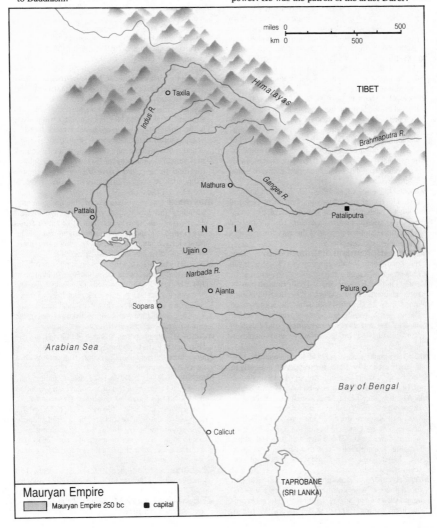

Mauryan Empire

▨ Mauryan Empire 250 bc   ■ capital

maximum and minimum

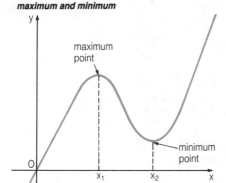

y

maximum point

minimum point

x_1 x_2 x

O

maximum and minimum in mathematics, points at which the slope of a curve representing a ◊function in ◊coordinate geometry changes from positive to negative (maximum), or from negative to positive (minimum). A tangent to the curve at a maximum or minimum has zero gradient.

maxwell former (◊c.g.s.) unit of magnetic flux (Mx), defined as the flux through 1 cm² perpendicular to a field of 1 gauss. It has been replaced by the SI unit, the ◊weber.

Maxwell (Ian) Robert 1923–1991. Czech-born British publishing and newspaper proprietor, chief executive of Maxwell Communications Corporation, and owner of several UK national newspapers, including the *Daily Mirror*. He was Labour member of parliament for Buckingham 1964–70. He died, by drowning at sea, in mysterious circumstances. It transpired that his empire carried debts of some $3.9 billion.

Maxwell James Clerk 1831–1879. Scottish physicist. He contributed to every branch of physical science, particularly gases, optics, colour sensation, electricity, and magnetism. His theoretical work in magnetism prepared the way for wireless telegraphy and telephony.

Maxwell–Boltzmann distribution basic equation concerning the distribution of velocities of the molecules of a gas.

May Thomas Erskine 1815–1886. English constitutional jurist. He was Clerk of the House of Commons from 1871 until 1886, when he was created Baron Farnborough. He wrote a practical *Treatise on the Law, Privileges, Proceedings, and Usage of Parliament* 1844, the authoritative work on parliamentary procedure.

maya (Sanskrit 'illusion') in Hindu philosophy, particularly in the *Vedānta*, term applied frequently to the cosmos which Isvara, the personal expression of Brahman, or the Atman, has called into being.

Maya member of an American Indian civilization originating in the Yucatan Peninsula about 2600 BC, with late sites in Mexico, Guatemala, and Belize, and enjoying a classical period AD 325–925, after which it declined. The Maya constructed stone buildings and stepped pyramids without metal tools; used hieroglyphic writing and were skilled potters, weavers, and farmers.

Mayakovsky Vladimir 1893–1930. Russian futurist poet, who combined revolutionary propaganda with efforts to revolutionize poetic technique in his poems '150,000,000' 1920 and 'V I Lenin'

1924. His satiric play *The Bedbug* 1928 was taken in the West as an attack on philistinism in the USSR.

May Day first day of May, traditionally the beginning of summer, still marked in England by pre-Christian magical rites, for example, the dance round the maypole (an ancient fertility symbol). In many countries it is a public holiday in honour of labour (in the UK the first Monday in May); see also ◊Labour Day.

Mayer Julius Robert von 1814–1878. German physicist who in 1842 anticipated ◊Joule in deriving the mechanical equivalent of heat, and ◊Helmholtz in the principle of conservation of energy.

Mayflower the ship in which, in 1620, the ◊Pilgrims sailed from Plymouth, England, to found Plymouth in present-day Massachusetts, USA.

mayfly insect of the order Ephemeroptera (Greek *ephemeros* lasting for a day, an allusion to the very brief life of the adult). The larval stage, which can last a year or more, is passed in water, the adult form developing gradually through successive moults. The adult has transparent, net-veined wings.

Mayo county in Connacht province, Republic of Ireland

area 5,400 sq km/2,084 sq mi

towns administrative town Castlebar

products sheep and cattle farming; fishing

population (1991) 110,700

Mayo William James 1861–1939. US surgeon, founder with his brother, *Charles Horace* (1865–1939) of the Mayo Clinic for medical treatment 1889 in Rochester, Minnesota.

mayor title of head of urban administration. In England, Wales, and Northern Ireland, the mayor is the principal officer of a district council that has been granted district-borough status under royal charter. In certain cases the chair of a city council may (under a similar grant by letters patent) have the right to be called **Lord Mayor** (a usage also followed by Australian cities). In the USA a mayor is the elected head of a city or town.

mayweed several species of the daisy family, including the low annual *pineapple mayweed Matricaria matricarioides* and the *scentless mayweed Tripleurospermum inodorum*. The plants have branched, thread-like leaves and thrive as weeds in arable and waste places.

Mazarin Jules 1602–1661. French politician, who succeeded Richelieu as chief minister of France in 1642. His attack on the power of the nobility led to the ◊Fronde and his temporary exile, but his diplomacy achieved a successful conclusion to the Thirty Years' War, and, in alliance with Cromwell during the British protectorate, he gained victory over Spain.

mazurka a lively national dance of Poland from the 16th century. In triple time, it is characterized by foot-stamping and heel-clicking, together with a turning movement.

Mazzini Giuseppe 1805–1872. Italian nationalist. He was a member of the ◊Carbonari, and founded in exile the nationalist movement *Giovane Italia/ Young Italy* in 1832. Returning to Italy on the outbreak of the 1848 revolution, he headed a republican government established in Rome, but was forced into exile again on its overthrow 1849. He acted as a focus for the movement for Italian unity (see ◊Risorgimento).

Mbabane capital (since 1902) of Swaziland, 160 km/99 mi W of Maputo, in the Dalgeni Hills; population (1986) 38,000.

MBE abbreviation for *Member (of the Order) of the British Empire*.

Mboya Tom 1930–1969. Kenyan politician, a founder of the ◊Kenya African National Union (KANU), and minister of economic planning (opposed to nationalization) from 1964 until his assassination.

MDMA psychedelic drug, also known as ◊-ecstasy.

ME abbreviation for *Middle English*, the period of the English language 1050–1550.

ME abbreviation for *myalgic encephalomyelitis*, a debilitating condition still not universally accepted as a genuine disease. The condition is a diffuse one, with a range of symptoms including extreme fatigue, muscular pain, and weakness and anxiety attacks.

mead drink made from honey and water fermented with yeast. It was known in ancient times, and was drunk by the Greeks, Britons, and Norse.

Mead George Herbert 1863–1931. US philosopher and social psychologist, who helped to found the philosophy of pragmatism.

Mead Margaret 1901–1978. US anthropologist, who challenged the conventions of Western society with *Coming of Age in Samoa* 1928.

mean in mathematics, a measure of the average of a number of terms or quantities. The simple *arithmetic mean* is the average value of the quantities, that is, the sum of the quantities divided by their number. The *weighted mean* takes into account the frequency of the terms that are summed; it is calculated by multiplying each term by the number of times it occurs, summing the results and dividing this total by the total number of occurrences.

meander a loop-shaped curve in a river flowing across flat country. As a river flows, any curve in its course is accentuated by the current. The current is fastest on the outside of the curve where it cuts into the bank; on the curve's inside the current is slow and deposits any transported material. In this way the river changes its course across the floodplain.

mean deviation in statistics, a measure of the spread of a population from the ◊mean.

mean free path in physics, the average distance travelled by a particle, atom, or molecule between successive collisions. It is of importance in the ◊kinetic theory of gases.

measles a virus disease (rubeola), spread by airborne infection. Symptoms are severe catarrh, small spots inside the mouth, and a raised, blotchy red rash appearing after about a week's incubation. Prevention is by vaccination.

meat flesh of animals taken as food, in Western countries chiefly from cattle, sheep, pigs, and poultry. Major exporters include Argentina, Australia, New Zealand, Canada, USA, and Denmark (chiefly bacon). *Meat substitutes* are textured vegetable protein (TVP), usually ◊soya-based, extruded in fibres in the same way as plastics.

Meath county in the province of Leinster, Republic of Ireland
area 2,336 sq km/902 sq mi
county town Trim
population (1986) 104,000
products sheep, cattle.

Mecca (Arabic *Makkah*) city in Saudi Arabia and, as birthplace of Muhammad, the holiest city of the Islamic world; population (1974) 367,000. In the centre of Mecca is the Great Mosque, in whose courtyard is the ◊Kaaba.

mechanical equivalent of heat in physics, a constant factor relating the calorie (the ◊c.g.s. unit of heat) to the joule (the unit of mechanical energy), equal to 4.1868 joules per calorie. It is redundant in the SI system of units, which measures heat and all forms of energy in joules (so that the mechanical equivalent of heat is 1).

mechanics branch of applied mathematics dealing with the motions of bodies and the forces causing these motions, and also with the forces acting on

meat

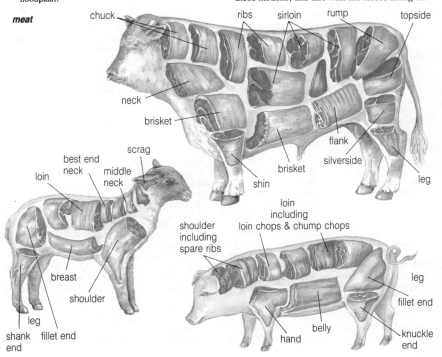

bodies in ◊equilibrium. It is usually divided into ◊dynamics and ◊statics.

mechanization use of machines as a substitute for manual labour or the use of animals. Until the 1700s there were few machines available to help people in the home, on the land, or in industry. The 1700s saw a long series of inventions, initially in the textile industry, that ushered in a machine age and brought about the ◊Industrial Revolution.

Mechnikov Elie 1845–1916. Russian scientist who discovered the function of white blood cells. In the course of studying digestion, Mechnikov discovered ◊phagocytes. After leaving Russia and joining ◊Pasteur in Paris, he described how these 'scavenger cells' can attack the body itself (autoimmune disease).

Mecklenburg historic name of an area of the Baltic coast of Germany. It was formerly the two grand duchies of Mecklenburg-Schwerin and Mecklenburg-Strelitz, which became free states of the Weimar Republic 1918–34, and were joined 1946 (with part of Pomerania) to form a region of East Germany. In 1952 it was split into the districts of Rostock, Schwerin, and Neubrandenburg.

Medawar Peter (Brian) 1915–1987. British immunologist, born in Brazil, who, with ◊Burnet, discovered that the body's resistance to grafted tissue is undeveloped in the newborn child, and studied the way it is acquired.

Mede member of a people of NW Iran who first appeared in the 9th century BC as tributaries to Assyria, with their capital at Ecbatana (now Hamadán). Allying themselves with Babylon, they destroyed the Assyrian capital of ◊Nineveh 612 BC, and extended their conquests into central Anatolia. In 550 BC the Persians, until then subject to them under their own King ◊Cyrus, successfully revolted. Cyrus ruled both peoples, who rapidly merged.

Medea in Greek mythology, the sorceress daughter of the king of Colchis. When ◊Jason reached the court, she fell in love with him, helped him acquire the golden fleece, and fled with him. When Jason married Creusa, Medea killed his bride with the gift of a poisoned garment, and also killed her own two children by Jason.

Medellín industrial town (textiles, chemicals, engineering, coffee) in the Central Cordillera, Colombia, 1,538 m/5,048 ft above sea level; population (1985) 2,069,000.

median in mathematics, the middle number of an ordered group of numbers. If there is no middle number (because there is an even number of terms), the median is the ◊mean (average) of the two middle numbers.

Medici noble family of Florence, the city's rulers from 1434 until they died out 1737. See also ◊Catherine de' Medici, Pope ◊Leo X, Pope ◊Clement VII, ◊Marie de' Medici.

Medici Cosimo de' 1389–1464. Italian politician and banker. Regarded as the model for Machiavelli's *The Prince*, he dominated the government of Florence from 1434 and was a patron of the arts.

Medici Lorenzo de' *the Magnificent* 1449–1492. Italian politician, ruler of Florence from 1469. He was also a poet and a generous patron of the arts.

medicine the science of preventing, diagnosing, alleviating, or curing disease, both physical and mental; also any substance used in the treatment of disease. The basis of medicine is anatomy (the structure and form of the body), and physiology (the study of the body's functions).

medicine, alternative forms of medical treatment which do not use synthetic drugs or surgery in response to the symptoms of a disease, but which aim to treat the patient as a whole (◊holism). The emphasis is on maintaining health (with diet and exercise) rather than waiting for the onset of illness. It involves the use of herbal drugs; and techniques such as ◊acupuncture, ◊homeopathy, and ◊osteopathy.

medieval art painting and sculpture of the Middle Ages in Europe and parts of the Middle East, dating roughly from the 4th century to the emergence of the Renaissance in Italy in the 1300s. This includes **early Christian, Byzantine, Celtic, Anglo-Saxon,** and **Carolingian** art. The **Romanesque** style was the first truly international style of medieval times, superseded by **Gothic** in the late 12th century. Religious sculpture and manuscript illumination proliferated; of murals little survives and panel painting came only towards the end of the period.

Medina (Arabic *Madinah*) Saudi Arabian city, about 355 km/220 mi N of Mecca; population (1974) 198,000. It is the second holiest city in the Islamic world, containing the tomb of Muhammad.

meditation act of spiritual contemplation, practised by members of many religions or as a secular exercise. It is important in Buddhism. The Sanskrit term is *dhyāna*. See also ◊transcendental meditation (TM).

Mediterranean inland sea separating Europe from N Africa, with Asia to the E; extreme length 3,700 km/2,300 mi; area 2,966,000 sq km/1,145,000 sq mi. It is linked to the Atlantic (at the Strait of Gibraltar), Red Sea, and Indian Ocean (by the Suez Canal), Black Sea (at the Dardanelles and Sea of Marmara). The main subdivisions are the Adriatic, Aegean, Ionian, and Tyrrhenian seas.

Mediterranean climate a climate characterized by hot dry summers and warm wet winters. Mediterranean zones are situated in either hemisphere on the western side of continents, between latitudes of 30° and 60°.

medlar small European shrub or tree *Mespilus germanica* of the family Rosaceae, with fruits resembling a small brown-green pear or quince, eaten when decay has set in.

Medusa in Greek mythology, a mortal woman who was transformed into a ◊Gorgon. The winged horse ◊Pegasus was supposed to have sprung from her blood.

Medvedev Vadim 1929– . Soviet politician. He was deputy chief of propaganda 1970-78, was in charge of party relations with communist countries 1986–88, and in 1988 was appointed by the Soviet leader Gorbachev to succeed the conservative Ligachev as head of ideology. He adheres to a firm Leninist line.

Mee Margaret 1909–1988. English botanical artist. In the 1950s, she went to Brazil, where she depicted the many exotic species of plants in the Amazon basin.

mega- prefix denoting multiplication by a million. For example, a megawatt (MW) is equivalent to a million watts.

megalith prehistoric stone monument of the late Neolithic or early Bronze Age. Megaliths include single, large uprights (**menhirs**, for example the Five Kings, Northumberland, England); rows (for example, Carnac, Brittany, France); **circles,** generally with a central 'altar stone' (for example Stonehenge, Wiltshire, England); and the remains of burial chambers with the covering earth removed, looking like

medicine: chronology

c.400 BC	Hippocrates recognized disease had natural causes.
c.200 AD	Galen, the authority of the Middle Ages, consolidated the work of the Alexandrian doctors.
1543	Andreas Versalius gave the first accurate account of the human body.
1628	William Harvey discovered the circulation of the blood.
1768	John Hunter began the foundation of the experimental and surgical pathology.
1785	Digitalis used to treat heart disease; the active ingredient was isolated in 1904.
1798	Edward Jenner published his work on vaccination.
1882	Robert Koch isolated the tuberculosis bacillus.
1884	Edwin Klebs, German pathologist, isolated the diphtheria bacillus.
1885	Louis Pasteur produced the rabies vaccine.
1890	Joseph Lister demonstrated antiseptic surgery.
1897	Martinus Beijerinck, Dutch botanist, discovered viruses.
1899	Felix Hoffman developed aspirin; Sigmund Freud founded psychiatry.
1910	Paul Ehrlich synthesized the first specific bacterial agent, salvarsan (cure for syphilis).
1922	Insulin was first used to treat diabetes.
1928	Alexander Fleming discovered the antibiotic penicillin.
1930s	Electro-convulsive therapy (ECT) was developed.
1932	Gerhard Domagk, German bacteriologist and pathologist, began work on the sulphonamide drugs, a kind of antibiotic.
1950s	Major development of antidepressant drugs and also beta blockers for heart disease; Medawar's work on the immune system.
1950–75	Manipulation of the molecules of synthetic chemicals, the main source of new drugs.
1954	Vaccine for polio developed by Jonas Salk.
1960s	Heart transplant surgery began with the work of Christiaan Barnard; new generation of minor tranquillizers called benzodiazepines was developed.
1971	Viroids, disease-causing organisms smaller than viruses, isolated outside the living body.
1978	Birth of the first 'test-tube baby', Louise Brown, on 25 July in England.
1980s	AIDS (Acquired Immune Deficiency Syndrome) first recognized in the USA.
1980	Smallpox declared eradicated by the World Health Organization.
1984	Vaccine for leprosy developed; discovery of the Human Immuno-deficiency Virus (HIV) responsible for AIDS, at the Institut Pasteur in Paris and in the USA.
1987	World's longest-surviving heart transplant patient died, 18 years after his operation.
1990	Gene for maleness discovered by UK researchers.
1991	First successful use of gene therapy (to treat severe combined immune deficiency) was reported in the USA.

a hut (***dolmens***, for example Kits Koty House, Kent, England).

megamouth filter-feeding deep-sea shark *Megachasma pelagios*, first discovered 1976. It has a bulbous head with protruding jaws and blubbery lips, is 4.5 m/15 ft long, and weighs 750 kg/1,650 lb.

megapode large (70 cm/2.3 ft long) ground-living bird of the family Megapodidae, found mainly in Australia, but also in SE Asia. They lay their eggs in a pile of rotting vegetation 4 m/13 ft across, and the warmth from this provides the heat for incubation. The male bird feels the mound with his tongue and adjusts it to provide the correct temperature.

megatherium extinct giant ground sloth of America. Various species lived from about 7 million years ago until geologically recent times. They were planteaters, and some grew to 6 m/20 ft long.

megaton one million (10^6) tons. Used with reference to the explosive power of a nuclear weapon, it is equivalent to the explosive force of one million tons of trinitrotoluene (TNT).

Meghalaya NE state of India
area 22,429 sq km/8,658 sq mi
capital Shillong
products potatoes, cotton, jute, fruit
minerals coal, limestone, white clay, corundum, sillimanite.
population (1991) 1,760,000, mainly Khasi, Jaintia, and Garo
religion Hindu 70%.

Megiddo site of a fortress town in N Israel, where Thothmes III defeated the Canaanites *c.* 1469 BC; the Old Testament figure Josiah was killed in battle *c.* 609 BC; and in World War I the British field marshal Allenby broke the Turkish front 1918.

Mehemet Ali 1769–1849. Pasha (governor) of Egypt from 1805, and founder of the dynasty that ruled until 1953. An Albanian in the Ottoman service, he had originally been sent to Egypt to fight the French. As pasha, he established a European-style army and navy, fought his Turkish overlord 1831 and 1839, and conquered Sudan.

Meiji era in Japanese history, the reign of Emperor ◊Mutsuhito 1867–1912.

Meikle Andrew 1719–1811. Scottish millwright who designed and built the first practical threshing machine for separating corn from straw, in 1785.

Mein Kampf (German 'my struggle') book written by Adolf ◊Hitler 1924 during his jail sentence for his part in the abortive 1923 Munich beerhall putsch. Part autobiography, part political philosophy, the book outlines Hitler's ideas of German expansion, anti-communism, and anti-semitism.

meiosis in biology, a process of cell division in which the number of ◊chromosomes in the cell is halved. It only occurs in ◊eukaryotic cells, and is an important part of a life cycle that involves sexual reproduction, because it allows the genes of two parents to be combined without the total number of chromosomes increasing.

Meir Golda 1898–1978. Israeli Labour (*Mapai*) politician, born in Russia. She was foreign minister 1956–66 and prime minister 1969–74, resigning after criticism of the Israelis' lack of preparation for the 1973 Arab-Israeli War.

Meistersinger (German 'master singer') one of a group of German lyric poets, singers, and musicians of the 14th–16th centuries, who formed guilds for the revival of minstrelsy. Hans ◊Sachs was a noted Meistersinger, and Richard Wagner's opera, *Die Meistersinger von Nüremberg* 1868 depicts the tradition.

Mekong river rising as the Za Qu in Tibet and flowing to the South China Sea, through a vast delta (about 200,000 sq km/77,000 sq mi); length 4,500 km/2,800 mi. It is being developed for irrigation and hydroelectricity by Kampuchea, Laos, Thailand, and Vietnam.

Melanchthon Philip. Assumed name of Philip Schwarzerd 1497–1560. German theologian, who helped Luther prepare a German translation of the New Testament. In 1521 he issued the first systematic formulation of Protestant theology, and composed the *Confession of ◊Augsburg* 1530.

Melanesia islands in the SW Pacific between Micronesia to the north and Polynesia to the east, embracing all the islands from the New Britain archipelago to Fiji.

melanoma mole or growth containing the dark pigment melanin. Malignant melanoma is a type of skin cancer developing in association with a pre-existing mole. Once rare, this disease is now increasing, possibly due to depletion of the ozone layer, which provides some protection against ultra-violet radiation from the Sun. Most at risk are those with fair hair and light skin.

Melbourne capital of Victoria, Australia, near the mouth of the river Yarra; population (1986) 2,943,000. Industries include engineering, shipbuilding, electronics, chemicals, food processing, clothing, and textiles.

Melchite or *Melkite* member of a Christian church in Syria, Egypt, Lebanon, and Israel. The Melchite Church was founded in Syria in the 6th–7th centuries after accepting Byzantine rule at the council of Chalcedon 451 (unlike the ◊Maronites). In 1754 some Melchites broke away to form a ◊Uniate Church with Rome; the remainder belong to the Orthodox Church.

meiosis

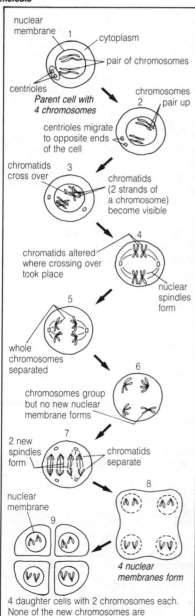

nuclear membrane 1
cytoplasm
pair of chromosomes
centrioles
chromosomes
Parent cell with 4 chromosomes
2 pair up
centrioles migrate to opposite ends of the cell
chromatids 3 cross over
chromatids (2 strands of a chromosome) become visible
chromatids altered where crossing over took place
4
nuclear spindles form
5
whole chromosomes separated
6
chromosomes group but no new nuclear membrane forms
2 new spindles form
7
chromatids separate
nuclear membrane
8
9
4 nuclear membranes form
4 daughter cells with 2 chromosomes each. None of the new chromosomes are exactly like the original chromosomes

Meir Israeli prime minister Golda Meir, 1970.

Memlinc St John the Baptist and St Lawrence *National Gallery, London.*

melodrama originally, a play accompanied by music. The early melodramas used extravagant theatrical effects to heighten violent emotions and actions artificially, and were frequently played against a Gothic background of mountains or ruined castles. By the end of the 19th century, a melodrama was a popular form of stage play with romantic and sensational plot elements, often unsubtly acted. Today the term is often derogatory.

melon twining plant of the family Cucurbitaceae. The musk melon *Cucumis melo* and the watermelon *Citrullus vulgaris* are two of the many edible varieties.

meltdown a very serious type of accident in a nuclear reactor. If the reactor's cooling system fails and a major part of the core reaches its melting point (about 2,900°C/5,200°F), the metal reactor vessel may also melt, burn through the concrete floor beneath and release radioactive material into the atmosphere through ◊fallout. A meltdown was narrowly avoided at Three Mile Island, Pennsylvania, USA 1979, but occurred in a reactor at ◊Chernobyl 1986, spreading radiative fallout over a large area of N Europe.

Melville Henry Dundas, Viscount Melville 1742–1811. British Tory politician, born in Edinburgh. He entered Parliament 1774, and as home secretary 1791–94 persecuted the parliamentary reformers. He received a peerage 1802 and was 1st Lord of the Admiralty 1804–05. His impeachment for malversation (misconduct) 1806 was the last in English history.

Melville Herman 1819–1891. US writer, whose ◊*Moby Dick* 1851 was inspired by his whaling experiences in the South Seas, the setting for other fiction, such as *Typee* 1846 and *Omoo* 1847. He published several volumes of verse, and short stories (*The Piazza Tales* 1856). *Billy Budd* was completed just before his death and published 1924.

membrane in living things, a continuous layer, made up principally of fat molecules, which encloses a ◊cell or a part of a cell (organelle). Certain small molecules can pass through the cell membrane, but most must enter or leave the cell via channels in the membrane made up of special proteins. The ◊Golgi apparatus within the cell produces certain membranes.

Memlinc (or *Memling*) Hans *c.* 1430–1494. Flemish artist, born near Frankfurt-am-Main, Germany, but active in Bruges. He painted religious subjects and portraits. Some of his works are in the Hospital of St John, Bruges, including *Adoration of the Magi* 1479.

Memorial Day in the USA, a day of remembrance (formerly Decoration Day) instituted 1868 for those killed in the US Civil War. It is now observed as a public holiday on the last Monday in May in remembrance of all Americans killed in war.

memory in computing, any device, collection of devices, or components in a computer system used to store data and programs either permanently or temporarily. There are two main types: internal memory and external memory. All computer memory stores information in binary code (using the ◊binary number system). Memory capacity is measured in K (kilobytes).

memory ability to store and recall observations and sensations. Memory does not seem to be based in any particular part of the brain; it may depend on changes to the pathways followed by nerve impulses as they move through the brain. Memory can be improved by regular use as the connections between ◊nerve cells (neurons) become 'well-worn paths' in the brain. Events stored in *short-term memory* are forgotten quickly, whereas those in *long-term memory* can last for many years, enabling recognition of people and places over long periods of time. Human memory is not well understood.

Memphis ruined city beside the Nile, 19 km/12 mi south of Cairo, Egypt. Once the centre of the worship of Ptah, it was the earliest capital of a united Egypt under King Menes about 3200 BC, but was superseded by Thebes under the new empire 1570 BC. It was later used as a stone quarry, but the 'cemetery city' of Sakkara survives, with the step pyramid built for King Zoser by ◊Imhotep, probably the world's oldest stone building.

Memphis industrial city (pharmaceuticals, food processing, cotton, timber, tobacco) on the Mississippi River, in Tennessee, USA; population (1986) 960,000.

Menander *c.* 342–291 BC. Greek comic dramatist, born in Athens. Of his 105 plays only fragments (many used as papier-mâché for Egyptian mummy cases) and Latin adaptations were known prior to the discovery 1957 of the *Dyscholos/The Bad-tempered Man*.

Mencken H(enry) L(ouis) 1880–1956. US essayist and critic, known as 'the sage of Baltimore'. His unconventionally phrased, satiric contributions to *Smart Set* and *US Mercury* (both of which periodicals he edited) aroused great controversy. His book *The American Language* 1918 is often revised.

Mende person of the Mende culture, from central-east Sierra Leone and W Liberia. They number approximately 1,000,000, and their language belongs to the Niger-Congo family.

Mendel Gregor Johann 1822–1884. Austrian biologist, founder of genetics. His experiments with successive generations of peas gave the basis for his theory of organic inheritance, governed by dominant and recessive characters (genes). His results, published 1865–69, remained unrecognized until early this century.

mendelevium an artificially-made element, symbol Md, atomic number 101. One of the ◊actinide series, it is a radioactive element produced by bombardment of einsteinium-253.

Mendeleyev Dmitri Ivanovich 1834–1907. Russian chemist, who framed the periodic law in chemistry which states that the chemical properties of the elements depend on their relative atomic masses. This law is the basis of the ◊periodic table of elements.

Mendelism in genetics, the theory of inheritance originally outlined by Gregor Mendel. He suggested that, in sexually reproducing species, characters (such as hair colour) are inherited through indivisible 'factors' (now identifed with ◊genes) contributed by each parent to its offspring.

Mendelssohn (-Bartholdy) (Jakob Ludwig) Felix 1809–1847. German composer, also a pianist and conductor, whose works include *A Midsummer Night's Dream* 1827; the *Fingal's Cave* overture 1832; chamber music (including string quartets); and the Italian (1833) and Scottish (1842) symphonies.

Mendès-France Pierre 1907–1982. French prime minister and foreign minister 1954–55. He extricated France from the war in Indochina, and prepared the way for Tunisian independence.

mendicant order religious order dependent on alms. In the Roman Catholic Church there are four orders of mendicant friars: Franciscans, Dominicans, Carmelites, and Augustinians. Hinduism has similar orders.

Mendoza Antonio de 1490–1552. First Spanish viceroy of New Spain (Mexico) 1535–51. He attempted to develop agriculture and mining, and supported the church in their attempts to convert the Indians. The system he established lasted until the 19th century. He was subsequently viceroy of Peru 1551–52.

Menelik II 1844–1913. Negus (emperor) of Abyssinia (now Ethiopia) from 1889. He defeated the Italians 1896 at ◊Adowa, and thereby retained the independence of his country.

Menes *c.* 3200 BC. traditionally, the first king of the first dynasty of ancient Egypt. He is said to have founded Memphis and organized worship of the gods.

menhir (Breton 'long stone') a prehistoric standing stone (see ◊megalith).

Ménière's disease (or syndrome) a recurring condition of the inner ear affecting mechanisms both of hearing and balance. It develops usually in the middle or later years. Symptoms, which include ringing in the ears, nausea, vertigo, and loss of balance, may be relieved by drugs.

meningitis inflammation of the meninges (membranes) surrounding the brain caused by bacterial or viral infection. The severity of the disease varies from mild to rapidly lethal, and symptoms include fever, headache, nausea, neck stiffness, delirium,

Mendelssohn German composer Felix Mendelssohn.

meniscus

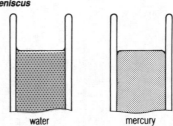

water   mercury

and (rarely) convulsions. Many common viruses can cause the occasional case of meningitis, although not usually in its more severe form. The treatment for viral meningitis is rest. Bacterial meningitis, though treatable by antibiotics, is a much more serious threat. Diagnosis is by ◊lumbar puncture.

meniscus in physics, the curved shape of the surface of a liquid in a thin tube, caused by the cohesive effects of ◊surface tension. Most liquids adopt a concave curvature (viewed from above), although with highly viscous liquids (such as mercury) the meniscus is convex. Meniscus is also the name given to a concavo-convex or convexo-concave ◊lens.

Mennonite member of a Protestant Christian sect, originating in Zürich 1523. Members refuse to hold civil office or do military service, and reject infant baptism. They were later named Mennonites after Menno Simons (1496–1559), leader of a group in Holland.

menopause in women, the cessation of reproductive ability, characterized by ◊menstruation becoming irregular and eventually ceasing. The onset is about the age of 45, but often varies greatly. Menopause is usually uneventful, but some women suffer from complications such as flushing, excessive bleeding, and nervous disorder. Since the 1950s, hormone replacement therapy (HRT), using ◊oestrogen alone or with ◊progesterone, has been developed to counteract such effects.

menorah a seven-branched candlestick used in Jewish ritual, a symbol of Judaism and of the state of Israel.

Menshevik member of the minority (Russian *menshinstvo* 'minority') of the Russian Social Democratic Party, who split from the ◊Bolsheviks 1903. The Mensheviks believed in a large, loosely organized party, and that before socialist revolution could occur in Russia, capitalism, industrialization, and bourgeois democracy must develop further. During the Russian Revolution, they were part of Kerensky's provisional government, and succeeded in setting up a government in Georgia, but were suppressed 1922.

menstrual cycle the cycle that occurs in female mammals of reproductive age, in which the body is prepared for pregnancy. At the beginning of the cycle, a Graafian (egg) follicle develops in the ovary, and the inner wall of the uterus forms a soft spongy lining. The egg is released from the ovary, and the lining of the uterus becomes vascularized (filled with blood vessels). If fertilization does not occur, the corpus luteum (remains of the Graafian follicle) degenerates, and the uterine lining breaks down, and is shed. This is what causes the loss of blood which marks menstruation. The cycle then begins again. Human menstruation takes place from puberty to menopause, occurring about every 28 days.

mental illness abnormal working of the mind. Since normal working cannot be defined, the

menstrual cycle

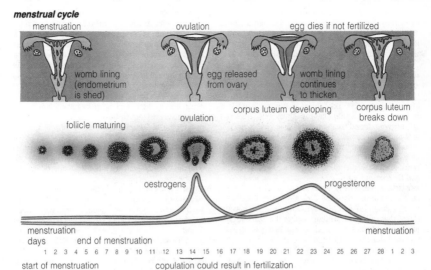

menstruation · ovulation · egg dies if not fertilized

womb lining (endometrium is shed) · egg released from ovary · womb lining continues to thicken

corpus luteum developing · corpus luteum breaks down

follicle maturing · ovulation

oestrogens · progesterone

menstruation · menstruation

days · end of menstruation

1 2 3 4 5 6 7 8 9 10 11 12 13 14 15 16 17 18 19 20 21 22 23 24 25 26 27 28 1 2 3

start of menstruation · copulation could result in fertilization

borderline between mild mental illness and normality is a matter of opinion. Mild forms are known as *neuroses*, affecting the emotions, while severe forms, *Psychoses*, distort conscious reasoning.

menthol peppermint camphor $C_{10}H_{19}OH$, an alcohol derivative of menthone. It occurs in peppermint and is responsible for the plant's odour.

menu in computing, a list of options, displayed on screen, from which the user may choose in order to operate a program, for example the choice of services offered by a bank cash dispenser: withdrawal, deposit, balance, and statement.

Menuhin Yehudi 1916– . US violinist and conductor. A child prodigy, he achieved great depth of interpretation, and was often accompanied on the piano by his sister Hephzibah (1921–81). He founded schools in England and Switzerland for training young musicians.

Menzies Robert Gordon 1894–1978. Australian conservative politician, prime minister 1939–41 and 1949–66. In 1944, he founded the Australian Liberal Party, uniting all anti-Labor groups except the Country Party.

Meo or *Miao* member of a SE Asian highland people (also known as Hmong). They are predominantly hill farmers, cultivating rice and maize, rearing pigs, and many are involved in growing opium. Their language belongs to the Sino-Tibetan family.

MEP abbreviation for *Member of the ◊European Parliament*.

Mercalli scale scale used to measure the intensity of an ◊earthquake. It differs from the ◊Richter scale, which measures *magnitude*. It is named after the Italian seismologist Giuseppe Mercalli (1850–1914).

mercantilism economic theory held 16th–18th centuries, that a nation's wealth (in the form of bullion or treasure) was the key to its prosperity. To this end, foreign trade should be regulated to obtain a surplus of exports over imports, and the state should intervene where necessary (for example subsidizing exports and taxing imports). The bullion theory of wealth was demolished by Adam ◊Smith in Book IV of *The Wealth of Nations* 1776.

Mercator Gerardus 1512–1594. Latinized form of the name of the Flemish map-maker Gerhard Kremer, who devised the first modern atlas, show-

ing *Mercator's ◊projection* in which the parallels and meridians on maps are drawn uniformly at 90°. The true area of countries is increasingly distorted the further N or S they are from the equator. For other types, see ◊map projection.

mercenary form of military service originating in the 14th century, when cash payment on a regular basis was the only means of guaranteeing loyalty. The term came to be restricted to a soldier hired by a foreign army. In the 20th century mercenaries have been common in wars and guerrilla activity in Asia, Africa, and Latin America.

Merchant Ismael 1936– . Indian film producer, known for his stylish collaborations with James ◊Ivory on films including *Shakespeare Wallah* 1985, *The Europeans* 1979, *Heat and Dust* 1983, *A Room with a View* 1986, *Maurice* 1987, and *Howards End* 1992.

merchant bank a bank which developed from the existence of merchant houses trading in various parts of the world. As such houses became known, they found that a remunerative way to finance trade was to accept bills of exchange from lesser-known traders. Originally developed in the UK in the 19th century, merchant banks now offer many of the services provided by the commercial banks.

merchant navy the passenger and cargo ships of a country. Most are owned by private companies. To avoid strict regulations on safety or union rules on crew wages, and so on, many ships are today registered under 'flags of convenience', that is, those of countries which do not have such rules.

Merchant of Venice, The a comedy by William Shakespeare, first performed 1596–97. Antonio, a rich merchant, borrows money from Shylock, a Jewish moneylender, promising a pound of flesh if the sum is not repaid; when Shylock presses his claim, the heroine, Portia, disguised as a lawyer, saves Antonio's life.

Merchants Adventurers trading company founded 1407 and consisting of guilds and traders in many N European ports. In direct opposition to the Hanseatic League, it came to control 75 per cent of English overseas trade by 1550.

Mercia an Anglo-Saxon kingdom which emerged in the 6th century, and by late the 8th dominated all England south of the Humber, but from about

825 came under the power of ◊Wessex. Mercia eventually came to denote an area bounded by the Welsh frontier, the Humber river, East Anglia, and the River Thames.

Merckx Eddie 1945– . Belgian cyclist known as 'The Cannibal'. He won the Tour de France a joint record five times 1969-74.

mercury chemical element, the only common liquid metal at ordinary temperatures; symbol Hg, atomic number 80, relative atomic mass 200.61. It is a dense, mobile, silvery liquid (also called quicksilver), found free in nature. The chief source is the mineral cinnabar, HgS. Its alloys with other metals are called amalgams. It is used in drugs and chemicals, for mercury vapour lamps, arc rectifiers, power-control switches, barometers, and thermometers.

Mercury in astronomy, the closest planet to the Sun, at an average distance of 58,000,000 km/36,000,000 mi. Its diameter is 4,880 km/3,030 mi, its mass 0.056 that of Earth. Mercury orbits the Sun every 88 days, and spins on its axis every 59 days. On its sunward side the surface temperature reaches over 400°C, but on the 'night' side it falls to –170°C. Mercury has an atmosphere with minute traces of argon and helium. The US space probe Mariner 10 1974 discovered that its surface is cratered by meteorite impacts. Mercury has no moons.

Mercury Roman god, identified with the Greek Hermes, and like him represented with winged sandals and a winged staff entwined with snakes. He was the messenger of the gods.

mercury fulminate highly explosive compound used in detonators and percussion caps. It is a grey, sandy powder, and extremely poisonous.

Meredith George 1828–1909. English novelist and poet. He published the first realistic psychological novel *The Ordeal of Richard Feverel* 1859.

merganser type of diving duck with a saw-bill for catching fish. It is widely distributed in the N hemisphere.

Mergenthaler Ottmar 1854–1899. German-American who invented a typesetting method. He went to the USA in 1872 and developed the first linotype machine (for casting metal type in complete lines – hence the name) 1876–86.

merger the linking of two or more companies, either by creating a new organization by consolidating the original companies, or by absorption by one of the others. Unlike a takeover, which is not always a voluntary fusion of the parties, a merger is the result of an agreement.

Mérida capital of Yucatán state, Mexico, a centre of the sisal industry; population (1986) 580,000.

meridian half a ◊great circle drawn on the Earth's surface passing through both poles, and thus through all places with the same longitude. Terrestrial longitudes are usually measured from the Greenwich Meridian.

Mérimée Prosper 1803–1870. French author. Among his works are *Colomba* 1841, *Carmen* 1846, and *Lettres à une inconnue/Letters to an Unknown Girl* 1873.

merino breed of sheep. Its close-set, silky wool is of extremely good quality, and the merino, now found all over the world, is the breed on which the Australian wool industry is built.

meristem a region of plant tissue containing cells which are actively dividing to produce new tissues (or have the potential to do so). Meristems found in the tip of roots and stems, the apical meristems, are responsible for the growth in length of these organs.

meritocracy a system (of for example education or government) in which selection is by performance (in education, in competitive examinations), which therefore favours intelligence and ability rather than social position or wealth. The result is the creation of an elite group. The term was coined by Michael Young in his *The Rise of the Meritocracy* 1958.

Merlin legendary magician and counsellor to King Arthur. Welsh bardic literature has a cycle of poems attributed to him, and he may have been a real person. He is said to have been buried in a cave in the park of Dynevor Castle, Dyfed.

merlin a small ◊falcon.

mermaid mythical sea creature (the male is a *merman*), having a human upper part, and a fish's tail. The dugong and seal are among suggested origins for the idea.

Meroe ancient city in Sudan, on the Nile near Khartoum, capital of Nubia from about 600 BC to 350 AD. Tombs and inscriptions have been excavated, and iron-smelting slag heaps have been found.

Merovingian dynasty a Frankish dynasty, named after its founder, Merovech (5th century AD). His descendants ruled France from the time of Clovis (481–511) to 751.

Merseyside former (1974–86) metropolitan county of NW England, replaced by a residuary body in 1986 which covers some of its former functions
area 652 sq km/252 sq mi
towns administrative headquarters Liverpool; Bootle, Birkenhead, St Helens, Wallasey, Southport
products chemicals, electrical goods, vehicles
population (1991) 1,376,800
famous people the Beatles.

Merv oasis in Turkmenistan, a centre of civilization from at least 1200 BC, and site of a town founded by Alexander the Great. Old Merv was destroyed by the emir of Bokhara 1787, and the modern town of Mary, founded by the Russians in 1885, lies 29 km/18 mi west.

mesa (Spanish 'table') a steep-sided plateau, particularly those found in the desert areas of the USA and Mexico. A small mesa is called a butte.

mescalin drug derived from a turnip-shaped cactus (*Lophophora williamsii*), known locally as ◊peyote. The tops, which scarcely appear above ground, are dried and chewed, or added to alcoholic drinks.

Mesmer Friedrich Anton 1733–1815. Austrian physician, who was an early experimenter in ◊hypnosis, which was formerly (and popularly) called *mesmerism* after him.

Mesolithic the Middle Stone Age period of ◊prehistory.

meson unstable fundamental particle with mass intermediate between those of the electron and the proton, found in cosmic radiation and emitted by nuclei under bombardment by very high-energy particles.

mesophyll the tissue between the upper and lower epidermis of a leaf blade (◊lamina), consisting of parenchyma-like cells containing numerous ◊chloroplasts.

Mesopotamia the land between the rivers Euphrates and Tigris, part of modern Iraq. Here the civilizations of Sumer and Babylon flourished, and some consider it the site of the earliest civilization.

mesosphere layer in the Earth's ◊atmosphere above the stratosphere and below the thermosphere. It lies between about 50 km/31 mi and 80 km/50 mi above the ground.

Mesozoic era of geological time 248–65 million years ago, consisting of the Triassic, Jurassic, and Cretaceous periods. The continent were joined together as Pangaea, dinosaurs were abundant, other giant reptiles dominated the sea and air, and ferns, horsetails, and cycads thrived in a warm climate worldwide. By the end of the Mesozoic era, many of the large reptiles and marine fauna were extinct.

Messalina Valeria c. 22–48 AD. Third wife of the Roman emperor ◊Claudius, whom she dominated. She was notorious for her immorality, forcing a noble to marry her in 48 AD, although still married to Claudius, who then had her executed.

Messerschmitt Willy 1898–1978. German plane designer, whose ME-109 was a standard Luftwaffe fighter in World War II, and whose ME-262 (1942) was the first mass-produced jet fighter.

Messiaen Olivier 1908– . French composer and organist. He was an innovator both with tone and rhythm and his teaching influenced contemporary composers including Boulez and Stockhausen. Among his better-known works are the *Quatuor pour la fin du temps* 1941, the large-scale *Turangalîla Symphony* 1949, and several organ pieces.

messiah a saviour or deliverer. Jews from the time of the Old Testament exile in Babylon have looked forward to the coming of a messiah. Christians believe that the messiah came in the person of ◊Jesus Christ.

Messier Charles 1730–1817. French astronomer, who discovered 15 comets and in 1781 published a list of 103 star clusters and nebulae. Objects on this list are given M (for Messier) numbers which astronomers still use today, such as M1, the Crab Nebula, and M31, the Andromeda Galaxy.

Messina, Strait of channel in the central Mediterranean separating Sicily from mainland Italy; in Greek legend a monster (Charybdis), who devoured ships, lived in the whirlpool on the Sicilian side, and another (Scylla), who devoured sailors, in the rock on the Italian side. The classical hero Odysseus passed safely between them.

metabolism the chemical processes of living organisms: a constant alternation of building up (**anabolism**) and breaking down (**catabolism**). For example, green plants build up complex organic substances from water, carbon dioxide, and mineral salts (photosynthesis); by digestion animals partially break down complex organic substances, ingested as food, and subsequently resynthesize them in their own bodies.

metal a type of element with certain chemical characteristics and physical properties. Metals are good conductors of heat and electricity; opaque, but reflect light well; malleable, which enables them to be cold-worked and rolled into sheets; and ductile, which permits them to be drawn into thin wires. Sixty to seventy metals are known; their many uses include engineering and jewellery.

metal detector an electronic device for detecting metal, usually below ground, developed from the wartime mine detector. In the head of the metal detector is a coil, which is part of an electronic circuit. The presence of metal causes the frequency of the signal in the circuit to change, setting up an audible note in the headphones worn by the user.

metal fatigue a condition in which metals fail or fracture under relatively light loads, when these loads are applied repeatedly. Structures that are subject to flexing, such as the airframes of aircraft, are prone to metal fatigue.

metalloid (or *semimetal*) an element, such as arsenic, with some metallic properties; metalloids are thus usually electrically semiconducting. The term is also used for nonmetallic elements, such as carbon, which can form an alloy with a metal.

metallurgy the science and technology of metals. Extractive or *process metallurgy* is concerned with the extraction of metals from their ◊ores, and refining and adapting them for use. *Physical metallurgy* is concerned with their properties and application.

metamorphic rock a rock altered in structure and composition by pressure and/or heat although it does not melt (if it melts it is termed igneous rock).

metamorphism geological term referring to the changes that have occurred in rocks of the Earth's crust (◊metamorphic rocks are those changed by metamorphism as opposed to ◊igneous rocks).

metamorphosis a period during the life cycle of many invertebrates, most amphibians, and some fish, during which the individual's body changes from one form to another through a major reconstitution of its tissues. For example, adult frogs are produced by metamorphosis from tadpoles, and butterflies are produced from caterpillars following metamorphosis within a pupa.

metaphor a figure of speech whose name in Greek means 'transfer' and implies the use of an analogy or close comparison between two things that are not normally treated as if they had anything in common. Metaphor is a common means of extending the uses and references of words. See also ◊simile.

metaphysical in English literature, a term applied to a group of 17th-century poets, whose work is characterized by conciseness, ingenious, often highly intricate word-play, and striking imagery. The best-known exponents of this genre are ◊Donne, ◊Herbert and ◊Cowley.

metaphysics a branch of philosophy that deals with first principles, especially 'being' (ontology) and 'knowing' (epistemology), and which is concerned with the ultimate nature of reality. It has been maintained that no certain knowledge of metaphysical questions is possible.

Metaxas Joannis 1870–1941. Greek soldier and politician, born in Ithaca. He restored ◊George II (1890–1947) as king of Greece, under whom he established a dictatorship as prime minister from 1936, and introduced several important economic and military reforms. He led resistance to the Italian invasion of Greece in 1941, refusing to abandon Greece's neutral position.

metempsychosis another name for ◊reincarnation.

meteor a flash of light in the sky, popularly known as a *shooting* or *falling star*, caused by a particle of dust, a *meteoroid*, entering the atmosphere at speeds up to 70 km/45 mi per sec and burning up by friction. Several times each year the Earth encounters swarms of dust shed by comets, which give rise to a *meteor shower*. This usually comes from one particular point in the sky, after which the shower is named; the Perseid meteor shower in August appears in the constellation Perseus.

meteorite a piece of rock or metal from space that reaches the surface of the Earth, Moon, or other body. Meteorites are thought to be fragments from asteroids, although some may be pieces from the heads of comets. Most are stony, although some are made of iron and a few have a mixed rock-iron composition. Meteor Crater in Arizona, about 1,200 m/4,000 ft in diameter and 200 m/650 ft deep, is the site of a meteorite impact about 50,000 years ago.

meteorology the scientific observation and study of the ◊atmosphere, to enable weather to be accurately forecast. Data from meteorological stations and weather satellites is collated by computer at central agencies such as the Meteorological Office in Bracknell, near London, and a forecast and ◊weather maps based on current readings are issued at regular intervals.

meter an instrument used for measurement; the term is often compounded with a prefix to denote a specific type of meter, for example, ammeter, voltmeter, flowmeter, or pedometer. Some meters may not only indicate but also integrate and/or record measurements.

methanal HCHO (common name *formaldehyde*) a gas at ordinary temperatures, condensing to a liquid at −21°C. It has a powerful penetrating smell. In aqueous solution it is used as a biological preservative. It is used in manufacture of plastics, dyes, foam (for example urea-formaldehyde foam, used in insulation), and in medicine.

methane the simplest hydrocarbon, CH_4, of the paraffin series. Colourless, odourless, and lighter than air, it burns with a bluish flame, and explodes when mixed with air or oxygen. It is the chief constituent of natural gas and also occurs in the explosive firedamp of coal mines, and in marsh gas formed from rotting vegetation, which results by spontaneous combustion in the pale flame seen over marshland, and known as will-o'the-wisp or ignis fatuus.

methanogenic bacteria one of a group of primitive bacteria (◊archaebacteria). They give off methane gas as a by-product of their metabolism, and are common in sewage-treatment plants and hot springs, where the temperature is high and oxygen is absent.

methanoic acid HCOOH (common name *formic acid*) a colourless, slightly fuming liquid that melts at 8°C and boils at 101°C. It occurs in stinging ants, nettles, sweat, and pine needles, and is used in dyeing, tanning, and electroplating.

methanol CH_3OH (common name *methyl alcohol*) the simplest of the alcohols. It can be made by the dry distillation of wood (hence it is also known as wood alcohol), but today is usually made from coal or natural gas. When pure, it is a colourless, flammable liquid with a pleasant odour, and is highly poisonous. It is used to produce formaldehyde (from which resins and plastics can be made), methyl-tert-butyl ether (MTB) (a replacement for lead as an octane-booster in petrol), vinyl acetate (largely used in paint manufacture); and petrol.

Method the US adaptation of ◊Stanislavsky's teachings on acting and direction, in which importance is attached to the psychological building of a role rather than the technical side of its presentation.

Methodism evangelical Protestant Christian movement which was founded by John ◊Wesley in 1739 within the Church of England, but which became a separate body in 1795. The church government is presbyterian in Britain and episcopal in the USA. There are over 50 million Methodists in 1988.

Methuselah in the Old Testament, Hebrew patriarch who lived before the Flood; his supposed age of 969 years made him a byword for longevity.

methyl alcohol another name for ◊methanol.

methylated spirit alcohol which has been rendered undrinkable, and is free of duty for industrial purposes.

methyl benzene another name for ◊toluene.

metonymy a figure of speech whose Greek name suggests a transferred title. When people speak or write metonymically they work by association. They may refer to the theatrical profession as 'the stage', or call journalists 'the press', See also ◊synecdoche.

metre SI unit of length (m), equivalent to 1.094 yards. It is defined as the length of the path travelled by light in a vacuum during a time interval of 1/299,792,458 of a second.

metric system system of weights and measures developed in France in the 18th century and recognized by other countries including the UK in the 19th century. In 1960 an international conference on weights and measures recommended the universal adoption of a revised International System (Système International d'Unités, or SI), with seven prescribed 'base units', the metre 'm' for length, kilogram 'kg' for mass, second 's' for time, ampere 'A' for electric current, kelvin 'K' for thermodynamic temperature, candela 'cd' for luminous intensity, and mole 'mol' for quantity of matter.

metropolitan in the Christian church generally, a bishop who has rule over other bishops (termed **suffragans**). In the Church of England, the archbishops of York and Canterbury are both metropolitans. In the Eastern Orthodox Church, a metropolitan has a rank between an archbishop and a ◊patriarch.

metropolitan county in England, a group of six counties (1974–86) established under the Local Government Act 1972 in the major urban areas outside London: Tyne and Wear, South Yorkshire, Merseyside, West Midlands, Greater Manchester, and West Yorkshire. Their elected assemblies were abolished 1986 when their areas of responsibility reverted to district councils.

Metropolitan Opera Company foremost opera company in the USA, founded 1883 in New York. The Metropolitan Opera House (opened 1883) was demolished 1966, and the company transferred to the Lincoln Center.

Metternich Klemens (Wenzel Lothar), Prince von Metternich 1773–1859. Austrian foreign minister from 1809 until the 1848 revolution forced him to flee to the UK. At the Congress of Vienna of 1815 he advocated cooperation by the great powers to suppress democratic movements.

Mexican Empire short-lived empire 1822–23 following the liberation of Mexico from Spain. The empire lasted only eight months, under the revolutionary leader ◊Iturbide.

Mexican War war between the USA and Mexico 1846–48, begun when Gen Zachary Taylor invaded New Mexico. Mexico City was taken in 1847, and under the Treaty of Guadaloupe-Hidalgo, Mexico lost Texas, New Mexico, and California (half its territory) to the USA for $15 million compensation.

Mexico country in Central America, bordered N by the USA, E by the Gulf of Mexico, SE by Belize and Guatemala, and SW and W by the Pacific Ocean.

Mexico City (Spanish *Ciudad de México*) capital, and industrial (iron, steel, chemicals, textiles) and cultural centre of Mexico, 2,255 m/7,400 ft above sea level on the S edge of the central plateau; population (1985) 15,667,000.

Meyerbeer Giacomo. Adopted name of German composer Jakob Liebmann Beer 1791–1864. He became best known for his spectacular operas, including *Robert le Diable* 1831 and *Les Huguenots* 1836.

mezuzah in Judaism, a small box containing a parchment scroll inscribed with a prayer, the Shema,

Mexico
United States of
(*Estados Unidos Mexicanos*)

0 miles 500
0 km 1000

area 1,979,650 sq km/763,944 sq mi
capital Mexico City
towns Guadalajara, Monterrey; port Veracruz
physical partly arid central highlands flanked by
Sierra Madre mountain ranges E and W; tropical
coastal plains
head of state and government Carlos Salinas de
Gortari from 1988

political system federal democratic republic
exports silver, gold, lead, uranium; oil, natural gas,
traditional handicrafts, fish
currency peso
population (1990 est) 88,335,000 (60% mixed
descent, 30% Indian, 10% Spanish descent; 50%
under 20 years of age); annual growth rate 2.6%
life expectancy men 67, women 73
language Spanish (official); Indian languages
include Nahuatl, Maya, and Mixtec
religion Roman Catholic 97%
literacy 92% male/88% female (1989)
GNP $126 bn (1987); $2,082 per head
chronology
1821 Mexico achieved independence from Spain.
1846–48 Mexico at war with USA.
1848 Maya Indian revolt suppressed.
1917 New constitution introduced, designed to
establish permanent democracy.
1983–84 Financial crisis.
1985 Institutional Revolutionary Party (PRI)
returned to power. Earthquake in Mexico City.
1986 IMF loan agreement signed to keep the
country solvent until at least 1988.
1988 The PRI candidate, Carlos Salinas, won the
presidency amid allegations of election fraud.
1991 PRI won general election. President Salinas
promised constitutional reforms.
1992 Public outrage following Guadalajara gas-
explosion disaster.

---

which is found on the doorpost of every room in a
Jewish house except the bathroom.

mezzanine architectural term (derived from the
diminutive of the Italian *mezzano*, middle) for a
storey with a lower ceiling placed between two
higher storeys, usually between the ground and
first floors of a building.

mezzo-soprano female singing voice halfway
between soprano and contralto.

mezzotint a print produced by a method of etching
in density of tone rather than line, popular in the 18th
and 19th centuries. A copper or steel plate is
worked with a tool that raises a burr (rough edge),
which will hold ink. The burr is then scraped away to
produce a range of lighter tones.

MFA abbreviation for ◊*Multi-Fibre Agreement.*

Mfecane in African history, a series of disturbances
in the early 19th century among communities in
what is today the eastern part of South Africa. They
arose when chief ◊Shaka conquered the Nguni
peoples between the Tugula and Pongola rivers,
then created by conquest a centralized, militaristic
Zulu kingdom from several communities, resulting
in large-scale displacement of people. These had
repercussions as far north as modern Tanzania.

mg abbreviation for *milligram.*

Mgr in the Roman Catholic Church, the abbreviation for *Monsignor.*

MHD abbreviation for ◊magnetohydrodynamics.

mho SI unit of electrical conductance, now called
the ◊siemens; equivalent to a reciprocal ohm.

mi abbreviation for *mile.*

Maimi city and port in Florida, USA; population
(1990) 358,500. It is the hub of finance, trade,
and air transport for Latin America and the Caribbean.

mica a group of silicate minerals that split easily into
thin flakes along lines of weakness in their crystal
structure (perfect basal cleavage). They are glossy

and have a pearly lustre, and are found in schists,
gneisses, and granites. Their good thermal and
electrical insulation quality makes them valuable in
industry.

Michael in the Bible, an archangel, referred to as
the guardian angel of Israel. In the New Testament Book of Revelation he leads the hosts of
heaven to battle against Satan. In paintings he is
depicted with a flaming sword and sometimes a pair
of scales. Feast day 29 Sept (Michaelmas). Michael
is also mentioned in the Koran as the 'friend of the
Jews'.

Michael Mikhail Fyodorovich Romanov 1596–
1645. Tsar of Russia from 1613. He was elected tsar
by a national assembly, at a time of anarchy and
foreign invasion, and was the first of the house of
Romanov, which ruled until 1917.

Michael 1921– . King of Romania 1927–30 and
1940–47. The son of Carol II, he succeeded his
grandfather as king in 1927, but was displaced when
his father returned from exile in 1930. In 1940 he
was proclaimed king again on his father's abdication,
and in 1944 overthrew the fascist dictatorship of Ion
Antonescu (1882–1946) and enabled Romania to
share in the victory of the Allies at the end of the
World War II. He abdicated and left Romania in
1947.

michaelmas daisy popular name for species of
◊*Aster,* family Compositae, and also for the sea
aster or starwort.

Michaelmas Day in church tradition, the festival
of St Michael and all Angels, observed on 29 Sept,
and one of the English ◊quarter days.

Michelangelo Buonarroti 1475–1564. Italian sculptor, painter, architect, and poet, active in his native
Florence and in Rome. His giant talent dominated
the High Renaissance. The monumental *David*
1501–04 (Accademia, Florence) set a new standard
in nude sculpture. His massive figure style was
translated into fresco in the Sistine Chapel 1508–12

(Vatican). Other works in Rome include the dome of St Peter's basilica.

Michelson Albert Abraham 1852–1931. German-born US physicist. In conjunction with Edward Morley, he performed in 1887 the *Michelson-Morley experiment* to detect the motion of the Earth through the postulated ◊ether (a medium believed to be necessary for the propagation of light). The failure of the experiment indicated the non-existence of the ether, and led ◊Einstein to his theory of ◊relativity.

Michigan state of the USA, bordered by the Great Lakes, Ohio, Indiana, Wisconsin, and Canada; nickname Great Lake State or Wolverine State,
area 150,777 sq km/58,216 sq mi, including inland water
capital Lansing
towns Detroit, Grand Rapids, Flint
products cars, iron, cement, oil
population (1983) 9,069,000
famous people General Custer, Edna Ferber, Henry Ford
history explored by the French from 1618, it became British in 1763, and a US state in 1837.

Michigan, Lake lake in north central USA, one of the Great Lakes; area 58,000 sq km/22,390 sq mi. Chicago and Milwaukee are its main ports.

Mickiewicz Adam 1798–1855. Polish revolutionary poet, whose *Pan Tadeusz* 1832–34 is Poland's national epic. He died at Constantinople while raising a Polish corps to fight against Russia in the Crimean War.

micro- prefix denoting one millionth part (10^{-6}) (symbol μ). For example a micrometre, μm, is one millionth of a metre.

microbe another word for ◊microorganism.

microbiological warfare use of harmful microbes as a weapon. See ◊biological warfare.

microbiology the study of organisms that can only be seen under the microscope, mostly single-celled organisms such as viruses, bacteria, protozoa, and yeasts. The practical applications of microbiology are in medicine (since many microorganisms cause disease); in brewing, baking, and so on, where the microorganisms carry out fermentation; and in genetic engineering, which is making microbiology an increasingly important field.

microchip popular name for the ◊silicon chip or ◊integrated circuit.

microcomputer or *micro* a small desktop or portable computer, typically built around a single printed circuit board and including a microprocessor chip. It normally consists of a processor unit with built-in disk drives, a keyboard, and a VDU (screen).

microscope

eyepiece lens
light paths
coarse focusing adjustment
fine focusing adjustment
barrel
alternative objective lenses
objective lens
slide
moves slide
stage light source
condenser
stage
mirror   stand   condenser focus adjuster

microeconomics the division of economics concerned with the study of individual decision-making units within an economy: a consumer, firm, or industry. Unlike macroeconomics, it looks at how individual markets work and how individual producers and consumers make their choices and with what consequences. This is done by analysing how relevant prices of goods are determined and the quantities that will be bought and sold. The operation of the market is therefore a central concern of microeconomics.

microform any of the media on which printed text is photographically reduced to a size unreadable by the naked eye.

microlight aircraft very light aircraft, with small engines, rather like powered hang-gliders.

micrometer instrument for measuring minute lengths or angles with great accuracy; different types of micrometer are used in astronomical and engineering work.

micrometre one millionth of a ◊metre.

microminiaturization the reduction in size and weight of electronic components. The first size

micrometer

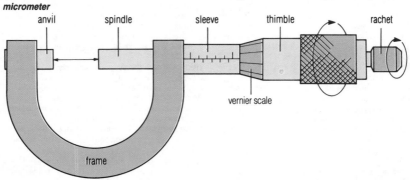

anvil   spindle   sleeve   thimble   rachet
vernier scale
frame

reduction in electronics was brought about by the introduction of the ◊transistor. Further reductions were achieved with ◊integrated circuits and the ◊silicon chip.

Micronesia islands in the Pacific Ocean lying N of ◊Melanesia, including the Federated States of Micronesia, Belau, Kiribati, the Mariana and Marshall Islands, Nauru, and Tuvalu.

Micronesia, Federated States of self-governing island group (Kosrae, Ponape, Truk, and Yap) in the W Pacific; capital Kolonia, on Ponape; population (1984) 88,500. It is part of the US Trust Territory.

microorganism or *microbe* a living organism invisible to the naked eye but visible under a microscope. Most are single-celled; they include bacteria, protozoa, yeasts, viruses, and some algae. The term has no taxonomic significance in biology. The study of microorganisms is known as microbiology.

microphone the first component in a sound-reproducing system, whereby the mechanical energy of sound waves is converted into electrical energy. One of the simplest is the telephone receiver mouthpiece, invented by Alexander Graham Bell in 1876, and other well-known examples are those used with broadcasting and sound-film apparatus.

microprocessor a computer's central processing unit (◊CPU) contained on a single ◊integrated circuit. The appearance of the first microprocessors in 1971 heralded the introduction of the ◊microcomputer. The microprocessor has led to a dramatic fall in the size and cost of computers.

microscope instrument for magnification with high resolution for detail. Optical and electron microscopes are the ones chiefly in use; other types include acoustic and X-ray. Laser microscopy is under development.

microwave an ◊electromagnetic wave with a wavelength in the range 0.1 to 30 cm (between radio waves and ◊infrared radiation). They are used in radar, as carrier waves in radio broadcasting, and in microwave heating and cooking.

microwave heating heating by means of ◊microwaves. Microwave ovens use this form of heating for the rapid cooking and reheating of foods, where heat is generated throughout the food simultaneously. Industrially, microwave heating is used for destroying insects in grain and enzymes in processed food; for pasteurizing and sterilizing liquids; and drying timber and paper.

Midas in Greek legend, a King of Phrygia who was granted the gift of converting all he touched to gold, and who, for preferring the music of Pan to that of Apollo, was given ass's ears by the latter.

MIDAS acronym for Missile Defence Alarm System.

Mid-Atlantic Ridge the ◊ocean ridge, formed by the movement of plates described by ◊plate tectonics, that runs along the centre of the Atlantic Ocean, parallel to its edges, for some 14,000 km/8,800 mi – almost from the Arctic to the Antarctic.

Middle Ages the period of European history between the fall of the Roman Empire in the 5th century to the Renaissance in the 15th. Among the period's distinctive features were the unity of W Europe within the Roman Catholic church, the feudal organization of political, social, and economic relations, and the use of art for largely religious purposes.

Middle East indeterminate area now usually taken to include the Balkan States, Egypt, and SW Asia. Until the 1940s, this area was generally called the

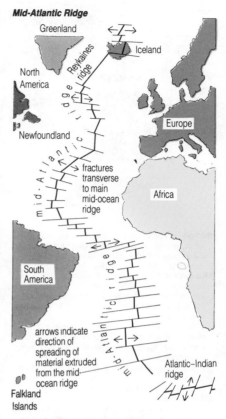

Mid-Atlantic Ridge

Greenland
Iceland
Reykjanes ridge
North America
Newfoundland
Europe
fractures transverse to main mid-ocean ridge
Africa
South America
arrows indicate direction of spreading of material extruded from the mid-ocean ridge
Atlantic–Indian ridge
Falkland Islands

Near East, and the term Middle East referred to the area from Iran to Burma.

Middle English the period of the ◊English language from about 1050 to 1550.

Middle Kingdom *Egyptian* a period of Egyptian history extending from the late 11th to the 13th dynasty (roughly 2040–1670 BC);
Chinese Chinese term for China and its empire up to 1912, describing its central position in the Far East.

Middlemarch, A Study of Provincial Life a novel by George Eliot, published 1871–72. Set in the fictitious provincial town of Middlemarch, the novel has several interwoven plots played out against a background of social and political upheaval.

Middlesex former English county, absorbed by Greater London in 1965. Contained within the Thames basin, it provided good agricultural land before it was built over. It was settled in the 6th century by Saxons, and its name comes from its position between the kingdoms of the East and West Saxons.

Middleton Thomas c. 1570–1627. English dramatist. He produced numerous romantic plays and realistic comedies, both alone and in collaboration. The best known are *A Fair Quarrel* and *The Changeling* 1622 with Rowley; *The Roaring Girl* with Dekker; and *Women Beware Women* 1621.

Middle Way the path to enlightenment, taught by Buddha, which avoids the extremes of indulgence and asceticism.

Middx abbreviation for ◊*Middlesex*.

migration

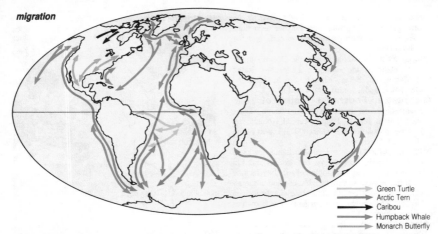

> Green Turtle
> Arctic Tern
> Caribou
> Humpback Whale
> Monarch Butterfly

midge popular name for many ◊gnat-like insects, generally divided into biting midges (family Ceratopogonidae) that suck blood, and non-biting midges (family Chironomidae).

Mid Glamorgan county of S Wales
area 1,019 sq km/393 sq mi
towns administrative headquarters Cardiff; resort Porthcawl; Aberdare, Merthyr Tydfil, Bridgend, Pontypridd
products the north was formerly an important coal (Rhondda) and iron and steel area; Royal Mint at Llantrisant; agriculture in the S; Caerphilly noted for mild cheese
population (1983) 536,400, largest of the Welsh counties
language 8% Welsh-speaking, English.

MIDI abbreviation for *Musical Instrument Digital Interface*, a device which enables signals to be transferred from an electronic keyboard to a computer or to other digital instruments. Pitch, dynamics and decay rate can all be transmitted. The information-sending device is called a controller and the reading device (such as a computer) the sequencer.

Midi-Pyrénées region of SW France, consisting of the *départements* of Ariège, Aveyron, Haute-Garonne, Gers, Lot, Haute-Pyrénées, Tarn, and Tarn-et-Garonne; area 45,348 sq km/17,510 sq mi; population (1984) 2,340,000.

Midlands area of England corresponding roughly to the Anglo-Saxon kingdom of ◊Mercia
E Midlands Derbyshire, Leicestershire, Northamptonshire, Nottinghamshire *W Midlands* parts of Staffordshire, Warwickshire, and Worcestershire; and (often included) *S Midlands* Bedfordshire, Buckinghamshire, and Oxfordshire.

midnight Sun the constant appearance of the Sun within the Arctic circle above the horizon during the summer.

Midrash the ancient Jewish commentaries on the Bible, in the form of sermons in which allegory and legendary illustration are used. They were compiled mainly in Palestine between 400 and 1200 AD.

midsummer the summer ◊solstice, about 21 Jun. *Midsummer Day* is 24 Jun, a quarter day and the festival of St John the Baptist.

Midsummer Night's Dream, A a comedy by William Shakespeare, first performed 1595–96. Hermia, Lysander, Demetrius, and Helena in their various romantic endeavours are subjected to the playful manipulations of fairies in a wood near Athens.

Midway Islands two islands in the Pacific, 1,800 km/1,110 mi NW of Honolulu; area 5.5 sq km/2.2 sq mi. They were annexed by the USA in 1867, and are now administered by the US Navy. The naval *Battle of Midway* 3–6 Jun 1942, between the USA and Japan, was the turning point in the Pacific in World War II.

Midwest or *Middle West* a large area of N central USA. It is a loosely defined, but is generally taken to comprise the states of Ohio, Indiana, Illinois, Michigan, Iowa, Wisconsin, Minnesota, and sometimes Nebraska. It tends to be conservative socially and politically, and isolationist. Traditionally its economy is divided between agriculture and heavy industry.

Mies van der Rohe Ludwig 1886–1969. German architect, born in Aachen who practised in the USA from 1937. He was director of the ◊Bauhaus 1929–33. He became professor at the Illinois Technical Institute 1938–58, for which he designed new buildings on characteristically functional lines from 1941. He also designed the bronze-and-glass Seagram building in New York 1956–59.

mignonette sweet-scented plant *Reseda odorata*, native to N Africa, bearing yellowish-green flowers in racemes (along the main stem), with abundant foliage.

migraine acute, sometimes incapacitating headaches which recur, often with advance symptoms such as flashing lights, and accompanied by nausea. No cure has been discovered, but ◊ergotamine normally relieves the symptoms. Some sufferers learn to avoid particular foods (such as chocolate), which suggests an allergic factor.

migrant labour people who leave their homelands to work elsewhere, usually because of economic or political pressures.

migration the movement, either seasonal or as part of a single life cycle, of certain animals, chiefly birds and fish, to distant breeding or feeding grounds.

Mihailović Draza 1893–1946. Yugoslav soldier, leader of the guerrilla ◊Chetniks of World War II against the German occupation. His feud with Tito's communists led to the withdrawal of Allied support and that of his own exiled government from 1943. He turned for help to the Italians and Germans, and was eventually shot for treason.

mikado (Japanese 'honourable palace gate') title until 1867 of the Japanese emperor, when it

Milan *The Gothic cathedral (c. 1450).*

was replaced by the term 'tenno' (heavenly sovereign).

Milan (Italian *Milano*) industrial city (aircraft, cars, locomotives, textiles), financial and cultural centre, capital of Lombardy, Italy; population (1984) 1,534,000.

mildew minute fungi which appear as a destructive growth on plants, paper, leather, or wood, when exposed to damp; they form a thin white coating.

mile Imperial measure of length. A statute mile is equal to 1.60934 km/1,760 yd , and an international nautical mile is equal to 1,852 m/2,026 yd.

Miles Bernard (Baron Miles) 1907– . English actor and producer. He appeared in *Thunder Rock* 1940 and *Othello* 1942, and his films include *Great Expectations* 1947. He founded a trust which built the City of London's first new theatre for 300 years, the Mermaid 1959.

Miletus ancient Greek city in SW Asia Minor, with a port which eventually silted up. It carried on an important trade with Egypt and the Black Sea.

milfoil another name for the herb ◊yarrow. Water milfoils, plants of the genus *Miriophyllum*, are unrelated; they have whorls of fine leaves.

Milhaud Darius 1892–1974. French composer, a member of the group of composers ◊*Les Six*. His work includes the operas *Christophe Colombe* 1928 and *Bolivar* 1943, and the jazz ballet *La Création du monde* 1923.

Militant Tendency a faction formed within the British Labour Party, aligned with the newspaper *Militant*. It became active in the 1970s, with radical socialist policies based on Trotskyism (see ◊Trotsky), and gained some success in local government, for example in the inner-city area of Liverpool. In the mid-1980s the Labour Party considered it to be an organization within the party and banned it.

Military–Industrial Complex, The phrase used by US president and former general, Dwight D Eisenhower, in his 1961 farewell address to warn Americans of the potential misplacement of power that might arise from the conjunction of a military establishment and arms industry both inflated by Cold War demands.

military law articles or regulations that apply to members of the armed services.

militia a body of civilian soldiers, usually with some military training, who are on call in emergencies, distinct from professional soldiers. In Switzerland, the militia is the national defence force, and every able-bodied man is liable for service in it. In the UK the ◊*Territorial Army* and in the USA the ◊*National Guard* have supplanted earlier voluntary militias.

milk the secretion of the ◊mammary glands of female mammals, with which they suckle their young

(during ◊lactation). The milk of cows, goats, or sheep is that most usually consumed by humans; over 85 per cent is water, the remainder comprising protein, fat, lactose (a sugar), calcium, phosphorus, iron, and vitamins. Milk composition varies between species, depending on the nutritional requirements of the young; human milk contains less protein and more lactose than that of cows.

milking machine a machine that uses suction to milk cows. A suction milking machine was invented in the USA by L O Colvin in 1860. Later it was improved so that the suction was regularly released by a pulsating device, since it was found that continuous suction is bad for the cow. Modern milking machines also work by suction and pulsation.

Milky Way the faint band of light crossing the night sky, consisting of stars in the plane of our Galaxy. The name Milky Way is often used for the Galaxy itself. It is a spiral ◊galaxy, about 100,000 light years in diameter, containing at least 100 billion stars. It is a member of a small cluster, the ◊Local Group. The Sun is in one of its spiral arms, about 25,000 light years from the centre.

Mill James 1773–1836. Scottish philosopher and political thinker who developed the theory of ◊utilitarianism. He is remembered for his political articles, and for the rigorous education he gave his son John Stuart Mill.

Mill John Stuart 1806–1873. English philosopher and economist, who wrote *On Liberty* 1859, the classic philosophical defence of liberalism, and *Utilitarianism* 1863, a version of the 'greatest happiness for the greatest number' principle in ethics.

Millais John Everett 1829–1896. British painter, a founder member of the ◊Pre-Raphaelite Brotherhood (PRB) in 1848. One of his works, *Christ in the House of His Parents* 1850 (Tate Gallery, London) caused an outcry on its first showing, since its realistic detail was considered unfitting to the sacred subject. By the late 1850s Millais had dropped out of the PRB and his style became more fluent and less detailed.

Miller Arthur 1915– . US playwright. His plays deal with family relationships and contemporary American values, and include *All my Sons* 1947, *Death of a Salesman* 1949,and *The Crucible* 1953. He was married 1956–61 to Marilyn ◊Monroe, for whom he wrote the film *The Misfits* 1960.

Miller Glenn 1904–1944. US trombonist and, as bandleader, exponent of the big-band 'swing' sound from 1938. He composed his signature tune 'Moonlight Serenade'. He disappeared without trace on a flight between England and France during World War II.

millet type of grass, family Gramineae, of which the grains are used as a cereal food, and the stems as fodder.

Millet Jean François 1814–1875. French painter, a leading member of the ◊Barbizon school, painting scenes of peasant life and landscapes. *The Angelus* 1859 (Musée d'Orsay, Paris) brought him great success and was widely reproduced in his day.

Millett Kate 1934– . US radical feminist lecturer, writer and sculptor, whose book *Sexual Politics* 1970 was a landmark in feminist thinking. She was a founding member of the *National Organization of Women* (NOW). Later books include *Flying* 1974, *The Prostitution Papers* 1976, and *Sita* 1977.

millibar unit of pressure, equal to one thousandth of a ◊bar.

Millikan Robert Andrews 1868–1953. US physicist, awarded a Nobel prize in physics in 1923 for his determination of the ◊electric charge on an

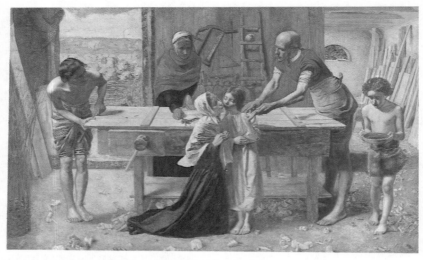

Millais Christ in the House of His Parents *(1850) Tate Gallery, London.*

electron by his oil-drop experiment (which took him five years up to 1913 to perfect).

millilitre on thousandth of a litre (ml), equivalent to 1 cm³ (cc).

millimetre of mercury unit of pressure, used in medicine for measuring blood pressure, defined as the pressure exerted by a column of mercury 1 millimetre high, under the action of gravity.

millipede arthropod of worldwide distribution, of the class Diplopoda. It has a segmented body, each segment usually bearing two pairs of legs, and the distinct head bears a pair of short clubbed antennae. Certain orders have silk glands. Millipedes live in damp dark places, feeding mainly on rotting vegetation. Some species injure crops by feeding on tender roots, and some produce a poisonous secretion in defence. Most are a few cm long; a few in the tropics are 30 cm/12 in.

Mills C Wright 1916–1962. US sociologist, whose concern for humanity, ethical values, and individual freedom led him to criticize the US Establishment.

Miller US playwright Arthur Miller, photographed in Sept 1956.

Milne A(lan) A(lexander) 1882–1956. British writer. His books for children were based on the teddy bear and other toys of his son Christopher Robin (*Winnie-the-Pooh* 1926 and *The House at Pooh Corner* 1928). He also wrote children's verse (*When We Were Very Young* 1924 and *Now We Are Six* 1927), and plays, including an adaptation of Kenneth Grahame's *The Wind in the Willows* as *Toad of Toad Hall* 1929.

Milosevic Slobodan 1941– . Serbian communist politician, party chief and president of Serbia from 1986; re-elected Dec 1990 in multiparty elections. Milosevic wielded considerable influence over the Serb-dominated Yugoslav federal army during the 1991–92 civil war and has continued to back Serbian militia in ◊Bosnia-Herzegovina 1992–93, although publicly disclaiming any intention to carve up the newly independent republic.

Milosz Czeslaw 1911– . Polish writer, born in Lithuania. He became a diplomat before defecting and taking US nationality. His poetry in English translation includes *Selected Poems* 1973 and *Bells in Winter* 1978.

Milton John 1608–1674. English poet. His early poems include the pastoral *L'allegro* and *Il penseroso* 1632, the masque *Comus* 1633, and the elegy *Lycidas* 1637. His later works include *Paradise Lost* 1667, *Paradise Regained* 1677, and the classic drama, *Samson Agonistes* 1677.

Milwaukee industrial (meatpacking, brewing, engineering, textiles) port in Wisconsin, USA, on Lake Michigan; population (1990) 628,100.

mime in ancient Greece, a crude, realistic comedy with speech and exaggerated gesture, but in common usage, acting in which gestures, movements, and facial expressions replace dialogue. It has developed as a form of theatre, particularly in France, where ◊Marceau and ◊Barrault have continued the traditions established in the 19th century by Deburau, and the practices of the ◊commedia dell'arte in Italy.

mimicry the imitation of one ◊species (or group of species) by another. The most common form is *Batasian mimicry* (named after H W ◊Bates), where the mimic resembles a

millet

mimicry

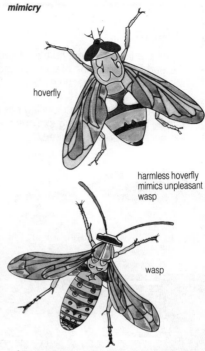

hoverfly

harmless hoverfly mimics unpleasant wasp

wasp

model that is poisonous or unpleasant to eat, and has ◊aposematic coloration; the mimic thus benefits from the fact that predators learn to avoid the model. Hoverflies which resemble bees or wasps are an example. In *Mullerian mimicry*, two or more equally poisonous or distasteful species have a similar colour pattern, thereby reinforcing the warning each gives to predators. In some cases, mimicry is not for protection, but allows the mimic to prey on, or parasitize, the model. While appearance is usually the basis for mimicry, calls, songs, scents, and other signals can also be mimicked.

mimosa plant of the family Leguminosae, found in tropical and subtropical regions. It ranges from herb to large tree size, and bears small, fluffy, golden ball-like flowers, tufts of stamens, and pinnate leaves, divided into a multiplicity of small leaflets.

Minangkabau people of W Sumatra in Indonesia. In addition to approximately 3,000,000 Minagkabau in W Sumatra, there are sizeable communities in the major Indonesian cities. The Minangkabau language belongs to the Austronesian family.

minaret a slender turret or tower attached to a Muslim mosque. It has one or more balconies, from which the *muezzin* calls the people to prayer five times a day.

mind in philosophy, the presumed mental or physical being or faculty that enables a person to think, will, and feel; the seat of the intelligence and of memory; sometimes only the cognitive or intellectual powers as distinguished from the will and the emotions. The relation of mind to matter may be variously regarded. Traditionally, materialism identifies the two together; mental and physical phenomena are to be explained equally in terms of matter and motion. Dualism holds that mind and matter exist independently side by side. Idealism maintains that mind is the ultimate reality, and that matter is the creation of intelligence, and does not exist apart from it.

Mindanao the second-largest island of the Philippines
area 94,627 sq km/36,526 sq mi
towns Davao, Zamboanga
physical mountainous rainforest
products pineapples, coffee, rice, coconut, rubber, hemp, timber, nickel, gold, steel, chemicals, fertilizer
population (1980) 10,905,250.

mine explosive charge on land or sea, or in the atmosphere, designed to be detonated by contact, vibration (for example from an enemy engine), magnetic influence, or a timing device. Countermeasures include metal detectors (useless for plastic types), specially equipped helicopters, and (at sea) ◊minesweepers.

mineral a naturally formed inorganic substance with a particular chemical composition and usually a well-defined crystal structure. Either in their perfect crystalline form or otherwise, minerals are the constituents of rocks. In more general usage, a mineral is any substance economically valuable for mining (including coal and oil, despite their organic origins).

mineral dressing preparing a mineral ore for processing. Ore is seldom in a fit state to be processed when it is mined; it often contains unwanted rock and dirt. Therefore it is usually crushed into a uniform size, and then separated from the dirt, or gangue. This may be done magnetically (some iron ores), by washing (gold), by treatment with chemicals (copper ores), or by ◊flotation.

mineralogy the study of minerals. The classification of minerals is chiefly based on their chemical nature: metallic, ionic, or molecular. The mineralogist also studies their crystallographic and physical characters, occurrence, and mode of formation. For minerals of economic importance, a knowledge of mining and metallurgy is needed.

mineral water water with mineral constituents gathered from the rocks over which it flows, and classified by these into earthy, brine, and oil mineral waters; or water with artificially added minerals and, sometimes, carbon dioxide.

Minerva in ancient Roman mythology, the goddess of intelligence, and of the handicrafts and arts, counterpart of the Greek ◊Athena. From the

mining

Since prehistoric times, humans have dug into the earth to obtain the materials needed to help sustain life. In the resources-hungry 20th century, power, mineral, and building needs are being met by an ever-increasing range of mining methods, allowing exploration and extraction wherever required.

Traditional ways of raising hand-hewn coal are being replaced by safer and more efficient computer-controlled operations. (1) MINOS, the Mine-Operating System, has a control centre on the surface. (2) FIDO continuously monitors underground teams. (3) MIDAS surveys seams and adjusts the shearer automatically. (4) IMPACT monitors the machinery, to save on maintenance and avoid breakdown. (5) Transport is also monitored to minimise delays. (6) Coal is graded and washed under electronic control.

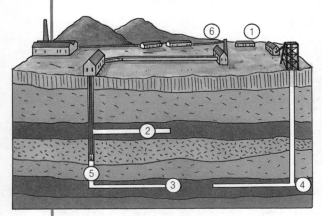

The discovery of oil and gas under the sea is not the only one to attract commercial exploitation. Mineral nodules have been found on the sea bed, and despite technical and legal problems, dredging of mineral-rich mud from the bottom of the Red Sea may soon be viable.

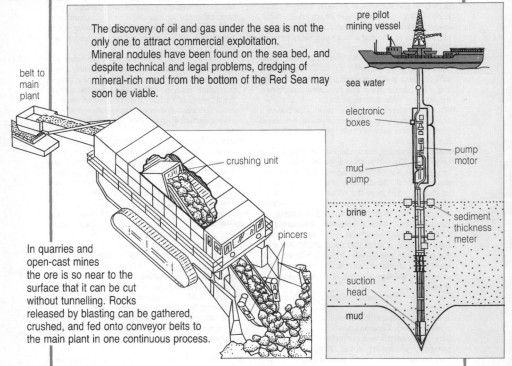

belt to main plant

crushing unit

pincers

In quarries and open-cast mines the ore is so near to the surface that it can be cut without tunnelling. Rocks released by blasting can be gathered, crushed, and fed onto conveyor belts to the main plant in one continuous process.

pre pilot mining vessel

sea water

electronic boxes

pump motor

mud pump

brine

sediment thickness meter

suction head

mud

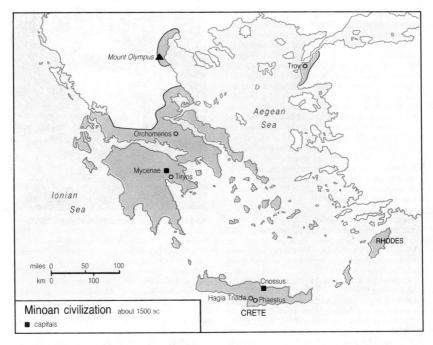

Minoan civilization about 1500 BC

CRETE

■ capitals

earliest days of ancient Rome, there was a temple to her on the Capitol.

minesweeper small sea vessel for locating mines by sonar and destroying them. A typical modern minesweeper weighs about 725 tonnes, and is built of reinforced plastic (immune to magnetic and acoustic mines). Remotely controlled miniature submarines may be used to destroy the mines by laying charges alongside them.

Mingus Charles 1922–1979. US bass player and composer. He was influential for his experimentation with atonality and dissonant effects, opening the way for the new style of free collective jazz improvisation of the 1960s.

miniature painting painting on a very small scale, notably early manuscript paintings, and later miniature portraits, sometimes set in jewelled cases. The art of manuscript painting was developed in classical times in the West, and revived in the Middle Ages. Several Islamic countries, for example Persia and India, developed strong traditions of manuscript art. Miniature portrait painting enjoyed a vogue in France and England in the 16th–19th centuries.

minicomputer a computer whose size and processing power are between those of a ⟨⟩mainframe and a ⟨⟩microcomputer.

Minimalism a movement from the late 1960s in abstract art and music towards a severely simplified composition. In *painting*, it emphasized geometrical and elemental shapes. In *sculpture*, Minimalists such as Carl André focused on industrial materials. In *music*, Minimalists such as Philip Glass and Steve Reich attempted to depart from complexity with repetitive rhythms and harmonies.

mining extraction of minerals from under the land or sea for industrial or domestic use. Exhaustion of traditionally accessible resources has led to development of new mining techniques, for example extraction of oil from under the North Sea

and from land shale reserves. Technology is also under development for the exploitation of minerals from entirely new sources such as mud deposits and mineral nodules on the sea bed.

mink two species of carnivorous mammal of the weasel family, usually found in or near water. They have rich brown fur, and are up to 50 cm/1.6 ft long with bushy tails 20 cm/8 in long. They live in Eurasia and North America.

Minnesinger German lyric poets of the 12th and 13th centuries, who in their songs dealt mainly with the theme of courtly love without revealing the identity of the object of their affections. Minnesingers included Dietmar von Aist, Friedrich von Hausen, Heinrich von Morungen, Reinmar, and Walther von der Vogelweide.

Minnesota N midwest state of the USA; nickname North Star or Gopher State
area 217,735 sq km/84,068 sq mi
capital St Paul
towns Minneapolis, Duluth
products cereals, potatoes, livestock products; pulpwood; iron ore (60% of US output); farm and other machinery
population (1983) 4,145,500
famous people F Scott Fitzgerald, Sinclair Lewis, William and Charles Mayo
history the first Europeans to explore were French fur traders in the 17th century; part was ceded to Britain in 1763, and part passed to the USA under the Louisiana Purchase in 1803; it became a territory 1849 and a state 1858.

minnow abundant small fish *Phoxinus phoxinus* of the carp family found in streams and ponds worldwide. Most species are small and dully-coloured, but some are brightly-coloured. They feed on larvae and insects.

Minoan civilization Bronze Age civilization on the Aegean island of Crete. The name is derived from Minos, the legendary king of Crete, reputed to be the son of the god Zeus. The civilization is divided into three main periods: Early Minoan, about 3000–2200 BC, Middle Minoan, about 2200–1580 BC; and Late Minoan, about 1580–1100 BC.

minor the legal term for those under the age of majority, which varies from country to country but is usually between 18 and 21. In Britain (since 1970), the USA (from 1971 for voting, and in some states for all other purposes) and certain European countries the age of majority is 18. Most civic and legal rights and duties only accrue at the age of majority; for example, the rights of vote, to make a will, and (usually) to make a fully binding contract, and the duty to act as a juror.

Minorca (Spanish *Menorca*) second largest of the ◊Balearic Islands in the Mediterranean
area 689 sq km/266 sq mi
towns Mahon, Ciudadela
products copper, lead, iron, tourism
population (1985) 55,500

Minotaur in Greek mythology, a monster, half man and half bull, offspring of Pasiphaë, wife of King Minos of Crete, and a bull. It lived in the labyrinth at Knossos and its victims were seven girls and seven youths, sent in annual tribute by Athens, until ◊Theseus slew it, with the aid of Ariadne, the daughter of Minos.

Minsk industrial city (machinery, textiles, leather; a centre of the Russian computer industry) and capital of Belarus; population (1987) 1,543,000.

minster in the UK, a church formerly attached to a monastery, for example, York Minster. Originally the term meant a monastery, and in this sense it is often preserved in place names, such as Westminster.

mint a place where coins are made under government authority. In Britain, the official mint is the *Royal Mint*; the US equivalent is the *Bureau of the Mint*.

mint in botany, an aromatic plant, genus *Mentha*, of the family Labiatae, widely distributed in temperature regions. The plants have square stems, creeping rootstocks, and flowers, usually pink or purplish, that grow in a terminal spike. Mints include *Garden mint Mentha spicata* and *peppermint Mentha piperita*.

Minto Gilbert, 4th Earl of 1845–1914. British colonial administrator, who succeeded Curzon as Viceroy of India 1905–1910. With John Morley, Secretary of State for India, he co-sponsored the Morley Minto reforms of 1909. The reforms increased Indian representation in government at provincial level, but also created separate Muslim and Hindu electorates which, it was believed, helped the British Raj in his policy of divide and rule.

Mintoff Dom (Dominic) 1916– . Labour prime minister of Malta 1971–84. He negotiated the removal of British and other foreign military bases 1971–79, and made treaties with Libya.

Minton Thomas 1765–1836. British potter. He first worked at the Caughley porcelain works, but in 1789 established himself at Stoke-on-Trent as an engraver of designs (he originated the 'willow pattern') and in the 1790s founded a pottery there, producing high-quality bone china, including tableware.

minuet European courtly dance of the 17th century, later used with the trio as the third movement in a classical symphony.

minuteman in weaponry, a US three-stage intercontinental ballistic missile, with a range of about 8,000 km/5,000 mi. In US history, it was a member

Mishima *Japanese novelist Yukio Mishima, 1970.*

of the citizens' militia in New England who fought in the War of Independence; they pledged to be ready at a minute's notice.

Miocene fourth epoch of the Tertiary period of geological time 25–5 million years ago. The name means 'middle recent'. At this time the grasslands spread over much of the continents, and hoofed mammals became numerous.

Mir Soviet space station, launched on 20 Feb 1986; an improved version of the earlier ◊Salyut.

Mirabeau Honoré Gabriel Riqueti, Comte de 1749–1791. French politician, leader of the National Assembly in the French Revolution.

miracle an event which cannot be explained by the known laws of nature and which is therefore attributed to divine intervention.

miracle play another name for ◊mystery play.

Miró Joan 1893–1983. Spanish Surrealist painter, born in Barcelona. In the mid-1920s he developed a distinctive abstract style with amoeba-like shapes, some linear, some highly coloured, generally on a plain ground.

mirror any polished surface that reflects light; often made from 'silvered' glass (in practice, a mercury alloy coating of glass). A plane (flat) mirror produces a same-size, erect 'virtual' image located behind the mirror at the same distance from it as the object is in front of it. A spherical concave mirror produces a reduced, inverted real image in front or an enlarged, erect virtual image behind it (as with a shaving mirror), depending on how close the object is to the mirror. A spherical convex mirror produces a reduced, erect virtual image behind it (as with a car's rear-view mirror).

MIRV abbreviation for *multiple independently targeted re-entry vehicle*, used in ◊nuclear warfare.

misdemeanour in English law, an obselete term for an offence less serious than a ◊felony. In the USA, a misdemeanour is an offence punishable only by a fine or short term in prison, while a felony carries a term of imprisonment of a year or more.

misericord or *miserere* in architecture, a projection on the underside of a hinged seat of the choir stalls in a church, used as a rest for a priest when standing during long services. Misericords are often decorated with carvings.

Mishima Yukio 1925–1970. Japanese novelist, whose work often deals with sexual desire and perversion, as in *Confessions of a Mask* 1949, and *The Temple of the Golden Pavilion*

1956. He committed hara-kiri (ritual suicide) as a demonstration against the corruption of the nation and the loss of the samurai warrior tradition.

Mishna a collection of commentaries on written Hebrew law, consisting of discussions between rabbis handed down orally from their inception in 70 AD until about 200, when, with the Gemara, the discussions in schools of Palestine and Babylon on law, it was committed to writing to form the Talmud.

missal in the Roman Catholic Church, a service book containing the complete office of Mass for the entire year. A simplified missal in the vernacular was introduced 1969 (obligatory from 1971), the first major reform since 1570.

missile rocket-propelled weapon, which may be nuclear-armed (see ◊nuclear warfare). The first long-range missiles used in warfare were the ◊V1 and V2 launched by Germany against Britain in World War II.

mission an organized attempt to spread a religion. Throughout its history Christianity has been the most influential missionary religion; Islam has also played had a missionary role. Missionary activity in the Third World, has frequently been criticized for its political, economic, and cultural effects on indigenous peoples.

Mississippi river in the USA, the main arm of the great river system draining the USA between the Appalachian and the Rocky mountains. The length of the Mississippi is 3,780 km/2,350 mi; of the Mississippi-Missouri 6,020 km/3,740 mi.

Mississippi state of the S USA; nickname Magnolia State
area 123,584 sq km/47,703 sq mi
capital Jackson
towns Biloxi
products cotton, sweet potatoes, sugar, rice; canned sea food at Biloxi; timber and pulp; oil and natural gas, chemicals
population (1983) 2,587,000
famous people William Faulkner, Elvis Presley, Eudora Welty
history settled in turn by French, English, and Spanish until passing under US control 1798; statehood achieved in 1817. After secession from the Union during the Civil War, it was readmitted 1870.

Mississippian US term for the Lower ◊Carboniferous period of geological time, named after the state of Mississippi.

Missouri state of the central USA; nickname Show Me State
area 180,445 sq km/69,652 sq mi
capital Jefferson City
towns St Louis, Kansas City, Springfield, Independence
products meat and other processed food; aerospace and transport equipment; lead, clay, coal
population (1982) 4,951,000
famous people T S Eliot, Joseph Pulitzer, Mark Twain
history explored by de Soto 1541; acquired under the ◊Louisiana Purchase; achieved statehood 1821.

Missouri Compromise, The in US history, the solution by Congress (1820–21) of a sectional crisis caused by the 1819 request from Missouri for admission to the union as a slave state, despite its proximity to existing non-slave states. The compromise was the simultaneous admission of Maine as a non-slave state.

Missouri River river in central USA, a tributary of the Mississippi, which it joins at St Louis; length 3,725 km/2,328 mi.

mistletoe parasitic evergreen unisexual plant *Viscum album*, native to Europe. It grows on trees as a branched bush, with translucent white berries, and is used as a Christmas decoration. See ◊Druidism.

mistral cold, dry, northerly wind that occasionally blows during the winter on the Mediterranean coast of France. It has been known to reach a velocity of 145 kph/90 mph.

Mistral Gabriela. Pen name of Lucila Godoy Alcayaga 1889–1957. Chilean poet, known for her *Sonnets of Death* 1915. Nobel Prize for Literature 1945.

Mitchell Margaret 1900–1949. US novelist, born in Atlanta, Georgia, which is the setting for her one book *Gone With the Wind* 1936, a story of the US Civil War.

Mitchell R(eginald) J(oseph) 1895–1937. British aircraft designer, whose Spitfire fighter was a major factor in winning the Battle of Britain.

mite minute animal belonging to the Arachnida, related to spiders. Mites may be free living scavengers or predators.

Mithraism the ancient Persian worship of ◊Mithras. His cult was introduced into the Roman Empire in 68 BC, spread rapidly particularly among soldiers, and by about 250 AD rivalled Christianity in strength.

Mithras in Persian mythology, the god of light. Mithras represented the power of goodness, and promised his followers compensation for present evil after death. Mithras was said to have captured and killed the sacred bull, from whose blood all life sprang.

Mithridates VI Eupator known as *the Great* 132–63 BC. King of Pontus (NE Asia Minor, on the Black Sea) from 120 BC. He massacred 80,000 Romans in over-running the rest of Asia Minor, and went on to invade Greece. He was successively defeated by ◊Sulla in the First Mithridatic War 88–84; by ◊Lucullus in the Second 83–81; and by ◊Pompey in the Third 74–64. He was killed by a soldier at his own order rather than surrender to captivity.

mitochondria rodlike or spherical bodies within ◊eukaryotic cells, containing enzymes responsible for energy production. They are thought to be derived from free-living bacteria that, at a very early stage in the history of life, invaded larger cells and took up a symbiotic (mutually beneficial) way of life there. Each still contains its own small loop of DNA, and new mitochondria arise by division of existing ones.

mitosis in biology, the process of cell division. The genetic material of ◊eukaryotic cells is carried on a number of ◊chromosomes. To control their movements during cell division so that both new cells get a full set, a system of protein tubules, known as the spindle, organizes the chromosomes into position in the middle of the cell before they replicate. The spindle then controls the separation of the daughter chromosomes as the cell divides in two.

mitre in the Christian church, the headdress worn by bishops, cardinals, and mitred abbots at solemn services. There are mitres of many different shapes, but in the Western church they usually take the form of a tall cleft cap.

Mitre Bartólomé 1821–1906. Argentinian president 1861–68. In 1852 helped overthrow the dictatorial regime of Juan Manuel de Rosas. In 1861 he was

mitosis

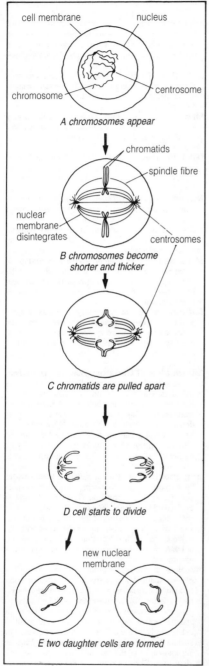

cell membrane   nucleus

chromosome   centrosome

A chromosomes appear

chromatids

spindle fibre

nuclear
membrane
disintegrates   centrosomes

*B chromosomes become
shorter and thicker*

C chromatids are pulled apart

D cell starts to divide

new nuclear
membrane

E two daughter cells are formed

elected president of a unified Argentina. As president, Mitre encouraged immigration and favoured growing commercial links with Europe. He is seen as a symbol of national unity.

Mitterrand François 1916– . French socialist politician, president from 1981. He held ministerial posts in 11 governments between 1947 and 1958.

He founded the French Socialist Party (PS) in 1971. In 1985 he introduced proportional representation, allegedly to weaken the growing opposition from left and right.

Mizoram a union territory of NE India; area 21,230 sq km/8,195 sq mi; population (1981) 493,755.

m.k.s. system system of units in which the base units metre, kilogram, and second replace the centimetre, gram, and second of the ◊c.g.s. system.

ml abbreviation for *millilitre*.

mm abbreviation for *millimetre*.

mmHg abbreviation for *millimetre of mercury*.

moa extinct kiwi-like bird, order Dinornithoformes, 19 species of which lived in New Zealand. They varied from 0.5–3.5 m/2–12 ft, with strong limbs, a long neck, and no wings. The last moa was killed in the 1800s.

Moab an ancient country in Jordan E of the S part of the river Jordan and the Dead Sea. The inhabitants were closely akin to the Hebrews in culture, language, and religion, but were often at war with them, as recorded in the Old Testament.

Mobutu Seso-Seko-Kuku-Ngbeandu-Wa-Za-Banga 1930– . Zaïrean politician, president from 1965. He assumed the presidency by coup, and created a unitary state under his centralized government. The harshness of some of President Mobutu's policies has attracted widespread international criticism of Zaïre. In 1983 amnesty was offered to all political exiles. Mobutu was re-elected for a third term in 1984.

Moby Dick classic American novel by Herman Melville, published 1851. Its story of the conflict between the monomaniac Captain Ahab and the great white whale explores both the mystery and destructiveness of nature's power.

Moche or *Mochica* a pre-Inca people who lived in the coastal area of Peru 100–800 AD. Remains include massive platform tombs (*adobe*) and pottery.

mocking bird American bird *Mimus polyglottos*, related to the thrushes, brownish grey, with white markings on the black wings and tail. It is remarkable for its ability to mimic.

mock orange deciduous shrub of the genus *Philadelphus*, family Philadelphaceae, including *Philadelphus coronarius* which has white, strongly scented flowers, resembling those of the orange; it is sometimes referred to as ◊syringa.

mod a youth sub-culture that originated in London and Brighton in the early 1960s; revived in the late

Mitterrand French socialist president François Mitterrand, 1988.

Mobutu *President Mobutu of Zaïre.*

1970s. Mods were fashion-conscious, speedy, and upwardly mobile; they favoured scooters and soul music.

MOD abbreviation for *Ministry of ◊Defence*.

Model Parliament English ◊parliament, set up 1295 by Edward I; it was the first to include representatives from outside the clergy and aristocracy, and was established because Edward needed the support of the whole country against his opponents: Wales, France, and Scotland. His sole aim was to raise money for defence, and the parliament did not pass any legislation.

modem (*mo*dulator–*dem*odulator) an electronic device for converting digital (discrete) signals from a computer into analogue (continuous) signals on a telecommunications network, and vice versa.

Moderator in the Church of Scotland, the minister chosen to act as president of the annual General Assembly.

moderator in a nuclear reactor, the material such as graphite used to reduce the speed of neutrons. Neutrons produced by nuclear fission are fast-moving and must be slowed for them to initiate further fission, so that nuclear energy continues to be released, and at a controlled rate.

Modernism in the arts, a general term used to describe various tendencies in the first three-quarters of the 20th century. It refers mainly to a conscious attempt to break away from the artistic traditions of the 19th century, and also to a concern with form and the exploration of technique as opposed to content and narrative.

Modigliani Amedeo 1884–1920. Italian artist. He is best known as a painter and sculptor of graceful nudes and portrait studies. His paintings, while influenced by Picasso and Henri Rousseau, had a soft, elongated, linear style all his own.

modular course in education, a course, usually leading to a recognized qualification, which is divided into short and often optional units which are assessed as they are completed.

modulation in ◊radio, the intermittent change of frequency, or amplitude, of a radio carrier wave, in accordance with the audio-frequency, speaking voice, music, or other signal being transmitted.

modulation in music, movement from one ◊key to another.

module in construction, a part which governs the form of the rest, for example Japanese room sizes are traditionally governed by multiples of standard tatami floor mats; modern prefabricated buildings are mass-produced in a similar way. The components of a spacecraft are designed in coordination, for example for the Apollo Moon landings the craft comprised a command module (for working, eating, sleeping), service module (electricity generators,

oxygen supplies, manoeuvring rocket), and lunar module (to land and return the astronauts).

modulus in mathematics, the positive value of a ◊real number, irrespective of its sign, indicated by a pair of vertical lines. Thus $|3|$ is 3; and $|-5|$ is 5.

modus operandi (Latin) a method of operating.

modus vivendi (Latin 'way of living') a compromise between opposing points of view.

Mogadishu or *Mugdisho* capital and chief port of Somalia; population (1983) 600,000. It is a centre for oil refining, food processing, and uranium mining.

Mohács, Battle of Austro-Hungarian defeat of the Turks 1687 which effectively marked the end of Turkish expansion into Europe. It is also the site of an earlier Turkish victory, in 1526.

mohair hair of the Angora goat. The fine, white, lustrous fibre is manufactured into fabric. Commercial mohair is now obtained from cross-bred animals, pure-bred supplies being insufficient.

Mohamad Mahathir bin 1925– . Prime minister of Malaysia from 1981 and leader of the United Malays' National Organization (UMNO). His 'look east' economic policy emulates Japanese industrialization.

Mohammed alternative form of ◊Muhammad, founder of Islam.

Mohammedanism misnomer for ◊Islam, the religion founded by Muhammad.

Mohenjo Daro site of a city *c.* 2500–1600 BC on the lower Indus, Pakistan, where excavations from the 1920s have revealed the ◊Indus Valley civilization.

Moholy-Nagy Laszlo 1895–1946. US photographer. Through his theories and practical experiments in photography he had great influence on 20th-century photography.

Mohorovičić discontinuity (or *Moho*) boundary that separates the Earth's crust and mantle. It follows the variations in the thickness of the crust and is found approximately 32 km/20 mi below the continents and about 10 km/6 mi below the oceans.

Modigliani *Nude (c.1916) Courtauld Galleries, London.*

Moldova
Republic of

area 33,700 sq km/13,012 sq mi
capital Chişinău (Kishinev)
towns Tiraspol, Beltsy, Bendery
physical hilly land between rivers Prut and
Dniester; plain of the Beltsy Steppe and uplands in N.
head of state Mircea Snegur from 1989
head of government Valerin Murovsky from 1992
political system emergent democracy
products wine, tobacco, canned goods
population (1990) 4,400,000 (Moldavian 64%,
Ukrainian 14%, Russian 13%, Gagauzi 4%,
Bulgarian 2%)
language Moldavian, allied to Romanian
religion Russian Orthodox

chronology
1940 Bessarabia in the E became part of the Soviet
Union whereas the W part remained in Romania.
1941 Bessarabia taken over by Romania–Germany.
1944 Red Army reconquered Bessarabia.
1946–47 Widespread famine.
1988 A popular front, the Democratic Movement
for Perestroika, campaigned for accelerated
political reform.
1989 May: Moldavian Popular Front established.
July: Snegur became head of state. Aug:
Moldavian language granted official status
triggering clashes between ethnic Russians and
Moldavians. Nov: Gagauz-Khalky People's
Movement formed to campaign for Gagauz
autonomy.
1990 Feb: Popular Front polled strongly in
supreme soviet elections. June: economic and
political sovereignty declared; renamed Republic
of Moldova. Oct: Gagauzi held unauthorized
elections to independent parliament in self-
proclaimed republic; state of emergency declared
after inter-ethnic clashes. Trans-Dniester region
declared its sovereignty. Nov: state of emergency
declared in Trans-Dniester region after inter-
ethnic killings.
1991 March: Moldova boycotted the USSR's
constitutional referendum. Aug: independence
declared after abortive anti-Gorbachev coup;
Communist Party outlawed. Dec: Moldova joined
new Commonwealth of Independent States (CIS).
1992 Possible union with Romania discussed.
March: state of emergency imposed; admitted into
United Nations (UN). May: Trans-Dniester region
fighting intensified. July: Andrei Sangheli became
premier; Moldova agreed to outside peacekeeping
force. Aug: Russian peacekeeping force
reportedly deployed in Trans-Dniester region.

It is named after the Yugoslav geophysicist Andrija
Mohorovičić (1857–1936).

Mohs Friedrich 1773–1839. German mineralogist,
who in 1812 devised the **Mohs scale** of minerals
classified in order of hardness.

Moi Daniel arap 1924– . Kenyan politician, president from 1978. Minister of home affairs from 1964,
he was Kenyatta's vice president from 1967.

Mojave Desert arid region in S California, USA,
part of the Great Basin; area 38,500 sq km/15,000
sq mi.

moksha (Sanskrit 'liberation') in Hinduism, liberation from the cycle of reincarnation and from the
illusion of ◊maya. In Buddhism, enlightenment.

Moldova or *Moldovia* country in E central Europe,
bounded N, S, and E by Ukraine, and W by Romania.

mole burrowing mammal of the family Talpidae.
Moles grow to 18 cm/7 in, and have acute senses of
hearing, smell, and touch, but poor vision. They
have strong, clawed front feet, and eat insects,
grubs, and worms.

mole basic unit in the ◊SI system, unit symbol *mol*,
indicating amount of substance. The mole is the
amount of substance of a system which contains as
many elementary entities as there are atoms in 0.012
kg of the ◊isotope carbon-12. The entities must be
specified as atoms, molecules, ions, electrons, etc.

mole a mechanical device for boring horizontal
holes underground without the need for digging
trenches. It is used for laying pipes and cables.

mole a person working subversively within an
organization. The term has come to be used broadly
for someone who gives out ('leaks') secret information in the public interest; it originally meant a per-

son who spends several years working for a government department or a company with the intention of
ultimately passing secrets to a rival or enemy.

molecular biology the study of the molecular
basis of life including the biochemistry of molecules
such as DNA, RNA, and proteins, and the structure
and function of the various parts of living cells.

molecular clock the use of rates of ◊mutation in
genetic material to calculate the length of time
elapsed since two related species diverged from
each other during evolution. The method can be
based on comparisons of the DNA or of widely
occurring proteins, such as haemoglobin.

molecular weight another name for ◊relative
molecular mass.

molecule smallest particle of any substance that
can exist freely yet still exhibit all the chemical
properties of the substance. Molecules are composed of ◊atoms, ranging in size from one atom in,
for example, a helium molecule to many thousands
of atoms in the macromolecules of complex organic
substances. The composition of the molecule is
determined by the nature of the ◊bonds, which hold
the atoms together.

Molière Pen name of French satirical playwright
Jean Baptiste Poquelin 1622–1673. One of the
founders of the *Illustre Théâtre* in 1643, he was later
its leading actor, and in 1655 wrote his first play,
L'Etourdi. His satirical masterpieces include *L'Eco-
le des femmes* 1662, *Le Misanthrope* 1666, *Le
Bourgeois gentilhomme* 1670, and *Le Malade imagi-
naire* 1673.

Molinos Miguel de 1640–1697. Spanish mystic
and Roman Catholic priest. He settled in Rome

molecule

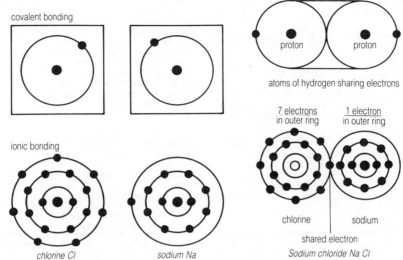

covalent bonding

ionic bonding

chlorine Cl   sodium Na

shared path of electron

proton   proton

atoms of hydrogen sharing electrons

7 electrons in outer ring   1 electron in outer ring

chlorine   sodium

shared electron
Sodium chloride Na Cl

and wrote several devotional works in Italian, including the *Guida spirituale/Spiritual Guide* 1675 which aroused the hostility of the Jesuits. He was sentenced to life imprisonment 1687. His doctrine is known as quietism.

Molise mainly agricultural region of S central Italy, comprising the provinces of Campobasso and Isernia; area 4,437 sq km/1,713 sq mi; population (1984) 332,500. Its capital is Campobasso.

mollusc invertebrate animal of the phylum Mollusca. The majority are marine animals, but some inhabit fresh water, and a few are terrestrial. They include shell-fish, snails, slugs, and cuttles. The body is soft, limbless, and cold-blooded. There is no internal skeleton, but most species have a hard shell covering the body.

Molly Maguires, The in US history, a secret Irish coalminers' organization in the 1870s which staged strikes and used violence against coal company officials and property in the anthracite fields of Pennsylvania, prefiguring a long period of turbulence in industrial relations.

Molnár Ferenc 1878–1952. Hungarian novelist and playwright. His play *Liliom* 1909, a study of a circus barker, was adapted as the musical *Carousel*.

Moloch or *Molech* in the Old Testament, a Phoenician deity worshipped in Jerusalem in the 7th century BC, to whom live children were sacrificed in fire.

Molotov Vyacheslav Mikhailovich. Assumed name of V M Skryabin 1890–1986. Soviet communist politician. He was chair of the Council of People's Commissars (prime minister) 1930–41, and foreign minister 1939–49, during which period he negotiated a nonaggression treaty with Germany (the ◊Hitler-Stalin pact), and again 1953–56. In 1957 he was expelled from the government for Stalinist activities.

molotov cocktail home-made weapon consisting of a bottle of petrol fired by a wick. Used by Resistance groups during World War II, it was named after the Soviet foreign minister Molotov.

Moltke Helmuth Carl Bernhard, Count von Moltke 1800–1891. Prussian general. He entered the Prussian army 1821, became chief of the general staff

1857, and was responsible for the Prussian strategy in the wars with Denmark 1863–64, Austria 1866, and France 1870–71. He was created a count 1870 and a field marshal 1871.

Moltke Helmuth Johannes Ludwig von Moltke 1848–1916. German general (nephew of Count von Moltke), chief of the German general staff 1906–14. His use of ◊Schlieffen's plan for a rapid victory on two fronts failed and he was superseded.

Moluccas another name for the ◊Maluku islands, Indonesia.

molybdenite molybdenum disulphide, MoS_2, the chief ore mineral of molybdenum. It possesses a hexagonal crystal structure, and has a metallic lustre resembling graphite.

molybdenum a very hard white metallic element, symbol Mo, atomic number 42, relative atomic mass 95.975. It is important in making special steels, and it is also used for electrodes (since it is easily welded to soda and Pyrex glass, and to other metals), and for filaments (alloyed with tungsten) in thermionic valves.

Mombasa industrial port (oil refining, cement) in Kenya (serving also Uganda and Tanzania), built on Mombasa Island and adjacent mainland; population (1984) 481,000.

moment of a force in physics, product of the force and the perpendicular distance from the point to the line of action of the force; it measures the turning effect or torque produced by the force.

moment of inertia in physics, the sum of all the point masses of a rotating object multiplied by the squares of their respective distances from the axis of rotation. It is analagous to the ◊mass of a stationary object or one moving in a straight line.

momentum in physics, the product of the mass of a body and its linear velocity; *angular momentum* (of a body in rotational motion) is the product of its moment of inertia and its angular velocity. The momentum of a body does not change unless it is acted on by an external force.

Monaco small sovereign state, forming an enclave in southern France, with the Mediterranean to the S.

Monaco
Principality of

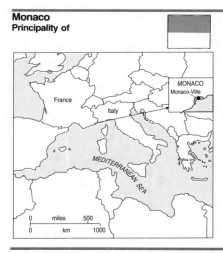

MONACO
Monaco-Ville

France

Italy

MEDITERRANEAN SEA

| 0 | miles | 500 |
| 0 | km | 1000 |

area 1.5 sq km/0.575 sq mi
capital Monaco-Ville
towns Monte Carlo, La Condamine
physical steep and rugged
head of state Rainier III from 1949
head of government Jean Ausseil from 1986
government constitutional monarchy under French protectorate
exports some light industry, but economy depends on tourism and gambling
currency French franc
population (1989) 29,000; annual growth rate −0.5%
language French (official)
religion Roman Catholic 95%
literacy 99% (1985)
chronology
1861 Became an independent state, under French protection.
1918 France given a veto over succession to the throne.
1949 Prince Rainier III ascended the throne.
1962 New constitution adopted.

monad a philosophical term deriving from the philosophy of Leibniz, suggesting a soul or metaphysical unit which has a self-contained life. The monads are independent of each other, but coordinated by a 'pre-established harmony'.

Monaghan (Irish *Mhuineachain*) county of the NE Republic of Ireland, province of Ulster
area 1,290 sq km/498 sq mi
towns county town Monaghan
physical low and rolling
products cereals, linen, potatoes, cattle
population (1991) 51,300.

monasticism devotion to religious life under vows of poverty, chastity, and obedience, known to Judaism (for example ◊Essenes), Buddhism, and other religions, before Christianity. In Buddism, the Sufis formed monastical orders from the 12th century.

Mondale Walter 'Fritz' 1928– . US Democrat politician, unsuccessful presidential candidate 1984. He was a senator 1964–76 for his home state of Minnesota, and vice president to Jimmy Carter 1977–81.

Mondrian Piet (Pieter Mondriaan) 1872–1944. Dutch abstract painter. He lived in Paris 1919–38, then in London, and from 1940 in New York. He was a founder member of the de ◊Stijl movement and chief exponent of Neo-Plasticism, a rigorous abstract style based on the use of simple geometric forms and pure colours.

Monet Claude 1840–1926. French painter, a pioneer of Impressionism and a lifelong exponent of its ideals; his painting *Impression, Sunrise* 1872 gave the movement its name. In the 1870s he began painting the same subjects at different times of day to explore the effects of light on colour and form; the *Haystacks* and *Rouen Cathedral* series followed in the 1890s, and from 1899 a series of *Waterlilies* painted in the garden of his house at Giverny.

monetarism an economic policy, advocated by the economist Milton Friedman and others, which proposes control of a country's money supply to keep it in step with the country's ability to produce goods, with the aim of curbing inflation. Cutting government spending is advocated, and the long-term aim is to return as much of the economy as possible to the private sector, allegedly in the interests of efficiency.

monetary policy an economic policy which sees control of both the money supply and liquidity as important determinants of the level of employment and inflation. By influencing interest rates, the policy aims to ease balance of payment problems.

money any common medium of exchange acceptable in payment for goods or services or for the settlement of debts. Today money is usually coinage (invented by the Chinese in the second millenium BC) or paper notes (used by the Chinese from about 800 AD). Developments such as the cheque and credit card now fulfil many of the traditional functions of money.

money market an institution that deals in gold and foreign exchange, and securities in the short term. Long-term transactions are dealt with on the capital market. There is no physical market place, and many deals are made by telephone or telex.

money supply the quantity of money present in an economy at a given moment.

Mongol Empire Empire established by Genghis Khan, who extended his domains from Russia to North China and became khan of the Mongol tribes in 1206. His grandson Kublai Khan conquered China and used foreigners such as Marco Polo as well as subjects to administer his empire. In 1367 the Mongols lost China and suffered defeats in the

Monet The Water Lily Pond *(1899) National Gallery, London.*

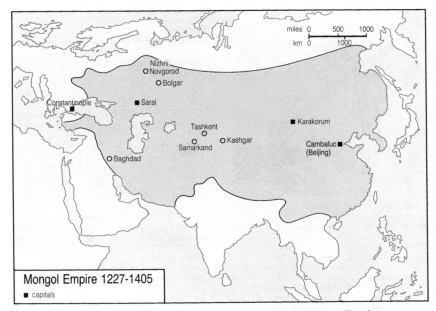

Mongol Empire 1227-1405
■ capitals

West in 1380; the empire soon broke up.

Mongolia country in E Central Asia, bounded N by Russia and S by China.

Mongolia, Inner (Chinese *Nei Mongol*) autonomous region of NE China from 1947.

mongoose carnivorous mammal of the family Viverridae. The *Indian mongoose Herpestes mungo* is greyish in colour, about 50 cm/1.5 ft long, with a long tail. It may be tamed, and is often kept for its ability to kill snakes.

monism in philosophy, the theory that reality is made up of only one substance. This view is usually contrasted with ◊dualism, which divides reality into two substances, matter and mind. Spinoza saw the one substance as God or Nature.

monitor type of lizard of the family Varanidae, found in Africa, S Asia, and Australia. Monitors are generally large and carnivorous, with well-developed

---

Mongolia
State of
(*Outer Mongolia* until 1924;
*People's Republic of
Mongolia* until 1991)

area 1,565,000 sq km/604,480 sq mi
capital Ulaanbaatar (formerly Ulan Bator)
towns Darkhan, Choybalsan
physical a high plateau with steppe (grasslands)
head of state Punsalmaagiyn Ochirbat from 1990
head of government Puntsagiyn Jasray from 1992
political system emergent democracy

exports meat, butter, varied minerals, furs
currency tugrik
population (1990 est) 2,185,000; annual growth rate 2.8%
language Khalkha Mongolian (official), Chinese, Russian, and Turkic languages.
religion officially none
literacy 89% (1985)
GNP $3.6 bn (1986); $1,820 per head
chronology
1911 Mongolia gained autonomy from China.
1915 Chinese sovereignty reasserted.
1921 Chinese rule overthrown with Soviet help.
1924 People's Republic proclaimed.
1946 China recognized Mongolia's independence.
1966 20-year friendship, cooperation and mutual-assistance pact signed with USSR; deterioration in relations with China.
1984 Yumjaagiyn Tsedenbal, effective leader, deposed and replaced by Jambyn Batmonh.
1987 Soviet troop numbers reduced; Mongolia's external contacts broadened.
1989 Further major Soviet troop reductions.
1990 Mongolian Democratic Union launched democratization campaign; Gombojavyn Ochirbat's Mongolian People's Revolutionary Party elected in free multi-party elections.
1991 Privatization programme launched as part of move towards market economy.
1992 New constitution introduced. Economic situation worsened.

monkey-puzzle tree

legs and claws, and a long powerful tail which can be swung in defence.

monk member of a male religious order; see ◊monasticism.

Monk or *Monck*, George, 1st Duke of Albemarle 1608–1669. English soldier. During the Civil War he fought for King Charles I, but after being captured changed sides and took command of the Parliamentary forces in Ireland. Under the commonwealth he became commander in chief in Scotland, and in 1660 he led his army into England and brought about the restoration of Charles II.

monkey the smaller, mainly tree-dwelling primates, excluding humans and the anthropoid ◊apes.

monkey-puzzle tree or *Chilean pine* evergreen tree *Araucaria araucana*, native to Chile; it has whorled branches covered in prickly leaves of a leathery texture.

Monmouth James Scott, Duke of Monmouth 1649–1685. Claimant to the English crown, the illegitimate son of Charles II and Lucy Walter. After James II's accession in 1685, he raised a rebellion, which was crushed at ◊Sedgemoor in Somerset. Monmouth was executed with 320 of his accomplices.

Monmouthshire former county of Wales, which in 1974 became, minus a small strip on the border with Mid Glamorgan, the new county of *Gwent*.

monocarpic or *hapaxanthic* describing plants which flower and produce fruit only once during their lifecycle, after which they die. Most ◊annual and ◊biennial plants are monocarpic, but there are also a small number of monocarpic ◊perennial plants which flower just once, sometimes after as long as 90 years, dying shortly afterwards, for example, century plant (*Agave*) and some species of bamboo (*Bambusa*). See also ◊semelparity.

monoclonal antibodies (MABs) antibodies produced by cloned cells which can be reproduced in quantity for use in research and in the diagnosis and treatment of disease.

monocotyledon angiosperm (flowering plant) with a single cotyledon, or seed-leaf (as opposed to ◊dicotyledons, which have two). Monocotyledons usually have narrow leaves with parallel veins and smooth edges, and hollow or soft stems. Their flower parts are arranged in threes. Most are small plants such as orchids, grasses, and lilies, but some are trees such as palms.

Monod Jacques 1910–1976. French biochemist who shared the 1965 Nobel Prize for Medicine with two colleagues.

monody in music, declamation by accompanied solo voice, used at the turn of the 16th and 17th centuries.

monogamy the practice of having only one husband or wife at a time in ◊marriage.

Monophysite a member of a group of Christian heretics of the 5th–7th centuries who taught that Jesus had one nature, rather than two natures, the human and the divine. Monophysitism developed as a reaction to ◊Nestorianism and led to the formal secession of the Coptic and Armenian churches from the rest of the Christian church. Monophysites survive today in Armenia, Syria, and Egypt.

Monopolies and Mergers Commission (MMC) UK government body re-established in 1973 under the Fair Trading Act and, since 1980, embracing the Competition Act. Its role is to investigate and report when there is a risk of creating a monopoly following a company merger or takeover, or when a newspaper or newspaper assets are transferred. It also investigates companies, nationalized industries, or local authorities which are suspected of operating in a non-competitive way. The US equivalent is the *Federal Trade Commission* (FTC).

monopoly in economics, the domination of a market for a particular product or service by a single company, which can therefore restrict competition and keep prices high. In practice, a company can be said to have a monopoly when it controls a significant proportion of the market (technically an ◊oligopoly).

monorail a railway that runs on a single rail. It was invented in 1882 to carry light loads, and when run by electricity was called a *telpher*. The Wuppertal Schwebebahn, which has been running in Germany since 1901, is a suspension monorail, where the passenger cars hang from an arm that runs along the rail. Most modern monorails are of the straddle type, where the passenger cars run on top of the rail.

monosodium glutamate *MSG* $NaC_5H_8O_4$ the sodium salt of glutamic acid, an amino acid found widely in proteins which has an important role in the metabolism of plants and animals. It is used to enhance the flavour of many packaged and 'fast' foods, and in many Chinese dishes. Ill-effects may arise from its overconsumption.

monotheism the belief or doctrine that there is only one God, the opposite of polytheism. See also ◊religion.

Monothelite member of a group of Christian heretics of the 7th century who sought to reconcile the orthodox and ◊Monophysite theologies by maintaining that, while Christ possessed two natures, he had only one will.

monotreme member of the order Monotremata, the only living egg-laying mammals, found in Australasia. They include the echidna and platypus.

Monroe James 1758–1831. 5th president of the USA 1817–25, born in Virginia. He was minister to France 1794–96, and in 1803 negotiated the ◊Louisiana Purchase. He was secretary of state 1811–17. His name is associated with the ◊Monroe Doctrine.

Monroe Marilyn. Stage-name of Norma Jean Mortenson or Baker 1926–1962. US film actress, who made comedies such as *The Seven Year Itch* 1955, *Bus Stop* 1956, and *Some Like It Hot* 1959. Her second husband was baseball star Joe di Maggio, and her third Arthur ◊Miller.

Monroe Doctrine the declaration by President Monroe 1823 that any further European colonial

Monroe The filmstar Marilyn Monroe dancing with Truman Capote, 1955.

ambitions in the W hemisphere would be threats to US peace and security, made in response to proposed European intervention in newly independent former Spanish colonies in South America. In return the USA would not interfere in European affairs. The doctrine, subsequently broadened, has been a recurrent theme in US foreign policy, although it has no basis in US or international law.

Monrovia capital and port of Liberia: population (1985) 500,000. Industries include rubber, cement, and petrol processing.

Monsarrat Nicholas 1910–1979. English novelist, who served with the navy in the Battle of the Atlantic, subject of *The Cruel Sea* 1951.

monsoon (Old Dutch 'monçon') a wind system that dominates a climate, with seasonal reversals of direction; in particular, the wind in S Asia that blows towards the sea in winter and towards the land in summer, bringing heavy rain.

monstera or *Swiss cheese plant* evergreen climbing plant of the Arum family, Araceae, native to tropical America, cultivated as a house plant.

monstrance in the Roman Catholic Church, a vessel used to hold the Host (bread consecrated in the Eucharist) when exposed at benediction or in processions.

Montagnard member of a group in the legislative assembly and National Convention convened after the French Revolution. They supported the more extreme aims of the revolution, and were destroyed after the fall of Robespierre in 1794.

Montaigne Michel Eyquem de 1533–1592. French writer, regarded as the creator of the essay form. In 1580 he published the first two volumes of his *Essais*; the third volume appeared in 1588.

Montana state of the W USA on the Canadian border; nickname Treasure State
area 381,187 sq km/147,138 sq mi
capital Helena
*towns*Billings, Great Falls
physical mountainous forests in the west, rolling grasslands in the east
products wheat under irrigation; cattle, wool, copper, oil, and natural gas
population (1986) 819,000
famous people Gary Cooper
history first settled 1809; influx of immigrants pursuing gold; became a state 1889.

Montana Joe 1956– . US American footballer. He appeared in four winning Super Bowls with the San Francisco 49ers 1982, 1985, 1989, and 1990, winning the Most Valuable Player award in 1982, 1985, and 1990, and setting a record for passing yardage 1989. He threw a record five touchdown passes in the 1990 Super Bowl.

Mont Blanc (Italian *Monte Bianco*) the highest mountain in the ◊Alps, between France and Italy; height 4,807 m/15,772 ft.

montbretia plant *Tritonia crocosmiflora*, family Iridaceae, with orange flowers on long stems.

Montcalm Louis-Joseph de Montcalm-Grozon, Marquis de 1712–1759. French general, appointed military commander in Canada 1756. He won a series of victories over the British, but was defeated by Wolfe at Quebec, where both generals died.

Monte Carlo a town and resort in ◊Monaco, known for its gambling; population (1982) 12,000.

Montenegro (Serbo-Croat *Crna Gora*) constituent republic of Yugoslavia
area 13,812 sq km/5,337 sq mi
capital Titograd
town Cetinje
physical mountainous
population (1986) 620,000, including 40,000 Albanians
language Serbian variant of Serbo-Croat
religion Serbian Orthodox
history part of ◊Serbia from the late 12th century, it became independent (under Venetian protection) after Serbia was defeated by the Turks 1389. It was overrun by Austria in World War I, and voted in 1918 after the deposition of King Nicholas to become part of Serbia. In 1946 it became a republic of Yugoslavia. In a referendum 1992 Montenegrins voted to remain in the Yugoslav federation.

Monterrey industrial city (iron, steel, textiles, chemicals, food processing) in NE Mexico; population (1986) 2,335,000.

Montessori Maria 1870–1952. Italian educationalist. From her experience with mentally handicapped children, she developed the *Montessori method*, an educational system for all children incorporating instructive play and allowing children to develop at their own pace.

Monteverdi Claudio (Giovanni Antonio) 1567–1643. Italian composer. He is known for his contribution to the development of opera with *Orfeo* 1607 and *The Coronation of Poppea* 1642.

Montevideo capital and chief port (grain, meat products, hides) of Uruguay, on Rio de la Plata; population (1985) 1,250,000

Montezuma II 1466–1520. The last Aztec emperor 1502–19. When the Spanish conquistador Cortés invaded Mexico he was imprisoned and murdered, either by the Spaniards or by his own subjects.

Montfort Simon de, Earl of Leicester *c.* 1208–1265. English politician and soldier. From 1258 he led the baronial opposition to Henry III's misrule during the second ◊Barons' War and in 1264 defeated and captured the king at Lewes, Sussex. In 1265, as head of government, he summoned the first parliament in which the towns were represented; he was killed at the Battle of Evesham during the ◊Barons' Wars.

Montgolfier Joseph Michel 1740–1810 and Étienne Jacques 1745–1799 French brothers whose hot-air balloon was used for the first successful human flight 21 Nov 1783, following earlier experiments.

Montgomery Bernard Law, 1st Viscount Montgomery of Alamein 1887–1976. British field marshal.

Montgomery The British field marshal, Viscount Montgomery of Alamein, advances in the turret of a tank during the attack on El Alamein, Oct 1942.

In World War II he commanded the 8th Army in N Africa in the Second Battle of El ◊Alamein 1942. As commander of British troops in N Europe from 1944, he received the German surrender 1945.

month unit of time based on the motion of the Moon around the Earth. The time from one new or full Moon to the next (the *synodic month*) is 29.53 days. The time for the Moon to complete one orbit around the Earth relative to the stars (the *sidereal month*) is 27.32 days. The *calendar month* is a human invention, devised to fit the calendar year.

Montréal inland port, industrial city (aircraft, chemicals, oil and petrochemicals, flour, sugar, brewing, meat packing) of Quebec, Canada, at the junction of the Ottawa and St Lawrence rivers; population (1986) 2,921,000.

Montrose James Graham, 1st Marquess of Montrose 1612–1650. Scottish soldier. Son of the 4th earl of Montrose. He supported the ◊Covenanters against Charles I, but after 1640 changed sides. Defeated 1645 at Philiphaugh, he escaped to Norway. Returning in 1650 to raise a revolt, he was defeated and hanged.

Montserrat volcanic island in the West Indies, one of the Leeward group; capital Plymouth; area 101 sq km/39.5 sq mi; population (1985) 11,852.

Moon, the the natural satellite of Earth, 3,476 km/2,160 mi in diameter, with a mass an eighth that of Earth. Its average distance from Earth is 384,900 km/238,900 mi, and it orbits every 27.32 days (the *sidereal month*). The Moon spins on its axis so that it keeps one side permanently turned towards Earth. The Moon has no air or water.

Montreal The Hotel de Ville in Montreal, Canada.

Moore Family Group *bronze (1949) Tate Gallery,* London.

moon in astronomy, any small body that orbits a planet. Mercury and Venus are the only planets in the Solar System that do not have moons.

Moon Sun Myung 1920– . Korean industrialist and founder of the ◊Unification Church (*Moonies*) 1954. From 1973 he launched a major mission in the USA and elsewhere. The church has been criticized for its manipulative methods of recruiting and keeping members. He was convicted of tax fraud in the USA in 1982.

Moon William 1818–1894. English inventor of the Moon alphabet for the blind. Devised in 1847, it uses only nine symbols in different orientations.

Moonie popular name for a follower of the ◊Unification Church, a religious sect founded by Sun Myung Moon.

Moon probe spacecraft used to investigate the Moon. Early probes flew past the Moon or crash-landed on it, but later ones achieved soft landings or went into orbit. Soviet probes included the long Lunik/Luna series. US probes (Ranger, Surveyor, Lunar Orbiter) prepared the way for the Apollo manned flights.

Moor name (English form of Latin *Maurus*) originally applied to an inhabitant of the Roman province of Mauritania, in NW Africa. In current English usage the term is applied mainly to the Muslims who conquered Spain and occupied its southern part from 711 to 1492. They were of mixed Arab and Berber origin.

Moorcock Michael 1939– . British writer, associated with the 1960s new wave in science fiction, editor of the magazine *New Worlds* 1964–69. He is noted for the 'Jerry Cornelius' novels, collected as *The Cornelius Chronicles* 1977 and *Gloriana* 1978.

Moore George (Augustus) 1852–1933. Irish novelist, born in County Mayo. *A Modern Lover* 1883, sexually frank and banned in some quarters was followed by others, including *Esther Waters* 1894.

Moore Henry 1898–1986. English sculptor. As an official war artist during World War II he did a series of drawings of London's air-raid shelters. Many of his postwar works are in bronze or marble, including monumental semi-abstracts such as *Reclining Figure* 1957–58 (outside UNESCO, Paris), and often designed to be placed in landscape settings.

Moore John 1761–1809. British general, born in Glasgow. In 1808 he commanded the British army sent to Portugal in the Peninsular War. After advancing into Spain he had to retreat to Corunna in the NW, and was killed in the battle fought to cover the embarkation.

Moore Marianne 1887–1972. US poet. She edited the literary magazine *Dial* 1925–29, and published volumes of witty and intellectual verse including *Observations* 1924, *What are Years* 1941, and *A Marianne Moore Reader* 1961.

Moore Thomas 1779–1852. Irish poet, born in Dublin. Among his works are the verse romance, *Lalla Rookh* 1817, and the *Irish Melodies* 1807–35.

moorhen bird *Gallinula chloropus* of the rail family, common in swamps, lakes, and ponds in Eurasia, Africa, and North and South America. It is about 33 cm/13 in long, mainly brown and grey, but with a red bill and forehead, and a vivid white underside to the tail. The big feet are not webbed or lobed, but the moorhen can swim well.

moose North American name for ◊elk.

moraine rocky debris carried along and deposited by a ◊glacier. Material eroded from the side of a glaciated valley and carried along the glacier's edge is called lateral moraine; that worn from the valley and carried along the base of the glacier is called ground moraine

morality play didactic medieval verse drama, in part a development of the ◊mystery or miracle play, in which human characters are replaced by personified virtues and vices, the limited humorous elements being provided by the Devil. The morality play flourished in the 15th century, the most well-known example being *Everyman*. They exerted an important influence on the development of Elizabethan drama and comedy.

Moral ReArmament (MRA) international anti-communist movement calling for 'moral and spiritual renewal'. It was founded by the Christian evangelist F N D Buchman in 1938.

Morandi Giorgio 1890–1964. Italian still-life painter and etcher. He is noted for his subtle studies of bottles and jars.

Moravia (Czech *Morava*) district of central Europe, from 1960 two regions of Czechoslovakia (now Czech Republic):

South Moravia
area 15,022 sq km/5,800 sq mi
capital Brno
population (1991) 2,048,900
North Moravia
area 11,060 sq km/4,270 sq mi
capital Ostrava
population (1991) 1,961,500
products maize, grapes, wine in the S; wheat, barley, rye, flax, sugarbeet in the N; coal and iron
history part of the Avar territory since the 6th century; conquered by Charlemagne's Holy Roman Empire. In 874 the kingdom of Great Moravia was founded by the Slavic prince Sviatopluk. It was conquered by the Magyars 906, and became a fief of Bohemia 1029. It was passed to the Hapsburgs 1526, and became an Austrian crown land 1849. It was incorporated in the new republic of Czechoslovakia in 1918, forming a province until 1949.

Moravia Alberto, pen name of Italian novelist Alberto Pincherle 1907–1990. His first successful novel was *Gli indifferenti/The Time of Indifference* 1929. However, its criticism of Mussolini's regime

led to the government censoring his work until after World War II. Later books include *La romana/Woman of Rome* 1947, *La ciociara/Two Women* 1957, and *La noia/The Empty Canvas* 1961.

Moravian member of a Christian Protestant sect, the *Moravian Brethren*. It is an episcopal church and was founded in Bohemia 1457 as an offshoot of the Hussite movement (see John ◊Huss). Its followers were persecuted in the 17th and 18th centuries. There are about 63,000 Moravians in the USA, and small congregations in the UK and the rest of Europe.

Morazán Francisco 1792–1842. Central American politician, born in Honduras. He led the successful liberal-federalist revolt of the 1820s, and was elected president of the Central American Confederation 1830. In the face of secessions he attempted to hold the union together by force, but was driven out by the Guatemalan dictator Carrera, and eventually captured and executed 1842. He now symbolizes the movement for Central American unity.

More (St) Thomas 1478–1535. English politician and author. From 1509 he was favoured by ◊Henry VIII and employed on foreign embassies. He was a member of the privy council from 1518 and Lord Chancellor from 1529 but resigned over Henry's break with the pope. For refusing to accept the king as head of the church, he was executed. The title of his political book *Utopia* 1516 has come to mean any supposedly perfect society.

Moreau Gustave 1826–1898. French Symbolist painter. His works are biblical, mythological, and literary scenes, richly coloured and detailed.

Moreau Jean Victor Marie 1763–1813. French general in the Revolutionary Wars who won a brilliant victory over the Austrians at ◊Hohenlinden 1800; as a republican he intrigued against Napoleon, and, when banished, joined the Allies and was killed at the Battle of Dresden.

morel type of mushroom. The common morel, *Morchella esculenta*, grows abundantly in Europe and N America. The yellowish-brown edible cap is much wrinkled and about 2.5 cm/1 in long. It is used for seasoning gravies, soups, and sauces.

Morgagni Giovanni Battista 1682–1771. Italian anatomist. As professor of anatomy at Padua, Morgagni developed the view that disease was not an imbalance of the body's humours but a result of alterations in the organs. His work formed the basis of morbid anatomy and ◊pathology.

Morgan Henry *c.* 1635–1688. Welsh buccaneer in the Caribbean. He made war against Spain, capturing and sacking Panama in 1671. In 1674 he

More Portrait after Hans Holbein (1527) National Portrait Gallery, London.

Morocco
Kingdom of
(al-Mamlaka al-Maghrebia)

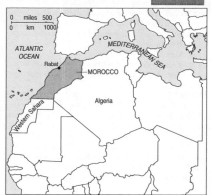

area 458,730 sq km/166,000 sq mi
capital Rabat
towns Marrakesh, Fez, Kenes; ports Casablanca, Tangier
physical mountain ranges NE–SW; plains in W
head of state Hassan II from 1961
head of government Mohamed Lamrani from 1992
political system constitutional monarchy
exports dates, figs, cork, wood pulp, canned fish, phosphates; tourism is important

currency dirham
population (1990 est) 26,249,000; annual growth rate 2.5%
life expectancy men 62, women 65
language Arabic (official); Berber, French, Spanish
religion Sunni Muslim 99%
literacy 45% male/22% female (1985 est)
GNP $18.7 bn (1988); $750 per head
chronology
1956 Achieved independence from France as the Sultanate of Morocco.
1957 Sultan restyled king of Morocco.
1961 Hassan II came to the throne.
1972 Major revision of the constitution.
1975 Western Sahara ceded by Spain to Morocco and Mauritania.
1976 Guerrilla war in the Sahara by the Polisario Front. Sahrawi Arab Democratic Republic (SADR) established in Algiers. Diplomatic relations between Morocco and Algeria broken.
1979 Mauritania signed a peace treaty with Polisario.
1983 Peace formula for the Sahara proposed by the Organization of African Unity (OAU) but not accepted by Morocco.
1984 Hassan signed an agreement for cooperation and mutual defence with Libya.
1987 Ceasefire agreed with Polisario but fighting continued.
1988 Diplomatic relations with Algeria restored.
1989 Diplomatic relations with Syria restored.
1992 Mohamed Lamrani appointed prime minister; new constitution approved in national referendum.

was knighted and appointed lieutenant-governor of Jamaica.

Morgan John Pierpont 1837–1913. US financier and investment banker whose company wielded great influence over American corporate economy after the Civil War, being instrumental in the formation of many trusts to stifle competition. He set up the US Steel Corporation in 1901.

Morgan Lewis Henry 1818–1881. US anthropologist. He studied American Indian culture, role of property, and was adopted by the Iroquois.

Morgan Thomas Hunt 1866–1945. US geneticist, awarded a Nobel prize in 1933 for his pioneering studies in classical genetics. He was the first to work on the fruit fly, *Drosophila*, which has since become a major subject of genetic studies. He helped to establish that the genes were located on the chromosomes, discovered sex chromosomes, and invented the techniques of genetic mapping.

Morgenthau Plan proposals orininated by Henry Morgenthau Jr (1891–1967), US secretary of the Treasury, for Germany after World War II, calling for the elimination of war industries in the Ruhr and Saar basins and the conversion of Germany 'into a country primarily agricultural and pastoral in character'. The plan for the pastoralization of Germany had already been dropped by the time the Allied leaders Churchill, Roosevelt, and Stalin met at Yalta, USSR, in Feb 1945.

Morisot Berthe 1841–1895. French Impressionist painter, who specialized in pictures of women and children. She was the granddaughter of the artist Jean Fragonard and she influenced Manet.

Morley Malcolm 1931– . British painter, active in New York from 1964. He coined the term *Superrealism* for his work in the 1960s.

Morley Thomas 1557–1602. English composer. A student of ◊Byrd. He was the most influential composer of the English madrigal school, and also wrote a large amount of polyphonic sacred music, songs for Shakespeare's plays, and a musical textbook, *Plaine and Easie Introduction to Practicall Musicke* 1597.

Mormon or *Latter-day Saint* member of a Christian sect, the *Church of Jesus Christ of Latter-day Saints*, founded at Fayette, New York, in 1830 by Joseph ◊Smith. According to Smith, Mormon was an ancient prophet in N America whose *Book of Mormon*, of which Smith claimed divine revelation, is accepted by Mormons as part of the Christian scriptures. In the 19th century the faction led by Brigham ◊Young was polygamous. It is a missionary church with headquarters in Utah and a worldwide membership of about 6 million.

morning glory plant *Ipomoea purpurea*, family Convolvulaceae, native to tropical America, with dazzling blue flowers. Small quantities of substances similar to ◊LSD are found in the seeds of one variety.

Moro Aldo 1916–1978. Italian Christian Democrat politician. Prime minister 1963–68 and 1974–76, he was expected to become Italy's president, but was kidnapped and shot by Red Brigade urban guerrillas.

Moroccan Crises Two periods of international tension 1905 and 1911 following German objections to French expansion in Morocco. Their wider purpose was to break up the Anglo-French Entente 1904, but both crises served to reinforce the entente and isolate Germany.

Morocco country in N Africa, bordered N and NW by the Mediterranean, E and SE by Algeria, and S by Western Sahara.

Moroni capital of the Comoros Republic, on Njazidja (Grand Comore); population (1980) 16,000.

Morpheus in Greek and Roman mythology, the god of dreams, son of Hypnos or Somnus, god of sleep.

morphine opium ◊alkaloid, prescribed for severe pain. Its use produces serious side effects, including nausea, constipation, tolerance, and addiction. Although it is a controlled substance in Britain, its effective ◊analgesia makes it highly valued in the treatment of terminal illness.

morphology in biology, the study of the physical structure and form of organisms, in particular their soft tissues.

Morris Henry 1889–1961. British educationalist. He inspired and oversaw the introduction of the 'village college' and ◊community school, which he saw as regenerating rural life.

Morris William 1834–1896. British designer, socialist, and poet, who shared the Pre-Raphaelite painters' fascination with medieval settings. His first book of verse was *The Defence of Guenevere* 1858. The prose romances *A Dream of John Ball* 1888 and *News from Nowhere* 1891 reflect his socialist ideology: he also lectured on socialism.

Morris dance an English folk-dance. In early times it was usually performed by six men, one of whom wore girl's clothing, while another portrayed a horse. The others wore a costume decorated with bells. It probably originated in pre-Christian ritual dances, and is still popular.

Morrison Herbert Stanley, Baron Morrison of Lambeth 1888–1965. British Labour politician. On leaving school he became a shop assistant. He was Secretary of the London Labour Party 1915–45, and a member of the London County Council 1922–45. He entered Parliament 1923, and in 1955 lost to Gaitskell in the contest for party leadership.

Morrison Toni 1931– . US novelist whose fiction records black life in the American South. Her works include *The Song of Solomon* 1978, *Tar Baby* 1981, *Beloved* 1987, which won the Pulitzer Prize 1988, and *Jazz* 1992.

Morse Samuel (Finley Breese) 1791–1872. US inventor. In 1835 he produced the first adequate electric ◊telegraph, and in 1843 was granted $30,000 by Congress for an experimental line between Washington and Baltimore. With his assistant Alexander Bain he invented the Morse code.

Morse code international code for transmitting message by wire or radio using signals of short (dots) and long (dashes) duration, originated by Samuel Morse for use on his ◊telegraph.

Morris William Morris, photographed by Abel Lewis (c. 1880).

Morse code

A .-	B -...	C -.-.	D -..	E .	F ..-.
G --.	H	I ..	J .---	K -.-	L .-..
M --	N -.	O ---	P .--.	Q --.-	R .-.
S ...	T -	U ..-	V ...-	W .--	X -..-
		Y -.--	Z --..		
1 .----	2 ..---	3 ...--	4 ....-	5	
6 -....	7 --...	8 ---..	9 ----.	0 -----	

Morte D'Arthur, Le a series of episodes from the legendary life of King Arthur by Thomas Malory, completed 1470, regarded as the first great prose work in English literature. Only the last of the eight books comprising the series is titled *Le Morte D'Arthur*.

mortgage a transfer of property – usually a house – as a security for repayment of a loan. The loan is normally repaid to a bank or building society over a period of years.

Mortimer John 1923– . British barrister and writer. His works include the plays *The Dock Brief* 1958 and *A Voyage Round My Father* 1970, the novel *Paradise Postponed* 1985, and the television series *Rumpole of the Bailey*, from 1978, centred on a fictional barrister.

Mortimer Roger de, 8th Baron of Wigmore and 1st Earl of March c. 1287–1330. English politician and adventurer. He opposed Edward II and with Edward's queen, Isabella, led a rebellion against him 1326, bringing about his abdication. From 1327 Mortimer ruled England as the queen's lover, until Edward III had him executed.

Morton Jelly Roll. Stage name of Ferdinand Joseph La Menthe 1885–1941. US jazz pianist, singer, and composer. Influenced by Scott Joplin, he played a major part in the development of jazz from ragtime to swing. His band from 1926 was called the Red Hot Peppers.

Morton William Thomas Green 1819–1868. US dentist who in 1846 introduced ether as an anaesthetic; his claim to be the first to do so was strongly disputed.

mosaic a design or picture, usually for a floor or wall, produced by inlay of small pieces of marble, glass, or other materials. Mosaic was commonly used by the Romans for their villas (for example Hadrian's Villa at Tivoli), and by the Byzantines.

Moscow (Russian *Moskva*) capital of Russia and the Moskva region, and formerly (1922–91) of the USSR, on the Moskva river 640 km/400 mi SE of Leningrad; population (1987) 8,815,000. Its industries include machinery, electrical equipment, textiles, chemicals, and many food products.

Moseley Henry Gwyn-Jeffreys 1887–1915. British physicist who, 1913–14, devised the series of atomic numbers, leading to the modern ◊periodic table.

Moses c. 13th century BC. Hebrew lawgiver and judge who led the Israelites out of Egypt to the promised land of Canaan. On Mount Sinai he claimed to have received from Jehovah the *Ten Commandments* engraved on tablets of stone.

mosaic A mosaic from the 1st or 2nd century AD, from Southern Italy.

The first five books of the Old Testament – in Judaism, the *Torah* – are ascribed to him.

Moses 'Grandma' (born Anna Mary Robertson) 1860–1961. US painter. She was self-taught, and began full-time painting in about 1927, after many years as a farmer's wife. She achieved great popularity with her naive and colourful scenes from rural American life.

Moslem alternative word for *Muslim*, a follower of ◊Islam.

Mosley Oswald Ernald 1896–1980. British politician, founder of the British Union of Fascists (BUF). He was a member of parliament 1918–31, then led the BUF until his interment from 1940–43, when he was released on health grounds. In 1946 Mosley was denounced when it became known that Italy had funded his pre-war efforts to establish fascism in Britain, but in 1948 he resumed fascist propaganda with his Union Movement, the revived BUF. See also ◊fascism.

mosquito fly of the family Culicidae. The female mosquito has needle-like mouthparts and sucks blood, needing a meal before egglaying. Males feed on plant juices. Some mosquitoes carry diseases such as malaria.

moss small non-flowering plant of the class Musci (10,000 species), forming with the ◊liverworts the order Bryophyta. The stem of each plant bears rhizoids which anchor it; there are no true roots.

motor car

Leaves spirally arranged on its lower portion have sexual organs at their tip. Most mosses flourish best in damp conditions where other vegetation is thin. The peat or bog moss *Sphagnum* was formerly used for surgical dressings.

Mossadeq Muhammad 1880–1967. Iranian prime minister 1951–53. He instigated a dispute with the Anglo-Iranian Oil Company over the control of Iran's oil production, and when he failed in his attempt to overthrow the shah he was imprisoned.

motet a form of sacred, polyphonic music for unaccompanied voices which originated in the 13th century.

moth one of the insects forming the greater part of the order Lepidoptera. The wings are covered with flat, microscopic scales. The mouth-parts are formed into a sucking proboscis, but certain moths have no functional mouth-parts, and rely upon stores of fat and other reserves built up during the caterpillar stage. In many cases the males are smaller and more brightly coloured than the females. At least 100,000 different species of moth are known.

mother of pearl the smooth lustrous lining in the shells of pearl-bearing molluscs; see ◊pearl.

motor a machine that provides mechanical power, particularly an ◊electric motor. Machines that burn fuel (petrol, diesel) are usually called engines.

motor boat small, water-borne craft for pleasure cruising or racing powered by a petrol, diesel, or gas turbine engine. For increased speed, especially in racing, motor boat hulls are designed to skim the water (aquaplane) and reduce frictional resistance, and plastics, steel, and light alloys are now used in construction as well as the traditional wood.

motor car a self-propelled vehicle with a petrol or diesel engine, for use on normal roads. Usually four wheeled, most cars have an engine at the front although one notable exception is the German Volkswagen 'Beetle', the first popular economy car. Racing cars have the engine situated in the middle for balance. Prior to World War II a car was a luxury item, but now 62% of households in Britain are car-owners.

motorcycle or *motorbike*, a two-wheeled vehicle propelled by a ◊petrol engine. The first successful

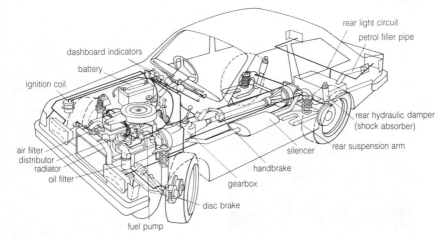

motor racing (Top left) Nigel Mansell 1988. (Top right) Ayrton Senna at the Belgian Grand Prix, 1988.

motorized bicycle was built in France in 1901, and British and American manufacturers first produced motorbikes in 1903.

motorcycle racing racing of motor cycles. It has many different forms: *road racing* over open roads, *circuit racing* over purpose built tracks, *speedway* over oval-shaped dirt tracks, *motor cross* over natural terrain, incorporating hill climbs, and *trials*, which are also over natural terrain, but with the addition of artificial hazards.

motoring law the law affecting the use of vehicles on public roads. It covers the licensing of vehicles and drivers, and the criminal offences which can be committed by the owners and drivers of vehicles.

motor nerves in anatomy, nerves which transmit impulses from the central nervous system to muscles or body organs. Motor nerves cause voluntary and involuntary muscle contractions, and stimulate glands to secrete hormones.

motor racing competitive racing of motor vehicles. It has many different forms as diverse as hill-climbing, stock-car racing, rallying, sports car racing, and Formula One Grand Prix racing. The first race was in 1894, from Paris to Rouen. It is now a popular spectator sport.

motorway main road for fast traffic, with separate carriageways for traffic moving in opposite directions. The first motorway (85 km) ran from Milan to Varèse and was completed 1924, and some 500 km of motorway were built in Italy by 1939. The first motorway in the UK was the M1, from London to Birmingham and Lancashire, opened 1955.

Motown the first black-owned US record company, founded in Detroit (*motor town*) 1959 by Berry Gordy Jr (1929–). Its distinctive, upbeat sound (exemplified by the Four Tops and the ◊Supremes) was a major element in 1960s' pop music.

Mott Nevill Francis 1905– . British physicist noted for his research on the electronic properties of metals, semiconductors, and noncrystalline materials. He shared the Nobel Prize for Physics 1977.

mouflon type of sheep *Ovis ammon* found wild in Cyprus, Corsica, and Sardinia. It has woolly underfur in winter, but this is covered by the heavy guard hairs. The coat is brown, with white belly and rump. Males have strong curving horns. The mouflon lives in rough mountain areas.

mould mainly saprophytic ◊fungi living on foodstuffs and other organic matter, a few being parasitic on plants, animals, or each other. Many are of medical or industrial importance, such as penicillin.

moulding a common method of shaping plastics, clays, and glass. In *injection moulding*, molten plastic, for example, is injected into a water-cooled

mould and takes the shape of the mould when it solidifies. In *blow moulding*, air is blown into a blob of molten plastic inside a hollow mould. In *compression moulding*, synthetic resin powder is simultaneously heated and pressed into a mould. When metals are used, the process is called ◊casting,

moulting the periodic shedding of the hair or fur of mammals, feathers of birds, or skin of reptiles. In mammals and birds, moulting is usually seasonal and is triggered by changes of daylength.

Moundbuilder a member of various N American Indian peoples who built earth mounds, linear and conical in shape for tombs, and 'platforms' for chiefs' houses, and temples from about 300 BC.

mountain a large natural upward projection of the Earth's surface. Orogenesis (the process of mountain building) consists of folding, faulting, and thrusting, resulting from the collision of two tectonic plates, deforming their rocks and compressing the sediment between them into mountain chains.

mountain ash or *rowan*, flowering tree *Sorbus aucuparia* of the family Rosaceae. It grows to 50 ft/15 m, and has pinnate leaves and large clusters of whitish flowers, followed by scarlet berries.

mountaineering the art and practice of mountain climbing. For major peaks of the Himalayas it was formerly thought necessary to have elaborate support from Sherpas, and fixed ropes and oxygen at high altitudes. In the 1980s the 'Alpine style' was introduced. This dispenses with these aids, and relies on human ability to adapt Sherpa-style to high altitude.

mountain lion another name for ◊puma.

Mountbatten Louis, 1st Earl Mountbatten of Burma 1900–1979. British admiral. In World War II he became chief of combined operations 1942 and commander in chief in SE Asia 1943. As last viceroy of India 1947 he oversaw the transition to independence, becoming first governor general of India until 1948. He was chief of UK Defence Staff 1959–65. Mountbatten was killed by an Irish Republican Army bomb aboard his yacht at Mullaghmore, County Sligo.

Mount St Helens volcanic mountain in Washington state, USA. When it erupted in 1980 after being quiescent since 1857, it devastated an area of 600 sq km/230 sq mi and its height was reduced from 2,950 m/9,682 ft to 2,560 m/8,402 ft.

mouse in computing, an input device, used to control a pointer on a computer screen. Moving the mouse across a desktop produces corresponding movement in the pointer. A mouse normally has one or more controlling buttons on its 'head' to instruct the computer when the pointer is superimposed on a menu option on the screen, and its connecting wire is its 'tail'.

mouse in zoology, name given to many small rodents, particularly those of the family Muridae.

motor car: chronology

1769	Nicholas-Joseph Cugnot in France built a steam tractor.
1801	Richard Trevithick built a steam coach.
1860	Jean Etienne Lenoir built a gas-fuelled internal combustion engine.
1865	The British government passed the 'Red Flag' Act, requiring a man to precede a 'horseless carriage' with a red flag.
1876	Nikolaus August Otto improved the gas engine, making it a practical power source.
1885	Gottlieb Daimler developed a lightweight petrol engine and fitted it to a bicycle to create the prototype of the modern motorbike; Karl Benz fitted his lightweight petrol engine to a three-wheeled carriage to pioneer the motor car.
1886	Gottlieb Daimler produced a four-wheeled motor car.
1891	René Panhard and Emile Levassor established the present design of cars by putting the engine in front.
1896	Frederick Lancaster introduced epicyclic gearing, which foreshadowed automatic transmission.
1901	The first Mercedes took to the roads. It was the direct ancestor of the present car; Ransome Olds in the USA introduced mass production on an assembly line.
1906	Rolls-Royce introduced the legendary Silver Ghost, which established their reputation for superlatively engineered cars.
1908	Henry Ford also used assembly-line production to manufacture his famous Model T.
1911	Cadillac introduced the electric starter and dynamic lighting.
1920	Duesenberg began fitting four-wheel hydraulic brakes.
1922	The Lancia Lambda featured unitary (all-in-one) construction and independent front suspension.
1928	Cadillac introduced the synchromesh gearbox, facilitating gear changing.
1934	Citroën pioneered front-wheel drive in their 7CV model.
1936	Fiat introduced their baby car, the Topolino, 500 cc.
1938	Germany produced its 'people's car', the Volkswagen 'beetle'.
1948	Jaguar launched the XK120 sports car, Michelin introduced the radial-ply tyre; Goodrich produced the tubeless tyre.
1950	Dunlop announced the disc brake.
1951	Buick and Chrysler introduced power steering.
1952	Rover's gas-turbine car set a speed record of 243 kph/152 mph.
1954	Bosch introduced fuel-injection for cars.
1955	Citroën produced the advanced DS-19 'shark-front' car with hydropneumatic suspension.
1957	Felix Wankel built his first rotary petrol engine.
1959	BMC (now Rover) introduced the Issigonis-designed Mini.
1966	California introduced legislation to reduce air pollution by cars.
1972	Dunlop introduced safety tyres, which sealed themselves after a burst.
1980s	Lean-burn engines were introduced to improve fuel consumption; electronic ignition and engine controls became widely available; on-board computers were introduced to monitor engine performance, speech synthesizers to issue audible warnings.
1987	The solar-powered *Sunraycer* travelled 3000 km/1,864 mi from Darwin to Adelaide, Australia, in six days.
1990	Fiat and Peugeot launched electric passenger cars on the market.
1992	Mazda and NEC of Japan developed a system for cars which views the road ahead through a video camera, and processes the information thus received.

mountain

Animals and plants that live on mountains are adapted to cope with low temperatures, strong winds, a thin, poor soil, and air with little oxygen.

With increasing altitude, the climate becomes bleaker. Temperature, for example, falls by roughly 1°C/2°F for every 150m/500ft. On high mountains near the equator, this usually produces distinct zones of vegetation (shown right) similar to those found as one travels from the tropics to the North Pole.

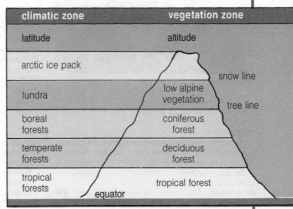

climatic zone	vegetation zone
latitude	altitude
arctic ice pack	snow line
tundra	low alpine vegetation
	tree line
boreal forests	coniferous forest
temperate forests	deciduous forest
tropical forests	tropical forest
equator	

Alpine wildlife 1. Brown bear 2. Alpine marmot 3. Chamois 4. Peregrine falcon 5. Golden eagle 6. Ibex.

7. Windflowers and gentians bloom in spring and last just a few weeks.

Plants of the alpine zone are small, compact and low-growing to survive the cold, strong winds. Most are perennial, continuing their growth over several years. Mountain animals tend to stay on the high slopes and peaks throughout the year. Many have a thick protective coat, and some of the hoofed mammals have soft pads on their feet that help them to cling to rocks.

Mountbatten Admiral Lord Louis Mountbatten 1943.

The house mouse *Mus musculus* is distributed worldwide. It is 75 mm/3 in long, with a naked tail of equal length, and a grey-brown body.

mousebird bird of the order Coliiformes, including the single family (Coliidae) of small crested birds peculiar to Africa. They have hair-like feathers, long tails and mouse-like agility. The largest is the *blue-naped mousebird Colius macrourus*, about 35 cm/14 in long.

Moustier, Le cave in the Dordogne, SW France, with prehistoric remains, giving the name *Mousterian* to the flint-tool culture of Neanderthal peoples; the earliest ritual burials are linked with Mousterian settlements.

mouth the cavity forming the entrance of the digestive tract. In mammals, it is also the entrance of the respiratory tract, and is enclosed by the jaws, cheeks and palate.

mouth organ another name for ◊harmonica, a musical instrument.

movement in music, a section of a large work, such as a symphony, which is often complete in itself.

Mozambique country in SE Africa, bordered to the N by Zambia, Malawi, and Tanzania, E by the Indian Ocean, S by South Africa, and E by Swaziland and Zimbabwe.

Mozart Wolfgang Amadeus 1756–1791. Austrian composer who showed astonishing precocity as a pianist and was trained by his father, Leopold Mozart (1719–87). From an early age he composed prolifically, his works including 25 piano concertos, 23 string quartets, 35 violin sonatas; some 50 symphonies, including the E flat K543, G minor K550, and C major K551 ('Jupiter') symphonies, all composed 1788. His operas include *Idomeneo* 1781, *Entführung aus dem Serail/The Abduction from the Seraglio* 1782, *Le Nozze di Figaro/The Marriage of Figaro* 1786, *Don Giovanni* 1787, *Così fan tutte/Thus do all Women*1790, and *Die Zauberflöte/The Magic Flute* 1791.

MP abbreviation for *member of parliament*.

MPLA (Portuguese *Movimento Popular de Libertacão de Angola*, Popular Movement for the Liberation of Angola) socialist organization founded in the early 1950s which sought to free

woodmouse

mudskipper

Angola from Portuguese rule 1961–75 before being involved in the civil war against its former allies ◊UNITA and ◊FNLA 1975–76. The MPLA took control of the country but UNITA guerrilla activity continues today, supported by South Africa.

Mubarak Hosni 1928– . Egyptian politician, president from 1981. He commanded the air force 1972–75 (he was responsible for the initial victories in the Egyptian campaign of 1973 against Israel), when he became an active vice president to Sadat, and succeeded him on his assassination. He has continued to pursue Sadat's moderate policies, and has significantly increased the freedom of the press and of political association.

mucous membrane thin skin found on all internal body surfaces of animals (for example, eyelids, breathing and digestive passages, genital tract). It secretes mucus, a moistening, lubricating and protective fluid.

mudpuppy brownish amphibian *Necturus maculosus*. It is about 20 cm/8 in long, and retains large external gills. It lives in streams in North America, and eats fish, snails, and other invertebrates.

mudskipper type of fish, genus *Periophthalmus*, found in brackish water and shores in the tropics, except for the Americas. It can walk or climb over mudflats, using its strong pectoral fins as legs, and has eyes set close together on top of the head. It grows up to 30 cm/12 in long.

muezzin (Arabic) a person whose job it is to perform the call to prayer five times a day from the minaret of a Muslim mosque.

mufti a Muslim legal expert who guides the courts in their interpretation. In Turkey the *grand mufti* had supreme spiritual authority until the establishment of the republic in 1924.

Mugabe Robert (Gabriel) 1925– . Zimbabwe politician, prime minister from 1980 and president from 1987. He was in detention in Rhodesia for nationalist activities 1964–74, then carried on guerrilla warfare from Mozambique. As leader of ◊ZANU he was in alliance with Joshua ◊Nkomo of ZAPU from 1976, and the two parties merged in 1987.

Mughal emperors North Indian dynasty 1526–1857, established by ◊Zahir ('Baber'). They were descendants of Tamerlane, the 14th-century Mongol leader, and ruled till the last Mughal emperor was dethroned and exiled by the British in 1857; they included ◊Akbar, ◊Aurangzeb, and ◊Shah Jehan. They were Muslims.

mugwump in US political history, a colloquial name for the Republicans who voted in the 1884 presidential election for Grover Cleveland, the Democratic candidate, rather than for their Republican nominee, James G Blaine (1830–93); hence the modern meaning of one who refuses to follow the official party line.

Muhammad or *Mohammed, Mahomet c.* 570–632. Founder of Islam, born in Mecca on the Arabian peninsula. In about 616 he claimed to be a prophet and that the *Koran* was revealed to him by God (it was later written down by his followers). He fled from persecution to the town now known as Medina in 622: the flight, *Hegira*, marks the beginning of the Islamic era.

Mozambique
People's Republic of (*República Popular de Moçambique*)

area 799,380 sq km/308,561 sq mi
capital and chief port Maputo
towns ports Beira, Nacala
physical mostly flat; mountains in W
head of state and government Joaquim Alberto Chissano from 1986

political system emergent democratic republic
exports prawns, cashews, sugar, cotton, tea
currency metical
population (1990 est) 14,718,000 (mainly indigenous Bantu peoples; Portuguese 50,000); annual growth rate 2.8%
language Portuguese (official)
religion animist 60%, Roman Catholic 18%, Muslim 16%
literacy 55% male/22% female (1985 est)
GDP $4.7 bn (1987); $319 per head
chronology
1962 Frelimo (liberation front) established.
1975 Independence achieved from Portugal as a Socialist republic, with Samora Machel as president and Frelimo as the sole legal party.
1983 Re-establishment of good relations with Western powers.
1984 Nkomati Accord signed with South Africa.
1986 Machel killed in air crash; succeeded by Joaquim Chissano.
1988 Tanzania announced complete withdrawal of its troops. South Africa provided training for Mozambiquan forces.
1989 Frelimo offered to abandon Marxist-Leninism; Chissano re-elected; Renamo continued to attack government facilities and civilians.
1990 One-party rule ended; partial ceasefire agreed.
1991 Peace talks resumed in Rome. Attempted coup thwarted.
1992 Peace accord agreed, but fighting continued.

Mujaheddin (Arabic *mujahid*, 'fighters', from *jihad*, 'holy war') Islamic fundamentalist guerrillas of contemporary Afghanistan and Iran.
Mujibur Sheik Rahman 1921–1975. Bangladeshi nationalist politician, president 1975. He was arrested several times for campaigning for the autonomy of

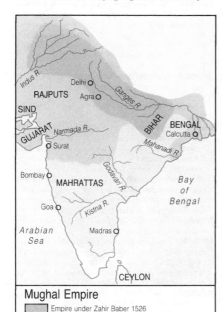

Mughal Empire
- Empire under Zahir Baber 1526
- expansion under Akbar to 1605
- expansion under Shah Jehan and Aurungzeb to 1707

East Pakistan. He won the elections of 1970 but was again arrested when negotiations with the Pakistan government broke down. After the civil war of 1971, he became prime minister of the newly independent Bangladesh. He was presidential dictator Jan–Aug 1975, when he was assassinated.
Mukden, Battle of the taking of Mukden (now Shenyang), NE China, the capital of the Manchu emperors, from Russian occupation by the Japanese, 20 Feb–10 Mar 1905, during the ◊Russo-Japanese War. Mukden was later the scene of a surprise attack 18 Sep 1931 by the Japanese on the Chinese garrison, which marked the beginning of their invasion of China.
mulberry tree, genus *Morus*, of the family Moraceae, consisting of a dozen species, including the *black mulberry Morus nigra*. Native to W Asia, it has heart-shaped toothed leaves, and spikes of whitish flowers. The fruit, made up of a cluster of small drupes, resembles a raspberry
Muldoon Robert David 1921–1992. New Zealand National Party politician, prime minister 1975–84. He sought to introduce curbs on trade unions, and was a vigorous supporter of the Western alliance.
mullah a teacher, scholar, or religious leader of Islam. It is also a title of respect given to various other dignitaries.
mullein plant of the genus *Verbascum*, family Scrophulariaceae. The *great mullein Verbascum thapsus* has lance-shaped leaves, 30 cm/21 in or more in length, covered in woolly down; in the second year of growth, a large spike of yellow flowers is produced. It is found in Europe and Asia, and is naturalized in N America.
Müller Johannes Peter 1801–1858. German comparative anatomist whose studies of nerves and sense organs opened a new chapter in physiology by demonstrating the physical nature of sensory perception.

mullet two types of fish. The *red mullet Mullus surmuletus* is found in the Mediterranean and warm Atlantic as far N as the English Channel. It is about 40 cm/16 in long, red with yellow stripes, and has long barbels round the mouth. The *grey mullet Crenimugil labrosus* lives in ponds and estuaries. It is greyish above, with longitudinal dark stripes, and grows to 60 cm/24 in.

Mulliken Robert Sanderson 1896–1986. US chemist and physicist, who received the 1966 Nobel Prize for Chemistry for his development of the molecular orbital theory.

Mulroney Brian 1939– . Canadian politician. Progressive Conservative party leader 1983–93, prime minister 1984–93. He won the 1988 election on a platform of free trade with the USA, but with a reduced majority. After continuing opposition to the Meech Lake agreement had caused his popularity to plummet in 1993 he resigned as party leader.

multi-cultural education a term used to describe education aimed at preparing children to live in a multi-racial society by giving them an understanding of the culture and history of different ethnic groups.

multilateralism trade between more than two countries without discrimination over origin or destination, and regardless of whether a large trade gap is involved.

multinational corporation company or enterprise operating in several countries, usually defined as one that has 25% or more of its output capacity located outside its country of origin.

multiple birth in humans, the production of more than two babies from one pregnancy. Multiple births can be caused by more than two eggs being produced and fertilized (often as the result of hormone therapy to assist pregnancy), or a single fertilized egg dividing more than once before implantation.

multiple sclerosis (MS) an incurable disease of the central nervous system, occurring in young or middle adulthood. It is characterized by degeneration of the myelin sheath which surrounds nerves in the brain and spinal cord. It is also known as disseminated sclerosis. Its cause is unknown.

multiplier in economics, the theoretical concept, formulated by J M Keynes, of the effect on national income or employment by an adjustment in overall demand. For example, investment by a company in new plant will stimulate new income and expenditure, which will in turn generate new investment, and so on, so that the actual increase in national income may be several times greater than the original investment.

multi-stage rocket a rocket launch vehicle consisting of a number of rocket stages joined together, usually end to end. See ◊step rocket.

Mumford Lewis 1895–1990. US sociologist, concerned with the effect of technology on modern society, as in *The Culture of Cities* 1938.

mummers' play or *St George play* British folk drama enacted in dumb show by masked performers, performed on Christmas Day to celebrate the death of the old year and its rebirth as the new year. The plot usually consists of a duel between St George and an infidel knight, in which one of them is killed but later revived by a doctor.

mummy human or animal body preserved after death, either naturally or artifically (for example, by drying or freezing – the science of cryonics). Examples are mammoths preserved in glacial ice from 25,000 years ago; shrunken heads preserved by the ◊Jivaro people in South America; the

Munch The Sick Child *(1907) Tate Gallery, London.*

mummies of ancient Egypt; and modern mummies such as Lenin and Eva Perón.

mumps virus infection marked by fever and swelling of the parotid salivary glands (under the ear). It is usually minor in children. It may cause sterility in adult males.

Munch Edvard 1863–1944. Norwegian painter. He studied in Paris and Berlin, and his best works date from 1892–1908, when he lived mainly in Germany. His style was expressive of emotional states, distorting faces and figures. The *Frieze of Life* 1890s, a sequence of highly charged, symbolic paintings, includes some of his best-known images, for example *Skriket/The Scream* 1893.

Münchhausen Karl Friedrich, Freiherr (Baron) von 1720–1797. German soldier, born in Hanover. He served with the Russian army against the Turks, and after his retirement in 1760 told exaggerated stories of his campaigning adventures. This idiosyncrasy was utilized by the German writer Rudolph Erich Raspe (1737–94) in his extravagantly fictitious *Adventures of Baron Munchausen* 1785, which he wrote in English while living in London.

Munich German *München* industrial city (brewing, printing, precision instruments, machinery, electrical goods, textiles), capital of Bavaria, Germany, on the river Isar; population (1986) 1,269,400.

Munich Agreement pact signed on 29 Sept 1938 by the leaders of the UK (N ◊Chamberlain), France (◊Daladier), Germany (Hitler), and Italy (Mussolini), under which Czechoslovakia was compelled to surrender its Sudeten-German districts (the *Sudetenland*) to Germany. Chamberlain claimed it would guarantee 'peace in our time', but it did not prevent Hitler from seizing the rest of Czechoslovakia in Mar 1939.

Munro H(ugh) H(ector) British author who wrote under the pen name ◊Saki.

Munster souther province of Republic of Ireland, comprising the counties of ◊Clare, ◊Cork, ◊Kerry, ◊Limerick, North and South ◊Tipperary, and ◊Waterford; area 24,128 sq km/9,319 sq mi; population (1991) 1,008,400.

muntjac small deer, genus *Muntiacus*, native to SE Asia. The buck has short spiked antlers and two sharp canine teeth forming tusks. They are sometimes called 'barking' deer because of their voices. Muntjac live mostly in dense vegetation and do not form herds.

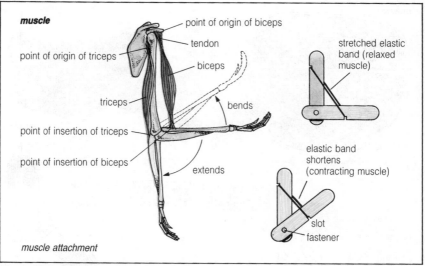

muscle

point of origin of biceps

point of origin of triceps

tendon

biceps

triceps

point of insertion of triceps

point of insertion of biceps

bends

extends

stretched elastic band (relaxed muscle)

elastic band shortens (contracting muscle)

slot

fastener

muscle attachment

Murasaki Shikibu *c.* 978–*c.* 1015. Japanese writer, a lady at the court. Her masterpiece of fiction, *The Tale of Genji*, is one of the classic works of Japanese literature, and may be the world's first novel.

Murat Joachim 1767–1815. King of Naples from 1808. An officer of the French army, he was made king by Napoleon, but deserted him in 1813 in the vain hope that the Allies would recognize him. in 1815 he attempted unsuccessfully to make himself king of all Italy, but when he landed in Calabria he was captured and shot.

Murcia autonomous region of SE Spain; area 11,313 sq km/4,368 sq mi; population (1986) 1,014,000. It includes the cities Murcia and Cartagena, and produces esparto grass, lead, zinc, iron, and fruit.

murder unlawful killing of one person by another. In British law murder is committed only when the killer acts with malice aforethought, that is, intending either to kill or to cause serious injury, or realizing that this would probably result.

Murdoch Iris 1919– . Irish novelist. Her novels combine philosophical speculation with often outrageous situations and tangled human relationships. They include *The Sandcastle* 1957, *The Sea, The Sea* 1978, and *The Book and the Brotherhood* 1987.

Murdoch Rupert 1931– . Australian entrepreneur and newspaper owner, with interests in Australia, Britain, and the USA. His Australian newspapers are the *Australian*, the *Daily Telegraph* and the *Daily Mirror*, and he controls the Melbourne-based *Herald and Weekly Times* publishing group. Among his British newspapers are the *Sun*, the *News of the World*, *The Times*, and the *Sunday Times*; in the USA, he has a 50% stake in 20th Century Fox, and he also owns publishing companies. He is chief executive of British Sky Broadcasting, the UK's satellite television service.

Murdock William 1754–1839. Scottish inventor who first used coal gas for domestic lighting, illuminating his house and office in 1792.

Murillo Bartolomé Esteban 1617–1682. Spanish painter, active mainly in Seville. He is perhaps best known for sweetly sentimental pictures of the Immaculate Conception; he also specialized in studies of street urchins.

Murmansk seaport in NW Russia, on the Barents Sea; population (1987) 419,000. It is the largest city in the Arctic, Russia's most important fishing port, and base of the icebreakers that keep open the North East Passage.

Murnau pseudonym of Friedrich Wilhelm Plumpe 1889–1931. German silent-film director, whose 'subjective' use of a moving camera to tell the story, through expressive images and without subtitles, in *Der letzte Mumm/The Last Laugh* 1924 made his famous.

Murray principal river of Australia, 2,575 km/1,600 mi long. It rises in the Australian Alps near Mount Kosciusko and flows west, forming the boundary between New South Wales and Victoria, and reaches the sea at Encounter Bay, South Australian. With its main tributary, the Darling, it is 3,750 km/2,330 mi long.

Murray James Augustus Henry 1837–1915. Scottish philologist. He was the first editor of the *Oxford English Dictionary* (originally the *New English Dictionary*) from 1878 until his death; the first volume was published 1884.

Murray James Stuart, Earl of Murray, or Moray 1531–1570. Regent of Scotland from 1567, an illegitimate son of James V. Murray was one of the leaders of the Scottish Reformation, and after the deposition of his half-sister ◊Mary, Queen of Scots, he became regent. He was assassinated by one of her supporters.

murray cod Australian freshwater fish *Maccullochella macquariensis* which grows to about 2 m/6 ft. It is named after the river in which it is found.

Muscat Arabic *Masqat* capital of Oman E Arabia, adjoining the port of Matrah, which has a deepwater harbour; combined population (1982) 80,000. It produces natural gas and chemicals.

muscle contractile animal tissue which produces locomotion and maintains the movement of body substances. Muscle is made of long cells which can contract to between one-half and one-third of their relaxed length. *Striped* muscles are activated by ◊motor nerves under voluntary control; they are attached to bones, except for those that form the tongue. *Involuntary* or *smooth* muscles are controlled by motor nerves of the ◊autonomic nervous system,

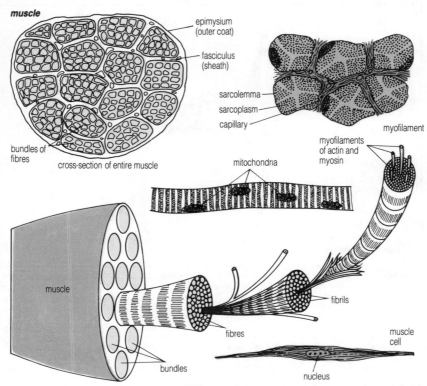

muscle

epimysium
(outer coat)

fasciculus
(sheath)

sarcolemma
sarcoplasm
capillary

myofilament

bundles of
fibres

cross-section of entire muscle

mitochondria

myofilaments
of actin and
myosin

muscle

fibrils

fibres

muscle
cell

bundles

nucleus

and located in the gut, blood vessels, iris, and ducts. *Cardiac* muscle only occurs in the heart, and is also controlled by the autonomic nervous system.

muscular dystrophy any of a group of inherited muscle disorders marked by weakening and wasting of muscle. Muscle fibres degenerate, to be replaced by fatty tissue, although the nerve supply remains unimpaired.

Muses in Greek mythology, the nine daughters of Zeus and Mnemosyne (goddess of memory) and inspirers of creative arts:
Calliope epic poetry;
Clio history;
Erato love poetry;
Euterpe lyric poetry;
Melpomene tragedy;
Polyhymnia hymns;
Terpsichore dance;
Thalia comedy;
Urania astronomy.

Museveni Yoweri Kaguta 1945– . Ugandan general and politician. He led the opposition to Idi Amin's regime (1971–78), and was then minister of defence 1979–80 but, unhappy with Milton Obote's autocratic leadership, formed the National Resistance Army (NRA), which helped to remove him. Museveni became president 1986, leading a broad-based coalition government.

mushroom fungus consisting of an upright stem and a spore-producing cap with radiating gills on the undersurface. There are many edible species belonging to the genus *Agaricus*, including the field mushroom *Agaricus campestris*. See also ♢toadstool.

music the art of combining sounds into a unified whole, typically in accordance with fixed patterns and for an aesthetic purpose.

musical recent form of popular dramatic musical performance, combining elements of song, dance, and the spoken word.

music hall a British light theatrical entertainment consisting of 'turns', in which singers, dancers, comedians, and acrobats perform in turn. Its heyday was at the beginning of the 20th century, with such artists as Marie Lloyd, Harry Lauder, and George Formby.

music theatre the staged performance of vocal music that deliberately sets out to get away from the grandiose style and scale of traditional opera.

musk perennial plant *Mimulus moschatus* of the family Scrophulariaceae; its small oblong leaves exude the musky scent from which it takes its name. Also any of several plants with a musky odour, including the **musk mallow** *Malva moschata* and the **musk rose** *Rosa moschata*.

musk ox

music: great composers

Giovanni Palestrina	c.1525–1594	Italian	motets, masses
Claudio Monteverdi	1567–1643	Italian	operas, vocal music
Henry Purcell	1659–1695	English	vocal music, operas
Antonio Vivaldi	1678–1741	Italian	concertos, chamber music
George Frideric Handel	1685–1759	German	oratorios, operas, orchestral music
Johann Sebastian Bach	1685–1750	German	keyboard, choral music, concertos
Joseph Haydn	1732–1809	Austrian	symphonies, oratorios, chamber music
Wolfgang Amadeus Mozart	1756–1791	Austrian	symphonies, operas, chamber music
Ludwig van Beethoven	1770–1827	German	symphonies, chamber music, opera
Carl Maria von Weber	1786–1826	German	operas, concertos
Gioacchino Rossini	1792–1868	Italian	operas
Franz Schubert	1797–1828	Austrian	songs, symphonies, chamber music
Hector Berlioz	1803–1869	French	operas, symphonies
Felix Mendelssohn	1809–1847	German	symphonies, concertos
Frédéric Chopin	1810–1849	Polish	piano music
Robert Schumann	1810–1856	German	piano, vocal music, concertos
Franz Liszt	1811–1886	Hungarian	piano, orchestral music
Richard Wagner	1813–1883	German	operas
Giuseppe Verdi	1813–1901	Italian	operas
César Franck	1822–1890	Belgian	symphony, organ works
Bedrich Smetana	1824–1884	Czech	symphonies, operas
Anton Bruckner	1824–1896	Austrian	symphonies
Johann Strauss II	1825–1899	Austrian	waltzes, operettas
Johannes Brahms	1833–1897	German	symphonies, concertos
Camille Saint-Saëns	1835–1921	French	symphonies, concertos, operas
Modest Mussorgsky	1839–1881	Russian	operas, orchestral music
Peter Ilyich Tchaikovsky	1840–1893	Russian	ballet music, symphonies
Antonin Dvořák	1841–1904	Czech	symphonies, operas
Edvard Grieg	1843–1907	Norwegian	concertos, orchestral music
Nikolai Rimsky-Korsakov	1844–1908	Russian	opera, orchestral music
Leos Janáček	1854–1928	Czech	operas, chamber music
Edward Elgar	1857–1934	English	orchestral music
Giacomo Puccini	1858–1924	Italian	operas
Gustav Mahler	1860–1911	Czech	symphonies
Claude Debussy	1862–1918	French	operas, orchestral music
Richard Strauss	1864–1949	German	operas, orchestral music
Carl Nielsen	1865–1931	Danish	symphonies
Jean Sibelius	1865–1957	Finnish	symphonies, orchestral music
Sergei Rachmaninov	1873–1943	Russian	symphonies, concertos
Arnold Schoenberg	1874–1951	Austrian	operas, orchestral and chamber music
Maurice Ravel	1875–1937	French	piano, chamber music
Béla Bartók	1881–1945	Hungarian	operas, concertos
Igor Stravinsky	1882–1971	Russian	ballets, operas
Anton Webern	1883–1945	Austrian	chamber, vocal music
Alban Berg	1885–1935	Austrian	operas, chamber music
Sergei Prokofiev	1891–1953	Russian	symphonies, ballets
George Gershwin	1898–1937	American	musicals, operas
Dmitri Shostakovich	1906–1975	Russian	piano music
Olivier Messiaen	1908–	French	piano, organ, orchestral music
Benjamin Britten	1913–1976	English	vocal music, operas
Karlheinz Stockhausen	1928–	German	electronic, vocal music

musk deer small deer *Moschus moschiferus* native to mountains of central Asia. It is about 50 cm/20 in high, sure-footed, with large ears, no antlers or horns, and is solitary.

musk ox hoofed mammal *Ovibos moschatus* native to the Arctic regions of North America. It displays characteristics of sheep and oxen, is about the size of a small domestic cow, and has long brown hair. At certain seasons it exhales a musky odour.

muskrat rodent *Ondatra zibethicus* about 30 cm/12 in long, living in watery regions of N America. It has webbed feet, a flattened tail, and shiny light brown fur. It builds up a store of food, plastering it over with mud, for winter consumption.

Muslim or *Moslem*, a follower of ◊Islam.

Muslim Brotherhood movement founded by members of the Sunni branch of Islam in Egypt in 1928. It aims at the establishment of a theocratic

Islamic state and is headed by a 'supreme guide'. It is also active in Jordan, Sudan, and Syria.

mussel popular name for a number of bivalve molluscs, some of them edible.

Musset Alfred de 1810–1857. French poet and playwright. He achieved success with the volume of poems *Contes d'Espagne et d'Italie/Stories of Spain and Italy* 1829. His *Confession d'un enfant du siècle/Confessions of a Child of the Century* 1835 recounts his broken relationship with George Sand.

Mussolini Benito 1883–1945. Italian dictator 1925–43. As founder of the Fascist Movement (see ◊fascism) 1919 and prime minister from 1922, he became known as *Il Duce* 'the leader'. He invaded Ethiopia 1935–36, intervened in the Spanish Civil War of 1936–39 in support of Franco, and conquered Albania in 1939. In Jun 1940 Italy entered World War II supporting Hitler. Forced by military and domestic setbacks to resign 1943,

Mussolini *Benito Mussolini greeting Adolf Hitler at Florence railway station, Italy, Oct 1940*

Mussolini established a breakaway government in N Italy 1944–45, but was killed trying to flee the country.

Mussorgsky Modest Petrovich 1839–1881. Russian composer, who was largely self-taught. His opera *Boris Godunov* was completed in 1869, although not produced in St Petersburg until 1874. Some of his works were 'revised' by Rimsky-Korsakov, and only recently has their harsh and primitive beauty been recognized.

Mustafa Kemal Turkish leader, who assumed the name of ◊Atatürk.

mustard annual plant of the family Cruciferae. The seeds of black mustard *Brassica nigra* and white mustard *Sinapis alba* are used in the production of table mustard. They are cultivated in Europe, North America, and England, where wild mustard or charlock *Sinapis arvensis* is also found.

mutation in biology, a change in the genes; more specifically, a change in the ◊DNA or ◊RNA that makes up the hereditary material of all living organisms. Mutations, the raw material of evolution, result from mistakes during replication (copying) of DNA molecules. Only a few improve the organism's performance and are therefore favoured by ◊natural selection. Mutation rates are increased by certain chemicals and by radiation.

mutiny a refusal by members of the armed services to obey orders given by a (usually military) authority.

Mutsuhito 1852–1912. Emperor of Japan from 1867, when he took the title *meiji tennō* ('enlightened sovereign'). During his reign Japan became a world military and naval power. He abolished the feudal system and discrimination against the lowest caste, established state schools, and introduced conscription, the Western calendar, and other measures in an attempt to modernize Japan, in-

Muzorewa *Zimbabwean politician and bishop of the Methodist Church, Abel Muzorewa, 1979.*

Mycenae *The Lion Gate, the main entrance to the Citadel.*

cluding a constitution 1889.

mutual fund another name for ◊unit trust, particularly in the USA.

mutual induction in physics, the production of an electromotive force (emf) or voltage in an electric circuit caused by a changing ◊magnetic flux in a neighbouring circuit. The two circuits are often coils of wire, as in a transformer, and the size of the induced emf depends largely on the numbers of turns of wire in each of the coils.

mutualism or ◊*symbiosis* an association between two organisms of different species whereby both profit from the relationship.

Muybridge Eadweard. Assumed name of Edward James Muggeridge 1830–1904. British photographer. He made a series of animal locomotion photographs in the USA in the 1870s and proved that, when a horse trots, there are times when all its feet are off the ground.

Muzorewa Abel (Tendekayi) 1925– . Zimbabwean politician and Methodist bishop. He was president of the African National Council 1971–85, and was prime minister of Rhodesia/Zimbabwe 1979. He was detained for a year in 1983–84. He is leader of the minority United Africa National Council (UANC).

MVD Soviet Ministry of Internal Affairs, name of the secret police 1946–53; later the ◊KGB.

Mwinyi Ali Hassan 1925– . Tanzanian socialist politician, president from 1985, when he succeeded Nyerere. He began a revival of private enterprise and control of state involvement and spending.

Myanmar formerly (until 1989) *Burma*; country in SE Asia, bounded NW by India and Bangladesh, NE by China, SE by Laos and Thailand, and SW by the Bay of Bengal.

mycelium an interwoven mass of threadlike filaments or ◊hyphae, forming the main body of most fungi. The reproductive structures, or 'fruiting bodies', grow from this mycelium.

Mycenae ancient Greek city in the E Peloponnese, which gave its name to the Mycenaean (Bronze Age) civilization. Its peak was 1400–1200 BC, when the Cyclopean walls (using close-fitting stones) were erected. The city ceased to be inhabited after about 1120 BC.

Mycenaean civilization one of several Bronze Age ◊Aegean civilizations, noted for its architecture and sophisticated artefacts, which flourished in Crete, Cyprus, Greece, the Aegean Islands, and W Anatolia *c.* 400–1000 BC. Originating in Crete, it spread into Greece *c.* 1600 BC, where it continued to thrive, with its centre at Mycenae, after the decline of Crete *c.* 1400. It was finally overthrown by the Dorian invasions, *c.* 1100.

mycorrhiza a mutually beneficial (mutualistic) association occurring between plant roots and a soil fungus. Mycorrhizal roots take up nutrients more efficiently, and the fungus benefits by obtaining carbohydrates from the tree.

myelin sheath insulating layer that surrounds nerve cells in vertebrate animals. It acts to speed up the passage of nerve impulses. It consists of up to 100 layers of membrane produced by the *Schwann cells*.

Myers F(rederic) W(illiam) H(enry) 1843–1901. English psychic investigator and writer, coiner of the word 'telepathy'. He was a founder of the Society for Psychical Research (1900).

My Lai massacre killing of 109 civilians in My Lai, a village in South Vietnam, by US troops commanded by Lt William Calley, Mar 1968.

mynah a number of starling species of SE Asia. The glossy black *hill mynah Gracula religiosa* of India is a mimic of sounds and human speech.

myoglobin a globular protein, closely related to ◊haemoglobin, which is located in vertebrate muscle.

myopia short-sightedness, caused either by an eyeball that is too long or a lens that is too strong. Nearby objects are sharply perceived, but distance vision is blurred.

myrmecophyte a plant that lives in association with a colony of ants, and possesses specialized organs in which the ants live. For example, *Myrmecodia* develops root tubers containing a network of cavities, which are inhabited by ants.

Myron *c.* 500–440 BC. Greek sculptor. His *Discobolus/Discus-Thrower* and *Athene and Marsyas*, are known through Roman copies. They confirm his ancient reputation.

myrrh gum resin produced by a small tree, *Commiphora myrrha*, found in Abyssinia and Arabia. In ancient times it was used for incense and perfume, and in embalming.

myrtle evergreen shrub of the genus *Myrtus*, family Myrtaceae. The common Mediterranean myrtle *Myrtus communis* has fragrant oval leaves, white flowers and purple berries.

mystery play or *miracle play* a medieval religious drama based on stories from the Bible which were performed at church festivals.

mystery religion any of various cults of the ancient world, open only to the initiated, for example the cults of Demeter (see ◊Eleusinian Mysteries), Dionysus, Cybele, Isis, and Mithras.

mysticism religious belief based on personal spiritual experience, not necessarily involving an orthodox deity, though found in all the major religions.

mythology the study and interpretation of the stories inherent in a given culture and how they relate to similar stories told in other cultures. These stories of gods and other supernatural beings are devised to explain the operation of the universe and history.

myxoedema thyroid deficiency developing in adult life, most commonly in middle-aged women. The symptoms are loss of energy and appetite, inability to keep warm, mental dullness, and dry, puffy skin. It is completely reversed by giving the thyroid hormone, thyroxine.

Myanmar, Union of (*Thammada Myanmar Naingngandaw***, formerly Burma)**

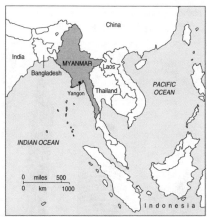

area 676,577 sq km/261,159 sq mi
capital and chief port Yangon (formerly Rangoon)
towns Mandalay, Karbe
physical over half is forested; rivers Irrawaddy and Chindwin; mountains in N, W, and E
head of state and government Than Shwe from 1992
political system military republic

exports rice, rubber, jute, teak, jade, rubies
currency kyat
population (1990 est) 41,279,000; annual growth rate 1.9%
language Burmese
religion Hinayana Buddhist 85%, animist, Christian
literacy 66% (1989)
GNP $9.3 bn (1988); $210 per head
chronology
1886 United as province of British India.
1937 Became crown colony in the British Commonwealth.
1942–45 Occupied by Japan.
1948 Independence achieved from Britain.
1962 Gen Ne Win assumed power in army coup.
1973–74 Adoption of presidential-style 'civilian' constitution.
1975 Formation of opposition National Democratic Front.
1988 The government resigned after violent demonstrations. Two changes of regime later, Gen Saw Maung seized power in a military coup Sept. Over 1,000 killed.
1989 Martial law declared; thousands arrested.
1990 Breakaway opposition group formed 'parallel government' on rebel-held territory.
1991 Martial law and human rights abuse continued. Opposition leader, Aung San Suu Kyi, received Nobel Prize for Peace.
1992 Pogrom against Muslim community in W Myanmar carried out with army backing. Martial law lifted.
1993 Constitutional convention held to discuss adoption of new constitution.

N abbreviation for *north*, ◊*newton*, and the symbol for *nitrogen*.

NAACP abbreviated name of US civil-rights organization ◊*National Association for the Advancement of Colored People*.

NAAFI acronym for *Navy, Army, and Air Force Institutes*. Non-profitmaking association providing canteens for HM British Forces.

Nabis, Les a group of French artists, active in the 1890s in Paris, united in their admiration of Gauguin. Bonnard and Vuillard were members.

Nabokov Vladimir 1899–1977. US writer, who left his native Russia in 1917; he began writing in English in the 1940s. His principal work is *Lolita* 1955, the story of the infatuation of middle-aged Humbert Humbert with a precocious child of 12.

Nadar Pen name of Gaspard-Félix Tournachan 1820–1910. French photographer and designer. He took the first aerial photographs (from a balloon in 1858), and the first flash photographs (using magnesium bulbs) in the Paris Métro in 1860.

Nader Ralph 1934– . Us lawyer. The 'scourge of corporate morality', he had led many major consumer campaigns. His book *Unsafe at Any Speed* 1965 led to US car-safety legislation.

nadir the point in the sky vertically 'below' the observer (that is, beneath the Earth), and hence diametrically opposite to the *zenith*.

Nagaland state of NE India, bordering Myanmar on the east
area 16,488 sq km/6,366 sq mi

Nader *US consumer campaigner Ralph Nader at a press conference, 1971.*

capital Kohima
products rice, tea, coffee, paper, sugar
population (1989) 1,215,600
history formerly part of Assam, it was seized by Britain from Burma 1826. The British sent 18 expeditions against the Naga peoples in the north 1832–87. After India attained independence in 1947, there was Naga guerrilla activity against the Indian government; the state of Nagaland was established in 1963 in response to demands for self-government, but fighting continued sporadically.

Nagasaki industrial port (coal, iron, shipbuilding) on Kyushu island, Japan; population (1990) 444,600. An atom bomb was dropped on it 9 Aug 1945.

Nagorno-Karabakh autonomous region of Azerbaijan
area 4,400 sq km/1,700 sq mi
capital Stepanakert
products cotton, grapes, wheat; silk
population (1987) 180,000 (76% Armenian, 23% Azeri), the Christian Armenians forming an enclave within the predominantly Shi'ite Muslim Azerbaijan
history an autonomous protectorate after the Russian revolution 1917, Nagorno-Karabakh was annexed to Azerbaijan 1923 against the wishes of the largely Christian-Armenian population. Since the local council promised to transfer control of the region to Armenia 1989, the enclave has been racked by fighting between Armenian and Azeri troops, both attempting to assert control. By Feb 1992, the conflict had caused the loss of at least 1,000 lives and the displacement of some 270,000 people.

Nagoya industrial seaport (cars, textiles, clocks) on Honshu island, Japan; population (1990) 2,154,700.

Nagpur industrial city (textiles, metals) in Maharashta, India; population (1981) 1,298,000.

Nagy Imre 1896–1958. Hungarian politician and prime minister 1953–5, 1956. He led the Hungarian revolt against Soviet domination in 1956, for which he was executed.

Nahua indigenous American people of Central Mexico. Historically, the best-known group were

Nairobi *Kimathi Street and the Hilton Hote in Kenya's capital of Nairobi.*

Namibia
Republic of
(formerly South West Africa)

area 824,300 sq km/318,262 sq mi
capital Windhoek
physical mainly desert; includes the enclave of
Walvis Bay (area 1,120 sq km/432 sq mi)
head of state Sam Nujoma from 1990
head of government Hage Geingob from 1990
political system democratic republic
exports diamonds, uranium, copper, lead
currency South African rand
population (1990 est) 1,372,000 (85% black
African, 6% European).

language Afrikaans, German, English (all official)
religion 51% Lutheran, 19% Roman Catholic, 6%
Dutch Reformed Church, 6% Anglican
literacy 100% whites, 16% non-whites
GNP $1.6 bn (1988); $1,300 per head
chronology
1915 German colony seized by South Africa.
1920 Administered by South Africa, under League
of Nations mandate, as British South Africa (SWA).
1946 Full incorporation in South Africa refused by
United Nations (UN).
1958 South West African People's Organization
(SWAPO) set up to seek racial equality and full
independence.
1966 South Africa's apartheid laws extended to the
country.
1968 Redesignated Namibia by UN.
1978 UN Security Council Resolution 435 to grant
full sovereignty accepted by South Africa, then
rescinded.
1988 Peace talks between South Africa, Angola
and Cuba led to agreement on full independence
for Namibia.
1989 Unexpected incursion by SWAPO guerrillas
from Angola into Namibia threatened agreed
timetable for independence from South Africa;
transitional constitution created by elected
representatives; SWAPO dominant party.
1990 Liberal multi-party 'independence'
constitution adopted; Independence achieved
from South Africa; Sam Nujoma elected president.
1992 Agreement between Namibia and South
Africa on establishment of Walvis Bay Joint
Administrative Body to administer this
commercially important enclave.

---

the Aztecs. The Naua language, a member of the
Uto-Aztecan family, is spoken by over one million
people today.

Naipaul V(idiadhar) S(urajprasad) 1932– . British
writer. Born in Trinidad of Hindu parents, his novels
include *A House for Mr Biswas* 1961, *Mr Stone and
the Knights Companion* 1963, and *A Bend in the
River* 1979. His brother *Shiva(dhar) Naipaul*
1940–85 was also a novelist (*Fireflies* 1970) and
journalist.

Nairobi capital of Kenya, in the central highlands at
1,660 m/5,450 ft; population (1985) 1,100,000. It
has light industry and food processing, and is the
headquarters of the United Nations Environment
Programme (UNEP).

Najibullah Ahmadzai 1947– . Afghan communist
politician, state president 1986–92. A member of
the Politburo from 1981, he was leader of the ruling
People's Democratic Party of Afghanistan (PDPA)
from 1986. Although his government initially survived the withdrawal of Soviet troops Feb 1989,
continuing pressure from the mujaheddin forces
resulted in his eventual overthrow.

Nakasone Yasuhiro 1917– . Japanese conservative politician, leader of the Liberal Democratic
Party (LDP) and prime minister 1982–87. He stepped up military spending and increased Japanese
participation in international affairs, with closer ties
in the USA. He was forced to resign his post 1989 as
a result of the Recruit financial scandal. After
serving a two-year period of atonement, he rejoined
the LDP 1991.

Namib Desert coastal desert region in Namibia
between the Kalahari Desert and the Atlantic
Ocean.

Namibia country in S W Africa, bounded on the N
by Angola and Zambia, on the E by Botswana and
South Africa and on the W by the Atlantic Ocean.

Nana Sahib Popular name for Dandhu Panth.
1820–*c.* 1859. Adopted son of a former *peshwa*
(chief minister) of the ◊Mahrattas in central
India; he joined the rebels in the ◊Indian Mutiny
1857–58, and was responsible for the massacre at
Kanpur when safe conducts given to British civilians were broken and many women and children
massacred.

Nanchang industrial (textiles, glass, porcelain,
soap) capital of Jianqxi province, China, about 260
km/160 mi SE of Wuhan; population (1989)
1,330,000.

Nanjing (formerly *Nanking*) capital of Jiangsu
province, China 270 km/165 mi NW of Shanghai;
centre of industry (engineering, shipbuilding, oil
refining), commerce, and communications; population (1989) 2,470,000. The bridge 1968 over the
Chang Jiang river is the longest in China at 6,705 m/
22,000 ft.

Nanning industrial river port, capital of Guangxi
autonomous region, China, on the You Jiang; population (1989) 1,050,000. It was an important supply
town during the Vietnam war and the Sino-
Vietnamese confrontation 1979.

nano- prefix used in ◊SI units of measurement,
equivalent to one thousand millionth part (10^{-9}) For
example, a nanosecond is one thousand millionth of a
second.

Nansen Fridtjof 1861–1930. Norwegian explorer
and scientist. In 1893, he sailed to the Arctic in the
Fram, which was deliberately allowed to drift north
with an iceflow. Nansen, accompanied by F J

Johansen, continued northward on foot, and reached 86°14′ North, the highest latitude then attained. After World War I, Nansen became League of Nations High Commissioner for refugees; Nobel Peace Prize 1923.

Nantes, Edict of decree by which Henry IV of France granted religious freedom to the ◊Huguenots in 1598. It was revoked in 1685 by Louis XIV.

napalm fuel used in flame-throwers and incendiary bombs. Produced from jellied petrol, it is a mixture of naphthenic and palmitic acids. It was widely used by the US Army during the Vietnam War. Extensive burns are caused by napalm, because it sticks to the skin even when alight.

naphtha originally applied to naturally occurring liquid hydrocarbons, the term is now used for the mixtures of hydrocarbons obtained by destructive distillation of petroleum, coal-tar and shale oil. It is a major raw material for the petrochemicals and plastics industry.

naphthalene a solid, aromatic hydrocarbon $C_{10}H_8$ obtained from coal-tar. A white, shiny, solid with a smell of moth-balls, it is used in making indigo and certain azo-dyes, and as a mild disinfectant and insecticide.

Napier John 1550–1617. Scottish mathematician who invented ◊logarithms in 1614, and 'Napier's bones', an early logarithmic calculating device for multiplication and division.

Naples (Italian *Napoli*) industrial port (shipbuilding, cars, textiles, paper, food processing) and capital of Campania, Italy, on the Tyrrhenian Sea; population (1984) 1,207,000. To the south is the Isle of Capri, and behind the city is Mount Vesuvius, with the ruins of Pompeii at its foot.

Napoleon I Bonaparte 1769–1821. Emperor of the French 1804–14 and 1814–15. A general from 1796 in the ◊Revolutionary Wars, in 1799 he overthrew the Directory (see ◊French Revolution) and made himself dictator. From 1803 he conquered most of Europe (see ◊Napoleonic Wars) and installed his brothers as puppet kings (see ◊Bonaparte). After the ◊Peninsular War and retreat from Moscow 1812, he was forced to abdicate 1814 and banished to Elba. In Mar 1815 he reassumed power (the

Napoleon I Portrait by Emile-Jean-Horace Vernet (1815) National Gallery, London.

Napoleon III Napoleon III, emperor of the French 1852-70.

◊hundred days), but was defeated at ◊Waterloo and exiled to the island of St Helena.

Napoleon II 1811–1832. Title given by the Bonapartists to the son of ◊Napoleon I and ◊Marie Louise; until 1814 he was known as *the king of Rome*, and after 1818 as the duke of Reichstadt. After his father's abdication in 1814 he was taken to the Austrian court, where he spent the rest of his life. By Hitler's order his body was removed from Vienna in 1940 and reinterred in the Hôtel des Invalides, Paris.

Napoleon III 1808–1873. Emperor of the French 1852–70, known as *Louis-Napoleon*. After two attempted coups (1836 and 1840) he was jailed and went into exile, returning for the revolution of 1848, when he became president of the Second Republic, but soon turned authoritarian. He had military victories in Europe but in Mexico sponsored the unsuccessful ◊Maximilian. Manoeuvred by the German chancellor Bismarck in 1870 into war with Prussia, he was forced to surrender at Sedan, NE France, and the empire collapsed.

Napoleonic Wars 1803–15 a series of European wars which followed the ◊Revolutionary Wars.

narcissism in psychology, an exaggeration of normal self-respect and pride in oneself, which may amount to mental disorder when it precludes relationships with other people.

Narcissus in Greek mythology, a beautiful youth, who rejected the love of the nymph ◊Echo, and as a punishment was condemned to fall in love with his own reflection in a stream. He eventually pined away for love of himself, and in the place where he died a flower sprang up which was named after him.

narcissus genus of bulbous plants of the family Amaryllidaceae, of which the best-known are the daffodil, jonquil, and narcissus.

narcolepsy a rare disorder characterized by bouts of overwhelming sleepiness, occurring

narcissus

narwhal

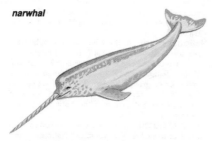

inappropriately during the day, and loss of muscle power. It is controlled by drugs.

narcotic pain-relieving and sleep-inducing drug. The principal narcotics induce dependency and include opium; its derivatives and synthetic modifications (such as morphine and heroin); alcohols (for example paraldehyde and ethyl alcohol); and barbiturates.

Narodnik member of a secret Russian political movement, active 1873–76 before its suppression by the tsarist authorities. Its main purpose was to convert the peasantry to socialism.

narwhal whale *Monodon monoceros*, found only in the Arctic Ocean. It grows to 5 m/16 ft long, has a grey and black body, a small head, and short flippers. The male has a single spirally fluted tusk which may be up to 2.7 m/9 ft long.

NASA National Aeronautics and Space Administration, the US government agency, founded 1958, for spaceflight and aeronautical research. Its headquarters are in Washington DC and its main installation is at the ◊Kennedy Space Center.

Naseby, Battle of decisive battle of the English Civil War 14 Jun 1645, when the Royalists led by Prince Rupert were defeated by Oliver Cromwell and Gen Fairfax. Named after the nearby village of Naseby, 20 km/12 mi NNW of Northampton.

Nash (Richard) 'Beau' 1674–1762. British dandy. As master of ceremonies at Bath from 1705, he made the town the most fashionable watering-place in England, and did much to introduce a more polished code of manners.

Nash John 1752–1835. British architect. He laid out Regent's Park, London, and its approaches. Between 1813 and 1820 he planned Regent Street (later rebuilt), repaired and enlarged Buckingham Palace (for which he designed Marble Arch), and rebuilt Brighton Pavilion in flamboyant oriental style.

Nash Ogden 1902–1971. US poet. He published numerous volumes of humorous verse of quietly puncturing satire, with unorthodox rhymes, assembled in *Collected Verses* 1961.

Nash Paul 1889–1946. British painter, an official war artist in World Wars I and II. In the 1930s

he was one of a group of artists promoting avant-garde styles in the UK. Two of his most celebrated works are *Totes Meer/Dead Sea* and *The Battle of Britain*.

Nash(e) Thomas 1567–1601. English poet, dramatist and pamphleteer. Author of the first English picaresque novel, *The Unfortunate Traveller* 1594.

Nash Walter 1882–1968. New Zealand Labour politician. Born in England, he emigrated to New Zealand in 1909. He held ministerial posts 1935–49, was prime minister 1957–60, and leader of the Labour Party until 1963.

Nashville port on the Cumberland river and capital of Tennessee, USA; population (1980) 455,651. It is a banking and commercial centre and has large printing, music-publishing, and recording industries.

Nassau capital and port of the Bahamas, on New Providence island; population (1980) 135,000. English settlers founded it 1629.

Nasser Gamal Abdel 1918–1970. Egyptian politician; prime minister 1954–56 and from 1956 president of Egypt (the United Arab Republic 1958–71). In 1952 he was the driving power behind the Neguib coup, which ended the monarchy. His nationalization of the Suez Canal 1956 (see ◊Suez Crisis) and his ambitions for an Egyptian-led Arab union led to disquiet in the Middle East and in the West.

nastic movement a plant movement that is caused by an external stimulus, such as light or temperature, but which is directionally independent of its source, unlike ◊tropisms. Nastic movements occur due to changes in water pressure within specialized cells, or as a result of differing rates of growth in parts of the plant. Examples include the opening and closing of *crocus* flowers following an increase or decrease in temperature (thermonasty), and the opening and closing of evening primrose *Oenothera* flowers on exposure to dark and light (photonasty).

Nasser Egyptian politician and prime minister, Gamal Abdel Nasser, Oct 1964.

Nash Battle of Britain (Aug/Oct 1940) Imperial War Museum, London.

nasturtium genus of plants of the family Cruciferae, including **watercress**, *Nasturtium officinale*, a perennial aquatic plant of Europe and Asia, grown as a salad crop. Also plants of the S American Tropaeolaceae family, including the garden species, *Tropaeolum majus*, with orange or scarlet flowers.

Natal province of South Africa, NE of Cape Province, bounded on the E by the Indian Ocean
area 91,355 sq km/35,273 sq mi
capital Pietermaritzburg
towns Durban
physical slopes from the Drakensberg to a fertile subtropical coastal plain
products sugar cane, black wattle (*Acacia mollissima*), maize, fruits, vegetables, tobacco, coal
population (1985) 2,145,000.

Nataraja 'Lord of the Dance' in Hinduism, a title of ◊Siva.

Natchez member of a North American Indian people of the Mississippi area, one of the ◊Moundbuilder group of peoples. They had a highly developed caste system, headed by a ruler priest (the 'Great Sun'), unusual in North America. This lasted until the near genocide of the Natchez by the French in 1731: only a few survive in Oklahoma.

national accounts the organization of a country's finances. In the UK the economy is divided into the *public sector* (central government, local authorities, and public corporations), the *private sector* (the personal and company sector), and the *overseas sector* (transactions between residents and non-residents of the UK).

national assistance in the UK, former term 1948–66 for a weekly allowance, paid by the state to ensure a national minimum income (◊supplementary benefit until 1988).

National Association for the Advancement of Colored People NAACP US civil-rights organization, dedicated to ending black inequality and segregation through nonviolent protest. Founded 1910, its first aim was to eradicate lynching, which was largely achieved by the 1950s. The NAACP was noted particularly for its long campaign to end segregation in state schools; it funded test cases which eventually led to the Supreme Court decision 1954 outlawing school segregation. In 1987 it had about 500,000 members, black and white.

National Book League former name of ◊*Book Trust*.

National Country Party former name for the Australian ◊National Party.

national debt debt incurred by the central government of a country to its own people and institutions and also to overseas creditors. If it does not wish to raise taxes to finance its activities, a government can borrow from the public, by means of selling interest bearing bonds, for example, or from abroad. Traditionally a major cause of incurring national debt was the cost of war but in recent decades governments have borrowed heavily in order to finance development or nationalized industries, to support an ailing currency, or because it is preferred to raising taxation. On Mar 31 1988 the UK National Debt was £97,295 million, or £3,465 per head of population.

National Economic Development Council (NEDC) (known as '*Neddy*') the UK forum for economic consultation between government, management, and trade unions. Established 1962, it examines the country's economic and industrial performance, both in the public and private sectors, and seeks agreement on ways to improve efficiency. Its role has diminished under the Thatcher administration.

National Front in the UK, extreme right-wing political party founded in 1967. It was formed from a merger of the League of Empire Loyalists and the British National Party. In 1980 dissension arose and splinter groups formed. Electoral support in the 1983 general election was minimal. Some of its members had links with the National Socialist Movement of the 1960s: see under ◊Nazi Party.

National Guard a ◊militia force recruited by each state of the USA. The volunteer National Guard units are under federal orders in emergencies, and are now an integral part of the US Army. The National Guard have been used against demonstrators and on one occasion shot four demonstrating students at Kent State University, Ohio, in 1970.

National Health Service (NHS) UK government medical scheme; see under ◊health service.

national income the total income of a state in one year, comprising both the wages of individuals and the profits of companies. It is equal to the value of the output of all goods and services during the same period. National income is equal to gross national product (the value of a country's total output) minus an allowance for replacement of ageing capital stock.

national insurance in the UK, state social security scheme which provides child allowances, maternity benefits and payments to the unemployed, sick, and retired, and also covers medical treatment. It is paid for by weekly contributions from employees and employers.

nationalism in politics, a feeling of solidarity with other people sharing one's ethnic origins, traditional culture, or language; the term is used especially to describe a movement which consciously aims to unify a nation or to liberate it from foreign rule.

nationalization policy of bringing a country's essential services and industries under public ownership. It was pursued, for example, by the UK Labour government 1945–51. In recent years the trend towards nationalization has slowed and in many countries (the UK, France, and Japan) reversed (◊privatization). Assets in the hands of foreign governments or companies may also be nationalized, for example Iran's oil industry (see ◊Abadan), the ◊Suez Canal, and US-owned fruit plantations in Guatemala, all in the 1950s.

National Party, Australian Australian political party representing the interests of the farmers and people of the smaller towns. It developed from about 1860 as the *National Country Party*, and holds the power balance between Liberals and Labour. It gained strength following the introduction of proportional representation in 1918, and has been in coalition with the Liberals since 1949.

National Research Development Council (NERC) UK corporation exploiting inventions derived from public or private sources, usually jointly with industrial firms. It was set up in 1967.

National Security Agency agency handling US security communications worldwide. Known popularly as the Puzzle Palace, its headquarters are at Fort Meade, Maryland (with a major facility at Menwith Hill, England).

National Socialism official name for the ◊Nazi movement in Germany; see ◊fascism.

National Sound Archive department of the British Library since 1983. It was founded 1947 as the British Institute of Recorded Sound, and now has

Nauru
Republic of

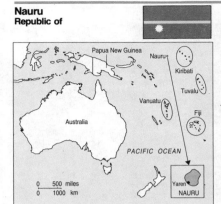

area 21 sq km/8 sq mi
capital Yaren
physical island country in W Pacific
head of state and government Bernard Dowiyogo
from 1989

political system liberal democracy
exports phosphates
currency Australian dollar
population (1990 est) 8,100 (mainly Polynesian; Chinese 8%, European 8%); annual growth rate 1.7%
language Nauruan (official), English
religion Protestant 66%, Roman Catholic 33%
literacy 99%
GNP $160 million (1986); $9,091 per head
chronology
1888 Annexed by Germany.
1920 Administered by Australia, New Zealand, and UK until independence, except 1942–45, when it was occupied by Japan.
1968 Full independence achieved. Hammer DeRoburt elected president.
1976 Bernard Dowiyogo elected president.
1978 DeRoburt returned to power.
1986 DeRoburt resigned when his budget plans were not approved, and the opposition leader Kenneth Adeang took over.
1987 After fresh parliamentary elections DeRoburt returned to power. Adeang, again in opposition, established the Democratic Party of Nauru.
1989 DeRoburt replaced by Kensas Avoi, who was succeeded by Bernard Dowiyogo.
1992 Dowiyogo re-elected.

over 750,000 discs and over 40,000 hours of tapes, ranging from wildlife to grand opera, and from jazz to National Theatre performances.

National Theatre British national theatre company established 1963, and the complex which houses it on London's South Bank, opened 1976.

National Trust British trust founded in 1895 for the preservation of land and buildings of historic interest or beauty, incorporated by Act of Parliament in 1907. It is the largest private landowner in Britain. The National Trust for Scotland was established in 1931.

native metal a mineral consisting of the metal uncombined with any other element. Copper and silver can be found as native metals.

nativity a Christian festival celebrating a birth: *Christmas* celebrated 25 Dec from 336 AD in memory of the birth of Jesus Christ in Bethlehem; *Nativity of the Virgin Mary* celebrated by the Catholic and Eastern Orthodox churches, 8 Sept; *Nativity of John the Baptist* celebrated by the Catholic, Eastern Orthodox, and Anglican churches, 24 Jun.

NATO abbreviation for ◊*North Atlantic Treaty Organization*.

Natural Environment Research Council British organization established by Royal Charter 1965 to undertake and support research in the earth sciences, to give advice both on exploiting natural resources and on protecting the environment, and to support education and training of scientists in these fields of study. Research areas include geothermal energy, industrial pollution, waste disposal, satellite surveying, acid rain, biotechnology, atmospheric circulation, and climate.

natural gas a mixture of flammable gases found in the Earth's crust, which is now one of the world's three main fossil fuels (with coal and oil). Natural gas is a mixture of ◊hydrocarbons, notably methane, ethane, butane and propane. Before the gas is piped to homes butane and propane are removed and liquefied to form 'bottled gas'.

natural logarithms in mathematics, the exponent of a number expressed to base *e*, where *e* represents the ◊irrational number 2.71828...

natural selection the process whereby gene frequencies in a population change through certain organisms producing more descendants than others, because they are better able to survive and reproduce. The accumulated effect of natural selection is to produce ◊adaptations such as the thick coat of a polar bear or the spadelike forelimbs of a mole. It was recognized by the British scientist Charles Darwin as the main process driving ◊evolution.

Nature Conservancy Council (NCC) UK government agency established by Act of Parliament 1973 (Nature Conservancy created by Royal Charter 1949) to oversee nature conservation. It is responsible for national nature reserves and other conservation areas, advising government ministers on policies, providing advice and information, and for relevant scientific research.

nature-nurture controversy or *environment-heredity controversy* a long-standing dispute among philosophers and psychologists over the relative importance of inheritance ('nature') and experience ('nurture').

nature reserve area set aside to protect a habitat and the wildlife that lives within it, with only restricted admission for the public. The world's largest is Etosha Reserve, Namibia; area 99,520 sq km/38,415 sq mi.

Naukratis city of Greek traders in ancient Egypt, in the Nile delta, rediscovered by the British archaeologist William ◊Petrie 1884.

Nauru island country in the SW Pacific, in ◊Polynesia, W of Kiribati.

nautical mile unit of distance used in navigation, equalling the average length of one minute of arc on a great circle of the Earth. In the UK it was formerly defined as 1,853 m/6,080 ft; the international nautical mile is now defined as 1,852 m.

nautilus type of ◊cephalopod found in the Indian and Pacific oceans. The *pearly nautilus Nautilus pompilius* has a chambered spiral shell about 20 cm/8 in in diameter. Its body occupies the outer chamber. The nautilus has a large number of short, grasping tentacles surrounding a sharp beak.

Navajo North American Indian people, related to the ◊Apache. They were defeated by Kit ◊Carson and

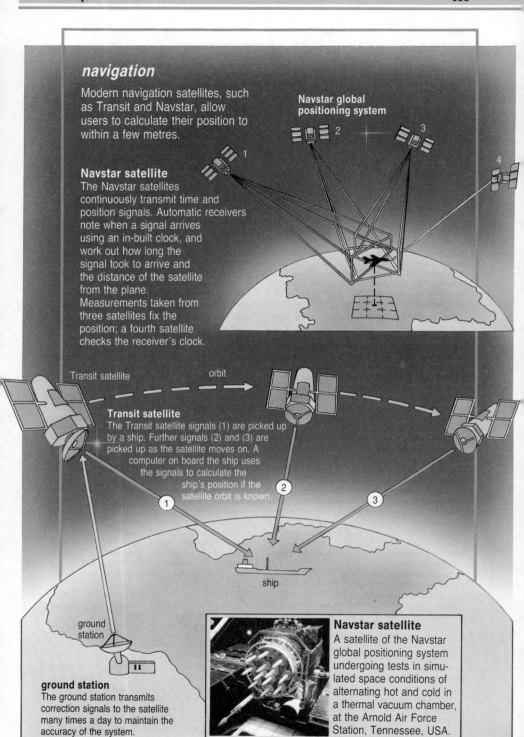

navigation

Modern navigation satellites, such as Transit and Navstar, allow users to calculate their position to within a few metres.

Navstar global positioning system

Navstar satellite

The Navstar satellites continuously transmit time and position signals. Automatic receivers note when a signal arrives using an in-built clock, and work out how long the signal took to arrive and the distance of the satellite from the plane. Measurements taken from three satellites fix the position; a fourth satellite checks the receiver's clock.

Transit satellite   orbit

Transit satellite

The Transit satellite signals (1) are picked up by a ship. Further signals (2) and (3) are picked up as the satellite moves on. A computer on board the ship uses the signals to calculate the ship's position if the satellite orbit is known.

ship

ground station

ground station

The ground station transmits correction signals to the satellite many times a day to maintain the accuracy of the system.

Navstar satellite

A satellite of the Navstar global positioning system undergoing tests in simulated space conditions of alternating hot and cold in a thermal vacuum chamber, at the Arnold Air Force Station, Tennessee, USA.

US troops 1864, and were rounded up and exiled. Their reservation, created 1868, is the largest in the USA (65,000 sq km/25,000 sq m), mostly in Arizona.

Navarino, Battle of a decisive naval action off Pylos in the Greek war of liberation 20 Oct 1827, which was won by the combined fleets of the English, French, and Russians under Vice-Admiral Edward Codrington (1770–1851), over the Turkish and Egyptian fleets.

Navarre (Spanish *Navarra*) autonomous mountain region of N Spain
area 10,421 sq km/4,023 sq mi
capital Pomplona
population (1986) 513,000.

Navarre, Kingdom of former kingdom comprising the Spanish province of Navarre and part of the French *département* of Basses-Pyrénées. It resisted the Moors' conquest, and was independent until it became French 1284 on the marriage of Philip IV to the heiress of Navarre. In 1479 Ferdinand of Aragon annexed Spanish Navarre, with French Navarre going to Catherine of Foix (1483–1512), who kept the royal title. Her grandson became Henry IV of France, and Navarre was absorbed in the French crown lands 1620.

nave in architecture, the central part of a church, between the choir and the entrance.

navigation the means of finding the position, course, and distance travelled by a ship, plane, or other craft. Traditional methods include the magnetic ◊compass and ◊sextant. Today the gyrocompass is usually used, together with highly sophisticated electronic methods, such as *Decca*, *Loran*, and *Omega*. These employ beacons that beam out radio signals. Satellite navigation employs satellites that broadcast time and position signals.

Navigation Acts a series of acts passed from 1381 to protect English shipping from foreign competition, and to ensure monopoly trading between Britain and its colonies. The last was repealed 1849. The Navigation Acts were enormously influential in establishing England as a major sea power. They ruined the Dutch merchant fleet in the 17th century, and were one of the causes of the War of ◊American Independence.

navigation, biological the ability of animals or insects to navigate. Although much animal navigation consists of following established routes or piloting via known landmarks, many animals can navigate without such aids; for example, birds can fly several thousand miles back to their nest site, over unknown terrain. Such feats may be based on compass information derived from the position of the Sun, Moon, or stars, or on the characteristic patterns of Earth's magnetic field.

Navratilova Martina 1956– . Czechoslovakian tennis player, who became a naturalized American 1981. The most outstanding woman player in the 1980s, she has 50 Grand Slam victories, including 17 singles titles. She has won the Wimbledon singles title eight times, including six in succession 1982–87.

navy a fleet of ships, usually a nation's warships and the organization to maintain them.

Naxalite member of an Indian extremist communist movement named after the town of Naxalbari, W Bengal, where a peasant rising was suppressed 1967. The movement was founded by Charu Mazumdar (1915–72).

Nazareth town in Galilee, N Israel, SE of Haifa; population (1981) 64,000. According to the New Testament, it was the boyhood home of Jesus.

Nazi Party German ◊fascist political party. The name is derived from the full name, *Nationalsozialistiche Deutsche Arbeiterpartei* (National Socialist German Workers' Party). It was formed from the German Workers' Party (founded 1919), and led by Adolf ◊Hitler 1921–45. The ideology was based on racism, nationalism, and the supremacy of the state over the individual. During the 1930s, many similar parties were created throughout Europe, although only those of Austria and Sudetenland were of any major importance. These parties collaborated with the German occupation of Europe 1939–45. After the Nazi atrocities of World War II (see ◊SS, ◊concentration camp), the party was banned in Germany, but there are parties with Nazi or neo-Nazi ideologies in many countries.

N'djamena capital of Chad, at the confluence of the Chari and Logone rivers, on the Cameroon border; population (1988) 594,000.

Ne Win 1911– . Myanmar (Burmese) nationalist socialist politician. A general, he was prime minister 1958–60 and, after a military coup 1962, effectively ruled the country until 1988 (as president 1974–81), pursuing an isolationist foreign policy.

Neagh, Lough lake in Northern Ireland, 25 km/15 mi W of Belfast; area 396 sq km/153 sq mi. It is the largest lake in the British Isles.

Neanderthal hominid of the Palaeolithic period originating 120,000 years ago (named from a skeleton found in the Neanderthal valley in the Rhineland 1857). Extinct from 30,000 years ago, they were replaced through Europe by, or possibly interbred with, modern *Homo sapiens*. See ◊primate.

Nebraska plains state of the central USA; nickname Cornhusker State
area 200,036 sq km/77,214 sq mi
capital Lincoln
towns Omaha
products cereals, livestock, processed foods, fertilizers, oil, natural gas
population (1990) 1,578,400
famous people Fred Astaire, Willa Cather, Henry Fonda, Gerald Ford, Harold Lloyd, Malcolm X.

Nebuchadnezzar or *Nebuchadrezzar II*. King of Babylonia from 604 BC. He defeated the Egyptians and brought Palestine and Syria into his empire. He captured Jerusalem twice 596 and 587–586 BC and carried many Jews into captivity. He largely rebuilt Babylon and constructed the hanging gardens.

nebula a cloud of gas and dust in space. Nebulae are the birthplace of stars. An *emission nebula*, such as the ◊Orion nebula, glows brightly because its gas is energized by stars that have formed within it. In a *reflection nebula*, starlight reflects off grains of dust in the nebula, such as surrounds the

Nazi Party Brown-shirted girls giving the Nazi salute, 1940.

nebula *The Orion nebula is located 1,600 light years from Earth and its fan-shaped cloud is 15 light years across.*

stars of the ◊Pleiades cluster. A *dark nebula* is a dense cloud, composed of molecular hydrogen, which partially or completely absorbs light behind it. Examples include the Coalsack nebula in ◊Crux, and the Horsehead nebula in Orion. Some nebulae are produced by gas thrown off from dying stars; see ◊planetary nebula; ◊supernova.

neck the structure between the head and the trunk in animals. In humans its bones are the upper seven vertebrae, and it has many powerful muscles which support and move the head. In front, it contains the pharynx and trachea, and behind these the oesophagus. Within it are the large arteries (carotid, temporal, maxillary) and veins (jugular) which supply the brain and head.

Necker Jacques 1732–1804. French politician. As finance minister 1776–81, he attempted reforms but was dismissed. Recalled 1788, he persuaded Louis XVI to summon the States General (parliament), which earned him the hatred of the court, and in Jul 1789 he was banished. The French Revolution forced his reinstatement, but he resigned Sep 1790.

necrosis death of body tissue, usually due to bacterial poisoning or loss of blood supply.

nectar a sugary liquid secreted by some plants from a nectary, a specialized gland usually situated near the base of the flower. Nectar often accumulates in special pouches or spurs, not always in the same location as the nectary. It attracts insects, birds, bats, and other animals to the flower for ◊pollination, and is the raw material used by bees in the production of honey.

nectarine smooth, shiny-skinned peach, usually smaller than other peaches and with firmer flesh.

NEDC abbreviation for ◊*National Economic Development Council*.

née (French 'born') followed by a surname, indicates the name of a woman before marriage.

needlefish long thin-bodied fish of the ◊garfish type with needle teeth.

Nefertiti or *Nofretète* 14th century BC. queen of Egypt, who ruled *c.* 1372–1350 BC. She was the wife of ◊Ikhnaton.

negative/positive in photography, a reverse image, which when printed is again reversed, restoring the original scene. It was invented by Fox ◊Talbot about 1834.

Negev desert in S Israel which tapers to the port of Eilat. It is fertile under irrigation, and minerals include oil and copper.

Nehru *Pandit Jawaharlal Nehru (left) with Mohammed Ali Jinnah, the founder of Pakistan.*

negligence in law, negligence consists in doing some act which a 'prudent and reasonable' person would not do, or omitting to do some act which such a person would do. Negligence may arise in respect of a person's duty towards an individual or towards other people in general. *Contributory negligence* is a defence sometimes raised where the defendant to an action for negligence claims that the plaintiff by his own negligence contributed to the cause of the action.

Negro term formerly used to refer to a member of the indigenous people of Africa south of the Sahara, today distributed around the world. The term generally preferred today is ◊black.

Nehemiah 5th century BC. Jewish governor of Judaea under Persian rule, who rebuilt Jerusalem's walls 444 BC, and made religious and social reforms.

Nehru Jawaharlal 1889–1964. Indian nationalist politician, prime minister from 1947. Before partition he led the socialist wing of the ◊Congress Party, and was second in influence only to Mahatma ◊Gandhi. He was imprisoned nine times 1921–45 for political activities. As prime minister from the creation of the dominion (later republic) of India Aug 1947, he originated the idea of ◊nonalignment. His daughter was Indira Gandhi.

Nelson Horatio, Viscount Nelson 1758–1805. British admiral. In the Revolutionary Wars against France he lost the sight in his right eye 1794, and his right arm 1797. He became a national hero, and rear-admiral, after the victory off Cape St Vincent,

Nelson *British admiral Horatio Nelson won the Battle of Trafalgar 1805, but was mortally wounded.*

Nepal
Kingdom of
(Nepal Adhirajya)

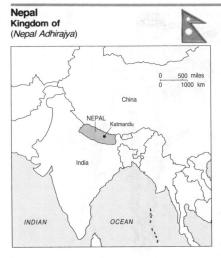

area 141,400 sq km/54,600 sq mi
capital Katmandu
physical descends from the Himalaya mountain range in the N to the river Ganges plain in the S
head of state King Birendra Bir Bikram Shah Dev from 1972
head of government Girija Prasad Koirala from 1991
political system constitutional monarchy

exports jute, rice, timber, oilseed
currency Nepalese rupee
population (1990 est) 19,158,000 (mainly known by the name of the predominant clan, the Gurkhas; the Sherpas are a Buddhist minority of NE Nepal); annual growth rate 2.3%
life expectancy men 50, women 49
language Nepali (official)
religion Hindu, with Buddhist minority
literacy 39% male/12% female (1985 est)
GNP $3.1 bn (1988); $160 per head
chronology
1768 Nepal emerged as unified kingdom.
1846–1951 Ruled by the Rana family.
1951 Monarchy restored.
1959 Constitution created elected legislature.
1960–61 Parliament dissolved by king and political parties banned.
1980 Constitutional referendum held following popular agitation.
1981 Direct elections held to national assembly.
1983 Overthrow of monarch-supported prime minister.
1986 New assembly elections returned a majority opposed to *panchayat* system.
1988 Strict curbs placed on opposition activity.
1989 Border blockade imposed by India in treaty dispute.
1990 *Panchayat* system collapsed after mass demonstrations. New constitution introduced.
1991 Nepali Congress Party won the general election.
1992 Communists led anti-government demonstrations.

Portugal. In 1798 he tracked the French fleet to Aboukir Bay, and almost entirely destroyed it in the Battle of the Nile. In 1801 he won a decisive victory over Denmark at ◊Copenhagen, and in 1805, after two years of blockading Toulon, another over the Franco-Spanish fleet at ◊Trafalgar, near Gibraltar.

nematode unsegmented worm of the phylum Aschelminthes. It is pointed at both ends, and with a tough smooth outer skin. Nematodes include some soil and water forms, but a large number are parasites, such as the roundworms and pinworms that live in humans, or the eelworms that attack plant roots.

Nemerov Howard 1920– . US poet, critic, and novelist. In 1977 his *Collected Poems* won both the National Book Award and the Pulitzer Prize.

Nemesis in Greek mythology, the goddess of retribution, especially punishing hubris (Greek *hybris*), arrogant self-confidence.

nemo me impune lacessit (Latin 'no one injures me with impunity') the motto of Scotland.

Nennius *c.* 800. Welsh historian, believed to be the author of a Latin *Historia Britonum*, which contains the earliest reference to King Arthur's wars against the Saxons.

neo- a prefix denoting a new development of an older form, often in a different spirit. Examples include *Neo-Marxism* and ◊*Neo-Classicism*.

Neo-Classical economics a school of economic thought based on the work of 19th-century economists such as Alfred Marshall, using ◊marginal theory to modify classical economic theories.

Neo-Classicism movement in art and architecture in Europe and North America about 1750–1850, a revival of classical art, which superseded the Rococo style. It was partly inspired by the excavation of the Roman cities of Pompeii and Herculaneum. The architect Piranesi was an early Neo-Classicist;

in sculpture Canova and in painting David were exponents.

Neo-Colonialism a disguised form of ◊imperialism, by which a country may grant independence to another country, but continue to dominate it by control of markets for goods or raw materials.

Neo-Darwinism the modern theory of ◊evolution, built up since the 1930s by integrating ◊Darwin's theory of evolution through natural selection with the theory of genetic inheritance founded on the work of ◊Mendel.

Neo-Impressionism movement in French painting in the 1880s, an extension of the Impressionists' technique of placing small strokes of different colour side by side. Seurat was the chief exponent; his minute technique became known as *pointillism*.

Neolithic last division of the ◊Stone Age. It lasted in SW Asia 9000–6000 BC, and in Europe 4000–2400 BC. Flint weapons and tools were used, and the earliest organized agriculture dates from this period.

neon a chemically inert gaseous element, symbol Ne, atomic number 10, relative atomic mass 20.183. It is extracted by liquefaction and fractional distillation. It glows bright orange-red in a ◊discharge tube, and is used in lights such as advertisement signs, and in lasers.

neoplasm literally, a new growth. It is any lump or tumour, which may be benign or malignant (cancerous).

neoprene a ◊synthetic rubber, developed in the USA 1931. It is made from acetylene and hydrogen chloride. It is much more resistant to heat and petrol than ordinary rubber.

Neo-Realism a film-making movement that emerged in Italy in the 1940s. Neo-Realism was characterized by its naturalism; problems, such as poverty and deprivation, were depicted, and visual authenticity was achieved by shooting the

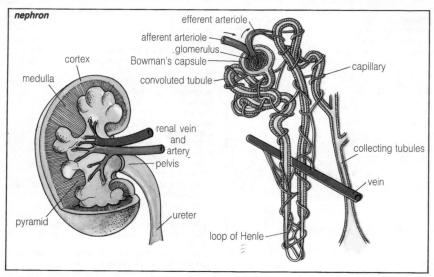

nephron

efferent arteriole
afferent arteriole
glomerulus
Bowman's capsule
cortex
medulla
convoluted tubule
renal vein and artery
pelvis
pyramid
ureter
capillary
collecting tubules
vein
loop of Henle
loop of Henle

films on location. Important exponents of the movement were the directors ◊De Sica, ◊Visconti, and ◊Rossellini.

neoteny in biology, the retention of some juvenile characteristics in an animal that seems otherwise mature. An example is provided by the axolotl, a salamander that can reproduce sexually although still in its larval form.

Nepál landlocked country in the Himalayan mountain range, bounded to the N by Tibet, to the E by Sikkim, and to the S and W by India.

neper unit used in telecommunications to express a ratio of powers and currents. It gives the attenuation of amplitudes as the natural logarithm of the ratio.

nephrectomy surgical removal of a kidney.

nephritis inflammation of the kidneys, usually due to bacterial infection. The degree of illness varies, and it may be acute or chronic, requiring a range of treatments from antibiotics to ◊dialysis.

nephron a microscopic unit in an animal's kidneys which forms *urine*. Each nephron consists of a filter cup surrounding a knot of blood capillaries and a long narrow collecting tubule in close association with more capillaries. Waste materials and water pass from the bloodstream into the filter cup and essential minerals and some water are reabsorbed from the tubule back into the blood.

Neptune in Roman mythology, god of the sea, the equivalent of the Greek ◊Poseidon.

Neptune in astronomy, the eighth planet from the Sun, located 1846 by Galle after calculations by Adams and Leverrier had predicted its existence on the basis that another body must be disturbing the orbit of Uranus. Neptune orbits the Sun every 164.8 years at an average distance of 4,497,000,000 km/2,794,000,000 mi. It is a giant gas planet with a diameter of 48,600 km/30,200 mi and a mass 17.2 times that of Earth. It is believed to have a central rocky core covered by a layer of ice, and a deep atmosphere composed mainly of hydrogen and helium, with methane clouds. Neptune has two moons, Nereid and Triton, and partial rings. The planet was surveyed by ◊Voyager 2 in Aug 1989.

neptunium an artificially made element, symbol Np, atomic number 93. Neptunium is a member of the actinide series produced in nuclear reactors by neutron bombardment of uranium. It is radioactive and chemically highly reactive.

NERC abbreviation for ◊*Natural Environment Research Council*.

Nereid in Greek mythology, a minor sea goddess who sometimes mated with mortals.

Nergal Babylonian god of the sun, war, and pestilence, ruler of the underworld, symbolized by a winged lion.

Nero 37–68 AD. Roman emperor from 54. He is said to have murdered his stepfather ◊Claudius'

nerve cell

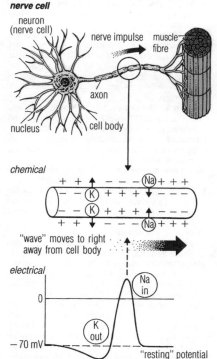

neuron (nerve cell)
nerve impulse
muscle fibre
axon
nucleus
cell body

chemical

"wave" moves to right away from cell body

electrical

Na in
K out
0
−70 mV
"resting" potential

K = potassium   Na = sodium

son Britannicus, his own mother, his wives Octavia and Poppaea, and many others. After the great fire of Rome 64, he persecuted the Christians, who were suspected of causing it. Military revolt followed 68; the senate condemned Nero to death, and he committed suicide.

Neruda Pablo. Pen name of Neftalí Ricardo Reyes Basoalto 1904–1973. Chilean poet and diplomat. His work includes the epic of the American continent *Canto General* 1950. Nobel prize 1971.

Nerva (Marcus Cocceius Nerva) *c.* 35–98 AD. Roman emperor. He was proclaimed emperor on Domitian's death 96 AD, and introduced state loans for farmers, family allowances, and allotments of land to poor citizens.

Nerval Gérard de, pen name of Gérard Labrunie 1808–1855. French writer. One of the first French symbolists and surrealists, he lived a wandering life, darkened by periodic insanity. His writings include the travelogue *Voyage en Orient* 1851; short stories, including the collection *Les Filles du feu* 1854; poetry; a novel *Aurélia* 1855; and drama. He committed suicide.

nerve a strand of ◊nerve cells enclosed in a sheath of connective tissue connecting the ◊central nervous system with receptor and effector organs. A single nerve may contain both ◊motor and sensory nerve cells, but they act independently.

nerve cell an elongated cell (neuron), part of the ◊nervous system, that transmits electrical impulses. A nerve impulse is a travelling wave of chemical and electrical changes which affects the surface membrane of the nerve fibre. Sequential changes in the permeability of the membrane to positive sodium (Na) ions and negative potassium (K) ions, produce electrical signals called action potentials. Impulses are received by the cell body and passed, as a pulse of electric charge, along the ◊axon. At the far end of the axon, there

are ◊synapses where the impulse triggers the release of the chemical ◊neurotransmitter, which stimulates another nerve cell or the action of an effector organ (for example, a muscle).

Nervi Pier Luigi 1891–1979. Italian architect, who used soft steel mesh within concrete to give it flowing form, for example Turin exhibition hall 1949, UNESCO building in Paris 1952.

nervous system the system of interconnected ◊nerve cells of most invertebrates and all vertebrates. It is comprised of the ◊central and ◊autonomic nervous systems.

Nesbit Edith 1858–1924. English author of children's books, including *The Treasure-Seekers* 1899 and *The Railway Children* 1906.

Nestorianism Christian doctrine held by the Syrian ecclesiastic Nestorius (died *c.* 457), patriarch of Constantinople 428–431. He asserted that Jesus Christ had two natures, human and divine. He was banished for maintaining that Mary was the mother of the man Jesus only, and therefore should not be called the Mother of God. His followers survived as the Assyrian church in Syria, Iraq, Iran, and as the Christians of St Thomas in S India.

Netherlands, the country in W Europe on the North Sea, bounded to the E by Germany and to the S by Belgium.

Netherlands Antilles two groups of Caribbean islands, part of the Netherlands with full internal autonomy, comprising ◊Curaçao and Bonaire off the coast of Venezuela (◊Aruba is considered separately), and St Eustatius, Saba, and the S part of St Maarten in the Leeward Islands, 800 km/500 mi NE.
area 797 sq km/308 sq mi
capital Willemstad on Curaçao
products oil from Venezuela is refined here
language Dutch (official), Papiamento, English
population (1983) 193,000.

Netherlands
Kingdom of the (*Koninkrijk der Nederlanden*), popularly known as **Holland**

```
0    miles    500
0    km    1000
         NORTH
         SEA
    NETHERLANDS
              Amsterdam
              Germany
    Belgium
```

area 34,000 sq km/13,020 sq mi
capital Amsterdam
towns The Hague (seat of government); chief port Rotterdam
physical almost completely flat; rivers Rhine,

Schelde (*Scheldt*), Maas; Frisian Islands
territories Aruba, Netherlands Antilles
head of state Beatrix Wilhelmina Armgard from 1980
head of government Ruud Lubbers from 1989
political system constitutional monarchy
exports dairy products, flowers bulbs, vegetables, petrochemicals, electronics
currency guilder
population (1990 est) 14,864,000; annual growth rate 0.5%
life expectancy men 73, women 80
language Dutch
religion Roman Catholic 40%, Protestant 31%
literacy 99% (1989)
GNP $223 bn (1988); $13,065 per head
chronology
1940–45 Occupied by Germany during World War II.
1947 Joined Benelux Union.
1948 Queen Juliana succeeded Queen Wilhelmina to the throne.
1949 Founder member of NATO.
1958 Joined European Community.
1980 Queen Juliana abdicated in favour of her daughter Beatrix.
1981 Opposition to cruise missiles averted their being sited on Dutch soil.
1991 Treaty on political and monetary union signed by EC members at Maastricht.
1992 Maastricht Treaty ratified.

netsuke toggle of ivory, wood, or other materials, made to secure a purse or tobacco pouch, for men wearing Japanese traditional costume. Made especially in the Edo period in Japan 1601–1867, the miniature sculptures are now valued as works of art in their own right.

nettle plants of the genus *Urtica*, family Urticaceae. Stinging hairs on the generally ovate leaves can penetrate the skin, causing inflammation. The *common nettle Urtica dioica* grows in Europe and in North America.

network in computing, a pattern of communication links between computers and their ◊peripheral (input and output) devices. The main types are classified by the pattern of the connections, for example, star or ring network; or by the degree of geographical spread allowed, for example, local area networks (LANs) for communication within a room or building, and wide area networks (WANs) for more remote systems.

Neumann John von 1903–1957. Hungarian-born scientist and mathematician, known for his pioneering work on computer design. He invented his 'rings of operators' (called von Neumann algebras), contributed to set theory, games theory, cybernetics, and the development of the atomic and hydrogen bombs.

neuralgia pain originating in a nerve. Trigeminal neuralgia is a severe pain on one side of the face.

neuritis nerve inflammation caused by injury, poisoning, or disease.

neurology the branch of medicine concerned with disease of, or damage to, the brain, spinal cord, and peripheral nerves.

neurosis in psychology, a general term referring to emotional disorders, such as anxiety, depression, and obsessions. The main disturbance tends to be one of mood; contact with reality is relatively unaffected, in contrast to ◊psychosis.

neuroticism a personality dimension described by the German psychologist Hans Jurgen Eysenck, (who developed an alternative form of psychoanalysis known as ◊behaviour therapy). People with high neuroticism are worriers, emotional and moody.

neurotoxin any substance which destroys nervous tissue.

neurotransmitter a chemical which diffuses across a ◊synapse, and thus transmits impulses between ◊nerve cells, or between nerve cells and effector organs (for example, muscles). Common neurotransmitters are norepinephrine (which also acts as a hormone) and acetylcholine, the latter being most frequent at junctions between nerve and muscle.

neutrality the legal status of a country that decides not to take part in a war. Certain states, notably Switzerland and Austria, have opted for permanent neutrality. Neutrality always has a legal connotation. Neutrality towards the big power alliances is usually called *nonalignment* (see ◊nonaligned movement).

neutrino a very small uncharged ◊elementary particle of minute mass, very difficult to detect and of great penetrating power, emitted in all radioactive disintegrations which give rise to ◊beta rays. Nuclear reactors emit neutrinos.

neutron one of the three chief subatomic ◊particles (the others being the ◊proton and the ◊electron). Neutrons have about the same mass as protons but no electric charge, and occur in the nuclei of all ◊atoms except hydrogen. They contribute to the mass of atoms but do not affect their chemistry, which depends on the proton or electron numbers. For instance, ◊isotopes of a single element (with different masses) differ only in the number of neutrons in their nuclei and have identical chemical properties.

neutron beam machine a nuclear reactor or accelerator producing a stream of neutrons, which can 'see' through metals. It is used in industry to check molecular changes in metal under stress.

neutron bomb hydrogen bomb that kills by radiation. See ◊nuclear warfare.

neutron star a very small, 'superdense' star composed mostly of ◊neutrons. They are thought to form when massive stars explode as ◊supernovae, during which the ◊protons and ◊electrons of the star's atoms merge to make neutrons. A neutron star may have the mass of up to three Suns, compressed into a globe only 20 km/12 mi in diameter. If its mass is any greater, its gravity will be so strong that it will shrink even further to become a ◊black hole. Being so small, neutron stars can spin very quickly. The rapidly 'flashing' radio stars called ◊pulsars are believed to be neutron stars.

Nevada state of the W USA; nickname Sagebrush, Silver, or Battleborn State
area 286,427 sq km/110,561 sq mi
capital Carson City
towns Las Vegas, Reno
physical Mojave Desert, Lake Tahoe, mountains and plateaus alternating with valleys
products mercury, barite, gold, copper, oil; gaming machines
population (1986) 1,008,000
history ceded to the USA after the Mexican War 1848; the first permanent settlement 1858; discovery of silver the same year led to rapid population growth; became a state 1864; huge water projects and military installations 20th century.

New Age a type of instrumental pop music of the 1980s, often semi-acoustic or electronic; less insistent than rock.

New Brunswick maritime province of E Canada
area 72,919 sq km/28,147 sq mi
capital Fredericton
towns Saint John, Moncton
products cereals; wood, paper; fish; lead, zinc, copper, oil and natural gas
population (1986) 709,000, 37% French-speaking
history first reached by Europeans (Cartier) in 1534; explored by Champlain 1604; remained a French colony as part of Nova Scotia until ceded to England 1713; after American Revolution, many United Empire Loyalists settled there, and it became a province 1784; one of the original provinces of Confederation 1867.

New Caledonia island group, a French overseas territory in the S Pacific
area 18,576 sq km/7,170 sq mi
capital Nouméa on New Caledonia
products world's third largest producer of nickel; chrome, iron
population (1983) 145,300; Kanak (Melanesian) 43%, European 37%, Polynesian 7%
history visited by ◊Cook 1774; under French control 1853; French overseas territory 1958; independence movement started, but with Kanaks boycotting the referendum 1987, independence was defeated.

Newcastle-upon-Tyne industrial port (coal, shipbuilding, marine and electrical engineering, chemicals, metals), commercial and cultural centre, in Tyne and Wear, NE England, administrative headquarters of Tyne and

Wear and Northumberland; population (1981) 278,000.

Newcomen Thomas 1663–1729. British inventor of an early steam engine.

New Deal in US history, programme introduced by President F D Roosevelt 1933 to counter the Depression of 1929, including employment on public works and farm loans at low rates, and social reforms such as old-age and unemployment insurance; prevention of child labour; protection of employees against unfair practices by employers; and loans to local authorities for slum clearance. Many of its provisions were declared unconstitutional by the Supreme Court 1935–36.

New Democratic Party (NDP) Canadian political party, moderately socialist, formed 1961 by a merger of the Labour Congress and the Cooperative Commonwealth Federation. Its leader from 1975, *Edward Broadbent* (1936–), resigned 1989.

New Economic Policy (NEP) economic policy of the USSR 1921–29 devised by the Soviet leader Lenin. Rather than requisitioning all agricultural produce above a stated subsistence allowance, the state requisitioned only a fixed proportion of the surplus; the rest could be traded freely by the peasant.

New England region of NE USA, comprising the states of Maine, New Hampshire, Vermont, Massachusetts, Rhode Island, and Connecticut, originally settled by Pilgrims and Puritans from England.

Newfoundland breed of dog. Males can grow to 70 cm/2.3 ft tall, and weigh 65 kg/145 lbs, the females slightly smaller. They are gentle in temperament, and their fur is dense, flat and usually dull black.

Newfoundland and Labrador Canadian province on Atlantic Ocean
area 405,664 sq km/156,586 sq mi
capital St John's
towns Corner Brook, Gander
physical Newfoundland island and the coast of Labrador on the other side of the Straits of Belle Isle; rocky
products newsprint, fish products, hydroelectric power; iron, copper, zinc, uranium, and oil offshore
population (1986) 568,000
history colonized by Vikings about AD 1000; the English, under ◊Caboto, reached Newfoundland 1497; colony established 1583; France also made settlements and British sovereignty not recognized until 1713; internal self-government 1855; joined Canada 1949.

New Guinea island in the SW Pacific, N of Australia, comprising Papua New Guinea and Irian Jaya (administered by Indonesia); area 775,213 sq km/229,310 sq mi; population (1980) 1,174,000. Part of the Dutch East Indies from 1828, it was ceded by the UN to Indonesia in 1963. Its tropical rainforest is under threat from logging companies and resettlement schemes.

New Hampshire state of the NE USA; nickname Granite State
area 24,039 sq km/9,279 sq mi
capital Concord
towns Manchester, Nashua
products electrical machinery, gravel, apples, maple syrup, livestock
population (1985) 998,000
famous people Mary Baker Eddy, Robert Frost
history first settled in 1623, it was the first colony to declare its independence of Britain. It became

a state in 1788, one of the original Thirteen States.

New Hebrides former name (until 1980) of ◊Vanuatu.

New Ireland Forum a meeting between politicians of the Irish Republic and Northern Ireland in May 1983. It offered three potential solutions to the Northern Irish problem, but all were rejected by the UK the following year.

New Jersey state of NE USA; nickname Garden State
area 20,174 sq km/7,787 sq mi
capital Trenton
towns Newark, Jersey City, Paterson, Elizabeth
products asparagus, fruit, potatoes, tomatoes, poultry, chemicals, metal goods, electrical machinery, clothing
population (1985) 7,562,000
famous people Aaron Burr, James Fenimore Cooper, Stephen Crane, Thomas Edison, Alexander Hamilton, Thomas Paine, Paul Robeson, Frank Sinatra, Bruce Springsteen
history colonized in the 17th century by the Dutch, it was ceded to England in 1664, and became a state in 1787, one of the original Thirteen States.

newly industrialized country (NIC) a developing country which has in recent decades experienced a breakthrough into manufacturing and rapid export-led economic growth. The prime examples are in Asia: Taiwan, Hong Kong, Singapore, and South Korea. Their vast economic and social development during the 1970s and 1980s is partly due to a rapid increase of manufactured goods in their exports.

Newman John Henry 1801–1890. British Roman Catholic theologian. While still an Anglican, he wrote a series of *Tracts for the Times*, which gave their name to the Tractarian Movement (subsequently called the ◊Oxford Movement). He became a Catholic in 1845 and was made a cardinal in 1879.

Newman Paul 1925– . US actor, Hollywood's leading male star of the 1960s and 1970s. His films include *The Hustler* 1962, *Butch Cassidy and the Sundance Kid* 1969, *The Sting* 1973, and *The Color of Money* 1986 (for which he won an Academy Award).

New Mexico state of the SW USA; nickname Land of Enchantment
area 315,008 sq km/121,593 sq mi
capital Santa Fé
towns Albuquerque
physical more than 75% of the area is over 1,200 m/4,000 ft above sea level; plains, mountains, caverns
products uranium, oil, natural gas, cotton, cereals, vegetables
population (1987) 1,500,000
famous people Kit Carson
history explored by Spain in the 16th century; most of it was ceded to the USA by Mexico in 1848, and it became a state in 1912.

New Model Army army created in 1645 by Oliver Cromwell to support the cause of Parliament during the English Civil War. It was characterized by organization and discipline. Thomas Fairfax was its first commander.

New Orleans commercial and industrial city (banking, oil refining, rockets) and Mississippi river port in Louisiana, USA; population (1980) 557,500. It is the traditional birthplace of jazz.

news agency agency handling news stories and photographs which are then sold to newspapers and

newt

magazines. Major world agencies include Associated Press (AP), Agence France-Presse (AFP), United Press International (UPI), Telegraphic Agency of the Soviet Union (TASS), and Reuters.

New South Wales   state of SE Australia
area 801,600 sq km/309,418 sq mi
capital Sydney
towns Newcastle, Wollongong, Broken Hill
physical Great Dividing Range (including Blue Mountains) and part of the Australian Alps (including Snowy Mountains and Mount Kosciusko); Murray, Darling, Murrumbidgee river system irrigates the Riverina district
products cereals, fruit, sugar, tobacco, wool, meat, hides and skins, gold, silver, copper, tin, zinc, coal; hydroelectric power from the Snowy river
population (1986) 5,402,000; 60% living in Sydney
history convict settlement 1788–1850, and opened to free settlement by 1819; received self-government 1856; became a state of the Commonwealth of Australia 1901.

newspaper   a daily or weekly publication in the form of folded sheets containing news and comment. News-sheets became commercial undertakings after the invention of printing and were introduced 1609 in Germany, 1616 in the Netherlands. In 1622 the first newspaper appeared in English, the *Weekly News*. By 1645 there were 14 news weeklies on sale in London. Improved ◊printing (steam printing 1814, the rotary press 1846 USA and 1857 UK), newsprint (paper made from woodpulp, used in the UK from the 1880s), and a higher literacy rate led to the growth of newspapers. In recent years, production costs have fallen with the introduction of new technology.

newt   a salamander, one of the tailed ◊amphibians of the genus *Triturus*, found in Europe, Asia, and North America.

New Testament   the second part of the ◊Bible, recognized by the Christian church from the 4th century as canonical. The New Testament includes the Gospels, which tell of the life and teachings of Jesus Christ, the history of the early church, teachings of St Paul, and mystical writings. It was written in Greek during the 1st and 2nd centuries AD, and the individual sections have been ascribed to various authors.

newton   SI unit of force, being the amount of force required to accelerate a mass of 1 kg by 1 metre per second. It is named after Isaac Newton, and has the unit symbol N.

Newton   Isaac 1642–1727. English physicist and mathematician, who discovered the law of gravity, created calculus, discovered that white light is composed of many colours, and developed the three standard laws of motion still in use today. During 1665–66, he discovered the binomial theorem, differential and integral calculus, and also began to investigate the phenomenon of gravitation. In 1685, he expounded his universal law of gravitation.

Newton's laws of motion   in physics, three laws that form the basis of Newtonian mechanics. 1) unless acted upon by a net force, a body at rest stays at rest, and a moving body continues moving at the same speed in the same straight line. 2) a net force applied to a body gives it a rate of change of ◊momentum proportional to the force and in the direction of the force. 3) when a body A exerts a force on a body B, B exerts an equal and opposite force on A, that is, to every action there is an equal and opposite reaction.

Newton's rings   in optics, an ◊interference phenomenon seen (using white light) as concentric rings of spectral colours where light passes through a thin film of transparent medium, such as the wedge of air between a large-radius convex lens and a flat glass plate. With monochromatic light (light of a single wavelength), the rings take the form of alternate light and dark bands. They are caused by interference (interaction) between light rays reflected from the plate and those reflected from the curved surface of the lens.

new town   in the UK, a town either newly established or greatly enlarged after World War II, when the population was rapidly expanding and city centres had either decayed or been destroyed.

New Wave   in pop music, a style that evolved parallel to punk in the second half of the 1970s. It shared the urban aggressive spirit but was musically and lyrically more sophisticated; examples are the early work of Elvis Costello in the UK and Talking Heads in the USA.

New Wave (French *nouvelle vague*)   French literary movement of the 1950s, a cross-fertilization of the novel (Marguerite Duras, Alain Robbe-Grillet, Nathalie Sarraute) and film (directors Jean-Luc Godard, Alain Resnais and François Truffaut).

New World   the Americas, so called by Europeans who reached them later than other continents. The term is used as an adjective to describe animals and plants that live in the western hemisphere.

New York   state of the NE USA; nickname Empire State
area 127,233 sq km/49,108 sq mi
capital Albany
towns New York, Buffalo, Rochester, Yonkers, Syracuse
physical Adirondack and Catskill mountains; Lake Placid; bordering on lakes Erie and Ontario; Hudson river; Niagara Falls; ◊Long Island
products clothing, printing, Steuben glass, titanium concentrate, cereals, apples, maple syrup, poultry, meat, dairy products, wine
population (1985) 17,783,000

Newton *Portrait of Isaac Newton by Godfrey Kneller (1702) National Portrait Gallery, London.*

New York *The New York skyline, showing the twin towers of the World Trade Center.*

famous people Henry and William James, Herman Melville, Walt Whitman

history explored by Champlain and Hudson 1609, colonized by the Dutch from 1614, and annexed by the English 1664. The first constitution was adopted in 1777, when New York become one of the original Thirteen States.

New York largest city in USA, industrial port (printing, publishing, clothing), cultural and commercial centre in New York State, at the junction of the Hudson and East rivers; comprises the boroughs of the Bronx, Brooklyn, Manhattan, Queens, and Staten Island; population (1990) 7,322,600.

New Zealand country in the S Pacific, SE of Australian.

Ney Michael, Duke of Elchingen, Prince of Ney 1769–1815. Marshal of France under ◊Napoleon I, who commanded the rearguard of the French army during the retreat from Moscow.

Nguyen Van Linh 1914– . Vietnamese communist politician, member of the Politburo 1976–81 and from 1985; party leader 1986–91. He began economic liberalization and troop withdrawal from Kampuchea and Laos.

NHS abbreviation from *National Health Service*, the UK state-financed ◊health service.

Niagara Falls two waterfalls on the Niagara river, on the Canada–USA border, separated by Goat Island. The *American Falls* are 51 m/167 ft high, 330 m/1,080 ft wide; *Horseshoe Falls*, in Canada, are 49 m/160 ft high, 790 m/2,600 ft across.

Niamey river port and capital of Niger; population (1983) 399,000. It produces textiles, chemicals, pharmaceuticals, and foodstuffs.

Nicaea, Council of Christian church council held in Nicaea (modern *Iznik*, Turkey) in 325, called by the Roman emperor Constantine, in which Arianism was condemned as heretical and the doctrine of the Trinity was established under Athanesius as the Nicene ◊Creed.

Nicaragua country in Central America, between the Pacific Ocean and the Caribbean, bounded N by Honduras and S by Costa Rica.

Nicaraguan Revolution the revolt 1978–79 in Nicaragua, led by the socialist *Sandinistas* against

---

New Zealand
Dominion of

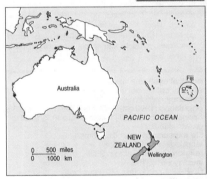

area 268,675 sq km/103,736 sq mi
capital Wellington
towns Hamilton, Palmerston North, Christchurch Dunedin; ports Wellington, Auckland
physical comprises North and South islands, Stewart and Chatham islands; mainly mountainous
territories overseas comprise Tokelau Island (three atolls transferred 1926 from the former Gilbert and Ellice Islands colony) and Niue Island (one of the Cook Islands, but separately administered from 1903; chief town Alafi). The Cook Islands are internally self-governing, but share common citizenship with New Zealand. The Ross Dependency is in the Antarctic
head of state Elizabeth II from 1952 represented by governor general
head of government Jim Bolger from 1990

political system constitutional monarchy
exports lamb, beef, wool, leather, dairy products and other processed foods, kiwi fruit, seeds and breading stock, timber, paper, pulp, light aircraft
currency New Zealand dollar
population (1990 est) 3,397,000; annual growth rate 0.9%
life expectancy men 72, women 78
language English (official); Maori
religion Protestant 50%, Roman Catholic 15%
literacy 99% (1989)
GNP $37 bn (1988); $11,040 per head
chronology
1947 Full independence within the Commonwealth confirmed by the New Zealand parliament.
1972 National Party government replaced Labour Party, with Norman Kirk as prime minister.
1974 Kirk died and was replaced by Wallace Rowling.
1975 National Party returned, with Robert Muldoon as prime minister.
1984 Labour Party returned under David Lange.
1985 Non-nuclear defence policy created disagreements with France and the USA.
1987 National Party declared support for the Labour government's non-nuclear policy. Lange re-elected. New Zealand officially became a 'friendly' rather than 'allied' country in the eyes of the USA, because of its non-nuclear defence policy.
1988 Free-trade agreement with Australia signed.
1989 Lange resigned and was replaced by Geoffrey Palmer.
1990 Palmer replaced by Mike Moore. National Party won general election and Jim Bolger became prime minister.
1991 Formation of amalgamated Alliance Party to challange two-party system.
1992 Ban on US warships lifted. Constitutional change agreed upon.

New Zealand

	Area sq km
North Island	114,688
South Island	150,460
Stewart Island	1,735
Chatham Islands	963
Minor Islands	320
	268,675

Island Territories:

Niue Island	260
Tokelau Islands	10
Cook Islands	230
Ross Dependency	453,250

the US-supported right-wing dictatorship established by the father of the president Anastasio 'Tacho' Somoza. Somoza was forced into exile and assassinated in Paraguay in 1980. The Sandinist National Liberation Front (FSLN) is named after Augusto César Sandino, a guerrilla leader killed by the US-trained National Guard in 1934.

Nice city of the French Riviera; population (1990) 345,700. Founded in the 3rd century BC, it repeatedly changed hands between France and the Duchy of Savoy until 1860.

Nicene Creed one of the fundamental ◊creeds of Christianity, promulgated by the Council of ◊Nicaea in 325.

niche in ecology, the 'place' occupied by a species in its habitat, including all chemical, physical and biological requirements, such as food, the time of day at which it feeds, temperature, moisture, and the parts of the habitat that it uses (for example, trees or open grassland).

Nichiren 1222–1282. Japanese Buddhist monk, founder of the sect that bears his name. It bases its beliefs on the *Lotus Sūtra*, which stresses the need for personal effort to attain enlightenment. Sōka Gakkai is a form of Nichiren Buddhism.

Nicholas two tsars of Russia:

Nicholas II Tsar Nicholas II of Russia in his youth.

Nicholas I 1796–1855. Tsar of Russia from 1825. His Balkan ambitions led to war with Turkey 1827–29 and the Crimean War 1853–56.

Nicholas II 1868–1918. Tsar of Russia 1894–1917. He was dominated by his wife, Princess Alix of Hesse, who in turn was under the influence of ◊Rasputin. His mismanagement of the ◊Russo-Japanese War, and of internal affairs led to the revolution of 1905, which he suppressed, although he was forced to grant limited constitutional reforms. He took Russia into World War I in 1914, was forced to abdicate in 1917, and was shot with his family by the Bolsheviks at Ekaterinburg in Jul 1918.

Nicholas, St also known as *Santa Claus* 4th century. In the Christian church, patron saint of Russia, children, merchants, and sailors; bishop of Myra (now in Turkey). His legendary gifts of dowries to poor girls led to the custom of giving gifts to children on the eve of his feast day, 6 Dec, still retained in some countries, such as the Netherlands, although elsewhere now transferred to Christmas Day. His emblem is three balls.

Nicaragua
Republic of (*República de Nicaragua*)

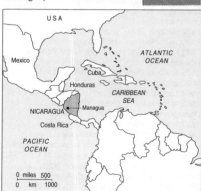

area 148,000 sq km/57,150 sq mi
capital Managua
physical volcanic mountain ranges; lakes Nicaragua and Managua
head of state and government Violeta Barrios de Chamorro from 1990

political system emergent democracy
exports coffee, cotton, sugar, bananas
currency cordoba
population (1990 est) 3,606,000 (70% mesitzo, 15% Spanish descent, 10% Indian or black); annual growth rate 3.3%
life expectancy men 61, women 63
language Spanish (official)
religion Roman Catholic 95%
literacy 66%˙ (1986)
GNP $2.1 bn (1988); $610 per head
chronology
1838 Achieved full independence.
1962 Sandinista National Liberation Front (FSLN) formed to fight Somoza regime.
1979 Somoza government ousted by FSLN.
1982 Subversive activity against the government promoted by the USA.
1985 FSLN won big victory in assembly elections.
1987 Central American peace agreement co-signed by Nicaraguan leaders.
1988 Peace agreement failed. Nicaragua held talks with Contra rebel leaders. Hurricane left 180,000 people homeless.
1989 Demobilization of rebels and release of former Somozan hostages; cease-fire ended.
1990 Violeta Barrios de Chamorro elected president. Antigovernment riots.
1991 First presidential state visit to USA for over 50 years.
1992 US aid suspended because of concern over role of Sandinistas in the government. About 16,000 people made homeless by earthquake.

Niger

Republic of
(*République du Niger*)

area 1,187,000 sq km/459,000 sq mi
capital Niamey
physical mountains in centre; arid except in S

(savanna) and SW (river Niger)
head of state Ali Saibu from 1987
head of government to be elected
political system military republic
exports peanuts, livestock, gum arabic, uranium
currency CFA franc
population (1990 est) 7,691,000; annual growth
rate 2.8%
life expectancy men 48, women 50
language French (official), Hausa, Djerma
religion Sunni Muslim 86%, animist 15%
literacy 19% male/9% female (1985 est)
GNP $2.2 bn (1987); $310 per head
chronology
1960 Achieved full independence from France with
Hamani Diori elected president.
1974 Diori ousted in an army coup led by Seyni
Kountché.
1977 Cooperation agreement signed with France.
1987 Kountché replaced by Ali Saibu.
1989 Ali Saibu elected president without opposition.
1990 Multiparty politics promised.
1991 Saibu stripped of executive power;
transitional government formed.
1992 Transitional government collapsed.
Constitutional change allowing for multiparty
politics approved in referendum.

Nicholson Ben 1894–1982. British abstract artist. After early experiments influenced by Cubism and de Stijl, he developed a style of geometrical reliefs, notably a series of white reliefs (from 1933).

Nicholson Jack 1937– . US film actor, who captured the mood of non-conformist, young Americans in such films as *Easy Rider* 1969. He subsequently became a Hollywood star in *Chinatown* 1974, *One Flew over the Cuckoo's Nest* 1975, *The Shining* 1979, and *Batman* 1989.

Nicholson John 1822–1857. British general and colonial administrator in India. He was administrative officer in the Punjab 1851–56. Promoted to brigadier general 1857 on the outbreak of the ◊Indian Mutiny, he defeated resistance in the Punjab, but was killed during the storming of Delhi.

nickel a lustrous white metallic element, symbol Ni, atomic number 28, relative atomic mass 58.71. It has a high melting point, low electrical and thermal conductivity, and can be magnetized. Nickel may be forged readily when hot, and is tough, malleable, and ductile when cold. It is used in coinage, in the chemical and food industries because of its resistance to corrosion, in electronics, and for electroplating. The most important use, however, is in alloys with iron, steel, copper, and chromium, including nickel steel for armour plating and safes.

nickel ore mineral ore from which nickel is obtained. Its main minerals are the arsenides kupfernickel, NiAs, and chloanthite, $NiAs_2$, and the sulphides millerite, NiS, and pentlandite, $(Fe,Ni)_9^c$, the commonest ore.

Nicklaus Jack William 1940– . US golfer, nicknamed 'the Golden Bear'. He has won a record 20 major titles, including 18 professional 'majors' 1962–86.

Nicosia capital of Cyprus, with leather, textiles, and pottery industries; population (1987) 165,000.

nicotine an ◊alkaloid (nitrogenous compound) obtained from the dried leaves of the tobacco plant (*Nicotiana tabacum*) and used as an insecticide. A colourless oil, soluble in water, it turns brown on exposure to the air.

nielsbohrium alternative name for the element ◊unnilpentium.

Nielsen Carl (August) 1865–1931. Danish composer. His works are notable for their progressive tonality, as in his opera *Saul and David* 1902 and six symphonies. His compositions also include concertos for violin, 1911, and clarinet, 1928, and chamber and piano works.

Niemeyer Oscar 1907– . Brazilian architect, joint designer of the United Nations headquarters in New York, and of many buildings in ◊Brasilia.

Niemöller Martin 1892–1984. German Christian Protestant pastor. He was imprisoned in a concentration camp 1938–45 for compaigning against Nazism in the German church. President of the World Council of Churches 1961–68.

Niepce Joseph Nicéphore 1765–1833. French pioneer of ◊photography.

Nietzsche Friedrich Wilhelm 1844–1900. German philosopher, who rejected the accepted absolute moral values and the 'slave morality' of Christianity. He argued that 'God is dead', and therefore people were free to create their own values. His ideal was

Nightingale *A pencil drawing of Florence Nightingale by George Scharf, 1857.*

Nigeria
Federal Republic of

area 924,000 sq km/357,000 sq mi
capital and chief port Lagos
towns administrative headquarters Abuja; Ibadan, Ogbomosho, Kano; ports Port Harcourt, Warri, Calabar
physical the arid N becomes savanna and farther S tropical rainforest, with mangrove swamps along the coast; river Niger
head of state and government Ibrahim Babangida from 1985
political system military republic pending transition to civilian rule
exports petroleum (richest African country in oil resources), cocoa, peanuts, palm oil, cotton, rubber, tin
currency naira
population (1991 est) 88,514,500. Yoruba in W, Ibo in E, and Hausa-Fulani in N); annual growth rate 3.3%
life expectancy men 47, women 49
language English (official), Hausa, Ibo, Yoruba
religion Sunni Muslim in the N, Christian in the S
literacy 54% male/31% female (1985 est)
GNP $78 bn (1987); $790 per head
chronology
1960 Achieved full independence within the Commonwealth.
1963 Became a republic, with Nnamdi Azikiwe as president.
1966 Military coup, followed by a counter-coup led by Gen Yakubu Gowon. Slaughter of many members of the Ibo tribe in the N.
1967 Conflict about oil revenues leads to declaration of an independent state of Biafra and outbreak of civil war.
1970 Surrender of Biafra and end of civil war.
1975 Gowon ousted in military coup; a second coup puts Gen Obasanjo in power.
1979 Shehu Shagari becomes civilian president.
1983 Shagari's government overthrown in a coup by Maj-Gen Buhari.
1985 Buhari replaced in a bloodless coup led by Maj-Gen Ibrahim Babangida.
1989 Babangida promised a return to pluralist politics.
1991 Nine new states created.
1992 Multiparty elections won by Babangida's SDP. Primary elections to be introduced; transition to civilian rule delayed.

the *Übermensch* or 'Superman' who would impose his will on the weak and worthless. Nietzsche claimed that knowledge is never objective, but always serves some interest or unconscious purpose.

Niger third longest river in Africa, 4,185 km/2,600 mi from the highlands bordering Sierra Leone and Guinea NE through Mali, then SE through Niger and Nigeria to an inland delta on the Gulf of Guinea. Its flow has been badly affected by the expansion of the Sahara Desert

Niger landlocked country in W Africa, bounded to the N by Nigeria and Libya, to the E by Chad, to the S by Nigeria and Benin, and to the W by Burkina Faso and Mali.

Nigeria country in W Africa on the Gulf of Guinea, bounded to the N by Niger, to the E by Chad and Cameroon, and to the W by Benin.

nightingale songbird of the thrush family. About 16.5 cm/6.5 in long, it is dull brown, lighter below, with a reddish-brown tail. It feeds on insects. It is a summer visitor to Europe and winters in Africa.

Nightingale Florence 1820–1910. English nurse, the founder of nursing as a profession. She took a team of nurses to Scutari in 1854 and reduced the ◊Crimean War hospital death rate from 42% to 2%. In 1856 she founded the Nightingale School and Home for Nurses, attached to St. Thomas's Hospital, London.

nightjar nocturnal bird *Caprimulgus europaeus* with a large bristle-fringed beak that catches moths and other flying insects in the air. About 28 cm/11 in long, it is patterned in shades of brown, and well camouflaged. It is a summer visitor to Europe, and winters in tropical Africa.

Night Journey or *Al-Miraj* (Arabic 'the ascent') the journey of the prophet Muhammad, guided by the archangel Gabriel, from Mecca to Jerusalem, where he met the earlier prophets, including Adam, Moses, and Jesus Christ; he then ascended to paradise, where he experienced the majesty of Allah, and was also shown hell.

nightshade several plants in the family Solanaceae, of which the best known are the black nightshade *Solanum nigrum*, bittersweet or woody nightshade *Solanum dulcamara*, and deadly nightshade ◊belladonna.

Nihilist member of a group of Russian revolutionaries in the reign of Alexander II 1855–81. The name, popularized by the writer Turgenev, means one who approves of nothing (Latin *nihil*) belonging to the existing order. In 1878 the Nihilists launched a guerrilla campaign which culminated in the murder of the tsar in 1881.

Nijinsky Vaslav 1888–1950. Russian dancer and choreographer. Noted for his powerful but graceful technique, he was a legendary member of ◊Diaghilev's *Ballets Russes*, for whom he choreographed Debussy's *L'Après-midi d'un faune* 1912 and *Jeux* 1913 and Stravinsky's *The Rite of Spring* 1913

nil desperandum (Latin) never despair.

Nile river in Africa, the world's longest, 6,695 km/4,160 mi. The Blue Nile rises in Lake Tana, Ethiopia, the White Nile at Lake Victoria, and they join at Khartoum, Sudan. It enters the Mediterranean at a vast delta in N Egypt.

Nile, Battle of the alternative name for the Battle of Aboukir Bay Aug 1 1798, in which Nelson defeated Napoleon's fleet, thus ending the projected French conquest of the Middle East.

Nin Anaïs 1903–1977. US novelist and diarist. Her impressionistic diaries, published 1966–76, show her interest in dreams, which along with psychoanalysis are recurring themes of her gently erotic novels (such as *House of Incest* 1936 and *A Spy in the House of Love* 1954).

Nineteen Eighty-Four a futuristic novel by George Orwell, published 1949, which tells of an individual's battle against, and eventual surrender to, a totalitarian state where Big Brother rules. It is a dystopia (the opposite of utopia) and many of the words and concepts in it have passed into common usage (newspeak, doublethink, thought police).

Nineteen Propositions demands presented by the English Parliament to Charles I in 1642, designed to limit the powers of the crown. Their rejection represented the final breakdown of peaceful negotiations and the effective beginning of the Civil War.

Nineveh capital of the Assyrian Empire from the 8th century BC until its destruction by the Medes under King Cyaxares in 612 BC, as forecast by the Old Testament prophet Nahum. It was situated on the Tigris (opposite the modern city of Mosul, Iraq) and was adorned with splendid palaces.

Ningxia or *Ningxia Hui* autonomous region (formerly Ninghsia-Hui) of NW China
area 170,000 sq km/65,600 sq mi
capital Yinchuan
physical desert plateau
products cereals and rice under irrigation; coal
population (1990) 4,655,000, including many Muslims, and nomadic hersdmen.

niobium light-grey metal closely allied to tantalum, symbol Nb, atomic number 41, relative atomic mass 92.91. Occurring in a number or rare minerals, it is generally obtained from an African ore, and is a valuable addition to stainless steels. It is also used for canning high-temperature nuclear fuel elements, for example in fast breeder-reactors, especially when liquid sodium is the coolant.

Nippon English transliteration of the Japanese name for ◊Japan

nirvana in Buddhism, the attainment of perfect serenity by the eradication of all desires. To some Buddhists it means complete annihilation, to others it means the absorption of the self in the infinite.

Nixon *The Watergate scandal led Richard Nixon to become the first US president to resign from office.*

nitrate any salt of nitric acid, containing the NO_3^- ion. Nitrates are widely used in explosives, in the chemical and drugs industries, and as fertilizers. Run-off from fields results in nitrates polluting rivers and reservoirs. Excess nitrate in drinking water may be a health hazard.

nitric acid or *aqua fortis* an acid, HNO_3, obtained by the oxidation of ammonia, or the action of sulphuric acid on potassium nitrate. It is a strong oxidizing agent, dissolves most metals, and is used for nitration and esterification of organic substances, for explosives, plastics, and dyes, and in making sulphuric acid and nitrates.

nitrite any salt or ester of nitrous acid containing the nitrite ion (NO^{2-}). Nitrites are used as a preservative (for example, to prevent the growth of botulism spores) and as colouring in cured meats, such as bacon and sausages.

nitrogen a colourless, odourless, inert gas, symbol N, atomic number 7, relative atomic mass 14.008. Nitrogen is a constituent of many organic substances, particularly proteins. It is obtained for use in industry by liquefaction and fractional

nitrogen cycle

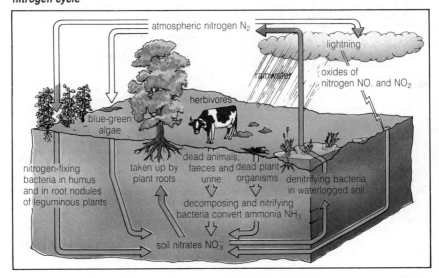

atmospheric nitrogen N_2

lightning

rainwater

oxides of nitrogen NO. and NO_2

herbivores

blue-green algae

nitrogen-fixing bacteria in humus and in root nodules of leguminous plants

taken up by plant roots

dead animals, faeces and urine

dead plant organisms

denitrifying bacteria in waterlogged soil

decomposing and nitrifying bacteria convert ammonia NH_3

soil nitrates NO_3^-

Nkomo *Zimbabwean politician and cabinet member, Joshua Nkomo.*

Nkrumah *The first president of Ghana, Kwame Nkrumah.*

distillation of air. Nitrogen is used in the Haber process to make ammonia, NH_3, and to provide an inert atmosphere for certain chemical reactions.

nitrogen cycle in ecology, the process of nitrogen passing through the ecosystem. Nitrogen, in the form of inorganic compounds (such as nitrates) in the soil, is absorbed by plants and turned into organic compounds (such as proteins) in plant tissue. A proportion of this nitrogen is eaten by ◊herbivores and used for their own biological processes, with some of this in turn being passed on to the carnivores, which feed on the herbivores. The nitrogen is finally returned to the soil, either as excreta or when the organisms die, to be returned to inorganic form by bacterial decomposers.

nitrogen fixation the process by which nitrogen in the atmosphere is converted into nitrogenous compounds by the action of microorganisms, such as cyanobacteria and bacteria, in conjunction with certain ◊legumes. Several chemical processes reproduce nitrogen fixation to produce fertilizers; see ◊nitrogen cycle.

nitroglycerine a substance produced by the action of nitric and sulphuric acids on glycerol. It is very poisonous and explodes with great violence if heated in a confined space. It is used in the preparation of dynamite, cordite, and other high explosives.

nitrous oxide or *dinitrogen oxide* (N_2O) a gass which produces analgesia. In higher doses, it is an anaesthetic. Well-tolerated, but less potent than some other anaesthetic gases, it is often combined with other drugs to allow lower doses to be used.

nitrous acid (HNO_2) a weak acid which, in solution with water, decomposes quickly to form nitric acid and nitrogen dioxide.

Nixon Richard (Milhous) 1913– . 37th president of the USA 1969–74, a Republican. He attracted attention as a member of the Un-American Activities Committee 1948, and was vice president to Eisenhower 1953–61. As president he was responsible for US withdrawal from Vietnam, and forged new links with China, but at home his culpability in the cover-up of the ◊Watergate scandal and the existence of a 'slush fund' for political machinations during his re-election campaign 1972 led to his resignation 1974.

Nizhny Novgorod formerly (1932–90) Gorky, city in central Russia; population (1987) 1,425,000. Cars, locomotives, and aircraft are manufactured here.

Nkomati Accord a non-aggression treaty between South Africa and Mozambique concluded 1984, under which they agreed not to give material aid to opposition movements in each other's countries.

Nkomo Joshua 1917– . Zimbabwean politician, president of ZAPU (Zimbabwe African People's Union) from 1961, and a leader of the black nationalist movement against the white Rhodesian regime. He was a member of Robert ◊Mugabe's cabinet 1980–82 and from 1987.

Nkrumah Kwame 1909–1972. Ghanaian nationalist politician, prime minister of the Gold Coast 1952–57 and of independent Ghana 1957–60, and Ghana's first president 1960–66. His policy of 'African socialism' led to links with the communist bloc.

NKVD (Russian 'People's Commissariat of Internal Affairs') the Soviet secret police 1934–38, replaced by the ◊KGB. The NKVD was responsible for the infamous ◊purges of Stalin.

No or *Noh* the classical, aristocratic Japanese drama, which developed in the 14th–16th centuries and is still performed.

Noah in the Old Testament or Hebrew Bible, the son of Lamech and father of Shem, Ham, and Japheth, who built an ark so that he and his family and specimens of all existing animals might survive the ◊Flood; there is also a Babylonian version of the tale.

Nobel Alfred Bernhard 1833–1896. Swedish chemist. He invented dynamite 1867, and ballistite, a smokeless gunpowder, 1889. He amassed a large fortune from the manufacture of explosives and the exploitation of the Baku oilfields in Russia. He left this fortune in trust for the endowment of five Nobel prizes.

nobelium metallic, radioactive element of the ◊actinide series, symbol No, atomic number 102. It is obtained by bombarding curium, and was first produced 1958. It is named after Alfred Nobel.

Nobel prize annual international prize, first awarded 1901, for achievement in chemistry, physics, medicine, literature, and the promotion of peace. The first four are awarded by academic committees based in Sweden, while the peace prize is awarded by a committee of the Norwegian parliament. A sixth prize, for economics, financed by the Swedish National Bank, was first awarded 1969.

Noble Savage, the influential Enlightenment idea of the virtuous innocence of 'savage' peoples, often embodied in the American Indian, and celebrated by J J Rousseau, Chateaubriand (in *Atala* 1801), and James Fenimore Cooper.

nocturne in music, a lyrical, dreamy piece, often for piano, introduced by John Field (1782–1837) and adopted by Chopin.

nodule in geology, a lump of mineral or other matter found within rocks or formed on the seabed

Nobel Prizes

Peace
1988 The United Nations peacekeeping forces
1989 The Dalai Lama (Tibet)
1990 President Mikhail Gorbachev (USSR)
1991 Aung San Suu Kyi (Myanmar)
1992 Rigoberta Menche (Guatemala)

Economics
1988 Maurice Allais (France)
1989 Trygve Haavelmo (Norway)
1990 Harry Markowitz, Merton Miller & William Sharpe (USA)
1991 Ronald H Coase (USA)
1992 Gary S Becker (USA)

Physiology and Medicine
1988 Gertrude Elion (USA), George Hitchins (USA), & James Black (UK)
1989 Michael Bishop (USA), & Harold Varmus (USA)
1990 Joseph Murray & E Donnall Thomas (USA)
1991 Erwin Neher (Germany)
1992 Edmond Fisher (USA)

Literature
1988 Naguib Mahfouz (Egypt)
1989 Camilo José Cela (Spain)
1990 Octavio Paz (Mexico)
1991 Nadine Gordimer (South Africa)
1992 Derek Walcott (St Lucia)

Chemistry
1988 Johann Deisenhofer, Robert Huber, & Hartmut Michel (Germany)
1989 Sidney Altman (USA), Thomas Cech (USA)
1990 Elias James Corey (USA)
1991 Richard R Ernst (Switzerland)
1992 Rudolf A Marcus (USA)

Physics
1988 Leon Lederman, Melvin Schwartz, & Jack Steinberger (USA)
1989 Norman Ramsey (USA), Hans Dehmelt (USA), & Wolfgang Paul (Germany)
1990 Richard Taylor (Canada), Jerome Friedman, & Henry Kendall (USA)
1991 Pierre-Gilles de Gennes (France)
1992 Georges Charpak (France)

---

surface; ◊mining technology is developing to exploit them.

Nolan Sidney 1917–1992. Australian artist. He created atmospheric paintings of the outback, exploring themes from Australian history such as the life of the outlaw Ned Kelly and the folk heroine Mrs Fraser.

Nolde Emil. Adopted name of Emil Hansen 1867–1956. German Expressionist painter. He studied in Paris and Dachau, joined the group of artists known as *die Brücke* 1906–07, and visited Polynesia 1913; he then became almost a recluse in NE Germany.

Nollekens Joseph 1737–1823. British sculptor, specializing in portrait busts and memorials. He worked in Rome 1759–70.

Nom Chinese-style characters used in writing the Vietnamese language. Nom characters were used from the 13th century for Vietnamese literature, but were replaced in the 19th century by a romanized script known as Quoc Ngu. The greatest Nom writer was the poet Nguyen Du.

nom de plume (French 'pen name') a writer's pseudonym.

nominative in the grammar of some inflected languages such as Latin, Russian, and Sanskrit, the form of a word used to indicate that a noun or pronoun is the subject of a finite verb.

nonaligned movement strategic and political position of neutrality ('nonalignment') towards major powers, specifically the USA and USSR. Although originally used by poorer states, the nonaligned position was later adopted by oil-producing nations too.

Nonconformist in religion, originally a member of the Puritan section of the Church of England clergy who, in the Elizabethan age, refused to conform to certain practices, for example the wearing of the surplice and kneeling to receive Holy Communion. After 1662 the term was confined to those who left the church rather than conform to the Act of Uniformity requiring the use of the Prayer Book in all churches. It is now applied mainly to members of the Free churches.

Nonjurors priests of the Church of England who after the revolution of 1688 refused to take the oaths of allegiance to William and Mary. They continued to exist as a rival church for over a century, and consecrated their own bishops, the last of whom died 1805.

non-renewable resource natural resource, such as coal or oil, that cannot be replaced once it is consumed. The main energy sources used by humans are non-renewable resources.

non sequitur (Latin 'it does not follow') a statement which has little or no relevance to that which preceded it.

Nordenskjöld Nils Adolf Erik, Baron Nordenskjöld 1832–1901. Swedish explorer. He made voyages to the Arctic with the geologist Torell, and in 1878–79 discovered the North-East Passage.

Nordic ethnic designation formerly used to describe the Germanic peoples mainly of Scandinavia.

Norman Invasion of England
- dependency   ✕ battle
- possessions (England after 1066)

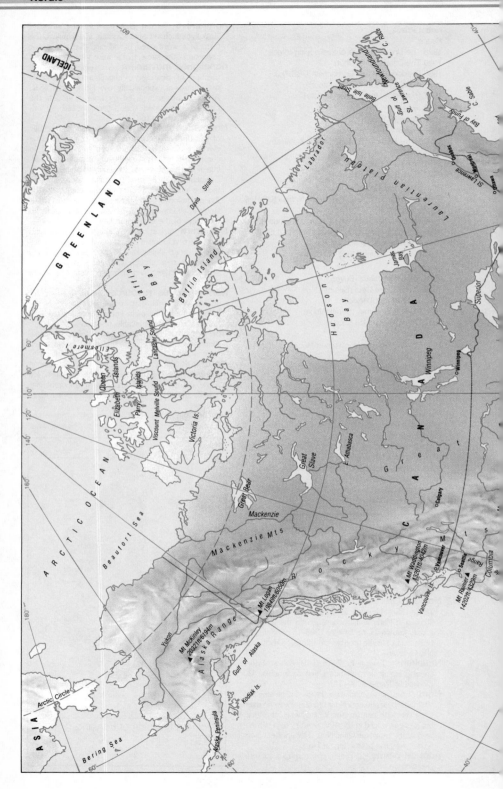

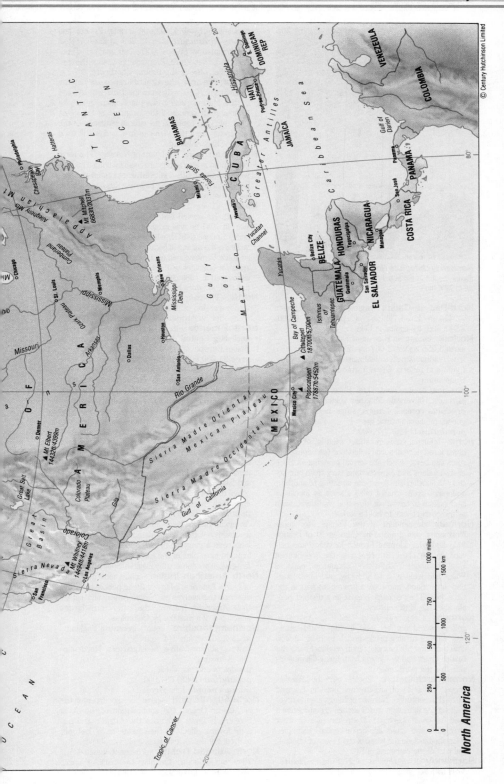

North America

Norman architecture *Norman tower at Hedingham, Essex, begun in the late 11th century. It is 22 m/72 ft high.*

Nord-Pas-de-Calais region of N France; area 12,414 sq km/4,792 sq mi; population (1986) 3,932,000. Its capital is Lille.

Norfolk county on E coast of England
area 5,355 sq km/2,067 sq mi
towns administrative headquarters Norwich; King's Lynn, and resorts Great Yarmouth, Cromer, and Hunstanton
physical rivers Ouse, Yare, Bure, Waveney; the ◊Broads; Halvergate Marshes wildlife area
products cereals, turnips, sugar beet, turkeys, geese, offshore natural gas
population (1986) 728,000.

norm informal guideline about what is, or is not, considered normal social behaviour (as opposed to rules and laws, which are formal guidelines). Such shared values and expectations vary from one society to another and from one situation to another, and range from crucial taboos such as incest or cannibalism to trivial customs and traditions, such as the correct way to hold a fork.

Norman descendant of the Vikings, to whom Normandy was granted by Charles III of France 911, and who adopted French language and culture. In the 11th–12th centuries they conquered England (under William the Conqueror), parts of Wales and Ireland, S Italy, Sicily, and Malta, settled in Scotland, and took a prominent part in the Crusades. They ceased to exist as a distinct people after the 13th century.

Norman Greg(ory) John 1955– . Australian golfer ranked number one in the world within ten years of turning professional. In 1986 he won nine tournaments (six consecutively) including the British Open and the World Matchplay Championship (for the third time).

Norman architecture English term for ◊Romanesque, the style of architecture used in England 11th–12th centuries. Norman buildings are massive, with arches (although trefoil arches are sometimes used for small openings). Buttresses are of slight projection, and vaults are barrel-roofed. Examples in England include the Keep of the Tower of London, and part of the cathedral of Ely.

Normandy two regions of N France: *Haute-Normandie* area 12,317 sq km/4,754 sq mi;

population (1986) 1,693,000; capital Rouen; and *Basse-Normandie* area 17,589 sq km/6,789 sq mi; population (1986) 1,373,000; capital Caen. Its main towns are Alençon, Bayeux, Dieppe, Deauville, Lisieux, Le Havre, Cherbourg.

Norman French the form of French used by the Normans in Normandy from the 10th century, and by the Norman ruling class in England after the Conquest. It remained the language of the court until the 15th century, the official language of the law courts until the 17th century, and is still used in the Channel Islands.

Norseman early inhabitant of Norway. The term Norsemen is also applied to Scandinavian ◊Vikings who during the 8th–11th centuries raided and settled in Britain, Ireland, France, Russia, Iceland, and Greenland.

North Oliver 1943– . US Marine lieutenant-colonel. He served with distinction in the Vietnam War. In 1981 he was inducted into the National Security Council (NSC), where he supervised actions including the mining of Nicaraguan harbours 1983, an air-force bombing raid on Libya 1986, and an illegal arms-for-hostages deal with Iran 1985 which, when uncovered in 1986 (◊Irangate), forced his dismissal and trial, at which he was found guilty.

North Thomas 1535–1601. English translator, whose version of ◊Plutarch's *Lives* 1579 was the source for Shakespeare's Roman plays.

North America third largest of the continents (including Central America), and over twice the size of Europe
area 24,000,000 sq km/9,500,000 sq mi
largest cities (population over 1 million) Mexico City, New York, Chicago, Toronto, Los Angeles, Montreal, Guadalajara, Monterrey, Philadelphia, Houston, Guatemala City, Vancouver, Detroit
physical mountain belts to the E (Appalachians) and W (see ◊Cordilleras), the latter including the Rocky Mountains and the Sierra Madre; coastal plain on the Gulf of Mexico, into which the Mississippi river system drains from the central Great Plains; the St Lawrence and the Great Lakes form a rough crescent (with the Great Bear and Great Slave lakes, and lakes Athabasca and Winnipeg) around the exposed rock of the great Canadian/Laurentian Shield, into which Hudson Bay breaks from the North.
population (1981) 345 million; the aboriginal American Indian, Inuit, and Aleut peoples are now a minority within a population predominantly of European immigrant origin. Many Africans were brought in as part of the slave trade.
language predominantly English, Spanish, French.

North American Indian indigenous inhabitant of North America. Many of these people prefer to describe themselves as 'Native Americans' rather than 'American Indians', the latter term having arisen out of a mistake by Columbus.

Northamptonshire county in central England
area 2,367 sq km/914 sq mi
towns administrative headquarters Northampton; Kettering
products cereals, cattle
population (1986) 554,000
famous people John Dryden.

North Atlantic Drift warm ocean ◊current in the N Atlantic Ocean, the continuation of the ◊Gulf Stream. It flows E across the Atlantic and has a mellowing effect on the climate of W Europe, particularly the British Isles and Scandinavia.

North Atlantic Treaty agreement signed 4 Apr 1949 by Belgium, Canada, Denmark, France, Iceland, Italy, Luxembourg, Netherlands, Norway,

Portugal, UK, USA; later accessions Greece, Turkey in 1952; West German in 1955; Spain in 1982. They agreed that 'an armed attack against one or more of them in Europe or North America shall be considered an attack against them all'. The North Atlantic Treaty Organization is based on this treaty.

North Atlantic Treaty Organization (NATO) association set up 1949 to provide for the collective defence of the major W European and North American states against the perceived threat from the USSR. Its chief body is the Council of Foreign Ministers (who have representatives in permanent session), and there is an international secretariat in Brussels, Belgium, and also the Military Committee consisting of the Chiefs of Staff. The military headquarters SHAPE (Supreme Headquarters Allied Powers, Europe) is in Chièvres, near Mons, Belgium. After the E European ◊*Warsaw Pact* was disbanded 1991, an adjunct to NATO, the *North Atlantic Cooperation Council* was established, including all the former Soviet republics, with the aim of building greater security in Europe.

North Carolina state of the USA; nicknamed the Tar Heel or Old North state
area 136,448 sq km/52,669 sq mi
capital Raleigh
towns Charlotte, Greensboro, Winston-Salem
products tobacco, maize, soybeans; livestock, poultry and dairy products; textiles and clothing, funiture, computers; mica, feldspar, bricks
population (1990) 6,628,600
famous people Billy Graham, O Henry
history The first permanent settlement in the state was made in 1663; it was one of the original Thirteen States in 1789.

Northcliffe Alfred Charles William Harmsworth, 1st Viscount Northcliffe 1865–1922. British newspaper proprietor born in Dublin. Founding the *Daily Mail* 1896, he revolutionized popular journalism, and with the *Daily Mirror* 1903 originated the picture paper: in 1908 he also obtained control of *The Times*.

North Dakota prairie state of the USA; nicknamed Sioux or Flickertail State
area 183,070 sq km/70,665 sq mi
capital Bismarck
towns Fargo, Grand Forks
products cereals, meat products, farm equipment, oil, coal
population (1990) 638,800
famous people Maxwell Anderson, Louis l'Amour
history acquired by the USA partly in the ◊Louisiana Purchase 1803, and partly by treaty with Britain in 1813; it became a state in 1889.

North-East India area of India (Meghalaya, Assam, Mizoram, Tripura, Manipur, and Nagaland, and the union territory of Arunachal Pradesh) linked with the rest of India only by a narrow corridor. There is opposition to immigration from Bangladesh and the rest of India, and demand for secession.

North-East Passage sea route from the N Atlantic, around Asia, to the N Pacific, pioneered by ◊Nordenskjöld 1878–79, and developed by the USSR in settling N Siberia from 1935. The USSR owns offshore islands, and claims it as an internal waterway; the USA claims that it is international.

Northern Rhodesia former name (until 1964) of ◊Zambia.

Northern Territory territory of Australia
area 1,356,165 sq km/523,620 sq mi
capital and chief port Darwin
towns Alice Springs
exports beef cattle; prawns; bauxite (Gove), gold

and copper (Tennant Creek), uranium (Ranger)
population (1987) 157,000
government there is an administrator and legislative assembly, and the territory is also represented in the federal parliament
history originally part of New South Wales, it was annexed in 1863 to South Australia, but 1911–78 (when self-government was granted) was under the control of the Commonwealth of Australia government.

North Korea see ◊Korea, North.

North Pole the north point where an imaginary line penetrates the Earth's surface by the axis about which it revolves; see also ◊Poles and ◊Arctic.

North Rhine-Westphalia (German *Nordrhein-Westfalen*) administrative *Land* of Germany
area 34,150 sq km/13,110 sq mi
capital Düsseldorf
towns Cologne, Essen, Dortmund, Duisberg, Wuppertal
products iron and steel, coal and lignite, electrical goods, fertilizers, synthetic textiles
population (1988) 16,700,000
religion Roman Catholic 53%, Protestant 42%
history see ◊Westphalia.

North Sea sea to the E of Britain and bounded by the coasts of Belgium, the Netherlands, Germany, Denmark, and Norway; area 523,000 sq km/202,000 sq mi; average depth 55 m/180 ft, greatest depth 660 m/2165 ft. In the NE it joins the Norwegian Sea, and in the S it meets the Strait of Dover. It has fisheries, oil and gas.

Northumberland county in N England
area 5,032 sq km/1,942 sq mi
towns administrative headquarters Morpeth; Berwick-upon-Tweed, Hexham
products sheep
population (1991) 300,600
famous people Thomas Bewick, Bobby Charlton.

Northumberland John Dudley, Duke of Northumberland *c.* 1502–1553. English politician, chief minister until Edward VI's death 1553. He then tried to place his daughter-in-law Lady Jane ◊Grey on the throne, and was executed on Mary's accession.

Northumbria Anglo-Saxon kingdom which covered NE England and SE Scotland, comprising the 6th-century kingdoms of Bernicia (Forth–Tees) and Deira (Tees–Humber), united in the 7th century. It accepted the supremacy of Wessex in 827, and was conquered by the Danes in the later 9th century.

North-West Passage Atlantic-Pacific sea route around the north of Canada. Canada, which owns offshore islands, claims it as an internal waterway; the USA insists that it is international and sent an icebreaker through without permission 1985.

Northwest Territories territory of Canada
area 3,426,300 sq km/1,322,552 sq mi
capital Yellowknife
physical extends to the North Pole, to Hudson's Bay in the E, and in the W to the edge of the Canadian Shield
products oil and natural gas, zinc, lead, gold, tungsten, silver
population (1991) 54,000, over 50% native American peoples (Indian, Inuit)
history the area was the northern part of Rupert's Land, bought by the Canadian government from the Hudson's Bay Company in 1869.

North Yorkshire county in NE England
area 8,317 sq km/3,210 sq mi
towns administrative headquarters Northallerton; York, Harrogate, Scarborough, and Whitby

Norway
Kingdom of
(Kongeriget Norge)

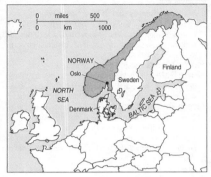

area 324,220 sq km/125,065 sq mi
capital Oslo
towns Bergen, Trondheim
physical mountainous; forests cover 25%; extends N of Arctic Circle
territories dependencies in the Arctic (Svalbard and Jan Mayen) and in the Antarctic (Bouvet and Peter I Island, and Queen Maud Land)
head of state Harald V from 1991

head of government Gro Harlem Brundtland from 1990
political system constitutional monarchy
exports petrochemicals from North Sea oil and gas, paper, wood pulp, furniture, iron ore and other minerals, high-tech goods, sports goods, fish
currency krone
population (1990 est) 4,214,000; annual growth rate 0.3%
life expectancy men 73, women 80
language Norwegian (official); Saami- and Finnish-speaking minorities
religion Evangelical Lutheran (endowed by state)
literacy 100% (1989)
GNP $89 bn (1988); $13,790 per head
chronology
1814 Independent from Denmark.
1905 Links with Sweden ended.
1940–45 Occupied by Germany.
1949 Joined NATO.
1952 Joined Nordic Council.
1957 Haakon VII succeeded by his son, Olaf V.
1960 Joined EFTA.
1972 Accepted into membership of the European Community but application withdrawn after a referendum.
1989 Jan P Syse became prime minister.
1990 Brundtland returned to power.
1991 Olaf V succeeded by his son, Harald V.
1992 Norway defied whaling ban to resume whaling industry. Formal application made for EC membership.

products cereals, wool and meat from sheep, dairy products, coal, electrical goods
population (1986) 700,000
famous people Alcuin, W H Auden.

Norway country in NW Europe, on the Scandinavian peninsula, bounded E by Sweden, NE by Finland and Russia, S by the North Sea, W by the Atlantic Ocean, and N by the Arctic Ocean.

Norwich industrial city (shoes, clothing, chemicals, confectionery, engineering, printing) in Norfolk, England; population (1989) 121,000. It has a university, a cathedral (founded 1096) and Norman castle.

nose in humans, the upper entrance of the respiratory tract; the organ of the sense of smell. The external part is divided down the middle by a septum of ◊cartilage. The nostrils contain plates of cartilage which can be moved by muscles and have a growth of stiff hairs at the margin to prevent foreign objects from entering. They contain cells sensitive to smell. The whole nasal cavity is lined with a ◊mucous membrane which warms and moistens the air and ejects dirt.

Nostradamus Latinized name of Michel de Notredame 1503–1566. French physician and astrologer, who was consulted by Catherine de Medici and was physician to Charles IX. His book of prophesies in rhyme, *Centuries* (1555), has had a number of interpretations.

notation in music, the use of symbols to represent individual sounds (such as the notes of the chromatic scale) so that they can be accurately interpreted and reproduced.

notation in dance, notation is the recording of dances by symbols. There are several dance notation systems, prominent among which is ◊labanotation.

Nottingham industrial city (engineering, coal-mining, cycles, textiles, knitwear, pharmaceuticals, tobacco, lace, electronics) and administrative

headquarters of Notthinghamshire, England; populantion (1989) 261,500.

Nottinghamshire county in central England
area 2,164 sq km/836 sq mi
towns administrative headquarters Nottingham; Mansfield, Worksop
products cereals, cattle, sheep, light engineering, footwear, limestone, ironstone and oil
population (1991) 980,600
famous people D H Lawrence, Alan Sillitoe.

Nouakchott capital of Mauritania; population (1985) 500,000. Products include salt, cement and insecticides.

noun the grammatical ◊part of speech referring to words that name certain classes of words as persons, animals, objects, qualities, ideas and so on. Nouns can refer to objects such as house, tree (concrete nouns); abstract ideas such as love, anger (abstract nouns); and in English many simple words are both noun and verb (jump, reign, rain). Adjectives are sometimes used as nouns (a local man, one of the locals).

nova a faint star that suddenly erupts in brightness, becoming visible in binoculars or to the naked eye. They are believed to occur in close ◊double star systems, where gas from one star flows to a companion ◊white dwarf. The gas ignites, and is thrown off in an explosion, the star increasing in brightness by 10,000 times or more. Unlike a ◊supernova, the star is not completely disrupted by the outburst.

Novalis pen name of Freiherr von Hardenburg 1772–1801. Pioneer German Romantic poet, best known for his *Hymnen an die Nacht/Hymns to the Night* 1800.

Nova Scotia province of E Canada
area 55,490 sq km/21,065 sq mi
capital and chief port Halifax
towns Dartmouth

nose

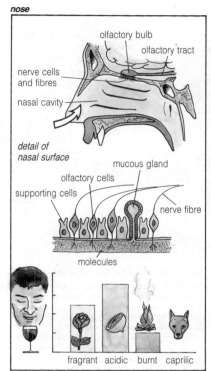

fragrant   acidic   burnt   caprilic

Novgorod *The theatre, the monument to the thousandth anniversary of the foundation of the Russian state (862), and the cathedral of St Sophia (11th century) inside the Novgorod kremlin.*

products coal, gypsum; dairy products, poultry, fruit; forest products; fish products, including scallop and lobster

population (1991) 897,500

history England and France contended for possession of the territory until Nova Scotia (which then included present-day New Brunswick and Prince Edward Island) was ceded to Britain in 1713; Cape Breton Island remained French until 1763.

novel an extended fictitious prose narrative, often incuding some sense of the psychological development of the central characters and of their relationship with a broader world. The modern novel took its name and inspiration from the Italian *novella*, the short tale of varied character popular in the late 13th century. As the main form of narrative fiction in the 20th century, the novel is frequently classified according to genres and sub-genres such as the ◊historical novel, ◊detective fiction, ◊fantasy, and ◊science fiction.

Novello Ivor 1893–1951. British composer and actor-manager. Stage name of I(vor) N(ovello) Davies. He is best remembered for the musical play spectaculars in which he often appeared as the romantic lead, including *Glamorous Night* 1925, *The Dancing Years* 1939, and *Gay's the Word* 1951.

November criminals name given by right-wing nationalists in post-1918 Germany to the socialist politicians who had taken over the government after the abdication of Kaiser Wilhelm II and had signed the armistice with the Western Allies in Nov 1918.

Noverre Jean-Georges 1727–1810. French choreographer, writer, and ballet reformer. He promoted ◊*ballet d'action* and simple, free movement and is often considered the creator of modern classical ballet.

Novgorod industrial (chemicals, engineering, clothing, brewing) city on the Volkhov River, NW Russia, a major trading city in medieval times; population (1987) 228,000.

Novi Sad industrial and commercial (pottery and cotton) city, capital of the autonomous province of Vojvodina, in N Serbia, Yugoslavia on the river Danube; population (1981) 257,700. Products include leather, textiles, and tobacco.

Novocaine trade name for *procaine hydrochloride,* a synthetic drug widely used as a local anaesthetic.

Novosibirsk industrial city (engineering, textiles, chemicals, food processing) in W Siberia, Russia on the river Ob; population (1987) 1,423,000. Winter lasts eight months.

NPA abbreviation for *New People's Army* (Philippines).

NSAID abbreviation for *non-steroidal anti-inflammatory drug.* It is effective in the long-term treatment of rheumatoid ◊arthritis and osteoarthritis. It acts to reduce swelling and pain in soft tissues. Bleeding into the digestive tract is a serious side effect; its use is contra-indicated in persons who have a peptic ulcer.

NSPCC abbreviation for *National Society for the Prevention of Cruelty to Children* (UK).

NTP (*N*ormal *T*emperature and *P*ressure) former name for ◊STP (*S*tandard *T*emperature and *P*ressure).

Nuba the peoples of the Nuba mountains, W of the White Nile, Sudan. Their languages belong to the Nubian branch of the Chari-Nile family.

nuclear arms verification the process of checking the number and types of nuclear weapons held by a country. The chief means are:

reconnaissance satellites which detect submarines or weapon silos, using angled cameras to give 3-D pictures of installations, penetrating camouflage by means of scanners, and partially seeing through cloud and darkness by infrared devices; *telemetry* (radio transmission of instrument readings);

interception to get information on performance of weapons under test;

radar tracking of missiles in flight;

seismic monitoring of underground tests, in the same way as with earthquakes; this is not accurate

nuclear energy

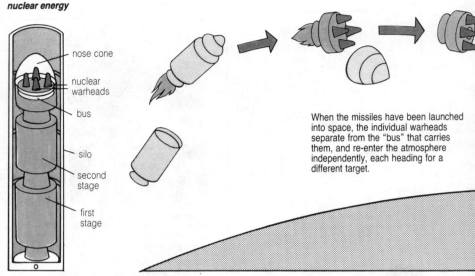

- nose cone
- nuclear warheads
- bus
- silo
- second stage
- first stage

When the missiles have been launched into space, the individual warheads separate from the "bus" that carries them, and re-enter the atmosphere independently, each heading for a different target.

and on-site inspection is needed. Tests in the atmosphere, space, or the oceans are forbidden, and the ban is accepted because explosions are not only dangerous to all, but immediately detectable.

nuclear energy energy from the inner core or ◊nucleus of the atom, as opposed to energy released in chemical processes, which is derived from the electrons surrounding the nucleus. Energy may be released by nuclear fission, in which a uranium atom is split when bombarded with neutrons, or nuclear fusion, in which helium nuclei are formed from hydrogen nuclei. *Nuclear reactors* produce energy by nuclear fission, and may be gas-cooled, advanced gas-cooled, water-cooled, or pressurized water reactors. A major danger with any type of reactor is the possibility of ◊meltdown, which can result in the release of radioactive material. Problems also arise over the reprocessing of nuclear fuel and disposal of nuclear waste.

nuclear fission is achieved by allowing a neutron to strike the nucleus of an atom of uranium-235, which then splits apart to release other neutrons. A chain reaction is set up when these neutrons in turn strike other nuclei, resulting in a tremendous burst of energy. However, the process can be controlled inside a nuclear power plant by absorbing excess neutrons in 'control rods' (which may be made of steel alloyed with boron), and slowing down the speed of those neutrons allowed to act.

nuclear fusion is the release of thermo-nuclear energy by the conversion of hydrogen nuclei to helium nuclei, which occurs in the hydrogen bomb and, as a continuing reaction, in the Sun and other stars. It avoids the loss of much of the energy produced which occurs in the original atom bomb, so that it is correspondingly more powerful. Attempts to harness it for commercial power production have so far not succeeded. In 1989, it was alleged that nuclear fusion had occurred in a test tube at room temperature, but this has not been verified.

nuclear reactors in a gas-cooled reactor, a circulating gas (such as carbon dioxide) under pressure removes heat from the core of the reactor, which usually contains natural uranium and has neutron-absorbing control rods made of boron. An advanced gas-cooled reactor (AGR) generally

has enriched uranium oxide as its fuel. A water-cooled reactor has water circulating through the hot core. The water is converted to steam which drives turbo-alternators for generating electricity. In a pressurized water reactor (PWR), the coolant consists of a sealed system of pressurized water (deuterium oxide), which heats water to form steam in heat exchangers in an external circuit. The spent fuel from either type of reactor contains some plutonium, which can be extracted and used as a fuel for the ◊fast breeder reactor. This produces more plutonium than it consumes (hence its name) by converting uranium placed in a blanket round the main core. The usual coolant is liquid sodium, a substance that is difficult to handle.

nuclear accidents the most recent was **Chernobyl**, Ukraine, USSR. In Apr 1986, there was a leak, caused by overheating, from a non-pressurized boiling-water reactor, one of the largest in the Soviet Union. The resulting clouds of radioactive isotopes were traced as far away as Sweden; many people were killed, and thousands of square kilometres of land were contaminated.

Three Mile Island, Harrisburg, Pennsylvania, USA. In 1979, a combination of mechanical and electrical failure, as well as operator error, caused a PWR to leak radioactive matter.

Church Rock, New Mexico, USA. In Jul 1979, 100 million gallons of radioactive water containing uranium tailings leaked from a pond into the Rio Puerco, causing the water to become over 6,500 times as radioactive as safety standards allow for drinking water.

Windscale, now Sellafield, Cumbria, England. In 1957, fire destroyed the core of a reactor, releasing large quantities of lethal radioactive fumes into the atmosphere.

nuclear physics the study of the properties of the nucleus of the ◊atom.

nuclear warfare war involving the use of nuclear weapons. Nuclear-weapons research began in Britain 1940, but was transferred to Los Alamos, New Mexico, USA, after the USA entered the war. It was known as the Manhattan Project, and was directed by J Robert Oppenheimer. The worldwide total of nuclear weapons is about 50,000.

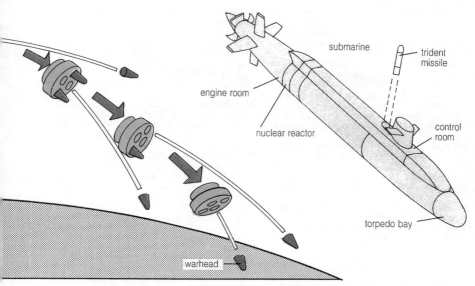

engine room

nuclear reactor

submarine

trident missile

control room

torpedo bay

warhead

atom bomb The original weapon relied on use of a chemical explosion to trigger a chain reaction. The first test explosion was at Alamogordo, New Mexico, 16 Jul 1945; the first use in war was 6 Aug 1945 over Hiroshima and three days later at Nagasaki, Japan.

hydrogen bomb A much more powerful weapon, it relies on the release of thermonuclear energy by the condensation of hydrogen nuclei to helium nuclei (as happens in the Sun). The first detonation was at Eniwetok Atoll, Pacific Ocean 1952 by the USA.

neutron bomb or enhanced radiation weapon (ERW) It is a very small hydrogen bomb which has relatively high radiation but relatively low blast, designed to kill (in up to six days) by a brief neutron radiation which leaves buildings and weaponry intact.

nuclear methods of attack now include aircraft bombs, rocket-propelled missiles with nuclear warheads (long- or short-range, surface-to-surface, and surface-to-air), depth charges, and high-powered landmines ('atomic demolition munitions' to blast craters in the path of an advancing enemy army). The major subjects of Soviet-US negotiation are: **intercontinental ballistic missiles** (ICBMs) which have from 1968 been equipped with clusters of warheads (which can be directed to individual targets), and are known as multiple independently targetable re-entry vehicles (MIRVs).

methods of defence include:

antiballistic missile (ABM) earth-based systems, with two types of missile, one short-range with high acceleration, and one comparatively long-range for interception above the atmosphere; **Strategic Defense Initiative** (announced by the USA 1983 to be operative from 2000, and popularly known as the 'Star Wars' programme) 'Directed energy weapons' firing laser beams would be mounted on space stations, and by burning holes in incoming missiles would either collapse them or detonate their fuel tanks.

nuclear waste the toxic by-products of the nuclear energy industry. Reactor waste is of three types: high-level spent fuel, or the residue when nuclear fuel has been removed from a reactor and reprocessed; intermediate, which may be long- or short-lived; and low-level, but bulky, waste from reactors, which has only short-lived radioactivity. Disposal, by burial on land or at sea, raises problems of safety, environmental pollution, and security.

nuclear winter term for the expected effects after a protracted nuclear war. Although much of the life on Earth would be destroyed by nuclear blasts and the subsequent radiation, it has been suggested that the atmosphere would be so full of dust, smoke, soot, and ash that the Sun would be blotted out for a significant period of time, sufficient to eradicate most plant life on which other life depends. The cold would be intense, and there would be a significant

nuclear energy The Sellafield nuclear plant, Cumbria, England.

increase in snow and ice worldwide. Once the ash finally settled, the Sun's rays would be reflected so much that there would not be enough heat to warm up the planet. Insects and grasses would have the best prospects of survival.

nucleic acid a complex organic acid made up of a long chain of nucleotides. The two types, known as DNA (deoxyribonucleic acid) and RNA (ribonucleic acid), form the basis of heredity in living organisms.

nucleolus in biology, a structure found in the nucleus of ◊eukaryotic cells. It produces the RNA that makes up the ◊ribosomes, from instructions in the DNA.

nucleus in physics, the positively-charged central part of an ◊atom. Except for hydrogen, the nuclei contain ◊neutrons as well as ◊protons. Surrounding the nuclei are ◊electrons, which contain a negative charge equal to the protons, thus giving the atom a neutral charge.

nucleus in biology, the central part of a ◊eukaryotic cell, containing the chromosomes.

Nuffield William Richard Morris, Viscount Nuffield 1877–1963. British manufacturer and philanthropist. Starting with a small cycle-repairing business, he designed in 1910 a car that could be produced cheaply, and built up Morris Motors Ltd at Cowley, Oxford.

nugget piece of gold found as a lump of the ◊native ore. Nuggets occur in ◊alluvial deposits where river-borne particles of the metal have adhered to one another.

nuisance in law, interference with enjoyment of, or rights over, land. In English law there are two kinds of nuisance. *Private nuisance* affects a particular occupier of land, such as noise from a neighbour; the aggrieved occupier can apply for an ◊injunction and claim ◊damages. *Public nuisance* affects an indefinite number of members of the public, such as obstructing the highway; it is a criminal offence. In this case, an individual can only claim damages if he is affected more than the general public.

Nujoma Sam 1929– . Namibian politician, president from 1990, founder and leader of ◊SWAPO from 1959. He was exiled in 1960 and controlled guerrillas from Angolan bases until the first free elections were held 1989, taking office early the following year.

Nukau'lofa capital and port of Tonga on Tongatapu; population (1986) 29,000.

numbat Australian banded anteater *Myrmecobius fasciatus*. It is brown with white stripes on the back, and has a long tubular tongue to gather termites and ants. The body is about 25 cm/10 in long, and the tongue can be extended 10 cm/4 in.

number a symbol used in counting or measuring. In mathematics, there are various kinds of numbers. The everyday number system is the decimal system, using the base 10. Real numbers include all rational numbers (integers, or whole numbers, and fractions), and irrational numbers (those not expressible as fractions). Complex numbers include the real and unreal numbers (real number multiples of the square root of -1). The ◊binary number system, used in computers, has 2 as its base.

Numidia Roman N African territory ('nomads' land'), modern E Algeria.

numismatics the study of ◊coins and medals.

nun a woman belonging to a religious order under the vows of poverty, chastity, and obedience, and living under a particular rule. Christian convents are ruled by a superior (often elected), who is subject to the authority of the bishop of the diocese or sometimes directly to the pope. See ◊monasticism.

nuncio a diplomatic representative of the pope, from the 16th century performing the functions of a papal ambassador.

Nuremberg (German *Nürnberg*) industrial city (electrical and other machinery, precision instruments, textiles, toys) in Bavaria, Germany; population (1988) 467,000. From 1933 the Nuremberg rallies were held here, and in 1945 the Nuremberg trials.

Nuremberg rallies the annual meetings of the German ◊Nazi Party. They were characterized by extensive marches in party formations and mass rallies addressed by Nazi leaders such as Hitler and Goebbels.

Nuremberg Trials after World War II, the trials of the 24 chief ◊Nazi war criminals Nov 1945–Oct 1946 by an international military tribunal consisting of four judges and four prosecutors: one of each from the UK, USA, USSR, and France. An appendix accused the German cabinet, general staff, high command, Nazi leadership corps, ◊SS, ◊Sturm Abteilung, and ◊Gestapo of criminal responsibility.

Nureyev Rudolf 1938–1993. Russian dancer and choreographer. A soloist with the Kirov Ballet, he defected to the West during a visit to Paris 1961. Mainly associated with the Royal Ballet, and Margot ◊Fonteyn's principal partner, he was one of the most brilliant dancers of the 1960s and 1970s.

nursery rhyme jingle current among children. Usually limited to a couplet or quatrain with strongly marked rhythm and rhymes, nursery rhymes have often been handed down by oral tradition.

nursing supervision of health as well as care of the sick, the very young, the very old, and the disabled. Organized training first originated 1836 in Germany, and was developed in Britain by the work of Florence ◊Nightingale who, during the Crimean War, established standards of scientific, humanitarian care in military hospitals.

nut the common name for a dry, single-seeded fruit that does not split open to release the seed. It is formed from more than one carpel, but only one seed becomes fully formed, the remainder aborting. The wall of the fruit, the pericarp, becomes hard and woody, forming the outer shell. The term is also popularly used to describe various hard-shelled fruits and seeds, including almonds and walnuts, which are really the stones of ◊drupes, and Brazil nuts and shelled peanuts, which are both seeds. The kernels of most nuts provide a concentrated food with about 50% fat, and a protein content of 10–20%, though a few, such as chestnuts, are high in carbohydrates and have only a moderate (5%) protein content. Most nuts are produced by perennial trees and bushes. While the majority are obtained from plantations, considerable quantities of Brazil and pecan nuts are still collected from the wild. Current estimates suggest that world production in the mid-1980s was about four million tonnes per year. They aso provide edible and industrial oils.

nutation in astronomy, a slight 'nodding' of the Earth in space, caused by the varying gravitational pulls of the Sun and Moon. Nutation changes the angle of the Earth's axial tilt (average 23.5°) by about 9 seconds of arc to either side of its mean position, a complete side-to-side nodding taking just over 18.5 years.

nutation in botany, the spiral movement exhibited by the tips of certain stems during growth; it enables a climbing plant to find a suitable support. The direction of the movements, clockwise or

nuthatch

European
nuthatch

Nyerere Tanzanian politician and premier Dr Julius
Nyerere, 1960.

anticlockwise, is usually characteristic for particular species. Nutation sometimes also occurs in tendrils and flower stalks.

nutcracker bird *Nucifraga caryocatactes* of the crow family found in areas of coniferous forest in Asia and parts of Europe, particularly mountains. About 33 cm/1.1 ft long, it has a speckled plumage and powerful beak. It feeds particularly on conifer seeds.

nuthatch European bird *Sitta europaea* about the size of a sparrow, with a blue-grey back and buff breast. It is a climber, and feeds chiefly upon nuts. The nest is built in a hole in a tree, and five to eight white eggs with reddish-brown spots are laid in early summer.

nutmeg kernel of the seed of the evergreen tree *Myristica fragrans*, native to the Moluccas. Both the nutmeg and its secondary covering known as mace are used as a spice in cookery.

nutrition the science of food, and its effect on human life and health.

Nuuk Greenlandic for ◊Godthaab, capital of Greenland.

nyala antelope *Tragelaphus angasi* found in the thick bush of S Africa. About 1 m/3 ft at the shoulder, it is greyish-brown with thin vertical white stripes. Males have horns up to 80 cm/2.6 ft long.

Nyasa former name for Lake ◊Malawi.

Nyasaland former name (until 1964) for ◊Malawi.

Nyerere Julius (Kambarage) 1922– . Tanzanian socialist politician, president 1964–85. Originally

a teacher, he devoted himself from 1954 to the formation of the Tanganyika African National Union and subsequent campaigning for independence. He became chief minister 1960, was prime minister of Tanganyika 1961–62, president of the newly formed Tanganyika Republic 1962–64, first president of Tanzania 1964–85, and head of the Organization of African Unity 1984.

nylon a synthetic fibre-forming plastic, which is similar in chemical structure to protein. It is used in the manufacture of toilet articles, textiles, and medical sutures. Nylon is particularly suitable for hosiery and woven goods, simulating other materials such as silks and furs; it is also used in carpets.

nymph in Greek mythology, a guardian spirit of nature. *Hamadryads* or *dryads* guarded trees; *naiads*, springs and pools; *oreads*, hills and rocks; and *nereids*, the sea.

nymph in entomology, the immature form of insects which do not have a pupal stage, for example, grasshoppers and dragonflies. Nymphs generally resemble the adult (unlike ◊larvae), but do not possess fully formed reproductive organs or wings.

o/a abbreviation for **on account**.

oak tree and shrub of the genus *Quercus*, family Fagaceae, with over 300 known species widely distributed in temperate zones. They are valuable for their timber, the wood being durable and straight grained. Their fruits are called acorns.

Oakley Annie (Phoebe Annie Oakley Mozee) 1860–1926. American sharpshooter, member of Buffalo Bill's Wild West Show (see William ◊Cody).

Oaks horse race, one of the English classics. Run at Epsom racecourse in Jun (normally two days after the ◊Derby) it is for three-year-old fillies only. The race is named after the Epsom home of the 12th Earl of Derby.

oarfish oceanic fish *Regalecus glesne*, in the family of ribbon-fishes. Occasionally up to 9 m/30 ft long, it has no scales, a small mouth, large eyes, and a compressed head.

OAS abbreviation for ◊*Organization of American States*.

oasis area of land made fertile by the presence of water in an otherwise arid region. The occurrence of oases dictates the distribution of plants, animals, and people in the desert regions of the world.

Oastler Richard 1789–1861. British social reformer, born in Leeds. He opposed child labour and the ◊Poor Law of 1834, winning the nickname of 'the Factory King', and was largely responsible for securing the Factory Act of 1833 and the Ten Hours Act of 1847.

oat type of grass, genus *Avena*, and an important cereal food. The plant has long, narrow leaves, and a stiff straw stem; the panicles of flowers, and later of grain, hang downwards. The cultivated oat *Avena sativa* is produced for human and animal food.

Oates Titus 1649–1705. British conspirator. A priest, he entered the Jesuit colleges at Valladolid, Spain, and St Omer, France, as a spy in 1677–78, and on his return to England announced he had discovered a 'Popish Plot' to murder Charles II and re-establish Catholicism. Although this story was almost entirely false, many innocent Roman Catholics were executed during 1678–80 on Oates's evidence. In 1685 he was flogged, pilloried, and imprisoned for perjury. He was pardoned and granted a pension after the revolution of 1688.

oath a solemn promise to tell the truth or perform some duty, combined with an appeal to a deity or something held sacred.

OAU abbreviation for ◊*Organization of African Unity*.

Ob river in Asian Russia, flowing 3,380 km/2,100 mi from the Altai mountains through the W Siberian Plain to the Gulf of Ob in the Arctic Ocean. With its main tributary, the *Irtysh*, it is 5,600 km/3,480 mi.

OBE Order of the British Empire, a British order of knighthood.

Oberammergau village in Bavaria, West Germany, where a Christian passion play has been performed every ten years (except during the world wars) since 1634 to commemorate the ending of the plague.

Oberon king of the elves or fairies, and, according to a 13th-century French romance *Huon of Bordeaux*, an illegitimate son of Julius Caesar. Shakespeare used the character in *A Midsummer Night's Dream*.

obesity condition of being overweight (generally, 20% or more above the desirable weight for your sex and height).

obi or **obeah** a form of witchcraft practised in the West Indies. It combines elements of Christianity and African religions, such as snake worship.

obit (Latin 'he/she died') found, for example, in inscriptions on tombstones, followed by a date.

oboe a musical instrument of the ◊woodwind family. Played vertically, it is a wooden tube with a

oat

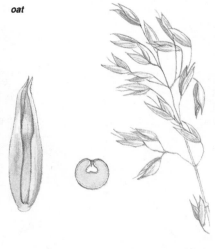

oak

bell, is double-reeded, and has a yearning, poignant tone. The range is almost three octaves.

Obote (Apollo) Milton 1924– . Ugandan politician who led the independence movement from 1961. He became prime minister 1962 and was president 1966–71 and 1980–85, being overthrown by first Idi ◊Amin and then Brig Tito Okello.

Obrenovich a Serbian dynasty which ruled 1816–42 and 1859–1903. The dynasty engaged in a feud with the rival house of Karageorgevich, which obtained the throne by the murder of the last Obrenovich in 1903.

obscenity laws in Britain, laws prohibiting the publishing of any material which tends to deprave or corrupt. Obscene material can be, for example, pornographic, violent, or encourage drug taking. Publishing includes distribution, sale, and hiring of the material. There is a defence of public good, if the defendant can produce expert evidence to show that publication was in the interest of, for example, art, science or literature.

observation in science, the perception of a phenomenon, for example, examining the Moon through a telescope, watching mice to discover their mating habits, or seeing how a plant grows.

observatory a site or facility for observation of natural phenomena. The earliest recorded observatory was at Alexandria, built by Ptolemy Soter, *c.* 300 BC. The modern observatory dates from the invention of the telescope. Most were near towns, but with the advent of big telescopes, clear skies, and hence high, remote sites, became essential. The most powerful optical telescopes covering the sky from the northern hemisphere are Mount ◊Palomar; Kitt Peak, Arizona; La Palma, Canary Islands; and Mount Semirodniki, Caucasus, USSR. Radio astronomy observatories include ◊Jodrell Bank; the Mullard, Cambridge, England; ◊Arecibo; Effelsberg, West Germany; and ◊Parkes. In the 1970s optical telescopes were established at Cerro Tololo, Las Campanas, and La Silla, Chile; and ◊Siding Spring. Observatories are also carried on aircraft or sent into orbit as satellites, in space stations, and in the Space Shuttle.

obsession repetitive unwanted thought that is often recognized by the sufferer as being irrational, but which nevertheless causes distress. It can be associated with a compulsion where the individual feels an irresistible urge to carry out a repetitive series of actions.

obsidian a glassy volcanic rock, chemically similar to ◊granite, but formed by cooling rapidly on the Earth's surface at low pressure.

obstetrics the medical specialty concerned with the management of pregnancy, childbirth, and the immediate post-natal period.

O'Casey Sean 1884–1964. Irish dramatist. His first plays are tragi- comedies, blending realism with symbolism and poetic with vernacular speech: *The Shadow of a Gunman* 1922, and *Juno and the Paycock* 1925 were followed by *The Plough and the Stars* 1926. Later plays include *The Star Turns Red* 1940, *Oak Leaves and Lavender* 1946 and *The Drums of Father Ned* 1960.

occultation in astronomy, the temporary obscuring of a star by a body in the Solar System. Occultations are used to provide information about changes in an orbit, and the structure of objects in space, such as radio sources.

occupational psychology the study of human behaviour at work. It includes dealing with problems in organizations, advising on management difficulties, and investigating the relationship between humans and machines (as in the design of aircraft controls). Another important area is ◊psychometrics and the use of assessment to assist in selection of personnel.

ocean great mass of salt water. There are strictly three oceans – ◊Atlantic, ◊Indian, and ◊Pacific – to which the Arctic is usually added. They cover approximately 70 per cent of the total surface area of the Earth: 363,000,000 sq km/140,000,000 sq mi.

oceanarium large display tank in which aquatic animals and plants live together much as they would in their natural environment.

Oceania the islands of the S Pacific (◊Micronesia, ◊Melanesia, ◊Polynesia). The term is sometimes taken to include ◊Australasia and the ◊Malay archipelago, in which case it is considered as one of the seven continents.

ocean ridge topographical feature of the seabed indicating the presence of a constructive plate margin (produced by the movements of ◊plate tectonics). It can rise many thousands of metres above the surrounding abyssal plain.

ocean trench topographical feature of the seabed indicating the presence of a destructive plate margin (produced by the movements of ◊plate tectonics). The subduction or dragging downwards of one plate of the ◊lithosphere beneath another means that the ocean floor is pulled down.

Oceanus in Greek mythology, the god (one of the ◊Titans) of a river supposed to encircle the earth. He was the progenitor of other river gods, and the nymphs of the seas and rivers.

ocelot wild ◊cat of Central and South America, up to 1 m/3 ft long with a 45 cm/1.5 ft tail. It weighs about 18 kg/40 lbs, and has a pale yellow coat marked with longitudinal stripes and blotches.

O'Connell Daniel 1775–1847. Irish politician, called 'the Liberator'. In 1823 he founded the Catholic Association to press Roman Catholic claims. Although ineligible as a Roman Catholic to take his seat, he was elected MP for County Clare in 1828, and so forced the government to grant Catholic emancipation. In Parliament he cooperated with the Whigs in the hope of obtaining concessions until 1841, when he launched his campaign for repeal of the union.

O'Connor Feargus 1794–1855. Irish parliamentary follower of ◊O'Connell. He sat in parliament 1832–35 and as editor of the *Northern Star* became the most influential figure of the Chartist movement (see ◊Chartism).

O'Connor Flannery 1925–1964. US Southern novelist and story writer. Her works have a great sense of evil and sin, and often explore the religious sensibility of the Deep South. Her powerful short stories are collected in *A Good Man Is Hard to Find* 1955 and *Everything That Rises Must Converge* 1965.

OCR (*optical character recognition*) the technology for transforming written material directly into computer-readable codes. A scanning light beam is reflected from the text onto photoreceptors which convert it into electrical signals.

Octans constellation containing the southern celestial pole. It represents the octant.

Octavian original name of ◊Augustus, the first Roman emperor.

October Revolution the second stage of the ◊Russian Revolution 1917.

Octobrists a group of Russian liberal constitutional politicians who accepted the reforming October

ocean

Wildlife in oceans ultimately depends on the tiny floating plants, the phytoplankton, that live in the lighted surface waters (the euphotic zone).

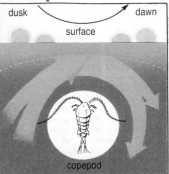

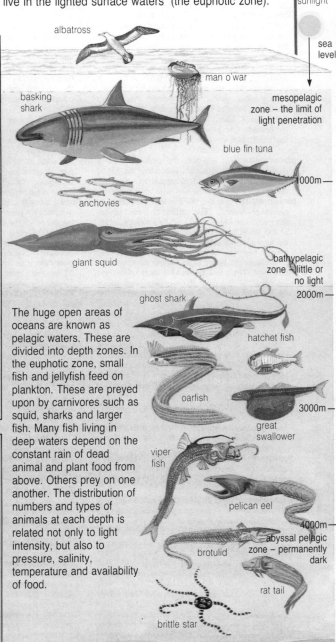

Phytoplankton cease photosynthesizing at dusk and at night use the food they have produced for growth. By dawn each day, their mass may have doubled. Small floating animals, the zooplankton, such as copepods, migrate to the surface at dusk to feed on the plants when these are most nutritious. They return to deep water at dawn, allowing the phytoplankton to regenerate.

Snaggle tooth fish, such as this, live in deep waters, where their luminous skin spots lure small fish, squid, and shrimps into their mouths.

The huge open areas of oceans are known as pelagic waters. These are divided into depth zones. In the euphotic zone, small fish and jellyfish feed on plankton. These are preyed upon by carnivores such as squid, sharks and larger fish. Many fish living in deep waters depend on the constant rain of dead animal and plant food from above. Others prey on one another. The distribution of numbers and types of animals at each depth is related not only to light intensity, but also to pressure, salinity, temperature and availability of food.

octopus

Manifesto instituted by Tsar Nicholas II after the 1905 revolution and rejected more radical reforms.

octopus type of ◊cephalopod having a round or oval body, and eight arms with rows of suckers on each. They occur in all temperate and tropical seas, where they feed on crabs and other small animals. They can vary their coloration according to their background, and can swim with their arms or by a type of jet propulsion by means of their funnel. They are as intelligent as some vertebrates.

ODA abbreviation for *Overseas Development Adminstration*.

ode lyric poem of complex form and charged emotion, originally chanted in ancient Greece to a musical accompaniment. Exponents include Sappho, Pindar, Horace and Catullus, and among English poets: Spenser, Milton and Dryden.

Odessa seaport in the Ukraine, USSR, on the Black Sea, capital of Odessa region; population (1985) 1,126,000. Products include chemicals, pharmaceuticals, and machinery. Odessa was founded by Catherine II in 1795 near the site of an ancient Greek settlement.

Odin chief god of Scandinavian mythology, the **Woden** or **Wotan** of the Germanic peoples. A sky god, he is resident in Asgard, at the top of the world-tree, and receives the souls of heroic slain warriors from the Valkyries, the 'divine maidens', feasting with them in his great hall, Valhalla. The wife of Odin is ◊Frigga or Freya, and ◊Thor is their son. Wednesday is named after him.

Odoacer 433–493. King of Italy from 476, when he deposed Romulus Augustulus, the last Roman emperor. He was a leader of the barbarian mercenaries employed by Rome. He was overthrown and treacherously killed by Theodoric the Great, king of the Ostrogoths.

Odysseus the chief character of Homer's *Odyssey*, mentioned also in the *Iliad* as one of the most prominent leaders of the Greek forces at the siege of Troy. He is said to have been the ruler of the island of Ithaca. Among the Greek heroes Odysseus was distinguished for his sagacity.

Odyssey Greek epic poem in 24 books, probably written before 700 BC, attributed to Homer. It describes the voyage of Odysseus after the fall of Troy and the vengeance he takes on the suitors of his wife Penelope on his return. During his ten-year wanderings he has many adventures including encounters with the Cyclops, Circe, Scylla and Charybdis, and the Sirens.

OE abbreviation for *Old English*; see ◊English language.

OECD abbreviation for ◊*Organization for Economic Cooperation and Development*.

oedema waterlogging of the tissues due to excessive loss of plasma through the capillary walls into the tissues. It may be generalized (the condition once known as dropsy) or confined to one area, such as the ankles.

Oedipus in Greek legend, king of Thebes. Left to die at birth because his father Laius had been warned by an oracle that his son would kill him, he was saved and brought up by the King of Corinth. Oedipus killed Laius in a quarrel (without recognizing him) and married his mother Jocasta. After four children had been born, the truth was discovered. Jocasta hanged herself, Oedipus blinded himself, and as an exiled wanderer was guided by his daughter, Antigone.

Oedipus complex in psychology, term coined by ◊Freud for the unconscious antagonism of a son to his father, whom he sees as a rival for his mother's affection. For a girl antagonistic to her mother for the same reason, the term is *Electra complex*.

oersted ◊c.g.s. unit of magnetic field strength (Oe), defined as the field strength that would exert a force of 1 dyne on a unit magnetic pole in a vacuum; equal to $\frac{1}{4}\pi \times 10^3$ amperes per metre (SI system). It is named after Hans Christian ◊Oersted.

Oersted Hans Christian 1777–1851. Danish physicist who founded the science of electromagnetism. He discovered the ◊magnetic field associated with an electric current in 1820.

oesophagus the passage by which food travels from mouth to stomach. The human oesophagus is about 23 cm/9 in long. Its upper end is at the bottom of the ◊pharynx, immediately behind the windpipe.

oestrogen a group of hormones produced by the ◊ovaries of vertebrates, the term is also used for various synthetic hormones which mimic their effects. The principal oestrogen in mammals is oestradiol. Oestrogens promote the development of female secondary sexual characteristics in mammals, stimulate egg production, and prepare the lining of the uterus for pregnancy.

oestrus in mammals, the period during a female's reproductive cycle (also known as the oestrus cycle or ◊menstrual cycle) when mating is most likely to occur. It usually coincides with ovulation.

Offa died 796. King of Mercia, England from 757. He conquered Essex, Kent, Sussex, and Surrey, defeated the Welsh and the West Saxons, and established Mercian supremacy over all England S of the Humber.

Offaly county of the Republic of Ireland, in the province of Leinster, between Galway on the W and Kildare on the E; area 1,997 sq km/771 sq mi; population (1981) 58,300.

Offa's Dyke a defensive earthwork along the Welsh border, of which there are remains from the mouth of the river Dee to that of the river Severn. It represents the boundary secured by ◊Offa's wars with Wales.

Offenbach Jacques 1819–1880. French composer. He wrote light opera, initially for presentation at the Bouffes-Parisiens, of which he held the lease. His most widely known works are *Orphée aux enfers/Orpheus in the Underworld* 1858, *La Belle Hélène* 1864, and *Les Contes d'Hoffmann/The Tales of Hoffmann* 1881.

office automation the introduction of computers and other electronic equipment to support an office routine. Increasingly, over the past decade, computers have been used to support administrative tasks such as document processing, filing, mail, and diary management; project planning and management accounting have also been computerized. All these are now being integrated.

oil oil refinery at Stanlow, near Ellesmere Port, Cheshire, UK.

Official Secrets Act UK act of Parliament of 1911, which superseded that of 1889 and introduced new sections making it an offence for anyone who had ever served the crown to communicate to any person information acquired in that service, whether it is harmful to the state or not.

offset litho the most common method of ◊printing, which uses smooth printing plates. It works on the principle of ◊lithography, that grease and water repel one another. The printing plate is prepared using a photographic technique, resulting in a type image which attracts greasy printing ink. On the printing press the plate is wrapped around a cylinder and wetted and inked in turn. The ink adheres only to the type area, and this image is then transferred via an intermediate blanket cylinder to the paper.

O'Flaherty Liam 1897–1984. Irish author whose novels of ◊Fenian activities in county Mayo include *The Neighbour's Wife* 1923, *The Informer* 1925, and *Land* 1946.

Ogbomosho city and commercial centre in W Nigeria, 80 km/50 mi NE of Ibadan; population (1981) 590,600.

Ogden C(harles) K(ay) 1889–1957. British writer and scholar. With I A ◊Richards he developed the simplified form of English known as ◊Basic English. Together they wrote *Foundations of Aesthetics* 1921 and *The Meaning of Meaning* 1923.

Oglethorpe James Edward 1696–1785. English soldier. He joined the Guards, and in 1732 obtained a charter for the colony of Georgia, intended as a refuge for debtors and for European Protestants.

OGPU name 1923–34 of the Soviet secret police, later the ◊KGB.

O'Higgins Bernardo 1776–1842. Chilean revolutionary. He was a leader of the struggle for independence from Spanish rule 1810–17, and head of the first permanent national government 1817–23.

Ohio midwest state of the USA; nicknamed Buckeye State
area 106,714 sq km/41,222 sq mi
capital Columbus
towns Cleveland, Cincinnati, Toledo, Akron, Dayton, Youngstown
products coal, cereals, livestock, machinery, chemicals, steel
population (1990) 10,847,100

famous people Thomas Edison, John Glenn, Paul Newman, Gen Sherman, Orville Wright; six presidents (Garfield, Grant, Harding, Harrison, Hayes, and McKinley)
history ceded to Britain by France in 1763, and first settled by Europeans 1788, it became a state in 1803.

Ohm Georg Simon 1787–1854. German physicist who promulgated what is known as Ohm's law 1827. It states that the steady current in a metallic circuit is directly proportional to the constant total ◊electromotive force in the circuit.

OHMS abbreviation for *On Her (His) Majesty's Service*.

oil inflammable substance, usually insoluble in water, and chiefly composed of carbon and hydrogen. Oils may be solids (fats) or liquids. There are three main types: *essential oils*, used in perfumes and for flavouring; *fixed oils* obtained from both animals and plants (oil crops); and *mineral oils* obtained chiefly from petroleum.

oil crop plant from which vegetable oils are pressed from the seeds. All arable agricultural regions have their characteristic oil crops. Cool temperate areas grow rapeseed and linseed; warm temperate regions produce sunflowers, olives, and soyabeans; tropical regions produce groundnuts, oil palm, and coconuts. Some of the major vegetable oils such as soyabean oil, groundnut oil, and cottonseed oil are derived from crops grown primarily for other purposes. Most vegetable oils are used as both edible oils and ingredients in industrial products such as soaps, varnishes, printing inks, and paints.

oil palm type of ◊palm tree *Elaeis guineensis*, the fruit of which yields valuable oils, used as food or processed into margarine, soaps, and livestock feeds.

okapi animal *Okapia johnstoni* of the giraffe family, though with much shorter legs and neck, found in the tropical rainforests of central Africa. Purplish brown with creamy face and black and white stripes on the legs and hindquarters, it is excellently camouflaged. Unknown to Europeans until 1901, only a few hundred are thought to survive.

O'Keeffe Georgia 1887–1986. US painter, based mainly in New York and New Mexico, known for her large, semi-abstract studies of flowers and skulls.

Okhotsk, Sea of arm of the N Pacific between the Kamchatka Peninsula and Sakhalin, and bordered southward by the Kurile Island; area 937,000 sq km/361,700 sq mi. Free of ice only in summer, it is often fogbound.

Okinawa largest of the Japanese ◊Ryukyu Islands in the W Pacific

okapi

female okapi

oil drilling

Offshore rigs are used to extract oil from the seabed. These are some of the largest structures ever built and can contain living quarters for 300 workers.

The largest rigs are floating platforms called semi-submersible rigs. They are anchored to the seabed by cables and chains. Large air tanks below the surface keep the rig stable.

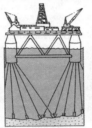

The simplest and earliest kind of rig is the fixed-leg platform. This stands on rigid legs which are fixed to the seabed. Some of these fixed-leg rigs are as tall as the Empire State Building in New York.

Trapped gas or water may exert sufficient pressure on oil-bearing rocks to force oil up to the surface. Pumps, such as 'nodding donkey' pumps, may have to be used to raise the oil.

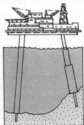

The gravity platform has large concrete tanks at its base. Oil from several wells is collected in the tanks. The great weight pins it to the seabed and no piles are needed to secure it.

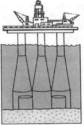

'nodding donkey' pumps

gas well

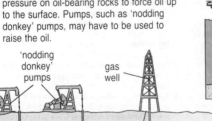

sedimentary rock layers

fault

oil wells

Oil, water and natural gas are found in certain formations of layered rock. Impermeable rock layers stop the oil rising and a pool is formed containing water covered by a layer of oil and a layer of gas.

impervious layer

gas

impervious layer

oil

oil

water

impervious layer

impervious layer

area 2,250 sq km/869 sq mi
capital Naha
population (1990) 3,145,500
history captured by the USA in the *Battle of Okinawa* 1 Apr–21 Jun 1945 with 47,000 US casualties (12,000 dead) and 60,000 Japanese (only a few hundred survived as prisoners); the island was returned to Japan 1972.

Oklahoma SW state of the USA; nicknamed Sooner State
area 181,088 sq km/69,919 sq mi
capital Oklahoma City
towns Tulsa
products cereals, peanuts, cotton, livestock, oil, natural gas, helium, machinery and other metal products
population (1990) 3,145,600
famous people Woody Guthrie, Will Rogers
history the region was acquired with the ◊Louisiana Purchase in 1803.

Oklahoma City industrial city (oil refining, machinery, aircraft, telephone equipment), capital of Oklahoma, USA, on the Canadian river; population (1990) 444,700.

okra type of ◊hibiscus plant, with edible fruit known as *bhindi* or ladies' fingers.

Okubo Toshimichi 1831–1878. Japanese ◊samurai leader whose opposition to the Tokugawa shogunate made him a leader in the Meiji restoration (see ◊Mutsuhito) 1866–68.

Okuma Shigenobu 1838–1922. Japanese politician and prime minister. Helping to found the Jiyuto (Liberal party) in 1881, but became prime minister briefly in 1898 and again in 1914 when he presided over Japanese pressure for territorial concessions in China before retiring in 1916.

Olaf five kings of Norway including:

Olaf I, Tryggvesson 969–1000. King of Norway from his election 995. He began the conversion of Norway to Christianity, and was killed in a sea battle against the Danes and Swedes.

Olaf II, Haraldsson 995–1030. King of Norway from 1015. He offended his subjects by his centralizing policy and zeal for Christianity, and was killed in battle by Norwegian rebel chiefs backed by ◊Canute of Denmark. He was declared the patron saint of Norway in 1164.

Olav V 1903–1991. King of Norway from 1957, when he succeeded his father Haakon VII; a well-loved monarch, Olaf was succeeded by his son Harald V.

Olbrich Joseph Maria 1867–1908. Viennese architect who worked under Otto ◊Wagner and was opposed to the over-ornamentation of Art Nouveau. His most important buildings, however, remain Art Nouveau in spirit: the Vienna Sezession 1897–98, the Hochzeitsturm 1907, and the Tietz department store in Düsseldorf, Germany.

Old Bailey popular name for the Central Criminal Court in London, situated in a street of that name in the City of London, off Ludgate Hill.

Old Catholic one of various breakaway groups from Roman Catholicism, including those in Holland (such as the *Church of Utrecht*, who separated from Rome 1724 after accusations of ◊Jansenism) and groups in Austria, Czechoslovakia, Germany, and Switzerland, who rejected the proclamation of ◊papal infallibility of 1870. Old Catholic clergy are not celibate.

Oldenbarnvelt Johan van 1547–1619. Dutch politician, a leading figure in the Netherlands struggle for independence from Spain, who helped William I negotiate the Union of Utrecht 1579.

Oldenburg Claes 1929– . US pop artist, known for *soft sculptures*, gigantic replicas of every-day objects and foods, made of stuffed canvas or vinyl.

Old English another term for ◊Anglo-Saxon; see also ◊English language.

Oldfield Bruce 1950– . Engish fashion designer. He set up his own business in 1975. His evening wear has been worn by the royal family and other well-known personalities.

Old Moore's Almanac annual publication in the UK containing prophecies of the events of the following year. It was first published in 1700, under the title *Vox Stellarum/Voices of the Stars*, by Francis Moore (1657–*c*. 1715).

Old Pretender nickname of ◊James Francis Edward Stuart, the son of James II of England.

Old Testament Christian term for the Hebrew ◊Bible, which is the first part of the Christian Bible. It contains 39 (according to Christians) or 24 (according to Jews) books, which include the history of the Jews and their covenant with God, prophetical writings and religious poetry. The first five books are traditionally ascribed to Moses and known as the Pentateuch (by Christians) or the Torah (by Jews).

Olduvai Gorge deep cleft in the Serengeti steppe, Tanzania, where the ◊Leakeys found prehistoric stone tools in the 1930s. They discovered 1958–59 Pleistocene remains of prehumans and gigantic animals. The gorge has given its name to the *Olduvai culture*, a simple stone-tool culture of prehistoric hominids, dating from 2–0.5 million years ago.

Old Vic theatre in south London, former home of the National Theatre (1963–76).

oleander or *rose bay* an evergreen Mediterranean shrub *Nerium oleander*, family Apocynaceae, with pink or white flowers and leaves which secrete the poison oleandrin.

O level, General Certificate of Education in the UK, formerly the examination usually taken at 16 by the most able children. It was superseded by the ◊GCSE in 1988.

Oligocene third epoch of the Tertiary period of geological time, 38–25 million years ago. The name, from Greek, means 'a little recent', referring to the presence of some modern types of animals at that time.

oligopoly in economics, a situation in which few companies control the major part of a particular market and concert their actions to perpetuate such control. This may include an agreement to fix prices (a ◊cartel).

Olivares Count-Duke of (born Gaspar de Guzmán) 1587–1645. Spanish prime minister 1621–43. He overstretched Spain in foreign affairs, and unsuccessfully attempted domestic reform. He committed Spain to recapturing the Netherlands and to involvement in the Thirty Years' War 1618–48, and his efforts to centralize power led to revolts in Catalonia and Portugal, which brought about his downfall.

olive evergreen tree *Olea europaea* of the family Oleaceae. Native to Asia but widely distributed in Mediterranean and subtropical areas, it grows up to 15 m/50 ft high, with twisted branches and opposite, lance-shaped leaves. The white flowers are followed by bluish-black oval fruits, which are eaten or pressed to make olive oil.

olive branch an ancient symbol of peace; in the Bible (Genesis 9), the dove brings back an olive branch to Noah to show that the flood has abated.

Oman
Sultanate of
(*Saltanat 'Uman*)

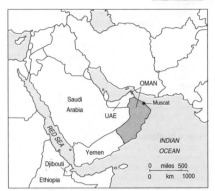

area 212,000 sq km/82,000 sq mi
capital Muscat
towns Salalah

physical mountains and a high arid plateau; fertile coastal strip
head of state and government Qaboos bin Said from 1970
political system absolute monarchy
exports oil, dates, silverware, copper
currency Omani rial
population (1990 est) 1,305,000; annual growth rate 3%
life expectancy men 55, women 58
language Arabic (official)
religion Ibadhi Muslim 75%, Sunni Muslim, Shi'ite Muslim, Hindu
literacy 20% (1989)
GNP $7.5 bn (1987); $5,070 per head
chronology
1951 The Sultanate of Muscat and Oman achieved full independence. Treaty of friendship with Britain signed.
1970 After 38 years' rule, Sultan Said bin Taimur replaced in coup by his son Qaboos bin Said. Name changed to Sultanate of Oman.
1975 Left-wing rebels in the S defeated.
1982 Memorandum of Understanding with the UK signed, providing for consultation on international issues.
1985 Diplomatic ties established with USSR.
1991 Sent troops to Operation Desert Storm as part of the coalition opposing Iraq's occupation of Kuwait.

Oliver Isaac *c.* 1556–1617. British painter of miniatures, originally a Huguenot refugee, who studied under Nicholas ◊Hilliard. He became a court artist in the reign of James I. Famous sitters include the poet John Donne.

Olives, Mount of a range of hills E of Jerusalem, important in the Christian religion: a former chapel (now a mosque) marks the traditional site of Jesus Christ's ascension to heaven, and the Garden of Gethsemane was at its foot.

Olivier Laurence Kerr, Baron Olivier 1907–1989. British actor-director. For many years associated with the Old Vic, he was director of the National Theatre company 1962–73, and the Olivier Theatre (part of the National Theatre on the South Bank, London) was named after him. His major stage roles include Henry V, Hamlet, Richard III and Archie Rice in *The Entertainer*. His acting and direction of filmed versions of Shakespeare's plays received outstanding critical acclaim, for example *Henry V* 1944 and *Hamlet* 1948. Famous early films include *Wuthering Heights* and *Rebecca*.

olivine or *chrysolite* a greenish mineral, magnesium iron silicate, $(Mg,Fe)_2SiO_4$. It is an important rock-forming mineral in such rocks as gabbro and basalt.

olm cave-dwelling aquatic salamander *Proteus anguinus* found along the E Adriatic seaboard in Italy and Yugoslavia. About 25 cm/10 in long the 'adult' is permanently larval in form, with external gills. See ◊neoteny.

Olympia sanctuary in the W Peloponnese, ancient Greece, with a temple of Zeus, and the stadium (for foot races, boxing, wrestling) and hippodrome (for chariot and horse races), where the original ◊Olympic games were held.

Olympic Games sporting contests originally held in Olympia, ancient Greece, every four years during a sacred truce; records were kept from 776 BC. Women were forbidden to be present and the male contestants were naked. The ancient games were abolished 394 AD. The modern games were revived in 1896 by Frenchman Pierre de Fredi, Baron de Coubertin (1863–1937).

Olympus (Greek *Olimbos*) several mountains in Greece and elsewhere, the most famous being *Mount Olympus* in N Thessaly, Greece, a group of hills in which the high point is 2,918 m/9,570 ft. In ancient Greece it was considered the abode of the gods.

OM abbreviation for ◊*Order of Merit*.

Om sacred word in Hinduism, which is used to begin prayers and is placed at the beginning and end of

Olympic Games Bas relief on the base of a statue c. 510 BC, Athens Museum, showing a pair of wrestlers practising, a runner in the start position, and a javelin thrower.

books. It is composed of three syllables, symbolic of the Hindu Trimurti, or trinity of gods.

Oman country on the Arabian peninsula, bounded to the W by the United Arab Emirates, Saudi Arabia, and South Yemen.

Omar 581–644. Adviser of the prophet Muhammad. In 634 he succeeded Abu Bakr as caliph (civic and religious leader of Islam), and conquered Syria, Palestine, Egypt, and Persia. He was assassinated by a slave. The Mosque of Omar in Jerusalem is attributed to him.

Omar Khayyam *c.* 1050–1123. Persian astronomer and poet. Born in Nishapur, he founded a school of astronomical research and assisted in reforming the calendar. The result of his observations was the *Jalāli* era, begun in 1079. In the West, Omar Khayyam is chiefly known as a poet through ◊Fitzgerald's version of the *The Rubaiyat of Omar Khayyam* 1859.

Omayyad dynasty Arabian dynasty of the Islamic empire who reigned as caliphs 661–750. They were overthrown by Abbasids, but a member of the family escaped to Spain and in 756 assumed the title of emir of Córdoba. His dynasty, which took the title of caliph in 929, ruled in Córdoba until the early 11th century.

ombudsman person appointed to safeguard citizens' rights against encroachment by the government or its employees. The post is of Scandinavian origin: it was introduced in Sweden 1809, Denmark 1954, and Norway 1962, and spread to other countries in the 1960s. The ombudsman investigates complaints of injustice that would otherwise have no hope of redress.

The first Commonwealth country to appoint an ombudsman was New Zealand 1962; the UK followed 1966 with a parliamentary commissioner; and Hawaii was the first US state to appoint an ombudsman, 1967. The UK Local Government Act 1974 set up a local ombudsman, or commissioner for local administration, to investigate maladministration by local councils, police, health or water authorities.

Omdurman city in the republic of Sudan, on the White Nile, opposite Khartoum; population (1983) 526,500.

omnibus a road conveyance for several passengers, more commonly known as a ◊bus.

omnivore an animal which feeds on both plant and animal material. Omnivores have digestive adaptations intermediate between those of ◊herbivores and ◊carnivores, with relatively unspecialized digestive systems and gut microorganisms which can digest a variety of foodstuffs.

Omsk industrial city (agricultural and other machinery, food processing, sawmills, oil refining) in Russia, capital of Omsk region, W Siberia; population (1987) 1,134,000. The refineries are linked with Tuimazy in Bashkiria by a 1,600 km/1,000 mi pipeline.

onager type of wild ass *Equus hemionus* found in W Asia. They are sandy brown, lighter underneath, and about the size of a small horse.

Onassis Aristotle (Socrates) 1906–1975. Turkish-born Greek shipowner. During the 1950s he was one of the first shipbuilders to build supertankers. In 1968 he married Jacqueline Kennedy, widow of US president John F Kennedy.

oncology the branch of medicine concerned with the diagnosis and treatment of cancer.

O'Neill Eugene (Gladstone) 1888–1953. US playwright, widely regarded as the leading US dramatist between World Wars I and II. His best plays are characterized by a down-to-earth quality, although often experimental in form, and include *Anna Christie* 1922, *Desire under the Elms* 1924, *The Iceman Cometh* 1946, and the posthumously produced autobiographical drama *Long Day's Journey into Night* 1956 (written 1940). Nobel prize 1936.

O'Neill Terence, Baron O'Neill of the Maine 1914–1990. Northern Irish Unionist politician. In the Ulster government he was minister of finance 1956–63, prime minister 1963–69. He resigned when opposed by his party on measures to extend rights to Roman Catholics, including a universal franchise.

onion bulbous plant *Allium cepa* of the family Liliaceae. Cultivated from ancient times, it may have originated in Asia. The edible part is the bulb, containing an acrid volatile oil and having a strong flavour.

online system in computing, a system that allows the computer to work interactively with its users, responding to each instruction as it is given and prompting users for information when necessary, as opposed to a ◊batch system. Since the fall in the cost of computers in the 1970s, online operation has become increasingly attractive commercially.

o.n.o. abbreviation for *or near(est) offer.*

onomatopoeia a ◊figure of speech whose Greek name means 'name-making', on the principle of copying natural sounds. Thus, the word or name 'cuckoo' arises out of imitating the sound that the cuckoo makes.

Ontario central province of Canada
area 1,068,587 sq km/412,582 sq mi
capital Toronto
towns Hamilton, Ottawa (federal capital), London, Windsor, Kitchener, Sudbury
products nickel, iron, gold, forest products, motor vehicles, iron and steel, paper, chemicals, copper, uranium
population (1986) 9,114,000
history an attempt in 1841 to form a merged province with French-speaking Quebec failed, and Ontario became a separate province of Canada in 1867.

Ontario, Lake smallest and easternmost of the Great Lakes, on the US-Canadian border; area 19,200 sq km/7,400 sq mi. It is connected to Lake Erie by the Welland Canal, and drains into the St Lawrence River. Its main port is Toronto.

ontogeny the process of development of a living organism, including the part of development that takes place after hatching or birth. The idea that 'ontogeny recapitulates phylogeny', proposed by the German scientist Haeckel, is now discredited.

onus (Latin) a burden or responsibility.

onyx a semiprecious variety of the mineral ◊silica in which the crystals are too fine to be detected microscopically (cryptocrystalline). It has straight parallel bands of different colours: milk-white, black, and red.

oolite a limestone made up of tiny spherical structures. Called ooliths, these structures can be up to 2 mm in diameter and have a concentric structure – under the microscope they have an aniseed ball appearance. They were formed by chemical accretion on an ancient sea floor.

Oort Jan Hendrik 1900–1992. Dutch astronomer. In 1927, he calculated the mass and size of the Galaxy, and the Sun's distance from its centre, from the observed movements of stars around the Galaxy's centre. In 1950 Oort proposed that comets exist in a vast swarm, now called the *Oort Cloud*, at the edge of the Solar System.

oosphere another name for the female gamete or ◊ovum of certain plants such as algae.

ooze ◊sediment of fine texture consisting mainly of organic matter found on the ocean floor at depths greater than 2,000 m/6,700 ft. Several kinds of ooze exist, each named after its constituents.

opal a non-crystalline form of ◊silica, often occurring as stalactites and found in many types of rock. The common opal is opaque, milk-white, yellow, red, blue, or green, and lustrous. The precious opal is colourless, having innumerable cracks from which emanate brilliant colours produced by minute crystals of cristobalite.

Op art movement in modern art, especially popular in the 1960s. It uses scientifically based optical effects that confuse the spectator's eye. Precisely painted lines or dots are arranged in carefully regulated patterns that create an illusion of surface movement. Exponents include Victor Vasarely and Bridget Riley.

op. cit. abbreviation for *opere citato* (Latin 'in the work cited').

OPEC abbreviation for ◊*Organization of the Petroleum Exporting Countries.*

opencast mining also called open-pit mining, it is mining at the surface rather than underground. Coal, iron ore, and phosphates are often extracted by opencast mining. Often the mineral deposit is covered by soil, which must first be stripped off, usually by huge excavators, such as walking draglines and bucketwheel excavators. Then the ore deposit is broken up by explosives.

Open College in the UK, an initiative launched by the Manpower Services Commission (now the ◊Training Commission) to enable people to gain and update technical and vocational skills by means of distance teaching, such as correspondence, radio, and television.

open-door policy economic philosophy of equal access by all nations to another nation's markets.

open-hearth furnace once the most important method of steelmaking, now largely superseded by the ◊basic-oxygen process. The open-hearth furnace was developed in England by German-born William and Friedrich Siemens and improved by Pierre and Emile Martin in 1864. In the furnace molten pig iron and scrap are packed into a shallow hearth and heated by overhead gas burners using preheated air.

open shop factory or other business employing men and women not belonging to trades unions, as opposed to the ◊closed shop, which employs trades unionists only.

Open University an institution established in the UK in 1969 to enable mature students without qualifications to study to degree level without regular attendance. Open University teaching is based on a mixture of correspondence courses, TV and radio lectures and demonstrations, personal tuition organized on a regional basis, and summer schools.

opera dramatic work in which singing takes the place of speech. In opera the music accompanying the action has paramount importance, although dancing and spectacular staging may also play their part. Opera originated in late 16th-century Florence when a number of young poets and musicians attempted to reproduce in modern form the musical declamation, lyrical monologues, and choruses of classical Greek drama.

opera buffa (Italian 'comic opera') a type of humorous opera, with characters taken from everyday life; it is contrasted with ◊opera seria. The form began as a musical intermezzo in the 18th century, which was then adopted in Italy and France for complete operas. An example is Rossini's *The Barber of Seville.*

opéra–comique (French 'comic opera') opera which includes text to be spoken, not sung; thus, Bizet's *Carmen* is an example. The distinction was important since of the two Paris opera houses in the 18th–19th centuries, the *Opéra* (which aimed at setting a grand style) allowed no spoken dialogue, unlike the *Opéra–Comique.*

opera seria (Italian 'serious opera') a type of opera distinct from opera buffa, or humorous opera. Common in the 17th-18th centuries, it tended to formality and frigidity. Examples include many of Handel's operas.

operating system (OS) in computing, a program that controls the routine operations of a computer. It is sometimes called DOS (disc operating system) when the program also controls the disc. The operating system looks after the computer's filing system and handles the input and output of data and programs between the processor unit, external memory devices (such as disc drives), and input and output devices (such as keyboard and screen).

operations research a business discipline which uses logical analysis to find solutions to managerial and administrative problems, such as the allocation of resources, inventory control, competition, and the identification of information needed for decision-making.

operetta a light opera, which may use spoken dialogue.

operon a group of genes that are found next to each other on a chromosome, and are turned on and off as an integrated unit. They usually produce enzymes that control different steps in the same biochemical pathway. Operons were discovered (by the French biochemists F Jacob and J Monod) in bacteria; they are less common in higher organisms where the control of metabolism is a more complex process.

Ophiuchus large constellation of the equatorial region of the sky, known as the serpent bearer. The Sun passes through Ophiuchus each Dec, although the constellation is not part of the zodiac. Ophiuchus contains ◊Barnard's Star.

ophthalmia inflammation of the eye.

ophthalmology the medical specialty concerned with diseases of the eye and its surrounding tissues.

opiates, endogenous naturally produced chemicals in the body which have effects similar to morphine and other opiate drugs. These include ◊endorphins and encephalins.

opinion poll attempt to measure public opinion by taking a survey of the views of a representative sample of the electorate. The first accurately sampled opinion poll was carried out by the statistician George ◊Gallup during the US presidential election 1936. Opinion polls have encountered criticism on the grounds their publication influence the outcome of an election.

opium drug extracted from the unripe seeds of the opium poppy *Papaver somniferum* of SW Asia. An addictive narcotic, it contains several alkaloids, the most important being *morphine*, one of the most powerful natural painkillers and addictive narcotics known, and *codeine*, a milder painkiller.

Opium Wars wars waged in the mid-19th century by the UK against China to enforce the opening of Chinese ports to trade in opium. Opium from British India paid for Britain's imports from China, such as porcelain, silk, and,

Oppenheimer US physicist J Robert Oppenheimer.

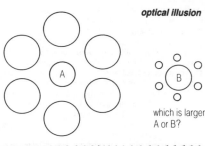

which is larger A or B?

are the two inner lines parallel?

above all, tea, then obtainable in bulk only from China.

The *First Opium War 1839–42*, between Britain and China, resulted in the cession of Hong Kong to Britain and the opening of five treaty ports, licensed for foreign trade. Other European states were also subsequently given concessions.

A *Second Opium War 1856–60* followed between Britain and France in alliance against China, when there was further Chinese resistance, notably in Canton, one of the treaty ports. At its close the Summer Palace in Beijing was set on fire. China was forced to ratify the treaty of Tientsin 1858 which gave the European states even more trading privileges at the expense of the Chinese.

Oporto (Portuguese *Porto*) industrial city (textiles, leather, pottery) in Portugal, on the Douro, 5 km/3 mi from its mouth; known for the export of port; population (1984) 327,500.

opossum the only marsupial native to North America, of the family Didelphidae. Opossums are arboreal, nocturnal animals, with prehensile tails, and hands and feet well adapted for grasping. They can grow to the size of a cat, are carnivorous and insectivorous.

Oppenheimer Robert 1904–1967. US physicist. As director of the Los Alamos Science Laboratory 1943–45, he was in charge of the development of the atomic bomb (the ◊Manhattan Project). He objected to the development of the H-bomb, and was declared a security risk in 1953 by the US Atomic Energy Commission.

opportunity cost in economics, that which has been foregone in order to achieve an objective. A family may choose to buy a new television and forego their annual holiday; the holiday represents the opportunity cost.

opposition in astronomy, the moment at which the longitude of a body in the solar system differs from

that of the Sun by 180°, so that it lies opposite the Sun in the sky and crosses the meridian at about midnight. The term also applies to the alignment of the two bodies at this moment.

Opposition, Leader of His/Her Majesty's in British politics, official title (from 1937) of the leader of the largest opposition party in the House of Commons.

optical computer a computer in which both light and electrical signals are used in the CPU (central processing unit). The technology is still not fully developed, but such a computer promises to be faster and less vulnerable to outside electrical interference than one that relies solely on electricity.

optical contouring computerized monitoring of a light pattern projected onto a patient to detect discrepancies in movements during breathing.

optical fibre very fine optically pure glass fibre through which light can be reflected to transmit an image or information from one end to the other. Bundles of such fibres are used in ◊endoscopes to inspect otherwise inaccessible parts of machines or of the living body. Optical fibres are increasingly being used to replace copper wire in telephone cables, the messages being coded as pulses of light rather than a fluctuating electric current.

optical illusion a scene or picture that fools the eye. An example of a natural optical illusion is that the moon appears bigger when it is on the horizon than it does when it is high in the sky, due to the ◊refraction of light rays by the Earth's atmosphere.

optics scientific study of light and vision, for example shadows and mirror images, and lenses, microscopes, telescopes, and cameras. Light rays travel for all practical purposes in straight lines, although ◊Einstein has demonstrated that they may be 'bent' by a gravitational field. On striking a surface they are reflected or refracted with some attendant absorption of energy, and the study of these facts is the subject of geometrical optics.

option in business, a contract giving the owner the right (as opposed to the obligation, as with ◊futures contracts) to buy or sell a specific quantity of a particular commodity or currency at a future date and at an agreed price, in return for a premium. The buyer or seller can decide not to exercise the option if it would prove disadvantageous.

opto-electronics a branch of electronics concerned with the development of devices (based on the semiconductor gallium arsenide) which

optical fibre spray of glass fibre optics consisting of 2,000 individual strands each measuring 60 microns thick.

orang-utan

respond not only to the ◊electrons of electronic data transmission, but also to ◊photons.

opuntia   genus to which the ◊prickly pear belongs.

opus   (Latin 'work') in music, a term, used with a figure, to indicate the numbering of a composer's works, usually in chronological order.

opus anglicanum   ecclesiastical embroidery produced in England from *c.* 900–*c.* 1500. It was characterized by its use of rich materials.

Opus Dei   a Roman Catholic institution aiming at the dissemination of the ideals of Christian perfection, particularly in intellectual and influential circles. Founded in Madrid in 1928, and still powerful in Spain, it is now international. Its members may be of either sex, and lay or clerical.

oracle   Greek sacred site where answers (also called oracles) were given by a deity to enquirers about future events; these were usually ambivalent, so that the deity was proved right whatever happened. The earliest was probably at Dodona (in ◊Epirus), where priests interpreted the sounds made by the sacred oaks of ◊Zeus, but the most celebrated was that of Apollo at ◊Delphi.

Oracle   the ◊teletext system operated in Britain by Independent Television, introduced in 1973. See also ◊Ceefax.

oral literature   stories which are or have been transmitted in spoken form, such as public recitation, rather than through writing or printing. Most preliterate societies seem to have had a tradition of oral literature, including short 'folk tales', legends, proverbs, and riddles as well as longer narrative works; and most of the ancient epics – such as the Greek *Odyssey* and the Mesopotamian *Gilgamesh* – seem to have been composed and added to over many centuries before they were committed to writing.

Oran   (Arabic **Wahran**)   seaport in Algeria; population (1984) 663,500. Products include iron, textiles, footwear, and processed food. It was part of the Ottoman Empire except 1509–1708 and 1732–91 under Spanish rule.

Orange, House of   the royal family of the Netherlands. The title is derived from the small principality of Orange, in S France, held by the family from the 8th century to 1713. They held considerable possessions in the Netherlands, to which, after 1530, was added the German county of Nassau.

orange   evergreen tree of the genus *Citrus*, remarkable for bearing blossom and fruit at the same time. Thought to have originated in SE Asia, they are commercially cultivated in Spain, Israel, Brazil, S Africa, USA, and elsewhere. The *sweet orange*

Citrus sinensis is the one commonly eaten fresh; the Jaffa, blood, and navel orange are varieties within this species. Oranges yield several essential oils.

Orange Free State   province of the Republic of South Africa
area 129,152 sq km/49,866 sq mi
capital Bloemfontein
products grain, wool, cattle, gold, oil from coal, cement, pharmaceuticals
population (1985) 1,775,500 (1,445,000 ethnic Africans)
history Original settlements from 1810 were complemented by the ◊Great Trek, and it was recognized by Britain as independent in 1854.

Orangeman   member of the Ulster Protestant *Orange Society* established 1795 in opposition to the United Irishmen and the Roman Catholic secret societies. It was a revival of the Orange Institution 1688, formed in support of William (III) of Orange, the anniversary of whose victory over the Catholic James II at the Battle of the Boyne 1690 is commemorated by Protestants in parades on 12 Jul.

Orange, Project   plan 1980 for a white South African 'homeland' (Projek Oranje) to be established on the border between Orange Free State and the Northern Cape. No black person would be allowed to live or work there.

orang-utan   anthropoid ape *Pongo pygmaeus*, found solely in Borneo and Sumatra. Up to 1.65 m/5.5 ft in height, it is covered with long red-brown hair, and mainly lives a solitary, arboreal life, feeding chiefly on fruit. Now an endangered species, it is officially protected, and is threatened by habitat destruction (logging, forest clearance for farming).

Orasul Stalin   name 1948–56 of the Romanian town ◊Braşov.

Oratorian   a member of the Roman Catholic order of secular priests, called in full *Congregation of the Oratory of St Philip Neri*, formally constituted by Philip Neri in 1575 in Rome, and characterized by the degree of freedom allowed to individual communities. The churches of the Oratorians are noted for their music.

oratorio   musical setting of religious texts, scored for orchestra, chorus, and solo voices, on a scale more dramatic and larger than a cantata.

orbit   the path of one body in space around another, such as the orbit of Earth around the Sun, or the Moon around Earth. When the two bodies are similar in mass, as in a ◊double star, both bodies move around their common centre of mass. The movement of objects in orbit follows ◊Kepler's laws, which apply to artificial satellites as well as to natural bodies.

orchestra   A group of musicians playing together, usually on a variety of different instruments. In contemporary Western music, the term orchestra is commonly applied to an ensemble containing bowed string instruments with more than one player to a part, which may also include wind, brass, and percussion instruments. The format varies considerably according to the needs of composers.

orchestration   the scoring of a composition for orchestra.

orchid   plant of the family Orchidaceae containing some 18,000 species, distributed throughout the world except in the coldest areas, and most numerous in damp equatorial regions. The flowers have three sepals and three petals and are sometimes solitary, but more usually borne in spikes, racemes or panicles, either erect or drooping.

orchid

Orczy Baroness Emmusca 1865–1947. Hungarian-born novelist, best remembered for *The Scarlet Pimpernel* 1905.

ordeal in medieval times, method of testing guilt of an accused person based on a belief in heaven's protection of the innocent. Examples of such ordeals are walking barefoot over glowing ploughshares, dipping the hand into boiling water, and swallowing consecrated bread (causing the guilty to choke).

order in classical architecture, the column (including capital, shaft, and base) and the entablature, considered as an architectural whole. The five orders are Doric, Ionic, Corinthian, Tuscan, and Composite. See also ◊column.

order in biological classification, a group of related ◊families. For example, the horse, rhinoceros, and tapir families are grouped in the order Perissodactyla, the odd-toed ungulates, because they all have either one or three toes on each foot. The names of orders are not shown in italic (unlike genus and species names) and by convention they all have the ending -formes (birds and fish), -a (mammals, amphibians, reptiles, and other animals), or -ales (fungi and plants). Related orders are grouped together in a ◊class.

order in council in the UK, an order issued by the sovereign with the advice of the Privy Council; in practice it is issued only on the advice of the cabinet. Acts of Parliament often provide for the issue of orders in council to regulate the detailed administration of their provisions or they may be used to introduce wartime emergency legislation.

Order of Merit British order of chivalry founded in 1902 by Edward VII and limited in number to 24.

ordination religious ceremony by which a person is accepted into the priesthood or monastic life in various religions. Within the Christian church, ordination authorizes a person to administer the sacraments. The Roman Catholic and Eastern Orthodox churches refuse to ordain women.

Ordnance Survey official department for the mapping of Britain, established 1791.

Ordovician period of geological time 505–438 million years ago; the second period of the Palaeozoic era. Animal life was confined to the sea: reef-building algae and the first jawless fish.

ore deposit of ◊sediment or a body of ◊rock worth mining for the economically valuable minerals it contains.

Oregon Pacific state of the USA; nickname Beaver State
area 251,180 sq km/96,981 sq mi
capital Salem
towns Portland, Eugene
products wheat, livestock, timber, gold, silver, nickel, electronics
population (1990) 2,842,300
famous people Linus Pauling

history the Oregon Trail (3,200 km/2,000 mi from Independence, Missouri, to the Columbia river) was the pioneer route across the USA 1841–60.

Orestes in Greek legend, the son of Agamemnon and ◊Clytemnestra.

orfe fish *Leuciscus idus* of the carp family. It grows up to 50 cm/1.7 ft, and feeds on small aquatic animals. Generally greyish-black, an ornamental variety is orange. It lives in rivers and lakes of Europe and NW Asia.

Orff Carl 1895–1982. German composer; best remembered for his scenic cantata *Carmina Burana* 1937, and his operas, including *Antigone* 1949.

Organ musical wind instrument of ancient origin. It developed from the Pan-pipe and hydraulus, and is mentioned as early as the 3rd century BC. Organs were imported to France from Byzantium in the 8th and 9th centuries, after which their manufacture in Europe began. The superseding of the old drawslides by the key system dates from the 11th–13th century, the first chromatic keyboard from 1361. The more recent designs date from the 1809 composition pedal. The modern organ produces sound from varying-sized pipes under applied pressure.

organ in biology, part of a living body, such as the liver, or brain, that has a distinctive function or set of functions.

organelle a discrete and specialized structure in a living cell; organelles include *mitochondria, chloroplasts, lysosomes, ribosomes,* and the *nucleus.*

organic chemistry the chemistry of carbon compounds, particularly the more complex carbon compounds.

organic farming a type of agriculture without synthetic chemicals or fertilizers.

Organisation de l'Armée Secrète (OAS) guerrilla organization formed 1961 by French settlers devoted to perpetuating their own rule in Algeria (Algérie Française). It collapsed on the imprisonment 1962–68 of its leader Gen Raoul Salan.

Organization for Economic Co-operation and Development (OECD) Paris-based international organization of 24 industrialized countries which co-ordinates member states' economic policy strategies. It was founded 1961. Its headquarters are in Paris. The OECD's subsidiary bodies include the International Energy Agency, set up 1974 in the face of a world oil crisis.

Organization of African Unity (OAU) association established 1963 to eradicate colonialism and improve economic, cultural, and political cooperation in Africa; headquarters Addis Ababa, Ethiopia. The French-speaking *Joint African and Mauritian Organization/Organisation Commune Africaine et Mauritienne: OCAM* (1962) works within the framework of the OAU for African solidarity; headquarters Yaoundé, Cameroon.

Organization of American States (OAS) association established 1948, largely concerned with the social and economic development of Latin America; headquarters Washington DC, USA. It is based on the International Union of American Republics 1890–1910 and Pan-American Union 1910–1948, set up to encourage friendly relations between countries of North and South America.

Organization of Central American States (*Organización de Estados Centro Americanos: ODECA*) International association promoting common economic, political, educational, and military aims in Central America. The first organization of this name, established in 1951, was

organic chemistry
common organic molecule groupings

formula	name	atomic bonding
CH_3	Methyl	H—C— with H above and H below
CH_2CH_3	Ethyl	H H / C—C—H / H H
CC	Double bond	C=C
CHO	Aldehyde	—C with H and double-bond O
CH_2OH	Alcohol	—C—OH with H above and H below
CO	Ketone	C=O
COOH	Acid	—C with double-bond O and OH
CH_2NH_2	Amine	H H / —C—N / H H
C_6H_6	Benzene ring	benzene ring structure

superseded by a new one in 1962; membership: Costa Rica, El Salvador, Guatemala, Honduras, and Nicaragua, provision being made for Panama to join at a later date. The permanent headquarters is in Guatemala City.

Organization of the Petroleum Exporting Countries (OPEC) body established in 1961 to co-ordinate price and supply policies of oil-producing states. OPEC members include: Iran, Iraq, Kuwait, Saudi Arabia, Venezuela, Indonesia, Libya, Qatar, United Arab Emirates, Nigeria, Ecuador, and Gabon.

organizer in embryology, a part of the embryo that causes changes to occur in another part, through ◊induction, thus 'organizing' development and ◊differentiation.

orienteering sport of cross-country running and route-finding. Competitors set off at one minute intervals and have to find their way, using map and compass, to various check points (approximately 0.8 km/0.5 mi apart), where their control cards are marked. World championships have been held since 1966.

origami art of folding paper into forms such as dolls and birds, originating in Japan in the 10th century.

Origen c. 185–c. 254. Christian theologian, born in Alexandria, who produced a fancifully allegorical interpretation of the Bible.

original sin Christian doctrine that Adam's fall rendered humankind able to achieve salvation only through divine grace.

Orinoco river in S America, flowing for about 2,400 km/1,500 mi through Venezuela and forming for about 320 km/200 mi the boundary with Colombia; tributaries include the Guaviare, Meta, Apure, Ventuari, Caura, and Caroni. It is navigable by large steamers for 1,125 km/700 mi from its Atlantic delta; rapids obstruct the upper river.

oriole name given to birds, often brightly coloured, of two families. In Africa and Eurasia, orioles belong to the family Oriolidae, such as the golden oriole *Oriolus oriolus*; in the Americas to the Icteridae, such as the bobolink and the Baltimore oriole.

Orion in Greek mythology, a giant of ◊Boeotia, famed as a hunter.

Orion in astronomy, a very prominent constellation in the equatorial region of the sky, representing the hunter of Greek mythology. It contains the bright stars Betelgeuse and Rigel, as well as a distinctive row of three stars that make up Orion's Belt. Beneath the belt, marking the sword of Orion, is the Orion nebula; nearby is one of the most distinctive dark nebulae, the Horsehead.

Orion nebula a luminous cloud of gas and dust 1,500 light years away, in the constellation Orion, from which stars are forming. It is about 15 light years in diameter, and contains enough gas to make a cluster of thousands of stars. At the nebula's centre is a group of hot young stars, called the *Trapezium*, which make the surrounding gas glow. It is visible to the naked eye as a misty patch below the Belt of Orion.

Orissa state of NE India
area 155,782 sq km/60,132 sq mi
capital Bhubaneswar
towns Cuttack, Rourkela
products rice, wheat, oilseed, sugar, timber, chromite, dolomite, graphite and iron
population (1981) 26,370,500
language Oriya (official)
religion Hindu 90%
history administered by the British 1803–1912 as a subdivision of Bengal, it joined with Bihor to become a province; in 1936 Orissa became a separate province and 1948–49 its area was almost doubled before its designation as a state 1950.

Orkney Causeway construction in N Scotland put up in World War I, completed in 1943 during World War II, joining four of the Orkney Islands, built to protect the British fleet from intrusion through the eastern entrances to Scapa Flow. It links Kirkwall and the island by road.

Orkney Islands a group of islands off the N E coast of Scotland.
area 984 sq km/380 sq mi
towns administrative headquarters Kirkwall, on Mainland (Pomona)
products fishing and farming, wind power (Burgar Hill has the world's most productive wind generator; blades 60 m/197 ft diameter)
population (1981) 18,900
history Harold I (Fairhair) of Norway conquered the islands in 876; they were pledged to James III of Scotland 1468 for the dowry of Margaret of

Denmark, and annexed by Scotland (the dowry unpaid) in 1472.

Orlando Vittorio Emanuele 1860–1952. Italian politician, prime minister 1917–19. He attended the Paris Peace Conference after World War I, but dissatisfaction with his handling of the Adriatic settlement led to his resignation. He initially supported Mussolini, but was in retirement 1925–46, when he returned first to the assembly and then the senate.

Ormuzd another name for *Ahura Mazda*, the good god of ◊Zoroastrianism.

ornithology in zoology, the study of birds. It covers scientific aspects relating to their structure and classification, their habits, song, flight, and their value of agriculture as destroyers of insect pests.

ornithophily the ◊pollination of flowers by birds. Ornithophilous flowers are typically brightly coloured, often red or orange. They produce copious quantities of thin, watery nectar, and are scentless because most birds do not respond well to smell. They are found mostly in tropical areas, with hummingbirds being the chief pollinators in N and S America, and the sunbirds in Africa and Asia.

orogeny formation of mountains, by such processes as folding, faulting, and upthrusting (by the action of ◊plate tectonics).

Orozco José Clemente 1883–1949. Mexican painter, known for his murals inspired by the Mexican revolution of 1910, such as the series in the Palace of Government, Guadalajara, 1949.

Orpheus mythical Greek poet and musician. The son of Apollo and a muse, he married Eurydice, who died from the bite of a snake. Orpheus went down to Hades to bring her back and her return to life was granted on condition that he walked ahead of her without looking back. He broke this condition, and Eurydice was irretrievably lost. In his grief, he despised the Maenad women of Thrace, and was torn in pieces by them.

Orphism ancient Greek mystery cult, of which the Orphic hymns formed part of the secret rites which, accompanied by an ascetic regime, were aimed at securing eventual immortality.

orrery a mechanical device for demonstrating the motions of the heavenly bodies. Invented in about 1710 by George Graham, it was named after his patron, the 4th Earl of Orrery. It is the forerunner of the modern ◊planetarium.

orris root the underground stem of a species of iris grown in S Europe. Violet-scented, it is used in perfumery.

Orsini Felice 1819–1858. Italian political activist, a member of the ◊Carbonari secret revolutionary group, who attempted unsuccessfully to assassinate Napoleon III in Paris in Jan 1858. He was subsequently executed, but the Orsini affair awakened Napoleon's interest in Italy and led to a secret alliance with Piedmont at Plombières 1858, directed against Austria.

Ortega (Saavedra) Daniel 1945– . Nicaraguan socialist politician, a member of the Sandinista Liberation Front (FSLN) (which overthrew the regime of Anastasio Somoza in 1979), and head of state 1981–90; he was defeated, after eight years of US-backed opposition from the right-wing Contra guerrillas, by Violeta Chamorro, whose election campaign was heavily supported by the US.

orthochromatic a photographic film or paper of decreased sensitivity, which can be processed with a red safe-light. Bue objects appear lighter and red ones darker because of increased blue sensitivity.

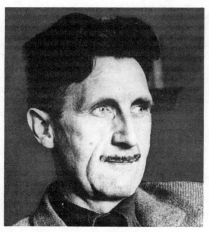
Orwell Novelist and social critic, George Orwell.

orthodontics branch of ◊dentristry, mainly dealing with correction of malocculusion (faulty position of teeth).

Orthodox Church also known as *Eastern Orthodox Church* or *Greek Orthodox Church*, a federation of self-governing Christian churches mainly found in E Europe and parts of Asia. The centre of worship is the Eucharist. There is a married clergy, except for bishops; the Immaculate Conception is not accepted. The highest rank in the church is that of Ecumenical Patriarch, or Bishop of Istanbul. There are approximately 130 million adherents.

orthopaedics the branch of medicine concerned with the surgery of bones and joints.

ortolan bird *Emberiza hortulana* of the bunting family, common in Europe and W Asia, migrating to Africa in the winter. It is brownish, with a grey head, and nests on the ground.

Orton Joe 1933–1967. British dramatist, whose plays include *Entertaining Mr Sloane* 1964, *Loot* 1966, and *What the Butler Saw* 1968. His diaries deal frankly with his personal life. He was murdered by his flatmate Kenneth Halliwell.

Orwell George, pen name of Eric Arthur Blair 1903–1950. British author. His best-known books are the satire *Animal Farm* 1945 and the prophetic

Osaka Osaka Castle, completed 1586, but destroyed several times, took 40,000 workmen three years to construct.

Nineteen Eighty-Four 1949, portraying state control of existence carried to the ultimate extent.

oryx type of large African desert antelope with large horns. The Arabian oryx *Oryx leucoryx* was extinct in the wild, but bred in captivity and has been successfully reintroduced into the wild. The scimitar-horned oryx of the Sahara is also rare. Beisa oryx in East Africa and gemsbok in the Kalahari are more common.

Osaka industrial port (iron, steel, shipbuilding, chemicals, textiles) on Honshu island; population (1985) 2,636,000, metropolitan area 8,000,000. It is the oldest city of Japan, and was at times the seat of government in the 4th–8th centuries.

Osborne John (James) 1929–   . English dramatist and actor. He became well known as an 'angry young man' when his first play, *Look Back in Anger* 1956, in which the hero rebels against middle-class life, was produced.

Osborne House preferred residence of Queen Victoria, for whom it was built in 1845, on the Isle of Wight, England. It was presented to the nation by Edward VII.

Oscar in cinema, popular name for ◊Academy Award.

Oscar two kings of Sweden and Norway:

Oscar I 1799–1859. King of Sweden and Norway from 1844, when he succeeded his father, Charles XIV.

Oscar II 1829–1907. King of Sweden and Norway 1872–1905, king of Sweden until 1907. Younger son of Oscar I. He abandoned the title of king of Norway on the separation of the two kingdoms in 1905.

oscillator generator producing a desired oscillation (vibration). There are many types of oscillator for different purposes involving various arrangements of valves or components such as ◊transistors, ◊inductors, ◊capacitors, and ◊resistors. It is an essential part of a radio transmitter, generating the high-frequency carrier signal necessary for radio communication.

oscillograph instrument for recording oscillations, electrical or mechanical. An *oscilloscope* shows variations in electrical ◊potential on the screen of a ◊cathode-ray tube, by means of deflection of a beam of ◊electrons.

Oshogbo city and trading centre on the river Niger, in W Nigeria, 200 km/125 mi NE of Lagos; population (1986) 405,000. Industries include cotton and brewing.

osier tree or shrub of the willow genus *Salix*, cultivated for basket making, in particular *Salix viminalis*.

Osiris ancient Egyptian god, the embodiment of goodness, who went to rule the underworld, after being killed by ◊Set. The sister-wife of Osiris was ◊Isis or Hathor and their son ◊Horus captured his father's murderer.

Oslo capital and industrial port (textiles, engineering, timber) of Norway; population (1985) 447,500. The first recorded settlement was made by Harald III, but after a fire in 1624, it was entirely replanned by Christian IV and renamed *Christiania* 1624–1924.

Osman I or *Othman I* 1259–1326. Turkish ruler from 1299. He began his career in the service of the ◊Seljuk Turks, but in 1299 he set up a kingdom of his own in Bithynia, NW Asia, and assumed the title of sultan. He conquered a great part of Anatolia, so founding a Turkish empire. His successors were known as 'sons of Osman', from which the term *Ottoman Empire* is derived.

osmosis

before osmosis

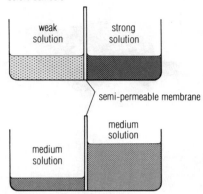

after osmosis

osmium a bluish-white, hard, crystalline metallic element, very heavy and infusible, symbol Os, atomic number 76, relative atomic mass 190.2. It is used for lamp filaments, with iridium to form a very hard alloy suitable for pen-nibs and fine machine bearings, and as a catalyst.

osmoregulation the process whereby the water content of living organisms is maintained at a constant level. If the water balance is disrupted, the concentration of salts will be too high or too low and vital functions, such as nerve conduction, will be adversely affected. In mammals, loss of water by evaporation is counteracted by increased intake and by mechanisms in the kidneys that enhance the rate at which water is resorbed before urine production. Both these responses are mediated by hormones, primarily those of the adrenal cortex (see under ◊adrenal gland).

osmosis movement of solvent (liquid) through a semipermeable membrane separating solutions of different concentrations. The solvent passes from the more dilute solution to the more concentrated solution until the two concentrations are equal. Many cell membranes behave as semipermeable membranes, and osmosis is an important mechanism in the transport of fluids in living organisms, for example in the transport of water from the roots up the stems of plants.

osprey bird of prey *Pandion haliaetus*, known in America from its diet as the fish hawk. Dark brown above and a striking white below, it measures 60 cm/2 ft with a 2 m/6 ft wingspan.

Ossian (Celtic *Oisin*) Irish hero and poet. He is traditionally represented as the son of Finn Mac Cumhaill, *c.* 250, and as having lived to tell the tales of Finn and the Ulster heroes to St Patrick, about 400. The publication from 1760 onwards of the poems of the Scottish writer J Macpherson, attributed to Ossian, made Ossian's name familiar throughout Europe.

ossification the process whereby bone is formed in vertebrate animals by special cells (*osteoblasts*) that secrete layers of ◊extracellular matrix on the surface of the existing ◊cartilage. This matrix is then converted to bone by the deposition within it of calcium phosphate crystals.

osteomalacia literally a softening of the bones, a condition caused by lack of vitamin D in adult life. It results in pain and cramping, bone deformity, and a tendency to spontaneous fracture.

ostrich

otter

petrochemical and other industries. Nobel prize 1909.

Oswald, St *c.* 605–642. King of Northumbria from 634, after killing the Welsh king Cadwallon. Oswald had become a Christian convert during exile on the Scottish island of Iona. With the help of St Aidan he furthered the spread of Christianity until he was defeated and killed by King Penda of Mercia.

Oswiecim (German ◊*Auschwitz*) town in S Poland, site of the World War II concentration and extermination camp.

OT abbreviation for ◊*Old Testament.*

Othello a tragedy by William Shakespeare, first performed 1604–05. Othello, a commander in the Venetian army, is persuaded by Iago that his wife Desdemona is having an affair with his friend Cassio. Othello murders Desdemona; on discovering her innocence, he kills himself.

Othman *c.* 574–656. Arabian caliph (leader of the Islamic empire) from 644, when he was elected; he was a son-in-law of the prophet Muhammad. Under his rule the Arabs became a naval power and captured Cyprus, but Othman's personal weaknesses led to his assassination. He oversaw the final editing of the Koran, the sacred book of Islam.

Othman I another name for the Turkish sultan ◊Osman.

Otho I 1815–1867. King of Greece 1832–62. The 17-year-old son of King Ludwig I of Bavaria, he was selected by the European powers as the first king of independent Greece. He was overthrown by a popular revolt.

otitis inflammation of the ear.

otosclerosis overgrowth of bone in the middle ear causing progressive deafness. This inherited condition is gradual in onset, developing usually before middle age. It is twice as common in women.

Ottawa capital of Canada, in the province of Ontario, on the hills overlooking the river Ottawa, and divided by the Rideau Canal into the Upper (western) and Lower (eastern) Town. Industries include timber, pulp and paper, engineering, food processing, publishing; population (1986), 301,000, metropolitan area (with adjoining Hull, Quebec) 819,000. Founded 1826–32 as Bytown (in honour of John By (1781–1836) whose army engineers were building the Rideau Canal), it was renamed 1854 after the Outaouac Indians.

otter aquatic carnivore of the weasel family found on all continents except Australia. It has thick, brown fur, a long, flattened tail, short limbs, and webbed toes. It is social, playful, and agile.

Otto Nikolaus August 1832–1891. German engineer, who in 1876 patented an effective internal combustion engine.

Otto four Holy Roman Emperors, including:

Otto I 912–973. Holy Roman emperor from 936. He restored the power of the empire, asserted his authority over the pope and the nobles, ended the Magyar menace by his victory at the Lechfeld in 955, and refounded the

---

osteomyelitis infection of bone, with spread of pus along the marrow cavity. Now quite rare, it may ensue from a compound fracture (where broken bone protrudes through the skin), or from infectious disease elsewhere in the body.

osteopathy system of alternative therapy using physical manipulation to treat mechanical stress. It claims to relieve not only postural problems and muscle pain, but asthma and other disorders.

osteoporosis thinning and weakening of bone substance. It is common in older people, affecting more women than men. It may occur in women whose ovaries have been removed unless hormone replacement therapy (HRT) is instituted. Osteoporosis may occur as a side effect of long-term treatment with ◊corticosteroids.

Ostia ancient Italian town and harbour near the mouth of the Tiber. Dating from about 330 BC, it was the port of Rome and at one time had a population of about 100,000; in modern times a seaside resort, *Ostia Mare*, has been established nearby.

Ostpolitik West German chancellor ◊Brandt's policy of reconciliation with the communist bloc from 1971, pursued to a modified extent also by his successors Schmidt and Kohl. Its goal was attained with the reunification of Germany 1990.

ostracism ancient Athenian political device to preserve public order. Votes on pieces of broken pot (Greek *ostrakon*) were used to exile unpopular politicians for ten years.

Ostrava industrial city (iron works, furnaces, coal, chemicals) in the Czech Republic, capital of Severomoravsky region, NE of Brno; population (1991) 327,600.

ostrich flightless bird *Struthio camelus* found in Africa. The male may be about 2.5 m/8 ft tall and weigh 135 kg/300 lb, and is the largest extant bird. It has exceptionally strong legs and feet (two-toed) which enable it to run at high speed, and are also used in defence. It lives in family groups of one cock with several hens.

Ostrogoth member of a branch of the E Germanic people, the ◊Goths.

Ostrovsky Alexander Nikolaevich 1823–1886. Russian playwright, founder of the modern Russian theatre. He is known for *A Family Affair* 1850 and *The Snow Maiden* 1873.

Ostwald Wilhelm 1853–1932. German chemist whose work on catalysts laid the foundations of the

East Mark, or Austria, as a barrier against them.

Otto IV *c.* 1182–1218. Holy Roman emperor, elected 1198. He engaged in controversy with Pope Innocent III, and was defeated by the Pope's ally, Philip of France, at Bouvines in 1214.

Otto cycle the correct name for the ◊four-stroke cycle, introduced by the German engineer Nikolaus Otto in 1876. It improved upon existing engine cycles by compressing the fuel mixture before it was ignited.

Ottoman Empire Muslim empire of the Turks 1300–1920, the successor of the ◊Seljuk Empire. It was founded by ◊Osman I and reached its height with ◊Suleiman in the 16th century. Its capital was Istanbul (formerly Constantinople). At its greatest extent its bounds were Europe as far as Hungary, part of S Russia, Iran, the Palestinian coastline, Egypt, and N Africa. From the 17th century it was in decline. There was an attempted revival and reform under the Young Turk party in 1908, but the regime crumbled when Turkey took the German side in World War I. The sultanate was abolished by Atatürk in 1922; the last sultan was Muhammad VI.

Ouagadougou capital and industrial centre of Burkina Faso; population (1985) 442,000. Products include textiles, vegetable oil, and soap.

Oudh region of N India, now part of Uttar Pradesh. An independent kingdom before it fell under Mogul rule, Oudh regained independence 1732–1856, when it was annexed by Britain. Its capital was Lucknow, centre of the ◊Indian Mutiny 1857–58. In 1877 it was joined with Agra, from 1902 as the United Provinces of Agra and Oudh, renamed Uttar Pradesh 1950.

Oujda industrial and commercial city (lead and coalmining) in N Morocco, near the border with Algeria; population (1982) 260,802.

ounce snow leopard *Panthera uncia* which lives in the mountains of central Asia. It has light cream or grey fur with large black spots, and is similar in size to the leopard.

ounce unit of weight, in ◊avoirdupois the 16th part of a pound which is equal to 437.5 grains (28.3g); also the 12th part of a pound troy which is equal to 480 grains. The *fluid ounce* is a measure of capacity, in the UK equivalent to one twentieth of a pint.

ousel or *ouzel* ancient name of the blackbird. The ring ouzel *Turdus torquatus* is similar to a blackbird, but has a white band across the breast. It is found in Europe in mountainous and rocky country. Water ouzel is another name for ◊dipper.

outback the inland region of Australia.

outlawry in medieval England, a declaration that a criminal was outside the protection of the law, with his or her lands and goods forfeited to the Crown, and all civil rights being set aside. It was a lucrative royal 'privilege'; Magna Carta restricted its use and under Edward III it was further modified. Some outlaws became popular heroes, for example, ◊Robin Hood.

output device in computing, any device for displaying, in a form intelligible to the user, the results of processing done by a computer. The most common output devices are the VDU (visual display unit, or screen) and the printer.

Oval, the a cricket ground in Kennington, London. The home of Surrey County Cricket Club. It was the venue for the first test match between England and Australia in 1880.

ovary in female animals, an organ which generates the ◊ovum. In humans, the ovaries are two whitish rounded bodies about 25 mm/1 in by 35 mm/1.5 in,

located in the abdomen near the ends of the ◊Fallopian tubes. Every month, from puberty to the onset of the ◊menopause, an ovum is released from the ovary. This is called ovulation, and forms part of the ◊menstrual cycle.

In botany, an ovary is the expanded basal portion of the ◊carpel of flowering plants, containing one or more ◊ovules. It is hollow with a thick wall to protect the ovules. Following fertilization of the ovum, it develops into the fruit wall or pericarp.

overdraft in banking, a loan facility on a current account. It allows the account holder to overdraw on his or her account up to a certain limit and for a specified time, and interest is payable on the amount borrowed.

overhead in economics, fixed costs in a business which do not vary in the short term. These might include property rental, heating and lighting, insurance, and administration costs.

overlander one of the Australian drovers who in the 19th century opened up new territory by driving their cattle to new stations, or to market, before the establishment of regular stock routes.

overland telegraph the cable erected 1870–72 linking Port Augusta in S Australia and Darwin in Northern Territory, and the latter by undersea cable to Java: it ended the communications isolation of the Australian continent.

Overlord, operation the Allied invasion of Normandy on 6 Jun 1944 during World War II.

Overseas Development Administration (ODA) UK official body which deals with development assistance to overseas countries, including financial aid on concessionary terms and technical assistance, usually in the form of sending specialists abroad and giving training in the UK.

Ovid full name Publius Ovidius Naso 43–17 BC. Roman poet. His poetry deals mainly with the themes of love *Amores, Ars amatoria*, mythology *Metamorphoses*, and exile *Tristia*.

ovipary a method of animal reproduction in which eggs are laid by the female and develop outside her body, in contrast to ◊ovovivipary and ◊vivipary. It is the most common form of reproduction.

ovule a structure found in seed plants which develops into a seed after fertilization. It consists of an ◊embryo sac containing the female gamete (◊ovum or egg cell), surrounded by nutritive tissue, the nucellus. Outside this there are one or two coverings which provide protection, developing into the testa or seed coat following fertilization. In flowering plants (◊angiosperms) the ovule is within an ◊ovary, but in ◊gymnosperms (conifers and their allies) the ovules are borne on the surface of an ovuliferous (or ovule-bearing) scale, usually with a cone, and are not enclosed by an ovary.

ovum the female gamete (sex-cell) before fertilization. In animals, it is called an egg, and is produced in the ovaries. In plants, where it is also known as an egg-cell or oosphere, the ovum is produced in an ovule. The ovum is non-motile. It must be fertilized by a male gamete before it can develop further, except in cases of ◊parthenogenesis.

Owen David 1938– . British politician, Labour foreign secretary 1977–79. In 1981 he was one of the founders of the ◊Social Democratic Party (SDP), and in 1983 became its leader. Opposed to the decision of the majority of the party to merge with the Liberals 1987, Owen stood down, but emerged 1988 as leader of a rump SDP, which was eventually disbanded 1990. In 1992 he was chosen to replace Lord Carrington as EC mediator in the peace talks on Bosnia-Herzegovina. Together with

owl

barn owl

UN mediator Cyrus Vance, he was responsible for devising a peace plan dividing the republic into 10 semi-autonomous provinces.

Owen Robert 1771–1858. British socialist. He became manager in 1800 of a mill at New Lanark, Scotland, where by improving working and housing conditions and providing schools he created a model community. His ideas did much to stimulate the ◊co-operative movement.

Owen Wilfred 1893–1918. British poet of World War I. His poetry, owing much to encouragement of Siegfried ◊Sassoon, expressed his hatred of war, for example *Anthem for Doomed Youth*, published 1921 after his death.

Owens (James Cleveland) 'Jesse' 1913–1980. US track and field athlete, who excelled in the sprints, hurdles, and the long jump. At the 1936 Olympics he won four gold medals.

owl bird of the order Strigiformes, found worldwide. They are mainly nocturnal birds of prey, with mobile heads, soundless flight, acute hearing, and forward-facing eyes, set round with rayed feathers. All species lay white eggs, and begin incubation as soon as the first is laid. They disgorge indigestible remains of their prey in pellets (castings).

ox the castrated male of domestic species of ◊cattle, used in Third World countries for ploughing and other agricultural purposes; also the extinct wild ox or aurochs of Europe, and extant wild species.

oxalic acid $(COOH)_2.2H_2O$ a white, poisonous solid, soluble in water, alcohol, and ether. Oxalic acid is found in rhubarb, and its salts (oxalates) occur in wood sorrel and other plants. It is used in the leather and textile industries, in dyeing and bleaching, ink manufacture, metal polishes, and for removing rust and ink stains.

oxbow lake curved lake found on the floodplain of a river. Oxbows are caused by the loops of

Owens *The US track and field athlete Jesse Owens during an exhibition of the long jump at White City, London, 1936.*

◊meanders being cut off at times of flood and the river subsequently adopting a shorter course. The US term is bayou.

Oxbridge generic term for Oxford and Cambridge, the two oldest universities in the UK.

OXFAM (*Ox*ford Committee for *Fam*ine Relief) established in the UK 1942 by Canon Theodore Richard Milford (1896–1987), initially to assist the starving people of Greece, and subsequently to relieve poverty and famine worldwide, and fund long-term aid projects.

Oxford and Asquith Earl of title of British Liberal politician Herbert Henry ◊Asquith.

Oxford Movement known also as the *Tractarian Movement* or *Catholic Revival* a movement that attempted to revive Catholic religion in the Church of England. Cardinal Newman dated the movement from the Anglican cleric John Keble's sermon in Oxford in 1833. The Oxford Movement by the turn of the century had transformed the face of the Anglican communion, and is represented today by Anglo-Catholicism.

Oxfordshire county in S central England
area 2,608 sq km/1,006 sq mi
towns administrative headquarters Oxford; Abingdon, Banbury, Henley-on-Thames, Witney, Woodstock
products cereals, cars, paper, bricks, cement
population (1991) 553,800
famous people Flora Thompson, Winston Churchill.

oxide a compound of oxygen and another element, for example nitrous oxide, N_2O ('laughing gas').

Oxon. abbreviation for *Oxoniensis* (Latin 'of Oxford').

oxpecker African bird, genus *Buphagus*, of the starling family. It clambers about the bodies of large mammals, feeding on ticks and other parasites.

oxyacetylene torch a gas torch that burns acetylene in pure oxygen, producing a high-temperature (3000°C) flame. It is widely used in welding to fuse metals. In the cutting torch, a jet of oxygen burns through metal already melted by the oxyacetylene flame.

oxygen a colourless, odourless, tasteless, gaseous element, slightly soluble in water, symbol O, atomic number 8, relative atomic mass 16.00. The only gas able to support respiration, it is just as essential for almost all combustion, and is used in high-temperature welding and improving blast-furnace working.

oxymoron a ◊figure of speech, whose Greek name means 'sharply dull' or 'pointedly foolish'. It is the bringing together of two words or phrases that are normally kept apart as opposites, in order to startle. 'Bittersweet' is an oxymoron, as are 'cruel to be kind' and 'beloved enemy'.

oxytocin a hormone which stimulates the uterus in late pregnancy to initiate and sustain labour. After birth, it stimulates the uterine muscles to contract, reducing bleeding at the site where the placenta was attached.

oyster bivalve mollusc with the upper valve flat, the lower concave, hinged by an elastic ligament. The mantle, lying against the shell, protects the inner body, which includes respirative, digestive, and reproductive organs. Oysters are distinguished by their change of sex, which may alternate annually or more frequently, and by the number of their eggs – a female may discharge up to a million eggs during a spawning period.

oyster catcher wading bird allied to the plovers. The common oyster catcher of European coasts,

Haemotopus ostralegus, is black and white, with a long red beak to open shellfish.

oz abbreviation for ◊*ounce*.

ozalid process a copying process used, for example, to produce printing proofs from film images. The film is placed on top of chemically treated paper, and then exposed to ultraviolet light. The image is developed using ammonia.

Ozark Mountains area in USA (shared by Arkansas, Illinois, Kansas, Mississippi, Oklahoma) of ridges, valleys, and streams, highest point only 700 m/2,300 ft; area 130,000 sq km/50,000 sq mi.

ozone O_3 a highly reactive blue gas, comprising three atoms of oxygen. It is formed when the molecule of the stable form of oxygen (O_2) is split by ultraviolet radiation or electrical discharge. It forms a layer in the upper atmosphere, which protects life on Earth from ultraviolet rays, a cause of skin cancer. At lower levels it contributes to the ◊greenhouse effect.

p in music, abbreviation for *piano* (Italian 'softly').

pace (Latin) with deference to, followed by a name, used to acknowledge contradiction of the person named.

pacemaker a medical device fitted to patients whose hearts beat irregularly. It delivers minute electric shocks to stimulate the heart muscles at certain times. The latest ones are powered by radioactive ◊isotopes for long life, and are implanted in the patient's body.

Pachomius, St 292–346. Egyptian Christian, the founder of the first Christian monastery, near Dendera on the river Nile. Originally for Copts, the monastic movement soon spread to the Greeks.

Pacific Islands United Nations trust territory in the W Pacific comprising over 2,000 islands and atolls, under Japanese mandate 1919–47, and administered by the USA 1947–80, when all its members, the ◊Carolines, ◊Marianas (except ◊Guam), and ◊Marshall Islands, became independent.

Pacific Ocean world's largest ocean, extending from Antarctica to the Bering Strait; area 166,242,500 sq km/64,170,000 sq mi; average depth 4,188 m/13,745 ft; greatest depth of any ocean 11,034 m/36,214 ft in the ◊Mariana Trench.

Pacific Security Treaty military alliance agreement between Australia, New Zealand, and USA, signed 1951 (◊ANZUS).

Pacific War war 1879–83 by an alliance of Bolivia and Peru against Chile. Chile seized Antofagasta and the coast between the mouths of the rivers Loa and Paposo, rendering Bolivia completely landlocked, and also annexed the southern Peruvian coastline from Arica to the mouth of the Loa, with the nitrate fields of the Atacama Desert.

pacifism belief that violence, even in self-defence, is unjustifiable under any condition, and that arbitration is preferable to war as a means of solving disputes.

Packer Kerry (Francis Bullmore) 1937– . Australian media proprietor, currently chair of Consolidated Press Holdings Ltd in Australia. He is involved in promoting Australian sport and in 1977 was instrumental in contracting Australian Test cricketers to make up a world series cricket team.

Padua (Italian *Padova*) city in N Italy, 45 km/25 mi W of Venice; population (1988) 224,000. The astronomer Galileo taught at the university, founded 1222.

paediatrics or *pediatrics* the medical specialty concerned with the care of children.

paedomorphosis in biology, an alternative term for ◊neoteny.

Paestum ancient Greek city, near Salerno in S Italy, founded about 600 BC. There are a number of temple ruins.

Pagan archaeological site in Myanmar with the ruins of the former capital (founded 847, taken by Kublai Khan 1287). These include Buddhist temples with wall paintings of the great period of Burmese art (11th–13th centuries).

Paganini Niccolò 1782–1840. Italian violinist, a soloist from the age of nine. He composed works for the violin which ingeniously exploit every potential of the instrument.

Page Earle (Christmas Grafton) 1880–1961. Australian politician. He represented Australia in the British war cabinet 1941–42, and as minister of health 1949–56 introduced Australia's health scheme 1953.

Page Frederick Handley 1885–1962. British aircraft engineer, founder of one of the earliest aircraft-manufacturing companies 1909, and designer of long-range civil aeroplanes and multi-engined bombers in both World Wars.

pageant originally the wagon on which medieval ◊mystery plays were performed. The term was later applied to the moving, spectacular procession of songs, dances, and tableaux which became fashionable during the 1920s.

Paganini *A drawing by Ingres of the Italian violinist and composer Paganini.*

Paine *Portrait after George Romney (c. 1880) National Portrait Gallery, London.*

Pakistan
Islamic Republic of

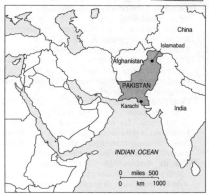

area 796,100 sq km/307,295 sq mi; one-third of Kashmir is under Pakistani control
capital Islamabad
towns Karachi (largest city and port), Lahore
physical fertile Indus plain in E; Baluchistan plateau in W, mountains in N and NW
head of state Ghulam Ishaq Khan from 1988
head of government Nawaz Sharif from 1990
political system emergent democracy
exports cotton textiles, rice, leather, carpets
currency Pakistan rupee

population (1990 est) 113,163,000 (66% Punjabi, 13% Sindhi); annual growth rate 3.1%
language Urdu and English (official); Punjabi, Sindhi, Pashto, Baluchi, local dialects
religion Sunni Muslim 75%, Shi'ite Muslim 20%, Hindu 4%
literacy 40% male/19% female (1985 est)
GDP $39 bn (1988); $360 per head
chronology
1947 Independence achieved from Britain; Pakistan formed following partition of India.
1956 Proclaimed a republic.
1958 Military rule imposed by Gen Ayub Khan.
1971 Secession of East Pakistan (Bangladesh); after civil war, power transferred to Zulfiqar Ali Bhutto.
1977 Bhutto overthrown in military coup by Gen Zia ul-haq; martial law imposed.
1979 Bhutto executed.
1981 Islamization process expedited.
1985 Non-party elections held, amended constitution adopted, martial law and ban on political parties lifted.
1986 Agitation for free elections launched by Benazir Bhutto.
1988 Zia introduced Islamic legal code, the *Shariah*. He was killed in a military air crash Aug; Benazir Bhutto elected prime minister Nov.
1989 Pakistan rejoined the Commonwealth.
1990 Army mobilized in support of Muslim separatists in Indian Kashmir; Bhutto dismissed.
1991 Privatization and economic deregulation programme launched.
1992 Floods devastated N of the country. Pakistan elected to UN Security Council 1993–95.

Pahlavi dynasty Iranian dynasty founded by Riza Khan (1877–1944), an army officer who seized control of the government 1921, and was proclaimed Shah 1925. During World War II Britain and the USSR were nervous of his German sympathies, and occupied Iran 1941–46. They compelled him to abdicate in favour of his son Mohammed Riza Shah Pahlavi, who was deposed in the Islamic revolution 1979.

Paine Thomas 1737–1809. British left-wing political writer, active in the American and French revolutions. His influential pamphlets include *Common Sense* 1776, *The Rights of Man* 1791, and *The Age of Reason* 1793. He advocated republicanism, deism, the abolition of slavery, and the emancipation of women.

paint material used to give a protective and decorative finish to surfaces. Paints consist essentially of a pigment suspended in a vehicle, or binder, sometimes with added solvents. It is the vehicle that dries and hardens to form an adhesive film of paint. Among the most common kinds are cellulose paints (or lacquers), oil-based paints, emulsion paints, and special types such as enamels and primers.

painting the application of colour, pigment, paint to a surface. The chief methods of painting are:
tempera emulsion painting, with a gelatinous (for example egg yolk) rather than oil base; known in ancient Egypt;
fresco watercolour painting on plaster walls; the palace of Knossos, Crete, contains early examples;
ink developed in China from calligraphy in the Sung period and became highly popular in Japan from the 15th century;
oil ground pigments in linseed, walnut, or other oil; spread from N to S Europe in the 15th century;

watercolour pigments combined with gum arabic and glycerine, which are diluted with water; the method was developed in the 15th–17th centuries from wash drawings;
acrylic synthetic pigments developed after World War II; the colours are very hard and brilliant.

Pakhtoonistan independent state desired by the ◊Pathan people.

Pakistan country in S Asia, stretching from the Himalayas to the Arabian Sea, bounded to the W by Iran, to the NW by Afghanistan, to the NE by China, and to the E by India.

Palaeocene first epoch of the Tertiary period of geological time, 65–55 million years ago. Many types of mammals spread rapidly after the disappearance of the great reptiles of the Mesozoic. The name means 'the ancient part of the early recent'.

Palaeolithic earliest division of the Stone Age; see ◊prehistory.

palaeontology in geology, the study of ancient life that encompasses the structure of ancient organisms, their environment, evolution, and ecology as revealed by their ◊fossils.

Palaeozoic era of geological time 590–248 million years ago. It comprises the Cambrian, Ordovician, Silurian, Devonian, Carboniferous, and Permian periods. Plants and invertebrates such as insects covered the land, and amphibians were the first vertebrates to walk on land. The earliest identifiable fossils date from this era. The climate was mostly warm with short ice ages.

Palatinate a historic division of Germany, dating from before the 8th century. It was ruled by a *count palatine* (a count with royal prerogatives) and varied in size.

Palermo capital and seaport of Sicily; population (1988) 729,000. Industries include shipbuilding, steel, glass, and chemicals. It was founded by the Phoenicians 8th century BC.

Palestine (Arabic *Falastin* 'Philistine') geographical area at the eastern end of the Mediterranean sea, also known as the Holy Land because of its historic and symbolic importance for Jews, Christians and Muslims. In ancient times Palestine extended E of the river Jordan, though today it refers to the territory of the State of Israel and the two Israeli-occupied territories of the West Bank and the Gaza Strip. Early settlers included the Canaanites, Hebrews, and Philistines. Over the centuries it became part of the Egyptian, Assyrian, Babylonian, Macedonian, Ptolemaic, Seleucid, Roman, Byzantine, Arab, and Ottoman empires.

Many Arabs refuse to recognize a Jewish state in Palestine, where for centuries Arabs constituted the majority of the population. Today, Jews form the majority of Palestine's population. Palestinian Arabs include over 1 million in the West Bank, E Jerusalem and the Gaza Strip; 1.2 million in Jordan; 750,000 in Israel; 300,000 in Lebanon; and 100,000 in the USA.

history
c. 1000 BC Hebrew leader King David formed a united Kingdom of Israel.
922 Kingdom of Israel split into Israel in the north and Judah in the south after the death of King Solomon.
722 Israel conquered by Assyrians.
586 Judah conquered by Babylonians who destroyed Jerusalem and forced many Jews into exile in Babylon.
539 Palestine became part of Persian empire.
536 Jews allowed to return to Jerusalem.
332 Conquest by Alexander the Great.
168 Maccabean revolt against Seleucids restored independence.
63 Conquest by Roman empire.
AD 70 Romans destroyed Jerusalem following Jewish revolt.
636 Conquest by the Muslim Arabs made Palestine a target for the Crusades.
1516 Conquest by the Ottoman Turks.
1880–1914 Jewish immigration increased sharply as a result of pogroms in Russia and Poland.
1897 At the first Zionist Congress, Jews called for a permanent homeland in Palestine.
1909 Tel Aviv, the first all-Jewish town in Palestine was founded.
1917 The Balfour Declaration expressed the British government's support for the establishment of a Jewish national homeland in Palestine.
1917–18 The Turks were driven out by the British under field marshal Allenby in World War I.
1922 A League of Nations mandate (which incorporated the Balfour Declaration) placed Palestine under British administration.
1936–39 Arab revolt took place, protesting against Jewish immigration (300,000 people 1920–39).
1937 The Peel Commission report recommended the partition of Palestine into Jewish and Arab states.
1939–45 Arab and Jewish Palestinians served in the Allied forces in World War II.
1946 Resentment of immigration restrictions led to acts of anti-British violence by Jewish guerrilla groups.
1947 The United Nations (UN) approved plan for partition.
1948 A Jewish state of Israel was proclaimed 14 May (eight hours before Britain's renunciation of the mandate was due). A series of Arab-Israeli Wars resulted in Israeli territorial gains and the occupation of other parts of Palestine by Egypt and Jordan. Many Palestinian Arabs were displaced.

Palestine Liberation Organization (PLO) Arab organization founded 1964 to bring about an independent state in Palestine. It consists of several distinct groupings, the chief of which is al-◊Fatah, led by Yassir ◊Arafat, the president of the PLO from 1969. The PLO's original main aim was the destruction of the Israeli state, but over time it has changed to establishing a Palestinian state alongside that of Israel.

Palestrina Giovanni Pierluigi da 1525–1594. Italian composer. He wrote secular and sacred choral music, his religious work gaining him a reputation as the master of polyphonic vocal music. Apart from motets and madrigals, he also wrote 105 masses, including *Missa Papae Marcelli*.

Palladio Andrea 1518–1580. Italian architect. His country houses (for example, Malcontenta, and the Villa Rotonda near Vicenza) were designed from 1540 for patrician families.

palladium in chemistry, a white metal of the platinum family, symbol Pd, atomic number 46, relative atomic mass 106.4. Palladium does not tarnish in air, can absorb up to 3,000 times its volume of hydrogen, and is used as a catalyst, in alloys, and in delicate machinery.

palm plant of the family Palmae, characterized by a single tall stem bearing a thick cluster of large palmate or pinnate leaves at the top. The majority of the numerous species are tropical or subtropical.

Palma (Spanish *Palma de Mallorca*) industrial port (textiles, cement, paper, pottery), resort, and capital of the Balearic Islands, Spain, on Majorca; population (1991) 308,600. Palma was founded 276 BC as a Roman colony.

Palmas, Las see under ◊Las Palmas.

Palme (Sven) Olof 1927–1986. Swedish social-democratic politician. He entered government 1963, holding several posts before coming leader of the Social Democratic Labour Party (SD) and prime minister 1969–76 and 1982–86. He was assassinated.

Palmer Samuel 1805–1881. British painter and etcher. He lived 1826–35 in Shoreham, Kent, with a group of artists who were all followers of William Blake and called themselves *the Ancients.*

Palmerston Henry John Temple, 3rd Viscount Palmerston 1784–1865. British politician. Initially a Tory, in Parliament from 1808, he was secretary-at-war 1809–28. He broke with the Tories 1830 and sat in the Whig cabinets of 1830–34, 1835–41 and 1846–51 as foreign secretary. He was prime minister 1855–58 and 1859–65.

Palm Sunday in the Christian calendar, the Sunday before Easter, and first day of Holy Week, which commemorates Jesus' entry into Jerusalem, when the crowd strewed palm leaves in his path.

Palmyra ancient city and oasis in the desert of Syria, about 240 km/150 mi NE of Damascus. Palmyra, the Biblical Tadmor, was flourishing by about 300 BC. It was destroyed 272 AD after Queen Zenobia had led a revolt against the Romans. Extensive temple ruins exist, and on the site is a village called Tadmur.

Palumbo Peter 1935– . British property developer. Appointed chairman of the Arts Council 1988, he advocated a close partnership between public and private funding of the arts, and a greater role for the regions.

Pamirs central Asian plateau mainly in Tajikistan, but extending into China and Afghanistan, traversed

Panama
Republic of (*República de Panamá*)

area 77,100 sq km/29,768 sq mi
capital Panama City
towns Cristóbal, Balboa, Colón
physical mountain ranges, tropical rainforest; Pearl Islands in Gulf of Panama
head of state and government Guillermo Endara from 1989
political system emergent democratic republic
exports bananas, petroleum products, copper
currency balboa

population (1990 est) 2,423,000; annual growth rate 2.2%
language Spanish (official), English
religion Roman Catholic 93%
literacy 87% (1989)
GNP $4.2 bn (1988); $1,970 per head
chronology
1903 Independence achieved from Colombia.
1974 Agreement to negotiate a full transfer of the Panama Canal from the USA to Panama.
1977 USA–Panama treaties transferred the canal to Panama, effective 1999; USA guaranteed its protection and an annual payment.
1984 Nicolas Ardito Barletta elected president.
1985 Barletta resigned to be replaced by Eric Arturo del Valle, but effectively by Gen Manuel Noriega, army commander in chief.
1987 Gen Noriega successfully resisted calls for his removal, despite suspension of US military and economic aid.
1988 Noriega, charged with drug smuggling by US federal court, declared state of emergency.
1989 Noriega declared election results invalid when opposition won; coup attempts failed; 'state of war' with USA announced; US invasion deposed Noriega, installed Guillermo Endara, winner of earlier elections; Noriega taken to USA for trial.
1991 Attempted coup foiled. Army abolished.
1992 Noriega found guilty of drug offences. Referendum voted down government's constitutional changes, including abolition of the army.

by mountain ranges. Its highest peak is Kommunizma Pik (Communism Peak, 7,495 m/24,600 ft) in the Akademiya Nauk range.

Pampas flat, treeless, Argentinian plains, lying between the Andes and the Atlantic, and rising gradually from the coast to the lower slopes of the mountains. The E Pampas contain large cattle ranches and the flax- and grain-growing area of Argentina; the W Pampas are arid and unproductive.

pampas grass grass, genus *Cortaderia*, native to South America. *Cortaderia argentea* is grown in gardens, and has tall leaves and large panicles of white flowers.

Pan in Greek mythology, god (Roman *Sylvanus*) of flocks and herds, shown as a man with horns, ears, and hoofs of a goat, and playing a shepherd's pipe.

panacea a remedy for all known disease; a cure-all.

Pan-Africanist Congress (PAC) militant South African nationalist group, which broke away from the African National Congress 1959. More radical than the ANC, the Pan-Africanist Congress has a black-only policy for Africa. Its military wing is called Poqo ('we alone'). PAC was outlawed from 1960 to 1990. Since the 1970s, it has been weakened by internal dissent.

Panama country in Central America, on a narrow isthmus between the Caribbean and the Pacific Ocean, bounded to the W by Costa Rica and to the E by Colombia.

Panama Canal canal across the Panama isthmus in Central America, connecting the Pacific and Atlantic oceans; length 80 km/50 mi, with 12 locks. Built by the USA 1904–14 after an unsuccessful attempt by the French, it was formally opened 1920. The ***Panama Canal Zone*** was acquired 'in perpetuity' by the USA 1903, comprising land extending about 5 km/3 mi on either side of the canal. The Zone passed to Panama 1979, but the USA retains control of the management and defence of the canal itself until 1999, and the use of about 25% of the Zone's former land area.

Panama City capital of the Republic of Panama, near the Pacific end of the Panama Canal; population (1990) 584,800. Products include chemicals, plastics, and clothing.

Pan-American Union former name 1910–48 of the ◊Organization of American States.

Panchen Lama 10th incarnation 1935–1989. Tibetan spiritual leader, second in importance to the ◊Dalai Lama. A protégé of the Chinese since childhood, he is not indisputably recognized. When the Dalai Lama left Tibet 1959, the Panchen Lama was deputed by the Chinese to take over, but stripped of power for subversion 1964, and held in China 1965–78.

panchromatic in photography, a highly sensitive black-and-white film made to render all visible spectral colours in correct grey tones. It is always developed in total darkness.

lesser panda

Pankhurst *The result of Emmeline Pankhurst demonstrating outside Buckingham Palace 1914.*

pancreas in vertebrates, a gland between the spleen and duodenum. When stimulated by ◊secretin, it secretes enzymes into the duodenum which digest starch, proteins, and fats. In humans, it is about 18 cm/7 in long, and lies behind and below the stomach. It contains groups of cells called the islets of Langerhans, which secrete the hormones insulin and glucagon which regulate the blood sugar level.

panda mammal of NW China and Tibet. The *giant panda Ailuropoda melanoleuca* has black and white fur with black eye patches, and feeds solely on bamboo shoots. It can grow up to 1.5 m/4.5 ft long, and weigh up to 140 kg/300 lbs. The *lesser panda Ailurus fulgens*, 50 cm/1.5 ft long, is black and chestnut, with a long tail. Destruction of their natural habitats have made their extinction possible in the wild. They are both members of the raccoon family.

Pandora in Greek mythology, the first woman. Zeus sent her to Earth with a box of evils (to counteract the blessings brought to mortals by ◊Prometheus' gift of fire); she opened it, and they all flew out. Only hope was left inside as a consolation.

pangolin or *scaly anteater* African and Asian toothless, long-tailed mammal, order Pholidota, up to 1 m/3 ft long. The upper part of the body is covered with horny plates for defence. It is nocturnal, and eats ants and termites.

Pankhurst Emmeline (born Goulden) 1858–1928. British suffragette. Founder of the Women's Social and Political Union 1903, she launched the militant suffragette campaign 1905. In 1926 she joined the Conservative Party, and was a prospective parliamentary candidate.

pansy perennial garden flower, also known as *heartsease*, derived from the European wild pansy *Viola tricolor*, and including many different varieties and strains. The flowers are usually purple, yellow, cream, or a mixture, and there are many highly developed varieties bred for size, colour, or special markings.

pantheism a mode of thought which regards God as omnipresent, identical to the Universe or nature. It

pansy

Papandreou Greek prime minister Andreas Papandreou in Brussels, Feb 1988.

is expressed in Egyptian religion and Brahmanism; stoicism, Neo-Platonism, Judaism, Christianity, and Islam can be interpreted in pantheistic terms. Pantheistic philosophers have included Bruno, Spinoza, Fichte, Schelling, and Hegel.

pantheon originally a temple for worshipping all the gods, such as that in ancient Rome, rebuilt by ◊Hadrian and still used as a church. In more recent times, it is a building where famous people are buried (Panthéon, Paris).

panther another name for ◊leopard.

pantomime in the British theatre, a traditional Christmas entertainment with its origins in the harlequin spectacle of the 18th century and burlesque of the 19th century, which gave rise to the tradition of the principal boy being played by an actress and the dame by an actor. The harlequin's role faded as themes emerged from folktales with additional material such as popular songs, topical comedy, and audience participation.

panzer German mechanized divisions and regiments in World War II, used in connection with armoured vehicles.

Paolozzi Eduardo 1924– . British sculptor, a major force in the Pop art movement in London in the mid-1950s.

papacy the office of the ◊pope or bishop of Rome, as head of the Roman Catholic Church.

papal infallibility doctrine formulated by the Roman Catholic Vatican Council 1870, which stated that the pope, when speaking officially on certain doctrinal or moral matters, was protected from error by God and such rulings, therefore, could not be challenged.

Papal States area of central Italy in which the pope was temporal ruler 756–1870, when Italy became a united state.

Papandreou Andreas 1919– . Greek socialist politician, founder of the Pan-Hellenic Socialist Movement (PASOK), and prime minister from 1981–89, when he was implicated in the alleged embezzlement and diversion to the Greek government of $200 million from the Bank of Crete, and so lost the election. A trial in 1992 cleared Papandreou of all charges.

papaya another name for ◊pawpaw, a tropical fruit tree.

Papeete capital and port of French Polynesia on Tahiti; population (1983) 79,000.

Papen Franz von 1879–1969. German right-wing politician. As chancellor 1932, he negotiated the Nazi-Conservative alliance which made Hitler chan-

cellor 1933. He was envoy to Austria 1934–38 and ambassador to Turkey 1939–44. Although acquitted at the ◊Nuremberg trials, he was imprisoned by a German denazification court for three years.

paper a sheet of vegetable fibre. The name comes from ◊papyrus, a form of writing material made from water reed, used in ancient Egypt. The invention of true paper, originally made of pulped fishing nets and rags, is credited to Tsai Lun, Chinese minister of agriculture 105 AD.

papier mâché a craft technique which involves building up layer upon layer of pasted paper which is then baked or left to harden. Used for a variety of decorative objects, it is often painted, lacquered, or decorated with mother of pearl.

pappus (plural *pappi*) a modified ◊calyx comprising a ring of fine, silky hairs, or sometimes scales or small teeth, which persists after fertilization. Pappi are found in members of the daisy family, Compositae such as the dandelions *Taraxacum*, where they form a parachute-like structure which aids dispersal of the fruit.

Papua New Guinea country in the SW Pacific, comprising the E part of the island of New Guinea, the New Guinea islands, the Admiralty islands, and part of the Solomon islands.

papyrus type of paper made by the ancient Egyptians from the stem of the papyrus or paper reed *Cyperus papyrus* family Cyperaceae.

parabola in mathematics, a curve formed by cutting a right circular cone with a plane parallel to the sloping side of the cone; one of the family of curves known as ◊conic sections.

Paracelsus original name Theophrastus Bombastus von Hohenheim 1493–1541. Swiss physician, alchemist, and scientist. He developed the idea that minerals and chemicals might have medical uses (iatrochemistry). He introduced the use of ◊laudanum (which he named) for pain-killing purposes. His rejection of the ancients and insistence on the value of experimentation made him an important figure in early science.

paracetamol analgesic, particularly effective for musculoskeletal pain. It is as effective as aspirin in reducing fever, and less irritating to the stomach, but has little anti-inflammatory action. An overdose can cause severe, often irreversible, liver damage.

parachute umbrella-shaped device, basically consisting of some two dozen panels of nylon with shrouded lines to a harness. It is used to slow down

parabola

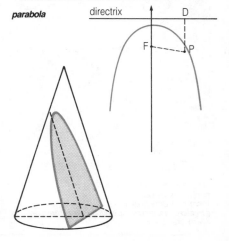

Papua New Guinea

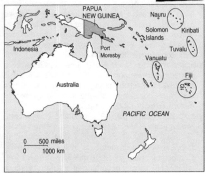

area 462,000 sq km/178,260 sq mi
capital Port Moresby (on E New Guinea)
physical mountains in centre; thickly forested
head of state Elizabeth II represented by governor
general
head of government Paias Wingti from 1992
political system liberal democracy
exports copra, coconut oil, palm oil, tea, copper
currency kina
population (1989 est) 3,613,000 (Papuans,
Melanesians, Negritos, various minorities); annual
growth rate 2.6%

life expectancy men 53, women 54
language English (official)
religion Protestant 63%, Roman Catholic 3%, local
faiths
literacy 55% male/36% female (1985 est)
GNP $2.5 bn (1987); $730 per head
chronology
1883 Annexed by Queensland, and soon became
known as the Australian Territory of Papua.
1884 NE New Guinea annexed by Germany; SE
claimed by Britain.
1914 NE New Guinea occupied by Australia.
1921–42 Held as a League of Nations mandate.
1942–45 Occupied by Japan.
1975 Achieved full independence, within the
Commonwealth, with Michael Somare as prime
minister.
1980 Julius Chan became prime minister.
1982 Somare returned to power.
1985 Somare challenged by deputy prime minister,
Paias Wingti, who later formed a five-party
coalition government.
1988 Wingti defeated on no-confidence vote and
replaced by Rabbie Namaliu, who established a
six-party coalition government.
1989 State of emergency in Bougainville in
response to separatist violence.
1991 Peace accord signed with Bougainville
secessionists. Economic boom as gold
production doubled.
1992 Wingti elected premier. Killings by outlawed
secessionists reported.

the descent of a human being, or supplies, from a
plane or missile to a safe speed for landing, or
sometimes to aid (through braking) the landing of a
plane or missile itself. Modern designs enable the
parachutist to exercise considerable control of
direction, as in ◊skydiving, and ◊freefalling.

paradigm term used by the US historian of science T S ◊Kuhn to describe all those factors,
both scientific and otherwise, which influence the
research of the scientist. The term has subsequently spread to the areas of social studies and
politics.

Paraguay
Republic of (*República del Paraguay*)

area 406,752 sq km/157,042 sq mi
capital Asunción
town port Concepción
physical mostly flat; divided by river Paraguay;
river Paraná in S

head of state and government Gen Andrés
Rodriguez from 1989.
political system emergent democratic republic
exports cotton, soya beans, timber, tung oil, maté
currency guaraní
population (1990 est) 4,660,000 (95% of mixed
Guaraní Indian-Spanish descent); annual growth
rate 3.0%
life expectancy men 67, women 72
language Spanish 6% (official), Guaraní
religion Roman Catholic 97%
literacy 91% male/85% female (1985 est)
GNP $7.4 bn (1987); $1,000 per head
chronology
1811 Independent from Spain.
1865–70 At war with Argentina, Brazil and
Uruguay. Much territory lost.
1932–35 Much territory won from Bolivia during
the Chaco War.
1940–48 Gen Higino Moriñigo president.
1948–54 Political instability with six different
presidents.
1954 Gen Alfredo Stroessner seized power. He
was subsequently re-elected seven times, despite
increasing opposition and accusations of human-
rights violations.
1989 Stroessner ousted in coup led by Gen Andrés
Rodriguez. Rodriguez elected president in free
elections. Colorado Party won congressional
elections.
1991 Colorado Party successful in assembly
elections.

Paris (Top left) the Pompidou Centre of art and culture (1977). (Top right) the Basilica of Sacré Coeur (1919).

paradise in various religions, a place or state of happiness. Examples are the Garden of Eden and the Messianic kingdom; the Islamic paradise of the Koran is a place of sensual pleasure.

Paradise Lost an epic poem by John Milton, first published 1667. The poem describes the Fall of Man and the battle between God and Satan, as enacted through the story of Adam and Eve in the Garden of Paradise. A sequel, *Paradise Regained*, was published 1671.

paraffin a general term for hydrocarbons of the paraffin series, general formula CnH_2n+_2. The lower members are gases, for example methane (marsh or natural gas). The middle ones (mainly liquid) form the basis of petrol (gasolene), kerosene, and lubricating oils, while the higher ones (paraffin waxes) are used in ointment and cosmetic bases.

Paraguay landlocked country in S America, bounded to the NE by Brazil, to the S by Argentina, and to the NW by Bolivia.

parallax the change in the apparent position of an object against its background when viewed from two different positions. In astronomy, nearby stars show a shift due to parallax when viewed from different positions on the Earth's orbit around the Sun. A star's parallax is used to deduce its distance.

parallel computing or *parallel processing* an emerging computer technology that allows more than one computation at the same time. Currently, this means having a few computer processors working in parallel, but in future the number could run to thousands or millions.

parallel lines and parallel planes in mathematics, straight lines or planes that always remains the same perpendicular distance from one another no matter how far they are extended. This is a principle of Euclidean geometry and has been important in everyday consequences as well as for mathematics and science.

parallelogram in mathematics, a quadrilateral (four-sided plane figure) with opposite pairs of sides equal in length and parallel, and opposite angles equal. In the special case when all four sides are equal in length, the parallelogram is known as a rhombus, and when the internal angles are right angles, it is a rectangle or square.

parallelogram of forces in physics and applied mathematics, a method of calculating the resultant (combined effect) of two different forces acting together on an object. Because a force has both magnitude and direction it is a ◊vector quantity and can be represented by a straight line. A second force acting at the same point in a different direction is represented by another line drawn at an angle to the first. By completing the parallelogram (of which the two lines are sides) a diagonal may be drawn from the original angle to the opposite corner to represent the resultant force vector.

paralysis loss of voluntary movement due to failure of nerve impulses to reach the muscles involved. It may result from almost any disorder of the nervous system, including brain or spinal cord injury, ◊stroke, and progressive conditions such as tumour or ◊multiple sclerosis.

Paramaribo port and capital of Surinam, South America, 24 km/15 mi from the sea on the river Surinam; population (1980) 68,000. Products include coffee, fruit, timber, and bauxite. It was founded by the French 1540 and placed under Dutch rule 1816.

Paraná river in South America, formed by the confluence of the Rio Grande and Paranaiba; the Paraguay joins it at Corrientes, and it flows into the Rio de la Plata with the Uruguay; length 4,500 km/2,800 mi. It is used for hydroelectric power by Argentina, Brazil, and Paraguay.

paranoia mental disorder marked by a single-channelled delusion, for example, that the patient is someone of great importance, the subject of a conspiracy, etc. This dominates the whole way of life, sometimes to the danger of the patient or others.

paraplegia paralysis of the lower limbs, usually due to spinal injury.

parapsychology study of phenomena, for example, extra-sensory perception, which are not within (Greek *para* 'beside') the range explicable by established science. The faculty allegedly responsible for them, and common to humans and other animals, is known as *psi* (23rd letter of the Greek alphabet).

parasite an organism which lives on or in another organism (called the 'host'), feeding on the host without immediately killing it, and dependent on it to some degree. Parasites that live inside the host, such as liver flukes and tapeworms, are called *endoparasites*; those that live on the outside, such as fleas and lice, are called *ectoparasites*.

Parcae in Roman mythology, the three Fates of ancient Rome, whose Greek counterparts are the Moirai.

Paré Ambroise 1509–1590. French surgeon who introduced modern principles into wound treatment. As a military surgeon, Paré developed new ways of treating wounds and amputations. He abandoned the practice of cauterization (sealing with heat), using balms and soothing lotions instead. He also used ligatures to tie off blood vessels.

parenchyma a plant tissue composed of loosely packed, more or less spherical cells, with thin cellulose walls. Although parenchyma often has no specialized function, it is usually present in large amounts, forming a packing or ground tissue. It usually has many intercellular spaces.

parental care in biology, the time and energy spent by a parent in order to rear its offspring to maturity. Among animals, it ranges from the simple provision of a food supply for the young which are abandoned after the eggs are laid (for example, many wasps) to feeding and protection of the young after hatching or birth, as in birds and mammals. In the more social species, parental care may include the teaching of skills, such as female cats teaching their kittens to hunt.

Pareto Vilfredo 1848–1923. Italian economist and political philosopher, born in Paris. A vigorous opponent of socialism and liberalism, Pareto justified inequality of income on the grounds of his empirical observation (Pareto's law) that income distribution remained constant whatever efforts were made to change it.

Paris port and capital of France, on the River Seine; *département* in the Île de France region; area 105 sq km/40.5 sq mi; population (1982, metropolitan area) 8,707,000. Products include metal, leather and luxury goods; chemicals, glass, and tobacco. The Champs-Elysées leading to the Arc de Triomphe, the Place de la Concorde, and the Eiffel Tower are amongst the city's notable features. Paris was the centre of the revolutions of 1789–94, 1830, and 1848.

Paris in Greek legend, a prince of Troy whose abduction of Helen, wife of King Menelaus of Sparta, caused the Trojan war.

Paris Henri d'Orléans, Comte de Paris 1908– . Head of the royal house of France. He served in the Foreign Legion under an assumed name 1939–40, and in 1950, on the repeal of the *loi d'exil* 1886 banning pretenders to the French throne, returned to live in France.

Paris Club an international forum dating from the 1950s for the rescheduling of debts granted or guaranteed by official bilateral creditors; it has no fixed membership nor an institutional structure. In the 1980s it has been closely involved in seeking solutions to the serious debt crisis affecting many developing countries.

Paris Commune two periods of government in France:

The Paris municipal government 1789–94 was established after the storming of the Bastille, and remained powerful in the French Revolution until after the fall of Robespierre.

The provisional national government 18 Mar–May 1871 consisting of socialists and left-wing republicans, often considered the first socialist government in history. Elected after the right-wing National Assembly at Versailles tried to disarm the National Guard, it fell when the Versailles troops captured Paris and massacred about 20,000 people 21–28 May.

parish the smallest territorial subdivision in church administration, served by a parish church.

parish council unit of local government in England and Wales, based on church parishes. In Wales they are commonly called *community councils*.

Paris, Treaty of any of various peace treaties signed in Paris; they include:

1763 ending the ◊Seven Years' War

1783 recognizing ◊American Independence

1814 and *1815* following the abdication and final defeat of ◊Napoleon I

1856 ending the ◊Crimean War

1898 ending the ◊Spanish-American War

1919–20 the conference preparing the Treaty of ◊Versailles at the end of World War I was held in Paris

1946 after World War II the peace treaties between the ◊Allies and Italy, Romania, Hungary, Bulgaria, and Finland.

1973 concluding the ◊Vietnam War

parity in economics, equality of price, rate of exchange, wages, and buying power. In the US, agricultural output prices are regulated by a parity system. Parity ratios may be used in the setting of wages to establish similar status to different work groups. Parity in international exchange rates means that those on a par with each other share similar buying power.

Park Merle 1937– . British ballerina, born in Rhodesia. She joined Sadler's Wells in 1954, and by 1959 was a principal soloist with the Royal Ballet. She combined elegance with sympathetic appeal in such roles as *Cinderella*.

Park Mungo 1771–1806. Scottish explorer. He traced the course of the Niger 1795–97, and probably drowned during a second expedition in 1805–06. He published *Travels in the Interior of Africa* 1799.

Park Chung Hee 1917–1979. President of South Korea 1963–79. Under his rule South Korea had the world's fastest-growing economy and the wealth was widely distributed, but recession and his increasing authoritarianism led to his assassination 1979.

Parker 'Charlie', 'Bird', 'Yardbird' (Charles Christopher) 1920–1955. US alto saxophonist and jazz composer, associated with the trumpeter Dizzy Gillespie in developing the bebop style. His mastery of improvisation influenced performers on all jazz instruments.

Parker Dorothy (born Rothschild) 1893–1967. US poet and wit. She reviewed for the magazines *Vanity Fair* and the *New Yorker*, and wrote wittily ironic verses, collected in several volumes including *Not So Deep As A Well* 1940.

Parkes the site in New South Wales of the Australian National Radio Astronomy Observatory, featuring a radio telescope of 64 m/210 ft aperture, run by the Commonwealth Scientific and Industrial Research Organization (CSIRO). Astronomers here discovered the first quasars.

Parkes Henry 1815–1896. Australian politician, born in the UK. He promoted education and the cause of federation, and suggested the official name Commonwealth of Australia. He was five times premier of New South Wales 1872–91.

Parkinson Cecil (Edward) 1931– . British Conservative politician. As chair of the party 1981–83, he masterminded the electoral victory of 1983, and was created minister for trade and industry, but resigned in Oct 1984 following disclosure of an affair with his secretary. In 1987 he rejoined the cabinet as secretary of state for energy.

Parr Portrait by an unknown artist (c. 1545) National Portrait Gallery, London.

Parkinson's disease (Parkinsonism, paralysis agitans) a degenerative disease of the brain characterized by slowness and loss of mobility, muscular rigidity, tremor, and speech difficulties. It is a progressive condition, mainly seen in people over the age of 50.

parliament the legislative body of a country. The world's oldest parliament is the Icelandic Althing from about 930. The UK Parliament is usually dated from 1265. The Supreme Soviet of the USSR, with 1,500 members, may be the world's largest legislature.

In the UK, Parliament is the supreme legislature, comprising the House of Commons and the House of Lords. There are 650 Members of Parliament in the Commons, each representing a geographical constituency. The origins of Parliament are in the 13th century, but its powers were not established until the late 17th century. The powers of the Lords were curtailed in 1911, and the duration of parliaments was fixed at five years, but any parliament may extend its own life, as happened during both World Wars. It meets in the Palace of Westminster, London.

parliamentary paper in UK politics, an official document, such as a White Paper or report of a select committee, which is prepared for the information of Members of Parliament. Many are also published.

Parliament, European governing body of the European Community; see ◊European Parliament.

Parliament, Houses of the building where the British legislative assembly meets. The present Houses of Parliament in London, designed in Gothic

parrot

Revival style by the architects Charles Barry and A W Pugin, were built in 1840–60, the previous building having burned down in 1834. It incorporates portions of the medieval Palace of Westminster. The Commons debating chamber was destroyed by incendiary bombs in 1941: the rebuilt chamber (opened 1950) is the work of G G Scott and preserves its former character.

Parnassiens, Les school of French poets including Leconte de Lisle, Mallarmé, and Verlaine, which flourished 1866–76. Named from the review *Parnasse Contemporain*, it advocated 'art for art's sake' in opposition to the ideas of the Romantics.

Parnassus mountain in central Greece; height 2,457 m/8,062 ft, revered as the abode of Apollo and the Muses. Delphi lies on its S flank.

Parnell Charles Stewart 1846–1891. Irish nationalist politician. He supported a policy of obstruction and violence to attain Home Rule, and became the president of the Nationalist Party in 1877. In 1879 he approved the ◊Land League, and his attitude led to his imprisonment in 1881. His career was ruined 1890 when he was cited as co-respondent in a divorce case.

parody in literature and the other arts, a work that imitates the style of another work, usually with mocking or comic intent; it is related to ◊satire.

Parr Catherine 1512–1548. Sixth wife of Henry VIII of England. She had already lost two husbands when in 1543 she married Henry VIII. She survived him, and in 1547 married Lord Seymour of Sudeley (1508–49).

parrot bird of the order Psittaciformes, abundant in the tropics, especially in Australia and South America. The smaller species are commonly referred to as parakeets. They are mainly vegetarian, and range in size from the 8.5 cm/3.5 in pygmy parrot to the 100 cm/40 in Amazon parrot. The plumage is very colourful, and the call is commonly a harsh screech. The talent for imitating human speech is most marked in the grey parrot *Psittacus erithacus* of Africa.

parsec in astronomy, a unit used for distances to stars and galaxies. One parsec is equal to 3.2616 light years. It is the distance at which a star would have a ◊parallax of one second of arc, taking the baseline as the Earth's distance from the Sun.

Parsee or *Parsi* a follower of the religion ◊Zoroastrianism. The Parsees fled from Persia after its conquest by the Arabs, and settled in India in the 8th century AD. About 100,000 now live mainly in Bombay state, maintaining their rituals of the sacred fire and the exposure of their dead.

Parsifal in Germanic legend, the father of ◊Lohengrin and one of the knights who sought the Holy Grail.

parsley biennial herb *Petroselinum crispum*, cultivated for flavouring. Up to 45 cm/1.5 ft high, it has pinnate, aromatic leaves and yellow umbelliferous flowers.

parsnip temperate Eurasian biennial *Pastinaca sativa*, family Umbelliferae, with a fleshy edible root.

Parsons Charles Algernon 1854–1931. British engineer, who invented the Parsons steam ◊turbine 1884, a landmark in marine engineering and later universally used in electricity generation (to drive an alternator).

parthenocarpy the formation of fruits without seeds. This phenomenon, of no obvious benefit to the plant, occurs naturally in some plants, such as bananas. It can also be induced in some fruit

grey parrot

Parthenon The West Front of the Parthenon, on the Acropolis at Athens, Greece.

crops, either by breeding or by applying certain plant hormones.

parthenogenesis the development of an ovum (egg) without any genetic contribution from a male. Parthenogenesis is the normal means of reproduction in some plants (for example, dandelions) and animals (for example, certain fish). Some sexually reproducing species, such as aphids, show parthenogenesis at some stage in their life cycle.

Parthenon temple of Athena Parthenos ('the Virgin') on the Acropolis at Athens; built 447–438 BC under the supervision of Phidias, and the most perfect example of Doric architecture (by Callicrates and Ictinus). In turn a Christian church and Turkish mosque, it was then used as a gunpowder store, and reduced to ruins when the Venetians bombarded the Acropolis in 1687. Greek sculptures from the Parthenon were removed by Lord Elgin in the early 19th century; popularly known as the ◊Elgin marbles.

Parthia ancient country in W Asia in what is now NE Iran, capital Ctesiphon. Originating about 248 BC, it reached the peak of its power under Mithridates I in the 2nd century BC, and was annexed to Persia under the Sassanids in 226 AD. Parthian horsemen feigned retreat and shot their arrows unexpectedly backwards, hence 'Parthian shot', a remark delivered in parting.

participle a form of the verb, in English either a *present participle* ending in *-ing* (for example, 'work*ing*' in 'They were working', 'working men', and 'a hard-working team') or a *past participle* ending in *-ed* in regular verbs (for example, 'train*ed*'

in 'They have been trained well', 'trained soldiers', and 'a well-trained team').

particle physics the study of elementary particles that make up all atoms. Atoms are made up of positively charged protons and, except for hydrogen, neutrons (which have no charge) in the nucleus, surrounded by negatively charged electrons. Nuclei do not split apart easily; they usually need to be bombarded by particles such as protons, raised to very high kinetic energies by particle accelerators.

particle, subatomic any of the subdivisions of the ◊atom. They are frequently classified in groups of ◊elementary particles: baryons, which include the massive particles (proton, neutron, antiproton, antineutron); mesons, which include the intermediate-mass particles (pion); leptons, which include the light particles (electron, positron, neutrino); and the ultra-elementary particles, ◊quarks.

partisan member of an armed group that operates behind enemy lines or in occupied territories during wars. The name 'partisans' was first given to armed bands of Russians who operated against Napoleon's army in Russia during 1812, but has since been used to describe Russian, Yugoslav, and Polish ◊Resistance groups against the Germans during World War II. In Yugoslavia the communist partisans under ◊Tito played a major role in defeating the Germans.

partnership in English law, two or more persons carrying on a common business for shared profit. The business can be of any kind, for instance solicitors, shop owners or window cleaners. A partnership differs from a limited company in that the individuals remain separate in identity and are not protected by limited liability, so that each partner is personally responsible for any debts of the partnership. Absolute mutual trust is therefore essential.

part of speech a category of words, as defined in the ◊grammar of Western languages which has described Greek and Latin over the centuries since classical times. The 'part of speech' of a word is its grammatical function. The four major parts of speech are the ◊noun, ◊verb, ◊adjective, and ◊adverb; the minor parts of speech vary according to schools of grammatical theory, but include the ◊article, ◊conjunction, ◊preposition, and ◊pronoun.

particle, subatomic The drift chamber of the Mark II particle detector at the Stanford Linear Accelarator Center. California. USA.

Pasteur French chemist and scientist Louis Pasteur.

particle: major fundamental (subatomic) particles

Name	Symbol	Category	Mass (electron = 1)	Charge	Spin	Parity
electron	e	lepton	1	−1	1/2	
graviton	g	quantum	0	0	2	
K meson (kaon)	K	meson	998	−1,0,+1	0	−1
lambda particle	Λ	baryon	2231	0	1/2	+1
muon	μ	lepton	211	−1	1/2	
neutrino	ν	lepton	0	0	1/2	
neutron	n	baryon	1880	0	1/2	+1
omega particle	Ω	baryon	3345	−1	3/2	+1
photon	α	quantum	0	0	1	−1
pion	π	meson	280	−1,0,+1	0	−1
proton	p	baryon	1876	+1	1/2	+1
sigma particle	Σ	baryon	2380	−1,0,+1	1/2	+1
xi particle	Ξ	baryon	2644	−1,0	1/2	+1

More than one charge in the Charge column indicates that there is more than one particle of that type, which differ in charge (there may also be slight differences in mass). Certain particles with a single charge have antiparticles of opposite charge. Thus the positron resembles the electron in every respect except that its charge is +1; similarly, the antiproton has a charge of −1.

Lambda, omega, sigma, and xi particles are known collectively as hyperons.
Baryons and mesons togther make up the type termed hadrons.

partridge gamebird of the family Phasianidae which includes pheasants and quail. Two species common in the UK are the grey partridge *Perdix perdix*, with mottled brown back, grey speckled breast, and patches of chestnut on the sides, and the French partridge *Alectoris rufa*, distinguished by its red-legs, bill, and eyelids.

Parvati in Hinduism, the consort of Siva in one of her gentler manifestations, and the mother of Ganesa; she is said to be the daughter of the Himalayas.

parvenu (French) a social upstart.

PASCAL a high-level computer-programming language. Designed by Niklaus Wirth (1934–) in the 1960s as an aid to teaching programming, it is still widely used as such in universities, but is also recognized as a good general-purpose programming language.

Pascal Blaise 1623–1662. French philosopher and mathematician. He contributed to the development of hydraulics, the ◊calculus, and the mathematical theory of ◊probability.

pas de deux a dance for two performers. A *grand pas de deux* is danced by the prima ballerina and the premier danseur.

Pashto or Pushtu an Indo-European language, officially that of Afghanistan, and also spoken in another dialect in N Pakistan.

Pasolini Pier Paolo 1922–1975. Italian poet, novelist, and film director, an influential figure of the

Pascal's triangle

```
                    1
                 1     1
              1     2     1
           1     3     3     1
        1     4     6     4     1
     1     5    10    10     5     1
  1     6    15    20    15     6     1
1     7    21    35    35    21     7     1
```

post-war years. His writings (making much use of Roman dialect) include *Una vita violenta/A Violent Life* 1959, and his films include *Il vangelo secondo Mateo/The Gospel According to St Matthew* 1964, and *I racconti de Canterbury/The Canterbury Tales* 1972.

pasque flower plant *Pulsatilla vulgaris* of the buttercup family. A low-growing hairy perennial, it has feathery leaves and large purple bell-shaped flowers which start erect then droop. Found in Europe and Asia, it is characteristic of grassland on limy soil.

Passchendaele village in W Flanders, Belgium, near Ypres. The Passchendaele ridge before Ypres was the object of a costly, but unsuccessful, British offensive in World War I, Jul–Nov 1917; British casualties numbered nearly 400,000.

passé (French) out of date.

passim (Latin 'in many places') indicates that what is referred to occurs repeatedly throughout the work.

passion flower climbing plant of the tropical American genus *Passiflora*, family Passifloraceae. It bears distinctive flowerheads comprised of a saucer-shaped petal base, a fringe-like corona and a central stalk bearing the stamens and ovary. Some species produce edible fruit.

passion play play representing the death and resurrection of a god, as of Osiris, Dionysus, and Christ; it has its origins in medieval ◊mystery plays. Traditionally, a passion play takes place every ten years at ◊Oberammergau, West Germany.

Pass Laws South African laws that required the black population to carry passbooks (identity documents) at all times and severely restricted freedom of movement. The laws, a major cause of discontent, formed a central part of the policies of ◊apartheid. They were repealed 1986.

Passover in Judaism, a spring festival, dating from ancient times, which commemorates the exodus from Egypt.

pasteurization

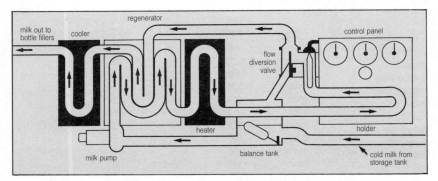

passport document issued by a government authorizing the bearer to go abroad and guaranteeing the bearer the state's protection. Some countries require an intending visitor to obtain a special endorsement or **visa**. Uniform European Community passports were progressively introduced from 1978.

Pasternak Boris Leonidovich 1890–1960. Russian poet and novelist. His volumes of lyric poems include *A Twin Cloud* 1914, and *On Early Trains* 1943, and he translated Shakespeare's tragedies. His novel *Dr Zhivago* 1958, dealing with a scientist's disillusion with the Russian revolution, was followed by a Nobel prize (which he declined), and the novel was banned in the USSR as 'a hostile act'.

Pasteur Louis 1822–1895. French chemist and microbiologist who discovered that fermentation was caused by microorganisms. He also developed a vaccine for ◊rabies, which led to the foundation of the Institut Pasteur in Paris 1888.

pasteurization treatment of food to reduce the number of microorganisms it contains, and so protect consumers from disease. A temperature of between 62.8°C and 65.5°C is maintained for at least 30 minutes, then the food is rapidly cooled to 10°C or lower. Harmful bacteria are killed and the development of others is delayed.

pastiche a term applied in the arts to a work which imitates another's style, or a medley composed of fragments from an original. The intention is normally homage, rather than ridicule as in parody.

Patagonia geographic area of South America, south of latitude 40° S, with sheep farming, coal and oil resources. Sighted by Magellan 1520, it was claimed by both Argentina and Chile until divided between them 1881.

paten flat dish of gold or silver used in the Christian church for holding the consecrated bread at the Eucharist.

patent letters patent, more usually known as a patent, are documents conferring the exclusive right to make, use, and sell an invention (ideas are not eligible, neither is anything not new) for a limited period. The earliest known patent for an invention in England is dated 1449.

Paternoster in the Roman Catholic Church, the Lord's Prayer. The opening words of the Latin version are *Pater noster*.

Pathan Muslim people of NW Pakistan and Afghanistan. Formerly a constant threat to the British Raj, the Pakistani Pathans now claim independence, with the Afghani Pathans, in their own state of Pakhtoonistan.

pathogen any disease-causing organism.

pathology the medical specialty concerned with the study of disease processes.

Patinir (also Patenier, Patinier) Joachim *c.* 1485–*c.* 1524. Flemish painter, active in Antwerp, noted for the inspired landscape backgrounds that dominate his religious subjects. He worked with Matsys (1464–1530) and painted landscape backgrounds for other artists' works.

Paton Alan 1903–1988. South African writer. His novel *Cry, the Beloved Country* 1948 touched the heart of South Africa's problems: later books include the study *Land and People of South Africa* 1956, *The Long View* 1968, and his autobiography *Towards the Mountain* 1980.

Patras (Greek *Patrai*) industrial city (hydroelectric installations; textiles and paper) in the NW Peloponnese, Greece, on the Gulf of Patras; population (1981) 141,500. The ancient *Patrae*, it is the only one of the 12 cities of ◊Achaea to survive.

patriarch in the Old Testament or Hebrew Bible, one of the ancestors of the human race, especially of the Jews from Adam to the sons of Jacob. In the Eastern Orthodox Church, the term refers to the leader of a national church.

patricians privileged class in ancient Rome, descended from the original citizens. After the 4th century BC the patricians' formerly exclusive rights were open to the plebeians.

Patrick, St 389–*c.* 461. Patron saint of Ireland. Born in Britain, probably in S Wales, he was carried off by pirates to six years' slavery in Antrim before escaping either to Britain or Gaul – his poor Latin suggests the former – to train as a missionary. He is variously said to have landed again in Ireland in 432 or 456, and his work was a vital factor in the spread of Christian influence there. His symbols are snakes and shamrocks; feast day 17 Mar.

Patten Chris(topher) Francis 1944– . British Conservative politician, governor of Hong Kong from 1992. He was Conservative Party chair 1990–92, orchestrating the party's campaign for the 1992 general election, in which he lost his parliamentary seat. He accepted the governorship of Hong Kong for the crucial five years prior to its transfer to China.

Patton George (Smith) 1885–1945. US general in World War II, known for his fiery daring as 'Blood and Guts' Patton. He commanded the 2nd Armoured Division in 1940, and in 1942 led the Western Task Force which landed at Casablanca.

Morocco. After commanding the 7th Army, he led the 3rd Army in France, Belgium, and Germany, and in 1945 took over the 15th Army.

Paul Les, adopted name of Lester Polfuss 1915– . US inventor of the solid-body electric guitar in the early 1940s, and a pioneer of recording techniques including overdubbing and electronic echo. The *Gibson Les Paul guitar* was first marketed 1952 (the first commercial solid-body guitar was made by Leo ◊Fender).

Paul 1901–1964. King of the Hellenes from 1947, when he succeeded his brother George II. He was the son of Constantine I. He married in 1938 Princess Frederika (1917–), daughter of the Duke of Brunswick, whose involvement in politics brought her under attack.

Paul six popes, including:

Paul VI, Giovanni Battista Montini 1897–1978. Pope from 1963. His encyclical *Humanae Vitae/Of Human Life* 1968 reaffirmed the church's traditional teaching on birth control, thus following the minority report of the commission originally appointed by Pope John, rather than the majority view.

Paul I 1754–1801. Tsar of Russia from 1796, in succession to his mother Catherine II. Mentally unstable, he pursued an erratic foreign policy, and was assassinated.

Pauli Wolfgang 1900–1958. Austrian physicist, who originated *Pauli's exclusion principle*: in a given system no two ◊electrons, ◊protons, ◊neutrons, or other particles of half-integrated spin can be characterized by the same set of ◊quantum numbers. He also predicted the existence of neutrinos.

Pauling Linus Carl 1901– . US chemist, noted for his fundamental work on the nature of the chemical bond and on the discovery of the helical structure of many proteins.

Paulinus died 644. Roman missionary to Britain who joined St ◊Augustine in Kent in 601, converted the Northumbrians in 625, and became the first archbishop of York. Excavations 1978 revealed a church he built in Lincoln.

Paul, St *c.* 3–*c.* 68 AD. Christian missionary and martyr; in the New Testament, one of the apostles and author of 13 epistles. He was converted by a vision on the road to Damascus. His emblems are a sword and a book; feast day 29 Jun.

Paulus Friedrich von 1890–1957. German field marshal in World War II, commander of the forces that besieged Stalingrad (now Volgograd) in the USSR 1942–43; he was captured and gave evidence at the Nuremberg trials before settling in East Germany.

Pavarotti Luciano 1935– . Italian operatic tenor, whose roles include Rodolfo in *La Bohème*, Cavaradossi in *Tosca*, the Duke of Mantua in *Rigoletto*, and Nemorino in *L'Elisir d'amore*.

Pavia, Battle of battle 1525 between France and the Holy Roman Empire. The Hapsburg emperor Charles V defeated and captured Francis I; it signified the onset of Hapsburg dominance in Italy.

Pavlov Ivan Petrovich 1849–1936. Russian physiologist who studied conditioned reflexes in animals. His work greatly influenced behavioural theory (see ◊behaviourism) and ◊learning theory. See also ◊conditioning.

Pavlova Anna 1881–1931. Russian dancer. Prima ballerina of the Imperial Ballet from 1906, she left Russia in 1913, going on to become the world's most famous classical ballerina.

pawnbroker one who lends money on the security of goods held. The traditional sign of the premises is three gold balls, the symbol used in front of the houses of the medieval Lombard merchants.

pawpaw or *papaya* tropical tree *Carica papaya*, originating in South America and grown in many tropical countries. The edible fruits resemble a melon, with orange-coloured flesh and numerous blackish seeds in the central cavity; they may weigh up to 9 kg/20 lb.

Pax Roman goddess of peace; Greek counterpart ◊Irene.

Paxton Joseph 1801–1865. British architect, garden superintendent to the Duke of Devonshire from 1826 and designer of the Great Exhibition building of 1851 (◊Crystal Palace), revolutionary in its structural use of glass and iron.

PAYE or *Pay As You Earn* in the UK, a system of tax collection in which a proportional amount of income tax is deducted on a regular basis by the employer before wages are paid and transferred to the Inland Revenue, reliefs due being notified to the employer by a code number for each employee. In the USA it is called withholding tax.

paymaster-general head of the Paymaster-General's Office, the British government department (established 1835) that acts as paying agent for most other departments.

Paysandú city in Uruguay, capital of Paysandú department, on the River Uruguay; population (1985) 74,000. Tinned meat is the main product. The city dates from 1772, and is linked by bridge 1976 with Puerto Colón in Argentina.

Pays de la Loire agricultural region of W France, comprising the *départements* of Mayenne, Sarthe, Vendée, Loire-Atlantique, and Maine-et-Loire; capital Nantes; area 32,082 sq km/12,387 sq mi; population (1986) 3,018,000. Industries include shipbuilding and wine.

Paz Octavio 1914– . Mexican poet, whose *Piedra del Sol/Sun Stone* 1957 takes the ◊Aztec Calendar Stone as a symbol of the loneliness of individuals, and their search for union. Nobel Prize for Literature 1990.

Paz Estenssoro Victor 1907– . President of Bolivia 1952–56, 1960–64, and 1985–89. He founded and led the left-wing *Movimiento Nacionalista Revolucionario* which seized power in 1952. His regime gave the vote to Indians, nationalized the country's largest tin mines, began a programme of agrarian reform, and controlled inflation.

PC abbreviation for *police constable; Privy Councillor; personal computer*.

PCP abbreviation for *phencyclidine*, a drug popularly known as ◊angel dust.

pea climbing plant *Pisum sativum*, family Leguminosae, with pods of edible seeds.

Peace Corps a body of trained men and women, established in the USA by President Kennedy in 1951, providing skilled workers for the developing countries, especially in the fields of teaching, agriculture, and health. Living among the country's inhabitants, volunteers are paid only a small allowance to cover their basic needs and maintain health. The Peace Corps was inspired by the British programme Voluntary Service Overseas.

peace movement the collective opposition to war. The Western peace movements of the 1980s can trace their origins to the pacifists of the 19th century and conscientious objectors of World War I. The campaigns after World War II have tended to concentrate on nuclear weapons, but there are numerous organizations, some wholly pacifist, some merely opposed to nuclear proliferation.

peach tree *Prunus persica*, family Rosaceae. It has ovate leaves and small, usually pink flowers. The yellowish edible fruits have thick velvety skins; the ◊nectarine is a smooth-skinned variety.

peacock bird of the pheasant family, native to S Asia. The common peacock *Pavo cristatus* is rather larger than a pheasant. The male has a large fan-shaped tail, brightly coloured with blue, green, and purple 'eyes' on a chestnut ground. The peahen is brown with a small tail.

Peacock Thomas Love 1785–1866. British satirical novelist and official of the East India Company. His works include *Headlong Hall* 1816, and *Nightmare Abbey* 1818.

Peake Mervyn (Lawrence) 1911–1968. British writer and illustrator, best known for the grotesque fantasy trilogy *Titus Groan* 1946, *Gormenghast* 1950, and *Titus Alone* 1959, which deals with the inhabitants of a great isolated house.

peanut another name for ◊groundnut.

pear tree *Pyrus communis*, family Rosaceae, native to temperate regions of Eurasia. It has a succulent edible fruit, less hardy than the apple.

pearl calcareous substance (nacre) secreted by many molluscs, and deposited in thin layers on the inside of the shell around a parasite, a grain of sand, or some other irritant body. After several years of the mantle (the layer of tissue between the shell and the body mass) secreting this calcium carbonate, a pearl is formed.

Pearl Harbor US Pacific naval base in Oahu, chief of the islands forming Hawaii, USA, the scene of a Japanese attack on 7 Dec 1941, which brought America into World War II. It took place while Japanese envoys were holding so-called peace talks in Washington. The local commanders Admiral Kummel and Lt-Gen Short were relieved of their posts and held responsible for the fact that the base, despite warnings, was totally unprepared at the time of the attack. More than 2000 US servicemen were killed, and a large part of the US Pacific fleet was destroyed or damaged during the attack.

Pearse Patrick Henry 1879–1916. Irish poet prominent in the Gaelic revival, and leader of the Easter Rebellion of 1916. Proclaimed president of the provisional government, he was court-martialled and shot after its suppression.

Pearson Lester Bowles 1897–1972. Canadian politician, leader of the Liberal Party from 1958, prime minister 1963–68. As foreign minister 1948–57, he effectively represented Canada at the United Nations. Nobel Peace Prize 1957.

Peary Robert Edwin 1856–1920. US Polar explorer. At his seventh attempt, he was the first person to reach the North Pole, on 6 Apr 1909.

Peasants' Revolt the rising of the English peasantry in Jun 1381. Led by Wat ◊Tyler the rebels occupied London and forced Richard II to abolish serfdom, but after Tyler's murder were compelled to withdraw. The movement was then suppressed, and the king's concessions revoked.

peat fibrous organic substance found in ◊bogs and formed by the incomplete decomposition of plants such as sphagnum moss. The USSR, Canada, Finland, Ireland, and other places have large deposits, which have been dried and used as fuel from ancient times. Peat can also be used as a soil additive.

pecan nut-producing tree *Carya pecan*, native to southern USA and N Mexico, and now widely cultivated. The tree grows to over 45 m/150 ft, and the edible nuts are smooth-shelled, the kernel resembling a smoothly ovate walnut.

Pécs city in SW Hungary, the centre of a coalmining area on the Croatian frontier; population (1988) 182,000. Industries include metal, leather and wine. The town dates from Roman times, and was under Turkish rule 1543–1686.

pedicel the stalk of an individual flower, which attaches it to the main floral axis, often developing in the axil of a bract.

pediment in architecture, the triangular part crowning the fronts of buildings in classic styles. The pediment was a distinctive feature of Greek temples.

pedometer small portable instrument for measuring the approximate distance covered by its wearer. Each step taken by the walker sets in motion a swinging weight within the instrument, causing the mechanism to rotate, and the number of rotations are registered on the instrument face.

Pedro two emperors of Brazil:

Pedro I 1798–1834. Emperor of Brazil 1822–31. The son of John VI of Portugal, he escaped to Brazil on Napoleon's invasion, and was appointed regent in 1821. He proclaimed Brazil independent in 1822 and was crowned emperor, but abdicated in 1831 and returned to Portugal.

Pedro II 1825–1891. Emperor of Brazil 1831–89. He proved an enlightened ruler, but his anti-slavery measures alienated the landowners, who in 1889 compelled him to abdicate.

Peeblesshire former county of S Scotland, included from 1975 in Borders region; Peebles was the county town.

Peel Robert 1788–1850. British Conservative politician. As home secretary 1822–27 and 1828–30, he founded the modern police force and in 1829 introduced Roman Catholic emancipation. He was prime minister 1834–35 and 1841–46, when his repeal of the ◊Corn Laws caused him and his followers to break with the party.

Peenemünde fishing village in East Germany, used from 1937 by the Germans to develop the V2 rockets used in World War II.

peepul an Indian tree. See under ◊fig and ◊bo tree.

peerage in the UK, holders of the titles of duke, marquess, earl, viscount, and baron. Some of these titles may be held by a woman in default of a male heir. In the later 19th century they were augmented by the Lords of Appeal in Ordinary (life peers), and from 1958 by a number of specially created life peers of either sex (usually long-standing members' of the Commons). Since 1963 peers have been able to disclaim their titles (for example Lord Home and Tony Benn), usually to take a seat in the Commons (where peers are disqualified from membership).

peer group in the social sciences, people who have a common identity based on such characteristics as similar social status, interests, age, or ethnic group. The concept has proved useful in analysing the power and influence of workmates, school friends, and ethnic and religious groups in socialization and social behaviour.

Pegasus in astronomy, a constellation of the northern hemisphere, near Cygnus, representing the winged horse of Greek mythology. It is the seventh-largest constellation in the sky, and its main feature is a square outlined by four stars, one of which is actually part of the adjoining constellation Andromeda.

Pegasus in Greek mythology, the winged horse which sprang from the blood of Medusa. Hippocrene, the spring of the Muses on Mount Helicon, is said to have sprung from a blow of his hoof. He was transformed to a constellation.

pegmatite a coarse-grained igneous rock found in veins usually associated with large granite masses.

Pegu city in S Myanmar on the river Pegu, NE of Yangon; population (1983) 254,762. It was founded 573 AD and is noted for the Shwemawdaw pagoda.

Péguy Charles 1873–1914. French Catholic socialists, who established a socialist publishing house in Paris. From 1900 he published on political topics *Les Cahiers de la Quinzaine/Fortnightly Notebooks* and poetry, including *Le Mystère de la charité de Jeanne d'Arc/The Mystery of the Charity of Joan of Arc* 1897.

Pel Ieoh Ming 1917– . Chinese-born American Modernist/high-tech architect. His buildings include the Bank of China Tower, Hong Kong, 1987, and the glass pyramid in front of the Louvre, Paris, 1989.

pekan or *fisher marten* North American marten (carnivorous mammal) about 1.2 m/4 ft long, with a doglike face, and brown fur with white patches on the chest.

Peking former name of ◊*Beijing*, capital of China.

pekingese long-haired toy dog with a flat skull and flat face.

Peking man early type of human, *homo erectus*. Carbon dating indicates that they lived between 500,000 and 1,500,000 years ago.

pelargonium flowering plant of the genus *Pelargonium*, grown extensively in gardens, where it is familiarly known as *geranium*. It is related to the true geranium, being also a member of the family Geraniaceae. Ancestors of the garden hybrids came from S Africa.

Pelé adopted name of Edson Arantes do Nascimento 1940– . Brazilian footballer who appeared in four World Cup competitions 1958–70 and won three winner's medals.

Pelham Henry 1696–1754. British Whig politician. He held a succession of offices in Walpole's cabinet 1721–42, and was prime minister 1743–54.

pelican type of water bird remarkable for the pouch beneath the bill used as a fishing net and temporary store for its catches of fish. Some species grow up to 1.8 m/6 ft, and have wingspans of 3 m/10 ft.

Peloponnese Greek *Peloponnesos* peninsula forming the S part of Greece; area 21,549 sq km/8,320 sq mi; population (1989) 1,077,000. It is joined to the mainland by the narrow isthmus of Corinth, and is divided into the nomes of Argolis, Arcadia, Achaea, Elis, Corinth, Lakonia, and Messenia, representing its seven ancient states.

Peloponnesian War conflict between Athens and Sparta and their allies, 431–404 BC, originating in suspicions of 'empire-building' ambitions of Pericles. It was ended by ◊Lysander's destruction of the political power of Athens.

pelota very fast ball game (the name means 'ball') of Basque derivation, also known as *jai alai* ('merry festival'), popular in Latin-American countries. It is played in a walled court or *cancha*, and resembles squash, but the players use a long, curved wickerwork basket or *cesta*, strapped to the hand, to hurl the ball (about the size of a baseball) against the walls.

Peltier effect in physics, a change in temperature at the junction of two different metals produced when an electric current flows through them. The extent of the change depends on what the conducting metals are, and the nature of change (rise or fall

penicillin Penicillin notatum is a species of the fungus used as an early source of the antibiotic penicillin.

in temperature) depends on the direction of current flow. It is the reverse of the ◊Seebeck effect. Names after the French physicist Jean Charles Peltier (1785–1845) who discovered it in 1834.

Pembrokeshire former extreme SW county of Wales, which became part of Dyfed in 1974; the county town was Haverfordwest.

PEN literary association established in 1921 by C A Dawson Scott, to promote international understanding between writers. The initials stand for Poets, Playwrights, Editors, Essayists, Novelists.

penance a Roman Catholic sacrament, involving ◊confession of sins and the reception of absolution, and works performed or punishment self-inflicted in atonement for sin. Penance is worked out now in terms of good deeds rather than routine repetition of prayers.

Penang (Malay *Pulau Pinang*) state in W Malaysia, formed of Penang Island, Province Wellesley, and the Dindings on the mainland; area 1,034 sq km/400 sq mi; capital George Town, with port Penang; population (1990) 1,142,200. Penang Island was bought by Britain from the ruler of Kedah 1785; Province Wellesley was acquired 1800.

Penda king of Mercia from about 633. He raised Mercia to a powerful kingdom, and defeated and killed two Northumbrian kings, Edwin and ◊Oswald. He was killed in battle with Northumbria.

Pendleton Act, The in US history, a civil service reform bill (1883) sponsored by senator George Pendleton (1825–1889) of Ohio that was designed to curb the power of patronage exercised by new administrations over a swelling federal bureaucracy. Initially about 10% of civil service appointments were made subject to competitive examinations administered by an independent Civil Service Commission.

Penelope in Greek legend, wife of ◊Odysseus. During his absence after the siege of Troy she kept her many suitors at bay by asking them to wait until she had woven a shroud for her father-in-law, but undid her work nightly. When Odysseus returned, he killed her suitors.

penetration technology the development of missiles which 're low radar, infra-red and optical signatures, and can penetrate an enemy's defences undetected. In 1980 the USA announced that it had developed such piloted aircraft, known as *Stealth*.

penguin flightless, marine bird, usually black and white, found in the southern hemisphere. They range in size from 40 cm/1.6 ft to 1.2 m/4 ft tall, and have thick feathers to protect them from the intense cold. They are awkward on land, but their wings have evolved into flippers, making them excellent swimmers. Penguins congregate to breed in 'rookeries', and often spend many months incubating their eggs while their mates are out at sea feeding.

penicillin an ◊antibiotic, produced by fungus *Penicillium notatum*. The first antibiotic to be discovered, it kills a broad spectrum of bacteria, many of which cause disease in humans.

peninsula tongue of land surrounded on three sides by water but still attached to a larger landmass. Florida, USA, is an example.

Peninsular War the war of 1808–14 caused by the French emperor Napoleon's invasion of Portugal and Spain. British expeditionary forces, combined with Spanish and Portuguese resistance, succeeded in defeating the French at Vimeiro 1808, Talavera 1809, ◊Salamanca 1812, and Vittoria 1813. The results were inconclusive, and the war was ended by Napoleon's abdication.

penis male reproductive organ, used for internal fertilization; it transfers sperm to the female reproductive tract. In mammals, the penis is made erect by vessels which fill with blood, and in most mammals (but not men) is stiffened by a bone. It also contains the urethra, through which urine is passed. Snakes and lizards have two penises, other reptiles only one. A few birds, mainly ducks and geese, also have a type of penis, as do snails, barnacles, and some other invertebrates. Many insects have a rigid, non-erectile male organ, usually referred to as an intromittent organ.

Penn William 1644–1718. English Quaker, born in London. He joined the Quakers in 1667. In 1681 he obtained a grant of land in America, in settlement of a debt owed by the king to his father, on which he established the colony of Pennsylvania as a refuge for the persecuted Quakers.

Penney William, Baron Penney 1909–1991. British scientist. He worked at Los Alamos 1944–45, designed the first British atomic bomb, and developed the advanced gas-cooled nuclear reactor used in some power stations.

Pennines mountain system, 'the backbone of England', broken by a gap through which the river Aire flows to the E and the Ribble to the W; length (Scottish border to the Peaks in Derbyshire) 400 km/250 mi.

Pennsylvania sate of NE USA; nicknamed Keystone State
area 117,412 sq km/45,333 sq mi
capital Harrisburg
towns Philadelphia, Pittsburgh, Erie, Scranton
products mushrooms, fruit, flowers, cereals, tobacco, meat, poultry, dairy products, anthracite, electrical equipment
population (1990) 11,881,600
famous people Marian Anderson, Maxwell Anderson, Stephen Foster, Benjamin Franklin, George C Marshall, Robert E Peary, Gertrude Stein, John Updike
history There was a breakdown at the Three Mile Island nuclear reactor plant in Harrisburg 1979.

Pennsylvanian US term for the upper ◊Carboniferous period of geological time, named after the US state.

pension an organized form of saving for retirement. Pension schemes, which may be government-run or privately administered, involve regular payment for a qualifying period; when the person retires, a payment is made each week from the invested pension fund. Pension funds have today become influential investors in major industries. In the UK,

Pepys Portrait by John Hayls (1666) National Portrait Gallery, London.

the age at which pensions become payable is 65 for men and 60 for women.

Pentagon the headquarters of the US Department of Defense, Washington. One of the world's largest office buildings, it is constructed in five rings with a pentagonal central court. The *Pentagon Papers* were classified documents published by the American press in 1971 on US involvement in Vietnam.

pentanol $C_5H_{11}OH$ (common name *amyl alcohol*) in chemistry, a clear colourless oily liquid, usually having a characteristic choking odour.

Pentateuch Greek (and Christian) name for the first five books of the Bible, ascribed to Moses, and called the *Torah* by Jews.

pentathlon *Modern* pentathlon is a five sport competition involving former miltary training pursuits; swimming, fencing, running, horsemanship, and shooting. Formerly a five-event track and field competion for women, it was superseded by the ◊heptathlon in 1981.

Pentecost Jewish festival (50th day after ◊Passover) celebrating the end of the Palestinian grain harvest; in the Christian church, day on which the Holy Spirit descended, and commemorated on Whit Sunday.

Pentecostal Movement Christian revivalist movement inspired by the baptism in the Holy Spirit with 'speaking in tongues' experienced by the apostles at the time of Pentecost. It represents a reaction against rigid theology and formal worship of the traditional churches. Pentecostalists believe in the literal word of the Bible and disapprove of alcohol, tobacco, dancing, the theatre, and so on; worldwide membership is more than 10 million.

peony or *paeony* perennial plant of the family Paeoniaceae, remarkable for its brilliant flowers. Most popular are the common peony *Paeonia officinalis*, the white peony *Paeonia lactiflora* and the taller tree peony *Paeonia suffruticosa*.

Pepin the Short king of the Franks from 751. The son of Charles Martel, he acted as ◊mayor of the palace to the last Merovingian king, Childeric III, until he deposed him and assumed the royal title himself, founding the Carolingian line.

pepper climbing plant *Piper nigrum* native to the E Indies. When gathered green, the berries are crushed to produce the seeds for the condiment black pepper. When the berries are ripe the seeds are removed, and the outer skin discarded to produce white pepper. Sweet pepper comes from the ◊capsicum plant.

peppermint perennial herb *Mentha piperita*, with ovate aromatic leaves, and purple flowers. Oil of peppermint is used in medicine and confectionery.

peptide a molecule comprising two or more ◊amino acids joined by peptide bonds (bonds between nitrogen atoms and carbon atoms joined to an oxygen atom). The term 'peptide' is applied to the breakdown products of proteins, to the precursors of proteins, and to hormones such as vasopressin and oxytocin. The term 'polypeptide' generally refers to a longer-chain molecule.

Pepys Samuel 1633–1703. British diarist. He entered the navy office 1660, just after beginning his diary, written 1659–69 (when his sight failed) in shorthand. A unique record of both the daily life of the period and the intimate feelings of the man, it was not deciphered till 1825.

percentage a way of representing a number as a ◊fraction of 100. Thus 45 per cent (45%) equals $^{45}/_{100}$, and 45% of 20 is $^{45}/_{100} \times 20 = 9$.

Perceval Spencer 1762–1812. British Tory politician. He became chancellor of the Exchequer in 1807 and prime minister in 1809. He was shot in the lobby of the House of Commons in 1812.

perch freshwater fish, genus *Perca*, found in Europe, Asia, and North America. They have varied shapes, and are usually a greenish colour. They are very prolific, spawning when three years old, and have voracious appetites.

percussion instrument musical instrument played by being struck with the hand or stick. Percussion instruments can be divided into those which can be tuned to produce a sound of definite pitch, and those without pitch.

Examples of tuned percussion instruments include:

kettledrum a hemispherical bowl of metal with a membrane stretched across the top

tubular bells suspended on a frame

glockenspiel (German '*bell play*') using a set of steel bars

xylophone similar to a glockenspiel, but with wooden rather than metal bars.

Instruments without definite pitch include:

snare drum, which has a membrane across both ends, and a 'snare' which rattles when the drum is beaten

bass drum, which produces the lowest sound in the orchestra

tambourine a wooden hoop with a membrane stretched across it, and with metal plates inserted in the sides

triangle a triangular-shaped steel bar, played by striking it with a separate bar of steel. The sound produced remains distinctive even when played alongside a full orchestra

cymbals two brass plates struck together

castanets two round-shaped pieces of wood struck together

gong a heavy circular piece of metal struck with a soft hammer.

Percy family name of Dukes of Northumberland; seated at Alnwick Castle, Northumberland.

Percy Henry 'Hotspur' 1364–1403. English soldier, son of the 1st Earl of Northumberland. In repelling a border raid, he defeated the Scots at Homildon Hill in Durham 1402, and was killed at the battle of Shrewsbury 1403 while in revolt against Henry IV.

Perelman S(idney) J(oseph) 1904–1979. US humorist, born in New York. He wrote for the *New Yorker* magazine, and film scripts for the Marx

percussion instruments

bass drum

kettle drum

tambourine   snare drum

glockenspiel

cymbals

tubular bells

castanets

triangle

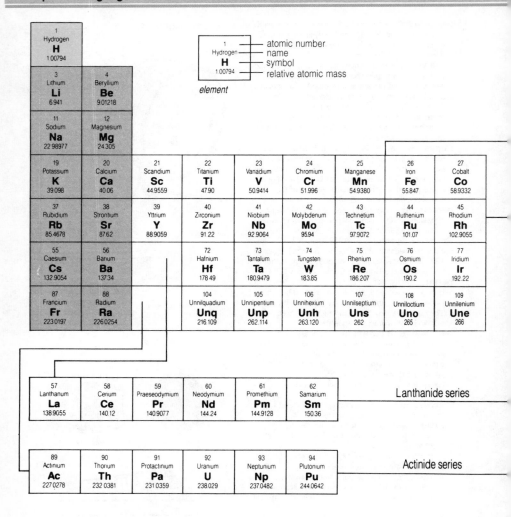

Brothers team of comedians; he shared the Academy Award for the film script *Around the World in 80 Days* 1956

perennating organ in plants, that part of a ◊biennial or herbaceous ◊perennial that allows it to survive the winter, usually a root, tuber, rhizome, bulb, or corm.

perennial plant a plant that lives for more than two years. Herbaceous perennials have aerial stems and leaves which die each autumn, and they survive the winter by means of an underground storage (◊perennating) organ, such as a bulb or rhizome. Trees and shrubs, or woody perennials, have stems which persist above ground throughout the year, and may be either ◊deciduous or ◊evergreen. *See also* ◊annual, ◊biennial.

Peres Shimon 1923– . Israeli socialist politician, prime minister 1984–86. Peres emigrated from Poland to Palestine in 1934, but was educated in the USA. In 1959 he was elected to the Knesset (Israeli parliament). He became leader of the Labour Party in 1977. Peres was prime minister under a power-sharing agreement with the leader of the Consolidation Party (Likud), Itzhak ◊Shamir. From 1989 to 1990 he was finance minister in a new Labour–Likud coalition.

perestroika (Russian 'restructuring') in Soviet politics, the wide-ranging economic and government reforms initiated from 1985 by Mikhail Gorbachev, finally leading to the demise of the Soviet Union.

Pérez de Cuellar Javier 1920– . Peruvian diplomat, secretary general of the United Nations 1982–91. He raised the standing of the UN by his successful diplomacy in ending the Iran–Iraq war 1988 and securing the independence of Namibia 1989.

Pérez Galdós Benito 1843–1920. Spanish novelist, born in the Canary Islands. His works include the 46 historical novels in the cycle *Episodios nacionales* and the 21-novel cycle *Novelas españolas contemporáneos*, which includes *Doña Perfecta* 1876 and the epic *Fortunata y Jacinta* 1886–87, his masterpiece. In scale he has been compared to Balzac and Dickens.

perfume fragrant essence used to scent the body, cosmetics, and candles. More than 100 natural aromatic materials may be blended from a range of 60,000 flowers, leaves, fruits, seeds, woods,

periodic table of the elements

								2 Helium **He** 4.00260
		5 Boron **B** 10.81	6 Carbon **C** 12.011	7 Nitrogen **N** 14.0067	8 Oxygen **O** 15.9994	9 Fluorine **F** 18.99840	10 Neon **Ne** 20.179	
		13 Aluminium **Al** 26.98154	14 Silicon **Si** 28.086	15 Phosphorus **P** 30.97376P	16 Sulphur **S** 32.06	17 Chlorine **Cl** 35.453	18 Argon **Ar** 39.948	

28 Nickel **Ni** 58.70	29 Copper **Cu** 63.546	30 Zinc **Zn** 65.38	31 Gallium **Ga** 69.72	32 Germanium **Ge** 72.59	33 Arsenic **As** 74.9216	34 Selenium **Se** 78.96	35 Bromine **Br** 79.904	36 Krypton **Kr** 83.80
46 Palladium **Pd** 106.4	47 Silver **Ag** 107.868	48 Cadmium **Cd** 112.40	49 Indium **In** 114.82	50 Tin **Sn** 118.69	51 Antimony **Sb** 121.75	52 Tellurium **Te** 127.75	53 Iodine **I** 126.9045	54 Xenon **Xe** 131.30
78 Platinum **Pt** 195.09	79 Gold **Au** 196.9665	80 Mercury **Hg** 200.59	81 Thallium **Tl** 204.37	82 Lead **Pb** 207.37	83 Bismuth **Bi** 207.2	84 Polonium **Po** 210	85 Astatine **At** 211	86 Radon **Rn** 222.0176

63 Europium **Eu** 151.96	64 Gadolinium **Gd** 157.25	65 Terbium **Tb** 158.9254	66 Dysprosium **Dy** 162.50	67 Holmium **Ho** 164.9304	68 Erbium **Er** 167.26	69 Thulium **Tm** 168.9342	70 Ytterbium **Yb** 173.04	71 Lutetium **Lu** 174.97

95 Americium **Am** 243.0614	96 Curium **Cm** 247.0703	97 Berkelium **Bk** 247.0703	98 Californium **Cf** 251.0786	99 Einsteinium **Es** 252.0828	100 Fermium **Fm** 257.0951	101 Mendelevium **Md** 258.0986	012 Nobelium **No** 259.1009	103 Lawrencium **Lr** 260.1054

barks, resins, and roots, linked by natural animal fixatives and various synthetics, the latter increasingly used even in expensive products.

Pergamum ancient Greek city in W Asia Minor, which became the capital of an independent kingdom in 283 BC. As the ally of Rome it achieved great political importance in the 2nd century BC, and became a centre of art and culture. Close to its site is the modern Turkish town of Bergama.

perianth a collective term for the outer whorls of the ◊flower which protect the reproductive parts during development. In most ◊dicotyledons the perianth is composed of two distinct whorls, the calyx of ◊sepals and the corolla of ◊petals, whereas in many ◊monocotyledons they are indistinguishable and the segments of the perianth are then known individually as tepals.

pericarp the wall of a ◊fruit. It encloses the seeds and is derived from the ◊ovary wall. In fruits such as the acorn, the pericarp becomes dry and hardened, forming a shell around the seed. In fleshy fruits the pericarp is typically made up of three distinct layers. The *epicarp* or *exocarp* forms the tough outer skin of the fruits, while the

mesocarp is often fleshy and forms the middle layers. The innermost layer or *endocarp*, which surrounds the seeds may be membranous, or may be thickened and hard, as in the ◊drupe (stone) of cherries, plums, and apricots.

Pericles *c.* 490–429 BC. Athenian politician, who dominated the city's affairs from 461 BC (as leader of the democratic party), and under whom Greek culture reached its climax. He created a confederation of cities under the leadership of Athens, but the disasters of the ◊Peloponnesian War led to his overthrow 430 BC. Although quickly reinstated, he died soon after.

perigee the point at which an object, travelling in an elliptical orbit around the Earth, is at its closest to the Earth.

perihelion the point at which an object, travelling in an elliptical orbit around the Sun, is at its closest to the Sun.

perinatal relating to the period shortly before, during, and after the birth of a child.

period a punctuation mark (.). The term 'period' is universally understood in English, and is the preferred usage in N America; the term 'full stop'

Pérez de Cuellar Peruvian diplomat, General Javier Pérez de Cuellar, Mexico City, 1984.

is the preferred form in the UK. Traditionally, the period has two functions: to mark the end of a properly formed sentence, and to indicate that a word has been abbreviated.

periodic table of the elements a classification of the elements following the statement by Mendeleyev in 1869, that 'the properties of elements are in periodic dependence upon their atomic weight'. There are striking similarities in the chemical properties of the elements in each of the main vertical groups, and a gradation of properties along the horizontal periods. These are dependent on the electronic and nuclear structure of atoms of the elements.

peripheral device in computing, any item of equipment attached to and controlled by a computer. Peripherals are typically for input from and output to the user (for example, keyboard, printer), storing data (for example, disk drive), communications (such as a modem) or for performing physical tasks (such as a robot).

periscope optical instrument designed for observation from a concealed position. In its basic form, it consists of a tube with parallel mirrors at each end inclined at 45° to its axis.

peristalsis contractions that pass along tubular organs, such as the intestines, in waves produced by the contraction of smooth ◊muscle. The same term describes the wavelike motion of earthworms and other invertebrates, in which part of the body contracts as another part elongates.

peritonitis inflammation within the peritoneum, the lining o f the abdominal cavity, due to infection or other irritation. It is sometimes seen following a burst appendix. Peritonitis would quickly prove fatal without treatment.

periwinkle in zoology, a snail-like marine mollusc found on the shores of Europe and E North America. It has a conical spiral shell, and feeds on algae.

periwinkle in botany, trailing blue-flowered evergreen plants of the genus *Vinca*, family Apocynaceae.

perjury the offence of deliberately making a false statement on ◊oath (or ◊affirmation) when appearing as a witness in legal proceedings, on a point material to the question at issue. In Britain it is punishable by a fine, imprisonment up to seven years, or both.

Perm industrial city (shipbuilding, oil refining, aircraft, chemicals, sawmills), capital of Perm region, N Russia, on the Kama near the Ural mountains;

Perón Eva (Evita) Perón used her talents as a broadcaster and speaker to gain support for her husband Juan Perón, the Argentinian leader.

population (1987) 1,075,000. It was called Molotov 1940–57.

permafrost condition in which a deep layer of ◊soil does not thaw out during the summer but remains at below 0°C/–32°F for at least two years, despite thawing of the soil above. It is claimed that 26 per cent of the world's land surface is permafrost.

Permian period of geological time 286–248 million years ago, the last period of the Palaeozoic era. Its end was marked by a significant change in marine life, including the extinction of many corals and trilobites. Deserts were widespread, and reptiles, amphibians, and theropods (mammal-like reptiles) flourished. Gymnosperms (cone-bearing plants) came to prominence.

permutation in mathematics, a specified arrangement of a group of objects. It is the arrangement of *a* distinct objects taken *b* at a time in all possible orders. It is given by $a!/(a-b)!$, where '!' stands for ◊factorial. For example, the number of permutations of four letters taken from any group of six different letters is $6!/2! = (1 \times 2 \times 3 \times 4 \times 5 \times 6)/(1 \times 2) = 360$.

Perón Eva ('Evita' Maria) 1922–1952. Argentinian populist leader. A successful actress, in 1945 she married Juan ◊Perón. When he was ousted from power and arrested she roused the trade unions to fight for his release and election as president. She gained popularity, and in 1951 stood for the post of vice president, but was opposed by the army and withdrew; she died soon afterwards.

Perón Isobel 1931– . President of Argentina 1974–76, and third wife of President Juan ◊Perón, who she succeeded after he died in office. However, labour unrest, inflation, and political violence pushed the country to the brink of anarchy. Accused of corruption, she was seized by air force officers and held under house arrest for five years. Later charged and convicted, she moved to Spain in 1985.

Perón Juan (Domingo) 1895–1974. Argentine politician, dictator 1946–55 and from 1973. He took part in the military pro-fascist coup of 1943, and his popularity with the *descamisados*, 'shirtless ones', led to his election as president in 1946. He lost

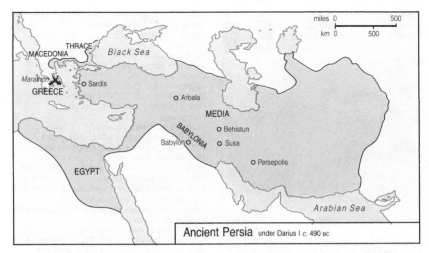

Ancient Persia under Darius I *c.* 490 BC

popularity after the death of his second wife Eva Perón, and was deposed in 1955, but returned from exile to the presidency in 1973. He was succeeded by his third wife Isobel Perón.

Perpendicular   a period of English Gothic architecture lasting from the end of the 14th to the mid-16th century. It is characterized by window tracery consisting chiefly of vertical members, two or four arc arches, lavishly decorated vaults and use of traceried panels. Examples include the choir and cloister of Gloucester Cathedral, and King's College Chapel, Cambridge.

Perrault   Charles 1628–1703. French author of the fairy tales *Contes de ma mère l'oye/ Mother Goose's Fairy Tales* 1697, including 'Sleeping Beauty', 'Red Riding Hood', 'Blue Beard', 'Puss in Boots', and 'Cinderella'.

Perry   Matthew Calbraith 1794–1858. US naval officer, commander of the expedition of 1853 that reopened communication between Japan and the outside world after 250 years' isolation. Military superiority enabled him to negotiate the *Treaty of Kanagawa* 1854 giving the USA trading rights with Japan.

per se   (Latin) in itself.

Persephone   Greek goddess, the daughter of Zeus and Demeter. She was carried off to the underworld by Pluto, who later agreed that she should spend six months of the year with her mother. The myth symbolizes the growth and decay of vegetation.

Persepolis   ancient capital of the Persian Empire, 65 km/40 mi NE of Shiraz. It was burned down after its capture in 331 BC by Alexander the Great.

Perseus   in Greek mythology, son of Zeus and Danaë. He slew ◊Medusa, the Gorgon; rescued ◊Andromeda; and became king of Tiryns.

Perseus   in astronomy, a constellation of the northern hemisphere, near Cassiopeia, representing the mythological hero. The eye of the decapitated Gorgon is represented by the variable star Algol. Perseus lies in the Milky Way and contains the Double Cluster, a twin cluster of stars. Every August the Perseid meteor shower radiates from its northern part.

Pershing   John Joseph 1860–1948. US general. He served in the Spanish War of 1898, the Philippines 1899–1903, and Mexico 1916–17. He commanded the American Expeditionary Force sent to France 1917–18.

Persia, ancient   kingdom in SW Asia. The early Persians were a nomadic Aryan people that migrated through the Caucasus to the Iranian plateau.

7th century BC   The Persians were established in the present region of Fars, which then belonged to the Assyrians.

550   ◊Cyrus the Great overthrew the empire of the Medes, to whom the Persians had been subject, and founded the Persian Empire.

539   Having conquered all Anatolia, Cyrus added Babylonia (including Syria and Palestine) to his empire.

529–485   ◊Darius I organized an efficient centralized system of administration and extended Persian rule east into Afghanistan and NW India and as far north as the Danube, but the empire was weakened by internal dynastic struggles.

499–449   The ◊*Persian Wars* with Greece ended Persian domination of the ancient world.

331   Alexander the Great drove the Persians under Darius III (died 330 BC) into retreat at Arbela on the Tigris, marking the end of the Persian Empire and the beginning of the Hellenistic period under the Seleucids.

226 AD   The ◊Sassanian Empire was established in Persia, and annexed Parthia.

637   Arabs took the capital, Ctesiphon, and introduced Islam in place of Zoroastrianism.

For modern history see ◊Iran.

Persian Gulf   shallow bay, area 233,000 sq km/90,000 sq mi, linked by the Strait of Hormuz and the Gulf of Oman to the Arabian Sea. Important oilfields lie on its shores.

Persian language   a member of the Indo-Iranian branch of the Indo-European language family and the official language of the state once known as Persia but now officially called Iran. Persian is known to its own speakers as *Farsi*, the language of the province of Fars (Persia proper). It is written in the Arabic script, from right to left, and has a large mixture of Arabic religious, philosophical, and technical vocabulary.

Persian Wars   a series of conflicts between the Greeks and the Persians 499 – 449 BC. The eventual victory of Greece was a turning point in the Persian domination of the ancient world and marked the beginning of Greek greatness.

Peru
Republic of (*República del Perú*)

area 1,285,200 sq km/496,216 sq mi
capital Lima, including port of Callao
towns Arequipa, Iquitos, Chiclayo
physical Andes mountains N–S cover 27%;
Amazon river-basin jungle in NE
head of state and government Alberto Fujimoro
from 1990
political system democratic republic
exports coffee, alpaca, llama and vicuna wool, fish
meal, lead, copper, iron, oil
currency new sol
population (1990 est) 21,904,000 (46% Indian,

mainly Quechua and Aymara; 43% of mixed
Spanish-Indian descent); annual growth rate
2.6% pa
life expectancy men 61, women 66
language Spanish 68%, Quechua 27% (both
official), Aymará 3%
religion Roman Catholic 90%
literacy 91% male/78% female (1985 est)
GNP $19.6 bn (1988); $940 per head
chronology
1824 Independence achieved from Spain.
1902 Boundary dispute with Bolivia settled.
1927 Boundary dispute with Colombia settled.
1942 Boundary dispute with Ecuador settled.
1948 Army coup installed a military government.
1963 Return to civilian rule.
1968 Return of military government in a bloodless
coup by Gen Juan Velasco Alvarado.
1975 Velasco replaced, in a bloodless coup, by Gen
Morales Bermúdez.
1980 Return to civilian rule.
1981 Boundary dispute with Ecuador renewed.
1987 President García delayed nationalizing
Peru's banks after proposal vigorously opposed.
1988 García under pressure to seek help from the
International Monetary Fund.
1989 Peru six months behind in debt repayments;
International Development Bank suspended
credit; annual inflation rate to Apr 4,329.4%.
1990 Alberto Fujimoro defeated Vargas Llosa in
presidential elections. Attempt to assassinate
Fujimoro failed.
1992 Fujimoro sided with army to avert coup, but
later promised a return to democracy. Sendero
Luminoso terrorists continued their campaign of
violence. A further coup attempt was foiled. A
single-chamber legislature replaced the two-
chamber system.

499 Revolt of the Ionian Greeks against Persian
rule.
490 Darius I of Persia defeated at Marathon.
480 Xerxes I victorious at Thermopylae (narrow
pass from Thessaly to Locris, which Leonidas, king
of Sparta, and 1,000 men defended to the death
against the Persians); Athens was captured, but the
Greek navy was victorious at ◊Salamis.
479 Greeks under Spartan general Pausanias (died
about 470) victorious at Plataea, driving the Persians from the country.
personal equity plan (PEP) investment scheme introduced in the UK 1987. Shares of public
companies listed on the UK stock exchange are
purchased by PEP managers on behalf of their
clients. Up to certain limits, individuals may purchase such shares and, provided they hold them for
at least a year, enjoy any capital gains and reinvested
dividents, tax-free.
personality an individual's characteristic way of
behaving across a wide range of situations.
personification a ◊figure of speech in which
animals, plants, objects, and ideas are treated as if
they were human or alive ('Clouds chased each
other across the face of the moon'; 'Nature smiled
on their work and gave it her blessing'.
Perspex trade name for a clear tough plastic widely
used for watch glasses, motorboat windscreens, and
protective shields, first produced in 1930. Its chemical name is polymethylmethacrylate (PMMA).
perspiration the excretion of water and dissolved substances from the ◊sweat glands of the

skin of mammals. Perspiration has two main functions: body cooling by the evaporation of water from
the skin surface; and excretion of waste products
such as salts.
Perth capital of Western Australia, with its port at
nearby Fremantle on the Swan river; population
(1990) 1,190,100. Products include textiles, cement, furniture, and vehicles. Founded in 1829, it is
the commercial and cultural centre of the state.
Perthshire former inland county of central Scotland, of which the major part was included in 1975
in Tayside, the SW being included in Central region;
Perth was the administrative headquarters.
Peru country in S America, on the Pacific, bounded
to the N by Ecuador and Colombia, to the E by Brazil
and Bolivia, and to the S by Chile.
Peru Current (formerly known as *Humboldt
Current*) cold ocean ◊current flowing N from the
Antarctic along the W coast of S America to S
Ecuador, then W.
Perugino Pietro. Assumed name of Pietro
Vannucci *c.* 1445–1523. Italian painter, active
chiefly in Perugia, the teacher of Raphael, who
absorbed his soft and graceful figure style. Perugino
produced paintings for the lower walls of the Sistine
Chapel 1481 (Vatican), and in 1500 decorated the
Sala del Cambio in Perugia.
perverting the course of justice in English
law, the criminal offence of acting in such a way as to
prevent justice being done. Examples are tamper-
ing with evidence or misleading the police.
Pesach the Jewish festival of ◊Passover.

Peshawar capital of North-West Frontier Province, Pakistan, 18 km/11 mi E of the Khyber Pass; population (1981) 555,000. Products include textiles, leather and copper.

Pestalozzi Johann Heinrich 1746–1827. Swiss educationalist who advocated Rousseau's 'natural' principles (of natural development and the power of example), and described his own theories in *Wie Gertrude ihre Kinder lehrt/How Gertrude Teaches her Children* 1801. He stressed the importance of mother and home in a child's education.

pesticide chemical used in farming and gardening to combat pests and diseases. Pesticides are of three main types – insecticides (to kill insects), fungicides (to kill fungal diseases), and herbicides (to kill weeds). The safest pesticides are those made from plants, such as the insecticides pyrethrum and derris. More potent are synthetic products, such as chlorinated hydrocarbons. These products, including DDT and dieldrin, are highly toxic to wildlife and human beings, so their use is now declining. Safer pesticides such as malathion are based on organic phosphorus compounds.

Pétain Henri Philippe 1856–1951. French general and right-wing politician. His defence of Verdun in 1916 during World War I made him a national hero. In World War II he became prime minister Jun 1940 and signed an armistice with Germany. Removing the seat of government to ◊Vichy, he established an authoritarian regime. He was imprisoned after the war.

petal part of a flower whose function is to attract pollinators such as insects or birds. They are frequently large and brightly coloured, and may also be scented. Some have a nectary at the base and markings on the petal surface, known as ◊honey guides, to direct pollinators to the source of the nectar. In wind-pollinated plants, however, the petals are usually small and insignificant, and sometimes absent altogether. Petals are derived from modified leaves, and are known collectively as a ◊corolla.

Peter three tsars of Russia:

Peter I *the Great* 1672–1725. Tsar of Russia from 1682 on the death of his brother Tsar Feodor, he assumed control of the government in 1689. He attempted to reorganize the country on Western lines: the army was modernized, a fleet was built, the administrative and legal systems were remodelled, education was encouraged, and the church was brought under state control. On the Baltic coast, where he had conquered territory from Sweden, Peter built his new capital, St Petersburg (now Leningrad).

Peter II 1715–1730. Tsar of Russia from 1727. Son of Peter the Great, he had been passed over in favour of Catherine I in 1725, but succeeded her in 1727. He died of smallpox.

Peter III 1728–1762. Tsar of Russia 1762. Weak-minded son of Peter I's eldest daughter, Anne, he was adopted 1741 by his aunt ◊Elizabeth and at her command married the future Catherine II in 1745. He was deposed in favour of his wife, probably murdered by her lover Alexius Orlov.

Peter I 1844–1921. King of Serbia from 1903. He was the son of Prince Alexander Karageorgevich, and was elected king when the last Obrenovich king was murdered in 1903. He took part in the retreat of the Serbian army in 1915, and in 1918 was proclaimed first king of the Serbs, Croats, and Slovenes.

Peter II 1923–1970. King of Yugoslavia 1934–45. He succeeded his father, Alexander I, and assumed the royal power after the overthrow of the regency

in 1941. He escaped to the UK after the German invasion, and married Princess Alexandra of Greece in 1944. He was dethroned in 1945.

Peterloo massacre name given, in analogy with the Battle of Waterloo, to the events in St Peter's Fields, Manchester, England, on 16 Aug 1819, when an open-air meeting in support of parliamentary reform was charged by yeomanry and hussars: 11 people were killed and 500 wounded.

Peter, St died 64 AD. Christian martyr, the author of two epistles in the New Testament and leader of the apostles. Tradition has it that he later settled in Rome; he is regarded as the first bishop of Rome, whose mantle the pope inherits. His emblem is two keys; feast day 29 Jun.

Peter's pence in the Roman Catholic Church, voluntary annual contribution to papal administrative costs; during the 10th–16th centuries it was a compulsory levy of one penny per household.

Peter the Hermit 1050–1115. French priest whose eloquent preaching of the First ◊Crusade sent thousands of peasants marching against the Turks, who massacred them in Asia Minor. Peter escaped and accompanied the main body of crusaders to Jerusalem.

petiole the stalk attaching the leaf blade, or ◊lamina, to the stem. Typically it is continuous with the midrib of the leaf and attached to the base of the lamina, but occasionally it is attached to the lower surface of the lamina (a peltate leaf), as in the nasturtium. Petioles that are flattened and leaf-like are termed phyllodes. Leaves that lack a petiole are said to be ◊sessile.

Petipa Marius 1818–1910. French choreographer. For the Imperial Ballet in Russia he created masterpieces such as *La Bayadère* 1877 *The Sleeping Beauty* 1890, *Swan Lake* 1895 (with Ivanov) and *Raymonda* 1898, which are still performed.

petition of right in British law, the procedure whereby, before the passing of the ◊Crown Proceedings Act 1947, a subject petitioned for legal relief against the crown, for example for money due under a contract, or for property of which the crown had taken possession. The most famous petition of right was that presented by Parliament and accepted by Charles I in 1628, declaring illegal taxation without parliamentary consent, imprisonment without trial, billeting of soldiers on private persons, and use of martial law.

Petra (Arabic *Wadi Musa*) ruined city carved out of the red rock at a site in modern Jordan, on the E slopes of the Wadi el Araba, 90 km/56 mi S of the Dead Sea. An Edomite stronghold, capital of the Nabataeans in the 2nd century, it was captured by the Roman emperor Trajan in 106 AD and wrecked by the Arabs in the 7th century. It was forgotten in Europe until in 1812 the Swiss traveller J L Burckhardt came across it.

Petrarch (Italian *Petrarca*) Francesco 1304–1374. Italian poet, a devotee of the classical tradition.

petrel two families of seabirds (Procellariidae and Hydrobatidae) which include albatrosses, fulmars, and shearwaters.

petrodollars in economics, dollar earnings of nations which comprise the ◊Organization of Petroleum Exporting Countries (OPEC).

Petrograd former name (1914–24) of St Petersburg, a city in Russia.

petrol engine the most commonly used source of power for cars and motorcycles, introduced by the German engineers Gottlieb Daimler and Karl Benz in 1885. The petrol engine is a complex piece of machinery made up of about 150 moving parts. It is

petroleum

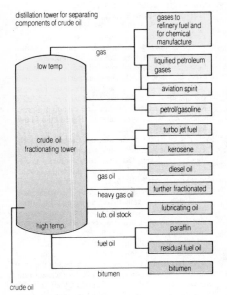

distillation tower for separating components of crude oil

gas

low temp

crude oil fractionating tower

gas oil

heavy gas oil

lub. oil stock

high temp.

fuel oil

bitumen

crude oil

gases to refinery fuel and for chemical manufacture

liquified petroleum gases

aviation spirit

petrol/gasoline

turbo jet fuel

kerosene

diesel oil

further fractionated

lubricating oil

paraffin

residual fuel oil

bitumen

a reciprocating piston engine, in which a number of pistons move up and down in cylinders. The motion of the pistons drive round a crankshaft, at the end of which is a heavy flywheel. From the flywheel the power is transferred to the car's driving wheels via the transmission system of clutch, gearbox, and final drive.

petroleum mineral oil, a thick greenish-brown liquid found underground in permeable rocks. Petroleum consists of hydrocarbons mixed with oxygen, sulphur, and so on, in varying proportions. It is thought to be derived from organic material which has been converted by, first, bacterial action, then heat and pressure, but its origin may be chemical rather than biological. From crude petroleum, or rock oil, various products are made by distillation and other processes, for example, fuel oil, gasoline (petrol), kerosene, diesel or gas oil, lubricating oil, paraffin wax, and petroleum jelly.

petrology branch of ◊geology that deals with the study of rocks, their mineral compositions, and their origins.

pewter an ◊alloy of tin and lead, known for centuries, once widely used for domestic utensils but now used mainly for ornamental ware.

peyote cactus *Lophophora williamsii* of Mexico and southern USA. Its white/pink flowers contain the hallucinogen *mescalin*, which is used by American Indians in religious ceremonies.

Pfalz German name of the historic division of Germany, the ◊Palatinate.

pH a scale for measuring acidity or alkalinity. A pH of 7.0 indicates neutrality, below 7 is acid, while above 7 is alkaline.

Phaethon in Greek mythology, the son of ◊Helios, who was allowed for one day to drive the chariot of the Sun. Losing control of the horses, he almost set the Earth on fire, and was killed by Zeus with a thunderbolt.

phage another name for a bacteriophage, a virus that attacks bacteria.

phagocyte a type of white blood cell, or ◊leucocyte, which can engulf a bacterium or other invading microorganism. They are found in blood, lymph, and other body tissues, where they also ingest foreign matter and dead tissue. A ◊macrophage differs in size and life span.

Phalangist member of a Lebanese military organization, since 1958 the political and military force of the ◊Maronite Church in the Lebanon. Its unbending right-wing policies and resistance to the introduction of democratic institutions helped contribute to the the civil war in ◊Lebanon.

phalarope genus of seabirds related to plovers and resembling sandpipers. They are native to North America, Britain, and polar regions of Europe.

phanerogam an obsolete name, once applied to plants which bore flowers or cones and reproduced by means of seeds, that is, ◊angiosperms and ◊gymnosperms, or ◊seed plants. Plants such as mosses, fungi, and ferns, were known as ***cryptogams***.

Phanerozoic eon in Earth history, consisting of the most recent 590 million years. It comprises the Palaeozoic, Mesozoic, and Cenozoic eras. The best fossils come from this eon, due to the evolution of skeletons and hard shells.

Pharaoh Hebrew form of the Egyptian royal title Per-'o. This term, meaning 'great house', was originally applied to the royal household, and after about 950 BC to the king.

Pharisee member of a Jewish sect that arose in the 2nd century BC in protest against all movements towards compromise with Hellenistic culture. They were devout adherents of the law both as found in the Torah and in the oral tradition known as the Mishnah.

pharmacology study of the origins, applications, and effects of chemical substances on living organisms. Products of the pharmaceutical industry range from aspirin to anti-cancer agents.

pharynx the interior of the throat, the cavity at the back of the mouth. Its walls are made of muscle strengthened with a fibrous layer and lined with mucous membrane. It has an opening into the back of each nostril, and downwards into the gullet and (through the epiglottis) into the windpipe. On each side, the Eustachian tube leads from it to the middle ear.

phase a physical state of matter: for example, ice and liquid water are different phases of water; a mixture of the two is termed a two-phase system. In physics, a stage in an oscillatory motion, such as a wave motion: two waves are in phase when their peaks and their troughs coincide. Otherwise, there is a phase difference, which has important consequences in ◊interference phenomena and ◊alternating current electricity.

phase in astronomy, the apparent shape of the Moon or a planet when all or part of its illuminated hemisphere is facing Earth. The Moon undergoes a full cycle of phases from new (when between Earth and the Sun) through first quarter (when at 90° eastern elongation from the Sun), full (when opposite the Sun), and last quarter (when at 90° western elongation form the Sun). The ◊inferior planets can also undergo a full cycle of phases as can an asteroid passing inside the Earth's orbit.

PhD abbreviation for *Doctor of Philosophy*.

pheasant bird of the family Phasianidae, which also includes quail and peafowl. The plumage of the male common pheasant *Phasianus colchicus* is richly tinted with brownish-green, yellow, and red markings, but the female is a camouflaged brownish

phenol

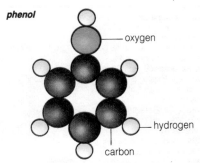

oxygen

hydrogen

carbon

colour. The nest is made in the ground, and the male is polygamous.

phenol also known as *carbolic acid* an aromatic compound, extracted from coal tar. Phenol, important industrially, is used to make dyes, drugs, nylon, and various plastics.

phenomenalism a philosophical position which argues that statements about objects can be reduced to statements about what is perceived or perceivable. Thus, J S Mill defined material objects as 'permanent possibilities of sensation'. Phenomenalism is closely connected with certain forms of ◊empiricism.

phenomenology the philosophical perspective, founded by ◊Husserl, which in the social sciences concentrates on phenomena as objects of perception (rather than as facts or occurrences which exist independently) in attempting to examine the ways people think about and interpret the world around them. It has been practised by the philosophers ◊Heidegger, Sartre, and Merleau-Ponty.

phenotype in genetics, the traits actually displayed by an organism. The phenotype is not a direct reflection of the ◊genotype because some alleles are masked by the presence of other, dominant alleles (see ◊dominance). The phenotype is further modified by the effects of the environment (for example, poor food stunting growth).

pheromone chemical signal that is emitted (like an odour) by one animal and affects the behaviour of others. Pheromones are used by many animal species to attract mates.

Phidias mid-5th century BC. Greek sculptor, one of the most influential of classical times. He supervised the sculptural programme for the Parthenon (most of it preserved in the British Museum, London, and known as the *Elgin marbles*). He also executed the colossal statue of Zeus at Olympia, one of the Seven Wonders of the World.

Philadelphia industrial city and port on the Delaware river in Pennsylvania, USA; population (1980) 1,688,000, metropolitan area 3,700,000. Products include refined oil, chemicals, textiles, processed food, printing and publishing. Founded 1682 as the 'city of brotherly love', it was the first capital of the USA 1790–1800.

philately the collection and study of postage stamps. It originated as a hobby in France about 1860.

Philby 'Kim' (Harold) 1912–1988. British intelligence officer from 1940 and Soviet agent from 1933. He was liaison officer in Washington 1949–51, when he was asked to resign. Named in 1963 as having warned Guy Burgess and Donald Maclean (similarly double agents) that their activities were known, he fled to the USSR, and became a Soviet citizen and general in the KGB. A fourth member of the ring was Anthony ◊Blunt.

Philip 1921– . Prince of the UK. A grandson of George I of Greece and a great-great-grandson of Queen Victoria, he was born in Corfu but raised in England. A naturalized British subject, taking the surname Mountbatten in Mar 1947, he married Princess Elizabeth (from 1952 Elizabeth II) in Westminster Abbey on 20 Nov 1947, having the previous day received the title Duke of Edinburgh.

Philip the Good 1396–1467. Duke of Burgundy from 1419. He engaged in the Hundred Years' War as an ally of England until he made peace with the French at the Council of Arras (1435). He made the Netherlands a centre of art and learning.

Philip six kings of France, including:

Philip II (Philip Augustus) 1165–1223. King of France from 1180. He waged war in turn against the English kings Henry II, Richard I (with whom he also went on the Third Crusade), and John (against whom he won the decisive battle of Bouvines in Flanders 1214) to evict them from their French possessions, and establish a strong monarchy.

Philip IV *the Fair* 1268–1314. King of France from 1285. He engaged in a feud with Pope Boniface VIII, and made him a prisoner in 1303. Clement V (1264–1314), elected pope through Philip's influence, moved to Avignon, and collaborated with Philip to suppress the ◊Templars, a powerful order of knights. Philip allied with the Scots against England, and invaded Flanders.

Philip VI 1293–1350. King of France from 1328, first of the house of Valois, elected by the barons on the death of his cousin, Charles IV. His claim was challenged by Edward III of England, who in 1346 defeated him at Crécy.

Philip II of Macedon 382–336 BC. King of ◊Macedonia from 359 BC. He seized the throne from his nephew, for whom he was regent, conquered the Greek city states and formed them into a league whose forces could be united against Persia. He was assassinated just as he was planning this expedition, and was succeeded by his son ◊Alexander the Great. His tomb was discovered at Vergina, N Greece, in 1978.

Philip five kings of Spain, including:

Philip I *the Handsome* 1478–1506. King of Castile from 1504, through his marriage 1496 to Joanna the Mad (1479–1555). Son of the Holy Roman emperor Maximilian I.

Philip II 1527–1598. King of Spain from 1556. Son of the Hapsburg emperor Charles V, he was born at Valladolid, and in 1554 married Queen Mary of England. On his father's abdication in 1556 he inherited Spain, the Netherlands, and the Spanish possessions in Italy and America, and in 1580 he annexed Portugal. His intolerance and lack of understanding of the Netherlanders drove them into

Philip II Philip II, King of Spain 1556-98.

Philippines
Republic of the (*Republika ng Pilipinas*)

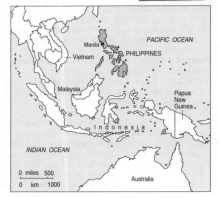

area 300,000 sq km/115,700 sq mi
capital Manila (on Luzon)
towns Quezon City
ports Cebu, Davao (on Mindanao) and Iloilo
physical comprises over 7,000 islands, with volcanic mountain ranges traversing the main chain N–S, and 50% of the area still forested.
head of state and government Fidel Ramos from 1992
political system emergent democracy

exports sugar, copra and coconut oil, timber, iron ore and copper concentrates
currency peso
population (1990 est) 66,647,000 (93% Malaysian); annual growth rate 2.4%
life expectancy men 63, women 69
language Tagalog (Filipino, official); English, Spanish
religion Roman Catholic 84%, Protestant 9%, Muslim 5%
literacy 88% (1989)
GNP $38.2 bn (1988); $667 per head
chronology
1565 Conquered by Spain.
1898 Ceded to the USA.
1935 Grant of internal self-government.
1942–45 Japanese occupation.
1946 Independence granted.
1965 Ferdinand Marcos elected president.
1983 Murder of Benigno Aquino.
1986 Overthrow of Marcos by Corazón Aquino's People's Power movement.
1987 New constitution approved in plebiscite; People's Power won majority in congressional elections. Attempted right-wing coup suppressed. Communist guerrillas active. Government in rightward swing.
1988 Diluted land-reform act gave favourable compensation to large estate holders.
1989 Marcos died in exile. Coup attempt suppressed with US aid.
1991 Mount Pinatubo erupted; hundreds killed. Senate voted to urge withdrawal of all US forces. Imelda Marcos returned.
1992 Fidel Ramos elected president to replace Aquino.

revolt. Political and religious reasons combined to involve him in war with England, and after 1589 with France. The defeat of the ◊Spanish Armada marked the beginning of the decline of Spanish power.

Philip V 1683–1746. King of Spain from 1700. A grandson of Louis XIV of France, he was the first Bourbon king of Spain. He was not recognized by the major European powers until 1713. See ◊Spanish Succession, War of the.

Philip Neri, St 1515–1595. Italian Roman Catholic priest who organized the Congregation of the Oratory (see ◊Oratorian). He built the oratory over the church of St Jerome, Rome, where prayer meetings were held and scenes from the Bible performed with music, originating the musical form ◊oratorio. Feast day 26 May.

Philippi ancient city of Macedonia founded by Philip of Macedon, 358 BC. Near Philippi, Antony and Octavius defeated Brutus and Cassius in 42 BC. It was the first European town where St Paul preached (about 53 AD), founding the congregation to which he addressed the Epistle to the Philippians.

Philippines country on an archipelago between the Pacific Ocean to the E and the South China Sea to the W.

Philip, St 1st century AD, in the New Testament, one of the 12 apostles. He was an inhabitant of Bethsaida (in N Israel), and is said to have worked as a missionary in Anatolia. Feast day 3 May.

Philistine member of a people of non-Semitic origin (possibly from Asia Minor) who founded city states on the Palestinian coastal plain in the 12th century BC, adopting a Semitic language and religion. They were at war with the Israelites in the 11th–10th centuries BC (hence the pejorative

use of their name in Hebrew records for anyone uncivilized in intellectual and artistic terms).

Phillip Arthur 1738–1814. British vice admiral, founder and governor of the convict settlement at Sydney, Australia, 1788–1792, and hence founder of New South Wales.

Phillips curve a graph showing the relationship between percentage changes in wages and unemployment, and indicating that wages rise faster during periods of low unemployment as employers compete for labour. The implication is that the dual objectives of low unemployment and low inflation are inconsistent. It was developed by A W Phillips.

philology a Greek term, meaning 'love of language'. In historical ◊linguistics, it refers to the study of the development of languages. It is also an obsolete term for the study of literature.

philosophy the branch of learning which includes metaphysics (the nature of Being), epistemology (theory of knowledge), logic (study of valid inference), ethics, and aesthetics. Originally, philosophy included all intellectual endeavour, but over time traditional branches of philosophy have acquired their own status as separate areas of study. Philosophy is concerned with fundamental problems, including the nature of mind and matter, perception, self, free will, causation, time and space, the existence of moral judgements, which cannot be resolved by a specific method. Contemporary philosophers are inclined to think of philosophy as an investigation of the fundamental assumptions that govern our ways of understanding and acting in the world.

phlebitis inflammation of a vein. It is sometimes associated with blockage by a blood clot (◊thrombosis), in which case it is more accurately described as thrombophlebitis.

philosophy: great philosophers

Name	Dates	Nationality	Representative work
Heraclitus	c.544–483 BC	Greek	On Nature (fragments)
Parmenides	c.510–c.450 BC	Greek	fragments
Socrates	469–399 BC	Greek	–
Plato	428–347 BC	Greek	Republic; Phaedo
Aristotle	384–322 BC	Greek	Nicomachean Ethics; Metaphysics
Epicurus	341–270 BC	Greek	fragments
Lucretius	c.99–55 BC	Roman	On the Nature of Things
Plotinus	205–270 AD	Greek	Enneads
Augustine	354–430	N African	Confessions; City of God
Aquinas	c.1225–1274	Italian	Summa Theologica
Duns Scotus	c.1266–1308	Scottish	Opus Oxoniense
William of Occam	c.1285–1349	English	Commentary of the Sentences
Nicholas of Cusa	1401–1464	German	De Docta Ignorantia
Giordano Bruno	1548–1600	Italian	De la Causa, Principio e Uno
Bacon	1561–1626	English	Novum Organum; The Advancement of Learning
Hobbes	1588–1679	English	Leviathan
Descartes	1596–1650	French	Discourse on Method; Meditations on the First Philosophy
Pascal	1623–1662	French	Pensées
Spinoza	1632–1677	Dutch	Ethics
Locke	1632–1704	English	Essay Concerning Human Understanding
Leibniz	1646–1716	German	The Monadology
Vico	1668–1744	Italian	The New Science
Berkeley	1685–1753	Irish	A Treatise Concerning the Principles of Human Knowledge
Hume	1711–1776	Scottish	A Treatise of Human Nature
Rousseau	1712–1778	French	The Social Contract
Diderot	1713–1784	French	D'Alembert's Dream
Kant	1724–1804	German	The Critique of Pure Reason
Fichte	1762–1814	German	The Science of Knowledge
Hegel	1770–1831	German	The Phenomenology of Spirit
Schelling	1775–1854	German	System of Transcendental Idealism
Schopenhauer	1788–1860	German	The World as Will and Idea
Comte	1798–1857	French	Cours de philosophie positive
Mill	1806–1873	English	Utilitarianism
Kierkegaard	1813–1855	Danish	Concept of Dread
Marx	1818–1883	German	Economic and Philosophical Manuscripts
Dilthey	1833–1911	German	The Rise of Hermeneutics
Peirce	1839–1914	American	How to Make our Ideas Clear
Nietzsche	1844–1900	German	Thus Spake Zarathustra
Bergson	1859–1941	French	Creative Evolution
Husserl	1859–1938	German	Logical Investigations
Russell	1872–1970	English	Principia Mathematica
Lukács	1885–1971	Hungarian	History and Class Consciousness
Wittgenstein	1889–1951	Austrian	Tractatus Logico–Philosophicus; Philosophical Investigations
Heidegger	1889–1976	German	Being and Time
Gadamer	1900–	German	Truth and Method
Sartre	1905–1980	French	Being and Nothingness
Merleau-Ponty	1908–1961	French	The Phenomenology of Perception
Quine	1908–	American	Word and Object
Foucault	1926–1984	French	The Order of Things

phloem a tissue found in vascular plants whose main function is to conduct sugars and other food materials from the leaves, where they are produced, to all other parts of the plant. Phloem is mainly composed of sieve elements and their associated companion cells, together with some ◊sclerenchyma and ◊parenchyma cell types. Sieve elements are long, thin-walled cells joined end to end forming sieve tubes; large pores in the end walls allow the continuous passage of nutrients. Phloem is usually found in association with ◊xylem, the water-conducting tissue, but unlike the latter it is a living tissue.

Phnom Penh capital of Kampuchea, on the Mekong, 210 km/130 mi NW of Saigon; population (1981) 400,000. Industries include textiles and food-processing.

phobia an excessive irrational fear of an object or situation, for example, agoraphobia (fear of open spaces and crowded places), acrophobia (fear of heights), claustrophobia (fear of enclosed places). Behaviour therapy is one form of treatment.

Phobos one of the two moons of Mars, discovered 1877 by the US astronomer Asaph Hall. It is an irregularly shaped lump of rock, cratered by ◊meteorite impacts. Phobos is 27 × 21 × 19 km/17 × 13 × 12 mi across, and orbits Mars every 0.32 days at a height of 9,400 km/5,840 mi. It is thought to be an asteroid captured by Mars' gravity.

Phoenicia ancient Greek name for Northern ◊Canaan on the E coast of the Mediterranean. The Phoenicians, c. 1200–332 BC, were seafaring traders and artisans, who are said to have circumnavigated Africa, and established colonies all round the Mediterranean. Their cities (Tyre, Sidon and Byblos were the chief ones), were independent states ruled by hereditary kings but dominated by merchant ruling classes. The fall of Tyre to Alexander the Great ended the separate history of Phoenicia.

Phoenix capital of Arizona, USA; industrial city (steel, aluminium, electrical goods, food processing) and tourist centre on the Salt river; population (1984) 866,500.

phosphorescence organic chemist working with phosphorescing solutions.

phoenix mythical Egyptian bird that burned itself to death on a pyre every 500 years, and rose rejuvenated from the ashes.

phon unit of loudness, equal to the intensity in decibels of a sound with a frequency of 1,000 hertz and a sound pressure of 20×10^{-6} pascals.

phonetics the identification, description, and classification of sounds used in articulate speech. These sounds are codified in the International Phonetic Alphabet (a highly modifed version of the Roman alphabet).

phonograph the name Thomas ◊Edison gave to his sound-recording apparatus, which developed into the modern ◊record player.

phosphate any salt of phosphorous oxy-acids, including hypophosphorous acid (H_3PO_2), phosphorous acid (H_3PO_3), hypophosphoric acid ($H_4P_2O_6$) and orthophosphoric acid (H_3PO_4). Phosphates are used as fertilizers.

phosphor a substance that gives out visible light when it is illuminated by a beam of electrons or ultraviolet light. The television screen is coated on the inside with phosphors which glow when beams of electrons strike them. Fluorescent lamp tubes are also phosphor-coated.

phosphorescence in physics, the emission of light by certain substances after they have absorbed energy, whether from visible light, other electromagnetic radiation such as ultraviolet rays or X-rays, or cathode rays (a beam of electrons). When the stimulating energy is removed phosphorescence ceases, although it may persist for a short time after (unlike ◊fluorescence, which stops immediately).

phosphorus an element, symbol P, atomic number 15, relative atomic mass 30.975. It occurs in several forms, the commonest being white phosphorus (a waxy solid emitting a greenish glow in air, burning spontaneously to phosphorus pentoxide, and very poisonous) and red phosphorus (neither igniting spontaneously nor poisonous). It is used in fertilizers, in matches, in the prevention of scale and corrosion in pipes and boiler tubes, and in certain organic chemicals.

photocell or *photoelectric cell* device for measuring or detecting light, or other electromagnetic radiation.

photocopier machine that uses some form of photographic process to reproduce copies of documents. Most modern photocopiers, as pioneered by the American Xerox Corporation, use electrostatic photocopying, or xerography ('dry writing'). This employs a drum coated with a light-sensitive material such as selenium, which holds a pattern of static electricity charges corresponding to the dark areas of an image projected on to the drum by a lens. Finely divided pigment (toner) of opposite electric charge sticks to the charged areas of the drum, and is transferred to a sheet of paper which is heated briefly to melt the toner and stick it to the paper.

photoelectric effect in physics, the emission of ◊electrons from a metallic surface when it is struck by ◊photons (quanta of electromagnetic radiation), usually those of visible light or ultraviolet radiation. The energy of the emitted electrons depends on the frequency of the incident radiation (which must exceed a characteristic threshold frequency); the higher the frequency, the greater the energy of its photons. The number of electrons emitted depends on the radiation's intensity (rate of transfer of energy per unit area). The theory of the photoelectric effect, a ◊quantum theory of radiation, was formulated in 1905, by ◊Einstein.

photofit system aiding the identification of wanted persons. Witnesses select photographs of a single feature (hair, eyes, nose, mouth), their choices resulting in a composite likeness, then rephotographed and circulated. It is a sophisticated development by Jacques Penry in 1970 for Scotland Yard of the identikit system evolved by an American, Hugh C McDonald (1913–).

photogram a picture produced on photographic material by means of exposing it to light, but without using a camera.

photography a process for producing images on sensitized materials by various forms of radiant energy, for example, visible light, ultraviolet, infrared, X-rays; radioactive radiation; electron beam.

photometer an instrument that measures luminous intensity. Bunsen's early greasespot photometer compares the intensity of a light source with a known source by each illuminating half of a translucent area. Modern photometers use ◊photocells, as in a photographer's exposure meter. A ◊photomultiplier can also be used as a photometer.

photomultiplier an instrument that detects low levels of electromagnetic radiation (usually visible light or ◊infrared radiation) and amplifies it to produce a detectable signal.

photon in physics, the smallest 'package', 'particle', or quantum of energy in which ◊light, or any other form of electromagnetic radiation, is emitted.

photoperiodism a biological mechanism that controls the timing of certain activities by responding to changes in day length. The flowering of many plants is initiated in this way. Photoperiodism in plants is regulated by a light-sensitive pigment, *phytochrome*. The breeding seasons of many temperate animals are also triggered by increasing or declining day length, as part of their ◊biorhythms.

photosphere the visible surface of the Sun, which emits light and heat. About 300 km/200 mi deep, it consists of incandescent gas at a temperature of 5,800K.

photosynthesis the process by which green plants, photosynthetic bacteria and cyanobacteria utilize light energy from the Sun to produce food molecules (◊carbohydrates) from carbon dioxide and water. There are two stages. During the *light reaction* sunlight is used to split water (H_2O) into oxygen (O_2), protons (hydrogen ions, H^+) and electrons, and Oxygen is given off as a by-product. In the second stage *dark reaction*, where sunlight is not required, the protons and electrons are used to convert carbon dioxide (CO_2) into carbohydrates

photography: chronology

1515	Leonardo da Vinci described the camera obscura.
1750	The painter Canaletto used a camera obscura as an aid to his painting in Venice.
1790	Thomas Wedgewood in England made photograms – placing objects on leather, sensitized using silver nitrate.
1826	Nicephore Niépce (1765–1833), a French doctor, produced the world's first photograph from nature on pewter plates with a camera obscura and an eight-hour exposure.
1835	Niépce and L J M Daguerre produced the first daguerreotype camera photograph.
1839	Daguerre was awarded an annuity by the French government and his process given to the world.
1841	Fox Talbot's calotype process was patented – the first multicopy method of photography using a negative/positive process, sensitized with silver iodide.
1843	Hill and Adamson began to use calotypes for portraits in Edinburgh.
1844	Fox Talbot published the first photographic book, *The Pencil of Nature*.
1851	Fox Talbot used a one-thousandth of a second exposure to demonstrate high-speed photography.
1855	Roger Fenton made documentary photographs of the Crimean War from a specially constructed caravan with a portable darkroom.
1859	Under the pseudonym Nadar, Gaspard-Felix Tournachan (1820–1910), French writer, caricaturist and photographer, made photographs underground in Paris using battery-powered arc lights.
1860	Queen Victoria was photographed by Mayall. Abraham Lincoln was photographed by Matthew Brady for political campaigning.
1861	The single lens reflex plate camera was patented by Thomas Sutton.
1862	Nadar took aerial photographs over Paris.
1870	Julia Margaret Cameron used long lenses for her distinctive portraits.
1878	In the USA Eadweard Muybridge analysed the movements of animals through sequential photographs, using a series of cameras.
1880	A silver bromide emulsion was fixed with hypo. Photographs were first reproduced in newspapers in New York using the half-tone engraving process. The first twin-lens reflex camera was produced in London.
1889	Eastman Company in the USA produced the Kodak No. 1 camera and roll film, facilitating universal, hand-held snapshots.
1902	In Germany Deckel invented a prototype leaf shutter and Zeiss introduced the Tessar lens.
1904	The autochrome colour process was patented by the Lumière brothers.
1905	Alfred Steiglitz opened the gallery '291' in New York promoting photography. Lewis Hine used photography to expose the exploitation of children in American factories, causing protective laws to be passed.
1907	The autochrome process began to be factory-produced.
1914	Oskar Barnack designed a prototype Leica camera for Leitz in Germany.
1924	Leitz launched the first 35 mm camera, the Leica, delayed because of World War I. It became very popular with photo-journalists because it was quiet, small, dependable and had a range of lenses and accessories.
1929	Rolleiflex produced a twin-lens reflex camera in Germany.
1935	In the USA, Mannes and Godowsky invented Kodachrome transparency film, which has great sharpness and rich colour quality. Electronic flash was invented in the USA. Social documentary photography received wide attention through the photographs of Dorothea Lange, Margaret Bourke-White, Arthur Rothstein, Walker Evans, and others taken for the US government's Farm Security Administration of the plight of the poor tenant farmers in the mid-West.
1936	*Life* magazine, noted for photo-journalism, was first published in the USA.
1938	*Picture Post* magazine was introduced in the UK.
1940	Multigrade enlarging paper by Ilford was made available in the UK.
1945	The Zone System of exposure estimation was explained in the book *Exposure Record* by Ansel Adams.
1947	Polaroid black and white instant process film was invented by Dr Edwin Land, who set up the Polaroid corporation in Boston, Massachusetts. The principles of holography were demonstrated in England by Dennis Gabor.
1955	Kodak introduced Tri-X, a black and white 200 ASA film.
1959	The zoom lens was invented in Germany by Voigtlander.
1960	Laser was invented in the USA, making holography possible. Polacolor, a self-processing colour film, was introduced by Polaroid, using a 60-second colour film and dye diffusion technique.
1963	Cibachrome, paper and chemicals for printing directly from transparencies, was made available by Ciba-Geigy of Switzerland. One of the most permanent processes, it is marketed by Ilford in the UK.
1969	Photographs were taken on the Moon by US astronauts.
1972	SX70 system, a single lens reflex camera with instant prints, was produced by Polaroid.
1980	Ansel Adams sold an original print *Moonrise: Hernandez* for $45,000, a record price, in the USA. Voyager 1 sent photographs of Saturn back to Earth across space.
1985	Minolta Corporation in Japan introduced the world's first body-integral autofocus single lens reflex camera.
1990	Kodak introduced Photo CD which converts 35 mm camera pictures (on film) into digital form and stores them on compact disc for viewing on TV.

photosynthesis

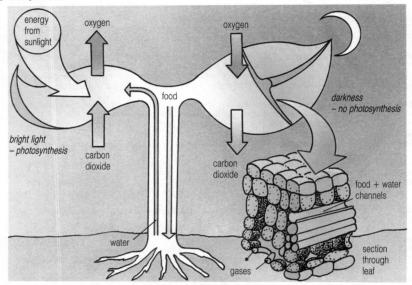

(CH₂O). Photosynthesis depends on the ability of ◊chlorophyll to capture the energy of sunlight and use it to split water molecules.

phrase structure grammar a theory of language structure which proposes that a given language has several different potential sentence patterns, consisting of various sorts of phrase, which can be expanded in various ways.

Phrygia former kingdom of W Asia covering the Anatolian tableland. It was inhabited in ancient times by an Indo-European people, and achieved great prosperity in the 8th century BC under a line of kings bearing in turn the names Gordius and Midas, but then fell under Lydian rule. From Phrygia the cult of ◊Cybele was introduced into Greece and Rome.

phyllotaxis the arrangement of leaves on a plant stem. Leaves are nearly always arranged in a regular pattern and in the majority of plants they are inserted singly, either in a *spiral* arrangement up the stem, or on *alternate* sides. Other principal forms are opposite leaves, where two arise from the same node, and whorled, where three or more arise from the same node.

phylloxera a genus of aphid-like lice.

phylogeny the historical sequence of changes that occurs in a given species during the course of evolution. It used to be erroneously associated with ontogeny (the process of development of a living organism).

phylum (plural *phyla*) a major grouping in biological classification. Mammals, birds, reptiles, amphibians, and fish belong to the phylum Chordata; the phylum Mollusca consists of snails, slugs, mussels and clams, squid and octopuses; the phylum Porifera contains sponges, and the phylum Echinodermata includes starfish, sea urchins, and sea cucumbers. Among plants there are between four and nine phyla depending on the classification used; all flowering plants belong to a single phylum, Angiospermata, and all conifers to another, Gymnospermata. Related phyla are grouped together in a ◊kingdom; phyla are subdivided into ◊classes.

physics the branch of science concerned with the ultimate laws that govern the structure of the Universe, and forms of matter and energy and their interactions. For convenience, physics is often divided into branches such as nuclear physics, solid and liquid state physics, electricity, electronics, magnetism, optics, acoustics, heat, and thermodynamics. Before this century, physics was known as *natural philosophy*.

physiology a branch of biology which deals with the functioning of living animals, as opposed to anatomy, which studies their structures.

physiotherapy treatment of injury and disease by physical means such as electrical stimulation, exercise, heat, manipulation, and massage.

Piaf (French slang 'sparrow'), Edith. Stage name of Edith Gassion 1915–1963. French Parisian singer and songwriter, best known for her defiant song 'Je ne regrette rien/I Regret Nothing'.

Piaget Jean 1896–1980. Swiss psychologist noted for his studies of the development of thought, concepts of space and movement, logic and reasoning in children.

piano (pianoforte) a stringed musical instrument, whose keyed hammers make it percussive and capable of soft (piano) or strong (forte) tones – hence its name.

Picabia Francis 1879–1953. French painter, a Cubist from 1909. On his second visit to New York, 1915–16, he joined with Marcel Duchamp in the Dadaist revolt and later took the movement to Barcelona. He associated with the Surrealists for a time. His work was generally provocative and experimental.

Picardy (French *Picardie*) region of N France, including Aisne, Oise, and Somme *départements*; area 19,399 sq km/7,490 sq mi; population (1982) 1,740,300. Industries include chemicals and metals. It was a major battlefield in World War I.

picaresque (Spanish *picaro* 'rogue') in literature, a genre of novels which take for their heroes rogues and villains, telling their story in a series of loosely linked episodes. Examples include Defoe's

physics: landmarks

c.400 BC	The first 'atomic' theory was put forward by Democritus.
c.250 BC	Archimedes' principle of buoyancy was established.
1600 AD	Magnetism was described by English physicist and physician William Gilbert (1544–1603).
c.1610	The principle of falling bodies descending to Earth at the same speed was established by Galileo.
1642	The principles of hydraulics were put forward by French mathematician, physicist, and philosopher Blaise Pascal (1623–62).
1643	The mercury barometer was invented by Italian physicist Evangelista Torricelli (1608–47).
1656	The pendulum clock was invented by Dutch physicist and astronomer Christiaan Huygens (1629–95).
c.1665	Newton put forward the law of gravity, stating that the Earth exerts a constant force on falling bodies.
1677	The simple microscope was invented by Dutch microscopist Antoni van Leeuwenhoek (1632–1723).
1690	The wave theory of light was propounded by Huygens.
1704	The corpuscular theory of light was put forward by Newton.
1714	The mercury thermometer was invented by German physicist (Gabriel) Daniel Fahrenheit.
1771	The link between nerve action and electricity was discovered by Italian anatomist and physiologist Luigi Galvani (1737–98).
1795	The metric system was adopted in France.
1798	The link between heat and friction was discovered by American-British physicist Count Benjamin Thomson Rumford (1753–1814).
1800	Volta invented the Voltaic cell.
1808	The 'modern' atomic theory was propounded by British physicist and chemist John Dalton (1766–1844).
1811	Avogadro's hypothesis relating volumes and numbers of molecules of gases was proposed by Italian physicist and chemist Amedeo Avogadro (1776–1856).
1815	Refraction of light was explained by French physicist Augustin Fresnel (1788–1827).
1819	The discovery of electromagnetism was made by Danish physicist Hans Oersted (1777–1851).
1821	The dynamo principle was described by British physicist and chemist Michael Faraday (1791–1867); the thermocouple was discovered by German physicist Thomas Seebeck (1770–1831).
1827	Ohm's law was established by German physicist GS Ohm; Brownian motion resulting from molecular vibrations was observed by British botanist Robert Brown (1773–1858).
1831	Electromagnetic induction was discovered by Faraday.
1842	The principle of conservation of energy was observed by German physician and physicist Julius von Mayer (1814–78).
c.1847	The mechanical equivalent of heat was described by Joule.
1849	A measurement of speed of light was put forward by French physicist Armand Fizeau (1819–96).
1851	The rotation of the Earth was demonstrated by Foucault.
1859	Spectrographic analysis was made by German chemist Robert Bunsen (1811–99) and German physicist Gustav Kirchhoff (1824–87).
1861	Osmosis was discovered.
1873	Light was conceived as electromagnetic radiation by British physicist James Clerk Maxwell.
1877	A theory of sound as vibrations in an elastic medium was propounded by British physicist John Rayleigh (1842–1919).
1887	The existence of radio waves was predicted by Hertz.
1895	X-rays were discovered by German physicist Wilhelm Röntgen (1845–1923).
1896	The discovery of radioactivity was made by French physicist Antoine Becquerel (1852–1908).
1897	The electron was discovered by J J Thomson.
1899	Rutherford discovered alpha and beta rays.
1900	Quantum theory was propounded by Planck; the discovery of gamma rays was made by French physicist Paul-Ulrich Villard (1860–1934).
1902	Heaviside discovered the ionosphere.
1904	The theory of radioactivity was put forward by Rutherford and British chemist Frederick Soddy (1877–1966).
1905	Einstein propounded his special theory of relativity.
1911	The discovery of the atomic nucleus was made by Rutherford.
1915	Einstein put forward his general theory of relativity; X-ray crystallography was discovered by William and Lawrence Bragg.
1922	The orbiting electron atomic theory was propounded by Bohr.
1924	Appleton made his study of the Heaviside layer.
1927	The uncertainty principle of atomic physics was established by German physicist Werner Heisenberg (1901–76).
1928	Wave mechanics was introduced by Schrödinger.
1931	The cyclotron was developed by American physicist Ernest Lawrence (1901–58).
1932	The discovery of the neutron was made by Chadwick; the electron microscope was developed by Soviet-American physicist Vladimir Zworykin (1889–1982).
1933	The position, the antiparticle of the electron, was discovered by Millikan.
1934	Artificial radioactivity was developed by Frédéric and Irène Joliot-Curie.
1939	The discovery of nuclear fission was made by Hahn and German chemist Fritz Strassman (1902–).
1942	The first controlled nuclear chain reaction was achieved by Fermi.
1956	The neutrino, a fundamental particle, was discovered.
1960	The Mössbauer effect of atom emissions was discovered by German physicist Rudolf Mössbauer (1929–); the first maser was developed by American physicist Theodore Maiman (1927–).
1963	Maiman developed the first laser.
1964	Murray Gell-Mann and George Zweig discovered the quark.
1973	Antony Hewish discovered pulsars.
1982	The discovery of the processes involved in the evolution of stars was made by Subrahmanyan Chandrasekhar and William Fowler.
1986	The first high-temperature superconductor was discovered.

Picasso The Three Dancers *(1925) Tate Gallery, London.*

Moll Flanders, Smollett's *Roderick Random*, and Fielding's *Tom Jones*.

Picasso Pablo 1881–1973. Spanish artist, active chiefly in France, one of the most inventive and prolific talents in 20th century art. His Blue Period 1901–04 and Rose Period 1905–06 preceded the revolutionary *Les Demoiselles d'Avignon* 1907 (Metropolitan Museum of Art, New York), which paved the way for Cubism. In the early 1920s he was considered a leader of the Surrealist movement. In the 1930s his work included metal sculpture, book illustration, and the mural *Guernica* 1937 (Casón del Buen Retiro, Madrid), a comment on the bombing of civilians in the Spanish Civil War. He continued to paint into his 80s.

Piccard August 1884–1962. Swiss scientist. In 1931–32, he and his twin brother Jean Félix made ascents to 16,800 m/55,000 ft in a balloon of his own design, resulting in important discoveries concerning such stratospheric phenomena as ◊cosmic rays. He also built and used, with his son Jacques Ernest, bathyscaphes for research under the sea.

piccolo a woodwind instrument, the smallest member of the ◊flute family.

picketing a gathering of workers and their trade union representatives, usually at the entrance to their place of work, to try to persuade others to support them in an industrial dispute.

Pickford Mary (born Gladys Smith) 1893–1979. American actress, the first star of the silent screen to be known by name. She and her second husband (from 1920), Douglas ◊Fairbanks senior, were known as 'the world's sweethearts'.

picric acid $C_6H_2(NO_2)_3OH$ a yellow crystalline solid (modern name 2,4,6-trinitrophenol). It is a strong acid, which is used to dye wool and silks yellow, for the treatment of burns, and in the manufacture of explosives.

Pict Roman term for a member of the peoples of N Scotland, possibly meaning 'painted' (tattooed). Probably of pre-Celtic origin, and speaking a non-Celtic language, the Picts were united with the Celtic Scots under the rule of Kenneth MacAlpin in 844.

PID abbreviation for *pelvic inflammatory disease*, an increasingly common gynaecological condition. It is characterized by lower abdominal pain, malaise, and fever; menstruation may be disrupted; infertility may result. The bacterium *Chlamydia trachomatis* has been implicated in a high proportion of cases. The incidence of the disease is twice as high in women using intrauterine contraceptive devices (IUDs).

pidgin English commonly and loosely used to mean any kind of 'broken' or 'native' version of the English language, pidgin English proper began as a trade jargon or contact language between the British and the Chinese in the 19th century.

pidgin languages trade jargons, contact languages, or lingua francas arising in ports and markets where people of different linguistic backgrounds meet for commercial and other purposes.

pièce de résistance (French) the most outstanding item in a collection.

Pieck Wilhelm 1876–1960. German communist politician. He was a leader of the 1919 Spartacist revolt and a founder of the Socialist Unity Party in 1946, and from 1949 was president of East Germany; the office was abolished on his death.

pied-à-terre (French 'foot on the ground') a convenient second home, usually small and in a town.

Piedmont (Italian *Piemonte*) region of N Italy, bordering Switzerland on the N and France on the W and surrounded, except on the E, by the Alps and the Apennines
area 25,399 sq km/9,804 sq mi
capital Turin
towns Alessandria, Asti, Vercelli, Novara
products fruit, grain, cattle, cars, textiles
population (1984) 4,412,000
history from Piedmont, under the house of Savoy, the movement for the unification of Italy started in the 19th century.

Pietism religious movement within Lutheranism in the 17th century which emphasized spiritual and devotional Christianity.

pietra dura Italian for 'hard stone', an Italian technique of inlaying furniture with semi-precious stone, such as agate or quartz, in different colours to create pictures or patterns.

piezoelectric effect property of some ◊crystals, for example, ◊quartz, which develop an electromotive force or voltage across opposite faces when subjected to a mechanical strain, and, conversely, which alter in size when subjected to an electromotive force. Piezoelectric crystal ◊oscillators are used as frequency standards, for example, replacing balance wheels in watches.

pig hoofed mammal of family Suidae. The European *wild boar Sus scrofa* is the ancestor of domesticated breeds; it is 1.5 m/4.5 ft long and 1 m/3 ft high, with formidable tusks, but not naturally aggressive. Pigs are omnivorous, with simple stomachs, and thick hides.

pigeon general term for members of the family Columbidae, sometimes also called doves, distinguished by their large crops which, becoming glandular in the breeding season, secrete a milky fluid ('pigeon's milk') which aids digestion of food for the young. They are found worldwide.

pigeon racing sport of racing pigeons against a clock. The birds are taken from their loft(s) and transported to a starting point, often hundreds of miles away. They have to return to their loft and a special clock times their arrival.

pig

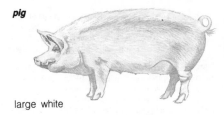

large white

saddle back

landrace

Piggott Lester 1935– . British jockey. He was regarded as a master tactician and adopted a unique high riding style. A champion jockey 11 times 1960-1982 he rode a record nine ◊Derby winners.

Pigs, Bay of inlet on the S coast of Cuba about 145 km/90 mi SW of Havana: the site of an unsuccessful invasion attempt by 1,500 US-sponsored Cuban exiles 17–20 Apr 1961; 1,173 were taken prisoner.

pike long, thin, freshwater fish *Esox lucius* family Esocidae, of Europe, Asia, and North America; it is a voracious feeder and may reach 2.2 m/7 ft, and 9 kg/20 lbs. Other types of pike include muskellunges and pickerels.

pike-perch freshwater fish *Stizostedion lucioperca*, related to the perch, common in Europe, W Asia, and North America. It reaches over 1 m/3 ft.

Pilate Pontius. Roman procurator of Judaea 26–36 AD. Unsympathetic to the Jews, his actions several times provoked riots, and in 36 AD he was recalled to Rome to account for disorder in Samaria. The New Testament Gospels describe his reluctant ordering of Jesus Christ's crucifixion. The Greek historian Eusebius says he committed suicide.

pilchard fish *Sardina pilchardus* of the herring family. Bluish-green above and silvery beneath, it grows to 25 cm/10 in long. It is most abundant in the W Mediterranean.

pilgrimage journey to sacred places inspired by religious devotion. For Hindus the holy places include Varanasi and the purifying river Ganges; for Buddhists the places connected with the crises of Buddha's career; for the ancient Greeks the shrines at Delphi and Ephesus among others; for the Jews, the sanctuary at Jerusalem; and for Muslims, Mecca. The great centres of Christian pilgrimages have been, or are, Jerusalem, Rome, the tomb of St James of Compostela in Spain, the shrine of Becket at Canterbury, and the holy places at La Salette and Lourdes in France.

Pilgrimage of Grace a rebellion against Henry VIII of England 1536–37, originating in Yorkshire and Lincolnshire. The rising, headed by Robert Aske (died 1537), was directed against the policies of the monarch (such as the dissolution of the monasteries and the effects of ◊enclosure).

Pilgrims name given to the emigrants who sailed from Plymouth, Devon, England, in the *Mayflower* on 16 Sept 1620 to found the first colony in New England at New Plymouth, Massachusetts. Of the 102 passengers less than a quarter were Puritan refugees.

Pilgrim's Progress an allegory by John Bunyan, published 1678–84, which describes a man's journey through life to the Celestial City. On his way through the Slough of Despond, the House Beautiful, Vanity Fair, Doubting Castle, and other landmarks, Christian meets a number of allegorical figures.

Pilgrims' Way track running from Winchester to Canterbury, England, which was the route of medieval pilgrims visiting the shrine of Thomas à Becket. Some 195 km/120 mi long, the Pilgrims' Way can still be traced for more than half its length.

pillory instrument of punishment consisting of a wooden frame set on a post, with holes in which the prisoner's head and hands were secured. Bystanders threw whatever was available at the miscreant. Its use was abolished in England in 1837.

pilotfish small sea fish *Naucrates ductor*, which hides below sharks, turtles, or boats, using the shade as a base from which to prey on smaller fish. It is found in all warm oceans and grows to about 36 cm/1.2 ft.

Pilsen German form of Czech town of ◊Plzeň.

Piłsudski Joseph 1867–1935. Polish nationalist politician, dictator from 1926. Born in Russian Poland, he founded the Polish Socialist Party in 1892, and was twice imprisoned for anti-Russian activities. During World War I he commanded a Polish force to fight for Germany, but fell under suspicion of intriguing with the Allies, and in 1917–18 was imprisoned by the Germans. When Poland became independent he was elected chief of state, and led an unsuccessful Polish attack on the USSR in 1920. He retired in 1923, but in 1926 led a military coup which established his dictatorship until his death.

pimento or *allspice*, tree found in tropical America. The dried fruits of the species *Pimenta dioica* are used as a spice.

Pincus Gregory Goodwin 1903–1967. US biologist who devised the contraceptive pill in the 1950s.

Pindar c. 552–442 BC. Greek poet, noted for his choral lyrics, 'Pindaric Odes', written in honour of victors of athletic games.

Pindling (Lynden) Oscar 1930– . Bahamian politician. After studying law in London, he returned to the island to join the newly formed Progressive Liberal Party, and then became the first black prime minister of the Bahamas 1967–92.

pine evergreen resinous tree of the genus *Pinus* with some 70–100 species, belonging to the Pinaceae, the largest family of conifers. The Scots pine *Pinus sylvestris* is grown commercially for soft timber and its yield of turpentine, tar, and pitch.

pineal body or *pineal gland* an outgrowth of the vertebrate brain. In some lower vertebrates, this develops a lens and retina, which show it to be derived from an eye, or pair of eyes, situated on the top of the head in ancestral vertebrates. The pineal still detects light (through the skull) in some fish, lizards, and birds. In fish that can change colour

piranha

*red
piranha*

to match the background, the pineal perceives the light level and controls the colour change. In birds, the pineal detects changes in daylight and stimulates breeding behaviour as spring approaches. Mammals also have a pineal gland, but it is located within the brain. It secretes a hormone-like substance, melatonin, which may influence rhythms of activity. In humans, it is a small piece of tissue attached to the posterior wall of the third ventricle of the brain.

pineapple plant *Ananas comosus*, native to S and Central America, but now cultivated in many other tropical areas, such as Queensland, Australia. The mauvish flowers are produced midway in the second year, and subsequently consolidated with their bracts into a fleshy fruit.

pink perennial plant of the genus *Dianthus*, including the maiden pink *Dianthus deltoides* found in dry grassy places. The stems have characteristically swollen nodes and the flowers range in colour from white through pink to purple. Garden forms include carnations, sweet williams and baby's breath *Gypsophila paniculata*.

Pinkerton Allan 1819–1884. US detective, born in Glasgow. He founded 1852 *Pinkerton's National Detective Agency*, and built up the federal secret service from the espionage system he developed during the American Civil War.

Pink Floyd British psychedelic rock group, formed 1965. The original members were Syd Barrett (1946–), Roger Waters (1944–), Richard Wright (1945–), and Nick Mason (1945–). Their albums include *The Dark Side of the Moon* 1973 and *The Wall* 1979.

pinnate leaf a leaf that is divided up into many small leaflets, arranged in rows along either side of a midrib, as in ash trees (*Fraxinus*). It is a type of compound ◊leaf. Each leaflet is known as a *pinna*, and where the pinnae are themselves divided, the secondary divisions are known as pinnules.

Pinochet (Ugarte) Augusto 1915– . Military ruler of Chile from 1973, when he led a CIA-backed coup that ousted and killed the Marxist president Salvador Allende. Pinochet took over the presidency and ruled ruthlessly, crushing all opposition. General elections were held 1989, and he was voted out of power, to remain head of the armed forces until 1997.

pint Imperial liquid or dry measure equal to 20 fluid ounces, ½ of a quart, ⅛ of a gallon, or 0.568 litre.

Pinter Harold 1930– . British dramatist and poet. He specializes in the tragicomedy of the breakdown of communication, broadly in the tradition of the theatre of the ◊absurd, for example, *The Birthday Party* 1958 and *The Caretaker* 1960. Later successes include *The Homecoming* 1965, *Old Times* 1971, *Betrayal* 1978, and *Mountain Language* 1988. He writes for radio and television, and his screenplays include *The Go-Between* 1969 and *The French Lieutenant's Woman* 1982.

Pinyin the Chinese phonetic alphabet approved 1956, and used from 1979 in transcribing all names of people and places from the Chinese language into foreign languages using the Roman alphabet. For example, Chou En-lai becomes Zhou Enlai, Hua Kuo-feng becomes Hua Guofeng, Teng Hsiao-ping becomes Deng Xiaoping, Peking becomes Beijing.

Pioneer probes a series of US space probes 1958–78. Pioneer 5, launched 1960, was the first of a series to study the ◊solar wind between the planets. Pioneer 10, launched Mar 1972, was the first probe to reach Jupiter (Dec 1973), and to leave the Solar System 1983. Pioneer 11, launched Apr 1973, passed Jupiter Dec 1974, and was the first probe to reach Saturn (Sept 1979), before also leaving the Solar System. Pioneers 10 and 11 carry plaques containing messages from Earth in case they are found by other civilizations among the stars. Pioneer Venus probes were launched May and Aug 1978. One orbited Venus, and the other dropped three probes onto the surface.

Piozzi Hester Lynch (born Salusbury) 1741–1821. British writer. She published *Anecdotes of the late Samuel Johnson* 1786, and their correspondence 1788. Johnson had been a constant visitor to her house when she was married to her first husband, Henry Thrale.

pipefish fish related to seahorses but long and thin like a length of pipe. The *great pipefish Syngnathus acus* grows up to 50 cm/1.6 ft, and the male has a brood pouch for eggs and developing young.

pipeline a pipe for carrying water, oil, gas, or other material over long distances. They are widely used in water-supply and oil- and gas-distribution schemes. The USA has over 300,000 km/200,000 mi of oil pipelines alone. One of the longest is the Trans-Alaskan Pipeline in Alaska.

pipit name for several birds in the family Motacillidae, related to the wagtails. The European meadow pipit *Anthus pratensis* is about the size of a sparrow and streaky brown, but has a slender bill. It lives in open country and feeds on the ground.

piracy the taking of a ship, aircraft, or any of its contents, from lawful ownership, punishable under international law by the court of any country where the pirate may be found or taken. The contemporary equivalent is ◊hijacking. Piracy is also used as a term for infringement of ◊copyright.

Pirandello Luigi 1867–1936. Italian writer. The novel *Il fu Mattia Pascal/The Late Mattia Pascal* 1904 was highly acclaimed, along with many short stories. His first play *La Morsa/The Vice* 1912, was followed by *Sei personaggi in cerca d'autore/Six Characters in Search of an Author* 1921, *Enrico IV/Henry IV* 1922, and others. The theme and treatment of his plays anticipated the work of Brecht, O'Neill, Anouilh, and Genet. Nobel Prize for literature 1934.

Piranesi Giovanni Battista 1720–1778. Italian artist, architect, and archaeologist. His powerful etchings of Roman antiquities evoked ruined grandeur and his *Vedute* (views of Rome), published from 1745, proved very popular. His book championing the superiority of Roman architecture was also influential. Only one of his designs was built, S Maria del Priorato, Rome.

piranha South American freshwater fish, genus *Serrusalmus*. It can grow to 60 cm/2 ft long. It has razor-sharp teeth, and some species may rapidly devour animals.

Piran, St *c.* 500 AD. Christian missionary sent to Cornwall by St Patrick. There are remains of his oratory at Perranzabuloe, and he is the patron saint

Pisa *The Leaning Tower of Pisa, Italy.*

of Cornwall and its nationalist movement; feast day 5 Mar.

pirouette a movement in dance comprising a complete turn of the body on one leg with the other raised.

Pirquet Clemens von 1874–1929. Austrian paediatrician and pioneer in the study of allergy.

Pisa city in Tuscany, Italy; population (1986) 104,000. The Leaning Tower is 55 m/180 ft high and is about 5 m/16.5 ft out of perpendicular.

Pisanello nickname of Antonio Pisano *c.* 1395–*c.* 1455. Italian artist active in Verona, Venice, Naples, Rome, and elsewhere. His panel paintings reveal a rich International Gothic style; his frescoes are largely lost. He was also an outstanding portrait medallist.

Pisano family of Italian sculptors, father and son, Nicola (died *c.* 1284) and his son Giovanni (died after 1314). They made decorated marble pulpits in churches in Pisa, Siena, and Pistoia. Giovanni also created figures for Pisa's baptistery and designed the façade of Siena Cathedral.

Pisano Andrea *c.* 1290–1348. Italian sculptor, best known for the earliest bronze doors for the Baptistery of Florence Cathedral, completed 1336.

Pisces faint constellation of the zodiac, mainly in the northern hemisphere near Pegasus, represented by two fish tied together by their tails. Pisces contains the **vernal ◊equinox**, the point at which the Sun's path around the sky (the ◊ecliptic) crosses the celestial equator. The Sun reaches this point around Mar 21 each year as it passes through Pisces from mid-Mar to late Apr.

Pisistratus *c.* 605–527 BC. Athenian politician. Although of noble family, he assumed the leadership of the peasant party, and seized power in 561 BC. He was twice expelled, but recovered power from 541 BC till his death. Ruling as a dictator under constitutional forms, he was the first to have the Homeric poems written down, and founded Greek drama by introducing the Dionysiac peasant festivals into Athens.

Pissarro Camille 1831–1903. French Impressionist painter, born in the West Indies. He went to Paris in 1855, met Corot, then Monet, and soon became a leading member of the Impressionist group. He experimented with various styles, including pointillism, in the 1880s.

pistachio deciduous Eurasian tree *Pistacia vera*, family Anacardiaceae, with edible green nuts which are eaten salted or used to flavour foods.

pistil a general term describing the female part of a flower, either referring to one single ◊carpel or a group of several fused carpels.

pistol small ◊firearm designed for one-hand use. Pistols were in use from the early 15th century. The problem of firing more than once without reloading was tackled by using many combinations of multiple barrels, both stationary and revolving. A breech-loading, multi-chambered revolver of 1650 still survives; the first practical solution was Samuel Colt's six-gun 1847. Behind a single barrel, a short six-chambered cylinder was rotated by cocking the hammer, and a fresh round brought into place. The automatic pistol, operated by gas or recoil, was introduced in Germany in the 1890s. Both revolvers and automatics are in widespread military use.

piston a barrel-shaped device used in reciprocating engines (◊steam, ◊petrol, ◊diesel) to harness power. Pistons are driven up and down in cylinders by expanding steam or hot gases. They pass on their motion via a connecting rod and crank to a ◊crankshaft, which turns the driving wheels. In a pump or ◊compressor, the role of the piston is reversed, being used to move gases and liquids.

Pitcairn Islands British colony in Polynesia, 5,300 km/3,300 mi NE of New Zealand
area 27 sq km/10 sq mi
capital Adamstown
exports fruit and souvenirs to passing ships
population (1982) 54
language English
government the governor is the British high commissioner in New Zealand
history The islands were first settled by nine mutineers from the *Bounty* together with some Tahitians, their occupation remaining unknown until 1808.

pitch in chemistry, a black substance, hard when cold, but liquid when hot, used as a sealant on roofs. It is made by the destructive distillation of wood or coal tar.

pitch the position of a note in the musical scale, dependent on the frequency of the predominant sound wave. In **standard pitch** A above middle C has a frequency of 440 Hz. **Perfect pitch** is an ability to name or reproduce any note heard or asked for; it does not necessarily imply high musical ability.

pitchblende an ore consisting mainly of uranium oxide U_3O_8, but also containing a radioactive salt of radium $RaBr_2$.

pitcher plant insectivorous plant of the genus *Nepenthes*, the leaves of which are shaped like a pitcher and filled with a fluid that traps insects.

Pitman Isaac 1813–1897. British inventor of Pitman's shorthand. A teacher, he studied Samuel Taylor's scheme for shorthand writing and published in 1837 his own system, *Stenographic Soundhand*, speedy and accurate, and adapted for use in many languages.

Pitot tube an instrument that measures fluid (gas and liquid) flow. Invented in the 1730s by Henri

Pitt William Pitt the Elder, also known as the 'Great Commoner'.

Pitot (1695–1771) in France. It is used to measure the airspeed of aircraft. It works by sensing pressure differences in different directions in the airstream.

Pitt William, the Elder, 1st Earl of Chatham 1708–1778. British Whig politician, 'the Great Commoner'. As paymaster of the forces 1746–55, he broke with tradition by refusing to enrich himself; he was dismissed for attacking Newcastle, the prime minister. He served effectively as prime minister in coalition governments 1756–61, successfully conducting the Seven Years' War, and 1766–68.

Pitt William, the Younger 1759–1806. British Tory politician, prime minister 1783–1801 and 1804–06. He raised the importance of the House of Commons and clamped down on corruption, carried out fiscal reforms and union with Ireland; he attempted to keep Britain at peace but underestimated the importance of the French Revolution and became embroiled in wars with France from 1793; he died on hearing of Napoleon's victory at Austerlitz.

Pitt-Rivers Augustus Henry 1827–1900. British general and archaeologist. He made a series of model archaeological excavations on his estate in Wiltshire, England, being among the first to recognize the value of everyday objects as well as art treasures. The *Pitt-Rivers Museum*, Oxford, contains the best of his collection.

Pittsburgh industrial city (machinery and chemicals) and inland port, where the Allegheny and Monongahela join to form the Ohio River in Pennsylvania, USA; population (1980) 423,940, metropolitan area 2,264,000. Established by the French as Fort Duquesne 1750, the site was taken by the British 1758 and renamed Fort Pitt.

pituitary gland the most important of the ◊endocrine glands of vertebrates, situated in the centre of the brain. The anterior lobe secretes hormones, some of which control the activities of other glands (thyroid, gonads, and adrenal cortex); others are direct-acting hormones affecting milk secretion, and controlling growth. Secretions of the posterior lobe control body water balance, and contraction of the uterus. The posterior lobe is regulated by the ◊hypothalamus, and thus forms a link between the nervous and hormonal systems.

Pius twelve popes, including:

Pius IV 1499–1565. Pope from 1559, of the Medici family. He reassembled the Council of Trent (see Counter-Reformation under ◊Reformation) and completed its work in 1563.

Pius V 1504–1572. Pope from 1566, who excommunicated Elizabeth I of England, and organized the expedition against the Turks that won the victory of ◊Lepanto.

Pius VI 1717–1799. Pope from 1775, strongly opposed the French Revolution, and died a prisoner in French hands.

Pius VII 1742–1823. Pope from 1800, who concluded a ◊concordat with France in 1801, and took part in Napoleon's coronation, but was a prisoner 1809–14. After his return to Rome in 1814 he revived the Jesuit order.

Pius IX 1792–1878. Pope from 1846. He never accepted the incorporation of the Papal States and of Rome in the kingdom of Italy, and proclaimed the dogmas of the Immaculate Conception of the Virgin 1854 and papal infallibility 1870; his pontificate was the longest in history.

Pius X 1835–1914. Pope from 1903, canonized 1954, who condemned Modernism (see under ◊Christianity) in a manifesto of 1907.

Pius XI 1857–1939. Pope from 1922, he signed the ◊concordat with Mussolini 1929.

Pius XII (Eugenio Pacelli) 1876–1958. Pope from 1939. He proclaimed the dogma of the bodily assumption of the Virgin Mary 1950 and in 1951 restated the doctrine (strongly criticized by many) that the life of an infant must not be sacrificed to save a mother in labour. He was also widely criticized for failing to speak out against atrocities committed by the Germans during World War II.

pixel (contraction of 'picture cell') on a computer screen (VDU), any one of the points in a matrix from which displayed images are constructed and illuminated (sometimes in colour) under the control of a computer.

Pizarro *c.* 1475–1541. Spanish conquistador. In 1526–27 he explored the NW coast of South America, and conquered Peru in 1530 with 180 followers. The Inca king Atahualpa was treacherously seized and murdered. In 1535 Pizarro founded Lima. Internal feuding led to his assassination. His half-brother *Gonzalo Pizarro* (*c.* 1505–48) explored the region east of Quito 1541–42. He made himself governor of Peru 1544, but was defeated and executed.

placenta

network of blood vessels in placenta

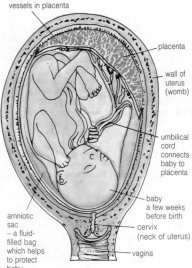

placenta

wall of uterus (womb)

umbilical cord connects baby to placenta

baby a few weeks before birth

cervix (neck of uterus)

vagina

amniotic sac – a fluid-filled bag which helps to protect baby

plane

pizzicato (Italian 'pinched') in music, an instruction to pluck a bowed stringed instrument (such as the violin) with the fingers.

Plaatje Sol 1876–1932. Pioneer South African nationalist who was the first secretary-general and founder (1912) of the ◊African National Congress.

placebo a harmless substance, often called a 'sugar pill', without any chemotherapeutic value which, nevertheless, produces physiological changes.

placenta the organ composed of maternal and embryonic tissue which attaches the developing ◊embryo or ◊fetus of placental mammals to the ◊uterus. Oxygen, nutrients, and waste products are exchanged between maternal and fetal blood over the placental membrane, but the two blood systems are not in direct contact. The placenta also produces hormones which regulate the progress of pregnancy. It is shed as part of the afterbirth.

plague disease transmitted by fleas (carried by the black ◊rat) which infect the sufferer with the bacillus *Pasturella pestis*. An early symptom is swelling of lymph nodes, usually in the armpit and groin; such swellings are called 'buboes', hence 'bubonic' plague. It causes virulent blood poisoning and the death rate is high.

plaice fish *Pleuronectes platessa* belonging to the flat-fish group, abundant in the N Atlantic. It is white beneath and brownish with orange spots on the 'eyed' side. It can grow to 75 cm/2.5 ft long, and weigh about 2 kg/4.5 lbs.

Plaid Cymru Welsh nationalist political party established 1925, dedicated to an independent Wales. In 1966 the first Plaid Cymru Member of Parliament was elected.

plain or grassland land, usually flat upon which grass predominates. The plains cover large areas of the Earth's surface, especially between the deserts of the tropics and the rainforests of the equator, and

have rain in one season only. In such regions the climate belts move north and south during the year, bringing rainforest conditions at one time and desert conditions at another. Well known plains include the North European Plain, the High Plains of the US and the Russian Plain also known as the ◊steppe.

Plains Indian any of the North American Indians of the High Plains, which run over 3,000 km/2,000 mi from Alberta to Texas. The various groups are ◊Blackfoot, Cheyenne, Comanche, Pawnee, and the Dakota or ◊Sioux.

plainsong ancient chant of the Christian Church first codified by Ambrose, bishop of Milan, and then by Pope Gregory in the 6th century. See ◊Gregorian chant.

plane tree of the genus *Platanus*. Species include the oriental plane *Platanus orientalis*, a favourite plantation tree of the Greeks and Romans; the hybrid London plane *Platanus hispanica*, with palmate, usually five-lobed leaves; and the American plane or buttonwood *Platanus occidentalis*.

planet a large body in orbit around a star, made of rock, metal, or gas. There are nine planets in the ◊Solar System.

planetarium optical projection device by means of which the motions of stars and planets are reproduced on a domed ceiling representing the sky.

planetary nebula a shell of gas thrown off by a star at the end of its life. After a star such as the Sun has expanded to become a ◊red giant, its outer layers are ejected into space to form a planetary nebula, leaving the core as a ◊white dwarf at the centre.

plankton small, often microscopic, forms of plant and animal life that drift in fresh or salt water, and are a source of food for larger animals.

plant an organism that carries out ◊photosynthesis, has ◊cellulose cell walls and complex ◊eukaryotic cells and is immobile. A few parasitic plants have lost the ability to photosynthesize, but are still considered as plants. See under ◊plant classification.

Plants are ◊autotrophs, that is they make carbohydrates from water and carbon dioxide, and are the primary producers in all ◊food chains, so that all animal life is directly or indirectly dependent on them. They play a vital part in the ◊carbon cycle, removing carbon dioxide from the atmosphere and generating oxygen. The study of plants is known as ◊botany.

Plantagenet English royal house, reigning 1154–1399, whose name comes from the nickname of Geoffrey, Count of Anjou (1113–51), father of Henry II, who often wore a sprig of broom, *planta genista*, in his hat. In the 1450s, Richard, duke of York, revived it as a surname to emphasize his superior claim to the throne over Henry VI.

planets

Planet	Main constituents	Atmosphere	Distance from Sun in millions of km	Time for one orbit in Earth-years	Diameter in thousands of km	Average density if density of water is 1 unit
Mercury	rocky, ferrous	–	5.8	0.24	4.9	5.4
Venus	rocky, ferrous	carbon dioxide,	108	0.61	12.1	5.2
Earth	rocky, ferrous	nitrogen, oxygen	150	1.00	12.8	5.5
Mars	rocky	carbon dioxide	228	1.88	6.8	3.9
Jupiter	liquid hydrogen, helium	–	778	11.86	142.8	1.3
Saturn	hydrogen, helium	–	1427	29.50	120.0	0.7
Uranus	icy, hydrogen, helium	hydrogen, helium	2875	84.00	51.1	1.2
Neptune	icy, hydrogen, helium	hydrogen, helium	4496	164.80	49.5	1.7
Pluto	icy, rocky	methane	5900	248.40	4.0	about 1

plain

Animals of the plains depend on grasses and occasional trees for sustenance. Plant-eaters graze (feed on growing grass), browse (eat leaves, twigs and sparse vegetation), or forage (rummage for bulbs, roots and fruits). They are preyed upon by the meat-eaters.

African plain (savannah) wildlife and plants. 1. Baboon 2. Acacia tree 3. Eland 4. Low-growing shrubs 5. Giraffe 6. Elephant 7. Steenbok 8. Topi 9. Warthog 10. Weaver bird nests 11. Termite mound 12. Baobab tree 13. Lions 14. Rhinoceros

Russian plain (steppe) wildlife and plants. 1. Shrubs and small trees 2. Grass snake 3. Lemmings 4. Field voles 5. Saiga antelope 6. Suslik 7. Marbled polecat 8. Black-bellied hamster

In temperate grasslands, where winter temperatures can fall far below freezing and summer temperatures rise to 40°C/104°F, many of the animals survive by living underground in burrows. In tropical grasslands, the climate is less extreme. Here a great variety of plants grow, and provide food for many more types of animals. The African grasslands support the world's largest wildlife populations.

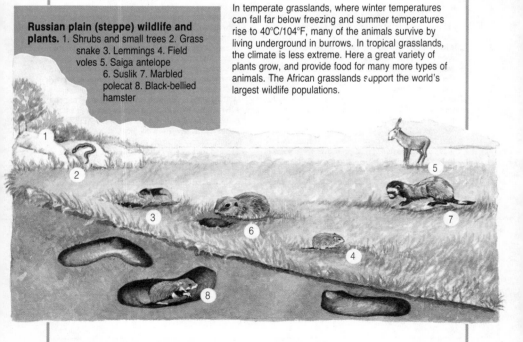

plant

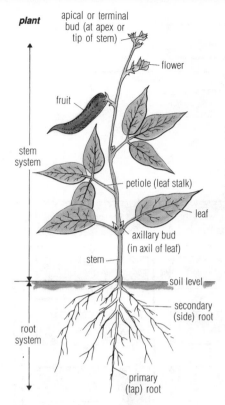

apical or terminal bud (at apex or tip of stem)

flower

fruit

stem system

petiole (leaf stalk)

leaf

axillary bud (in axil of leaf)

stem

soil level

secondary (side) root

root system

primary (tap) root

plantain plants of the genus *Plantago*. The great plantain *Plantago major* has oval leaves, grooved stalks and spikes of green flowers with purple anthers followed by seeds, which are used in bird food. The name plantain is also given to various types of ◊banana.

plant classification the taxonomy or ◊classification of plants. Originally the plant ◊kingdom included bacteria, diatoms, dinoflagellates, fungi and slime moulds, but these are not now thought of as plants. The groups that are always classified as plants are the ◊bryophytes (mosses and liverworts), ◊pteridophytes (ferns, horsetails, and clubmosses), ◊gymnosperms (conifers, yews, cycads, and ginkgos) and ◊angiosperms (flowering plants). The angiosperms are split into the ◊monocotyledons (for example, orchids, grasses, lilies) and the ◊dicotyledons (for example, oak, buttercup, geranium, and daisy).

The basis of plant classification was established by ◊Linnaeus. Among the angiosperms, it is largely based on the number and arrangement of the flower parts.

plant hormone a substance produced by a plant which has a marked effect on its growth, flowering, leaf-fall, fruit-ripening, or some other process. Examples include *auxin*, *gibberellin*, *ethylene*, and *cytokin*.

plasma in biology, the liquid part of the blood.

plasma in physics, an ionized gas produced at extremely high temperatures, as in the Sun and other stars, and which contains positive and negative charges in approximately equal numbers. It is affected by a magnetic field, and is a good electrical conductor.

plasmapheresis the removal from the body of large quantities of whole blood and its fractionization by centrifugal force in a continuous flow cell separator. Once separated, the elements of the blood are isolated and available for specific treatment.

plaster of Paris a form of calcium sulphate, mixed with water for making casts and moulds.

plastic any of the stable synthetic materials which are fluid at some stage in their manufacture, when they can be shaped and which later set to rigid or semi-rigid solids. Plastics today are chiefly derived from petroleum. Most are polymers, made up of long chains of identical molecules.

plastic surgery branch of surgery concerned with the repair of congenital disfigurement and the reconstruction of tissues damaged by disease or injury.

plastid a general name for a cell ◊organelle of plants that is enclosed by a double membrane and contains a series of internal membranes and vesicles. Plastids contain ◊DNA and are produced by division of existing plastids. They can be classified into two main groups, the *chromoplasts*, which contain pigments such as ◊carotenes and ◊chlorophyll, and the *leucoplasts*, which are colourless; however, the distinction between the two is not always clear-cut.

plateau an elevated area of fairly flat land, or a mountainous region in which the peaks are at the same height. An *intermontane plateau* is one surrounded by mountains. A *piedmont plateau* is one that lies between the mountains and low-lying land. A *continental plateau* rises abruptly from low-lying lands or the sea.

platelet the smallest cellular particle in the blood, essential to the clotting process.

plate tectonics concept that attributes ◊continental drift and ◊seafloor spreading to the continual formation and destruction of the outermost layer of the Earth. This layer is seen as consisting of major and minor plates, curved to the planet's spherical shape and with a jigsaw fit to each other. Convection currents within the Earth's ◊mantle produce upwellings of new material along joint lines at the surface. These lines are the ◊ocean ridges. The new material extends the plates at the surface and these move away from the ocean ridges. At the point of contact of two plates, one overrides the other and the lower is absorbed back into the mantle. These 'subduction zones' occur in the ◊ocean trenches.

Plath Sylvia 1932–1963. US poet and novelist. Plath's powerful, highly personal poems, often expressing a sense of desolation, are distinguished by their intensity and sharp imagery. Collections include *The Colossus* 1960, *Ariel* 1965, published after her death, and *Collected Poems* 1982. Her autobiographical novel, *The Bell Jar* 1961, deals with the events surrounding a young woman's emotional breakdown.

platinum a metallic element, symbol Pt, atomic number 78, relative atomic mass 195.09. It is greyish-white, untarnishable in air, and very resistant to heat and strong acids. Both pure and as an alloy, it is used extensively in jewellery, dentistry, and the chemical industry (in finely divided form, platinum acts as a catalyst). It is employed for switch contacts because of its durability, in car exhaust systems, where it helps the conversion of car fumes to non-toxic gases, and is valuable in scientific apparatus because platinum wires can be sealed gas-tight.

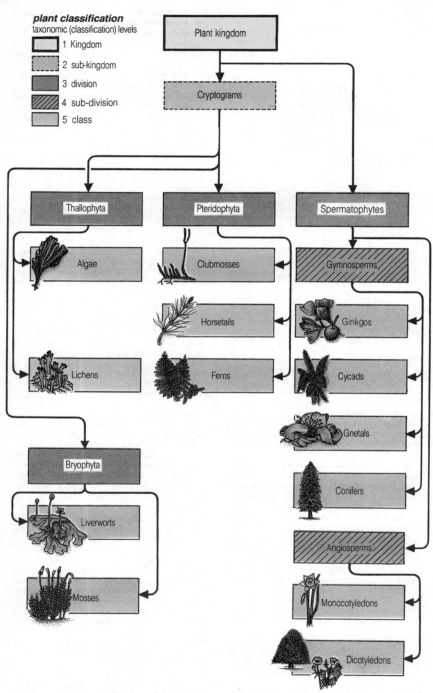

plant classification
taxonomic (classification) levels
1 Kingdom
2 sub-kingdom
3 division
4 sub-division
5 class

Plant kingdom

Cryptograms

Thallophyta — Pteridophyta — Spermatophytes

Algae — Clubmosses — Gymnosperms

Horsetails — Ginkgos

Lichens — Ferns — Cycads

Gnetals

Conifers

Bryophyta

Angiosperms

Liverworts — Monocotyledons

Mosses — Dicotyledons

Plato *c.* 428–347 BC. Greek philosopher, pupil of Socrates, teacher of Aristotle, and founder of the Academy. He was the author of philosophical dialogues on such topics as metaphysics, ethics, and politics. Central to his teachings is the notion of Forms, which are located outside the everyday world, timeless, motionless, and absolutely real.

platypus monotreme mammal *Ornithorhynchus anatinus*, found in Tasmania and E Australia. Semi-aquatic, it has naked jaws resembling a duck's beak, small eyes, and no external ears. It lives in long burrows along river banks, where it lays two eggs in a rough nest. It feeds on water worms and insects, and when full-grown is 60 cm/2 ft long.

plate tectonics
sea floor spreading

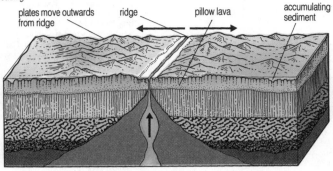

plates move outwards from ridge   ridge   pillow lava   accumulating sediment

rising magma

subduction zone

one plate slides under another   magma

collision zone

continental crust collides and is partly subducted   younger folded mountains   older folded mountains

Plautus Roman dramatist. He wrote at least 56 comedies, freely adapted from Greek originals, of which 20 survive. Shakespeare based *The Comedy of Errors* on his *Menoechmi*.

playgroup in the UK, a voluntary, usually part-time pre-school group, run by parents or sometimes by charitable organizations, to provide nursery education for children from three to five.

playing cards a set of small pieces of card with different markings, used in playing games. A standard set consists of 52 cards divided into four suits; hearts, clubs, diamonds, and spades. Within each suit there are 13 cards; numbered two to ten, three picture (or court) cards (jack, queen and king) and the ace.

Pleasance Donald 1919– . British actor. He has been acclaimed for roles in Pirandello's *The Rules of the Game*, in Pinter's *The Caretaker*, and also in the title role of the film *Dr Crippen* 1962,

conveying the sinister aspect of the outcast from society.

plebeians the unprivileged class in ancient Rome, composed of aliens and freed slaves, and their descendants. During the 5th–4th centuries BC they waged a long struggle with the patricians, until they secured admission to the offices formerly reserved for the patricians.

platypus

Plimsoll line

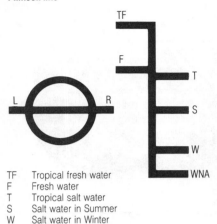

TF	Tropical fresh water
F	Fresh water
T	Tropical salt water
S	Salt water in Summer
W	Salt water in Winter
WNA	Winter in North Atlantic
LR	Lloyd's Register

plebiscite ◊referendum or direct vote by all the electors of a country or district on a specific question. Since the 18th century it has been employed on many occasions to decide to what country a particular area should belong, for example, in Upper Silesia and elsewhere after World War I, and in the Saar in 1935.

Pléiade, La group of seven poets in 16th-century France led by Pierre Ronsard (1524–1585), who were inspired by classical models to improve French verse. They were so called from the seven stars of the Pleiades group.

Pleiades in astronomy, a star cluster about 400 light years away in the constellation Taurus, representing the Seven Sisters of Greek mythology. Its brightest stars (highly luminous, very young blue-white giants only a few million years old) are visible to the naked eye, but there are many fainter ones.

Pleiades in Greek mythology, seven daughters of ◊Atlas, who asked to be changed to a cluster of stars to escape the pursuit of ◊Orion.

pleiotropy a process whereby a given gene influences several different observed characteristics of an organism.

Pleistocene epoch of geological time, beginning 1.8 million years ago and ending 10,000 years ago. Glaciers were abundant, altering the land. *Homo sapiens* appeared about 100,000 years ago.

Plekhanov Georgi Valentinovich 1857–1918. Russian Marxist revolutionary and theorist, founder of the Menshevik party. He led the first ◊populist demonstration in St Petersburg and left for exile in 1880. He became a Marxist and, with Lenin, edited the newspaper *Iskra* ('spark'). in 1903 his opposition to Lenin led to the Bolshevik-Menshevik split. In 1917 he returned to Russia.

pleurisy inflammation of the pleura, the secreting membrane which covers the lungs, and lines the space in which they rest. Nearly always due to bacterial or viral infection, it renders breathing painful.

Plimsoll Samuel 1824–1898. English social reformer. He sat in Parliament as a Radical 1868–80, and through his efforts the Merchant Shipping Act was passed in 1876, providing for Board of Trade

inspection of ships, and the compulsory painting of a *Plimsoll line*. This marking, painted on a ship's hull, shows the safe levels to which the hull can sink in waters at various times.

Pliny the Elder (Gaius Plinius Secundus) *c.* 23–79 AD. Roman scientist and historian; only his works on astronomy, geography, and natural history survive. He was killed in an eruption of Vesuvius.

Pliny the Younger (Gaius Plinius Caecilius Secundus) *c.* 61–113. Roman administrator, nephew of ◊Pliny the Elder, whose correspondence is of great interest. Among his surviving letters are those describing the eruption of Vesuvius, his uncle's death, and his correspondence with the emperor ◊Trajan.

Pliocene fifth and last epoch of the Tertiary period of geological time, 5–1.8 million years ago. Human-like apes developed in this epoch. The name means 'almost recent'.

Plisetskaya Maya 1925– . Russian ballerina and actress, who succeeded ◊Ulanova as prima ballerina of the Bolshoi Ballet.

PLO abbreviation for ◊*Palestine Liberation Organization*

plotter an ◊output device that draws pictures under computer control. *Flatbed plotters* move a pen up and down across a flat drawing surface, while *roller plotters* roll the drawing paper past the pen as it moves from side to side.

plough, the in astronomy, a popular name for the most prominent part of the constellation ◊Ursa Major.

plough the most important agricultural implement, used for tilling the soil. The plough dates from about 3500 BC, when oxen were used to pull a simple wooden blade, or ard. In about 500 BC the iron share came into use.

plover wading bird of the family Charadriidae, found worldwide. They are usually black or brown above, and white below. They have short bills.

plum tree *Prunus domestica*, bearing an edible fruit. There are many varieties, including the Victoria, Czar, egg-plum, greengage and damson; the sloe *Prunus spinosa* is closely related. The dried plum is known as a prune.

plumule the part of a seed embryo which develops into the shoot, bearing the first true leaves of the plant.

plur. in grammar, the abbreviation for *plural*.

pluralism in political science, the view that decision-making in contemporary liberal democracies is the outcome of competition among several interest

Plough *a camel ploughing a field on Lanzerote, one of the Canary Islands.*

groups in a political system characterized by free elections, representative institutions, and open access to the organs of power. This conception is opposed by corporatist and other approaches that perceive power to be centralized in the state and its principal elites.

plus ça change, plus c'est la même chose (French) the more things change, the more they stay the same.

Plutarch c. 46–120 BC. Greek biographer. He lectured on philosophy at Rome, and was appointed procurator of Greece by Hadrian. His *Parallel Lives* comprise biographies of pairs of Greek and Roman soldiers and politicians, followed by comparisons between the two. Thomas North's 1579 translation inspired Shakespeare's Roman plays.

Pluto in astronomy, the smallest and outermost planet, located by Clyde ◊Tombaugh 1930. It orbits the Sun every 248.5 years at an average distance of 5,800,000,000 km/3,600,000,000 mi. Its elliptical orbit occasionally takes it within the orbit of Neptune, such as 1979–99. Pluto has a diameter of about 3,000 km/2,000 mi, and a mass about 0.005 that of Earth. It is of low density, composed of rock and ice, with frozen methane on its surface. Charon, Pluto's moon, was discovered 1978.

Pluto in Roman mythology, the lord of Hades, the underworld. He was the brother of Jupiter and Neptune.

plutonic rock igneous rock derived from magma that has cooled and solidified deep in the crust of the Earth.

plutonium a synthetic element, symbol Pu, atomic number 94, relative atomic mass 242. Its most stable isotope, Pu-239 (discovered 1941), has a half-life of 24,000 years, undergoes nuclear fission, and is usually made in reactors by bombarding U-238 with neutrons. It is used in atom bombs, in reactors, and for enriching the abundant U-238. It has awkward physical properties, and is poisonous to animals, being absorbed into bone marrow.

Plymouth city and seaport in Devon, England, at the mouth of the river Plym, with dockyard, barracks, and naval base at Devonport; population (1981) 244,000.

Plymouth Brethren a fundamentalist Christian Protestant sect characterized by extreme simplicity of belief, founded in Dublin c. 1827.

An assembly was held in Plymouth in 1831 to celebrate its arrival in England, but by 1848 the movement had split into 'Open' and 'Close' Brethren. The latter refuse communion with all those not of their persuasion. The Plymouth Brethren are mainly found in the fishing villages of NE Scotland.

plywood a manufactured wood widely used in building. It is made up of thin sheets, or plies, of wood, which are stuck together so that the grain (direction of the wood fibres) of one sheet is at right-angles to the grain of the plies on either side. This construction gives plywood equal strength in every direction.

Plzeň (German *Pilsen*) industrial city (heavy machinery, cars, beer) in W Czechoslovakia, capital of Západočeský region; 84 km/52 mi SW of Prague; population (1984) 174,000.

p.m. abbreviation for *post meridiem* (Latin 'after noon').

PM abbreviation for *Prime Minister*.

pneumatic drill a drill operated by compressed air, used in mining and tunnelling, for drilling shot-holes (for explosives), and in road mending for breaking up pavements. It contains an air-operated piston which delivers hammer blows to the drill ◊bit many times a second. The French engineer Germain Sommeiller developed the pneumatic drill for tunnelling in the Alps in 1861.

pneumatophore an erect root that rises up above the soil or water and promotes gaseous exchange. Pneumatophores, or breathing roots, are formed by certain swamp-dwelling trees, such as mangroves, since there is little oxygen available to the roots in waterlogged conditions. They have numerous pores or ◊lenticels over their surface, allowing gas exchange.

pneumoconiosis disease of the lungs caused by dust, especially from coal, which causes the lung to become fibrous. The victim has difficulty breathing.

pneumonia inflammation of the lungs due to bacterial or viral infection. It is characterized by a build-up of fluid in the alveoli, the clustered air sacs (at the end of the air passages) where oxygen exchange takes place.

Pnom Penh alternative form of ◊Phnom Penh, capital of Kampuchea.

PO abbreviation for *Post Office*.

pochard type of diving duck found in Europe and N America. The male common pochard *Aythya ferina* has a red head, black breast, whitish body and wings with black markings, and is about 45 cm/1.5 ft long. The female is greyish-brown, with greyish-white below.

pod in botany, a type of ◊fruit that is characteristic of plants belonging to the Leguminosae family, such as peas and beans (technical name *legume*). It develops from a single ◊carpel and splits down both sides when ripe to release the seeds.

podesta in the Italian ◊communes, the highest civic official, appointed by the leading citizens, and often holding great power.

Poe Edgar Allan 1809–1849. US writer and poet. His short stories are renowned for their horrific atmosphere and acute reasoning, and include *The Fall of the House of Usher* 1839 and *The Murders in the Rue Morgue* 1841.

Poet Laureate poet of the British royal household, so called because of the laurel wreath awarded to eminent poets in the Graeco-Roman world. Early poets with unofficial status included Chaucer,

Poe Daguerreotype of US writer Edgar Allan Poe.

Skelton, Spenser, Daniel, and Jonson; the first official title-holder was Dryden. Successors have included Thomas Warton, Southey, Wordsworth, Tennyson, Bridges, Masefield, Cecil Day Lewis, Betjeman, and Ted Hughes. There is a stipend of £70 per annum, plus £27 in lieu of the traditional butt of sack (cask of wine).

poetry the imaginative expression of emotion, thought, or narrative, often in metrical form, and often in figurative language. Poetry has traditionally been distinguished from prose (ordinary written language), by rhyme or rhythmical arrangement of words, although the distinction is not always clear cut.

pogrom an unprovoked persecution or extermination of an ethnic group, particularly Jews, carried out with official connivance. The Russian pogroms began in 1881, and were common throughout the country. Later there were pogroms in E Europe and in Germany under Hitler.

poikilothermy the condition in which an animal's body temperature is largely dependent on the temperature of the air or water in which it lives. It is characteristic of all animals except birds and mammals which maintain their body temperatures by ◊homeothermy. Poikilotherms have some means of warming themselves up, such as basking in the sun, or shivering, and can cool themselves down by sheltering under a rock or by bathing in water.

Poincaré Raymond Nicolas Landry 1860–1934. French politician, prime minister 1912–13, president 1913–20, and again prime minister 1922–24 (when he ordered the occupation of the Ruhr, Germany) and 1926–29. He was a cousin of the mathematician Jules Henri Poincaré (1854–1912).

Poindexter John M 1936– . US retired rear admiral. In 1981 he joined the Reagan administration's National Security Cuncil (NSC) and became national security adviser 1985. As a result of the ◊Irangate scandal, Poindexter was forced to resign in 1986, with his assistant, Oliver North.

poinsettia winter flowering shrub *Euphorbia pulcherrima*, also known as Mexican flame-leaf and Christmas-flower, with large red leaves encircling small greenish-yellow flowers. It is native to Mexico and tropical America but is a popular pot plant in North America and Europe.

pointe (French 'toe of shoe'). In dance, the tip of the toe. A dancer *sur les pointes* is dancing on her toes in blocked shoes, as popularized by Marie ◊Taglioni in 1832.

Pointe-Noire chief port of the Congo, formerly (1950–58) the capital; population (1984) 297,000. Industries include oil refining and shipbuilding.

pointer breed of dog, often white mixed with black, tan, or liver, about 60 cm/2 ft tall, and weighing 28 kg/62 lbs.

pointillism technique in oil painting developed in the 1880s by the Neo-Impressionist Seurat. He used small dabs of pure colour laid side by side to create an impression of shimmering light when viewed from a distance.

Poiseuille's formula in physics, a relationship describing the rate of flow of a fluid through a narrow tube. For a capillary (very narrow) tube of length l and radius r with a pressure difference p between its ends, and a liquid of ◊viscosity ε, the velocity of flow expressed as the volume per second is $\pi p r^4/8l\varepsilon$. The formula was devised in 1843 by the French physicist Jean Louis Poiseuille (1799–1869).

poison a chemical substance which when intro-duced into or applied to the body is capable of injuring health or destroying life.

poison pill in business, a tactic to avoid hostile takeover by making the target unattractive. For example, a company may give a certain class of shareholders the right to have their shares redeemed at a very good price in the event of the company being taken over, thus involving potential predator in considerable extra cost.

Poitevin in English history, relating to the reigns of King John and King Henry III; derived from the region of France S of the Loire (*Poitou*), controlled by the English for most of this period.

Poitou-Charentes region of W central France, comprising the *départements* of Charente, Vienne, Charente-Maritime, and Deux-Sèvres; capital Poitiers; area 25,809 sq km/9,965 sq mi; population (1986) 1,584,000.

Pol Pot (also known as Saloth Sar, Tol Saut and Pol Porth) 1925– . Kampuchean politician and communist leader. As leader of the Khmer Rouge, he overthrew the government of general Lon Nol in 1975 and proclaimed a republic of Democratic Kampuchea with himself as prime minister. The policies of the Pol Pot government were to evacuate cities and put people to work in the countryside. The Khmer Rouge also carried out a systematic extermination of the educated and middle classes before the regime was overthrown by a Vietnamese invasion in 1979. Since then, Pol Pot has led a resistance group against the Vietnamese although he has been tried and convicted, in his absence, of genocide. He continued as a Khmer Rouge leader despite officially resigning from all positions 1989.

Poland country in E Europe, bounded to the E by the USSR, to the S by Czechoslovakia, and to the W by East Germany.

Polanski Roman 1933– . Polish film director, born in Paris. He suffered a traumatic childhood in Nazi-occupied Poland, and later his wife, actress Sharon Tate, was the victim of a brutal murder. His tragic personal life is reflected in a fascination with horror and violence in his work. His films include *Repulsion* 1965, *Cul de Sac* 1966, *Rosemary's Baby* 1968, *Tess* 1979, and *Frantic* 1988.

polar coordinates in mathematics, a way of defining the position of a point in terms of its distance r from a fixed point (the origin) and its angle gT to a fixed line or axis. The coordinates of the point are (r, gT).

Polaris or Pole Star the bright star closest to the north celestial pole, and the brightest star in the constellation Ursa Minor. Its position is indicated by the 'pointers' in ◊Ursa Major. Polaris is a yellow ◊supergiant about 700 light years away.

polarized light ordinary light which can be regarded as electromagnetic vibrations at right angles to the line of propagation but in different planes. Light is said to be polarized when the vibrations take place in one particular plane. Polarized light is used to test the strength of sugar solutions, to measure stresses in transparent materials, and to prevent glare.

Polaroid camera an instant-picture camera, invented by Edwin Land in the USA 1947. The original camera produced black-and-white prints in about one minute. Modern cameras can produce black-and-white prints in a few seconds, and colour prints in less than a minute. An advanced model has automatic focusing and exposure. It ejects a piece of film immediately after the picture has been taken. The film consists of layers of emulsion and colour dyes together with a pod of chemical developer.

Poland
Republic of (*Polska Rzeczpospolita*)

area 312,700 sq km/120,733 sq mi
capital Warsaw
towns Lódź, Kraków, Wroclaw, Poznań, Katowice, Bydogoszcz, Lublin; ports Gdánsk, Szczecin, Gdynia
physical comprises part of the great plain of Europe; Vistula, Oder and Neisse rivers; Sudeten, Tatra and Carpathian mountains.
head of state Lech Walesa from 1990
head of government Hanna Suchocka from 1992
political system emergent democratic republic
exports coal, softwood timber, chemicals, machinery, ships, vehicles, meat
currency zloty

population (1990 est) 38,363,000; annual growth rate 0.6%
language Polish (official), German
religion Roman Catholic 95%
literacy 98% (1989)
GNP $276 bn (1988); $2,000 per head
chronology
1918 Poland revived as independent republic.
1939 German invasion and occupation.
1944 Germans driven out by Soviet forces.
1945 Polish boundaries redrawn at Potsdam Conference.
1947 Communist people's republic proclaimed.
1956 Poznań riots; Gomulka installed as Polish United Workers' Party (PUWP) leader.
1970 Gdańsk riots; Gierek replaced Gomulka.
1980 Solidarity free trade union emerged.
1981 Imposition of martial law by Gen Jaruzelski
1983 Ending of martial law.
1984 Amnesty for political prisoners.
1985 Zbigniew Messner became prime minister.
1987 Referendum on economic reform rejected.
1988 Solidarity strikes and demonstrations called off after pay increases and government agreement to hold church-state-union conference; Messner resigned, replaced by reformist Mieczyslaw Rakowski.
1989 Agreement to re-legalize Solidarity and introduce new socialist pluralist constitution. Solidarity won national assembly elections (June). Jaruzelski elected presient (July). Grand coalition formed (Sept), headed by Solidarity's Mazowiecki. W Europe and USA created $1 bn aid package
1990 Lech Walesa élected head of state.
1991 Five-party centre-right coalition formed under Jan Olszewski. Treaty signed to complete withdrawal of Soviet troops.
1992 Hanna Suchocka became Poland's first female prime minister.

When the film is ejected the pod bursts, and processing begins in the light.

polar reversal changeover in polarity of the Earth's magnetic poles. Studies of the magnetism of rocks have shown that the Earth's N magnetic pole was once the S one and vice versa.

Pole Reginald 1550–1558. English cardinal from 1536, who returned from Rome as papal legatee on the accession of Mary in order to readmit England to the Catholic church. He succeeded Cranmer as archbishop of Canterbury 1556.

polecat species of weasel *Mustela putorius* with a brown back and dark belly. The body is about 50 cm/20 in long and it has a strong smell. It is native to Asia, Europe, and N America.

poles geographic N and S points of penetration of the Earth's surface by the axis about which it rotates. The magnetic poles are the points towards which a freely suspended magnetic needle will point, and they vary continually.

Pole Star ◊Polaris, the northern pole star.

police civil law-and-order force. In the UK it is under the Home Office, with 56 autonomous police forces, generally organized on a county basis; mutual aid is given in circumstances such as mass picketing in the 1984–85 miners' strike, but there is no national police force or police riot unit (such as the French CRS riot squad). London's Bow Street runners, introduced 1749 by Henry ◊Fielding, formed a model for the London police force established by ◊Peel's government 1829 (hence 'peelers'

or 'bobbies'); the system was introduced throughout the country from 1856.

Police Complaints Authority in the UK, a statutory body, set up in 1984, which supervises the investigation of complaints against the Police. It can order disciplinary action to be taken against police officers.

polio (poliomyelitis) once called infantile paralysis, a virus infection of the central nervous system affecting nerves which activate muscles.

Polish Corridor strip of land, designated under the Treaty of ◊Versailles 1919 to give Poland access to the Baltic. It cut off East Prussia from the rest of Germany. It was absorbed when Poland took over the southern part of East Prussia in 1945.

Polish language a member of the Slavonic branch of the Indo-European language family, spoken mainly in Poland. Polish is written in the Roman and not the Cyrillic alphabet and its standard form is based on the dialect of Poznań in W Poland.

Politburo contraction of 'political bureau', the executive committee (known as the Praesidium 1952–66) of the Supreme Soviet in the USSR, which laid down party policy. It consisted of 12 voting and 6 candidate (non-voting) members.

political action committee (PAC US organization which raises funds for political candidates and in return commits them to a particular policy. It also spends money on changing public opinion. There were 3,500 PACs in 1984, and they controlled 25 per cent of all funds spent in ◊Congress elections.

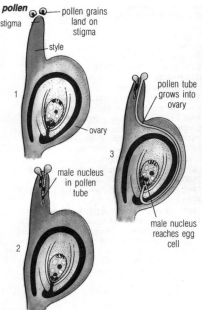

pollen

stigma — pollen grains land on stigma

— style

1

— ovary

male nucleus in pollen tube

2

3

pollen tube grows into ovary

male nucleus reaches egg cell

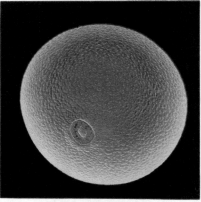

pollen Electron microscope picture of a pollen grain from cocksfoot grass, which is wind-pollinated.

1475 (National Gallery, London) is considered a joint work.

pollarding a type of pruning whereby the young branches of a tree are severely cut back, about 6–12 ft/2–4 m above the ground, to produce a stump-like trunk with a rounded, bushy head of thin new branches. It is often practised on willows, where the new branches or 'poles' are cut at intervals of a year or more, and used for fencing and firewood. Pollarding is also used to restrict the height of many street trees. See also ◊coppicing.

pollen the grains formed by seed plants that contain the male gametes. In ◊angiosperms pollen is produced within ◊anthers, in most ◊gymnosperms it is produced in male ◊cones. A pollen grain is typically yellow and, when mature, has a hard outer wall. Pollen of insect-pollinated plants (see ◊pollination) is often sticky and spiny, and larger than the smooth, light grains produced by wind-pollinated species.

pollen tube an outgrowth from a ◊pollen grain that grows towards the ◊ovule, following germination of the grain on the stigma. In ◊angiosperms (flowering plants) the pollen tube reaches the ovule

Polk James Knox 1795–1849. 11th president of the USA from 1845, a Democrat. Born in North Carolina. He admitted Texas to the Union, and forced the war on Mexico that resulted in the annexation of California and New Mexico.

polka folk dance in lively two-four time originating in Bohemia, fashionable in European society from about 1830.

pollack marine fish *Pollachius pollachius* of the cod family, growing to 75 cm/2.5 ft, and found inshore.

Pollaiuolo Antonio *c.* 1432–98 and Piero *c.* 1441–1496. Italian artists, active in Florence. Both brothers were painters, sculptors, goldsmiths, engravers, and designers. Antonio is said to have been the first Renaissance artist to make a serious study of anatomy. The *Martyrdom of St Sebastian*

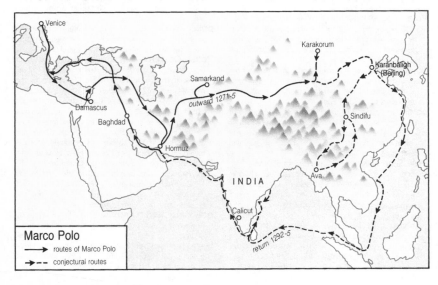

Venice

Karakorum

Karanbaligh (Beijing)

Samarkand

outward 1271–5

Damascus

Baghdad

Sindifu

Hormuz

Ava

INDIA

Calicut

return 1292–5

Marco Polo

→ routes of Marco Polo

-→- conjectural routes

by growing down through the ◊style, carrying the male gametes inside. The gametes are discharged into the ovule and one fertilizes the egg cell.

pollination the process by which ◊fertilization occurs in the sexual reproduction of higher plants. The male ◊gametes are contained in ◊pollen grains, which must be transferred from the ◊anther to the ◊stigma in ◊angiosperms, and from the male cone to the female cone in ◊gymnosperms. Self-pollination occurs when pollen is transferred to a stigma of the same flower, or to another flower on the same plant; cross-pollination occurs when pollen is transferred to another plant. This involves external pollen-carrying agents, such as wind (see ◊anemophily), water, insects, birds (see ◊ornithophily), bats or other small mammals.

Pollock Jackson 1912–1956. US painter, a pioneer of Abstract Expressionism and the foremost exponent of the dripping and splashing technique *action painting*, a style he developed around 1946.

poll tax or *community charge* tax levied on every individual, without reference to their income or property. Being simple to administer, it was among the earliest sorts of tax (introduced in England 1377), but because of its indiscriminate nature (it is a regressive tax, in that it falls proportionately more on poorer people) it has often proved unpopular. Poll tax was introduced in Scotland by the British Government in Apr 1989, and in England in 1990.

pollution the harmful effect on the environment of by-products of human activity, principally industrial and agricultural processes, for example, noise, smoke, gases, chemical effluents in seas and rivers, indestructible pesticides, sewage, and household waste. Natural disasters may also cause pollution: volcanic eruptions, for example, cause ash to be ejected into the atmosphere and deposited on the land surface. Failure to implement adequate pollution controls may result in long-term environmental damage and an increase in the incidence of diseases such as cancer.

Pollux in Greek mythology, the twin brother of ◊Castor.

polo game played between two teams of four on horseback, which originated in Iran, spread to India and was first played in England 1869. A game lasts about an hour, divided into 'chukkas' of 7½ minutes. A small ball is struck with a mallet through goals at each end of the ground.

Polo Marco 1254–1324. Venetian traveller and writer. He travelled overland to China 1271–75, and served under the emperor Kublai Khan until he returned to Europe by sea 1292–95. He was then captured while fighting for Venice against Genoa, and in prison wrote an account of his travels.

polonaise a Polish dance, in stately three-four time, which dates from the 16th century. Chopin developed the polonaise as a musical form.

polonium a radioactive element, symbol Po, atomic number 84, relative atomic mass 210. Polonium occurs naturally, but only in minute quantities. It has the largest number of isotopes of any element. One potential use for polonium is as a lightweight power source in satellites.

poltergeist (German 'noisy ghost') unexplained phenomenon that invisibly moves objects or hurls them about, starts fires, or causes other mischief.

polyandry system whereby a woman has more than one husband at the same time. It is found in many parts of the world, for example, in Madagascar, Malaysia, and certain Pacific isles, and among certain Inuit and South American Indian groups. In

polygon

	number of sides	sum of interior angles (degrees)
triangle	3	180
quadrilateral	4	360
pentagon	5	540
hexagon	6	720
heptagon	7	900
octagon	8	1,080
decagon	10	1,440
duodecagon	12	1,800
icosagon	20	3,240

Tibet and certain parts of India polyandry takes the form of the marriage of one woman to several brothers.

polyanthus garden variety of ◊primrose, with multiple flowers on one stalk.

polychlorinated biphenyls (PCBs) a group of dangerous industrial chemicals, valuable for their fire-resisting qualities, but an environmental hazard because of persistent toxicity. Since 1973, their use has been limited by international agreement.

polyester a type of thermosetting plastic, used in making synthetic fibres, such as Dacron and Terylene, and constructional plastics. With glass fibre added as reinforcement, polyesters are used in car bodies and boat hulls.

polyethylene a polymer of the gas ethylene (now called ethene, C_2H_4), best known under the tradename Polythene. It is a thermoplastic type of plastic, and was first made by the German chemist Ziegler (1898–1973). Either rigid or highly flexible, it is widely used for containers and protective wrapping. Because it may be made completely transparent and lends itself to colouring, it is also employed in decorative packaging.

polygamy the practice of having more than one husband or wife at the same time. It is found among many peoples, and is common in Africa. Normally it is confined to chiefs and nobles, as in ancient Egypt and among the primitive Teutons, Irish, and Slavs. Islam limits a man's legal wives to four. Certain Christian sects, for example, the Anabaptists of Münster, Germany, and the Mormons, have practised polygamy.

polygon in geometry, a plane (two-dimensional) figure with three or more straight-line sides. Common polygons have their own names, which define the number of sides (for example, triangle, quadrilateral, pentagon).

polygraph also called a *polygram*: an instrument that records graphically certain body activities, such as thoracic and abdominal respiration, blood pressure, pulse rate, and galvanic skin response (changes in electrical resistance of the skin). Changes in these activities when a person answers a question may indicate that the person is lying.

polyhedron in geometry, a solid figure with four or more plane faces. The more faces there are on a polyhedron, the more closely it approximates to a sphere. Knowledge of the properties of polyhedra is important in crystallography and stereochemistry in determining the shapes of crystals and molecules.

polymer a compound made up of large molecules composed of many repeated simple units (*monomers*), for example starch, nylon, and Perspex.

polymerization the chemical union of two or more (usually small) molecules of the same kind to form a new compound.

polymorphism in genetics, the coexistence of several distinctly different types in a ◊population. Examples include the different blood groups in humans, and different colour forms in some butterflies.

Polynesia those islands of Oceania E of 170° E latitude, including Hawaii, Kiribati, Tuvalu, Fiji, Tonga, Tokelau, Samoa, Cook Islands, and French Polynesia.

Polynesian languages see ◊Malayo-Polynesian languages.

polynomial in mathematics, algebraic expression that has only one ◊variable (denoted by a letter). A polynomial of degree one, that is, whose highest ◊power of x is 1, as in $2x + 1$, is called a linear polynomial; $3x^2 + 2x + 1$ is quadratic; $4x^3 + 3x^2 + 2x + 1$ is cubic.

polyp or *polypus* small 'stalked' benign tumour, most usually found on mucous membrane in the nose and bowel. Intestinal polyps are usually removed, as some have been found to be precursors of cancer.

polyphony music combining two or more 'voices' or parts, each with an individual melody.

polyploid in genetics, possessing three or more sets of chromosomes in cases where the normal complement is two sets (◊diploid). Polyploidy arises spontaneously and is common in plants (especially among the angiosperms), but rare in animals. Many crop plants are natural polyploids, including wheat, which has four sets of chromosomes per cell (durum wheat) or six sets (bread wheat). Plant breeders can induce the formation of polyploids by treatment with a chemical, colchicine.

polysaccharide a long-chain carbohydrate made up of hundreds or thousands of linked simple sugars (monosaccharides) such as glucose.

polystyrene a type of ◊plastic.

polytechnic in the UK, an institution for further education offering courses mainly at degree level and concentrating on full-time vocational courses, although many polytechnics provide a wide range of part-time courses at advanced levels. From Apr 1989 the 29 polytechnics in England became independent corporations.

polytheism the worship of many gods, as opposed to monotheism (belief in one god). Examples are the religions of ancient Egypt, Babylon, Greece and Rome, Mexico, and modern Hinduism.

polytonality in music, the simultaneous use of more than one ◊key. A combination of two keys is bitonality.

polyunsaturate a type of animal or vegetable fat whose molecules consist of long carbon chains with many double bonds. Polyunsaturated fats are considered healthier than saturated fats (such as butter), and are widely used in margarines and cooking oils. See also ◊fatty acid.

pome a type of ◊pseudocarp or false fruit typical of certain plants belonging to the Rosaceae family. The outer skin and fleshy tissues are developed from the ◊receptacle after fertilization and the five ◊carpels (the true ◊fruit) form the 'core' of the pome which surrounds the seeds. Examples of pomes are apples, pears, and quinces.

pomegranate fruit of a deciduous shrub or small tree *Punica granatum*, native to SW Asia but cultivated widely in tropical and subtropical areas. The seeds of the reddish-yellow fruit are eaten fresh or made into wine.

Pompeii *A street in Pompeii in 47 AD, inundated by ash, pumice and mud.*

pomeranian small breed of dog, about 15 cm/6 in, and 3 kg/6.5 lb. It has long straight hair with a neck frill, and the tail is carried over the back.

Pompadour Jeanne Antoinette Poisson, Marquise de Pompadour 1721–1764. Mistress of ◊Louis XV of France. Born in Paris, she became the king's mistress in 1744, and largely dictated the government's ill-fated policy of reversing France's anti-Austrian policy for an anti-Prussian one. She acted as the patron of the Enlightenment philosophers Voltaire and Diderot.

Pompeii ancient city in Italy, near ◊Vesuvius, 21 km/13 mi SE of Naples. In 63 AD an earthquake destroyed much of the city which had been a Roman port and pleasure resort; it was completely buried beneath lava when Vesuvius erupted in 79 AD. Over 2,000 people were killed. Pompeii was rediscovered in 1748 and the systematic excavation begun in 1763 still continues.

Pompey the Great (Gnaeus Pompeius Magnus) 106–48 BC. Roman soldier and politician. Originally a supporter of ◊Sulla and the aristocratic party, he joined the democrats when he became consul with ◊Crassus in 70 BC. He defeated ◊Mithridates of Pontus, and annexed Syria and Palestine. In 60 BC he formed the First Triumvirate with ◊Caesar (whose daughter Julia he married) and ◊Crassus, and when it broke down after 53 BC he returned to the aristocratic party. On the outbreak of civil war in 49 BC he withdrew to Greece, was defeated by Caesar at Pharsalus in 48 BC, and was murdered in Egypt.

Pompidou Georges 1911–1974. French conservative politician, president from 1969. An adviser on Gen de Gaulle's staff 1944–46, he held administrative posts until he became director-general of the French House of Rothschild in 1954, and even then continued in close association with de Gaulle. In 1962 he became prime minister, but resigned after the Gaullist victory in the elections of 1968, and was elected to the presidency on de Gaulle's resignation.

Ponce de León Juan 1460–1521. Spanish explorer who settled Puerto Rico in 1508–9 and was the first European to reach Florida in 1513.

Pondicherry union territory of SE India
area 492 sq km/186 sq mi
capital Pondicherry
products rice, groundnuts, cotton, sugar
language French, English, Tamil, Telegu, Malayalam
population (1981) 604,500
history Together with Karaikal, Yanam, and Mahé (on the Malabar Coast) it formed a French colony until 1954 when all were transferred to the government of India; since 1962 they have formed the union territory of Pondicherry.

pond-skater water ◊bug that rows itself across the surface using its middle legs. It feeds on smaller insects.

pondweed aquatic plant of the genus *Potamogeton* that either floats on the water or is submerged. The leaves of the floating pondweed are broad and leathery, while leaves of the submerged form are narrower and translucent; the flowers grow in green spikes.

Pontiac *c.* 1720–1769. North American Indian, chief of the Ottawa from 1755. He led in 1763–64 the 'Conspiracy of Pontiac' in an attempt to stop British encroachment on Indian lands. He achieved remarkable success against overwhelming odds, but eventually signed a peace treaty in 1766, and was murdered by an Illinois Indian at the instigation of a British trader.

Pontormo Jacopo Carucci 1494–1557. Italian painter, active in Florence. He had a dramatic Mannerist style, with lurid colours.

Pontus kingdom of NE Asia Minor on the Black Sea from about 300–65 BC when its greatest ruler, ◊Mithridates VI was defeated by ◊Pompey.

pony small horse under 1.47 m/58 in (14.2 hands) shoulder height.

poodle breed of dog, including standard (above 38 cm/15 in at shoulder), miniature (below 38 cm/15 in), and toy (below 28 cm/11 in) types. Their long curly coats, usually cut into elaborate styles, are mostly either black or white, although greys and browns are also bred.

pool game derived from ◊billiards and played in many different forms. Originally popular in US, it is now also played in Britain and Europe.

Poona former spelling of ◊Pune, city in India.

poor law English system for poor relief, established by the Poor Relief Act 1601. Each parish was responsible for its own poor, paid for by a parish tax. It was reformed in the 19th Century, parish functions being transferred to the Poor Law Commissioners 1834 and eventually to the Ministry of Health 1914. It is now superseded by rights to benefit payments, administered by the Department of Social Security.

Pop Iggy. Stage name of James Osterberg 1947– . US rock singer and songwriter, initially known as *Iggy Stooge* with a band called the Stooges (1967–74), and noted for his self-destructive proto-punk performances.

pop art movement of young artists in the 1950s and 1960s, reacting against the elitism of abstract art. Pop art used popular imagery drawn from advertising, comic strips, film, and television. It originated in the UK 1956 with Richard Hamilton, Peter Blake (1932–), and others, and broke through in the USA with the flags and numbers of Jasper Johns 1958 and the soup cans of Andy Warhol 1962.

pope the bishop of Rome as head of the Roman Catholic Church, which claims him as the spiritual descendant of St Peter. Elected by the Sacred College of Cardinals, a pope dates his pontificate from his coronation with the tiara, or triple crown, at St Peter's Basilica, Rome. The pope had great political power in Europe from the early Middle Ages until the Reformation.

Pope Alexander 1688–1744. British poet and satirist. He established his reputation with the precocious *Pastorals* 1709 and *Essay on Criticism* 1711, followed by a parody of the heroic epic *The Rape of the Lock* 1712–14, and *Eloisa to Abelard* 1717. Other works include a highly Neo-Classical translation of ◊Homer's *Iliad* and *Odyssey* 1715–26.

Popish Plot a supposed plot to murder Charles II; see under Titus ◊Oates.

poplar deciduous tree of the genus *Populus* with characteristically broad leaves. The white poplar *Populus alba* has a smooth grey trunk and leaves with white undersides. Other varieties are the aspen *Populus tremula*, and grey poplar *Populus canescens*. Most species are tall and often used as windbreaks in commercial orchards.

poplin a strong fabric, originally with a warp of silk and a weft of worsted, but now usually made from cotton, in a plain weave with a finely corded surface.

pop music short for popular music, umbrella term for modern music not classifiable as jazz or classical. Pop became distinct from folk music with the advent of sound-recording techniques, and incorporated blues, country and western, and music hall; electronic amplification and other technological innovations have played a large part in the creation of new styles.

Popocatépetl (Aztec 'smoking mountain') volcano in Amecameca, SE central Mexico; 5,340 m/17,520 ft.

Popov Alexander 1859–1905. Russian physicist who devised the first ◊aerial, in advance of ◊Marconi, (although he did not use it for radio communication), and a detector for radio waves.

Popper Karl (Raimund) 1902– . Austrian philosopher of science. His theory of falsificationism says that although scientific generalizations cannot be conclusively verified, they can be conclusively falsified by a counterinstance, and therefore science is not certain knowledge, but a series of 'conjectures and refutations', approaching, though never reaching, a definitive truth. For Popper, psychoanalysis and Marxism are unfalsifiable and therefore unscientific.

poppy plant of the genus *Papaver* that bears brightly coloured, often dark-centred, flowers and yields a milky sap. Species include the crimson field *Papaver rhoeas* and ◊opium poppies, found in Europe and Asia. Closely related are the Californian poppy *Eschscholzia californica*, and the yellow horned or sea poppy *Glaucium flavum*.

popular front a political alliance of liberals, socialists, communists, and other centre and left-wing parties against fascism. This policy was proposed by the Communist International in 1935, and was adopted in France and Spain, where popular-front governments were elected in 1936; that in France was overthrown in 1938, and in Spain in 1939. In Britain a popular-front policy was advocated by Sir Stafford Cripps and others, but rejected by the Labour Party. The resistance movements in the occupied countries during World War II represented a revival of the popular-front idea, and in postwar politics the term tends to recur whenever a strong right-wing party can be counterbalanced only by an alliance of those on the left.

population in biology and ecology, a group of animals of one species, living in a certain area and able to interbreed; the members of a given species in a ◊community of living things.

population cycle in biology, regular fluctuations in the size of a population, as seen in lemmings, for example. Such cycles are often caused by density-dependent mortality: high mortality due to overcrowding causes a sudden decline in the population, which then gradually builds up again. Population cycles may also result from an interaction between a predator and its prey.

population

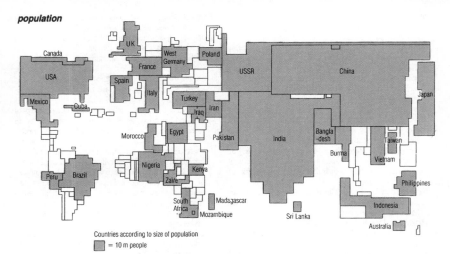

Countries according to size of population
◻ = 10 m people

population genetics the branch of genetics that studies the way in which the frequencies of different ◊alleles in populations of organisms change, as a result of natural selection and other processes, to give rise to evolution.

Populism in US history, a late 19th-century political movement that developed out of farmers' protests against economic hardship. The Populist, or People's, Party was founded in 1892 and fielded several presidential candidates. It failed however to reverse increasing industrialization and the relative decline of agriculture in the US.

porcelain (hardpaste) type of ◊ceramic material characterized by its hardness, ringing sound when struck, translucence, and shining finish, like that of a cowrie shell (Italian *porcellana*). It is made of kaolin and petuntse (fusible feldspar consisting chiefly of quartz, and reduced to a fine, white powder) and was first developed in China.

porcupine ◊rodent with sharp quills on its body. Porcupines of the family Hystricidae are terrestrial in habit. They are characterized by long spines in the coat. The colouring is brown with black and white quills. American porcupines constitute the family Erethizontidae and differ from the Old World varieties by living in trees, having a prehensile tail, and much shorter spines.

Porgy and Bess classic US folk opera 1935 by George and Ira Gershwin, based on the novel *Porgy* 1925 by DuBose Heyward, a story of the black residents of Catfish Row in Charleston, South Carolina.

pornography obscene literature, pictures, photos, or films of no artistic merit, intended only to arouse sexual desire. Standards are subjective about what is obscene, and about whether a particular work has artistic value, hence the difficulty in agreement over whether a work violates laws against obscenity.

porcupine

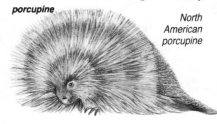

North American porcupine

porphyria rare hereditary metabolic disorder which may cause mental confusion. Other symptoms, for example, excessive growth of hair, contraction of muscles to reveal the teeth, sensitivity to sunlight, and a need for blood infusions, have been suggested as the basis for vampirism and werewolf legends.

porphyry any rock composed of large crystals in a purplish matrix.

porpoise smallest member of the whale group, distinguished from the dolphin by not having a 'beak', and being smaller. It can grow to 1.8 m/6 ft long, and feeds on fish and crustaceans.

Porsche Ferdinand 1875–1951. German car designer, for example, the Volkswagen (People's Car) marketed after World War II, and Porsche sports cars.

port sweet, fortified (with brandy) dessert wine (red, tawny, or white), from grapes grown in the Douro basin of Portugal and exported from Oporto, hence the name.

Port-au-Prince capital and industrial port (sugar, rum, textiles, plastics) of Haiti; population (1982) 763,000.

Port Elizabeth industrial port (engineering, steel, food processing) in Cape province, S Africa, about 710 km/440 mi E of Cape Town on Algoa Bay; population (1980) 492,140.

Porter Cole (Albert) 1891–1964. US composer and lyricist of musical comedies. His shows include *Gay Divorce* 1932 and *Kiss Me Kate* 1948.

Porter Eric 1928– . English actor. His numerous classical roles include title parts in *Uncle Vanya*, *Volpone*, and *King Lear*; on television he was noted for his role in *The Forsyte Saga*.

Porter Rodney Robert 1917–1985. British biochemist and Nobel prizewinner in 1972 for pioneering work on the chemical structure of antibodies.

Portland William Henry Cavendish Bentinck, 3rd Duke of Portland 1738–1809. British politician, originally a Whig, who in 1783 became nominal prime minister in the Fox–North coalition government. During the French Revolution he joined the Tories, and was prime minister 1807–09.

Port Louis capital of Mauritius, on the island's NW coast; population (1987) 139,000.

Port Moresby capital and port of Papua New Guinea on the S coast of New Guinea; population (1987) 152,000.

Portugal
Republic of (*República Portuguesa*)

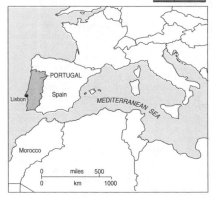

area 91,631 sq km/34,861 sq mi (including Azores and Madeira)
capital Lisbon
towns Coimbra, ports Oporto, Setúbal
physical mountainous in the N, plains in the S
head of state Mario Alberto Nobre Lopes Soares from 1986
head of government Aníbal Cavaco Silva from 1985
political system democratic republic
exports wine, olive oil, resin, cork, sardines, textiles, pottery, pulpwood

currency escudo
population (1990 est) 10,528,000; annual growth rate 0.5%
life expectancy men 71, women 78
language Portuguese
religion Roman Catholic 97%
literacy 89% male/80% female (1985)
GNP $33.5 bn (1987); $2,970 per head
chronology
1928–68 Military dictatorship under Antonio de Oliveira Salazar.
1968 Salazar succeeded by Marcello Caetano.
1974 Caetano removed in a military coup led by Gen Antonio Ribeiro de Spinola. Spinola was then replaced by Gen Francisco da Costa Gomes.
1975 Independence granted to African colonies.
1976 New constitution, providing for a gradual return to civilian rule, adopted. Minority government appointed, led by the Socialist Party leader Mario Soares.
1978 Soares resigned.
1980 Francisco Balsemão formed a centre-party coalition after two and a half years of political instability.
1982 Draft of new constitution approved, reducing the powers of the presidency.
1983 Centre-left coalition government formed.
1985 Cavaco Silva became prime minister.
1986 Mario Soares elected first civilian president for 60 years. Portugal joined the EC.
1987 Soares re-elected with large majority.
1988 Portugal joined the Western European Union.
1989 Constitution amended to allow major state enterprises to be denationalized.
1991 Soares re-elected president.

Port-of-Spain port and capital of Trinidad and Tobago, on Trinidad; population (1988) 58,000.

Porton Down site of the Chemical and Biological Defence Establishment of the Ministry of Defence in Wiltshire, SW England. Its prime role is to conduct research into means of protection from chemical attack.

Porto Novo capital of Benin, W Africa; population (1982) 208,258. A former Portuguese centre for the slave and tobacco trade with Brazil; it became a French protectorate 1863.

Port Rashid port serving ◊Dubai in the United Arab Emirates.

Port Said port in Egypt, on reclaimed land at the N end of the ◊Suez Canal; population (1983) 364,000. During the 1967 Arab-Israeli war the city was damaged and the canal was blocked; Port Said was evacuated by 1969, but by 1975 had been largely reconstructed.

Portsmouth city and naval port in Hampshire, England, opposite the Isle of Wight; population (1989) 174,000.

Portugal country in SW Europe, on the Atlantic, bounded to the N and E by Spain.

Portuguese East Africa former name of ◊Mozambique.

Portuguese Guinea former name of ◊Guinea-Bissau.

Portuguese language a member of the Romance branch of the Indo-European language family, the national language of Portugal, closely related to Spanish and strongly influenced by Arabic. It is also spoken in Brazil, Angola, Mozambique, and other former Portuguese colonies.

Portuguese man-of-war coelenterate with the appearance of a large jellyfish. There is a gas-filled float on the surface, below which hangs feeding, stinging, and reproductive individuals. The float can be 30 cm/1 ft long.

Portuguese West Africa former name of ◊Angola.

pos (short for 'point of sale') in business premises, the point where a sale is transacted, for example, a supermarket checkout. In conjunction with ◊EFT (electronic funds transfer), pos is part of the terminology of 'cashless shopping', enabling buyers to transfer funds directly from their bank accounts to the shop's.

Poseidon Greek god (Roman Neptune), the brother of Zeus and Pluto. The brothers dethroned their father, Kronos, and divided his

Poseidon The Temple of Poseidon (North-East corner), Cape Sounion, Greece.

realm, Poseidon taking the sea; he was also worshipped as god of earthquakes. His son was ◊Triton.

positivism a theory associated with the French philosopher Comte (1798-1857), and ◊empiricism, which confines genuine knowledge within the bounds of science and observation. The theory is hostile to theology and to metaphysics which oversteps this boundary. *Logical positivism* developed in the 1920s. It rejected any metaphysical world beyond everyday science and common sense, and confined statements to those of formal logic or mathematics. It was influential through the work of A J Ayer and the Vienna circle.

positron an ◊elementary particle, produced in some radioactive ◊decay processes, which is similar in every respect to an ◊electron, except that it carries a positive ◊electric charge. It is thus the ◊antiparticle to the electron. When a positron and electron collide they anihilate each other to produce gamma radiation.

postcard a card with a message, sent by post. The postcard's inventor was Emmanual Hermann, in Vienna, who proposed a 'postal telegram', sent at a lower fee to a normal letter with an envelope, in 1869. The first UK postcard dates from 1870; the first picture postcard was produced 1894.

poster advertising announcement for public display, often illustrated, first produced in modern form in France from the mid-19th century, when colour lithography came into its own, with the work of Jules Chéret (1836–1932).

poste restante (French) a system whereby mail is sent to a certain post office and kept there until collected by the addressee.

post hoc, ergo propter hoc (Latin) after this, therefore on account of this.

Post-Impressionism the various styles of painting that followed Impressionism in the 1880s and 1890s. The term was first used by the British critic Roger Fry in 1911 to describe the works of Cézanne, van Gogh, and Gauguin. These painters moved away from the spontaneity of Impressionism, attempting to give their work more serious meaning and permanence.

Post-Modernism a late 20th-century movement in the arts which rejects the preoccupation of ◊Modernism with form and technique rather than content. In the visual arts, and in architecture, it uses an amalgam of styles from the past, such as the classical and the baroque, whose slightly off-key familiarity has a more immediate appeal than the austerities of Modernism.

post mortem (Latin 'after death') dissection of a dead body to determine the cause of death. It is also known as ◊autopsy.

Post Office (PO) a government department or authority with responsibility for postal services and telecommunications.

post scriptum (PS) (Latin) something written below the signature on a letter.

potash general name for any potassium-containing mineral, most often applied to potassium carbonate (K_2CO_3). Potash, originally made by roasting plants to ashes in earthenware pots, is commercially produced from the mineral sylvite (potassium chloride, KCl) and is used mainly in making artificial fertilizers, glass, and soap.

potassium metallic element of the alkali group, symbol K, atomic number 19, relative atomic mass 39.1. It is a soft, silvery-bright metal which reacts violently with water, forming potassium hydroxide and hydrogen; this ignites and burns spontaneously with a violet flame. The element is therefore kept under kerosene or naphtha. The salts are important as essential constituents of fertilizers. Alloyed with sodium, it may be used as a coolant in nuclear reactors.

potato perennial plant *Solanum tuberosum*, family Solanaceae, with edible tuberous roots that are rich in starch. Used by the Andean Indians for at least 2,000 years, the potato was introduced to Europe by the mid-16th century, and reputedly to England by Walter Raleigh. The Irish *potato famine* 1845, caused by a parasitic fungus, resulted in many thousands of deaths, and led to large-scale emigration to the USA. See also *sweet potato* under ◊yam.

Potemkin Grigory Aleksandrovich, Prince Potemkin 1739–1791. Russian politician. He entered the army and attracted the notice of Catherine II, whose friendship he kept throughout his life. He was an active administrator who reformed the army, built the Black Sea Fleet, conquered the Crimea, developed S Russia, and founded the Kherson arsenal 1788 (the first Russian naval base on the Black Sea).

potential, electric the relative electrical state of an object. A charged ◊conductor, for example, has a higher potential than the earth, whose potential is taken by convention to be zero. An electric ◊cell has a potential in terms to e.m.f. (◊electromotive force) which can make current flow in an external circuit. The difference in potential between two points – the potential difference – is expressed in ◊volts; that is, a 12V battery has a potential difference of 12 volts between its negative and positive terminals.

potential energy ◊energy possessed by an object by virtue of its position or state. It is contrasted with ◊kinetic energy.

potentiometer in physics, an electrical ◊resistor that can be divided so as to compare or measure voltages. A simple type consists of a length of uniform resistance wire (about 1 m/3 ft long) carrying a constant current provided by a cell connected across the ends of the wire. The source of ◊potential difference (voltage) to be measured is connected (to oppose the cell) between one end of the wire, through a ◊galvanometer (instrument for measuring small currents), to a contact free to slide along the wire. The sliding contact is moved until the galvanometer shows no deflection. The ratio of the length of potentiometer wire in the galvanometer circuit to the total length of wire is then equal to the ratio of the unkown potential difference to that of the cell. In radio circuits, any rotary variable resistance (such as volume control) may be referred to as a potentiometer.

Potsdam Conference conference held at Potsdam in July 1945 between representatives of Britain, USSR, and USA. It established the political and economic principles governing the treatment of Germany in the initial period of Allied control at the end of World War II, and sent an ultimatum to Japan demanding unconditional surrender on pain of utter destruction.

Potter Beatrix 1866–1943. British writer and illustrator of children's books, beginning with *Peter Rabbit* 1900; her code diaries were published 1966. Her Lake District home is a museum.

Potter Paulus 1625–1654. Dutch painter, active in Delft, The Hague, and Amsterdam. He is known for paintings of animals, especially *The Young Bull* 1647 (Mauritshuis, The Hague).

Potter Stephen 1900–1969. British author of humorous studies in how to outwit and outshine others,

poultry

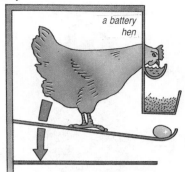

a battery hen

including *Gamesmanship* 1947, *Lifemanship* 1950, and *One Upmanship* 1952.

Potteries, the the centre of the china and earthenware industry in England, lying in the upper Trent basin of N Staffordshire. Wedgwood and Minton are factory names associated with the Potteries, which cover the area around Stoke-on-Trent, and include the formerly separate towns of Burslem, Hanley, Longton, Fenton, and Tunstall.

pottery a type of ◊ceramic ware in domestic and ornamental use ranging from opaque and porous earthenware through translucent bone china (5% calcined bone) to finest ◊porcelain.

potto arboreal, nocturnal, African mammal *Perodicticus potto* belonging to the loris family of primates. It has a thick body, strong limbs, grasping feet and hands, and grows to 40 cm/16 in long. It has horny spines along its backbone, which it uses in self-defence. It climbs slowly, and eats insects, snails, fruit, and leaves.

poujadists an extreme right-wing political movement in France led by Pierre Poujade which was prominent in French politics from 1954 until 1958. Known in France as the Union de Défence des Commercants et Artisands, it won 52 seats in the national election of 1956. Its voting strength come mainly from the lower-middle-class and petit-bourgeois sections of society but the return of ◊de Gaulle to power in 1958 and the foundation of the Fifth Republic led to a rapid decline in the movement's fortunes.

Poulenc Francis (Jean Marcel) 1899–1963. French composer and pianist. A self-taught composer of witty and irreverent music, he was a member of the group of French composers known as ◊Les Six. His works include the operas *Les Mamelles de Tirésias* 1947, and *Dialogues des Carmèlites* 1957, and the ballet *Les Biches* 1923.

Poulsen Valdemar 1869–1942. Danish engineer who in 1900 was the first to demonstrate that sound could be recorded magnetically – originally on a moving steel wire or tape; this was the forerunner of the tape recorder.

poultry domestic birds such as ducks, geese, turkeys, and chickens.

pound Imperial unit of weight. The commonly used avoirdupois pound (0.45 kg) differs from the troy pound (0.37 kg).

Pound Ezra 1885–1972. US poet, who lived in London from 1908. His verse *Personae* and *Exultations* 1909 established the principles of the ◊Imagist movement. His largest Modern work was the series of *Cantos* 1925–1969 (intended to number 100), which attempted a massive reappraisal of history.

poundal f.p.s. unit of force (pdl), defined as the force required to give a mass of 1 lb an acceleration of 1 ft/s². It is equivalent to 0.1383 newton, or 1.383 × 10⁴ dynes.

Poussin Nicolas 1594–1665. French painter, active chiefly in Rome; court painter to Louis XIII 1640–43. He was one of France's foremost landscape painters in the 17th century. He painted mythological and literary scenes in a strongly classical style, for example *Rape of the Sabine Women c.* 1636–37 (Metropolitan Museum of Art, New York).

poverty the condition that exists when the basic needs of human beings are not being met, particularly shelter, food, and clothing.

powder metallurgy a method of shaping heat-resistant metals such as tungsten. Metal powder is pressed into a mould and then sintered, or heated to very high temperatures.

Powell (John) Enoch 1912– . British politician. He was professor of Greek, University of Sydney, Australia 1937–39; he became a Conservative member of Parliament for Wolverhampton 1950, was minister of health 1960–63, and contested the party leadership 1965. Always controversial, he made a speech against immigration at Birmingham 1968 which led to his dismissal from the shadow cabinet. Declining to stand in the Feb 1974 election, he attacked the ◊Heath government and resigned from the party. From 1974 to 1987 he was Official Unionist Party member for S Down. He is an eloquent speaker.

Powell Anthony (Dymoke) 1905– . English novelist, whose chief work is the series of 12 volumes *A Dance to the Music of Time* 1951–75, which begins shortly after World War I and chronicles a period of 50 years in the lives of Nicholas Jenkins and his circle of upper-class friends.

Powell Cecil Frank 1903–1969. English physicist, awarded a Nobel prize 1950 for his use of photographic emulsion as a method of tracking charged nuclear particles.

Powell Michael 1905– . English film director, best known for his collaboration with screenwriter Emeric Pressburger (1902–88). Their work, often criticized for extravagance, is richly imaginative, and includes the films *A Matter of Life and Death* 1946, and *Black Narcissus* 1947.

power in mathematics, power, also called an index or exponent, is denoted by a superior small numeral. A number or symbol raised to the power 2, that is, multiplied by itself, is said to be squared (for example, 3^2, x^2) and something raised to the power three is said to be cubed (for example, 2^3, y^3).

power in physics, the rate of doing work or consuming energy. It is measured in watts, or other units of work per unit time.

power boat a ◊motorboat used for racing.

power of attorney in English law, legal authority to act on behalf of another, for a specific transaction, or for a particular period. From 1986 powers of attorney may, in certain circumstances, remain valid when the person who granted the power subsequently becomes mentally incapable.

Powys central county of Wales; area 5,077 sq km/1,960 sq mi; population (1981) 110,500. Products include agriculture, dairy cattle, and sheep.

Powys John Cowper 1872–1963. English novelist. His mystic and erotic books include *Wolf Solent* 1929 and *A Glastonbury Romance* 1933. He was one of three brothers (**Theodore Francis Powys** 1875–53 and **Llewelyn Powys** 1884–1939), all writers.

Poznań German *Posen* industrial city (machinery, aircraft, beer) in W Poland; population (1985) 553,000. Settled by German immigrants 1253, it passed to Prussia 1793, but was restored to Poland 1919.

pp abbreviation for *per procurationem* (Latin 'by proxy'); in music, the abbreviation for *pianissimo* (Italian 'very softly').

PR abbreviation for *public relations*, or *proportional representation*.

praesidium ◊Politburo, name (1952–66) of the executive committee of the Supreme Soviet in the former USSR.

praetor a Roman magistrate, elected annually, who assisted the ◊consuls and presided over the civil courts. The number of praetors was finally increased to eight, who after a year of office acted as provincial governors for a further year.

pragmatism a philosophical tradition which interprets truth in terms of the practical effects of what is believed, and in particular the usefulness of these effects.

Prague Czech *Praha* city and capital of the Czech Republic on the river Vltava; population (1991) 1,212,000. Industries include cars and aircraft, chemicals, paper and printing, clothing, brewing, and food processing. It became capital 1918.

Praia port and capital of the Republic of Cape Verde, on the island of Santiago; population (1980) 37,500. Industries include fishing and shipping.

prairie the central N American plains, formerly grass-covered, extending over most of the region between the Rockies on the W and the Great Lakes and Ohio river on the E, and northward into Canada.

prairie dog a burrowing rodent. See ◊marmot.

Prakrit a general name for the ancient Indo-European dialects of N India, contrasted with the sacred classical language Sanskrit. The word is itself Sanskrit, meaning 'natural', as opposed to *Sanskrit*, which means 'perfected'. The Prakrits are considered to be the ancestors of such modern N Indian languages as Hindi, Punjabi, and Bengali.

Prasad Rajendra 1884–1963. Bihari lawyer and politician. He was a member of the Indian National Congress and loyal follower of Mohandas Gandhi in Bihar. Prior to World War II, he succeeded Subhas Chandra Bose as national president of the Indian National Congress. He went on to become India's first president after independence.

praseodymium a silver-white metallic element, symbol Pr, atomic number 59, relative atomic mass 140,098. It is a member of the lanthanide series of elements, and occurs naturally in monazite and bastnasite. It is used in carbon-arc lights and as a pigment in glass.

prawn shrimplike member of the suborder Natantia ('swimming'), order Decapoda, as contrasted with lobsters and crayfish, which are able to 'walk'. The *common prawn Leander serratus*, of temperate seas has a long saw-edged spike or rostrum just in front of its eyes, and antennae much longer than its body length. It is distinguished from the shrimp not only by its larger size, but by having pincers on its second pair of legs.

Praxiteles mid-4th century BC. Greek sculptor, active in Athens. His best-known work, *Aphrodite of Knidos* (known through Roman copies), is thought to have begun the tradition of lifesize freestanding female nudes in Greek sculpture.

prayer address to divine power, ranging from a magical formula to attain a desired end, to selfless communication in meditation. Within Christianity

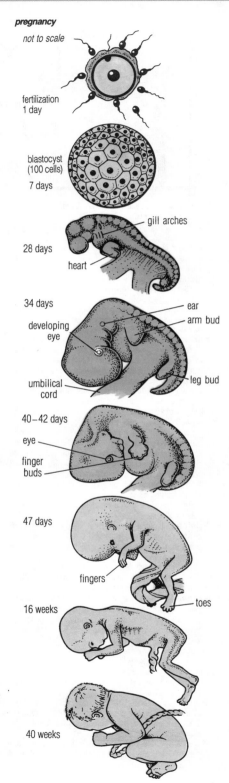

pregnancy

not to scale

fertilization
1 day

blastocyst
(100 cells)
7 days

gill arches

28 days

heart

34 days

ear

arm bud

developing
eye

umbilical
cord

leg bud

40–42 days

eye

finger
buds

47 days

fingers

16 weeks

toes

40 weeks

the Catholic and Orthodox churches sanction prayer to the Virgin, angels, and saints as intercessors, whereas Protestantism limits prayer to God alone, and does not provide for prayer for the dead.

preadaptation in biology, the fortuitous possession of a character that allows an organism to exploit a new situation. In many cases, the character evolves to solve a particular problem that a species encounters in its preferred habitat, but once evolved may allow the organisms to exploit an entirely different situation. Thus the ability to extract oxygen directly from the air evolved in some early fishes, probably in response to life in stagnant, deoxygenated pools; this later made it possible for their descendants to spend time on land, so giving rise eventually to the air-breathing amphibians.

Precambrian in geology, the time from the formation of Earth up to 590 million years ago. Its boundary with the succeeding Cambrian period marks the time when animals first developed hard skeletons and so left abundant fossil remains. It comprises about 85% of geological time and is divided into two periods: the Archaean and the Proterozoic.

precedent the ◊common law principle that, in deciding a particular case, judges are bound to follow any applicable principles of law laid down by superior courts in earlier reported cases.

precession a slow wobble of the Earth on its axis, like that of a spinning top. The gravitational pulls of the Sun and Moon on the Earth's equatorial bulge cause the Earth's axis to trace out a circle on the sky every 25,800 years.

precipitation meteorological term for water that falls to the Earth from the atmosphere. It includes ◊rain, ◊snow, sleet, ◊hail, ◊dew, and hoar frost.

predestination in Christian theology, the doctrine which asserts that God has determined all events beforehand, including the ultimate salvation or damnation of the individual human soul. Today Christianity in general accepts that humanity is free will, though some forms, such as Calvinism, believe that salvation can only be attained by the gift of God. The concept of predestination is also found in Islam.

pref. in grammar, the abbreviation for *prefix*.

prefect French government official who, under the centralized Napoleonic system 1800–1984, was responsible for enforcing government policy in each *département* and *région*. In 1984 prefects were replaced by presidents of elected councils (see government under ◊France.

prefix a letter or group of letters which can be added to the beginning of a word in order to make a new word.

pregnancy in humans, the period during which a fetus grows within the womb. It begins at conception and ends at birth, and the normal length is 40 weeks. ◊Menstruation usually stops on conception. After the second month, the breasts become tense and tender, and the area round the nipple becomes darker. Enlargement of the uterus can be felt at about the end of the third month, and thereafter the abdomen enlarges progressively. Pregnancy in animals is called ◊gestation.

prehistoric life the diverse organisms that inhabited the Earth from the origin of life about 3,500 million years ago to the time when humans began to keep written records in about 3500 BC. During the course of evolution, new forms of life developed and other forms, including the dinosaurs, became extinct.

prehistory human cultures before the use of writing. The classification system was devised 1816 by the Danish archaeologist Christian Thomsen, and is based on the materials used by early humans for tools and weapons.

Stone Age in which flint was predominant, divided into:

Old Stone Age (Palaeolithic) 3,500,000–5000 BC, in which the tools were chipped into shape; it includes ◊Neanderthal and ◊Cromagnon people; the only domesticated animals were dogs. Cave paintings were produced 20,000–8,000 years ago in many parts of the world, for example, ◊Altamira, Spain; ◊Lascaux, France; central Sahara; India; and Australia.

Middle Stone Age (Mesolithic) and *New Stone Age* (Neolithic), when tools were ground and polished, and, in Neolithic times, agriculture and domestication of cattle and sheep were practised. A Stone Age culture survived in Australia until the 19th century.

Bronze Age period of bronze tools and weapons beginning approximately 6000 BC in the Far East, and continuing in the Middle East until about 1200 BC; in Britain it lasted about 2000–500 BC, and in Africa the transition from stone tools to iron was direct. The heroes of the Greek poet Homer lived in the Bronze Age.

Iron Age when iron was hardened by the addition of carbon, so that it superseded bronze for tools and weapons; in the Old World generally from about 1000 BC.

prelude in music, a composition intended as the preface to further music, to set a mood for a stage work, as in Wagner's *Lohengrin*; as used by Chopin, a short piano work.

Premadasa Ranasinghe 1924–1993. Sri Lankan politician, a United National Party member of parliament from 1960, prime minister from 1978, and president from 1988, having gained popularity through overseeing a major housebuilding and poverty-alleviation programme.

prematurity in general, applied to an infant born before term. In ◊obstetrics, it is applied specifically where the birth weight is less than 2.5 kg/5.5 lbs.

premedication combination of drugs given before surgery to prepare a patient for general anaesthesia.

premenstrual tension or PMT popular name for *premenstrual syndrome*, a medical condition comprising a number of physical or emotional features which occur cyclically before menstruation, and which disappear with the onset of menstruation itself. Symptoms include mood changes, breast tenderness, a feeling of bloatedness, and headache.

Preminger Otto (Ludwig) 1906–1986. American film producer-director. Born in Vienna, he went to the USA in 1935. His films are characterized by an intricate technique of story-telling, and a masterly use of the wide screen and the travelling camera: they include *Margin for Error* 1942, *Skidoo* 1968, and *Rosebud* 1974.

Premonstratensian a Roman Catholic monastic order founded by St Norbert (*c.* 1080– 1134), a German bishop, at Prémontré, N France, in 1120. Members were known as White Canons. The rule was a stricter version of that of the Augustinian Canons.

Prempeh I chief of the Ashanti people in West Africa. He became king in 1888, and later opposed British attempts to take over the region. He was deported and in 1900 the Ashanti were defeated. He returned to Kumasi (capital of the

Presley Elvis in a scene from the film GI Blues, *1960.*

Ashanti region) in 1924 as head chief of the people.

preparatory school (prep school) a fee-paying independent school. In the UK, it is a junior school which prepares students for entry to a senior school at about age 13. In the USA, it is a school which prepares children for university entrance at about age 18.

preposition a grammatical ◊part of speech coming before a noun or pronoun in order to show a location ('in', 'on'), time ('during'), or some other relationship (for example figurative relationships in phrases like 'by heart' or 'on time').

Pre-Raphaelite Brotherhood group of British painters 1848–53: Dante Gabriel Rossetti, John Everett Millais, and Holman Hunt. They aimed to paint serious subjects, to study nature closely, and to shun the influence of painterly styles post-Raphael. Their subjects were mainly biblical and literary, painted with obsessive naturalism. Artists who came under their influence include Burne-Jones and William Morris.

Presbyterianism system of Christian Protestant church government, expounded during the Reformation by John Calvin, which gives its name to the established church of Scotland, and is also practised in England, Ireland, Switzerland, the USA, and elsewhere. There is no compulsory form of worship and each congregation is governed by presbyters or elders (clerical or lay), who are of equal rank, and congregations are grouped in presbyteries, synods, and general assemblies.

prescription in English law, the legal acquisition of title or right (such as an ◊easement) by uninterrupted use or possession.

prescription in medicine, an order written in a recognized form by a practitioner of medicine, dentistry, or veterinary surgery to a pharmacist for a preparation of drugs to be used in treatment.

present participle see ◊participle.

president · the usual title of the head of state in a republic; the power of the office may range from the equivalent of a constitutional monarch to the actual head of the government. For presidents of the USA, see ◊United States of America.

presidential medal of freedom highest peacetime civilian award in the USA, instituted in 1963, conferred annually on Independence Day by the president on those making significant contributions to the 'quality of American life'. It replaced the Medal of Freedom awarded from 1945 for acts and service aiding US security.

Presley Elvis (Aaron) 1935–1977. US singer and guitarist, born in Tupelo, Mississippi, the most influential performer of the rock-and-roll era. With his recordings for Sun Records in Memphis, Tennessee, 1954–55 and early hits such as 'Heartbreak Hotel' 1956, 'Hound Dog' 1956, and 'Love Me Tender' 1956, he created an individual vocal style, influenced by Southern blues, gospel music, country music, and rhythm and blues.

press the news media. See under ◊newspaper.

Pressburger Emeric 1902–1988. Hungarian director, producer, and screenwriter, known for his partnership with Michael ◊Powell.

Press Council in the UK, organization (established 1953) that aims to preserve the freedom of the press, to maintain standards, consider complaints, and report on monopoly developments.

press gang method used to recruit soldiers and sailors into the British armed forces in the 18th and early 19th centuries. In effect it was a form of kidnapping carried out by the services or their agents, often with the aid of armed men.

pressure in physics, force per unit area. In a fluid (liquid or gas) pressure increases with depth. At the edge of Earth's atmosphere, pressure is zero whereas at ground level it is about 1013.25 millibars (or 1 atmosphere). Pressure at a depth h in a fluid of density d is equal to hdg, where g is the acceleration due to ◊gravity. The SI unit of pressure is the ◊pascal (◊newton per square metre), equal to 0.01 millibars. Pressure has also been measured using a mercury column (see ◊Torricelli); 1 atmosphere equals 760 mm of mercury.

pressure cooker a closed pot in which food is cooked in water under pressure. Under pressure water boils at a higher temperature than normal boiling point (100°C/212°F), and therefore cooks food quicker. The modern pressure cooker has a quick-sealing lid and a safety valve which can be adjusted to vary the steam pressure inside.

pressure group (also called *interest group* or *lobby*) group that puts pressure on parties or governments to ensure laws and treatment favourable to its own interest. Pressure groups have played an increasingly prominent role in contemporary Western democracies. In general they fall into two types: groups concerned with a single issue, such as nuclear disarmament, and groups attempting to promote their own interest, such as oil producers.

Prestel the ◊viewdata service provided by British Telecom (BT), which provides information on the television screen via the telephone network. BT pioneered the service in 1975.

Prester John legendary Christian prince who, in the 12th–13th centuries, was believed to rule a powerful empire in Asia. In the 14th–16th centuries, Prester John was identified with the king of Ethiopia.

prêt-à-porter (French) ready-to-wear.

pretender a claimant to a throne. In British history, the term is widely used to describe the Old Pretender (◊James Francis Edward Stuart) and Young Pretender (◊Charles Edward Stuart).

Pretoria administrative capital of the Republic of South Africa from 1910 and capital of Transvaal province from 1860; population (1985) 741,300. Industries include engineering, chemicals, iron and steel. Founded 1855, it was named after Boer leader Andries Pretorius (1799–1853).

Previn André (George) 1929– . US conductor and composer born in Berlin. After a period working as a composer and arranger in the American film

Prime Ministers of Britain

Sir Robert Walpole	(Whig)	1721	Earl of Derby	(Conservative)	1866
Earl of Wilmington	(Whig)	1742	Benjamin Disraeli	(Conserative)	1868
Henry Pelham	(Whig)	1743	W E Gladstone	(Liberal)	1868
Duke of Newcastle	(Whig)	1754	Benjamin Disraeli	(Conservative)	1874
Duke of Devonshire	(Whig)	1756	W E Gladstone	(Liberal)	1880
Duke of Newcastle	(Whig)	1757	Marquess of Salisbury	(Conservative)	1885
Earl of Bute	(Tory)	1762	W E Gladstone	(Liberal)	1886
George Grenville	(Whig)	1763	Marquess of Salisbury	(Conservative)	1886
Marquess of Rockingham	(Whig)	1765	W E Gladstone	(Liberal)	1892
Duke of Grafton	(Whig)	1766	Earl of Roseberry	(Liberal)	1894
Lord North	(Tory)	1770	Marquess of Salisbury	(Conservative)	1895
Marquess of Rockingham	(Whig)	1782	Sir H Campbell-Bannerman	(Liberal)	1905
Earl of Shelbourne	(Whig)	1782	H HAsquith	(Liberal)	1908
Duke of Portland	(Coalition)	1783	H H Asquith	(Coalition)	1915
William Pitt	(Tory)	1783	D Lloyd George	(Coalition)	1916
Henry Addington	(Tory)	1801	A Bonar Law	(Conservative)	1922
William Pitt	(Tory)	1804	Stanley Baldwin	(Conservative)	1923
Lord Grenville	(Whig)	1806	Ramsay MacDonald	(Labour)	1924
Duke of Portland	(Tory)	1807	Stanley Baldwin	(Conservative)	1924
Spencer Percival	(Tory)	1809	Ramsay MacDonald	(Labour)	1929
Earl of Liverpool	(Tory)	1812	Ramsay MacDonald	(National)	1931
George Canning	(Tory)	1827	Stanley Baldwin	(National)	1935
Viscount Goderich	(Tory)	1827	N Chamberlain	(National)	1937
Duke of Wellington	(Tory)	1828	Sir Winston Churchill	(Coalition)	1940
Earl Grey	(Whig)	1830	Clement Attlee	(Labour)	1945
Viscount Melbourne	(Whig)	1834	Sir Winston Churchill	(Conservative)	1951
Sir Robert Peel	(Conservative)	1834	Sir Anthony Eden	(Conservative)	1955
Viscount Melbourne	(Whig)	1835	Harold Macmillan	(Conservative)	1957
Sir Robert Peel	(Conservative)	1841	Sir Alec Douglas-Home	(Conservative)	1963
Lord J Russell	(Liberal)	1846	Harold Wilson	(Labour)	1964
Earl of Derby	(Conservative)	1852	Edward Heath	(Conservative)	1970
Lord Aberdeen	(Peelite)	1852	Harold Wilson	(Labour)	1974
Viscount Palmerston	(Liberal)	1855	James Callaghan	(Labour)	1976
Earl of Derby	(Conservative)	1858	Margaret Thatcher	(Conservative)	1979
Viscount Palmerston	(Liberal)	1859	John Major	(Conservative)	1990
Lord J Russell	(Liberal)	1865			

industry, he concentrated on conducting. He was principal conductor of the London Symphony Orchestra 1968–79. In 1985 he was appointed music director of the Royal Philharmonic Orchestra (a post he relinquished the following year, staying on as principal conductor), and of the Los Angeles Philharmonic from 1986. He has done much to popularize classical music.

Prévost d'Exiles Antoine François 1697–1763. French novelist, known as Abbé Prévost, who sandwiched a military career into his life as a monk. His *Manon Lescaut* 1731 inspired operas by Massenet and Puccini.

Priam in Greek mythology, the last king of Troy. He was killed by Pyrrhus, son of Achilles, when Greeks entered the city of Troy concealed in a wooden horse.

Priapus Greek god of garden fertility, son of Dionysus and Aphrodite, represented as grotesquely ugly, with an exaggerated phallus. He was also a god of gardens, where his image was frequently used as a scarecrow.

prickly pear cactus of the genus *Opuntia*, native to America, especially Mexico and Chile, but naturalized in S Europe, N Africa, and Australia where it is a pest. The common prickly pear *Opuntia vulgaris* is low-growing, with bright yellow flowers, and prickly, oval fruit; the flesh and seeds of the peeled fruit have a pleasant taste.

Pride and Prejudice a novel by Jane Austen, published 1813. Mr and Mrs Bennet, whose property is due to pass to a male cousin, William Collins, are anxious to secure good marriage settlements for their five daughters. Central to the story is the romance between the witty Elizabeth Bennet and the proud Mr Darcy.

Pride's purge the removal of about 100 Royalists and Presbyterians of the English House of Commons from Parliament by a detachment of soldiers led by Col Thomas Pride (died 1658) in 1648. They were accused of negotiating with Charles I and were seen as unreliable by the army. The remaining members were termed the ◊Rump and voted in favour of the king's trial.

Priestley J(ohn) B(oynton) 1894–1984. English novelist and playwright. His first success was a novel about travelling theatre, *The Good Companions* 1929. He followed it with a realist novel about London life, *Angel Pavement* 1930; later books include *Lost Empires* 1965 and *The Image Men* 1968. As a playwright he was often preoccupied with theories of time, as in *An Inspector Calls* 1945, but had also a gift for family comedy, for example, *When We Are Married* 1938. He was also noted for his wartime broadcasts and literary criticism, as in *Literature and Western Man* 1960.

prima facie (Latin) at first sight.

primary in presidential election campaigns in the USA, an election to decide the candidates for the major parties. Held in some 35 states, primaries begin with New Hampshire in Feb and continue until Jun, and operate under varying complex rules. Generally speaking, the number of votes received by a candidate governs the number of delegates who will vote for that person at the national conventions in Jul/Aug, when the final choice of candidate for both Democratic and Republican parties is made.

primate in zoology, member of the order of mammals that includes monkeys, apes, and humans, as well as lemurs, bushbabies, lorises, and tarsiers. Generally, they have forward-directed eyes, gripping hands and feet, and opposable thumbs and big toes. They tend to have nails rather than claws, with gripping pads on the ends of the digits, all adaptations to the climbing mode of life.

primate in the Christian church, the official title of archbishops. The archbishop of Canterbury is the Primate of All England, and the archbishop of York the Primate of England.

prime minister or *premier* head of a parliamentary government, usually the leader of the largest party. The first in Britain is usually considered to have been Robert ◊Walpole, but the office was not officially recognized until 1905. In some countries, such as Australia, a distinction is drawn between the prime minister of the whole country, and the premier of an individual state. In countries with an executive president, such as France, the prime minister is of lesser standing.

prime number a number that can be divided only by 1 or itself, that is, having no other factors. There is an infinite number of primes, the first ten of which are 2, 3, 5, 7, 11, 13, 17, 19, 23 and 29. The number 2 is the only even prime (because all other even numbers have 2 as a factor).

prime rate the rate charged by commercial banks to their best customers. It is the base rate on which other rates are calculated according to the risk involved. Only borrowers who have the highest credit rating qualify for the prime rate.

Primo de Rivera Miguel 1870–1930. Spanish soldier and politician, dictator from 1923 as well as premier from 1925. He was captain-general of Catalonia when he led a coup against the ineffective monarchy and became virtual dictator of Spain with the support of Alfonso XIII. He resigned in 1930.

primrose woodland plant *primula vulgaris*, common to Europe, bearing pale yellow flowers in spring. Related to it is the cowslip, and the false oxlip is a hybrid of the two.

prince a royal or noble title. In Rome and medieval Italy it was used as the title of certain officials, for example, *princeps senatus* (Latin 'leader of the Senate'). The title was granted to the king's sons in 15th century France, and in England from Henry VII's time. The British sovereign's eldest son is normally created Prince of Wales.

Prince Stage name of Prince Rogers Nelson 1960– . US pop musician, who composes, arranges, and produces his own records, and often plays all the instruments. His albums, including *1999* 1982 and *Purple Rain* 1984, contain elements of rock, funk, and jazz.

Prince Edward Island province of Canada
area 5,657 sq km/2,184 sq mi
capital Charlottetown
products potatoes, dairy products, lobsters, oysters, farm vehicles
population (1987) 128,000.
history first recorded visit by Cartier 1534, who called it Isle St-Jean; settled by French; taken by British 1758; annexed to Nova Scotia 1763; separate colony 1769; settled by Scottish 1803; joined Confederation 1873.

princess royal title borne only by the eldest daughter of the British sovereign, granted by Royal declaration. It was first borne by Mary, eldest daughter of Charles I, probably in imitation

Prince *US pop star Prince in concert, 1986.*

of the French Court where the eldest daughter of the king was styled 'Madame Royale'. The title is currently held by Princess Anne.

print a picture or design that is printed using a plate (block, stone, or sheet) that holds ink or colour; for different techniques, see ◊engraving. The oldest type of print is the woodcut, popular in medieval Europe, followed by line engraving (from the 15th century), and etching (from the 17th); coloured woodblock prints flourished in Japan from the 18th century.

printed circuit board (PCB) an electrical circuit created by laying (printing) 'tracks' of a conductor such as copper onto one or both sides of an insulating board. The PCB was invented 1936 by the Austrian scientist Paul Eisler, and were first used on a large scale 1948.

printer in computing, an output device for producing printed copy of textual, numeric, and graphical data. Types include the *daisywheel*, which produces good-quality text but no graphics; the *dot matrix*, which creates character patterns from a matrix of small dots, producing text and graphics; and the *laser printer*, which produces high-quality text and graphics.

printing the reproduction of text or illustrative material on paper, as in books or newspapers, or on an increasing variety of materials, for example on tins and plastic containers. The first printing used moveable type and hand operated presses, but much current printing is effected by electronically controlled machinery. Current printing processes include ◊offset litho, ◊gravure print, and electronic phototypesetting.

prion an exceptionally small microorganism, a hundred times smaller than a virus. Composed

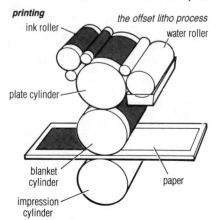

printing the offset litho process
ink roller
water roller
plate cylinder
blanket cylinder
paper
impression cylinder

printed circuit board   A typical microcomputer PCB

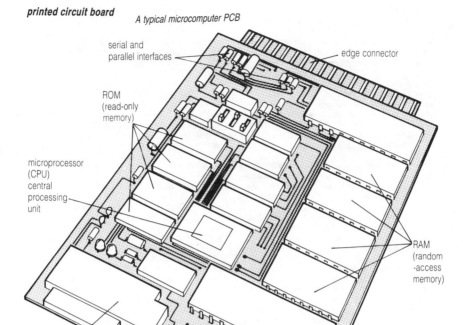

serial and
parallel interfaces

edge connector

ROM
(read-only
memory)

microprocessor
(CPU)
central
processing
unit

RAM
(random
-access
memory)

RF modulator
radio
frequency

ULA
(uncommitted logic
array)

expansion ports

of protein, and mysteriously without any detectable amount of nucleic acid (genetic material), it is thought to cause diseases such as scrapie in sheep, and some degenerative diseases of the nervous system in humans. How it can operate without nucleic acid is not yet known. The prion was claimed to have been discovered at the University of California 1982.

prior, prioress in a Christian religious community, either the deputy of an abbot or abbess, responsible for discipline. In certain Roman Catholic orders, it is the principal of a monastery or convent.

Prior James 1927– . British Conservative politician. He held ministerial posts from 1970. As employment secretary he curbed trade-union activity with the Employment Act 1980, and was Northern Ireland secretary 1981–84. After his resignation 1984 he became chairman of the General Electric Company (GEC).

prism in mathematics, a solid figure whose cross-section is constant in planes drawn perpendicular to its axis. A cylinder is a prism with a circular cross-section.

prism in optics, a triangular block of transparent material (plastic, glass, silica) commonly used to 'bend' a ray of light or split a beam into its spectral

prism white light passing through a triangular prism is split into its constituent wavelengths, forming colours of the rainbow.

colours. Prisms are used like mirrors to define the optical path in binoculars, camera viewfinders, and periscopes. The dispersive property of prisms is used in the ◊spectroscope.

prison place of confinement for those contravening the laws of the state; most countries claim to aim at rehabilitation. The average number of people in prison in the UK (1987) was 56,400, with almost 20% of these under the age of 21. About 22% were on remand (awaiting trial or sentence). Due to overcrowding in prisons, almost 2,000 prisoners were held in police cells (1988). 55% of male prisoners and 34% of female prisoners were reconvicted within 2 years of being discharged from prison (1984). The US prison population (1988) was 800,000.

Pritchett V(ictor) S(awdon) 1900– . English short story writer, novelist and critic, with an often witty and satirical style. His critical works include *The Living Novel* 1946 and a biography of the French novelist Balzac.

privacy the right of the individual to be free from secret surveillance (by scientific devices or other means), and from the disclosure to unauthorized persons of personal data, as accumulated in computer data banks. Always an issue complicated by considerations of state security, public welfare (in the case of criminal activity), and other factors, it has been rendered more complex by modern technology.

private enterprise business unit where economic activities are in private hands and are carried on for private profit, as opposed to national, municipal, or co-operative ownership.

privateer a privately owned ship commissioned by a state to attack enemy vessels. The crews of such ships were, in effect, legalized pirates; they were not paid but received a share of the spoils. Privateering existed from ancient times until the 19th century, when it was declared illegal by the Declaration of Paris 1856.

private limited company (plc) a registered company which has limited liability (the shareholders cannot lose more than their original shareholdings), and a minimum of two shareholders and a maximum of fifty. It cannot offer its shares or debentures to the public and their transfer is restricted; a shareholder may relinquish shares with the permission of the other shareholders.

private school alternative name for a fee-paying independent school.

privatization the selling or transfer into private hands of state-owned or public assets and services (notably nationalized industries). Privatization of services takes place by the contracting out to private firms of the rendering of services previously supplied by public authorities. The proponents of privatization argue for the public benefit from its theoretically greater efficiency in a competitive market, and the release of resources for more appropriate use by government. Those against privatization believe that it removes a country's assets from all the people to a minority, that public utilities such as gas and water become private monopolies, and that a profit-making state-owned company raises revenue for the government.

privet evergreen shrubs of the genus *Ligustrum*, family Oleaceae, with dark green leaves, including the wild *common privet Ligustrum vulgare*, with white flowers and black berries, and *hedge privet Ligustrum ovalifolium*.

Privy Council originally the chief royal officials of the Norman kings in Britain, which under the Tudors and early Stuarts became the chief governing body. It was replaced from 1688 by the ◊cabinet, originally a committee of the council, and the council itself now retains only formal powers, in issuing royal proclamations and orders-in-council. Cabinet ministers are automatically members, and it is presided over by the Lord President of the Council. The *Judicial Committee of the Privy Council*, once a final court of appeal for members of the Commonwealth, is almost completely obsolete.

privy purse the personal expenditure of the British sovereign, which derives from his/her own resources (as distinct from the ◊civil list which now finances only expenses incurred in pursuance of official functions and duties). The office that deals with this expenditure is also known as the Privy Purse.

Privy Seal, Lord until 1884, the British officer of state in charge of the royal seal to prevent its misuse. The honorary title is now held by a senior cabinet minister who has special nondepartmental duties.

Prix Goncourt French literary prize for fiction, given by the Académie ◊Goncourt from 1903.

probability the likelihood or chance an event will occur, often expressed as odds, or in mathematics, numerically as a fraction or decimal. In general, the probability that n particular events will happen out of a total of m possible events is n/m. A certainty has a probability of 1; an impossibility has a probability of 0. Empirical probability is defined as the number of successful events divided by the total possible number of events.

probate formal proof of a will. In the UK, if its validity is unquestioned, it is proven in 'common form'; the executor, in the absence of other interested parties, obtains at a probate registry a grant upon their own oath. Otherwise, it must be proved in 'solemn form': its validity established at a probate court (in the Chancery Division of the High Court), those concerned being made parties to the action.

probation in law, the placing of offenders under supervision in the community, as an alternative to prison. Juveniles are no longer placed on probation, but under a 'supervision' order.

procedure in computing, a part of a computer program describing the processing required to achieve a particular result. Most programming languages have a special notation to encourage the splitting of programs into small parts (procedures and functions), each of which, like a miniprogram, carries out a small part of the overall computation. This splitting of programs is called ◊structured programming.

processing cycle in computing, the sequence of steps performed repeatedly by a computer in the execution of a program. The computer's *processor* or ◊CPU (central processing unit) continuously works through a loop of fetching a program instruction from the memory, fetching any data it needs, operating on the data, and storing the result in the memory, before it fetches another program instruction.

processor in computing, another name for the central processing unit (◊CPU) or ◊microprocessor of a computer.

proconsul Roman ◊consul who went on to govern a province when his term ended.

Proconsul the prehistoric ape whose skull was found on Rusinga Island in Lake Victoria (Nyanza), E Africa, by the British archaeologist Mary

Leakey. It is believed to be 20 million years old.

procurator fiscal officer of a Scottish sheriff's court who (combining the role of public prosecutor and coroner) inquires into suspicious deaths and carries out the preliminary questioning of witnesses to crime.

Procyon the eighth-brightest star in the sky, and the brightest in the constellation Canis Minor. Procyon is a white star 11.3 light years away, with a mass of 1.7 Suns. It has a ◊white dwarf companion that orbits it every 40 years.

productivity, biological in an ecosystem, the amount of material in the ◊food chain produced by the primary producers (plants) that is available for consumption by animals. Plants turn carbon dioxide gas into sugars and other complex carbon compounds by means of photosynthesis. Their net productivity is defined as the quantity of carbon compounds formed, less the quantity used up by the plants' own respiration.

Profumo John (Dennis) 1915– . British Conservative politician, secretary of state for war 1960–Jun 1963, when he resigned on the disclosure of his involvement with Christine Keeler, mistress also of a Soviet naval attaché. In 1982 Profumo became administrator of the social and educational settlement Toynbee Hall in London.

progesterone a hormone which occurs in vertebrates. In mammals, it regulates the menstrual cycle and pregnancy.

prognosis in medicine, prediction of the course or outcome of illness or injury, especially the chance of recovery.

programme music term for music that tells a story, depicts a scene or painting, or illustrates a literary or philosophical idea, such as Richard Strauss' *Don Juan*.

programming in computing, the activity of writing statements in a programming language for the control of a computer. Applications programming is for end-user programs, such as accounts programs or word-processing packages. Systems programming is for operating systems and the like, which are concerned more with the internal workings of the computer.

programming language in computing, a special notation in which instructions for controlling a computer are written. Programming languages are designed to be easy for users to write and read, but must be capable of being mechanically translated (by a ◊compiler or ◊interpreter) into the ◊machine code that the computer can execute.

progression sequence of numbers each formed by a specific relationship to its predecessor. An *arithmetical progression* has numbers which increase or decrease by a common sum or difference (for example 2, 4, 6, 8), a *geometric progression* has numbers each bearing a fixed ratio to its predecessor (for example 3, 6, 12, 24), and a *harmonic progression* is a sequence with numbers whose ◊reciprocals are in arithmetical progression, for example 1, ½, ⅓, ¼.

progressive education teaching methods which take as their starting point children's own aptitudes and interests, and encourage them to follow their own investigations and lines of inquiry.

Progressivism in US history, the name of both a reform movement and a political party, active in the two decades before World War I. Mainly middle-class and urban-based, Progressives secured legislation at national, state, and local levels to improve the democratic

system, working conditions, and welfare provision.

Prohibition in US history, the period 1920–33 when alcohol was illegal, and which represented the culmination of a long campaign by church and women's organizations, temperance societies, and the Anti-Saloon League. This led to bootlegging (the illegal distribution of liquor, often illicitly distilled), to the financial advantage of organized crime, and public opinion insisted on repeal 1933.

projection in cartography, the means of depicting the spherical surface of the earth on a flat piece of paper. The theory is that, if a light were placed at the centre of a transparent earth,

projector an apparatus that projects a picture onto a screen. In a *slide projector*, a lamp shines a light through the photographic slide or transparency, and a projection ◊lens throws an enlarged image of the slide onto the screen. A *ciné projector* has similar optics, but incorporates a mechanism that holds the film still while light is shone through each frame (picture). A shutter covers the film when it moves between frames.

prokaryote in biology, an organism whose cells lack organelles (specialized structures such as nuclei, mitochondria, and chloroplasts). The prokaryotes comprise the *bacteria* and *cyanobacteria*; all other organisms are eukaryotes. Prokaryote DNA is not arranged in chromosomes but forms a simple loop.

Prokofiev Sergey (Sergeyevich) 1891–1953. Russian composer. His music includes operas such as *The Love of Three·Oranges* 1921; ballets for ◊Diaghilev, including *Romeo and Juliet* 1935; seven symphonies including the *Classical Symphony* 1916–17; music for films; pianoforte and violin concertos; songs and cantatas (for example, that for the 30th anniversary of the October Revolution); and *Peter and the Wolf* 1936.

prolapse the displacement of an organ due to the effects of strain in weakening the supporting tissues. The term is most often used with regard to the rectum (due to chronic bowel problems), or the uterus (following several pregnancies).

proletariat in Marxist theory, those classes in society which possess no property, and therefore depend on the sale of their labour or expertise (as opposed to the capitalists or bourgeoisie, who own the means of production, and the petty bourgeoisie, or working small-property owners). They are usually divided into the industrial, the agricultural, and the intellectual proletariat.

Prolog in computing, a programming language based on logic. Invented at the University of Marseilles 1971, it did not achieve widespread use until more than ten years later. It is used mainly for ◊artificial intelligence programming.

PROM (*p*rogrammable *r*ead-*o*nly *m*emory) in computing, a memory device in the form of a silicon chip that can be programmed to hold information permanently. PROM chips are empty of information when manufactured, unlike ROM chips, which have their memories built into them. Other memory devices are EPROM and RAM.

promenade concert originally a concert in which the audience walked about, now in the UK the name of any one of an annual BBC series (the Proms) at the Royal Albert Hall, London, at which part of the audience stands. They were originated by Henry Wood 1895.

Prometheus in Greek mythology, a ◊Titan who stole fire from heaven for the human race. In revenge, Zeus had him chained to a rock with an eagle preying on his liver, until he was rescued by ◊Hercules.

promethium an element of the ◊rare earth group, symbol Pm, atomic number 61. Several isotopes have been reported, obtained by fission of uranium or by neutron bombardment of neodymium. Its existence in nature is unconfirmed.

prominence a bright cloud of gas projecting from the Sun into space 100,000 km/60,000 mi or more. *Quiescent prominences* last for months, and are held in place by magnetic fields in the Sun's corona. *Surge prominences* shoot gas into space at speeds of 1,000 km/600 mi per sec. *Loop prominences* are gases falling back to the Sun's surface after a solar ◊flare.

promissory note a written promise to pay on demand, or at a fixed future time, a specific sum of money to a named person or bearer. Like a cheque, it is negotiable if endorsed by the payee. A commercial paper is a form of promissory note that can be bought and sold. These forms of payment are usually issued by large corporations at times when credit is otherwise difficult to obtain.

pronghorn hoofed herbivorous mammal *Antilocapra americana* of the W USA. It is light brown, and about 1 m/3 ft high. It sheds its horns annually, and can reach speeds of 100 kph/60 mph.

pronoun a grammatical ◊part of speech that is used in place of a noun, usually to save repetition of the noun (for example 'The people arrived around nine o'clock. *They* behaved as though we were expecting *them*').

pronunciation the way in which words are rendered into human speech sounds; either a language as a whole ('French pronunciation') or a particular word or name ('what is the pronunciation of *allophony*?'). The pronunciation of languages forms the academic subject of ◊*phonetics*.

propaganda literally, the spreading of information, used particularly with reference to the promotion of a religious or political doctrine. The word has acquired pejorative connotations because of its association with the use of propaganda by Nazi Germany and other regimes.

propane a gaseous hydrocarbon (C_3H_8), found in petroleum and used as fuel.

propanol another name for ◊propyl alcohol.

propanone (CH_3)$_2$CO (common name *acetone*) in chemistry, a colourless inflammable liquid used extensively as a solvent, as in nail-varnish remover. It boils at 56.5°C, mixes with water in all proportions, and has a characteristic odour.

propellant the substance burned in a rocket for propulsion. Two propellants are used; oxidizer and fuel are stored in separate tanks and pumped independently into the combustion chamber. Liquid oxygen (oxidizer) and liquid hydrogen (fuel) are common propellants, used for example in the Space Shuttle main engines.

propeller a screw-like device used to propel ships and some aeroplanes. A propeller has a number of curved blades, and accelerates fluid (liquid or gas) backwards when it rotates. Reaction to this backward movement of fluid sets up a propulsive thrust forwards. The marine screw propeller was developed by Francis Pettit Smith in Britain and Swedish-born John Ericsson in the USA.

propene CH_3CHCH_2 (common name *propylene*) second member of the alkene series of hydrocarbons. A gas, it is widely used by industry to make organic chemicals, including polypropylene plastics.

propenoic acid CH_2CHCO_2H (common name *acrylic acid*) obtained from the aldehyde propenal

(acrolein) derived from glycerol or fats. Glass-like thermoplastic resins are made by polymerizing ◊esters of propenoic acid or methyl propenoic acid, and used for transparent components, lenses, and dentures. Other acrylic compounds are used for adhesives, artificial fibres, and artists' acrylic paint.

proper motion the gradual change in the position of a star that results from its motion in orbit around the Galaxy. Proper motions are slight, undetectable to the naked eye, but can be accurately measured on telescopic photographs taken many years apart. ◊Barnard's Star is the star with the largest proper motion, 10.3 ◊arc seconds per year.

Propertius Sextus *c.* 47–15 BC. Roman elegiac poet, a member of ◊Maecenas' circle, who wrote of his love for his mistress 'Cynthia'.

property the right to control the use of a thing (such as land, a building, a work of art, or a computer program). In English law, a distinction is made between *real property*, which involves a degree of geographical fixity, and *personal property*, which does not. Property is never absolute, since any society places limits on an individual's property (such as the right to transfer that property to another). Different societies have held widely varying interpretations of the nature of property and the extent of the rights of the owner of that property.

prophet a person thought to speak from divine inspiration or who foretells the future. In Islam, ◊Muhammad is believed to be the last and greatest of a long line of prophets beginning with Adam and including Moses (both in the Old Testament or Hebrew Bible) and Jesus.

prophylaxis any measure taken to prevent disease, including exercise and ◊vaccination. Prophylactic (preventive) medicine is an increasingly important aspect of public health provision.

proportional representation (PR) electoral system in which distribution of party seats corresponds to their proportion of the total ◊votes cast, and minority votes are not wasted, (as opposed to a simple majority, or 'first past the post', system). Forms include:

party list or additional member system (AMS). As recommended by the Hansard Society 1976 for introduction in Britain, three-quarters of the members would be elected in single-member constituencies on the traditional majority-vote system, and the remaining seats be allocated according to the overall number of votes cast for each party (a variant of this is used in West Germany).

single transferable vote (STV), in which candidates are numbered in order of preference by the voter, and any votes surplus to the minimum required for a candidate to win are transferred to second preferences, as are second-preference votes from the successive candidates at the bottom of the poll until the required number of elected candidates is achieved (this is in use in the Republic of Ireland).

prop root a modified root that grows from the lower part of a stem or trunk down to the ground, providing a plant with extra support. Prop roots, also sometimes known as stilt roots, are common on some woody plants, such as mangroves, and also occur on a few herbaceous plants, such as maize. *Buttress roots* are a type of prop root found at the base of tree trunks, extended and flattened along the upper edge to form massive triangular buttresses; they are especially common on tropical trees.

propyl alcohol usually a mixture of two isomeric compounds, normal propyl alcohol and isopropyl alcohol ($CH_3CHOHCH_3$). The former is also known as 1-propanol, and the latter as 2-propanol. It is a colourless liquid which can be mixed with water, and is used in perfumery.

propylene common name for ◊propane.

pro rata (Latin) in proportion.

prose spoken or written language without metrical regularity; in literature, prose corresponds more closely to the patterns of everyday speech than ◊poetry. In modern literature, however, the distinction between verse and prose is not always clear-cut.

Prosecution Service, Crown body established by the Prosecution of Offences Act 1985, responsible for prosecuting all criminal offences in England and Wales. It is headed by the Director of Public Prosecutions (DPP), and brings England and Wales in line with Scotland (see ◊procurator fiscal) in having a prosecution service independent of the police.

Proserpina Roman equivalent of ◊Persephone, goddess of the underworld.

Prost Alain 1955– . French motor racing driver; world champion 1985, 1986, 1989, the first French world champion. By 1991 he had won a record 44 Grands Prix from 169 starts.

prostaglandin a complex fatty acid that acts as a messenger substance between cells. Effects include stimulating the contraction of smooth muscle (for example, of the womb during birth), regulating the production of stomach acid, and modifying hormonal activity. In excess, prostaglandins may produce imflammatory disorders such as arthritis. Synthetic prostaglandins are used to induce labour in humans and domestic animals.

prostate gland a gland surrounding, and opening into, the urethra at the base of the penis of male mammals. The prostrate gland produces an alkaline fluid, released during ejaculation which activates sperm, and prevents their clumping together.

prosthesis replacement of a body part with an artificial substitute. Prostheses in the form of artificial limbs, such as metal hooks for hands and wooden legs, have been used for centuries, although modern artificial limbs are more natural-looking and comfortable to wear. The latest myoelectric, or bionic, arms are electronically operated and are worked by minute electrical impulses from body muscles. Other prostheses include such things as hearing aids, false teeth and eyes, and for the heart, a ◊pacemaker, and plastic heart valves and blood vessels.

prostitution receipt of money for sexual acts. Society's attitude towards it varies according to place and period. In some countries, tolerance is combined with licensing of brothels and health checks on the prostitutes. In the UK a compromise system makes it legal to be a prostitute, but soliciting for customers publicly, keeping a brothel, living on 'immoral earnings', and 'procuring' (arranging to make someone into a prostitute) are illegal.

protactinium a rare element, symbol Pa, atomic number 91, relative atomic mass 231.04. One of the actinide series of elements, it is present in very small quantities in pitchblende.

protandry in a flower, the state where the male reproductive organs reach maturity before those of the female. This is a common method of avoiding self-fertilization. See also ◊protogyny.

prosthesis

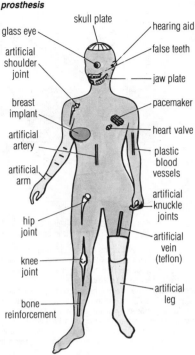

skull plate
glass eye
artificial shoulder joint
hearing aid
false teeth
jaw plate
breast implant
pacemaker
artificial artery
heart valve
artificial arm
plastic blood vessels
hip joint
artificial knuckle joints
knee joint
artificial vein (teflon)
bone reinforcement
artificial leg

protectionism in economics, the imposition of heavy duties or import quotas by a government as a means of discouraging the import of foreign goods likely to compete with domestic products. The opposite practice is ◊free trade.

protectorate formerly in international law, a small state under the direct or indirect control of a larger one. The modern equivalent is a ◊trust territory. In English history the rule of Oliver and Richard ◊Cromwell 1653–59 is referred to as the Protectorate.

protein a long chain molecule made up of ◊amino acids, joined together by ◊peptide bonds. Proteins are essential to all living organisms. As *enzymes* they regulate all aspects of metabolism. Structural proteins such as *keratin* and *collagen* make up the skin, claws, bones, tendons, and ligaments, while *muscle* proteins produce movement, *haemoglobin* transports oxygen, and *membrane* proteins regulate the movement of substances into and out of cells. For humans, protein is an essential part of the diet, and is found in greatest quantity in soya beans and other grain legumes, meat, eggs, and cheese.

pro tem abbreviation for *pro tempore* (Latin 'for the time being').

Proterozoic period of geological time, 2.5 billion to 590 million years ago, the second period of the Precambrian era. It is defined as the time of simple life, many rocks dating from this eon showing traces of biological activity.

Protestantism one of the main divisions of Christianity, which emerged from Roman Catholicism at the ◊Reformation. The chief sects are the Anglican Communion, Baptists, Christian Scientists, Lutherans, Methodists, Pentecostal Movement, Presbyterians, and Unitarians, with a total membership of about 320 million.

protein

amino acids, where R is one of many possible side chains

peptide
bond

peptide – this is one made of just three amino acid units. Proteins consist of very large numbers of amino acid units in long chains, folded up in specific ways

Proteus, in Greek mythology an old man, the warden of the sea beasts of Poseidon, who possessed the gift of prophecy, but could transform himself to any form he chose to evade questioning.

prothallus the short-lived gametophyte of many ferns and other ◊pteridophytes. It bears either the male or female sex organs, or both. Typically it is a small, green, flattened structure which is anchored in the soil by several ◊rhizoids and needs damp conditions to survive. The reproductive organs are borne on the lower surface close to the soil.

protist in biology, a single-celled organism which has a ◊eukaryotic cell, but which is not member of the plant, fungal, or animal kingdoms. The main protists are ◊protozoa. Single-celled photosynthetic organisms, such as diatoms and dinoflagellates, are classified as protists or algae. Recently the term has also been used for members of the kingdom Protoctista, which features in certain five ◊kingdom classifications of the living world. This kingdom may include slime moulds, all algae (seaweeds as well as unicellular forms) and protozoa.

Protocols of Zion forged document containing supposed plans for Jewish world conquest alleged to have been submitted by ◊Herzl to the first Zionist Congress at Basel 1897, and published in Russia 1905. They were proved to be a forgery by *The Times* 1921, but were used by Hitler in his anti-Semitic campaign.

protogyny in a flower, the state where the female reproductive organs reach maturity before those of the male. Like ◊protandry, this is a method of avoiding self-fertilization.

proton (Greek 'first') positively charged subatomic particle, a fundamental constituent of any atomic ◊nucleus. Most live for at least 10x^{32} years.

protonema the young ◊gametophyte of a moss, which develops from a germinating spore, see ◊alternation of generations. Typically it is a green, branched, threadlike structure which grows over the soil surface bearing several buds that develop into the characteristic adult moss plants.

Proton rocket a Soviet space rocket introduced 1965, used to launch heavy satellites, space probes, and the Salyut and Mir space stations.

protoplasm the contents of a living ◊cell. Strictly speaking it includes all the discrete structures (organelles) in a cell, but it is often used simply to mean the jelly-like material in which these float.

The contents of a cell outside the nucleus are called ◊cytoplasm.

prototype in technology, term used for the first few machines of a new design. Prototypes are tested for performance, reliability, economy, and safety; then the main design can be modified before full-scale production begins.

protozoa a group of single-celled organisms without rigid cell walls. Some, such as amoeba, ingest other cells, but most are ◊saprotrophs or parasites. The group is polyphyletic (containing organisms which have different evolutionary origins).

Proudhon Pierre Joseph 1809–1865. French anarchist, born in Besançon. He sat in the Constituent Assembly of 1848, was imprisoned for three years, and had to go into exile in Brussels. He published *Qu'est-ce que la propriété/What is Property?* 1840 and *Philosophie de la misère/Philosophy of Poverty* 1846. His most noted dictum is 'property is theft'.

Proust Marcel 1871–1922. French novelist and critic. He is best known for the autobiographical novel, *À la recherche du temps perdu/Remembrance of Things Past* 1913–37, the expression of his childhood memories coaxed from his subconscious; it is also a precise reflection of life in provincial France at the end of the 19th century.

Provençal language a member of the Romance branch of the Indo-European language family, spoken in and around Provence in SE France. It is now regarded as a dialect or patois.

Provence-Alpes-Côte d'Azur region of SE France, comprising the *départements* of Alpes-de-Haute-Provence, Hautes-Alpes, Alpes-Maritimes, Bouches-du Rhône, Var and Vaucluse; area 31,400 sq km/12,126 sq mi; capital Marseille; population (1982) 3,965,200. The *Côte d'Azur*, on the Mediterranean, is a tourist centre. Provence was an independent kingdom in the 10th century, and the area still has its own language, Provençal.

Provisions of Oxford issued by Henry III of England 1258 under pressure from Simon de Montfort (1208–65) and the baronial opposition, they provided for the establishment of a baronial council to run the government, carry out reforms, and keep a check on royal power.

provost chief magistrate of a Scottish burgh, approximate equivalent of an English mayor.

Proxima Centauri the closest star to the Sun, 4.3 light years away. It is a faint ◊red dwarf, visible only with a telescope, and is a member of the Alpha Centauri triple star system.

proxy in law, a person authorized to stand in another's place; also the document conferring this right. The term usually refers to voting at meetings, but there may be marriages by proxy.

Prunus genus of trees of the northern hemisphere, family Rosaceae, producing fruit with a fleshy, edible pericarp. The genus includes plums, peaches, apricots, almonds, and cherries.

Prussia a N German state 1618–1945. It was an independent kingdom until 1867 when it became a dominant part of the N German Confederation and part of the German empire in 1871 under the Prussian King Wilhelm I. West Prussia became part of Poland under the ◊Treaty of Versailles and East Prussia was largely incorporated into the USSR after 1945.

prussic acid an old name for ◊hydrocyanic acid.

PS abbreviation for *post scriptum* (Latin 'after writing').

psalm a sacred poem or song of praise. The best-known collection is the Book of Psalms in the Hebrew Bible (Christian Old Testament), which is divided into five books containing 150 psalms. They are traditionally ascribed to David, the second king of Israel.

PSBR abbreviation for ◊public sector borrowing requirement.

pseudocarp a fruit-like structure which incorporates tissue that is not derived from the ovary wall. The additional tissues may be derived from floral parts such as the ◊receptacle and ◊calyx. For example, the coloured, fleshy part of a strawberry develops from the ◊receptacle and the true fruits are small ◊achenes – the 'pips' embedded in its outer surface. Rose hips are a type of pseudocarp that consists of a hollow, fleshy receptacle containing a number of achenes within. Different types of pseudocarp include pineapples, figs, apples, and pears.

pseudocopulation the attempted copulation by a male insect with a flower. It results in ◊pollination of the flower and is common in the orchid family, where the flowers of many species resemble a particular species of female bee. When a male bee attempts to mate with a flower, the pollinia (see ◊pollinium) stick to its body. They are then transferred to the stigma of another flower, when the insect attempts copulation again.

PSFD abbreviation for public sector financial deficit; see under ◊public sector borrowing requirement.

psi in parapsychology, a hypothetical facility common to humans and other animals said to be responsible for extra-sensory perception (ESP) and telekinesis.

Psilocybe genus of mushroom with hallucinogenic properties, including the Mexican sacred mushroom *Psilocybe mexicana* which contains compounds with effects similar to LSD. A related species *Psilocybe semilanceata* is found in Britain.

psoriasis chronic skin inflammation resulting in raised, red, scaly patches, usually on the scalp, back, arms, and legs. The attacks are recurrent, but sometimes disappear of their own accord. Tar preparations are used to treat it.

Psyche late Greek personification of the soul as a winged girl or young woman. The goddess Aphrodite was so jealous of Psyche's beauty that she ordered her son Eros, the god of love, to make her fall in love with

pseudocopulation

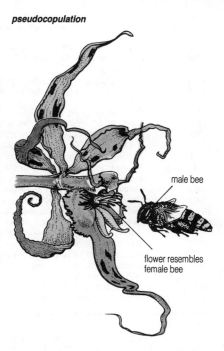

male bee

flower resembles female bee

the worst of men, but he fell in love with her himself.

psychedelic rock or *acid rock*, a type of pop music, with advanced electronic equipment for both light and sound, which began about 1966. The free-form improvisations and light shows of the hippie years had by the 1980s become stadium performances with lasers and other special effects.

psychiatry the branch of medicine dealing with the diagnosis and treatment of mental disorder.

psychic a person allegedly possessed of parapsychological, or paranormal, powers.

psychoanalysis a theory and treatment method for neuroses, developed by ◊Freud. The main treatment method involves the free association of ideas, and interpretation. It is typically expensive and prolonged and there is controversy about its effectiveness.

psychology the systematic study of human and animal behaviour. The first psychology laboratory was founded 1879 by Wilhelm ◊Wundt at Leipzig. The subject includes diverse areas of study and application, among them the roles of instinct, heredity, environment and culture; the processes of sensation, perception, learning and memory; the bases of motivation and emotion; and the functioning of thought, intelligence and language.

psychometrics the measurement of mental processes. This includes intelligence and aptitude testing to help in job selection and in the clinical assessment of cognitive deficiencies resulting from brain damage.

psychopathy a general term for a personality disorder characterized by chronic antisocial behaviour (violating the rights of others, often violently) and an absence of feelings of guilt about the behaviour.

psychosis or psychotic disorder. A general term for a serious ◊mental disorder where the individual commonly loses contact with reality and

psychology

1897	Wilhelm Wundt founded the first psychological laboratory, in Leipzig.
1890	William James published the first comprehensive psychology text, *Principles of Psychology.*
1895	Freud's first book on psychoanalysis was published.
1896	The first clinical psychology clinic was founded by Witner at the University of Pennsylvania.
1903	Pavlov reported his early studies on conditioned reflexes in animals.
1905	Binet and Simon developed the first effective intelligence test.
1908	A first textbook of social psychology was published by William McDougall.
1913	J B Watson published his influential work *Behaviourism.*
1926	Jean Piaget presented his first book on child development.
1947	Eysenck published *Dimensions of Personality*, a large scale study of neuroticism and extraversion.
1953	Skinner's *Science of Human Behaviour*, a text of operant conditioning, was published.
1957	Chomsky's *Syntactic Structures* which stimulated the development of psycho-linguistics, the study of language processes, was published.
1963	Milgram's studies of compliance with authority indicated conditions under which individuals behave cruelly to others when instructed to do so.
1967	Neisser's *Cognitive Psychology* marked renewed interest in the study of cognition after years in which behaviourism had been dominant.
1972	Newall and Simon simulated human problem solving abilities by computer, an example of artificial intelligence.
1989	Jeffrey Masson attacked the fundamental principles of Freudian analytic psychotherapy in his book *Against Therapy.*

may experience hallucinations (seeing or hearing things that do not exist) or delusions (fixed false beliefs). For example, in a paranoid psychosis, an individual may believe that others are plotting against him or her. A major type of psychosis is ◊schizophrenia.

psychosomatic a description applied to any physical symptom or disease arising from emotional or mental factors.

psychosurgery operation to achieve some mental effect, for example *leucotomy*/(US) *lobotomy* the separation of the white fibres in the prefrontal lobe of the brain, as a means of relieving a deep state of anxiety. It is irreversible, the degree of personality change is not predictable, and its justification is controversial.

psychotherapy treatment approaches for mental problems which involve talking rather than surgery or drugs. Examples of such approaches include ◊behaviour therapy, ◊cognitive therapy, and ◊psychoanalysis.

psychotic disorder another name for ◊psychosis.

pt abbreviation for *pint*.

ptarmigan a type of ◊grouse *Lagopus mutus* found in N Europe. About 36 cm/1.2 ft long, it has a white coat in winter.

pteridophyte a simple type of ◊vascular plant. The pteridophytes include four classes: the Psilosida, comprising the most primitive vascular plants, found mainly in the tropics; the Lycopsida, including the clubmosses and *Selaginella*; the Sphenopsida, including the horsetails; and the Pteropsida, including the ferns. They are mainly terrestrial, non-flowering plants characterized by the presence of a vascular system, the possession of true stems, roots and leaves, and by a marked ◊alternation of generations, with the sporophyte forming the dominant generation in the life-cycle. They do not produce seeds.

pterodactyl extinct flying reptile of the order Pterosauria, existing in the Mesozoic age.

Pterosaurs were formerly assumed to be smooth-skinned gliders, but recent discoveries show that at least some were furry, probably warm-blooded, and may have had strong flapping flight. They ranged from starling size to the largest with 17 m/50 ft wingspan.

PTFE *polytetrafluoroethylene*, a tough, waxlike and heat-resistant plastic, also known by the tradename Teflon, much used for the coating on non-stick kitchenware.

PTO abbreviation for *please turn over*.

Ptolemy (Claudius Ptolemaeus) *c.* 100–170 AD. Egyptian astronomer and geographer. The *Almagest* developed the theory that Earth is the centre of the universe, with the Sun, Moon, and stars revolving around it. In 1543 ◊Copernicus disproved the *Ptolemaic system*. His *Geography* was also a standard source of information until the 16th century.

Ptolemy dynasty of kings of Macedonian origin who ruled Egypt over a period of 300 years; they included:

Ptolemy I King of Egypt from 304 BC. He was one of ◊Alexander the Great's generals, and possibly

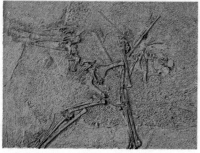

pterodactyl *Fossil remains of a pterodactyl, discovered in Würtemburg, West Germany.*

his half-brother (see also ◊Thaîs). He established the library at ◊Alexandria.

Ptolemy XIII 63–47 BC. Joint ruler of Egypt with his sister-wife Cleopatra; she put him to death.

ptomaine group of extremely toxic chemical substances produced as a result of decomposition.

puberty stage in human development when the individual becomes sexually mature. It may occur from the age of ten upwards. The sexual organs take on their adult form and pubic hair grows. In girls, menstruation begins, and the breasts develop; in boys, the voice breaks and becomes deeper, and a beard develops.

pubes the lowest part of the front of the human trunk, the region where the external generative organs are situated. The underlying bony structure, the pubic arch, is formed by the union in the midline of the two pubic bones, which are the front portions of the hip bones. In women it is more prominent than in men, to allow more room for the passage of the child's head at birth, and carries a pad of fat and connective tissue, the mons veneris (mountain of Venus), for its protection.

public corporation a company structure which is similar in organization to that of a public limited company but with no shareholder rights. Such corporations are established to carry out state-owned activities, but are financially independent of the state and are run by a board.

public house or *pub* in Britain a house licensed for consumption of intoxicating liquor, and either 'free' (when the licensee has free choice of suppliers), or 'tied' to a brewery company owning the house.

public lending right (PLR) method of paying a royalty to authors when books are borrowed from libraries, similar to a royalty on performance of a play or piece of music. Payment to the copyright holder for such borrowings was introduced in Australia in 1974 and in the UK in 1984.

public limited company (plc) a registered company in which shares and debentures may be offered to the public. It must have a minimum of seven shareholders and there is no upper limit. The company's financial records must be available for any member of the public to scrutinize, and the company's name must carry the words public limited company or initials *plc*. A public company can raise enormous financial resources to fuel its development and expansion by inviting the public to buy shares.

Public Order Act UK Act of Parliament 1986 to control ◊riots.

public school in England, a fee-paying independent school. In Scotland, the USA, and many other English-speaking countries, a 'public' school is a state-maintained school, and independent schools are generally known as 'private' schools.

public sector borrowing requirement (PSBR) money needed by a government to cover any deficit in financing its own activities (including loans to local authorities, and public corporations, and also the funds raised by local authorities and public corporations from other sources).

public spending expenditure by government, covering such things as national defence, health, education, infrastructure, development projects, and the cost of servicing overseas borrowing.

Puccini Giacomo (Antonio Domenico Michele Secondo Maria) 1858–1924. Italian opera composer, whose music shows a strong gift for melody and dramatic effect. His realist works include *Manon Lescaut* 1893, *La Bohème* 1896, *Tosca* 1900 and *Madame Butterfly* 1904.

puffin

Pudovkin Vsevolod Illationovich 1893–1953. Russian film director, whose greatest films were silent, for example *Mother* 1926, *The End of St Petersburg* 1927, and *Storm over Asia* 1928.

Pueblo generic name for North American Indians of SW North America, such as the ◊Hopi.

Puerto Rico the Commonwealth of
area 8,891 sq km/3,435 sq mi
capital San Juan
towns ports Mayagüez, Ponce
exports sugar, tobacco, rum, pineapples; textiles, plastics, chemicals, processed foods
currency US dollar
population (1980) 3,196,520, 62% urban
language Spanish and English (official)
religion Roman Catholic
government under the constitution of 1952, similar to that of the USA, with a governor elected for four years, and a legislative assembly with a senate and house of representatives
history visited in 1493 by Columbus, it was annexed by Spain 1509, ceded to the USA after the ◊Spanish-American War in 1898, and in 1952 achieved Commonwealth status with local self-government.

puffball globulous fruiting body of certain ◊fungi which cracks with maturity, releasing the enclosed spores, for example the *common puffball Lycoperdon perlatum*.

puffer fish name of many fish of the family Tetraodontidae. It can inflate its body with air or water as a means of defence. Puffer fish are mainly found in warm waters, where they feed on molluscs, crustaceans, and coral. They vary in size and grow to 50 cm/20 in. The skin of some puffer fish is poisonous.

puffin seabird *Fratercula arctica* of the ◊auk family, found in the N Atlantic. It is about 30 cm/1 ft long, with a white face and front, red legs, and a large deep bill, very brightly coloured in summer. It has short wings and webbed feet. It is a poor flyer, but an excellent swimmer. It nests in rock crevices, or makes burrows, and lays a single egg.

pug breed of small dog with short wrinkled face, chunky body, and tail curled over the hip.

Pugh Clifton Ernest 1925-1990. Leading Australian artist who won the Archibald Prize for portraiture three times. His studies of the Australian bush in early life formed the basis of his strongly regional style of painting.

Pugin Augustus Welby Northmore 1812–1852. British architect, collaborator with ◊Barry in the detailed design of the Houses of Parliament. He did much to revive Gothic architecture in England.

P'u-i Henry 1906–1967. Last emperor of China (as Hsuan Tung) from 1908 until his deposition

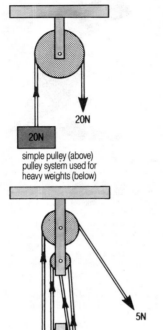

pulley

20N

20N

simple pulley (above)
pulley system used for
heavy weights (below)

5N

20N   N = newton,
a unit of force

pulsars are now known in our Galaxy, although a million may exist.

pulse crop such as peas and beans. They are grown primarily for their seeds which provide a concentrated source of vegetable protein, and make a vital contribution to human diets in poor countries where meat is scarce. Soya beans are the major temperate protein crop. Most are used for oil production or for animal feeds, though some are processed into 'meat substitutes'. Peanuts dominate pulse production in the tropical world, and are mostly consumed directly as human food.

pulse the impulse transmitted by the heartbeat throughout the arterial systems of vertebrates. When the heart muscle contracts, it forces blood into the ◊aorta. Because the arteries are elastic, the sudden rise of pressure causes a throb or sudden swelling through them. The actual flow of the blood is about 60 cm/2 ft a second in humans. The pulse rate is generally about 70 per minute. The pulse can be felt where the artery is near the surface, such as the wrist or the neck.

puma large wild cat found in the Americas, also called *cougar* or *mountain lion*. Tawny-coated, it is 1.5 m/4.5 ft long with a 90 cm/3 ft tail. They have been hunted nearly to extinction.

pumice a light volcanic rock produced by the frothing action of expanding gases during the solidification of lava. It has the texture of a hard sponge and is used as an abrasive both commercially and for personal toilet.

pump a device for moving liquids and gases, or compressing gases. Some pumps, such as the traditional *lift-pump* used to raise water from wells, work by a reciprocating (up-and-down) action. Movement of a piston in a cylinder with a one-way valve creates a partial vacuum in the cylinder, thereby sucking water into it. *Gear pumps*, used to pump oil in a car's lubrication system, have two meshing gears which rotate inside a housing, and the teeth move the oil. *Rotary pumps* contain a rotor with vanes projecting from it inside a casing, sweeping the oil round as they move.

pumped storage a type of hydroelectric plant which uses surplus electricity to pump water back into a high-level reservoir. In normal working the water flows from this reservoir through the ◊turbines to generate power for feeding into the national grid. At times of low power demand, electricity is taken from the grid to turn the turbines into pumps which then pump water back again. This ensures that there is always a maximum 'head' of water in the reservoir to give the maximum output when required.

pumpkin type of marrow *Cucurbita pepo* of the family Cucurbitaceae. The large spherical fruit has a thick, orange rind, pulpy flesh, and many seeds.

pun a ◊figure of speech, a play on words or double meaning that is technically known as *paronomasia* (Greek: 'adapted meaning'). Double meaning can be accidental or deliberate, often resulting from homonymy or the multiple meaning of words; puns, however, are intended as jokes or as clever and compact remarks.

Punch (shortened form of the name Punchinello) the hero of the traditional ◊puppet play *Punch and Judy*, in which he overcomes or outwits all opponents. Punch has a hooked nose, hunched back, and a squeaky voice. The play is performed by means of glove puppets, manipulated by a single operator concealed in a portable canvas stage frame. Punch originated in Italy, and was probably introduced to England at the time of the Restoration.

1912; he was restored for a week in 1917. He was president 1932–34 and emperor 1934–45 of the Japanese puppet state of Manchukuo (see ◊Manchuria); captured by the Russians, he was put on trial in 1950 after the Russians handed him over in 1949. Pardoned by Mao Zedong in 1959 he became a worker in a botanical garden in Beijing.

pūjā worship, in Hinduism, Buddhism, and Jainism.

Pulitzer Joseph 1847–1911. US newspaper proprietor, born in Hungary. He acquired the *New York World* 1883 and founded 1903 the school of journalism at Columbia University, which awards the annual Pulitzer prizes in journalism and letters.

pulley a simple machine consisting of a grooved wheel round which rope or chain can be run. A simple pulley serves only to change the direction of the applied effort (as in a simple hoist for raising loads). The use of more than one pulley results in a mechanical advantage, so that a given effort can raise a heavier load.

pulmonary pertaining to the lungs.

pulsar a celestial source that emits pulses of energy at very regular intervals, ranging from a few seconds to small fractions of a second. They were discovered 1967, and are thought to be rapidly rotating ◊neutron stars, which flash at radio and other wavelengths as they spin. Over 300 radio

punctuated equilibrium model an evolutionary theory which claims that periods of rapid change alternate with periods of relative stability (stasis), and that the appearance of new lineages is a separate process from the gradual evolution of adaptive changes within a species. The idea was developed in 1972 to explain discontinuities in the fossil record. The pattern of stasis and more rapid change is now widely accepted, but the second part of the theory remains unsubstantiated.

punctuation the system of conventional signs (*punctuation marks*) and spaces by means of which written and printed language is organized so as to be as readable, clear, and logical as possible.

Pune (formerly *Poona*) industrial city (chemicals, rice, sugar, cotton, paper, jewellery) in Maharashtra, India; population (1981) 1,202,848.

Punic (Latin *Punicus* a Phoenician) relating to ◊Carthage, ancient city in N Africa founded by the Phoenicians.

Punic Wars three wars between ◊Rome and ◊Carthage:
First 264–241 BC, resulted in the defeat of the Carthaginians under ◊Hamilcar Barca and the cession of Sicily to Rome
Second 218–201 BC, Hannibal invaded Italy, defeated the Romans under ◊Fabius Maximus at Cannae, capital of Crete, but was finally defeated by ◊Scipio at Zama (now in Algeria)
Third 149–146 BC ended in the destruction of Carthage, and her possessions becoming the Roman province of Africa
In 1985 Rome and modern Carthage signed a symbolic peace treaty.

Punjab name meaning 'five rivers' (the Indus tributaries Jhelum, Chnab, Ravi, Beas and Sutlej), for a former NW state of British India. See also ◊Punjab (Pakistan) and ◊Punjab (India).

Punjab state of NW India
area 50,362 sq km/19,440 sq miles
capital Chandigarh
towns Amritsar, Sikh holy city
population (1981) 16,669,755
language Punjabi
religion Sikhism 60%, Hinduism 30%; there is friction between the two groups.

Punjab state of Pakistan, the former W section of a state of British India formed after annexation by Britain in 1849 after the Sikh Wars 1845–46 and 1848–49
area 181,761 sq km/70,178 sq mi
capital Lahore
population (1981) 47,292,000
language Punjabi, Urdu
religion Muslim.

Punjabi language a member of the Indo-Iranian branch of the Indo-European language family, spoken in the Punjab provinces of India and Pakistan. It is considered by some to be a variety of Hindi, by others to be a distinct language.

punk a movement of disaffected youth of the late 1970s, manifesting itself, notably in Britain, in fashions and music designed to shock or intimidate. *Punk rock* stressed aggressive performance within a three-chord, three-minute format, for example, the Sex Pistols 1975–78, the Slits 1977–82, and Johnny Thunders (with the Heartbreakers from 1975).

pupa the non-feeding, largely immobile stage of some insect life-cycles, in which larval tissues are broken down, and adult tissues and structures are formed.

puppet figure manipulated on a small stage, usually by an unseen operator. Known from the 10th century BC in China, the types include *finger* or *glove puppets*, such as is ◊Punch; *string marionettes* (which reached a high artistic level in ancient Burma and Sri Lanka and in Italian princely courts 16–18th centuries, and for which ◊Haydn wrote his operetta *Dido* 1778 for performance in the Esterhazy theatre); *shadow silhouettes* (operated by rods and seen on a lit screen, as in Java); and *bunraku* (devised in Osaka, Japan), in which three or four black-clad operators on stage may combine to work each puppet about 1 m/3 ft high.

Purana one of a number of sacred Hindu writings dealing with ancient times and events, and dating from the 4th century AD onwards. There are 18 main texts, which include the popular Vishnu Parana and Bhagavata, which encourage devotion to Vishnu, especially in his incarnation as Krishna.

Purcell Henry 1659–1695. English composer. His work marks the high point of Baroque music in England, and can be highly expressive, for example, the opera *Dido and Aeneas* 1689 and music for Dryden's *King Arthur* 1691 and for *The Fairy Queen* 1692. He wrote more than 500 works, ranging from secular operas and incidental music for plays to cantatas and church music.

purchasing-power parity a system for comparing standards of living between different countries. Comparing the gross domestic product of different countries involves first converting them to a common currency (usually US dollars or sterling), a conversion which is subject to large fluctuations with variations in exchange rates. Purchasing power parity aims to overcome this by measuring how much money in the currency of those countries is required to buy a comparable range of goods and services.

purdah the seclusion of women practised by some Islamic and Hindu peoples. It had begun to disappear with the adoption of Western culture, but the fundamentalism of the 1980s revived it, for example, the wearing of the ◊chador, an all-enveloping black mantle, in Iran. The Koran actually requests only 'modesty' in dress.

Pure Land Buddhism the dominant form of Buddhism in China and Japan. It emphasizes faith in and love of Buddha, in particular Amitābha (Amida in Japan, Amituofo in China), the ideal 'Buddha of boundless light', who has vowed that all believers who call on his name will be reborn in his Pure Land, or Western Paradise. This also applies to women, who had been debarred from attaining salvation through monastic life. There are over 16 million Pure Land Buddhists in Japan.

purgatory in Roman Catholic belief, a purificatory state or place for the souls of those who have died in a state of grace to expiate their venial sins.

purge term usually applied to the removal of suspected opponents, especially by Joseph Stalin in the USSR during the 1930s. The purges were carried out by the secret police against political opponents, Communist Party members, minorities, civil servants, and large sections of the armed forces' officer corps. Some 10 million people were executed or deported to labour camps 1934–38.

Purim Jewish festival celebrated in Feb or Mar, commemorating ◊Esther, who saved the Jews from destruction.

Puritan from 1564, a member of the Church of England who wished to eliminate Roman Catholic survivals in ritual, or substitute a presbyterian for an episcopal form of church government. The term

Pushkin Portrait of Aleksandr Pushkin, by Vasily Tropinin, dated 1827.

also covers the separatists who withdrew from the church altogether. The Puritans were identified with the parliamentary opposition under James I and Charles I, and after the Restoration were driven from the church, and more usually known as ◊Dissenters or ◊Nonconformists.

Purple Heart, order of the the earliest American military award for distinguished service beyond the call of duty, established by Washington in 1782, when it was the equivalent of the modern Congressional Medal of Honour. Made of purple cloth bound at the edges, it was worn on the facings over the left breast. After the American Revolution it lapsed until revived by President Hoover 1932, when it was issued to those wounded in World War II and subsequently; the modern Purple Heart is of bronze and enamel.

purpura spontaneous bleeding beneath the skin localized in spots. It may be harmless, as sometimes with the elderly, or linked with disease.

pus yellowish liquid which forms in the body as a result of bacterial attack; it includes white blood cells (leucocytes) 'killed in battle' with the bacteria, plasma, and broken-down tissue cells. An enclosed collection of pus is an abscess.

Pusan or *Busan* chief industrial port of South Korea (textiles, rubber, salt, and fishing); population (1984) 3,495,500. It was invaded by the Japanese 1592, and opened to foreign trade 1883.

Pusey Edward Bouverie 1800–1882. British Church of England priest from 1828. He was Regius professor of Hebrew at Oxford University. In 1835 he joined J H ◊Newman in issuing the *Tracts for the Times*. After Newman's conversion to Catholicism, Pusey became leader of the High Church Party or Puseyites, striving until his death to keep them from conversion.

Pushkin Aleksandr 1799–1837. Russian poet and writer. He was exiled in 1820 for his political verse, and in 1824 was in trouble for his atheistic opinions. He wrote ballads such as *The Gypsies* 1827, and the novel in verse *Eugene Onegin* 1833. Other works include the tragic drama *Boris Godunov* 1825 and the prose pieces *The Captain's Daughter* 1836 and *The Queen of Spades* 1834. Pushkin's range was enormous, and his willingness to experiment freed later Russian writers from many of the archaic conventions of the literature of his time.

Pushtu another name for the ◊Pashto language.

putrefaction decomposition of organic matter by microorganisms.

putsch German term used to describe a military, paramilitary, or civilian coup d'état, such as Hitler and Ludendorff's abortive beer-hall putsch of Nov 1923, which attempted to overthrow the Bavarian government.

Puttnam David Terence 1941– . English film producer, largely influential in reviving the British film industry internationally. Notable successes include *Chariots of Fire* 1981 and *The Killing Fields* 1984.

Puvis de Chavannes Pierre Cécile 1824–1898. French Symbolist painter. His major works are vast decorative schemes, mainly on mythological and allegorical subjects, for public buildings such as the Panthéon and Hôtel de Ville in Paris. His work influenced Gauguin.

Pu-Yi former name of the last Chinese emperor Henry ◊P'u-i.

PWR *p*ressurized *w*ater *r*eactor, a nuclear reactor design extensively used in nuclear power stations in many countries, and in nuclear-powered submarines. In the PWR water under pressure is the coolant and ◊moderator. It circulates through a steam generator, where its heat boils water to provide steam to drive power ◊turbines.

pyelitis inflammation of the renal pelvis, the central part of the kidney where urine accumulates before discharge. Caused by bacterial infection, it is more common in women.

Pygmalion in Greek legend, a king of Cyprus who fell in love with an ivory statue he had carved, and when Aphrodite brought it to life as Galatea, he married her.

Pym Barbara 1913–1980. English novelist, born in Shropshire. She wrote a number of novels of manners, including *Some Tame Gazelle* 1950, treating a circumscribed life with comic irony and attention to detail. Her later books were *The Sweet Dove Died* 1978 and *A Few Green Leaves* 1980.

Pym John 1584–1643. English parliamentarian, largely responsible for the ◊Petition of Right in 1628. As leader of the Puritan opposition in the ◊Long Parliament from 1640, he moved the impeachment of Charles I's advisers Strafford and Laud, drew up the ◊Grand Remonstrance, and was the chief of five Members of Parliament singled out for by arrest by Charles I in 1642. The five took refuge in the City, from which they emerged triumphant when the King left London. Just before his death, with military stalemate threatening, he negotiated the alliance between Parliament and the Scots.

Pynchon Thomas 1937– . US novelist, who creates a bizarre, labyrinthine world in his books, which include *V* 1963, *The Crying of Lot 49* 1966, and *Gravity's Rainbow* 1973.

Pyongyang capital and industrial city (coal, iron, steel, textiles, chemicals) of North Korea; population 1,280,000 (1981).

pyramid in geometry, a solid figure with triangular side-faces meeting at a common vertex (point) and with a ◊polygon as its base. The volume of a

pyramid

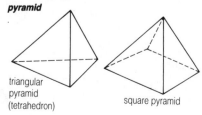

triangular
pyramid
(tetrahedron)

square pyramid

Pythagoras

for right-angled triangles

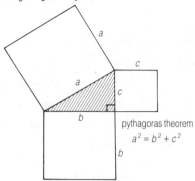

pythagoras theorem
$$a^2 = b^2 + c^2$$

pyramid, no matter how many faces it has, is equal to the area of the base multiplied by one-third of the perpendicular height.

pyramid pyramidal building used in ancient Egypt to enclose a royal tomb, for example the Great Pyramid of Khufu/Cheops at Gizeh, near Cairo; 230 m/755 ft square and 147 m/481 ft high. In Babylon and Assyria broadly stepped pyramids (ziggurats) were used as the base for a shrine to a god: the Tower of Babel (see also ◊Babylon) was probably one of these. Pyramidal temple mounds were also built by the ◊Aztecs and ◊Mayas, for example at Chichen Itza and Cholula, near Mexico City, which is the world's largest in ground area (300 m/990 ft base, 60 m/195 ft high).

Pyramus and Thisbe legendary Babylonian lovers whose story was retold by ◊Ovid. Pursued by a lioness, Thisbe lost her veil, and when Pyramus arrived at their meeting-place, he found it bloodstained. Assuming Thisbe was dead, he stabbed himself, and she, on finding his body, killed herself.

Pyrenees (French *Pyrénés*; Spanish *Pirineos*) mountain range in SW Europe between France and Spain; length about 435 km/270 mi; highest peak Aneto (French *Néthon*) 3,404 m/11,168 ft.

pyrethrum popular name for some flowers of the genus *Chrysanthemum*, family Compositae. The ornamental species *Chrysanthemum coccineum*, and hybrids derived from it, are commonly grown in gardens. Pyrethrum powder is a powerful contact herbicide for aphids and mosquitoes.

pyridine C_5H_5N a heterocyclic compound (see ◊cyclic compounds). It is a liquid with a sickly smell, and occurs in coal tar. It is soluble in water, acts as a strong base, and is used as a solvent, particularly in the manufacture of plastics.

pyrite a common iron ore, FeS. Its metallic lustre gives it its common name *fool's gold*.

pyrometer type of ◊thermometer used for measuring high temperatures.

pyroxene any one of a group of minerals, silicates of calcium, iron, and magnesium, found in igneous and metamorphic rocks.

Pyrrhon or *Pyrrho* c. 360–270 BC. Greek philosopher, founder of ◊Scepticism, who maintained that since certainty was impossible, peace of mind lay in renouncing all claims to knowledge.

Pyrrhus c. 318–c. 272 BC. King of ◊Epirus from 307, who invaded Italy in 280, as an ally of the Tarentines against Rome. He twice defeated the Romans, but with such heavy losses that a 'Pyrrhic victory' is a byword for one not worth winning, and he returned to Greece in 275 after his defeat at Beneventum.

Pythagoras c. 580–500 BC. Greek mathematician and philosopher, who formulated ◊Pythagoras' theorem.

Pythagoras' theorem in geometry, theorem stating that in a right-angled triangle, the area of the square on the hypotenuse (the longest side) is equal to the sum of the areas of the squares drawn on the other two sides. If the hypotenuse is *h* units long and the lengths of the other sides are *a* and *b*, then $h^2 = a^2 + b^2$.

Pytheas lived 4th century BC. Greek navigator from Marseille who explored the coast of W Europe at least as far as Denmark, sailed round Britain, and reached ◊Thule (possibly the Shetlands).

python type of constricting snake found in the tropics of Africa, Asia, and Australia, related to the boas but laying eggs rather than producing living young. Some species are small, but the reticulated python of SE Asia can grow to 10 m/33 ft.

pyx the container used in the Roman Catholic Church for the reservation of the wafers of the sacrament.

area 721,000 sq km/278,000 sq mi
capital Xining
products oil, livestock, medical products
population (1990) 4,457,000, including 90,000
Tibetans and other minorities.

Qisarya Mediterranean port N of Tel Aviv-
Jaffa, Israel, which has underwater remains of
the biblical port of Caesarea.

quadrathon a sports event in which the competitors must swim two miles, walk 30 miles,
cycle 100 miles, and run 26.2 miles (a
marathon) within 22 hours.

quadratic equation in mathematics, a poly-
nominal equation of second degree (that is, an equation containing as its highest power the square of a
single unknown variable, such as x^2). The general
formula of such equations is $ax^2 + bx + c = 0$, in
which a, b, and c are real numbers, and only the
coefficient a cannot equal 0. In ◊coordinate geometry, a quadratic function represents a ◊parabola.

Quadruple Alliance in European history,
three military alliances of four nations:
the Quadruple Alliance 1718 of Austria,
Britain, France, and the United Provinces
(Netherlands), to prevent Spain from annexing
Sardinia and Sicily;
the Quadruple Alliance 1813 of Austria,
Britain, Prussia, and Russia, aimed at defeating
the French emperor Napoleon; renewed 1815
and 1818. See Congress of ◊Vienna.
the Quadruple Alliance 1834 of Britain,
France, Spain, and Portugal, guaranteeing the
constitutional monarchies of Spain and Portugal
against rebels in the Carlist War.

quadrature the position of the Moon or an
outer planet where a line between it and the
Earth makes a right angle with a line joining the
Earth to the Sun.

quaestor a Roman magistrate whose duties
were mainly concerned with public finances. The
quaestors originated as assistants to the consuls. Both urban and military quaestors existed,
the latter being attached to the commanding
generals in the provinces.

quail smallest species of the partridge family. The
common quail *Coturnix coturnix* is about 18cm/7 in

Qaddafi alternative form of ◊*Khaddhafi*,
Libyan leader.

Qadsiya, Battle of battle fought in S Iraq 637.
A Muslim Arab force defeated a larger Zoroastrian
Persian army and ended the ◊Sassanian Empire.
The defeat is still resented in Iran, where mod-
ern Muslim Arab nationalism threatens to break
up the Iranian state.

qat shrub *Catha edulis* related to coffee; the
leaves are chewed as a mild narcotic in some Arab
countries. Its use was banned in ◊Somalia 1983.

Qatar country in the middle East, occupying
Qatar peninsula in the Arabian Gulf, bounded to
the SW by Saudi Arabia and to the S by United
Arab Emirates.

QC abbreviation for ◊*Queen's Counsel.*

QED abbreviation for *quod erat demonstrandum* (Latin 'which was to be proved').

Qin dynasty Chinese imperial dynasty 221–
206 BC. ◊Shi Huangdi was its most noted
emperor.

Qinghai formerly *Tsinghai* province, NW China

Qatar
State of (*Dawlat Qatar*)

QATAR
Doha
Bahrain
Saudi
Arabia
UAE
Oman
RED SEA
INDIAN
OCEAN
0 miles 500
0 km 1000

area 11,400 sq km/4,402 sq mi
capital and chief port Doha
towns Dukhan, centre of oil production

physical mostly flat desert with some salt flats
in the south
head of state and government Sheik Khalifa
bin Hamad al-Thani from 1972
political system absolute monarchy
exports oil, natural gas, petrochemicals,
fertilizers, iron, steel
currency riyal
population (1990 est) 498,000 (half in Doha);
annual growth rate 3.7%
language Arabic (official), English
religion Sunni Muslim 95%
literacy 60% (1987)
GNP $5.9 bn (1983); $35,000 per head
chronology
1970 Constitution adopted, confirming the
emirate as an absolute monarchy.
1971 Independence achieved from Britain; new
treaty of friendship signed with the UK.
1972 Emir Sheik Ahmad replaced in a
bloodless coup by his cousin, Crown Prince
Sheik Khalifa.
1991 Forces joined UN coalition in Gulf War
against Iraq.

long, reddish-brown, with a white throat and yellowish belly. It is found in Europe, Asia, and Africa, and has been introduced to North America.

Quaker popular name, originally derogatory, for a member of the Society of ◊Friends.

quango British term coined as an acronym from *q*uasi-*a*utonomous *n*on-*g*overnmental *o*rganization, for example the Equal Opportunities Commission (1975). They are nominally independent, but rely on government funding. Many (such as the Location of Offices Bureau) were abolished by the Thatcher government 1979–90.

Quant Mary 1934– . British fashion designer, whose clothes designs epitomized the 'swinging London' of the 1960s.

quantity theory of money economic theory claiming that an increase in the amount of money in circulation causes a proportionate increase in prices.

quant. suff. abbreviation for *quantum sufficit* (Latin 'as much as suffices').

quantum number in physics, one of a set of four numbers that uniquely characterize an ◊electron and its state in an ◊atom. The *principal quantum number* n (= 1, 2, 3, and so on) defines the electron's main energy level. The *orbital quantum number* l (= $n - 1$, $n - 2$, and so on to 0) relates to angular momentum. The *magnetic quantum number* m (= l, $l - 1$, $l - 2$, and so on to 0 and then on to ... $-(l - 2)$, $-(l - 1)$ and $-l$ describes the energies of electrons in a magnetic field. The *spin quantum number* m_s (= $+ \frac{1}{2}$ or $-\frac{1}{2}$) gives the spin direction of the electron.

quantum theory in physics, the theory that many quantities, such as ◊energy, cannot have a continuous range of values, but only a number of discrete (particular) ones, because they are packaged in 'quanta of energy'. Just as earlier theory showed how light, generally seen as a wave motion, could also in some ways be seen as composed of discrete particles (◊photons), quantum mechanics shows how atomic particles like electrons may also be seen as having wave- like properties. Quantum mechanics is the basis of ◊particle physics, modern theoretical chemistry, and the solid-state physics which describes the behaviour of the ◊silicon chips used in computers.

quarantine (from French *quarantaine* 40 days) any period for which people, animals, or vessels may be detained in isolation when suspected of carrying contagious disease.

quark any of at least five hypothetical elementary particles within atoms, which, together with their antiparticles, are believed to be fundamental constituents of mesons and baryons.

quart imperial liquid or dry measure, equal to 2 pints or 1.136 litres.

quarter day in the financial year, any of the four dates on which payments such as ground rents become due: in England, 25 Mar (Lady Day), 24 Jun (Midsummer Day), 29 Sept (Michaelmas), and 25 Dec (Christmas Day).

quarter session former local criminal court in England, replaced 1972 by crown courts (see also ◊law courts).

quartz a crystalline form of silica, SiO_2, one of the commonest minerals of the Earth's crust. It rates 7 on the Mohs scale of hardness. Quartz is used in jewellery and ornamental work, and its reaction to electricity makes it valuable in electronic instruments (see ◊piezoelectric effect). Quartz can also be manufactured.

quartzite a ◊metamorphic rock consisting of pure

quartz *well-formed crystals of quartz are usually pyramidal in shape.*

quartz sandstone that has recrystallized under pressure.

quasar (abbreviation of *quasi*- stell*ar*) in astronomy, an object that appears star-like. Quasars are thought to be the brilliant centres of distant galaxies, caused by stars and gas falling towards an immense ◊black hole at the galaxy's centre. Quasar light shows a large ◊red shift, placing quasars far off in the Universe, the most distant lying over 10 billion light years away. Although quasars are small, with diameters of less than a light year, they give out as much energy as hundreds of galaxies.

quasi (Latin 'as if') apparently but not actually.

Quasimodo Salvatore 1901–1968. Italian poet. His first book *Acque e terre/Waters and Land* appeared 1930. Later books, including *Nuove poesie/New Poetry* 1942, and *Il falso e vero verde/The False and True Green* 1956, reflect a growing preoccupation with contemporary political and social problems. Nobel prize 1959.

quassia trees native to tropical parts of the Americas, with a bitter bark and wood, including *Quassia amara*, family Simaroubaceae. The heartwood is a source of quassiin, an infusion of which was formerly used as a tonic; it is now used in insecticides.

Quaternary period of geological time that began 1.8 million years ago and is still in process. It is divided into the Pleistocene and Holocene epochs.

Quatre Bras, Battle of battle fought 16 Jun 1815 during the Napoleonic Wars, in which the British commander Wellington defeated French forces under Marshal Ney. It is named after a hamlet in Brabant, Belgium, 32 km/20 mi SE of Brussels.

Quayle (J) Dan(forth) 1947– . US Republican

Quayle *Vice president of the USA from 1989–93, Dan Quayle.*

politician, vice president 1989–93. A congressman for Indiana 1977–81, he became a senator 1981.

Québec   capital and industrial port (textiles, leather, timber, paper, printing and publishing) of Québec province, on the St Lawrence river, Canada; population (1986) 165,000, metropolitan area 603,000. It was founded 1608.

Québec   province of E Canada
area 1,540,680 sq km/594,700 sq mi
capital Québec
towns Montréal, Laval, Sherbrooke, Verdun, Hull, Trois-Rivières
products iron, copper, gold, zinc, cereals, potatoes, paper, textiles, fish; produces 70% of the world's maple syrup
population (1991) 6,811,800
language French is the only official language since 1974, although 17% speak English. Language laws 1989 prohibit the use of English on street signs.
history known as New France 1534–1763; captured by the British, and became province of Quebec 1763–90, Lower Canada 1791–1846, Canada East 1846–67, one of the original provinces 1867; nationalist feelings 1960s (despite existing safeguards for Quebec's French- derived civil law, customs, religon, and language) led to the foundation of the Parti Québecois by René Lévesque 1968; uprising by FLQ separatists 1970; referendum on 'sovereignty-association' (separation) defeated 1980. Parti Québecois defeated by Liberal Party 1989.

Québec Conference   conference in the city of Québec 1943, at which the Allied leaders Roosevelt, Churchill, Mackenzie King, and Tse-ven Soong approved the British admiral Mountbatten as supreme Allied commander in SE Asia, and made plans for the invasion of France, for which the US general Eisenhower was to be supreme commander.

Quechua   also *Quichua* or *Kechua* South American Indians of the Andean regions, whose ancestors include the Incas. The Quechua language is the second official language of Peru, and is also spoken in Ecuador.

Queensberry   John Sholto Douglas, 8th Marquess of Queensberry 1844–1900. British patron of boxing. In 1867 he formulated the *Queensberry Rules* which form the basis of modern-day boxing rules.

Queen's Counsel   or *QC* in England, a barrister appointed to senior rank by the Lord Chancellor.

Queensland   state in NE Australia
area 1,727,200 sq km/666,600 sq mi
capital Brisbane
towns Gold Coast-Tweed, Townsville, Sunshine Coast, Toowoomba, Cairns
exports sugar, pineapples, beef, cotton, wool, tobacco, copper, gold, silver, lead, zinc, coal, nickel, bauxite, uranium, natural gas
population (1987) 2,650,000
history part of New South Wales until 1859, it then became self-governing.

question mark   a punctuation mark (?), used to indicate enquiry or doubt.

quetzal   long-tailed Central American bird. The male is brightly coloured, with green, red, blue, and white feathers, and is about 1.3 m/4.3 ft long including tail. The female is smaller and lacks the tail and plumage. It eats fruit, insects, and small frogs and lizards. It is the national emblem of Guatemala, and was considered sacred by the Mayans and the Aztecs.

quince

Quetzalcoatl   feathered serpent god of air and water in the pre-columbian Aztec and Toltec cultures of Central America. In legendary human form, he was said to have been fair-skinned and bearded, and to have reigned on Earth during a golden age. He disappeared across the sea, with a promise to return; ◊Cortés exploited the coincidence of description when he invaded. Ruins of one of his temples survive at Teotihuacán in Mexico.

Quevedo y Villegas   Francisco Gómez de 1580–1645. Spanish novelist and satirist. His picaresque novel *La Vida del Buscón/The Life of a Scoundrel* 1626 follows the tradition of the roguish hero who has a series of episodic adventures.

Quezon City   former capital of the Philippines 1948–76, on Luzon Island, NE of Manila; population (1990) 1,166,800. It was named after the Philippines' first president, Manuel Luis Quezon (1878–1944).

quicksilver   former name for the element ◊mercury.

quid pro quo   (Latin 'something for something') an exchange of one thing in return for another.

quietism   a religious attitude, displayed periodically in the history of Christianity, consisting of passive contemplation and meditation to achieve union with God. The founder of modern quietism was the Spanish priest ◊Molinos who published a *Guida Spirituale/Spiritual Guide* 1675.

quilt   a padded bed-cover or the method used to make padded covers or clothing. The padding is made by sewing a layer of wool or other stuffing between two outer pieces of material in patterns, often diamond shapes or floral motifs.

quince   tree *Cydonia oblonga*, family Rosaceae, native to W Asia. The bitter, yellow, pear-shaped fruit is used in preserves.

quinine   an antimalarial drug, the first that was effective for its treatment. Peruvian Indians taught French missionaries how to use the bark of the cinchona tree 1630, but quinine was not isolated for another two centuries.

Quintero   Serafin Alvarez 1871–1938 and Joaquin Alvarez 1873–1945. Spanish dramatists. The brothers, born near Seville, always worked together and from 1897 produced some 200 successful plays, principally dealing with Andalusia. Among them are *Papá Juan: Centenario* 1909 and *Los Mosquitos* 1928.

Quintilian   Marcus Fabius Quintilianus *c.* 35–95 AD. Roman rhetorician, who taught rhetoric in Rome from 68 AD and later composed the *Institutio Oratorio/The Education of an Orator*, in which he advocated a simple and sincere style of public speaking.

Quirinal one of the seven hills on which ancient Rome was built. Its summit is occupied by a palace built 1574 as a summer residence for the pope and occupied 1870–1946 by the kings of Italy. The name Quirinal is derived from that of Quirinus, local god of the ◊Sabines.

Quisling Vidkun 1887–1945. Norwegian politician. Leader from 1933 of the Norwegian Fascist Party, he aided the Nazi invasion 1940 by delaying mobilization and urging nonresistance. He was made premier by Hitler 1942, and was arrested and shot as a traitor by the Norwegians 1945. His name became generic for a traitor who aids an occupying force.

Quito capital and industrial city (textiles, chemicals, leather, gold, silver) of Ecuador, about 3,000 m/9,850 ft above sea level; population (1982) 1,110,250. An ancient settlement, it was taken by the Incas about 1470 and by the Spanish 1534.

Quixote, Don novel by the Spanish writer ◊Cervantes, with a hero of the same name.

Qum holy city of Shi'ite Muslims, in central Iran, 145 km/90 mi south of Tehran; population (1986) 551,000.

Qumran or *Khirbet Qumran* ruined site, excavated from 1951, in the foothills on NW shores of the Dead Sea in Jordan. Originally an Iron Age fort (6th century BC) it was occupied in the late 2nd century BC by a monastic community, the ◊Essenes, until the buildings were burned down

68 AD. The monastery library contained the Dead Sea Scrolls, discovered 1947; the scrolls had been hidden for safekeeping and never reclaimed.

quod erat demonstrandum or *QED* (Latin 'which was to be proved') added at the end of a geometrical proof.

quod vide (qv) (Latin 'which see') indicates a cross-reference.

quoits game in which a rubber ring (quoit) is thrown towards an iron hob from a point 16.5 m/54 ft distant. A 'ringer', a quoit landing over the hob, gains two points, and one landing nearest the hob, within a circle 1 m/3 ft in diameter, gains one point.

quorum a minimum number of members required to be present for the proceedings of an assembly to be valid. The actual number required for a quorum may vary.

quota in international trade, a limitation on the quantities exported or imported. Restrictions may be imposed forcibly or voluntarily. The justification of quotas include protection of a home industry from an influx of cheap goods, prevention of a heavy outflow of goods (usually raw materials) because there are insufficient numbers to meet domestic demand, allowance for a new industry to develop before it is exposed to demand, or prevention of a decline in the world price of a particular commodity.

quo vadis? (Latin) where are you going?

qv abbreviation for ◊*quod vide*.

RA abbreviation for *Royal Academy* of Art, London, founded 1768.

Rabat capital of Morocco, industrial port (cotton textiles, carpets, leather goods) on the Atlantic coast, 177 km/110 mi W of Fez; population (1982) 519,000. Named after its original *ribat* or fortified monastery.

rabbi the chief religious minister of a synagogue; the spiritual leader of a Jewish congregation; or a scholar of Judaic law and ritual.

rabbit greyish- brown, long-eared, burrowing mammal *Oryctolagus cuniculus* of the family Leporidae in the order Lagomorpha (with hares and pikas). It has legs and feet adapted for running and hopping, large front teeth, and can grow up to 40 cm/16 in long. It is native to Europe and N Africa, but is now found worldwide.

Rabelais François 1495–1553. French satirist, monk, and physician, whose name has become synonymous with bawdy humour. He was educated in the Renaissance humanist tradition and was the author of satirical allegories, *La Vie inestimable de Gargantua/The Inestimable Life of Gargantua* 1535 and *Faits et dits héroïques du grand Pantagruel/Deeds and Sayings of the Great Pantagruel* 1533, the story of two giants (father and son) Gargantua and Pantagruel.

rabies disease of the central nervous system which can afflict all warm-blooded creatures. It is almost invariably fatal once symptoms have developed. Its transmission to a human being is almost always by a bite from a rabid dog.

Rabin Itzhak 1922– . Israeli prime minister 1974–77, succeeding Golda Meir, and from 1992 Minister of Defence under the Conservative Liberal coalition government 1984–90. His support for Palestinian self government in the occupied territories helped his party to victory in 1992.

Rabuka Sitiveni 1948– . Fijian soldier and politician. When the 1987 elections in Fiji produced an Indian-dominated government he staged a bloodless coup, kidnapping the prime minister and his cabinet and heading an interim government. He soon stood down, serving as home-affairs minister in a civilian administration. In May 1992 he was nominated as Fiji's new premier.

RAC abbreviation for the British *Royal Automobile Club.*

raccoon omnivorous nocturnal mammal of the Americas. The common raccoon *Procyon lotor* is about 60 cm/2ft long, with a grey-brown body, a black and white ringed tail, and a black 'mask' around its eyes. The crab-eating racoon *Procyon cancrivorus* of South America is slightly smaller, and has shorter fur.

race in anthropology, term sometimes applied to a physically distinctive group of people, on the basis of difference from other groups in skin colour, head shape, hair type, and physique. Formerly anthropologists divided the human race into three hypothetical racial groups: Caucasoid, Mongoloid, and Negroid. However, scientific studies have failed to indicate any absolute confirmation of genetic racial divisions.

raceme in botany, a type of ◊inflorescence.

Rachmaninov Sergei (Vasilevich) 1873–1943. Russian composer and pianist. After the 1917 Revolution he went to the USA. His dramatically emotional music has a strong melodic basis and includes operas, for example, *Francesca da Rimini* 1906, three symphonies, four piano concertos, piano pieces, and songs. Among his most familiar works are the *Prelude in C Minor* and *Rhapsody on a Theme of Paganini* 1934.

Racine Jean 1639–1699. French dramatist and greatest exponent of the classical tragedy in French drama. He was the friend of ◊Boileau, ◊La Fontaine, and ◊Molière. Most of his tragedies have women in the title role, for example *Andromaque* 1667, *Iphigénie* 1674, and *Phèdre* 1677. After the contemporary failure of the latter he no longer wrote for the secular stage, but influenced by Madame de ◊Maintenon wrote two religious dramas, *Esther* 1689 and *Athalie* 1691, which achieved considerable posthumous success.

racism or *racialism* a belief in, or set of implicit assumptions about, the superiority of one's own ◊race or ethnic group, often accompanied by prejudice against members of an ethnic group different from one's own. Racism may be used to justify ◊discrimination, verbal or physical abuse, or even genocide, as in Nazi Germany.

rackets or *racquets* (US spelling). Indoor game played on an enclosed court. It is regarded as the forerunner to many racket and ball games.

rack railway a railway used in mountainous regions, which uses a toothed pinion running in a toothed rack to provide traction. The rack usually runs between the rails. Ordinary wheels lose their grip even on quite shallow gradients, but rack railways, like that on Mount Pilatus in Switzerland, can climb slopes as steep as 1 in 2.1.

radar (from *radio direction and ranging*) a means of locating an object in space, direction finding, and navigation using high-frequency radio waves. Essential to navigation in darkness, cloud, and fog, it can be thwarted in warfare by: aircraft and missiles with a modified shape which reduces their radar cross-section; radar-absorbent paints; and electronic jamming. A countermeasure in pinpointing small targets is the use of ◊laser 'radar' instead of ◊microwaves. Chains of ground radar stations are used to warn of enemy attack, for example, North

raccoon

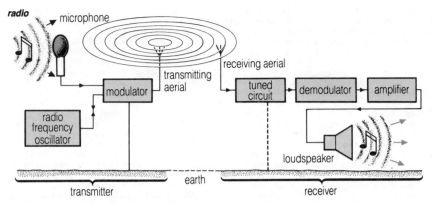

radio

microphone

transmitting aerial

receiving aerial

modulator

radio frequency oscillator

tuned circuit

demodulator

amplifier

loudspeaker

earth

transmitter   receiver

Warning System 1985, consisting of 52 stations across the Canadian Arctic and N Alaska. Radar is also used in ◊meteorology and ◊astronomy.

Radcliffe Anne (born Ward) 1764–1823. English novelist, a chief exponent of the Gothic novel or 'romance of terror', for example, *The Mysteries of Udolpho* 1794. She was one of the first novelists to include vivid descriptions of landscape and weather and her work was very popular in her day.

Radha in the Hindu epic ◊*Mahābhārata*, the wife of a cowherd who leaves her husband for love of Krishna. Her devotion to Krishna is seen by the mystical *bhakti* movement as the ideal of the love between humans and God.

radian in mathematics, an alternative unit to the ◊degree for measuring angles. It is defined as the angle subtended at the centre of a circle by an arc (length of circumference) equal in length to the radius of the circle. There are 2π (approximately 6.284) radians in a full circle (360°).

radiation in physics, the emission of radiant ◊energy as ◊particles or waves, for example, sound, light, alpha particles, and beta particles.

radiation biology the study of how living things are affected by radioactive (ionizing) emissions (see ◊radioactivity), and by electromagnetic (nonionizing) radiation (◊electromagnetic waves). Both are potentially harmful and can cause leukaemia and other cancers; even low levels of radioactivity are very dangerous. Both can be used therapeutically, for example to treat cancer, when the radiation dose is very carefully controlled (*radio therapy* or *X-ray therapy*).

radiation sickness sickness resulting from overlong exposure to radiation, including X-rays, gamma-rays, neutrons and other nuclear radiation. Such radiation ionizes atoms in the body and causes nausea, vomiting, diarrhoea, and other symptoms. The body cells themselves may be damaged, even by relatively small doses, causing ◊leukaemia, and genetic changes may also be induced.

radiation units units of measurement for the activity of radionuclides and the dose of ionizing radiation. Continued use of the units introduced earlier this century (the curie, rad, rem and roentgen) has been approved while the derived SI units become familiar. 1 curie = 3.7×10 becquerel (activity); 1 rad = 10^{-2} gray (absorbed dose); 1 rem = 10^{-2} sievert (dose equivalent); 1 roentgen = 2.58×10^{-4} coulomb/kg (exposure to ionizing radiation).

Radić Stjepan 1871–1928. Yugoslav nationalist politician. Born near Fiume, he led the Croat national movement within the Austro-Hungarian Empire, and supported union with Serbia in 1919.

His opposition to Serbian supremacy within Yugoslavia led to his murder in the parliament house.

Radical supporter of parliamentary reform in Britain before the Reform Bill of 1832. As a group the Radicals later became the advanced wing of the Liberal Party. During the 1860s (led by Cobden, Bright, and J S Mill) they campaigned for extension of the franchise, free trade, and ◊*laissez-faire*, but after 1870, under the leadership of J Chamberlain and Dilke, they adopted a republican and semi-socialist programme. With the growth of ◊socialism in the later 19th century, Radicalism ceased to exist as an organized movement.

radical anyone with political opinions more extreme than the main current of a country's major political party or parties. More often applied to those with left-wing opinions.

radical in chemistry, a group of atoms (for example the methyl radical, CH_3) forming part of a molecule, which takes part in chemical reactions without disintegration, yet often cannot exist alone.

radicle the part of a plant embryo that develops into the primary root. Usually it emerges from the seed before the embryonic shoot, or ◊plumule, its tip protected by a root cap, or calyptra, as it pushes through the soil. The radicle may form the basis of the entire root system, or it may be replaced by adventitious roots.

radio the transmission and reception of radio waves. In radio transmission a microphone converts ◊sound waves (pressure variations in the air) into an audiofrequency electrical signal which is then picked up by a receiving aerial and fed to a loudspeaker which reproduces sound waves.

radioactive decay the process of continuous disintegration undergone by the nuclei of radioactive elements, such as radium and various isotopes of uranium and the transuranic elements. Certain lighter artificially created isotopes also undergo radioactive decay. The associated radiation consists of alpha rays, beta rays, or gamma rays (or a combination of these) and it takes place with a characteristic half-life, which is the time taken for half of any mass of a radioactive isotope to decay completely.

The original nucleotide is known as the parent substance, and the product is a daughter nucleotide (which may or may not be radioactive).

radioactive tracer the radioactive isotope used in a labelled compound.

radioactive waste any waste that emits radiation in excess of the background level. See ◊nuclear waste.

radio astronomy the study of radio waves emitted naturally by objects in space. Radio emission comes from hot gas (*thermal radiation*), electrons spiralling in magnetic fields (*synchroton radiation*), and specific wavelengths (*lines*) emitted by atoms and molecules in space, such as the 21 cm line emitted by hydrogen gas. Radio astronomy began 1932 when Karl ◊Jansky detected radio waves from the centre of our Galaxy, but the subject did not develop until after World War II.

radio beacon a radio transmitter in a fixed location, used in marine and aerial navigation. Ships and aircraft pinpoint their position by reference to the signals given out by two or more beacons.

radiocarbon dating a method of dating organic materials (for example bone, wood) found by archaeologists. Plants take up carbon dioxide gas from the atmosphere and incorporate it into their tissues, and some of that carbon dioxide contains the radioactive isotope of carbon, carbon-14. On death, the plant ceases to take up carbon-14 and that already taken up decays at a known rate, allowing the time which has elapsed since the plant died. Animals take the carbon-14 into their own bodies from eating plant tissues and their remains can be similarly dated.

radio, cellular the use of a series of short-range transmitters at the centre of adjacent cells (each about 4 km/2.5 mi in diameter), using the same frequencies over and over again throughout the area covered. It is used for personal communication among subscribers via car phones, and portable units.

radiochemistry the chemical study of radioactive isotopes and their compounds (whether produced from naturally radioactive or irradiated materials) and their use in the study of other chemical processes.

radio frequencies and wavelengths classification of. In order to name them it is convenient to group frequencies and wavelengths together in bands, each band referring to waves having similar propagation characteristics, and for which similar techniques are used in the radio terminal equipment. For the internationally agreed radio frequency spectrum, see ◊electromagnetic waves.

radio galaxy a galaxy that is a strong source of electromagnetic waves of radio wavelengths. All galaxies, including our own, emit some radio waves, but radio galaxies are up to a million times more powerful.

radiography a branch of science concerned with the use of radiation (particularly ◊X-rays) to produce images on photographic film or fluorescent screens. X-rays penetrate matter according to its nature, density, and thickness. In doing so they can cast shadows on photographic film, producing a radiograph. Radiography is widely used in medicine for examining bones and tissues and in industry for examining solid materials to check welded seams in pipelines, for example.

radioisotope (radioactive ◊isotope) in physics, a radioactive form of an element. Most radioisotopes are made by bombarding an ordinary inactive material with neutrons in the core of a nuclear reactor. The radiations given off are easy to detect (hence their use as ◊tracers), can in some instances penetrate substantial thicknesses of materials, and may have profound effects on living matter. Radiosotopes are very useful in many fields of medicine, industry, agriculture, and research.

radioisotope scanning the use of radioactive materials (radioisotopes or radionuclides) to pinpoint disease.

radiometric dating a method of dating rock by assessing the degree of ◊radioactive decay of naturally occurring ◊isotopes. The dating of rocks often uses the gradual decay of uranium into lead. The ratio of the amounts of 'parent' to 'daughter' isotopes in a sample gives a measure of the time it has been decaying, that is, of its age. Once-living matter can often be dated by ◊radiocarbon dating, employing the decay of the isotope carbon-14, which is naturally present in living tissue.

radiosonde a balloon carrying a radio transmitter, used to 'sound' or measure conditions in the atmosphere. It carries instruments to measure temperature, pressure, and humidity. A radar target is often attached, allowing it to be tracked.

radio telescope an instrument for detecting radio waves from the Universe. Radio telescopes usually consist of a metal bowl which collects and focuses radio waves the way a concave mirror collects and focuses light waves. Other radio telescopes are shaped like long troughs, while some consist of simple rod-shaped aerials. Radio telescopes are much larger than optical telescopes, because the wavelengths they are detecting are much longer than the wavelength of light. A large dish such as that at ◊Jodrell Bank can see the radio sky less clearly than a small optical telescope sees the visible sky. The largest single dish is 305 m/1,000 ft across, at ◊Arecibo, Puerto Rico.

radiotherapy the treatment of disease by ◊radiation from X-ray machines or radioactive sources.

radish annual herb *Raphanus sativus*, family Cruciferae, grown for its fleshy, pungent, edible root, which is usually reddish, but sometimes white or black.

radium white, luminescent, metallic element, symbol Rd, atomic number 88, relative atomic mass 226.02. It is found in pitchblende in small quantities and in other uranium ores. Radium is used in radiotherapy, to treat cancer, and in luminous paints.

Radnorshire former border county of Wales, merged with Powys 1974. Presteign was the county town.

radon radioactive gaseous element, symbol Rn, atomic number 86. One of the inert gases, it is produced from the radioactive decay of radium, thorium and actinium. It is used in radiotherapy as a source of alpha particles.

Raeburn Henry 1756–1823. Scottish portrait painter, active mainly in Edinburgh. He developed a technique of painting with broad brush strokes directly on the canvas without preparatory drawing. He was knighted 1822 and appointed painter to George IV 1823.

RAF abbreviation for ◊*Royal Air Force*.

Raffles Thomas Stamford 1781–1826. British colonial administrator, born in Jamaica. He served in the East India Company, took part in the capture of Java from the Dutch in 1811, and while governor of Sumatra 1818–23 was responsible for the acquisition and foundation of Singapore in 1819. He was a founder and first president of the Zoological Society.

rafflesia parasitic plant without stems, family Rafflesiaceae, native to Malaysia. The largest flowers in the world are produced by *Rafflesia arnoldiana*. About 1 m/3 ft across, they exude a smell of rotting flesh, which attracts flies to pollinate them.

railway *(Left) A replica of Robert Stephenson's Rocket; the original was built for the Rainhill Trials in 1829. (Right) The French TGV passenger train, which travels at speeds of 260 kph. (Below) A locomotive on the line between Guayaquil and Quito in Ecuador, the last steam-worked crossing of the Andes.*

raga (Sanskrit *rāga* 'tone' or 'colour') in Indian music, a pattern of melody and rhythm associated with religious devotion. Ragas form the basis of improvised music; a composition may also be based on (and called) a raga.

Raglan FitzRoy James Henry Somerset, 1st Baron Raglan 1788–1855. English general. In the Peninsular War under Wellington, he was foremost in the storming of Badajoz, and at Waterloo lost his right arm. He commanded the British forces in the Crimean War from 1854. The *raglan sleeve*, with no shoulder seam but cut right up to the neckline, is named after him.

ragnarök in Norse mythology, the ultimate cataclysmic battle between gods and forces of evil from which a new order will come.

ragtime syncopated music ('ragged time') in two-four rhythm, developed among black American musicians in the late 19th century; it was influenced by folk tradition, minstrel shows, and marching bands, and later merged into jazz. Scott ◊Joplin was a leading writer of ragtime pieces, called rags.

ragwort perennial plant *Senecio jacobaea*, family ◊Compositae, prolific on waste ground; it has bright yellow flowers and is poisonous.

Rahman Tunku Abdul 1903– . Malaysian politician, the first prime minister of independent Malaya 1957–63 and of Malaysia 1963–70.

raï Algerian type of pop music developed in the 1970s from the Bedouin song form *melhoun*, using synthesizers and electronic drums.

Raikes Robert 1735–1811. English printer who started the first Sunday school (for religious purposes) in Gloucester in 1780.

rail general name for birds of the family Rallidae, including corncrakes, coots, moorhens, and gallinules.

railway method of transport in which trains convey passengers and goods along a twin rail track. Following the work of English steam pioneers such as ◊Watt, ◊Stephenson built the first public steam railway, from Stockton to Darlington, in 1825. This heralded extensive railway building in Britain as well as in Europe and North America, providing a fast and economic means of transport and communication nationally for the first time. After World War II steam was replaced by electric and diesel engines. At the same time the growth in car ownership and air services rapidly destroyed the supremacy of the railways.

rain precipitation in the form of separate drops of water that fall to the Earth's surface from clouds. The drops are formed by the accumulation of droplets that condense from water vapour in the air.

rainbow arch in the sky of the colours of the ◊spectrum formed by the refraction and reflection of the sun's rays through rain or mist.

rainbow alliance term applied from the mid-1980s to a political grouping of disparate elements who come together to further certain causes they have in common. It is typically used with reference to left-of-centre groups, and often encompasses sections of society that traditionally are politically under-represented, such as non-white ethnic groups.

Raine Kathleen 1908– . English poet. Her volumes of poetry include *Stone and Flower* 1943 and *The Lost Country* 1971 and reflect both the Northumberland landscape of her upbringing and the religious feeling which led her to the Roman Catholic Church in 1944.

rainforest dense forest found on or near the ◊equator where the climate is hot and wet. Over half the tropical rainforests are in Central and South America, the rest in SE Asia and Africa. Although covering approximately 8% of the Earth's land surface, they comprise almost half of all growing wood on the planet, and harbour at least two-fifths of the Earth's species (plants and animals). Rainforests are being destroyed at an alarming rate as their valuable timber is harvested and land cleared for agriculture, causing problems of ◊deforestation, soil ◊erosion, and flooding. By the late 1980s about 50% of the world's rainforest has been removed.

Rainier III 1923– . Prince of ◊Monaco from 1949. He was married to the US film actress Grace Kelly.

Rais Gilles de 1404–1440. French marshal who fought alongside Joan of Arc. In 1440 he was hanged for the torture and murder of 140 children, but the court proceedings were irregular. He is the historical basis of the ◊Bluebeard character.

raisin a dried grape; the chief kinds are the common raisin, the sultana or seedless raisin, and the currant. They are produced in the Mediterranean area, California, and Australia.

raison d'être (French) a reason for existence.

Rajasthan state of NW India

railways: chronology

1550s	Tramways – wooden tracks along which trolleys ran – were in use in mines.
1804	Richard Trevithick in England built the first steam locomotive and ran it on the track at the Pen-y-darren ironworks in South Wales.
1825	George Stephenson built the first public railway to carry steam trains – the Stockton and Darlington line.
1829	Stephenson designed his locomotive *Rocket*, which trounced its rivals at the Rainhill trials.
1830	Stephenson completed the Liverpool and Manchester Railway, the first steam passenger line; the first American-built locomotive, *Best Friend of Charleston*, went into service on the South Carolina Railroad.
1835	Germany pioneered steam railways in Europe, using *Der Adler*, a locomotive built by Stephenson.
1863	The Scotsman Robert Fairlie patented a locomotive with pivoting driving bogies, allowing tight curves in the track (this was later applied particularly in the Garratt locomotives); London opened the world's first underground railway.
1869	The first US transcontinental railway was completed at Promontory, Utah, when the Union Pacific and the Central Pacific Railroads met; George Westinghouse (USA) invented the compressed-air brake.
1879	Werner von Siemens demonstrated an electric train in Germany; Volk's Electric Railway along the Brighton seafront was the world's first public electric railway.
1883	Charles Lartique built the first monorail, in Ireland.
1885	The trans-Canada continental railway was completed, from Montreal in the east to Port Moody in British Columbia in the west.
1890	The first electric underground railway opened in London.
1901	The world's most successful monorail, the Wuppertal Schwebebahn, went into service.
1912	The first diesel locomotive took to the rails in Germany.
1926	The British steam locomotive *Mallard* set a steam rail speed record of 201 kph/125 mph.
1941	Swiss Federal Railways introduced a gas-turbine locomotive.
1964	Japan National Railways inaugurated the 512 km/320 mi New Tokaido line between Osaka and Tokyo, on which ran the 210 kph/130 mph 'bullet' trains.
1973	British Rail's High Speed Train (HST) set a diesel rail speed record of 229 kph/143 mph.
1979	Japan National Railways' maglev test vehicle ML-500 attained a speed of 517 kph/321 mph.
1981	France's TGV superfast trains began operation between Paris and Lyons, regularly attaining a peak speed of 270 kph/168 mph.
1987	Britian and France began work on the Channel tunnel, a railway link connecting the two countries running beneath the English Channel.

area 342,214 sq km/131,995 sq mi
capital Jaipur
products oilseed, cotton, sugar, asbestos, copper, textiles, cement, glass
population (1981) 34,262,000
language Rajasthani, Hindi
religion Hindu 90%, Muslim 3%
history formed 1948, enlarged 1956.

Rajneesh meditation a form of meditation based on the teachings of the Indian Shree Rajneesh, established in the early 1970s. Until 1989 he called himself *Bhagwan* (Hindi 'God'). His followers, who number about 0.5 million internationally, regard themselves as Sannyas, or Hindu ascetics: they wear orange robes and carry a string of prayer beads. They are not expected to observe any specific prohibitions, but to be guided by their instincts.

Raleigh or *Ralegh*, Walter *c.* 1552–1618. English adventurer, a favourite of Elizabeth I. He made colonizing and exploring voyages to North America 1584–87 and South America 1595 and naval attacks on Spanish ports. He was imprisoned by James I 1603–16 and executed on his return from an unsuccessful final expedition to South America.

RAM (random-access memory) an electronic memory device that can be written to and erased by a computer; a computer's internal memory. RAM comes in the form of ◊integrated circuits (chips). The size of RAM defines a computer's internal memory capacity. A modern microcomputer will have up to 4 Mb (megabytes, or million bytes) of RAM. Unlike ROM (read-only memory), RAM is volatile; it is erased when the machine is switched off.

Rama incarnation of ◊Vishnu, the supreme spirit of Hinduism. He is the hero of the epic poem, the Ramayana, and he is regarded as an example of morality and virtue.

Ramadan the ninth month of the Muslim year. Throughout Ramadan a strict fast is observed during the hours of daylight; Muslims are encouraged to read the whole Koran as a commemoration of the Night of Power, which falls during the month, and is when Muslims believe Muhammad first received his revelations from the angel Gabriel. (See also ◊Muslim Calendar).

Ramakrishna 1834–1886. A teacher and mystic (one dedicated to achieving oneness with or a direct experience of God or some force beyond the normal

rainforest

tropical rainforest habitat

Along the equator rising hot air draws winds in from the north and south. These winds, known as trade winds, are wet and their moisture falls as torrential rain as the air rises. The ensuing hot wet conditions encourage the prolific growth of thousands of plant species, giving rise to the tropical rainforest. The varied and abundant species of plant support many different species of animal. The rain runs off into huge rivers, such as the Amazon, the Zaïre and the Mekong.

The tropical rainforest runs in a belt along the equator, broken only by mountain ranges.

The tallest trees, the emergents, may be 100 m/325 ft high. They have buttresses, or stilt roots, to keep them upright.

The forest floor is a dark place where little grows. When a large tree falls there is a temporary pool of light. Saplings grow rapidly towards the light and quickly take the tree's place. Growth is so vigorous that some plants, epiphytes, grow on the branches of others.

Many of the tree-living animals have forward-pointing eyes, enabling them to judge distances when jumping and climbing; others are gliders, moving rapidly from branch to branch. On the forest floor, pig-size creatures are most common as there is little room between the trunks for larger animals to pass.

There is a continuous canopy of branches, all interlocked and reaching up towards the light.

key
1 flying squirrel
2 spider monkey
3 Wallace's flying frog
4 tapir
5 grey parrot

Alongside rivers the leafy growth comes right down to water level.

Raleigh Portrait of Walter Raleigh by Nicholas Hilliard (c.1585) National Portrait Gallery, London.

world). Ramakrishna claimed that mystical experience was the ultimate aim of religions, and that all religions which led to this goal were equally valid.

Ramayana Sanskrit epic *c.* 300 BC, in which Rama, an incarnation of the god ◊Vishnu and his friend Hanuman (the monkey chieftain) strive to recover Rama's wife, Sita, abducted by demon king Ravana.

Rambert Marie (born Cyvia Rambam) 1888–1982. British ballet dancer and teacher. Born in Warsaw, she was naturalized as a British citizen in 1918. One of the major innovative and influential figures in modern ballet, she was with the Diaghilev ballet 1912–13, opened the Rambert School in 1920, and in 1926 founded the *Ballet Rambert* which she directed (renamed Rambert Dance Company 1987).

Ram Das 1534–1581. Fourth guru (teacher) of Sikhism 1574–81, who founded the Sikh holy city of Amritsar.

Rameau Jean-Philippe 1683–1764. French organist and composer. He wrote an influential *Treatise on Harmony* 1722 and his varied works include keyboard and vocal music and many operas, such as *Castor and Pollux* 1737.

Rameses 11 kings of ancient Egypt, including:

Rameses II King of Egypt *c.* 1304–1236 BC, the son of Seti I. He campaigned successfully against the Hittites, and built two rock temples at ◊Abu Simbel in Upper Egypt.

Rameses III King of Egypt *c.* 1200–1168 BC. He won a naval victory over the Philistines and other peoples, and asserted his suzerainty over Palestine.

Ramilles, Battle of the British commander Marlborough's victory over the French on 23 May 1706, during the War of the ◊Spanish Succession, at a village in Brabant, Belgium, 21 km/13 mi N of Namur.

ram jet a simple kind of ◊jet engine used in some guided missiles. It only comes into operation at high speeds. Then air is 'rammed' into the combustion chamber, into which fuel is sprayed and ignited.

Ram Mohun Roy 1774–1833. Indian religious reformer, founder 1830 of ◊Brahma Samaj, Indian mystic cult.

Ramphal Shridath Surendranath ('Sonny') 1928– . Guyanese politician. He studied at the University of London and Harvard Law School, and was minister of foreign affairs and justice in Guyana 1972–75, and secretary-general of the Commonwealth 1975–90.

Rameses II The temple of Rameses II at Abu Simbel, showing the head of a giant statue.

Ramsay Allan 1686–1758. Scottish poet, born in Lanarkshire. He became a wig-maker and then a bookseller in Edinburgh. He published *The Tea-Table Miscellany* 1724–37, and *The Ever Green* 1724, collections of ancient and modern Scottish song including revivals of the work of such poets as ◊Dunbar and ◊Henryson.

Ramsay Allan 1713–1784. Scottish portrait painter. After studying in Edinburgh and Italy, he established himself as a successful portraitist in London, and became painter to George III in 1760. He was the son of the poet Allan Ramsay.

Ramsay William 1852–1916. Scottish chemist who, with Lord Rayleigh, discovered argon in 1894. In 1895 Ramsay manufactured helium, and in 1898, in cooperation with Morris Travers, identified neon, krypton, and xenon. With Frederick Soddy, he noted the transmutation of radium into helium in 1903, which led to the discovery of the density and atomic weight of radium.

rangefinder instrument for determining the range or distance of an object from the observer; used to focus a camera or to sight a gun accurately.

Rangoon former name (until 1989) of ◊Yangon, capital of Myanmar (Burma).

Ranjit Singh 1780–1839. Indian maharajah. He succeeded his father as a minor Sikh leader in 1792, and created a Sikh army that conquered Kashmir and the Punjab. In alliance with the British, he established himself as 'Lion of the Punjab', ruler of the strongest of the independent Indian states.

Ranke Leopold von 1795–1886. German historian whose quest for objectivity and attempts to explain 'how it really was' dominated historical thought beyond 1914. *Weltgeschichte/World History* (nine vols, 1881–88) exemplified his ideas.

Ransome Arthur 1884–1967. English writer. Once a journalist – he was correspondent in Russia for the *Daily News* during World War I and the Revolution – he is best known for his adventure stories for

Raphael An Allegory 'Vision of a Knight' *(c. 1504)* National Gallery, London.

children, such as *Swallows and Amazons* 1930 and *Peter Duck* 1932.

Ransome Robert 1753–1830. British ironfounder and agricultural engineer whose business, based in Ipswich, England, from 1789, earned a worldwide reputation in the 19th and 20th centuries.

Rao Raja 1909– . Indian writer, born at Hassan, Karnataka. He studied at Montpellier and the Sorbonne in France. He wrote about Indian independence from the perspective of a village in S India in *Kanthapura* 1938 and later, in *The Serpent and the Rope* 1960, about a young cosmopolitan intellectual seeking enlightenment.

Rapa Nui another name for ◊Easter Island, an island in the Pacific.

rape sexual intercourse with a woman without her consent. From 1976 in Britain the victim's name may not be published, her sex history should not be in question, and her 'absence of consent' rather than (as previously required) proof of her 'resistance to violence' is the criterion of the crime. The anonymity of the accused is also preserved unless he is convicted. In 1985, there were 22,900 reported cases of sexual assault in the UK. However, since victims are often unwilling to report what has happened, it is thought that there are perhaps some 10 times as many rapes as the reported figure.

rape in botany, two plant species of the mustard family, *Brassica rapa* and *Brassica napus*, grown for their seeds which yield a pungent edible oil. The *common turnip* is a variety of the former, and the *swede turnip* of the latter.

Raphael (Raffaello Sanzio) 1483–1520. Italian painter, one of the greatest of the High Renaissance, active in Perugia, Florence, and Rome (from 1508), where he painted frescoes in the Vatican and for secular patrons. His religious and mythological scenes are noted for harmonious composition; his portraits enhance his sitter's character and express dignity. Many of his designs were engraved, and his influence was soon widespread.

Rapid Deployment Force a military strike force established by the USA in 1979 (following the Iran and Afghan crises); headquarters Fort McDill, Tampa, Florida. It was extended by President Reagan in 1981 and from 1983, as the *US Central Command*, its potential operation area covers: Afghanistan, Arabia, Egypt, Ethiopia, Iran, Iraq, Jordan, Kenya, Pakistan, Somalia, Sudan, the Red Sea and Persian Gulf.

rap music a rapid, rhythmic chant over a prerecorded backing track. Rap emerged in New York in 1979 as part of the ◊hip-hop culture, although the usually macho, swaggering lyrics have roots in the Afro-American tradition of ritual boasts and insults. 'The Message' by Grandmaster Flash and the Furious Five 1982 expanded the content, and women rappers (Salt 'n' Pepa, the Cookie Crew, and others) have countered the sexism.

rare earth oxide of elements of the lanthanide series. They are found only in certain rare minerals. The term is sometimes also used for the lanthanide elements themselves.

rare gas another name for inert gas.

Rashdun the 'rightly guided ones', the first four caliphs (heads) of Islam: Abu Bakr, Umar, Uthman, and Ali.

raspberry prickly cane-plant *Rubus idaeus* of the Rosaceae family, with white flowers followed by red fruits. These are eaten fresh and used for jam and wine.

Rasputin Gregory Efimovich 1871–1916. Siberian wandering 'holy man', the illiterate son of a peasant. He acquired great influence over the tsarina, wife of ◊Nicholas II, because of her faith in his power to cure her son of his haemophilia. The control he exercised through the tsarina over political and ecclesiastical appointments, and his notorious debauchery (the nickname Rasputin means 'dissolute'), created a scandal which did much to discredit the monarchy. He was murdered by a group of nobles, who (when poison had no effect) dumped him in the river Neva after shooting him.

Rastafarianism religion originating in the West Indies, based on the ideas of Marcus ◊Garvey, who preached that the only way for black people to escape their poverty and oppression was to return to Africa. When Haile Selassie (*Ras Tafari*, the Lion of Judah) was crowned emperor of Ethiopia in 1930, this was seen as a fulfilment of prophecy, and Rastafarians acknowledged him as the Messiah, the incarnation of God (*Jah*). The use of ganja (marijuana) is a sacrament. There are no churches. There are currently about 1 million Rastafarians.

rat various large rodents, particularly the larger members of the family Muridae. They usually have pointed snouts and scaly tails. In urban environments rats are regarded as vermin. The brown rat *Rattus norvegicus* is now found worldwide.

rates in the UK, tax formerly levied on residential, industrial and commercial property by local authorities to cover their expenditure. (See ◊county council, ◊local government.) The ◊Thatcher government curbed high-spending councils by cutting the government supplementary grant aid to them and limiting the level of rate that could be levied (*ratecapping*), and replaced rates with a *community charge* or ◊poll tax on each individual (introduced in Scotland 1989 and England in 1990).

rate support grant an amount of money made available annually by central government in Britain to supplement rates as a source of income for local government. Introduced in 1967, it consists of a resources element, giving help to local authorities with small resources; a needs element, based on population size; and a domestic element, to reimburse local authorities for rate reductions for domestic ratepayers. Under the Conservative government 1979– , the system has been used as a method of curbing local authority spending by reducing or withholding the grant.

rattlesnake

*diamond backed
rattle snake*

Rathenau Walther 1867–1922. German Democrat politician. A leading industrialist, he was appointed economic director during World War I and developed a system of economic planning in combination with capitalism. After the war he founded the Democratic Party, and became foreign minister 1922. He signed the Rapallo Treaty of friendship with the USSR in 1922, and soon after was murdered by right-wing fanatics.

rationalism in theology, the belief that human reason rather than divine revelation is the correct means of ascertaining truth and regulating behaviour. In philosophy, rationalism takes the view that self-evident propositions deduced by reason are the sole basis of all knowledge (disregarding experience of the senses). It is usually contrasted with empiricism, which argues that all knowledge must ultimately be derived from the senses.

rationalized units units for which the defining equations conform to the geometry of the system. Equations involving circular symmetry contain the factor 2π; those involving spherical symmetry 4π. ◊SI units are rationalized, ◊c.g.s. units are not.

rational number in mathematics, any number that can be expressed as an exact fraction (with a denominator not equal to 0), that is, as $a \div b$ where a, b are integers. For example 2, $\frac{1}{4}$, $\frac{15}{4}$, $-\frac{3}{5}$ are all rational numbers, whereas π (= 3.141592 …) is not. Numbers such as π are called ◊irrational numbers.

rattle bird with a breastbone without the keel to which flight muscles are attached, for example, ostrich, rhea, emu, cassowary, and kiwi.

rat-tail type of fish, also known as **grenadier**, of the family Macrouridae. They have stout heads and bodies, and long tapering tails. They are common in deep oceanic waters on the continental slopes. Some species have a light-emitting organ in front of the anus.

Rattigan Terence 1911–1977. English naturalistic playwright, who portrayed the middle classes. His work ranged from the comedy *French Without Tears* 1936 to the psychological intensity of *The Winslow Boy* 1945. Other plays include *The Browning Version* 1948, *Separate Tables* 1954, and *Ross* 1960, based on T E ◊Lawrence.

rattlesnake snake of the North American genus *Crotalus*, and related genera, distinguished by the horny flat rings of the tail, which rattle when vibrated as a warning to attackers. They can grow to 2.5 m/8 ft long. The venom injected by some rattlesnakes can be fatal.

Ratushinskaya Irina 1954– . Soviet dissident poet. Sentenced 1983 to seven years in a labour camp, plus five years' internal exile, for criticism of the Soviet regime, she was released 1986. Her strongly Christian work includes *Grey is the Colour of Hope* 1988.

Rau Johannes 1931– . German socialist politician, member of the Social Democratic Party (SPD). In 1987 he stood for the chancellorship of W Germany but lost to the incumbent conservative coalition.

Raunkiaer system of classification a scheme devised by the Danish ecologist Christen Raunkiaer (1860–1938) whereby plants are divided into groups according to the position of their ◊perennating buds in relation to the soil surface. For example, plants in cold areas, such as the tundra, generally have their buds protected below ground, whereas in hot, tropical areas they are above ground and freely exposed. This method of plant classification is useful for comparing vegetation types in different parts of the world.

Rauschenberg Robert 1925– . US pop artist, a creator of happenings (art in live performance), incongruous multimedia works such as *Monogram* 1959 (Modern Muséet, Stockholm), a car tyre around the body of a stuffed goat daubed with paint.

Ravana in the Hindu epic *Rāmāyana*, the demon king of Lankā (Sri Lanka) who abducted Sita, the wife of Rama.

Ravel (Joseph) Maurice 1875–1937. French composer. His work is noted for its sensuousness, unresolved dissonances, and 'tone colour', as in the piano pieces *Pavane pour une infante défunte* 1899 and *Jeux d'eau* 1901, and the ballets *Daphnis et Chloë* 1912 and *Boléro* 1928.

raven bird *Corvus corax* of the crow family. It is about 60 cm/2ft long, and has black, lustrous plumage. It is a scavenger, found only in the northern hemisphere.

Raven, The one of the most famous of US poems, written 1845 by Edgar Allan Poe, about a bereaved poet haunted by a raven which sonorously warns 'Nevermore'.

Rawalpindi city in Punjab province, Pakistan, in the foothills of the Himalayas; population (1981) 928,400. Industries include oil refining, iron, chemicals, and furniture.

Rawlinson Henry Creswicke 1810–1895. English orientalist, political agent in Baghdad in the Ottoman Empire from 1844. He deciphered the Babylonian and Old Persian scripts of ◊Darius I's trilingual inscription at Behistun, Persia, continued the excavation work of A H Layard, and published a *History of Assyria* 1852.

Ray John 1627–1705. English naturalist who devised a classification system accounting for nearly 18,000 plant species. It was the first to divide flowering plants into ◊monocotyledons and ◊dicotyledons, with additional divisions made on the basis of leaf and flower characters and fruit types.

Ray Man. Adopted name of Emmanuel Rudnitsky 1890–1976. US photographer, painter, and sculptor, who lived most of his life in France; associated with the Dada movement. He is known for Surrealist images like the photograph *Le Violon d'Ingres* 1924.

Ray Satyajit 1921–1992. Indian film director, noted for his trilogy of life in his native Bengal: *Pather Panchali, Unvanquished*, and *The World of Apu* 1955–59. Later films include *The Chess Players* 1977 and *The Home and the World* 1984.

Raynaud's disease a condition in which the blood supply to the extremities is reduced by periodic spasm of the blood vessels on exposure to cold. It is most often seen in young women.

rayon artificial silk made from ◊cellulose. The most common type is ◊viscose, which consists of regenerated filaments of pure cellulose. Acetate and triacetate are kinds of rayon consisting of filaments of cellulose acetate and triacetate.

razorbill N Atlantic seabird *Alca torda*, of the auk family, which breeds on cliffs, and migrates to the Mediterranean in winter. It has a curved beak, and is black above and white below. It uses its wings as paddles when diving.

razorshell or *razor-fish*. Genera *Ensis* and *Solen* of bivalve molluscs, with narrow elongated shells, resembling an old-fashioned razor handle and delicately coloured. They are found in sand among rocks.

re abbreviation for Latin 'with regard to'.

reaction principle principle first stated by ◊Newton as his third law of motion: to every action, there is an equal and opposite reaction.

Reader's Digest world's best-selling magazine, founded 1922 in the USA to publish condensed articles and books, usually of an uplifting and often conservative kind, along with in-house features. It has editions in many different languages.

Reagan Ronald 1911– . US Republican politician, governor of California 1966–74, president 1981–89. A former Hollywood actor, Reagan was a popular president, who introduced deregulation of domestic markets and tax reform, and withstood criticism of his interventionist foreign policy, but failed to confront a mounting trade deficit. He was succeeded by George ◊Bush.

realism in the arts, a style of depicting life as we know it in everyday experience, as opposed to romanticism (an idealized portrayal), or to abstract or formalized representation. In medieval philosophy, it is the theory that 'universals' have existence, not simply as names for entities, but entities in their own right. It is thus opposed to nominalism. In contemporary philosophy, the term stands for the doctrine that there is an intuitively appreciated reality apart from what is presented to the consciousness. It is opposed to idealism.

real number in mathematics, any ◊rational (which include the integers) or ◊irrational number. Real numbers exclude ◊imaginary numbers, found in ◊complex numbers of the general form $a + bi$ where $i = \sqrt{-1}$, although these do include a real component a.

Realpolitik (German 'politics of realism') term coined in 1853 to describe ◊Bismarck's policies during the 1848 revolutions: the pragmatic pursuit of self-interest and power, backed up by force when necessary.

real tennis racket and ball game played in France, from about the 12th century, over a central net in an indoor court, but with a sloping roof let into each end and one side of the court, against which the ball may be hit. The term real in this sense means 'royal', not 'genuine'. Basic scoring is as for 'lawn' ◊tennis, but with various modifications.

real-time system in computing and information technology, a program that responds to events in the world as they happen, as, for example, an automatic pilot program in an aircraft must respond instantly to correct course deviations. Programs in process control, robotics, airline reservation, games, and many military applications are all dependent on a real-time system.

recall a process by which voters can demand the dismissal from office of elected officials, as in some states of the USA.

receiver in law, a person appointed by a court to collect and manage the assets of an individual, company, or partnership in serious financial difficulties. In the case of bankruptcy, the assets may be sold and distributed by a receiver to creditors.

receptacle the enlarged end of a flower stalk to which the floral parts are attached. Normally the receptacle is rounded but in some plants it is flattened or cup-shaped. The term is also used for the region on that part of some seaweeds that becomes swollen at certain times of the year and bears the reproductive organs.

recession in economics, a fall in business activity lasting more than a few months, causing stagnation in a country's output. A serious recession is called a *slump*.

recessivity in genetics, in a ◊diploid organism, a recessive allele (alternative form of a given gene) is one that can only produce a detectable effect on the organism bearing it when both chromosomes carry it, that is, when the same allele has been inherited from both parents. The individual is then said to be homozygous. In a heterozygous individual, the effect of a recessive allele will be masked by a dominant allele (see ◊dominance).

recherché (French 'sought after') rare.

Recife industrial seaport (cotton textiles, sugar refining, fruit canning, flour milling) and naval base in Brazil, capital of Pernambuco state, at the mouth of the river Capibaribe; population (1980) 1,184,215. It was founded 1504.

reciprocal in mathematics, of a quantity, that quantity divided into 1. Thus the reciprocal of 2 is $\frac{1}{2}$ (= 0.5); of $\frac{2}{3}$ is $\frac{3}{2}$; of x^2 is $\frac{1}{x^2}$ or x^{-2}.

recitative speech-like declamation of narrative episodes in opera.

recombination in genetics, any process which recombines or 'shuffles' the genetic material, so increasing genetic variation in the offspring. The two main processes of recombination are ◊*crossing over* (in which chromosome pairs exchange segments), and the random reassortment of the chromosomes that occurs during ◊*meiosis*, when each gamete (sperm or egg) receives only one of each chromosome pair.

Reconquista (Spanish 'reconquest') the Christian defeat of the Muslims 9th–15th centuries, and their expulsion from Spain.

Reconstruction in US history, the period 1865–77 after the Civil War during which the nation was reunited under the federal government after the defeat of the Southern Confederacy.

recorder in the English legal system, a part-time judge who usually sits in the ◊crown courts in less serious cases but may also sit in the county courts or the High Court. They are chosen from barristers of standing and also, since the Courts Act of 1971, from solicitors. Recorders may eventually become circuit judges.

recorder in music, an instrument of the ◊woodwind family, blown through one end, in which different notes are obtained by covering the holes in the instrument. A concert instrument until about the 18th century, when it was largely replaced by the flute, it was revived in the 20th century for teaching children and for performing early music.

Record Office, Public a government office containing the English national records since the Norman Conquest, brought together from courts of law and government departments, including the Domesday Book, the Gunpowder Plot papers, and the log of HMS *Victory* at Trafalgar. It was established in 1838 in Chancery Lane, London; modern records from the 18th century on have been housed at Kew from 1976.

record player device for reproducing sound recorded, usually in a spiral groove on a disc or record. A motor-driven turntable rotates the record at a constant speed, and a stylus or needle on the head of a pick-up is made to vibrate by the undulations in the record groove. These vibrations are then converted to electrical signals by a ◊transducer in the head (often a ◊piezoelectric crystal). After amplification, the signals pass to one or more loud-speakers which convert them into sound.

rectangle a quadrilateral (four-sided figure) with opposite sides equal and parallel, and with each interior angle a right angle (90°). Its area A is the product of the length l and breadth b; that is, $A = l \times b$. A rectangle with all four sides equal is a ◊square.

rectifier device which is necessary for obtaining one-directional current (DC) from an alternating source of supply (AC). Types include plate recti-fiers, thermionic ◊diodes, and ◊semiconductor diodes.

rector Anglican priest, formerly entitled to the whole of the ◊tithes levied in the parish, as against a *vicar* (Latin 'deputy') who was only entitled to part.

recycling the processing of industrial and house-hold waste (such as paper, glass, and some metals) so that it can be re-used, thus reducing pollution, saving expenditure on scarce raw materials, and slowing down the depletion of non-renewable re-sources. Also, the investment by oil-producing nations of surplus funds in the industries of oil-importing nations, so rectifying the shortfall in their profit-and-loss accounts.

red informal term for a leftist, revolutionary, or communist, which originated in the 19th century in the term 'red republican', meaning a republican who favoured a social as well as a political revolution, generally by armed violence. Red is the colour adopted by socialist parties.

Red Army former name of the army of the USSR. It developed from the Red Guards, volunteers who carried out the Bolshevik revolution, and received its name because it fought under the red flag. It was officially renamed the *Soviet Army* 1946. The Chinese revolutionary army was also called the Red Army.

Red Brigades extreme left-wing guerrilla groups active in Italy during the 1970s and early 1980s. They were implicated in many kidnappings and killings, including that of Christian Democrat leader Aldo Moro 1978.

Red Cross, the international relief agency founded by the Geneva Convention 1864 at the instigation of the Swiss doctor Henri Dunant (1828–1910) to assist the wounded and prisoners in war. Its symbol is a symmetrical red cross on a white ground. In addition to dealing with associated problems of war, such as refugees and the care of the disabled, the Red Cross is increasingly concerned with victims of natural disasters – floods, earthquakes, epidemics, and accidents.

redcurrant in botany, a type of ◊currant.

Redding Otis 1941–1967. US soul singer and song-writer. He had a number of hits in the mid-1960s such as 'My Girl' 1965, but was perhaps at his best in live performance (as in 'Respect', recorded at the Monterey Pop Festival in 1967). His biggest hit, '(Sittin' on the) Dock of the Bay' 1968, was released after his death in a plane crash.

red dwarf star that is cool, faint, and small (about ¹⁄₁₀ the mass and diameter of the Sun). They burn slowly, and have estimated lifetimes of 100 billion years. Red dwarfs may be the most abundant type of star, but are difficult to see because they are so faint. Two of the closest stars to the Sun,

red-hot poker

Proxima Centauri and ◊Barnard's Star, are red dwarfs.

red flag the international symbol of socialism. In France it was used as a revolutionary emblem from 1792 onward, and was adopted officially as its flag by the Paris Commune 1871. Since the Nov 1917 revo-lution, it has been the national flag of the USSR; as such it bears a golden hammer and sickle crossed, symbolizing the unity of the industrial workers and peasants, under a gold-rimmed five-pointed star, signifying peace between the five continents. The British Labour Party anthem called 'The Red Flag', was written 1889 by Jim ◊Connell.

red giant a large bright star, with a cool surface. It is thought to represent a late stage in the evolution of a star like the Sun, as it runs out of hydrogen fuel at its centre. Red giants have diameters between 10 and 100 times that of the Sun. They are very bright because they are so large, although their surface temperature is lower than that of the Sun, about 2,000–3,000K.

Redgrave Michael 1908–1985. English actor. His roles included Hamlet, Lear, Uncle Vanya, and the schoolmaster in *The Browning Version*.

Redgrave Vanessa 1937– . English actress. Daughter of Michael Redgrave, her roles include Shakespeare's Lady Macbeth and Cleopatra, and the title-part in the film *Julia* 1976 (Academy Award). She is active in left-wing politics.

Red Guards armed workers who took part in the ◊Russian Revolution of 1917. The name was also given to the school and college students, wearing red armbands, active in the Cultural Revolution in ◊China 1966–68.

red-hot poker plant of the African genus *Kniphofia*, family Liliaceae, in particular *Kniphofia uvaria*, with a flame-red spike of flowers.

Redmond John Edward 1856–1918. Irish politician, Parnell's successor as leader of the Nationalist Party 1890–1916. The 1910 elections saw him holding the balance of power in the House of Commons, and he secured the introduction of a ◊Home Rule bill, hotly opposed by Protestant Ulster.

Redon Odilon 1840–1916. French Symbolist painter, known for his use of fantastic symbols and images, sometimes mythological. From the 1890s he also produced still lifes and landscapes. His work was much admired by the Surrealists.

Redouté Pierre Joseph 1759–1840. French flower painter patronized by Empress Josephine and the

Bourbon court. He taught flower drawing at the Museum of Natural History in Paris and produced volumes of delicate, highly detailed flowers, notably *Les Roses* 1817–24.

Red Scare, the in US history, a campaign against radicals and dissenters that took place in the aftermath of World War I and the Russian revolution, and during a period of labour disorders and violence in the US. Mainly middle-class and urban-based, progressives secured legislation at national, state, and local levels to improve the democratic system, working conditions, and welfare provision.

Red Sea submerged section of the Great Rift Valley (2,000 km/1,200 mi long and up to 320 km/200 mi wide). Egypt, Sudan, and Ethiopia (in Africa) and Saudi Arabia (Asia) are on its shores.

redshank wading bird *Tringa totanus* of N Europe and Asia, a type of sandpiper. It nests in swampy areas, although most winter in the south. It is greyish and speckled black, and has long red legs.

red shift in astronomy, the lengthening of the wavelengths of light from an object as a result of the object's motion away from us. It is an example of the ◊Doppler effect. The red shift in light from galaxies is evidence that the Universe is expanding.

redstart bird of the genus Phoenicurus. A member of the thrush family, it winters in Africa and spends the summer in Eurasia. The male has a dark grey head (with white mark on the forehead and black face) and back, brown wings with lighter underparts, and a red tail.

red tape a derogatory term for bureaucratic methods, derived from the fastening for departmental bundles of documents in Britain.

red terror term used by opponents to describe the Bolshevik seizure and retention of power in Russia after Oct 1917.

redundancy rights in British law, the rights of employees to a payment (linked to the length of their employment) if they lose their jobs because they are no longer needed. The statutory right was introduced in 1965, but payments are often made in excess of the statutory scheme.

redwing type of thrush *Turdus iliacus*, smaller than the song thrush, with reddish wing and body markings. It breeds in the north of Europe and Asia, flying south in winter.

redwood giant coniferous tree. See ◊sequoia.

reed various perennial aquatic grasses, in particular several species of the genus *Phragmites*; also the stalk of any of these plants. The common reed *Phragmites australis* attains 3 m/10 ft, having stiff, erect leaves, and straight stems bearing a plume of purplish flowers.

Reed Lou 1942– . US rock singer, songwriter, and former member (1965–70) of the seminal New York garage band *Velvet Underground*. His solo work deals largely with urban alienation and angst, and includes the albums *Berlin* 1973, *Street Hassle* 1978, and *New York* 1989.

reeve in Anglo-Saxon England, an official charged with the administration of a shire or burgh, fulfilling similar functions to the later sheriff. After the Norman Conquest, the term tended to be restricted to the person elected by the villeins to oversee the work of the manor and to communicate with the manorial lord.

Reeves William Pember 1857–1932. New Zealand politician and writer. He was New Zealand minister of education 1891–96, and director of the London School of Economics 1908–19. He wrote poetry and the classic description of New Zealand, *Long White Cloud* 1898.

referee an arbitrator. The term is most commonly used of the official in charge of a game, such as football, but may also be applied in law to members of the court of referees appointed by the House of Commons to give judgment on petitions against private bills, and to the three official referees to whom cases before the high court may be submitted.

referendum the procedure whereby a decision on proposed legislation is referred to the electorate for settlement by direct vote of all the people. It is most frequently employed in Switzerland, but has also been used in Australia, New Zealand, Québec, and certain states of the USA. It was used in the UK for the first time in 1975 on the Common Market issue.

refining a process that purifies or converts something into a more useful form. Metals usually need refining after they have been extracted from their ores by such processes as ◊smelting. Petroleum, or crude oil, needs refining before it can be used; the process involves ◊fractionation: splitting up the substance into separate components.

reflection deflection of waves, such as ◊light or ◊sound waves, when they hit a surface. The *law of reflection* states that the angle of incidence (the angle between the ray and a perpendicular line drawn to the surface) is equal to the angle of reflection (the angle between the reflected ray and a perpendicular to the surface).

red shift

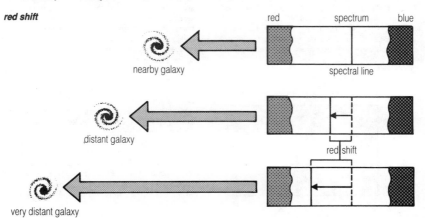

red   spectrum   blue

nearby galaxy   spectral line

distant galaxy   red shift

very distant galaxy

reflection

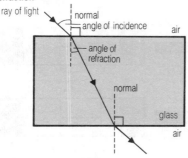

approaching or incident ray

angle of incidence   normal (at right angles to surface)
angle of reflection

reflected ray

mirror

refrigeration

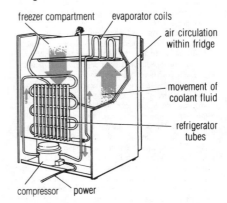

freezer compartment   evaporator coils

air circulation within fridge

movement of coolant fluid

refrigerator tubes

compressor   power

reflex an automatic response to a particular stimulus, controlled by the ◊nervous system. The receptor (for example, a sense organ) and the effector (such as a muscle) are linked directly (via the spinal ganglia or the lower brain, in vertebrates), making responses to stimuli very rapid. Reflex actions are more common in simple animals.

reflex camera a camera that uses a mirror and prisms to reflect light passing through the lens into the viewfinder, showing the photographer the exact scene which is being shot. When the shutter button is released the mirror springs out of the way, allowing light to reach the film. The commonest type is the single-lens reflex (SLR) camera. The twin-lens reflex (TLR) camera has two lenses; one has a mirror for viewing, the other is used for exposing the film.

Reformation movement in Christianity (anticipated from the 12th century by the Waldenses, Lollards, and Hussites) to reform the Catholic Church. It became effective in the 16th century when the absolute monarchies gave it support by challenging the political power of the papacy and confiscating church wealth.

refraction in physics, the bending of ◊light when it passes from one medium to another. Refraction occurs because light travels at different velocities depending on the medium. The *refractive index* is the measure of the extent to which a ray of light is bent as it passes from one transparent medium to another.

refractory in technology, a material that resists high temperature, including ◊ceramics made from clay, minerals, or other earthy materials. Furnaces are lined with silica and dolomite. Alumina (aluminium oxide) is an excellent refractory, often used for

refraction

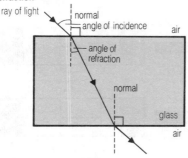

ray of light

normal
angle of incidence
air

angle of refraction

normal

glass

air

the bodies of spark plugs. Titanium and tungsten are often called refractory metals because they are temperature resistant. ◊Cermets are refractory materials made up of ceramics and metals.

refrigeration the process of absorbing heat at a low temperature and rejecting it at a higher temperature. *Refrigerators* are used in the food industry for preserving foodstuffs by chilling or freezing. The storage time that can be tolerated varies with the nature of the foodstuff and, in general, increases as the storage temperature is lowered. Refrigeration is also used in industrial processes and in air-conditioning.

refugee in general, a person fleeing from a problem, especially political persecution or war. At present there are an estimated 14 to 18 million refugees worldwide, whose resettlement and welfare are the responsibility of the United Nations.

regalia or *crown jewels* symbols of royal authority. The British set (except for the Ampulla and the Anointing Spoon) were broken up at the time of ◊Cromwell, and now date from the ◊Restoration. In 1671 Colonel ◊Blood attempted to steal them, but was captured, then pardoned and pensioned by Charles II. They are kept in the Tower of London in the Crown Jewel House (1967).

Regan Donald 1918– . US Republican political adviser to Ronald ◊Reagan. He was secretary of the Treasury 1981–85, and chief of White House staff 1985–87, when he was forced to resign because of complicity in ◊Irangate. He subsequently revealed that Reagan consulted an astrologer concerning decisions of state, and that Nancy Reagan exerted considerable influence over the president's decisions.

regelation phenomenon in which water re-freezes to ice after it has been melted by pressure, at a temperature below the freezing point of water. Pressure makes an ice skate, for example, form a film of water which re-forms ice after the skater has passed.

Regency in Britain, the years 1811–20 during which ◊George IV (then Prince of Wales) acted as regent for his father ◊George III.

Regency style style of architecture popular in England during the late 18th and early 19th century. The style is characterized by its restrained simplicity, and its imitation of ancient classical architecture, especially Greek. Architects of this period include Henry Holland (1746–1806), John ◊Nash, and Decimus Burton (1800–81).

regeneration in biology, the regrowth of a new organ or tissue after the loss or removal of the original. It is common in plants, where a new individual can often be produced from a 'cutting' of the original. In animals, regeneration of major organs is limited to 'lower' organisms; certain lizards can regrow their tails if these are lost, and new flatworms can grow from a tiny fragment of an old one. In mammals, regeneration is limited to the repair of tissue in wound-healing, and the regrowth of peripheral nerves following damage.

regent person discharging the royal functions during a sovereign's minority or incapacity, or during a lengthy absence from the country. In England since the time of Henry VIII, Parliament has always appointed a regent or council of regency when necessary.

Reger (Johann Baptist Joseph) Max(imilian) 1873–1916. German composer and pianist. He taught at Munich 1905–07, was professor at the Leipzig Conservatoire from 1907, and conductor of the Meiningen ducal orchestra 1911–14. His works include organ and piano music, chamber music, and songs.

reggae the predominant form of West Indian popular music of the 1970s and 1980s, characterized by a heavily accented onbeat. The lyrics often refer to Rastafarianism. Musicians include Bob Marley (1945–81), Lee 'Scratch' Perry (1940–) (performer and producer), and the group Black Uhuru 1974– .

Regina industrial city (oil refining, cement, steel, farm machinery, fertilizers), capital of Saskatchewan, Canada; population (1986) 175,000.

Regional Crime Squad in the UK, a local police force that deals with serious crime; see under ◊Scotland Yard, New.

register in computing, a location for storing data, program instructions, and intermediate results in a computer's central processing unit (CPU). A microcomputer will typically have only a few registers, a mainframe computer many thousands.

Rehoboam king of Judah *c.* 932–915 BC, son of Solomon. Under his rule the Jewish nation split into the two kingdoms of *Israel* and *Judah*: ten of the tribes revolted against him and took Jeroboam as their ruler, leaving him only the tribes of Judah and Benjamin.

Reich (German 'empire') the First Reich was the Holy Roman Empire 962–1806, the Second Reich the German Empire 1871–1918, and the ◊Third Reich Nazi Germany 1933–45.

Reich Wilhelm 1897–1957. Austrian doctor, who combined ◊Marxism and ◊psychoanalysis to advocate sexual freedom, for example in *Die Sexuelle Revolution/The Sexual Revolution* 1936–45, and *Die Funktion des Orgasmus/The Function of the Orgasm* 1948.

Reichstadt, Duke of another name of ◊Napoleon II, son of Napoleon I.

Reichstag German parliament building and lower legislative house during the German Empire 1871–1918 and Weimar Republic 1919–33.

Reichstag Fire the burning of the German parliament building in Berlin 27 Feb 1933, less than a month after the Nazi leader Hitler had become chancellor. The fire was used as a justification for the suspension of many constitutional guarantees, and also as an excuse to attack the communists. There is still debate over Nazi involvement in the crime, not least because they were the main beneficiaries.

Reign of Terror the period of the ◊French Revolution when the Jacobins were in power (Oct 1793–Jul 1794) under Robespierre and instituted mass persecution of their opponents. About 1,400 were executed.

Reims (English *Rheims*) capital of Champagne-Ardenne region, France; population (1982) 199,000. It is the centre of the champagne industry, and has textile industries. It was known in Roman times as *Durocorturum*. From 987 all but six French kings were crowned here. Ceded to England 1420 under the Treaty of Troyes, it was retaken by Joan of Arc, who had Charles VII consecrated in the 13th-century cathedral.

reincarnation the belief that the human soul or the spirit of a plant or animal after death may enter another human body or that of an animal. It is part of the teachings of many religions and philosophies, for example, Egyptian religion, Greek philosophy, Buddhism, Hinduism, Jainism, the philosophies of Pythagoras and Plato, certain Christian heresies (for example, ◊Cathars), and theosophy. It is also referred to as *transmigration* or metempsychosis.

reindeer (North American *caribou*) deer *Rangifer tarandus* of arctic and subarctic regions, common to both eastern and western hemispheres. About 120 cm/4 ft at the shoulder, it has a thick, brownish coat and broad hoofs well adapted to travel over snow. It is the only deer in which both sexes have antlers; up to 150 cm/5 ft long, they are shed in winter.

Reinhardt 'Django' (Jean Baptiste) 1910–1953. Belgian jazz guitarist and composer, who was co-leader, with Stephane Grappelli, of Quintet de Hot Club de France 1934–1939.

Reinhardt Max 1873–1943. Austrian producer and director, who helped to develop German theatre and film during the 1920s and 1930s through an expressionistic style. Directors, such as Murnau, Leni, and Lubitsch, and actors such as Veidt, Jannings, and Dietrich worked with him. He co-directed the US film *A Midsummer Night's Dream* 1935.

relative atomic mass or *atomic weight* the mass of an atom. It depends on the number of protons and neutrons in the atom, the electrons having negligible mass. It is calculated relative to one twelfth the mass of an atom of carbon-12. If more than one ◊isotope of the element is present, the relative atomic mass is calculated taking an average which takes account of the relative proportions of each isotope, resulting in values which are not whole numbers.

relative density or *specific gravity* in physics, the density (at 20°C) of a solid or liquid relative to (divided by) the maximum density of water (at

reindeer

Rembrandt (left) *Self-portrait*, an etching dated 1639; London. (right) *Girl Leaning on a Windowsill* (1645) Dulwich Picture Gallery, London.

4°C). The relative density of a gas is its density divided by the density of hydrogen (or sometimes dry air) at the same temperature and pressure.

relative humidity in physics, the concentration of water vapour in the air. It is expressed as a percentage of its moisture content to the moisture content of the air if it were saturated with water at the same temperature and pressure. The higher the temperature the more water vapour the air can hold.

relative molecular mass or *molecular weight* the mass of a molecule, calculated relative to one twelfth the mass of an atom of carbon-12. It is found by adding the relative atomic masses of the atoms which make up the molecule.

relativity two theories propounded by Albert ◊Einstein concerning the nature of space and time.

special theory (1905) starting with the premises that (1) the laws of nature are the same for all observers in unaccelerated motion, and (2) the speed of light is independent of the motion of its source, Einstein postulated that the time interval between two events was longer for an observer in whose frame of reference the events occur in different places than for the observer for whom they occur at the same place.

general theory of relativity (1915) the geometrical properties of space-time were to be conceived as modified locally by the presence of a body with mass. A planet's orbit around the Sun (as observed in three-dimensional space) arises from its natural trajectory in modified space-time; there is no need to invoke, as Newton did, a force of ◊gravity coming from the Sun and acting on the planet. Einstein's theory predicted slight differences in the orbits of the planets from Newton's theory, which were observable in the case of Mercury. The new theory also said light rays should bend when they pass by a massive object, owing to the object's effect on local space-time. The predicted bending of starlight was observed during the eclipse of the Sun 1919, when light from distant stars passing close to the Sun was not masked by sunlight.

relay in physics, an electromagnetic switch. A small current passing through a coil of wire wound round an iron core attracts an ◊armature whose movement closes a pair of sprung contacts to complete a secondary circuit, which can be carrying a large current. The solid-state equivalent is a thyristor switching device.

relic a part of some divine or saintly person, or something closely associated with them. Christian examples include the arm of St Teresa of Avila, the blood of St Januarius, and the ◊True Cross. Buddhist relics include the funeral ashes of the Buddha, placed in a number of stupas or burial mounds.

relief in architecture, a term applied to carved figures and other forms which project from the background. The Italian terms *basso-rilievo* (low relief), *mezzo-rilievo* (middle relief), and *alto-rilievo* (high relief) are used according to the extent to which the sculpture projects. The French term *bas-relief* is commonly used for low relief.

religion code of belief or philosophy which often involves the worship of a ◊god or gods. Belief in a supernatural power is not essential (absent in, for example, Buddhism, Confucianism), but faithful adherence is usually considered to be rewarded, for example by escape from human existence (Buddhism), by a future existence (Christianity, Islam), or by worldly benefit (Sōka Gakkai Buddhism). The word comes from the latin *religare* 'to bind'; perhaps referring to the binding of humans to God. The work of Charles Darwin in natural history and the growth of anthropology stimulated the investigation of religious beliefs, notably by the Sanskrit scholar Max Müller (1823-1900) and the Scottish anthropologists James Frazer and Andrew Lang.

Remarque Erich Maria 1898–1970. German novelist, a soldier in World War I, whose *All Quiet on the Western Front* 1929 led to his being deprived of German nationality. He lived in Switzerland 1929–39, and then in the USA.

Rembrandt Harmensz van Rijn 1606–1669. Dutch painter and etcher, one of the most prolific and influential artists in Europe of the 17th century. Between 1629 and 1669 he painted some 60 penetrating self-portraits. He also painted religious subjects, and produced about 300 etchings and over 1,000 drawings. His group portraits include *The Anatomy Lesson of Dr Tulp* 1632 (Mauritshuis, The Hague) and *The Night Watch* 1642 (Rijksmuseum, Amsterdam).

remedial education special classes, or teaching strategies, which aim to help children with learning difficulties to catch up with children within the normal range of achievement.

religion – festivals

Month	Festival	Religion	Commemorating
Jan 6th	Epiphany	Western Christian	coming of the Magi
6th–7th	Christmas	Orthodox Christian	birth of Christ
18th–19th	Epiphany	Orthodox Christian	coming of the Magi
Jan–Feb	New Year	Chinese	Return of Kitchen God to heaven
Feb–Mar	Shrove Tuesday	Christian	day before Lent
	Ash Wednesday	Christian	first day of Lent
	Purim	Jewish	story of Esther
	Mahashivaratri	Hindu	Siva
Mar–Apr	Palm Sunday	Western Christian	first day of Holy Week
	Good Friday	Western Christian	Crucifixion of Christ
	Easter	Western Christian	Resurrection of Christ
	Passover	Jewish	escape from slavery in Egypt
	Holi	Hindu	Krishna
	Holi Mohalla	Sikh	(coincides with Holi)
	Rama Naumi	Hindu	birth of Rama
	Ching Ming	Chinese	remembrance of dead
Apr 13th	Baisakhi	Sikh	founding of the Khalsa
Apr–May	Easter	Orthodox Christian	Resurrection of Christ
May–Jun	Shavuot	Jewish	giving of Ten Commandments to Moses
	Whitsun	Western Christian	filling of Jesus's followers with Holy Spirit
	Wesak	Buddhist	day of Buddha's birth, enlightenment and death
	Martyrdom of Guru Arjan	Sikh	death of fifth guru of Sikhism
Jun	Dragon Boat Festival	Chinese	Chinese martyr
	Whitsun	Orthodox Christian	filling of Jesus's followers with Holy Spirit
Jul	Dhammacakka	Buddhist	preaching of Buddha's first sermon
Aug	Raksha Bandhan	Hindu	family
Aug–Sept	Janmashtami	Hindu	birthday of Krishna
Sept	Moon Festival	Chinese	Chinese hero
Sept–Oct	Rosh Hashana	Jewish	start of Jewish New Year
	Yom Kippur	Jewish	day of fasting
	Succot	Jewish	Israelites' time in the wilderness
Oct	Dusshera	Hindu	goddess Devi
Oct–Nov	Divali	Hindu	goddeess Lakshmi
	Divali	Sikh	release of Guru Hargobind from prison
Nov	Guru Nanak's Birthday	Sikh	founder of Sikhism
	Advent	Western Christian	preparation for Christmas
Nov–Dec	Bodhi Day	Buddhist (Mahayana)	Buddha's enlightenment
Dec	Hanukkah	Jewish	recapture of Temple of Jerusalem
	Winter Festival	Chinese	time of feasting
25th	Christmas	Western Christian	birth of Christ
Dec–Jan	Birthday of Guru Gobind Singh	Sikh	last (tenth) human guru of Sikhism
	Martyrdom of Guru Tegh Bahadur	Sikh	ninth guru of Sikhism

Remembrance Sunday (known until 1945 as *Armistice Day*) in the UK, national day of remembrance for those killed in both World Wars and later conflicts, on the second Sunday of Nov. In Canada 11 Nov is *Remembrance Day*. The US equivalent is ◊Veterans Day.

Remington Philo 1816–1889. US inventor of the typewriter and breech-loading rifle that bear his name. He began manufacturing typewriters 1873, and made improvements that resulted five years later in the first machine with a shift key, thus providing lower-case letters as well as capital letters. The Remington rifle and carbine, which had a falling block breech and a tubular magazine, were developed in collaboration with his father.

remission temporary disappearance of symptoms during the course of a disease.

remora warmwater fishes which have an adhesive disc on the head, by which they attach themselves to whales, sharks, and turtles, which provide them with shelter, transport, and food in the form of parasites on the host's skin.

remote sensing gathering and recording information from a distance, developed as a result of space technology. Space probes have sent back photographs and data about planets as distant as Uranus. Satellites such as *Landsat* have surveyed all of the Earth's surface from orbit. Computer processing of data obtained by their scanning instruments, and the application of false-colours have made it possible to reveal surface features invisible in ordinary light. This has proved valuable in agriculture, forestry, and urban planning, and has led to the discovery of new deposits of minerals.

Renoir Les Parapluies 'Umbrellas' (1883) National Gallery, London.

REM sleep rapid-eye-movement sleep, a phase of sleep which recurs several times nightly in humans and is associated with dreaming. The eyes flicker quickly beneath closed lids.

Renaissance the period and intellectual movement in European history that is traditionally seen as ending the Middle Ages and beginning modern times. The Renaissance started in Italy in the 14th century, and flourished in W Europe until about the 17th century.

The aim of Renaissance education was to produce the 'complete human being' (**Renaissance man**), conversant in the humanities, mathematics and science (including their application in war), the arts and crafts, and athletics and sport; to enlarge the bounds of learning and geographical knowledge; to encourage the growth of scepticism and free-thought, and the study and imitation of Greek and Latin literature and art. The revival of interest in classical Greek and Roman culture inspired artists such as Leonardo da Vinci, Michelangelo, and Dürer; in literature the Renaissance began with the work of Dante; and scientists and explorers proliferated.

renal pertaining to the kidneys.

Renault Mary. Pen name of Mary Challans 1905–1983. British novelist who recreated the world of ancient Greece, with a trilogy on ◊Theseus, and two volumes on ◊Alexander: *The Persian Boy* 1972 and *The Nature of Alexander* 1975.

Rendell Ruth 1930– . British novelist and short story writer. She is the author of a detective series featuring Chief Inspector Wexford, and her psychological crime novels explore the minds of people who commit murder, often through obsession or social inadequacy, as in *A Demon in my View* 1976 and *Heartstones* 1987.

renewable resource environmental resources that are replaced by natural processes of growth, geology, or climatic change. Renewable resources include solar, wind, wave, and geothermal energy.

Reni Guido 1575–1642. Italian painter, active in Bologna and Rome (*c.* 1600–14), whose work includes the fresco *Phoebus and the Hours Preceded by Aurora* 1613 (Casino Rospigliosi, Rome). His successful workshop in Bologna produced numerous idealized religious images, including Madonnas. He was influenced by Caravaggio and the Carracci family.

Rennes industrial city (oil refining, chemicals, electronics, cars) and capital of Ille-et-Vilaine *département*, W France, at the confluence of the Ille and Vilaine, 56 km/35 mi SE of St Malo; population (1982) 234,000. It was the old capital of Britanny.

Rennie John 1761–1821. Scottish engineer who built the new Waterloo Bridge and old London Bridge (reconstructed in Arizona, USA).

Renoir (Pierre) Auguste 1841–1919. French Impressionist painter. He met Monet and Sisley in the early 1860s and together they formed the nucleus of the Impressionist movement. He developed a lively, colourful painting style with feathery brushwork and painted many voluptuous female nudes, such as *The Bathers c.* 1884–87 (Philadelphia Museum of Art). In his later years, he turned to sculpture.

Renoir Jean 1894–1979. French film director, son of the painter Auguste ◊Renoir, whose films include *La Grande Illusion/Grand Illusion* 1937, and *Règle du Jeu/The Rules of the Game* 1939.

Rentenmark currency introduced in Germany at the end of 1923 by the president of the Reichsbank, Hjalmar Schacht (1877–1970), to replace old Reichsmarks which had been rendered worthless by inflation.

reparation indemnity paid by countries defeated in war, as by Germany in both World Wars.

replication in biology, the production of copies of the genetic material, DNA; it occurs during cell division (◊mitosis and ◊meiosis), and depends for accuracy on the ◊base pair.

repression in psychology, the unconscious process said to protect a person from ideas, impulses, or memories that would threaten emotional stability were they to become conscious.

reprieve the legal temporary suspension of the execution of a sentence of a criminal court. It is usually associated with the death penalty. It is distinct from a pardon (extinguishing the sentence) and commutation (alteration) of a sentence (for example, from death to life imprisonment).

reproduction the process by which a living organism produces other organisms similar to itself. There are two kinds: ◊asexual reproduction and ◊sexual reproduction.

reproduction rate in ecology, the rate at which a population or species reproduces itself; also called ◊fecundity.

reptile class of vertebrates (Reptilia) including snakes, lizards, crocodiles, turtles, and tortoises. They breathe by means of lungs; this distinguishes them from ◊amphibians, the larvae of which breathe through gills. They are cold-blooded, produced from eggs, and the skin is usually covered with scales. The metabolism is slow, and in some cases (some large snakes) intervals between meals may be months. Reptiles date back over 300 million years.

republic a country where the head of state is not a monarch, either hereditary or elected, but usually a president whose role may or may not include political functions.

respiration

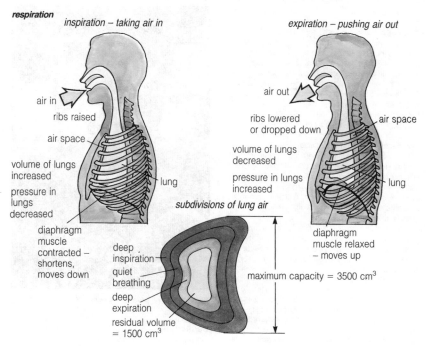

inspiration – taking air in

air in
ribs raised
air space
volume of lungs increased
pressure in lungs decreased
lung
diaphragm muscle contracted – shortens, moves down

expiration – pushing air out

air out
ribs lowered or dropped down   air space
volume of lungs decreased
pressure in lungs increased
lung
diaphragm muscle relaxed – moves up

subdivisions of lung air

deep inspiration
quiet breathing
deep expiration
residual volume = 1500 cm³

maximum capacity = 3500 cm³

Republican Party one of the USA's two main political parties, formed 1854 by a coalition of ◊slavery opponents, who elected their first president, Abraham ◊Lincoln, in 1860. The early Republican Party supported protective tariffs and favoured genuine settlers (homesteaders) over land speculators. Towards the end of the century the Republican Party was identified with US imperialism and industrial expansion. With few intermissions, the Republican Party controlled the legislature from the 1860s until defeated by the New Deal Democrats 1932. After an isolationist period before World War II, the Republican Party adopted an active foreign policy under ◊Nixon and ◊Ford, but the latter was defeated by Carter in the presidential election 1976. However, the party enjoyed landslide presidential victories for ◊Reagan and 1980–86 also carried the Senate. ◊Bush won the 1988 election, but faced the prospect of a Democratic Senate and Congress and in 1992 lost the presidency to the Democrat Bill Clinton.

requiem in the Roman Catholic church, the mass for the dead. Notable musical settings include those by Mozart and Berlioz.

reredos ornamental screen or wall-facing, behind a church altar.

research the primary activity in science, a combination of theory and experimentation directed towards finding scientific explanations of phenomena. It is commonly classified into two types: pure research involving theories with little apparent relevance to human concerns; and applied research concerned with finding solutions to problems of social importance, for instance in medicine and engineering. The two types are linked in that theories developed from pure research may eventually be found to be of great value to society.

reserve currency in economics, a country's holding of internationally acceptable means of payment (major foreign currencies or gold); central banks also hold the ultimate reserve of money for their domestic banking sector. On the asset side of company balance sheets, undistributed profits are listed as reserves.

resin substance exuded from pines, firs, and other trees in gummy drops which harden in air. Varnishes are common products of the hard resins, and ointments come from the soft resins.

resistance in physics, that property of a substance which restricts the flow of electricity through it, associated with conversion of electrical energy to heat; also the magnitude of this property. Resistance depends on many factors which may include any or all of the following: the nature of the material, its temperature, dimensions, and thermal properties; degree of impurity; the nature and state of illumination of the surface; and the frequency and magnitude of the current. The practical unit of resistance is the ohm.

Resistance movement an opposition movement in a country occupied by an enemy or colonial power. During World War II, resistance in E Europe took the form of ◊guerrilla warfare, for example in Yugoslavia, Greece, Poland, and by the ◊*partisan* bands behind the German lines in the USSR. In more industrialized countries, such as France (where the underground movement was called the *maquis*), Belgium, and Czechoslovakia, sabotage in factories and on the railways, propaganda, and the assassination of Germans and collaborators, were more important.

resistor in physics, any component in an electrical circuit used to introduce ◊resistance to a current. In electronics, resistors are often made from wire-wound coils or pieces of carbon. A variable resistor is a ◊rheostat or ◊potentiometer.

Resnais Alain 1922– . French film director, whose work is characterized by the themes of memory and unconventional concepts of time. His films include *Hiroshima mon amour* 1959, *L'Année Dernière* *à Marienbad/Last Year at Marienbad* 1961, and *Providence* 1977.

resources general term for things that can be used to provide the means to satisfy human wants. Because human wants are very diverse, and extend from basic physical requirements, such as food and shelter, through to ill-defined aesthetic needs, resources encompass a vast range of items. The intellectual resources of a society – its ideas and technologies – determine which aspects of the environment meet that society's needs, and therefore become resources. For example, in the 19th century uranium was used only in the manufacture of coloured glass. Today, with the advent of nuclear technology, it is a military and energy resource. Resources are often categorized into **human resources**, such as labour, supplies, and skills, and **natural resources**, such as climate, fossil fuels, and water. Natural resources are divided into ◊non-renewable resources and ◊renewable resources.

Respighi Ottorino 1879–1936. Italian composer, a student of ◊Rimsky-Korsakov, whose works include the symphonic poems *The Fountains of Rome* 1917 and *The Pines of Rome* 1924, operas, and chamber music.

respiration the biochemical process whereby food molecules are progressively broken down to release energy in the form of ◊ATP. In most organisms this is an aerobic process, so oxygen is required. In all higher organisms, respiration occurs in the ◊mitochondria. Respiration is also used to mean breathing, although this is more accurately described as ◊gas exchange.

respiratory distress syndrome (RDS) a condition, formerly known as hyaline membrane disease, in which a newborn baby's lungs are insufficiently expanded to permit adequate oxygenation. Premature babies are most at risk.

rest mass in physics, the mass of a particle at rest or moving at only a low velocity compared with that of light. According to the theory of ◊relativity, at very high velocities, there is a relativistic effect which increases the mass of the particle.

Restoration in English history, the period when the monarchy, in the person of Charles II, was re-established after the fall of the ◊Protectorate 1660.

Restoration comedy period in English theatrical history, which witnessed the first appearance of women on the English stage, most notably in the 'breeches part', specially created in order to costume the actress in male attire, thus revealing her figure to its best advantage. The genre is popular and naturalistic, placing much emphasis on sexual candour. Examples include Wycherley's *The Country Wife* 1675, Congreve's *The Way of the World* 1700, and Farquhar's *The Beaux' Strategem* 1707.

restrictive trade practices agreements between people in a particular trade or business which keep the cost of goods or services artificially high (for example an agreement to restrict output) or provide barriers to outsiders entering the trade or business. In British law these agreements are void unless they are registered with the Office of Fair Trading and are shown not to be contrary to the public interest.

resurrection in Christian, Jewish, and Muslim belief, the rising from the dead which all souls will experience at the Last Judgement. The Resurrection also refers to Jesus Christ rising from the dead on the third day after his crucifixion, which is a central belief of Christianity, celebrated at Easter.

resuscitation *A patient's eye-view of resuscitation techniques.*

resuscitation steps taken to revive anyone on the brink of death. The most successful technique for life-threatening emergencies, such as electrocution, near-drowning, or heart attack, is mouth-to-mouth resuscitation. Medical and paramedical staff are trained in cardiopulmonary resuscitation: the use of specialized equipment and techniques to restart the breathing and/or heart beat, and stabilize the patient long enough for more definitive treatment to be applied.

retail sale of goods and services to a consumer. The retailer is the last link in the distribution chain. A retailer's purchases are usually made from a wholesaler.

retail price index an indicator of variations in the ◊cost of living.

retail price maintenance (RPM) in the UK, exceptions to the general rule that shops can charge whatever price they choose for goods. The main areas where RPM applies are books (where the Net Book Agreement prevents booksellers charging less than the publisher's price) and some pharmaceutical products.

retriever type of dog. The commonest breeds are the Labrador retriever, large, smooth-coated, and usually black or yellow; and the golden retriever, with either flat or wavy coat. They can grow to 60 cm/2 ft high, and weigh 40 kg/90 lbs.

retrovirus a type of ◊virus containing the genetic material ◊RNA rather than the more usual ◊DNA.

Retz Jean François Paul de Gondi, Cardinal de Retz 1614–1679. French politician. A priest with political ambitions, he stirred up and largely led the insurrection of the ◊Fronde. After a period of imprisonment and exile he was restored to favour in 1662 and created abbot of St Denis.

Réunion French island of the Mascarenes group, in the Indian Ocean, 690 km/207 mi east of Madagascar
area 2,500 sq km/970 sq mi
capital St Denis

physical forested, rising in Piton de Neiges to 3,069 m/10,068 ft

products sugar, maize, vanilla, tobacco, rum

population (1985) 543,000

history the first European visitors were the Portuguese 1513; it was annexed by Louis XIII of France 1642. It became an overseas *département* of France 1946, and an overseas region 1972.

Reuter Paul Julius, Baron de Reuter 1816–1899. German founder of Reuters international news agency. He began a continental pigeon post in 1849, and in 1851 he set up a news agency in London. In 1858 he persuaded the press to use his news telegrams, and the service became worldwide.

Revelation last book of the New Testament, traditionally attributed to the author of the Gospel of St John but now generally held to be the work of another writer. It describes a vision of the end of the world, of the Last Judgement, and of a new heaven and earth ruled by God from Jerusalem.

revenons à nos moutons (French 'let us return to our sheep') let us get back to the subject.

revenue sharing in the US, federal aid to state and local government allocated under the State and Local Fiscal Assistance Act 1972.

Revere Paul 1735–1818. US nationalist, a Boston silversmith, who carried the news of the approach of British troops to Lexington and Concord (see ◊American Independence, War of) on the night of 18 Apr 1775. Longfellow's poem 'Paul Revere's Ride' commemorates the event.

reverse takeover in business, a ◊takeover situation where a company sells itself to another, to avoid being itself the target of a purchase by an unwelcome predator.

revisionism a political theory derived from Marxism which moderates one or more of the basic tenets of Marx, and which is hence condemned by orthodox Marxists. The first noted Marxist revisionist was Eduard ◊Bernstein, who in Germany in the 1890s questioned the inevitability of a breakdown in capitalism. After World War II the term became widely used by established Communist parties, both in Eastern Europe and Asia, to condemn movements (whether more or less radical) which threaten the official party policy.

revolution any rapid, far-reaching or violent change in the political, social, or economic structure of society. It has usually been applied to different forms of political change: the American Revolution (War of Independence), where colonists broke free from their colonial ties and established a sovereign, independent state; the French Revolution, where an absolute monarchy was overthrown by opposition from inside the country and a popular rising; and the Russian Revolution, where a repressive monarchy was overthrown by those seeking to institute widespread social and economic changes in line with a socialist model.

Revolutionary Wars a series of wars 1791–1802 between France and the combined armies of England, Austria, Prussia, and others, during the period of the French Revolution.

revolutions of 1848 a series of revolts in various parts of Europe against monarchical rule. While some of the revolutionaries had republican ideas, many more were motivated by economic grievances. The revolution began in France and then spread to Italy, the Austrian Empire, and to Germany, where the short-lived ◊Frankfurt Parliament put forward ideas about political unity in Germany. None of the revolutions enjoyed any lasting success, and most were violently suppressed within a few months.

revolver a small hand gun that has a revolving chamber that holds the bullets.

revue a stage presentation involving short satirical and topical items in the form of songs, sketches, and monologues. In Britain the first revue seems to have been *Under the Clock* 1893 by Seymour Hicks (1871–1949) and Charles Brookfield. The 1920s revues were spectacular entertainments, but the 'intimate revue' (such as *Sweet and Low* 1943) became increasingly popular under ◊Cochran, employing writers such as Noel ◊Coward. During the 1960s the satirical revue took off with the Cambridge Footlights' production *Beyond the Fringe*, firmly establishing the revue tradition among the young and at fringe theatrical events.

Reykjavik capital (since 1918) and chief port of Iceland, on the SW coast; population (1988) 93,000. Fish processing is the main industry. Reykjavik is heated by underground mains fed by volcanic springs.

Reynaud Paul 1878–1966. French prime minister in World War II, who succeeded Daladier in Mar 1940, but resigned in Jun after the German breakthrough. He was imprisoned by the Germans until 1945.

Reynolds Joshua 1723–1792. British portrait painter, active in London from 1752. He became the first president of the Royal Academy 1768 and was knighted 1769. His portraits of famous people of his day have striking and characterful compositions in a consciously grand manner and often borrow Classical poses, for example *Mrs Siddons as the Muse* 1784 (San Marino, California). His theories appear in *Discourses on Art* 1769–91.

Reynolds Albert 1933– . Irish politician, prime minister from 1992. He joined Fianna Fáil 1977, and held various government posts. He became prime minister when Charles Haughey was forced to resign Jan 1992, but his government was defeated on a vote of no confidence later that year. After an election, Reynolds succeeded in forming a Fianna Fáil-Labour coalition.

rhapsody in music, an instrumental fantasia, often based on folk melodies, such as Liszt's *Hungarian Rhapsodies*.

rhea flightless bird, family Rheidae, found only in South America. There are two species *Rhea americana* and the smaller *Pterocnemia pennata*. They differ from the ostrich in having a feathered neck and head and three-toed feet, no plume-like tail feathers, and in their smaller size (up to 1.5 m/5ft high, and 25 kg/55 lbs).

Rhea in Greek mythology, a fertility goddess, one of the Titans, wife of Kronos and mother of several gods, including Zeus.

Rhee Syngman 1875–1965. Korean right-wing politician. A rebel under Chinese and Japanese rule, he became president of South Korea from 1948 until riots forced him to resign and leave the country 1960.

rhenium metallic element: symbol Re, atomic number 75, relative atomic mass 186.22. It was identified in 1925 by Noddack, Tacke and Berg in the minerals columbite, tantalite, and wolframite. It is a hard grey metal, used in thermocouples, and as a catalyst.

rheostat in physics, a variable ◊resistor, usually consisting of a high-resistance wire-wound coil with a sliding contact. The circular type in electronics (which can be used, for example, as the volume control of an amplifier) is also known as a ◊potentiometer.

rhesus macaque monkey *Macaca mulatta*, also known as the bandar, found in N India and N Indo-China. It has long, straight, brown-grey hair, pinkish face, and red buttocks. It can

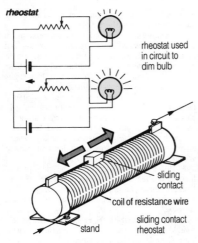

rheostat

rheostat used in circuit to dim bulb

sliding contact

coil of resistance wire

sliding contact rheostat

stand

grow up to 60 cm/2 ft long, with a 20 cm/8 in tail.

rhesus factor a ◊protein on the surface of red blood cells of humans, which is involved in the rhesus blood group system. Most individuals possess the main rhesus factor (Rh+), but those without (Rh−) will produce ◊antibodies if they come into contact with it. The name comes from rhesus monkeys, in whose blood the rhesus factors were first found.

rhetoric traditionally, the art of the orator (in Greek, *rhetor*) or of public speaking and debate. Rhetorical skills are valued in such occupations as politics, the law, preaching and broadcasting.

rhetorical question a question, often used by public speakers and debaters, which either does not require an answer or for which the speaker intends to provide his or her own answer ('Where else in the world can we find such brave young men as these?')

rheumatism a general term applied to a variety of ailments associated with inflammation of the joints and muscles. Acute rheumatism is better known as *Rheumatic fever*.

Rhine (German *Rhein*, French *Rhin*) European river rising in Switzerland and reaching the North Sea via West Germany and the Netherlands; length 1,320 km/820 mi. Tributaries include the Moselle and the Ruhr. The Rhine is linked with the Mediterranean by the Rhine-Rhône Waterway, and with the Black Sea by the Rhine-Main-Danube Waterway.

Rhine Joseph Banks 1895–1980. US parapsychologist. His work at Duke University, North Carolina, involving controlled laboratory experiments in telepathy, clairvoyance, precognition and psychokinesis, described in *Extra-Sensory Perception* 1934 made ESP a household word. See also ◊parapsychology.

Rhineland-Palatinate (German *Rheinland-Pfalz*) administrative region (German *Land*) of Germany
area 19,800 sq km/7,643 sq mi
capital Mainz
towns Koblenz, Trier, Ludwigshafen, Worms
physical wooded mountain country, river valleys of Rhine and Moselle
products wine (75% of German output), tobacco, chemicals, machinery, leather goods, pottery
population (1992) 3,702,000.

rhinoceros hoofed mammal of the family Rhinocerotidae. The one-horned Indian rhinoceros *Rhinoceros unicornis* is up to 2 m/6 ft at the shoulder, with a tubercled skin, folded into shield-like pieces; the African black rhinoceros *Diceros bicornis* is 1.5 m/5 ft high, with a prehensile upper lip for feeding on shrubs; the broad-lipped or 'white' rhinoceros *Ceratotherium simum* is slate-grey, with a squarish mouth for browsing grass. The latter two are smooth-skinned and two-horned. They are solitary and vegetarian, with poor eyesight but excellent hearing and smell. Needless slaughter has led to their near-extinction.

rhizoid a hair-like outgrowth found on the ◊gametophyte generation of ferns, mosses and liverworts. Rhizoids serve to anchor the plant to the substrate, and can absorb water and nutrients. They may be composed of many cells, as in mosses, where they are usually brownish, or unicellular as in liverworts, where they are usually colourless. Rhizoids fulfil the same basic functions as the ◊roots of higher plants but are simpler in construction.

rhizome a horizontal underground plant stem. It serves as a ◊perennating organ in some species, where it is generally thick and fleshy, while in other species it is mainly a means of ◊vegetative reproduction, and is therefore long and slender, with buds all along it that send up new plants. The potato is a rhizome which has two distinct parts, the tuber being the swollen end of a long, cord-like rhizome. See also ◊rootstock.

Rhode Island smallest state of the USA, in New England; nickname Little Rhody or the Ocean State
area 3,144 sq km/1,214 sq mi
capital Providence
products apples, potatoes, poultry (especially Rhode Island Reds), dairy products, jewellery (30% of the workforce), textiles, silverware, machinery, rubber, plastics, electronics
population (1987) 986,000
history founded 1636 by Roger Williams, exiled from Massachusetts Bay colony for religious dissent; one of the original Thirteen States.

Rhodes (Greek *Rodhos*) Greek island, largest of the Dodecanese, in the E Aegean Sea
area 1,412 sq km/545 sq mi
capital Rhodes
products grapes, olives
population (1981) 88,000
history settled by Greeks about 1000 BC; ◊Colossus of Rhodes (fell 224 BC) was one of the ◊Seven Wonders of the World; held by the Knights Hospitallers of St John 1306–1522; taken from Turkish rule by the Italian occupation 1912; ceded to Greece 1947.

Rhodes Cecil (John) 1853–1902. South African politician, born in the UK, prime minister of Cape Colony 1890–96. Aiming at the formation of a South African federation and of a block of British territory from the Cape to Cairo, he was largely responsible for the annexation of Bechuanaland (now Botswana) in 1885, and formed the British South Africa Company in 1889, which occupied Mashonaland and Matabeleland, thus forming *Rhodesia* (now Zambia and Zimbabwe).

Rhodes Wilfred 1877–1973. England cricketer. He was the game's most prolific wicket-taker, and took 4,187 wickets 1898–1930. An all-rounder, he also scored nearly 40,000 first class runs.

Rhodes Zandra 1940– . British fashion designer, known for the extravagant fantasy and luxury of her dress creations.

Rhodesia former name of ◊Zambia (North Rhodesia) and ◊Zimbabwe (South Rhodesia).

rhodium a silvery-white metal of the platinum family; symbol Rh, atomic number 45, atomic weight 102.91. It is used in thermocouples and in electroplating, and gives a corrosion-free, highly polished surface, superior to that of chromium.

rhododendron evergreen and deciduous shrub of the genus *Rhododendron*, family Ericaceae. The leaves are often dark and leathery, and the large racemes of flowers occur in all colours except blue.

rhombus a diamond-shaped plane figure, a parallelogram with four equal sides (opposite sides are equal in length and parallel) and no internal angle which is a right angle (otherwise it is a square). Its diagonals bisect each other at right angles. The area of a rhombus is half the product of the lengths of the two diagonals.

Rhône river of S Europe; length 810 km/500 mi. It rises in Switzerland and flows through Lake Geneva to Lyons in France, where at its confluence with the Saône the upper limit of navigation is reached. The river turns due south, passes Vienne and Avignon, and takes in the Isère and other tributaries. Near Arles it divides into the *Grand* and *Petit Rhône*, flowing respectively SE and SW into the Mediterranean west of Marseille.

rhubarb perennial plant *Rheum rhaponticum*, family Polygonaceae, grown for its red edible leaf stalks. The leaves are poisonous.

rhyme identity of sound, usually in the endings of lines of verse, such as 'wing' and 'sing'. Avoided as a blemish in Japanese, it is a common literary device in other modern Asian and European languages. Rhyme first appeared in western Europe in late Latin poetry, but was not used in classical Greek and Latin.

rhyolite an igneous rock, the fine-grained volcanic equivalent of granite.

Rhys Jean 1894–1979. British novelist, born in Dominica. Her works include *Wide Sargasso Sea* 1966, a recreation of the life of Rochester's mad wife in *Jane Eyre* by Charlotte Brontë.

rhythm and blues (R & B) a term covering all black US popular music of the 1940s–60s: it replaced the tag 'race music'. The music drew on swing and jump-jazz rhythms and blues vocals and was a progenitor of rock and roll. It diversified into soul, funk, and other styles. Singers include Bo Diddley (1928–), Jackie Wilson (1934–84), and Etta James (*c.* 1938–).

ria long narrow sea inlet, usually branching and surrounded by hills. A ria is deeper and wider towards its mouth, unlike a ◊fjord. It is formed by the flooding of a river valley due to either a rise in sea level or a lowering of a landmass.

rib a long, often curved bone that extends laterally from the ◊spine in vertebrates. Fish and some reptiles have ribs along most of the spine, but in mammals they are found in the chest only. In humans, there are 12 pairs of ribs. At the rear, each pair is joined to one of the vertebrae of the spine. The upper seven are joined by ◊cartilage directly to the breast bone/sternum. The next three are joined by cartilage to the rib above. The last two ('floating ribs') are not attached; they end in the muscles of the back. The ribs protect the lungs and heart, and at the same time allow the chest to expand and contract easily.

RIBA abbreviation for *Royal Institute of British Architects*.

Ribbentrop Joachim von 1893–1946. German Nazi leader. He served in World War I, and joined the

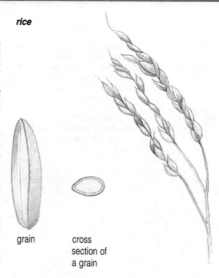

rice

grain   cross section of a grain

Nazi Party in 1932, acted as Hitler's adviser on foreign affairs, and was German ambassador to Britain 1936–38 and foreign minister 1938–45. He was tried at Nuremberg as a war criminal in 1946, and hanged.

Ribera José (Jusepe) de 1591–1652. Spanish painter, active in Italy from 1616 under the patronage of the viceroys of Naples. His early work shows the impact of Caravaggio, but his colours gradually lightened. His paintings include many full-length saints and mythological figures, and genre scenes, which he produced without preliminary drawing.

riboflavin a ◊vitamin of the B complex (B_2) whose absence in the diet causes stunted growth.

ribonucleic acid the full name of ◊RNA.

ribosome in biology, the protein-making machinery of the cell. Ribosomes are made of proteins and a special type of ◊RNA, ribosomal RNA. They receive messenger RNA (copied from the ◊DNA) and ◊amino acids, and 'translate' the messenger RNA by using its chemically coded instructions to link amino acids in a specific order, to make a strand of a particular protein.

Ricardo David 1772–1823. British classical economist, author of *Principles of Political Economy* 1817. Among his discoveries were the principle of ◊comparative advantage (that countries can benefit by specializing in goods they produce most efficiently and trading internationally to buy others), and the law of diminishing returns (that continued increments of capital and labour applied to a given quantity of land will eventually show a declining rate of increase in output).

rice principal cereal of the wet regions of the tropics; the yield is very large, and rice is said to be the staple food of one-third of the world population. It is derived from grass of the genus *Oryza sativa*, probably native to India and SE Asia.

Rice Elmer 1892–1967. US playwright, born in New York. His works include *The Adding Machine* 1923 and *Street Scene* 1929, which was made into an opera by Kurt Weill.

Rich Adrienne 1929– . US radical feminist poet, writer, and critic. Her poetry is both subjective and political, concerned with female consciousness, peace and gay rights. Her works include *The Fact* *of a Doorframe: Poems Selected and New* 1984 and *On Lies, Secrets and Silence* 1979.

Richard Cliff, stage name of Harry Roger Webb 1940– . British pop singer. In the late 1950s he was influenced by Elvis Presley, but soon became a Christian family entertainer, continuing to have hits in the UK through the 1980s. His original backing group were *the Shadows* (1958–68 and later re-formed).

Richard three kings of England:

Richard I 1157–1199. Known as *the Lionheart*, French *Coeur-de-Lion*. King of England from 1189. He was the third son of Henry II, against whom he twice rebelled. In the third ◊Crusade 1191–92 he showed courage and leadership, although he failed to recover Jerusalem. While returning overland he was captured by the Duke of Austria, who handed him over to the emperor Henry VI, and he was held prisoner until a large ransom was raised. His later years were spent in warfare in France, and he was killed while besieging Châlus. Himself a poet, he became a hero of romances after his death.

Richard II 1367–1400. King of England from 1377, effectively from 1389. Son of Edward the Black Prince. He reigned in conflict with Parliament; they executed some of his associates 1388 and he some of the opposing barons 1397, whereupon he made himself absolute. Two years later, forced to abdicate in favour of ◊Henry IV, he was jailed and probably assassinated.

Richard III 1452–1485. King of England from 1483. The son of Richard, Duke of York, he was created duke of Gloucester by his brother Edward IV, and distinguished himself in the Wars of the ◊Roses. On Edward's death in 1483 he became protector to his nephew Edward V, and soon secured the crown on the plea that Edward IV's sons were illegitimate. He proved a capable ruler, but the suspicion that he had murdered Edward V and his brother undermined his popularity. In 1485 Henry, Earl of Richmond, raised a rebellion, and Richard III was defeated and killed at ◊Bosworth.

Modern scholars tend to minimize the evidence for his crimes as Tudor propaganda.

Richards Frank. Pen name of British writer Charles Hamilton 1875–1961. Writing for the children's papers *Magnet* and *Gem*, he invented Greyfriars public school and the fat boy Billy Bunter.

Richards Gordon 1905–1986. British jockey who was champion on the flat a record 26 times 1925–1953.

Richards I(vor) A(rmstrong) 1893–1979. English literary critic. He collaborated with C K ◊Ogden and wrote the influential *Principles of Literary Criticism* 1924. In 1939 he went to Harvard, USA, where he taught detailed attention to the text and had a strong influence on contemporary American literary criticism.

Richardson Henry Handel. Pen name of Ethel Henrietta Richardson 1880–1946. Australian novelist. Born in Melbourne, she left Australia when only 18. Her work *The Fortunes of Richard Mahony* 1917–29 reflects her father's life.

Richardson Ralph David 1902–1983. British actor. He excelled in many parts including Falstaff, Peer Gynt, and Cyrano de Bergerac, as Dr Sloper in *The Heiress* (stage and screen 1949), and as Buckingham in ◊Olivier's film of *Richard III* 1956. Later stage successes include *Home* 1970 and *No Man's Land* 1976.

Richardson Samuel 1689–1761. British novelist, regarded as one of the founders of the modern novel. His *Pamela* 1740–41, written in the form of a series of letters, and containing much dramatic conversation, achieved a sensational vogue both in England and on the Continent, and was followed by *Clarissa* 1747–48, and *Sir Charles Grandison* 1753–54.

Richardson Tony 1928– . British director and producer. With George Devine he established the English Stage Company in 1955 at the Royal Court Theatre, where his productions included *Look Back in Anger* 1956. His films include *Saturday Night and Sunday Morning* 1960, *A Taste of Honey* 1961, and *Dead Cert* 1974.

Richelieu Armand Jean du Plessis de 1585–1642. French cardinal and politician, chief minister from 1624. He aimed to make the monarchy absolute; he ruthlessly crushed opposition by the nobility, and destroyed the political power of the ◊Huguenots, while leaving them religious freedom. Abroad he sought to establish French supremacy by breaking

Richard III Portrait by an unknown artist (c. 1518–23) Royal Collection, Windsor.

Richthofen German pilot Baron von Richthofen (centre) during World War I.

the power of the Hapsburgs; he therefore supported the Swedish king Gustavus Adolphus and the German Protestant princes against Austria, and in 1635 brought France into the Thirty Years' War.

Richler Mordecai 1931– . Canadian novelist, born in Montreal. His novels, written in a witty, acerbic style include *The Apprenticeship of Duddy Kravitz* 1959, *St Urbain's Horseman* 1971, and *Home Sweet Home* 1984.

Richter Charles Francis 1900–1985. US seismologist, deviser of the ◊Richter scale used to measure the strength of the waves from earthquakes.

Richter Johann Paul Friedrich 1763–1825. German author, commonly known as Jean Paul. He created a series of comic eccentrics in works such as the romance *Titan* 1800–03 and *Die Flegeljahre/ The Awkward Age* 1804–05.

Richter scale scale used to measure the magnitude of an ◊earthquake. The magnitude of an earthquake differs from the intensity, measured by the ◊Mercalli scale, which is subjective and varies from place to place for the same earthquake.

Richthofen Manfred, Freiherr von 1892–1918. German pilot. In World War I he commanded a crack fighter squadron, and shot down 80 aircraft before being killed in action.

ricin poison extracted from the seeds of the ◊castor oil plant.

rickets defective growth of bone in children due to lack of vitamin D. The bones, which do not harden adequately, are bent out of shape. Renal rickets, also a condition of malformed bone, is associated with kidney disease.

Ridley Nicholas *c.* 1500–1555. English Protestant bishop. He became chaplain to Henry VIII in 1541, and bishop of London in 1550. He took an active part in the Reformation and supported Lady Jane Grey's claim to the throne. After Mary's accession he was arrested and burned as a heretic.

Rie Lucie 1902– . Austrian-born potter who worked in England from the 1930s. Her pottery, exhibited all over the world, is simple and pure in form, showing a debt to Bernard ◊Leach.

Riefenstahl Leni 1902– . German film maker. Her film of the Nazi rallies at Nuremberg *Triumph des Willens/Triumph of the Will* 1934, vividly illustrated Hitler's charismatic appeal but tainted her career. After World War II her work was blacklisted by the Allies until 1952.

Riel Louis 1844–1885. French-Canadian rebel, a champion of the Métis (an Indian-French people); he established a provisional government in Winnipeg in an unsuccessful revolt 1869–70, and was

hanged for treason after leading a further rising in Saskatchewan 1884–85.

Rienzi Cola di *c.* 1313–1354. Italian political reformer. In 1347, he tried to re-establish the forms of an ancient Roman republic. His second attempt seven years later ended with his assassination.

Riesman David 1909– . US sociologist, author of *The Lonely Crowd: A Study of the Changing American Character* 1950.

Rietvelt Gerrit Thomas 1888–1964. Dutch architect, an exponent of De ◊Stijl. His best-known building is the Schroeder House at Utrecht 1924; he is also well known for colourful, minimalist chair design.

Riff ◊Berber people of N Morocco, who under ◊Abd el-krim long resisted the Spaniards and French.

rifle a ◊firearm that has spiral grooves (rifling) in its barrel. When a bullet is fired, the rifling makes it spin, thereby improving accuracy. Rifled guns came into use in the 1500s.

rift valley valley formed by the subsidence of a block of the Earth's ◊crust between two or more parallel ◊faults. Rift valleys are usually steep-sided and form where the crust is being pulled apart, as at ◊ocean ridges, or in the Great ◊Rift Valley.

Rift Valley, Great volcanic valley formed 10–20 million years ago by a crack in the Earth's crust, and running about 6,400km/4,000mi from the Jordan valley in Syria through the Red Sea to Mozambique in S East Africa. At some points its traces have been lost by erosion, but elsewhere cliffs rise thousands of metres. It is marked by a series of lakes, including Lake Turkana (formerly Lake Rudolph) and volcanoes, such as Mount Kilimanjaro.

Riga capital and port of Latvia; population (1987) 900,000. A member of the ◊Hanseatic League from 1282, Riga has belonged in turn to Poland 1582, Sweden 1621, and Russia 1710. It was the capital of independent Latvia 1918–40, and was occupied by Germany 1941–44, before being annexed by the USSR. It became capital again of independent Latvia 1991.

Rigel the brightest star in the constellation Orion. It is a blue-white supergiant, with an estimated diameter of over 50 Suns. It is 900 light years away, and is 50,000 times more luminous than our Sun.

Rigg Diana 1938– . British actress. Stage roles include Héloïse in *Abelard and Héloïse* 1970, and television roles, including Emma Peel in *The Avengers* 1965–67 and Lady Deadlock in *Bleak House* 1985.

right of way the right to pass over land belonging to another, such as a public right of way which can

rift valley

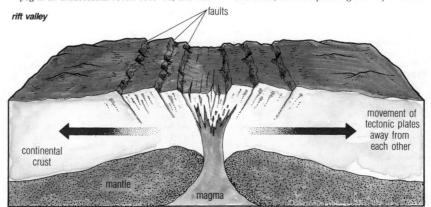

faults

movement of tectonic plates away from each other

continental crust

mantle

magma

be: a footpath; bridlepath, with horses permitted; or road, where vehicles are permitted. Other rights of way are licences (where personal permission is given) and ◊easements. In English law public rights of way are acquired by long use, by specific grant, or by statute. They are shown in definitive maps (which are conclusive evidence of the existence of the rights of way) maintained by the relevant local authority.

rights issue new shares offered to existing shareholders to raise new capital. Shareholders receive a discount on the market price while the company benefits from not having the costs of a re-launch of the new issue.

Rights of Man and the Citizen, Declaration of historic French document. According to the statement of the French National Assembly in 1789: representation in the legislature, equality before the law, equality of opportunity, freedom from arbitrary imprisonment, freedom of speech and religion, taxation in proportion to ability to pay, security of property. In 1946 were added: equal rights for women; right to work, join a union, and strike; leisure, social security, and support in old age; and free education.

right wing term applied to the more conservative or reactionary section of a political party or spectrum. It originated in the French national assembly in 1789, where the nobles sat in the place of honour on the president's right, whereas the commons were on his left (see under ◊left wing).

rigor the medical term for shivering. *Rigor mortis* is the stiffness which ensues in a corpse soon after death.

Rigveda the oldest of the ◊Vedas, the chief sacred writings of Hinduism. It consists of hymns to the Aryan gods, such as Indra, and to nature gods.

Riley Bridget (Louise) 1931– . British Op art painter. In the early 1960s she invented her characteristic style, arranging hard-edged black-and-white dots or lines in regular patterns that created disturbing effects of scintillating light and movement. She introduced colour in the late 1960s and experimented with silkscreen prints on Plexiglass.

Rilke Rainer Maria 1875–1926. Austrian poet, born in Prague. His prose works include the semi-autobiographical *Die Aufzeichnungen des Malte Laurids Brigge/Notebook of Malte Laurids Brigge* 1910, and his poetical works *Die Sonnette an Orpheus/Sonnets to Orpheus* 1923 and *Duisener Elegien/Duino Elegies* 1923. His verse is characterized by a form of mystic pantheism which seeks to achieve a state of ecstasy in which existence can be apprehended as a whole.

Rimbaud (Jean Nicolas) Arthur 1854–1891. French poet who was an important influence on ◊Symbolism. His verse was chiefly written before the age of 20 and includes *Les Illuminations* published in 1886.

Rimsky-Korsakov Nikolay Andreyevich 1844–1908. Russian composer. He made use of Russian folk idiom and rhythms, and excelled in orchestration. His operas include *The Maid of Pskov* 1873, *The Snow Maiden* 1882, *Mozart and Salieri* 1898 and *The Golden Cockerel* 1907, a satirical attack on despotism, banned till 1909.

ringworm a fungus infection of the skin, usually of the scalp and feet (athlete's foot). It is treated with ◊antifungal preparations.

Rinzai (Chinese *Lin-ch'i*) a school of Zen Buddhism introduced to Japan from China in the 12th century by the monk Eisai and others. It emphasizes rigorous monastic discipline and sudden

Río de Janeiro the Sugar Loaf peak in Rio de Janeiro.

enlightenment by meditation on a *kōan* (paradoxical question).

Río de Janeiro port and resort in Brazil; population (1980) 5,091,000, metropolitan area 10,217,000. The name commemorates the arrival of Portuguese explorers 1 Jan 1502, but there is in fact no river. Sugar Loaf Mountain stands at the entrance to the harbour. It was the capital of Brazil 1822–1960.

Río Grande river rising in the Rockies in S Colorado, USA, and flowing south to the Gulf of Mexico, where it is reduced to a trickle by irrigation demands on its upper reaches; length 3,050 km/1,900 mi. Its last 2,400 km/1,500 mi form the US-Mexican border.

Riom town on the river Ambène, in the Puy-de-Dôme *département* of central France. In World War II, it was the scene Feb–Apr 1942 of the 'war guilt' trials of several prominent Frenchmen by the ◊Vichy government. The accused included the former prime ministers ◊Blum and ◊Daladier, and Gen Gamelin (1872–1958). The occasion turned into a wrangle over the reasons for French unpreparedness for war, and at Hitler's instigation, the court was dissolved. The defendants remained in prison until released by the Allies in 1945.

Río Muni the mainland portion of ◊Equatorial Guinea.

riot disturbance caused by a potentially violent mob. In Britain, riots formerly suppressed under the ◊Riot Act are now governed by the Public Order Act 1986, which created a range of statutory offences (most of which were previously common law offences): riot, violent disorder (similar to riot but requiring only three people and no common purpose), affray (fights), threatening behaviour (shouting abuse), and disorderly conduct (minor acts of hooliganism). Riots in Britain include the Spitalfields weavers' riots 1736, the ◊Gordon riots 1780, the Newport riots 1839, and riots over the Reform Bill in Hyde Park, London, 1866; in the 1980s inner-city riots occurred in Toxteth, Liverpool; St Paul's, Bristol; and Broadwater Farm, Tottenham, London.

Modern methods of riot control include plastic bullets, stun bags (soft canvas pouches filled with buckshot which spread out in flight), water cannon, and CS gas (tear gas). Under the UK Public Order Act a person is guilty of riot if in a crowd of 12 or more, threatening violence; the maximum sentence is ten years' imprisonment. The act greatly extends police powers to control marches and demonstrations by rerouting them or restricting their size and duration.

Riot Act in the UK, an act passed in 1714 to suppress the ◊Jacobite disorders. If three or more persons assembled unlawfully to the disturbance of the public peace, a magistrate could read a proclamation ordering them to disperse ('reading the Riot Act'); after which they might be dispersed by force. It was superseded by the 1986 Public Order Act; see also ◊riot.

RIP abbreviation for *requiescat in pace* (Latin 'may he/she rest in peace').

ripple tank in physics, a shallow water-filled tray used to demonstrate various properties of waves, such as reflection, refraction, diffraction, and interference.

Rip Van Winkle legendary US character invented by Washington Irving in his 1819 tale of a man who falls into a magical 20-year sleep, and wakes to find he has slumbered through the War of Independence.

RISC (*reduced instruction-set chip*) in computing, a kind of processor on a single silicon chip that is faster and more powerful than those in common use today. By reducing the range of operations the processor can carry out, the chips are able to optimise those operations to execute more quickly. Computers based on RISC chips became commercially available in the late 1980s and considerably outperform their predecessors. See also ◊CPU .

risk capital or *venture capital* finance provided by venture capital companies, individuals and merchant banks, for medium or long-term business ventures which are not their own, and in which there is a strong element of risk.

Risorgimento movement for Italian national unity and independence from 1815. Uprisings failed 1848–49, but with French help, a war against Austria, including the Battle of Solferino 1859, led to the foundation of an Italian kingdom in 1861. Unification was finally completed with the addition of Venezia in 1866 and the Papal States in 1870. Three leading figures in the movement were ◊Cavour, ◊Mazzini, and ◊Garibaldi.

ritualization in ethology, the stereotype that occurs in certain behaviour patterns when these are incorporated into displays. For example, the exaggerated and stylized head toss of the goldeneye drake during courtship is a ritualization of the bathing movement used to wet the feathers; its duration and form have become fixed. Ritualization may serve to make displays clearly recognizable and unambiguous, so helping to ensure that individuals mate only with members of their own species.

river body of water, larger than a stream, that flows along a particular course. It originates at a point called its *source*, and enters the sea or a lake at its *mouth*. Along its length it may be joined by smaller rivers called *tributaries*. A river and its tributaries form a *river system*.

Rivera Diego 1886–1957. Mexican painter, active in Europe until 1921. He received many public commissions for murals exalting the Mexican revolution. A vast cycle on historical themes (National Palace, Mexico City) was begun 1929. In the 1930s he visited the USA and produced murals in the

roadrunner

greater roadrunner

Rockefeller Center, New York (later overpainted because he included a portrait of Lenin).

Rivera Primo de. Spanish politician. See ◊Primo de Rivera.

riveting a method of joining metal plates. A metal pin called a rivet, which has a head at one end, is inserted into matching holes in two overlapping plates and then the other end is struck and formed into another head, holding the plates tight. Riveting is used in building construction, boilermaking and shipbuilding.

Riviera the Mediterranean coast of France and Italy from Marseille to La Spezia.

Riyadh (Arabic *Ar Riyad*) capital of Saudi Arabia and of the Central Province, formerly the sultanate of Nejd, in an oasis, connected by rail with Damman on the Arabian Gulf; population (1984) 1,000.000.

Rizzio David 1533–1566. Italian adventurer at the court of Mary, Queen of Scots. After her marriage to ◊Darnley, Rizzio's influence over her incited her husband's jealousy, and he was murdered by Darnley and his friends.

RN abbreviation for *Royal Navy*; see under ◊navy.

RNA (*ribonucleic acid*) a nucleic acid involved in the construction of proteins from ◊DNA, the genetic material. It is usually single-stranded, unlike DNA, and consists of a large number of nucleotides strung together, each of which comprises the sugar ribose and one of four bases (uracil, cytosine, adenine, or guanine). RNA is copied from DNA by the formation of ◊base pairs, with uracil taking the place of thymine. Although RNA is normally associated only with the process of protein synthesis, it may be the hereditary material itself in some viruses.

RNLI abbreviation for *Royal National Lifeboat Institution*.

roach freshwater fish *Rutilus rutilus* of N Europe, dark green above, whitish below, and with reddish lower fins. It grows to 35 cm/1.2 ft.

roadrunner American bird *Geococcyx californianus* of the ◊cuckoo family that can run 25 kph/15 mph.

Robbe-Grillet Alain 1922–   . French writer. He is the leading theorist of *le nouveau roman* ('the new novel'), for example his own *Les Gommes/The Erasers* 1953, *La Jalousie/Jealousy* 1957, and *Dans le labyrinthe/In the Labyrinth* 1959, which concentrates on detailed description of physical objects. He also wrote the script for the film *L'Année dernière à Marienbad/Last Year in Marienbad* 1961.

robbery in English law, a variety of ◊theft: stealing from the person, using force, or the threat of force, to intimidate the victim. The maximum penalty is life imprisonment.

Robbia, della Italian family of sculptors and architects, active in Florence. *Luca della Robbia* (1400–82) executed a number of important works in Florence, notably the *cantoria* (singing gallery)

river landscape

A river can be regarded as having three stages – a youthful stage, a mature stage, and an old stage. Over millions of years it can develop from one stage to the next, or all three stages may be visible at one time along its length. Each stage is recognizable by the distinctive landscape it forms.

youthful stage

The river begins its descent through a narrow V-shaped valley. Falling steeply over a short distance, it follows a zig-zag course and produces interlocking spurs.

The current is strong, cutting a deep channel and wearing potholes through exposed rocks. Waterfalls and rapids form where it runs over hard rocks.

mature stage

The river flows through a broad valley, floored with sediments, and changes course quite frequently. It cuts into the bank on the outsides of the curves where the current flows fast and deep. Along the inside of the curves, sand and gravel deposits build up. When the river washes against a valley spur it cuts it back into a steep bank, or bluff.

old age

The river meanders from side to side across a flat plain on which deep sediments lie.

Loops and oxbow lakes form where the changing course of a river cuts off a meander.

Often the water level is higher than that of the plain. This is caused by the deposition of sand forming high banks and levees, particularly during times of flood. Crevasse splay deposits are left wherever the river overflows its banks.

Sand and mud deposited at the river mouth form sand banks and may produce a delta.

in the cathedral 1431–38 (Museo del Duomo), with lively groups of choristers. Luca also developed a characteristic style of glazed terracotta work that proved highly popular and provided the basis for the family business.

Robbins Jerome 1918– . US dancer and choreographer. He choreographed the musicals *The King and I* 1951, *West Side Story* 1957, and *Fiddler on the Roof* 1964. Robbins was ballet master of the New York City ballet 1969–83.

Robert two dukes of Normandy:

Robert I *the Devil* duke of Normandy from 1028. He was the father of William the Conqueror, and is the hero of several romances; he was legendary for his cruelty.

Robert II *c.* 1054–1134. Eldest son of William the Conqueror, succeeding him as duke of Normandy (but not on the English throne) in 1087. He took part in the First Crusade, and was deposed by his brother Henry I in 1106, remaining a prisoner in England until his death.

Robert three kings of Scotland:

Robert I *Robert the Bruce* 1274–1329. King of Scotland from 1306, and grandson of Robert de Bruce (1210–95). He shared in the national uprising led by William Wallace, and, after Wallace's execution in 1305, rose once more against Edward I and was crowned at Scone 1306. He defeated Edward II at ◊Bannockburn 1314. In 1328 the treaty of Northampton recognized Scotland's independence and Robert as king.

Robert II 1316–1390. King of Scotland from 1371. He was the son of Walter (1293–1326), steward of Scotland, who married Marjory, daughter of Robert I. He was the first king of the house of Stuart.

Robert III *c.* 1340–1406. King of Scotland from 1390. Son of Robert II. He was unable to control the nobles, and the government fell largely into the hands of his brother, Robert, duke of Albany (*c.* 1340–1420).

Roberts (Thomas William) 'Tom' 1856–1931. Australian painter, born in England, founder of the *Heidelberg School* which introduced Impressionism to Australia. He arrived in Australia in 1869, returning to Europe to study 1881–85. He received official commissions and painted the opening of the first Australian federal parliament, but his scenes of pioneering life are better known.

Roberts Frederick Sleigh, 1st Earl Roberts 1832–1914. British field marshal, known as 'Bobs'. During the Afghan War of 1878–80 he occupied Kabul, and subsequently made a victorious march to Kandahar. By his occupation of Bloemfontein and Pretoria in the Second South African War (1899-1902) he made possible the annexation of the Transvaal and Orange Free State.

Robertson Thomas William 1829–1871. British dramatist. At first an actor, he had his first success as a dramatist with *David Garrick* 1864, which set a new, realistic trend in English drama of the time; later plays included *Society* 1865 and *Caste* 1867.

Robeson Paul 1898–1976. US bass singer and actor. He graduated from Columbia University as a lawyer, but limited opportunities for blacks led him instead to the stage, for example, *The Emperor Jones* 1924 and *Showboat* 1928, in which he sang 'Ol' Man River'. He played *Othello* 1930, and his films include *Sanders of the River* 1935 and *King Solomon's Mines* 1937. An ardent advocate of black rights, he had his passport withdrawn 1950–58 because of his association with left-wing movements.

Robeson US singer and actor Paul Robeson testifies before committee in Washington, Jun 1948.

Robespierre Maximilien François Marie Isidore de 1758–1794. French politician in the ◊French Revolution. As leader of the ◊Jacobins in the National Convention he supported the execution of Louis XVI and the overthrow of the ◊Girondins, and in Jul 1793 was elected to the Committee of Public Safety. A year later he was guillotined.

robin migratory song-bird *Erithacus rubecula* of the thrush family, found in Europe, W Asia, Africa, and the Azores. About 13cm long, both sexes are olive brown, with a red breast. The nest is constructed in a sheltered place, and from five to seven white freckled eggs are laid. The larger North American robin belongs to the same family. In Australia members of several unrelated genera have been given the familiar name, and may have white, yellowish, or red breasts.

Robin Hood legendary English outlaw and champion of the poor against the rich. He feuded with the Sheriff of Nottingham, accompanied by Maid Marian and a band of followers, his 'merry men'. He appears in ballads from the 13th century, but his first datable appearance is in Langland's *Piers Plowman c.* 1377.

Robinson Edward G. Stage name of Emanuel Goldenberg 1893–1973. US film actor, born in Romania. He emigrated with his family to the USA in 1903. He was noted for his gangster roles, such as *Little Caesar* 1930.

Robinson Henry Crabb 1775–1867. British writer, whose diaries, journals, and letters are a valuable source of information on his friends ◊Lamb, ◊Coleridge, ◊Wordsworth, and ◊Southey.

Robinson W(illiam) Heath 1872–1944. British cartoonist and illustrator, known for his humorous drawings of bizarre machinery for performing simple tasks, such as raising one's hat.

Robinson Crusoe, The Life and strange and surprising Adventures of a novel by Daniel Defoe, published 1719, in which the hero is shipwrecked on an island and survives for years by his own ingenuity until rescued; based on the adventures of Alexander ◊Selkirk. The book had many imitators and is probably the first great English novel.

robot any computer-controlled machine that can be taught or programmed to do work. The most common types are mechanical 'arms'; when fixed to the floor or a workbench, they perform functions such as paint spraying or assembling parts in factories. Others include computer-controlled vehicles

robot arm on assembly line

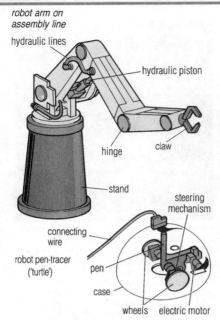

rock climbing Rock climbing in Scotland.

for carrying materials, and a miscellany of devices from cruise missiles, deep-sea and space-exploration craft to robotic toys.

Robson Flora 1902–1984. British actress. Her successes included Mrs Alving in *Ghosts* 1959, and Queen Elizabeth in the film *Fire Over England* (1931).

Rocard Michel 1930– . French socialist politician, prime minister 1988–91. A former radical, he joined the Socialist Party (PS) in 1973, emerging as leader of its moderate social-democratic wing. He held ministerial office under President Mitterrand 1981–85.

Roche Stephen 1959– . Irish cyclist. One of the outstanding riders on the continent in the 1980s, he was the first British winner of the Tour de France in 1987 and the first English-speaking winner of the Tour of Italy the same year, as well as the 1987 world professional road race champion.

Rochester John Wilmot, 2nd Earl of Rochester 1647–1680. British poet and courtier. He fought gallantly at sea against the Dutch, but chiefly led a debauched life at the court of Charles II. He wrote graceful lyrics, and his *A Satire against Mankind* (1675) rivals Swift.

rock the constitutent of the Earth's crust, either in its unconsolidated form as clay, mud, or sand, or consolidated into a hard mass as:

igneous rock, made from molten lava or magma solidifying on or beneath the Earth's surface, for example, basalt, dolerite, granite, obsidian

sedimentary rock, formed by deposition and compression at low temperatures and pressures, for example, sandstone from sand particles, limestone from the remains of sea creatures, or coal from those of plants; and

metamorphic rock, formed by changes in existing igneous or sedimentary rocks under high pressure or temperature, or chemical action, for example from limestone to marble.

rock and roll a type of pop music born of a fusion of rhythm and blues and country and western, and based on electric guitar and drums. In the mid-1950s, with the advent of Elvis Presley, it

became the heartbeat of Western teenage rebellion. It found perhaps its purest form in late-1950s *rockabilly*; the blanket term 'rock' later came to comprise a multitude of styles.

rock climbing originally an integral part of mountaineering, it is now a separate sport. It began as a form of training for alpine expeditions and is now divided into three categories: the *outcrop climb* for climbs of up to 30 m/100 ft; the *crag climb* on cliffs of between 30 m–300 m/100–1000 ft, and the *big wall climb* which is the nearest thing to Alpine climbing, but without the hazards of snow and ice.

Rockefeller John D(avison) 1839–1937. US millionaire, founder of Standard Oil in 1870 (which achieved control of 90% of US refineries), and of the philanthropic *Rockefeller Foundation* 1913, to which his son John D(avidson) Rockefeller Jr (1874–1960) devoted his life.

rocket projectile driven by the reaction of gases produced by a fast-burning fuel. Unlike the jet engine, which is also a reaction engine, the rocket carries its own oxygen supply to burn its fuel and is totally independent of any surrounding atmosphere. As rockets are the only form of propulsion available which can function in a vacuum, they are essential to exploration of outer space. Multi-stage, or ◊step rockets have to be used, consisting of a number of rockets joined together. In warfare, the head of the rocket carries an explosive device.

Rockwell Norman 1894–1978. US painter and illustrator, noted for magazine covers and cartoons portraying American life. His folksy view of the nation earned him huge popularity.

Rocky Mountains largest North American mountain system. They extend from the junction with the Mexican plateau, northward through the west central states of the USA, through Canada to the Alaskan border. The highest mountain is Mount McKinley (6,194 m/20,320 ft).

Rococo stylistic term describing the 18th century late ◊Baroque period in European art and architecture. The Rococo is characterized by light, deft patterns with much ornamentation; it is found chiefly in France, Spain, S Germany, and Austria. It was followed in the mid-18th century by ◊Neo-Classicism.

Roddick Anita 1943– . British entrepreneur, founder of the Body Shop, which now has branches worldwide. Roddick started with one shop in Brighton, England 1976, only selling natural products in refillable plastic containers.

rodent mammal of the worldwide order Rodentia. Besides ordinary 'cheek teeth', they have a single front pair of incisor teeth in both upper and lower jaw, which continue to grow as they are worn

the Saturn V moon rocket

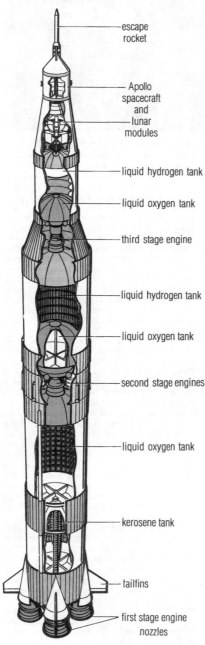

- escape rocket
- Apollo spacecraft and lunar modules
- liquid hydrogen tank
- liquid oxygen tank
- third stage engine
- liquid hydrogen tank
- liquid oxygen tank
- second stage engines
- liquid oxygen tank
- kerosene tank
- tailfins
- first stage engine nozzles

down. They are subdivided into three suborders, Myomorpha, Sciuromorpha, and Hystricomorpha, of which the rat, squirrel, and porcupine respectively are the typical members.

rodeo originally a practical means of rounding-up cattle in north America. It is now a popular side show and big-money sport in the US and Canada. Ranching skills such as broncobusting, bull riding, steer wrestling and calf roping are all part of the attraction of rodeo meetings.

Rodgers Richard (Charles) 1902–1979. US composer. He collaborated with librettist Lorenz Hart (1895–1943) in songs such as 'Blue Moon' 1934, and musicals such as *On Your Toes* 1936; and with Oscar Hammerstein II (1895–1960) in musicals such as *Oklahoma!* 1943, *South Pacific* 1949, *The King and I* 1951, and *The Sound of Music* 1959.

Rodin Auguste 1840–1917. French sculptor, considered the greatest of his time. His work freed sculpture from the current idealizing conventions by its realistic treatment of the human figure, introducing a new boldness of style and expression. It includes *Le Penseur/The Thinker* 1880, *Le Baiser/The Kiss* 1886 (marble version in the Louvre, Paris), and *Les Bourgeois de Calais/The Burghers of Calais* 1885–95 (copy in Embankment Gardens, Westminster, London).

Rodninia Irina 1949– . Russian ice skater. Between 1969-1980 she won 23 world, Olympic and European gold medals in pairs competitions. Her first partner was Alexei Ulanov and then Alexsandr Zaitsev, who became her husband in 1975.

Roeg Nicolas 1928– . British film director. His work is noted for its stylish visual appeal and imaginative, often off-beat, treatment of subjects. His films include *Walkabout* 1971, *Don't Look Now* 1973, and *The Witches* 1989.

Roethke Theodore 1908–1963. US poet. His father owned a large nursery business, and the greenhouses and plants of his childhood provide the detail and imagery of much of his lyrical, personal, and visionary poetry. Collections include *Open House* 1941, *The Lost Son* 1948, *The Waking* 1953 (Pulitzer Prize), and the posthumous *Collected Poems* 1968.

Rogation Day in the Christian calendar, one of the three days before Ascension Day which used to be marked by processions round the parish boundaries ('beating the bounds') and blessing of crops; now only rarely observed.

Rogers Carl 1902–1987. US psychologist who developed the client-centred approach to counselling and psychotherapy. This stressed the importance of clients making their own decisions and developing their own potential (self-actualization).

Rogers Richard 1933– . British architect. His works include the Centre Pompidou in Paris 1977 (jointly with Renzo Piano) and the Lloyd's building in London 1986.

Roget Peter Mark 1779–1869. British physician, one of the founders of the University of London, and author of a *Thesaurus of English Words and Phrases* 1852, a text constantly republished and still in use.

Röhm Ernst 1887–1934. German leader of the Nazi 'Brownshirts', the SA (◊Sturm Abteilung). On the pretext of an intended SA *Putsch* (uprising) some hundred of them, including Röhm, were killed 29–30 Jun 1934, sometimes referred to as 'the Night of the Long Knives'.

Rohmer Sax. Pen name of Arthur Sarsfield Ward 1886–1959. English crime writer who created the sinister Chinese character Fu Manchu.

Roh Tae-woo 1932– . South Korean right-wing politician. A general, he held ministerial office from 1981 under President Chun, and became chair of the ruling Democratic Justice Party 1985. He was elected president 1987, amid allegations of fraud and despite being connected with the massacre of about 2,000 anti-government demonstrators 1980.

Roland French hero of many romances, including the 11th-century *Chanson de Roland* and Ariosto's *Orlando Furioso*. Historically a soldier, killed in

Rolling Stones *The English rock band in 1963.*

roller brightly-coloured bird of the family Coraciidae, somewhat resembling crows but related to kingfishers, found in the Old World (eastern hemisphere). They grow up to 32 cm/13 in long. The name is derived from their habit of rolling over in flight.

rolling a common method of shaping metal. Rolling is carried out by giant mangles, consisting of several sets, or stands, of heavy rollers positioned one above the other. Red-hot metal slabs are rolled into sheet and also (using shaped rollers) girders and rails. Metal sheets are often cold-rolled finally to impart a harder surface.

Rolling Stones, the British band formed 1962, notorious as the 'bad boys' of rock. Original members were Mick Jagger (1943–), Keith Richards (1943–), Brian Jones (1942–69), Bill Wyman (1936–), Charlie Watts (1941–), and the pianist Ian Stewart (1938–85). In the 1970s they became a rock-and-roll institution and by the late 1980s Jagger and Richards were working separately.

Rollo 1st Duke of Normandy *c.* 860–932. Viking leader who was granted the province of Normandy by Charles III of France. He was its duke from 912 until his retirement to a monastery in 927.

Rolls-Royce industrial company manufacturing cars and aeroplane engines, founded 1906 by Henry ◊Royce and Charles Stewart Rolls (1877–1910). In 1906, the 'Silver Ghost' was designed, and produced until 1925, when the 'Phantom' was produced. In 1914, Royce designed the Eagle aircraft engine, which was used extensively in World War I. Royce designed the Merlin engine, which was used in Spitfires and Hurricanes in World War II. Jet engines followed, and became an important part of the company.

ROM (*read-only memory*) in computing, an electronic memory device; a computer's permanent store of important information or programs. ROM holds data or programs that will never need to be changed but must always be readily available, for example, a computer's operating system. It is an ◊integrated circuit (chip) and its capacity is measured in kilobytes (thousands of characters).

Romains Jules, pen name of Louis Farigoule 1885–1972. French novelist, playwright, philosopher, and poet. He developed the theory of Unanimism; this states that every group has a communal existence greater than that of the individual, which intensifies their perceptions and emotions. Of his plays, the farce *Knock, ou le triomphe de la médecine/Dr Knock* 1923 is best known.

Roman art sculpture, painting, and design in the Roman Empire. The Romans greatly admired Greek art. Realistic portrait sculpture was an original development from about 75 BC; narrative relief sculpture flourished; mosaics decorated

Rogers *The Lloyd's building in London (1987), by British architect Richard Rogers.*

778 with his friend Oliver and the twelve peers of France, at Roncesvalles (in the Pyrenees) by the ◊Basques. He had headed the rearguard during ◊Charlemagne's retreat from his invasion of Spain.

Roland de la Platière Jeanne Manon (born Philipon) 1754–1793. French intellectual politician, whose salon from 1789 was a focus of democratic discussion. Her ideas were influential after her husband Jean Marie Roland de la Platière (1734–93) became minister of the interior in 1792. As a supporter of the ◊Girondin party, opposed to Robespierre and Danton, she was condemned to the guillotine in 1793, without being allowed to speak in her own defence. Her last words were 'O liberty! What crimes are committed in thy name!'

role in the social sciences, the part a person plays in society, either in helping the social system to work or in fulfilling social responsibilities towards others. *Role play* refers to the way children learn adult roles by acting them out in play (mothers and fathers, cops and robbers). Everyone has a number of roles to play in a society: a woman may be a mother, a wife, and an employee at the same time, for example. *Role conflict* arises where two or more of a person's roles are seen as incompatible.

Rolfe Frederick 1860–1913. British writer, who called himself Baron Corvo. A Roman Catholic convert, frustrated in his desire to enter the priesthood, he wrote the novel *Hadrian the Seventh* 1904, in which the character of the title rose from being a poor writer to become pope. In *Desire and Pursuit of the Whole* 1934 he wrote about his homosexual fantasies and friends, earning the poet Auden's description of him as 'a master of vituperation'.

Romania

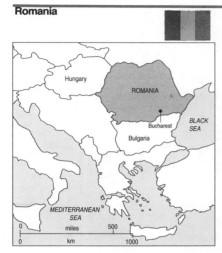

area 237,500 sq km/91,699 sq mi
capital Bucharest
towns Brasov, Timisoara, Cluj, Iasi; ports Galati, Constanta, Braila
physical mountains surrounding a plateau, with river plains S and E
head of state Ion Iliescu from 1989
head of government Theodor Stolojan from 1991
political system emergent democratic republic

exports petroleum products and oilfield equipment, electrical goods, cars
currency leu
population (1990 est) 23,269,000 (Romanians 89%, Hungarians 7.9%, Germans 1.6%; annual growth rate 0.5%
language Romanian (official), Hungarian; German
religion Romanian Orthodox 80%
literacy 98% (1988)
GNP $151 bn (1988) $6,400 per head
chronology
1944 Pro-Nazi government overthrown
1945 Communist-dominated government appointed.
1947 Boundaries redrawn; King Michael abdicated and People's Republic proclaimed.
1949 New constitution adopted; joined Comecon.
1952 New Soviet-style constitution.
1955 Romania joined Warsaw Pact.
1958 Soviet occupation forces removed.
1965 New constitution adopted.
1974 Ceausescu created president.
1985–86 Winters of austerity and power cuts.
1987 Workers' demonstrations against austerity.
1988–89 Relations with Hungary deteriorated over 'systematization programme'.
1989 Bloody overthrow of Ceausescu regime in 'Christmas Revolution' and power assumed by new military-dissident-reform communist National Salvation Front, headed by Ion Iliescu; Ceausescu tried and executed.
1990 Religious practices resumed.
1991 Treaty of friendship signed with USSR. New constitution endorsed by referendum.
1992 Iliescu re-elected in presidential runoff.

walls, vaults, and floors. very little painting has survived.

Roman Britain Roman relations with Britain began with Caesar's invasions of 55 and 54BC, but the actual conquest was not begun until 43 AD.

England was rapidly Romanized, but N of York fewer remains of Roman civilization have been found. After several unsuccessful attempts to conquer Scotland the N frontier was fixed at ◊Hadrian's Wall. During the 4th century Britain suffered from raids by the Saxons, Picts, and Scots. The Roman armies were withdrawn in 407 but there were partial re-occupations 417–c. 427 and c. 450 Roman towns include London, York, Chester, St Albans, Colchester, Lincoln, Gloucester, and Bath.

Roman Catholicism one of the main divisions of the Christian religion, separate from the Eastern Orthodox Church from 1054, and headed by the pope. For history and beliefs, see ◊Christianity. Membership 585 million worldwide, concentrated in S Europe, Latin America, the Philippines.

doctrine The Roman Catholic differs from the other Christian churches in that it acknowledges the supreme jurisdiction of the pope, infallible when he speaks *ex cathedra* 'from the throne'; in the doctrine of the Immaculate Conception (which states that the Virgin Mary, the mother of Jesus, was conceived without the original sin with which all other human beings are born); and in the allotment of a special place to the Virgin Mary.

organization The pope has (since the Second Vatican Council 1962–66) an episcopal synod of 200 bishops elected by local hierarchies to collaborate in the government of the church. Under John Paul II from 1978, power has been more centralized, and bishops and cardinals have been chosen from the more traditionally minded clerics, and from the Third World.

romance in literature, the term was first used for tales of love and adventure, in verse or prose, which became popular in France about 1200 and spread throughout Europe. There were Arthurian romances about the legendary King Arthur and his knights, and romances based on the adventures of Charlemagne and on classical themes. In the 20th century the term 'romantic novel' is often used disparagingly.

Romance languages the branch of Indo-European languages descended from the Latin of the Roman Empire ('popular' or 'vulgar' as opposed to 'classical' Latin). The present-day Romance languages with national status are French, Italian, Portuguese, Romanian, and Spanish.

Romanesque style of W European architecture of the 8th to 12th centuries, marked by rounded arches, solid volumes, and emphasis on perpendicular elements. In England the style was called ◊Norman.

Romania country in SE Europe, bounded to the N and E by Ukraine, to the E by Moldova, to the SE by the Black Sea, to the S by Bulgaria, to the SW by Yugoslavia, and to the NW by Hungary.

Romanian language a member of the Romance branch of the Indo-European language family, spoken in Romania, Macedonia, Albania, and parts of N Greece. It has been strongly influenced by the Slavonic languages and by Greek. The Cyrillic alphabet was used until the 19th century, when a variant of the Roman alphabet was adopted.

Roman law the legal system of ancient Rome which, in modern times, is the basis of ◊civil law, one of the main European legal systems.

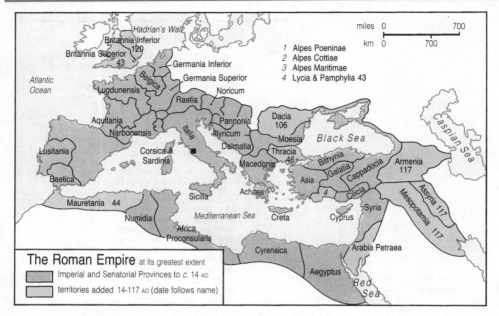

miles 0   700
km 0   700

Hadrian's Wall
Britannia Inferior
Britannia Superior 120
43
Atlantic Ocean
Germania Inferior
Germania Superior
Belgica
Lugdunensis
Noricum
Raetia
Aquitania
Pannonia
Dacia 106
Narbonensis
Italia
Illyricum
Moesia   *Black Sea*
Lusitania
Corsica & Sardinia
Dalmatia
Thracia
46
Bithynia
Armenia 117
Baetica
Macedonia
Galatia
Cappadocia
Asia
Cilicia
Assyria 117
Mauretania 44
Sicilia
Achaea
4
Syria
Mesopotamia 117
Numidia
Mediterranean Sea
Creta
Cyprus
Africa Proconsularis
Cyrenaica
Arabia Petraea
Caspian Sea
Aegyptus
Red Sea

1   Alpes Poeninae
2   Alpes Cottiae
3   Alpes Maritimae
4   Lycia & Pamphylia 43

The Roman Empire at its greatest extent
▨ Imperial and Senatorial Provinces to *c.* 14 AD
▢ territories added 14–117 AD (date follows name)

Roman numerals an old number system using different symbols from today's Arabic numerals (the ordinary numbers 1, 2, 3, 4, 5, and so on). The seven key symbols in Roman numerals as represented today (originally they were a little different) are I (= 1), V (= 5), X (= 10), L (= 50), C (= 100), D (= 500) and M (= 1,000). There is no zero. The first fifteen Roman numerals are I, II, III, IV (or IIII), V, VI, VII, VIII, IX, X, XI, XII, XIII, XIV and XV; the multiples of 10 from 20 to 90 are XX, XXX, XL, L, LX, LXX, LXXX and XC; and the year 1989 becomes MCMLXXXIX. Although addition and subtraction are fairly straightforward using Roman numerals, the absence of a zero makes other arithmetic calculations (such as multiplication) clumsy and difficult.

Romano Giulio see Giulio ◊Romano, Italian painter and architect.

Romanov dynasty which ruled Russia from 1613 to the ◊Russian Revolution 1917.

Roman religion a religion that retained early elements of reverence to stones and trees, and totemism (see ◊Romulus and Remus), and had a strong domestic base in the ◊lares and penates, the cult of Janus and Vesta. The main pantheon included Jupiter and Juno, Mars and Venus, Minerva, Diana, and Ceres, all of whom had their Greek counterparts, and many lesser deities.

Romanticism in literature, music, and art, a style that emphasizes the imagination, emotions, and creativity of the individual artist. The term Romanticism is often used to characterize the culture of 19th-century Europe, and contrasted with 18th-century ◊Classicism. Often linked with nationalistic feelings, the Romantic movement reached its height in the 19th century, as in the works of Schumann and Wagner.

Romany a nomadic people, also called *gypsy* (a corruption of 'Egyptian', since they were erroneously thought to come from Egypt). In the 14th century they settled in the Balkan peninsula, spread over Germany, Italy, and France, and arrived in England about 1500. The Romany language is a member of the Indo-European family.

Rome (Italian *Roma*) capital of Italy and ◊Lazio, on the Tiber, 27 km/17 mi from the Tyrrhenian Sea; population (1986) 2,815,000. Rome has few industries but is an important cultural, road, and rail centre. Remains of the ancient city include the Forum, Colosseum, and Pantheon. After the deposition of the last emperor Romulus Augustus 476, the papacy became the real ruler of Rome, and from the 8th century was recognized as such. In 1870 Rome became the capital of Italy, the pope retiring into the Vatican until 1929 when the Vatican City was recognized as a sovereign state.

Rome, ancient civilization around the Mediterranean Sea, based in Rome, which lasted for some 800 years. Traditionally founded in 753 BC, Rome became a self-ruling republic (and free of Etruscan rule) 510 BC. From then, the history of Rome is one of continual expansion, interrupted only by civil wars in the period 133–27 BC, until the murder of Julius ◊Caesar and foundation of the empire under ◊Augustus and his successors. At its peak under ◊Trajan, the Roman Empire stretched from Britain to Mesopotamia and the Caspian Sea. A long train of emperors ruling by virtue of military, rather than civil, power marked the beginning of Rome's long decline; under ◊Diocletian, the empire was divided into two parts although temporarily reunited under Constantine, the first emperor formally to adopt

Rome The Roman Forum showing the temple of Castor and Pollux.

Christianity. The end of the Roman Empire is generally dated by the sack of Rome by the Goths 410, or by the deposition of the last emperor in the West 476. The Eastern Empire continued until 1453 at Constantinople.

Romeo and Juliet a romantic tragedy by William Shakespeare, first performed 1594– 95. The play is concerned with the doomed love of Romeo and Juliet, victims of the bitter enmity between their respective families in Verona.

Rome, Sack of 410 AD. The invasion and capture of the city of Rome by the Goths. Generally accepted as marking the effective end of the Roman Empire.

Rome, Treaties of treaties establishing and regulating the ◊European Community.

Rommel Erwin 1891–1944. German field marshal. He served in World War I, later joining the Nazi Party. He played an important part in the invasions of central Europe and France, and was commander of the N African offensive from 1941 (when he was nicknamed 'Desert Fox') until defeated in the Battles of El ◊Alamein. He was commander in chief for a short time against the Allies in Europe 1944 but (as a sympathizer with the ◊Stauffenberg plot) was forced to commit suicide.

Romney George 1734–1802. British portrait painter, active in London from 1762. He painted several portraits of Lady Hamilton, Admiral Nelson's mistress.

Romulus in Roman mythology, the legendary founder and first king of Rome, the son of Mars by Rhea Silvia, daughter of Numitor, king of Alba Longa. He and his twin brother Remus were thrown into the Tiber by their great-uncle Amulius, who had deposed Numitor, but were suckled by a she-wolf and rescued by a shepherd. On reaching manhood they killed Amulius and founded Rome.

Romulus Augustus c. 461–c. 500. Last Roman emperor in the West. When about 14 he was made emperor by his soldier father Orestes in 475, but compelled to abdicate in 476 by Odoacer, leader of the barbarian mercenaries, who nicknamed him Augustulus. Orestes was executed and Romulus Augustus confined to a Neapolitan villa.

rondo a form of instrumental music where the principal section is repeated several times. Rondo form is often used for the last movement of a sonata or concerto.

Ronsard Pierre de 1524–1585. French poet, leader of the ◊Pléiade group of poets. Under the patronage of Charles IX, he published original verse in a lightly sensitive style, including odes and love sonnets, for example *Odes* 1550, *Les Amours/Lovers* 1552–53, and the 'Marie' cycle, *Continuation des amours/Lovers Continued*1555–56. He was fiercely opposed by the supporters of Marot.

Röntgen Wilhelm Konrad 1845–1923. German physicist who discovered X-rays 1895. While investigating the passage of electricity through gases, he noticed the ◊fluorescence of a barium platinocyanide screen. This radiation passed through some substances opaque to light, and affected photographic plates. Developments from this discovery have revolutionized medical diagnosis.

rood alternative name for the cross of Christ, especially applied to the large crucifix placed on a beam or screen at the entrance to the chancel of a church.

rook gregarious bird *Corvus frugilegus* of the crow family. The plumage is black and lustrous, the face bare, and it can grow to 45 cm/1.5 ft in length. Rooks nest in colonies at the tops of trees.

Roosevelt Franklin Roosevelt, president of the USA, was elected for an unprecedented fourth term of office.

Roon Albrecht Theodor Emil, Count von Roon 1803–1879. Prussian field marshal. As war minister from 1859, he reorganized the army and made possible the victories of 1866 over Austria, and 1870–71 in the ◊Franco-Prussian War.

Roosevelt (Anna) Eleanor 1884–1962. US social worker and lecturer; her newspaper column 'My Day' was widely syndicated, she was a delegate to the UN general assembly, and later chairwoman of the UN commission on human rights 1946–51. Within the Democratic Party she formed the left-wing Americans for Democratic Action group 1947. She was married to President Franklin Roosevelt.

Roosevelt Franklin Delano 1882–1945. 32nd president of the USA 1933–45, a Democrat. He served as governor of New York 1929–33. Becoming president amid the Depression, he launched the ◊*New Deal* economic and social reform programme, which made him popular with the people. After the outbreak of World War II he introduced ◊lend-lease for the supply of war materials to the Allies and drew up the ◊Atlantic Charter of solidarity, and once the USA had entered the war 1941 he spent much time in meetings with Allied leaders (see ◊Quebec, ◊Tehran, and ◊Yalta conferences).

Roosevelt Theodore 1858–1919. 26th president of the USA 1901–09, a Republican. After serving as governor of New York 1898–1900 he became vice president to ◊McKinley, whom he succeeded as president on McKinley's assassination 1901. He campaigned against the great trusts (combines that reduce competition), while carrying on a jingoist foreign policy designed to enforce US supremacy over Latin America. Alienated after his retirement by the conservatism of his successor Taft, Roosevelt formed the Progressive or 'Bull Moose' Party. As their candidate he unsuccessfully ran for the presidency 1912.

root the part of the plant that is usually underground, and whose primary functions are anchorage and the absorption of water and dissolved mineral salts. Roots are usually positively geotropic and hydrotropic (see ◊tropism), so they grow downwards and towards water. Plants, such as epiphytic orchids that grow above ground, produce aerial roots which absorb moisture from the atmosphere. Others, such as ivy, have climbing roots arising from the stems that serve to attach the plant to trees and walls.

root crop an ambiguous term which refers to several different types of crop; in agriculture, it refers to turnips, swedes, and beets, which are

root

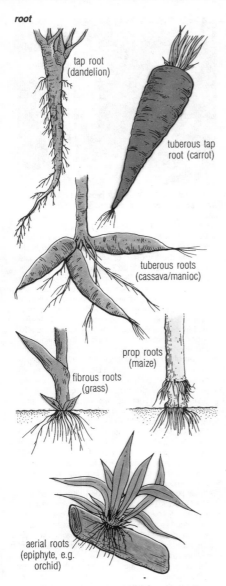

tap root
(dandelion)

tuberous tap
root (carrot)

tuberous roots
(cassava/manioc)

prop roots
(maize)

fibrous roots
(grass)

aerial roots
(epiphyte, e.g.
orchid)

actually enlarged hypocotyls and contain little root, while in trade statistics, it refers to the tubers of potatoes, cassava, and yams. Roots have a high carbohydrate content, but their protein content rarely exceeds 2%. Consequently, communities relying too heavily upon roots may suffer from protein deficiency. Potatoes, cassava, and yams are second in importance only to cereals as human food. Food production per hectare from roots is higher than for cereals.

root hair a tubular outgrowth from a cell on the surface of a plant root. It is a delicate structure which survives for a few days only, and does not develop into a root. New root hairs are continually being formed near the root tip to replace the ones that are lost. The majority of land plants possess root hairs, which serve greatly to increase the surface area available for the absorption of water and mineral salts from the soil. The layer of the root's epidermis that produces root hairs is known as the piliferous layer.

root-mean-square (*rms*) value obtained by taking the square root of the mean (average) of the squares of a set of values; for example the *rms* value of four quantities *a*, *b*, *c* and *d* is $\sqrt{1}$ (($a^2 + b^2 + c^2 + d^2$)/4). For an alternating current (AC), the *rms* value is equal to the peak value divided by the square root of 2.

roots music term originally denoting ◊reggae, later encompassing any music indigenous to a particular culture; also called **world music**. Examples are W African *mbalax*, E African *soukous*, S African *mbaqanga*, French Antillean *zouk*, Javanese gamelan, Latin American salsa, Cajun music, and European folk music.

rootstock another name for ◊rhizome.

rope stout cordage over 2.5 cm/1 in in circumference. Rope is made similarly to thread or twine, by twisting yarns together to form strands, which are then in turn twisted round each other in the direction opposite to that of the yarns. Although hemp is still the commonest material used to make rope, nylon is increasingly used.

Rorschach test in psychiatry, a method of diagnosis involving the use of ink-blot patterns which subjects are asked to interpret, to help indicate personality type, degree of intelligence, and emotional stability. It was invented by the Swiss psychiatrist Hermann Rorschach (1884–1922).

Rosa Salvator 1615–1673. Italian painter, etcher, poet, and musician, active in Florence 1640–49 and subsequently in Rome. He is known for wild, romantic, and sometimes macabre landscapes, seascapes, and battle scenes. He also wrote verse satires.

rosary string of beads used in a number of religions, including Buddhism, Christianity, and Islam. The term also refers to a form of prayer used by Catholics, consisting of 150 ◊Ave Marias and 15 ◊Paternosters and Glorias, or to a string of 165 beads for keeping count of these prayers; it is linked with the cult of the Virgin Mary.

Roscius Gallus Quintus *c.* 126–62 BC. Roman actor, originally a slave, so gifted that his name became proverbial for a great actor.

Roscommon county of the Republic of Ireland in the province of Connacht
area 2,463 sq km/951 sq mi
towns county town Roscommon
physical bounded on the east by the river Shannon; lakes Gara, Key, Allen; rich pastures
population (1986) 55,000.

rose shrubs and climbers of the genus *Rosa*, family Rosaceae. Numerous cultivated forms have been derived from the sweet briar *Rosa rubiginosa* and the dog-rose *Rosa canina*. There are many climbing varieties, but the forms more commonly cultivated are bush roses, and standards which are cultivated roses grafted on to a briar stem.

Roseau (formerly *Charlotte Town*) capital of ◊Dominica, in the West Indies; population (1981) 20,000.

rosemary evergreen shrub *Rosemarinus officinalis*, native to the Mediterranean and W Asia, with small scented leaves. It is widely cultivated as a culinary herb, and for the aromatic oil extracted from the clusters of pale purple flowers.

Rosenberg Alfred 1893–1946. German politician, born in Tallinn, Estonia. He became the chief Nazi ideologist, and was Reich minister for eastern

rose

*hybrid
tea rose*

occupied territories 1941-44. He was tried at Nuremberg in 1946 as a war criminal and hanged.

Rosenberg Isaac 1890–1918. English poet of the World War I period. Trained as an artist at the Slade school, Rosenberg enlisted in the Suffolk regiment in 1915 and was later transferred to the King's own Royal Lancaster regiment. He wrote about the horror of life on the front line, as in 'Break of Day in the Trenches'.

Rosenberg Julius 1918–53 and Ethel 1915–1953. US married couple, accused of being leaders of a nuclear-espionage ring passing information to the USSR; both were executed.

Roses, Wars of the name given in the 19th century by novelist Walter Scott to civil wars in England 1455–85 between the houses of ◊Lancaster (badge, red rose) and ◊York (badge, white rose):

1455 Opened with battle of St Albans on 22 May, a Yorkist victory (◊Henry VI made prisoner).

1459–61 War renewed until ◊Edward IV, having become king, confirmed his position by a victory at Towton on 29 Mar 1461.

1470 ◊Warwick (who had helped Edward to the throne) allied instead with Henry VI's widow, ◊Margaret of Anjou, but was defeated by Edward at Barnet on 14 Apr and by Margaret at Tewkesbury on 4 May.

1485 Yorkist regime ended with the defeat of ◊Richard III by the future ◊Henry VII at ◊Bosworth 22 Aug.

Rosetta Stone a slab of basalt with inscriptions from 197 BC, found near the town of Rosetta, Egypt, in 1799. It has the same text in Greek as in the hieroglyphic and demotic scripts, and was the key to deciphering other Egyptian inscriptions.

Rosh Hashana the two-day holiday that marks the start of the Jewish New Year (first new moon after the autumn equinox), traditionally announced by blowing a ram's horn.

Ross James 1800–1862. British explorer who discovered the magnetic North Pole in 1831. He also went to the Antarctic; Ross Island, Ross Sea, and Ross Dependency are named after him.

Ross Martin. Pen name of Violet Florence ◊Martin, Irish novelist.

Ross Ronald 1857–1932. British physician and bacteriologist. Born in India, he served 1881–99 in the Indian Medical Service, and 1895–98 identified the *Anopheles* mosquito as being responsible for the spread of malaria. Nobel prize 1902.

Ross Dependency all the Antarctic islands and territories between 160° E and 150° W longitude and south of 60° S latitude; it includes Edward

VII Land, Ross Sea and its islands, and parts of Victoria Land.

area 453,000 sq km/175,000 sq mi

population there are a few scientific bases with about 250 staff

history given to New Zealand 1923. It is probable that marine organisms beneath the ice shelf had been undisturbed from the Pleistoc ene period until drillings were made in 1976.

Rossellini Roberto 1906–1977. Italian film director, regarded as the leader of Italian ◊neo-Realism in films. His World War II theme trilogy of films, *Roma Città aperta/Rome, Open City* 1945, *Paisà/Paisan* 1946, and *Germania Anno Zero/Germany Year Zero* 1947, are considered landmarks in postwar European cinema.

Rossetti Christina (Georgina) 1830–1894. British poet, sister of Dante ◊Rossetti, and a devout High Anglican (see ◊Oxford movement). Her verse includes *Goblin Market and Other Poems* 1862 and expresses unfulfilled spiritual yearning and frustrated love. She was a skilful technician and made use of irregular rhyme and line length.

Rossetti Dante Gabriel 1828–1882. British painter and poet, a founder member of the ◊*Pre-Raphaelite Brotherhood* in 1848. Apart from romantic medieval scenes, he produced dozens of idealized portraits of women. His verse includes *The Blessed Damozel* 1850.

Rossini Gioachino (Antonio) 1792–1868. Italian composer. His first success was the opera *Tancredi* 1813. In 1816 his 'opera buffa' *Il barbiere di Siviglia/The Barber of Seville* was produced in Rome. During his fertile composition period, 1815–23, he produced 20 operas, and created (with ◊Donizetti and ◊Bellini) the 19th-century Italian operatic style. After the spectacular *Guillaume Tell/William Tell* 1829 he gave up writing opera and his later years were spent in Bologna and Paris.

Rostand Edmond 1869–1918. French dramatist, remembered for *Cyrano de Bergerac* 1897 and *L'Aiglon* 1900, based on the life of Napoleon III, in which the celebrated actress Sarah Bernhardt played a leading role.

Roth Philip 1933– . US novelist, noted for his portrayals of modern Jewish-American life. His best books include *Goodbye Columbus* 1959, *Portnoy's Complaint* 1969, and a series of novels about a writer, Nathan Zuckerman, including *The Ghost Writer* 1979, *Zuckerman Unbound* 1981, and *The Anatomy Lesson* 1984.

Rothko Mark 1903–1970. US painter, born in Russia, an Abstract Expressionist and a pioneer

Rosetta Stone *The Rosetta Stone, discovered 1799, has inscriptions dating from 196 BC.*

of ***Colour Field*** painting (abstract, dominated by areas of unmodulated, strong colour).

Rothschild a European family, noted for its activity in the financial world for two centuries. Mayer Anselm (1744–1812) set up as a moneylender in Frankfurt-am-Main, Germany, and important business houses were established throughout Europe by his ten children.

rotifer any of the tiny invertebrates, also called 'wheel animalcules' of the phylum Aschelminthes. Mainly freshwater, some marine, rotifers have a ring of cilia which carries food to the mouth, and also provides propulsion. Smallest of multicellular animals, few reach 0.05 cm/0.02 in.

rotten borough an English parliamentary constituency, before the Great Reform Act of 1832, which returned members to Parliament in spite of having small numbers of electors. Thus they could be easily manipulated by those with sufficient money or influence.

Rotterdam industrial port (brewing, distilling, shipbuilding, sugar and petroleum refining, margarine, tobacco) in the Netherlands and one of the foremost ocean cargo ports in the world, in the Rhine-Maas delta, linked by canal 1866–90 with the North Sea; population (1987) 1,031,000.

Rouault Georges 1871–1958. French painter, etcher, illustrator, and designer. Early in his career he was associated with the Fauves, but created his own style using heavy, dark colours and bold brushwork. His subjects included sad clowns, prostitutes, and evil lawyers; from about 1940 he painted mainly religious works.

Roubiliac or Roubillac, Louis François c. 1705–1762. French sculptor, a Huguenot who fled religious persecution to settle in the UK 1732. He soon became the most popular sculptor of the day, creating a statue of Handel for Vauxhall Gardens 1737 (Victoria and Albert Museum, London) and teaching at St Martin's Lane Academy from 1745.

roulette a gambling game of chance in which the players bet on a ball landing in the correct segment (numbered 0–36 and alternately coloured red and black) on a rotating wheel.

rounders bat and ball game similar to ◊baseball but played on a much smaller pitch. The first reference to rounders is in 1744.

Roundhead a member of the Parliamentary party during the English Civil War of 1640–60, opposing the royalist Cavaliers. The term referred to the short hair then worn only by the lower classes.

Rousseau Henri 'Le Douanier' 1844–1910. French painter, a self-taught naive artist. His subjects included scenes of the Parisian suburbs and exotic junglescapes, painted with painstaking detail, for example *Surprised! Tropical Storm with a Tiger* 1891 (National Gallery, London).

Rousseau Jean-Jacques 1712–1778. French philosopher. His *Discourse on the Origin and Foundations of Inequality amongst Men* 1754 denounced civilized society, but his most important work was the *Social Contract* 1762, which emphasized the rights of the people over those of the government. It was a significant influence on the French Revolution.

rowan another name for the ◊mountain ash tree.

Rowbotham Sheila 1943– . British socialist feminist, historian, lecturer, and writer. Her pamphlet *Women's Liberation and the New Politics* 1970 laid down the fundamental approaches and demands of the emerging British women's movement.

Rowe Nicholas 1674–1718. English dramatist and poet, formerly a lawyer. His best-known dramas

Rousseau *French philosopher and writer Jean-Jacques Rousseau.*

are *The Fair Penitent* 1702 and *Jane Shore* 1714, in which Mrs Siddons played. He edited Shakespeare, and was Poet Laureate from 1715.

rowing propulsion of a boat by oars, either by one rower with two oars (sculling) or by crews (two, four, or eight persons) with one oar each, often with a coxswain (steering).

Rowlandson Thomas 1756–1827. British painter and illustrator, a caricaturist of the social life of his times. His *Tour of Dr Syntax in Search of the Picturesque* 1809 and its two sequels 1812–21 proved very popular.

Rowley William c. 1585–c. 1642. English actor and dramatist, collaborator with ◊Middleton in *The Changeling* 1621 and with ◊Dekker and ◊Ford in *The Witch of Edmonton* 1658.

Rowling Wallace 'Bill' 1927– . New Zealand Labour politician, party leader 1969–75, prime minister 1974–75.

Rowse A(lfred) L(eslie) 1903– . British popular historian. He published a biography of Shakespeare in 1963, and in 1973 controversially identified the 'Dark Lady' of Shakespeare's sonnets as Emilia Lanier, half-Italian daughter of a court musician, with whom the poet is alleged to have had an affair 1593–95.

Roy Manabendra Nakh 1887–1954. Founder of the Indian Communist Party in exile in Tashkent in 1920. Expelled from the Comintern in 1929, he returned to India and was imprisoned for five years. A steadfast communist, he finally became disillusioned after World War II and developed his ideas on practical humanism.

rowan

Roy Rajah Ram Rohan 1770–1833. Bengali religious and social reformer. He was founder of the Brahma Samaj sect which formulated the creed of neo-Hinduism akin to Christian Unitarianism. He died in England in 1833 as emissary of the Great Mughal, who was still nominal sovereign in India.

Royal Academy of Dramatic Art (RADA) British college founded by actor-manager Herbert Beerbohm Tree 1904 to train young actors. Its headquarters have been in Gower Street, London, since 1905, and a royal charter was granted in 1920.

Royal Aeronautical Society the oldest British aviation body, formed in 1866. Its members discussed and explored the possibilities of flight long before its successful achievement.

Royal Air Force (RAF) the ◊air force of Britain. The RAF was formed in 1918 by the merger of the Royal Naval Air Service and the Royal Flying Corps.

Royal Ballet title under which the British Sadler's Wells Ballet (at Covent Garden), Sadler's Wells Theatre Ballet, and the Sadler's Wells Ballet School (Richmond, Surrey) were incorporated in 1956.

Royal Botanic Gardens, Kew a botanic garden, located in Richmond, Surrey. It was founded 1759 by the mother of George III as a small garden and passed to the nation by Queen Victoria 1840. By then it was almost at its present size of 149 hectares and since 1841 has been open daily to the public. It contains a collection of over 25,000 living plant species and many fine buildings. Much of its collection of trees was destroyed by a gale 1987. It is also a centre for botanical research.

Royal British Legion full name of the ◊British Legion, a nonpolitical body promoting the welfare of war veterans and their dependants.

Royal Canadian Mounted Police Canadian national police force known as the Mounties, with uniform of red jacket and broad-brimmed hat. Their Security Service, established 1950, was disbanded 1981, and replaced by the independent Canadian Security Intelligence Service.

royal commission in the UK and Canada, a group of people appointed by the government (nominally appointed by the sovereign) to investigate a matter of public concern and make recommendations on any actions to be taken in connection with it, including changes in the law. In cases where agreement on recommendations cannot be reached, a minority report can be submitted by dissenters. No royal commissions have been set up by the Thatcher administration since its election 1979.

Royal Greenwich Observatory the national astronomical observatory of the UK, founded 1675 at Greenwich, E London, England, to provide navigational information for seamen. After World War II, it was moved to Herstmonceux Castle, Sussex. It also operates telescopes on La Palma in the Canary Islands, including the 4.2 m/165 in William Herschel Telescope, commissioned 1987.

royal household the personal staff of a sovereign. In Britain the chief officers are the Lord Chamberlain, the Lord Steward, and the Master of the Horse. The other principal members of the royal family also maintain their own households.

Royal Institution of Great Britain organization for the promotion, diffusion, and extension of science and knowledge, founded in London 1799 by the physicist Count Rumford (1753–1814). ◊Faraday and ◊Davy were among its directors.

Royal Marines British military force trained for amphibious warfare. See under ◊Marines.

Royal Military Academy British military officer training college in Sandhurst, Berkshire, founded 1799. It is popularly known as *Sandhurst*, and its motto is 'Serve to Lead'.

Royal Opera House the leading British opera house, Covent Garden, London; the original theatre opened 1732 and the present building dates from 1858.

Royal Shakespeare Company (RSC) British professional theatre company that performs Shakespeare's and others' plays. It was founded 1961 from the company at the Shakespeare Memorial Theatre 1932 (now the Royal Shakespeare Theatre) at Stratford-upon-Avon, Warwickshire. Its first director was Peter Hall. A second large theatre in Stratford, the Swan, opened 1986 with an auditorium similar to theatres of Shakespeare's day. In 1982 it moved into a permanent London headquarters at the Barbican.

Royal Society the oldest and premier scientific society in Britain, originating 1645 and chartered 1660; Christopher ◊Wren and Isaac ◊Newton were prominent early members. Its Scottish equivalent is the Royal Society of Edinburgh 1783.

Royal Society for the Prevention of Cruelty to Animals (RSPCA) British organization formed 1824 to safeguard the welfare of animals; it promotes legislation, has an inspectorate to secure enforcement of existing laws, and runs clinics.

royalty in law, payment to the owner for rights to use or exploit literary or artistic copyrights and patent rights in new inventions of all kinds. Oil, gas, and other mineral deposits are also subject to royalty payments, but in these cases, royalties are paid by the owners (often government) to the exploiters of the deposits.

Royal Worcester Porcelain Factory see ◊Worcester Porcelain Factory.

Royce (Frederick) Henry 1863–1933. British engineer, who so impressed *Charles Stewart Rolls* (1877–1910) by the car he built for his own personal use 1904 that ◊Rolls-Royce Ltd was formed 1906 to produce cars and engines.

RPI abbreviation for *retail price index*; see ◊cost of living.

rpm abbreviation for *revolutions per minute*.

RSFSR abbreviation for ◊*Russian Soviet Federal Socialist Republic*, the largest constituent republic of the USSR.

RSPCA abbreviation for ◊*Royal Society for the Prevention of Cruelty to Animals*.

RSVP abbreviation for *répondez s'il vous plaît* (French 'please reply').

Rt Hon. abbreviation for *Right Honourable*.

Ruanda alternative spelling of ◊Rwanda, country in central Africa.

ruat coelum (Latin 'though the heavens may fall') whatever happens.

rubato a musical term, from *tempo rubato* (Italian 'robbed time'): a slight flexibility in the tempo for extra expressive effect.

rubber coagulated latex of a great range of plants, mainly from the New World. Most important is Para rubber, which derives from the tree *Hevea brasiliensis*. It was introduced from Brazil to SE Asia, where most of the world supply is now produced, the chief exporters being Malaysia, Indonesia, Sri Lanka, Kampuchea, Thailand, Sarawak, and Brunei. At about seven years the tree, which may grow to 20 m/60 ft, is ready for 'tapping'. Small incisions are made in the trunk and the latex drips into collecting cups.

rubber plant Asiatic tree *Ficus elastica*, family Moraceae, producing latex in its stem. With shiny, leathery, oval leaves, young plants are grown in the West as pot plants.

Rubbra Edmund 1901–1986. British composer. He studied under ◊Holst and was a master of contrapuntal writing, as exemplified in his study *Counterpoint* 1960. His compositions include 11 symphonies, chamber music, and songs.

rubella technical term for ◊German measles.

Rubens Peter Paul 1577–1640. Flemish painter, who became court painter to the archduke Albert and his wife Isabella in Antwerp. After a few years in Italy, he brought the exuberance of Italian Baroque to N Europe, creating, with an army of assistants, innumerable religious and allegorical paintings for churches and palaces. These show mastery of drama in large compositions, and love of rich colour and fleshy nudes. He also painted portraits and, in his last years, landscapes.

Rubicon ancient name of the small river flowing into the Adriatic which, under the Roman republic, marked the boundary between Italy proper and Cisalpine Gaul. When ◊Caesar led his army across it 49 BC he therefore declared war on the republic; hence to 'cross the Rubicon' means to take an irrevocable step. It is believed to be the present-day Fiumicino.

Rubik Erno 1944– . Hungarian architect, who invented the *Rubik cube*, a multicoloured puzzle which can be manipulated and rearranged in only one correct way, but about 43 trillion wrong ones. Intended to help his students understand three-dimensional design, it became a world craze.

Rubinstein Helena 1882–1965. Polish tycoon, who emigrated to Australia 1902, where she started up a face-cream business. She moved to Europe 1904, and later to the USA, opening salons in London, Paris, and New York.

Rubens The Descent from the Cross *(c. 1611) Courtauld Collection, London.*

Rublev (Rublyov) *c.* 1370–1430. Russian icon painter. Only one documented work survives, the *Holy Trinity c.* 1411 (Tretyakov Gallery, Moscow). This shows a basically Byzantine style, but with a gentler expression.

ruby the red transparent gem variety of the mineral ◊corundum. Small amounts of chromia, Cr_2O_3, substituting for alumina, give ruby its colour. The true ruby is found mainly in Burma, but rubies have been produced artificially and are widely used in ◊lasers.

rudd freshwater fish *Scardinius erythrophthalmus*, common in lakes and slow rivers of Europe. Brownish-green above and silvery below, with red fins and golden eyes, it can reach a length of 45 cm/1.5 ft, and a weight of 1 kg/2.2 lbs.

Rudolf former name of Lake ◊Turkana in E Africa.

Rudolph 1858–1889. Crown prince of Austria, the only son of Emperor Franz Joseph. From an early age he showed progressive views which brought him into conflict with his father. He conceived and helped to write a history of the Austro-Hungarian empire. In 1889 he and his mistress, Baroness Marie Vetsera, were found shot in his hunting lodge at Mayerling, near Vienna. The official verdict was suicide, although there were rumours that it was perpetrated by Jesuits, Hungarian nobles, or the baroness' husband.

Rudolph two Holy Roman emperors:

Rudolph I 1218–1291. Holy Roman emperor from 1273. Originally count of Hapsburg, he was the first Hapsburg emperor, and expanded his dynasty by investing his sons with the duchies of Austria and Styria.

Rudolph II 1552–1612. Holy Roman emperor from 1576, when he succeeded his father Maximilian II. His policies led to unrest in Hungary and Bohemia, which compelled Rudolph to surrender Hungary to his brother Matthias 1608, and to grant the Bohemians religious freedom.

Rudra early Hindu storm god, most of whose attributes were later taken over by ◊Siva.

rue shrubby perennial herb *Ruta graveolens*, family Rutaceae, native to S Europe and temperate Asia. It bears clusters of yellow flowers. An oil extracted from the strongly-scented blue-green leaves is used in perfumery.

ruff bird *Philomachus pugnax* of the snipe family. The name is taken from the frill of erectile feathers developed in breeding-time round the neck of the male. The ruff is found across N Europe and Asia, and migrates south in winter.

rugby a game that originated at Rugby school, England, 1823 when a boy, William Webb Ellis, picked up the ball and ran with it while playing football (now soccer). Rugby is played with an oval ball. It is now played in two forms: Rugby League and Rugby Union.

Rugby League the professional form of Rugby football founded in England 1895 as the Northern Union, when a dispute about pay caused northern clubs to break away from the Rugby Football Union. The game is similar to ◊Rugby Union but the number of players was reduced from 15 to 13 in 1906, and the scrum now plays a less important role as rule changes have made the game more open and fast-moving.

Rugby Union the amateur form of Rugby football, in which there are 15 players on each side. 'Tries' are scored by 'touching down' the ball beyond the goal-line or by kicking goals from penalties. The Rugby Football Union was formed 1871 and has its headquarters at Twickenham, Middlesex. The first World Cup was held in Australia and New Zealand 1987, and won by New Zealand.

Ruhr river in Germany; it rises in the Rothaargebirge and flows west to join the Rhine at Duisburg. The *Ruhr valley* (228 km/142 mi), a metropolitan industrial area (petrochemicals, cars; iron and steel at Duisburg and Dortmund) was formerly a coal-mining centre.

Ruisdael or *Ruysdael* Jacob van *c.* 1628–1682. Dutch landscape painter, active in Amsterdam from about 1655. He painted rural scenes near his native town of Haarlem and in Germany, and excelled in depicting gnarled and weatherbeaten trees. The few figures in his pictures were painted by other artists.

rule of law the doctrine that no individual, however powerful, is above the law. The principle had a significant influence on attempts to restrain the arbitrary use of power by rulers and on the growth of legally enforceable human rights in many Western countries. It is often used as a justification for separating legislative from judicial power.

rum spirit fermented and distilled from sugar cane. Scummings from the sugar-pans produce the best rum, molasses the lowest grade.

ruminant general name for an even-toed hoofed mammal with a rumen, the 'first stomach' of the complex digestive system. Plant food is stored and fermented before being brought back to the mouth for chewing (chewing the cud), and then is swallowed to the next stomach. Ruminants include cattle, antelopes, goats, deer, and giraffes.

rummy card game in which the players try to obtain either cards of the same denomination, or in sequence in the same suit, to score. It probably derives from ◊mahjong.

Rump, the English parliament formed between Dec 1648 and Nov 1653 after ◊Pride's Purge of the ◊Long Parliament to ensure a majority in favour of trying Charles I. It was dismissed 1653 by Cromwell, who replaced it with the ◊Barebones Parliament. Reinstated after the Protectorate ended 1659 and the full membership of the Long Parliament restored by ◊Monk 1660, it dissolved itself shortly afterwards and was replaced by the Convention Parliament which brought about the restoration of the monarchy.

Runcie Robert (Alexander Kennedy) 1921– . British cleric, archbishop of Canterbury 1980–91, the first to be appointed on the suggestion of the Church Crown Appointments Commission (formed 1977) rather than by political consultation. He favoured ecclesiastical remarriage for the divorced and the eventual introduction of the ordination of women.

Rundstedt Karl Rudolf Gerd von 1875–1953. German field marshal in World War II. Largely responsible for the German breakthrough in France 1940, he was defeated on the Ukrainian front 1941. As commander-in-chief in France 1942, he stubbornly resisted the Allied invasion 1944, and in Dec launched the temporarily successful Ardennes offensive. He was captured, but in 1949 war-crime charges were dropped owing to his ill health.

rune a character in the oldest Germanic script, chiefly adapted from the Latin alphabet, the earliest examples being from the 3rd century, and found in Denmark. Runes were scratched on wood, metal, stone, or bone.

runner in botany, an aerial stem which produces new plants, a type of ◊stolon.

Runyon Damon 1884–1946. US sports and crime reporter in New York, whose short stories *Guys*

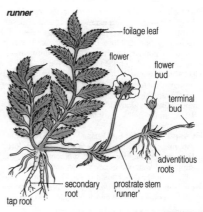

runner

foilage leaf
flower
flower bud
terminal bud
adventitious roots
secondary root
prostrate stem 'runner'
tap root

and Dolls 1932 deal wryly with the seamier side of the city's life in his own invented jargon.

Rupert Prince 1619–1682. English Royalist general and admiral, born in Prague, son of the Elector Palatine Frederick V (1596–1632) and James I's daughter Elizabeth. Defeated by Cromwell at ◊Marston Moor and ◊Naseby in the Civil War, he commanded a privateering fleet 1649–52, until routed by Admiral Robert Blake, and, returning after the Restoration, was a distinguished admiral in the Dutch Wars. He founded the ◊Hudson's Bay Company.

rupture synonym for ◊hernia.

rush plants of the genus *Juncus*, family Juncaceae, found in wet places in cold and temperate regions. The common rush has hollow stems which have been used for mats and baskets since ancient times.

Rushdie (Ahmed) Salman 1947– . British writer, born in India of a Muslim family. His novel *The Satanic Verses* 1988 (the title refers to verses deleted from the Koran) offended many Muslims with alleged blasphemy. In 1989 the Ayatollah Khomeini of Iran called for Rushdie and his publishers to be killed. Other books include *Midnight's Children* 1981 and for children, *Haroun and the Sea of Stories* 1990.

Rusk Dean 1909– . US Democratic politician. He was secretary of state to presidents Kennedy and Johnson 1961–69, and became unpopular through his involvement with the ◊Vietnam War.

Ruskin John 1819–1900. British art critic and social critic. He published five volumes of *Modern Painters* 1843–60, *The Seven Lamps of Architecture* 1849, in which he stated his philosophy of art, and *The Stones of Venice* 1851–53, in which he drew moral lessons from architectural history. His writings hastened the appreciation of painters considered unorthodox at the time, such as ◊Turner and the ◊Pre-Raphaelite Brotherhood. His later writings were concerned with social and economic problems.

Russell Bertrand (Arthur William), 3rd Earl 1872–1970. English philosopher and mathematician, who contributed to the development of modern mathematical logic, and wrote about social issues. Important works include *Principia Mathematica* 1910–13 (with A N Whitehead), in which he attempted to show that mathematics could be reduced to a branch of logic; *The Problems of Philosophy* 1912; and *A History of Western Philosophy* 1946. He was an outspoken liberal pacifist.

Russell Charles Taze 1852–1916. US religious figure, founder of the ◊Jehovah's Witness sect 1872.

Russell Dora (Winifred) (born Black) 1894–1986. English feminist, who married Bertrand ◊Russell 1921. The 'openness' of their marriage (she subsequently had children by another man) was a matter of controversy. She was a founder member of the National Council for Civil Liberties.

Russell George William 1867–1935. Irish poet and essayist. An ardent nationalist, he helped found the Irish national theatre, and his poetry, published under the pseudonym 'AE', includes *Gods of War* 1915, and reflects his interest in mysticism and theosophy.

Russell John, 1st Earl Russell 1792–1878. British Liberal politician, son of the 6th Duke of Bedford. He entered the House of Commons 1813, and supported Catholic emancipation and the Reform Bill. He held cabinet posts 1830–41, became prime minister 1846–52, and was again a cabinet minister until becoming prime minister again 1865–66. He retired after the defeat of his Reform Bill 1866.

Russell Ken 1927– . British film director, whose films include *Women in Love* 1969, *Altered States* 1979, and *Salome's Last Dance* 1988.

Russell Lord William 1639–1683. British Whig politician. Son of the 1st Duke of Bedford, he was among the founders of the Whig Party, and actively supported attempts in Parliament to exclude the Roman Catholic James II from succeeding to the throne. In 1683 he was accused, on dubious evidence, of complicity in the ◊Rye House Plot to murder Charles II, and was executed.

Russell of Liverpool Edward Frederick Langley Russell, 2nd Baron 1895–1981. British barrister. As deputy judge advocate-general, British Army of the Rhine 1946–47 and 1948–51, he was responsible for all war-crime trials in the British Zone of Germany 1946–50, and published *The Scourge of the Swastika* 1954 and *The Trial of Adolf Eichmann* 1962.

Russian Federation
formerly (until 1991)
Russian Soviet Federal Socialist Republic

area 17,075,500 sq km/6,591,100 sq mi
capital Moscow
towns St Petersburg (Leningrad), Nizhni-Novogorod (Gorky), Rostov-on-Don, Samara (Kuibyshev), Tver (Kalinin), Volgograd, Vyatka (Kirov), Ekaterinburg (Sverdlovsk)
physical fertile Black Earth district; extensive forests; the Ural Mountains with large mineral resources
head of state Boris Yeltsin from 1990/91
head of government Viktor Chernomyrdin from 1992
political system emergent democracy
products iron ore, coal, oil, gold, platinum, and other minerals, agricultural produce
currency rouble
population (1990) 148,000,000 (82% Russian, Tatar 4%, Ukrainian 3%, Chuvash 1%)
language Great Russian
religion traditionally Russian Orthodox
chronology
1945 Became a founding member of United Nations.
1988 Aug: Democratic Union formed in Moscow as political party opposed to totalitarianism. Oct: Russian language demonstrations in Leningrad and Tsarist flag raised.
1989 March: Boris Yeltsin elected to USSR Congress of People's Deputies. Sept:

conservative-nationalist Russian United Workers' Front established in Sverdlovsk.
1990 May: anticommunist May Day protests in Red Square, Moscow; Yeltsin narrowly elected RSFSR president by Russian parliament. June: economic and political sovereignty declared; Ivan Silaev became Russian prime minister. July: Yeltsin resigned his party membership. Aug: Tatarstan declared sovereignty. Dec: rationing introduced in some cities; private land ownership allowed.
1991 March: Yeltsin secured the support of Congress of Peoples' Deputies for direct election of an executive president. June: Yeltsin elected president under a liberal-radical banner. July: Yeltsin issued a sweeping decree to remove Communist Party cells from workplaces; sovereignty of the Baltic republics recognized by the republic. Aug: Yeltsin stood out against abortive anti-Gorbachev coup, emerging as key power-broker within Soviet Union; national guard established and pre-revolutionary flag restored. Sept: Silaev resigned as Russian premier. Nov: Yeltsin also named as prime minister; CPSU and Russian Communist Party banned; Yeltsin's government gained control of Russia's economic assets and armed forces. Oct: Checheno-Ingush declared its independence. Dec: Yeltsin negotiated formation of new confederal Commonwealth of Independent States (CIS); admitted into United Nations; Russian independence recognized by USA and EC.
1992 Jan: admitted into CSCE; assumed former USSR's permanent seat on UN Security Council; prices freed; Yeltsin proposed further major reductions in strategic nuclear weapons. Feb: Yeltsin-Bush summit meeting; Yeltsin administration rocked by neo-communist demonstrations in Moscow and criticism of vice president Rutskoi as living standards plummet. March: 18 out of 20 republics signed treaty agreeing to remain within loose Russian Federation; Tatarstan and Checheno-Ingush refused to sign. Aug: agreement with Ukraine on joint control of Black Sea fleet.
1993 March: Congress of People's Deputies attempted to limit Yeltsin's powers to rule by decree and cancel proposed referendum. Yeltsin declared temporary presidential 'special rule'. Results of referendum showed Russians in favour of Yeltsin's reforms.

Russian rulers 1547–1917

House of Rurik

Ivan IV 'the Terrible'	1547–84
Theodore I	1584–98
Irina	1598

House of Godunov

Boris Godunov	1598–1605
Theodore II	1605

Usurpers

Dimitri III	1605–6
Basil IV	1606–10

Interregnum 1610–13

House of Romanov

Michael Romanov	1613–45
Alexis	1645–76
Theodore III	1676–82
Peter I 'Peter the Great' and Ivan V (brothers)	1682–96
Peter I 'Peter the Great', as Tsar	1689–1721
as Emperor	1721–25
Catherine I	1725–27
Peter II	1727–30
Anna Ivanovna	1730–40
Ivan VI	1740–41
Elizabeth	1741–62
Peter III	1762
Catherine II 'Catherine the Great',	1762–96
Paul I	1796–1801
Alexander I	1801–25
Nicholas I	1825–55
Alexander II	1855–81
Alexander III	1881–94
Nicholas II	1894–1917

Russia originally the name of the pre-revolutionary Russian Empire (until 1917), and now accurately restricted to the Russian Federation.

Russian Federation or *Russia* country in N Asia and E Europe bounded by the Arctic Ocean, E by the Bering Sea and the Sea of Okhotsk, W by Norway, Finland, the Baltic States, Belarus, and Ukraine, and S by China, Mongolia, Georgia, Azerbaijan, and Kazakhstan.

Russian member of the majority ethnic group living in Russia. Russians are also often the largest minority in neighbouring republics. The Russian language is a member of the East Slavonic branch of the Indo-European language family and was the official language of the USSR, with 130–150 million speakers. It is written in the Cyrillic alphabet. The ancestors of the Russians migrated from central Europe between the 6th and 8th centuries AD.

Russian literature the modern period begins with Mikhail Lomonosov, who fused Church Slavonic and colloquial Russian. The 19th century was the golden age of Russian literature; its giants included novelists Ivan Turgenev, Fyodor Dostoievsky, and Leo Tolstoy; poets Alexander Pushkin and the Romantic Mikhail Lermontov; and Anton Chekhov brought his innovative genius to drama and the short story. Maxim Gorky was an exception to the pessimism of the 1880s. In the USSR (1917–91) censorship greatly impeded literary achievement. The few great writers of the period include poets Vladimir Mayakovsky, Osip Mandelshtam, Anna Akhmatova, and Nikolai Tikhonov, and Nobel-prizewinning novelists Boris Pasternak, Mikhail Sholokhov, and Alexander Sol-

zhenitsyn. Pasternak and Solzhenitsyn were disciplined for the views they expressed, and Solzhenitsyn, like many other writers, fled to the West.

Russian Revolution the two revolutions of Feb and Oct 1917 (Julian calendar) which began with the overthrow of the Romanov dynasty and ended with the establishment of a Soviet state. The *February Revolution* (Mar Western calendar) arose because of food and fuel shortages, the repressive nature of the tsarist government, and military incompetence in World War I. Riots in Petrograd led to the abdication of Tsar Nicholas II and the formation of a provisional government under Prince Lvov. They had little support as troops, communications, and transport were controlled by the Petrograd workers' and soldiers' council (soviet). ◊Lenin returned to Russia in Apr as head of the ◊Bolsheviks. Kerensky replaced Lvov as head of government in Jul. During this period, the Bolsheviks gained control of the soviets, and advocated land reform (under the slogan 'All power to the Soviets') and an end to the war. The *October Revolution* was a coup on the night of 25–26 Oct (6–7 Nov Western calendar). Bolshevik workers and sailors seized the government buildings and the Winter Palace, Petrograd. The second All-Russian Congress of Soviets, which met the following day, proclaimed itself the new government of Russia, and Lenin became leader. Bolsheviks soon took control of the cities, established worker control in factories, and nationalized the banks. The ◊Cheka (secret police) was set up to silence the opposition. The government concluded peace with Germany through the Treaty of ◊Brest-Litovsk, but civil war broke out as anti-Bolshevik elements within the army attempted to seize power; it lasted until 1920, when the Red Army, organized by ◊Trotsky, finally overcame 'White' opposition, with huge losses.

Russo-Japanese War war between Russia and Japan 1904–05, which arose from conflicting ambitions in Korea and ◊Manchuria, especially the Russian occupation of Port Arthur (modern Lüda) 1896 and of the Amur province 1900. Japan successfully besieged Port Arthur May 1904–Jan 1905, took Mukden 29 Feb–10 Mar, and on 27 May completely defeated the Russian Baltic fleet, which had sailed halfway around the world to Tsushima Strait. A peace was signed at Portsmouth, USA, 23 Aug. Russia surrendered her lease on Port Arthur, ceded S Sakhalin to Japan, evacuated Manchuria, and recognized Japan's interests in Korea.

russula type of fungus of the genus *Russula*, comprising many species. They are medium to large toadstools with flattened caps, and many are brightly coloured.

rust in chemistry, a reddish-brown oxide of iron (hydrated iron (III) or ferric oxide, $Fe_2O_3.H_2O$) formed by the action of moisture and oxygen on the metal.

rust in botany, common name for the minute parasitic fungi of the order Uredinales, which appear on the leaves of their hosts as orange-red spots, later becoming darker. The best-known is the wheat rust *Puccinia graminis*.

Ruth in the Old Testament or Hebrew Bible, Moabite (see ◊Moab) ancestress of David (king of Israel) by her second marriage to Boaz. When her first husband died, she chose to stay with her mother-in-law, Naomi.

Ruth Babe (George Herman) 1895–1948. US baseball player, regarded by many as the greatest of all time. He played in ten ◊World Series and hit 714 home runs, a record that stood from 1935 to 1974 and earned him the nickname 'Sultan of Swat'.

Rwanda
Republic of (*Republika y'u Rwanda*)

area 26,338 sq km/10,169 sq mi
capital Kigali
physical high savanna and hills, with volcanic mountains in NW
head of state and government Maj-Gen Juvenal Habyarimana from 1973

political system one-party military republic
exports tea, coffee, pyrethrum, tin, tungsten
currency Rwanda franc
population (1990 est) 7,603,000 (Hutu 90%, Tutsi 9%); annual growth rate 3.3%
life expectancy men 49, women 53
language Kinyarwanda, French
religion Christian (mainly Catholic) 66%, animist 23%, Muslim 9%
literacy 61% male/33% female (1985 est)
GNP $2.3 bn (1987); $323 per head
chronology
1962 Rwanda achieved full independence with Gregoire Kayibanda as president.
1962–65 Tribal warfare between the Hutu and the Tutsi.
1972 Renewal of tribal fighting.
1973 Kayibanda ousted in a military coup led by Maj-Gen Juvenal Habyarimana.
1978 New constitution approved but Rwanda remained a military-controlled state.
1980 Civilian rule adopted.
1988 Influx of refugees from Burundi.
1990 Government attacked by Rwanda Popular Front (FPR). Constitutional reforms promised.
1992 Peace accord with FPR.
1993 Power-sharing agreement with government repudiated by FPR.

Ruthenia or *Carpathian Ukraine* region of central Europe, on the south slopes of the Carpathian mountains, home of the Ruthenes or Russniaks. Dominated by Hungary from 10th century, it was part of Austria-Hungary until World War I. Divided among Czechoslovakia, Poland, and Romania 1918, it was independent for a single day in 1938, immediately occupied by Hungary, captured by the USSR 1944, and from 1945–47 was incorporated into Ukraine Republic, USSR. Ukraine became an independent republic 1991.

ruthenium element, symbol Ru, atomic number 44, relative atomic mass 101.06. It is a hard blue-white metal, a member of the platinum group, and used to harden platinum and palladium for use in electrical contacts. It is also a versatile catalyst.

Rutherford Ernest 1871–1937. New Zealand physicist. A pioneer of modern atomic science, his main research was in the field of radioactivity, and he was the first to recognize the nuclear nature of the atom.

rutherfordium artificially made element, symbol Rf, atomic number 104, named after Ernest Rutherford, but known in the USSR as kurchatovium (after scientist Igor Kurchatov). It is radioactive,

with a very short half-life, only 70 seconds for the most stable of the isotopes. It is now renamed unnilquadium.

rutile naturally occurring crystalline form of titanium (IV) oxide, TiO_2, from which titanium is extracted. It is also used as a pigment which gives a brilliant white to paint, paper, and plastics.

Rutland formerly the smallest English county, now part of ◊Leicestershire.

Ruyter Michael Adrianszoon de 1607–1676. Dutch admiral, who led his country's fleet in the wars against England. On 1–4 June 1666 he forced the British fleet under Rupert and Albemarle to retire into the Thames, but on 25 Jul was heavily defeated off the North Foreland, Kent. In 1667 he sailed up the Medway to burn three men-of-war at Chatham, and captured others.

Rwanda landlocked country in central Africa, bounded to the N by Uganda, to the E by Tanzania, to the S by Burundi, and to the W by Zaïre.

Ryder Cup golf tournament for professional men's teams from the United States and Europe. It is

rye

Rutherford New Zealand physicist Ernest Rutherford (right) with J Ratcliffe in Cambridge, 1935.

played every two years and the match is made up of a series of singles, foursomes, and fourballs played over three days.

rye a grain cereal *Secale cereale* grown extensively in N Europe. The flour is used to make black bread. In Britain, rye is grown principally as a forage crop, but the grain is used in the production of crispbread and some health cereals.

rye-grass perennial, rather wiry grass, *Lolium perenne*, common in pastures and waste places. It grows up to 60 cm/2 ft high, flowers in midsummer, and sends up abundant nutritious leaves, good for cattle. It is a Eurasian species but has been introduced to Australia and North America.

Rye House Plot conspiracy 1683 by English Whig extremists who had failed to stop the accession of the Catholic Charles II to the throne. They intended to murder Charles and his brother James, Duke of York, at Rye House, Hoddesdon, Hertfordshire, but the plot was betrayed. The Duke of ◊Monmouth was involved, and alleged co-conspirators, including Lord William ◊Russell and Algernon Sidney (1622–83) were executed for complicity.

Ryle Martin 1918–1984. English radioastronomer. At the Mullard Radio Astronomy Observatory, Cambridge, he developed the technique of sky-mapping using 'aperture synthesis', combining smaller dish aerials to give the characteristics of one large one.

Ryukyu Islands southernmost island group of Japan, stretching towards Taiwan and including Okinawa, Miyako, and Ishigaki

area 2,254 sq km/870 sq mi

capital Naha on Okinawa

products sugar, pineapples, fish

population (1985) 1,179,000

history originally an independent kingdom; ruled by China from the late 14th century until seized by Japan 1874; taken by USA 1945 (see under ◊Okinawa); northernmost group, Oshima, restored to Japan 1953, the rest 1972.

Ryzhkov Nikolai Ivanovich 1929– . Soviet communist politician. He held governmental and party posts from 1975 before being brought into the Politburo and made prime minister 1985–90 by Gorbachev. A low-profile technocrat, Ryzhkov was the author of unpopular economic reforms. In 1991 he unsuccessfully challenged Boris ◊Yeltsin for the Russian presidency.

S abbreviation for *south*.

SAARC abbreviation for *South Asian Association for Regional Co-operation*.

Saarinen Eero 1910–1961. Finnish-born US architect. His works include the US embassy, London, the TWA Terminal, New York, and Dulles Airport, Washington. He collaborated on a number of projects with his father, Eliel ◊Saarinen.

Saarinen Eliel 1873–1950. Finnish architect and town planner, founder of the Finnish Romantic school. In 1923 he emigrated to the USA, where he contributed to US skyscraper design by his work in Chicago, and later turned to functionalism.

Saarland (French *Saare*) *Land* (state) of Germany, crossed NW-S by the river Saar. Saarland is one-third forest.

area 2,569 sq km/992 sq mi

capital Saarbrücken

products former flourishing coal and steel industries survive only by government subsidy; cereals and other crops; cattle, pigs, poultry

population (1988) 1,034,000

history in 1919, the Saar district was administered by France under the auspices of the League of Nations; a plebiscite returned it to Germany 1935; Hitler gave it the name Saarbrücken; part of the French zone of occupation 1945, it was included in the economic union with France 1947; returned to Germany 1957.

Sabbath (from Hebrew *Shābath* 'to rest') the seventh day of the week, regarded as a sacred day of rest; in Judaism, from sunset Friday to sunset Saturday; in Christianity, Sunday (or, in some sects, Saturday).

Sabine a member of a people of ancient Italy from the mountains beyond the Tiber river, conquered by the Romans and amalgamated with them 3rd century BC. The rape of the Sabine women, which was a mythical attempt by Romulus in the early days of Rome to carry off the Sabine women to colonise the new city, is frequently depicted in art.

sable a carnivorous, nocturnal type of marten *Martes zibellina*, about 50 cm/20 in long, and usually brown. It is native to N Eurasian forests, but now found mainly in E Siberia.

saccharin sweet, white solid, ortho-sulpho benzimide, $C_7H_5NO_3S$, which is substituted for sugar as a slimming aid. In massive quantities it causes cancer in rats, but investigations in the USA led to no conclusive findings on its effect in humans.

Sacco-Vanzetti case murder trial in Massachusetts, USA, 1920–21. Italian immigrants Nicola Sacco (1891–1927) and Bartolomeo Vanzetti (1888–1927) were convicted of murder during an alleged robbery. The conviction was upheld on appeal, with application for retrial denied. Prolonged controversy delayed execution until 1927. In 1977 the verdict was declared unjust because of the judge's prejudice against the accuseds' anarchist views.

Sacher-Masoch Leopold von 1836–1895: Austrian novelist. His books dealt with the sexual pleasures to be obtained by having pain inflicted on oneself, hence ◊masochism.

Sachs Hans 1494–1576. German poet and composer who worked as a master shoemaker in Nuremberg. He composed 4,275 *Meisterlieder/mastersongs*, and figures prominently in ◊Wagner's opera *Die Meistersinger/The Mastersingers*.

sackbut musical instrument of the ◊brass family, a form of trombone, common from the 14th century.

Sackville Thomas, first Earl of Dorset 1536–1608. English poet, collaborator with Thomas Norton on *Gorboduc* 1561, written in blank verse and one of the earliest English tragedies.

sacrament in Christian usage, observances forming the visible sign of inward grace. In the Roman Catholic Church there are seven sacraments: baptism, Holy Communion (Eucharist or mass), confirmation, rite of reconciliation (confession and penance), holy orders, matrimony, and the anointing of the sick; only the first two are held to be essential by the Church of England.

Sacred Thread ceremony Hindu initiation ceremony which is a passage to maturity for boys of the upper three castes. It usually takes place between the ages of five and twelve, and is regarded as a second birth; the castes whose males are entitled to undergo the ceremony are called 'twice-born'.

Sadat Anwar 1918–1981. Egyptian politician. Succeeding ◊Nasser as president 1970, he restored morale by his handling of the Egyptian campaign in the 1973 war against Israel. In 1974 his plan for economic, social, and political reform to transform Egypt was unanimously adopted in a referendum. In 1977 he visited Israel to reconcile the two countries, and shared the Nobel Peace Prize with

Sadat President Anwar Sadat of Egypt, in Oct 1970.

Israeli Prime Minister Menachem Begin 1978. He was assassinated by Islamic fundamentalists.

Sadducee a member of an ancient Jewish sect opposed to the Pharisees. Sadducees denied the immortality of the soul and maintained the religious law in all its strictness.

Sade Marquis de 1740–1814. French soldier and author. He was imprisoned for sexual offences, and finally committed to an asylum. He wrote plays and novels dealing explicitly with a variety of sexual practices, including ◊sadism.

sadhu in Hinduism, a wandering holy man who devotes himself to the goal of *moksha*, or liberation from the cycle of reincarnation.

S'adi or Saadi pen name of Sheikh Moslih Addin *c.* 1184–*c.* 1291. Persian poet, author of *Bustan/Tree-garden* and *Gulistan/Flower-garden.*

sadism a tendency to derive pleasure (usually sexual) from inflicting physical or mental pain on others. The term is derived from the Marquis de ◊Sade, who used the theme in his works.

Sadler's Wells a theatre in Islington, N London, England. The original theatre was a music hall. Lilian Baylis developed a later theatre on the site 1931 as a northern annexe to the ◊Old Vic. For many years it housed the Sadler's Wells Opera Company, which moved to the London Coliseum 1969 (renamed English National Opera Company 1974), and the Sadler's Wells Ballet, which later became the ◊Royal Ballet.

Sadowa, Battle of (also known as the *Battle of Königgrätz*) Prussian victory over the Austrians 13 km/8 mi NW of Hradec Kralove (German Königgrätz) 3 Jul 1866, ending the ◊Seven Weeks' War. It confirmed Prussian hegemony over the German states, and led to the formation of the N German Confederation 1867. It is named after the nearby village of Sadowa (Czech *Sadová*) in Czechoslovakia.

s.a.e. abbreviation for *stamped addressed envelope.*

safety at work in British law all employers have a statutory duty under the Health and Safety at Work Act 1974 to ensure the safety, welfare, and health of their employees at work. This duty applies to all kinds of employment. Earlier legislation dealt with conditions of work only in particular kinds of employment.

safety glass glass that does not splinter into sharp pieces when smashed. *Toughened glass* is made by heating a glass sheet and then rapidly cooling it with a blast of cold air; it shatters into rounded pieces when smashed. *Laminated glass* is a 'sandwich' of a clear plastic film between two glass sheets; when this is struck, it simply cracks, the plastic holding the glass in place.

safety lamp a portable lamp designed for use in places where flammable gases such as methane may be encountered, for example in coal mines. The electric head lamp used as a miner's working light has the bulb and contacts in protected enclosures. The flame safety lamp, now used primarily for gas detection, has the wick enclosed within a strong glass cylinder surmounted by wire gauzes. Humphrey ◊Davy 1815 and George ◊Stephenson each invented flame safety lamps.

safflower Asian plant *Carthamus tinctorius*, family Compositae, resembling a thistle with reddish-orange flowers. It is widely grown for the oil from its seeds which is used in cooking, margarine, and paints and varnishes; the seed residue is used as cattle feed.

saffron plant *Crocus sativus*, probably native to SW Asia, and formerly widely cultivated in Europe; also the dried orange-yellow ◊stigmas of its purple flowers, used for colouring and flavouring.

saga prose narrative written down in the 11th–13th centuries in Norway and Iceland. The sagas range from family chronicles, such as the *Landnamabok* of Ari (1067–1148) to legendary and anonymous ones such as the *Njala* saga.

Sagan Françoise 1935– . French novelist. Her studies of love relationships include *Bonjour Tristesse/Hello Sadness* 1954, *Un certain sourire/A Certain Smile* 1956, and *Aimez-vous Brahms?/Do You Like Brahms?* 1959.

sage perennial herb *Salvia officinalis* with grey-green aromatic leaves used for flavouring. It grows up to 50 cm/1.6 ft high, and has bluish-lilac or pink flowers.

Sagittarius zodiac constellation representing a centaur aiming a bow and arrow at neighbouring Scorpius. The Sun passes through Sagittarius from mid-Dec to mid-Jan, including the winter solstice, when it is farthest south of the equator. The constellation contains many nebulae and ◊globular clusters, and some open ◊star clusters. The centre of the Galaxy is marked by the radio source Sagittarius A.

sago the starchy material obtained from the pith of the sago palm. It forms a nutritious food, and is used for manufacturing glucose.

Sahara the largest desert in the world, occupying 5,500,000 sq km/2,123,000 sq mi of N Africa from the Atlantic to the Nile, covering W Egypt, part of W Sudan, large parts of Mauritania, Mali, Niger, and Chad, and southern parts of Morocco, Algeria, Tunisia, and Libya. Small areas in Algeria and Tunisia are below sea level, but it is mainly a plateau with a central mountain system, including the Ahaggar Mountains in Algeria, the Aïr Massif in Niger and the Tibesti Massif in Chad, of which the highest peak is Emi Koussi 3,415 m/11,208 ft. The area of the Sahara has expanded by 650,000 sq km/251,000 sq mi in the last half century, but reafforestation is being attempted in certain areas.

saiga antelope *Saiga tartarica* of E European and W Asian steppes and deserts. Buff-coloured, whitish in winter, it stands 75 cm/2.5 ft at the shoulder, with a body about 1.5 m/5 ft long. The nose is large and swollen, with greatly developed bones and membranes, which may help warm and moisten the air inhaled, and keep out the desert dust. The saiga can run at 80 kph/50 mph.

Saigon former name of ◊Ho Chi Minh City, Vietnam.

Saigon, Battle of during the Vietnam War, battle 29 Jan–23 Feb 1968, when 5,000 Viet Cong were expelled by South Vietnamese and US forces. The city was finally taken by North Vietnamese forces 30 Apr 1975, after South Vietnamese withdrawal from the central highlands.

saint person eminently pious, especially one certified so in the Roman Catholic or Eastern Orthodox Church by ◊canonization. In the revised Calendar of Saints 1970 only 58 saints were regarded as of worldwide importance. The term is also used in Buddhism for individuals who have led a virtuous and holy life, such as Kukai (775–835), founder of the Japanese Shingon sect of Buddhism. For individual saints, see under forename, for example ◊Paul, St.

St Bartholomew, Massacre of religious murder of ◊Huguenots in Paris, 24 Aug–17 Sep 1572, and until 3 Oct in the provinces. When ◊Catherine

St Christopher (St Kitts)–Nevis

area 261 sq km/100 sq mi
capital Basseterre (on St Kitts)
towns Nevis (chief town of Nevis)
physical two islands in the Lesser Antilles

head of state Elizabeth II from 1983 represented by governor general
head of government Kennedy Alphonse Simmonds from 1980
political system federal constitutional monarchy
exports sugar, molasses, electronics, clothing
currency East Caribbean dollar
population (1990 est) 45,800; annual growth rate 0.2%
language English
religion Christian
literacy 90% (1987)
GNP $40 million (1983); $870 per head
chronology
1967 St Christopher, Nevis and Anguilla were granted internal self-government, within the Commonwealth, with Robert Bradshaw, Labour Party leader, as prime minister.
1971 Anguilla left the federation.
1978 Bradshaw died and was succeeded by Paul Southwell.
1979 Southwell died and was succeeded by Lee L Moore.
1983 St Christopher-Nevis achieved full independence within the Commonwealth.
1984 Coalition government re-elected.
1989 Prime minister Simmonds won a third successive term.

de Medici's plot to have ◊Coligny assassinated failed, she resolved to have all the Huguenot leaders killed, persuading her son Charles IX it was in the interests of public safety. 25,000 people were believed to have been killed. Catherine received congratulations from all the Catholic powers, and the pope ordered a medal to be struck.

St Bernard type of dog 70 cm/2.5 ft high at the shoulder, weight about 70 kg/150 lbs, named after the monks of St Bernard. They are squarely built, with pendulous ears and lips, large feet, and drooping lower eyelids.

St Christopher-Nevis country in the West Indies, in the Leeward Islands.

Sainte-Beuve Charles Augustin 1804–1869. French critic. He contributed to the *Revue des deux mondes/Review of the Two Worlds* from 1831. His articles on French literature appeared as *Causeries du lundi/Monday Chats* 1851–62, and his *Port Royal* 1840–59 is a study of ◊Jansenism.

St Elmo's fire harmless, flame-like electrical discharge, which occurs above ships' masts or about an aircraft in stormy weather. St Elmo (or St Erasmus) was a patron of sailors.

Saint-Exupéry Antoine de 1900–1944. French author, who wrote the autobiographical *Vol de nuit/Night Flight* 1931 and *Terre des hommes/Wind, Sand, and Stars* 1939. *Le petit prince/The Little Prince* 1943, a children's book, is also an adult allegory.

St George's port and capital of ◊Grenada; population (1986) 7,500, urban area 29,000.

St Helena island in the S Atlantic, 1,900 km/1,200 mi W of Africa, area 122 sq km/47 sq mi; population (1986) 5,700. Its capital is Jamestown, and it exports fish and timber. Ascension and Tristan da Cunha are dependencies.

St James's Palace a palace in Pall Mall, London, a royal residence 1698–1837.

St John, Order of (full title *Knights Hospitallers of St John of Jerusalem*) oldest order of Christian chivalry, named from the hospital at Jerusalem founded about 1048 by merchants of Amalfi for pilgrims, whose travel routes the knights defended from the Muslims. Today there are about 8,000 knights (male and female), and the Grand Master is the world's highest-ranking Roman Catholic layman.

St John's capital and chief port of Newfoundland, Canada; population (1986) 96,000, urban area 162,000. The main industry is cod fish processing.

St John's port and capital of Antigua and Barbuda, on Antigua; population (1982) 30,000.

Saint-Just Louis Antoine Léon Florelle de 1767–1794. French revolutionary. A close associate of ◊Robespierre, he became a member of the Committee of Public Safety 1793, and was guillotined with Robespierre.

St Kitts-Nevis contracted form of ◊St Christopher-Nevis.

Saint-Laurent Yves (Henri Donat Mathieu) 1936– . French couturier, partner to ◊Dior from 1954 and his successor 1957. He opened his own fashion house 1962.

St Lawrence river in E North America. From ports on the ◊Great Lakes, it forms, with linking canals (which also give great hydroelectric capacity to the river), the *St Lawrence Seaway* for ocean-going ships, ending in the *Gulf of St Lawrence*. It is 1,050 km/650 mi long, and is ice-bound for four months annually.

St Leger horse race held at Doncaster, England every September. It is a flat race over 2.8 km/1.7 mi, and is the last race of the season. First held 1776, it is the oldest of the English classic races.

St Louis city in Missouri, USA, on the Mississippi River; population (1990) 396,700, metropolitan area 2,444,100. Its industries include aerospace equipment, aircraft, vehicles, chemicals, electrical goods, steel, and beer.

Saint Lucia country in the West Indies, one of the Windward Islands.

St Moritz winter sports centre in SE Switzerland, which contains the Cresta Run (built 1885) for toboggans, bobsleighs, and luges. It was the site of the Winter Olympics 1928 and 1948.

St Lucia

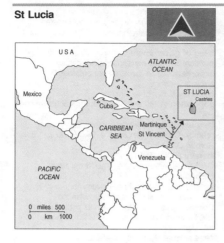

area 617 sq km/238 sq mi
capital Castries
towns Vieux-Fort, Soufrière
physical mountainous; mainly tropical forest

head of state Elizabeth II from 1979 represented by governor general
head of government John G M Compton from 1982
political system constitutional monarchy
exports coconut oil, bananas, cocoa, copra
currency E Caribbean dollar
population (1990 est) 153,000; annual growth rate 2.8%
language English; French patois
religion Roman Catholic 90%
literacy 78% (1989)
GNP $166 million (1987); $1,370 per head
chronology
1814 Became a British Crown Colony
1967 Granted internal self-government as a West Indies associated state.
1979 Independence achieved from Britain within the Commonwealth, with John Compton, leader of the United Workers' Party (UWP), as prime minister. Allan Louisy, leader of the Saint Lucia Labour Party (SLP), replaced Compton as prime minister.
1981 Louisy replaced by Winston Cenac.
1982 Compton returned to power at the head of a UWP government.
1987 Compton re-elected with reduced majority.
1991 Integration with Windward Islands proposed.
1992 UWP won general election.

St Petersburg capital of the St Petersburg region, Russia, at the head of the Gulf of Finland; population (1989 est) 5,023,500. Industries include shipbuilding, machinery, chemicals, and textiles. It was renamed Petrograd 1914 and was called Leningrad 1924–1991.

St Pierre and Miquelon territorial collectivity of France, eight small islands off the south coast of Newfoundland, Canada
area St Pierre group 26 sq km/10 sq mi; Miquelon-Langlade group 216 sq km/83 sq mi
capital St Pierre
products fish
currency French franc
population (1987) 6,300
language French
religion Roman Catholic
government French-appointed commissioner and elected local council; one representative in the National Assembly in France
history settled 17th century by Breton and Basque fishermen; French territory 1816–1976; overseas *département* until 1985; violent protests 1989 when France tried to impose its claim to a 200-mile fishing zone around the islands; Canada maintains that there is only a 12-mile zone.

Saint-Saëns (Charles) Camille 1835–1921. French composer, whose works include the symphonic poem *Danse macabre* 1875, the opera *Samson et Dalila* 1877, and the orchestral *Carnaval des animaux/Carnival of the Animals* 1886.

Saint-Simon Claude Henri, Comte de 1760–1825. French socialist, who fought in the American War of Independence and was imprisoned during the French Revolution. He advocated an atheist society ruled by technicians and industrialists in *Du Système industrielle/The Industrial System* 1821.

Saint-Simon Louis de Rouvroy, Duc de 1675–1755. French soldier, courtier, and politician, whose *Mémoires* 1691–1723 are unrivalled as a description of the French court.

Saint Vincent and the Grenadines country in the Windward Islands, West Indies.

St Vitus' dance former name for the disease ◊chorea. St Vitus, martyred under Diocletian, was the patron saint of dancers.

Sakhalin island in the Pacific, north of Japan, which since 1947 forms with the ◊Kurils a region of Russia; area 76,400 sq km/29,500 sq mi; population (1981) 650,000.

Sakharov Andrei Dmitrievich 1921–1989. Soviet physicist, known as the 'father of the Soviet H-bomb' and as an outspoken civil rights campaigner. He was elected to the Soviet parliament 1989.

Saki pen name of H(ugh) H(ector) Munro 1870–1916. British writer of ingeniously witty and bizarre short stories, often with surprise endings. He also wrote two novels. Born in Myanmar, where he served with the Military Police, he was foreign correspondent of the *Morning Post* 1902–08, and was killed in action in World War I.

Šatki the female principle in ◊Hinduism.

Šākyamuni the historical ◊Buddha, *Shaka* in Japan (because Gautama was of the Śakya clan).

Saladin or *Sala-ud-din* 1138–1193. Sultan of Egypt from 1175, in succession to the Atabeg of Mosul, on whose behalf he had conquered Egypt 1164–74. He conquered Syria 1174–87, and precipitated the third ◊Crusade by his recovery of Jerusalem from the Christians 1187. Renowned for knightly courtesy, Saladin made peace with Richard I of England 1192. He was a Kurd.

Salamanca, Battle of the British commander Wellington's victory over the French in the ◊Peninsular War, 22 Jul 1812.

salamander general name for a tailed amphibian, family Salamandridae, of the order *Caudata*, which

salamander

fire salamander

St Vincent and the Grenadines

area 389 sq km/150 sq mi, including N Grenadines 44 sq km/17 sq mi
capital Kingstown
physical volcanic mountains, thickly forested
head of state Elizabeth II from 1979 represented by governor general
head of government James Mitchell from 1984
political system constitutional monarchy
exports bananas, taros, sweet potatoes, arrowroot, copra
currency E Caribbean dollar
population (1990 est) 106,000; annual growth rate −4%
language English; French patois
religion Christian (Anglican 47%, Methodist 28%, Roman Catholic 13%)
literacy 85% (1989)
GNP $188 million (1989); $1,070 per head
chronology
1969 Granted internal self-government.
1979 Achieved full independence within the Commonwealth, with Milton Cato as prime minister.
1984 James Mitchell replaced Cato as prime minister.
1989 Mitchell decisively re-elected.
1991 Integration with Windward Isles proposed.

lives in the northern hemisphere. The European *spotted* or *fire salamander Salamandra salamandra*, is black with bright yellow, orange, or red markings, and up to 20 cm/8 in long. Other types include the *giant salamander* of Japan *Andrias japonicus*, 1.5 m/5 ft long, and the *Mexican salamander Ambystoma mexicanum*, or ◊*axolotl*.

Salamis ancient city on the E coast of Cyprus, the capital under the early Ptolemies until its harbour silted up about 200 BC, when it was succeeded by Paphos, in the southwest.

Salamis, Battle of naval battle off the coast of the island of Salamis in which the Greeks defeated the Persians 480 BC.

salat the daily prayers that are one of the Five Pillars of ◊Islam.

Salazar Antonio de Oliveira 1889–1970. Portuguese prime minister 1932–68, exercising a virtual dictatorship. A corporative constitution on the Italian model was introduced 1933, and until 1945 Salazar's National Union, founded 1930, remained the only legal party. Salazar was also foreign minister 1936–47, and during World War II maintained Portuguese neutrality.

Salic Law a law adopted in the Middle Ages by several European royal houses, excluding women from succession to the throne. In Sweden 1980 such a provision was abrogated to allow Princess Victoria to become crown princess. The name derives mistakenly from the Salian or northern division of the Franks who were supposed to have practised it.

salicylic acid the active chemical constituent of aspirin. The acid and its salts (salicylates) occur naturally in many plants; concentrated sources include willow bark and oil of wintergreen.

Salieri Antonio 1750–1825. Italian composer, who taught Beethoven, Schubert, and Liszt, and was the rival of Mozart, whom it has been suggested, without proof, he poisoned.

Salinger J(erome) D(avid) 1919– . US writer of the novel of adolescence *The Catcher in the Rye* 1951 and stories of a Jewish family, including *Franny and Zooey* 1961.

Salisbury former name of ◊Harare, capital of Zimbabwe.

Salisbury Robert Cecil, 1st Earl of Salisbury title conferred on Robert ◊Cecil, secretary of state to Elizabeth I of England.

Salisbury Robert Arthur Talbot Gascoyne-Cecil, 3rd Marquess of Salisbury 1830–1903. British Conservative politician. He entered the Commons 1853 and succeeded to his title 1868. As foreign secretary 1878–80, he took part in the Congress of Berlin, and as prime minister 1885–86, 1886–92, and 1895–1902 gave his main attention to foreign policy, remaining also as foreign secretary for most of this time.

saliva a secretion which aids the swallowing and digestion of food. In some animals, it contains the ◊enzyme ptyalin which digests starch, and in blood-sucking animals contains ◊anticoagulants.

Salk Jonas Edward 1914– . US physician and microbiologist. In 1954, he developed the original vaccine which led to virtual eradication of ◊polio in developed countries. He was director of the Salk Institute for Biological Studies, University of California, San Diego 1963–75.

Sallust Gaius Sallustius Crispus 86–c. 34 BC. Roman historian, a supporter of Julius ◊Caesar. He wrote accounts of Catiline's conspiracy and the Jugurthine War in an epigrammatic style.

salmon fish of the family Salmonidae. The normal colour is silvery with a few dark spots, but the colour changes at the spawning season. Salmon live in the sea, but return to spawn in the place they were spawned, often overcoming great obstacles to get there.

Salome 1st century AD. In the New Testament, granddaughter of the king of Judea, Herod the Great. Rewarded for her skill in dancing, she requested the head of John the Baptist from her stepfather ◊Herod Antipas.

salsa a Latin big-band dance music popularized by Puerto Ricans in New York in the 1980s and by, among others, the Panamanian singer Rubén Blades (1948–).

salsify hardy biennial *Tragopogon porrifolius*, family Compositae, often called *vegetable oyster*; its white fleshy roots and spring shoots are eaten as vegetables.

salt sodium chloride (NaCl), found in sea water, as rock salt, and in brine deposits. Common salt is used extensively in the food industry as a preservative and flavouring, and in the chemical industry to make chlorine and sodium. In chemistry, salts

Samoa, Western
Independent State of (*Samoa i Sisifo*)

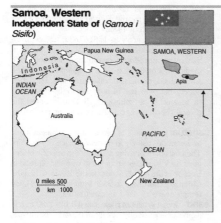

area 2,830 sq km/1,093 sq mi
capital Apia (on Upolu island)
physical comprises islands of Savai'i and Upolu, with two smaller tropical islands and islets; mountain ranges on the main islands
head of state King Malietoa Tanumafili II from 1962
head of government Tofilau Eti Alesana from 1988
political system liberal democracy
exports coconut oil, copra, bananas, cocoa
currency talà

population (1989 est) 169,000; annual growth rate 1.1%
life expectancy men 64, women 69 (1989)
language English, Samoan (official)
religion Christian
literacy 90% (1989)
GNP $110 million (1987); $520 per head
chronology
1959 Local government elected.
1961 Referendum favoured independence.
1962 Achieved full independence within the Commonwealth, with Fiame Mata'afa Mulinu'u as prime minister.
1975 Mata'afa died and was succeeded by Tupuola Taisi Efi, the first non-royal prime minister.
1982 Va'ai Kolone became prime minister, but was replaced the same year by Tupuola Efi. When the assembly failed to approve his budget, Tupuola Efi resigned and was replaced by Tofilau Eti Alesana.
1985 At the end of the year Tofilau Eti resigned over his budget proposals and the head of state refused to call a general election, inviting Va'ai Kolombe to return to lead the government.
1988 Elections produced a hung parliament, with first Tupuola Efi as prime minister and then Tofilau Eti.
1990 Universal adult suffrage introduced.
1991 Tofilau Eti Alesana re-elected. Fiame Naome became first woman in cabinet.

are compounds formed from an acid and a base; for example, hydrochloric acid and calcium carbonate form the salt sodium chloride, along with water and carbon dioxide.

SALT abbreviation for ◊*Strategic Arms Limitation Talks*, a series of US-Soviet negotiations 1969–79.

Salt Lake City capital of Utah, USA, on the river Jordan, 18 km/11 mi SE of the Great Salt Lake; population (1990) 159,900. Founded 1847, it is the headquarters of the ◊Mormon Church. Mining, construction, and other industries are being replaced by high technology.

saltpetre former name for potassium nitrate, KNO_3, the compound used in making gunpowder.

saluki breed of dog, also called the *gazelle hound*. It resembles the greyhound, is about 65 cm/26 in high, and has a light-coloured silky coat.

Salvador port and naval base in Bahia state, NE Brazil, on the inner side of a peninsula separating Todos Santos Bay from the Atlantic; population (1991) 2,075,400. Products include cocoa, tobacco, and sugar. Founded 1510, it was the capital of Brazil 1549–1763.

Salvador, El republic in Central America; see ◊El Salvador.

Salvation Army Christian evangelical, social-service, and social-reform organization, originating 1865 in London, England, with the work of William ◊Booth. Originally called the Christian Revival Association, it was renamed the East London Christian Mission 1870 and from 1878 has been known as the Salvation Army, now a worldwide organization. It has military titles for its officials, is renowned for its brass bands, and its weekly journal is the *War Cry*.

sal volatile another name for smelling salts.

Salyut a series of seven space stations launched by the USSR 1971–1982. Salyut was cylindrical in shape, 15 m/50 ft long, and weighed 19 tonnes. It

housed two or three cosmonauts at a time, for missions lasting up to eight months.

Salzburg capital of the state of Salzburg, W Austria, on the river Salzach, in W Austria; population (1981) 139,400. The city is dominated by the Hohensalzburg fortress. It is the seat of an archbishopric founded about 700, and has a 17th century cathedral.

samara in botany, a winged fruit, a type of ◊achene.

Samara formerly ◊Kuibyshev (1935–91). Capital of Kuibyshev region, W central Russia, and port at the junction of the rivers Samara and Volga, situated in the centre of the fertile middle Volga plain; population (1987) 1,280,000. Industries include aircraft, locomotives, cables, synthetic rubber, textiles, fertilizers, petroleum refining, and quarrying.

Samaria region of ancient Israel. The town of Samaria (modern *Sebastiyeh*) on the W bank of the river Jordan was the capital of Israel 10th–8th centuries BC, renamed Sebarte by Herod the Great. Extensive remains have been excavated.

Samaritan descendant of the colonists settled by the Assyrians in Samaria, after the destruction of the Israelite kingdom 722 BC. Samaritans adopted Judaism, but rejected all sacred books except the Pentateuch, and regarded their temple on Mount Gerizim as the true sanctuary.

Samaritans voluntary organization aiding those tempted to suicide or despair, established 1953 in the UK. Groups of lay people, often consulting with psychiatrists, psychotherapists, and doctors, offer friendship and counselling to those using their emergency telephone numbers, day or night.

Samarkand city in E Uzbekistan, capital of Samarkand region, near the river Zerafshan, 217 km/135 mi E of Bukhara; population (1987) 388,000. It was the capital of the empire of ◊Tamerlane, and was once an important city on the ◊Silk Road.

samizdat (Russian 'self-published') material circulated underground to evade censorship, especially in Eastern bloc countries, for example reviews of Solzhenitsyn's banned novel *August 1914* 1972.

Samoa volcanic island chain in the SW Pacific. It is divided into Western ◊Samoa and American ◊Samoa.

Samoa, American group of islands 2,600 miles S of Hawaii, administered by the US.
area 199 sq km/77 sq mi
capital Fagatogo on Tutuila
exports canned tuna, handicrafts
currency US dollar
population (1990) 46,800
language Samoan and English
religion Christian
government as a non-self-governing territory of the USA, under Governor A P Lutali, it is administered by the US Department of the Interior
history the islands were acquired by the United States Dec 1899 by agreement with Britain and Germany under the Treaty of Berlin. A constitution was adopted 1960 and revised 1967.

Samoa, Western country in the SW Pacific, in ◊Polynesia, NE of Fiji.

samovar (Russian 'self-boiling') an urn, heated by charcoal, used for making tea.

samoyed breed of dog, originating in Siberia. It is about 25 kg/60 lbs, and 50 cm/1.9 ft in height. It resembles a chow, but has a more pointed face and a white coat.

samphire also known as *glasswort* or *sea asparagus* perennial plant (*Crithmum maritimum*) found on sea cliffs in Europe. The aromatic leaves are fleshy and sharply pointed; the flowers grow in yellow-green umbels. It is used in salads, or pickled.

Samson in the Book of Judges in the Old Testament or Hebrew Bible, a hero of Israel. He was renowned for exploits of strength against the Philistines, which ended when his mistress Delilah cut off his hair.

Samuel in the Old Testament or Hebrew Bible, the last of the judges who ruled the ancient Israelites before their adoption of a monarchy, and the first of the prophets; the two books bearing his name cover the story of Samuel and the reigns of kings Saul and David.

samurai feudal military caste in Japan from the mid-12th century until 1869, when the feudal system was abolished and all samurai pensioned off by the government. A samurai was an armed retainer of a *daimyō* (large landowner) with specific duties and privileges, and a strict code of honour. A *rōnin* was a samurai without feudal allegiance.

San Hottentot name for hunter-gatherers of the Kalahari Desert. Found in Botswana, SW Africa and South Africa, they number approximately 50,000. Their languages belong to the Khoisan family.

San'a capital of Yemen, SW Arabia, 320 km/200 mi N of Aden; population (1986) 427,000. A walled city, with fine mosques and traditional architecture, it is rapidly being modernized. Weaving and jewellery are local handicrafts.

San Antonio city in S Texas, USA; population (1990) 935,900. A commercial and financial centre, industries include aircraft maintenance, oil refining, and meat packing. Founded 1718, it grew up around the site of the ◊Alamo fort.

sanction measure used to enforce international law, such as the attempted economic boycott of Italy during the Abyssinian War by the League of Nations; or Rhodesia, after its unilateral declaration of independence, by the United Nations; and the call for measures against South Africa on human rights grounds by the United Nations and other organizations from 1985.

Sanctorius Sanctorius 1561–1636. Italian physiologist who pioneered the study of ◊metabolism. Sanctorius introduced quantitative methods into medicine. For 30 years, he weighed both himself and his food, drink, and waste products. He determined that over half of normal weight-loss is due to 'insensible perspiration'. He also invented the clinical thermometer and a device for measuring pulse rate.

sanctuary a place of refuge from persecution or prosecution, usually in or near a place of worship. The custom of offering sanctuary in specific places goes back to ancient times and was widespread in Europe in the Middle Ages. In the 1980s in the UK, Christian churches, a Sikh temple, and a Hindu temple were all used as sanctuaries.

sand loose grains of rock, sized 0.02–2.00 mm in diameter, consisting chiefly of ◊quartz, but owing their varying colour to mixtures of other minerals. It is used in cement-making, as an abrasive, in glass-making, and for other purposes.

Sand George. Pen name of French author Amandine Aurore Lucie Dupin 1804–1876. Her prolific literary output was often autobiographical. After nine years of marriage, she left her husband 1831 and, while living in Paris as a writer, had love affairs with Alfred de ◊Musset, ◊Chopin, and others. Her first novel *Indiana* 1832 was a plea for women's right to independence.

sandbar ridge of sand lying in the water across the mouth of a river or bay, caused by a check on the current carrying sand. A sandbar may be entirely underwater or it may form an elongated island that breaks the surface. A sandbar stretching out from a headland is a *sand spit*.

Sandburg Carl August 1878–1967. US poet. He worked as a farm labourer, and a bricklayer, and his poetry celebrates ordinary US life, as in *Chicago Poems* 1916, and *The People, Yes* 1936. *Always the Young Strangers* 1953 is an autobiography. Both his poetry and his biography of Abraham Lincoln won Pulitzer prizes.

sandgrouse bird of the family Pteroclidae related to the pigeons. It lives in warm, dry areas of Europe and Africa and has long wings, short legs, and hard skin.

sandhopper crustacean *Talitrus saltator* about 1.6 cm/0.6 in long, without a shell. It is found above the high-tide mark on seashores. The term is also used to refer to some other amphipod crustaceans.

San Diego city and military and naval base in California, USA; population (1990) 1,110,500. Industries include bio-medical technology, aircraft missiles, and fish canning. Tijuana adjoins San Diego across the Mexican border.

sandpiper type of bird belonging to the snipe family Scolopacidae. The common sandpiper *Tringa hypoleucos* is a small graceful bird with long slender bill and short tail, drab above and white below. It is common in the N hemisphere.

Sandringham House private residence of the British sovereign, built by the Prince of Wales (afterwards Edward VII) 1869–71 on the estate which he had bought in Norfolk, NE of Kings Lynn, in 1863. The house is named after the nearby village of Sandringham. George V and George VI both died in the house, and Elizabeth II completely modernized both it and the estate.

sandstone *Torridonian Sandstone rock, shaped by the action of the waves at Loch Broom, Ross-shire, Scotland.*

sandstone rocks formed from the consolidation of sand, with sand-sized grains in a matrix or cement. The principal component is quartz. Sandstones are classified according to the matrix or cement material: whether derived from clay or silt, for example.

Sandwich John Montagu, 4th Earl of Sandwich 1718–1792. British politician. He was an inept 1st Lord of the Admiralty 1771–82 during the American War of Independence, his corrupt practices being held to blame for the British navy's inadequacies.

Sandwich Islands former name of ◊Hawaii, a group of islands in the Pacific.

San Francisco Pacific port of the USA, in California; population (1990) 724,000, metropolitan area of San Francisco-Oakland 3,192,000. The city stands on a peninsula, south of the Golden Gate 1937, the world's second longest single-span bridge, 1,280 m/4,200 ft. The strait gives access to San Francisco Bay. Industries include meat-packing, fruit canning, printing and publishing, and the manufacture of metal goods.

Sanger Frederick 1918– . English biochemist, the first to win a Nobel Prize for Chemistry twice: first for his elucidation of the structure of insulin 1958; and second, shared with two US scientists, for his work on the chemical structure of genes and the decoding of DNA, 1980.

Sangha in Buddhism, the monastic orders, one

San Francisco *Powell Street in San Francisco, USA.*

of the Three Treasures of Buddhism (the other two are Buddha and the law, or *dharma*). The term Sangha is sometimes used more generally by Mahāyāna Buddhists to include all believers.

San José capital of Costa Rica; population (1989) 284,600. Products include coffee, cocoa, and sugar cane. Founded in 1737, and capital since 1823.

San José city in Santa Clara Valley, California, USA; population (1990) 782,200. Industries include aerospace research and development, electronics, flowers, fruit canning, and wine making.

San Juan capital of Puerto Rico; population (1990) 437,750. It is a port and industrial city. Products include sugar, rum, and cigars.

San Luis Potosí silver-mining city and capital of San Luis Potosí state, central Mexico; population (1986) 602,000. It was founded 1586 as a Franciscan mission, and became the colonial administrative headquarters.

San Marino landlocked country within N central Italy.

San Martin José de 1778–1850. South American nationalist. Born in Argentina, he served in the Spanish army during the Peninsular War, but after 1812 he devoted himself to the South American struggle for independence, playing a large part in

San Marino
Republic of
(Republica di San Marino)

area 58 sq km/22.5 sq mi
capital San Marino
physical on the slope of Mount Titano
head of state and government two captains-regent, elected for a six-month period
political system direct democracy
exports wine, ceramics, paint, chemicals
currency Italian lira
population (1990 est) 23,000; annual growth rate 0.1%
language Italian
religion Roman Catholic 95%
literacy 97% (1987)
chronology
1862 Treaty with Italy signed, recognizing its independence and providing for its protection.
1947–86 Governed by a series of left-wing and centre-left coalitions.
1986 Formation of Communist and Christian Democrat 'grand coalition'.
1992 Joined the United Nations.

Santiago The Opera House in Santiago, Chile.

the liberation of Argentina, Chile, and Peru from Spanish rule.

sannyasin in Hinduism, a person who has renounced worldly goods in order to live a life of asceticism and seek *moksha*, or liberation from reincarnation, through meditation and prayer.

San Salvador capital of El Salvador, 48 km/30 mi from the Pacific, at the foot of San Salvador volcano 2,548 m/8,363 ft; population (1984) 453,000. Industries include food processing and textiles. Since its foundation 1525, it has suffered from several earthquakes.

sansculotte (French 'without knee breeches') in the French Revolution a member of the working classes, who wore trousers, as opposed to the aristocracy and bourgeoisie, who wore knee breeches.

Sanskrit the dominant classical language of the Indian subcontinent, a member of the Indo-Iranian group of the Indo-European language family, and the sacred language of Hinduism. The oldest form of sanskrit is *Vedic*, the variety used in the Vedas and Upanishads (*c.* 1500–700 BC).

sans souci (French) without cares or worries.

Santa Ana periodic warm California ◊wind.

Santa Anna Antonio Lopez de 1795–1876. Mexican revolutionary. A leader in achieving independence from Spain 1821, he pursued a chequered

career of victory and defeat, and was in and out of office as president or dictator for the rest of his life; he led the attack on the ◊Alamo 1836.

Santa Claus another name for Father Christmas; see under St ◊Nicholas.

Santa Fé Trail US trade route 1821–80 from Independence, Missouri, to Santa Fé, New Mexico.

Sant'Elia Antonio 1888–1916. Italian architect. His drawings convey a Futurist vision of a metropolis with skyscrapers, traffic lanes, and streamlined factories.

Santiago capital of Chile; population (1990) 4,385,500. Industries include textiles, chemicals, and food processing.

Santo Domingo capital and chief sea port of the Dominican Republic; population (1982) 1,600,000. Founded 1496 by Bartolomeo, brother of Christopher Columbus, it is the oldest colonial city in the Americas.

Sānusī Sidi Muhammad ibn 'Ali as' 1787–1859. Algerian-born Muslim religious reformer. He preached a return to the puritanism of early Islam and met with much success in Libya, where he made Jaghbub his centre and founded the sect called after him.

San Yu 1919– . Myanmar (Burmese) politician. A member of the Revolutionary Council which came to power 1962, he became president 1981 and was re-elected 1985. He was forced to resign 1988.

São Paulo city in Brazil, 72 km/44 mi NW of its port Santos; population (1991) 9,700,100, metropolitan area 15,280,000. It is 900 m/3,000 ft above sea level, and 2° S of the Tropic of Capricorn. It is South America's leading industrial city, producing electronics, steel, and chemicals, has meat-packing plants, and is the centre of Brazil's coffee trade.

São Tomé e Príncipe country in the Gulf of Guinea, off the coast of W Africa.

sap milky fluid exuded by certain plants, for example the rubber tree and opium poppy. The sap contains alkaloids, protein, and starch.

sapphire the blue transparent gem variety of the mineral ◊corundum. Small amounts of iron and titanium give it its colour.

Sappho *c.* 612–580 BC. Greek lyric poet, friend of the poet ◊Alcaeus, and leader of a female literary coterie at Mytilene (modern *Lesvos*, hence ◊lesbianism); legend says she committed suicide when her love for the boatman Phaon was

---

São Tomé e Príncipe
Democratic Republic of

area 964 sq km/372 sq mi
capital São Tomé

physical comprises the two main islands and several smaller ones, all of volcanic origin; thickly forested and fertile
head of state and government Miguel Trovoada from 1991
political system emergent democratic republic
exports cocoa, copra, coffee, palm
currency dobra
population (1990 est) 125,000; annual growth rate 2.5%
language Portuguese (official), Fang
religion Roman Catholic 80%; animist
literacy 73% male/42% female (1981)
GNP $32 million (1987); $384 per head
chronology
1973 Granted internal self-government.
1975 Achieved full independence, with Manuel Pinto da Costa as president.
1984 Formally declared itself a nonaligned state.
1987 President now popularly elected.
1988 Unsuccessful coup attempt.
1990 New constitution approved.
1991 First multiparty elections; Trovada replaced Pinto da Costa.

sapphire macrophotograph of sapphire or corundum.

unrequited. Only fragments of her poems have survived.

Sapporo capital of ◊Hokkaido, Japan; population (1990) 1,671,800. Industries include rubber and food processing. It is a winter sports centre, and was the site of the 1972 Winter Olympics.

saprophyte in botany, an obsolete term for a saprotroph.

saprotroph (formerly **saprophyte**) an organism that feeds on the products (such as excreta) or dead bodies of others. They include most fungi (the rest being parasites), many bacteria and protozoa, animals such as dung beetles and vultures, and a few unusual plants, including several orchids. Saprotrophs cannot make food for themselves, so they are a type of ◊heterotroph. They are useful scavengers, and in sewage farms and refuse dumps break down organic matter into nutrients easily assimilable by green plants.

Saracen ancient Greek and Roman term for an Arab, used in the Middle Ages by Europeans for all Muslims. The equivalent term used in Spain was Moor.

Saragossa (Spanish *Zaragoza*) industrial city in Aragon, Spain; population (1991) 614,400. It produces iron, steel, chemicals, plastics, canned food, and electrical goods. The medieval city walls and bridges over the Ebro survive, and there is a 15th-century university.

Sarajevo capital of Bosnia-Hercegovina population (1982) 448,500. Industries include engineering, brewing, chemicals, carpets, and ceramics. It was the site of the 1984 Winter Olympics. Since 1992 the city has been besieged by Serb militia units.

Sarawak state of Malaysia, on the island of Borneo
area 124,450 km/48,050 mi
capital Kuching
products forestry, rubber, coconuts
population (1991) 1,669,000
history granted by the Sultan of Brunei to James Brooke 1841, who became 'Rajah of Sarawak'; the region remained British (although captured by the Japanese in World War II) to 1963, when it became part of Malaysia.

sardine name for several small fish in the herring family.

Sardinia (Italian *Sardegna*) mountainous island, special autonomous region of Italy.
area 24,090 sq km/9,299 sq mi
capital Cagliari
exports cork, petrochemicals
population (1990) 1,664,400
recent history after centuries of foreign rule, it became linked with Piedmont 1720, and this dual kingdom became the basis of a united Italy 1861.

Sardou Victorien 1831–1908. French dramatist. He wrote plays with roles for Sarah Bernhardt and Henry Irving, for example *Fédora* 1882, *Madame Sans-Gêne* 1893, and *La Tosca* 1887 (the basis for the opera by Puccini). George Bernard Shaw coined the expression 'Sardoodledom' to express his disgust with the contrivances of the 'well-made' play – a genre of which Sardou was the leading exponent.

Sargasso Sea part of the N Atlantic (between 40° and 80° W, and 25° and 30° N) left static by circling ocean currents, and covered with floating weed *Sargassum natans*.

Sargent John Singer 1856–1925. US society portrait painter. Born in Florence of American parents, he studied there and in Paris, then settled in London about 1885. He was prolific and highly fashionable in his day.

Sargeson Frank 1903–1982. New Zealand writer of short stories and novels including *The Hangover* 1967 and *Man of England Now* 1972.

Sargon I King of Akkad *c.* 2370–2230 BC, and founder of the first Babylonian empire. His story resembles that of Moses in that he was said to have been found floating in a cradle on the river Euphrates.

Sargon II died 705 BC. King of Assyria from 722 BC, who assumed the name of his famous predecessor. To keep conquered peoples from rising against him, he had whole populations moved from their homelands, including the Israelites from Samaria.

Sark one of the ◊Channel Islands, 10 km/6 mi E of Guernsey; area 5 sq km/2 sq mi; there is no town or village. It is divided into Great and Little Sark, linked by an isthmus, and is of great natural beauty. The Seigneurie of Sark was established by Elizabeth I, the ruler being known as Seigneur/Dame, and has its own parliament, the Chief Pleas. There is no income tax and cars are forbidden; immigration is controlled.

Sarney José 1930 –. President of Brazil 1985–90, member of centre-left Brazilian Democratic Movement (PMDB).

Sarraute Nathalie 1920 –. Russian-born French novelist whose books include *Portrait d'un inconnu/Portrait of a Man Unknown* 1948, *Les Fruits d'or/The Golden Fruits* 1964, and *Vous les entendez? Do You Hear Them?* 1972. Sarraute bypasses plot, character, and style for the half-conscious interaction of minds.

sarsaparilla drink prepared from the long twisted roots of plants in the genus *Smilax*, native to Central and South America.

Sartre Jean-Paul 1905–1980. French author and philosopher, one of the leading proponents of existentialism in post-war philosophy. He published his first novel *La Nausée/Nausea* 1937, followed by the trilogy *Les Chemins de la liberté/Roads to Freedom* 1944–45, and many plays, including *Huis Clos/In Camera* 1944. *L'Être et le néant/Being and Nothingness* 1943, his first major philosophical

satellite *satellite image of the continent of North America.*

work, is important for its radical doctrine of human freedom. In the later work *Critique de la raison dialectique/Critique of Dialectical Reason* 1960 he tried to produce a fusion of Existentialism and Marxism.

Sary-Shagan weapons-testing area in Kazakhstan, near the Chinese border. In 1980 beam weapons were detected on trial there.

SAS abbreviation for ◊*Special Air Service, Scandinavian Airlines System*.

Saskatchewan province of W Canada.
area 652,330 sq km/251,800 sq mi
capital Regina
towns Saskatoon, Moose Jaw, Prince Albert
physical prairies in the south; to the north forests, lakes and subarctic tundra
products more than 60% of Canada's wheat; oil, natural gas, uranium, zinc, potash (world's largest reserves), copper, the only western reserves of helium outside the USA
population (1991) 995,300.
history French trading posts established about 1750; owned by Hudson's Bay Company, first permanent settlement 1774; ceded to Canadian government 1870 as part of Northwest Territories; became a province 1905.

Sassanian Empire Persian empire founded 224 AD by Ardashir, a chieftain in the area of modern Fars in Iran, who had taken over ◊Parthia; it was named for his grandfather, Sasan. The capital was Ctesiphon, near modern Baghdad. After a rapid period of expansion, when it contested supremacy with Rome, it was destroyed 637 by Muslim Arabs at the Battle of Qadisiyah.

Sassoon Siegfried 1886–1967. English writer. Educated at Cambridge, he enlisted in 1915, serving in France and Palestine. He published many volumes of poetry, three novels, and an autobiography.

sat in Hinduism, true existence or reality: the converse of illusion (*maya*).

Satan a name for the ◊devil.

satellite any small body that orbits a larger one, either natural or artificial. Natural satellites that orbit planets are called moons. The first *artificial satellite*, Sputnik I, was launched into orbit around the Earth by the USSR 1957. Artificial satellites are used for scientific purposes, communications, weather forecasting, and military purposes. The largest artificial satellites can be seen by the naked eye.

satellite television transmission of broadcast signals through artificial communications satellites. Mainly positioned in ◊geostationary orbit, satellites have been used since the 1960s to relay television pictures around the world. Higher power satellites have more recently been developed to broadcast signals to cable systems or directly to people's homes.

satellite town new town planned and built to serve a particular local industry, or as a dormitory or overspill town for people who work in a nearby metropolis. New towns in Britain include Port Sunlight near Birkenhead, Cheshire, built to house workers at Lever Brothers soap factories. More recent examples include Welwyn Garden City 1948, Cumbernauld 1955, and Milton Keynes 1967.

Satie Erik (Alfred Leslie) 1866–1925. French composer. His piano pieces, such as *Gymnopédies* 1888, often combine wit and melancholy. His orchestral works include *Parade* 1917, amongst whose bizarre sound effects is a typewriter. He was the mentor of the group of composers known as ◊*Les Six*.

satire a poem or piece of prose, which uses wit, humour, or irony, often through ◊allegory or extended metaphor, to ridicule human pretensions or expose social evils. Satire is related to *parody* in its intention to mock, but satire tends to be more subtle and to mock an attitude or a belief, whereas parody tends to mock a particular work such as a poem by imitating its style, often with purely comic intent.

Sato Eisaku 1901–1975. Japanese politician. He opposed the policies of Hayato Ikeda (1899–1965) in the Liberal Democratic Party, and succeeded him as prime minister 1964–72, pledged to a more independent foreign policy. He shared a Nobel Peace Prize 1974 for his rejection of nuclear weapons. His brother *Nobosuke Kishi* (1896–1987) was prime minister of Japan 1957–60.

satori in Zen Buddhism, awakening, the experience of sudden ◊enlightenment.

satrap title of a provincial governor in ancient Persia. The Persian Empire was divided into some 20 of these under Darius I, each owing allegiance only to the king. Later the term was used to describe any local ruler, often in a derogatory way.

Saudi Arabia
Kingdom of (al-Mamlaka al-'Arabiyaas-Sa'udiya)

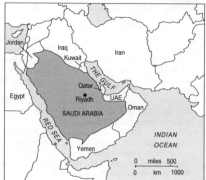

area 2,200,518 sq km/849,400 sq mi
capital Riyadh
towns Mecca, Medina; ports Jidda, Dammam
physical desert, sloping to the Persian Gulf from a height of 2,750 m/9,000 ft in the W
head of state and government King Fahd Ibn Abdul Aziz from 1982
political system absolute monarchy

exports oil, petroleum products
currency rial
population (1990 est) 16,758,000 (16% nomadic): annual growth rate 3.1%
life expectancy men 64, women 67
language Arabic
religion Sunni Muslim, with a Shi'ite minority
literacy men 34%, women 12% (1980 est)
GNP $70 bn (1988); $6,170 per head
chronology
1926–32 Territories united and kingdom established.
1953 King ibn-Saud died and was succeeded by his eldest son, Saud.
1964 King Saud forced to abdicate and was succeeded by his brother Faisal.
1975 King Faisal assassinated by a nephew and succeeded by his half-brother Khalid.
1982 King Khalid died of a heart attack and was succeeded by his brother Crown Prince Fahd.
1990 Iraq troops invaded and occupied Kuwait, then gathered on Saudi Arabian border. King Fahd called for help; US, UK and other multinational forces rallied in Saudi Arabia.
1991 King Fahd provided military and financial assistance to the Allies in the Gulf War. Calls from religious leaders for 'consultative assembly' to assist in government.
1992 Formation of a consultative council.

saturated solution in physics, a solution obtained when a solvent (liquid) can dissolve no more of a solute (usually a solid) at a particular temperature.

Saturn in astronomy, the second largest planet in the Solar System, sixth from the Sun, and encircled by bright rings. Viewed through a telescope it is white, but appears lemon-coloured when seen at closer range. Saturn orbits the Sun every 29.46 years at an average distance of 1,427,000,000 km/886,700,000 mi. Its equatorial diameter is 120,000 km/75,000 mi, but its polar diameter is 12,000 km/7,450 mi smaller, a result of its fast rotation and low density (70% of water, the lowest of any planet). Saturn spins on its axis every 10 hr 14 min at its equator, slowing to 10 hr 40 min at high latitudes. Its mass is 95 times that of Earth, and its magnetic field 1,000 times stronger. Saturn is believed to have a small core of rock and iron, encased in ice and topped by a deep layer of liquid hydrogen. There are over 20 known moons, its largest being ◊Titan. The visible rings, made of ice and rock, are 275,000 km/170,000 mi from rim to rim, but only 100 m/300 ft thick. The ◊Voyager probes showed that the rings actually consist of thousands of closely spaced ringlets, looking like the grooves in a gramophone record.

Saturn in Roman mythology, the god of agriculture (Greek **Kronos**), whose period of rule was the ancient Golden Age. He was dethroned by his sons Jupiter, Neptune, and Pluto. At his festival, the Saturnalia in Dec, gifts were exchanged, and slaves were briefly treated as their masters' equals.

Saturn rocket a family of large US rockets, developed by Wernher von Braun for the ◊Apollo project.

satyr in Greek mythology, a woodland being characterized by pointed ears, two horns on the forehead, and a tail, who attended Dionysus. Roman writers confused satyrs with goat-footed fauns.

Saudi Arabia country on the Arabian peninsula, stretching from the Red Sea to the Arabian Gulf, bounded to the N by Jordan, Iraq, and Kuwait, to the E by Qatar and United Arab Emirates, to the SE by Oman, and to the S by Yemen.

Saul died c. 1010 BC. In the Old Testament or Hebrew Bible, the first king of Israel, who was anointed by Samuel and warred successfully against the Ammonites and Philistines (neighbouring peoples). He turned against Samuel and committed suicide as his mind became unbalanced.

sauna a steamy heat bath consisting of a small room or cabinet in which the temperature is raised to about 90°C/200°F. The occupant typically stays in it for only a few minutes and then follows it with a cold shower.

savanna or **savannah** extensive open tropical grasslands, with scattered bushes and trees. Savannahs cover large areas of Africa, North and South America, and N Australia.

Savery Thomas c. 1650–1715. British engineer who invented the steam driven water pump, precursor of the steam engine. First built 1696 for use in mines, and patented two years later, it used a boiler to raise steam which was condensed (in a separate condenser) by an external spray of cold water. The partial vacuum created sucked water up a pipe from the mine shaft; steam pressure was then used to force the water away, after which the cycle was repeated.

savings unspent income, after deduction of tax. In economics a distinction is made between ◊investment, involving the purchase of capital goods, such as buying a house, and saving (where capital goods are not directly purchased, for example, buying shares).

savings and loan association in the USA, an institution which makes loans for home improvements, construction, and purchase. It also offers financial services such as insurance and annuities. It is not solely dependent on individual deposits for funds but may borrow from other institutions and on ◊money markets.

Savonarola Girolamo 1452–1498. Italian reformer, a Dominican friar whose eloquent preaching made him very popular. In 1494 he led a revolt in Florence which expelled the ruling Medici family and established a democratic republic. However, his denunciations of Pope ◊Alexander VI led to his excommunication 1497, and in 1498 he was arrested, tortured, hanged, and burned for heresy.

Savoy area of France between the Alps, Lake Geneva, and the river Rhône. A medieval duchy, it was formed into the *départements* of Savoie and Haute-Savoie, in Rhône-Alpes region.

sawfish fish of the ◊ray order. The *common sawfish Pristis pectinatus*, family Pristidae, is more than 6 m/19 ft long. It resembles a shark and has some 24 teeth along an elongated snout (2 m/6 ft) which can be used as a weapon.

sawfly type of insect of the order Hymenoptera, related to bees, wasps, and ants, but lacking a 'waist' on the body. The egg-laying tube (ovipositor) of the female has a saw edge which she uses to make a slit in a plant stem to lay her eggs.

Saxe Maurice, Comte de 1696–1750. Soldier, illegitimate son of the Elector of Saxony, who served under Prince Eugène of Savoy and was created marshal of France 1743 for his exploits in the War of the Austrian Succession.

Saxe-Coburg-Gotha Saxon duchy. Albert, the Prince Consort of Queen Victoria, was a son of the 1st Duke (Ernest 11784–1844), who was succeeded by Albert's elder brother, Ernest II (1818–93). It remained the name of the British royal house until 1917, when it was changed to Windsor.

saxifrage plant of the family Saxifragaceae, occuring in rocky, mountainous, and alphine situations. London Pride *Saxifraga umbrosa x spathularis* is a common garden hybrid, with rosettes of fleshy leaves and clusters of white to pink star-shaped flowers.

Saxon member of a Teutonic people who invaded Britain in the early Middle Ages; see under ◊Anglo-Saxon.

Saxony (German *Sachsen*) administrative *Land* (state) of Germany.
area 17,036 sq km/6,580 sq mi
capital Dresden
towns Leipzig, Chemnitz, Zwickau
physical on the plain of the river Elbe north of the Erzgeburge mountain range
products electronics, textiles, vehicles, machinery, chemicals, coal
population (1990) 5,000,000
history conquered by Charlemagne 792, Saxony became a powerful medieval German duchy. The electors of Saxony were also kings of Poland 1697–1763. Saxony was part of East Germany 1946–90.

Saxony-Anhalt administrative *Land* (state) of Germany.
area 20,450 sq km/10,000 sq mi
capital Magdeburg
towns Halle, Dessau
products chemicals, electronics, rolling stock, footwear, cereals, vegetables.
population (1990) 3,000,000
history A duchy 1863, Anhalt joined the North German Confederation 1866. With Saxony, it was a region of East Germany 1946–90.

saxophone a type of woodwind musical instrument made of metal. It was invented by the Belgian Adolphe Sax (1814–94) about 1840. Several varieties (soprano, alto, tenor, baritone, bass) of saxophone exist.

Sayers Dorothy L(eigh) 1893–1957. English writer of crime novels featuring detective Lord Peter Wimsey and heroine Harriet Vane, including *Strong Poison* 1930, *The Nine Tailors* 1934, and *Gaudy Night* 1935.

Say's Law in economics, the 'law of markets' enunciated by Jean-Baptiste Say (1767–1832) to the effect that supply creates its own demand and that resources can never be under-used.

scables contagious infection of the skin caused by the mite *Sarcoptes scaboi*. Treatment is by antiparasitic creams and lotions.

scabious Mediterranean plant of the family Dipsacaceae, with many small, usually blue, flowers borne in a single head. The *small scabious Scabiosa columbaria* and the *field scabious Knautia arvensis* are common species.

scalawag or *scallywag* in US history, a derogatory term for white Southerners who, during and after the Civil War of 1861–65, supported the Republican Party, and black emancipation.

scale in music, progression of notes which varies according to the musical system being used, for example, the seven notes of the ◊diatonic scale, the 12 notes of the ◊chromatic scale. Major and minor scales derive from the Ionian and Aeolian modes respectively, two of the 12 modes or scales of ancient music.

scallop marine ◊mollusc of the family Pectinidae, with a bivalve fan-shaped shell. Scallops use 'jet propulsion' to move through the water to escape predators such as starfish.

scampi (Italian 'shrimps') small lobster *Nephrops norwegicus* up to 15 cm/6 in long.

Scandinavia peninsula in NW Europe, comprising Norway and Sweden; politically and culturally it also includes Denmark and Finland.

scandium a scarce metallic element, symbol Sc, atomic number 21, relative atomic mass 44.96. It is one of the lanthanide series of elements and was discovered 1879 in the Scandinavian mineral euxenite.

scanner a device, usually electronic, used to sense and reproduce an image. In medicine scanners are used in diagnosis to provide images of internal organs.

scanning in medicine, the non-invasive examination of body organs to detect abnormalities of structure of function. Detectable waves, for example ◊ultrasound, ◊magnetic, or ◊X-rays, are passed through the part to be scanned. Their absorption pattern is recorded, analysed by computer, and displayed pictorially on a screen.

scarab name for the dung-beetles of the family Scarabeidae.

Scargill Arthur 1938– . English trade-union leader, a member of the Labour Party from 1966 and president of the Yorkshire miners' union 1973–81. Elected president of the National Union of Miners (NUM) 1981, he soon embarked on a collision course with the Conservative government of Margaret Thatcher. The damaging strike of 1984–85 split the miners' movement.

Scarlatti (Giuseppe) Domenico 1685–1757. Italian composer, eldest son of Alessandro ◊Scarlatti, who lived for most of his life in Portugal and Spain in the service of the Queen of Spain. He wrote highly original harpsichord sonatas.

Scarlatti (Pietro) Alessandro (Gaspare) 1660–1725. Italian Baroque composer, Master of the Chapel at the court of Naples, who developed the opera form (arias interspersed with recitative), writing more than 100 operas, such as *Tigrane* 1715, as well as much church music, including oratorios.

scarlet fever more correctly *scarlatina*, an infectious disease caused by the bacterium *Streptococcus pyogenes*. It is marked by a sore throat and a bright red rash spreading from the upper to the lower part of the body. The rash is followed by the skin peeling in flakes. It is treated with antibiotics.

scarp and dip in geology, the two slopes formed when a sedimentary bed outcrops as a landscape feature. The scarp is the slope that cuts across the bedding plane; the dip is the opposite slope which follows the bedding plane. The scarp is usually steep, the dip a gentle slope.

scent gland a gland that opens at the skin surface of animals, producing odorous compounds which are used in communication (◊pheromones).

Scepticism an ancient philosophical view that absolute knowledge of things is ultimately unobtainable, hence the only proper attitude is to suspend judgement. Its origins lay in the teachings of the Greek philosopher Pyrrho, who maintained that peace of mind lay in renouncing all claims to knowledge.

Scheer Reinhard 1863–1928. German admiral in World War I, commander of the High Sea Fleet 1916 at the Battle of Jutland.

scherzo in music, a lively piece, usually in rapid triple time, often the third movement of a symphony or sonata.

Schiaparelli Elsa 1896–1973. Italian couturier. Born in Rome, she emigrated to the USA and in the early 1920s went to Paris, where her modernistic knitwear designs made a great impact. She became known for her innovative fashion ideas, such as padded shoulders, colours ('shocking pink'), and the pioneering of zips and synthetic fabrics.

Schiele Egon 1890–1918. Austrian Expressionist artist. Originally a landscape painter, he was strongly influenced by Art Nouveau and developed a contorted linear style. His subject matter included portraits and nudes. In 1911 he was arrested for alleged obscenity.

Schiller Johann Christoph Friedrich von 1759–1805. German dramatist, poet and historian. He wrote *Stürm und Drang* (storm and stress) verse and plays, including the dramatic trilogy *Wallenstein* 1796–99. Much of his work concerns the desire for political freedom, and for the avoidance of mediocrity. He was a close friend of ◊Goethe.

Schinkel Karl Friedrich 1781–1841. Prussian architect of the Neo-Classical style. Major works include the Old Museum, Berlin 1823–30, the Nikolaikirche at Potsdam 1830–37, and the Roman Bath 1833 in the park of Potsdam.

schipperke (Dutch 'little boatman' from its use on canal barges), tailless watchdog, bred in Belgium. It has black fur and erect ears, is about 30 cm/1 ft high, and weighs about 7 kg/16 lbs.

schism a formal split over a doctrinal difference between religious believers, as in the Roman Catholic Church in the ◊Great Schism; that of the Old Catholics in 1870 over the doctrine of papal infallibility; and over use of the Latin Tridentine mass 1988.

schist a foliated (laminated) ◊metamorphic rock presenting layers of various minerals, for example mica, which easily split off into thin plates. Schist is formed by great pressure applied from one direction.

schizocarp a type of dry ◊fruit that develops from two or more carpels, and which splits, when mature, to form separate one-seeded units known as mericarps. The mericarps may be dehiscent, splitting open to release the seed when ripe, as in *Geranium*, or indehiscent, as in mallow *Malva* and plants of the Umbelliferae family, such as the carrot *Daucus carota* and parsnip *Pastinaca sativa*.

schizophrenia a mental disorder, a psychosis of unknown origin. It may develop in early adulthood and can lead to profound changes in personality and behaviour, including paranoia and hallucinations. Modern treatment approaches include drugs, family therapy, stress reduction, and rehabilitation.

Schlegel August Wilhelm von 1767–1845. German Romantic author, translator of Shakespeare, whose *Über dramatische Kunst und Literatur/Lectures on Dramatic Art and Literature* 1809–11 broke down the formalism of the old classical criteria of literary composition. Friedrich von Schlegel was his brother.

Schlegel Friedrich von 1772–1829. German critic, who (with his brother August) was a founder of the Romantic movement, and a pioneer in the comparative study of languages.

Schleswig-Holstein *Land* (state) of Germany.
area 15,727 sq km/6,071 sq mi
capital Kiel
towns Lübeck, Flensburg, Schleswig
products shipbuilding, mechanical and electrical engineering, food processing
population (1988) 2,613,000
religion Protestant 87%; Catholic 6%
history Schleswig (Danish *Slesvig*) and Holstein were two duchies held by the kings of Denmark from 1460, but were not part of the kingdom; a number of the inhabitants were German, and Holstein was a member of the German Confederation formed 1815. Possession of the duchies had long been disputed by Prussia, and when Frederick VII of Denmark died without an heir 1863, Prussia, supported by Austria, fought and defeated the Danes 1864, and in 1866 annexed the two duchies. A plebiscite held 1920 gave the N part of Schleswig to Denmark, which made it the province of Haderslev and Aabenraa; the rest, with Holstein, remained part of Germany.

Schlieffen Plan military plan produced by chief of the German general staff, Gen Count Alfred von Schlieffen (1833–1913) Dec 1905 which formed the basis of German military planning before World War I. It involved a simultaneous attack on Russia and France, the object being to defeat France quickly and then deploy all available resources against the Russians. A modified version of the plan was implemented 1914, and it also inspired Hitler's plans for the conquest of W Europe in World War II.

Schliemann Heinrich 1822–1890. German archaeologist. In 1871 he began excavating at Hissarlik, which he established as the site of Troy, although the 'palace and treasure of Priam' which he discovered belong to an earlier settlement than the one which Homer describes. His most important later excavations were at Mycenae.

Schmidt Helmut 1918–. West German socialist politician, member of the Social Democratic Party (SPD), chancellor 1974–83. He introduced social reforms and continued Brandt's policy of ◊Ostpolitik. With the French president Giscard d'Estaing, Schmidt introduced annual world and European economic summits. He was a firm supporter of ◊NATO and of the deployment of US

Schoenberg *Arnold Schoenberg teaching at the University of California.*

nuclear missiles in West Germany during the early 1980s.

Schoenberg Arnold (Franz Walter) 1874–1951. Austro-Hungarian composer. After romantic early work such as *Gurrelieder/Songs of Gurra* 1900–11) he flirted briefly with ◊atonality, producing such works as *Pierrot Lunaire* 1912, for chamber ensemble and voice, before developing the ◊*12-note system* of musical composition for which he is best known. This was further developed by his pupils ◊Berg and ◊Webern.

Scholasticism the theological and philosophical system of Christian Europe in the medieval period as studied in the schools. Principally, scholasticism sought to integrate Christian teaching with Platonic and Aristotelian philosophy.

Schopenhauer Arthur 1788–1860. German philosopher, whose *The World as Will and Idea* 1818 expounded an atheistic and pessimistic world view: an irrational will is considered as the inner principle of the world, producing an ever-frustrated cycle of desire, of which the only escape is aesthetic contemplation, or absorption into nothingness.

Schreiner Olive 1862–1920. South African novelist and supporter of women's rights. Her autobiographical *The Story of an African Farm* 1883 describes life on the South African veld.

Schubert Franz (Peter) 1797–1828. Austrian composer. He was only 31 when he died of syphilis, but his musical output was prodigious. He wrote ten symphonies, including the incomplete eighth in B minor (the 'Unfinished') and the 'Great' in C major 1829, chamber and piano music, and over 600 *Lieder* (songs) combining the romantic expression of emotion with pure melody. They include the cycles *Die schöne Müllerin/The Beautiful Maid of the Mill* 1823 and *Die Winterreise/The Winter Journey* 1827.

Schumacher Ernst Friedrich 'Fritz' 1911–1977. German writer and economist, whose *Small is Beautiful: Economics as if People Mattered* 1973 makes a case for small-scale economic growth without great capital expenditure.

Schuman Robert 1886–1963. French politician. He was prime minister 1947–48, and as foreign minister 1948–53 he proposed in May 1950 a common market for coal and steel (the *Schuman Plan*), which was established as the European Coal and Steel Community 1952, the basis of the European Community.

Schumann Robert Alexander 1810–1856. German composer. He was an influential member of the Romantic movement, and many of his works,

particularly his songs and short piano pieces, show simplicity combined with an ability to portray mood and emotion. His works include four symphonies, a piano concerto, sonatas and song cycles including *Dichterliebe/Poet's Love* 1840.

Schuschnigg Kurt von 1897–1977. Austrian chancellor 1934, in succession to ◊Dollfuss. In Feb 1938 he was forced to accept a Nazi minister of the interior, and a month later Austria was occupied and annexed by Germany. He was imprisoned in Germany until 1945, when he went to the USA.

Schütz Heinrich 1585–1672. German composer, music director to the Elector of Saxony from 1614. His works include *The Seven Last Words* about 1645, *Musicalische Exequien* 1636 (funeral pieces), and the *Deutsch Magnificat/German Magnificat* 1671.

Schwitters Kurt 1887–1948. German artist, a member of the Dada movement. He moved to Norway 1937 and to the UK 1940. From 1918 he developed a variation on collage, using discarded rubbish such as buttons and bus tickets to create pictures and structures.

sciatica persistent pain along the sciatic nerve which runs from the hip, down the back of the thigh, and, in its branches, to the toes. Causes of sciatica include inflammation of the nerve itself, or pressure on, or inflammation of, a nerve root leading out of the lower spine.

science broad term which can be applied to any systematic field of study or body of knowledge which aims, through experiment, observation and deduction, to produce reliable explanation of phenomena, with reference to the material and physical world. Modern science is divided into separate areas of study, such as astronomy, biology, chemistry, mathematics, and physics, although more recently attempts have been made to synthesize traditionally separate disciplines under such headings as ◊life sciences and ◊earth sciences. These areas are sometimes jointly referred to as the **natural sciences**. The **physical sciences** comprise mathematics, physics, and chemistry. The application of science for practical purposes is called **technology**. **Social science** is the systematic study of human behaviour, and includes such

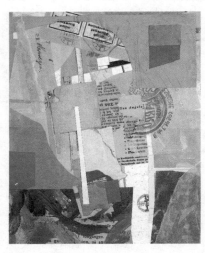

Schwitters Opened by Customs *(1937-38) Tate Gallery, London.*

areas as anthropology, economics, psychology, and sociology.

science fiction also known as *SF* or *Sci-Fi* prose fantasy based on an imaginary scientific and technological future. The genre is sometimes held to have its roots in the works of Mary Shelley, notably *Frankenstein* 1818. Often taking its ideas and concerns from current ideas in science and the social sciences, SF aims to shake up standard perceptions of reality.

Science Museum British museum of science and technology in South Kensington, London. Founded 1853 as the National Museum of Science and Industry, it houses exhibits from all areas of science.

science park site on which high-technology industrial businesses are housed near a university, so that they can benefit from the research expertise of the university's scientists. Science parks originated in the USA in the 1950s in North Carolina, California, Boston, and Cambridge. By 1985 the UK had 13, beginning with Heriot-Watt in Edinburgh.

scientific law in science, principles which are taken to be universally applicable.

Scientology an 'applied religious philosophy', based on ◊dianetics, founded in California 1954 by L Ron ◊Hubbard as the *Church of Scientology*. It claims to 'increase man's spiritual awareness', but its methods of recruiting and retaining converts have been criticized. Its headquarters from 1959 were in Sussex, England.

scilla bulbous plant of the family Liliaceae, bearing blue, pink, or white flowers, and including the spring squill *Scilla verna*.

Scilly Islands group of 140 islands and islets lying 40 km/25 mi SW of Land's End, England; administered by the Duchy of Cornwall; area 16 sq km/6.3 sq mi; population (1981) 1,850. The five inhabited islands are *St Mary's*, the largest, on which is Hugh Town, capital of the Scillies; *Tresco*, the second largest, with sub-tropical gardens; *St Martin's*, noted for beautiful shells; *St Agnes*, and *Bryher*.

scintillation counter an instrument for measuring very low levels of radiation. The radiation strikes a scintillator (a device which outputs a unit of light when a charged elementary particle collides with it), whose small light output is 'amplified' by a ◊photomultiplier; the current pulses of its output are in turn counted or summed by a scaler.

Scipio Publius Cornelius   died 211 BC. Roman general, father of Scipio Africanus Major. Elected consul 218, during the 2nd Punic War, he was defeated by Hannibal at Ticinus and killed by the Carthaginians in Spain.

Scipio Africanus Major 237–*c.* 183 BC. Roman general . He defeated the Carthaginians in Spain 210–206 BC, invaded Africa 204 BC, and defeated Hannibal at Zama 202 BC.

Scipio Africanus Minor *c.* 185–129 BC. Roman general, the adopted grandson of Scipio Africanus Major, also known as *Scipio Aemilianus*. He destroyed Carthage 146 BC, and subdued Spain 134 BC. He was opposed to his brothers-in-law, the Gracchi (see under ◊Gracchus), and his wife is thought to have shared in his murder.

SCLC abbreviation for US civil-rights organization ◊Southern Christian Leadership Conference.

sclerenchyma a plant tissue whose function is to strengthen and support, composed of thick-walled cells that are heavily lignified (see ◊lignin). On maturity the cell inside dies, and only the cell walls remain. Sclerenchyma may be made up of one or two types of cells: *Sclereids* can occur singly or

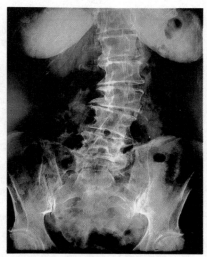

scoliosis X-ray of the spine of a woman, aged 80, showing a prominent scoliosis (lateral curve).

in small clusters, and are often found in the hard shells of fruits, in seed coats, bark, and the stem cortex. *Fibres*, frequently grouped in bundles, are elongated cells, often with pointed ends, associated with the vascular tissue (◊xylem and ◊phloem) of the plant.

Scofield Paul 1922–   . English actor. His wideranging lead roles include the drunken priest in Greene's *The Power and the Glory*, Harry in Pinter's *The Homecoming*, and Salieri in *Amadeus*. He appeared as Sir Thomas More in both stage and film versions of *A Man for All Seasons*.

scoliosis curvature of the spine. Correction by operation to insert a bone graft (thus creating only a rigid spine) has been replaced by insertion of an electronic stimulative device in the lower back to contract the muscles.

scorched earth in warfare, the policy of burning and destroying everything that might be of use to an invading army. The policy was used to great effect in Russia against invading armies, both in 1812 against the invasion of the French emperor Napoleon and again during World War II to hinder the advance of German forces 1941.

Scorpio another term for ◊Scorpius.

scorpion member of the order Scorpiones, class Arachnida. Common in the tropics and sub-tropics, the scorpion has a segmented body with a long tail ending in a poisonous sting, though the venom is not usually fatal to a healthy adult. Some species reach 25 cm/10 in. They produce live young rather than eggs, and hunt chiefly by night.

scorpion fly insect of the order Mecoptera. They have a characteristic downturned beak with jaws at the tip, and many males have a turned-up tail, giving

scorpion

Scotland: history

1st cent.	Romans prevented by Picts from penetrating far into Scotland.
5th–6th cent.	Christianity introduced from Ireland.
9th cent.	Kenneth MacAlpin united kingdoms of Scotland.
946	Malcolm I conquered Strathclyde.
1015	Malcolm II conquered Lothian.
1263	Defeat of Haakon, king of Norway at Battle of Largs.
1266	Scotland gained Hebrides from Norway at Treaty of Perth.
1292	Scottish throne granted by Edward I (attempting to annexe Scotland) to John Baliol.
1297	Defeat of England at Stirling Bridge by Wallace.
1314	Robert Bruce defeated English at Bannockburn.
1328	Scottish independence recognized by England.
1371	First Stuart king, Robert II.
1513	James IV killed at Battle of Flodden.
1540s–50s	Knox introduced Calvinism to Scotland.
1565	Mary Queen of Scots married Darnley.
1566	Rizzio murdered.
1567	Darnley murdered.
1568	Mary fled to England.
1578	James VI took over government.
1587	Mary beheaded.
1592	Presbyterianism established.
1603	James VI became James I of England.
1638	Scottish rebellion against England.
1643	Solemn League and Covenant.
1651–60	Cromwell conquered Scotland.
1679	Covenanters defeated at Bothwell Brig.
1689	Jacobites defeated at Killiecrankie.
1692	Massacre of Glencoe.
1707	Act of Union with England.
1715, 1745	Failed Jacobite risings against England.
1945	First Scottish nationalist member of parliament elected.
1979	Referendum on Scottish directly elected assembly fails.
1989	Local rates replaced by "poll tax" against wide opposition.

them their common name. Most feed on insects or carrion.

Scorpius or *Scorpio* zodiac constellation in the southern hemisphere, representing a scorpion. The Sun passes briefly through Scorpius in the last week of Nov. The heart of the scorpion is marked by the red supergiant star Antares. Scorpius contains rich Milky Way star fields, plus the strongest ◊X-ray source in the sky, Scorpius X-1.

Scorsese Martin 1942– . US director, whose films concentrate on complex characterization and the theme of alienation, and include *Taxi Driver* 1976, *Raging Bull* 1979, *After Hours* 1987, and *The Last Temptation of Christ* 1988.

Scotland country in N Europe, part of the British Isles
area 78,762 sq km/30,422 sq mi
capital Edinburgh
towns Glasgow, Dundee, Aberdeen
industry electronics, aero and marine engines, oil and natural gas, chemicals, textiles and clothing, food processing, tourism
currency pound sterling
population (1981) 5,121,000
language English; Gaelic spoken by 1.3%, mainly in the Highlands
religion Presbyterian (the Church of ◊Scotland), Roman Catholic
famous people Robert Bruce, Walter Scott, Robbie Burns, Robert Louis Stevenson, Adam Smith

government Scotland sends members to the UK parliament at Westminster. Local government is on similar lines to that of England (see under ◊provost), but there is a differing legal system (see ◊Scots Law). There is a growing movement for an independent or devolved Scottish assembly.

Scotland Yard, New headquarters of the ◊Criminal Investigation Department (CID) of the London Metropolitan Police, established 1878. It is named

Scotland: regions

Regions	Administrative headquarters	Area sq km
Borders	Newtown St Boswells	4,662
Central	Stirling	2,590
Dumfries and Galloway	Dumfries	6,475
Fife	Glenrothes	1,308
Grampian	Aberdeen	8,550
Highland	Inverness	26,136
Lothian	Edinburgh	1,756
Strathclyde	Glasgow	13,856
Tayside	Dundee	7,668
Island Authorities:		
Orkney	Kirkwall	974
Shetland	Berwick	1,427
Western Islands	Stornoway	2,901
		78,303

Scotland: kings and queens

(from the unification of Scotland to the union of the crowns of Scotland and England)

Celtic Kings

Malcolm II	1005
Duncan I	1034
Macbeth	1040
Malcolm III Canmore	1057
Donald Ban	1093
Duncan II	1094
Donald Ban (restored)	1095
Edgar	1097
Alexander I	1107
David I	1124
Malcolm IV	1153
William the Lion	1165
Alexander II	1214
Alexander III	1249
Margaret of Norway	1286–90

English Domination

John Balliol	1292–96
Annexed to England	1296–1306

House of Bruce

Robert I Bruce	1306
David II	1329

House of Stuart

Robert II	1371
Robert III	1390
James I	1406
James II	1437
James III	1460
James IV	1488
James V	1513
Mary	1542
James VI	1567
Union of Crowns	1603

from its original location in Scotland Yard off Whitehall.

Scots language the form of the English language as traditionally spoken and written in Scotland, regarded by some scholars as a distinct language.

Scots law the legal system of Scotland. Owing to its separate development, Scotland has a system differing from the rest of the UK, being based on ◊civil law. Its continued separate existence was guaranteed by the Act of Union with England 1707.

Scott (George) Gilbert 1811–1878. English architect. As the leading practical architect in the mid-19th-century Gothic revival in England, Scott was responsible for the building or restoration of many public buildings, including the Albert Memorial, the Foreign Office, and St Pancras Station, all in London.

Scott Giles Gilbert 1880–1960. English architect, grandson of George Gilbert Scott. He designed Liverpool Anglican Cathedral, Cambridge University Library, and Waterloo Bridge, London 1945. He supervised the rebuilding of the House of Commons after World War II.

Scott Paul (Mark) 1920–1978. English novelist, author of *The Raj Quartet* comprising *The Jewel in the Crown* 1966, *The Day of the Scorpion* 1968, *The Towers of Silence* 1972 and *A Division of the Spoils* 1975, dealing with the British Raj in India.

Scott Robert Falcon 1868–1912. '*Scott of the Antarctic*.' English Antarctic explorer, who commanded two Antarctic expeditions, 1901–04 and 1910–12. On 18 Jan 1912 he reached the South Pole, shortly after ◊Amundsen, but on the return journey he and his companions died, only a few miles from their base camp.

Scott Walter 1771–1832. Scottish novelist and poet. His first works were translations of German ballads, followed by poems such as 'The Lady of the Lake' 1810, and 'Lord of the Isles' 1815. He gained a European reputation for his historical novels such as *Heart of Midlothian* 1818, *Ivanhoe* 1819 and *The Fair Maid of Perth* 1828. His last years were marked by frantic writing to pay off his debts.

Scout member of a youth organization, originated (as the Boy Scouts) in England 1907 by Robert ◊Baden-Powell. His book *Scouting for Boys* 1908 led to the incorporation of the Boy Scout Association by royal charter in 1912. There are four branches: Beaver Scouts (aged 6–8), Cub Scouts (aged 8–11), Scouts (11–15), and Venture Scouts (15–20). About ⅓ of all Venture Scouts are girls; see also ◊Girl Guides. In 1987 there were 560,000 cubs and scouts and 640,000 brownies and guides.

Scrabble board game for two to four players, based on the crossword puzzle, in which 'letter' counters of varying point values are used to form words.

scrambling circuit in radio-telephony, a transmitting circuit which renders signals unintelligible unless received by the corresponding unscrambling circuit.

scraper an earth-moving machine used in road construction. Self-propelled or hauled by a ◊bulldozer, a scraper consists of an open bowl, with a cutting blade at the lower front edge. When moving, the blade bites into the soil, which is forced into the bowl.

scrapie fatal disease of sheep and goats, which attacks the central nervous system, causing deterioration of the brain cells. It is believed to be caused by a submicroscopic organism known as a prion.

screamer South American marsh-dwelling bird of the family Anhimidae, of which there are only three species. They are about 80 cm/2.6 ft long, with large bodies, short curved beaks, dark plumage, spurs on the front of the wings, and a crest or a horn on the head.

screening testing large numbers of apparently healthy people to detect early signs of disease, or checking into their backgrounds for security purposes.

screw thread cylindrical or tapering piece of metal or plastic (or formerly wood) with a helical groove

Scott *Robert Falcon Scott writing his journal during his second, fateful expedition to the Antarctic.*

cut into it. Each turn of a screw moves it forward or backwards by a distance equal to the pitch (the spacing between neighbouring threads). It can be thought of as an inclined plane (wedge) wrapped round a cylinder or cone.

Scriabin alternative spelling of the name of the Russian composer ◊Skryabin.

Scribe Augustin Eugène 1791–1861. French dramatist. He achieved fame with *Une Nuit de la garde nationale/Night of the National Guard* 1815, and with numerous assistants produced many plays of technical merit but little profundity, including *Bertrand et Raton/The School for Politicians* 1833.

scrip issue or *subscription certificate* a free issue of new shares to existing shareholders based on their holdings. It does not involve the raising of new capital as in a ◊rights issue.

Scudamore Peter 1958– . English National Hunt jockey. He was champion jockey 1982 (shared with John Francome), 1986, 1987, 1988, and 1989. In the 1988–89 season he became the third jockey to ride 1,000 National Hunt winners; in Feb 1989 he became the first man to ride 150 winners in a season.

Scullin James Henry 1876–1953. Australian Labor politician. He was leader of the Federal Parliamentary Labor Party 1928–35, and prime minister and minister of industry 1929–31.

sculpture the artistic shaping in relief or in the round of materials such as wood, stone, metal, and, more recently, plastic and other synthetics. All ancient civilizations, including the Assyrian, Egyptian, Indian, Chinese, and Maya, have left examples of sculpture, for the most part by unknown artists. Traditional European sculpture descends through that of Greece, Rome, and Renaissance Italy. The indigenous tradition of sculpture in Africa (see ◊African art), South America, and the Caribbean has particularly influenced modern sculpture.

scurvy a disease caused by lack of vitamin C which is contained in fresh vegetables, fruit, and milk. The signs are bleeding into the skin, swelling of the gums, and drying up of the skin and hair.

scurvy grass plant *Cochlearia officinalis* of the cabbage family, growing on salt marshes and banks by the sea. Shoots may grow low, or more erect up to 50 cm/2.6 ft, with rather fleshy heart-shaped leaves; flowers are white or mauve and four-petalled. The edible, sharp-tasting leaves are a good source of vitamin C and were formerly eaten by sailors as a cure for scurvy.

scutage in medieval times, a feudal tax imposed on knights as a substitute for military service.

Scylla and Charybdis in classical mythology, a sea-monster and a whirlpool, between which Odysseus had to sail. Later writers placed them in the Straits of Messina, between Sicily and Italy.

scythe harvesting tool with long wooden handle and sharp, curving blade. It was in common use in Britain from at least the Roman period through to the early 20th century, by which time it had generally been replaced by machinery.

Scythia region N of the Black Sea between the Carpathians and the river Don, inhabited by the Scythians 7th–1st centuries BC. Darius I of Persia made an unsuccessful attempt to conquer the Scythians 6th century BC; from the middle of the 4th century BC they were slowly superseded by the Sarmatians. They produced ornaments and vases in gold and electrum with animal decoration.

SDI abbreviation for ◊*Strategic Defense Initiative*.

SDLP abbreviation for ◊*Social Democratic and Labour Party* (Northern Ireland).

SDP abbreviation for ◊*Social Democratic Party*.

SDR abbreviation for ◊*special drawing right*.

sea anemone invertebrate sea-dwelling animal of the class Cnidaria with a tubelike body attached by the base to a rock or shell. The other end has an open 'mouth' surrounded by stinging tentacles, which capture crustaceans and other small organisms. Many sea anemones are beautifully coloured, especially those in tropical waters.

sea cucumber echinoderm of the class Holothuroidea with a cylindrical body which is tough-skinned, knobbed, or spiny. The body may be several feet in length. Sea cucumbers are sometimes called 'cotton-spinners' from the sticky filaments they eject from the anus in self-defence.

seafloor spreading growth of the ocean ◊crust outwards (sideways) from ◊ocean ridges. The concept of seafloor spreading has been combined with that of continental drift and incorporated into ◊plate tectonics.

sea-horse fish of one of several genera, of which *Hippocampus* is typical. The body is small and compressed and covered with bony plates raised into tubercles or spines. The tail is prehensile, and the tubular mouth sucks in small animals as food.

seakale perennial plant *Crambe maritima* of the family Cruciferae. In Europe it is cultivated as a vegetable, the young shoots being forced and blanched.

seal marine mammal of the family Phocidae. Streamlined in body shape, they have thick blubber for insulation, no external earflaps, and small front flippers. The hind flippers provide the thrust for swimming, but they cannot be brought under the body for walking on land. They feed on fish, squid, or crustaceans, and are most commonly found in Arctic and Antarctic waters, but are also found in Mediterranean, Caribbean, and Hawaiian waters.

seal a mark or impression made in a block of wax to authenticate letters and documents. In medieval England, the *great seal* was kept by the chancellor. The *privy seal* was initially kept for less serious matters, but by the 14th century it had become the most important seal.

sea law laws dealing with fishing areas, ships, and navigation; see ◊maritime law.

sea-lily deep-water echinoderm of the class Crinoidea. The rayed, cup-like body is borne on a stalk, and has feathery arms in multiples of five encircling the mouth.

sea lion marine mammal of the family Otariidae which also includes the fur seals. This streamlined animal has large fore flippers which it uses to row itself through the water. The hind flippers can be turned beneath the body to walk on land. A small earflap is present.

sea-mouse marine bristle worm *Aphrodite aculeata*, up to 20 cm/8 in long, with an oval body, flattened beneath and covered above with a mat of grey bristles, with iridescent bristles showing at the edges. It is usually found on soft sea beds.

Sea Peoples unidentified seafaring warriors who may have been ◊Achaeans, ◊Etruscans, or ◊Philistines, who ravaged and settled the Mediterranean coasts in the 12th–13th centuries BC. They were defeated by Rameses III of Egypt 1191.

seaplane an aeroplane capable of taking off from, and alighting on, water. There are two major types,

season

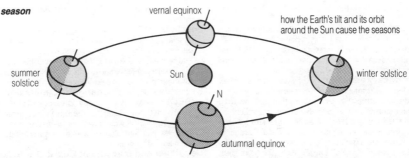

vernal equinox

how the Earth's tilt and its orbit
around the Sun cause the seasons

summer
solstice

Sun

winter solstice

N

autumnal equinox

float-planes and flying-boats. The float-plane is similar to an ordinary aeroplane but has floats in place of wheels; the flying-boat has a broad hull shaped like a boat, and may also have floats attached to the wing tips. Seaplanes depend on smooth water for a good landing and since World War II few have been built.

sea-potato yellow-brown sea-urchin *Echinocardium cordatum* covered in short spines, and found burrowing in sand from the lower shore downwards.

Searle Ronald 1920– . English cartoonist and illustrator, creator of the schoolgirls of St Trinian's 1941 and cartoons of cats.

sea-slug marine gastropod mollusc in which the shell is reduced or absent. Nudibranch sea-slugs include some very colourful forms, especially in the tropics. Tentacles on the back help take in oxygen. They are largely carnivorous, feeding on hydroids and sponges. Most are under 2.5 cm/1 in long, and live on the sea bottom or on vegetation.

season climatic type, at any place, associated with a particular time of the year. The change in seasons is mainly due to the change in attitude of the Earth's axis in relation to the Sun, and hence the position of the Sun in the sky at a particular place. In temperate latitudes four seasons are recognized: spring, summer, autumn (fall), and winter. Tropical regions have two seasons – the wet and the dry. Monsoon areas around the Indian Ocean have three seasons – the cold, the hot, and the rainy.

seasonal adjustment in statistics, an adjustment of figures designed to take into account influences which are purely seasonal, and relevant only for a short time.

seasonal unemployment unemployment arising from the seasonal nature of some economic activities. An example is agriculture, which uses a smaller labour force in winter. Seasonal employment can be created, however, as in the example of the retail sector in Western countries over the Christmas period.

sea-squirt ◊chordate of the class Ascidiacea. The adult is a pouch-shaped animal attached to a rock or other base, and drawing in food-carrying water through one siphon, and expelling it through

another after straining through the gills. The young are free-swimming tadpole-shaped organisms.

SEATO abbreviation for ◊*South-East Asia Treaty Organization.*

Seattle port (grain, timber, fruit, fish) of the state of Washington, USA, situated between Puget Sound and Lake Washington; population (1980) 494,000, metropolitan area 1,601,000. It is a centre for the manufacture of jet aircraft (Boeing), and also has shipbuilding, food processing, and paper industries.

sea-urchin name for a type of Echinoderm with a globular body enclosed with plates of lime and covered with spines. Sometimes the spines are holding-organs, and they also assist in locomotion. Sea-urchins feed on seaweed and the animals frequenting them, and some are edible.

seaweed common name for a vast collection of lower plant forms belonging to the ◊Algae and found growing from about high-water mark to depths of 100–200 m/300–600 ft. The plants have stalks or fronds, sometimes with air bladders to keep them afloat, and are green, blue-green, red, or brown.

Sebastiano del Piombo *c.* 1485–1547. Italian painter, born in Venice. He moved to Rome 1511, where his friendship with Michelangelo (and rivalry with Raphael) inspired him to his greatest works, such as the *Flagellation* (San Pietro in Montorio, Rome). He also painted portraits.

Sebastian, St died *c.* 288. Roman soldier, traditionally a member of Emperor Diocletian's bodyguard until his Christian faith was discovered. He was martyred by being shot with arrows; feast day 20 Jan.

secant in trigonometry, the function of an angle in a right-angled triangle obtained by dividing the length of the hypotenuse (the longest side) by the length of the side adjacent to the angle. It is the ◊reciprocal of the cosine (*sec* = 1/*cos*).

secession (Latin *secessio*) in politics, the withdrawal from a federation of states by one or more of its members, as in the secession of the

seaweed

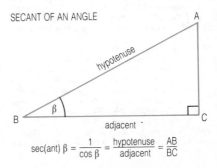

sea lettuce

dulse

sugar kelp

bladderwrack

SECANT OF AN ANGLE

A

hypotenuse

β

B

adjacent

C

$$\sec(\text{ant})\ \beta = \frac{1}{\cos \beta} = \frac{\text{hypotenuse}}{\text{adjacent}} = \frac{AB}{BC}$$

Confederate states from the Northern states in the USA 1860.

second basic ◊SI unit of time, one-sixtieth of a minute. It is defined as the duration of 9,192,631,770 periods of the radiation corresponding to the transition between two hyperfine levels of the ground state of the caesium-133 isotope.

secondary emission in physics, an emission of electrons from a surface of certain substances when they are struck by electrons or other particles from an external source. See also ◊photomultiplier.

secondary growth or *secondary thickening* the increase in diameter of the roots and stems of certain plants (notably shrubs and trees) that results from the production of new cells by the ◊cambium. It provides the plant with additional mechanical support and new conducting cells, the secondary ◊xylem and ◊phloem. Secondary growth is generally confined to ◊gymnosperms and, among the ◊angiosperms, to the dicotyledons. With just a few exceptions, the monocotyledons (grasses, lilies) exhibit only primary growth, resulting from cell division at the apical ◊meristems.

secondary market market for resale of purchase of shares, bonds, and commodities outside of organized stock exchanges and primary markets.

secondary modern school the secondary school which normally takes children who have failed to gain a ◊grammar school place, in those few areas of the UK which retain academic selection at 11 or 12.

secondary sexual character in biology, an external feature of an organism which is characteristic of its gender (male or female), but not the genitalia themselves. They include facial hair in men and breasts in women, combs in cockerels, brightly coloured plumage in many male birds, and manes in male lions. In many cases, they are involved in displays and contests for mates and have evolved by ◊sexual selection. Their development is stimulated by sex hormones.

secretary bird long-legged, mainly grey-plumaged bird of prey *Sagittarius serpentarius*, about 1.2 m/ 4 ft tall, with an erectile head crest. It is protected in S Africa because it eats poisonous snakes.

Secretary of State originally the title given under Elizabeth I of England to each of two officials conducting the royal correspondence. It is now a title held in the UK by a number of the more important ministers, for example, the Secretary of State for Foreign and Commonwealth Affairs. In the USA the Secretary of State deals with foreign affairs.

secretin a ◊hormone produced by the small intestine of vertebrates which stimulates the production of digestive secretions by the pancreas and liver.

secretion in biology, any substance (normally a fluid) produced by a cell or specialized gland, for example, sweat, saliva, enzymes, and hormones. The process whereby the substance is discharged from the cell is also known as secretion.

Secret Service government ◊intelligence organization.

secret society society with membership by invitation only, often involving initiation rites, secret rituals, and dire punishments for those who break the 'code'. Originally often founded for religious reasons or mutual benefit, they can become the province of corrupt politicians or gangsters. They include the ◊Mafia, ◊Ku Klux Klan, ◊Opus Dei, ◊Freemasonry, and the ◊Triad.

sect a small ideological group, usually religious in nature, aspiring to personal perfection and claiming a monopoly of access to truth or salvation.

secularization the process through which religious thinking, practice, and institutions lose their social significance. The concept is based on the theory, held by some sociologists, that as societies become industrialized their religious morals, values, and institutions give way to secular ones.

Securities and Exchange Commission (SEC) official US agency created 1934 to ensure full disclosure to the investing public and protection against malpractice in the securities (stocks and shares) and financial markets (such as insider trading).

Securities and Investment Board UK body with the overall responsibility for policing financial dealings in the City of London. Introduced 1987 following the deregulation process of the so-called ◊Big Bang, it acts as an umbrella organization to such self-regulating bodies as the Stock Exchange.

sedan chair an enclosed chair for one passenger carried on poles by two bearers, said to have been invented at Sedan, France. It was introduced to England by James I.

sedative drug (minor tranquillizer) with a calming effect. It will induce sleep in larger doses.

Seddon Richard John 1845–1906. New Zealand Liberal politician, prime minister 1893–1906.

seder meal that forms part of the Jewish festival of Passover, or Pesach.

sedge perennial grass-like plants of the genus *Carex*, family Cyperaceae, with three-cornered solid stems, common on wet and marshy ground.

Sedgemoor, Battle of battle which took place 6 Jul 1685, on a tract of marshy land 5 km/3 mi SE of Bridgwater, Somerset, England, in which ◊Monmouth's rebellion was crushed by the forces of James II of England.

sediment any loose material that has 'settled' – deposited from suspension in water or by wind, generally as the water or wind speed decreases. Typical sediments are, in order of increasing coarseness, clay, mud, silt, sand, gravel, pebbles, cobbles, and boulders.

sedimentary rock a rock formed by the accumulation and cementation of particles.

sedition in the UK, the offence of inciting unlawful opposition to the Crown and Government. It includes attempting to bring into contempt or hatred the person of the reigning monarch, the lawfully established Government, or either house of Parliament; inciting a change of government by other than lawful means; and raising discontent between different sections of the sovereign's subjects. Today any criticism aimed at reform is allowable. Unlike ◊treason, sedition does not carry the death penalty.

Seebeck effect in physics, the generation of a voltage in a circuit containing two different metals, or semiconductors, by keeping the junctions between them at different temperatures. Discovered by the German physicist Thomas Seebeck (1770–1831), it is also called the thermoelectric effect, and is the basis of the ◊thermocouple.

seed the reproductive structure of higher plants (◊angiosperms and ◊gymnosperms). It develops from a fertilized ovule and consists of an embryo and a food store, surrounded and protected by an outer seed coat, called the testa. The food store is contained either in a specialized nutritive tissue, the ◊endosperm, or in the ◊cotyledons of the embryo itself. In angiosperms the seed is enclosed within a

seed

castor (dicotyledon)

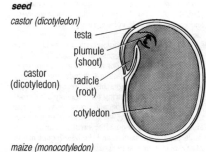

castor
(dicotyledon)

testa
plumule
(shoot)
radicle
(root)
cotyledon

maize (monocotyledon)

soft
endosperm
hard
endosperm
scutellum
plumule
radicle

maize
(monocotyledon)

◊fruit, whereas in gymnosperms it is usually naked and unprotected, once shed from the female cone. Following ◊germination the seed develops into a new plant.

seed drill   a machine for sowing cereals and other seeds, developed by Jethro ◊Tull in England 1701, although simple seeding devices were known in Babylon 2000 BC. The seed is stored in a hopper and delivered by tubes into furrows made in the ground by a set of blades called coulters attached in front. A ◊harrow is drawn behind the drill to cover up the seeds.

seed plant   any seed-bearing plant; also known as a spermatophyte. The seed plants are subdivided into two classes, the ◊angiosperms, or flowering plants, and the ◊gymnosperms, principally the cycads and conifers. Together, they comprise the major types of vegetation found on land. Angiosperms are the largest, most advanced, and most successful group of plants at the present time, occupying a highly diverse range of habitats. There are estimated to be about 250,000 different species.

Seferis   George. Assumed name of Greek poet-diplomat Georgios Seferiades 1900–1971. Ambassador to Lebanon 1953–57 and then to the UK 1957–62, he helped to resolve the Cyprus crisis. He published his first volume of lyrics 1931 and *Collected Poems* 1950, his work having a deep feeling for the Hellenic world and showing the influence of the French symbolists and of T S Eliot, whose *The Waste Land* he translated into modern Greek. Nobel prize 1963.

Seifert   Jaroslav 1901– . Czech poet, who won state prizes, but became an original member of the Charter 77 human rights movement. Works include *Mozart in Prague* 1970 and *Umbrella from Piccadilly* 1978. Nobel prize 1984.

Seine   French river rising on the Langres plateau NW of Dijon, and flowing 774 km/472 mi in a NW direction to join the English Channel near Le Havre, passing through Paris and Rouen.

seismology   study of earthquakes and how their shock waves travel through the Earth. By examining the global pattern of waves produced by an earthquake, seismologists can deduce the nature of the materials through which they have passed. This leads to an understanding of the Earth's internal structure.

Sekhmet   Egyptian goddess of heat and fire. She was represented with the head of a lioness, and worshipped at Memphis as the wife of Ptah.

select committee   name for several long-standing committees of the UK House of Commons. The former Estimates Committee, called the Expenditure Committee from 1970, was replaced 1979 by 14 separate committees, each with a more specialized function, such as the Environment Committee, and the Treasury and Civil Service Committee. These were intended to restore parliamentary control of the executive, improve the quality of legislation, and scrutinize public spending and the work of government departments. Departmental ministers attend to answer questions, and if information is withheld on a matter of wide concern, a debate of the whole House may be called. Select committees represent the major parliamentary reform of the 20th century, and a possible means – through their all-party membership – of avoiding the automatic repeal of one government's measures by its successor.

Selene   in Greek mythology, the goddess of the Moon. She was the daughter of Titan, and the sister of Helios and Eos. In later times she was identified with ◊Artemis.

selenium   an element, symbol Se, atomic number 34, atomic weight 78.96, associated with telurium and the sulphur family. It occurs as selenides and in many sulphide ores, and is used in making red glasses and enamels. As a semiconductor it is used extensively in photocells and rectifiers.

Seleucus I   Nicator *c.* 358–280 BC. Macedonian general under Alexander the Great and founder of the *Seleucid Empire*. After Alexander's death 323 BC, Seleucus became governor, and then ruler of Babylonia 321, founding the city of Seleucia on the river Tigris. He conquered Syria and had himself crowned king 306, but his expansionist policies brought him into conflict with the Ptolemies, and he was assassinated by Ptolemy Ceraunus. He was succeeded by his son Antiochus I.

self induction   or *self inductance*. In physics, the creation of a back e.m.f. (◊electromotive force) in a coil because of variations in the current flowing through it.

Selfridge   Harry Gordon 1857–1947. US businessman, who in 1909 founded the Selfridge Store in London, the first large department store in Britain.

Seljuk Empire   empire of the Turkish people, converted to Islam from the 7th century, under the leadership of the invading Tatars or Seljuk Turks. The Seljuk Empire 1055–1243 included all Anatolia and most of Syria. It was succeeded by the Ottoman Empire.

Sellafield   site of an atomic power station on the coast of Cumbria, NW England. It was formerly known as Windscale.

Sellers   Peter 1925–1980. English comedian and film actor, whose ability as a mimic often allowed him to take several parts. He made his name in the British radio comedy series *Goon Show* 1949–60, and his films include *Dr Strangelove* 1964, *Being There* 1979, and five *Pink Panther* films 1964–78 (as the bumbling Inspector Clouseau).

seller's market   market in which sellers prosper because there is a strong demand for their goods or services, thus pushing up the price.

selvas equatorial rainforest, especially that in the Amazon basin in South America.

Selwyn Lloyd John, Baron 1904–1978. British Conservative politician. He was foreign secretary 1955–60, and chancellor of the Exchequer 1960–62, responsible for the creation of the National Economic Development Council, but the unpopularity of his policy of wage restraint in an attempt to defeat inflation forced his resignation. He was Speaker of the House of Commons 1971–76.

Selznick David O(liver) 1902–1965. US film producer. His independent company Selznick International made such films as *King Kong* 1933, *Gone With the Wind* 1939, *Rebecca* 1940, and *Duel in the Sun* 1946.

semantics branch of ◊linguistics dealing with the meaning of words.

semaphore a visual signalling system in which the relative positions of two movable pointers or hand-held flags stand for different letters or numbers.

Semarang port in N Java, Indonesia; population (1980) 1,027,000. There is a shipbuilding industry and exports include coffee, teak, sugar, tobacco, kapok, and petroleum from nearby oilfields.

Semele in Greek mythology, mother of Dionysus by Zeus. At Hera's suggestion she demanded that Zeus should appear to her in all his glory, but when he did so she was consumed by lightning.

semelparity in biology, the occurrence of a single act of reproduction during an organism's lifetime. Most semelparous species produce very large numbers of offspring when they do reproduce, and normally die soon afterwards. Examples include the Pacific salmon and the pine looper moth. Many plants are semelparous, or ◊monocarpic. Repeated reproduction is called iteroparity.

semicolon a punctuation mark (;) with a function halfway between the separation of sentence from sentence by means of a full stop or period (.) and the gentler separation provided by a comma (,).

semaphore

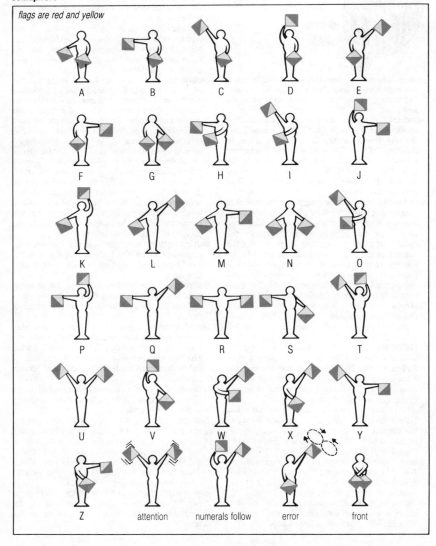

flags are red and yellow

Senegal
Republic of (*République du Sénégal*)

area 197,000 sq km/76,000 sq mi
capital and chief port Dakar
towns Thies, Kaolack
physical plains; swamp and tropical forest in SW
head of state and government Abdou Diouf from 1981
political system emergent socialist democratic republic
exports peanuts, cotton, fish, phosphates
currency CFA franc
population (1990 est) 7,740,000; annual growth rate 3.1%
life expectancy men 51, women 54
language French (official); African dialects
religion Muslim 80%, Christian 10% (chiefly Roman Catholic), animist 10%
literacy men 37%, women 19% (1985 est)
GNP $2 bn (1987); $380 per head
chronology
1960 Achieved full independence, with Léopold Sedar Senghor, leader of the Senegalese Progressive Union (UPS), as president.
1966 UPS declared the only legal party.
1976 UPS reconstituted as the Senegalese Socialist Party (PS). Abdou Diouf nominated as Senghor's successor.
1980 Senghor retired and was succeeded by Diouf. Troops sent to defend The Gambia.
1981 Military help again sent to The Gambia.
1982 Confederation of Senegambia came into effect.
1983 Diouf re-elected. Post of prime minister abolished.
1988 Diouf decisively re-elected.
1989 Violent clashes between Senegalese and Mauritanians in Dakar and Nouakchott.
1992 Diplomatic links with Mauritania re-established.

semiconductor a crystalline material with an electrical conductivity between that of metals (good) and insulators (poor).

semiology or *semiotics* the study of the function of signs and symbols in human communication, both in language and by various non-linguistic means. Beginning with the notion of the Swiss linguist Ferdinand de Saussure (1857–1913), that no word or other sign (*signifier*) is intrinsically linked with its meaning (*signified*), it was developed as a scientific discipline, especially by ◊Lévi-Strauss and ◊Barthes. See also ◊structuralism.

Semite a member of one of the ancient peoples of the Near and Middle East, traditionally said to be descended from Shem, a son of Noah in the Bible. Ancient Semitic peoples include the Israelites, Ammonites, Moabites, Edomites, Babylonians, Assyrians, Chaldaeans, Carthaginians, Phoenicians, and Canaanites. The Semitic peoples founded the religions of Judaism, Christianity, and Islam.

Semitic languages a branch of the ◊Hamito-Semitic family of languages.

Semtex a plastic explosive, manufactured in the Czech Republic. It is safe to handle (it can only be ignited by a detonator), and is difficult to trace, since it has no smell. It has been used by extremist groups in the Middle East, and by the IRA in Northern Ireland.

Senanayake Don Stephen 1884–1952. First prime minister of independent Sri Lanka (formerly Ceylon) 1947–52.

Senanayake Dudley 1911–1973. Prime minister of Sri Lanka 1952–53, 1960, and 1965–70; son of Don Senanayake.

senate the Roman 'council of elders'. Originally consisting of the heads of patrician families, it was recruited from ex-magistrates and persons who had rendered notable public service, but was periodically purged by the censors. Although nominally advisory, it controlled finance and foreign policy.

The US senate consists of 100 members, two from each state, elected for a six-year term. 'Senate' also refers to the upper house of the

Canadian parliament, equivalent to the House of Lords, the upper chambers of Italy and France, and also the governing bodies in some universities.

Sendai city in NE Honshu, Japan; population (1990) 918,400. Industries include metal goods (a Metal Museum was established in 1975), textiles, pottery, and food processing.

Seneca Lucius Annaeus *c.* 4 BC–AD 65. Roman Stoic playwright, author of essays and nine tragedies. Born at Córdoba, Spain, he was Nero's tutor, but lost favour after his accession and was ordered to commit suicide. His tragedies were accepted as classical models by 16th-century dramatists.

Seneca Falls Convention a meeting in New York state 1848 of women campaigning for rights.

Senegal country in W Africa, on the Atlantic, bounded to the N by Mauritania, to the E by Mali, to the S by Guinea and Guinea-Bissau, and enclosing Gambia on three sides.

Senghor Léopold 1906– . First president of independent Senegal 1960–80.

senile dementia a general term associated with old age; see ◊dementia.

Sennacherib died 681 BC. King of Assyria from 705. Son of ◊Sargon II, he rebuilt the city of Nineveh on a grand scale, sacked Babylon 689, and crushed ◊Hezekiah, king of Judah.

Seoul or *Soül* capital of South Korea, near the Han river, and with its chief port at Inchon; population (1985) 9,646,000. Industries include engineering, textiles, and food processing.

sepal part of a flower, usually green, which surrounds and protects the flower in bud. The sepals are derived from modified leaves, and collectively known as the ◊calyx. In some plants, such as the marsh marigold *Caltha palustris*, where the true ◊petals are absent, the sepals are brightly coloured and petal-like, taking over the role of attracting insect pollinators to the flower.

Sephardim Jews descended from those expelled from Spain and Portugal in the 15th century, or from those forcibly converted to Christianity (Marranos) at that time. Many settled in N Africa, and some in other Mediterranean countries or in England.

sepsis a general term for infection either on the surface of the body or within.

septicaemia ◊blood poisoning, the spread of ◊sepsis due to bacteria circulating in the bloodstream.

Septuagint the oldest Greek version of the Old Testament or Hebrew Bible, traditionally made by 70 scholars.

sequoia two species of conifer in the family Taxodiaceae, native to California, USA. The redwood *Sequoia sempervivens* is a long-lived timber tree, and one variety, the Howard Libbey redwood, is the world's tallest tree at 110 m/361 ft, with a circumference of 13.4 m/44 ft. The *Sequoiadendron giganteum* is the world's largest tree, up to 30 m/100 ft in circumference at the base, and almost as tall as the redwood. It is also, except for the bristlecone pine, the oldest living tree, some specimens having lived more than 3,000 years.

seraph (plural *seraphim*) in Christian and Judaic belief, an ◊angel of the highest order, as mentioned in the book of Isaiah in the Old Testament.

Serapis Graeco-Egyptian god, a combination of Hades and Osiris, invented by the Ptolemies; his finest temple was the Serapeum at Alexandria.

Serbia (Serbo-Croatian *Srbija*) constituent republic of Yugoslavia, which includes Kosovo and Vojvodina

area 88,400 sq km/34,122 sq mi

capital Belgrade

physical fertile Danube plains in the north, mountainous in the south

population (1986) 9,660,000

language the Serbian variant of Serbo-Croatian

religion Serbian Orthodox

history The Serbs settled in the Balkans in the 7th century and became Christians in the 9th century. They were united as one kingdom about 1169; the Serbian hero Stephan Dushan (1331–1355) founded an empire covering most of the Balkans. After their defeat at Kosovo 1389 they came under the domination of the Turks, who annexed Serbia 1459. Uprisings 1804–16, led by Kara George and Milosh Obrenovich, forced the Turks to recognize Serbia as an autonomous principality under Milosh. The assassination of Kara George on Obrenovich's orders gave rise to a long feud between the two houses. After a war with Turkey 1876–78, Serbia became an independent kingdom. On the assassination of the last Obrenovich 1903 the Karageorgevich dynasty came to the throne. The two Balkan Wars 1912–13 greatly enlarged Serbia's territory at the expense of Turkey and Bulgaria. Serbia's designs on Bosnia and Herzegovina, backed by Russia, led to friction with Austria, culminating in the outbreak

of war 1914. Serbia was overrun 1915–16 and was occupied until 1918, when it became the nucleus of the new kingdom of the Serbs, Croats, and Slovenes, and subsequently ◊Yugoslavia. Rivalry between Croats and Serbs continued within the republic. During World War II Serbia was under a puppet government set up by the Germans; after the war it became a constituent republic of Yugoslavia. From 1986 Slobodan Milosević as Serbian party chief and president waged a populist campaign to end the autonomous status of the provinces of Kosovo and Vojvodina. Despite a violent Albanian backlash in Kosovo 1989–90 and growing pressure in Croatia and Slovenia to break away from the federation, Serbia formally annexed Kosovo Sept 1990. Milosević was re-elected by a landslide majority Dec 1990, but in March 1991 there were anticommunist and anti-Milosević riots in Belgrade. The 1991 civil war in Yugoslavia arose from the Milosević nationalist government attempting the forcible annexation of Serb-dominated regions in Croatia, making use of the largely Serbian federal army. In Oct 1991 Milosević renounced territorial claims on Croatia pressured by threats of EC and UN sanctions, but the fighting continued until a cease-fire was agreed Jan 1992. EC recognition of Slovenia's and Croatia's independence in Jan 1992 and Bosnia-Herzegovina's in April left Serbia dominating a greatly reduced 'rump' Yugoslavia. A successor Yugoslavia, announced by Serbia and Montenegro April 1992, was rejected by the USA and EC, who remained concerned about serious human rights violations in Kosovo and Serbia's continued attempted partition of Bosnia-Herzegovina. In March 1992, and again in June, thousands of Serbs marched through Belgrade, demanding the ousting of President Milosević and an end to the war in Bosnia-Herzegovina.

SERC abbreviation for *Science and Engineering Research Council*.

sere a type of plant ◊succession developing in a particular habitat. A *lithosere* is a succession starting on the surface of bare rock. A *hydrosere* is a succession in shallow freshwater, beginning with planktonic vegetation and the growth of pondweeds and other aquatic plants, and ending with the development of swamp. A *plagiosere* is the sequence of communities that develops following the clearing of the existing vegetation.

serenade a piece for chamber orchestra or wind instruments in several movements, originally intended for evening entertainment, such as Mozart's *Eine Kleine Nachtmusik/A Little Night Music*.

Sergius, St of Radonezh 1314–1392. Patron saint of Russia, who founded the monastery of the Blessed Trinity near Moscow 1334.

serialism in music, another name for the ◊twelve-note system of composition.

Serpens constellation of the equatorial region of the sky, representing a serpent coiled around the body of Ophiuchus. It is the only constellation divided into two halves, *Serpens Caput*, the head (on one side of Ophiuchus), and *Serpens Cauda*, the tail (on the other side). Its main feature is the Eagle Nebula.

serpentine a group of minerals, hydrated magnesium silicate, $Mg_3Si_2O_5.2H_2O$, occuring in soft rocks. The fibrous form chrysotile is a source of ◊asbestos; other forms are antigorite, talc, and meerschaum.

SERPS abbreviation for State Earnings Related Pension Schemes, the UK state ◊pension scheme. Pension schemes operated by private companies

sequoia

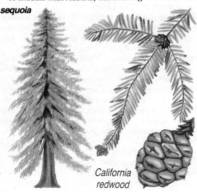

California
redwood

may now be run in conjunction with SERPS; if they are, they are called 'contracted in', and part of an employee's National Insurance contributions go towards the pension, which is linked to final salary.

serum   a clear fluid that remains after blood clots. It is blood plasma with the anti-coagulant proteins removed, and contains ◊antibodies and other proteins, as well as the fats and sugars of the blood. It can be produced synthetically, and is used to protect against disease.

serval   African wildcat *Felis serval*. It is a slender, long-limbed cat, about 1 m/3 ft long, with a yellowish-brown, black-spotted coat. It has large, sensitive ears, with which it locates its prey, mainly birds and rodents.

Servetus   Michael 1511–1553. Spanish Christian theologian and Anabaptist. He was burned alive by the church reformer Calvin in Geneva, Switzerland, for his unitarian views. As a physician, he was a pioneer in the study of the circulation of the blood.

Service   Robert (William) 1874–1938. Canadian author, born in England. He was popular for his ballads of the Yukon in the days of the Gold Rush, for example 'The Shooting of Dan McGrew' 1907.

service industry   commercial activity that provides and charges for various services to customers (as opposed to manufacturing or supplying goods), such as restaurants, the tourist industry, cleaning, hotels, and the retail trade (shops and supermarkets).

service tree   deciduous Eurasian tree *Sorbus domestica*, family Rosaceae, with alternate leaves, white flowers, and small oval fruit. The wild service tree *Sorbus torminalis* has lobed leaves.

servo system   an automatic control system used in aircraft, motor cars, and other complex machines. A specific input, such as moving a lever or joystick, causes a specific output, such as feeding current to an electric motor that moves, for example, the rudder of the aircraft. At the same time the position of the rudder is detected and fed back to the central control, so that small adjustments can continually be made to maintain the desired course.

set

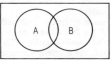

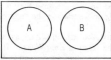

A and B are overlapping sets

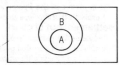

A and B are disjoint sets

B

A

A is the subset of B

sesame   annual plant *Sesamum indicum* of the family Pedaliaceas, probably native to SE Asia. It produces oily seeds used for food and soap making.

sessile   in botany, a leaf, flower, or fruit that lacks a stalk and sits directly on the stem, as with the acorns of sessile oak *Quercus petraea*. In zoology, it is an animal that normally stays in the same place, such as a barnacle or mussel. The term is also applied to the eyes of crustaceans when these lack stalks and sit directly on the head.

Session, Court of   one of the civil courts in Scotland.

Sessions   Roger (Huntingdon) 1896–1985. US composer, whose dense and dissonant works include *The Black Maskers* incidental music 1923, eight symphonies, and *Concerto for Orchestra* 1971.

Set   in Egyptian mythology, the god of night, the desert, and of all evils. He was the murderer of ◊Osiris, and is portrayed as a grotesque animal.

set   in mathematics, any collection of defined things (elements), provided the elements are distinct and

Seurat The Bathers, Asnières *(1883-84)* National Gallery, London.

that there is a rule to decide whether an element is a member of a set. It is usually denoted by a capital letter and indicated by curly brackets .

setter breed of dog, about 60 cm/2 ft high, and weighing about 25 kg/55 lbs. It has a long, smooth coat, a feathered tail, and a spaniel-like face. The *Irish setter* is a rich red, the *English setter* is usually white with black, tan, or liver markings, and the *Gordon setter* is black and brown. They are called 'setters' because they were trained in crouching or 'setting' on the sight of game to be pursued.

Settlement, Act of in Britain, a law passed 1701 during the reign of King William III, designed to ensure a Protestant succession to the throne by excluding the Roman Catholic descendants of James II in favour of the Protestant House of Hanover. Elizabeth II still reigns under this Act.

settlement out of court a compromise reached between the parties to a legal dispute. Most civil legal actions are settled out of court, reducing legal costs, and avoiding the uncertainty of the outcome of a trial.

Seurat Georges 1859–1891. French artist. He originated, with ◊Signac, the Neo-Impressionist technique of pointillism (painting will small dabs rather than long brushstrokes), in part inspired by 19th-century theories of colour and vision. He also departed from Impressionism by evolving a more formal type of composition.

Seventh Day Adventist a member of the Protestant Christian religious sect of the same name. It has its main following in the USA, and distinctive tenets are that Saturday is the Sabbath, and that Jesus' second coming is imminent.

Seven Weeks' War war 1866 between Austria and Prussia, engineered by the German chancellor Bismarck. It was nominally over the possession of ◊Schleswig-Holstein (by the Treaty of Prague, Prussia took both Holstein, previously seized by Austria, and Schleswig), but it was actually to confirm Prussia's superseding Austria as the leading German state. The Battle of ◊Sadowa was the culmination of von ◊Moltke's victories.

Seven Wonders of the World in antiquity, the pyramids of Egypt, the hanging gardens of Babylon, the temple of Artemis at Ephesus, the statue of Zeus at Olympia, the mausoleum at Halicarnassus, the Colossus of Rhodes, and the Pharos (lighthouse) at Alexandria.

Seven Years' War war 1756–63 between Britain and Prussia on the one hand, and France, Austria, Spain, and Russia on the other. Politically, Britain gained control of many of France's colonies, including Canada. Fighting against great odds, Frederick II of Prussia was eventually successful, establishing Prussia as one of the great European powers.

Severn river of Wales and England, rising on the NE side of Plynlimmon, N Wales, and flowing some 338 km/210 mi through Shrewsbury, Worcester, and Gloucester to the Bristol Channel. The *Severn bore* is a tidal wave up to 2 m/6 ft high.

Severus Lucius Septimus 146–211 AD. Roman emperor. Born in North Africa, he held a command on the Danube when in 193 the emperor Pertinax was murdered. Proclaimed emperor by his troops, Severus proved an able administrator. The only African to become emperor, he died at York while campaigning against the Caledonians.

Sévigné Marie de Rabutin-Chantal, Marquise de Sévigné 1626–1696. French writer, born in Paris. In her letters to her daughter, the Comtesse de

Sèvres *A characteristic piece of Sèvres porcelain.*

Grignan, she gives a vivid picture of contemporary customs and events.

Seville (Spanish *Sevilla*) city in Andalucia, Spain, on the Guadalquivir river, 96 km/60 mi N of Cádiz, population (1981) 654,000. Industries include machinery, spirits, porcelain, pharmaceuticals, silk, and tobacco.

Sèvres fine porcelain produced at a factory in Sèvres, France since the early 18th century. It is characterized by the use of intensely coloured backgrounds (such as pink and royal blue), against which flowers are painted in elaborately embellished frames, often in gold. It became popular after the patronage of Louis XV's mistress, Madame de ◊Pompadour.

sewage disposal the disposal of human excreta and other water-borne waste products from houses, streets, and factories. It is conveyed through sewers to sewage works where it is supposed to be treated so that it is clean enough to be discharged into rivers or the sea. In 1987, Britain dumped more than 4,700 tonnes of sewage sludge into the North Sea, and 4,200 tonnes into the Irish Sea and other coastal areas. Also dumped in British coastal waters, other than the Irish Sea, were 6,462 tonnes of zinc, 2,887 tonnes of lead, 1,306 tonnes of chromium, and 8 tonnes of arsenic. Dumped into the Irish Sea were 916 tonnes of zinc, 297 tonnes of lead, 200 tonnes of chromium, and 1 tonne of arsenic.

Sewell Anna 1820–1878. English author, whose only published work tells the life story of a horse, *Black Beauty* 1877. Although now read as a children's book, it was written to encourage sympathetic treatment of horses by adults.

sewing machine apparatus for the mechanical sewing of cloth, leather, and other materials by a needle, powered by hand, treadle, or belted electric motor. The popular lockstitch machine, using a double thread, was invented independently in the USA by both Walter Hunt 1834 and Elias Howe 1846. Howe's machine was the basis of the

sewing machine

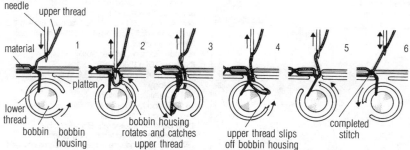

machine patented 1851 by Isaac ◊Singer. In the latest microprocessor-controlled sewing machines, as many as 25 different stitching patterns can be selected by pushbutton.

sex determination the process by which the sex of an organism is determined. In many species, the sex of an individual is dictated by the two sex chromosomes (X and Y) it receives from its parents. In mammals, some plants, and a few insects, males are XY, and females XX; in birds, reptiles, some amphibians, and butterflies the reverse is the case. In bees and wasps, males are produced from unfertilized eggs, females from fertilized eggs. Environmental factors can affect some fish and reptiles, such as turtles, where sex is influenced by the temperature at which the eggs are kept before hatching.

sexism belief in (or set of implicit assumptions about) the superiority of one's own sex, often accompanied by a ◊stereotype or preconceived idea about the opposite sex. Sexism may also be accompanied by ◊discrimination on the basis of sex.

sex linkage in genetics, the tendency for certain characteristics to occur exclusively, or predominantly, in one sex only. Human examples include red-green colour blindness and haemophilia, both found predominantly in males. In both cases, these characteristics are recessive (see ◊recessive) and are determined by genes on the ◊X chromosome. Since females possess two X chromosomes, any such recessive ◊allele on one of them is likely to be masked by the corresponding allele on the other. In males (who have only one X chromosome paired with an inert Y chromosome) any gene on the X chromosome will automatically be expressed.

Sex Pistols, the UK punk rock group (1975–78) who became famous under the guidance of their manager, Malcolm McLaren. They released one album, *Never Mind the Bollocks, Here Come the Sex Pistols* 1977. Members included Johnny Rotten (real name John Lydon, 1956–   ) and Sid Vicious (John Ritchie, 1957–79).

sextant navigational instrument for determining latitude by measuring the angle between some heavenly body and the horizon. Invented by John Hadley (1682–1744) in 1730, it can only be used in clear weather. When the horizon is viewed through the right-hand side *horizon glass*, which is partly clear and partly mirrored, the light from a star can be seen at the same time in the mirrored left-hand side by adjusting an *index mirror*. The angle of the star to the horizon can then be read on a calibrated scale.

Sexton Anne 1928–1974. US poet. She studied with Robert Lowell and wrote similarly confessional poetry, as in *All My Pretty Ones* 1962.

She committed suicide, and her *Complete Poems* appeared posthumously 1981.

sexual reproduction a reproductive process in living creatures which requires the union, or ◊fertilization, of the gametes (such as eggs and sperm). These are generally produced by two different individuals, although self-fertilization can occur in ◊hermaphrodites. Most organisms other than bacteria and cyanobacteria show some sort of sexual process. Except in some lower organisms, the gametes are of two distinct types. The organisms producing the eggs are called females, and those producing the sperm, males. The fusion of a male and female gamete produces a *zygote*, from which a new individual develops. The alternatives to sexual reproduction are ◊parthenogenesis and ◊spores.

sexual selection competition between males to mate with females, leading to the evolution of particular characteristics in the males. Examples include the antlers of male deer (used in combat for females) and the bright plumage of many male birds (used to attract females and warn off rival males). In

female reproductive system

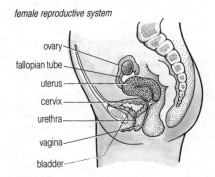

male reproductive system

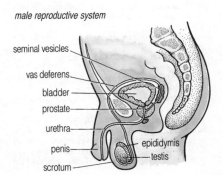

Seychelles
Republic of

India

INDIAN OCEAN

Somalia

Kenya

SEYCHELLES

Victoria

0   miles   500
0   km   1000

area 404 sq km/156 sq mi
capital Victoria on Mahé
physical comprises two distinct island groups,
one concentrated, the other widely scattered,
totalling over 100 islands and islets
head of state and government France-Albert René
from 1977
political system one-party socialist republic

exports copra, cinnamon
currency Seychelles rupee
population (1990 est) 71,000; annual growth 2.2%
language creole, spoken by 95%, English and
French (all official)
religion Roman Catholic 90%
literacy 80% (1989)
GNP $175 million (1987); $2,600 per head
chronology
1794 Captured by British.
1814 Ceded by France to Britain; incorporated as a
dependency of Mauritius.
1903 Became a separate British colony.
1975 Internal self-government granted.
1976 Full independence achieved as Commonwealth
republic with Mancham as president.
1977 René ousted Mancham in an armed coup and
took over the presidency.
1979 New constitution adopted, making the
Seychelles People's Progressive Front (SPPF) the
only legal party.
1981 Attempted coup by South African
mercenaries thwarted.
1984 René re-elected.
1987 Coup attempt foiled.
1989 René re-elected.
1991 Multiparty politics promised.
1992 Mancham returned from exile. Referendum
on constitutional reform received insufficient
support.

---

some species, the females compete for mates, and
sexual selection then operates on the females, as
in phalaropes (a sea bird) where the female is more
brightly coloured than the male. The process was
first noted by Charles Darwin.

Seychelles country in the Indian Ocean, off E
Africa, N of Madagascar.

Seyfert galaxy a type of galaxy whose small,
bright centre is caused by hot gas moving at high
speed around a massive central object, possibly a
◊black hole. Almost all Seyferts are spiral galaxies.
They seem to be closely related to ◊quasars, but
about 100 times fainter. They are named after
discoverer Carl Seyfert (1911–60).

Seymour Jane c. 1509–1537. Third wife of Henry
VIII, whom she married 1536. She died soon after
the birth of her son, Edward VI.

Sezession various groups of German and Austrian artists in the 1890s who 'seceded' from official
academic art institutions in order to found modern
schools of painting. The first was in Munich, 1892;
the next, linked with the paintings of Gustav
◊Klimt, was the Vienna Sezession 1897; the Berlin
Sezession followed in 1899.

Sforza Italian family which ruled the duchy of Milan
1450–99 and 1522–35. Their court was a centre
of Renaissance culture, and **Ludovico Sforza**
(1451–1508) was patron of the artist ◊Leonardo da
Vinci.

Shaanxi (formerly **Shensi**) province of NW
China.
area 157,100 sq km/60,641 sq mi
capital Xi'an
physical mountains; Huang He valley, one of the
earliest settled areas of China
products iron, steel, mining, textiles, fruit, tea,
rice, wheat
population (1990) 32,882,000.

Shackleton Ernest 1874–1922. Irish Antarctic
explorer. In 1907–09, he commanded an expedition
which reached 88° 23' S latitude, located the south
magnetic pole and climbed Mount ◊Erebus. He

died on board the *Quest* on another expedition
1921–22 to the Antarctic.

Shad marine fish, largest (2.7 kg/6 lbs) of the
herring family. They migrate in shoals to breed in
rivers. They are Atlantic fish but have been introduced to the Pacific.

Shadow Cabinet the chief members of the
British parliamentary opposition, each of whom is
responsible for commenting on the policies and
performance of a government ministry.

shaduf a machine for lifting water, consisting
typically of a long wooden pole acting as a lever, with
a weight at one end. The other end is positioned
over a well, for example. The shaduf was in use in
Ancient Egypt, and is still used in Arab countries
today.

Shadwell Thomas 1642–1692. English dramatist
and poet. His plays include *Epsom-Wells* 1672 and
Bury-Fair 1689. He was involved in a violent feud
with the poet ◊Dryden whom he attacked in 'The
Medal of John Bayes' 1682, and succeeded as Poet
Laureate.

SHAEF abbreviation for *Supreme Headquarters
Allied Expeditionary Force* World War II military centre established 1944, London, where final
plans for the Allied invasion of Europe (under US
general Eisenhower) were worked out.

Shaffer Peter 1926– . English playwright. His
plays include *Five Finger Exercise* 1958, *The Royal
Hunt of the Sun* 1964, *Equus* 1973, and *Amadeus*
1979.

Shaftesbury Anthony Ashley Cooper, 1st Earl of
Shaftesbury 1621–1683. English politician, a supporter of the Restoration of the monarchy. He
became lord chancellor 1672, but went into opposition 1673 and began to organize the ◊Whig Party.
He headed the demand for the exclusion of the
future James II from the succession, secured the
passing of the ◊Habeas Corpus Act 1679 and, when
accused of treason 1681, fled to Holland.

Shaftesbury Anthony Ashley Cooper, 7th Earl of
Shaftesbury 1801–1885. British Tory politician. A

strong supporter of the Ten Hours Act 1847 and other factory legislation, he was largely responsible for the 1842 act forbidding the employment of women and children underground in mines. He was also associated with the movement for the establishment of ragged schools to provide free education for the poor.

shag type of small ◊cormorant, *Phalacrocorax aristotelis*.

shah (more formally, *Shahanshah* 'king of kings') traditional title of ancient Persian rulers, and also of those of the recent ◊Pahlavi dynasty in Iran.

Shah Jehan 1592–1666. ◊Mughal emperor of India from 1627, when he succeeded his father Jehangir. He conquered the Deccan plateau in SE India, but was less fortunate in his campaigns against the Persians. From 1658 he was a prisoner of his son Aurangzeb. He built the ◊Taj Mahal.

Shahn Ben 1898–1969. US artist, born in Lithuania, a Social Realist painter. His work included drawings and paintings on the ◊Dreyfus case and ◊Sacco and Vanzetti. As a mural artist he worked at the Rockefeller Center, New York (with the Mexican artist Diego Rivera) and the Federal Security Building, Washington, 1940–42.

Shaka or *Chaka* 1787–1828. Zulu leader who formed a Zulu empire in S Africa. The illegitimate son of a minor Zulu chief, he seized power from his half-brother 1816, and then embarked on a campaign to unite the Nguni (the area that today forms the South African province of Natal), initiating the period of warfare known as the ◊Mfecane; his success was the result of almost permanent mobilization and constant fighting.

Shaker popular name for a member of the Christian sect of the *United Society of Believers in Christ's Second Appearing*. This was founded by James and Jane Wardley in England about 1747, and taken to North America 1774 by Ann Lee (1736–84), the wife of a Manchester blacksmith. The name was applied because of their ecstatic shakings in worship. They anticipated modern spiritualist beliefs, but their doctrine of celibacy led to their virtual extinction. *Shaker furniture* has been revalued in the 20th century for its simplicity and robustness.

Shakespeare William 1564–1616. English dramatist and poet. Established in London by 1589 as an actor (in the Chamberlain's Men) and a playwright, he was England's unrivalled dramatist until his death, and is considered the greatest English playwright. His plays can be broadly divided into lyric plays *Romeo and Juliet, Midsummer Night's Dream*; comedies including *Comedy of Errors, As You Like It, Much Ado About Nothing, Measure For Measure*; historical plays such as *Henry VI* (the three parts) *Richard III, Henry IV* (parts I and II), which often showed cynical political wisdom; and tragedies such as *Hamlet, Macbeth*, and *King Lear*. He also wrote numerous celebrated sonnets.

shale a fine-grained black sedimentary rock which splits into thin beds. It can be thought of as consolidated mud, and differs from mudstone in that the latter splits into flakes.

shallot type of onion *Allium cepa* in which bulbs multiply freely; used for cooking and in pickles.

Shalmaneser III King of Assyria 859–824 BC, who pursued an aggressive policy, and brought Babylon and Israel under the domination of Assyria.

shaman a ritual figure who acts as intermediary between society and the supernatural world in

Shakespeare: the plays

Title	Performed
Early Plays	
Henry VI Part I	1589–92
Henry VI Part II	1589–92
Henry VI Part III	1589–92
The Comedy of Errors	1592–93
Titus Andronicus	1593–94
The Two Gentlemen of Verona	1594–95
The Taming of the Shrew	1593–94
Love's Labour's Lost	1594–95
Romeo and Juliet	1594–95
Histories	
Richard III	1592–93
Richard II	1593–96
Henry IV Part I	1597–98
Henry IV Part II	1597–98
King John	1596–97
Henry V	1599
Roman Plays	
Julius Caesar	1599–1600
Antony and Cleopatra	1607–08
Coriolanus	1607–08
The 'Great' or 'Middle' Comedies	
The Merry Wives of Windsor	1600–01
Much Ado About Nothing	1598–99
The Merchant of Venice	1596–97
As You Like It	1599–1600
Twelfth Night	1601–02
A Midsummer Night's Dream	1595–96
The Great Tragedies	
Hamlet	1600–01
Othello	1604–05
King Lear	1605–06
Macbeth	1605–06
Timon of Athens	1607–08
The 'Dark' Comedies	
Troilus and Cressida	1601–02
All's Well That Ends Well	1602–03
Measure for Measure	1604–05
Late Plays	
Pericles	1608–09
Cymbeline	1609–10
The Winter's Tale	1610–11
The Tempest	1611–12
Henry VIII	1612–13

Shakespeare *Portrait attributed to John Taylor* (*c.* 1610) National Portrait Gallery, London.

Shanghai The commercial centre of Shanghai, China.

many indigenous cultures of Asia, Africa, and the Americas. Also known as a *medicine man, seer* or *sorcerer*, the shaman uses magic powers to cure illness and control good and evil spirits.

Shamir Yitzhak 1915–. Israeli politician, born in Poland. Prime minister 1983–84 and 1986–92; leader of the Likud (Consolidation Party) until 1993. He was foreign minister under Menachem Begin 1980–83, and again foreign minister in the Peres unity government 1984–86.

shamrock several trifoliate plants of the family Leguminosae. One is said to have been used by St Patrick to illustrate the doctrine of the Holy Trinity, and it was made the national badge of Ireland.

Shamyl c. 1797–1871. Caucasian soldier. He led the people of Dagestan in a fight for independence from Russia from 1834 until he was captured 1859, when the Russians were able to deploy greater forces after the Crimean War.

Shan a member of a people of the mountainous borderlands between Thailand, Myanmar, and China. They are related to the Laos and Thais, and their language belongs to the Sino-Tibetan family.

Shandong (formerly *Shantung*) province (formerly *Shantung*) of NE China
area 153,300 sq km/59,174 sq mi
capital Jinan
towns ports Yantai, Weihai, Qingdao, Shigiusuo
products cereals, cotton, wild silk, varied minerals.
population (1990) 84,393,000.

Shanghai port on the Huang-pu and Wusong rivers, Jiangsu province, China, 24 km/15 mi from the Chang Jiang estuary; area 5,800 sq km/2,240 sq mi; population (1986) 6,980,000; the largest city in China. Industries include textiles, paper, chemicals, steel, agricultural machinery, precision instruments; shipbuilding, flour and vegetable-oil milling, and oil refining. It handles about 50% of China's imports and exports.

Shankar Ravi 1920–. Indian composer and musician. A virtuoso of the ◊sitar, he has composed film music and founded music schools in Bombay and Los Angeles.

Shankara 799–833. Hindu philosopher who wrote commentaries on some of the major Hindu scriptures, as well as hymns and essays on religious ideas. Shankara was responsible for the final form of the Advaita Vedanta school of Hindu philosophy, which teaches that Brahman, the supreme being, is all that exists in the Universe; everything else is illusion. Shankara was fiercely opposed to Buddhism, and may have been largely responsible for its decline in India.

Shannon longest river in Ireland, rising in County Cavan and flowing 260 km/161 mi through Loughs

Allen and Ree and past Athlone, to reach the Atlantic through a wide estuary below Limerick. It is also the major source of electric power in the republic, with hydroelectric installations at and above Ardnacrusha, 5 km/3 mi N of Limerick.

Shanxi (formerly *Shansi*) province of NE China.
area 157,100 sq km/60,640 sq mi
capital Taiyuan
products coal, iron, fruit
population (1990) 28,759,000

SHAPE acronym for *Supreme Headquarters Allied Powers Europe*, situated near Mons in Belgium and the headquarters of NATO's *Supreme Allied Commander Europe* (SACEUR).

Shapley Harlow 1885–1972. US astronomer, whose study of ◊globular clusters showed that they were arranged in a halo around the Galaxy, and that the Galaxy was much larger than previously thought. He realized that the Sun was not at the centre of the Galaxy as then assumed, but two-thirds of the way out to the rim.

share in finance, that part of the capital of a company held by a member (shareholder). Shares may be numbered and are issued as units of definite face value; shareholders are not always called on to pay the full face value of their shares, though they bind themselves to do so.

Shari'a the law of ◊Islam believed by Muslims to be based on divine revelation, and drawn from a number of sources, including the Koran, the Hadith and the consensus of the Muslim community. From the latter part of the 19th century, the role of the Shari'a courts in the majority of Muslim countries began to be taken over by secular courts, and the Shari'a to be largely restricted to family law. Modifications to Koranic maxims have resulted from the introduction of Western law; for example, compensation can now be claimed only after a conviction by a criminal court.

Sharjah or *Shariqah* third largest of the seven member states of the ◊United Arab Emirates, situated on the Arabian Gulf NE of Dubai; area 2,600 sq km/1,004 sq mi; population (1985) 269,000. Since 1952 it has included the small state of Kalba. In 1974 oil was discovered offshore. Industries include ship repair, cement, paint, and metal products.

shark the bigger members of the Pleurotremata, a large group of marine fish with cartilaginous skeletons. They are found worldwide. They have streamlined bodies, and high-speed manoeuvrability, and their eyes, though lacking acuity of vision or sense of colour, are highly sensitive to light. Their sense of smell is so acute that one-third of the brain is given up to interpreting its signals; it can detect blood in the water up to 1 km/0.6 mi away. They also respond to electrical charges emanating from other animals.

Sharp Granville 1735–1813. English philanthropist. He was prominent in the anti-slavery movement, and in 1772 secured a legal decision 'that as soon as any slave sets foot on English territory he becomes free'.

Sharpeville black township in South Africa, 65 km/40 mi S of Johannesburg and N of Vereeniging; 69 people were killed here when police fired on a crowd 21 Mar 1960, during a campaign launched by the Pan-Africanist Congress against the pass laws (laws requiring nonwhite South Africans to carry identity papers). On the anniversary 1985, during funerals of protesters against unemployment who had been killed, 19 people were shot by the police at Langa near Port Elizabeth.

Sharpey-Schäfer Edward Albert 1850–1935. English physiologist and one of the founders of endocrinology. He discovered the powerful effects of the product of the adrenal gland, later identified as ◊adrenaline, and went on to make important discoveries relating to the ◊pituitary and other ◊endocrine or ductless glands.

Shastri Lal Bahadur 1904–1966. Indian politician who succeeded Nehru as prime minister of India 1964. He emerged as a major figure in the process of national integration because of his firm stand against Pakistani attempts to capture Kashmir 1965. At the Tashkent peace conference 1966, he persuaded Pakistan's leader, Ayaub Khan, to sign a declaration agreeing never to use force again.

Shatt-al-Arab 'river of Arabia', the waterway formed by the confluence of the ◊Euphrates and ◊Tigris; length 190 km/120 mi to the Arabian Gulf. Basra, Khorramshar and Abadan stand on it.

Shaw George Bernard 1856–1950. Irish dramatist. A debater, critic, and novelist, he is most famous for his plays which combine comedy with political, philosophical, and polemic aspects, aiming to make an impact on his audience's social conscience as well as their emotions. His plays include *Arms and the Man* 1894, *Devil's Disciple* 1897, *Man and Superman* 1905, *Pygmalion* 1913, and *St Joan* 1924.

Shchedrin N. Pen name of Russian writer Mikhail Evgrafovich Saltykov 1826–1889. A uniquely pessimistic writer, he wrote *Fables* 1884–85, in which Saltykov depicts misplaced 'good intentions', and the novel *The Golovlevs* 1880.

shearwater sea bird related to petrels and albatrosses.

Sheba ancient name for modern South ◊Yemen (Sha'abijah). It was once renowned for gold and spices. According to the Old Testament, its queen visited Solomon; the former Ethiopian royal house traced its descent from their union.

Shechem ancient town in Palestine, capital of Samaria. In the Old Testament, it is the traditional burial place of Joseph; nearby is Jacob's well. Shechem was destroyed about 67 AD by the Roman emperor Vespasian; on its site stands Nablus (a corruption of Neapolis) built by ◊Hadrian.

sheep genus *Ovis* of ruminant hoofed mammals of the family Bovidae. Wild species survive in the uplands of central Asia, and their domesticated descendants are reared worldwide for meat, wool, milk, and cheese, and for rotation on arable land to maintain its fertility.

sheepdog rough-coated breed of dog. The Old English sheepdog is grey or blue-grey, with white markings, and is about 56 cm/1.8 ft tall. The Shetland sheepdog is much smaller, 36 cm/1.2 ft tall, and shaped more like a long-coated collie. Border collies are considered the best dogs for tending sheep.

Sheffield industrial city on the Don river, South Yorkshire, England; population (1986) 538,700. From the 12th century, iron smelting was the chief industry, and by the 14th century Sheffield cutlery, silverware, and plate were famous. During the Industrial Revolution the iron and steel industries developed rapidly. It now produces alloys and special steels, cutlery of all kinds, permanent magnets, drills, and precision tools. Other industries include electroplating, type-founding, and the manufacture of optical glass.

sheik the leader or chief of an Arab family or village.

sheep

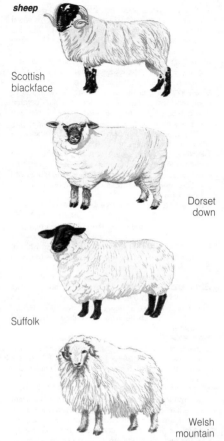

Scottish blackface

Dorset down

Suffolk

Welsh mountain

Shelburne William Petty FitzMaurice, 2nd Earl of Shelburne 1737–1805. British Whig politician. He was an opponent of George III's American policy, and as prime minister in 1783, he concluded peace with the USA.

shelduck duck *Tadorna tadorna* with dark green head and red bill, with the rest of the plumage strikingly marked in black, white, and chestnut. Widely distributed in Europe and Asia, it lays 10–12 white eggs in rabbit burrows in sandy coasts, and is usually seen on estuary mudflats.

shelf sea relatively shallow sea, usually no deeper than 200 m/650 ft, overlying the continental shelf around the coastlines. Most fishing and marine mineral exploitations are carried out in shelf seas.

shellac a resin derived from the ◊lac insect.

Shelley Mary Wollstonecraft 1797–1851. English writer, the daughter of Mary Wollstonecraft and William Godwin. She eloped 1814 with the poet Percy Bysshe ◊Shelley, whom she married 1816. In 1818 she published *Frankenstein*, a story of a scientist who created a man-monster and gave it life.

Shelley Percy Bysshe 1792–1822. English lyric poet, a leading figure in the Romantic movement. Expelled from Oxford for atheism, he fought all his life against religion and for political freedom. This is reflected in his early poems such as *Queen Mab* 1813. He later wrote tragedies including *The Cenci* 1818, lyric dramas such as *Prometheus Unbound*

1820 and lyrical poems such as 'Ode to the West Wind'. His first wife, Harriet Westbrook drowned herself, and he lived in Italy from 1817 with his second wife Mary Shelley. He drowned while sailing near the Italian coast 1822.

shellfish popular name for molluscs and crustaceans, including the whelk and periwinkle, mussel, oyster, lobster, crab, and shrimp.

shell-shock name given during World War I to various forms of mental disorder, also called combat neurosis, which affects soldiers exposed to heavy explosions or extreme ◊stress. It shares many symptoms with disorders brought on by other non-military forms of stress.

Shema Jewish prayer from the Torah, recited every morning and evening, which begins with the words 'Hear, O Israel, the Lord your God, the Lord is One' and affirms the special relationship of the Jews with God.

Shenyang industrial city and capital of Liaoning province, China; population (1990) 4,500,000. It was the capital of the Manchu emperors 1644–1912.

Shepard E(rnest) H(oward) 1879–1976. English illustrator, celebrated for his illustrations to books by A A Milne (*Winnie-the-Pooh* 1926) and Kenneth Grahame (*The Wind in the Willows* 1908).

Shepard Sam 1943– . US dramatist and actor. His work, which combines colloquial American dialogue with striking visual imagery, includes *Buried Child* 1978, for which he won the Pulitzer prize, and *Seduced* 1979.

Sheraton Thomas *c.* 1751–1806. English designer of elegant inlaid furniture, as in his *Cabinet-maker's and Upholsterer's Drawing Book* 1791. He was influenced by his predecessors ◊Hepplewhite and ◊Chippendale.

Sheridan Philip Henry 1831–1888. US Union general in the ◊Civil War. Gen Ulysses S ◊Grant gave him command of his cavalry 1864, and soon after of the army of the Shenandoah Valley, Virginia, which he cleared of Confederates. In the final stage of the war, Sheridan forced Gen Lee to retreat to Appomattox, and surrender.

Sheridan Richard Brinsley 1751–1816. Irish dramatist, born in Dublin. His first social comedy *The Rivals*, 1775 was celebrated for the character of Mrs Malaprop. In 1776 he became lessee of the Drury Lane Theatre, where he produced *The School for Scandal* 1777 and *The Critic* 1779. He became a member of Parliament 1780.

sheriff in England and Wales, the Crown's chief executive officer in a county for ceremonial purposes. In Scotland, the equivalent of the English county court judge, but also dealing with criminal cases; and in the USA the popularly elected head law-enforcement officer of a county, combining judicial authority with administrative duties.

Sherman William Tecumseh 1820–1891. US Union general in the ◊Civil War. In 1864 he captured and burned Atlanta, from where he marched to the sea, laying Georgia waste, and then drove the Confederates northwards. He was US Army chief of staff 1869–83.

Sherman Anti-Trust Act in US history, an act of Congress 1890, named after senator John Sherman (1823–1900) of Ohio, designed to prevent powerful corporations from monopolizing industries and restraining trade for their own benefit. Relatively few prosecutions of such trusts were successful under the act.

Sherpa member of a people in NE Nepál of Mongolian origin, renowned for their mountaineering skill. A Sherpa, Norgay Tensing, was one of the two men to conquer Mount Everest for the first time.

Sherrington Charles Scott 1857–1952. English neurologist and neurophysiologist. He studied the nervous system and made fundamental contributions to our understanding of its structure and function.

Sherwood Forest a hilly stretch of parkland in W Nottinghamshire, England, area about 520 sq km/200 sq mi. Formerly a royal forest, it is associated with the legendary ◊Robin Hood.

Shetland islands off N coast of Scotland
area 1,429 sq km/552 sq mi
towns administrative headquarters Lerwick, on Mainland, largest of 19 inhabited islands
physical comprise over 100 islands; Muckle Flugga (latitude 60° 51′ N) is the most northerly of the British Isles
products Europe's largest oil port is Sullom Voe, Mainland; processed fish, handknits from Fair Isle and Unst; miniature ponies
population (1988 est) 22,900
language the dialect is derived from Norse, the islands having been under Scandinavian rule 875–1468.

Shevardnadze Eduard 1928– . Georgian politician, Soviet foreign minister 1985–91, head of state of Georgia from 1992. A supporter of ◊Gorbachev, he was first secretary of the Georgian Communist Party from 1972 and an advocate of economic reform. In 1985 he became a member of the Politburo, working for détente and disarmament. In July 1991, he resigned from the Communist Party (CPSU) and, along with other reformers and leading democrats, established the Democratic Reform Movement. In March 1992 he was chosen as chair of Georgia's ruling military council, and in October elected speaker of parliament.

Shiah alternative form of *Shi'ite*, one of the two main sorts of ◊Islam.

Shidehara Kijuro 1872–1951. Japanese politician and diplomat who as foreign minister 1924–27 and 1929–31, promoted conciliation with China, and economic rather than military expansion. In 1945, he was recognised by the USA as prime minister and acted as speaker of the Japanese Diet (parliament) until his death.

shield in geology, another name for ◊craton, the ancient core of a continent.

shield any material used to reduce the amount of radiation (electrostatic, electromagnetic, heat, nuclear) reaching from one region of space to another, or any material used as a protection against falling debris, as in tunnelling. Electrical conductors are used for electrostatic shields, soft iron for electromagnetic shields, and poor conductors of heat for heat shields. Heavy materials such as lead and concrete are used for protection against X-ray and nuclear radiation. See also ◊biological shield, and ◊heat shield.

Shi Huangdi (formerly *Shih Huang Ti*) 259–210 BC. Emperor of China. He succeeded to the throne of the state of Qin 246 BC, and reunited the country as an empire by 228 BC. He burned almost all existing books 213 BC to destroy ties with the past; built the ◊Great Wall; and was buried in a tomb complex guarded by 10,000 individualized, life-size pottery warriors (still being excavated in the 1980s). He had so overextended his power that the dynasty and the empire collapsed at the death of his feeble successor 207 BC.

Shi'ite member of a Muslim sect prominent in Iran and Lebanon who are doctrinally opposed to the

Sunni Muslims or the successors of Muhammad; see also ◊Islam.

Shikoku smallest of the four main islands of Japan, S of Honshu, E of Kyushu; area 17,790 sq km/6,869 sq mi; population (1986) 4,226,000; chief town Matsuyama. Products include rice, wheat, soya, sugar cane, orchard fruits, salt and copper.

shingles popular name for infection with ◊herpes zoster.

Shinkansen (Japanese 'New Trunk Line'); the fast railway network operated by Japanese National Railways, on which the bullet trains run. The network, opened 1964, uses specially built straight and level track, on which average speeds of 160 kph/100 mph are attained.

Shinto the Chinese transliteration of the Japanese *Kami-no-Michi*, the Way or Doctrine of the Gods, the indigenous religion of Japan. This mingles an empathetic oneness with natural forces and loyalty to the reigning dynasty as descendants of the Sungoddess, Amaterasu-Omikami. Sectarian Shinto consists of 130 sects, each founded by a historical character; the sects are officially recognized, but are not state-supported, as was State Shinto until its disestablishment after World War II and Emperor Hirohito's disavowal of his divinity 1946. Traditional Shinto stressed obedience and devotion to the emperor and an aggressive nationalist aspect was developed by the Meiji rulers. Modern Shinto has discarded these aspects.

shinty a winter ball game played in the Scottish Highlands between teams of 12 players with sticks; it resembles hockey and lacrosse.

ship large sea-going vessel. The Greeks and Phoenicians, Romans and Norsemen used ships extensively for exploration and warfare. The 14th century was the era of European exploration by sailing ship – largely aided by the invention of the compass. In the 15th century Britain's Royal Navy was first formed, but from the 16th–19th centuries Spanish and Dutch ships reigned supreme. The ultimate sailing ships, the fast tea clippers, were built in the 19th century, at the same time as iron was first used for some shipbuilding instead of wood. Steam propelled ships of the late 19th century were followed by compound engine and turbine propelled boats from the early 20th century.

ship money tax for support of the navy, levied on the coastal districts of England in the Middle Ages. Ship money was declared illegal by Parliament 1641.

shire a county in Britain. *The Shires* are the Midland counties of England.

shock circulatory failure or sudden fall of blood pressure, resulting in pallor, sweating, fast (but weak) pulse, and possibly complete collapse. Causes include disease, injury, and psychological trauma.

Shockley William 1910–1989. US physicist, who worked with ◊Bardeen and ◊Brattain on the invention of the ◊transistor. They were jointly awarded a Nobel prize 1956.

shoebill or *whale-headed stork* large, long-legged, swamp-dwelling African bird *Balaeniceps rex*. It is grey, up to 1.5 m/5 ft tall, and has a large wide beak 20 cm/8 in long, with which it scoops fish, molluscs, reptiles, and carrion out of the mud.

Shoemaker William Lee 'Bill' 1931– . US jockey, who was the most successful of all time. He rode 8,833 winners from 40,351 mounts He retired 1990, and became a successful trainer, until he was paralysed in a car accident 1991.

shofar in Judaism, a ram's horn blown in the synagogue as a call to repentance at the festivals of Rosh Hashanah and Yom Kippur.

shogun in Japanese history, the hereditary commander in chief of the army. Though nominally subject to the emperor, he was the real ruler of Japan 1192–1867, when the emperor reassumed power.

Sholokhov Mikhail Aleksandrovich 1905–1984. Soviet novelist. His *And Quiet Flows the Don* 1926–40, depicts the Don Cossacks through World War I and the Russian Revolution. Nobel prize 1965.

Shona person of Shona culture, comprising approximately 80% of the population of Zimbabwe. They also occupy the land between the Save and Pungure rivers in Mozambique, and smaller groups are found in South Africa, Botswana, and Zambia. The Shona language belongs to the Bantu branch of the Niger-Congo family.

shoot in botany, a general term for parts of a vascular plant growing above ground, comprising a stem bearing leaves, buds, and flowers. The shoot develops from the ◊plumule of the embryo.

shop steward trade union representative in a 'shop' or department of a factory, who recruits for the union, inspects contribution cards, and reports grievances to the district committee. This form of organization originated in the engineering industry and has spread to all large industrial undertakings.

shorthand any system of rapid writing, such as the abbreviations practised by the Greeks and Romans. The first perfecter of an entirely phonetic system was Isaac ◊Pitman, by which system speeds of about 300 words a minute are said to be attainable.

Short Parliament the English parliament that was summoned by Charles I 13 Apr 1640 to raise funds for his war against the Scots. When it became clear that the parliament opposed the war and would not grant him any money, he dissolved it 5 May and arrested some of its leaders. It was succeeded later in the year by the even more intransigent ◊Long Parliament.

short story a short work of prose fiction, which typically either sets up and resolves a single narrative point or which depicts a mood or an atmosphere. Short story writers include Chekhov, Kipling, Maupassant, Mansfield, Henry, Saki, and Borges.

Shostakovich Soviet composer Dmitry Shostakovich, 1954.

Shostakovich Dmitry 1906–1975. Soviet composer. His music, tonal and expressive, and sometimes highly dramatic, was not always to official Soviet taste. He wrote 15 symphonies, chamber music, ballets and operas, the latter including *Lady Macbeth of Mtsensk* 1934, which was suppressed as 'too divorced from the proletariat', but revived as *Katerina Izmaylova* 1963.

shoveler fresh-water duck *Anas clypeata*, so named from its long and broad flattened beak. The male has a green head, white and brown body plumage, and can grow up to 50 cm/1.7 ft long. The female is speckled brown. Spending the summer in N Europe or North America, it winters further south.

Shovell Cloudesley *c.* 1650–1707. English admiral. He took part, with George Rooke (1650–1709), in the capture of Gibraltar 1704. In 1707 his flagship *Association* and four other ships of his home-bound fleet were wrecked off the Isles of Scilly. He was strangled for his rings by an islander when he came ashore.

Shrapnel Henry 1761–1842. British army officer who invented shells containing bullets, to increase the spread of casualties, first used 1804; hence the word *shrapnel* to describe shell fragments.

shrew insectivorous mammal of the family Soricidae, found in Eurasia and the Americas. It is mouse-like, but with a long nose and pointed teeth. Its high metabolic rate means that it must eat almost constantly.

shrike 'butcher-bird' of the family Laniidae, of which there are over 70 species, living mostly in Africa, but also in Eurasia and North America. They can grow to 35 cm/14 in long, and have grey, black, or brown plumage. They often impale insects and small vertebrates on thorns.

shrimp a crustacean related to the ◊prawn. It has a cylindrical, semi-transparent body, with ten jointed legs. Some shrimps grow as large as 25 cm/10 in long.

Shropshire county in W England
area 3,490 sq km/1,347 sq mi
towns administrative headquarters Shrewsbury, Telford, Oswestry, Ludlow
products chiefly agricultural: sheep and cattle
population (1991) 401,600

shroud of Turin see ◊Turin shroud.

Shrove Tuesday in the Christian calendar, the day before the beginning of Lent. It is also known as *Mardi Gras* and, in the UK, *Pancake Tuesday*, for the custom of eating rich things before the Lenten fast.

shrub a perennial, woody plant that typically produces several separate stems, at or near ground level, rather than the single trunk of most trees. A shrub is usually smaller than a tree, but there is no clear distinction between large shrubs and small trees.

Shultz George P 1920– . US Republican politician, economics adviser to President ◊Reagan 1980–82, and secretary of state 1982–89.

Shute Nevil. Pen name of Nevil Shute Norway 1899–1960. English novelist, who wrote *A Town Like Alice* 1949 and *On the Beach* 1957.

shuttle diplomacy a form of international diplomacy prominent in the 1970s where an independent mediator would travel between belligerent parties in order to try and achieve a compromise solution.

SI abbreviation for *Système International (d'Unités)* (French 'International System (of Metric Units)').

sial in geochemistry and geophysics, term denoting the substance of the Earth's continental ◊crust, as distinct from the ◊sima of the ocean crust. The name is derived from *si*lica and *al*umina, its two main chemical constituents.

siamang the largest ◊gibbon *Symphalangus syndactylus*, native to Malaysia and Sumatra. They are black-haired, up to 90 cm/3 ft tall, with very long arms (a span of 150 cm/5ft). Siamangs have a large throat pouch to amplify the voice making the territorial 'song' extremely loud.

Sibelius Jean (Christian) 1865–1957. Finnish composer. He studied the violin and composition at Helsinki and went on to Berlin and Vienna. His works include nationalistic symphonic poems such as *En Saga* 1893, *Finlandia* 1900, *Tapiola* 1926, the Violin Concerto 1904, and seven symphonies.

Siberia Asian region of Russia, extending from the Urals to the Pacific.
area 12,050,000 sq km/4,650,000 sq, mi
towns Novosibirsk, Omsk, Krasnoyarsk, Irkutsk
products hydroelectric power from rivers Lena, Ob, and Yenisei; forestry; mineral resources, including gold, diamonds, oil, natural gas, iron, copper, nickel, cobalt
history overrun by Russia 17th century, it was used from the 18th to exile prisoners. The first *Trans-Siberian Railway* 1892–1905 from St Petersburg (via Omsk, Novosibirsk, Irkutsk and Khabarovsk) to Vladivostok, approximately 8,700 km/5,400 mi, began to open it up.

Sibyl in Roman mythology, priestess of Apollo. She offered to sell ◊Tarquinius nine collections of prophecies, the *Sibylline Books*, but the price was too high. When she had destroyed all but three, he bought those for the identical price, and these were kept for consultation in emergency at Rome.

sic (Latin 'thus' 'so') sometimes found in brackets within a printed quotation to show that an apparent error is in fact an error in the original.

Sichuan (formerly *Szechwan*) province of central China
area 569,000 sq km/220,000 sq mi
capital Chengdu
towns Chongqing
products rice, coal, oil, natural gas
population (1990) 107,218,000

Sicily (Italian *Sicilia*) largest Mediterranean island, an autonomous region of Italy
area 25,708 sq km/9,923 sq mi
capital Palermo
towns ports Catania, Messina, Syracuse, Marsala
exports Marsala wine, olives, citrus, refined oil and petrochemicals, pharmaceuticals, potash, asphalt, marble
population (1990) 5,196,000.

Sickert Walter (Richard) 1860–1942. German-born English artist, the son of a Danish painter. He painted Impressionist cityscapes of London and Venice, portraits, and domestic interiors.

sickle harvesting tool of ancient origin characterized by a curving blade with serrated cutting edge and short wooden handle. It was widely used in Britain for cutting corn from at least Roman times to the 19th century.

sickle-cell disease a hereditary blood disorder common among people of black African descent. It is characterized by distortion and fragility of the red blood cells, which are lost too rapidly from the circulation. This results in ◊anaemia. A curious effect of sickle-cell disease is to give protection against ◊malaria.

Siddons Sarah 1755–1831. Welsh actress. Her majestic presence made her most suited to tragic

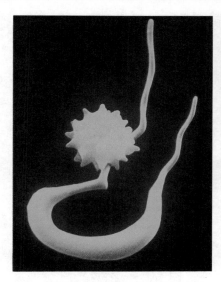

sickle-cell disease Scanning electron micrograph of the abnormal type of red blood cell that causes sickle-cell anaemia.

and heroic roles such as Lady Macbeth, Zara in Congreve's *The Mourning Bride*, and Constance in *King John*.

sidewinder type of rattlesnake *Crotalus cerastes* which lives in the deserts of the SW USA and Mexico, and moves by throwing its coils into a sideways 'jump' across the sand. It can grow up to 75 cm/2.5 ft long.

Siding Spring Mountain peak 400 km/250 mi NW of Sydney, site of the 3.9 m/154 in Anglo-Australian Telescope, opened 1974, the first big telescope to be fully computer controlled.

Sidney Philip 1554–1586. English poet and soldier, author of the sonnet sequence *Astrophel and Stella* 1591, *Arcadia* 1590, and *Apologie for Poetrie* 1595, the earliest work of English literary criticism.

Siegfried legendary Germanic hero. It is uncertain whether his story has a historical basis, but it was current about 700 AD. In the poems of the Norse Elder Edda and in the prose Völsunga Saga, Siegfried appears under the name of Sigurd. A version is in the German *Nibelungenlied*.

Siegfried Line in World War I the defensive line established 1918 by the Germans in France; in World War II the name given by the Allies to the West Wall, the German defensive line established along its western frontier.

Siemens family of four brothers, creators of a vast industrial empire. The eldest, Ernst Werner von Siemens (1812–92), founded the original electrical firm of *Siemens und Halske* 1847 and made many advances in telegraphy. William (Karl Wilhelm) (1823–83) perfected the open-hearth production of steel (now superseded), pioneered the development of the electric locomotive, the laying of transoceanic cables, and improvements in the electric generator.

siemens ◊SI unit of electrical conductance (S), defined as the conductance of a circuit or element with a resistance of 1 ohm. Named after William Siemens, it was formerly called the mho or reciprocal ohm.

Sienkiewicz Henryk 1846–1916. Polish author. His books include *Quo Vadis?* 1895, set in Rome at

Sidney Renaissance man Philip Sidney was a poet, politician, courtier, and soldier.

the time of Nero, and the 17th-century historical trilogy *With Fire and Sword, The Deluge* and *Pan Michael* 1890–93.

Sierra Leone country in W Africa, on the Atlantic, bounded to the N and E by Guinea and to the SE by Liberia.

Sierra Madre chief mountain system of Mexico, consisting of three ranges, enclosing the central plateau of the country: highest point Pico de Orizaba 5,700 m/18,700 ft. The Sierra Madre del Sur ('of the south') runs along the SW Pacific coast.

sievert ◊SI unit of dose equivalent (Sv). It is defined as the absorbed dose of ionizing radiation (with certain dimensionless factors to account for different types of radiation causing different effects in biological tissue) of 1 joule/kg.

Sigismund 1368–1437. Holy Roman emperor from 1411. He convened and presided over the council of Constance 1414–18, where he promised protection to the religious reformer ◊Huss, but imprisoned him after his condemnation for heresy, and acquiesced in his burning. King of Bohemia from 1419, he led the military campaign against the Hussites.

Signac Paul 1863–1935. French artist. In 1884 he joined with ◊Seurat in founding the Société des Artistes Indépendants and developing the technique of ◊*pointillism*.

signal a sign, gesture, sound, or action which conveys information. Examples include the use of flags (◊semaphore), light (traffic and railway signals), radio telephony, radio telegraphy (◊Morse code), and electricity (telecommunications and computer networks).

Signorelli Luca *c.* 1450–1523. Italian painter, active in central Italy. About 1483 he was called to the Vatican to complete frescoes on the walls of the Sistine Chapel.

Sigurd in Norse mythology, a hero who appears in both the ◊*Nibelungenlied* (under his German name of ◊Siegfried) and the ◊*Edda*.

Sihanouk Norodom 1922– . Cambodian politician, king 1941–55, prime minister 1955–70, when his government was overthrown by a military coup led by Lon Nol. With Pol Pot's resistance front, he overthrew Lon Nol 1975, and again became prime minister 1975–76, when he was forced to resign by the Khmer Rouge. He returned from exile 1991 under the auspices of a UN-brokered peace settlement, to head the Supreme National Council, a coalition of all Cambodia's warring factions.

Sikhism the religion professed by 16 million Indians, living mainly in the Punjab. Sikhism was founded by

Sierra Leone
Republic of

0 miles 500
0 km 1000

area 73,325 sq km/27,925 sq mi
capital Freetown
towns Bo, Kenema, Makeni
physical mountains in E; hills and forest; coastal mangrove swamps
head of state and government military council headed by Capt Valentine Strasser from 1992
political system transitional
exports palm kernels, cocoa, coffee, ginger, diamonds, bauxite, rutile

currency leone
population (1990 est) 4,168,000; annual growth rate 2.5%
life expectancy men 41, women 47 (1989)
language English (official); local languages
religion animist 52%, Muslim 39%, Protestant 6%, Roman Catholic 2%
literacy men 38%, women 21%
GNP $965 million (1987); $320 million per head
chronology
1962 Achieved full independence as a constitutional monarchy within the Commonwealth, with Milton Margai, leader of the Sierra Leone People's Party (SLPP), as prime minister.
1964 Milton succeeded by his half-brother Albert Margai.
1967 The army set up a National Reformation Council and forced the governor general to leave.
1968 Another army revolt made Siaka Stevens, leader of the All-People's Congress (APC), prime minister.
1971 Sierra Leone became a republic, Stevens its president.
1978 APC declared the only legal party. Stevens sworn in for another seven-year term.
1985 Stevens retired at the age of 80 and was succeeded by Maj-Gen Joseph Momoh.
1989 Attempted coup foiled.
1991 Referendum endorsed multiparty politics.
1992 Military take-over; Momoh fled. National Provisional Ruling Council (NPRC) established under Capt Strasser.

Nanak (1469–*c.* 1539). Its basis is the Unity of God and the equality of all human beings; Sikhism is strongly opposed to caste divisions. Guru Gobind Singh (1666–1708) instituted the Khanda-di-Pabul, the Baptism of the Sword, and established the *Khalsa* ('the pure'), the company of the faithful. The Khalsa wear the five Ks: *kes*, long hair; *kangha*, a comb; *kirpan*, a sword; *kachh*, short trousers; and *kara*, a steel bracelet. Sikh men take the last name 'Singh' ('lion'), and women 'Kaur' ('princess'). Sikhs believe in a single God, who is the immortal creator of the universe, and who has never been incarnate in any form. Human beings can make themselves ready to find God by prayer and meditation, but can only achieve closeness to God as a result of God's nadar or grace. Sikhs believe in ◊reincarnation, and that the ten human gurus were teachers through whom the spirit of Guru Nanak was passed on, and lives today in the Guru Granth Sahib (holy book) and the Khalsa. Sikhs avoid the use of all non-medicinal drugs, and in particular tobacco.

Sikh Wars two wars in India between the Sikhs and the British:
First Sikh War 1845–46 following an invasion of British India by Punjabi Sikhs. The Sikhs were defeated and part of their territory annexed.
Second Sikh War 1848–49 arising from a Sikh revolt in Multan. They were defeated and the British annexed the Punjab.

Sikkim or *Denjong* NE state of India; formerly a protected state, it was absorbed by India 1975, the monarchy being abolished. China does not recognize India's sovereignty.
area 7,298 sq km/2,817 mi
capital Gangtok
products rice, grain, tea, fruit, soyabeans, carpets, cigarettes, lead, zinc, copper
population (1991) 403,600
language Bhutia, Lepecha, Khaskura (Nepáli) (all official)
religion Mahayana Buddhism, Hinduism.

Sikorski Wladyslaw 1881–1943. Polish general and politician. In 1909, he formed the nationalist military organization which during World War I fought for the central powers. He was prime minister 1922–23 and war minister 1923–25. In Sep 1939 he became prime minister of the exiled Polish government, which transferred to London 1940. He was killed in an air crash.

Sikorsky Igor 1889–1972. Ukrainian engineer, who built the first successful helicopter. He emigrated to the US 1918 where he first constructed multi-engined flying boats. His first helicopter (the VS300) flew 1939 and a commercial version (the R3) went into production 1943.

silage fodder preserved through controlled fermentation in a silo, an airtight structure which presses green crops. The term also refers to stacked crops which may be preserved indefinitely.

Silbury Hill steep, rounded artificial mound (40 m/130 ft high) of the Bronze Age 2660 BC, in Wiltshire, near ◊Avebury, England. Excavation has shown it not to be a barrow (grave), as was previously thought.

Silchester archaeological site, a major town in Roman Britain. It is 10 km/6 mi N of Basingstoke, Hampshire.

silencer (North American *muffler*) a device in the exhaust system of cars and motorbikes. Gases leave the engine at supersonic speeds, and the exhaust system and silencer are designed to slow them down, thereby silencing them. Some silencers use baffle plates (plates with holes, which disrupt the airflow), others use perforated tubes and an expansion box (a large chamber which slows down airflow).

Silesia long-disputed region of Europe, Austrian 1675–1745: Prussian/German 1745–1919 (following its seizure by ◊Frederick II); and in 1919 divided among newly formed Czechoslovakia, revived Poland, and Germany, which retained the major part. In 1945 all German Silesia east of the Oder-Neisse line was transferred to Polish administration; about 10 million inhabitants of German origin, both there and in Czechoslovak Silesia, were expelled.

silhouette a profile or shadow portrait filled in with black or a dark colour. A popular pictorial technique in the late 18th and early 19th centuries, it was named after Etienne de Silhouette (1709–67), a French finance minister who made paper cut-outs.

silica silicon dioxide, SiO_2, the commonest mineral, of which the most familiar form is quartz. Other silica types are flint, jasper, and opal. Chalcedony is a semiprecious form, varieties of which are agate, onyx, sardonyx, and carnelian.

silicon a non-metallic element, symbol Si, atomic number 14, relative atomic mass 78.09. It is used in glass-making, as a hardener in steel alloys, and in silicon chips for microcomputers.

silicon chip popular term for an ◊integrated circuit with microscopically small electrical components on a piece of silicon crystal only a few millimetres square. Often with more than a million components, it is mounted in a rectangular plastic package and linked via gold wires to metal pins so that it can be connected to a printed circuit board for electronic devices such as computers, calculators, televisions, car dashboards, and domestic appliances.

Silicon Valley nickname given to Santa Clara county, California, since the 1950s, the site of many high-technology electronic firms, whose prosperity is based on the silicon chip.

silicosis disease of miners and stone cutters who inhale flint dust, which makes lung tissue fibrous, less capable of aerating the blood, and less resistant to tuberculosis.

silk fine soft thread produced by the larva of the ◊silkworm moth, and used in the manufacture of textiles. The introduction of synthetics originally harmed the silk industry, but rising standards of living have produced an increased demand for real silk. China and Japan are the largest silk producers.

Silk Road ancient route by which silk was brought from China to Europe in return for trade goods; it ran via the Gobi Desert, Samarkand, Mount Ararat, and Transylvania.

silk-screen printing a method of printing using treated silk as a kind of stencil. It can be used to print on most surfaces, including paper, plastic, cloth, and wood. In the printing process, the silk is treated with a kind of varnish so that ink can only pass through where the image is required.

silkworm usually the larva of the *common silkworm moth Bombyx mori*. After hatching from the egg and maturing on the leaves of white mulberry trees (or a synthetic substitute), it 'spins' a protective cocoon of fine silk thread 275 m/900 ft long. It is killed before emerging as a moth to keep the thread intact, and several threads are combined to form the commercial silk thread woven into textiles.

silo in farming, an airtight tower in which ◊silage is made by the fermentation of freshly cut grass and other forage crops. In military technology, a silo is an underground chamber for housing and launching a ballistic missile.

Silurian period of geological time 438–408 million years ago, the third period of the Palaeozoic era. Silurian sediments are mostly marine, and consist of shales and limestone. The first land plants began to evolve during this period, and there were many jawless fish.

silver lustrous metal, extremely malleable and ductile, symbol Ag (Latin *argentum*), atomic number 47, relative atomic mass 107.873. The chief ores are sulphides, from which the metal is extracted by smelting with lead. It is one of the best metallic conductors of both heat and electricity, and its most important compounds are the chloride and bromide which darken on exposure to light, the basis of photographic emulsions. Silver is used for tableware, jewellery, coinage, electrical contacts, electroplating, and as a solder. It has been known since prehistoric times. The world's greatest producer of silver is Mexico (approximately 40,000,000 troy ounces per annum), followed by the USA, Canada, Peru, the USSR, Australia, and Japan.

silverfish wingless insect, a type of ◊bristletail.

sima in geochemistry and geophysics, term denoting the substance of the Earth's ocean ◊crust, as distinct from the ◊sial of the continent crust. The name is derived from *si*lica and *ma*gnesia, its two main chemical constituents.

Simenon Georges 1903–1989. Belgian crime writer. Initially a pulp fiction writer, in 1931 he created Inspector Maigret of the Paris Sûreté who appeared in a series of detective novels.

Simeon Stylites, St *c.* 390–459. Syrian Christian ascetic, who practised his ideal of self-denial by living for 37 years on a platform on top of a high pillar. Feast day 5 Jan.

simile a ◊figure of speech whose Latin name means 'likeness' and which in English uses the conjunctions 'like' and 'as' to express imaginative comparisons ('run like the devil'; 'as deaf as a post'). It is sometimes confused with ◊metaphor.

Simon Claude 1913– . French novelist. Originally an artist, he abandoned the 'time structure' in such novels as *La Route de Flandres/The Flanders Road* 1960. Other novels include *Le Palace* 1962, *Histoire* 1967, and *Les Géorgiques* 1981. Nobel prize 1985.

Simon Herbert 1916– . US social scientist. He researched decision-making in business corporations, and argued that maximum profit was seldom the chief motive. Nobel Prize for Economics 1978.

Simon John Allsebrook, Viscount Simon 1873–1954. British Liberal politician. He was home secretary 1915–16, but resigned over the issue of conscription. He was foreign secretary 1931–35, home secretary again 1935–37, chancellor of the Exchequer 1937–40, and lord chancellor 1940–45.

Simon (Marvin) Neil 1927– . US playwright. His plays include the comic *Barefoot in the Park* 1963, *The Odd Couple* 1965, and *The Sunshine Boys* 1972, and the more serious, autobiographical *Brighton Beach Memoirs* 1983. He has also written screenplays, and co-written musicals.

Simon Paul 1942– . US pop singer and songwriter. In a folk-rock duo with Art Garfunkel (1942–), he had hits such as 'Mrs Robinson' 1968 and 'Bridge Over Troubled Water' 1970. His solo work includes the album *Graceland* 1986, for which he drew on Cajun and African music.

Simone Martini Sienese painter; see ◊Martini, Simone.

si monumentum requiris, circumspice (Latin 'if you seek his monument, look about you') the epitaph of Christopher Wren in St Paul's Cathedral, London.

simony in the Christian church, the buying and selling of church preferments, now usually regarded as a sin. The term is derived from *Simon Magus* (Acts 8) who offered money to the Apostles for the power of the Holy Ghost.

Sinatra US singer and actor Frank Sinatra.

simple harmonic motion (SHM) oscillatory or vibrational motion in which an object (or point) moves so that its acceleration towards a central point is proportional to its distance from it. A simple example is a pendulum, which also demonstrates another feature of SHM, that the maximum deflection is the same on each side of the central point.

Simpson Wallis Warfield, Duchess of Windsor 1896–1986. US socialite, who married Earl Winfield Spencer 1916 (they divorced 1927), Ernest Simpson 1928 (they divorced 1936), and the Duke of Windsor (formerly ◊Edward VIII) 1937.

simultaneous equations in mathematics, one of two or more algebraic equations that contain two or more unknown quantities which may have a unique solution. For example, in the case of two linear equations with two unknown variables, such as (i)$x + 3y = 6$ and (ii) $3y - 2x = 4$, the solution will be those unique values of x and y that are valid for both equations. Linear simultaneous equations can be solved using algebraic manipulation to eliminate one of the variables, ◊co-ordinate geometry, or matrices (see ◊matrix).

sin disobedience to the will of God or the gods, as revealed in the moral code laid down by a particular religion. In Roman Catholic theology, a distinction is made between *mortal sins*, which, if unforgiven, result in damnation, and *venial sins*, which are less serious. In Islam, the one unforgivable sin is *shirk*, denial that Allah is the only god.

Sinai Egyptian peninsula, at the head of the Red Sea; area 65,000 sq km/25,000 sq mi. Resources include oil, natural gas, manganese, and coal; irrigation water from the Nile is carried under the Suez Canal.

SINE OF AN ANGLE

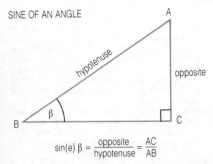

$$\sin(e)\ \beta = \frac{\text{opposite}}{\text{hypotenuse}} = \frac{AC}{AB}$$

Sinai, Battle of battle 6–24 Oct 1973. An Egyptian surprise attack across the Suez canal 6 Apr had initiated the Yom Kippur War with Israel. The first counter-attack was heavily defeated but, after one of the longest tank battles ever, the Israelis crossed the Suez canal 16 Oct cutting off the Egyptian 3rd Army.

Sinan 1489–1588. Ottoman architect, chief architect from 1538 to ◊Suleiman the Magnificent. Among the hundreds of buildings he designed are the Suleimaniye in Istanbul, a mosque complex, and the Topkapi Saray, palace of the Sultan (now a museum).

Sinatra Frank (Francis Albert) 1915– . US singer and film actor. He achieved fame with the Tommy Dorsey band with songs such as 'Night and Day' and 'You'd Be So Nice To Come Home To'. After a slump in his career, he established himself as an actor. *From Here to Eternity* 1953 won him an Academy Award. His later songs include 'My Way'.

Sinclair Clive 1940– . British electronics engineer, who produced the first widely available pocket calculator, pocket and wristwatch televisions, a series of popular home computers, and the innovative but commercially disastrous 'C5' personal transport (a low cycle-like three-wheeled device powered by a washing-machine motor).

Sinclair Upton 1878–1968. US novelist. His concern for social reforms is reflected in *The Jungle* 1906, which exposed the horrors of the Chicago stockyards and led to a change in food-processing laws, *Boston* 1928, and his Lanny Budd series 1940–53, including *Dragon's Teeth* 1942, which won a Pulitzer prize.

sine in trigonometry, a function of an angle in a right-angled triangle defined as the ratio of the length of the side opposite the angle to the length of the hypotenuse (the longest side).

sine wave

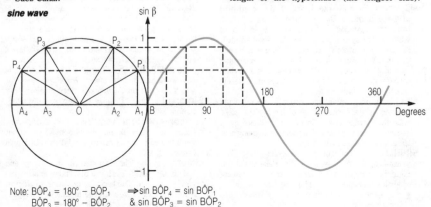

Note: $B\hat{O}P_4 = 180° - B\hat{O}P_1$ $\Rightarrow \sin B\hat{O}P_4 = \sin B\hat{O}P_1$
$B\hat{O}P_3 = 180° - B\hat{O}P_2$ & $\sin B\hat{O}P_3 = \sin B\hat{O}P_2$

Singapore
Republic of

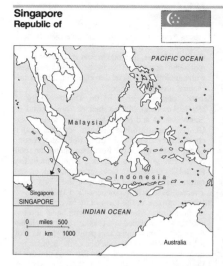

area 620 sq km/239 sq mi
capital Singapore City in the S of the island, a major world port and financial centre
physical comprises Singapore Island, which is low and flat, and 57 small islands
head of state Wee Kim Wee from 1985

head of government Goh Chok Tong from 1990
political system liberal democratic republic with strict limits on dissent
exports electronics, petroleum products, rubber, machinery, vehicles
currency Singapore dollar
population (1990 est) 2,703,000 (Chinese 75%, Malay 14%, Tamil 7%); annual growth rate 1.2%
language Malay, Chinese, Tamil, English (all official)
religion Buddhist, Taoist, Muslim, Hindu, Christian
literacy men 93%, women 79% (1985 est)
GDP $19.9 bn (1987); $7,616 per head
chronology
1819 Singapore leased to British East India Co.
1858 Placed under crown rule.
1942 Invaded and occupied by Japan.
1945 Japanese removed by British forces.
1959 Independence achieved from Britain; Lee Kuan Yew became prime minister.
1963 Joined new Federation of Malaysia.
1965 Left federation to become independent republic.
1984 Opposition made advances in parliamentary elections.
1986 Opposition leader convicted of perjury, prohibited from standing for election.
1988 The ruling conservative party elected to all but one of the available assembly seats; increasingly authoritarian rule.
1990 After 25 years in office Lee Kuan Yew stepped down as prime minister, succeeded by Goh Chok Tong.
1991 People's Action Party (PAP) and Goh Chok Tong re-elected.

Various properties in physics vary sinusoidally, that is, they can be represented diagrammatically by a sine wave (a graph obtained by plotting values of angles against the values of their sines). Examples include ◊simple harmonic motion, such as the way alternating current (AC) electricity varies with time.

Sinfonietta an orchestral work which is of a shorter, lighter nature than a symphony.

Singapore country in SE Asia, off the tip of the Malay Peninsula.

Singer Isaac Bashevis 1904–1991. Polish novelist and short story writer, who became a US citizen 1942. His works, written in Yiddish, often portray traditional Jewish life in Poland, and the loneliness of old age. They include *Gimpel the Fool* 1957, *The Slave* 1960, and *Old Love* 1979. Nobel prize 1978.

Singer Isaac Merit 1811–1875. US inventor of domestic and industrial sewing machines. Within a few years of opening his first factory 1851, he became the world's largest manufacturer (despite charges of patent infringement by Elias ◊Howe), and by the late 1860s more than 100,000 Singer sewing machines were in use in the USA alone.

Singh Vishwanath Pratar 1931– . Indian politician, prime minister 1989–90. As a member of the Congress (I) Party, he held ministerial posts under Indira Gandhi and Rajiv Gandhi, and from 1984 led an anti-corruption drive. When he unearthed an arms-sales scandal 1988, he was ousted from the government and party, and formed a broad-based opposition alliance, the **Janata Dal**. He was overthrown as prime minister by Chandra Shekhar.

Singh, Gobind see ◊Gobind Singh, Sikh guru.

Singapore *The skyline of Singapore.*

Singer *Writer Isaac Bashevis Singer.*

siphon

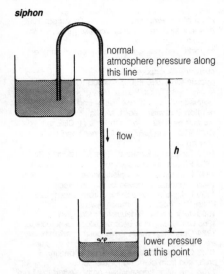

normal atmosphere pressure along this line

flow

h

lower pressure at this point

single sideband transmission radio wave transmission using either the frequency band above the carrier wave frequency, or below, instead of both (as now).

Sinhalese member of the majority population of Sri Lanka. The Sinhalese language belongs to the Indo-Iranian branch of the Indo-European family.

sinking fund money set aside for the repayment of debt. For a company, a sinking fund is used to allow annually for ◊depreciation; in the case of a nation, a sinking fund pays off a part of the national debt.

Sinn Féin Irish nationalist party ('We ourselves'), founded by Arthur Griffith (1872–1922) in 1905; in 1917 ◊de Valera became its president. It is the political wing of the Irish Republican Army, and is similarly split between comparative moderates and extremists. In 1985 it gained representation in 17 out of 26 district councils in Northern Ireland.

Sino-Japanese Wars wars waged by Japan against China to secure expansion on the mainland.

First Sino-Japanese War 1894–95. Under the treaty of Shimonoseki, Japan secured the 'independence' of Korea, cession of Taiwan and the nearby Pescadores Islands, and of the Liaodong peninsula (for a naval base). France, Germany, and Russia pressured Japan into returning the last-named, which Russia occupied 1896 to establish Port Arthur (now Lüda), leading to the Russo-Japanese War.

Second Sino-Japanese War 1931–45
1931–32 The Japanese occupied Manchuria, which they formed into the puppet state of Manchukuo. They also attacked Shanghai, and moved into NE China.

1937 Chinese leaders Chiang Kai-shek and Mao Zedong allied to fight the Japanese; war was renewed as the Japanese overran NE China and seized Shanghai and Nanjing.

1938 Japanese capture of Wuhan and Guangzhou was followed by the transfer of the Chinese capital to Chongqing; a period of stalemate followed.

1941 Japanese attack on Britain and the USA (see ◊Pearl Harbor) led to the extension of lend-lease aid to China.

1944 A Japanese offensive threatened Chongqing.

1945 Chinese received the Japanese surrender at Nanjing in Sep.

sinusitis inflammation of one of the sinuses, or air spaces, which surround the nasal passages. It most frequently involves the maxillary sinuses, within the cheek bones, to produce pain around the eyes, toothache, and a nasal discharge. Most cases clear with antibiotics and nasal decongestants, but some require surgical drainage.

Sioux principal group of the Dakota family of North American ◊Plains Indians, now found in South Dakota and Nebraska. They defeated Gen George Custer at Little Bighorn, Montana (under chiefs Crazy Horse and Sitting Bull); as a result, Congress abrogated the Fort Laramie treaty 1868 (which had given the Indians a large area in the Black Hills of Dakota). Gold, uranium, coal, oil and natural gas are found there, and the Sioux were awarded $160 million compensation 1980.

siphon a tube in the form of an inverted U with unequal arms. When it is filled with liquid and the shorter arm is placed in a tank or reservoir, liquid flows out of the longer arm provided that its exit is below the level of the surface of the liquid in the tank. It works on the principle that the pressure at the liquid surface is atmospheric pressure, whereas at the lower end of the longer arm it is less than atmospheric pressure, causing flow to occur.

siren in Greek mythology, a sea nymph who lured sailors on to rocks by her singing. ◊Odysseus, in order to hear the sirens safely, tied himself to the mast and stuffed his crews' ears with wax; the Argonauts escaped them because the singing of Orpheus surpassed that of the sirens.

Sirius or *Dog Star* the brightest star in the sky, 8.7 light years away in the constellation Canis Major. Sirius is a white star with a mass of 2.35 Suns, diameter 1.8 times that of the Sun, and a luminosity of 23 Suns. It is orbited every 50 years by a white dwarf, Sirius B.

sirocco a hot, normally dry and dust-laden wind that blows from the highland of Africa to N Africa, Malta, Sicily, and Italy. It occurs mainly in the spring. The name sirocco has been applied to southerly winds in the east of the USA.

sisal strong fibre made from various species of ◊agave, such as *Agave sisalina*.

siskin greenish-yellow bird *Carduelis spinus* in the finch family Fringillidae, about 12 cm/5 in long, found in Eurasia.

Sisley Alfred 1839–1899. French Impressionist painter, known for his views of Port-Marly and the Seine, which he painted during floods 1876.

Sistine Chapel a chapel in the Vatican, Rome, begun under Pope Sixtus IV 1473 by Giovanni del Dolci, and decorated by (among others) Michelangelo. It houses the conclave which meets to select a new pope.

Sisyphus in Greek mythology, king of Corinth who, after his evil life, was condemned in the underworld to roll a huge stone uphill, which always fell back before he could reach the top.

Sita in Hinduism, the wife of Rama, an avatar (manifestation) of the god Vishnu; a character in the ◊*Rāmāyana* epic, characterized by chastity and kindness.

sitar Indian instrument, similar to a ◊lute, with seven metal strings, a gourd body, and long neck with movable frets.

sitatunga herbivorous antelope *Tragelaphus spekei* found in several swamp regions in Central Africa. The hooves are long and splayed to help progress on soft surfaces. Males are dark greyish-brown, females and young are chestnut, all with whitish markings on the rather shaggy fur. They are up to about 1.2 m/4 ft high at the shoulder; the males have thick horns up to 90 cm/3 ft long.

Sitting Bull *c.* 1834–1893. North American Indian chief, who led the ◊Sioux onslaught against Gen ◊Custer.

Sitwell Edith 1887–1964. English poet, whose series of poems *Façade* was performed as recitations to the specially written music of ◊Walton from 1923.

Sitwell Osbert 1892–1969. English poet and author, elder brother of Edith and Sacheverell Sitwell.

SI units (French *Système International d'Unités*) accepted standard system of scientific units used by scientists worldwide. Originally proposed in 1960, it replaces the ◊m.k.s., ◊c.g.s., and ◊f.p.s. systems. It is based on seven basic units: the metre (m) for length, kilogram (kg) for weight, second (s) for time, ampere (A) for electrical current, kelvin (K) for temperature, mole (mol) for amount of substance, and candela (cd) for luminosity.

Siva or *Shiva* (Sanskrit 'propitious') the third person in the Hindu triad. As Mahadeva (great lord), he is the creator, symbolized by the phallic *lingam*, who restores what as Mahakala he destroys. He is often sculptured as Nataraja, performing his fruitful cosmic dance. His consort or female principle (*sakti*), is Parvati, otherwise known as Durga or Kali.

Six, The the original six signatory countries to the Treaty of Rome which created the ◊European Community.

Six Articles an act introduced by Henry VIII in England 1539, to settle disputes over dogma in the English Church. See ◊Anglican Communion.

Six Counties the six counties which form Northern Ireland, namely Antrim, Armagh, Derry (Londonderry), Down, Fermanagh, and Tyrone.

Six, Les a group of French 20th-century composers; see ◊Les Six.

sixth form in UK education, an inclusive term used for pupils staying on for one or two years

skeleton

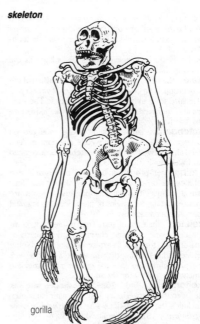

gorilla

fish (perch)

crab
(carapace and exoskeleton)

stag beetle (exoskeleton)

skating British skaters Christopher Dean and Jayne Torvill at the World Championships, Helsinki, 1983.

of study beyond school-leaving age in order to gain ◊A Level or other post-15 qualifications. In many areas, sixth-form education is concentrated in sixth-form colleges.

Skara Brae preserved Neolithic village in the Orkney Islands, Scotland, on Mainland.

skate the name of several species of flatfish of the ray group. The *common skate Raja batis* is up to 1.8 m/6 ft, greyish, with black specks. The egg-cases ('mermaids purses') are often washed ashore by the tide.

skateboard single flexible board mounted on wheels, and steerable by weight positioning. As a land alternative for surfing, skateboards developed in California in the 1960s.

skating self-propulsion on ice by means of bladed skates, or on other surfaces by skates with four small rollers. The chief competitive events are figure skating, for singles or pairs, ice-dancing, and simple speed skating.

skeleton the rigid or semi-rigid framework, composed of bone, cartilage, chitin, and calcium carbonate or silica, found in all vertebrate animals and some invertebrates. It supports the animal's body, as well as protecting the internal organs and providing anchorage points for the muscles.

Skelton John *c*. 1460–1529. English poet, who was tutor to the future Henry VIII. His satirical poetry includes the rumbustious *The Tunnyng of Elynor Rummynge* 1516, and political attacks on Wolsey, such as *Colyn Cloute* 1522.

skiffle a style of British popular music, introduced by the singer and banjo player Lonnie Donegan (1931–) in 1956, using improvised percussion instruments such as tea chests and washboards.

skiing self-propulsion on snow by means of elongated runners for the feet, slightly bent upward at the tip. Events include downhill (with speeds up to 125 km/80 mi per hour); slalom, in which a series of turns between flags have to be negotiated; cross-country racing; and ski jumping

when jumps of over 150 m/400 ft are achieved from ramps up to 90 m/295 ft high.

skin the covering of the body of a vertebrate. In mammals its outer layer (epidermis) is dead and protective, and the cells of this are constantly being rubbed away and replaced from below. The lower layer (dermis) contains blood vessels, nerves, hair roots, and the sweat and sebaceous glands and is supported by a network of fibrous and elastic cells.

skink lizard of the family Scincidae, a large family of about 700 species found throughout the tropics and subtropics. There is a range of body form but in many the body is long, and the legs reduced. Some are actually legless and rather snake-like. Many are good burrowers, or can 'swim' through sand, like the *sandfish* genus *Scincus* of N Africa. Some skinks lay eggs, others bear live young.

Skinner B(urrhus) F(rederic) 1903–1990. US psychologist, a radical behaviourist, who rejected mental concepts, and saw the organism as a 'black box' in which internal processes are not important in predicting behaviour. He studied operant conditioning and stressed that behaviour is shaped and maintained by its consequences.

skittles or *ninepins* game in which nine pins are arranged in a diamond-shaped frame at the end of an alley. The pins have to be knocked down in three rolls from the other end of the alley with a wooden ball. Two or more players can compete. Skittles resembles ◊tenpin bowling.

Skopje capital and industrial city of Macedonia, Yugoslavia; population (1981) 506,547. Industries include iron, steel, chromium mining, and food processing.

Skryabin Alexander (Nikolayevich) 1872–1915. Russian composer and pianist, born in Moscow whose powerfully emotional tone poems such as *Prometheus* 1911, and symphonies, such as *Divine Poem* 1903, employed strange harmonies to express his mystical feelings.

skin

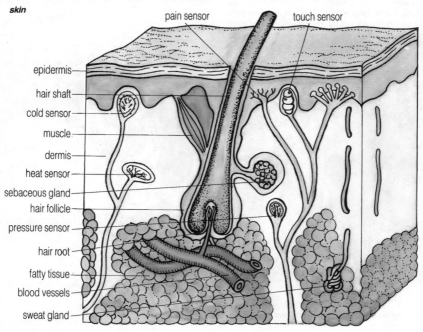

pain sensor touch sensor

epidermis
hair shaft
cold sensor
muscle
dermis
heat sensor
sebaceous gland
hair follicle
pressure sensor
hair root
fatty tissue
blood vessels
sweat gland

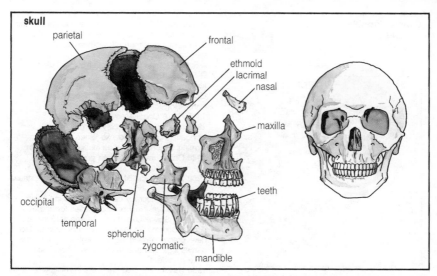

skull

parietal
frontal
ethmoid
lacrimal
nasal
maxilla
occipital
temporal
sphenoid
zygomatic
mandible
teeth

skua dark-coloured gull-like seabird living in arctic and antarctic waters. They can grow up to 60 cm/2 ft long, and are good fliers. They are aggressive scavengers, and will seldom fish for themselves but force gulls to disgorge their catch, and will also eat chicks of other birds.

skull in vertebrates, the collection of flat and irregularly-shaped bones (or cartilage) which enclose and protect the brain. In mammals, it consists of 22 plates of bone joined by sutures. The floor of the skull is pierced by a large hole for the spinal cord and a number of smaller apertures through which other nerves and blood vessels pass.

skunk North American mammal of the weasel family. The *common skunk Mephitis mephitis* has a long, arched body, short legs, a bushy tail, and black fur with white streaks on the back. In self-defence, it discharges a foul-smelling fluid.

skydiving the sport of freefalling from an aircraft at up to 3,650 m/12,000 ft, performing aerobatics, and then opening a parachute when 600 m/2,000 ft from the ground.

Skye largest island of the Inner ◊Hebrides, Scotland; area 1,665 sq km/643 sq mi; population (1981) 8,000. It is separated from the mainland by the Sound of Sleat. The chief port is Portree.

Skylab US space station, launched 14 May 1973, made from the adapted upper stage of a Saturn V rocket. At 75 tonnes, it was the heaviest object ever put into space, and was 25.6 m/84 ft long. Skylab contained a workshop for carrying out experiments in weightlessness, an observatory for monitoring the Sun, and cameras for photographing Earth's surface.

skylark a type of ◊lark.

skyscraper a building so tall that it appears to 'scrape the sky', first developed 1868 in New

skyscraper

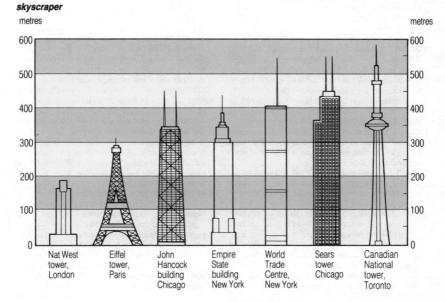

metres

600
500
400
300
200
100
0

Nat West tower, London
Eiffel tower, Paris
John Hancock building Chicago
Empire State building New York
World Trade Centre, New York
Sears tower Chicago
Canadian National tower, Toronto

Slovak Republic
(*Slovenská Republika*)

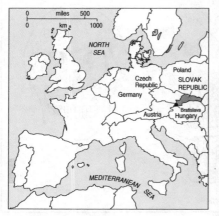

area 49,035 sq km/18,940 sq mi
capital Bratislava
towns Kosice, Nitra, Presov, Banská Bystrica
physical Carpathian Mountains including Tatra and Beskids in N; fine beech and oak forests; Danube plain in S
head of state Michal Kovak from 1993
head of government Vladimir Meciar from 1993
political system emergent democracy
exports iron ore, copper, mercury, magnesite, armaments, chemicals, textiles, machinery
currency new currency based on koruna

population(1991) 5,268,900 (with Hungarian and other minorities); growth rate 0.4% p.a.
life expectancy men 68, women 75
language Slovak (official)
religion Roman Catholic (over 50%), Lutheran, Reformist, Orthodox
literacy 100%
GDP $10,000 m (1990); $1,887 per head
chronology
1906–1918 Under Magyar domination.
1918 Independence achieved from Austro-Hungarian Empire; Slovaks joined Czechs in forming Czechoslovakia as independent nation.
1948 Communists assumed power in Czechoslovakia.
1968 Slovak Socialist Republic created under new federal constitution.
1989 Pro-democracy demonstrations in Prague and Bratislava. New political parties formed, including Slovak-based People Against Violence (PAV). Communist Party stripped of powers. Dec: new 'grand coalition' government formed, political parties legalized and Václav Havel appointed state president.
1990 Havel re-elected president in multiparty elections.
1991 Evidence of increasing Czech and Slovak separatism. Soviet troops withdrawn.
1992 March: PAV renamed Civic Democratic Union (CDU). June: Havel resigned following Slovak gains in assembly elections. Aug: agreement on creation of separate Czech and Slovak states from Jan 1993.
1993 Jan: Slovak Republic became sovereign state, with Vladimir Meciar, leader of the MFDS, as prime minister. Feb: Michal Kovak became president.

York, USA, where land prices were high, and the geology adapted to such methods of construction. Skyscrapers are to be found in cities throughout the world. In Manhattan, New York, are the Empire State Building (1931), 102 storeys and 381 m/1,250 ft high, and the twin towers of the World Trade Center 415m/1,361 ft; these were surpassed by the ◊Sears Tower 443m/1,454 ft in Chicago. The world's tallest free-standing structure is the CN (Canadian National) Tower Toronto, 555 m/1,821 ft.

slander spoken defamatory statement, although if broadcast on radio or television it constitutes ◊libel. In the UK slander is generally only actionable if pecuniary loss has been suffered except where, for example, the slander imputes that a person is inadequate in his or her profession. As in the case of libel, the slander must be made to some person other than the person defamed for it to be actionable.

slate a fine-grained, bluish-purple ◊metamorphic rock which splits readily into thin slabs. Its single prominent cleavage is due to the alignment of platy mineral such as ◊mica.

slavery the involuntary servitude of one person to another, or one group to another. Slavery goes back to prehistoric times, but declined in Europe after the fall of the Roman Empire. In the imperialism of Spain, Portugal, and Britain in the 16th–18th centuries, slavery became a mainstay of the economy, with millions of Africans abducted to work on plantations in the New World colonies. Millions more died in the process, but the profits from this trade were enormous. Slavery was abolished in the British Empire 1833 and in the USA 1863–65, but continues today in some countries.

Slavonic languages or *Slavic languages* a branch of the Indo-European language family spoken in Central and Eastern Europe, the Balkans, and parts of N Asia. The family comprises the *southern group* (Serbo-Croat, Slovene and Macedonian in Yugoslavia, and Bulgarian in Bulgaria); the *western group* (Czech and Slovak, Sorbian in Germany, and Polish and its related dialects); and the *eastern group* (Russian, Ukrainian and Byelorussian).

Slavophile intellectual and political group in 19th century Russia which promoted the idea of an eastern orientation for the empire in opposition to those who wanted the country to adopt western methods and ideas of development.

SLD abbreviation for ◊Social and Liberal Democrats.

sleep a state of reduced awareness and activity that occurs at regular intervals in most mammals and birds, though there is considerable variation in the amount of time spent sleeping. Sleep differs from hibernation in occurring daily rather than seasonally, and involving less drastic reductions in metabolism. The function of sleep is unclear. People deprived of sleep become irritable, uncoordinated, forgetful, hallucinatory and even psychotic.

sleeping sickness an infectious disease of tropical Africa. Once the ◊trypanosome has entered the bloodstream, early symptoms include fever, headache, and chills, followed by ◊anaemia and joint pains. Later, the disease attacks the central nervous system, causing drowsiness, lethargy, and if left untreated, death. Control is by eradication of the tsetse fly which transmits the disease to humans.

slide rule a mathematical instrument having pairs of logarithmic sliding scales, used for rapid

Slovenia
Republic of

area 20,251 sq km/7,817 sq mi
capital Ljubljana
towns Maribor, Kranj, Celji; chief port: Koper
physical mountainous; rivers: Sava, Drava
head of state Milan Kucan from 1990
head of government Janez Drnovsek from 1992
political system emergent democracy
products grain, sugarbeet, livestock, timber, cotton and woollen textiles, steel, vehicles
currency tolar
population (1990) 2,000,000 (91% Slovene, 3% Croat, 2% Serb)
language Slovene, resembling Serbo-Croat, written in Roman characters

religion Roman Catholic
chronology
1918 United with Serbia and Croatia.
1929 The kingdom of Serbs, Croats, and Slovenes took the name of Yugoslavia.
1945 Became a constituent republic of Yugoslav Socialist Federal Republic.
mid-1980s The Slovenian Communist Party liberalized itself and agreed to free elections. The Yugoslav counterintelligence (KOV) began repression.
1989 Jan: Social Democratic Alliance of Slovenia launched as first political organization independent of Communist Party. Sept: constitution changed to allow secession from federation.
1990 Feb: Slovene League of Communists, renamed as the Party of Democratic Reform, severed its links with the Yugoslav League of Communists. April: nationalist DEMOS coalition secured victory in first multiparty parliamentary elections; Milan Kucan became president. July: sovereignty declared. Dec: independence overwhelmingly approved in referendum.
1991 June: independence declared; 100 killed after federal army intervened; cease-fire brokered by EC. July: cease-fire agreed between federal troops and nationalists. Oct: withdrawal of Yugoslav army completed. Dec: DEMOS coalition dissolved.
1992 Jan: European Community recognized Slovenia's independence. April: Janez Drnovsek appointed prime minister designate; independence recognized by USA. May: admitted into UN. Dec: Liberal Democrats and Christian Democrats won assembly elections; Kucan re-elected president.
1993 Drnovsek re-elected prime minister.

---

calculations, including multiplication, division, and the extraction of square roots.

Sligo county in the province of Connacht, Republic of Ireland, situated on the Atlantic coast of NW Ireland; area 1,796 sq km/693 sq mi; population (1991) 54,700. The country town is Sligo; there is livestock and dairy farming.

Slim William Joseph, 1st Viscount Slim 1891–1970. British field marshal in World War II. A veteran of Gallipoli, Turkey, in World War I, he commanded the 14th 'forgotten' army 1943–45, stemming the Japanese invasion of India at Imphal and Kohima, and then recovered Burma. He was governor general of Australia 1953–60.

slime mould or **myxomycete** an extraordinary organism which shows some features of ◊fungi and some of ◊protozoa. Slime moulds are not closely related to any other group, although they are often classed, for convenience, with the fungi. *Cellular slime moulds* go through a phase of living as single cells, looking like amoebae, and feed by engulfing the bacteria found in rotting wood, dung, or damp soil. When a food supply is exhausted, up to 100,000 of these amoebae form into a colony resembling a single slug-like animal and migrate to a fresh source of bacteria. The colony then takes on the aspect of a fungus, and forms long-stalked fruiting bodies which release spores. These germinate to release amoebae, which repeat the life cycle. *Plasmodial slime moulds* have a more complex life cycle involving sexual reproduction. They form a slimy mass of protoplasm with no internal cell walls, which slowly spreads over the bark or branches of trees.

sloe fruit of the ◊blackthorn.

sloth South American mammal, about 70 cm/2.3 ft long, of the order Edentata. Sloths are greyish-brown, and have small rounded heads, rudimentary tails, and prolonged forelimbs. Each foot has long curved claws adapted for clinging to trees and hanging upside down. They are vegetarian.

Slovakia one of the two republics that formed the Federative Republic of Czechoslovakia. Settled in the 5th-6th centuries by Slavs; it was occupied by the Magyars in the 10th century, and was part of the kingdom of Hungary until 1918, when it became a province of Czechoslovakia. Slovakia was a puppet state under German domination 1939–45, and was abolished as an administrative division in 1949. Its capital and chief town is Bratislava. It was re-established as a sovereign state after the breakup of the Czechoslovak Republic in 1993.

Slovak Republic country in E central Europe, bounded N by Poland, W by Ukraine, S by Hungary, SW by Austria, and NW by the Czech republic.

Slovenia or *Slovenija* country in S central Europe bounded N by Austria, E by Hungary, W by Italy, and S by Croatia.

slow-worm harmless species of lizard *Anguish fragilis*, common in Europe. Superficially resembling a snake, it is distinguished by its small mouth and movable eyelids. It is about 30 cm/1 ft long, and eats worms and slugs.

SLR abbreviation for *single-lens reflex*, a type of camera in which the image is seen in the taking lens.

slug air-breathing gastropod related to snails, but with absent or much-reduced shell.

Sluter Claus *c.* 1380–1406. N European sculptor, probably of Dutch origin. His work shows an expressive Gothic style.

small arms one of the two main divisions of firearms, guns that can be carried by hand. The first small arms were portable hand-guns in use in the late 14th century, supported on the ground and ignited by hand. Modern small arms range from breech-loading single shot rifles and shotguns to sophisticated automatic and semi-automatic weapons. In 1980, 11,522 deaths in the USA were caused by hand guns; in the UK, there were 8.

Small Claims Court in the USA, a court which deals with small civil claims, using a simple procedure. In Britain, similar bodies introduced experimentally in London and Manchester have now ceased. The term is sometimes used for the arbitration procedure in county courts in the UK, where a simplified procedure applies for small claims.

smallpox contagious viral disease, marked by fever and skin eruptions leaving pitted scars. Widespread vaccination programmes have almost eradicated this disease.

smart pill in medicine, a peanut-sized pill containing a computer and sensors to take measurements as it passes through the body. The information is transmitted, by ultrasound, to an external computer. The pill can discharge drugs, for example, it can detect stones in the gallbladder and release chemicals to dissolve them.

smelling salts or **sal volatile** a mixture of ammonium carbonate, bicarbonate, and carbamate. They were once used to arouse people who had fainted, their strong and unpleasant smell having a marked stimulant effect.

smelt small fish, usually marine, although some species are freshwater, and some live in lakes. They occur in Europe and North America.

smelting processing a metallic ore in a furnace to produce the metal. Oxide ores such as iron ore are smelted with coke (carbon), which reduces the ore into metal and also provides fuel for the process. A substance such as limestone is often added during smelting to facilitate the melting process and to form a slag which dissolves many of the impurities present.

Smetana Bedřich 1824–1884. Czech composer, conductor at the National Theatre of Prague 1866–74. His music has a distinct national character, for example, the operas *The Bartered Bride* 1866, *Dalibor* 1868, and the symphonic suite *My Country* 1875–80. Deaf from 1874, he became insane in 1883.

Smith Adam 1723–1790. Scottish economist and philosopher, the founder of modern political economy. His *The Wealth of Nations* 1776 defined national wealth in terms of labour, as the only real measure of value, expressed in terms of wages. The cause of wealth is explained by the **division of labour** – dividing a production process into several repetitive operations, each carried out by different workers. Smith advocated the free working of individual enterprise, and the necessity of 'free trade' rather than the protection offered by a mercantile system.

Smith Bessie 1894–1937. US jazz and blues singer, born in Chattanooga, Tennessee. She established herself in the 1920s, but her popularity waned in the Depression, and she died after a car crash when she was refused admission to a whites-only hospital. She was known as the Empress of the Blues.

Smith Ian Douglas 1919– . Rhodesian politician. He was a founder of the Rhodesian Front 1962 and prime minister 1964–79. In 1965 he made a unilateral declaration of Rhodesia's independence, and despite United Nations sanctions, maintained his regime with tenacity. He was suspended from the Zimbabwe parliament Apr 1987 and resigned in May as head of the white opposition party.

Smith John 1580–1631. English colonist. After an adventurous early life he took part in the colonization of Virginia, acting as president of the colony 1608–09. He explored New England 1614, which he named, and published pamphlets on America and an autobiography.

Smith John Maynard 1920– . British biologist, whose work in evolutionary theory resulted in the theory of the **evolutionarily stable strategy** (◊ESS), which explains animal aggression as part of a ritual and suggests that evolution prevents animals from attacking each other.

Smith John 1938– . British labour politician, party leader from 1992. He was secretary of stake for trade 1978–79 and from 1979 held various shadow cabinet posts, culminating in shadow chancellor 1987–92.

Smith Joseph 1805–1844. US founder of the ◊Mormon religious sect.

Smith Maggie (Margaret Natalie) 1934– . English actress. Her roles include the title part (winning an Oscar) in the film *The Prime of Miss Jean Brodie* 1969. Other films include *California Suite* 1978, *A Private Function* 1984, and *A Room with a View* 1986.

Smith 'Stevie' (Florence Margaret) 1902–1971. English poet, whose books include *Novel on Yellow Paper* 1936, and the poems *A Good Time was had by All* 1937, and *Not Waving but Drowning* 1957.

smoker vent on the ocean floor, associated with an ◊ocean ridge, through which hot, mineral-rich groundwater erupts into the sea, forming thick clouds of suspension. The clouds may be dark or light, depending on the mineral content, thus producing 'white smokers' or 'black smokers'.

smoking inhaling the fumes from burning leaves, generally tobacco, in the form of ◊cigarettes. The practice can be habit-forming, and is dangerous to health. A direct link between lung cancer and smoking was established 1950; there is also a link between smoking and respiratory and coronary diseases. Today smoking is increasingly forbidden in public places because of the risk of **passive smoking**, the inhaling of fumes from other people's cigarettes. The first successful claim in the USA for health damages against a US cigarette company was made 1988.

smut parasitic ◊fungus, which infects flowering plants, particularly cereals.

Smuts Jan Christian 1870–1950. South African politician, field marshal, and lawyer; prime minister 1919–24 and 1939–48. He supported the Allies in both world wars and was a member of the British imperial war cabinet 1917–18.

snail air-breathing gastropod mollusc, with a spiral shell. Thousands of species exist, on land and in water.

snake reptile of the suborder Serpentes of the order Squamata which also includes lizards. Snakes are characterized by an elongated limbless body, possibly evolved because of subterranean ancestors. One of the striking internal modifications is the absence or greatly reduced size of the left lung. The skin is covered in scales which are markedly wider underneath where they form. There are 3,000 species found in the tropic and temperate zones, but none in New Zealand, Ireland, Iceland, and near the poles.

snapdragon perennial herbaceous plant of the genus *Antirrhinum*, family Scrophulariaceae, with spikes of brightly coloured two-lipped flowers.

snipe European marsh bird of the family Scolopacidae, order Charadriiformes; species include **common snipe** *Gallinago gallinago*, and

snow a snow crystal.

the rare **great snipe** *Gallinago media*, of which the males hold spring gatherings to show their prowess. It is closely related to the ◊woodcock.

snooker indoor game derived from ◊billiards (via ◊pool). It is played with 22 balls: 15 reds, one each of yellow, green, brown, blue, pink and black, and a white cue-ball. Red balls when potted are worth one point while the coloured balls have ascending values from two points for the yellow to seven points for the black.

snoring a loud noise during sleep made by vibration of the soft palate (the rear part of the ceiling of the mouth) caused by streams of air entering the nose and mouth at the same time. It is most common when the nose is blocked.

snow precipitation in the form of flaked particles caused by the condensation in air of excess water vapour below freezing point. Light reflecting in the crystals, which have a basic hexagonal (six-sided) geometry, gives the snow a white appearance.

Snow C(harles) P(ercy), Baron Snow 1905–1980. English novelist. His sequence of novels *Strangers and Brothers* 1940–64 portrayed English life from 1920 onwards. His *Two Cultures* (Cambridge Rede lecture 1959) discussed the absence of communication between literary and scientific intellectuals in the West, and added the phrase 'the two cultures' to the language.

Snowden Philip, 1st Viscount Snowden 1864–1937. British right-wing Labour politician, chancellor of the Exchequer 1924 and 1929–31. He entered the coalition National Government in 1931 as Lord Privy Seal, but resigned in 1932.

Snowdon Anthony Armstrong-Jones, Earl of Snowdon 1930– . British photographer specializing in portraits, who married Princess Margaret in 1960, was granted his peerage in 1961, and divorced in 1978.

snowdrop bulbous plant *Galanthus nivalis*, family Amaryllidaceae, with white bell-shaped flowers, tinged with green, in spring.

snow leopard a type of ◊leopard.

snowdrop

snuff finely powdered ◊tobacco for sniffing up the nostrils as a stimulant or sedative. Snuff taking was common in 17th-century England and the Netherlands, and spread in the 18th century to other parts of Europe, but was then superseded by cigarette smoking.

Soames Christopher, Baron Soames 1920–1987. British Conservative politician. He held ministerial posts 1958–64, was vice president of the Commission of the European Communities 1973–77 and governor of (Southern) Rhodesia in the period of its transition to independence as Zimbabwe, Dec 1979–Apr 1980. He was created a life peer in 1978.

Soane John 1753–1837. British architect. His individual Neo-Classical style resulted in works anticipating modern taste. Little remains of his extensive work at the Bank of England, London. Other buildings include his own house in Lincoln's Inn Fields, London, now the Soane Museum.

soap a mixture of the sodium salts of various fatty acids: palmitic, stearic, or oleic acid. It is made by the action of caustic soda or caustic potash on fats of animal or vegetable origin. Soap makes grease and dirt disperse in water in a similar manner to a ◊detergent.

soap opera a television series or radio melodrama. It originated in the USA as a series of daytime programmes sponsored by washing-powder manufacturers. The popularity of the genre has led to major soap operas being shown at peak viewing times. Notable television soap operas include: *Coronation Street* (UK, 1960–); *Crossroads* (UK, 1964–88); *Dallas* (USA, 1978–91); *Dynasty* (USA, 1981–); *Neighbours* (Australia, 1983–) *Eastenders* (UK, 1985–).

soapstone a type of rock from which talc is derived.

Soares Mario 1924– . Portuguese politician. Exiled in 1970, he returned to Portugal in 1974, and as leader of the Portuguese Socialist Party (PSP) was prime minister 1976–78. He resigned as party leader in 1980, but in 1986 he was elected Portugal's first socialist president.

Sobers Garfield St Aubrun 'Gary' 1936– . West Indian test cricketer. One of the game's great allrounders he scored more than 8000 test runs, took over 200 wickets, held more than 100 catches, and holds the record for the highest test innings, 365 not out.

Sobieski John 1642–1696. Alternative name for ◊John III, king of Poland.

soca Latin Caribbean music, a mixture of *soul* and *ca*lypso.

socage Anglo-Saxon term for the free tenure of land by the peasantry. Sokemen, holders of land by this tenure, formed the upper stratum of peasant society at the time of the ◊Domesday Book.

Social and Liberal Democrats official name for new British political party formed 1988 from the former Liberal Party and most of the Social Democratic Party. Its leader (from Jul 1988) is Paddy ◊Ashdown. The common name for the party is *Liberal Democrats*.

social behaviour in zoology, behaviour concerned with altering the behaviour of other individuals of the same species. Social behaviour allows animals to live in groups and form alliances within their group against other members (for example, subordinate animals can group together to prevent dominant individuals from monopolizing food). It may be aggressive or submissive (for example, cowering and other signals of appeasement), or designed

snooker

black
score 7

reds score 1

rack

pink
score 6

Snooker is played on a table measuring approximately 1.83m/6ft by 3.66m/12ft. The bed of the table is made of slate and covered by a stretched green cloth. The inside of the playing area (cushions) are rubberised.

The game is played with one white cue-ball, fifteen reds and six coloured balls (yellow, green, brown, blue, pink and black). Reds are worth one point when potted while the colours are rated in ascending order from two to seven points.

angles
The use of angles is an important feature of snooker. In this example, the cue-ball, after potting the ball into the middle pocket, travels around the table using the natural angles to get into position for the shot on the next ball.

blue
score
5

bridges
The hand should form a natural support, or bridge, for the cue. A good bridge is essential. However, there are times when the hand cannot get near enough to the ball to make a natural bridge and a variety of aids are then utilised.

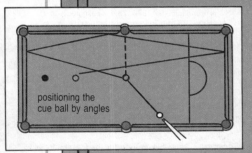

positioning the cue ball by angles

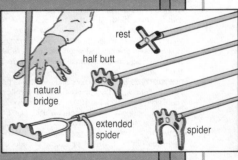

rest

half butt

natural bridge

extended spider

spider

green
score 3

brown score 4

yellow
score 2

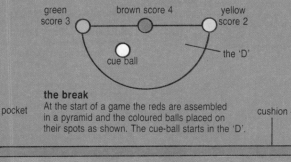

the 'D'

cue ball

the break
At the start of a game the reds are assembled in a pyramid and the coloured balls placed on their spots as shown. The cue-ball starts in the 'D'.

pocket

cushion

to establish bonds (such as social grooming or preening).

social contract the idea that government authority derives originally from an agreement between ruler and ruled in which the former agrees to provide ◊order in return for obedience from the latter. It has been used to support either absolutism (◊Hobbes) or democracy (◊Locke, ◊Rousseau, and ◊Rawls). The term was revived in the UK in 1974 when a head-on clash between the Conservative government and the trade unions resulted in a general election which enabled a Labour government to take power. It now denotes an unofficial agreement (hence also called 'social compact') between a government and organized labour that, in return for control of prices, rents, and so on, the unions would refrain from economically disruptive wage demands.

social democracy a political ideology of belief in the gradual evolution of a democratic ◊socialism within existing political structures. The earliest was the German *Sozialdemokratische Partei* (SPD), today one of the two major West German parties, created in 1875 from August Bebel's earlier German Social Democratic Workers' Party, itself founded 1869. The British Labour Party is in the social democratic tradition.

Social Democratic Labour Party (SDLP) Northern Irish left-wing political party, formed in 1970. It aims ultimately at Irish unification, but distances itself from the violent tactics of the Irish Republican Army (IRA), adopting a constitutional, conciliatory role. The SDLP, led by John Hume (1937–), was responsible for setting-up the ◊New Ireland Forum in 1983.

Social Democratic Party (SDP) British political party 1981–90, formed by members of parliament who resigned from the Labour Party and took a more centrist position. The 1983 and 1987 general elections were fought in alliance with the Liberal Party as the *Liberal/SDP Alliance* (1983, six seats, 11.6% of the vote; 1987, five seats, 9.8% of the vote). The SDP voted for a merger of the two parties in 1987, and the new party became the ◊Social and Liberal Democrats, leaving a rump SDP that folded 1990.

socialism movement aiming to establish a classless society by substituting public for private ownership of the means of production, distribution, and exchange. The term has been used to describe positions as widely apart as anarchism and social democracy. Socialist ideas appeared in classical times; in early Christianity; among later Christian sects such as the ◊Anabaptists and ◊Diggers; and, in the ferment of the revolutionary period at the end of the 18th and early 19th centuries, were put forward as systematic political aims by ◊Rousseau, ◊Saint Simon, ◊Fourier, and ◊Owen, among others. ◊Marx (*Communist Manifesto* 1848) and ◊Engels.

'socialism in one country' concept proposed by ◊Stalin in 1924. In contrast to ◊Trotsky's theory of the permanent revolution, Stalin suggested that the emphasis be changed away from promoting revolutions abroad to the idea of building socialism, economically and politically, in the USSR without help from other countries.

socialist realism artistic doctrine set up by the Soviet Union during the 1930s setting out the optimistic, socialist terms in which society should be portrayed in works of art (including music and painting as well as prose fiction).

socialization the process, beginning in childhood, by which a person learns how to become a member of a particular society, learning its norms, customs, laws, and ways of living. The main agents of socialization are the family, school, peer groups, work, religion, and the mass media. The main methods of socialization are direct instruction, rewards and punishment, imitation, experimentation, role play, and interaction.

Social Realism in painting, the branch of Realism concerned with poverty and deprivation. The French artist Courbet provides a 19th-century example of the genre. Subsequently, in the USA, the Ashcan school and Ben Shahn are among those described as Social Realists.

social science the group of academic disciplines which investigate how and why people behave the way they do, as individuals and in groups. The term originated with the 19th-century French thinker Auguste ◊Comte. The academic social sciences are generally listed as sociology, economics, anthropology, political science, and psychology. A current debate is whether the study of people can or should be a science.

social security state provision of financial aid to alleviate poverty. The term 'social security' was first applied officially in the USA, in the Social Security Act 1935. It was first used officially in Britain in 1944, and following the ◊Beveridge Report in 1942 a series of acts was passed from 1945 to widen the scope of social security. Basic entitlements of those paying National Insurance contributions in Britain include an old-age pension, unemployment benefit, widow's pension, and payment during a period of sickness in one's working life. Other benefits include Family Credit, Child Benefit, and Attendance Allowance for those looking after sick or disabled people. Entitlements under National Insurance, such as Unemployment Benefit, are paid at flat rates regardless of need; other benefits, such as Income Support, are 'means-tested', that is, claimants' income must be below a certain level. Most payments, with the exception of Unemployment Benefit, are made by the Department of Social Security.

In the USA the term 'social security' usually refers specifically to old-age pensions, which have a contributory element, unlike 'welfare'. The federal government is responsible for social security (medicare, retirement, survivors', and disability insurance); unemployment insurance is covered by a joint federal-state system for industrial workers, but few in agriculture are covered; and welfare benefits are the responsibility of individual states, with some federal assistance.

Socinianism form of 17th-century Christian belief which rejects such traditional doctrines as the Trinity and original sin, named after *Socinus*, the Latinized name of Lelio Francesco Maria Sozzini (1525–62), Italian Protestant theologian. Socinianism denies the divinity of Jesus while emphasizing his virtues. It is an early form of ◊Unitarianism.

sociobiology the study of the biological basis of all social behaviour, including the application of ◊population genetics to the evolution of behaviour. It builds on the concept of ◊inclusive fitness. Contrary to some popular interpretations, it does not assume that all behaviour is genetically determined.

sociology the systematic study of society, in particular of social order and social change, social conflict and social problems. It studies institutions such as the family, law, and the church, as well as concepts such as norm, role, and culture. Sociology attempts to study people in their social environment according to certain underlying moral, philosophical, and political codes of behaviour.

Socrates c. 469–399 BC. Athenian philosopher. He wrote nothing but was immortalized in the dialogues of his pupil, Plato. In his desire to combat the scepticism of the ◊sophists, Socrates asserted the possibility of genuine knowledge. In ethics, he put forward the view that the good person never knowingly does wrong. True knowledge emerges through dialogue and systematic questioning, and an abandoning of uncritical claims to knowledge.

Socratic method way of teaching used by Socrates, in which he aimed to guide pupils to clear thinking on ethics and politics by asking questions and then exposing their inconsistencies in cross-examination.

soda ash former name for ◊sodium carbonate (Na_2CO_3).

soda lime mixture of calcium hydroxide and sodium hydroxide or potassium hydroxide, used in medicine and as a drying agent.

Soddy Frederick 1877–1956. English physical chemist, pioneer of research into atomic disintegration who coined the term 'isotope'. Nobel Prize 1921.

sodium a metallic element, symbol Na (Latin *natrium*), atomic number 11, relative atomic mass 22.991. It is a soft, bright, silvery, reactive metal tarnishing quickly on exposure to air, and reacting violently with water to form sodium hydroxide. Important sodium compounds include common salt, sodium carbonate (Na_2CO_3 – washing soda), and hydrogencarbonate ($NaHCO_3$ – bicarbonate of soda), sodium hydroxide or caustic soda ($NaOH$), sodium nitrate or Chile saltpetre ($NaNO_3$ – fertilizer), sodium thiosulphate or hypo ($Na_2S_2O_3$ – photographic fixer).

Sodom and Gomorrah two ancient cities in the Dead Sea area of the Middle East, recorded in the Old Testament or Hebrew Bible (Genesis) as destroyed by fire and brimstone for their wickedness.

Sofia or *Sofiya* capital of Bulgaria since 1878; population (1981) 1,070,000. Industries include textiles, rubber, machinery, and electrical equipment. It lies at the foot of the Vitosha Mountains.

softball outdoor bat and ball game. It is like a smaller version of ◊baseball; the main differences are that the pitching of the ball in softball must be delivered underarm, and that the bases are closer together.

soft currency a vulnerable currency which tends to fall in value on foreign exchange markets because of political or economic uncertainty. Governments are unwilling to hold soft currencies in their foreign exchange reserves, preferring

solar energy *Solar dishes at the Themis experimental solar power station in the French Pyrenees.*

strong or hard currencies which are easily convertible.

software in computing, any kind of program or programs (as opposed to hardware, that is, the mechanical and electrical components of a computer), without which no computer can function. Even to execute a program a computer first needs another program to guide it (an ◊operating system). This may be built into the hardware or may need to be loaded on ◊disk. This loading is called 'booting' or 'bootstrapping' the system.

software project lifecycle in computing, the various stages of development in the writing of a major program (◊software), from the identification of a requirement to the installation and support of the finished program. The most common pattern for the project lifecycle is the 'waterfall' model. The process includes systems analysis and systems design.

softwood a coniferous tree, or the wood from it. In general this type of wood is softer and easier to work, but in some cases less durable, than wood from ◊deciduous trees.

soil loose covering of broken rocky material and decaying organic matter overlying the rocks of the Earth's surface. Various types of soil develop under different conditions: deep soils form in hot wet climates and in valleys, and shallow soils form in cool dry areas and on slopes. Pedology, the study of soil, is significant because of the relative importance of different soil types to agriculture.

soil creep gradual movement of soil down a slope. As each soil particle is dislodged by a raindrop it moves slightly further downhill. This results eventually in a mass downward movement of soil on the slope.

soil erosion the wearing away of the Earth's soil layer. It is caused by the action of water, wind, and ice, and also by exploitative methods in ◊agriculture. If unchecked, soil erosion results in the formation of ◊deserts.

soil mechanics a branch of engineering that studies the nature and properties of the soil. Soil is investigated during construction work to ensure that it has the mechanical properties necessary to support the foundations of dams, bridges, and roads.

solan goose another name for the ◊gannet.

solar energy energy derived from the Sun's radiation. Solar heaters have industrial or domestic uses. They usually consist of a black (heat-absorbing) panel containing pipes through which air or water, heated by the Sun, is circulated, either by thermal ◊convection or by a pump. Solar energy may also be harnessed indirectly using solar cells made of panels of ◊semiconductor material (usually silicon) which generate electricity when illuminated by sunlight. Although it is difficult to generate a high output from solar energy compared to sources such as nuclear or fossil fuel energy, it is an important non-polluting and renewable energy source used as far north as Scandanavia as well as in Mediterranean countries.

solar pond natural or artificial 'pond', for example the Dead Sea, in which salt becomes more soluble in the Sun's heat. Water at the bottom becomes saltier and hotter, and is insulated by the less salty water layer at the top. Temperatures at the bottom reach about 100°C/200°F and can be used to generate electricity.

Solar System the Sun and all the bodies orbiting around it: the nine planets (Mercury, Venus, Earth, Mars, Jupiter, Saturn, Uranus, Neptune,

Solar System

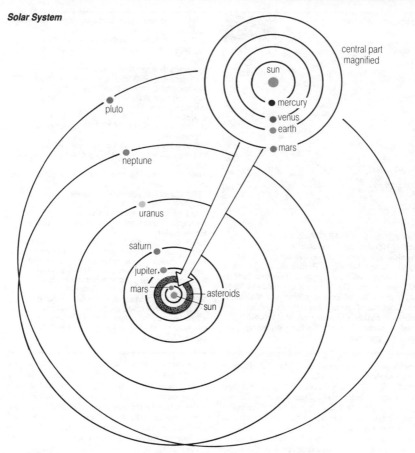

and Pluto), their moons, asteroids, and comets. It is thought to have formed from a cloud of gas and dust in space about 4,600,000,000 years ago. The Sun contains 99% of the mass of the solar system. The edge of the Solar System is not clearly defined, marked only by the limit of the Sun's gravitational influence, which extends about 1.5 light years, almost halfway to the nearest star.

solar wind a stream of atomic particles, mostly protons and electrons, from the Sun's corona, flowing outwards at speeds of 300–1,000 km per second.

solder alloy used for joining metals such as copper, its common alloys (brass and bronze) and tin-plated steel as used for making food cans. Soft solders (usually alloys of tin and lead, sometimes with added antimony) melt at low temperatures (about 200°C), and are widely used in the electrical industry for joining copper wires. Hard solders, such as silver solder (an alloy of copper, silver and zinc), melt at much higher temperatures, and form a much stronger joint. ◊Brazing is another method of joining metals.

sole flatfish found in temperate and tropical waters.

solenodon rare insectivorous shrew-like mammal, genus *Solenodon*. There are two species, one each on Cuba and Hispaniola, and they are threatened with extinction due to introduced predators. They are about 30 cm/1 ft long with a 25 cm/10 in

tail, slow-moving, and they produce venomous saliva.

sole trader or *sole proprietor* one person who runs a business, receiving all profits and responsible for all liabilities. Many small businesses are sole traders.

sol-fa short for tonic sol-fa, a method of teaching music, usually singing, systematized by John Curwen (1816–1888).

Solferino, Battle of Napoleon III's victory over the Austrians 1859, at a village near Verona, N Italy, 8 km/5 mi S of Lake Garda.

solicitor in the UK, a member of one of the two branches of the English legal profession, the other being a ◊barrister. A solicitor is a lawyer who provides all-round legal services (making wills, winding up estates, conveyancing, divorce, and litigation). A solicitor cannot appear in court at Crown Court level, but must brief a barrister on behalf of his client. Solicitors may become circuit judges and recorders. In the USA the general term is lawyer or ◊attorney.

Solicitor General in the UK, a law officer of the Crown, deputy to the ◊Attorney General, a political appointee with ministerial rank.

solid in physics, a state of matter which holds its own shape (as opposed to a liquid, which takes up the shape of its container, or a gas, which totally fills its container). According to ◊kinetic theory, the atoms or molecules in a solid are not free to

Solomon Islands

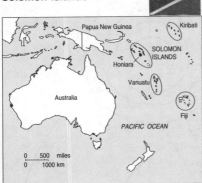

area 27,556 sq km/10,637 sq mi
capital Honiara on Guadalcanal
physical comprises all but the northernmost
islands (which belong to Papua New Guinea) of
a Melanesian archipelago that stretches nearly
1,500 km/900 mi. The largest is Guadalcanal (area
6,475 sq km/2,500 sq mi); others are Malaita,
San Cristobal, New Georgia, Santa Isabel,
Choiseul; mainly mountainous and forested
head of state Elizabeth II, represented by
governor general

head of government Solomon Mamaloni from
1989
political system constitutional monarchy
exports fish products, palm oil, copra, cocoa,
timber
currency Solomon Island dollar
population (1990 est) 314,000 (the majority
Melanesian); annual growth rate 3.9%
language English (official); local dialects
religion Christian
literacy 60% (1989)
GNP $141 million (1987); $7420 per head
chronology
1978 Achieved full independence, within the
Commonwealth, with Peter Kenilorea as prime
minister.
1981 Solomon Mamaloni replaced Kenilorea as
prime minister.
1984 Kenilorea returned to power, heading a
coalition government.
1986 Kenilorea resigned after allegations of
corruption, and was replaced by his deputy,
Ezekiel Alebua.
1988 Kenilorea back as deputy prime minister.
The Solomon Islands joined Vanuatu and
Papua New Guinea to form the Spearhead
Group, aiming to preserve Melanesian cultural
traditions and secure independence for the
French territory of New Caledonia.
1989 Solomon Mamaloni (People's Action
Party; PAP returned as prime minister
1990 Mamaloni resigned as PAP party leader,
but continued as head of government of
national unity.

move but merely vibrate about fixed positions –
such as those in crystal lattice.

Solidarity (Polish *Solidarnosc*) the national confederation of Independent Trade Unions in Poland,
formed under the leadership of Lech ◊Walesa in
Sept 1980. It emerged from a summer of industrial
disputes caused by the Polish government's
attempts to raise food prices. The strikers created a
trade union movement independent of the Communist Party, and protracted negotiations with the
government led to recognition of Solidarity in exchange for an acceptance of the leading role of the
Communist Party in Poland. Continuing unrest and
divisions in Solidarity's leadership led government
to ban the movement 1981–89. In 1989 it was
elected to head the Polish government. Divisions
soon emerged in the leadership. Solidarity had 2.8
million members in 1991.

solid-state circuit a circuit where all the components (resistors, capacitors, transistors, and
diodes) and interconnections are made at the same
time, and by the same processes, in or on one piece
of single crystal silicon. The small size of this
construction accounts for its use in electronics for
space vehicles and aircraft. See also ◊integrated
circuit and ◊silicon chip.

solipsism in philosophy, a view which maintains
that the self is the only thing that can be known to
exist. It is an extreme form of ◊scepticism. The
solipsist sees himself or herself as the only individual
in existence, assuming other people to be a reflection of his or her own consciousness.

soliton non-linear wave which does not widen and
disperse in the normal way. Such behaviour is
characteristic of the waves of ◊energy which constitute the particles of atomic physics, so that the
mathematical equations which sum up the behaviour
of solitons are being used to further research in
nuclear ◊fusion and ◊superconductivity.

Solomon *c.* 974–*c.*937 BC. In the Old Testament
or Hebrew Bible, king of Israel, son of David by
Bathsheba. He was famed for his wisdom, the much
later biblical Proverbs, Ecclesiastes, and Song of
Songs being attributed to him. He built the temple
in Jerusalem with the aid of heavy taxation and
forced labour. The so-called *King Solomon's
Mines* at Aqaba, Jordan (copper and iron), are of
later date.

Solomon Islands country in the W Pacific, E of
New Guinea, comprising many hundreds of islands,
the largest of which is Guadalcanal.

Solomon's seal perennial plant *Polygonatum
multiflorum*, family Liliaceae, found growing in
moist shady woodland areas. It has bell-like white
flowers drooping from the leaf axils of its arching
stems, followed by blue-black berries.

Solon *c.* 638–558 BC. Athenian statesman. As one
of the chief magistrates *c.* 594 BC who carried out the
revision of the constitution which laid the foundations of Athenian democracy.

solstice either of the points at which the Sun is
farthest north or south of the celestial equator each
year. The *summer solstice*, when the Sun is
farthest north, occurs around Jun 21; the *winter
solstice* around Dec 22.

Solti George 1912– . Hungarian-born British
conductor. He was music director at Covent Garden
1961–71, and of the Chicago Symphony Orchestra
from 1969. He was also principal conductor of the
London Philharmonic Orchestra 1979–83.

solubility in physics, a measure of the amount of
solute (usually a solid or gas) that will dissolve in a
given amount of solvent (usually a liquid) at a particular temperature. Solubility may be expressed as
grams of solute per 100 grams of solvent or, for a
gas, in parts per million of solvent.

Solyman I alternative form of ◊Suleiman, Ottoman sultan.

Somalia
Democratic Republic of
(*Jamhuriyadda Dimugradiga Somaliya*)

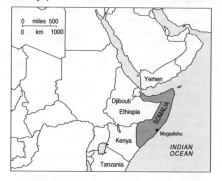

area 700,000 sq km/270,000 sq mi
capital Mogadishu
towns Hargeisa, Kismayu, port Berbera
physical mainly flat, with hills in the N
head of state and government Ali Mahdi Mohammed from 1991

political system one-party socialist republic
exports livestock, skins, hides, bananas
currency Somali shilling
population (1990 est) 8,415,000; annual growth rate 3.1%
life expectancy men 53, women 53
language Somali, Arabic (both official)
religion Sunni Muslim 99%
literacy 40% (1986)
GNP $1.5 bn (1987); $290 per head
chronology
1960 Achieved full independence.
1963 Border dispute with Kenya.
1969 Maj-Gen Mohamed Siad Barre suspended the constitution.
1978 Defeated in eight-month war with Ethiopia. Armed insurrection began in N.
1979 New constitution for a socialist one-party state adopted.
1990 Civil war intensified.
1991 Mogadishu captured by rebels; Barre fled. Secession of NE Somalia, as the Somaliland Republic. Heavy fighting in the capital.
1992 Famine relief efforts severely hampered by unstable political situation. UN peacekeeping troops sent in.
1993 Leaders of armed factions agreed to federal system of government. US-led UN forces destroyed headquarters of war lord, Gen Aideed, after the shooting of Pakistani UN troops.

Solzhenitsyn Alexander 1918– . Soviet novelist. After distinguished military service, he revolted against Stalinism and was in prison and exile 1945–57. Much of his writing is semi-autobiographical and highly critical of the system as in, for example, *One Day in the Life of Ivan Denisovich* 1962, *The Gulag Archipelago* 1973. This led to his expulsion from the USSR 1974.

Somalia country in the Horn of Africa, on the Indian Ocean.

Somaliland region of Somali-speaking peoples in E Africa including the former British Somaliland Protectorate and Italian Somaliland, which both became independent 1960 as the Somali Democratic Republic, the official name for ◊Somalia; and former French Somaliland which was established 1892, became known as the Territory of the Afars and Issas 1967, and became independent as ◊Djibouti 1977.

Somerset county in SW England
area 3,460 sq km/1,336 sq mi
towns administrative headquarters Taunton; Wells, Bridgwater, Glastonbury, Yeovil
physical rivers Avon, Parret, and Exe; marshy coastline on the Bristol Channel: Mendip Hills (including Cheddar Gorge and Wookey Hole, a series of limestone caves where Old Stone Age flint implements and bones of extinct animals have been found); the Quantock Hills; Exmoor
products engineering, dairy products, cider, Exmoor ponies
population (1991) 459,100
famous people Ernest Bevin, Henry Fielding.

Somerset Edward Seymour, 1st Duke of Somerset c. 1506–1552. English politician. Created Earl of Hertford, after Henry VIII's marriage to his sister Jane, he became Duke of Somerset and Protector (regent) for Edward VI in 1547. His attempt to check ◊enclosure offended landowners and his moderation religious upset the Protestants. He was beheaded on a fake treason charge 1549.

Somerset House government office in the Strand, London, built in 1775. It is used by the Inland Revenue, Principal Probate Registry, where wills are kept, and by the University of London. Somerset House is also the new home of the ◊Courtauld Gallery.

Somme, Battle of the Allied offensive in World War I Jul–Nov 1916 at Beaumont-Hamel Chaulnes, on the river Somme in N France, during which severe losses were suffered by both sides. It was the first battle in which tanks were used. The German offensive around St Quentin Mar–Apr 1918 is sometimes called the Second Battle of the Somme.

Somosa Anastasio 1896–1956. Nicaraguan politician and head of the army. Elected president 1937, he remained in office, except for the period 1947–50, until his assassination. He exiled most of his political opponents and amassed a considerable fortune in land and businesses. Members of his family retained control of the country until 1981 when they were overthrown by popular forces.

sonar or *echo-sounder* a method of locating underwater objects by the reflection of ultrasonic waves. The time taken for an acoustic beam to travel to the object and back to the source enables the distance to be found since the velocity of sound in water is known. The process was developed 1920.

sonata term originally used to describe a composition for instruments, as opposed to the cantata, which is a composition for voices. The sonata is usually written for one or two instruments, one of which is usually a piano, and consists of a series of related movements.

sonata form in music, the structure of a movement, typically involving division into exposition, development, and recapitulation sections. It is the framework for much of classical music, including ◊sonatas, ◊symphonies, and ◊concertos.

Sondheim Stephen (Joshua) 1930–. US composer and lyricist. He achieved success first as a witty and sophisticated lyricist of Leonard Bernstein's *West Side Story* 1957, and later as a composer of musicals, including *Company* 1970, *A Little Night Music* 1973, *Pacific Overtures* 1976, and *Sweeney Todd* 1979.

son et lumière French 'sound and light', the outdoor night-time dramatization of the history of a notable building, town, and so on, using theatrical lighting effects, sound effects, and narration; invented by Paul Robert Houdin, curator of the Château de Chambord.

song composition for one or more singers, often with instrumental accompaniment, such as madrigals, and chansons. Popular forms include folk song and ballad. The term song is usually used for secular music, whereas motet and cantata tend to be forms of sacred music.

Songhai Empire a former kingdom of NW Africa, founded in the 8th century, which developed into a powerful Muslim empire under the rule of Sonni Ali (reigned 1464–92). It superseded ◊Mali and extended its territory, occupying an area that includes present-day Senegal, Gambia, Mali, and parts of Mauretania, Niger, and Nigeria. In 1591 it was invaded and overthrown by Morocco.

sonic boom a noise like a thunderclap that occurs when an aircraft passes through the ◊sound barrier, or begins to travel faster than the speed of sound. It is caused by shock waves set up by the aircraft.

sonnet fourteen-line poem of Italian origin introduced to England by Thomas ◊Wyatt in the form used by Petrarch (rhyming abba abba cdcdcd or cdecde), as followed by Milton and Wordsworth; Shakespeare used the form abab cdcd efef gg.

Sons of Liberty in American colonial history, the name adopted by those colonists opposing the ◊Stamp Act of 1765. Merchants, lawyers, farmers, artisans and labourers joined what was an early instance of concerted resistance to British rule, causing the repeal of the Act in Mar 1766.

Soong Ching-ling 1892–1981. Chinese politician, wife of the Guomindang founder ◊Sun Yat-sen; she remained a prominent figure in Chinese politics after his death, being vice chair of the republic from 1959, but came under attack 1967 during the Cultural Revolution. After the death of Zhu De (1886–1976), she served as acting head of state.

Sophia Electress of Hanover 1630–1714. Twelfth child of Frederick V, elector palatine of the Rhine and king of Bohemia, and Elizabeth, daughter of James I of England. She married the Elector of Hanover 1658. Widowed in 1698, she was recognized in the succession to the throne 1701, and when Queen Anne died without issue in 1714, her son George I founded the Hanoverian dynasty.

sophist one of a group of 5th century BC lecturers on culture, rhetoric, and politics. Sceptical about the possibility of achieving genuine knowledge, they were noted for their bogus reasoning and concern with winning arguments rather than establishing the truth. ◊Plato regarded them as dishonest and 'sophistry' came to mean fallacious reasoning.

Sophocles 495–406 BC. Greek dramatist, the second of the three great tragedians who included Aeschylus and Euripides. He modified the form of tragedy by introducing a third actor and greatly developed stage scenery. He wrote some 120 plays, of which seven tragedies survive. These are *Antigone* 441, *Oedipus Tyrannus*, *Electra*, *Ajax*, *Trachiniae*, *Philoctetes* 409, and *Oedipus at Colonus* 401.

soprano in music, the highest range of female voice.

Sopwith Thomas Octave Murdoch 1888–1989. British designer of the Sopwith Camel biplane used in World War I, and joint developer of the Hurricane in World War II.

sorbic acid a tasteless acid found in the fruit of the rowan or mountain ash, widely used in the preservation of food, for example cider, wine, soft drinks, animal feedstuffs, bread, and cheese.

Sorbonne alternative name for the University of Paris, originally a theological institute founded 1253 by Robert de Sorbon.

Sorel Georges 1847–1922. French philosopher, who believed that socialism could only come about through a general strike; his theory of the need for a 'myth' to sway the body of the people was used by fascists.

sorghum cereal grass, also called great millet or guinea-corn, native to Africa but cultivated widely in India, China, USA, and S Europe. The seeds are used for making bread.

sorority a club or society for university women in the USA; the men's equivalent is a fraternity.

sorrel species of plants in the genus *Rumex*, family Polygonaceaec. *Rumex acetosa* is grown for its bitter salad leaves.

sorus in ferns, a group of sporangia, the reproductive structures that produce ◊spores. They occur on the lower surface of fern fronds.

SOS internationally recognized distress signal; forming part of the ◊Morse code.

soul according to many religions, an intangible part of a human being which survives the death of the physical body.

soul music style of ◊rhythm and blues, influenced by gospel music, and sung by, among others, Sam Cooke (1931–1964), Aretha Franklin (1942–), and Al Green (1946–).

Soult Nicolas Jean de Dieu 1769–1851. Marshal of France. He held commands in Spain in the Peninsular War, when he sacked the port of Santander 1808, and was chief of staff at the Battle of ◊Waterloo. He was war minister 1830–40.

sound physiological sensation received by the ear, originating in a vibration (pressure variation in the air), which communicates itself to the air, and travels in every direction, spreading out as an expanding sphere. All sound waves in air travel with a speed dependent on the temperature; under ordinary conditions, this is about 330 m/1,070 ft per second. The pitch of the sound depends on the number of vibrations imposed on the air per second, but the speed is unaffected. The loudness of a sound is dependent primarily on the amplitude of the vibration of the air.

sound barrier the concept that the speed of sound, or sonic speed, (about 1,220 kph/760 mph at sea level) constitutes a speed limit to flight through the atmosphere, since a badly designed aircraft suffers severe buffeting at near sonic speed due to the formation of shock waves. (Chuck) Yeager first flew through the 'barrier' in 1947 in a Bell X-1 rocket plane. Now, by careful design, aircraft such as Concorde can fly at supersonic speed with ease, though they create in their wake a ◊sonic boom.

sound synthesis the generation of sound (usually music) by electronic means. The use of electrical ◊oscillators to drive loudspeakers can be coupled with the information processing power of a computer to generate all kinds of sounds from pure tones to human speech. Synthesized music emerged as a popular medium for musicians of all kinds in the 1970s.

sound track a band at one side of a cine film on which the accompanying sound is recorded. Usually it takes the form of an optical track, a pattern of light and shade. The pattern is produced on the film when signals from the recording microphone are made to

South Africa: territorial divisions

Provinces and Capitals	Area sq km
Cape of Good Hope *Cape Town*	721,000
Natal *Pietermaritzburg*	86,965
Transvaal *Pretoria*	286,064
Orange Free State *Bloemfontein*	129,152
	1,223,181

vary the intensity of a light beam. During playback, a light is shone through the track onto a photocell which converts the pattern of light falling on it into appropriate electrical signals. These signals are then fed to loudspeakers to recreate the original sounds.

Souphanouvong Prince 1912– .Laotian politician. After an abortive revolt against French rule in 1945, he led the guerrilla Pathel Lao, and in 1975 became first president of the Republic of Laos.

South Africa
Republic of
(*Republiek van Suid-Afrika*)

area 1,223,181 sq km/472,148 sq mi
capital Cape Town (legislative), Pretoria (administrative), Bloemfontein (judicial)
towns Johannesburg, ports Cape Town, Durban, Port Elizabeth, East London
physical the southern end of a large plateau, fringed by mountains and a lowland coastal area
territories Prince Edward Island in the Antarctic
head of state and government F W de Klerk from 1989
political system nationalist republic, restricted democracy
exports maize, sugar, fruit, wool, gold, platinum (world's largest producer), diamonds
currency rand
population (1990 est) 39,550,000 (73% black: Zulu, Xhosa, Sotho, and Tswana, 18% white, 3% mixed, 3% Asian): growth rate 2.5% pa
life expectancy whites 71, Asians 67, blacks 58
language Afrikaans and English (both official); various Bantu languages
religion Dutch Reformed Church 40%, Anglican 11%, Roman Catholic 8%, other Christian 25%, Hindu, Muslim

South Africa country on the S tip of Africa, bounded to the N by Namibia, Botswana, and Zimbabwe, and to the NE by Swaziland and Mozambique.
South African Wars two wars between the Boers (settlers of Dutch origin) and the British; essentially fought for the gold and diamonds of the Transvaal.
War of 1881 was triggered by the attempt of the Boers of the ◊Transvaal to reassert the independence surrendered 1877 in return for British aid against African peoples. The British were defeated at Majuba, and the Transvaal again became independent.
War of 1899–1902, also known as the *Boer War*, was preceded by the armed ◊Jameson Raid into the Boer Transvaal, a failed attempt, inspired by the Cape Colony prime minister Rhodes, to precipitate a revolt against Kruger, the Transvaal president. The *uitlanders* (non-Boer immigrants)

literacy whites 99%, Asians 69%, blacks 50% (1989)
GNP $81 bn (1987); $ 1,890 per head
chronology
1910 Union of South Africa formed from two British colonies and two Boer republics.
1912 African National Congress (ANC) formed.
1948 Apartheid system of racial discrimination initiated by prime minister Daniel Malan.
1955 Freedom Charter adopted by ANC.
1958 Malan succeeded by Hendrik Verwoerd.
1960 ANC banned
1961 South Africa withdrew from the Commonwealth and became a republic.
1962 ANC leader Nelson Mandela jailed.
1964 Mandela and other ANC leaders sentenced to life imprisonment.
1966 Verwoerd assassinated and succeeded by B J Vorster.
1976 Soweto uprising.
1977 Death in custody of Pan African Congress activist Steve Biko.
1978 Vorster replaced by Pieter W Botha.
1984 New constitution adopted, giving segregated representation to coloureds and Asian and making Botha president; nonaggression pact with Mozambique signed but not observed.
1985 Growth of violence in black townships.
1986 Commonwealth agreed on limited sanctions; US Congress voted to impose sanctions; some major multinational companies announced closure of South African operations.
1987 Government formally acknowledged presence of its military forces in Angola.
1988 Peace agreement with Angola and Cuba, recognising independence for Namibia.
1989 Botha gave up NP leadership and state presidency. Democratic Party (DP) launched; F W de Klerk became president. Some ANC activists released.
1990 ANC ban lifted; Nelson Mandela released from prison. Membership opened to all races.
1991 Mandela elected ANC president. De Klerk announced repeal of remaining apartheid laws. South Africa readmitted to international sport.
1992 New constitution leading to all-races majority rule approved by whites-only referendum. Massacre of civilians at the black township of Boipathong by Inkatha (the Zulu movement rivalling the ANC), aided by the police, threatened constitutional talks.
1993 De Klerk and Mandela agreed to formation of government of national unity after free elections. ANC leading member Chris Hani assassinated.

were still not given the vote by the Boers, negotiations failed, and the Boers invaded British territory, besieging Ladysmith, Mafeking (now Mafikeng), and Kimberley.

South America fourth largest of the continents, nearly twice as large as Europe
area 17,854,000 sq km/6,891,644 sq mi
largest cities (over 3.5 million inhabitants) Buenos Aires, São Paulo, Rio de Janeiro, Bogotá, Santiago, Lima, Caracas
exports coffee, cocoa, sugar, bananas, oranges, wine, meat and fish products, cotton, wool, handicrafts, minerals including oil, silver, iron ore, copper
population (1985) 263,300,000, originally ◊American Indians, who survive chiefly in Bolivia, Peru, and Ecuador, and are increasing in number; in addition there are many mestizo (people of mixed Spanish or Portuguese and Indian ancestry) elsewhere; many people originally from Europe, largely Spanish, Italian and Portuguese; and many of African descent, originally imported as slaves;
language many American Indian languages; Spanish; Portuguese is the main language in Brazil
religion Roman Catholic; American Indian beliefs.

Southampton port in Hampshire, England; population (1981) 204,604. Industries include engineering, chemicals, plastics, flourmilling, and tobacco; it is also a passenger and container port.

Southampton Henry Wriothesley, 3rd Earl of Southampton 1573–1624. English courtier, patron of Shakespeare who dedicated *Venus and Adonis* and *The Rape of Lucrece* to him, and may have addressed him in the sonnets.

South Asia Regional Cooperation Committee (SARC) organization established 1983 by India, Pakistan, Bangladesh, Nepál, Sri Lanka, Bhutan and the Maldives to cover agriculture, telecommunications, health, population, sport, art, and culture.

South Australia state of the Commonwealth of Australia
area 984,377 sq km/379,970 sq mi
capital and chief port Adelaide
towns Whyalla, Mount Gambier
products meat and wool (80% of area cattle and sheep grazing), wines and spirits, dried and canned fruit, iron (Middleback Range), coal (Leigh Creek), copper, uranium (Roxby Downs), oil and natural gas in the NE, lead, zinc, iron, opals, household and electrical goods, vehicles
population 1,346,000, including 13,300 Aborigines
history possibly known to the Dutch in the 16th century; surveyed by ◊Tasman 1644; first European settlement 1834; province 1836; state 1901.

South Carolina state of the SE USA; nicknamed Palmetto State.
area 80,604 sq km/31,113 sq mi
capital Columbia
towns Charleston, Greenville
physical large areas of woodland; subtropical climate in coastal areas
products tobacco, cotton, fruit, soybeans; meat products; textiles, clothing, paper and woodpulp, furniture, bricks, chemicals, machinery
population (1986) 3,376,000
history first Spanish settlers 1526; Charles I gave the area (known as Carolina) to Robert Heath (1575–1649), attorney general 1629; Declaration of Independence, one of the original Thirteen states

1776; joined the Confederacy 1860; re-admitted to Union 1868.

South Dakota state of the USA; nicknamed Coyote or Sunshine State.
area 199,782 sq km/77,116 sq mi
capital Pierre
towns Sioux Falls
physical Great Plains; Black Hills (which include granite Mount Rushmore, on whose face giant relief portrait heads of former presidents Washington, Jefferson, Lincoln and T Roosevelt are carved); Badlands
products cereals, livestock, gold (greatest USA producer)
population (1986) 708,000
famous people Crazy Horse, Sitting Bull, Ernest O Lawrence
history claimed by French 18th century; first white settlements 1794; state 1889.

South-East Asia Treaty Organization (SEATO) collective defence system analogous to NATO established 1954. Participating countries are Australia, France, New Zealand, Pakistan, the Philippines, Thailand, UK, and USA, with Vietnam, Cambodia, and Laos as protocol states. It originated in ◊ANZUS. After the Vietnam War SEATO was phased out by 1977, and its nonmilitary aspects assumed by the ◊Association of South-East Asian Nations (ASEAN).

Southern Christian Leadership Conference (SCLC) US civil rights organization founded 1957 by Martin Luther ◊King and led by him until his assassination 1968. It advocated nonviolence and passive resistance, and sponsored the 1963 march on Washington DC that focused national attention on the civil-rights movement.

Southern Cross popular name for the constellation ◊Crux.

Southey Robert 1774–1843. British poet and author, friend of Coleridge and Wordsworth. In 1813 he became Poet Laureate, but his verse is little read today. He is better known for his *Life of Nelson* 1813, and his letters.

South Georgia island 1,300 km/800 mi SE of the Falkland Islands, of which it is a dependency; area 3,775 sq km/1,450 sq mi. The British Antarctic Survey has a station here.

South Glamorgan county of S Wales
area 416 sq km/161 sq mi
towns administrative headquarters Cardiff; Barry, Penarth
products dairy farming, with industry (steel, plastics, engineering) in the Cardiff area
population (1986) 396,000
language 6% Welsh; English.

South Korea see ◊Korea, South.

South Sea Bubble a financial crisis in Britain in 1720. The South Sea Company, founded 1711, which had a monopoly of trade with South America, offered in 1719 to take over more than half the national debt in return for further concessions. Its £100 shares rapidly rose to £1,000, and an orgy of speculation followed. When the 'bubble' burst, thousands were ruined. The discovery that cabinet ministers had been guilty of corruption led to a political crisis. Horace Walpole became prime minister, protected the royal family and members of the government from scandal, and restored financial confidence.

South West Africa former name (until 1968) of ◊Namibia.

Soutine Chaim 1894–1943. Lithuanian-born French Expressionist artist. He painted landscapes and

UNITED STATES
OF AMERICA

Tropic of Cancer

BAHAMAS

MEXICO

CUBA

Greater

HAITI   DOMINICAN REP.

JAMAICA

Antilles

GUATEMALA

HONDURAS
San Salvador
EL
SALVADOR NICARAGUA
Managua

Caribbean Sea

COSTA San José
RICA
PANAMA

Gulf of Panama

Lesser Antilles

Maracaibo
L. Maracaibo
Gulf of Sta Marta
Darien 19028ft/5800m
Panama

TRINIDAD AND TOBAGO
Port of Spain

Caracas

Llanos

Orinoco

Georgetown

VENEZUELA

Paramaribo
FRENCH
GUIANA
SURINAME

GUYANA

Guiana Highlands

Bogota

COLOMBIA

Serra de
Tumucumaque

Quito

ECUADOR

Negro

Equator

Guayaquil

Putumayo

Manaus   *Amazon*

Marajo I.   Belém

Madeira

Tapajos

Xingú

Araguaia

Parnaiba

Plateau of
Borborema

▲Huascaran
22204ft/6768m

PERU

Andes

B R A Z I L

Recife

Lima

Paraguay

Plateau of
Mato Grosso

Brazilian Highlands

Salvador

L. Titicaca   La Paz

BOLIVIA

Chaco

Gran

Serra da Mantiqueira

Tropic of Capricorn

PARAGUAY

Asunción

Parana

Serra do Mar

Rio de Janeiro

São Paulo

PACIFIC

OCEAN

Atacama Desert

Sierra de Cordoba

Salado

Entre Rios

Pampas

URUGUAY

Lagoa dos
Patos

Juan Fernández Is.

Santiago

Aconcagua
22834ft/9960m

Sierra de Cordoba

C
H
I
L
E

A
R
G
E
N
T
I
N
A

Buenos Aires

Montevideo

Rio de la Plata

SOUTH

Colorado

Negro   Bahia Blanca

ATLANTIC

Chiloé I.

Patagonia

Gulf of San
Matias

OCEAN

Chonos
Archipelago

G. of San
Jorge

Gulf of Peñas S. Valentin
13313ft/4058m

West Falkland
Magellan's Strait East Falkland

Falkland Islands

Scotia Sea

Tierra del Fuego

Cape Horn

Drake Passage

South Georgia

South Orkney Is.

South Sandwich Islands

Graham
Land

Antarctic Circle

Weddell Sea

Antarctic
Peninsula

South America

0   500   1000 miles
0   500   1000   1500 km

© Century Hutchinson Limited

Soutine The Road up the Hill *(c. 1924) Tate Gallery, London.*

Soyuz Soyuz 37 crew before launch, 23 Jul 1980. (Left) Soviet cosmonaut Vikto Gorbatko, (right) Pham Tuan, the first Vietnamese in space.

portraits, including many of painters active in Paris in the 1920s and 1930s. He had a distorted style, using thick application of paint (impasto) and brilliant colours.

sovereign British gold coin, introduced by Henry VII, which became the standard monetary unit in 1817. Minting ceased for currency purposes in the UK in 1914, but the sovereign continued to be used as 'unofficial' currency in the Middle East. It was minted for the last time in 1987 and has now been replaced by the *Britannia*.

sovereignty absolute authority within a given territory. The possession of sovereignty is taken to be the distinguishing feature of the state, as against other forms of community. The term has an internal aspect, in that it refers to the ultimate source of authority within a state such as a parliament or monarch, and an external aspect, where it denotes the independence of the state from any outside authority.

soviet (Russian 'council') originally a strike committee elected by Russian workers in the 1905 revolution; in 1917 these were set up by peasants, soldiers, and factory workers. The soviets sent delegates to the All-Russian Congress of Soviets to represent their opinions to a future government. They were later taken over by the ◊Bolsheviks.

Soviet Central Asia former name (until 1991) of the ◊Central Asian Republics.

Soviet Union alternative name for the former ◊Union of Soviet Socialist Republics (USSR).

sovkhoz state-owned farm in the USSR where the workers were state employees (such farms are still widespread in ex-Soviet republics). The sovkhoz can be contrasted with the *kolkhoz* where the farm is run by a ◊collective.

Soweto (*So*uth *We*st *To*wnship) racially segregated urban settlement in South Africa, SW of Johannesburg; population (1983) 915,872. It has experienced civil unrest over the years due to the apartheid regime.

soya bean leguminous plant *Glycine max*, native to E Asia, in particular Japan and China. Originally grown as a forage crop, it is increasingly used for human consumption in cooking oils and margarine, as a flour, or processed and extruded as textured vegetable protein (TVP).

Soyinka Wole 1934– . Nigerian author, who was a political prisoner in Nigeria 1967–69. His works include the play *The Lion and the Jewel* 1963, his prison memoirs *The Man Died* 1972, and *Aké, The Years of Childhood* 1982, an autobiography. He was the first African to receive the Nobel Prize for Literature, in 1986.

Soyuz Soviet spacecraft, capable of carrying up to three cosmonauts. Soyuz spacecraft consist of three parts: a rear section containing engines; the central crew compartment; and a forward compartment that gives additional room for working and living space. They are now used for ferrying crews up to space stations; they were originally used for independent flight.

Spaak Paul-Henri 1899–1972. Belgian socialist politician. From 1936 to 1966 he held office almost continuously as foreign minister or prime minister. He was an ardent advocate of international peace.

space the void that exists above Earth's atmosphere. Above 120 km/75 mi, very little atmosphere remains, so objects can continue to move quickly without extra energy. The space between the planets is not entirely empty, but filled with the tenuous gas of the ◊solar wind as well as dust specks. The space between stars is also filled with thin gas and dust. There is even evidence of highly rarefied gas in the space between clusters of galaxies, and also between individual galaxies.

Spacelab a small space station built by the European Space Agency, carried in the cargo bay of the Space Shuttle, in which it remains throughout each flight, returning to Earth with the Shuttle. Spacelab consists of a pressurized module in which astronauts can work, and a series of *pallets*, open to the vacuum of space, on which equipment is mounted.

space probe any instrumented object sent beyond Earth, to other parts of the Solar System, and on into deep space. The first probe was the Soviet Lunik 1, which flew past the Moon 1959. Other probes include ◊Giotto, ◊Mariner, the ◊Moon probes, ◊Pioneer, ◊Viking, and ◊Voyager.

space shuttle reusable US manned spacecraft, first launched 12 Apr 1981. It takes off vertically like a conventional rocket, but glides back to land on a runway. The space shuttle orbiter, the part that goes into space, is 37.2 m/122 ft long and weighs 68 tonnes. Two to eight crew members occupy the orbiter's nose section, and missions last up to ten days. In its cargo bay the orbiter can carry up to 29 tonnes of satellites, scientific equipment, ◊Spacelab, or military payloads. In 1986 the space shuttle *Challenger* blew up on take-off, killing all seven crew members.

space station any large structure designed for human occupation in space for extended periods

space flight: chronology

1903	Russian scientist Konstantin Tsiolkovsky published the first practical paper on aeronautics.
1926	US engineer Robert Goddard launched the first liquid-fuel rocket.
1937–45	·In Germany, Wernher von Braun developed the V2 rocket.
1957	4 Oct: The first space satellite, *Sputnik 1* (USSR, Russian 'fellow-traveller'), orbited the Earth at a height of 229–898 km/142–558 mi in 96.2 min. 3 Nov: *Sputnik 2* was launched carrying a dog, 'Laika'; it died on board seven days later.
1958	31 Jan: *Explorer 1*, the first US satellite, discovered the Van Allen radiation belts.
1961	12 April: the first crewed spaceship, *Vostok 1* (USSR), with Yuri Gagarin on board, was recovered after a single orbit of 89.1 min at a height of 142–175 km/88–109 mi.
1962	20 Feb: John Glenn in *Friendship 7* (USA) became the first American to orbit the Earth. *Telstar* (USA), a communications satellite, sent the first live television transmission between the USA and Europe.
1963	16–19 June: Valentina Tereshkova in *Vostok 1* (USSR) became the first woman in space.
1967	24 April: Vladimir Komarov was the first person to be killed in space research, when his ship, *Soyuz 1* (USSR), crash-landed on the Earth.
1969	20 July: Neil Armstrong of *Apollo 11* (USA) was the first person to walk on the Moon.
1970	10 Nov: *Luna 17* (USSR) was launched; its space probe, *Lunokhod* took photographs and made soil analyses of the Moon's surface.
1971	19 April: *Salyut 1* (USSR), the first orbital space station, was established; it was later visited by the *Soyuz 11* crewed spacecraft.
1973	*Skylab 2*, the first US orbital space station, was established.
1975	15–24 July: *Apollo 18* (USA) and *Soyuz 19* (USSR) made a joint flight and linked up in space.
1979	The European Space Agency's satellite launcher, *Ariane 1*, was launched.
1981	12 April: The first reusable crewed spacecraft, the space shuttle *Columbia* (USA), was launched.
1986	Space shuttle *Challenger* (USA) exploded shortly after take-off, killing all seven crew members.
1988	US shuttle programme resumed with launch of *Discovery*. Soviet shuttle *Buran* was launched from the rocket *Energiya*. Soviet cosmonauts Musa Manarov and Vladimir Titov in space station *Mir* spent a record 365 days 59 min in space.
1990	April/June: Hubble Space Telescope (USA) and X-ray and ultraviolet astronomy satellite *ROSAT* (USA/Germany/UK) were launched from Cape Canaveral. 2 Dec: *Astro-1* ultraviolet observatory and the Broad Band X-ray Telescope were launched from the space shuttle *Columbia*. Japanese television journalist Toyohiro Akiyama was launched with Viktor Afanasyev and Musa Manarov to the space station *Mir*.
1991	5 April: The Gamma Ray Observatory was launched from the space shuttle *Atlantis* to survey the sky at gamma-ray wavelengths. 18 May: Astronaut Helen Sharman, the first Briton in space, was launched with Anatoli Artsebarsky and Sergei Krikalek to *Mir* space station, returning to Earth 26 May in *Soyuz TM-11* with Viktor Afanasyev and Musa Manarov. Manarov set a record for the longest time spent in space, 541 days, having also spent a year aboard *Mir* 1988.
1992	European satellite *Hipparcos*, launched 1989 to measure the position of 120,000 stars, failed to reach geostationary orbit and went into a highly elliptical orbit, swooping to within 500 km/308 mi of the Earth every ten hours. The mission was later retrieved. 16 May: Space shuttle *Endeavor* returned to Earth after its maiden voyage. During its mission, it circled the Earth 141 times and travelled 4 million km/2.5 million mi. 23 Oct: *LAGEOS II* (Laser Geodynamics Satellite) was released from the space shuttle *Columbia* into an orbit so stable that it will still be circling the Earth in billions of years.

of time. Space stations are used for carrying out astronomical observations and surveys of Earth, as well as for biological studies and the processing of materials in weightlessness. The first space station was ◊Salyut 1, and the US has launched ◊Skylab. The USA plans to build a larger space station in orbit during the 1990s, in cooperation with other countries.

spadix a type of inflorescence consisting of a long fleshy axis bearing many small, stalkless flowers. It is partially enclosed by a large bract or ◊spathe. A spadix is characteristic of plants belonging to the family Araceae, including arum lilies *Zantedeschia aethiopica*.

Spain country in SW Europe, on the Iberian Peninsula between the Atlantic and the Mediterranean, bounded to the N by France and to the W by Portugal.

Spandau suburb of Berlin, Germany. The chief war criminals condemned at the Nuremberg Trials in 1946 were imprisoned in the fortress here. The last of them was the Nazi leader Rudolf Hess.

spaniel type of dog, characterized by large, drooping ears and a long, silky coat. The

Space Shuttle *Launch of the space shuttle Discovery, mission STS-26, from the Kennedy Space Center, Florida, Sept 29 1988.*

Spain: former colonies

Current name	Colonized	Independent
Paraguay	1537	1811
Argentina	16th cent.	1816
Chile	1541	1818
Costa Rica	1563	1821
Mexico	16th cent.	1821
Peru	1541	1824
Bolivia	16th cent.	1825
Ecuador	16th cent.	1830
Venezuela	16th cent.	1830
Honduras	1523	1838
El Salvador	16th cent.	1839
Guatemala	16th cent.	1839
Dominican Republic	16th cent.	1844
Cuba	1512	1898
Colombia	16th cent.	1903
Panama	16th cent.	1903
Philippines	1565	1946

cocker spaniel (English and American) weighs 12 kg/25 lb, and is 40 cm/15 in tall.

Spanish–American War war 1898 by Cuban revolutionaries (with US backing) against Spanish rule. The Treaty of Paris ceded Cuba, the Phillippines, Guam, and Puerto Rico to the USA.

Spanish Armada the fleet sent by Philip II of Spain against England in 1588. Consisting of 130 ships, it sailed from Lisbon, and carried on a running fight up the Channel with the English fleet of 197 small ships under Howard of Effingham and Francis ◊Drake. The Armada anchored off Calais, but was forced to put to sea by fireships, and a general action followed off Gravelines. What remained of the Armada escaped round the N of Scotland and W of Ireland, suffering many losses by storm and shipwreck on the way. Only about half the original fleet returned to Spain.

Spanish Civil War 1936–39. See ◊Civil War, Spanish.

Spanish Guinea former name of the Republic of ◊Equatorial Guinea.

Spanish language a member of the Romance branch of the Indo-European language family, traditionally known as Castilian and originally spoken only in NE Spain. As the language of the court it has been the standard and literary language of the Spanish state since the 13th century. It

Spain
(*España*)

area 504,879 sq km/194,883 sq mi
capital Madrid
towns Bilbao, Valencia, Saragossa, Murcia; ports Barcelona, Seville, Málaga
physical a central plateau with mountain ranges; lowlands in the S
head of state Juan Carlos I from 1975
head of government Felipe González Marquez from 1982
political system constitutional monarchy
exports fruit, vegetables, wine, olive oil, tinned fruit and fish, iron ore, cork.
currency peseta
population (1990 est) 39,623,000 annual growth rate 0.2%
life expectancy men 74, women 80
language Spanish (Castilian, official), Basque, Catalan, Galician, Valencian, and Majorcan
religion Roman Catholic 99%
literacy 97% (1989)
GNP $288 bn (1987); $4,490 per head
chronology
1936–39 Civil war. Gen Francisco Franco became head of state and government. The fascistic Falange party became the only legal political organization.
1947 Gen Franco announced a return to the monarchy after his death.
1975 Franco died and was succeeded by King Juan Carlos I as head of state.
1978 New constitution adopted with Adolfo Suárez, leader of the Democratic Centre Party, as prime minister.
1981 Suárez succeeded by Calvo-Sotelo.
1982 Socialist Workers' Party (PSOE), led by Felipe González, won a sweeping electoral victory.
1986 Referendum confirmed NATO membership. Spain joined the European Community.
1989 PSOE lost seats to hold only parity after general election. Talks between government and the Basque terrorist movement ETA collapsed and their truce ended.
1992 Summer Olympics held in Barcelona. ETA 'armed struggle' resumed. Maastricht Treaty ratified by parliament.

Spain 1270-1492

is now a world language, spoken in all South and Central American countries, except Brazil, Guyana, Suriname and French Guiana, as well as in the Philippines.

Spanish Main term often used to describe the Caribbean in the 16th–17th centuries, but more properly the South American mainland between the river Orinoco and Panama.

Spanish Sahara former name for ◊Western Sahara.

Spanish Succession, War of the a war 1701–14 between Britain, Austria, the Netherlands, Portugal, and Denmark (the Allies) and France, Spain, and Bavaria. It was caused by Louis XIV's acceptance of the Spanish throne on behalf of his grandson, Philip V of Spain, in defiance of the Partition Treaty of 1700, under which it would have passed to Archduke Charles of Austria (later Holy Roman emperor Charles VI). Peace was made by the Treaties of Utrecht 1713 and Rastatt 1714 and Philip V was recognized as king of Spain, thus founding the Spanish branch of the Bourbon dynasty.

Spain: territorial divisions

	Area in sq km
Andalusia	87,268
Aragón	47,669
Asturias	10,565
Basque	17,682
Castilla la Nueva	72,363
Castilla la Vieja	49,976
Catalonia	31,930
Extremadura	41,602
Galicia	29,434
Murcia	26,175
Léon	54,594
Valencia	23,305
Balearic Islands	5,014
Canary Islands	7,273
	504,750

Britain received Gibraltar, Minorca, and Nova Scotia; and Austria received Belgium, Milan, and Naples.

spark chamber electronic device for recording tracks of atomic ◊particles. In combination with a stack of photographic plates, a spark chamber enables the point where an interaction has taken place to be located, within a cubic centimetre. At its simplest, it consists of two smooth thread-like ◊electrodes which are positioned 1–2 cm apart, the space between being filled by gas.

spark plug a plug that produces an electric spark in the cylinder of a petrol engine to ignite the fuel mixture. It consists essentially of two electrodes insulated from one another. High-voltage (18,000 V) electricity is fed to a central electrode via the distributor. At the base of the electrode, inside the cylinder, the electricity jumps to another electrode earthed to the engine body, and creates a spark. See also ◊ignition coil.

sparrow term for many small thick-beaked birds. They are generally brown and grey, up to 18 cm/7 in long, and are found worldwide.

sparrow-hawk woodland bird of prey *Accipiter nisus* found in Eurasia and N Africa. It has a long tail and short wings. The male grows to 28 cm/1.1 ft long, and the female 38 cm/1.5 ft. It hunts small birds.

Sparta ancient Greek city state in the S Peloponnese (near modern Sparte), developed from Dorian settlements in the 10th century BC. The Spartans, noted for their military discipline and austerity, took part in the Persian and Peloponnesian wars.

Spartacist member of a group of left-wing radicals in Germany at the end of World War I, founders of the *Spartacus League*, which became the German Communist party in 1919. The league participated in the Berlin workers' revolt of Jan 1919 which was suppressed by the Freikorps on the orders of the socialist government. The agitation ended with the murder of Spartacist leaders Karl ◊Liebknecht and Rosa ◊Luxemburg.

Spartacus died 71 BC. Thracian gladiator who in 73 BC led a popular revolt of gladiators and slaves at ◊Crassus.

spastic a person with ◊cerebral palsy. The term is also applied generally to limbs with impaired movement, stiffness, and resistance to passive movement.

spathe in flowers, the single large bract surrounding the type of inflorescence known as a ◊spadix. It is sometimes brightly coloured and petal-like, as in the brilliant scarlet spathe of the flamingo plant (*Anthurium andreanum*) from South America; this serves to attract insects.

speakeasy a bar that illegally sold alcohol during the ◊Prohibition period in the USA. The term is probably derived from the need to speak quickly or quietly to the doorkeeper in order to gain admission.

Speaker the presiding officer charged with the preservation of order in the legislatures of various countries. In the UK the Speaker in the House of Lords is the Lord Chancellor; in the House of Commons the Speaker is elected for each parliament, usually on an agreed basis among the parties, but often holds the office for many years. The original appointment dates from 1377.

special relationship the belief that ties of common language, culture and shared aims of the defence of democratic principles should sustain a political relationship between the USA and the UK, and that the same would not apply to relationships between the USA and other European states.

Special Air Service (SAS) specialist British regiment recruited mainly from Parachute Regiment volunteers. It has served in Malaysia, Oman, Northern Ireland, and against international terrorists, as in the siege of the Iranian embassy in London 1980.

Special Branch section of the British police established 1883 to deal with Irish 'Fenian' terrorists. All 42 police forces in Britain now have their own Special Branches. They act as the executive arm of MI5 (British intelligence) in its duty of preventing or investigating espionage, subversion and sabotage; carry out duties at air and sea ports in respect of naturalization and immigration, and provide armed bodyguards for public figures.

special drawing right (SDR) the right of a member state of the ◊International Monetary Fund to apply for money to finance its balance of payments deficit. Originally, the SDR was linked to gold and the US dollar. After 1974 SDRs were defined in terms of a 'basket' of the 16 currencies of countries doing 1% or more of the world's trade. In 1981 the SDR was simplified to a weighted average of US dollars, French francs, German marks, Japanese yen and UK sterling.

special education education, often in separate 'special schools', for children with specific physical or mental problems or disabilities.

speciation the emergence of a new species during evolutionary history. One cause of speciation is the geographical separation of populations of the parent species, followed by their reproductive isolation, so that they no longer produce viable offspring unless they interbreed. Other, less common causes are ◊assortative mating and the establishment of a ◊polyploid population.

species in biology, a distinguishable group of organisms, which resemble each other or consist of a few distinctive types (as in ◊polymorphism), and which can all interbreed (actually or potentially) to produce fertile offspring. Species are the lowest level in the system of biological classification. Examples include lions, Douglas firs, cabbage white butterflies, humans, and sperm whales.

specific gravity alternative term for ◊relative density.

specific heat capacity in physics, quantity of heat required to raise unit mass (1 kg) of a substance by one degree ◊kelvin (1°C). The unit of specific heat capacity is the ◊joule per kilogram kelvin (J kgh^{-1} Kh^{-1}).

spectacles a pair of lenses fitted in a frame and worn in front of the eyes to correct or assist defective vision. Common defects of the eye corrected by spectacle lenses are short sight (myopia) by using concave (spherical) lenses, long sight (hypermetropia) by using convex (spherical) lenses, and astigmatism by using cylindrical lenses. Spherical and cylindrical lenses may be combined in one lens. For convenience bi-focal spectacles provide for correction both at a distance and for reading by combining two lenses of different curvatures in one piece of glass.

Spector Phil 1940– . US record producer, known for the *Wall of Sound*, created using a large orchestra, distinguishing his work in the early 1960s with vocal groups such as the Crystals and the Ronettes. He withdrew into semi-retirement in 1966.

spectroscopy in physics, the study of spectra associated with ◊atoms or ◊molecules in solid, liquid, or gaseous phase. Spectroscopy can be used to identify unknown compounds and is an invaluable tool to scientists, industry (especially pharmaceuticals for purity checks), and medical workers.

spectrum in physics, an arrangement of frequencies or wavelengths when electromagnetic radiations are separated into their constituent parts. Visible light is part of the electromagnetic spectrum and most sources emit waves of a range of wavelengths which can be broken up or 'dispersed'; white light can be separated into red, orange, yellow, green, blue, indigo, and violet.

Spee Maximilian, Count von Spee 1861–1914. German admiral, born in Copenhagen. He went down with his flagship in the 1914 battle of the Falkland Islands, and the *Graf Spee* battleship was named after him.

speech recognition a computer-based technology for analysing and recognizing speech. Speech 'recognizers' must be 'trained' for particular users, as speaker-independent speech recognition is not yet possible.

speech synthesis a computer-based technology for the generation of speech sounds. A speech synthesizer is controlled by a computer which supplies strings of codes representing basic speech sounds (phonemes) and these together make up words. Speech-synthesis applications include children's toys and car and aircraft warning systems.

speed common name for ◊amphetamine, a stimulant drug.

speedometer instrument attached to the gear-box of a vehicle by a flexible drive, which indicates the speed of the vehicle in miles or kilometres per hour on a dial easily visible to the driver.

speedway the sport of motorcycle racing on a dirt track. Four riders compete in each heat over four laps. A series of heats make up a match or competition. In Britain there are two Leagues, the British League and the National League. World championships exist for individuals, pairs, four-man teams, long-track racing, and ice speedway.

Spencer Christ Carrying the Cross (1920) Tate Gallery, London.

speedwell flowering plant, genus *Veronica*, of the figwort family. Of the many wild species, most are low-growing with small bluish flowers. The creeping *Common speedwell Veronica officinalis* grows in dry grassy places, heathland and open woods throughout Europe, with oval leaves and spikes of lilac flowers.

Speenhamland system method of poor relief in England started by Berkshire magistrates in 1795, whereby wages were supplemented from the poor-rates. However, it encouraged the payment of low wages and was superseded by the 1834 ◊Poor Law.

speleology scientific study of caves, their origin, development, physical structure, flora, fauna, folklore, exploration, surveying, photography, cave-diving, and rescue work. Potholing, which involves following the course of underground rivers or streams, has become a popular sport.

Spence Basil 1907–1976. British architect. He was professor of architecture at the Royal Academy, London, 1961–68, and his works include Coventry Cathedral, Sussex University, and the British embassy in Rome.

Spencer Stanley 1891–1959. British painter. He was born and lived in Cookham-on-Thames, Berkshire, and recreated the Christian story in a Cookham setting. His detailed, dreamlike compositions had little regard for perspective and used generalized human figures.

Spencer-Churchill family name of Dukes of Marlborough; seated at Blenheim Palace, Oxon.

Spender Stephen (Harold) 1909– . English poet and critic. His earlier poetry has a left-wing political content, as in *Twenty Poems* 1930, *Vienna* 1934, *The Still Centre* 1939, and *Poems of Dedication* 1946. Other works include the verse drama *Trial of a Judge* 1938, the autobiography *World within World* 1951, and translations. His *Journals 1939–83* were published 1985.

Spenser Edmund c. 1552–1599. English poet, who has been called the 'poet's poet' because of his rich imagery and command of versification. He is known for his moral allegory *The Faerie Queene* to Elizabeth I, of which six books survive (three published in 1590 and ·three in 1596). Other books include *The Shepheard's Calendar* 1579, *Astrophel* 1586, the love sonnets *Amoretti* and the *Epithalamion* 1595.

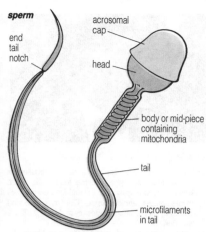

sperm in biology, the male ◊gamete of animals. Each sperm cell has a head capsule containing a nucleus, a middle portion containing ◊mitochondria (which provide energy), and a long tail (flagellum).

spermatophyte in botany, another name for a ◊seed plant.

Sperry Elmer Ambrose 1860–1930. American engineer who developed various devices using ◊gyroscopes, such as gyrostabilizers (for ships and torpedoes) and gyro-controlled autopilots. The first gyrostabilizers dated from 1912, and during World War I Sperry designed a pilotless aircraft that could carry up to 450 kg/990 lb of explosives a distance of 160 km/100 miles (the first flying bomb) under gyroscopic control. By the mid-1930s Sperry autopilots were standard equipment on most large ships.

SPF abbreviation for *South Pacific Forum*.

sphere in mathematics, a circular solid figure with all points on its surface the same distance from the centre. For a sphere of radius r, the volume $V = \frac{4}{3}\pi r^3$ and the surface area $A = 4\pi r^2$.

Sphinx a mythological creature, represented in Egyptian, Assyrian and Greek art as a lion with a human head. In Greek myth the Sphinx was female, and killed travellers who failed to answer a riddle; she killed herself when ◊Oedipus gave the right answer.

sphygmomanometer instrument for measuring blood pressure, particularly of the arteries. Consisting of an inflatable arm cuff joined by a rubber tube to a column of mercury scale, it is used, together with a stethoscope, to measure blood pressure.

Sphinx The avenue of Ram Sphinxes at the temple of Karnak in Luxor, Egypt.

Spielberg US film director Steven Spielberg.

spice any aromatic vegetable substance used as a condiment and for flavouring food. Spices are obtained from tropical plants, and include pepper, nutmeg, ginger, and cinnamon. They have little food value, but increase the appetite, and may facilitate digestion.

spider jointed-legged animal of the class Arachnida. Unlike insects, the head and breast are merged to form the cephalothorax, connected to the abdomen by a characteristic narrow waist. There are eight legs, and up to eight eyes. On the under-surface of the abdomen are spinnerets which exude a viscid fluid. This hardens on exposure to the air to form silky threads, used to spin webs in which the spider nests and catches its prey. Its fangs inject substances to subdue and digest prey, the juices of which are then sucked in by the spider.

Spielberg Steven 1947– . US director, whose highly successful films, including *Jaws* 1975, *Close Encounters of the Third Kind* 1977, *Raiders of the Lost Ark* 1981, and *ET* 1982 are renowned for their special effects.

spikelet in botany, one of the units of a grass ◊inflorescence. It comprises a slender axis on which one or more flowers are borne.

spikenard Himalayan plant *Nardostachys jatamansi*, family Valerianaceae; its underground stems give a perfume used in Eastern aromatic oils.

spina bifida a congenital defect in which part of the spinal cord and its membranes are exposed due to incomplete development of the spine.

spinach annual plant *Spinacia oleracea* of the family Chenopodiaceae. A native of Asia, it is cultivated for its leaves which are eaten as a vegetable.

spine the backbone of vertebrates. In most mammals, it contains 26 small bones called vertebrae, which enclose and protect the spinal cord (which links the peripheral nervous system to the brain). The spine connects with the skull, ribs, back muscles, and pelvis.

spinel a group of minerals possessing cubic symmetry and consisting chiefly of magnesia and alumina, for example $MgAl_2O_4$ and $FeAl_2O_4$.

spinet a keyboard instrument, similar to a harpsichord but smaller, which has only one string for each note.

spinning the art of drawing out and twisting fibres (originally wool or flax) into threads, by hand or machine. Synthetic fibres are extruded as a liquid through the holes of a spinneret.

spinning machine machine for spinning—drawing out fibres and twisting them into a long thread, or yarn. Spinning was originally done by hand, then with the spinning wheel, and in about 1767 James ◊Hargreaves in England built the spinning jenny, a machine that could spin eight, then sixteen, bobbins at once. Later came Samuel ◊Crompton's spinning mule 1779, which has a moving carriage carrying the spindles and is still used today. Also used is the

spine

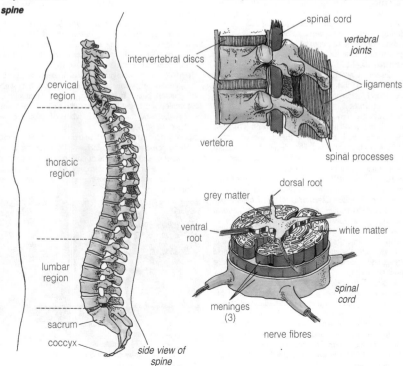

side view of spine

ring-spinning frame introduced in the USA in 1828 where sets of rollers moving at different speeds draw out finer and finer thread, which is twistd and wound onto rotating bobbins.

Spinoza Benedict or Baruch 1632–1677. Dutch philosopher who believed in a rationalistic pantheism that owed much to Descartes' mathematical appreciation of the Universe. Mind and matter are two modes of an infinite substance which he called God or Nature, good and evil being relative. He was a determinist, believing that human action was motivated by self-preservation.

spiracle in insects, the opening of a ◊trachea, through which oxygen enters the body and carbon dioxide is expelled. In cartilaginous fish, the same name is given to a circular opening that marks the remains of the first gill slit.

spiraea herbaceous plant and shrubs of the genus *Spiraea*, family Rosaceae, which includes many cultivated species with ornamental panicles of flowers.

spiral a common curve such as that traced by a flat coil of rope. Various kinds of spiral can be generated mathematically, for example, an equiangular or logarithmic spiral (in which a tangent at any point on the curve always makes the same angle with it) and an ◊involute. It also occurs in nature as a normal consequence of accelerating growth, such as the spiral shape of the shells of snails and some other molluscs.

spit ◊sandbar (sand ridge) projecting into a body of water and growing out from land, formed by a current carrying material from one direction to another across the mouth of an inlet.

Spitsbergen the main island in the Norwegian archipelago of ◊Svalbard.

Spitz Mark Andrew 1950– . US swimmer. He won a record seven gold medals at the 1972 Olympic Games, all in world record times.

spleen organ in vertebrates, part of the lymphatic system, which helps to process ◊lymphocytes. It also regulates the number of red blood cells in circulation by destroying old cells, and stores iron. It is situated behind the stomach.

splenectomy surgical removal of the spleen.

Split (Italian *Spalato*) port in Yugoslavia, on the Adriatic; population (1981) 236,000. Industries include engineering, cement, and textiles, and it is also a tourist resort.

Spock Benjamin McLane 1903– . US paediatrician and writer on child care. His *Common Sense Book of Baby and Child Care* 1946 urged less rigidity in bringing up children than had been advised by previous generations of writers on the subject, but was popularly misunderstood as advocating complete permissiveness.

Spode Josiah 1754–1827. British potter, son of Josiah Spode the elder (an apprentice of Thomas Whieldon who started his own works at Stoke-on-Trent 1770), and his successor in the new firm in 1797. He developed bone porcelain (bone ash, china stone, and china clay) around 1800, which was produced at all English factories in the 19th century, and became potter to King George III in 1806.

spoils system in the USA, the granting of offices and favours among the supporters of a party in office. The spoils system, a type of ◊patronage, was used by Jefferson, and was enlarged in scope by the 1820 Tenure of Office Act which gave the President and Senate the power to reappoint posts which were the gift of the government after each four-yearly election. The system reached a peak under the presidency of Ulysses S Grant (1869–77).

The practice remained common in this century in US local government, where civil service posts in large cities were often filled on the recommendation of newly elected political leaders. The system was epitomized by the Democratic Party 'machine' of Richard Daley (1902–76), mayor of Chicago 1955–76.

sponge very simple animal of the phylum Porifera, usually marine. A sponge has a hollow body, its cavity lined by cells bearing flagellae, whose whip-like movements keep water circulating, bringing a stream of food particles. The body walls are strengthened with protein (as in the bath-sponge) or small spikes of silica.

spontaneous generation the erroneous belief that living organisms can arise spontaneously from non-living matter, which survived until the mid-19th century, when the French chemist Louis Pasteur demonstrated that a nutrient broth would not generate microorganisms if it was adequately sterilized. The theory of ◊biogenesis holds that spontaneous generation cannot occur.

spoonbill type of bird, of the family Threskiornithidae, characterized by a long, flat bill, dilated at the tip in the shape of a spoon. They are usually white, and up to 90 cm/3 ft tall.

Spoonerism a form of expression not unlike a slip of the tongue, arising from the exchange of elements in a flow of words. The result can often be amusing and even ridiculous (for example 'a troop of Boy Scouts' becoming 'a scoop of Boy Trouts'). Dr William Spooner (1844–1930), gave his name to the phenomenon.

sporangium a structure in which ◊spores are produced.

spore a small reproductive or resting body, usually consisting of just one cell. Unlike a ◊gamete, it does not need to fuse with another cell in order to develop into a new organism. Spores are produced by the lower plants, most fungi, some bacteria, and certain protozoa. They are generally light and easily dispersed by wind movements. Plant spores are haploid and are produced by the sporophyte, following meiosis; see ◊alternation of generations.

sporophyte the diploid spore-producing generation in the life cycle of a plant that undergoes ◊alternation of generations.

sport an activity pursued for exercise or pleasure, performed individually or in a group, often involving the testing of physical capabilities and often taking the form of a competitive game.

spreadsheet in computing, a program displaying a matrix of numbers with row and column headings, allowing complex numerical analyses. The users can 'program' each cell of the matrix; for example, the last cell in a column may be defined as the sum of the cells above it. Spreadsheets are used primarily for financial calculations and forecasting analyses (changing values to see what effect this might have).

spring a device, usually a metal coil, which returns to its original shape when stretched or compressed. Springs are used in some machines (such as clocks) to store energy, which can be released at a controlled rate. In other machines (such as engines) they are used to close valves. In vehicle suspension systems springs are used to cushion passengers from road shocks. These springs are used in conjunction with ◊dampers, to limit their amount of travel.

spring in geology, a natural flow of water from the ground, formed at the point of intersection of the water table and the ground's surface. The source

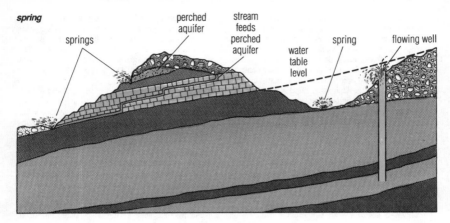

spring

springs — perched aquifer — stream feeds perched aquifer — water table level — spring — flowing well

of water is rain that has fallen on the overlying rocks and percolated through. During its passage the water may have dissolved mineral substances which may then be precipitated at the spring.

Spring Richard 1950– . Irish Labour Party leader from 1982, who entered into coalition with ◊FitzGerald's Fine Gael 1982 as deputy prime minister (and minister for the environment 1982–83 and minister for energy 1983–87). He was deputy premier and minister for foreign affairs in a Fianna Fáil–Labour coalition formed 1993.

springbok S African antelope *Antidorcas marsupialis* about 80 cm/2.6 ft at the shoulder, with head and body 1.3 m/4 ft long. They may leap 3 m/10 ft or more in the air when startled or playing, and have a fold of skin along the middle of the back which is raised to a crest in alarm. They once migrated in herds of over a million, but are now found only in a small numbers where protected.

Springsteen Bruce 1949– . US rock singer, song-writer, and guitarist, born in New Jersey. His music combines traditional rock melodies and reflective lyrics of working-class life on albums such as *Born to Run* 1975, *Born in the USA* 1984 and in concerts with the E Street Band.

spruce coniferous tree of the genus *Picea*, found over much of the northern hemisphere. Pyramidal in shape, spruces have harsh needles and drooping leathery cones. Some are important forestry trees, such as the *Sitka spruce Picea sitchensis* originally from W North America, and the *Norway spruce* or *Christmas tree Picea abies*.

Sputnik a series of ten Soviet Earth-orbiting satellites. *Sputnik 1* was the first artificial satellite, launched 4 Oct 1957. It weighed 84 kg/185 lb, with a 58 cm/23 in diameter, and carried only a simple radio transmitter which allowed scientists to track it as it orbited Earth. It burned up in the atmosphere 92 days later. *Sputnik 2*, launched 3 Nov 1957, weighed about 500 kg/1,100 lb including the dog Laika, the first living creature in space. Unfortunately, there was no way to return the dog to Earth, and it died in space.

Spycatcher the controversial memoirs (published 1987) of former UK intelligence officer Peter ◊Wright. The Law Lords unanimously rejected the UK government attempt to prevent allegations of MI5 misconduct being reported in the British media.

sq abbreviation for *square* (measure).

square in geometry, a quadrilateral (four-sided plane figure) with all sides equal and each angle a right-angle. Its diagonals also bisect each other at right-angles. The area A of a square is the length, l of one side multiplied by itself; $A = l^2$. Similarly, any quantity multiplied by itself, is also a square, represented by an index (power) of 2; for example, $4^2 = 16$ and $6.8^2 = 46.24$.

square root in mathematics, a number, which when squared (multiplied by itself) equals another given number. For example, the square root of 25 (written $\sqrt{25}$) is ± 5, because $5 \times 5 = 25$, and $(-5) \times (-5) = 25$. As an ◊index, a square root is represented by ½, for example, $16^{1/2} = 4$.

springbok

spruce

squash

An indoor racket and ball game played on an enclosed court. The use of walls is important and plays an integral part in the game. Squash is played by two players. Play continues until one player reaches nine points.

the court

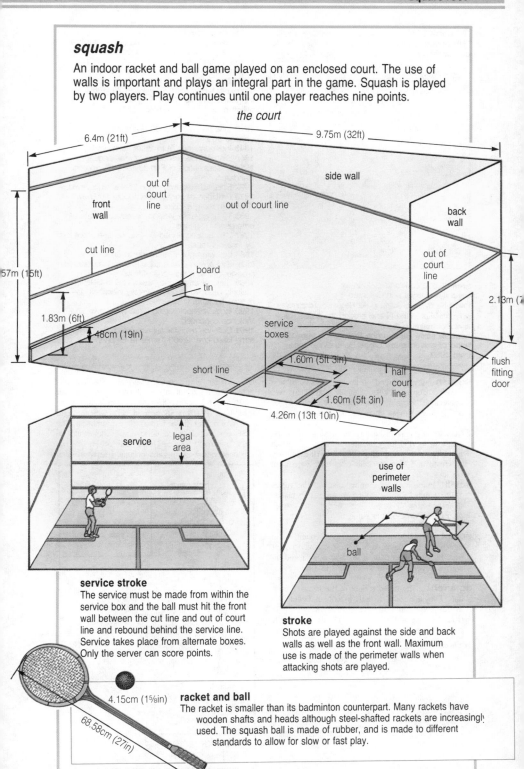

6.4m (21ft)

9.75m (32ft)

out of court line

side wall

front wall

out of court line

back wall

cut line

out of court line

57m (15ft)

board

tin

2.13m (7

1.83m (6ft)

48cm (19in)

service boxes

1.60m (5ft 3in)

short line

half court line

flush fitting door

1.60m (5ft 3in)

4.26m (13ft 10in)

service

legal area

use of perimeter walls

ball

service stroke
The service must be made from within the service box and the ball must hit the front wall between the cut line and out of court line and rebound behind the service line. Service takes place from alternate boxes. Only the server can score points.

stroke
Shots are played against the side and back walls as well as the front wall. Maximum use is made of the perimeter walls when attacking shots are played.

4.15cm (1⅝in)

68.58cm (27in)

racket and ball
The racket is smaller than its badminton counterpart. Many rackets have wooden shafts and heads although steel-shafted rackets are increasingly used. The squash ball is made of rubber, and is made to different standards to allow for slow or fast play.

Sri Lanka
Democratic Socialist Republic
of (*former name* Ceylon)

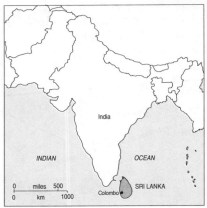

area 65,000 sq km/25,332 sq mi
capital and chief port Colombo
towns Kandy; ports Jaffna, Galle, Negombo, Trincomalee
physical flat in the N and around the coast; hills and mountains in the S
head of state Ranasinghe Premadasa from 1989
head of government Dingiri Banda Wijetunge from 1989

political system liberal democratic republic
exports tea, rubber, coconut products, graphite, sapphires, rubies, precious stones
currency Sri Lanka rupee
population (1990 est 17,135,000 including 2,500,000 Tamils); annual growth rate 1.8%
life expectancy men 67, women 70 (1989)
language Sinhalâ, Tamil, English
religion Buddhist 69% Hindu 15%
literacy 87% (1988)
GNP $7.2 bn (1988); $400 per head
chronology
1948 Independence from Britain achieved.
1956 Sinhalâ established as official language.
1959 Assassination of Prime Minister Solomon Bandaranaike.
1972 Socialist Republic of Sri Lanka proclaimed.
1978 Presidential constitution adopted by new Jayawardene government.
1983 Tamil guerrilla violence escalated: state of emergency imposed.
1987 Violence continued despite ceasefire policed by Indian troops.
1988 Left-wing guerrilla campaign against the Indo–Sri Lankan peace pact. Premadasa elected president amid allegations of fraud.
1989 State of emergency lifted. Ruling UNP majority reduced in parliamentary elections marred by terrorist violence.
1990 Indian peacekeeping force withdrawn. Violence continued.
1991 Defence minister assassinated. Sri Lanka army killed over 2,500 Tamils at Elephant Pass.

---

squash game played on an enclosed court and derived from ◊rackets. Usually played by two players, it became a popular sport in the 1970s and is now a fitness craze as well as a competitive sport.

Squatter person illegally occupying someone else's property, for example, some of the urban homeless in contemporary Britain. In 19th-century Australia and New Zealand squatters were legal tenants of Crown grazing land.

squill bulb-forming perennial plant of the genus *Scilla*, family Liliaceae, found growing in dry places near the sea in W Europe. Cultivated species usually bear blue flowers either singly or in clusters at the top of the stem.

squint or *strabismus* a common condition, in which one eye deviates in any direction. A squint may be convergent (with the bad eye turned inward), divergent (outward), or, in rare cases, vertical.

squirrel bushy-tailed rodent of the family Sciuridae. They are about 20 cm/8 in long, and generally live in trees, but some are ground dwellers.

Sri Lanka island in the Indian Ocean, off the SE coast of India.

squirrel

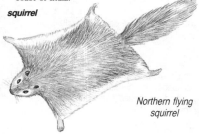

Northern flying
squirrel

SS Nazi elite corps (German *Schutz-Staffel* 'protective squadron') established 1925. Under ◊Himmler its 500,000 membership included the full-time **Waffen-SS** (armed SS), which fought in World War II, and spare-time members. The SS performed police duties, and was brutal in its treatment of the Jews and others in the concentration camps and occupied territories; it

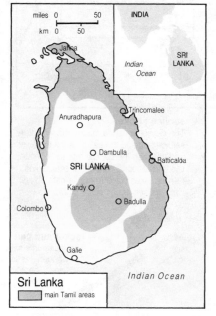

Sri Lanka
main Tamil areas

was condemned at the Nuremberg Trials of war criminals.

stabilizer one of a pair of fins fitted to the sides of a ship and governed automatically by ◊gyroscope mechanism, designed to reduce side-to-side rolling of the ship in rough weather.

stadholder or *stadtholder* the leader of the United Provinces of the Netherlands from the 15th to the 18th century. Originally provincial leaders appointed by the central government, stadholders were subsequently elected in the newly independent Dutch republic. For much of their existence they competed with the States General (parliament) for control of the country. The stadholders later became dominated by the house of ◊Orange-Nassau.

Staël Anne Louise Germaine Necker, Madame de Staël 1766–1817. French author, daughter of the financier ◊Necker. She was banished from Paris by Napoleon in 1803 because of her advocacy of political freedom. She wrote semi-autobiographical novels such as *Delphine* 1802 and *Corinne* 1807, and the critical work *De l'Allemagne* 1810, on German literature.

Staffordshire county in W central England
area 2,716 sq km/1,054 sq mi
towns administrative headquarters Stafford; Stoke-on-Trent
products coal in north; china and earthenware
population (1986) 1,021,000.

Staffordshire porcelain pottery from Staffordshire, England, one of the largest pottery producing regions in the world, built up around an area rich in clay. Different companies, the first of which was Longton, have produced stoneware and earthenware from the 17th century onwards. See also the ◊Potteries, and ◊pottery and porcelain.

stagflation economic condition (experienced in Europe in the 1970s) in which rapid inflation is accompanied by stagnating, even declining, output and by increasing unemployment. Its cause is often sharp increases in costs of raw materials and/or labour.

stained glass term applied to coloured pieces of glass which are joined by lead strips to form a pictorial window design.

stainless steel a widely used ◊alloy of iron, chromium and nickel that resists rusting.

Stakhanov Aleksei 1906–1977. Soviet miner who exceeded production norms, and who gave his name to the *Stakhanovite* movement of the 1930s, when workers were encouraged to simplify and reorganize work processes in order to increase production.

stalactite and stalagmite cave structures formed by the deposition of calcite dissolved in groundwater. *Stalactites* grow downwards from the roofs or walls and can be icicle-shaped, straw-shaped, curtain-shaped, or formed as terraces. *Stalagmites* grow upwards from the cave floor and can be conical, fir-cone-shaped, or resemble a stack of saucers. Growing stalactites and stalagmites may meet to form a continuous column from floor to ceiling.

Stalin adopted name (Russian 'steel') of Joseph Vissarionovich Djugashvili 1879–1953. Soviet politician. A member of the October Revolution Committee 1917, Stalin became General Secretary of the Communist party 1922. After Lenin's death 1924, Stalin sought to create 'socialism in one country' and clashed with ◊Trotsky, who denied the possibility of socialism inside Russia until revolution had occurred in W Europe. Stalin won this ideological

Stalin *Soviet leader Stalin taking the salute in Red Square, Moscow, 1932.*

struggle by 1927, and a series of five-year plans was launched to collectivize industry and agriculture from 1928. All opposition was eliminated by the Great Purge 1936–38 by which Stalin disposed of all real and fancied enemies. During World War II, Stalin intervened in the military direction of the campaigns against Nazi Germany. His role was denounced after his death by Khrushchev and other Soviets.

Stalingrad name (1925–1961) of the Russian city of ◊Volgograd.

Stalker affair an inquiry begun 1984 by John Stalker, deputy chief constable in Manchester, into the killing of six unarmed men in 1982 by Royal Ulster Constabulary (RUC) special units in Northern Ireland. The inquiry was halted and Stalker suspended from duty in 1986. Although he was later reinstated, the inquiry did not reopen, and no reason for his suspension was given.

Stamboul the old part of the Turkish city of ◊Istanbul, the area formerly occupied by ◊Byzantium.

stamen the male reproductive organ of a flower. The stamens are collectively referred to as the ◊androecium. A typical stamen consists of a stalk, or *filament* with an *anther*, the pollen-bearing organ, at its apex, but in some primitive plants, such as *Magnolia*, the stamen may not be markedly differentiated. The number and position of the stamens are important characters in the classification of flowering plants. Generally the more advanced plant families have fewer stamens, but they are often positioned more effectively so that the likelihood of successful pollination is not reduced.

Stamp Act an act of Parliament in 1765 which taxed (by requiring an official stamp) all publications and legal documents published in British colonies. A blockade of British merchant shipping proved so effective that the act was repealed the following year. It was a precursor of the War of ◊American Independence.

standard deviation in statistics, a measure of the spread of data. The deviation (difference) of each of the data items from the mean is found, and their values squared. The mean value of these

stamen

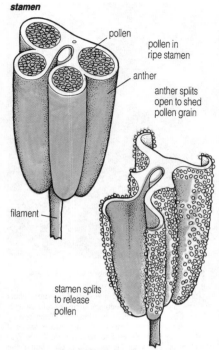

pollen

pollen in
ripe stamen

anther

anther splits
open to shed
pollen grain

filament

stamen splits
to release
pollen

squares is then calculated. The standard deviation
is the square root of this mean.

standard of living in economics, the measure
of consumption and welfare of a country, community, class, or person. Individual standard of living
expectations are heavily influenced by the income
and consumption of other people in similar jobs.

standing committee a committee of the UK
House of Commons which examines parliamentary bills (proposed acts of parliament) for detailed
correction and amendment. Several standing committees may be in existence at any time, each
usually created for a particular bill. The committee
comprises members of parliament from the main
political parties, with a majority usually held by the
government.

standing crop in ecology, the total number of
individuals of a given ◊species alive in a particular
area at any moment. It is sometimes measured as
the weight (or ◊biomass) of a given species, usually
calculated by weighing the vegetation growing in a
sample section.

standing order in banking, an instruction (banker's
order) by a depositor with the bank to pay a certain
sum of money at regular intervals. In some cases,
the bank may be billed by a third party such as a
supplier of gas or electricity, who is authorized by
the depositor to invoice the bank directly, which
in turn will pay out the sum demanded (known as
direct debit).

Stanford Charles Villiers 1852–1924. British composer and teacher, born in Ireland. A leading figure
in the late-19th-century renaissance of British music, his many works include operas such as *Shamus
O'Brien* 1896, seven symphonies, chamber music,
and church music. His pupils included Vaughan
Williams, Holst, and Bridge.

Stanislavsky Konstantin Sergeivich 1863–1938.
Russian actor, director, and teacher. He founded

the Moscow Art Theatre in 1898 and directed
productions of Chekhov and Gorky. He was the
originator of ◊Method acting, described in *My Life
in Art* 1924 and other works. It had considerable
influence on acting techniques in Europe and the
USA (resulting in the founding of the ◊Actors'
Studio). He rejected the declamatory style of acting
in favour of a more realistic approach concentrating
on the psychological development of character.

Stanley family name of Earls of ◊Derby.

Stanley town on E Falkland, capital of the
◊Falkland Islands; population (1986) 1,200.

Stanley Henry Morton 1841–1904. US explorer
and journalist, born in Wales, who made four
expeditions in Africa. He and ◊Livingstone met
at Ujiji 1871, and explored Lake Tanganyika. He
traced the course of the Zaïre (Congo) to the
sea 1874–77, established the Congo Free State
(modern Zaïre) 1879–84, and charted much of the
interior 1887–89.

Stanton Elizabeth Cady 1815–1902. US feminist,
who with Susan B ◊Anthony, founded the National Woman Suffrage Association 1869, the first
women's movement in the USA. She and Anthony
wrote and compiled the *History of Women's Suffrage*
1881–86. Stanton also worked for the abolition of
slavery.

staple in medieval Europe, a riverside town where
merchants had to offer their wares for sale before
proceeding to their destination, a practice which
constituted a form of toll; such towns were particularly common on the Rhine.

star a luminous globe of gas, producing its own
heat and light by nuclear reactions. They are born
from ◊nebulae, and consist mostly of hydrogen
and helium gas. Surface temperatures range from
2,000°C to above 30,000°C, and the corresponding colours from blue-white to red. For most of a
star's life, energy is produced by the fusion of
hydrogen into helium at its centre. The brightest
stars have masses 100 times that of the Sun, and
emit as much light as millions of suns. They live
for less than a million years before exploding as
◊supernovae. The faintest stars are the ◊red
dwarfs, less than one-thousandth the brightness
of the Sun. The smallest mass possible for a star is
about 8% that of the Sun (80 times the mass of the
planet Jupiter), otherwise nuclear reactions do not
take place. Objects with less than this critical mass
shine only dimly, and are termed **brown dwarfs**.
There is no firm distinction between a small brown
dwarf and a large planet. Towards the end of its life,
a star like the Sun swells up into a ◊red giant, before losing its outer layers as a ◊planetary nebula,
and finally shrinking to become a ◊white dwarf. See
also ◊supergiant, ◊binary star, ◊Hertzsprung-
Russell diagram, ◊variable star.

starch a widely distributed long-chain carbohydrate
(or polysaccharide), produced by plants as a food
store. It occurs in granular form in cereals, pulses,
and various tubers, including potatoes.

Star Chamber a civil and criminal court in England,
so-named because of the star-shaped ceiling decoration of the room in the Palace of Westminster, London, where its first meetings were held. Created in
1487 by Henry VII, the Star Chamber comprised
some 20 or 30 judges. It was abolished 1641 by the
◊Long Parliament. Under the Thatcher government the term was revived for private ministerial
meetings, at which disputes between the Treasury
and high-spending departments are resolved.

star cluster a group of related stars, usually held
together by gravity. Members of a star cluster are

starfish

*crown of thorns
starfish*

thought to form together from one large cloud of gas in space. *Open clusters* such as the Pleiades contain from a dozen to many hundreds of young stars, loosely scattered over several light years. ◊Globular clusters are larger and much more densely packed, containing perhaps 100,000 old stars.

starfish an echinoderm with arms radiating from a central body. Usually there are five arms, but some species have more. They are covered with spines and small pincer-like organs. There are also a number of small tubular processes on the skin surface which assist in respiration. Starfish are predators, and vary in size from 1.2 cm/0.5 in to 90 cm/3 ft.

starling bird *Sturnus vulgaris* common in N Eurasia and naturalized in North America from the late 19th century. The black, speckled plumage is glossed with green and purple. Its own call is a bright whistle, but it is a mimic of the songs of other birds. It is about 20 cm/8 in long.

Starling Ernest Henry 1866–1927. English physiologist who discovered ◊secretin, and coined the word 'hormone' to describe chemicals of this sort. He formulated Starling's Law, which states that the force of the heart's contraction is a function of the length of the muscle fibres.

Star of David or *Magen David* (Hebrew 'shield of David') six-pointed star, a symbol of Judaism and used on the flag of Israel.

START phase in peace discussions dealing with disarmament, initially involving the USA and the Soviet Union, and from 1992 the USA and Russia. It began with talks in Geneva 1983 leading to the signing of the Intermediate Nuclear Forces (INF) treaty 1987. Reductions of about 30% in strategic nuclear arms were agreed 1991 (START) and more significant cuts Jan 1993 (START II).

Star Wars popular term for the ◊Strategic Defence Initiative (SDI) announced by US President Reagan in 1983.

state a territory which forms its own domestic and foreign policy, acting through laws which are typically decided by a government and carried out, by force if necessary, by agents of that government. Although most states are members of the United Nations Organization, this is not a completely reliable criterion: some are not members by choice, like Switzerland; some have been deliberately excluded, like Taiwan; and some are members but do not enjoy complete national sovereignty, like Byelorussia, which forms part of the USSR. It can be argued that growth of regional international bodies such as the European Community means that states no longer enjoy absolute sovereignty.

State Department (Department of State) US government department responsible for ◊foreign relations.

States General the former French parliament which consisted of three estates – nobility, clergy, and commons. First summoned in 1302, it declined in importance as the power of the Crown grew. It was not called at all between 1614 and 1789 when the Crown needed to institute fiscal reforms to avoid financial collapse. Once called, the demands made by the States General formed the first phase in the ◊French Revolution. The term States General is also the name of the Dutch parliament.

static electricity ◊electric charge acquired by a body by means of electrostatic induction or friction. Rubbing different materials can produce static electricity, seen in the sparks produced on combing one's hair, or removing a nylon shirt. In some processes, static electricity is useful, as in paint spraying where the parts to be sprayed are charged with electricity of opposite polarity to that on the paint droplets, and in ◊xerography.

statics branch of mechanics concerned with the behaviour of bodies at rest and forces in equilibrium, and distinguished from ◊dynamics.

Stationery Office, Her (His) Majesty's (HMSO) office established in 1786 to supply books and stationery to British government departments, and to superintend the printing of government reports and other papers, and books and pamphlets on subjects ranging from national works of art to industrial and agricultural processes. The corresponding establishment in the USA is the Government Printing Office.

Stations of the Cross in the Christian church, a series of 14 crosses, usually each with a picture or image, depicting the 14 stages in Jesus Christ's journey to the crucifixion.

statistics the branch of mathematics concerned with the meaningful collection and interpretation of data. For example, to determine the ◊mean age of the children in a school, a statistically acceptable answer might be obtained by calculating an average based on the ages of a representative sample, consisting, for example, of a random tenth of the pupils from each class. Probability is the branch of statistics dealing with predictions of events.

status in the social sciences, an individual's social position, or the esteem in which he or she is held by others in society. Both within and between most occupations or social positions there is a status hierarchy. *Status symbols*, such as insignia of office or an expensive car, often accompany high status.

Staudinger Hermann 1881–1965. German organic chemist, founder of macro-molecular chemistry, who did pioneering research into the structure of albumen and cellulose.

Stauffenberg Claus von 1907–1944. German colonel in World War II, who planted a bomb in Hitler's headquarters conference room in the Wolf's Lair at Rastenburg, E Prussia, 20 Jul 1944. Hitler was injured, and Stauffenberg and some 200 others were later executed.

STDs abbreviation for *sexually transmitted diseases*, a term encompassing not only traditional ◊venereal disease, but also a growing list of conditions, such as ◊AIDS and scabies, which are known to be spread primarily by sexual contact.

Stead Christina 1902–1983. Australian writer, who lived in Europe and the US 1928–53. Her novels include *The Man Who Loved Children* 1940, *For Love Alone* 1944 and *Cotter's England* 1966.

steady state theory theory that the Universe is in a steady state: it appears the same wherever (and whenever) viewed. It seems to be refuted by the existence of cosmic background radiation.

steam in chemistry, a dry, invisible gas formed by vaporizing water. The visible cloud which normally

Steen The Harpsichord Lesson *Wallace Collection, London.*

forms in the air when water is vaporized is due to minute suspended water particles. Steam is widely used in chemical and other industrial processes, and for the generation of power.

stearic acid $CH_3(CH_2)_{16}CO_2H$ a saturated long-chain fatty acid, soluble in alcohol and ether but not in water. It is found in many fats and oils, and used to make soap and candles, and as a lubricant.

steel alloy or mixture of iron and up to 1.7% carbon, sometimes with other elements, such as manganese, phosphorus, sulphur, and silicon. The USA, Russia, Ukraine, and Japan are the main steel producers. Steel has innumerable uses, including ship and automobile manufacture, skyscraper frames, and machinery of all kinds.

Steel David 1938– . British politician, leader of the Liberal Party 1976–88. He entered into a compact with the Labour government 1977–78, and into an alliance with the Social Democratic Party (SDP) 1983. Having supported the Liberal–SDP merger, he resigned the leadership in 1988.

steel band type of musical ensemble popular in the West Indies, especially Trinidad, consisting mostly of percussion instruments made from oil drums.

Steele Richard 1672–1729. Irish essayist, who founded the journal *The Tatler* 1709–11, in which ◊Addison collaborated. They continued their joint work in *The Spectator*, also founded by Steele, 1711–12, and *The Guardian* 1713. He also wrote plays, such as *The Conscious Lovers* 1722.

Steen Jan 1626–1679. Dutch painter. Born in Leiden, he was also active in The Hague, Delft, and Haarlem. He painted humorous genre scenes, mainly set in taverns or bourgeois households, as well as portraits and landscapes.

Steer Philip Wilson 1860–1942. British painter, influenced by the French Impressionists, known for seaside scenes such as *The Beach at Walberswick* (Tate Gallery, London).

Stein Gertrude 1874–1946. US writer. She influenced writers such as ◊Hemingway and Scott ◊Fitzgerald by her cinematic technique, use of repetition and absence of punctuation: devices to convey immediacy and realism. Her works include the self-portrait *The Autobiography of Alice B Toklas* 1933.

Steinbeck John (Ernst) 1902–1968. US novelist, whose works include *Tortilla Flat* 1935, *Of Mice and Men* 1937, *The Grapes of Wrath* 1939, *Cannery Row* 1945, and *East of Eden* 1952. Nobel prize 1962.

stem the main supporting axis of a ◊vascular plant that bears the leaves, buds, and reproductive structures: it may be simple or branched. The plant stem usually grows above ground, although some grow underground, including ◊rhizomes, ◊corms, ◊rootstocks, and ◊tubers. Stems contain a continuous vascular system that conducts water and food to and from all parts of the plant. The point on a stem from which a leaf or leaves arise is called a node, and the space between two successive nodes is the internode.

Stendhal pen name of Marie Henri Beyle 1783–1842. French novelist. His two major novels *Le Rouge et le Noir*/*Red and Black* 1830 and *La Chartreuse de Parme*/*The Charterhouse of Parma* 1839 were pioneering works in their treatment of disguise and hypocrisy, and gained their reputation with a review of the latter by ◊Balzac 1840.

stenosis narrowing of a body vessel, duct, or opening, usually due to disease.

Stephen, St died *c.* 35 AD, the first Christian martyr; he was stoned to death. Feast day 26 Dec.

Stephen I, St 975–1038. King of Hungary from 997, when he succeeded his father. He completed the conversion of Hungary to Christianity, and was canonized 1003.

Stephen *c.* 1097–1154. King of England from 1135. A grandson of William I, he was elected king 1135, although he had previously recognized Henry I's daughter ◊Matilda as heiress to the throne. Matilda landed in England 1139, and civil war disrupted the country until 1153, when Stephen acknowledged Matilda's son, Henry, as his own heir.

Stephen Leslie 1832–1904. English critic, first editor of the *Dictionary of National Biography* and father of novelist Virginia ◊Woolf.

Stephens John Lloyd 1805–1852. US explorer in Central America, with Frederick Catherwood. He recorded his findings of the ruined Mayan cities in his two volumes of *Incidents of Travel* 1841–43.

Stephenson George 1781–1848. English engineer, who built the first successful steam locomotive, and who also invented a safety lamp 1815. He was appointed engineer of the Stockton and Darlington Railway, the world's first public railway, in 1821, and of the Liverpool and Manchester Railway 1826. In 1829 he won a £500 prize with his locomotive, *Rocket*.

Stephenson Robert 1803–1859. English civil engineer, who constructed railway bridges such as the high level bridge at Newcastle, and the Menai and Conway tubular bridges in North Wales. He was the son of George Stephenson.

steppe the temperate grassland of Europe and Asia. Sometimes the term refers to other temperate grasslands and semi-arid desert edges.

step rocket also called ***multi-stage rocket*** a rocket launch vehicle made up of several rocket stages (often three) joined end to end. The bottom stage fires first, boosting the vehicle to high speed, then it falls away. The next stage fires, thrusting the now lighter vehicle even faster. The remaining stages fire and fall away in turn, boosting the vehicle's payload (cargo) to an orbital speed that can reach 28,000 kph/17,500 mph.

Steptoe Patrick Christopher 1913–1988. English obstetrician who pioneered *in vitro* or 'test-tube' fertilization. Steptoe, together with biologist Robert Edwards, was the first to succeed in implanting in the womb an egg fertilized outside the body.

stereophonic sound a system of sound reproduction using two loudspeakers, which give a more natural 'depth' to the sound. See ◊hi-fi.

stereotype a one-sided, exaggerated, and preconceived idea about a particular group or society. It is based on prejudice rather than fact, but by repetition stereotypes become fixed in people's minds, resistant to change or to factual evidence to the contrary.

sterilization an operation to terminate the power of reproduction. In women, this is normally achieved by sealing or tying off the ◊Fallopian tubes (tubal ligation) so that fertilization can no longer take place. In men, the transmission of sperm is blocked by ◊vasectomy. Sterilization is also used to describe the cleansing of medical equipment and materials.

sterling silver an ◊alloy containing 925 parts of silver and 75 parts of copper. The copper hardens the metal, making it more useful for jewellery.

Sterne Laurence 1713–1768. Irish writer, creator of the comic anti-hero Tristram Shandy. *The Life and Opinions of Tristram Shandy, Gent* 1760–67, an eccentrically whimsical and bawdy novel, foreshadowed many of the techniques and devices of 20th-century novelists, including Joyce. His other works include *A Sentimental Journey through France and Italy* 1768.

Stern Gang (formal name 'Fighters for the Freedom of Israel') a Zionist guerrilla group founded 1940 by Abraham Stern (1907–42). The group carried out anti-British attacks during the UK mandate rule in Palestine, both on individuals and on strategic targets. Stern was killed by British forces, but the group survived until 1948, when it was outlawed with the creation of the independent state of Israel.

steroid in biology, a type of lipid (fat), derived from sterols, with a complex molecular structure consisting of four carbon rings. Steroids include the sex hormones, such as ◊testosterone, the corticosteroid hormones produced by the ◊adrenal gland, and ◊cholesterol. The term is also commonly used to refer to ◊anabolic steroid.

sterol one of a group of organic alcohols, with a complex structure, consisting of four carbon rings. Steroids are derived from sterols, and have the same ring structure, but with various other chemical groups attached. They are physiologically very active.

stethoscope instrument used to ascertain the condition of the heart and lungs by listening to their action. It consists of two earpieces connected by flexible tubes to a small plate which is placed against the body. It was invented 1819 by René Théophile Hyacinthe Laënnec (1781–1826).

Stevens Wallace 1879–1955. US poet. His volumes of poems include *Harmonium* 1923, *The Man with the Blue Guitar* 1937, and *Transport to Summer* 1947. *The Necessary Angel* 1951 is a collection of essays. An elegant and philosophical poet, he won a Pulitzer prize 1954 for his *Collected Poems*.

Stevenson Adlai 1900–1965. US Democrat politician. As governor of Illinois 1949–53 he campaigned vigorously against corruption in public life, and as Democratic candidate for the presidency 1952 and 1956 was twice defeated by Eisenhower. In 1945 he was chief US delegate at the founding conference of the United Nations.

Stevenson Robert Louis 1850–1894. Scottish novelist and poet. Early works included *An Island Voyage* 1878 and *Travels with a Donkey* 1879, but he achieved fame with his adventure novel *Treasure Island* 1883. Later works included the novels *Kidnapped* 1886, *The Master of Ballantrae* 1889, *Dr Jekyll and Mr Hyde* 1886, and the anthology *A Child's Garden of Verses* 1885. In 1890 he settled at Vailima, in Samoa, where he sought a cure for the tuberculosis of which he died.

Stewart James 1908– . US actor. Gangling, and speaking with a soft drawl, he specialized in the role of the stubbornly honest, ordinary American in such films as *You Can't Take It With You* 1938, *The Philadelphia Story* 1940, *Harvey* 1950, *Rear Window* 1954, and *The FBI Story* 1959.

Stewart John Young 'Jackie' 1939– . Scottish motor racing driver. Until surpassed by Alain ◊Prost (France) 1987, Stewart held the record for the most Formula One Grand Prix wins (27).

stick insect insect of the order Phasmida, closely resembling a stick or twig. Many species are wingless. The longest reach a length of 30 cm/1 ft.

stickleback fish of the family Gasterosteidae, found in the N hemisphere. It has a long body which can grow to 18 cm/7 in. It has spines along the back which take the place of the first dorsal fin, and which can be raised to make the fish difficult to eat for predators.

stigma in a flower, the receptive surface at the tip of a ◊carpel which receives the ◊pollen. It often has short outgrowths, flaps, or hairs to trap pollen, and may produce a sticky secretion to which the grains adhere.

stigmata impressions or marks corresponding to the five wounds Jesus received at his crucifixion, which are said to have appeared spontaneously on St Francis and others.

Stijl, de a group of 20th-century Dutch artists and architects led by ◊Mondrian from 1917. They believed in the concept of the 'designer', that all life, work, and leisure should be surrounded by art; and that everything functional should be aesthetic as well. The group had a strong influence on the ◊Bauhaus school.

Stilicho Flavius 359–408 AD. Roman general, of ◊Vandal origin, who campaigned successfully against the Visigoths and Ostrogoths. He virtually ruled the western empire as guardian of Honorius (son of ◊Theodosius I), but was executed on the orders of Honorius when he was suspected of wanting to make his own son successor to another son of Theodosius in the eastern empire.

Stilwell Joseph Warren 1883–1946. US general, nicknamed 'Vinegar Joe'. In 1942 he became US military representative in China, when he commanded the Chinese forces cooperating with the British (with whom he quarrelled) in Burma; he later commanded all US forces in the Chinese, Burmese, and Indian theatres until recalled to the USA 1944 after differences over nationalist policy with the Guomindang leader Chiang Kai-shek. Subsequently he commanded the US 10th Army on the Japanese island of Okinawa.

Stimson Henry Lewis 1867–1950. US politician. He was war secretary in Taft's cabinet 1911–13, Hoover's secretary of state 1929–33, and war secretary 1940–45.

stimulant a drug which acts on the brain to increase alertness and activity. When given to children, it may have a paradoxical, calming effect. Stimulants have limited therapeutic value and are now given only to treat ◊narcolepsy.

stinkhorn species of fungus (*Phallus impudicus*); it first appears as a white ball.

stinkwood various trees with unpleasant-smelling wood. The S African tree *Ocotea bullata*, family Lauraceae, has offensive-smelling wood when newly felled, but fine, durable timber used for furniture. Another stinkwood is *Gustavia augusta* from tropical America.

stipule an outgrowth arising from the base of a leaf or leaf stalk in certain plants. Stipules usually occur in pairs, or fused into a single semicircular structure. They may have a leaf-like appearance, as

Stirling The Staatsgalerie, Stuttgart, by Stirling and Wilford.

in goosegrass *Galium aparine*, be spiny, as in false acacia *Robina*, or look like small scales. In some species they are large, and contribute significantly to the photosynthetic area, as in the garden pea *Pisum sativum*.

Stirling James 1926– . British architect associated with collegiate and museum architecture. His works include the engineering building at Leicester University, and the Clore Gallery (the extension to house the Tate's ◊Turner collection) at the Tate Gallery, London, opened 1987.

Stirling engine a hot-air engine invented by Scottish priest Robert Stirling 1876. It is a piston engine that uses hot air as a working fluid.

stoat carnivorous mammal *Mustela erminea* of the weasel family, about 37 cm/15 in long including black-tipped tail. It has a long body and a flattened head. Stoats live in Europe, Asia, and North America. In the colder regions, the coat turns white (ermine) in winter.

stock UK term for the fully paid-up capital of a company. It is bought and sold by subscribers not in units or shares, but in terms of its current cash value. In US usage the term stock generally means an ordinary share.

stock in botany, herbaceous plants of the genus *Matthiola*, commonly grown as garden ornamentals. Many cultivated varieties, including simple-stemmed, queen's and ten-week, have been derived from the wild stock *Matthiola incana*; night-scented stock is *Matthiola bicornis*.

stock car racing sport popular in the UK and USA, but in two different forms. In the UK, the cars are old 'bangers' which attempt to force the others cars off the track or to come to a standstill. In the USA, the cars are high-powered sports cars which race on purpose-built tracks, normally over 400-500 miles.

stock exchange institution for the buying and selling of stocks and shares (securities). The world's largest stock exchanges are London, New York (Wall Street), and Tokyo. London's is the oldest stock exchange in the world, opened 1801. The former division on the London Stock Exchange between brokers (who bought shares from jobbers to sell to the public) and jobbers (who sold them only to brokers on commission, the 'jobbers' turn') was abolished 1986.

Stock Exchange Automation System (SEAQ) a computerized system of share price monitoring. From October 1987, SEAQ began displaying market maker's quotations for UK stocks, having only been operational previously for overseas equities.

Stockhausen Karlheinz 1928– . German composer of avant-garde music, who has continued to explore new musical sounds and compositional techniques since the 1950s. His major works include *Klavierstücke* 1952–85, *Momente* 1961–64, revised 1972, *Mikrophonie I* 1964, and *Mikrophonie II* 1965. Since 1977 all his works have been part of *Licht*, a cycle of seven musical ceremonies, intended for performance on the evenings of a week. He has completed *Donnerstag* 1980, *Samstag* 1984, and *Montag* 1988.

Stockholm capital and industrial port of Sweden; population (1986) 663,000. It is built on a number of islands. Industries include engineering, brewing, electrical goods, paper, textiles, and pottery.

stocks wooden device used until the 19th century to confine the legs or arms of minor offenders, and expose them to public humiliation. The ◊pillory had a similar purpose.

stoicism a Greek school of philosophy, founded about 300 BC by Zeno of Citium. The stoics were pantheistic materialists who believed that happiness lies in accepting the law of the Universe. They emphasized human brotherhood, denounced slavery, and were internationalist.

Stoker Bram (Abraham) 1847–1912. Irish novelist, actor, theatre manager, and author of the novel

stoma

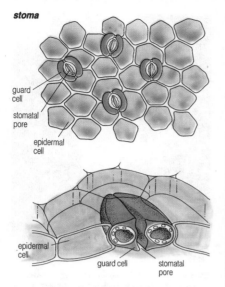

guard cell
stomatal pore
epidermal cell

epidermal cell
guard cell
stomatal pore

stomach

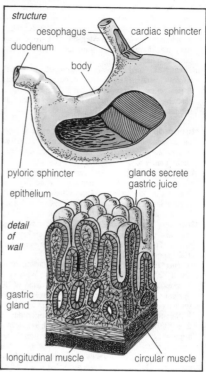

structure
oesophagus — cardiac sphincter
duodenum
body
pyloric sphincter
epithelium
glands secrete gastric juice
detail of wall
gastric gland
longitudinal muscle   circular muscle

◊*Dracula* 1897, which crystallized most aspects of the traditional vampire legend and became the source for all subsequent popular fiction and films on the subject.

Stokes   George Gabriel 1819–1903. Irish physicist. During the late 1840s, he studied the ◊viscosity (resistance to relative motions) of fluids. This culminated in Stokes' law, which applies to a sphere falling under gravity through a liquid. It states that if a sphere of radius r falls with a velocity v through a liquid of viscosity ε, the force acting on it $F = 6\pi\varepsilon rv$.

STOL   *S*hort *T*ake *O*ff and *L*anding. A type of aircraft, STOL craft are fitted with special devices on the wings (such as sucking flaps), which increase aerodynamic lift at low speeds. Small passenger and freight STOL craft are likely to become common with the demand for city centre airports.

stolon   a type of ◊runner.

stoma   (plural stomata) in botany, a pore in the epidermis of a plant.

stomach   the first cavity in the digestive system of animals. In mammals, it is a bag of muscle situated just below the diaphragm. Food enters it from the oesophagus, is digested by the acid and ◊enzymes secreted by the stomach lining, and then passes into the duodenum. Some plant-eating (herbivorous) mammals have multi-chambered stomachs, which harbour bacteria in one of the chambers to assist in the digestion of ◊cellulose.

stomata   (singular stoma) pores in the epidermis of a plant; each stoma is surrounded by a pair of guard cells that are crescent-shaped when the stoma is open, but can collapse to an oval shape, thus closing off the opening between them. They allow the exchange of carbon dioxide and oxygen (needed for ◊photosynthesis and ◊respiration) between the internal tissues of the plant and the outside atmosphere. They are also the main route by which water is lost from the plant, and they can be closed to conserve water, the movements being controlled by changes in turgidity of the guard cells.

stone   British unit of weight used to express bodyweight (st). 14 lbs comprise 1 stone, which is equivalent to 6.35 kg.

Stone   Lucy 1818–1893. US feminist orator and editor. Married to the radical Henry Blackwell 1855 after a mutual declaration rejecting the legal superiority of the man in marriage, she gained wide publicity when she chose to retain her own surname despite her marriage. The epithet 'Lucy Stoner' was coined to mean a woman who advocated doing the same.

Stone Age   the period in ◊prehistory before the use of metals, when tools and weapons were made

Stonehenge *The local sandstone or 'sarsen' was used for the uprights, which measure 5.5 by 2m/18 by 7ft, and each weigh some 26 tonnes.*

chiefly of flint. The Stone Age is subdivided into the Old or Palaeolithic, the Middle or Mesolithic and the New or Neolithic. The people of the Old Stone Age were hunters, whereas the Neolithic people progressed to making the first steps in agriculture, domestication of animals, weaving, and pottery making.

stonechat bird *Saxicola torquata* of the thrush family (Turdidae) frequently found in Eurasia and Africa on open land with bushes. The male has a black head and throat, tawny breast, and dark back; the female is browner. They are about 12 cm/5 in long.

stonecrop different species of the genus *Sedum*, family Crassulaceae, with fleshy leaves and clusters of star-like flowers. They are characteristic of dry rocky places and some grow on walls.

stonefish fish *Synanceia verrucosa* that lives in shallow waters of the Indian and Pacific Oceans. It is about 35 cm/14 in long, and camouflaged to resemble encrusted rock. It has poisonous spines that can inflict painful venom.

stonefly insect of the order Plecoptera, with long tails and antennae and two pairs of membranous wings. They live near fresh water. There are over 1300 species.

Stonehenge megalithic monument dating from about 2000 BC on Salisbury Plain, ·Wiltshire, England. It consisted originally of a circle of 30 upright stones, their tops linked by lintelstones to form a continuous circle about 30 m/100 ft across. Within the circle was a horseshoe rrangement of five trilithons (two uprights plus a lintel, set as five separate entities), and a so-called 'altar stone' – an upright pillar – on the axis of the horseshoe at the open, NE end, which faces in the direction of the rising sun. It has been suggested that it served as an observatory.

stoneware a very hard opaque pottery made of non-porous clay with a high silica content, fired at high temperature.

stoolball an ancient game, considered the ancestor of cricket, the main differences being that in stoolball bowling is underarm, and the ball is soft, the bat is wooden, and shaped like a tennis racket.

Stopes Marie (Carmichael) 1880–1958. Scottish birth-control campaigner. With her husband H V Roe (1878–1949), an aircraft manufacturer, she founded a London birth-control clinic 1921. The Well Woman Centre in Marie Stopes House, London, commemorates her work. She wrote plays and verse as well as the best-selling manual *Married Love* 1918.

Stoppard Tom 1937– . Czechoslovakian-born British playwright, whose works use wit and word-play to explore logical and philosophical ideas. He achieved fame with *Rosencrantz and Guildenstern are Dead* 1967. This was followed by comedies including *The Real Inspector Hound* 1968, *Jumpers* 1972, *Travesties* 1974, *Dirty Linen* 1976 and *The Real Thing* 1982.

Storey David Malcolm 1933– . English dramatist and novelist. His plays include *In Celebration* 1969, *Home* 1970, and *Early Days* 1980. Novels include *This Sporting Life* 1960.

stork carnivorous wading bird of the mainly tropical order Ciconiiformes, with a long beak, slender body, long, powerful wings, and long thin neck and legs. Some species grow up to 150 cm/5 ft tall.

Storting the Norwegian parliament, which consists of 150 representatives, elected every four years.

Stopes *Scottish birth control campaigner Marie Stopes.*

Stoss Veit. Also known as *Wit Stwosz* c. 1450–1533. German sculptor and painter, active in Nuremberg and 1477–96 in Poland. He carved a wooden altarpiece with high relief panels in St Mary's, Krakow, a complicated design with numerous figures which centres on the Death of the Virgin.

Stowe Harriet Beecher 1811–1896. US suffragist, abolitionist, and author of of the anti-slavery novel ◊*Uncle Tom's Cabin*, first published as a serial 1851–52.

STP (Standard Temperature and Pressure) in physics, a standard for comparing the properties of gases equal to a temperature of 273.15K/0°C and a pressure of 101,325 pascals (760 mm of mercury). Formerly called normal temperature and pressure, or NTP.

Strachey (Giles) Lytton 1880–1932. English critic and biographer, a member of the Bloomsbury group of writers and artists. He wrote *Landmarks in French Literature* 1912. The mocking and witty treatment of Cardinal Manning, Florence Nightingale, Thomas Arnold, and General Gordon in *Eminent Victorians* 1918 won him recognition. His biography of *Queen Victoria* 1921 was more affectionate.

Stradivari Antonio 1644–1737. Italian violin maker, generally considered the greatest of all violin makers. He was born in Cremona, and studied there with Nicolo ◊Amati.

Strafford Thomas Wentworth, 1st Earl of Strafford 1593–1641. English politician, originally an opponent of Charles I, but from 1628 on the Royalist side. He ruled despotically as Lord Deputy of Ireland 1632–39, when he returned to England as Charles's chief adviser and received an earldom. He was impeached 1640 by Parliament, abandoned by Charles as a scapegoat, and beheaded.

straits question the 19th and 20th century international and diplomatic debate over Russian naval access to the Mediterranean from the Black Sea via the Bosporus.

Straits Settlements former province of the ◊East India Company 1826–58, and British Crown colony 1867–1946: it comprised Singapore, Malacca, Penang, Cocos Islands, Christmas Island, and Labuan.

Stralsund, Peace of in 1369, the peace between Waldemar IV of Denmark and the Hanse (association of N German trading towns) which concluded the Hanse war 1362–69.

Strand Paul 1890–1976. US photographer, who used large format cameras for his strong, clear, close-up photographs of natural objects.

strange attractor in physics, point that moves irregularly within a given region at all times. Such movement describes, for example, the motion of turbulent fluids.

Strasberg Lee 1902–1982. US actor and director of ◊Actors Studio from 1948, who developed 'method' acting from ◊Stanislavsky's system; pupils have included Jane Fonda, John Garfield, Sidney Poitier, and Paul Newman.

Strasbourg city on the river Ill, in Bas-Rhin *département*, capital of ◊Alsace, France; population (1990) 255,900. Industries include car manufacture, tobacco, printing and publishing, and preserves. The ◊Council of Europe meets here, and sessions of the European Parliament alternate between Strasbourg and Luxembourg.

Strategic Arms Limitation Talks (SALT) US–Soviet talks suggested by President Johnson 1967 for the mutual limitation and eventual reduction of nuclear weapons. They were delayed by the Soviet invasion of Czechoslovakia but began 1969. They were superseded 1983 by START (Strategic Arms Reduction Talks).

US–Soviet summits
1969 SALT talks begin in Helsinki
1972 Nixon and Brezhnev sign SALT I accord
1973 Brezhnev meets Nixon in Washington
1974 (Jun) Nixon meets Brezhnev in Moscow
1974 (Nov) Ford meets Brezhnev in Vladivostok
1975 Ford and Brezhnev at 35-nation meeting in Helsinki
1979 Carter and Brezhnev sign SALT II accord in Vienna
1983 Strategic Arms Reduction Talks (START) in Geneva
1986 Reagan and Gorbachev meet in Iceland
1987 Intermediate Nuclear Forces treaty signed in Washington.
1989 Cuts of short-range missiles in Europe proposed conditional on reduction of conventional forces.

Strategic Defense Initiative (SDI) also called *Star Wars*. An attempt by the USA to develop a defence system against foreign nuclear missiles based in part outside Earth's atmosphere. It was announced by President Reagan Mar 1983, and had cost by 1990 over $16.5 billion. In 1988, it was announced that only 30% of incoming missiles could be intercepted. Scientists maintain that the system is unworkable.

strategic Islands islands (Azores, Canary Islands, Cyprus, Iceland, Madeira, and Malta) of great political and military significance likely to affect their stability; they held their first international conference 1979.

Stratford-upon-Avon market town on the river Avon, in Warwickshire, England; population (1986) 20,900. It is the birthplace of William ◊Shakespeare.

Strathclyde region of Scotland
area 13,856 sq km/5,348 sq mi
towns administrative headquarters Glasgow; Paisley, Greenock, Kilmarnock, Clydebank, Hamilton, Coatbridge, Prestwick

products dairy, pig, and poultry products; shipbuilding and engineering; coal from Ayr and Lanark; oil-related services
population (1991) 2,218,200, almost half the population of Scotland.

stratigraphy branch of ◊geology that deals with the sequence of formation of ◊sedimentary rocks and the conditions under which they were formed.

stratosphere that part of the atmosphere beyond 10 km/6 mi from Earth, wherein the temperature is constant. After the minimum −55°C/−67°F is reached, there is even a slight rise up to 40 km/25 mi in the extremely rarefied air.

Strauss Franz-Josef 1915–1988. West German conservative politician, leader of the Bavarian Christian Social Union (CSU) party 1961–88, premier of Bavaria 1978–88.

Strauss Johann (Baptist) 1825–1899. Austrian composer, the son of Johann Strauss (1804–49), a composer of waltz music. In 1872 he gave up conducting to compose, and wrote operettas, such as *Die Fledermaus* 1874 and numerous waltzes, such as 'The Blue Danube' and 'Tales from the Vienna Woods', which gained him the title 'The Waltz King'.

Strauss Richard (Georg) 1864–1949. German composer and prominent conductor. He was influenced by the German Romantic heritage but had a strongly personal style, particularly in his use of bold, colourful orchestration. His reputation was established with tone poems such as *Don Juan* 1889, *Till Eulenspiegel's Merry Pranks* 1895, and *Also sprach Zarathustra* 1896. He then moved on to operatic success with *Salome* 1905, and *Elektra* 1909, both of which have elements of polytonality, followed by a reversion to a more traditional style with *Der Rosenkavalier* 1911.

Stravinsky Igor 1882–1971. Russian composer, later of French (1934) and US (1945) nationality. He studied under ◊Rimsky-Korsakov and wrote the music for the Diaghilev ballets *The Firebird* 1910, *Petrushka* 1911, and *The Rite of Spring* 1913 (controversial at the time for their unorthodox rhythms and harmony). His versatility ranges from his Neo-Classical ballet *Pulcinella* 1920, the choral-orchestral *Symphony of Psalms* 1930, and his later use of serial techniques in works such as the *Canticum Sacrum* 1955 and the ballet *Agon* 1953–57.

strawberry low-growing perennial plant of the genus *Fragaria*, family Rosaceae, widely cultivated for its red fruit which is rich in vitamin C. Commercial cultivated forms bear one crop of fruit in summer and multiply by runners. Alpine garden varieties are derived from the wild strawberry *Fragaria vesca* which has small aromatic fruit.

streaming in education, the practice of dividing pupils for all classes according to an estimate of their overall ability, with arrangements for 'promotion' and 'demotion' at the end of each academic year.

streamlining shaping a body so that it offers the least resistance when travelling through an element, usually air or water. Aircraft, for example, must be carefully streamlined to reduce air resistance, or ◊drag.

stream of consciousness narrative technique in which a writer presents directly the uninterrupted flow of a character's thoughts, impressions, and feelings, without the conventional devices of dialogue and description. It first came to be widely used in the early 20th century, leading exponents have included Virginia Woolf and James Joyce.

Streep Meryl 1949– .US actress noted for her strong character roles. Her films include *The Deer Hunter* 1978, *Kramer vs Kramer* 1979, *Out of Africa* 1985, and *Ironweed* 1988.

street hockey form of hockey played on roller skates. At one time played mostly on streets, notably in the USA, it is now played in indoor arenas. It rapidly increased in popularity in the UK in the late 1980s.

streptomycin ◊antibiotic discovered 1944, used to treat tuberculosis, influenzal meningitis, and other infections, some of which are unaffected by ◊penicillin.

stress in psychology, a wide range of situations or events which can tax the individual's physical or mental ability to cope. Examples of stress include excessive noise, marital conflict, and overwork. Individual reactions to stress are varied, including irritability, fatigue, anxiety, or physical health problems, such as stomach ulcers and high blood pressure. Stress is treated by health psychology.

stress and strain in the science of materials, measures of the deforming force applied to a body and of the resulting change in its shape. For a perfectly elastic material, stress is proportional to strain (◊Hooke's law).

stridulatory organs in insects, organs that produce sound when rubbed together. Crickets rub their wings together, but grasshoppers rub the hind-leg against the wing. Stridulation is considered to be used for attracting mates, but may also be used to mark territory.

strike and lockout a *strike* is a stoppage of work by employees, often as members of a trade union, to obtain or resist change in wages, hours, or conditions. *Lockout* is a weapon of an employer to enforce such change by preventing employees working. Another measure is *work to rule*, when production is virtually brought to a halt by strict observance of union rules.

Strindberg August 1849–1912. Swedish playwright. His plays were influential in the development of dramatic technique, and are in a variety of styles including historical plays, symbolic dramas, and 'chamber plays'. They include *The Father* 1887, *Miss Julie* 1888, *The Dance of Death* 1901, and *The Ghost (or Spook) Sonata* 1907.

stringed instrument musical instrument which produces a sound by making a stretched string vibrate. Types include: *bowed* violin family, viol family; *plucked* guitar, ukelele, lute, sitar, harp, banjo, lyre; *plucked mechanically* harpsichord; *struck mechanically* piano, clavichord; *hammered* dulcimer.

strobilus in botany, a reproductive structure found in most ◊gymnosperms and some pteridophytes, notably the clubmosses. In conifers the strobilus is commonly known as a ◊cone.

stroboscope instrument for studying continuous periodic motion using light flashing at the same frequency as that of the motion; for example, rotating machinery can be 'stopped' by illuminating it with a stroboscope flashing at the exact rate of rotation.

Stroessner Alfredo 1912– . Military leader and president of Paraguay 1954–89. Accused by his opponents of harsh repression, his regime spent heavily on the military in order to preserve his authority. He was overthrown by a military coup and gained asylum in Brazil.

***Stubbs** John Gascoigne with Bay Horse* (1791) Royal Collection, Windsor.

stroke a sudden episode involving the blood supply to the brain. It may also be termed a cerebrovascular accident (CVA) or apoplexy.

strontium metallic element, symbol Sr, atomic number 38, relative atomic mass 87.63. Isolated electrolytically by ◊Davy 1808, it is widely distributed in small quantities as sulphate and carbonate. The silver-white ductile metal, which is used in electronics, resembles calcium.

Strophanthus genus of tropical plants of Afro-Asia, family Apocynaceae. Seeds of the handsome climber *Strophanthus gratus* yield a poison, used on arrows in hunting, and in medicine as a heart stimulant.

structuralism a 20th-century philosophical movement which has been influential in such areas as linguistics, anthropology, and literary criticism. Inspired by the work of the Swiss linguist Ferdinand de Saussure (1857–1913), structuralists believe that objects should be analysed as systems of relations, rather than as positive entities.

structured programming the process of writing a computer program in small, independent parts. This allows a more easily controlled program development and the individual design and testing of the component parts. Structured programs are built up from units called modules which normally correspond to single procedures or functions. PASCAL was the forerunner of today's structured programming languages such as Modula 2 and ADA.

strychnine $C_{21}H_{22}O_2N_2$ a bitter-tasting poisonous alkaloid. It is a violent poison, causing muscular spasms.

Stuart, house of or *Stewart* royal family who inherited the Scottish throne 1371 and the English 1603.

Stubbs George 1724–1806. English artist, best known for paintings of horses. After the publication of his book of engravings *The Anatomy of the Horse* 1766, he was widely commissioned as an animal painter and group portraitist.

Stud, National British establishment founded 1915, and since 1964 located at Newmarket, where stallions are kept for visiting mares. It is now maintained by the Horserace Betting Levy Board.

sturgeon fish of sub-class Chondrostei. They are large, have five rows of bony plates, small mouths, and four barbels. They are voracious feeders.

Sturluson Snorri 1179–1241. Icelandic author of the Old Norse poems called ◊Eddas, and the *Heimskringla*, a saga chronicle of Norwegian kings until 1177.

Sturm Abteilung (SA) terrorist militia, also known as *Brownshirts*, of the ◊Nazi Party, established 1921 under the leadership of E ◊Röhm,

submersible

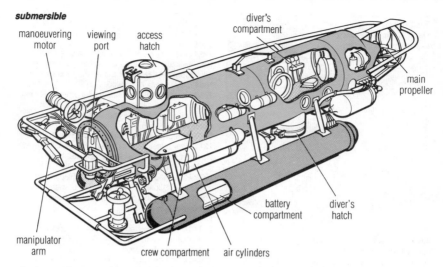

manoeuvering motor · viewing port · access hatch · diver's compartment · main propeller · manipulator arm · crew compartment · air cylinders · battery compartment · diver's hatch

in charge of physical training and political indoctrination.

Sturm und Drang (German 'storm and stress') German early Romantic movement in literature and music, from about 1775, concerned with depiction of extravagant passions. Writers associated include Herder, Goethe, and Schiller. The name is taken from a play by Friedrich von Klinger 1776..

Stuttgart capital of Baden-Württemberg, Germany; population (1988) 565,000. Industries include publishing and the manufacture of vehicles and electrical goods.

style in flowers, the part of the ◊carpel bearing the ◊stigma at its tip. In some flowers it is very short or completely lacking, while in others it may be long and slender, positioning the stigma in the most effective place to receive the pollen. Usually the style withers after fertilization but in certain species, such as traveller's joy *Clematis vitalba*, it develops into a long feathery plume which aids dispersal of the fruit.

Styx in Greek mythology, the river surrounding the underworld.

Suárez González Adolfo 1933– . Spanish politician, prime minister 1976–81. A friend of King Juan Carlos, he worked in the National Movement for 18 years, but in 1975 became president of the newly established Unión del Pueblo Español (UPE). He took office as prime minister at the request of the king, to speed the reform programme. He suddenly resigned 1981.

subatomic particle see ◊particle, subatomic, and ◊elementary particle.

sub judice (Latin 'under a judge') not yet decided by a court of law.

subliminal message a message delivered beneath the level of human consciousness. It may be visual (words or images flashed between the frames of a cinema or TV film), or aural (a radio message broadcast constantly at very low volume).

submarine an underwater ship, especially a warship. The first underwater boat was constructed for James I of England by the Dutchman Cornelius van Drebbel 1620. The first naval submarine, or submersible torpedo boat, the *Gymnote*, was launched by France 1888. The conventional submarine of World War I was driven by diesel engine on the surface and by battery-powered electric motors underwater. The diesel engine also drove a generator that produced electricity to charge the batteries. In 1954 the USA launched the first nuclear-powered submarine, the *Nautilus*. The nuclear submarine *Ohio*, USA, in service from 1981, is 170 m/560 ft long, weighs about 18,700 tonnes, and carries 24 Trident missiles, each with a dozen independently-targetable nuclear warheads. Operating depth is usually up to 300 m/1,000 ft, and nuclear power speeds of 30 knots (55 kph/34 mph) are reached. As in all nuclear submarines, propulsion is by steam ◊turbine driving a propeller. The steam is raised using the heat given off by the nuclear reactor (see ◊nuclear energy).

submersible a small submarine used by engineers and research scientists, and as a ferry craft to support diving operations. The most advanced submersibles are the so-called lock-out type, which have two compartments: one for the pilot, the

succession

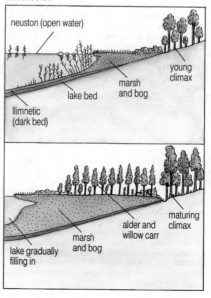

neuston (open water) · young climax · marsh and bog · lake bed · llimnetic (dark bed)

lake gradually filling in · marsh and bog · alder and willow carr · maturing climax

Sudan
Democratic Republic of
(*Jamhuryat es-Sudan*)

area 2,505,800 sq km/967,489 sq mi
capital Khartoum
towns Omdurman, Juba, Wadi Medani, al-Obeid, Kassala, Atbara, al-Qadarif, Kosti; chief port Port Sudan
physical fertile valley of the Nile River separates Libyan Desert in W from high rocky Nubian Desert in E
head of state and government Gen Omar Hassan Ahmed el-Bashir from 1989
political system military republic
exports cotton, gum arabic, sesame, groundnuts, durra
currency Sudanese pound
population (1990 est) 25,164,000; annual growth rate 2.9%
life expectancy men 51, women 55 (1989)
language Arabic 51% (official), local languages
religion Sunni Muslim 73%, animist 18%, Christian 9% (in S)
literacy 30% (1986)
GNP 8.5 bn (1988); $330 per head

chronology
1955 Civil war between Muslim north and non-Muslim south
1956 Sudan became an independent republic.
1958 Military coup replaced civilian government with Supreme Council of the Armed Forces.
1964 Civilian rule reinstated.
1969 Coup led by Col Gaafar Mohammed Nimeri established Revolutionary Command Council (RCC); country's name changed to Democratic Republic of Sudan.
1970 Agreement in principle on union with Egypt
1971 New constitution adopted; Nimeri confirmed president; and the Sudanese Socialist Union (SSU) declared the only legal party.
1972 Proposed Federation of Arab Republics; comprising Sudan, Egypt, and Syria, abandoned; Addis Ababa conference proposed autonomy for S provinces.
1974 National assembly established
1983 Nimeri re-elected amid growing opposition to his social, economic and religious policies; *Sharia* (Islamic law) introduced
1985 Nimeri deposed in a bloodless coupled by Gen Swar al Dahab, who set up a transitional military council; state of emergency declared.
1986 More than 40 political parties fought general election; coalition government formed
1987 Virtual civil war with Sudan People's Liberation Army (SPLA).
1988 Al-Mahdi formed new coalition; civil war between N and S created tens of thousands of refugees; floods made 1.5 million people homeless; peace pact signed with SPLA.
1989 Sadiq Al-Mahdi overthrown in coup led by Gen Omar Hasan Ahmed el-Bashir.
1990 Civil war continued with new SPLA offensive.
1991 Federal system introduced with division of country into nine states.
1993 SPLA leaders announced unilateral ceasefire after ten years war with central government.

---

other to carry divers. The diving compartment is pressurized and provides access to the sea.

subpoena in law, a writ requiring someone who might not otherwise come forward of his or her own volition to give evidence before a court or judicial official at a specific time and place.

subsidiary a company which is legally controlled by another company having 50% or more of its shares.

subsidy government payment or concession granted to a state, private company, or individual. A subsidy may be provided to keep prices down, to stimulate the market for a particular product, or because it is perceived to be in the public interest.

subsistence farming term used for farming when the produce is enough to feed only the farmer and family.

subway North American term for ◊underground railway.

succession in ecology, series of changes that occur in the structure and composition of the vegetation in a given area from the time it is first colonized, or after it has been disturbed (for example, by fire, flood, or clearance).

Succot or *sukkoth* Jewish festival celebrated in Oct, also known as the *Feast of Booths*, which commemorates the period when the Israelites

lived in the wilderness during the ◊Exodus from Egypt.

succubus a female spirit; see ◊incubus.

succulent plant a thick, fleshy plant that stores water in its tissues, for example cacti and stonecrops (*Sedum*). Succulents live either in areas where water is very scarce, such as deserts, or in places where it is not easily obtainable due to the high concentrations of salts in the soil, as in salt marshes. See also ◊xerophyte.

Suckling John 1609–1642. English poet and dramatist. He was an ardent Royalist who tried to effect ◊Strafford's escape from the Tower of London. On his failure, he fled to France and may have committed suicide. His chief lyrics appeared in *Fragmenta Aurea* and include 'Why so pale and wan, fond lover?'

Sucre legal capital and judicial seat of Bolivia; population (1988) 95,600. It stands on the central plateau at an altitude of 2,840 m/9,320 ft.

Sucre Antonio José de 1795–1830. Bolivian revolutionary leader. As chief lieutenant of Simon ◊Bolivar, he won several battles in freeing the colonies of South America from Spanish rule, and in 1826 became president of the new republic of Bolivia. After a mutiny by the army and invasion by Peru, he resigned 1828 and left the country to join

Bolivar. While crossing the Andes he was killed by thieves.

Sudan country in NE Africa, S of Egypt, with a Red Sea coast; it is the largest country in Africa.

Sudbury city in Ontario, Canada; population (1985) 154,000. A buried ◊meteorite yields 90% of the world's nickel.

sudden infant death syndrome (SIDS) formal term for ◊cot death, or crib death.

Sudetenland mountainous region of Czechoslovakia (now the Czech Republic), annexed by Germany under the ◊Munich Agreement 1938–45.

Suetonius (Gaius Suetonius Tranquillius) *c.* AD 69–140. Roman historian, author of *Lives of the Caesars* (Julius Caesar to Domitian).

Suez Canal artificial waterway, 160 km/100 mi long, from Port Said to Suez, linking the Mediterranean and Red seas, separating Africa from Asia, and providing the shortest sea route from Europe eastwards. It was opened 1869, nationalized 1956, blocked by Egypt during the Arab–Israeli war 1967, and not re-opened until 1975.

Suez Crisis incident Oct–Dec 1956 following the nationalization of the ◊Suez Canal by President Nasser of Egypt. In an attempt to reassert international control of the canal, Israel launched an attack towards the canal, after which British and French troops landed. Widespread international censure (Soviet protest, US non-support, and considerable opposition within Britain) soon led to withdrawal of the troops and the resignation of British prime minister Eden.

suffix a letter or group of letters added to the end of a word in order to form a new word. For example, the suffix 'ist' can be added to 'sex' to form the word 'sexist'.

Suffolk county of eastern England.
area 3,797 sq km/1,466 sq mi
towns administrative headquarters Ipswich, Bury St Edmunds, Lowestoft, Felixstowe
physical low undulating surface and flat coastline; rivers Waveney, Alde, Deben, Orwell, Stour; part of the Norfolk Broads
products cereals, sugar beet, working horses (Suffolk punches), fertilizers, agricultural machinery
population (1991) 629,900.

suffragette a woman fighting for the right to vote; in the USA, the preferred term was *suffragist*. In the UK, women's suffrage bills were repeatedly introduced and defeated in Parliament between 1886 and 1991, and a militant campaign was launched 1906 by Emmeline ◊Pankhurst and her daughters. In 1918 women were granted limited franchise; in 1928 it was extended to all women over 21. In the USA the 19th amendment to the constitution 1920 gave women the vote in federal and state elections.

suffragist US term for ◊suffragette.

Sufism a mystical movement of ◊Islam which originated in the 8th century. Sufis believe that deep intuition is the only real guide to knowledge. The movement has a strong strain of asceticism. The name derives from the *suf*, a rough woollen robe worn as an indication of their disregard for material things. There are a number of groups or brotherhoods within Sufism, each with its own method of meditative practice, one of which is the whirling dance of the ◊dervishes.

sugar sweet, soluble carbohydrate, either a monosaccharide or disaccharide. The major sources are tropical cane sugar, which accounts for about two-thirds of production, and temperate sugar beet. Cane, which is a grass, usually yields over 20 tonnes of sugar per hectare per year, while sugar

Sugar British businessman and entrepreneur Alan Sugar.

beet rarely exceeds 7 tonnes per hectare per year. Beet sugar is more expensive to produce, and is often subsidised by governments which wish to support the agricultural sector and avoid overdependence on the volatile world sugar market. Minor quantities of sugar are produced from the sap of maple trees, and from sorghum and date palms. Sugar is a major source of energy, but can also contribute to tooth decay.

monosaccharides are the simplest of sugars; examples include fructose and glucose, both obtained from fruit and honey.

disaccharides are sugars which, when hydrolysed by dilute acids, give two of either the same or different simple sugars (monosaccharides). An example is sucrose from sugar cane.

Sugar Alan 1947– . British businessman, founder of the Amstrad electronics company 1968 which holds a major position in the European personal computer market.

sugar maple North American ◊maple tree *Acer saccharum.*

Suger 1081–1151. Abbot of St Denis, Paris, elected 1122; counsellor to, and biographer of, Louis VI; regent of France during the Second Crusade. He rebuilt St Denis as the first large-scale Gothic building.

Suharto Raden 1921– . Indonesian politician and general. He ousted Sukarno to become president 1967. He ended confrontation with Malaysia, invaded East Timor 1975, and reached a cooperation agreement with Papua New Guinea 1979. His authoritarian rule has met domestic opposition from the left. He was re-elected 1973, 1978, 1983, 1988, and 1993.

suicide self-murder. Until 1961 it was a criminal offence in English law, if committed while of sound mind. In earlier times it was punished by the confiscation of the suicide's possessions. Even until 1823 burial was at night, without burial service, and with a stake through the heart. To aid and abet another's suicide is an offence, and euthanasia or mercy killing may amount to aiding in this context. In 1987, there were 4,000 suicides in England and Wales.

suite in music, formerly a grouping of old dance forms. The term has more recently been used to describe a set of instrumental pieces, sometimes assembled from a stage work, such as Tchaikovsky's *Nutcracker Suite.*

Sukarno Achmed 1901–1970. Indonesian nationalist, president 1945–67. During World War II he cooperated in the local administration set up by the Japanese, replacing Dutch rule. After the war he became the first president of the new Indonesian

Suharto General Suharto, president of Indonesia.

republic, becoming president-for-life 1966; he was ousted by ◊Suharto.

Sulawesi (formerly *Celebes*) island in E Indonesia, one of the Sunda Islands; area (with dependent islands) 190,000 sq km/73,000 sq mi; population (1980) 10,410,000. It is mountainous and forested, and produces copra and nickel.

Suleiman or *Solyman* 1494–1566. Ottoman sultan from 1520, known as *the Magnificent* and *the Lawgiver*. Under his rule the Ottoman Empire flourished and reached its largest extent. He made conquests in the Balkans, the Mediterranean, Persia, and N Africa, but was defeated at Vienna 1529 and Valletta 1565. He was a patron of the arts, a poet, and administrator.

Sulla Lucius Cornelius 138–78 BC. Roman general and politician, a leader of the senatorial party. Forcibly suppressing the democrats 88 BC, he departed for a successful campaign against ◊Mithridates VI of Pontus. The democrats seized power in his absence, but on his return Sulla captured Rome and massacred all opponents. As dictator, his reforms, which strengthened the senate, were backward-looking and shortlived. He retired 79 BC.

Sullivan Arthur (Seymour) 1842–1900. English composer, who wrote operettas in collaboration with William Gilbert, including *HMS Pinafore* 1878, *The Pirates of Penzance* 1879, and *The Mikado* 1885. Their partnership broke down 1896. Sullivan also composed oratorios.

Sully Maximilien de Béthune, Duc de Sully 1560–1641. French politician, who served with the Protestant ◊Huguenots in the wars of religion, and, as Henry IV's superintendent of finances 1598–1611, aided French recovery.

Sully-Prudhomme Armand 1839–1907. French poet, who wrote philosophical verse including *Les Solitudes/Solitude* 1869, *La Justice/Justice* 1878, and *Le Bonheur/Happiness* 1888. Nobel prize 1901.

sulphonamide drug any of a group of compounds containing the chemical group sulphonamide SO_2NH_2, or its derivatives, which were, and still are in places, used to treat bacterial diseases.

sulphur a non-metallic element, symbol S, atomic number 16, relative atomic mass 32.066. It is a pale yellow, odourless, brittle solid. Insoluble in water, but soluble in carbon disulphide, it is a good electrical insulator. It is widely used in the manufacture of sulphuric acid and in chemicals, explosives, matches, fireworks, dyes, fungicides, drugs, and in vulcanizing rubber, particularly for tyres.

sulphuric acid H_2SO_4 (also called *oil of vitriol*) a dense, oily, colourless liquid which gives out heat when added to water. It is used extensively in the chemical industry, petrol refining, and in manufacturing fertilizers, detergents, explosives, and dyes.

Sumatra or *Sumatera* second largest island of Indonesia, one of the Sunda Islands; area 473,600 sq km/182,800 sq mi; population (1980) 28,016,000. East of a longitudinal volcanic mountain range is a wide plain; both are heavily forested. Products include rubber, rice, tobacco, tea, timber, tin, and petroleum.

Sumer area of S Iraq where the Sumerian civilization was established; part of Babylonia.

Sumerian civilization the world's earliest civilization, which arose about 3400 BC in lower Mesopotamia (modern Iraq); it is known to have had a city-state, with priests as secular rulers, and a common culture. Cities included Lagash, Eridu, and Ur.

summer time practice (introduced in the UK 1916) whereby legal time from spring to autumn is an hour in advance of Greenwich mean time. Continental Europe 'puts the clock back' a month earlier than the UK in autumn. British *summer time* was permanently in force Feb 1940–Oct 1945 and Feb 1968–Oct 1971. Double summer time (2 hours in advance) was in force 1941–45 and 1947. In North America and Australia the practice is known as *daylight saving time*.

summons in law, a court order officially delivered, requiring someone to appear in court on a certain date. It is used for appearances at ◊Magistrates Courts, County Courts and for procedural matters in higher courts.

sumo wrestling national sport of Japan. Fighters of larger than average size (rarely less than 130 kg/21 st) try to push, pull, or throw each other out of a circular ring.

sumptuary law a law restraining excessive individual consumption, such as expenditure on dress, or attempting to control religious or moral conduct. The Romans had several sumptuary laws;

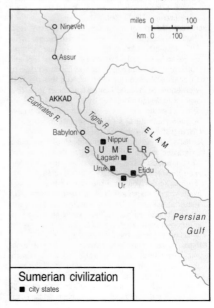

Sumerian civilization
■ city states

sumo wrestling *A sumo wrestling exhibition match in Paris, France 1986.*

for example the *lex Orchia* in 181 BC limited the number of dishes at a feast. In England sumptuary laws were introduced by Edward III and Henry VII.

Sun the ◊star at the centre of the ◊Solar System. Its diameter is 1,392,000 km/865,000 mi, its temperature at the surface about 6,000K, and at the centre 15,000,000K. It is composed of about 70% hydrogen and 30% helium, with other elements making up less than 1%. The Sun generates energy by nuclear ◊fusion reactions that turn hydrogen into helium at its centre. It is about 4,700,000,000 years old, with a predicted lifetime of 10,000,000,000 years. At the end of its life, it will expand to become a ◊red giant the size of Mars' orbit, and then shrink to become a ◊white dwarf. The Sun spins on its axis every 25 days near its equator, but more slowly towards the poles.

sundew insectivorous plant, genus *Drosera*, with viscid hairs on the leaves for catching prey.

sundial instrument measuring time by means of a shadow cast by the Sun. Almost completely superseded by the invention of clocks, it survives ornamentally in gardens. The dial is marked with the hours at graduated distances, and a style or gnomon (parallel to Earth's axis and pointing to the north) casts the shadow.

sunfish marine fish *Mola mola* with disc-shaped body 3 m/10 ft long found in all temperate and tropical oceans. The term also applies to fish of the North American freshwater Centrarchidae family, which have compressed, almost circular bodies, up to 80 cm/2.6 ft long, and are nestbuilders and avid predators.

sunflower plant of the genus *Helianthus*, family Compositae. The **common sunflower** *Helianthus annuus* probably native of Mexico, grows to 4.5 m/15 ft in favourable conditions. It is commercially cultivated in central Europe and the USSR for the oil-bearing seeds which follow the yellow-petalled flowers.

Sunni a member of the larger of the two main sects of ◊Islam, with about 680 million adherents. Sunni Muslims believe that the first four caliphs were all legitimate successors of the prophet Muhammad, and that guidance on belief and life should come from the Koran and the Hadith, and from the

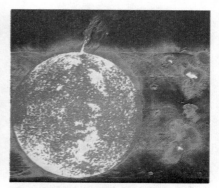

Sun *Ultraviolet image of the solar disc and solar prominence, recorded by the Skylab space station in 1973.*

Shari'a, not from a human authority or spiritual leader. Imams in Sunni Islam are educated lay teachers of the faith and prayer leaders. The name derives from the *Sunna*, Arabic 'rule', the body of traditional law evolved from the teaching and acts of Muhammad.

Sunningdale Agreement an agreement reached by the UK and Irish governments, together with the Northern Ireland executive, Dec 1973 in Sunningdale, England. The agreement included provisions for a power-sharing executive in Northern Ireland. However, the executive lasted only five weeks before the UK government was defeated in a general election, and a subsequent general strike May 1974 brought down the Northern Ireland government. The experiment has not been repeated.

sunspot a dark patch on the surface of the Sun, actually an area of cooler gas, thought to be caused by strong magnetic fields that block the outward flow of heat to the Sun's surface. Sunspots consist of a dark central **umbra**, about 4,000K, and a lighter surrounding **penumbra**, about 5,500K. They last from several days to over a month, ranging in size from 2,000 km to groups stretching for over 100,000 km. The number of sunspots visible at a given time varies from none to over 100 in a cycle averaging 11 years.

Sun Yat-sen or *Sun Zhong Shan* 1867–1925. Chinese nationalist politician, founder of the ◊Guomindang 1894, president of China 1912 after playing a vital part in deposing the emperor, and president of a breakaway government from 1921.

Sun Yat-sen *The founder of the Nationalist Guomindang party and guiding force behind the Chinese revolution in 1911.*

Sun Zhong Shan Pinyin transliteration of ◊Sun Yat-sen.

supercomputer the fastest, most powerful type of computer, capable of performing its basic operations in picoseconds (thousand-billionths of a second), rather than nanoseconds (billionths of a second) which is typical of most other computers.

superconductivity in physics, increase in electrical conductivity at low temperatures. The resistance of some metals and metallic compounds decreases uniformly with decreasing temperature until at a critical temperature (the superconducting point), within a few degrees of absolute zero (0K/–273°C), the resistance suddenly falls to zero. In this superconducting state, an electric current will continue indefinitely after the magnetic field has been removed, provided that the material remains below the superconducting point. In 1986 IBM researchers achieved superconductivity with some ceramics at –243°C; Paul Chu at the University of Houston achieved superconductivity at –179°C, a temperature which can be sustained using liquid nitrogen.

supercooling in physics, the lowering in temperature of a ◊saturated solution without crystallization taking place, forming a supersaturated solution. Usually crystallization rapidly follows the introduction of a small (seed) crystal or agitation of the supercooled solution.

superego in Freudian psychology, the element of the human mind concerned with the ideal, responsible for ethics and self-imposed standards of behaviour. It is characterized as a form of conscience, restraining the ◊ego, and responsible for feelings of guilt when the moral code is broken.

supergiant the largest and most luminous type of star known, with a diameter of up to 1,000 times that of the Sun and absolute magnitudes of between –5 and –9.

Superior, Lake largest of the ◊Great Lakes, and the second largest lake in the world; area 83,300 sq km/32,000 sq mi.

superior planet a planet that is farther away from the Sun than the Earth.

supermarket a large self-service shop selling food and household goods. The first was introduced by US retailer Clarence Saunders in Memphis, Tennessee, 1919.

supernova the explosive death of a star, which temporarily attains a brightness of 100 million Suns or more, so that it can shine as brilliantly as a small galaxy for a few days or weeks. *Type I* supernovae are thought to occur in ◊binary star systems in which gas from one star falls on to a white dwarf, causing it to explode. *Type II* supernovae occur in stars ten times or more as massive as the Sun, which suffer runaway internal nuclear reactions at the ends of their lives, leading to an explosion. These are thought to leave behind ◊neutron stars and ◊black holes. Gas ejected by the explosion causes an expanding radio source, such as the ◊Crab Nebula. Supernovae are thought to be the main source of elements heavier than hydrogen and helium.

superpower term used to describe the USA and the USSR from the end of World War II, when they emerged as significantly stronger than all other countries.

supersonic speed speed greater than that at which sound travels, measured in ◊Mach numbers. In dry air at 0°C, it is about 1,170 kph/727 mph, but decreases with altitude until, at 12,000 m/39,000 ft, it is only 1,060 kph, remaining constant above that height.

supplementary benefit in Britain, former name (1966–88) for *income support*, weekly payments by the state to low earners.

supply in economics, the production of goods or services for a market in anticipation of an expected ◊demand. There is no guarantee that supply will match actual demand.

supply and demand one of the fundamental approaches to economics, which examines and compares the supply of a good with its demand (usually in the form of a graph of supply and demand curves plotted against price). For a typical good, the supply curve is upward sloping (the higher the price, the more the manufacturer is willing to sell), while the demand curve is downward-sloping (the cheaper the good, the more demand there is for it). The point where the curves intersect is the equilibrium at which supply equals demand.

support environment in computing, a collection of programs (◊software) used to help people to design and write other programs. At its simplest, this includes an editor (word-processing software) and a ◊compiler for translating programs into executable form; but can also include interactive debuggers for locating faults, data dictionaries for keeping track of the data used, and rapid prototyping tools for producing quick, experimental mock-ups of programs.

Supremacy, Acts of two acts of the English Parliament 1534 and 1559, which established Henry VIII and Elizabeth I respectively as head of the English church in place of the pope.

Suprematism Russian art movement developed about 1913 by ◊Malevich, inspired in part by Futurist and Cubist ideas. The Suprematist paintings gradually became more severe, until in 1918 the *White on White* series showed white geometrical shapes on a white ground.

Supreme Court highest US judicial tribunal, composed of a chief justice (William Rehnquist from 1986) and eight associate justices. Vacancies are filled by the president, and members can be removed only by impeachment. In Britain, the Supreme Court of Judicature is made up of the Court of Appeal and the High Court.

Supremes, the US vocal group, pioneers of the ◊Motown sound, formed 1959 in Detroit, from 1962 a trio comprising, initially, Diana Ross (1944–), Mary Wilson (1944–), and Florence Ballard (1943–76). The most successful female group of the 1960s, they had a string of pop hits beginning with 'Where Did Our Love Go?' 1964 and 'Baby Love' 1964. Diana Ross left the group 1969.

Surabaya port on the island of Java, Indonesia; population (1980) 2,028,000. It has oil refineries and shipyards, and is a naval base.

Suraj-ud-Dowlah 1728–1757. Nawab of Bengal, India. He captured Calcutta from the British 1756 and imprisoned some of the British in the ◊Black Hole of Calcutta, but was defeated 1757 by Robert ◊Clive, and lost Bengal to the British at the Battle of ◊Plassey. He was killed in his capital, Murshidabad.

surd term for the mathematical root of a quantity that can never be exactly expressed because it is an ◊irrational number, for example, $\sqrt{3}$ = 1.73205....

Sûreté the criminal investigation department of the French police.

Surinam
Republic of
(*Republiek Suriname*)

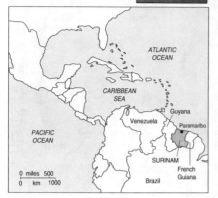

area 163,265 sq km/63,250 sq mi
capital Paramaribo
physical hilly and forested, with flat coast
head of state and government Ronald Venetiaan
from 1991

political system emergent democratic republic
exports alumina, bauxite, rice, timber
currency Suriname guilder
population (1990 est) 408,000 (Hindu 37%, Creole
31%, Javanese 15%); annual growth rate 1.1%
life expectancy men 66, women 71 (1989)
language Dutch (official), Creole, English
religion Christian 30%, Hindu 27%, Muslim 20%
literacy 65% (1989)
GNP $1.1 bn (1987); $2,920 per head
chronology
1954 Granted internal self-government as Dutch
Guiana.
1975 Achieved full independence with Dr Johan
Ferrier as president. About 40% of the population
emigrated to the Netherlands.
1980 Government overthrown in an army coup but
President Ferrier refused to recognize the military
regime and appointed Dr Henk Chin A Sen to lead a
civilian administration.
1982 Army, led by Lt-Col Desi Bouterse, seized
power, setting up a Revolutionary People's Front.
1985 Ban on political activities lifted.
1987 New constitution approved.
1988 Ramsewak Shankar elected president.
1989 Bouterse rejected peace accord reached with
guerrilla insurgents and vowed to continue fighting.
1990 Shankar deposed in army coup.
1991 New Front for Democracy won assembly
majority. Venetiaan elected president.
1992 Peace accord with guerrilla groups.

surface tension in physics, the property that
causes the surface of a liquid to behave as if it
were covered with a weak elastic skin; this is
why a needle can float on water. It is caused by
cohesive forces between ◊molecules of a liquid.
Allied phenomena include the formation of droplets
and the ◊capillary action by which water soaks into a
sponge.

surfing sport of riding on the crest of large waves
while standing on a narrow, keeled surfboard,
usually of light synthetic material, about 1.8 m/5 ft
long, as first developed in Hawaii and Australia.
Boardsailing is a recent development.

surgeon fish fish of the tropical marine family
Acanthuridae. It has a flat body up to 50 cm/1.7 ft
long, is brightly coloured, and has a moveable spine
on each side of the tail which can be used as a
weapon.

surgery in medicine, originally the removal of
diseased parts or foreign substances from the body.
The surgeon now uses not only the scalpel and
electric cautery, but beamed high-energy ultrasonic
waves, binocular magnifiers for microsurgery, and
the intense light energy of the laser.

Suriname country on the N coast of South
America, on the Atlantic coast, between Guyana
and French Guiana.

Surrealism movement in art, literature, and film,
which developed out of Dada about 1922. Led
by André ◊Breton, who produced the *Surrealist Manifesto* 1924, the Surrealists were inspired
by the thoughts and visions of the subconscious
mind. They explored highly varied styles and
techniques, and the movement was a dominant
force in Western art between World Wars I and
II. Surrealists include Buñuel, Dali, Arp, Ernst, and
Aragon.

Surrey county in S England
area 1,679 sq km/648 sq mi
towns administrative headquarters Kingston-
upon-Thames, Guildford, Woking

products market garden vegetables, agricultural
products, service industries
population (1991) 997,000
famous people John Galsworthy.

Surrey Henry Howard, Earl of Surrey *c.* 1517–
1547. English courtier and poet, executed on a
poorly-based charge of high treason. With ◊Wyatt,
he introduced the sonnet to England, and was a
pioneer of blank verse.

surrogacy the practice whereby a woman becomes pregnant with the intention of the resultant
child being handed over to a couple (of whom the
man may be the natural father, usually by artificial
insemination), usually in return for payment. It is
illegal in the UK.

surveying the accurate measurements of the
Earth's crust, or of land features or buildings.
It is used to establish boundaries, and to evalu-
ate the topography for engineering work. The
measurements used are both linear and angular,
and geometry and trigonometry are applied in the
calculations.

Sūrya in Hindu mythology, the Sun god, son of the
sky god Indra. His daughter, also named Sūrya, is a
female personification of the Sun.

suslik type of ground ◊squirrel.

suspension in physics, a ◊colloidal state consisting of a small solid particle dispersed in a liquid or
gas.

Sussex former county of England, on the south
coast, now divided into ◊East Sussex and ◊West
Sussex.

sustained yield cropping in ecology, the
removal of surplus individuals from a ◊population of
organisms so that the population maintains a constant size. This usually requires selective removal
of animals of all ages and both sexes to ensure a
balanced population structure.

Sutcliff Rosemary 1920–1992. British historical
novelist, who wrote for both adults and children.
Her books include *The Eagle of the Ninth* 1954,

Sutherland *Study for* Origins of the Land *(1950) Courtauld Collection, London.*

Tristan and Iseult 1971.

Sutherland Graham (Vivian) 1903–1980. English painter, active mainly in the south of France from the late 1940s. He is noted for portraits, landscapes, and religious subjects. His landscapes of the 1930s show a strong Surrealist influence.

Sutherland Joan 1926– . Australian soprano, who made her debut in England in 1952 in *The Magic Flute*; later roles included *Lucia di Lammermoor*, Donna Anna in *Don Giovanni*, and Desdemona in *Otello*. She retired in 1990.

sūtra in Buddhism, discourse attributed to the Buddha. In Hinduism, the term generally describes any sayings that contain moral instruction.

suttee Hindu custom whereby a widow committed suicide on her husband's funeral pyre. It was banned in the 17th century by the Moghul emperors and made illegal under British rule from 1829. There have been sporadic revivals. In 1988 a public ceremony took place in Rajasthan and a temple was erected on the site.

Sutton Hoo village near Woodbridge, Suffolk, England, where in 1939 a Saxon ship burial was excavated. It is the funeral monument of Raedwald, king of the East Angles, who died about 624 or 625. The jewellery, armour, and weapons discovered were placed in the British Museum, London.

suture a surgical stitch used to draw together the edges of a wound.

Suzhou (formerly *Soochow* and *Wuhsien* 1912–49) city on the ◊Grand Canal, in Jiangsu province, China; population (1983) 670,000. It has embroidery and jade-carving traditions, and Shizilin and Zhuozheng gardens. The city dates from about 1000 BC, the name Suzhou from the 7th century AD.

Suzuki Zenko 1911– . Japanese politician. A socialist member of the Diet 1947, he became a Liberal Democrat 1949, and prime minister 1980–82.

Svalbard Norwegian archipelago in the Arctic Ocean. The main island is Spitsbergen; other islands include North East Land, Edge Island, Barents Island, and Prince Charles Foreland.

area 62,000 sq km/24,000 sq mi

towns Long Year City on Spitsbergen

products coal, phosphates, asbestos, iron ore, and galena are mined by the USSR and Norway

population (1982) 4,000, including 2,500 Russians

Suzhou *The Tiger Hill Pagoda near Suzhou, China. Built in 961, it is five degrees out of perpendicular, making the top two metres out.*

Swaziland
Kingdom of
(*Umboso weSwatini*)

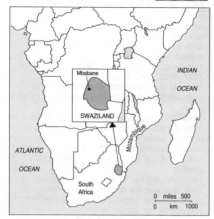

area 17,400 sq km/6704 sq mi
capital Mbabane
physical central valley; mountains in W
head of state and government King Mswati III from 1986
political system near-absolute monarchy

exports sugar, citrus, timber, asbestos, iron ore
currency lilangeni
population (1990 est) 779,000; annual growth rate 3%
life expectancy men 47, women 54
language Swazi 90%, English (both official)
religion Christian 57%, animist
literacy men 70%, women 66%
GNP $539 million (1987); $750 per head
chronology
1967 Granted internal self-government.
1968 Achieved full independence from Britain, within the Commonwealth, as the Kingdom of Swaziland, with King Sobhuza II as head of state.
1973 The king assumed absolute powers.
1978 New constitution adopted.
1982 King Sobhuza died and his place was taken by one of his wives, Dzeliewe, until his son, Prince Makhosetive, reached the age of 21.
1983 Queen Dzeliewe ousted by another wife, Ntombi
1984 It was announced that the crown prince would become king at the age of 18.
1986 Crown prince formally invested as King Mswati III.
1987 A power struggle developed between the advisory council Liqoqo and Queen Ntombi over the accession of the king. Mswati dissolved parliament and a new government was elected with Sotsha Dlamini as prime minister.
1991 Calls for democratic reform.
1992 Mswati dissolved parliament, assuming 'executive powers'.

---

history under the *Svalbard Treaty* 1925, Norway has sovereignty, but allows free scientific and economic access to others.

Sverdlovsk former name 1924–91 of Ekaterinberg, a town in Russia.

Svetambara ('white-clad') member of a sect of Jain monks (see ◊Jainism) who wear a white loincloth.

Svevo Italo. Pen name of Italian novelist Ettore Schmitz 1861–1928. His books include *As a Man Grows Older* 1898 and *Confessions of Zeno* 1923.

Swabia (German *Schwaben*) historic region of SW Germany, an independent duchy in the Middle Ages. It includes Augsburg and Ulm, and forms part of the *Länder* (states) of Baden-Württemberg, Bavaria, and Hessen.

Swahili people living along the coast of Kenya and Tanzania. The Swahili are not an isolated group, but are part of a mixed coastal society engaged in fishing and trading.

Swahili language a language of Bantu origin and strongly influenced by Arabic, a widespread ◊lingua franca of E Africa and the national language of Tanzania (1967) and Kenya (1973).

swallow insect-eating bird of the family Hirundinidae, found worldwide. It has a dark blue back, brown head and throat, and pinkish breast. Its tail feathers are forked, and its wings are long and narrow.

swami title of respect for a Hindu teacher.

swamp low-lying, permanently waterlogged tract of land, often overgrown with plant growth.

swamp cypress species of tree of the genus ◊*Taxodium*.

swan large long-necked bird of the duck family. The *mute swan Cygnus olor* is up to 150 cm/5 ft long, has white plumage, an orange bill with a black knob surmounting it, and black legs; the voice is a harsh hiss.

Swan Joseph Wilson 1828–1914. English inventor of the incandescent filament electric lamp, and of bromide paper for use in photography.

SWAPO (*South West African People's Organization*) organization formed 1959 in South West Africa (now ◊Namibia) to oppose South African rule. SWAPO guerrillas, led by Sam Nujoma, began attacking with support from Angola. Since 1966 SWAPO was recognized by the United Nations as the legitimate government of Namibia and won the first independent election 1989.

swastika cross in which the bars are extended at right angles, in the same clockwise or anti-clockwise direction. An Aryan and Buddhist mystic symbol, it was adopted by Hitler, first as the emblem of the Nazi Party, and then incorporated in the German national flag 1935–45.

Swazi kingdom Southern African kingdom, established by Sobhuza (died about 1840) as a result of the ◊Mfecane disturbances, and named after his successor Mswati (ruled 1840–75).

Swaziland country in SE Africa, bounded E by Mozambique and SE, S, W and N by South Africa.

sweat gland a ◊gland within the skin of mammals which produces surface perspiration. Primatial sweat glands are distributed over the whole body, but in most mammals are more localized; in cats and dogs they are normally restricted to the feet and around the face.

sweatshop a workshop or factory where employees work long hours for poor wages. Conditions are generally poor and employees may be under the legal working age. Exploitation of labour in this way is associated with unscrupulous employers, who often employ illegal immigrants in their labour force, or children in less developed economies.

Sweden
Kingdom of
(*Konungariket Sverige*)

area 450,000 sq km/173,745 sq mi
capital Stockholm
towns Göteborg, Malmö, Uppsala, Norrköping, Västerås
physical mountains in the NW; plains in the S: much of the land is forested
head of state Carl XVI Gustaf from 1973
head of government Carl Bildt from 1991
political system constitutional monarchy
exports aircraft, vehicles, ballbearings, drills, missiles, electronics, petrochemicals, textiles, furnishings.
currency krona

population (1990 est) 8,407,000 (including 17,000 Saami and 1,200,000 postwar immigrants from Finland, Turkey, Yugoslavia, Greece, Iran and other Nordic countries); annual growth rate 0.1%
language Swedish; Finnish- and Saami-speaking minorities
religion Lutheran 95%
literacy 99% (1989)
GNP $179 bn (1989); $11,783 per head
chronology
12th century United as an independent nation.
1397–1520 Under Danish rule.
1914–45 Neutral in both World Wars.
1951–76 Social Democratic Labour Party (SAP) in power.
1969 Olof Palme became SAP leader and premier.
1971 Constitution amended, creating a single-chamber parliament.
1975 Monarch's constitutional powers reduced.
1976 Thorbjörn Fälldin headed centre-right coalition.
1982 SAP, led by Palme, returned to power.
1985 SAP won the largest number of seats in parliament and formed a minority government, with communist support.
1986 Olof Palme murdered in Stockholm; Ingvar Carlsson became prime minister and SAP party leader.
1988 SAP re elected with reduced majority; Green Party increased its vote dramatically.
1990 SAP government resigned.
1991 Formal application for EC membership. New cralition government.
1992 Across-parties agreement to solve economic problems.

---

swede annual or biennial plant *Brassica napus*, widely cultivated for its edible root which is purple, white or yellow. The yellow variety is commonly known as *rutabaga*. It is similar to the turnip but is of greater food value, firmer fleshed, and longer keeping.

Sweden country in N Europe bounded W by Norway, NE by Finland and the gulf of Bothnia, SE by the Baltic Sea, and SW by the Kattegat.

Swedenborg Emanuel 1688–1772. Swedish theologian and philosopher. He trained as a scientist, but from 1747 concentrated on scriptural study, and in *Divine Love and Wisdom* 1763 concluded that the Last Judgment had taken place 1757, and that the *New Church*, of which he was the prophet, had now been inaugurated. His writings are the scriptures of the sect popularly known as Swedenborgians, and his works are kept in circulation by the Swedenborg Society, London.

Swedish language a member of the Germanic branch of the Indo-European language family, spoken in Sweden and Finland and closely related to Danish and Norwegian.

sweet cicely plant *Myrrhis odorata*, family Umbelliferae, native to S Europe: the root is eaten as a vegetable and the aniseed-flavoured leaves are used in salads.

sweet pea see ◊pea.

sweet potato tropical American plant *Ipomoea batatas*, family Convolvulaceae; the white/orange tuberous root is used as a source of starch and alcohol, and eaten as a vegetable.

sweet william biennial to perennial plant *Dianthus barbatus*, family Caryophyllaceae, native to S Europe and also known as the *bearded pink*. It is grown for its fragrant red, white, and pink flowers.

Sweyn I died 1014. King of Denmark from *c.* 986, and nicknamed 'Forkbeard'. He raided England, finally conquered it 1013, and styled himself king, but his early death led to the return of ◊Ethelred II.

swift fast-flying, short-legged bird of the family Apodidae, of which there are about 75 species, found largely in the tropics. They are 9–23 cm/4–11 in long, with brown or grey plumage, and a forked tail. They are capable of flying at 110 kph/70 mph.

Swift Jonathan 1667–1745. Irish satirist and Anglican cleric, known as the author of *Gulliver's Travels*, 1726, an allegory describing travel to lands inhabited by giants, miniature people, and intelligent horses. Other works include *The Tale of the Tub* 1704, attacking corruption in religion and learning: contributions to the Tory paper *The Examiner* of which he was editor 1710–11; *A Modest Proposal* 1729 which suggested that children of the poor should be eaten; and many essays and pamphlets.

swim bladder a thin-walled air-filled sac found in bony fishes, between the gut and the spine. Air enters the bladder from the gut or from surrounding ◊capillaries, and changes of air pressure within the bladder maintain buoyancy whatever the water depth.

swimming self-propulsion of the body through water. As a competitive sport there are four strokes; freestyle, breast-stroke, backstroke, and butterfly. Distances of races vary between

swingwing

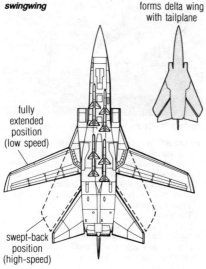

forms delta wing with tailplane

fully extended position (low speed)

swept-back position (high-speed)

50–1500 m. Olympic-size pools are 50 m/55 yd long and have eight lanes.

swimming, synchronized   a swimming discipline which demands artistry as opposed to speed. Competitors, either individual (solo) or in pairs, perform rhythmic routines to music. Points are awarded for interpretation and style. It was introduced into the Olympic swimming programme 1984.

Swinburne   Algernon Charles 1837–1909. English poet. He attracted attention with the choruses of his Greek-style tragedy *Atalanta in Calydon* 1865, but he and ◊Rossetti were attacked 1871 as leaders of 'the fleshly school of poetry', and the revolutionary politics of *Songs before Sunrise* 1871 alienated others.

swing music   jazz style popular in the 1930s–40s, with a simple harmonic base of varying tempo from the rhythm section (percussion, guitar, piano), and superimposed solo melodic line, for example from trumpet, clarinet, or saxophone. Exponents included Benny Goodman, Duke Ellington, and Glenn Miller.

swing-wing   correctly called a variable-geometry wing; an aircraft wing that can be moved during flight to provide a suitable configuration for both low-speed and high-speed flight. The British engineer Barnes ◊Wallis developed the idea of the swing-wing, now used in several aircraft, including the European *Tornado* and the American *F-111*. These craft have their wings projecting nearly at right-angles for take-off and landing and low-speed flight, but swing them back for high-speed flight.

Swiss cheese plant   common name for ◊*Monstera*, plant of the Arum family.

Swithun, St   died 862. English priest, chancellor of King Ethelwolf and bishop of Winchester from 852. According to legend, the weather on his feast day (15 Jul) is said to continue as either wet or fine for 40 days.

Switzerland   landlocked country in W Europe, bounded to the N by Germany, to the E by Austria, to the S by Italy, and to the W by France.

sword-fish   fish of the family Xiphiidae, characterized by the long sword-like beak protruding from the upper jaw. They may reach 4.5 m/ 15 ft in length, and weigh 450 kg/1000 lbs.

sycamore   tree *Acer pseudoplatanus*, native to Europe. The leaves are five-lobed, and the hanging racemes of flowers are followed by winged fruits. The timber is used for furniture making.

Sydney   capital and port of New South Wales, Australia; population (1990) 3,656,900. Industries include engineering, oil refining, electronics, scientific equipment, chemicals, clothing, and furniture.

syllogism   a set of philosophical statements devised by Aristotle in his work on logic. It establishes the conditions under which a valid conclusion follows or does not follow by deduction from given premises. The following is an example of a valid syllogism:

Switzerland
Swiss Confederation (German *Schweiz*, French *Suisse*)

area 41,288 sq km/15,941 sq mi
capital Bern
towns Zürich, Geneva, Lausanne; river port Basel

physical most mountainous country in Europe
head of state and government Adolf Ogi from 1993
political system federal democratic republic
exports electrical goods, chemicals, pharmaceuticals, watches, precision instruments, confectionery
currency Swiss franc
population (1990 est) 6,628,000, annual growth rate 0.2%
life expectancy men 74, women 82 (1989)
language German 65%, French 18%, Italian 12% Romansch 1% (all official)
religion Roman Catholic 50%, Protestant 48%
literacy 99% (1989)
GNP $111 bn (1988); $26,309 per head
chronology
1648 Became independent of the Holy Roman Empire.
1798–1815 Helvetic Republic established
1847 Civil war resulted in greater centralization.
1971 Women given the vote in federal elections.
1984 First female cabinet minister appointed.
1986 Referendum rejected a proposal for membership of United Nations.
1989 Referendum supported abolition of citizen army and military service.
1991 18-year-olds allowed to vote in national elections.
1992 Closer ties with EC rejected in national referendum.

sycamore

Sydney The Opera House in Sydney, Australia.

'All men are mortal, Socrates is a man, therefore Socrates is mortal'.

symbiosis any close relationship between two organisms of different species, and one where both partners benefit from the association. A well-known example is the pollination relationship between insects and flowers, where the insects feed on nectar and carry pollen from one flower to another. This is sometimes known as ◊mutualism. Symbiosis in a broader sense includes ◊commensalism and ◊parasitism.

symbol in general, something that stands for something else. A symbol may be an aesthetic device, or a sign used to convey information visually, thus saving time, eliminating language barriers, or overcoming illiteracy.

symbolic processor a computer purpose-built to run so-called symbol-manipulation programs rather than programs involving a great deal of numerical computation. Mostly, they exist for the ◊artificial intelligence language ◊Lisp, although some have also been built to run ◊Prolog.

symbolism in the arts, the use of symbols as a device for concentrating or intensifying meaning. In particular, the term is used for a late 19th-century movement in French poetry, associated with Verlaine, Mallarmé, and Rimbaud, who used words for their symbolic rather than concrete meaning.

Symington William 1763–1831. Scottish engineer who built the first successful steamboat. He invented the steam road locomotive 1787 and a steamboat engine 1788. His steamboat, the *Charlotte Dundas* was completed 1802.

Symons Arthur 1865–1945. Welsh critic, follower of ◊Pater, and friend of Toulouse-Lautrec, Mallarmé, Beardsley, Yeats, and Conrad. He introduced Eliot to the work of Laforgue and wrote *The Symbolist Movement in Literature* 1900.

symphonic poem in music, a term originated by Liszt for his 13 one-movement orchestral works which interpret a story from literature or history, and used by many other composers. Richard Strauss preferred the title *tone poem*.

symphony a musical composition for orchestra, traditionally in four separate but closely related movements. It developed from the smaller ◊sonata form, the Italian overture, and the dance suite of the 18th century.

symptom any change or manifestation in the body suggestive of disease as perceived by the sufferer. Symptoms are subjective phenomena.

synagogue a Jewish place of worship, also (in the USA) called a temple. As an institution it dates from the destruction of the temple in Jerusalem 70 AD.

synapse the junction between two ◊nerve cells of an animal, or between a nerve cell and a muscle. The two cells involved are not in direct contact but separated by a narrow gap called the synaptic cleft. Across this gap flow chemical ◊neurotransmitters, which have a specific effect on the receiving cell when they bind to special receptors on its surface. The response may be a nervous impulse in a nerve cell, for example contraction in a muscle cell.

synapsida mammal-like reptiles living 315–195 million years ago, whose fossil record is largely complete, and who were for a long time the dominant land animals.

syncline geological term for a fold in the rocks of the Earth's crust in which the layers or ◊beds dip inwards, thus forming a trough-like structure with a sag in the middle. The opposite, with the beds arching upwards, is an ◊anticline.

syncopation in music, the deliberate upsetting of rhythm by shifting the accent to a beat that is normally unaccented.

syncope a temporary loss of consciousness, as in ◊fainting.

syndicalism political movement that rejected parliamentary activity in favour of direct action, culminating in a revolutionary general strike to secure worker ownership and control of industry. The idea originated under Robert ◊Owen's influence in the 1830s, acquired its name and its more violent aspects in France from the philosopher ◊Sorel, and also reached the USA (IWW). After 1918 syndicalism was absorbed in communism, although it continued to have an independent existence in Spain until the late 1930s.

syndrome a collection of signs and symptoms which always occur together, thus characterizing a particular condition or disorder.

synecdoche a ◊figure of speech whose Greek name means 'accepted together' and which either uses the part to represent the whole ('There were some new faces at the meeting', rather than *new people*), or the whole to stand for the part ('The West Indies beat England at cricket', rather than naming the national teams in question).

synergy (Greek 'combined action') in medicine, the 'co-operative' action of two or more drugs, muscles, or organs; in architecture, the augmented strength of systems, where the strength of a wall is greater than the added total of its individual units.

Synge J(ohn) M(illington) 1871–1909. Irish playwright, a leading figure in the Irish dramatic revival of the early 20th century. His six plays reflect the speech patterns of the Aran Islands and W Ireland. They include *In the Shadow of the Glen* 1903, *Riders to the Sea* 1904, and *The Playboy of the Western World* 1907, which caused riots at the Abbey Theatre, Dublin, when first performed.

synodic period the interval between successive oppositions of a superior planet (those from Mars outwards) or inferior ◊conjunctions of an inferior planet (Venus or Mercury).

synonymy near or identical meaning between or among words. There are very few strict synonyms in any language, although there may be many near-synonyms, depending upon the contexts in which the words are used. Thus, 'brotherly' and 'fraternal' are synonyms in English, but a 'brotherhood' is not exactly the same as a 'fraternity'.

synovial fluid a viscous yellow fluid which bathes movable joints between the bones of vertebrates. It nourishes and lubricates the ◊cartilage at the end of each bone.

synthesizer device which uses electrical components to produce sounds, such as conventional musical instruments, or in free creativity. In *pre-set synthesizers*, the sound of various instruments is produced by a built-in computer-type memory. In *programmable synthesizers* any number of new instrumental or other sounds may be produced at the will of the performer. *Speech synthesizers* can break down speech into 128 basic elements (allophones), which are then combined into words and sentences, as in the voice of electronic teaching aids.

synthetic an artificial material made from chemicals. Many of the materials used in everyday life are artificial, including plastics (polythene, polystyrene), synthetic fibres (nylon, acrylics, polyesters), synthetic resins, and synthetic rubber. Plastics are made mainly from petroleum chemicals by the process of ◊polymerization, in which small molecules are joined to make very large ones.

synthetic in philosophy, a term employed by Immanuel ◊Kant to describe a judgment in which the predicate is not contained within the subject,

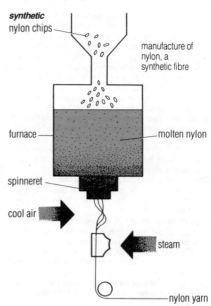

synthetic manufacture of nylon, a synthetic fibre

- nylon chips
- furnace
- molten nylon
- spinneret
- cool air
- steam
- nylon yarn

for example: 'The flower is blue' is synthetic, since every flower is not blue. It is the converse of ◊analytic.

synthetic fibre an artificial fibre, unknown in nature. There are two kinds of artificial fibres. One is made from natural materials that have been

---

Syria
Syrian Arab Republic (*al-Jamhouriya al-Arabia as-Souriya*)

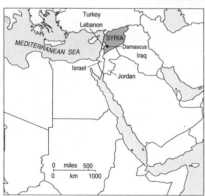

area 186,000 sq km/72,000 sq mi
capital Damascus
towns Aleppo, Homs, Hama; chief port Lattakia
physical mountains alternate with fertile plains and desert areas; river Euphrates
head of state and government Hafiz al-Assad from 1971
political system socialist republic
exports cotton, cereals, oil, phosphates
currency Syrian pound
population (1990 est) 12,471,000; annual growth rate 3.5%

life expectancy men 67, women 69 (1989)
language Arabic (official)
religion Sunni Muslim 74%; ruling minority Alawite and other Islamic sects 16%, Christian 10%
literacy men 76%, women 43% (1985)
GNP $17 bn (1986); $702 per head
chronology
1946 Achieved full independence from France.
1958 Merged with Egypt to form the United Arab Republic (UAR).
1961 UAR disintegrated.
1967 Six-Day War resulted in the loss of territory to Israel.
1970–71 Syria supported Palestinian guerrillas against Jordanian troops.
1971 Following a bloodless coup, Hafiz al-Assad became president.
1973 Israel consolidated its control of the Golan Heights after the Yom Kippur War.
1976 Troops committed to the civil war in Lebanon.
1981–82 Further military engagements in Lebanon.
1982 Islamic militant uprising suppressed.
1984 Presidents Assad and Gemayel approved a plan for government of national unity in Lebanon.
1985 Assad secured the release of US hostages hijacked by an extremist Shi'ite group.
1987 Improved relations with USA and attempts to secure the release of western hostages in Lebanon.
1989 Diplomatic relations with Morocco and Egypt restored.
1990 Diplomatic relations with Britain restored.
1991 Syria fought against Iraq in the Gulf War. President Assad agreed to Middle East peace plan. Assad re-elected as president.

chemically processed in some way. ◊Rayon, for example, is made by processing the cellulose in woodpulp. The other type is the true synthetic fibre, made entirely from chemicals. ◊Nylon was the original synthetic fibre, made from chemicals obtained from petroleum (crude oil). Fibres are drawn out into long threads or filaments, usually by so-called 'spinning' methods, melting or dissolving the parent material and then forcing it through the holes of a perforated plate, or spinneret.

syphilis a venereal disease caused by the spiral-shaped bacterium (spirochete) *Treponema pallidum*. Untreated, it runs its course over many years, starting with a hard sore, or chancre, develops on the genitals within a month of infection, and leads to blindness, insanity, and death.

Syria country in W Asia, on the Mediterranean, bounded to the N by Turkey, to the E by Iraq, to the S by Jordan, and to the SW by Israel and Lebanon.

Syriac language an ancient Semitic language, originally the Aramaic dialect spoken in and around Edessa (now in Turkey) and widely used in W Asia about 700 BC–700 AD. From the 3rd to 7th centuries it was an important Christian liturgical and literary language.

syringa genus of shrubs, including ◊lilac *Syringa vulgaris*. It is also the common name for the ◊mock orange.

Système international d'Unité see ◊SI units.

systemic in medicine, relating to or affecting the body as a whole. A systemic disease is one whose effects are present throughout the body, as opposed to local disease, such as ◊conjunctivitis, which is confined to one part.

systems analysis in computing, an early stage in the process of constructing software, concerned with the analysis of the problem that the program is intended to solve. It involves developing a formalized model of the problem using diagrams and formal languages (part of the ◊software project lifecycle).

systems design in computing, a stage in the development of a program, concerned with its detailed design. It typically involves the use of diagramming conventions (such as ◊flow charts) and formalized language (pseudocode) to express the logic of the design. See also ◊software project lifestyle and ◊systems analysis.

Szczecin (German *Stettin*) industrial (shipbuilding, fish processing, synthetic fibres, tools, iron) port on the river Oder, in NW Poland; population (1985) 391,000.

Szymanowski Karol (Maliej) 1882–1937. Polish composer of orchestral works, operas, piano music, and violin concertos. He was director of the Conservatoire in Warsaw from 1926.

of the Roman Empire, *Historiae* and *Annales*, covering the years 96BC–AD69 and AD14–68 respectively.

taekwon-do Korean ◊martial art similar to ◊karate which includes punching and kicking. It officially became part of Korean culture 1955 and was included as a demonstration Olympic sport 1988.

Tafawa Balewa Alhaji Abubakar 1912–1966. Nigerian politician, prime minister from 1957. Entering the House of Representatives 1952, he was minister of works 1952–54 and transport 1954–57. He was assassinated in the coup of Jan 1966.

Taft William Howard 1857–1930. 27th president of the USA 1909–13, a Republican. Born in Cincinnati. He was secretary of war 1904–08 in Theodore Roosevelt's administration, but as president his conservatism provoked Roosevelt to stand against him in the 1912 election. Taft served as chief justice of the Supreme Court 1921–30.

Tagliacozzi Gaspare 1546–1599. Italian surgeon who pioneered plastic surgery. He was first to repair noses lost in duels or through ◊syphilis, and also repaired ears.

Taglioni Marie 1804–1884. Italian dancer. The most important ballerina of the Romantic era, acclaimed for her ethereal style and exceptional lightness, she was the first to use ◊pointe work, or dancing on the toes, as an expressive part of ballet rather than sheer technique. She created many roles, including the title role in her father's ballet *La Sylphide* 1832, first performed at the Paris Opéra.

Tagore Rabindranath 1861–1941. Indian writer in Bengali. One of the most influential Indian authors of the 20th century. Nobel prize 1913.

Tahiti largest of the Society Islands, in ◊French Polynesia; capital Papeete; area 1,040 sq km/402 sq mi; population (1983) 116,000. Tahiti was visited by Capt James ◊Cook 1769 and by Bligh of the *Bounty* 1788. It came under French protection 1843, becoming a colony 1880.

t abbreviation for *tonne*.

table tennis indoor ball game played on a rectangular table by two or four players. It was developed in Britain about 1880 and derived from lawn tennis. It is popularly known as *ping-pong*.

tachograph combined speedometer and clock which records a vehicle's speed on a small card disk, magnetic disk or tape, and also the length of time the vehicle is moving or stationary. It is used to monitor a lorry-driver's working practice.

Tacitus Publius or Gaius Cornelius *c.* AD 55–120. Roman historian. A public orator in Rome, he was consul under Nerva (97) and governor of Asia 112–13. He wrote a life of Agricola (whose daughter he married in 77) and a description of the German tribes (*Germania* 98), but is better known for his histories

---

Tajikistan
Republic of

area 143,100 sq km/55,251 sq mi
capital Dushanbe
towns Khodzhent (formerly Leninabad), Kurgan-Tyube, Kulyab
physical mountainous, mostly lying above 3,000 m/10,000 ft; huge mountain glaciers are the source

of many rapid rivers
head of state Imamoli Rahmanov (acting)
head of government Abdumalik Abdulojonov from 1992
political system emergent democracy
products fruit, cereals, cotton, cattle, sheep, silks, carpets, coal, lead, zinc, chemicals, oil, gas
population (1990) 5,300,000 (63% Tajik, 24% Uzbek, 8% Russian, 1% Tatar, 1% Kyrgyz, 1% Ukrainian)
language Tajik, similar to Farsi (Persian)
religion Sunni Muslim
chronology
1921 Part of Turkestan Soviet Socialist Autonomous Republic.
1929 Became a constituent republic of USSR.
1990 Ethnic Tajik/Armenian conflict in Dushanbe resulted in anti-government rioting.
1991 March: maintenance of Union endorsed in referendum. Aug: President Makhkamov forced to resign after failed anti-Gorbachev coup. Sept: declared independence; Nabiyev elected president; state of emergency declared. Dec: joined new Commonwealth of Independent States (CIS).
1992 Jan: Nabiyev temporarily ousted; state of emergency lifted. Feb: joined the Muslim Economic Cooperation Organization (ECO). March: admitted into United Nations (UN). May: coalition government formed. Sept: Nabiyev forced to resign; replaced by Akbasho Iskandrov; Abdumalik Abdulojonov became prime minister.
1993 Civil war between communist forces and Islamic and pro-democracy groups continued.

Taiwan
Republic of China (*Chung Hua Min Kuo*)

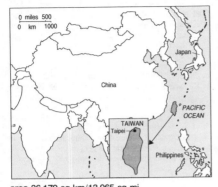

area 36,179 sq km/13,965 sq mi
capital Taipei
towns ports Keelung, Kaohsiung
physical island (formerly Formosa) off the coast of the People's Republic of China; mountainous, with lowlands in the W
head of state Lee Teng-hui from 1988
head of government Lien Chan from 1993

political system emergent democracy
exports textiles, steel, plastics, electronics, foodstuffs
currency New Taiwan dollar
population (1990) 20,454,000 (84% Taiwanese, 14% mainlanders); growth rate 1.4% p.a.
language Mandarin Chinese (official); Taiwan, Hakka dialects
religion officially atheist. Taoist, Confucian, Buddhist, Christian
literacy 89% (1983)
GNP $119.1 bn (1984); $6,200 per head
chronology
1683 Taiwan (Formosa) annexed by China.
1895 Ceded to Japan.
1945 Recovered by China.
1949 Flight of Nationalist government to Taiwan after Chinese Communist revolution.
1954 US–Taiwainese mutual defence treaty.
1971 Expulsion from United Nations.
1975 President Chiang Kai-Shek died; replaced as Kuomintang leader by his son Chiang Ching-kuo.
1979 USA severed diplomatic relations.
1986 Democratic Progressive Party (DPP) formed as opposition party to the Nationalist Kuomintang (KMT).
1988 New president Lee Teng-hui accelerated political liberalization.
1991 End to civil war with China; KMT won assembly elections.
1993 Lien Chan became premier.

Tai   speakers of Tai languages, all of which belong to the Sino-Tibetan family. There are over 60 million speakers of Tai languages.

Tai Chi   series of 108 complex slow-motion movements, designed to ensure effective circulation of the 'chi' or intrinsic energy of the Universe through the mind and body. It derives partly from the Shaolin ◊martial arts of China, and partly from ◊Taoism.

taiga   Russian name for the heavily forested territory, some of it in the ◊permafrost zone, in Siberia. There is rich and varied fauna and flora, in delicate balance because conditions are precarious; this ecology is threatened by railway construction, mining, and forestry. The name is also applied to similar regions elsewhere.

taipan   type of small-headed cobra *Oxyuranus scutellatus* found in NE Australia and New Guinea. Some 3 m/10 ft long, it has a brown back and yellow belly. Its venom is fatal within minutes.

Taipei   (*mainland spelling Taibei*) capital and commercial centre of Taiwan; population (1990) 2,719,700. Industries include electronics, plastics, textiles, and machinery.

Taiwan   country in SE Asia, officially the Republic of China, occupying the island of Taiwan between the E China Sea and the S China Sea.

Talyuan   capital of Shanxi province, NE China; population (1989) 1,900,000. Industries include iron, steel, agricultural machinery, and textiles.

Tajik   (or *Tadzhik*) speakers of any of the Tajik dialects which belong to the Iranian branch of the Indo-European family.

Tajikistan   (formerly until 1992 *Tadzhikistan*) country in central Asia, bounded by Kyrgyzstan and Uzbekistan, E by China, and S by Afghanistan and Pakistan.

Taj Mahal   a white marble mausoleum built on the river Jumna near Agra, India. Built by Shah Jehan to the memory of his favourite wife, it is a celebrated example of Indo-Islamic architecture, the fusion of Muslim and Hindu styles.

takahe   bird *Notornis mantelli* of the rail family and native to New Zealand. A heavy flightless species,

about 60 cm/2 ft tall, with blue and green plumage and a red beak, the takahe was thought to have become extinct at the end of the 19th century, but in 1948 small numbers were rediscovered in the tussock grass of a mountain valley on South Island.

Takeshita   Noboru 1924– . Japanese right-wing politician. He was elected to parliament as a Liberal Democratic Party (LDP) deputy 1958, and was minister of finance 1982–86. He became president of the LDP and prime minister in Oct 1987. His administration was undermined by the Recruit insider-trading scandal, which came to light in June 1988 and in April 1989 he resigned because of his involvement.

Talbot   William Henry Fox 1800–1877. British pioneer of photography. He invented the ◊calotype process, the first ◊negative/positive method, and had made ◊photograms several years before Daguerre's invention was announced.

talc   a mineral, hydrated magnesium silicate, $Mg_3Si_4O_{11}.H_2O$). It occurs in crystals, but the

***Taj Mahal** Perhaps the most famous monument in Asia, the Taj Mahal was built over a period of 20 years by more than 20,000 labourers (1634–56).*

massive form, known as *steatite* or *soapstone*, is more common. Talc is very soft, rated 1 on the Mohs scale of hardness. It is used in cosmetics, for lubricants, and as an additive in paper manufacture.

Talleyrand Charles Maurice de Talleyrand-Périgord 1754–1838. French politician, bishop of Autun 1789–91. A supporter of moderate reform in the ◊French Revolution, he fled to the USA during the Reign of Terror (persecution of anti-revolutionaries), but became foreign minister under the Directory 1797–99 and under Napoleon 1799–1807. He represented France at the Congress of ◊Vienna 1814–15, and was ambassador to London 1830–34.

Tallinn (German *Reval*) naval port and capital of Estonia; population (1987) 478,000. Industries include electrical and oil drilling machinery, textiles, and paper. Founded 1219, it was a ◊Hanseatic port, passed to Sweden 1561, and to Russia 1750.

Tallis Thomas *c.* 1505–1585. English composer. A master of the polyphonic style, he wrote masses, anthems, and other church music, including a setting for five voices of the *Lamentations of Jeremiah*, and for 40 of *Spem in alium*.

tallith four-cornered, fringed shawl worn by Jewish men during morning prayers.

Talmud chief work of Jewish post-Biblical literature, providing a compilation of ancient Jewish law and tradition, based on the ◊*Mishna*. To this was added the *Gemara*, discussions centring on its texts, during the 3rd and 4th centuries AD.

tamandua tree-living toothless anteater *Tamandua tetradactyla* found in tropical forests and tree savannah from S Mexico to Brazil. About 56 cm/1.8 ft long with a prehensile tail of equal length, it has strong foreclaws with which it can break into nests of tree ants and termites, which it licks up with its narrow tongue.

Tamar in the Old Testament, the sister of ◊Absalom. She was raped by her half-brother Amnon, who was then killed by Absalom.

tamarind evergreen tropical tree *Tamarindus indica*, family Leguminosae, with pinnate leaves, and reddish-yellow flowers, followed by pods. The pulp surrounding the seeds is used as a flavouring and medicinally.

tamarisk shrub of the genus *Tamarix*, flourishing in warm, salty barren deserts regions. *The common tamarisk Tamarix gallica* has scale-like leaves and spikes of very small, pink flowers.

Tambo Oliver 1917–1993. South African nationalist politician, in exile from 1960, president of the African National Congress (ANC) 1977–91, when owing to poor health, he took the honorary post of national Chair, and the presidency passed back to Nelson ◊Mandela.

tambourine musical percussion instrument of ancient origin consisting of a shallow drum with a single and loosely set jingles in the rim.

Tamerlane or *Timur i Leng* 1336–1405. Mongol ruler of ◊Samarkand from 1369, who conquered Persia, Azerbaijan, Armenia, Georgia; defeated the ◊Golden Horde 1395; sacked Delhi 1398; invaded Syria and Anatolia, and captured the Ottoman Sultan in Ankara 1402; and died invading China. He is the subject of Christopher Marlowe's play *Tamburlaine the Great c.* 1587.

Tamil person of Tamil culture. The majority of Tamils live in the Indian state of Tamil Nadu (formerly Madras), though there are approximately 3 million Tamils in Sri Lanka.

Tamil language a Dravidian language of SE India, spoken principally in the state of Tamil Nadu and also in N Sri Lanka. It is written in its own distinctive script.

Tamil Nadu state of SE India; former name to 1968 *Madras State*
area 130,069 sq km/50,207 sq mi
capital Madras
products mainly industrial (cotton, textiles, silk, electrical machinery, tractors, rubber, sugar refining)
population (1991) 55,638,300
language Tamil
history the present state was formed in 1956.

Taming of the Shrew, The a comedy by William Shakespeare, first performed 1593–94. Bianca, who has many suitors, must not marry before her sister Katherina (the shrew). Petruchio agrees to woo Katherina so that his friend Hortensio may marry Bianca. Petruchio succeeds in taming Katherina but Bianca marries another.

Tammany Hall Democratic Party organization in New York. It originated in 1789 as the Society of St Tammany, named after an American Indian chief. It was dominant from 1800 until the 1930s and gained a reputation for gangsterism; its domination was broken by Mayor ◊La Guardia.

Tammuz in Sumerian legend, a vegetation god, who died at midsummer and was brought back from the underworld in spring by his lover Ishtar. His cult spread over Babylonia, Syria, Phoenicia, and Palestine. In Greek mythology Tammuz appears as ◊Adonis.

Tampa port and resort in W Florida, USA; population (1990) 280,000. Industries include fruit and vegetable canning, shipbuilding, and the manufacture of fertilizers, clothing, and cigars.

Tampere (Swedish *Tammerfors*) city in SW Finland; population (1990) 172,600. The second largest city in Finland; industries include textiles, paper, footwear, and turbines.

Tanabata Japanese 'star festival' celebrated annually on 7 Jul, introduced from China in the 8th century. It is dedicated to Altair and Vega, two stars in the constellation Aquila, which are united once yearly in the Milky Way. According to legend they represent two star-crossed lovers allowed by the gods to meet on that night.

tanager bird of the family Emberizidae, related to buntings. There are about 230 species in forests of Central and South America, all brilliantly-coloured. They are 10–20 cm/4–8 in long, with plump bodies and conical beaks.

Tanagra ancient Greek city in ◊Boeotia. Sparta defeated Athens here 457 BC, and it is also noted for terracotta statuettes excavated here in the 19th century.

Tanaka Kakuei 1918– . Japanese right-wing politician, leader of the dominant Liberal Democratic Party (LDP) and prime minister 1972–74. In 1976 he was charged with corruption and resigned from the LDP but remained a powerful faction leader.

Tananarive former name for ◊Antananarivo, the capital of Madagascar.

Tanganyika lake 772 m/2,534 ft above sea level in the Great Rift Valley, E Africa, with Zaïre to the W and Tanzania and Burundi to the E. It is about 645 km/400 mi long; area 31,000 sq km/12,700 sq mi, and is the deepest lake in Africa (1,435 m/4,708 ft). The mountains round its shores rise to some 2,700 m/9,000 ft. The chief ports are

Tanzania
United Republic of (*Jamhuri*
ya Muungano wa Tanzania)

area 945,000 sq km/ 364,865 sq mi
capital Dodoma (since 1983)
towns chief port Dar es Salaam, Zanzibar; Mwanza
physical a central plateau with lakes in the W and
coastal plains
head of state and government Ali Hassan Mwinyi

from 1985
political system one-party socialist republic
exports coffee, cotton, sisal, cloves, tea, tobacco
currency Tanzanian shilling
population (1990) 26,070,000; growth rate 3.5%
p.a.
life expectancy men 49, women 53 (1989)
language Kiswahili, English (both official)
religion Muslim 35%, Christian 35%, traditional
30%
literacy 85% (1987)
GNP $4.9 bn (1987); $258 per head
chronology
1961 Tanganyika achieved full independence,
within the Commonwealth, with Julius Nyerere as
prime minister.
1962 Tanganyika became a republic with Nyerere
as president.
1964 Tanganyika and Zanzibar became the United
Republic of Tanzania with Nyerere as president.
1967 East African Community (EAC) formed.
Arusha Declaration.
1977 Revolutionary Party of Tanzania (CCM)
proclaimed the only legal party. EAC dissolved.
1984 Nyerere announced his retirement but stayed
on as CCM leader.
1985 Ali Hassan Mwinyi elected president.
1990 Nyerere handed over CCM leadership to
Mwinyi.
1992 CCM agreed to abolish one-party rule.

Bujumbura (Burundi), Kigoma (Tanzania), and
Kalémié (Zaîre).

Tanganyika former British colony in E Africa,
which now forms the mainland of ♦Tanzania.

Tange Kenzo 1913– . Japanese architect. His
works include the National Gymnasium, Tokyo, for
the 1964 Olympics, and the city-plan of ♦Abuja,
the capital of Nigeria.

tangent in trigonometry, a function of an angle in a
right-angled triangle, defined as the ratio of the
length of the side opposite the angle (not the right
angle) to the length of the side adjacent to it; a way
of expressing the slope of a line. In geometry, a
tangent is a straight line that touches a curve and
has the same slope as the curve at the point of
contact. At a maximum or minimum, the tangent
to a curve has zero slope.

tangerine type of small ♦orange *Citrus reticulata*.

Tangier (or *Tangiers* or *Tanger*) port in N
Morocco, on the Strait of Gibraltar; population
(1982) 436,227.
   history an important Phoenician trading centre in
the 15th century BC, Tangier was ruled successively by many states until the city and surrounding

area became an international zone in 1923. In 1956 it
was transferred to independent Morocco, and became a free port 1962.

tango slow dance in two-four time of partly African
origin which came to Europe via South America,
where it had blended with Spanish elements (such as
the ♦habanera).

Tanguy Yves 1900–1955. French Surrealist painter, who lived in the USA from 1939. His semi-
abstract forms suggest living creatures in a barren
landscape.

Tanizaki Jun-ichirō 1886–1965. Japanese novelist. His works include a modern version of ♦Mura-
saki's *The Tale of Genji* 1939–41, *The Makioka
Sisters* in three volumes 1943–48, and *The Key*
1956.

tank an armoured fighting vehicle that runs on tracks
and is fitted with weaponry capable of defeating
other tanks. The term was originally a code name
given to the first effective tracked armoured fighting
vehicle used in the battle of the Somme in 1916,
invented by the British soldier Ernest Swinton.

tanker ship with tanks for carrying mineral oil,
liquefied gas, and molasses in bulk.

Tannenberg, Battle of two battles, named after
a village in N Poland:
   1410 the Poles and Lithuanians defeated the
Teutonic Knights, establishing Poland as a major
power;
   1914, during World War I, when Tannenberg was
part of East Prussia, ♦Hindenburg defeated the
Russians here.

tanning treating animal skins to preserve them and
make them into leather. This may be done by
vegetable tanning: soaking the prepared skins in
tannic acid or *tannin*, a substance obtained from
the bark, wood, and galls (growths) on certain
trees, such as the oak. Chrome tanning, which is
much quicker, uses solutions of chromium salts.

TANGENT OF AN ANGLE

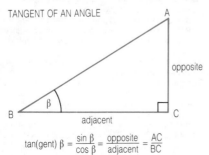

$$\tan(\text{gent}) \; \beta = \frac{\sin \beta}{\cos \beta} = \frac{\text{opposite}}{\text{adjacent}} = \frac{AC}{BC}$$

tansy perennial herb *Tanacetum vulgare*, family Compositae, native to Europe. The yellow flowerheads grow in clusters and the aromatic leaves are used in cookery.

tantalum a metallic element, symbol Ta, atomic number 73, relative atomic mass 180.95. Tantalum can be drawn into wire with a very high melting point and great tenacity (useful for filament lamps subject to vibration). It is also used in alloys, for corrosion-resistant laboratory apparatus and chemical equipment, as a catalyst in the manufacture of synthetic rubber, in tools and instruments, and in rectifiers and capacitors.

tant mieux (French) so much the better.

tant pis (French) so much the worse.

Tantrism forms of Hinduism and Buddhism that emphasize the division of the Universe into male and female forces which maintain its unity by their interaction; this gives women equal status. Tantric Hinduism is associated with magical and sexual yoga practices that imitate the union of Siva and Sakti, as described in religious books known as the *Tantras*. In Buddhism, the *Tantras* are texts attributed to the Buddha describing methods of attaining enlightenment.

Tanzania country in E Africa, on the Indian Ocean, bounded to the N by Uganda and Kenya, to the S by Mozambique, Malawi, and Zambia, and to the W by Zaïre, Burundi, and Rwanda.

Taoiseach Gaelic name for the prime minister of the Irish Republic.

Taoism Chinese philosophical system, traditionally founded by the philosopher Lao Zi 6th century BC, though the scriptures, *Tao Te Ching*, were apparently compiled 3rd century BC. The 'tao' or 'way' denotes the hidden Principle of the Universe, and less stress is laid on good deeds than on harmonious interaction with the environment, which automatically ensures right behaviour. The second important work is that of Zhuangzi (*c.* 389–286 BC), *The Way of Zhuangzi*. The magical side of Taoism is illustrated by the *I Ching* or *Book of Changes*, a book of divination.

tap dancing a rapid step dance, derived from clog dancing. Its main characteristic is the tapping of toes and heels. It was popularized in ◊vaudeville and in films by dancers such as Fred ◊Astaire and Ginger Rogers.

tape recording, magnetic method of recording electric signals on a layer of iron oxide, or other magnetic material, coating a thin plastic tape. The electrical impulses are fed to the electromagnetic recording head, which magnetizes the tape in accordance with the frequency and amplitude of the original signal, and may be audio (for sound recording), video (for television), or data (for computer). For playback, the tape is passed over the same or another head to convert magnetic into electrical impulses, which are then amplified for reproduction. Tapes are easily demagnetized (erased) for re-use, and come in cassette, cartridge, or reel form.

tapestry ornamental woven textile used for wall-hangings, furniture, and curtains. The tapestry design is threaded into the warp with various shades of wool.

tapeworm flat parasitic worm in the class Cestoda, of the phylum Platyhelminthes (flatworms), with no digestive or sense organs. It can reach a length of 15 m/50 ft, and attaches itself to its host's intestines by means of hooks and suckers. Tapeworms usually reach humans in imperfectly cooked meat or fish, causing anaemia and intestinal disorders.

tapioca a starch used in cooking, produced from the ◊cassava root.

tapir mammal of the ancient family Tapiridae, which grows to a maximum of 1 m/3 ft at the shoulder, and weighs 350 kg/770 lbs. They have thick, hairy, black skin, short tails and trunks, and no horns. They are vegetarian, harmless, shy inhabitants of the forests of Central and South America, and also Malaysia. Their survival is in danger because of destruction of the forests.

taproot in botany, a single, robust, main ◊root which is derived from the embryonic root, or ◊radicle, and grows vertically downwards, often for some considerable depth. Taproots are often modified for food storage and are common in biennial plants such as the carrot, *Daucus carota*, where they act as ◊perennating organs.

tar a dark brown or black viscous liquid, obtained by the destructive distillation of coal, shale, and wood. Tars consist of a mixture of hydrocarbons, acids, and bases. Creosote and paraffin are produced from wood tar. See also ◊coaltar.

tarantella a peasant dance from S Italy, which gives its name to a piece of music composed for or in the rhythm of this dance in fast six-eight time.

Taranto naval base and port in Apulia region, SE Italy; population (1981) 244,000. An important commercial centre, its steelworks are part of the new industrial complex of S Italy.

tarantula poisonous spider *Lycosa tarantula* with a 2.5 cm/1 in body. It spins no web, relying on its speed in hunting to catch its prey.

tare alternative common name for ◊vetch.

tariff a tax on imports or exports from a country. Tariffs have generally been used by governments to protect home industries from lower-priced foreign goods, and have been opposed by supporters of free trade. For a tariff to be successful, it must not provoke retaliatory tariffs from other countries. Organizations such as the European Community, EFTA, and the General Agreement on Tariffs and Trade (GATT) 1948, have worked towards mutual lowering of tariffs between countries.

Tarkovsky Andrei 1932–1986. Soviet film director, whose work is characterized by unorthodox

tapeworm *Electron microscope picture of the head of a tapeworm showing the hooks which cling to the host's tissues. (×200).*

cinematic techniques and visual beauty. His films include the science-fiction epic *Solaris* 1972, *Mirror* 1975, and *The Sacrifice* 1986.

taro, cocco or *eddo* plant *Colocasia esculenta* of the family Araceae, native to tropical Asia; the tubers are edible.

tarot cards fortune-telling aid of unknown, probably medieval origin, consisting of 78 cards: the *minor arcana* in four suits (resembling modern playing cards) and the *major arcana*, 22 cards with densely symbolic illustrations that have links with astrology and Kabbala.

tarpon marine herring-like fish *Tarpon atlanticus*. It reaches 2 m/6 ft, and may weigh 135 kg/300 lb. It lives in warm Atlantic waters.

Tarquinius Superbus legendary last king of Rome 534–510 BC. He was deposed when his son Sextus violated ◊Lucretia.

tarragon perennial bushy herb *Artemisia dracunculus* of the daisy family, growing to 1.5 m/5 ft, with narrow leaves and small green-white flowerheads arranged in groups. Tarragon contains an aromatic oil; its leaves are used as a culinary flavouring.

tarsier Malaysian primate *Tarsius spectrum* about the size of a rat. It has thick, brown fur, very large eyes, and long feet and hands. It is nocturnal, arboreal, and eats insects and lizards.

tartan woollen cloth woven in specific chequered patterns individual to Scottish clans, with stripes and squares of different widths and colours crisscrossing, and used in making plaids, kilts, and trousers. Developed in the 17th century, tartan was banned after the 1745 ◊Jacobite rebellion, and not legalized again until 1782.

Tartar a variant spelling of ◊Tartar, member of a Turkic people now living mainly in the autonomous region of Tartastan, Russia.

Tartarus in Greek mythology, a part of ◊Hades.

Tasaday a people of the rainforests of Mindanao in the ◊Philippines.

Tashkent capital of Uzbekistan; population (1990) 2,100,000. Industries include the manufacture of mining machinery, chemicals, textiles, and leather goods. Founded in the 7th century, it was taken by the Turks in the 12th century, and captured by Tamerlaine in 1361. In 1865 it was taken by the Russians.

Tasman Abel Janszoon 1603–1659. Dutch navigator. In 1642, he was the first European to see Tasmania. He also made the first European sightings of New Zealand, Tonga, and Fiji.

Tasmania island off the S coast of Australia, a state of the Commonwealth of Australia
area 68,331 sq km/26,383 sq mi
capital Hobart
towns chief port Launceston
products wool, dairy products, fruit, timber, iron, tin, coal, copper, silver
population (1987) 448,000
history the first European to visit Tasmania was Abel ◊Tasman 1642; it joined the Australian Commonwealth as a state 1901. The last of the Tasmanian Aboriginals died in 1876.

Tasmanian devil bear-like marsupial *Sarcophilus harrisii*. About 65 cm/2.1 ft long with a 25 cm/10 in bushy tail, it has a large head, strong teeth, and is blackish with white patches on the chest and hind parts. It is nocturnal, carnivorous, and can be ferocious.

Tasmanian tiger/wolf carnivorous marsupial *Thylacinus cynocephalus* also called thylacine; it is

dog-like in appearance and can be nearly 2 m/6 ft from nose to tail tip. It was hunted to probable extinction in the 1930s.

Tasman Sea the Pacific Ocean between SE Australia and NW New Zealand. It is named after the explorer Abel ◊Tasman.

Tass *Telegrafnoye Agentstvo Sovyetskovo Soyuza*, international news agency of the former Soviet Union.

Tasso Torquato 1544–1595. Italian poet, author of the romantic epic poem of the First Crusade *La Gerusalemme Liberata/Jerusalem Delivered* 1574, followed by the *Gerusalemme Conquistata/Jerusalem Conquered*, written during the period from 1576 when he was mentally unstable.

Tatar member of a Turkic, mainly Muslim people, the descendants of the followers of ◊Genghis Khan, called the Golden Horde because of the wealth they gained by plunder. They now live mainly in the Russian autonomous republic of Tatarstan, W Siberia, Turkmenistan and Uzbekistan (where they were deported from the Crimea 1944). Their language belongs to the Altaic family.

Tatarstan autonomous republic of E Russia
capital Kazan
area 68,000 sq km/26,250 sq mi
population (1986) 3,537,000
products oil, chemicals, textiles, and timber
history it was conquered by Russia 1552, and became an autonomous republic in 1920. In 1990 it gave itself full republic status and stopped participating in Russian political affairs.

Tate Nahum 1652–1715. Irish poet. Born in Dublin, he wrote an adaptation of Shakespeare's *King Lear* with a happy ending. He also produced a version of the psalms, and hymns; noted among his poems is 'While shepherds watched'. He became Poet Laureate in 1692.

Tate Phyllis (Margaret) 1911–1987. British composer. Her works include *Concerto for Saxophone and Strings* 1944, the opera *The Lodger* 1960, based on the story of Jack the Ripper, and *Serenade to Christmas* for soprano, chorus and orchestra 1972.

Tati Jacques, stage name of Jacques Tatischeff 1908–1982. French actor. A brilliant comic, he is remembered for his portrayal of Monsieur Hulot (for example in *Les Vacances de M Hulot/Monsieur Hulot's Holiday* 1953), a character embodying polite opposition to modern mechanization.

Tatum Edward Lawrie 1909–1975. US microbiologist. He shared a Nobel Prize in 1958 for his work on biochemical genetics with G W Beadle.

Taube Henry 1915– . US chemist, who established the basis of modern inorganic chemistry by his study of the loss or gain of electrons by atoms during chemical reactions.

Taurus zodiac constellation in the northern hemisphere near Orion, represented as a bull. The Sun passes through Taurus from mid-May to late June. Its brightest star is Aldebaran, seen as the bull's red eye. Taurus contains the Hyades and Pleiades open ◊star clusters, and the Crab Nebula.

Taussig Helen Brooke 1898–1986. US cardiologist who developed surgery for 'blue' babies. Such babies are born with one or more congenital deformities, which cause the blood to circulate in the body without first passing through the lungs. The babies are chronically short of oxygen and may not survive.

tautology repetition of the same thing in different words, or the ungrammatical use of unnecessary words: for example, it is tautologous to say something is *most unique* as something unique cannot by definition be comparative.

Tavener John (Kenneth) 1944– . British composer, whose individual and sometimes abrasive works include the dramatic cantata *The Whale* 1968 and the opera *Thérèse* 1979. He has also composed music for the Eastern Orthodox Church.

Taverner John 1495–1545. English organist and composer. He wrote masses and motets in polyphonic style, showing great contrapuntal skill, but as a Protestant renounced his art. He was imprisoned in 1528 for heresy, and, as an agent of Thomas Cromwell, assisted in the dissolution of the monasteries.

taxation the raising of money from individuals and organizations by the state in order to pay for the goods and services it provides. Taxation can be *direct* (a deduction from income) or *indirect* (added to the purchase price of goods or services, that is, a tax on consumption). The standard form of indirect taxation in Europe is *value-added tax (VAT)*. *Income tax* is the most common form of direct taxation.

tax avoidance the conducting of financial affairs in order to keep tax liability to a minimum within the law.

tax deductible an item which may be offset against tax liability, such as the cost of a car where it is required as an integral part of a job.

tax evasion failure to meet tax liabilities by illegal action, such as non-declaration of income. Tax evasion is a criminal offence.

tax haven a country or state where taxes are much less than elsewhere. It is often used by companies of another country which register in the tax haven to avoid tax. Any business transacted is treated as completely confidential. Tax havens include the Channel Islands, Switzerland, Bermuda, the Bahamas, and Liberia.

taxis or *tactic movement* in botany, the movement of a single cell, such as a bacterium, protozoan, single-celled alga, or gamete, in response to an external stimulus (plural *taxes*). A movement directed towards the stimulus is described as positive taxis, and away from it as negative taxis. The alga *Chlamydomonas*, for example, demonstrates positive *phototaxis* by swimming towards a light source to increase the rate of photosynthesis. *Chemotaxis* is a response to a chemical stimulus, as seen in many bacteria that move towards higher concentrations of nutrients.

Taxodium tree genus of the family Taxodiaceae. The American deciduous swamp cypress, *Taxodium distichum*, grows in or near water, and is a valuable timber tree.

taxonomy another name for the ◊classification of living organisms.

tax shelter an investment opportunity designed to reduce the tax burden on an individual or group of individuals, but at the same time to stimulate finance in the direction of a particular location or activity. Such shelters might be tax exempt or lightly taxed securities in government or a local authority, or forestry or energy projects.

Taylor Elizabeth 1932– . US actress, born in England, whose films include *Butterfield 8* 1960 (Academy award), *Cleopatra* 1963, and *Who's Afraid of Virginia Woolf?* 1966. Her eight husbands have included the actors Michael Wilding and Richard ◊Burton (twice).

Taylor Elizabeth (born Coles) 1912–1975. British novelist. Her books include *At Mrs Lippincote's* 1946 and *Angel* 1957.

Taylor Frederick Winslow 1856–1915. US engineer and management consultant, the founder of scientific management. His ideas, published in *Principles of Scientific Management* 1911, were based on the breakdown of work to the simplest tasks, the separation of planning from execution of tasks, and the introduction of time and motion studies. His methods were most clearly expressed in assembly-line factories, but have been criticized for degrading and alienating workers and producing managerial dictatorship.

Tay-Sachs disease an inherited disorder, caused by a defective gene, leading to blindness, retardation, and death in childhood. It is most common in people of Jewish descent.

Tayside region of Scotland
area 7,511 sq km/2,899 sq mi
towns administrative headquarters Dundee; Perth, Arbroath, Forfar
products beef and dairy products; soft fruit from the fertile Carse of Gowrie, SW of Dundee
population (1991) 385,300
famous people James Barrie

TB abbreviation for ◊*tuberculosis*.

Tbilisi (formerly *Tiflis*) capital of the Republic of Georgia; population (1987) 1,194,000. Industries include textiles, machinery, ceramics, and tobacco. Dating from the 5th century AD, it is a centre of Georgian culture, with fine medieval churches. Public demonstrations, following rejected demands for autonomy from Abkhazia enclave, were quashed here by troops 1989, resulting in 19 deaths and 100 injured.

Tchaikovsky Pyotr Ilyich 1840–1893. Russian composer. His strong sense of melody, personal expression and brilliant orchestration are clear throughout his large output, which includes six symphonies; three piano concertos and a violin concerto; operas (for example *Eugene Onegin* 1879 and *The Queen of Spades* 1890); ballets (*Swan Lake* 1877, *The Sleeping Beauty* 1890, and *The Nutcracker* 1892); and orchestral fantasies (*Romeo and Juliet* 1870, *Francesca da Rimini* 1877, and *Hamlet 1888*); and chamber and vocal music.

TD abbreviation for *Teachta Dála* (Irish 'a Member of the Irish Parliament').

tea evergreen shrub *Camellia sinensis*, of which the fermented, dried leaves are infused to make a beverage of the same name. Known in China as early as 2737 BC, tea was first brought to Europe in 1610 AD where it rapidly became a fashionable

Tchaikovsky Russian composer Pyotr Ilyich Tchaikovsky.

drink. In 1823 it was found growing wild in N India and plantations were later established in Assam and Sri Lanka; modern producers include Africa, South America, USSR, Indonesia, and Iran.

teak tropical Asian timber tree *Tectona grandis*, family Verbenaceae, used in furniture and shipbuilding.

teal small freshwater duck *Anas crecca* of the N hemisphere, about 35 cm/14 in long. The drake has a reddish-brown head with green and buff markings on either side, and a black and white line on the wing. The female is buff and brown.

Teapot Dome Scandal US political scandal which revealed the corruption of the Harding administration. It centred on the leasing of naval oil reserves in 1921 at Teapot Dome, Wyoming, without competitive bidding as a result of bribing the secretary of the interior, Albert B Fall (1861–1944). Fall was tried and imprisoned in 1929.

tear gas lacrimatory and irritant vapour used as a riot-control agent. The gas is delivered in pressurized, liquid-filled canisters or grenades, thrown by hand or launched from a specially adapted rifle. Gases such as Mace cause violent coughing and blinding tears, which pass when the victim breathes fresh air, and there are no lasting effects. Blister gases (such as mustard gas) and nerve gases are more harmful and may cause permanent injury or death.

teasel erect, prickly biennial herb *Dipsacus fullonum*, family Dipsacaceae, native to Eurasia; the dry seed heads were once used industrially to tease, or raise the nap of, cloth.

Tebbit Norman 1931– . British Conservative politician. His first career was as an airline pilot, when he held various trade-union posts. He was minister for employment 1981–83, for trade and industry 1983–85, chancellor of the Duchy of Lancaster 1985–87, and chair of the party 1985–87. He was injured in a bomb blast during the 1985 Conservative Party conference in Brighton.

technetium the first artifically made element (Greek *technetos*, artificial), symbol Tc, atomic number 43. Originally produced by Perrier and Segré in 1937 by bombarding molybdenum with deuterons or neutrons, it was later isolated in large amounts from the fission products of uranium. It is used as a hardener in steel alloys.

Technicolor trade name for a film colour process using three separate negatives, invented by Daniel F Comstock and Herbert T Kalmus in the USA 1922. Originally, Technicolor was a two-colour process in which superimposed red and green images were thrown on to the screen by a special projector. This proved expensive and imperfect, but when the three-colour process was introduced in 1932 (producing separate negatives of blue, green, and red images) the system came to be widely adopted, culminating in its use in *Gone with the Wind* 1939. Despite increasing competition, Technicolor remains the most commonly used colour process for cinematography.

technocracy a society controlled by technical experts such as scientists and engineers. The term was invented by Californian engineer W H Smyth in 1919 to describe his proposed 'rule by technicians', and was popularized by James Burham (1903–   ) in *Managerial Revolution* 1941.

technology the practical application of science in industry and commerce. Britain's industrial revolution preceded that of Europe by half a century, and its prosperity stimulated countries to encourage technological education. France established the École Polytechnique, the first technological university, in 1794, and Germany founded the Technische Hochschulen in Berlin in 1799. Britain founded the mechanics institutes for education in technology, notably the University of Manchester Institute of Science and Technology (founded 1824) which, together with the Imperial College of Science and Technology (established 1907), still forms the focus of technological work.

tectonics in geology, the study of the movements of rocks. On a small scale tectonics involves the formation of ◊folds and ◊faults, but on a large scale ◊plate tectonics deals with the movement of the Earth's surface as a whole.

Tecumseh 1768–1813. North American Indian chief of the Shawnee. He attempted to unite the Indian peoples from Canada to Florida against the encroachment of white settlers, but the defeat of his brother Tenskwatawa, 'the Prophet', at the battle of Tippecanoe in Nov 1811 by Gov W H ◊Harrison, largely destroyed his confederacy.

Teesside industrial area at the mouth of the river Tees, Cleveland, NE England; population (1981) 382,700. Industries include high-technology, capital-intensive steelmaking, chemicals, an oil fuel terminal, and the main North Sea natural-gas terminal. Middlesbrough is a major port.

tefillin or *phylacteries* two leather boxes worn by Jewish men during weekday prayer. They contain small scrolls from the Torah and are strapped to the left arm and the forehead.

Teflon a trade name for the plastic ◊PTFE.

Teg Bahadur 1621–1675. Ninth guru (teacher) of Sikhism 1664–75, executed for refusing to renounce his faith.

Tegucigalpa capital of Honduras, population (1985) 571,400. It has textile and food processing industries, and was a gold and silver mining centre.

Tehran capital of Iran; population (1983) 5,784,200. Industries include textiles, chemicals, engineering, and tobacco. It became the capital 1788.

Tehran Conference conference held in Tehran in 1943: the first meeting of World War II Allied leaders Stalin, Roosevelt, and Churchill.

Teilhard de Chardin Pierre 1881–1955. French Jesuit mystic. Publication of his *Le Phénomène humain/The Phenomenon of Man* 1955 was delayed until after his death by the embargo of his superiors. He envisaged humanity as eventually in charge of its own evolution, and developed the concept of the *noosphere*, the unconscious union of thought among human beings.

Te Kanawa Kiri 1944-   . New Zealand opera singer. Her first major role was the Countess in Mozart's *The Marriage of Figaro* at Covent Garden, London, 1971.

tektite small, rounded glassy stone, found in certain regions of Earth, such as Australasia. They are probably the scattered drops of molten rock thrown out by the impact of a large ◊meteorite.

Tel Aviv (official name *Tel Aviv-Jaffa*) city in Israel, on the Mediterranean Sea, with its port at Ashdod to the S; population (1982) 325,700. Industries include textiles, chemicals and sugar.

history Tel Aviv was founded 1909 as a Jewish residential area in the Arab town of Jaffa, with which it was combined 1949; their ports were superseded by Ashdod 1965.

telecommunications communications over a distance. Long-distance voice communication was pioneered in 1876 by Alexander Graham Bell, when he invented the telephone as a result of Faraday's discovery of electromagnetism. Today it is possible to communicate with most countries by

telecommunications chronology

1794	Claude Chappe in France built a long-distance signalling system using semaphore.
1839	Charles Wheatstone and William Cooke devised an electric telegraph in England.
1843	Morse transmitted the first message along a telegraph line in the USA.
1858	The first transatlantic telegraph cable was laid.
1876	American Alexander Graham Bell invented the telephone.
1877	Edison invented the carbon transmitter for the telephone.
1894	Marconi pioneered wireless telegraphy in Italy, later moving to England.
1900	Fessenden in the USA first broadcast voice by radio.
1901	Marconi transmitted the first radio signals across the Atlantic.
1904	Fleming invented the thermionic valve.
1907	American Charles Krumm introduced the forerunner of the teleprinter.
1920	Stations in Detroit and Pittsburgh began regular radio broadcasts.
1922	The BBC began its first radio transmissions, for the London station 2LO.
1932	The Post Office introduced the Telex in Britain.
1956	The first transatlantic telephone cable was laid.
1962	Telstar pioneers transatlantic satellite communications, transmitting live TV pictures.
1966	Charles Kao advanced the idea of using optical fibres for telecommunications.
1969	Live TV pictures were sent from astronauts on the moon back to Earth.
1975	The Post Office announced Prestel, the world's first viewdata system.
1986	Voyager 2 transmitted images of Uranus some 3,000 million km/2,000 million mi, the signals taking 2 hours 45 minutes to reach Earth.

telephone cable, or by satellite or microwave link, with several hundred simultaneous conversations being carried. Integrated service digital network (ISDN) is a system that transmits voice and image data on a single transmission line by changing them into digital signals, making videophones and high-quality fax possible; the world's first large-scale centre of ISDN began operating in Japan 1988. The chief method of relaying long-distance calls on land is microwave radio transmission.

Telecom Tower building in London, 189 m/620 ft high. Completed in 1966, and formerly known as the Post Office Tower, it is a microwave relay tower capable of handling up to 150,000 simultaneous telephone conversations and over 40 television channels.

telegraphy the transmission of coded messages along wires by means of electrical signals. The first modern form of telecommunication, it now uses printers for the transmission and receipt of messages. Telex is an international telegraphy network.

Telemann Georg Philipp 1681–1767. German Baroque composer, organist, and conductor at the Johanneum, Hamburg, from 1721. He composed operas, over 600 church cantatas, and other vocal and instrumental works.

telemetry measurement at a distance. It refers particularly to the systems by which information is obtained and sent back by instruments on board a spacecraft. See ◊remote sensing.

telepathy 'the communication of impressions of any kind from one mind to another, independently of the recognized channels of sense', as defined by F W H ◊Myers who coined the term.

telephone an instrument for communicating by voice over long distances, invented by Alexander Graham ◊Bell in 1876. The transmitter (mouthpiece) consists of a carbon microphone, with a diaphragm that vibrates when a person speaks into it. The diaphragm vibrations compress grains of carbon to a greater or lesser extent, altering their resistance to an electric current passing through them. This sets up variable electrical signals, which travel along the telephone lines to the receiver of the person being called. There they cause the magnetism of an electromagnet to vary, making a diaphragm above the electromagnet vibrate and give out sound waves, which mirror those that entered the mouthpiece originally.

telephone tapping method of listening in on a telephone conversation; in the UK a criminal offence if done without a warrant or the consent of the person concerned. Warrants are issued by the foreign secretary and home secretary (and those for Northern Ireland and Scotland), chiefly for the collection of military or political intelligence about other countries, defence of national security, and detection of crime.

telephoto lens a photographic lens of longer focal length than normal, taking a very narrow view, and giving a large image through a combination of telescopic and ordinary photographic lenses.

teleprinter or **teletypewriter** a transmitting and receiving device used in telecommunications to handle coded messages. Teleprinters are like automatic typewriters. They convert typed words into electrical signals (using a 5-unit Baudot code, see ◊baud) at the transmitting end, and signals into typed words at the receiving end.

telescope a device for collecting and focusing light and other forms of ◊electromagnetic radiation (such as a ◊radio telescope). A telescope produces a magnified image, which makes the object seem nearer, and it shows objects fainter than can be seen by the eye alone. A telescope with a large **aperture**, or opening, can distinguish finer detail and fainter objects than one with a small aperture. There are two main types of optical telescope: the **refracting telescope**, which uses lenses, and the

telephone

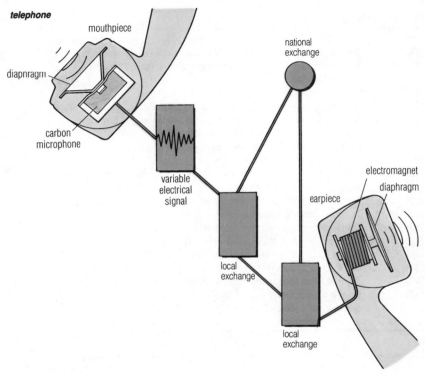

mouthpiece

diapnragm

carbon microphone

variable electrical signal

national exchange

local exchange

earpiece

electromagnet

diaphragm

local exchange

reflecting telescope, which uses mirrors. A third type, the *catadioptric telescope*, with a combination of lenses and mirrors, is used increasingly.

teletext broadcast system of displaying information on television screens (entertainment, sport, finance) which is constantly updated. It is a form of ◊videotext, pioneered in Britain by the British Broadcasting Corporation with

◊Ceefax and by Independent Television with ◊Oracle.

television the reproduction at a distance by radio waves of visual images. For transmission, a television camera converts the pattern of light it takes in into a pattern of electrical charges. This is scanned line-by-line by a beam of electrons from an electron gun, resulting in variable electrical signals that represent the visual picture. These vision signals are combined with a radio carrier wave and broadcast. The TV aerial picks up the wave and feeds it to the receiver (TV set). This separates out the vision signals, which pass to a cathode-ray tube. The vision signals control the strength of a beam of electrons from an electron gun, aimed at the screen and making it glow more or less brightly. At the same time the beam is made to scan across the screen line-by-line, mirroring the action of the gun in the TV camera. The result is a recreation, spot-by-spot, line-by-line, of the pattern of light that entered the camera. Twenty-five pictures are built up each second with interlaced scanning (30 in US), with a total of 625 lines in Europe, or 525 lines in the US and Japan.

telex an international telecommunications network that handles telegraph messages in the form of coded signals. It uses ◊teleprinters for transmitting and receiving, and makes use of land lines (cables), radio and satellite links to make connections between subscribers. The word 'telex' is an acronym for '*tel*etypewriter *ex*change service'.

Telford Thomas 1757–1834. Scottish civil engineer who opened up N Scotland by building roads and waterways. He constructed many aqueducts and canals including the Caledonian (1802–23), and erected the Menai road suspension bridge (1819–26).

telescope

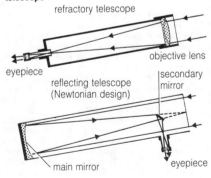

refractory telescope

objective lens

eyepiece

reflecting telescope (Newtonian design)

secondary mirror

main mirror

eyepiece

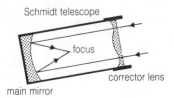

Schmidt telescope

focus

corrector lens

main mirror

television

television transmitter (essentials)

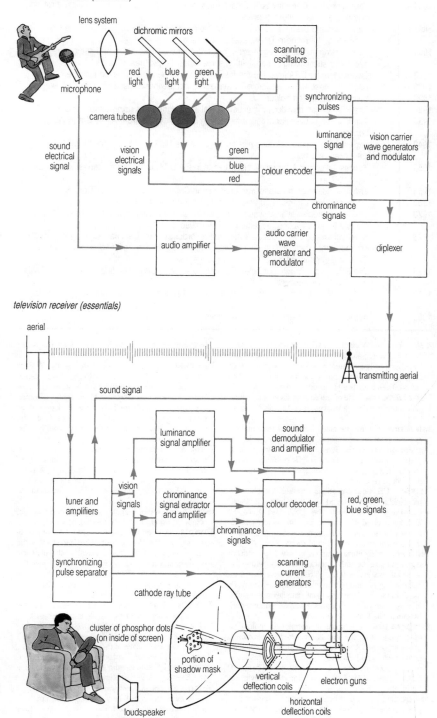

television receiver (essentials)

television chronology

1878	William Crookes in England invented the Crookes tube, which produced cathode rays.
1884	Paul Nipkow in Germany built a mechanical scanning device, the Nipkow disc, a rotating disc with a spiral pattern of holes in it.
1897	Karl Ferdinand Braun, also in Germany, modified the Crookes tube to produce the ancestor of the modern TV receiver picture tube.
1906	Boris Rosing in Russia began experimenting with the Nipkow disc and cathode-ray tube, eventually succeeding in transmitting some crude TV pictures.
1923	Zworykin in the USA invented the first electronic camera tube, the iconoscope.
1926	Baird demonstrated a workable TV system, using mechanical scanning by Nipkow.
1928	Baird demonstrated colour TV.
1929	The BBC began broadcasting experimental TV programmes using Baird's system.
1936	The BBC began regular broadcasting using Baird's system from Alexandra Palace, London.
1940	Experimental colour TV transmission began in the USA, using the modern system of colour reproduction.
1953	Successful colour TV transmissions began in the USA, using the modern system of colour reproduction.
1956	The first videotape recorded was produced in California by the Ampex Corporation.
1962	TV signals were transmitted across the Atlantic via the Telstar satellite.
1970	The first videodisc system was announced by Decca in Britain and AEG-Telefunken in Germany, but it was not perfected until the 1980s.
1975	Sony introduced their videocassette tape recorder system, Betamax, for domestic viewers, six years after their professional U-Matic system; the British Post Office (now British Telecom) announced their Prestel viewdata system.
1973	The BBC and Independent Television introduced the world's first teletext systems, Ceefax and Oracle, respectively.
1979	Matsushita in Japan developed a pocket-sized flat-screen TV set, using a liquid-crystal display (LCD).
1989	Introduction of satellite television in Britain.

Tell Wilhelm (William) 14th century. Legendary Swiss archer, said to have refused to salute the Hapsburg badge at Altdorf on Lake Lucerne. Sentenced to shoot an apple from his son's head, he did so, then shot the tyrannical Austrian ruler.

Tell el Amarna site of the ancient Egyptian capital ◊Akhetaton. The ◊Amarna tablets were found there.

tellurium a semi-metallic element of the sulphur group, symbol Te, atomic number 52, relative atomic mass 127.61. It is used in colouring glass (blue to brown), in the electrolytic refining of zinc, and in electronics. It is also used as a catalyst in petroleum refining.

Telstar US communications satellite, launched 10 Jul 1962, which relayed the first live television transmissions between the USA and Europe. Telstar orbited the Earth in 158 minutes, and so had to be tracked by ground stations, unlike the geostationary satellites of today.

tempera a painting medium in which powdered pigments are bound together, usually with egg yolk and water. A form of tempera was used in ancient Egypt, and egg tempera was the foremost medium for panel painting in late medieval and early Renaissance Europe. It was gradually superseded by oils in the late 15th century.

temperature the state of hotness or coldness of a body, and the condition which determines whether or not it will transfer heat to, or receive heat from, another body according to the laws of ◊thermodynamics. It is measured in degrees Celsius (before 1948 called centigrade), Kelvin, or Fahrenheit.

tempering a kind of heat treatment used for improving the properties of metals, particularly steel alloys. It involves heating the metal to a certain temperature and then cooling it suddenly in a water or oil bath.

Tempest, The a romantic drama by William Shakespeare, first performed 1611–12. Prospero, usurped as duke of Milan by his brother Antonio, lives on a remote island with his daughter Miranda and Caliban, a deformed creature. Prospero uses magic to shipwreck Antonio and his party on the island and with the help of the spirit Ariel regains his dukedom.

Templar member of a Christian military order, founded in Jerusalem in 1119, the **Knights of the Temple of Solomon**. The knights took vows of poverty, chastity, and obedience and devoted themselves to the recovery of Palestine from the Muslims.

temple a place of religious worship. In US usage, temple is another name for synagogue.

Temple the centre of Jewish national worship in Jerusalem. The Western or **Wailing Wall** is the surviving part of the western wall of the platform of the enclosure of the Temple of Herod. Since the destruction of the Temple in 70 AD, Jews have come here to pray and to mourn their dispersion and the loss of their homeland.

Temple Shirley 1928– . US actress, who became the most successful child star of the 1930s. Her films include *Bright Eyes* 1934, in which she sang 'On the Good Ship Lollipop'. As Shirley T Black, she was active in the Republican Party, and was US Chief of Protocol 1976–77. She was appointed US ambassador to Czechoslovakia (now the Czech and Slovak Republics) 1989.

tench European freshwater fish *Tinca tinca*. A member of the carp family, it is about 45 cm/18 in long, weighing 2 kg/4.5 lbs, with olive-green above and grey beneath. The scales are small,

tennis, lawn (Top left) Boris Becker (Germany), 1987. (Top right) Gabriela Sabatini (Argentina), 1988.

and there is a barbel at each side of the mouth.

Ten Commandments in the Old Testament or Hebrew Bible, the laws given by God to the Israelite leader Moses on Mount Sinai, engraved on two tablets of stone. They are: to have no other gods besides Jehovah; to make no idols; not to misuse the name of God; to keep the sabbath holy; to honour one's parents; not to commit murder, adultery, or theft; not to give false evidence; not to be covetous. They form the basis of Jewish and Christian moral codes; the 'tablets of the Law' given to Moses are also mentioned in the Koran.

tendon a type of connective tissue which joins muscle to bone in vertebrates. Tendons are largely composed of the protein collagen, and because of their inelasticity are very efficient at transforming muscle power into movement.

tendril in botany, a slender, threadlike structure that supports a climbing plant by coiling around suitable supports, such as the stems and branches of other plants. It may be a modified stem, leaf, leaflet, flower, or leaf stalk, and may be simple or branched.

Tenerife largest of the ◊Canary Islands, Spain; area 2,060 sq km/795 sq mi; population (1981) 557,000. *Santa Cruz* is the main town, and *Pico de Teide* is an active volcano.

Teng Hsiao-ping former spelling of ◊Deng Xiaoping, Chinese politician.

Teniers family of Flemish painters, active in Antwerp. The most successful was *David Teniers the Younger* (David II, 1610–90), who became court painter to Archduke Leopold William, governor of the Netherlands, in Brussels. He painted scenes of peasant life.

Tennessee state of the E central USA; nickname Volunteer State
area 109,412 sq km/42,224 sq mi
capital Nashville
towns Memphis, Jackson, Knoxville, Chattanooga
products cereals, cotton, tobacco, timber, coal, zinc, pyrites, phosphates, iron, steel, and chemicals
population (1986) 4,803,000
famous people Davy Crockett
history first settled 1757, it became a state 1796.

Tenniel John 1820–1914. British illustrator and cartoonist, known for his illustrations for Lewis Carroll's *Alice's Adventures in Wonderland* 1865 and *Through the Looking-Glass* 1872. He joined the satirical magazine *Punch* in 1850, and for over 50 years he was one of its leading cartoonists.

tennis, lawn a racket and ball game invented in England towards the end of the 19th century It derived from ◊real tennis. Although played on different surfaces (grass, wood, shale, clay, and concrete) it is still called 'lawn tennis'. The aim of the two or four players is to strike the ball into the prescribed area of the court, with oval-headed rackets (strung with gut or nylon), in such a way that it cannot be returned.

Tennyson Alfred, 1st Baron Tennyson 1809–1892. British poet, poet laureate 1850–96, noted for the majestic musical language of his verse. His works include 'The Lady of Shalott', 'The Lotus Eaters', 'Ulysses', 'Break, Break, Break', 'The Charge of the Light Brigade'; the longer narratives *Locksley Hall* 1832, and *Maud* 1855; the elegy *In Memoriam* 1850; and a long series of poems on the Arthurian legends *The Idylls of the King* 1857–85.

tenor in music, the highest range of adult male voice not using falsetto (singing in the female register).

tenpin bowling indoor sport popular in US. Like skittles, the object is to bowl a ball down an alley at pins (ten as opposed to nine). The game is usually between two players or teams. A game of ten pins is made up of ten 'frames'. The frame is the bowler's turn to play and in each frame he or she may bowl twice. One point is scored for each pin knocked down, with bonus points for knocking all ten pins down in either one ball or two. The player or team making the greater score wins.

tenure employment terms and conditions. Security of tenure is often granted to the judiciary, civil servants, and others in public office, where impartiality and freedom from political control are considered important.

Tenzing Norgay, popularly known as *Sherpa Tenzing* 1914–1986. Tibetan mountaineer. In 1953, he was the first, with Edmund Hillary, to reach the summit of Mount Everest.

Teotihuacan ancient city in central Mexico, capital and religious centre of the ◊Toltec civilization.

tequila Mexican alcoholic drink made from the ◊agave plant and named from the place, near Guadalajara, where the conquistadors first developed it from Aztec pulque, which would keep for only a day.

teratogen any agent causing malformation in the fetus. Teratogens known to cause human malformations include some drugs (notably ◊thalidomide), and other chemicals, certain disease organisms, and high-level radiation.

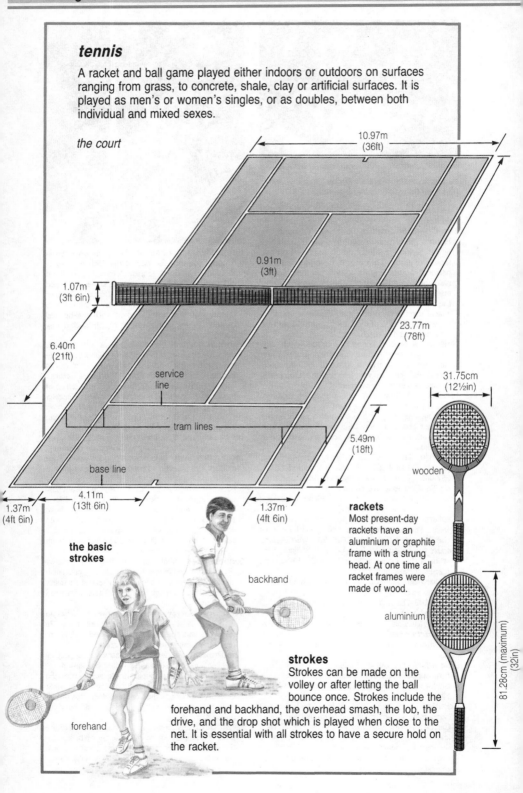

tennis

A racket and ball game played either indoors or outdoors on surfaces ranging from grass, to concrete, shale, clay or artificial surfaces. It is played as men's or women's singles, or as doubles, between both individual and mixed sexes.

the court

10.97m
(36ft)

0.91m
(3ft)

1.07m
(3ft 6in)

23.77m
(78ft)

6.40m
(21ft)

service line

tram lines

5.49m
(18ft)

base line

4.11m
(13ft 6in)

1.37m
(4ft 6in)

1.37m
(4ft 6in)

31.75cm
(12½in)

wooden

rackets

Most present-day rackets have an aluminium or graphite frame with a strung head. At one time all racket frames were made of wood.

aluminium

the basic strokes

backhand

81.28cm (maximum)
(32in)

strokes

Strokes can be made on the volley or after letting the ball bounce once. Strokes include the forehand and backhand, the overhead smash, the lob, the drive, and the drop shot which is played when close to the net. It is essential with all strokes to have a secure hold on the racket.

forehand

termite

termite – a typical termite mound

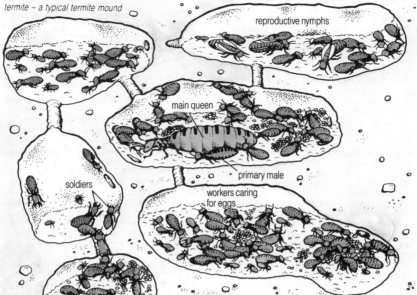

reproductive nymphs

main queen

soldiers

primary male

workers caring
for eggs

terbium a metallic element, symbol Tb, atomic number 65, relative atomic mass 158.93. One of the lanthanide series, it is used in lasers, semiconductors, and television tubes.

Terence (Publius Terentius Afer) 190–159 BC. Latin dramatist, born at Carthage, and brought as a slave to Rome where he was freed and came under ◊Scipio's patronage. The surviving six subtly characterized comedies (including *The Eunuch* 161 BC) are based on Greek models.

Teresa Mother, born Agnes Bojaxhiu 1910– . Indian Roman Catholic nun. She was born in Skopje, Albania and at 18 entered a Calcutta convent and became a teacher. In 1948 she became an Indian citizen, and founded the Missionaries of Charity, an order for men and women based in Calcutta, which especially helps abandoned children and the dying. Nobel Peace Prize 1979.

Teresa, St 1515–1582. Spanish mystic. Born at Avila, she became a Carmelite nun, and in 1562 founded a new and stricter order. She was subject to fainting fits, during which she saw visions. She wrote *The Way to Perfection* 1583, and an autobiography, *Life of the Mother Theresa of Jesus* 1611. In 1622 she was canonized, and became the first woman Doctor of the Church in 1970.

Tereshkova Valentina (Vladimirovna) 1937– . Soviet cosmonaut, the first woman to fly in space. In Jun 1963 she made a three-day flight in Vostok 6, orbiting the Earth 48 times.

term in architecture, a pillar in the form of a pedestal supporting the bust of a human or animal figure. Such objects derive from Roman boundary-marks sacred to *Terminus*, the god of boundaries.

terminal in computing, a keyboard and ◊VDU (screen) for communicating with a computer. Originally, 'terminal' or 'terminal equipment' was any input or output device connected to a computer, but today the word ◊peripheral is used.

termite soft-bodied social insect, of the tropical order Isoptera, living in large colonies, comprising one or more queens (of relatively enormous size and producing an egg every two seconds), much smaller kings, and still smaller soldiers, workers, and immature forms. Termites build galleried nests of soil particles which may be 6 m/20 ft high.

tern lightly built gull-like seabird, between 20–50 cm/8–20 in long, characterized by long pointed wings and a forked tail. They are white, black, or a combination.

terracotta (Italian 'baked earth') brownish-red baked clay used in building, sculpture, and pottery. It was first used in ancient times in countries where there was no stone available. The term is specifically applied to small figures or figurines, such as those found at ◊Tanagra. Recent excavations at Xian, China, have revealed life-size terracotta figures of the army of the Emperor Qin dating from the 3rd century.

terrapin fresh-water tortoises, found in North America and Australia.

terrier type of highly intelligent, active, and mostly small dog. They include the bull, cairn, fox, Irish, Scottish, Sealyham, Skye, and Yorkshire terriers.

Territorial Army British force of volunteer soldiers, created from volunteer regiments (incorporated 1872) as the *Territorial Force* 1908. It was raised and administered by county associations, and intended primarily for home defence. It was renamed Territorial Army 1922. Merged with the Regular Army in World War II, it was revived 1947, and replaced by a smaller, more highly trained Territorial and Army Volunteer Reserve, again renamed Territorial Army 1979.

territorial behaviour in biology, the active defence of a ◊territory. It may involve aggressively driving out intruders, marking the boundary (with dung piles or deposits from special scent glands), conspicuous visual displays, characteristic songs, or loud calls. In general, the territory-owner repels only individuals of its own species.

territorial waters an area of sea over which the adjoining coastal state claims territorial rights. This is most commonly a distance of 12 nautical miles from the coast, but, increasingly, states claim fishing and other rights up to 200 miles.

territory in animal behaviour, an area that is actively defended by an individual or group. Animals may hold territories for many different reasons, for example, to provide a constant food supply, to monopolize potential mates, or to ensure access to refuges or nest sites. The size of a territory depends in part on its function: some nesting and mating territories may be only a few square metres, whereas feeding territories may be as large as hundreds of square kilometres.

terrorism systematic violence in the furtherance of political aims, especially by small ◊guerrilla groups.

Terry (John) Quinlan 1937– . British architect. His work includes country houses in the Neo-Classical style, for example Merks Hall, Great Dunmow, Essex, 1982, and the larger scale Richmond riverside project commissioned 1984.

Tertiary period of geological time 65–1.8 million years ago, divided into into five epochs: Palaeocene, Eocene, Oligocene, Miocene, and Pliocene. During the Tertiary mammals became the important land animals, and grasslands expanded.

tertiary in the Roman Catholic church, a member of a 'third order' (see under ◊Holy Orders), a layman who, while marrying and following a normal employment, attempts to live in accordance with a modified version of the rule of one of the religious orders. The first such order was founded by St ◊Francis 1221.

tertiary college in the UK, a college for students over 16 which combines the work of a ◊sixth form and a ◊further education college.

Tertullian Quintus Septimius Florens 155–222 AD. Latin name **Tertullianus**. Carthaginian Father of the Church, the first important Christian writer in Latin; he became involved with ◊Montanism in 213.

Terylene trade name for a polyester synthetic fibre produced by ICI. It is made by polymerizing ethylene glycol and terephthalic acid. Cloth made from Terylene keeps its shape after washing and is hard-wearing.

terza rima a poetical metre used in ◊Dante's *Divine Comedy*, consisting of three-line stanzas in which the second line rhymes with the first and third of the following stanza. Shelley's 'Ode to the West Wind' is a good example.

Tesla Nikola 1856–1943. Croatian electrical engineer, who emigrated to the US 1884. He invented fluorescent lighting, the Tesla induction motor, the Tesla coil, and developed the ◊alternating current (AC) electrical supply system.

Test Ban Treaty a treaty signed by the USA, USSR, and Britain on 5 Aug 1963 which agreed to test nuclear weapons only underground. In the following two years 90 other nations signed the treaty, the only major non-signatories being France and China who continued underwater and ground-level tests.

testis (plural *testes*) the organ that produces ◊sperm in male (and hermaphrodite) animals. In most animals it is internal, but in mammals (other than marine mammals), the paired testes descend from the body cavity during development, to hang outside the abdomen in a scrotal sac.

testosterone a hormone secreted chiefly by the testes of vertebrates. It promotes the development of secondary sexual characteristics in males. In animals with a breeding season, the onset of breeding behaviour is accompanied

tetra

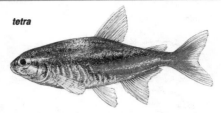

by a rise in the level of testosterone in the blood.

tetanus or *lockjaw* an acute disease caused by the bacillus, *Clostridium tetani*, entering a wound. The bacterium is chiefly found in richly manured soil. Untreated, tetanus produces muscular spasm, convulsions, and death. There is a vaccine.

tête-à-tête (French 'head-to-head') a private meeting between two people,

Tet Offensive in the Vietnam War, a prolonged attack mounted by the Vietcong against Saigon in Jan and Feb 1968. Although the communist Vietcong were forced to withdraw, the attack on the South Vietnamese capital brought into question the ability of the South Vietnamese and their US allies to win the war.

tetra a brightly coloured tropical fish of the family Characidae.

tetrahedron in geometry, a solid figure (◊polyhedron) with four triangular faces; that is, a ◊pyramid on a triangular base. A regular tetrahedron has equilateral triangles as its faces.

tetrapod a type of ◊vertebrate. The group includes mammals, birds, reptiles, and amphibians. Although the name tetrapod means 'four-legged', birds are included because they evolved from four-legged ancestors, the forelimbs having become modified to form wings.

Tetuán (or *Téouan*) town in NE Morocco, near the Mediterranean coast, 64 km/40 mi SE of Tangier; population (1982) 199,615. Products include textiles, leather, and soap. It was settled by Moorish exiles from Spain in the 16th century.

Teutonic Knight member of a German Christian military order, founded 1190 by Hermann of Salza in Palestine. They crusaded against the pagan Prussians and Lithuanians from 1228, and controlled Prussia until the 16th century.

Texas state of the SW USA; nickname Lone Star State
area 692,407 sq km/267,339 sq mi
capital Austin
towns Houston, Dallas, San Antonio, Fort Worth, El Paso

tetrahedron

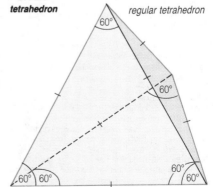

regular tetrahedron

60° 60° 60° 60° 60° 60° 60° 60°

Thailand
Kingdom of (*Prathet Thai* or *Muang-Thai*)

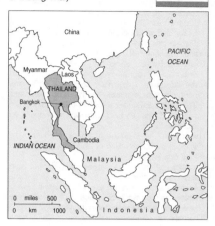

area 513,115 sq km/ 198,108 sq mi
capital and chief port Bangkok
towns Chiangmai

physical central valley flanked by highlands
head of state King Bhumibol Adulyadej from 1946
head of government Chuan Leekpai from 1992
political system military-run emergent democracy
exports rice, rubber, tin, rubies, sapphires
currency baht
population (1990 est) 54,890,000 (Thai 75%, Chinese 14%); growth rate 2% p.a.
life expectancy men 62, women 68
language Thai and Chinese (both official)
religion Buddhist 95% Muslim 4%
literacy 89% (1988)
GNP $52bn (1988); $771 per head
chronology
1782 Siam absolutist dynasty commenced.
1932 Constitutional monarchy established.
1939 Name of Thailand adopted.
1947 Military seized power in coup.
1973 Military government overthrown.
1976 Military reassumed control.
1988 Prime Minister Prem resigned and was replaced by the conservative Chatichai Choonhavan.
1991 Military seized power in coup. Interim civilian government formed.
1992 March: general election produced five-party coalition; new premier removed after a month; April: appointment of Gen. Suchinda Krapayoon as premier provoked mass riots; May: Suchinda stood down; Sept: new coalition government.

products rice, cotton, sorghum, peanuts, pecans, vegetables, fruit, meat products, oil (a third of the needs of the USA), natural gas, asphalt, graphite, sulphur, salt, helium, chemicals, oil products, processed food, machinery, transport equipment
population (1980) 14,229,191
history settled by the Spanish 1682, Texas was part of Mexico 1821–36, and an independent republic 1836–45. In 1845 it became a state of the USA.

The area won independence from Mexico in 1821, and American immigration followed with resultant friction. Santa Anna massacred the Alamo garrison 1836, but was defeated by Sam Houston at San Jacinto the same year. Houston then became president of the Texas Republic 1836–45. Texas is the only state in the USA to have previously been an independent republic.

texte intégral (French 'the complete text') unabridged.

textile formerly only a material woven (Latin *texere* to weave) from natural spun thread, now loosely extended to machine-knits and spun-bonded fabrics (in which a web of fibre is created and then fuse-bonded by passing it through controlled heat).

textured vegetable protein a manufactured foodstuff, see ◊TVP.

TGV *train á grande vitesse*, a superfast French train that operates the world's fastest rail service between Paris and Lyon. Introduced in 1981 and electrically powered, the TGV covers the 425 km/ 264 mile journey in just two hours.

Thackeray William Makepeace 1811–1863. British novelist, author of *Vanity Fair*. He was a regular contributor to *Fraser's Magazine* and *Punch*. *Vanity Fair* 1847–48 was his first novel, followed by *Pendennis* 1848, *Henry Esmond* 1852 (and its sequel *The Virginians* 1857–59), and *The Newcomes* 1853–55, in which Thackeray's tendency to sentimentality is most marked. Other works include the fairy tale. *The Rose and the Ring* 1855 and *The Book of Snobs* 1848.

Thailand country in SE Asia on the Gulf of Siam, bounded to the E by Laos and Kampuchea, to the S by Malaysia, and to the W by Myanmar.

Thais 4th century BC. Greek courtesan, mistress of ◊Alexander the Great and later wife of ◊Ptolemy I king of Egypt. She allegedly instigated the burning of ◊Persepolis.

thalassaemia a hereditary blood disorder (also known as Cooley's anaemia) which is widespread in the Mediterranean countries especially, also in Africa and Asia. It is characterized by an abnormality in the red blood cells and bone marrow, with enlargement of the spleen.

thalidomide ◊hypnotic developed in the 1950s. When taken in early pregnancy, it caused malformation of the fetus in over 5,000 recognized cases, and the drug was withdrawn. It has limited use in the treatment of leprosy.

thallium a metallic element, symbol Tl, atomic number 81, relative atomic mass 204.39. It is a soft, bluish-grey metal which tarnishes in air, is malleable but of low tenacity. It is a poor conductor of electricity and its compounds are poisonous, being used as rat poison and insecticide. Other compounds are used in optical and infrared glass making, and in photoelectric cells.

thallus any plant body that is not divided into true leaves, stems and roots. It is often thin and flattened, as in the body of a seaweed, lichen or liverwort and the gametophyte generation (◊prothallus) of a fern. Some flowering plants (◊angiosperms) that are adapted to an aquatic way of life may have a very simple plant body which is described as a thallus (for example duckweed, *Lemna*).

Thames river in SE England; length 338 km/210 mi. It rises in the Cotswolds above Cirencester, and is tidal as far as Teddington. Below London there is protection from flooding by means of the Thames barrier.

Thames barrier a moveable barrier built across the River Thames at Woolwich, London, as part of that city's flood defences. Completed in 1982,

Thatcher The Iron Lady: British Conservative politician and prime minister 1979-1990, Margaret Thatcher.

the barrier comprises curved flood gates which can be rotated 90° into position from beneath the water to form a barrier against high tides.

Thanksgiving (Day) national holiday in the USA (fourth Thursday in Nov) and Canada (second Monday in Oct), first celebrated by the Pilgrim settlers in Massachusetts on their first harvest 1621.

Thant U 1909–1974. Burmese diplomat, secretary-general of the United Nations 1962–71. He helped to resolve the US-Soviet crisis over the Soviet installation of missiles in Cuba, and he made the controversial decision to withdraw the UN peacekeeping force from the Egypt–Israel border 1967 (◊Arab-Israeli Wars).

Thatcher Margaret Hilda (born Roberts) 1925– . British Conservative politician, in Parliament from 1959, party leader from 1975, and prime minister 1979-90. Landmarks of the Thatcher government include the independence of Zimbabwe, the ◊Falklands conflict; the 1984–85 miners' strike; reduction of inflation; large-scale privatization; the attempt to suppress the publication of ◊*Spycatcher* and other measures to limit civil liberties; the Anglo-Irish Agreement of 1985; a large rise in unemployment; depletion of the ◊welfare state; the introduction of the community charge or ◊poll tax in Scotland 1989, England 1990; active opposition to the Iraqi invasion of Kuwait 1990; and resistance to practical integration with Europe. She resigned in acknowledgement of deep divisions within her party in Nov 1990.

thaumatrope in photography, a disc with two different pictures at opposite ends of its surface. They combine into one when rapidly rotated because of the persistence of visual impressions.

theatre broad term applied to a performance by actors for an audience, which may include ◊drama, dancing, music, ◊mime, ◊puppetry and so on. The term is also used for the place or building in which dramatic performances take place. Theatre history can be traced to Egyptian religious ritualistic drama as far back as 3200 BC.

Theatre Museum museum in London opened in ◊Covent Garden, London, on 23 Apr 1987 to commemorate Shakespeare's birthday. It houses the largest collections of memorabilia from the world of the theatre, opera, ballet, dance, circus, puppetry, pop, and rock and roll.

thebaine highly poisonous extract of ◊opium.

Thebes capital of Boeotia in ancient Greece. In the Peloponnesian War it was allied with Sparta against Athens, and for a short time after 371 BC it was the most powerful state in Greece. Alexander the Great destroyed it in 336 BC and although it was restored it was never again important.

Thebes Greek name of an ancient city (Niut-Ammon) in Upper Egypt, on the Nile, probably founded under the first dynasty, centre of the worship of Ammon, and the Egyptian capital under the New Kingdom about 1600 BC. Temple ruins survive near the modern villages of Karnak and Luxor, and in the nearby *Valley of the Kings* the 18th–20th dynasty kings, including Tutankhamen and Amenhotep III, are buried.

theft in Britain, under the Theft Act 1968, the dishonest appropriation of another's property with the intention of depriving him/her of it permanently: maximum penalty ten years imprisonment. The act placed under a single head forms of theft which had formerly been dealt with individually, for example burglary and larceny.

thegn an Anglo-Saxon hereditary nobleman rewarded by the granting of land for service to the king or a lord.

theism belief in the existence of gods, but more especially in that of a single personal God, made known to the world in a special revelation.

theme in music, a basic melody or musical figure, which often occurs with variations.

Themis in Greek mythology, one of the ◊Titans, the daughter of Uranus and Gaia. She was the personification of law and order.

Themistocles 525–460 BC. Greek soldier. Largely responsible for the ostracizing of ◊Aristides in 483 BC, he held almost supreme power in Athens for ten years, created its navy and strengthened its walls, and fought with distinction in the Battle of ◊Salamis 480 BC during the Persian War. Banished by Spartan influence about 470 BC, he fled to Asia, where Artaxerxes, the Persian king, received him with favour.

Theocritus born *c.* 270 BC– . Greek poet. Probably born at Syracuse, he spent much of his life at Alexandria. His *Idylls* became models for later pastoral poetry.

theodolite instrument used in surveying for the measurement of horizontal and vertical angles. It consists of a small telescope mounted so as to move on two graduate circles, one horizontal and the other vertical, while its axes pass through the centre of the circles. See also ◊triangulation.

Theodora 508–548. Byzantine empress from 527, originally the mistress of Emperor Justinian, and his consort from about 523. She earned a reputation for charity and courage.

Theodorakis Mikis 1925– . Greek composer, imprisoned 1967–70 for attempting to overthrow the military regime.

Theodoric *the Great* 455–526. King of the Ostrogoths from 474 in succession to his father. He invaded Italy 488, overthrew King Odoacer (whom he murdered) and established his own Ostrogothic kingdom there, with its capital in Ravenna. He had no strong successor, and his kingdom eventually became part of the Byzantine Empire of Justinian.

Theodosius II 401–450. Byzantine emperor from 408, who defeated the Persians 421 and 441, and from 441 bought off Attila's Huns with tribute.

theology the study of God or gods, either by reasoned deduction from the natural world, or through revelation, as in the scriptures of Christianity, Islam, or other religions.

theorbo a form of ◊lute.

theosophy any religious or philosophical system based on intuitive insight into the nature of the divine, but especially that of the Theosophical Society founded in New York in 1875 by Madame Blavatsky and Colonel II S Olcott, based on Hindu ideas of ◊Karma and ◊reincarnation, with ◊Nirvana as the eventual aim.

Theravāda one of the two major forms of ◊Buddhism, common in S Asia (Sri Lanka, Thailand, Kampuchea, and Myanmar); the other is the later ◊Mahāyāna.

Thérèse of Lisieux 1873–1897. French saint. Born at Alençon, she entered a Carmelite convent at Lisieux at 15, where her holy life induced her superior to ask her to write her spiritual autobiography. She advocated the Little Way of Goodness in small things in everyday life, and is known as Little Flower of Jesus. She died of tuberculosis and was canonized 1925.

therm unit of energy defined as 10^5 British thermal units; equivalent to 1.055×10^8 joules. It is no longer in scientific use.

thermal conductivity in physics, the ability of a substance to conduct heat. Good thermal conductors, like good electrical conductors, are generally materials with many free electrons (such as metals). Thermal conductivity is expressed in units of ◊joules per second per metre per degree ◊Kelvin ($Js^{-1}m^{-1}K^1$).

thermal expansion or *expansivity* in physics, expansion due to a rise in temperature, expressible in terms of linear, area, or volume expansion.

thermal reactor nuclear reactor in which the neutrons released by fission of uranium-235 nuclei are slowed down in order to increase their chances of capture by other uranium-235 nuclei, inducing further fission. Those slowed to a speed matching the surrounding material's thermal (heat) energy are called *thermal neutrons*, and these are the most likely to induce fission and ensure the continuation of the chain reaction.

thermic lance cutting tool consisting of a tube of mild steel, enclosing tightly-packed small steel rods and fed with oxygen. On ignition temperatures above 3000°C are produced and the thermic lance becomes its own sustaining fuel. It rapidly penetrates walls and a 23 cm/9 in steel door can be cut through in less than 30 seconds.

Thermidor 11th month of the French Revolutionary calendar, which gave its name to the period after the fall of the Jacobins and the proscription of Robespierre by the National Convention on 9 Thermidor 1794.

thermionics branch of electronics dealing with the emission of electrons from matter under the influence of heat.

thermite process a process used in incendiary devices and welding operations. It uses a powdered mixture of aluminium and (usually) iron oxide, which, when ignited, gives out enormous heat. The oxide is reduced to iron, which is molten at the high temperatures produced. This can be used to make a weld. The process was discovered by German chemist Hans Goldschmidt in 1895.

thermocouple electric temperature-measuring device consisting of a circuit having two wires made of different metals welded together at their ends. A current flows in the circuit when the two junctions are maintained at different temperatures (◊Seebeck effect). The electromotive force generated – measured by a millivoltmeter – is proportional to the temperature difference.

thermodynamics branch of physics dealing with the transformation of heat into other forms of energy, on which is based the study of the efficient working of engines, such as the steam and internal combustion engines. The three laws of thermo-

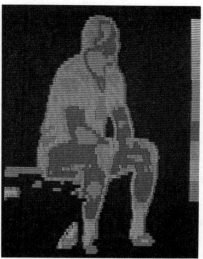

thermography Thermogram, or heat image, of a man. The warmest parts of his body show as spots of red; the cooler areas are blue, green, and purple.

dynamics are: (1) energy can be neither created nor destroyed, heat and mechanical work being mutually convertible; (2) it is impossible for an unaided self-acting machine to convey heat from one body to another at a higher temperature; (3) it is impossible by any procedure, no matter how idealized, to reduce any system to the ◊absolute zero of temperature (0K/-273°C) in a finite number of operations. Put into mathematical form, these have widespread applications in physics and chemistry.

thermography the photographic recording of heat patterns. It is used medically as an imaging technique to identify 'hot spots' in the body, for example tumours, where cells are more active than usual.

thermoluminescence light released by a material which is heated after it is exposed to ◊irradiation. It occurs with most crystalline substances to some extent. It is used in archaeology to date pottery, and by geologists in studying terrestrial rocks and meteorites.

thermometer instrument for measuring temperature. Expansion of a liquid is employed in common liquid-in-glass thermometers, such as those containing mercury or alcohol. The more accurate gas thermometer uses the effect of temperature on the pressure of a gas held at constant volume. A resistance thermometer takes advantage of the change in resistance of a conductor (such as a platinum wire) with variation in temperature. These are many types, designed to measure temperature ranges and to varying degrees of accuracy. Each makes use of a different physical effect of temperature. Another electrical thermometer is the ◊thermocouple. Mechanically, temperature change can be indicated by the change in curvature of a bimetallic strip (as commonly used in a ◊thermostat).

Thermopylae, Battle of battle during the ◊Persian wars in 480 BC when Leonidas, king of Sparta, and 1,000 men defended the pass of Thermopylae to the death against the Persians. The pass led from Thessaly to Locris in central Greece.

Thermos trade name for a type of ◊vacuum flask.

thermosphere the layer in the Earth's ◊atmosphere above the mesosphere and below the exosphere. Its lower level is about 80 km/50 mi above

thermometer

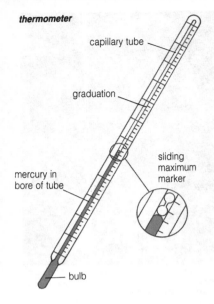

capillary tube

graduation

mercury in bore of tube

sliding maximum marker

bulb

the ground but its upper level is undefined. The ionosphere is located in the thermosphere. In the thermosphere the temperature rises with increasing height, to a maximum of several thousand degrees C. However, because of the thinness of the air, very little heat is present.

thermostat a temperature-controlling device that makes use of feedback. It employs a temperature sensor (often a bimetallic strip) to operate a switch or valve to control electricity or fuel supply. Thermostats are used in central heating, ovens, and car engines.

thesaurus (Greek 'treasure') a collection of synonyms or words with related meaning. Early thesaurus compilers include ◊Pliny, Francis ◊Bacon, and Comenius (1592–1670), but the best-known is Peter Mark ◊Roget, whose work was published in 1852.

Theseus legendary hero of ◊Attica, supposed to have united the states of the area under a constitutional government at Athens. Ariadne, whom he later abandoned on Naxos, helped him find his way through the labyrinth to kill the ◊Minotaur. He also fought the Amazons and was one of the Argonauts.

Thespis 6th century BC. Legendary Greek poet, said to have introduced the first actor into plays (previously presented by choruses only), hence the word 'thespian' for an actor. He was also said to have invented tragedy and to have introduced the wearing of linen masks.

Thessaloniki English *Salonica* port in Macedonia, NE Greece, at the head of the Gulf of Thessaloniki, the second largest city of Greece; population (1981) 706,200. Industries include textiles, shipbuilding, chemicals, brewing, and tanning.

history Founded by the Romans 315 BC, captured by the Saracens 904 AD, by the Turks 1430, it was restored to Greece 1912.

Thessaly Greek *Thessalia* region of E central Greece, on the Aegean; area 14,037 sq km/5,395 sq mi; population (1981) 695,650. It is a major area of cereal production.

history An independent state in ancient Greece, it later formed part of the Roman province of ◊Macedonia. It was Turkish from the 14th century until incorporated in Greece 1881.

Thetford Mines site of the world's largest asbestos deposits, Quebec, Canada.

thiamine a ◊vitamin of the B complex (B_1). Its absence from the diet causes the disease beri-beri.

Thiers Louis Adolphe 1797–1877. French politician and historian. He held cabinet posts under Louis Philippe, led the parliamentary opposition to Napoleon III from 1863, and as head of the provisional government in 1871 negotiated peace with Prussia and suppressed the Paris ◊Commune. He was first president of the Third Republic 1871–73.

Thimbu or *Thimphu* capital since 1962 of the Himalayan state of ◊Bhutan; population (1982) 15,000.

thing an assembly of freemen in the Norse lands (Scandinavia) during the medieval period. It could encompass a meeting of the whole nation (*Althing*) or of a small town or community (*Husthing*).

Think Tank popular name for *Central Policy Review Staff*, a consultative body to the UK government 1970–83, set up to provide Cabinet ministers with informed background advice on major policy decisions.

Third Reich a term coined by the German writer Moeller van den Bruck (1876–1925) in the 1920s and used by the Nazis to describe the years of Hitler's dictatorship after 1933, although they later dropped the term. The idea of the Third Reich (Third Empire) was based on the existence of two previous German empires, the medieval Holy Roman Empire and the second empire 1871–1918.

Third World developing countries defined by the World Bank as the world's hundred poorest countries, as measured by their income per capita; they are concentrated in Asia, Africa, and Central America. They are divided into low-income countries, including China and India, and middle-income countries such as Nigeria, Indonesia, and Brazil. Problems associated with developing countries include high population growth and mortality rates, poor educational and health facilities, heavy dependence on agriculture and commodities for which prices and demand fluctuates, high levels of underemployment and, in some cases, political instability. Third World countries account for over 75% of all arms imports. The economic performance of developing countries in recent years has been mixed, with sub-Saharan Africa remaining in serious difficulties and others, in Asia, making significant progress. Failure for many developing countries to meet their enormous debt obligations has led to more stringent terms being imposed on loans by industrialized countries, as well as rescheduling (deferring payment).

Thirteen Colonies the 13 colonies of the USA that signed the ◊Declaration of Independence from Britain in 1776. Led by George Washington, they defeated the British army in the War of American Independence 1776–81 to become the original 13 United States of America. They were: Connecticut, Delaware, Georgia, Maryland, Massachusetts, New Hampshire, New Jersey, New York, North Carolina, Pennsylvania, Rhode Island, South Carolina, and Virginia.

38th parallel the demarcation line between North and South Korea, first agreed at the Yalta Conference in 1945 and largely unaltered by the Korean War of 1950–53.

35 mm a width of photographic film, the most popular format for the modern camera. The 35

thistle

mm camera falls into two categories, the ◊SLR and the rangefinder.

Thirty-Nine Articles a set of articles of faith defining the doctrine of the Anglican Church; see under ◊Anglican Communion.

Thirty Years' War major war in central Europe 1618–48. Beginning as a conflict between Protestants and Catholics, it gradually became transformed into a struggle to determine whether the ruling Austrian Hapsburg family would gain control of all Germany.

1618–20 A Bohemian revolt against Austrian rule was defeated. Some Protestant princes continued the struggle against Austria.

1625–27 Denmark entered the war on the Protestant side.

1630 Gustavus Adolphus of Sweden intervened on the Protestant side, overrunning N Germany.

1631 The Catholic commander Tilly stormed Magdeburg.

1632 Tilly defeated at Breitenfeld and the Lech, and died. The German general Wallenstein defeated at Battle of Lützen; Gustavus Adolphus killed.

1634 When the Swedes were defeated at Nördlingen, ◊Richelieu brought France into the war to inflict several defeats on Austria's Spanish allies. Wallenstein assassinated.

1648 The Treaty of Westphalia gave France S Alsace, and Sweden certain Baltic provinces, the emperor's authority in Germany becoming only nominal. The mercenary armies of Wallenstein, Tilly, and Mansfeld devastated Germany.

thistle species of prickly plant of several genera, such as *Carduus* and *Cirsium*, in the family Compositae, found in the N hemisphere. The stems are spiny, the flowerheads purple and cottony, and the leaves deeply indented. The thistle is the Scottish national emblem.

Thistle, Order of the a Scottish order of ◊knighthood.

Thomas Dylan (Marlais) 1914–1953. Welsh poet. His poems include the celebration of his 30th birthday 'Poem in October' and the evocation of his youth 'Fern Hill' 1946. His radio play *Under Milk Wood* 1954 and the short stories of *Portrait of the Artist as a Young Dog* 1940 are autobiographical. He died in New York where he had made a number of reading and lecture tours.

Thomas à Kempis 1380–1471. German Augustinian monk who lived at the monastery of Zwolle. He took his name from his birthplace Kempen; his real surname was Hammerken. His *Die Imitatione Christi/Imitation of Christ* is probably the most widely known devotional work ever written.

Thomas, St in the New Testament, one of the 12 Apostles, said to have preached in S India, hence the ancient churches there were referred to as the 'Christians of St Thomas'. He is not the author of

the Gospel of St Thomas, the Gnostic collection of Christ's sayings.

Thompson Flora 1877–1948. English novelist, whose trilogy *Lark Rise to Candleford* 1945 deals with late Victorian rural life.

Thompson Francis Morgan 'Daley' 1958– . English decathlete, who broke the world record four times, and won two Olympic titles, one world title, three European titles, and three Commonwealth titles. He retired 1992.

Thompson John Taliaferro 1860–1940. US colonel, and inventor of the Thompson sub-machine-gun (see ◊machine gun).

Thomson Elihu 1853–1937. US inventor. He founded, with E J Houston, the Thomson-Houston Electric Company in 1882, later merging with the Edison Company to form the General Electric Company. He made important advances into the nature of the ◊electric arc, and invented the first high-frequency ◊dynamo and ◊transformer.

Thomson George Paget 1892–1975. British physicist, son of Joseph ◊Thomson. His work on ◊interference phenomena in the scattering of electrons by crystals helped to confirm the wave-like nature of particles. He shared a Nobel Prize with C J ◊Davisson 1937, and was knighted 1943.

Thomson James 1700–1748. Scottish poet, whose descriptive blank verse poem *The Seasons* 1726–30 was a forerunner of the Romantic movement. He also wrote the words of 'Rule, Britannia'.

Thomson Joseph John 1856–1940. British physicist, who discovered the ◊electron. He was responsible for organizing the Cavendish atomic research laboratory. His work inaugurated the electrical theory of the atom, and his elucidation of positive rays and their application to an analysis of neon led to ◊Aston's discovery of ◊isotopes.

Thomson Virgil 1896–1989. US composer. His large body of work, characterized by a clarity and simplicity of style, includes operas such as *Four Saints in Three Acts* (libretto by Gertrude Stein) 1934, orchestral, choral, and chamber music, and film scores.

Thor in Norse mythology, son of Odin and Frigga, god of thunder (his hammer), and represented as a man of enormous strength defending humanity against demons. Thursday is named after him.

thorax in vertebrates, the part of the body containing the heart and lungs, and protected by the rib cage; in arthropods, the middle part of the body, between the head and abdomen.

Thoreau Henry David 1817–1862. US author and naturalist. His work *Walden, or Life in the Woods* 1854 stimulated the back-to-nature movement, and he completed some 30 volumes based on his daily nature walks. His essay 'Civil Disobedience' 1849, advocating peaceful resistance to unjust laws, had a wide impact.

thorium a dark grey, naturally radioactive metal, widely distributed throughout the world in minerals, particularly monazite beach sands; symbol Th, atomic number 90, atomic weight 232.05. Discovered by Berzelius (1828), it has a half-life 1.39×10^{10} years, and its greatest potential use is breeding from it uranium-233, a fuel for nuclear power reactors.

thorn apple annual plant *Datura stramonium*, also called *jimsonweed*, growing to 2 m/6 ft in N temperate and subtropical areas. It bears white or violet trumpet-shaped flowers and capsule-like fruit that splits to release black seeds. All parts of the plant are poisonous.

throwing events Fatima Whitbread throwing the javelin.

Thorpe Jeremy 1929– . British Liberal politician, leader of the Liberal Party 1967–76.

Thorwaldsen Bertel 1770–1844. Danish sculptor in the Neoclassical style. He went to Italy on a scholarship in 1796 and stayed in Rome for most of his life, producing highly successful portraits, monuments, religious and mythological works.

Thoth in Egyptian mythology, god of wisdom and learning. He was represented as a scribe with the head of an ◊ibis, the bird sacred to him.

Thothmes four Egyptian kings of the 18th dynasty, including:

Thothmes I king of Egypt 1540–1501 BC. He founded the Egyptian empire in Syria.

Thothmes III king of Egypt c. 1500–1446 BC. He extended the empire to the Euphrates, and conquered Nubia. He was a grandson of Thothmes I.

Thousand and One Nights a collection of Oriental tales, known also as the ◊*Arabian Nights*.

thousand days the period of office of US president John F Kennedy from 20 Jan 1961 to his assassination on 22 Nov 1963.

Thrace Greek *Thráki* ancient empire (6000 BC–300 AD) in the Balkans, SE Europe, formed by parts of modern Greece, Bulgaria. It was held successively by the Greeks, Persians, Macedonians, and Romans.

threadworm a form of ◊nematode.

three-day week the policy adopted by British prime minister Edward Heath in Jan 1974 to combat an economic crisis and coal miners' strike. A shortage of electrical power led to the allocation of energy to industry for only three days each week. A general election was called in Feb 1974 during the ◊winter of discontent.

threshing agricultural process of separating the grain of corn from the ear. Traditionally, the work was carried out by hand in the winter months using the flail, a jointed beating stick. Today, threshing is carried out inside the combine harvester at the time of cutting.

thrips tiny insect with feathery wings, of the order Thysanoptera.

throat in engineering, any narrowing entry, such as the throat of a carburettor; in humans, the passage that leads from the back of the nose and mouth to the ◊trachea and ◊oesophagus. It includes the ◊pharynx and the ◊larynx, the latter being at the top of the trachea. The word 'throat' is also used to mean the front part of the neck, both in humans and other vertebrates, for example, in describing the plumage of birds.

thrombosis a condition in which the blood clots in a vein or artery, causing loss of circulation to the area served by the vessel.

throwing events field athletic contests. There are four at major international track and field meetings; hammer throw (men only), javelin, discus throw, and shot putt. Caber tossing is also a throwing event but found only at Highland Games.

thrush bird of the family Turdidae, found worldwide, noted for its song. They are usually brown with speckles of other colours. They are between 12–30 cm/5–12 in long.

thrush infection usually of the mouth, but also sometimes of the vagina, caused by a yeast-like fungus. It is seen as white patches on the mucous membrane.

Thrust 2 jet-propelled car in which British driver Richard Noble set a new world land speed record in the Black Rock Desert of Nevada, USA, in Oct 1983. The record speed was 1,019.4 kph/633.468 mph.

Thucydides 460–400 BC. Athenian historian, who exercised command in the ◊Peloponnesian War in 424 with so little success that he was banished till 404. In his *History of the Peloponnesian War* he attempted a scientific impartiality.

thug originally a member of a Hindu sect who strangled travellers as sacrifices to ◊Kali the goddess of destruction; suppressed about 1830.

Thule Greek and Roman name for the most northerly land known. It was applied to the Shetlands, the Orkneys, and Iceland, and by later writers to Scandinavia.

thulium a metallic element, symbol Tm, atomic number 69, relative atomic mass 168.94. One of the lanthanide series of elements, it is used in arc lighting. The isotope Tm-170 is used as an X-ray source.

Thurber James (Grover) 1894–1961. US humorist. His short stories, written mainly for the *New Yorker* magazine, include 'The Secret Life of Walter Mitty' 1932, and his doodle drawings include fanciful impressions of dogs.

thylacine another name for the ◊Tasmanian tiger/wolf.

thyme herb, genus *Thymus*, of the family Labiatae. Garden thyme *Thymus vulgaris*, a native of the Mediterranean, grows to 30 cm/1 ft high, with aromatic leaves used for seasoning, and pinkish flowers.

thymus an organ in vertebrates, situated in the upper chest cavity in humans. The thymus processes the ◊lymphocyte cells to produce T-lymphocytes (T denotes 'thymus-derived'), which are responsible for binding to specific invading organisms and killing them, or rendering them harmless. The thymus reaches full size at puberty, and shrinks thereafter; the stock of T-lymphocytes is built up early in life, so this function diminishes in adults, but the thymus continues to function as an ◊endocrine gland, producing the hormone thymosin, which stimulates the activity of the T-lymphocytes.

thyroid an ◊endocrine gland of vertebrates, situated in the neck. It secrets thyroxin, a hormone containing iodine. This stimulates growth, metabolism, and other functions of the body. Abnormal action produces Graves' disease, with bulging eyeballs, while deficient action produces ◊myxoedema in adults and dwarfism in juveniles.

thyrotoxicosis a synonym for ◊hyperthyroidism.

Tianjin formerly *Tientsin* port and industrial and commercial city, and a special municipality in Hubei province, central China: city population (1989) 5,620,000. Its handmade silk and wool carpets are renowed. Dagan oilfield is nearby. Tianjin was opened to foreign trade 1860, and occupied by the Japanese 1937.

Tian Shan (Chinese *Tien Shan*) mountain system in central Asia. The highest peak is *Pik Pobedy* on the Xinjiang/Kyrgyz border 7,439 m/24,415 ft.

tiara the triple crown worn by the pope, or a semi-circular headdress worn by women for formal occasions. The term was originally applied to a headdress worn by the ancient Persians.

Tiberius Claudius Nero 42 BC–37 AD. Roman emperor, the stepson, adopted son, and successor of Augustus from 14 AD. A distinguished soldier, he was a conscientious ruler under whom the empire prospered.

Tibet autonomous region of SW China (Pinyin form *Xizang*)
area 1,221,600 sq km/471,540 sq mi
capital Lhasa
products wool, borax, salt, horn, musk, herbs, furs, gold, iron, pyrites, lapis lazuli, mercury, textiles, chemicals, agricultural machinery. Industrialization (textiles, chemicals, agricultural machinery) has been encouraged and many Chinese have settled in the country.
population (1991) 2,190,000 including 2,090,000 Tibetan nationalists
government Tibet is an autonomous region of ◊China with its own People's Government and People's Congress. The controlling force in Tibet is the Communist Party of China, represented locally by First Secretary Wu Jinghua (1985).
history Tibet was an independent kingdom from the 5th century AD. It came under nominal Chinese suzerainty c. 1700. Independence was regained after a revolt in 1912. China regained control in 1951 when the historic ruler, the ◊Dalai Lama, was driven from the country and the monks (who formed 25% of the population) were forced out of the monasteries. Between 1951–59 the Chinese People's Liberation Army (PLA) controlled Tibet, although the Dalai Lama returned as nominal spiritual and temporal head of state. In 1959 a Tibetan uprising spread from bordering regions to Lhasa and was supported by the Tibet local government. The rebellion was suppressed by the PLA, prompting the Dalai Lama and 9,000 Tibetans to flee to India. The Chinese proceeded to dissolve the Tibet local government, abolish serfdom, collectivize agriculture and suppress ◊Lamaism. In 1965 Tibet became an autonomous region of China. Chinese rule continued to be resented, however, and the economy languished. The country is one of immense strategic importance to China, being the site of 200,000 troops and a nuclear missile base at Nagchuka. In 1989 many anti-China demonstrators were shot and all foreigners were expelled.

tide

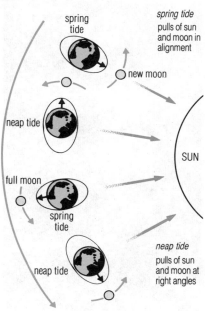

spring tide

spring tide pulls of sun and moon in alignment

new moon

neap tide

SUN

full moon

spring tide

neap tide pulls of sun and moon at right angles

neap tide

Tibetan person of Tibetan culture. The majority of Tibetans live in Tibet, though there are refugee communities in India, and Nepál. The Tibetan language belongs to the Sino-Tibetan language family.

tick arachnid allied to the ◊mites; ticks are bloodsucking, disease-carrying parasites on humans, animals, and birds.

tidal power station a kind of ◊hydroelectric power plant that uses the 'head' of water created by the rise and fall of the ocean tides to spin the water turbines.

tidal wave a misleading name for a ◊tsunami.

tide rise and fall of sea level due to the gravitational forces of the Moon and Sun. High water occurs at an average interval of 12 hr 24 min 30 sec. The highest or *spring tides* are at or near new and full Moon, and the lowest or *neap tides* when the Moon is in the first or third quarter. Some seas, such as the Mediterranean, have very small tides.

Tieck Johann Ludwig 1773–1853. German Romantic poet and collector of folk-tales, some of which he dramatized, for example 'Puss in Boots'.

Tientsin former name for ◊Tianjin, an industrial city in NE China.

Tiepolo Giovanni Battista 1696–1770. Italian painter, born in Venice, he created huge Rococo decorative schemes in palaces and churches in NE Italy, SW Germany, and in Madrid (1762–70). The style is light-hearted, the palette light and warm, and he made great play with illusionism.

Tierra del Fuego island group divided between Chile and Argentina. It is separated from the mainland of South America by the Strait of Magellan, and Cape Horn is at the southernmost point. Ushuaia (Argentina) is the chief town, and the world's most southerly town. Industries include oil and sheep farming.

Tiffany Louis Comfort 1848–1933. US artist and glassmaker, son of Charles Louis Tiffany who

Tiepolo The Immaculate Conception *(commissioned 1767) Courtauld Collection, London.*

founded the New York jewellers. He produced stained glass windows, iridescent Favrile (Latin *faber* 'craftsman') glass, and lampshades. He used glass which contained oxides of iron and other impurities to produce rich colours.

tiger largest of the great cats *Panthera tigris*, formerly found in much of Central and S Asia but nearing extinction due to hunting, and the destruction of their natural habitat. The tiger can grow to 3.6 m/12 ft long, and 300kg/660 lbs, and has a yellow-orange coat with black stripes. It is solitary, and feeds on deer or cattle. It is a good swimmer.

Tigris (Arabic *Shatt Dijla*) river flowing through Turkey and Iraq (see also ◊Mesopotamia), joining the ◊Euphrates above Basra; length 1,600 km/1,000 mi.

Tihuanaco site of a Peruvian city, 24 km/15 mi S of Lake Titicaca, which gave its name to the 8th–14th century civilization that preceded the Inca.

Tijuana city and resort in NW Mexico; population (1980) 461,257; noted for horse races and casinos. ◊San Diego adjoins it across the US border.

Tikhonov Nikolai 1905– . Soviet politician. Once a locomotive engineer, he became a close associate of President Brezhnev, joining the Politburo in 1979. He was prime minister (chair of the Council of Ministers) 1980–85. In Apr 1989 he was removed from the central committee.

till or *boulder clay* a deposit of clay, mud, gravel, and boulders left by a glacier. Till is unsorted, all sizes of fragment are mixed up together, and it shows no stratification, that is, it does not form clear layers or ◊beds.

Tilly Jan Tserklaes, Count Tilly 1559–1632. Flemish commander of the army of the Catholic League and imperial forces in the ◊Thirty Years' War. Notorious for his storming of Magdeburg, E Germany, in 1631, he was defeated by the Swedish king Gustavus Adolphus at Breitenfeld, and at the river Lech in SW Germany, where he was mortally wounded.

timber wood used in construction, furniture and paper pulp. *Hardwoods* include tropical mahogany, teak, ebony, rosewood, temperate oak, elm, beech, and eucalyptus. Most are slow-growing and world supplies are near exhaustion. *Softwoods* are comprised of the ◊conifers (pine, fir, spruce, and larch) which are quick to grow and easy to work, but inferior in quality of grain. *White woods* include ash, birch, and sycamore; all have light-coloured timber, are fast-growing, and can be used through modern methods as veneers on cheaper timber.

timbre in music, the tone colour of an instrument.

Timbuktu or *Tombouctou* town in Mali; population (1976) 20,500. A camel caravan centre from the 11th century on the fringe of the Sahara, since 1960 it has been surrounded by the southward movement of the desert, and the former canal link with the Niger is dry. Products include salt.

time the continuous passage of existence, recorded by division into hours, minutes, and seconds. Formerly measurement of time was based on the Earth's rotation on its axis, but this was found to be irregular. Therefore the second, the standard ◊SI unit of time, was redefined first, in 1956, in terms of the Earth's annual orbit of the Sun, and subsequently, in 1967, in terms of a radiation pattern of the element caesium.

time and motion study process of analysis applied to a job or number of jobs to check the efficiency of the work method, equipment used, and the worker. Its findings are used to improve performance.

Timor largest and most easterly of the Sunda islands, part of Indonesia; area 33,610 sq km/12,973 sq mi. West Timor (capital Kupang) was formerly Dutch and was included in Indonesian independence. East Timor (capital Dili) was an overseas province of Portugal until it was annexed by Indonesia 1975. Guerrilla warfare by local people seeking independence continues. Products include coffee, maize, rice, and coconuts.

Timothy in the New Testament, companion to St ◊Paul, both on his missionary journeys and in prison. Two of the Pauline epistles are addressed to him.

tin a silver-white, crystalline metal, malleable and somewhat ductile, which crumbles to a greyish powder at low temperatures; symbol Sn (Latin *stannum*), atomic number 50, atomic weight 118.70. It is used in alloys and containers. Tin is found chiefly in the mineral cassiterite, SnO_2, in Malaysia, Indonesia, and Bolivia.

tinamou South American bird of the order *Tinamiformes*, of which there are some 45 species. They are up to 40 cm/16 in long, and their drab colour provides good camouflage. They may be related to the flightless birds, and are themselves poor flyers. They are mainly vegetarian, but sometimes eat insects. They escape predators by remaining still, or by burrowing through dense cover.

Tinbergen Jan 1903–1988. Dutch economist. He shared a Nobel Prize 1969 with Ragnar Frisch for his work on ◊econometrics (the mathematical-statistical expression of economic theory).

tinnitus internal sounds, inaudible to others, which are heard by sufferers from malfunctions of hearing, from infection of the middle or inner ear.

tinplate the metal used for most 'tin' cans. They are not made of tin itself, but of tinplate which is mild steel coated with tin. The steel provides the strength and the tin provides the corrosion resistance, ensuring that the food inside is not contaminated. Tinplate may be made by ◊electroplating, or by dipping in a bath of molten tin.

Tintoretto Jacopo. Real name Jacopo Robusti 1518–1594. Italian painter, active in Venice. His dramatic religious paintings are spectacularly lit and full of movement, such as his enormous canvases of the lives of Christ and the Virgin in the Scuola di San Rocco, Venice, 1564–88. A student of Titian, his painting foreshadowed the ◊Baroque movement.He was so named because his father was a dyer (*tintore*).

Tipperary county in the Republic of Ireland, province of Munster, divided into north and south regions (administrative headquarters Nenagh and Clonmel respectively), and includes part of the Golden Vale, a major dairy farming region; total area 4,255 sq km/1,642 sq mi; population (1986) 136,500.

Tippett Michael (Kemp) 1905– . British composer, whose works include the operas *The Midsummer Marriage* 1952, *The Knot Garden* 1970, and *The Ice Break* 1977; four symphonies; *Magnificat and Nunc Dimittis* and *Songs for Ariel* 1962.

Tirana (Albanian *Tiranë*) capital (since 1920) of Albania; population (1983) 206,000. Industries include metallurgy, cotton textiles, soap, and cigarettes. It was founded in the early 17th century by Turks when part of the Ottoman Empire. Though now mainly modern, some older districts and mosques have been preserved.

Tirol former province (from 1363) of the Austrian Empire, divided 1919 between Austria and Italy (see ◊Trentino-Alto Adige). The modern Austrian state of Tirol (capital Innsbruck) produces diesel engines, optical instruments, and hydroelectric power; area 12,647 sq km/4,882 sq mi; population (1986) 606,000.

Tirpitz Alfred von 1849–1930. German admiral. As secretary for the Navy 1897–1916, he created the modern German navy, and planned the World War I U-boat campaign.

Tirso de Molina Pen name of Gabriel Telléz 1571–1648. Spanish dramatist and monk, who wrote more than 400 plays, of which eight are extant, including comedies, historical and biblical dramas, and a series based on the legend of Don Juan.

Tiryns ancient Greek city in the Peloponnesus on the plain of Argos, with remains of the ◊Mycenaean culture.

Tissot James (Joseph Jacques) 1836–1902. French painter, who produced detailed portraits of fashionable Victorian society during a ten-year spell in England.

tissue in biology, a general term for any kind of cellular fabric that occurs in an organism's body. Several kinds of tissue can usually be distinguished, each consisting of cells of a particular kind bound together by cell walls (in plants) or extracellular matrix (in animals). Thus, nerve and muscle are different kinds of tissue in animals, as are ◊parenchyma and ◊sclerenchyma in plants.

tissue culture a process in which cells from a plant or animal are removed from the organism, and grown under carefully controlled conditions in a sterile medium containing all the necessary nutrients. Tissue culture can provide information on cell growth and differentiation, and is also used in plant propagation and drug production. See also ◊meristem.

tit or *titmouse* insectivorous, acrobatic bird of the family Paridae, of which there are 65 species. They are 8–20 cm/3–8 in long, have grey or black plumage, often with blue or yellow markings. They are found in Eurasia and Africa, and also in North America, where they are called *chickadees*.

Titan in astronomy, largest moon of the planet Saturn, with a diameter of 5,150 km/3,200 mi, and a mean distance from Saturn of 1,222,000 km/759,000 mi. It was discovered 1655 by Christiaan Huygens. Titan is the only moon in the Solar System with a substantial atmosphere (mostly nitrogen), topped with smoggy orange clouds that obscure the surface, which may be covered with liquid ethane lakes. Its surface atmospheric pressure is greater than Earth's.

Titan in Greek mythology, any of the giant children of Uranus and ◊Gaia, who included Kronos, Rhea, Themis (mother of Prometheus and personification of law and order) and Oceanus. Kronos and Rhea were in turn the parents of Zeus, who ousted Kronos as the ruler of the world.

Titanic British liner, supposedly unsinkable, which struck an iceberg off the Grand Banks of Newfoundland, Canada, on its maiden voyage 14–15 Apr 1912; 1,513 lives were lost. In 1985 it was located by robot submarine 4 km/2.5 mi down in an ocean canyon.

titanium a lustrous, steel-like white metal resembling iron, burning in air, and the only metal to burn in nitrogen; symbol Ti, atomic weight 47.90, atomic number 22. It is very strong and resistant to corrosion, and is used in many high-speed aeroplanes and spacecraft.

Titan rocket a family of US space rockets, developed from the Titan intercontinental missile. Two-stage Titan rockets launched the ◊Gemini manned missions. More powerful Titans, with additional stages and strap-on boosters, were used to launch spy satellites and space probes, including ◊Viking and ◊Voyager.

tithe formerly, a payment exacted from the inhabitants of a parish for the maintenance of the church and its incumbent; some religious groups continue the practice by giving 10% of members' incomes to charity.

Titian Anglicized form of the name of Tiziano Vecellio *c.* 1487–1576. Italian painter, active in Venice. In 1533 he became court painter to Charles V, Holy Roman emperor, whose son Philip II of Spain later became his patron. Titian's work is richly coloured, with inventive composition. He created a vast output of portraits, religious paintings, and mythological scenes, including *Bacchus and Ariadne* 1520–23, *Venus and Adonis* 1554, and the *Entombment of Christ* 1559.

Titicaca lake in the Andes, 3,810 m/12,500 ft above sea level; area 8,300 sq km/3,200 sq mi, the largest lake in South America. It is divided between Bolivia (port at Guaqui) and Peru (ports at Puno and Huancane). It has huge edible frogs.

Tito Adopted name of Josip Broz 1892–1980. Yugoslav soldier and communist politician. In World War II he organized the National Liberation Army to carry on guerrilla warfare against the German invasion 1941, and was created marshal 1943. As prime minister 1946–53 and president from

Tito Marshal Tito, the former president of Yugoslavia.

1953, he followed a foreign policy of 'positive neutralism'.

Titograd formerly *Podgorica* capital of Montenegro, Yugoslavia; population (1981) 132,300. Industries include metal working, furniture making, and tobacco. It was damaged in World War II, and after rebuilding was renamed 1948 in honour of Tito. It was the birthplace of the Roman emperor Diocletian.

Titus Flavius Sabinus Vespasianus 39–81 AD. Roman emperor from 79. Eldest son of ◊Vespasian, he stormed Jerusalem 70 to end the Jewish revolt. He finished the Colosseum, and enjoyed a peaceful reign, except for ◊Agricola's campaigns in Britain.

Tlatelolco, Treaty of international agreement signed 1967 in Tlatelolco, Mexico, prohibiting nuclear weapons in Latin America (not ratified by Argentina); it was signed also by countries responsible for territories in the area (UK, USA, France, Netherlands).

Tlingit North American Indian people, living on the SE coast and nearby islands. They carved wooden totem poles bearing animals: the mythical 'thunderbird', raven, whale, octopus, beaver, bear, and wolf.

TLR camera a twin lens reflex camera, which has a viewing lens mounted above and parallel to the taking lens, of the same angle of view and focal length.

TM abbreviation for ◊*transcendental meditation*.

TNT trinitrotoluene, $CH_3C_6H_2(NO_3)_3$, a powerful high explosive. It is a yellow solid, prepared from toluene using sulphuric and nitric acids.

toad general name for over 2,500 species of tailless amphibians which are slow-moving, stout, and have dry warty skins. They live in cool, moist places, lay their eggs in water, and grow up to 25 cm/10 in long.

toad

western spadefoot toad

toadstool inedible or poisonous type of ◊fungus with a fleshy gilled fruiting body on a stalk.

tobacco large-leaved plant *Nicotiana tabacum*, family Solanaceae; native to tropical parts of the Americas, it is widely cultivated as an annual in warm, dry climates for use in cigars and cigarettes, and in powdered form as snuff. The worldwide profits of the tobacco industry are estimated to be over £4 billion annually.

Tobago island in the West Indies; part of the republic of ◊Trinidad and Tobago.

Tobruk Libyan port; population (1984) 94,000. Occupied by Italy 1911, it was taken by Britain 1941, and unsuccessfully besieged by Axis forces Apr–Dec 1941. It was captured by Germany Jun 1942 after the retreat of the main British force to Egypt, and this precipitated the replacement of Auchinleck by Montgomery as British commander.

toccata in music, a display piece for keyboard instruments, particularly the organ.

Tocqueville Alexis de 1805–1859. French politician and political scientist, author of the first analytical study of the US constitution *De la Démocratie en Amérique/Democracy in America* 1835, and of a penetrating description of France before the Revolution, *L'Ancien Régime et la Révolution/The Old Regime and the Revolution* 1856.

tog measure of thermal insulation used in the textile trade. The tog-value of an object is equal to ten times the temperature difference (in °C) between its two surfaces when the flow of heat is equal to one watt per square metre.

Togliatti Palmiro 1893–1964. Founder of the Italian Communist Party 1921, and influential member of the Comintern. Returning to Italy 1944 after years of exile in Moscow, he became party leader, and was a member of the government 1944–46.

Togo country in W Africa, bounded to the W by Ghana, to the E by Benin, and to the N by Burkina Faso.

Togo Heihachiro 1846–1934. Japanese admiral who commanded the fleet at the battle of Tsushima Strait 27 May 1905 when Japan decisively defeated the Russians and effectively ended the Russo-Japanese war of 1904–05.

Tojo Hideki 1884–1948. Japanese general and prime minister 1941–44. Promoted to chief of staff of the Guangdong army 1937, he served as minister for war 1938–39 and 1940–41. He was held responsible for defeats in the Pacific 1944 and forced to resign. He was hanged as a war criminal.

tokamak an experimental machine designed to investigate nuclear fusion. It consists of a chamber surrounded by electromagnets capable of exerting very powerful magnetic fields. The fields are generated to confine very hot (millions of degrees) ◊plasma, keeping it away from the chamber walls. See also ◊JET.

Tokugawa the military family that controlled Japan 1603–1867. *Iyeyasu* or *Ieyasu Tokugawa* (1542–1616) was the Japanese general and politician who established the Tokugawa shogunate. They were feudal lords who ruled about one-quarter of Japan.

Tokyo capital of Japan, on ◊Honshu Island; population (1985) 8,354,000, the metropolitan area of Tokyo-to over 12,000,000. The Sumida river delta separates the city from its suburb of Honjo. It is Japan's main cultural and industrial centre (engineering, chemicals, textiles, electrical goods). Founded in the 16th century as Yedo, it was renamed when the emperor moved his court there from Kyoto

Togo
Republic of (*République Togolaise*)

area 56,800 sq km/21,930 sq mi
capital Lomé
physical two savanna plains, divided by a range of hills NE–SW
head of state Etienne Gnassingbé Eyadéma from 1967

head of government Joseph Kokou Koffigoh from 1991
political system transitional
exports cocoa, coffee, coconuts, copra, phosphate, bauxite
currency franc CFA
population (1990 est) 3,566,000; annual growth rate 3%
life expectancy men 53, women 57 (1989)
language French (official) Ewe, Kabre
religion animist 46%, Christian 37%, Muslim 17%
literacy men 53%, women 28% (1985 est)
GNP $1.3bn (1987); $240 per head
chronology
1960 Achieved full independence as the Republic of Togo with Sylvanus Olympio as head of state.
1963 Olympio killed in a military coup. Nicolas Grunitzky became president.
1967 Grunitzky replaced by Lt-Gen Etienne Gnassingbé Eyadéma in a bloodless coup.
1973 The Assembly of Togolese People (RPT) formed as the only legal political party.
1979 Eyadéma returned in election.
1986 Unsuccessful coup attempt.
1991 Eyadéma legalized opposition parties.

1868. An earthquake 1923 killed 58,000 people. The city was severely damaged by Allied bombing in World War II. The subsequent rebuilding has made it into one of the world's most modern cities.

Toledo city on the river Tagus, central Spain; population (1982) 62,000. It was the capital of the Visigoth kingdom 534–711 (see ◊Goths), then became a Moorish city, and was the Castilian capital 1085–1560.

Tolkien J(ohn) R(onald) R(euel) 1892–1973. English writer, who created the fictional world of Middle Earth in *The Hobbit* 1937 and the trilogy *The Lord of the Rings* 1954–55, fantasy novels peopled with hobbits, dwarves, and strange magical creatures. His work became a cult in the 1960s and had many imitations.

Tolpuddle Martyrs six farm labourers of Tolpuddle, near Dorchester, England, who in 1834 were transported to Australia for forming a trade union. After nationwide agitation they were pardoned two years later.

Tolstoy Leo (Nikolaievich) 1828–1910. Russian novelist, who wrote *Tales from Sebastopol* 1856, *War and Peace* 1863–69, an epic set in the Napoleonic wars, and *Anna Karenina* 1873–77. From 1880 Tolstoy underwent a profound spiritual crisis and took up moral positions including passive resistance to evil, rejection of authority (religious or civil) and of private ownership, and a return to basic mystical Christianity. He was excommunicated by the Orthodox Church, and his later works banned.

Toltec member of an American Indian people who ruled much of Mayan central Mexico in the 10th–12th centuries, with their capital at Tula. Their religious centre was at Teotihuacán, where there are temples of the Sun and Moon, and to ◊Quetzalcoatl.

toluene $C_6H_5CH_3$ (also called *methyl benzene*) a colourless, inflammable liquid, insoluble in water, derived from petroleum. It is used as a solvent, in aircraft fuels, in preparing phenol (carbolic acid, used in making resins for adhesives, pharmaceuticals, and as a disinfectant),

and the powerful high explosive TNT (trinitrotoluene).

Tomasi Giuseppe, Prince of Lampedusa. Italian writer; see ◊Lampedusa.

tomato annual plant *Lycopersicon esculentum*, family Solanaceae; native to South America, it is widely cultivated for the many-seeded red fruit, used in salads and cooking.

Tombaugh Clyde (William) 1906– . US astronomer, who discovered the planet ◊Pluto 1930.

Tombstone former silver-mining town in the desert of SE Arizona, USA. The *gunfight at the OK Corral*, deputy marshal Wyatt Earp, his brothers, and 'Doc' Holliday against the Clanton gang, took place here 26 Oct 1881.

Tom Jones, The History of novel by Henry Fielding, published 1749. It describes the complicated, and not always reputable, early life of Tom Jones, an orphan, who is good-natured but hot-headed.

tommy gun informal name for Thompson submachine gun; see ◊machine gun.

Tom Sawyer, The Adventures of novel by Mark Twain written 1876. It describes young Tom Sawyer, his friend Huckleberry Finn, and their comic adventures by the Mississippi River before the American Civil War.

ton former imperial measure of weight, the *long ton* of 2,240 lb, equivalent to 1.016 metric ◊tonnes; also the North American *short ton* of 2,000 lb, equivalent to 0.907 metric tonnes.

tonality in music, the observance of a key structure, that is, the recognition of the importance of a tonic or key note, and of the diatonic scale built upon it. See also ◊atonality and ◊polytonality.

Tone (Theobald) Wolfe 1763–1798. Irish nationalist, called to the Bar 1789, and prominent in the revolutionary society of the United Irishmen. In 1798 he accompanied the French invasion of Ireland, was captured and condemned to death, but slit his own throat in prison.

tone poem in music, another name for ◊symphonic poem, as used, for example, by Richard Strauss.

Tonga
Kingdom of or Friendly Islands
(Pule'anga Fakatu'i 'o Tonga)

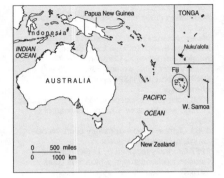

area 748 sq km/289 sq mi
capital Nuku'alofa on Tongatapu
physical comprises three groups of islands in the SW Pacific, mostly coral formations
head of state King Taufa'ahau Tupou IV from 1965
head of government Baron Vaea from 1991
political system constitutional monarchy
currency Tongan dollar or pa'anga
population (1988) 95,000; p.a. growth 2.4%
languages Tongan (official) English
religion Wesleyan 47%, Roman Catholic 14%, Free Church of Tonga 14%, Mormon 9%, Church of Tonga 9%
literacy 93% (1988)
GNP $65 million (1987); $430 per head
chronology
1965 Queen Salote died; succeeded by her son, King Tupou IV.
1970 Achieved full independence within the Commonwealth.
1990 Three prodemocracy candidates elected. Calls for reform of absolutist power.

Tonga country in the SW Pacific, in ◊Polynesia.

tongue in tetrapod (four-limbed) vertebrates, a muscular organ usually attached to the floor of the mouth. It has a thick root attached to a U-shaped bone (hyoid) behind. It is covered with ◊mucous membrane containing nerves and 'taste buds'. It directs food and drink to the teeth and into the throat for chewing and swallowing. In humans, it is important for speech; in other animals, for lapping up water and for grooming.

tonic in music, the first degree or key note of a scale, for example C in C major.

Tonkin Gulf Incident clash that triggered US entry into the Vietnam War. After a minor skirmish 2 Aug 1964, two US destroyers reported a night attack 4 Aug by North Vietnamese torpedo boats (radar and sonar effects were possibly misinterpreted, or invented as an excuse to get the USA into the war). A retaliatory air attack was made on North Vietnam which led to the eventual despatch of over 1 million US troops to battle in South Vietnam to prevent a North Vietnamese annexation.

Tonkin resolution act passed by the US Congress 7 Aug 1964 after the Tonkin Gulf Incident. It allowed President Johnson 'to take all necessary steps, including the use of armed forces' to help SEATO (South-East Asia Treaty Organization) members 'defend their freedom'. This resolution formed the basis for the considerable increase in US military involvement in the Vietnam War.

tonne the metric ton of 1,000 kg/2,204.6 lb; equivalent to 0.9842 of an imperial ton.

Tönnies Ferdinand 1855–1936. German social theorist and philosopher, one of the founders of the sociological tradition of community studies and urban sociology through his key work, ◊*Gemeinschaft–Gesellschaft* 1887.

tonsil a lump of lymphatic tissue situated at the back of the mouth and throat in higher vertebrates. The tonsils contain many ◊lymphocytes and are part of the body's defence system against infection.

tonsillectomy surgical removal of the tonsils.

tonsillitis an inflamation of the ◊tonsils.

tonsure the shaving of the hair of the head as a symbol of being a priest. Until 1973 in the Roman Catholic Church, the crown was shaved (leaving a surrounding fringe to resemble Christ's crown of thorns); in the Eastern Orthodox Church the hair is merely shorn close.

Tontons Macoutes death squads organized by François ◊Duvalier, president of Haiti 1959–71.

Tony Award any of the annual awards by the League of New York Theaters to playwrights, performers, and technicians in ◊Broadway plays. It is named after the US actress and producer Antoinette Perry (1888–1946).

tool an implement such as a hammer or a saw; a *machine tool* is a tool operated by power. Tools are the basis of industrial production; the chief machine tool is the ◊lathe. The industrial potential of a country is often calculated by the number of machine tools available. Automatic control of machine tools,

tooth

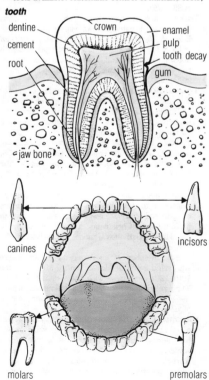

an important modern development, is known as ◊automation.

tooth in vertebrates, a hard structure in the mouth, used for biting and chewing food, and in defence and aggression. In humans, the first set (20 milk teeth) appear from age six months to two-and-a-half years. The permanent dentition replaces these from the sixth year onwards, the wisdom teeth (third molars) sometimes not appearing until the age of 25 or 30. Adults have 32 teeth: two incisors, one canine (eye tooth), two premolars, and three molars on each side of each jaw. The tooth is hollow, and filled with a highly sensitive pulp made of nerves and blood vessels. It has a root or roots set in a socket of fine bone, a neck covered by the ◊gum, covered with a crown of a bony substance (dentine) and hard white enamel.

topaz a mineral, fluosilicate of aluminium, $Al_2SiO_4(F,OH)_2$. It is usually yellow, or pink if it has been heated, and is used as a gemstone. It rates 8 on the Mohs scale of hardness.

tope slender shark *Galeorhinus galeus* ranging through temperate and tropical seas. Dark grey above and white beneath, it reaches 2 m/6 ft. The young are born well-formed, sometimes 40 at a time.

tope type of tumulus found in India and SE Asia; a Buddhist monument usually built over a relic of Buddha or his disciples. They date from 400–300 BC, including ones at Sanchi, near Bhilsa, central India.

topi or *korrigum* antelope *Damaliscus korrigum* of equatorial Africa, head and body about 1.7 m/5.5 ft long, 1.1 m/3.5 ft high at the shoulder, with a chocolate-brown coat.

topiary the clipping of trees and shrubs into ornamental shapes, originated by the Romans in the 1st century and revived in the 16th–17th centuries in formal gardens.

topology the branch of geometry that deals with those properties of a figure which remain unchanged even when the figure is transformed (bent or stretched), for example when a square painted on a rubber sheet is deformed by distorting the sheet. Topology has scientific applications, as in the study of turbulence in fluids. The map of the London Underground system is an example of the topological representation of the rail network.

topsoil the upper, cultivated layer of soil which may vary in depth from 8–45 cm/3–18 in. It contains organic matter, the decayed remains of vegetation, which plants need for active growth.

tor isolated mass of rock, usually granite, left upstanding on a moor after the surrounding rock has been worn away. Erosion takes place along the joints in the rock, wearing the outcrop into a mass of rounded lumps.

Torah in ◊Judaism, the first five books of the Hebrew Bible (Christian Old Testament), which are ascribed to Moses. It contains a traditional history of the world from the Creation to the death of Moses; it also includes rules and guidelines for religious observance and social conduct, including the Ten Commandments.

Torgau town in Leipzig county, Germany; population 20,000. In 1760, during the Seven Years' War Frederick II of Prussia defeated the Austrians nearby, and in World War II the US and Soviet forces first met here.

tornado extremely violent revolving storm with swirling, funnel-shaped clouds, caused by a rising column of warm air propelled by strong wind. A tornado can rise to a great height, but with a diameter of only a few hundred metres or less. Tornadoes moving at speeds of up to 400 kph/250 mph are common in the Mississippi basin of the USA.

Toronto port on Lake Ontario, capital of Ontario, Canada; metropolitan population (1985) 3,427,000. It is Canada's main industrial and commercial centre (banking, shipbuilding, cars, farm machinery, food processing, publishing), and also a cultural centre, with theatres and a film industry. A French fort was established 1749, and the site became the provincial capital (then named York) 1793; it was renamed Toronto (North American Indian 'place of meeting') 1834, when incorporated as a city.

torpedo type of ray (fish) whose electric organs between the pectoral fin and the head can give a powerful shock. They can grow to 180 cm/6 ft in length.

torpedo self-propelled underwater missile, invented in 1866 by the British engineer Robert ◊Whitehead. Modern torpedos are homing missiles; some resemble mines in that they lie on the seabed until activated by the acoustic signal of a passing ship. A television camera enables them to be remotely controlled, and in the final stage of attack they lock on to the radar or sonar signals of the target ship.

torque converter a device similar to a turbine, filled with oil, used in automatic transmission systems in cars, locomotives, and other vehicles to transmit power between the engine and the gearbox.

Torquemada Tomás de 1420–1498. Spanish Dominican friar, confessor to Queen Isabella I. In 1483 he revived the ◊Inquisition on her behalf, and at least 2,000 'heretics' were burned; Torquemada also expelled the Jews from Spain with a resultant decline of the economy.

torr unit of pressure used in high vacuum technology, equal to 1/760 of an ◊atmosphere. It is equivalent to 133.322 pascals, and for practical purposes the same as the millimetre of mercury. It is named after Evangelista Torricelli.

Torricelli Evangelista 1608–1647. Italian physicist and pupil of ◊Galileo, who devised the mercury ◊barometer.

tort in law, a wrongful act for which someone can be sued for damages in a civil court. It includes such acts as libel, trespass, injury done to someone (whether intentionally or by negligence), and inducement to break a contract (although breach of contract itself is not a tort). In general a tort is distinguished from a crime in that it affects the interests of an individual rather than of society at large, but some crimes can also be torts (for example, ◊assault).

tortoise reptile of the order Chelonia. Its shell consists of a curved upper carapace and flattened lower plastron joined at the sides. The head and limbs may

tortoise

toucan

be withdrawn into it when the tortoise is in danger. Most land tortoises are herbivorous and have no teeth. The mouth forms a sharp-edged 'beak'. Eggs are laid in warm earth in great numbers, and are not incubated by the mother. Some tortoises are known to live for 150 years, and range in size from 10 to 150 cm/4 in to 5 ft.

torture infliction of bodily pain, to extort evidence or confession. Legally abolished in England about 1640, torture was allowed in Scotland until 1708 and until 1789 in France. In the 20th century torture is widely, though in most countries unofficially, used.

Tory Party name applied about 1680–1830 to the forerunner of the British ◊Conservative Party. They were the party of the squire and parson, as opposed to the Whigs (supported by the trading classes and Nonconformists). The name is still applied colloquially to the Conservative Party. In the USA a Tory was an opponent of the break with the UK in the War of American Independence 1775– 83.

totalitarianism government control of all activities within a country, overtly political or otherwise, as in fascist or communist dictatorships.

totemism belief in individual or clan kinship with an animal, plant, or object. This totem is sacred to those concerned, and they are forbidden to eat or desecrate it; marriage within such a clan is usually forbidden.
Totem poles are used on the Pacific coast of North America, and incorporate totem objects (carved and painted) as a symbol of the people, or to commemorate the dead. A similar belief occurs among Australian Aborigines, and was formerly prevalent in Europe and Asia.

Totenkopfverbände the 'death's head' units of the Nazi ◊SS organization. Originally used to guard concentration camps after 1935, they later became an elite fighting division attached to the Waffen-SS during World War II.

Totila died 522. King of the Ostrogoths, who warred with the Byzantine emperor Justinian for Italy, and was killed by Gen Narses at the battle of Taginae in the Apennines.

toucan South and Central American forest-dwelling birds of the family Ramphastidae. They have very large, brilliantly coloured beaks, and often have handsome plumage. They live in small flocks, eat fruits, seeds, and insects, and lay their eggs in holes in trees. They grow to 64 cm/2 ft in length.

touch screen in computing, an input device allowing the user to communicate with the computer by touching a display screen with a finger. ◊Software in the device then calculates the centre-point of the finger and communicates the coordinates (grid reference) to the computer. Touch screens are used in financial computer systems where a spreadsheet of data is displayed on the screen.

touch sensor in a computer-controlled ◊robot, a device used to give the robot a sense of touch, allowing it to manipulate delicate objects or move automatically about a room. Touch sensors provide the *feedback* necessary for the robot to adjust the force of its movements and the pressure of its grip. The main types include the strain gauge and microswitch.

Toulon port and capital of Var *département*, SE France, on the Mediterranean Sea, 48 km/30 mi SE of Marseilles; population (1983) 190,000. It is the chief Mediterranean naval station of France. Industries include oil refining, chemicals, furniture, and clothing.
history the Roman *Telo Martius*, Toulon was made a port by Henry IV. In World War II the French fleet was scuttled here to avoid its passing to German control.

Toulouse capital of Haute-Garonne *département*, S France, on the river Garonne SE of Bordeaux; population (1982) 354,800. The chief industries are textiles and aircraft construction (Concorde was built here). Toulouse was the capital of the Visigoths (see ◊Goth), and later of Aquitaine 781–843. The university was founded 1229 to combat heresy.

Toulouse-Lautrec Henri Raymond de 1864–1901. French artist, associated with the Impressionists and Post- Impressionists. He was active in Paris, where he painted entertainers and prostitutes. From 1891 his lithograph posters were a great success.

touraco fruit-eating African bird of the family Musophagidae. They have short, rounded wings, long tails, and erectile crests. The largest are 70 cm/28 in long.

Toulouse-Lautrec The Two Friends *(1894)* Tate Gallery, London.

tour de force (French 'feat of strength') a remarkable accomplishment.

Tour de France French road race for professional cyclists held annually over approximately 4,800 km/3,000 mi of French roads. The race takes about three weeks to complete and the route varies each year, often taking in adjoining countries, but always ending in Paris. A separate stage is held every day, and the overall leader at the end of each stage wears the coveted leader's 'yellow jersey' (French *maillot jaune*).

tourmaline a hard, brittle mineral, a complex of various metal silicates, containing aluminium and boron.

Tourneur Cyril 1575–1626. English dramatist. Little is known about his life but *The Atheist's Tragedy* 1611 and *The Revenger's Tragedy* 1607 (now thought by some scholars to be by ◊Middleton) are among the most powerful of Jacobean dramas.

Toussaint L'Ouverture Pierre Dominique 1746–1803. Haitian revolutionary leader, born a slave. He joined the insurrection of 1791 against the French colonizers and was made governor by the revolutionary French government. He expelled the Spanish and British, but when the French emperor Napoleon reimposed slavery, he revolted, was captured, and died in prison in France. In 1983 his remains were returned to Haiti.

tout de suite (French) immediately.

tout ensemble (French 'all together') the overall effect.

Tower John 1925–1991. US Republican politician, a Texas senator 1961–83. Despite having been a paid arms-industry consultant, he was selected in 1989 by President Bush to serve as defence secretary, but the Senate refused to approve the appointment because of Tower's previous heavy drinking. He died in a plane crash.

Tower of London fortress on the Thames bank to the E of the City. The keep, or White Tower, was built about 1078 by Bishop Gundulf on the site of British and Roman fortifications. It is surrounded by two strong walls and a moat (now dry), and was for centuries a royal residence and the principal state prison.

town planning the design of buildings or groups of buildings in a physical and social context, concentrating on the relationship between various buildings and their environment, as well as on their uses. See also ◊garden city; ◊new town.

Townsend Sue 1946– . British humorous novelist, author of *The Secret Diary of Adrian Mole, aged 13¾* 1982 and later sequels.

Townshend Pete 1945– . UK rock musician, former member of the ◊Who.

Townshend Viscount 'Turnip' 1674–1738. A pioneer of the Agricultural Revolution, Townshend was erroneously credited with the introduction of turnips and clover into what became known as the Norfolk four-course rotation system.

Townswomen's Guilds, National Union of in the UK, an urban version of the ◊Women's Institute. It was founded in 1929.

toxaemia blood poisoning. In general terms, it is the presence of toxins in the blood derived from a bacterial infection in some part of the body.

toxocariasis infection of humans by a canine intestinal worm, which results in a swollen liver and sometimes eye damage.

Toynbee Arnold 1852–1883. British economic historian, who coined the term 'industrial revolution' in his *Lectures on the Industrial Revolution* published

1884. Toynbee Hall, an education settlement in the East End of London, was named after him.

Toynbee Arnold Joseph 1889–1975. British historian, whose *A Study of History* 1934–61 was an attempt to discover the laws governing the rise and fall of civilizations. He was the nephew of the economic historian Arnold Toynbee.

trace element a chemical element necessary for the health of a plant or animal, but only in minute quantities.

tracer in science, a small quantity of a radioactive ◊isotope (form of an element) used to follow the path of a chemical reaction or a physical or biological process. The location (and possibly concentration) of the tracer is usually detected using a Geiger-Muller counter.

trachea tube which forms an airway in air-breathing animals. In land-living ◊vertebrates, including humans, it is known as the *windpipe* and is the largest airway, running from the larynx to the upper part of the chest. It is about 1.5 cm/0.58 in diameter and 10 cm/3.94 in length, and is strong and flexible, reinforced by rings of ◊cartilage. In the upper chest, the trachea branches into two tubes - the left and right bronchi - which enter the lungs. Insects have a branching network of tubes, the trachea, which conduct air from holes in the body surface (◊spiracles) to all the body tissues. The finest branches of the trachea are called tracheoles.

tracheid a type of cell found in the water-conducting tissue (◊xylem) of many plants, particularly gymnosperms (conifers) and pteridophytes (ferns). It is long and thin with pointed ends. The cell walls are thickened by ◊lignin except for numerous small rounded areas, or pits, through which water and dissolved minerals pass from one cell to another. Once it is mature, the cell itself dies and only the cell walls remain.

tracheostomy the creation of an opening in the windpipe (trachea) into which a tube is inserted to

trachea

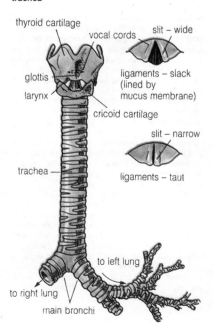

thyroid cartilage
vocal cords
slit – wide
glottis
larynx
ligaments – slack (lined by mucus membrane)
cricoid cartilage
slit – narrow
trachea
ligaments – taut
to left lung
to right lung
main bronchi

enable the patient to breathe. It is done either to bypass the airway impaired by disease or injury, or to safeguard it during surgery or a prolonged period of mechanical ventilation.

trachoma a chronic eye infection, in effect severe ◊conjunctivitis. The conjunctiva becomes inflamed, with scarring and formation of pus, and there may be damage to the cornea, the delicate front 'window' of the eye.

tracked vehicle a vehicle, such as a tank or bulldozer, that runs on tracks (known as ◊caterpillar tracks) it lays itself.

Tractarianism another name for the ◊Oxford Movement, 19th-century movement for Catholic revival within the Church of England.

tractor in agriculture, a four-wheeled motor vehicle commonly having two very large rear wheels, used in cultivation. It is usually powered by a diesel engine and has a power-take-off (PTO) mechanism for driving machinery, and hydraulic lift for raising and lowering implements.

Tracy Spencer 1900–1967. US actor, noted for his understated, seemingly effortless natural performances. His films include *Captains Courageous* 1937 and *Boys' Town* 1938 (for both of which he won Academy Awards), and he starred with Katharine Hepburn in *Adam's Rib* 1949 and *Guess Who's Coming to Dinner* 1967.

trade cycle or *business cycle* period of time which includes a peak and trough of economic activity, as measured by a country's national income. In Keynesian economics, one of the main roles of the government is to smooth out the peaks and troughs of the trade cycle, by intervening in the economy, thus minimizing 'overheating' and 'stagnation' in the economy.

trade description the description of the characteristics of goods, including their quality, quantity, and fitness for the purpose for which they are required. False trade descriptions are illegal in English law.

trade mark a name or symbol which is distinctive of a marketed product. The owner may register the mark to prevent its unauthorised use.

Tradescant John 1570–1638. English gardener and botanist, who travelled widely in Europe and may have introduced the cos lettuce to England, from the Greek Island bearing the same name. He was appointed as gardener to Charles I and succeeded by his son, John Tradescant the Younger (1608–1662), after his death. The younger Tradescant undertook three plant-collecting trips to Virginia, USA, and Linnaeus named the genus *Tradescantia* in his honour.

tradescantia genus of plants of the family Commelinaceae, native to North and Central America. The *spiderwort Tradescantia virginiana* is a cultivated garden plant; the *wandering jew Tradescantia albiflora* is a common houseplant, with green oval leaves tinged with pink or purple or silver-striped.

Trades Union Congress voluntary organization of trade unions, founded in the UK in 1868, in which delegates of affiliated unions meet annually to consider matters affecting their members. In 1988 there were some 100 affiliated unions, with an aggregate membership of about 11 million.

trade union organization of employed workers formed to undertake collective bargaining with employers and to try to achieve improved working conditions for its members. Attitudes of government to unions and of unions to management vary greatly from country to country. Probably the most effective trade-union system is that of Sweden, and the best-known union is the banned Polish ◊Solidarity.

trade unionism, international worldwide cooperation between unions. Modern organizations are the International Confederation of Free Trade Unions (ICFTU 1949), including the American Federation of Labor and Congress of Industrial Organizations and the UK Trades Union Congress, and the World Federation of Trade Unions (WFTU 1945).

trade wind prevailing wind that blows towards the equator from the NE and SE. Trade winds are caused by hot air rising at the equator and the consequent movement of air from N and S to take its place. The winds are deflected towards the W because of the Earth's W-to-E rotation. The unpredictable calms known as the ◊Doldrums lie at their convergence.

trading stamp a stamp given by retailers to customers according to the value of goods purchased; when a sufficient number has been collected, the stamps can be redeemed for goods or money.

Trafalgar, Battle of battle on 21 Oct 1805 in the ◊Napoleonic Wars. The British fleet under Nelson defeated a Franco-Spanish fleet; Nelson was mortally wounded. Named after Cape Trafalgar, low headland in SW Spain, near the W entrance to the Straits of Gibraltar.

tragedy in theatrical terms, a play dealing with a serious theme, traditionally one in which a character falls to disaster either as a result of personal failings or circumstances beyond his or her control. Historically the Greek view of tragedy, as defined by Aristotle and expressed by the great tragedians Aeschylus, Euripides, and Sophocles, has been the most influential. In the 20th century tragedies in the narrow Greek sense of dealing with exalted personages in an elevated manner have virtually died out. Tragedy has been replaced by dramas with 'tragic' implications or overtones, as in the work of Ibsen, Pinter, and Osborne, for example, or by the hybrid tragi-comedy.

tragi-comedy a drama which contains elements of tragedy and comedy; for example, Shakespeare's 'reconciliation' plays such as *The Winter's Tale*, which reaches a tragic climax but then lightens to a happy conclusion. A tragi-comedy is the usual form for plays in the tradition of the Theatre of the ◊Absurd, such as *En attendant Godot/Waiting for Godot* 1953 by Beckett and *Rosencrantz and Guildenstern are Dead* 1967 by Stoppard.

tragopan type of short-tailed pheasant of which there are several species living in wet forests along the S Himalayas. Tragopans are brilliantly coloured, with arrays of spots. They have long crown feathers and two blue erectile crests.

trahison des clercs (French 'the treason of the intellectuals') the involvement of intellectuals in active politics.

train vehicle which moves on a ◊railway.

Training Agency British government-sponsored organization responsible for retraining of unemployed workers. Founded as the *Manpower Services Commission* in 1974, it was renamed the *Training Commission* in 1988 and later the same year restructured under the Employment Secretary, and again renamed. The organization operated such schemes as the Training Opportunities Scheme (TOPS), the Youth Opportunities Programme (YOP) 1978, the Youth Training Scheme (YTS) 1983, and the Technical and Vocational Initiative (TVEI).

Training Commission in the UK, official body appointed by the government to oversee training for employment. The training division runs the Youth Training Scheme (YTS) and training services for adults both in and out of work.

Trajan Marcus Ulpius (Trajanus) 52–117 AD. Roman emperor. Born in Seville, he distinguished himself as a soldier and was adopted as heir by ◊Nerva, whom he succeeded in 98 AD. He was a just and conscientious ruler, corresponded with ◊Pliny about the Christians, and conquered Dacia (approximately modern Romania) 101–07 and much of ◊Parthia. *Trajan's Column*, Rome, commemorates his victories.

trampolining gymnastics performed on a sprung canvas sheet which allows the performer to reach great heights before landing again. Marks are gained for carrying out difficult manoeuvres. Synchronized trampolining and tumbling are also popular forms of the sport.

tramway a transport system, particularly popular in Europe from the late 19th–mid 20th century, where wheeled vehicles run along parallel rails. It originated in collieries in the 18th century, and the earliest passenger system was in 1832, in New York. Trams are powered either by electric conductor rails below ground or conductor arms connected to overhead wires, but their use on public roads is very limited because of their lack of manoeuvrability. Greater flexibility can be achieved with the *trolleybus*, similarly powered by conductor arms overhead, but without tracks.

trance mental state in which the subject loses the ordinary perceptions of time and space, and even of his or her own body.

tranquillizer ◊anxiolytic. Antipsychotic drugs are not tranquillizers.

Trans-Alaskan Pipeline Scheme one of the world's greatest civil engineering projects, the construction of a 1,285 km/805 mi long pipeline to carry petroleum (crude oil) from the North Slope of Alaska to the icefree port of Valdez. It was completed in 1977 after three years' work. The engineers had to elevate nearly half of the pipeline on supports above ground level to avoid thawing the permanently frozen ground which would have caused much environmental damage. They also had to cross 600 rivers and streams, two mountain ranges and allow for earthquakes.

Transcendental Meditation (TM) a technique of focusing the mind based in part on Hindu meditation, introduced to Britain by the Maharishi Mahesh Yogi and popularized by the Beatles in the late 1960s. Such meditation is believed to bring benefit to the practitioner in the form of release from stress; devotees claim that if even as few as one per cent of the population meditated in this way, it would create peace in the world. Meditators are given a mantra (a special word or phrase) to chant. This mantra is never written down or divulged to anyone else. The Maharishi believes that through the practice of meditation special powers, such as levitation, precognition and control over bodily functions can be developed.

transcription in living cells, the process by which the information for the synthesis of a protein is transferred from the ◊DNA strand on which it is carried to the messenger ◊RNA strand involved in the actual synthesis. It occurs by the formation of ◊base pairs between the DNA molecule and the nucleotides that make up the new RNA strand.

transducer power-transforming device which enables ◊energy in any form (electrical, acoustical,

transfer orbit

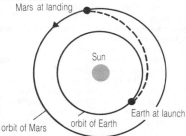

mechanical) to flow from one transmission system to another.

transfer orbit the elliptical path followed by a spacecraft moving from one orbit to another, designed to save fuel by moving for most of the journey in ◊free fall.

transformational grammar a theory of language structure initiated by Noam ◊Chomsky, which proposes that below the actual phrases and sentences of a language (its *surface structure*) there lies a more basic layer (its *deep structure*), which is processed by various transformational rules when we speak and write.

transformer device in which, by ◊electromagnetic induction, an alternating or intermittent current of one voltage is transformed to another voltage, without change of ◊frequency. Transformers are widely used in electrical apparatus of all kinds, and in particular in power transmission where high voltages and low currents are utilized.

transfusion the delivery of blood or blood products (plasma, red cells) into a patient's circulation to make good deficiencies due to disease, injury or surgical intervention.

transistor electronic component, made of ◊semiconductor material, with three or more ◊electrodes, that can regulate a current passing through it. A transistor can act as an amplifier, ◊oscillator, ◊photocell, or switch, and usually operates on a very small amount of power. Transistors commonly consist of a tiny sandwich of ◊germanium or ◊silicon, alternate layers having different electrical properties. A crystal of pure germanium or silicon would act as an insulator (non-conductor). By introducing impurities in the form of atoms of other materials (for example, boron, arsenic, or indium) in minute amounts, the layers may be made either *n-type*, having an excess of electrons, or *p-type*, having a deficiency of electrons. This enables electrons to flow from one layer to another in one direction only.

transit the passage of a smaller object across the visible disc of a larger one. Transits of the ◊inferior planets occur when they pass directly between the Earth and Sun, and are seen as tiny dark spots against the Sun's disc.

transition metal one of a group of metals with variable valency, for example cobalt, copper, iron, and molybdenum. They are excellent conductors of electricity, and generally form highly coloured compounds.

Transkei largest of South Africa's Bantu Homelands, extending NE from the Great Kei River, on the coast of Cape Province, to the border of Natal; self-governing 1963, full 'independence' 1976
area 43,800 sq km/16,910 sq mi
capital Umtata
towns port Mnganzana

products coffee, tea, sugar, maize, sorghum
population (1984) 2,927,400
language Xhosa
government president (paramount chief Tutor Nyangelizwe Vulinolela Ndamase 1986–) and single-chamber national assembly.

translation in literature, the rendering of words from one language to another.
240 BC the *Odyssey* translated into Latin by Livius Andronicus, the first recorded named translator
3rd century BC–1st century AD ◊Septuagint: Greek translation of Old Testament and Apocrypha
4th century ◊Vulgate: Latin translation of Bible by St ◊Jerome: first complete translation direct from Hebrew
8th–9th centuries Arabic scholars, mostly based in Baghdad, translate many of the Greek classics into Arabic
12th century translations from Arabic to Latin, centred in Toledo, Spain (school of translators founded by Archbishop Raymund I 1126–51): translations of Aristotle, Avicenna, by, for example, Gerard of Cremona, John of Seville, Adelard of Bath
1382 ◊Wycliffe: first translation of Bible into English
1522 ◊Luther's translation of New Testament into German
1525 ◊Tyndale's English translation of the New Testament
1537 ◊Coverdale's translation of the Bible into English
1579 ◊North's translation of Plutarch (actually from French)
1598–1616 ◊Chapman's translations of *Iliad* and *Odyssey* of Homer
1603 ◊Florio's translation of Montaigne's Essays
1603–11 Authorized Version of Bible
1693 Dryden: Juvenal
1697 Dryden: Virgil
1715–26 Pope: *Iliad* and *Odyssey*
1859 Edward Fitzgerald, *Rubaiyat of Omar Khayyam.*
1966 The Jerusalem Bible (from the original languages).

translation in living cells, the process by which proteins are synthesized. During translation, the information coded as a sequence of nucelotides in messenger ◊RNA is transformed into a sequence of amino acids in a peptide chain. The process involves the 'translation' of the ◊genetic code. See also ◊transcription.

transmigration of souls another name for ◊reincarnation.

transpiration the loss of water from a plant by evaporation. Most of the water is lost from the leaves through pores known as ◊stomata, whose primary function is to allow gas exchange between the internal plant tissues and the atmosphere. Only a very small percentage of the total water loss occurs through the epidermis, which generally has a waxy ◊cuticle to make it waterproof. Transpiration from the leaf surfaces causes a continuous upward flow of water from the roots via the ◊xylem, which is known as the transpiration stream.

transplantation in medicine, the transfer of a tissue or organ from one human being to another. In most organ transplants, the operation is life-saving (although kidney patients have the alternative of ◊dialysis).

Transport and General Workers Union UK trade union founded in 1921 by the amalgamation of a number of dockers' and road-transport workers' unions, previously associated in the Transport Workers' Federation. It is the largest trade union in Britain.

transportation in the UK, a former punishment which involved sending convicted persons to overseas British territories either for life or for shorter periods. It was introduced in England towards the end of the 17th century and was abolished in 1857 after many thousands had been transported, especially to Australia. Also used for punishment of criminals by France, until 1938.

transputer an electronic device being introduced in computers to increase computing power. In the circuits of a standard computer the processing of data takes place in sequence. In a transputer's circuits processing takes place in parallel, greatly reducing computing time.

transsexual a person who identifies himself/herself completely with the opposite sex, believing that the wrong sex was assigned at birth. Unlike *transvestitism*, which is the desire to dress in clothes typically worn by the opposite sex, transsexuals think and feel emotionally in a way typically considered appropriate to members of the opposite sex, and may undergo surgery to modify external sexual characteristics.

Trans-Siberian Railway railway line connecting the cities of European Russia with Omsk, Novosibirsk, Irkutsk, and Khabarovsk, and terminating at Vladivostok on the Pacific. It was built 1891–1905; from Leningrad to Vladivostok is about 8,700 km/5,400 mi. A 3,102 km/1,927 mi northern line was completed in 1984 after ten years' work.

transubstantiation in Christian theology, the doctrine that the whole substance of the bread and wine changes into the substance of the body and blood of Christ when consecrated in the ◊Eucharist.

transuranic element or *transuranium element* a chemical element with an atomic number of 93 or more, that is, with a greater number of protons in the nucleus than uranium. Apart from neptunium and plutonium, none of these has been found in nature, but they have been created in nuclear reactions.

Transvaal province of NE South Africa, bordering Zimbabwe in the N
area 286,064 sq km/110,450 sq mi
capital Pretoria
towns Johannesburg, Germiston
history settled by *Voortrekkers* who left Cape Colony in the Great Trek from 1831. Transvaal was made a British colony after the South African War 1899–1902, and in 1910 became a province of the Union of South Africa.

Transylvania mountainous area of central and NW Romania, bounded to the S by the Transylvanian Alps (an extension of the ◊Carpathians), formerly a province, with its capital at Cluj. It was part of Hungary from about 1000 until its people voted to unite with Romania 1918.

trapezium (North American *trapezoid*) in geometry, a four-sided plane figure (quadrilateral) with two of its sides parallel. If the parallel sides have lengths a and b and the perpendicular distance between them is h (the height of the trapezium), its area $A = [\frac{1}{2}(a + b) \times h]$.

Trappist member of a Roman Catholic order of monks and nuns, renowned for the strictness of their rule, which includes the maintenance of silence. It originated in 1664 at La Trappe, in Normandy, as a reformed version of the

transpiration

During photosynthesis, carbon dioxide enters the leaves of a plant through the stomata. A leaf that is permeable to carbon dioxide is also permeable to water vapour. Therefore, water is lost from the plant. The evaporation of water from the leaves is called transpiration. It produces a transpiration stream, which is a tension that draws water up the vessels of the stem. The tension can be sufficiently great to draw water up trees 100 m/328 ft tall.

Transpiration rates can be measured using a potometer.

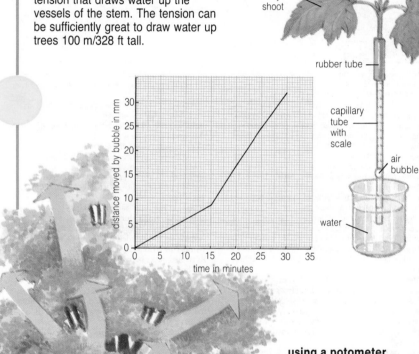

large leafy shoot

rubber tube

capillary tube with scale

air bubble

water

A typical plant transpires about 50 ml of water per square metre of leaf surface every hour.

using a potometer

A shoot is cut from a tree and placed in the top of a length of rubber tubing. A calibrated capillary tube, filled with water, is inserted in the bottom of the tubing and the whole arrangement is placed in a beaker of water. If a small air bubble is created in the tube, the rate of movement of the water due to transpiration is indicated by the speed with which the bubble moves up the tube.

Transylvania

◊Cistercian rule, under which it is now once more governed.

trasformismo the practice of government by coalition, using tactics of reforming new cabinets and political alliances, often between conflicting interest groups, in order to retain power. The term was first used to describe the way the Italian nationalist leader Cavour held on to power.

trauma a powerful shock which may have a long-term effect; also any physical damage or injury.

travelator a moving walkway, rather like a flat ◊escalator.

traveller an itinerant wanderer; the term is usually applied to the◊Romany people.

Traven Ben, pen name of Herman Feige 1882–1969. US novelist, whose true identity was unrevealed until 1979. His books include the bestseller *The Death Ship* 1926, and *The Treasure of Sierra Madre* 1934, which was filmed in 1948 starring Humphrey Bogart.

Travers Morris William 1872–1961. English chemist who, with William Ramsay, first identified the inert gases krypton, xenon, and radon (1894–1908).

treason an act of betrayal, generally used of acts against the sovereign or the state to which the offender owes allegiance. It is punishable in Britain by death.

treasure trove in England, any gold or silver, plate or bullion found concealed in a house or the ground, the owner being unknown. Normally, treasure originally hidden, and not abandoned, belongs to the Crown, but if the treasure was casually lost or intentionally abandoned, the first finder is entitled to it against all but the true owner. Objects buried with no intention of recovering them, for example in a burial mound, do not rank as treasure trove, and belong to the owner of the ground.

treaty a written agreement between two or more states. Treaties take effect either immediately on signature or, more often, on ratification. Ratification involves a further exchange of documents and usually takes place after the internal governments have approved the terms of the treaty. Treaties are binding in international law, the rules being laid down in the Vienna Convention on the Law of Treaties 1969.

tree a perennial plant with a woody stem, usually a single stem or 'trunk'; this is made up of ◊wood, and protected by an outer layer of ◊bark. There is

no clear dividing line between ◊shrubs and trees, but sometimes a minimum height of six metres is used to define a tree.

tree-creeper small, short-legged bird of the family Certhiidae, that spirals with a mouse-like movement up tree trunks searching for food with its thin downcurved beak.

trefoil several plants of the genus *Trifolium*, family Leguminosae, the leaves of which appear to be divided into three lobes.

trematode a parasitic flatworm with an oval non-segmented boyd, of the class Trematoda, including the ◊fluke.

tremor minor ◊earthquake.

Trenchard Hugh Montague, 1st Viscount Trenchard 1873–1956. British aviator and police commissioner. He commanded the Royal Flying Corps in World War I 1915–17, and 1918–29 organized the Royal Air Force, becoming first marshal of the Royal Air Force 1927. As commissioner of the Metropolitan Police, he established the Police College at Hendon and carried out the Trenchard Reforms, which included the application of more scientific methods of detection. He was nicknamed 'Boom' because of his loud voice.

Trent, Council of 1545–1563. Council held by the Roman Catholic Church at Trento, N Italy; initiating the ◊Counter-Reformation; see also ◊Reformation.

Trentino-Alto Adige autonomous region of N Italy, comprising the provinces of Bolzano and Trento; capital Trento for the Italian-speaking southern area, and Bolzano-Bozen for the northern German-speaking area of South ◊Tirol (the region was Austrian until ceded to Italy 1919); area 13,613 sq km/5,256 sq mi; population (1981) 873,413.

trespass going on to the land of another without authority. In English law, a landowner has the right to eject a trespasser by the use of reasonable force, and can sue for any damage caused. A trespasser who refuses to leave when requested may, in certain circumstances, be committing a criminal offence under the Public Order Act 1986 (designed to combat convoys of caravans trespassing on farm land). A trespasser injured on another's land cannot usually recover damages from the landowner unless the latter did him or her some positive injury.

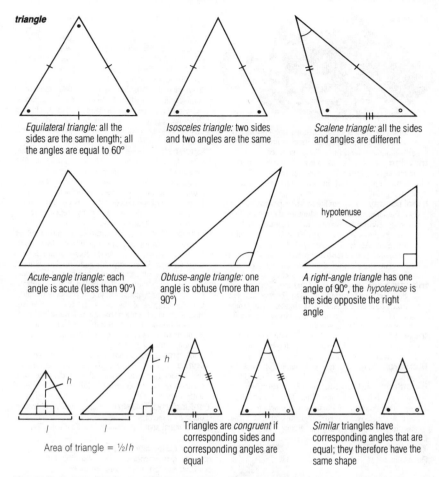

triangle

Equilateral triangle: all the sides are the same length; all the angles are equal to 60°

Isosceles triangle: two sides and two angles are the same

Scalene triangle: all the sides and angles are different

Acute-angle triangle: each angle is acute (less than 90°)

Obtuse-angle triangle: one angle is obtuse (more than 90°)

A right-angle triangle has one angle of 90°, the *hypotenuse* is the side opposite the right angle

Area of triangle = ½*lh*

Triangles are *congruent* if corresponding sides and corresponding angles are equal

Similar triangles have corresponding angles that are equal; they therefore have the same shape

Tressell Robert. Pseudonym of Robert Noonan 1868–1911. British author, whose *The Ragged Trousered Philanthropists*, published after his death in an abridged form in 1914, gave a detailed account of working people's lives.

Trevdyan George Otto 1838–1928. British politician and historian, a nephew of the historian Lord Macaulay, whose biography he wrote in 1876.

Trevithick Richard 1771–1833. British engineer, constructor of a steam road locomotive 1801 and the first steam engine to run on rails 1804.

Triad secret society, founded in China as a Buddhist cult in 36 AD. It became known as the Triad because the triangle played an important part in the initiation ceremony. Later it became political, aiming at the overthrow of the Manchu dynasty, and backed the Taiping Rebellion 1851 and Sun Yat-sen's establishment of a republic 1912. Today it has a reputation for organized crime (drugs, gambling, prostitution) among overseas Chinese. Its headquarters are alleged to be in Hong Kong.

trial by ordeal a system of justice used in the Middle Ages, by which the accused could prove innocence by emerging unscathed from an ordeal (typically involving fire or water). The practice originated with the Franks in the 8th century, and survived until the 13th century.

triangle in geometry, a three-sided plane figure. A *scalene triangle* has no sides of equal length; an *isosceles triangle* has two equal sides (and two equal angles); an *equilateral triangle* has three equal sides (and three equal angles of 60°). A right-angled triangle has one angle of 90°. If the length of one side of a triangle is *l* and the perpendicular distance from that side to the opposite corner is *h* (the height or altitude of the triangle), its area *A* = ½ *l* × *h*.

triangulation a technique used in surveying to determine distances, using the properties of the triangle. In triangulation, surveyors measure a certain length exactly to provide a base line. From each end of this line they then measure the angle to a distant point, using a ◊theodolite. They now have a triangle in which they know the length of one side and the two adjacent angles. By simple trigonometry they can work out the lengths of the other two sides.

Trianon two palaces in the park at ◊Versailles, France: Le Grand Trianon built for Louis XIV, and Le Petit Trianon for Louis XV.

Triassic period of geological time 248–213 million years ago, the first period of the Mesozoic era. The continents were fused together to form the supercontinent ◊Pangaea, and the climate was

trigger-fish

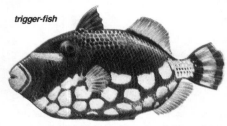

generally dry: desert sandstones are typical Triassic rocks. Triassic sediments contain remains of early dinosaurs and other large reptiles.

triathlon a test of stamina involving three sports: swimming 3.8 km/2.4 mi, cycling 180 km/112 mi, and running a marathon, each one immediately following the last.

tribal society a way of life in which people govern their own affairs as independent local communities without central government organisations or states, in parts of SE Asia, New Guinea, South America and Africa. People in tribal societies share in the production of food and other necessities and learn basic skills rather than specializing in certain tasks and developing elaborate technologies.

tribunal strictly, a court of justice, but used in English law for a body appointed by the government to arbitrate in disputes, or investigate certain matters. They usually consist of a lawyer as chair, sitting with two lay assessors.

triceratops rhinoceros-like dinosaur with three horns and a neck frill. Up to 8 m/25 ft long, it lived in the Cretaceous period.

trichloromethane modern name for ◊chloroform.

tricouleur the French national flag of three vertical bands of red, white, and blue. The red and blue were the colours of Paris and the white represented the royal house of Bourbon. The flag was first adopted during the French Revolution,

three days after the storming of the Bastille, on 17 Jul 1789.

Trieste port on the Adriatic, opposite Venice, capital of Friuli-Venezia-Giulia, Italy; population (1988) 237,000 including a large Slovene minority. It is the site of the International Centre for Theoretical Physics, established 1964.

history under Austrian rule from 1382 (apart from Napoleonic occupation 1809–14) until transferred to Italy 1918, Trieste was claimed after World War II by Yugoslavia, and the city and surrounding territory were divided 1954 between Italy and Yugoslavia.

trigger-fish marine fish of the family Balistidae, with a laterally compressed body, up to 60 cm/2 ft long, and deep belly. They have small mouths but strong jaws and teeth. The first spine on the dorsal fin locks into an erect position, which can enable them to lock themselves into crevices for protection, and can only be moved by depressing the smaller third ('trigger') spine.

trigonometry branch of mathematics that solves problems relating to plane and spherical triangles. Its principles are based on the fixed proportions of sides for a particular angle in a right-angled triangle, the simplest of which are known as the ◊sine, ◊cosine, and ◊tangent (so-called trigonometrical ratios). Using trigonometry, it is possible to calculate the lengths of the sides and the sizes of the angles of a right-angled triangle as long as one angle and one side are known. It is of practical importance in navigation, surveying, and ◊simple harmonic motion in physics.

triiodomethane modern name for ◊iodoform.

trilobite extinct, marine, invertebrate arthropod of the Palaeozoic era, with a flattened, oval, segmented body, 1–65 cm/0.4–26 in long, covered with a shell.

Trinidad and Tobago country in the W Indies, off the coast of Venezuela.

Trinitarianism a belief in the Christian Trinity.

Trinidad and Tobago
Republic of

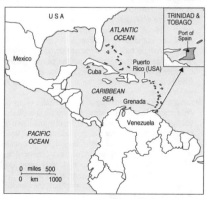

area Trinidad 4,828 sq km/1,864 sq mi and Tobago 300 sq km/116 sq mi
capital Port-of-Spain
towns San Fernando, Arima, Scarborough
physical comprises the two main islands, and some smaller ones; coastal swamps and hills E–W

head of state Noor Hassanali from 1987
head of government Patrick Manning 1991
political system democratic republic
exports oil, petroleum, chemicals, sugar, cocoa
currency Trinidad and Tobago dollar
population (1990 est) 1,270,000 (40% African descent, 16% European, 2% others); growth rate 1.6% p.a
life expectancy men 68, women 72
language English (official), Hindi, French, Spanish
religion Christian 47%, Hindu 25%, Muslim 6%
literacy 97% (1988)
GNP 4.5 (1983); $3,371 per head
chronology
1956 The People's National Movement (PNM) founded.
1959 Granted internal self-government, with PNM leader Eric Williams as chief minister.
1967 Achieved full independence, within the Commonwealth, with Williams as prime minister.
1976 Became a republic, with Ellis Clarke as president and Williams as prime minister.
1981 Williams died and was succeeded by George Chambers, with Arthur Robinson as leader of the opposition.
1986 Arthur Robinson became prime minister.
1987 Noor Hassanali became president.
1991 PNM won election; Patrick Manning became prime minister.

Trinity in the Christian religion, the threefold union of three persons in one godhead, namely Father, Son, and Holy Ghost/Spirit. The precise meaning of the doctrine has been the cause of unending dispute, and was the chief cause of the split between the Eastern Orthodox and Roman Catholic churches. *Trinity Sunday* occurs on the Sunday after Whit Sunday.

triode a three-electrode thermionic valve containing an anode and a cathode (as does a ◊diode) with an additional negatively biased control grid. Small variations in voltage on the grid bias result in large variations in the current. The triode was thus commonly used in amplifiers until largely superseded by the ◊transistor. The valve was invented by the American radio engineer Lee De Forest (1873–1961).

Tripitaka (Pāli 'three baskets') the canonical texts of Theravāda Buddhism, divided into three parts.

Triple Alliance an alliance from 1882 between Germany, Austria-Hungary, and Italy to offset the power of Russia and France. It was last renewed in 1912 but during World War I, Italy's initial neutrality gradually changed, and it denounced the alliance in 1915. The term also refers to other alliances: 1668 England, Holland, and Sweden; 1717 Britain, Holland, and France (joined 1718 by Austria); 1788 Britain, Prussia, and Holland; 1795 Britain, Russia, and Austria.

Triple Entente alliance of Britain, France, and Russia 1907–17. In 1911 this became a military alliance and formed the basis of the Allied powers in World War I against the Central Powers, Germany and Austria-Hungary. The failure of the alliance system to create a stable balance of power, coupled with universal horror of the carnage created by World War I, led to attempts to create a new international order with the League of Nations.

Tripoli (Arabic *Tarabulus*) capital and chief port of Libya, on the Mediterranean; population (1980) 980,000. Products include olive oil, fruit, fish, and textiles.
history Tripoli was founded around the 7th century BC by the Phoenicians. It was an important base for Axis powers during World War II. In 1986 it was bombed by US Air Force in response to international guerrilla activity.

Tripura state of NE India since 1972, formerly a princely state, between Bangladesh and Assam.
area 10,477 sq km/4,044 sq mi
capital Agartala
products rice, cotton, tea, sugar cane
population (1981) 2,060,000
language Bengali
religion Hindu.

trireme ancient Greek warship with three banks of oars as well as sails, 38 m/115 ft long. They were used at the battle of ◊Salamis, and by the Romans until the 4th century AD.

Tristan hero of Celtic legend, who fell in love with Iseult, the bride he was sent to win for his uncle King Mark of Cornwall; the story became part of the Arthurian cycle, and is the subject of Wagner's opera *Tristan and Isolde*.

Tristan Flora 1803–1844. French socialist writer and activist, author of *Promenades dans Londres/The London Journal* 1840, a vivid record of social conditions, and *L'Union ouvrière/Workers' Union* 1843, an outline of a workers' utopia.

Tristram Shandy a novel by Laurence Sterne, published 1759–67. The work, a forerunner of the 20th-century stream-of-consciousness novel, has no coherent plot and uses typographical devices to

emphasize the author's disdain for the structured novels of his contemporaries.

triticale cereal crop of recent origin which is a cross between wheat and rye. It can produce heavy yields of high-protein grain principally for use as an animal feed.

tritium unstable isotope of hydrogen, with two neutrons as well as one proton in its nucleus.

Triton in astronomy, the larger of the two moons of Neptune. It has a diameter of about 3,800 km/2,350 mi, and orbits Neptune in 5.9 days. It was discovered 1846.

triumvir one of a group of three magistrates sharing power in ancient Rome, as in the *First Triumvirate* 60 BC: Caesar, Pompey, Crassus; and *Second Triumvirate* 43 BC: Augustus, Antony, and Lepidus.

troglodyte Greek term for a cave-dweller, designating certain peoples in the ancient world. The troglodytes of S Egypt and Ethiopia were a pastoral people.

trogon tropical bird, up to 50 cm/1.7 ft long, with resplendent plumage, living in the Americas and Afro-Asia, order Trogoniformes.

trolleybus type of bus driven by electric power collected from overhead wires. They have greater manoeuvrability than a ◊tram, but their obstructiveness in modern traffic conditions led to their being abandoned, since they are less efficient in their use of energy than diesel buses. However, their quietness in operation and freedom from pollution make them attractive, and Germany has developed new types which operate, by means of three tonnes of batteries, for 10 km/6 mi without drawing current from an overhead wire.

Trollope Anthony 1815–1882. British novelist, who delineated provincial English middle-class society in his popular Barchester series of novels. He became a post office clerk 1834, introduced the pillar box 1853, and achieved the position of surveyor before retiring 1867. *The Warden* 1855 began the Barchester series, which includes *Barchester Towers* 1857, *Doctor Thorne* 1858, and *The Last Chronicle of Barset* 1867.

trombone a ◊brass wind musical instrument developed from the sackbut. It consists of a tube bent double, varied notes being obtained by an inner sliding tube. Usual sizes are alto, tenor, bass, and contra-bass.

Tromp Maarten Harpertszoon 1597–1653. Dutch admiral. He twice defeated the occupying Spaniards in 1639. He was defeated by the British admiral Blake in May 1652, but in Nov triumphed over Blake in the Strait of Dover. In Feb–June 1653 he was defeated by Blake and Monk, and was killed off the Dutch coast. His son, *Cornelius Tromp* (1629–91), also an admiral, won fame in 1673 for his battle against the English and French fleets.

trompe l'oeil painting that gives a convincing illusion of reality. It has been popular in most periods in the West, from classical Greece through the Renaissance.

trophic level in ecology, the position occupied by a ◊species (or group of species) in a ◊food chain. The main levels are *primary producers* (for example, plants), *primary consumers* (for example, herbivores), *secondary consumers* (for example, carnivores), and *decomposers*.

tropics the tropics of Cancer and Capricorn, defined by the parallels of latitude 23°30′ N and S of the equator, are the limits of the area of Earth's surface in which the Sun can be directly overhead.

Trotsky *Leon Trotsky in 1917, the year of the Russian Revolution.*

tropism or *tropic movement* the directional growth of a plant, or part of a plant, in response to an external stimulus. If the movement is directed towards the stimulus it is described as positive, if away from it, as negative. *Geotropism*, the response of plants to gravity, causes the root, (positively geotropic), to grow downwards, and the stem (negatively geotropic) to grow upwards. *Phototropism* occurs in response to light, *hydrotropism* to water, *chemotropism* to a chemical stimulus, and *thigmotropism*, or *haptotropism*, to physical contact, as in the tendrils of climbing plants when they touch a support and then grow around it.

troposphere lower part of the Earth's ◊atmosphere extending about 10.5 km/6.5 mi from the Earth's surface, in which temperature decreases with height except in local layers of temperature inversion. The *tropopause* is the upper boundary of the troposphere above which the temperature is constant or even increases slightly with height.

Trotsky Leon. Adopted name of Lev Davidovitch Bronstein 1879–1940. Russian revolutionary. He joined the Bolshevik party and took a leading part in the seizure of power and raising the Red Army which fought the Civil War 1918–20. In the struggle for power that followed Lenin's death in 1924, ◊Stalin defeated him, and this and other differences with the Communist Party led to his exile in 1929. Trotsky settled in Mexico, where

Truman *US politician and president, Harry Truman.*

he was assassinated with an ice pick, possibly at Stalin's instigation.

Trotskyism the form of Marxism advocated by Leon Trotsky. Its central concept is that of *permanent revolution*. In his view, a proletarian revolution, leading to a socialist society, could not be achieved in isolation, so it would be necessary to spark off further revolutions throughout Europe and ultimately worldwide. This was in direct opposition to the Stalinist view that socialism should be built and consolidated within individual countries.

troubadour one of a group of poet-musicians in Provence and S France, in the 12th–13th centuries, which included both nobles and wandering minstrels. The troubadours originated a type of lyric poetry devoted mainly to themes of courtly love and the idealization of women, and to glorifying the deeds of their patrons, reflecting the chivalric ideals of the period. Little is known of the music, which was normally passed down orally.

trout fish closely related to the salmon. It has a thick body and a blunt head, and varies in colour. It is native to the northern hemisphere, usually in fresh waters.

Troy ancient city (Latin name *Ilium*) of Asia Minor, which the poet Homer in the *Iliad* described as besieged in the ten-year Trojan War (mid-13th century BC), falling to the Greeks by the stratagem of leaving behind, in a feigned retreat, a wooden horse containing armed infiltrators to open the gates. Believing it to be a religious offering, the Trojans took it within the walls.

troy system system of units used for precious metals and gems. The troy pound (0.37 kg) consists of 12 ounces (each of 120 carats) or 5,760 grains (each equal to 65 mg).

Trudeau Pierre (Elliott) 1919– . Canadian Liberal politician. He was prime minister 1968–79 and won again by a landslide in Feb 1980. In 1980 he defeated the Quebec independence movement in a referendum and gained control over the constitution 1982, but by 1984 had so lost support that he resigned.

True Cross the instrument of Christ's crucifixion, supposedly found by St Helena, the mother of the emperor Constantine, on Calvary in 326.

Truffaut François 1932–1984. French film director, whose gently comic films include *Jules et Jim* 1961, and *La Nuit américaine/Day for Night* 1973 (for which he won an Academy Award). His work was greatly influenced by Hitchcock, and also draws on Surrealist and comic traditions.

truffle subterranean fungus of the order Tuberales. Certain species are valued as edible delicacies, in particular *Tuber melanosporum*, native to to the Perigord region of France and generally found growing under oak trees; it is rounded, blackish brown, covered with warts externally, and with blackish flesh.

Trujillo city in NW Peru, with its port at Salaverry; population (1981) 354,557. Industries include engineering, copper, sugar milling, and vehicle assembly.

Trujillo Molina Rafael (Leonidas) 1891–1961. Dictator of the Dominican Republic from 1930 until his death, he controlled political life as commander-in-chief of the army. His suppression of opponents resulted in his assassination.

Truman Harry S 1884–1972. 33rd president of the USA 1945–53, a Democrat. In Jan 1945 he became vice president to F D Roosevelt, and president when Roosevelt died in Apr that year. He used the atom bombs against Japan, launched the ◊Marshall Plan to restore W Europe's economy, and nurtured the European Community and NATO (including the rearmament of West Germany).

Truman Doctrine US president Harry Truman's 1947 doctrine that the USA would 'support free peoples who are resisting attempted subjugation by armed minorities or by outside pressures'. It was used to justify sending US troops abroad, for example, to Korea.

trumpet ◊brass wind musical instrument; a doubled tube with valves.

trumpeter South American bird, up to 50 cm/20 in tall, genus *Psophia*, related to the cranes. It has long legs, a short bill, and dark plumage. It is also a type of ◊swan.

trust an arrangement whereby a person or group of people holds property for the benefit of others entitled to the beneficial interest.

trust territory territory formerly held under the United Nations trusteeship system to be prepared for independence, either former ◊mandates, territories taken over by the Allies in World War II, or those voluntarily placed under the UN by the administering state.

Truth Sojourner (born Isabella Baumfree, subsequently Isabella Van Wagener) 1797–1883. US antislavery campaigner. Born a slave, she obtained her freedom and that of her son and became involved with religious groups. In 1843 she was 'commanded in a vision' to adopt the name Sojourner Truth. She published an autobiography, *The Narrative of Sojourner Truth* in 1850.

trypanosomiasis collection of debilitating long-term diseases caused by infestation with the microscopic single-celled *Trypanosoma*. They include sleeping sickness (nagana) in Africa, transmitted by the bites of ◊tsetse flies, and Chagas' disease in the Americas, spread by assassin-bugs.

Ts'ao Chan former name for the Chinese novelist ◊Cao Chan.

Tsar the Russian imperial title, derived from Latin *Caesar*.

tsetse African fly of the genus *Glossina*, related to the house fly, which transmit the disease nagana to cattle and sleeping sickness to human beings. It grows up to 1.5 cm/0.6 in long.

Tsiolkovsky Konstantin 1857–1935. Russian scientist. He published the first practical paper on astronautics in 1903, covering rocket space travel using liquid propellants, such as liquid oxygen.

tsunami giant wave generated by an undersea ◊earthquake or other disturbance. In the open ocean it may take the form of several successive waves, travelling at tens of kilometres per hour but with an amplitude (height) of only a metre or so. In the coastal shallows, however, they slow down and build up, producing towering waves tens of metres high that can sweep inland and cause great loss of life and property.

Tsvetaeva Marina 1892–1941. Russian poet, born in Moscow. She wrote mythic, romantic, frenetic verse, including *The Demesne of the Swans*.

TT abbreviation for *Tourist Trophy*; *teetotal*; *tuberculin tested*.

Tuareg nomadic ◊Hamite people of the Sudan.

tuatara lizard-like reptile *Sphenodon punctatus*, found only on a few islands off New Zealand. It grows up to 70 cm/2.3 ft long, is greenish or black, and has a spiny crest down its back. On the top of its head is the pineal organ, or so-called 'third eye', linked to the brain, which probably acts as a kind of light meter.

tuba a ◊brass wind musical instrument.

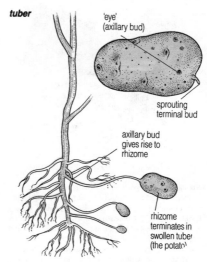

tuber

'eye'
(axillary bud)

sprouting
terminal bud

axillary bud
gives rise to
rhizome

rhizome
terminates in
swollen tuber
(the potato)

tuber a swollen region of an underground stem or root which is usually modified for storing food. The potato is a *stem tuber*, as shown by the presence of terminal and lateral buds, the 'eyes' of the potato. *Root tubers*, developed from adventitious roots, lack these. Both types of tuber can give rise to new individuals and so provide a means of ◊vegetative reproduction. New shoots grow directly from the buds of stem tubers, while root tubers (for example dahlias) are attached to a portion of stem with buds, and these develop into new plants.

tuberculosis (TB) an infectious disease caused by the bacillus *Mycobacterium tuberculosis*. It takes several forms, of which pulmonary tuberculosis (formerly known as consumption or phthisis) is by far the most common.

Tubman Harriet Ross 1821–1913. US abolitionist. Born a slave in Maryland, she escaped to Philadelphia (where slavery was outlawed) in 1849. She set up the *Underground Railroad* to help slaves escape to freedom in the Northern states and Canada. During the Civil War she served as a spy for the Union army. A noted speaker against slavery and for women's rights, she founded schools for freed slaves after the Civil War.

Tubman William V S 1895–1971. Liberian politician. The descendant of American slaves, he was a lawyer in the USA. After his election to the presidency of Liberia in 1944 he concentrated on uniting the various ethnic groups. Re-elected several times, he died naturally in office despite frequent assassination attempts.

TUC abbreviation for ◊*Trades Union Congress*.

Tucana constellation of the southern hemisphere, represented as a toucan. It contains the second most prominent ◊globular cluster in the sky, called 47 Tucanae, and the Small ◊Magellanic Cloud.

tucu-tuco S American burrowing rodent, genus *Ctenomys*, about 20 cm/8 in long with a 7 cm/3 in tail. It has a large head, sensitive ears, and huge incisor teeth.

Tudor English dynasty descended from the Welsh Owen Tudor (*c.* 1400–61), the second husband of Catherine of Valois, the widow of Henry V of England. Their son Edmund married Margaret Beaufort (1443–1509), the great-granddaughter of ◊John of Gaunt, and was the

tulip

father of Henry VII, who ascended the throne in 1485.

tufa a soft, porous rock, white in colour, consisting of calcium carbonate, $CaCO_3$, deposited from solution in spring water or percolating ground water.

Tu Fu 712–770. Chinese poet, who wrote about the social injustices of his time, peasant suffering, and war, as in 'The Army Carts'.

Tukano indigenous American people of the Vaupés Region on the Colombian-Brazilian border, numbering approximately 2,000.

tulip plant of the genus *Tulipa*, family Liliaceae, with usually single goble-shaped flowers on the end of an upright stem and leaves of a narrow oval shape with pointed ends. It is widely cultivated as a garden ornamental.

Tull Jethro 1674–1741. British agriculturist who, about 1701, developed a drill enabling seeds to be sown mechanically and spaced so that cultivation between rows was possible in the growth period.

tuna fish of the mackerel family *Thunnus thynnus*, up to 2.5 m/8 ft long and 200 kg/440 lbs. It is also known as *tunny*.

tundra region of high latitude almost devoid of trees, resulting from the presence of ◊permafrost. The term, formerly applied to part of N Russia, is now used for all such regions.

tungsten a metallic element, symbol W, atomic number 74, relative atomic mass 183.86. A grey hard metal, it is insoluble except in a mixture of nitric and hydrofluoric acids, and has the highest melting point (3,370°C) of any metal. Tungsten is used in alloy steels for armour plate, projectiles, high-speed cutting tools, lamp filaments, and thermionic valves. Its salts are used in the paint and tanning industries.

tunicate any ◊chordate of the sub-phylum Tunicata (Urochordata), for example the ◊sea-squirt.

Tunis capital and chief port of Tunisia; population (1984) 597,000. Industries include chemicals and textiles. Founded by the Arabs, it was occupied by the French 1881, and by the Axis powers 1942–43. The ruins of ancient ◊Carthage are to the NE.

Tunisia country in N Africa, on the Mediterranean, bounded to the SE by Libya and to the W by Algeria.

tunnel an underground passageway. Tunnelling is an increasingly important branch of civil engineering in mining and transport. In the 19th century there were two major advances: the use of compressed air within the tunnel to balance the external pressure of water, and of the tunnel shield to support the face and assist excavation. In recent years there have been notable developements in linings, for example concrete segments and steel liner plates; in the use of rotary diggers and cutters; and of explosives. See ◊Channel Tunnel.

Túpac Amaru (adopted name of José Gabriel Condorcanqui) 1743–1781. Peruvian Indian revolutionary leader, executed for his revolt in 1780 against Spanish rule; he claimed to be descended from the last of the Incas.

Tupamaros urban guerrilla movement operating in Uruguay, named after the 18th-century revolutionary Túpac Amaru. Its aim is to create a Marxist revolution, and it has been responsible for a number of bank robberies, kidnappings, and attacks on government buildings and institutions. Active in the 1960s, the movement became less evident after a government clampdown in 1972.

Tunisia
Republic of (*al-Jumhuriya at-Tunisiya*)

area 164,000 sq km/63,300 sq mi
capital and chief port Tunis
towns ports Sfax, Sousse, Bizerta
physical arable and forested land in the N graduates towards desert in the S

head of state and of government Zine el Abidine Ben Ali from 1987
political system emergent democratic republic
exports oil, phosphates, chemicals, textiles
currency dinar
population (1990 est) 8,094,000; growth rate 2% p.a.
life expectancy men 68, women 71
language Arabic (official), French
religion Sunni Muslim 95%; Jewish, Christian
literacy 68% men 41% women (1985 est)
GNP $9.6 bn (1987) $1,163 per head
chronology
1955 Granted internal self-government.
1956 Achieved full independence as a monarchy, with Habib Bourguiba as prime minister.
1957 Became a republic with Bourguiba as president.
1975 Bourguiba made president for life.
1985 Diplomatic relations with Libya severed.
1987 Bourguiba removed Prime Minister Rashed Sfar and appointed Zine el Abidine Ben Ali. Ben Ali declared Bourguiba incompetent and seized power.
1988 Constitutional changes towards democracy announced. Diplomatic relations with Libya restored.
1989 RDC (government party) won all assembly seats in general election.

tundra habitat

The landscape around the ice caps at the North and South Poles consists of an open treeless plain called tundra, or muskeg in North America. Winters last for about eight or nine months and the temperature can fall to −30°C (−86°F). The ground is frozen for most of the year, and in the summer there is only time for the topmost layer of soil to thaw. The meltwater cannot drain away and this gives rise to a waterlogged landscape where only low stunted plants grow. Insects flourish

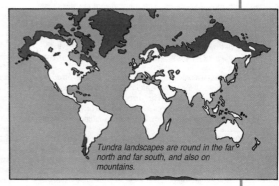

Tundra landscapes are round in the far north and far south, and also on mountains.

during the short summer, and birds migrate into the area to feed on them. Other animals winter in the forests in warmer latitudes and migrate into the region in the summer.

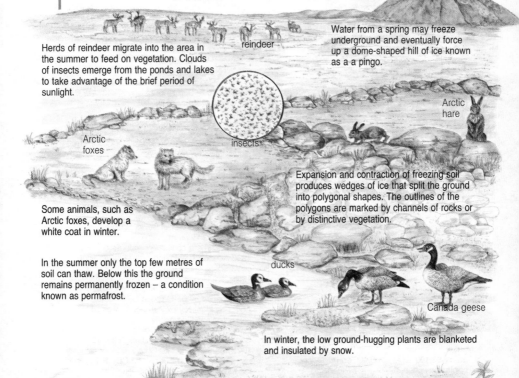

Herds of reindeer migrate into the area in the summer to feed on vegetation. Clouds of insects emerge from the ponds and lakes to take advantage of the brief period of sunlight.

reindeer

Water from a spring may freeze underground and eventually force up a dome-shaped hill of ice known as a a pingo.

Arctic hare

Arctic foxes

insects

Some animals, such as Arctic foxes, develop a white coat in winter.

Expansion and contraction of freezing soil produces wedges of ice that split the ground into polygonal shapes. The outlines of the polygons are marked by channels of rocks or by distinctive vegetation.

In the summer only the top few metres of soil can thaw. Below this the ground remains permanently frozen – a condition known as permafrost.

ducks

Canada geese

In winter, the low ground-hugging plants are blanketed and insulated by snow.

turbine an engine in which steam, water or gas is made to spin a rotating shaft by pushing on angled blades, like a fan. Turbines are among the most powerful machines. Steam turbines are used to drive generators in power stations and ships' propellers; water turbines spin the generators in hydroelectric power plants; and gas turbines, in the guise of jet engines, power most aircraft, and drive machines in industry.

turbocharger a turbine-driven device fitted to engines to force more air into the cylinders, producing extra power. The turbocharger consists of a 'blower' or ◊compressor, driven by a turbine, which in most units is driven by the exhaust gases leaving the engine.

turbojet a type of jet engine, which derives its thrust from a jet of hot exhaust gases. Pure turbojets can be very powerful but use a lot of fuel.

turboprop a jet engine that derives its thrust partly from a jet of exhaust gases, but mainly from a propeller powered by a turbine in the jet exhaust. Turboprops are more economical than turbojets, but can only be used at relatively low speeds.

turbot carnivorous flat-fish *Scophthalmus maximus* found in European waters. It grows up to 1 m/3 ft long and weighs up to 14 kg/30 lb. It is brownish above and whitish underneath.

Turgenev Ivan Sergeievich 1818–1883. Russian writer, noted for his poetic realism, his pessimism, and his skill at characterization. Major works include the play *A Month in the Country* 1849, and the novels *A Nest of Gentlefolk* 1858, *Fathers and Sons* 1862, and *Virgin Soil* 1877.

Turin (Italian *Torino*) capital of Piedmont, NW Italy, on the river Po; population (1988) /1,025,000. Industries include iron, steel, cars, silk and other textiles, fashion goods, chocolate, and wine. It was the first capital of united Italy 1861–64.

Turing Alan Mathison 1912–1954. British mathematician credited with laying the theoretical foundations of modern computing. In 1936 he published a paper describing theoretical computing devices (later known as 'Turing machines') which could perform any kind of 'effective' computation. The modern digital computer is, in effect, a realization of such a machine.

Turin shroud ancient piece of linen bearing the image of a body, claimed to be that of Jesus Christ. Independent tests carried out in 1988 by scientists in Switzerland, the USA, and the UK showed that the cloth of the shroud dated from between 1260 and 1390. The shroud, property of the pope, is kept in Turin Cathedral, Italy.

Turkana, Lake (formerly *Lake Rudolf*) lake in the Great Rift Valley, 375 m/1,230 ft above sea level, with its northernmost end in Ethiopia and the rest in Kenya; area 9,000 sq km/3,500 sq mi. It is saline and is shrinking by evaporation. Its shores were an early human hunting ground, and valuable remains have been found which are accurately datable because of undisturbed stratification.

turkey bird related to the pheasants. The wild turkey reaches a length of 1.3 m/4.3 ft, and is native to North and Central American woodlands. The domesticated turkey *Meleagris gallopavo* derives from the American wild species.

Turkey country between the Black Sea and the Mediterranean, bounded to the E by Armenia, Georgia, and Iran, to the S by Iraq and Syria.

Turkish language a language of central and W Asia, the national language of Turkey. Originally written in Arabic script, the Turkish of Turkey has since 1928 been written in a variant of the Roman alphabet. Varieties of Turkish are spoken in NW Iran and several central Asian Republics, and all have been influenced by Arabic and Persian.

Turkmenistan
Republic of

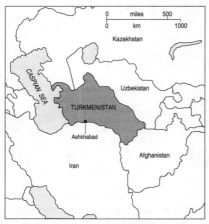

area 488,100 sq km/188,406 sq mi
capital Ashkhabad
towns Chardzhov, Mary (Merv), Nebit-Dag, Krasnovodsk
physical some 90% of land is desert including the Kara Kum 'Black Sands' desert (area 310,800 sq km/120,000 sq mi)

head of state Saparmurad Niyazov from 1991
head of government Sakhat Muradov from 1992
political system socialist pluralist
products silk, karakul, sheep, astrakhan fur, carpets, chemicals, rich deposits of petroleum, natural gas, sulphur, and other industrial raw materials
population (1990) 3,600,000 (72% Turkmen, 10% Russian, 9% Uzbek, Kazakh 3%, Ukrainian 1%)
language West Turkic, closely related to Turkish
religion Sunni Muslim
chronology
1921 Part of Turkestan Soviet Socialist Autonomous Republic.
1925 Became a constituent republic of USSR.
1990 Aug: economic and political sovereignty declared.
1991 Jan: Communist Party leader Niyazov became state president. March: endorsed maintenance of the Union in USSR referendum. Aug: President Niyazov initially supported attempted anti-Gorbachev coup. Oct: independence declared. Dec: joined new Commonwealth of Independent States (CIS).
1992 Jan: admitted into Conference for Security and Cooperation in Europe (CSCE). Feb: joined the Muslim Economic Cooperation Organization (ECO). March: admitted into United Nations (UN); US diplomatic recognition achieved. May: new constitution adopted. Nov–Dec: 60-member parliament popularly elected with Sakhat Muradov as prime minister.

Turkey
Republic of (*Türkiye Cumhuriyeti*)

area 779,500 sq km/300,965 sq mi
capital Ankara
towns ports Istanbul and Izmir
physical central plateau surrounded by mountains
head of state to be appointed
head of government Suleyman Demirel from 1991
political system democratic republic
exports cotton, yarn, hazelnuts, citrus fruits, tobacco, dried fruit, chromium ores
currency Turkish lira
population (1990 est) 56,549,000 (85% Turkish, 12% Kurdish); growth rate 2.1% p.a.

language Turkish (official), Kurdish Arabic
religion Sunni Muslim 98%
literacy men 86% women 62% (1985)
GNP $62 bn (1987); $1,160 per head (1986)
chronology
1919–22 Turkish War of Independence provoked by Greek occupation of Izmir; Mustafa Kemal (Atatürk), leader of nationalist congress, defeated Italian, French and Greek forces.
1923 Treaty of Lausanne established independent Turkish republic under Kemal; westernization began.
1950 First free elections; Adnan Menderes became prime minister.
1960 Menderes executed after military coup.
1965 Suleyman Demirel became prime minister.
1971 Army forced Demirel to resign.
1973 Civilian rule returned under Bulent Ecevit.
1975 Demirel returned at the head of a right-wing coalition.
1978 Ecevit returned, in the face of economic difficulties and factional violence.
1979 Demeril returned; violence grew.
1980 Army took over; Bulent Ulusu became prime minister. Harsh repression of political activists attracted international criticism.
1982 New constitution adopted.
1983 Ban on political activity lifted; Turgut Ozal became prime minister.
1987 Ozal retained majority in general election.
1989 Turgot Ozal elected president; Turkey's application for EC membership refused.
1991 Mesut Yilmaz became prime minister. Coalition government formed under Suleyman Demirel after inconclusive election result.
1993 Ozal died of heart attack

Turkmenistan country in Central Asia, bounded N by Kazakhstan and Uzbekistan, W by The Caspian Sea, and S by Iran and Afghanistan.

Turkoman person of Turkoman culture. They live around the Kara Kum desert, to the E of the Caspian Sea, and straddle the borders of Afghanistan and Iran. Their language belongs to the Turkic branch of the Altaic family.

Turks and Caicos Islands a British Crown Colony in the W Indies
area 430 sq km/166 sq mi
capital Cockburn Town on Grand Turk
exports crayfish and conch (flesh and shell)
currency US dollar
population (1980) 7,500, 90% of African descent
language English, French Creole
religion Christian
government governor, with executive and legislative councils (chief minister from 1985 Nathaniel Francis, Progressive National Party)
history secured by Britain 1766 against French and Spanish claims, the islands were a Jamaican dependency 1873–1962, and in 1976 attained internal self-government. The chief minister, Norman Saunders, resigned 1985 after his arrest in Miami on drugs charges, on which he was convicted.

turmeric perennial plant *Curcuma longa* of the ginger family, native to India; also the ground powder from its tuberous rhizomes, used in curries to give a yellow colour, and as a dyestuff.

Turner John Napier 1929– . Canadian Liberal politician, prime minister 1984. Elected to the House of Commons 1962, he served in Pierre Trudeau's Cabinet. He succeeded Trudeau 1984 as

party leader and premier, but lost the 1984 and 1988 elections, and resigned as party leader 1989.

Turner Joseph Mallord William 1775–1851. British landscape painter. He travelled widely in Europe, and his landscapes became increasingly Romantic, with the subject often transformed in scale and flooded with brilliant, hazy light. His brushwork became very free, so that many later works appear to anticipate Impressionism.

Turner Nat 1800–1831. US slave and Baptist preacher, who led 60 slaves in the most important US slave revolt – the **Southampton Insurrection** of 1831 – in Southampton County, Virginia. Before he and 16 of the others were hanged, at least 55 people had been killed.

Turner Tina (born Annie Mae Bullock) 1938– . US rhythm-and-blues singer who recorded 1960–76 with her husband as *Ike and Tina Turner*, notably *River Deep, Mountain High* 1966 produced by Phil Spector. Tina Turner had success in the 1980s as a solo performer, as on *Private Dancer* 1984.

turnip biennial plant *Brassica rapa* cultivated in temperate regions for its edible white or yellow-fleshed root and the young leaves, which are used as a green vegetable. Closely allied to it is the ◊swede *Brassica napus*.

turnstone wading bird *Arenaria interpres* which breeds in the Arctic and migrates to the S hemisphere. It is about 23 cm/9 in long, has a summer plumage of black and chestnut above, white below, and is duller in winter. It is seen on rocky beaches, searching for small crustaceans and insects.

turpentine solution of resins distilled from the sap of conifers, used in varnish and as a paint

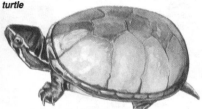

common mud turtle

turtle

Turner US rock star Tina Turner, 1986.

solvent, but now largely replaced by ◊white spirit.

Turpin Dick 1706–1739. English highwayman. Born
at Hempstead, Essex, the son of an innkeeper, he
turned to highway robbery, cattle-thieving, and
smuggling, and was hanged in York.

turquoise a mineral, hydrous phosphate of aluminium and copper. Opaque and blue-green, it is
used as a gem; it is found in Iran, Turkestan, and
Mexico.

turtle marine species of ◊tortoise, some of which
grow up to a length of 2.5 m/8 ft. They are excellent swimmers, having legs which are modified to
oar-like flippers, but which make them awkward on
land. They often travel long distances to lay their
eggs on the beaches where they were born.

Tuscany (Italian *Toscana*) region of central
Italy
capital Florence
area 22,990 sq km/8,876 sq mi

population (1981) 3,581,745
towns Pisa, Livorno, and Siena
products grapes, lignite and iron mines, marble
quarries
language the Tuscan dialect has been adopted as
the standard form of Italian *history* Tuscany was
formerly the Roman *Etruria*. In medieval times the
area was divided into small states, united under
Florentine rule during the 15th–16th centuries. It
became part of united Italy 1861.

Tussaud Madame (born Anne Marie Grosholtz)
1760–1850. French wax-modeller. In 1802 she
established an exhibition of wax models of famous
people in the Strand, London. It was transferred
to Baker St in 1883 and to Marylebone Rd in 1884
(destroyed by fire 1925, but reopened 1928).

Tutankhamen King of Egypt of the 18th dynasty *c.*
1360–1350 BC. A son of Ikhnaton or of Amenhotep
III, he was probably about 11 at his accession. In
1922 his tomb was discovered by the British archaeologists Lord Carnarvon and Howard Carter in the
Valley of the Kings at Luxor, almost untouched by
tomb robbers. The contents included many works
of art and his solid-gold coffin.

Tutu Desmond (Mpilo) 1931– . South African
priest, Anglican archbishop of Johannesburg and
general secretary of the South African Council of
Churches. He is one of the leading figures in the
struggle against apartheid in the Republic of South
Africa. Nobel Peace Prize 1984.

Turner Fighting Téméraire *(1838) by J M W Turner, National Gallery, London.*

Tuvalu
South West Pacific State of
(formerly *Ellice Islands*)

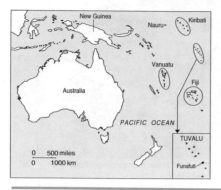

area 24.6 sq km/9.5 sq mi
capital Funafuti
physical low coral atolls in Polynesia
head of state Elizabeth II from 1978 represented by governor general
head of government Bikenibeu Paeniu from 1989
political system liberal democracy
exports copra, handicrafts, stamps
currency Australian dollar
population (1990 est.) 9,000 (Polynesian 9.6%); growth rate 3.4% p.a.
language Tuvaluan and English
religion Christian, chiefly Protestant
literacy 96% (1985)
GDP $6.1 million (1983); $711 per head
chronology
1978 Achieved full independence.
1986 Islanders rejected republican status.
1989 Bikenibeu Paeniu elected prime minister.

Tuva (Russian *Tuvinskaya*) autonomous republic of Russia, NW of Mongolia
capital Kyzyl
area 170,500 sq km/65,800 sq mi
population (1985) 278,000
history declared a Russian protectorate 1914, after the 1917 revolution it became the independent Tannu-Tuva republic 1920, until incorporated in the USSR as an autonomous region 1944. It was made the Tuva Autonomous Republic in 1961.

Tuvalu country in the SW Pacific, on the former Ellice Islands; part of ◊Polynesia.

TVP *T*exturized *V*egetable *P*rotein, a meat substitute made usually from soya beans. In manufacture, the soya-bean solids (what remains after oil has been removed) are ground finely and mixed with a binder to form a sticky mixture. This is forced through a spinneret and extruded into fibres, which are treated with salts and flavourings, wound into hanks and then chopped up to resemble meat chunks.

Twain Mark. Pen name of Samuel Langhorne Clemens 1835–1910. US humorous writer. He established his reputation with the comic masterpiece *The Innocents Abroad* 1869, and two children's books, *The Adventures of Tom Sawyer* 1876 and *The Adventures of Huckleberry Finn* 1885. He also wrote satire, as in *A Connecticut Yankee at King Arthur's Court* 1889.

Twain US novelist Mark Twain.

tweed cloth made of woollen yarn, usually of several shades, but in its original form without regular pattern and woven on a hand loom in the remoter parts of Ireland, Wales, and Scotland.

Twelfth Day the 12th and final day of the Christmas celebrations, 6 Jan; the feast of the ◊Epiphany.

Twelfth Night a comedy by William Shakespeare, first performed 1601–02. The plot builds on misunderstandings and mistaken identity, leading to the successful romantic unions of Sebastian and his twin sister Viola with Duke Orsino and Olivia respectively, and the downfall of Olivia's steward Malvolio.

twelve-note system or *twelve-tone system* a system of musical composition in which the 12 notes of the chromatic scale are arranged in a particular order, called a 'series' or 'note-row'. A work using the system consists of restatements of the series in any of its formations. ◊Schoenberg and ◊Webern were exponents of this technique.

Twelver member of a Shi'ite Muslim sect who believe that the 12th imam (Islamic leader) did not die, but is waiting to return towards the end of the world as the Mahdi, the 'rightly guided one', to establish a reign of peace and justice on Earth.

twin one of two young produced from a single pregnancy. Human twins may be genetically identical, having been formed from one fertilized egg which split into two cells, both of which became implanted. Non-identical twins are formed when two eggs are fertilized at the same time.

twitch alternative common name for ◊couch grass.

two-stroke cycle an operating cycle for internal combustion piston engines. The engine cycle is completed after just two strokes (movement up or down) of the piston unlike the more common ◊four-stroke cycle. All lightweight motorbikes use two-stroke petrol engines, which are cheaper and simpler than four-strokes.

tycoon a person who has acquired great wealth through business achievements. Examples include J Pierpont Morgan (1837–1913) and J D Rockefeller (1839–1937).

Tyler John 1790–1862. 10th president of the USA 1841–45, succeeding Benjamin ◊Harrison, who died after only a month in office. His government annexed Texas 1845.

Tyler Wat died 1381. English leader of the *Peasants' Revolt* of 1381. He was probably born in Kent or Essex, and may have served in the French wars. After taking Canterbury he led the peasant army to Blackheath and occupied London. At Mile End King Richard II met the rebels and promised to redress their grievances, which included the imposition of a poll tax. At a further conference at Smithfield, Tyler was murdered.

Tyndale William 1492–1536. English translator of the Bible. The printing of his New Testament (basis of the Authorized Version) was begun in 1525 in Cologne, and (after he had been forced to flee) completed in Worms. He was strangled and burnt as a heretic at Vilvorde in Belgium.

Tyndall John 1820–1893. Irish physicist, who in 1869 studied the scattering of light by invisibly small suspended particles. Known as the *Tyndall effect*, it was first observed with ◊colloidal solutions, in which a beam of light is made visible when it is scattered by minute colloidal particles (whereas a pure solvent does not scatter light). Similar scattering of blue wavelengths of sunlight by particles in the atmosphere makes the sky look blue (beyond the atmosphere, in outer space, the sky is black).

Tyne and Wear metropolitan county in NE England, created 1974, originally administered by an elected metropolitan council; its powers reverted to district councils 1986.
area 540 sq km/209 sq mi
towns administrative headquarters Newcastle-upon-Tyne; South Shields, Gateshead, Sunderland
products once a centre of heavy industry, it is now being redeveloped and diversified
population (1991) 1,087,000.

Tynwald the parliament of Isle of ◊Man.

typeface a style of printed lettering. Books, newspaper and other printed matter are produced in different styles of lettering; examples include Times and Baskerville. These different 'families' of alphabets have been designed over the centuries since printing was invented and each has distinguishing characteristics.

type metal an ◊alloy of tin, lead, and antimony, used for making the metal type printers use.

typesetting the means by which text is prepared for ◊printing, now usually carried out by computer. Text is keyed on a typesetting machine in a similar way to typing. Laser or light impulses are projected onto light-sensitive film which when developed can be used to make plates for printing.

typewriter a hand-operated machine for producing characters on paper. The first practicable typewriter was built at Milwaukee, Wisconsin, by C L Sholes, C Glidden and S W Soulé in 1867, and by 1874 E Remington and Sons, the gun makers whose name was soon given to the typewriters, produced under contract the first machines for sale.

typhoid fever infectious disease caused by the bacterium *Salmonella typhi*, and usually contracted through contaminated food or fluids. It is characterized by fever and damage to internal organs, mainly the spleen and intestine. Treatment is with antibiotics.

typhoon violently revolving storm, a type of ◊cyclone.

typhus an infectious disease, often fatal, caused by a microbe carried in the excreta of lice, fleas, mites, and ticks. Symptoms include fever, headache, and rash. It enters the body usually by abrasions in the

Tyson US boxer and heavyweight champion of 1987, Mike Tyson.

feet, and is epidemic among human beings in overcrowded conditions. Treatment is by antibiotics.

typography the design and layout of the printed word. Typography began with the invention of writing and developed as printing spread throughout Europe following the invention of metal moveable type by Johann ◊Gutenberg around 1440. Early type designs resembled the handwritten letters of the scribes – a heavy, angular, gothic style – but in about 1470 the Frenchman Nicholas Jensen (*c.* 1420–1480) is thought to have produced the first popular roman typeface (style of lettering), the capital letters being based on Roman inscriptions. Hundreds of variations have followed, but the basic design, with a few modifications, is still in use as the ordinary ('roman') type used in printing.

Tyr in Norse mythology, the god of battles, whom the Anglo-Saxons called Týw, hence 'Tuesday'.

tyrannosaurus largest known meat-eating dinosaur which lived in North America about 70 million years ago. Bipedal, it was up to 15 m/50 ft long, 6.5 m/20 ft tall, weighed 10 tonnes, and had teeth 15 cm/6 in long.

tyre (US *tire*) the rubber hoop fitted round the rims of bicycle, car, and other road-vehicle wheels. The first pneumatic rubber tyre was patented by R W Thompson in 1845, but it was John Boyd Dunlop of Belfast who independently re-invented pneumatic tyres for use with bicycles 1888–89.

Tyrone county of Northern Ireland
area 3,155 sq km/1,218 sq mi
towns county town Omagh; Dungannon, Strabane, Cookstown
products mainly agricultural
population (1981) 144,000.

Tyson Mike 1966– . US boxer, undisputed world heavyweight champion 1987–90. He won the WBC heavyweight title 1986 when he beat Trevor Berbick to become the youngest world heavyweight champion. He beat James 'Bonecrusher' Smith for the WBA title 1987 and later that year he became the first undisputed champion since 1978 when he beat Tony Tucker for the IBF title. He lost the title 1990 in an upset to James 'Buster' Douglas.

Tzu-Hsi former spelling of ◊Zi Xi, dowager empress of China.

dominate his later pictures. His works include the *Nativity* fresco (Florence) and three battle pictures for the Palazzo Medici.

Udall Nicholas 1504–56. English schoolmaster and playwright. He was the author of *Ralph Roister Doister c.* 1553, the first known English comedy.

UDI (*Unilateral Declaration of Independence*). Usually applied to the declaration of Ian Smith's Rhodesian Front government on 11 Nov 1965 announcing the independence of Rhodesia (now Zimbabwe) from the British Crown.

Udmurt (Russian *Udmurtskaya*) autonomous republic in the W Ural foothills, central Russia
area 42,100 sq km/16,200 sq mi
capital Izhevsk
products timber, flax, potatoes, peat, quartz
population (1985) 1,559,000; Udmurt 33%, Tatar 7%, Russian 58%
history conquered in the 15th–16th centuries; constituted the Votyak Autonomous Region 1920; name changed to Udmurt 1932; Autonomous Republic 1934; part of the independent republic of Russia 1991.

U-2 a US military reconnaissance aeroplane, used in clandestine flights over the USSR from 1956 to photograph military installations. In 1960 a U-2 was shot down over the USSR and the pilot, Gary Powers, captured and imprisoned; he was exchanged for a Soviet agent two years later.

U2 Irish rock group formed 1978 by singer Bono Vox (1960–), guitarist Dave 'The Edge' Evans (1961–), bassist Adam Clayton (1960–), and drummer Larry Mullen (1961–). Radical Christians, they play socially concerned stadium rock, and their albums include *The Unforgettable Fire* 1984 and *The Joshua Tree* 1987.

uakari rare South American monkey, genus *Cacajao*, of which there are three species. They have bald faces and long fur. About 55 cm/1.8 ft long in head and body, and with a comparatively short 15 cm/6 in tail, they rarely leap, but are good climbers, remaining in the tops of the trees in swampy forests and feeding largely on fruit.

Ubangi-Shari former name for the ◊Central African Republic.

U-boat German submarine. In both World Wars they were named U followed by a number.

Uccello Paolo. Adopted name of Paolo di Dono 1397–1475. Italian painter, active in Florence, celebrated for his early use of perspective. He is recorded as an apprentice in Ghiberti's workshop in 1407, but his surviving paintings date from the 1430s onwards. Decorative colour and detail

Uelsman Jerry 1934– . US photographer, noted for his dream-like images, created by synthesizing many elements into one with great technical skill.

Uganda landlocked country in E Africa, bounded to the N by Sudan, to the E by Kenya, to the S by Tanzania and Rwanda, and to the W by Zaïre.

Ugarit ancient trading city kingdom (modern Ras Shamra) on the Syrian coast. It was excavated by the French archaeologist Claude Schaeffer (1898–1982) from 1929, finds ranging from about 7000 to 15–13th centuries BC. They include numerous cuneiform documents and an early Ugaritic alphabet of 22 letters (the earliest alphabet known, and closely related to the Phoenician, from which the Roman is ultimately derived).

UHF *U*ltra *H*igh *F*requency, referring to radio waves of very short wavelength, used, for example, for television broadcasting.

uitlander (Dutch 'foreigner') in South African history, term applied by the Boer inhabitants of the Transvaal to immigrants of non-Dutch origin (mostly British) in the late 19th century. The *uitlanders'* inferior political position in the Transvaal led to the Second ◊South African War 1899–1902.

UK abbreviation for ◊*United Kingdom*.

UKAEA abbreviation for *United Kingdom Atomic Energy Authority*.

Ukraine Country in E central Europe, bounded E by Russia, N by Belarus, S by Moldova, Romania, and the Black Sea, and W by Poland, the Slovak Republic, and Hungary.

uakari

Uccello St George and the Dragon *(c. 1460) National Gallery, London.*

Uganda
Republic of

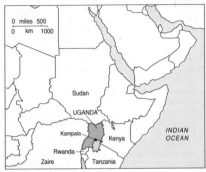

area 236,000 sq km/93,980 sq mi
capital Kampala
towns Jingar, M'Bale, Entebbe
physical plateau with mountains in W; forest and grassland; arid in N
head of state and government Yoweri Museveni from 1986
political system emergent democratic republic
exports coffee, cotton, tea, copper
currency Uganda new shilling
population (1990 est) 17,593,000 (the largest ethnic group is the Baganda; others include the Langi and Acholi, and a few surviving Pygmies); annual growth rate 3.3%
life expectancy men 49, women 51 (1989)
language English (official); Kiswahili and other African languages
religion Roman Catholic 33%, Protestant 33%, Muslim 16%, animist minority
literacy Men 70%, women 45% (1985)
GNP $3.6 bn (1987); $220 per head
chronology
1962 Achieved independence within the Commonwealth with Milton Obote as prime minister.
1963 Proclaimed a federal republic with King Mutesa II as president.
1966 King Mutesa ousted in a coup led by Obote, who ended the federal status and became executive president.
1969 All opposition parties banned after an assassination attempt on Obote.
1971 Obote overthrown in an army coup led by Maj-Gen Idi Amin, who established a ruthlessly dictatorial regime, expelling nearly 49,000 Ugandan Asians. Up to 300,000 opponents of the regime are said to have been killed.
1978 After heavy fighting, Amin was forced to leave the country. A provisional government was set up with Yusuf Lule as president. Lule was replaced by Godfrey Binaisa.
1978–79 Fighting with Tanzanian troops.
1980 Binaisa overthrown by the army. Elections held and Milton Obote returned to power.
1985 After years of opposition, mainly by the National Resistance Army (NRA), and uncontrolled indiscipline in the regular army, Obote was ousted by Brig Basilio Okello, who entered a power-sharing agreement with the NRA leader, Yoweri Museveni.
1986 Agreement ended and Museveni became president, heading a broad-based coalition government.
1992 Announcement made that East African cooperation pacts with Kenya and Tanzania would be revived.

Ukrainian language a member of the Slavonic branch of the Indo-European language family, spoken in Ukraine. It is closely related to Russian and is sometimes referred to by Russians as 'Little Russian'. Communities speaking Ukrainian are also found in Canada and the United States.

ukulele a type of small four-stringed ◊guitar.

Ulaanbaatar (formerly *Ulan Bator*, until 1924 *Urga*) capital of the Mongolian Republic, a trading centre producing carpets, textiles, vodka; population (1991) 575,000.

Ulbricht East German politician Walter Ulbricht (front row, third from right).

Ulanova Galina 1910– . Soviet dancer. Prima ballerina of the Bolshoi Theatre Ballet 1944–61, she excelled as Juliet and Giselle, and created the principal role of Katerina in Prokofiev's *The Stone Flower*. She continued as ballet mistress to the company.

Ulbricht Walter 1893–1973. East German politician. After exile in the USSR during Hitler's rule, he became first secretary of the Socialist Unity Party in East Germany in 1950 and (as chair of the Council of State 1960–73) was instrumental in the building of the Berlin Wall in 1961. He established East Germany's economy and recognition outside the E European bloc.

ulcer a persistent breach in a body surface (skin or mucous membrane). It may be caused by infection, ischaemia, irritation, or tumour.

Ulster former kingdom in Northern Ireland, annexed by England 1461, from Jacobean times a centre of English, and later Scottish, settlement on land confiscated from its owners; divided 1921 into Northern Ireland (counties Antrim, Armagh, Down, Fermanagh, Londonderry, and Tyrone) and Cavan, Donegal, and Monaghan in the Republic of Ireland.

Ultra abbreviation of Ultra Secret, used by the British from spring 1940 in World War II to denote intelligence gained by deciphering German signals at the interception centre at Bletchley Park, Buckinghamshire. Failure to use such information in the Battle of ◊Anzio meant that Allied troops were stranded for a time.

ultra (Latin) extreme.

Ultramontanism in the Roman Catholic Church,

Ukraine

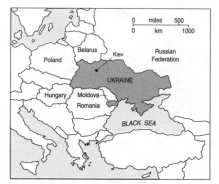

area 603,700 sq km/233,089 sq mi
capital Kiev
towns Kharkov, Donetsk, Odessa,
Dnepropetrovsk, Lugansk (Voroshilovgrad), Lviv
(Lvov), Matiupol (Zbdanov), Krivoi Rog,
Zaporozhye
physical Russian plain: Carpathian and Crimean
Mountains; rivers: Dnieper (with the Dnieper dam
1932), Donetz, Bug
head of state Leonid Kravchuk from 1990
head of government Leonid Kuchma from 1992
political system emergent democracy
products grain, coal, oil, various minerals
currency grivna
population (1990) 51,800,000 (73% Ukrainian, 22%
Russian, 1% Byelorussian, 1% Russian-speaking
Jews – some 1.5 million have emigrated to the
USA, 750,000 to Canada)
language Ukrainian (Slavonic)

religion traditionally Ukrainian Orthodox; also
Ukrainian Catholic
chronology
1918 Independent People's Republic proclaimed.
1920 Conquered by Soviet Red Army.
1921 Poland alloted charge of W Ukraine.
1932–33 Famine caused the deaths of more than
7.5 million people.
1939 W Ukraine occupied by Red Army.
1941–44 Under Nazi control: Jews massacred at
Babi Yar; more than five million Ukrainians and
Ukrainian Jews deported and exterminated.
1944 Soviet control re-established.
1945 Became a founder member of the United
Nations.
1946 Ukrainian Uniate Church proscribed and
forcibly merged with Russian Orthodox Church.
1986 April: Chernobyl nuclear disaster.
1989 Feb: Ukrainian People's Movement (Rukh)
established. Ban on Ukrainian Uniate Church
lifted.
1990 July: voted to proclaim sovereignty; Leonid
Kravchuk indirectly elected as president;
sovereignty declared.
1991 Aug: demonstrations against the abortive
anti-Gorbachev coup; independence declared,
pending referendum; Communist Party (CP)
activities suspended. Dec: Kravchuk popularly
elected president; independence overwhelmingly
endorsed in referendum; joined new
Commonwealth of Independent States (CIS).
1992 Jan: pipeline deal with Iran to end
dependence on Russian oil; prices freed. Feb:
prices 'temporarily' re-regulated. March: agreed
tactical arms shipments to Russia suspended.
May: Crimean sovereignty declared, but
subsequently rescinded. Aug: joint control of
Black Sea fleet agreed with Russia. Oct: Kuchma
became prime minister. Production decline by
20% during 1992.
1993 Inflation at 35% a month in early part of year,
budget deficit at 44% of GDP.

---

the tenets of the Italian party which stresses papal
authority rather than nationalism in the church.

ultrasound physical vibrations in matter occurring at frequencies above 20,000 hertz (cycles per
second), the approximate limit of human hearing.
Nearly all practical applications are in liquids or
solids.

ultraviolet radiation light rays invisible to the
human eye, of wavelengths from about 4×10^{-7} to
5×10^{-9} metres (where the ◊X-ray range begins).
Physiologically, they are extremely powerful, producing sunburn and causing the formation of vitamin
D in the skin; they are strongly germicidal and may
be produced artificially by mercury vapour and arc
lamps for therapeutic use.

Ulysses Roman name for ◊Odysseus, Greek
mythological hero.

Ulysses a novel by James Joyce, published 1922. It
employs stream of consciousness, linguistic experiment, and parody to describe in enormous detail a
single day (16 June 1904) in the life of its characters
in Dublin. It was first published in Paris but, because
of obscenity prosecutions, not until 1936 in the UK.

Ulmar died AD 644. 2nd caliph (head of Islam, noted
as a strong disciplinarian. Under his rule Islam spread
to Egypt and Persia. He was assassinated in Medina.

Umayyad alternative spelling for ◊Omayyad dynasty.

Umberto two kings of Italy:

Umberto I 1844–1900. King of Italy from 1878,
who joined the Triple Alliance 1882 with Germany

and Austria-Hungary; his colonial ventures included
the defeat at Aduwa, Abyssinia, 1907. He was
assassinated by an anarchist.

Umberto II 1904–1983. Last king of Italy, 1946.
On the abdication of his father, Victor Emmanuel III,
he ruled from 9 May to 13 June 1946, when he also
abdicated and left the country.

umbilical cord the connection between the
◊embryo and the ◊placenta of placental mammals.
It has one vein and two arteries, transporting
oxygen and nutrients to the developing young, and
removing excretory products. At birth, the connection between the young and the umbilical cord is
severed, leaving a scar called the navel.

umbrella portable protection against the rain –
when used in the sun usually called a parasol or
sunshade. In use in China for more than a thousand
years, umbrellas were also held over the rulers of
ancient Egypt and Assyria as symbols of power, and
had a similar significance for Aztec and African
rulers, as well as in the Roman Catholic church.

Umm al Qalwain one of the ◊United Arab
Emirates.

Umtata capital of the South African Bantu homeland of ◊Transkei.

UN abbreviation for ◊*United Nations*.

Unamuno Miguel de 1864–1936. Spanish writer
of Basque origin. He was exiled 1924–30 for criticism of the military directorate of Primo de ◊Rivera.
His works include the mystic poem on survival of

death 'El Cristo de Velázquez/The Velazquez Christ' 1920, and the philosophical prose study *Del sentimiento trágico de la vida/The Tragic Sense of Life* 1913, about the conflict of reason and belief in religion.

uncertainty principle or *indeterminacy principle* in quantum mechanics, the principle that it is meaningless to speak of a particle's position, momentum, or other parameters, except as results of measurements; measuring, however, involves an interaction (such as a ◊photon of light bouncing off the particle under scrutiny), which must disturb the particle, though the disturbance is noticeable only at an atomic scale. The principle implies that one cannot, even in theory, predict the moment-to-moment behaviour of such a system.

Uncle Sam nickname for the US government. It originated during the War of 1812, probably from the initials U S placed on government property.

Uncle Tom's Cabin best-selling US novel by Harriet Beecher Stowe, written 1851–52, a sentimental but powerful portrayal of the cruelties of slave life on Southern plantations which promoted the call for Abolition. The heroically loyal slave Uncle Tom has in the 20th century become a byword for black subservience.

unconformity in geology, a break in the sequence of ◊sedimentary rocks. It is usually seen as an eroded surface, with the ◊beds above and below lying at different angles. An unconformity represents an ancient land surface, where exposed rocks were worn down to sea level and later covered with deposited sediments.

unconscious an absence of awareness. In psychoanalysis it refers to part of the personality of which the individual is unaware, and which contains impulses or urges that are held back, or repressed, from conscious awareness. Emotional problems and irrational actions are believed by psychoanalysts to stem from unconscious conflicts.

UNCTAD abbreviation for *UN Commission on Trade and Development*.

underground (USA *subway*) a rail service that runs underground. The first underground line in the world was in London. Opened in 1863, it was essentially a roofed-in trench. The London Underground is still the longest, with over 400 km/250 mi of routes. Many major cities throughout the world have similar systems, and Moscow's Underground, the Metro, handles up to six and a half million passengers a day.

Underground Railroad in US history, a network established in the northern states before the Civil War to provide sanctuary and assistance for black slaves on the run from their owners. Safe houses, transport facilities, and conductors existed to lead the slaves to safety in the north, although the number of fugitives who secured their freedom by these means may have been exaggerated.

Undset Sigrid 1882–1949. Norwegian novelist, born in Denmark. Author of *Kristin Lavransdatter* 1920–22, a strongly Catholic novel set in the 14th century. Nobel Prize for Literature 1928.

unemployment an involuntary lack of paid employment. Unemployment is generally subdivided into *frictional unemployment*, the inevitable temporary unemployment of those moving from one job to another; *cyclical unemployment*, caused by a downswing in the trade cycle; *seasonal unemployment*, in an area where there is high demand only during holiday periods, for example; and *structural unemployment*, where changing technology or other long-term change in

the economy results in large numbers without work. Periods of widespread unemployment in Europe and the USA this century include 1929–1930s, and the years since the mid-1970s.

UNESCO *United Nations Educational, Scientific, and Cultural Organization*. Agency of the United Nations, established in 1946, with its headquarters in Paris. The USA, contributor of 25 per cent of its budget, withdrew in 1984 on grounds of its over-politicization, and Britain followed in 1985.

Ungaretti Giuseppe 1888–1970. Italian poet, born in Alexandria, and later living in Paris and São Paulo. His lyrics show a cosmopolitan independence of Italian poetic tradition.

ungulate general name for any hoofed mammal.

UNHCR abbreviation for *United Nations High Commission for Refugees*.

Uniate (united Greek or Eastern Orthodox and Roman Catholic Church) those Christian churches which accept the full Catholic faith and the supremacy of the Pope, and are in full communion with the Roman Catholic Church, but retain their own liturgy and separate organization.

UNICEF abbreviation for *United Nations International Children's Emergency Fund*.

unicorn mythical animal referred to by classical writers, said to live in India and to be like a horse but with one straight horn.

unidentified flying object (UFO) any light or object seen in the sky whose immediate identity is not apparent. The term *flying saucer* was coined 1947.

Unification Church or *Moonies* church founded in Korea in 1954 by the Reverend Sun Myung ◊Moon. World membership is about 200,000. The theology unites Christian and Taoist ideas, and is based on Moon's book *Divine Principle* which teaches that the original purpose of creation was to set up a perfect family, in a perfect relationship with God.

unified field theory in physics, the theory which attempts to explain the four natural forces (strong, weak, electromagnetic, and gravitational) in terms of a single unified force.

uniformitarianism in geology, the principle that processes that can be seen to occur on the Earth's surface today are the same as those that have occurred throughout geological time. For example, desert sandstones containing sand-dune structures must have been formed under conditions similar to those present in deserts today. The principle was formulated by James ◊Hutton and expounded by Charles ◊Lyell.

Union, Act of act of 1707 that effected the union of England and Scotland; that of 1801 united England and Ireland. The latter was abrogated when the Irish Free State was constituted in 1922.

union flag the British national ◊flag.

Union Movement British political group. Beginning as the New Party founded by Sir Oswald ◊Mosley and a number of Labour Members of Parliament in 1931, it developed into the British Union of Fascists in 1932. In 1940 the organization was declared illegal and its leaders interned, but at the end of World War II it was revived as the Union Movement, characterized by racist doctrines including anti-Semitism.

Union of Soviet Socialist Republics (USSR) former country in N Asia and E Europe that reverted to independent states after Mikhail Gorbachev's resignation 1991.

UNITA abbreviation for *National Union for the Total Independence of Angola* an Angolan nationalist movement backed by South Africa, which continued to wage guerrilla warfare against the ruling MPLA regime after the latter gained control of the country.

Unitarianism a Christian denomination which rejects the orthodox doctrine of the Trinity, asserts the Fatherhood of God and the Brotherhood of Man, and gives a pre-eminent position to Jesus Christ as a religious teacher, while denying his Deity. Unitarians believe in individual conscience and reason as a guide to right action, rejecting the doctrines of original sin, the atonement, and eternal punishment. The various congregations are linked in the General Assembly of Unitarian and Free Christian Churches. See also ◊Arianism and ◊Socinianism. It is widely spread in England and North America.

United Arab Emirates federation in SW Asia, on the Arabian Gulf, bounded to the SW by Saudi Arabia and to the SE by Oman.

United Arab Republic union formed 1958, broken 1961, between Egypt and Syria. Egypt continued to use the name after the breach until 1971.

United Australia Party Australian political party formed by J A ◊Lyons in 1931 from the right-wing Nationalist Party (founded by W M Hughes and in power 1917–29). It was led by Robert Menzies after the death of Lyons. Considered to have become too dominated by financial interests, it lost heavily to the Labor Party in 1943, and was reorganized as the ◊Liberal Party in 1944.

United Democratic Front moderate political organization in South Africa, the main focus of anti-apartheid action within South Africa since the African National Congress and Pan-Africanist Congress were declared illegal by that country.

United Kingdom (UK) country in NW Europe off the coast of France.

United Nations (UN) association of states (successor to the ◊League of Nations) for international peace, security, and cooperation, with its headquarters in New York. Its charter was drawn up at the San Francisco Conference 1945, based on proposals drafted at the Dumbarton Oaks conference. It comprises:

General Assembly one member from each of 159 member states who meet annually; decisions on important questions require a two-thirds majority, while on minor ones, a simple majority suffices;

Security Council five permanent members (UK, USA, USSR, France, China, who exercise a veto in that their support is requisite for all decisions), plus six others elected for two years by the General Assembly. It may undertake investigations into disputes and make recommendations to the parties concerned, and may call on all members to take economic or military measures to enforce its decisions;

Economic and Social Council 18 members elected for three years. It initiates studies of international economic, social, cultural, educational, health, and related matters, and may make recommendations to the General Assembly. It operates largely through specialized commissions of international experts on economics, transport and communications, human rights, status of women, and so on. It coordinates the activities of the ◊*Food and Agriculture Organization* (FAO);

General Agreement on Tariffs and Trade (GATT) established 1948, headquarters in Geneva; reduction of trade barriers, anti-dumping code, assistance to trade of developing countries;

◊*International Atomic Energy Agency* (IAEA);

International Bank for Reconstruction and Development (IBRD) popularly known as the ◊World Bank;

International Civil Aviation Organization (ICAO) established 1947, headquarters in Montreal; safety and efficiency, international facilities and air law;

International Development Association (IDA) administered by the World Bank;

International Finance Corporation (IFC) established 1956; affiliated to the World Bank, it encourages private enterprise in less developed countries;

International Fund for Agricultural Development (IFAD) established 1977, headquarters in Rome; additional funds for benefiting the poorest in developing countries;

◊*International Labour Organization* (ILO);

International Maritime Organization (IMO) established 1958, headquarters in London; safety at sea, pollution control, abolition of restrictive practices;

◊*International Monetary Fund* (IMF);

International Telecommunication Union (ITU) established 1934, headquarters in Geneva; allocation of radio frequencies; promotes low tariffs and life-saving measures for, for example, disasters at sea;

United Nations Educational, Scientific, and Cultural Organization (◊UNESCO);

◊*Universal Postal Union* (UPU);

◊*World Health Organization* (WHO);

World Intellectual Property Organization (WIPO) established 1974, headquarters in Geneva; protection of copyright in the arts, science, and industry;

World Meteorological Organization (WMO) established 1951, headquarters in Geneva;

Trusteeship Council consisting of members administering ◊trust territories, other permanent members of the Security Council, plus sufficient other elected members to balance the administering powers;

International Court of Justice at The Hague, with 15 judges elected by the General Assembly and Security Council; United Nations members are pledged to accept decisions;

Secretariat headed by a secretary general who is elected for five years by the General Assembly.

United States of America (USA) country in North America, extending from the Atlantic to the Pacific, bounded by Canada to the N and Mexico to the S, and including the outlying states of Alaska and Hawaii.

United World Colleges six colleges worldwide with admission by scholarship for students aged 16–18. Its curriculum demands both academic achievement and service to the community.

unit trust a company which invests its clients' funds in other companies. The units it issues represent holdings of shares, which means unit shareholders have a wider spread of capital than if they bought shares on the stock market.

universal joint a flexible coupling used to join rotating shafts, for example, the propeller shaft in a car. In a typical universal joint the ends of the shafts to be joined end in U-shaped yokes. They dovetail into each other and pivot flexibly about an X-shaped spider. This construction allows side-to-side and up-and-down movement, while still transmitting rotary motion.

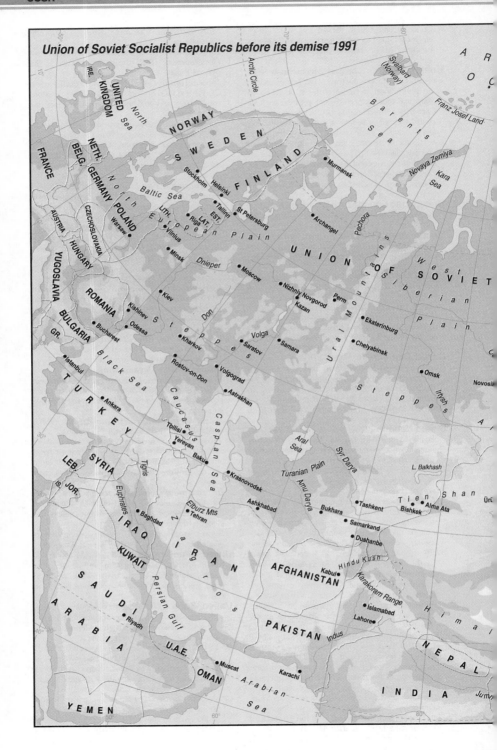

Union of Soviet Socialist Republics before its demise 1991

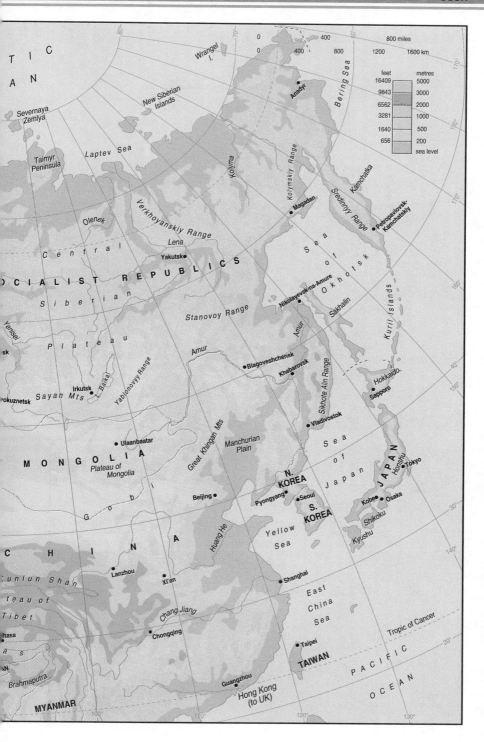

C T I C
A N

Wrangel I.

0   400
0   400   800

800 miles

1200   1600 km

New Siberian
Islands

Severnaya
Zemlya

Bering Sea

feet   metres
16409   5000
9843   3000
6562   2000
3281   1000
1640   500
656   200
            sea level

Taimyr
Peninsula

Laptev Sea

Anadyr

Kolyma

Kolymskiy Range

Kamchatka

Magadan

Sredinnyy Range

Olenek

Verkhoyanskiy Range

Lena

Petropavlovsk-
Kamchatskiy

Yakutsk

C e n t r a l

Sea
of
Okhotsk

O C I A L I S T   R E P U B L I C S

S i b e r i a n

Nikolayevsk-na-Amure

Stanovoy Range

Amur

Sakhalin

Kuril Islands

Yenisei

P l a t e a u

Amur

Blagoveshchensk

Khabarovsk

Hokkaido

Sikhote Alin Range

sk

Sayan Mts

Irkutsk

L. Baikal

Yablonovyy Range

Sapporo

rokuznetsk

Vladivostok

Great Khingan Mts

Manchurian
Plain

Sea
of

Ulaanbaatar

M O N G O L I A

Plateau of
Mongolia

N.
KOREA

Japan

J A P A N

Sea
of
Japan

Honshu

Tokyo

Pyongyang

Seoul

Beijing

S.
KOREA

G o b i

Kobe

Osaka

Shikoku

Kyushu

C H I N A

Yellow
Sea

unlun Shan

Lanzhou

Xi'an

teau of

Tibet

Chang Jiang

Shanghai

East
China
Sea

hasa

Chongqing

a s

Tropic of Cancer

Taipei

Brahmaputra

TAIWAN

P A C I F I C

MYANMAR

Guangzhou

Hong Kong
(to UK)

O C E A N

United Kingdom

Shetland Is

Orkney Is
Pentland Firth

North Minch

Outer Hebrides

Inner Hebrides

West Highlands

North Highlands

Skye

Rhum
Coll
Tiree
Mull

Jura
Islay

Arran

L. Ness

Ben Nevis
4402ft/1342m

Grampian Mts

Dee

Tay

Forth

Clyde

Tweed

Southern Uplands

Cheviot Hills

Pennines

Tyne

Tees

ATLANTIC

OCEAN

NORTH

SEA

Mts of Antrim

Sperrin Mts

L. Neagh

L. Erne

North Channel

Cumbrian Mts

Scafell Pike
3208ft/978m

North York
Moors

L. Mask

L. Corrib

Central Plain

Shannon

Wicklow
Mts

Barrow

Macgillycuddys Reeks
3415ft/1041m
Mts of Kerry

Blackwater

I. of Man

IRISH SEA

Liverpool Bay

Ribble

Mersey

Trent

The
Wash

Snowdon
3559ft/1085m

Cardigan Bay

St. George's Channel

Cambrian Mts

Severn

Avon

Welland

The Fens

Ouse

London

Thames

North Downs

South Downs

Cotswolds

Bristol Channel

Exmoor

Dartmoor

Str. of Dover

Isles of Scilly

ENGLISH CHANNEL

Alderney

Guernsey

Channel Is.
(Br.)
Jersey

FRANCE

0   50   100   150 miles
0   100   200 km

United Kingdom

ATLANTIC

OCEAN

SHETLAND

ORKNEY

-58°

The districts of Northern Ireland
1 Londonderry
2 Limavady
3 Coleraine
4 Ballymoney
5 Moyle
6 Larne
7 Ballymena
8 Magherafelt
9 Cookstown
10 Strabane
11 Omagh
12 Fermanagh
13 Dungannon
14 Craigavon
15 Armagh
16 Newry and Mourne
17 Banbridge
18 Down
19 Lisburn
20 Antrim
21 Newtownabbey
22 Carrickfergus
23 North Down
24 Arda
25 Castlereagh
26 Belfast

WESTERN

ISLES

NORTH

SEA

HIGHLAND

GRAMPIAN

S C O T L A N D

TAYSIDE

FIFE

STRATHCLYDE

CENTRAL

Edinburgh

LOTHIAN

BORDERS

DUMFRIES
AND GALLOWAY

NORTHUMBERLAND

TYNE AND WEAR

DONEGAL

CUMBRIA

DURHAM

CLEVELAND

ISLE
OF MAN

NORTH YORKSHIRE

SLIGO

N

I R E L A N D

MONAGHAN

CAVAN

LOUTH

LANCASHIRE

W
YORKS

HUMBERSIDE

MAYO

ROSCOMMON

LONGFORD

WEST
MEATH

MEATH

GREATER MANCHESTER

MERSEYSIDE

S
YORKS

NOTT

LINCOLNSHIRE

GALWAY

I R E L A N D

OFFALY

KILDARE

Dublin

CHESHIRE

DERBYSHIRE

GHAM

CLARE

LAOIS

WICKLOW

GWYNEDD

CLWYD

SHROP
SHIRE

STAFFORD
SHIRE

LEICESTERSHIRE

NORFOLK

LIMERICK

TIPPERARY

KILKENNY

CARLOW

WEXFORD

W A L E S

WEST MIDLANDS

WARWICK
SHIRE

CAMBRIDGE
SHIRE

SUFFOLK

KERRY

CORK

WATERFORD

POWYS

HEREFORD
AND WORCESTER

BEDFORD
SHIRE

St. George's Channel

DYFED

GLOUCESTER
SHIRE

GWENT

BUCKS

HERTFORD

ESSEX

WEST GLAMORGAN
MID GLAMORGAN
SOUTH GLAMORGAN

Cardiff

AVON

OXFORD
SHIRE

BERKSHIRE

GREATER
LONDON

London

KENT

WILTSHIRE

SURREY

SOMERSET

HAMPSHIRE

WEST
SUSSEX

EAST
SUSSEX

Str. of Dover

DEVON

DORSET

ISLE OF WIGHT

CORNWALL

E N G L I S H   C H A N N E L

-50°

Isles of Scilly

Alderney

Guernsey

Channel Is.
(Br.)

Jersey

ATLANTIC   OCEAN

FRANCE

0   50   100   150 miles
0   100   200 km

United Kingdom
of Great Britain and
Northern Ireland (UK)

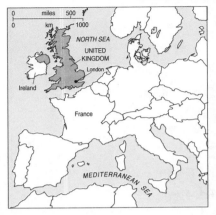

area 243,363 sq km/93,938 sq mi
capital London
towns Birmingham, Glasgow, Leeds, Sheffield, Liverpool, Manchester, Edinburgh, Bradford, Bristol, Belfast, Newcastle-upon-Tyne, Cardiff
physical rolling landscape, becoming increasingly mountainous towards the N, with the Grampian Mountains in Scotland and Snowdon in Wales. Rivers include Thames and Severn
territories Anguilla; Bermuda; British Antarctic Territory; British Indian Ocean Territory; British Virgin Islands; Cayman Islands; Falkland Islands (disputed by Argentina); Gibraltar; Hong Kong (until 1997); Montserrat; Pitcairn Islands; St Helena and Dependencies (Ascension, Tristan da Cunha); Turks and Caicos Islands
head of state Elizabeth II from 1952
head of government John Major from 1990
political system liberal democracy
exports agricultural (cereals, rape, sugar beet, potatoes); meat and meat products, poultry, dairy products; electronic and telecommunications equipment; engineering equipment and scientific instruments; North Sea oil and gas, petrochemicals, pharmaceuticals, fertilizers; film and television programmes; tourism is a major industry
currency pound sterling
population (1990 est) 57,121,000; annual growth rate 0.1%
life expectancy men 72, women 78 (1989)
religion mainly Christian (55% Protestant, 10% Roman Catholic); Muslim, Jewish, Hindu, Sikh minorities
language English, Welsh, Gaelic
literacy 99% (1989)
GNP $758 bn (1988); $13,329 per head
chronology
1707 Act of Union between England and Scotland under Queen Anne.
1721 Walpole unofficially the first prime minister under George I.
1783 Loss of the N American colonies.
1801 Act of Union united Britain and Ireland.
1832 Great Reform Bill became law, shifting political power from upper to middle class.
1848 Chartist working-class movement formed.

1867 Second Reform Bill, extending the franchise, introduced by Disraeli and passed.
1906 Liberal victory: programme of social reform.
1911 Powers of House of Lords curbed.
1920 Home Rule Act incorporated the NE of Ireland (Ulster) into the United Kingdom of Great Britain and Northern Ireland.
1921 Ireland, except for Ulster, became a dominion (Irish Free State, later Eire, 1937).
1924 First Labour government led by Ramsay Macdonald.
1926 General Strike.
1931 National government; unemployment reached 3 million.
1940 Churchill became head of coalition government.
1945 Labour government under Attlee; birth of welfare state.
1951 Conservatives defeated Labour.
1956 Suez crisis.
1964 Labour victory under Wilson.
1970 Conservatives under Heath defeated Labour.
1972 Parliament prorogued in Northern Ireland; direct rule from Westminster began.
1973 Britain joined EEC.
1974 Three-day week, coal strike; Wilson replaced Heath.
1979 Victory for Conservatives under Thatcher.
1981 Formation of Social Democrat Party (SDP). Riots in inner cities.
1982 Unemployment over 3 million. Falklands War.
1984–85 Coal strike, the longest in British history.
1986 Abolition of metropolitan counties.
1987 Thatcher re-elected for third term.
1988 Liberals and most of SDP merged into Democrats, leaving a splinter group. Inflation rose sharply.
1989 SDP ceases to operate as a national party. Green Party polled 2 million votes in the European election.
1990 Riots as poll tax introduced in England. Challenge to Thatcher's leadership led to her resignation and replacement by John Major.
1991 British troops took part in US-led war against Iraq under UN umbrella. Support was given to the USSR during the dissolution of communism and the restoration of independence to the republics. John Major visited Beijing to sign agreement with China on new Hong Kong airport. At home, Britain suffered severe economic recession and rising unemployment.
1992 April: Conservative Party, led by John Major, won fourth consecutive general election, but with reduced majority. Neil Kinnock resigned. July: John Smith became new Labour leader. Sept: sterling devalued and UK withdrawn from ERM. Oct: drastic pit-closure programme encountered massive public opposition; subsequently reviewed. John Major's popularity at unprecedentedly low rating. Nov: government motion in favour of ratification of Maastricht Treaty narrowly passed. Revelations of past arms sales to Iraq implicated senior government figures, including the prime minister.
1993 Heavy losses by the Conservative Party in local elections. The chancellor of the Exchequer, Norman Lamont, resigned and was replaced by Kenneth Clarke.

Universal Postal Union   an agency of the United Nations responsible for collaboration of postal services. It was first established in 1875, with headquarters in Berne, Switzerland.

Universe   all of space and its contents, the study of which is called cosmology. The Universe is thought to be between 10,000 million and 20,000 million years old, and is mostly empty space, dotted with ◊galaxies for as far as telescopes can see. The most distant detected galaxies and ◊quasars lie 10,000 million light years away. The Universe is expanding, with the galaxies moving apart from each other (as revealed by the ◊red shift in their light) and the space between them getting larger. The speed of recession of the galaxies (◊Hubble's constant) increases in proportion with their distance apart, an effect known as *Hubble's law*.

university   an institution of higher learning for those who have completed primary and secondary education. There are now 45 universities in the UK which are funded directly by the government through the University Grants Committee. The USA has both state universities (funded by the individual states) and private universities. The oldest universities in the USA are all private: Harvard 1636, William and Mary 1693, Yale 1701, Pennsylvania 1741, and Princeton 1746. Recent innovations include universities serving international areas, for example, the Middle East Technical University 1961 at Ankara, supported by the United Nations; the United Nations university in Tokyo 1974; and the British ◊Open University 1969.

Unix   an ◊operating system designed for minicomputers but becoming increasingly popular on large microcomputers. Developed by Bell Laboratories in the late 1960s, it is now widely used in universities and is closely related to the programming language C. Its wide functionality and flexibility have also made it popular with commercial software developers.

unknown soldier   unidentified dead soldier, for whom a tomb is erected as a memorial to other unidentified bodies killed in war.

unnilennium   a synthetically made element, symbol Une, atomic number 109. It was first synthesized in 1974.

unnilhexium   a synthetically made element, symbol Unh, atomic number 106. It was first synthesized in 1974.

unniloctium   a synthetically made element, symbol Uno, atomic number 108. It was first synthesized in 1981.

unnilpentium   a synthetically made element, symbol Unp, atomic number 105. Credit for its discovery is disputed between the USA (who named it *hahnium*) and the USSR (who named it *nielsbohrium*).

unnilquadium   a synthetically made element, symbol Unq, atomic number 104. Also named *kurchitovium* and ◊*rutherfordium* by teams in the USSR and USA respectively.

unnilseptium   a synthetically made element, symbol Uns, atomic number 107. It was first synthesized in 1976.

untouchable   the lowest Indian ◊caste, whom members of the other castes were formerly forbidden to touch.

Unwin   Raymond 1863–1940. English town planner. He put the Garden City ideals of Sir Ebenezer Howard into practice, overseeing Letchworth (begun 1903), Hampstead Garden Suburb (begun 1907) and Wythenshawe outside Manchester (begun 1927).

Upanishad   one of a collection of Hindu sacred treatises, written in Sanskrit, connected with the ◊Vedas but composed later, about 800–200 BC. Metaphysical and ethical, they exposed a monistic, pantheistic doctrine equating the atman (self) with the Brahman (supreme spirit): *'Tat tvam asi (Thou art that)'*, and developed the theory of the transmigration of souls.

Updike   John (Hoyer) 1932– . US writer. Associated with the *New Yorker* magazine from 1955, he soon established a reputation for polished prose, poetry, and criticism. His novels include *Couples* 1968 and *Roger's Version* 1986 and deal with contemporary US middle-class life.

United Arab Emirates
(UAE) federation of the emirates of **Abu Dhabi, Ajman, Dubai, Fujairah, Ras al Khaimah, Sharjah, Umm al Qaiwain**

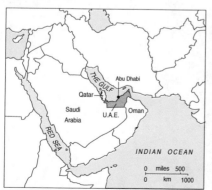

total area 83,000 sq km/32,000 sq mi
capital Abu Dhabi
towns chief port Dubai
physical mainly desert; mountains in E

head of state and of government Zayed Bin Sultan Al-Nahayan from 1971
political system absolutism
exports oil, natural gas, fish, dates
currency UAE dirham
population (1990 est) 2,250,000 (10% are nomadic); annual growth rate 6.1%
life expectancy men 68, women 72
language Arabic (official); Farsi, Hindi, Urdu, English
religion Muslim 96%, Christian, Hindu
literacy 68% (1989)
GNP $22 bn (1987); $1,900 per head
chronology
1952 Trucial Council established.
1971 Federation of Arab Emirates came into being but was later dissolved. Six of the Trucial States formed the United Arab Emirates, with the ruler of Abu Dhabi, Sheik Zayed, as president.
1972 The seventh state joined.
1976 Sheik Zayed threatened to relinquish presidency unless progress towards centralization became more rapid.
1985 Diplomatic and economic links with the USSR and with China established.
1990–91 Iraqi invasion of Kuwait opposed: UAE fought in UN coalition.
1991 Bank of Credit and Commerce International (BCCI), controlled by Abu Dhabi's ruler, collapsed.

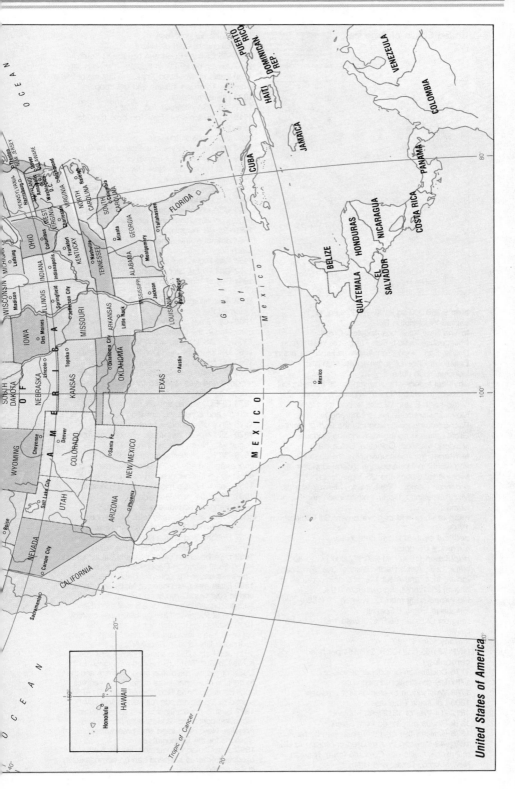

United States of America

United States of America (USA)

area 9,368,900 sq km/3,618,770 sq mi

capital Washington DC

towns New York, Los Angeles, Chicago, Philadephia, Detroit, San Francisco, Washington, Dallas, San Diego, San Antonio, Houston, Boston, Baltimore, Phoenix, Indianapolis, Memphis, Honolulu, San José

physical topography and vegetation from tropical (Hawaii) to arctic (Alaska); mountain ranges parallel with E and W coasts, and the Rocky Mountains separate rivers emptying into the Pacific from those flowing into the Gulf of Mexico; Great Lakes in north; rivers include Hudson, Missippi, Missouri, Colorado, Columbia

territories the commonwealths of Puerto Rico, and Northern Marianas; the federated states of Micronesia; Guam, the US Virgin Islands, American Samoa, Wake Island, Midway Islands, Marshall Islands, Belau, and Johnson and Sand Islands

head of state and of government Bill Clinton from 1993

political system liberal democracy

currency US dollar

population (1990 est) 250,372,000 (white 80%, black 12%, Asian/Pacific islander 3%, American Indian, Inuit, and Aleut 1%, Hispanic [included in above] 9%); annual growth rate 0.9%

life expectancy men 72, women 79 (1989)

language English, Spanish

religion Christian 86.5%, Jewish 1.8%, Muslim 0.5%

literacy 99% (1989)

GNP $3,855 bn (1983); $13,451 per head

chronology

1776 Declaration of Independence.

1787 US constitution drawn up.

1789 Washington elected as first president.

1803 Louisiana Purchase.

1812–14 War of 1812 with England.

1819 Florida purchased from Spain.

1836 Battle of the Alamo, Texas, won by Mexico.

1846–48 Mexican War resulted in cession to USA of Arizona, California, Colorado (part), Nevada, New Mexico, Texas, and Utah.

1848 California gold rush.

1860 Lincoln elected president.

1861–65 Civil War between North and South.

1867 Alaska bought from Russia.

1890 Battle of Wounded Knee, the last major battle between American Indians and US troops.

1898 Hawaii annexed.

1917–18 USA entered World War I.

1919–21 Wilson's 14 Points become base for League of Nations.

1920 Women won the vote.

1924 American Indians made citizens by Congress.

1929 Wall Street stock-market crash.

1933 F D Roosevelt's New Deal to alleviate the Depression put into force.

1941–45 The Japanese attack on Pearl Harbor Dec 1941 precipitated US entry into World War II.

1945 USA ended war in the Pacific by dropping A-bombs on Hiroshima and Nagasaki, Japan.

1950–53 US involvement in Korean war; McCarthy anti-Communist investigations (HUAC) became a 'witch hunt'.

1954 Civil Rights legislation began.

1957 Civil Rights bill on voting.

1961 Bay of Pigs abortive CIA-backed invasion of Cuba.

1963 Assassination of Kennedy; L B Johnson assumed the presidency.

1964–68 'Great Society' civil-rights and welfare measures in the Omnibus Civil Rights bill.

1964–75 US involvement in Vietnam War.

1965 US intervention in Dominican Republic.

1969 US first to land a person on the moon.

1973–74 Watergate scandal. President Nixon resigned and was replaced by Gerald Ford, who 'pardoned' Nixon.

1973 OPEC oil embargo almost crippled US industry and consumers; inflation began.

1975 Final US withdrawal from Vietnam.

1979 US-Chinese diplomatic relations normalized; began with Nixon visit to China 1972.

1979–80 Iranian hostage crisis; relieved by concessions made by President Reagan and released on his inauguration day Jan 1981.

1981 Space Shuttle mission was successful.

1983 US invasion of Grenada.

1986 'Irangate' scandale over secret US government arms sales to Iran, with proceeds to anti-government Contra guerrillas in Nicaragua.

1987 Reagan and Gorbachev (for USSR) signed INF treaty; Wall Street stock-market crash.

1988 USA becomes world's largest debtor nation, owing $532 billion, in Republican bid to control Congress under Reagan and Bush.

1989 Bush met Gorbachev at Malta and declared end to cold war. Large troop reductions and budget cuts announced for US military; US invasion of Panama: Noriega taken into custody.

1990 Bush and Gorbachev met again. USA opposed Iraq's invasion of Kuwait, sending troops to support UN force in Saudi Arabia.

1991 Jan-Feb: US-led assault drove Iraq from Kuwait in Gulf War. US support was given to the USSR during the dissolution of communism and the recognition of independence of the Baltic republics. July: Strategic Arms Reduction Treaty (START) signed at US-Soviet summit held in Moscow.

1992 Bush's popularity slumped as economic recession continued. Widespread riots in Los Angeles. Nov: Bill Clinton won presidential elections for the Democrats.

1993 Jan: Clinton inaugurated. He delayed executive order to suspend ban on homosexuality in the armed forces.

United States of America: Presidents

Name	Party	Took office
1. George Washington	(Federalist)	1789
2. John Adams	(Federalist)	1797
3. Thomas Jefferson	(Dem. Republican)	1801
4. James Madison	(Dem. Republican)	1809
5. James Monroe	(Dem. Republican)	1817
6. John Quincy Adams	(Dem. Republican)	1825
7. Andrew Jackson	(Democrat)	1829
8. Martin Van Buren	(Democrat)	1837
9. William Henry Harrison	(Whig)	1841
10. John Tyler	(Whig)	1841
11. James Knox Polk	(Democrat)	1845
12. Zachary Taylor	(Whig)	1849
13. Millard Fillmore	(Whig)	1850
14. Franklin Pierce	(Democrat)	1853
15. James Buchanan	(Democrat)	1857
16. Abraham Lincoln	(Republican)	1861
17. Andrew Johnson	(Democrat)	1865
18. Ulysses Simpson Grant	(Republican)	1877
19. Rutherford Birchard Hayes	(Republican)	1877
20. James Abram Garfield	(Republican)	1881
21. Chester Alan Arthur	(Republican)	1881
22. Grover Cleveland	(Democrat)	1885
23. Benjamin Harrison	(Republican)	1889
24. Grover Cleveland	(Democrat)	1893
25. William McKinley	(Republican)	1897
26. Theodore Roosevelt	(Republican)	1901
27. William Howard Taft	(Republican)	1909
28. Woodrow Wilson	(Democrat)	1913
29. Warren Gamaliel Harding	(Republican)	1921
30. Calvin Coolidge	(Republican)	1929
31. Herbert C Hoover	(Republican)	1929
32. Franklin Delano Roosevelt	(Democrat)	1933
33. Harry S Truman	(Democrat)	1945
34. Dwight D Eisenhower	(Republican)	1953
35. John F Kennedy	(Democrat)	1961
36. Lyndon B Johnson	(Democrat)	1963
37. Richard M Nixon	(Republican)	1969
38. Gerald R Ford	(Republican)	1974
39. James Earl Carter	(Democrat)	1977
40. Ronald Reagan	(Republican)	1981
41. George Bush	(Republican)	1989
42. Bill Clinton	(Democrat)	1993

universities in the United Kingdom

Name	Date founded	No of students
Aberdeen	1945	5.700
Aston	1966	3.900
Bath	1966	3.700
Belfast	1908	7.200
Birmingham	1900	9.000
Bradford	1966	4.200
Bristol	1966	7.200
Brunel	1966	2.900
Buckingham	1983	700
Cambridge	13th cent.	9.800
City	1966	3.200
Dundee	1967	3.800
Durham	1832	5.100
East Anglia	1963	4.400
Edinburgh	1583	10.100
Essex	1964	3.000
Exeter	1955	5.000
Glasgow	1451	10.500
Heriot-Watt	1966	3.800
Hull	1954	4.800
Keele	1962	2.400
Kent	1965	4.200
Lancaster	1964	4.600
Leeds	1904	10.300
Leicester	1957	4.900
Liverpool	1903	7.600
London	1836	50.200
Loughborough	1966	5.800
Manchester	1851	11.100
Newcastle upon Tyne	1852	7.800
Nottingham	1948	7.000
Open University	1969	149.500
Oxford	12th cent.	9.700
Reading	1926	5.900
Salford	1967	3.800
Sheffield	1905	8.000
Southampton	1952	6.400
St Andrews	1411	3.800
Stirling	1967	2.900
Strathclyde	1964	7.500
Surrey	1966	3.400
Sussex	1961	4.600
Ulster	1984	7.600
Wales	1893	21.300
Warwick	1965	5.900
York	1963	3.400

Upper Volta former name (until 1984) of ◊Burkina Faso.

Ur an ancient city of the Sumerian civilization, now in Southern Iraq. Excavations by the British archaeologist Leonard Woolley show that it was inhabited 3500 BC. He discovered evidence of a flood that may have inspired the biblical account, and remains of ziggurats, or step pyramids, as well as social and cultural relics.

uraemia an excess of the waste product known as urea in the blood due to kidney impairment. It may be due to damage, poisoning, circulatory disturbance, or other conditions which undermine kidney function.

Ural Mountains (Russian *Ural'skiy Khrebet* mountain system running from the Arctic to the Caspian Sea, traditionally separating Europe from Asia. The highest peak is Naradnaya 1,894 m/ 6,214 ft. It has vast mineral wealth.

uranium a metallic element, symbol U, atomic number 92, relative atomic mass 338.07. It is a lustrous white metal, malleable and ductile, tarnishing in air. The chief ore is uranite (pitch-blende, U_3O_8), and recent technological advances have made possible its extraction from low-grade ores. Its chief use is in the form of the radioactive isotope uranium -235, used as a source of nuclear energy (both for nuclear weapons and for generating power). Small amounts of its compounds are used in the ceramics industry to give yellow glazes, and as a mordant in dyeing.

Uranus in Greek mythology, the sky-god. He was responsible for for the sun and rain, and was the son and husband of ◊Gaia the goddess of the earth, by whom he fathered the ◊Titans.

Uranus the seventh planet from the Sun, discovered by William ◊Herschel 1781. Uranus has a diameter of 50,000 km/31,600 mi and a mass 14.5 times that of Earth. It orbits the Sun in 84 years at an average distance of 2,870 million km/1,783 million mi. Uranus is thought to have a large rocky core overlain by ice, with a deep atmosphere mostly of hydrogen and helium, plus traces of methane which give the planet a greenish tinge. The spin axis of Uranus is tilted at 98°, so that at times its poles point towards the Sun, giving extreme seasons. It has 15

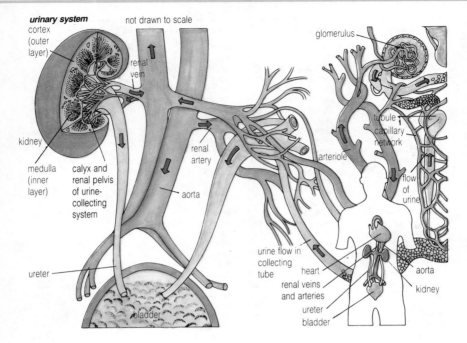

urinary system   not drawn to scale

cortex (outer layer)

renal vein

glomerulus

kidney

tubule capillary network

arteriole

medulla (inner layer)   calyx and renal pelvis of urine-collecting system

renal artery

aorta

flow of urine

ureter

urine flow in collecting tube   heart

renal veins and arteries

aorta

kidney

ureter

bladder

bladder

moons, and in 1977 astronomers discovered that Uranus has thin rings around its equator.

Urban II c. 1042–1099. Pope 1088–99. He launched the First Crusade at the Council of Clermont in France in 1095.

urbanization the process by which the proportion of a population living in or around towns and cities increases through migration. The growth of urban concentrations is a relatively recent phenomenon, dating back only about 150 years, although the world's first cities were built more than 5,000 years ago.

urban renewal the adaptation of existing buildings in towns and cities to meet changes in economic, social, and environmental requirements, rather than their demolition.

urbi et orbi (Latin 'to the city and to the world') a papal proclamation.

Urdu language a member of the Indo-Iranian branch of the Indo-European language family, related to Hindi and written not in Devanagari but in Arabic script. Strongly influenced by Persian and Arabic, Urdu is the official language of Pakistan and a language used by Muslims in India.

urea $CO(NH_2)_2$ waste product formed when nitrogen compounds are broken down by mammals. It is excreted in urine. When purified, it is a white, crystalline solid. It is used in industry to make urea-formaldehyde plastics (or resins), pharmaceuticals and fertilizers.

Urey Harold Clayton 1893–1981. US chemist. In 1932 he isolated heavy water and discovered deuterium; Nobel prize 1934.

uric acid $C_5H_4N_4O_3$ a nitrogen-containing waste substance, formed from the breakdown of food and body protein. It is a normal constituent of urine in reptiles and birds, but not in most mammals. Humans and other primates produce some uric acid, in place of urea, the normal nitrogen-waste product. If formed in excess and not excreted it may be deposited in sharp crystals in the joints and other

tissues, causing gout; or it may form stones in the kidneys or bladder (calculi).

urinary system the system of organs which removes nitrogenous excretory products and excess water from the bodies of animals. In mammals, it consists of a pair of ◊kidneys, ureters which drain the kidneys, and a bladder, which stores urine before its discharge through the urethra.

urine an amber-coloured fluid made by the kidneys from the blood. It contains excess water, salts, protein, waste products, a pigment, and some acid. The kidneys pass it through two fine tubes (ureters) to the bladder, which may act as a reservoir for up to 0.7l/1.2pt at a time. It then passes into the urethra, which opens to the outside by a sphincter (constricting muscle) under voluntary control.

urology branch of medicine concerned with diseases of the urinary tract.

Ursa Major the third-largest constellation in the sky, in the north polar region, representing the great bear. Its seven brightest stars make up the familiar shape of the *Big Dipper* or *Plough*. The second star of the 'handle' of the dipper, called Mizar, has a companion star, Alcor. Two stars in the 'bowl' act as pointers to the north pole star, Polaris.

Ursa Minor constellation representing the little bear. It is shaped like a little dipper, with the north pole star Polaris at the end of the handle.

Ursula, St English legendary saint, supposed to have been martyred with 11 virgins (misread as 11,000 in the Middle Ages), by the Huns in the Rhineland, in the 4th century.

Ursuline a Roman Catholic religious order, founded at Brescia, by St Angela Merici in 1537; it is renowned for its educational work among girls.

urticaria nettle-rash: an irritant skin condition characterized by the spontaneous appearance of weals. Treatment is usually by soothing lotions and, in severe cases, by antihistamines or steroids. Its causes are varied, and may include ◊allergy or ◊stress.

urine

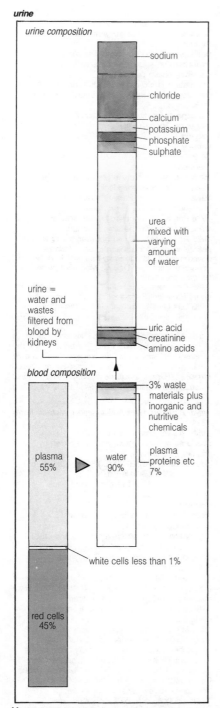

urine composition

—sodium

—chloride

—calcium
—potassium
—phosphate
—sulphate

urea
mixed with
—varying
amount
of water

urine =
water and
wastes
filtered from
blood by
kidneys

—uric acid
—creatinine
—amino acids

blood composition

—3% waste
materials plus
inorganic and
nutritive
chemicals

plasma
55%

water
90%

plasma
—proteins etc
7%

white cells less than 1%

red cells
45%

Uruguay country in South America, on the Atlantic, bounded N by Brazil and W by Argentina.

Urumqi (formerly *Urumchi*) industrial city (cotton textiles, cement, chemicals, iron, steel), capital of Xinjiang Uygur autonomous region, China, at the N foot of the Tyan Shan mountains; population (1989) 1,110,000.

US abbreviation for *United States*.

USA abbreviation for the ◊*United States of America*.

user interface in computing, the parts of a program with which users come into contact, by means of which they control the program; information is passed in both directions. For example, a menu may be displayed on the screen and the user asked to choose an option, which then instructs the computer to continue its task in only one of several ways.

Usher James 1581–1656. Irish priest, Archbishop of Armagh from 1625. He was responsible for the dating of creation as the year 4004 BC, a figure which was inserted in the margin of the Authorized Version of the Bible until the 19th century.

Ushuaia southernmost town in the world, at the tip of Tierra del Fuego, Argentina, less than 1,000 km from Antarctica; population (1991) 29,700. It is a free port and naval base.

Ussher alternative spelling of James ◊Usher.

USSR abbreviation for the former ◊*Union of Soviet Socialist Republics*.

Ustinov Peter 1921– . British actor. His plays include *The Love of Four Colonels* 1951 and *Beethoven's Tenth* 1983. His many films include *Death on the Nile* 1978 and *Evil under the Sun* 1981. He published his autobiography *Dear Me* in 1983.

usury former term for charging interest on a loan of money. In medieval times, usury was held to be a sin, and Christians were forbidden to lend (although not to borrow).

Utah state of the W USA; nickname Beehive State

area 219,931 sq km/84,915 sq mi

capital Salt Lake City

towns Provo, Ogden

physical Colorado Plateau to the East; mountains in centre; Great Basin to the West; Great Salt Lake

products wool, gold, silver, uranium, coal, salt, steel

population (1989) 1,722,850

famous people Brigham Young, religious leader

history part of the area ceded by Mexico 1848; developed by Mormons, still the largest religious sect in the state; territory 1850, but not admitted to statehood until 1896 because of Mormon reluctance to relinquish plural marriage.

Utamaro Kitagawa 1753–1806. Japanese artist of the *ukiyo-e* ('floating world') school, known for his muted colour prints of beautiful women, including informal studies of prostitutes.

UTC abbreviation for Coordinated Universal Time, the standard measurement of ◊time.

uterus a hollow muscular organ of female mammals, lying between the bladder and rectum, and connected to the Fallopian tubes and vagina. The embryo develops within it, and is attached via the ◊placenta and ◊umbilical cord after implantation. The lining of the uterus changes during the ◊menstrual cycle. The outer wall of the uterus is composed of smooth muscle, capable of powerful contractions (induced by hormones) during childbirth. In humans and other higher primates, it is a single structure, but in other mammals is paired.

Uthman died 656 AD. 3rd caliph (head) of Islam, son-in-law of the prophet Muhammad. He was responsible for the compilation of the authoritative

Uruguay
Oriental Republic of (*República Oriental del Uruguay*)

0 miles 500
0 km 1000

area 196,945 sq km/72,180 sq mi
capital Montevideo

physical grassy plains (pampas)
head of state and of government Luis Lacalle Herrera from 1989
political system democratic republic
exports meat, leather, wool, textiles
currency nuevo peso
population (1990 est) 3,002,000 (Spanish, Italian, mestizo, mulatto, and black); annual growth rate 0.7%
life expectancy men 68, women 75 (1989)
language Spanish
religion Roman Catholic 66%
literacy 96% (1984)
GNP $7.5 bn (1988); $2,470 per head
chronology
1956 The Blanco party in power, with Jorge Pacheco Areco as president.
1972 The Colorado Party returned, with Juan Maria Bordaberry Arocena as president.
1976 Bordaberry deposed by the army and Dr Méndez Manfredini became president.
1985 Agreement reached between the army and political leaders for a return to constitutional government. Colorado Party narrowly won the general election and Dr Julio Maria Sanguinetti became president.
1986 A government of national accord established under President Sanguinetti's leadership.
1989 Luis Lacalle Herrera elected president.

version of the Koran. During his caliphate large areas of N Africa came under Muslim rule. He was killed by rioters.

utilitarianism a philosophical theory of ethics outlined by the philosopher Jeremy Bentham, and developed by J S Mill. According to utilitarianism, an action is morally right if it has consequences which lead to happiness, and wrong if it brings about the reverse of happiness. Thus, society should aim for the greatest happiness of the greatest number.

Utopia (Greek 'no place') Thomas More's ideal commonwealth in his book *Utopia* 1516, which has

Uzbekistan
Republic of

0 miles 500
0 km 1000

area 447,400 sq km/172,741 sq mi
capital Tashkent
towns Samarkand, Bukhara, Namangan
physical oases in the deserts: rivers: Amu Darya, Syr Darya; Fergana Valley; rich in mineral deposits
features more than 20 hydroelectric plants; three natural gas pipelines
head of state Islam Karimov from 1990

head of government Abdul Hashim Mutalov from 1991
political system socialist pluralist
products rice, dried fruit, vines (all grown by irrigation); cotton, silk
population (1990) 20,300,000 (71% Uzbek, 8% Russian, 5% Tajik, 4% Kazakh)
language Uzbek, a Turkic language
religion Sunni Muslim
chronology
1921 Part of Turkestan Soviet Socialist Autonomous Republic.
1925 Became constituent republic of the USSR.
1944 Some 160,000 Meskhetian Turks forcibly transported from their native Georgia to Uzbekistan by Stalin.
1989 June: Tashlak, Yaipan, and Ferghana were the scenes of riots in which Meskhetian Turks were attacked; 70 killed and 850 wounded.
1990 June: economic and political sovereignty declared.
1991 March: Uzbek supported 'renewed federation' in USSR referendum. Aug: anti-Gorbachev coup in Moscow initially accepted by President Karimov; later, Karimov resigned from Soviet Communist Party (CPSU) Politburo; Uzbek Communist Party (UCP) broke with CPSU; pro-democracy rallies dispersed by militia; independence declared. Dec: joined new Commonwealth of Independent States (CIS).
1992 Jan: admitted into Conference on Security and Cooperation in Europe (CSCE); violent food riots in Tashkent. March: joined the United Nations (UN); US diplomatic recognition achieved.

Utrillo Street at Sannois *(1913) Courtauld Collection, London.*

given its name to any ideal state in literature. Other similar inventions include Plato's *Republic*, Bacon's *New Atlantis* 1626, and the Renaissance *City of the Sun* by Tommaso Campanella (1568–1639). Utopias are a common subject in ◊science fiction.

Utrecht industrial city (metallurgy, chemicals, textiles), capital of Utrecht province in central Netherlands, on the Kromme Rijn (crooked Rhine) 35 km/22 mi SE of Amsterdam; population (1985) 230,000.

Utrecht, Treaty of treaty signed 1713 which ended the War of the ◊Spanish Succession. Philip V was recognized as the legitimate king of Spain, thus founding the Spanish branch of the Bourbon dynasty; the Netherlands, Milan, and Naples were ceded to Austria; Britain gained Gibraltar; the duchy of Savoy was granted Sicily.

Utrecht, Union of in 1579, the union of seven provinces of the N Netherlands: Holland, Zeeland, Friesland, Groningen, Utrecht, Gelderland, and Overijssel, which became the basis of opposition to the Spanish crown and the foundation of the modern Dutch state.

Utrillo Maurice 1883–1955. French artist, known

for townscapes of his native Paris, especially Montmartre, often painted from postcard photographs, but capturing a certain atmosphere. His earlier work, from 1908–14, is considered his best.

Uttar Pradesh state of N India
area 294,413 sq km/113,643 sq mi
capital Lucknow
towns Varanasi
population (1991) 138,760,400
famous people Indira Gandhi, Ravi Shankar
language Hindi
religion Hindu 80%, Muslim 15%
history formerly the heart of the Mogul Empire, and generating point of the ◊Indian Mutiny of 1857 and subsequent opposition to British rule; see also the ◊United Provinces of ◊Agra and ◊Oudh.

Uzbek person of Uzbek culture. They comprise approximately 70% of the population of Uzbekistan. The Uzbek language belongs to the Turkic branch of the Altaic family.

Uzbekistan country in central Asia, bounded N by Kazakhstan and the Aral Sea, E by Kyrgyzstan and Tajikistan, S by Afghanistan, and W by Turkmenistan.

V1, V2 the designation of Hitler's revenge weapons (*Vergeltungswaffe*) of World War II, launched against Britain 1944 and 1945. The V1, also called the doodle-bug and buzz bomb, was a flying bomb powered by a simple kind of jet engine called a pulse jet. The V2, a rocket bomb, was the first long-range ballistic missile. It was a formidable weapon against which there was no defence. It was 14 m/47 ft long, carried a 1-tonne warhead and dropped onto its target at a speed of 5,000 kph/3,000 mph.

vaccination the use of specially prepared microbes (bacteria and viruses) to confer immunity to the diseases with which they are associated. When injected or taken by mouth, a vaccine stimulates the production of antibodies to protect against that particular disease. Vaccination is the oldest form of ◊immunization.

vacuole in biology, a fluid-filled, membrane-bound cavity inside a ◊cell. It may be a reservoir for fluids that the cell will secrete to the outside, or filled with excretory products or essential nutrients that the cell needs to store. In amoebae (single-cell animals) vacuoles are formed around food particles. Plant cells usually have a large central vacuole for storage.

vacuum in general, a region completely empty of matter; in physics, any enclosure in which the gas pressure is considerably less than atmospheric pressure (101,325 pascals).

vacuum cleaner cleaning device invented 1901 by Scotsman Hubert Cecil Booth (1871–1955). Having seen an ineffective dust-blowing machine, he reversed the process so that his machine (originally on wheels, and operated from the street by means of tubes running into the house) operated by suction.

vacuum flask or *Dewar Flask* a container for keeping things either hot or cold, often called a Thermos flask. It consists of a double-walled container made of glass, containing a vacuum, and the insides of the walls are silvered. This reduces heat loss through the walls. The vacuum flask was invented by James Dewar (1842-1923) about 1872 to store liquefied gases.

Vaduz capital of the European principality of Liechtenstein; population (1984) 5,000. Industry includes engineering and agricultural trade.

vagina the front passage in a woman linking the womb to the exterior. It admits the penis during sexual intercourse, and is the birth canal down which the fetus passes during delivery.

Vairochana the cosmic Buddha, *Dainichi* in Japan; central to esoteric Buddhism.

Valdemar alternative spelling of ◊Waldemar, name of four kings of Denmark.

Valencia industrial city (wine, fruit, chemicals, textiles, ship repair) in Valencia region, E Spain; population (1981) 752,000.

valency the measure of an element's ability to combine with other elements, expressed as the number of atoms of hydrogen (or any other standard univalent element) capable of uniting with (or replacing) its atoms.

Valentine, St died 270. According to tradition a bishop of Terni martyred at Rome, now omitted from the calendar of saints' days as probably nonexistent. His festival was 14 Feb, but the custom of sending 'valentines' to a loved one on that day seems to have arisen because the day accidentally coincided with the Roman mid-Feb festival of ◊Lupercalia.

Valentino Rudolf 1895–1926. Italian film actor, the archetypal romantic lover of the Hollywood silent movies. His films include *The Four Horsemen of the Apocalypse* 1921, *The Sheik* 1922, and *Blood and Sand* 1922.

Valera Éamon de. Irish politician. See ◊de Valera.

valerian perennial plant of either of two genera, *Valeriana* or *Centranthus*, native to the N hemisphere, with clustered heads of fragrant tubular flowers in red, white or pink. The root of the common valerian *Valeriana officinalis* is used medicinally as a carminative and sedative.

Valéry Paul 1871–1945. French mathematician, philosopher, and poet, author of philosophical verse, for example *La Jeune Parque/The Young Fate* 1917, *Le Cimetière marin/The Graveyard by the Sea* 1920, and *Charmes* 1922.

Valhalla in Norse mythology, the hall in Odin's palace where he feasts with the souls of the heroes killed in battles.

Valkyrie in Norse mythology, any of the female attendants of ◊Odin. They select those who die in battle and escort them to ◊Valhalla.

Valladolid industrial town (food processing, vehicles, textiles, engineering), capital of Valladolid province, Spain; population (1981) 330,245.

Valle d'Aosta autonomous region of NW Italy; area 3,263 sq km/1,260 sq mi; population (1984) 113,500, many of whom are French-speaking. It

vacuum flask

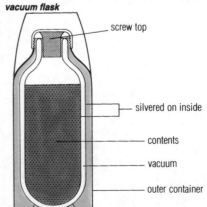

- screw top
- silvered on inside
- contents
- vacuum
- outer container

Van Allen belts

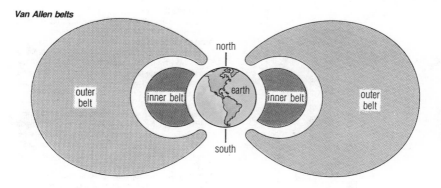

produces wine and livestock, and its capital is Aosta.

Valle-Inclán Ramón Maria de 1866–1936. Spanish author of erotic and symbolist works including *Sonatas* 1902–05 and, set in South America, the novel *Tirano Banderas/The Tyrant* 1926.

Valletta capital and port (with large repair yards) of Malta; population (1987) 9,000, urban harbour area 214,000.

Valley Forge site in Pennsylvania 32 km/20 mi NW of Philadelphia, USA, where Washington's army spent the winter of 1777–78 in terrible hardship during the War of ◊American Independence.

Valley of Ten Thousand Smokes valley in Alaska, USA, where in 1912 Mount Katmai erupted in one of the largest volcanic explosions ever known, though without loss of life since the area was uninhabited. It was dedicated 1918 as the Katmai National Monument. The many fissures on the valley floor still emit steam jets.

Valley of the Kings burial place of ancient kings opposite ◊Thebes, Egypt, on the left bank of the Nile.

Valmy, Battle of battle 1792 in which the army of the French Revolution under Gen ◊Dumouriez defeated the Prussians at the French village.

Valois branch of the Capetian dynasty (see Hugh ◊Capet) in France, members of which occupied the French throne from Philip VI 1328 to ◊Henry III 1589.

value-added tax (VAT) the standard form of tax in Europe on goods produced for sale. VAT is applied at each stage of the production of a commodity and is charged only on the value added at that stage. It is not levied, unlike purchase tax, on the sale of the commodity itself, but at this stage, the VAT paid at earlier stages of the good's manufacture cannot be reclaimed.

vampire in Slav demonology, an 'undead' corpse which returns to 'life' by sucking the blood of the living (such as ◊Dracula; see ◊porphyria).

vampire bat South and Central American bat of the family Desmodontidae, of which there are three species. The ***common vampire Desmodus***

vampire bat

rotundus is found from N Mexico to central Argentina, its head and body grow to 9 cm/3.5 in. Vampires feed on the blood of mammals; they slice a piece of skin from a victim with their sharp incisor teeth and lap up the flowing blood.

vanadium a silver-white hard metal, discovered by Del Rio 1801, and isolated by Rosco 1869; symbol V, atomic number 23, atomic weight 50.95. It occurs in the rare minerals, vanadinite and patronite; its chief use is in alloying steel to which it imparts toughness, elasticity and tensile strength.

Van Allen belts two doughnut-shaped zones of atomic particles around Earth, discovered 1958 by James Van Allen (1914–). The atomic particles come from the Earth's upper atmosphere and the ◊solar wind, and are trapped by the Earth's magnetic field. The inner belt lies between 1,000–5,000 km/620–3,100 mi above the Earth, and contains ◊protons and ◊electrons. The outer belt lies from 15,000–25,000 km/9,300–15,500 mi above the equator, but is lower around the magnetic poles. It contains mostly electrons from the solar wind.

Vanbrugh John 1664–1726. English Baroque architect and dramatist. He designed Blenheim Palace, Oxfordshire, and Castle Howard, Yorkshire and was assisted in both projects by ◊Hawksmoor. His written works include translations, adaptations, and the comedy plays *The Relapse* 1696 and *The Provok'd Wife* 1697.

Van Buren Martin 1782–1862. 8th president of the USA. Secretary of state 1829–31 and then minister to England, he was elected President on the Democratic ticket 1837 and held office until 1841.

Vance Cyrus 1917– . US Democratic politician, secretary of state 1977–80. He resigned because he did not support President Carter's abortive mission to rescue the US hostages in Iran. In 1992 he was chosen as UN negotiator in the peace talks on ◊Bosnia-Herzegovina. Together with EC negotiator Lord Owen, he devised the Vance–Owen peace plan for dividing the republic into 10 semi-autonomous provinces.

Vancouver industrial city (oil refining, engineering, shipbuilding, aircraft, timber, pulp and paper, textiles, fisheries) in Canada, its main Pacific seaport, on the mainland of British Columbia; population (1986) 1,381,000.

Vancouver George c. 1758–1798. British navigator who made extensive exploration of the W coast of North America.

Vancouver Island island off the W coast of Canada, part of British Columbia
area 32,136 sq km/12,405 sq mi

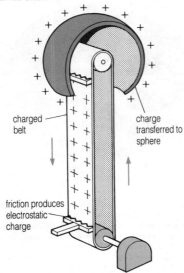

van de Graaff

charged belt

charge transferred to sphere

friction produces electrostatic charge

towns Victoria, Nanaimo, naval base Esquimalt
products coal, timber, fish.

Vandal member of a Germanic people related to the ◊Goths. In the 5th century AD the Vandals moved from N Germany to invade Roman Gaul and Spain, many settling in Andalusia (formerly Vandalitia) and others reaching N Africa 429. They sacked Rome 455 but accepted Roman suzerainty in the 6th century.

van de Graaff Robert Jemison 1901–1967. US physicist who from 1929 developed a high-voltage generator, which in its modern form can produce more than a million volts. It consists of an endless vertical conveyer belt which carries electrostatic charges (resulting from friction) up to a large hollow sphere supported on an insulated stand. The lower end of the belt is earthed, so that charge accumulates on the sphere. The size of the voltage built up in air depends on the radius of the sphere, but can be increased by enclosing the generator in an inert atmosphere, such as nitrogen.

Vanderbilt Cornelius 1794–1877. US industrialist, who made a fortune in steamships and (from the age of 70) by financing railways.

Van der Post Laurens (Jan) 1906– . South African writer. His books, many of them autobiographical, are concerned with the duality of human existence, which is symbolized in Africa by the tension between black and white, Boer and Briton, city and veld, as in the novel *Flamingo Feather* 1955.

Van der Waals Johannes Diderik 1837–1923. Dutch physicist who was awarded a Nobel prize 1910 for his theoretical study of gases. He emphasized the forces of attraction and repulsion between atoms and molecules in describing the behaviour of real gases, as opposed to the ideal gases dealt with in ◊Boyle's law and ◊Charles' law.

van Dyck Anthony see ◊Dyck, Anthony van.

Vane Henry 1613–1662. English politician. He was elected a member of the ◊Long Parliament 1640 and was prominent in the impeachment of Bishop ◊Laud. He was in effect the civilian head of the Parliamentary government 1643–53. At the Restoration he was executed.

Vane John 1923– . British pharmacologist, who discovered the wide role of prostaglandins in the human body, produced in response to illness and stress. He shared a Nobel prize 1982.

van Eyck Jan see ◊Eyck, Jan van.

van Gogh Vincent see ◊Gogh, Vincent van.

vanilla genus of climbing orchids, native to Mexico but cultivated elsewhere, with large white or yellow flowers. The dried and fermented fruit, or pods, of *Vanilla planifolia* in particular, are the source of the vanilla flavouring used in confectionery. Vanilla flavouring can now also be produced artificially.

Vanity Fair a novel by William Makepeace Thackeray, published 1847–48. It deals with the contrasting fortunes of the tough orphan Becky Sharp and the soft-hearted, privileged Amelia Sedley, who first meet at Miss Pinkerton's Academy for young ladies.

Vanuatu group of islands in the S Pacific, part of ◊Melanesia.

vapour density density of a gas, expressed as the ◊mass of a given volume of the gas divided by the mass of an equal volume of a reference gas (such as hydrogen or air) at the same temperature and pressure. It is equal to half the relative molecular weight (mass) of the gas.

Vanuatu
Republic of

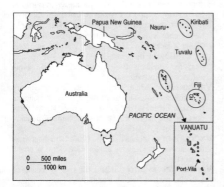

area 14,750 sq km/5,700 sq mi
capital Vila on Efate
physical comprises about 70 islands, including Espiritu Santo, Malekala, and Efate
head of state Fred Timakata from 1989
head of government Maxime Carlot from 1991
political system democratic republic
exports copra, fish, coffee, cocoa
currency vatu
population (1989) 152,000 (90% Melanesian); annual growth rate 3.3%
language Bislama, English, French
religion Presbyterian 40%, Roman Catholic 16%, animist 15%, Anglican 14%
chronology
1975 Representative assembly established.
1978 Government of national unity formed
1980 Revolt on the island of Espiritu Santo delayed independence but it was achieved, within the Commonwealth, with George Sokomanu as president and Father Walter Lini as prime minister.
1989 Sokomanu succeeded by Fred Timakata.
1991 Lini voted out. General election produced a coalition government under Maxime Carlot.

vapour pressure pressure of a vapour given off by (evaporated from) a liquid or solid, caused by vibrating atoms or molecules continuously escaping from its surface. In an enclosed space, a maximum value is reached when the number of particles leaving the surface is in equilibrium with those returning to it; this is known as the saturated vapour pressure.

Varanasi or *Benares* holy city of the Hindus in Uttar Pradesh, India, on the Ganges; population (1981) 794,000. There are 1,500 golden shrines, and a 5 km/3 mi frontage to the Ganges with sacred stairways (ghats) for purification by bathing.

Varangians Swedish vikings in E Europe and the Balkans, and more particularly the Byzantine imperial guard founded 988 by Vladimir of Kiev (955–1015), which lasted until the fall of Constantinople 1453.

Varèse Edgard 1885–1965. French avant-garde composer. He studied with d'Indy and Busoni, and settled in New York 1916, where he founded the New Symphony Orchestra 1919 to advance the cause of modern music. His own work is experimental and often dissonant, combining electronic sounds with orchestral instruments and includes *Hyperprism* 1923, *Intégrales* 1931, and *Poème Electronique* 1958.

Vargas Getulio 1883–1954. President of Brazil 1930–45 and 1951–54. He overthrew the republic 1930 after being defeated as reform candidate for the presidency. In 1937 he set up a totalitarian state known as the *Estado Novo*. His pro-fascist regime made concessions to workers while industry developed rapidly and agrarian reform was left alone. He was overthrown by a military coup 1945, and returned as president 1951. Amidst mounting opposition and political scandal, he committed suicide.

Vargas Llosa Mario 1937– . Peruvian novelist (*La ciudad y los perros*/trans. as *The Time of the Hero* 1963, and *La guerra del fin del mundo/The War at the End of the World* 1982), who attacks both right and left in politics. *La tía Julia y el escribidor/Aunt Julie and the Scriptwriter* 1977 is autobiographical.

variable in mathematics, a changing quantity (one that can take various values), as opposed to a ◊constant. For example, in the algebraic expression $y = 4x^3 + 2$, the variables are x and y, whereas 4 and 2 are constants. A variable may be dependent or independent.

variable-geometry wing technical name for what is popularly termed a ◊swing-wing, a moveable aircraft wing.

variable star a star whose brightness changes, either regularly or irregularly, over a period ranging from a few hours to months or even years. The ◊Cepheid variables regularly expand and contract in size every few days or weeks.

variations in music, a series of different developments of one self-contained theme, such as *Variations on the St Anthony Chorale* by Brahms.

varicose veins a condition where the veins become distended and tortuous. The superficial veins of the leg are most often affected, although other vulnerable sites include the rectum (◊haemorrhoids) and testes.

variegated a description of plant leaves or stems that exhibit patches of different colours. The term is most commonly applied to plants that show white, cream or yellow on their leaves, caused by areas of tissue that lack the green pigment ◊chlorophyll. Variegated plants are bred for their decorative value, but are often considerably weaker than the normal all-green plant. Many will not breed true and can be propagated only vegetatively.

Varna port in Bulgaria, on an inlet of the Black Sea; population (1983) 295,000. Industries include shipbuilding and the manufacture of chemicals.

varnish resins or resinous gums dissolved in linseed oil, turpentine, and other solvents, and to synthetic equivalents. It is used to give a shiny, sealed surface to furniture and interior fittings.

Varuna sky god and king of the universe in early Hindu mythology.

Vasarely Victor 1908– . French Op artist, born in Hungary. In the 1940s he developed his precise geometric compositions, full of visual puzzles and effects of movement, which he created with complex arrangements of hard-edged geometric shapes and subtle variations in colours.

Vasari Giorgio 1511–1574. Italian art historian, architect, and painter, author of *Lives of the Most Excellent Architects, Painters and Sculptors* 1550 (enlarged and revised 1568), in which he proposed the theory of a Renaissance of the arts beginning with Giotto and culminating with Michaelangelo. His architectural masterpiece is the Uffizi Palace, Florence.

vascular bundle a strand of primary conducting tissue (a 'vein') in vascular plants, consisting mainly of water-conducting tissue, ◊xylem, and nutrient-conducting tissue, ◊phloem. It extends from the roots to the stems and leaves. Typically the phloem is situated nearest to the epidermis and the xylem towards the centre of the bundle. In plants exhibiting ◊secondary growth, the xylem and phloem are separated by a thin layer of vascular ◊cambium, which gives rise to new conducting tissues.

vascular plant a plant with specialized conducting tissues, the ◊xylem and ◊phloem, which transport water and nutrients from one part of the plant to another. Pteridophytes (ferns, horsetails and clubmosses), gymnosperms (conifers and cycads) and angiosperms (flowering plants) are all vascular plants.

vasectomy sometimes known as male sterilization, an operation to cut and tie the vessels which carry sperm from the testes to the penis. Vasectomy does not interfere with sexual performance, but the semen produced at ejaculation no longer contains sperm.

vassal term used from the 9th century to refer to one who paid homage to a superior lord, and who promised to give him military service in return for a grant of land.

VAT abbreviation for ◊value-added tax, a form of indirect taxation.

Vatican City State St Peter's Square in the Vatican City State, central Rome, Italy.

Vatican City State
(Stato della Città del Vaticano)

area 0.4 sq km/109 acres
physical forms an enclave in the heart of Rome, Italy
head of state and government John Paul II from 1978
government absolute Catholicism
currency Vatican City lira; Italian lira
population (1985) 1,000
language Latin (official), Italian
religion Roman Catholic
chronology
1947 New Italian constitution confirmed the sovereignty of the Vatican City State.
1978 John Paul II became the first non-Italian pope for more than 400 years.
1985 New concordat signed under which Roman Catholicism ceased to be the state religion.

Vatican City State sovereign area in central Rome, Italy.

Vatican Councils the Roman Catholic ecumenical councils called by Pope Pius IX 1869 (which met 1870) and by Pope John XXIII 1959 (which met 1962). These councils considered major elements of church policy.

Vauban Sébastien le Prestre de 1633–1707. French marshal and military engineer. In Louis XIV's wars he conducted many sieges, and rebuilt many of the fortresses on France's eastern frontier.

vaudeville variety entertainment popular in the USA from 1890s to 1920s in the same tradition as ◊music hall in Britain.

Vaughan Henry 1622–1695. Welsh poet and physician, born in Brecknockshire. He published several volumes of religious verse and prose devotions. A disciple of Donne, Vaughan is classed as a metaphysical poet, and his mystical outlook on nature influenced later poets including Wordsworth.

Vaughan Williams Ralph 1872–1958. English composer. His style was always tonal, and often evocative of the English countryside, particularly through the use of folk song.

vb in grammar, the abbreviation for ◊*verb*.

VDU (visual display unit) an electronic output device for displaying the data processed by a computer on a screen. The oldest and the most popular type is the ◊cathode ray tube (CRT), which uses essentially the same technology as a television screen. Other types use plasma display technology and ◊liquid crystal displays.

vector any physical quantity that has both magnitude and direction, such as the velocity or acceleration of an object, as distinct from a scalar quantity which has magnitude but no direction, such as speed, density, or mass. A vector is represented geometrically by an arrow whose length corresponds to its magnitude, and in an appropriate direction. Vectors can be added graphically by constructing a triangle of vectors (such as the triangle of forces commonly employed in physics and engineering).

Veda (Sanskrit, divine knowledge) the most sacred of the Hindu scriptures, hymns written in an old form of Sanskrit; the oldest may date from 1500 or 2000 BC. The four main collections are: the *Rigveda* (hymns and praises); *Yajurveda* (prayers and sacrificial formulae); *Sâmaveda* (tunes and chants); and *Atharvaveda*, or Veda

of the Atharvans, the officiating priests at the sacrifices.

Vedānta school of Hindu philosophy which developed the teachings of the *Upanishads*. Its best-known teacher was Śamkara, who lived in S India in the 8th century AD and is generally regarded as a manifestation of Siva. He taught that there is only one reality, Brahman, and that knowledge of Brahman leads finally to *moksha*, or liberation from reincarnation.

Vedda person of Vedda culture, a distinct group who are thought to be descendants of the people who inhabited Sri Lanka prior to the arrival of the Aryans about 550 BC. They live mainly in the central highlands of Sri Lanka, and many practice shifting cultivation.

Vega the fifth-brightest star in the sky, and the brightest in the constellation Lyra. It is a blue-white star, 27 light years away, with a luminosity of 50 Suns.

vegetarianism the practice of restricting diet to foods obtained without slaughter, for humanitarian, aesthetic, or health reasons.

vegetative reproduction a type of ◊asexual reproduction in plants that relies not on ◊spores, but on multicellular structures formed by the parent plant. Some of the main types are ◊stolons and runners, ◊gemmae, sucker shoots produced from the roots of some species, such as creeping thistle (*Cirsium arvense*), ◊tubers, ◊bulbs, ◊corms, and ◊rhizomes. Vegetative reproduction has long been exploited in horticulture and agriculture, with various methods employed to multiply stocks of plants.

Veil Simone 1927– . French politician. A survivor of Hitler's concentration camps, she was minister of health 1974–79, and framed the French abortion bill. In 1979–81 she was president of the European Parliament.

vein in animals with a circulatory system, a vessel which carries blood from the body to the heart. Veins contain valves which prevent the blood from running back when moving against gravity. They always carry deoxygenated blood, with the exception of the veins leading from the lungs to the heart in birds and mammals, which carry newly oxygenated blood.

Vela constellation of the southern hemisphere, representing the sails of a ship. It contains large wisps

Venezuela
Republic of (*República de Venezuela*)

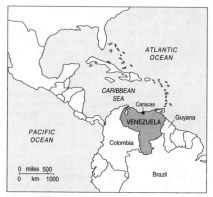

area 912,068 sq km/ 352,150 sq mi
capital Caracas
towns Barquisimeto, Valencia; port Maracaibo
physical valleys and delta of river Orinoco flanked by mountains
head of state and of government Carlos Andrés Pérez from 1988

political system federal democratic republic
exports coffee, cocoa, timber, oil, aluminium, iron ore, petrochemicals
currency bolivar
population (1990 est) 19,753,000 (70% mestizos, 32,000 American Indians); annual growth rate 2.8%
life expectancy men 67, women 73
religion Roman Catholic
language Spanish (official), Indian languages 2%
literacy 88% (1989)
GNP $47.3 bn (1988); $2,629 per head
chronology
1961 New constitution adopted.
1964 Dr Raúl Leoni became president.
1969 Dr Rafael Caldera became president.
1974 Carlos Andrés Pérez Rodriguez became president.
1979 Dr Luis Herrera became president.
1984 Dr Jaime Lusinchi became president. He tried to solve the nation's economic problems through a social pact between the government, trade unions, and business, and by rescheduling the national debt.
1987 Widespread social unrest triggered by inflation; student demonstrators shot by police.
1988 Andrés Pérez elected president.
1989 Economic austerity programme enforced by $4.3 billion loan from International Monetary Fund
1991 Protests against austerity programme continued.
1992 Attempted coups failed. Pérez promised constitutional changes.

of gas called the Gum Nebula, believed to be the remains of one or more ◊supernovae. Vela also contains the second optical ◊pulsar (a pulsar that flashes at a visible wavelength) to be discovered.

Velázquez Diego Rodriguez de Silva y 1599–1660. Spanish painter, born in Seville, the outstanding Spanish artist of the 17th century. In 1623 he became court painter to Philip IV in Madrid, where he produced many portraits of the royal family, as well as occasional religious paintings, genre scenes, and other subjects. *Las Meninas/The Ladies-in-Waiting* 1655 is a complex group portrait which includes a self-portrait, but nevertheless focuses clearly on the doll-like figure of the Infanta Margareta Teresa.

Velde, van de family of Dutch artists. Both *Willem van de Velde* the Elder 1611–93 and his son *Willem van de Velde* the Younger 1633–1707 painted sea battles for Charles II and James II (having settled in London 1672). Another son *Adriaen van de Velde* 1636–72 is known for his landscapes.

veldt subtropical grassland in South Africa, equivalent to the ◊Pampas of South America.

vellum a type of parchment made from the skin of a calf, kid, or lamb. It was used during the Middle Ages, and occasionally later, for exceptionally important documents and the finest manuscripts. It is currently used to describe thick, high-quality paper which resembles fine parchment.

velvet a fabric of silk, cotton, nylon, or other textiles, with a short, thick pile. Utrecht and Genoa are traditional centres of manufacture.

Venda Black National State from 1979, near Zimbabwe border, in South Africa
area 6,500 sq km/2,510 sq mi
capital Thohoyandou
towns MaKearela
government executive president (paramount chief P R Mphephu in office from Sep 1979) and national assembly

products coal, copper, graphite, construction stone
population (1980) 343,500
language Luvenda, English.

Vendée, Wars of the in the French Revolution, a series of peasant risings against the Revolutionary government that began in the Vendée *département* in W France 1793 and spread to other areas of France, lasting until 1795.

vendetta any prolonged feud, in particular the practice that existed until recently in Corsica, Sardinia, and Sicily of exacting revenge for the murder of a relative by killing a member of the murderer's family.

Vendôme Louis Joseph, Duc de Vendôme 1654–1712. Marshal of France, who lost his command after defeat by the British commander Marlborough at Oudenaarde, Belgium 1708, but achieved successes in the 1710 Spanish campaign during the War of the ◊Spanish Succession.

venereal disease (VD) any disease mainly transmitted by sexual contact, although commonly, the term is used specifically for gonorrhea and syphilis, both occurring worldwide, and chancroid ('soft sore') and lymphogranuloma venerum, seen mostly in the tropics.

Veneto region of NE Italy, comprising the provinces of Belluno, Padova (Padua), Treviso, Rovigo, Venezia (Venice), and Vicenza
area 18,377 sq km/7,094 sq mi
capital Venice
towns Padua, Verona, Vicenza
products cereals, fruit, vegetables, wine, chemicals, shipbuilding, textiles
population (1990) 4,398,100.

Venezuela country in N South America, on the Caribbean Sea, bounded E by Guyana, S by Brazil, and W by Colombia.

Venice (Italian *Venezia*) city, port, and naval base, capital of Veneto, Italy, on the Adriatic; population (1990) 79,000. The old city is built on piles

Venus flytrap

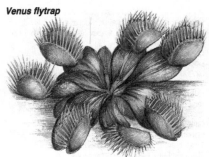

on low-lying islands. Apart from tourism, industries include glass, jewellery, textiles, and lace. Venice was an independent trading republic from the 10th century, ruled by a doge, or chief magistrate, and was one of the centres of the Italian Renaissance.

veni, vidi ,vici (Latin 'I came, I saw, I conquered') Julius ◊Caesar's description of his victory over King Pharnaces II (63–47 BC) at Zela 47 BC.

Venizelos Eleutherios 1864–1936. Greek politician. Born in Crete, he came to prominence as one of the Cretan movement against Turkish rule, aiming at union with Greece. He was prime minister of Greece 1910–15, 1917–20, 1924, 1928–32, and 1933, and was exiled 1935.

Venn diagram in mathematics, a diagram representing a ◊set or sets and the logical relationships between them. Sets are drawn as circles. An area of overlap between two circles (sets) contains elements that are common to both sets, and thus represents a third set. Circles that do not overlap represent sets with no elements in common (disjoint sets). The method is named after the British logician John Venn (1834–1923).

Ventris Michael George Francis 1922–1956. English archaeologist. Deciphering Minoan Linear B, the language of the tablets found at Knossos and Pylos, he showed that it was a very early form of Greek, thus revising existing views on early Greek history.

venture capital or *risk capital* money put up by investors such as merchant banks to fund a new company or expansion of an established company. The organization providing the money receives a share of the company's equity and seeks to make a profit by rapid growth in the value of its stake, as a result of expansion by the start-up company or 'venture'.

Venturi Robert 1925– . US architect. He pioneered Post-Modernism through his books, *Complexity and Contradiction in Architecture* 1967 and *Learning from Las Vegas* 1972. In 1986 he was commissioned to design the extension to the National Gallery, London.

Venus the second planet in order of distance from the Sun. It orbits the Sun every 225 days at an average distance of 108.2 million km/67.2 million mi and can approach the Earth to within 38 million km/24 million mi, closer than any other planet. Its diameter is 12,100 km/7,500 mi and its mass is 0.82 that of Earth. Venus rotates on its axis more slowly than any other planet, once every 243 days and from east to west, the opposite direction to the other planets (except Uranus). Venus is shrouded by clouds of sulphuric acid droplets which sweep across the planet from east to west every four days. The atmosphere is almost entirely carbon dioxide, which traps the Sun's heat by the ◊greenhouse effect to raise the planet's surface temperature to 480°C, with an atmospheric pressure 90 times that at Earth's surface.

Venus in Roman mythology, the goddess of love (Greek *Aphrodite*).

Venus flytrap North American insectivorous plant *Dionaea muscipula*, the leaf of which folds together to trap insects.

verb the grammatical part of speech for what someone or something does (*to go*), experiences (*to live*), or is (*to be*). Verbs involve the grammatical categories known as number (singular or plural: 'He *runs*; they *run*'), voice (active or passive: 'She *writes* books; it *is written*'), mood (statements, questions, orders, emphasis, necessity, condition), aspect (completed or continuing action: 'She *danced*; she *was dancing*'), and tense (variation according to time: simple present tense, present continuous/progressive tense, simple past tense, and so on).

types of verb A *transitive* verb takes a direct object ('he saw *the house*'). An *intransitive* verb has no object ('She laughed'). An *auxiliary or helping* verb is used to express tense and/or mood ('He *was* seen'; 'They *may* come'). A *modal* verb or *modal auxiliary* generally shows only mood; common modals are *may/might, will/would, can/could, shall/should, must*. The *infinitive* of the verb usually includes 'to' (*to go, to run*, and so on), but may be a bare infinitive (for example, after modals, as in 'She may *go*'). A *regular* verb forms tenses in the normal way (*I walk, I walked, I have walked*); irregular verbs do not (*swim, swam, swum; put, put, put*; and so on). Because of their conventional nature, regular verbs are also known as weak verbs, while some irregular verbs are strong verbs with special vowel changes across tenses, as in *swim, swam, swum*; and *ride, rode, ridden*. A *phrasal verb* is a construction in which a particle attaches to a usually single-syllable verb (for example, *put* becoming *put up*, as in 'He put up some money for the project', and *put up with*, as in 'I can't put up with this nonsense any longer').

verbena genus of plants, family Verbenaceae, of about 100 species, mostly found in the American tropics. The leaves are fragrant and the tubular flowers arranged in close spikes in colours ranging from white to rose, violet, and purple. The garden verbena is a hybrid annual.

Vercingetorix died *c*. 45 BC. Gallic chieftain. Leader of a revolt against the Romans 52 BC,

Verdi Giuseppe Verdi, the great Italian opera composer.

Vermeer A Young Woman standing at a Virginal
(c. 1670) National Gallery, London.

he was displayed in Caesar's triumph 46 BC, and later executed.

Verdi Giuseppe (Fortunino Francesco) 1813–1901. Italian opera composer of the Romantic period, who brought his native operatic style to new heights of dramatic expression. In 1842 he first achieved success with his opera *Nabucco*, followed by *Ernani* 1844 and *Rigoletto* 1851. Other works include *Il travatore* and *La traviata* both 1853; *Aida* 1871, and the masterpieces of his old age *Otello* 1887 and *Falstaff* 1893. His *Requiem* 1874 commemorates Alessandro ◊Manzoni.

Verdun fortress town in NE France on the Meuse. During World War I it became the symbol of French resistance, withstanding a German onslaught 1916.

vérité (French) realism, as in the phrase *cinéma-vérité*, used to describe a realistic or documentary style.

Verlaine Paul 1844–1896. French lyrical poet who was influenced by the poets Baudelaire and Rimbaud. His volumes of verse include *Poèmes saturniens/Saturnine Poems* 1866, *Fêtes galantes/Amorous Entertainments* 1869, and *Romances sans paroles/Songs without Words* 1874. In 1873 he was imprisoned for attempting to shoot Rimbaud. His later works reflect his attempts to lead a reformed life and he was acknowledged as leader of the ◊Symbolist poets.

Vermeer Jan 1632–1675. Dutch painter, active in Delft. Most of his pictures are genre scenes, with a limpid clarity and distinct air of stillness, and a harmonious palette often focusing on yellow and blue. He frequently depicted single women in domestic settings, such as *The Lacemaker* (Louvre, Paris).

Vermont state of the USA in New England; nickname Green Mountain State
area 24,907 sq km/9,614 sq mi
capital Montpelier
products apples, maple syrup, dairy products, china clay, asbestos, granite, marble, slate, business machines, furniture, paper
population (1986) 541,000
history explored by Champlain from 1609; settled 1724; state 1791. The **Green Mountain Boys** were irregulars who fought to keep Vermont from New York interference.

vermouth a white wine flavoured by the maceration of bitter herbs and fortified by alcohol. It is made in France and Italy.

vernal equinox see ◊equinox.

vernalization the stimulation of flowering by exposure to cold. Certain plants will not flower unless subjected to low temperatures during their development. For example, winter wheat will flower in summer only if planted in the previous autumn. However, by placing partially germinated seeds in low temperatures for several days, the cold requirement can be supplied artificially, allowing the wheat to be sown in the spring.

Verne Jules 1828–1905. French author. Born in Nantes, he went to Paris and established a reputation as a writer of tales of adventure which anticipate future scientific developments: *Five Weeks in a Balloon* 1862, *Journey to the Centre of the Earth* 1864, *Twenty Thousand Leagues under the Sea* 1870, and *Around the World in Eighty Days* 1873.

Verney Edmund 1590–1642. English courtier, knight-marshal to Charles I from 1626. He sat as a Member of both the Short and Long parliaments and, though sympathizing with the parliamentary position, remained true to his allegiance: he died at his post as royal standard bearer at the Battle of ◊Edgehill.

vernier device for taking readings on a graduated scale to a fraction of a division. It consists of a short divided scale which carries an index or pointer and is slid along a main scale. It was invented by Pierre Vernier (*c.* 1580–1637).

Verona industrial city (printing, paper, plastics, furniture, pasta) in Veneto, Italy, on the Adige; population (1986) 259,000.

Veronese Paolo *c.* 1528–1588. Italian painter, born in Verona, active mainly in Venice (from about 1553). He specialized in grand decorative schemes, such as his ceilings in the Doge's Palace in Venice, with *trompe l'oeil* effects and inventive detail. The subjects are religious, mythological, historical, and allegorical.

Veronica, St a woman of Jerusalem who, according to tradition, lent her veil to Jesus to wipe the sweat from his brow on the road to Calvary, whereupon the image of his face was printed upon it. What is alleged to be the actual veil is preserved in St Peter's, Rome.

Verrocchio Andrea del 1435–1488. Italian painter, sculptor, and goldsmith, born in Florence, where

Verne French writer and science fiction novelist Jules Verne.

Veronese Allegory of Love, III *(1570s) National Gallery, London* .

he ran a large workshop and received commissions from the Medici family. The vigorous equestrian statue of Bartolommeo Colleoni, begun 1481 (Campo SS Giovanni e Paolo, Venice), was his last work.

verruca growth on the skin. See ◊wart.

Versailles city in N France, capital of Les Yvelines *département*, on the outskirts of Paris; population (1982) 95,240. It grew up around the palace of Louis XV. Within the palace park are two small châteaux, Le Grand and Le Petit ◊Trianon, built for Louis XIV (by Hardouin ◊Mansart) and Louis XV (by Gabriel 1698–1782), respectively.

Versailles, Treaty of peace treaty after World War I between the Allies and Germany, signed 28 Jun 1919. It established the League of Nations. Germany surrendered Alsace-Lorraine to France, large areas in the east to Poland, and made smaller cessions to Czechoslovakia, Lithuania, Belgium, and Denmark. The Rhineland was demilitarized, German rearmament was restricted, and Germany agreed to pay reparations for war damage. The treaty was never ratified by the USA, which made a separate peace with Germany and Austria 1921.

verse arrangement of words in rhythmic pattern, which may depend on the length of syllables (as in Greek or Latin verse), or on stress, as in English.

vertebrate any animal with a backbone. The 41,000 species of vertebrates include mammals, birds, reptiles, amphibians, and fishes. They include most of the larger animals, but in terms of numbers of species are only a tiny proportion of the world's animals. The zoological taxonomic group Vertebrata is a sub-group of the ◊phylum Chordata.

vertical take-off aircraft an aircraft that can take off and land vertically (VTOL). The helicopter, airship, and balloon can do this, as can a few fixed-wing aeroplanes like the Harrier.

vertigo dizziness; a whirling sensation accompanied by a loss of any feeling of contact with the ground. It may be due to temporary disturbance of the sense of balance (as in spinning for too long on one spot), disease, or intoxication.

Verulamium Roman-British town whose remains have been excavated close to St Albans.

Verwoerd Hendrik (Frensch) 1901–1966. South African right-wing Nationalist Party politician, prime minister from 1958. As minister of native affairs 1950–58, he was the chief promoter of apartheid legislation. He made the country a republic 1961.

He was assassinated in the House of Assembly by a parliamentary messenger, Dimitri Tsafendas.

Very Large Array (VLA) one of the world's most powerful radio telescopes, located on the Plains of San Augustine, near Socorro, New Mexico, USA. It consists of 27 dish antennae, 25 m/82 ft in diameter, which can move along a Y-shaped rail track.

Vesalius Andreas 1514–1564. Belgian physician who revolutionized anatomy. His great innovations were to perform postmortem dissections, and to make use of illustrations in teaching anatomy.

Vespasian (Titus Flavius Vespasianus) 9–79 AD. Roman emperor from 69 AD. He had a distinguished military career and was proclaimed emperor by his soldiers while he was campaigning in Palestine. He reorganized the eastern provinces, and was a capable administrator.

vespers the seventh of the eight canonical hours in the Catholic Church.

Vespucci Amerigo 1454–1512. Florentine merchant. The Americas were named after him as a result of the widespread circulation of his accounts of his explorations, but evidence suggests that he never made the voyages.

Vesta in Roman mythology, the goddess of the hearth (Greek *Hestia*). In Rome, the sacred flame in her shrine in the Forum was kept constantly lit by the six *Vestal Virgins*.

vestigial organ in biology, an organ that remains in diminished form after it has ceased to have any significant function in the adult organism. In humans, the appendix is vestigial, having once had a digestive function in our ancestors.

Vesuvius (Italian *Vesuvio*) active volcano SE of Naples, Italy; height 1,277 m/4,190 ft. In 79 BC it destroyed the cities of Pompeii, ◊Herculaneum, and Oplonti.

vetch trailing/climbing plants of several genera, family Leguminosae, with pinnate leaves and purple, yellow or white flowers, including the fodder crop lucerne *Vicia sativa*.

Veterans Day in the USA the name adopted for *Armistice Day* in 1954, and from 1971 observed by most states on the fourth Monday in Oct. The equivalent in the UK and Canada is ◊Remembrance Sunday.

veterinary science the prevention and cure of disease in animals. More generally, it covers their anatomy, breeding, and relations to humans. Professional bodies: Royal College of Veterinary Surgeons 1844 in the UK, and the American Veterinary Medical Association 1883 in the USA.

veto (Latin *'I forbid'*) exercise by a sovereign, branch of legislature, or other political power, of the right to prevent the enactment or operation of a law, or the taking of some course of action.

Veuster Joseph de 1840–1889. Belgian missionary, known as Father Damien. He entered the order of the Fathers of the Sacred Heart at Louvain, went to Hawaii, and from 1873 was resident priest in the leper settlement at Molokai. He eventually became infected and died there.

VHF *Very High Frequency*, referring to radio waves. VHF waves, which also have very short wavelengths, are used for interference-free ◊FM (frequency-modulated) transmissions. VHF transmitters have relatively short range because the waves cannot be reflected over the horizon like longer radio waves.

vibrato in music, a slight but rapid fluctuation of pitch, in voice or instrument.

viburnum genus of temperate and subtropical trees and shrubs, family Caprifoliaceae, including the *wayfaring* tree, the *laurustinus* and the *guelder rose*.

vicar a Church of England clergyman, originally one who acted as deputy to a ◊rector, but now also a parish priest.

viceroy the chief officer of the crown in many Spanish and Portuguese South American colonies who had ultimate responsibility for administration and military matters. The office of viceroy was also used by the British crown to rule India.

vice versa (Latin) the other way around.

Vichy health resort with thermal springs, known to the Romans, on the river Allier in Allier *département*, central France. During World War II it was the seat of ◊Pétain's government 1940–44.

Vico Giambattista 1668–1744. Italian philosopher, considered the founder of the modern philosophy of history. He rejected Descartes' emphasis on the mathematical and natural sciences, and argued that we can understand history more adequately than nature, since it is we who have made it. He believed that the study of language, ritual and myth was a way of understanding earlier societies. His cyclical theory of history (the birth, development and decline of human societies) was put forward in *New Science* 1725.

Victor Emmanuel three kings of Italy including:

Victor Emmanuel II 1820–1878. First king of united Italy from 1861. He became king of Sardinia on the abdication of his father Charles Albert 1849. In 1855 he allied Sardinia with France and the UK in the Crimean War. In 1859 in alliance with the French he defeated the Austrians and annexed Lombardy. By 1860 most of Italy had come under his rule, and in 1861 he was proclaimed king of Italy. In 1870 he made Rome his capital.

Victor Emmanuel III 1869–1947. King of Italy from the assassination of his father Umberto I 1900. He acquiesced in the Fascist regime of Mussolini but cooperated with the Allies; he abdicated 1946.

Victoria 1819–1901. Queen of the UK from 1837, when she succeeded her uncle William IV, and empress of India from 1876. In 1840 she married Prince ◊Albert of Saxe-Coburg and Gotha. Her relations with her prime ministers ranged from the affectionate (Melbourne and Disraeli) to the stormy (Peel, Palmerston, and Gladstone). Her golden jubilee 1887 and diamond jubilee 1897 marked a waning of republican sentiment, which had developed with her withdrawal from public life on Albert's death.

Victoria state of SE Australia
area 227,620 sq km/87,861 sq mi
capital Melbourne
towns Geelong, Ballarat, Bendigo
physical part of the Great Dividing Range runs E–W and includes the larger part of the Australian Alps; Gippsland lakes, shallow lagoons on the coast; the ◊mallee shrub region
products sheep, beef cattle, dairy products, tobacco, wheat; vines for wine and dried fruit, orchard fruits, vegetables, gold, brown coal (Latrobe Valley), oil and natural gas in Bass Strait
population (1986) 4,165,000; 71% live in the Melbourne area
history annexed for Britain by Cook 1770; settled in the 1830s; after being part of New South Wales, it became a separate colony 1851, named after the queen; became a state 1901.

Victoria industrial port (shipbuilding, chemicals, clothing, furniture) on Vancouver Island, capital of British Columbia, Canada; population (1986) 256,000.

Victoria port and capital of the Seychelles, on Mahé island; population (1985) 23,000.

Victoria, Lake or *Victoria Nyanza* largest lake in Africa, over 69,400 sq km/27,000 sq mi (410 km/255 mi long) on the equator at an altitude of 1,136 m/3,728 ft. It lies between Uganda, Kenya, and Tanzania, and is a source of the Nile.

Victoria and Albert Museum a museum of decorative arts in South Kensington, London, opened 1909, inspired by Henry Cole (1808–1882) and Prince ◊Albert.

Victoria Cross British decoration for conspicuous bravery in wartime, instituted by Queen Victoria 1856. It is bronze, with a 4 cm/1.5 in diameter, and has a crimson ribbon.

Victoria Falls or *Mosi-oa-tunya* waterfall on the river Zambezi, on the Zambia–Zimbabwe border. The river is 1,700 m/5,580 ft wide, and drops 120 m/400 ft to flow through a 30 m/100 ft wide gorge.

Victorian a term applied to the mid and late 19th century in England, covering the reign of Queen Victoria. Victorian style was often very ornate, markedly so in architecture, and Victorian Gothic harked back to the original Gothic architecture of medieval times. It was also an era when increasing machine mass-production threatened the existence of crafts and craftsmanship.

Victorian Order, Royal one of the fraternities carrying with it the rank of Knight; see ◊knighthood.

vicuna ruminant mammal *Lama vicugna* of the camel family which lives in herds on the Andean plateau. They can run at speeds of 50 kph/30 mph. They have good eyesight, fair hearing, and a poor sense of smell. They have been hunted close to extinction for their meat and soft brown fur, which is used in textile manufacture.

Vidal Gore 1925– . US writer and critic. Much of his work deals satirically with history and politics and includes the novels *Myra Breckinridge* 1968, *Burr* 1973, and *Empire* 1987, plays and screenplays, including *Suddenly Last Summer* 1958, and essays, such as *Armageddon?* 1987.

video camera a portable television camera that takes 'movie' pictures electronically. It produces an electrical output-signal corresponding to rapid line-by-line 'scanning' of the field of view. The output is recorded on videotape and is played back on a television screen via a videotape recorder.

video disc a method of recording pictures (and sounds) on disc. The video disc (originated by Baird 1928; commercially available from 1978) is chiefly used to provide commercial films for personal viewing. The Philips *Laservision* system uses a 30 cm/12 in rotating vinyl disc coated with a reflective material. Laser scanning recovers picture and sound signals from the surface where they are recorded as a spiral of microscopic pits. The video disc works in the same way as a ◊compact disc.

video games or *telegames* games played, by means of special additional or built-in components, on the screen of a home television set. The first commercially sold was a simple bat and ball game developed in the USA 1972, but complex variants are now available in colour and with special sound effects.

videography filming with a lightweight video camera, producing a videotape that can immediately be played back in colour and sound on a television set. The tape can be wiped and reused.

Vietnam
Socialist Republic of (*Công Hòa Xã Hội Chu Nghĩa Việt Nam*)

area 336,000 sq km/129,000 sq mi
capital Hanoi
towns ports Ho Chi Minh City (formerly Saigon), Da Nang, and Haiphong
physical Red River and Mekong deltas; some tropical rainforest; the rest is mountainous

head of state Le Duc Anh from 1992
head of government Vo Van Kiet from 1992
political system communism
exports rice, rubber, coal, iron, apatite
currency dong
population (1990 est) 68,488,000 (some 750,000 Chinese refugees left the country 1975–79, some settling in SW China, others fleeing by sea – the 'boat people' – to Hong Kong and elsewhere); annual growth rate 2.4%
life expectancy men 62, women 66 (1989)
language Vietnamese (official); French, English, Khmer, Chinese
religion Buddhist, Taoist, Confucian, Christian
literacy 78% (1989)
GNP $12.6 bn (1987); $180 per head
chronology
1945 Japanese removed from Vietnam.
1946 Commencement of Vietminh war against French.
1954 France defeated at Dien Bien Phu. Vietnam divided along 17th parallel.
1964 USA entered Vietnam War.
1973 Paris ceasefire.
1975 Saigon captured by North.
1976 Socialist Republic of Vietnam proclaimed.
1978 Invasion of Kampuchea (now Cambodia).
1979 Sino-Vietnamese border war.
1986 Retirement of old-guard leaders.
1988–89 Troop withdrawals from Cambodia.
1991 Vo Van Kiet became prime minister. Cambodia peace agreement signed.
1992 Le Duc Anh elected president. USA eased 30-year-old trade embargo.

videotape recorder (VTR) a device for recording television programmes for later viewing, or linked by cable with a video camera. A *cam-corder* is a portable videotape recorder with a built-in camera.

videotext a system in which information (text) is displayed on a television (video) screen. There are two basic systems, known as ◊teletext and ◊viewdata. In the teletext system information is broadcast with the ordinary television signals, while in viewdata information is relayed to the screen from a central data bank via the telephone network. Both systems require

Vietnam War US troops of the 1st Cavalry Division, Vietnam 1967.

the use of a television receiver with special decoder.

Vidocq Françoise Eugène 1775–1857. French criminal who, in 1809, became a spy for the Paris police, and rose to become chief of the detective department.

Vienna (German *Wien*) capital of Austria, on the river Danube at the foot of the Wiener Wald (Vienna Woods); population (1986) 1,481,000. Industries include engineering and the production of electrical goods and precision instruments.

Vienna, Congress of the international congress held 1814–15, which effected the settlement of Europe after the Napoleonic Wars. National representatives included the Austrian foreign minister Metternich, Alexander I of Russia, the British foreign secretary Castlereagh and military commander Wellington, and the French politician Talleyrand.

Vientiane capital and chief port of Laos on the Mekong river; population (1985) 377,000.

Viet Cong (Vietnamese *Vietnamese Communists*) in the Vietnam War, the members of the National Front for the Liberation of South Vietnam, founded 1960, who fought the South Vietnamese and US forces. The name was coined by the South Vietnamese government to differentiate these communist guerrillas from the ◊Vietminh.

Vietminh the Vietnam Independence League, founded 1941 to oppose the Japanese occupation of Indochina and later directed against the French colonial power. The Vietminh was instrumental in achieving Vietnamese independence through military victory at Dien Bien Phu 1954.

Vietnam country in SE Asia, on the South China Sea, bounded N by China and W by Cambodia and Laos.

Vietnam War 1954–75. War between the communist North Vietnam and the US-backed South Vietnam. 200,000 South Vietnamese soldiers, 1,000,000 North Vietnamese soldiers, and 500,000

Viking

In their narrow, shallow-draughted and highly manoeuvrable longships, the Vikings spread from their Scandinavian homelands to fight, trade and settle through most of the coastal regions of 8th to 11th-century Europe. They established kingdoms in the British Isles, Normandy, and Russia. As Normans they founded a kingdom in Sicily and in 1066 achieved a second conquest of England. They are believed to have sailed to North America and as far south as the Byzantine Empire where Swedish Vikings (Varangians) formed the imperial guard.

A stone cross (below) from Middleton, Yorkshire, depicting a well-armed Viking warrior. His weapons include a spear, sword, axe and dagger.

The vikings in Northern Europe: their major trade routes and areas of raiding and settlement. Viking longships, weapons and armour combined practicality and craftsmanship.

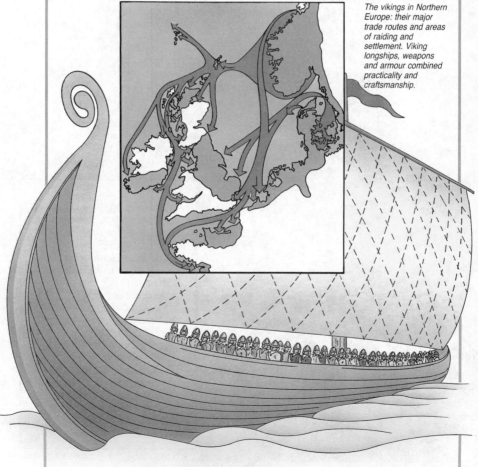

Viking probes

Most of the Viking experiments were performed by the three-legged landers. As well as cameras, the 1.9m (6ft) tall lander carried a range of instruments for chemical, biological and geological experiments. The orbiter, which circled the planet at a height of 1,500 km (930 mi), carried infra-red scanners and cameras. It also relayed messages between the lander and Earth. Transmissions continued until the early 1980s.

(1) After reaching Mars, Viking spends a month orbiting the planet while the best landing site is selected. (2) The lander and orbiter separate. (3) The lander aligns itself for descent. (4) The lander enters atmosphere at 243,800 m (800,000 ft). (5) A parachute is deployed to slow the descent at 5913 m (19,400 ft). (6) The parachute is jettisoned and descent engines start at 1,402 m (4,600 ft). Sensors on the legs cut off the engines when the craft lands.

(1) Descent engine fuel tank. (2) Roll engine to stabilize descent. (3) Low-gain ratio antenna. (4) UHF antenna. (5) Seismometer to measure ground tremors. (6) High-gain dish antenna. (7) One of two high-resolution black and white, and colour, cameras. (8) Meterology sensors to measure atmospheric pressure, wind direction and speed, and temperature. (9) Mechanical scoop to collect soil for chemical and biological tests which were carried out inside the body of the lander. (10) Descent engine.

civilians were killed. 56,555 US soldiers were killed 1961–1975, a fifth of which were killed by their own troops.

1954 Under the Geneva Convention the former French colony of Indochina was divided into the separate states of North Vietnam and South Vietnam. Within South Vietnam the communist Vietcong, supported by North Vietnam and China, attempted to seize power. The USA provided military aid to support the South Vietnamese.

1964 The ◊Tonkin Gulf Incident.

1967 Several large-scale invasion attempts by North Vietnam were defeated by indigenous and US forces.

1968 ◊My Lai massacre.

1973 The unpopularity of the war within the USA led to the start of US withdrawal. A peace treaty was signed between North Vietnam and South Vietnam.

1975 South Vietnam was invaded by North Vietnam in Mar.

1976 South Vietnam was annexed by North Vietnam, and the two countries were renamed the Socialist Republic of Vietnam.

viewdata a system of displaying information on a television screen in which the information is extracted from a computer data bank and transmitted via the telephone lines. It is one form of ◊videotext. The British Post Office (now British Telecom) developed the world's first viewdata system, ◊Prestel, in 1975, and similar systems are now in widespread use in other countries. Viewdata users have access to an almost unlimited store of information, presented on the screen in the form of 'pages'.

vigilante in US history, originally a member of a 'vigilance committee', a self-appointed group to maintain public order in the absence of organized authority. Early examples included the 'Regulators' in South Carolina in the 1760s, and in Pennsylvania 1794 during the Whiskey Rebellion. Many more appeared in the 19th century in frontier towns. Once authorized police forces existed, vigilante groups such as the ◊Ku Klux Klan operated outside the law, often as perpetrators of mob violence such as lynching. The vigilante tradition continues with present-day urban groups patrolling subways to deter muggers and rapists.

Vigny Alfred, Comte de 1797–1863. French romantic writer, whose works include the historical novel *Cinq-Mars* 1826, the play *Chatterton* 1835, and poetry, for example, *Les Destinées/Destinies* 1864.

Viking or **Norseman** Scandinavian sea warrior, who raided Europe in the 8th–11th centuries, and often settled.

Viking art sculpture and design of the Vikings. Viking artists are best known for woodcarving and metalwork, and for an intricate interlacing ornament similar to that found in Celtic art.

Viking probes two US space probes to Mars, each one consisting of an orbiter and a lander. They were launched 20 Aug and 9 Sep 1975. They transmitted colour pictures, and analysed the soil.

village college a type of ◊community school.

Villa-Lobos Heitor 1887–1959. Brazilian composer. His national style was based on folk tunes collected on his travels in the country, for example, *Bachianas Brasileiras*, in which he treats them in the manner of Bach. He used orchestras of hundreds, choirs of thousands, and produced 2,000 works, including 12 symphonies.

Villehardouin Geoffroy de *c.* 1160–1213. French historian, the first to write in the French language.

He was born near Troyes, and was a leader of the Fourth ◊Crusade, of which his *Conquest of Constantinople c.* 1209 is an account.

villeinage the system of serfdom that prevailed in Europe in the Middle Ages. A villein was a peasant who gave dues and services to his lord in exchange for land.

Villiers de l'Isle Adam Philippe Auguste Mathias, comte de Villiers de l'Isle Adam 1838–1889. French poet, the inaugurator of the Symbolist movement. He wrote the drama *Axel* 1890; *Isis* 1862, a romance of the supernatural; verse, and short stories.

Villon François 1431–1485. French poet, noted for his satiric humour, pathos, and lyric power in works which used the *argot* (slang) of the time. Very little of his work survives; it includes the *Ballade des dames du temps jadis/Ballad of the ladies of former times*, the *Petit Testament* 1456, and the *Grand Testament* 1461.

Vilnius capital of Lithuania; population (1987) 566,000. Industries include engineering, and the manufacture of textiles, chemicals, and foodstuffs.

Vimy Ridge hill in N France, a spur of the ridge of Nôtre Dame de Lorette, 8 km/5 mi NE of Arras, taken in World War I by Canadian troops during the battle of Arras, Apr 1917, costing 11,285 lives.

Vincent de Paul, St *c.* 1580–1660. French Roman Catholic priest and founder of the two charitable orders of Dazarists 1625 and Sisters of Charity 1634. Born in Gascony, he was ordained 1600, then captured by Barbary pirates and was a slave in Tunis until he escaped 1607. He was canonized 1737; feast day 19 Jul.

Vincent of Beauvais *c.* 1190–1264. French scholar, encyclopedist, and Dominican priest. A chaplain to the court of Louis IX, he is mainly remembered for his encyclopedia *Speculum majus/Great Mirror* 1220–44.

vincristine an ◊alkaloid extracted from the blue periwinkle plant. Developed as an anticancer agent, it has revolutionized the treatment of childhood acute leukaemias; it is also included in ◊chemotherapy regimens for some lymphomas (cancers arising in the lymph tissues), lung and breast cancers. Side effects, such as nerve damage and loss of hair, are severe but usually reversible.

vine climbing plant *Vitis vinifera* of the family Vitaceae. It is native to Asia Minor and cultivated from antiquity for its fruit, which is eaten or made into wine or other fermented drinks; dried fruits of certain varieties are known as raisins and currants. Other species of climbing plant are sometimes termed vines.

vinegar a 4% solution of acetic acid produced by the oxidation of alcohol, used to flavour food and as a preservative in pickles. *Malt vinegar* is brown and made from malted cereals; *white vinegar* is distilled from it. Other sources of vinegar include cider, inferior wine, and honey.

Vinland Norse name for the area of North America, probably on the east coast of Nova Scotia or

violet

violin family

bow

viola

violin

cello

double bass

New England, which the Viking Leif ◊Ericsson visited. It was named for the wild grapes that grew there.

viola a bowed string musical instrument of the ◊violin family.

violet plant of the genus *Viola*, family Violaceae, with toothed leaves and mauve, blue or white flowers, such as the **heath dog violet** *Viola canina* and **sweet violet** *Viola odorata*. **Pansies** are very close relatives.

viol family bowed musical instruments of the 16th–18th centuries, similar to the violin (which superseded them), but having frets and (normally) six strings, instead of four, tuned in fourths, and with a flatter back.

violin family musical instruments played with a bow drawn against a stretched string. There are four members: *violin, viola, violoncello* or *cello,* and *double bass.* Each of the instruments consists of a resonant hollow body, a neck with fingerboard attached, and four catgut strings, stretched over the body, tuned in fifths above the lowest note, G below middle C.

violoncello or *cello* a bowed string musical instrument of the ◊violin family.

VIP abbreviation for *very important person.*

viper front-fanged venomous snake of the family Viperidae. They range in size from 30 cm/1 ft to 3 m/9.8 ft, and often have diamond or jagged markings. Most give birth to live young.

Virchow Rudolf Ludwig Carl 1821–1902. German pathologist and founder of cellular pathology. Virchow was the first to describe ◊leukemia. In his book *Die Cellulare Pathologie/Cellular Pathology* 1858, he proposed that disease is the cell's response to altered and abnormal conditions within the body. It is not due to sudden invasions or changes, but to slow processes in which normal cells give rise to abnormal ones.

Virgil Publius Vergilius Maro 70–19 BC. Roman poet, patronized by Maecenas. He wrote the *Eclogues* 37 BC, a series of pastoral poems, the *Georgics* 30 BC, four books on the art of farming and his masterpiece, the ◊*Aeneid,* an epic in 12 books which describes the wanderings of ◊Aeneas after he fled from the sack of Troy, and glorifies the Roman Empire.

virginal a small type of ◊harpsichord.

Virginia state of the S USA; nickname Old Dominion
area 105,614 sq km/40,767 sq mi
capital Richmond
towns Norfolk, Newport News, Hampton, Portsmouth
products sweet potatoes, corn, tobacco, apples, peanuts, coal, furniture, paper, chemicals, processed food, textiles,
population (1986) 5,787,000
famous people Richard E Byrd, Patrick Henry, Meriwether Lewis and William Clark, Edgar Allan Poe, Booker T Washington
history named in honour of Elizabeth I; Jamestown first permanent English settlement in the New World 1607; took a leading part in the American Revolution, and was one of the original Thirteen States; joined the Confederacy in the Civil War.

Virgin Islands group of about 100 small islands, northernmost of the Leeward Islands in the Antilles, West Indies. Tourism is the main industry. They comprise the *US Virgin Islands* St Thomas (with the capital, Charlotte Amalie), St John, and St Croix; area 352 sq km/136 sq mi; population (1985) 111,000; and the *British Virgin Islands* Tortola (with the capital, Road Town), Virgin Gorda, Anegada, Jost van Dykes; area 153 sq km/59 sq mi; population (1980) 12,000.

Virgo constellation of the zodiac, and the second largest in the sky, representing a maiden holding an ear of wheat. The Sun passes through Virgo from late Sep to the end of Oct. Virgo's brightest star is the first-magnitude Spica, a blue-white star about 250 light years away. Virgo contains the nearest large cluster of galaxies to us, 50 million light years away, consisting of about 3,000 galaxies centred on the giant elliptical galaxy M87. Also in Virgo is the nearest ◊quasar, 3C 273, an estimated 3 billion light years distant.

virion a single mature ◊virus particle.

virus an infectious particle consisting of a core of nucleic acids (DNA or RNA) enclosed in a protein shell. Viruses are acellular, able to function and reproduce only if they can force their way into a living cell to use the cell's system to replicate themselves. In doing so, they may disrupt or alter the host cell's own DNA. The healthy human body reacts by producing an antiviral protein, ◊interferon, which prevents the infection spreading to adjacent cells.

virus in computing, a hidden piece of software within a legitimate program which is inserted maliciously and carries a set of instructions that can destroy

viper

common viper

other programs and files. It can spread from computer to computer along telephone links and is very difficult to eradicate.

vis-à-vis (French 'face-to-face') with regard to.

Visby town and bishopric on the island of Gotland in the Baltic. In the 12th and 13th centuries, it was an important centre in the Hanseatic League.

viscacha Argentinian pampas and scrubland-dwelling rodent *Lagostomus maximus* of the chinchilla family. It is up to 66 cm/2.2 ft long with a 20 cm/8 in tail, and weighs 7 kg/15 lbs. It is grey and black, and has a large head and small ears. Viscachas live in warrens of up to 30 individuals. They are nocturnal, and feed on grasses, roots, and seeds.

viscera a general term for the organs contained in the chest and abdominal cavities.

Visconti Luchino 1906–1976. Italian film and theatrical director. The film *Ossessione* 1942 pioneers his work with Neo-Realist theories; later works include *The Leopard* 1963 and *Death in Venice* 1971. His powerful social comment in documentaries led to clashes with the Italian government and Roman Catholic Church.

Visconti, Dukes of Milan rulers of Milan 1277–1447. They originated as N Italian feudal lords who attained dominance over the city as a result of their alliance with the Holy Roman emperors. By the mid-14th century, they ruled 15 other major towns in N Italy.

viscose the most common type of ◊rayon, made by dissolving the cellulose in ◊woodpulp and regenerating it in an acid bath in the form of continuous filament or fibres.

viscosity in physics, the resistance of a fluid to flow. It applies to the motion of an object moving through a fluid as well as the motion of a fluid passing by an object.

viscount in the UK peerage, the fourth degree of nobility, between earl and baron.

Vishnu in ◊Hinduism, the second in the triad of gods representing three aspects of the supreme spirit. He is the Preserver, and is believed to have assumed human appearance in nine avataras or incarnations, in such forms as Rama and Krishna. His worshippers are the Vaishnavas.

Visigoths branch of ◊Goths, an E Germanic people.

vision system a computer-based device for interpreting visual signals from a video camera. Computer vision is important in robotics where sensory abilities would considerably increase the flexibility and usefulness of a robot.

vitalism the idea that living organisms derive their characteristic properties from a universal life force. The view is associated in the present century with the philosopher Henri Bergson.

vitamin any of several organic substances present in differing amounts in various types of food. Various characteristic diseases and disturbances arise if vitamins are absent or deficient in the diet. Vitamins are only needed in small amounts; a balanced diet usually provides an adequate intake of the 20 known vitamins required for normal function. Many act as coenzymes, small molecules which enable ◊enzymes to function effectively. Vitamins are either *water-soluble* (B, C, P) or *fat-soluble* (A, D, E, K).

vitamin C another name for ◊ascorbic acid.

vitriol any of a number of sulphate salts. Blue, green, and white vitriols are copper, ferrous, and zinc sulphate respectively. Oil of vitriol is sulphuric acid.

Vitus, St Christian saint, probably Sicilian, who was martyred at Rome early in the 4th century.

Vivaldi Antonio (Lucio) 1678–1741. Italian Baroque composer of 23 symphonies, 75 sonatas, over 400 concertos, over 40 operas, and much sacred music. His work was largely neglected until the 1930s.

vivipary in animals, a method of reproduction in which the embryo develops inside the body of the female from which it gains nourishment (in contrast to ◊ovipary and ◊ovovivipary). Vivipary is best developed in mammals, but also occurs in some arthropods, fish, amphibians, and reptiles. In plants, it is the formation of young plantlets or bulbils instead of flowers. The term also describes seeds which germinate prematurely, before falling from the parent plant. This is common in mangrove trees where the seedlings develop sizeable spear-like roots before dropping into the swamp below; this prevents then being washed away by the tide.

vivisection literally, cutting into a living animal. Used originally to mean experimental surgery or dissection practised on a live subject, it is now often used by ◊anti-vivisection campaigners to include any experiment on animals, surgical or otherwise.

viz abbreviation for *videlicet* (Latin 'that is to say', 'namely').

Vladimir I St 956–1015. Russian saint and grand duke of Kiev. Converted to Christianity 988, he married Anna, Christian sister of the Byzantine emperor ◊Basil II, and established Orthodox Christianity as the Russian national faith. Feast day 15 Jul.

Vladivostok port (naval and commercial) in E Siberian Russia at the Amur Bay on the Pacific coast; population (1987) 615,000. It is kept open by ice-breakers during winter. Industries include shipbuilding, and the manufacture of precision instruments.

Vlaminck Maurice de 1876–1958. French painter, who began painting in brilliant colour as an early member of the Fauves, mainly painting landscapes. Later he abandoned Fauve colour. He also wrote poetry, novels, and essays.

VLSI *very large-scale integration* the current level of advanced technology in the microminiaturization of ◊integrated circuits, and an order of magnitude smaller than ◊LSI.

vocal cords folds of tissue within a mammal's larynx, and a bird's syrinx. Air passing over them makes them vibrate, producing sounds. Muscles in the larynx change the pitch of the sound by adjusting the tension of the vocal cords.

vocational education education relevant to a specific job or career and referring to medical and legal education in the universities as well as further education courses in craft skills.

vocative in the grammar of certain inflected languages, for example, Latin, the form of a word, especially a name, that is used to indicate that a person or thing is being addressed.

vodka a strong colourless alcoholic liquor distilled from rye, potatoes, maize, or barley.

volcanic rock ◊igneous rock formed at the surface of the Earth. It is usually fine-grained unlike other types of igneous rocks such as plutonic rocks. Basalt and andesite are the main types of volcanic rock.

volcano vent in the Earth's ◊crust from which molten rock, lava, ashes, and gases are ejected. Usually it is cone-shaped with a pit-like opening at the top called the crater. Some volcanoes, for example Stromboli and Vesuvius in Italy, eject the material with explosive violence; others are quiet

volcanoes

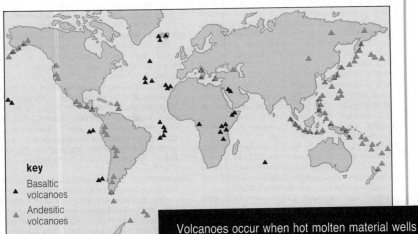

key

▲ Basaltic volcanoes

▲ Andesitic volcanoes

Andesitic volcanoes are found where areas of the Earth's surface are being pushed together. They take their name from the Andes mountains in South America. Basaltic volcanoes form where areas of the Earth's surface are pulling apart, and usually erupt from the ocean floor.

Volcanoes occur when hot molten material wells up from the interior of the Earth. The molten material is generated by the movements of plate tectonics and is known as lava when it appears at the surface. The volcanic mountain is formed by the build-up of solidified lava and ash around the vent or crack in the Earth's surface.

andesitic formation

ash and dust

built on contorted mountain rock layers

steep sides

thick, slow lava

There are two main types of volcano. The more violent is the andesitic volcano which is typical of island arcs and coastal mountain chains. The molten rock is mostly derived from plate material and is rich in silica. This makes it very stiff and it solidifies to form high, steep-sided volcanic mountains.

The stiff lava of an andesitic volcano often clogs the volcanic vent. Eruptions can be violent as the blockage is blasted free, as in the eruption of Mount Saint Helens in North America in 1980.

The black silica-poor lava from a basaltic volcano, such as those in Hawaii or Iceland, often forms wrinkled ropy surfaces before it sets.

The quieter type of volcano is the basaltic type which is found along rift valleys and ocean ridges, and also over 'hot spots' beneath the Earth's crust. The molten material is derived from the Earth's mantle and is quite runny. It flows for some distance over the surface before it sets and so forms broad low volcanoes.

basaltic formation

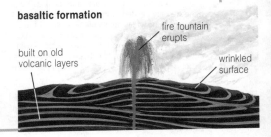

fire fountain erupts

built on old volcanic layers

wrinkled surface

volcano *Kilauea volcano, Hawaii 1983.*

and the lava rises up into the crater and flows over the rim; and some may be quiescent for long periods.

vole rodent of the family Cricetidae, distributed over Europe, Asia, and North America, and related to hamsters and lemmings. They have brown or grey fur, blunt noses, and some species reach a length of 30 cm/2 ft. They feed on grasses, seeds, aquatic plants, and insects.

Volga longest river in Europe; 3,685 km/2,290 mi, 3,540 km/2,200 mi of which are navigable. It drains most of the central and eastern parts of European Russia, rises in the Valdai plateau and flows into the Caspian Sea 88 km/55 mi below Astrakhan.

Volgograd formerly (until 1925) Tsaritsyn and (1925–61) Stalingrad industrial city (metal goods, machinery, sawmills, oil refining) in SW Russia, on the river Volga; population (1987) 988,000.

Völkerwanderung (German 'nations wandering') the migration of tribes, usually with reference to Slavic and Germanic movement in Europe 2nd–11th centuries AD.

Volkswagen 'the people's car'. The original VW, with its distinctive beetle shape, was produced in Germany 1938, a design of Ferdinand ◊Porsche. It was still in production in Latin America in the late 1980s, by which time it had exceeded 20 million sales.

volleyball an indoor team game played on a court between two teams of six players each. A net is placed across the centre of the court, and players hit the ball with their hands over it, the aim being to ground it in the opponents' court.

volt in physics, unit of potential difference, electromotive force, or electric potential. When 1 coulomb of electric charge generates 1 joule of energy (in c.g.s units, when the current is 1 amp and the power dissipated 1 watt) between two points in an electrical circuit, the potential difference between them is 1 volt.

Volta main river in Ghana, about 1,600 km/1,000 mi long, with two main upper branches, the Black and White Volta.

Volta, Upper name until 1984 of ◊Burkina Faso.

Volta Alessandro 1745–1827. Italian physicist. He invented the voltaic pile (the first battery), the electrophorus (an early electrostatic generator), and an ◊electroscope.

Voltaire Pen name of François-Marie Arouet 1694–1778. French writer, who believed in ◊deism, and devoted himself to tolerance, justice, and humanity. He was threatened with arrest for *Lettres philosophiques sur les anglais/Philosophical Letters on the English* 1733, a panegyric of English ways, thought, and political practice, and had to take refuge. Other writings include *Le Siècle de Louis*

Voltaire *French writer and philosopher Voltaire.*

XIV/The Age of Louis XIV 1751; *Candide* 1759, a parody on ◊Leibniz's 'best of all possible worlds'; and *Dictionnaire Philosophique* 1764.

voltmeter instrument for measuring potential difference (voltage). It has a high internal resistance (so that it passes only a small current), such as a sensitive moving-coil ◊galvanometer in series with a high-value resistor. To measure an alternating voltage, the circuit also includes a rectifier. A moving-iron instrument can be used to measure AC (◊alternating current) voltages without the need for a rectifier.

volume in geometry, the space occupied by a three-dimensional solid object. A cube, cuboid, other prismatic figure, or cylinder has a volume equal to the area of the base multiplied by the height. For a pyramid or cone, the volume is equal to one-third of the area of the base multiplied by the perpendicular height. The volume of a sphere is equal to $\frac{4}{3}\pi r^3$. Volumes of irregular solids may be calculated by the technique of ◊integration.

vomiting the expulsion of the contents of the stomach through the mouth. It may have very many causes, including direct irritation of the stomach, severe pain, dizziness, and emotion. Sustained or repeated vomiting is always a serious symptom, both because it may indicate serious disease, and because dangerous loss of water, salt, and acid may result.

von Braun Wernher 1912–1977. German rocket engineer, who developed German military rockets (V1 and V2) during World War II, and later worked for ◊NASA in the USA.

Vonnegut Kurt, Jr 1922– . US writer, whose work generally has a fantasy element; his novels include *The Sirens of Titan* 1958, *Cat's Cradle* 1963, *Slaughterhouse-Five* 1969, which draws on his World War II experience of the fire-bombing of Dresden, Germany, and *Galapagos* 1985.

voodoo a set of magical beliefs and practices, followed in some parts of Africa and the West Indies, especially Haiti. It arose in the 17th century on slave plantations as a combination of Roman Catholicism and W African religious traditions; believers retain membership in the Roman Catholic church. Beliefs include the existence of *loas*, spirits who involve themselves in human affairs, and who are invoked alongside Christian saints by the priest or priestess at ceremonies, during which loas take possession of the worshippers, and can be identified by the characteristic behaviour of the possessed person.

Voroshilov Klement Efremovich 1881–1969. Marshal of the USSR. He joined the Bolsheviks 1903 and was arrested many times and exiled, but escaped. He became a member of the central committee 1921, commissar for war 1925, member of the

Politburo 1926, marshal 1935. He was removed as commissar 1940 after defeats on the Finland front. He was a member of the committee for defense 1941–44, and president of the Presidium of the USSR 1953–60.

Vorster Balthazar Johannes 1915–1983. South African Nationalist politician, prime minister 1966–78, in succession to Verwoerd, and president 1978–79. During his premiership some elements of apartheid were allowed to lapse, and attempts were made to improve relations with the outside world. He resigned when it was discovered that the Department of Information had made unauthorized use of public funds during his premiership.

Vorticism a short-lived movement in British painting, begun 1913 by Wyndham ◊Lewis. Influenced by Cubism and Futurism, he believed that painting should reflect the complexity and pace of the modern world. It was the first organized movement towards abstraction in British art.

Voskhod (Russian 'ascent') a Soviet spacecraft used in the mid-1960s, modified from the single-seat Vostok, capable of carrying two or three cosmonauts. During the During the second Voskhod flight 1965, Alexei Leonov made the first space walk.

Vostok (Russian 'east') the first Soviet spacecraft, capable of carrying one cosmonaut, used 1961–63, which made flights lasting up to five days. Vostok was a metal sphere 2.3 m/7.5 ft in diameter.

vote expression of opinion by ballot, show of hands, or other means. For direct vote, see ◊plebiscite and ◊referendum. In parliamentary elections the results can be calculated in a number of ways. The main electoral systems are:

first past the post, with single-member constituencies in which the candidate with most votes wins (UK, Canada, USA);

◊proportional representation (PR), in which seats are shared by parties according to their share of the vote;

preferential vote, in which the voter indicates first and second choices either by **alternative vote** (AV), in which, if no candidate achieves over 50% of the votes, voters' second choices are successively transferred from the least successful candidates until one candidate does achieve 50% (Australia); or by **second ballot**, when no candidate has an absolute majority on the first count (France).

Voyager probes two US space probes, originally ◊Mariners. Voyager 1, launched 5 Sep 1977, passed Jupiter Mar 1979, and reached Saturn Nov 1980. Voyager 2 was launched earlier, 20 Aug 1977, on a slower trajectory that took it past Jupiter Jul 1979 and Saturn Aug 1981; it then flew past Uranus Jan 1986, and Neptune Aug 1989. Both Voyagers will ultimately leave the Solar System, and both carry long-playing records called 'Sounds of Earth' for the enlightenment of any other civilizations that might find them. See also ◊Pioneer.

Voysey Charles Francis Annesley 1857–1941. English architect and designer. He designed country houses which were characteristically asymmetrical with massive buttresses, long sloping roofs, and rough-cast walls. He is also noted for textile and wallpaper design.

Vries Hugo de 1848–1935. Dutch botanist, who con-

vulture

ducted important research on osmosis in plant cells and was a pioneer in the study of plant evolution. His work led to the rediscovery of ◊Mendel's laws and the formulation of the theory of mutation.

Vuillard (Jean) Edouard 1886–1940. French painter and printmaker, a founder member of **Les ◊Nabis**. His work is mainly decorative, with an emphasis on surface pattern reflecting the influence of Japanese prints. With Bonnard he produced numerous lithographs and paintings of simple domestic interiors, works that are generally categorized as *intimiste*.

Vulcan in Roman mythology, the god of fire and destruction, later identified with the Greek god ◊Hephaestus.

vulcanization technique for hardening ◊rubber by heating it with, and chemically combining it with, sulphur. The process also makes the rubber stronger and more elastic. If the sulphur content is increased to as much as 30%, the product is the inelastic solid known as ebonite. More expensive alternatives to sulphur, such as selenium and telurium, are used to vulcanize rubber for specialized products such as vehicle tyres. The process was discovered accidentally by US inventor Charles ◊Goodyear 1839.

vulcanology study of ◊volcanoes and the geological phenomena that cause them.

Vulgate the Latin translation of the Bible, mostly by St Jerome 4th century, so called because of its vulgar (common) use in the Roman Catholic Church.

Vulpecula small constellation in the northern hemisphere of the sky, in the shape of a fox. It contains a major planetary ◊nebula (interstellar gas and dust), the Dumb-bell, and the first ◊pulsar (pulsating radio source) to be discovered.

vulture a carrion-eating bird with keen senses of sight and smell. It is up to 1 m/3.3 ft long, with a wingspan of up to 3.5 m/11.5 ft. It has a bare head and neck, shaggy black or brown plumage, and hooked beak and claws. True vultures occur only in the Old World; the New World forms include the ◊condor and turkey buzzard.

Vyshinsky Andrei 1883–1954. Soviet politician. As commissar for justice he acted as prosecutor at the treason trials 1936–38. He was foreign minister 1949–53, and often represented the USSR at the United Nations.

Maori recognition of British right to govern. The treaty lapsed from 1877 until 1975, when the Treaty of Waitangi Act enshrined its principles in law.

Wajda Andrzej 1926– . Polish film director, one of the major figures in postwar European cinema. His films deal with the predicament of individuals caught up in political events. His works include *Ashes and Diamonds* 1958, *Man of Marble* 1977 and *Danton* 1982.

Wakhan Salient narrow strip of territory in Afghanistan bordered by Tajikistan, China, and Pakistan. It was effectively annexed by the USSR in 1980 to halt alleged arms supplies to Afghan guerrillas from China and Pakistan.

Waksman Selman Abraham 1888–1973. US biochemist, born in the Ukraine. He coined the word 'antibiotic' for bacteria-killing chemicals derived from microorganisms, and won the 1952 Nobel prize for the discovery of streptomycin.

Waldemar or *Valdemar* four kings of Denmark including:

Waldemar I *the Great* 1131–1182. King of Denmark from 1157, who defeated rival claimants to the throne, and overcame the Wends on the Baltic island of Rügen in 1169.

Waldemar II *the Conqueror* 1170–1241. King of Denmark from 1202. He was the second son of Waldemar I, and succeeded his brother Canute VI. He gained control of land N of the river Elbe (which he later lost), as well as much of Estonia, and he completed the codification of Danish law.

Waldemar IV 1320–1375. King of Denmark from 1340, responsible for reuniting his country by capturing Skåne (S Sweden) and the island of Gotland in 1361. However, the resulting conflict with the Hanseatic League led to defeat by them, and in 1370 he was forced to submit to the Peace of Stralsund.

Waldenses (also known as *Waldensians or Vaudois*) Protestant religious sect, founded *c.* 1170 by Peter Waldo, a merchant of Lyons. They were allied to the ◊Albigenses. They lived in voluntary poverty, refused to take oaths or take part in war, and later rejected the doctrines of transubstantiation, purgatory, and the invocation of saints. Although subjected to persecution until the 17th century, they spread in France, Germany, and Italy, and still survive in Piedmont.

Waldheim Kurt 1918– . Austrian politician and diplomat. He was secretary general of the United Nations 1972–81, having been Austria's representative there 1964–68 and 1970–71. In 1986 he was elected president of Austria, but his tenure of office

wadi in Arab countries, an irrigation canal, normally dry except in the rainy season.

Wafd the main Egyptian nationalist party between World Wars I and II. Under Nahas Pasha it formed a number of governments in the 1920s and 1930s. Dismissed by King Farouk in 1938, it was reinstated by the British in 1941. The party's pro-British stance weakened its claim to lead the nationalist movement and the party was again dismissed by Farouk in 1952, shortly before his own deposition. Wafd was banned in Jan 1953.

wafer in microelectronics, a 'super-chip' some 8–10 cm/3–4 in in diameter, for which wafer-scale integration (WSI) is used to link the equivalent of many individual ◊silicon chips, improving on reliability, speed, and cooling.

Wagner Otto 1841–1918. Viennese architect. Initially designing in the Art Nouveau style, for example Vienna Stadtbahn 1894–97, he later rejected ornament for rationalism, as in the Post Office Savings Bank, Vienna, 1904–06. He influenced Viennese architects such as Josef Hoffmann and Adolf Loos.

Wagner Richard 1813–1883. German opera composer. He revolutionized the 19th-century conception of opera, envisaging it as a wholly new art form in which musical, poetic and scenic elements should be unified; and through such devices as the *Leitmotiv*. His early operas include *Tännhauser*, and *Lohengrin* (produced by ◊Liszt in Weimar in 1850). He fled Germany to escape arrest for his part in the 1848 revolution but in 1861 was allowed to return, and in 1872 he founded the festival theatre in Bayreuth. His masterpiece *Der Ring des Nibelungen/The Ring of the Nibelung*, a sequence of four operas, was first performed there in 1876.

Wagram, Battle of battle in Jul 1809 when the French emperor Napoleon defeated the Austrians under Archduke Charles.

wagtail slim narrow-billed bird *Motacilla*, about 18 cm/7 in long, with a characteristic flicking movement of the tail. There are about 30 species, mostly in Eurasia and Africa.

Wahabi the purist Saudi Islamic sect founded by Muhammad ibn-Abd-al-Wahab (1703–92), which regards all other sects as heresies and whose followers are liable to the death penalty.

Waitangi Treaty New Zealand treaty between the Maoris and white settlers, signed in 1840, in which the British granted the Maoris rights over their lands, villages, forests and fisheries, in return for

Wagner *German composer Richard Wagner.*

Wales: Counties

	Administrative headquarters	Area sq km
Clwyd	Mold	2,424
Dyfed	Carmarthen	5,767
Mid-Glamorgan	Cardiff	1,019
South Glamorgan	Cardiff	416
West Glamorgan	Swansea	815
Gwent	Cwmbran	1,377
Gwynedd	Caernarvon	3,865
Powys	Llandrindod Wells	5,079
		20,762

was clouded by allegations that during World War II he had been an intelligence officer in an army unit responsible for transporting Jews to death camps. His election led to some diplomatic isolation of Austria, and he announced 1991 that he would not run for reelection.

Wales (Welsh *Cymru*) Principality of
area 20,762 sq km/8,030 sq mi
capital Cardiff
towns Swansea, Newport, Carmarthen
exports traditional industries (coal and steel) have declined, but varied modern and high-technology ventures are being developed: Wales has the largest concentration of Japanese-owned plant in the UK. It also has the highest density of sheep in the world and a dairy industry; tourism is important
currency pound sterling
population (1991) 2,835,073
language English; Welsh-speaking 19% (1991)
religion Nonconformist Protestant denominations; Roman Catholic minority
government returns 38 members to the British Parliament
chronology
c. 200 AD The Celts of Wales became Christian.
c. 450–600 Wales became chief Celtic stronghold to the W as a result of the Saxon invasions of S Britain.
8th century Frontier pushed back to ◊Offa's Dyke.
9th–11th centuries Vikings raided the coasts. At this time Wales was divided into small states organized on a clan basis, although princes such as Rhodri (844–78), Howel the Good (*c.* 904–49), and Griffith ap Llewelyn (1039–63) temporarily united the country.
11th–12th centuries Continual pressure from across the English border (resisted notably by ◊Llewelyn I and II).
1277 Edward I of England accepted as overlord.
c. 1350–1400 Nationalist uprisings against the English, the most notable of which were led by Owen ◊Glendower 1400–02.
1535 Act of Union united Wales with England.
18th century Evangelical revival made Nonconformity a powerful factor in Welsh life. A strong coal and iron industry developed in the S.
19th century The miners and ironworkers were militant supporters of Chartism, and Wales became a stronghold of trade unionism and socialism.
1893 University of Wales founded.
1920s–30s Wales suffered from industrial depression; unemployment reached 21% in 1937, and a considerable exodus of population took place.
post-1945 Growing nationalist movement and a revival of the language, earlier suppressed or discouraged (there is a Welsh television channel).
1966 ◊Plaid Cymru, the Welsh National Party, returned its first member to Westminster.
Wales, Prince of title conferred on the eldest son of Great Britain's sovereign. Prince ◊Charles was

Walesa Polish trade unionist and leader of Solidarity, Lech Walesa was elected president in Dec 1990.

invested as 21st prince of Wales at Caernavon in 1969 by his mother, Elizabeth II.

Walesa Lech 1943– . Polish president from 1990. Trade-union leader, founder of ◊Solidarity 1980, an organization, independent of the Communist Party, which forced substantial political and economic concessions from the Polish government during 1980–81. Nobel Peace Prize 1983.

Wales, Church in the Welsh Anglican Church, independent from the ◊Church of England.

Waley Arthur 1889–1966. British orientalist, who translated from both Japanese and Chinese, including such works as the Japanese classics *The Tale of Genji* 1925–33 and *The Pillow-book of Sei Shonagon* 1928, and the 16th-century Chinese novel *Monkey* 1942.

walkabout word used by European settlers in Australia for the Aborigines' nomadic ritual excursion into the bush. The term was adopted in 1970, during tours of Australia and New Zealand by Elizabeth II, for informal public-relations walks by politicians and royalty.

Walker Alice 1944– . US poet, novelist, critic, and essay writer. She was active in the civil-rights movement in the USA in the 1960s, and as a black woman has written about the double burden for women of racist and sexist oppression. Her novel *The Color Purple* 1983 won the Pulitzer Prize.

Walker Peter (Edward) 1932– . British Conservative politician, energy secretary 1983–87, secretary of state for Wales 1987–90.

Walker William 1824–1860. US adventurer who for a short time established himself as president of a republic in NW Mexico, and was briefly president of Nicaragua 1856–57, but was eventually executed. He is regarded as the symbol of US imperialism in Central America.

wallaby name for several small members of the ◊kangaroo family.

Wallace Lewis 1827–1905. US general and novelist. He served in the Mexican and Civil wars, and subsequently became governor of New Mexico and minister to Turkey. He wrote the historical novel *Ben Hur* 1880.

Wallace Alfred Russel 1823–1913. British naturalist who collected animal and plant specimens in South

walnut

walrus

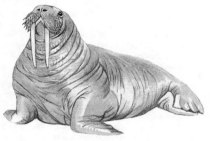

America and the Far East, and independently arrived at a theory of evolution by ◊natural selection similar to that of Charles Darwin.

Wallace Edgar 1875–1932. British writer of thrillers. His prolific output includes *The Four Just Men* 1905; a series set in Africa and including *Sanders of the River* 1911; crime novels such as *A King by Night* 1926; and melodramas such as *The Ringer* 1926.

Wallace George 1919– . US right-wing politician, governor of Alabama 1962–66. He contested the presidency in 1968 as an independent, and in 1972 campaigned for the Democratic nomination, but was shot at a rally and became partly paralysed.

Wallace William 1272–1305. Scottish nationalist who led a revolt against English rule in 1297, won a victory at Stirling, and assumed the title 'governor of Scotland'. Edward I defeated him at Falkirk in 1298, and Wallace was captured and executed.

Wallace line an imaginary line running down the Lombok Strait in SE Asia, between the island of Bali and the islands of Lombok and Sulawesi. It was identified by the naturalist A R Wallace as separating the Asian and Australian biogeographical regions, each of which has its own distinctive animals.

Wallachia independent medieval principality, under Turkish rule 1387–1861, when it was united with Moldavia to form Romania.

Wallenstein Albrecht Eusebius Wenzel von 1583–1634. German general who, until his defeat at Lützen in 1632, led the Hapsburg armies in the Thirty Years' War. He was assassinated in 1634.

Wallis Barnes (Neville) 1887–1979. British aeronautical engineer who designed the airship R-100 and perfected the 'bouncing bombs' used against the German Möhne and Eder dams in 1943 by the Royal Air Force Dambusters Squadron. He also assisted the development of the Concorde supersonic airliner, and developed the swing-wing aircraft.

Walloon member of a French-speaking people of SE Belgium, and adjacent areas of France.

Wall Street street in Manhattan, New York, on which the stock exchange is situated, and a synonym for stock dealing in the USA. It is so called from a stockade erected 1653.

walnut tree *Juglans regia*, probably originating in SE Europe. It can reach 30 m/100 ft, and produces a full crop of nuts about a dozen years from planting; the timber is used in furniture making.

Walpole Horace, 4th Earl of Orford 1717–1797. English novelist and politician, the son of Robert Walpole. He was a Whig member of parliament 1741–67. He converted his house at Strawberry Hill, Twickenham, into a Gothic castle; his *The Castle of Otranto* 1764 established the genre of the ◊gothic novel.

Walpole Hugh 1884–1941. British novelist, born in New Zealand. His books include *The Cathedral* 1922 and *The Old Ladies* 1924. He also wrote the historical 'Lakeland Saga' of the *Herries Chronicle* 1930–33.

Walpole Robert, 1st Earl of Orford 1676–1745. British Whig politician, the first 'prime minister' as 1st Lord of the Treasury and chancellor of the Exchequer 1715–17 and 1721–42. He managed Parliament, encouraged trade by his pacific foreign policy (until forced into the War of Jenkins's Ear with Spain in 1739), and received an earldom when he eventually retired in 1742. His son was the writer Horace Walpole.

Walpurga, St English nun who preached Christianity in Germany. *Walpurgis Night* the night before 1 May, one of her feast days, was formerly associated with witches' sabbaths. Her main feast day is 25 Feb.

walrus seal-like marine mammal *Odobenus rosmarus* of the Arctic. It can reach 4 m/13 ft in length, and weigh up to 1,400 kg/3,000 lb. It has webbed flippers, a bristly moustache, and large tusks. It is gregarious except at breeding time, and feeds mainly on shellfish. It has been hunted close to extinction for its ivory tusks, hide, and blubber.

Walsingham Francis c. 1530–1590. English politician who, as secretary of state from 1573, both advocated a strong anti-Spanish policy and ran the efficient government spy system that made it work.

Walter Lucy c. 1630–1658. Mistress of ◊Charles II, whom she met while a Royalist refugee at The Hague in 1648; the Duke of ◊Monmouth was their son.

Walther von der Vogelweide c. 1170–c. 1230. German poet, greatest of the ◊Minnesingers. Of noble birth, he lived in his youth at the Austrian ducal court in Vienna, adopting a wandering life after the death of his patron in 1198. His lyrics deal mostly with love, but also with religion and politics.

Walton Izaak 1593–1683. English author of the classic *Compleat Angler* 1653. He was born in Stafford, and settled in London as an ironmonger. He also wrote short biographies of the poets George Herbert and John Donne, and the theologian Richard Hooker.

Walton William (Turner) 1902–1983. British composer. His music is tonal, harmonically rich, often sensuous and energetic. Among his works are *Façade* 1923 a series of instrumental pieces designed to be played in conjunction with the recitation of poems by Edith Sitwell, a viola concerto

1929; the oratorio *Belshazzar's Feast* 1931; two symphonies 1935; a violin concerto 1939; a sonata for violin and pianoforte 1950 and *Variations on a Theme by Hindemith* 1963.

waltz a ballroom dance in three-four time evolving from the Austrian *Ländler* (traditional peasants' country dance), and later made popular by the ◊Strauss family in Vienna.

Wandering Jew in medieval legend, a Jew (named Ahasuerus) said to have induced Christ on his way to Calvary, and been condemned to wander the world till the second coming.

Wankel engine a rotary petrol engine developed by the German engineer Felix Wankel (born 1902) in the 1950s. It operates according to the same stages as the ◊four-stroke petrol engine cycle, but these stages take place in different sectors of a figure-of-eight chamber in the space between the chamber walls and a triangular rotor. Power is produced once on every turn on the rotor. The Wankel engine is simpler in construction than the normal piston petrol engine, and produces rotary power directly (instead of via a crankshaft). Problems with rotor seals have prevented its widespread use.

wapiti or **elk** species of deer *Cervus canadensis*, native to North America, Europe, and Asia. It is reddish-brown in colour, about 1.5 m/5 ft at the shoulder, weighs up to 450 kg/1,000 lb, and has antlers up to 1.2 m/4 ft long. It is becoming increasingly rare.

war an act of force, usually on behalf of the state, intended to compel a declared enemy to obey the will of the other. The aim is to render the opponent incapable of further resistance by destroying his capability and will to bear arms in pursuit of his own aims. War is therefore a continuation of political intercourse carried on with other means, or as an instrument of policy.

waratah Australian shrub or tree, of the family Proteaceae, especially the crimson-flowered *Telopea speciosissima*, emblem of New South Wales.

Warbeck Perkin *c.* 1474–1499. Flemish pretender to the English throne. Claiming to be Richard, brother of Edward V, he led a rising against Henry VII in 1497, and was hanged after attempting to escape from the Tower of London.

War Between the States, the another (usually Southern) name for the ◊American Civil War 1861–65 (but now seldom used in standard histories).

warbler family of songbirds, order Passeriformes. The Old World birds are drab-coloured, and the New World birds are brightly plumed in the spring. They are up to 25 cm/10 in long, and feed on berries and insects.

war crime act (such as murder of a civilian or a prisoner of war) that contravenes the internationally agreed laws governing the conduct of wars, particularly the Hague Convention 1907 and the Geneva Convention 1949. Nazi war criminals were tried after World War II at the ◊Nuremberg Trials.

Ward Mrs Humphry (born Mary Augusta Arnold) 1851–1920. British novelist, who wrote serious didactic books, such as *Robert Elsmere* 1888, a study of religious doubt. She was an opponent of women's emancipation.

warfarin an anticoagulant which works by inhibiting the action of vitamin K. It can be taken by mouth and begins to act several days after the initial dose.

Warhol Andy 1928–1987. US pop artist and filmmaker. He made his name in 1962 with paintings of Campbell's soup tins, Coca-Cola bottles, and

wart hog

dollar bills. His films include the semi-documentary *Chelsea Girls* 1966 and *Trash* 1970. In the 1970s and 1980s he was primarily a society portraitist, although his activities remained diverse.

warlord in China, any of the local leaders in the provinces who, between 1916 and 1928, took advantage of central government weakness to organize their own private armies and fiefdoms.

warning coloration in biology, an alternative term for ◊aposematic coloration.

War of 1812, the a war between the USA and Britain caused by British interference with American trade as part of the economic warfare against Napoleonic France. US forces failed twice to invade Canada, but achieved important naval victories, while in 1814 British forces occupied Washington DC and burned many public buildings. A treaty signed at Ghent in Dec 1814 ended the conflict.

War Office former British government department controlling military affairs. The Board of Ordnance, which existed in the 14th century, was absorbed into the War Department after the Crimean War and the whole named the War Office. In 1964 its core became a subordinate branch of the newly established *Ministry of Defence*.

War Powers Act legislation passed 1973 enabling the US president to deploy US forces abroad for combat without prior Congressional approval. The president is nevertheless required to report to both Houses of Congress within 48 hours of having taken such action. Congress may in turn restrict the continuation of troop deployment despite any presidential veto.

warrant officer rank between commissioned and senior noncommissioned officer (SNCO) in the British army, and the highest noncommissioned rank in ground trades of the Royal Air Force and the RAF regiment.

Warren Earl 1891–1974. US jurist and politician. As Chief Justice of the US Supreme Court 1953–69 he took a stand against racial discrimination, ruling that segregation in schools was unconstitutional. He headed the commission that investigated President Kennedy's assassination 1964 which made the controversial finding that Lee Harvey Oswald acted alone.

Warsaw (Polish *Warszawa*) capital of Poland, on the river Vistula; population (1985) 1,649,000. Industries include engineering, food processing, printing, clothing, and pharmaceuticals.

Warsaw Pact military alliance established in 1955 between the USSR and E European communist states as a response to the admission of West Germany into NATO.

warship a fighting ship armed and crewed for war. The supremacy of the battleship at the beginning of the 20th century was superseded during World War I by the development of ◊submarine attack,

Washington US educationist Booker T Washington.

Washington George Washington, first president of the newly independent USA.

and was rendered obsolete in World War II with the growth of long-range air attack. ◊Aircraft carriers and submarines are now considered the most important warships.

wart protuberance composed of a local overgrowth of skin. The common wart (*verruca vulgaris*) is due to a virus infection, and usually disappears spontaneously within two years, but can be treated with peeling applications, burning away (cautery) or freezing (cryosurgery).

wart hog species of African wild pig *Phacochoerus aethiopicus* which has a large head with a bristly mane, fleshy pads beneath the eyes, and four large tusks. It has short legs, and can grow to 75 cm/2.5 ft at the shoulder.

Warwick Richard Neville, Earl of Warwick 1428–1471. English politician, called the King-maker. During the Wars of the ◊Roses he fought at first on the Yorkist side, and was largely responsible for placing Edward IV on the throne. Having quarrelled with him, he restored Henry VI in 1470, but was defeated and killed by Edward at Barnet, Hertfordshire.

Warwickshire county in central England
area 1,981 sq km/765 sq mi
towns administrative headquarters Warwick; Leamington, Nuneaton, Rugby, Stratford-upon-Avon
products mainly agricultural, engineering, textiles
population (1986) 479,700
famous people George Eliot, William Shakespeare.

Washington state of the NW USA; nickname Evergreen State
area 176,615 sq km/68,191 sq mi
capital Olympia
towns Seattle, Spokane, Tacoma
products apples, cereals, livestock, processed food, timber, chemicals, cement, zinc, uranium, lead, gold, silver, aircraft, ships, road transport vehicles
population (1983) 4,300,000, including 61,000 Indians, mainly of the Yakima people
famous people Bing Crosby, Jimi Hendrix, Frances Farmer.

Washington Booker T(aliaferro) 1856–1915. US educationist, pioneer in higher education for black people in the southern USA. He was the founder and first principal of Tuskegee Institute, Alabama, in 1881, originally a training college for blacks, which became a respected academic institution. He maintained that economic independence was the way for blacks to achieve social equality.

Washington George 1732–1799. First president of the USA 1789–97. As a strong opponent of the British government's policy, he sat in the ◊Continental Congresses of 1774 and 1775, and on the outbreak of the War of ◊American Independence was chosen commander in chief. After the war he retired to his Virginia estate, Mount Vernon, but in 1787 he re-entered politics as president of the Constitutional Convention. Although he attempted to draw his ministers from all factions, his aristocratic outlook alienated his secretary of state, Thomas Jefferson, with whose resignation in 1793 the two-party system originated.

Washington Convention an alternative name for ◊*CITES*, the international agreement which regulates trade in endangered species.

Washington DC (District of Columbia) national capital of the USA, on the Potomac river.
area 178 sq km/68.7 sq mi
capital the District of Columbia covers only the area of the city of Washington
population (1983) 623,000 (metropolitan area, extending outside the District of Columbia, 3 million)
history the District of Columbia, initially land ceded from Maryland and Virginia, was established by Act of Congress 1790–91, and was first used as the seat of Congress 1800. The right to vote in national elections was not granted to residents until 1961.

Wash, the bay of the North Sea between Norfolk and Lincolnshire, England.

wasp stinging insect of the order Hymenoptera, characterized by a thin join between the thorax and the abdomen. Wasps can be social or solitary. Among social wasps, the queens devote themselves

Washington DC The Capitol, Washington DC, national capital of the USA.

wasp

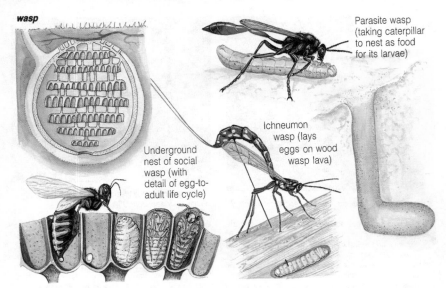

Parasite wasp (taking caterpillar to nest as food for its larvae)

Underground nest of social wasp (with detail of egg-to-adult life cycle)

Ichneumon wasp (lays eggs on wood wasp lava)

to egg-laying, the fertilized eggs producing female workers; the males arise from unfertilized. eggs, and have no sting. The larvae are fed on insects, but the mature wasps feed mainly on fruit and sugar. In winter, the fecundated queens hibernate, but the other wasps die.

waste materials that are no longer needed and are discarded. Examples are industrial and household waste, pathological waste which may contain organisms that cause disease, and nuclear waste. By ◊recycling, some materials in waste can be reclaimed for further use.

waste disposal depositing waste. Methods of waste disposal vary according to the materials in the waste, and include incineration, burial at designated sites, and dumping at sea. Organic waste can be treated and reused as fertilizer; sewage can be recycled in this way. Nuclear and other toxic waste is usually buried or dumped at sea.

Waste Land, The a poem by T S Eliot, first published 1922. It expressed the prevalent mood of depression after World War I, and is a key work of Modernism in literature.

watch a personal portable timepiece. In the 20th century increasing miniaturization, mass production, and the need for accurate timekeeping in World War I led to the migration of the watch from the pocket to the wrist. Watches were given further refinements, such as being made antimagnetic or self-winding, or given shock resistance. In 1957 the electric watch was developed, and in the 1970s came the digital watch, in which all moving parts are dispensed with.

water (H_2O) a liquid without colour, taste, or odour. It is an oxide of hydrogen. Water begins to freeze solid at 0°C or 32°F, and to boil at 100°C or 212°F. When liquid, it is virtually incompressible; frozen, it expands by $\frac{1}{11}$ of its volume. 1 cubic cm weighs 1 gram at 4°C, its maximum density, forming the unit of specific gravity. It has the highest known specific heat, and acts as an efficient solvent, particularly when hot.

water boatman water bug of the family Corixidae that feeds on plant debris and algae. It has a flattened body 1.5 cm/0.6 in long, with oar-like legs. The name is also for the backswimmers,

genus *Notecta*, which are superficially similar.

waterbuck African antelope *Kobus ellipsiprymnus* with characteristic white ring marking on the rump. It is about 2 m/6 ft long and 1.4 m/4.5 ft at the shoulder, and has long, coarse, brown fur. The males have big horns with corrugated surfaces.

water closet (WC) flushing lavatory which works by siphon action. The first widely used WC was produced in the 1770s by Alexander Cummings in London. The modern type dates from Davis Bostel's invention of 1889, which featured a ballcock valve system to refill the flushing cistern.

watercolour painting method of painting with pigments mixed with water, known in China as

wasp *Head of a hornet showing the biting mouthparts, large compound eyes, and branched antennae.*

early as the 3rd century. The art as practised today began in England with the work of Paul Sandby (1725–1809). Other excellent watercolourists were Turner, Cézanne, and Paul Nash.

watercress perennial aquatic plant *Nasturtium officinale*, found in Europe and Asia, and cultivated as a salad crop. It requires 4.5 million litres/1 million gallons of running water daily per hectare/2.5 acres in cultivation.

water cycle in ecology, the natural circulation of water through the ◊biosphere. Water is lost from the Earth's surface to the atmosphere either by evaporation from the surface of lakes, rivers, and oceans or through the transpiration of plants. This atmospheric water forms clouds which, under the appropriate conditions, condense to deposit moisture on the land and sea as rain or snow.

waterflea any aquatic crustacean in the order Cladocera, of which there are over 400 species. The commonest species is *Daphnia pulex*.

Waterford county in Munster province, Republic of Ireland
area 1,839 sq km/710 sq mi
towns county town Waterford
physical rivers Suir and Blackwater; Comeragh and Monavallagh mountain ranges in the N and centre
products cattle, beer, whiskey, glassware
population (1981) 89,000.

waterfowl order of birds, Anseriformes, which includes ducks, geese, and swans.

Watergate US political scandal, named after the building in Washington DC that housed the Democrats' campaign headquarters in the 1972 presidential election. Five men, hired by the Republican Committee to Re-elect the President (CREEP), were caught inside the Watergate with electronic surveillance equipment. Over the next two years, investigation by the media and a Senate committee revealed that the White House was implicated in the break-in, and that there was a 'slush fund', used to finance unethical activities. In Aug 1974, President ◊Nixon was forced to surrender to Congress tape recordings of conversations he had held with administration officials, and these indicated his complicity in a cover-up. Nixon resigned, the only president to have left office through resignation.

water glass common name for the colourless, jellylike substance sodium metasilicate (Na_2SiO_3). It dissolves readily in water to give a solution that is used for preserving eggs and fireproofing porous materials such as cloth, paper, and wood. It is also used as an adhesive for paper and card, and in the manufacture of soap and the desiccant substance silica gel.

Waterhouse Alfred 1830–1905. English architect. He was a leading exponent of Victorian Neo-Gothic using, typically, multicoloured tiles and bricks. His works include the Natural History Museum in London 1868.

water hyacinth tropical aquatic plant, *Eichhornia crassipes*, of the family Pontederiaceae. It is liable to choke waterways, but is valued as a purifier of sewage-polluted water, and is used in making methane gas, compost, concentrated protein, paper, and baskets.

water lily aquatic plant of the family Nymphaeaceae. The fleshy roots are embedded in mud and the large round leaves float on the water. The cup-shaped flowers may be white, pink, yellow, or blue.

Waterloo, Battle of battle on 18 Jun 1815 in which the British commander Wellington defeated the French emperor Napoleon near the village of

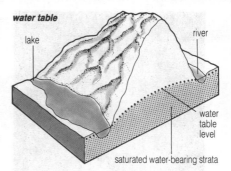

water table

lake

river

water table level

saturated water-bearing strata

Waterloo, 13 km/8 mi S of Brussels, Belgium. Wellington had 68,000 men, of whom 24,000 were British, the remainder being German, Dutch, and Belgian, and Napoleon had 72,000. During the last stage of the battle Wellington was supported by the Prussians under Gen Blücher.

watermelon a type of large ◊melon with green rind and red flesh.

water mill a machine that harnesses the energy in flowing water to produce mechanical power, typically for milling (grinding) grain. Water from a stream is directed against the paddles of a water wheel and makes it turn. Simple gearing transfers this motion to the millstones. The modern equivalent of the water wheel is the water turbine, used in ◊hydroelectric power plants.

water pollution see ◊pollution and ◊sewage disposal.

water polo a water sport developed in England in 1869, originally called 'soccer-in-water'. The Swimming Association of Great Britain recognized the game in 1885. The idea is to score goals, as in soccer, at each end of a swimming pool.

water skiing a watersport in which a person is towed across water on a ski, or skis, wider than those used for skiing on snow, by means of a rope (23 m/75 ft long) attached to a speedboat. In competitive water skiing, competitions are for overall performances, slalom, tricks, and jumping.

water softener a substance or unit that removes the hardness from water. Hardness is caused by the presence of calcium and magnesium ions, which combine with soap to form an insoluble scum and prevent lathering, and cause pipes and kettles to fur up. A water-softener replaces these ions by sodium ions, which are fully soluble and cause no scum.

water table level of ground below which the rocks are saturated with water. Thus, above a water table, water will drain downwards, and where a water table cuts the surface of the ground, a spring results. The water table usually follows surface contours, and varies with rainfall.

Watling Street a Roman road running from London to Wroxeter (*Viroconium*) near Chester, via St Albans (*Verulanium*). Its name comes from *Waetlingacaester*, the Anglo-Saxon name for St Albans.

Watson James Dewey 1928– . US biologist whose researches on the molecular structure of DNA (the genetic code), in collaboration with Francis ◊Crick, earned him a shared Nobel Prize 1962.

Watson John B(roadus) 1878–1958. US psychologist, founder of behaviourism. He rejected introspection (observation by an individual of his or her own mental processes) and regarded psychology

Watteau Gilles and his family *(c. 1717) Wallace Collection, London.*

as the study of observable behaviour, within the scientific tradition.

Watson-Watt Robert Alexander 1892–1973. Scottish physicist who developed a forerunner of ◊radar.

watt unit of power equal to the expenditure (or consumption) of energy at a rate of 1 joule per second. In electricity, the flow of 1 amp of current through a conductor whose ends are at a potential difference of 1 volt requires 1 watt of power (watts = volts × amps). Named after the British scientist James Watt.

Watt James 1736–1819. Scottish engineer who developed the steam engine. He made ◊Newcomen's steam engine vastly more efficient by cooling the used steam in a separate condenser.

Watteau Jean-Antoine 1684–1721. French Rococo painter. He developed a new category of genre painting known as the *fête galante*, a kind of aristocratic pastoral fantasy world. One of these pictures, *The Embarkation for Cythera* 1717 (Louvre, Paris), won him membership of the French Academy.

wattle a certain species of acacia in Australia, where its fluffy golden flowers are the national emblem. Adapted to drought conditions, the tough leaves of the wattle further avoid loss of water through transpiration by turning their edges to the direct rays of the sun. Wattles are used for tanning and in fencing. *Wattle day*, a national day, is celebrated in Australia on 1 Aug or 1 Sept.

wattle and daub a method of constructing walls consisting of upright stakes bound together with withes (strong flexible shoots or twigs, usually of willow), and covered in mud or plaster. It was the usual way of building houses in the Middle Ages.

Watts G(eorge) F(rederic) 1817–1904. English painter and sculptor. He painted allegorical, biblical, and classical subjects, investing his work with a solemn morality.

Watts Isaac 1674–1748. British Nonconformist writer of hymns including 'O God, our help in ages past'.

Waugh Evelyn (Arthur St John) 1903–1966. British novelist. He made his name with social satire, for example *Decline and Fall* 1928, *Vile Bodies*

1930, and *The Loved One* 1948. A Roman Catholic convert from 1930, he developed a serious concern with such issues in *Brideshead Revisited* 1945. *The Ordeal of Gilbert Pinfold* 1957 is largely autobiographical.

wave in physics, a disturbance travelling through a medium (or space). There are two types: in a ***longitudinal wave*** (such as a ◊sound wave) the disturbance is parallel to the wave's direction of travel; in a ***tranverse wave*** (such as an ◊electromagnetic wave) it is perpendicular. The medium (for example the Earth, for seismic waves) is not permanently displaced by the passage of a wave.

wave in the oceans, the formation of a ridge or swell by wind or other causes. Freak or 'episodic' waves form under particular weather conditions at certain times of the year, travelling long distances in the Atlantic, Indian, and Pacific oceans. They are considered responsible for the sudden disappearance, without distress calls, of many ships. A ◊tsunami is a type of freak wave.

Wavell Archibald, 1st Earl Wavell 1883–1950. British field marshal in World War II, appointed commander in chief Middle East in Jul 1939. He conducted the North African war against Italy 1940–41, and achieved notable successes there as well as in Ethiopia. He was transferred as commander in chief in India in Jul 1941, and succeeded Lord Linlithgow as viceroy 1943–47.

wave power power obtained by harnessing the energy of water waves. Various schemes have been advanced since 1973, when oil prices rose dramatically and the prospect of an energy shortage became serious. Few wave power schemes have yet proved economical, and a major breakthrough will be required if wave power is ever to contribute significantly to the world's energy needs.

wax solid fatty substance of animal, vegetable, or mineral origin. The most important modern waxes are mineral waxes obtained from petroleum. They vary in hardness from the soft petroleum jelly (also called petrolatum) used in ointments to the hard paraffin wax employed for making candles and waxed paper for drinks cartons.

waxbill small African seed-eating bird, genus *Estrilda*. They grow to 15 cm/6 in long, are brown and grey with yellow, red or brown markings, and have waxy-looking red or pink beaks.

waxwing bird *Bombycilla garrulus* found in the northern hemisphere. It is about 18 cm/7 in long, and is greyish-brown above with a reddish-chestnut crest, black streak at the eye, and variegated wings. It undertakes mass migrations in some years.

wayfaring tree shrub *Viburnum lantana*, with clusters of fragrant white flowers, found on limy soils.

Wayne John 1907–1979. Stage name of US actor Marion Morrison, nicknamed 'Duke' from the name of a dog he once owned. Wayne was the archetypal western star, and his films include *Stagecoach* 1939 and *True Grit* 1969 (for which he won an Academy Award).

WCC abbreviation for *World Council of Churches*.

weapon an implement used for attack and defence, from simple clubs and bows and arrows in prehistoric times to machine guns and nuclear bombs in modern times. The first revolution in warfare came with the invention of ◊gunpowder and the development of handguns and cannons. Many other weapons now exist, such as grenades, shells, torpedoes, rockets, and guided missiles.

Wayne US film actor John Wayne in The Man Who Shot Liberty Valance, 1961.

The ultimate in explosive weapons are the atomic (fission) and hydrogen (fusion) bombs. They release the enormous energy produced when atoms split or fuse together. There are also chemical and bacteriological weapons. See ◊nuclear warfare.

weasel mammal of the family Mustelidae, which feeds mainly on mice, voles, and rats. It has a long body (20 cm/8 in, with 5 cm/2 in tail) and neck, short ears and legs, and dense fur, brownish above and white below. It is found in Eurasia, N Africa, and the Americas.

weather the day-to-day variations of meteorological and climatic conditions at a particular place. See ◊metereology and ◊climate.

weather areas divisions of the sea around the British Isles for the purpose of weather forecasting for shipping, particularly to indicate where strong and gale-force winds are expected.

weathering process by which exposed rocks are broken down by the action of rain, frost, wind, and other elements of the weather. Two types of weathering are recognized, physical and chemical. They usually occur together.

weaver any small bird of the family Ploceidae, mostly about 15 cm/6 in, which includes the house sparrow. The majority of weavers are African, a few Asian. The males use grasses to weave elaborate globular nests in bushes and trees. Males are often more brightly coloured than females.

weaving the production of ◊textile fabric by means of a loom. The basic process is the interlacing at right angles of longitudinal threads (the warp) and crosswise threads (the weft), the latter being carried across from one side of the loom to the other by a type of bobbin called the shuttle.

Webb (Martha) Beatrice (born Potter) 1858–1943 and Sidney (James), Baron Passfield 1859–1947

weaver

Webb Sidney Webb, who influenced socialist thought in Britain.

English social reformers and writers. Together they founded the London School of Economics 1895; argued for social insurance in their minority report (1909) of the Poor Law Commission, and wrote many influential books, including The History of Trade Unionism 1894. In later life Beatrice Webb wrote My Apprenticeship 1926 and Our Partnership 1948.

Webb Philip 1831–1915. English architect. He mostly designed private houses, including the Red House for William ◊Morris, and was one of the leading figures, with Richard Norman ◊Shaw and C F A ◊Voysey, in the revival of domestic English architecture in the late 19th century.

Webber Andrew Lloyd. British composer of musicals: see ◊Lloyd Webber.

weber SI unit of magnetic flux (Wb), defined as the flux that, linking a circuit of one turn, produces in it an electromotive force of 1 volt as it is reduced to zero at a uniform rate over 1 second; the equivalent of 10^8 maxwells. It is named after Wilhelm ◊Weber.

Weber Carl Maria Friedrich Ernst von 1786–1826. German composer. He became Kapellmeister at Breslau 1804–06, Prague 1813–16, and Dresden 1816. He established the romantic school of opera with Der Freischütz 1821, Euranthe 1823, and Oberon 1826; his work influenced Richard Wagner.

Weber Max 1864–1920. German sociologist, one of the founders of modern sociology. He emphasized cultural and political factors as key influences on economic development and individual behaviour.

Weber Wilhelm Eduard 1804–1891. German physicist, who studied magnetism and electricity. Working with Karl Gauss he made sensitive magnetometers to measure magnetic fields, and instruments to measure direct and alternating currents. He also built an electric telegraph. The SI unit of magnetic flux, the weber, is named after him.

Webern Anton (Friedrich Wilhelm von) 1883–1945. Austrian composer. A pupil of ◊Schoenberg, whose twelve-note technique he adopted. He wrote works of extreme brevity, for example, the oratorio Das Augenlicht 1935 and songs to words by Stefan George and Rilke.

Webster Daniel 1782–1852. US politician and orator, born in New Hampshire. He sat in the House of Representatives from 1813 and in the Senate from 1827, at first as a Federalist and later as a Whig. He was secretary of state 1841–43 and

weathering

Frost, wind, rain and sunshine all have a part to play in the gradual wearing away of the landscape. As soon as an area of rock is exposed on the surface of the Earth, it is attacked over time by the weather, which reduces it to sand and rubble. This material is carried downwards by gravity, rivers and glaciers and redeposited in low areas. Eventually it may be turned back into solid rock.

Frost shattering produces spiky peaks.

In mountainous areas the water that collects in rock cracks freezes regularly. As it does so, it expands, forcing the rocks apart.

A combination of temperature, moisture and chemical effects can wear away the outer skin of a rock. As a result it may peel off, layer by layer. This process is known as onion-skin weathering.

ice

The debris broken off the peaks by the frost piles up as slopes of scree.

Soft soil may be washed away by the rain. Where a boulder provides protection, only the surrounding soil may be washed away, leaving the boulder on a soil pedestal.

The debris produced by weathering forms the basis of soil. It can work its way downhill in a process known as soil creep, causing trees to bend and posts to lean.

The carbon dioxide in rainwater produces weak carbonic acid. This reacts with some minerals, and causes spheroidal weathering of dolerite, the opening up of cracks called grykes in limestone, and the decay of granite into china clay.

Soil creep may give rise to a stepped appearance – terracettes – on a hillside.

1850–52, and negotiated the Ashburton Treaty 1842, which fixed the Maine–Canada boundary. His celebrated 'seventh of March' speech in the Senate in 1850 helped secure a compromise on the slavery issue.

Webster John *c.* 1580–1634. English dramatist, who ranks after Shakespeare as the greatest tragedian of his time and the Jacobean whose plays are most frequently performed today. His two great plays *The White Devil* 1608 and *The Duchess of Malfi* 1614 are dark, violent tragedies obsessed with death and decay, and infused with poetic brilliance.

Webster Noah 1758–1843. US lexicographer, whose books on grammar and spelling and *American Dictionary of the English Language* 1828 standardized American English.

Weddell Sea an arm of the S Atlantic Ocean that cuts into the Antarctic continent SE of Cape Horn; area 8,000,000 sq km/3,000,000 sq mi. Much of it is covered with thick pack ice for most of the year. It is named after the British explorer James Weddell (1787–1834).

Wedekind Frank 1864–1918. German dramatist. He was a forerunner of expressionism with *Frühlings Erwachen/The Awakening of Spring* 1891, and *Der Erdgeist/The Earth Spirit* 1895 and its sequel *Der Marquis von Keith. Die Büchse der Pandora/Pandora's Box* 1904 was the source for Berg's opera *Lulu.* Many of Wedekind's writings were considered shocking because of their earthy sexuality.

wedge a block of triangular cross-section which can be used as a simple machine. An axe is a wedge; it splits wood by redirecting the energy of the downward blow sideways, where it exerts the force needed to split the wood.

Wedgwood Josiah 1730–1795. English pottery manufacturer. He set up business in Burslem, Staffordshire, in the early 1760s, to produce his unglazed blue or green stoneware decorated with white Neo-Classical designs, using pigments of his own invention.

weedkiller common term for *herbicide.* The widespread use of herbicides in agriculture has led to a dramatic increase in crop yield. Selective herbicides are effective with cereal crops, as they kill all broad-leaved plants without affecting the grasslike leaves. Some weedkillers, such as sodium chlorate and paraquat, kill all plants. See also ◊Agent Orange.

weever fish European fish, genus *Trachinus,* with poison glands on dorsal fin and gill cover that can give a painful sting. It grows up to 5 cm/2 in long, has eyes near the top of its head, and lives on sandy seabeds.

weevil superfamily of beetles, Curculionoidea, in the order Coleoptera, which are usually less than 6 mm/0.25 in long. The head has a prolonged rostrum, which is used for boring into plant stems and trees for feeding, and in the female's case for depositing eggs.

Wegener Alfred Lothar 1880–1930. German meteorologist and geophysicist, whose theory of ◊continental drift, expounded in *Origin of Continents and Oceans* 1915, was originally known as Wegener's hypothesis; it is now attributed to the movements of ◊plate tectonics.

weightlessness condition in which there is no gravitational force acting on a body, either because gravitational force is cancelled out by equal and opposite acceleration, or because the body is so far outside a planet's gravitational field that it exerts no force on it.

weevil *Electron microscope picture of a grain weevil emerging from a wheat grain. (×12)*

weightlifting the sport of lifting the heaviest possible weight above one's head to the satisfaction of judges. In international competitions there are two standard lifts, **snatch** and **jerk**.

weights and measures see under ◊c.g.s. system, ◊f.p.s. system, ◊MKS system, ◊SI units.

Weil Simone 1909–1943. French writer, who became a practising Catholic after a mystical experience in 1938. Apart from essays, her works (advocating political quietism) were posthumously published, including *Waiting for God* 1951, *The Need for Roots* 1952, and *Notebooks* 1956.

Weill Kurt (Julian) 1900–1950. German composer, US citizen from 1943. He wrote chamber and orchestral music, and collaborated with ◊Brecht in operas such as *Die Dreigroschenoper/The Threepenny Opera* 1928, and *Aufsteig und Fall der Stadt Mahagonny/The Rise and Fall of the City of Mahagonny* 1930, which attacks social corruption and caused a riot at its premiere in Leipzig. He tried to evolve a new form of musical theatre, using subjects with a contemporary relevance and the simplest possible musical means.

Weil's disease an infectious disease of animals (also known as leptospirosis) which is occasionally transmitted to human beings. It is characterized by acute fever, and infection may spread to the liver, kidneys, and heart muscle.

Weimar Republic the constitutional republic in Germany 1919–33, which was crippled by the election of antidemocratic parties to the ◊Reichstag, and then subverted by the Nazi leader Hitler after his appointment as Chancellor in 1933 . It took its name from the city where in Feb 1919 a constituent assembly met to draw up a democratic constitution.

Weinberger Caspar ('Cap' Willard) 1917– . US Republican politician. He served under Presidents Nixon and Ford, and was Reagan's defence secretary 1981–87.

Weir Peter 1938– . Australian film director. His films have an atmospheric quality and often contain a strong spiritual element. They include *Picnic at Hanging Rock* 1975, *Witness* 1985, *Mosquito Coast* 1986 and *Dead Poets' Society* 1989.

Weizmann Chaim 1874–1952. Zionist leader (president of Israel 1948–52) and chemist, born in Russia. He became a naturalized British subject, and

Welles US actor and director, Orson Welles.

Wellington Arthur Wellesley, 1st Duke of Wellington, known as the Iron Duke.

as director of the Admiralty laboratories 1916–19 discovered a process for manufacturing acetone, a solvent. He conducted the negotiations leading up to the ◊Balfour Declaration. He was head of the Hebrew University in Jerusalem, and in 1948 became the first president of the new republic of Israel.

welding joining pieces of metal (or non-metal), at faces rendered plastic or liquid by heat or pressure (or both). Forge, or hammer, welding, employed by blacksmiths since early times, was the only method available until near the end of the 19th century. The principal modern processes are gas and electric-arc welding, in which the heat from a gas flame or an electric arc melts the faces to be joined. Additional 'filler metal' is usually added to the joint.

Weldon Fay 1931– . British novelist and dramatist, whose work deals with feminist themes, often in an ironic or comic manner. Novels include *The Fat Woman's Joke* 1967, *Female Friends* 1975, *Remember Me* 1976, *Puffball* 1980, and *The Life and Loves of a She-Devil* 1984. She has also written plays for the stage, radio, and television.

Welensky Roy 1907– . Rhodesian right-wing politician. He was instrumental in the creation of a Federation of N and S Rhodesia and Nyasaland in 1953 and was prime minister 1956–63. His Federal Party was defeated by Ian Smith's Rhodesian Front in 1964.

Welles (George) Orson 1915–1985. US actor and director. He produced a radio version of H G Wells' *The War of the Worlds* 1938, and then produced, directed, and starred in *Citizen Kane* 1941, a landmark in the history of cinema, yet he directed very few films subsequently in Hollywood. Later films as an actor include *The Lady from Shanghai* 1948, and *The Third Man* 1949.

Wellington capital and industrial port (woollen textiles, chemicals, soap, footwear, bricks) of New Zealand in North Island on Cook Strait; population (1987) 351,000. The city was founded 1840, and became the seat of government 1865.

Wellington Arthur Wellesley, 1st Duke of Wellington 1769–1852. British soldier and Tory politician. As commander in the ◊Peninsular War, he expelled the French from Spain in 1814. He defeated Napoleon Bonaparte at Quatre-Bras and Waterloo in 1815, and was a member of the Congress of Vienna. As prime minister 1828–30, he was forced to concede Roman Catholic emancipation.

Wells H(erbert) G(eorge) 1866–1946. British writer. He first made his name with 'scientific romances' such as *The Time Machine* 1895, and *The War of the Worlds* 1898. Later novels had an anti-establishment, anti-conventional humour remarkable in its day, for example *Kipps* 1905 and *Tono-Bungay* 1909. Of his many other books, his *Outline of History* 1920 and *The Shape of Things to Come* 1933, from which a number of his prophecies have since been fulfilled, are notable; he wrote many short stories.

Welsh corgi breed of dog, with a foxlike head and pricked ears. The coat is dense and there are several varieties of colouring. Corgis are about 30 cm/1 ft at the shoulder, and weigh up to 12 kg/27 lbs.

Welsh language or *Cymraeg* a member of the Celtic branch of the Indo-European language family, spoken chiefly in the rural N and W of Wales; it is the strongest of the surviving Celtic languages.

Weltpolitik (German) world politics. Term applied to German foreign policy after about 1890, which represented Emperor Wilhelm II's attempt to make Germany into a world power through a more aggressive foreign policy on colonies and naval building combined with an increase in nationalism at home.

Wenceslas, St 907–929. Duke of Bohemia who attempted to Christianize his people and was murdered by his brother. He is patron saint of Czechoslovakia and the 'good King Wenceslas' of the carol. Feast day 28 Sept.

Wells British journalist and novelist, H G Wells.

Wends the NW slavonic tribes who settled the east of the rivers Elbe and Saale 6th–8th centuries. By the 12th centuries most had been forcibly Christianized and absorbed by invading Germans; a few preserved their indentity and survive as the Sorbs of Lusatia (East Germany/Poland).

Wentworth William Charles 1790–1872. Australian politician, the son of D'Arcy Wentworth (c. 1762–1827), surgeon of the penal settlement at Norfolk Island. In 1855 he was in Britain to steer the New South Wales constitution through Parliament, and campaigned for Australian federalism and self-government.

werewolf in folk belief, a human being either turned by spell into a wolf, or having the ability to assume either human or wolf form. The symptoms of ◊porphyria may have fostered the legends.

Werfel Franz 1890–1945. Austrian poet, dramatist, and novelist, a leading Expressionist. His works include the poems 'Der Weltfreund der Gerichtstag'/'The Day of Judgment' 1919; the plays *Juarez und Maximilian* 1924, and *Das Reich Gottes in Böhmen/The Kingdom of God in Bohemia* 1930; and the novels *Verdi* 1924 and *Das Lied von Bernadette/The Song of Bernadette* 1941.

Wergeland Henrik 1808–1845. Norwegian lyric poet born at Christiansand. He was the greatest leader of the Norwegian revival, and is known for his epic *Skabelsen, Mennesket, og Messias/Creation, Humanity, and Messiah* 1830.

wergild or *wergeld* (Old English 'man' and 'yield') in the Middle Ages, the compensation paid by a murderer to the relatives of the victim, its value dependent on the social rank of the deceased.

Werner Abraham Gottlob 1750–1815. German geologist, one of the first to classify minerals systematically. He also developed the theory of neptunianism – that the Earth was initially covered by water, with every mineral in suspension. As the water receded, layers of rocks 'crystallized'.

Werner Alfred 1866–1919. Swiss chemist. He was awarded a Nobel prize in 1913 for his work on ◊valency theory.

Wesker Arnold 1932– . British playwright. His socialist beliefs were reflected in the successful trilogy *Chicken Soup with Barley, Roots, I'm Talking about Jerusalem* 1958–60. He established a catchphrase with *Chips with Everything* 1962.

Wesley Charles 1707–1788. brother of John ◊Wesley and one of the original Methodists at Oxford. He became a principal preacher and theologian of the Wesleyan Methodists. He wrote some 6,500 hymns, including 'Jesu, lover of my soul'.

Wesley John 1703–1791. British founder of ◊Methodism. When the pulpits of the established church were closed to him and his followers, he took the gospel to the people. For 50 years he rode about the country on horseback, preaching daily, largely in the open air, and often several times a day. His sermons became the doctrinal standard of the Wesleyan Methodist Church.

Wessex the kingdom of the West Saxons in Britain, said to have been founded by Cerdic about 500 AD, covering present day Hampshire, Dorset, Wiltshire, Berkshire, Somerset, and Devon. In 829 Egbert established West Saxon supremacy over all England.

West Benjamin 1738–1820. American painter, active in London from 1763. He enjoyed the patronage of George III for many years and became president of the Royal Academy in 1792. He painted historical pictures, including *The Death of Wolfe* 1770 (National Gallery,

Ottawa), and many early American artists studied with him.

West Mae 1892–1980. US vaudeville and film actress. She wrote her own dialogue, sending herself up as a sex symbol. Her films include *She Done Him Wrong* 1933; two of her often quoted lines are 'Come up and see me some time', and 'Beulah, peel me a grape'.

West Nathanael. Pen name of Nathan Weinstein 1904–1940. US black-humour novelist, born in New York. West's surrealist influenced novels capture the absurdity and extremity of modern American life and the dark side of the American dream. *The Day of the Locust* 1939, his finest book, explores the violent fantasies induced by Hollywood, where West was a screenwriter.

West Rebecca. Pen name of Cicily Isabel Fairfield 1892–1983. British journalist and novelist. *The Meaning of Treason* 1949 deals with the spies Burgess and Maclean. Her novels include *The Fountain Overflows* 1956.

West African Economic Community international organization established 1975 to end barriers in trade and cooperation in development; members in 1988 include: Burkina Faso, Ivory Coast, Mali, Mauritania, Niger, and Senegal; Benin and Togo have observer status.

West, American the Great Plains region of the USA to the E of the Rocky Mountains from Canada to Texas.

1250 Unidentified epidemic weakened American Indian civilization.

1650 Horses introduced by Spanish conquistadors.

1775 Wilderness Road opened by Daniel ◊Boone.

1805 Zebulon Pike (see ◊Pikes Peak) explored the Mississippi.

1819 Maj Stephen Long, a US government topographical engineer, explored the Great Plains.

1822 ◊Santa Fe Trail established.

1824 Great Salt Lake discovered by Jim Bridger, 'mountain man', trapper and guide.

1836 Defeat of Davy Crockett and other Texans by Mexicans at Alamo.

1840–60 ◊Oregon Trail in use.

1846 Mormon trek to Utah under Brigham ◊Young.

1846–48 ◊Mexican War.

1849–56 ◊California gold rush.

1860 Pony Express (St Joseph, Missouri–San Francisco, California) 3 Apr–22 Oct; superseded by the telegraph.

1863 On 1 Jan the first homestead was filed; followed by the settlement of the Western Prairies and Great Plains.

1865–90 Period of the Indian Wars, accompanied by rapid extermination of the buffalo, upon which much of Indian life depended.

1867–80s Period of the 'cattle kingdom', and cowboy trails such as the Chisholm Trail from Texas to the railheads at Abilene, Wichita, Dodge City.

1869 First transcontinental railroad completed by Central Pacific company, building eastward from Sacramento, California, and Union Pacific company, building westward from Omaha, Nebraska.

1876 Battle of Little Bighorn; see Gen ◊Custer and ◊Plains Indians.

1890 Battle of ◊Wounded Knee; official census declaration that the West no longer had a frontier line.

West Bank the area on the W bank of the river Jordan occupied by the Israelis after the Six-Day

Western Australia Wave Rock at Hyden, Western Australia, which resulted from sea action when the land was submerged.

War 5–10 Jun 1967. The continuing Israeli occupation has created tensions with the Arab population, especially as a result of Israeli (Jewish) settlements in the area.

West Bengal   state of NE India
area 88,563 sq km/33,829 sq mi
capital Calcutta
towns Durgarpur
physical occupies the W part of the vast alluvial plain created by the Ganges and Brahmaputra, with the Hooghly river; annual rainfall in excess of 250 cm/100 in
products rice, jute, tea, coal, iron, steel, cars, locomotives, aluminium, fertilizers
population (1981) 54,485,500.

Westerlies   prevailing winds from the W that occur in both hemispheres between latitudes of about 35° and 60°. Unlike the ◊trade winds, they are variable and produce stormy weather.

western   genre of popular fiction and film based on the landscape and settlement of the US west. It developed in American ◊dime novels and ◊frontier literature. The western became established in written form with novels such as *The Virginian* 1902 by Owen Wister (1860–1938) and *Riders of the Purple Sage* 1912 by Zane Grey. The movies extended the western mythology and, in Italian *spaghetti westerns* and Japanese westerns, made it an international form.

Western Australia   state of Australia
area 2,527,632 sq km/975,920 sq mi
capital Perth
towns main port Fremantle, Bunbury, Geraldton, Kalgoorlie-Boulder, Albany
products wheat, fresh and dried fruit, meat and dairy products; natural gas (NW Shelf) and oil (Canning Basin), iron (the Pilbara), copper, nickel, uranium, gold, diamonds
population (1986) 1,496,000
history a short-lived convict settlement at King George Sound 1826; Captain James Stirling (1791–1865) founded the modern state at Perth 1829; self-government 1890; state 1901.

Western European Union   (WEU) organization established 1955 as a consultative forum for military issues among the W European governments, Belgium, France, Holland, Italy, Luxembourg, the UK, West Germany, and (from 1988) Spain and Portugal.

Western Isles   island area of Scotland, comprising the Outer Hebrides (Lewis, Harris, North and South Uist, and Barra); unofficially the Inner and Outer Hebrides generally
area 2,901 sq km/1,120 sq mi
towns administrative headquarters Stornoway on Lewis
products Harris tweed, sheep, fish, cattle
population (1986) 31,500.

Western Sahara   disputed territory in NW Africa
area 266,000 sq km/102,000 sq mi
capital La'Youn (Arabic *El Aaiún*)
towns phosphate mining town of Bou Craa
exports phosphates
currency peseta
population about 1,000,000 in the area occupied by Polisario; 400,000 in Algeria and Libya, and (1970) 76,500 in Morocco
language Arabic
religion Sunni Muslim
government within the fortified wall Morocco rules, and outside, Polisario
recent history a Spanish possession until 1976, when two-thirds was taken over by Morocco and one-third by Mauritania (withdrew in 1979). The Popular Front for the Liberation of Saguia al Hamra and Rio de Oro (Polisario) proclaimed the Saharan Arab Democratic Republic in 1976, and is supported by Algeria and Libya; it currently controls the area formerly occupied by Mauritania.

Western Samoa   see ◊Samoa, Western.

West Germany   see ◊Germany, West.

West Glamorgan   county in SW Wales
area 817 sq km/315 sq mi
towns administrative headquarters Swansea, Port Talbot, Neath
products tinplate, copper, steel, chemicals
population (1986) 363,400
language English, 16% Welsh-speaking.

West Indies   archipelago of about 1,200 islands, dividing the Atlantic from the Gulf of Mexico and the Caribbean. The islands are divided into:
Bahamas
Greater Antilles Cuba, Hispaniola (Haiti, Dominican Republic), Jamaica, Puerto Rico
Lesser Antilles Aruba, Netherlands Antilles, Trinidad and Tobago, the Windward Islands (Grenada, Barbados, St Vincent, St Lucia, Martinique, Dominica, Guadeloupe), the Leeward Islands (Montserrat, Antigua, St Christopher (St Kitts)–Nevis, Barbuda, Anguilla, St Martin, British and US Virgin Islands), and many smaller islands.

West Indies, Federation of   federal union 1958–62 comprising Antigua, Barbados, Dominica, Grenada, Jamaica, Montserrat, St Christopher (St Kitts)-Nevis and Anguilla, St Lucia, St Vincent, and Trinidad and Tobago. This federation, of which the federal parliament was at Port-of-Spain, Trinidad, came to an end when first Jamaica and then Trinidad and Tobago withdrew.

Westland affair   the events surrounding the takeover of the British Westland helicopter company in 1985–86. There was much political acrimony in the cabinet and allegations of malpractice. The affair led to the resignation of two cabinet ministers: Michael Heseltine, minister of defence, and the secretary for trade and industry, Leon Brittan.

Westmeath   inland county of Leinster province, Republic of Ireland
area 1,764 sq km/681 sq mi
town county town Mullingar
physical rivers Shannon, Inny, and Brosna; lakes Ree, Sheelin, and Ennell

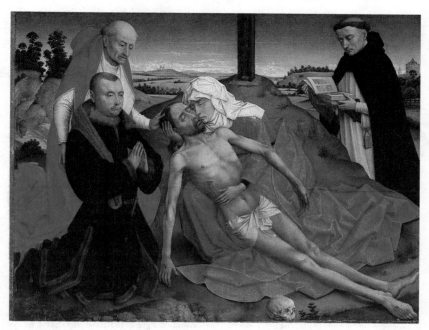

Weyden Pietà *National Gallery, London.*

products agricultural and dairy products, limestone, textiles
population (1981) 61,500.

West Midlands metropolitan county in central England, created 1974, originally administered by an elected council; its powers reverted to district councils from 1986
area 899 sq km/347 sq mi
towns administrative headquarters Birmingham
products manufacturing industrial goods
population (1986) 2,632,000.

Westminster Abbey Gothic church in central London, officially the Collegiate Church of St Peter. It was built 1050–1745 and consecrated under Edward the Confessor in 1065. The west towers are by ◊Hawksmoor 1740. Since William I nearly all English monarchs have been crowned in the abbey, and several are buried there; many poets are buried or commemorated at Poets' Corner.

Westphalia an independent medieval duchy, incorporated in Prussia by the Congress of Vienna 1815, and made a province 1816 with Münster as its capital. Since 1946 it has been part of the West German *Land* (region) of ◊North Rhine–Westphalia.

Westphalia, Treaty of agreement 1648 ending the ◊Thirty Years' War.

West Point former fort in New York State, on the Hudson, 80 km/50 mi N of New York City, site of the US Military Academy (commonly referred to as West Point), established in 1802. Women were admitted 1976. West Point has been a military post since 1778.

West Sussex county on the S coast of England
area 1,989 sq km/768 sq mi
towns administrative headquarters Chichester; Crawley, Horsham, Haywards Heath; resorts Worthing, Littlehampton, Bognor Regis; port Shoreham
physical the Weald, South Downs; rivers Arun, West Rother, Adur

population (1986) 695,000.

West Virginia state of the E USA; nickname Mountain State
area 62,629 sq km/24,180 sq mi
capital Charleston
towns Huntington, Wheeling
physical Allegheny Mountains; Ohio river
products fruit, poultry, dairy and meat products, timber, coal, natural gas, oil, chemicals, synthetic fibres, plastics, steel, glass, pottery
population (1984) 1,952,000
famous people Pearl Buck, Thomas 'Stonewall' Jackson
history mound builders 6th century; explorers and fur traders 1670s; German settlements 1730s; industrial development early 19th century; on the secession of Virginia from the Union in 1862, West Virginians dissented, and formed a new state 1863; industrial expansion accompanied by labor strife early 20th century.

West Yorkshire metropolitan county in NE England, created 1976, originally administered by an elected metropolitan council; its powers reverted to district councils from 1986
area 2,039 sq km/787 sq mi
towns administrative headquarters Wakefield; Leeds, Bradford, Halifax, Huddersfield
products coal, woollen textiles
population (1986) 2,053,000
famous people the Brontës, David Hockney, Henry Moore, J B Priestley.

wet in politics a derogatory term used to describe a moderate or left-wing supporter of the British Conservative Party who opposes the monetary or other hard-line policies of its leader Margaret Thatcher.

weta flightless insect *Deinacrida rugosa*, resembling a large grasshopper (8.5 cm/3.5 in long), found on offshore islands of New Zealand.

Wexford county in the Republic of Ireland, province of Leinster

whale

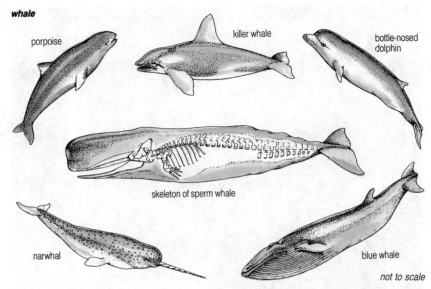

porpoise

killer whale

bottle-nosed dolphin

skeleton of sperm whale

narwhal

blue whale

not to scale

area 2,352 sq km/908 sq mi
towns county town Wexford; Rosslare
products fish, livestock; oats, barley, potatoes
population (1981) 99,000.

Weyden Rogier van der *c.* 1399–1464. Dutch painter, official painter to the city of Brussels from 1436. He painted portraits and religious subjects, such as *The Last Judgement c.* 1450 (Hôtel-Dieu, Beaune). His refined style had considerable impact on Dutch painting.

Weygand Maxime 1867–1965. French general. In 1940, as French commander in chief, he advised surrender to Germany, and was subsequently high commissioner of N Africa 1940–41. He was a prisoner in Germany 1942–45, and was arrested after his return to France; he was released in 1946, and in 1949 the sentence of national infamy was quashed.

whale large marine mammal of the order Cetacea, with internal vestiges of hind limbs. When they surface to breathe, they eject exhausted air in a 'spout' through the blowhole or nostril in the top of the head. There were hundreds of thousands of whales at the beginning of the century, but they have been hunted close to extinction.

Wharton Edith (born Jones) 1862–1937. US novelist. Her work was influenced by her friend Henry James, and mostly set in New York society. It includes *The House of Mirth* 1905, the rural *Ethan Frome* 1911, *The Custom of the Country* 1913, and *The Age of Innocence* 1920.

wheat cereal plant derived from the wild *Triticum*, a grass native to the Middle East. It is the chief cereal used in bread making and is widely cultivated in temperate climates suited to its growth. Wheat is killed by frost, and damp renders the grain soft; warm dry regions therefore produce the most valuable grain.

Wheatley Dennis (Yates) 1897–1977. British thriller and adventure novelist. He is known for his series dealing with black magic and occultism, but also wrote crime novels in which the reader was invited to play the detective, as in *Murder off Miami* 1936, with real clues such as ticket stubs.

Wheatstone Charles 1802–1875. British physicist and inventor. With William Cooke, he patented a railway telegraph 1837, and, developing an idea of Samuel Christie's, devised the *Wheatstone bridge*, an electrical network for measuring resistance. He invented the harmonica and the concertina.

wheel and axle a simple machine with a rope wound round an axle connected to a larger wheel with another rope attached to its rim. Pulling on the wheel rope (applying an effort) lifts a load attached to the axle rope. The velocity ratio of the machine (load divided by effort) is equal to the ratio of the wheel radius to the axle radius.

Wheeler Mortimer 1890–1976. British archaeologist. While he was keeper of the London Museum 1926–44, his digs included Caerleon in Wales 1926–27 and Maiden Castle in Dorset 1934–37. As director-general of archaeology in India 1944–48 he revealed the Indus Valley civilization.

whelk type of marine gastropod with a thick spiral shell. Whelks are scavengers, and will eat other shellfish. The largest grow to 40 cm/16 in long. Tropical species are very colourful.

wheat

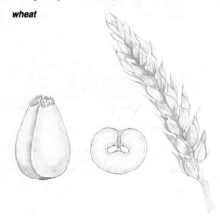

Whig Party In the UK predecessor of the Liberal Party. The name was first used of rebel ◊Covenanters and then of those who wished to exclude James II from the English succession (as a Roman Catholic). They were in power continuously 1714–60 and pressed for industrial and commercial development, a vigorous foreign policy, and religious toleration. During the French Revolution, they demanded parliamentary reform in Britain, and from the passing of the Reform Bill in 1832 became known as Liberals.

Whig Party in the USA, political party opposed to the autocratic presidency of Andrew Jackson from 1834. They elected the presidents W H Harrison, Taylor, and Fillmore. The party diverged over the issue of slavery 1852; the Northern Whigs joined the Republican party; the Southern or 'Cotton' Whigs joined the Democrats. The title was taken from the British Whig Party which supported Parliament against the king. During the War of American Independence, American patriots described themselves as Whigs, while those remaining loyal to Britain were known as Tories.

whimbrel wading bird *Numenius phaeopus* related to the curlew but with a shorter down-curved bill, streaked brown plumage, and head stripes. About 40 cm/1.3 ft long, it breeds in the arctic, and winters in Africa, South America, and S Asia.

whip in UK politics, the member of parliament who ensures the presence of colleagues in the party when there is to be a vote in Parliament at the end of a debate. The written appeal sent by the whips to MPs is also called a whip; this letter is underlined once, twice, or three times to indicate its importance. A *three-line whip* is the most urgent, and every MP is expected to attend and vote with their party.

whiplash injury damage to the neck vertebrae and their attachments caused by a sudden backward jerk of the head and neck. It is most often seen in vehicle occupants as a result of the rapid deceleration experienced in a crash.

whippet breed of dog resembling a small greyhound. It grows to 56 cm/22 in at the shoulder, and 9 kg/20 lb in weight.

Whipple Fred Lawrence 1906– . US astronomer, whose hypothesis in 1949 that the nucleus of a comet is like a dirty snowball was confirmed 1986 by space-probe studies of ◊Halley's Comet.

whippoorwill North American insectivorous nightjar *Caprimulgus vociferus*, so called from its cry. It is about 25 cm/10 in long, and is mottled brown.

Whipsnade a zoo in Bedfordshire, England, 5 km/3 mi S of Dunstable, where wild animals and birds are bred and exhibited in conditions resembling their natural state. It was opened to the public 1931.

whisky or *whiskey* a distilled spirit made from malted barley or other grain. American whiskey or bourbon is made from rye. Scotch is usually blended; pure malt whisky is more expensive.

whist predecessor of ◊bridge, a card game for four, in which the partners try to win a majority of the 13 tricks (the highest card played being the winner).

Whistler James Abbott McNeill 1834–1903. US painter and etcher, active in London from 1859. His riverscapes and portraits show subtle composition and colour harmonies, for example *Arrangement in Grey and Black: Portrait of the Painter's Mother* 1871 (Louvre, Paris).

Whitby, Synod of council summoned by King Oswy of Northumbria in 664, which decided to

Whistler Miss Cicely Alexander, harmony in grey and green *(1872) Tate Gallery, London.*

adopt the Roman rather than the Celtic form of Christianity for Britain.

White a counter-revolutionary, especially during the Russian civil wars 1917–21. Originally the term described the party opposing the French Revolution, when the royalists used the white lily of the French monarchy as their badge.

White Gilbert 1720–1793. English cleric and naturalist, born at Selborne, Hampshire, and author of *Natural History and Antiquities of Selborne* 1789.

White Patrick 1912– . Australian novelist. Born in London, he settled in Australia in the 1940s. His novels (with allegorical overtones) include *The Aunt's Story* 1948, *Voss* (based on the 19th-century explorer Leichhardt) 1957, and *The Twyborn Affair* 1979. Nobel Prize 1973.

White T(erence) H(anbury) 1906–1964. British writer, who retold the Arthurian legend in four volumes of *The Once and Future King* 1938–58.

whitebait the young of the ◊herring.

whitebeam tree *Sorbus aria*, native to S Europe, usually found growing on chalk or limestone. It can reach 20 m/60 ft. It takes its name from the leaves, which are elliptical and toothed, and have a dense coat of short white hairs on the underside.

white dwarf a small, hot star, the last stage in the life of a star such as the Sun. White dwarfs have a mass similar to that of the Sun, but are only 1% of the Sun's diameter, similar in size to the Earth. Most have surface temperatures of 8,000°C or more, hotter than the Sun. Yet, being so small, their overall luminosities are 1% that of the Sun or less.

White House The official residence of the president of the USA, in Washington DC.

whitefish name applied to freshwater fishes of the salmon family, belonging to the genus *Coregonus*. They live in deep lakes and rivers of North America, Europe, and Asia.

Whitehall street in central London, between Trafalgar Square and the Houses of Parliament, with many government offices and the Cenotaph war memorial.

Whitehead Robert 1823–1905. British engineer who invented the self-propelled torpedo 1866.

Whitehorse capital of Yukon Territory, Canada; population (1981) 18,000.

White Horse any of several hill figures in England, including the one on Bratton Hill, Wiltshire, said to commemorate Alfred the Great's victory over the Danes at Ethandun 878.

White House official residence of the president of the USA, in Washington DC. It was built in the Italian Renaissance style 1792–99 to the designs of James Hoban, who restored it after it was burned by the British 1814; it was then painted white to hide the scars.

Whitehouse Mary 1910– . British activist. She founded the National Viewers' and Listeners' Association, campaigning to censor radio and television in their treatment of sex and violence.

white knight in business, a company invited by the target of a takeover bid to make a rival bid.

Whitelaw William, Viscount Whitelaw 1918– . British Conservative politician. As secretary of state for Northern Ireland he introduced the concept of power sharing, then became secretary of state for employment Dec 1973–74, but failed to conciliate the unions. He was chair of the Conservative Party 1974, and home secretary 1979–83, when he was made a peer. He resigned 1988.

whiteout 'fog' of grains of dry snow caused by strong winds in temperatures of between –18°C/0°F to –35°C/–30°F. The uniform whiteness of the ground and air causes disorientation.

white paper in the UK and some other countries, name of an official document that expresses government policy on an issue. It is usually preparatory to the introduction of a parliamentary bill (a proposed act of Parliament). Its name derives from its having fewer pages than a government 'blue book', and therefore needing no blue paper cover.

White Patrick 1912– . Australian novelist. Born in London, he settled in Australia in the 1940s. His novels (with allegorical overtones) include *The Aunt's Story* 1948, *Voss* (based on the 19th-century explorer Leichhardt) 1957, and *The Twyborn Affair* 1979. Nobel prize 1973.

White Russia English translation of ◊Belorussia, republic of the USSR.

white spirit a colourless liquid derived from petrol; it is used as a solvent and in paints and varnishes.

white terror general term used by socialists and Marxists to describe a right-wing counter-revolution, for example, the attempts by the Chinese Guomindang to massacre the communists 1927–1931.

whitethroat bird *Sylvia communis* of the warbler group, found in scrub, hedges, and wood clearings of Eurasia in summer, migrating to Africa in winter. It is about 14 cm/5.5 in long. The female is dull brown, but the male is reddish-brown, with a grey head and white throat, and performs an acrobatic aerial display during courtship.

whiting predatory fish *Merlangius merlangus* common in shallow sandy N European waters. It grows to 70 cm/2.3 ft.

Whitlam (Edward) Gough 1916– . Australian politician, leader of the Labor Party 1967–78 and prime minister 1972–75. He cultivated closer relations with Asia, attempted redistribution of wealth, and raised loans to increase national ownership of industry and resources.

Whitman Walt(er) 1819–1892. US poet, who published *Leaves of Grass* 1855, which contains the symbolic 'Song of Myself'. It used unconventional ◊free verse and scandalized the public by its frank celebration of sexuality.

Whitney Eli 1765–1825. US inventor who in 1793 patented the cotton gin, a device for separating cotton fibre from its seeds.

Whit Sunday Christian church festival held seven weeks after Easter, corresponding to the Jewish Pentecost and commemorating the descent of the Holy Spirit on the Apostles. The name is probably derived from the white garments worn by candidates for baptism at the festival.

Whittle Frank 1907– . British engineer who invented the jet engine in 1930. In the Royal Air Force he worked on jet propulsion 1937–46. In May 1941 the Gloster E 28/39 aircraft first flew with the Whittle jet engine.

WHO abbreviation for ◊*World Health Organization*.

Who, The English rock group (1964–83) with a hard, aggressive sound, high harmonies, and a stage show that often included destroying their instruments. Their albums include *Tommy* 1969, *Quadrophenia* 1971, and *Who's Next* 1971. Originally a mod band, the Who comprised Pete Townshend (1945–), guitar and songwriter; Roger Daltrey (1944–), vocals; John Entwhistle (1944–), bass; Keith Moon (1947–78), drums.

wholesale the business of selling merchandise to anyone other than the final customer. Most manufacturers or producers sell in bulk to a wholesale organization which distributes the smaller quantities required by retail outlets.

whooping cough or *pertussis* an infectious disease, mainly seen in children, caused by colonization of the air passages by the bacterium *Haemophilus pertussis*. There may be catarrh, mild fever, and loss of appetite, but the main symptom is paroxysmal coughing, associated with the sharp intake of breath which is the characteristic 'whoop', and often followed by vomiting and severe nose bleeds. The cough may persist for weeks.

whortleberry a form of ◊bilberry.

whydah African bird, genus *Vidua*, of the weaver family. It lays its eggs in the nest of the waxbill, a small seed-eating bird, which rears the young. Males have long tail feathers used in courtship displays.

Whymper Edward 1840–1911. British mountaineer. He made the first ascents of many Alpine peaks, including the Matterhorn 1865, and in the Andes scaled Chimborazo and other mountains.

Wicklow county in the Republic of Ireland, province of Leinster
area 2,025 sq km/782 sq mi
towns county town Wicklow
physical Wicklow Mountains; rivers Slane and Liffey.
population (1991) 97,300.

wide-angle lens a photographic lens of shorter focal length than normal, taking in a wider angle of view.

Wiener Werkstätte (German *Vienna Workshops*). A group of Viennese craftsmen and artists, founded in 1903 by Josef ◊Hoffmann and Kolo Moser who were both members of the Vienna ◊Sezession. They designed objects ranging from furniture and jewellery to metal and books, in a rectilinear Art Nouveau style influenced by Charles Rennie ◊Mackintosh. The workshop, financed by Fritz Wärndorfer, closed in 1932.

Wiesel Elie 1928– . US academic and human-rights campaigner, born in Romania. He was held in Buchenwald concentration camp during World War II, and has assiduously documented wartime atrocities against the Jews, in an effort to alert the world to the dangers of racism and violence. 1986 Nobel Peace Prize.

wig artificial head of hair, either real or synthetic, worn as an adornment, disguise, or to conceal baldness. Wigs were known in the ancient world, and have been found on Egyptian mummies. The 16th-century periwig imitated real hair, and developed into the elaborate peruke. Today they remain part of the uniform of judges, barristers, and some parliamentary officials in the UK and certain Commonwealth countries.

wigeon wild duck *Anas penelope* about 45 cm/18 in long. The male has a red-brown head with cream crown, greyish-pink breast and white beneath. The bill is blue-grey. The female is brown with a white belly and shoulders. It breeds in N Eurasia, and winters in Africa or S Asia.

Wight, Isle of island and county in S England
area 381 sq km/147 sq mi
towns administrative headquarters Newport; resorts Ryde, Sandown, Shanklin, Ventnor
economy agriculture, tourism
population (1991) 126,600.

Wightman Cup annual lawn tennis competition between international women's team from the USA and the UK. The trophy, first contested in 1923, was donated by Hazel Wightman (born Hotchkiss) (1886–1974) a former US lawn tennis player who won singles, doubles, and mixed doubles titles at the US Championships 1909–1911.

Wilberforce William 1759–1833. British reformer, born in Hull. He began his attacks on slavery while at school, and from 1788 devoted himself to its abolition. He entered Parliament in 1780; in 1807 his bill for the abolition of the slave trade was passed, and in 1833, largely through his efforts, slavery was abolished throughout the British Empire.

Wild Jonathan *c.* 1682–1725. English criminal, who organized the thieves of London and ran an office which, for a payment, returned stolen goods to their owners. He was hanged at Tyburn.

Wilde Oscar (Fingal O'Flahertie Wills) 1854–1900. Irish writer. Famed for his flamboyant style and quotable conversation, he published his only novel *The Picture of Dorian Gray* 1891, followed by witty

Wilde Irish writer and poet Oscar Wilde, a leading figure of the Aesthetic Movement.

comedies including *A Woman of No Importance* 1893 and *The Importance of Being Earnest* 1895. In 1895 he was imprisoned for two years for homosexual practices (see Edward ◊Carson) and wrote his *Ballad of Reading Gaol* 1898 and *De Profundis* 1905.

wildebeest another name for ◊gnu.

Wilder Billy 1906– . US film director, who worked with Charles Brackett on film scripts such as *Ninotchka* 1939. He directed and collaborated on the script of *Double Indemnity* 1944, The *Lost Weekend* 1945, *Sunset Boulevard* 1950, and *Some Like it Hot* 1959.

Wilder Thornton (Niven) 1897–1975. US playwright and novelist. He won the Pulitzer Prize for the novel *The Bridge of San Luis Rey* 1927, and for the plays *Our Town* 1938 and *The Skin of Our Teeth* 1942. His play *The Matchmaker* appeared at the Edinburgh Festival in 1954, and as the hit musical entitled *Hello Dolly!* in New York, in 1964, and in London the following year.

wild type in genetics, the naturally occurring gene for a particular character that is typical of most individuals of a given species, as distinct from new genes that arise by mutation.

Wilhelm (English *William*) two emperors of Germany:

Wilhelm I 1797–1888. King of Prussia from 1861 and emperor of Germany from 1871; the son of Frederick William III. He served in the Napoleonic Wars 1814–15 and helped to crush the 1848 revolution. After succeeding his brother Frederick William IV in 1861, his policy was largely dictated by his chancellor ◊Bismarck, who secured his proclamation as emperor.

Wilhelm II 1859–1941. Emperor of Germany from 1888, the son of Frederick III and Victoria, daughter of Queen Victoria. In 1890 he forced Chancellor Bismarck to resign and began to direct foreign policy himself, which proved disastrous. In 1914 he first approved Austria's ultimatum to Serbia and then, when he realized war was inevitable, tried in vain to prevent it. In 1918 he fled to Holland.

Wilkes John 1727–1797. British Radical politician, imprisoned for his political views; member of parliament 1757–64 and from 1774. He championed parliamentary reform, religious toleration, and American independence.

Wilkie David 1785–1841. Scottish genre and portrait painter, active in London from 1805. His paintings are in the 17th-century Dutch tradition.

Wilkins William 1778–1839. English architect. He pioneered the Greek Revival in England with his design for Downing College, Cambridge. Other works include the main block of University College London 1827–28, and the National Gallery, London, 1834–38.

will in law, declaration of how a person wishes his or her property to be disposed of after death. It also appoints administrators of the estate (◊executors), and may contain wishes on other matters, such as place of burial or use of organs for transplant. Wills must comply with formal legal requirements.

Willem Dutch form of ◊William.

William 1143–1214. King of Scotland from 1165, known as *William the Lion*. He was captured by Henry II while invading England in 1174, and forced to do homage, but Richard I abandoned the English claim to suzerainty for a money payment in 1189. William was forced by John I in 1209 to renounce his claim to Northumberland.

William 1533–1584. Prince of Orange from 1544, known as *William the Silent* because of his absolute discretion. He was appointed governor of Holland by Philip II of Spain in 1559, but joined the revolt of 1572 against Spain's oppressive rule, and, as a Protestant from 1573, became the national leader. He briefly succeeded in uniting the Catholic south and Protestant northern provinces.

William four kings of England:

William I the Conqueror *c.* 1027–1087. King of England from 1066. He was the illegitimate son of Duke Robert the Devil, and succeeded his father as duke of Normandy 1035. Claiming that his kinsman Edward the Confessor had bequeathed him the English throne, William invaded the country 1066, defeating ◊Harold II at Hastings, Sussex, and was crowned king of England (as depicted in the Bayeux Tapestry).

William II Rufus, 'the Red' *c.* 1056–1100. King of England from 1087, the third son of William I. He spent most of his reign attempting to capture Normandy from his brother Robert. His extortion of money led his barons to revolt and caused confrontation with Bishop Anselm. He was killed while hunting in the New Forest.

William III (William of Orange) 1650–1702. King of Great Britain and Ireland from 1688, the son of William II of Orange. He was offered the English crown by the parliamentary opposition to James II. He invaded England 1688 and in 1689 became joint sovereign with his wife Mary. He spent much of his reign campaigning, first in Ireland, where he defeated James II at the ◊Boyne 1690, and later against the French in Flanders.

William IV 1765–1837. King of the United Kingdom from 1830, and third son of George III. He was created Duke of Clarence 1789, and married Adelaide of Saxe-Meiningen (1792–1849) 1818. During the Reform Bill crisis he secured its passage by agreeing to create new peers to overcome the hostile majority in the House of Lords.

William (full name William Arthur Philip Louis) 1982– . Prince of the United Kingdom, first child of the Prince and Princess of Wales.

William three kings of the Netherlands:

William I 1772–1844. King of the Netherlands 1815–40. He lived in exile during the French occupation 1795–1813, and fought against the emperor Napoleon at Jena and Wagram. The Austrian Netherlands were added to his kingdom by the Allies 1815, but secured independence (recognized by the major European states 1839) by the revolution of 1830. William's unpopularity led to his abdication 1840.

William II 1792–1849. King of the Netherlands 1840–49, son of William I. He served with the British army in the Peninsular War and at Waterloo. In 1848 he averted revolution by conceding a liberal constitution.

William III 1817–1890. King of the Netherlands 1849–90, the son of William II. In 1862 he abolished slavery in the Dutch East Indies.

William of Malmesbury *c.* 1080–*c.* 1143. English historian and monk. He compiled the *Gesta regum/Deeds of the Kings c.* 1120–40 and *Historia novella*, which together formed a history of England to 1142.

Williams John (Christopher) 1942– . Australian guitarist, whose extensive repertoire includes contemporary music and jazz.

Williams Roger *c.* 1604–1684. British founder of Rhode Island colony in North America 1636, on a basis of democracy and complete religious freedom.

Williams Shirley 1930– . British Social Democrat Party politician. She was Labour minister for prices and consumer protection 1974–76 and education and science 1976–79. She became a founder member of the SDP in 1981 and its president in 1982. In 1983 she lost her parliamentary seat. She is the daughter of Vera ◊Brittain.

Williams Tennessee (Thomas Lanier) 1911–1983. US playwright, born in Mississippi. His work is characterized by fluent dialogue and searching analysis of the psychological deficiencies of his characters. His plays, usually set in the Deep South against a background of decadence and degradation, include *The Glass Menagerie* 1945 and *A Streetcar Named Desire* 1947.

Williams William Carlos 1883–1963. US poet. His spare images and language reflect everyday American speech. His epic poem *Paterson* 1946–58 celebrates his home town in New Jersey. His *Pictures from Brueghel* 1963 won a Pulitzer Prize. His work had great impact on younger American poets.

Williams-Ellis Clough 1883–1978. British architect, designer of the fantasy resort of Portmeirion, N Wales.

Williamson Henry 1895–1977. British author, who wrote stories of animal life such as *Tarka the Otter* 1927.

Williamson Malcolm (Benjamin Graham Christopher) 1931– . Australian composer, pianist, and organist, who settled in Britain in 1953. His works include operas (*Our Man in Havana* 1963), symphonies, and chamber music. He became Master of the Queen's Music 1975.

will-o'-the-wisp light sometimes seen over marshy ground, believed to be burning gas containing methane from decaying organic matter.

willow tree or shrub of the genus *Salix*, family Salicaceae, which flourishes in damp places. The

willow

Wilson Woodrow Wilson, president of the USA during World War I.

leaves are often lance-shaped, and the male and female catkins are found on separate trees.

willowherb plant of either of two genera, *Epilobium* or *Chamaenerion*; it is a perennial weed. The rose-bay willowherb or fireweed *Chamaenerion angustifolium* is common in woods and waste places. It grows to 1.2 m/4 ft with long terminal racemes of red or purplish flowers.

willow-warbler bird *Phylloscopus trochilus* which migrates from N Eurasia to Africa. It is about 11 cm/4 in long, similar in appearance to the chiffchaff, but with a distinctive song, and found in woods and shrubberies.

Wilms' tumour one of the rare cancers of infancy, arising in the kidneys, and also known as nephroblastoma. Often the only symptom is abdominal swelling. Treatment is by removal of the affected kidney (nephrectomy), followed by radiotherapy and ◊cytotoxic drugs.

Wilson Angus (Frank Johnstone) 1913–1991. British novelist, whose acidly humourous books include *Anglo-Saxon Attitudes* 1956 and *The Old Men at the Zoo* 1961.

Wilson Colin 1931– . British author of *The Outsider* 1956, and of thrillers, including *Necessary Doubt* 1964. Later works such as *Mysteries* 1978 are about the occult.

Wilson Edward O 1929– . US zoologist, whose books have stimulated interest in ◊biogeography

and the evolution of behaviour, or ◊sociobiology. His works include *Sociobiology* 1975 and *On Human Nature* 1978.

Wilson (James) Harold, Baron Wilson of Rievaulx 1916– . British Labour politician, prime minister 1964–70 and 1974–76. His premiership was dominated by the issue of UK admission to EEC membership, the ◊social contract (unofficial agreement with the trade unions), and economic difficulties.

Wilson Richard 1714–1782. British painter, whose English and Welsh landscapes are infused with an Italianate atmosphere and recomposed in a Classical manner. They influenced the development of an English landscape-painting tradition.

Wilson (Thomas) Woodrow 1856–1924. 28th president of the USA 1913–21, a Democrat. He kept the USA out of World War I until 1917, and in Jan 1918 issued his ◊Fourteen Points as a basis for a just peace settlement. At the peace conference in Paris he secured the inclusion of the ◊League of Nations in individual peace treaties, but these were not ratified by Congress, so the USA did not join the League. Nobel Peace Prize 1919.

Wiltshire county in SW England
area 3,480 sq km/1,482 sq mi
towns administrative headquarters Trowbridge, Salisbury, Swindon, Wilton
physical Marlborough Downs, Savernake Forest; rivers Kennet, and Salisbury and Bristol Avons; Salisbury Plain, including Stonehenge
products wheat, cattle, carpets, rubber, engineering
population (1990) 553,300.

wind lateral movement of the Earth's atmosphere from high-to low-pressure areas. Although modified by features such as land and water, there is a basic worldwide system of ◊trade winds, ◊Westerlies, and ◊monsoons.

Windermere largest lake in England, in Cumbria, 17 km/10.5 mi long and 1.6 km/1 mi wide.

Windhoek capital of Namibia; population (1988) 115,000. It is just north of the Tropic of Capricorn, 290 km/180 mi from the W coast.

wind instrument musical instrument which uses a performer's breath to make a column of air vibrate. The pitch of the note is controlled by the length of the column. The main types are ◊woodwind instruments and ◊brass instruments.

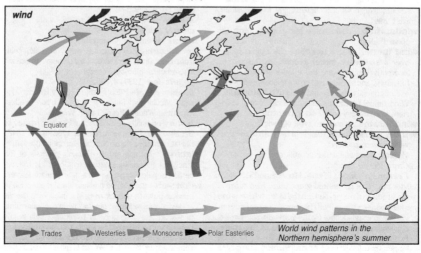

World wind patterns in the Northern hemisphere's summer

Trades   Westerlies   Monsoons   Polar Easterlies

wing   *comparison of wing shapes*

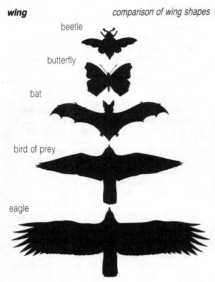

beetle

butterfly

bat

bird of prey

eagle

windmill a mill with sails or vanes which by the action of wind upon them drive machinery for grinding corn or pumping water, for example. Modern wind turbines, designed to use wind power on a major scale, usually have a propeller-type rotor mounted on a tall shell tower. The turbine drives a generator for producing electricity.

Windsor, House of official name of the British royal family since 1917, adopted in place of Saxe-Coburg-Gotha. Since 1960 those descendants of Elizabeth II not entitled to the prefix HRH have borne the surname Mountbatten-Windsor.

Windsor Duchess of. Title of Wallis Warfield ◊Simpson.

Windsor Duke of. Title of ◊Edward VIII.

Windsor Castle British royal residence in Windsor, Berkshire, founded by William the Conqueror on the site of an earlier fortress. It includes the Perpendicular Gothic St George's Chapel and the Albert Memorial Chapel, beneath which George III, George IV, and William IV are buried. In the Home Park adjoining the castle is the Royal Mausoleum where Queen Victoria and Prince Albert are buried.

windsurfing trade name and popular term for ◊boardsailing.

wind tunnel a test tunnel in which air is blown over a stationary model aircraft, car, truck, or locomotive to simulate the effects of movement. Lift, drag, and air-flow patterns are observed by the use of special cameras and sensitive instruments. Wind-tunnel testing assesses the aerodynamic design, preparatory to full-scale construction.

wind turbine a modern type of ◊windmill.

Windward Islands islands in the path of the prevailing wind, notably:
West Indies see under ◊Antilles
Cape Verde Islands
French Polynesia (Tahiti, Moorea, and Makatea).

wine liquor of fermented grape pulp. *Red wine* is the product of the grape with the skin; *white wine* of the inner pulp only. The sugar content is converted to ethyl alcohol by the yeast *Saccharomyces ellipsoideus* which lives on the skin of the grape. For *dry wine* the fermentation is allowed to go on longer than for *sweet* or *medium*; ◊champagne is bottled while still fermenting, but other sparkling wines are artificially carbonated. The world's largest producers are Italy, France, the USSR, and Spain; others include Germany, Australia, South Africa, California, and Chile; a small quantity of wine is produced in the UK.

wing in biology, the modified forelimb of birds and bats, or the membranous outgrowths of the ◊exoskeleton of insects, which give the power of flight. Birds and bats have two wings. Birds' wings have feathers, while bats' wings consist of skin stretched between the digits ('fingers') of the limb. Most insects have four wings, which are strengthened by wing veins. The wings of butterflies and moths are covered with wing scales.

Winnipeg capital and industrial city (sawmills, textiles, meat packing) in Manitoba, Canada, on the Red River, south of Lake Winnipeg; population (1986) 623,000.

Winnipeg, Lake lake in S Manitoba, Canada, draining much of the Canadian prairies; area 24,500 sq km/9,460 sq mi.

wintergreen plant of the genus *Pyrola*, family Pyrolaceae. *Pyrola minor*, with rounded white flowers, is a woodland plant. Oil of wintergreen, used in treating rheumatism, is extracted from the leaves of the North American *Gaultheria procumbens*.

winter of discontent the winter of 1978–79 in Britain, which was marked by a series of strikes that contributed to the defeat of the Labour government in the general election of spring 1979. The phrase is from Shakespeare's *Richard III*: 'Now is the winter of our discontent/Made glorious summer by this sun of York.'

Winter War the USSR's invasion of Finland 30 Nov 1939–12 Mar 1940.

wire a thread of metal, made by drawing a rod through progressively smaller-diameter dies. Fine-gauge wire is used for electrical power transmission; heavier-gauge wire is used to make load-bearing cables.

wireless original name for a radio receiver. In early experiments with transmission by radio waves, notably by ◊Marconi in Britain, signals were sent in ◊Morse code, as on the telegraph. Unlike the telegraph, no wires were used for transmission, and the means of communication was termed wireless telegraphy.

Wisconsin state of the north central USA; nickname Badger State
area 145,477 sq km/56,154 sq mi
capital Madison
towns Milwaukee, Green Bay, Racine
products premier dairying state, cereals, coal, iron, zinc, lead, agricultural machinery, precision instruments, plumbing equipment
population (1987) 4,795,000
famous people Edna Ferber, Harry Houdini, Joseph McCarthy, Spencer Tracy, Orson Welles, Thornton Wilder, Frank Lloyd Wright
history originally settled by the French; passed to Britain 1763; became American 1783; state 1848.

wisent another name for the European ◊bison.

wisteria climbing shrub *Wistaria sinensis* of the family Leguminosae, native to China. It has racemes of pale mauve flowers, and pinnate leaves.

witchcraft the alleged possession and exercise of magical powers (*black magic* if used with the aid of devils, and *white* if benign, as in the 'charming' of warts). Its origins lie in traditional beliefs and religions. Practitioners of witchcraft have often had considerable skill in herbal medicine and traditional remedies; in 1976 the World Health Organization recommended the integration of traditional healers into the health teams of African states.

witch hazel flowering shrub *Hamamelis virginiana*, native to E Asia and North America. An astringent extract prepared from the bark or leaves is used in medicine.

witch-hunt general term used to describe the persecution of minority or opposition political groups without any regard for their guilt or innocence. Witch-hunts are often accompanied by a degree of public hysteria, for example the ◊McCarthy anticommunist hearings during the 1950s in the USA.

withholding tax personal income tax on wages, salaries, dividends, or other income which is taxed at source or by a bank to ensure that it reaches the tax authority. Those not liable to the tax have to reclaim it. In the UK, the withholding of taxes on wages and salaries is known as PAYE (Pay As You Earn).

witness in law, a person who was present at some event (such as an accident, a crime, or the signing of a document) or who has relevant special knowledge (such as a medical expert), and who can be called on to give evidence in a court of law.

Witt Johann de 1625–1672. Dutch politician, and virtual prime minister of Holland from 1653. His skilful diplomacy ended the Dutch Wars of 1652–54 and 1665–67, and in 1668 he formed a triple alliance with England and Sweden against Louis XIV of France. He was murdered by a rioting mob.

Wittelsbach Bavarian dynasty, who ruled Bavaria as dukes from 1180, electors from 1623, and kings 1806–1918.

Wittgenstein Ludwig 1889–1951. Austrian philosopher. *Tractatus Logico-Philosophicus* 1922 postulated the 'picture theory' of language, that words represent things according to social agreement. He subsequently rejected this idea, and developed the idea that usage was more important than convention.

Wizard of Oz, The Wonderful classic US children's tale of Dorothy's journey by the yellow brick road to an imaginary kingdom, written by L Frank Baum 1900, with many sequels, and made into a musical film 1939 with Judy Garland.

Wodehouse P(elham) G(renville) 1881–1975. British novelist, whose humourous novels portray the accident-prone world of such characters as the socialite Bertie Wooster and his invaluable and impeccable manservant Jeeves, and Lord Emsworth of Blandings Castle with his pig, the Empress of Blandings.

Woden (or Wodan) the foremost Anglo-Saxon god, whose Norse counterpart is ◊Odin.

Wöhler Friedrich 1800–1882. German chemist, who synthesized the first organic compound (urea) from an inorganic compound (ammonium cyanate). He also isolated the elements aluminium, beryllium, yttrium, and titanium.

wolf largest wild member *Canis lupus* of the dog family, found in Eurasia and North America. It is gregarious, grows to 90 cm/3 ft at the shoulder, and can weigh 45 kg/100 lb.

Wolf Hugo (Filipp Jakob) 1860–1903. Austrian composer, whose songs are in the German *Lieder* tradition. He also composed the opera *Der Corregidor* 1895 and orchestral works, such as *Italian Serenade* 1892.

Wolfe James 1727–1759. British soldier. He fought at the battles of ◊Dettingen, Falkirk, and ◊Culloden. In 1758 he served in Canada, and played a conspicuous part in the siege of the French stronghold of Louisburg. He was promoted to major-general 1759, and commanded a victorious expedition against Québec in which he lost his life.

Wolfe Thomas 1900–1938. US novelist. He wrote four long and powerful autobiographical novels: *Look Homeward, Angel* 1929, *Of Time and the River* 1935, and the posthumous *The Web and the Rock* 1939 and *You Can't Go Home Again* 1940.

Wolfe Tom 1931– . US journalist and novelist. In the 1960s a founder of the 'New Journalism', which brought fiction's methods to reportage, Wolfe recorded American mores and fashions in pop style in *The Kandy-Kolored Tangerine-Flake Streamline Baby* 1965. His sharp social style is applied to the New York of the 1980s in his novel *The Bonfire of the Vanities* 1988.

wolfram another name for ◊tungsten.

Wollongong industrial city (iron, steel) in New South Wales, Australia, 65 km/40 mi south of Sydney; population (1985, with Port Kembla) 238,000.

Wollstonecraft Mary 1759–1797. British feminist, member of a group of radical intellectuals called the English Jacobins, whose book *Vindication of the Rights of Women* 1792 demanded equal educational opportunities for women. She married William Godwin and died in giving birth to a daughter, Mary, who later, as Mary ◊Shelley, wrote the gothic novel *Frankenstein*.

Wolsey Thomas *c.* 1475–1530. English cardinal and politician. Under Henry VIII he became both cardinal and lord chancellor 1515, and began the dissolution of the monasteries. His reluctance to further Henry's divorce from Catherine of Aragon, partly because of his ambitions to be pope, led to his downfall 1529. He was charged with high treason 1530 but died before being tried.

Wolverhampton industrial city (metalworking, chemicals, tyres, aircraft, commercial vehicles) in West Midlands, England, 20 km/12 mi NW of Birmingham; population (1984) 254,000.

wolverine carnivorous bear-like mammal *Gulo gulo* found in Europe, Asia, and North America. It is the largest member of the weasel family, Mustelidae. It is about 1 m/3.3 ft long, and has long, thick fur, a dark brown back and belly, and lighter sides. It covers food it is unable to consume with an unpleasant secretion.

wombat herbivorous, nocturnal marsupial of the family Vombatidae, native to Tasmania and S Australia. It is about 1 m/3.3 ft long, heavy, with a big head, short legs and tail, and coarse fur.

Women's Institute local organization in country districts in the UK for the development of mutual fellowship, community welfare, and the practice of rural crafts.

Women's Land Army organization founded 1916 for the recruitment of women to work on farms during World War I. At its peak, in Sep 1918, it had 16,000 members. It re-formed Jun 1939, before the

wombat

outbreak of World War II. Many 'Land Girls' joined up to help the war effort, and by Aug 1943, 87,000 were employed in farm work.

women's movement the campaign for the rights of women, including social, political, and economic equality with men. Early campaigners fought for women's right to own property, to have access to higher education, and to vote (see ◊suffragette). Once women's suffrage was achieved, the emphasis of the movement shifted to the goals of equal social and economic opportunities for women, including employment. A current area of concern is the contradiction between the now generally accepted principle of equality and the demonstrable inequalities between the sexes that remain, both in state policies and in everyday life.

women's services the organized military use of women on a large scale, a comparatively recent development. First, women replaced men in factories and on farms during wartime, and in noncombat tasks; they are now found in combat units in many countries, including the USA, Cuba, the UK, and Israel.

Wonder Stevie. Stage name of Steveland Judkins Morris 1950– . US pop musician, singer, and songwriter, associated with Motown Records. His hits include 'My Cherie Amour' 1973, 'Master Blaster (Jammin)' 1980, and the album *Innervisions* 1973.

wood the hard tissue beneath the bark of many perennial plants; it is composed of water-conducting cells, or secondary ◊xylem, and gains its hardness and strength from deposits of ◊lignin. It has commercial value as a structural material and for furniture (**hardwoods** such as oak, and **softwoods** such as pine).

Wood Grant 1892–1942. US painter, a 'regionalist' based mainly in his native Iowa. Though his work is highly stylized, he struck a note of hard realism in his studies of farmers, such as *American Gothic* 1930 (Art Institute, Chicago).

Wood Mrs Henry (born Ellen Price) 1814–1887. British novelist, a pioneer of crime fiction, who wrote the melodramatic *East Lynne* 1861.

wood carving an art form practised since prehistoric times, including W Africa where there is a long tradition, notably in Nigeria, but surviving less often than sculpture in stone or metal because of the comparative fragility of the material.

woodcock Eurasian wading bird *Scolopax rusticola*, about 35 cm/14 in long, with mottled plumage, a long bill, short legs, and a short tail. It searches for food in boggy ground in woods.

woodcut and *wood engraving* print made by a woodblock in which a picture or design has been cut in relief. The woodcut is the oldest type of print, invented in China in the 5th century AD. In the Middle Ages woodcuts became popular in Europe, illustrating early printed books and broadsheets.

woodpecker

green woodpecker

woodwind instrument

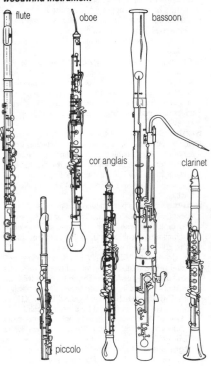

woodland area in which trees grow more or less thickly together, generally smaller than a forest. Temperate climates, with four distinct seasons per year, tend to support a mixed woodland habitat, most trees being broad-leaved and deciduous, shedding their leaves in autumn and regrowing them in spring. In the Mediterranean region and parts of the southern hemisphere, the trees are mostly evergreen.

woodlouse name given to certain crustaceans of the order Isopoda. They have segmented bodies and flattened undersides. The eggs are carried by the female in a pouch beneath the thorax.

woodpecker bird of the family Picidae, which drills holes in trees to obtain insects. There are about 200 species worldwide.

wood pitch a by-product of charcoal manufacture, made from *wood tar*, the condensed liquid produced from burning charcoal gases. The wood tar is boiled to produce the correct consistency. It has been used since ancient times for caulking wooden ships (filling in the spaces between the hull planks to make them watertight).

woodpulp wood that has been processed into a pulpy mass of fibres. Its main use is for making paper, but it is also used in making ◊rayon and other cellulose fibres and plastics.

Woodstock location near Bethel, New York state, USA, site of one of the first and largest rock festivals Aug 1969. It was attended by 400,000 people, and performers included Joan Baez; Richie Havens; Crosby, Stills and Nash; Joe Cocker; Santana; The Who; and Jimi Hendrix. The festival was a landmark in the youth culture of the 1960s.

woodwind instrument musical instrument from which sound is produced by blowing into a tube,

woodland

Northern temperate woods support huge populations of insects, slugs, snails and worms, on which prey birds, amphibians and mammals.

In an oak wood, there are several distinct small environments, or micro-habitats. High among the foliage, in the tree canopy, are animals that feed on the leaves, flowers and fruits. The open branches and the tree trunk support beetles and warps that search for food or lay eggs in bark crevices. On the ground, in the shade of the trees grow various flowering plants, as well as ferns, mosses and fungi. A fallen tree provides a home for fungi and invertebrates. Within the soil live insect larvae, worms and ants.

1. Jay 2. Oak tortrix
3. Sparrowhawk 4. Wren 5. Purple hairstreak 6. Gall warp 7. Oak bush cricket 8. Acorns 9. Bumble bee 10. Wood ant 11. Tree creeper 12. Beard lichen 13. Grey squirrel 14. Bluebell 15. Centipede 16. Fox 17. Roe-deer 18. Hornet 19. Wood anemone 20. Violet 21. Pot worm 22. Tiger moth larva 23. Cockchafer 24. Wireworm 25. Starling 26. Primrose 27. Hart's tongue fern 28. Woodwarbler 29. Red underwing 30. Badger 31. Longicorn larva 32. Ground beetle 33. Woodlouse 34. Dogs mercury 35. Fly agaric 36. Horn of plenty

World War I George V touches his cap to infantrymen in Fouquerueil, Aug 1916.

causing the air within to vibrate. They are no longer always made from wood (the modern flute, for example, is commonly made from stainless steel). In Western music the term is used mainly for wind instruments not made of brass, namely members of the flute, oboe, clarinet, bassoon, and saxophone families.

woodworm the common name for the larval stage of certain wood-boring beetles. Dead or injured trees are their natural target, but they also attack structural timber and furniture.

Wookey Hole natural cave near Wells, Somerset, England, in which flint implements of Old Stone Age people and bones of extinct animals have been found.

wool the natural fibrous covering of the sheep, and also of the llama, angora goat, and other animals. The domestic sheep *Ovis aries* provides the great bulk of the fibres used in commerce. Lanolin is a byproduct.

Woolf Virginia (born Virginia Stephen) 1882–1941. British novelist and critic. Her first novel *The Voyage Out* 1915 explored the tensions experienced by women who want marriage and a career. In *Mrs Dalloway* 1925 she perfected her 'stream of consciousness' technique. Among her later books are *To the Lighthouse* 1927, *Orlando* 1928, and *The Years* 1937, which considers the importance of economic independence for women.

Woolworth Frank Winfield 1852–1919. US businessman. He opened his first successful 'five and ten cent' store in Lancaster, Pennsylvania, 1879, and, together with his brother C S Woolworth (1856–1947), built up a chain of similar shops throughout the USA, Canada, Great Britain, Ireland, and Europe.

Worcester Porcelain Factory English porcelain factory, since 1862 the Royal Worcester Porcelain Factory. The factory was founded 1751, and produced a hard-wearing type of softpaste porcelain, mainly as tableware and decorative china.

Worcestershire former Midland county of England, merged 1974 with Herefordshire in the new county of Hereford and Worcester, except for a small projection in the north, which went to West Midlands. Worcester was the county town.

word in computing, a set of ◊bits of information processed by a computer in a single operation. A ◊byte corresponds to one character of the word.

word processor in computing, a program that allows the input, amendment, manipulation, storage, and retrieval of text; or a computer system

which runs such software. Since word-processing programs became available to microcomputers, the method is rapidly replacing the typewriter for producing letters or other text.

Wordsworth William 1770–1850. British Romantic poet. In 1797 he moved with his sister Dorothy to Somerset to be near ◊Coleridge, collaborating with him on *Lyrical Ballads* 1798 (which included 'Tintern Abbey'). From 1799 he lived in the Lake District, and later works include *Poems* 1807 (including 'Intimations of Immortality') and *The Prelude* (written by 1805, published 1850). He was appointed poet laureate 1843.

work in physics, a measure of the result of transferring energy from one system to another to cause an object to move. Work should not be confused with ◊energy (the capacity to do work, which is also measured in ◊joules), or ◊power (the rate of doing work, measured in joules per second).

World Bank popular name for the *International Bank for Reconstruction and Development*, established 1945 under the 1944 Bretton Woods agreement which also created the International Monetary Fund. The World Bank is a specialized agency of the United Nations which borrows in the commercial market and lends on commercial terms. The *International Development Association* is an arm of the World Bank.

World Cup quadrennial sporting competitions in football, cricket, rugby union, and other sports. The 1990 football World Cup was won by Germany, the 1992 cricket World Cup by Pakistan, and the 1991 rugby World Cup by Australia.

World Health Organization (WHO) an agency of the United Nations established 1946 to prevent the spread of diseases, and to eradicate them. Its headquarters are in Geneva, Switzerland.

World Intellectual Property Organization (WIPO) specialist agency of the United Nations established 1974 to coordinate the international protection (initiated by the Paris convention 1883) of inventions, trademarks, and industrial designs, and also literary and artistic works (as initiated by the Berne convention 1886).

World Meteorological Organization agency, part of the United Nations since 1950, that promotes the international exchange of weather information through the establishment of a worldwide network of meteorological stations. It was founded as the International Meteorological Organization 1873, and its headquarters are now in Geneva.

World War II The liberation of Paris by the Allies in June 1944; Gen de Gaulle leads jubilant Parisians down the Champs-Elysées.

World War I 1914–1918. war between the Central European Powers (Germany, Austria-Hungary, and allies), against the Triple Entente (Britain and the British Empire, France, and Russia), their allies, including the USA (who entered 1917). An estimated 10 million lives were lost and twice that number were wounded.

outbreak On 28 Jun the heir to the Austrian throne was assassinated at Sarajevo; on 28 Jul Austria declared war on Serbia; as Russia mobilized, Germany declared war on Russia and France, and invaded Belgium; on 4 Aug Britain declared war on Germany.

1914 Western Front The German advance reached within a few miles of Paris, but an Allied counterattack at Marne drove them back to the river Aisne; the opposing lines then settled to trench warfare.

Eastern Front The Prussian commander Hindenburg halted the Russian advance at the Battle of Tannenberg.

Africa On 16 Sep all Germany's African colonies were in Allied hands.

Middle East On 1 Nov Turkey entered the war.

1915 Western Front Several offensives on both sides resulted in insignificant gains. Haig became British commander in chief.

Eastern Front The German field marshal Mackensen and Hindenburg drove back the Russians and took Poland.

Middle East British attacks against Turkey in Mesopotamia (Iraq), the Dardanelles, and at Gallipoli were all unsuccessful.

Italy declared war on Austria; Bulgaria joined the Central Powers.

war at sea Germany declared all-out U-boat war, but the sinking of the liner *Lusitania* (with Americans among the 1,198 lost) led to demands in the USA to enter the war.

1916 Western Front German attack on the Verdun salient, countered by the Allies on the Somme and at Verdun.

Eastern Front Romania joined the Allies but was soon overrun by Germany.

Middle East Kut-al-Imara, Iraq, was taken from the British by the Turks.

war at sea The Battle of Jutland between England and Germany which, although indecisive, put a stop to further German naval participation in the war.

1917 USA entered the war.

1918 Eastern Front On 3 Mar Russia signed the Treaty of Brest-Litovsk with Germany.

Western Front Germany began a final offensive. In Apr the Allies appointed Foch supreme commander, but by Jun (when the first US troops went into battle) the Allies had lost all gains since 1915, and the Germans were on the Marne. The battle at Amiens marked the launch of the Allied victorious offensive.

Italy At Vittorio Veneto the British and Italians finally defeated the Austrians.

German capitulation began with naval mutinies at Kiel, followed by uprisings in the major cities. Kaiser Wilhelm II abdicated, and on 11 Nov the armistice was signed.

1919 18 Jun, peace treaty of Versailles.

World War II 1939–1945. War between Germany, Italy, and Japan (the Axis powers) on one side, and Britain, the Commonwealth, France, the USA, USSR, and China (the Allied powers) on the other.

An estimated 55 million lives were lost, 20 million of them citizens of the USSR.

1939 Sep German invasion of Poland; Britain and France declared war on Germany; USSR invaded Poland; fall of Warsaw (Poland divided between Germany and USSR).

Nov USSR invaded Finland.

1940 Mar Soviet peace treaty with Finland.

Apr Germany invaded Denmark, Norway, Netherlands, Belgium, and Luxembourg. In Britain, a coalition government was formed under Churchill.

May Germany outflanked the defensive Maginot Line.

May–Jun Evacuation of 337,131 Allied troops from Dunkirk.

Jun Italy declared war on Britain and France; Germans entered Paris; the French prime minister Pétain signed the armistice with Germany and moved the seat of government to Vichy.

Jul–Oct Battle of Britain between British and German air forces.

Sep Japanese invasion of French Indochina.

Oct Abortive Italian invasion of Greece.

1941 Apr Germany overran Greece and Yugoslavia.

Jun Germany invaded USSR; Finland declared war on USSR.

Jul Germans entered Smolensk.

Dec Germans within 40 km/25 mi of Moscow, with Leningrad under siege. First Soviet counteroffensive. Japan attacked Pearl Harbor and declared war on USA and Britain. Germany and Italy declared war on USA.

1942 Jan Japanese conquest of Philippines.

Jun Naval battle of Midway, the turning point of the Pacific War.

Aug German attack on Stalingrad.

Oct–Nov Battle of El Alamein in N Africa, turn of the tide for the Western Allies.

Nov Soviet counteroffensive on Stalingrad.

1943 Jan Casablanca conference issued Allied demand of unconditional surrender; Germans surrender at Stalingrad.

Mar USSR drove Germans back to the river Donetz.

May End of Axis resistance in N Africa.

Aug Beginning of campaign against Japanese in Burma.

Sep Italy surrendered to Allies; Allied landings at Salerno; USSR retook Smolensk.

Oct Italy declared war on Germany.

Nov–Dec Allied leaders met at Tehran Conference.

1944 Jan Allied landing in Italy: Battle of Anzio.

Mar End of German U-boat campaign in the Atlantic.

May Fall of Monte Cassino, S Italy.

6 Jun D-day: Allied landings in Normandy.

Jul Bomb plot against Hitler failed.

Aug Romania joined Allies.

Sep Battle of Arnhem on the Rhine; Soviet armistice with Finland.

Oct The Yugoslav guerrilla leader Tito and Soviets entered Belgrade.

Dec German counteroffensive, Battle of the Bulge.

1945 Feb Soviets reached German border; Yalta conference; Allied bombing campaign over Germany (Dresden destroyed); Americans landed on Iwo Jima.

Apr Hitler committed suicide.

May German surrender to the Allies.

Jul Potsdam Conference issued Allied ultimatum to Japan.

Aug Atom bombs dropped on Hiroshima and Nagasaki; Japan surrendered.

World Wide Fund for Nature (WWF, formerly the World Wildlife Fund) an international organization established 1961 to raise funds for conservation by public appeal. Its headquarters are at Gland, Switzerland. Projects include conservation of particular species (for example, the tiger and giant panda) or special areas (such as the Simen Mountains, Ethiopia).

worm term popularly used for various elongated limbless creatures. Worms include the flatworms, such as ◊flukes and ◊tapeworms; the roundworms or ◊nematodes, such as the potato eelworm and the hookworm, an animal parasite; the marine ribbon worms or nemerteans; and the segmented worms or ◊annelids.

Worms industrial town in Rhineland-Palatinate, Germany, on the Rhine; population (1984) 73,000. Liebfraumilch wine is produced here. Luther appeared before the *Diet* (Assembly) *of Worms* 1521, and was declared an outlaw by the Roman Catholic church.

wormwood aromatic herb *Artemisia absinthium*, family Compositae; the leaves are used in ◊absinthe.

Wounded Knee site on the Oglala Sioux Reservation, South Dakota, USA, of a confrontation between the US Army and American Indians. Sitting Bull was killed, supposedly resisting arrest, on 15 Dec 1890, and on 29 Dec a group of Indians involved with him in the Ghost Dance Movement (aimed at resumption of Indian control of North America with the aid of the spirits of dead braves) were surrounded and 153 killed.

wrack any of the large brown seaweeds characteristic of rocky shores. The *bladder wrack Fucus vesiculosus* has narrow dichotomously branched fronds up to 1 m/3.3 ft long, with oval air bladders, usually in pairs on either side of the midrib or central vein.

wrasse fish of the family Labridae, found in temperate and tropical seas. They are slender, and often brightly coloured, with a single long dorsal fin. They have elaborate courtship rituals, and some species can change their colouring and sex. Species vary in size from 5–200 cm/2 in–6.5 ft.

wren small brown bird *Troglodytes troglodytes* with a cocked tail, found in North America, Europe, and N Asia. It is about 10 cm/4 in long, has a loud trilling song, and feeds on insects and spiders. The male constructs a domed nest of moss, grass, and leaves.

Wren Christopher 1632–1723. English architect, designer of St Paul's Cathedral, London, built 1675–1710; many London churches including St Bride's, Fleet Street, and St Mary-le-Bow, Cheapside; the Royal Exchange; Marlborough House; and the Sheldonian Theatre, Oxford.

wrestling sport popular in ancient Egypt, Greece, and Rome, and included in the Olympics from 704 BC. The two main modern international styles are *Graeco-Roman*, concentrating on above-waist holds, and *freestyle*, which allows the legs to be used to hold or trip; in both the aim is to throw the opponent to the ground.

Wright Frank Lloyd 1869–1959. US architect, who rejected Neo-Classicist styles for 'organic architecture', in which buildings reflected their natural surroundings. Among his buildings are his Wisconsin home Taliesin East 1925; Falling Water, Pittsburgh, Pennsylvania, 1936; and the Guggenheim Museum, New York, 1959.

Wright Joseph 1734–1797. British painter, known as *Wright of Derby* from his birthplace. He painted portraits, landscapes, and scientific experiments. His work is often dramatically lit, by fire, candle-light, or even volcanic explosion.

Wright Joseph 1855–1930. British philologist. He was professor of comparative philology at Oxford 1901–25, and recorded English local speech in his six-volume *English Dialect Dictionary* 1896–1905.

Wright Judith 1915– . Australian poet, author of *The Moving Image* 1946 and *Alive* 1972.

Wright Orville 1871–1948 and Wilbur 1867–1912 US brothers who pioneered powered flight. Inspired by ◊Lilienthal's gliding, they perfected their piloted glider 1902. In 1903 they built their first powered machine, and became the first to make a successful powered flight, near Kitty Hawk, North Carolina.

Wright Peter 1917– . British intelligence agent. His book *Spycatcher* 1987, written after his retire-ment, caused a major international stir when the British government tried unsuccessfully to block its publication anywhere in the world because of its damaging revelations about the secret service.

Wright Richard 1908–1960. US novelist. He was one of the first to depict the condition of blacks in 20th-century US society with *Native Son* 1940 and the autobiography *Black Boy* 1945.

writ in English law, a document issued in the name of an executive officer of the crown, such as the lord chancellor or a judge, commanding some act from a subject. A writ of summons is the first step in legal proceedings, in the High Court.

writing a written form of communication using a set of symbols: see ◊alphabet, ◊cuneiform, ◊hi-eroglyphic. The last two used ideographs (picture writing) and phonetic word symbols side by side, as does modern Chinese. Syllabic writing, as in Japanese, develops from the continued use of a symbol to represent the sound of a short word. 8,000-year-old inscriptions, thought to be picto-graphs, were found on animal bones and tortoise shells in Henan province, China, at a Neolithic site at Jiahu. They are thought to pre-date the oldest known writing (Mesopotamian) by 2,500 years.

Wroclaw industrial river port in Poland, on the river Oder; population (1985) 636,000. Under the Ger-man name of Breslau, it was the capital of former German Silesia. Industries include shipbuilding, en-gineering, textiles, and electronics.

wrought iron fairly pure iron containing beads of slag, widely used for construction work before the days of cheap steel. It is strong, tough, easy to ma-chine, and is made in a so-called puddling furnace.

Wuhan river port and capital of Hubei province, China, at the confluence of the Han and Chang Jiang, formed 1950 as one of China's greatest industrial areas by the amalgamation of Hankou, Hanyang, and Wuchang; population (1986) 3,400,000. It produces iron, steel, machine tools, textiles, and fertilizer.

Wundt Wilhelm Max 1832–1920. German physi-ologist, who regarded psychology as the study of internal experience or consciousness. His main psychological method was introspection; he also studied sensation, perception of space and time, and reaction times.

Wuthering Heights a novel by Emily Brontë, published 1847, which chronicles the tumultuous relationship of Heathcliff and Catherine.

Wyatt James 1747–1813. English architect, con-temporary of the Adam brothers, who designed in the Neo-Gothic style. His over-enthusiastic 'res-torations' of medieval cathedrals earned him the nickname 'Wyatt the Destroyer'.

Wycherley William 1640–1710. English Restora-tion playwright. His first comedy *Love in a Wood* won him court favour 1671, and later bawdy works include *The Country Wife* 1675 and *The Plain Dealer* 1676.

Wycliffe John *c.* 1320–1384. English religious re-former. Allying himself with the party of John of Gaunt, which was opposed to ecclesiastical influ-ence at court, he attacked abuses in the Church, holding that the Bible rather than the Church was the supreme authority. About 1378 he criticized such fundamental doctrines as priestly absolution, confession, and indulgences. He set disciples to work on translating the Bible into English.

Wyeth Andrew (Newell) 1917– . US painter, whose portraits and landscapes, usually in water-colour or tempera, are naturalistic and minutely detailed.

Wyndham John. Pen name of John Wyndham Parkes Lucas Beynon Harris 1903–1969. Eng-lish science fiction writer who wrote *The Day of the Triffids* 1951, *The Chrysalids* 1955, and *The Midwich Cuckoos* 1957. A recurrent theme in his work is human response to disaster, whether caused by nature, aliens, or mankind's own mis-takes.

Wyoming state of W USA; nickname Equality State
area 253,595 sq km/97,888 sq mi
capital Cheyenne
towns Casper, Laramie
products oil, natural gas, tin, sodium salts, coal, phosphates, sulphur, uranium, sheep, beef
population (1986) 485,000
famous people Buffalo Bill Cody
history part of the ◊Louisiana Purchase; first settled by whites 1834; granted women the vote 1869; state 1890.

Wyss Johann David 1743–1818. Swiss author of the children's classic *Swiss Family Robinson* 1813.

xenon gaseous element, symbol Xe, atomic number 54, relative atomic mass 131.30. It is a heavy, inert gas, used in lasers, incandescent lamps, and electronic flash lamps. It is a fission product of uranium nuclear reactors. Radioactive xenon has been used to measure the flow of blood to the brain when testing the effects of supersonic speeds on humans.

Xenophon *c.* 430–354 BC. Greek historian, philosopher, and soldier. He was a disciple of ◊Socrates (described in Xenophon's *Symposium*). In 401 BC he joined a Greek mercenary army aiding the Persian prince Cyrus, and on Cyrus' death, took command. His *Anabasis* describes how he led 10,000 Greeks in a 1,000-mile march home across enemy territory. His other works include *Memorabilia* and *Apology*.

xerography a dry, non-chemical method of producing images without the use of negatives or sensitized paper, invented in the USA by Chester Carlson in 1938 and applied in the Xerox ◊photocopier.

xerophyte a plant that is adapted to live in dry conditions. Common adaptations to reduce the rate of ◊transpiration include a reduction of leaf size, sometimes to spines or scales; a dense covering of hairs over the leaf to trap a layer of moist air (as in edelweiss); and permanently rolled leaves or leaves that roll up in dry weather (as in marram grass). Many desert cacti are xerophytes.

Xerxes *c.* 519–465 BC. King of Persia from 485 BC, when he succeeded his father Darius, and, after several years' preparation, continued the Persian invasion of Greece. In 480 BC, at the head of an army of some 400,000 men and supported by a fleet of 800 ships, he crossed the Hellespont over

Xavier, St Francis 1506–1552. Spanish Jesuit missionary. He went as a Catholic missionary to the Portuguese colonies in the Indies, arriving at Goa in 1542. He was in Japan 1549–51, establishing a Christian mission which lasted for 100 years. He returned to Goa in 1552, and sailed for China, but died of fever there. He was canonized in 1621.

X-chromosome the larger of the two sex chromosomes, the smaller being the ◊Y-chromosome. These two chromosomes are involved in ◊sex determination. Genes carried on the X-chromosome produce the phenomenon of ◊sex linkage.

xerophyte

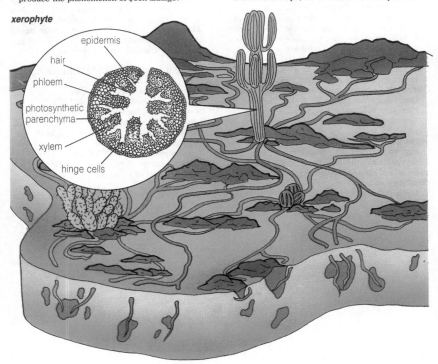

epidermis
hair
phloem
photosynthetic parenchyma
xylem
hinge cells

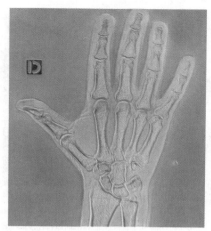

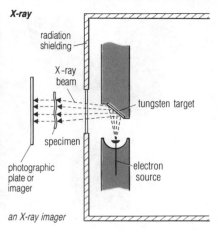

X-ray

radiation shielding

X-ray beam

tungsten target

specimen

photographic plate or imager

electron source

an X-ray imager

X-ray X-ray of a normal human hand and wrist, obtained using xerography.

a bridge of boats. He defeated the Greek fleet at Artemisium and, having stormed the pass of Thermopylae, captured and burned Athens, but Themistocles annihilated the Persian fleet at Salamis and Xerxes was forced to retreat.

Xhosa people of South Africa, living mainly in the Black National State of ◊Transkei. Their Bantu language belongs to the Niger-Congo family.

Xi'an industrial city and capital of Shaanxi province, China; population (1986) 2,330,000. It produces chemicals, electrical equipment, and fertilizers.

Xian Incident kidnapping of the Chinese generalissimo and politician ◊Chiang Kai-shek 12 Dec 1936, by one of his own generals, to force his cooperation with the communists against the Japanese invaders.

Xi Jiang (formerly *Si-Kiang*) river in China, which rises in Yunnan and flows into the South China Sea; length 1,900 km/1,200 mi. Guangzhou lies on the N arm of its delta, and Hong Kong island at its mouth. The name means West River.

Xinhua official Chinese news agency.

Xining (formerly *Sining*) industrial city, capital of Qinghai province, China; population (1982) 873,000.

Xinjiang Uygur (formerly *Sinkiang Uighur*) autonomous region of NW China
area 1,646,800 sq km/635,665 sq mi
capital Urumqi
products cereals, cotton, fruit in valleys and oases; uranium, coal, iron, copper, tin, oil
population (1985) 13,440,000
religion 50% Muslim
history under Manchu rule from the 18th century; large sections ceded to Russia 1864 and 1881; China has raised the question of their return and regards the 480 km/300 mi frontier between Xinjiang Uygur

and Soviet Tadzikistan as undemarcated.

X-ray electromagnetic radiation in the wavelength range 10^{-11} to 10^{-9} m (shorter wavelengths are gamma rays; see ◊electromagnetic waves). Applications of X-rays make use of their short wavelength (such as X-ray crystallography) or their penetrating power (as in medical X-rays of internal body tissues). High doses of X-rays are dangerous, and can cause cancer.

X-ray astronomy detection of ◊X-rays from intensely hot gas in the Universe. Such X-rays are prevented from reaching the Earth's surface by the atmosphere, so detectors must be placed in rockets and satellites. The first celestial X-ray source, Scorpius X-1, was discovered by a rocket flight in 1962.

xylem a tissue found in ◊vascular plants, whose main function is to conduct water and dissolved mineral nutrients from the roots to other parts of the plant. Xylem is composed of a number of different types of cell, and may include long, thin, usually dead cells known as ◊tracheids, fibres, thin-walled ◊parenchyma cells, and conducting vessels. In most flowering plants water is translocated through the vessels.

xylophone musical ◊percussion instrument in which a number of wooden bars of varying lengths are arranged in rows over resonators to produce sounds when struck with hammers.

XYZ Affair, The an incident (1797–8) in which the French were accused of demanding a $250,000 bribe before agreeing to negotiate with American envoys in Paris in an attempt to resolve a crisis in Franco-American relations caused by the war in Europe. Three French agents (referred to by President John Adams in 1797 as X, Y and Z) held secret talks with the envoys over the money. Publicity fuelled anti-French feelings in the US and led to increased defence spending.

Y

yachting *Wyvern, a 19th century yacht under sail in the North Sea off Stavanger, Norway.*

yachting pleasure cruising or racing a small light vessel, whether sailing or power-driven. At the Olympic Games, seven categories exist. They are: Soling, Flying Dutchman, Star, Finn, Tornado, 470, and Boardsailing (Windsurfing), which was introduced at the 1984 Los Angeles games. The Finn and Boardsailing are solo events, the Soling Class is for three-person crews, while all other classes are for crews of two.

yak wild *ox Bos grunniens* which lives in herds at high altitudes in Tibet. It stands about 2 m/6 ft at the shoulder, and has long shaggy hair on the underparts. It has large, upward curving horns and humped shoulders. The yak is in danger of becoming extinct.

Yakut (Russian *Yakutskaya*) Autonomous Soviet Socialist Republic in Siberian Russia
area 3,103,000 sq km/1,197,760 sq mi
capital Yakutsk
products furs; gold, natural gas, some agriculture
population (1986) 1,009,000; Yakuts 37%, Russians 50%
history the nomadic Yakuts were conquered by Russia 17th century; Yakut became a Soviet republic 1922.

Yakuza Japanese criminal organization, the equivalent of the Italian Mafia. Some 110,000 are registered Yakuza; they are identifiable by tattooing and a missing fingertip.

Yalta Conference conference at which the Allied leaders Churchill, Roosevelt, and Stalin completed plans for the defeat of Germany and the foundation of the United Nations in 1945. It took place at Livadia (summer palace built by Nicholas II 1910–11), in Yalta, a Soviet holiday resort in the Crimea.

yam tuber of tropical plant, genus *Dioscorea*, of the family Dioscoreaceae, cultivated in wet regions and eaten as a vegetable. The *Mexican yam Dioscorea composita* contains a chemical used in the manufacture of the contraceptive pill.

Yamagata Aritomo 1838–1922. Japanese soldier and politician. He was prime minister (1890–91 and 1898–1900) and chief of staff in the 1870s, 1880s, and during the Russo-Japanese war of 1904–05.

Yamamoto Gombei 1852–1933. Japanese admiral and politician. As prime minister 1913–14, he began Japanese expansion on the Chinese mainland and initiated reforms in the political system. He again became premier in the aftermath of the Tokyo earthquake 1923, but resigned later that year.

Yamoussoukro capital of ◊Ivory Coast (Côte d'Ivoire); population (1983) 70,000. The economy is based on tourism and agricultural trade.

Yangon capital and chief port of Myanmar (Burma) on the Yangon River, 32 km/20 mi from the Indian Ocean; population (1983) 2,459,000. Products include timber, oil and rice. The city *Dagon* was founded on the site AD 746; it was given the name Rangoon ('end of conflict') by King Alaungpaya 1755.

Yang Shangkun 1907– . Chinese communist politician. He held a senior position in the party 1956–66, but was demoted during the Cultural Revolution. He was rehabilitated 1978, elected to the Politburo 1982, and to the position of state president 1988.

Yangtze-Kiang former name for ◊Chang Jiang, greatest Chinese river.

Yalta Conference *The Allied leaders: Churchill Roosevelt, and Stalin at the Yalta Conference, 1945.*

yak

yachting

Yachting takes various forms ranging from the use of large sailing yachts as seen in major international events like the America's Cup, to dinghy racing, and indeed boardsailing. In all cases power is provided by wind and sail(s), and the ability to utilise both to the full is important.

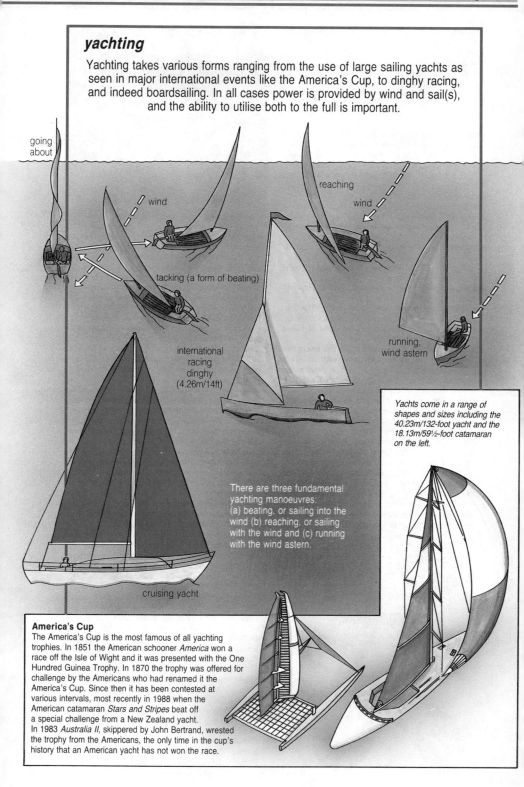

going about

wind

reaching

wind

tacking (a form of beating)

international racing dinghy (4.26m/14ft)

running, wind astern

Yachts come in a range of shapes and sizes including the 40.23m/132-foot yacht and the 18.13m/59½-foot catamaran on the left.

There are three fundamental yachting manoeuvres: (a) beating, or sailing into the wind (b) reaching, or sailing with the wind and (c) running with the wind astern.

cruising yacht

America's Cup
The America's Cup is the most famous of all yachting trophies. In 1851 the American schooner *America* won a race off the Isle of Wight and it was presented with the One Hundred Guinea Trophy. In 1870 the trophy was offered for challenge by the Americans who had renamed it the America's Cup. Since then it has been contested at various intervals, most recently in 1988 when the American catamaran *Stars and Stripes* beat off a special challenge from a New Zealand yacht.
In 1983 *Australia II*, skippered by John Bertrand, wrested the trophy from the Americans, the only time in the cup's history that an American yacht has not won the race.

Yankee colloquial (sometimes disparaging) term for an American. Outside the USA it is used for any American. In the northern USA it is applied to a person from the New England states, while in the southern states it refers to a person from any of the northern states.

Yaoundé capital of Cameroon, 210 km/130 mi E of the port of Douala; population (1984) 552,000. Industry includes tourism, oil refining, and cigarette manufacturing.

yapok nocturnal fish-eating marsupial *Chironectes minimus* found in tropical South and Central America. The head and body are about 33 cm/1.1 ft long, with a 40 cm/1.3 ft tail. It has webbed hind feet and thick fur, and is the only aquatic marsupial. The female has a watertight pouch. It feeds on fish and crayfish.

yard imperial measure of length (yd), equivalent to 3 ft. It was defined by the UK 1963 Weights and Measures Act as being equivalent to 0.9144 metre.

yardang ridge formed by wind erosion from a dried-up river bed or similar feature, as in Chad, China, Peru, USA. They occur on the planet Mars on a more massive scale.

yarmulke or *kippa* a skullcap worn by Jewish men.

yarrow or *milfoil* perennial herb *Achillea millefolium* of the family Compositae, with feathery scented leaves and flat-topped clusters of white or pink flowers.

Y-chromosome the smaller of the two sex chromosomes. It only ever occurs paired with the other type of sex chromosome (X), which carries far more genes. Thus individuals are either XY (male) or XX (female); see ◊sex determination. The Y-chromosome is the smallest of all the mammalian chromosomes and considered to be inert (without direct effect on the physical body).

yd abbreviation for *yard*.

year a unit of time measurement, based on the orbital period of the Earth around the Sun. The *tropical year*, from one vernal ◊equinox to the next lasts 365.2422 days. It governs the occurrence of the seasons, and is the period on which the ◊calendar year is based. The *sidereal year* is the time taken for the Earth to complete one orbit relative to the fixed stars, and lasts 365.2564 days (about 20 minutes longer than a tropical year).

yeast

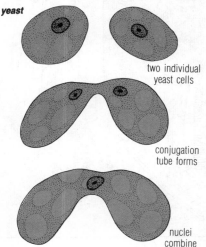

two individual yeast cells

conjugation tube forms

nuclei combine

Yeats *Irish poet and dramatist W B Yeats.*

The difference is due to the effect of ◊precession, which slowly moves the position of the equinoxes. The calendar year consists of 365 days, with an extra day added at the end of Feb each *leap year*. Leap years occur in every year that is divisible by 4, except that a century year is not a leap year unless it is divisible by 400. Hence 1900 was not a leap year, but 2000 will be. A historical year begins on 1 Jan but up to 1752 in England the civil or legal year began on 25 Mar. The English *fiscal/financial year* still ends on 5 Apr, which is 25 Mar plus 11 days added under the reform of the ◊calendar in 1752. The *regnal year* begins on the anniversary of the sovereign's accession; it is used in the dating of Acts of Parliament.

yeast mass of minute circular or oval fungal cells, each of which is a complete fungus capable under suitable conditions of reproducing new cells by budding. When placed in a sugar solution they multiply and convert the sugar into alcohol and carbon dioxide. Yeasts are used as fermenting agents in baking, brewing, and the making of wine and spirits. *Brewer's yeast Saccharomyces cerevisiae* is a rich source of vitamin B.

Yeats Jack Butler 1871–1957. Irish artist, brother of the poet W B Yeats. His vivid scenes of Irish life, for example *Back from the Races* (Tate Gallery, London), and Celtic mythology reflected a new consciousness of Irish nationalism.

Yeats W(illiam) B(utler) 1865–1939. Irish poet. He was a leader of the Celtic revival and a founder of the Abbey Theatre in Dublin. His early work was romantic and lyrical, as in the poem 'The Lake Isle of Innisfree' and plays *The Countess Cathleen* 1892 and *The Land of Heart's Desire* 1894. His later books of poetry include *The Wild Swans at Coole* 1919 and *The Winding Stair* 1933. He was a senator of the Irish Free State 1922–28. Nobel prize 1923.

Yedo name for ◊Tokyo, Japan, until 1868.

Yellow Book 1894–1897. Illustrated literary and artistic quarterly to which the artists Aubrey Beardsley and Walter Sickert and the writers Max Beerbohm and Henry James contributed.

yellow fever or *yellow jack* tropical viral fever, prevalent in the Caribbean area, Brazil, and the W coast of Africa. Its symptons are a high fever and jaundice (possibly leading to liver failure); the heart and kidneys may also be affected.

yellowhammer bird *Emberiza citrinella* of the bunting family, found in open country across Eurasia. About 16.5 cm/6.5 in long, the male has a bright yellow head and underside, a chestnut

Yemen
Republic of Yemen
(al Jamhuriya al Yamaniya)

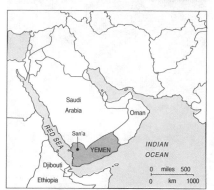

area 531,900 sq km/205,367 sq mi
capital San'a
towns Ta'iz; and chief port Aden
physical hot moist coastal plain, rising to plateau and desert
head of state and of government Ali Abdullah Saleh from 1978
political system authoritarian republic
exports cotton, coffee, grapes, vegetables
currency rial
population (1990 est), 11,000,000; growth rate 2.7% p.a.
language Arabic
religion Sunni Muslim 63%, Shi'ite Muslim 37%
literacy men 20%, women 3% (1985 est)
GNP $4.9 bn (1983); $520 per head

chronology
1962 North Yemen declared Yemen Arab Republic (YAR), with Abdullah al-Sallal as president; civil war between royalists and republicans.
1967 Civil war ended with republican victory; Sallal deposed and replaced by Republican Council; The People's Republic of South Yemen was formed.
1971–72 War between South Yemen and YAR; union agreement signed but not kept.
1974 Ibrahim al-Hamadi seized power in North Yemen and Military Command Council set up.
1977 Hamadi assassinated and replaced by Ahmed ibn Hussein al-Ghashmi.
1978 Constituent People's Assembly appointed and the Military Command Council dissolved; Ghashmi killed by an envoy from South Yemen and succeeded by Ali Abdullah Saleh; war broke out again between the two Yemens. Yemen Socialist Party (YSP) formed.
1979 Ceasefire agreed with commitment to a future union.
1983 Saleh elected president of North Yemen for a further five-year term.
1984 Joint committee on foreign policy for the two Yemens met in Aden.
1988 President Saleh re-elected.
1989 Draft constitution for single Yemen state published.
1990 Border with South Yemen opened. Countries formally united as Republic of Yemen.
1993 Multiparty parliamentary elections set.

rump, and a brown-streaked back. The female is duller.

Yellowknife capital of Northwest Territories, Canada, on the north shore of Great Slave Lake; population (1984) 11,000. It was founded 1935 when gold was discovered in the area, and became the capital 1967.

Yellow River English name for the ◊Huang He river, China.

Yellow Sea gulf of the Pacific Ocean between China and Korea; area 466,200 sq km/180,000 sq mi. It receives the Huang He (Yellow River) and Chang Jiang.

Yellowstone National Park largest US nature reserve, established 1872, on a broad plateau in

yellowhammer

the Rocky Mountains, Wyoming. 1 million of its 2.2 million acres have been destroyed by fire since Jul 1988.

Yeltsin Boris Nikolayevich 1931– . Russian politician, president of the Russian Soviet Federative Socialist Republic (RSFSR) 1990–91, and president of the Russian Federation from 1991. He directed the Federation's secession from the USSR and the formation of a new, decentralized confederation, the ◊Commonwealth of Independent States (CIS). An international advocate of nuclear disarmament, at home he deregulated prices and accelerated privatization. Faced with severe economic problems, civil unrest and threats of a communist backlash, he consistently requested international aid to bring his country out of recession.

Yemen two countries (North Yemen and South Yemen) between which union was agreed in 1979. Unification was proclaimed in May 1990, with a 30-month period of implementation. The capital of the new republic of Yemen is San'a. A democratic system of government is promised.

Yenisei river in Asiatic Russia, rising in Tuva region and flowing across the Siberian plain into the Arctic Ocean; length 4,100 km/2,460 mi.

yeoman small English landowner who farmed his own fields between the break-up of the feudal system and the agricultural revolution of the 18th–19th centuries.

Yeomanry English volunteer cavalry organized 1794, and incorporated into volunteer regiments which became first the Territorial Force 1908 and then the ◊Territorial Army 1922.

Yeomen of the Guard English military corps founded by Henry VII in 1485 since when it has constituted the bodyguard of the English sovereign. Its duties are now purely ceremonial.

Yerevan industrial city (tractor parts, machine tools, chemicals, bricks, bicycles, wine, fruit canning), capital of Armenia a few miles north of the Turkish border; population (1987) 1,168,000. It was founded 7th century, and was alternately Turkish and Persian from the 15th century until ceded to Russia 1828. Armenia became an independent republic 1991.

Yerkes Observatory astronomical centre in Wisconsin, USA, founded by George Hale in 1897. It houses the world's largest refracting optical ◊telescope, with a lens of diameter 102 cm/ 40 in.

Yersin Alexandre Emile Jean 1863–1943. Swiss bacteriologist, who discovered the bubonic plague bacillus in Hong Kong in 1894 and prepared a serum against it.

Yesenin Sergei 1895–1925. Alternative form of ◊Esenin, Russian poet.

yeti Tibetan name for the ◊abominable snowman.

Yevtushenko Yevgeny Aleksandrovich 1933– . Russian poet, born in Siberia. He aroused controversy by his anti-Stalinist 'Stalin's Heirs' 1956, published with Khrushchev's support, and 'Babi Yar' 1961. His *Autobiography* was published 1963.

yew evergreen coniferous tree *Taxus baccata* of the family Taxaceae, native to the N hemisphere. The leaves and bright red berry-like seeds are poisonous; the wood is hard and close-grained.

Yiddish language a member of the Germanic branch of the Indo-European language family, deriving from Rhineland German and spoken by Polish and Russian Jews, who have carried it to Israel, the USA, and elsewhere.

yin and yang (Chinese 'dark' and 'bright') respectively, the interdependent passive (thought of as feminine, negative, intuitive) and active (thought of as masculine, positive, intellectual) principles of nature are said to correspond to the two halves of the brain. In ◊Taoism and ◊Confucianism, they are represented by two interlocked curved shapes within a circle, one white, one black, but having a spot of the contrasting colour within the head of each.

Yinchuan capital of Ningxia-Hui autonomous region, NW China; population (1989) 576,000.

yoga Hindu philosophic system (Sanskrit 'union') attributed to Patanjali, who lived about 150 BC at Gonda, Uttar Pradesh, India. He preached mystical union with a personal deity

Yevtushenko A master of the conversational, confessional style, the Russian poet Yevtushenko walked a thin line between Communist idealism and raising sensitive issues.

by the practice of hypnosis and rising above the senses by meditation, adoption of special postures, and ascetic practices. As practised in the West, yoga is more a system of relaxation.

yoghurt or *yogurt* or *yoghourt* food made from milk fermented with bacteria, often with fruit or other flavourings added.

Yokohama Japanese port on Tokyo Bay: population (1990) 3,220,350. Industries include shipbuilding, oil refining, engineering, textiles, glass, and clothing.

yolk a store of food, mostly in the form of fats and proteins, found in the ◊eggs of many animals: it provides nourishment for the growing embryo.

yolk sac the sac containing the yolk in the egg of most vertebrates. The term is also used for the membrane surrounding the developing mammalian embryo.

Yom Kippur the Jewish Day of ◊Atonement.

Yom Kippur War the 1973 *October War* between the Arabs and Israelis; see ◊Arab–Israeli Wars. It is named after the Jewish holiday on which it began.

York cathedral and industrial city (railway rolling stock, scientific instruments, sugar, chocolate, and glass) in North Yorkshire, N England; population (1991) 100,600.

York English dynasty founded by Richard, duke of York (1411–60).

York Frederick Augustus, Duke of York 1763–1827. Second son of George III. He was an unsuccessful commander in the Netherlands 1793–99, and British commander in chief 1798– 1809.

York, Archbishop of Metropolitan of the northern province of the Anglican Church in England and Primate of England, next in rank to the Lord High Chancellor.

York, Duke of second son of Queen Elizabeth II of the UK; see ◊Andrew.

Yorkshire county in NE England on the North Sea, formerly divided into north, east, and west ridings (thirds), but in 1974 reorganized to form a number

yew

Yugoslavia
Socialist Federal Republic of (*Socijalistička Federativna Republika Jugoslavija*)

area 255,800 sq km/98,739 sq mi
capital Belgrade
towns Podgorica (Titograd) Kraljevo, Leskovac, Novi Sad
physical mountainous, with river Danube plains in N and E; limestone (Karst) features in NW
head of state Dobrica Cosic from 1992
head of government Radoje Kontic from 1993
political system socialist pluralist republic
exports machinery, electrical goods, chemicals
currency dinar

population (1990) 12,420,000 (53% Serb, 15% Albanian, 11% Macedonian, 5% Montenegrin, 3% Muslim, 2% Croat)
language Serbian variant of Serbo-Croatian Macedonian, Slovenian.
religion 41% Orthodox (Serbs), 29% Roman Catholic (Croats), 3% Muslim
literacy 90% (1989)
GNP $154.1bn; $6,540 per head (1988)
chronology
1917–18 Creation of Kingdom of the Serbs, Croats and Slovenes.
1929 Name of Yugoslavia adopted.
1945 Tito formed communist federal republic.
1948 Split with USSR.
1953 Self-management principle enshrined in constitution.
1980 Tito died; collective leadership in power.
1988 massive economic difficulties: inflation over 250%, unemployment near 20%; ethnic unrest led to the resignation of the government.
1989 Reformist Croatian Ante Markovic became prime minister; ethnic riots in Kosovo province, state of emergency imposed; annual inflation to May 490%.
1990 Multi-party systems established in Slovenia and Croatia.
1991 Slovenia and Croatia declared independence, resulting in armed clashes; Slovenia accepted EC-sponsored peace pact.
1992 Bosnia-Herzegovina and Macedonia declared independence; Slovenian, Croatian, and Bosnia-Herzegovinan independence recognized by EC and USA. Bloody civil war ensued in Bosnia. UN membership suspended.
1993 Radoje Kontic became prime minister.

of new counties: the major part of *Cleveland* and *Humberside*; *North Yorkshire, South Yorkshire*, and *West Yorkshire*. Small outlying areas also went to Durham, Cumbria, Lancashire, and Greater Manchester.

Yoruba person of Yoruba culture from SW Nigeria and E Benin. They number approximately 20,000,000, in all and their language belongs to the Kwa branch of the Niger-Congo family.

Yoshida Shigeru 1878–1967. Japanese politician, leader of the Liberal party, who was prime minister for most of the 1946–54 period.

Young Arthur 1741–1820. Prolific writer and publicizer of the new farm practices associated with the Agricultural Revolution. When the board of Agriculture was established in 1792, Young was appointed secretary, and directed a county-by-county survey of British agriculture.

Young Brigham 1801–1877. US ◊Mormon religious leader, born in Vermont. He joined the Mormon Church 1832, and three years later was appointed an apostle. After a successful recruiting mission in Liverpool, he returned to the USA, and as successor of Joseph Smith, who had been murdered, led the Mormon migration to the Great Salt Lake in Utah 1846, founded Salt Lake City, and ruled the colony until his death.

Young David Ivor (Baron Young of Graffham) 1932– . British Conservative politician, chair of the Manpower Services Commission (MSC) 1982–84, secretary for employment from 1985, trade and industry secretary 1987–89, when he retired.

Young John Watts 1930– . US astronaut, the first person to make six space flights. He became

chief of the NASA Astronaut Office in 1975. His first flight was on Gemini 3 in 1965, followed by Gemini 10 in 1966. He flew on Apollo 10 in 1969 and landed on the Moon with Apollo 16 in 1972. He was commander of the first flight of the Space Shuttle 1981, and the ninth Shuttle flight 1983.

Young Lester (Willis, 'Press') 1909–1959. US tenor saxophonist and jazz composer. He was a major figure in the development of his instrument for jazz music from the 1930s.

Young Ireland Irish nationalist organization, founded 1840 by William Smith O'Brien (1830–64), who rejected the nonviolent policies of Daniel ◊O'Connell's Repeal Association. It attempted an abortive insurrection of the peasants against the British at Tipperary in 1848.

Young Italy Italian nationalist organization, founded 1831 by Giuseppe ◊Mazzini while in exile in Marseille. The movement, which was immediately popular, was followed the next year by Young Germany, Young Poland, and similar organizations.

Young Pretender nickname of ◊Charles Edward Stuart, claimant to the Scottish and English thrones.

Young Turk member of a reformist movement of young army officers in the Ottoman Empire founded 1889. The movement was instrumental in the constitutional changes of 1908 and gained prestige during the Balkan Wars 1912–13; it also encouraged Turkish links with the German empire. Its influence diminished after 1918. The term is now used for a member of any radical faction.

Young Women's Christian Association
(YWCA) organization for women and girls, formed

in 1887 when two organizations, both founded in 1855 – one by Emma Robarts, the other by Lady Kinnaird – combined their work.

Yourcenar Marguerite. Pen name of Marguerite de Crayencour 1903–1987. French writer, who achieved a reputation as a novelist in France in the 1930s (for example *La Nouvelle Euridyce/The New Euridyce* 1931), but after World War II settled in the USA. Novels such as *Les Mémoires d'Hadrien/The Memoirs of Hadrian* 1951 and *L'Oeuvre au noir/The Work in Black* 1968 (translated as *The Abyss*) won her acclaim as a historical novelist. In 1980 she was the first woman to be elected to the French Academy.

Ypres (Flemish *Ieper*) Belgian town in W Flanders, 40 km/25 mi S of Ostend, a centre of fighting in World War I. The Menin Gate 1927 is a memorial to British soldiers lost in the great battles fought round the town 1914–18.

YTS the *Youth Training Scheme* in the UK, a mandatory one-or two-year course of training and work experience for unemployed school leavers aged 16 and 17. Opponents argue that it is a form of extremely cheap forced labour for employers, does not provide young people with the high-technology skills that will be needed in the future, and does not pay well enough.

ytterblum metallic element, symbol Yb, atomic number 70; a member of the ◊lanthanide series. It is used in steelmaking.

yttrium silvery metallic element, symbol Yt, atomic number 39. A member of the ◊lanthanide series, it occurs in monazite; it is used to reduce steel corrosion.

Yucatán peninsula in Central America, divided between Mexico, Belize, and Guatemala; area 180,000 sq km/70,000 sq mi. Tropical crops are grown. It is inhabited by ◊Maya Indians and contains the remains of their civilization.

Yucca plant of the genus *Yucca*, family Liliaceae, with some 40 species found in Mexico and SW USA. The leaves are stiff and sword-shaped, and the flowers white and bell-shaped.

Yugoslavia country in SE Europe, on the Adriatic Sea, bounded W by Bosnia-Herzegovina, NW by Croatia, E by Romania and Bulgaria, and S by Greece and Albania.

Yukawa Hideki 1907–1981. Japanese physicist, who predicted the existence of the ◊meson in 1935. Nobel prize 1949.

Yukon territory of NW Canada
area 483,500 sq km/186,631 sq mi
towns capital Whitehorse; Dawson City
products oil, natural gas, gold, silver, coal
population (1991) 26,500
history settlement dates from the gold rush 1896– 1910, when 30,000 people moved to the ◊Klondike river valley (silver is now worked there); became separate from Northwest Territories 1898, with Dawson City as the original capital.

Yunnan province of SW China, adjoining Myanmar, Laos, and Vietnam
area 436,200 sq km/168,370 sq mi
capital Kunming
physical Chang Jiang, Salween, and Mekong rivers; crossed by the Burma Road; mountainous and well forested
products rice, tea, timber, wheat, cotton, rubber, tin, copper, lead, zinc, coal, salt.
population (1990) 36,973,000.

Zadkine Ossip 1890–1967. French Cubist sculptor, born in Russia, active in Paris from 1909. He represented the human figure in dramatic, semiabstract forms, as in the monument *To a Destroyed City* 1953 (Rotterdam).

Zagreb industrial city (leather, linen, carpets, paper, and electrical goods), capital of Croatia, on the Sava river; population (1981) 1,174,512.

Zahir ud-din Mohammed 1483–1530. First Great Mogul of India from 1526, called Baber (Arabic 'lion'). He was the great-grandson of the Mongol conqueror Tamerlane and, at the age of 12, succeeded his father, Omar Sheikh Mirza, as ruler of Ferghana (Turkestan). In 1526 he defeated the emperor of Delhi at Panipat in the Punjab, captured Delhi and ◊Agra, and established

a dynasty which lasted until 1858.

Zahir Shah Mohammed 1914– . King of Afghanistan 1933–73. Zahir, educated in Kabul and Paris, served in the government 1932–33 before being crowned king. He was overthrown in 1973 by a republican coup led by his cousin General Daud Khan, and went into exile in Rome. He has been a symbol of national unity for the ◊Mujaheddin resistance groups.

zaibatsu (Japanese 'financial clique') large monopolistic or cartelized industries (see ◊cartel) or combines in Japan.

Zaïre country in central Africa.

Zaïre (formerly *Congo*, until 1971) second longest river in Africa, rising near the Zambia-Zaïre border (and known as the Lualaba river in the upper reaches) and flowing 4,500 km/2,800 mi to the Atlantic, running in a great curve which crosses the Equator twice. The chief tributaries are the Ubangi, Sangha, and Kasai.

Zama site of battle fought in 202 BC in Numidia (now Algeria) in which the Carthaginians under Hannibal were defeated by the Romans under Scipio, so ending the Second Punic War.

Zambezi river in central and SE Africa; length 2,575 km/1,600 mi from NW Zambia through Mozambique to the Indian Ocean, with a wide delta near Chinde. Major tributaries include the Kafue in Zambia.

Zambia landlocked country in central Africa.

ZANU (*Zimbabwe African National Union*) political organization founded in Aug 1963 by Ndabaningi Sithole with Robert Mugabe as secretary general. It was banned 1964 by Ian Smith's Rhodesian Front government, against which it conducted a guerilla war from Zambia until the free elections of 1980, when the ZANU (PF) party, led by Mugabe, won 63% of the vote. In 1987 it merged with ◊ZAPU in preparation for making Zimbabwe a one-party state.

Zaïre
Republic of (*République du Zaïre*) (formerly *Congo*)

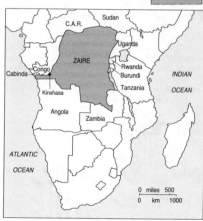

0 miles 500
0 km 1000

area 2,344,900 sq km/905,366 sq mi
capital Kinshasa
towns Lubumbashi, Kananga, Kisangani; ports Matadi, Boma
physical Zaïre river basin has tropical rainforest and savanna; mountains in E and W
head of state Mobuto Sésé Séko Kuku Ngbendu

wa Zabanga from 1965
head of government Faustin Birindwa from 1993
political system socialist pluralist republic
exports coffee, copper, cobalt (80% of world output), industrial diamonds
currency zaïre
population (1990 est.) 35,330,000; annual growth rate 2.9%
language French (official), African dialects
religion Christian 70% Muslim 10%
literacy 79% men 45% women (1985 est)
GNP $5 bn (1987), $127 per head
chronology
1960 Independence from Belgium; civil war between central government and Katanga province.
1963 Katanga war ended.
1967 New constitution adopted.
1970 Col Mobutu elected president.
1971 Country became the Republic of Zaïre, with the Popular Movement of the Revolution (MPR) the only legal political party.
1974 Foreign-owned businesses seized by Mobutu and given in political patronage.
1977 Owners of confiscated properties invited back; Mobutu re-elected; Zaïrians invaded Katanga province from Angola, repulsed by Belgian paratroops.
1978 Second unsuccessful invasion from Angola.
1984 Mobutu re-elected.
1990 Ban on multiparty politics lifted after internal dissent.
1991 Mobutu agreed to share power with opposition after antigovernment riots.
1992 Interim opposition parliament formed after renewed rioting.
1993 Army mutiny: French ambassador shot dead.

Zambia
Republic of

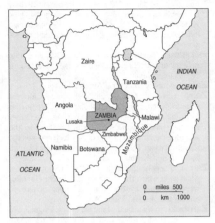

0   miles 500
0   km   1000

area 752,620 sq km/ 290,586 sq mi
capital Lusaka
towns Kitwe, Ndola, Kabwe, Chipata, Livingstone
physical a forested plateau cut through by rivers

head of state and government Frederick Chiluta from 1991
political system socialist pluralist republic
exports copper, emeralds, tobacco
currency kwacha
population (1990 est) 8,119,000; annual growth rate 3.3%
life expectancy men 54, women 57 (1989)
language English (official); Bantu dialects
religion Christian 66%, animist, Hindu, Muslim
literacy 54% (1988)
GNP $2.1 bn (1987); $304 per head
chronology
1964 Achieved full independence as the Republic of Zambia with Kenneth Kaunda as president.
1972 United Independence Party (UNIP) declared the only legal party.
1976 Support for the Patriotic Front in Rhodesia.
1980 Unsuccessful coup against Kaunda.
1985 Kaunda elected chair of the Front Line States.
1987 Kaunda elected chair of the Organization of African Unity (OAU).
1988 Kaunda re-elected unopposed for sixth term.
1990 Multiparty system announced for 1991.
1991 Movement for Multiparty Democracy won landslide election victory. Chiluta became president.
1992 Food and water shortages caused by severe drought.

Zanzibar   island region of Tanzania
area 1,658 sq km/640 sq mi (80 km/50 mi long)
towns Zanzibar
products cloves, copra
population (1985) 571,000
history Arab traders settled in the 7th century, and Zanzibar became a sultanate; under British protection 1890–1963; together with the island of Pemba, some nearby islets, and a strip of mainland territory, it became a republic; merged with Tanganyika as Tanzania 1964.

Zapata   Emiliano 1877–1919. Mexican Indian revolutionary guerrilla leader. He led a revolt against dictator Porfirio Diaz (1830–1915) from 1911 under the slogan 'Land and Liberty', attempting to repossess for the indigenous Mexicans the land that had been taken by the Spanish. He was driven into retreat by 1915, and was assassinated by an opponent at Puebla.

Zapotec   indigenous American people of S Mexico, numbering approximately 250,000, living mainly in Oaxaca. The Zapotec language, which belongs to the Oto-Mangean family, is divided into nine dialects. The ancestors of the Zapotec built the city of Monte Albán 1000–500 BC.

ZAPU   (*Zimbabwe African People's Union*) political organization founded by Joshua Nkomo in 1961 and banned 1962 by the Rhodesian government. It engaged in a guerrilla war in alliance with ◊ZANU against the Rhodesian regime until late 1979. In the 1980 elections ZAPU was defeated and was then persecuted by the ruling ZANU (PF) party. In 1987 the two parties merged.

Zaragoza   Spanish spelling of ◊Saragossa, industrial city in Aragon.

zazen   formal seated meditation in Zen Buddhism. Correct posture and breathing are important. The term is also used for the Buddhist practice of constant awareness and attention.

zebra   black-and-white striped members of the horse family found in Africa; the stripes serve as camouflage against their mountain or plains habitat,

or dazzle and confuse predators. They are about 1.5 m/5 ft high at the shoulder, with a stout body, and a short, thick mane. They live in herds, and can run at up to 60 kph/40 mph.

zebu   ox *Bos indicus* found in E Asia, India, and Africa. It is usually light-coloured, with large horns and a large fatty hump near the shoulders. It is used for pulling loads, and is held by some Hindus to be sacred.

Zedekiah   in the Old Testament, last king of Judah 597–586 BC. Placed on the throne by Nebuchadnezzar, he died a blinded captive in Babylon.

Zeebrugge   small Belgian ferry port on the North Sea, linked to Bruges by 14 km/9 mi canal (built 1896–1907). In Mar 1987 it was the scene of a disaster in which over 180 passengers lost their lives when the car ferry *Herald of Free Enterprise* put to sea from Zeebrugge with its car loading doors not properly closed.

Zeffirelli   Franco 1923– . Italian theatre and film director and designer, noted for his lavish designs

zebra

and stylish productions. His films include *Jesus of Nazareth* 1977 and *La Traviata* 1983.

Zeiss Carl 1816–1888. German optician. He opened his first workshop in Jena in 1846, and in 1866 joined forces with Ernst Abbe (1840–1905) producing cameras, microscopes, and field glasses.

zemstvo Russian provincial or district councils established by Tsar Alexander II in 1864. They were responsible for local administration until the revolution of 1917.

Zen abbreviation of Japanese *zenna*, 'quiet mind concentration', a form of ◊Buddhism introduced from India to Japan via China in the 12th century.

Zendavesta the sacred scriptures of ◊Zoroastrianism, today practised by the Parsees. They comprise the *Avesta* (liturgical books for the use of the priests); the *Gathas* (the discourses and revelations of Zoroaster); and the *Zend* commentary upon them.

zenith the upper pole of the celestial horizon, the point immediately above the observer; the ◊nadir is the point diametrically opposite. See ◊celestial sphere.

Zenobia queen of Palmyra 266–272 AD. She assumed the crown in the Syrian desert as regent for her sons, after the death of her husband Odenathus, and in 272 was defeated at Homs by Aurelian and taken as a captive to Rome.

Zeno of Elea *c.* 490–430 BC. Greek philosopher, whose paradoxes raised 'modern' problems of space and time. For example, motion is an illusion, since an arrow in flight must occupy a determinate space at each instant, and therefore must be at rest.

zeolite any of the silica-rich minerals of sodium, calcium, barium, strontium, and potassium, which can readily absorb and give up water, and have a high ion-exchange capacity. They can be used to make petrol, benzene, and toluene from low-grade raw materials, such as coal and methanol.

Zeppelin Ferdinand, Count von Zeppelin 1838–1917. German ◊airship pioneer. On retiring from the army in 1891, he devoted himself to the study of aeronautics, and his first airship was built and tested in 1900. During World War I a number of Zeppelin airships bombed England; they were also used for passenger transport. Zeppelin also helped to pioneer large multi-engine bomber planes.

Zeus in Greek mythology, chief of the gods (Roman Jupiter). He was the son of Kronos, whom he overthrew; his brothers and sisters included Demeter, Hades, Hera, and Poseidon. As the supreme god he dispensed good and evil and was the father and ruler of all mankind. His emblems are the thunderbolt and aegis (shield), representing the thunder cloud.

Zhangjiakou (formerly *Changchiakow*) city and trade centre in Hebei province, 160 km/100 mi NW of Beijing, on the Great Wall; population (1980) 1,100,000. It was the centre of the the overland tea trade from China to Russia.

Zhao Ziyang 1918– . Chinese politician, a member of the Politburo 1977–89, prime minister 1980–87, and secretary of the Chinese Communist Party (CCP) 1987–89. He introduced an economic programme based on self-management and material incentives for workers and factories. He lost all his posts after the Tiananmen Square massacre in Beijing 1989.

Zhejiang (formerly *Chekiang*) province of SE China
area 101,800 sq km/39,295 sq mi
capital Hangzhou
products rice, cotton, sugar, jute, maize; timber on the uplands
population (1990) 41,446,000.

Zhao Ziyang An economic expert with a pragmatic outlook.

Zhengzhou (formerly *Chengchow*) industrial city (light engineering, cotton textiles, foods), capital of Henan province (from 1954), China, on the Huang He; population (1989) 1,660,000.

Zhivkov Todor 1911– . Bulgarian Communist Party leader 1954–89, prime minister 1962–71, president 1971–89. His regime was cautious and conservative. He was tried for gross embezzlement 1991.

Zhou Enlai formerly *Chou En-lai* 1898–1976. Chinese politician. Zhou, a member of the Chinese Communist Party from the 1920s, was prime minister 1949–76 and foreign minister 1949–58. He was a moderate Maoist, and weathered the Cultural Revolution. He played a key role in foreign affairs.

Zhu De formerly *Chu Teh* 1886–1976. Chinese Red Army leader from 1931. He devised the tactic of mobile guerrilla warfare and organized the Long March to Shaanxi 1934–36. He was made a marshal 1955.

Zhukov Grigory Konstantinovich 1896–1974. Marshal of the USSR in World War II, and minister of defence 1955–57. As chief of staff from 1941, he defended Moscow 1941, counterattacked at Stalingrad, organized the relief of Leningrad 1943, and led the offensive from the Ukraine in Mar 1944 which ended in the fall of Berlin. He headed the Allied delegation

Zhou Enlai Chinese politician and prime minister, Zhou Enlai, 1971.

zinnia

Zia ul-Haq *Former Pakistani president General Mohammad Zia ul-Haq.*

that received the German surrender, and subsequently commanded the Soviet occupation forces in Germany.

Zia ul-Haq Mohammad 1924–1988. Pakistani general, in power from 1977 until his assassination. He was a career soldier from a middle-class Punjabi Muslim family, and became army chief of staff in 1976. He led the military coup against Zulfiqar Ali ◊Bhutto in 1977 and became president in 1978. Zia introduced a fundamentalist Islamic regime and restricted political activity.

ziggurat in ancient Babylonia and Assyria, a step pyramid of sun-baked brick faced with glazed bricks or tiles on which stood a shrine to a deity. The Tower of Babel described in the Bible may have been a ziggurat.

Zimbabwe extensive ruins near Victoria in Mashonaland, Zimbabwe. They were probably the work of a highly advanced Bantu-speaking people from Zaïre or Ethiopia, smelters of iron, who were in the area before 300 AD. The new state of Zimbabwe took its name from these ruins, and the national emblem is a bird derived from soapstone sculptures of fish eagles found in them.

Zimbabwe landlocked country in central Africa.

zinc a bluish-white metallic element, symbol Zn, atomic number 30, relative atomic mass 65.38. Ores occur in many parts of the world, but the principal source is the USA. Its chief modern uses are in the production of galvanized iron and in alloys, especially brass. Its compounds include zinc oxide, used in ointments and cosmetics, as well as in the manufacture of paint, glass, and printing ink. Zinc sulphide is used in television screens and X-ray apparatus.

zinnia annual plants of the family Compositae, native to Mexico, especially the cultivated hybrids of *Zinnia elegans*, with brightly coloured daisy-like flowers.

Zinoviev Grigory 1883–1936. Russian politician. A prominent Bolshevik, he returned to Russia in 1917 with Lenin and played a leading part in the Revolution. As head of the Communist ◊International 1919, his name was linked with a forged letter, inciting Britain's communists to rise, which helped to topple the Labour government in 1924. As one of the 'Old Bolsheviks', Stalin saw him as a threat. He was accused of complicity in the murder of the Bolshevik leader Kirov, and shot.

Zion Jebusite (Amorites of Canaan) stronghold in Jerusalem on which King David built the Temple, symbolic of Jerusalem and of Israel as a homeland for the Jews.

Zionism a Jewish movement for the establishment in Palestine of a Jewish homeland, the 'promised land' of the Bible, with its capital Jerusalem, the 'city of Zion'.

zip fastener a fastening device used in clothing, invented in the USA by Whitcomb Judson in 1891, originally for doing up shoes. It has two sets of interlocking teeth which are meshed by means of a slide.

Zircon codename for a British signals-intelligence satellite originally intended to be launched in 1988. The revelation of the existence of the Zircon project (which had been concealed by the government), and the government's subsequent efforts to suppress a programme about it on BBC television, caused much controversy in 1987.

zirconium a metallic element, symbol Zr, atomic number 40, relative atomic mass 91.22. It is used in highly corrosion-resistant ceramic oxide coatings in, for example, chemical plant, and also in nuclear plant where its low neutron absorption is advantageous. In steelmaking it is used as a deoxidizer.

zither a musical instrument, best known as an Austrian Alpine folk instrument, consisting of up to 34 strings, which are plucked, stretched across a flat wooden soundbox about 60 cm/24 in long. Five of the strings are used for melody, and pass over frets, while the rest are used for harmonic accompaniment.

Zi Xi (formerly *Tzu-Hsi*) 1836–1908. Dowager empress of China (formerly Tzu-Hsi). She was presented as a concubine to the emperor Hsien-Feng. On his death 1861 she became regent for her son T'ung Chih, and, when he died in 1875, for her nephew Guang Xu (1871–1908).

zodiac name given by the ancient Greeks to the zone of the heavens containing the paths of the Sun, Moon and the five planets then known. It was about 16° wide, and the stars contained in it were grouped into 12 signs each of 30° in extent: Aries, Taurus, Gemini, Cancer, Leo, Virgo, Libra, Scorpius, Sagittarius, Capricornus, Aquarius, and Pisces. Because of the ◊precession of the equinoxes, the modern constellations do not cover the same areas of sky as the zodiacal signs of the same name.

zodiacal light a cone-shaped light sometimes seen extending from the Sun along the ecliptic, visible after sunset or before sunrise. It is due to thinly spread dust particles in the central plane of the ◊Solar System. It is very faint, and requires a dark, clear sky to be seen.

Zoffany Johann 1733–1810. German-born British portrait painter, based in London from about 1761.

Zimbabwe
Republic of

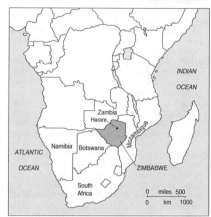

area 390,300 sq km/150,695 sq mi
capital Harare
towns Bulawayo, Gweru, Kwekwe, Mutare, Hwange
physical high plateau, central high veld, mountains in E
head of state and government Robert Mugabe from 1987
political system effectively one-party socialist republic
exports tobacco, asbestos, cotton, gold, silver
currency Zimbabwe dollar
population (1990 est) 10,205,000 (Shona 80%, Ndbele 19%; 100,000 whites); annual growth rate 3.5%
language English (official); Shona, Sindebele
religion Christian, Muslim, Hindu, animist

literacy men 81%, women 67% (1985 est)
GNP $5.5 bn (1988); $275 per head
chronology
1961 Zimbabwe African People's Union (ZAPU) formed, with Joshua Nkomo as leader.
1962 ZAPU declared illegal.
1963 Zimbabawe African National Union (ZANU) formed, with Robert Mugabe as secretary general.
1964 Ian Smith became prime minister. Nkomo and Mugabe imprisoned.
1965 ZANU banned; Smith declared unilateral independence.
1966–68 Abortive talks between Smith and UK prime minister Harold Wilson.
1974 Nkomo and Mugabe released.
1975 Geneva conference set a date for constitutional independence.
1979 Smith produced new constitution; the government he established with Bishop Abel Muzorewa as prime minister was denounced by Nkomo and Mugabe; London conference decided arrangements for independence in Lancaster House Agreement.
1980 Independence achieved from Britain, with Robert Mugabe as prime minister.
1981 Rift between Mugabe and Nkomo.
1982 Nkomo dismissed from cabinet.
1984 ZANU-People's Front (PF) Party Congress agreed to create a one-party state in the future.
1985 Mugabe/Nkomo relations improved.
1986 Joint ZANU-PF rally amid merger plans.
1987 Abolition of white-roll seats in assembly; President Banana retired. Mugabe became executive president – both head of state and prime minister.
1988 Nkomo returned to cabinet; appointed vice president.
1989 Opposition party, the Zimbabwe Unity Movement, formed by Edgar Tekere; constitution drafted renouncing Marxist-Leninist ideology; ZANU and ZAPU formally merged.
1990 ZANU-PF re-elected. Opposition to creation of one-party state.
1992 United Front formed to oppose ZANU-PF. Mugabe declared drought and famine a national disaster.

Under the patronage of George III he painted many portraits of the royal family. He spent several years in Florence (1770s) and India (1780s).

Zog Ahmed Beg Zogu 1895–1961. King of Albania 1928–39. He became prime minister of Albania 1922, president of the republic 1925, and proclaimed himself king 1928. He was driven out by the Italians in 1939, and settled in England.

Zola Emile Edouard Charles Antoine 1840–1902. French novelist and social reformer. With *La Fortune des Rougon/The Fortune of the Rougons* 1867 he began a series of some 20 naturalistic novels, portraying in realistic and sometimes sordid detail the fortunes of a French family under the Second Empire. In 1898 he published *J'accuse/I Accuse*, indicting the persecutors of ◊Dreyfus, for which he was prosecuted for libel but later pardoned.

zombie a corpse believed (especially in Haiti) to be reanimated by a spirit. The idea possibly arose from voodoo priests using the nerve poison tetrodotoxin (from the puffer fish) to produce a semblance of death, from which the victim afterwards physically recovers, and is enslaved.

Zone System in photography, a system of exposure estimation invented by Ansel ◊Adams which groups infinite tonal gradations into ten zones, zone 0 being black and zone 10 being white.

zoo short for *zoological gardens*, a place where animals are kept in captivity, whether as a spectacle or for scientific study.

zoology the branch of biology concerned with the study of animals. It includes description of present-day animals, the study of evolution of animal forms,

Zola French novelist and reformer Emile Zola.

anatomy, physiology, embryology, and geographical distribution.

zoom lens a photographic lens which by variation of focal length allows speedy transition from long-shots to close-ups.

zoonosis any infectious disease which can afflict both human beings and animals. Probably the most feared example is ◊rabies, which is the subject of stringent controls in some countries.

Zoroaster or Zarathustra c. 628–c. 551 BC. Persian prophet and religious teacher, founder of Zoroastrianism.

Zoroastrianism religion founded by Zoroaster, and still practised by the Parsees, who fled from Persia after the Arab conquest in the 8th century AD, and settled in India, especially in Bombay. The ◊Zendavesta are the sacred scriptures of the faith. The theology is dualistic, *Ahura Mazda* or *Ormuzd* (the Good God) being in conflict with *Ahriman* (the Evil God), but the former is assured of eventual victory.

Zorrilla y Moral José 1817–1893. Spanish poet and playwright. Born at Valladolid, he based his plays chiefly on national legends, such as the *Don Juan Tenorio* 1844.

Zouave member of a corps of French infantry soldiers, first raised in Algeria in 1831 from the Berber Kabyle people of Zouaves. The term came to be used for soldiers in other corps modelled on the French Zouaves.

ZST abbreviation for *Zone Standard Time*.

zucchini alternative common name for the courgette, a type of ◊marrow.

Zuider Zee former sea inlet in Holland, cut off from the North Sea by the closing of a dyke in 1932, much of which has been reclaimed as land. The remaining lake is called the ◊IJsselmeer.

Zulu an ethnic group from Natal, South Africa. The modern homeland, Kwazulu, represents the nucleus of the old Zulu kingdom. The Zulu language belongs to the Bantu branch of the Niger-Congo family.

Zululand region in Natal, South Africa, largely corresponding to the Black National State, Kwazulu. It was formerly a province, annexed to Natal 1897.

Zurbarán Francisco de 1598–1664. Spanish painter, based in Seville. He painted religious subjects in a powerful, austere style, often focusing on a single figure in prayer.

Zürich financial centre and industrial city (machinery, electrical goods, textiles) on Lake Zürich, capital of Zürich canton, chief city in Switzerland; population (1984) 352,358.

Zweig Arnold 1887–1968. German novelist, playwright and poet. He is remembered for his realistic novel of a Russian peasant in the German army *Der Streit um den Sergeanten Grischa/The Case of Sergeant Grischa* 1927.

Zweig Stefan 1881–1942. Austrian writer, noted for plays, poems, and many biographies of writers (Balzac, Dickens) and historical figures (Marie Antoinette, Mary Stuart). He and his wife, exiles from the Nazis from 1934, despairing at what they saw as the end of civilization and culture, committed suicide in Brazil.

Zwingli Ulrich 1484–1531. Swiss Protestant, born in St Gall. He was ordained a Roman Catholic priest in 1506, but by 1519 was a Reformer, and led the Reformation in Switzerland with his insistence on the sole authority of the Scriptures. In a war against the cantons that had not accepted the Reformation he was killed in a skirmish at Kappel.

Zworykin Vladimir Kosma 1889–1982. Russian-born American electronics engineer who invented a television camera tube and the ◊electron microscope.

zygote the name given to an ◊ovum (egg) after ◊fertilization but before it undergoes division at the start of its development.

Weights and Measures

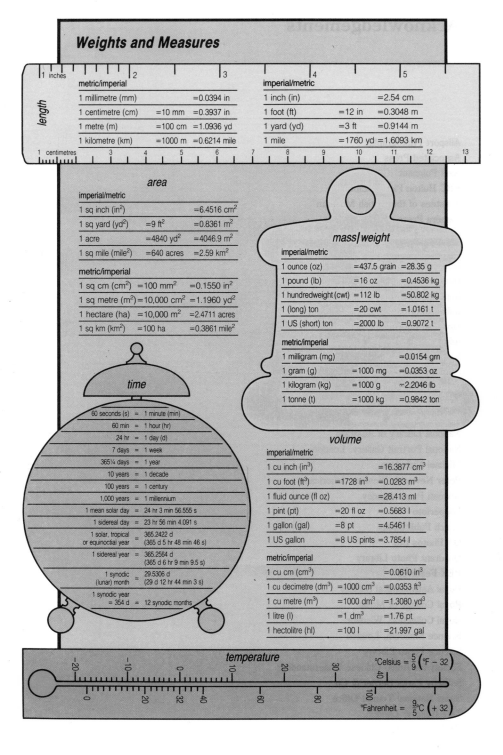

length

metric/imperial

1 millimetre (mm)		=0.0394 in
1 centimetre (cm)	=10 mm	=0.3937 in
1 metre (m)	=100 cm	=1.0936 yd
1 kilometre (km)	=1000 m	=0.6214 mile

imperial/metric

1 inch (in)		=2.54 cm
1 foot (ft)	=12 in	=0.3048 m
1 yard (yd)	=3 ft	=0.9144 m
1 mile	=1760 yd	=1.6093 km

area

imperial/metric

1 sq inch (in^2)		=6.4516 cm^2
1 sq yard (yd^2)	=9 ft^2	=0.8361 m^2
1 acre	=4840 yd^2	=4046.9 m^2
1 sq mile (mile^2)	=640 acres	=2.59 km^2

metric/imperial

1 sq cm (cm^2)	=100 mm^2	=0.1550 in^2
1 sq metre (m^2)	=10,000 cm^2	=1.1960 yd^2
1 hectare (ha)	=10,000 m^2	=2.4711 acres
1 sq km (km^2)	=100 ha	=0.3861 mile^2

mass/weight

imperial/metric

1 ounce (oz)	=437.5 grain	=28.35 g
1 pound (lb)	=16 oz	=0.4536 kg
1 hundredweight (cwt)	=112 lb	=50.802 kg
1 (long) ton	=20 cwt	=1.0161 t
1 US (short) ton	=2000 lb	=0.9072 t

metric/imperial

1 milligram (mg)		=0.0154 grn
1 gram (g)	=1000 mg	=0.0353 oz
1 kilogram (kg)	=1000 g	≈2.2046 lb
1 tonne (t)	=1000 kg	=0.9842 ton

time

60 seconds (s)	=	1 minute (min)
60 min	=	1 hour (hr)
24 hr	=	1 day (d)
7 days	=	1 week
365¼ days	=	1 year
10 years	=	1 decade
100 years	=	1 century
1,000 years	=	1 millennium
1 mean solar day	=	24 hr 3 min 56.555 s
1 sidereal day	=	23 hr 56 min 4.091 s
1 solar, tropical or equinoctial year	=	365.2422 d (365 d 5 hr 48 min 46 s)
1 sidereal year	=	365.2564 d (365 d 6 hr 9 min 9.5 s)
1 synodic (lunar) month	=	29.5306 d (29 d 12 hr 44 min 3 s)
1 synodic year	= 354 d =	12 synodic months

volume

imperial/metric

1 cu inch (in^3)		=16.3877 cm^3
1 cu foot (ft^3)	=1728 in^3	=0.0283 m^3
1 fluid ounce (fl oz)		=28.413 ml
1 pint (pt)	=20 fl oz	=0.5683 l
1 gallon (gal)	=8 pt	=4.5461 l
1 US gallon	=8 US pints	=3.7854 l

metric/imperial

1 cu cm (cm^3)		=0.0610 in^3
1 cu decimetre (dm^3)	=1000 cm^3	=0.0353 ft^3
1 cu metre (m^3)	=1000 dm^3	=1.3080 yd^3
1 litre (l)	=1 dm^3	=1.76 pt
1 hectolitre (hl)	=100 l	=21.997 gal

temperature

$$°\text{Celsius} = \frac{5}{9}\left(°F - 32\right)$$

$$°\text{Fahrenheit} = \frac{9}{5}°C \left(+32\right)$$

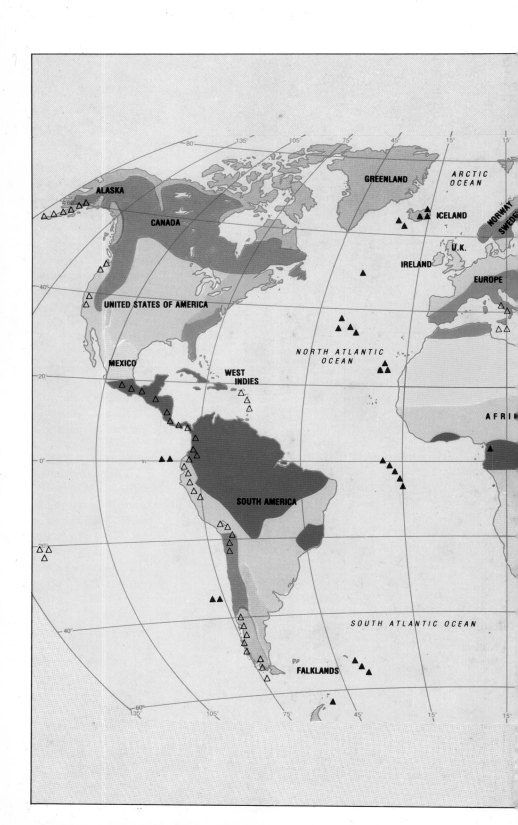